ENCYCLOPAEDIA
JUDAICA

ENCYCLOPAEDIA JUDAICA

SECOND EDITION

VOLUME 17
Ra–Sam

Fred Skolnik, *Editor in Chief*
Michael Berenbaum, *Executive Editor*

MACMILLAN REFERENCE USA
An imprint of Thomson Gale, a part of The Thomson Corporation

IN ASSOCIATION WITH
KETER PUBLISHING HOUSE LTD., JERUSALEM

THOMSON
GALE

Detroit • New York • San Francisco • New Haven, Conn. • Waterville, Maine • London

THOMSON GALE

ENCYCLOPAEDIA JUDAICA, Second Edition

Fred Skolnik, *Editor in Chief*
Michael Berenbaum, *Executive Editor*
Shlomo S. (Yosh) Gafni, *Editorial Project Manager*
Rachel Gilon, *Editorial Project Planning and Control*

Thomson Gale
Gordon Macomber, *President*
Frank Menchaca, *Senior Vice President and Publisher*
Jay Flynn, *Publisher*
Hélène Potter, *Publishing Director*

Keter Publishing House
Yiphtach Dekel, *Chief Executive Officer*
Peter Tomkins, *Executive Project Director*

Complete staff listings appear in Volume 1

For more information, contact
Macmillan Reference USA
An imprint of Thomson Gale
27500 Drake Rd.
Farmington Hills, MI 48331-3535
Or you can visit our internet site at
http://www.gale.com

LIBRARY OF CONGRESS CATALOGING-IN-PUBLICATION DATA

Encyclopaedia Judaica / Fred Skolnik, editor-in-chief ; Michael Berenbaum, executive editor. -- 2nd ed.
v. cm.
Includes bibliographical references and index.
Contents: v.1. Aa-Alp.
ISBN 0-02-865928-7 (set hardcover : alk. paper) -- ISBN 0-02-865929-5 (vol. 1 hardcover : alk. paper) -- ISBN 0-02-865930-9 (vol. 2 hardcover : alk. paper) -- ISBN 0-02-865931-7 (vol. 3 hardcover : alk. paper) -- ISBN 0-02-865932-5 (vol. 4 hardcover : alk. paper) -- ISBN 0-02-865933-3 (vol. 5 hardcover : alk. paper) -- ISBN 0-02-865934-1 (vol. 6 hardcover : alk. paper) -- ISBN 0-02-865935-X (vol. 7 hardcover : alk. paper) -- ISBN 0-02-865936-8 (vol. 8 hardcover : alk. paper) -- ISBN 0-02-865937-6 (vol. 9 hardcover : alk. paper) -- ISBN 0-02-865938-4 (vol. 10 hardcover : alk. paper) -- ISBN 0-02-865939-2 (vol. 11 hardcover : alk. paper) -- ISBN 0-02-865940-6 (vol. 12 hardcover : alk. paper) -- ISBN 0-02-865941-4 (vol. 13 hardcover : alk. paper) -- ISBN 0-02-865942-2 (vol. 14 hardcover : alk. paper) -- ISBN 0-02-865943-0 (vol. 15: alk. paper) -- ISBN 0-02-865944-9 (vol. 16: alk. paper) -- ISBN 0-02-865945-7 (vol. 17: alk. paper) -- ISBN 0-02-865946-5 (vol. 18: alk. paper) -- ISBN 0-02-865947-3 (vol. 19: alk. paper) -- ISBN 0-02-865948-1 (vol. 20: alk. paper) -- ISBN 0-02-865949-X (vol. 21: alk. paper) -- ISBN 0-02-865950-3 (vol. 22: alk. paper)
1. Jews -- Encyclopedias. I. Skolnik, Fred. II. Berenbaum, Michael, 1945-
DS102.8.E496 2007
909'.04924 -- dc22

2006020426

ISBN-13:

978-0-02-865928-2 (set)
978-0-02-865929-9 (vol. 1)
978-0-02-865930-5 (vol. 2)
978-0-02-865931-2 (vol. 3)
978-0-02-865932-9 (vol. 4)
978-0-02-865933-6 (vol. 5)
978-0-02-865934-3 (vol. 6)
978-0-02-865935-0 (vol. 7)
978-0-02-865936-7 (vol. 8)
978-0-02-865937-4 (vol. 9)
978-0-02-865938-1 (vol. 10)
978-0-02-865939-8 (vol. 11)
978-0-02-865940-4 (vol. 12)
978-0-02-865941-1 (vol. 13)
978-0-02-865942-8 (vol. 14)
978-0-02-865943-5 (vol. 15)
978-0-02-865944-2 (vol. 16)
978-0-02-865945-9 (vol. 17)
978-0-02-865946-6 (vol. 18)
978-0-02-865947-3 (vol. 19)
978-0-02-865948-0 (vol. 20)
978-0-02-865949-7 (vol. 21)
978-0-02-865950-3 (vol. 22)

This title is also available as an e-book
ISBN-10: 0-02-866097-8
ISBN-13: 978-0-02-866097-4
Contact your Thomson Gale representative for ordering information.
Printed in the United States of America

10 9 8 7 6 5 4 3 2

TABLE OF CONTENTS

Initial letter "R" of Recordare, *the first word of a prologue to the apocryphal book of Baruch, in a Latin Bible written and illuminated in France, c. 1300. Princeton University Library, Med. and Ren. Mss., Garrett no. 29, vol. II fol. 79v.*

RA-RZ

RAAB, ESTHER (1894–1981), Hebrew poet. Raab, born in Petaḥ Tikvah, is considered the first Hebrew poetess in Ereẓ Israel. Her father, Judah *Raab, had immigrated from Hungary and helped found the first moshavah, where she grew up in poverty and hardship. After a short stay in Deganyah, she worked in Ben Shemen and returned home. In 1921 she married her cousin, the merchant Yitzhak Green and spent five years with him in Cairo and in Paris. Back in Tel Aviv, the couple's home became a meeting place for writers and painters. Her first poems appeared in *Hedim* in the beginning of the 1920s. In 1930, shortly before the publication of her first collection of poems, *Kimshonim* (*Thistles*, 2002), her husband died. Two years later, Raab married the painter Arieh Alweil. Her second collection, *Shirei Esther Raab*, appeared more than 30 years later, in 1964. Her late poems appeared in the volume *Tefillah Aḥaronah* ("Last Prayer," 1972). *Yalkut Shirim*, published in 1982, includes a lengthy introduction by Reuven Shoham. A collection of stories, *Gan she-Ḥarav*, with stories depicting her childhood and youth in the moshavah and her vivid impressions of her stay in Egypt, appeared in 1983. Her nephew, the writer Ehud Ben Ezer, edited *Kol ha-Shirim* (1988) and *Kol ha-Prozah* (2001) and wrote her biography *Yamim shel La'anah u-Devash* ("Days of Gall and Honey" – including a bibliography, 1998). The landscape of Ereẓ Israel and the Orient, colors, shades, and smells, and particularly the flora of the homeland make up her poetic texture. Raab expresses a genuine love for the country, the soil, the space, and writes passionate lyrical poetry, expressing yearning, pain, disappointment, and loneliness. The growing interest in Hebrew women writers and their oeuvre has also given rise to a rediscovery and re-appreciation of Esther Raab and her poetry. In addition to the English collection *Thistles*, to which the translator Harold Schimmel added an Introduction, single poems and stories appeared in foreign anthologies. For translations see the ITHL website at www.ithl.org.il.

BIBLIOGRAPHY: E. Sharoni, "Edenic Energy: E. Raab's Unmediated Vision of Nature," in: *Modern Hebrew Literature* 8:3–4 (1983), 62–69; D. Melamed, "Requiem for a Landscape," in: *Modern Hebrew Literature*, 9:3–4 (1984), 69–72; A. Lerner, "'A Woman's Song': The Poetry of E. Raab," in: *Gender and Text in Modern Hebrew and Yiddish Literature* (1992), 17–38; idem, "The Naked Land: Nature in the Poetry of E. Raab," in: *Women of the Word* (1994), 236–57; B. Mann, "Framing the Native: E. Raab's Visual Poetics," in: *Israel Studies*, 4:1 (1999), 234–57; H. Zamir, "*Ahavat Moledet ve-Si'aḥ Ḥershim*," in: *Theory and Criticism*, 7 (1995), 125–45; E. Ben Ezer, "*E. Raab ve-ha-Aravim*," in: *Nativ*, 9:5 (1996), 72–78; Z. Luz, *E. Raab, Monografiyyah* (1997); E. Ben Ezer, "*Or Ḥadash al E. Raab ve-Y. Luidor*," in: *Iton 77*, 255 (2001), 17–20; Sh. Zayit, "'*Ani Amarti et Kol ha-Emet, Ani Nishba'at': Ha-Model ha-Biografi shel E. Raab*," in: *Masad*, 2 (2004), 21–29.

[Anat Feinberg (2nd ed.)]

RAAB (Ben-Ezer), JUDAH (1858–1948), pioneer and one of the first Jewish guards in Ereẓ Israel. Born in the village of Szent István in western Hungary into a farming family which had contacts with the Jewish community in Ereẓ Israel, Raab went to Ereẓ Israel with his father in 1876. He joined the group of Jerusalemites who founded Petaḥ Tikvah and plowed the first furrow in its fields in 1878. He was one of the first guards and was responsible for the settlement's security during its early years. When Petaḥ Tikvah was abandoned during the sabbatical year (*shemittah*) of 1882, Raab became an instructor for new settlers in Rishon le-Zion and the Bilu settlers. In 1883, when Petaḥ Tikvah was resettled, he returned and instructed new immigrants ("the Byalistokites") in agricultural techniques. Raab was appointed a foreman by Baron de *Rothschild's officials and struggled to maintain the agricultural character of Petaḥ Tikvah. His memoirs, *Ha-Telem ha-Rishon* (1956) recorded by his son, B. Ben-Ezer, constitute valuable material on the early history of Jewish settlement in Ereẓ Israel. His daughter Esther *Raab (1894–1981) was born in Petaḥ Tikvah and joined kibbutz Deganyah in her youth. After her marriage she lived in Egypt for five years and then in Tel Aviv, returning afterward to Petaḥ Tikvah. Her early lyric poetry, characterized by its descriptions of the landscape of Ereẓ Israel, is collected in *Kimshonim* (1930). Her collected poems were published in *Kol ha-Shirim* (1988).

BIBLIOGRAPHY: Y. Yaari and M. Ḥarizman, *Sefer ha-Yovel shel Petaḥ Tikvah* (1929), 126–9, 187–92; Tidhar, 1 (1947), 119–21.

[Yehuda Slutsky]

RA'ANANNAH (Heb. רַעֲנַנָּה), urban community with municipal council status in central Israel, N.E. of Herzliyyah. Ra'anannah was established in 1922 as a village (moshavah) by a group of American Jews who founded Aḥuzzat New York A Inc. (1912). The land was bought through the Palestine Land Development Company. Initially there were many economic difficulties. An attempt was made to raise cattle as the mainstay of the economy. Ra'anannah progressed in the later 1920s and in the 1930s when a rich groundwater table was tapped, the citrus branch introduced, and middle-class immigrants of the Fourth Aliyah and later newcomers were absorbed. With the crisis in the citrus branch during World War II, the settlers changed over to mixed farming and made beginnings in industry. In the 1940s, two housing quarters for Yemenite and other immigrants were built with contributions from Zionists in the United States and South Africa. In 1947, Ra'anannah had 3,800 inhabitants and grew quickly after the War of Independence (1948) when *ma'barot* (immigrant transit camp) inhabitants were given permanent housing (1953 – 9,000 inhabitants; 1968 – 11,900). Ra'anannah belonged to the outer ring of the Tel Aviv conurbation and developed various industries as well as agriculture. Over the years, most of Ra'anannah's farmland became built-up areas. In 1981 Ra'anannah received city status, with an area of about 6 sq. mi. (15 sq. km.). In the mid-1990s the population was approximately 56,900, rising to 68,900 in 2002. The city had a large community of immigrants from English-speaking countries. Its expansion reached the outskirts of *Herzliyyah in the south. In 1996 a high-tech industrial area was established, housing such big companies as Amdocs. Ra'anannah was one of the few Israeli cities to receive ISO 9002 certification for the quality of its public services. Income among residents was much higher than the national average.

WEBSITE: www.raanana.muni.il.

[Efraim Orni / Shaked Gilboa (2nd ed.)]

RABAN, AVNER (1937–2004), Israeli underwater archaeologist. Born in kibbutz Ramat David in the Jezreel Valley, Raban's interest in underwater activities began after completing his military service while fishing with nets along the coast of Israel and accidentally discovering archaeological artifacts. Raban studied fine arts at the Oranim Teachers College from 1958 to 1960. In 1961 he became one of the founders of the Underwater Exploration Society of Israel, together with Dr. Elisha Linder. The society eventually joined the International Confederation of Underwater Activity (CMAS), headed by Jacques Cousteau, and Raban in time took part in a number of underwater expeditions working in the Mediterranean area, notably on the excavation of the Yassi Ada shipwreck off the coast of Turkey. Raban was co-director and staff member of various underwater expeditions in Israel: Akhziv (1961); surveys along the northern coast of Israel (1964); Acre (1965); and Athlit (1966). In 1966 Raban began his academic studies at the Hebrew University of Jerusalem, studying archaeology and geography. To qualify for his B.A. Raban participated in a number of excavations on land, at Megiddo and Hazor. During the Six-Day War (1967), he discovered several shipwrecks in the Red Sea while combing the Straits of Tiran and Snapir for mines. In 1968 he directed his first underwater excavation at Sharm el-Sheikh, which led to an interdisciplinary survey of the Gulf of Eilat and a survey of the east coast of Sinai in 1969–70, the excavation of the "Mercury Wreck" in the Red Sea in 1972, and the excavation of a wreck in the Na'ama Gulf of the Red Sea in 1973. In 1981 Raban received his Ph.D. degree from the Hebrew University of Jerusalem, subsequently teaching in the Department of Maritime Civilizations and the Center of Maritime Studies at Haifa University, where eventually he became a full professor. From the mid-1970s Raban concentrated on the archaeological study of the harbors along the coast at Israel, namely at Acre, Dor, Athlit, and Caesarea, as well as further afield in Crete and Sicily. Between 1972 and 1992 Raban also conducted work on land, with a survey of the Jezreel Valley, and digging at Tell Abu-Hawam. From the 1980s on Raban dedicated many years to the study of Caesarea Maritima, but, unfortunately, was unable to complete the two-volume report *The Harbors of Caesarea*, when he unexpectedly died while visiting London during a sabbatical at Oxford.

BIBLIOGRAPHY: R. Gertwagen, "Obituary: Avner Raban (1937–2004)," in: *Bulletin of the Anglo-Israel Archaeological Society,* 22 (2004), 79–82.

[Shimon Gibson (2nd ed.)]

RABB, MAXWELL MILTON (1910–2002), U.S. attorney, government official, and Jewish community leader. Rabb, who was born in Boston, graduated from Harvard Law School and was admitted to the Massachusetts bar in 1935. He subsequently became an administrative assistant to Senators Henry Cabot Lodge (1937–43) and Sinclair Weeks (1944). After naval service, Rabb became a legal and legislative consultant to Secretary of the Navy James Forrestal in 1946. He later served as associate counsel to President Dwight Eisenhower (1953–54), and was secretary to Eisenhower's cabinet from 1954 to 1958. Rabb was sent as chairman of the U.S. delegation to the tenth session of UNESCO in Paris in 1958, later serving on the executive committee of the United States Committee for UNESCO (1959–60). President Johnson appointed Rabb to the Commission on Income Maintenance Programs (the Heineman Commission on welfare and related programs, 1968–70). He was a trustee of the American Health Foundation (1969–74) and served on the Council of Foreign Relations (1978). Between 1981 and 1989 he was American ambassador to Italy.

Among other posts, Rabb was a director of several corporations and a member of the board of directors of the NAACP Legal Defense and Educational Fund. He also served as president of the United States Committee for Refugees, a private group organized in 1958 that dealt with refugee resettlement and immigration. Active in Jewish community affairs, Rabb was chairman of the government division of the UJA (1953–57), a member of the board of governors of the Hebrew Union College-Jewish Institute of Religion, and vice chairman of the New York executive committee of the Anti-Defamation League, among many other posts. Rabb was a member of the New York law firm of Stroock, Stroock and Lavan from 1958.

John Cabot University established the Maxwell Rabb Scholarship in honor of Rabb, who was the longest-serving American ambassador to Italy. The partial-tuition scholarship is granted to a degree-seeking student from the U.S. or Italy who demonstrates a commitment to community service and/or civic involvement.

[Rohan Saxena and Ruth Beloff (2nd ed.)]

RABBA, MENAHEM (16th century), preacher in Padua. Rabba wrote *Beit Mo'ed* (Venice, 1605), a homiletic work containing sermons for every religious occasion during the year. A large number of his sermons deal with the concept of repentance (*teshuvah*) to which he ascribes a metaphysical dimension. Although the work exhibits certain philosophic influences, no specific philosophic thought is dominant. The book was published posthumously by Rabba's son, Elijah, who in the introduction lists other works of his father similar in style to *Beit Mo'ed: Ot ha-Berit, Ḥavvat Rabba, Netivot Olam, Kelil Tekhelet, Ma'aneh Rakh*, and *Kiryat Arba*, none of which was published.

RABBA BEN MATNAH (late fourth–early fifth century), Babylonian *amora*. The Talmud relates that he was a pupil of *Rabbah and *Sheshet and a colleague of *Abbaye b. Avin and Ḥanina (Pes. 34a). On the death of R. Joseph he was a candidate, together with Abbaye, Rava, and Zera II, for the post of head of the Pumbedita academy. They decided on a contest to see which of them could make a statement that the others could not refute. Abbaye succeeded and was appointed. The rabbis, in discussing the relative merits of the intellectual characteristics of Zera and Rabba ben Matnah, described the former as "keen witted, and sharp intellectually," whereas Rabba ben Matnah was "slow in deliberation, and so able to arrive at firm conclusions" in deciding a law (Hor. ad fin). Strangely enough, though he was apparently a very great scholar, none of his teaching has survived. However if he is to be identified with R. Abba II much of his wisdom has been recorded under the latter name.

BIBLIOGRAPHY: Halevy, Dorot, 2 (1923), 460–1; Hyman, Toledot, s.v.

RABBAH (**Ha-Rabbah**; Heb. רַבָּה, הָרַבָּה).

(1) An abbreviation for *Rabbath-Ammon.

(2) A town in Judah mentioned with Kiriath-Jearim as part of the inheritance of the tribe of Judah in the hill country (Joshua 15:60). It is probably identical with a city called *Rbt* near Gezer in Thutmosis III's list of Canaanite cities (no. 105). It may also be mentioned in a cuneiform letter found at Taanach. According to two el-Amarna letters (289, 290) sent by the king of Jerusalem to the pharaoh, Milkilu, the king of Gezer, together with Shuwardata captured Rubutu with the aid of mercenaries. The name appears for the last time in Shishak's list of conquered towns, after Gezer and before Aijalon. Some scholars, following the Septuagint, identify Rabbah with Soba (Ar. Sūbā) near Jerusalem, but the recently discovered site of Khirbat Bīr (Bi'r) al-Ḥilū fits the descriptions in the ancient sources remarkably well.

(3) An abbreviation for the city of Rabbath-Moab, now Khirbat al-Rabba, 14 mi. (c. 22 km.) south of the River Arnon. Alexander Yannai conquered it with other cities in Moab; after his death it was restored to the Nabateans by Hyrcanus II (Jos., Ant., 14:18). It is called Rabbathmoba by Ptolemy (5:16, 4) and appears thus on the coins of his time. Rabbah appears as a district capital in one of the Babatha letters found in the Naḥal Hever in 1961. Eusebius refers to it as Areopolis, the town of the war god Ares (Onom. 124:15 ff.). In the fourth century it was identified with the Ar of Moab of Numbers 21:28; recently, the remains of a Canaanite-Moabite city (Early and Late Bronze ages) were found at al-Mishna in the vicinity of Khirbat al-Rabba. In late Roman times, Rabbah was a post of the Equites Mauri Illyriciani (*Notitia Dignitatum* 80:5); remains of a temple, walls, and a citadel have been noticed here. A sumptuous Jewish synagogue was destroyed there in the fifth century by the fanatical monk Bar-Sauma. After the Arab conquest, Rabbah, sometimes called Moab by Arab geographers, continued in existence. It is mentioned in 1321 as a village in the district of Karak and as a station on the Damascus-al-Karak road.

BIBLIOGRAPHY: Glueck, in: AASOR, 14 (1934), 62; Press, Ereẓ, s.v.; Abel, Geog, 2 (1938), 23–5; Aharoni, Land, index; idem, in: VT (1969).

[Michael Avi-Yonah]

RABBAH (**Mar-Rava**), *gaon* of Pumbedita from 651, contemporary of *Huna, *gaon* of Sura. Rabbah and Huna were jointly responsible for one of the earliest and most important of post-talmudic *takkanot*, the *takkanah* of the *Moredet* ("the obstreperous wife"). According to the Talmud, a Jewish wife could demand a divorce only in certain exceptional cases specified in talmudic law (as for instance when her husband was stricken with a repulsive disease). The new *takkanah* extended the reasons and made it possible for some women to obtain dissolution of their marriages by the local courts obliging the husband to issue a divorce, without her forfeiting the amount of her *ketubbah* or suffering any loss of property which she had brought into the marriage. Moreover, the period of waiting was reduced from the usual 12 months to as short as one to four weeks.

BIBLIOGRAPHY: Baron, Social², 6 (1958), 132f.; Ḥ. Tykocinski, *Takkanot ha-Ge'onim* (1960), 11–29.

[Meir Havazelet]

RABBAH BAR BAR ḤANA (second half of the third century), *amora*. As his father's name was also Rabbah, it is thought his patronymic referred to his grandfather (see *Rabbah bar Ḥana). Born in Babylonia, he went to Ereẓ Israel to study in the academy of R. Johanan, and many years after returned to his native land, where he disseminated the teachings of Johanan, transmitting in his name close to 200 *halakhot* in all spheres. The heads of the Babylonian academies, such as R. Judah of Pumbedita and his distinguished disciples, Rabbah, and R. Joseph, transmitted in his name *halakhot* they had learned from him. He suffered from the persecutions of the Sassanids who even broke into his house, and he complained: "Merciful One! Either in Thy shadow or in the shadow of Esau [= Rome]" (Git. 17a). It is possible that in consequence of these sufferings he decided to return to Ereẓ Israel (Pes. 51a), but there is no evidence that he did so.

Rabbah achieved great renown for his remarkable legends (known as the "*aggadot* of Rabbah bar Bar Ḥana" and chiefly found in the tractate *Bava Batra* (73a–74a). These tales purport to relate what he saw and heard during his many journeys by sea and land. They are marked by hyperbole, and excited the wonder of contemporary scholars. Some of them spoke out sharply against him: "Every Abba is an ass and every bar Bar Ḥana is a fool" (BB 74a). Rabbah ascribes some of his stories to sailors and Arabs, but begins most of them with the words, "I myself saw." The following is a typical one: "We were once traveling in a desert and an Arab joined us.… He said to me: 'Come and I will show you where the men of Korah were swallowed up' (cf. Num. 16:23ff). I saw two cracks that emitted smoke. I took a piece of clipped wool, dipped it in water, attached it to the point of a spear, and inserted it there, and when I took it out it was singed. He said to me: 'Listen carefully! What do you hear?' I heard them crying out: 'Moses and his Torah are true and we are liars!' The Arab said to me 'Every 30 days Gehenna returns them here as meat turns on a spit,' and they cry out: 'Moses and his Torah are true and we are liars'" (BB 74a).

The expositors of the Talmud, aware of the strangeness of these stories, sought to rationalize them. Yom Tov b. Abraham *Ishbili stated: "The stories in this chapter deal with subjects that are strange to people because they are unfamiliar with them, but they are very plausible to those with a knowledge of nature, such as the size of sea monsters and the size of waves in a storm. They also contain allusions to matters which were not seen with the eye but in a vision. For when the sages went on ocean voyages they saw there God's wonders … and during their sleep they experienced remarkable visions in the context of their meditations. The *geonim* wrote that wherever the words 'I myself saw' occur, it was in a dream while on a voyage." Some regard these tales and *aggadot* as ethical and national allegories, while others see them as intimations and cryptic sayings (see Maharsha (Samuel Eliezer b. Judah *Edels), ad loc.).

BIBLIOGRAPHY: Hyman, Toledot, 1076–78; Bacher, Bab Amor, 87–93; idem, *Ergaenzungen und Berichtigungen…* (1913), 10; Bacher, Trad, 699, s.v.

[Abraham Arzi]

RABBAH BAR ḤANA (TJ, **Abba bar Hana**, e.g., in BM 5:5; early third century), Babylonian *amora*. In Babylon Rabbah studied under his uncle, Ḥiyya (MK 16b), whom he subsequently accompanied to Ereẓ Israel (MK 21a). Before they left to return to Babylon, Ḥiyya asked the *nasi* to give Rabbah permission to decide matters of ritual law, monetary cases, and defects in a firstborn animal which could render its slaughter permissible. Although such permission was rarely granted, the *nasi* acceded to the request (Sanh. 5a). Rabbah's closest colleague was Rav (TJ, BM 5:7, 10c), in whose company he is found both in Ereẓ Israel and in Babylon (MK 21a; Ḥul. 44b), with whom he held halakhic discussions (Ḥul. 8b), and in whose name he transmitted teachings (Shab. 50a; Nid. 47a). It is related that when Rabbah was once in mourning and thought that he ought not to give his regular lecture, Rav said, "We have learned, 'if the public have need of him, he does not refrain'" (MK 21a). Little is known of Rabbah's personal life, other than that he traded in wine (BM 83a, see Dik. Sof. *ibid.*) and that his wife died before him (BB 52a). His only known pupil was Hananel (MK 19a). Rabbah b. Ḥana is frequently confused with *Rabbah b. Bar Ḥana who, some believe, was his son. They can be distinguished only by context and chronology.

BIBLIOGRAPHY: Hyman, Toledot.

RABBAH BAR HUNA (in TJ, **Abba bar Huna** or **Bar bar Huna**; d. 322 C.E.), Babylonian *amora*. Rabba was a disciple of both Samuel (Er. 49a), and Rav (BB 136b), in whose names he transmitted sayings and decisions (Ber. 25a; Shab. 97a). His main teacher, however, was his father, Huna (Me'il. 15b), the head of the academy at Sura (cf. Git. 35a). His father urged him to attend Ḥisda's lectures diligently. Initially, however, Rabbah found some of the matters discussed (such as personal hygiene) alien to his earnest nature (Shab. 82a). Only in later life did he develop a close association with Ḥisda, and served with him as a judge (Shab. 10a). Indeed, his eventual respect for Ḥisda was such that he accepted his advice not to introduce the Decalogue in the statutory daily prayers (Ber. 12a; see Dik. Sof. thereto). He publicly acknowledged Ḥisda's correction of another of his decisions, instructing his *amora* to deliver a discourse on the theme that "no one can fully understand the words of the Torah until he has been mistaken in their interpretation" (Git. 43a). The two are also known to have studied *aggadah* together (Pes. 110a; 117a; Sot. 39a).

After Ḥisda's death Rabbah was appointed head of the academy of Sura (*Iggeret Sherira Gaon*, p. 82). Rabbah was particularly friendly with the exilarch, frequenting his home (Shab. 157b, Suk. 10b, etc.), and the exilarch used to address halakhic queries to him (Shab. 115b). Nevertheless, Rabbah insisted on his complete independence of him, and in a dispute with the members of the exilarch's household, he emphasized that he had received authority to act as judge from his father and not from the exilarch, and was therefore not bound by their views (Sanh. 5a). Rabbah was distinguished by his piety (Shab. 31a–b), and by his modesty which his colleague Rava once prayed that he might emulate (MK 28a). Among his maxims and sayings are many which stress this virtue: "An insolent person is considered a transgressor" (Ta'an. 7b). He also taught that he who possesses knowledge of the Torah but is without the fear of God is like a steward who, although in possession of the inner keys of the treasure house, is unable to gain access to it, because he does not possess the outer keys (Shab. 31a–b). He also said: "When a man loses his temper, even the Divine Presence is unimportant in his eyes" (Ned. 22b). Rabbah died in Babylon, but his remains were taken to Ereẓ Israel, where funeral orations were delivered for him (MK 25b).

BIBLIOGRAPHY: Bacher, Bab Amor, 62f.; Hyman, Toledot, 1071–74.

RABBAH BAR NAḤAMANI (c. 270–330; d. 321/22 according to *Iggeret R. Sherira Ga'on*, ed. by B.M. Lewin (1921), 87; according to Hyman c. 260–340), Babylonian *amora*. Rabbah was the scion of a priestly family, which traced its lineage to the high priest Eli (RH 18a). He studied under *Huna at Sura, and under *Judah b. Ezekiel at Pumbedita (Er. 17a). To such an extent did Huna respect him that he seldom decided a question of importance without consulting him (Git. 27a; BM 18b; BB 172b, et al.). On one occasion his contemporaries in Ereẓ Israel suggested that he join them and study under *Johanan, maintaining that he would learn more with a guide than by studying by himself (Ket. 111a). From *Nedarim* 59a, it would appear that he took their advice, although Bacher maintains that he never left Babylonia. He certainly spent most of his life in Babylonia, where his most constant colleague was Joseph (BB 114a). Rabbah's main interest was in the *halakhah*, and he was renowned for his interpretation of the Mishnah and for his elucidation and clarification of the apparent contradictions contained in various texts. He was particularly versed in the regulations concerning ritual purity, in which he was regarded as an authority (BM 86a). Whereas Joseph's encyclopedic knowledge of traditions earned him the title "Sinai," Rabbah was known as *oker harim* ("uprooter of mountains"), for his exceptionally skillful dialectic ability (Ber. 64a.). Only ten aggadic sayings are quoted in his name (e.g., Shab. 64a; Pes. 68b; Meg. 15b; et al.), and there is no foundation for the statement of Abraham ibn Daud in the *Sefer ha-Kabbalah* that he was the author of such aggadic compilations as *Genesis Rabbah*.

Judah's death left the post of the head of the academy of Pumbedita vacant. Joseph declined the office, whereupon Rabbah was elected. He held the post for 22 years, until his death (Ber. 64a; *Iggeret R. Sherira Ga'on*, 85–86), and under his leadership the academy achieved its greatest renown. The number of regular students rose to 400 (Ket. 106a), and during the **kallah* months of Adar and Elul, the audiences numbered 12,000 (BM 86a). Rabbah's own contribution as a teacher was significant. He used to put his audience in a receptive mood by beginning his lectures with witty aphorisms and interesting anecdotes (Shab. 30b), and he would frequently invite comment on paradoxical *halakhot* and deliberately captious decisions (Ber. 33b). However, although highly esteemed by scholars, he was intensely disliked by the members of the Pumbedita community, whose behavior he frequently and severely denounced (Shab. 153a and Rashi *ibid.*).

Little is known of his private life other than that he was poor. The Talmud explicitly contrasts his poverty with Ḥisda's comfortable economic position (MK 28a). Rabbah died in tragic circumstances. Charged with aiding his large audiences to avoid paying poll tax during the *kallah* months, Rabbah was forced to flee the bailiffs who had been sent to seize him. He wandered about in the vicinity of Pumbedita, and it was there, in a thicket, that his body was ultimately found (BM 86a; *Iggeret R. Sherira Ga'on* 78–87). According to the *aggadah*, it was on that day that the Heavenly Academy was debating whether, if the bright spot appeared after the white hair (cf. Lev. 13:1–3), the leper was clean or unclean. The Almighty maintained that he was clean, the Heavenly Academy that he was unclean. Rabbah was asked for his opinion, and, as he called out "Clean, clean," he expired. At that moment, a heavenly voice was heard to declare, "Happy art thou, O Rabbah b. Naḥamani, whose body is pure, and whose soul has departed in purity" (BM 86a). According to *Rosh Ha-Shanah* 18a (MK 28a) he was only 40 years old at his death. However, this figure is unacceptable on chronological grounds and has generally been emended to 60. He was survived by a son also called Rabbah (Shab. 123a). *Abbaye, who grew up in his house (Ber. 48a), was his nephew and pupil.

BIBLIOGRAPHY: Halevy, Dorot, 2 (1923), 435–40; Hyman, Toledot.

RABBAH BEN AVUHA, Babylonian *amora* of the second half of the third century C.E. Rabbah's first teacher was Rav, in whose name he transmitted many sayings (Shab. 129b; Er. 85a). After the latter's death, he continued his studies at Samuel's academy at Nehardea. When Nehardea was destroyed in 259 by the Palmyrenes, he moved to Maḥoza, where he was appointed a judge (Yev. 115b) and head of the academy (Shab. 59b). According to Sherira Gaon he was of the family of the exilarch, and Sherira himself claimed to be a descendant of his (*Iggeret R. Sherira Ga'on*, ed. by B.M. Lewin (1921), 82). The Talmud (Ber. 21a; BM 91b) records halakhic decisions in his name. He, however, stated that his knowledge extended only to four orders of the Mishnah (according to Rashi, *Mo'ed, Nashim, Nezikin*, and *Kodashim*; not *Zera'im* and *Tohorot*; but according to *tosafot*, the reference is to those four orders in the Tosefta; BM 114b). A legendary account is given of the manner in which Rabbah was miraculously relieved of his poverty. He was privileged to meet the prophet Elijah, and to discuss *halakhah* with him. Elijah gave him some leaves from paradise which, although discarded by Rabbah (in order not to consume his portion in the world to come), left such a pleasant fragrance on his robe, that he sold it for 12,000 denarii (BM 114a–b).

He had a son named R. Kamma (Er. 3a); however his main pupil and (probably) his son-in-law was R. Naḥman (b. Jacob), who transmits many of his sayings (Yev. 80b). Among his teachings were that the commandment to love one's neighbor as oneself (Lev. 19:18) applies even in the execution of a criminal, and is fulfilled by granting him as easy a death as possible (Ket. 37b).

BIBLIOGRAPHY: Hyman, Toledot, 1070–71.

RABBAH BEN SHILAH (fl. late third early fourth century C.E.), Babylonian *amora*. His teacher was Ḥisda (Shab. 81a). Because of his aversion to bribery, Rabbah declared a judge unfit to try a case involving neighbors from whom he had borrowed anything (Ket. 105b). He was quick to defend others. According to an *aggadah*, Elijah appeared to Rabbah on one occasion, and told him that God mentions *halakhot* in the name of the sages but not in that of R. Meir, because he had been taught by *Elisha b. Avuyah who had denied the existence of God. Rabbah said to Elijah: "Meir found a pomegranate, ate the fruit, and threw away the peel," i.e., he had extracted only what was good from Elisha's teachings, whereupon Elijah replied that henceforward God would mention Meir's name (Ḥag. 15b).

BIBLIOGRAPHY: Hyman, Toledot, 1083–84; Bacher, Bab Amor, 140–1.

[Moshe Beer]

RABBAH TOSFA'AH (middle of the fifth century), Babylonian *amora*. He was a pupil of *Ravina (I) (Suk. 32a; BK 119a), and a colleague of the latter's nephew, *Ravina (II) (Yev. 75b; MK 4a). He succeeded Mar Bar Rav Ashi as head of the Sura Academy, a position he held for six years until his death in 474 (Ibn Daud, *Book of Tradition*, 36). Although among the last of the *amoraim*, he still gave original rulings. He declared a child legitimate although born to a woman whose husband had gone overseas 12 months before the birth, assuming that a pregnancy may extend as long as that period (Yev. 80b; for another example see Ber. 50a). Some claim that his name, Tosfa'ah ("the amplifier"), reflects the activity of making additions of brief, explanatory remarks, through which he clarified talmudic themes and decided between the conflicting opinions of earlier *amoraim* (Halevy, Dorot, 3 (1923), 19; but see Ḥ. Albeck, in: *Sinai, Sefer Yovel* (1958), 72). He is in fact mentioned by name in the Talmud only in nine places.

BIBLIOGRAPHY: Hyman, Toledot, 1086f.; Ḥ. Albeck, *Mavo la-Talmudim* (1969), 448.

[Aaron Rothkoff]

RABBANITES, name and definition current from approximately the tenth century applied to Jews accepting the Oral Law (*Torah she-be-al peh*) as binding and normative in the same degree as Scripture (*Torah she-bi-khetav*). As with many party definitions the term is used with pride by the Rabbanites themselves and with derision and contempt by their opponents the *Karaites.

RABBATH-AMMON (**Rabbah**; Heb. רַבַּת בְּנֵי עַמּוֹן, רַבָּה), the capital of the Ammonites, present-day Amman, capital of the Hashemite Kingdom of *Jordan. The earliest settlement, dating from the Chalcolithic period until the end of the early Bronze Age (c. 2200 B.C.E.), was centered on a sacred rock on the acropolis. After a gap, occupation was resumed with the establishment of the Ammonite kingdom. Its strong fortifications prevented its capture by the Israelites (Josh. 13:25). The bedstead of the giant *Og, king of Bashan, in Rabbath-Ammon is mentioned in the Bible (Deut. 3:11). In the time of David, Joab captured the "royal city" and the "city of waters" (probably the acropolis and the water installations in the valley below), but he postponed conquest of the entire city until David's arrival (II Sam. 11–12; cf. I Chron. 20:1). Shobi, the son of Nahash (an Ammonite king) of Rabbath-Ammon, succored David when he fled before Absalom (II Sam. 17:27–29). Soon after David's death, however, the city again became the capital of an independent kingdom, and it is denounced as such by the prophets Amos (1:14), Jeremiah (49:2–3), and Ezekiel (21:25; 25:5). Remains of tombs and temples containing figurines and seals inscribed in Ammonite have been found there. The main temple was erected over the "sacred" rock on the acropolis.

In the Hellenistic period, Rabbath-Ammon was again a flourishing city and was known as Philadelphia in honor of Ptolemy II and his wife Arsinoe. It was besieged and taken by Antiochus III in 218 B.C.E. by a stratagem similar to that used earlier by *Joab (see I Chron. 19:10ff.). The city successfully resisted Alexander Yannai under its ruler Zeno Cotylas. It became a city of the *Decapolis in Roman times and later developed into a great and prosperous center of the caravan trade in Provincia Arabia. It was mentioned by Eusebius (*Onom.* 146). It was captured by the Arabs in 635 and became the capital of the Belqa' district. A Jewish community existed there in the 11th–12th centuries, as is known from the Scroll of *Abiathar. In the time of the Crusaders, Rabbath-Ammon, then known as Ahamant, was temporarily in the possession of the prince of Transjordan. It was subsequently abandoned until resettled by Circassians in 1878, who were relocated there by the Ottoman Turks. In 1921 it became the capital of the emirate of Transjordan and later of the Hashemite Kingdom of Jordan. Its population, greatly increased by Palestinian refugees, numbered approximately 200,000 in 1970. By 2006 its population was over 1.7 million.

The site was surveyed and photographed by a British team led by C. Warren in 1867 for the Palestine Exploration Fund. Since then Amman was frequently visited by scholars and explorers, notably by H.C. Butler in 1921. In 1927 an Italian expedition directed by G. Guidi worked at the site; the excavations continued in 1929–33 under the direction of R. Bartoccini. From 1945 G.L. Harding investigated Amman on behalf of the Department of Antiquities, and in 1966 J.B. Hennessy excavated the Late Bronze Age temple on behalf of the British School of Archaeology in Jerusalem. Numerous excavations have taken place in recent years in Amman, particularly in the area of the acropolis/citadel (Jebel Qal'a).

BIBLIOGRAPHY: H.C. Butler, *Architecture* (1909), 34ff.; Avi-Yonah, Geog, index; L. Harding, in: QDAP, 11 (1945), 67ff.; 14 (1950), 44ff.; idem, in: ADAJ, 3 (1956), 80; Maayah, *ibid.*, 4–5 (1960), 114–5; Ward, *ibid.*, 8–9 (1964), 47ff. **ADD. BIBLIOGRAPHY:** G.M. Landes, "The Material Civilization of the Ammonites," in: *Biblical Archaeologist*, 24 (1961), 65–86; A. Almagro and E. Olavarri, "A New Umayyad Palace at the Citadel of Amman," in: A. Hadidi (ed.), *Studies in the History and Archaeology of Jordan* 1 (1982), 305–21; L.G. Herr, *The Amman Airport Excavations, 1976*. ASOR Annual 48 (1983); A. Northedge, *Studies on Roman and Islamic Amman* (1992); J.B. Humbert and F. Zayadine, "Trois campagnes de fouilles à Ammân (1988–1991)," in: *Revue Biblique*, 99 (1992), 214–60; G.S.P. Grenville, R.L. Chapman and J.E. Taylor, *Palestine in the Fourth Century. The Onomasticon by Eusebius of Caesarea* (2003), 81.

[Michael Avi-Yonah / Shimon Gibson (2nd ed.)]

RABBI, RABBINATE. The title rabbi is derived from the noun *rav*, which in biblical Hebrew means "great" and does not occur in the Bible; in its later sense in mishnaic Hebrew, however, the word *rav* means a master as opposed to a slave (e.g., "does a slave rebel against his *rav*" – Ber. 10a; "It is like a slave who filled a cup for his *rav* and he poured the water over his face" – Suk. 2:9). It was only during the tannaitic period, in the generation after Hillel, that it was employed as a title for the sages. The passage in the New Testament (Matt. 23:7) in which the Scribes and Pharisees are criticized because they "love… to be called of men, Rabbi, Rabbi" probably reflects the fact of its recent introduction. The word "rabbi" therefore means literally "my master," although the Sephardim point it and pronounce it *ribbi*, the suffix therefore not being a pronominal one. In any case it lost its significance, and rabbi became simply the title accorded to a sage. Since the title was accorded only to those who had been properly ordained, and such ordination was not granted in talmudic times outside Ereẓ Israel (see *Semikhah*), it was not borne by the Babylonian sages (the *amoraim*) who adopted, or were granted, the alternative title of *rav*. In the Talmud, therefore, the title rabbi refers either to a *tanna* or to a Palestinian *amora*, while *rav* refers to a Babylonian *amora*. The rabbi of the Talmud was therefore completely different from the present-day holder of the title. The talmudic rabbi was an interpreter and expounder of the Bible and the Oral Law, and almost invariably had an occupation whence he derived his livelihood. It was only in the Middle Ages that the rabbi became – in addition to, or instead of, the interpreter and decisor of the law – the teacher, preacher, and spiritual head of the Jewish congregation or community, and it is with this meaning of the word that this article deals. For the talmudic rabbi see Sages. In modern usage the word "rabbi" in Hebrew has sometimes become the equivalent of "mister." Thus every Jew called up to the reading of the Torah is invited to do so as "Rabbi So-and-So the son of Rabbi So-and-So," and for the rabbi as spiritual head the title *ha-rav* is employed.

[Louis Isaac Rabinowitz]

Middle Ages

In medieval times, the title *ha-rav* denoted great scholarly standing and social reputation unconnected with the hierarchical structure of the yeshivot and *geonim*. In this sense it appears, for example, in various letters of the 10th–12th centuries, and in the Chronicle of Ahimaaz is used to describe the mysterious Aaron, while the chronicler Abraham ibn Daud employs these terms and their derivatives to define the generations of scholars – *rabbanim* – after the death of Hai Gaon. Relatively early in these centuries, the term *rabbanim* (now translated into English as Rabbanites) came to designate the mainstream of Orthodoxy in Judaism, which based itself on the authority of the Talmud and the *geonim*, as against the minority of the Karaites. Centralistic tendencies in the leadership of the gaonate and exilarchs are revealed in the tendency for one of these institutions to appoint from above the scholar who led the local community and in the main carried out the functions of judge (*dayyan*), bringing with him as his letter of appointment a "writ of judgeship" (*pitka de-dayyanuta*). What is known of their actual functioning, however, shows both that such appointees were in reality much more than judges only and that in fact local opinion had a say in their appointment. By the end of the 10th and beginning of the 11th century there were more and more cases of open local election by the community of a spiritual and moral leader.

Through their social functions rabbi and rabbinate carried over into the Middle Ages a medley of concepts and attitudes, the active elements being scholarship, judgeship, social-spiritual leadership, and example. A certain measure of religious authority attached to the concept of rabbi and to his person, deriving from the authority invested in the geonic academies and the outlook of their scholars, and also from the distant memories of the supreme authority of the mishnaic rabbi ordained by *semikhah* – the ordination of ancient times. These titles and designations never carried with them priestly or semi-priestly authority or functions. Prayer and leading in prayer, blessing of the people, and officiating in marriage and burial ceremonies never became an integral part of the conception of rabbinical office until the beginning of the 19th century, with the Reform movement. Some rabbis led in prayer and blessed the people, but until modern times this was no more than a matter of personal inclination. The supervision of marriage, and even more so of divorce proceedings, became an integral part of the rabbinic office, both because the payment for performing such functions became part of the stipend of the local rabbi, and because legal acumen was required, especially in the case of divorce. It would seem that from its earliest days preaching to the people was an integral part of the rabbinic function, the rabbi being both the authoritative scholarly expositor of law and morals, and the moral and spiritual leader of the people. At certain times and in certain regions scholarly exposition was regarded as the main part of preaching, while in others moral exhortation was seen as its main burden; both elements were always present in rabbinical preaching, though in varying proportions.

The weakening of centralistic institutions, as well as the continuing growth of Jewish communities in countries which had never known such leadership, increasingly augmented the importance of the local rabbi. Although the activities of many rabbis are known, in most cases neither income nor status are clearly apparent. Over the years the ideal has developed of the scholarly charisma of the rabbi asserting itself without recourse to official definitions. Ideally all rabbis are equal as officeholders; the only hierarchy ideally obtaining between them is that of personal intellectual and moral preeminence.

The office of rabbi was originally an honorary one on the principle that the Torah had to be taught free of charge. It was not until the 14th century that there is the first clear evidence of a rabbi receiving emoluments. When Simeon b. Zemah Duran fled from the anti-Jewish riots in Spain in 1391 and arrived in Algiers the local community wished to appoint him as rabbi. He pleaded inability to accept as he was penniless and had to earn a livelihood. In order to enable him to accept the position, a formula was worked out whereby instead of a salary for his services he was to receive *sekhar battalah*, i.e., compensation for loss of time due to his preoccupation with his rabbinic office. This remained the legal basis in Jewish law for a rabbi receiving a salary, even though in the modern period the rabbi's salary is generally regarded as in the category of a professional wage with contracts written between rabbis and their congregations.

In outward recognition of such preeminence, the various communities applied to a particular local rabbi for his personal responsa on different legal and theoretical matters. He would thus be given, de facto and personally, the authority vested in the *geonim* ex officio.

In both Ashkenazi and Sephardi centers rulers became aware relatively early of this new development in Jewish society. In the story of the Four Captives, Abraham ibn Daud describes the satisfaction of a local ruler in late tenth-century Muslim Spain, at having a scholarly Jewish authority in his country, independent of the *geonim* in Baghdad. The office of the *rab de la corte* in Castille and *Arraby moor* in Portugal, as well as appointments known from the 13th century of a Jewish *Hochmeister* for some regions of the German Empire (see, e.g., Meir Baruch of Rothenburg), and also similar appointments in France – all are related phenomena. They are manifestations both of the gradual institutionalization of the office of rabbi, and of the attempts by rulers and community leaders to structure a formal and fixed hierarchy out of fluid relationships based on scholarly and personal charisma. The responsa of the Sephardi Isaac b. Sheshet Perfet disclose a conflict surrounding the appointment to the office of rabbi of France in the 14th century, while other contemporary writings reveal the views of the Ashkenazi scholar Meir ha-Levi of Vienna on the nature of the rabbinate. All demand proven and attested knowledge, as well as integrity and excellence in character and conduct; and on these grounds candidates are approved and disqualified. The Ashkenazi scholar reveals a conception of a well-defined written diploma attesting to the knowledge and qualifications for a rabbi – the so-called *semikhah* diploma. For about a century – mainly in the 15th – Ashkenazi rabbis were titled *manhig* ("leader"), which shows their centrality in community life at that time. Sephardi society had its own ways of attesting these qualifications, without instituting such a diploma (see below). When Sephardim and Ashkenazim came in close contact after the expulsion from the Iberian Peninsula (1492–97), the institution of this diploma became a bone of contention, as is evidenced in the writings of Isaac Abrabanel. Ironically enough, the abortive attempt to resurrect the *semikhah*, made in 1538 by Jacob Berab and enthusiastically accepted by Joseph Caro, served to strengthen the Ashkenazi type of *semikhah* diploma and the medieval line of development of the office of rabbi, and also gave impetus to the development of the Shulḥan Arukh, the combined work of Joseph Caro and the Ashkenazi-Polish Moses Isserles (who was himself a royal appointee to the central rabbinate in Poland).

From the 14th century onward there emerged the concept of one rabbi for one locality – the *mara de-atra* ("the master of the locality"). Other scholars in his community were to submit to his authority, ex officio, a concept that took a long time to establish. In Poland-Lithuania of the 16th–17th centuries rabbinical office was linked to being a *rosh yeshivah*, thereby deriving much of its authority and prestige. In its main outline, though with various changes in details, this conception of the rabbi and his office remains to the present day that which in fact dominates the society and communities of *Mitnaggedim* wherever they are found, the religious establishment in the State of Israel, and communities of Hungarian and German Orthodoxy and Neo-Orthodoxy. In these circles the office and conception of the rabbi are those which have emerged from the Middle Ages: he is seen as scholar and teacher, judge and spiritual leader. His livelihood comes either from a fixed salary or from payments for functions performed, or from a combination of both. His rights and duties are often defined in a *ketav rabbanut* (letter of appointment to and acceptance of the rabbinic office, sometimes written as two separate documents), a custom deriving from the late Middle Ages. In the frame of this traditional rabbinate there have appeared in modern times centralistic trends, manifested, e.g., in the

British office of chief rabbi for the U.K. and the dominions and the Chief Rabbinate in Ereẓ Israel. On the other hand, in the huge concentrations of Jewish population in modern cities, in the U.S. in particular, the concept of the *mara de-atra* is on the point of vanishing and the rabbi there is mainly the rabbi of a synagogue congregation. In regions and communities where Ḥasidism prevails, the status and function of the rabbi as such have in many ways become subordinate to those of the *ẓaddik*.

The Reform movement, with its progressive rejection of traditionally received *halakhah*, has changed the very concept of rabbi. The Reform rabbi is judge no longer: he has become to a large degree, for the first time in the history of the rabbinate, a priest ordering the prayer service and leading it. In the U.S. in particular he is also becoming the social and even the socialite director of his synagogue congregation. The Conservative wing of Judaism, in particular in the U.S., is trying to combine both concepts of the rabbinate.

The Jewish Religious Leadership in the Muslim East

There is a scarcity of information concerning the religious leadership of the early Middle Ages in eastern lands. Extant fragments of records pertaining to such leadership date back only to the 12th century. Sources become more extensive beginning in the 16th century, after the expulsion of the Jews from Spain, and are found in the responsa of the eastern lands, especially from the Ottoman Empire. In this section the religious leadership will be discussed starting with the geonic era, although the title of "rabbi," in its usual sense of a scholar appointed over a community to decide and teach its religious regulations, was not used until the 12th century.

The *geonim* served as spiritual heads of the Babylonian or Palestinian communities, and in Babylonia they ruled alongside the exilarchs, who served as secular heads. The authority of the *geonim* extended over the borders of the Arabian caliphate due to their religious authority. Previously the exilarch had reserved the right to appoint judges, either alone or in consultation with the *gaon*. But during the decline of the exilarchate, the *geonim* appointed judges for most of Babylonia, granting them a "certificate of justiceship" (*pitka de-dayyanuta*).

In Ereẓ Israel the religious head of a community was known as a *ḥaver* (associated member of the Academy) and was ordained in the Palestinian academy. The *ḥaver* served as head of the community's rabbinical court once he had been empowered by the head of the academy. The Palestinian academies granted to ordained scholars the title of *ḥaver be-Sanhedrin ha-Gedolah* (member of the Great Sanhedrin); in Babylonia it was customary to call similar appointees *alluf*. At the same time the title of *rav* (rabbi) was common in Egypt, North Africa, and Spain.

The decline of the gaonate and the Palestinian Academy in the 11th century created some confusion regarding the rabbinate as a communal institution. There was no sufficient religious authority capable of continuing the traditional ordination (*semikhah*) or appointment of judges. Consequently, ordination was discontinued. In Spain, however, some religious heads of communities would grant their students a "writ of ordination" (*ketav masmikh*). Judah ben Barzillai al-Bargeloni declared in his *Sefer ha-Shetarot* that this writ was only reminiscent of the ancient ordination and that no actual *semikhah* could be given outside Ereẓ Israel. This type of document, he maintained, was awarded only for the purpose of encouraging students.

In the 1130s R. Joseph ibn Migash ordained Joseph *ben* Mamal by means of a *ketav minnui* (writ of appointment). Maimonides opposed the institution of the professional rabbi in the sense of a paid official; he preferred the ideal of the scholar who earns his living independently but serves as a communal teacher. Even in the geonic period in North Africa, there were scholars who received "appointments" to the rabbinate. R. Hushi'el b. Elhanan of Kairouan ordained his son Hananel and Nissim b. Jacob b. Nissim (Ibn Shahin). Abraham ibn Daud mentioned in his *Sefer ha-Kabbalah* that after the deaths of Hananel and Nissim b. Jacob the tradition was discontinued, although judges officiated in Mahdia and Qalat Hammad without ordination. In the geonic period the title of *ha-rav ha-rosh* (chief rabbi) was widespread in North Africa. It was awarded by the academy in Pumbedita to designate the head of a famous rabbinical court.

In Spain the rank of *dayyan* (judge) was higher than that of rabbi. Certain individuals were empowered to punish offenders and bore the right to judge alone. Important authorities, such as Maimonides and his father Maimon, were called *dayyan*. The position of *dayyan* was more highly regarded in Spain than in the eastern lands after the expulsion. In those countries the *hakham* ("scholar") gained prominence, although the *dayyan* reserved the right to appoint a *hakham* or to empower even ordinary individuals with the right to judge. Two examples are known of appointment of rabbis by the government in the 14th and 15th centuries: Joseph Sasportas who was invested with judicial powers in the kingdom of Tlemcen and Isaac b. Sheshet Perfet, who was appointed by the government of Algiers. Isaac b. Sheshet Perfet (second half of the 14th century) wrote that in Germany, as well, it was customary to award a "writ of ordination," although in Spain it was considered sufficient if a teacher gave permission to his student to act as congregational religious leader.

The arrival of Spanish and Portuguese refugees in eastern lands aroused a serious conflict concerning "ordination" as practiced by the native Ashkenazim and Romaniots. An example of this was the controversy about Messer David ben Judah Leon, an "ordained" scholar and leader in Jewish education in Avilona (Valona), Albania, in the early 16th century. Rabbi David Cohen of Corfu supported Leon and stated that the method of ordination in use at least served to deter those not fit to decide the *halakhah*. David Cohen himself had received "ordination." Elijah Mizraḥi opposed the Sephardi refugees who claimed that no one could ordain once the Sanhedrin no longer existed. Nonetheless, the Ashkenazim did influence some Eastern Sephardi communities to practice "ordination."

However the significance of the ordination was completely different from the Ashkenazi ordination. The responsa cite several examples of writs of appointment containing the phrase "*yoreh, yoreh, yadin, yadin*" ("he will teach, he will judge"), sometimes adding "*yattir, yattir*" ("he will permit"); this was the text of ordination customary in the talmudic period. One factor which soothed the conflict was the public's reluctance to accept Ashkenazi ordination as an automatic qualification for communal leadership. The idea of reinstituting the traditional ordination as known in ancient times continued to excite scholars until the 16th century, when Jacob Berab relied on the words of Maimonides in his attempt to ordain certain scholars. This act aroused negative reactions and a fresh conflict continued for two generations.

When the Spanish and Portuguese refugees reached the Ottoman Empire, they organized communities according to their origins, each preserving its own traditions. Due to the absence of ordination, the spiritual leader in these communities was mainly called *ḥakham* or *marbiẓ Torah* ("teacher of the Torah"). Other titles in use were *dayyan, ḥaver beit ha-din, kaḥin ve-rosh, moreh ẓedek*, and *moreh hora'ah*; these titles were not limited to congregational leaders in the strict sense. In *Erez Israel*, Egypt, and Syria, however, the title *marbiẓ Torah* was replaced by *ḥakham* and in North Africa by *moreh ẓedek*. A rabbi in charge of all or most congregations in a city was called *ha-rav ha-kolel* ("the 'supreme' rabbi").

The *marbiẓ Torah* or *ḥakham* was the highest religious authority in his district. To qualify for his office he had to be expert in all fields of *halakhah*. He preached publicly on Sabbaths and holidays. Frequently he acted as chief controller over foundations and bequests and organized the redemption of hostages. In small communities he often served as a scribe or notary. The *marbiẓ Torah* judged in matters of marriage, divorce, *ḥaliẓah*, and monetary disputes generally alone but sometimes joined by two laymen to strengthen the verdict as having been passed in a court of three. Claims between people of different communities were judged by the *marbiẓ Torah* of the defendant's community. He was also responsible for judging in matters of ritual fitness and maintaining standards of morality in the city. Generally, his office was not inherited.

The *marbiẓ Torah* was usually treated with respect and admiration. He was paid an ample wage and honored with set marks of etiquette; the congregation stood when he entered and allowed him to pass first through the synagogue or street. He occupied a fixed seat in the synagogue and when he died he was buried with special marks of honor. Certain congregations purposely left the late leader's office vacant for a considerable period to show deference to their loss.

On the other hand there is record of conflicts between the *marbiẓ Torah* and members of his congregation. Sometimes his knowledge of *halakhah* was questioned or sometimes competition between two scholars for the same office would cause conflicts or a split in the community; many *marbiẓei Torah* are known to have been dismissed from their positions. An *ḥakham* who was disregarded or dishonored could excommunicate his opponents, and sometimes members of his congregation took measures to curb his powers of excommunication if used too freely.

From the late 15th century the Eastern communities felt the need for a central rabbinate that would assume the overall religious and administrative leadership that lay beyond the province of the local *marbiẓei Torah*. In the late 15th and early 16th centuries this office had already been filled by the two chief rabbis of the Romaniots, Moses Capsali and Elijah Mizraḥi, both in Constantinople, who were called *rav kolel, ha-rav ha-manhig* ("leading rabbi"), or *ha-rav ha-gadol* ("grand rabbi"). They were appointed by the government and given a permit known as the *hurman* to collect Jewish taxes. For the privilege of maintaining this office, the community had to pay a special tax, known as *rav aqchesi* ("white (i.e., silver) coin for the permit to have a rabbi"). This tax had to be paid even in the 17th century long after the office of chief rabbi had been discontinued. After the death of Elijah Mizraḥi, there was no longer any one figure who filled this position; rabbinical councils, however, frequently met in various cities on important matters. At this time there was a growing feeling among the *Sephardim* to grant high office to great rabbis of the generation. Samuel de Medina was recognized as chief rabbi in Salonika, and Jacob Berab filled the same office in Safed. In almost every large community there was a *rav kolel* who was not appointed by the government but by the Jews themselves. The *rav kolel* performed all tasks of the *marbiẓ Torah* and was also head of the rabbinical court or of a yeshivah. Often he was called *reish mata* (Aramaic: "head of the city"). In Izmir (Smyrna) it was customary for two chief rabbis to serve simultaneously, one in charge of civil law, the other in charge of ritual; both were called *ha-rav ha-gadol*. Their subordinate rabbis were called *morei ẓedek*. In this city there was a time when four chief rabbis ruled simultaneously. The *ḥakhamim* devoted all their time to the study of Torah and as such were exempt from taxes; an ordinance which fixed this exemption was drafted in Jerusalem in the early 16th century. The exemption applied to any *ḥakham rashum* ("recorded rabbi") who served as *marbiẓ Torah* or filled a spiritual position.

In other eastern countries, additional titles were awarded attesting the outstanding scholarship or eminence of the leader. The names *navon* ("understanding") or *maskil* ("wise, erudite") were used generally for young scholars who had acquired a fair knowledge of *halakhah*. The term *ḥakham vatik* ("senior" or "conscientious scholar"), despite its literal meaning, was also used for younger leaders. The name *he-ḥakham ha-shalem* was used to distinguish well-known important rabbis, *marbiẓei Torah*, heads of academies, and rabbinical courts.

Beginning in 1836 the Ottoman regime established the office of *ḥakham bashi* (head of the rabbis) in Constantinople. The incumbent had to be a citizen of the empire. Eventually similar offices were established in the capitals of big provinces. The exact duties and privileges of the *ḥakham bashi* were fixed in 1864. The *ḥakham bashi* of Constantinople exercised authority over all other rabbis in the empire (including the *rishon le-Zion* in Ereẓ Israel). In Egypt the *ḥakham bashi* was the only authority to decide ritual matters and was accompanied by a judge who had the right to sit alone. The Jewish community in Ereẓ Israel appointed a chief rabbi known as the *rishon le-Zion* ("first of Zion"). Although this title existed from the 17th century, it was not officially recognized until 1842, when the incumbent *rishon le-Zion* was named *ḥakham bashi* of Ereẓ Israel. In 1874 a *ḥakham bashi* was appointed in Tripoli (North Africa) and soon the title became so popular that almost every North African community had its *ḥakham bashi*.

There were also chief rabbis who were heads of rabbinical courts in Tunis, Djerba, in Algeria and Morocco.

In smaller cities in Morocco, which did not possess rabbinical courts, a *rabbin délégué* was appointed who acted as a one-man court and a community representative before the government. In Morocco there were some families who reserved the dynastic right (*serarah*) to serve as rabbis and judges. No parallel custom is found in any other land. Soleiman Kareh was appointed in 1872 *ḥakham bashi* of Yemen by the Turkish regime. In that country the *ḥakham bashi* was the highest legal and religious authority. After Kareh the position of *ḥakham bashi* was held intermittently and for short durations. In each village and town in Yemen, the *mori* served as rabbi, judge, and teacher. The Yemenite rabbis earned their livings mainly as slaughterers, goldsmiths, and teachers.

[Leah Bornstein-Makovetsky]

Modern Period

Since the emancipation era, the functions of the rabbi, particularly in Western countries, have undergone a radical change to which various factors contributed. In the first place, the governments of the various countries abolished the right of jurisdiction previously granted to the Jews in civil law, in consequence of which the function of the rabbi as judge in civil litigation and the need to study *Ḥoshen Mishpat* (the Jewish civil code) for practical purposes no longer existed. Moreover, even matters of ritual and matrimonial law which remained within the sphere of Jewish jurisdiction were dealt with, in these countries, not by the individual rabbi, but by a central *bet din*, these functions being fulfilled by the *dayyan*. In the second place, with the entry of the Jews into general life the need became increasingly felt for the rabbis to be equipped with a wider knowledge than was regarded as necessary for the medieval rabbi in the Jewish community, in both Jewish spheres – Jewish history, literature, homiletics, and *Juedische Wissenschaft* generally – and in purely secular branches. This need, felt internally, was powerfully reinforced when the governments of various countries, commencing with Emperor Franz Joseph in Austria in 1848 and extending to other countries, demanded a certain standard of general education as a condition of recognizing rabbis. When the existing yeshivot refused to countenance any change in their traditional syllabus, which was almost wholly confined to Talmud and the codes, the need was met by the establishment of rabbinical seminaries which provided a comprehensive curriculum of Jewish studies (with a lessened stress on Talmud and codes), which was generally supplemented by a university education. The modern rabbi, whether Orthodox, Conservative, or Reform, was largely the product of these institutions. A major transformation in the makeup of the rabbinate in liberal denominations (Reform, Conservative, and Reconstructionist) from the 1970s into the 21st century has been the ordination of women.

FUNCTIONS OF THE RABBI. The function of the modern rabbi varied somewhat in the various countries according to local conditions. Thus in England he approximated until recently more to the cantor than in any other country. His official title in the United Synagogue was "minister-preacher," while his colleague was the "minister-reader," both sharing the conduct of the weekly and Sabbath services and the reading of the Torah. In England, France, and Germany the wearing of canonicals was obligatory, while in France the organizational aspects of the rabbinate was largely determined by the Consistory. Nevertheless there are general lines of similarity which applied equally to all. Preaching, of course in the vernacular, occupied a place of prime importance, out of all proportion to the old-fashioned rabbi who generally limited his public discourses to two halakhic-aggadic addresses per year (see Preaching). The modern rabbi was expected to devote much of his time to pastoral work, establishing a personal bond between himself and his congregants, visiting the sick, officiating at benei mitzvahs, marriages, funerals, and houses of mourning as a matter of course. He was expected to take part in all social, educational, and philanthropic activities of the congregation. Above all he was looked to as the spokesman of the Jewish community to the larger community, though the extent of this participation varied in different countries, being most extensive in the United States. The influence of the larger denominations, particularly the Protestant Church, was marked. Until recent times in England it was de rigueur for the rabbi to wear a clerical collar, while the garb of the French rabbi in synagogue was identical with that of the Protestant pastor. In England Chief Rabbis Adler and Hertz donned the gaiters and the silk hat with cockade of the Anglican bishop at official functions. Recent years have witnessed a departure from those models to a considerable extent, and a closer proximation to those of the old school, partly under the influence of the yeshivot and the revival of Orthodoxy.

In England particularly, as in the countries which constituted the British Empire for which it served as a model, it was not even regarded as essential that the rabbi should acquire the rabbinical diploma (it was actually forbidden by Chief Rabbi Herman Adler, who essayed to establish the principle that he was the only rabbi for the British Empire) and the title "reverend" was coined for them. This situation changed considerably, but a student of Jews College still graduates and is qualified to accept a position on obtaining the minister's diploma, which is less than the rabbinical diploma and carries with it the title "reverend." In all other countries, without exception, and among Reform and Conservative, as well as Orthodox, the only title borne by the spiritual leader is rabbi, apart from the *Sephardi* congregations where he is called Haham (*ḥakham*). In England, France, and South Africa, in which the various congregations are united in one roof organization, the rabbi tended more and more to become a local congregational functionary, the chief rabbi alone representing the community as a whole both in religious matters and vis-à-vis the non-Jewish world. In the United States (see below) and Canada, where the tendency is for each congregation to be an independent unit, his sphere of activities was much wider. In the United States, Canada, and England, and in other countries where yeshivah education developed, a return to the old conception of the classic Eastern European rabbi in appearance, outlook, and function is apparent within limited pockets of strict Orthodox Judaism.

Jacqueline Tabick, the first female rabbi in the United Kingdom, was ordained in 1975 by Leo Baeck College, an institution under the joint sponsorship of the Reform Synagogues of Great Britain and the Union of Liberal and Progressive Synagogues.

[Louis Isaac Rabinowitz]

Germany

Some special features characterized the German rabbinate until the *Holocaust*. In the debates on emancipation the question of the training and functions of the rabbis played an important part. In Prussia, which had the largest number of Jews, successive legislation beginning with the "Religionsedikt" of 1788 to the community law of 1847, had more or less ignored the position of the rabbi, leaving it to the communities whether to appoint rabbis at all, and if they did, they were shorn of their traditional authority, becoming mere functionaries, whose opinion in religious matters could be ignored by the lay leaders. Opinions given by prominent Jews such as Gumpert, Muhr, Rubo, and even Zunz had declared the rabbinical office to be altogether dispensable; rabbis were considered mere "Kauscherwaechters" (Kashrut Supervisors) and protests to the contrary remained ineffective. Their rabbinical jurisdiction had been abolished in 1811 (in Altona-Schleswig-Holstein as late as 1863) and when the last chief rabbi of Berlin, Hirschel Lewin, appointed under the "General Juden Reglement" of 1750, died in 1800, his position was not filled again. Yet rabbis of the old school were in positions of religious authority to the middle of the century, such as Akiva Eger (d. 1837) and his son Solomon (d. 1852) in Posen. The Law of 1847 required government confirmation of rabbinical appointments, though they were not considered public functionaries. The constitution of the Bismarckian Reich gave rabbis equal status with Christian clergy in some respects. States like Hanover, Electoral Hesse, and Schleswig-Holstein, which were later incorporated in Prussia, retained their previously adopted Jewish community organization in which rabbis had the official status of Landrabbiner, Provinzialrabbiner, etc. Even where rabbis possessed no legal status, they were in fact recognized as the representatives and spokesmen of the Jewish faith and community, sat on the advisory educational boards, were given chaplaincy commissions, etc. In most other German states the new laws regulating the life of Jewish communities (Bavaria, 1813; Wurtemberg, 1828; Baden, 1809; grand-duchy of Hesse, 1841) recognized the official position of rabbis providing for offices of Landrabbiner, Konferenzrabbiner, Bezirksrabbiner or just local rabbis, regulating their qualifications, duties, emoluments, garb, etc. In several of these states they had to face examinations before specially appointed government boards. The new type of rabbi who emerged spoke High German and possessed besides rabbinical training a higher and often university education. This was not limited to Liberal and Reform rabbis; it applied to the Orthodox rabbinate as well as exemplified by such men as J. Ettlinger, I. Bernays, M. Sachs, S.R. Hirsch, and A. Hildesheimer. The transition from the new to the old was not without struggle as shown by the controversy about A. Geiger's appointment in Breslau. The emerging Wissenschaft des Judentums was both creative of and created by this modern type of rabbi. At first, at least, their individual and collective authority within the community was paramount, while rabbinical conferences and synods were shaping a new non-Orthodox Judaism. Rabbinical seminaries of the three main religious trends (Breslau, Hildesheimer, and Hochschule) trained these modem rabbis. Their students could not always be clearly classified. Orthodox ones could be found at Breslau and the Hochschule, while some non-Orthodox rabbis qualified at the Hildesheimer Seminary. A large part of the future rabbis hailed from Germany's eastern provinces or from East European countries where they had received the traditional yeshivah training. Toward the end of the 19th century and after World War I new yeshivot (the last of the old yeshivot was closed in 1865) were established in Germany itself, while some rabbinical students enrolled in eastern yeshivot. This raised both the qualifications and standing of the Orthodox rabbinate.

With this went a general lowering of their status and authority, with the lay leadership, qualified by mere professional or financial success, in the ascendancy. Most rabbis were no longer given a "call," but had to apply for advertised positions. They were now officials rather than leaders, without a vote and even a voice on their communities' administration. Even by 1922 there was only one congregation in Germany on whose board the rabbi had a seat and later became its chairman. Vigorous protests from within the rabbinate were of no avail. Only the Nazi persecutions brought about some belated change.

The rabbi usually taught at the community's religious school as well as to Jewish pupils in the state high schools. Adult education emerged gradually after World War I and became an important function in the Nazi period. Public relations with the non-Jewish community, such as lecturing, participation in public functions and social and educational work in general, occupied a considerable part of the rabbi's time. His relations to his congregation were regulated by private contract; his salary was usually adequate for maintaining a middle-class standard of living, incidental fees being paid into the community's funds.

In the larger communities with several synagogues a division developed between the community rabbi and the synagogue rabbi. In many parts of Germany, where rural, rabbi-less communities survived in great number, district rabbis, with their seat in state or provincial capitals, were in charge of their religious needs. Even after 1918, when the separation of church and state had led to the abolition of the 19th-century laws, the titles of Oberrabiner, Landesrabbiner, or Provinzialrabbiner survived as a historical relic, without much significance, unless it meant the care of rural communities. There was at no time a German chief rabbi. When, under the Nazis, Leo Baeck became president of the Reichsvertretung der deutschen Juden, his being a (liberal) rabbi was incidental.

Regina *Jonas, the first woman to receive rabbinic ordination, was a 1930 graduate of the Hochschule fuer die Wisenschaft des Judentums (College of Jewish Studies) in Berlin. She received private ordination in 1935 from Max Dienemann, one of the rabbinic leaders of German Liberal Judaism.

From the Franco-Prussian War of 1870 until World War I, many German rabbis served as army chaplains. The needs of German Jewry under the Nazi regime produced the office of Youth Rabbi; the social – and educational – responsibilities of the rabbi in this tragic period increased manifold.

In 1884 German rabbis united in the "Verband der Rabbiner Deutschlands," which in 1896 became the "Allgemeiner Rabbinerverband in Deutschland," though some Orthodox rabbis refused to join. The Orthodox, on their side, established in 1897 their own "Vereinigung traditionell-gesetzestreuer Rabbiner" while an "Orthodoxer Rabbinerverband" excluded those rabbis who served in "mixed" Reform-Orthodox communities. Another source of controversy was emerging Zionism; the great majority of German Jews were anti-Zionist and their assimilated leaders even more so; a great number of rabbis had signed the famous protest against the holding of the First Zionist Congress (see Protestrabbiner). This led to a head-on conflict with some of the younger rabbis who had embraced Zionism, as in the case of Emil Bernard Cohn, who was dismissed from his post by the Berlin Jewish community board for propagating Zionism.

[Alexander Carlebach]

In the U.S.

The status and role of the contemporary rabbi in North America exhibit some unique features which can best be understood in the light of the historical development of the synagogue as the central institution in the Jewish community.

The North American cultural and social development accepted the concept of differences based on faith, but has resisted differences based on other criteria. A full treatment of this sociological phenomenon can be found in W. Herberg's *Protestant-Catholic-Jew* (1955). The Eastern European community, from which most North American Jews and their ancestors emigrated, was based on ethnic and other national minority differences. In the "melting pot" process, allowances were made for such concepts as Jewish nationality on the one hand, while on the other various ethnic minorities that make up the North American community (with the possible growing exception of the French-Canadian and the black-American separatists) assimilated to a cultural climate in which only differences of faith are recognized and where each community is given equal status and dignity unrelated to the number of its adherents.

Insofar as earlier immigrant generations attended churches and synagogues, they probably preferred those where the language and customs of their countries of origin were used in worship and pulpit. Norwegian Lutherans attended churches where Norwegian was used, Italian Catholics where Italian was used. Their children and grandchildren however chose to affiliate with a place of worship which was American in loyalty and composition. The place of worship became a center around which gravitated social and cultural activities which previously had been the functions of societies and clubs of a strong ethnic flavor. In the Jewish community particularly, many of the functions previously performed by Hebrew communal schools, Zionist youth movements, philanthropic activities, and social action committees, became increasingly centered in the synagogue which developed into the comprehensive Jewish Center. The latter often was the only functioning Jewish institution in the community with adequate building, constituency, and professional leadership. Besides being spiritual leader, interpreter of Jewish law, and preacher, the rabbi tended more and more to become the senior Jewish professional in the community. This was equally true of the rabbi of a Conservative, Orthodox, Reform, or unaffiliated congregation. He came to interpret the Jewish tradition not only to the members of his congregation, but also to their Christian neighbors. He had to assume responsibility for all aspects of Jewish education. National and international Jewish organizations looked to him for influence. During the first decades of this century, the Reform rabbi tended to represent the total Jewish community to its neighbors. This function later came to be performed by rabbis of all denominations. The field of counseling has become a part of the modern rabbi's schooling. In the U.S. both the Reform and Conservative rabbinical training schools include courses in pastoral psychiatry for their students. These institutions also maintain pastoral psychiatry centers for research, marriage counseling, etc.

In recent years, the modern rabbi has played an increasing role in the general field of human relations or civil rights, and organizations dealing with them as a general rule increasingly tend to have a rabbi either on their staff or as an elected president. For example, the American Jewish Congress has almost invariably elected a rabbi as president, after the election of Stephen Wise, its first rabbi president. One of the reasons is that when they participate in government or communal affairs, they often prefer that a rabbi represent them since their counterparts are likely to be Protestant or Catholic clergymen.

The modern rabbi tends to model himself after the paradigm (and often the founders) of his rabbinical seminary and professional associations, e.g., Sabato Morais and Isaac Meyer Wise, the first presidents of the Jewish Theological Seminary and the Hebrew Union College respectively, who took forthright, if different, positions on the merits of the American Civil War. Alumni of all the American Jewish seminaries played central roles as social activists, Zionists or anti-Zionist leaders.

The status of the modern rabbi is probably best reflected in the number of institutions established by the different Jewish denominations to educate future rabbis (see *Rabbinical Seminaries).

[Wolfe Kelman]

The ordination of women as rabbis has transformed the rabbinate in North America. In 1972, in response to changing public attitudes and social realities, the leadership of the Reform movement approved the ordination of Sally *Priesand by Hebrew Union College-Jewish Institute of Religion. By the beginning of the 21st century, several hundred women had been ordained as rabbis in North America, the United Kingdom, and Israel, and as many as half of rabbinical students in seminaries of liberal denominations of Judaism, including those of the Conservative/Masorti and Reconstructionist movements, were female. The paths of rabbis who are women have not been free of obstacles. Many female clergy hold subordinate positions in larger synagogues, or work as educators or chaplains, rather than senior leaders of congregations. These occupational patterns are a not only a reflection of persistent cultural prejudices towards women as religious authority figures, but also of many women's choices of rabbinic options that allow them time for the demands of home and family.

[Judith R. Baskin (2nd ed.)]

In Israel

The rabbinate and the functions of the rabbi in modern Israel differ fundamentally from their counterparts in any other part of the Jewish world, whether ancient or modern. A number of factors have contributed toward this unique state of affairs. In the first place there is the law of the State of Israel which establishes the *halakhah* as state law in all matters affecting personal status, which includes marriage, divorce, legitimacy, and conversion and affords the rabbinical courts the status of civil courts of law within that wide sphere. This, coupled with the fact that the Ministry of Religious Affairs was, apart from one brief interregnum, the prerogative of the (Orthodox) National Religious Party, has had the effect of making Orthodox Judaism to all intents and purposes the "established church" of the state, to the virtual exclusion of other religious trends in Judaism, Conservative and Reform, which have only a handful of congregations, mostly composed of recently arrived immigrants belonging to those trends in the countries of their origin.

A second factor determining the complexion and the functions of the rabbinate is the establishment of the twin Orthodox chief rabbinate (Ashkenazi and Sephardi) which are state appointments, and similar twin chief rabbinates in the larger cities. These local rabbinates and chief rabbinates are administered by the local religious councils, which are nominated through a complicated system of political party representation and the Ministry of Religious Affairs, and it is to all intents controlled by the ministry. These councils consist of Orthodox Jews. All appointments of rabbis must be confirmed by the chief rabbis and the Ministry of Religious Affairs.

A third factor is the fact that almost without exception the *rashei yeshivot*, who exercise a powerful influence in Israel, as well as the other rabbis who belong to the Agudat Israel (to which the *rashei yeshivot* also mostly belong), regard the National Religious Party and the chief rabbis who owe their appointments to their support as tending toward heterodoxy, a charge which they are at great pains to disprove or dispel. As a result, they are unduly apprehensive of any move which might be regarded as progressive or "reform." To these considerations must be added two others. The Ashkenazi rabbinate continues wholly the tradition of the classical Eastern European rabbinate, and the new incumbents to the rabbinate are wholly the products of the yeshivot, while the Sephardi rabbinate equally continues in their old traditions. Lastly, the synagogue in Israel is, with only a handful of exceptions, not a congregational entity with fixed membership but a place for worship and study.

All these factors add up to the distinctive features of the rabbinate and the functions of the rabbis in Israel. Next to the chief rabbis the hierarchy consists of the *dayyanim* of the Supreme Bet Din of Appeal, followed by the *dayyanim* of the district courts. They are classified as civil judges with the emoluments and privileges of judges, and their functions are wholly judicial and not pastoral. Next in importance, and in receipt of salaries from the religious councils, are a host of rabbis who act as religious functionaries with specific and limited duties such as inspection of *kashrut*, of *mikva'ot*, of the *eruv*, of the adherence to the various agricultural laws, etc. They also, by nature of their functions, perform no pastoral duties. Next in the scale come district rabbis, also appointed by the religious councils. In theory they are charged with the welfare of the community within the district over which they have been appointed, but with few exceptions they regard their position as a sinecure. Lowest on the scale come, what in theory is the nearest approach to the Western rabbi, the rabbi of a synagogue. In the absence of a regularly constituted congregation, however, and with no official source of income, they are financially the least rewarded. Few synagogues pay anything approaching a living wage to these rabbis. They mostly depend upon one of the other rabbinic functions referred to for their livelihood, and their appointments largely commence as de facto ones which sometimes develop into uneasy de jure ones. In the absence of the congregational unit with its duly paid-up membership, and the consequent lack of personal bond between rabbi and worshiper, there is nothing in the rabbinate in Israel which approaches the pastoral aspect of the work of the modern rabbi. Marriages are performed by duly appointed officials of the local religious councils, funerals by the various *ḥevra kaddisha* organizations. Visiting the sick is not regarded as the function of the rabbi of a synagogue; cultural activities apart from the *shi'urim* in rabbinics are undertaken by other agencies, as is youth work and philanthropic activity. The virtual nonexistence of regular preaching should be noted.

The cumulative effect of this situation is that the Western-trained rabbi even of Orthodox Jewry finds it hard to find a place in the rabbinate in Israel. Of all those who have immigrated few have been appointed to a rabbinical position in Israel, and most find their livelihood in other spheres.

[Louis Isaac Rabinowitz]

BIBLIOGRAPHY: Middle Ages: Baron, Community, index; Baron, Social², index volume to vols. 1–8 (1960), 126; S. Assaf, in: *Reshumot*, 2 (1927), 259–99; Neuman, Spain, 2 (1942), index; Finkelstein, Middle Ages; S. Schwarzfuchs, *Études sur l'origine et le developpement de Rabbinat au Moyen-Age* (1957); H.H. Ben-Sasson, *Hagut ve-Hanhagah* (1959), 160–228; J. Katz, *Masoret u-Mashber* (1958), index, s.v. *Rav, Rabbanut*; idem, in: *Sefer Zikkaron… B. de Vries* (1968), 281–94; S. Spitzer, in: *Bar Ilan Sefer ha-Shanah*, 7–8 (1970), 261–79. Muslim East: Rosanes, Togarmah; Mann, Texts; Mann, Egypt; idem, in: JQR, 7 (1916/17), 457ff.; D. Revel, in: *Horeb*, 5 (1939), 1–26; H.Z. Hirschberg, in: *Religion in the Middle East*, 1 (1969), 119–225; Hirschberg, Afrikah, index; Baer, Spain, index; Baer, Urkunden, 2 (1936), index; H.H. Ben-Sasson, *Toledot Am Yisrael bi-Ymei ha-Beinayim* (1969); Neuman, Spain, index; M. Benayahu, *Marbiz Torah* (1953); idem, in: *Sefer… Baer* (1961), 248–69; S. Assaf, *Le-Korot ha-Rabbanut* (1943); idem, *Battei ha-Din…* (1924); Assaf, Geonim; Neubauer, Chronicles; Ibn Daud, Tradition; J.M. Landau, *Ha-Yehudim be-Mizrayim ba-Me'ah ha-Tesha Esreh* (1967); A. Elmaleh, *Ha-Rishonim le-Ẓiyyon* (1970); *Saloniki Ir va-Em be-Yisrael* (1967); I.S. Emmanuel, *Maẓẓevot Saloniki*, 2 vols. (1963–68); Ashtor, Korot; Ashtor Toledot; A. Ben-Jacob, *Yehudei Bavel* (1965); M.S. Goodblatt, *Jewish Life in Turkey in the XVIth Century…* (1952); M. Zadoc, *Yehudei Teiman* (1967); S.D. Goitein, *Sidrei Ḥinnukh* (1965). Modern Period: *Sulamith*, 2 (1809), 300–5; S. Holdheim, *Ueber die Autonomie der Rabbiner…* (1847²); L. Auerbach, *Das Judentum und seine Bekenner* (1890), 284ff.; B. Jacobs, *Die Stellung des Rabbiners* (1910); *Paul Lazarus Gedenkbuch* (1961); M.S. Gelber, *Failure of the American Rabbi* (1962); M.M. Berman, *The Role of the Rabbi, What Was, What Is, and What Shall the Rabbi Be* (1941); A.Y. Feldman, *The American Reform Rabbi* (1962); L.M. Franklin, *The Rabbi, the Man and his Message* (1938); R. Hertz, *The Rabbi Yesterday and Today* (1943); G.D. Cohen, *Studies in the Variety of Rabbinic Cultures* (1991); J.R. Marcus and A.J. Peck (eds.), *The American Rabbinate; a Century of Continuity and Change*, 1883–1980 (1985); I.H. Sharfman, *The First Rabbi: Origins of Conflict between Orthodox and Reform* (1988); S. Schwarzfuchs, *A Concise History of the Rabbinate* (1993); R. Patai and E.S. Goldsmith (eds.), *Thinkers and Teachers of Modern Judaism*, 1994); L. Bernstein, *Challenge and Mission: the Emergence of the English Speaking Orthodox Rabbinate* (1982). **ADD. BIBLIOGRAPHY:** P. Nadell, *Women Who Would Be Rabbis* (1998); S. Sheridan, *Hear Our Voice: Women Rabbis Tell Their Stories* (1994).

RABBI BINYAMIN (pseudonym of **Yehoshua Radler-Feldmann**; 1880–1957), Hebrew journalist. Born in Zborov, Galicia, Rabbi Binyamin published his first essay in 1903, and in 1906 moved to London, where he joined J.Ḥ. *Brenner in the publication of *Ha-Me'orer*. Arriving in Palestine in 1907, he first worked as a laborer in Petaḥ Tikvah, then as secretary of Herzlia, the first Hebrew high school in Tel Aviv. He left this position to join in the founding of kevutzat *Kinneret. In 1910 he moved to Jerusalem, taught at the Reḥavyah Hebrew high school, and later at the Taḥkemoni religious school. After World War I he was active in the Mizrachi Party and edited the religious national monthly *Ha-Hed* (1926–53). In 1925 he was among the founders of the *Berit Shalom association, which advocated a binational state for Arabs and Jews.

Rabbi Binyamin published thousands of articles and essays, often expressing individualistic viewpoints. He did much to introduce Brenner and Agnon to the Hebrew reading audiences. His critical essays include surveys and analyses of the great figures of ancient and modern European civilization, Asian cultures, and modern Hebrew literature. His works include *Al ha-Gevulin* (1923) and *Parzufim* (2 vols., 1934, 1936), a volume of memoirs, *Mi-Zborov ve-ad Kinneret* (1950), and essays on writers and scholars, *Mishpeḥot Soferim* (1960) and *Keneset Ḥakhamim* (1961).

BIBLIOGRAPHY: *Rabbi Binyamin, Zikhrono li-Verakhah* (1958), contains bibliography and a collection of evaluations; Waxman, Literature, 4 (1960), 427–9; I. Cohen, *Demut el Demut* (1949), 225–33; D. Sadan, *Bein Din le-Ḥeshbon* (1963), 358–63; J. Fichmann, *Ruḥot Menaggenot* (1952), 285–311; Kressel, Leksikon, 2 (1967), 831–3.

[Getzel Kressel]

RABBINER-SEMINAR FUER DAS ORTHODOXE JUDENTUM, the Rabbinical Seminary for Orthodox Judaism, founded in 1873 in Berlin by Azriel (Israel) *Hildesheimer to promote *Torah im Derekh Erez* (the combination of loyalty to Judaism with awareness of modern culture and method). For the next seven decades rabbinic and lay leaders emerged from that institution whose influence extended over four continents. Throughout his career Hildesheimer had to fight opponents from the left and the right. He inspired his disciples by his life and learning. After having headed the seminary for 26 years, Hildesheimer was followed by David *Hoffmann, Joseph *Wohlgemuth, and Jehiel Jacob *Weinberg. The students attended classes both at the seminar and at the university, and the curriculum included Bible, Talmud, Jewish philosophy, and other subjects. Hildesheimer's faculty was made up of distinguished scholars. Among them were Jacob *Barth, Abraham *Berliner, Hirsch *Hildesheimer (son of the founder), Simon *Eppenstein, Moses Auerbach, and Samuel *Gruenberg. The seminary's annual reports (*Jahresberichte*, 1873–1915; 1935–36) contained a series of important scholarly studies by the members of its teaching staff. The seminary was the center of modern Orthodoxy, which combined loyalty to traditional Judaism with the recognition of the need for scientific method (most of the graduates obtained a doctorate in philosophy). Many graduates, among them Joseph *Carlebach and Leo *Deutschlander, attained continental fame through their educational work in Eastern Europe, while many others built *Torah im Derekh Erez* congregations in Germany, France, and beyond their frontiers. The seminary, which started as a German-Hungarian enterprise, was greatly enriched in its last two decades by two Lithuanian scholars on its faculty: Abraham Elijah *Kaplan, who died at a young age, and Jehiel Jacob Weinberg, a great talmudist. In 1934 plans were prepared to transfer the seminary to Palestine, but the proposal had to be abandoned owing to the opposition of extreme Orthodox elements there to the concept of a modern rabbinical seminary. The institution closed in November 1938 shortly after the *Kristallnacht* pogrom. The greater part of its library was transferred to Tel Aviv. The principal fruits of the seminary's work was the training of German rabbis to counter the tide of religious liberalism.

BIBLIOGRAPHY: S. Goldschmidt, in: *Jeschurun*, 7 (1920), 216–55; J. Wohlgemuth, *Das Rabbiner-Seminar zu Berlin* (1923); H. Schwab, *History of Orthodox Jewry in Germany* (1950), 54–57; M.A. Shulvass (Szulvas), in: S.K. Mirsky (ed.), *Mosedot Torah be-Eiropah* (1956), 689–713; Y. Aviad (Wolfsberg), *Deyokena'ot* (1962), 40–51; I.J. Eisner, in: YLBI, 12 (1967), 32–52.

[Leo Jung]

RABBINICAL ALLIANCE OF AMERICA (Iggud ha-Rabbonim). Founded in 1942 as an association of Orthodox rabbis, the RAA "seeks to promulgate the cause of Torah-true Judaism through an organized rabbinate that is consistently Orthodox." In its early years, most of its members were ordained by Yeshivah Torah Vodaath in Brooklyn. By 1965 the group had a membership of 250, of whom 100 occupied pulpits. In 2005 membership reached 834, of whom slightly more than half occupied pulpits. It has always been common for members of the RAA who occupy significant pulpits to also hold membership in the preexisting *Rabbinical Council of America (RCA). As early as 1949, there was discussion about an amalgamation with the RCA, which heightened during the RCA presidency of Theodore L. Adams and his counterpart at the RAA, Ralph Pelcovitz, yet nothing ever materialized from these discussions. At a joint press conference in New York City on December 3, 1954, the RCA and RAA teamed up to protest the Conservative movement's innovations regarding the *ketubbah* (marriage contract). This was noteworthy since the other major Orthodox rabbinic body, the Union of Orthodox Rabbis of the United States and Canada (Agudat ha-Rabbonim), refused to join the RCA in this endeavor. A defining feature of the RAA has been its refusal to recognize non-Orthodox streams of Judaism, although some of their rabbis are members of Jewish ecumenical bodies such as the New York Board of Rabbis. From its founding, the RAA has maintained its own **bet din* in Brooklyn, New York, headed (2005) by Rabbi Herschel Kurzrock, who was also the chairman of the RAA's halakhic committee. The RAA publishes an occasional periodical by the name of *Zikhron Meyer*. Since 1972 Rabbi Abraham B. Hecht has served as president of the RAA, although prior to the assassination of Yitzhak Rabin, Hecht called for the death of any Jewish leader who would concede portions of the land of Israel for peace. Later he expressed remorse for his comments.

BIBLIOGRAPHY: Louis Bernstein, *Challenge and Mission: The Emergence of the English Speaking Rabbinate* (1982).

[Asher Oser (2nd ed.)]

RABBINICAL ASSEMBLY (RA), the international association of Conservative rabbis. The Rabbinical Assembly was founded in Philadelphia in June 1901, as the Alumni Association of the Jewish Theological Seminary, with Rabbi Henry M. Speaker as its first president. The name was changed to the Rabbinical Assembly in 1918, when graduates of other institutions were admitted as members. The RA, as it is known, functions on two levels – as a professional organization serving the needs of its members, and as an organization which seeks to promote the observance of Conservative Judaism, working closely with the Jewish Theological Seminary of America, the United Synagogue of Conservative Judaism, and other arms of the Conservative Movement.

In 2005, the organization had 1,564 members, 1,290 of them serving in the United States. Members served in 25 countries, with 151 in Israel, and 52 in Latin America. First admitting female rabbis in 1985, the group had 204 women members in 2005.

As a professional organization, the RA has always sought to improve the status of the Conservative rabbi; and its achievements have benefited the rabbis of other movements as well. Thanks to the efforts of its long-time executive director, Rabbi Wolfe Kelman, who served from 1951 to 1989, and his successor, Rabbi Joel Meyers, many rabbis now receive benefits such as pensions, medical insurance, and convention allowances. Working with other arms of the movement on the Joint Placement Commission, the RA has sought to create fair and standardized procedures for rabbinic placement. RA members serve not only as pulpit rabbis, but also as educators, academics, Hillel directors, and chaplains, and hold other positions in the Jewish community.

In seeking to promote the practice of Conservative Judaism and the study of the Torah, the RA has had an active publications program, headed from 1961 to 1994 by Rabbi Jules Harlow. It has published weekday, Sabbath, and holiday prayerbooks, a Passover *haggadah*, a commentary on the Torah, a Holocaust *Megillah*, rabbis' manuals, and other learned works that reflect the Conservative ideology. Through its Law Committee, the RA has sought to grapple with halakhic issues such as the plight of the **agunah* (deserted wife), the observance of the Sabbath and the dietary laws under modern conditions, and the role of women in the synagogue. At the start of the 21st century, the RA was also dealing with the issues of outreach to intermarried families and the role of homosexuals in Jewish life.

BIBLIOGRAPHY: R.E. Fierstein (ed.), *A Century of Commitment: One Hundred Years of the Rabbinical Assembly* (2000); P.S. Nadell, *Conservative Judaism in America: A Biographical Dictionary and Sourcebook* (1988); Rabbinical Assembly, *Proceedings* (1927–).

[Robert E. Fierstien (2nd ed.)]

RABBINICAL CONFERENCES. The idea of a *synod to provide authoritative guidance and meet the current needs of Jews in the era of *Emancipation led to the holding of rabbinical conferences in Germany in the mid-19th century. A convention was called by Abraham *Geiger in Wiesbaden in 1837 to discuss his proposals for *Reform, but had no practical results. Subsequently a conference initiated by Ludwig *Philippson met in Brunswick in 1844, and was attended by 25 Reform rabbis, including Geiger and Samuel *Holdheim. However, no substantial resolutions were passed, and the conference was attacked by all sectors: the Orthodox protested against the rejection of Jewish tradition, Philippson regretted the theorizing instead of practical solutions, and Zacharias *Frankel criticized the discussions and results. Following the conference 116 Orthodox rabbis declared that nobody could "abrogate the least of the religious laws." In 1845, 31 rabbis, this time including Frankel, met at Frankfurt on the Main. As laid down in a memorandum delivered to the Frankfurt conference by three representatives of the Reform Association of Berlin, their stated purpose was to strengthen Judaism by rescuing it from legalistic stagnation and adapting it to modern needs, thus making it attractive to the new generation. When Frankel was overruled on the retention of Hebrew prayers, he withdrew. Heinrich *Graetz expressed a similar view. Other proposed reforms referred to the messianic portions of the prayers, the supplication for the restoration of sacrifices, the triennial cycle of Torah readings, and the use of the organ in the synagogue. A third conference took place in 1846 at Breslau, attended by 25 rabbis only. While Holdheim suggested that the Sabbath should be transferred to the civil day of rest, the majority was satisfied with minor reform in Sabbath observance, and the abolition of the second day of holidays and many mourning customs. Several resolutions dealt with the supervision of circumcision from the hygienic aspect. A number of radical reformers, dissatisfied with the conservative line taken by the conference, demanded that laymen should participate in future meetings.

In 1868 24 rabbis met in Kassel to prepare such a "synod" and to decide on a number of liturgical reforms. The "synod" assembling at Leipzig in 1869 consisted of 49 lay and 34 rabbinical delegates from 60 communities. Presided over by Moritz *Lazarus, it dealt with Jewish education, liturgical reforms, and other questions. The Orthodox and Frankel's sympathizers were not represented. Two years later, the "synod" of Augsburg was attended by representatives from only 30 communities. Its resolutions dealt with marriage, *ḥaliẓah*, and other subjects, but the stand taken on the Sabbath was more conservative than before. Again, 133 Orthodox rabbis published a strong protest, asserting that the participants were unfit to hold religious office. Neither "synod" came up to the expectations of its own promoters, and no further meeting of this kind was convened in Germany.

[Ze'ev Wilhelm Falk]

Nevertheless, agitation for synods continued especially in America, by Isaac Mayer *Wise in 1881, and at three sessions of the Central Conference of American Rabbis in 1904–06. Solomon *Schechter, leader of U.S. *Conservative Jewry, opposed synods as encouraging sacerdotalism and creating the danger of a schism within Orthodoxy. The Reform movement in the United States, nevertheless, adopted in 1887 its Pittsburgh *Platform, laying down the principles of classic Reform. It reversed its stance in 1937 in Columbus, when it reaffirmed its adherence to Hebrew, Zionism, and other traditional values. In 1961 the Federation of *Reconstructionist Congregations and Fellowships, at a conference of lay and rabbinic delegates, adopted a guide for Jewish ritual in line with their humanist philosophy of Judaism. Among certain Orthodox circles there has been agitation for a Sanhedrin to legislate for world Jewry, but the difficulties involved appeared insuperable.

[Isaac Levitats]

See also *Bet Din; *Chief Rabbi; *Synods.

BIBLIOGRAPHY: D. Philipson, *Reform Movement in Judaism* (1931^2, repr. 1967), 140–224; W.G. Plaut, *Rise of Reform Judaism* (1963).

RABBINICAL COUNCIL OF AMERICA (RCA; Histadrut Harabanim). Founded in 1923 (as the Rabbinical Council of the Union of Orthodox Jewish Congregations), in 1935 the RCA merged with the Rabbinical Association of the Rabbi Isaac Elchanan Theological Seminary (Yeshiva University) and took its present name. The goal of the RCA is "to advance the cause and the voice of Torah and the rabbinic tradition" by "promoting the welfare, interests, and professionalism of Orthodox rabbis all around the world"; it is the rabbinic counterpart of the Union of Orthodox Jewish Congregations. The RCA has offices in New York and Jerusalem and sponsors various yeshivot and educational institutions in Israel. In 2005 the RCA claimed an international membership of over 1,000 members, of whom 600 occupied pulpits and one hundred were in chaplaincy, the remainder were in educational or communal positions. Most of its members are graduates of the Rabbi Isaac Elchanan Theological Seminary.

Since 1960, the RCA has sponsored the independent Beth Din of America, which, in addition to dealing with questions of personal status, also addresses issues arising from commercial disputes and keeps records of prenuptial agreements that are promulgated through the RCA. In 2005 The Beth Din of America was headed by Rabbi Gedalia Schwartz and its director was Rabbi Jonathan Reiss. Until his death in 1993, Rabbi Joseph B. *Soloveitchik was the "guiding spirit and mentor" of the RCA and chaired its *halakhah* commission, which Rabbi Asher Bush was coordinating in 2005. While eschewing inter-religious activities that include discussions of theology, the RCA has sent representatives to the International Jewish Committee for Interreligious Consultations (IJCIC), which is under the auspices of the World Jewish Congress. The RCA publishes two journals, a quarterly, *Tradition* (1958–) and a halakhic journal in Hebrew, *Hadarom.* (1957–). From 2002 the executive vice president of the RCA was Rabbi Basil Herring.

BIBLIOGRAPHY: Leibman, in: AJYB, 66 (1965), 21–97; Davis, in: L. Finkelstein, *The Jews: Their History, Culture, and Religion*, 1 (1960^3), 559f.; L. Bernstein, *Challenge and Mission: The Emergence of the English Speaking Rabbinate* (1982).

[Asher Oser (2nd ed.)]

RABBINICAL LITERATURE, a modern scientific term used to describe the literature of *halakhah* which is based upon the Oral Law, its traditions and methodology in its different periods, its changing languages, and its varied forms. This definition excludes from its purview such sacred literature as liturgy, *piyyutim*, and other liturgical compositions, pure Kabbalah works, philosophical bible exegesis, theology, and grammar. On the other hand it frequently includes what appear at first sight to be purely secular topics, such as the works on astronomy – inasmuch as their aim is to clarify topics connected with the calendar, such as laws of the determination of the New Moon and its intercalation; "chronologies of the *tannaim* and *amoraim*", which are strictly chronographies, but whose main purpose is to determine according to which authority the *halakhah* is to be established; homiletic ethical and aggadic works, which aim at giving the practical *halakhah* and guidance for everyday living, and other similar works. Despite this, or perhaps because of this, the term also includes books on the laws of the Temple and its appurtenances, the laws of ritual cleanness and uncleanness, which will be actual only in the messianic future, since their purpose was regarded as "practical" in view of the ever-present faith in the imminent redemption. Combined with this was the concept of "interpret and receive reward," i.e., the study of Torah for its own sake without regard to its application to practical life, as an independent discipline which was part of the concept of *talmud torah*, and therefore this literature too is included in the term "rabbinical literature." It must be clearly emphasized that, despite the formal name, the term does not indicate books written by rabbis but works whose subject matter and aim belong to the sphere that concerns rabbis in their function as teachers of Judaism. Works on grammar may have an important halakhic bearing, for instance in connection with the laws of reading the Torah, but in most cases such was not the intention of their authors, whose purpose was primarily to teach grammar for its own sake or as an aid to biblical exegesis. These books are therefore not included in the term "rabbinical literature." The name rabbinical literature is also used in an entirely different sense since it also describes literature written by Rabbanites against the *Karaites in all eras – even if it deals with theology or other non-halakhic topics.

Rabbinical literature can be divided, according to its contents, into several basic categories: exposition of the *Talmud; *responsa; codes and their commentaries; *minhagim; halakhic monographs; rules of conduct and ethical wills, and the like. This formal division, however, was adopted in practice long after the inception of this literature. The term is commonly accepted to indicate every category of this literature as defined above, from Saadiah *Gaon, who was the first rabbinical scholar to write "books" in the present sense of the word. According to this usage rabbinical literature constitutes a stage following the period of talmudic and midrashic literature, which, as is usually accepted, came to a close at the end of the geonic period. No books in the present sense of the word were written, however, from the close of this period until Saadiah, with the possible sole exception of the *She'iltot* of Aḥa of *Shabḥa. Saadiah was also a very prolific writer, and the many fragments extant of his various works bear evidence to his creativity in every branch of rabbinical literature.

The formal division begins to emerge in the 11th and 12th centuries, and, with the general development of literary expression, it became progressively more refined and defined. In its historical development rabbinical literature may be divided into three periods:

(1) The geonic period;

(2) The period of the *rishonim*;

(3) The period of the *aḥaronim* (the subdivisions of each period are dealt with under their separate headings). In its fate and its preservation in manuscripts in libraries or in the *genizah*, there is not much difference between rabbinical literature and other branches of Jewish literary creativity. It is likewise very difficult to indicate lines of development which are unique or specially characteristic of it. Research into rabbinical literature, as a branch of the study of Jewish literature in general, is still in its infancy, and the basic groundwork toward it has not yet been done. There are as yet no reliable and comprehensive catalogs of Hebrew manuscripts in the different libraries and erroneous identification of books belonging to it is still widespread.

[Israel Moses Ta-Shma]

RABBINICAL SEMINARIES. Until the first quarter of the 19th century the only source for the training of rabbis was the *yeshivot. These were not rabbinical training institutions in the strict sense, but institutions of higher rabbinic learning designed for the education of the people as a whole. The curriculum was thus strictly limited to Talmud and its commentaries and the codes. A student wishing to enter the rabbinate obtained *semikhah* and thus became an ordained rabbi.

With the advent of the era of emancipation and the consequent demolition of the ghetto walls in Western Europe, and under the influence of the *Haskalah and the development of the Wissenschaft des *Judentums, the demand became increasingly heard for the establishment of institutions specifically for the training of rabbis. These institutions would produce a new type of modern rabbis, equipped with a thorough mastery of the vernacular and a knowledge of both secular and extra-talmudic Jewish subjects. An added incentive to the establishment of such institutions was the regulation enacted by Franz Joseph I of Austria-Hungary in 1848 requiring secular knowledge of an academic standard for rabbis in his country.

The proposed seminaries were bitterly contested by the rabbis and heads of the yeshivot of the old school as a dangerous innovation, with the result that where they dominated the religious life of the community these seminaries never struck root and consequently they played no significant part in Russia and Poland. This opposition, which still exists, is the cause of the curious fact that in Israel there is no institution specifically set up for the training of rabbis. It was only in Central and Western Europe and in the United States that such seminaries flourished.

The first rabbinical seminary was the Instituto Convitto Rabbinico, established in Padua by I.S. *Reggio in 1829, in which Lelio Della *Torre and Samuel David *Luzzatto were the first teachers. It served as the model for all future seminaries. It was closed in 1871 but reopened in 1887 in Rome as the Collegio Rabbinico Italiana. In 1899 it moved to Florence where it remained until 1932, when again it moved to Rome remaining there until it was closed down under the Fascist regime in 1939. In 1928 a branch was established for Sephardi communities on the Island of Rhodes, but it was also closed down at the outbreak of World War II.

The Ecole Centrale Rabbinique was established in Metz in 1830 and a year later it received a state subsidy. It moved to Paris in 1859 as the Seminaire Israelite de France and later was given the name of the Ecole Rabbinique. Probably the most famous rabbinical seminary in Europe was the Juedisch-Theologisches Seminar of Breslau founded by Zacharias *Frankel in 1854. Among its professors were H. *Graetz, Immanuel *Loew, J. *Guttman, and Yiẓḥak *Heinemann. Jews' College was founded in London in 1855. Its most prominent principals were Michael *Friedlaender (1865–1907), Adolph *Buechler (1907–39), and Isidore *Epstein (1948–62). In Berlin the Juedische Hochschule was established in 1872. Its name was changed to the Lehranstalt fuer die Wissenschaft des Judentums in 1883, but it resumed its old name in 1920. A year after the establishment of the Hochschule the strictly Orthodox Rabbiner Seminar fuer das Orthodoxe Judentum was established in Berlin by Azriel *Hildesheimer, and is usually referred to as Hildesheimer's Seminar.

The bitter opposition of Hungarian Orthodox circles to the establishment of a rabbinical seminary in that country caused a delay in its opening for over a quarter of a century. In 1850 the Emperor Franz Joseph I devoted a million talers, derived from the fine imposed upon the Jews of Hungary for their participation in the rebellion of 1849, to a fund for Jewish education, but the rabbinical seminary was not established until 1877 in Budapest. Among its prominent teachers were Wilhelm *Bacher, M. *Guttmann, and I. *Goldziher. The Israelitisch-theologische Lehranstalt of Vienna, established by A. *Jellinek in 1862, did not make much progress until 1893 when it moved to the Jewish quarter of Leopoldstadt and Adolph Schwarz was appointed its rector.

An outstanding example of the complete failure of a rabbinical seminary was provided by Poland. Established in 1826 and strongly supported by the government, in the 36 years of its existence, it did not produce a single rabbi. The fact is not surprising since both its principal, A. *Eisenbaum, and its main teacher, A. *Buchner, were pronounced assimilationists. Buchner actually published a book, *Der Talmud in seiner Nichtigheit* ("The Worthlessness of the Talmud", 1848). Not much more successful was the Russian seminary which was opened in 1847 in Vilna and in Zhitomir. It was regarded with suspicion by the Jews as an instrument of the government's anti-Jewish educational policy and was closed down in 1873.

On the other hand the *Makhon le-Ḥokhmat Yisrael*, whose name was later changed to the *Makhon le-Madda'ei ha-Yahadut*, established by M. *Schorr, the chief rabbi of Warsaw and its first principal, served as the rabbinical seminary for Poland until the outbreak of World War II.

The United States has rabbinical seminaries for all three trends in religious Jewry. The first to be established, the Reform Hebrew Union College, was founded by Isaac Mayer *Wise in Cincinnati in 1875. In 1922 Stephen *Wise established the Jewish Institute of Religion in New York which merged with the Hebrew Union College in 1950.

The rabbinical seminary of the Conservative movement, the Jewish Theological Seminary, was established in 1886. Orthodox seminaries are represented by the Rabbi Isaac Elchanan Theological Seminary, later a unit of the Yeshiva *University, established in 1897; and the Talmudical College of Chicago, in 1922. As a result of the Holocaust, all the seminaries in Central and Eastern Europe, with the exception of the Budapest seminary have ceased to exist. The only seminaries still functioning in Europe are the Ecole Rabbinique, Jews' College, and the Reform Leo Baeck College in London.

See also the articles on the individual seminaries.

BIBLIOGRAPHY: D. Prato, in: *Relazione sul biennio 1899–1900* (1901); A. Toaff, in: RMI, 12, nos. 7–9 (1937/38), 194f.; *Jews' College Jubilee Volume* (1906); P. Smolenskin, in: *Ha-Shaḥar*, 9 (1876/77), 57–61; *Sefer ha-Zikkaron le-Veit-ha-Midrash le-Rabbanim be-Vinah* (1946); *Sefer ha-Yovel li-Melot 50 Shanah le-Veit-ha-Midrash ha-Rabbanim be-Budapest* (partly in Ger. and Hung.; 1927); A. Geiger, in: WZJT, 2 (1836), 1–21; M. Brann, *Geschichte des juedisch-theologischen Seminars… in Breslau* (1904); J. Elbogen, in: *Festschrift… der Hochschule fuer die Wissenschaft des Judentums in Berlin* (1922), 101–44; J. Bauer, *L'Ecole rabbinique de France 1830–1930* (1930); J. Heinemann, in: *Bericht des juedischtheologischen Seminars… in Breslau* (1929), 34–48; *Festschrift zum 50-jaehrigen Bestehen des Rabbinerseminars zu Berlin 1873–1923* (1924); G. Kisch (ed.), *Das Breslauer Seminar* (partly in Heb. and Eng.; 1963). IN THE U.S.: M. Davis, in: L. Finkelstein (ed.), *Jews, Their History, Culture, and Religion*, 1 (1960^3), 488–587.

[Louis Isaac Rabinowitz]

RABBINICAL TRAINING, AMERICAN.

Background

When the *Hebrew Union College and the *Jewish Theological Seminary were established in the late 19th Century as the first institutions for the education of rabbis on American soil, the founders did not establish these schools of higher learning in a vacuum. Men like Isaac Mayer Wise of Hebrew Union and Sabato Morais of JTS did not confront the task of imagining a modern rabbinical seminary *de novo*. Instead, their aim was to house "places of Jewish learning" comparable to the models provided by schools such as the Positive-Historical Breslau Jewish Theological Seminary (see Breslau *Juedisch-Theologisches Seminar), the Liberal Berlin *Hochschule fuer die Wissenschaft des Judentums, and the Orthodox Berlin Rabbinerseminar (see *Rabbiner-Seminar fuer das

Orthodoxe Judentum) that had been established in Europe just years before.

All of these schools – even the Orthodox Rabbinerseminar – were marked by a dual devotion to classical Judaica and rabbinic sources on the one hand and modern critical scholarship on the other. This twofold commitment to classical rabbinic sources and the canons of academic inquiry reflects an era and intellectual setting in which it was deemed imperative that texts be understood and interpreted in light of the historical contexts that formed them.

While this ethos did not take hold at the Orthodox Rabbi Isaac Elchanan Theological Seminary (RIETS) of Yeshiva University in New York, this approach did shape the curricula and courses of training designed for rabbis in the American Reform and Conservative movements for the next 75 years. Indeed, this heritage remains prominent at JTS and HUC-JIR as well as other liberal rabbinical schools even today. Events and currents from the mid-1970s, however, have challenged the exclusive monopoly this particular vision previously enjoyed in shaping rabbinical education in North America and these events and currents have changed and informed the nature of rabbinical education for North American rabbis across denominational lines at the onset of a new century. A few words about these currents and patterns, as well as an appreciation of the western European heritage mentioned above that shaped the initial manifestations of the American rabbinical seminary, will provide a fitting backdrop and framework for the description and analysis of rabbinical education for the North American Jewish community at the onset of the 21st Century.

In the 1960s and 1970s, many of the sociological factors that became seminal in shaping the contours of contemporary American Judaism today started to emerge. The American Jewish community was no longer an immigrant community seeking to adjust to the United States. Old ethnic patterns that formerly preserved and divided the Jewish religious community were no longer present and the rivalry that had existed between American Jews of German and Eastern European descent was no more than an historical memory – if that – for most American Jews.

Jews were now completely accepted into American life, and Jews of all stripes and ethnic backgrounds were now full participants in the cultural and economic spheres of the United States. As a result, the attitudes and beliefs that had so sharply divided Reform from Conservative Jews in the first half of the 20th century were now blurred for many of these people. A permeability was emerging, one that would allow for crossover between the disparate movements.

Larger societal developments going on in the greater American culture also promoted this crossover. With the rise in the 1960s of what came to be known as "the new ethnicity" in the larger culture, an expression of ethnic allegiances unprecedented in this nation's history appeared, and a religious revival and a renewed search for religious and spiritual meaning accompanied this expression. These forces had a decisive impact in promoting a renewed interest in Judaism among many, as did the exhilarating 1967 Israeli victory in the Six-Day War. Trips to Israel and programs there now became a staple of American Jewish life. All these dynamics propelled many Jews to seek out Jewish community and religion in an intensive manner that was unknown to their parents earlier in the century.

The *Havurah Movement of the late 1960s and 1970s ran parallel to and was a result of these developments, and the appearance and influence of what is today called "Jewish renewal" owes its origins to those years. This "movement" envisioned a non-hierarchical brand of Judaism and promoted an "expressive individualism that featured the activism of all participants." The inroads of feminism in organized Jewish religious life also appeared for the first time in American Jewish religious life. Jewish day school attendance in the United States rose as well, and the explosion of Jewish studies programs in American universities also began at this time. This phenomenon has caused there to be an ever-burgeoning number of serious academics devoted to the many fields of Jewish Studies. A number of these scholars are the products of previous rabbinical training. The opportunity for employment academia now provides these rabbis contrasts sharply to the reality that obtained in earlier generations, for rabbis who were scholars and gravitated to an academic environment prior to the 1960s were generally compelled either to choose Hillel or the pulpit as there were few academic positions available. Today the opportunities abound for rabbis and non-rabbis alike. Many Jewish Studies scholars today are not rabbis, and many among this non-rabbinic group now populate the teaching ranks of Jewish religious institutions as well as the secular academy.

At the same time, the reality of acculturation among American Jews fostered Jewish assimilation. As Jews became fully accepted by gentiles as social equals and as traditional Jewish attitudes that opposed exogamy weakened, intermarriage rates soared. While significant numbers of Israeli, Russian, Iranian, and South African Jewish immigrants came to the United States during the latter years of the 20th Century, they entered a well-established and fully organized American Jewish community that was largely composed of fourth-, fifth-, and sixth-generation American Jews who are an integral part of every sector of American society.

It is small wonder that Charles Liebman, in his influential landmark study, "The Training of American Rabbis," written in 1968, would give voice to the need for change in rabbinical education brought on by all these transformations. The events and trends that were then unfolding led him to critique the contemporary state of rabbinical education in the United States for its inability to inculcate practical rabbinical skills in its graduates. While Liebman acknowledged that many of the graduates of these schools were well educated Jewishly, all too few were able to explain the relevance of Jewish knowledge to their congregants nor were they able to inspire and guide their laity spiritually and religiously in this transformed setting. The point of his critique was not to assert that classical

Jewish knowledge was not vital for the modern rabbi. Indeed, no Jewish educational institution or seminary would dissent from this posture. All are agreed that such knowledge must serve as the foundation for the authority and authenticity of the rabbi. However, American rabbinical training centers at the current moment do resonate to his call that this knowledge be taught in such a way that modern rabbis can apply this knowledge to the spiritual life and interests of modern persons. As Ismar Schorsch, the retiring chancellor of Jewish Theological Seminary has stated, the changed world of contemporary America brought on by all the factors enumerated above, has signaled a move in the present day from an accent upon historical context to an emphasis upon the immediacy and spiritual intensity associated with text devoid of content in the education and formation of American rabbis. The cultural, religious, and intellectual climate of the day has caused the institutions charged with educating rabbis for the Jewish community of 21st-century America to restructure their programs as they rethink their priorities and reshape their educational offerings in light of these concerns and this reality. This survey and analysis of rabbinical education in America at the turn of the 21st century will indicate how this is so; elements of discontinuity as well as continuity in the training of American rabbis and the curricula of the institutions and schools that educate American rabbis will be highlighted in this essay.

Conservative Institutions

JEWISH THEOLOGICAL SEMINARY OF AMERICA. In turning at the outset of this survey to the Jewish Theological Seminary of America of the Conservative Movement, it must be said that devotion to Talmud and classical rabbinical texts taught in accord with a modern critical-academic spirit still resides at the heart of the curriculum – just as it has since the institution was established in 1886. Indeed, JTS affirms a long seminary tradition of academic rigor and devotion to Jewish scholarship as a religious value. The seminary remains committed to the belief that knowledge of rabbinic literature *and* mastery of academic scholarship remain the *sine qua non* that establishes the grounds for exercising legitimate rabbinic leadership. Talmud constitutes the central core of the curriculum, and courses in other areas of rabbinic literature as well as in academic disciplines such as history, literature, and philosophy occupy the bulk of the course of instruction throughout the years spent in study at JTS.

There was a period in American Jewish history when most of the students at JTS came from Orthodox Jewish homes and their backgrounds in Talmud were strong and their commitment to Jewish observance could be taken for granted. This is not the case today, and JTS increasingly accepts students who lack the knowledge and preparation in Judaica that was true of earlier generations. While Solomon Schechter Day Schools, Camp Ramah, and United Synagogue Youth provide fertile training grounds for many Conservative movement rabbis and professionals, their level of commitment to *halakhah* cannot always be assumed. Consequently, JTS stipulates that candidates for admission to the rabbinical school are "expected to be living according to Jewish tradition." This means that "*mitzvot* must guide the lives of the students," and while JTS – like other non-Orthodox rabbinical programs – admits women to rabbinical study, the women are obligated – no less than the men – to observe "even those mitzvoth from which women have traditionally been exempt – *tallit*, *tefillin*, and *tefillah*." However, there is an acknowledgement "that persons may be in the process of deepening their religious commitment" as they apply, and JTS encourages such students to explore JTS as an option for their rabbinic careers.

On an academic level, students are required to have completed at least the equivalent of four semesters of college-level Hebrew prior to their admission, and they must be prepared to enroll in a six-year course of study. For students with minimal background in Jewish sources, the first year is labeled as *Mechinah* (Preparation). The student is then introduced to the richness and depth of the Jewish textual tradition and required to master ten folios of Talmud prior to admission to the second year of study. Students with advanced backgrounds in Talmud at the time of admission can proceed – depending upon their talmudic skills and erudition – immediately to the second or third year.

What is noteworthy at JTS is that the curriculum now pays significant attention – particularly in the final years – to the task of "spiritual formation" and the rabbi is consciously trained for the role he/she will play as a mediator of the tradition for those whom he/she will serve. There is a recognition that scholarly goals alone are no longer the most appropriate way to educate rabbis for their future vocation, one in which the rabbi will be asked to mediate the knowledge of Torah to their congregants so that these Jews can make the legacy of the tradition relevant to their lives as contemporary American Jews. This requires the modern Conservative rabbi to "develop a more collaborative style of leadership," one that will demand them to be "leaders of inquiry," not "suppliers of answers." Bible, history, electives, and professional skills are thus given much more emphasis in the prescribed course of study at JTS than was true in earlier generations, and the administration recognizes that the modern Conservative rabbi "is a member of a profession dedicated to addressing the needs of the individual."

This means that JTS aspires to devote serious attention to the inner religious growth of the student, and seminars and internships during the last two years of study seek to allow the student to develop the ability to teach, inspire, and transform the lives of others by articulating a compelling vision of Jewish life. Students should serve as mediators of tradition, and the curriculum is now designed to foster the analytical-synthetic skills of the students. While the vast majority of courses remain devoted to Jewish texts, the description of rabbinic training at JTS today as reflected in catalogues and articles by JTS professors and staff indicate that in accord with the changing spirit of the time there is an effort to have students "grow in wisdom and piety" as well as knowledge as they prepare for the rabbinate.

THE ZIEGLER SCHOOL OF RABBINIC STUDIES AT THE UNIVERSITY OF JUDAISM. Of course, JTS no longer has a monopoly on Conservative rabbinical ordination. The Ziegler School of Rabbinic Studies at the University of Judaism (UJ) in Los Angeles now serves as a second center for Conservative ordination. While the *University of Judaism housed the *Mechinah* program of JTS for many years, the UJ expanded to a full rabbinic program in 1995. The parallels between the course of study at the Ziegler School and JTS are many. Both programs emphasize the study of Talmud and classical rabbinic texts. However, the UJ is distinct in that the attempt to sensitize the rabbinical student "to the affective and spiritual dimensions of Jewish identity and faith" is even more pronounced than at JTS. There is also a decided emphasis on preparing the students to provide such an approach to the laypersons they will one day serve. Consequently, all UJ students are required to take a ten-hour per week Senior Internship that is integrated into a Senior Seminar co-taught by a Rabbi/M.B.A. and a congregational rabbi so that the graduates are prepared to do the actual work of a congregational rabbi. The congregational rabbinate is thus privileged as the normative option for UJ students in a way that it is not for students at JTS. Finally, classes in Kabbalah and *ḥasidut* are required for all UJ students. This literature involves study of texts and genres that focus on the mystical and personal elements in Jewish tradition, and their assignment as a required part of rabbinical training surely reflects the intense personalism and turn towards spirituality that marks American religion today.

THE INSTITUTE OF TRADITIONAL JUDAISM. The Union for Traditional Judaism established The *Institute of Traditional Judaism (ITJ), also known as the Metivta, in 1990 in Monroe, New York. The founders of ITJ were drawn principally, though not exclusively, from graduates and faculty of JTS who were disturbed by the decision of JTS to ordain women as rabbis. They believed that that the ordination of homosexuals would soon follow. Former JTS professor of Talmud David Weiss *Halivni, who moved to a position at Columbia University in the wake of his not being appointed as rector of JTS after the death of his mentor Professor Saul Lieberman, was the principal academic-religious spirit behind the establishment of ITJ, and he continues to serve as rector. Rabbi David Novak of the University of Toronto as well as Sephardi Hakham Isaac Sassoon from the Syrian Community are members of the Metivta Faculty, whose members range from graduates of the Mir Yeshiva and the Rabbi Isaac Elchanan Theological Seminary of Yeshiva University to ordinands of JTS. The ITJ motto is, "*Emunah ẓerufah ve-yosher da'at* – Genuine Faith and Intellectual Honesty." ITJ strives to create rabbis who are halakhic traditionalists. At the same time, the Metivta opposes an Orthodox Judaism that is seen as becoming increasingly "triumphalist and separatist." ITJ therefore seeks to create rabbis who will "be fully committed to halakhic observance while facing the non-halakhic community with warmth and willingness to work with all Jews regardless of affiliation."

The ITJ, in keeping with its Conservative Movement roots, is comfortable with the critical method of Talmudic study employed by Rabbi Halivni, who said that "our library will have Wellhausen in it, but not on the top shelf." The leadership sees the school as a transdenominational halakhic rabbinical school. In 1995 the school moved to Teaneck, New Jersey, and in 2005 opened a satellite site on the Upper West Side of Manhattan. In addition to rabbinical ordination, the school offers an MPA in Jewish communal service in conjunction with Fairleigh Dickinson University as well as a *mekhinah* or preparatory program in textual study for men and women.

Reform Institutions

HEBREW UNION COLLEGE-JEWISH INSTITUTE OF RELIGION. The oldest rabbinical college in North America, the Reform seminary Hebrew Union College-Jewish Institute of Religion (HUC-JIR) was formed from a merger of Hebrew Union College (1875) in Cincinnati with the Jewish Institute of Religion (1922) in New York in 1950; it has been informed by the same contemporary cultural-religious forces and sentiments that have influenced the parameters of the JTS and UJ curricula described above. The College-Institute has engaged in a Core Curriculum Project that has caused the curriculum to focus on three key areas – academic, professional, and spiritual – in the education of a new generation of Reform rabbis. While this curriculum has been designed to "foster greater appreciation of practical skills," every effort has been made to strengthen the "academic integrity" of the course of study. For the first time in the history of HUC-JIR, students cannot be admitted unless they have completed at least two years of college-level Hebrew. It is hoped that this minimal level of Hebrew competency for entering students will allow them to advance to "a scholarly mastery of sources."

The HUC-JIR course of study for the rabbinate is five years, and the first-year student is required to study at the HUC campus in Jerusalem. The College-Institute is absolutely committed on an ideological level to the notion of Jewish peoplehood, the first year program in Israel is designed to instill – in addition to Hebrew and textual skills – a sense of solidarity with the Jewish people and the reborn Jewish state. Commitment to *kelal Yisrael* (the Jewish community as a whole) is viewed as a prerequisite for the rabbinic office. While students with little Judaica background are often accepted, HUC-JIR is in the process of raising its requirements in this area (beyond the Hebrew requirement mentioned above) and the establishment of a *mekhinah* year was being contemplated. All students who will be ordained must possess suitable qualities of "character, leadership, personality, and academic capacity" to serve in the rabbinical office, though unlike JTS and in keeping with the non-halakhic character of the Reform Movement, there are no minimal requirements for observance that are demanded.

While the current curriculum of HUC-JIR does display a greater emphasis on classical textual competency than previous curricula did, it would be incorrect to assert that the HUC-JIR curriculum – even as it is refashioned – privileges Talmud. Students can often leave with as little as three classes in Talmud, as required rabbinic literature is construed much more broadly to include commentaries, liturgy, Midrash, and responsa than it would be in more traditional settings. Bible remains a central subject in the curriculum of the College-Institute and the academic orientation of the program is reflected in the scholarly thesis that is required for ordination.

Interestingly, the professors at HUC-JIR today are drawn from every part of the Jewish world, and a number of faculty have received their rabbinic and academic training at both Yeshiva University and the Jewish Theological Seminary as well as secular universities throughout North America, Europe, and Israel. These professors are asked to help equip their students with "the ability to elicit religious values and meanings from the texts they study." Furthermore, there has been a concerted effort to foster the individual spiritual growth of the student as well as the student body as a whole. After all, the student will be striving to create such community after graduation. This necessitates spiritual growth in the seminary years, and the creation of a spiritual community during this period can serve as a model of what the student can aspire to create in the years ahead. In articulating these concerns and themes, HUC-JIR reflects the educational ethos and cultural-spiritual concerns of the day.

Reconstructionist Institution

Such concerns are present at the *Reconstructionist Rabbinical College (RRC) as well. The RRC asserts that its curriculum "embodies a new approach to rabbinic education. The approach understands rabbinical studies as necessarily combining aspects of academic study with a personal encounter with Judaism." Citing the work of Rabbi Mordecai *Kaplan, the RRC contends that a rabbinical school should furnish its students with extensive knowledge of the Jewish heritage, of human nature and social conditions, and with the ability to synthesize situations with which they will have to deal as rabbis. In so doing, the RRC consciously rejects the ideal of rabbis as authority figures. Instead, the rabbi is envisioned as a guide who will help people explore Jewish life for themselves. The rabbi, as part of the community, will work in an egalitarian spirit of cooperation with others to shape the future of Jewish life. Indeed, the RRC teaches its rabbis "to work closely with lay people to build democratic communities." While there is undoubtedly a unique Reconstructionist emphasis at play at the RRC, the themes that are articulated in these descriptions echo comparable accounts found at JTS, UJ, and HUC. The influence of larger cultural trends on all these major institutions of non-Orthodox rabbinical education is readily apparent.

Academically, the program is based on the Reconstructionist notion of Judaism as an evolving, dynamic religious civilization. Each year focuses on biblical, rabbinic, medieval, modern, and contemporary eras of Jewish civilization in succession. By studying the texts, history, thought, and culture of the Jewish heritage in this way, the student gains an appreciation of the constantly evolving nature of Jewish belief and practice. There is also a practical rabbinics program with three main components – course work, fieldwork, and group supervision. The RRC offers five programs of study in this program, and encourages the student to specialize in one – congregational life; campus and Hillel; chaplaincy in hospital, hospice, and geriatric centers; community organization; and education. For people who specialize in education, there is a joint master's degree in education from *Gratz College. The curriculum is designed to have the students appreciate and understand the nature of a rapidly changing world. The RRC is a self-described "warm, caring" community, and its rabbis are educated for the entire Jewish community – in both the synagogue and beyond. In its early years, the RRC insisted that its students pursue a Ph.D. at either Temple University or the University of Pennsylvania alongside their course of study for ordination. However, the demands this imposed on the students were soon seen as too strenuous and such academic training and aspirations were seen as unnecessary for the rabbinic careers they were choosing. The notion of the scholar-rabbi that the American rabbinical seminary had inherited from their German seminary models was no longer culturally compelling.

Transdenominationalism and Spirituality

The dual themes of transdenominationalism and spirituality find strong expression in both the Rabbinical School at Hebrew College in Greater Boston (Newton Centre) (BHC) and the Academy for Jewish Religion (AJR) in California and New York.

RABBINICAL SCHOOL AT HEBREW COLLEGE IN GREATER BOSTON. Led by Rabbi Arthur *Green, a scholar of Ḥasidism, the founder of Havurat Shalom in 1968 during the era of Jewish renewal, and the former dean and president pf the RRC, the Boston Hebrew College Rabbinical School has built upon the Hebrew College's "84-year legacy of transdenominational Jewish studies." Boston Hebrew sees itself as devoted to *kelal Yisrael* and notions of inclusion and spirituality. Indeed, BHC emphasizes that it accepts men and women, gays and heterosexuals, and it requires that candidates display "a love of Jews as well as Judaism." Applicants must have a B.A. and three years of college Hebrew to qualify for admission. The standard program is five years, though BHC specifies that there is a possible *mekhinah* year for students who are in need of remedial work in Judaica and texts. All students are required to study for at least one semester and one summer in Israel.

The emphasis at BHC is upon the study of primary texts. However, these texts focus upon "themes of Jewish living and daily rabbinic practice," and the curriculum is structured around cycles of Torah study and Jewish religious life. The school states that it is a blend of "academy and *yeshivah" –

formal academic study is combined with traditional *ḥevruta*-style learning. Emphasis is placed upon the historic contexts, but a personal religious point of view is cultivated in every class, and there is a strong emphasis on ḥasidic and kabbalistic sources. BHC hopes that the transdenominational setting will prepare rabbis for service in a wide variety of congregational and non-congregational settings, and the college intends to support its graduates should they apply for membership in particular denominations (including possible Orthodox *semikhah*).

ACADEMY FOR JEWISH RELIGION. The Academy for Jewish Religion in California is also designed to be transdenominational and successful completion of its program leads to the title "Rabbi and Teacher in Israel" as well as a Master's Degree in Rabbinic Studies, for its graduates. The program is designed for five years of full-time study, with part-time options available. A supervised internship is required as well as an M.A. thesis prior to ordination. The school, in a manner reminiscent of HUC-JIR, intends to offer "in-depth studies in Bible, Hebrew, History, Liturgy, Philosophy and Theology," as well as rabbinic literature. According to Rabbi Mel Gottlieb, dean of the Rabbinical School, the AJR attempts to revitalize Judaism and seeks to train rabbis who "reflect a deep respect for all denominations" and who engage in "outreach to the unaffiliated." Its motto, "To serve as a bridge between the pillars of Judaism," reflects the aspirations of its founders. The AJR in California also emphasizes spirituality by focusing on mysticism and spirituality and the classics of those traditions – Musar, Ḥasidic thought, and kabbalistic teachings.

Its sister institution, the Academy for Jewish Religion in New York, also seeks to train rabbis who have a deep understanding of all the streams of modern Judaism. There is a focus on "texts and tradition," and there is an effort to cultivate "an appreciation for the historical forces that have shaped our people." At the same time, there is a recognition that Jews in the contemporary period "are in search of meaning and authentic guidance in spirituality." Therefore, considerable time and attention is devoted in the curriculum to "meditation and prayer," in addition to courses in Bible, Hebrew, history, liturgy, and philosophy.

Orthodox Institutions

The Orthodox schools for rabbinic education are all centered on the intensive study of Talmud, and critical academic study is completely eschewed in virtually every one of them. Nevertheless, the institutions and programs that educate rabbis for the North American Orthodox rabbinate display a great deal of variety in their approaches and emphases, and their offerings are surely influenced by the larger environment of North America in ways that parallel the impacts this environment have upon non-Orthodox rabbinical settings.

RABBI ISAAC ELHANAN THEOLOGICAL SEMINARY. Rabbi Isaac Elchanan Theological Seminary of Yeshiva University (RIETS) remains the premiere rabbinical educational institution of Orthodox Judaism in North America. The curriculum is "firmly set in Talmud, Codes, and Halakhah," and there is no attempt to introduce a critical approach to talmudic scholarship into its course of study. While the motto of Yeshiva University may be "*Torah u'madda* – Torah and Academic Study," the latter does not intrude upon the former within the walls of RIETS. As Rabbi Samuel Belkin, the late president of Yeshiva University and head of RIETS, phrased it, "Modern Jewish scholarship has tried to explain Judaism in terms which are alien and do not apply to it, and has attempted to force even those practices and rituals which define the relationship of man to God into the molds of current sociological and economic theories." Though Belkin made this statement decades earlier, critical academic scholarship still has no place at RIETS, which views itself as "heir to, and modeled after, the traditional yeshivot of Europe." This vision is the mirror opposite of the models that the liberal programs have embraced.

The prescribed course of study at RIETS is four years. All students accepted at RIETS must possess an undergraduate academic degree, and they must also have studied Talmud in a post-high school *yeshivah environment for a significant period of time. Virtually all of the students come from intense Orthodox educational backgrounds, and no more than a quarter of the students aspire to the pulpit rabbinate. Study of Talmud for its own sake constitutes the *raison d'être* for this yeshivah and the trend towards ever-greater levels of piety and traditional observance that mark contemporary Orthodoxy have only intensified this ethos within the walls of RIETS. While enrolled in RIETS, students study Talmud a minimum of six hours daily. During the last two years, more emphasis is placed on the codes of the Shulḥan Arukh that deal with dietary laws, family purity, and Sabbath and holiday observance, topics that have constituted the core of classical rabbinic training for centuries.

Students may also then elect an additional four hours of Talmud study daily, work towards a Master's Degree in Judaic Studies, education, or social work, or attend classes sponsored by RIETS in traditional Jewish thought. All students must pass an examination demonstrating mastery of Hebrew as well.

To be sure, a host of classes that hone practical skills have been added to the curriculum in recent years and students may do a year's internship in a synagogue under the guidance of an experienced pulpit rabbi. The rabbis educated by RIETS are essentially prepared to deal almost exclusively with an Orthodox audience of Jews. RIETS has therefore "developed programs to meet the communal and personal needs of our time and place – business ethics, bioethics, and technology." The description indicates that RIETS remains modeled upon the traditional yeshivah, and these other topics are in effect supplements to the study of Talmud that occupies the central place in the curriculum of the yeshivah. This allows the ordainee of RIETS who elects congregational work "to present a more sophisticated, culturally contoured side of Judaism" to congregants who are increasingly Jewishly knowledgeable and halakhically observant.

Interestingly, RIETS was legally separated decades earlier from Yeshiva University itself, because then President Belkin wanted RIETS to be unencumbered by the legal requirements the federal government might impose upon the university itself when the university applied for federal grants. He feared that federal requirements in areas such as housing for men and women and treatment of homosexuals might compromise the religious integrity of RIETS. However, both Rabbi Belkin and his successor rabbi Norman Lamm served both as president of Yeshiva University and *rosh ha-yeshivah* at RIETS. When layman Richard Joel was appointed as president of Yeshiva University, Rabbi Lamm remained formal head of RIETS, inasmuch as Joel faced stiff opposition from many faculty members at RIETS because he was not a rabbi and a suitable religious authority.

HEBREW THEOLOGICAL COLLEGE. A parallel trajectory to that of RIETS is displayed by the Hebrew Theological College (HTC) in Skokie, Illinois. HTC was created in 1922 to provide Orthodox rabbis for an expanding Midwestern Jewish population. Its popular name, "The Skokie Yeshiva," seems to best capture its sectarian nature. Its three-year course of study focuses almost exclusively on traditional Jewish texts and topics and a wide range of classical commentaries on those texts. The student is expected to master the same halakhic texts that the RIETS student is, and the parts of the Shulḥan Arukh that deal with the Sabbath, dietary law, family purity, and mourning are emphasized. The students possess the same type of backgrounds that RIETS students do, though the flavor of the school is even more traditional.

In addition to the intensive three-year cycle of Talmud and *halakhah* study program, "students are also involved in academic areas addressing the particular needs of the chosen specialized area of rabbinic activity, such as education, public speaking, homiletics, and psychology." These students are also assigned to internships with rabbinical mentors in these practical areas.

There is also a *Rav u-Manhig* Program, begun in 1995, which includes 30 semester hours of Talmud study and completion of exams in *Oraḥ Ḥayyim* that "form the cornerstone of the life of a religious Jew." This program is designed to assist students who wish to pursue advanced programs of talmudic studies and is a further sign of the rightward drift that marks the Orthodox world today.

Ironically, the late Rabbi Eliezer *Berkovits, who taught for many years at the Skokie Yeshiva, wrote in a 1975 article in *Tradition: A Journal of Orthodox Jewish Thought*, that the traditional Orthodox rabbinical curriculum had to reshape itself so that the modern Orthodox rabbi would be more capable of connecting traditional Jewish learning to the demands of the modern world in which most North American Jews live.

YESHIVA CHOVEVEI TORAH. While HTC did not heed Rabbi Berkovits's word, Yeshiva Chovevei Torah Rabbinical School (YCT), founded by activist Orthodox Rabbi Avi *Weiss of Riverdale, New York, has donned this mantle. YCT consciously seeks "to promote an inclusive modern Orthodoxy that requires respectful interaction with all Jewish movements" and that expands "the role of women in religious life and leadership." YCT has a four-year program, and intensive study of Talmud and *halakhah* form the focus of the curriculum, as is the case at both HTC and RIETS. However, *Tanakh* (Bible) is a separate discipline as is Jewish Thought (labeled *Maḥshevet Yisrael*). There is an attempt to nurture students "both intellectually and spiritually," and to encounter the texts as an act of "*avodat Hashem*" – service to God. Here YCT adopts the language of religious personalism and spirituality that is the hallmark of all the more liberal non-Orthodox programs.

YCT is distinct among Orthodox yeshivot in other ways as well. In studying Talmud, the curriculum is designed to "address historical and source critical concerns." In *Tanakh*, academic issues of authorship are addressed, while the literary-theological message, as well as classical commentaries, are consulted and considered. This openness to integrating critical, scientific approaches with traditional ones in the study of Jewish texts makes YCT unique in the Orthodox world.

YCT is also a yeshivah that emphasizes the value and religious significance of the State of Israel, and requires a year of study there prior to ordination. In Jewish Thought, ḥasidic and kabbalistic literatures are studied, and two required courses are "The Rise and Development of Jewish Denominations" and "The Challenges of Modern Orthodoxy," which addresses issues of faith and doubt, dogma, authority of the modern rabbi, and gender issues. As its literature proclaims, YCT is "a yeshiva not afraid of ideas," and promotes "academic excellence, *ahavat HaTorah* (love of Torah), and ahavat *Yisrael* (love of the Jewish people)" in its graduates who go out to serve in a wide variety of Orthodox synagogues and communal and educational settings.

OHR TORAH STONE (JOSEPH STRAUSS RABBINICAL SEMINARY). In completing this review of institutions and programs that produce Orthodox rabbis to serve the North American Jewish community, it is important to take note of Ohr Torah Stone (Joseph Strauss Rabbinical Seminary) in Efrat, Israel. Headed by Rabbi Shlomo *Riskin and Rabbi Chaim Brovender, this Israeli-based Orthodox rabbinical program aims at training "a new generation of rabbinic leaders who combine their halakhic knowledge with an understanding of the particular needs of contemporary Jewish life." After completing a four-year course of study, students are expected to return to the Diaspora. Ohr Torah Stone views Torah as a "unifying force rather than a divider," and is "attentive to the importance of tolerance and openness, without compromising religious commitment." There is "sensitivity towards the situation of Jews in the Diaspora." Thus, when laws of conversion, for example, are taught, considerable attention is paid to issues of assimilation and intermarriage in the Diaspora. Similarly, in studying laws relating to Sabbath observance, the focus is placed upon how a community of Sabbath-observant Jews might be established.

There is also a program called Amiel – Rabbi Emanuel Rackman Program for Practical Rabbinics, attached to the yeshivah. Directed by R. Eliyahu Birnbaum, it is open to both JSRS students and qualified candidates from other Israeli yeshivot. This program is designed to train rabbis to work with the non-observant in Jewish communities throughout the Diaspora and desires to meet the challenges posed by assimilation. A number of these students come to America for at least two years, and they focus on "Communal Leadership."

ULTRA-ORTHODOX YESHIVOT. *Ḥaredi* (Ultra-Orthodox) yeshivot that focused almost exclusively on the study of Torah for its own sake during the first 80 years of the 20th century began to change direction as a result of a speech Rabbi Moshe Sherer, the president of Agudath Israel in America, delivered in 1978. In an appeal to yeshivah students, Rabbi Sherer stated that if *ḥaredi* rabbis did not enter "into the rabbinate to save," assimilated American Jews, then "millions of *neshamos* (souls)… will enter churches." While ultra-Orthodox seminaries remain firm in their commitment to "Torah for Torah's sake," there has been movement towards the pulpit in many of them during the last two decades.

In The Rabbinical Seminary of America, Chofetz Chaim Yeshiva, Kew Gardens Hills, New York, which follows the Lithuanian model of the Musar (Ethical-Pietistic) yeshivah, a great deal of emphasis is placed upon *middos*, the formation of spiritual and ethical character. In addition to classical rabbinic texts, time is devoted each day to the study of *musar* literature. Its students can earn a master's degrees in education or business while they study at the yeshiva a novel turn for such institutions. Baltimore's Ner Israel Rabbinical College has such cooperative programs as well.

Chofetz Chaim also sends its students into the public schools each week for an outreach activity labeled JEP – Jewish Educational Programs. Here, the yeshivah students offer programs in Jewish cultural literacy to non-observant Jews. In this yeshivah, students study from the age of 18 to 30 or 35 before they complete their studies and receive ordination. Hence, they are in school 8 to 12 years more than their counterparts at other Orthodox rabbinical schools. As of 2006, there were over 300 students in Chofetz Chaim yeshivot, and branches have been established in Milwaukee, Cherry Hills, Los Angeles, and San Diego. The *rosh yeshivah* (head of the yeshivah) assigns ordainees to communities where he feels there is the greatest need, and these rabbis are instructed to establish day schools. These rabbis also go in a group, not as individuals, and an infrastructure is thereby established to sustain religious life for these men and their families. The influence of these rabbis in a number of communities is quite pronounced, and they are marked by a significant missionary zeal.

At the Maor Program, in Silver Spring, Maryland, a course consisting of two three-week sessions is offered in two consecutive summers to train graduates of *ḥaredi* yeshivot for the pulpit rabbinate. Established by Rabbi Shaya Milikowsky, a Ner Israel ordainee, the program is similar in its aim to the Amiel Program of Ohr Torah, and it reflects a shift in the right-wing Orthodox world and the determination of the leadership of that world to speak to non-observant as well as observant Jewish populations. The students come from places such as Ner Israel and Beth Midrash Ha-Gavohah in Lakewood and Philadelphia. The classes meet five days a week, eight hours a day, and the courses aim to prepare their graduates for service in communities with heavy Jewish populations where no Orthodox synagogues exist. Maor does not seek students who have undergraduate degrees, and even looks askance upon them.

Rabbinical Ordination/Leadership Program (ROLP) (Aish Hatorah) was established in 1975 by Rabbi Noah Weinberg. This yeshivah also aims to educate rabbis who will bring non-observant and weakly affiliated Jews to embrace traditional Judaism, and the program attempts to foster an "Aish Culture." In contrast to other Orthodox yeshivot, the course of study is relatively short and less textually demanding. Furthermore, it is focused on outreach. Thus, even courses in Talmud and Codes center on what one needs to know in order to be an effective outreach rabbi. The course of study is one and a half to two years. Three components mark the curriculum – traditional rabbinic learning, practical rabbinics, and vocational training. In addition to study of Talmud and Codes, there is a great deal of emphasis placed upon Bible, as this is seen as vital for outreach to non-observant American Jews. Students also engage in practical programs where they work with such people during their time in the yeshivah, and they then take courses "dedicated to the daily responsibilities of the rabbi." This constitutes 40% of the curriculum, and the graduates are expected to work one day in Aish centers, principally in North America.

Finally, *Chabad constitutes the other formal program designed for the education of rabbis who will serve the North American Jewish community. Chabad rabbis have to complete three years of post-high school study in Chabad yeshivot. They are then permitted to study the traditional Codes required to receive ordination, and they center their efforts in these years on those sections that deal with dietary laws, the Sabbath, and prayer. However, most of these rabbis began their formation for the Chabad rabbinate long before they entered advanced Chabad yeshivot. Indeed, the average Chabad rabbi began serving as a *shali'aḥ* (emissary) at the age of 14. Hence, by the time they are ordained, most have spent eight years as *sheliḥim*, teaching Jewish men how to don *tefillin* and women to light Shabbat candles. They have a great deal of exposure to non-observant Jews and unlike other Orthodox yeshivot, their graduates intend to stay in whatever community they have been assigned permanently. They often serve as Orthodox rabbis to non-observant Jews and will sometimes begin their work as the only observant Jews in their new homes. The difference here between the ideology and program that animates Chofetz Chayim – where graduates go to a community in a group – and Chabad is pronounced.

Conclusion

The venues where rabbis are educated to serve the North American Jewish community are thus many and highly variegated. Furthermore, there are a number of rabbis who are ordained privately as well and these men and women serve the North American Jewish community in a wide variety of settings. While the student of North American Judaism must be keenly mindful of this variety, there is no question that the religious and cultural environment of 21st-century America has had a profound impact upon the course of study that these many programs and institutions of higher Jewish education provide and the coming years will undoubtedly witness an ongoing vitality and diversity in the education of rabbis who will serve the contemporary American Jewish community.

BIBLIOGRAPHY: E. Berkovits, "A Contemporary Rabbinical School for Orthodox Jewry," in: *Tradition: A Journal of Orthodox Jewish Thought*, 13 (1971), 5–20; D. Ellenson and L. Bycel, "A Seminary of Sacred Learning: The JTS Rabbinical Curriculum in Historical Perspective," in: J. Wertheimer (ed.), *Tradition Renewed: A History of the Jewish Theological Seminary of America* (1997), 525–91; A. Ferziger, "Training American Orthodox Rabbis to Play a Role in Confronting Assimilation: Programs, Methodologies, and Directions," in: *Rappaport Center for Assimilation Research: Research and Position Papers Series*, vol. 4 (2003), 7–72; C. Liebman, "The Training of American Rabbis," in: *American Jewish Year Book*, 69 (1968), 3–114.

[David Ellenson (2nd ed.)]

RABBINOVICZ (Rabinovitz), RAPHAEL NATHAN NATA (1835–1888), talmudic scholar. Born in Novo-Zhagory, district of Kovno, at the age of 16 he wrote a bibliographical treatise, *Siftei Yeshenim Gimmel*. Several years later he gave it to the bibliographer Isaac *Benjacob, who used it in compiling his *Ozar ha-Sefarim*. Rabbinovicz lived for a time in Lemberg, Galicia, where he published a volume of responsa by R. Meir of Rothenburg (1860) and *Ge'on Ya'akov* (1863), novellae on the tractate of *Eruvin* by R. Jacob Kahana of Vilna. Moving on to Pressburg, he published *Kunteres Ikkarei ha-Avodah* (1863) by his teacher R. Joseph b. Israel Issar of Vilkomir. About that time he learned from Adolph *Jellinek in Vienna of the 14th-century manuscript of the Babylonian Talmud preserved in the Royal Library of Munich. He proceeded to that city, and with the encouragement of R. Joseph Saul *Nathanson, the rabbi of Lemberg, devoted himself to copying the variant readings in order to publish them. In 1864 he published a small booklet, *Alim le-Mivḥan* (lithographed from his handwriting), containing samples of the variant readings found in the Talmud manuscript. The following year he published a similar, but more detailed, treatise, *Kunteres Dikdukei Soferim*, in the Hebrew weekly *Ha-Maggid*.

Between 1867 and 1886 he published 15 volumes of *Dikdukei Soferim*, containing the variant readings on all the tractates of the orders of *Zera'im*, *Mo'ed*, and *Nezikin*, and on the tractates of *Zevaḥim*, and *Menaḥot*. The variant readings are accompanied by explanatory notes in which readings found in other manuscripts – in the writings of early authorities and in old printed editions – are recorded. In his introduction to *Dikdukei Soferim* Rabbinovicz gave a history of the printing of the Babylonian Talmud. A revised and much enlarged version of this essay *Ma'amar al Hadpasat ha-Talmud* appeared later in volume 8 (1877). In the course of his work he traveled widely to consult manuscripts and early printed editions in various libraries. He was aided greatly in his efforts by the Munich Jewish banker Abraham *Merzbacher, who supported him materially and permitted him to buy at his expense all the books and manuscripts he needed. After the death of Merzbacher, Rabbinovicz compiled, at the request of the banker's son, a catalog (*Ohel Avraham*, 1888) of the rich library he had amassed for his father. Its treasures included 156 manuscripts and 43 incunabula.

Despite the material support he received, Rabbinovicz was forced to engage in the selling of books and manuscripts. He died in Kiev, while on one of his business journeys to Russia. Shortly before his death he began printing *Dikdukei Soferim* on the tractate of *Ḥullin*. The work on the volume was completed by Heinrich Ehrentreu and appeared in 1897.

Rabbinovicz also wrote *Moreh ha-Moreh* (1871), a critique of D.B. *Zomber's *Moreh Derekh*, about Rabbenu Gershom's and Rashi's commentaries on the tractate *Mo'ed Katan*, and published a small part of the medieval *Yiḥusei Tanna'im va-Amora'im* (1874). He also contributed to *Ha-Maggid*, where his notes on Jehiel M. Zunz's *Irha-Ẓedek* appeared (vols. 19–20, 1875–76).

BIBLIOGRAPHY: R.N. Rabbinovicz, *Ma'amar al Hadpasat ha-Talmud*, ed. by A.M. Habermann (1952²), 261–7; A. Schischa, in: *Aresheth*, 3 (1961), 376–91; Y. Raphael, *ibid.*, 392–4.

[Tovia Preschel]

RABBINOWICZ, ISRAEL MICHEL (1818–1893), writer and scholar. Born in Gorodets, Lithuania, Rabbinowicz, whose father was rabbi in Gorodets and from 1828 in Antopol, received a traditional education. His brother, Joshua Jacob, also rabbi in Gorodets, was the author of several talmudic works. At the yeshivah in Brest-Litovsk Rabbinowicz began his study of the philosophers, especially Maimonides. Deciding to widen his field of study, he learned German in Brody and Greek and Latin (with D. Chwolson) in Breslau, where he subsequently entered the university as a student of philology. In 1851 he published a Hebrew grammar, *Hebraeische Grammatik nach neuen, sehr vereinfachten Regeln und Grundsaetzen*, followed by *Hebraeische Schulgrammatik...* in 1853 (French translation by J.J. Clement-Mullet), selling the books himself in order to earn a living. Later he took up medicine and in 1854 went to Paris, where he continued his studies in hospitals until 1865. In that year he obtained his M.D. with his *Etudes historiques de l'empoisonnement*, which consisted in the main of a translation of Maimonides' "Treatise on Poisons." However, he rarely practiced medicine, preferring to devote himself, in solitude and poverty, to scholarship. Too poor to heat his room, he wrote his books in a café. As well as extending his grammatical methods to other languages (*Nouveaux principes comparés de la prononciation Anglaise...*, 1874; *Vergleichende Gramma-*

tik der polnischen Sprache, 1877; *Grammaire de la langue française d'après de nouveaux principes…* 1886, 1889²), he defended Jewish tradition against its detractors, publishing *Le rôle de Jésus et des apôtres* (1866), a critique of Renan; *La religion nationale des anciens Hébreux* (1873), a criticism of Jules Soury; and *Histoire Sainte: Ancien Testament* (1877). However his main work was his condensed translation, with commentary, of talmudic legislation, *La législation criminelle du Thalmud* (1876) and *La législation civile du Thalmud* (1–5, 1877–80). A Zionist from the early days of the movement, he took part in the Kattowitz Conference of 1884 and presided over the Benei Zion of Paris. He went to Russia in 1889 with the intention of trying to have his books republished, and subsequently lived in London, where he was assisted until his death by Chief Rabbi N.M. Adler and other benefactors.

BIBLIOGRAPHY: *Ha-Maggid*, 32 (1888), 153–5; Reines, in: *Oẓar ha-Sifrut*, 5 (1896), 117–23; M. Schwab, *Le Docteur I.M. Rabbinowicz* (1903).

[Moshé Catane]

RABBINOWITZ, SAUL PHINEHAS (acronym, **SHePHeR**; 1845–1910), East European Hebrew writer and historian. Rabbinowitz, who was born in Tavrogi, Lithuania, to a family of rabbis, received *semikhah* from Israel Salanter (Lipkin), while also becoming interested in Haskalah and teaching himself German and Russian. Rabbinowitz first worked as a private tutor in Vilna and other Lithuanian towns before settling in Warsaw in 1875 where he wrote for the Hebrew press. During this period he inclined toward socialist cosmopolitanism, which brought him into contact with A.S. *Liebermann's circle of Jewish Socialists. In 1881 Rabbinowitz was among those who reported on the Russian pogroms to Western Jewry. He accompanied S. *Mohilever to Brody, where they organized help for the refugees; he also took part in the St. Petersburg Conference of Notables (1882), calling for mass emigration from Russia. At first, Rabbinowitz advocated emigration to the U.S. but he soon joined Ḥovevei Zion, became secretary of the important Warsaw branch, and attended the Kattowitz Conference (1884). During 1886–88 he published the annual *Keneset Yisrael*, an organ for national revival and Ḥibbat Zion, and published documents on the history of Russian-Polish Jewry in a supplement (*Orot me-Ofel*). In 1890 he was among the founders of the Warsaw office of Aḥad Ha-Am's order *Benei Moshe and tried to defend the interests of religious tradition within its ranks. In 1891 he joined an abortive Ḥovevei Zion mission to the West. A member of the Zionist movement, Rabbinowitz attended the first Zionist Congresses, although he criticized aspects of the movement in *Al Ẓiyyon ve-al Mikra'eha* (1898).

Rabbinowitz's great scholarly achievement was his Hebrew translation of H. Graetz's *History of the Jews* (1890–99), in which the author had given him a free hand. Rabbinowitz introduced many changes in the text, also omitting passages that might offend the Orthodox and the Russian censors. The translation includes his own notes and those of A. Harkavy and other scholars. Rabbinowitz's work, which was in fact a new "Graetz," had a tremendous impact on Eastern Jewry, despite its *meliẓah* style, and was reprinted in many editions. Other writings by Rabbinowitz include biographies of L. *Zunz (1896), Z. *Frankel (1898), and *Joseph (Joselman) of Rosheim (1902), and a study on the Jews expelled from Spain, published on the 400th anniversary of the Expulsion (*Moẓe'ei Golah*, 1894). He contributed articles to the newly founded (1896) Hebrew periodical *Ha-Shilo'aḥ*, participated in the early *Eshkol* Hebrew encyclopedia (1888), and completed S.J. *Fuenn's Hebrew dictionary *Ha-Oẓar* (1900–03).

Beset by poverty and family misfortunes, and having suffered great hardship during and after the 1905 revolution, Rabbinowitz left Russia for Frankfurt where, however, he found little recognition and had to live on charity. His proposed three-volume modern Jewish history did not advance beyond the publication of a few chapters. His biography was written by his son-in-law, the historian J. *Meisl.

BIBLIOGRAPHY: J. Meisl, *Rabbi Sha'ul Pinḥas Rabbinowitz (Shefer); ha-Ish u-Fo'olo* (1943), incl. bibl.; A. Druyanow (ed.), *Ketavim le-Toledot Ḥibbat Ẓiyyon* 1–3 (1919–32), index.

[Yehuda Slutsky]

RAB DE LA CORTE ("court rabbi"), an office common in Navarre and Castile until the expulsion of the Jews from Spain in 1492. He was appointed by the crown to supervise the Jewish communal leadership and the apportionment of taxes among the communities. Because of this task he is referred to as *repartidor de todas las aljamas* and was considered "Judge in Chief" of the Jewish communities. The office was established in these kingdoms during the middle of the 13th century. Attempts to introduce it into Aragon, Catalonia, and Valencia, mainly at the end of the 13th century, failed. The beginnings of this office are unknown. As judge in chief, *juez mayor* ("chief justice"), he served as a kind of a court of appeals for the Jews. Generally those appointed to this position were Jews close to the kings or crown princes, serving as physicians, interpreters, or fiscal agents. The majority were not distinguished for their learning, and Solomon b. Abraham ibn *Adret complained that "in our country there are rabbis appointed by the king who do not know how to read properly." Some, however, were scholars, for instance Abraham *Benveniste. The Rab de la Corte presided over meetings of representatives of the communities who were convened when necessary and supervised the drafting of the *askamot* ("communal regulations") and the tax apportionment. Sometimes, he acted as arbitrator in intercommunal disputes. The last Rab de la Corte in Castile was Abraham *Seneor, who became converted to Christianity shortly before the expulsion. The office of Araby *Mor in Portugal largely corresponds to that of Rab de la Corte.

BIBLIOGRAPHY: Baer, Spain, index; Baer, Urkunden, index; Neuman, Spain, index; Suárez Fernández, Documentos (1964), 108–9, 162–3, 243–5, 246–7, 297–9, 375–7.

RABI, ISIDOR ISAAC (1898–1988), U.S. physicist and Nobel Prize winner. Rabi was born at Rymanow, Austro-Hungary, and taken to the United States when he was a year old. He became a tutor in physics at City College, New York, and won fellowships to various European universities. In 1937 he returned to lecture at Columbia, where he was appointed a full professor in 1950. Meanwhile, he continued his own researches in nuclear physics, quantum mechanics and magnetism. He realized that the essential step was to determine the nature of the force that holds together the protons within the nucleus of the atom, overcoming the mutual repulsion that must exist between them, as all are positively charged. When Otto *Stern discovered how to measure this force by means of a "molecular beam," Rabi followed up the discovery, which he found more effective than fission for elucidating the structure of the atom. His most distinguished work was the development of a method of receiving and interpreting such beams, and it was this that won him the Nobel Prize for physics in 1944, four years after he had become associate director of the radiation laboratory at the Massachusetts Institute of Technology. During the remainder of World War II Rabi served as a civilian investigator for the Office of Scientific Research and Development. From 1953 he was chairman of the general advisory committee of the Atomic Energy Commission, but he was active among those opposing the strict military control of atomic energy proposed by Congress, and he deplored what he saw as a tendency for pure science to be subordinated to industrial needs. He was involved with building the cyclotron as well as with other work at the Brookhaven National Laboratory for Atomic Research. Rabi was a member of the UN Science Committee and on the Atomic Energy agency, among other international agencies. He was a member of the board of governors of the Weizmann Institute in Israel. Two autobiographical lectures, published under the title *My Life and Times as a Physicist*, appeared in 1960.

BIBLIOGRAPHY: T. Levitan, *Laureates, Jewish Winners of the Nobel Prize* (1960), 89–92; *Current Biography Yearbook 1948* (1949), 509–10.

[J. Edwin Holmstrom]

RABĪʿ IBN ABI AL-ḤUQAYQ (end of the 6th century). Jewish poet from the Jewish tribe of Banī *Naḍīr in Yathrib, Arabia. A short poem of his is included in the anthology of Arabic poetry by al-Jumaḥī, in the chapter on the Jews of *Medina (pp. 70–74). Except for al-*Samaw'al ibn ʿĀdiyah, he is the only poet in pre-Islamic Arabia mentioned by Moses Ibn Ezra in his book on Hebrew medieval poetry, probably based on Arab sources. Ibn Ezra raises the possibility that both Samaw'al and Rabīʿ were Arabs converted to Judaism. Rabīʿ took part in intertribal wars and in poetic contests with other famous Arab poets, such as al-Nābighah.

BIBLIOGRAPHY: Al-Jumaḥī, *Ṭabaqāt al-Shuʿarāʾ*, ed. J. Hell (1913), 71; Moses Ibn Ezra, *Kitāb al-Muḥāḍārah, wa-al-Mudhākarah* ed. A.Sh. Halkin (1975), 31; H.Z. Hirschberg, *Israel ba-Arav* (1946), 129, 172, 250–251.

[Yosef Tobi (2nd ed.)]

RABIN, family of scholars. ISRAEL ABRAHAM RABIN (1882–1951) was born in Proskurov, Ukraine. After the *Kishinev pogrom of 1903, he was entrusted to accompany the orphans to Austria (in the post-World War I Ukrainian pogroms his own parents were murdered). From 1909 he taught at the Ezra teachers' seminary in Jerusalem, and in 1911 was called to head the Odessa Rabbinical Seminary. Detained in Germany by the outbreak of World War I, he subsequently took up a teaching position in post-biblical Jewish literature and history at Giessen University, taught at Frankfurt University (1918–21), and at the Jewish Theological Seminary, Breslau. From 1929 Rabin also taught Semitics and post-biblical literature at Breslau University. In 1935 he left Nazi Germany for Palestine where he headed a Mizrachi elementary school at Haifa and was chairman of the Haifa Religious Council. Rabin was an early supporter of religious Zionism (Mizrachi) and as its delegate attended all Zionist Congresses from the sixth – at which he voted against acceptance of the Uganda offer – to the twenty-first. While teaching at Jerusalem (1909–11), he was among the members of the *Academy of the Hebrew Language.

Rabin's published work ranges over a wide field of Jewish scholarship. His historical studies are devoted to the Jews of Silesia (*Beitraege zur Rechts-und Wirtschaftsgeschichte…* 1, 1932; *Rechtskampf der Juden in Schlesien*, 1927; *Juden in Dyhernfurth*, 1929; in *Zuelz*, 1926) and also deal with general problems of historiography (*Stoff und Idee…, in Festschrift… Dubnow*, 1930, 41–56). His *Studien zur Vormosaischen Gottesvorstellung (Festschrift zum 75 = jaehrigen Bestehen des Juedisch-Theologischen Seminars*, 2, 1929) deal critically with the hypotheses of higher biblical criticism and anticipate some of the ideas on Israel's monotheism later developed by Y. *Kaufmann. Of special importance to rabbinics is the critical edition of *Mekhilta*, prepared by S. Horovitz but completed and published by Rabin (1931, repr. 1960).

One son was the Hebraist and linguist Chaim Menachem *Rabin. Israel's younger son was Michael Oser *Rabin.

RABIN, MICHAEL OSER (1931–), Israeli mathematician. Rabin was born in Breslau, Germany, and was brought to Ereẓ Israel in 1935. After graduating from the Hebrew University he taught mathematics from 1956 to 1958 at Princeton, where he obtained his doctorate and was a member of the Institute for Advanced Study. Returning to Israel in 1958 he became associate professor at the Hebrew University in 1961 and full professor in 1965. Rabin's field of study was mathematical logic, autotheory, and the mathematical theory of computations, and he is credited with a number of inventions in the field of computers. From 1972 to 1975 Rabin was the rector of the Hebrew University of Jerusalem and in 1980 was awarded the Harvey Prize of the Haifa Technion (jointly with S.D. *Goitein and E. *Racker). He was rewarded the Israel Prize in 1995.

RABIN, OSCAR (1928–), Russian painter. Rabin, both of whose parents were doctors, was born in Moscow and studied music before turning to art. He is an extraordinary case of an artist refused recognition in the Soviet Union, who nevertheless became known as an outstanding painter outside his native country. Since he was not a member of the Artists' Union he was not officially recognized as an artist or allowed to exhibit and had to work as an exhibition designer from his home in a suburb of Moscow. He first gained a reputation outside the U.S.S.R. when his work was seen in London at the Grosvenor Gallery in 1964 in a mixed show of Soviet painters, and later the same gallery mounted his first ever one-man exhibition. Rabin's work was Expressionistic in character, having much in common with Soutine and Rouault, using dark somber colors and heavy outlines – almost in the manner of stained glass. He painted his native Moscow in street scenes and often depicted Western cities he has never visited. On the day of President Kennedy's assassination, Nov. 22, 1963, he painted a canvas to commemorate the event. Rabin was a prolific painter and despite official lack of recognition his work was popular both in the Soviet Union and among foreign visitors.

Both Rabin's status as a leader of young, dissident Soviet painters and his connections with foreign journalists and diplomats came to the fore in the remarkable effort to hold a "free" exhibition in September 1974. The exhibition was organized by Rabin and his son, together with a group of unorthodox artists. Their first effort was literally destroyed by the police, but as a result of international publicity the authorities relented and allowed some 60 painters to exhibit their work in an informal display at Moscow's Izmailovo Park.

In July 1978 the Soviet authorities canceled his Soviet citizenship "in view of his systematic activity incompatible with the status of Soviet citizen." He continued to work in Paris

[Charles Samuel Spencer]

RABIN, SAM (1903–1991), British painter. Rabin was born in Manchester as Samuel Rabinovitch, the son of an impoverished cap cutter who had migrated from Vitebsk. His children were artistically gifted and Rabin was taught draughtsmanship by an elder brother. At the age of eleven he was the youngest pupil ever to win a scholarship to the Manchester School of Art, and later won a scholarship to the Slade School in London, where, at the age of 15, he was the youngest student and where he was befriended and influenced by the artist Barnett *Freedman. On the completion of his studies Rabin spent some time in Paris and took up modeling under the influence of the famous French sculptor Charles Despiau. His portrait head of Barnett Freedman is in the Tate Gallery, London. Rabin, however, devoted most of his career to working in pastels and to the subject of sport. A physically powerful man, Rabin won a bronze medal in wrestling at the 1928 Olympics and later, to make ends meet, became a professional wrestler. Wrestling and boxing became the principal subjects of his work, which depicted the atmosphere of the ring and the figures of the combatants with a mixture of brilliant realism and graceful movement. Rabin was also an actor, and played boxers and wrestlers in several films, including *The Scarlet Pimpernel* (1934), where he had the role of Daniel *Mendoza, the famous Jewish boxer. He taught at the Goldsmith School of Art from 1949 to 1965, where Mary Quant was one of his students, and then at the Bournemouth College of Art. His work is represented in leading public collections; the British Museum obtained a group of his drawings.

ADD. BIBLIOGRAPHY: ODNB online; J. Sheeran, *Introducing Sam Rabin* (1965).

[Charles Samuel Spencer / William D. Rubinstein (2nd ed.)]

RABIN, YITZHAK (1922–1995), military commander and politician, seventh chief of staff of the Israel Defense Forces, and prime minister in the years 1974–77 and 1992–95, member of the Eighth to Thirteenth Knessets. Rabin was born in Jerusalem. His mother was known as "Red Rosa." He graduated from the Kadoorie Agricultural School. He joined the *Palmaḥ in 1941, and participated in the Allied invasion of Syria that year. In 1944, as second in command of a Palmaḥ battalion, he participated in underground activities against the British Mandatory Government. On Black Saturday, June 29, 1946, he was arrested and imprisoned in the Rafa detention camp for six months. After his release he was appointed deputy to Yigal *Allon, who was commander of the Palmaḥ from 1945. In the early days of the *War of Independence, Rabin was appointed commander of the Harel Brigade on the Jerusalem front. Later in 1948 he was responsible, as Allon's second in command, for the occupation of Lydda and Ramleh, and the expulsion of their Arab inhabitants. He was next appointed chief of operations of the Southern Command until the armistice agreement with Egypt, and was a member of the Israeli delegation to the Rhodes armistice talks. However, he objected to the agreement reached, and left before it was signed. After the War of Independence Rabin was given various assignments, and graduated from the British Staff College in 1953. In the years 1956–59 he served as commander of the Northern Command, and in the years 1959–63 served as head of the Operations Branch in the General Staff, and deputy chief of staff. Rabin was appointed chief of staff in January 1964, and served for four years. As a heavy smoker on the eve of the outbreak of the *Six Day War he suffered from nicotine poisoning but recovered to lead the IDF in its major victory over the Egyptian, Syrian, and Jordanian forces. Immediately after the war he was awarded an honorary degree by the Hebrew University at a ceremony on Mount Scopus, and delivered an impressive acceptance speech, noted for its humane spirit. He retired from active military service in January 1968, and was appointed ambassador to the U.S. Upon his return to Israel in March 1973 he decided to enter politics, and was elected to the Eighth Knesset on the Alignment list, right after the *Yom Kippur War. He was appointed minister of labor in the short-lived government formed by Golda *Meir, and when Meir decided to resign following the publication of the Interim Report of the *Agranat Commission in April 1974, he won the first of numerous contests for the leadership of the *Israel Labor Party against Shimon *Peres. The fact that he had not been involved in any way in the Yom Kippur War was the main reason for his victory. Rabin formed a new government in June 1974. Even though his first premiership was generally viewed as mediocre, during his term as prime minister, with U.S. assistance, the IDF was rehabilitated, and the economy picked up, even though the rate of inflation rose. After disengagement agreements were signed with Egypt and Syria in January and May 1974 with the help of the "shuttle diplomacy" of Secretary of State Henry *Kissinger, an interim agreement was signed with Egypt in September 1975, together with a memorandum of understanding with the U.S. The Entebbe operation also took place in the course of his premiership. Towards the end of 1976 Rabin fired the ministers from the *National Religious Party, after they had abstained in a vote on a motion of no-confidence in the government, over the arrival of F-15 planes from the U.S. to Israel on a Friday afternoon, and the holding of a ceremony that allegedly resulted in the desecration of the Sabbath by those who participated in it. However, the historic coalition with the NRP was in trouble even before this event, due to a shift to the right by the young guard in the national religious camp. As a result of pressure by Attorney General Aharon *Barak, Rabin was forced to resign from the premiership in March 1977, following the revelation by journalist Dan *Margalit that his wife, Leah, continued to hold a bank account in Washington, D.C. from the time of his service as ambassador, contrary to the Israeli foreign exchange regulations. In the elections for the Ninth Knesset held in May 1977, Shimon *Peres led the Alignment and suffered a bitter defeat, in what came to be known as "the political upheaval." In 1979 Rabin published his memoirs, in which his bitterness against Peres emerged. Following the death of Yigal *Allon, Rabin decided to contend again for the leadership of the Labor Party against Peres, but at the Party Conference held in December 1980 he gained only 29% of the votes. In the National Unity Government that was in office from 1984 to 1990 Rabin served as minister of defense. In this capacity he got the IDF out of Lebanon, canceled the Lavi fighter project, and led Israel's fight against the first Intifada. Even though his policy in the territories was viewed as a "hard fist" policy, he realized soon after the outbreak of the Intifada that there could be no military solution to the conflict with the Palestinians. Prior to the elections to the Twelfth Knesset in 1988, he formulated a plan for holding elections in the West Bank and Gaza Strip. This plan was adopted by the National Unity Government in May 1989 as part of the Shamir-Rabin peace initiative. Even though he favored the continued existence of the government led by Yitzhak *Shamir, he supported Peres' initiative to bring down the government in March 1990, following problems within the Likud in advancing the peace initiative. However, after Peres failed to form an alternative government, he called the ploy "the stinking ploy." In February 1992 he contested the leadership of the Labor Party with Peres for the third time, gaining over 40 percent of the votes to Peres' 34 percent (there were two additional contestants). In the Knesset he supported the adoption of the law for the direct election of the prime minister, but he won the elections to the Thirteenth Knesset under the old system. After forming a government with *Meretz and *Shas, he concentrated on changing Israel's economic priorities from massive support of the settlements in the territories to Israel's periphery, and on efforts to further the peace process. Though the Oslo process was initiated by Yossi *Beilin (who in the past Rabin had called "Peres' poodle") he gave the negotiations his backing in its latter stages, and on September 13, 1993, signed the Declaration of Principles (DOP) with PLO chairman Yasser *Arafat, which led to Israel's handing over to a "Palestinian entity" the city of Gaza and the Jericho area. This agreement was followed by two additional agreements, under which Israel handed over the Arab towns and cities in the territories to the Palestinians, and agreed to the establishment of a *Palestinian Authority. However, the talks with the Palestinians at this stage did not deal with the future of the Jewish settlements, Jerusalem, or the Palestinian refugees. Very close relations also developed at this time between Rabin and King *Hussein of Jordan, and a peace treaty was signed between Israel and Jordan in October 1994. Formal relations were also established with Morocco, Tunisia, and several Gulf states, and Israel participated in a succession of economic conferences held in various Arab capitals. Talks were also held with Syria, but despite Rabin's willingness to make substantial concessions, these talks led to naught. For his efforts toward regional peace, Rabin was the recipient, along with Peres and Arafat, of the Nobel Prize for Peace in December 1994.

However, right-wing circles in Israel objected to Rabin's peace initiatives, and willingness to give up control over parts of Ereẓ Israel. Demonstrations against him became increasingly vicious and threatening, but despite warnings by the General Security Services, Rabin refused to wear a bulletproof vest. On November 4, 1995, at the end of a mass demonstration in Kikar Malkhei Yisrael in Tel Aviv, which he addressed, Rabin was shot in the back by Yigal Amir, a Jewish right-wing fanatic, who acted on his own, with only his brother being privy to his plans. Rabin's coffin was placed at the entrance of the Knesset, and his funeral was attended by numerous heads of state and prime ministers, including King Hussein of Jordan and President Hosni *Mubarak of Egypt, who had never previously set foot in Israel. It was President Bill Clinton who coined the term "*Shalom Ḥaver*" ("farewell, friend") that continues to appear on stickers on many cars in Israel to the present day. The assassination was a major failure for the GSS, which changed its entire strategy of protecting VIPs in Israel. Ten years after his assassination the people of Israel were still divided over Rabin's heritage.

Rabin's daughter DALIA RABIN-PELOSSOF entered the Fifteenth Knesset on the Center Party list, and joined the One Israel (Labor) parliamentary group in May 2001. She did not run in the elections to the Sixteenth Knesset.

Among his books are *The Rabin Memoirs* (1979) and a collection of his peace speeches *Ne'umei ha-Shalom shel Rosh ha-Memshalah Yiẓhak Rabin* (1995).

BIBLIOGRAPHY: Z. Galili, *Yiẓhak Rabin 1922–1995* (Heb., 1996); D.P. Horowitz (ed.), *Shalom Friend: The Life and Legacy of*

Yitzhak Rabin (1996); A. Kapelyuk, *Rabin: Reẓaḥ Politi be-Ezrat ha-Shem* (1996); M. Na'or, *Yiẓḥak Rabin: Ha-Ish, ha-Mefaked, ha-Medina'i, ha-Mazbi, ha-Shalom* (1996); R. Slater, *Rabin of Israel: Warrior for Peace* (1996); L. Rabin, *Our Life, His Legacy* (1997); M. Karpin, *Murder in the Name of God: The Plot to Kill Yitzhak Rabin* (1998); D. Kurzman, *Soldier of Peace: The Life of Yitzhak Rabin* (1998); Y. Pery (ed.), *The Assassination of Yitzhak Rabin* (2000); E. Inbar, *Rabin and Israel's National Security* (2001); A. Dalal, *Ma'arekhet ha-Emunot shel Yiẓḥak Rabin Kelappei ha-Aravim ve-ha-Sikhsukh ha-Yisra'eli* (2003).

[Susan Hattis Rolef (2nd ed.)]

RABINOFF, GEORGE W. (1893–1970), pioneer of U.S. professional Jewish communal service. Rabinoff, born in New York City, graduated from the New York School of Social Work (1914), one of the first trained Jewish social workers. After serving various Jewish communities and the Jewish Welfare Board, he became associate executive director of the Bureau of Jewish Social Research (1928–32), where he was instrumental in founding the Council of Jewish Federations and Welfare Funds, serving as its first executive (1932–35) and, after the merger of the Council and the Bureau, as its associate director. He was associate director of Chicago's Jewish Charities and Jewish Welfare Fund during World War II and served UNRRA as deputy director of the Division of Welfare and Displaced Persons in Europe. From 1947 to 1951 he directed the training bureau for Jewish Communal Service, reflecting his concern for Jewish communal professionalism. He then became associate director of the National Social Welfare Assembly (1951–61), afterward spending a year aiding the development of social work in Australia. Throughout his career Rabinoff was a leader of the National Conference on Jewish Communal Service, serving as secretary (1929–33) and president (1949). His influence on Jewish communal service and its professional practitioners was extensive.

BIBLIOGRAPHY: Bernstein, in: *Journal of Jewish Communal Service*, 46 (1970), 351–3.

[Robert S. Goldman]

RABINOVICH, ISAAC JACOB ("Itzele Ponovezher"; 1854–1919), Lithuanian rabbi. Rabinovich was born in Shershov, Grodno district. Contrary to the prevailing custom, his father, a wealthy and learned merchant, did not send him to a yeshivah but engaged private tutors for him. Supported by his father-in-law, both before and after his marriage, he was able to devote himself entirely to study, including two years with R. Ḥayyim Soloveichik in Brest-Litovsk.

In 1889, after teaching Talmud for a year in Bialystok, he was appointed a teacher at the famous Slobodka Yeshivah, a center of the *musar* movement. Rabinovich, whose system of study was similar to that of Soloveichik, maintained that priority should be given to the study of Talmud and not to *musar*, and the popularity of his courses-at the expense of the *musar* aspect-brought about some tension between him and the head of the yeshivah, R. Nathan Ẓevi Finkel. As a result, in 1899 Rabinovich left the yeshivah and, after serving for a year as rabbi of the small town Gorzd, moved to Panevezys. There he established in 1911 the *Kolel "Kibbutz le-Meẓuyyanei ha-Yeshivot," which was financed by Miriam Gavronsky, daughter of the tea magnate and philantropist Kalonymus *Wissotzky. The venture was an outstanding success and made Panevezys a major center of Talmud study in Lithuania. Forced to leave Panevezys during World War I Rabinovich moved the Kolel first to Luzin in the Vitebsk district and then to Mariopol. After the Bolshevik Revolution he returned to Panavezys, where he died.

Rabinovich was one of the few rabbis of his time who knew Russian and modern Hebrew literature, which he mastered during an illness. Originally a supporter of the *Ḥibbat Ẓion movement, he later became one of the founders of the *Agudat Israel. He was almost unique among contemporary rabbis in his support of the workers' and socialist movements; in 1917 he made a passionate but unavailing appeal at a meeting of the Orthodox association *Masoret ve-Ḥerut*, to persuade its member to come out in support of expropriation of the lands of the nobility and their redistribution to the peasants. As a result he was popular among the *Bundists, and even among the *Yevsektsiya, who did not attack him as they had other rabbis. Despite this they refused to allow him to reopen his yeshivah, and he died brokenhearted.

Famed as an outstanding *posek*, especially after the death of R. Isaac Elḥanan *Spektor, and in his decisions tending to leniency, he committed little to writing and what there was, was lost in World War I. In 1948, however, a small collection of his commentaries and responsa was published under the title *Zekher Yitzhak*. About the same time a former student, D. Zachs, published a volume consisting of notes he had taken of his master's lectures on tractates *Kiddushin* and *Baba Meẓia*.

BIBLIOGRAPHY: Rivkind, in: *Lite* (1951), 577–83; M.S. Shapiro, in: *Lite* (1951), 645–53; J. Marck, *Bi-Meḥiẓatan shel Gedolei ha-Dor* (1958), 115–19; *Yahadut Lita* (1960), 394–98.

[Shaul Stampfer]

RABINOVICH, ISAAK MOSEYEVICH (1886–1977), Russian construction engineer. Rabinovich, who attained the rank of major-general in the Red Army, taught at several Soviet institutes of higher education. He was appointed professor at the Military Engineering Academy in 1932 and at the Moscow Construction Engineers' Institute in 1933. From 1946 he was a corresponding member of the Academy of Sciences. He wrote several books on construction mechanics.

RABINOVICH, ITAMAR (1942–), president of Tel Aviv University. Born in Jerusalem, Rabinovich received his B.A. degree from the Hebrew University in 1960; in 1966 he completed his M.A. degree at Tel Aviv University; and in 1971 he received his Ph.D. from the University of California. In 1971 he joined Tel Aviv University. He was the director of the Shiloh Center, dean of the Faculty of Humanities, and rector of the university. He also served as senior research fellow at the Moshe Dayan Center for Middle Eastern and African Studies and as incumbent of the Yona and Dina Ettinger Chair in Contemporary History of the Middle East at Tel Aviv University as well as Andrew White Professor at Large at Cornell University. Between 1993 and 1996 Rabinovich was the chief negotiator with Syria and ambassador in Washington. He served as a board member of the International Crisis Group and was a member of the Trilateral Commission and a lecturer at the World Economic Forum. He was elected president of Tel Aviv University in 2003.

Rabinovich published a number of articles and books, including *Syria Under the Ba'th* (1972); *The War for Lebanon* (1984); *The Road Not Taken: Early Arab-Israeli Negotiations* (1991); *The Brink of Peace: Israel and Syria* (1998); *Waging Peace: Israel and the Arabs at the End of the Century* (1999); and *Waging Peace: Israel and Arabs, 1948–2003* (2004).

[Shaked Gilboa (2nd ed.)]

RABINOVICH, JOSÉ (1903–1978), Yiddish and Spanish author, playwright, and poet. Born in Bialystok, in 1924 Rabinovich arrived in Argentina, where he made his living in the printing business. Before his emigration he had written a number of texts in Yiddish and continued to do so in Argentina; part of these works were translated into Spanish, the language he adopted at a later stage. Influenced by the hardships of his life in Russia, by the difficulties faced by Jewish immigrants in Argentina and, later, by the Holocaust, all his writing is haunted by an atmosphere of hostility, material and moral misery, poverty, and fear. His Jewish characters often face the religious aporia of God's indifference and injustice. Many of his themes deal with proletarian issues and come under the rubric of leftist social-realist literature. His works include the following: novels and short stories: *Cabizbajos* ("Lowered Heads," 1943); *Tercera clase* ("Third Class," 1944); *Pan duro* ("Hard Bread," 1953); *El perro de Maidanek* ("The Dog of Majdanek," 1968); *Cuentos de pico y pala* ("Stories of Pick and Shovel," 1971); and the autobiographical *Sobras de una juventud* ("Youth Leftovers," 1977); dramas: *Con pecado concebida* ("Conceived in Sin," 1975); *El gran castigo* ("The Great Punishment," 1976); poetry: *Hombre escatimado* ("Skimped-on Man," 1969); *Rapsodia judía* ("Jewish Rhapsody," 1969); *El violinista bajo el tejado* ("The Fiddler under the Roof," 1970); *Rapsodia rusa* ("Russian Rhapsody," 1971); *Misa de un play boy* ("A Playboy Mass," 1972); *Dios mediante* ("With God's Help," 1976).

BIBLIOGRAPHY: R.A. Arrieta, *Historia de la literatura argentina*, vol. 4 (1959); D.W. Foster, *Cultural Diversity in Latin American Literature* (1994); N. Lindstrom, *Jewish Issues in Argentine Literature: From Gerchunoff to Szichman* (1989); D.B. Lockhart, *Jewish Writers of Latin America. A Dictionary* (1997); L. Senkman, *La identidad judía en la literatura argentina* (1983); A. Weinstein and M. Nasatsky, *Escritores judeo-argentinos: bibliografía 1900–1987* (1994).

[Florinda F. Goldberg (2nd ed.)]

RABINOVICH, JOSEPH (1837–1899), missionary in *Kishinev, Bessarabia, and founder of a Jewish-Christian sect. Born into a ḥasidic family, Rabinovich was attracted by the *Haskalah movement. During the early 1880s he joined the *Ḥibbat Zion movement and visited Palestine. He returned disappointed in the new movement and at the end of 1883, under the influence of a missionary named Faltin, he founded a new sect called The Children of Israel of the New Testament (this sect should not be confused with the sect called Novy Izrail (*New Israel) founded by Jacob Priluker of Odessa). Adherents of the sect were to accept the basic precepts of Christianity, while at the same time retaining their Jewish nationalism and observing Jewish traditions such as circumcision, the Sabbath, Jewish festivals, etc. On Christmas Day, 1884, a prayer house Bethlehem, in which prayers were recited in Hebrew and sermons delivered in Yiddish, was opened in Kishinev. In 1885 Rabinovich converted to Protestantism and continued his work in Kishinev with the support of Protestant missionaries whose funds allowed him to open a small printing press where he published prayer books and sermons. Among his publications were *Tefillah ve-Ikkerei Emunah li-Venei Yisrael Benei Berit Ḥadashah* ("Prayers and Principles of Faith of the Children of Israel of the New Testament," 1892), and *Divrei Niḥumim* ("Words of Comfort," 1897). His activities had no influence on Russian Jewry and he remained an inefficient instrument in the hands of the German Protestant mission.

BIBLIOGRAPHY: J. Dunlop, *Memories of Gospel Triumphs among the Jews* (1894), 445–8; J. Rabinowitsch, *Neue Dokumente der suedrussischen Christentumbewegung* (1887), includes autobiography.

[Yehuda Slutsky]

RABINOVICH, OSIP ARONOVICH (1817–1869), Russian author and publicist, founder and editor of *Razsvet, the first Jewish journal in Russian. Born in Kobelyaki, Ukraine, the son of a well-to-do businessman, he studied both Jewish and secular subjects under private tutors. He settled in Odessa in 1845 and developed a successful practice as an adviser and pleader at the commercial court, and later, as a notary. Rabinovich's literary career also began in Odessa. In 1847 he translated Jacob *Eichenbaum's Hebrew poem on chess, *Ha-Kerav*, into Russian and contributed articles and feuilleton-type fiction to local publications. Later his works were published by leading Russian journals. Although published after the abolition of certain laws regarding recruitment of Jews into the Russian army, his story, "*Shtrafnoy*" (in *Russkiy Vestnik*, 1859), was considered a bitter reflection of the abuse perpetuated on Jews under the rule of *Nicholas I. It was a tale of the anguish suffered by a fine, public-spirited, middle-aged Jew recruited for a lifetime into the Russian army in partial payment for communal indebtedness. In 1860–61 Rabinovich published *Razsvet*. He was the mainstay of the journal, writing articles and stories for it and setting its tone by his weekly editorials. Maintaining a high standard, Rabinovich concentrated in the journal on the relationship of Jewish life to outside forces, i.e., to Russian society, and in particular to the Russian authorities. He relegated to others the concern for the inner aspects of Jewish life. He pleaded for the recognition of Jews as Russian citizens and for their integration step by step into Russian society as useful, contributing human beings. If inner reforms were needed to prepare Jews for their role in society, it was no less important to rid them of the outward vestiges of medieval segregation and discrimination they were suffering in Russia. Rabinovich felt that a first step must be the removal of such vestiges from the law and from state and public institutions. As Rabinovich saw it, the major obstacle toward citizenship for Jews was the *Pale of Settlement. He contended that not only Jews but the country as a whole suffered from this system which closed off most of the state from Jewish settlement. He believed that the humanist and reformist tendencies during the early years of the reign of *Alexander II, which culminated in the abolition of serfdom (1861), should also lead to reforms for Russian Jews, enabling them to emulate the progress of Western Europe. Rabinovich insisted that the coercive administrative measures sometimes urged by westernizers would not help to better the conditions of the Jewish masses and should not be applied. He believed that a progressive modernization among the Jews would be evoked primarily by improving social and legal conditions. Full equality was due to Jews as human beings, irrespective of the degree to which they might be considered modern, i.e., westernized. Under oppressive Russian censorship, Rabinovich decided to discontinue the publication of *Razsvet*. He died in Merano, Italy. His complete works were published in three volumes in 1880–88.

BIBLIOGRAPHY: Yu. I. Gessen, *Gallereya yevreyskikh deyateley*, 1 (1898), 5–72; N.A. Buchbinder, *Literaturnye etyudy* (1927); Perlmann, in: JSOS, 24 (1962), 162–82; Waxman, Literature, index.

[Mark Perlman]

RABINOVICH, YEHUDAH LEIB (Leon; 1862–1937), Hebrew writer, editor, and physicist; known by his pen name, Ish Yehudi. Born in Brestovitz, Russia, Rabinovich studied medicine and physics. In 1887 he began to write popular articles on science etc. in *Ha-Meliẓ and *Keneset Yisrael*. In 1890 he won a gold medal at the Paris Exhibition for his inventions.

A collection of his articles appeared in *Ha-Yerushah ve-ha-Ḥinnukh* (1903), and *Yesod Leshon ha-Mikra* (1939). In 1903 he published a Yiddish newspaper *Bleter fun a Togbukh*. Later he served as editor of *Ha-Meliẓ* but was unable to adapt it to the spirit of the times, and had to discontinue it in 1904. In his later years he lived in poverty in Leningrad and contributed articles to the Jewish press in the United States. His memoirs appeared in *Hadoar*, 3 (1924), no. 1, pp. 7–8; no. 3, pp. 5–6).

BIBLIOGRAPHY: Kressel, Leksikon, 2 (1967), 816–7; R. Malachi, in: *Hadoar*, 17 (1938), 182–3.

[Yehuda Slutsky]

RABINOVICZ, HAIM BEN ZION (1888–1976), *ḥazzan*. Rabinovicz was born in Kiev to a family of Tomashover ḥasidim. As a child he sang at the synagogue of the Tomashover rebbe. In 1917 he moved to Odessa and studied in the conservatory. When Pinḥas Minkovsky moved to the United States, Rabinovicz took his place in the Brody Synagogue in Odessa. In 1927 he moved to Antwerp and was appointed chief cantor at the "Shomre Hadass" Synagogue there. In 1951 he immigrated to Israel. He refused to perform in concerts and only in his old age did he agree to make recordings of some portions of the prayer service that attest to his talents.

[Akiva Zimmerman]

RABINOVICZ, PINCHAS (1947–), *ḥazzan*. Rabinovicz was born in Lodz, and at the age of three immigrated to Israel with his family and was educated in *yeshivot*. In 1968 he began to serve as a cantor in the Gevurat Yisrael Synagogue in Tel Aviv. He has appeared in concerts and on radio and television programs. In 1973 he moved to Montreal and continued his studies in music and voice development in McGill University. His voice is a lyric tenor, and he soon became famous throughout Canada and appeared in broadcasts of the Canadian Broadcasting Authority. He served as a cantor in the Beth Ora Synagogue in Montreal and was president of the Cantors' Association. In 1983 he moved to Los Angeles and was appointed chief cantor of the largest Orthodox congregation in the Western United States, Beth Jacob Synagogue of Beverly Hills. He has composed music to portions of the prayer service and ḥassidic songs. Rabinovicz's website made available many new and original compositions for downloading.

[Akiva Zimmerman]

RABINOVITZ, ALEXANDER SISKIND (known by acronym **Azar**; 1854–1945), Hebrew author. Born in Lyady, Belorussia, Rabinovitz became affiliated with the *Ḥibbat Zion movement during a stay in Moscow. In 1888 he became a teacher in Poltava, where his pupils included D.B. *Borochov and Izhak *Ben-Zvi. It was in Poltava that he was elected a delegate to the First Zionist Congress (1897). Settling in Ereẓ Israel in 1906, he alternately taught and worked as a librarian.

From 1888 the Hebrew language was his medium of expression, although he also wrote occasionally in Yiddish. He contributed articles to *Ha-Meliẓ* (1899) and to *Sefer ha-Sharon* (1891), a children's book. From that time on, he concentrated on storywriting, and was among the first to write stories of social content in Hebrew. These were published successively in the books *Be-Ẓel ha-Kesef* (1894), *Ḥattat ha-Ẓibbur* (1896), *Bat he-Ashir* (1898), and in various Hebrew literary journals, such as *Ha-Shiloaḥ* and *Luaḥ Aḥiasaf*. His writings were a synthesis of his affinity with the common people, his interest in socialism and Russian literature, and of his strong attachment to the Jewish tradition and its cultural values – an attachment which, upon his arrival in Ereẓ Israel, expressed itself both in his personal ties with Rabbi A.I. *Kook and in his own inclination to religious observance.

In its entirety, Rabinovitz's prolific and varied output numbers over 100 books and pamphlets, including original works, translations, and adaptations. He popularized scientific subjects in Hebrew, and for many years also wrote "*Hirhurim*," a regular column in *Kunteres* and *Davar*, which dealt with matters of concern to the labor movement. The first collection of his stories and articles was published in 1904; the second and third volumes were published, in Ereẓ Israel, in 1914–22. Some of his stories were also published separately at various times. Among his monographs are *Jean Jacques Rousseau* (1899); *Keter Torah* (1911), on Rabbi Kook; *Yosef Ḥayyim Brenner* (1922); and *Ḥayyei L.N. Tolstoi* (1924). He also wrote *Toledot ha-Sifrut ha-Ivrit li-Venei ha-Ne'urim* (1906–10), a literary history for youth; *Toledot ha-Pedagogikah* (1913) a history of pedagogy from early times to the present; textbooks for Jewish history; original and translated books for children and youth; and *Ha-Islam* (1927) and *Ha-Inkviziẓyah* (1930), popular histories. Encouraged by Bialik, he worked for many years on the translation of the works of W. Bacher, among them *Aggadot ha-Tanna'im* (3 vols., 1920–23) and *Aggadot Amora'ei Ereẓ Yisrael* (1916–17, 2 pts.; 1925–30², 5 vols.). In addition he edited several literary collections, notably *Yizkor* (1912), commemorating Jewish laborers who fell in the course of their work in Ereẓ Israel. On his 80th birthday his collected works were published in five volumes (1934–36).

BIBLIOGRAPHY: Z. Fishman, in: *Sefer Zikkaron le-Yovel ha-Shivim shel A.S. Rabinovitz* (1924), 3–23 (incl. bibl.). **ADD. BIBLIOGRAPHY:** D. Hoshen, "*Ma'aseh Tefillat ha-Em: Keriah Mashvah bein 'Tefillat ha-Em' shel Azar le-'Ma'aseh' shel 'Agnon,*" in: *Mabu'a* 35 (2001), 65–75; 36 (2001), 69–85.

[Getzel Kressel]

RABINOWICH (Rabinowitsch), ELIYAHU AKIVA (1861–1917), Russian rabbi. Born in Silale, Lithuania, Rabinowich studied in various Lithuanian yeshivot, including Eisiskes, where he obtained *semikhah*, at the same time becoming proficient in secular studies and foreign languages. After marriage he engaged in business, but was unsuccessful, and on his father's death in 1888 he succeeded him as rabbi of Pyantiza. In 1892 he was appointed as rabbi of Kinishin but following a communal dispute he was expelled by the authorities, who were informed that he had no right of residence there. In 1893 he was appointed rabbi of Poltava, where he remained until his death.

Rabinowich became famous as a result of his attitude toward Zionism and the resulting controversy. Influenced by R. Samuel *Mohilewer, he attended the first Russian Zionist Conference in Warsaw in 1898 and was a delegate to the Second Zionist Congress in Basle in the same year. Like many other rabbis, Rabinowich was uneasy about associating himself with Zionism, and the parting of the ways came over the question of "Culture." Rabinowich, like R.J.L. *Zirelson, objected to the Zionist movement engaging in culture and education, urging that it confine itself to political and economic activity, and that if it did deal with such matters it should at least be under rabbinic supervision. When his proposal was rejected, the disappointed Rabinowich, on his return to Poltova from the Congress, launched a vehement attack against the Zionist Movement. In 1899 he published a pamphlet, *Ẓiyyon be-Mishpat*, which raised a storm in both the Zionist and the Orthodox world. He was attacked by both the secular elements in the Zionist Movement (*Ha-Meliẓ*. 1899, 218–9) and its Orthodox members, such as Rabbis S.J. *Rabinowitz (*ibid.*, 153–73) and David Solomon Slouschz (*Mikhtav le-David*, 1899). A bitter personal note was injected into the controversy. Rabinowich replied in his pamphlet *Ve-Anta Bi Ẓidkati* (1899). Thereafter he became one of the leading opponents of Zionism, and was associated with the Lishkah Sheḥorah (see *Zionism: In Russia) which had its headquarters in Kovno (Kaunas). From 1901 to 1905 he edited *Ha-Peles* and from 1910 to 1914 *Ha-Modi'a* which were the main vehicles for his polemics. In 1912 Rabinowich participated in the founding conference of the Agudat Israel in Kattowice. He also participated in various rabbinical conferences, including the one in Cracow in 1903, whose proceedings he edited.

Among his literary works were *Ḥesed li-Meshiḥo*, a commentary on the Book of Ruth. The first edition (1898), unlike later ones, also included halakhic responsa. His son, J.Z. Rabinowich, published a selection of his sermons (1943).

BIBLIOGRAPHY: J. Barnai, in: *Sinai*, 70 (5–6), 1972, 282–8; *Oẓar Yisrael*, 9:242–3 (the article was written by Rabinowich himself).

[Jacob Barnai]

RABINOWICH, SARAH (**Sonia**; married name – **Margolin**; 1880–1918), publicist, daughter of S.P. *Rabbinowitz. Born in Berezin, province of Minsk, Sarah graduated in Germany in 1902 as a doctor of social sciences, her thesis dealing with the organization of the Jewish working class in Russia. In 1903 she was sent to Galicia on behalf of women's organizations against white slavery, and together with Bertha *Pappenheim she wrote a study on the situation of Galician Jewry and possible steps towards an improvement of its social conditions. During 1904–05 she organized illegal political activities by workers against the military in Odessa and was arrested. Released after a short time, she left for Germany where she continued her political and publicistic work, writing in Russian, German, and Yiddish. In her writings Rabinowich showed a special interest in the Jewish working class in Russia, the women's question within Jewry, Jewish education, and statistics. Her published works include "Zur Lage des juedischen Proletariats in Mohilew am Dnjepr," in: *Die Welt* (15.8.1902), no. 33:6–7 (Aug. 22,1902), no. 34, 4–6 (an extract of her Ph.D. thesis); "The Life of the Trade and Handcraft Classes in the Representation of Peretz," in: *Yevreyski Mir* (1909, 69–79); "On the Jewish Question within Jewry," in: *Yevreyski Mir* (1909); "On the Question of the Training of Jewish Female Teachers," in: *Vestnik obshchestva rasprostraneniya prosveshcheniya mezhdu evreyami v Rossii* (1911), no. 5, 28–46); "*Die Heiraten von Juden im Europaeischen Russland vom Jahre 1867 bis 1902,*" in: *Zeitschrift fuer Demographie und Statistik der Juden* (5 (1909), nos. 10, 11, 12); "Die Heiraten von Juden in Russisch-Polen," *ibid.* (6 (1910), no. 4, 61–64); "*Zur Statistik der juedischen Schulen in Russland,*" *ibid.* (7 (1911), nos. 9, 121–30); "Zur Bildungsstatistik der juedischen Arbeiter in Rußland," *ibid.* (9 (1913), no. 11, 153–60). During World War I Sarah was active in the German Independent Labor Party and was again arrested. In a seizure of depression she committed suicide in prison.

BIBLIOGRAPHY: Rabbinowitz, in: *Yidishe Shriftn*, 3 (1939), 345–6.

RABINOWICZ (Kwasnik), OSKAR K. (1902–1969), financier, author, and Zionist. Born in Aspern, Austria, Rabinowicz studied at Brno, Prague, and Berlin, later engaging in the gold business. He was active in the Zionist Revisionist movement and after 1933 became chairman of the Czechoslovak committee to boycott Nazi Germany. When the Germans occupied Prague in 1939, he barely managed to escape, though he had helped 3,000 Jews leave Czechoslovakia for Palestine. He went to England, living mainly in London, and became active in communal life, being on the councils of Jews' College and the Jewish Historical Society. He was director of the Anglo-Federal Banking Corporation from 1946 to 1956. In 1956 he settled in the U.S., where he was active in communal affairs, particularly in the Jewish Theological Seminary and the Jewish Publication Society of America.

In his Prague period Rabinowicz wrote, among other works, *Einleitung in die Probleme des rituellen Schlachtens* (1937), in defense of *sheḥitah* and edited his father's *Makor Niftaḥ* (1938), a lexicographical Bible index. In England he wrote *Vladimir Jabotinsky's Conception of a Nation* (1946), submitted Chaim *Weizmann's autobiography *Trial and Error* to a searching factual criticism in his *Fifty Years of Zionism* (1950), and championed Herzl as the great figure in Zionism in his *Herzl, Architect of the Balfour Declaration* (1958). Among his other works is *Winston Churchill on Jewish Problems* (1956, 1960^2) and the posthumously published *Arnold Toynbee on Judaism and Zionism: A Critique* (1974). He was one of the initiators of the Society for the History of Czechoslovak Jews and co-editor of *The Jews of Czechoslovakia* (vol. 1, 1968). His literary work was based on his extensive library, which was particularly rich in periodicals and works on Zionist and contemporary history. This was bequeathed to the National and University Library, Jerusalem. Rabinowicz was a departmental editor of the *Encyclopaedia Judaica* for Czech Jewish history.

His son, THEODORE K. RABB (1937–), was a professor of history at Princeton, specializing in 16th- and 17th-century European history. His works include *Enterprise and Empire* (1967), a study of merchant and gentry investment in early English maritime ventures; *The Struggle for Stability in Early Modern Europe* (1975); *Industrialization and Urbanization* (1981); *Renaissance Lives* (1993); *Origins of the Modern West* (1993); and the audiobook *What If?* (with J. Ober, 2001). He co-edited *Action and Conviction in Early Modern Europe* (1969); *The New History, the 1980s and Beyond* (1982); and *The Making and Unmaking of Democracy* (2002).

BIBLIOGRAPHY: A. Hertzberg, in: JSOS, 32 (1970), 99–100.

[Cecil Roth / Ruth Beloff (2nd ed.)]

RABINOWITCH, EUGENE (1901–1973), U.S. biochemist and biophysicist. Born in St. Petersburg, Russia, Rabinowitch worked in the Kaiser Wilhelm Institute of Physical Chemistry at Dahlem, Berlin (1926–29), and at the University of Goettingen until the Nazis came to power. In 1933 he was Rask-Orsted Fellow of the Royal Academy of Sciences in Copenhagen and from 1934 worked in London. In 1939 he went to the United States, where he was attached to the Massachusetts Institute of Technology and associated with the Manhattan Atomic Bomb Project. In 1947 he became professor of botany at the University of Illinois, and in 1960 professor of biophysics. In 1968 he was appointed professor of chemistry and biology, and adviser to the Center for Science and Human Affairs, at the State University of New York (Albany). His major scientific papers were on photochemistry, photobiology and reaction kinetics.

He wrote *Periodisches System* (1930) and *Photosynthesis and Related Processes* (3 vols., 1945–56), edited *The Bulletin of Atomic Scientists* (1945–); *Minutes to Midnight* (1950); *The Chemistry of Uranium* (1951); and *Dawn of a New Age* (1963), and co-edited *The Atomic Age* (1963).

[Samuel Aaron Miller]

RABINOWITZ, ELIAHU WOLF (1853–1932), Hebrew writer. Born in Stawiski, Poland, he went to Germany in his youth. Rabinowitz joined the Socialist movement, was also involved in the Hebrew Socialist Circle and became friendly with Morris *Vinchevski. In 1876, after contributing to the journal *Ha-Shaḥar*, he became the assistant of M.L. *Rodkinson, owner of *Ha-Kol*. As a result of the persecution of German Socialists he moved to Paris and then to London (1880). A member of Ḥibbat Zion from its early days, he conducted a correspondence with Judah L. *Levin regarding the social prospects of Palestinian settlement in Ereẓ Israel (*Ha-Maggid* (1883), no. 20). In his later years he published chapters from his memoirs, in *Haolam* (1927), nos. 52, 53, and in *Iyyim*, 1 (1927). His autobiographical notes appeared in *Davar* (July 7, 1933).

BIBLIOGRAPHY: S.L. Zitron, *Drey Literarishe Doyres*, 2 (1921), 129–32; Klausner, Sifrut, 6 (1958^2), index.

[Yehuda Slutsky]

RABINOWITZ, JOEL (1828–1902), one of the first Jewish ministers in South Africa. Born in Lublin, Poland, Rabinowitz was second minister to the synagogue in Birmingham, England. He came to Cape Town in 1859, when the congregation was struggling to keep alive. Largely as a result of Rabinowitz' efforts, the congregation was able to erect its first synagogue in 1863, which still stands. Taking the small Jewish communities scattered over the whole *Cape Province and beyond as his parish, Rabinowitz corresponded with outlying families and traveled long distances by post-cart to officiate at marriages or circumcisions, thus contributing greatly to the preservation of Judaism. He was also a tireless collector for charitable causes, Jewish or non-Jewish, at home and abroad.

After serving the Cape Town community for 23 years he returned to England, but was back in Cape Town in 1886. His modest investments having failed because of a depression at the Cape, he took a course in metallurgy at the South African College in Cape Town and opened an assay laboratory on the Witwatersrand. He remained involved in communal life, raised funds for building the first synagogue in *Johannesburg and officiated at High Holy Day services. Two years later ill health forced him to retire to Cape Town, where he continued to devote himself to communal affairs. Rabinowitz wrote a series of articles about the early Jewish settlers in South Africa for the London *Jewish Chronicle* (1895).

BIBLIOGRAPHY: L. Herrman, *History of the Jews in South Africa* (1935), index; G. Saron and L. Hotz, *The Jews in South Africa* (1955), index; I. Abrahams, *The Birth of a Community* (1955), index. **ADD. BIBLIOGRAPHY:** J. Simon, *The Reverend Joel Rabinowitz, and Other Adventures of a Library Chairman* (1996).

[Lewis Sowden]

RABINOWITZ, LOUIS ISAAC (1906–1984), rabbi. Born in Edinburgh, he served as rabbi in the London communities of Shepherd's Bush, South Hackney, and Cricklewood, successively. During World War II he was a senior Jewish chaplain with the British army in the Middle East and Normandy. In 1945 he became chief rabbi of the United Hebrew Congregation of Johannesburg and the Federation of Synagogues of Transvaal and the Orange Free State. He was appointed professor of Hebrew at the University of Witwatersrand and head of the Johannesburg *bet din*. In 1947, in protest against British policy in Palestine, he discarded his war decorations in public. An eloquent preacher, he was also outspoken in his criticism of the South African government's apartheid policy. Retiring in 1961, he settled in Israel and became deputy editor in chief of the *Encyclopaedia Judaica* (first edition). He was also a *Gaḥal* representative in the Jerusalem municipality from 1969 and in 1976 was appointed a deputy mayor of Jerusalem. He did not stand for re-election in the elections held in October 1978. In 1980 he was made a Yakir Yerushalayim ("Worthy Citizen of Jerusalem"), and in November of that year he was given the title of Chief Rabbi Emeritus of the Federation of Synagogues of South Africa.

Rabinowitz is the author of *The Social Life of the Jews of Northern France* (1938), *Ḥerem Hayyishub* (1945), and *Jewish Merchant Adventurers* (1948). His other books include *Soldiers from Judea* (1942), *Far East Mission* (1952), *Torah and Flora* (1977), and volumes of sermons.

[Lewis Sowden]

RABINOWITZ, LOUIS MAYER (1887–1957), U.S. manufacturer and philanthropist. Rabinowitz, who was born in Rosanne, Lithuania, immigrated to the U.S. in 1901. In 1916 he established a corset manufacture company in New York. Rabinowitz subsequently became chairman of the corset industry (1934) and director of the Business Men's Council (1935).

Active in Jewish community affairs, he was vice president of the Hebrew National Orphan Home (1921), the Jewish Hospital of Brooklyn, the American Jewish Historical Society, the New York chapter of the America-Israel Society, and director of the Federation for the Support of Jewish Philanthropic Societies of New York City (1935). A collector of books, manuscripts, and paintings, he gave much of his collection to the New York Public Library, Library of Congress, Jewish Theological Seminary, and Yale University. Donating the Rabinowitz Fund for Judaica Research at Yale, he established a chair there in Semitic languages and literature (1955). Rabinowitz served as director of the Yale University Association of Fine Arts and as honorary trustee of the Yale Library Associates. A director of the Jewish Theological Seminary, he established the Louis M. Rabinowitz Institute for Research in Rabbinics at the seminary in 1951 and donated many rare books to its library. The Louis M. Rabinowitz Foundation (1953) sponsored a five-year archaeological exploration in Israel in conjunction with the Hebrew Union College of Cincinnati.

RABINOWITZ, SAMUEL JACOB (1857–1921), Lithuanian rabbi and Zionist leader. Born in Kelme, Rabinowitz held rabbinical posts at Ivye, Aleksot, and Sopotskin and was esteemed as a writer of responsa and novellae, some of which were collected in his *Sefer Oraḥ Yashar* (1903). An early member of the Ḥovevei Zion, Rabinowitz attended the Second Zionist Congress, where he made a deep impression on both Theodor Herzl and the delegates; he was elected to the Zionist General Council, later serving as one of the first directors of the *Jewish Colonial Trust. In 1899 Rabinowitz led the Lithuanian Zionists in their battle against the Lishkah Sheḥorah, a group of violently anti-Zionist rabbis. As a result of his vigorous efforts, over 100 East European rabbis wrote letters in support of the Zionist movement. His own essays on the religious aspects of Zionism appeared in *Ha-Dat ve-ha-Le'ummiyyut* (1900). After the Fourth Zionist Congress Rabinowitz accompanied Isaac J. *Reines on a mission to the Warsaw area, where their efforts to gain the support of leading ḥasidic rabbis for the Zionist cause met with some success.

In 1906 Rabinowitz was appointed rabbi of Liverpool, where he did much to promote traditional observance and communal harmony, despite the early hostility of more Anglicized members of the local community. Together with Reines, he founded the *Mizrachi world movement of religious Zionists in 1902, and he maintained his Zionist activity in England, being elected president of the British Mizrachi organization at its first conference in 1918.

A volume of his essays and addresses, *Li-Tekufot ha-Yamim* ("The Cycle of Seasons," 1918), was sponsored by *Aḥad Ha-Am, and a supplementary work, *Sefer Yashresh Ya'akov* (1925), appeared as Liverpool Jewry's memorial tribute, with a preface written by Rabinowitz's successor, Isser Yehudah *Unterman. He inspired the character of "Reb Shemu'el" in Herzl's novel *Altneuland*.

BIBLIOGRAPHY: JC (June 17 and 24, 1921); G. Kressel, in: *Kaẓir* (1964), 123–39; J.L. Maimon, *Sarei ha-Me'ah*, 6 (1956), 217–21; L.P. Gartner, *Jewish Immigrant in England* (1960), 193–6, 216, 249; G.E. Silverman, in: *Jewish Review* (May 31, 1961); idem, in: *Niv ha-Midrashiyyah* (Spring, 1970), 74–81 (Eng. section).

[Godfrey Edmond Silverman]

RABINOWITZ, STANLEY (1917–), U.S. rabbi and president of the Rabbinical Assembly. Born in Duluth, Ia., Rabinowitz received his B.A. from the State University of Iowa in 1939 and was ordained by the Jewish Theological Seminary

(1943). He began his career as an itinerant rabbi of congregations whose rabbis were away serving in the Armed Forces; as director of the Midwest office of the Jewish Theological Seminary; and then as director of field services for the United Synagogue of America. For a time, he served as acting director of the United Synagogue.

In 1947 Rabinowitz assumed the pulpit of B'nai Jacob Congregation in New Haven, Connecticut, where he served for five years, and then moved to Congregation Adath Jeshurun in Minneapolis (1953–60) before coming to Adas Israel Congregation in Washington, D.C., where he served for 26 years. As the rabbi of the largest Conservative congregation in Washington, Rabinowitz often had Israeli ambassadors and prominent national leaders in the pews. A champion of women's rights in Conservative Judaism, he initiated the bat mitzvah ceremony at his three congregations and counted women in the *minyan* at Adas Israel well before it was sanctioned by the Rabbinical Assembly.

He was instrumental in pushing for the desegregation of Washington, D.C., encouraging building owners in his congregation to desegregate their facilities. He allowed and encouraged Adas Israel to hold multiple services on Shabbat morning including a Havurah service and an Orthodox *minyan*. Adas Israel also did not follow the lead of many other inner city synagogues that moved to the suburbs following the 1968 riots.

Rabinowitz was also a national leader. Handsome and charismatic, he was a well-respected orator; he chaired the Committee on Synagogue Standards for the Rabbinical Assembly; and was later vice president of the Rabbinical Assembly in 1974–76 and then president in 1976–78. He represented the Conservative movement in its confrontations with Prime Minister Menaḥem Begin over an amendment to the *Law of Return regarding non-Orthodox conversions. He also traveled to Egypt soon after Anwar Sadat's path-breaking trip to Jerusalem.

His national career was thwarted by a technicality of the Rabbinical Assembly bylaws that limited the presidency to two one-year terms. A leading candidate to be chairman of the Conference of Presidents of Major American Jewish Organization and thus *the* major spokesman of American Jews, his nomination hinged on his remaining a third year as president of the RA, at least until he secured the chairmanship of the Conference. The timing was not propitious and Rabinowitz became ineligible to serve as chairman since he was no longer president of a major American Jewish organization. Rabbi Alexander *Schindler had used the bully pulpit of the chair to advance his movement's prominence. Since then no Conservative movement figure has had comparable influence.

Rabinowitz' experience with the Israeli prime minister convinced him that Conservative Judaism needed a strong presence in Israel. He thus became founding president of the Zionist Organization of the Conservative Movement (MERCAZ) (1977–1985) and chaired the Rabbinic Cabinet of United Jewish Appeal (1986). He retired in 1986 and was named rabbi emeritus of Adas Israel.

BIBLIOGRAPHY: M. Berenbaum, "Stanley Rabinowitz Reflects on Five Decades of Leadership," *Washington Jewish Week* (June 26, 1986).

RABINOWITZ, YA'AKOV (1875–1948), Hebrew journalist and author. Born in Volkovysk, Poland, Rabinowitz, after teaching for several years in Vitebsk, left in 1900 for Switzerland, where he started to write. Upon his return to Russia in 1904, he became active in Zionist affairs and began his long career as journalist and author. From 1907 until his departure for Ereẓ Israel in 1910, he was active in the *Odessa Committee, becoming M.M. *Ussishkin's principal aide. In Ereẓ Israel he first settled in Petaḥ Tikvah, but moved to Tel Aviv in 1923.

Rabinowitz became a regular contributor to *Ha-Po'el ha-Ẓa'ir*. Together with A. *Barash he founded the literary journal *Hedim* (1922), which became a forum for both the old and young generations of writers and an outstanding expression of the literary milieu in Ereẓ Israel from the time of the Third Aliyah. His own contributions consisted of monographs on various authors. In addition, he wrote a regular column for *Davar*, contributed to many literary periodicals, and published translations. Among Rabinowitz' books are *Be-Ein Shoresh* (1914), a historical novel; *Or va-Ed* (1922), stories; *Setav* (1926), poems; *Nedudei Amasai ha-Shomer* (2 vols., 1929), a story of the Second Aliyah period; *Neveh Kayiẓ* (1934), a novel; and *Hassagot* (1935), articles and essays. Y. Har-Even edited Rabinowitz's essays and published them with a biographical essay under the title *Maslulei Sifrut* (1971).

BIBLIOGRAPHY: Kressel, Leksikon, 2 (1967), 3–8. **ADD. BIBLIOGRAPHY:** Y. Keshet, "*Y. Rabinowitz, Mesapper shel Dor Ma'avar*," in: *Moznayim*, 32 (1971), 45–51; Y. Hanani, "*Iyyun ba-Nose ha-Ereẓ Yisraeli be-Sippurei Y. Rabinowitz*," in: *Katif*, 8 (1971), 137–152; G. Shaked, *Ha-Sipporet ha-Ivrit*, 1 (1977), 467–77; N. Govrin, *Aggadah u-Meẓiut be-'Nedudei Amasai ha-Shome'*," in: *Bikkoret u-Farshanut*, 9–10 (1977), 47–91; N. Tamir-Smilanski, *Tekhanim ve-Izzuvim be-Sippurei Ya'akov Rabinowitz* (1991).

[Getzel Kressel]

RABINOWITZ, YEHOSHUA (1911–1979), Israeli politician. Rabinowitz was born in Vishnevets, Poland, where his father was a well-to-do merchant. He studied at the Tarbut school and graduated from the Teachers' Seminary in Vilna. He was appointed director of a Hebrew school in Poland, where he was active in the He-Ḥalutz movement.

Immigrating to Ereẓ Israel in 1934 Rabinowitz was employed in the Department of Industry of Hamashbir Hamerkazi, eventually becoming head of the Consumers' Cooperative of Israel.

Elected to the municipal council of Tel Aviv in 1956, he succeeded Mordekhai Namir as mayor in 1969. The Israel Labor Party, which he represented, was defeated in the elections held in 1973, and he was not reelected. A member of the Central Bureau of the Labor Party, he was regarded as a key figure in the movement and wielded enormous influence in it councils.

In March 1974 Rabinowitz was appointed minister of housing in the short-lived government of Golda Meir, but when Pinḥas Sapir decided not to serve in the government formed on June 3, by Yiẓḥak Rabin, Rabinowitz was appointed to succeed him as minister of finance, remaining in office until the elections held in May 1977.

RABINOWITZ, ẒEVI HA-COHEN (1832–1889), science popularizer. Born in Linkavo, in the Kaunas district of Lithuania (then Russia), Rabinowitz early showed an inclination for mathematics and physics, and from 1852 began to prepare a comprehensive Hebrew work which was to encompass all the fields of physics, with his own notes.

Because of financial difficulties, he only published one volume, *Sefer ha-Menuḥah ve-ha-Tenu'ah* (1867). He later wrote other books on mathematics, magnetism, chemistry, and steam engines, thus enriching Hebrew terminology in these fields and bringing them to the attention of Hebrew readers. He also published many articles on these subjects in *Ha-Meliẓ*, and in Russian in several newspapers and periodicals which he edited and published between the late 1870s and 1885. Even after the pogroms of the 1880s he remained convinced that education was the solution to the Jewish problem in Russia. He died in St. Petersburg.

BIBLIOGRAPHY: Kressel, Leksikon, 2 (1967), 821; Waxman, Literature, 3 (1960^2), 331.

[Getzel Kressel]

RABINOWITZ, ZINA (1895–1965), Hebrew writer. Born in Bendery, Bessarabia, she went to Ereẓ Israel in 1913. With the outbreak of World War I she returned to Bessarabia and later continued her studies at Moscow University. After living in the U.S., Canada and Palestine, she permanently settled in Israel in 1961.

Her poems and stories first appeared in *Ha-Shilo'aḥ* during World War I, after which she continued to publish stories and travel articles in Hebrew and Yiddish. Her books include *Ma'aseh be-Makkel* (1960), *Ba-Derekh la-Ḥerut* (1962), and *Be-Ahavatam Nitgallu* (1963).

BIBLIOGRAPHY: Kressel, Leksikon, 2 (1967), 816.

[Getzel Kressel]

RABINOWITZ-TEOMIM, ELIJAH DAVID BEN BENJAMIN (ADeReT; 1842/43–1905), Ashkenazi chief rabbi of Jerusalem. Elijah David was born in Pikeln, Lithuania. His father Benjamin Rabinowitz, who was rabbi of Zamosc and later of Wilkomierz, was called "Benjamin the righteous" because of his great piety; it was said that he never slept the night through and never ate a meal before completing the study of a tractate. As Elijah David was a twin, his brother being Ẓevi Judah, the name Teomim ("twins") was added to the family surname. Elijah David was known from his youth as an unusual genius and in 1874 was chosen rabbi of the community of Ponevezh. In 1893 he was appointed rabbi of Mir which, though smaller than Ponevezh, was renowned for its large yeshivah. His decision to move to Mir started a controversy, and the leaders of Ponevezh sent "an open letter" to Mir asking that their rabbi be "freed," but the appeal was ignored. His period at Mir was regarded as the creative period of his life. There he published the most notable of his works, as well as articles which appeared in many periodicals – *Ha Tevunah, Ha-Me'assef, Kevod ha-Levanon, Ha-Ẓofeh, Ha-Maggid, Keneset Ḥakhmei Yisrael, Ittur Soferim, Keneset ha-Gedolah*, etc. In Mir he wrote no less than a hundred works, especially notes and glosses to the Talmud, Maimonides' *Mishneh Torah*, the *Tur* of Jacob b. Asher, the Shulḥan Arukh, and responsa. His novellae and glosses on the Jerusalem Talmud entitled *Tuv Yerushalayim* appeared in the Romm-Vilna edition (1922) and those on the *Tur Ḥoshen Mishpat* entitled *Et Devar ha-Mishpat* in the *El ha-Mekorot* (1959) edition of the *Turim*. His extraordinary erudition is discernible in his novellae and notes, and his great knowledge of historical matters from his correspondence on these subjects with Jacob Reifmann, Isaac Hirsch Weiss and others.

The following of his works may be mentioned: *Oholei David, Matta'ei Hadar*, and *Heshiv Davar*, responsa; *Gefen Adderet*, on the Babylonian and Jerusalem Talmud; *Seder ha-Mo'adot*, on the festivals and special seasons; *Ma'as la-Melekh*, on Maimonides' *Mishneh Torah; Ẓiyyunim la-Torah*, source references; and *Kelei ha-Ro'im*, on the *aggadot* of the rabbis. Among his published works are *Zekher le-Mikdash* (1889), on *Hakhel; Aḥarit ha-Shanim* (1893); *Over Oraḥ*, appended to N. Cahana, *Orḥot Ḥayyim* (pt. 2, 1898); notes and glosses on the *Mishneh Torah* of Maimonides (1900); *Teshuvah mi-Yirah* (1906), on all topics in which Maimonides employs the phrase *Yireh Li* ("it seems to me"); *Zahav Sheva* (appended to *Tosefot ha-Rashba*, 1956), notes on the *tosafot* to *Pesaḥim* by Samson b. Abraham of Sens.

In 1899 a new period of his life commenced. When Samuel *Salant reached an advanced age and asked for a successor to be appointed chief rabbi of Jerusalem, extended negotiations with rabbis of the Diaspora began. At the recommendation of Ḥayyim Ozer *Grodzinski of Vilna, Elijah David was officially appointed in 1901. He succeeded in uniting the Jerusalem community, which was split into various **kolelim* and suffered from inner dissension between the *perushim* (the non-ḥasidic Ashkenazi community) and the **Ḥasidim*, and in forming a single organization for *sheḥitah*. He was also active in many communal spheres. He was the first treasurer of the Bikkur Ḥolim hospital, made regulations for institutions of learning and charity – particularly in the yeshivah Eẓ Ḥayyim – and arranged strict supervision of shops and merchants. His local regulations and customs are still in force, included in the annual calendar which is published by the Eẓ Ḥayyim yeshivah. The most famous of his sons-in-law, Abraham Isaac ha-Kohen *Kook, published a special brochure entitled *Eder ha-Yakar* (1906, 1967^2) describing his father-in-law's personality and quoting his testament, which shows the extraordinary humility and modesty of its author, and 20 of his letters.

BIBLIOGRAPHY: A.I. Kook, *Eder ha-Yakar* (1906, 1967²); J. Gelis, *Mi-Gedolei Yerushalayim* (1967), 116–35.

[Itzhak Alfassi]

RABON (Rubin), ISRAEL (1900–1941), Yiddish poet and novelist. Born in Govertshev, Poland, Rabon lived most of his life in Lodz. He was murdered by the Nazis at Ponary, near Vilna. He wrote his works of raw power and imaginative force under several pseudonyms including Yisrolik der Kleyner, Rut Vintsigster, Shabtai Tsiter, and Y. Rozental. His books include poetry, *Hintern Ployt fun der Velt* ("Behind the World's Fence," 1928) and *Groer Friling* ("Grey Spring," 1933), and two novels, *Di Gas* ("The Street," 1928), and *Balut, Roman fun a Forshtot* ("Balut, Novel of a Suburb," 1934).

BIBLIOGRAPHY: J.J. Trunk and A. Zeitlin (eds.), *Antologie fun der Yidisher Proze in Poyln* (1946), 611–8, 637; Fuks, in: *Fun Noentn Over* (1957), passim; Shnapper, in: *Literarishe Bleter* (Jan. 1, 1938). **ADD. BIBLIOGRAPHY:** Reyzen, Leksikon, 4, s.v. "Rubin, Yisrol" (1929), 272; Y. Goldkorn, *Lodzher Portretn* (1963), 33–57.

[Leonard Prager / Marc Miller (2nd ed.)]

RABOY, ISAAC (Yitskhok; 1882–1944), Yiddish novelist, poet, and playwright. Born into a ḥasidic family in rural Podolia and raised in northern Bessarabia where he came in contact with maskilic circles and read Russian literature, in 1904, following the Kishinev pogroms and seeking to avoid conscription into the czarist army, he immigrated to New York where he worked in a hat factory. Dovid *Ignatov, a fellow worker, and *Mani Leyb, a neighbor, introduced him to the literary group Di *Yunge, in whose anthologies Raboy published his first stories. He studied agriculture with the financial support of the Baron de Hirsch Fund (1908–10) and subsequently worked on a horse-breeding ranch in North Dakota. On his return to the East in 1913, he failed both at farming in Connecticut and in a business venture in New York and was compelled to work in factories for the rest of his life. Many of his short stories and his two best-known novels, *Her Goldnbarg* ("Mr. Goldenberg," 1923) and *Der Yidisher Kauboy* (1942; *Jewish Cowboy*, 1989) reflect his farming experiences. The lightly veiled autobiographical protagonists exult in the freedom of the prairies – a world hitherto unknown to Yiddish literature. They empathize with Native Americans, are compassionate to animals, but experience antisemitic prejudice and long to till the soil of Palestine. In his lyrical and often humorous prose, Raboy celebrates the Jewish discovery of the New World, not only the vast spaces of the Midwest but also, in a manner comparable to those works of Sholem *Asch set in New York, as in *Iz Gekumen a Yid keyn Amerike* ("A Jew Came to America," 1929), the sweatshops and tenements of Delancey Street at the turn of the century.

BIBLIOGRAPHY: Rejzen, Leksikon, 4 (1929), 1–8; D. Ignatov, *Opgerisene Bleter* (1957), 52–6; Y. Yeshurin, in: Sh. Rozhanski (ed.), *Pionern in Amerike* (1963), 305–9 (bibl.); S. Liptzin, *Maturing of Yiddish Literature* (1970), 5–9. **ADD. BIBLIOGRAPHY:** LNYL, 8 (1981), 278–82; N. Meisel, *Forgeyer un Mittsaytler* (1946), 289–303; H. Leivik, *Eseyen un Redes* (1963), 261–4; C. Madison, *Yiddish Literature* (1968), 300–1; Sh. Niger, *Yidishe Shrayber fun Tsvantsikstn Yorhundert*, 2 (1973), 251--6.

[Sol Liptzin / Hugh Denman (2nd ed.)]

RAB-SARIS AND RAB-MAG (Heb. רַב־סָרִיס; רַב מָג), titles of high ranking Assyrian and Babylonian officials. An economic bilingual document in Akkadian and Aramaic attests the title Rab-Saris as held by an Assyrian eponym. In that document, however, the corresponding Akkadian term is absent and it is as yet unattested elsewhere. Further a מרסרס of Sargon is found in Aramaic. The meaning of all these is "chief of the king's attendants." Though the *saris* – in Akkadian *ša rēši* – was often a *eunuch (in contradistinction to the *ša ziqni*, "the bearded one"), there is no indication that the Rab-Saris was always castrated. In the story of Daniel, the Rab-Saris Ashpenaz trained certain aristocratic Jewish youths for service in the court of Nebuchadnezzar (Dan. 1:3 ff.). The Rab-Saris is among the Assyrian officials leading the siege of Jerusalem in the days of Hezekiah (II Kings 18:17). In Jeremiah 39:3–13, the Rab-Saris Nebushazban is mentioned together with other Babylonian officials. Among these was Nergalsharezer the Rab-Mag. In late Assyrian and late Babylonian texts the *rab-mugi* (or *rab-mungi*) is described as a high official who performed military, administrative, and diplomatic duties, although the precise significance of the title is unclear.

BIBLIOGRAPHY: M. Sprengling, in: AJSLL, 49 (1932), 53–54; E. Weidner, in: AFO, 17 (1954–56), 293; J. Nougayrov, *Le Palais royal d'Ugarit*, 3 (1955), 16:162; H. Tadmor, in: BIES, 31 (1967), 77.

[S. David Sperling]

RAB-SHAKEH (Heb. רַבְשָׁקֵה; Akk. *rab šāqî*), title of a high Assyrian and Babylonian official. Akkadian texts indicate that he was in charge of territories. In the Assyrian eponym succession, this official was fourth in line from the king. In Middle Assyrian texts the *šāqû* ("butler") is mentioned as a member of the domestic staff of the palace. The *rab-šāqî* was thus originally "chief butler." The development calls to mind the English "chamberlain." At the siege of Jerusalem by Sennacherib the Rab-Shakeh addresses the leaders and the people in an effort to secure their surrender (II Kings 18:19; Isa. 36–37).

BIBLIOGRAPHY: L. Waterman, *Royal Correspondence of the Assyrian Empire* (1930), pt. 1, 353, r. 9; E. Weidner, in: AFO, 17 (1954–56), 290; R. Labat, in: *Fischer Weltgeschichte*, 5 (1970), 36.

[S. David Sperling]

RACAH, GIULIO (Yoel; 1909–1965), Israeli physicist, born in Florence, Italy. On his mother's side, Racah's family claimed to trace its ancestry in Italy back to the destruction of the Second Temple. Racah studied in Rome under Enrico Fermi and in Pisa under Wolfgang Pauli. At the age of 28 he was appointed professor at the University of Pisa. An ardent Zionist, he placed his farm outside Pisa for use by the Zionist Organization as an agricultural training center. He first visited Palestine in 1934, and on settling in Jerusalem in 1939 headed the department of theoretical physics of the Hebrew University. Here, Racah began his studies of atomic spectroscopy which gained the department an international reputation. During the Israel War of Independence he served as deputy commander of the Haganah on Mount Scopus and led research on munitions that could be produced from the raw materials available in the besieged city. The "Racah method" of spectroscopy has been recognized as one of the most effective methods of studying all types of nuclear structure. His "Racah coefficient W" has wide application in research on nuclear radiations, and it is the basis of books of tables published by many of the world's leading scientific institutions. In 1958 Racah was awarded the Israel Prize for natural sciences. His reputation attracted notable scientists to Israel, and the department of nuclear physics at the Weizmann Institute of Science was built up mainly by graduates trained by Racah. In 1961 Racah was elected rector of the Hebrew University. He died while visiting Florence.

BIBLIOGRAPHY: PIASH, section of sciences, no. 2 (1966); I. Talmi, in: *Nuclear Physics*, 83 (1966), 1–8, incl. bibl.; *Journal of the Optical Society of America*, 56 (Feb. 1966), 268.

RACCAH, MAS'ŪD BEN AARON (1690–1768), rabbi in *Tripoli. Raccah appears to have been descended from the Venetian Raccah family. Isaac Raccah, whose daughter he married, and Solomon Raccah, wealthy uncles of his, and his brother-in-law Mas'ūd lived in Venice. These relatives encouraged him and lent him their support. He studied principally in Smyrna under R. Ḥayyim Abulafia the Elder and R. Isaac ha-Kohen Rapoport, the author of *Battei Kehunnah*. Raccah immigrated to Ereẓ Israel, settled in *Jerusalem, and was sent from there as an emissary to Tripoli. The leaders of the Tripoli community invited him to become their spiritual leader. Accepting their proposal, he was appointed *av bet din*. During his stay in Tripoli he founded a yeshivah and trained many disciples who later became rabbis and community leaders. They included R. Shalom Flus, R. Moses Lahmias, R. Nathan Adadi, who married his daughter, R. Benjamin Vaturi, and others. During the years 1731–36 he appears to have been in Leghorn, where he corresponded on halakhic matters with the rabbi of Leghorn, R. Abraham Rodriguez. While there, he gave his *haskamah* ("approval") in 1736 to the responsa of R. David b. Zimra, which were then published there.

Raccah wrote the following works:

(1) *Ma'aseh Roke'aḥ* ("Works of the Apothecary," a pun on his own name), a commentary in four parts on Maimonides' *Mishneh Torah* (parts 1–2, Venice, 1742; part 3, Leghorn, 1863; part 4, Tel Aviv, 1964). In this work he compares the texts of the various editions of *Mishneh Torah* in order to determine the correct version;

(2) *Divrei ha-Baraita* ("Words of the *Baraita*"), commentaries on the *beraitot*, which is extant in manuscript;

(3) various sermons which are extant in manuscript;

(4) a commentary on the Five Scrolls; and

(5) a collection of commentaries on several of the tractates of the Talmud.

BIBLIOGRAPHY: R. Attal, in: *Sefunot*, 9 (1965), 384ff., incl. bibl.; Va'ad Kehillot Luv be-Yisrael, *Yahadut Luv* (1960), 67 and passim; M. Raccah, *Ma'aseh Roke'aḥ*, ed. by S.A. Schlesinger, 4 (1964), introd.

[Haiim Bentov]

RACE, THEORY OF. In the 18th century the "founding fathers" of anthropology almost all believed that the human races differed in innate intelligence, or even in virtue. Obviously the idea of such racial differences is far older than the first attempts at their scientific classification.

Early Beliefs

Primitive tribes who laid claim to particular genealogies, going back to legendary ancestors, developed these ideas in their own way. In classical Greece, philosophers like Plato and Aristotle were "racists" in the modern sense of the word: according to Aristotle, the Greeks were born to be free while the barbarians were slaves by nature. However, in the melting pot of Alexander's empire and later in the Roman empire, belief in ethnocentrism faded; this was especially true of Stoic philosophy. The Jewish tradition, with its majestic story of Adam which furnished all men with a common ancestor, can be considered the first historical example of a fundamentally "antiracist" conception. On this subject the Talmud states: "for the sake of peace among creatures, the descent of all men is traced back to one individual, so that one may not say to his neighbor, my father is greater than yours" (Sanh. 4:5). Belief in a common descent from Adam was taken over by Christianity and became one of the fundamentals of the Christian principle of the equality of all men before God. However, at the same time, medieval society was divided into three estates – commoners, clergy, and nobility – superiority being ascribed to the "blue blood" of the latter. As most of Europe's reigning monarchs were of Germanic origin, there was a tendency apparent from the earliest days to accord a measure of preeminence to "Germanic blood." Conflicts between such conceptions of degree and the Christian universalist principle were particularly acute in the 16th-century Spanish empire. It was only after lengthy struggles and theological discussions that the Spaniards recognized the native races they found in America as men endowed with souls. At the same time, through statutes dealing with racial purity (*limpieza de sangre*), a system of racial discrimination was instituted in Spain, applying to the descendants of Jews and Moors who had been converted to Christianity. In spite of their baptism, the blood of these "new Christians" was considered impure and their race inferior.

Eighteenth-Century Anthropological Theories

So, during the whole of European history, it is possible to speak of latent, or even open, racial prejudice. The establishment of the anthropological sciences in the 18th century enabled these prejudices to be expressed systematically, and the systems of classification worked out by the scientists Buffon and Linnaeus were typical in this respect. Both men coupled features (color of skin, type of hair, etc.) with mental and moral characteristics, which were interpreted in favor of the white man of Europe. Buffon, whose system was more overtly racial than Linnaeus', even considered the white man as the norm, the "king of the creation," and colored men as members of degenerate races. The tendency to regard the white race as superior characterized the majority of anthropological systems elaborated during the 18th and 19th centuries. The rejection of biblical anthropology favored this trend, because then it became possible to attribute different origins to different races. Thus, according to *Goethe, Adam was the ancestor of the Jews only, while *Voltaire believed that black men were an intermediate species between white men and apes. In the 18th century the major systems of classification (of which the best known and least marred by racial value judgments was that of Blumenbach) distinguished between only four or five principal races. The Jews were usually included in the white race, in whose midst they were supposed to form a nation *sui generis*. But at the beginning of the 19th century, with the emergence of nationalist struggles, writers began to multiply the number of races, to distinguish between different European races and even to set one against the other. There was continuous interaction in this field between the mental climate of the time, itself closely related to political upheavals, and the current intellectual theories.

Nineteenth-Century Nationalism

From then on racist or quasiracist notions took root, especially in Germany where nationalist agitators like E.M. Arndt and F.L. Jahn extolled the merits and qualities of the Teutonic race. The philosopher *Fichte elaborated a patriotic theory postulating that German was the original language (*Ursprache*) of Europe and the Germans its original people (*Urvolk*). After 1815, many German students and academics propounded these opinions as part of the Pan-Germanic movement. Ideas of the same type also spread in other countries. After the restoration of the monarchy in France some bourgeois intellectuals, reacting against the pretensions of the "Frankish" nobility, claimed to belong to the native "Gallic" race. In Britain "Germanism" or "Teutonism" found influential supporters in Carlyle and Thomas Arnold. In more enlightened English circles the "Hebrew race," which had given the West its spiritual values, was championed by Benjamin *Disraeli: "All is race, there is no other truth" was his maxim. In that age the concept of "race" was espoused by numerous authors as a substitute for divine providence as the determining factor in history. Germany continued to be the principal nursery of race theories reinforced by scientific pretensions, partly because its political divisions before 1871 stimulated nationalist fervor, and partly because according to the most prevalent notions the Germans were the only European nation which could claim to be a wholly "pure" race, that is, purely Teutonic. Heinrich *Heine commented ironically: "We Germans are the strongest and wisest race; descendants of our princely house sit on all European thrones; our Rothschilds control all the world's stock markets; our scholars lead in all sciences; we know it all."

"Aryan" and "Semite"

It is obvious that from then on the Jews were considered as a race apart, an Oriental one, and the spectacle of their success in all walks of life after emancipation strengthened the tendency to attribute to them certain specific – and detrimental – racial characteristics. In intellectual spheres the race theories of the 19th century received a powerful impetus and gained a new orientation from the linguistic discovery of the Indo-European group of languages. A confusion arose between languages and races, a mistake which had grave consequences. It was believed that the nations that spoke European languages, which were thought to have derived from Sanskrit, belonged to the Indo-European or "Aryan" race. In opposition to them was a "Semitic" race, represented by the Jews and the Arabs. Typically enough, German scholars used the term "Indo-Germanic" instead of Indo-European. Of course it was also taken for granted that the "Aryan" race was morally superior to the "Semitic" one. Thus, according to the famous Orientalist scholar Lassen, "the Semites do not possess that harmonious equilibrium between all the powers of the intellect which characterized the Indo-Germans." His well-known French colleague Ernest *Renan spoke of the "appalling simplicity of the Semitic mind." All original creations of the human spirit – with the possible exception of religion – were attributed to the "Aryans." Moreover, many authors considered that, to preserve their special qualities, the Aryan nations must avoid intermingling with the people of an "inferior race." They accorded the Germans the distinction of being the purest Aryans.

Such were the opinions, which, pushed to their limits, were developed and popularized by Comte de *Gobineau in his infamous *Essai sur l'Inégalité des Races Humaines* (1853–55). The racial theories of the 19th century tended to establish a double hierarchy: the superiority of the "Aryans" over "Semites" and other "inferior races"; and the superiority of the "Germans" over other "Aryans." The political and economic success (especially after 1871) of the nations that spoke Germanic languages and that therefore considered themselves as belonging to the Teutonic race helped to sanction these opinions. In Latin countries efforts were made to set up a rival hierarchy (which gave rise to the myths of "Latinity" and "Celticity") or, especially in France, to proclaim the superiority of a "racial mixture" over "racial homogeneity." Similarly, in the United States, the adherents of the "melting-pot" conception of the country (limited to the white race) were in conflict with the acolytes of the "Anglo-Saxon race." All these notions continued to be based on the tenacious confusion, typical of the materialist orientation of anthropological science in the 19th century, between "races" and languages or cultures.

However, during the same century, progress in anthropology, ethnography, and prehistory made most specialists gradually abandon these simplified conceptions. Thus the distinguished philologist Max Mueller, although he had previously supported such theories, announced in 1871 that it was absurd to speak of an "Aryan race" or of a "grammar based on the size of the head." However, the "Aryan theory" continued to gain adherents among the general public. It was propagated in every country in school textbooks, which usually summarily repeated ancient opinions and classified Europeans as "Aryans," all except the "Semitic" Jews. The anti-Jewish campaigns, from then on styled "antisemitic," made their contribution to the spread of the theory. As a result of all this, by 1900 the existence of an "Aryan race" was firmly established in the public mind as a scientific truth. Usually, this only implied a vague belief in the intellectual or moral superiority of the "Aryans" over the "Semites," and a more marked superiority of the "whites" over the "yellows" and especially the "blacks." But in the arena of the violent antisemitic campaigns of the time, some fanatics worked out elaborate eschatological systems in which the struggle between the Aryan and Semitic races was the counterpart of the final struggle between Good and Evil. The most influential of these writers was the Anglo-German Houston Stewart *Chamberlain, who stated that the original sin of the Jews was that from ancient times they had been a mixed race opposed to Aryan purity. Ingenuously, in the time of King Cyrus, the Aryans had committed the fatal blunder of protecting the Jews: "…under the protection of Aryan tolerance was planted the seed from which Semitic intolerance spread its poison over the earth for thousands of years, a curse on all that was noble and a shame to Christianity."

From the second quarter of the 20th century scientific anthropology rid itself almost entirely of the dangerous error of dividing the human races into "superior" and "inferior," or even "good" and "bad." At that same time, however, in a defeated and disoriented Germany, gripped by unemployment, this same error helped to weld a political party and then grew into a state dogma. Thus, from 1933 the theory of race was nothing but a kind of totemistic mythology, serving to justify an imperialistic and murderous expansionism.

In the later part of the 20th century, all such theories of race, whether applied to Jews or other groups, had been largely dicredited by the scientific community.

BIBLIOGRAPHY: M.F. Ashley Montagu, *Man's Most Dangerous Myth: The Fallacy of Race* (1942); H. Kohn, *Idea of Nationalism* (1944); G.W. Allport, *Nature of Prejudice* (1954); UNESCO, *Race Question in Modern Science* (1957); L.L. Snyder, *Idea of Racialism* (1962); L. Poliakov, *Histoire de l'Antisémitisme de Voltaire à Wagner* (1968); S. Conn and E.E. Hunt, *Living Race of Man* (1965); idem, *The Origin of Races* (1962); idem, *The Races of Europe* (1939); idem, *The Story of Man* (19622); A.R. Jensen, in: *Harvard Educational Review*, 39, no. 1 (Winter 1969), 1–123; 39, no. 2 (Spring 1969), 273–356; L. Edson, in: *The New York Times Magazine* (August 31, 1969), 10–11; M. Deutsch, in: *Harvard Educational Review*, 39, no. 3 (Summer 1969), 523–57.

[Léon Poliakov]

RACHEL (Heb. רָחֵל), matriarch of Israel, wife of *Jacob and the mother of *Joseph and Benjamin. Her name means "ewe," while that of her sister *Leah means "cow." She was the younger daughter of *Laban, brother of Rebekkah.

Rachel first appears as a shepherdess who happened to come in sight just when Jacob had arrived at a well near Haran in his flight from his brother Esau. The two seem to have fallen in love at once, and Jacob made an agreement with his uncle to work for him for seven years in return for receiving Rachel in marriage. However, when the time of the nuptials arrived, Laban cheated Jacob and gave him Leah, his older daughter, instead. Laban, however, agreed to deliver Rachel in advance if Jacob undertook to serve him for another seven years as the bride-price for Rachel (Gen. 29:4–30).

Rachel is described as "shapely and beautiful" (29:17) and was more beloved of Jacob than Leah (29:30). She was, however, barren and became very jealous of her sister's fecundity. In her desperation, she resorted to the device of concubinage, used earlier by Sarah under similar circumstances (16:2–4; see *Patriarchs). She gave her maid Bilhah to Jacob and looked upon the offspring of the union, Dan and Naphtali, as her own children (30:1–8). On one occasion, she yielded her conjugal rights to Leah in return for some mandrakes that Reuben had collected (30:14–16), apparently sharing the widespread belief that this "love apple" could cure barrenness in women. It was only after Leah had borne seven children that Rachel finally gave birth, naming her son Joseph, noting with satisfaction that God had taken away (*ʾasaf*) her disgrace and expressing the wish that the Lord might give her an additional (*yosef*) son (30:22–24).

Jacob consulted with Rachel and her sister about his plan to return to his homeland and he received their consent. Before the family's precipitate flight, Rachel stole her father's household idols, unbeknown to her husband. The exact significance of this act is uncertain (see *Teraphim). Three days later, Laban caught up with Jacob and searched his effects. Rachel, however, managed to outwit her father and to conceal the idols (31:4–35).

When Jacob prepared for the encounter with Esau on his return home, he took care to place Rachel and Joseph last in the receiving line (33:1–7), apparently to ensure that they would have a chance to escape should the meeting prove to be hostile.

Rachel died in childbirth on the way from Beth-El to Ephrath. As she lay dying she named her son Ben-Oni, "son of my suffering," although her husband called him Benjamin. Jacob did not bury her in the ancestral, patriarchal vault at Machpelah, but interred her at the place of her death and set up a monument over the grave (35:16–21; cf. 48:7). These traditions of burial in Bethlehem are in conflict with I Samuel 10:2 and Jeremiah 31:14 (15), which locate the tomb in Benjamin (see below).

Rachel appears again only twice in biblical literature. She is mentioned, together with Leah, as a matriarch of Israel, in the marriage blessing of Ruth (Ruth 4:11), and Jeremiah poetically visualizes her weeping in Ramah for her children (the tribes of Ephraim and Manasseh descended from Joseph), who are in exile (Jer. 31:15).

The traditions about Rachel in Genesis are generally regarded as reflections of Israelite tribal history – though there is no unanimity as to the period involved. It is assumed that at some stage in the development of the 12-tribe league, the tribes associated with Rachel (Benjamin, Ephraim, and Manasseh) and Bilhah (Dan and Naphtali) constituted a distinct confederation. The territory of Benjamin is, as a matter of fact, contiguous with that of Ephraim. The attribution of two tribes to the concubine Bilhah probably reflects their inferior status within the smaller confederation, while the birth of Benjamin in Canaan would imply a late association of that tribe with the others in the group. The very name can be interpreted as "son of the south," which correctly describes the location of Benjamin's territory in Israel in relation to that of the other members of the groups.

[Nahum M. Sarna]

In the Aggadah

Rachel warned Jacob that her cunning father would try dishonestly to wed her elder sister, Leah, to him. Jacob and Rachel therefore agreed upon a sign by which he would recognize her on the nuptial night. Nevertheless, when Laban actually sent Leah into the bridal chamber, Rachel revealed the sign to her sister lest she be put to shame. As a reward for this act, Rachel was vouchsafed to be the ancestress of King *Saul (Meg. 13b).

Rachel began to envy her sister after Leah had borne Jacob four sons because she attributed this good fortune to her sister's piety (Gen. R. 71:6). After she implored Jacob to pray for the termination of her barrenness, he hinted that Sarah was only blessed with Isaac because "she brought her rival [Hagar] into her home." Rachel thereupon gave her maidservant, Bilhah, to Jacob (Gen. R. 71:7). When she finally bore a son, she was doubly thankful because she had feared that Laban would permit only Leah to accompany Jacob to Ereẓ Israel, and would detain the childless wife (Gen. R. 73:3). She was a prophetess and thus knew that Jacob was destined to have only 12 sons. Since Joseph was the 11th, she prayed for only one more son (Tanḥ. Va-Yeẓe, 20). One opinion is that she stole her father's teraphim in order to conceal the knowledge of Jacob's flight (PdRE 36); another is that the purpose was to turn her father away from idolatry (Gen. R. 74:5). Jacob's unintentional curse against her on that occasion caused Rachel's premature death. The curse would have taken effect at once were it not that she was destined to bear Jacob his youngest son (Gen. R. 74:9; PdRE 36).

She was not vouchsafed burial next to her husband in the cave of Machpelah because of her indelicate request to Leah in the mandrake incident (Gen. R. 72:3). Jacob buried her at Ephrath because he foresaw that the exiles would pass this place when they were exiled to Babylon. As they passed, Rachel would entreat God's mercy for them (Gen. R. 82:10). Indeed, it was only Rachel who was able to obtain God's promise that Israel would ultimately be restored after she pleaded with Him to recall her kindness to Leah on the night that should have been her own nuptial celebration (Lam. R., Proem 24).

[Aaron Rothkoff]

Tomb of Rachel

According to Genesis (35:19–20), Rachel was buried "on the road to Ephrath, which is Beth-Lehem"; according to I Samuel (10:–2) the tomb of Rachel was situated "within the border of Benjamin, in Zelzah." The words of the prophet Jeremiah (31:15) allude to the tomb of Rachel as being in the portion of Benjamin. The rabbis who sought to correct this contradiction saw an error in the order of the words in the construction of the verse in the Book of Samuel. Among others, they suggested the following correction: "When thou goest from me today to the border of Benjamin, to Zelzah, thou shalt find two men by the tomb of Rachel" (Gen. R. 82:10; Tosef., Sot. 11:11; Sif. Deut. 352). Some modern scholars read: "When thou goest from me today, thou shalt find two men within the border of Benjamin, in Zelzah, and they shall say to thee: the she-asses which thou went to seek by the tomb of Rachel have been found."

The tombstone near Beth-Lehem is mentioned by the first Christians, e.g., Eusebius; the most ancient Jewish source on the tomb of Rachel is the *Guide to Jerusalem* of the tenth century, which was found in the Cairo **Genizah*. According to the descriptions of Jewish travelers, from R. Benjamin of Tudela (c. 1170) until the 18th century, the tombstone consisted of 11 stones which were laid by the 11 sons of Jacob on the grave; a large stone was placed over them, that of Jacob. The tomb was roofed over with a dome which was supported by four pillars. At the end of the 18th century the tomb was surrounded by a closed structure. In 1841 this structure was renovated with funds which were supplied by Sir Moses Montefiore. This is attested by an inscription engraved on a marble tablet inside the structure.

The tomb is especially visited on the new moons, during the whole of the month of Elul, and on the 14th of Marheshvan, the traditional anniversary of the death of "Our Mother Rachel." Jews donated oil, sacred curtains, and charity for the tomb structure. They were also accustomed to inscribing their names on the tombstone and measuring it with red woolen threads, which were tied onto children and the sick as a remedy for good health and healing. During the Jordanian occupation, the area around the tomb was converted into a Muslim cemetery. After the Six-Day War, the structure was renovated by the Israel Ministry of Religions and adapted to mass pilgrimage. A picture of the Tomb of Rachel was commonly used as a decoration in Jewish homes throughout the world.

[Joseph Braslavi (Braslavski)]

In the Arts

Of the four matriarchs Rachel has inspired the most original work in literature and art. In many instances she figures largely as the wife of Jacob, but in others she appears as the central character, often in connection with the theme of Jeremiah 31:15 – "A voice is heard in Ramah, Lamentation, and bitter weeping, Rachel weeping for her children; She refuseth to be comforted for her children, Because they are not." The account of Rachel's marriage to Jacob forms the basis of three early literary works, the German dramatist Christian Weise's

Jacobs doppelte Heyrath (1683), the Swiss German Johann Jacob Bodmer's epic *Jacob und Rachel* (1752), and an anonymous Spanish allegorical play, *La mas hermosa Rachel pastora de las almas* (c. 1780). Probably the outstanding 19th-century treatment of the subordinate theme was *Rachel* ("Rachel's Lament," 1851), a verse allegory of the fate of his homeland by the Hungarian nationalist poet János Arany. Among works on the subject written in the 20th century are *Plach Rakhili* ("Rachel's Lament," c. 1923), by the Russian writer Nikolai Alexandrovich Krasheninnikov; "Rahel," a lyrical ballad by the German poet Max Barthel, who later became sympathetic to the Nazis; and *Jacob's Ladder*, one of Laurence Housman's *Old Testament Plays* (1950), in which Rachel and Leah unendearingly squabble over their claims to Jacob's affection. A Jewish treatment was that by the Hebrew poet *Raḥel, whose *Shirat Raḥel* ("Song of Rachel," 1935) includes the phrase "Her voice sings in mine..." In medieval Christian iconography, the two wives of Jacob, Leah and Rachel, were associated with the New Testament figures of Martha and Mary (representing the active and the contemplative life), since Rachel was preferred by Jacob as Mary was preferred by Jesus. However, Rachel was not a popular subject among artists of the Middle Ages. Interest revived in the 15th century, when the meeting of Jacob and Rachel (Gen. 29:10ff.) was the subject of a pen-and-wash drawing by the Flemish painter Hugo van der Goes (Christ Church, Oxford). During the Renaissance, Palma Vecchio painted Jacob kissing Rachel (Gen. 29:11), and there is a study of Jacob and Rachel by Raphael in the Loggia of the Vatican. A painting by Hendrik Terbrugghen (National Gallery, London) shows Jacob asking Laban for Rachel's hand (Gen. 29:18). Claude Lorrain painted an idyllic landscape with Jacob and Rachel (Hermitage, Leningrad). The robust nude by *Rembrandt, known as *Danaë* (Hermitage, Leningrad), may have been intended to represent Jacob's unintended marriage to Rachel's sister, Leah. Jacob's appropriation of Laban's household idols, which were taken and hidden by Rachel (Gen. 31:30–35), is depicted in the seventh-century *Ashburnham Pentateuch* (Bibliothèque Nationale, Paris). This subject later appeared in the Vatican Loggia frescoes by Raphael and in a tapestry by Barend van Orley, one of a series recounting the story of Jacob. It was also a popular subject in the 17th century. There are examples by the French painter Sébastien Bourdon (Louvre), by the Spanish master Murillo (Duke of Westminster Collection, London), by the Dutch genre painter Jan Steen, and by Rembrandt's teacher Pieter Lastman. Among works of the 18th century is a painting by Gabriel de Saint-Aubin in the Louvre; and the subject was included by Tiepolo in his wall paintings for the archbishop's palace at Udine, Italy.

In Music

Rachel has attracted rather less attention in music, although she and Jacob have together inspired some compositions, notably a 16th-century motet by Joachim à Burck (1599), some 17th-century Spanish songs, and a comic opera by Johann Philipp Krieger (1649–1725). The oratorio *Rachel* was composed by Jean François Lesueur (1760–1837), and in the 20th century Lazare *Saminsky wrote a ballet on the theme. *Raḥel Mevakkah al Baneha* (Jer. 31:15–17) has been a favorite subject for composers of cantorial music, and settings have been recorded by several leading *ḥazzanim*, including Josef (Yossele) *Rosenblatt; there are also modern interpretations by singers such as Jan Peerce and Richard Tucker. David Roitman's extended version of *Raḥel Mevakkah al Baneha* (Jer. 31:15; Jer. 25:30; Isa. 20:12; Lam. 1:16; and Isa. 33:7) was arranged for voice and piano by A.W. Binder (1930).

See also: *Jacob in the Arts.

[Bathja Bayer]

BIBLIOGRAPHY: B. Stade, in: ZAW, 1 (1881), 112–4; B. Luther, *ibid.*, 21 (1901), 37ff.; CH Gordon, in: RB, 44 (1935), 35, 36; J. Bright, *Early Israel in Recent History Writing* (1956), 115ff.; for further bibliography see *Genesis, *Patriarchs. IN THE AGGADAH: Ginzberg, Legends, index. TOMB OF RACHEL: Eshtori ha-Parḥi, *Kaftor va-Feraḥ*, ed. by A.M. Luncz (1897), 221, 229, 299; J. Schwarz, *Tevu'ot ha-Areẓ*, ed. by A.M. Luncz (1900), 131–5; A. Yaari, *Masot Ereẓ Yisrael* (1946), index; A. Schlesinger, in: *Sefer Neiger* (1959), 19–26; Z. Vilnay, *Maẓẓevot Kodesh be-Ereẓ Yisrael* (19632), 98–107; J. Braslavi, in: *Eretz-Israel*, 7 (1964), 76. **ADD. BIBLIOGRAPHY:** W. Holladay, *Jeremiah 2* (1989), 186–89; M. Dijkstra, in: DDD, 683–84; T. Lewis, in: *ibid.*, 844–50.

RACHEL (first century C.E.), wife of R. *Akiva. The daughter of *Kalba Savua, one of the three richest men of Jerusalem, Rachel secretly married Akiva, who was ignorant and her father's shepherd, because she saw in him a man of modest and noble character. When her father found out about the secret betrothal, he took a vow against her deriving any benefit from his estate. Akiva and Rachel lived in straitened circumstances, but Akiva promised her a gift of a golden ornament with an engraving of Jerusalem on it. According to legend, the prophet *Elijah once came to them disguised as a poor man and begged them for some straw for a bed for his wife who had just given birth, in order to make them realize that there were people worse off than they (Ned. 50a). Akiva later decided to study Torah. Encouraged by Rachel he stayed away for 24 years (Finkelstein assumes that this absence did not last more than three years). He returned home with 24,000 disciples to whom he said, "mine and yours are hers," i.e., the credit for all our achievements is hers. When Akiva was able to fulfill his promise and give Rachel the "Jerusalem of Gold," Rabban *Gamaliel's wife envied her and told her husband of Akiva's generosity. He replied, "Did you do what she did, selling her hair in order that he might study?" (TJ, Sot. 9:16,24c). Akiva's love for Rachel is reflected in his saying, "who is wealthy?... He who has a wife comely in deeds" (Shab. 25b).

When Akiva's daughter became secretly betrothed to *Simeon ben Azzai, the Talmud concluded that this was indeed an illustration of the proverb "Ewe (Heb. *raḥel*) follows ewe; a daughter acts like her mother" (Ket. 63a). Two major traditions are preserved in the Talmud about Rachel. One is that it was she who encouraged Akiva to study (Ket. 62b, 63a; see also Ned. 50a, which is a more legendary source), while the other presents the stimulus as coming from himself and his gift to his wife as a compensation for her suffering during his absence (ARN[1] 6, 29).

BIBLIOGRAPHY: L. Finkelstein, *Akiba; Scholar, Saint, and Martyr* (1936), 22ff., 79ff.

RACHEL, the stage name of **Eliza Rachel Felix** (1821–1858), French actress and one of the world's greatest tragediennes. Born in Switzerland, Rachel was the daughter of a peddler, Jacob Felix, who took his large family to Paris. She was singing with her sisters in the streets when she was heard by the singing master, Etienne Choron, who undertook to give her free instruction. Under his sponsorship, she attended drama classes and the conservatoire, and at the age of 17 played at the Théâtre Gymnase. The leading Paris critic, Jules Janin of the *Journal de Débats*, was the only one to perceive her quality, and saw his enthusiasm vindicated when, in 1838, she entered the Comédie-Française and achieved success in Corneille's *Horace*. Thereafter her career was one of fame and notoriety. Rachel was slight of build and by some considered plain; but on the stage she had beauty, charm, and power. Though she had little formal education, her supreme dramatic achievement was in the French classics, especially Corneille and Racine, in which she replaced the declamatory style of the period with vitality and passion. She appeared in some contemporary plays, including *Adrienne Lecouvreur*, written for her by Legouvé and Scribe. Her greatest performance was in Racine's *Phèdre*; it was described as "an apocalypse of human agony."

The notoriety attending Rachel's name arose from her private life. She never married, but she had two children, one by Count Colonna-Walewski, an illegitimate son of Napoleon. She was also the mistress at different times of the poet Alfred de Musset, the Prince de Joinville, and a nephew of Napoleon, Prince Jerome. She first appeared in London in 1841 and subsequently toured the Continental capitals, including St. Petersburg. Her tour of the United States in 1855 proved to be the end of her career, for the tubercular condition from which she suffered became worse, and she never acted again. At her funeral, the chief rabbi of the Consistory of Paris delivered an oration in Hebrew.

Rachel's brother RAPHAEL (1825–1872), and her sisters SARAH (1819–1877), LIA (1828–1908), REBECCA (1829–1854), and DINAH (1836–1909) all had theatrical careers of varying success.

BIBLIOGRAPHY: J.E. Agate, *Rachel* (Eng., 1928); B. Falk, *Rachel the Immortal* (1936); J. Richardson, *Rachel* (Eng., 1956).

[Ravelle Brickman]

RACHMAN, PETER (c. 1920–1962), British property tycoon and racketeer. He was born Perec Rachman in Lvov, Poland, the son of a dentist. His parents perished in the Holocaust and he survived the war as a slave laborer, migrating to Britain around 1946. After working as a dishwasher, in the 1950s Rachman built up a property empire in London by methods which later made him nationally notorious. Due to the war, there had been an extreme housing shortage in London. Resident tenants were protected by rent control, but the owner of a property was free to raise rents to their market level once the previous occupant had vacated a building. Rachman hired thugs, mainly recent West Indian migrants, to intimidate tenants, often elderly, into leaving, using threats and other unacceptable tactics. It is believed that Rachman was one of the main progenitors of the race riots in Notting Hill and elsewhere in west London in the late 1950s. Rachman dealt almost exclusively in cash, operating from no fixed premises, which made him immune from prosecution. He also became notorious for his lifestyle of ostentatious luxury, philandering, and gambling. In 1960 he was denied British citizenship on police advice, which resulted in his moving into more upmarket property pursuits just before his death of a heart attack at the age of about 42. After his death, when his methods became public knowledge, Harold Wilson coined the term "Rachmanism" to describe his racketeering, a term which has passed into common British usage. Rachman was among the most notorious businessmen in modern British history.

BIBLIOGRAPHY: ODNB online.

[William D. Rubinstein (2nd ed.)]

RACHMILEWITZ, MOSHE (1899–1985), Israeli hematologist. Born in Mstislavl (Russia) and educated in Berlin, he reached Palestine in 1926. He joined the Hadassah Department of Internal Medicine in Jerusalem in 1931 and became its head in 1939. One of the architects of the Hebrew University-Hadassah Medical School, he became professor in 1950 and served as dean from 1957 to 1961. From 1960 he headed the Israel Association for Hematology and Blood Transfusions and in 1964 was president of the first Congress of the Asian and Pacific Society of Hematology to be held in Israel. His research work has centered on the metabolism of vitamin B-12 and folic acid, Mediterranean fever, liver diseases, the mechanisms regulating blood creation, and nutritional anemia. He made a significant contribution to the formulation of Israel's health policies as vice chairman of the National Health Council, and internationally as a member of the World Health Organization's Expert Committee on Nutritional Anemia. In 1964, he was awarded the Israel Prize in Medicine.

[Lucien Harris]

°**RACINE, JEAN** (1639–1699), French tragic dramatist. Racine's reputation rests on nine tragedies in Alexandrine verse written between 1667 and 1691. There is no record of his having any personal knowledge of Jews, but the heroine's speech in *Esther* (1689) makes his sympathy for them clear enough. A reference in the preface to *Esther* to the modern celebration of Purim also shows an awareness of Jewish customs. Racine's profound knowledge of the Scriptures and its application to his work can be traced to his Jansenist education at Port-Royal (1655–58), where he first met Blaise *Pascal and enjoyed semi-private tutoring by such scholars as Louis-Isaac Le Maître de Saci (1615–84), the translator and Bible commentator, and Jean

Hamon (1618–87), author of a four-volume commentary on the *Song of Songs* (1708). Racine obtained the most thorough grounding in the Scriptures then available in France, but did not learn Hebrew. His knowledge of *Midrash* and *Targum* and Jewish traditions were derived from the works of the contemporary Christian Hebraists Matthew Poole, John *Lightfoot, and Richard *Simon. Racine's *Phèdre* (1677), though based on classical myth, involves Judeo-Greek syncretism. Phaedra's pangs of conscience can only be understood within the framework of biblical law and a biblical conception of man's relationship to the Deity. The biblical tragedies (*Esther*, 1689; *Athalie*, 1691) are less religious in implication than *Phèdre*, and partake of the rationalist spirit that pervaded French intellectual society at the end of the 17th century. Like most of Racine's plays, *Esther* depicts only the last part of the story, stressing midrashic, apocryphal, and original elements – Ahasuerus' dream, Esther's prayer, and an intimate conversation between Haman and his wife. Haman's pathetic supplication to the queen, Esther's refusal of pardon, and her silence when the king falsely accuses Haman of attempting to rape her are given far more emphasis in Racine's play than in the biblical narrative. David *Franco-Mendes, who pointed out that Racine's last great tragedy supports Queen Athaliah in her struggle against God, intended his Hebrew melodrama *Gemul Atalyah* (Amsterdam, 1770) as a reply to the French author. Racine makes the high priest Joad (the biblical Jehoiadah) a prophet of heroic faith, who foresees on stage the criminal career of his Davidic protégé, yet unflinchingly sacrifices his own son to his messianic hopes.

A Hebrew verse translation of *Esther* by Solomon Judah *Rapoport, entitled *She'erit Yehudah*, was published in Vienna in 1827 in *Bikkurei ha-Ittim*, 7, 171–254. *Athalie* was twice translated into Hebrew, first by Meir ha-Levi *Letteris (1835), and a century later by Elijah Meitus (1950). A two-volume English translation by Samuel Solomon of Racine's complete plays appeared in New York in 1968.

BIBLIOGRAPHY: L.-C. Delfour, *La Bible dans Racine* (1891); J. Lichtenstein, *Racine, poète biblique* (1934); G. Spillebout, *Le vocabulaire biblique de Racine* (1968); Salomon, in: *Cahiers raciniens*, 15 (1964); 23 (1968); idem, in: *Etudes françaises*, 1 (June 1965), 131–5; C. Lehrmann, *L'Elément juif dans la littérature française*, 1 (1960²), 97–113; J.M. Cohen, *History of Western Literature* (1956), 190–5; L. Goldmann, *Le Dieu Caché* (1955); idem, *Jean Racine dramaturge* (1956).

[Herman Prins Salomon]

RACKER, EFRAIM (1913–1991), U.S. biochemist Racker was born in Neu Sandez, Poland, and, after a brief period in the Vienna Academy of Art studied at the University of Vienna, where he received his M.D. in 1938. However, art remained a lifelong passion and later in life he sold his own brilliant acrylics to benefit the fund he had established to help needy students. He left Austria after Nazi occupation for Great Britain, where his interest in psychiatry led him to work on the metabolism of the brain at the Cardiff City Mental Hospital. The general ignorance of normal cell metabolism motivated his change from physician to biochemist after he moved to New York University Medical School in 1944 and Yale Medical School in 1952. In 1954–66 he was head of the Nutrition and Physiology Department at the Public Health Research Institute, New York City, before moving to Cornell University, where he became the Albert Einstein Professor of Biochemistry and remained a working scientist until his death. His research interests concerned photosynthesis and energy production with the major discovery that oxidative phosphorylation is mediated by a transmembrane proton gradient. His world leadership in this field was recognized by many honors, including the National Medal of Science (1976), the Gairdner Award (1980), and the Harvey Prize of the Israel Technion (1980).

[Michael Denman (2nd ed.)]

RACKMAN, EMANUEL (1910–), U.S. Orthodox rabbi, educator, and author. Rackman was born in Albany, New York. His father, Rabbi David Rackman, was an early *rosh yeshivah* at the Rabbi Isaac Elchanan Theological Seminary (RIETS). Rackman studied at Columbia University where he received his B.A. Phi Beta Kappa, his law degree, and a Ph.D. in political science, and at the Rabbi Isaac Elchanan Theological Seminary (see *Yeshiva University) where he was ordained in 1934. He served congregations in Glen Cove (1930–36) and Lynbrook (1936–43), New York, and was a chaplain in the U.S. Air Force (1943–46), later attaining the rank of colonel in the reserves. He was in Europe at the time of the liberation of the concentration camps, an experience that shaped his desire to make use of his rabbinical ordination to rebuild the Jewish people. In 1946 he became the rabbi of Congregation Shaarey Tefila of Far Rockaway, New York, and in 1967 succeeded to the rabbinate of Manhattan's Fifth Avenue Synagogue, replacing Rabbi Immanuel Jacobwitz, who had been named chief rabbi of the United Kingdom. Rackman was prominently identified with the modern Orthodox group within American Orthodoxy, and was particularly concerned with understanding the meaning of the *halakhah* in order to find contemporary applications. He took issue with those who he claimed have frozen Jewish law and refused to solve current problems within its framework. Rackman also held that Orthodox rabbis and institutions should cooperate with the non-Orthodox and could participate in organizations which contained all the divisions of American Jewry. Rackman was also a leading figure in the Far Rockaway Jewish community and was instrumental in making it an important center for Orthodoxy. He also taught political science and served as assistant to the president of Yeshiva University (1962–70), a professor of political science and jurisprudence, and later a University Professor at Yeshiva where he served as provost, and professor of Jewish studies at the City University of New York (1971–77). Rackman was president of the New York Board of Rabbis (1955–57) and the Rabbinical Council of America (1958–60), and a member of the executive of the Jewish Agency. In 1977 Rackman was appointed president of Bar-Ilan University and became chancellor of the institution in 1986. Under his leadership Bar-Ilan expanded dramatically and became the focal point of contact between Orthodox Jews and secular education. It took shape as a critical institution in what remained of Modern Orthodoxy. Well into his 90s, he was not afraid to tackle difficult issues and, despite great controversy, he worked with Agunot International to free women trapped in dead marriages by recalcitrant husbands who refuse to grant a *get*, serving on a *bet din* that invokes the halakhic concepts of *kiddushei ta'ut* and *umdenah* to annul the marriage. He was the author of *Israel's Emerging Constitution* (1955) and *One Man's Judaism* (1970), which included some of his previously published essays. Among his many acts of service, he was a member of the Board of Higher Education of the City of New York. Rackman received the Jerusalem Prize for Community Spiritual Leadership. The prestigious honor was awarded to him by Israel President Moshe Katzav, on Rackman's 90th birthday. The Jerusalem Prize is awarded annually to leading international figures dedicated to the education and preservation of the Jewish people. The prize is awarded by the Center of Jewish Relations in the Diaspora of the World Zionist Organization.

BIBLIOGRAPHY: M.R. Konvitz, in: *Midstream* (June–July 1995), 33–36; D. Rackman, *Kiryat Ḥannah David* (1967), 29–33; C. Liebman, in: AJYB, 66 (1965), 48–49; 69 (1968), 70, 74.

[Aaron Rothkoff / Stanley Wagner (2nd ed.)]

°**RAD, GERHARD VON** (1901–1971), German Bible scholar. Born in Nuremberg, Von Rad was a disciple of A. Alt. He was professor in Jena (1934), Goettingen (1945), and Heidelberg (from 1949).

His earliest research was concerned with the theological aspects of certain books of the Bible (*Das Gottesvolk im Deuteronomium*, 1929; *Das Geschichtsbild des chronistischen Werkes*, 1930; *Die Priesterschrift im Hexateuch*, 1934). Later he applied the form-critical method to the entire Hexateuch, whose nucleus he saw in confessional summaries of the Exodus and the entrance into Canaan, like Deuteronomy 26:5–9 ("short historical credo"), which had their "*Sitz im Leben*" in the cult (*Das formgeschichtliche Problem des Hexateuchs*, 1938). His *Theologie des Alten Testaments* (2 vols., 1957–60) tries to let the biblical texts speak for themselves ("*Nacherzaehlung*"), and traces a history of the tradition, in continuity and discontinuity, through to the New Testament. Von Rad was particularly concerned with Wisdom Literature, in which he found a possible relevance to contemporary thought (*Weisheit in Israel*, 1970).

BIBLIOGRAPHY: *Probleme biblischer Theologie* (1971), jubilee volume in honor of G. Von Rad's 70th birthday.

[Rudolf Smend]

RADANIYA (**Radhanites**), Jewish merchants of the ninth century C.E., who, according to the contemporary report of the Arab geographer Ibn Khurradādhbih, spoke Arabic, Persian, Greek, Frankish, Spanish, and Slavonic, and traveled from the farthest west to the farthest east and back again. Their starting point is stated to have been in Spain or France. They crossed the Mediterranean to Egypt, and transferred their merchandise on camelback across the isthmus of Suez to the Red Sea, whence by ship they eventually reached India and China. They returned by the same route with musk, aloeswood, camphor, cinnamon, and other products of the Oriental countries. From the west they brought eunuchs, slave girls and boys, brocade, beaver and marten skins, and swords. Some of them sailed to Constantinople to sell their goods. Others visited the residence of the Frankish king for the same purpose. Sometimes, instead of using the Red Sea route to the East, they disembarked at Anṭākiya (Antioch) and crossed Syria to the Euphrates, whence they passed to Baghdad. Then they descended the Tigris to the Persian gulf, and so reached India and China. These journeys could also be made by land. Thus the Jewish merchants might proceed to the east via Tangier, Kairouan, and the other North African towns, reaching Cairo, Damascus, Kufa, Basra, Ahwaz, Persia, and India, and finally, as before, attaining by this land route their destination in China.

Another of their routes lay across Europe, "behind Rome," through the country of the Ṣaqāliba (Slavonians) to Khamlīj, the capital of the *Khazars, another name for *Atil. Thence they passed to the sea of Jurjan (i.e., down the Volga to the Caspian), then to Balkh and Transoxiana, and so to the Far East. Since Ibn Khurradādhbih relates that the Russian merchants, when passing through the Khazar capital, were tithed by the Khazar ruler, the Radaniya in similar circumstances were no doubt also liable.

The name occurs in two forms: Rādhāniya (as recorded by Ibn Khurradādhbih) and Rāhdāniya (by Ibn al-Faqīh). Since the research of J.-T. Reinaud it has been customary to explain the latter form as Persian, from *rāhdān*, "knowing the way," but it is not certainly the more original. Other suggestions have been that the name is connected with Latin Rhodanus, i.e., the river Rhone, and that in the Letter of Ḥasdai (see *Khazars) the people called *sheluḥei Ḥorasan ha-soḥarim*, apparently "merchant-envoys of Khurasan" (not very probably), are the Radaniya.

BIBLIOGRAPHY: *Bibliotheca Geographicorum Arabicorum*, 5 (1885), 270ff.; 6 (1889), 153–5 (Ar. section), 114ff. (Fr. section); L. Rabinowitz, *Jewish Merchant Adventurers* (1948), bibl. 202–4; Dunlop, Khazars, 138ff.; M.I. Artamonov, *Istoriya Khazar* (1962), 404; Baron, Social^2, 4 (1957), 328–9; C. Cahen, in: REJ, 123 (1964), 499–505.

[Douglas Morton Dunlop]

RADAUTI (Rom. **Rădăuți**, Ger. **Radautz**), city in Bukovina, N. Romania, near the Ukrainian border. The first Jews to settle there came from Bohemia in the late 18th century and were later joined by others from Galicia and Russia. Three Jewish families were listed in the tax register of 1807. The Jews of Radauti were at first affiliated to the community of the district capital *Suceava. They opened their own synagogue in 1830, when a *talmud torah* was also founded. Subsequently land for a cemetery was acquired (until then the cemetery at *Siret had been used). After Radauti became an independent community it established its own institutions. The Jewish population numbered 3,452 in 1880 (30.9% of the population), and 6,000 in 1914. In 1888 there were in Radauti eight prayer-houses (*shtiblekh*) in addition to the central synagogue. In that year 523 heads of families were registered in the community.

Ḥasidism had a strong influence on Jewish life in Radauti, especially the *Vizhnitz, *Bojan, and *Sadagora dynasties. The Ḥasidim held services in their own *kloyzen* and were frequently the cause of local disputes in their opposition to Zionism. There had been adherents of Zionism in Radauti from the beginning of the *Bilu movement, and in 1892 a local group Ahavat Zion was founded. The movement gained headway in the early 20th century. When the city was incorporated in Romania (1918) the Zionist parties began to exert an active influence on municipal and communal affairs. Members of the *Bund were also active on the municipal and community councils. A Hebrew school, which maintained a kindergarten and adult courses, was supported by the community. From 1919 to 1926 a private Jewish high school also functioned in Radauti. In 1930 the community numbered 5,647 (about 31% of the total population). Among rabbis of Radauti were Eliezer Lipmann Kunstadt (officiated 1894–1907); Jacob Hoffmann (1912–23); and the Hebrew author and scholar Jacob Nacht (1925–28).

Holocaust and Contemporary Periods

Romanian antisemites increased their agitation in 1939, and in October 1941 the Jews of Radauti, numbering 4,763 (32% of the total population), were deported to death camps. In 1942 there were only 42 Jews remaining in the city.

Some survivors made their way back in 1944, and by 1947 there were as many as 6,000 Jews living in the city. The Zionist movement regained strength after World War II (until the government decided to dissolve it in 1949). New communal and welfare institutions were established with the aid of overseas organizations, such as *OSE, the American Jewish Joint Distribution *Committee, and the World Jewish *Congress, but their activities gradually decreased. From 1948 the community dwindled through emigration to Israel and other countries. In 1971 only 700 Jews remained in the city (3.5% of the total population). Some communal activity continued, however, including the holding of Sabbath and holiday services in the central synagogue.

BIBLIOGRAPHY: H. Gold (ed.), *Geschichte der Juden in der Bukowina*, 2 vols. (1958–62), index.

[Yehouda Marton]

RADEK (Sobelsohn), KARL (1885–1939?), Russian revolutionary and publicist. Born in Lemberg, Radek was a member of the Polish Social Democratic Party, for which he wrote many articles. Before World War I he was also active as a publicist for the left wing of the German Social Democratic Party. During the war he played a prominent part in the Zimmerwald and Kintal pacifist conferences. After the Russian Revolution broke out in February 1917, Radek was one of those who accompanied Lenin on his famous journey from Switzerland through Germany to Sweden in a sealed railroad car. He remained in Sweden as a representative of the Bolshevik Party, but after the October Revolution he returned to Russia and became head of the Central European section of the Foreign Affairs Commissariat. In 1918, when revolution broke out in Germany, Radek entered the country secretly and helped to organize the first congress of the German Communist Party. In 1920 he proposed and supported the idea of a "united front" of the German Communists and Social Democrats. He was arrested in February 1919 but was released at the end of the year. He was one of the leaders of the group which opposed the Brest-Litovsk agreement with Germany. He returned to the U.S.S.R. and in 1922 became a leading official of the Communist International. In this capacity he maintained contact with communist-oriented Zionists of the "left *Po'alei Zion faction" who applied for admission into and recognition by the Communist International. In 1924, however, he joined the Trotskyite opposition and in 1927 was expelled from the party and banished to the Ural mountains. He was readmitted in 1930 on renouncing his adherence to the Trotskyists. Just before his banishment he had served for a year as rector of the Sun Yat-Sen University for Chinese students in Moscow.

In the 1930s Radek was an influential writer and speaker on international affairs and was a regular contributor to *Pravda* and *Izvestia*. He was the coauthor of the draft of the so-called "Stalin constitution" of the U.S.S.R. (1936). Radek's writings include *In den Reihen der deutschen Revolution 1909–1919* (1921) and many articles on literature and the theater. In 1937 Radek was arrested and charged with complicity in plots against the Soviet government. At a show trial which received worldwide publicity, with the prisoners compelled to make dramatic and abject confessions, he was convicted of being "an enemy of the people" and was sentenced to ten years' imprisonment. On May 19, 1939, he was killed by criminal prisoners in the prison, probably by the order of the leadership. In 1988 he was rehabilitated by the Supreme Court of the U.S.S.R. A selection of his works, *Portraits and Pamphlets*, appeared in 1935.

BIBLIOGRAPHY: L. Schapiro, *The Communist Party of the Soviet Union* (1960), index; E.H. Carr, *The Bolshevik Revolution 1917–1923*, 3 (1966), index; idem, *Socialism in One Country*, 3, Pt. 2 (1964), index; D. Collard, *Soviet Justice and the Trial of Radek and Others* (1937); R. Conquest, *Great Terror* (1968), index.

°**RADEMACHER, FRANZ** (1906–1973), German diplomat; from 1940–43 head of Section Deutschland III of the German Foreign Office, which dealt with "Jewish Affairs" and cooperated closely with *Eichmann. The son of a railroad engineer, he was a lawyer and joined the Nazi party only in 1933. He joined the Foreign Office in 1937 and served abroad. Like many ambitious civil servants, Rademacher carved out an area of expertise, choosing to view the Jewish situation within the context of Germany's war aims and its expected triumph. It is in this context that Rademacher wrote a memorandum on the

"*Madagascar Plan" – one of a number of territorial solutions to the Jewish problem that were overtaken by the Final Solution. When Germany did not defeat Great Britain, the plan became impossible to implement and therefore non-operative. He exerted personal influence on the German representatives in the satellite states to facilitate the "Final Solution" (see *Holocaust, General Survey). In the autumn of 1941 he was sent to speed up the killing of 8,000 Serbian Jews (see *Yugoslavia). His task was in part to minimize the foreign policy complications of the Final Solution. After the war he was sentenced to only five months' imprisonment by a German court in 1952, but skipped bail and escaped to Syria. In 1966 he returned to Germany and was sentenced in May of that year to five years' imprisonment for aiding in the murder of Romanian, Bulgarian, and Yugoslav Jews, but was released from prison for medical reasons.

BIBLIOGRAPHY: G. Reitlinger, *Final Solution* (1968²), index; L. Poliakov and J. Wulf, *Das dritte Reich und seine Diener* (1956), passim; Billig, in: *Le Monde Juif*, 24 no. 50 (1968), 27–36; R. Hilberg, *Destruction of the European Jews* (1967²), index s.v. *Rademacher, Karl.* **ADD. BIBLIOGRAPHY:** C.R. Browning, *The Final Solution and the German Foreign Office: A Study of the Referat D3 of the Abetilung Deutschland 1940–43* (1978).

[Yehuda Reshef /Michael Berenbaum (2nd ed.)]

RADIN, ADOLPH MOSES (1848–1909), U.S. rabbi and communal worker. Radin, born in Neustadt-Schirwindt, Lithuania, served as rabbi in Prussia and Poland, and then immigrated to the United States in 1886, becoming rabbi in Elmira, New York. There he was appointed visiting Jewish chaplain of the State Reformatory, but soon accepted a position as rabbi of Congregation Gates of Hope in New York City. A pioneer among American rabbis in working with Jewish inmates, Radin was named chaplain of all penal institutions in New York and Brooklyn (1890), serving until his death. In 1905 he assumed the pulpit of the People's Synagogue of the Educational Alliance, from which he assisted immigrants on the Lower East Side, and founded the Russian American Hebrew Association, which he considered his greatest achievement. Radin was an active philanthropic fund raiser and a champion of Zionism.

He wrote *Offener Brief eines polnischen Juden an Heinrich von Treitschke* (1885³); *Asirei Oni u-Varzel* (1893), a report on the Jews in New York prisons; and other works, and contributed to Hebrew, German, Polish, and American Jewish periodicals.

BIBLIOGRAPHY: S.A. Neuhausen, *Telishat Asavim al Kever A.M. Radin* (1910); AJYB, 5 (1903/04), 87; CCARY, 19 (1909), 424–31.

RADIN, MAX (1880–1950), U.S. jurist, teacher, and legal historian. Son of Adolph *Radin, he was born in Kempen, Russian Poland. He taught in public schools and then at Columbia University (1918–19). He was professor of law at the University of California at Berkeley from 1919 to 1948. Among his many offices and positions, he was Commissioner on Uniform State Laws for California 1941–48. Upon his death his library went to the Hebrew University of Jerusalem. Radin's work as a scholar and teacher ranged through law, philosophy, history, linguistics, anthropology, and literature. He was known as one of the chief proponents of "legal realism."

The principal works in which he propagated his views are *The Law and You* (1947); *Stability in Law* (1944); *Law as Logic and Experience* (1940); and *The Law and Mr. Smith* (1938). His first interest was in the relationship of morals and ethics to commercial occupations. One of his first publications was *The Legislation of the Greeks and Romans on Corporations* (1909). Related works are *Lawful Pursuit of Gain* (1931) and *Manners and Morals of Business* (1939). Radin was deeply concerned with the political events of his time. In *The Day of Reckoning* (1943), he expounded his thoughts on the war crimes trials, then in the planning stage, and he also wrote on the treatment of the Nisei (American-born citizens of Japanese descent) of California during World War II. His pervasive interest in legal history found expression in his *Handbook of Anglo-American Legal History* (1936) and *Handbook of Roman Law* (1927), and numerous works on Jewish law and history, including: *The Life of the People in Biblical Times* (1929), *The Trial of Jesus of Nazareth* (1931), and his unpublished *Bibliography of Jewish Law.*

BIBLIOGRAPHY: *American Historical Review*, 56 (1950), 58.

[Albert A. Ehrenzweig]

RADIN, PAUL (1883–1959), U.S. anthropologist. Born in Lodz, Russian Poland, Paul Radin was the youngest son of Adolph *Radin, a rabbi, and brother of Herman, a physician, and of Max *Radin, an eminent legal scholar. He studied first in Europe, then in New York, coming to anthropology via zoology and history. A student of Franz Boas and James Harvey Robinson, he did his first field work with the Winnebago Indians, and during the next five decades explored this group intensively. He advocated the outlook of a natural scientist for the study of human cultures. Like his mentor Boas, he represented the humanistic approach to the understanding of preliterate societies.

A member of the Boas School, he differed from it principally in holding that Boas' quantitative and distributional treatment of culture data leads to inadequate and faulty histories of the societies concerned. With his historicist perspective, Radin interpreted Boas' work in terms of the latter's intellectual antecedents, showed how changes in Boas' intellectual perspective influenced his interpretation of the primitive, and how his positions became the framework and presupposition for subsequent American anthropology. Radin taught at various universities including Cambridge, Chicago, Brandeis, and California.

His contributions to linguistics are impressive, comprising texts of Winnebago and various other American Indian languages, and work in historical linguistics (*The Genetic Relationship of the North American Indian Languages*, 1919). He also endeavored to produce a systematic ethnological theory in such works as *The Method and the Theory of Ethnology* (1933, 1966[2]).

Radin's life style was that of a liberated cosmopolitan intellectual, and evinced humanistic skepticism toward our culture-bound arrogance vis-à-vis the primitives. His Enlightenment perspective stimulated his immersion in the intellectual world of the primitive and his defense of the primitive mentality as against denigration of it by *Levy-Bruhl as "prelogical." While admitting, in *Primitive Man as Philosopher* (1927), that primitive mentality differs in degree, he noted that its reaction patterns evince regularity, uniqueness, individuality, and depth, and betray neither linguistic nor conceptual inadequacy. He devoted much study to the phenomena of religion, especially the God concept among primitives, as in *Primitive Religion* (1937) and *The Trickster: A Study in American Indian Mythology* (1956).

His synthesis of the objective and subjective worlds of the primitive culminated in an apologia for pristine civilizations, and he stressed the virtues found therein – viz., their respect and concern for the individual and their impressive social and political organization.

His deeply felt insight that the universal human drama is enacted in primitive societies was set forth in *The Road of Life and Death: A Ritual Drama of the American Indians* (1945) and in his other studies of the Winnebago Indians.

BIBLIOGRAPHY: S. Diamond (ed.), *Culture in History, Essays in Honor of Paul Radin* (1960).

[Ephraim Fischoff]

RADISH, a vegetable, the *Raphanus raphanistrum*; not mentioned in the Bible, despite the fact that it is one of the ancient plants of the Mediterranean region. Herodotus reports that the large sum spent on radishes for the pyramid workers was inscribed on the pyramid of Cheops. In Israel it is found as a weed. In the Mishnah it is called *ẓenon* and in the *Gemara* it is called *pugla* (Akk., *puglu*). The radish tuber was regarded as a healthy vegetable but its leaves as harmful (Er. 56a). It is a winter plant difficult to grow in Israel in the summer, and it is therefore related of the emperor Antoninus and Judah ha-Nasi that radish was not absent from their tables even in summer (Ber. 57b). From the radish seeds an oil was extracted which the Mishnah (Shab. 2:2) declares invalid as fuel for the Sabbath lamp. In the Tosefta (*ibid.*) however, a *tanna* contends against those forbidding its use: "What shall the people of Alexandria do who possess only radish oil?" The radish is very like the rape, called *nafos* or *nafoẓ* in the Mishnah. According to the Jerusalem Talmud (Kil. 1:5, 27a) they are regarded as belonging to different species in spite of their similarity.

BIBLIOGRAPHY: Loew, Flora, 1 (1926), 511–5; J. Feliks, *Kilei Zera'im ve-Harkavah* (1967), 76–79. **ADD. BIBLIOGRAPHY:** Feliks, Ha-Tzome'aḥ, 103, 134.

[Jehuda Feliks]

RADNER, GILDA (1946–1989), U.S. comedian and actress. Radner was born to Herman Radner and Henrietta Dworkin in Detroit, Michigan. Her father was a Canadian brewery owner and during the Prohibition earned enough from smuggling to the United States to invest in the Detroit hotel The Seville, where performers stayed while entertaining in local theaters. Known for his humor and magic tricks, he died of a brain tumor when she was 14. Radner joined the drama club at the Liggett School, an all-girls high school in Detroit, and later studied in the theater department at the University of Michigan, which she attended over a six-year period without graduating. In 1972, she joined a Toronto production of *Godspell*, which included Paul Shaffer and Eugene Levy. After the show ended, she joined the comedy troupe Second City in Toronto, where she was discovered by producer Lorne Michaels, who asked her to join the cast of the *National Lampoon Radio Hour*. In 1975 she was the first cast member Michaels hired for *Saturday Night Live*. Radner would go on to create such memorable characters as Lisa Loopner, Emily Litella, and Babwa Wawa, a parody of Barbara *Walters. In 1979, she appeared on Broadway in a solo show, *Gilda Radner Live from New York*, which featured many of her well-established characters. She left *Saturday Night Live* in 1980, the same year she married its bandleader, G.E. Smith. Radner had small parts in a variety of feature films, including *The Rutles* (1978) and *First Family* (1980), but her first major role was in *Hanky Panky* (1982), a film directed by and co-starring Gene *Wilder. After she divorced Smith in 1982, Wilder and Radner married in 1984. The couple went on to star in two other films together, *Woman in Red* (1984) and *Haunted Honeymoon* (1986). Radner was diagnosed with ovarian cancer in 1986. She used her celebrity status to call attention to the Wellness Community, a cancer support group, and to start her own, Gilda's Club. In 1988, she earned an Emmy nomination for her appearance on *It's Garry Shandling's Show*. In 1989, she detailed her fight with cancer in her autobiography *It's Always Something*. She died in Los Angeles shortly after the book's publication.

[Adam Wills (2nd ed.)]

RADNÓTI, MIKLOS (1909–1944), Hungarian poet. Radnóti, born in Budapest and an orphan from childhood, was converted to Christianity. He trained to become a teacher, but because of his Jewish origin was prevented from taking up a post. He spent his last years in Hungarian army labor camps. Radnóti's writings are overshadowed by World War II and the social crises of the Horthy regime. His early poetry is filled with surrealistic influences, but over the years, as the atrocities of the Holocaust increased, it became pure enough to be defined as neoclassicist.

His verse collections include *Pogány köszöntő* ("Pagan Salute," 1930), *Újhold* ("New Moon," 1935), *Meredek út* ("Steep Way," 1938), and the autobiographical *Ikrek hava* ("Under the Sign of Gemini," 1940). Two verse collections that appeared after World War II were *Radnóti. Miklós versei* ("The Poems of Miklós Radnóti," 1948), and *Radnóti, Miklós összes versei és műfordításai* ("Translations and Poems of Miklós Radnóti," 1963).

His last book, *Tajtékos ég* ("Stormy Skies"), published in 1946, contains poems found in his pocket as he lay in a mass grave at Abda. They accurately prophesy the circumstances of his death. Radnóti, who has come to be considered one of the most important Hungarian lyric poets, was also a skilled translator.

BIBLIOGRAPHY: *Magyar Irodalmi Lexikon*, 2 (1965), 543–9; L. Madácsi, *Radnóti Miklós* (Hung., 1954).

[Itamar Yaos-Kest]

RADÓ, ANTAL (1862–1944), Hungarian journalist and translator. Born in Mór, Radó wrote for newspapers during his student days and in 1885 became a parliamentary stenographer. He eventually became director of the stenographic bureau. Known mainly as a translator of classics of Western literature, he wrote many books: *A magyar müforditás története, 1772–1831* ("History of Hungarian Literary Translation," 1883), *Az olasz irodalom történte* ("History of Italian Literature," 1896), and a biography of Dante (1907). When Germany occupied Hungary, Radó committed suicide.

RADO, SANDOR (1890–1972), psychoanalyst. Born in Hungary, Rado became secretary of the Hungarian Psychoanalytic Society in 1913 during the presidency of Sandor *Ferenczi. In 1922 he was analyzed by Karl *Abraham in Berlin and from 1926 to 1930 was secretary of the German Psychoanalytic Society, playing an active part in organizing the training curriculum there. Sigmund *Freud appointed him managing editor of the *Internationale Zeitschrift fuer Psychoanalyse* in 1924 and three years later managing editor of *Imago.* In 1931, at the invitation of A.A. *Brill, Rado moved to the U.S., where he organized the New York Psychoanalytical Institute on the Berlin model. In 1944 Rado was appointed professor of psychiatry and head of Columbia University's pioneering psychoanalytic institute. He was subsequently professor of psychiatry at New York State University (1956–58) and from 1958 he organized a progressive teaching program in the New York School of Psychiatry.

Rado's contributions to psychiatry were threefold: in the sphere of classical psychodynamics; the quest for a basic conceptual system of mind; and the development of adaptational psychodynamics. In his early writings, which included two works on the problem of melancholia, Rado revealed his search for psychological realities rather than abstractions. His research into drug addiction developed the concept of "alimentary orgasm" (later, "narcotic elation") replacing genital satisfaction. During the years 1933–45, in his search for generally valid conceptual schemata, Rado wrote papers on the fear of castration in women (*Die Kastrationsangst des Weibes*, 1934) and the concept of bisexuality. His work culminated in his writings on adaptational psychodynamics. Rado questioned the therapist's exclusive preoccupation with the patient's past. He felt that the exploration of the past should be the beginning of an "emotional reeducation" of the patient in relation to his past and his adaptation to present reality.

His *Collected Papers* (*Psychoanalysis of Behavior*) appeared in 1956 and 1962 and *Adaptational Psychodynamics: Motivation and Control* in 1969. Rado also co-edited *Changing Concepts of Psychoanalytic Medicine* (1956).

BIBLIOGRAPHY: F. Alexander, in: F. Alexander et al. (eds.), *Psychoanalytic Pioneers* (1966), 240–8 (incl. bibl.); *New Perspectives in Psychoanalysis: Sandor Rado Lectures 1957–1963* (1965), vi–viii. **ADD. BIBLIOGRAPHY:** P. Roazen and B. Swerdloff, *Heresy: Sandor Rado and the Psychoanalytic Movement* (1995).

[Louis Miller / Ruth Beloff (2nd ed.)]

RADOM, city in Kielce province, Poland. The first Jews to visit Radom mainly traveled there as representatives of the Jewish communities at the sessions of the Polish Sejm (Diet) or to negotiate with the tribunal of the treasury, which met at Radom between 1613 and 1764. Jewish residence in the city was banned in 1633, 1724, and 1746; a few Jews settled in the suburbs and numbered 67 by 1765. They were later permitted to reside in a special quarter. The settlement began to develop after 1814, and an organized community was formed; a cemetery was established in 1831 and the first synagogue built in 1884. The community increased from 413 in 1815 (about 16% of the total population) to 1,495 in 1856 (23%); 11,277 in 1897 (37.6%); 24,465 in 1921 (39.7%); and 25,159 in 1931 (23.3%). Before World War I and during the period between the two world wars Jews played a considerable role in the development of commerce and industry in Radom, both as entrepreneurs and employed workers. Jewish organizations in 1925 included a merchants' and artisans' bank and trade unions; there were numerous welfare institutions, including the hospital, founded in 1847, and an old age home, founded in 1913. Religious and secular educational and cultural needs were met by yeshivot, the first founded in 1908, the *talmud torah*, and prayer houses (*shtiblekh*) for the ḥasidic community, as well as schools of various types, including a high school, and five libraries. Periodicals published in Radom during the inter-war period were the Yiddish daily *Radomer Tsaytung* until 1925; the weekly *Radomer Lebn*, later *Radomer-Keltser Lebn; Radomer Shtime*; and *Trybuna* (in Polish). The first rabbi of the community officiated at the beginning of the 19th century. Rabbis of note were Samuel *Mohilewer and Simḥah Treistman (1904–13), later rabbi of Lodz.

[William Glicksman]

Holocaust Period

In 1939 over 30,000 Jews, comprising 30% of the total population, lived in Radom. During the German occupation it was the capital of the Radom District in the General Government. The German army entered the city on Sept. 8, 1939, and immediately subjected the Jewish population to persecution. During the first months of German occupation, about 2,000 Jews from the Poznan and Lodz provinces were expelled to Radom. In turn, 1,840 Jews from Radom were expelled to the smaller towns in the Kielce Province (December 1939). In August about 2,000 young men and women were deported to slave labor camps, where almost all of them perished. In March

1941 a decree for the establishment of the ghetto was issued and by April 7, 1941, the entire Jewish population was concentrated in two separate ghettos. At the beginning of 1942 the Nazis conducted a number of terror actions within the ghettos, among them an action of February 19 ("bloody Thursday") when 40 men were shot, and on April 28, when 70 men were killed and hundreds deported to the concentration camp in *Auschwitz. On Aug. 5, 1942, the smaller ghetto was liquidated and its inhabitants (almost 10,000 people) were deported to *Treblinka death camp. On Aug. 6–17, 1942, the larger ghetto was liquidated and its 20,000 Jews dispatched for extermination. Within the part of the ghetto that was transformed into a slave labor camp (the "small ghetto"), only about 4,000 Jews remained. On Dec. 4, 1942, about 800 inmates of this camp were deported to Szydlowiec and afterward exterminated. On Jan. 13, 1943, another 1,500 prisoners were deported to Treblinka. On Nov. 8, 1943, the prisoners of the "small ghetto" were transferred to the newly established forced labor camp in the town. On July 26, 1944, all but 300 prisoners were deported to Auschwitz, where only a handful survived. The last 300 prisoners were liberated on Jan. 16, 1945.

At the time of the mass deportations in August 1942, hundreds of Jews fled to the forests to organize guerrilla units. Such units were composed mostly of persons who escaped from Radom. All the partisans fell in battles with the Germans. Many who escaped from Radom reached Warsaw and took part in the Polish Warsaw uprising (August 1944). In the whole Radom District 380,000 Jews lost their lives during the German occupation, according to figures of the Radom Regional Commission to investigate Nazi Crimes. A few hundred Jews settled in Radom for a short time after World War II, but soon left due to the hostility of the Polish population. Organizations of former Radom residents exist in Israel, the United States, Canada, France, and Australia. There were seven Jews living in Radom in 1965.

[Stefan Krakowski]

BIBLIOGRAPHY: Halpern, Pinkas, index; A. Rutkowksi, in: BŻIH, 15–16 (1955), 75–182; 17–18 (1956), 106–8; *Sefer Milḥamot ha-Getta'ot* (1954^2), index; *Sefer Radom* (1961), a memorial book published in Heb. and Yid.

RADOMSKO (Radomsk), town in Lodz province, S. central Poland. In 1643 King Ladislaus IV granted the city the privilege *de non tolerandis Judaeis* excluding Jews from its bounds, which remained in force until 1862. Although the city council complained about the presence of Jews on the nobles' estates and in neighboring villages during the 17th and 18th centuries Jewish settlement there continued. The establishment of a Jewish cemetery in the city was permitted in 1816, and by 1822 a synagogue committee existed which levied taxes for the engagement of religious functionaries. The census of 1827 recorded 369 Jews of the total 1,792 inhabitants. In 1834 the community engaged Solomon ha-Kohen Rabinowich of Włoszczowa as rabbi and *av bet din*, who in 1843 established a ḥasidic court and founded the *Radomsko ḥasidic dynasty.

After the opening of the Vienna-Warsaw railroad in 1846, the community developed rapidly. By 1857 there were 1,162 Jews living in Radomsko (about 39% of the total population). The 1897 census showed 5,054 Jews (43%). They were mainly occupied in carpentry, weaving, and dealing in timber and grain. Well-to-do Jews established factories, hotels, and restaurants which employed some 500 Jews. In this period the community expanded its activities in all spheres. Ḥovevei Zion (see *Ḥibbat Zion) groups formed Zionist parties. In 1899 the Great Synagogue was completed. Jewish workers organized in the *Po'alei Zion, *Bund, etc., from 1905 to 1907. In 1906 the Jews in Radomsko organized *self-defense against pogroms.

During World War I the Jews in Radomsko suffered from the depredations of Russian soldiers and economic depression. The historian M. *Balaban visited the city in 1916 and established a Jewish youth group, Kultura.

In 1919, after Poland became independent, there were attempts at pogroms, but they were prevented by the Jewish self-defense organization. The Jewish population rose from 7,774 in 1921 (41.5%) to 12,371 in 1935 (55%). During this period the number of Jewish workers doubled in the large industrial plants for furniture, metal goods, and printing. Of the 24 members of the city council elected in 1926, eight were Jews. Jewish educational institutions included a high school (from 1916), two *talmud torah* schools, the Keter Torah yeshivah, a *bet midrash*, and two government elementary schools. There were also guilds of craftsmen and small businessmen, and a cooperative commercial bank. In 1926 a library named for *Shalom Aleichem was opened, and there were Ha-Po'el and Ha-Ko'aḥ sports clubs. In 1930 a commune preparing for immigration to Ereẓ Israel was established named Vitkinyah.

[Arthur Cygielman]

Holocaust Period

Under the German occupation, Radomsko was incorporated into the *Radom district of the General Government. When the German army entered the city on Sept. 3, 1939, they immediately began a campaign of terror against the Jewish population. On Dec. 20, 1939, a decree was issued establishing a closed ghetto in Radomsko into which all the Jews from the surrounding districts were also concentrated. In consequence, the Jewish population of the Radomsko ghetto increased despite the high mortality due to starvation and epidemics. Two especially severe epidemics of typhus broke out during the early winter of 1940 and in January 1941. In June 1941 the authorities reduced the area of the ghetto, thus aggravating the living conditions there. On Oct. 9, 1942, an *Aktion* was carried out, and in the course of the following three days almost the entire Jewish population was deported to *Treblinka death camp where they perished. About 500 Jews and seven houses remained in the Radomsko ghetto (including some 200 Jews living there "illegally"). During the deportations hundreds of Jews from Radomsko and thousands from the surrounding districts escaped to the forests, many joining Jewish guerrilla groups which rapidly organized. They encountered severe obstacles: lack of arms, an inimical local peasant population, and no possibility of a food supply for the great number of Jews who had escaped. In November 1942 the Germans established a "second ghetto" in Radomsko, and promised security for all who voluntarily left the forests. About 4,500 Jews unable to survive the winter there returned to resettle in the ghetto. On Jan. 5, 1943, the Germans liquidated the ghetto in a surprise *Aktion*; hundreds of Jews who resisted were murdered on the spot while the rest were deported to Treblinka. A number of Jews who escaped from Radomsko were active in partisan units and resistance organizations. Some of them won recognition for bravery, including Tuvia Borzykowski, who became a member of the staff of the Jewish Fighting Organization in the *Warsaw ghetto; the three brothers Sabatowski (Ḥayyim, Mordekhai, and Herzke) who fought together in a guerrilla unit in the Konskie forest (all three were murdered in a treacherous attack by antisemitic Polish nationalists); and Rosa Szapiro, who managed to make her way out of Radomsko to the Yugoslav partisans under Tito.

After the war the community was not renewed in Radomsko. Organizations of former Radomsko residents were formed in Israel, Argentina, the United States, Canada, and France. A memorial book, *Sefer Yizkor li-Kehillat Radomsk ve-ha-Sevivah*, was published in 1967 (Heb. and Yid.).

[Stefan Krakowski]

BIBLIOGRAPHY: B. Wasiutyński, *Ludność żydowska w Polsce w wiekach XIX i XX* (1930), 29, 51, 52, 71, 75, 78; *Almanach gmin żydowskich w Polsce* (1939), 209–11; *Novoradomsker Almanakh* (1939); Gelber, in: *Beit Yisrael be-Polin*, 1 (1948), 110–27.

RADOMSKO (Radomsk), SOLOMON HA-KOHEN RABINOWICH OF (1803–1866), ḥasidic *ẓaddik*. Solomon studied in the yeshivah of Piotrkow under Abraham Ẓevi, author of the responsa *Berit Avraham* (1819). His father educated him in Ḥasidism. In his youth he joined Meir of *Apta, leader of the popular trend in Polish Ḥasidism after the death of *Jacob Isaac ha-Ḥozeh ("the Seer") of Lublin. In 1834 Solomon was appointed rabbi of Radomsk, and from 1843 he was accepted as an ḥasidic rabbi. Solomon's teachings were in the spirit of the popular trend of Polish Ḥasidism. He engaged in public affairs and worked on behalf of the poor of his town. His striking personality, his enthusiastic way of praying, and his witty sayings attracted to him many disciples, among them the Ḥasid and philosopher Aaron *Marcus (Verus) and the physician Ḥayyim David Bernard of Piotrkow. Solomon's book, *Tiferet Shelomo* (1867–69), is considered one of the classic works of Polish Ḥasidism. His successor was ABRAHAM ISSACHAR HA-KOHEN (d. 1892), author of *Ḥesed le-Avraham* (1893–95), who in turn was succeeded by his son EZEKIEL HA-KOHEN (d. 1911), author of *Keneset Yeḥezkel* (1913). The last of the ḥasidic rabbis of Radomsk in Poland before the Holocaust was SOLOMON ENOCH HA-KOHEN (d. 1942), famous for his establishment of a network of yeshivot called Keter Torah. He was murdered in the Warsaw ghetto. His novellae and those of his son-in-law David Moses, who was killed at the same time, were collected in the book *Shivḥei Kohen* (1953).

BIBLIOGRAPHY: I.M. Rabinowitz, *Ohel Shelomo* (1924); idem, *Ateret Sholomo* (1926); A. Marcus (Verus), *Der Chassidismus* (1901), 363–5; *Sefer Yizkor le-Kehillat Radomsk ve-ha-Sevivah* (1967), 22–26, 75–106, 110–4.

[Zvi Meir Rabinowitz]

RADOMYSHL, city in Zhitomir district, Ukraine. The Jewish community of Radomyshl was established in the 18th century. In 1792 it numbered 1,424 (80 percent of the total population), in 1847 2,734, and it increased to 7,502 (67 percent) in 1897. There were 161 Jewish artisans out of a total of 198. The community maintained a *talmud torah* and three secular schools. The district of Radomyshl included the communities of *Chernobyl near *Korosten (4,160), Brusilov (3,575), Malin (2,547), and others. The entire region was influenced by the teaching of the ḥasidic rabbis of Chernobyl. In May 1919 bands of peasants of the *hetman* Sokolovski organized pogroms in the Jewish communities of Radomyshl and neighboring towns. Hundreds (more than 400) of Jews were massacred and many others fled to the big cities. Under the Soviet regime, Jewish community life stopped and the town declined. In 1926 there were 4,637 Jews (36 percent of the total population) in Radomyshl, their number declining by 1939 to 2,348 (20 percent of the total population). The Germans entered the town on July 9, 1941, and established an open ghetto, where 15 persons were crowded per room. In August they killed 389, and on September 6 a unit of Sonderkommando 4A murdered 1,107 adults, and the Ukrainian auxiliary police murdered 561 children. Six mass graves mark the murder of Jews in the vicinity. Later, Jews were prohibited from gathering at the graves, since the militia claimed that for them to do so was to cause a "demonstration." Jews were also forbidden to erect a monument to the dead. In 1970 the Jewish population was estimated at about 250.

BIBLIOGRAPHY: *Yidishe avtonomye un der Natsyonaler Sekretaryat in Ukraine* (1920), 176, 180; E. Tcherikower, *Di Ukrainer Pogromen in Yor 1919* (1965), 220–3.

[Yehuda Slutsky / Shmuel Spector (2nd ed.)]

RADOSHITSER (of Radoszyce), ISSACHAR BAER (1765–1843), ḥasidic *ẓaddik* whose popularity is attested by his nickname, "the holy old man"; famous as a miracle healer. At first he lived in great poverty as a village schoolmaster (*melammed*) in Checiny (Chantchin) and Chmielnik. He frequented the courts of numerous *ẓaddikim* and was among the disciples of *Jacob Isaac ha-Ḥozeh (The Seer) of Lublin, Jacob Isaac "the holy Jew of *Przysucha", Joshua Heshel of *Apta, and Israel the *Maggid* of *Kozienice. From 1815 he became a *ẓaddik* in his own right in Radoszyce. He was a *tärnik*, i.e., one of those who believed that 1840 (ת״ר) would be the year of the redemption.

BIBLIOGRAPHY: R.H. Tshernoḥa, *Nifla'ot ha-Sava Kaddisha* (1937); I. Alfasi, *Ha-Sava ha-Kadosh mi-Radoshitz* (1957); M. Buber,

Tales of the Hasidim, 2 (1966), 200–5; R. Mahler, *Ha-Ḥasidut ve-ha-Haskalah* (1961), 303–5,307–11.

[Esther (Zweig) Liebes]

RADOSHKOVICHI (Pol. **Radoszkowice**), town in Molodechno district, Belarus; within Poland until the partitions and between the two world wars. The Jewish community was established in the 16th century. The Jews numbered 455 in 1765; 1,701 in 1847; 1,519 (58.9 percent of the total population) in 1897; and 1,215 (49.4 percent) in 1925. The Jews earned their livelihood from trading at the annual fair, dealing in wood and cereals (exported to Germany and even Hungary), local retail trade, and crafts. In the town there was also a brewery, a brick factory, flour mills, and small tanneries. Many families earned their living from cultivating orchards on behalf of non-Jewish farmers and landowners. In the 1920s and 1930s the Jewish economy suffered and there was considerable poverty as a result of the poor returns, the heavy taxes, and the competition of non-Jews who were supported by the Polish government. The local Jewish people's bank made considerable efforts to assist the community in its economic struggle. The members of the community were largely **Mitnaggedim*, but local Ḥasidim had two prayer rooms. Pioneers from Radoshkovichi were among the first members of the Third *Aliyah. After World War I, Zionist youth movements were very active and a *He-Ḥalutz training farm was established. In 1921–22 Radoshkovichi (then on the Polish-Russian border) was a transit station for the Jewish refugees returning from Soviet Russia to their homes in Poland. Communal institutions included a *Tarbut school, and a Hebrew library named after the poet Mordecai Ẓevi *Manne, a native of Radoshkovichi. Among the community's rabbis were Abraham b. Judah Leib *Maskileison, Meir b. Joshua Ẓevi Rabinsohn, who settled in Palestine in his old age, and his son, Joseph Zundel, the last rabbi of Radoshkovichi. Notable natives of the town included Israel Rivka'i-Rubin, educator and author; Mordecai Rabinsohn, Hebrew critic; and Naphtali Maskileison, poet and Talmud scholar.

[Dov Rabin]

Holocaust Period

At the outbreak of World War II there were about 1,200 Jews in Radoshkovichi. On Sept. 18, 1939, the Red Army entered the town and a Soviet administration was established there. The Germans occupied the town on June 25, 1941. A Judenrat was appointed and the Jews were compelled to pay heavy contributions. An *Aktion* took place on March 11, 1942, when 800 Jews were killed, 200 escaped, and 50 were shot while trying to flee; 110 were left as skilled artisans. After this *Aktion*, a ghetto was established for the remaining Jews. The Jewish community was liquidated on March 7, 1943, when the remaining 260 Jews were burned alive in a barn. During the liquidation, about 50 Jews succeeded in escaping to the nearby forests, where they joined the "Revenge" partisan unit. After the war the Jewish community of Radoshkovichi was not reconstituted.

BIBLIOGRAPHY: I. Rubin and M. Rabinsohn (eds.), *Radoshkovich, Sefer Zikkaron* (1965); *Unzer Hilf* (1932). **ADD. BIBLIOGRAPHY:** Sh. Spector (ed.), *Pinkas Kehilot Poland*, vol. 8, *Northeast* (2005).

RADUN (Pol. **Raduń**; Yid. **Radin**), a town in Grodno district, Belarus. Originally a Polish royal estate, Radun became important in the 16th century because it was situated on the main road between Cracow and Vilna. Jews were still forbidden to live there in 1538 and Jewish farmers who cultivated lands in the vicinity exerted their influence to have Radun granted municipal status so that they would not be expelled. In 1623 the Council of the Province of Lithuania (see Councils of the *Lands) made the Radun community subordinate to that of Grodno. In 1765 there were 581 poll tax-paying Jews in Radun and district; in the town itself there were 283 Jews in 1847; 896 (53.3 percent of the total population) in 1897; and 671 (53.5 percent) in 1925. The center of Radun spiritual life was the yeshivah founded in 1869 by *Israel Meir ha-Kohen (the Ḥafez Ḥayyim). Its fame was widespread and the 300 students came from far and near. In 1940 most of the yeshivah students were transferred to United States via Japan. The Jews of Radun earned their livelihood from commerce, crafts, and agriculture; in the 1920s, 12 percent of the 200 members of the Jewish cooperative bank were farmers. In 1922 the *Yekopo relief society in Vilna gave loans to 19 farms, covering an area of 420 dessiatines (1,134 acres).

[Dov Rabin]

Holocaust Period

Before the outbreak of World War II, there were about 800 Jews in Radun. In September 1939 the Red Army entered the town and a Soviet administration was established there until the outbreak of the German-Soviet war. The Germans occupied the town on June, 30, 1941. In October a ghetto was established containing 1,700 persons, from neighboring towns: Dowgielishki, Zablocie, Zirmun and Nacha. A large-scale *Aktion* took place on May 10, 1942, when 1,000 Jews were killed, 300 escaped to the forests, some joining partisan units; the remaining skilled artisans were sent to Szczuczyn and from there, after a while, to their deaths in an unknown place. After the war the Jewish community of Radun was not reconstituted.

BIBLIOGRAPHY: S. Dubnow (ed.), *Pinkas ha-Medinah* (1925), 17–18; A. Rivkes, in: *Life*, 1 (1951), 653; *Unzer Hilf*, 1–3 (1921–23); *Yahadut Lita*, 3 (1967), 57–58.

[Shmuel Spector (2nd ed.)]

RADYMNO (Yid. **Redem**), town in Rzeszow province, S.E. Poland; between the two world wars in the province of Lvov. The town was founded in the 14th century by the Polish king Casimir the Great. In 1640 King Ladislaus IV granted it the privilege *de non tolerandis Judaeis*, excluding Jews from the town. Subsequently Jewish settlement was discontinued until the first partition of Poland and the incorporation of Radymno into Austria in 1772, although during this period a few Jews were granted the right of residence. In 1644 the Jew Benko was granted the right by the owners of the town to settle in Radymno with his family and trade there. When a survey of the population carried out in 1711 showed some Jews living there, they were expelled on the demand of the townsmen. Jews who settled in the town from the close of the 18th century engaged in commerce. The Jewish population gradually increased, and around 1880 numbered 898 (46.8% of the total population). During World War I the number declined, and in 1921 there were 808 (42.3%). After World War I and the incorporation of Radymno into independent Poland, it lost its importance. The Jewish population became impoverished, Jewish communal activities, particularly in the sphere of social relief, began to wane. Elections to the community council were held in 1927, and Jews also took part in the municipal elections of 1934. The community came to an end during the Holocaust.

[Shimshon Leib Kirshenboim]

RADZINOWICZ, SIR LEON (1906–1999), British criminologist. Born in Poland to affluent parents, Radzinowicz lectured at the University of Geneva from 1928 to 1931. In 1932 he began teaching at the Free University of Warsaw and in 1936 was appointed an assistant professor. Two years later he made a study of the English penal system on behalf of the Polish Ministry of Justice. He and his wife remained in England at the outbreak of World War II, living in Cambridge. In 1946 he was named assistant director of research at the University of Cambridge and in 1949 director of the department of criminal science, a post he held for ten years. From 1959 to 1973, he was Wolfson professor of criminology at Cambridge, and from 1960 was director of the Institute of Criminology which he had founded.

Radzinowicz held many important offices in the field of law and criminology, among them, head of the Social Defense Section of the United Nations and a member of the Royal Commission on Capital Punishment in the Advisory Council on the Penal System of the Home Office and president of the British Academy of Forensic Sciences (1960–61). He served on many British inquiries and committees into crime and prison policy and was knighted in 1970. Radzinowicz made a major contribution by his research in the trends of legal thought which led to modern concepts in the administration of justice which were adopted in many of the democratic countries. Among his most significant works are *History of English Criminal Law* (4 vols. 1948–68), *In Search of Criminology* (1961), *The Need for Criminology* (1965), and *Ideology and Crime* (1966). From 1940 he was the editor of 33 volumes of *English Studies in Criminal Science*, called later *Cambridge Studies in Criminology*. Radzinowicz converted to Christianity prior to World War II. He was generally regarded as the most influential British academic criminologist and historian of crime of his time. Radzinowicz wrote an autobiography, *Adventures in Criminology* (1999).

ADD. BIBLIOGRAPHY: ODNB online.

RADZIWILLOW (since 1940, **Chervonoarmeisk**), town in Volhynia, today in Rovno district, Ukraine. A Jewish community existed in Radziwillow from the end of the 16th century. In 1787 the owner of the town, K. Miączyński, obtained permission from King Stanislaus II Augustus (Poniatowski) to establish a printing press for Hebrew books. At that time Jewish merchants and contractors founded an explosives factory in the town. From 298 Jews who paid poll tax in 1765, the community increased to 3,064 in 1857 and 4,322 (59 percent of the total population) in 1897. The majority were shopkeepers, tailors, and furriers, but some Jews also engaged in tanning, joinery, manufacture of building materials, and transportation; the wealthy traded in timber and grain. Branches of the Jewish labor movement and of the Zionist movement were first organized in 1905–06. The Jewish population of Radziwillow suffered heavily during World War I and the civil war between Ukrainian nationalists and Bolsheviks. In 1920 the town was incorporated into independent Poland. By 1921 the number of Jews had declined to 2,036 (48 percent). Jews dominated the grain trade between the world wars. Jewish cultural and educational institutions functioned until 1939, among them a Hebrew Tarbut school with 300 pupils.

[Arthur Cygielman]

Holocaust Period

In 1939 the Jewish population numbered more than 3,000. As a result of the Soviet-German partition of Poland, the Red Army entered the city on Sept. 19, 1939. The Soviet authorities conducted a survey to determine how many of the refugees wished to return to the German-occupied zone. All those who declared that they wished to do so were deported in the summer of 1940 to the Soviet interior. After June 22, 1941, when war broke out between Germany and the U.S.S.R., groups of Jews retreated with the Red Army, but were turned back by the Soviet border patrol at the old Soviet-Polish border. Most of these Jews returned to Radziwillow.

On June 27, 1941, the city was captured by the Germans. In the first few weeks the Jewish population suffered damage to life and property at the hands of the Ukrainian police and population. On July 15, 1941, 28 Jews were killed for being "dangerous Communists." The following day the Germans set the synagogue aflame and burned the Torah scrolls. On April 9, 1942, a ghetto was established for 2,600 Jews, and divided into two categories: "fit" and "unfit" for labor. Only about 400 persons were found to be "fit." On May 29, 1942, an *Aktion* took place and some 1,500 persons were killed near the city. After this *Aktion* the youth attempted to organize; at the head of one of these underground organizations was Asher Czerkaski. A second *Aktion* took place on Oct. 5, 1942, and hundreds of persons were killed in Suchodoly. Under the assumption that this was a final *Aktion* mass suicides were committed and some 500 Jews broke out of the ghetto and succeeded in reaching the forests, but only 50 of them survived; some reached Brody, where a ghetto still existed, but later they also perished.

[Aharon Weiss]

BIBLIOGRAPHY: B. Wasiutański, *Ludność żydowska w Polsce w wiekach XIX i XX* (1930), 85; I. Schiper, *Dzieje handlu żydowskiego na ziemiach polskich* (1937), index; *Radzivilov; Sefer Zikkaron* (Heb. and Yid., 1966).

RADZYMIN (Rus. **Radimin**), town in Warszawa province, E. central Poland. Founded during the middle of the 17th century as a private town by a privilege granted by King Ladislaus IV of Poland, it grew rapidly during the 19th century as a result of Jewish enterprise. The synagogue was erected in 1840. There were 432 Jews (about 33% of the total population) in Radzymin in 1827, 1,278 (c. 70%) in 1856, 2,133 (c. 53%) in 1897, 2,209 (55% of the population) in 1921, and 3,559 (52.6%) in 1931. Radzymin was a center of Ḥasidism, and during the 19th century it was the home of Jacob Aryeh Guterman, founder of the *Radzymin dynasty of *ẓaddikim*. A yeshivah which gained renown was also established by the dynasty in Radzymin. Zionists played an important role in the public life of the town and in the municipal elections of 1927 they won seven of the ten seats reserved for Jews. The community council, elected in 1931, included six Zionists and two members of Agudat Israel. Among religious, educational, and charitable institutions in Radzymin was the *Linat ha-Ẓedek* ("Hospice for the Poor") established in 1910.

[Shimshon Leib Kirshenboim]

Holocaust Period

Before the outbreak of World War II there were 3,900 Jews living in Radzymin. The Jewish community was liquidated on Oct. 3, 1942, when all the Jews were deported to *Treblinka death camp. After the war the Jewish community was not reconstituted.

RADZYMIN, dynasty of ḥasidic *ẓaddikim* in central Poland. The founder of the dynasty, JACOB ARYEH BEN SOLOMON GUTERMAN OF RADZYMIN (1792–1874), was a pupil of the *ẓaddikim* *Simḥah Bunem of Przysucha and Isaac Kalish of Worky (see *Warka). Jacob Aryeh was rabbi in Rychwal and Radzymin. He became famous as a miracle worker and attracted a large ḥasidic followership. His teachings were published in *Divrei Aviv* (1924) and *Bikkurei Aviv* (1936). Jacob Aryeh's son, SOLOMON (d. 1903), followed his father in the rabbinate of Radzymin and in the ḥasidic leadership. The third *ẓaddik* of the Radzymin dynasty was AARON MENAHEM MENDEL (d. 1934). During World War I he moved to Warsaw, where he also remained after the war. He was active in Jewish communal affairs in Poland. He visited Ereẓ Israel in 1929 and on his initiative a separate section for women was established at the Western Wall. This served as a pretext for the Arabs in the bloody anti-Jewish riots which occurred in 1929. Aaron Menahem Mendel was the author of *Ḥinnukh ha-Banim* (1913) and *Alim li-Terufah* (1936).

[Avraham Rubinstein]

RADZYN (Pol. **Radzyń-Podlaski**; Rus. **Radin**), district capital in the province of Lublin, E. Poland. Founded in 1468, the town was first named Koźirynek. Although no reliable evidence is available, it has been assumed that Jews lived in Radzyn from its foundation. In 1765 there were 537 Jews living there. The town developed during the 19th century. There were 1,301 Jews (about 53% of the total population) by 1856 and 2,853 (53.5% of the total population) in 1897. During World War I the general population decreased, but in 1921 there were still 2,895 Jews (59.7%) in Radzyn, and an estimated 3,000 on the eve of World War II.

The synagogue, a single-story stone building, was erected at the beginning of the 19th century. Among the outstanding personalities of the community was Gershon Ḥanokh Leiner, founder of the Radzyn dynasty of Ḥasidim, who reintroduced the interweaving of the blue thread among the *ẓizit* and established a laboratory for producing the proper color. His grandson, Samuel Solomon Leiner, also a leader of the Radzyn Ḥasidim, perished in the Holocaust. Prominent rabbis of Radzyn were Simeon Deutsch, who held office during the first half of the 19th century, and Ḥayyim Fein (d. during World War II). Jewish economic life was affected by a fire which destroyed many homes in 1929, and many Jewish families became dependent on support from their coreligionists in other communities. During the 1930s an economic crisis and the anti-Jewish economic *boycott proclaimed by Polish antisemites also undermined Jewish economic life. In the democratic elections to the community's council (1931) two Zionists, two Ḥasidim, two representatives of the craftsmen, one of the socialist craftsmen, and two representatives of the *battei midrash* were elected.

[Shimshon Leib Kirshenboim]

Holocaust Period

On Sept. 9, 1939, the Jewish quarter of Radzyn was heavily bombarded by the German air force. At the end of the month, just before the German army entered the town, several hundred Jews, mostly young men and women, left for Soviet-occupied territory. In December 1939 the Germans sent most of the Jews to Sławatycze and Miedzyrzec, but after a few months most returned to Radzyn. In the summer of 1940 an open ghetto was established in Radzyn. Considerable underground activities were conducted, mainly by *Ha-Shomer ha-Ẓa'ir, which organized several smaller partisan groups. On Aug. 20, 1942, the first deportation of Jews to the *Treblinka death camp took place, and on Dec. 20, 1942, the second, when the Jewish community was "liquidated."

[Stefan Krakowski]

BIBLIOGRAPHY: *Sefer Radzyn* (Heb. and Yid., 1957).

RADZYNSKI, JAN (1950–), composer, born in Warsaw, Poland. Radzynski immigrated to Israel in 1969 and studied at the Tel Aviv Rubin Academy of Music with Leon *Schidlowsky. From 1977 he continued his studies at Yale University in the U.S. with Krzysztof Penderecki and Jacob Druckman and received his doctorate in 1984. He settled in the U.S.

Radzynski's music is characterized by the utilization of contemporary techniques in contexts rich of stylistic elements from the past. It is carried by expressive melodies of long chromatic lines and features rich textures and carefully composed structures, paying special attention to the links and interrelations between movements of a single work. Radzynski's virtuoso writing offers technical challenges to the performing musicians and is often witty and full of verve. By embedding East European-Jewish (cantorial) and Middle-Eastern (heterophonic) musical elements in compositions committed to the past masters, Radzynski aims at a musical language timeless and contemporary alike, culturally unique and universal.

His works have been performed by such orchestras as the Cleveland, Columbus, New Haven Symphony, the Mexico National, the West German and the Saarländische Radio Symphony Orchestras, the Cracow Philharmonic, the Russian Federal, the Moscow Bolshoi Theater Chamber Orchestra; the Israel Philharmonic, Jerusalem and Haifa Symphony and Israel Chamber Orchestras and Israel Sinfonietta. He was composition professor at Yale between 1981 and 1994 and was professor at the Ohio State University in Columbus.

Radzynski's list of compositions include *String Quartet* (1977); *Kaddish for the Victims of the Holocaust* for four amplified flutes, six percussion players, piano and strings (1979); *Homage to Itzik Manger* for mixed ensemble of nine players (1979); *Canto* for piano (1981); *Psalms* for viola and eight celli (1983); *Take Five*, brass quintet (1984); *Hebrew Melodies*, piano quintet; Violin/Viola Sonata (1985); *David – Symphony in One Movement* (1987); *Encounters* for chamber ensemble (1988); *Viola Concerto* (1990); *Time's Other Beat* for symphony orchestra (1990); Cello Concerto (1990–92); *Serenade*, Wind Quintet; String Trio (1995); *Fanfare*; *Shirat Ma'ayan* for mezzo-soprano, tenor and orchestra (1997); *Summer Charms Rag* for violin and piano (1998); *Personal Verses* for violin and piano (1999); *Serenade for Strings* (2000); *Concert Duos* for clarinet and cello (2004).

Among the many awards Radzynski received are the ASCAP Standard Awards (1989 and 1997), the Mellon Fellowship (1985), the Research and Creative Work Grant of the Rothschild Foundation (1995), and the Distinguished Scholar Award given by the Ohio State University (1996). In 1983 he was in residence at the Foundation Artists' House in Boswil, Switzerland.

[Yuval Shaked (2nd ed.)]

RAFA (Ar. **Rafah**; Heb. **Rafi'aḥ**), town, near the Mediterranean coast, 22 mi. (35 km.) S. of Gaza. Rafa is first mentioned in an inscription of the pharaoh Seti I (c. 1300 B.C.E.) as Rph; it also appears in other Egyptian sources, in Papyrus Anastasi I and in the inscription of Shishak. As a border town on the way to Egypt and a point of sharp transition from desert to cultivated land, it is frequently referred to as the site of conflicts between the armies of Egypt and its neighbors. In 721 B.C.E. Sargon of Assyria defeated at Rapihu (Rafa) Sib'e of Egypt and Hanno of Gaza; the Assyrians burned the city and deported 9,033 inhabitants. Rafa does not appear in the Bible; the Targums (on Deut. 2:23) identify it with Hazerim. It was the center of important operations in the Hellenistic period during the wars of the Diadochi. Antigonus attacked it in 306 B.C.E. and in 217 B.C.E. Antiochus III of Syria was defeated there by the army of Ptolemy V of Egypt (Polybius 5:82–86). The town was conquered by Alexander Yannai and held by the Hasmoneans until it was rebuilt in the time of Pompey and Gabinius; the latter seems to have done the actual work of restoration for the era of the town dates from 57 B.C.E. Rafa is mentioned in Strabo (16:2, 31), the Itinerarium Antonini, and is depicted on the Madaba Map. It was the seat of worship of Dionysius and Isis (*Papyrus Oxyrrhynchus*, 1380). It was the seat of an Episcopal see in the fifth-sixth centuries. A Jewish community settled there in the geonic period; it flourished in the ninth to tenth centuries and again in the 12th, although in the 11th century it suffered a decline and in 1080 the Jews of Rafa had to flee to Ashkelon. A Samaritan community also lived there at this period. Like most cities of southern Ereẓ Israel, ancient Rafa had a landing place on the coast (now Tell Rafāḥ), while the main city was inland.

[Michael Avi-Yonah]

Modern Period

Between 1905 and 1913 Ereẓ Israel Jews and Zionist groups in Central and Eastern Europe made repeated but futile attempts to buy land and establish settlements in the area. The town was reestablished in the 1920s under the British Mandate, and built for the most part on the Palestinian side but also on the Egyptian side of the border. Rafa's population grew around the time of World War II, when the British army established large military camps there, providing the Arab inhabitants with employment. In the late 1940s, before the *War of Independence, members and leaders of Jewish settlements, *Haganah, *Irgun Ẓeva'i Le'ummi, and the *yishuv* were detained in British detention camps at Rafa. After the battles of 1948 Arab refugees settled in the former British camps at Rafa, which was under Egyptian administration in the *Gaza Strip. Taken by Israel forces in the Sinai Campaign (1956), Rafa was evacuated by them in March 1957. During the *Six-Day War, on June 5, 1967, Israel again took the town. In 1931 the town had 1,400 inhabitants, in 1945 2,500, and according to the Israel census of the fall of 1967, 49,812, almost all Muslim Arabs, 39,000 of whom lived in refugee camps. In 1971 many inhabitants worked as farm laborers and in small trades, but the percentage of those subsisting on relief was particularly high. After the signing of the Declaration of Principles in 1993, the town was handed over to the Palestinian Authority.

[Efraim Orni]

BIBLIOGRAPHY: J. Mann, *The Jews in Egypt*, 2 (1922), 71–72; S. Klein (ed.), *Sefer ha-Yishuv* (1939), s.v.; Abel, in: RB, 49 (1940), 73ff. **ADD. BIBLIOGRAPHY:** Y. Tsafrir, L. Di Segni, and J. Green, *Tabula Imperii Romani. Iudaea – Palaestina. Maps and Gazetteer.* (1994), 212, s.v. "Raphia."

RAFALIN, DAVID SHLOMÓ (1899–1979), rabbi of the Ashkenazi community of Mexico. He was born in Suwalki, Poland, and studied in the yeshivot of Slobodka and Mir. Rabbi Rafalin immigrated to New York and in 1929 to Havana, Cuba, where he was appointed rabbi of the Orthodox Ashkenazi congregation Adath Israel and was active in the Zionist Union of Cuba. In 1933 Rafalin immigrated to Mexico where he became the rabbi of the Ashkenazi community Nidchei Israel, serving until his death. Besides his rabbinic functions, Rafalin developed many public activities in the community. As an active Zionist he presided over the Jewish National Fund (1938–39); he founded and was the leader of the Mexican branch of the religious Zionist party, the Mizrachi; he headed many fundraising efforts in support of the government in its campaign for the nationalization of oil resources (1938) and for the aid to Holocaust survivors. Rafalin also collaborated in the foundation of the Jewish religious school Yavneh (1942).

[Efraim Zadoff (2nd ed.)]

RAFELSON, ROBERT (1933–), U.S. director, producer, writer. Born in Manhattan, Rafelson worked at a rodeo at 15, followed by a stint as a deckhand on an ocean liner, and later tried his hand as a jazz drummer. At Dartmouth College, Rafelson was an Armed Forces radio deejay. He was a producer on the TV series *The Wackiest Ship in the Navy* (1965–66) before becoming writer, director, and producer for the television series *The Monkees* (1966–67) for which he won an Emmy. Rafelson's film debut was *Head* (1968), a Monkees movie which he directed and produced. He cowrote the screenplay with Jack Nicholson, and coproduced *Easy Rider* (1969). Rafelson directed, produced, and cowrote *Five Easy Pieces*, in which Nicholson starred, earning four Academy Award nominations, including Best Film and Best Original Screenplay. Rafelson and Nicholson also worked together on *The King of Marvin Gardens* (1972). *Stay Hungry* (1976), which Rafelson directed and produced, featured Arnold Schwarzenegger in one of his first roles. Nicholson also starred in Rafelson's 1981 hit *The Postman Always Rings Twice*, a remake of the 1946 film based on the James M. Cain novel, with a screenplay by David *Mamet. *Mountains of the Moon* (1990) was a biographical account of Sir Richard Burton and John Speke's search for the origin of the Nile. In 1994, Rafelson returned to television and directed the "Armed Response" episode of the miniseries *Picture Window*. Rafelson also directed the television films *Poodle Springs* (1998) and *Afterthoughts* (2002), a documentary about independent Hollywood filmmakers. Other Rafelson films include *Brubaker* (1980), *Black Widow* (1987), *Man Trouble* (1992), *Wet* (1995), *Blood and Wine* (1996), and *The House on Turk Street* (2002). Rafelson is playwright Samson *Raphaelson's nephew.

[Susannah Howland (2nd ed.)]

RAFES, MOSES (1883–1942), leading member of the Russian Bund. Rafes, born into a family of merchants, was associated in his youth with revolutionary circles and in 1902–03 joined the *Bund in Vilna, where he had some connection with the terrorist act of Hirsch *Lekert. He was also active in *Gomel (1906) and St. Petersburg and was a Bund delegate to the London convention of the Social Democratic Workers' Party of Russia (1907). In 1912 he was coopted to the central committee of the Bund. During World War I he supported the "defensist" wing of the Social Democrats, which preferred the victory of Russia. Together with H. *Erlich he represented the Bund on the "industrial war committees." After the revolution of February 1917 he was a member of the Executive Council of the Petrograd Soviet and was later active within the Ukrainian Bund. He was at first an extremist of the right and anti-Bolshevist wing, then turned toward the center, and after the revolution in Germany made a sharp turn toward communism. He played a central role in the divisions in the Bund, creation of the Kombund and Komfarband, and the amalgamation of its majority with the Communist Party in Soviet Russia, and he was then also sent to work for the liquidation of the Bund in Poland. In a 1919 memorandum he appealed to the Kommissariat of Interior Affairs to immediately liquidate all Jewish institutions, organizations, and parties, claiming that they were a danger to the Soviet state. He acted with particular energy as the head of the Liquidation Committee for Jewish Affairs of the *Yevsektsiya, subsequently adhering to the assimilationist trend and abandoning Jewish activities. After having served as a commissar in the Red Army, he worked in the government in Moscow, and also for the Comintern and the Soviet Foreign Service (Chinese affairs). He was finally transferred to the sphere of cinema work. He was arrested in May 1938, and sentenced to 10 years imprisonment, and died in the camps of Komi ASSR.

Before World War I, he contributed to the Bundist press and continued to write from time to time in the Soviet Yiddish press. He published some works on the history of the Bund which, in spite of their bias, are of some historiographic value. These include (in Russian): "Two Years of Revolution in the Ukraine" (1920) and "Chapters on the History of the Bund" (1923). He edited the anthology *Der Yidisher Arbeter* (4 vols., 1925–28) of A. *Kirzhnitz.

BIBLIOGRAPHY: Ch. Shmeruk (ed.), *Pirsumim Yehudiyyim bi-Verit ha-Mo'aẓot* (1961), index; Rejzen, Leksikon, 4 (1929), 237–43; I.S. Hertz et al. (eds.), *Geshikhte fun Bund* 1–3 (1960–66), index; M. Altschuler (ed.), *Russian Publications on Jews and Judaism in the Soviet Union* (1970), index.

[Moshe Mishkinsky]

RAFFALOVICH, ARTHUR GERMANOVICH (1853–1921), Russian economist. Born in Odessa, Raffalovich lived in Paris where his lucid and pertinent explanations of, and comments on, contemporary economic issues such as cartels and other commercial agreements, brought him in close contact with leading French publications and journalists. He became a regular contributor to *Le Temps* and *Le Journal des Débats*. Having acquired the confidence of the Russian authorities, particularly of Prime Minister Witte and Finance Minister Kokovtsev, whom he successfully advised on commercial and financial affairs, he became the major Russian publicity agent in France, and was particularly concerned with press relations and their effect on the placement of Russian government bonds in France. His assignment included guidance to the Russian authorities on the allocation of advertising in the French press. This exposed him to the charge of bribery. After having attacked Bolshevism, Raffalovich became the object of relentless charges by *L'Humanité*, the Communist daily, which published his confidential reports to St. Petersburg after their release by the Soviet government. Most of these publications, however, did not prove conclusively the bribery charge.

[Joachim O. Ronall]

RAFFALOVICH, ISAIAH (1870–1956), rabbi and author who promoted the development of Brazil's Jewish community. Born in Bogopol, Podolia, Raffalovich was taken in 1882 by his parents to Ereẓ Israel. He became interested in Jewish settlement schemes on both sides of the Jordan and worked for nine months at Es-Salt in Transjordan, trying to encourage young Jews in Jerusalem to follow his example. Together with M.E. Sachs, he published an album of his own photographs, *Views from Palestine and its Jewish Colonies* (1898). Raffalovich left for Europe, where he studied in Berlin and London, obtaining his rabbinical diploma at the Hildesheimer Seminary in Berlin. He served congregations in Manchester and Wales and the Hope Place Synagogue in Liverpool (1904–24).

While on a mission to South America in 1923, he was invited by the *Jewish Colonization Association (ICA) to go to Brazil as its representative, promote immigration to that country, and serve as a spiritual guide to the Jewish community. In this capacity he toured the country, established welfare institutions and improved already existing ones, and helped the newly established communities and synagogues. Raffalovich appealed to the common heritage of the Ashkenazi and Sephardi immigrants in working for the coordination of Jewish life in Brazil, and it was through his personal efforts that more than 30 Jewish schools and teachers' training courses were firmly established. His publications include: *Rudiments of Judaism* (1906); *Anglo-Hebrew Modern Dictionary* (1926); and *Our Inheritance* (1932), a volume of sermons and addresses. He also published in 1927 a Portuguese version of Paul *Goodman's popular short *History of the Jews* (1911) and the first Jewish sermons in Portuguese printed in modern times, *Rudimentos de judaismo* (1926^2). In 1935 he retired to Ereẓ Israel and five years later was appointed senior Jewish chaplain to the British forces in the Middle East. A Hebrew edition of his collected sermons (*Ma'gelei Yosher*) appeared in 1950 and his autobiography, *Ẓiyyunim ve-Tamrurim*, in 1952. His brother SAMUEL REFAELI (1867–1927), a numismatist, was director of the numismatic department of the Department of Antiquities in Palestine (under the British) and left his coin collection to the Bezalel Museum.

BIBLIOGRAPHY: Tidhar, 1 (1947), 216–7; JC (June 8, 1956); G.E. Silverman, in: *Niv ha-Midrashiyyah* (Spring, 1970), 74–81, Eng. section.

[Godfrey Edmond Silverman]

RAFI (abbreviation of Heb. *Reshimat Po'alei Yisrael*, "Israel Labor List"), founded in 1965 as the result of a split in *Mapai. The original split was the outcome of *Ben-Gurion's political fight against Levi *Eshkol over the *Lavon Affair and of the struggle for succession to the leadership between a group of younger men, headed by Moshe *Dayan and Shimon *Peres, supported by Ben-Gurion, and the party veterans, headed by Levi Eshkol and Golda *Meir. At the Mapai convention in February 1965, the rebels supported Ben-Gurion's demand for an inquiry into the Lavon Affair and opposed the proposed political alignment with Aḥdut ha-Avodah. After their defeat at the convention, they proposed Ben-Gurion's return to the premiership in place of Eshkol. In July, seven Mapai Knesset members (later joined by Dayan) formed a new list, called Rafi, which obtained 12% of the votes at the Histradrut elections in September and ten Knesset seats in November.

At its founding convention in May 1966, representing 23,000 members, Rafi called for electoral reform, self-reliance in the field of defense, national health insurance, free secondary education, and modernization of the economy, with particular emphasis on the full utilization of science. It became part of the parliamentary opposition, especially in defense and foreign affairs, sometimes cooperating with *Gaḥal. In May 1967, during the prewar tension and the discussions on the appointment of Dayan as minister of defense, Rafi offered to return to Mapai bodies, and when the government was reformed after the 1969 elections Peres joined it. The elections were also contested by the State (or National) List (*Reshimah Mamlakhtit*), headed by Ben-Gurion, which consisted mainly of Rafi supporters and won four seats. In February 1971 (after Ben-Gurion's resignation from the Knesset) it decided to call itself Rafi-State List. Negotiations after the *Six-Day War led to agreement between Mapai, Rafi, and Aḥdut ha-Avodah. When the united Israel Labor Party was formed on Jan. 21, 1968, Rafi received 21.5 percent of the places on its governing bodies. In 1973 the State List ran for the Knesset as part of the Likud.

[Misha Louvish]

RAGEN, NAOMI (1949–), author. Born in New York, Ragen earned a bachelor's degree in English from Brooklyn College and a master's in English from the Hebrew University of Jerusalem. In January 1971 she moved with her husband to Israel. The translation of her books into Hebrew made her one of Israel's best-loved writers. Blending history, Jewish religious themes and their relation to the modern-day world, she had six international bestsellers: *Jephte's Daughter* (1989); *Sotah* (1992), her first book translated into Hebrew; *The Sacrifice of Tamar* (1995); *Chains Around the Grass* (2001); *The Ghost of Hannah Mendes* (2002); and *The Covenant.* (2004) Her play, *Women's Minyan*, commissioned by Israel's National Theater, Habimah, premiered in Israel in 2000 and became one of Habimah's longest-running hits. Its American premiere in English took place in 2005 at Duke University's Reynolds Theatre. She is an outspoken advocate of gender equality and human rights. One of the most influential and widely read columnists on the Internet, with thousands of subscribers, Ragen served as Israel's delegate to the Council of Europe's International Conference on Women's Rights in September 2000. Caught along with her family in the Netanyah Passover massacre, she used the experience to write passionately about the dangers of terror organizations and their supporters, as well as the experience of innocent civilians who find themselves on the front lines. A frequent contributor to op-ed pages, she was also a columnist for *The Jerusalem Post*. The Israeli government honored her in 2002 for outstanding achievement in literature.

[Stewart Kampel (2nd ed.)]

RAGER, BRACHA (1938–), Israeli microbiologist. Born in Tel Aviv, Rager obtained her M.Sc. in microbiology from Tel Aviv University in 1963 and received her Ph.D. from the School of Hygiene and Tropical Medicine, London University, London, England in 1973. Between 1973 and 1976, she was a postdoctoral research fellow in the Department of Microbiology and Immunology, Albert Einstein College of Medicine, New York, where later she was appointed visiting professor, a position she held until 1987. In 1977 she joined the newly established Faculty of Health Sciences, Ben-Gurion University of the Negev, and was one of the founders of the department of microbiology and immunology, where she was appointed full professor in 1997. From 1997 to 2001 she was chief scientist of the Ministry of Health and from 2005 the president of the Israel Society of Microbiology. Rager was a member of the Higher Council of Education (MALAG) and served on the board of directors of Teva Pharmaceuticals. As an expert in virology and immunology, Rager conducted extensive research on mechanisms of defense against virus infections and cancer. She was a recipient of many prestigious awards and wrote numerous papers, which were published in professional journals. She also published articles on medical research policy and of scientific interest in national newspapers and was much involved in promoting medical research, women's health, and biotechnology. Throughout her professional life, Rager was extremely active in community and education projects related to the scientific education of the young. She was the academic consultant to gifted children and science for youth programs at Ben-Gurion University and a board member of the Blumfield Science Museum in Jerusalem. She was also a member of the board of directors of ORT, Israel. Rager was co-editor of the science section of the 2nd edition of the *Encyclopedia Judaica* and the widow of Itzhack *Rager, the late mayor of Beersheba.

RAGER, (IJO) ITZHACK, (1932–1997), Israeli journalist, diplomat, businessman, and mayor. Rager was born in Egypt and came to Israel in his infancy in 1932. He was a graduate of the David Yellin Teacher's College, the Hebrew University (in international affairs), Hunter College (in Soviet studies), and the City University of New York Graduate Center (in cross-system analysis). After his army service, in 1955, he was a bureau chief for the minister of interior, Israel Rokach, and in 1958 he joined the Israel Broadcasting Authority (IBA) as a parliamentary correspondent, later becoming chief news editor. In 1962, he was appointed chief European correspondent of IBA in Paris, and upon his return from Paris (1966) was appointed secretary general of the Broadcasting Authority. In 1969 he was chief editor of the *Ha-Yom* national daily newspaper. From 1971 to 1976 he was consul in London and New York and in 1980–83 was president of the worldwide State of Israel Bonds agency. In 1976 he settled in Beersheba, and in 1983 was appointed chairman of the Eilat Development Company. After building the first shopping mall in Beersheba (1984–89), he was elected mayor of Beersheba. Rager is remembered for numerous achievements during his lifetime. As an IDF officer (colonel, reserve), during the Six-Day War he commanded the battalion that liberated *Gush Etzyon and was the first to enter the city of Bethlehem. As a counselor in London and consul in New York he was an active leader for the freedom of Soviet Jews and participated in the creation of the "35s" Women's Campaign for Soviet Jewry. During his time as mayor of Beersheba, the city's population grew by 50 percent; he attracted industrial investments and revolutionized the educational system. Rager died of cancer in 1997 during his second term as mayor.

[Bracha Rager (2nd ed.)]

RAGOLER, ABRAHAM BEN SOLOMON (18th century), Lithuanian rabbi and preacher, brother of *Elijah b. Solomon Zalman Gaon of Vilna. Abraham was born in Vilna, but because of the controversy between *Ḥasidim and *Mitnaggedim* he moved to Ragola and was thereafter called Abraham of Ragola or "the Ḥasid ("righteous one") of Ragola." He was appointed preacher in Shklov.

He was the author of the *Ma'alot ha-Torah* (1828), a collection of rabbinic dicta dealing with the virtue of those who occupy themselves with the study of Torah. While explaining in detail the precepts of Torah study, he stressed that it is not sufficient "merely to study the text superficially, but it is also essential to carry it out in practice." He left in manuscript a kabbalistic commentary to the tractate *Megillah* and a commentary to the Book of Esther.

BIBLIOGRAPHY: S.J. Fuenn, *Kiryah Ne'emanah* (1915^2), 206; S.M. Chones, *Toledot ha-Posekim* (1929), 53; *Yahadut Lita*, 1 (1959), 355; 3 (1967), 24; E. Landau, *Toledot u-Mifalot ha-Gra u-Mishpaḥto*, in: *Minḥat Eliyahu* (1927).

[Yehoshua Horowitz]

RAGOLER, ELIJAH BEN JACOB (1794–1850), Lithuanian talmudist. Ragoler was born in Sogindat in the Zamut region. His only teacher was his father Jacob, a distinguished scholar and wealthy merchant. In his youth Elijah acquired a comprehensive knowledge of the Talmud, the *rishonim*, and the *posekim* – which he regarded as the essential elements of study in contrast to the prevalent methods of *pilpul* and hairsplitting unconnected with the definitive *halakhah*. He was renowned throughout Lithuania for his encyclopedic talmudic knowledge, and his contemporaries said of him that he had gone over the whole of the Talmud more than 400 times. He devoted himself to considerable study of the Kabbalah, in which he also became renowned. Nevertheless, he refused throughout his life to have any dealings with mystic exercises, despite the many appeals for prayers, amulets, etc. made to him by scholars and the common people. In his youth he spent some months with *Isaac of Volozhiner for the purpose of learning Kabbalah from him in accordance with the traditions which Isaac had received from *Elijah of Vilna. When, however, he lost hope of this he returned home. At that time, his father and father-in-law failed in business and Elijah was compelled to accept a rabbinical post. He first served as rabbi of the small town of Schatt near Keidany. From 1821 to 1824 he was rabbi of Ragola (Eiragola) where he gained his main reputation and from which he derived his name. From 1824 to 1840 he was rabbi of Slobodka and from 1840 until his death rabbi of Kalisz in Poland.

In addition to his great reputation as a *posek* and scholar in *halakhah* and Kabbalah, Elijah was distinguished for his diligence and application, and for his shrewdness and sincerity. During his last years he suffered from ill health as well as from the opposition of a group of members of the Kalisz community to whom the Lithuanian ways of their rabbi were strange. Despite this he did not hesitate to take a decisive attitude in his leadership of the community, and sided with Akiva *Lehren of Amsterdam in his violent opposition to the Reform conference of Brunswick (1844), organized by A. *Geiger. Ragoler's letter to Lehren differs from the many other letters of contemporary Orthodox rabbis in its exceptionally moderate tone. In contrast to them, Elijah held that the weapon of excommunication, prohibition of marriage, etc., should not be followed because of the grave danger it held for the whole of the Jewish community. In his view a sharp and unequivocal dissociation from the path of reform, and a warning to the public against it were necessary, but not a "war of destruction."

Ragoler left many manuscripts in all spheres of Torah study. According to the members of his family their number exceeded 35. Of these only one has been published: *Yad Eliyyahu* (1900), pt. I, 120 responsa and a methodology of the Talmud in alphabetical order, pt. II, talmudic novellae. Among his pupils were many great Lithuanian talmudists, including Mordecai Eliasberg and Joshua Heshel *Lewin. Many of his novellae are to be found in the works of other scholars, particularly in those of his pupils, including the *Ilana de-Ḥayyei* (1860–65) of Gershon Tanḥum. The *Keneset ha-Gedolah*, pt. 4 (1892), of Isaak *Suwalski cites many of his sayings on prayer.

Ragoler's brother, SAMUEL KELMER, was also a renowned scholar who went to Ereẓ Israel in the closing years of his life. Samuel was the father of Aryeh Leib *Frumkin.

BIBLIOGRAPHY: A.L. Frumkin, *Toledot Eliyyahu* (1900); Urbach (ed.), in: *Kovez al Yad*, 6 (16) pt. 2 (1966), 535–53.

[Israel Moses Ta-Shma]

RAHAB (Heb. רָחָב), the prostitute (Heb. *zonah* – see below), mentioned in the Book of Joshua as a central figure in Joshua's conquest of Jericho (Josh. 2–6). When Joshua sent two of his men to Jericho on a reconnaissance mission, they came to the house of Rahab and spent the night there (2:1–2). When the king of Jericho learned about the two spies, he sent word to Rahab ordering her to surrender them (2:3). However, she hid them on the roof under stalks of flax, and declared that they had already left (2:4–6). In return for the kindness that she had shown them and her promise to keep the entire affair confidential, the spies took an oath that she and her family would be spared when Joshua conquered the land (2:12–14). They further stipulated that when the conquest began, she was to gather her entire family into her home and bind a cord of crimson thread in the window, which would serve to identify her house (2:17–21). This cord of crimson thread was the same one which had been used to let the spies down through the window when they left Rahab's house (2:18). Rahab did as she was bidden, and so when Joshua did conquer the land, she and her entire family were saved (6:22–23, 25). After the total destruction of Jericho, it is stated that Rahab and her family elected to reside with the Israelites, who accepted her into their camp (6:25).

There are two somewhat conflicting Jewish traditions concerning Rahab's profession and later life among the Israelites. The first (e.g., Meg. 14b; Ginzberg, Legends, 4 (1954), 5–8) maintains that she married Joshua after becoming a proselyte, and became the ancestress of eight prophets and priests among whom were the prophet Jeremiah and the prophetess Huldah. According to this tradition, the fact that a proselyte and former prostitute could achieve such a name for herself in the annals of Jewish history proved that repentance can work salvation for anyone no matter how great his past sins. The second tradition contends that Rahab was not a prostitute at all but an innkeeper. This tradition (e.g., Rashi on Josh. 2:1) is based on the Targum's rendering of *zonah* as *pundekita* (*pundeqita*), the assumption being that this word means, like *pundakit* (*pundaqit*) in Hebrew, "hostess, innkeeper," and the derivation of the word *zonah* (normally "prostitute") from the same stem as *mazon* (מָזוֹן, "food"). If Rahab had been merely an innkeeper, then the shame of considering a former prostitute to be the ancestress of some of Israel's most important figures would cease to be a problem. However, as first noted by Kimḥi (on Josh. 2:1), the adherents of this theory simply misunderstood the Targum, for the Targum to the Prophets in various passages also renders *zonah* by *pundeqētā*, plural *pundeqāyān* or *pundeqāʾān* (e.g., I Kings 3:16; Ezek. 23:44), in which it cannot possibly have been understood to mean anything but "prostitute." Therefore, the Targum's rendering of Hebrew "prostitute" with Aramaic "innkeeper" is to be understood either as a euphemism or as an intended double entendre, implying that there is a connection between bars or inns and prostitutes.

[Chayim Cohen]

In the Aggadah

Rahab was one of the four most beautiful women in history. The mere mention of her name sufficed to excite desire (Meg. 15a). At the age of ten Rahab became a prostitute. There was not a prince or ruler who did not have relations with her. Because of this, she was well informed about events outside of Jericho (Zeb. 116b). Rahab became a righteous proselyte and married Joshua. She was the ancestress of eight prophets, among them Jeremiah, who were also priests, and of the prophetess Huldah (Meg. 14b). Her conversion is regarded as more complete than that of Jethro and Naaman for, unlike them, she acknowledged that the God of Israel is the only God both in heaven and on earth (Deut. R. 2:26–27).

BIBLIOGRAPHY: Y. Kaufmann, *Sefer Yehoshu'a* (1959). IN THE AGGADAH: Ginzberg, Legends, index.

RAHABI, EZEKIEL (1694–1771), merchant and community leader in Cochin (*Kochi), India. In 1726, after the death of his father, Rahabi was appointed by the Dutch East India Company as "chief merchant and agent," and invested with a monopoly of the trade in pepper and other commodities in Malabar. He rose to a position of remarkable influence and prestige; for almost 50 years he was connected with all the company's major financial transactions in Malabar, and undertook for it diplomatic assignments to the king of Travancore (1734–42), to the zamorin of Calicut (1751), and to other native rulers.

Rahabi was also an outstanding leader of the Jewish community. He purchased land for the Black Jews near Cranganore and in 1756 built a synagogue there for ten Jewish families, supporting it until it was closed in 1761; improved and embellished the Parathesi synagogue of the White Jews in Cochin; and imported Hebrew books from Holland. Through his efforts to decipher the ancient copperplate inscriptions in Cochin, Ezekiel Rahabi also became the historian of his community. His letter of 1768 to the Dutch banker Tobias Boas remains a major source of information about Cochin Jewry. Rahabi's tombstone is preserved in the courtyard of the Parathesi synagogue. The changed economic and political conditions in Malabar after the English occupation of Cochin (1795) caused the decline of the Rahabi family.

BIBLIOGRAPHY: S.S. Koder, in: *Journal of the Rama Varma Archaeological Society*, 15 (1949), 1–6; W.J. Fischel, *Ha-Yehudim be-Hodu* (1960), 97–111; idem, in: PAAJR, 30 (1962), 37–59; A. Das Gupta, *Malabar in Asian Trade* (1967), index. **ADD. BIBLIOGRAPHY:** J.B. Segal, *A History of the Jews of Cochin* (1993).

[Walter Joseph Fischel]

RAHABI (Raby), NAPHTALI ELIAHU (1863–1951), "white" Jewish scholar of Cochin (*Kochi), India. He is the author of *Divrei Yemei ha-Yehudim be-Cochin* ("History of the Jews of Cochin"; Sasson Ms. 268), and of *Toledot Beit Rahabi be-Cochin* ("History of the Rahabi Family"), both unpublished. He edited *Ḥuppat Ḥatanim* (1917), a collection of songs and hymns for weddings, etc. Like many Cochin leaders, Rahabi had strong Zionist sympathies.

BIBLIOGRAPHY: D.S. Sassoon, *Ohel Dawid*, 1 (1932), 370; 2 (1932), 844, 967; A. Yaari, *Ha-Defus ha-Ivri be-Arẓot ha-Mizraḥ*, 2 (1940), 70; W.J. Fischel, *Ha-Yehudim be-Hodu* (1960), 97–111; idem, in: *Herzl Yearbook*, 4 (1961–62), 309–28.

[Walter Joseph Fischel]

RAHAMIMOFF, RAMI (1937–), Israeli physiologist. He was born in Sofia and immigrated to Israel in 1949. He received his M.D. from the Hebrew University-Hadassah Medical School (1963) and, after deciding on a research career, worked with Sir Bernard *Katz as a British Council Research Fellow (1965–66) and lecturer in biophysics (1966–68) in the department of biophysics of University College, London. He returned to the Hadassah Medical School as a senior lecturer in physiology (1969), where he was appointed professor of physiology from 1975, chairman of the division of basic medical sciences (1974–81), Jacob Gitlin Professor of Physiology from 1985, chairman of the department of physiology (1986–89), and director of the Bernard Katz Minerva Center for Cell Biophysics (1994–2005). Rahamimoff's research interests developed with the undergraduate teaching he received from Jonathan Magnes and Joseph Dobkin. It concerns the regulation of the chemical transmitters in the nervous system which pass information from one nerve cell to another. He and his collaborator Fred Dodge developed a theory of cooperation between factors governing neuro-transmission that has been highly influential in progress in this field. Subsequently his laboratory has helped to clarify the significance of calcium and the functional significance of the fine anatomical details involved in neuro-transmission. His findings also have important implications for understanding the mechanisms that account for many diseases of the nervous system and their therapeutic control. Rahamimoff's teaching distinction was recognized by his regular nomination as distinguished university lecturer, the many physiologists he trained, and his contributions to many prestigious international courses. He also made important contributions to scientific education and research as chairman and council member of national and international committees concerned with the neuro-sciences and physiology in general. He served as dean (1981–85) and director of the Center for Medical Education (1985–88) of the Hebrew University-Hadassah Medical School (1981–85). From 2001 he was chief scientist of the Israel Ministry of Health and chairman of the committee responsible for the establishment of an Israeli Medical Research Council in 2002. His achievements were recognized by the award of the 1998 Israel Prize in life sciences.

[Michael Denman (2nd ed.)]

RAḤBAH, AL-, town situated on the W. bank of the Euphrates, S. of Kirkisiya. Founded in the first third of the ninth century by Mālik ibn Ṭauq, al-Raḥbah was named Raḥbat Mālik ibn Ṭauq to differentiate it from other towns bearing the name Al-Raḥbah. Onkelos, and after him R. *Saadiah Gaon, identify the town with the biblical Rehoboth by the River (Gen. 36:37), while the Arab geographer Yāqūt reports an ancient tradition, according to which Al-Raḥbah was founded by Namrūd (Nimrod) b. Kūsh. It was, at any rate, one of the large cities on the Euphrates – as confirmed by another Arab geographer, al-Mukaddasī, writing at the end of the tenth century – and it had a large Jewish community. Obadiah the proselyte was in this town at the beginning of the 12th century. *Benjamin of Tudela, the 12th-century traveler, found a Jewish community of 2,000 there. In a letter (*iggeret*) written by R. *Samuel b. Ali, head of the *Baghdad academy, in 1191, Al-Raḥbah heads the list of the communities of northern *Babylonia and *Syria. There were also *Karaites living in the town, as is known from a list appearing at the end of a manuscript of Japheth b. Ali's commentary on Numbers, dedicated by Moses b. Japheth al-Raḥbī to the Karaite community in *Jerusalem. By the 14th century the ancient town had been destroyed and its site had been moved further to the west. At the time that the town was included within the *Mamluk kingdom, Jews still lived there, as may be inferred from an inscription found in the synagogue of Tadef (a village near *Aleppo), dating apparently from about 1400, which mentions the name "Obadiah b. Moses … b. Abraham al-Raḥbī." During Ottoman rule Jews from al-Raḥbah moved to *India, and some of them (e.g., a prominent family that lived in Cochin in the 18th century), bore the name of their ancient home.

BIBLIOGRAPHY: Yāqūt, *Muʿjam al-Buldān* s.v.; J. Obermeyer, *Die Landschaft Babylonien* (1929), 36f; Mann, Texts, 2 (1935), 28f; Ashtor, Toledot, 1 (1944), 278; 2 (1951), 120; S.D. Goitein, in: JJS, 4 (1953), 83; A. Ben-Jacob, *Yehudei Bavel* (1965), 56.

[Eliyahu Ashtor]

RAHBAR, SAMUEL (1929–), Iranian immunologist. Rahbar was born in Hamadan, Iran, and studied medicine at the University of Teheran, obtaining his doctorate in 1953. After doing hemoglobin research at the Albert Einstein College of Medicine, New York, he was appointed professor of immunology at the University of Teheran. In 1963, he established the university's Abnormal Hemoglobin Research Laboratory of which he became the director; a number of new abnormal hemoglobins were discovered there. In addition to numerous contributions on the subject in international scientific journals, Rahbar published *Principles of Molecular Biology* (Persian, 1972). His most important achievement is the discovery of HbA1c in diabetic patients, which was published in 1968. HbA1c became one of the most important biochemical values to be measured in diabetic patients, its measurement being a major contribution to the quality of care of diabetic patients. At the beginning of the Islamic Revolution, he was fired from the University of Tehran and immigrated to U.S. As a professor of diabetes at the City of Hope National Medical Center in Duarte, California, he worked on the development of "inhibitors of glycation," compounds that may prevent diabetic complications in the kidneys, eyes, and nervous system.

RAḤEL (pseudonym of **Rahel Bluwstein**, 1890–1931), Hebrew poet in Ereẓ Israel. Raḥel was born in Saratov, on the Volga in northern Russia, and raised in Poltava. She began writing poetry in Russian at the age of 15 and also studied painting. In 1909 she emigrated to Ereẓ Israel, settling in Reḥovot. She abandoned her native Russian idiom and learned Hebrew. Under the influence of the pioneer Zionist Hannah Maisel (Shoḥat) she became a pioneer and was one of the first trainees at the young women's training farm at Kinneret. At Kinneret she met Aaron David *Gordon, the philosopher of Zionist agrarianism, and to him she dedicated her first Hebrew poem, "*Halokh Nefesh*" ("Mood"), in *Ha-Shiloʾaḥ*, 37 (1920). Having decided on an agricultural life, she studied agronomy at the University of Toulouse (1913). Unable to return to Ereẓ Israel because of World War I, she went to Russia, where she taught Jewish refugee children. After the war she settled in Deganyah. However, having contracted tuberculosis during the war, she soon became too ill for farm life and had to spend the rest of her life in hospitals and sanatoria.

Raḥel is among the first modern Hebrew poets who wrote in a conversational style. Her knowledge of Hebrew was drawn from both the developing spoken idiom and the Bible. She was also influenced by the conversational school which then prevailed in Russian poetry (Blok, Akhmatova, and Yesenin). Her poems are characterized by a clear, uncomplicated lyrical line and a musicality, then rare in Hebrew poetry. Invariably short, her poems are elegiac and nostalgic in tone, many of them reflecting the pessimism of a young writer on the brink of death. These qualities made her writings very popular with younger Hebrew readers and with the general public. Many of the poems, including the widely sung "*Kinneret*," have been put to music. Raḥel also translated Russian, Yiddish, and French poetry and wrote occasional pieces of criticism. Two volumes of her verse appeared in her lifetime: *Safiʾaḥ* ("Aftergrowth," 1927), *Mi-Neged* ("From Opposite," 1930), and one posthumously, *Nevo* (1932). These were collected in *Shirat Raḥel* ("The Poetry of Raḥel," 1935), the eighth edition (1961) of which also contains her other works as well as a biography by Bracha *Ḥabas and a bibliography of her poems and their translations. Uri Milstein edited a collection of Raḥel's poems, letters, and articles with a biographical essay (1985) and Z. Yafit published all of her poems accompanied by a biographical note (2000). An unknown short play written in Deganyah 1919/1920, in which Rahel depicts with a grain of irony the life of the pioneers and the gap between ideals and daily life, was discovered by Dana Olmert and published in the literary supplement of *Haaretz* (November 19, 2004). Rahel's poems have been translated into many languages and information is available at the ITHL website at www.ithl.org.il.

BIBLIOGRAPHY: Kressel, Leksikon, 1 (1965), 243–4; R. Wallenrod, *Literature of Modern Israel* (1956), 54–59; Goell, Bibliography, for list of her poetry translated into English. **ADD. BIBLIOGRAPHY:** R. Kritẓ, *Al Shirat Raḥel* (1969; 1987); idem, *Shirei Raḥel, Shirat Raḥel* (with biographical notes and bibliography, 2003); A. Bar, *Ha-Meshoreret mi-Kinneret: Sippurah shel Raḥel* (1993); M. Zur, "Rahel," in: Y. Bartal and Z. Zahor (eds.), *Ha-Aliyah ha-Sheniyah*, 3 (1998) 336–46; E. Zadik, *Aliyah la-Regel le-Kever Raḥel ha-Meshoreret: Semalim ve-Dat Ezraḥit ba-Ḥevrah ha-Yisraelit* (2000); R. Lapidus, "Between 'Reeds' and 'New Growths': On the Influence of Anna Akhmatova on the Poetry of Rahel," in: *Trumah*, 13 (2003), 227–37; Y. Peles, "*Kol Mah she-Raẓita la-Daʿat al Lev Koreʾa, Einayim Meshavʾot vi-Ydei Gaʿagu'im*," in: *Haaretz* (June 25, 2004).

[Ezra Spicehandler]

RAHV, PHILIP (1908–1973), U.S. editor and critic. Born in Russia and named Ivan Greenberg, Rahv (literally, teacher) came to the United States after living in Palestine. One of the founders of the *Partisan Review*, Rahv helped to turn the magazine into an anti-Stalinist organ. He was also known for his helping other writers find their audience. His later magazine was called *Modern Occasions*. His critical works include *Image and Idea* (1949), *Literature in America* (1957), and *Myth and the Powerhouse* (1965). His *Literature and the Sixth Sense* was published in 1969. Of note is his *Essays on Literature and Politics, 1932–1972*, edited by Arabel Porter and Andrew Dvosin (1978). He also edited anthologies of U.S., British, and Russian fiction. During the 1940s Rahv did much to revive interest in the works of Henry James.

RAILROADS. Jewish financiers played a considerable role in the construction of railroads in France and in Central and Eastern Europe from the 1830s until the beginning of the 20th century. These Jewish financiers were the only investors – besides the British – among the private bankers dominant in Europe until the second half of the 19th century (see also *Banking) who were prepared to risk their capital in the pioneer stage of railroad construction. In the second half of the 19th century, when large banking joint-stock firms sprang up and expanded, private banks were increasingly pressed into the background, and the share of private Jewish capital in railroad investment diminished accordingly. In the majority of European countries this tendency became linked to nationalization of the railroads when financial crises occurred in private railroad companies. The nationalization of Prussian railroads was organized on the financial side by Bismarck's adviser Gerson von *Bleichroeder. In the 19th-century era of "railroad fever" former *court Jews who had become private bankers with considerable funds took part in furthering the industrial revolution through their investments in railroad construction.

The *Rothschilds were urged by Nathan Mayer Rothschild soon after the opening of the first successful railroad in England (1825) to invest money on the continent in railroad construction. Salomon Rothschild of Vienna sent Professor F.X. Riepel from the Vienna Institute of Technology to England to study the new means of transportation with Rothschild's secretary, Leopold von Wertheimstein. Subsequently they proposed the construction (1829) of a first line to run straight through the Hapsburg Empire, connecting Vienna with Galicia and Trieste. The July Revolution postponed the execution of Rothschild's plans. It was only in 1836, after overcoming many obstacles (especially the rivalry of the Viennese banking houses of *Arnstein and *Eskeles) that he began construction of the northern line from Vienna to Bochnia, in Galicia. The railroad was only completed in 1858. The house of Rothschild sold the shares on the stock market mainly to small investors.

James Rothschild of Paris was encouraged to construct the local line between Paris and St. Germain (opened in 1837) by Emile *Pereire. Emile Pereire and his brother Isaac viewed the railroad as the salvation of the future, producing work for the masses, connecting nations, and conducive to world welfare and peace. The two brothers could later boast that through their efforts more than 6,000 miles (10,000 km.) of railroads had come into existence. In the 1840s they were the rivals of the Rothschilds in this field.

After the success of the Paris-St. Germain line, James Rothschild and the *Fould brothers (apostate Jews), were eager to receive the concession for the Paris-Versailles line. The government eventually approved two plans, so that Rothschild constructed his line on the left bank of the River Seine and the Foulds on the right bank. In 1839 the railroad was opened, and in 1840 the two companies merged. This did not diminish the rivalry between them and the Pereire brothers. James Rothschild also succeeded in obtaining the concession for the construction of a northern line connecting Paris with England and the industries of northern France. The financial means of the Rothschilds were thereby severely strained, but the line was at last opened in 1846.

Nathan Mayer Rothschild and his sons helped finance the state-constructed railroad network in Belgium in the years 1834 to 1843. The Antwerp-Ghent line was built by the first private railway company in Belgium formed by Leopold *Koenigswarter. The Rothschilds were the chief financiers of the world-spanning railroad politics of Leopold I. They also raised funds for building railroads in Italy, Spain, and Brazil.

The Pereire brothers were second only to the Rothschilds in the first stage of railroad network development on the continent until 1869. The first half of their organizational activity was spent on a substantial part of the French railroad network. While the Rothschilds constructed the "northern" line in the 1840s, the Pereires were responsible for the "southern" one. The 1848 revolution plunged the railroads into a severe crisis (the "southern" line, managed by Isaac Pereire, was also financially ruined). The Pereire brothers wished to overcome this crisis by diverting to plans for a "railroad bank," a bank that would solve all the current financial difficulties of the French economy. The Crédit Mobilier (1852) also was intended not only to finance railroad construction but also heavy industry. Pereire introduced a new type of railroad security, the 500-franc capital bond (*obligation*), paying 15 francs annual interest and issued at whatever the market would bring, generally between 300 and 400 francs. With interest guaranteed by the state these bonds were ideally suited to the investor of moderate means. They quickly replaced other types of railroad borrowing and greatly facilitated railroad finance.

In the first years of its establishment the Crédit Mobilier financed (through advance payments and increased circulation of bonds) the "southern" line, the "grand central," the French "eastern" line, and many others in their first years. Through its contribution the railroad network expanded from 2,000 miles (3,600 km.) in 1852 to 11,000 miles (18,000 km.) in 1870. The Pereire brothers did not neglect to finance railroad construction and industrial ventures abroad. They contributed to the predominance of French finance in the development of foreign railroads in the post-1850 decade: in Austria, where there was fierce competition between the Pereires and the Rothschilds, the Pereires founded the important Austrian State-Railroad Company, in conjunction with Sina, Arnstein, and Eskeles, while the Rothschilds were successful in buying the Lombard-Venetian and the Central Italian Railway (1856). In Spain there was lively rivalry between the Rothschilds, Pereires, and Jules Isaac *Mirès; and in Hungary they built the "Franz-Joseph" line (1857). The Crédit Mobilier also financed Swiss railroads.

The importance of railroads was grasped in Russia only after its defeat in the Crimean War. The Grande Société des Chemins de fer Russes (1857) had, besides the Pereires, other Jewish bankers as founders: Alexander *Stieglitz of St. Petersburg, S.A. Fraenkel of Warsaw, and the *Mendelssohns of Berlin. An important figure in Russian railroad construction in the 1860s and 1870s was Samuel *Polyakov. He built railroads of supreme importance for the Russian grain export trade, and also wrote on the political aspect of railroad construction. He and other Jewish entrepreneurs succeeded in attracting foreign capital (Leopold *Kronenberg, J.J. Sack, Gerson von Bleichroeder, Sulzbach Brothers, etc.) without which their plans would have been unattainable. Railroad construction by Jewish bankers in Russia created employment for numbers of Jews, who filled technical and administrative posts. The advent of the railroad brought many changes in Jewish economic and social life, described, for instance, in the poem *Shenei Yosef ben Shim'on* of J.L. *Gordon.

Bethel Henry *Strousberg started by working for English firms, and when he had accumulated enough capital, founded railway companies in Prussia and later in Hungary. He also acquired locomotive factories and rolling mills for rails, and subsequently coal mines. A careless venture into Romanian railroad construction ruined his enterprise. His bankruptcy influenced public opinion in favor of nationalization of railroad lines in Germany. It also revealed malpractices and bribery, which were given a prominent place in antisemitic propaganda.

Jewish bankers were large-scale investors in railroad construction outside Europe. Baron Maurice de *Hirsch bought, in 1869, the concession for railroad building in Turkey from the bankrupt International Land Credit Company. His connection by marriage with the Jewish banking enterprise Bischoffsheim and Goldschmidt aided him initially. In 1869 he began the first stage of extending the Austro-Hungarian lines southward. However, before beginning construction on the Oriental Railroad, he took steps to secure financial backing, and chose a new type of 3% government loan. "Turkish lottery bonds," which attracted small investors in France and Germany, were offered on the general market. Hirsch concluded his project in 1888.

At first Jewish financiers, mainly of German origin, acted as intermediaries between foreign finance and the United States. When the Civil War broke out in 1861, railway bonds, mainly distributed by Jewish bankers in Europe, served as a means of payment for munitions bought in Europe. The Speyer, Stern, and *Seligman New York banking houses all dealt in railway shares. A leading personality in late 19th and early 20th century American financing was Jacob H. *Schiff. In 1875 he became a member of the banking firm of Kuhn, Loeb & Company (a firm long engaged in railroad financing) which he eventually dominated. In 1897 he reorganized the Union Pacific Railroad, which was described in the period as being "battered, bankrupt and decrepit." According to financial authorities the Harriman-Schiff railway combination became the most powerful and most successful that America had ever known. Schiff was one of the first supporters and associates of James Hill, who, by building the Great Northern Railway, virtually became the founder of a vast empire in the northwest. His firm aided other railroads by financial operations until the end of World War I. Schlesinger-Trier in Berlin, together with other Jewish banks, imported the shares of the Canadian Pacific railroad and offered them on the Berlin stock market.

A position similar to that of Schiff in financing railway companies in the United States was held by Sir Ernest *Cassel in England. He had a share in developing Swedish, American, and Mexican railway companies. The Vickers and Central London Railway Company was connected with his name.

BIBLIOGRAPHY: K. Grunwald, in: YLBI, 12 (1967), 163–212; 14 (1969), 119–61; idem, *Tuerkenhirsch* (1966); R.E. Cameron, *France and the Economic Development of Europe, 1880–1914* (1961); E.C. Corti, *Rise of the House of Rothschild* (1928); idem, *Reign of the House of Rothschild* (1928); P.H. Emden, *Money Powers of Europe* (1937); J. Plenge, *Gruendung und Geschichte des Crédit Mobilier* (1903); AJYB, 23 (1921). **ADD. BIBLIOGRAPHY:** J.M. Landau, *The Hejaz Railway and the Muslim Pilgrimage* (1971).

[Michael Graetz]

RAIN (Heb. מָטָר, גֶּשֶׁם). The large number of quotations referring to rain in the biblical and talmudic sources may be attributed to the fact that rain is the most important climatic element for the agriculture of Israel, particularly in non-irrigated areas. In comparing these quotations with modern knowledge of rainfall in Israel it is evident that although part of the quotations are in the realm of folklore, many of them are valid and correspond to contemporarily measured data, although the descriptions of rain in the Bible and talmudic literature are mainly qualitative. This correspondence not only shows the keen observations of weather phenomena made in ancient times, but also indicates that during the last 3,000 years there were fluctuations but not fundamental changes in the climate of Israel. The importance of a normal rainfall regime, i.e., an appropriate seasonal distribution of rainfall, for the success of agricultural crops is clearly stated in the Bible on several occasions (Lev. 26:4; Deut. 28:12; Ezek. 34:26), sometimes with special emphasis on the first and last rains of the season (the *yoreh* and the *malkosh*) whose importance for agriculture is particularly great (Deut. 11:14; Jer. 5:24). The local nature of

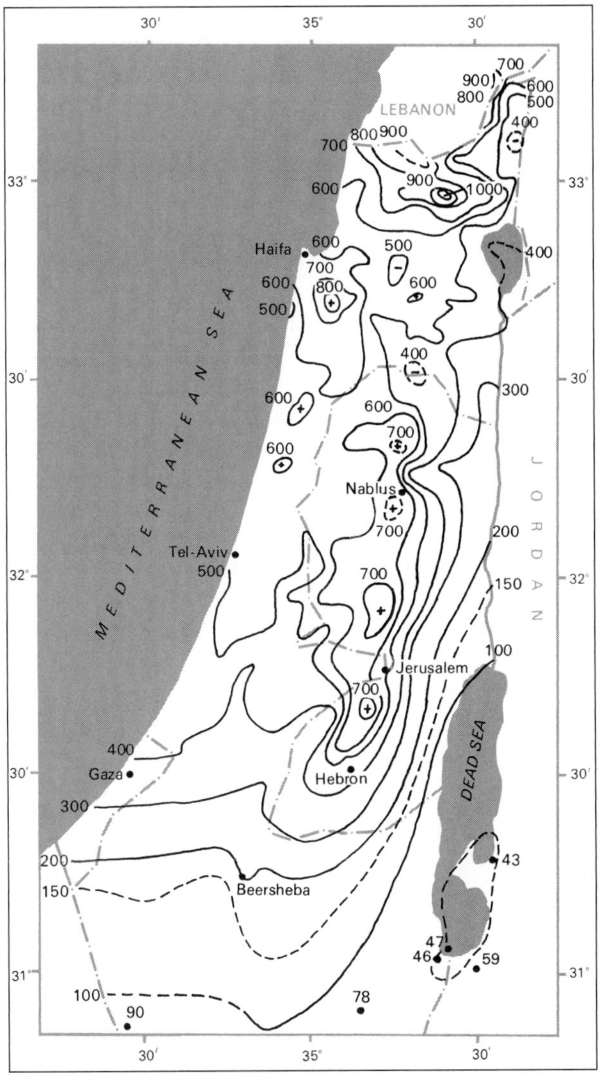

Map 1. Average annual rainfall, amounts in mm. (1921–1950).

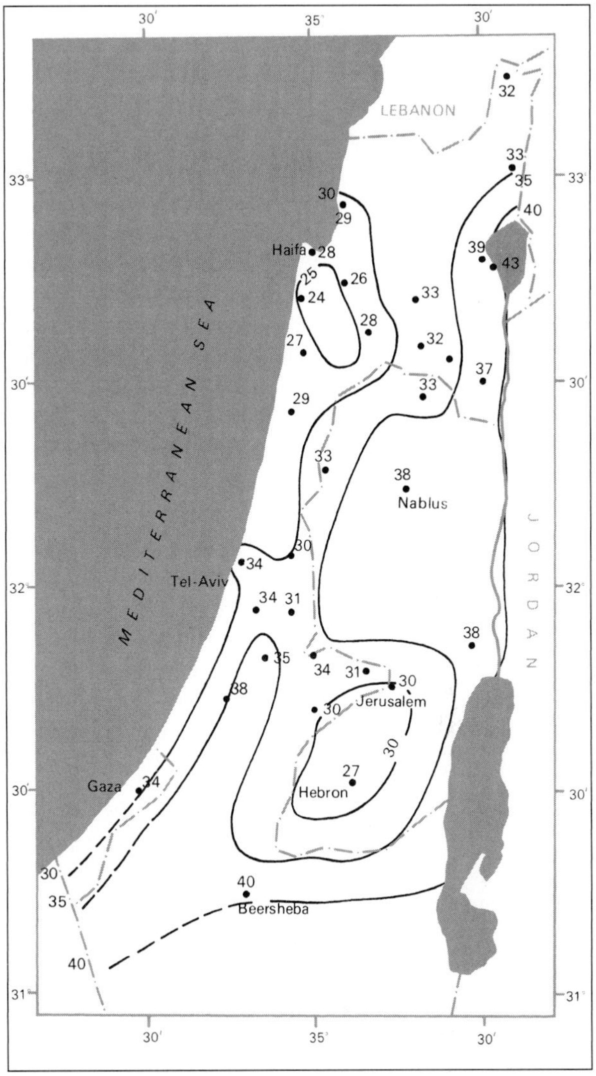

Map 2. Interannual variability of rainfall amount, as a percentage of the average for the period 1921/22–1950/51.

rainfall, expressed in Ereẓ Israel particularly at the beginning and end of the rainfall season, is also mentioned (Amos 4:7; cf. Ta'an. 6b). An impressive description of the results of droughts is available in Jeremiah 14:1–6. Late and strong rains at the beginning of June are as rare and notable nowadays as they were at the time of Samuel (1 Sam. 12:16–18). Similarly, three consecutive drought years in the region of Samaria are as rare and notable in the last 50 years of rainfall measurements (1931/32, 1932/33, and 1933/34) as they were at the time of Elijah and Ahab (1 Kings 18:1).

In the Talmud and Midrashim

Rain is referred to on many occasions in the Talmud and midrashic literature, particularly in tractate *Ta'anit* (Mishnah, Tosefta, and the Babylonian and Jerusalem Talmuds). In the Mishnah there is a quantitative definition of drought (Ta'an, 3:1). The following references are examples of keen observations of weather phenomena: R. Eleazar b. Perata paid attention to the variations from year to year in both amounts and times of rain occurrence (Ta'an. 19b). R. Johanan and R. Papa determined that thin clouds under thick clouds are a sign of rainfall (*ibid.* 9b); the ragged fragments of low clouds, known as scud (nautical term) or stratus fractus (meteorological term), often moving rapidly below rain clouds, indicate rainy weather (which is also the case today). On the same page in the Babylonian Talmud a weather forecast is given by R. Ulla, using the above-mentioned sign. Even a forecast for the rainfall of a whole year is given in the Jerusalem Talmud (Ta'an. 2:1, 65b). The dates of the beginning and end of the rainfall season in Israel also fit modern conditions (Ta'an. 1:1; Ned. 8:5; see also Yal., Num. 29). As for rain intensities, there are various expressions for slight, moderate, and heavy rains in the Bible (e.g., 1 Kings 18:45; Ezek. 13:11; 34:26; Ps. 68:10; Prov. 28:3; for the Mishnah see Ta'an. 3).

In Contemporary Israel

Israel is situated on the boundary of two different climatic regions: its northern half belongs to the southern part of a region having the so-called "Mediterranean" type of climate, whose main feature is that the greatest part of the annual rainfall occurs during the moderately cold winter months, while in the warm summer practically no rain falls; the southern half of Israel, the Negev, is situated on the northern boundary of a hot desert. Like every country with a Mediterranean climate Israel also lies near the limit of the cyclonic rains. Most of the rain-bearing cold lows (barometric depressions) arriving or forming in the eastern Mediterranean during the rainfall season are situated in the northeastern part of this sea (the "Cyprus Low"). Such a depression in the lower layers of the atmosphere is generally associated with a cold barometric trough in the higher layers (upper trough). The great majority of rainfall in Israel is due to this combination, even in the southern Negev – which is far away from the center of the Cyprus Low. Rains usually fall in Israel when cold air masses arrive mainly from Russia, the Balkans, or Turkey. These air masses are cold and dry, but in passing over the relatively much warmer waters of the Mediterranean they are heated in their lower layers, absorb much moisture, and reach Israel in a state of marked instability. Then, the land areas of Israel serve as a "trigger" to induce rainfall.

REGIONAL DISTRIBUTION OF RAINFALL. For the areal distribution of rainfall over Israel four rules can be stated:

(1) rainfall decreases with increasing distance from the sea, i.e., from west to east (continental effect);

(2) rainfall increases with increasing elevation (orographic effect);

(3) rainfall depends on exposure: of two localities at the same elevation, other conditions being equal, the windward slope facing ascending air (anabatic effect) receives more rainfall than the leeward slope with descending air (katabatic effect);

(4) rainfall decreases from north to south, i.e., with increasing distance from the Cyprus Low and decreasing distance from the planetary desert.

A good example for the first rule is the Valley of Jezreel where the average annual rainfall decreases gradually from west to east (650 mm.–400 mm.), and for the fourth rule – the Coastal Plain (650 mm.–200 mm., north to south). In each of these regions there are no significant differences in elevation. The second and third rules are clearly demonstrated on the Carmel range (600 mm.–850 mm.), where the isolines of rainfall (isohyets) are somewhat similar to those of elevation (isohypses), demonstrating the importance of the height factor. The same applies to two other compact and continuous ranges, namely, Upper Galilee, which is the highest and most northerly region in Israel and therefore the rainiest one (600 mm.–1000 mm.), and the Judean Hills (450 mm.–700 mm.); whereas the Samarian Hills and those of Lower Galilee are broken up and scattered, so that their isohyets do not take a markedly topographic course. The Samarian Hills, which generally become higher from north to south, demonstrate the prevalence of height over latitude when the latter factor is opposed to the former: this is the only region in Israel where rainfall increases from north to south (500 mm.–700 mm.). In the Jordan Rift Valley, on the other hand, the combined influence of southward progress and falling elevation is seen in the rapid decrease of the average annual rainfall from 570 mm. in the northern part of the Ḥuleh Area to 90 mm. at the northern edge of the Dead Sea. Further south, the Arabah between the Dead Sea and the Gulf of Eilat, forming the eastern border of the Negev, is the driest region in the country (25 mm.–50 mm.). Even the highest hills of the Negev do not enjoy 100 mm. while the northwestern Negev receives 200 mm. as an annual average.

SEASONAL DISTRIBUTION OR REGIMEN OF RAINFALL. In effect rains fall in Israel only during the period October through May, which is called "the rainfall season." The three central rainy months – the "winter" of the temperate climates, December, January, and February – contribute two-thirds to three-quarters of the annual rainfall in most regions of the country. The remaining 30% is distributed among the first and last months of the rainfall season: the "autumn" months October and November and the "spring" months March, April, and May, although in the Coastal Plain the percentage of rainfall in autumn is greater than in the hill region, while in the hills and other regions of the interior the percentage of spring rains is larger than near the coast. In addition to this west-east variation of the rainfall regime there is a north-south variation: while the northern half of the country has a Mediterranean rainfall regime with the characteristic steep increase from the beginning of the season toward the peak month and a rapid decrease from then to the end of the season, no specific month can be singled out in the central and southern Negev as having a marked maximum, and the curve typical for the Mediterranean regime becomes ill-defined. All the preceding facts are true with respect to a normal rainfall regime, i.e., a seasonal distribution of rainfall in which each month receives its average value. But in fact there are large variations from year to year in the seasonal rainfall, and particularly in its monthly distribution, so that it is difficult to find a season in which each of its months has even approximately received its average amount.

VARIABILITY OF RAINFALL. There are several statistical methods for measuring quantitatively the variations of annual rainfall from year to year. One measure, called Relative Variability, is defined as the percentage ratio between the mean deviation of individual annual totals from their average and the average; another measure, Relative Interannual Variability, relates, in percent, the mean value of absolute differences between successive annual totals to the average. The values of each of these measures of variability are relatively low (20%–26% RV; 25%–37% RIV) in regions with much rainfall (the hill region and Coastal Plain) and higher (≥ 27% RV; ≥ 38% RIV) in regions with less rainfall (the Jordan Valley and Negev). This property is of important consequence to non-irrigated areas in the eastern and southern parts of Israel in drought years. For charts, tables, and further details see bibliography.

See *Rain, Prayer for; *Israel, Land of (Climate).

BIBLIOGRAPHY: D. Ashbel, in: *Aklim Ereẓ Yisrael la-Azoreha* (1951); idem, in: *Leksikon Mikra'i*, 1 (1965), 94–103; N. Shalem, in: *Desert Research…* (1953), 153–64; N. Rosenan, in: IEJ, 5 (1955), 137–53; idem, in: UNESCO (ed.), *Symposium on Changes of Climate…* (1963), 67–73; idem, in: *Atlas of Israel* (1970), sheet IV/2; J. Katsnelson, in: *Archiv fuer Meteorologie, Geophysik und Bioklimatologie*, 13 (1963/65), 163–72; idem, in: *Ha-Enẓiklopedyah le-Ḥakla'ut*, 1 (1966), 27–62; idem, in: *Gishmei Ereẓ Yisrael ke-Gorem Yesod be-Meshek ha-Mayim shel ha-Areẓ* (1968/69).

[Jacob Katsnelson]

RAIN, PRAYER FOR (Heb. תְּפִלַּת גֶּשֶׁם, *Tefillat Geshem* (Ashkenazi); תִּקּוּן הַגֶּשֶׁם, *Tikkun ha-Geshem* (Sephardi)), prayers offered on various occasions, in which God is acknowledged as the power causing rain and the change of seasons, and which contain petitions for the fertility of the fields and for preservation from famine.

The principal prayer for rain is recited during the *Musaf* service on the eighth day of Sukkot (*Shemini Aẓeret) as part of the second benediction in the reader's repetition of the **Amidah* (Ashkenazi tradition). The Sephardim recite it before the Additional Service. The *piyyutim* of which this prayer is composed vary according to the different rites. Those in the Ashkenazi rite are by Eliezer *Kallir; the last of the six *piyyutim* invokes the remembrance of Abraham, Isaac, Jacob, Moses, Aaron, and the Twelve Tribes, and culminates in the invocation: "In their merit favor us with abundant water (rain)… For a blessing and not for a curse, for life and not for death, for plenty and not for famine. Amen." From this service on Shemini Aẓeret until that of the first day of Passover when the prayer for *dew is said, the sentence *mashiv ha-ru'aḥ u-morid ha-geshem* ("cause the wind to blow and the rain to fall") is included in every *Amidah* prayer at the beginning of the second benediction (Sh. Ar., OḤ 114). This insertion is called by the Mishnah (Ta'an. 1:1) *gevurot* (meaning "the Powers of God"). In traditional synagogues following the customs of Eastern Europe the *ḥazzan* officiates in the *kitel at the *Musaf* service when the prayer for rain is read as on the Day of Atonement, and recites the *Kaddish* before the *Musaf* service to a solemn melody. In Israel, the *Tefillat Geshem* is recited after the Torah scrolls have been returned to the ark and before the *Musaf* service so as to avoid an "interruption" in the statutory *Amidah*; however, the ḥasidic rite in Israel recites it in the reader's repetition of the *Amidah*. The *Tefillat Geshem* (like the prayer for dew) is part of the service in all Jewish rituals including the *Conservative and *Reform where it appears in a shortened version.

Another prayer for rain is the petition (*she'elah*) "and give dew and rain for a blessing" (*ve-ten tal u-matar li-verakhah*; in the Sephardi rite this is a different and longer petition) inserted in the ninth benediction of the *Amidah for weekdays. This petition is recited only from a date two weeks or more after the *Tefillat Geshem* on Shemini Aẓeret because the pilgrims in Temple times had to return from Jerusalem to their homes and traveling during a rainy season would have caused them hardship. Thus, in Ereẓ Israel the insertion is made from the evening prayer of the seventh of Ḥeshvan (Ta'an. 1:3; Ta'an. 4b); elsewhere, from the 60th day after the autumnal equinox, that is, from the fifth or sixth of December. This petition for rain appears in the ninth benediction (the "Blessing of the Years"), rather than in the second benediction of the *Amidah*, because the first three benedictions of the *Amidah* should contain the praise of God only and no petitions.

Prayers for rain are among the earliest liturgical texts and withholding of rain is regarded in the Bible as a punishment from God (cf. Deut. 11:11–17; I Kings 17:1). In the time of the Second Temple, the high priest recited a special prayer for rain on the *Day of Atonement (Yoma 53b) based upon Solomon's prayer (I Kings 8:35–36; II Chron. 7–13). During periods of drought, special prayers and supplications combined with fasting (see Fast *Days) were ordained (Ta'an. 1:4–3:9). These prayers entered the liturgy as it evolved in the time of the Mishnah and thereafter.

The dates for the special fasts and prayers for rain were fixed by the rabbis with a view to the climate and agricultural needs of Palestine; later rabbinic authorities decreed that wherever rain is beneficial during the summer, appropriate prayers for rain may be inserted, even during this season, in the 16th benediction of the *Amidah, Shome'a Tefillah* (Ta'an. 14b; Maim. Yad, Tefillah, 2:17; Sh. Ar., OḤ 117:2).

BIBLIOGRAPHY: Elbogen, Gottesdienst, 44–45, 214–5; Davidson, Oẓar, 1 (1924), 322 (no. 7091), 324 (no. 7128), 337 (no. 7419); 2 (1929), 209 (no. 91), 418 (no. 3466); 3 (1930), 528 (no. 267); *Union Prayer Book*, 1 (1927²), 268–9 (Reform); Silverman, Prayer, 210–1 (Conservative); E. Levy, *Yesodot ha-Tefillah* (1952²), 161–2; ET, 5 (1953), 65–79.

RAINBOW, "bow" (Heb. קֶשֶׁת), "in the cloud" (Gen. 9:13–14, 16; Ezek. 1:28). In the sequel to the Flood Story (Gen. 9:8–17) God sets His bow in the clouds as a sign to the people and as a reminder to Himself that no deluge shall again destroy the earth. According to the rabbis this rainbow was created during the eve of the Sabbath of Creation at twilight (Pes. 54a). Naḥmanides similarly explained that the rainbow had existed previously but was now designated to serve as this symbol (to Gen. 9:12). However, Ibn Ezra held that the bow was first created by God after the Flood (to Gen. 9:13). The bow symbolized that God s wrath had ceased since the end of the bow pointed downward just as the warrior lowers his bow on declaring peace (Naḥmanides to Gen. 9:12).

The rabbis held that the rainbow need not appear in the lifetime of a saint whose merit alone is sufficient to save the world from destruction (Ket. 77b and Rashi ad. loc.). Since the rainbow was the reflection of "the glory of the Lord" (Ezek. 1:28), it was considered injurious to gaze directly at it (Hag.

16a). It was reported that R. Joshua b. Levi declared that upon seeing the rainbow one should fall on his face as did Ezekiel (Ezek. 1:28). Nevertheless, in Ereẓ Israel, the rabbis disapproved of such action since it appeared as if the person was bowing down to the rainbow. They, however, approved of reciting a blessing upon the rainbow's appearance. The text of this blessing as it is today recited is "Blessed are Thou O Lord our God, King of the Universe, Who remembers the Covenant, is faithful to His Covenant, and keeps His promise" (Ber. 59a; Sh. Ar. OḤ 229:1). The blessing is to be recited even if a rainbow is seen twice within 30 days *Mishnah Berurah* to Sh. Ar., loc. cit.).

BIBLIOGRAPHY: Idelsohn, Liturgy, 126, note j; ET, 4 (1952), 358.

RAINER, LUISE (1910 –), German actress. Born in Dusseldorf, Germany, into a prosperous Jewish family, Rainer began her career in 1928. She later joined Max Reinhardt's company in Vienna, Austria. As part of his company, Rainer became a popular stage actress in Berlin and Vienna in the early 1930s, appearing in such plays as *Saint Joan* and *Six Characters in Search of an Author.* In 1935 she went to Hollywood and became famous for her performance in the films *Escapade* (1935); *The Great Ziegfeld* (Oscar for Best Actress, 1936); and *The Good Earth* (Oscar for Best Actress, 1937). These were followed by less notable roles in *The Emperor's Candlesticks* (1937); *The Big City* (1937); *The Toy Wife* (1938); *The Great Waltz* (1938); *Dramatic School* (1938); and *Hostages* (1943). Ultimately disillusioned with the superficial quality of Hollywood and frustrated at not being able to attain the more substantial roles, Rainer retired from the screen in 1943. She made a brief comeback decades later when she starred in the Swiss TV movie *A Dancer* (1988) and appeared in the Hungarian film *The Gambler* (1997), based on the story by Dostoievsky; and the German film *Poem: I Set My Foot upon the Air and It Carried Me* (2003).

Amassing a string of "firsts" to her credit, Rainer was the first actor/actress to achieve the perfect Oscar track record of two nominations, two wins; she was the first to receive double Oscars consecutively; she was the first to obtain two Oscars before turning 30; she was the first (and as of 2005 the only) German actress to win an Academy Award; and she was the first actress to win an Academy Award for portraying a real-life person – Anna Held in the biopic *The Great Ziegfeld.*

Her first role on the English stage was in *Behold the Bride* (London, 1939) and, on the New York stage, *A Kiss for Cinderella* (1942), followed by *The Lady from the Sea* (1950).

Clifford *Odets, the playwright, was her first husband; they were married from 1937 to 1940. Rainer wed publisher Robert Knittel in 1944, to whom she remained married until his death in 1989.

[Ruth Beloff (2nd ed.)]

RAISA, ROSA (née **Raisa Burchstein**; 1893–1963), dramatic soprano. Born in Bialystok, Poland, Raisa fled from there following the 1907 pogroms and settled on Capri. She studied at the Conservatorium of Naples with Barbara Marchisio, the famous 19th-century "bel canto" contralto. Conductor Cleofonte Campanim, the director of the Chicago Opera, contracted the 20-year-old Raisa for a debut in Parma's Teatro Regio in Verdi's first opera, *Oberto, Conte di San Bonifacio,* inaugurating a special festival of operas commemorating the hundredth anniversary of Verdi's birth. Her immediate success prompted him to take Raisa to the United States for her North America debut. Her first professional seasons witnessed debuts at London's Covent Garden singing Aida opposite Enrico Caruso as well as appearances in Paris, at the Rome Opera, and La Scala, Milan.

Raisa spent the major part of her career with the Chicago Opera as principal dramatic soprano from 1913 to 1937. Her best known roles were as Aida, Gioconda, Norma, Santuzza, Maliella in *Jewels of the Madonna* and Rachel in *La Juive.* She also appeared on the stages of South America (Buenos Aires, Montevideo, Rio do Janeiro, and Sao Paulo) and Mexico. Arturo Toscanini, whose admiration for her voice and art, led him to name her in 1916 the "Tamagno of dramatic sopranos," brought her back to La Scala (1924–1926) and cast her in the world premieres of Boito's posthumous *Nerone* and Puccini's posthumous *Turandot.* Raisa sang numberous concerts throughout the United States with her husband, the Italian baritone, Giacomo Rimini. Her programs often included Russian and Yiddish art and folk songs. She made numerous appearances for Jewish charities and causes. Upon her retirement in 1938 she and Rimini opened a voice school in Chicago.

Raisa was noted for her large and richly colored voice with its brilliant upper register, the technical control and ease of her delivery, as well as the emotionalism, sincerity, and beauty of her stage portrayals.

[Charles B. Mintzer]

RAISIN, JACOB ZALMAN (1877–1946), rabbi and writer. After emigrating from Poland to the United States, he served as a Reform rabbi in Charleston, South Carolina, for many years (1915–44).

An author of Hebrew poems and articles on English literature in Hebrew, his books – in English – include *Sect, Creed and Custom in Judaism* (1907), *Centennial Booklet Commemorating the Introduction of Reform Judaism in America* (1925), and the posthumously published *Gentile Reactions to Jewish Ideals* (1953). His volume *The Haskalah Movement in Russia* (1913) is still an important contribution to the literature of Haskalah.

BIBLIOGRAPHY: M. Raisin, *Mi-Sefer Ḥayyai* (1956), 117–20; Lefkowitz, in: *Central Conference of American Rabbis Yearbook,* 56 (1946), 267–8.

[Eisig Silberschlag]

RAISIN, MAX (1881–1957), rabbi and author, the younger brother of Jacob *Raisin. Born in Poland, he arrived in the United States as a boy of 12. He was ordained as rabbi at the Hebrew Union College in Cincinnati in 1903. He served as rabbi of Congregation B'nai Jeshurun of Paterson, New Jersey (1921–53).

A prolific writer in Hebrew, English, and Yiddish, Raisin dealt with contemporary problems, with the history of the Reform movement, and with Hebrew literature, on both a popular and a scholarly level. His books included: *Mordecai Manuel Noah: Zionist, Author and Statesman* (1905); *John Milton* (1924); *Israel in America* (1947); and *A History of the Jews in Modern Times* (1919) which was published as a supplement to *Graetz's *History of the Jews*. An ardent Zionist when Zionism was unpopular in the Reform movement, his views were influenced by *Aḥad Ha-Am. A number of his works were autobiographical: *Dappim mi-Pinkaso shel Rabbi* (1941); *Out of My Life* (1956); and *Great Jews I have Known* (1959).

BIBLIOGRAPHY: Morgenstern, in: Central Conference of American Rabbis, *Yearbook*, 67 (1957), 154f.; Kressel, Leksikon, 2 (1967), 861f.

[Eisig Silberschlag]

RAISMAN, SIR (Abraham) JEREMY (1892–1978), British economist and banker. Born in Leeds, in 1916 he entered the Indian Civil Service, first in Bihar and Orissa, then with the customs department in Bombay and Calcutta, and as commissioner for income tax in the Punjab and the Northwest Frontier Province. In 1931 he joined India's central government as joint secretary in the Commerce Department. In 1938 he was appointed secretary to the Finance Department, and from 1939 to 1945 served as finance member of the government of India. In 1944 he led India's delegation to the International Monetary Conference at Bretton Woods (New Hampshire) which resulted in the formation of the International Monetary Fund and the International Bank for Reconstruction and Development. In 1939 he was knighted, and in 1945 resigned from service in India, where he had been helpful to many Jewish refugees from Europe. After his retirement he served as an adviser to several newly independent countries including Pakistan, Rhodesia, Nigeria, and East African countries.

[Joachim O. Ronall]

RAISZ, ERWIN J. (1893–1968), U.S. geographer and authority on cartography. Raisz was born in Hungary, where he studied architecture and engineering. He settled in New York City in 1923 and studied geology at Columbia University. From 1925 to 1931 he was an instructor in this field, but during this period turned his attention to geography and cartography. He instituted Columbia's first course in cartography. From 1931 to 1950 he was a lecturer at the Institute of Geographical Exploration at Harvard. In 1945 he founded the cartography group of the Association of American Geographers and was its chairman until 1952.

Raisz was the author of *General Cartography* (1938); the *Atlas of Global Geography* (1944); *Mapping the World* (1956); *Principles of Cartography* (1962); and *Atlas of Florida* (1964).

BIBLIOGRAPHY: *New York Times* (Dec. 5, 1968).

RAJAK, TESSA (1946–), British historian of Hellenistic and Roman-era Judaism. Born in London and educated at Oxford, Rajak became professor of ancient history at the University of Reading, a leading historian of the cultural history of the Jews in the Hellenistic and Roman periods. She is particularly known for her work on *Josephus, and is the author of *Josephus: The Historian and His Society* (1982) as well as *The Jewish Dialogue With Greece and Rome: Studies in Cultural and Social Interaction* (2000) and other works. She was the editor of *The Journal of Jewish Studies*.

[William D. Rubinstein (2nd ed.)]

RAJPURKAR, JOSEPH EZEKIEL (1834–1905), scholar of the *Bene Israel community in Bombay. After studying at the Free Assembly School, he became a teacher in the David Sassoon Benevolent Institution, Bombay, in 1856 and after five years its headmaster, a post which he occupied for 40 years. In 1871 he was appointed Hebrew examiner at the University of Bombay, which elected him a fellow in 1879. A master of Hebrew as well as of Marathi, the vernacular of Bombay, he translated over 20 works of the Hebrew liturgy and many English works of Jewish interest into Marathi.

His translations of Hebrew liturgical works include the Daily Prayer Book (1889, 1924), the *maḥzor, piyyutim*, and *seliḥot*. In 1887 he published *Kuttonet Yosef* – a handbook of Hebrew abbreviations, a Hebrew grammar in Marathi, a Hebrew primer for children, and prayers for various occasions.

BIBLIOGRAPHY: H.S. Kehimkar, *History of the Bene Israel of India* (1937); *The Israelite*, 9 (1925), 97ff.; A. Yaari, *Ha-Defus ha-Ivri be-Arẓot ha-Mizraḥ*, 2 (1940), 54n, 73–79, 82. **ADD. BIBLIOGRAPHY:** S.B. Isenberg, *India's Bene Israel. A Comprehensive Inquiry and Source Book* (1988

[Walter Joseph Fischel]

RÁKOSI, MÁTYÁS (1892–1971), Hungarian Communist dictator. Born in Ada (then Hungary), Rákosi was the son of a small shopkeeper. He completed his studies at the Budapest Oriental Academy and after working as a bank clerk in Budapest and Hamburg, went to England where he became active in the socialist movement. During World War I he fought in the Austro-Hungarian army until 1915 when he was taken prisoner by the Russians. Following the October Revolution of 1917, Rákosi joined the Red Army and the Communist Party and returned to Hungary with Béla *Kun. He was made deputy commissioner of trade in Kun's Hungarian soviet republic (1919) and with the suppression of the regime in the same year, fled to the Soviet Union. He returned to Hungary secretly in 1924 to organize the illegal Communist Party, and was arrested and sentenced to death. Following the intervention of leading intellectuals abroad such as Romain Rolland his sentence was commuted to life imprisonment. In 1940 he was released and settled in the Soviet Union where he became the leading figure and propagandist among the Hungarian exiles in Moscow.

Rákosi returned to Hungary in 1944, and reorganized the Hungarian Communist Party. Between 1945 and 1948 he served as deputy leader of a coalition government, but step by step he removed the other parties from political life and assumed dictatorial powers. From 1949 he removed all traces of the former regime, among them leaders of the Catholic Church, Social Democrats, and even Communists and secret police chiefs. Rákosi conducted his policy in strict conformity with the Stalinist line. After Stalin's death (1953) he was summoned to Moscow and severely criticized for the failure of his economic policy. He resigned but was recalled to the premiership in the following year and remained in power until the summer of 1956, shortly before the outbreak of the Hungarian revolution. Once again, he was obliged to flee to the Soviet Union but after the rebellion's suppression did not return to Hungary until shortly before his death. Rákosi did not take any interest in Jewish affairs and tried to hide his Jewish origins. His policy of trials against Zionists, the confiscation of private enterprises, and the transfer of populations from the large cities caused great suffering to many Jews.

BIBLIOGRAPHY: M.M. Drachkovits and B. Lazitch (eds.), *The Comintern: Historical Highlights* (1966); T. Aczél and M. Méray, *The Revolt of the Mind* (1959).

[Baruch Yaron]

RAKOUS, VOJTĚCH (pseudonym of **Vojtěch Oesterreicher**; 1862–1935), Czech writer. Born in Velký Brázdim, Bohemia, Rakous was a prominent representative of the Czech-Jewish assimilation movement in literature. He published some short stories in a serious vein, such as Doma ("At Home," 1897) and *Na rozcestí* ("At the Crossroads," 1914). Nevertheless, he is best remembered as a writer with a sense of comedy or the tragicomic, as in the sketch *Strýc Václav* ("Uncle Wenceslas"). In the four volumes of humorous tales entitled *Vojkovičtí a přespolní* ("Those from Vojkovice and Those from Elsewhere," 1910), Rakous vividly portrayed Jewish life in the Czech villages. The volume featuring the *schlemiel*, Modche, and his domineering wife, Rézi, became a popular classic and was later dramatized and filmed. The stories also shed important light on Jewish-Christian relations in Czech villages at the turn of the 19th century. *Výbor ze spisů* 1–3 ("Selected Works") appeared in 1925, other editions continuously.

BIBLIOGRAPHY: O. Donath, *Židé a židovství v české literatuře* (1930); F. Kafka, in: *Židovská ročenka* (1967/68), 106–15. **ADD. BIBLIOGRAPHY:** *Českožidovští spisovatelé v literatuře 20. století* (2000); H. Krejčová, "Příběhy plné vášní a rámusu," in: *Židovská ročenka* (1990–91), 35–39; *Lexikon české literatury*, 3/11 (2000); A. Mikulášek et al., *Literatura s hvězdou Davidovou*, 1 (1998); M. Otruba, "Předmluva," in: V. Rakous, *Vojkovičtí a přespolní* (1986); *Slovník českých spisovatelů* (2000).

[Avigdor Dagan /Milos Pojar (2nd ed.)]

RAKOVSKY, PUAH (1865–1955), feminist activist, Zionist, educator, and translator. Born in Bialystok into a middle-class religiously observant family, Rakovsky was educated by private tutors in Bible, Hebrew, and rabbinics, in addition to receiving a general education in Polish schools. Fluent in Russian, Polish, German, French, Hebrew, and Yiddish, Rakovsky made her debut as a translator at 15, when her translation of a Russian poem by Shimon Frug was published in the Hebrew journal *Ha-Ẓefirah*. Rakovsky had a son and a daughter in her unhappy first marriage to Shimon Machlin, arranged when she was 16. She ultimately left her husband to be trained as a teacher, and they were divorced while she was teaching Hebrew in a Jewish girls' school in Lomza, Poland. Two years later, under the auspices of Bnei Moshe, the cultural arm of the Zionist movement *Ḥibbat Zion, Rakovsky founded "Yehudiah," a Jewish school for girls in Warsaw, which was pathbreaking in the prominence given to Hebrew in its curriculum. Rakovsky married twice more; her second husband, Abraham Krislavin, died of pleurisy after six years of marriage. Rakovsky and her third husband, Mordechai Birnbaum (1875–1934), whom she married in 1901, had a daughter.

World War I drove Rakovsky to close her school and flee Warsaw. Now drawn to Socialist Zionism, Rakovsky joined the Ze'irei Zion faction, and she became well-known as a Zionist and feminist advocate. Her first pamphlet, *Di Yiddishe Froy* ("The Jewish Woman"), published by Bnos Tsyion ("Daughters of Zion"), called for Jewish women's greater activism in Zionist affairs. In 1920, at the age of 55, Rakovsky emigrated to Palestine, but remained there for only one year. Rakovsky attended the 1920 founding meeting of *WIZO and became the first secretary of its Palestinian branch. She also established a vocational school for girls in Jerusalem before returning to Warsaw.

Known for her mastery as a Hebrew writer, highly unusual for a Polish Jewish woman of her generation and social class, Rakovsky also strongly supported the Yiddish language; during the 1920s, she increasingly turned to Yiddish in her writing, publishing, and translations. As a leader of the Jewish Women's Association in Poland, she coedited the *Froyenshtim* ("Women's Voice"), a journal which gave women a forum for public commentary that the general Yiddish press denied them. In this publication, as well as in her second Yiddish pamphlet, *Di moderne froyen-bavegung* ("The Modern Women's Movement"), Rakovsky encouraged women to organize separately and independently for equal participation in Zionist and Jewish communal affairs.

In 1935, Rakovsky moved permanently to Palestine. Between 1940 and 1942, she wrote her memoirs, published in both Hebrew and Yiddish. In her autobiography, Rakovsky labeled herself a "Radical Jewish Woman," an appellation which accurately reflected the revolutionary nature of her break from the traditional heritage of her family, her devotion to Zionism, and her advocacy for women's equality in modern Jewish life.

BIBLIOGRAPHY: Puah Rakovsky, P.E. Hyman; trans. B. Harshav (ed.), *My Life as a Radical Jewish Woman: Memoirs of a Zionist Feminist in Poland*, (2002).

[Tracy Sivitz (2nd ed.)]

RALL, YISRAEL (1830–1893), Hebrew writer and translator. Born in Brody, Galicia, he became interested in the Haskalah and studied classical and European languages. He lived for many years in Odessa where he published a collection of translations from classical Latin poetry, *Shirei Romi* (1876), which established his reputation. After years of wandering in Western Europe he settled in Lemberg, where he founded the periodical *Shem ve-Yafet* (1887). He also published booklets in German and French in which he rebutted antisemitic libels. Rall contributed to **Ha-Meliẓ*, **Ha-Maggid*, and also to the German press.

BIBLIOGRAPHY: Lachower, Sifrut, 2 (1963), 171–6; Waxman, Literature, 3 (1960^2), 262.

[Yehuda Slutsky]

RAM, MOSHE (1895–1975), Israel hydrological engineer. Born in Tatarsk, Russia, Ram was educated at California and in Moscow. He went to Palestine in 1925, and worked on the Naharayim hydroelectric station. Ram was chief engineer of the Jewish Agency water resources bureau from 1936, and with the establishment of the State in 1948 he became director of the water utilization division of the Israel Ministry of Agriculture until 1960. He wrote several books, including *Surface Irrigation* (1964). He was one of the leading thinkers of Israel water planning.

[Bracha Rager (2nd ed.)]

RĀMA, AL-, Christian-Arab and Druze village in Upper Galilee, Israel, at the foot of Mt. Ha-Ari. Reported uninhabited and in ruins in 1729, the village thrived in the 20th century, and as in antiquity, is one of the principal olive-growing centers in the country. In the Israel War of *Independence, al-Rāma fell to Israel forces in October 1948. The number of inhabitants increased from about 1,100 in 1947 to 3,570 in 1968, with a majority of Christians (mostly Greek-Orthodox and Greek-Catholic), and about one-third Druze. In 1954 al-Rāma received municipal council status. In 2002 the population of al-Rāma was 7,280 in an area of 2.5 sq. mi. (6 sq. km.). Among the inhabitants, 51.5% were Christian, 29% Druze, and 18% Muslims. Income in the village was much lower than the national average.

[Efraim Orni / Shaked Gilboa (2nd ed.)]

RAMAH or **HA-RAMAH** or **HA-RAMATHAIM-ZOPHIM** (Heb. הָרָמָתַיִם־צוֹפִים, הָרָמָה, רָמָה; "height"), the designation of several places located on high ground (see also Ramoth).

(1) A town in the territory of Benjamin, mentioned together with Gibeon and Beeroth in Joshua 18:25 and with Gibeah on the main road north of Jerusalem in Judges 19:13, Isaiah 10:29, and Hosea 5:8. Baasha, king of Israel, tried to fortify the place against Judah, but Asa of Judah dismantled the fort and used the materials to strengthen Gebah and Mizpeh (I Kings 15:17ff.; II Chron. 16:1, 5–6). Jeremiah, following the tradition of the north, located the tomb of Rachel in Ramah (31:15). There the Babylonians concentrated the captives taken from Jerusalem before exiling them (Jer. 40:1). After the return from exile, the place was resettled by Judeans (Ezra 2:26; Neh. 7:30; 11:33). Later authors place it 6 mi. (c. 9 km.) north of Jerusalem (Eusebius, Onom. 144:14; Jerome, Hosea 5:8, and Zephaniah 1:15), a location corresponding to the village of al-Rām, which was a fief of the Holy Sepulcher in the Middle Ages.

(2) A town in the territory of Naphtali, mentioned together with Adamah and Hazor in Joshua 19:36. It is identified with Khirbet al-Jūl, near al-Rāma in the valley of Beth-Cherem in Galilee. In 1933 I. Ben-Zvi discovered a synagogue lintel with an Aramaic inscription there.

(3) A town in the territory of Asher (Josh. 19:29). Its identification with Rāmiya, southeast of Tyre, is controversial.

(4) The hometown of Samuel (I Sam. 1:1; as Ramathaim-Zophim) and possibly the residence of Deborah (Judg. 4:5). There Samuel judged Israel (I Sam. 7:17; 8:4) and was later buried (I Sam. 25:1; 28:3); his school of prophets was located in Naioth in Ramah (I Sam. 19:22–24). In the Septuagint, it is identified with ha-Ramatha or Arimathea, which is described in I Maccabees 11:34 as the headquarters of a Samaritan toparchy transferred to Judea in 145 B.C.E.; this place was the home town of Joseph, a Jerusalem councilor, in whose tomb Jesus was buried (Matt. 27:57, et al.). It was called Remphthis by Eusebius (Onom. 144:28) and is the present-day Rantis, northeast of Lydda. However, the identification of this site with Samuel's birthplace is controversial. Various scholars view that both names of Zuph on the border of the territories of Benjamin and Ephraim (I Sam. 1:1; 9:4).

BIBLIOGRAPHY: Abel, Geog, 2 (1938), 427; Abel and Ben-Zvi, in: JPOS, 13 (1933), 94ff.; Alt, in: PJB, 24 (1928), 70; Aharoni, Land, index.

[Michael Avi-Yonah]

RAMALLAH (Rām Allāh; al-Bīra), twin towns in the northern Judean Hills, 9 mi. (15 km.) N. of Jerusalem. While al-Bīra is supposed to stand on the site of biblical *Beeroth, Ramallah is generally identified with *Ramah. The twin towns occupy a strategic position at 2,854 ft. (870 m.) above sea level, where the Judean upfold broadens, and at a crossroads. During the British Mandate, Ramallah was preponderantly Christian-Arab with 4,710 Christian and 650 Muslim inhabitants in 1946. The proportion was reversed in al-Bīra, then a village with 2,100 Muslims and 150 Christians. Because of Ramallah's elevation, the authorities chose it as the site for the country broadcasting transmitters. The clear, brisk climate encouraged the development of the town as a summer resort, which gained impetus under Jordanian rule when wealthy citizens built summer houses there and tourists came from other Arab countries to spend the summer. In the *Six-Day War, Ramallah was taken by Israeli forces. The census taken by the Israeli authorities in the fall of 1967 revealed that the population of both towns had greatly increased since 1948, mainly through the opening of refugee camps, while the relative strength of the Christian communities had diminished. Ramallah in 1967 had 12,134 inhabitants, of whom 6,966 (57.4%) were Christians, while al-Bīra, with a population of 13,037, was larger than Ramallah and was almost exclusively Muslim. Following the Oslo Agreements and the transfer of the city to the Palestinians, the Palestinian Authority located its government institutions there. Against a background of undiminished terrorism, Yasser *Arafat was confined to his headquarter compound in the city (the Muqata) by Israeli forces from 2003 until his death in 2004, and was also buried there. According to the Palestinian Bureau of Statistics, in 1997 the population of Ramallah was 18,017 and that of Al-Bīra was 27,972.

[Efraim Orni / Shaked Gilboa (2nd ed.)]

RAMAT DAVID (Heb. רָמַת דָּוִד), kibbutz in northern Israel, near Nahalal, affiliated with Iḥud ha-Kevuẓot veha-Kibbutzim, founded in 1926 by two groups of Third Aliyah pioneers, "Ayanot" and "Ha-Sharon," from Eastern Europe. The kibbutz economy was based on field and fodder crops and dairy cattle. The kibbutz also housed one of the biggest disco clubs in the north of the country, called Vertigo. The village is named after David *Lloyd George who was prime minister of the British War Cabinet which issued the *Balfour Declaration. In 2002 its population was 238.

[Efram Orni / Shaked Gilboa (2nd ed.)]

RAMAT GAN (Heb. רָמַת גַּן; "Garden Height"), city in central Israel adjoining Tel Aviv. In 1914, 20 settlers from Eastern Europe formed a group called Ir-Gannim ("garden city"); they envisaged a garden suburb where they could enjoy a country-like life without having to relinquish the amenities of a city. The group resolved to carry out the building without the use of any hired labor and forbade the establishment of factories within the settlement's boundaries. The project became feasible only in December 1921. The proximity of Jaffa and expanding Tel Aviv engendered Ramat Gan's quick growth. In 1922 it had 140 inhabitants, but in 1926 already rated municipal council status with A. *Krinitzi as its first mayor. In the 1930s relatively large industrial enterprises, instead of choosing Tel Aviv, preferred to establish themselves in Ramat Gan where land prices were cheaper. In 1939, the community had 5,000 inhabitants and grew vigorously. In 1948 its population was 19,000. Care was taken to preserve the design of the town. Avenues of trees were planted and many public gardens were laid out, utilizing mainly the slopes of the low sandstone hills. In 1948 the municipal area covered about 3 sq. mi. (7.92 sq. km.). After 1948 Ramat Gan's growth accelerated and city status was obtained in 1950. Population growth was most rapid in the early 1950s. In 1953 there were 42,000 inhabitants, in 1958, 71,500, and by 1963, 95,800. In 1961 *Bar-Ilan University and the Tel ha-Shomer hospital were affiliated to Ramat Gan. By 1968 the city's population totaled 106,800. In 2002 it was 126,000, making it the 11th largest city in Israel.

Bordering on Tel Aviv in the west and north, on Givatayim in the southwest, on Bene-Berak in the east and on Ramat ha-Sharon in the northeast, Ramat Gan, whose municipal area expanded to 4.7 sq. mi (12.2 sq. km.) in 2004, occupies a central position in the country's largest conurbation. The city has been one of Israel's foremost manufacturing centers (food preserves, chocolate, cigarettes, textile spinning, weaving, dyeing and finishing, metals, building materials, and wood). In 1968 the Israel Diamond Bourse was opened in Ramat Gan. Hotels and recreation sites constituted another branch of the city's economy. The largest of the city's network of gardens was the 494 acre (200 ha.) national park to the south with tropical tree species, a rose garden, and a large artificial lake with boating facilities. A quarter of the city's area is green. Ramat Gan has the country's largest sport stadium with a capacity of 60,000 and Israel's most important sports center. The Safari, a large zoo without bars, is also located in Ramat Gan, as is the *Maccabiah Village and many other installations and children's playgrounds belong to its municipal area. It has many cultural institutions (municipal library, museum, and lecture halls), and a chamber orchestra as well as the Beit-Zvi acting school and the Shenkar School of Engineering and Design.

WEBSITE: www.ramat-gan.muni.il.

[Efraim Orni / Shaked Gilboa (2nd ed.)]

RAMAT HA-GOLAN (Heb. רָמַת הַגּוֹלָן; the "Golan Heights" or "Plateau"), comprises practically the whole Golan region of N. Transjordan which forms the western section of the *Bashan. Ramat ha-Golan borders on the upper Jordan Rift Valley and Lake Kinneret in the west, on the Yarmuk Valley in the south, on the Ruqqād stream in the east, and on the Hermon Massif in the north. In the last stage of the Six-Day War (1967), nearly the entire region was occupied by the Israeli army and came under Israeli administration. Together with the southeast portion of Mount Hermon – also occupied by Israeli forces – it measures about 480 sq. mi. (1,250 sq. km.). The origin of the name Golan is not clear; A.J. Brawer proposes that it is derived from *golah* ("exile") as the biblical "Golan in Bashan" (Deut. 4:43; I Chron. 6:56) was a city of refuge for expatriates (see below History and Archaeology).

Three subregions are distinguished: the southern Golan, a plain area with land suitable for farming, characterized by a hot, dry climate and an average annual rainfall of 10 in. (250 mm.); the central Golan, moderate slope with altitudes of up to 3,000 ft. (700 m.), with rocky lands and deep gulleys; and the northern Golan, rising to altitudes of 2,000–3,000 ft. (600–900 m.), with a number of hilltops attaining 3,600–4,040 ft. (1,100–1,226 m.). This last area is characterized by low temperatures and large amounts of rain (about 40 in. or 1,000 mm. a year). The dominant characteristics of the Golan's topography were created through volcanism, which continued into the Middle Pleistocene period, i.e., until approximately 500,000 years ago, with lava pouring out from fissures and craters and covering the plateau with a continuous layer of basalt and strings of volcanic cones, the largest being Tel Avital (Tell Abu al-Nadā', 1,204 m.). The plateau rises gently from south to north and dominates the rift valley to the west and south with abrupt escarpments. Stream courses, mainly in the southern section, have cut deep ravines, laid bare light-colored chalks, marls, and limestones underneath the black basalt, and separated small portions of the plateau from each other. Soils are mostly dark, fertile, and deep grumusols and are covered with basalt boulders in the north.

The Lower Golan has been farming country throughout most of its historic past, with grain crops as the principal branch; the ample rainfall and resulting stronger erosion make the Upper Golan a region of brush, forest, and pastures, rather than tilled fields, and biblical expressions such as the "cows" or "cattle of Bashan" (Amos 4:1; Ezek. 39:18) and "oaks of Bashan" (Isa. 2:13; Ezek. 27:6) seem to refer to this section. Deforestation by man has left only stunted remnants of ancient forests in the northern Golan; flocks of sheep and herds of cattle, however, continued to be the region's economic mainstay until the recent past.

[Efraim Orni]

History and Archaeology

The name "Golan" is first mentioned in the Bible as a settlement in the region of the Bashan (Deut. 4:43; Josh. 20:8), within the territory allocated to the tribe of Manasseh (Deut.4:43). It is referred to as a free city (Josh. 20:8) and later as a Levitical city (I Chron.6:7), thought to be Sahem ed-Djolan (Eusebius, *Onom.* 64:7), beyond the eastern border formed by the river Rukkad. The name of the entire region appears to have derived from this site. In the Persian period the region was included in the satrapy of *Karnaim, which encompassed the Golan and the *Bashan.

In the early Hellenistic period, the Golan formed a separate district under the name of Gaulanitis. The writings of *Josephus help to trace the history of the entire area (Antiq. 4:5, 3; 8: 2, 3; 13:15, 4; Wars 2:20, 6; 3:3, 1–5; 3:10, 10; 4:1,1). Early in the reign of the Hasmonean Alexander Jannaeus, the cities of Golan, Gamala and Seleucia were conquered (83–81 B.C.E., and the Golan was annexed to the Hasmonean kingdom (Antiq. 16:9, 2). After the conquest of Palestine by Pompey (63 B.C.E.) the Golan was populated by the *Itureans, but when Herod the Great came to the throne it came into his possession (23 B.C.E.). It remained part of his descendants' kingdom until the death of Agrippa II. It was then annexed to the Roman Provincia Judaea and later in the Roman period it formed part of Palaestina Secunda. The more important large villages were Seleucia, Sogane, Bethsaida, and Gamla, and these were fortified by Josephus who had been proclaimed Jewish rebel commander of the Galilee (Wars 2:20, 6). The revolt was crushed by the Romans in 67 C.E. During the Roman and Byzantine periods the Gaulanitis was a prosperous rural area but devoid of large towns. At the end of the 5th century C.E., the emperor Anastasius made use of the Ghassanids, a Monophysite Christian Arab tribe from the Yemen that had moved into Syria, as frontier guards, particularly against the Lakhimids who were nomads in the Upper Euphrates. The Golan in the sixth century was populated by two groups: a well-established community of Jews and the Christian Ghassanids. Following the Arab invasion of 636 C.E., the region was slowly depopulated. The Mamluk and Ottoman authorities initiated enforced resettlement.

L. Oliphant was one of the first to record the archaeological sites in the Golan during his visits to the region between 1879 and 1886. At Khirbat Kānif Oliphant found the remains of a synagogue with a lintel bearing an incomplete Aramaic inscription: "… remembered be for good Yose son of Ḥalfu son of Ḥana[n]."

A large number of sites were recorded and described by G. Schumacher following his work in the area between 1883 and 1885, and until 1914. Schumacher also prepared the first proper map of the region. He investigated at least a dozen sites with stones bearing Jewish symbols, such as the seven-branched *menorah* and other motifs, and attributed these to the remains of ancient synagogues. These sites include Fīq, Umm al-Qanāṭir, Khan-Bandaq, Lawiyya, al-Dikkī (Dikke), al-Rafīd, al-Aḥmadiyya, al-Burayka – most of them in southwestern Golan near the shores of the Sea of Galilee. In the village of Fīq a basalt column was found incised with a seven-branched *menorah* and under it an Aramaic inscription: "I, Judah, the cantor."

Since 1967 numerous surveys and excavations have been carried out in the region, notably a general survey of the region by S. Gutman and C. Epstein in 1967–1968, a more methodical general survey by D. Urman in 1968–1972, surveys of Chalcolithic sites and of dolmen fields by C. Epstein in 1973–2000, various investigations by Z. Maoz since 1977, a study of settlements and their landscapes by C. Dauphin in 1978–1988, and a study of "Iturean" settlements by M. Hartal since 1983. Since the late 1970s surveys and excavations have been undertaken on Mount Hermon by S. Dar.

Prehistoric evidence (Upper Paleolithic) comes mostly from Berkehat Ram with flints and basalt implements, and from Biq'at Kuneitra. A site from the southern Golan, Mjhiyyeh, has been dated to the Pre-Pottery Neolithic period. At least 30 Chalcolithic unwalled settlements from the first half of the 4th millennium B.C.E. have been investigated. Houses were broad rooms built in chain formation. The settlers engaged in agriculture and stock breeding and placed basalt pillar-shaped house gods in their houses and courtyards. Their material culture was quite distinctive. The Early Bronze I is barely represented in the Golan, but more than 40 sites from the Early Bronze Age II have been identified, including settlements (e.g., Gamla) and enclosures (e.g., Mitham Leviah). The enigmatic megalithic structure at Rujm el-Hiri with concentric circles and a tumulus at its center is also dated to this period.

Early Bronze Age IV settlements have only been identified in the southern Golan. Elsewhere there are very extensive fields of dolmens and tumuli/cairns. The earliest material found in the dolmens is dated to the Early Bronze IV. However, it is likely that these finds represent the final use of these structures, which may date back to the Early Bronze II. In the Middle Bronze Age IIB, settlement was concentrated mainly in the southern and northern parts of the region. Many of the sites controlled roads and were probably built for strategic purposes. Fewer settlements of the Late Bronze Age were found. Settlement was renewed in the Iron Age I, especially above earlier Middle Bronze II sites. A lion's head carved on an orthostat, discovered not *in situ*, was dated on stylistic grounds to the 9th century B.C.E. It was probably originally placed at the entrance of a citadel of a local ruler. Numerous Iron Age II sites are known from the Golan and particularly at sites along the shores of the Sea of Galilee (see *En-Gev; Tel Hadar).

From the Hellenistic period there are agricultural villages and fortified towers. Two sites (Ḥorvat Zemel and Ḥorvat Namra) are identified as "Iturean" on the basis of the discovery of a distinctive pottery ("Golan Ware") within these settlements. Early Roman sites were scattered throughout the Golan. One major site was Gamla which fell to the Romans in 67 C.E. Numerous sites from the Late Roman period are known (2nd–early 4th centuries C.E.), with exceptional remains at the site identified as Hippos (Sussita) and Banias. Villages were built in the Golan, many of which were of pagan character, judging by the discovery of statue fragments and altars. Roads were built criss-crossing the region, linking the land of Israel with Damascus.

The Byzantine period saw an enormous increase of sites in the Golan to close to one hundred. Numerous large villages are known but the region did not have towns or cities. A project led by C. Dauphin has traced the growth of four settlements (Kafr Naffakh, Na'aran, Farj, and Er-Ramthaniyyeh) between the Hellenistic and Ottoman periods, focusing particularly on the Byzantine period. Olive oil production (but not exclusively) was undertaken in the western parts of the Golan. Viticulture was also practiced. The agricultural landscapes surrounding the four above settlements were also investigated. Remains of numerous churches and synagogues have been found. An ongoing debate exists among scholars as to whether the ethnic divide between the Jewish and Christian populations in the Golan in this period was sharply defined or whether some or many of the settlements had mixed populations as well as to the extent of the Jewish-Christian element in the population between the 1st and 5th centuries C.E. Some agricultural villages were abandoned prior to the Umayyad period (7th century), but others survived, notably Kaẓrin, until the earthquake of 749 C.E.

[Shimon Gibson (2nd ed.)]

Modern Period

One of Syria's backward provinces, Golan entered modern history in the 1880s, when the Turkish authorities settled Circassians there to ward off Bedouin robbers. The regional center, *al-Qunaytira, came into being at that time. Shortly afterward, Jews made attempts to found settlements in the Golan, initially at Rumsaniyya, south of al-Qunaytira; then at Benei Yehudah east of Lake Kinneret; and finally, in 1908, in the Bet Ẓayyada (al-Buṭayḥa) Valley (a much larger enterprise, at Benei Binyamin and Jilīn, was undertaken with Baron E. de Rothschild's aid in the Bashan, further east). Prior to 1967, the Golan's population included Sunnite Muslims, as well as Circassians, Druze, Alawids (Nusayris), a small Christian minority, and others. In the 1950s and 1960s, the Syrians covered the Golan with a network of artillery positions and fortifications to harass Israeli settlements in Upper Galilee and the Lake Kinneret area, and geared the region's entire economy to military needs. In the last two days of the Six-Day War (June 9–10), almost the entire population took to flight together with the Syrian army, with the exception of the Druze who stayed on in six villages in the north (in the September 1967 census they numbered over 6,000). The remaining Druze villagers in the area quickly made contact with their kinsmen in Israel and developed friendly relations with the Israeli administration and their new Jewish neighbors.

The first initiative for new Jewish settlement in the region was taken in July 1967 by a group of Ha-Kibbutz ha-Me'uḥad, which founded Kibbutz Merom Golan. By 1970 the number of Golan settlements had increased to 12, including Ramat Banias (Senir; of Ha-Shomer ha-Ẓa'ir), Merom Golan and Ein Zivan (Ha-Kibbutz ha-Me'uḥad) in the north; Naḥal Geshur (Ha-Shomer ha-Ẓa'ir) in the center; Ramot Magshimim (moshav shittufi of Ha-Po'el ha-Mizrachi), Givat Yo'av (Tenu'at ha-Moshavim), Ne'ot Golan (moshav shittufi of Ha-Oved ha-Ẓiyyoni), El Al (Tenu'at ha-Moshavim), Mevo Ḥammah (Iḥud ha-Kibbutzim), Naḥal Golan, and Ramot (Tenu'at ha-Moshavim) in the south Hermon. In 1977 *Kaẓrin, an urban community, was established. Subsequently, other settlements were founded, bringing the total up to 33 at the beginning of the new millennium, with a total population of 37,000, including 18,300 Druze (see *Israel, State of, under Religious Life). After 1967, land reclamation was carried out on a large scale and the first storage ponds were installed to retain runoff and ease the problem of water shortage, which is serious despite the relatively ample rainfall. The main economic branches in the area are agriculture, tourism, and industry. Farming is based on citrus groves, orchards, vineyards, and vegetables crops. Tourism includes 1,000 guest rooms and other tourist attractions. Ramat ha-Golan industry is located in three industrial zones, in Katzrin, Benei Yehudah, and the Technological Center. It includes the Golan Heights Wineries and the Eden natural mineral water bottling plants.

Since the 1990s there have been sporadic negotiations between Israel and Syria about the future of the area in a political settlement, and various Israeli prime ministers have reportedly expressed a willingness to return most of it to Syria. In 1999 the Knesset passed the Golan Law, requiring an absolute majority of 61 Knesset votes to confirm the return of any Golan land.

[Efraim Orni / Shaked Gilboa (2nd ed.)]

BIBLIOGRAPHY: G. Schumacher, *The Jaulan* (1888); S. Klein, *The Jewish Transjordan* (1925); C. Epstein and S. Gutman, "The Golan," in: M. Kochavi (ed.), *Judaea, Samaria and the Golan* (1972), 243–98; Z. Ilan, *The Jewish Settlement and Synagogues in the Golan* (1980); idem, *Ereẓ ha-Golan* (1980); Z.U. Maoz, "The Art and Architecture of the Synagogues of the Golan," in: L.I. Levine (ed.), *Ancient Synagogues Revealed* (1981), 98–115; C.M. Dauphin, "Jewish and Christian Communities in the Roman and Byzantine Gaulanitis: A Study of Evidence From Archaeological Surveys," in: PEQ (1982), 129–42; Y. Roth, *Survey of the Southern Golan* (1984); Z. Ilan, *Attempts at Jew-*

ish Settlement in TransJordan, 1871–1947 (1984); C. Epstein, "Dolmens Excavated in the Golan," in: *Atiqot*, 17 (1985), 20–58; D. Urman, *The Golan: A Profile of a Region During the Roman and Byzantine Periods* (1985; cf. Dauphin, AJA, 91 [1987], 156–57; S. Gibson, *Institute of Archaeology Bulletin* [1988]: 87–88); Z.U. Maoz, *Ramat Ha-Golan in Antiquity: A Geographical-Historical Study* (1986); M. Anbar and E. Schiller (eds.), *Ramat Ha-Golan* (1987); Z.U. Maoz and A. Killebrew, "Ancient Qasrin Synagogue and Village," in: BAR, 51 (1988), 5–19; I. Cohen, *Daily Life in the Druze Villages in the Hermon and on its Slopes* (1989); M. Hartal, *Northern Golan Heights* (1989); Vinitsky, "The Date of the Dolmens in the Golan and the Galilee – A Reassessment," *Tel Aviv*, 19 (1992), 100–12; C. Dauphin and S. Gibson, "Ancient Settlements in their Landscapes: the Results of Ten years of Survey on the Golan Heights (1978–1988)," in: *Bulletin of the Anglo-Israel Archaeological Society*, 12 (1992–93), 7–31; S. Dar, *Settlements and Cult Sites on Mount Hermon, Israel* (1993); A. Degani and M. Inbar (eds.), *Golan Heights and Mount Hermon*, 2 vols. (1993); S. Gutman, *Gamla – A City in Rebellion* (1994); R. Gersht and S. Dar, "A Roman Cuirassed Basalt Torso from Khirbet-Beida," in: *ARAM*, 7 (1995), 369–78; R.C. Gregg and D. Urman, *Jews, Pagans and Christians in the Golan Heights* (1996; cf. B. Isaac, in J.H. Humphrey (ed.), *The Roman and Byzantine Near East*, vol. 2 [1999] 179–88); D. Urman, "Additional Jewish Inscriptions from Dabura and Qisrin in the Golan," in: *Tarbiz*, 65 (1996), 515–21; C. Dauphin, S. Brock, R.C. Gregg, and A.F.L. Beeston, "Païens, Juifs, Judéo-Chrétiens, Chrétiens et Musulmans en Gaulanitide," in: *Proche-Orient Chrétien*, 46 (1996), 305–40; S. Dar, "The Material Culture of the Ituraeans," in: *Michmanim* (1998), 23–44; C. Epstein, *The Chalcolithic Culture of the Golan* (1998). **WEBSITE:** www2.golan.org.il

RAMAT HA-KOVESH (Heb. רָמַת הַכּוֹבֵשׁ), kibbutz in central Israel, N.E. of *Kefar Sava, affiliated with Ha-Kibbutz ha-Me'uḥad. It was founded in 1932 by pioneers from Eastern Europe who, before setting up their own kibbutz, had worked in Kefar Sava's citrus groves. In the 1936–39 Arab riots, the kibbutz was the easternmost outpost of Jewish settlement in the southern Sharon and suffered attacks, losing 15 of its members. Similarly, the kibbutz found itself in the front line during the Israel *War of Independence (1948), and again suffered losses. In 1970 Ramat ha-Kovesh had 520, rising to 586 in 2002. Its economy was based on citrus groves and irrigated crops, etc., as well as on a large bakery. The kibbutz also opertated a factory for rubber products and an events garden. The name, "Height of the Conqueror," symbolizes the settlers' early history as "conquerors of labor" in Kefar Sava

[Efram Orni / Shaked Gilboa (2nd ed.)]

RAMAT HA-SHARON (Heb. רָמַת הַשָּׁרוֹן; "Sharon Height"), urban community with municipal council status, in central Israel, N. of Tel Aviv. Ramat ha-Sharon was founded in 1923 as a middle-class village (moshavah) primarily based on citriculture. Following the crisis in citrus exports during World War II, the settlers turned to other branches, including vegetable growing. In the late 1940s, industrial enterprises were opened. By 1947 the population reached 1,150. After the War of Independence (1948), a large *ma'barah* was included in Ramat ha-Sharon's area which covers 4,250 acres (1,700 ha.). The population increased quickly as the *ma'barah* inhabitants were gradually transferred to permanent housing and numerous veteran Israelis settled in Ramat ha-Sharon. It became a town within the Tel Aviv conurbation. Over the years, the moshavah changed its character from rural to urban. The number of inhabitants grew to 8,200 in 1958 and 17,600 in 1970. By 2002 it had reached 35,600, occupying a municipal area of 8.5 sq. mi. (22 sq. km.). Its population was well-educated, with high income and a high mean age level. Most residents earned their livings in the Tel Aviv conurbation. Some of Israel biggest industries, such Israel Military Industries and Elco, were located in Ramat ha-Sharon.

WEBSITE: www.ramat-hasharon.muni.il.

[Efraim Orni / Shaked Gilboa (2nd ed.)]

RAMAT HA-SHOFET (Heb. רָמַת הַשּׁוֹפֵט), kibbutz in central Israel, on the Manasseh Hills near Ein ha-Shofet, affiliated with Kibbutz Arẓi ha-Shomer ha-Ẓa'ir. It was founded by pioneers from Lithuania, Poland, Hungary, and Bulgaria in 1941, with the aim of reinforcing the "bridge" of Jewish settlements between the Sharon and the Jezreel Valley. In 1970 the kibbutz had 530 inhabitants, increasing to 710 in the mid-1990s but then dropping to 557 in 2002. Farming included field crops (with Kibbutz *Ramot Menasheh), avocado plantations, poultry, and dairy cattle. The kibbutz also manufactured plastic and wood products and operated guest rooms. The local Beit Rishonim museum focuses on the history of the kibbutz. The name Ramat ha-Shofet, meaning "Height of the Judge," commemorates Judge Julian W. *Mack, U.S. Zionist leader.

[Efraim Orni / Shaked Gilboa (2nd ed.)

RAMAT RAḤEL (Heb. רָמַת רָחֵל), ancient tell (Khirbat Ṣāliḥ) located on a hilltop (2,683 ft. (818 m.) above sea level) within Israel's international 1947–48 border, in the western part of Kibbutz Ramat Raḥel, about midway between the Old City of Jerusalem and Bethlehem. The site is strategically situated, overlooking the junction of two important roads – the one that in ancient times was the major route from Jerusalem southwards, and the road connecting Jerusalem to the west, via Beth-Shemesh in the Shephelah, through the Rephaim valley, where the old Turkish railway, as well as the modern one, runs to Jerusalem.

The name and the site's biblical identity are still enigmatic. Y. Aharoni identified the site as *Bet-Cherem, and hypothesized that it had been built on a former vineyard of the king, hence its name. He based the assumption on the reference in the LXX supplement to Joshua 15:59a, as a site near Bethlehem. It was also mentioned in Nehemiah 3:14 as a center of one of the districts in the province of Yehud. B. Mazar, however, identified the Ramat Raḥel site with Netofah, a place mentioned in the OT near Bethlehem (II Sam. 23:28; I Chr. 2:54ff. and cf. Ezra 2:22; Neh. 7:26; 12:28). G. Barkay identified the site with *MMŠT* – one of the places mentioned on the *lmlk* stamp impressions. He regarded it as one of the four local centers in Judah (together with Hebron, Sochoh, and Ziph). Lipschits has suggested identifying the site with

Geruth Chimham, mentioned in Jeremiah 41:17 as a place "near Bethlehem."

Already in 1930–31, B. Mazar and M. Stekelis, working on behalf of the Israel Exploration Society, excavated a Jewish burial cave some 200 m. south of the hilltop of the site. Y. Aharoni began excavating the site in 1954 and later conducted four successive seasons there, between 1959 and 1962, on behalf of the Israel Department of Antiquities and Museums, the Israel Exploration Society, the Hebrew University of Jerusalem, and the University of Rome. G. Barkay made a few soundings at the site in 1984 on behalf of the Institute of Archaeology of Tel Aviv University, the Israel Exploration Society, the Israel Department of Antiquities and Museums, and the American Institute of Holy Land Studies on Mount Zion. In the course of the site's restoration and reconstruction as an Archaeological Park, trial excavations were made by Gideon Suleimanny on behalf of the Israel Antiquities Authority. Excavations on behalf of the Institute of Archaeology of Tel Aviv University and the University of Heidelberg were resumed at the site in 2004 under the direction of O. Lipschits, M. Oeming, and Y. Gadot, as part of a major excavation project.

As at other hilly archaeological sites, differentiating between the strata at Ramat Raḥel has been difficult. The generally accepted view, however, is that there were seven periods of occupation:

1. The site was first settled in the time of the kings of Judah at the end of the eighth and early seventh centuries B.C.E. (Stratum VB). Scanty architectural remains have been found, and a large number of storage jar handles, stamped with royal seal impressions of the *lmlk* type. Aharoni assumed that during this period there was a royal fortress at the site (though only scanty architectural remains were assigned to this stratum, and most of them were found in the fillings of stratum VA, out of any clear archaeological context). Some agricultural terraces and private dwellings are the main structural finds from this stratum; in one of the houses Aharoni found seal impressions of "Shebnah [son of] Shaḥar." The same seal impressions have also been discovered at Lachish and Mizpah. Lipschits, Oeming, and Gadot assigned to this same stratum another private seal impression – "Ahaziahu [son of] Tanhum." The same seal impressions are known at Mizpah, Lachish, and Beth-Shemesh.

2. In the next stratum (VA), dated to the seventh century B.C.E., an imposing palace stood on top of the mound. This is the first palace from the period of the kingdom of Judah that has so far been found in archaeological excavations. The palace walls were built of ashlar blocks, uniquely in Judean architecture, and it was decorated with proto-Aeolic capitals. Ten of these were found in Ramat Raḥel, and other than one found in Kenyon's excavations in the city of David (dated by her to the 10th–9th centuries), this is the only example found in Judah. Lipschits, Oeming, and Gadot have suggested that the capitals may have been first used in the palace of stratum VB. Among the other main finds were window balustrades of the palace (cf. Jer. 22:14), a painted potsherd depicting a king (?) seated on a throne, and a seal impression of "Eliakim, steward of Yokhan," also known from Beth-Shemesh and Tell Beit Mirsim. Aharoni assumed that the palace was built at the end of the seventh century and assigned it to king *Jehoiakim son of Josiah (608–598 B.C.E.), whose palace is described by Jeremiah (22:13–19). This date is, however, not justified, at least from the archaeological point of view. Aharoni assumed that the palace was surrounded by a wide fortified courtyard extending over an area of about 20 dunams (five acres). However, the 2005 excavation season at the site revealed that this courtyard, if it existed, was much smaller and confined to the western side of the mound. As a result of the recent work it is possible to reconstruct a small citadel that stood west of the palace, next to its western wall, and a system of wide, open pools adjacent to the southwestern corner of the palace. However, the architectural and chronological connections between the palace and the citadel with the pools and water system are still unclear.

3. The next settlement (Stratum IVB), was dated to the long time-span extending between the Persian and Hasmonean periods. Numerous small finds from these periods have been found, with unclear and segmented architectural finds. Hundreds of seal impressions on jar handles were attributed to the Persian and Hellenistic occupation. The site was the main center of the Yehud seal impressions (of all types), as nearly 200 impressions were found. Many jar-handle impressions with the name *yršlm* (Jerusalem) were found at the site, dated to the Hasmonean occupation. Other seal impressions were stamped with the names of royal officials or governors of the province, two of whom – Jehoezer and Ahiyab (new reading by Lipschits and Vanderhooft) – could have been previously unknown Jewish governors. We may accept Aharoni's assumption that a new citadel was built at the site during the post-Exilic period, and served as one of the main administrative centers in Judah. So far, however, no significant architectural finds from the Persian and Hellenistic periods have been found.

4. A small unfortified village from the Early Roman period (Stratum IVA), dated to the first century B.C.E.–first century C.E. After its destruction ca. 70 C.E., the site remained abandoned until the third century. The main find from this period are tomb caves containing ossuaries with Jewish names written in Aramaic and Greek.

5. After a gap of more than a century, a Roman-style house with a well-built bathhouse was erected on the hill, probably for the Tenth Roman Legion, as confirmed by bricks stamped LXFR (*Legio X Fretensis*). The many small remains from this stratum (Stratum III) are dated to the third and fourth centuries C.E.

6. Between the middle of the fifth century and the sixth century, a Christian church was built on the tell with an attached monastery complex and a large settlement around it (Stratum II). There are clear two phases in this period. This church should be connected to the other, larger, church of the "Kathisma" ("the Seat"), that was excavated close by, about

300 m. from the tell and just beside the main road leading from Jerusalem to Bethlehem. This last church was often mentioned in Byzantine sources as the place where Mary, mother of Jesus, rested during her journey to Bethlehem, where she gave birth.

7. Scanty remains were found upon the ruined Byzantine stratum dating from the Umayyad and the early Abbasid periods (7th–8th centuries C.E.). The finds from this period (Stratum I) consisted of poorly built structures. This was the last occupation of the tell.

[Oded Lipschits (2nd ed.)]

Modern Period

The founders of Kibbutz Ramat Raḥel originated from Eastern Europe. They came with the Third Aliyah to the country and belonged to *Gedud ha-Avodah ("Labor Legion"). In 1921 they were sent to Jerusalem as an "urban work group" and set up a temporary camp on the site of Jerusalem's Reḥavyah quarter. The first houses in this quarter were built by the work group, who became construction workers and stone dressers. In 1926 the kibbutz was transferred to its present site on a dominating hill overlooking a wide expanse of the Judean Desert to the east, *Herodium, and the town of *Bethlehem with Rachel's Tomb to the south (from which the settlement took its name). Ramat Raḥel joined Ha-Kibbutz ha-Me'uḥad at the end of the 1920s. In the 1929 Arab riots a large armed mob stormed Ramat Raḥel and completely destroyed it. The kibbutz was rebuilt in 1930. Ramat Raḥel again came under repeated attacks in the 1936–39 Arab riots. As the settlement's cultivable area was then severely limited, its economy was partly based on outside work in which the members performed important pioneering tasks, e.g., in the potash works near the Dead Sea, the railway service, and in enterprises established in the kibbutz, notably a laundry and bakery for Jerusalem customers. In 1946 additional land was allocated and the deciduous fruit orchards and vegetable gardens were enlarged. In the Israel *War of Independence (1948), Ramat Raḥel constituted one of Jewish Jerusalem's forward defense positions and the battles around it were decisive for the city's fate. In May 1948 the kibbutz was attacked by the Arab Legion and irregulars advancing from the east and by an Egyptian tank force simultaneously attacking from the Bethlehem road in the west. In the following battles, the place changed hands several times and was completely destroyed, but finally remained in Israel hands. The armistice border was drawn around it to the east, south, and southwest. The village was rebuilt and received farmland in the nearby demilitarized zone around the former high commissioner's palace and in the Coastal Plain. A seminary was opened at the kibbutz. In the 1951–52 split in Ha-Kibbutz ha-Me'uḥad, Ramat Raḥel joined Iḥud ha-Kevuzot ve-ha-Kibbutzim, while a part of its members went to Ein Karmel. In the autumn of 1956 nearby Jordanian positions opened fire on a party of the Israel Exploration Society congress visiting the local excavations and killed four persons. In the *Six-Day War (1967), the kibbutz again found itself in the front line, when the way to Bethlehem and the Hebron Hills was opened by Israel forces on June 6–7, by the capture in a hard battle of fortifications around the nearby monastery of Mar Elias.

In 2002 the population of the kibbutz was 308. Its economy was based mainly on tourism, including a hotel, archaeological garden, and conferences and sports centers. Its farming branches were field crops, fruit orchards, citrus groves, and poultry.

[Efraim Orni]

BIBLIOGRAPHY: Y. Aharoni, et al., *Excavations at Ramat Rahel 1, seasons 1959 and 1960* (1962); Y. Aharoni, et al., *Excavations at Ramat Rahel 2, Seasons 1961 and 1962* (1964); Y. Aharoni, "Ramat Rahel," in: IEJ, 9 (1959), 272–74; "Ramat Rahel," in: ibid., *10*, (1960), 261–62; "Ramat Rahel," in: RB, 67 (1960), 398–400; "Ramat Rahel," in: IEJ, 11 (1961), 193–95; "Excavations at Ramat Rahel," in: BA, 24 (1961), 98–118; "Ramat Rahel," in: RB, 69 (1962), 401–4; "Ramat Rahel," in: Ruth Beloff (2nd ed.), 70 (1963), 572–74; "The Citadel of Ramat Rahel," in: *Archaeology*, 18 (1965), 15–25; idem, "Beth Hacherem," in: D.W. Thomas (ed.), *Archaeology and Old Testament Study* (1967), 171–85; S. Geva, in: IEJ, 31 (1981), 186–89; N. Na'aman, "An Assyrian Residence at Ramat Rahel," in: TAU, 28 (2001), 260–81; R. Reich, "On Assyrian Presence at Ramat Rahel," in: TAU, 30 (2003), 124–30.

RAMAT RAZIEL (Heb. רָמַת רָזִיאֵל), moshav in Israel's Judean Hills, on the Ẓobah-Eshtaol road, affiliated with the Ḥerut movement. Ramat Raziel was founded in 1948 as one of the first settlements designed to secure the Jerusalem Corridor that had been opened in the fighting in the Israel *War of Independence in the preceding months. The terrain conditions were particularly difficult and all the farming land had to undergo heavy reclamation. Ramat Raziel was therefore included in the work village scheme. The population, in spite of this scheme, changed several times. In 1970 the moshav had 135 inhabitants. In 2002 the population was 382. Farming was based on deciduous fruit orchards, vineyards, and poultry. A well-known boutique winery by the name of Kastel was owned by one of the settlers. The village bears the name of David *Raziel, the *Irgun Ẓeva'i Le'ummi commander.

[Efram Orni / Shaked Gilboa (2nd ed.)]

RAMAT YISHAI (Heb. רָמַת יִשַׁי), semirural settlement in N. Israel, in the Tivon Hills. It was founded in 1925 by industrialists from Poland as a textile center. Abandoned with the outbreak of the Arab riots in 1936, Ramat Yishai was resettled in 1943. In 1958 the settlement received municipal council status. In 1970, it had 800 inhabitants and medium-size factories for textiles and leather. In the mid-1990s the population was approximately 2,990, increasing to 5,280 in 2002 on an area of nearly a square mile (2.3 sq. km.). The majority of residents found work in the Haifa conurbation. Income was much higher than the national average. The town is named after the writer and teacher Yishai Adler, whose contribution was instrumental in rebuilding the settlement in 1943.

[Efraim Orni / Shaked Gilboa (2nd ed.)]

RAMAT YOḤANAN (Heb. רָמַת יוֹחָנָן), kibbutz in N. Israel, in the Haifa Bay area, E. of Kiryat Ata, affiliated with Iḥud ha-

Kevuẓot ve-ha-Kibbutzim, founded in 1932 by pioneers from Eastern Europe. In 1939 an ideological split brought about an exchange of members with *Bet Alfa, with those in favor of *Ha-Shomer ha-Ẓa'ir concentrating in the latter kibbutz, while the members who supported the *Mapai Party stayed in Ramat Yoḥanan. In the Israel *War of Independence, the kibbutz was attacked by a strong unit of Druze irregulars, but held out and counterattacked successfully (April 13–16, 1948). After this battle, the Druze in Israel ceased to side with the Arabs. In 1970 Ramat Yoḥanan had 500 inhabitants, increasing to 700 in 2002. The kibbutz's economy was based on highly intensive farming (field crops, orchards, citrus groves, and dairy cattle) and on a plastics factory. Ramat Yoḥanan had among its members several painters and writers. The ancient tradition of gathering the *Omer* ("sheaf") during the Passover week was first renewed in Ramat Yoḥanan. The name, "Height of Yoḥanan," commemorates Gen. Jan (Yoḥanan) *Smuts.

[Efraim Orni]

RAMAT ẒEVI (Heb. רָמַת צְבִי), moshav in N. Israel, on the Kokhav Plateau of Lower Galilee, affiliated with Tenu'at ha-Moshavim. It was founded in 1942 by a group of veteran farm laborers, who had previously set up a temporary settlement, based on auxiliary holdings at Shimron, near Nahalal. They were later joined by demobilized soldiers from World War II. After 1948 the population changed when most of the veteran settlers left and were replaced by new immigrants. Farming at Ramat Ẓevi consisted mainly of field crops and dairy cattle. The village is named after Ẓevi (Henry) Monsky, B'nai B'rith president. Its population in 1970 was 180. In 2002 its population was 388.

[Efraim Orni]

RAMBERT, DAME MARIE (1888–1982), British ballet teacher and founder director of the Ballet Rambert. Born in Warsaw as Miriam Rambach, she studied eurythmics and was invited by Serge Diaghilev to teach in his company. While she influenced Diaghilev's most famous dancer, Nijinsky, in his choreographic work, she was herself won over to classical ballet, became a pupil of Enrico Cecchetti, the Italian ballet dancer and teacher, and followed his principles when she opened a school in London in 1920. By 1930 the school had developed into the Ballet Club which, as the Ballet Rambert, became famous for its performances at the Mercury Theater, a former parish hall at Notting Hill rebuilt by Rambert's husband, the author, Ashley Dukes. Rambert had a great flair for discovering new talent and inspired choreographers, designers, and dancers. She was the first to present a whole group of young dancers under British names, and she drew the public with ballets like *A Tragedy of Fashion, Lilac Garden, Lady into Fox*, and *Death and the Maiden*. In 1966 she became co-director with Nathan Morrice of the New Ballet Rambert Company. She was made a Dame of the British Empire in 1962.

BIBLIOGRAPHY: W. Gore (ed.), *Ballet Rambert 1926–1946* (Eng., 1946); L.J.H. Bradley, *Sixteen Years of Ballet Rambert* (1946); M. Clarke, *Dancers of Mercury* (1960); Haskell, in: *Ballet* (Eng., 1938), 137–41.

[Lewis Sowden]

RAMERUPT, village in the Aube department, N.E. central France. No single extant non-Jewish source confirms the existence of a Jewish community in Ramerupt during the Middle Ages, but Jewish sources mention a community which existed from at least around 1100 until the latter half of the 12th century. It was renowned for its yeshivah, headed by *Meir b. Samuel, Rashi's son-in-law, who was succeeded by his sons, Jacob *Tam and *Samuel b. Meir. The chronicle of *Ephraim b. Jacob of Bonn records an attack made by crusaders on the community of Ramerupt on the second day of Shavuot, 1147, but only describes in detail the ill-treatment of R. Jacob Tam. His house was looted, a Torah Scroll was desecrated, and he would have been murdered in the fields had not a passing nobleman tricked the crusaders into releasing him.

BIBLIOGRAPHY: Gross, Gal Jud, 634–8; A.M. Habermann, *Sefer Gezerot Ashkenaz ve-Ẓarefat* (1946), 121.

[Bernhard Blumenkranz]

RAMLEH (Heb. רַמְלָה, **Ramlah**), city in Israel, situated on the Jerusalem–Tel Aviv highway, approximately 28 mi. (45 km.) from Jerusalem.

The Old City

Ramleh was founded in 716 by the Umayyad caliph Suleiman ibn ʿAbd al-Malik and is the only city in the country established by Arabs. The name means "sand" in Arabic and refers to the sandy ground on which the city arose. Ramleh was the administrative capital of the country under the *Umayyads and the *Abbasids. Although originally founded as a town for Muslims, it had from the beginning a large population of Christians, Jews, and Samaritans. Hārūn al-Rashīd, the Abbasid ruler in the late eighth century, increased the Samaritan farming population. Due to its advantageous location on the crossroads of the Egypt–Damascus and Jerusalem–Jaffa highways, the city prospered until the time of the Crusades.

Among the Jewish community, Ramleh was called Gath or Gath-Rimmon or Ramathaim-Zophim, after the biblical towns with which it was identified. The temporary transfer of the Jerusalem academy to Ramleh in the tenth century greatly strengthened the Jewish population. At that time, a Karaite and a Rabbanite community, the latter divided into Palestinians and Babylonians, existed in the town; there were also synagogues for the Jerusalemites and the Damascenes. In the 11th century the flourishing communities of Ramleh suffered from a series of blows: a disastrous Bedouin raid in 1025 and two devastating earthquakes in 1033 and 1067 (in the latter, 25,000 people reportedly perished). During the Crusader occupation, beginning in 1099, the Jewish and Samaritan communities were dispersed. When Benjamin of Tudela visited there in 1170–71, he recorded a Jewish population of only three dyers, living in the midst of extensive cemeteries.

During the 12th and 13th centuries, the city was often attacked by Muslims. It was finally captured by the *Mamluk sultan Baybars and as the capital of a province, it regained some of its former importance. By the 14th century, it was again the largest town in Palestine and a Jewish community was reestablished there. With the Ottoman conquest, it once more declined, although most pilgrims passed through the town, at the time called Rames, on their way to Jerusalem. The tax records for 1690–91 show no Jews living there. The main buildings of the early city which still stand are the Cathedral of St. John (now the Great Mosque), the White Mosque and its minaret (completed in 1318) and the ʿUnayziyya cistern (dating from the eighth century).

[Michael Avi-Yonah]

The New Town

In 1890 Ramleh had 9,611 inhabitants, the majority of whom were Muslim Arabs, with a sizable minority of Arab and non-Arab Christians, and a small Jewish community of 66 people. Under the British Mandate (1917–48), the town's economy benefited only slightly from its location near a principal highway. Christian institutions helped raise the local educational level. In the 1930s Ramleh still had five Jewish families; they left, however, in 1936, with the outbreak of the Arab riots.

During the Israel *War of Independence, when Ramleh was occupied by Israel forces in July 1948, most of the town's Arabs abandoned it, causing the population to shrink to 1,547 persons by the November 1948 census. At the beginning of the 1950s the town absorbed a large number of Jewish immigrants from various countries, raising the population to 20,548 in 1961. Initially the newcomers were housed in three *ma'barot* ("immigrant transit camps"); but, with housing construction proceeding rapidly, Ramleh's built-up area expanded, principally to the west and southwest, until it covered an area of about 4 sq. mi. (10 sq. km.). In 1969 about 4,200 families lived in the new sections, compared to 3,000 in the town's older areas, where numerous structures were earmarked for leveling and reconstruction. Of its 30,800 inhabitants in 1970, 27,000 were Jews and 3,800 Arabs. In the mid-1990s the population was approximately 55,000, including 9,020 non-Jews. By 2002 the population of Ramleh increased to 62,800, consisting of 80.5% Jews, 15.4% Muslims, and 4% Christians. A third of the population consisted of immigrants from the former Soviet Unions. In earlier years the Arabs were for the most part well integrated in the city's economy and cultural life and satisfactory social relations existed between the Jewish and Arab communities, with a Jewish-Arab Friendship League in operation. However, in the course of time, relations became tense. Most Arabs remained in the old city, nicknamed the Ghetto, while the Jews lived in the new areas of the city. When the "al-Aqsa" Intifada erupted in 2000 a few synagogues were set on fire and Jews tried to burn a mosque.

The city's economy was based mainly on industry, which benefited from its location at one of the country's major highway and railroad junctions and its relative proximity to the port of Ashdod. In 1969, 23 of the larger industrial enterprises employed about 2,000 workers. Products included cement (in the country's largest cement factory), wood products, metal pipes, motors, refrigerators and miscellaneous metal products, prefabricated houses, and canned foods. There were two industrial zones. Until June 1971, the Tel Aviv–Jerusalem traffic artery intersected the town from northwest to southeast, with the number of vehicles passing through Ramleh averaging 17,000 a day. The local market mainly serviced rural settlements around Ramleh, and provided an outlet for its farm produce. The city also provided health services to the villages in the vicinity. During the 1980s the city became known for its various disco clubs. According to Israel's Central Bureau of Statistics, income in Ramleh was much lower than the national average in 2002 and a third of the population was on welfare

[Shlomo Hasson / Shaked Gilboa (2nd ed.)]

BIBLIOGRAPHY: B. Segal, in: *Zion*, 5 (1933), 12–18; S. Klein, *Toledot ha-Yishuv ha-Yehudi be-Ereẓ Yisrael* (1935), index; S. Assaf and L.A. Mayer (eds.), *Sefer ha-Yishuv*, 2 (1944), 56–63; Mayer-Pinkerfeld, *Principal Muslim Religious Buildings in Israel* (1950), 25–30; J. Braslavski, *Le-Ḥeker Arẓenu* (1954), index; Hirschberg, in: *Yerushalayim*, 4 (1953), 123–8; Shapira, *ibid.*, 118–22; J. Kaplan, in: *ʿAtiqot*, 2 (1958), 106–15; Z. Vilnay, *Ramleh* (1961); I. Ben-Zvi, *She'ar Yashuv* (1965), 316–21; Ben-Zvi, Ereẓ Yisrael, index; M. Rosen-Ayalon, in: IEJ, 16 (1966), 148–50. **WEBSITE:** www.ramla.muni.il.

°**RAMON, LULL** (**Raimundus Lullus**; c. 1234–1315), Catalan Christian preacher, mystic, and philosopher. As a youth Lull grew up in *Majorca, where a substantial Muslim majority had remained even after this island's conquest (1229–32) by King James I. This enabled him, besides the traditional education imparted to the sons of Spanish nobility, to familiarize himself with Muslim culture and the Arabic language. When he was 30, Lull turned to ascetic life. Besides his immersion in mystical contemplation, he considered it his vocation to preach and propagate Christianity among nonbelievers, Muslims, and Jews in Aragon and, chiefly, in Majorca. To this end, Lull devoted many years to the study of Arabic language, philosophy, and theology, and some of his initial works were written in that language. In comparison, his knowledge of Judaism was scant and superficial, some works by Jewish thinkers being known to him through Arabic philosophy, or from Maimonides *Guide of the Perplexed*. In about 1272 Lull wrote in Arabic and translated into Catalan the widely circulated *Libre del gentil e los tres savis*, which was subsequently translated into Latin, French, and probably Hebrew. It is a work of apologetic character, drawn up in a form frequent in those times. A man, either a nonbeliever or a pagan, consults three sages – a Jew, a Christian, and a Muslim – and asks them the basic principles of their respective creeds. This furnishes the starting point of a peaceful debate between the three, which finally remains inconclusive, although the author does not conceal his sympathy for the Christian. There has been speculation as to the possible influence of *Judah Halevi s *Kuzari* over this work, but there is nothing to warrant it. In 1305 Lull wrote a second apologetic work chiefly directed against the Jews, *Liber de Trinitate et In-*

carnatione adversus Judaeos et sarracenos, better known under its shorter appellation *Liber Predicationis Contra Judaeos* (scholarly edition published in Madrid-Barcelona, 1957). The book comprises 52 sermons, one for each week of the year, preceded by a verse from the Bible. In these Lull strives to demonstrate, against Jewish and Muslim arguments as to the irrationality of Christianity, that the Christian truth is not only rational but also borne out by common sense.

Lull was also active as a preacher. In 1299 James II (1291–1327) allowed him to give sermons on Saturdays and Sundays in the synagogues and on Fridays and Sundays in mosques. In his important *Ars Magna* (c. 1274) Lull reduces all knowledge to a few basic metaphysical principles. The theory of the attributes of God occupies the central part of this work and it is interesting to compare the *dignitates* of Lull with the *Sefirot* of the kabbalists. The similarity between the two categories possibly stems from Neoplatonic influence common to the kabbalists and to Lull; the latter maintained friendly relations with a circle of Jewish religious thinkers in Catalonia, such as Solomon b. Abraham *Adret and R. Aaron ha-Levi of Barcelona, author of *Sefer ha-Ḥinnukh*; Lull presumably learned about the foundations of *Kabbalah from them.

BIBLIOGRAPHY: Baer, Spain, index; J.M. Millás Vallicrosa, in: *Sefarad*. 18 (1958), 241–53; idem, in: S. Ettinger et al. (eds.), *Sefer Yovel le-Yiẓḥak Baer* (1961), 186–90; R.J.Z. Werblowsky, in: *Tarbiz*, 32 (1962/63), 207–11; A. Llinares, *Raymond Lulle...* (Fr., (1963), bibl.: 455–81.

[José Maria Millas-Vallicrosa]

RAMON, HAIM (1950–), Israeli politician, member of the Knesset from the Tenth Knesset. Ramon was born in Jaffa. He served in the air force in the years 1967–73 and received a law degree from Tel Aviv University. He started his political life as national secretary of the *Israel Labor Party Young Guard in 1978, serving in this capacity until 1984. He first entered the Knesset in 1983, replacing MK Danny Rosolio, who resigned. In the course of the Eleventh Knesset he was the Labor Alignment's coordinator in the Knesset Finance Committee, and in the course of the Twelfth Knesset served as chairman of the Labor parliamentary group. In 1985 he established together with Nissim Zvili the Kefar ha-Yarok circle – a dovish political group made up of younger members of the Labor Party that succeeded in getting several members into the Twelfth Knesset. It was generally believed at the time that some of Labor's future leaders would emerge from this circle, but in 2005 Ramon and Amir *Peretz were the only two members of this group still in the Knesset.

In March 1990 Ramon was actively involved, in full coordination with Labor Party chairman Shimon *Peres, and in consultation with his friend Aryeh *Deri from Shas, in the plan to bring down the National Unity Government headed by Yitzhak *Shamir, of which the Labor Party was a member, in a vote on a motion of no confidence. However, Peres failed to form an alternative government. Prior to the fifth Labor Party Conference, at the end of 1991, Ramon considered leaving the Labor Party and forming a joint dovish party with the CRM, Mapam and Shinui. However, in light of his success, together with some of his colleagues, in getting the Conference to adopt many of their positions in connection with the peace process and religion and state, he decided to remain. In the primaries for the elections of Labor's leader in February 1992 Ramon supported Yitzhak *Rabin rather than Peres, and in the government formed by Rabin in July he was appointed minister of health. In this position he started, much to the chagrin of many of his Labor colleagues, to prepare a National Health Insurance bill that would, inter alia, break the link between the *Histadrut and Israel's largest health fund, Kuppat Ḥolim Kelalit. Ramon supported the candidature of Amir Peretz as Labor's candidate in the election for secretary general of the Histadrut against that of Haim Haberfeld, and when Peretz failed, stood himself for election against Haberfeld at the head of his own list, called Ḥayyim Ḥadashim la-Histadrut. Before deciding to run, Ramon gave a well-publicized speech at a special session of the Labor Party Conference in which he compared the party to a whale swimming towards the beach to its death, arguing that with his meager power he was trying to push the party back into the living water. Several days later he resigned from the government. As a result of his decision to run against the Labor candidate for the Histadrut, he was removed from the party, but nevertheless remained part of the Labor parliamentary group.

In May 1994 Ramon was elected secretary general of the Histadrut, and changed his title to chairman. He set off immediately to make drastic organizational and functional changes in the bankrupt Histadrut, and managed to enact the National Health Insurance Law. Before Rabin's assassination in November 1995 Ramon was reinstated in the party, and was invited by Rabin to return to the government. However, it was only in December that he entered the government formed by Peres, as minister of the interior, and Peretz took over the leadership of the Histadrut. Ramon was in charge of Labor's propaganda strategy in the elections to the Fourteenth Knesset, and was largely responsible for the decision to minimize mention of the Likud's role in creating the atmosphere that led up to Rabin's assassination. He was thus blamed by many Laborites for Labor's defeat in the elections, in which Binyamin *Netanyahu beat Peres by only 30,000 votes. Ramon considered running against Ehud *Barak in the primaries for the Labor Party leadership in June 1997, but when his proposal that open primaries be held, rather than primaries among Labor Party members only, was rejected, he decided not to run. In the government formed by Barak after the elections to the Fifteenth Knesset Ramon was appointed minister in the Prime Minister's office. He was not a member of the National Unity Government formed by Ariel *Sharon after he defeated Barak in the election for prime minister in 2001.

In 2004–5 Ramon played an active role in the negotiations for the formation of a new National Unity Government, after the government formed by Sharon following the 2003 elections disintegrated against the background of his disengagement plan. However, after doing poorly in the vote that took place in the Labor Party Central Committee for ministerial posts in the new government formed in January 2005, he was appointed minister without portfolio. At the end of 2005, when Sharon left the Likud and formed the new Kadimah Party, Ramon left the Labor Party to join him, along with Shimon Peres and others. After the 2006 elections he was appointed minister of justice.

BIBLIOGRAPHY: A. Barzilai, *Ramon: Biographia Politit* (1996).

RAMON, ILAN (1954–2003), colonel in the Israel air force, the first Israeli astronaut. Ramon was killed on board the U.S. space shuttle *Columbia* in its ill-fated 2003 mission. Ramon served in the IDF as a combat pilot and was among those who participated in the bombardment of the Iraqi nuclear reactor in 1981. From 1983 to 1987 he studied computer science and electronic engineering at Tel Aviv University. From 1990 to 1992 he served as an F-16 squadron commander. Later, with rank of colonel, he served as head of the Department of Operational Requirements for Weapons Development and Acquisition. In 1995 Israel and the United States agree to send an Israeli astronaut into space, and Ramon was chosen in 1997 after a lengthy selection process. He and his alternate, Yiẓḥak Mayo, were sent with their families to the U.S. to start training at the NASA Space Agency. Four years later, in 2003, as the only payload specialist on board, he was part of the crew that lifted off on the *Columbia* shuttle mission. During the 16-day journey in space, he carried out a number of scientific experiments. During re-entry, a technical problem caused the *Columbia* to disintegrate, and all its crew members, including Ramon, lost their lives. After his death, asteroid 51828 was named after him.

[Shaked Gilboa (2nd ed.)]

RAMONE, JOEY (**Jeffrey Hyman**; 1951–2001), co-founder, vocalist, and songwriter for the influential U.S. punk rock group The Ramones (1974–96); member of the Rock & Roll Hall of Fame. Ramone was born in Forest Hills, Queens, to Charlotte and Noel, who divorced when he was young. His mother encouraged an interest in music in both Joey and his younger brother Mitchell (who later adopted the name Mickey Leigh). Ramone took up drums at 13, playing throughout his teen years at Forest Hills High School, where he met his future band mates. The 6 ft. 6 in., gangly Ramone was originally the drummer for the Ramones, but eventually moved to vocalist and frontman for the band. Described as a "cartoon family," The Ramones played fast, furious, and funny primal pop songs, with titles like "Teenage Lobotomy" and "I Wanna Be Sedated," and chants like "Hey ho let's go" and "Gabba gabba hey!" that became rallying cries for disaffected youth. The other original Ramones were Tommy, Johnny, and Dee Dee, who like Ramone, all adopted the stage surname of Ramone and wore matching "non-uniforms" of black leather jackets, black t-shirts, and ripped jeans – what became standard attire for a generation of musicians. They led a movement of no-frills bands that were based in the seedy Bowery club CBGB in New York. Rules that The Ramones eponymous 1976 debut album instated into a bloated mid-1970s rock world were no song needed to be more than two minutes long, include more than three chords, or needed a guitar solo – guidelines the band stuck to closely for their entire career. During their career, The Ramones played over 2,000 shows. Diagnosed with lymphoma in 1995, and given three to six months to live, Joey maintained his health and spirits for five years until a broken hip led to a decline. His death was treated as the end of an era, and given almost the same amount of coverage as the deaths of rock icons John Lennon and Jerry Garcia. Ramone's first solo album – *Don't Worry About Me* – was posthumously released in 2002, the same year he entered the Rock & Roll Hall of Fame as a member of The Ramones. In November 2003, the city of New York named the corner of 2nd St. and the Bowery near CBGB as Joey Ramone Place. In September 2005, Ramone was awarded the Heeb Magazine Lifetime Achievement Award at the inaugural Jewish Music Awards.

[David Brinn (2nd ed.)]

RAMOT, BRACHA (1927–2006), physician and medical researcher. Ramot was born in Raseinei, Lithuania. In 1941, after the occupation of Lithuania by the Soviets, she was transferred to Komi in North Russia, where she studied to become a practical nurse (*felsher*) and substituted for a family physician. Simultaneously, she also graduated from an evening high school. She arrived in Israel illegally via Poland and Cyprus in 1947, to be joined by her family 27 years later. During the Israel War of Independence she served in the *Palmaḥ as a nurse. She then studied at the Hebrew University-Hadassah Medical School, from which she graduated in 1952. She did her internship and residency in medicine at the Tel Hashomer (now Sheba) Hospital.

In 1954–56 Ramot trained with Karl Singer in hematology at the Michael Reese Hospital, Chicago, and in 1956–57 at the Albert Einstein College of Medicine with Irving London. Upon her return to Israel, she established the Institute of Hematology at Tel Hashomer Hospital and took an active part in the founding of the Sackler Faculty of Medicine of Tel Aviv University. From 1971 until her retirement in 1994 she was professor and head of the Hematology Section at the Postgraduate School of Medicine, Tel Aviv University. In 1975–79 she was head of the Blood Service of *Magen David Adom and in 1991–96 she was medical director of the Maccabi Health Services. She educated an entire generation of hematologists who became leaders in the field in Israel. In 2001 she was awarded the Israel Prize in medical sciences.

Ramot was involved in a number of fields of basic and clinical research. They included red cell enzymes and cell aging, circadian rhythms of enzymes, variants of glucose-6-phospahate dehydrogenase (G6PD), genetic variants of serum proteins in Jewish ethnic groups and Arabs, and effects of genetic and environmental factors on the hematologic malignancies. She described the clinical and pathologic entity of small intestinal lymphoma with malabsorption in Arab and non-Ashkenazi Jewish young adults.

[Bracha Rager (2nd ed.)]

RAMOTH (Heb. רָאמוֹת), Levitical city in the territory of Issachar (I Chron. 6:58), called Jarmuth in one of the lists apportioning territory to the Levites (Josh. 21:29). In the city list of Issachar, the town is called Remeth (Josh. 19:21). It seems to have been the center of the mountainous district of Yarmutu, which was inhabited by Ḫabiru even before the Israelite conquest; Seti I, in one of his stelae found at Beth-Shean, describes his victory over them in approximately 1300 B.C.E. The suggested identification is with Kokhav ha-Yarden (Ar. Kawkab al-Hawā, the Crusader "Belvoir"), a dominating height (895 ft., 275 m.) overlooking the Jordan Valley; it is possibly identical with the fortress of *Agrippina. The topographical position of the site justifies the name Ramoth ("the Heights").

BIBLIOGRAPHY: Abel, Geog, 2 (1938), 435; Aharoni, Land, index.

[Michael Avi-Yonah]

RAMOT HA-SHAVIM (Heb. רָמוֹת הַשָּׁבִים; "Heights of the Returning"), moshav with municipal council status, in central Israel, near Hod ha-Sharon, affiliated with Ha-Mo'eẓah ha-Ḥakla'it. It was founded in 1933 by middle-class immigrants from Germany, who chose to become farmers although they had been merchants and members of the free professions abroad. As the area initially available for farming was extremely limited, poultry breeding became the principal farming branch. In 1970, Ramot ha-Shavim had 450 inhabitants, growing to around 890 in the mid-1990s and 1,100 in 2002.

[Efraim Orni]

RAMOTH-GILEAD (Heb. רָמוֹת גִּלְעָד), levitical city of refuge in the territory of the tribe of Gad in N. Transjordan, which was held by the family of Merari (Deut. 4:43; Josh. 20:8; 21:38). Ramoth-Gilead was chosen by Solomon as the capital of his sixth district, which included the villages of Jair and the region of Argob in Bashan (I Kings 4:13), thus strengthening the assumption that the levitical cities served as administrative centers from the time of David. Its fall to the Arameans in the days of the divided monarchy was regarded as a grievous blow. Ahab, king of Israel, tried to retake it with the help of Jehoshaphat, king of Judah, but fell in the battle (I Kings 22; II Chron. 18); his son Joram was wounded in another attempt (II Kings 8:28ff.; II Chron. 22:5ff.). Jehu was anointed and proclaimed king by a messenger of the prophet Elisha in the camp before Ramoth-Gilead (II Kings 9). Josephus calls the city Arimanon or Aramatha(h) (Ant., 4:173; 8:399; 9:105). Eusebius identified it with the village al-Rāmm on the Jabbok (Onom. 144:4). Modern scholars locate it at Ḥuṣn ʿAjlūn or at Tell Ramīth south of Edrei, near the village of al-Ramta. A fortress of the Israelite period was discovered at the latter site in recent excavations.

BIBLIOGRAPHY: Abel, Geog, 2 (1938), 430–1; Aharoni, Land, index; N. Glueck, in: AASOR, 25–28 (1951), 96ff.; H.J. Stoebe, in: ZDPV, 82 (1966), 27.

[Michael Avi-Yonah]

RAMOT MENASHEH (Heb. רָמוֹת מְנַשֶּׁה; *ramot*, "heights"), kibbutz in the Manasseh Hills, Israel, affiliated with Kibbutz Arẓi ha-Shomer ha-Ẓa'ir. It was founded in 1948 by young immigrants from Poland, including ghetto fighters of World War II, and Bulgaria. Later, immigrants from Chile and Uruguay joined the kibbutz and became the majority among the settlers. In 1970 the kibbutz had 500 inhabitants; in 2002, 447. Its economy was based on partly intensive farming, including field crops in partnership with Kibbutz Ramat ha-Shofet, and dairy cattle. It also manufactured water gauges and was a partner in a metal factory at nearby *Daliyyah.

[Efram Orni / Shaked Gilboa (2nd ed.)]

RAMOT NAFTALI (Heb. רָמוֹת נַפְתָּלִי; *ramot*, "heights"), moshav E. of the Israel-Lebanese border, Israel, affiliated with Tenu'at ha-Moshavim. It was founded by a group of veteran soldiers called "Irgun Wingate." Originally a moshav shittufi, Ramot Naftali was the first settlement of demobilized soldiers from World War II. In the *War of Independence (1948), the settlers were in a highly dangerous position and in one instance drove off Lebanese attacking forces after they had already broken into the settlement's perimeter. Although after the war moshav-born youth, and later new immigrants joined the village, it made little progress, due to a number of difficulties: access to the site, the pumping of water, and reclamation of the mountainous terrain for farming. Deciduous fruit trees and vineyards constituted its prominent agricultural branches. Later, guest rooms became another source of income in the face its declining farm economy. Large areas in the vicinity have been afforested. In 2002 the population of Ramot Naftali was 414.

[Efraim Orni]

RAMSES (Raamses, Rameses; Heb. רַעְמְסֵס, רַעַמְסֵס), ancient city in Lower Egypt. The second but the more important of the two treasury cities which the Hebrews built in Egypt (Ex. 1:11), Ramses is mentioned four further times in the Bible (see also *Pithom). In Genesis 47:11 *Joseph established his family in the land (i.e., region) of Ramses, and in Exodus 12:37 and Numbers 33:3, 5 Ramses was the Israelites' point of departure from Egypt. Ramses can be hardly any city other than the Delta residence of the Ramessid kings of the Egyptian 19th dynasty, Per-Rameses-Miʿamunpa-ka-aʿo-en-preʿ-Ḥorakhty ("The House of Rameses-Beloved-of-Amun, the-Great-Ka-Soul-of-Re-Ḥorakhty"), the identification of which was long a subject of controversy among modern scholars. Since it was certainly situated within the eastern Delta, its exact location would shed light on the possible route of the Exodus. It was first thought to have been Pelusium, but the identification was then narrowed down to either Tanis (biblical *Zoan) or Qantir, with the weight of scholarly opinion favoring the latter.

BIBLIOGRAPHY: E.P. Uphill, in: jnes, 27 (1968), 291–316; 28 (1969), 15–39.

[Alan Richard Schulman]

RAMSES (Egyptian **Rʿ-ms-sw**; "Re is he that has borne him"; name of several Egyptian rulers of the 19th and the 20th dynasties. Connected with the sun god of Heliopolis, the name is significant for the orientation toward Lower Egypt that accompanied the attempt to regain power over Asia, which had been lost in the Amarna period. Ramses I (c. 1306–1305 B.C.E.) rose to become founder of the 19th dynasty from a non-royal position as vizier. It was left to his grandson Ramses II (c. 1290–1223 B.C.E.) to restore Egypt to her former greatness. His long reign, splendid building activities (additions to the Karnak and Luxor temples, the Ramesseum, the monumental rock-cut temple at Abu Simbel), and numerous offspring (over 100 children) made him a legendary figure for later times. The enlargement of his residence at Tanis, renamed Per-Ramses in his honor, agrees with the biblical record (Ex. 1:11) of the building of *Ramses and *Pithom (Tell el-Maskhouta in the eastern Delta) by the Israelites, and makes him the probable *pharaoh of the Exodus. A battle with the Hittites at Kadesh in his fifth year ended in a stalemate. Campaigns in Palestine, southern Phoenicia, and Edom are attested for the following years. In year 21 of his reign a treaty with Hatti was drawn up in the face of the new common menace embodied in the advancing Sea Peoples. The full impact of these peoples fell on Ramses III (c. 1188–1157 B.C.E.), the son of the founder of the 20th dynasty. He warded off their attack in his eighth year, after they had overrun the Hittites. He also managed to check the Libyans and maintained authority over Palestine. However, after his death by a harem intrigue, Palestine, now settled by Philistines and the Israelites, was forever lost to Egypt. A list of his temple donations shows that increasing wealth accumulated in the hands of the priests of Amun at Thebes. Under his successors (Ramses IV–XI, c. 1157–1085 B.C.E.), political influence was also taken over by the priests, while the might of the rulers steadily declined in a country lacking foreign influence and troubled by poverty and inflation.

BIBLIOGRAPHY: M.B. Rowton, in: *Journal of Egyptian Archaeology*, 34 (1948), 57–74; J.A. Wilson, *The Burden of Egypt* (1951), 239ff.; P. Montet, *Géographie de l'Egypte ancienne*, 1 (1957), 214; O. Eissfeldt, in: CAH², vol. 2, ch. 26, 17–19; R.O. Faulkner, *ibid.*, ch. 23.

[Irene Grumach]

RAN, SHULAMIT (1949–), composer. Born in Tel Aviv, already by age nine she studied composition with Alexander U. *Boskovich and Paul *Ben-Haim and piano with Emma Gorochov. At the age of 14 she moved with her mother to New York on a piano scholarship to the Mannes College of Music where she studied composition with Norman Dello-Joio and piano with Nadia Reisenberg. She continued her studies with Dorothy Taubman (1970–76) and Ralph Shapey (1977). In 1971 she premiered her *Concert Piece* for piano and orchestra as soloist with the Israel Philharmonic Orchestra conducted by Zubin *Mehta. In 1973, she joined the faculty of the University of Chicago, where she became the William H. Colvin Professor in the department of music. She was visiting professor at Princeton University in 1987.

Ran's music shows a diversity of styles and flexibility maintained in the process of composing. Her early works are more indebted to modernism than her later ones. Though the emphasis is on the comprehensibility of the music, the result is often an overt expression of a large gamut of sentiments, at times extravagantly so. Being mostly fantasy-like, the works feature great contrasts and have a sharply dramatic profile. Ran explores the dramatic potential of a certain compositional idea or of specific musical instruments and sets musical elements in action similar to theatrical personae in a play.

Her list of works includes *O the Chimneys* for mezzo-soprano, chamber ensemble and magnetic tape (1968); *For an Actor*, monologue for clarinet (1978); *Private Games* for clarinet and cello (1979); *Verticals* for piano (1982); *Amichai Songs* for mezzo-soprano, oboe/English horn, viola da gamba and harpsichord (1985); *Concerto da Camera I & II* (1985 and 1987); *String Quartet No. 2 "Vistas"* (1988/89); *Concerto for Orchestra* (1986); *Inscriptions* for violin (1991); *Legends* for orchestra (1992/93); *Invocation* for horn, timpani and chimes (1994); *Soliloquy* for violin, cello and piano (1997); *Between Two Worlds (The Dybbuk)*, opera (1997); *Vessels of Courage and Hope* for orchestra (1998); and *Voices* for flute and orchestra (2000).

Ran's numerous honors include an award from the Rockefeller Fund (1968), Ford Foundation (1972), and the Guggenheim Foundation (1977 & 1990). From 1990–97 she served as composer-in-residence with the Chicago Symphony Orchestra and from 1994–97 with the Lyric Opera of Chicago. Her *Symphony* (1989/90) earned her the 1991 Pulitzer Prize in Music and the 1992 Kennedy Center Friedheim Award. In 1998 she received the Koussevitsky Foundation Grant. In 2003 she was elected to the American Academy of Arts and Letters.

[Yuval Shaked (2nd ed.)]

RAND, AYN (**Alissa Zinovievna Rosenbaum**; 1905–1982), writer and philosopher. Born in St. Petersburg, Russia, she displayed a strong interest in literature and films from an early age. Her mother taught her French and subscribed to a magazine featuring stories for boys, where Rand found her first childhood hero, an Indian army officer in a Kipling-style story. She expressed a passionate enthusiasm for the Romantic Movement and fell deeply in love with the novels of Victor Hugo at the age of 13. She studied philosophy and history at the University of Petrograd. In her diary she expressed intensely anti-Soviet ideas. She loved the philosophical ideas of Nietzsche, and embraced his exaltation of the heroic and independent individual who embraced egoism and rejected altruism in *Thus Spake Zarathustra*. She eventually became critical of Nietzsche, believing his philosophy emphasized emotion over reason. She considered Aristotle her greatest influence by far.

She entered the State Institute for Cinema Arts in 1924 to study screenwriting. The following year, she was granted a visa to visit American relatives and in 1926, after a brief stay in Chicago, she resolved never to return to the Soviet Union. She set out for Hollywood to become a screenwriter, changing her name to Ayn (rhymes with pine) Rand, a variant spelling of the name of a Finnish writer. While working as an extra in Cecil B. DeMille's *King of Kings*, she met an aspiring actor, Frank O'Conner. They married in 1929. Rand became a naturalized citizen of the United States in 1931. The following year she achieved literary success with the sale of her fist screenplay, *Red Pawn*, to Universal Studios. In 1934 she wrote the play *The Night of January 16th*; it was highly successful. She then published two novels, *We the Living* (1936) and *Anthem* (1938).

Her first major professional success came with the best-selling novel *The Fountainhead* (1943), which she wrote over a period of seven years. The theme of *The Fountainhead* is "individualism and collectivism in man's soul." The hero is Rand's ideal, a noble soul, an architect who is firmly and serenely devoted to his own ideals and believes that no man should copy the style of another. The other characters demand that he renounce his values, but the hero maintains his integrity.

Rand's *Atlas Shrugged* (1957), her most extensive statement of her Objectivist philosophy in any of her fiction, became an international bestseller. In the appendix, she asserted: "My philosophy, in essence, is the concept of man as a heroic being, with his own happiness as the moral purpose of his life, with productive achievement as his noblest activity, and reason as his only absolute." Along with Nathaniel Branden, a young philosophy student, his wife, Barbara, Alan *Greenspan, the future head of the Federal Reserve System, and others, members of The Collective, she launched the Objectivist movement to promote her philosophy of individual ability and laissez-faire capitalism. After several years, Rand and Branden's relationship blossomed into an intense romance, despite the fact that both were married. Eventually, the affair led to the Brandens' divorce.

Rand's political views were radically pro-capitalist, anti-statist, and anti-Communist. She had a strong dislike for mysticism, religion, and compulsory charity, all of which she believed helped foster a crippling culture of resentment towards individual human happiness and success. Although she became a cult figure in libertarian circles, her view of selfishness as a virtue and altruism as a vice was a reversal of the traditional Judeo-Christian ethic. In 1985, Leonard Peikoff, a surviving member of The Collective and Rand's designated heir, established the Ayn Rand Institute: The Center for the Advancement of Objectivism.

[Stewart Kampel (2nd ed.)]

RAND, YA'AKOV (1926–), professor of education, specializing in special education. His research contributed to the development of cognitive teaching techniques. Rand was born in Romania, and left for Israel in 1947. Seized by the British, he was sent to Cyprus and finally arrived to Israel in 1948. In 1964 he graduated in psychology and special education from the Hebrew University of Jerusalem and in 1971 he received his Ph.D. from the Sorbonne. From 1971 he served as a lecturer in the School of Education of Bar-Ilan University, serving as head of the school in 1972. In 1978 he was named dean of the Faculty of Social Sciences, a position he held until 1982. From 1980 until 1983 he was the chairman of the public committee for retarded children. In 1983 he served as the chairman of the committee for advanced studies in Bar-Ilan. In 1989 he became a professor. From 1990 until 1996 he was a member of the Council for Higher Education and from 1991 chairman of its regional college committee. From 1997 he served as academic consultant for Touro College and rector of the Academic Education College Talpiyyot. During these years he was also a visiting professor in universities in the United States and Canada. Rand is a member of many professional and academic associations and societies. He published numerous articles and 10 books. In 2001 he was awarded the Israel Prize for education.

BIBLIOGRAPHY: cms.education.gov.il/EducationCMS/Units/PrasIsrael/Tashsa/YaacovRand/NimokyHsoftim.htm

[Shaked Gilboa (2nd ed.)]

RANDALL, TONY (**Leonard Rosenberg**; 1920–2004). Born in Tulsa, Okla., Randall enrolled as a speech and drama major at Northwestern University in Evanston, Ill., but dropped out after a year and moved to New York, where he studied acting at the Neighborhood Playhouse. In the early 1940s he got a start in radio, appearing in mysteries; his distinctive voice was heard on soap operas like *Portia Faces Life*. He made his New York stage debut in an adaptation of the 13th-century Chinese fantasy *A Circle of Chalk* and later that year appeared in Shaw's *Candida*. After his discharge from the army in 1946, he returned to New York. By 1950 he was appearing in *Caesar and Cleopatra* and two years later he won a role as a teacher in *Mr. Peepers*, playing opposite Wally Cox as his posturing, swaggering sidekick. His portrayal earned him an Emmy nomination and his career took off. He appeared in three Doris Day-Rock Hudson movies: *Lover Come Back*, *Pillow Talk*, and *Send Me No Flowers*, often as the foil to Hudson's romantic leads. He had similar roles in *Let's Make Love* (with Marilyn Monroe) and *Boys Night Out* (with Kim Novak).

Randall was best known for comedy, particularly his signature role as the fussbudget Felix Unger in the classic television series *The Odd Couple* (1970–75), based on Neil *Simon's play and movie. Randall's roommate and temperamental opposite on the show was the slovenly, unkempt, cigar-smoking sportswriter, played by Jack *Klugman. Randall had a great love for repertory theater, and in 1991, with a million dollars of his own money and much more from friends and moneyed associates, he founded the National Actors Theater in New York. Its purpose was to keep the works of playwrights like Ibsen, Chekhov and Arthur *Miller before the public, at a reasonable price. As he gained fame as an actor, Randall became active in a number of causes, including a futile effort to save the old Metropolitan Opera House in New York. He was national chairman of the Myasthenia Gravis Foundation for

30 years, and supported medical and artistic organizations. A member of Congregation Rodeph Shalom in New York, he was also prominent in many Jewish scientific and educational philanthropies.

[Stewart Kampel (2nd ed.)]

RANK, OTTO (original surname – **Rosenfeld**; 1884–1939), psychoanalyst. Born in Vienna, Rank met *Freud in 1906 and became a member of his inner circle. Rank edited with H. *Sachs the psychoanalytic journal *Imago* and with S. Ferenczi and E. Jones *International Zeitschrift fuer Psychoanalyse* (1912–24). He founded and directed the Internationale Psychoanalytische Verlag (1919–24). He had a special flair for interpreting myths, legends, and dreams. His vast erudition was evident in his great work on incest myths, *Das Inzest Motiv in Dichtung und Sage* (1912). He spent the war years in Cracow. E. Jones notes the change that had occurred in him as a reaction to the melancholia he suffered there. He eventually broke with Freud after his book *Das Trauma der Geburt* (1923; *The Trauma of Birth*, 1929) appeared. Freud opposed what he finally considered to be Rank's error in attributing to birth trauma the determination of anxiety and his underemphasis of the role of incest drives and the Oedipus complex. After the split with Freud he left Vienna, finally settling in the U.S. in 1935. Rank applied psychoanalytic theory to the arts and to mythology in his works *Der Kuenstler* (1907; *Art and Artist*, 1932) and *Der Mythus von der Geburt des Helden* (1909; *The Myth of the Birth of the Hero*, 1914).

BIBLIOGRAPHY: E. Jones, *Sigmund Freud*, 3 (1957), 45ff. **ADD. BIBLIOGRAPHY:** J. Taft, *Otto Rank* (1958); A. Zottl, *Otto Rank* (1982); E. Menaker, *Otto Rank* (1982); E.J. Lieberman, *Acts of Will* (1985); E. Menaker, *Separation, Will, and Creativity* (1996).

[Louis Miller]

RANKIN, HARRY (1920–2002), Canadian lawyer and politician. Rankin was born and raised in Vancouver, British Columbia, and became one of the city's most beloved and controversial public figures. During World War II, Rankin served in the Canadian Army Seaforth Highlanders and was twice wounded. Returning to civilian life, he completed a B.A. and law degree in just five years at the University of British Columbia. Staunchly left-wing, Rankin was nearly prevented from taking the bar because he had belonged to the Communist University Club. He went on to become treasurer and a life member of the BC Law Society and was appointed Queen's Counsel. In addition to helping establish the province's first system of legal aid, much of Rankin's work as a lawyer was performed without charge. He was a tireless advocate for tenant rights, the working class, Aboriginals, Vancouver's downtown east side, and many disadvantaged groups and individuals. He and his first wife, Jonnie (Ottwell) Rankin, were early members of the city's People's Cooperative Bookstore, and their Vancouver home was a well-known meeting place for leftist political and labor activists. In 1966 Rankin was elected as a City Council alderman, a position that he held for 24 years. In 1968 he co-founded the Coalition of Progressive Electors (COPE), a socialist municipal political party that eventually broke the conservative domination of city government. Rankin retired from the City Council in 1993, but he continued to pursue high-profile progressive causes and cases until his death. His second wife and widow, Connie Fogal-Rankin, is also a prominent Vancouver lawyer and politician. Following Rankin's death, the BC chapter of the Canadian Bar Association established an annual award in his memory as recognition of Rankin's outstanding contributions in pro bono work.

[Barbara Schober (2nd ed.)]

RANSCHBURG, BEZALEL BEN JOEL (1760–1820), rabbinical author. In accordance with the imperial decree of 1787 (see *Names) he adopted the name "Daniel Rosenbaum" but was later called Ranschburg, the Yiddish pronunciation of the town Ronsperg, the German name for *Pobezovice where he was born. He attended yeshivot at Schwabach, Fuerth, and Prague, where he was a pupil of Leib Fischels and also studied under Ezekiel *Landau. He never held an official appointment and was supported by his wife and her father, but acted as *rosh yeshivah* in Prague. Ranschburg fought Reform (Resp. Ḥatam Sofer). Among his pupils was Zacharias *Frankel (MGWJ, 45 (1901), 220).

He devoted himself to commenting on those tractates of the Talmud on which there are few commentaries, such as his *Horah Gever* on *Horayot (Prague, 1802) and *Pitḥei Niddah* (1957; published in Jerusalem 1928 under the title *Hokhmat Beẓalel*). His *Sedeh Ẓofim* on *Asher b. Jehiel's *halakhot* was appended to the Prague Talmud edition (1839–46). His *Ma'aseh Rav* (Prague, 1823) deals partly with tractate *Nazir*. *Haggahot based on it are included in all subsequent editions of the Talmud. Many letters on halakhic subjects which he wrote to the censor Carolus Fischer (partly signed "Ilan Shoshan") are preserved in the Prague University Library (MGWJ, 62 (1918), 49–56).

BIBLIOGRAPHY: B. Ranschburg, *Horah Gever* (1802), introd.; idem, *Ma'aseh Rav* (1823), introd.; S. Kauder, *Ahavat Emet* (1828), 47b–50b; O. Muneles, *Bibliographical Survey of Jewish Prague* (1952), index.

[Meir Lamed]

RANSOM (Heb. כֹּפֶר, *kofer*), the compensation required to avoid bodily punishment or to free one's self from an undesirable state or condition (Isa. 43:3). The term *kofer* is related to the Akkadian *kapāru* ("to wipe off") or *kuppuru* ("to expiate"). The substitution of a penal sum for corporal punishment was widespread in the ancient world. Thus, the Hittite Code provides for fixed damages for bodily harm; and the Bedouin, too, allowed for ransom as an alternative to blood vengeance. Except in the case of murder (Num. 35:31–34), the Israelites followed this practice too, though fixed sums do not seem to have existed in early times. Instead the principle of "measure for measure" was employed (Ex. 21:36; Lev. 24:18), together with specific standards for determining the compensation

(Ex. 21:19; 22:16). Later, set amounts were established (Deut. 22:29), such as the "redemption" fees for those consecrated to YHWH (Lev. 27). To be distinguished from *kofer* in the sense of "ransom," which is paid to an aggrieved party, is *kofer* in the sense of "bribe," which is paid to a judge in the hope of influencing his decision (I Sam. 12:3; Amos 5:12).

BIBLIOGRAPHY: Pedersen, Israel, 1–2 (1926), 398–99; Pritchard, Texts, 189–90; E.A. Speiser, in: JBL, 182 (1963), 301–6.

[David L. Lieber]

°**RAOUL (Rodulphus) GLABER** (before 1000–1049?), Benedictine chronicler. In his very comprehensive account of the anti-Jewish persecutions perpetrated in France (and in Germany) at the beginning of the 11th century, Glaber confirms or completes many details of the Hebrew report concerning the same events, in which Jacob b. Jekuthiel of Rouen had become involved. His narrative gives a clearer insight than the Hebrew report as to what extent this persecution gave rise to the idea of the *Crusades. He is also the source of information on a Judaizing movement promoted by Raynaud, Duke of Sens, from 1009, and a similar Judaizing heresy in Lombardy in 1024.

BIBLIOGRAPHY: B. Blumenkranz, *Auteurs chrétiens latins...* (1963), 256–9.

[Bernhard Blumenkranz]

RAPAPORT, DAVID (1911–1960), U.S. clinical psychologist. Born in Hungary, he interrupted his studies in 1933 and for two years lived in a kibbutz in Palestine. He moved to the U.S. and from 1940 to 1948 was a leading figure at the Menninger Foundation, Topeka, Kansas, first as chief clinical psychologist and then as director of research. From 1948 he worked at the Austen Riggs Center, Stockbridge, Massachusetts.

He wrote *Emotions and Memory* (1950) which reflects his continuous attempts at demonstrating the close interaction between the affective and cognitive spheres in mental functioning; *Diagnostic Psychological Testing* (with M.M. Gill and R. Schafer, 2 vols. 1948–49; rev. ed. 1968) presenting his pioneering work in clinical psychology and reflecting the revolutionary transition of psychologists from psychometricians to clinicians; and *Organization and Pathology of Thought* (1951), a monumental annotated source book, in which his copious critical footnotes to excellent translations into English of important contributions to psychology and psychiatry from Europe attempted to create a conceptual framework linking ideas and findings of different thinkers. A visit to Israel in 1953 resulted in his paper "Study of Kibbutz Education and Its Bearing on the Theory of Development" (1957). His works extend from clinical research on the etiology of the psychosis of dementia paralytica to the analysis of different psychodiagnostic instruments. His attempt at systematization of psychoanalytic theory appeared as *The Structure of Psychoanalytic Theory: A Systematizing Attempt* (1960). He was also concerned with the professional status of the clinical psychologist and his training. With David Shakow he wrote *The Influence of Freud on American Psychology* (1964). His collected papers, edited by M.M. Gill, were published in 1967.

BIBLIOGRAPHY: R.P. Knight, in: *Psychoanalytic Quarterly*, 30 (1961), 262–4; M.M. Gill, in: *Rapaport, Collected Papers* (1967), 3–7; M.M. Gill and G.S. Klein, *ibid.*, 8–31, incl. bibl.

[Avraham A. Weiss]

RAPAPORT, DAVID HA-KOHEN (second half of 17th century), rabbi and Jerusalem emissary. Rapaport's family originated in Lublin. He emigrated to Ereẓ Israel and settled in Jerusalem, where he served as a *dayyan* in the *bet din* of Moses *Galante. A responsum to a halakhic query from Mordecai ha-Levi, chief rabbi of Egypt, signed by Rapaport, Abraham *Amigo, and Moses ibn Ḥabib, is mentioned in Ha-Levi's *Darkhei No'am* (*Even ha-Ezer*, no. 18), where he refers to Rapaport as "one of the three great men of Ereẓ Israel" (*ibid.*, 17, 31). In 1679, apparently, Rapaport went as an emissary to Germany, and his mission seems to have terminated in 1682. When he passed through Belgrade he appended his signature in approval to two rulings of Joseph b. Isaac *Almosnino (see *Edut bi-Yhosef*, pt. 1 (Constantinople, 1716), nos. 1 and 3), who refers to him in the most laudatory words, stating that "his decision is final since the *halakhah* is according to him" (*ibid.*, no. 23).

His responsum on the subject of a will in the town of Arta in 1675 is no longer extant, but it was seen by Moses b. Jacob Shilton of Constantinople, who agreed with his decision (Resp. *Benei Moshe* (Constantinople, 1712), no. 4). Rapaport's responsum is also mentioned in *Shenei ha-Me'orot ha-Gedolim* of Elijah Covo (Constantinople, 1739), pt. 1, nos. 21–22). In 1700 Rapaport signed in Jerusalem the authentication of a Safed bill of debt (*Mishkenot ha-Ro'im* of Uzziel Al-Haïk, 1860, 153c). He was the author of *Da'at Kedoshim* (Leghorn, 1809), source references to the *posekim* – both *rishonim* and *aharonim* – on the four sections of the Shulḥan Arukh, arranged alphabetically and published by his grandson Jacob David Jekuthiel, who added his own commentary, entitled *Shelal David*. Rapaport's novellae together with the sermons and memorial addresses he delivered on various occasions were published under the title *Ben He He* (Leghorn, 1821).

His son JACOB was rabbi of Safed. His daughter married her relative Judah ha-Kohen Rapaport of Lublin, who emigrated to Jerusalem. Their son ISAAC HA-KOHEN, author of the *Battei Kehunnah*, was rabbi of Smyrna.

BIBLIOGRAPHY: Azulai, 2 (1852), 30, no. 36; Frumkin-Rivlin, 2 (1928), 86f.; 3 (1929), 61; S.M. Chones, *Toledot ha-Posekim* (1910), 165; Rosanes, Togarmah, 4 (1934–35), 320; Yaari, Sheluḥei, 299f., 705.

[Yehoshua Horowitz]

RAPAPORT, NATHAN (1911–1987), Israel sculptor, born in Warsaw. Rapaport studied in Warsaw, Italy, and France, went to Russia, and settled in Israel in 1948. Among his best-known works are his majestic monument in Warsaw to the *Heroes of the Warsaw Ghetto* and his statue of their commander, Mordecai *Aniliewicz, at Kibbutz Yad Mordekhai, Israel. His monument to the *Defenders of Kibbutz Negbah* is also famous. Rapaport is a conservative sculptor whose rhetorical, patriotic monuments are characterized by idealization and pathos. In later works he experimented with abstract form.

RAPE (Heb. אֹנֶס, *ones*), sexual intercourse with a woman against her will. Unless the contrary be proved by the testimony of witnesses, intercourse with a woman in a place where no one could have come to her aid even if she had cried out ("in the open country," Deut. 22:25, 27) will be presumed to have occurred against her will. If, however, it happened in a place where she could have summoned help ("in the town," Deut. 23), but there are no witnesses to testify that she did so, she will be presumed to have been seduced, i.e., to have consented to intercourse (*ibid.* and Sif. Deut. 242:5 and commentaries; Yad, Na'arah Betulah 1:2 and *Hassagot Rabad* thereto). If intercourse took place while she was asleep and thus unaware, she is considered to have been raped because of the absence of her free will. Intercourse with a female minor is always regarded as rape since she has no will of her own (Yev. 33b, 61b; Sh. Ar., EH 178:3 and Beit Shemu'el n.3, thereto). If intercourse began as a forcible violation but terminated with the woman's consent, she will nevertheless be regarded as having been raped since in such circumstances her passions and nature have compelled her to acquiesce (Ket. 51b; Yad, Issurei Bi'ah 1:9).

Legal Consequences

IN CIVIL MATTERS. A person who violates a virgin *na'arah* (between the ages of 12 years and one day and 12 years and six months) must pay a fine at the fixed amount of 50 shekels of silver (Deut. 22:28–29), as well as compensation for pain and suffering, shame, and blemish, which is to be assessed according to the circumstances in each case (Yad, Na'arah Betulah 2:1–6; see *Damages). If the *na'arah* is seduced, the seducer is liable to pay the same fine and compensation, but in view of her consent is not liable for compensation for pain and suffering (*za'ar*; *ibid.*). Since when laying down the liability for the fine the pentateuchal law speaks of a *na'arah* only, there is no liability for a fine upon the rape or seduction of a *bogeret* i.e., a girl above the age of 12 years and six months (Yad, *ibid.* 1:8), but compensation for pain and suffering, shame, and blemish is due if she was raped (Tur, EH 177, contrary to Yad, *ibid.* 2:10, 11). The seducer of a *bogeret* is exempt from all financial liability toward her since, having consented to the intercourse, she is presumed to have waived all such claims (Ket. 42a; Yad, *ibid.*; *Beit Yosef*, EH 177).

IN PERSONAL LAW MATTERS. In addition to the financial liabilities mentioned above, the violator of a *na'arah* is compelled to marry her, "She shall be his wife… he cannot put her away all his days" (Deut. 22:29), unless marriage between them is prohibited by the pentateuchal or rabbinic law (see *Marriage, Prohibited). However, for the reasons set out above concerning the fine, this obligation does not apply if the victim is a *bogeret* (Ket. 39a; Yad, *ibid.* 1:3; 5:7; Resp. Radbaz, no. 63; Glosses (*haggahot*) of Akiva Eger to Sh. Ar., EH 177:2). The *na'arah* or her father may refuse her marriage to the violator, in which event the transgressor will be exempt from the obligation to marry her and be liable only for the fine and the other payments (Yad, *ibid.* 1:3; Sh. Ar., EH 177:3). A person who seduces a *na'arah* has no obligation to marry her (Yad, *ibid.*). A married woman who has been raped does not become prohibited to her husband unless he is a priest, in which case he must divorce her (Yev. 56b; Yad, Ishut 24:19, 21; Sh. Ar., EH 6:10, 11; see also *Marriage, Prohibited). The outraged wife's pecuniary rights toward her husband, in particular her **ketubbah*, remain unaffected in both cases since there is no blameworthiness on her part (Yad, *ibid.* 24:22; Sh. Ar., EH 115:6).

In suits concerning matters of rape and seduction the court must be composed of three competent ordained judges (*mumḥim semukhim*), and, therefore, in strict law the fine (see above) is no longer recoverable since today there are no *semukhim* (see *Bet Din); in various *takkanot*, however, the scholars have nevertheless regulated for recovery of the fine, "lest the sinner be rewarded" (Tur, EH 177; Sh. Ar., EH 117:2; Resp. Radbaz, no. 63; see also *Fine).

In the State of Israel

Of practical significance is the *halakhah* concerning the effect of rape on the marital relationship between the victim and her husband, since this is a matter of personal law which for Jews is governed by Jewish law. The purely civil-law aspects, such as the question of compensation, are governed before the civil courts by the general law of the state, i.e., the Civil Wrongs Ordinance, 1946 (NV 1968). The provision that a person must marry the *na'arah* he has violated is rendered unenforceable by the provisions of the Marriage Age Law, 1950, as amended in 1960.

BIBLIOGRAPHY: ET, 1 (1951^3), 166–72; 2 (1949), 60–63, 295f.; B. Schereschewsky, *Dinei Mishpaḥah* (1967^2), 49–51, 316. **ADD. BIBLIOGRAPHY:** M. Elon, *Ha-Mishpat ha-Ivri* (1988), 1:72, 287, 290, 790ff.; 2:842, 1070; idem, *Jewish Law* (1994), 1:80, 339ff., 344ff.; 2:969ff.; 3:1030, 1291; M. Elon and B. Lifshitz, *Mafte'aḥ ha-She'elot ve-ha-Teshuvot shel Ḥakhmei Sefarad u-Ẓefon Afrikah* (legal digest), (1986), 3–5; B. Lifshitz and E. Shochetman, *Mafte'aḥ ha-She'elot ve-ha-Teshuvot shel Ḥakhmei Ashkenaz, Ẓarefat ve-Italyah* (legal digest) (1997), 4–5.

[Ben-Zion (Benno) Schereschewsky]

RAPHAEL, one of the chief angels. The name occurs in the Bible (I Chron. 26:7) but not yet as an angelic name, first appearing as such in the Apocrypha (Tob. 12:15 and I En. 20:3), where he is one of the seven archangels. In angelological systems built upon four archangels, he is one of the four; the others are Michael, *Gabriel, and *Uriel or Suriel (I En. 9:1–3). He defeats the demon Asmodeus (Tob. 3:17) and binds *Azazel, chief of the demons, throwing him into the abyss (I En. 10:4). As his name implies ("God is healing"), he is the angel set over all kinds of healing and this is his main function. The Talmud (Yoma 37a; BM 86) knows of him as one of the three angels who came to visit Abraham after he had circumcised himself. From the second century on, Jewish traditions referring to Raphael were taken over by both Christian angelology and syncretistic magic. His name occurs frequently in magical papyri in Greek and Coptic, on amulets, and in many Jewish and Mandean incantations. As a planetary angel he governs the sun, and in the division of the four corners of the world he commands the west. He is one of the four angels of the Presence who stand on the four sides of God, a notion taken over into the prayer at bedtime: "to my right Michael and to my left Gabriel, in front of me Uriel and behind me Raphael, and over my head God's *Shekhinah* ["the presence of God"]." According to esoteric Midrashim, his original name was Laviel or Buel but the name was changed to Raphael when he defended against the other angels God's decision to create man. In kabbalistic literature he keeps his high rank and is credited with many missions and functions. Among the four elements he governs earth; in the colors of the rainbow he represents green. M. Recanati even sees him as the angel who governs primordial matter before it divides up into the four elements. According to others, he commands the host of angels known as the *ofannim*. He is also ordained over one of the four rivers coming out of paradise. In the Zohar he is the angel who dominates the morning hours which bring relief to the sick and suffering.

BIBLIOGRAPHY: M. Schwab, *Vocabulaire de l'angélologie* (1897), 10, 249; A. Kohuth, *Die juedische Angelologie* (1866), 35; C. Preisendanz, *Papyri graecae magicae*, 3 (1928), index; G. Davidson, *A Dictionary of Angels* (1967), 240–2; R. Margolioth, *Malakhei Elyon* (1945), 184–92.

[Gershom Scholem]

RAPHAEL, ALEXANDER (1775–1850), English merchant. Born in Madras (India) of Persian Jewish parentage, Raphael settled in England and built up a considerable fortune as a stockbroker in the City of London. Having become converted to Roman Catholicism, he was sheriff of London in 1834 and was elected to the House of Commons as a Liberal in 1835 and again in 1847–50. He was one of the two Roman Catholic M.P.s who opposed Jewish emancipation, notwithstanding the fact that their own religious disabilities had been removed so recently. Although he was not the first person born a Jew to be elected to the English parliament, his career is of interest as typifying the assimilatory potentialities of even an Oriental Jew in early 19th century England. There is some doubt about his ancestry: it is possible that his mother was not Jewish.

BIBLIOGRAPHY: A.M. Hyamson, in: JHSET, 16 (1952), 225–6.

[Cecil Roth]

RAPHAEL, CHAIM (1908–1994), author and scholar. Born in Middlesborough, he lectured in post-biblical Hebrew at Oxford (1932–39), became a civil servant, and was head of the information division of the British Treasury (1959–68) before returning to academic life as a Jewish social historian. Raphael wrote thrillers such as *The Naked Villany* (1958) under the pen-name of Jocelyn Davey; the autobiographical *Memoirs of a Special Case* (1962); and several books on Jewish history and practice, including *The Walls of Jerusalem* (1968), on the destruction of the Temple in history and legend, *The Springs of Jewish Life* (1983), and *The Sephardi Story* (1991).

RAPHAEL, FREDERIC (1931–), English novelist and scriptwriter. Born in Chicago of an American mother and a British father, Raphael was taken to England by his parents in 1938. His first novel, *Obbligato*, was published in 1956 and *The Earlsdon Way*, a study of suburban life, in 1958. Other books included *Orchestra and Beginners* (1967) and *Like Men Betrayed* (1970).

Jewish themes dominate two of Raphael's novels, *The Limits of Love* (1960) and *Lindmann* (1963). The former traces the development of three children of a lower-middle-class London Jewish shopkeeper from the years immediately after World War II up to the Suez Campaign and the Hungarian Revolt in 1956. A family chronicle in form, this novel touches vividly upon a number of social themes. *Lindmann* is different in form and conception. It is a brilliant tour de force, based on the tragic fate of the SS Struma which sank in Turkish waters with its cargo of "illegal" immigrants during 1941.

Raphael won an Academy Award for best screenplay for the 1975 film *Darling*, one of many film scripts he wrote. Later books included *Richard's Things* (1973), *California Time* (1975), *The Glittering Prizes* (1976) – which became a popular television serial – and *Heaven and Earth* (1985). These too evince Raphael's perpetual preoccupation with Jewish themes such as antisemitism, the specter of the Holocaust, and the pull toward assimilation. He also wrote a biography, *Somerset Maugham and His World* (1977), and several books of short stories. Raphael wrote most of the screenplay for Stanley Kubrick's controversial last film, *Eyes Wide Shut* (1999), and a book about his dealings with the filmmaker, *Eyes Wide Open: A Memoir of Stanley Kubrick* (1999).

BIBLIOGRAPHY: F.P.W. McDowell, in: *Novel* (Brown University), 2 (1969), 288–90.

[Shulamit Nardi / Rohan Saxena (2nd ed.).]

RAPHAEL, GIDEON (1913–), Israeli civil servant. Raphael was born in Berlin and immigrated to Ereẓ Israel in 1934. Prior to the establishment of the State of Israel he served in the Political Department of the Jewish Agency, and after its establishment he joined the Ministry for Foreign Affairs and was a member of its Israeli delegation to the United Nations until 1953. In September of that year he returned to Jerusalem on his appointment as head of the Department of the Middle East and of United Nations Affairs in the Foreign Ministry. In 1957 he was appointed ambassador to Belgium and Luxembourg, and from 1960 to 1965 was a deputy director-general of the Foreign Office. From September 1965 to April 1966, Raphael served as Israel's representative to the European Office of the United Nations in Geneva, and in February 1967 was appointed permanent representative of Israel to the United Nations. In 1968 he was appointed director-general of the Ministry for Foreign Affairs. From 1972 until January 1974 he served as senior adviser to the foreign minister, when he was appointed ambassador to England and Israel's first nonresident ambassador to Ireland. Upon his return to Israel in 1977 he was appointed political adviser to the foreign minister, retiring in 1978. In 1981 he published his memoirs *Destination Peace*.

RAPHAEL, JOHN (**Nathaniel**, known as "**Percival**"; 1868–1917), author, critic, and journalist. He reported the *Dreyfus case for *The Daily Mail* and was Paris correspondent for various British periodicals. Raphael's plays include *The Uninvited Guest* (1911), based on a drama by Tristan *Bernard, and a French adaptation of *Potash and Perlmutter* by Montague *Glass (1916). He also wrote books about Paris and made translations from the French.

RAPHAEL, MARK (**Marco**; c. 1460–after 1534), Italian rabbi converted to Christianity by Francesco *Giorgio, who acted as his godfather. Raphael played an important role in the theological controversy engendered by the divorce suit brought by Henry VIII against his wife Catherine of Aragon and instituted at Venice by the secret envoy of the king, Richard Croke. Associated with the kabbalistic circles which were influential at the time, as well as with the most erudite of the hebraizing humanists in Venice, Raphael entered the service of the Venetian republic in 1525, which made him a grant for having invented an improved invisible ink. He ranged himself on the side of the king in 1529. Although many eminent rabbis of Venice had been consulted, including Kalonymus b. David, Elijah Menahem *Ḥalfan, and Baruch (Bendit) Axelrod ben Eleazar, as well as Solomon *Molcho, Henry VIII attached the greatest weight to Raphael s opinion. Raphael wrote a number of theological treatises in Hebrew, still not discovered, at the instigation of Giorgio, who translated them for the king. The quality of his arguments, which varied according to need, and his vast erudition were feared by the king's opponents. Warmly recommended by Giorgio to Henry VIII, Raphael was invited to England in 1530, and he remained in the king's service for several years, accompanying him on his visit to France in 1532, serving him in the most diverse capacities and receiving substantial rewards. Henry VIII even sent him on a mission of investigation to the Welsh silver and iron mines. He was still alive in 1534, when he complained about his lack of means to his protector Thomas Cromwell.

BIBLIOGRAPHY: J.S. Brewer and J. Gairdner (eds.), *Letters and Papers of the Reign of Henry VIII*, 4, 3; *ibid.*, 5 and 6; *ibid.*, Addenda 1, 1; *Calendar of State Papers in Spanish*, 3 and 4,4; L. Wolf, in: *Papers Read at the Anglo-Jewish Historical Exhibition* (1888), 53; D. Kaufmann, in: REJ, 27 (1893) and 30 (1895); C. Roth, *History of the Jews in Venice* (1930); J.F. Maillard, in: RHR (1972), 157.

[J.-F. Maillard]

RAPHAEL, RALPH ALEXANDER (1921–1998) British organic chemist. Raphael was born in Croydon, Greater London, and educated at Wesley College, Dublin and Tottenham County School, where he was inspired to study science by Edgar Ware. He graduated B.Sc. (1941), Ph.D. (1943, under the supervision of I. Heilbron and E.R.H. Jones), and D.Sc. (1952) from Imperial College of Science and Technology, University of London. Raphael was head of the chemotherapy research unit of the pharmaceutical company May and Baker (1943–46) and then ICI research fellow at Imperial College (1946–49). He was lecturer in chemistry at Glasgow University (1949–54) before his appointment as the first professor of organic chemistry at Queen's University, Belfast (1954–57), where he established a new department. He returned to Glasgow University as Regius Professor of Chemistry (1957–1972). Later, he was appointed professor of organic chemistry at Cambridge University and Fellow of Christ's College (1972–88). Raphael's research started with his Ph.D. thesis and mainly concerned the chemistry of acetylenic compounds and their application to the synthesis of a wide range of novel products derived from natural substances. He was the first to synthesize penicillinic acid and linoleic acid. He synthesized novel compounds related to carbohydrate synthesis and many other compounds of great theoretical and practical importance. He also developed new pathways for synthesizing histamine and many alkaloids. He was an outstanding teacher and he established thriving research and teaching departments in the universities where he held chairs. He served on the governing committees of his own and other universities and of the societies with which he was associated. His many honors included election to the Royal Society of London (1962) and the award of its Davy Medal (1981), the Ciba-Geigy Award for Synthetic Chemistry (1975), and appointment as C.B.E. (1982). He was visiting professor at the Haifa Technion and the Hebrew University of Jerusalem (1981). He married the violinist and violist Prudence Gaffikin (1944). He was passionately interested in music and the improvement of violin tone by utilizing his chemical expertise. He was a noted raconteur of Jewish humor.

[Michael Denman (2nd ed.)]

RAPHAEL, WILLIAM (1833–1914), artist and teacher. Raphael is Canada's first known professional Jewish artist. He was born into a religious home in East Prussia and studied at the Royal Academy of Berlin and emigrated first to New York and then to Montreal in 1857. Here he produced mainly genre scenes, landscapes, and portraits in the Biedermeier realist tradition. His earliest livelihood derived from portrait commissions in Montreal, Quebec City, and Trois Rivières and from photography-based art for William Notman. In Jewish public spaces, portraits remain of Dr. Aaron David Hart, ophthalmologist, and Dr. Abraham David *de Sola, rabbi of the Spanish and Portuguese Synagogue. Raphael loved the Canadian landscape and its indigenous peoples and habitants, both of which became part of his lively genre scenes and site-specific landscapes. He created artistically rendered drawings in *Behind Bonsecours Market, Montreal*, 1866, (where he includes himself as the immigrant artist clutching his portfolio and family menorah), *Habitants Attacked by Wolves*, 1870 (made into the first Canadian chromolithograph for distribution by the Art Association), and his Murray Bay Indian Encampment scenes. Raphael painted religious subjects for Catholic institutions and taught in those institutions as well. Canadian artist Wyatt Eaton received his first art lessons with him before 1867. Raphael also taught at Montreal High School; the Art Association of Montreal (the first teacher of "Figure Painting and Drawing" there, 1881); the Sisters of St. Anne Convent (where he trained nuns to teach art); and the Villa Maria Convent and society pupils at Raphael's private art school from 1885. One of his nine children, Samuel, became an artist in New York. Raphael was a charter member of the Royal Canadian Academy and the Society of Canadian Artists. He was a member of the Art Association of Montreal; the Ontario Society of Artists; the Pen and Pencil Club of Montreal; and the Council of Arts and Manufacturers of Quebec. Raphael was also a founder of the National Gallery of Canada and of Montreal's first Reform temple, Temple Emanuel.

BIBLIOGRAPHY: S.R. Goelman, *William Raphael (1833–1914)* (1996).

[Sharon Goelman (2nd ed.)]

RAPHAEL (Werfel), YITZHAK (1914–1999), Israeli religious politician, member of the Second to Eighth Knessets. Born in Sasov, East Galicia, Raphael went to a *heder*, and then studied at a yeshivah in Lublin. Raphael moved to Lvov in 1929, where he studied in a gymnasium. He was one of the founders of the *Bnei Akiva movement and a member of the Torah va-Avodah leadership in Galicia. Raphael settled in Palestine in 1935. He received a second degree from the Hebrew University in the arts, and a doctorate from the Jewish Theological Seminary in New York. In the years 1940–46 he edited the weekly *Bamishor*. In the Jewish Agency he was director of the department for small businesses. In 1944 he became a member of the Va'ad Le'ummi. In the years 1947–48 he was a member of the Jerusalem Committee, and in 1948 was the director of the office that provided for those wounded in the course of the War of Independence. In the years 1948–53 he was a member of the *Jewish Agency Executive, and head of its Aliyah Department during the period of mass immigration. He was a member of Ha-Po'el ha-Mizrachi, and later of the *National Religious Party. Raphael was first elected to the Second Knesset. In the Knesset he was a member of the Foreign Affairs and Defense Committee. In the years 1961–65 he served as deputy minister of health. During this period he started to edit *Sinai*, a monthly on Judaica. In 1965 he was implicated in an affair involving one of his employees, who was imprisoned on charges of extortion, and resigned from his ministerial post in 1965. He was finally acquitted of complicity in this affair by the Tel Aviv District Court. In the years 1974–76 he was minister of religious affairs. After abstaining in a vote on a motion of no confidence in the government, against the background of the alleged desecration of the Sabbath as a result of an official ceremony held when new fighter aircraft arrived from the U.S. on Friday afternoon, the National Religious Party ministers, including Raphael, were dismissed from the government.

Raphael was chairman of Mossad ha-Rav Kook and Yad ha-Rav Maimon, and a member of the Party Executive and of the World Center of ha-Mizrachi-ha-Po'el ha-Mizrachi. In 1979 he received the Bialik prize for Jewish knowledge.

Among his writings are an autobiography *Lo Zakhiti ba-Or min ha-Hefker* (1981) and a book on Ḥasidism. He was also an encyclopedia editor on religious Zionism in the *Enẓiklopedyah shel ha-Ẓiyyonut ha-Datit*, 3 vols. (1958–65), and on Ḥasidism, in the *Enẓiklopedyah le-Ḥasidut* (2000).

[Susan Hattis Rolef (2nd ed.)]

RAPHAEL OF BERSHAD (d. between 1816 and 1826), ḥasidic *ẓaddik*. Raphael was a close disciple and successor of Phinehas of *Korets, who thought highly of him. After Phinehas' death many of his followers became Raphael's disciples. He introduced several customs and liturgical elements ("the Bershad liturgy") that differed from the accepted ḥasidic style and came closer to the Ashkenazi rite. His followers remained a distinct group after his death, although he had no successor. There are many legends about him and some of his sayings were published in *Midrash Pinḥas* (1872), most of which is still in manuscript.

BIBLIOGRAPHY: Horodezky, Ḥasidut, 1 (1951³), 150, 155f.; N. Huberman, *Bershad* (Heb., 1956), 8, 21, 23–39.

[Adin Steinsalz]

RAPHAELSON, SAMSON (1894–1983), U.S. playwright and screenwriter. After graduating from the University of Illinois, the Manhattan-born Raphaelson worked at various jobs, including English literature professor at his alma mater, advertising account executive, and crime reporter at the *New York Times*. *The Jazz Singer* (1926) was Raphaelson's first and best-known play. A story of assimilation, it told how a young Jew breaks with his family's tradition of being cantors to become a jazz singer. In 1927, Raphaelson adopted *The Jazz Singer* for the screen and it became the first "talkie." Raphaelson's 1934 play, *Accent on Youth*, was turned into a film in 1935. It was redone in 1950 as *Mr. Music* and in 1959 as *But Not for Me*. Other Raphaelson plays that later became movies include *Skylark* (1941), *Bannerline* (1951), from his play *A Rose Is Not a Rose*, and *Hilda Crane* (1956). In 1941, Raphaelson wrote the Alfred Hitchock classic *Suspicion*. Raphaelson characterized his work as "sophisticated comedy," which went well with director Ernst *Lubitsch's style. The two often worked together, and Raphaelson was the screenwriter for *The Smiling Lieutenant* (1931), *Broken Lullaby* (1932), *One Hour with You* (1932), *Trouble in Paradise* (1932), *The Merry Widow* (1934), *Angel* (1937), *The Shop Around the Corner* (1940), and *Heaven Can Wait* (1943). Other Raphaelson films include *Caravan* (1934), *Ladies Love Danger* (1935), *Green Dolphin Street* (1947), and *That Lady in Ermine* (1948). From 1978 to 1982, Raphaelson taught screenwriting at Columbia University. Raphaelson was Robert *Rafelson's uncle.

[Susannah Howland (2nd ed.)]

RAPHALL, MORRIS JACOB (1798–1868), rabbi. Raphall, who was born in Stockholm, Sweden, settled in England in 1825. He quickly became prominent in British Jewry and one of its chief exponents to the Christian world, fighting for the political rights of Jews and against defamations of Judaism. He published *Hebrew Review and Magazine of Rabbinical Literature* (3 vols., October 1834–July 1836), the first Jewish periodical in England, and, with David Aaron de *Sola, he produced the first translation of parts of the Mishnah into English, *Eighteen Treatises from the Mishna* (1843; 1845²). In 1849 Raphall went to the U.S. to serve as rabbi of B'nai Jeshurun Synagogue in New York. There he associated himself with Isaac *Leeser and S.M. *Isaacs and preached against Reform. His lectures on Jewish history attracted large crowds, including many Christians. In 1860 he gave the first invocation by a rabbi before the House of Representatives.

At the peak of the secession crisis, on Jan. 4, 1861, a day President Buchanan had proclaimed a National Fast Day, Raphall delivered what became the most highly publicized rabbinical statement on the "Bible and Slavery." Placing Judaism squarely in opposition to abolitionism, he denied that any statement in the Bible could be interpreted to prohibit slavery, and insisted that, on the contrary, biblical law granted the right to own slaves. He did distinguish between biblical slavery and the southern system; the Bible, he said, regarded the slave as a person, whereas Southerners treated the slave as a thing. But he directed his major attack against the abolitionists for their misrepresentation of the Bible and their agitation against the legitimate right of slaveholding. The sermon was widely reprinted, drawing praise throughout the South and criticism from Jewish and non-Jewish abolitionists in the North. A notable reply came from the Reform leader and abolitionist Rabbi David *Einhorn.

An active fund-raiser on behalf of the needy, Raphall was particularly concerned for the poor of Palestine. His books include *Ruhama: Devotional Exercises for the Use of the Daughters of Israel* (1852), *Post-Biblical History of the Jews* (2 vols., 1855), and *Path to Immortality* (1859).

BIBLIOGRAPHY: DAB, s.v.; I. Goldstein, *Century of Judaism in New York* (1930), 111–5, 148–53; H.S. Morais, *Eminent Israelites of the Nineteenth Century* (1880), 287–91; E.M.F. Mielziner, *Moses Mielziner* (Eng., 1931), 212–50; M. Davis, *Emergence of Conservative Judaism* (1963), 356–58.

[Jack Reimer]

RAPKINE, LOUIS (1904–1948), biochemist. Rapkine was born in Russia, taken to Canada in 1911, and settled in France in 1924. As early as 1932 he became involved with the plight of European victims of racial and political discrimination and in 1934 set up in France the "Comité d'accueil des savants étrangers" to find work for academic refugees. During the war he went to the United States, where he worked tirelessly and managed to rescue a group of men of science and their families. When American legislation made it difficult for this group of foreign scientists to work for the allied war effort, Rapkine arranged for them to be transferred to the United Kingdom, where he became head of a French Scientific Mission. In 1946 he followed his group back to France to continue his research in a department of cellular chemistry created for him at the Pasteur Institute. He also devoted much of his energy to getting French science back on its feet.

BIBLIOGRAPHY: Crowther, in: *Nature*, 163 (1949), 162–3, 458–9.

RAPOPORT (**Rappoport**; also **Rapaport** or **Rappaport**), common surname among Jews in Italy, Germany, Poland, and Russia. The family was descended from Abraham Menahem b. Jacob ha-Kohen Rapa who lived in Porto, Italy, at the beginning of the 16th century. The name Rapa originated in the German *Rabe* (*Rappe* in Middle High German), i.e., a raven. In order to distinguish themselves from other members of the Rapa family, the members of this family added the name of the town of Porto, and thus the name Rapoport was formed. (According to another version, this came about by a marriage between the Rapa and Porto families.) The family escutcheon of Abraham Rapa of Porto shows a raven surmounted by two hands raised in blessing (indicating the family's priestly descent). In the course of time other families, including some who were not *kohanim*, took the name of Rapoport.

Known from the 17th century were David ha-Kohen *Rapaport of Lublin and SOLOMON BEN NAḤMAN HA-KOHEN, who officiated as a rabbi in Dubno, Grodno, and Lublin. In the 18th century there were ḤAYYIM BEN SIMḤAH HA-KOHEN RAPOPORT (c. 1700–1771), rabbi in Slutsk and Lvov, who took part in the disputation with the Frankists in Lvov in 1759 and was the author of *Zekher Ḥayyim* (Lemberg, 1865), responsa and funeral orations. His brother, BENJAMIN BEN SIMḤAH HA-KOHEN RAPOPORT, a *Maggid* in the community of Brzezany (Berezhany), Galicia, wrote *Gevulot Binyamin* (Lemberg, 1789), containing novellae on the Torah, and a commentary on the Passover *Haggadah*. Isaac ben Judah ha-Kohen *Rappaport officiated as rabbi at Smyrna. He died in Jerusalem, having published responsa and homilies *Battei Kehunnah* (Smyrna, 1736; Salonika, 1754²). In the 19th century Benjamin Ze'ev Wolf ha-Kohen ben Isaac *Rapoport (1754–1837) officiated as rabbi in Papa, Hungary. He was known for the lenient decisions in his responsa, which caused the extreme Orthodox Mordecai *Banet and Moses *Sofer to demand his dismissal. He opposed Kabbalah and Ḥasidism. He wrote *Simlat Binyamin* (Dyhernfurth, 1788), *Simlah Sheniyyah* (Vienna, 1800), and responsa *Edut le-Yisrael* (Pressburg, 1839).

The most important member of the Rapoport family in the 19th century was Solomon Judah Leib *Rapoport ("Shir"). His grandson, ARNOLD RAPOPORT (b. 1840), a leader of the assimilationists in Galicia, was a deputy of the Austrian Reichsrat from 1879 to 1907 representing the Polish party. He was popular among the Jewish masses in Galicia for founding relief organizations. In 1890 he was ennobled, receiving the title von Porada.

Members of the family well known in Russia in modern times were the Russian-Yiddish journalist SIMON RAPA-

PORT; the author and folklorist Solomon Zainwil Rapoport (S. *An-ski); and the socialist leader and writer Charles *Rappoport. ALEXANDER RAPOPORT (1862–1928), a publisher in Russia, was the last owner of the Hebrew newspaper *Ha-Meliẓ* as well as the publisher of *Der Fraynd*, the first Yiddish daily in Russia.

BIBLIOGRAPHY: E. Carmoly, *Ha-Orevim u-Venei ha-Yonah* (1861); J. Reifmann, in: *Ha-Shaḥar*, 3 (1872), 353–76; I.T. Eisenstadt and S. Wiener, *Da'at Kedoshim* (1897–98), 135–81.

[Yehuda Slutsky]

RAPOPORT, ABRAHAM BEN ISRAEL JEHIEL HAKOHEN (1584–1651), Polish talmudist and halakhic authority. Abraham was born in Cracow, and studied in the yeshivah there under Meshullam Feivush of Zbarazh. He married the daughter of Mordecai Schrenzilsh, a wealthy man of distinguished ancestry from Lvov, and adopted his surname, becoming known as Abraham Schrenzel of Schrenzilsh. In Lvov he studied under Joshua ben Alexander *Falk. Although one of the outstanding scholars of his time, Abraham did not take up a rabbinical position, and taught in a voluntary capacity for more than 40 years in the yeshivah of Lvov. He was prominent in the *Council of the Four Lands, and was placed in charge of the collection of funds for the needy in Ereẓ Israel.

Rapoport's most important work is his *Eitan ha-Ezraḥi*, published by his grandson Abraham, the rabbi of Baslov (Ostrow, 1796). It is divided into two parts, the first containing more than 50 responsa, and the second including sermons arranged according to the weekly sections of the Pentateuch, together with a commentary on the Five Scrolls and parts of Psalms and Proverbs. Rapoport's genealogy appears at the end of the work. In addition to its halakhic value, *Eitan ha-Ezraḥi* contains much important historical material, biographies of rabbis and heads of yeshivot, and details of the economic and moral state of the Polish communities of the time. Some responsa shed light on the Chmielnicki massacre (1648–49) which occurred during his lifetime. From the introduction to *Eitan ha-Ezraḥi* it appears that Rapoport left many writings in manuscript, which were destroyed during various upheavals which occurred after his death.

BIBLIOGRAPHY: A. Harkavy, *Ḥadashim Gam Yeshanim*, 2, pt. 3 (1899), 40f.; Rubashov (Shazar), in: *Historish Shriftn*, 1 (1929), 172f.; Halpern, Pinkas, 67, 74 n. 6, 220; Markon, in: *Festschrift… J. Freimann* (1937), 93–104 (Heb. section).

[Shlomo Eidelberg]

RAPOPORT, BENJAMIN ZE'EV WOLF HA-KOHEN BEN ISAAC (1754–1837), Hungarian rabbi. His father Isaac and his grandfather came from Fuerth in Germany to Nikolsburg, where Benjamin was born. In 1771 Rapoport went, as was the custom with many Moravians, to nearby Hungary in order to evade the ban on Jewish marriages of other than the eldest son in force at the time in Moravia (see *Familiants Laws). He settled in Obuda (now part of Budapest) and married the daughter of David Boskovitz, one of the leaders of the community. He lived with his father-in-law for ten years, engaging in studying and teaching. In 1781 he was appointed rabbi of the community of Pápa in Hungary, where he served until his death. This community, founded in 1749, made considerable progress during the period of his office. Because of his comparatively liberal attitude, differences between him and the influential rabbis of the time, particularly Moses *Sofer and Mordecai *Banet, increased. These two rabbis were opposed to his methods of study and teaching as well as to his halakhic rulings, even attempting to oust him from his rabbinic office. Rapoport was opposed to *Ḥasidism and to the study of *Kabbalah. A dispute, which exercised Jewish communities in Central Europe for many years, also developed between him and Moses Sofer with regard to Jonathan Alexandersohn, rabbi of Hejőcsaba in Hungary. Like R. *Schwerin-Goetz, Rapoport supported the attacked Alexandersohn, while Moses Sofer was opposed to him, even invoking the secular government, but his community supported him.

Rapoport published during his lifetime, *Simlat Binyamin u-Vigdei Kehunnah* (Dyhrenfurth, 1788) on the Shulḥan Arukh *Yoreh De'ah*, but he left a number of works in manuscript, some of which were published after his death, among them *Edut le-Yisrael* on tractate *Makkot* with additions by his son (Pressburg, 1839). It constitutes the third part of his *Masat Binyamin*.

BIBLIOGRAPHY: E. Carmoly, *Ha-Orevim u-Venei ha-Yonah* (1861); P.Z. Schwartz, *Shem ha-Gedolim me-Ereẓ Hagar* 1 (1914), 28bf., no. 13.

[Yehouda Marton]

RAPOPORT (Rappaport), SAMUEL (1871–1943), rabbi, folklorist, and religious Zionist. Born in Lemberg, Rapoport studied in Germany and then returned to Galicia where he managed the family estate at Kalinka near Zloczow. An ardent (pre-Herzlian) Zionist from his youth, he was active and prominent in the Zionist movement from its beginning, participating in Zionist Congresses from 1898. Rapoport was co-founder of the *Mizrachi and the leader of its East Galician branch. During World War I, the Austrian government appointed him honorary rabbi of Zloczow, in which post he remained to the end. He was a victim of the Holocaust. His scholarly interests were in Jewish folklore, Ḥasidism, and Kabbalah.

In 1906 he published in Polish a work on the psychology of Ḥasidism, and also wrote a historical study in German on the Ḥanukkah festival (1912). His main work, *Werdegang und Charakteristik des religioesen Lebens der Ostjuden*, was not completed, but a number of chapters appeared in M. Buber's *Der Jude* from 1917–23. These gave western Jews an insight into the rich religious and cultural life of Eastern Jewry. Rapoport also wrote the articles on Jewish folklore for the *Juedisches Lexikon*.

BIBLIOGRAPHY: N.M. Gelber, in: S.K. Mirsky (ed.), *Ishim u-Demuyyot be-Ḥokhmat Yisrael…* (1959), 353–6.

RAPOPORT (Rappaport), SOLOMON JUDAH LEIB (known by his acronym **Shir**; 1790–1867), rabbi and scholar, pioneer of Haskalah and *Wissenschaft des Judentums. Rapoport, born in Lemberg, Galicia, received a traditional education and became known for his brilliance as a talmudist. Under the influence of Nachman *Krochmal he took an early interest in Haskalah and secular learning, studying classical, Semitic, and modern languages, as well as science. Supported at first by his father-in-law Aryeh Leib *Heller, who was one of the leading talmudists of his time, Rapoport later had to take the position of a manager of the government kosher-meat tax. Without income again in 1832, Rapoport tried unsuccessfully to obtain a rabbinical position in Berlin and in Italy through recommendations by L. Zunz and S.D. Luzzatto, but his German was poor and he had no university education. After a period in business in Brody, he became rabbi of Tarnopol (1837), where he had to contend with the violent opposition of the Ḥasidim, whom he had attacked in a pamphlet (*Ner Mitzvah*, in: *Naḥalat Yehudah*, 1868) in defense of Haskalah in 1815 (see also his introduction to *She'erit Yehudah*, in: *Bikkurei ha-Ittim*, 8, 1827). Rapoport was appointed chief rabbi of Prague in 1840, successfully opposing the candidacy of Ẓevi Hirsch *Chajes for the same position.

After some youthful efforts at poetry and drama, including a paraphrase of Racine's *Esther* entitled *She'erit Yehudah* ("The Remnant of Judah," first published in *Bikkurei ha-Ittim*, 8, 1827), Rapoport turned to Jewish scholarship, publishing articles in *Bikkurei ha-Ittim* and *Kerem Ḥemed*. Dealing with biblical subjects, he considered the Book of Judges a composite work, certain Psalms to be post-Davidic, and some chapters in Isaiah as belonging to a later prophet. His real mark on Jewish scholarship was made in a series of bibliographical studies of the geonic leaders Saadiah, Hai, Hananel b. Ḥushi'el, Nissim b. Jacob, and Ḥefeẓ b. Yaẓli'aḥ, and of Eleazar ha-Kallir and Nathan b. Jehiel of Rome, author of the *Arukh* (published in *Bikkurei ha-Ittim*, 1828–31; and also separately and posthumously under the title *Yeri'ot Shelomo*, 1904, repr. 1913 and 1960). These studies illuminated a relatively obscure period of Jewish history and paved the way for later research; moreover, they set a new standard of critical methodology to be applied to the history of rabbinics. In them Rapoport traced the migration of rabbinic scholarship and tradition from Ereẓ Israel through italy to Central and Western Europe, and from Babylonia through North Africa to Spain.

Of importance, too, was his *Erekh Millin*, a talmudic encyclopedia dealing mainly with historical and archaeological aspects of the Talmud (vol. 1 (1852); the rest, 1914). Rapoport also wrote an introduction to Abraham b. Ḥiyya's ethical treatise *Hegyon ha-Nefesh* (ed. by Freimann, 1860, reprint 1967). Rapoport wrote articles for Abraham Geiger's *Wissenschaftliche Zeitschrift*, Julius Fuerst's *Orient*, and Zacharias Frankel's *Zeitschrift fuer die religioesen Interessen des Judentums* and became editor of *Kerem Ḥemed*. He was in close contact with these and other leading figures of the Wissenschaft des Judentums (see his correspondence in A. Harkavy, *Zikkaron la-Rishonim* (vol. 2, pt. 1, 1881); *Iggerot Shir*, ed. by S.E. Graeber (1885); M.S. Ghirondi, *Peletat Soferim* (1890); and B.Z. Dinaburg-Dinur (in KS, 3 (1927), 222–35; 306–19). Rapoport took a moderate line against radical writers such as Geiger (see his *Or Torah*, a detailed criticism of the latter's *Urschrift*, in: *Naḥalat Yehudah*, published posthumously in 1868 by Rapoport's son David). He strongly opposed the decisions of the Rabbinical Conferences held by the German Reform rabbis (1844–46), both for the divisive character of the proposed reforms and for the assimilationist tendencies which inspired them, but even so did not exclude the reformers from the Jewish people as long as they considered themselves Jewish (*Tokhaḥat Megullah*, with German translation by R. Kirchheim, 1845). Like Krochmal and Luzzatto, he wanted to see the national character of Judaism preserved. When Frankel's *Darkhei ha-Mishnah* was attacked by Samson Raphael *Hirsch and others on dogmatic grounds, Rapoport came to his defense (*Divrei Shalom ve-Emet*, 1861, repr. 1969; see Hirsch's reply in his *Gesammelte Schriften*, 6, 419–34).

BIBLIOGRAPHY: E. Barzilay, *Shelomo Yehudah Rapoport* (Eng., 1969), incl. bibl.; A. Kurlaender, *Biographie S.J. Rapoports* … (1878^3); S. Bernfeld, *Toledot Shir* (1899); Kressel, Leksikon, 2 (1967), 874–6, incl. bibl.; Waxman, Literature, index.

[Victor A. Mirelman]

RAPPAPORT, ARMIN H. (1916–1983), U.S. historian. Rappaport was born in New York City. He taught briefly at Stanford University and then for nearly two decades at the University of California, Berkeley, where he gained recognition as one of the foremost scholars of American diplomatic history. He also served as assistant dean of students from 1957 to 1967.

He was then appointed professor of history and, from 1967, provost of the Third College, University of California, San Diego. He was one of the founding members of the UCSD history department and served as its chairman. He was editor of the journal of *Diplomatic History* and president of the Society of Historians of American Foreign Relations. Rappaport was also involved in La Jolla, California, Jewish community affairs.

UCSD established the Rappaport Prize, which is awarded annually for the best history essay.

Rappaport's major works include *The British Press and Wilsonian Neutrality* (1951), *The Navy League of the United States* (1962), *Henry L. Stimson and Japan* (1963), *Patterns in American History* (with A. De Conde and W. Steckel, 1965), *Present in the Past* (with R. Traina, 1972), and *A Short History of American Diplomacy* (1975). He also edited several books of sources and issues in American diplomacy.

[Ruth Beloff (2nd ed.)]

RAPPAPORT, HENRY (1913–2003), U.S. pathologist. Born in Austria, where he obtained his doctorate in medicine, Rappaport trained in both Europe and the U.S. In the late 1940s he was assistant professor of pathology at George Washington University School of Medicine and pathologist and chief of laboratories at Mount Alto Veterans Administration Hospital, Washington, D.C. He headed the reticulo-endothelial pathology and hematology section of the Armed Forces Institute of Pathology, Washington, D.C., from 1949 to 1954. Rappaport moved to the University of Chicago, where he became professor of pathology and director of surgical pathology. He was a member of the WHO committee for nomenclature and histopathologic classification of leukemias and lymphomas. He wrote *Tumors of the Hematopoietic System* (1966).

RAPPAPORT, ISAAC BEN JUDAH HA-KOHEN (d. 1755), rabbi in *Jerusalem and Smyrna, and rabbinic emissary of Safed. His father emigrated from Lublin to Jerusalem, where Isaac studied at the yeshivah Beit Ya'akov Pereira, headed by *Hezekiah da Silva. Because of the difficult circumstances then prevailing in Jerusalem, Isaac accepted the assignment of rabbinic emissary of Safed to Turkey and the Balkans (1702–12). Arriving in Constantinople in 1709, he joined Abraham *Yiẓhaki, who was there as the emissary of Jerusalem, in issuing a proclamation against the Shabbatean, Nehemiah Ḥiyya *Ḥayon, and engaged there in halakhic discussions with Aaron *Alfandari. He arrived in Salonika in 1712. At the conclusion of his mission, because of the straitened circumstances in Jerusalem, he accepted the position of rabbi at Smyrna, a position he held for 36 years, though he originally intended to stay only a short time. In this capacity, he greatly assisted Ereẓ Israel emissaries who visited Smyrna, and in 1732–33 saw through the press in Constantinople and Smyrna *Zera Abraham*, responsa by Abraham Yiẓhaki, then the chief rabbi in Jerusalem. In 1749 he returned to Jerusalem, where he became the chief rabbi. Unable to trace the old record book of the local *takkanot*, he published many of them from memory, but was unwilling to issue new ones of his own accord. A collection of his responsa, novellae, and homilies, entitled *Battei Kehunnah*, was published in two volumes, the first in Constantinople, 1736, and the second at Salonika, 1754.

BIBLIOGRAPHY: Rivkind, in: *Reshummot*, 4 (1925), 341–2; Frumkin-Rivlin, 3 (1929), 61–4; Yaari, Sheluḥei, 423–5.

[Avraham Yaari]

RAPPAPORT, JACOB (1890–1943), *ḥazzan*. Rappaport was born in Telenesht, Bessarabia. As the son of a rabbi and a seventh generation descendant of the Ba'al Shem Tov, he enjoyed a strong ḥasidic upbringing. As a child he was apprenticed to the great Zeidel Rovner. In Hungary, at the age of 18, he made his debut as a cantor. Two years later he emigrated to America, where he held various positions and devoted himself to composing, becoming a master of the ḥazzanic recitative. Among those who turned to him for their materials were *Hershman, Shlisky, and *Ganchoff, as well as operatic singers Richard *Tucker and Jan *Peerce. Amongst his famous recitatives are *Ellu Devarim, Modim anahnu lakh* and *Atta noten yad*. He also served as president of the Jewish Ministers Cantors Association.

[Raymond Goldstein (2nd ed.)]

RAPPAPORT, ROY (1926–1997), U.S. anthropologist. A native of New York City, Rappaport enlisted in the U.S. Army at the age of 17, seeing combat duty with the Infantry in World War II, for which he received the Purple Heart. He earned his bachelor's degree in hotel administration from Cornell University in 1949; in 1951 he opened Avaloch Inn, near Tanglewood in Lenox, Massachusetts. He then studied anthropology at Columbia University, receiving his doctorate in 1966.

Rappaport joined the faculty of the University of Michigan at Ann Arbor as an assistant professor in 1965, becoming associate professor in 1968 and professor of anthropology in 1972, eventually serving as chair of the department of anthropology. An internationally respected scholar, his work explored the relationship between religion, society, and ecology, and his many professional activities reflected these interests. His early work, *Pigs for the Ancestors: Ritual in the Ecology of a New Guinea People* (1968), based on his fieldwork among the Maring people, established his reputation. Another notable work, *Ecology, Meaning and Religion*, was published in 1979. His last book, *Holiness and Humanity: Ritual in the Making of a Religious Life*, completed shortly before his death in 1997, was published in 1999; it is considered to represent the scope of his academic work, and it was described as a milestone in the anthropology of religion.

Rappaport served as a consultant for educational, anthropological, and environmental projects, including the National Academy of Sciences Task Force. He was a consultant to the state of Nevada and to Nye County concerning the storage of nuclear waste at Yucca Mountain, and he advised the federal government regarding oil leasing on the outer continental shelf. He contributed numerous articles to academic journals, including *American Anthropologist*, *Ethnology*, *Scientific American*, and the *Journal of the Polynesian Society*. He was a member of the American Association for the Advancement of Science, the American Academy of Arts and Sciences, and the American Ethnological Society. Rappaport was president of the American Anthropological Association, and he served on several national committees on environmental issues.

[Dorothy Bauhoff (2nd ed.)]

RAPPOPORT, CHARLES (1865–1941), socialist politician and writer. Born in Doukshty (Dukštos), Lithuania, Rappoport joined the social revolutionary movement in Vilna as a youth. In 1887 he took part in a conspiracy together with Lenin's brother Alexander Ulyanov, to assassinate Czar Alexander II. Ulyanov was apprehended and hanged. Rappoport fled to France where he joined the Socialist Party and became a prominent Marxist, in opposition to the moderate doctrines of the Socialist leader, Jean Jaurès (1858–1914). Rappoport opposed France's participation in World War I and was present at the left-wing anti-war conferences at Kienthal and Zimmerwald and was arrested in 1917 on charges of making defeatist speeches. Sentenced to three months' imprisonment, his pamphlet *Devant les juges militaires*, describing how he conducted his own defense, created a sensation. In 1921 Rappoport joined the French Communist Party and edited the *Revue Communiste* and the official party organ *Humanité*. Already disillusioned by the evolution of communism in Russia, and shocked by the Moscow trials, Rappoport resigned from the Communist Party in 1938. He condemned the Munich pact and expressed his great sympathy for the Jewish victims of Nazism, regretting that he had not fought more often for Jewish rights.

Rappoport published several works on politics and history including *La Philosophie de l'histoire comme science de l'évolution* (1925^2), *Jean Jaurès, L'homme, le penseur, le socialiste* (1916, 1925), and *La revolution mondiale* (1921). His autobiography was published in the Paris Yiddish newspaper, *Arbeter Shtime.*

BIBLIOGRAPHY: A. Kriegel, *Aux origines du communisme français*, 2 vols. (1954), index.

RAQQA (**al-**), city on the Euphrates in N.E. Syria, founded in 722 by the *Abbasid caliph al-Manṣūr. The Jews identified al-Raqqa with the Calneh of Genesis 10:10. According to the Arab geographer al-Muqaddasī (late 10th century) the city was an important commercial center during his lifetime. Throughout the period of caliphal rule there was a large Jewish community in al-Raqqa and its environs. The philosopher David *al-Mukammis was from this city. An 11th-century letter from a *ḥaver* (rabbi) to a *rosh yeshivah* in *Jerusalem is extant which states that he will go to Calneh the following day to pacify the community, where a dispute had arisen over the appointment of a successor to the deceased *dayyan*. The Jewish community of al-Raqqa also prospered during the period of the Crusades. In the latter half of the 12th century, the traveler *Benjamin of Tudela found about 700 Jews there. In 1191 the head of the Baghdad academy, Samuel b. 'Ali, addressed an *iggeret* ("letter") to al-Raqqa and other important communities in northern Babylonia and Syria. A letter from the last decade of that century, from a Jewish scholar in al-Raqqa to *Cairo, is extant; he sends greetings to *Maimonides and tells about his contacts with the Jews of *Aleppo. At the beginning of the 13th century Judah *Al-Ḥarizi visited the city and complained about the miserliness of the Jews living there, deriding them bitterly.

BIBLIOGRAPHY: Al-Harizi, Juda b. Solomon, *Taḥkemoni*, ed. by A. Kaminka (1899), 189, 367, 399, 411, 417, 453; Mann, Egypt, 1 (1920), 201, 245f.; Assaf, in: *Tarbiz*, 1 pt. 1 (1930), 102–30; 1 pt. 2 (1930), 43–84; 1 pt. 3 (1930), 15–80.

[Eliyahu Ashtor]

RASEINIAI (Rus. **Rossieni**), city in W. central Lithuania. The community there, which included *Karaites, numbered 4,247 in 1797, 2,649 in 1847, and 3,484 in 1897 (46.7% of the total population). Raseiniai was one of the centers of the *Haskalah movement in Lithuania. Abraham *Mapu and Senior *Sachs lived there. According to the 1923 census, there were 2,305 Jews living in Raseiniai (43.7% of the total), most of whom were occupied in small trade and crafts, with a number in business on a larger scale. The Jewish People's Bank had 600 members. Communal institutions included a Yavneh primary school, a Hebrew secondary school, and a yeshivah. Raseiniai was occupied by the Germans a few days after the outbreak of the German-Soviet war in 1941. The more prominent Jews were murdered first, followed by the men, and ultimately the women and children. A few families who managed to escape survived until the liberation.

BIBLIOGRAPHY: Z. Kadish, in: *Lite*, 1 (1951), 1383–86; N. Ben-Ḥayyim, *ibid.*, 1576–77; *Lite*, 2 (1965), index; *Yahadut Lita*, 1 (1959), index; 2 (1967), 359–60.

[Joseph Gar]

RASHI (**Solomon ben Isaac**; 1040–1105), leading commentator on the Bible and Talmud.

His Life

Rashi was born at Troyes, France. (See Chart: Rashi Family). His mother was the sister of the liturgical writer, *Simeon b. Isaac. His father was a scholar whom Rashi quoted in his writings (Av. Zar. 75a). Few facts are known about his early life, although many legends are told about this period. A legend tells that his father cast a precious gem into the sea rather than surrender it to Christians who desired it for idolatrous purposes. A heavenly voice then foretold the birth of a son who would enlighten the world with his wisdom. It is also related that his mother was imperiled in a narrow street during her pregnancy. She pressed against a wall which formed a niche to rescue her.

Troyes was then the capital city of Champagne which attracted merchants from many countries. Rashi learned about different currency standards, banking, and trade. He knew of soldering, engraving, weaving figures into material, and the embroidering of silk with gold. He also learned much about agriculture and husbandry. After his initial education in Troyes, Rashi was attracted to the great academies of Mainz and Worms where he studied after his marriage. His main teachers were *Jacob b. Yakar and *Isaac b. Judah at Mainz, and *Isaac b. Eleazar ha-Levi at Worms. At about the age of 25, Rashi returned to Troyes. He maintained close relations with his teachers, occasionally returning to the academies to discuss unclear talmudic texts with them.

Rashi's return to Troyes was notable, since, due to his influence, henceforth the schools of Champagne and northern France were destined to rival and finally supplant those of the Rhenish provinces. Around 1070, he founded a school which attracted many pupils and became even more important after the death of his own teachers. His most gifted pupils were his relatives, *Simḥah b. Samuel of Vitry, Shemaiah, *Judah b. Abraham, Joseph b. Judah, and *Jacob b. Samson. Nothing is known about Rashi's wife. Although the couple had no sons, they are generally believed to have had three daughters, all of whom married prominent scholars. One of them, Jochebed, married R. *Meir b. Samuel who attended the Mainz academy with Rashi. Four sons were born to Jochebed and Meir and they all became famous scholars: *Samuel (Rashbam), *Isaac

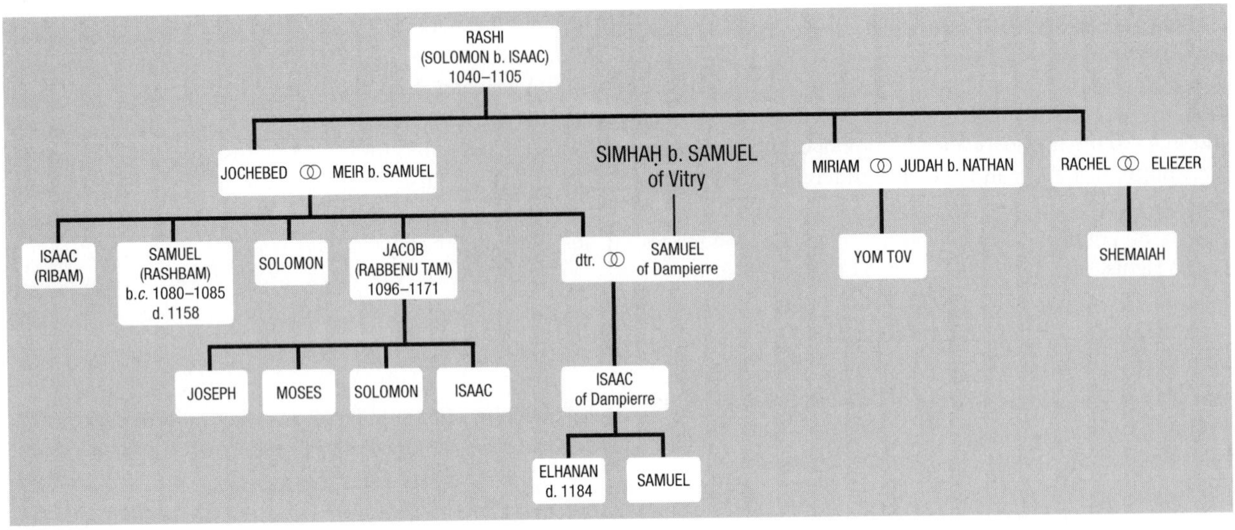

(Ribam), *Jacob, popularly known as Rabbenu Tam, and *Solomon (the actual birth order is unclear, although Jacob was certainly younger than Samuel). They all belonged to the outstanding group of French scholars of the following generation who founded the school of **tosafot*. Another daughter, Miriam, was married to *Judah b. Nathan, whose commentary to the end of *Makkot* is included in all editions of the Talmud (19b–24b). This couple also had a learned son, Yom Tov, and a daughter, from whom *Dulcea, the wife of R. Eleazar of Worms, was descended. A third daughter, Rachel, was known as Belle Assez. Her marriage to a certain Eliezer (Jocelyn or Vasselin in the vernacular) ended in divorce.

Rashi's last years were aggrieved by the massacres committed at the outset of the First Crusade (1095–96), in which he lost relatives and friends. Tradition relates that he foretold the defeat of the expedition of Godfrey of Bouillon, correctly predicting that Godfrey would return to his native city with only three horses remaining from his entire massive army. It is only a legendary tradition that during this period Rashi transferred his school to Worms; there the house called his *bet ha-midrash*, which was located next to the city's synagogue, is a construction of the 16th century. He is reported to have died while writing the word "pure" in his commentary to *Makkot*, (19b) on 29 Tammuz. His burial place is not known.

[Aaron Rothkoff]

Biblical Exegesis

Rashi commented on most, if not all, the books of the Bible. The comments ascribed to him on Job, from 40:25, on Ezra, Nehemiah, and Chronicles are not his, being different in style and method of exegesis. According to Poznański, Rashi did not manage to comment on these, since in writing his commentary he followed the order of the books in the Bible. Lipschuetz, however, contends that the exegesis on these books is substantially Rashi's but was recast and augmented by his pupils. Comments of pupils of Rashi, who studied with him, are embodied in his biblical commentary, which contains (1) explanations that Rashi himself accepted and included in his commentary, and (2) annotations written alongside Rashi's commentary by others, and later interpolated into the text by copyists.

Rashi incorporated in his comments that of *Samuel b. Meir (Rashbam) on Exodus 15:6 ("Thy right hand, O Lord, glorious in power"), even referring to this and other verses expounded by the latter as "the verses of Samuel" (Tosafists' Commentary on the Pentateuch, in Ms.). Writing to the rabbis of Auxerre in connection with his commentary on Ezekiel, Rashi declared: "At all events I made a mistake in that comment… I have now gone through it with our brother Shemaiah and have corrected it" (A. Geiger, *Melo Chofnajim* (1840), Heb. pt. 36). A third pupil whose explanations are embodied in Rashi's commentary is Joseph *Kara (the passages are enumerated by A. Berliner in *Peletat Soferim* (1872)). There is evidence that the latter two, Shemaiah and Joseph Kara, studied the Book of Ezekiel under Rashi, while he was writing his commentary to it. The copyists' interpolations, now part of Rashi's commentary, can be identified by the aid of manuscripts, in which these are written between the lines, accompanied by the word "addition."

Main Characteristics of His Commentary

The main distinguishing characteristic of Rashi's commentary is a compromise between the literal and the midrashic interpretations; to the latter, which was the principal method of exposition in French biblical exegesis, he added the former. At least three-quarters of Rashi's comments are based on rabbinic sources. The few that are original are mainly philological explanations. When basing his comment on the Midrashim, Rashi chose from the available material those that were closest to the literal interpretation of the biblical text, or solved the difficulties presented by it. Thus, for example, in commenting on Leviticus 19:3 ("Ye shall fear every man his mother, and his father"), Rashi, instead of using the *Sifra*, the halakhic Midrash on Leviticus, as he had done in interpreting the preceding verses, now resorted to the *Mekhilta*, the halakhic Midrash on Exodus. The latter explains the twofold difficulty in the verse, namely, the prior mention of the mother and the use of the verb "fear" rather than "honor" as in the Ten Commandments, whereas the *Sifra* explains only the first difficulty.

Another characteristic aspect of Rashi's exegesis is the manner in which he formulated his comment. In many instances he did not quote a Midrash literally but either augmented or abridged it, or even altered its wording (cf. Gen. 1:5, 6, 7 with Gen. R.), his aim being to make for easier understanding and lucidity, and to adapt the language of the Midrash to that of the text. In this way Rashi obviated a patchwork impression and instead achieved a uniform style. The criterion on which he based his choice of comment is clearly stated by him: "As for me, I am only concerned with the literal meaning of the Scriptures and with such *aggadot* as explain the biblical passages in a fitting manner" (Gen. 3:8). In many instances where he departs from this latter principle he adds the comment that these *aggadot* do not give the literal interpretation. But it is not to be assumed that where he failed to add this comment he regarded such Midrashim as providing a literal exposition of the text (thus, for example, the Midrash quoted without this comment in his explanation on Gen. 1:6 ("Let there be a firmament") does not accord with his exegesis of Gen. 1:1). While Rashi based his comment on the halakhic part of the Pentateuch on talmudic literature, his purpose was not to lay down the *halakhah*, and he therefore quoted only some of the many *halakhot* dealing with the subject in question. Sometimes he states that the halakhic Midrash does not give the literal interpretation of a passage (Ex. 16:29, 22:8); at others he interprets a verse contrary to the decided *halakhah* (Lev. 13:6). His partiality for the literal explanation is further attested by the fact that, having revised his commentary several times, he wished at the end of his days to improve it "on the basis of the plain meanings which appear daily" (Rashbam, to Gen. 37:2).

Generally, Rashi did not state his sources but these have been given in detail by Zunz in his book on Rashi, the most important of his sources being the Targums. In his Pentateuch commentary, Rashi derived much help from Targum Onkelos. Not only did he expound many verses according to it, but on occasion dwelt at length on its rendering (Gen. 49:24; Ex. 24:14); interpreted the words of Targum Onkelos; quoted from the Talmud in support of them, and dealt with the etymology of some Aramaic word in the Targum (Deut. 14:5). He laid down general rules explaining Onkelos' choice of words (Gen. 43:15), but in many instances rejected his translation where he found this unacceptable (Gen. 15:11). On several passages Rashi had a different version of Targum Onkelos (Gen. 27:36; Ex. 23:27), which was subsequently emended by publishers in accordance with his version. In his commentary on the Prophets and the Hagiographa he made much use of Targum Jonathan and even quotes Targum Sheni on Esther but apparently did not know the Palestinian Targum on the Pentateuch nor the Targum on the Hagiographa. Some of his sources he heard from others (Deut. 29:3). On one occasion he even declared: "I have had no one to help me, nor a teacher, in all this edifice, but it is as revealed to me from Heaven."

[Avraham Grossman]

Rashi as Grammarian

Rashi centers his commentaries on meticulous analysis of the language of the text. He was both philologist and linguist and derived his grammatical principles from rabbinic literature and the Hebrew works of the Spanish grammarians, *Menahem b. Jacob ibn Saruq and *Dunash b. Labrat (Ps. 39:7, 55:22). Since he knew no Arabic, Rashi never learned of Judah b. David Ḥayyuj's and Jonah *Ibn Janaḥ's work on triconsonantalism. Like Menahem, Rashi sometimes assumes the existence of roots of one consonant (like *hoga*), although, following Dunash, he generally regards the verbs primae *waw* as being tri-consonantal. Verbs tertiae *he* are in his view biconsonantal. To support this view Rashi calls attention to the nominal derivation from the root (such as *ẓadah-ẓedi'ah* in Ex. 21:13). Verbs primae *nun* are bi-consonantal (e.g., *niḥatu*, Ps. 38:3), as are those mediae *waw* as the middle letter, and the geminates like *yegudennu* (Gen. 49:19). By turns, he utilizes the terms *yesod, ikkar*, and *shoresh* to indicate the root; *yesod nofel* (omitted root) to represent a consonantal root which falls away in conjugation; and *pa'ol* and *asoh* to indicate the conjugation of the verb. For the names of vowels he utilizes *pathaḥ* (a), *pathaḥ qatan* or *segol* (e (or: ae)), *ḥireq* (i), *qameṣ* or *qameṣ gadol* (a), *ṣereh* (e), *melopum* (o), *šuruq* (u). Scattered throughout his commentaries are many remarks on syntax, tenses, moods, conjugations (such as the privative use of the *pi'el* – Ex. 27:3), collective nouns (Gen. 32:6), deletion of parts of the sentence, prepositions required by certain verbs (Judg. 6:32), and changes in word order (Gen. 2:19). Occasionally he formulates rules on linguistic usage (Jer. 51:12), and discusses the shades of meaning of various synonyms (Gen. 1:11; Micah 5:7). He discriminates clearly between biblical Hebrew and mishnaic Hebrew (e.g., Ps. 76:11), even though he sometimes interprets the verse in accordance with the rabbinic literature (Ex. 12:7), for which he was criticized by his grandson, Samuel b. Meir. Rashi often resorts to the vernacular French in order to explicate difficult words and phrases, for example, about 1,000 such words and phrases are so explained in his commentary on the Bible. This practice has proven invaluable for the study of Old French glosses (see *La'az). He wrote a small number of glosses in German. However, some of the existing German glosses, and all of the Slavonic glosses, were added by other scholars in subsequent generations (1 Kings 6:7).

[Menahem Zevi Kaddari]

His language is concise and straightforward. At times his terseness is due to his assuming that the reader is fully acquainted with the relevant details (Deut. 1:3, 18), and it is therefore a mistake to hold, as some do, that his commentary was intended for the masses. He explained many difficult problems with a word or a mere hint. Thus, for example, he did not deal explicitly with the difficulty raised (in view of the belief in the giving of the Torah at Mt. Sinai) by the passage "And the Canaanite was then in the land" (Gen. 12:6), but contented himself with the brief comment: "He [i.e., the Canaanite] was increasingly conquering Ereẓ Israel from the descendants of Shem." In many instances he even refrained from entering into the detailed proof of his comments hinted at in the verses he cites. A thorough study of his statements is thus necessary to reveal the problems that faced him, his manner of solving them, and the support for his comments that he derived from scriptural verses and rabbinic sources. His honesty led him in many instances to declare: "I do not know what it is" (Ex. 22:28; Is. 13:21).

Other Characteristic Aspects of Rashi's Commentary

(1) He placed great reliance on the cantillation signs: "Had I not seen the accent *zakef gadol* on the word *u-feneihem*, I would not have been able to explain it" (Ezek. 1:11), but also on occasion he disagreed with them (Gen. 20:16).

(2) Sometimes he combined verses (Deut. 4:44), or explained apparently superfluous details in order to throw light on events mentioned elsewhere (Ex. 13:18), two methods that were later developed and elaborated by his French pupils in their exegesis.

(3) On occasion, as at the beginning of his commentary on Zechariah and Song of Songs, he prefaced his comments with the principles underlying his exegesis, or added illustrations for greater clarity (1 Kings 6:31), some of which were omitted by copyists and publishers (*Rashbam* Num. 34:2: "Our teacher, my grandfather, explained and made a drawing of the borders").

(4) He refrained from dealing with problems associated with philosophy which had not penetrated into German Jewish culture, and thus the question of reconciling philosophy with the biblical concept of the universe did not arise. In many instances he did not even deal with moralistic appreciations of the Patriarchs' actions, e.g., the driving out of Hagar), nor was he concerned with mysticism.

(5) On various occasions he referred to contemporary events (Ex. 28:41; Job 19:24). Here and there one can detect in his comments an echo of the persecution of the Jews in his day (Isa. 53:9; Ps. 38:18). He also disputed the christological interpretation of biblical passages (e.g., Isa. 9:6), a course also adopted by his pupils in Germany in their exegesis.

Rashi's commentary on the Bible, and particularly that on the Pentateuch, enjoyed an enormous circulation. More than 200 supercommentaries were written on his Pentateuch commentary, some even by distinguished halakhists, such as, for example, Joseph *Caro, the author of the Shulḥan Arukh. Of particular importance is Elijah Mizraḥi's supercommentary. The study of Rashi's commentary spread to such an extent that he was accorded the title of "Parshandata" ("the expounder of the law," "the commentator par excellence," a pun on Esther 9:7). It was even laid down in the *halakhah* that the reading of the weekly portion with his commentary could take the place of the obligatory reading "twice in the original and once in the Targum." Christian scholars were also influenced by his commentary. As early as the 12th century Nicholas of Manjacoria mentions him. Nicholas de Lyra (1279–1340) in particular was so greatly influenced by him that his critics called him "the ape of Rashi." This interest of Christian scholars in Rashi grew in the 15th century, and from the 17th century onward his commentary began to be translated into other languages. Rashi's commentary on the Pentateuch is the first known Hebrew work to have been printed (1475), and since then hardly an edition of the Hebrew Bible for Jewish use has appeared without his commentary. An excellent edition was issued by A. Berliner (1905[2]) who examined more than a hundred manuscripts and printed books, indicated Rashi's sources, and added annotations of his own. Part of Rashi's commentary to the Prophets and Hagiographa was edited by I. Maarsen, Isaiah (Jerusalem, 1933), the Minor Prophets (Amsterdam, 1932), and Psalms (Jerusalem, 1936). I. Elbogen published fragments from his commentary to Ezekiel from manuscripts in the S. Poznański jubilee volume (Warsaw, 1927) and by A. Levy in Rashi's commentary on Ezekiel (Philadelphia, 1931). J. Rosenthal edited his commentary to Song of Songs, on the basis of manuscripts and various printed versions (S. Mirsky jubilee volume (New York, 1958), 130–88). An English translation of Rashi's commentary on the Pentateuch was made by M. Rosenbaum and A.M. Silbermann (5 vols., London, 1929–34).

Commentary to the Babylonian Talmud

The summit of Rashi's creative work was his commentary to the Babylonian Talmud. His commentary on most of the tractates of the Talmud has been preserved, but those to tractates *Ta'anit, Nedarim, Nazir,* and *Horayot* ascribed to him are not his. The commentary to *Mo'ed Katan* which bears his name is not by him, but his commentary to this tractate has been published by A. Kupfer (1961). His commentary to *Bava Batra* was completed by his grandson and pupil, Samuel b. Meir (Rashbam), and to *Makkot* by his pupil, *Judah b. Nathan. Rashi's commentary to the Talmud was published with the first printed edition of the Talmud, and except for modern editions of a few tractates no edition of the Talmud has appeared without it. There are extant whole or fragmentary manuscripts of his commentary on most tractates but no critical and scientific edition of his commentary to even one tractate had appeared by the end of the 1960s. Rashi's commentary on the Talmud had been preceded by others, both of the Franco-German school, including his own teachers, and of other centers. His commentary, however, superseded them all and caused them to be virtually forgotten. The language of his commentary is variegated but nevertheless accurate. In his explanations of words he does not confine himself to dry lexicographical data; his explanation is often colorful and the commentary is replete with realistic concrete descriptions. He adduces reasons for *halakhot* and talmudic argumentations, and often provides psychological and realistic backgrounds to talmudic times. In manifold ways he aids the student in the understanding of the text. He provides introductions to themes, intersperses the commentary with the words of the text, and combines recurring statements. With an excellent feeling for the methodology of the Talmud, he points out difficulties in the construction of the passages and unusual terminology. In all this his commentary is unique. In Rashi's view, the only acceptable explanation of the Mishnah is that given to it by the *Gemara* (see BM 33a and b et al.), with the result that he does not give an independent explanation of the Mishnah. Rashi did not write commentaries to those tractates that have no Babylonian Talmud (the commentary to *Avot* ascribed to him is not his).

Although carefully planned, the linguistic variety led many scholars to point to inconsistencies and contradictions, but most of these have no real substance and can be explained against the background of his methods. From the statements of medieval scholars it is known that Rashi emended his commentary here and there after it had already been issued. However, there are only a few emendations which are definitely from Rashi's pen and an examination of the manuscripts proves that Rashi did not write his commentary more than once, i.e., there were no revised editions of it. The commentary circulated rapidly, and from the beginning of the 13th century almost every talmudic scholar made use of it and pointed out difficulties which he answered or explained. Some even worked over his commentary to various tractates, e.g., to *Sukkah, Ketubbot, Bava Kamma*, and *Sanhedrin*. Rashi's corrections of the Talmud text were for the most part introduced into the standard editions and became the accepted text.

[Jona Fraenkel]

As a Halakhist

Despite the fact that Rashi's main aim in his commentary to the Talmud was not to determine the *halakhah*, practical halakhic rulings are scattered here and there, and at times even at length, and he was regarded as a halakhic authority of the first rank in Germany during a very long period. In the same way as his commentary on the Talmud became the basis for all later literary activity in this field in France and Germany, even though his pupils and their pupils did not hesitate to query his comments, disagree with them, and suggest alternatives, so with regard to his halakhic rulings. They based themselves upon his oral teachings and his practices as testified to by those who witnessed them, though they did not hesitate to differ from him in practice from time to time. His grandson Jacob already disagreed with him on *halakhah*, and did not even refrain from criticizing him sharply (cf. *Sefer ha-Yashar*, novellae no. 449). To such an extent was he regarded as a halakhic authority that shortly after his death his responsa, teachings, communications, and practices were assembled in different collections. This literature, the greater part of which has survived, both published and in manuscript, is very ramified, and has acquired the general title of "the school of Rashi." The published collections are: *Sefer ha-Pardes* (Constantinople, 1807, ed, by H.L. Ehrenreich, 1924), *Sefer ha-Orah* (ed. by S. Buber, 1905), *Siddur Rashi* (ed. by S. Buber, 1911), *Maḥzor Vitry* (ed. by S. Hurwitz, 1923²), *Likkutei ha-Pardes* (Venice, 1519), *Sefer Issur ve-Hetter* (printed in part c. 1925), and the one published by Urbach (see bibl.). The connection of the *Sefer ha-Sedarim* (ed. by S. Elfenbein, in: *Horeb*, 11 (1951), 123–56) with Rashi is very much closer. Apart from all these there are extant about 350 of Rashi's responsa, collected from various sources by S. Elfenbein (1943). On the other hand, the works of "the school of Rashi" include additions of a very varied and diversified nature, from the teaching of the *geonim*, from the great Spanish scholars (chiefly in accordance with the *Sefer ha-Ittim* of *Judah b. Barzillai al-Bargeloni), as well as from the early teaching of Ereẓ Israel. It is still somewhat of a riddle how the teaching of Ereẓ Israel was preserved and in what manner it found its way into various works of "the school of Rashi."

The special character of the books of "the school of Rashi" as halakhic collections caused them to pass through many hands, involving additions and omissions, so that the traditions and the practices have become confused. The many parallels existing among these books themselves show considerable differences. Rashi's influence as a ruling authority is also discernible upon the Italian authorities, both among the pupils of *Isaiah di Trani I and also upon Zedekiah *Anav, whose *Shibbolei ha-Leket* depends upon the work of Rashi and his school.

[Israel Moses Ta-Shma]

Rashi's Daughters

Legends about the exceptional piety and learning of Rashi's daughters include the claim that they wore *tefillin*. There is no direct evidence for this assertion but it may have arisen from the likelihood that Rashi's daughters, like other daughters of learned men who had no sons, were better educated than most women in the Jewish communities of their time. Moreover, Jewish women of medieval Ashkenaz, who played a significant role in the economic success of their households and community, had an unusually elevated social position. As A. Grossman has demonstrated, this high status was reflected, in part, by women's increased involvement in Jewish religious life, including their voluntary assumption of religious practices from which they were exempt in talmudic Judaism. Certainly, Rashi's grandson, Rabbenu Tam, knew of women who chose to recite blessings over the performance of time-bound commandments, including donning *tefillin*. Like many contemporaneous sages in Ashkenaz, he accepted these practices (Tosafot to Er. 96a, s.v. *dilma*).

A legend also survives that one of Rashi's daughters had significant rabbinic scholarship. This may be based on a report in *Shem ha-Gedolim* that when Rashi fell ill he called upon his daughter to write an involved responsum. While this reading was accepted by the 19th-century historian Heinrich *Graetz, most contemporary scholars believe it stems from a scribal error which made its way into *Sefer ha-Pardes*. They suggest that instead of "*ve-lakhen bitti karati*" ("and thus I called my daughter"), the text should be read "*u-le-ven bitti karati*" ("and

I called the son of my daughter") (Berger, 167, n. 46). The claim that one of Rashi's daughters wrote a commentary on *Nedarim* probably stems from confusion over the commentary on that tractate written by Judah b. Nathan, Miriam's husband.

However, Rashi's daughter Miriam is cited as an authoritative source on ritual practice in the *Teshuvot Maimoniot* of R. Isaac b. Samuel (the Ri) to *Hilkhot Kedushah, Ma'akhalot Asurot*, par. 5, which states, "This is how it was done at the home of Miriam, the daughter of our teacher Solomon." The citation adds, "We rely upon our logic and upon the testimony of the daughters of the leading lights of the generation." (See E. Urbach, *Ba'alei ha-Tosafot* (1955), 1:38, who cites manuscript evidence that "daughter," not "granddaughter," is the correct reading.) In medieval and early modern Ashkenaz, women were often invoked as authoritative witnesses of the domestic practices of their learned fathers and husbands.

[Judith R. Baskin (2nd ed.)]

BIBLIOGRAPHY: A. Marx, in: *Rashi Anniversary Volume* (1941), 9–30; A. Owen, *Rashi, his Life and Times* (1952); H. Hailperin, *Rashi and his World* (1957); M.W. Glenn, in: *Rashi, his Teachings and Personality*, ed. by S. Federbush (1958), 131–55; S.A. Poznański, *Mavo al Ḥakhmei Ẓarefat Mefareshei ha-Mikra*, in: idem (ed.), *Perush al Yeḥezkel u-Terei Asar le-Rabbi Eliezer mi-Belganẓy*, introd. (1913), xiii–xxii (extensive bibl. in xiii n. 2); Sonne, in: HUCA, 15 (1940), Heb. pt. 37–56; M. Liber, *Rashi* (Eng., 1906); E.M. Lipschuetz, *R. Shelomo Yiẓḥaki* (1912); J.L. Maimon (Fishman) (ed.), *Sefer Rashi* (1940[1], 1956[2]); (American Academy for Jewish Research), *Rashi Anniversary Volume* (1941); M. Waxman, in: S. Federbush (ed.). *Rashi, his Teaching and Personality* (1958), 9–47; J. Bloch, *ibid.*, 49–61; H. Englander, *Rashi's View of the Weak* ע"ע *and* פ"ן *Roots*, in: HUCA, 7 (1930), 399–437; idem, *Grammatical Elements and Terminology in Rashi's Biblical Commentaries*, in *ibid.*, 11 (1936), 367–89; 12–13 (1937–38), 505–521; 14 (1939), 387–429; N. Šapira, *Die grammatische Terminologie des Solomon be Isaak (Raschi)* (1930?); J. Pereira-Mendoza, *Rashi as Philologist* (1940); Ḥ. Yalon, in: *Sefer Rashi* (1956), 515–22; Urbach, *ibid.*, 322–65; I. Schapiro in: *Bitzaron*, 2 (1940), 426–37 (published separately with additions, same year); D.S. Blondheim, in: REJ, 91 (1931); Epstein, in: *Tarbiz*, 4 (1933), 189–92; Shunami, Bibl. 755–757; J. Fraenkel, "Rashi's Methodology in his Exegesis of the Babylonian Talmud" (Ph.D. thesis, Hebrew University, Jerusalem, 1969); S.N. Blumenfeld, in: S. Noveck (ed.), *Great Jewish Personalities in Ancient and Medieval Times* (1959), 233–52; H. Hailperin, *Rashi and the Christian Scholars* (1963); Y. Avineri, *Heikhal Rashi* (4 vols. 1940–60). **ADD. BIBLIOGRAPHY:** I. Berger, "*Rashi be-Aggadah ha-Am*," in: S. Federbush (ed.), *Rashi: Torato ve-Ishiyyuto* (1958); A. Grossman, *Pious and Rebellious* (Heb. 2001, Eng. 2004); E. Shereshevsky, *Rashi: The Man and His World* (1982).

RASHID AL-DIN (**Fazlallah Tabib al-Hamdani**, "the physician from Hamadan"; 1247–1318). He was born to Jewish parents in *Hamadan. He was the son of ʿImād al-Dawla b. Abu al-Khayr, a pharmacist by profession. We do not have any knowledge of the early periods of his life until we hear of him entering the service of the Ilkhan Abaqa (r. 1265–1282), the second *Mongol Emperor, as a physician. We are informed from some early sources that he had embraced Islam around the year 1278, when he was 30 years old. Twenty years later, namely around 1298, Rashid al-Din became a deputy to Sadr al-Din Zanjāni, the vizier of Arghun's son, Ghazan Khan (r. 1295–1304). A few months later, Sadr al-Din was put to death and his place was taken by Saʿd al-Din Sāvaji who made Rashid al-Din his associate. In this capacity Rashid al-Din introduced substantial administrative reforms during Ghazan's reign. He amassed tremendous power and wealth and owned property in almost every corner of the Mongol Empire. Eight of his 14 sons were appointed governors of provinces. As the associate of the Sāhib Divān, mostly using his fortune he built *madrasas*, hospitals, and other public and educational institutions in many places in the empire, especially in the capital city of *Tabriz and in the nearby city, Sultāniyya. In the suburb of Tabriz he constructed a little town, called by his name Rabʿ-i Rashidi, to which he brought intellectuals and artists from different Islamic lands.

In *Tārikh-i Uljeitu*, composed by ʿAbdallah Kāshāni (d. 1337), we read about a bitter debate which took place between Rashid al-Din and Saʿd al-Din Sāvaji in the presence of the Uljeitu. Saʿd al-Din vilified Rashid al-Din with abusive words and called him a Jew (1969:121ff.). For this impudent behavior, Saʿd al-Din was dismissed from the office of the Sāhib Divān and was put to death on February 19, 1312. Rashid al-Din almost experienced the same fate.

Soon afterwards, Tāj al-Din ʿAli-Shāh was appointed by the Emperor Uljeitu to replace Saʿd al-Din. From that time, because of the deep hatred and rivalry between ʿAli-Shāh and Rashid al-Din, the vast Mongol Empire was divided and administered by the two Sāhib Divāns. Thus ʿAli Shāh became responsible for northwestern *Persia, Mesopotamia, and Asia Minor, and Rashid al-Din took charge of central and southern Persia. Eventually, the enmity between the two viziers brought disaster to Rashid al-Din when he was accused of having poisoned the Uljeitu. In an interesting account, related mostly by Kāshāni, Rashid al-Din was charged with murdering the emperor by prescribing the wrong medicine. During his trial, his Jewish background was mentioned very often. Rashid al-Din, when defending himself against the accusation that he had poisoned Uljeitu, said: "How could I do such a thing? I was a Jewish pharmacologist, a physician, a weak person who rose to a high rank" (Suqāʿi 1974:183). Rashid al-Din and his 16-year-old son, Ibrahim, were put to death in 1318 by the new emperor, Abu Saiʿd, the son of Uljeitu. Consequently, Rashid al-Din's property was confiscated and Rabʿ-i Rashidi was looted. Later on, one of Rashid al-Din's sons, Ghiyāth al-Din, was appointed vizier to Abu Saʿīd (r. 1316–1335).

Rashid al-Din is considered one of the greatest scholars in Persia. Besides Persian, he knew Arabic, Hebrew, Turkish, and Mongolian languages. He produced several monumental books, the most important of which was *Jāmiʿ al-Tavārīkh*. The latter includes the history of the Mongols and accounts relating to the history of many nations including the European peoples. His production of the history of the Mongol and Turkish tribes remains a single, uniquely valuable source until now. Regarding his writings, including a commentary on *Koran, see S.H. Nasr et al. in the bibliography below. About

80 years later, Rashid al-Din's body was transferred from the Muslim graveyard and buried in the Jewish cemetery.

BIBLIOGRAPHY: E. Blochet, *Introduction à l'histoire des Mongols* (1910); W.J. Fischel, "Ueber Raschid ad-Daulas juedischen Ursprung," in: MGWJ, 81 (1937), 145–53; J. Karl, *Die Geschichte der Kinder Israels des Rašid ad-Din* (1973; ʿAbdallah Kāshāni, *Tarikh-i Uljeitu* (1969), in Persian; S.H. Nasr et al. (eds), *Proceedings of the Colloquium on Rashid al-Din* (1971), in Persian; A. Netzer, "Rashid al-Din and His Jewish Background," in: Sh. Shaked and A. Netzer (eds.), *Irano-Judaica*, 3 (1994), 118–26; B. Spuler, *Die Mongolen in Iran* (1939); F. Suqaʿi, *Tāli kitāb wafayāt al-aʿyān ibn al-Suqāʿi* (1974).

[Amnon Netzer (2nd ed.)]

RASHKIN, LEYB (**Leib Raskin**, born **Shoyl Fridman**; 1905–1942), Yiddish writer. Born in Kazimierz Dolny (Kuzmir), Poland, where he managed a cooperative bank and was a hardwareman, Rashkin started writing stories in his early youth. His major work is a searingly satirical anatomy of the *shtetl* Godlbozhits (patently the author's Kuzmir) between the two world wars. Completed in 1934 and published in Warsaw in 1935, *Di Mentshn fun Godlbozhits* ("The People of Godlbozhits") is an epic portrait of the disintegrating Polish Jewish *shtetl*. The author draws his townsfolk with acerbic pungency, animating a large crosscut of the town's inhabitants in a broad-canvas *comedie humaine*. The Polish Jewish Pen Club divided the 1938 Peretz Prize among Aaron *Zeitlin, Joshua *Perle, and Rashkin. Y.-Y. *Trunk wrote of the novelist: "*Er iz geven … di letste atraktsye fun a nayem yidishn shriftshteler in Poyln*" ("He was the last new Jewish writer to attract attention in Poland"). The novel still attracts readers, one recent study hailing it as "a lasting work of European literature" (Clifford). His *ershtling* ("firstling"), as he calls his novel in a dedication to Abraham *Reisen (University of Haifa Library copy), had no fellows since he was killed by the Nazis in the Brest ghetto extermination while still in the prime of life. A daughter survived and raised a family in Israel.

BIBLIOGRAPHY: D. Clifford, in: G. Estraikh and M. Krutikov, *The Shtetl: Image and Reality* (2000), 115–32; Ch. Shmeruk, in: *Polin*, 1 (1986), 176–95; Y.-Y. Trunk, *Di Yidishe Proze in Poyln* (1949), 97–101; N. Meisel, in: *Literarishe Bleter*, 4 (Jan. 1938), 56–7.

[Leonard Prager (2nd ed.)]

RASKIN, JUDITH (1928–1984), U.S. lyric soprano. Born in New York City, she grew up as the only child of teachers Harry A. Raskin and Lillian Mendelson Raskin. She studied both violin and piano as a child, but discovered singing and sang in the glee club of Roosevelt High School in Yonkers. She studied voice with Anna Hamlin and acting with Ludwig Donath at Smith College, graduating in 1949 with a B.A. Smith College also awarded her an honorary M.A. in 1963. She won the Marian Anderson Scholarship in 1952 and 1953, and in 1956 won an award from the Musician's Club of New York. That same year, she sang the title role in *The Ballad of Baby Doe*, which premiered in Central City, Colorado. Raskin married the psychiatrist Dr. Raymond A. Raskin, a distant relative, in 1948. They had two children.

Raskin sang with the New York Oratorio Society and was soloist with the Symphony of the Air. She joined the New York City Opera Company in 1959, making her debut at City Center as Despina in *Cosi fan Tutte*. From her debut at the Metropolitan Opera in 1962 as Susanna in *The Marriage of Figaro*, Raskin's repertoire ranged over about 20 operatic roles, especially baroque opera. She stayed at the Met 10 years until 1972. She also sang at the Chicago Lyric and other opera houses.

In 1964, Raskin received a Ford Foundation grant for a solo recital where she premiered pieces by Hugo Weisgall and Miriam Gideon. While she enjoyed an active recital life, especially in baroque music, unfortunately the amount of recital work that she would have preferred did not materialize during her mature career years. She took advantage of other opportunities and recorded for numerous record labels. She also turned to teaching, becoming an instructor at Manhattan School of Music, the 92nd Street Y, and at Mannes College. Raskin served on the music panel of the National Endowment of the Arts and as a judge for the Metropolitan Opera auditions. Raskin continued singing until just before her death from ovarian cancer at the age of 56. Her voice was often described as ravishing.

[Judith S. Pinnolis (2nd ed.)]

RASKIN, SAUL (1878–1966), illustrator, painter, printmaker, critic. Born in Nogaisk, Russia, Raskin studied lithography in Odessa, and attended art academies in Germany, Switzerland, France, and Italy. In 1904, he emigrated to the U.S. He worked in many media and garnered a reputation for his draftsmanlike attention to detail and his realistic approach. His imagery depicted scenes of Jewish life, especially that of New York's Lower East Side. His trips to Palestine yielded many representations of that country's Jewish population, among them twenty lithographs of Jerusalem. Raskin also illustrated many Hebrew texts, including *Pirke Aboth* (1940), the *Haggadah* (1941), Psalms (1942), the *Siddur* (1945), *Kabbalah in Word and Image* (1952), and other works with Jewish content, such as *Hebrew Rhapsody* (1959). *Pirke Aboth* demonstrates Raskin's wonderful sense of design; he makes dramatic use of blank space as a component of his compositions as well as underscores the meaning of each of the book's sections with a powerful combination of human and fantastic forms, each revealing carefully rendered details of expression. Raskin was the art and theater critic for the Yiddish weekly magazine *Does Neie Land*. In 1911, Raskin's "The Future of Jewish Art," appeared in the magazine. In the article, Raskin bemoans the inability to find common Jewish attributes in the works of such artists as Antokolsky, Israels, Liebermann, and Pissarro. Raskin postulated that a Jewish Art (sic) might emerge through the identification of common themes and subjects in the work of his contemporaries, specifically in genre and history paintings, rather than through an examination of the widely varied techniques, forms, and styles used by artists of Jewish heritage. Raskin's work has been exhibited at the Art Institute of Chicago, the National Academy of Design, and the Pennsylvania Academy.

His work has been collected by many major museums and galleries, including the Brooklyn Museum.

BIBLIOGRAPHY: A. Kampf, *Jewish Experience in the Art of the Twentieth Century* (1984); S. Raskin, *Pirke Aboth in Etchings* (1969).

[Nancy Buchwald (2nd ed.)]

RASKY, HARRY (1928–), Canadian film maker, producer, director, author. Rasky was born in Toronto, one of eight children in a Yiddish-speaking Russian immigrant home. Harry, whose father was a cantor and *shoḥet*, spoke only Yiddish until he began public school. In 1949 he graduated from the University of Toronto with a B.A. in arts and began looking for a job in the media, a field not always welcoming to Jews. He found a first job as a reporter in Kirkland Lake in northern Ontario but soon moved back to Toronto to work as editor for a local radio station and also wrote copy for popular newscaster Lorne *Greene. In 1952 Rasky began to write and direct news programs for the new CBC television network and in 1955 he moved to New York to work for Edward R. Murrow. In 1970, already an accomplished documentary film maker and winner of an Emmy award for his film *Hall of Kings*, a documentary on Westminster Abbey, Rasky returned to Toronto, where he continued his career as freelance filmmaker.

Rasky regards his more than 40 films as infused with Jewishness – about half of his documentaries deal directly with Jewish themes and many of the rest are informed by his Jewish roots. His unique, innovative documentary films, often dubbed "Raskymentaries" for their combination of documentary and fiction-film elements, include: *Homage to Chagall: The Colours of Love* (1975), *Arthur Miller on Home Ground* (1979), *Karsh: The Searching Eye* (1986), and the autobiographical *Nobody Swings on Sunday* (2003). His work has chronicled the lives of people as diverse as Shaw and Tennessee Williams, Northrop Frye and Robertson Davies, Leonard Cohen and Henry Moore. In 2005 he was preparing a film on Italian-Jewish artist Amedeo Modigliani.

Rasky's art has been honored with more than 200 international prizes and citations, including the Venice Film Award, the Golden Eagle, several Peabody Awards, an Emmy, and two Oscar Nominations. In 1992, he was given the lifetime award of the Association of Canadian Television and Radio Artists. The Denver International Film Festival called Harry Rasky "the world's most acclaimed nonfiction filmmaker." Rasky has also published a number of books on his life, his art, and some of those he has documented on film, including *Nobody Swings on Sunday, The Many Lives and Films of Harry Rasky* (1980), and *The Three Harrys* (1999).

[Joel Greenberg (2nd ed.)]

RASMINSKY, LOUIS (1908–1998), economist, governor of the Bank of Canada. Rasminsky was born in Montreal and grew up in Toronto. He was active in Jewish life at the University of Toronto, where, despite his outstanding record in the Economics Department, he was unable to attract postgraduate funding. Jewish community leaders established a scholarship allowing him to attend the London School of Economics in 1928. He was soon drawn to Geneva, where he worked at the League of Nations specializing in monetary and banking matters. By the late 1930s he was devoting a large portion of his salary to aiding refugees from Nazism to escape to England.

A man of formidable intellect, Rasminsky joined the Bank of Canada in 1940, becoming executive assistant to the governor in 1943. He organized the research and statistical section of Canada's Foreign Exchange Control Board and played a key role at the 1944 Bretton Woods Conference. John Maynard Keynes credited him with helping shape the consensus that gave birth to the postwar system of international finance and trade. In 1954, Rasminsky was deeply disappointed to be passed over for the position of governor of the Bank of Canada, a snub which reflected antisemitism in the civil service and banking sector of the day. Nevertheless, he continued to hold important positions at the Bank and in 1955 was appointed deputy governor and finally in 1961 governor of the Bank of Canada. In 1973 Rasminsky resigned to spend more time with his ailing wife. However, he remained active, chairing the Board of Governors of the International Development Research Institute in 1973–78 and re-immersing himself in Jewish communal activities.

Although a member of the small circle that comprised Ottawa's postwar bureaucratic elite, Rasminsky was initially denied membership in the Rideau Club, the bastion of Ottawa's establishment. Due to his influence, the club's membership policies were altered, but Rasminsky chose not to join until he completed his term as governor. Among his many honors, Rasminsky received eight honorary doctorates and the Outstanding Achievement Award of the Public Service, Canada's highest recognition of a public servant. He was named a Companion of the Order of Canada in 1968.

BIBLIOGRAPHY: B. Muirhead, *Against the Odds. The Public Life and Times of Louis Rasminsky* (1999).

[Paula Draper (2nd ed.)]

RASSEGNA MENSILE DI ISRAEL, LA, Italian Jewish review founded by Alfonso *Pacifici in 1925 as a monthly supplement to the weekly newspaper *Israel*. It dealt with Jewish history and contemporary Jewish life from the traditional point of view. Its editor until 1938 was Guido *Bedarida, but it became most effective under the direction, until 1965, of Dante *Lattes. From 1965 the review was directed by Yoseph *Colombo. The *Rassegna* was closed by the Fascist government in 1938, but reappeared in 1948 and in time regained its importance. For the centenary of Samuel David *Luzzatto in 1966, a special number of 300 pages was issued.

[Yoseph Colombo]

It was followed by another special number of 400 pages for the centenary of Dante Lattes' birth in 1976. In the course of the years the *Rassegna* tried to express in the best possible way the cultural recrudescences of an Italian Hebraism during a process of radical transformation under the influence of new

Jewish migratory waves coming mostly from Libya, on the one hand, and the influence of circumstances that are extrinsic to the local Jewish situation. These phenomena were specifically connected to Italian political and social life, mostly involving, in broad terms, the vicissitudes of Italian public opinion in the context of the Arab-Israeli conflict. After the editorship of Augusto Segre (1975–1979) the *Rassegna* was distinguished chiefly as a publication with a high-quality scholarly content, published by the Italian Jewish Communities Union.

[Massimo Longo Adorno (2nd ed.)]

BIBLIOGRAPHY: I. Zolli, *Il giornalismo israelitico in Italia* (1924); A. Milano, in: RMI, 12 (1937/38), no. 7–9. **ADD. BIBLIOGRAPHY:** B. Di Porto, *La Rassegna Mensile di Israel in Epoca Fascista*, in: RMI, 61 (1995), no. 1, 7–60.

RAT (Heb. חֹלֶד, *ḥoled*, mod. Heb. חֻלְדָּה, *ḥuldah*, JPS and AV "weasel"), rodent. Two species of rat are found in Israel, *Rattus rattus* and *Rattus norvegicus*. The second only reached the country in approximately the 18th century. *Ḥuldah* occurs as the name of a prophetess (II Kings 22:14, the same verse including two other names taken from the world of fauna: *shafan* ("coney") and *akhbar* ("mouse")). In the Torah *ḥoled* is mentioned with the *akhbar* among the unclean creeping things, from which it seems that *ḥoled* is the same as *ḥuldah* (so rendered by Onkelos) where the Palestinian Targum (cf. Meg. 14b) has *kirkushta*, "rat." The name *ḥuldah* is derived from *ḥalod* ("to undermine"); "*ḥuldah* that undermines the foundations of the houses" (Pes. 118b in Ms. Munich). The *ḥuldah* is frequently mentioned in rabbinic literature. It is said to drag food into its nest for storage (Pes. 1:2; TJ, Shab. 14:1, 14c; Lev. R. 6:2). There is a well-known legend of "the rat [*ḥuldah*] and the pit," in which the *ḥuldah* bit the child of a man who did not keep faith with a maiden and married another (see Rashi, Ta'an. 8a). These characteristics do not apply to the cat or the polecat (*Mustela nivalis*), with which some have identified the *ḥuldah*. The polecat is not found in Israel, neither does it store up its food.

BIBLIOGRAPHY: Lewysohn, Zool, 101f. (no. 135), 107f. (no. 139); F.S. Bodenheimer, *Animal and Man in Bible Lands* (1960), 227 (index), s.v. *Rattus*; J. Feliks, *Animal World of the Bible* (1962), 42; M. Dor, *Leksikon Zo'ologi* (1965), 122. **ADD. BIBLIOGRAPHY:** Feliks, Ha-Ẓome'aḥ, 226.

[Jehuda Feliks]

RATH, MESHULLAM (1875–1963), talmudist and rabbinic authority. Rath's father and earlier forebears had occupied the rabbinate of Kolomyya for 150 years consecutively. Rath, who had a remarkable memory and a rapid grasp of essentials, was ordained at the age of 12 by Isaac *Schmelkes and Jacob Teomim. In 1895 he was appointed rabbi of Molniza and in 1899 rabbi to his native town Horoskov and then to Ushbuza. Rath was an active community leader. He founded a yeshivah for outstanding students, was elected to the Romanian senate, and was one of the first rabbis to join the Mizrachi movement openly. He spent part of World War I in Vienna, where his renown spread. On returning to Galicia after the war, he was considered for the Lvov rabbinate but withdrew his candidacy when asked to give up his Zionist work. He was then appointed rabbi of Chernovtsy. In 1944 he settled in Ereẓ Israel and became a member of the chief rabbinate. There he was consulted by the Supreme Rabbinic Court, and examined candidates for the post of *dayyan*.

Some of his responsa were published under the title *Kol Mevasser* (2 vols., 1955–62). These deal with such topical matters as the permissibility of a bat mitzvah ceremony for girls and of the wording of the *ketubbah* in Hebrew instead of Aramaic. He ruled that *Hallel* with blessings and the *She-Heḥeyanu* should be recited on Israel Independence Day.

BIBLIOGRAPHY: O. Feuchtwanger, *Righteous Lives* (1965), 98–101; S.N. Gottlieb, *Oholei Shem* (1912), 407; Kaniel, in: *Shanah be-Shanah* (1963), 493–7.

[Mordechai Hacohen]

RATHAUS, KAROL (1895–1954), composer. Born in Poland, Rathaus studied composition in Vienna and in Berlin, where he taught at the Hochschule fuer Musik. In 1934 he moved to London, and in 1938 to New York. He taught at Queen's College, New York, from 1940 until his death.

His music was very individual in style. It was atonal and intellectual, showing skill in contrapuntal development and at the same time brooding and romantic. Among his works are three symphonies; an opera *Fremde Erde* describing the modern American city; a ballet; chamber and piano music; incidental music to films; a setting of Psalm 23; and stage music, including, for the Habimah Theater, the music for *Uriel Acosta, Jacob's Dream*, and *Herod and Mariamne*.

BIBLIOGRAPHY: Riemann-Gurlitt; Grove, Dict; MGG, incl. bibl.; Baker, Biog Dict, incl. bibl.; Sendrey, Music, index.

°**RATHBONE, ELEANOR** (1872–1946), British philo-semite and champion of Jewish refugees. Born to a family of wealthy and influential Unitarian shipowners in Liverpool, Rathbone was educated at Somerville College, Oxford, and became a champion of feminism and other social causes. She was an early and important advocate of family allowances – benefits paid to the wife rather than the husband – and of state pensions for widows, and was very active in the anti-colonial movement. From 1929 until her death she was an Independent Member of Parliament. Beginning in 1934, when she visited Palestine, Rathbone became probably the foremost gentile champion of Jewish refugees from Nazism in Britain, constantly raising their plight in the House of Commons, and was a determined opponent of the appeasement of Hitler. In 1942, with Victor *Gollancz and others, she was the founder and head of the National Committee for Rescue from Nazi Terror, the main British body working on behalf of rescuing Jews from the Nazis. It constantly lobbied government ministers to do more to save the lives of Jews in Nazi-occupied Europe and produced a number of widely distributed pamphlets advocating plans of action. The committee met with little success, in large part because of the near impossibility of rescue from the

Nazi death machine, but was very influential in arousing British public opinion on behalf of Hitler's victims.

BIBLIOGRAPHY: ODNB online; S. Pedersen, *Eleanor Rathbone and the Politics of Conscience* (2004); J. Alberti, *Eleanor Rathbone* (1996); M.D. Stocks, *Eleanor Rathbone: A Biography* (1946); W.D. Rubinstein, *Great Britain*, index.

[William D. Rubinstein (2nd ed.)

RATHENAU, EMIL MORITZ (1838–1915), German industrialist and engineer. Emil Rathenau was born in Berlin into a family of businessmen and entrepreneurs. Through his mother he was related to the painter Max *Liebermann. After leaving school before the final examination he started his education as an engineer and technician, which lasted until 1862. Afterwards he worked in different companies in Germany and Great Britain. In 1865 he bought an engineering plant in Berlin. One year later he married Sabine Mathilde Nachmann, with whom he had three children Walther (1867), Erich (1871), and Edith (1883). Shortly after the foundation of the German Reich, Rathenau's company was closed. After some years living independently on his own resources, he established the Deutsche Edison Gesellschaft in 1883. In 1887 it was enlarged and named Allgemeine Elektrizitaets-Gesellschaft (AEG). By the turn of the century the AEG became Germany's second-largest electrical company, topped only by Siemens. The AEG was active worldwide. Rathenau was an obsessive and brilliant entrepreneur. He was creative in finding new ways of marketing and creating new needs for products of the AEG. Thanks to his close contacts with banks, with which the AEG cooperated (especially the Deutsche Bank, later the Berliner Handelsgesellschaft under Carl *Fuerstenberg), he invented new systems of financing his business projects by founding his own company banks (i.e., the Elektrobank in Zurich). Buying licenses for innovative technical products he carefully applied scientific advances to the purposes of the AEG. As a Jew, Rathenau followed the path of acculturation. He avoided any kind of close religious or cultural contacts with the Jewish community. He assumed that a Jewish state could never be self-supporting and thus rejected Zionism. In spite of all this Rathenau was an opponent of the conversion of Jews. Early in his life, he was confronted with antisemitism, including antisemitic comments by his competitors. Being a National Liberal Rathenau always remained faithful to the constitutional monarchy. He was one of the few unbaptized Jews who could come into close contact with German Emperor Wilhelm II. When World War I broke out Rathenau initially expected that it would last only a short time. As an entrepreneur he followed traditional and patriarchal social patterns even though he was able to think in modern abstract terms of building up a modern world-wide company. In the years before his death Emil Rathenau succeeded in placing his son Walther *Rathenau at the helm of the AEG.

BIBLIOGRAPHY: Riedler, *Emil Rathenau und das Werden der Großwirtschaft* (1916), containing an autobiographic fragment by Emil Rathenau from 1908; AEG (ed.), *50 Jahre AEG: Als Manuskript gedruckt* (1956), M. Pohl, *Emil Rathenau und die AEG* (1988), W. Knopp, *Ein Industrieller im Strom der Zeit: Emil Rathenau (1838–1915)*, in: *Jahrbuch Preußischer Kulturbesitz*, vol. 26 (1989), 339–54, U. Wengenroth, *Emil Rathenau*, in: W. Treue et al. (ed.), *Berlinische Lebensbilder: Techniker* (1990), 193–209, P. Strunk, *Die AEG: Aufstieg und Niedergang einer Industrielegende* (1999).

[Christian Schoelzel (2nd ed.)]

RATHENAU, WALTHER (1867–1922), German statesman, writer, and industrialist; son of Emil *Rathenau and his wife, Mathilde. Walther Rathenau's father became the founder of the Allgemeine Elektrizitäts-Gesellschaft (AEG) in the 1880s. After his studies in physics, chemistry, and philosophy in Berlin and Strasbourg, Walther Rathenau wrote his Ph.D. thesis on the "Absorption of Light in Metals." Afterwards he completed a postdoctorate course in electro-chemistry in Munich and then started practical work in the field of industry. Step by step Rathenau developed into an industrialist on the world stage. In 1899 he became a member of the governing body of the AEG. From 1902 to 1907 Rathenau was co-proprietor of the Berliner Handels-Gesellschaft. At the same time he went back to the AEG as a member of its board of directors. In 1912 he became chairman of the board. Rathenau was one of Europe's leading entrepreneurs and an expert on global finance. As an innovative "system-builder" he not only created new organizational structures in the AEG, but also thought of new ways to develop processes for both heavy and light industry. During the last pre-war years Rathenau made some attempts at attaining a political role. A few days after the outbreak of World War I he started to organize the German war economy as the leader of the newly created Kriegs-Rohstoff-Abteilung (Raw Material Department) in the Prussian War-Ministry. When Emil Rathenau died in 1915, Walther became president of the AEG, a newly created directorial function. During the war Walther Rathenau became increasingly an informal advisor to politicians and high-ranking military personnel. After the war he was one of the official German experts at the financial conference in Spa in 1920. Here he created, with other members of the German delegation such as Moritz Julius *Bonn and Carl *Melchior, the idea of a cooperative "fulfillment policy." In 1921, Rathenau was appointed minister for reconstruction (*Wiederaufbauminister*). In this capacity he signed the Treaty of Wiesbaden with his French colleague Louis Loucheur. This treaty foresaw partial payment by Germany of its reparations not in money but in goods. The agreement helped German industry regain the French foreign market. In 1922 Rathenau was appointed foreign minister. Increasingly despairing of French diplomacy Rathenau was tempted to abandon his concept of a "cooperative revisionism" of the Versailles Treaty. He still planned to cooperate in the reconstruction of the Soviet economy with the Western powers. Rathenau signed the Treaty of Rapallo, which set the frame for further closer political and economic German-Soviet-Russian cooperation.

During his career as an industrialist, banker, and politician Rathenau also revealed a strong desire to be a man of letters. In this he opposed his father's wishes to see his son exclusively in the world of money and technology. His publications number more than 150 titles, monographs, essays, poems, and plays. Rathenau wrote about politics, economics, financial affairs, aesthetics, social matters, the arts, literature, and philosophy. He developed a philosophy of world history which was based on the antagonism of two types of human beings, the "*Furchtmensch*" (as a symbol for a mechanistic and rational capitalism) and the "*Mutmensch*" (as a symbol for the world of art, social progress, and morality). Both were fighting for dominance in the world. The ideal, which only the "*Mutmensch*" could reach was Rathenau's "*Reich der Seele*" – a way of living characterized by love, freedom, and transcendent spirituality. Out of his experiences as an industrialist and also with the ideal aim of reaching the "*Reich der Seele*," after the war Rathenau also developed his theory of a cooperative economy ("*Gemeinwirtschaft*"). However, Rathenau was a staunch opponent of socialism. For him the question of a constitutional monarchy or a democracy (which he demanded in opposing the feudal structures in Prussia until 1918) was not as important as having all institutions run by capable and moral people. In foreign affairs Rathenau had an international perspective strongly influenced by his business interests. During the war he became increasingly nationalistic, which also reflects the development of his ideas for creating a "Mitteleuropa" under German hegemony. From the end of the World War I until 1920 Rathenau turned towards a "cooperative revisionism" of the Versailles Treaty.

Rathenau revealed a complex relationship towards his own Jewishness. He internalized antisemitic stereotypes with the idea of escaping discrimination by identifying with the perpetrators. Rathenau regarded Jews as a "race" and demanded their physical and spiritual transformation ("*Höre Israel!*" (1897) published in *Die Zukunft*). He opposed Zionism and all kinds of Jewish organizations (e.g., the Centralverein). Beneath these tendencies Rathenau also displayed more hidden, positive attitudes towards Jewishness: He refused to leave the Jewish community. The baptism of Jews seemed to him only possible for religious reasons, not for reasons of social opportunism. He was interested in Ḥasidism and started to re-learn Hebrew. In his belief Rathenau tried to find parallels between Jewishness and Christianity. After World War I he tried to create his own religion integrating the ideal of the "*Reich der Seele*" in it.

Rathenau suffered severely from constant attacks by antisemites from his early years on. From 1918 there were warnings about assassination plots against him and, indeed, in 1922 he was assassinated by members of the "Organization Consul," an antisemitic, antidemocratic, "volkish" secret organization. The murderers killed Rathenau as a symbol of the Republic of Weimar and as a Jew. Rathenau became a symbol of the Weimar democracy, and remains one of its most-read authors.

BIBLIOGRAPHY: SOURCES: W. Rathenau, *Gesammelte Reden* (1924); *ibid., Gesammelte Schriften in fünf Bänden* (1925); ibd., *Neue Briefe* (1927); *ibid., Briefe: Neue Folge* (1928); ibd., *Nachgelassene Schriften*, 2 vol. (1928); *ibid., Politische Briefe* (1929); ibd., *Schriften aus Kriegs- und Nachkriegszeit* (1929); *ibd., Briefe: Neue Ausgabe in drei Bänden* (1930, volumes 1 and 2 have been published 1926 the first time); H.W. Richter (ed.), *Walther Rathenau: Schriften und Reden* (1964, 1986[2]); H. Pogge von Strandmann (ed.), *Walther Rathenau: Tagebuch 1907–1922* (1967). **ADD. BIBLIOGRAPHY:** E. Schulin (ed.), *Walther Rathenau: Hauptwerke und Gespräche* (1977, 1992[2]); H.-D. Hellige (ed.), *Walther Rathenau: Maximilian Harden: Briefwechsel 1897–1920* (1983). LITERATURE: H. Graf Kessler, *Walther Rathenau: Sein Leben und sein Werk* (1928, 1988); P. Loewenberg, "Walther Rathenau and German Society" (Ph.D. diss., Univ. of California, Berkeley, 1966); P. Berglar, *Walther Rathenau* (1970, 1987[2]); R. Kallner, *Herzl und Rathenau: Wege juedischer Existenz an der Wende des 20. Jahrhunderts* (1976); E. Schulin, *Walther Rathenau: Repraesentant, Kritiker und Opfer seiner Zeit* (1979, 1992[2]); H. Wilderotter et al. (ed.), *Walther Rathenau 1867–1922: Die Extreme berühren sich* (1993); M. Sabrow, *Der Rathenaumord: Rekonstruktion einer Verschwörung gegen die Republik von Weimar* (1994); C. Schoelzel, *Walther Rathenau: Industrieller. Schriftsteller. Politiker* (2004); idem, *Walther Rathenau. Eine Biographie* (2005).

[Christian Schoelzel (2nd ed.)]

RATISBONNE BROTHERS, two French Jews who converted to Christianity and who became prominent in the Catholic Church in the 19th century. The Ratisbonne brothers were sons of a Strasbourg Jewish banker who was president of the Consistoire of Alsace. His second eldest son, THEODORE RATISBONNE (1802–1884) was born in Strasbourg and practiced law in his native city. He devoted much of his time to the improvement of the social and economic plight of the Jews in the Strasbourg ghetto. However, his study of the Bible and church history led him to be baptized secretly. He adopted the name Marie and was hereafter known as Marie Théodore Ratisbonne. After being ordained a priest in 1830 he taught at a church school in Strasbourg and in 1840 went to Paris to work for the archconfraternity of the parish Notre-Dame des Victoires. In 1843, together with his brother Alphonse, he founded the Congregation of Notre Dame de Sion for women and in 1852 the Fathers of Zion. Marie Théodore Ratisbonne's avowed aims in founding these religious societies were to bring about a better understanding between Jews and Christians and to convert Jews. He wrote profusely, and among his principal works are *Histoire de Saint Bernard et de son siècle* (2 vols., 1840; 1903[11]) *Manuel de la mère chrétienne* (1859; 1926[22]).

ALPHONSE RATISBONNE (1812–1884), the ninth child of the family, was also born in Strasbourg and began his career as a lawyer and banker. Like his brother Théodore he was filled with fervor to help his fellow Jews. At first he found it difficult to forgive his brother's conversion and felt hatred toward Christendom for its persecution of Jews. However, an experience during a visit to a church in Rome in which he reportedly saw a vision of Mary (January 20, 1842) moved him so powerfully that he had himself baptized eleven days later. He took the name of Marie, became a Jesuit, as Marie Alphonse

Ratisbonne, and in 1848 was ordained a priest. He left the Society of Jesus in 1852 to collaborate with Théodore in Paris, but in 1855 went to Palestine, where he spent the rest of his life working for the conversion of Jews and Muslims. In 1856 he established the Ecce Homo convent for the Sisters of Zion in the Old City of Jerusalem and, subsequently, two orphanages. He wrote *Monument à la gloire de Marie* (1847).

The Ratisbonne Congregations

The Sisters of Zion benefited from the fact that in the middle of the 19th century there was a prodigious development in the education of girls, particularly in France, and that the French teaching congregations were spreading throughout the world. A congregation whose aim was the conversion of the Jews would have attracted a very limited number of candidates, whereas the movement toward teaching and the establishment of boarding schools made it possible to reach young ladies attracted to religious life. The development deflected the primitive orientation of the congregation: if in their life of prayer their objects remained unchanged the sisters made no efforts at proselytizing. The Fathers of Zion who did not constitute a canonically erected religious congregation during the lifetime of the Ratisbonne brothers were at the beginning primarily chaplains and spiritual directors to the Sisters and their pupils. Until the end of World War I both congregations had little contact with Jews and Judaism. With the rise of Hitlerism Fathers and Sisters were among its most prominent opponents on the Catholic side and insisted in their publications on the necessity of common action by Jews and Christians against neo-paganism. In the countries occupied by Nazi Germany Sisters and Fathers made efforts to provide Jews with shelter and a passage to safety, although they themselves were closely observed by the Gestapo. After World War II they were active in the development of the mentality which led to the Declaration *"Nostra Aetate"* by the second Vatican Council. Both Congregations now hold that proselytizing must be entirely abandoned and they considered themselves pioneers of a new era of Jewish-Christian understanding. The Sisters and Fathers of Zion have taken a positive attitude toward the State of Israel.

BIBLIOGRAPHY: J. Guitton, *Le conversion de Ratisbonne* (1964); L.M. Leggatt (tr.), *A Nineteenth Century Miracle* (1922); M.J. Egan, *Our Lady's Jew, Father M.A. Ratisbonne* (1953); idem, *Christ's Conquest: The Coming of Grace to Theodore Ratisbonne* (1945).

[Marie Joseph Stiassny]

RATNER, BRUCE C. (1945–), U.S. developer. Ratner was born in Cleveland, Ohio, part of the second generation of a prominent realestate family that left Poland in 1920. The original family name, Ratowczer, was changed to Ratner. A family lumberyard business built by Ratner's three uncles and an aunt grew into a national real estate enterprise, Forest City Enterprises, now publicly owned, with Albert Ratner, Bruce's cousin, as its chairman. Bruce Ratner graduated from Harvard University in 1967 and earned a law degree from the Columbia University School of Law in 1970. His interest at first was public service, and his first job out of school was as a lawyer for the Model Cities program in Queens. In 1978, he became head of the city's consumer-protection division. He taught law for four years at New York University Law School before being named commissioner of consumer affairs for New York City. He quit government at the end of 1981 to fortify his net worth in real estate development. He formed the Forest City Ratner Companies, an affiliate of Forest City Enterprises, in 1982. He picked unlikely places to develop, like little-known poor areas of Brooklyn. He built an office building in Brooklyn and then the Metrotech office complex in downtown Brooklyn, which proved to be major factors in raising the vitality of the area. From there he built hotels in Manhattan and spread his projects across Harlem, Queens, the Bronx, and Staten Island. In 2004 he bought the New Jersey Nets, a professional basketball team, and was engaged in extensive negotiations with New York City and others to build an arena at Brooklyn Atlantic Yards for the team and to create a cultural-business center there, with Frank *Gehry as the architect. He was also a partner with the New York Times Company in building the newspaper's new headquarters, with Renzo Piano as architect. He was a member of the board of the Museum of Jewish Heritage.

[Stewart Kampel (2nd ed.)]

RATNER, DOV BAER (1852–1917), Lithuanian talmudic scholar. Born in Kalvarija, Lithuania, Ratner studied at the yeshivot of Mir and Volozhin, and acquired a wide secular knowledge by independent study. In St. Petersburg and Vilna he engaged in commerce, but later devoted himself entirely to scholarly research.

Having made his literary debut at the age of 16, he contributed studies, learned notes, and book reviews to a variety of publications, particularly to *Ha-Meliẓ*. In 1894 his *Mavo le-Seder Olam Rabbah* appeared in Vilna and was followed three years later by a critical edition of the text of the *Seder Olam Rabbah*. From 1901 until his death, he published 12 parts of *Ahavat Ẓiyyon vi-Yrushalayim*, on the entire orders of *Zera'im* and *Mo'ed* of the Jerusalem Talmud, except for the tractate *Eruvin*, containing variant readings and explanations culled from the writings of early authorities. Selections from this work were subsequently included in the Vilna (Romm) edition of the Jerusalem Talmud. An early adherent of the Zionist movement, Ratner was among the Vilna community notables who welcomed Theodor Herzl on his visit to the city in 1903. He left his books to the Straschun Library of Vilna, of which he had been a director.

BIBLIOGRAPHY: L. Slonimski, in: *Vilner Zamelbukh*, 2 (1918), 186–91; T. Preschel, in: D.B. Ratner (ed.), *Midrash Seder Olam* (1966), bio-bibliography.

[Tovia Preschel]

RATNER, LEONARD (1896–1975), U.S. business executive and Jewish community leader. Ratner, who was born in Bialystok, Poland, went to the U.S. and settled in Shaker Heights, Ohio. He was founder and chairman of the board of directors of Forest City Enterprises, Inc., a national real estate development firm with interests in retail stores and building materials.

Ratner served a wide variety of community organizations and educational institutions in the United States and Israel. He was a member of the board of overseers of the Jewish Theological Seminary from 1953, a member of the board of the American Committee for the Weizmann Institute of Science in Israel, and former vice president and board member from 1965 of the American Friends of the Hebrew University. He worked for many charitable organizations, including the Jewish Community Federation of Cleveland, the UJA, and the American Jewish Joint Distribution Committee.

RATNER, MARC BORISOVICH (1871–1917), Russian lawyer and socialist. Born in Kiev, Ratner was brought up in an assimilated environment. He was expelled from high school because of clandestine Socialist activities. As a law student he was arrested and exiled for two years, but later graduated as a lawyer. In his student days he attracted attention with his articles in *Russkoye Bogatstvo* on the agrarian problem, Marxism, political economy, and labor legislation. He appeared as counsel for the defense in political trials and as civil prosecutor in the pogrom trials. The Kishinev pogrom brought him closer to Jewish affairs. He was among the leaders of the *Vozrozhdeniye and later the *Jewish Socialist Workers' Party, in which, with Chaim *Zhitlowsky, he represented the populist socialist-revolutionary trend. He fought for the inclusion of Yiddish in the curriculum of the *Society for the Promotion of Culture among the Jews of Russia, and was a candidate to the second *Duma. As a result of his activities during the 1905 revolution, he was compelled to leave Russia. Ratner was the initiator of the convention of the socialist parties of oppressed nations in Russia (1907). He represented the Jewish Socialist Workers' Party at the Congress of the Socialist International in Copenhagen (1910) and initiated the campaign for the recognition of a Jewish section of the International. The hardships of emigration (Switzerland, Vienna) ruined his health. A short while before his death he settled in Jassy, Romania.

In his works on the national question he rejected assimilationism and supported the idea of a national-personal, exterritorial, autonomy. Noteworthy are his "*Evolyutsiya natsionalno-politicheskoy mysli v russkom yevreystve*" ("The Evolution of National-Political Thought among Russian Jewry," in *Serp*, vol. 2, 1907); "*Natsionalny vopros v svete sotsialisticheskago mirovozzreniya*" ("The National Question in Light of the Socialist Weltanschauung," in *Russkoye Bogatstvo*, nos. 2–5, 1908); and articles on autonomism in *Yevreyskiy Mir*, nos. 6, 9, and 10 (1909).

BIBLIOGRAPHY: Rejzen, Leksikon, 4 (1929), 187–93; O.I. Janowsky, *Jews and Minority Rights* (1933), index; *Kniga o russkom yevreystve* (1960), index; B. Borochov, *Ketavim…* 2 (1958), index.

[Moshe Mishkinsky]

RATNER, SIDNEY (1908–1996), U.S. economic historian. Born in New York City, Ratner was appointed professor of economic history at Rutgers University, New Brunswick, New Jersey, in 1958. He was active in U.S. civil liberties and civil rights movements. Ratner's major scholarly work concerned the interaction between government and the economy, with particular focus upon American taxation problems.

Among other books, he was the author of *Taxation, Its History as a Social Force in Democracy* (1942), *Taxation and Democracy in America* (1967), and *The Evolution of the American Economy* (with J. Soltow and R. Sylla, 1979).

RATNER, YOHANAN (1891–1965), Israel architect and a commander in the *Haganah and the *Israel Defense Forces. Born in Odessa into an assimilated family, Ratner completed university studies in Germany and served in the Czar's army during World War I and, despite being a Jew, was employed in planning campaigns on various fronts. Ratner went to Palestine in 1923 and was appointed a professor at the *Technion in Haifa. He played an important role in establishing the faculty of architecture, which he headed from 1930 until his retirement in 1963. Parallel to his career as a teacher, Ratner worked as an architect and drew up the plans for many public buildings, including the *Jewish Agency building in Jerusalem, the Eden Hotel, Jerusalem, the aeronautics building for the Technion in Haifa, the Kefar ha-Yarok Agricultural School, and Bet Berl at *Ẓofit.

Ratner joined the Haganah upon arrival in Palestine, became a member of the Haganah Committee in Haifa, and participated in the defense of Jerusalem during the riots of August 1929. He supported a more efficient and compact organization of the Haganah, and when the decision was made to appoint a head of the territorial command of the Haganah, Ratner was the first to occupy the position, which he held in 1938–39. During the German advance on Egypt (1941–42), he was among the creators of the "Carmel Plan," the main aim of which was to concentrate the Jewish armed forces in the Haifa region to fight the invaders. In 1947 Ratner became a member of the Haganah's high command, and, when the Israel Defense Forces were formed, became head of a department of general headquarters with the rank of *alluf* ("brigadier general"). In 1948 he was appointed military attaché to the Israel embassy in Moscow and filled the post until 1951.

BIBLIOGRAPHY: Dinur, Haganah, 2, pt. 3 (1963), index.

[Yehuda Slutsky]

RATOSH, YONATHAN (originally **Uriel Halperin**; 1908–1981; pseudonym: **Uriel Shelaḥ**), Hebrew poet and journalist. Born in Russia, the son of Yehiel *Halperin, he was brought up in an exclusively Hebrew-speaking environment. Ratosh went to Palestine in 1921. In the mid-1930s, he worked on the staff of two daily newspapers, first *Haaretz* and then the right-wing *Ha-Yarden*. In 1938 he left the country to avoid imprisonment by the Mandatory authorities for his political activities, but returned with the outbreak of World War II.

Ratosh published several volumes of poetry; the first, *Ḥuppah Sheḥorah* ("Black Canopy," 1941), caused a scandal because of its sensuality, its innovations of language, and the *Canaanite motifs intrinsic to the writer's political-cultural thought. He translated many books into Hebrew, including such classics as *Cyrano de Bergerac* (1965) and the *Fables* of La Fontaine. Ratosh founded a political movement, originally called the Young Hebrews, but dubbed the "Canaanites" by its opponents, and he published articles on politics. He coined many new Hebrew words, worked in Hebrew literature and linguistics, and advocated the use of the Latin alphabet for Hebrew.

Ratosh was distinguished by his political-cultural philosophy. His insistence on being defined as a "Hebrew" rather than as a "Jew" reflects his conviction that the population developing an identity in Palestine/Israel is a new nation – as the descendants of immigrants in a country of immigration invariably become. Through its choice of the Hebrew language and culture, the new nation is defining itself as the cultural descendant of the ancient Hebrew-Canaanite nation, indigenous to what is generally known as the Fertile Crescent, which produced such cultural documents as the Ugaritic tablets and the body of literature that, extensively and tendentiously edited, has come down as the Hebrew Bible. The terms "Jew" and "Jewish" are, in Ratosh's opinion, to be reserved for the adherents of the religion of that name, developed by a group of Judean emigrés during the Babylonian Exile and imposed on the people of the land when part of them returned there in the time of Ezra and Nehemiah. To apply the term now as a national determinant is in his view a distortion, and the resulting identification between the old-new Hebrew nation and the Jewish communities of different persuasions in the rest of the world runs counter to history. In addition, Ratosh believed that the identification is injurious to the Hebrew nation and to the role that it must play in the national revival of the lands of the Euphrates. Ratosh had considerable influence on contemporary Hebrew poetry. The vicissitude of his early work, which provoked violent opposition when it first appeared, and was accepted ten years later and held up as a standard 20 years later, is perhaps characteristic. Devices and principles which he was the first to use were later taken for granted as part of the Hebrew poet's tools. This is true at all levels, from such purely technical matters as the use of an indention and dash pattern instead of punctuation, to structural techniques such as the near-repetition of phrases and refrains to obtain a counterpoint effect, to the recourse to local mythology as a vivifying poetic element. It seems likely that later works, particularly his verse in *Ha-Holkhi ba-Ḥoshekh* ("Who Walketh in Darkness," 1965) will, in time, be found to have had a similar influence. His collected poetry was published 1975–77, followed by a number of collections, among them *Shirei Ahavah* (1983), *Ḥuppah Sheḥorah* (1988), and *Shirei Ḥeshbon* (1988), as well as the letters (1937–80), which were edited by Y. Amrami (1986). D. Laor supervised the publication of Ratosh's essays (1983). Aharon *Amir edited (with a bibliography) a collection of Ratosh's poems (*Yalkut Shirim*), to which he and Dan Miron added essays (1991). For English translations of Ratosh's works see Goell, Bibliography and the ITHL website at www.ithl.org.il.

BIBLIOGRAPHY: D. Meron, *Arba'ah Panim ba-Sifrut ha-Ivrit Bat Yameinu – Iyyunim bi-Yẓirot Alterman, Ratosh, Yizhar, Shamir* (1962); S. Burnshaw et al. (eds.), *Modern Hebrew Poem Itself* (1966), 92–105. **ADD. BIBLIOGRAPHY:** B. Evron, "*Uriel Shelah and Yonatan Ratosh*," in: *Modern Hebrew Literature*, 7:1–2 (1981/1982), 37–40; Y. Bronowski, "*Y. Ratosh, Poet and Ideologist*," in: *Modern Hebrew Literature*, 9:3–4 (1984), 5–12; J.S. Diamond, *Homeland or Holy Land? The "Canaanite" Critique of Israel* (1986); J. Shavit, *The New Hebrew Nation: A Study in Israeli Heresy and Fantasy* (1987); Y. Porat, *Shelaḥ ve-Et be-Yado: Sippur Ḥayyav shel Uriel Shelaḥ (Yonatan Ratosh)* (1989); Z. Shamir, *Lehatḥil mi-Alef: Shirat Ratosh – Mekoriyyutah u-Mekorotehah* (1993); S. Zeevi, *Livtei Ma'avar ba-Poetikah shel Yonatan Ratosh* (1998); E. Rabin, "'Hebrew' Culture': The Shared Foundations of Ratosh's Ideology and Poetry," in: *Modern Judaism*, 19:2 (1999), 119–32; M. Ephratt, *Shirat Ratosh u-Leshono* (2002).

[David Saraph]

RATSHESKY, ABRAHAM CAPTAIN (1864–1943), U.S. banker and civic leader. Ratshesky was born in Boston. He became a state Republican leader and was state senator in 1892–94. In 1895 he left career politics and founded the U.S. Trust Company, of which he served as president and board chairman. Subsequently, Ratshesky held numerous civic posts, including Massachusetts food administrator during World War I and U.S. minister to Czechoslovakia (1930–33). He was chairman of the Massachusetts Department of Public Welfare for ten years. Ratshesky served as first president of the Federated Jewish Charities of Boston (1909–19) and was prominent in many civic and Jewish endeavors. He formed the A.C. Ratshesky Charity Foundation in 1916.

[Edward L. Greenstein]

RATTNER, ABRAHAM (1893–1978), U.S. painter and sculptor. An expressionist artist who painted many biblical subjects imbued with subjective elements, Rattner was born in Poughkeepsie, New York, to Russian immigrant parents. He studied at George Washington University and the Corcoran School of Art in Washington, D.C., and attended the Pennsylvania Academy of Fine Arts in Philadelphia. His studies were interrupted by service in the army during World War I as a camouflage artist. Upon his return from war Rattner re-enrolled at the Pennsylvania Academy and soon won a fellowship to travel in Europe. After his travels, Rattner lived in Paris (1920–39), only returning to the United States because of Germany's invasion of France. While in Paris, Rattner received additional art instruction at École des Beaux-Arts, Grand Chaumière, and Académie Ranson. He had his first one-man show at the Galerie Bonjean in Paris (1935), from which the French government bought *Card Party* for the Louvre. At this time Rattner exhibited paintings influenced by Cubism and Futurism. Later that year Rattner had a one-man exhibition in New York at the Julien Levy Gallery, establishing the artist as a progenitor of the avant-garde in contrast to the Social Realist imagery popular in New York at the time. Much of Rattner's early work was abandoned when he hurriedly left France and was destroyed before the artist could return after the war.

Soon after settling in New York, Rattner toured the eastern and southern United States with Henry Miller in 1940. Their travels resulted in the book *The Air-Conditioned Nightmare*, with text by Miller and drawings by Rattner. Distraught by the war, Rattner responded with a series of Crucifixion paintings conceived in what would become known as his signature style. *Descent from the Cross* (1940, Art Institute of Chicago) shows a cubistically rendered Jesus helped down from a bright red cross by two geometrically delineated figures. The segmented figures, painted with exaggerated limbs and oversized features, are colorful in conception with thick black lines separating the juxtaposition of warm and cool hues. Many of Rattner's later paintings, which are often pictured in multiple versions of biblical themes – such as Moses, Ezekiel, and Job – employ a heavy paint application and stronger abstraction.

He designed mosaics and a tapestry column for Fairmount Temple in Cleveland, Ohio (1957), and a stained-glass window, *And God Said Let There Be Light*, for the Chicago Loop Synagogue (1958). In 1968, Rattner exhibited his canvas *Victory – Jerusalem the Golden* (1967–68, collection unknown) to honor the celebration of Israel's 20th anniversary of independence. In 1969, he painted *The Gallows of Baghdad* series to protest the hanging of nine Jews in Iraq. Opened in 2002, the Leepa-Rattner Museum on the Tarpon Springs campus of St. Petersburg College contains the largest holdings of Rattner's work in the world.

BIBLIOGRAPHY: A.S. Weller, *Abraham Rattner* (1956); A. Leepa, *Abraham Rattner* (1974); R. Henkes, *The Spiritual Art of Abraham Rattner: In Search of Oneness* (1998).

[Samantha Baskind (2nd ed.)]

RAU, HEINZ (1896–1965), Israel architect. Rau was born in Berlin, where he specialized in interiors, among which were several for Berlin University. When Hitler came to power in 1933 he immigrated to Ereẓ Israel, where he entered the office of Richard *Kaufmann. From 1949 to 1953 he worked for the Israel Government Planning Department. In 1962 he went to England to become assistant professor in the Department of Town and Country Planning, Manchester. Among Rau's designs in Jerusalem were the Hebrew Union College, the Mathematics Institute, and the domed synagogue at the Hebrew University of Jerusalem (in collaboration with Reznik). A feature of his buildings in Israel is the small intake of light, which he regarded as most suited to the climatic conditions.

RAUCH, EDUARDO (1940–2002), Jewish educator. Rauch was born in Chile to a family that fled Romania before the Holocaust. He was raised and educated in Santiago, receiving a master's degree in biochemistry from the Universidad de Chile. In his student years he was deeply affected by Zionism, partially through meeting the charismatic Argentinean Jewish educator Jaime *Barylko, and in the wake of the Six-day War, led a delegation of Latin American volunteers to Israel. He spent three years in Israel working in the No'ar ve-He-Ḥalutz department of the Jewish Agency under Shelomo Dinur and Mordechai (Morele) Bar-On. In Israel he met and married his wife.

Rauch was elected secretary general of the World Union of Jewish Students (WUJS) and relocated to the WUJS headquarters in London, where he stayed from 1970 to 1973. After his term at WUJS ended, Rauch moved to America so that he could work on a doctorate in education at Harvard. He completed his degree in 1978 and accepted a position at the Melton Research Center for Jewish education at the Jewish Theological Seminary of America.

Two years later he and Barry W. Holtz became co-directors of Melton, serving in that position for 12 years. Rauch taught on the Seminary's education faculty, was the co-creator and editor of *The Melton Journal* (in its time one of the liveliest publications in the field), invented innovative educational projects such as the Melton Teacher Retreat Program, and helped build the Melton Center as a national force in American Jewish education. He published numerous reviews, poems, and essays on a wide range of topics. In a language that was not his native tongue, he was a powerful writer and a remarkable editor. His history of American Jewish education, *The Education of Jews and the American Community*, was published by Tel Aviv University Press posthumously in 2004.

[Barry W. Holtz (2nd ed.)]

RAUH, FRÉDÉRIC (1861–1909), French philosopher. He was born at St. Martin-le-Vinoux, was professor at Toulouse and later (1901) at the Sorbonne (where he replaced *Bergson) and at the Ecole Normale Supérieure.

His main philosophical interest was in morality, which he treated apart from metaphysics and empirical facts. He held that moral thought is like invention, and finds its verification in action. Moral certitude is possible, and man's true guide is reflection upon instinct, rather than either just reflection or just instinct. Individual conscience in which active moral belief manifests itself is all important. His main works were *Essai sur le fondement métaphysique de la morale* (1890); *L'experience morale* (1903); *Psychologie appliquée à la morale et à l'éducation*, with R. d'Allones (1900–17); and *Etudes de Morale* (posthumous, 1911). He was a brilliant teacher. He was actively involved in the Dreyfus case.

BIBLIOGRAPHY: L. Brunschwicg, in: *Revue Philosophique* (1928), 5–32; H. Daudin, in: *Revue de Métaphysique et de Morale* (1910), 185–218, 318–44 (contains complete bibliography); R. Junod, *Frédéric Rauh, Essai de biographie intellectuelle* (1932).

[Richard H. Popkin]

RAUH, JOSEPH L., JR. (1911–1992), U.S. lawyer. Rauh, who was born in Cincinnati, Ohio, graduated from Harvard Law School. He was law secretary to U.S. Supreme Court Justice Benjamin *Cardozo and counsel to various government agencies, including the Wage and Hour Administration and the Federal Communications Commission (1935–42). Rauh served in the U.S. Army as a commissioned officer in the Pacific during World War II and was discharged with the rank of lieutenant colonel. He was a founder of the Americans for Democratic Action in 1947, which presented a liberal, non-Communist alternative to the then-conservative domination of both the Republican and Democratic parties. He was chairman of the ADA executive committee (1947–52), vice chairman (1952–55 and 1957), and national chairman (1955–57). Rauh was a delegate to all Democratic National Conventions from 1948, when he fought for the inclusion of the first strong civil rights plank in that party's platform, through 1964, when he strongly advocated seating the blacks representing the Mississippi Freedom party as the official Democratic delegation from that state. He served for many years on the board of the NAACP and as general counsel to the Leadership Conference on Civil Rights. Rauh was the Washington counsel (1951–63 and again from 1966) and general counsel (1963–66) for the United Automobile Workers. He also served as attorney for the insurgent United Mineworkers Union group led by Joseph Yablonski, who opposed incumbent Tony Boyle for the union's presidency in 1969.

Rauh was instrumental in the founding of the District of Columbia's public law school. In 1999, the Joseph L. Rauh, Jr. Chair of Public Interest Law was established at the University of the District of Columbia's David A. Clarke School of Law.

Regarded as one of the foremost civil rights and civil liberties lawyers of his time, Rauh was awarded the Presidential Medal of Freedom, posthumously, by President Bill Clinton in 1993.

°**RAUTER, HANNS ALBIN** (1895–1949), Austrian *SS officer and *Himmler's principal representative in the occupied *Netherlands. One of the founders of the fascist Steirischer Heimatschutz ("Styrian Homeguard"), he became its chief. In 1933 he adhered with his organization to the Austrian branch of the Nazi Party. Himmler appointed him in 1940 Higher SS and Police leader in the Netherlands. In this capacity he won Himmler's praise for precisely and zealously carrying out the persecution of Dutch Jewry and their deportation to the camps in Poland. Rauter was considered the chief executor of the "Final Solution" (see *Holocaust, General Survey) of the Jews of the Netherlands. He was sentenced to death by a Dutch court and executed in 1949.

BIBLIOGRAPHY: *Het proces Rauter* (Dutch, 1952); J. Presser, *Ashes in the Wind* (1968); G. Reitlinger, *Final Solution* (1953), index.

[Yehuda Reshef]

RAV (third century C.E.), leading Babylonian *amora* and founder of the academy at *Sura. His name was Abba b. Aivu, but he was also called Abba Arikha ("Abba the Tall") because of his tall stature (Nid. 24b). He is generally known as Rav by reason of being "the teacher [*rav*] of the entire Diaspora" (Beẓah 9a, and Rashi thereto). Born at Kafri in southern Babylonia in the latter half of the second century C.E., he belonged to a very distinguished family; he was related to Ḥiyya through both his parents (Sanh. 5a; Pes. 4a and Rashi) and traditionally was descended either from Shimei, brother of David (Ket. 62b), or from Shephatiah, the son of Abital and David (TJ, Ta'an. 4:2, 68a). It is not known who were Rav's teachers in Babylonia, but he immigrated to Ereẓ Israel and studied under his uncle Ḥiyya (MK 16b), was a member of his household (Shab. 66b), and assisted him in his business affairs (TJ, BM 6:1, 10d). Ḥiyya introduced him into the home of Judah ha-Nasi (Ber. 46b), where he discussed *halakhah* under Ḥiyya's guidance (Ḥul. 16a). Extremely diligent in his studies (cf. Suk. 26b), Rav joined the academy of Judah ha-Nasi, with whom he debated halakhic topics (Ḥul. 137b) and whose *bet din* he joined (Git. 59a). He knew and entered into halakhic discussions with the greatest of the last generation of *tannaim*, being in contact with Ishmael b. Yose (Pes. 112b, according to R. Hananel's version; see Dik. Sof. *ibid.*), Symmachus (Ket. 81a), Bar Kappara (Yoma 87b), Eleazar b. Simeon (Zev. 102b), as well as with Levi (Beẓah 24b) and Ḥanina b. Ḥama (Yoma 87b).

He learnt the Torah of Ereẓ Israel, and prior to leaving the country was ordained by Judah ha-Nasi and was authorized to give decisions in ritual law and in civil cases (Sanh. 5a–b; TJ, Ḥag. 1:8, 76c). Some hold that after going back to Babylonia, he returned several times to Ereẓ Israel (see TJ, Pe'ah 6:3, 19c) before finally deciding to settle in Babylonia, apparently in 219 C.E. (*Iggeret R. Sherira Ga'on*, ed. by B.M. Lewin (1921), 78). He encountered some difficulties in Nehardea (Shab. 108a), which was an important center of sages and Torah, and where Shila, Samuel, and Karna flourished at the time. Rav first served as an interpreter in Shila's *bet midrash* (Yoma 20b), and subsequently the exilarch appointed him *agoranomos* ("market commissioner," TJ, BB 5:11, 15a), whose duties in Babylonia comprised superintending market measures and prices; in keeping with the prevailing *halakhah* in Ereẓ Israel, however, he refused to regulate prices. Compelled to resign his position, he left Nehardea and went to Sura, whose inhabitants were not distinguished for their knowledge of the Torah (Ḥul. 110a); there he established a *bet din* and academy which in time attained such eminence that it was regarded as "a little sanctuary" (Meg. 29a) and attracted hundreds of pupils from Sura and its neighborhood. Its permanent pupils numbered 1,200 (Ket. 106a).

The Jews of Sura and its neighboring towns accepted his religious leadership and jurisdiction (*ibid.* 54a). Not only the Babylonian sages, foremost among them Samuel, acknowledged his considerable religious authority (Git. 36b), but Johanan, the head of the academy at Tiberias and one of the outstanding sages of Ereẓ Israel at the time, counted Rav as his teacher in *halakhah* (Ḥul. 95b). Perhaps the most conspicuous recognition of his signal religious authority is the statement: "Rav is a *tanna* and differs" (Ket. 8a), that is, Rav has the right to differ from a *tanna* without sustaining or basing his view on that of another *tanna*, a privilege accorded only to him among all the Babylonian sages of that generation. Returning to Babylonia equipped with the teachings of Judah ha-Nasi and with a profound, comprehensive knowledge of the Torah of Ereẓ Israel, Rav introduced into Babylonia several *halakhot* previously not practiced there. Thus Huna, one of Rav's distinguished pupils, declared: "From the time Rav arrived in Babylonia, we in Babylonia have put ourselves on the same footing as Ereẓ Israel with regard to the breeding of small cattle" (which was prohibited there; BK 80a), as well as "with regard to bills of divorce" (the bearers of which in Ereẓ Israel were exempted from stating, "In my presence it was written and in my presence it was signed"; Git. 6a). Rav enacted regulations relating to matrimony (Yev. 52a; Kid. 12b) and the education of children (Ket. 50a), and frequently visited different communities in Babylonia to institute various ordinances there and to raise their religious and social standard (the sources have been collected by J. Umanski, notes 140/1).

That he relied on his independent judgment, unrestrained by other authorities, when issuing regulations and arriving at decisions, shows the extensive authority enjoyed by him in Babylonia and recognized, according to all indications, also by the exilarch and his officials. Rav was a member of the exilarch's *bet din* (Kid. 44b) and his daughter married into the exilarch's family (Ḥul. 92a). The fact that Rav was economically independent (Ber. 57b), owning landed property (Kid. 59a) and enjoying an income from the manufacture and sale of beer (Pes. 107a), helped to sustain his eminent status. Although there is evidence that he was in some contact with Artabanus V, the last of the royal Arsacid dynasty (Ar. Zar. 10b), unlike Samuel, he did not maintain close relations with the authorities or with non-Jews, his chief activity being directed to internal affairs, to the religious welfare of the members of the Babylonian Jewish community. In addition to his labors in his *bet din* and the academy, Rav was one of the most eminent and prolific Babylonian aggadists and frequently delivered public discourses. In his addresses, greatly influenced by the Ereẓ Israel *aggadah*, he urged his audiences to observe the *mitzvot* and to study the Torah.

In explaining the reason for the *mitzvot* and for their observance he declared: "The *mitzvot* were given only as a means of refining men. For what difference does it make to God whether one slaughters an animal from the front or from the back of the neck?" (Gen. R. 44:1). Of the study of the Torah he said that it "is more important than the offering of the daily sacrifices" (Er. 63b), that it "is superior to the building of the Temple" (Meg. 16b), that "whoever departs from the words of the Torah is consumed by fire" (BB 79a), and that "he who says, 'I shall rise early to study this chapter or this tractate,' has vowed a great vow to the God of Israel" (Ned. 8a). In his solicitude for the status and dignity of scholars he asserted that anyone who insults a scholar is a heretic (*eppikoros*; Sanh. 99b) and "has no remedy for his wounds" (Shab. 119b). Urging scholars to be diligent in teaching the Torah, he declared that "whoever withholds a *halakhah* from a disciple is as though he has robbed him of his ancestral heritage" (Sanh. 91b), and "that whoever teaches Torah to his neighbor's son will be privileged to sit in the Heavenly Academy… if he teaches it to an ignorant man's son, even if the Holy One blessed be He decrees adversely, He annuls it for his sake" (BM 85a). From the examples quoted and their emphasis, it is evident that Rav regarded the teaching of the Torah and the spreading of the knowledge of the Torah as one of the most important spheres of his communal activities.

Of the Jews of Babylon who had refused to grant a certain Shabbetai b. Marinus facilities for earning a livelihood and had not given him any food either, Rav said: "These are the descendants of the 'mixed multitude' (Ex. 12:38), for it is written (Deut. 13:18). 'And [He will] show thee mercy, and have compassion upon thee.' Whoever is merciful to his fellowmen is decidedly of the children of our father Abraham, and whoever is not merciful to his fellowmen is decidedly not of the children of our father Abraham" (Beẓah 32b). Rav warned his audiences against quarreling (Sanh. 110a), against slander and its grave consequences (BB 164b), against paying heed to slander (Shab. 56b), and against boastfulness (Pes. 66b), and was solicitous for the position and welfare of workers (BM 83a).

In some of Rav's homilies a tendency to a certain mystical thinking is discernible. Describing, for example, the difference between this and the next world, he said: "In the future world there is no eating nor drinking, no propagation nor business, no jealousy nor hatred nor competition, but the righteous sit with their crowns on their heads feasting on the Divine Glory" (Ber. 17a). Rav expounded God's names and their pronunciation (Kid. 71a), the purpose of creation (Shab. 77b) and the process of creation (Ḥag. 12a), the divine providence of the world and its creatures (Sot. 2a; Ḥag. 5b), and warned against criticizing God's attributes (Men. 29b). Rav composed several prayers, the best known being *Teki'ata de-Rav* which is recited during the *Amidah* on Rosh Ha-Shanah (TJ, RH 1:3, 57a) and whose contents express his outlook on God's providence over the nations and of Israel.

Opposed to a life of abstinence and mortification, Rav asserted: "Man is destined to render an account for all that his eye has seen and he has not eaten" (TJ, Kid. 4:12, 66d). To *Hamnuna he declared: "My son, if you have anything, derive what benefit you can from it, for there is no enjoyment in the grave nor does death delay. And should you say, 'I would leave a portion for my children,' who will tell you in the grave? The children of men are like the grasses of the field, some blossom and some fade" (Er. 54a, based on Ecclus. 14:12–14). The Jews of Babylonia had great esteem for Rav and grieved deeply at his death. Samuel rent his garments (MK 24a), as did Rav's pupils (Ber. 42b–43a) who mourned him for a long time (Shab. 110a). People took earth from his grave for medicinal purposes (Sanh. 47b). Rav and Samuel are the founders of the Babylonian Talmud, and their discussions and debates both in *halakhah* and *aggadah* are one of its prominent features. Where Samuel, who probably never visited Ereẓ Israel, and his academy in Nehardea reflect the Babylonian tradition, Rav and the academy of Sura which he founded reflect that of Ereẓ Israel.

BIBLIOGRAPHY: Bacher, Bab Amor; Hyman, Toledot, 15–42; Kohut, Arukh, 1 (19262) 6–10; 7 (19262), 236–9; Weiss, Dor, 3 (19044), 129–43; Halevy, Dorot, 2 (1923), passim; Graetz-Rabbinowitz, 2 (1893), 350–6; I.S. Zuri, *Rav* (Heb., 1925); J. Umanski, *Ḥakhmei ha-Talmud, Sefer Rav* (1931); M. Beer, in: *Divrei ha-Congress ha-Olami ha-Revi'i le-Madda'ei ha-Yahadut*, 1 (1967), Heb. pt., 99–101; Epstein, Mishnah, 1 (1948), 166–211; S. Rosenthal, in: *Sefer Ḥ. Yalon* (1963), 281–337; Ḥ. Albeck, *Mavo la-Talmudim* (1969), 170f.

[Moshe Beer]

RAVA (d. 352 C.E.), Babylonian *amora*. Rava is an abbreviation of R. Abba, and his full name was R. Abba b. Joseph b. Ḥama (Er. 54a). He lived at *Maḥoza. His teachers were *Ḥisda, the head of the academy at Sura, whose daughter he married (BB 12b), but principally *Naḥman b. Jacob (Shab. 4a) and R. Joseph, head of the academy at Pumbedita (Ḥul. 133a). His main halakhic discussions were with his companion *Abbaye, and their statements and controversies are found throughout the Babylonian Talmud. In their many debates the *halakhah* follows Rava's view except in six instances (for which the mnemonic יע״ל קג״ם was given) in which the *halakhah* is according to Abbaye (BM 22b). After R. Joseph's death in 323 (*Iggeret Sherira Ga'on*, ed. by B.M. Lewin (1921), 85–86), Abbaye was chosen in preference to the other candidates (Rava, Zera, and Rabbah b. Matna) as the head of the Pumbedita academy. Rava thereupon left that city and returned to Maḥoza, where be established a *bet midrash* which attracted many pupils (BB 22a). Rava ascribed overriding weight to logical reasoning and inference in the study and comprehension of the Torah; this approach is reflected in his statement that "one grain of pungent pepper is better than a basketful of pumpkins" (Ḥag. 10a) and in his assertion that he was "like Ben Azzai," who was noted for his mental keenness (Er. 29a). His educational approach was popular with Rava's pupils, one of whom, addressing the pupils of Abbaye, who in his teaching preferred a thorough knowledge and comprehension of halakhic discussions, said: "Instead of gnawing bones in the school of Abbaye, why do you not eat fat meat in the school of Rava?" (BB 22a). Those who had studied under Rava found no great satisfaction in other sages' discourses (Ta'an. 9a). Rava's academy became the principal one after Abbaye's death in 338, the sages and pupils of Abbaye's academy moving to Maḥoza (*Iggeret Sherira Ga'on* pp. 88–89).

For 14 years, until his death, Rava was the head of the academy, during which time his intellectual powers and economic position so expanded as to enable him to assert that he had been granted the wisdom of *Huna and the wealth of Ḥisda, though not the modesty of *Rabbah b. Huna (MK 28a). He owned fields and vineyards (BM 73a) and traded in wine (Ber. 56a), cooperated in public and administrative matters with the exilarch's officials (BB 22a; Git. 31b), and negotiated with the Persian authorities. He was on friendly terms with the exilarch (Beẓah 21b; Ber. 50a; Pes. 74b), and there is illuminating information on his contacts with *Shapur II. When the sages of the academy complained that Rava had established too close relations with the royal court, he replied by telling them what he had to endure there and the large sums with which he bribed the court (Ḥag. 5b). Apparently much money was demanded from the Jews, as from the rest of the population, to finance Shapur's wars against the Romans. Rava also maintained close ties with Ifra Hormuz, the king's mother, who sent him money for distribution among the poor (BB 10b) and a calf to be sacrificed on her behalf (Zev. 116b). She told her son of Rava's greatness when the king wished to punish him for having sentenced a man to flogging which proved fatal (Ta'an. 24b). Maḥoza's geographic proximity to Be-Ardashir, one of the country's capitals, may have facilitated Rava's contacts with the authorities there.

Rava's main activity, however, lay in teaching and in spreading knowledge of the Torah. He instituted various regulations for the people of Maḥoza (Beẓah 30a; Er. 40a; MK 22a; Nid. 66b). He denounced for their pursuit of pleasure (RH 17a), many among the well-to-do (BK 119a) who ate and drank to excess (Shab. 109a) and whose wives did no work (Shab. 32b–33a). On the other hand, he praised the industry of the workers of Maḥoza (BM 77a). Large audiences gathered on Sabbaths to hear Rava's discourses (Er. 44b), and in numerous statements he stressed the signal religious value of studying the Torah. Once, when he noticed a disciple of the sages praying at great length, he said: "They forsake eternal life and occupy themselves with temporal life" (Shab. 10a). He declared that whoever occupies himself with the study of the Torah has no need of sacrifices (Men. 110a) and is superior to a high priest who enters into the innermost part of the sanctuary (Sot. 4b), that the Torah is an antidote to the evil inclination (BB 16a), that suffering comes upon a man for neglecting the study of the Torah (Ber. 5a), and that King Asa was punished for having imposed forced labor on the disciples of the sages who were thus compelled to neglect the study of the Torah (Sot. 10a). He claimed exemption from government taxes for disciples of the sages (Ned. 62b), to whom he gave the right to sell their goods in the market (BB 22a). To uphold their honor and prevent them from wasting their time, which should be devoted to the study of the Torah, he allowed them to disclose that they were disciples of the sages so that they might be judged or give evidence without having to wait for the cases of others to be finished (Ned. 62a). But he also demanded of them that they be worthy of the name, declaring that "any disciple of the sages whose inside is not like his outside is not a disciple of the sages" (Yoma 72b).

Yet despite its great importance Rava did not regard the study of the Torah as an end in itself. Thus a favorite saying of his was, "The goal of wisdom is repentance and good deeds, so that a man should not study the Torah and Mishnah and then despise his father and mother, his teacher, and his superior in wisdom and rank" (Ber. 17a). In like manner, when describing what is demanded of man in this world, he said: "When man is brought in for judgment [in the next world] he is asked, 'Did you deal faithfully, fix times for studying the Torah, did you engage in procreation, hope for salvation, did you search after wisdom, infer one thing from another?' Yet, even so, if 'the fear of the Lord is his treasure' (Isa. 33:6) it is well; if not, it is not well" (Shab. 31a). Rava's special outlook can be better comprehended when compared with Hamnuna's statement that "the first matter for which a man is called to render account in the hereafter is with regard to the study of the Torah" (Sanh. 7a). Rava likewise said: "Jerusalem was destroyed only because men of integrity ceased therein" (Shab. 119b). An illuminating view of his is that "length of life, children, and sustenance depend not on merit but on luck" (MK 28a). He had many affinities with mysticism and performed miracles (see Sanh. 65b). On one occasion he even wished to discourse in the *bet midrash* on the mystery of the Tetragrammaton but was stopped by a certain old man (Pes. 50a). On Rava's death the academy at Maḥoza was divided in two, *Naḥman b. Isaac, the head of the **kallah* at Maḥoza, succeeding Rava as head of the academy there, while R. *Papa, a pupil of Rava, established one at Naresh.

BIBLIOGRAPHY: Bacher, Pal Amor; Hyman, Toledot, s.v.; Ḥ. Albeck, *Mavo la-Talmudim* (1969), 374–6.

[Moshe Beer]

RAVA, MAURIZIO (1878–after 1935), Italian colonial administrator and traveler. Born in Milan, Rava studied painting. Due to poor health he moved to warmer climates, traveling in Africa and Asia. He published his impressions in Italian magazines and geographical periodicals. In 1909 he founded *Il Carrocio*, a political literary periodical, staunchly supporting the new Italian Nationalist Party. Rava strongly advocated Italian colonial expansion. He served in the Libyan campaign and was decorated for valor. In 1927 Rava was appointed secretary-general of the *Tripoli government and from 1932 to 1935 was governor of Italian Somaliland. Rava published many studies on Italian administration in *Libya, East Africa, and Ethiopia.

RAVAYA (**Ravalia, Ravaylla**), family of courtiers in 13th-century Spain, originating from Gerona in Aragon. Its prominent members included ASTRUG RAVAYA, bailiff of Gerona from 1276 to 1281. In the 1260s Astrug and his son JOSEPH (d. 1282) loaned large sums to King James I, and also farmed the royal revenues. Joseph was the treasurer of King Pedro the Great (1276–85). In the reign of Pedro's father, James I, Joseph had served as the infante's banker and for a time managed all the latter's property. From 1268 Joseph was bailiff of Besalú and from 1271 also of Gerona and district. Apart from the king and the infante, Joseph was the only person in the kingdom of Aragon whose functions enabled him to act in the three states of the crown (Aragon, Catalonia, and Valencia). The general local bailiffs as well as various other officials were all subordinated to his authority. Muca de *Portella, Aaron Abinafia, and Joseph's brother, Moses (see below), served under him as district commissioners, their functions being similar to those of the general bailiffs in later periods. As king's treasurer, Joseph had to supervise the royal accounts and manage the crown revenues. In 1279 he is mentioned by the title *thesaurarius* ("treasurer"). Joseph had a part in the appointment or dismissal of royal officials and often served Pedro in an advisory capacity. He accompanied the king at the siege of Balaguer against the rebel Catalonian nobles (1280) and during the campaign against Sicily (1282). Various state documents contain Joseph's signature in Hebrew and other administrative notes in this language.

Joseph's brother, MOSES, headed the crown administration of Catalonia until his dismissal (before February 1283). In that year, when he was about to inherit his brother's office in charge of the three states of the kingdom, the king ordered that Moses' functions should be restricted to Catalonia only, while for the first time Christian officials were appointed to these posts in Aragon and Valencia. Moses also continued his activities under Alfonso III (1285–91), despite the laws of 1283 which barred Jews from holding public office in the kingdom.

BIBLIOGRAPHY: Baer, Spain, index; *Sefarad*, index; D. Romano, *Los funcionarios judíos de Pedro el Grande de Aragón* (1970).

RAVEN (Heb. עוֹרֵב), bird. Mentioned in the Pentateuch among the unclean birds is "every raven after its kind" (Lev. 11:15). The reference is to the genus *Corvus* of which four species are found in Israel, three black (cf. Song 5:11) and one, very prevalent near inhabited areas, the hooded crow, *Corvus corone*, which has a gray back and belly and a black head and wings. It is commonly found in Jerusalem where it nests in high trees. Metal spikes were placed on the roof of the Temple to prevent ravens, undoubtedly attracted by the remains of sacrifices, from sitting on these (Mid. 4:6) and disturbing the Temple service with their raucous cries. These sounds are particularly strident during hot spells at the beginning of summer, when the "young ravens" leave the nest. Although already grown, the young are incapable of finding food, and since they have a voracious appetite, their parents fly to and fro in search of food for them, the air being filled with their cries, and hence the description: "He giveth to the beast his food, and to the young ravens which cry" (Ps. 147:9). These young ravens cry, as it were, to God to satisfy their hunger, as it says in Job (38:41): "Who provideth for the raven his prey, when his young ones cry unto God…?" The hooded crow is found in flocks which with great devotion defend their companions and especially the young, and hence the saying: "Three love one another, proselytes, slaves, and ravens" (Pes. 113b). The black raven, *Corvus corax*, preys on small animals and feeds on carcasses and corpses (cf. Prov. 30:17). Although folklore represents the raven as presaging evil (cf. Isa. 34:11), it is once mentioned in a favorable context, ravens having fed *Elijah when he hid in the brook *Cherith (I Kings 17:2–6). The raven is endowed with a highly developed sense of orientation, and in eastern countries mariners took with them ravens to direct them to dry land; the story of the raven in the ark (Gen. 8:7) is reminiscent of this.

BIBLIOGRAPHY: Lewysohn, Zool, 172–5, nos. 205–8; F.S. Bodenheimer, *Animal and Man in Bible Lands* (1960), 57; J. Feliks, *Animal World of the Bible* (1962), 88. **ADD. BIBLIOGRAPHY:** Feliks, Ha-Ẓome'aḥ, 258.

[Jehuda Feliks]

RAVENNA, city in Emilia Romagna, N. central Italy. There is evidence that a Jewish settlement existed in Ravenna in the third and fourth centuries, probably the earliest Jewish community in the region. A piece of an amphora with the word "Shalom" written on it attests physically the Jewish presence, when Ravenna was the capital of Byzantine Italy. Around the beginning of the sixth century Ravenna became the capital of the kingdom of the Ostrogoths under Theodoric, who was well disposed toward the Jews. Thus in 519, after the Christian populace incited by the clergy burnt down the synagogue in Ravenna, Theodoric ordered that those responsible should pay compensation: persons who refused were to be publicly flogged. The early medieval Jewish community of Byzantine Ravenna probably consisted of merchants engaged in overseas commerce.

In 1352 there is mention of the first loan bank owned by Jews. When the Republic of Venice took control of Ravenna, a number of Jews immigrated. Ravenna Jews were goldsmiths, wine merchants, and hemp merchants. When Ravenna passed under the rule of the pope the situation of the Jews worsened. The vigilance committee of the Italian Jewish communities met at Ravenna in 1443 to consider measures to counteract the restrictive papal bull recently issued. The original nucleus had by now been joined by loan-bankers, whose lucrative activities continued until 1492 when a public loan-bank (*Monti di Pietà) was opened. In the same year the first expulsion occurred. The previous year the synagogue had been destroyed by the populace incited by the preaching of the *Franciscans, and the Jews had been attacked. Since Ravenna was now under the sovereignty of the Church, the anti-Jewish regulations issued by the popes in the second half of the 16th century were all enforced, and the Talmud was burned in 1553. Jews came back to Ravenna; thus in 1515 the General Council decreed the erection of a ghetto in the area where Via Luca Lunghi stands today. The Jews also erected a small synagogue. The Jews were expelled once more in 1555. In 1569, when Pope *Pius V ordered the Jews to leave the minor centers of the Papal States, the Jews were expelled from Ravenna. Thirty loan-bankers returned following the concessions made by *Sixtus V in 1587. In 1593, the Jews were again expelled by Clement VIII.

The Biblioteca Classense includes various manuscripts in Hebrew and a printed book, *Sefer Kol Bo*, dated to 1525. The book was printed in the workshop of Gershon Soncino at Rimini.

Not far from Ravenna at Piangipane, there is the Allied War Cemetery. Part of the burial ground includes the graves of the 34 soldiers of the Jewish Brigade Group who fought in the Senio area at Alfonisine di Romagna and Brisighella between March and April 1945.

BIBLIOGRAPHY: L. Ruggini, *Ebrei e orientali nell'Italia settentrionale…* (= *Studia et Documenta Historiae et Juris*, 25 (1959), 186–308), index; A. Balletti, *Gli ebrei e gli Estensi* (1930²), 18ff.; Roth, Italy, index; Milano, Italia, index; Loevinson, in: REJ, 94 (1933), 173–5. **ADD. BIBLIOGRAPHY**: M. Perani, "Frammenti di manoscritti ebraici medievali negli Archivi di Stato di Imola e Ravenna," in: *La Bibliofilia*, 13 (1991), 1–20; R. Segre, "Gli ebrei a Ravenna nell'eta' veneziana," in: *Ravenna in eta' veneziana* (1986), 155–70; A. Tedeschi Falco, *Emilia Romagna, Jewish Itineraries, Places, History and Art* (1992), 126.

[Ariel Toaff / Samuele Rocca (2nd ed.)]

RAVENSBRUECK, Nazi concentration camp for women. This camp, the only one of its kind, was located near Fuerstenberg in Mecklenburg (in the former East Germany). Its construction by prisoners from *Sachsenhausen, begun in the fall of 1938, was completed in the spring of 1939. The first camp commandant, Max Koegel, was replaced in 1942 by Fritz Suhren, who remained in charge until the evacuation of the camp (April 30, 1945). The key posts were held by men, but the *SS staff was mostly female and excelled in its cruel treatment of the inmates. Originally intended as a prison camp for political prisoners, Ravensbrueck's role changed with the start of World War II, eventually becoming a concentration camp and finally, in 1944, with the addition of a gas chamber, an extermination camp.

On May 15, 1939 the first prisoner transport arrived from Lichtenburg, a concentration camp for women in Saxony that closed in May 1939. The women were "Bibelforscher" (Jehovah's Witnesses) or criminals. On May 18, 1939, 867 women who were political prisoners (some were coincidentally Jewish, arrested for their political activities, not because they were Jewish), arrived from Germany and Austria. By late May 1939 there were 974 women imprisoned in Ravensbrueck including 137 Jews. In the summer of 1939 a transport of gypsies arrived from Austria. The camp's original purpose was the imprisonment and punishment of political prisoners. After the war began its prisoners served as a pool for slave labor. The outbreak of World War II also brought thousands of Polish women (many with their children) and Czech women to Ravensbrueck. Later on other prisoners came, especially resistance fighters from all over Europe. Women wore color-coded triangles that designated them as political prisoners, criminals, asocials, Jehovah's Witnesses, or Jews. With the war and the increasing numbers of incarcerated women came a swift deterioration in living conditions due to overcrowding, malnutrition, and hard labor. The escalation of the war brought continually harsher and demanding work conditions in jobs that ranged from hard physical labor such as road building to factory work in the network of satellite camps. A clothing industry, especially for furs, operated in the camp. Work was required of everyone. Older women who were too weak to do hard labor were used to make clothes for the army or clean the barracks and latrines. The "Bunker" – as the camp prison was known – was completed in 1939 and became the site where women were regularly subjected to solitary confinement and torture. In 1941 the sick prisoners were included in the *Euthanasiaaktion* involving the killing of the mentally ill. The steadily growing death rate was caused by overwork and deteriorating living conditions. In the fall of 1944 a gas chamber was constructed (until then prisoners had been sent for gassing to other camps), and it is likely that the first female prisoners were murdered there in January 1945.

Ravensbrueck prisoners served as guinea pigs for pseudomedical experiments carried out by the *Auschwitz physicians, August Horst and Karl Clauberg. The surviving victims were often crippled for life. Ravensbrueck also became a training site for women SS auxiliary guards who went on to work in Auschwitz or *Majdanek. The rising number of Jewish inmates was concentrated in a special Jewish block, where the worst living conditions prevailed. With the implementation of the "Final Solution," all Jewish prisoners were sent to Auschwitz or Majdanek in October 1942. In the summer of 1944 Hungarian Jewish women arrived, followed later by others from other camps. Due to the intervention of *Himmler's favorite, the Finnish Dr. Kersten, and of the representatives of the World Jewish Congress in Sweden, together with the activities of *Bernadotte, on April 21 Himmler gave his consent to release thousands of women from Ravensbrueck and two other camps nearby. They were transferred by the Red Cross to Sweden and Denmark. Among them were at least 1,000 Jewish women. This rescue action had been decisively influenced by the personal intervention of Norbert Masur (d. 1971), a member of the Swedish section of the World Jewish Congress, who flew with Kersten to Berlin on April 19 and conferred with Himmler in a meeting arranged by Kersten, during the night of April 20 to 21. With the approach of the Soviet army, evacuation of Ravensbrueck was ordered by Himmler and 15,000 women were sent on a forced death march. Up to this time, 132,000 women and children had passed through the camp, of whom 92,000 died or were murdered in the camp. When the Red Army reached the camp on April 30, 1945, they found 3,000 gravely ill and dying prisoners there.

No armed resistance was possible in Ravensbrueck, but other examples of "illegal" and punishable activities are noteworthy. Those of a political nature include attempts by women working in the nearby Siemens factory to sabotage its manufacture of rocket components, to steal newspapers, or to keep lists of prisoners. Women also taught clandestinely and attempted small theatrical productions. Acts that offered reminders of home and emotional reassurance to the imprisoned women are also important. Women secretly created cookbooks, artwork, and other small items. These artistic and hand-crafted gifts that prisoners fashioned from scraps and threads of clothing and exchanged among themselves were unique ways in which women were able to resist the dehumanizing and deadly conditions.

BIBLIOGRAPHY: W. Machlejd (ed.), *Experimental Operations on Prisoners of Ravensbrueck Concentration Camp* (1960); M. Buber-Neumann, *Under Two Dictators* (1950), passim; IMT, *Trial of the Major War Criminals*, 23 (1949), index s.v. *concentration camps*; E.N. Masur, *En Jude Talar med Himmler* (1945); L. Yahil, in: *Yad Vashem Studies*, 6 (1967), 210–20; E. Buchmann (ed.), *Die Frauen von Ravensbrueck* (1959); D. Dufournier, *Ravensbrueck: the Women's Camp of Death* (1948); M. Maurel, *An Ordinary Camp* (1958); *Ravensbrueck: German Concentration Camp for Women* (1961). **ADD. BIBLIOGRAPHY:** R. Saidel, *The Jewish Women of Ravensbrück Concentration Camp* (2004).

[Yehuda Reshef / Beth Cohen (2nd ed.)]

RAVENSBURG, city in Wuerttemberg, Germany. A Jewish community existed there in the first half of the 14th century and had a synagogue. From 1330 to 1343 ten Jews are listed in the burgher rolls, including a rabbi or teacher (referred to as Ysak *scholasticus*) and a miller. The Jewish *oath (a brief dignified formula) was administered in the synagogue. The Jews' street was near the northern wall. During the *Black Death persecutions, the Jews fled to the imperial bailiff's castle where most of them were burned to death by the populace early in 1349. A survivor was admitted as a burgher in *Esslingen in 1385. Jews again appear in Ravensburg in 1380; in 1385 two Jewish masons are mentioned. In 1427 a Jew was imprisoned on charges of forgery but released upon proving his innocence. In 1429, when a young lay brother's body was found hanging from a tree in a nearby wood, two Jewish couples, one of them with their son, were accused of murder and imprisoned; they made a public declaration of innocence, which was signed by the Swabian imperial bailiff, his deputy, and others. However, the social unrest in the area caused the *blood libel to spread, and Jews in the communities on Lake *Constance were also arrested. In 1430 the imprisoned Jews in Ravensburg were burned to death and the rest banished from the city. The decision was reaffirmed by King Ferdinand I in 1588. Both King Sigismund II at the end of 1430 and Bishop Henry of Constance in 1441 vigorously opposed attempts to venerate the dead boy. Nevertheless, in local tradition the blood libel fable prevailed, as crystalized in a chronicle written c. 1770.

In the 18th century some Jews attended fairs held in Ravensburg, and by 1835 a few Jews had moved to the city. They numbered 40 in 1900 and 27 between 1925 and 1933. Of these 12 emigrated, five moved elsewhere, and 13 were deported to death camps in Eastern Europe in 1941–42. There were 32 liberated Jewish survivors of the Holocaust living in Ravensburg by 1947–48; 17 Jews remained by 1965. In 1968 eight Jews were affiliated with the *Stuttgart community. In 2005 there were three Jews living in Ravensburg who were members of the Jewish community in Stuttgart.

BIBLIOGRAPHY: M. Stern, in: ZGJD, 1 (1887), 301 (15a), 303 (2), 307 (16); 7 (n.s. 1937), 248; *Der Israelit*, 50, nos. 30, 31, 33 (1909); H. Maor, *Ueber den Wiederaufbau der juedischen Gemeinden in Deutschland seit 1945* (1961), 59; A. Dreher, in: *Wuerttembergisches Staedtebuch* (1962), 407; idem, in: *Zeitschrift fuer Wuerttembergische Landeskunde*, 12 (1962), 453–5; P. Sauer (ed.), *Dokumente ueber die Verfolgung der juedischen Bevoelkerung in Baden-Wuerttemberg 1933–1945* (1966), index; Stadtarchiv Ravensburg: Urkunden nos. 943, 945. Reportorium, vol. 2, 92d, 864f., 23a; Germ Jud, 2 (1968), 676–8. **ADD. BIBLIOGRAPHY:** *Germania Judaica*, vol. 3, 1350–1514 (1987), 1173–77.

[Toni Oelsner]

RAVIKOVITCH, DALIA (1936–2005), Hebrew poet. Born in Ramat Gan, Ravikovitch was sent after her father's death to live on a kibbutz. She studied at the Hebrew University, worked as journalist and teacher, and began publishing poetry in 1955. Her first collection, *Ahavat Tappuaḥ ha-Zahav*, with the title alluding to Prokofiev's burlesque opera, appeared in 1959. Nearly a dozen volumes of poetry followed, including *Ha-Sefer ha-Shelishi* ("The Third Book," 1969), *Ahavah Amitit* ("True Love," 1987), *Kol ha-Shirim ad Ko* ("All the Poems Till Now," 1995), *Merov Ahavah* ("Because of Love," 1998) and *Ḥazi Sha'ah lifnei ha-Monsun* ("Half an Hour before the Monsoon," 1998). The often very intimate poetry addresses the theme of loss and loneliness. Typical is the way in which Ravikovitch sets the personal experience in a wider context, the emotion in a collective historical or mythological frame of reference (as, for example, in the poem "*Ha-Historyah shel ha-Perat*"). Dreams and hallucinations evoke the vulnerability of the feminine speaker in the poems, the sense of yearning and anticipation, frequently alluding to a thwarted eroticism (as in "Clockwork Doll"). Motherhood and commitment, bodily decrepitude, and the mysterious life-driving force are some of the recurring themes. Another keynote is the political one: poems in which the speaker protests in the tradition of the biblical prophet against injustice and oppression. Ravikovitch depicts the fate of an infant who was killed in his mother's womb ("Mother Walks Around"), delineates with sarcasm the picture of terror and death in the Palestinian refugee camps of Sabra and Shatilla ("One Doesn't Kill a Baby Twice"), tells of an Arab who was burned to death, reflects on Palestinian youth throwing stones, robbed of the innocence of childhood ("Stones"), or portrays the Israeli mother whose son died in the army ("But She Had a Son"). A sense of futility and resignation marks many of the confessional poems speaking of existence – both private and collective – on the verge of an abyss. "We are a plan that has gone awry," she writes.

In addition to her own collections of poetry, Ravikovitch translated the poetry of W.B. Yeats and T.S. Eliot into Hebrew. She is the author of children's books in verse and prose, including *Mekhonit ha-Pela'im* ("The Magic Car," 1959), *Kalman shel Rami* ("Rami's Kalman," 1961), *Imma Mevulbelet* ("Absent-Minded Mommy," 1978). She also published two collections of short stories: *Mavet ba-Mishpaḥah* ("Death in the Family," 1976) and *Kevuẓat ha-Kaduregel shel Winnie Mandela* ("Winnie Mandela's Soccer Team," 1997). The typical protagonist is generally a woman or a girl who does not fit into normative social frameworks, a sensitive individual who remains an outsider, whether in the family, in the group, or in the kibbutz. In 2005 Ravikovitch published a collection of fifty mini-stories, oscillating between the melancholy and the humorous, under the title *Ba'ah ve-Halkhah* ("She Came and Went"). Ravikovitch was awarded the Bialik Prize (1987) and the Israel Prize (1998). Her poems have been translated into many languages. The English collection *Dress of Fire* appeared in 1978, followed by *The Window* in 1989. For information concerning translations into other languages see the ITHL website at www.ithl.org.il.

Ravikovitch was found dead in her apartment on August 21, 2005, apparently by her own hand.

BIBLIOGRAPHY: R. Gurfein, *Mi-Karov u-me-Raḥok* (1964), 247–50; A. Cohen, *Soferim Ivriyyim Benei Zemannenu* (1964), 296–7; G. Yardeni-Agmon, in: *Haaretz* (Jan. 30, 1970), 14–15; M. Shalev, in: *Haaretz* (27 Sivan 1969); Y. Zemora, in: *Moznayim*, 43 (1976), 418–24; A. Feinberg, "*Mavet ba-Mishpaḥah*," in: *Moznayim*, 42 (1976), 145–46; M. Baruch, *Iyyun be-Shirei D. Ravikovitch* (1973); D. Ben-Shem, in: *Ma'alot*, 8:4 (1977), 48–50; J. Hassine, *Shirah ve-Mitos bi-Yẓiratah shel D. Ravikovitch* (1989); R.E. Sherwin, "Two New Translations: The Poems of L. Goldberg and D. Ravikovich," in: *Modern Hebrew Literature*, 3:1–2 (1977), 38–42; A. Hirschfeld, "*Ravikovitch aḥarei Asor*," in: *Yedioth Aharonoth* (January 9, 1987); I. Pincas, "Leaving Traces," in: *Modern Hebrew Literature*, 1 (1988), 36–38; N. Carmel-Yonatan, "*Tafnit Amitit*," in: *Moznayim*, 61:5–6 (1988), 71–73; Y. Oppenheimer, "*Al Litikah u-Politikah be-Shirat D. Ravikovitch*," in: *Siman Keriah*, 22 (1991), 415–30; O. Yaglin, "*Al Sheloshah Shirim shel D. Ravikovitch*," in: *Reḥov*, 2 (1995), 71–81; Y. Mazor, "*Al Shirat D. Ravikovitch*," in: *Iton 77*, 206 (1997), 16–19; D. Meirovitz, in: *Haaretz* (April 29, 1998); M. Gluzman, "*Ha-Kinah ha-Olezet*," in: *Helikon*, 26 (1998), 19–26; R. Wichert, "*Ha-Em, ha-Ahavah, ha-Milḥamah*," in: *Moznayim*, 72:9 (1998), 34–36; H. Zamir, "*Ha-Metim ve-ha-Ḥayyim, ha-Ma'aminim ve-ha-Akurim*," in: *Mikan*, 1 (2000), 44–63; M. Ben-Naftali, "*Keri'ah*," in: *Resling*, 7 (2000), 65–79; E. Feliu, "*Dahlia Ravikovitch o la libertat de la imaginacio*," in: *Tamid*, 4 (2002–2003), 147–86; N. Keren, "*Ẓa'akatah ha-Kevusha shel ha-Em ha-Alumah*," in: *Teoriyah u-Vikoret*, 21 (2002), 193–200.

[Anat Feinberg (2nd ed.)]

RAVINA (abbreviation of Rav Avina), the name of several Babylonian *amoraim*, some of whom are mentioned with their patronymics and some without. At times it is difficult to identify the particular Ravina. The two best known are: RAVINA I (d. 422), who studied under Rava (Ber. 20b; 38a, et al.), and also maintained contact with Rava's other pupils, Naḥman b. Isaac, Papa, and Huna b. Joshua (Pes. 105a; BM 74b; Sanh. 69a). He had frequent discussions with R. Ashi, who was his junior. He attended his academy in *Mata Meḥasya and referred to himself as a pupil-colleague of Ashi (Er. 63a; et al.). He gave rulings on various occasions (Er. 40a, 63a). The statement, "Ravina and R. Ashi conclude the [authoritative] teaching [of the Talmud]" (BM 86a), may refer to him (Ravina's name occurs before that of Ashi in many manuscripts and early sources; see bibl., *Sinai Sefer Yovel*, 60, n. 6). He was renowned for his devotion to study and it was said of him that "he made nights as days in study of the Torah" (MK 25b; see Dik. Sof., *ibid.*). He had a son and daughter (BM 104b; Nid. 66a), and lived to an advanced age ("*Seder Tanna'im ve-Amora'im*" in *Maḥzor Vitry*, p. 483). Lavish eulogies were delivered at his death (MK 25a).

Ravina II (d. 499), Ravina b. Huna, apparently a nephew of Ravina I (Ket. 100b). His father, who was a scholar since he transmitted sayings of R. Papi (Ned. 90a) and of R. Joseph (Ned. 60b), died while Ravina was still young and his mother reported some of his father's customs in a number of *halakhot* that were in dispute (Ber. 39b; Men. 68b). Maremar was his main teacher and Ravina frequently discussed halakhic problems with him (Shab. 81b; et al.). Ravina served as *dayyan* in Mata Meḥasya and helped Ashi's daughter collect the portion of her father's property that was her due from the property of her brother Mar (Ket. 69a). On the death of Rabbah Tosfa'ah in 474, Ravina succeeded him as head of the academy of Sura (*Iggeret R. Sherira Ga'on*, ed. by B.W. Lewin (1921), 95; and see Abraham ibn Daud, *Sefer ha-Kabbalah – Book of Tradition*, ed. by G.D. Cohen, 1942). During that period the Babylonian government issued harsh decrees against the Jewish community; synagogues were closed and Jewish children compelled to apostasize (*Iggeret R. Sherira Ga'on*, p. 97). According to Sherira Gaon it is this Ravina who together with Ashi "concluded the teaching" (see above). The death of Ravina marks the end of the era of *amoraim* in Babylonia and the beginning of the age of the *savoraim*.

BIBLIOGRAPHY: Halevy, Dorot, 2 (1923), 536–51; 3 (1923), 74–85; Hyman, Toledot s.v.; B.M. Lewin, *Rabbanan Savora'im ve-Talmudam* (1937), 2–6; S. Albeck, in: *Sinai Sefer Yovel* (1958), 57ff.; Ḥ. Albeck, *ibid.*, 73 ff.

[Moshe Beer / Yitzhak Dov Gilat]

RAVINA (Rabinowitz), MENASHE (1899–1968), composer and writer. Menashe Ravina was born in Pereyaslavl, Ukraine, went to Palestine in 1924, and became active as a music educator, choral organizer, music critic (for *Davar*, from 1925 until his death), and composer. He pioneered in music popularization as well as in the arranging of music and singing courses for workers. Ravina's writings include *Yo'el Engel ve-ha-Musikah ha-Yehudit* (1947); and an exercise book for solfège, *Organum and the Samaritans* (1963). His songs include *Ha-Shekediyyah Poraḥat* (text by Israel Dushman), *Alei Giv'ah* (A. Broides), and many others.

RAVITCH, MELECH (pseudonym of **Zekharye Khone Bergner**; 1893–1976), Yiddish poet and essayist. Born in Radymno, East Galicia, Ravitch left home at 14 and lived in various cities, including, for long periods, Vienna (1912–21) and Warsaw (1921–34), later emigrating to Australia (1936–38), Argentina, the U.S., and Mexico (1939–40), before settling in Montreal in 1941 for the rest of his life (excepting 1954–56 in Israel). His earliest lyrics appeared in *Der Yudisher Arbeter* (1910); his first volume of verse was *Oyf der Shvel* (1912). He worked in a bank before serving in the Austrian army during World War I. His *Spinoza* (1918) is a tribute to the philosopher whom he ranked with Moses and Jesus. From the early 1920s he was an active contributor of poems and essays to major Yiddish periodicals in Eastern Europe and beyond. He co-founded *Literarishe Bleter* (1924) and the Yiddish Pen Club. In Vienna he felt the impact of expressionistic poets such as F. *Werfel and E. *Lasker-Schüler and began to experiment with expressionistic technique. In his *Nakete Lider* ("Naked Songs," 1921), he gave up rhyme, regular meter, and stanzas. Impressed by the Yiddish revival in postwar Poland, he settled in Warsaw in 1921. There he joined Uri Ẓevi *Greenberg and Peretz *Markish, a triumvirate branded the *Khalyastre ("Gang"), in the struggle against realism in art. Ravitch reached the climax of his expressionistic striving in the poems "Dos Gezang tsum Mentshlekhn Kerper" ("Song to the Human Body"), "Gezang tsu der Zun" ("Song to the Sun"), "Dos Gezang fun Has un Libe tsum Yidishn Folk" ("Song of Hate and Love for the Jewish People"), and "Efntlekher Mishpet Ibern Toyt" ("Public Judgment of Death"), all four of which, having initially appeared in periodicals, were published in book form in *Di Fir Zaytn fun Mayn Velt* ("The Four Sides of My World," 1929). Ravitch's retreat from expressionism was reflected in the song and ballads of *Kontinentn un Okeanen* ("Continents and Oceans," 1937), a volume which embodied his moods and experiences of the restless decade that preceded his two years in Melbourne (1936–37). Instead of trying to shock and mystify his readers, he aimed at maximum clarity, proclaiming himself a citizen of the world, a poet beyond nationalism. In 1946 he and his brother H. *Bergner published the memoirs of their family as recorded by their mother Hinde Bergner (1870–1942) on the eve of World War II. In Montreal he served as a catalyst of Yiddish literary, educational, and cultural activities. During his active association there with the *Yidishe-folksbyblotek* (Jewish Public Library), he revived the *Yidishe-folksuniversitet* (Jewish People's Popular University) to offer adult education programming in Jewish and non-Jewish topics from 1941 to 1954. Soon after he settled in Montreal, Ravitch embarked on a project to immortalize the Jewish cultural figures he had known in Poland, Israel, and America, and other countries and produced five encyclopedic volumes, *Mayn Leksikon* (1945–82). He also wrote three autobiographical volumes (*Dos Mayse-bukh fun Mayn Lebn* (1962–75), which appeared in Hebrew as *Sefer ha-Ma'asiyot shel Ḥayai* (1976).

Ravitch was one of the world's leading Yiddish literary figures after the Holocaust. His poetry and essays appeared in the international Yiddish press and in anthologies, as well as in translation. Ravitch published numerous collections of poetry, including *67 Lirishe, Satirishe, Natsyonale, Sotsyale un Filozofishe Lider fun di Letste Finf-zeks Yor* (1946), *Di Kroynung fun a Yungn Yidishn Dikhter in Amerike: Poeme* (1953), *Di Lider fun Mayne Lider* (1954), and *Iker Shokhakhti: Lider un Poemes fun di Yorn 1954–1969* (1969), as well as in Hebrew translation (*Ḥamishim Shirim*, 1969). His essays appeared in *Eynems Yidishe Makhshoves in Tsvantsikstn Yorhundert* (1949), and posthumously in *Eseyen* (1992). Ravitch edited and co-edited numerous collective projects, including the weekly literary supplement of the *Keneder Odler* (1943–49), *Almanakh Yidish* (1961), and *Dos Amolike Yidishe Varshe biz der Shvel fun Dritn Khurbn* (1966). During his long career, he was awarded numerous literary prizes including the prestigious L. Lamed, Yud Yud Segal, and Itzik Manger Prizes.

ADD. BIBLIOGRAPHY: C.L. Fuks (Fox) (ed.), *Hundert Yor Yidishe un Hebreyishe Literatur in Kanade* (Montreal, 1982), 264–71; S. Niger et. al. (eds.), *Leksikon fun der Nayer Yidisher Literatur*, vol. 8, 314–18; E.H Jeshurin and W. Ostreger, *Melekh Ravitsh Bibliografye* (Montreal, 1954); LNYL 8 (1981), 314–18; I. Bruce, in: *Traduction, Terminologie, Redaction*, 7/2 (1994), 35–62; A. Eidherr, in: *Informationen zur Deutschdidaktik*, 2 (2001), 66–75.

[Sol Liptzin / Jerold C. Frakes and Rebecca Margolis (2nd ed.)]

RAVITZ, SHELOMO (c. 1886–1980), *ḥazzan* and composer. Born in Novogrudok, Russia, Ravitz studied music from the age of 15 and received his diploma in Vienna. He officiated in various European communities, including Riga, and in Johannesburg before moving to Ereẓ Israel in 1932. He became *ḥazzan* of the Ohel Shem Synagogue in Tel Aviv and his reputation spread through his singing together with his own choir, at the weekly *oneg shabbat* organized there by Ḥ.N. *Bialik. He subsequently became *ḥazzan* of the Tel Aviv Great Synagogue, where his expressive, yet unexaggerated, style of singing brought him admiration and popularity. As director of the Selah Seminary for *ḥazzanim*, Ravitz was the teacher of many present-day *ḥazzanim*.

His compositions and arrangements of traditional melodies were published in *Yalkut Zemirot* (1954) and *Kol Yisrael*, 2 vols. (1964), edited by M.S. Geshuri. Ravitz also edited the music section in each volume of Y.L. Baruch and Y.T. Levinsky (eds.), *Sefer ha-Mo'adim*, 8 vols. (1946–67), which serves as a popular source of Jewish musical tradition in Israeli homes and schools.

BIBLIOGRAPHY: M.S. Geshuri (ed.), *Kol Yisrael*, 1 (1954), xxii–xxv; idem, in: *Dukhan*, 3 (1962), 31–38; *Yedi'ot ha-Makhon ha-Yisre'eli le-Musikah Datit*, 5 (1963), 23–25; S. Samet, in: *Haaretz* (April 10, 1970), 18.

[David M.L. Olivestone]

RAVITZKY, AVIEZER (1945–), Israeli philosopher and professor. Born in Jerusalem, Ravitzky was raised in a religious-Zionist family and in his youth led the Bnei Akiva youth movement in Tel Aviv. As a graduate student in Jewish philosophy at the Hebrew University he headed the university's student union. His Ph.D. dissertation dealt with the early commentators on Maimonides' *Guide of the Perplexed*, a subject of his continued scholarly interest. In 1980 he joined the faculty of the department of Jewish Thought at the Hebrew University of Jerusalem, eventually becoming department chairman and head of the Institute of Jewish Studies. Ravitzky was an active member of the Israel Council for Higher Education, and from 1995 served as a senior fellow at the Israel Democracy Institute, where he headed research projects dealing with religion and state, the subject of some of his own publications. Ravitzky also served on the National Committee for Bio-Ethics. In 2001 he was awarded the Israel Prize for Jewish Thought.

His research has led to new ways of understanding Jewish philosophy in the Middle Ages and 20th-century Jewish thought. Ravitzky's medieval studies cast new light on *Maimonides and Ḥasdai *Crescas, and showed how a continuous Maimonidean–Ibn *Tibbon school of thought shaped Jewish philosophy in subsequent generations, thereby influencing research into the esoteric doctrines found in the manuscripts of Maimonides' early followers and commentators. Ravitzky's work also provided a new conceptual framework for understanding Jewish political philosophy, clarifying the ideological tensions relating to messianism and the Land of Israel. His research investigating the roots of contemporary Orthodox theological responses to nationalist movements, presented these diverse perspectives in an overall conceptual model, and thereby led to new ways of understanding religious thought and its relation to modernity, Zionism, and the State of Israel. Many of Ravitzky's publications focus on the connection between classical Jewish thought and existential issues, including war and peace, exile and redemption, religion and state.

Ravitzky rejected the increasingly right-wing orientation of the national-religious movement and its emphasis on settlement activity, in favor of an ideology balancing these values with the sanctity of life and the search for peace. From the early 1970s he was a founder and leader of the religious peace movements in Israel.

Among Ravitzky's books are *Messianism, Zionism and Jewish Religious Radicalism* (1996); *History and Faith: Studies in Jewish Philosophy* (1996); *The Land of Israel in Jewish Thought* (Heb., 3 vols., 1990, 1998, 2005), *Religion and State in Jewish Thought* (Heb., 2 vols., 1998, 2005; Eng., 2000); and *Argument on Faith and Philosophy with Yeshayahu Leibowitz* (Heb., 2006).

[Raphael Jospe (2nd ed.)]

RAWET, SAMUEL (1929–1984), Brazilian author. Rawet was born in Klimontow, Poland; in 1936 his family immigrated to Brazil, where his parents settled in the suburbs of Rio de Janeiro. Rawet earned a degree in engineering, and he made significant contributions to the design and building of Brasília. He early on decided to establish a career as an author and in 1956 published his first volume of short stories, *Contos do imigrante*, which contains stories he had previously published between 1949 and 1953 in a variety of magazines and literary supplements. Subsequent works of fiction include: *Diálogo* (1963), *Abama* (1964), *Os sete sonhos* (1967), *O terreno de uma polegada quadrada* (1970), *Viagens de Ahasverus* (1970), and *Que os mortos enterrem os seus mortos* (1981). An anthology of his stories has also been published in English under the title *The Prophet and Other Stories* (1998). In addition to his fiction, Rawet also wrote two plays (never published) and a number of nonfiction works such as *Alienação e realidade* (1970), *Homossexualismo, sexualidade e valor* (1970), and *Angústia e conhecimento* (1978).

Rawet's works began to receive critical attention in the 1990s. Most critics point to his adherence to a nostalgic portrayal of *Yiddishkeit* in his early fiction to a rather violent rejection of Jewishness is his later works. To be sure, his work reflects the author's changing attitudes over the course of his life. He was at times controversial. His characters are in a constant struggle to define and find their place in the world. Displacement, exile, tragedy, solitude, suffering, incomprehension, anguish, insecurity, and memory persist in his literature as inherent to the human condition. The trope of the wandering Jew, most overt in *Viagens de Ahasverus*, is a persistent leitmotif in his works. Problematic and inconsistent, his works represent a major contribution to Brazilian literature.

[Darrell B. Lockhart (2nd ed.)]

RAWICZ (Ger. **Rawitsch**), town in Poznan province, W. Poland. The first settlement of Jews in Rawicz took place soon after the founding of the town in 1639. In 1648 complaints were lodged against Jewish merchants who were then expelled. They returned soon thereafter, only to be expelled again in 1674. By 1698 an organized community was in existence and in 1719 it received a *Freibrief* ("letter of privileges") regulating the rights and taxes of its members. By then the community totaled 12 families. A *ḥevra kaddisha* was founded in 1728 and the first rabbi, Menahem Mendel Gradenwitz, was appointed in 1755. Its *bet din* was headed by learned talmudic authorities, including R. Solomon b. Dov Baer (1786–93), later to be the community's rabbi. In 1774 a *bet midrash* was founded. Services were held in a private house until a synagogue was built in 1783. The community (35 families in 1739) flourished, and after a fire in *Leszno (1790) absorbed many refugees, including R. Akiva *Eger, who lived there for one year. The local Jews were mainly shopkeepers, tailors, livestock merchants, and artisans. In 1797 the community had 198 families, and by 1835 there were 401 families (a total of 1,574 persons, or about 50% of the total population). A new synagogue was built in 1889 when the community was at its economic peak and served by a long line of scholarly rabbis, including its last one, the scholar John Cohn (1893–1920). The Jewish population subsequently declined to 363 in 1905. The town suffered during World War I, and under Polish rule the community was subjected to discrimination which induced many to leave for Germany; only 15 remained in 1933. The cemetery and synagogue were both destroyed by the Nazis during World War II. Markus *Brann, the historian, and Arthur *Ruppin, the Zionist leader, were both born in Rawicz.

BIBLIOGRAPHY: J. Cohn, *Geschichte der juedischen Gemeinde Rawitsch* (1915); A.B. Posner, *The Annals of the Community of Rawitsch* (Heb. and Eng., 1962).

RAWIDOWICZ, SIMON (1896–1957), Jewish scholar, philosopher, Hebraist, and ideologue. Born in Grajewo, then in Russia, Rawidowicz received a traditional Jewish education, during the course of which he became attracted to the Haskalah and Modern Hebrew literature. After the outbreak of World War I in 1914, he moved with his family to Bialystok, where he became active in the Hebrew cultural life of the city. In 1919, he left for Berlin, where he obtained a Ph.D. in philosophy in 1926 for his dissertation on Ludwig Feuerbach, which he expanded into *Ludwig Feuerbachs Philosophie: Ursprung and Schicksal* ("Ludwig Feuerbach's Philosophy: Sources and Influence," 1931; 1964^2). Concomitantly, he made his mark as a scholar of Judaica with the publication of *Kitvei Ranak* ("The Writings of Nahman Krochmal," 1924; 1961^2), and volume seven of the Jubilee Edition of the writings of Moses Mendelssohn (1930; 1971^2). Additionally, he established the Hebrew Ayanot Publishing Company (1922–25) and the *Brit Ivrit Olamit (World Hebrew Union, 1931), and edited the Hebrew miscellany *Ha-Tekufah* (1928–30) with Saul Tchernikowsky and Ben-Zion Katz. In 1933, he left Berlin and after looking unsuccessfully for a position in Ereẓ Israel, went to London, where he continued his research in Jewish philosophy, primarily on Saadiah, Maimonides, Krochmal, and Mendelssohn.

From his youth, Rawidowicz had been a staunch supporter of the development of the Jewish community in the Land of Israel and of the political aims of the Zionist movement, but in the early 1930s he also became concerned with the future of Hebrew creativity in the Diaspora. This led him to criticize the accepted Zionist position that the Land of Israel was to serve as the spiritual center for world Jewry and to reject the concept of the "Negation of the Diaspora." He believed that realistically the Jewish Diaspora would continue to exist for the foreseeable future, and that as long as it did, it should be accepted as a fact and encouraged to maintain its own creativity. Consequently, Rawidowicz formulated his concept of "partnership" which posited that rather than being relegated to the inferior role of imitating the spiritual center, the Diaspora should be considered an equal partner. Rejecting the dominant ideology expressed symbolically by a circle with a center and circumference representing the Land of Israel and the Diaspora, respectively, instead he adopted the figure of an ellipse with two foci, the Land of Israel and the Diaspora, with the ellipse itself representing the entirety of the united Jewish people. As historical precedent for the coexistence of two such creative centers, Rawidowicz invoked the experience of the Land of Israel and Babylonia during the talmudic period.

In 1941, Rawidowicz accepted a newly created position in Medieval and Modern Hebrew at Leeds University, eventually becoming head of the department of Hebrew language and literature in 1946. During World War II, he established the Ararat Publishing Company as an affirmation of Hebrew creativity in the only country in Europe in which it was still possible to publish Hebrew books. Ararat's publications edited by Rawidowicz included the Hebrew miscellany *Meẓudah* (7 vols. in 5; 1943–54) and *Sefer Dubnow* (1954). He additionally edited *Sefer Sokolow* (1942).

In 1948, Rawidowicz left Leeds for the College of Jewish Studies in Chicago, and in 1951 accepted a new position in Jewish Philosophy and Hebrew literature at Brandeis University. There, he served as the first chair of the department of Near Eastern and Judaic Studies until his death in 1957. At the time, he was in the final stage of proofreading *Bavel vi-Yrushalayim* ("Babylon and Jerusalem," 1957), the final and most elaborate formulation of his ideology which also contained a chapter from his projected introduction to the philosophy of Jewish history.

Rawidowicz's overall approach was to stress the importance of the Hebrew language for continued Jewish creativity and to emphasize the ongoing internal process of interpretation within the realm of Jewish thought rather than the influence of external factors. While his philosophical research remains important for the field of Jewish thought, he is increasingly remembered for his ideological approach and insights, which despite the acknowledgment of his great erudition were widely and sharply criticized during his lifetime but in recent years have attracted growing favorable attention.

Many of Rawidowicz' essays and articles have been reissued in four books: *Shriftn* ("The Yiddish Writings of Simon Rawidowicz"), ed. A. Golumb (Buenos Aires, 1962); *Iyyunim Be-Maḥashevet Yisrael: Hebrew Studies in Jewish Thought by Simon Rawidowicz*, ed. B. Ravid, 2 vols. (Jerusalem, 1969–71), with biography and bibliography; and with translations from Hebrew and Yiddish, *Studies in Jewish Thought,* ed. N.N. Glatzer (Philadelphia, 1974), 3–42, and *Israel: The Ever-Dying People and Other Essays by Simon Rawidowicz,* ed. B. Ravid (Rutherford, NJ, 1986), with biography, reissued in expanded version in paperback under title of *State of Israel, Diaspora and Jewish Continuity* (Hanover, NH, 1998).

BIBLIOGRAPHY: "Simon Rawidowicz," in: *American National Biography*, 18 (1999), 194–96; A. Greenbaum, *History of the Ararat Publishing Society* (1998); D.N. Myers, "A Third Guide for the Perplexed: Simon Rawidowicz 'On Interpretation,'" in: W. Cutter and D.C. Jacobson (eds.), *History and Literature: New Readings of Jewish Texts in Honor of Arnold J. Band* (2002), 75–87; B. Ravid, "Simon Rawidowicz and the 'Brit Ivrit Olamit': A Study in the Relationship Between Hebrew Culture in the Diaspora and Zionist Ideology" (Heb.), in: *Studies and Essays in Hebrew Language and Literature: Berlin Congress: Proceedings of the 16th Hebrew Scientific European Congress* (2004), 119–54.

[Benjamin Ravid (2nd ed.)]

RAWNITZKI, YEHOSHUA ḤANA (1859–1944), Hebrew journalist and publisher. Born in Odessa, Rawnitzki began his journalistic career – in which he continued for most of his life – in 1879, by contributing first to *Ha-Kol,* and then to other periodicals. His articles, first in Hebrew and later in Yiddish, were largely the result of his activities in the *Ḥibbat Zion movement. He was the editor and publisher of the literary collection *Pardes* (3 vols., 1892–96), a forum for the outstanding Hebrew writers of the time and a forerunner of *Ha-Shilo'aḥ. With his publication of Ḥ.N. *Bialik's first poem, "*El ha-Ẓippor,*" in *Pardes*, Rawnitzki became Bialik's first patron, thus initiating a lifelong association with the poet. Some of his own works appeared in *Pardes* and subsequently in *Ha-Shilo'aḥ*, as well as other periodicals. Special recognition was aroused by a series of feuilletons, "*Kevurat Soferim*" ("The Burial of Writers"), which were written with Shalom Aleichem under the pseudonyms of Eldad (Shalom Aleichem) and Medad (Rawnitzki). As a result of his teaching experience and interest in pedagogical problems, he established the Moriah publishing house in Odessa in 1901, together with S. *Ben-Zion and Bialik, having influenced the latter to move to Odessa. The publishing house, the first of his joint endeavors with Bialik, began with the publication of textbooks (e.g., *Sippurei ha-Mikra*, 1903–05), followed by the influential aggadic anthology *Sefer ha-Aggadah* (1908–11), and many other books. This partnership between the two continued until the poet's death. Bialik frequently complained that Rawnitzki's role was not sufficiently appreciated. Settling in Ereẓ Israel in 1921, Rawnitzki, together with Bialik and S. *Levin, founded the Devir publishing house, where he published the works on which he and Bialik had cooperated (e.g., the commentary on the poems of Moses *Ibn Ezra and Solomon ibn *Gabirol).

Later, he published *Dor ve-Soferav* (2 vols., 1926–37), a collection of his articles and memoirs on Bialik, Mendele Mokher Seforim, and other writers of his time, and *Mikhtavim le-Vat Yisrael* (2nd ed., 1923), on educational problems. A collection of his articles, *Be-Sha'arei Sefer* (1961), was published by S. Kremer, together with a comprehensive introduction by the editor. Rawnitzki also published Yiddish books and edited various Yiddish periodicals.

BIBLIOGRAPHY: Kressel, Leksikon, 2 (1967), 828–9.

[Getzel Kressel]

RAY, MAN (1890–1976), U.S. photographer and painter. Born in Philadelphia and moving to Paris in 1921, Ray is known as a founder of the dadaist-surrealist movement in painting, and in photography circles he is famous for his abstract prints made in the darkroom without a camera, to which he gave the name of "Rayograph." Ray added beams and moving pencils of light to the original technique of spreading objects on photographic sensitized papers which were exposed and then developed. He also contributed other facets to creative photography, making effective use of solarization by giving a momentary second exposure to his negative before developing it. The prints he produced from film treated this way showed strong secondary black lines along the major contours of the subject. Ray's portfolio of portraits records the celebrities of the 1920s. Ray fled from France in 1940 on the Nazi invasion and went to Hollywood, where he remained for the duration of World War II, after which he returned to Paris. His autobiography, *Self Portrait* (1963), explains a great deal of his artistry and his personality.

BIBLIOGRAPHY: *Current Biography Yearbook 1965* (1965), 336–8; J.I.H. Baur (ed.), *New Art in America* (1957), 88–91.

[Peter Pollack]

RAYKIN, ARKADI ISAAKOVICH (1911–1987), Soviet Russian vaudeville actor and director. After theatrical training in Leningrad, Raykin became widely known in the U.S.S.R. for his mime and impersonations. In 1939 he established the Variety and Miniature Theater in Leningrad, becoming its director. One of his most popular impersonations was that of Charlie Chaplin. He also appeared as Don Quixote and caricatured many types in his act *Intourist Hotel.* In later years his satire of bureaucrats and pseudointellectuals became more caustic. In 1962 Raykin appeared at the International Festival of Pantomime in West Berlin, and in 1964 in England. His wife, Ruth Joffe-Raykin, was a writer and an actor, as were his daughter Yekaterina and his son Konstantin.

°RAYMOND DE PENAFORTE (d. 1275), Dominican monk, one of the initiators of anti-Jewish activities in Catalonia during the reign of James I (1213–76). Raymond was born in Peñaforte, Catalonia, and studied law at the University of Bologna, completing his studies in 1216. In 1222 he founded the

Dominican monastery of Barcelona. He was a favorite of Pope *Gregory IX and, among other duties, he served as the Pope's confessor beginning in 1230. When the heresy of the *Albigenses spread to northern Catalonia from Provence, Raymond influenced the king of Aragon to establish the Papal *Inquisition in the district of *Tarragona. As initiator of missionary activities in his order, he made great efforts to convert Jews to Christianity, founding Hebrew and Arabic schools for this purpose. He was the moving spirit of the anti-Jewish legislation of James I in 1228. He was also among the initiators and most prominent participants of the *Barcelona disputation of 1263. The accusation before the royal tribunal of Barcelona against *Naḥmanides, in 1265, that he had "blasphemed Christianity," was also instigated by Raymond and the Christian anti-Jewish literature written after the disputation of Barcelona was a product of his school. He was canonized in 1601.

BIBLIOGRAPHY: Baer, Spain, 1 (1961), 152, 156f., 161; F. Valls-Taberner, *San Ramón de Penyafort* (1953), incl. bibl., 372–80.

RAYNAL, DAVID (1841–1903), French politician. Born in Paris, Raynal founded the firm of Astruc and Raynal in Bordeaux in 1862 and there made the acquaintance of the French leader, Léon Gambetta. He was elected deputy for Bordeaux in 1879 and two years later became minister of works in the government of Gambetta. From 1883 to 1885 Raynal was again minister of public works, from 1893 to 1894 he was minister of the interior. While in office he was accused of underhand dealings in his handling of the railways, but his successful libel action against the journal *La Cocarde* in 1893 cleared him of all suspicion. He was made a senator in 1897 and was president of a commission to reform the merchant navy.

[Shulamith Catane]

RAYNE, SIR MAX, BARON (1918–2003), British businessman and financier. The son of a tailor in London's East End, Rayne was educated at University College London and served in the Royal Air Force during World War II. Rayne was was one of the most successful of post-World War II property developers and was chairman from 1961 of the property company London Merchant Securities. He was also chairman or director of other property and industrial companies. Rayne was active in support for the arts as a governor of the Royal Ballet School, chairman of its London Trust (1967–75) and of the National Theatre Board from 1971 to 1988. His support for medical work included the post of special trustee of St. Thomas's Hospital. He was an honorary vice president of the (London) Jewish Welfare Board and served on other bodies concerned with social service, including the King Edward VII Hospital Fund for London and St. Thomas's Medical School. Rayne was knighted in 1969 and created a life peer in 1976. In 1962 he established the Rayne Foundation, a charity devoted to helping the disadvantaged, the arts, and education.

[Vivian David Lipman]

RAYNER, ISIDOR (1850–1912), U.S. lawyer and politician. Rayner was born in Baltimore, where his Bavarian immigrant father William Solomon Rayner had been one of the founders of the Har Sinai Congregation. He studied law at the University of Virginia and was admitted to the Baltimore bar in 1870. After several years of legal practice he entered Democratic Party politics and was elected to the Maryland state legislature in 1878 and to the state senate in 1885. In 1886 he was elected to the first of three terms in the U.S. House of Representatives, and after serving a term as Maryland attorney general (1899–1903), he was elected to the U.S. Senate in 1904 and again in 1910. Politically, Rayner was a moderate liberal. While still in the state legislature, he was a vigorous opponent of black disenfranchisement laws and Jim Crow, and his 1904 senatorial campaign was undertaken in defiance of the corrupt Democratic machine. In the Senate Rayner was particularly active on the Foreign Relations Committee, which he used as a forum to eloquently criticize President Theodore Roosevelt's imperialist policies toward Latin America. He also helped lead successful Senate efforts to abrogate the treaty with Russia in 1911 in protest against czarist antisemitism and discrimination against U.S. Jewish travelers. A nominal member of his father's congregation, Rayner married a Christian and was buried in a Unitarian ceremony.

[Hillel Halkin]

RAYNOR, BRUCE (1950–), U.S. labor leader. Raynor was born and raised on Long Island, New York, the son of a truck driver and a department store worker. He joined the labor movement shortly after graduating from Cornell University in Ithaca, N.Y., in 1973, rose to become president of UNITE, the apparel and textile workers union, then became the first president of the organization formed in 2004 by the merger of UNITE and HERE, the hotel and restaurant employees union. Raynor entered Cornell on a scholarship, majoring in biochemistry, but found himself stirred by the Vietnam antiwar and civil rights movements. He gave up his chemistry scholarship and enrolled in Cornell's School of Industrial and Labor Relations. After graduation, Raynor joined the education department of the Textile Workers Union, which in a few years would merge with the Amalgamated Clothing Workers Union and became the ACTWU. His first assignment was to help lead a six-month strike at Oneida Knitting Mills. It resulted in the union's first contract with that company. Raynor became an associate organizing director and soon found himself taking part in a bigger fight, one that had begun in 1963. This was an effort to organize J.P. Stevens, the giant textile company, a struggle dramatized in the 1979 movie *Norma Rae*. Raynor was said to have been the inspiration for the union organizer portrayed by actor Ron Leibman. In 1980, the ACTWU finally won a contract at Stevens. A year later, Raynor was named Southern Regional Director of the union and in 1993 was appointed executive vice president. He held the same post when the ACTWU and the International Ladies Garment Workers Union merged in 1995 to create UNITE. Three years later, he was named secretary-treasurer of UNITE and in 2001 he became president, succeeding Jay *Mazur. Although many Jewish garment workers had been replaced by other ethnic groups by then, Raynor said, "This is still a Jewish union – in terms of its beliefs and ideals. It views itself as much more than wages and benefits. It's deeply rooted in the traditions of social justice and concern for the least of us. When I say 'Jewish union,' that's what I mean." Raynor had already led an organizing drive that expanded UNITE's membership to include industrial laundry workers. From 5,000 such members in 1998, the number grew to more than 40,000 in 2000. As UNITE's president, Raynor continued to focus on building its membership. At the same time, he helped reform abusive labor practices by overseas contractors of major U.S. brands. Raynor, who was also a vice president of the AFL-CIO, then played a key role in the merger with HERE. At the time of the merger, the combined organization had 440,000 members and an annual operating budget in excess of $60 million.

BIBLIOGRAPHY: *Women's Wear Daily* (Feb. 17, 1998); *The Forward* (July 20, 2001).

[Mort Sheinman (2nd ed.)]

RAYSS, TSCHARNA (1890–1965), Israel botanist. Born in Vinnitsa, Russia, Rayss was in charge of research at the department of botany at the universities of Odessa and Bucharest, 1918–29, and deputy director of the phytopathology department of the Institute for Agricultural Research, Romania. An enthusiastic Zionist she joined the newly formed botany department of the Hebrew University in Jerusalem in 1934 and was appointed professor in 1951.

Her research on the lower plants dealt with the taxonomy and ecology of algae of the Mediterranean and the Red Sea; mycoflora of Israel; taxonomy and biology of fungi in Romania, France, and Israel, with special emphasis on their pathogenicity to crops and wild plants. She built up the herbarium and library of cryptogamic plants in the Hebrew University.

BIBLIOGRAPHY: Viennot Bourgin, in: *Bulletin de la Société Mycologique de France*, 81 no. 2 (1965), 113–5.

[Shira Borut]

RAZA RABBA, SEFER (Aram. סֵפֶר רָזָא רַבָּא; "The Book of the Great Secret"), a work of *Merkabah mysticism which is no longer extant as a separate entity. That it existed, however, cannot be doubted. Several Near Eastern, Palestinian, and Babylonian authors of the ninth, tenth, and 11th centuries who attest to its existence were discovered by Jacob Mann (Mann, Texts, 2 (1935), 74–83). In the polemical works of the leading Karaite sage of Jerusalem, *Daniel b. Moses al-Qumisi (late ninth century), the work is described as having magical content. Another Karaite author writes about the magical acts described in the book: "for love and hate, miraculous shortcuts, and questions in dreams." *Raza Rabba* is also mentioned in a responsum of *Hai Gaon (B.M. Lewin (ed.), *Oẓar ha-Ge'onim*, on *Ḥagigah* (1931), 21). In *Sefer Raza Rabba* magical content is intertwined with an exposition on the Merkabah, including speculations on the names of angels and demons known from magical literature on oaths, formulations of amulets by Babylonian Arabs from the fifth to eighth centuries, and *gematriot* which afterward passed on to the *Ḥasidei Ashkenaz.

Raza Rabba differs in character from Midrashim written in France and in Narbonne and apparently derived from an Eastern or Babylonian source which reached Germany and groups of Ḥasidim. However, it is not clear whether either *Judah he-Ḥasid or *Eleazar of Worms knew the work.

Portions of *Raza Rabba* were found in a manuscript of a commentary on *Sefer *Shi'ur Komah* written in the late 13th century by Moses (Azriel) b. Eleazar ha-Darshan ("the preacher"), son of Moses ha-Darshan (the husband of Judah b. Samuel he-Ḥasid's granddaughter in Wuerzburg), and have been published by G. *Scholem. Moses cites a work which he calls *Ha-Sod ha-Gadol* ("The Great Secret") and quotes other works which leave no doubt that he saw several versions of *Raza Rabba* or parts of it; he cites Sefer ha-*Bahir as a separate source.

In contrast to extant visionary Merkabah texts, *Raza Rabba* was a Merkabah Midrash and some elements in it are clearly and unquestionably linked to *Sefer ha-Bahir*, although they appear in different versions. While *Raza Rabba* contains no definitely Gnostic homilies, the *Sefer ha-Bahir* develops the same motifs in a new direction, a kabbalistic-Gnostic one. *Sefer ha-Bahir* contains the oldest enumeration of the ten *Sefirot* interpreted kabbalistically; an older, though incomplete, list is found in *Raza Rabba*, which was one of the literary sources for the editing of the *Bahir*. The homiletic symbolism of the *Sefirot* developed in the *Bahir* does not occur in *Raza Rabba*. Other matters treated in the *Bahir*, such as **gilgul*, are not present in the extant portions of *Raza Rabba*.

BIBLIOGRAPHY: G. Scholem, *Reshit ha-Kabbalah* (1948), 195–238; idem, *Ursprung und Anfaenge der Kabbala* (1962), 94–109.

[Esther (Zweig) Liebes]

RAZIEL, an important angel who, according to his name, is connected with "the mysteries of God." In midrashic and magical literature he is mentioned only in sources going back to the esoteric teachings of the talmudic period, where he appears in three sources. When Moses is ascending to heaven in order to receive the Torah, he encounters on his way the angel Gallizur ("he who reveals the hidden reasons of the Rock"; i.e., God), who is also called Raziel because he hears from behind the divine curtain all that is going to happen in the world, and this he reveals to Elijah, who "spreads the voice" over all the world. The angel Raziel also appeared to Adam three days after he had been expelled from paradise and had fallen into despair. Then Raziel revealed to him a magical textbook containing the mysteries of the workings of creation. This version of an old esoteric *aggadah* was incorporated into a collection of cosmological and angelological material culled mainly from the writings of *Eliezer b. Isaac of Worms and some other 13th-century kabbalists, and published in Amsterdam in 1701 under the title, "This is the book of the first Adam which the angel Raziel delivered to him," commonly called "*Sefer Razi'el*" (see below). It had a wide circulation, being reprinted nearly 40 times. The third source is the apocryphal Sefer *ha-Razim, known in manuscript form in post-talmudic times. This purported to be the book of mysteries which the angel Raziel taught to Noah in the year he entered the ark and which Noah later wrote down on tablets of sapphire. It is a handbook of magic, both Jewish and syncretistic, giving a detailed account of the angels in the seven heavens and the magical practices connected with them and their conjuration. Whereas the first part is of a strictly Jewish character, the magical practices contain strong pagan elements. In the opinion of the editor, Mordecai Margalioth (1966), the text goes back to the talmudic period, perhaps even to the earlier part, especially because of its close connection with some texts in the Greek magical papyri. The age of the book is still a matter of controversy. According to the Zohar, Adam received his book while he was still in paradise, and the angel Raziel was none other than the archangel *Uriel who revealed the deep mysteries of the Torah. The numerical value of the Hebrew name is 248, corresponding to the number of the positive commandments of the Torah and the name Abraham. The kabbalist Abraham b. Samuel *Abulafia used this name as a pseudonym in several of his books.

BIBLIOGRAPHY: M. Margalioth, *Sefer ha-Razim* (a newly recovered book of magic from the talmudic period) (1966[9]); M. Schwab, *Vocabulaire de l'angélologie* (1897), 246; R. Margalioth, *Malakhei Elyon* (1945), 280–2; J. Dan, in: Tarbiz, 37 (1967/68), 208–14; F. Secret, in: REJ, 128 (1969), 223–45.

[Gershom Scholem]

RAZIEL, BOOK OF, collection of mystical, cosmological, and magical Hebrew works and portions of works. First printed in Amsterdam in 1701, it was reprinted many times, because of the popular belief that the book protected its owner's home from fire and other dangers. There are some manuscripts of, at least, parts of this work which date back to the 16th century. However, in its printed form, it was not compiled much earlier than the 17th century. Many manuscript collections of material of the same sort are extant, and *Raziel* is not unique among them in any way. The material included in the collection can be divided into three distinct categories or strata:

(1) Works, or parts of works, which belong to *Heikhalot* and *Merkabah mysticism, the mystical and cosmological literature of the talmudic and geonic periods. Of these, *Raziel* contains a version of the *Sefer ha-Malbush*, a magical work; *baraita* of *Ma'aseh Bereshit*, a cosmological and astrological description of the Creation, which has some mystical overtones; and a major part of the *Sefer ha-Razim* ("Book of Magical Secrets"), which is a collection of magical formulas and angelological material from talmudic times. The introduction to *Sefer ha-*Razim* probably gave the whole collection its name. In this introduction, the angel Raziel is claimed to have revealed the secrets described to Adam. In this category, there is some importance to a long version of the early anthropomorphic work, the **Shi'ur Komah*, describing the members and secret names of the Creator.

(2) Material which belongs to literature of the 13th-century *Ḥasidei Ashkenaz. To this category belong the introduction and the first half of *Eleazar of Worms' work, *Sod Ma'aseh Bereshit* ("The Secret of the Creation"), which formed the first part of his *Sodei Rezaya*. Some exegetical works on the Holy Names of God, and some magical formulas which conclude the collection, also belong to the literary heritage of the Ḥasidei Ashkenaz.

(3) A few portions of kabbalistic literature, descriptions of the *Sefirot* and exegeses of Holy Names, mostly reflecting kabbalistic theology of pre-Lurianic periods. A critical analysis of the work by Elyakim Melsack (Milzahagi) is preserved in a manuscript in Jews' College, London.

BIBLIOGRAPHY: M. Margalioth, *Sefer ha-Razim* (1966), introduction; J. Dan, *Torat ha-Sod shel Ḥasidei Ashkenaz* (1968), 83, 208.

[Joseph Dan]

RAZIEL, DAVID (1910–1941), commander of the *Irgun Ẓeva'i Le'ummi (IẒL). Born in Smorgon, near Vilna, Raziel was taken to Ereẓ Israel at the age of three by his parents. From an early age he displayed literary ability, writing essays and plays on biblical themes. During the 1929 Arab riots he joined the *Haganah, becoming one of the first members of the IẒL, which seceded from the Haganah in 1931. He soon became known as a gifted instructor and leader and produced manuals of military instruction. About a year after the first split in IẒL (1937), he became commander of the organization, and during that tense year led it in its reprisal activities against the Arabs. On May 19, 1939, he was captured by the British authorities, and sent to a prison camp, from which he was released at the end of October as a result of the outbreak of World War II and the IẒL's readiness to cooperate in the war effort against the Axis. He continued to serve as commander of the IẒL and leader of *Betar in Palestine even after the June 1940 split in IẒL. On May 17, 1941, in cooperation with British Army intelligence, he led a group of IẒL members to Ḥabbāniyya, Iraq, to sabotage the oil depots on the outskirts of Baghdad, which were serving the German Luftwaffe; but on May 20, in a German bombing attack, the car in which he was traveling was hit and he and a British officer were killed. Buried in the British military cemetery at Ḥabbāniyya, his remains were transferred to Nicosia, Cyprus, in 1955 and finally interred on Mount Herzl in Jerusalem in 1961. Ramat Raziel, a moshav in the Judean Mountains, is named after him.

BIBLIOGRAPHY: S. Katz, *Days of Fire* (1968), index; Jabotinsky Institute in Israel, *David Raziel* (Heb., 1956); D. Niv, *Ma'arekhot ha-Irgun ha-Ẓeva'i ha-Le'ummi*, 3 (1967), index; Dinur, Haganah, 2 pt. 3 (1963), index.

[David Niv]

RAZIM, SEFER HA- (Heb. סֵפֶר הָרָזִים; "Book of Secrets"), early work of Jewish mystical literature. *Sefer ha-Razim* is remarkable for its systematic treatment of magic, witchcraft, incantations, and supernatural remedies, on which no special works have otherwise been preserved in Hebew literature. In the midst of deliberations on the angels, their names, and their functions in the six heavens which precede the supreme heaven, the book interweaves about 30 magical counsels for suppliants – who might include those seeking to know the future, to sway the hearts of the great, to have their enemies overtaken by misfortune, to be healed, to have their dreams interpreted, to overcome an enemy or a wild animal, to see the sun during the day or the night, or to speak with the moon and the stars. The general contents of this work have long been known, especially from the extracts scattered in the *Book of *Razi'el*, but most of its magical terms became known only through Mordecai Margalioth's discovery, as he probably succeeded in restoring *Sefer ha-Razim* to its original form. On the basis of fragments from the *genizah* and Hebrew, Latin, and Arabic manuscripts, he organized the work into a preface and seven short chapters describing the Seven Heavens. The work is relatively short (about 800 lines), but it is of considerable literary and historic interest. Written in a beautiful midrashic Hebrew containing hardly any Aramaic, it is however inlaid with transliterated Greek words – some of which are *termini technici* of Greek magic – as well as a short Greek prayer. The names of about 700 angels are listed (some having a Greek etymology); several have specified "characters" (symbolic figures, which form a quasi-magical alphabet). The chapter on the Seventh Heaven, dealing with the Divine Throne, the Throne of the Great Light, praises God in an exalted liturgical style. The chapters dealing with the heavens are skillfully constructed to form one unit (but it cannot be ascertained if the preface in the Margalioth edition belongs to the work because it differs widely in content from the seven chapters). Nor is it at all certain that the original name of the work in its original context was *Sefer mi-Sifrei ha-Razim*. It may perhaps have been entitled *Razi'el ha-Malakh* or possibly *Razei Ḥokhmah*, or some other name.

In this work, Raziel is mentioned as the angel who stands on the seventh step of the Second Heaven. Scholars differ on the extent of the role and influence which mystical doctrines wielded over the rabbis and their schools, but it may definitely be assumed that these doctrines, which were accepted in the Orient as well as by the Greeks and Romans, were not basically foreign to the Jews of Palestine during the Second Temple period and the generations which followed the destruction of the Temple. According to *Origen (third century), such Hebrew names as Ẓeva'ot, Eloha, etc. were mentioned along with the names of the archons, and Gabriel, Raphael, Michael, and Soriel with the demons of the Gnostic sect of the Ophites (*Contra Celsum* I, 22, 26; II, 6; IV, 33–34; V. 9, 42, 45, etc.). Those engaged in magic recited the prayer to the God of Abraham, Isaac, and Jacob while invoking demons (*Contra Celsum*, IV, 33). Greek amulets which have been preserved show a marked relation to Jewish concepts. The pagans even attributed the worship of the sun and the moon to the Jews, but Origen pointed out their error. Some of the themes of the *Sefer ha-Razim* are also discussed in the apocryphal books of the Bible, especially in II *Enoch (the Slavonic version), and in the Apocalypse of *Baruch: others are mentioned in talmudic literature (Seven Heavens, dreams, amulets in Shab. 8:2; remedies in Ber. 40a; and "Hezekiah burned the Book of Remedies" in Pes. 4:8), while parallels to them can be found in various Midrashim, *Heikhalot*, *Merkabah, and *Ma'aseh Bereshit* literature.

On the grounds of contents and style, his work should be dated to no later than the talmudic period, a dating corroborated by the chronology of Greek kings mentioned in it, which A.S. Rosenthal explained as referring to the *Indictio* of the middle or possibly the beginning of the fourth century. However, further study may perhaps reveal the later inclusion of Greco-Egyptian magical texts to eighth-century Arabic literature.

BIBLIOGRAPHY: M. Margalioth (ed.), in: *Sefer ha-Razim* (1966), 1–62; H. Merhavia, in: KS, 42 (1967), 297–303; E.E. Urbach, in: *Studies in Mysticism and Religion presented to G.G. Scholem* (1968); G. Scholem, *Jewish Gnosticism, Merkabah Mysticism and Talmudic Tradition* (1965^{2}), 101–17; idem, *Kitvei Yad be-Kabbalah* (1930), 12; J. Dan, in: *Tarbiz*, 37 (1968), 208.

[Chen Merchavya]

RAZIN, AHARON (1935–), Israeli biochemist. Born in Tel Aviv, Israel, he received his Ph.D. in biochemistry from the Hebrew University of Jerusalem in 1967, continuing his postdoctoral studies at the California Institute of Technology from 1968 to 1970. From 1971 he taught cell biochemistry and human genetics at the Hebrew University and held the Dr. Jacob Grunbaum Chair in Medical Science from 1988. His career included research and teaching posts at Cambridge University, the Beckman Cancer Research Center, and the NIH. Between 1994 and 2000, he was a member of the advisory committee on human genome research of the Israeli Academy of Sciences. Razin was awarded the Israel Prize in 2004 for his research in biochemistry and was among the outstanding figures in this field in Israel and internationally. His studies made significant contributions to the furtherance of the understanding of gene-expression control mechanisms, and he was a pioneer in the understanding of the biological role of DNA methylation.

[Ruth Rossing (2nd ed.)]

RAZON, JACKO (1921–), Greek boxer. Born in Salonika, Razon had to terminate his studies when the Germans occupied Salonika in 1941 and was left without a profession. He learned boxing in Maccabi and in 1939 was the middleweight boxing champion of Greece. He was also goalkeeper for the Salonikan soccer team Olympiakos in the Greek National Football League. In 1943, he was deported by the Germans to Auschwitz. After two months, he was transferred to the Buna labor camp where he organized the boxing at the camp. He had 12 pairs of boxers – Jews and non-Jews, professionals and amateurs, among them Jung Perez, the former Tunisian world lightweight boxing champion. During the day he worked in the kitchen and after working hours he trained the boxers. Razon had to box weekly, often against heavyweights, winning most of his matches. Due to his kitchen connections, he was able to help many prisoners and hundreds owed their lives to him. This ended when Buna was evacuated and the "death march" began.

After a short stay in Gleiwitz, where Jung Perez died, Jacko was moved to Dora. He boxed also there but received little extra food for his talent and managed to feed only a few individuals at most. Transferred to Bergen-Belsen, he found the way to return to kitchen duty and helped Greek Jews in their most dire hour, when the camp was full of living skeletons and food was scarce. He was liberated by the British in May 1945.

After returning to Greece, Razon was a leader of Holocaust survivors who planned to immigrate to Palestine "illegally." They sailed on the *Henrietta Szold*, with 356 passengers, which was met by British warships in Haifa port. Razon led a revolt against the British navy, which was eventually overcome, and he and the other passengers were deported to Cyprus where they were interned for several months.

Eventually he arrived in Palestine and participated in Israel's War of Independence; he was one of the founders of the Organization of Greek Concentration Camp Survivors in Israel.

BIBLIOGRAPHY: S. Raphael (ed.). *Binitivei Shaol: Yehudei Yavan Beshoa – Pirkei Aidout* (1988), 454–458.

[Yitzhak Kerem]

RAZOVSKY (Davidson), CECILIA (1891–1968), U.S. social worker and expert on immigration. Born in St. Louis, she worked there as a volunteer at the Jewish Educational Alliance, teaching English to foreigners. In 1917 she moved to Washington, D.C. and served as an inspector in the U.S. Children's Bureau. She was secretary in the immigration department of the National Council of Jewish Women and in 1932 became associate director of the council. Razovsky traveled widely to study the conditions of Jewish refugees, and in Cuba she set up a social service program for the refugees.

Razovsky was head of a group of experts assigned by Secretary of Labor Perkins to study conditions on Ellis Island and was on several U.S. immigration committees. She also served as assistant to the executive director of the National Refugee Service.

From 1922 to 1930 she was editor of *The Immigrant* and she wrote articles, plays, and pamphlets on immigration. Her pamphlet *Handicaps in Naturalization* (1932) investigated the effects of the 1929 amendment to the Naturalization Law, raising the fee from five to twenty-five dollars. Her *Making Americans* (1938), a manual prepared for the National Council of Jewish Women, contains information on the naturalization process and suggests ways of organizing communal naturalization aid programs.

RAZRAN, GREGORY (1901–1973), U.S. psychologist. Razran was born in a village near Slutsk, Russia. He immigrated to the United States in 1920 and graduated from Columbia University in 1927, receiving his doctorate in 1933. He was a lecturer in psychology at Columbia from 1930 to 1938 and a research associate from 1938 to 1946. In 1946, he was appointed chairman of the Psychology Department of Queens College, and on his retirement in 1966 was appointed emeritus professor. He served as statistical consultant to the Office of Strategic Services in World War II. In 1952, he took a year's leave to serve as visiting professor at the Hebrew University of Jerusalem, where he helped to establish the Department of Psychology. In 1961 he was co-chairman of the International Pavlovian Conference on Higher Nervous Activity, which was held in Israel.

Razran's main contribution to psychology was twofold. His interest in conditioning led him early in his career (1933) to pioneering work in the study of conditioning of young infants. His later work on adults focused on the study of the meaning of words by a conditioning technique (1939). Other areas of conditioning theory to which he contributed were the transposition problem (1938) and conditioning to compound stimuli, particularly as an aid in analyzing perception (1965). Much of his activity consisted in bringing to the attention of his colleagues the work of the Russian school of conditioning, especially the use of conditioned stimuli of the internal organs in interoceptive conditioning. Razran served as president of the division on general psychology of the American Psychological Association and chairman of the psychology section of the New York Academy of Sciences. His only book *Mind Evolution: An East-West Synthesis* (1971) represents the culmination of his activities. He met his death by drowning.

[Helmut E. Adler (2nd ed.)]

RAZSVET (Rus. "Dawn"), name of four Russian-Jewish weeklies that appeared in Russia and abroad.

(1) The first *Razsvet* was published in Odessa (May 1860–May 1861). The first Jewish periodical in Russian, it was founded in an era when knowledge of the Russian language was rare even among "enlightened" Jews. Although a few *maskilim* in Vilna and Minsk regarded the promotion of Russian among the Jews as a step toward social integration in Russia (see *Haskalah), Odessa was the only Russian-speaking Jewish community of any considerable size. Among the founders of *Razsvet* were Osip *Rabinovich and Joachim (Ḥayyim) *Tarnopol, who in 1856 appealed to the ministry of education through N.I. Pirogov, inspector of education for the Odessa region, to allow them to publish a weekly. The purpose of this weekly was to spread Russian among the masses, thus helping to eliminate prejudices and enlighten the Jews. Rabinovich and Tarnopol also claimed that the periodical would serve to clarify Jewish problems to the Russian public and combat defamation of the Jews and attacks against them. After considerable effort permission was received to publish the weekly. Soon after the first issues a disagreement arose among the founders as to whether *Razsvet* should include Jewish self-criticism and a public airing of internal Jewish problems. It was feared that

a lack of discretion might provoke antisemitic reaction. Those who opposed self-criticism, led by Tarnopol, left the staff, and Rabinovich remained as sole editor. Among those who contributed to *Razsvet* were the writer L. *Levanda, the physician and communal leader E. Soloveychik, and the jurist and historian Hermann *Baratz, as well as the Russian professor A.I. Georgiyevski and the German-Jewish historian I.M. *Jost. From the outset *Razsvet* encountered difficulties from the censors, who forbade all reference to emancipation for the Jews, and from the apathy of the Jewish public toward the Russian language. The number of subscribers never exceeded 640. After a year's publication, Rabinovich was forced to relinquish editorship to L. *Pinsker and Soloveychik, who for technical reasons changed the periodical's name to *Sion*. *Razsvet* was a first step in an effort to encourage an active Russian-speaking Jewish intelligentsia and a Jewish literature in Russian.

(2) The second *Razsvet*, published in St. Petersburg (September 1879–January 1883), was founded by a group of young intellectuals seeking ways to attract more enlightened Jews back to their national values. Publication rights were acquired from the journalist Alexander *Zederbaum, who had been granted them by the authorities. The editors were Jacob Rosenfeld and G.I. *Bogrov, and the staff was filled by such writers as S. *Wengeroff, L. *Slonimski, A. Tenenbaum, S.Z. Luria, A. *Volynski (A.L. Flexer), and M.B.H. Ha-Kohen, and the poets N. *Minski (Vilenkin) and S. *Frug. *Razsvet* called for Jewish patriotism and the development of Jewish literature in Russian, closer association with the Jewish masses, and a positive approach to Jewish national values, the Jewish religion, the Hebrew language, and the settlement of Ereẓ Israel. The solution of the Jewish problem would be for large numbers of Jews to take up agriculture. The publication soon attained a circulation of 3,400. However, the wave of pogroms and antisemitism in 1881 caused severe disillusionment among the staff, and after several weeks of indecision they reached the conclusion that the sole solution to the Jewish problem was emigration. Hence *Razsvet* became the outstanding spokesman for organized emigration and the proponent of the *Ḥibbat Zion movement. The January 16, 1882, edition of *Razsvet* contained an interview between a staff member, I. Orshanski, and the minister of the interior, N. Ignatiev, in which the latter announced that "the western borders were open to the Jews." The Zionist writings of Levanda and M.L. *Lilienblum appeared in *Razsvet*, as well as a translation of Pinsker's *Autoemanzipation*. Bogrov left the staff, and Rosenfeld departed for Constantinople to examine the possibilities of Jewish immigration into, and settlement in, Ereẓ Israel. Opponents of mass emigration sought all possible ways to fight *Razsvet's* policies. The two other Russian-Jewish periodicals, *Russky Yevrey* and *Voskhod, attacked *Razsvet*, and letters were sent to the provinces to discourage further subscriptions; by 1883 circulation fell to 900. Financial support was not forthcoming and *Razsvet* closed down. Its staff dispersed, some withdrawing from public life and some joining Ḥibbat Zion; others turned their attention from Jewish affairs to find their places in Russian literature and public activity. Despite its brief existence *Razsvet* opened up a new direction in Jewish life and thought in Russia, especially among the intellectuals.

[Yehuda Slutsky]

(3) The third *Razsvet* was a weekly journal of topical political and literary content, published in St. Petersburg by the Zionist Organization of Russia from 1907, when it replaced the weeklies *Khronika Yevreyskoy Zhizni* ("Chronicle of Jewish Life") and *Yevreyskiy Narod* ("The Jewish People"), which had been suppressed by the czarist administration. The editor of *Razsvet* was A.D. *Idelson, assisted by an editorial staff consisting of S. Gepstein, A. *Goldstein, V. *Jabotinsky, A. Seidenman, and M. Soloveichik (*Solieli). Questions of major policy were decided upon by the Zionist Central Committee. *Razsvet* played an outstanding part in molding and disseminating the ideology and program of the Zionist movement in Russia. Strictly adhering to Herzl's political Zionism, the journal also advocated immediate practical colonizing work in Ereẓ Israel and active Zionist participation in the defense of the rights and interests of the Russian-Jewish community. It laid the foundation of what later became known as "synthetic Zionism," a concept which harmoniously combined the traditional Zionist negation of *Galut with the struggle for Jewish survival and national organization in the countries of dispersion. *Razsvet's* militant nationalist crusade against all forms of assimilation contributed essentially to the defeat of assimilationist tendencies and groups in Russian Jewry and made it the most widely read Jewish publication in the Russian language. Early in its career its circulation reached 10,000. In July 1915 the weekly was closed down, and in its stead appeared in Moscow the *Yevreyskaya Zhizn*. In July 1917 *Razsvet* again appeared in Petrograd, and its circulation rose to 25,000. After the Bolshevik Revolution of November 1917, the Zionist press was allowed to exist for a time. But in September 1918 *Razsvet* was closed by the Cheka. In its place appeared the *Khronika Yevrevskoy Zhizni*, edited by Y. Klebanov, which was also closed down on July 18, 1919.

(4) The fourth *Razsvet* reappeared in 1922 in Berlin as the organ of the Federation of Russian-Ukrainian Zionists in exile. It was headed by an editorial board nominated by the Federation and consisting of S. Gepstein (editor), J. *Schechtman (secretary), M. Aleinikov, Ḥayyim Greenberg, M. Hindes, and V. *Jacobson. Soon after V. Jabotinsky's resignation from the Zionist executive (February 1923), *Razsvet* endorsed his criticism of the official Zionist political line and his concept of an activist Zionist policy; it strongly disapproved, however, of Jabotinsky's later decision to leave the World Zionist Organization. Soon Jabotinsky, J. *Brutzkus, Y. Klinov, M. Schwartzman, and I. Trivus joined the reconstructed editorial board and *Razsvet* became the spokesman of the Zionist Revisionists. Financial difficulties led to the periodical's brief discontinuance in May 1924, but by the end of the year publication was resumed in Paris, with Jabotinsky as editor-in-chief and M. Berchin and J. Schechtman as acting editors.

The first issue of the Paris edition sold 1,000 copies; the tenth issue, 2,500. The ideology, program, and tactical line of the Zionist-Revisionist World Union, founded in April 1925, was largely molded by the *Razsvet* group. Although the readership of the journal largely consisted of Jewish émigrés from Russia in West European countries and groups in Ereẓ Israel, and of the Jewish communities in east and southeast Europe which had a Russian cultural background, *Razsvet's* influence reached far beyond its immediate audience. Its articles were frequently translated and reprinted in other periodicals and widely commented upon by Zionists and non-Zionists alike. Stressing that *Razsvet* was the only Russian-language journal serving the Russian-Jewish diaspora, a group of noted non-Revisionist and non-Zionist émigré leaders in Paris, headed by Henry *Sliozberg, and including I. *Naiditsch, M. Goldstein, G. Vishnyak, and the sculptor N. *Aronson, formed in the spring of 1933 the "Society of Friends of Razsvet." The editorial policy in Zionist affairs remained unaffected by the agreement between the editorial board and the "Friends," but the coverage of matters of general topical Jewish interest – cultural, economic, and political – was expanded. The financial position of the paper steadily deteriorated, however, as the circle of the Jewish Russian-reading public shrank. *Razsvet* had to be converted from a weekly to a biweekly, and even in this form it appeared irregularly; the periodical was discontinued in 1935.

[Joseph B. Schechtman]

BIBLIOGRAPHY: M.L. Lilienblum, *Derekh La'avor Ge'ulim* (1899); M. Kagan, in: *Perezhitoye*, 3 (1911), 151–7; M. Ha-Kohen, *Olami*, 1 (1927), 112–206; 2 (1927), 42–46; S. Zinberg, *Istoriya yevreyskoy pechati* (1915); S. Ginzburg, *Amolike Peterburg* (1944), 155–69; B. Shochetman, in: *He-Avar*, 2 (1954), 61–72; J.B. Schechtman, *The Vladimir Jabotinsky Story*, 1 (1956), index; M. Perlmann, in: JSOS, 24 (1962), 162–82; idem, in: PAAJR, 33 (1965), 21–50; J. Slutsky, *Ha-Ittonut ha-Yehudit-Rusit ba-Me'ah ha-19* (1970), 102–15, 122–7.

RAZUMNI, EPHRAIM ZALMAN (Solomon; 1866–1904), *ḥazzan* and composer. Born in Nikolayev, Russia, Razumni became *ḥazzan* there at the age of nineteen. After serving in Kishinev, he moved to Odessa where he spent the rest of his life. An unpredictable character, Razumni was a lyric tenor with an unusually fine faculty for improvisation. He officiated as guest cantor in many communities and gave concerts throughout Eastern Europe, gaining a huge popular following and becoming a legend in his own lifetime. His rendition of *El Male Raḥamim after the *Kishinev pogrom became the standard musical version of the prayer in the East European Ashkenazi area and its sphere of influence. A collection of his recitatives, *Shirei Razumni*, was published by S. *Alman in 1930.

BIBLIOGRAPHY: Y. Icht, in: *Khazonim Velt* (March, 1934), 11–12, 23; H.H. Harris, *Toledot ha-Neginah ve-ha-Ḥazzanut be-Yisrael* (1950), 448–9.

[David M.L. Olivestone]

RAZUMNY, MARK (1896–1988), Yiddish writer. Born in the *shtetl* of Zhager, he grew up in Riga, where he received a traditional Jewish and general secular education and became a Labor Zionist. In 1919, after brief service in the Red Army, he emigrated to Germany, living in Hamburg, where he worked at a bank and studied at the university. His first publication, a story in German, appeared in the Hamburg *Israelitisches Familienblatt*. In 1921 he returned to Riga and began to work for various Yiddish periodicals, some edited by his cousin, journalist Moshe-Mikhl Kitay (1886–194?). From 1924 he was a correspondent for the New York *Forverts*, and in January–March 1925, he edited the shortlived *Riger Moment*. In 1926–34 he worked for the democratic newspaper *Frimorgn*, cofounded by Kitay. Newspapers published his numerous travelogues, some of which later appeared in book form, e.g. *Dos Land fun Toyznt Geshtaltn: a Rayze in Norvegye* ("The Country of a Thousand Images: A Trip to Norway," 1929) and *Eyner Tsvishn Milyonen: fun an Amerikaner Nesie* ("Alone among Millions: From an American Trip," 1931). He was a prolific translator from German and Russian. From 1937 until World War II, he edited the popular magazine *Yidishe Bilder* ("Jewish Pictures"). When Riga became the capital of Soviet Latvia, Razumny became secretary of the Jewish Cultural Society and wrote for the newspaper *Kamf* and the journal *Ufboy*. After World War II he continued to write short stories and fables, which appeared in the Warsaw-based *Yidishe Shriftn* and *Folks-shtime*, and after 1961 the Moscow journal *Sovetish Heymland* and its affiliated book publications. Among his other books are *Hintergeslekh* ("Backalleys," 1929), *Breyter di Trit* ("Longer Steps," 1975), and *A Velt mit Vunder* ("A World of Wonders," 1986; German tr. 1985).

[Gennady Estraikh (2nd ed.)]

READING, family of British statesmen and lawyers. RUFUS DANIEL ISAACS (1860–1935), first marquess of Reading, British statesman, advocate and lord chief justice. Born in London into a family of fruit merchants, and a relative of the famous boxer Daniel *Mendoza, Isaacs went to sea as a ship's boy at the age of 16. He returned to England two years later and in 1879 went into the London Stock Exchange in an attempt to make his fortune. In 1884, however, he was unable to meet his obligations and was "hammered" (suspended from the exchange). Isaacs planned to sail to Panama to recoup his losses but was persuaded by his mother to study for the bar instead and was admitted in 1887. His knowledge of the commercial world enabled him to establish himself as a leading commercial counsel and in 1898 he was made a queen's counsel. Subsequently he was involved in a series of cases which brought him before the public eye. His ability to master complicated facts and his magnificent cross-examination of the financier Whittaker Wright on charges of fraud and of Frederick Seddon on charges of murdering his lodger won him the reputation as one of the greatest advocates of all time. Isaacs' success at the bar was phenomenal. He amassed a considerable fortune and honors were heaped upon him. He was elected to parliament as a Liberal Imperialist in 1904 and was made solicitor-general in 1910. In the same year Isaacs was given a knighthood and appointed attorney-general. Nevertheless, he was passed over for the appointment of lord chancellor because of his involvement in the Marconi scandal in which he was one of four ministers accused of attempting to make financial gain out of a government contract with the English Marconi Company. In 1913 Isaacs was made lord chief justice of England, the first Jew ever to hold this post, and took the title of Lord Reading. He presided over several famous criminal cases, among them the trial of the Irish nationalist, Roger Casement, on charges of treason. Yet although he was well known for his humanity and impartiality he was not considered a great judge.

Following the outbreak of World War I, Isaacs became increasingly involved in problems of government finance and introduced the scheme by which the state guaranteed all bills of exchange, thereby preventing a panic in the London bill market. In 1915 he went to the United States as president of the Anglo-French mission and secured a loan of 500 million dollars. Isaacs returned to the U.S. two years later as special envoy with the object of persuading America to join the Allies. In the following spring he went to the U.S. for a third time as high commissioner and special ambassador to convince the American government to send half a million American troops to France immediately. Isaacs remained lord chief justice until 1920 when he was made viceroy of India, ruler of India on behalf of the British crown, the only Jew ever to hold this post. His appointment was hailed as a move to reconcile warring factions in India and also to assuage the growing hostility toward British rule. Isaacs succeeded in initiating the widespread reforms embodied in the Montagu-Chelmsford report (1918), establishing a form of self-government in most of the Indian provinces and introducing improvements in agriculture and housing. He was much admired for the genuine sympathy he and his wife showed for the people of India but he failed, nevertheless, to obtain the cooperation of Mahatma Gandhi and the Hindu nationalists and was eventually obliged to arrest Gandhi for incitement to civil disobedience and to call in the army to keep order. Isaacs returned to England in 1926 and was given the title of marquess, the only Jew to be so honored. He held numerous company directorships and remained a prominent figure in the Liberal Party, representing the party at the Indian Round Table Conference of 1930. For a short period in 1931 he was foreign secretary in the national government headed by J. Ramsay Mac-Donald and he retired in 1934 from public life with the honorary post of lord warden of the Cinque ports.

Rufus Isaacs was one of the outstanding figures of his age and in Anglo-Jewish history. He showed considerable interest in Jewish and Zionist affairs toward the end of his life and in 1926 became chairman of the Palestine Electric Corporation. He visited Palestine in 1932 and associated himself with various Zionist projects. After the advent of Hitler, Isaacs resigned the presidency of the Anglo-German Fellowship and spoke in the House of Lords against the persecution of the Jews in Germany.

GERALD RUFUS ISAACS (1889–1960), second marquess of Reading, British statesman and lawyer. Born in London, he was the only son of Rufus Isaacs and succeeded to his father's titles in 1935. He was admitted to the bar and was a bencher of the Middle Temple from 1936, becoming treasurer in 1958. Isaacs was chairman of several government committees and was undersecretary of state for foreign affairs from 1951 to 1953. He served as minister of state for foreign affairs from 1953 until his retirement in 1957. Isaacs was active in Jewish affairs as chairman of the Council for German Jewry and president of the London Jewish Hospital.

EVA VIOLET, MARCHIONESS OF READING (1895–1973), English social worker. The daughter of Alfred *Mond, first Lord Melchett, she married Gerald Rufus Isaacs in 1914. Eva Reading devoted her life to problems of nursing and child care and was adviser to the ministry of health on child care during World War II. From 1957 to 1959 she was president of the National Council of Women. Though brought up as a Christian, Eva Reading reverted to Judaism in the 1930s and became a staunch Zionist; she toured the United States on behalf of the *United Jewish Appeal in 1939, and later served as chairman of the British section of the *World Jewish Congress. She should not be confused with Stella Isaacs, marchioness of Reading (1894–1971), the second wife of Rufus Isaacs, first marquess of Reading, who was not Jewish. She was the founder of the Women's Royal Voluntary Service, and, in 1958, was the first woman to be given a life peerage and to sit in the House of Lords, where she took the title of Baroness Swanborough.

BIBLIOGRAPHY: H.M. Hyde, *Lord Reading; the Life of Rufus Isaacs, First Marquess of Reading* (1968); D. Walker Smith, *Lord Reading and his Cases* (1934); L. Broad, *Advocates of the Golden Age; Their Lives and Cases* (1958); P.H. Emden, *Jews of Britain* (1943), 295–316; N.B. Birkett, *Six Great Advocates* (1962); I. Butler, *The Viceroy's Wife* (1970). **ADD. BIBLIOGRAPHY:** ODNB online; (G.R. Isaacs) Marquess of Reading, *Rufus Isaacs, First Marquess of Reading* (2 vols, 1942–45); D. Judd, *Lord Reading* (1982).

READING, FANNY (1884–1974), Australian communal leader. Born Fanny Rabinowich near Minsk, she migrated with her family to Victoria, Australia, in 1889. Active from her youth in Melbourne Jewish communal affairs, she was originally a music teacher but in 1916–22 studied medicine and became a physician, moving to Sydney and changing her name to Reading in 1918. She was one of the first Jewish women physicians in Australia. In 1923 she was instrumental in founding the Council of Jewish Women of New South Wales, serving as its president from 1923 to 1931. Unlike many mainstream Australian Jewish organizations of the time, it was keenly Zionistic, despite communal pressures to moderate its stance. In 1929 it changed its name to the National Council of Jewish Women of Australia. Reading remained its life president until her death. In 1947 she sued *Smith's Weekly*, a populist Australian tabloid, for libel when it alleged that her fundraising was being used to fight the British in Palestine. Although she lost the case on a technicality, the verdict, delivered "with regret" by the judge, was regarded as a moral victory for the Jewish community. In 1957 a settlement in Israel, Neve Zipporah, was named in her honor. The National Council of Jewish Women of Australia continues as one of the most important Jewish women's organizations in the country.

BIBLIOGRAPHY: ADB, 11, 343–44; M. Newton, *Making a Difference: The History of the National Council of Jewish Women of Australia* (2000).

[William D. Rubinstein (2nd ed.)]

°**REAGAN, RONALD WILSON** (1911–2005), 40th president of the United States. Born in Tampico, Illinois, Reagan became an actor, serving as president of the Screen Actor's Guild (1947–52, 1959–60) and the Motion Picture Industry Council. From 1967 to 1975 he was governor of California, home to America's second largest Jewish community.

In 1948 he resigned from the Lakeside Country Club in Los Angeles because of its refusal to permit a Jew to take out membership. In 1967 he strongly supported Israel during the *Six-Day War and was the featured speaker at a pro-Israel rally in the Hollywood Bowl in Los Angeles.

During his governorship he was instrumental in having a law passed in the California legislature in which banks and savings institutions were authorized to purchase and invest in State of Israel Bonds. During the mid-1970s Reagan had a weekly column in the *Jewish Press* newspaper, whose readers were mainly Orthodox Jews in New York and other parts of the U.S.A.

His closest Jewish advisor was Theodore E. Cummings of Los Angeles. Cummings served in the Reagan inner circle for a number of years. During the presidential campaign in 1980 Los Angeles businessman Albert Spiegel headed the Jewish Coalition for Reagan. Additional figures with access to Reagan were Max *Fisher, *Maxwell Rabb, George Klein, Gordon Zacks, and Jacob Stein. Neo-conservative Jewish intellectuals, such as Eugene V. Rostow, Max Kempelman, Irving Kristol, and Norman Podhoretz were active in the Reagan election campaign and many became influential in the Reagan Administration.

In the 1980 election 40 percent of the Jews who voted chose Reagan, another 40 percent voted for the incumbent President Jimmy Carter, the lowest percentage for a Democrat in the past 80 years, and 20 percent for John Anderson, indicating that the Democratic party could no longer take the Jewish vote for granted. Orthodox Jews in Brooklyn voted overwhelmingly for Reagan, the first time that the Jewish vote split along religious divides within the United States.

Reagan saw the early raw footage of the liberation of the concentration camps and referred to this during his Yom Hashoah address in the White House in 1981. None of this, however, was any guarantee that at the helm of the nation he would be particularly sensitive to the cause of Israel.

Upon assuming office Reagan's Middle East position could be summarized as follows: First, a militarily strong Israel, which is both democratic and anti-Soviet, is "the only remaining strategic asset in the region on which we can rely" (*Washington Post*, August 1979); second, opposition to the terrorist PLO and rejection of the notion of a PLO state because it would be a surrogate to the Soviet Union; third, strong support for Israel as America's most reliable ally in the Middle East and unequivocal support for Egyptian and Israeli peacemakers as the best way to attract other Arab states to the peace process.

Interestingly, one of the first crises affecting Israel, which was to have tremendous ramifications for the region, revolved around the June 7, 1981, bombing of the Iraqi nuclear reactor at Osirak by Israeli jet fighters. Only the newly appointed U.S. Ambassador to the United Nations Jeane J. Kirkpatrick stood in the way of an anti-Israel vote. Realizing that the word "aggression" had terrible consequences for Israel as it would make it appear that the attack was unprovoked and that the attacked party, Iraq, might now legitimately undertake unspecified self-defense measures, she strenuously argued that the U.S. should abstain from voting for that resolution, unless the word "aggression" was deleted. In the end, after taking the matter directly to President Reagan, her efforts prevailed and "aggression" was deleted from the resolution allowing the U.S. to half-heartedly join in the condemnation. This set the tone for much that was to follow at the UN during the years of the Reagan presidency.

In this context, and especially as concerned UN activities relative to Israeli-Arab relations, Reagan understood that charges of illegality aimed at Israel's conduct in the West Bank and Gaza had nothing to do with allegiance to rule of law in the sense of objective jurisprudence. Rather, it had everything to do with using law as a weapon in order to isolate Israel on the diplomatic front as a prelude to legitimating terrorism and other hostilities against Israel as a pariah state. The formula that Reagan repeatedly espoused was that "the settlements are not unlawful."

Similarly, when it came to Arab efforts to characterize East Jerusalem as "occupied territory," President Reagan instructed his delegates to the UN to veto such resolutions on the grounds that the final status on Jerusalem was to be negotiated, and not subject to resolution by legal fiat. He authorized a U.S. veto – the only veto cast – on April 19, 1982, of a Security Council resolution which sought to condemn the 1982 shooting of Palestinian worshippers at the Dome of the Rock by a deranged Israeli gunman – even though the U.S. was revolted by the shooting – because of the insertion of a paragraph equating Jerusalem with occupied Arab territory.

The Israeli invasion of Lebanon on June 6, 1982, created unique challenges for the Reagan Administration, with many White House advisors wanting Israel out of Lebanon as quickly as possible. Their views prevailed, but only up to a point. Although the United States joined in a UN Security Counsel resolution on June 6 that called for "unconditional withdrawal of Israeli forces (paragraph 1) while calling (paragraph 2) for cessation of all cross border attacks," the U.S. made clear in its explanation of its vote that "paragraphs 1 and

2 are inextricably linked… there can be no Israeli withdrawal before there is a cessation of all cross border hostilities. One cannot be without the other." This set the tone for the U.S. position throughout the war.

U.S. Ambassador Phillip Habib conducted a mission for peaceful evacuation of the PLO from Beirut. Its success led in turn to termination of the Lebanon war, and made it propitious for President Reagan to launch a major peace initiative in his speech of September 1, 1982. That initiative, also known as the Reagan Plan, called for direct negotiations between the Israel and the Arab states; Palestinian autonomy, but not an independent Palestinian state; and, for maintaining Jerusalem as an undivided city, with its final status to be negotiated.

A byproduct of Ronald Reagan's meetings with U.S.S.R.'s President Mikhail Gorbachev in 1985 aimed at creating a thaw in the Cold War led to conditions for the liberation of Ethiopian Jews who were rescued and brought to Israel in Operation Moses between November 19, 1984, and January 5, 1985, with some covert U.S. assistance.

In July through September of 1985, Israel had undertaken the sale of arms to Iran through the "Arms for Hostages Deal." Although the Iran Contra Affair, which resulted from exposure of the illicit sale of U.S. arms to Iran resulted in a major embarrassment to the Reagan Administration, it did not impair U.S.-Israeli relations.

Reagan's consistent record in identifying with the cause of Israel was somewhat marred by his decision to go to Germany's Bitburg Cemetery in 1985 (see *Bitburg Controversy), despite the knowledge that this was the burial ground for SS officers who committed the most heinous crimes. In hindsight, the President's visit – controversial as it was – caused no lasting damage to the cause of remembrance.

[David Geffen / Allan Gerson (2nd ed.)]

REBBETZIN, Yiddish honorific for the wife of a rabbi. Although no such title existed in ancient Judaism, its emergence in medieval and early modern Central and Eastern Europe indicates that rabbis' wives frequently assumed an elevated status in Jewish society deriving from their husbands' religious roles and from their own activities. Rabbis tended to marry daughters of elite families who had often received Jewish educations superior to those of most women. Many learned *rebbetzins*, such as the 12th-century *Dulcea of Worms, took on a variety of spiritual and communal functions. These could include leading worship in the women's section of the synagogue and teaching prayers and responses to other women as well as coordinating bridal arrangements, preparing corpses for burial, and dispensing charity. *Rebbetzins* were regarded as reliable witnesses of their husbands' rulings on ritual matters, particularly related to Jewish dietary laws, and they might be consulted for legal testimony as to their husbands' customary practices.

In a social setting which honored scholarship above economic success, the *rebbetzin* frequently supported her family financially while her husband devoted himself to study. In some European communities the *rebbetzin* had a monopoly on the sale of yeast; she might also be compensated for providing refreshments following religious events at which her husband officiated. Literary portrayals of the *rebbetzin* in East European Jewish culture can be found in the writings of such authors as Chaim *Grade (*Rabbis and Wives*, 1982) and Isaac Bashevis *Singer (*In My Father's Court*, 1966).

In more recent times, the *rebbetzin* in all denominations of Judaism was expected to fulfill a number of social, communal, and educational functions within her husband's congregation. Prior to the introduction of female ordination in non-Orthodox forms of Judaism, some women who became *rebbetzins* built on their husbands' positions to achieve their own independent roles as teachers and representatives of Jewish life within their communities and the larger non-Jewish world. With changing social mores and increased professional opportunities for Jewish women in many fields, it had become less common by the early 21st century for rabbis' spouses in Reform, Reconstructionist, and Conservative Judaism to follow these patterns. However, within Orthodox Jewish communities, the *rebbetzin*, more frequently known by the Hebrew designation *rabbanit*, continued to fulfill traditional expectations, serving as a domestic hostess to her husband's congregation and as an educator and counselor to female congregants. Some *rebbetzins* continued to achieve renown on their own terms, as inspirational teachers and charismatic counselors for women in their communities.

BIBLIOGRAPHY: I.I. Etkes, "Marriage and Torah Study among the *Lomdim* in Lithuania in the Nineteenth Century," in: D. Kraemer (ed.), *The Jewish Family: Metaphor and Memory* (1989), 153–78; S.J. Landau-Chark, "Whither the Rebbetzin in the Twenty-First Century?," http://www. utoronto.ca/wjudaism/contemporary/articles/a_landauchark.html; S.R. Schwartz, *The Rabbi's Wife: The Rebbetzin in American Jewish Life* (2006).

[Judith R. Baskin (2nd ed.)]

REBECCA BAT MEIR TIKTINER (16th century), Yiddish author, probably from Prague. Two texts are attributed to her: *Meneket Rivkah* (*Meynekes Rivko*) ("The Nursemaid of Rebecca"), which was published posthumously in 1609, and *Eyn Simkhas Touro Lid* ("A Simḥat Torah Song"), to be sung by women in the synagogue.

While Rebecca bat Meir's place and date of birth are unknown, her tombstone inscription in Prague indicates that her learned father was from Tykocin, Poland. She probably acquired her knowledge of Hebrew and rabbinic literature in her childhood home. The inscription also relates that Rebecca "taught (or preached) day and night to women in every pious neighborhood." The titles, *darshanit ve-rabbanit* (preacher and teacher), with which she was eulogized on the title page of *Meneket Rivkah*, appear to be honorifics reflecting her instruction to women in Prague and elsewhere. Rebecca bat Meir was married; her husband is mentioned in her entry in the *Memorbukh* of the Altneushul as *ha-rav rabbi*, a title uncommon for an officiating rabbi in Prague.

Meneket Rivkah, published posthumously in Prague in 1609 (a second edition appeared in Cracow in 1618) and consisting of 36 folios, was written for a female readership, and belongs to the genre of Yiddish **musar* literature. The book is divided into seven chapters, six of which deal with a particular domestic relationship in the life of a married woman (her husband, her parents, her parents-in-law, her children, her daughter-in-law, and servants and guests). In the first chapter, the author develops a comprehensive ethical system, in which she lists important profane and religious commandments related to the body. These include healthy nutrition and the laws of **niddah*, labeled as *ḥokhmat ha-guf* (wisdom of the body), and the enumeration of social and practical-religious ideals and commandments, termed *ḥokhmat ha-neshamah* (wisdom of the soul).

Rebecca's many practical instructions paint a vivid picture of Jewish women's daily lives in the early modern period. They are accompanied by long homiletical and exegetical passages demonstrating her erudition. She provides biblical citations in Hebrew, as well as quotations from contemporary Hebrew and Yiddish *musar* literature. Rebecca also includes Yiddish adaptations of stories from the Talmud and midrash, and adopts terms and techniques of rabbinical exegesis. *Meneket Rivkah* is probably the first substantive published book in Yiddish written by a Jewish women. The only other extant Yiddish works by Jewish women from this period are personal supplicatory prayers (**tkhines*). It is significant, too, because it contains homiletics and exegeses, genres which had hitherto been written exclusively by learned men.

Rebecca also wrote a rhymed Yiddish hymn for the holiday of Simḥat Torah, entitled *Eyn Simkhas Touro Lid*, which describes an eschatological, festive banquet for men and women alike. The poem, which survives in two separate undated 17th century printings, consists of 40 rhyming couplets (with acrostic), in which each verse is followed by the refrain *hallelujah*.

BIBLIOGRAPHY: J. Baumgarten, *Introduction to Old Yiddish Literature* (2005), 273–74; J.C. Frakes, *Early Yiddish Texts: 1100–1750* (2004), 510–19, 648–51; F. von Rohden (ed.), *Rivkah bat Meir Tikotin, Meneket Rivkah: Introduction, Text and Translation* (2007); Ch. Shmeruk. *Sifrut Yidish be-Polin* (1981), 56–69, 101–2.

[Frauke von Rohden (2nd ed.)]

REBEKAH (Heb. רִבְקָה), wife of *Isaac, daughter of Bethuel, and granddaughter of Nahor, a brother of *Abraham (Gen. 22:23; 24:15, 24, 47). Rebekah is also described as "the sister of *Laban" (24:29, 50; 25:20). When Abraham sought a wife for his son he sent his servant to his homeland, Aram-Naharaim, for he wanted to avoid marriage with the Canaanites. The episode is described in detail in Genesis 24, which makes clear the providential nature of the union of Isaac with Rebekah (verses 7, 14, 27, 48, 50).

The text provides an insight into Rebekah's character by stressing her hospitality to strangers and her kindness to animals (verses 14, 18, 20), as well as her beauty and chastity (24:16; 26:7). That she is willing to expend considerable energy on watering camels is a testament to her virtue. The same feature may reflect an eighth century B.C.E. date for the origin of this element of the tradition. On one occasion Isaac felt that his life was in danger because of Rebekah's great beauty and he felt constrained to claim that she was his sister (26:6–11). Isaac's age at the time of the marriage is given as 40 (25:20); Rebekah's is not recorded. She is said to have remained childless for 20 years until, in divine response to her husband's prayers, she gave birth to twins: Esau and Jacob. During a difficult pregnancy, she received an oracle about the future relationships between, and destinies of, her unborn children (25:21–26). On the biblical account she displayed favoritism toward Jacob (25:28).

When Isaac in his old age expressed his intention of bestowing his farewell blessing on Esau, Rebekah skillfully induced Jacob to supplant his brother so as to obtain it for himself. When Esau, in his bitter disappointment, threatened to kill Jacob, Rebekah arranged Jacob's flight to the house of Laban in Haran (Gen. 27), using as a pretext her bitterness and disgust over Esau's marriage to local women and her determination that Jacob marry within the family (26:34–35; 27:46; 28:1).

The death of Rebekah is not recorded in the Bible, but only the fact that she was buried in the cave of Machpelah together with the Patriarchs and *Sarah and *Leah (49:31).

[Nahum M. Sarna]

In the Aggadah

The description of Rebekah as the "daughter of Bethuel the Aramean, of Padan-Aram, the sister of Laban the Aramean" (Gen. 25:20) is taken to indicate her righteousness. Despite the fact that her father and brother were scoundrels and she came from a land where deceit was rife, she succeeded in being pious (a play on the Hebrew *arammi* which by a transposition of letters is read as *ramai*, "scoundrel" or "cheat"; Gen. R. 63:4). Eliezer immediately perceived her greatness since the water of the well rose to greet her when she came to draw water (Gen. R. 60:5). The blessings of her mother and brother when she left with Eliezer were not sincere, and they were considered the "blessings of the impious which are curses." This caused Rebekah to remain barren for years (60:13). Rebekah was either three or fourteen years old at the time of her marriage (Tos. to Yev. 61b). When she entered Sarah's tent, the divine cloud that had overhung it during Sarah's lifetime immediately reappeared (Gen. R. 60:16). Nevertheless, their marriage was not entirely happy, as a result of Rebekah's barrenness. Together they prayed for children. Finally, God acceded to the prayers of Isaac since the prayer of a pious man who is the son of a pious man is far more efficacious than the prayer of one who descends from a godless father (Yev. 64a). While pregnant, Rebekah suffered agonizing pains because her twin sons had already begun their lifelong quarrel in her womb. If she walked near a synagogue, Jacob tried to break forth from her womb, while Esau attempted to get out when she passed an idolatrous temple (Gen. R. 63:6). Finally she went to consult in the *bet midrash* of Shem and Eber where she was informed that two opposing nations were in her womb (63:6, 7).

The children Esau and Jacob seemed alike, yet Rebekah already perceived Jacob's greatness. The more often she heard his voice (engaged in study), the deeper grew her affection for him (63:10). Rebekah was not present when Isaac requested Esau to bring him savory food so that he would bless him; Isaac's charge was revealed to her through the holy spirit since she was a prophetess (67:9). She thereupon insisted that Jacob receive Isaac's blessing. She was not only actuated by love for Jacob, but also by the wish to keep Isaac from committing a detestable act by blessing the wicked Esau (65:6). She agreed to bear the possible imprecation of Isaac just as the curse of Adam fell upon "his mother," the earth (65:15). Rebekah died a short time after the death of her nurse Deborah. Her death was not mentioned explicitly in the Scripture, but is implied by the words *allon bakhut* (Allon-Bacuth; Gen. 35:8) which the Midrash renders "weeping for another," *allon* being connected with the Greek ἄλλον "another" (Gen. R. 81:5). There was no public mourning for Rebekah. Since Abraham was dead, Isaac blind, and Jacob away from home, only Esau remained to represent the family in public. It was feared that onlookers might say, "Cursed be the breasts that sustained thee." To avoid this, Rebekah was buried at night (PdRK 23; PR 12:48b).

BIBLIOGRAPHY: Noth, Personennamen. 10; H. Bauer, in: ZDMG, 67 (1913), 344; idem, in: ZAW, 48 (1930), 78; See Commentaries on *Genesis. IN THE AGGADAH: Ginzberg, Legends, index.

REBELLIOUS SON. "If a man have a stubborn and rebellious son, that will not hearken to the voice of his father and [not "or"] the voice of his mother and though they chasten him, will not hearken unto them, then shall his father and his mother lay hold of him and bring him out unto the elders of his city… They shall say unto the elders of his city: This our son is stubborn and rebellious, he doth not hearken to our voice, he is a glutton and a drunkard. And all the men of his city shall stone him with stones that he die; so shalt thou put away the evil from the midst of thee; and all Israel shall hear, and fear" (Deut. 21:18–21).

It appears that this law was intended to limit the powers of the *pater familias*: the head of the household could no longer punish the defiant son himself, according to his own whim, but had to bring him before the elders (i.e., judges) for punishment. In earlier laws (eg., Hammurapi Code, nos. 168, 169) only the father had to be defied; in biblical law it must be both father and mother, and the father cannot act without the mother's concurrence. If either was dead (Sif. Deut. 219) or refused to join in the prosecution, the son could not be indicted (Sanh. 8:4), but it was not necessary that father and mother should be validly married to each other (Sanh. 71a).

There is no record of a rebellious son ever having been executed, except for a dictum of R. Jonathan stating that he had once seen such a one and sat on his grave (Sanh. 71a). However, it is an old and probably valid tradition that there never had been, nor ever will be, a rebellious son, and that the law had been pronounced for educational and deterrent purposes only, so that parents be rewarded for bringing their children up properly (*ibid.*; Tosef. Sanh. 11:6).

Interpreting every single word of the biblical text restrictively, the talmudic jurists reduced the practicability of this law to nil. The "son" must be old enough to bear criminal responsibility, that is 13 years of age (see *Penal Law), but must still be a "son" and not a man: as soon as a beard grows ("by which is meant the pubic hair, not that of the face, for the sages spoke euphemistically") he is no longer a "son" but a man (Sanh. 8:1). The period during which he may thus be indicted as a "son" is three months only (Sanh. 69a; Yad, Mamrim 7:6), or, according to another version, not more than six months (TJ, Sanh. 8:1). The term "son" excludes a daughter (Sanh. 8:1; Sif. Deut. 218), though daughters are no less apt to be rebellious (Sanh. 69b–70a).

The offense is composed of two distinct elements: repeated (Sif. loc. cit.) disloyalty and defiance, consisting in repudiating and reviling the parents (Ex. 21:17), and being a "glutton and drunkard." This second element was held to involve the gluttonous eating of meat and drinking of wine (in which sense the same words occur in Prov. 23:20–21), not on a legitimate occasion (Sanh. 8:2), but in the company of loafers and criminals (Sanh. 70b; Yad, Mamrim 7:2) and in a ravenous manner (Yad, Mamrim 7:1). There are detailed provisions about the minimum quantities that must be devoured to qualify for the use of the term (cf. Yad, Mamrim 7:2–3). As no "son" can afford such extravagance, the law requires that he must have stolen money from his father and misappropriated it to buy drinks and food (Sanh. 8:3, 71a; Yad, Mamrim 7:2). "Who does not heed his father and mother" was interpreted as excluding one who does not heed God: thus, eating pork or other prohibited food, being an offense against God, would not qualify as gluttony in defiance of parents (*ibid.*). But it was also said that one who in his use of the stolen money performed a precept and thus heeded his Father in heaven could not be indicted (TJ, Sanh. 8:2).

As father and mother have to be "defied," to "take hold of him," to "say" to the elders, and to show them "this" is our son, neither of them may be deaf, dumb, blind, lame, or crippled, or else the son cannot be indicted as rebellious (Sanh. 8:4; Sif. Deut. 219). Either of them could condone the offense and withdraw the complaint at any time before conviction (Sif. Deut. 218; Sanh. 88b; TJ, Sanh. 8:6; Yad, Mamrim 7:8).

The son had first to be brought before a court of three judges (see *Bet Din) where, when he was convicted, he would be flogged and warned that unless he desisted from his wanton conduct he would be indicted as a rebellious son and liable to be stoned; if he did not desist, he would be brought before a court of 23, including the three judges who had warned him (Sanh. 8:4; 71b; Mid. Tan. to 21:18; Yad, Mamrim 7:7). If he escaped before sentence was passed, and in the meantime his hair had grown, he had to be discharged; but if he escaped after sentence, he would be executed if caught (Sanh. 71b; Yad, Mamrim 7:9).

The sentence passed upon a rebellious son had to be published far and wide, so that "all Israel will hear and be afraid" (Sanh. 89a; Mid. Tan. to 18:21). According to one view, the sentence was to be passed and executed at Jerusalem, at the time of mass pilgrimages, when all the people would be there to see and to hear (Tosef. Sanh. 11:7). It is said that the rebellious son is executed, not because of what he has actually done, but because of what he was foreseen to be prone to do were he allowed to live. His conduct showed that eventually he would have ruined his parents and become a robber and murderer (Sanh. 72a; TJ, Sanh. 8:7), so God considered it better for him to die innocent than to die guilty (Sanh. 8:5).

"In our times, we pay no attention to gluttonous and defiant sons, and everybody covers up the sins of his children; even where they might be liable to flogging or to capital punishment under the law, they are not even reprimanded. Many such children are leading purposeless lives and learn nothing – and we know that Jerusalem was destroyed because children loafed around and did not study" (Shab. 119b; Samuel Eliezer Edels, *Ḥiddushei Halakhot ve-Aggadot*, Sanh. 71a).

BIBLIOGRAPHY: J.S. Zuri, *Mishpat ha-Talmud*, 6 (1921), 88; ET, 3 (1951), 362–7; A.Ch. Freimann, in: EM, 2 (1954), 160–2; **ADD. BIBLIOGRAPHY:** M. Elon, *Ha-Mishpat ha-Ivri* (1988), 1:305ff.; 3:1408; *ibid.*, *Jewish Law* (1994), 1:365; 4:1677; *Enziklopedyah Talmudit*, vol. 3, s.v. *"ben sorer u-moreh,"* 362–27; index.

[Haim Hermann Cohn]

REBREANU, village in Transylvania, central Romania. Jews settled in the villages Lusça and Entrádám which later became part of Rebreanu. There was a Jewish community in Lusça dating from the early 18th century, while the population of Entrádám was entirely Jewish and its Romanian name was Jidovița, from the Old Romanian word *jidov* of Slavic origin (a pejorative ethnonym meaning "Jew"). The Jews engaged mainly in commerce and agriculture and operated water mills. With the abolition of the settlement restrictions in Transylvania in 1848 many Jews from Entrádám moved to the nearby city of Nasaud, founding the community there. The population of the village was almost wholly Jewish in 1900. In 1930 the 135 Jews formed over 60% of the total population. The administration of the village remained in Jewish hands, and Rebreanu was popularly known as "Klayn Erez Israel" ("little Erez Israel"). The community was Orthodox with a strong ḥasidic influence.

During World War II, in 1944, the Jews were moved by the Hungarian Fascists first to Nasaud, then to Bistrita, then finally deported to *Auschwitz. In 1947 there were 17 Jews living in Rebreanu, but they left soon afterward. There was no Jewish community in Rebreanu in the early 21st century

[Yehouda Marton]

REBUKE AND REPROOF (Heb. *tokhaḥah*), admonition and chastisement for the purpose of restraint or correction. The biblical source for the duty to rebuke the wrongdoer is: "You shall not hate your kinsman in your heart. Reprove your neighbor, but incur no guilt because of him" (Lev. 19:17). In the view of the rabbis the duty to reprove one's neighbor has two applications: the first, to confront one's fellow with personal grievances held against him, and the second, to chastise evildoers in the hope of bringing about their regeneration (Maim. Yad, De'ot 6:6, 7). The duty to openly confront one's neighbor with personal grievances is entailed in the injunction against hatred of one's brother, insofar as the silent harboring of resentments leads to hatred (Ch. B. Chavel (ed.), *Sefer ha-Ḥinnukh* (1961), 297). Thus the behavior of Absalom toward his brother Amnon ("Absalom spoke unto his brother Amnon neither good nor bad, for Absalom hated Amnon…," II Sam. 13:22) is cited as an example of the wickedness of bearing unexpressed grievances (see Gersonides on this verse; and also Yad, De'ot 6:6, 7). The duty to chastise sinners and wrongdoers stems from the view that everyone is charged with the responsibility of bringing about the correction of the sins of his fellowman. Failure to discharge this responsibility is tantamount to bearing the same sins and faults (cf. Targum Onkelos and commentary of Naḥmanides on Lev. 19:12).

Because the intention behind the rebuking of the evildoer is his rehabilitation, a number of qualifications are imposed upon this commandment. One is prohibited from rebuking another to the point of embarrassment (Ar. 16b). According to Maimonides, admonition must be carried out in private (Yad, De'ot 6:7). In fact, rebuke must be effected with such delicacy that R. Eleazar b. Azariah doubted that there were any in his generation sufficiently capable in this regard (Ar. 16b). Furthermore, the Talmud, in accordance with the dictum "Reprove not a scorner lest he hate thee" (Prov. 9:8), prohibits admonition where there is a foregone conclusion that it will be rejected and merely increase enmity (Yev. 65b). Certain later rabbinic authorities maintain that in cases where it may safely be assumed that rebuke will be disregarded, it is preferable not to rebuke people for violating prohibitions that are not explicit in the Torah, for it is preferable that they transgress unknowingly rather than deliberately (Sh. Ar., OḤ 608:2).

Procedures of Rebuke

It is not sufficient to rebuke the wrongdoer once, rather one must rebuke him incessantly so long as he is recalcitrant. According to R. Johanan, a person should persist in rebuking his neighbor until the wrongdoer insults him; according to Samuel, until he curses him; and according to Rav, until he is ready to strike him (Ar. 16b). The obligation to rebuke one's neighbor falls even upon one who is generally intellectually and morally inferior to the person at fault, so that the disciple, for instance, must rebuke his teacher where necessary (BM 31a). Every community must appoint a wise and respected person whose function it is to publicly chastise wrongdoing and call for repentance (Yad, Teshuvah 4:2).

The role of admonition is central in Jewish ethical thought. The rabbis proclaim that there exists no love or peace where there is no admonition, citing as an example the peace covenant between Abimelech and Abraham which resulted from Abraham's reproving Abimelech (Gen. R. 54:3). The duty of admonition extends not only to individuals, but to the community at large, and even to the entire world, to the extent that if one does not fulfill the commandment of rebuke, the guilt of all those he might have reformed accrues to him (Shab. 54b). Some rabbis of the Talmud maintain that the Second Temple was destroyed, despite the presence of the righteous, because the righteous did not fulfill their obligation to rebuke the wrongdoers of their time, and thus shared their guilt (Shab. 119b). In the opinion of Judah ha-Nasi, the most righteous course for a man to choose is the love of admonition: "As long as there is admonition in the world there is satisfaction, goodness, and blessing in the world… as it is written [Prov. 24:25] 'To them that rebuke shall be delight, and a good blessing shall come upon them'" (Tam. 28a).

BIBLIOGRAPHY: Ḥ.N. Bialik, and Y.Ḥ. Rawnitzki (eds.), *Sefer ha-Aggadah*, 2 (1960), 541–3; J.D. Eisenstein, *Oẓar Musar u-Middot* (1941).

[Joshua H. Shmidman]

RECANATI, town in the Marches, central Italy. Already by the 13th century there was a Jewish community in Recanati, trading in wine, oil, and cereals. Around the end of the following century Jewish loan-bankers settled in Recanati. In the 15th and 16th centuries Recanati became the most important Jewish center in the Marches, and in 1448 delegates of the Jewish communities in the region were summoned to assemble there to consider ways of defending themselves against the prevailing anti-Jewish agitation. Other meetings took place in 1480, 1509, and 1515. In 1558 the apostate Fra Filippo (formerly Joseph Moro) burst into the synagogue during the Day of Atonement service and profaned the Ark. After he had been driven out of the synagogue by the furious congregation, he appealed to the ecclesiastical authorities and obtained a severe sentence against the Jewish community. In 1569, following a bull by Pius v, the Jews were expelled from Recanati, as they were from all other centers in the Papal States, except Rome and Ancona. They returned for a brief period under Sixtus *v (1587) and opened loan-banks once again until 1593. The famous mystical exegete, Menahem (of) *Recanati, may have lived here in the 14th century.

BIBLIOGRAPHY: Kaufmann, in: REJ, 23 (1891), 249–55; Servi, in: *Vessillo Israelitico*, 47 (1899), 79–81, 117f.; Ghetti, in: *Atti e memorie della Regia deputazione di storia patria delle Marche*, 4 (1907), 11–39; Milano, Bibliotheca, index; A. Bravi, *Reminiscenze recanatesi* (1878), 71–78.

[Ariel Toaff]

RECANATI, Italian family, originally from *Spain, which produced scholars, physicians, merchants, and financiers. The name derives from the town of *Recanati. The family rose into special prominence in the 17th century, but earlier members of the family are Menahem *Recanati in the 13th century and AMADEO (Jedidiah) in the 16th century who translated Maimonides' *Guide of the Perplexed* into Italian, under the title *Erudizione dei Confusi*, which he dedicated to Menahem Azariah da *Fano.

The main branch of the family begins with SHABBETAI ELHANAN (early 17th century), rabbi of Ferrara when the ghetto was established there (1624). He founded a dynasty of rabbis that continued for at least six generations. MENAHEM, his son, succeeded him as a rabbi in Ferrara. He wrote a number of responsa. Some of these are included in *Piskei Recanati ha-Aḥaronim* of Jacob Ḥayyim Recanati (nos. 4, 6, 33; see below). JUDAH ḤAYYIM (late 17th century), Menahem's son, was rabbi of the Sephardi community of Ferrara. He wrote a number of responsa and his name appears often with the other rabbis of the city on rabbinical decrees. One of his responsa appears in *Piskei Recanati ha-Aḥaronim* (no. 5). SHABBETAI ELHANAN (d. 1738), his son, continued as rabbi of the Sephardi community of Ferrara. He was a contemporary of Mordecai *Ẓahalon and his name appears often together with Ẓahalon's and those of the other rabbis of Ferrara on regulations (*takkanot*) and approvals (*haskamot). He wrote responsa at a very early age. One of them is found in *Devar Shemu'el* (p. 280) of Samuel Aboab. He is mentioned in the *Paḥad Yiẓḥak* of Lampronti, *Reshit Bikkur Kaẓir* of Jacob Daniel Olmo, and *Shemesh Ẓedakah* of Samson Morpurgo. His son MOSES was also a rabbi in Ferrara as early as 1730.

JACOB ḤAYYIM BEN ISAAC SAMUEL (1758–1824), his grandson, born in Pesaro. At first an elementary school teacher in Ferara, he later served as rabbi in Siena, Acqui, Moncalvo, Finale, Carpi, Verona, and Venice. In Verona he also acted as head of a rabbinical school. He is best known for his *Piskei Recanati ha-Aḥaronim* (Leghorn, 1813) a collection of responsa, and for *Ya'ir Nativ* (Dessau, 1818) a responsum on the Hamburg Temple and its use of an organ. He was one of the four rabbis who took the liberal view. He was a man of wide interests, being also a grammarian and mathematician, poet and preacher. He published a treatise on arithmetic at Siena. Unpublished are books of sermons entitled *Afikei Mayim, Oholei Ya'akov*, and *Neveh Ya'akov*. He also wrote a compendium on Judaism (Verona, 1813), a number of Hebrew poems, and *Har ha-Tov*, quotations from *Ein Ya'akov*. Emanuele (Menahem; 1796–1864), the son of Jacob Ḥayyim, was physician in Verona. He wrote *Grammatica Ebraica in Lingua Italiana* (Verona, 1842); and *Dizionario Ebraico-Caldaico ed Italiano e Italiano ed Ebraico* (2 vols., *ibid*., 1854–56). Other branches of the family are found in various Italian cities. In the 20th century branches of the family spread to Greece, Israel, and the U.S.

[Isaac Klein]

In *Greece, Yehudah Leib Recanati (1890–1945) was a noted banker. Born in *Salonika, Recanati was a leader of Greek Jewry for many years and became the president of the Greek communities in 1934, representing them on the Jewish Agency council. In 1935 he settled in Tel Aviv and established the Discount Bank of which he became chairman of the board of directors. This bank became one of the largest in the country and contributed substantially to the economic development of Israel. Recanati was the chairman of the Sephardi community council in Tel Aviv and was active in a large number of public institutions and bodies. His sons, Harry Rafael (1918–) and Daniel (1921–1984), were both directors of the Discount Bank and developed wide banking and commercial interests in Israel and elsewhere. They were dedicated to public and social needs in Israel (see Israel: *Banking).

[Benjamin Jaffe]

BIBLIOGRAPHY: Ghirondi-Neppi, 127, 155–7, 225–7, 319, 335; I. Sonne, in: *Horeb*, 6 (1941), 79–95.

RECANATI, ABRAHAM SAMUEL (1888–1980), Greek Zionist and journalist. A member of the *Recanati family, Abraham Samuel was born and educated in Salonika. He wrote in the local Jewish Judeo-Spanish press. In the Balkan wars, as a correspondent for the *Jewish Chronicle* and *Die Welt* (Berlin) he brought the suffering of the Jewish community of Salonika to the attention of the Jewish world and to the general European public.

In 1911 he became the head of Maccabi Federation in Salonika, transforming it from a sports organization to a mass youth movement.

Among his writings are *La Poriza dela Familia Judia, Ke es el Tsionismo,* and *Los Judios de Rusia Sofrin Eyos Como Judios.* He also translated *The Jewish State* by Theodor Herzl into French.

Owing to tactical and ideological differences, Abraham Recanati and a group of friends left Maccabi and in 1917 founded the French weekly newspaper *Pro Israel*, which Recanati edited during the ten years in which it appeared. The newspaper had widespread influence on the development of the Zionist movement in Salonika. The connections which developed at that time between Vladimir *Jabotinsky and Recanati brought about the molding of the core group of *Pro Israel* into a branch of the Revisionist Zionists in Salonika.

In 1919, Recanati formed the Histadrut ha-Mizrachi (Mizrachi Organization) in Greece and served as its leader. In 1923 he formed "Ha-Shomer," which was founded to use legal and "illegal" means to work for a Jewish state in Ereẓ Israel.

He was a delegate to various Zionist Congresses and was among the founders of the World Revisionist Organization and a member of its world executive committee. The Jews always had a small representation in the municipality of Salonika and in 1929 Recanati was appointed assistant mayor of the city.

In 1934 Recanati immigrated to Palestine. He was one of the founders of "Ha-Mizrachi Ha-Mekori," which was a faction in the Tel Aviv branch of the Mizrachi. In 1935 he obtained immigration certificates for Salonikan portworkers, sailors, and fishermen.

In Tel Aviv most of the Salonikan immigrants settled in the Florentin Quarter. Recanati served as vice chairman of the neighborhood committee under Rabbi Iẓḥak Yedidiah Frenkel and helped in the areas of health, sanitation, education, commerce, and the crafts. During the period of the Holocaust he participated in the formation of the Va'ad ha-Haẓẓalah (Rescue Committee) for Greek Jewry.

As a veteran Revisionist he was elected to the First Knesset in Israel representing the Ḥerut party. He was chairman of the public services committee of the Knesset.

In the last years of his life, he spent much time collecting material and writing for the Salonika memorial book, *Zikhron Salonika* (vol. 1, 1972; vol. 2, 1986).

He was the brother of the banker Yehudah Leib (Leon) Recanati.

[Yitzhak Kerem]

RECANATI, LEON (Yehuda) (1890–1945), banker. Born in Salonika, Recanati was one of the earliest Zionist activists in Salonika. After the outbreak of the Young Turk revolution in 1908, he was one of the first Zionist leaders who acted in the open. In the same year he began to function as a correspondent of the local Zionist movement to the Central Zionist Bureau in Cologne. After the death of his older brother Zacharia, Leon took over the family business of commercial representation for foreign firms in Salonika.

When the Young Turks began to ban official Zionist activities, Leon channeled his public endeavors through his involvement with B'nai B'rith, of which he was one of the founding members in Salonika (1911). One of the first results of his B'nai B'rith work was his initiative in founding a women's organization, B'not Israel.

Recanati's principal business was as owner of the tobacco factory Fumero. He provided work for some 600 Jewish breadwinners in times of economic stress.

In 1929 he was the Greek Jewish representative at the gathering which founded an extended Jewish Agency and subsequently was Greek Jewry's representative to the World Jewish Congress in Geneva. In 1933 the Zionist slate won the local Jewish community elections, and Leon Recanati was elected president of the Jewish community of Salonika.

In 1934 he moved to Palestine and in 1935 founded the Israel Discount Bank. He continued his concern with the welfare of his fellow Salonikan Jews. During the period of Nazi occupation in Greece, Recanati tried to take measures to help save his fellow Jews. He persuaded the Jewish agency to rent a small boat that sailed secretly at night between Zakalos, on the eastern coast of the Euboean peninsula in Greece, and Gesme, Turkey. Hundreds of Greek Jews fleeing Nazi terror were saved in this manner and later arrived in Palestine. Hundreds of Greek officers escaped from Greece in these same boats in order to join the Greek army stationed in the Middle East.

In Palestine, Recanati cared for the few refugees who succeeded in escaping and granted them loans for initial rehabilitation. He also participated in the building of a residential area for Greek Jewish immigrants in Yad Eliyahu in the Tel Aviv region.

He was also actively involved in public life in Palestine. He was chairman of the Greek-Jewish Kadima club, leader of the Organization of Greek Immigrants which ran a kitchen for the needy as well as a welfare fund for Greek immigrant women, and was president of the settlement company Banimli-Gevulam, which founded and strengthened the settlements of Kefar Hittim, Bet Hanan, Zur Moshe, and Bet Halevi, all inhabited mostly by Sephardi Jews. He also set up a scholarship fund to enable Sephardi youth to obtain high school, technical, agricultural, and particularly university training.

BIBLIOGRAPHY: D.A. Recanti, *Zikhron Saloniki* (1986), 11:487–94; H. Recanti, Recanti, *Av u-Ven* (1984).

RECANATI, MENAHEM BEN BENJAMIN (late 13th–early–14th centuries), Italian kabbalist and halakhic authority. No information whatsoever is available on Recanati's life, although according to family tradition mentioned in *Shalshelet ha-Kabbalah* he was once an ignorant man who miraculously became filled with wisdom and understanding.

He wrote three kabbalistic works: *Perush al ha-Torah* (Venice, 1523); *Ta'amei ha-Mitzvot* (Constantinople, 1544); and *Perush ha-Tefillot* (*ibid.*, 1544); and one halakhic work, *Piskei Halakhot* (Bologna, 1538). Two commentaries on the *Perush al ha-Torah* were written during the 16th century: one by Mattathias Delacrut (Neubauer, Cat, nos. 1615, 1623, 3); and *Be'ur Levush Even Yekarah* by Mordecai Jaffe (Lublin, 1605; Lemberg, 1840–41). An important part of the *Ta'amei ha-Mitzvot*, in which Recanati deals with the problem of the nature of the *Sefirot*, still remains in manuscript. According to Recanati, the *Sefirot* are not the essence of God but coverings in which God enfolds Himself and instruments through which He acts. This entire extract is quoted by Judah *Ḥayyat in his commentary to **Ma'arekhet ha-Elohut*, and in their discussions of this question other 16th-century kabbalists (notably Isaac Mor Ḥayyim, Elhanan Sagi Nahor, Solomon *Alkabeẓ, and Moses *Cordovero) refer to Recanati's views. Even those who oppose his theory refer to him with admiration and respect, with the exception of David Messer *Leon, who attacks him harshly in *Magen David* (MS Montefiore 290).

With the exception of his discussion on the essence of the *Sefirot*, where his conclusion is the result of his own speculations, Recanati's doctrine is drawn mainly from written sources. He cannot be regarded as the recipient of "revelations from heaven" (despite Guedemann; see bibl.), and in few places indeed does he tell of his dreams and visions. Thanks to him the doctrines of many kabbalists whose writings are otherwise unknown have been preserved. He made use of many sources, which he usually does not mention by name, and was especially indebted to *Naḥmanides, whom he refers to as "the great rabbi." Another kabbalist he mentions frequently is R. Ezra (whose name is occasionally changed to R. Azriel), and he made use of the writings of Jacob b. Sheshet Gerondi, *Asher b. David, Joseph *Gikatilla, and *Moses b. Shem Tov de Leon. Recanati was acquainted with two large works on the reasons for the precepts which were written during his lifetime: one by R. Joseph from Shushan (then attributed to Isaac ibn Farḥi) and another by an unknown author. An important part of his commentaries on Naḥmanides' esoteric mysticism derives from *Keter Shem Tov* by Shem Tov *Ibn Gaon. Other important sources were Sefer ha-*Bahir and the Zohar, which he quotes often although he had access to only a limited number of sections.

BIBLIOGRAPHY: Zunz, Lit Poesie, 369ff.; Guedemann, Gesch Erz, 2 (1884), 180–2; I. Sonne, in: KS, 11 (1934/35), 530; G. Scholem, *ibid.*, 185; Scholem, Mysticism, index s.v. *Menahem of Recanati*; idem, *Ursprung und Anfaenge der Kabbala* (1962), index; idem, *Von der mystischen Gestalt der Gottheit* (1962), index; idem, *On the Kabbalah and its Symbolism* (1965), index; Y. Nadav, in: *Tarbiz*, 26 (1956/57), 440–58; J. Ben-Shelomo, *Torat ha-Elohut shel R. Moshe Cordovero* (1965), index; E. Gottlieb, *Ha-Kabbalah be-Khitvei Rabbenu Baḥya ben Asher* (1970), 259–63.

[Efraim Gottlieb]

°**RECCARED,** Visigothic king of Spain (586–601). He succeeded his father Leovigild and shortly thereafter converted from Arianism to orthodox Christianity. This conversion was followed in 589 by the Third Council of Toledo, where it was decreed that all Arians must become orthodox. His preoccupation with religious matters seems to have led Reccared to reaffirm and modify existing anti-Jewish legislation. He forbade Jews to own Christian slaves and decreed that if a Jew circumcised a Christian slave, the latter was to be set free and the owner was himself to be enslaved. Jews were further forbidden to have Christian wives or mistresses and any children born from such a union were to be baptized. This is the earliest example of compulsory conversion of Jews in Visigothic Spain. Aside from the enactment requiring the forced baptism of offspring from mixed marriages, Reccared's legislation did not go beyond that which had existed under his Arian predecessors. In fact the punishment for converting one's own slaves was reduced from death to slavery. Like his predecessors, moreover, Reccared was lax in enforcing the anti-Jewish laws. Not only did Jews continue to own and trade Christian slaves, but the pope felt compelled to indicate his wrath at this state of affairs. This had little effect, however, and the Jews seem to have been little bothered by Reccared's legislation against them.

BIBLIOGRAPHY: S. Katz, *Jews in the Visigothic and Frankish Kingdoms of Spain and Gaul* (1937), index; B. Blumenkranz, *Juifs et Chrétiens dans le monde occidental*, 430–1096 (1960), index; E.A. Thompson, *The Goths in Spain* (1969).

[Bernard Bachrach]

RECHAB AND BAANAH (Heb. רֵכָב, "rider"; and בַּעֲנָה, cf. Ugaritic *bnʿna*, "son of Ana"), sons of Rimmon from Beeroth, one of the four cities which constituted the Gibeonite (or Hivite) league, and which has been identified as the site of el-Bire, lying northwest of Jerusalem just outside the territory of the tribe of Benjamin. Rechab and Baanah, captains of the army of Saul's son Ish-Bosheth (II Sam. 4:2), murdered their king (verse 7). Entering Ish-Bosheth's house undetected, they decapitated him while he was sleeping (verse 7) and took his head to David, claiming to have carried out the will of God (verse 8). David, anxious to clear himself of the suspicion of complicity, had them summarily executed, reminiscent of the way he treated the man who brought the news of Saul's suicide. The assassins' bodies were mutilated and hanged beside the pool in Hebron, while the head of Ish-Bosheth was honorably buried in Abner's grave in the same town (verse 12). Several possible motives may explain the captains' regicide: the hope of being rewarded by David; the desire to realize Abner's plan for a united kingdom with David as king, by eliminating David's most dangerous opponent; and revenge for Saul's conquering the confederacy of the Hivite cities (cf. Josh. 9:17).

Saul's conquering of the confederacy explains why the Beerothites, including the sons of Rimmon, fled to Gittaim, where they lived as aliens (II Sam. 4:3). In the course of time the sons of Rimmon became officers of Ish-Bosheth and at an opportune moment murdered him as an act of blood revenge.

BIBLIOGRAPHY: M.H. Segal, in: JQR, 8 (1917/18), 98–99.

RECHABITES (Heb. בְּנֵי הָרֵכָבִים), a small religious sect first identified as such in Jeremiah 35 in an incident dated in the reign of *Jehoiakim, but tracing their descent to Jonadab son of Rechab, who was a contemporary of *Jehu (II Kings 10:15–17 where he is called Jehonadab; see below). Jeremiah was commanded by God to take the Rechabites to one of the chambers in the Temple and serve them wine. The Rechabites, however, refused to drink the wine, citing the charge of their ancestor Jonadab son of Rechab, which forbade them to drink wine, to cultivate or even to own fields or vineyards or to build houses. They had remained pastoral tent-dwellers until the invasion of Nebuchadnezzar, when they had taken refuge in Jerusalem. It is not known whether this was when Nebuchadnezzar merely occupied the West and Jehoiakim became his vassal (604 B.C.E.) or during Jehoiakim's rebellion (601–598), nor whether the Rechabites had been able to continue to dwell in tents while residing in Jerusalem, but at any rate they continued to abstain from wine. Jeremiah, while he did not necessarily demand this Nazirite-like asceticism, extolled their strict observance of these commandments, contrasting it with the evil ways of the people of Judah. He promised the Rechabites that they would continue to serve before God: "Jonadab son of Rechab shall never lack a man to stand before me" (35:19).

"Ben Rechab" may mean not literally "son of Rechab" but "Rechabite," in which case Jonadab may have won over his clansmen as well as his descendants to his way of life. He was not necessarily the physical ancestor of all the Rechabites of Jeremiah's day, but he was in any case their lawgiver and spiritual ancestor. Whether the Rechabites had peculiar religious observances (e.g., letting the hair grow) other than those enumerated above is not known.

Opposition to the Monarchy of Omri

Jonadab son of Rechab sided with Jehu against the House of Ahab. From a fragmentary text (II Kings 10:15–17) it appears that Jonadab, riding in Jehu's chariot from Jezreel to Samaria, gave his blessing to the slaughter of the royal family, and that Jehu was interested in proving to him his zealousness on behalf of God. Jonadab also participated at Jehu's side in the slaughter of the prophets of Baal in the House of Baal in Samaria (II Kings 10:23). There is no evidence in the text that other men of the family of Rechab participated with Jonadab or that he acted as a representative of the sect. However, although Jonadab was accepted by Jehu on the strength of his personality, it may be assumed that his reputation as a zealous supporter of the God of Israel, who would tolerate no compromises, derived from his position as a head of a family that was completely opposed, because of its zealous faith and unique social character, to the rule of the House of Omri. Jonadab may have promulgated his rules as a reaction to the policies of Ahab, which notoriously provoked the opposition of the prophets and the sons of prophets headed by *Elijah and *Elisha. It appears that even at that time the Rechabites were distinguished from the prophets by their asceticism and extreme zealousness on behalf of the God of Israel (there is no sign that the prophets also participated in the slaughter of the worshipers of Baal in Samaria).

Origin of the Group

There is no definite information concerning the origins of the Rechabites. From a vague verse in I Chronicles 2:55 – "These are the Kenites who came from Hammath, the father of the house of Rechab" – it follows that the house of Rechab (as far as it is possible to identify it with "the house of the Rechabites" in Jer. 35 and "the son of Rechab" in II Kings 10) was related to the *Kenites. This verse mentions the Rechabites only in passing, in connection with the lineage of the Kenites. It goes on to say that the Kenites, or at least some of them, were among the inhabitants of Jabez, implying that they established a permanent settlement there, which cannot of course refer to the Rechabites. Even if "the house of Rechab" is also a place-name, identical with the name of the family, as is usually the case in the genealogies of Chronicles, there is no proof that it refers to a permanent settlement. If preference is given to the text of the Septuagint: "these are the men of Rechab," over that of I Chronicles 4:12: "these are the men of Recah," it is seen that, in accordance with the genealogical context in I Chronicles 4:11–15, the Rechabites were related to the Kenazites and the Calebites. Indeed, if these above verses reflect the process of settlement of the desert tribes in Judah in the period of the united monarchy in Israel, it may be estimated that the Rechabites were known, many years before Jonadab, as a special family in Judah. It is reasonable to suppose that, like the Kenites and the Kenazites, the Rechabites were absorbed in Judah at the time of the united monarchy, and in any case their territory was adjacent to the permanent settlements in the hill country of Judah. But their character as a religious sect dates only from the time of Jonadab.

Seminomadic Shepherds

Not engaging in agriculture and living in tents, the Rechabites must have subsisted by raising sheep and goats (cf. Gen. 4:20; 25:27). It follows that the Rechabites were among the nomads and herdsmen who dwelt in proximity to the permanent settlements in Israel and Judah, and even wandered further to the Wilderness of Judah. From the verses describing the meeting between Jonadab and Jehu – which took place between Jezreel and Samaria – it may be inferred that Jonadab's settlement was in the neighborhood of the cities in Israel. But their wanderings in the different periods ranged over Israel and Judah.

Relation to Society at Large

It appears that, in contrast to the deeds of Jonadab in the days of Jehu, the Rechabites in the following generations did not participate in the practical life of the kingdom and were essentially not a rebellious sect. The impression is that they did not set out to preach a way of life to the whole people, but, as is generally the case with a separatist group unified by family ties and stringent communal restrictions, it served in its very existence as a challenge to the conventions of the agrarian society and culture; in this respect it was analogous to some of the ascetic sects in the Wilderness of Judah in Second Temple times.

Second Temple Period

There are allusions to the existence of the family of the Rechabites in the days of the Second Temple. In Nehemiah reference is made to Malchijah son of Rechab, officer of the district of Beth-Cherem who held the Dung Gate (3:14), but there is no mention of his being unique among the other officers. Diodorus Siculus (19:9), in the name of Jerome of Cardia, speaks of the asceticism of the early Nabateans at the end of the fourth century B.C.E. in terminology almost exactly like that which Jeremiah used in describing the Rechabites, and he too placed special emphasis on the prohibition against drinking wine. There is no way of knowing of any connection between the Rechabites and the Nabateans, but it is probable that there were parallels to biblical asceticism, such as that of the house of Rechab, among other ethnic groups that settled in the south and Transjordan. According to the Mishnah (Ta'an. 4:5), "the children of Jonadab son of Rechab" had (in Second Temple times) a fixed day in the year for bringing wood for the altar of the Temple. They were probably descended from the tent-dwelling Rechabites, but they hardly constituted a separate sect. There were "water-drinking" sacrificers, and the Midrash traces their descent to Jonadab (Gen. R. 98:10; Sif. Num. 78, 81, et al.; cf. Ta'an. 28a; TJ, Ta'an. 4:2, 68a), but this merely indicates that sects of teetotalers existed in the Second Temple period. The designation which connects them with the pre-Exilic Rechabites may very well be typological rather than truly genealogical.

BIBLIOGRAPHY: E. Meyer, *Die Israeliten und ihre Nachbarstaemme* (1906), 40–409, 444ff.; J.W. Flight, in: JBL, 42 (1923), 158–226 (incl. bibl.); S. Klein, in: *Ẓiyyon Me'assef*, 2 (1927), 9; J.A. Montgomery, in: JBL, 51 (1932), 183–213; H. Schmoekel, *Jahwe und die Fremdvoelker…* (1934), 212–22; S. Talmon, in: *Eretz Israel*, 5 (1958), 111–3; N. Glueck, *Rivers in the Desert* (1959), 142–5; Kaufmann Y., Toledot, 2 (1960), 232, 338, 625–6; S. Abramsky, in: *Eretz-Israel*, 8 (1967), 255–64, incl. bibl. For the Rechabites in the Second Temple period see: Y. Baer, *Yisrael ba-Ammim*, 1 (1955), 45, 125.

[Samuel Abramsky]

RECHITSA, city in Gomel district, Belarus. Rechitsa had one of the oldest Jewish communities in Belorussia. In 1648 the rampaging Cossacks murdered many of its Jews. The Jewish population in 1766 numbered 133, increasing to 1,268 in 1800 (two thirds of the total population), and 2,080 in 1847. The city was a center for Chabad *Ḥasidism. At the end of the 19th century Rechitsa had a yeshivah led by Rabbi Ḥayyim Shelomo Kumm and was the residence of the ḥasidic leader, R. Shalom Dov Ber *Schneersohn. Rechitsa's Jews included petty merchants in lumber and agricultural produce, artisans, a few wholesalers, and the owner of a match factory. In 1897 the 5,334 Jews of Rechitsa constituted 57 percent of the population. On October 23, 1905 the peasants of the surrounding area participated in a pogrom which killed 6 Jews and wounded 12, most of them members of the Jewish self-defense force. On the eve of World War I the Jewish population numbered about 7,500. Jewish communal and religious life began to decline under Soviet rule. There existed a Yiddish section in the court of law and two Jewish elementary schools. In 1926 there were 7,386 Jews, and 7,237 in 1939 (24 percent of the total population). The Germans occupied the town on August 23, 1941. In November 1941 all 3,000 remaining Jews were gathered in a ghetto, and on November 25 they were murdered. A few Jews returned after the war. They had no synagogue, and in 1970 the Jewish population was estimated at about 1,000. In the 1990s most remaining Jews emigrated to Israel and the West.

BIBLIOGRAPHY: I. Halpern, *Sefer ha-Gevurah*, 3 (1950), 186–90; *Die Judenpogrome in Russland*, 2 (1909), 465–7; *Prestupleniya nemetsko-fashistskikh okkupantov v Belorussii* (1963), 268–71.

[Yehuda Slutsky / Shmuel Spector (2nd ed.)]

RECHTER, Israeli architects. ZE'EV RECHTER (1899–1960) was born in Russia and went to Palestine in 1919, working in an engineering office in Jerusalem. He worked for many years as a draughtsman and surveyor, later studying architecture and engineering in Italy and France. After his studies, he returned to Tel Aviv. He had a considerable influence in formulating the types of urban dwelling houses in Israel as a whole, and in Tel Aviv in particular. He introduced the house built on piles, with the lower floor open to the street, which determined the look of residential streets in Tel Aviv and other towns. The first building of this type was Bet Engel in the Rothschild Boulevard in Tel Aviv built by Rechter in 1934–36. Among other public buildings built or designed by Rechter are Binyenei ha-Ummah in Jerusalem, the Meir Hospital at Kefar Sava, the Elisha Hospital in Haifa, the Tel Aviv law courts (in partnership with Dov *Karmi), and the School of Archaeology at the Hebrew University. Rechter was one of the leaders of the modernist movement in Israel, simple forms characterizing his architecture.

His son, YA'AKOV RECHTER (1924–2001), was born in Tel Aviv and served as an officer during the War of Independence. In 1951 he became partner in his father's firm. He worked on a number of private buildings and public projects such as the F.R. Mann Auditorium in Tel Aviv (in collaboration with D. Karmi). On the death of his father, he ran the office with his brother-in-law, Zarchi. The designs emerging from the reorganized office shifted from a solid sobriety to lively sculptural forms blending with the natural surroundings. In the Zikhron Ya'akov Rest Home, Rechter repeated the cellular pattern of his Tel Aviv Hilton. In a different mood, Rechter experimented with concrete and glass at the Polyclinic in Haifa. Rechter worked on a town-planning scheme for the development of the Tel Aviv seafront. One of his most famous buildings is the Stage Arts building in Tel Aviv, a monumental structure that includes a small piazza, two large entrance gateways, and a large hall. Rechter was awarded the Israel Prize for arts in 1972.

The Ministry of Education and Culture awards the Rechter Prize for excellence and creativity in architecture.

[Abraham Erlik / Shaked Gilboa (2nd ed.)]

RECIFE, city in northeast Brazil, capital of the state of Pernambuco; population: 1,486,869 (2004); Jewish population estimated at 1,300.

Colonial Period

When Recife became a prosperous center for sugar production in the 16th and 17th centuries, Portuguese New Christians were already living in the city and its environs and in many regions of the Brazilian Nordeste (North East). They worked mainly in sugar production and commerce. The significant number of New Christians in Recife took part in a variety of activities, and some bound themselves through intermarriage to prestigious Old Christian families.

The Inquisition dispatched an official inspector (*visitator*) and an inquisitional commission was established in 1593–1595 in Olinda, the port of Recife. New Christians were tried and arrested; some were taken to Lisbon and handed over to the inquisitional tribunal. After the inspector had left, surveillance of New Christians was continued by the bishop of Brazil, with the assistance of the local clergy. Thus the New Christian Diego Fernandez, husband of Branca Dias, was accused by the Inquisition of being a "Judaizer" and of keeping an "esnorga," a secret place to pray.

Two New Christian writers lived in Recife and stood out in the colonial period with works that reveal elements of Jewish expression: Bento Teixeira, author of *Prosopopéia* – one of the most important Portuguese-Brazilian colonial poems – published in Lisbon on 1601, and Ambrósio Fernandes Brandão, author of *Diálogos das Grandezas do Brasil*, in 1618.

Dutch Period

The first organized Jewish community in Brazil was established in Recife during the period of Dutch colonial occupation (1630–1654) that brought Jews among other Dutch colonists and permitted religious freedom. The West India Company came to Brazil attracted by the sugar plantations and more than 120 engenhos (sugar mills) in Pernambuco.

In 1636–1640 the Dutch Jews founded the first Brazilian synagogue in Recife, the first on American soil: Kahal Kadosh Ẓur Israel. Later they founded the synagogue Kahal Kadosh Magen Abraham in Maurícia. Both were unified in 1648, with the signatures of 172 members both from Recife and Maurícia. The Jewish community was very well organized along the same lines as the mother community in Amsterdam. Ẓur Israel maintained a synagogue, the religious schools Talmud Torah and Eẓ Ḥayim, and a cemetery. In Recife there was a "Rua dos Judeus" (Jodenstraat or Jewish street) in 1636.

In 1642 Rabbi Isaac Aboab da Fonseca arrived from Holland, accompanied by the *ḥakham* Moses Rafael de Aguilar. Jews from Recife addressed an inquiry regarding the proper season to recite the prayers for rain to Rabbi Ḥayyim Shabbetai in Salonika, the earliest American contribution to rabbinic responsa literature. Despite official tolerance, however, the Jews were subjects of some hostility at the hands of Calvinists.

The estimates of the Jewish population at Recife vary greatly. According to Arnold Wiznitzer, it reached 1,450 members in 1645. Egon and Frieda Wolff's research indicated around 350 Jews.

By 1639 Dutch Brazil had a flourishing sugar industry with more than 120 sugar cane mills, six of which were owned by Jews. Jews also had an important role in commerce, tax farming, and finances. Jews were also engaged in the slave trade, worked in agriculture, in the Dutch militia and as artisans and physicians. The contacts with the local population – including many New Christians – was permanent, due to the economic activities. During Dutch domination in the Nordeste, New Christians came closer to Judaism.

As early as 1642 the Portuguese began preparations for the liberation of northeastern Brazil. In 1645 they began a war that lasted nine years. Jews joined the Dutch ranks, and some were killed in action. Famine had set in and conditions were desperate when, on June 26, 1649, two ships arrived from Holland with food. On that occasion, Rabbi Isaac Aboab wrote the first Hebrew poem in the Americas, "*Zekher Asiti le-Nifle'ot El*" ("I Have Set a Memorial to God's Miracles").

It was stipulated in the capitulation protocol of Jan. 26, 1654, that all Jews, like the Dutch, were to leave Brazil within three months and had the right to liquidate their assets and to take all their movable property with them. The majority left for Amsterdam, but some sailed to the Caribbean Islands (Curaçāo, Barbados, and so on). Wiznitzer maintained that a group of 23 Brazilian Jews arrived in New Amsterdam (old name of New York), then under Dutch rule, on the *Saint Catherine* at the beginning of September 1654 and that they were the founding fathers of the first Jewish community in New York. Egon and Frieda Wolff rejected this historical connection and argued that there is no documentary basis to assume that the Jews who arrived in New York were the same that had left Recife during the expulsion of the Dutch.

New Christians continued to live in Recife. Two decades after the departure of the Dutch, the Inquisition was also acquainted with and persecuted the New Christians who had converted to Judaism during the Dutch occupation and had remained in Pernambuco. Many reports reached the Lisbon

Inquisition in the second half of the 17th century and during the 18th century regarding their clandestine observance of Jewish rituals. Portuguese policy in the middle of the 18th century eventually enabled the New Christians to mingle with the rest of the population, until their traces disappeared as they became completely assimilated.

Modern Period

The contemporary immigration of Jews from Eastern Europe to Recife started in the 1910s, and in 1910 a synagogue was established in a private house. The Centro Israelita de Pernambuco and the local Ídishe Shul were founded in 1918. Synagoga Israelita da Boa Vista and the Jewish cemetery were created in 1927. In 1930 Sephardi immigrants built their synagogue. The Jewish community was very active with a network of institutions, including six schools, the assistance organization Relief, a sports club, a library, a Yiddish theater group, youth and Zionist groups, and women organizations such as WIZO and Pioneiras. The community, which reached a population of 1,600, lived mostly in the neighborhoods of Boa Viagem and Boa Vista.

In 1992 the Arquivo Histórico Judaico de Pernambuco (Historic Jewish Archive of Pernambuco) was founded. In 1994 the Associação para a Restauração da Memória Judaica das Américas (Association for the Restoration of Jewish Memory in the Americas) was established and in 2000 the building where the synagogue Kahal Kadosh Ẓur Israel had been founded in the Dutch period was recognized as a "national historical patrimony" by Instituto do Patrimônio Histórico e Artístico Nacional – Iphan, a federal agency, and a memorial-museum was opened. Together with the old "Rua dos Judeus" the memorial figures in the tourist tours of the city of Recife.

BIBLIOGRAPHY: A. Dines, F. Moreno de Carvalho & N. Falbel (eds.), *A Fênix ou o Eterno Retorno* (2001); A. Wiznitzer, *Os judeus no Brasil colonial* (1960); E. & F. Wolff, *A odisséia dos judeus no Recife* (1979); J.A. Gonçalves de Mello, *Gente da Nação: cristãos-novos e judeus em Pernambuco 1542–1654* (1990); T. Neumann Kaufman, *Passos perdidos – história recuperada. A presença judaica em Pernambuco* (2001).

[Roney Cytrinowicz (2nd ed.)]

RECKENDORF, HERMANN SOLOMON (1863–1923), German Orientalist. Reckendorf's father, also named HERMANN (Ḥayyim Ẓevi; 1825–1875), taught Semitic languages at Heidelberg University, and wrote a Hebrew translation of the Koran (1857). Inspired by E. Sue's *Les Mystères de Paris*, he also wrote *Die Geheimnisse der Juden* (5 vols., 1856–57), a fictionalized recounting of Jewish history. Several Hebrew versions of this work were published; the one by A.S. Friedberg (*Zikhronot le-Veit David*, 1893–1900) is still popular with Israel youth. Hermann Solomon Reckendorf studied Semitics under T. Noeldeke and at the Berlin rabbinical seminary, but later abandoned Orthodoxy. Reckendorf became professor at Freiburg University, specializing in Arabic syntax.

His *Die syntaktischen Verhaeltnisse des Arabischen* (1895–98) outlines the problems of Arabic syntax; his *Arabische Syntax* (1921) is important for its collection of material. The two works remain outstanding. In his *Ueber Paronomasie in den semitischen Sprachen* (1909) Reckendorf covers a wider field, dealing with a well-defined syntactic phenomenon in most Semitic languages. Another of his works is *Mohammed und die Seinen* (1907).

BIBLIOGRAPHY: J. Fueck, *Arabische Studien in Europa* (1955), 312–3.

[Joseph L. Blau]

RECKLINGHAUSEN, town in Westphalia, Germany, where the presence of Jews is attested as early as 1305. The financier Gottschalk of Recklinghausen, who carried on extensive business from Lochern (in Dutch Gelderland), was killed during the disturbances caused by the Black Death in 1349–50. No organized community, however, came into being in medieval times, and there is no record of one in Recklinghausen until 1828. In the course of time, an active Jewish life developed and the community established a synagogue, communal center, elementary school, *mikveh*, and a variety of Jewish societies. Eastern European immigrants founded their own society and *minyan*. The Jewish population of Recklinghausen grew from 72 in 1880 to 298 in 1905. It dropped to 280 (5% of the total population) in 1933. From 1903 until 1922 and again from 1934 to 1938, Recklinghausen was the seat of a district rabbi. The last incumbent was Selig Auerbach, who later immigrated to the U.S. During the Nazi persecutions, many members of the community succeeded in emigrating from Recklinghausen, principally to Holland. On Nov. 9/10, 1938, the synagogue was destroyed, and subsequent deportations of the remaining Jews brought the community to an end. A new community of 52 Jews was established in Recklinghausen after World War II in conjunction with *Bochum and Herne, numbering 76 persons in 1962. In 1960 and 1961 the "Synagoga" exhibition of Jewish art and folklore was held in Recklinghausen and was subsequently shown throughout Germany. In 1974 there were 60 Jews residing in the city. In 1997 a new synagogue was consecrated. Due to the immigration of Jews from the former Soviet Union, the community grew so that it was divided in 1999. The new Jewish community of Recklinghausen numbered 624 in 2004.

BIBLIOGRAPHY: H.C. Meyer (ed.), *Aus Geschichte und Leben der Juden in Westfalen* (1962), 125–33, 165, 187, 255; Germ Jud, 2 (1968), 678–9; *Monumenta Judaica*, 2 (1963), 369, 379, 653. **ADD. BIBLIOGRAPHY:** W. Schneider, *Juedische Heimat im Vest. Gedenkbuch der juedischen Gemeinden im Kreis Recklinghausen* (1983); *1829–2004. 175 Jahre Juedische Kultusgemeinde Recklinghausen. Festschrift* (2004).

[Larissa Daemmig (2nd ed.)]

RECONSTRUCTIONISM, ideology and movement in U.S. religious life. Both the idea and the movement owe their inspiration to Mordecai Menahem *Kaplan (1881–1983). Raised Orthodox in Eastern Europe, Kaplan came to America at age eight. He saw his generation responding to this radically different setting in two ways: struggling to maintain Jewish identity while acclimating to America, or abandoning Jewish identity altogether. Kaplan believed that with the breakdown of belief in the Torah as the revealed word of God, in the authority of *halakhah* (Jewish law), in a supernatural conception of God, and in the notion of the Jews as a separated and "chosen people," a new rationale for maintenance of Jewish identity was needed. Kaplan argued that in pre-modern times, Jews had remained loyal to their identity despite hardship and suffering because they believed that adherence to Judaism assured them of salvation in the next world. Before the French Revolution (1789) Europe's Jews also lived in segregated communities; with the entry of Jews into citizenship in the countries where they resided, the social and sociological constraints that kept them apart from the larger culture were removed, however imperfectly. Kaplan argued that Jews had to learn to live in two civilizations: the Jewish one and the larger culture of which they were now a part.

When Kaplan began his career, there was widespread disagreement among Jews about how to define Judaism and what comprised Jewish identity. Reform Judaism defined Judaism as a religion only, and Jews as a community of faith. Zionist theoreticians defined Judaism as a nationality, and Jews as citizens (in exile, perhaps, but citizens nonetheless) of the Jewish nation. Secular Jews saw Judaism as a culture and Jews as an ethnic group. Kaplan sought definitions that could encompass this diversity. He decided that Judaism should be understood as the evolving religious civilization of the Jewish people, and that the Jews should share a common sense of peoplehood. Judaism, like any other civilization, comprised a history, a language, a religion, a social organization, standards of conduct, and spiritual and social ideals. Under the influence of modern sociology, Kaplan stated that whatever is an object of collective concern takes on all the traits of a religion, which in its turn functions in order to hold up to the individual the value of the group and the importance of his complete identification with it. For Kaplan, belonging to the Jewish people came before behaving according to Jewish practice or believing according to Jewish religion.

Kaplan believed that Judaism had to be transformed from an "other-worldly" civilization into a "this-worldly" one. He rejected supernaturalism in all of its manifestations. For Kaplan, the Torah was a human document recording the Jewish people's earliest record of their search for God and for the behaviors that would lead to human responsibility. What tradition called *mitzvot* (divine commandments) were for Kaplan "folkways" (*minhagim*) that had been created by the Jewish people, and thus were subject to adaptation, change, and/or rejection in response to the changing needs of the Jewish people. The Jewish religion, said Kaplan, exists for the Jewish people, not the Jewish people for the Jewish religion. Where Reform Judaism saw ethical monotheism as the unbroken line of continuity throughout Jewish history, and Orthodox Judaism saw the Torah and *halakhah* as the unchanging constants, Kaplan held that it was Jewish peoplehood that was the sole constant throughout the evolving history of Judaism.

Many Jewish intellectuals were attracted to Kaplan's program for a Jewish life. Since Judaism was a civilization, Kaplan argued that its parts could best function in interrelationship with one another. Kaplan sought to replicate the model of the European Jewish *kehillah* as what he called an "organic community," in which the basic unit of Jewish life would be the entire aggregate of a given community's synagogues, educational institutions, Zionist organizations, agencies, and organizations, linked into a single structure with a democratically elected leadership. In Kaplan's vision, one would join the local Jewish community, pay dues to that community, and in return have access to all the services of that community from birth to death. While this model was never implemented in the way Kaplan envisioned, it did have an influence on the emergence and development of the Jewish Federations and Jewish Community Relations Councils, each of which sought to embrace the entire spectrum of the communities they represented.

Kaplan was also a pioneer in conceiving of the synagogue as a Jewish center, in which social, intellectual and athletic activities would be as much a part of the institutional program as the synagogue and the religious school. This vision not only influenced the development of Jewish congregational life in the period before World War II, but it also helped inspire the creation and development of the Jewish Community Center movement.

The most controversial aspect of Kaplan's thinking was his theology. The conception of God as a supernatural personality became for Kaplan a conception of God as force or process, or, in his preferred formulation, "the Power that makes for salvation." Salvation was understood by Kaplan as self-fulfillment on a social and individual basis. It meant the progressive improvement of the human personality and the establishment of a free, just, and cooperative social order. Kaplan maintained that there were adequate resources in the world and capacities in humans to achieve such salvation. Since we sense a power that orients us to this life and elicits from us the best of which we are capable, this notion of God conforms to our experience. Kaplan distinguished between conceptions of God and belief in God. He felt that Judaism offered many different conceptions of God, from rational to mystical, and from personal to non-personal. It was belief in God as that force or power in creation and in human life that supported salvation, what Kaplan later called "transnaturalism," that he felt was essential; the conception of God that a Jew might choose was less important. Some early Reconstructionists, such as Milton *Steinberg, rejected Kaplan's naturalistic theology while accepting the rest of Kaplan's program.

Until the founding of the Reconstructionist Rabbinical College (RRC) in 1968, Reconstructionist ideology was essentially defined by Kaplan and his immediate circle of disciples and followers. Once the RRC began to ordain Reconstructionist rabbis, and as the number of Reconstructionist congregations began to grow in the 1980s and 1990s, Reconstructionism itself began to evolve, adapt and change to meet new circumstances. The inclusion of ḥasidic, kabbalistic and meditative practices and teachings broadened the spectrum of Reconstructionist spirituality in ways that the primarily rational approach of Kaplan might not have accommodated. As an independent movement, Reconstructionism had to grapple with creating positions and practices that, if not exactly couched as a return to *halakhah*, meant a serious engagement with *halakhah*. The rise of literary analysis and appreciation of biblical scripture in the last quarter of the 20th century provided a new opportunity to reengage the Torah and other biblical writings as myth and poetry, and not only as an historical document.

Reconstructionism in the 21st century remains firmly grounded in Kaplan's essential insight, that Judaism is the product of the historical experience of the Jewish people, and is not the revealed word of God or an inspired reaction to revelation. The traditional sources and practices of Judaism still have, in Kaplan's famous formulation, a "vote but not a veto." The organic Jewish community may never have actually been created, but the institutions of the movement and the congregations affiliated with the Jewish Reconstructionist Federation (JRF) try to operate with Kaplan's principles of democracy, egalitarianism, and openness. In particular, the concept of values-based decision-making has become integral to Reconstructionism, as has inclusivity, the bringing into the Jewish community of intermarried Jews, single Jews, gay and lesbian Jews, single Jewish parents and elderly Jews, among others. Kaplan's emphasis on belonging over behaving and believing remains central to Reconstructionism; what has changed is that it is as much the belonging to a Jewish community (congregation or havurah) as to the Jewish people that is now central.

The founding of the Reconstructionist movement may be dated from the establishment by Mordecai Menahem *Kaplan of the Society for the Advancement of Judaism (SAJ) in January 1922. The society served both as a synagogue center and as a forum for Kaplan's ideas. Several months after the publication of Kaplan's *Judaism as a Civilization* (1934), he launched the magazine *The Reconstructionist* in collaboration with his closest associates, of whom Milton Steinberg, Eugene *Kohn, and Kaplan's son-in-law, Ira *Eisenstein, formed the nucleus. In 1941 the *New Haggadah* and *A Guide to Jewish Ritual* were published. In the *Guide*, ritual was viewed not as law but a means to group survival and the spiritual growth of the individual Jew. The individual was to be the arbiter of which rituals or folkways would be followed, though when making such choices, a balance between one's own needs and those of the group was optimal. Preserving the integrity of the tradition, while being responsive to contemporary needs, was fundamental.

In 1945 the Reconstructionist Sabbath Prayer Book appeared, which resulted in a ban (*ḥerem*) against Kaplan by the Agudat ha-Rabbonim, a small Orthodox association, although such an attempt was largely ignored. But several of Kaplan's colleagues on the faculty of the Jewish Theological Seminary published an adverse "statement of opinion" (*gillui da'at*) in the Hebrew publication *Hadoar*. In accordance with Kaplan's ideology, the prayerbook excised references to the Jews as the "chosen people," and to such concepts as God's revelation of the Torah to Moses, the parting of the Red Sea, and belief in the coming of a personal Messiah. Some passages of the traditional prayerbook were retained despite Kaplan's rejection of the concepts which lay behind them. In such cases the editors suggested to the reader how the passages were to be understood. Thus, prayers for the restoration of Israel were retained, but readers were told this should not be construed as the return of all Jews to Palestine. Kaplan was a Zionist of the American school, ardent in his support for the colonization of Palestine, but opposed to concepts implying the "negation of the Diaspora" and to emphasis on the necessity of *aliyah*. The entire second half of the prayerbook contained a major innovation for the time: supplementary readings intended to allow for variety in the structure of weekly services.

Kaplan's greatest success was in his impact on Jewish educators, social workers, and rabbis, especially students of the Jewish Theological Seminary, where he taught from 1909 to 1963. Because he himself preferred to think of Reconstructionism as a school of thought rather than a separate movement, and because he was resistant to further dividing the Jewish community, Kaplan's followers were constrained from building on his intellectual and liturgical efforts. Only with the establishment in 1968 of the Reconstructionist Rabbinical College (RRC) in Philadelphia did Kaplan finally give his blessing to the development of Reconstructionism as an independent denomination. Ira Eisenstein, who had been Kaplan's closest collaborator, and had served as the editor of *The Reconstructionist* magazine since the 1940s, became the first president of the RRC, serving until his retirement in 1981. Without Eisenstein's dedication to the creation of the RRC, Kaplan's legacy would have been one primarily of ideas, and not of institutions.

Once Reconstructionism began to train its own rabbinic leaders, the movement began to grow, slowly at first, but then in the 1980s and 1990s, the number of affiliated Reconstructionist congregations and havurot grew rapidly. From ten affiliates in 1968, the movement counted 105 members of the Jewish Reconstructionist Federation (JRF) in 2005. As of 2005, the RRC had graduated 265 rabbis who served in congregations, agencies, schools, on campuses and in chaplaincy settings, and as writers, lecturers and teachers, so that the influence of Reconstructionism continued to be disproportionate to the size of the movement.

In the 1990s, the Reconstructionist movement issued a new series of prayerbooks and a new *Haggadah*. This second generation of Reconstructionist liturgy was unique in being the work of an editorial committee comprised of rabbis, academics, and laypeople, and in reflecting the contributions of many of the graduates of the RRC, who were also rapidly moving into positions of leadership on the faculty and administration of the RRC, the staff of the JRF, and of the Reconstructionist Rabbinical Association (RRA, established in 1974). In 1996 the RRA published the first Reconstructionist rabbi's manual.

A new magazine, *Reconstructionism Today,* was established in 1994. In 2005, *The Reconstructionist,* now a journal, published its 70th anniversary issue. The initial publication of a projected three-volume *Reconstructionist Guide to Jewish Practice* appeared in 2000. In 2003, a Reconstructionist youth movement, No'ar Hadash, was established. That same year, the first Reconstructionist summer camp opened (Camp JRF); in 2005, the camp purchased a permanent home in the Pocono mountains in Pennsylvania, which will also serve as a year-round conference and retreat center for the movement.

After Kaplan and Eisenstein, the most important and influential leader of the Reconstructionist movement has been David *Teutsch, who served as vice president of the Jewish Reconstructionist Foundation (1980–82), executive vice president of the Federation of Reconstructionist Congregations and Havurot (1982–86), president of the Reconstructionist Rabbinical College (1993–2002), editor-in-chief of the *Kol Haneshamah* prayerbook series (1989–2002), and director of the Center for Jewish Ethics at the RRC (2002–).

The intellectual history of the Reconstructionist movement came full circle with the publication in 2002 of the first volume of excerpts from the daily journal kept by Kaplan from 1913 until the late 1970s. Edited by Kaplan's biographer, Mel Scult, the journals helped to bring to a new generation of Reconstructionists and to all interested in the history of American Judaism in the 20th-century, the insights of the founder of Reconstructionism as he worked out the ideas, principles, and positions that would become Reconstructionist Judaism.

BIBLIOGRAPHY: R.T. Alpert and J.J. Staub, *Exploring Judaism: a Reconstructionist Approach* (2000); E.S. Goldsmith, M. Scult, and R.M. Seltzer (eds.), *The American Judaism of Mordecai M. Kaplan* (1990); *Communings of the Spirit: The Journals of Mordecai M. Kaplan, 1913–1934* (2001); M. Scult, *Judaism Faces the Twentieth Century: A Biography of Mordecai M. Kaplan* (1993); I. Eisenstein, *Reconstructing Judaism: An Autobiography* (1986).

[Richard Hirsch (2nd ed.)]

RECONSTRUCTIONIST RABBINICAL COLLEGE. The Reconstructionist Rabbinical College (RRC) was founded in 1968 in Philadelphia to carry on the ideals of the founder of Reconstructionist Judaism, Rabbi Mordecai *Kaplan. The decision to open the school was made by the lay-led organization of the movement, the Federation of Reconstructionist Congregations and Havurot (today the Jewish Reconstructionist Federation) meeting in Montreal in June 1967. Kaplan previously had resisted establishing a seminary that would mark Reconstructionism as a denomination rather than a school of thought. He maintained a life-long allegiance to the Jewish Theological Seminary where he taught for decades. However Reconstructionist congregations, insufficiently served by Reform and Conservative rabbis, pushed Rabbi Ira Eisenstein and lay leaders to make this decision.

Eisenstein became the RRC's first president. The college included two unique features. Reflecting Kaplan's vision of living in two civilizations, students were to pursue doctoral studies in religion simultaneously at a secular university. (However this dual-studies program would later be dropped.) Second, the curriculum would be based on Kaplan's concept of Judaism as an evolving Jewish civilization, studying each period sequentially and integrating history and literature from each time period. The five-year rabbinic curriculum devotes a year each to the biblical, rabbinic, medieval, modern, and contemporary periods. Open to both men and women, from the beginning RRC included faculty from diverse Jewish backgrounds.

The college opened in September 1968 in Philadelphia near Temple University, as the college was to collaborate with the Temple religion department and provide access to other graduate programs. Given the existence of only a handful of Reconstructionist congregations, for many students their first exposure to the movement in practice came as students. In 1974, the second graduating class included Sandy Eisenberg Sasso, the second woman rabbi in the United States.

In 1984 the college moved from its inner-city location to its current home in a former mansion in suburban Wyncote. Around that time, the college leadership wanted to enrich the curriculum and increase the Hebrew level of students. The number of RRC courses increased, including courses by visiting non-Jewish scholars. In 1983 RRC became the first rabbinical seminary to officially admit openly gay students. A *mekhinah* (preparatory) year for some students was also added. The college continued to expand in the late 1980s as faculty and student enrollment significantly increased, and the Israel study program expanded. The college received full academic accreditation in 1990.

In the 1990s and early 2000s the college strengthened its financial base and expanded its programs, publications, and facilities. Cantorial studies and a masters program in Jewish studies were added. Three academic centers were established to support research, publications, and education in the wider community: Jewish ethics; Kolot, a center on Jewish women's and gender studies; and Hiddur, a center on aging.

By 2005, RRC had graduated 283 rabbis and two cantors. Of these, 153 were male and 132 were female. Enrollment in 2005 was 76 rabbinical students, two cantorial students, and two masters' candidates. RRC publishes the *Reconstructionist* journal (1935–).

BIBLIOGRAPHY: M. Kaplan, "Why a Reconstructionist Rabbinical College?" in: *Reconstructionist*, 35:14 (Jan. 2, 1970); R. Alpert, "The Making of American Rabbis: Reconstructionist Rabbis," in: *EJ Yearbook* 1983–85; D. Teutsch, "Rabbis for the 21st Century," in: *Sh'ma* (January 2003).

[Robert P. Tabak (2nd ed)]

RECORDS, PHONOGRAPH. The earliest "talking machine" was patented by Thomas A. Edison in 1878 as a vertical cylinder device. In 1887 Emile *Berliner produced a lateral flat disc mechanism, bringing the disc "gramophone" into competition with the cylinder "phonograph." By 1891 recordings were introduced to public entertainment as coin-in-slot machines, and soon included some Jewish monologues, skits, and songs.

One of the most widespread Jewish subjects on recordings was cantorial music. Gershon *Sirota was the first cantor to record liturgicals commercially. He was widely criticized because recordings were played in cabarets and on the Sabbath. Then Zavel *Kwartin recorded and other cantors followed in a "golden cantorial age." In the 1920s such favorites as Mordecai *Hershman, David *Roitman, and Berele *Chagy were presented on discs and cylinders. Cantor Josef (Yossele) *Rosenblatt put 82 different liturgical selections on 10 labels. Since World War II revival of interest in European-style cantorials has resulted in re-pressings and reissues of old liturgical performances, as well as recordings of modern cantors such as Moshe *Koussevitzky and Leib *Glantz, and the cantorial records of such prominent concert and opera artists as Jan *Peerce and Richard Tucker. In the U.S. congregations have honored their own cantor with a recording issue of his performances. In the 1960s recordings of the devotional music of ḥasidic groups, such as the Lubavitcher, Modzhitzer, and Gerer, on their own labels or Jewish companies, added to the number of Jewish liturgical recordings.

Theatricals

Edison cylinders early captured such voices as the Yiddish artist Madame Regina Prager (1874–1949) and the Jewish entertainer Sophie *Tucker. Among the Jewish performances early in this century on single-side small discs were a folk melody *Min ha-Meẓar* and a popular ditty *Kum Yisrulik, Kum Aheym*. Shalom Aleichem read his works for cylinders, and the comic monologuist, Ikey Eisenstein, was a great favorite on discs. Especially in the U.S. dance music recordings sold well, particularly of Jewish wedding *freylekhs, shers, kazatskis*, and *horas*. By the end of World War I every recording company had a roster of all types of Jewish performers. With the rise of radio in the 1920s, records dropped in sales. Jewish records especially lost their audiences with the changing tastes of the U.S. Jewish public for "Anglicized" entertainment and with the appearance of Jewish "stars" on the general stage, in radio, and "talking pictures." Some recordings include Yiddish theatrical personalities of the era between the two world wars, such as Joseph Rumshinsky (1881–1956), Aaron Lebedeff (1873–1960), Ludwig Satz (1891–1944), Moishe Oysher (1907–1958), and Menasha Skulnick (1892–1970). The aftermath of the Holocaust in Europe and the establishment of the State of Israel stimulated wider interest for popular performances of Yiddish and Hebrew folk music. Prominent among recorders of this postwar Jewish expression have been the actor-singer Theodore Bikel, the ḥasidic performer Shlomo Carlebach, the Israel entertainer Shoshana Damari, and the Yiddish actress Molly Picon. With the rise of the "youth market" in the 1960s, such phenomena as folk-rock liturgicals and rock-ballads in Hebrew with electronic instrumentation have appeared in the U.S. and Israel.

At the turn of the century, in St. Petersburg, Russia, the Jewish proprietor of Rappaport's "listening shop" encouraged and assisted his supplier of discs to present in 1902 a roster of higher quality selections on a special "red seal" label. The entire industry followed over the next decade with "quality labels" on larger double-side discs, upon which were available the performance of concert artists, many of them Jewish. In the worldwide growth of better quality recordings over the decades to the 1970s, Jewish participation has been outstanding. In 1969 the *Service Technique pour l'Education* (STE) of the Alliance Israélite Universelle in Paris published a selective listing of all types of Jewish recordings available on the Continent at the time.

Folk Music

Use of cylinder recording for collection of Jewish folk materials was made at the turn of this century by collectors in Russia. Before World War I the Jewish musicologist Abraham Ẓevi *Idelsohn made use of recording apparatus in assembling liturgical materials in Jerusalem for his 10-volume *Thesaurus of Hebrew-Oriental Melodies*. Such scholars in Israel and America as Edith *Gerson-Kiwi and Johanna *Spector used recording equipment in their work among groups in the field.

Jewish Recording Companies

By 1920 there were about 30 different companies each issuing several labels, all of which had some Jewish materials in addition to rosters of Jewish performers. The decade of the 1920s was an era of consolidation into "big business" concerns in the recording industry, as well as much technological expansion. The oldest continually operating record shop into 1971 has been the Metro Music Shop, which was established in 1918 on the Lower East Side of Manhattan in the Yiddish theatrical area of Second Avenue by Henry Lefkowitch (1892–1959), a composer and publisher of Jewish music. A number of specifically Jewish recording companies have been formed since World War II. In 1939 Moses Asch (d. 1986) formed Asch Record Company to supply Jewish recordings for the all-Jewish radio station WEVD in New York. Expanded to Ethnic-Folkways Records in 1947, its scope of Jewish materials was broadened to include recordings of Sephardim, Beta Israel, Yemenites, and other Oriental Jewish groups, much of it based on field collections by researchers, in addition to folk music in Yiddish and Hebrew Zionist songs. Formed after the war, Banner Records has made a specialty of Jewish variety and theatrical presentations by more recent artists. Ḥasidic music has been issued by smaller companies as well as by the larger Jewish companies. Menorah Records features recordings for children, holiday albums, and other educational releases. Since 1947, Tikva Records has manufactured and distributed a wide variety with an active market catalog of about 130 different issues. It has been especially successful in presenting Jewish folk dance records with instructions for the performances of the dances. In 1962 Greater Recording Company was formed to locate and re-issue on long-playing records rare Jewish performances done originally in the early decades of this century on cylinders and discs. Some recent performances of ḥasidic music and cantorials are included in its roster. Benedict Stambler (1903–1967) formed Collectors Record Guild and began in 1955 to re-press for commercial sale many of the old Jewish recordings from his large personal collection. He also produced new ḥasidic recordings. In 1971 the Stambler collection of recorded Jewish music, comprising 4,000 different selections, was donated to the Rogers and Hammerstein Archives of Recorded Sound, housed in the New York Public Library at Lincoln Center. This collection, recorded on approximately 150 labels and starting with materials from 1902, is available for study on the library premises. Among the leading Israel recording companies were Hed Arẓi, for light Israel entertainers and folk ensembles; Ha-Taklit, with folk music presentations; Israeli Music Foundation, for serious compositions as well as folk dances; and CBS-Israel, which produced light popular, classical, musical and drama, educational material, and "small disc specials" for children. All went over to compact disks in the 1990s.

See also *Music: Archives and Important Collections of Jewish Music.

BIBLIOGRAPHY: R. Gelatt, *Fabulous Phonograph: From Edison to Stereo* (1966²); S. Rosenblatt, *Yossele Rosenblatt* (1954); Catalogs of: Folkways, Banner, Tikva, Menorah, Greater Recording, Collectors Record Guild, CBS, Hed Arẓi, Ha-Taklit; *Schwann Record and Tape Guide* (1971–); Alliance Israélite Universelle, *Service Technique pour l'Education*, Catalogs (1961; 1969).

[Irene Heskes]

REDEMPTION, salvation from the states or circumstances that destroy the value of human existence or human existence itself. The word "redeemer" and its related terms "redeem" and "redemption" appear in the Bible some 130 times and are derived from two Hebrew roots, *pdh* (פדה) and *g'l* (גאל). Though used to describe divine activity as well, they arose in ordinary human affairs and it is in this context in which they must first be understood. *Pdh* is the more general of the two, with cognates of related meaning in Akkadian, Arabic, and Ethiopic. It belongs to the domain of commercial law, and refers to the payment of an equivalent for what is to be released or secured. The verb *pdh*, unlike *g'l*, indicates nothing about the relation of the agent to the object of redemption, which in the Bible is always either a person or another living being. Its usage does not differ in cultic activity from that of a normal commercial transaction. In both cases a person or an animal is released in return for money or an acceptable replacement (cf. Ex. 13:13; 34:20; Lev. 27:27; I Sam. 14:45 with Ex. 21:7–8; Lev. 19:20; Job 6:23). *G'l* is more restricted in usage and does not appear to have cognates in other Semitic languages. It is connected with family law and reflects the Israelite conception of the importance of preserving the solidarity of the clan. The *go'el* ("redeemer") is the next of kin who acts to maintain the vitality of his extended family group by preventing any breaches from occurring in it. Thus, he acquires the alienated property of his kinsman (Lev. 25:25) or purchases it when it is in danger of being lost to a stranger (cf. Jer. 32:6ff.). Possibly, too, he is required to support the widow of his next of kin in the event of her being dependent on this estate for her livelihood (cf. Ruth 4:4ff.). In any event, he redeems a clansman who has been reduced to slavery by poverty (Lev. 25:47ff.), and avenges his blood when it has been shed (cf., e.g., Num. 35:17–19). Whether he actually was duty bound to perform these acts was contested by early rabbinic authorities (cf. Kid. 21a), but it seems likely that he was expected to do so, unless there was a good reason to the contrary (cf. Ruth 4:6).

When applied to divine activity, a slight shift occurs in the use of both these terms. Thus, *pdh* takes on the general meaning of "deliver" and does not involve the notion of the payment of an equivalent. God is, after all, the Lord of the universe and everything belongs to Him. Indeed the only place in Scripture when the possibility of such an exchange is even suggested is obviously rhetorical and *pdh* is not used (cf. Isa. 43:3–4). God's purpose is not to retain the right of possession, but to liberate people, both individuals and groups, from their woes (cf. II Sam. 4:9; I Kings 1:29), including bondage (e.g., Deut. 7:8; 13:6), oppression (e.g., Isa. 1:27; Ps. 119:134), and death (e.g., Hos. 13:14; Ps. 49:16). In the Torah, the Deuteronomist uses *pdh* to characterize God's acts at the time of the Exodus as redemptive (e.g., Deut. 9:26; 15:15; 21:8; 24:18). This usage is extended by later writers to describe Israel's eschatological redemption as well (cf., e.g., Isa. 1:27; 35:10; Jer. 31:11) and even, on one occasion, its deliverance from its sins (Ps. 130:8). Though *g'l*, like *pdh*, loses its strictly juridical connotation when describing divine activity, and takes on the meaning of "deliver" pure and simple (cf., e.g., Gen. 48:16), it still does retain some of its original overtones even when referred to God. Thus, Proverbs (23:10–11) speaks of God as the *go'el* of ("the next of kin," duty bound to protect) orphans, and Job similarly believes Him to be the *go'el* of the persecuted (19:25; cf. 19:21–22). In the same spirit the Psalmist calls Him the "father of orphans, defender of widows" (68:6). What better way, then, for the prophet to reassure his people that God has a special reason to redeem them, for He is their *go'el* (Isa. 41:14; 43:14; 44:6, 24; 47:4; 48:17, etc.) and an intimate relationship exists between Him and them (41:89; 43:10, 20; 44:1–2; 45:4; 54:10; 55:3). It must be no accident also that the prophet uses *pdh* only twice (50:2; 51:11) and in both instances it appears in earlier expressions that concern the Exodus. For, though the two terms were used interchangeably when separated from their life context, the poet was aware of their broader connotations and exploited them to create a more receptive mood for his message. Possibly, too, he wanted to distinguish between the earlier redemption from Egypt and the later one to come, by using a term for the latter that had only infrequently been associated with the Exodus (e.g., Ex. 6:6; 15:13).

While the king is described as a deliverer of the poor in a royal Psalm (72:4, 14), and Ezekiel prophesies that David will be established as the shepherd of God's flock (34:23), the national hope for redemption was centered on God. Only He – not the messianic king or other divine being – was the Redeemer. And though some biblical passages stipulated that His deliverance is conditional upon repentance, many simply state that He Himself would take the initiative because of His boundless love (e.g., Isa. 54:8) and passionate concern for justice (cf., e.g., Isa. 59:15–20). An end would come to all pain and suffering, and Israel would be restored to its land to live in safety, protected by an everlasting covenant and the Divine Presence (Jer. 32:37–44; cf. Ezek. 11:17–21). Israel's Redeemer would then be manifest through His great acts of redemption and "the redeemed of the Lord" give thanks to him (Ps. 107:1–2).

[Donald Daniel Leslie]

Dead Sea Sect

The idea of redemption had a special character among sects in the Judean desert. Although the word *ge'ullah* itself has not yet been found in their works, nor does the root *ga'al* appear there, yet a redemptive function was at the very heart of the beliefs of the sect, which in their view was the remnant of Israel of whom the prophets had spoken. They are "the basis for that which God chose. He appointed them as a permanent estate and will possess them the portion of the holy ones" (Manual of Discipline, 11:6–7; cf. Col. 1:12). Entry into the sect is an act of divine grace that atones for all iniquities and purifies the associate "from human impurity and the sin of men" (*ibid.*, 11:14). Despite this the sect believed also in the perfect redemption of the end of time. "And then God with His truth will clarify all the deeds of a man… to purify him with a holy spirit of truth free of any abomination of falsehood" (*ibid.*, 2:20–22, cf. Mark 1:8). In keeping with the sect's regard of itself as the subject of redemption, the Messiah served merely a minor role in their religious system.

In the Talmud

While the Bible uses both *padah* and *ga'al* for redemption, the Talmud applies *padah* to ransom (see *Ransom) and *ga'al* to redemption. The sages know nothing of a miraculous redemption of the soul by external means. There is no failing in man, whether collectively or as an individual, which requires special divine intervention and which cannot be remedied, with the guidance of the Torah, by man himself. As a result, the term *ge'ullah* is applied almost exclusively to national redemption, and became a synonym for national freedom. This idea of national freedom from subjection to other states is the main element in the yearnings of the people for the redemption of Israel, and it became even more pronounced during the period of Roman domination. Redemption is dependent upon repentance and good deeds (Shab. 118b; Yoma 86b; BB 10b; Sanh. 97b), and all attempts to calculate the exact date of the redemption by means of transcendental or cosmic factors were opposed, at times even sharply, even though in all eras such calculators – for understandable psychological reasons – were never wanting (Sanh. 97b). Despite the prominence of the image of the Messiah as a redeemer, his role in the process of redemption is no different from those of Moses and the other redeemers in the past; he is merely an instrument in the hands of God. The view is also found that in contrast to past redemptions that were effected by human agency and were therefore only temporary redemptions, the final redemption will be accomplished by God Himself and will be eternal (Mid. Ps. to 31:2).

A quasi-transcendental and mystical element was introduced into the concept of redemption with the notion that it served the "needs of the Most High," since "wherever [Israel] was exiled the Divine Presence was exiled with them" (Sif. Num. 161; Meg. 29a). God therefore, so to speak, redeems Himself with the redemption (Mekh. Bo 14). There are contradictory statements and inconsistent popular aggadic descriptions about the redemption. At one extreme is found the view that even proselytes will not be accepted in the time of the Messiah (Yev. 24b) – a saying that is probably to be explained by the unfortunate personal experience of its author. At the other are the many descriptions of the redemption of Israel bringing with it the redemption of the world (Song R. 2:2, no. 3); the gentiles will become proselytes and all will call on the name of the Lord (cf. Tosef., Ber. 7:2); God himself will bring all of them "beneath the wings of the Divine Presence" (Tanḥ. B., Gen. 108).

[David Flusser]

Medieval Philosophy

As in the biblical and talmudic systems that preceded them, the medieval philosophers generally regarded man's finite condition as the primary state from which he required redemption. The state of finiteness was not the result of human action or sin, but a cosmic circumstance ultimately due to the nature of creation. The creation of the universe is attributed ultimately by almost all medieval Jewish philosophers to the goodness and grace of God, yet despite the divine goodness, man was so formed that he is finite, a state in which he is subject to despair and death, spiritual and physical annihilation. Open thus to annihilation, man stands in need of redemption. Owing to the divine goodness, redemption is available to him, but he must participate in the redemptive process. If he adheres to true beliefs and performs right actions, he is accounted righteous and worthy of redemption, otherwise he is a sinner and condemned either to eternal torment or physical annihilation. Hence sin does not produce the unsaved state, as does original sin, for example, in the Christian view; sin rather serves to prevent the redemption of man from the spiritual or physical consequences of his finite condition.

Despite broad agreement among the medieval Jewish philosophers on the general understanding of redemption, significant differences appear among them in their various individual soteriologies. Two major approaches, which may be termed traditional supernaturalism and philosophic naturalism, can be distinguished. The former retains the basic features of talmudic soteriology, while the latter is strongly influenced by Aristotelian and Neoplatonic concepts. Saadiah *Gaon (*Book of Beliefs and Opinions*), whose view is representative of traditional supernaturalism, states the position this way. God created the world out of his goodness. Man, though created finite, is the ultimate purpose of creation. God intended from the beginning that man should attain redemption from his finite condition. To enable man to merit such redemption, God revealed to him His will through Moses at Sinai. Thus man could come to know the divine commandments and by obedience to them earn salvation. Although the Jews are the chosen of God, salvation is attained by the righteous of all peoples. There are two major stages of redemption, both of which will arise miraculously: the Messianic Age and the world to come. In the Messianic Age the Jewish people will be restored to the Land of Israel and the first of two resurrections will occur, that of the righteous Jews. When the Messianic Age ends, the world to come will emerge, then all the dead will be resurrected and final judgment rendered. All who ever lived will now be infinite in time, the righteous enjoying eternal reward and the wicked eternal punishment. Included among those who subscribe to the view of traditional supernaturalism are Judah *Halevi (*Kuzari*), Ḥasdai *Crescas (*Or Adonai*), and Joseph *Albo (*Sefer ha-Ikkarim*).

*Maimonides (*Guide of the Perplexed*) is the foremost exponent of a philosophic, naturalistic soteriology among the medieval Jews. In Maimonides' view, the creation of the world is also the result of God's goodness, but the universe was not created for the sake of man nor is he the direct creation of the Godhead. The universe comes from God through a successive series of emanations in the course of which the world of man (sublunar world) and man himself are created out of matter. All that is formed of matter is necessarily finite. Hence matter is the principle of human finity, and redemption is attained, therefore, by man overcoming his material nature. This is accomplished naturally, by the actualization of the hylic intellect to an acquired intellect through metaphysical and scientific studies. The acquired intellect enables man to gain ascendancy over his material desires during the life of his body, and at the time of death gives him immortality, since the acquired intellect exists separate from the body and is unaffected by its states or finity. Among those who subscribe to such a view of redemption are Solomon ibn *Gabirol (*Mekor Ḥayyim*), Abraham ibn *Ezra, and Levi b. *Gershom (*Milḥamot Adonai*). The Christian notion that mankind requires redemption owing to the guilt of original sin, which is incurred by every person as a consequence of Adam's disobedience in Eden, is completely foreign to the medieval Jewish thinkers. Judah Halevi manifests the spirit of the Jewish position when he presents Adam as a paradigm of religious excellence whose spiritual genius was ultimately inherited by the Jews, the chosen people.

[Alvin J. Reines]

In the Kabbalah

The kabbalists make no additions to the historic aspects of the doctrine of redemption as developed in rabbinic tradition. Their original contribution to this concept is bound up with its inner "hidden" aspect. As in all things, there is an inner aspect or "mystery" in the course of redemption, which is intimated and expressed in a symbolic manner. The basic tenet of their outlook is derived from the verse "On that day the Lord shall be One and his Name One" (Zech. 14:9), which was often interpreted in the *Zohar as indicating the lack of perfection in the unity of God during the time of exile. As long as iniquity has caused a fissure in the mystery of the Godhead, i.e., between His *Sefirot* which constitute the totality of His manifestation to created beings, His Name is not one; for the "Name" is, in the opinion of the kabbalists, the symbol of the Divine *Sefirot* when they are joined in complete unity. The exile is indicative of a state of creation in which this unity has, "so to speak," become impaired. (Many kabbalists took care always to add the qualifying phrase "so to speak" in order to intimate the symbolic character of their daring expressions.) Consequently, redemption is bound up with a certain change in the regulating mechanism at the heart of creation: If exile is expressed, in the language of symbols, as a temporary separation between the king and the queen, between God and His *Shekhinah*, so that their union is not perfect and continuous, then redemption will be expressed in restoration of this uninterrupted union. The return of the people of Israel to its land at the time of redemption symbolizes the inner process of the return of the "Congregation of Israel" or the *Shekhinah* ("the Matron") to a continuous attachment to her husband. The secret meaning of the messianic redemption was already defined in this way by the Gerona school of Kabbalah (*Naḥmanides and his colleagues), and this definition was accepted by the author of the Zohar. Views more far-reaching than this were expressed in the *Ra'aya Meheimna* and the *Tikkunei Zohar*, where a new set of symbols appears. During exile, the world is conducted in accordance with the mystery of the "Tree of Knowledge of Good and Evil" from which Adam and Eve ate and brought sin and separation upon the world; redemption will reveal a conduct of the world in accordance with the mystery of the "Tree of Life." These two trees were once of one root, but were separated by the original sin of Adam, as were "the king and the matron" in the earlier symbolism. Consequently, during the exile there are separate spheres of good and evil, holiness and impurity, etc., but at the time of redemption the pure spiritual essence of all the worlds will become manifest. The Divine Life will spread to every sphere and this will cause a deep change in the state of the entire creation. In this view the kabbalists are aligned with those who regard redemption as a metaphysical concept. It is not only the oppression of Israel by the nations of the world which distinguishes exile and redemption, but also a deep and even utopian change in the structure of creation.

In Lurianic Kabbalah a new element is added to these ideas which relates redemption and exile not only to original sin, but also to the inner structure of every act of creation and to situations and events in the world of emanation. The "breaking of the vessels" (see *Kabbalah) caused, in all the worlds, a state which has in it something of a general exile of all creation, a disturbance in the harmony destined for the worlds. The disturbance, however, was inevitable, and the entire substance of the process of creation in all its manifestations, including the history and mission of the people of Israel within it, are nothing but stages through which this harmony will be restored and achieve the perfection for which it was destined from the beginning. Redemption is here defined as the manifestation of that state in which the breaking of the vessels is completely "mended." Every other manifestation of redemption serves only as symbol of this fundamental meaning.

An important problem in the doctrine of redemption arose regarding the role of the Jew in bringing it about. There were two contradictory opinions on this point.

(1) Essentially, redemption will come miraculously, and flesh and blood creatures shall have no part in bringing it about: this is the opinion of the majority of the Spanish kabbalists.

(2) Redemption is no more than the external manifestation of the inner state of *tikkun* ("restitution") which depends on the deeds of Israel and a realization of the way of life which the Kabbalah preaches. The fact of *tikkun* is not something which depends on a miracle, but rather on human action.

According to the first view, the Messiah's coming will not bear any essential relationship to men's deeds; according to the second view, his coming is conditional upon the accomplishment of the task of Israel in the "*tikkun* of the world." According to this latter view, there is a human and historical preparation for redemption and the Messiah will come automatically if this preparation is completed. This belief is widespread among the disciples of Isaac *Luria, and it follows logically from the basic assumptions of Lurianic Kabbalah. Only after the triumph of these ideas had brought about the deep historical crisis of Shabbateanism did the Ḥasidic doctrine appear, which distinguished between "general redemption" (of the people of Israel; redemption in its literal meaning) and "individual redemption" (the mystical redemption of the soul, which has no messianic connotation). This distinction is intended to limit human initiative to the realm of individual redemption and make general redemption once again dependent solely on the power of God. This distinction removed the dangerous and utopian sting contained in the Lurianic view of redemption.

[Gershom Scholem]

Modern Jewish Thought

In modern Jewish thought redemption has been viewed as referring to the eventual triumph of good over evil, to the striving of individuals to self-fulfillment, to the achievement of social reforms, and also in terms of the reestablishment of a sovereign Jewish state. Hermann *Cohen, for example, regarded redemption as man's conquering his impulse to sin. The idea of God is that which ensures the eternal existence of mankind as a whole in order that His program for the future ethical world can become real. The individual who commits sin feels that he has strayed from the rest of mankind and detracted from the common goal, and that he must be redeemed back to humanity. God then becomes the indicator of individual man's triumph over sin (cf. *Der Begriff der Religion im System der Philosophie* (1915), 64). This conception of God the Redeemer is an aid to the individual in helping him to repent. The individual who contemplates this relationship with God may be led to improve his character.

Other thinkers who deal with redemption as the triumph over evil are Martin *Buber and A.J. *Heschel. Buber speaks of redemption as the eradication of man-caused evil in human history. The means of achieving this is to sanctify daily life in order to redeem evil. This sanctification comes about in the greater context of the encounter of man and God, "Who enters into a direct relation with us men in creative, revealing, and redeeming acts, and thus makes it possible for us to enter into a direct relation with him" (*I and Thou* (1958^2), 135). This encounter is characterized by a turning away from evil and toward God. In addition God comes toward us "The Thou meets me through grace – it is not found by seeking" (*ibid.*, 11) – and when this grace of His becomes manifest – redemption begins. Repentance is the spur to the attitude of redemption, but is not to be confused with it. Buber saw in Ḥasidic teaching the kernel of this doctrine of redeeming evil. "If you direct the undiminished power of your fervor to God's world-destiny… you will bring about the union between God and *Shekhinah*, eternity and time… All that is necessary is to have a soul united within itself and indivisibly directed to its divine goal. The world in which you live affords you that association with God, which will redeem you and whatever divine aspect of the world you have been entrusted with" (*Tales of the Ḥasidim; the Early Masters* (1947), 4). Heschel also speaks in these terms: "The world is in need of redemption, but the redemption must not be expected to happen as an act of sheer grace. Man's task is to make the world worthy of redemption. His faith and his works are preparation for ultimate redemption" (*God in Search of Man* (1959), 380). In the manner of Ḥasidic thought Heschel sees man's task in preparing the world for redemption as separating evil from good. "All of history is a sphere where good is mixed with evil. The supreme task of man, his share in redeeming the work of creation, consists in an effort to separate good from evil and evil from good. Since evil can only exist parasitically on good, it will cease to be when that separation will be accomplished. Redemption, therefore, is contingent upon the separation of good and evil" (*The Insecurity of Freedom* (1966), 135). Heschel does not emphasize the state of actual redemption but the task of separating good and evil – which leads to redemption.

For Franz *Rosenzweig, redemption is the process by which the world and man are united in one perfect harmony with God – and thereby partake of God's eternity. Rosenzweig dealt with the relationship between God, man, and the world pointing to certain key words as standing for those relationships. The words are creation (God – world), revelation (God – man), and redemption (man – world). Traditionally, philosophy held that these three items had basically one being – that all existence was a unity. For Rosenzweig that conception, a basic premise of much of Western philosophy, was the conclusion of his philosophy. Man, God, and the world have three separate beings which unite into one only under the force of redemption. The revelation of God to man implies God's love. Man's feeling of God's love "redeems" man from his state of isolation and indeed from the supreme form of isolation – death, and its concomitant fear. This love also awakens the response of love in man, and the binding together of man and God in love is the first step toward redemption of the world for the love spreads and is applied to other men. This first redemption applies to man. Rosenzweig also held that the world had a special spiritual relationship to God and that it, too, could be redeemed. In the second stage God acts to unite man and the world. When this is achieved God, too, is redeemed. "For God is not only the redeemer but also the redeemed. In this redemption God redeems the world by the means of man and redeems man by the means of the world. He also redeems Himself" (*Kokhav ha-Ge'ulllah* (1970), 267). "For then true unity is created – God-man-world. Eternity enters into being and death is pushed off and the living become immortals in eternal praise of redemption" (*ibid.*, 280).

Mordecai *Kaplan uses the term salvation instead of redemption. He links redemption with the concept of the other world and asserts that until modern times the Jewish concept of salvation was other-worldly. Kaplan maintains that it is impossible in modern times to continue this belief and that we must see salvation in terms of this world. Furthermore Kaplan speaks of God as "the power that makes for salvation," i.e., an inherent force in the universe which enables man to achieve salvation. He points out that salvation must have both a personal and social significance. "In its personal aspect it represents the faith in the possibility of achieving an integrated personality" (*The Meaning of God in Modern Jewish Religion* (1937), 53). Social salvation is the natural concomitant of personal salvation for "we cannot think of ourselves except in relation to something not ourselves" (*ibid.*)... Social salvation is "the pursuit of common ends in a manner which shall afford to each the maximum opportunity for creative self-expression" (*ibid.* 54). "Salvation must be conceived mainly as an objective of human action, not as a psychic compensation for human suffering" (*ibid.*) "Salvation means deliverance from those evils, external and internal, which prevent man from realizing his maximum potentialities. It is deliverance from frustration..." (*Questions Jews Ask* (1956), 126).

Joseph B. *Soloveichik, the modern Orthodox thinker, describes redemption in terms of faith and performance of *mitzvot*, but also includes the idea that the human capability of renewal and self-transformation manifests itself especially in times of human distress. Being redeemed is a mode of existence, not an attribute. "Even a hermit can live a redeemed life" (i.e., as a mode of existence, redemption is an individual thing and not dependent upon society. "The Lonely Man of Faith" in: *Tradition*, vol. 7, no. 2, Summer 1965). Furthermore redemption is a function of man's control over himself. "A redeemed life is ipso facto a disciplined life" (*ibid.*). As opposed to dignity which is man's triumph over nature and the feeling of success, redemption is when man is "overpowered by the creator of nature," and it is discovered in the "depth of crisis and failure" (*ibid.*, 23–24).

Zionist thought represents another aspect of modern Jewish thought about redemption. To the extent that Zionism was considered a messianic movement dealing with the redemption of the Jewish people, its theorists talked in terms of redemption. A. *Hertzberg characterizes Zionist thought by saying that classical Judaism saw redemption as a confrontation between the Jew and God, but Zionism "in its most revolutionary expression... is between the Jew and the nations of the earth" (*The Zionist Idea* (1959), 18). Religious Zionist thinkers saw redemption as at least beginning in temporal terms with the return of the Jews to Ereẓ Israel and the building of the land. Rabbi Y. *Alkalai writes "Redemption must come slowly. The land must, by degrees, be built up and prepared" (*ibid.*, 105). Some religious Zionists such as A.I. *Kook added another dimension to this idea: "The hope for the return to the Holy Land is the continuing source of the distinctive nature of Judaism. The hope for the redemption is the force that sustains Judaism in the Diaspora; the Judaism of Ereẓ Israel is the very redemption" (*ibid.*, 420). Redemption in Kook's thought thus becomes not only a physical reality by the return to Ereẓ Israel, but a metaphysical underpinning for Jewry everywhere. Even nonreligious Zionist thinkers, while not necessarily using the term redemption, spoke in messianic terms or expressed themselves by concepts traditionally connected with redemption. J. *Klatzkin for example states "Zionism pins its hopes, in one sense, on the general advance of civilization and its national faith is also a faith in man in general – faith in the power of the good and the beautiful" (*ibid.*, 327). Here the element of the triumph over evil and the advance of social good, topics connected with redemption, are assumed as an integral part of the Zionist hope.

[Michael J. Graetz]

BIBLIOGRAPHY: G.B. Gray, *Numbers* (ICC, 1903), 470–1; S.R. Driver, *Exodus* (1911), 43–44, 109; J. Pederson, in: ZAW, 49 (1931), 175; J.J. Stamm, *Erloesen und Vergeben im Alten Testament* (1940), 7–46; M. Burrows, in: JBL, 59 (1940), 445–54; N.H. Tur-Sinai, *Ha-Lashon ve-ha-Sefer*, 2 (1950), 290; L. Koehler, *Theologie des Alten Testaments* (1953^3), 225ff.; A.R. Johnson, in: VT *Supplement*, 1 (1953), 66–77; T. and D. Thomson, in: VT, 18 (1968), 98–99. IN KABBALAH: I. Tishby, *Torat ha-Ra ve-ha-Kelippah be-Kabbalat ha-ARI* (1942), 113–43; G. Scholem, *Ra'yon ha-Ge'ullah ba-Kabbalah* (1946); Scholem, Mysticism, index.

REDER, BERNARD (1897–1963), U.S. painter, printmaker. Born in Czernowitz, Bukovina, Austria, a center of Hasidic culture before WWII, Reder studied at the Academy of Fine Arts in Prague, after which he returned to his hometown to work as a carver of cemetery monuments while also pursuing stonecarving. In 1935, he returned to Prague, enjoying his first exhibition at the Manes Gallery. Reder moved to Paris in 1937, where he met the sculptor Aristide Maillol, even exhibiting at the prestigious Wildenstein Gallery in 1940. However, the Nazi occupation of France forced Reder to flee to Spain, passage to which Maillol secured for Reder and his wife. The Nazis destroyed the contents of Reder's studio. Sometime later, Reder traveled to Cuba, where he concentrated on woodcuts and drawings, such as the both haunting and whimsical woodcut *The Complaining Ravens* (1950). A recurring subject in Reder's art was that of musicians, such as the one depicted in the bronze sculpture *The Trumpeter* (1955). He settled in New York in 1943, where he enjoyed great success: he won a Guggenheim fellowship and exhibited at the Whitney Museum and the Philadelphia Museum of Art (1949). In 1954, Reder studied sculpture in Rome and Florence; two years later, he had a solo exhibition at Galleria d'arte Moderno l'Indiano. Reder attained American citizenship in 1948. The artist worked in both bronze and stone. For instance, the bronze sculpture *The Conquerer*, a work depicting a military figure astride a tiny horse balanced on a circular object, suggests to the viewer both the pompousness and precarious nature of leadership. As his career progressed, Reder moved from realism to a rhythmic abstraction, as expressed in the stone sculptures *Centaur's Head* and *The Fantastic Bird*. One of Reder's better-known sculptures is the bronze *Aaron with Tabernacle* (1959), now in the Israel Museum in Jerusalem. This large-scale sculpture combines biblical history, Jewish folklore, and references to mysticism and magic in a magisterial figure which seems rooted and blossoming like a tree. Reder was a recipient of a Ford Foundation Grant in 1960, and a year later the Whitney Museum presented a solo exhibition of his work. In 1969, the State of Israel gave Denmark a sculpture entitled *Wounded Woman*. Made by Reder, it is sited behind the Museum of Jewish Resistance, as a symbol of gratitude for Denmark's efforts on behalf of persecuted Jews during WWII. Reder's prints and sculptures have a wide range of subject matter, including figures, both human and fantastic, and subjects with Jewish themes, often infused with what many critics refer to as a baroque, Rabelaisian spirit. He also worked as an illustrator, fashioning woodcuts for such publications as *Yiddish Proverbs* by Hanan J. Ayalti (1949). His work is in the collections of the Art Institute of Chicago, the Brooklyn Museum, the Hofstra Museum, the Jewish Museum, New York, the National Gallery of Art, and the Whitney Museum.

BIBLIOGRAPHY: A. Kampf, *Jewish Experience in the Art of the Twentieth Century* (1984); C. Roth, *Jewish Art: An Illustrated History*, revised edition by Bezalel Narkiss (1971).

[Nancy Buchwald (2nd ed.)]

RED HEIFER (Heb. פָּרָה אֲדֻמָּה), the animal whose ashes were used in the ritual purification of persons and objects defiled by a corpse (Num. 19). While the English term heifer means a young cow that has not had a calf, the Bible (Num. 19:2) speaks simply of a cow (Heb. *parah*). The Bible prescribes that the red cow be without blemish (Heb. *temimah*), that it should have no defect (Heb. *mum*), and that it should never have been yoked (Num. 19:2). The first of these requirements applies also to burnt offerings (Lev. 1:3, 10), peace offerings (Lev. 3:1, 6), and sin offerings (Lev. 4:3). The second regulation, which applies to all sacrifices (Lev. 22:19, 21; Deut. 17:1), is explained in Leviticus 22:22. The third stipulation applies also to the calf whose neck is broken to atone for the blood-guilt of the unidentified manslayer (Deut. 21:3).

Unlike ordinary sacrifices, which could be slaughtered only at the entrance of the Tent of Meeting (Lev. 17:5), the red heifer was to be slaughtered outside the camp (Num. 19:3). Not slaughtered in the camp are likewise the scapegoat (Lev. 16:10), the calf whose neck is broken (Deut. 21:4), and the birds used in the purification of the recovered leper (Lev. 14:7). The red heifer was more like an ordinary sacrifice than these, however, in that some of its blood was sprinkled seven times toward the front of the Tent of Meeting (Num. 19:4). In the other two rites there was no sprinkling of blood at the sanctuary. The red heifer ritual resembled the purification of the recovered leper in that cedar wood, crimson stuff, and hyssop were used in the preparation of the purificatory substances in both rites. While it was the blood of a bird that was mixed with these in the purification of the leper, these were combined with the ashes of the red heifer in the purification of persons and objects defiled by a corpse. Like the bull used in the induction of Aaron and his sons (Ex. 29:14; Lev. 8:17), the bull for the sin offering of the anointed priest (Lev. 4:11), and the goat and the bull for the sin offering of the Day of Atonement (Lev. 16:27), the red heifer was burned outside the camp along with its flesh and dung. In the red heifer ritual the greater part of the blood as well was burned outside the camp (Num. 19:5). In all of these rituals the performance of certain acts outside the camp clearly indicates a degree of ritual impurity that somehow threatens the holiness of the sanctuary itself. If the scapegoat which assumed Israel's impurities had to be removed from the camp, and if the birds which revived the leper from his temporary symbolic death (cf. Ned. 64b) had to be subjected to the appropriate ritual outside the camp, it is logical that the ritual purification of those in contact with death itself, the source of the highest degree of ritual impurity (cf. Kel. 1:4), should be performed outside the camp. In the books of Numbers and Deuteronomy the Israelite community is often pictured as an armed camp. Wherever the camp is located God's Presence is found. The area outside the camp is the sphere of uncleanness to which lepers, gonorrheal persons, and those defiled by contact with the dead are sent (Num. 5:2), as are men who have had nocturnal emissions (Deut. 23:11 [10]). Excrement likewise was to be buried outside the camp (Deut. 23:14 [13]). The stoning to death of the man who gathered sticks on the Sabbath also took place outside the camp (Num. 15:35). The Book of Leviticus (Lev. 14:45) speaks of the domain of the unclean as "outside the town" rather than as "outside the camp" but there is no practical difference, since the camp of the wilderness period actually represents the towns of the settled period.

The law of the red heifer addressed to Moses and Aaron (Num. 19:1) prescribes that the slaughtering and burning of the animal be carried out by Eleazar (19:4), Aaron's heir apparent (after the death of his two older brothers; Lev. 10:1–3, 12). Some modern commentators suggest that Eleazar was given the role so as not to defile Aaron the high priest. The ashes were gathered by a ritually clean man (Num. 19:9) and placed outside the camp in a ritually pure place (cf. Lev. 6:4). The gatherer of the ashes could evidently be a layman as could also the slaughterer of a freewill offering (Lev. 1:5). Both the priest and the gatherer became unclean until evening, as did a person who carried the carcass of an animal from a species that is forbidden for food and as did a person who ate or carried the carcass of a permissible animal that was not properly slaughtered (Lev. 11:28, 39).

The ashes of the red heifer were combined with spring water (Heb. *mayim ḥayyim*) in a vessel (Num. 19:17) to produce a mixture called "water of lustration" (Heb. *me niddah*). The mixture was applied by dipping into it and sprinkling (19:18) on the third and seventh days after defilement (19:19). This defilement was acquired by touching a corpse, a grave, or a human bone, or by being under the same roof with any of these. That the priest, the gatherer of the ashes, the sprinkler (19:21), and the one who touched the water of lustration (19:22) became unclean until evening has been explained both as uncleanness attached to the handling of sacred objects and as contamination by association. The second explanation means that the red heifer caused uncleanness because of its association with death. The first explanation finds its analogy in the defiling of the hands by sacred scrolls (Yad. 3–4), while the latter has no analogue. In addition, the red heifer has not yet come into contact with the dead during the time of its preparation. Furthermore, the assumption that the red heifer defiles because of its association with human death ignores the distinction between the seven days of uncleanness consequent on contact with the dead (Num. 19:14) and the shorter period noted for the priest, the gatherer of the ashes, the lustrator, and the one who touched the water of lustration according to the law of the red heifer.

Baumgarten elaborates on the first explanation by showing that normality results from equilibrium. On the one hand, the dead are the most potent source of defilement. On the other hand, the ashes of the heifer with their ability to reverse that defilement are equally potent. As a result, those who come into contact with the ashes, which are especially holy, have subverted the equilibrium required for normality and are therefore impure. The apparent paradox as to how the red heifer purifies the defiled and defiles the pure is no paradox. Too much sanctity is dangerous and leads to impurity. The same conception underlies Rabban Yohanan b. Zakkai's explanation (Yad. 4:5–6) that sacred Scripture defiles the hands because of their precious character. The ancient of sanctity though, conveys a lesser impurity than corpse contagion. The uncleanness of the red heifer is only until evening, but it affects the priest, the gatherer, the lustrator, whoever touches the water of lustration, and indeed the man who is purified by it from the more severe defilement. Thus, after his purification from the latter by the application of water of lustration, he, like the lustrator, must wash his clothes, bathe in water, and remain unclean until evening (Num. 19:19b).

The burning of the red heifer with its blood, the crimson that was combined with it, and the red color of the animal itself may allude to the power of blood to overcome the power of death which threatens both the sanctity and the existence of the Israelite camp (cf. Ex. 12:22–23). While blood is mostly a source of purity, innocent blood that has been shed is a pollutant. In such a case, the red of the heifer might be seen as symbolic of the sin (cf. Isa. 1:18) that caused the death, which is banished from the camp.

[Mayer Irwin Gruber / S. David Sperling (2nd ed.)]

In the Talmud

The entire tractate *Parah* is devoted to the laws of the red heifer. The accepted opinion in talmudic law is that a cow which has been mounted by a bull may not be used for the ritual (Par. 2:4). The Mishnah specifies that the cow be at least three or four years old; younger than three is termed "calf" (Heb. *eglah*) rather than "cow" (Par. 1:1). Furthermore, R. Meir asserts that theoretically the animal may be aged. In practice, he explains, a younger one is more likely to fulfill the other biblical specifications (Par. 1:1). Since the red heifer is called a sin offering (*Ḥattat*; Num. 19:9), the rabbis applied to it the laws appertaining to this offering. The mixture of the heifer's ashes with water is called consecrated water. Some of the rites connected with the red heifer were instituted by the Pharisees in order to refute the view of the Sadducees. The Sadducees claimed that only those who were in a state of complete ritual purity were entitled to burn the heifer. According to the Pharisees, however, even a *tevul yom* (an unclean person who has already undergone ritual immersion but still has to wait until sunset to be declared clean; see *Tevul Yom*) is qualified to burn it. As a result, the priest who was assigned to burn the heifer was deliberately rendered unclean and afterward immersed himself (Par. 3:7–8). This procedure was not carried out without opposition. One tradition tells about a Sadducean high priest who attempted to burn the red heifer according to the ritual of his faction and was prevented by *Johanan b. Zakkai, who told him to immerse himself. The priest answered rudely, and the story continues that as a punishment the Sadducee died three days later (Tosef., Par. 3:8). In reference to another law, R. Yose recommended being less strict, saying, "Do not give the Sadducees an opportunity to cavil at us" (Par. 3:3; cf. Tosef., Par. 3:3). According to the Mishnah, only the high priests could be qualified (Par. 4:1; cf. Yoma 42b). Some talmudic authorities (Yoma 42b; Sif. Num. 123) insist that the assistant to the high priest be in charge; others suggest that it may be any priest.

According to R. Meir in all of Jewish history only seven heifers were burned, but according to the rabbis there were nine (Par. 3:5), and the tenth and last will be prepared by the Messiah (Yad, Parah Adummah 3:4). If two hairs of the animal were not red, it was invalid. As a result, the red heifer was rare and costly, and several stories are told in the Talmud about the exorbitant price demanded for it (TJ, Pe'ah 1:1, 15c; Kid. 31a). Although it was impossible to prepare the ashes of the red heifer after the destruction of the Temple, its use did not cease with the destruction, since there was still a supply of the ashes. As late as the amoraic period, those who had become ritually unclean through contact with the dead still used to cleanse themselves with it (see Nid. 6b, Y. Gilat, *Mishnato shel R. Eliezer b. Hyrcanus* (1968), 252; Neusner (1987), 146ff.; and Sussmann, 306–16).

Even after it ceased entirely, however, the rabbis still regarded its regulations as of importance in teaching a profound lesson. With its contradictory "regulations" rendering the unclean clean and the clean unclean, it was regarded as a classic example of a *ḥukkah* (i.e., a statute for which no rational explanation can be adduced, but which must be observed because it is divinely commanded). It is one of the laws about which "the evil inclination and the gentile nations" deride the Jews and weaken their religious loyalties (Num. R. 19:5–6). Even Solomon, the wisest of men, was baffled by it (Eccles. R. 7:23 no. 4). Similarly, although an *aggadah* relates that Rabban Joḥanan b. Zakkai once replied to a gentile that the sprinkling of the holy water of the heifer's ashes can be compared to exorcising a demon from a person (Num. R. 19:8), it goes on to tell that he nevertheless told his students that he was merely "putting him off with a straw," and that in truth the law of the red heifer should be understood as a *ḥukkah* which must not be questioned (*ibid.*). It is even stated that the reason was not revealed to Moses himself (Eccles. R. 8:1 no. 5). Several homiletical interpretations of the red heifer are given, one being that it was to atone for the sin of the golden calf, so that the mother – the red heifer – should purify the defilement caused by her offspring, the golden calf (PR 14:65a and see the whole chapter). Nevertheless, the rabbis of the talmudic period never really solved these problems (Urbach, see bibl.). The portion of *Parah* constitutes the reading of the third of the four special *Sabbaths, and one of the reasons given is that an unclean person could not celebrate the paschal sacrifices without first being purified by the consecrated water of the red heifer.

[Arie Strikovsky]

BIBLIOGRAPHY: G.B. Gray, *Numbers* (ICC, 1903), 241–56; N.H. Snaith, *Leviticus and Numbers* (1967), 270–4. **ADD. BIBLIOGRAPHY:** J. Milgrom, *JPS Torah Commentary Numbers* (1990), 438–43; S.D. Sperling, in: ABD I, 761–63; D. Wright, in: ABD III, 115–16; G. Anderson, in: ABD V, 870-86; A. Baumgarten, in: VT 43 (1993), 442–51; B. Levine, *Numbers 1–20* (AB; 1993), 457–79; J. Jaech, "A Socio-Political Study of the Role of the Biblical Red Heifer in Tannaitic and Amoraic Literature" (unpublished rabbinic thesis, Hebrew Union College, 2003). IN THE TALMUD: E.E. Urbach, *Ḥazal; Pirkei Emunot ve-De'ot* (1969), 333; S.H. Kook, in: *Sinai*, 30 (1952), 29–34. **ADD. BIBLIOGRAPHY:** J. Sussman, "Babylonian Sugiyot to the Orders of Zera'im and Tohorot" (Heb., Ph.D. diss., 1969), 306–16; J. Neusner, *A History of the Mishnaic Laws of Purities*, vol. 9–10 (1974–77); idem, *From Mishnah to Scripture* (1984), 59–66; idem, *The Mishnah Before 70* (1987), 143–68; idem, *The Philosophical Mishnah*, 3 (1989), 63–74; idem, *Purity in Rabbinic Judaism* (1994), 157–69.

REDL, FRITZ (1902–1988), child psychologist. Redl was born in Klaus, Austria, and trained at the Vienna Psychoanalytic Institute. In 1936 he emigrated to the United States, where he was a research associate at the Rockefeller Foundation. From 1941 to 1953 he was a professor of social work at Wayne State University, Detroit, and from 1953 to 1959 he was chief of the Child Research Branch of the National Institute of Mental Health. From 1948 to 1957 he was the principal investigator on a research project for clinical work with disturbed children, and from 1959 was professor of behavioral science at Wayne State.

In 1959 Redl published *Mental Hygiene in Teaching* (with William Wattenberg; 1959²) and *Children Who Hate* (with David Wineman; 1951; 1969²). In the latter book, Redl contributed to understanding the abnormal psychology of antisocial behavior. Redl made an essential contribution to understanding delinquency, especially in groups and gangs, and the use of group methods in its treatment. In his paper *The Psychology of Gang Formation and the Treatment of Juvenile Delinquents* (1945) he distinguishes four types of delinquents: those protesting against wrong handling; those basically nondelinquent who drift into delinquency because of growth confusion; delinquency as a part of neurosis; and "genuine delinquency" in which there are disturbances of impulse or personality structure. On the issue of treatment, Redl wrote *Psychoanalysis and Group Therapy: A Developmental Point of View* (1963).

He also co-wrote with David Wineman *Controls from Within* (1952), *The Aggressive Child* (1966), and *When We Deal with Children* (1966).

ADD. BIBLIOGRAPHY: W. Morse (ed.), *Crisis Intervention in Residential Treatment: The Clinical Innovations of Fritz Redl* (1991).

[Louis Miller]

REDLICH, FREDERICK C. (1910–2004), U.S. psychiatrist and psychoanalyst. Redlich was born in Vienna. Raised as a Catholic, he discovered his Jewish ancestry at age 24. After working at a psychiatric hospital in Vienna, he left for the United States in 1938. In 1940 he joined the staff of the New Haven Hospital and in 1948 was appointed its chief psychiatrist. From 1942 he taught at Yale University, where in 1950 he became professor of psychiatry. He served as head of the department of psychology from 1950 to 1967 and was dean of the Yale School of Medicine from 1967 to 1972. During that time, he helped to establish a new department of molecular biophysics and biochemistry and to create a new program of medical education. In 1972 he returned to Yale's department of psychiatry for five more years before retiring. He subsequently taught for five years at the University of California, Los Angeles. He returned to New Haven in 1999.

Redlich was the co-founder and first director of the Yale-Connecticut Mental Health Center. He was also instrumental in inspiring the founders of the Western New England Institute of Psychoanalysis to locate in New Haven, and was president of the foundation's Fund for Research in Psychiatry throughout its existence.

Redlich published *Psychotherapy with Schizophrenics* (1952, joint ed.), *The Inside Story* (1953, 1955², compiler, written by J. Bingham), *Social Class and Mental Illness* (1958, with August B. Hollingshead), and *Theory and Practice of Psychiatry* (with Daniel Freedman, 1966). *Social Class and Mental Illness* is a report on research conducted in 1957 by Redlich and Yale sociologist August Hollingshead into the relation of social class and the distribution of mental illness and its relation to the ways mentally ill persons are treated by psychiatrists. Redlich also wrote *Hitler: Diagnosis of a Destructive Prophet* (1998), in which he attempts to determine whether Hitler's actions were the result of physical and mental illnesses. It is novel in that it may well be the first book in which these questions were examined by a practicing psychiatrist.

[Louis Miller / Ruth Beloff (2nd ed.)]

REDLICH, HANS FERDINAND (1903–1968), musicologist. Born in Vienna, Redlich conducted opera in Berlin and Mainz, and after 1931 devoted himself to research and writing. In 1939 he settled in Britain, where he lectured at Cambridge University from 1942 and at Edinburgh University from 1955. He was an authority on Monteverdi and edited some of his works. His writings include *Gustav Mahler* (1919), *Claudio Monteverdi* (1949; Eng., 1952), *Bruckner and Mahler* (1955), and *Alban Berg* (1957). He composed a concerto grosso (1927) and *Hoelderlin Trilogy* for tenor and orchestra (1946).

REDLICH, JOSEPH (1869–1936), Austrian constitutional lawyer and politician. Born in Goeding, Moravia, Redlich was acknowledged as an outstanding authority on Austrian and British parliamentary procedure. He was made assistant professor at the University of Vienna in 1905 and full professor in 1908. Redlich was active in politics and, from 1906 to 1918, was a Liberal member of the Moravian Landtag (provincial legislature) and the Austrian Reichstrat. His support for the Western Allies before World War I barred him from the Austrian government until 1918 when shortly before the fall of the empire he was made minister of finance in the last Hapsburg government. Redlich was an authority on American legal education on which he had written a study in 1905. He was invited to lecture in the United States at the Institute of Politics at Williamstown, Massachusetts, and at Harvard. In 1929 he was appointed professor of comparative law at the latter university but in 1931 was recalled to Austria to become minister of finance for a second time during the Austrian financial crisis. Redlich retained this post until the advent of the Dolfuss regime in 1934. He was baptized in 1903.

Redlich's many works include *The Procedure of the House of Commons* (3 vols., 1908); *The Common Law and the Case Method in American University Law Schools* (1914); and *Das Wesen der oesterreichischen Kommunalverfassung* (1910) as well as a number of important books on Austrian political history, such as *Das oesterreichische Staats- und Reichsproblem* (1920) and *Oesterreichische Regierung und Verwaltung im Weltkriege* (1925). He also wrote a history of English local government, *Englische Lokalverwaltung* (1901; trans. by F.W. Hirst, *Local Government in England*, 1903; vol. 1, republished 1958) in which he traced the growth of democratic institutions in English local government.

BIBLIOGRAPHY: J. Redlich and F.W. Hirst, *History of Local Government in England* (1958²), introd. by B. Keith-Lucas, 7–15.

[Josef J. Lador-Lederer]

REDLICH, NORMAN (1925–), U.S. jurist. Redlich received his LL.B. from Yale Law School in 1950 and served as the executive editor of the *Yale Law Journal* from 1949 to 1950. He received his LL.M. from New York University in 1955. He was in private practice and business from 1950 to 1959. He was a lecturer at the New York University School of Law (1957–60), and then associate professor (1960–62), and professor of law from 1962 to 1988. In 1974 he was appointed associate dean, and then served as dean from 1975 to 1988. He taught the subjects of constitutional law, professional responsibility, federal income taxation, state and municipal finance, and urban law.

An outspoken opponent of capital punishment, he has been counsel to the New York Committee to Abolish Capital Punishment. He served from 1963 to 1964 as assistant counsel to the President's Commission on the Assassination of President Kennedy (the Warren Commission), and as special consultant to the state of Vermont on Revision of Vermont's Income Tax Law (1965–66). In 1966 he was given a leave of absence from the New York University School of Law to become Executive Assistant Corporation Counsel to the City of New York. In 1972 Mayor John Lindsay named him corporation counsel of the City of New York, the city's highest legal office. Redlich was active in the organized bar, having served as chair of the American Bar Association's Section of Legal Education and Admissions to the Bar (1989 to 1990). He was a member of the House of Delegates of the American Bar Association. He was also a member of the board, and of its executive committee, of the NAACP Legal Defense and Education Fund, and cochair of the Commission on Law and Social Action of the American Jewish Congress.

Redlich served as counsel to the law firm of Wachtell, Lipton, Rosen, & Katz. He continued to teach at the NYU Law School as an adjunct professor, offering a course in professional responsibility. Greatly concerned with professional ethics, Redlich believes there is "deficiency in legal education concerning what a lawyer's role is to his client, his adversary, and the legal system." He has written extensively on taxation and civil liberties. From 1960 to 1966 he was editor of the *Tax Law Review.*

Redlich wrote or co-authored such books as *Professional Responsibility: A Problem Approach* (1976), *Constitutional Law* (1983), *Standards of Professional Conduct for Lawyers and Judges* (1984), *Understanding Constitutional Law* (1995), and *Understanding Contracts* (2004).

[Julius J. Marcke / Ruth Beloff (2nd ed.)]

RED SEA (Heb. יַם סוּף, *yam suf*; lit. "Sea of Reeds"). The Hebrew term *yam suf* denotes, in some biblical references and in most later sources, the sea known as the Red Sea (as in Gr. Ἐρυθρά θάλασσα; Lat. Sinus Arabicus, Mare Rubrum; Ar. Baḥr or al-Baḥr al-Aḥmar). The Red Sea is a long narrow strip of water separating the Arabian Peninsula from the northeastern corner of Africa (Egypt, Sudan, Ethiopia) and forming the northwestern arm of the Indian Ocean to which it is connected by the Bāb al-Mandib Straits (whose narrowest point is 21 mi. (33 km.) wide). In the northern part of the Red Sea are the Gulf of Elath (Aqaba) and the Gulf of Suez which enclose the Sinai Peninsula. With the opening of the Suez Canal, the Red Sea was connected with the Mediterranean. Its total area is 176,061.6 sq. mi. (456,000 sq. km.) and its length about 1,240 mi. (2,000 km., excluding the gulfs in the north). For most of its length it is 124–155 mi. (200–250 km.) wide and about 223 mi. (360 km.) at its widest point, near Massawa. Its mean depth measures approximately 1,640 ft. (500 m.); about 70% of its area is more than 656 ft. (200 m.) deep and its maximum depth, 7,741 ft. (2,360 m.), is northeast of Port Sudan. The Red Sea is the warmest and most saline of all open seas. The temperature of the surface water reaches 30°–33° C (86°–91° F) in July–September (near the shores it rises to 36° C (97° F) and drops to 23°–27° C (73°–81° F) in December-February. The average salinity near the surface is 40–41% which increases to 43% on the northern side, in the gulfs of Elath and Suez. Because of the wasteland nature of the area, the shores of the Red Sea are sparsely settled. Its port sites are few and for the most part small; the principal ones are Joba, Suez, Port Sudan, and Hudida.

History

In the Bible the Red Sea, apart from its problematical appearance in the route of the Exodus (see below), is clearly identified in the description of the borders of the land promised to Israel (Ex. 23:31) and in other passages describing the maritime activities of Solomon (I Kings 9:26) and later kings. In antiquity the two gulfs at its northern tip served as important navigation routes. The Gulf of Clysma (Suez) was used by the rulers of Egypt as the shortest route to the Mediterranean above the Isthmus of Suez. It was connected via the Bitter Lakes with the Nile and the Mediterranean by a canal which already existed in the days of Necoh and which was repaired by Darius I, the Ptolemies, and the Romans. The Gulf of Elath was a vital outlet to the south for the kings of Israel and Judah and their Phoenician allies. David acquired access to the sea and this was maintained by his successors until the division of the kingdom; it was later regained by Jehoshaphat and Uzziah. Still later the Nabateans used it for their maritime trade and overland transport to Petra and Gaza. In the Hellenistic period the discovery of the monsoon wind systems revived direct trade with India via the Red Sea; this trade continued throughout the Roman period. During the Byzantine period the Red Sea was the only trade route to the East open to the empire, which explains the tenacity with which the Byzantines fought for its control against the Jewish kings of Ḥimyar. From the seventh century onward the Arabs dominated the Red Sea, except for a brief period during which Elath was held by the crusaders. The discovery of the sea route to India and Turkish domination put an end to international trade on the Red Sea; it was revived with the inauguration of the Suez Canal in 1869.

The Red Sea and the Problem of the Exodus

Tradition has identified the sea which engulfed Pharaoh's army with the Red Sea ever since the Septuagint translation of the Bible in the third century B.C.E. This identification was adopted by Josephus and the Christian pilgrims and is still accepted by some scholars. They place the crossing of the Red Sea in the vicinity of Suez and point out the high tides in the Red Sea (up to 6½ ft.), but they fail to explain how an east wind could have driven the waters back at this point (Ex. 14:21). Most of the scholars who accept the southern route of the Exodus maintain that the Red Sea was crossed at the Great Bitter Lake, but here too an east wind could lower the water level by only a few inches at the utmost. This theory, furthermore, is unable to account for the places Pi-Hahiroth, Migdol, and Baal-Zephon which the Israelites passed. The majority opinion today identifies the Red Sea of the Exodus with one of the lagoons on the shores of the Mediterranean. Some locate it at Baḥr Manzala (Gardiner, Loewenstamm) or the Sirbonic Lake (Jarvis, Mazar, Noth) and identify Pi-Hahiroth with Tell al-Khayr, Migdol with Pelusium, and Baal-Zephon with the sanctuary of Zeus Cassius on the isthmus dividing the lake from the sea, the former being occasionally inundated by waves from the latter when an east wind is blowing (cf. also *Exodus).

[Moshe Brawer and Michael Avi-Yonah]

In the Aggadah

While the Israelites were threatened by the Egyptians' closing in on them and driving them toward the sea, the angels wanted to sing a song of praise, but God did not permit them to do so, saying: "My sons are in distress and you want to praise Me?" (Tanḥ. Ex. 60; Ex. R. 23:7; the version quoted in Meg. 10b, "The work of My hands are about to drown in the sea," also referred originally to the Israelites, not the Egyptians). Even after the sea was parted and Israel had crossed it safely, God again told the angels to wait, for He desired to hear first the song sung by Israel (Tanḥ *ibid.*; Ex. R. *ibid.*). When Moses raised the rod over the sea and commanded it to be parted, the sea refused at first to obey the orders of a human being; it only submitted when it saw the Divine Name engraved on the rod, or – according to another version – when God Himself rebuked it (Mekh. Be-Shallaḥ 4; Ginsburger, *Fragmententhargum*, Ex. 14:29). In spite of the miracle, the people were at first afraid to enter the receding waters, until *Naḥshon of the tribe of Judah descended first; but another version relates that all were eager to obey the Divine command, competing among themselves until eventually the tribe of Benjamin succeeded in being the first to enter the sea (Mekh. *ibid.* 5; Sot. 36bff.). When the Egyptians had drowned, the sea tossed their bodies to the shore, but the earth, too, refused to receive them until God swore an oath not to punish it for receiving the corpses (Mekh. Shirata 9; Pseudo-Jon.; Ex. 15:12). According to another version the sea refused to give up the corpses and only agreed to do so when God promised to compensate it in the days of Sisera (Pes. 118b). God's decision that the Egyptians should not be swallowed up by the sea was either in order to give the Israelites the satisfaction of seeing their former masters lying dead at their feet (Mekh. Be-Shallaḥ 6) or because in spite of all they deserved burial in the ground (Mekh. Shirata 9; PdRE 39).

[Joseph Heinemann]

BIBLIOGRAPHY: Abel, Geog, 2 (1938), 209ff.; Servin, in: *Bulletin de l'Institut d'Egypte*, 31 (1949), 315ff.; C.S. Jarvis, *Yesterday and Today in Sinai* (1931), 158ff.; Gardiner, Onomastica, 2 (1947), 201ff.; EM, s.v. (incl bibl.); M. Harel, *Masei Sinai* (1968). In the Aggadah: Ginzberg, Legends, 3 (1947[3]), 14–36; 5 (1947[5]), 4–12; J. Heinemann, in: *Bar-Ilan Sefer ha-Shanah*, 7–8 (1970), 80–84.

REDSTONE, SUMNER MURRAY (Ostrovsky; 1923–), U.S. entertainment executive. Born in Boston, Massachusetts, Redstone attended Boston Latin School, the oldest public high school in the United States, graduating at the top of his class in 1940. While attending Harvard University, Redstone studied German and Japanese. In 1943, he was selected to join a team that successfully broke a secret Japanese code. After a two-year stint in the Army, Redstone entered Harvard Law School in 1947. After law school, he worked first as special assistant to U.S. attorney general Tom Clark before joining private practice. In 1954 he joined the family business, Redstone Management, which owned movie theaters, building up the company's drive-ins. In the early 1960s, he served as president of the Theater Owners of America. In 1968, as president and CEO of the growing family business, which had been renamed National Amusements, Redstone began converting his properties into multi-screen theaters, which he called "multiplexes," a term he trademarked. In 1977, he purchased a 5 percent stake in 20th Century Fox after viewing the film *Star Wars*; the investment netted him $20 million when he sold the stock in 1981. In 1979, he was caught in a fire at Boston's Copely Plaza Hotel, during which he suffered third-degree burns over 45 percent of his body. He underwent five operations, which lasted 60 hours. Redstone went on to invest in Columbia Pictures and MGM/UA, earning $40 million. In 1987, Redstone bought Viacom Pictures for $3.2 billion and then took the company public the next day. Throughout the 1980s and 1990s, he battled for control of studios, finally acquiring Paramount. In 1996, Redstone was elected CEO of Viacom, and by 2000 National Amusements' holdings would include CBS, Blockbuster, Simon and Schuster, Showtime Networks, 18 television stations, and movie theaters in 12 countries. In 2001, he released his biography, *A Passion to Win*. In 2004, Redstone announced he was stepping down as CEO of Viacom by 2006. Redstone also served in leadership roles for various nonprofits, including the Combined Jewish Philathropies of Greater Boston, and was a visiting professor at Brandeis University.

[Adam Wills (2nd ed.)]

RÉE, HARTVIG PHILIP (1778–1859), manufacturer, merchant, and religious reformer. He was born and brought up in Fredericia (Denmark), where in his young days, he tried to introduce religious reform but was unsuccessful. In 1810 he moved to Aarhus, establishing there a business empire and became known as "King Rée." In Aarhus he also founded a synagogue and officiated as rabbi, introducing choir hymns, psalms in German, and sermons in Danish; however his reforms were not imitated throughout Denmark, as he had hoped. He also wrote many hymns in Hebrew and German, with melodies, and made frequent contributions to Jewish and general periodicals. Rée was the author of several books, including *Forschungen ueber die Ueberschriften der Psalmen* (1846).

BIBLIOGRAPHY: J. Fischer, *Hartvig Philip Rée og hans Slaegt* (Danish, Fr., and Ger., 1912); *Dansk Biografisk Leksikon*, s.v.

REED. Three species of reed grow in Israel on the banks of rivers and swamps. Two of them, *Phragmites communis* and *Arundo donax*, are the *kaneh* of the Bible and rabbinical literature; the third, *Saccharum biflorum*, seems to be the biblical *agmon*. These species also grow on the banks of the Nile. In the scriptural parable "the bruised reed" that cannot be depended on and even inflicts harm symbolizes treacherous Egypt (Isa. 36:6; Ezek. 29:6–7), and it is mentioned as withering during the drying-up of the Nile. The *Behemoth dwells "in the covert of the reed and the fens" (Job 40: 21), and is therefore called "the wild beast of the reeds" (Ps. 68:31). The reed standing in the water and shaking in the wind in the prophecy of *Ahijah symbolized the Israelite nation shaking from the many blows inflicted upon it (I Kings 14:15). According to the Midrash: "The curse with which Ahijah of Shiloh cursed Israel is preferable to the blessing of the wicked Balaam. Balaam praised them as cedars (Num. 24:6) while Ahijah cursed them as 'the reed which is shaken.' The reed stands in water and, although bruised and bent, recovers. It has many roots so that even if all the winds of the world blow upon it, they do not move it from its place, but it sways with them and when the wind ceases it remains standing in its place." Hence, concludes the moralist, "a man should always be as pliant as a reed and not as hard as the cedar." As a result, the reed merited that the scroll of the law be written with it.

Reeds had many uses: for roofing (Gen. R. 1:8), for making partitions (Tosef., Er. 2:4), mats (Kel. 17:17), scales (Kel. 17:16), flutes (Tosef., Ar. 2:3), and pens (*kolmos*, "pen" is derived from *calamus*, "reed," Ta'an, 20b). Some grew it in gardens (Tosef., Dem. 7, end). The pay for cutting reeds was low, hence the designation *katla kanya be'agma* ("cutter of reeds") for a person of little worth (Sanh. 33a, et al.). Reeds were much used for making arrows, the Midrash noting that Israel lacks nothing – "even reeds for arrows" (Eccles. R. 2:8, no. 2). In this connection the words of Pliny are instructive: "The peoples of the East wage war with the aid of the reed, they strengthen their arrowheads with it and give wings to death by putting feathers into the reeds" (*Natural History*, 16:159).

Agmon is mentioned a number of times in the Bible as a slender plant, shaking in the wind and bowing its head, its head being the thick inflorescence shaped like a tail (Isa. 9–13). Its thin stalk was used for stringing fish (Job 40:26). The word is connected with *agam* ("swamp"). The scriptural descriptions of *agmon* fit *Saccharum biflorum*, the slenderest of the reeds common in Israel.

BIBLIOGRAPHY: Loew, Flora, 1 (1928), 662–85; H.N. and A.L. Moldenke, *Plants of the Bible* (1952), index; J. Feliks, *Olam ha-Ẓome'aḥ ha-Mikra'i* (1968²), 288–93. **ADD. BIBLIOGRAPHY:** Feliks, Ha-Ẓome'aḥ, 146.

[Jehuda Feliks]

REED, LOU (Lewis Allen; 1942–), U.S. guitarist, songwriter, founder of the influential art rock band The Velvet Underground; often referred to as the "Godfather of Punk." Born into a middle-class Jewish family in Freeport, New York, Reed played guitar in several high school bands. He attended Syracuse University, but dropped out after two years and moved to New York City, where he became a songwriter for Pickwick records. There, Reed met John Cale, with whom he formed The Primitives, a band which evolved to become The Velvet Underground in 1964. Later managed by Andy Warhol, The Velvet Underground was considered groundbreaking for their lyrical tales of urban decay, heroin addiction, and social realism, as well as for their droning sound and experiments in noise. Although the band was never a commercial success, The Velvet Underground is considered one of the most influential rock bands of all time. Reed left the band in 1970, and after spending a short musical hiatus working for his father's Long Island accounting firm, he released an eponymous solo album that was mostly rehashed Velvet Underground tunes. It wasn't until Reed recruited David Bowie and Mick Ronson to produce his 1972 album *Transformer* that Reed achieved widespread success: a Top-20 hit in the U.S., and a Top-Ten hit in the U.K. for "Walk on the Wild Side," a tribute song to the transsexuals, misfits, and hustlers at Andy Warhol's Factory. Reed followed *Transformer* with *Berlin*, which though artistically impressive, failed to make a mark commercially. Reed, who adopted a public persona of an androgynous junkie, followed *Berlin* with *Rock and Roll Animal* and *Sally Can't Dance*, both albums aimed at commercial success, and then in 1975, *Metal Machine Music*, a double album of pure guitar feedback. As Reed wrestled with drug and alcohol problems, his releases, while prolific, remained inconsistent. On 1976's *Rock and Roll Heart*, Reed delivered an album of pure guitar pop, only to follow up with raw punk on 1978's *Street Hassle*. The 1980s saw a sober, drug-free, and more focused Reed releasing critically acclaimed albums such as 1983's *The Blue Mask* and 1989's *New York*, a love letter and sharp criticism of the state of his adored city. After a 25-year estrangement, Reed reunited with John Cale in 1990 and released *Songs for Drella*, a musical biography and tribute to Andy Warhol. The Velvet Underground temporarily reunited in 1993. Reed and his bandmates from The Velvet Underground were inducted into the Rock and Roll Hall of Fame in 1996.

[Harry Rubenstein (2nd ed.)]

REESE, JIMMIE (James Hymie Solomon; 1901–1994), U.S. baseball player and coach for 78 years. Reese first became involved with baseball in 1917 as a mascot and then batboy for the Los Angeles Angels in the Pacific Coast League, for whom he played briefly in 1920 and 1924. Reese had changed his given name from Solomon, and no one knew that he was Jewish. Reese was invited to play in a celebrity exhibition game in Los Angeles against a team with songwriter Harry Ruby pitching and Ike Danning – brother of N.Y. Giants star Harry – as the catcher. Clowning around, the battery mates opted to forgo the traditional hand signals and instead call out their pitches in Yiddish, certain that nobody on the other team would understand. Reese got four hits in the game, and afterward Danning said, "I didn't know you were so good," to which Reese replied, "You also didn't know that my name was Hymie Solomon." Reese played fulltime with the PCL's Oakland Oaks from 1924 to 1928, when he was sold to the New York Yankees. Reese, who made his Major League debut on April 19, 1930, played second base for the Yankees in 1930 and 1931 – when he was the roommate of Babe Ruth on the road – and then with the St. Louis Cardinals in 1932, finishing with a .278 batting average in 742 at bats. Reese returned to the Pacific Coast League, finishing a 14-year minor league career hitting .289 in 1,673 games, and setting the PCL record for most put-outs by a second baseman (4,771) as well as most assists (5,119). Reese served as a coach with four minor league teams and managed two others, and then joined the California Angels in 1972, where he remained as scout and coach until he died. Reese was known for his ability to hit fungos, and for being known as "the nicest guy in baseball" – indeed, two pitchers he worked with named their sons Reese.

[Elli Wohlgelernter (2nd ed.)]

REESE, MICHAEL (1815–1878), U.S. realtor and philanthropist. Reese, whose place of birth is unknown, made his fortune as a realtor during the California gold rush, but lived alone in miserly frugality. Reese's estate was worth ten million dollars at the time of his death and he was the second-largest real-estate owner in San Francisco. He bequeathed $30,000 to his nephews in Chicago for use in a charitable cause. They, in turn, donated the money toward the rebuilding of a Jewish hospital destroyed in the Chicago fire, with the stipulation that it be called the Michael Reese Hospital. Reese also left portions of his estate to the University of California and to various Jewish charities.

REEVE, ADA (1874–1966), British actress. Born in London to an acting family, Ada Reeve played Willie in *East Lynne* at the age of six and toured the music halls with a light comedy group. She appeared in the West End in 1894, and played the title role in *San Yoy*, 1901. In subsequent years she visited Australia five times between 1896 and 1935, and South Africa five times between 1906 and 1913. She acted in many plays during World War II. In 1954 she appeared in the television show *Life Begins at 80* and at the age of 90 she took part in a TV film. In 1954 she published her autobiography *Take it for a Fact*. Some sources give her birthdate as 1870 or 1876.

REFORMATION. Like most revolutions the Reformation within the Christian Church in 16th-century Europe combined ultraconservative trends with a drive for change. In his attitude toward the Jews, Martin *Luther moved from a conscious attempt at a form of reconciliation, through a missionary effort, to a most extreme, abusive outlook aimed at putting an end to their very existence in Christian states. His more benevolent approach finds expression in his *Das Jesus Christus eyn geborner Jude sey* (1523), while his *Von den Jueden und jren Luegen* (1543) exemplifies his most vehement attitude. This vacillation between extremes was typical of Luther's personal approach to many problems (e.g., toward the peasant revolt and toward toleration in general); more than that, however, it was also an expression of, on the one hand, the reform movement's feeling that their revolutionary return to a "pure" biblical Christianity would make a greater appeal to the Jews – the earlier missionary attempts having failed because they were made in the name of corrupt Christianity – and, on the other, the deeply ingrained fear and hatred of the Jews which characterized most of the Reformation leaders. As their mission to the Jews failed too, they felt deeply insulted; the deep layers of their baleful image of the Jew came to the fore in Luther's scurrilous attacks. His work is described by Joseph b. Gershon of *Rosheim as "such a boorish and inhuman book, containing curses and vilification hurled at us, hapless Jews, such as by the will of God can truly never be found in our beliefs and Judaism generally" (ZGJD, 5 (1892), 331). Of the legal and social measures vis-à-vis the Jews proposed by Luther toward the end of his life, Joseph b. Gershom said that the like "never has… been contended by any scholar, that we Jews ought to be treated with violence and great tyranny, that none was bound to honor any obligation toward us" (*ibid.*, 332).

Less abuse and violence but a similar mixture of innovation and hatred marked the attitude to the Jews of John *Calvin – in his "*Ad quaestiones et obiecta Judaei cuiusdam Responsio*" (*Opera quae supersunt omnia*, 9 (1900), 653–74), of Martin *Bucer – in many of his writings and public appearances, and especially in the *Ratschlag ob die Christliche Oberkait gebueren muege, dass sye die Juden undter den Christen zu wonen gedulden, und wa sye zu gedulden welche gestalt und mass* of 1539 (in his *Deutsche Schriften*, 7 (1964), 319–94), and of many of their followers and imitators. Exceptions to the rule were Wolfgang Fabricius *Capito of Strasbourg and the Bavarian Andreas *Osiander, who dared to give the lie to one of the basic elements of popular hatred of the Jews, the blood *libel, in: *Ob es war vn-glaublich sey dass die Juden der Christen kinder heymlich erwuergen, und jr blut gebrauchen, ein treffenlich schrifft, auff eines yeden urteyl gestelt. Wer menschen blut vergeusst, des blut sol auch vergossen werde* (written in 1529; published in 1893). Here is an eloquent and well-reasoned treatise against this appalling accusation.

For the Jews, the Reformation brought humiliation and suffering and an additional burden because of Catholic Counter-Reformation claims that they were responsible for its "Judaizing" tendencies. There is also the impression that, at a far later date, Luther's teaching of the submission of the individual to his rulers, combined with his latter-day virulent antisemitism, were one of the root causes of racist Nazism, preparing the soil for the acceptance of the Holocaust in the German mind and society. Yet in spite of all these elements (some certain and some arguable), in Jewish history the Reformation was not only, nor even largely, negative and harmful. Not only were many elements of Catholic faith changed in a way that removed the grounds for anti-Jewish accusations – e.g., charges of desecration of the *Host disappeared in Protestant circles because of the change in beliefs about transubstantiation – but many of the reformers' innovations removed some differences between Jews and Christians in the Reformation environment. About 1524, Jews coming from Europe described with joy to the kabbalist Abraham b. Eliezer *ha-Levi in Jerusalem the iconoclastic and anti-clerical tendencies of the reformers. On the basis of this much exaggerated report the kabbalists regarded Luther as a kind of *Crypto-Jew who was trying gradually to educate Christians away from the bad elements of their faith (Abraham's letter of 1525; see KS, 7 (1930/31), 444–5).

Of more importance and real impact for the future relationship with Christians – and for that matter for the relationship with Christians of other denominations in the post-Reformation period – was the great weight the Reformation gave to the Bible in Hebrew and to Hebrew in general. Although it had originated with the Renaissance, this tendency was given major religious sanction in the Reformation. According to Abraham b. Eliezer ha-Levi, this was one of the mysteries of "God's mind, who decreed this beforehand… when He turned the hearts of many nations in the lands of the uncircumcised toward the study of the Hebrew language and writing. And they delve into these, each according to his powers of attainment" (*ibid.*, 445). Later, in many Protestant groups and sects, this was combined with the appreciation of the law and values of ancient Jewish society which were seen as the proper basis for the life of a model sectarian society. Away from the individualistic spiritual path of the evangelists, they looked to the Hebrew Bible for the modes of justice and moral way of life appropriate to a closely knit group. Many of them – both before and after him – would have agreed with Samuel Langdon, president of Harvard, when he declared in his election sermon delivered in 1775 that "the Jewish government, according to the original constitution which was divinely established, if considered merely in a civil view was a perfect republic" (in J. Wingate Thornton, *Pulpit of the American Revolution* (1860), 239). This sums up the attitude of many settlers in New England from the time it was first expressed by John Cotton in his *Moses, His Judicials* (1641). The great debate in Reformation countries, in Cromwellian and Restoration England in particular, about the divine right of kings and regicide was conducted to a large degree on the basis of texts and ideas from the Old Testament, which were taken as valid paradigms for actual Christian society. In many such circles, from the Netherlands to the eastern boundaries of Reformation Europe, Jews and Judaic ways came to be considered respectable and exemplary. Gradually this appreciation of the Jewish past developed into an appreciation of the Jews of the day, as abundantly shown by the paintings of *Rembrandt and a great deal of literary and social evidence.

Yet the main importance of the Reformation for Jewish history lies more in what it failed to achieve than in its direct attitudes and achievements. No less fervently than the pope, its leaders wanted to have one Christian, all-embracing, orthodox Church. In the clash between the various strands of the Reformation and between all of them and the Catholic Counter-Reformation, this concept of an all-inclusive orthodoxy had perforce gradually to be abandoned. Through the fire and blood of the wars of religion (at least up to 1648), toleration reluctantly dawned in European culture. The centuries-old reality of a fixed religious, legal, and social attitude toward the Jews vanished; many established attitudes were now reexamined. Toleration embraced only very reluctantly the notion of including a non-Christian, let alone a Jew, within its permissive outlook. An anonymous Jew began to urge this change in Luther's lifetime. To the demand for apostasy he advised that the Jew reply with a polite refusal based on historical continuity and loyalty. Jews will not listen: "now, in our [the Jewish] old age, after we have suffered the servitude to the kingdoms and the hand of our enemies… God forbid that we should relinquish what our fathers left to us, a tradition in our hands, with proof, more than the other nations of the world." This refusal is addressed to the "very few men of reason who ply their words mildly" (published from Ms. by H.H. Ben-Sasson, in HTR, 59 (1966), 388). Yet by implication, and through forces inherent in the very logic of its birth, toleration had to relate to the Jews. This move was first made only by small splinter groups like some Puritan sectarians in the Netherlands and England. But the attitude of the eminent lawyer and theologian Hugo *Grotius in his memorandum of 1616 (as member of a committee of two appointed by the municipality of Amsterdam to regulate the status of the newly admitted Jews) shows the considerable change in the thought of the Calvinist Netherlands. He assumes the right of the Jews to basic equality, while advocating many specific legal disabilities; thus, much of medieval practice was to remain without the medieval frame of mind. Oliver Cromwell's readmission of Jews into England was intended to be on a similar basis; in the end popular opposition resulted in factual readmission without explicit legal formulation. The pro-Jewish trend continued both in England and the Netherlands, widening to embrace more and more sectors of the population. By 1697 the city of London had demanded that Jews be admitted as members of the London Stock Exchange. The writings of men like John *Toland and Roger Williams give an explicit edge to the reform attitude of toleration toward Jews, providing a weapon for its advocates. Thus the fluid situation following on the Reformation offered the chance of a change (both for better and worse) in the status and image of the Jews in Europe.

As noted, Jewish reaction to the Reformation was related from the beginning to the actions and expressions of the movement, but from the very first moment the Jews appreciated the element of revolutionary breakthrough, as they had done much earlier in relation to other heretical and revolutionary movements in Christianity, as evident in their disputations and in their attitude toward the *Hussites. Old traditions and ideas looked to a change in Christianity that would bring back its beliefs to the right Jewish way that they had erroneously departed from. Some made an extreme evaluation of the reports of the new leader and his acts. In a "prophecy" ascribed to "the sage and astronomer R. Abraham *Zacuto," Abraham b. Eliezer includes "what a great astrologer in Spain, named R. Joseph, wrote in a forecast on the significance of the sun's eclipse in the year 1478. He states: 'Having no desire to favor any particular religion or mores I say that a man will arise who will be great, valiant, and mighty. He will pursue justice and loathe butchery. He will marshal vast armies, originate a religion, and destroy the houses of worship and clergy. In his days Jerusalem shall be rebuilt.'" Abraham b. Eliezer adds that "at first glance we believed that the man foreshadowed by the stars was Messiah b. Joseph [see *Messiah]. But now it is evident that he is none other than the man mentioned [by all; i.e., Luther, according to the general trend of Abraham b. Eliezer's thought at this time], who is exceedingly noble in all his undertakings and all these forecasts are realized in his person" (in H.H. Ben-Sasson, *Yehudim mul ha-Reformaẓyah* (1969/70), Eng. translation in bibl.).

Admiration for Luther vanished in many Jewish circles, in particular in Germany, in view of his later enmity and cruelty. To Joseph b. Gershon of Rosheim, Luther is the archenemy of the Jews, a second Haman. But some still retained their sympathy for the Reformation movement if not for Luther himself. The growing diversity within the Reformation camp encouraged the rationalist Abraham ibn Migash, physician to the sultan in the 16th century, to think that "their faith has reverted to a state of primeval flux. Where there are a thousand of them one cannot find 10 men willing to rely upon a single doctrine or consent to a given line of reasoning. Thus they are in a state of formlessness, ready to take shape, since faith has departed and no longer finds expression in their utterances. But they have been made ready to assume form when they will find favor with God, after being scourged for their sins and the sins of their fathers, for all that they and their fathers have perpetrated against Israel. And when they find favor with God they will be ready to accept the faith" (*Kevod Elohim* (Constantinople, 1586), essay no. 3, ch. 3, fols. 127v.–128r.). Even from afar, the capital of the Ottoman Empire, Ibn Migash recognized that the Protestant camp was splintered because it was ardently striving for true faith; they had lost their form in the Aristotelian sense of the term. He could not understand their remaining outside of the true Jewish form except through accepting that this is a temporary withholding of grace to enable them to expiate their sins in persecuting Jews in former generations. To Samuel *Usque the Reformation was a revolt of descendants of Jewish *anusim who had naturally taken the opportunity to avenge their forced conversion: "For since throughout Christendom Christians have forced Jews to change their religion, it seems to be divine retribution that the Jews should strike back with the weapons that were put into their hands; to punish those who compelled them to change their faith, and as a judgment upon the new faith, the Jews break out of the circle of Christian unity, and by such actions seek to reenter the road to their faith, which they abandoned so long ago" (*Consolation for the Tribulations of Israel*, trans. by M.A. Cohen (1965), 193). Another Jewish chronicler, Joseph *ha-Kohen – born in Avignon but living and writing in Italy – wholeheartedly supported the Reformation camp and described events and personalities consistently from this point of view. To him Luther was the sage among the Christians; the Council of Trent failed because the Lutherans did not come and, left to themselves, the Catholics could only do foolish things. His sympathy goes out to the Reformation fighters of southern France in particular. He describes their plight in a way that shows that he made use of their information and sources. The death of the heads of the population of a Protestant city in the province is described as true *kiddush ha-Shem*: "the leaders of the populace they [the Catholic forces] took along with them, torturing them and burning them alive… But they [the Reformation martyrs] exclaimed: 'This indeed is the day we have hoped for – our souls shall return to God while our bodily clods return to dust'" (*Divrei ha-Yamim* (Sabbioneta, 1554), pt. 2, fol. 289v.). Joseph ha-Kohen was happy to witness and describe the sack of Rome in 1527, but when a Protestant church in Metz was destroyed by the Catholics and some of the people killed, he commented that the Catholics had "polluted the land with blood" (in H.H. Ben-Sasson, op. cit., 284). Perceiving the hope of toleration emerging from the wars of religion, he felt that the essential factor to emerge from a peace pact between reformers and Catholics in France was "that each man could worship his God according to his wish without fear. So all the people were exceedingly pleased" (*ibid.*). This is quite in the spirit of the middle-of-the-road party in France.

With sectarian existence under Catholic rule in Bohemia and Moravia, Hungary, and Poland-Lithuania, ties between Protestants and Jews became closer, for there was a growing similarity between their modes of existence. In the 1530s there were complaints in Poland that Jews exploited the Reformation disquiet for proselytizing. Much more clear are the contacts – both through disputations and through direct influence – between anti-trinitarians and Jews, as, e.g., in Poland between Isaac b. Abraham of *Troki and Szymon *Budny, and between Marcin Czechowic and Jacob of *Bełżyce. In the thought of Judah Loew b. *Bezalel of Prague and his circle, there is much evidence of contacts with sectarians. Judah Loew's plea against censorship on books – antedating *Milton's *Areopagitica* by about 50 years (Judah Loew's plea was printed in 1598) – has the marks of sectarian pleading for tolerance. Yet his brother *Ḥayyim felt constrained to warn "the Jews that… when they slacken in their regard for the Torah and its commandments, God bestows His bounty upon the unclean cattle. So that even if Israel subsequently repents, it is difficult for God to reject that nation on their account. This is all due to the fact that we, in our manifold sinfulness, are daily drawing farther away from the truth, whereas they, on the contrary, realize day by day that they are in the grip of falsehood. A different spirit is manifesting itself to some extent in their midst, bringing them nearer to truth, since they, too, for the most part are descended from the true seed" (*Sefer ha-Ḥayyim, Sefer Ge'ullah vi-Yshu'ah*, ch. 7, fol. 46v.). Ḥayyim feared that the new and eager spirit of the Reformation was endangering the covenant between the Jewish people and the Torah.

In modern times some Reformation patterns of worship and behavior and modes of thought influenced not only the *Reform trend in Judaism but also some of the *Orthodox communities, in particular in Anglo-Saxon countries. The ideology of religious pluralism accepted in the U.S., and welcomed by Jews, is a direct result of Reformation development. On the other hand, Nazism reawakened in Europe all the scars and problems of the Reformation's antisemitic inclination. In modern Jewish *historiography and thought, the 19th century may be described mainly as the pro-Reformation period, while in the 20th century some pro-Catholic and anti-Reformation historiography and ideas emerged and developed.

BIBLIOGRAPHY: H.H. Ben-Sasson, "The Reformation in Contemporary Jewish Eyes," in: PIASH, 4 (1970); S.W. Baron, in: *Diogenes*, 16, no. 61 (1968), 32–51.

[Haim Hillel Ben-Sasson]

REFORM JUDAISM, first of the modern interpretations of Judaism to emerge in response to the changed political and cultural conditions brought about by the *Emancipation.

The Reform movement was a bold historical response to the dramatic events of the 18th and 19th centuries in Europe. The increasing political centralization of the late 18th and early 19th centuries undermined the societal structure that perpetuated traditional Jewish life. At the same time, Enlightenment ideas began to influence not only a small group of intellectuals but also wider circles. The resulting political, economic, and social changes were profound. From a religious point of view, many Jews felt a tension between Jewish tradition and the way they were now leading their lives.

Many responded to this new situation by observing less and less of that tradition. As the insular religious society that reinforced such observance disintegrated, it was easy to fall away from vigilant observance without deliberately breaking with Judaism. Over the course of a few decades, a large percentage of the Jews of central Europe were no longer sure exactly how much of the traditional belief they subscribed to. Some tried to reconcile their religious heritage with their new social surroundings by reforming traditional Judaism to meet their new needs and to express their spiritual yearnings. Gradually these efforts became a movement with a set of religious beliefs, with practices that were considered expected as well as practices regarded as antiquated, and with an identity as a coherent and cohesive modern Jewish religious stream or denomination.

Usually viewed in contrast with Orthodoxy, Reform Judaism was the first of the modern responses to the emancipation of the Jews, a political process that occurred over an extended period. Because of its stress on autonomy – both of the individual and of the congregation – Reform Judaism has manifested itself differently in various countries. Nevertheless, Reform communities throughout the world share certain characteristics. Reform Jews believe that religious change is legitimate and that Judaism has changed over the centuries as society has changed. While in the past this evolutionary process was subconscious and organic, in the modern world it has become deliberate. The guiding principal of the contemporary Reform movement is that it can adapt Jewish religious beliefs and practices to the needs of the Jewish people from generation to generation.

The first Reformers – long identified as "German" Jews but, in fact, Jews from many European countries – were seeking a middle course between halakhic Judaism, which they wanted to break away from, and conversion to Christianity, which they wanted to avoid. Looking for a way to remain Jewish while adapting to the prevailing social customs, they hoped that by introducing modern aesthetics and strict decorum, they could make worship services more attractive to the many central European Jews who were drifting away from traditional Judaism but had not become Christians. Most of the early reforms focused on minor cosmetic changes: They abbreviated the liturgy and added a sermon in the vernacular, a mixed male and female choir accompanied by an organ, and German along with Hebrew prayers. From the point of view of Jewish law, reading some additional prayers in German was a relatively minor divergence. But for the congregants eager to create a synagogue service that would look respectable to their neighbors and at the same time feel authentic to themselves, such a change carried great import.

By the early 1840s, a trained Reform rabbinic leadership had emerged in central Europe. Abraham Geiger, called to the Breslau Jewish community in 1839, developed into the most distinguished intellectual defender of Reform Judaism in 19th-century Europe. Reform rabbinical conferences in Brunswick in 1844, Frankfurt in 1845, and Breslau in 1846 gave rabbis an opportunity to clarify their beliefs and the practices that could follow from them. A debate over the use of Hebrew in the services led Zacharias *Frankel to walk out of the 1845 conference, a moment many see as the beginning of the historical school, which advocated positive-historical Judaism. Frankel accepted the evolutionary character of the Jewish religion but insisted that the "positive" dimensions of Jewish tradition needed to be preserved. This perspective later evolved into Conservative Judaism. Although most of the rabbis at these conferences were much less traditional than Frankel, they taught in the established Jewish community, the *Einheitsgemeinde*, and therefore had to remain sensitive to and conversant with traditional rituals and observances.

A number of radical Reform rabbis, in particular Samuel Holdheim, made strong anti-traditional statements that shocked many of the more traditionally inclined. Geiger himself has been quoted as seeming to repudiate the circumcision rite as "a barbaric act." Yet the practice of most German Reform rabbis remained far more traditional than their rhetoric. They worked to remain a part of Kelal Israel, the totality of the Jewish people, and did not fully accept the radical Reform groups in Berlin and Frankfurt.

Reform Arrives in the United States

The history of Reform Judaism in the United States differs profoundly from that in Europe. Whereas in Europe the movement developed under the shadow of antisemitism and the threat of conversion to Christianity, in the United States a much freer and more pluralistic, more heterodox atmosphere prevailed. There was no established religious community and no support from the state. Over 200 years, the U.S. Reform movement has changed significantly and has seen substantial regional and even local variation among individual congregations. Nevertheless, it can point to a surprisingly high degree of continuity.

The first attempt at Reform occurred in Charleston, South Carolina, in 1824, when 47 members of Congregation Beth Elohim signed a petition requesting that their congregational leadership institute certain ritual reforms, including the introduction of prayers in English. The congregational board rejected the request, and a small group of intellectuals decided to form a new congregation, to be based on enlightened liberal values. On November 21, 1824, the Reformed Society of Israelites came into being, and the group published the first American Reform prayer book, *The Sabbath Service and Miscellaneous Prayers Adopted by the Reformed Society of Israelites*. Although the original group disbanded in 1833, due in part to the relocation and subsequent death of one of its more dynamic leaders, an interesting Sephardi intellectual named Isaac *Harby, Mother Congregation Beth Elohim soon began to move toward Reform under the leadership of its *hazzan*, Gustavus Poznanski.

One of the most fascinating episodes in American Jewish history, the Charleston Reform attempt was an isolated phenomenon. Far more important for the development of the Reform movement in the United States was the arrival of large numbers of central European Jews beginning in the 1830s, later mistakenly referred to as "German" Jews. For the most part, they were central Europeans. The Jewish population of the United States jumped from approximately 3,000 in 1820 to 15,000 in 1840 and 150,000 in 1860. Although many scholars have assumed that these immigrants brought Reform Judaism with them from Germany, Leon Jick has argued persuasively that American Reform was not "imported" but rather developed in the United States in response to the American socioreligious environment of the antebellum period. While Jick overstates his argument, his book was a much needed corrective to the earlier historical consensus.

Jewish immigrants settled throughout the United States. As they established businesses and built homes, local Jews began to put more effort into building a community. They consecrated cemeteries and held High Holy Day services, usually in a private home or a hotel meeting room. Eventually, they erected synagogue buildings and, if the community was large enough, engaged a religious leader with training in religious matters in the old country who could read the Hebrew prayers and perform the required rituals. For the congregations in Fort Wayne, Indiana, or Lexington, Kentucky, this was sufficient. As the immigrants gradually acculturated, they wanted their synagogue practice to reflect American norms. They wanted to use English as well as Hebrew in the services and to create an atmosphere to which they could bring Christian neighbors, who would come away impressed with the propriety and nobility of the ritual. Thus they moved their congregations toward Reform, not out of an intellectually based theological commitment, but as a practical response to daily life in the United States. Most of the functionaries went along with that trend. They were not theologically motivated but rather saw the practical benefits of adapting religious practices to the American patterns of living and enabling Jews to remain Jewish.

But ideologically motivated reformers also existed. One group of liberal religious intellectuals in Baltimore formed a *verein* in 1842, a small religious group that met to discuss theology and conduct services based on that theology, the Har Sinai Verein. In 1845 a similar group founded Emanu-El in New York City, which developed into the largest and most prestigious Reform congregation in the country. These groups, dedicated to Reform Judaism in ideological terms, differed from the vast majority of congregations in the United States, whose members were more concerned with the realities of everyday life in America than with the intricacies of Judaic theological debate.

Isaac Mayer Wise and the Development of the American Reform Movement

As more congregations developed in the antebellum period, the need for strong rabbinic leadership grew. Not all congregations felt this need; many treasured their independence and many local lay leaders enjoyed dominating communal affairs. Despite the difficulties, rabbis carved out a leadership niche for themselves. Numerous immigrant teachers and ritual functionaries were interested in serving in the rabbinate and, in some cases, in assuming leadership roles on a regional or national level. One of the best known was Isaac *Leeser of Philadelphia. A traditionalist minister who published an influential newspaper, *The Occident*, Leeser also promoted many other intellectual, social, and educational projects. But it was Isaac Mayer *Wise who had the charisma and determination to develop into a national Jewish religious leader and to actively work to build American Jewish institutions and organizations.

Isaac Mayer Wise arrived from Bohemia in 1846, and although he was advised to become a peddler, Rabbi Max Lilienthal encouraged him to consider the pulpit rabbinate and sent Wise in his stead to dedicate a number of synagogues. This led to an opportunity for Wise to begin serving as rabbi in Albany, New York, where there was a famous confrontation between Wise and the congregation's president, the first of so many clashes between rabbis and lay leaders. When he was offered a life contract in 1854 to become the rabbi of Congregation B'ne Jeshurun in Cincinnati, Wise accepted, and the pulpit became his base for building the American Reform movement.

Wise established a newspaper, *The Israelite* – later *The *American Israelite* – and edited a *siddur* called *Minhag Amerika: Tefillot Beney Yeshurun/Daily Prayers*. Credited with establishing or being the driving force behind the founding of all three major institutions of the Reform movement, he inspired one of his lay leaders to establish the Union of American Hebrew Congregations (UAHC, later *Union for Reform Judaism (URJ)) and himself founded the *Hebrew Union College (HUC) and the *Central Conference of American Rabbis (CCAR).

Although Wise had hoped to build an American Judaism that included all American Israelites rather than just the more liberal elements, a moderate form of Judaism that combined some ritual reforms with traditional elements, this vision proved unworkable especially after the incident of the *Treife Banquet*, in which forbidden foods were served as the post ordination reception of the first ordination of Hebrew Union College. The Reform movement, however, was the first Jewish religious movement in the United States to organize itself on a denominational basis. Reform Judaism includes three types of organizations, each with its own territorial parameters: the congregational organization, today represented nationally by the UAHC; the four campuses of the *Hebrew Union College–Jewish Institute of Religion (HUC-JIR); and the rabbinate, represented by the CCAR. The movement pioneered this "tripartite polity" – a congregational body, a rabbinic organization and a seminary – as Lance Sussman refers to it, subsequently adopted by the other major denominations of American Judaism.

In the early 1870s, Wise, who had been trying for many years to create a national association of U.S. congregations, encouraged Moritz Loth, the president of Wise's Congregation B'ne Jeshurun, to issue a call to congregations to meet in Cincinnati for the purpose of establishing a Hebrew theological college. In July 1873, representatives from 34 congregations from 28 cities, mostly in the Midwest and the South, came together to found the organization. The following year, 21 additional temples joined. By the end of the decade, 118 congregations belonged to the UAHC, more than half of all identified synagogues in the United States.

The UAHC dealt with congregational issues and strategies for working together as an organized congregational movement. Its first goal was to create a rabbinical school. Wise had been trying to create such a school for many years and had actually opened one shortly after his arrival in Cincinnati in 1855, Zion College, which lasted for only one year. But Wise did not give up on the idea. He was further encouraged when Henry Adler of Lawrenceburg, Indiana, offered a $10,000 gift toward the establishment of an American rabbinical college. With the UAHC's establishment in 1873, Wise saw a new opportunity to build a successful school. That same year, the University of Cincinnati was founded, presenting the possibility for rabbinical students to attend the university simultaneously and graduate from rabbinical school with a university degree as well. At the UAHC annual meeting in July 1874, congregational representatives voted unanimously for such a college to be established, with Wise as president. In 1875 the Hebrew Union College was founded. Wise served as president until his death in 1900. A number of distinguished Reform rabbis followed him in this role: Kaufmann *Kohler (1903–1921), Julian *Morgenstern (1921–1947), Nelson *Glueck (1947–1971), Alfred *Gottschalk (1971–1996), Sheldon *Zimmerman (1996–2000), and David *Ellenson (2001–). Since its founding, the college has educated the professionals who would assume leadership roles in the congregations, as well as many of the women who would marry future rabbis.

A long period of tension and conflict between the theologically oriented radical Reformers in the East and the more moderate Reformers in the Midwest had created a great deal of bitterness between the two groups as they attempted to influence the direction of American Judaism. Because of this divisiveness, Wise waited until HUC had graduated a sufficient number of rabbis and only then moved forward with the establishment of a permanent rabbinical association. David Philipson, an early HUC graduate and rabbi at Congregation Bene Israel in Cincinnati, helped Wise issue a call to rabbis planning to attend the 1889 UAHC conference to meet separately to establish their own organization. The rabbis created the Central Conference of American Rabbis, then elected Wise president by unanimous vote; he continued to serve until his death 11 years later.

By 1890 90 rabbis had affiliated with the CCAR, which dealt with rabbinical issues, including controversial religious questions. Membership was open to any rabbi who was serving or had served a synagogue as spiritual leader. After the first year, membership would be open to those from several categories, not only those with ordination from HUC, but also a wide variety of religious functionaries. As time went on, more and more members were HUC graduates. Today the CCAR has a membership of more than 1,800.

Despite his successful leadership, Wise was considered an uneducated and unworthy colleague by some of the "German" Reform rabbis who arrived in the 1850s and 1860s with doctorates from prestigious central European universities. Primary among them was David *Einhorn, who immigrated to the United States in 1855. Einhorn wrote a number of scathing attacks on Wise for abrogating Reform theology and turning what he saw as a consistent and principled approach to modern Judaism into a jumble of incoherent beliefs. The issue debated by Wise and Einhorn has remained a relevant theme throughout the history of the Reform movement. Is it more important to be theologically unswerving, or to respond effectively to changing societal trends? Most of the time, the movement has favored pragmatism over theological consistency.

Wise represented a pragmatic approach to American Judaism. He was primarily an institution builder who attempted to use ideology as a tool for compromise and consensus. Wise succeeded as an organizational leader in building an entire American religious movement from scratch, under very difficult circumstances.

The Classical Reform Period

Classical Reform was the type of Reform Judaism that developed in the late 19th century. American Jews, most of whom were of central European background, saw the tremendous influence that liberal religion had on their Protestant neighbors and wanted to develop a form of Judaism equivalent to Episcopalianism, Presbyterianism, and especially Unitarianism.

As presented in the 1885 *Declaration of Principles*, known as the 1885 *Pittsburgh Platform, Classical Reform Judaism minimized Judaic ritual and emphasized ethics in a universalist context, stressing universalism while reaffirming the Reform movement's commitment to Jewish particularism through the expression of the religious idea of the mission of Israel. The document defined Reform Judaism as a rational and modern form of religion in contrast with traditional Judaism on one hand and universalist ethics on the other.

Motivated by his concern that persuasive personalities were urging American Jews to embrace these alternatives, Kohler, the platform's principal author and a son-in-law of David Einhorn, wanted to present in a formal manner what distinguished Reform Judaism from traditional Judaism as well as what was Jewish about Reform Judaism. Earlier in 1885, he had debated in a series of public forums with Alexander *Kohut, a Hungarian rabbi recently arrived in New York who espoused the traditionalist approach. Their debates had attracted wide attention in the synagogues and the press. That the founder of the Society for Ethical Culture, Felix *Adler, was the son of Samuel *Adler, the rabbi of Congregation Emanu-El in New York, particularly galled Kohler. The rabbi's son, who had returned from rabbinic studies in Germany advocating a philosophical approach to ethics in a universalistic framework, was attracting to his philosophy and organization many Reform Jews who wanted both to express their conviction that ethics was important and to loosen or break their particularistic ties with Jewish ethnic identity. Adler placed himself on the extreme of the continuum between particularism and universalism, emphasizing the individual's connection with and commitment to humanity as a whole, rather than to any one ethnic or religious grouping.

Kohler chose a middle road, as this excerpt from the *Declaration* indicates:

> We hold that all such mosaic and rabbinical laws as regulate diet, priestly purity and dress originated in ages and under the influence of ideas altogether foreign to our present mental and spiritual state. They fail to impress the modern

> Jew with a spirit of priestly holiness; their observance in our days is apt rather to obstruct than to further modern spiritual elevation.

Reform Judaism has historically emphasized what it interpreted as the central message of the prophets: the need to fight for social justice. The Reformers believed deeply in working with their Christian neighbors to help make the world a place of justice and peace, and this belief was a central part of the religious worldview. The platform emphasized the prophetic mandate to work tirelessly for the rights of the downtrodden, and the term "prophetic Judaism" described the Reform vision of following the dictates of the prophets to create a just society on earth. Coupled with the emphasis on its interpretation of prophetic Judaism, the early Reformers in particular spoke frequently about the mission of Israel, which presented the idea that the prophets of the Bible served as advocates of ethical monotheism. Ethical monotheism combined the Jewish belief in one God with rational thought and modern innovations in scientific knowledge.

The mission of Israel was to stand as an example of the highest standards of ethics and morals and to help bring the world to an awareness of and commitment to ethical monotheism.

American Jews who embraced Reform were greatly influenced by the popular belief in the sovereign self. They started with their own religious feelings and tried to place their personal understanding of what we would today call "spirituality" in a Judaic context. When Emil G. Hirsch of Chicago Sinai Congregation in 1925 entitled one of his books *My Religion*, he was making a statement about the source of his religious inspiration. Still, the Reformers understood that American Judaism could not stand solely on the basis of personal inspiration but needed a connection to Jewish history through a religious concept not "nationalistic" in orientation, but pure and holy.

They believed that the prophets stressed universalism rather than particularism, and therefore the Reformers felt justified in likewise stressing the universal over the particular. At the same time, the concept of the mission of Israel justified the continued existence of the Jewish people by arguing that their ongoing survival as a religious group was essential if the Jews were to bring their universalistic message of ethical monotheism to the world. David Einhorn used a version of this argument to oppose intermarriage with non-Jews, since "the small Jewish race [a term acceptable at that time]" needed to preserve itself as a separate entity to fulfill their religious mission on earth. Taken to its extreme, the mission of Israel concept helped Reform leaders present Judaism as the ultimate expression of ethical monotheism.

As the purest form of monotheistic religion, Judaism was therefore the strongest theological argument for ethical behavior. As such, it deserved to be taken seriously as a way of thought and a way of life by all individuals committed to finding a true understanding of God and God's place in the world. This allowed Reform leaders such as Wise to declare that Judaism was destined to become the faith of all humankind, or at least of all Americans who held liberal religious beliefs.

Reform leaders believed that as time passed, humankind would be better able to understand the will of God, and thus society was certain to become a better place. This belief became most pronounced in Classical Reform.

The theology of the Classical Reform rabbis is only part of the story. Yaakov Ariel has argued that historians have portrayed the Reform movement of this period in stereotypical terms taken from eastern European Jewish perceptions of the German Jewish elite. Specifically, such historians have presented the Reform movement as having divorced itself completely from the national as well as the ethnic components of Jewish identity. Ariel argues that there was an "astonishing gap" between the ideals of the Reform movement as expressed by rabbinic leaders, and the attitudes held by the vast majority of members in the congregations:

> The Reform movement held a character almost diametrically opposed to its universalistic aspirations. As an ethnically oriented, parochial, and tribal group, Reform Jews were concerned with Jewish matters on local, national, and international levels, and were strongly involved with their non-Reform Jewish brethren.

Classical Reform Judaism had developed during a period of heady optimism, beginning with the 1885 Pittsburgh Platform, but as early as 1881, Jews began fleeing to the United States to escape the pogroms of eastern Europe. By the time the Nazi Party rose to power in 1933, it was increasingly difficult to see the world as a place where Jew and gentile could continue to work side-by-side to make the world a better place and to bring justice and peace to all in the spirit of the prophets.

The 1930s brought signs that at least some of the Reform movement's leaders felt the need for a return to tradition. Jews increasingly believed that the world was profoundly hostile to them. Rather than universal goals, they yearned for a Jewish homeland that could absorb the hundreds of thousands or even millions of Jews who faced prejudice, persecution, and murder. While no one imagined the enormity of the tragedy that would befall European Jewry, the possibilities were apparent. In response to the changing political environment, the Reform movement began to accept and eventually embrace a more particularistic understanding of Jewish identity, including political Zionism. The Reformers began to accept a definition of Judaism centered on Jewish peoplehood. Nevertheless, Reform rabbis continued to speak of ethical monotheism, which stressed that the Jewish belief in one God would lead to the highest ethical behavior.

The Changing Character of the Reform Movement

The Reform movement changed its direction as a consequence of the increasingly brutal nature of the 20th century. World War I jump-started the process of reexamining the liberal sense that had propelled Reform religious thought until that time. The movement's optimistic view of human progress in collaboration with God underwent further change after the rise of the Nazi movement in Germany and the subsequent murder of six million Jews. In the aftermath of that tragedy, the Reform movement veered away from its universalistic triumphalism toward a more ethnically based cultural identity. But the breakdown of this optimism did not mean the end of either Reform Judaism or the Reform movement. Congregations continued to attract new adherents as sociological patterns shifted. Many Jews found that the Reform temple met their need for a nominal religious identification, while allowing them to join the stew in the American melting pot.

From 1881 until 1920, the Reform movement grew slowly relative to the increase in the American Jewish population, with 99 congregations consisting of 9,800 members in 1900 and 200 congregations with 23,000 in 1920 while the American Jewish population increased 14-fold. The Reform movement went from being the single most important voice of the Jewish American community to being a small minority. Although the elite nature of many Reform Jews meant they retained a high profile, they were swamped by the eastern European organizations and ideologies.

The eastern European mass immigrations increased the American Jewish population from 250,000 in 1880 to 1 million by 1900 and 3.5 million by 1920. The bulk of the immigrants came from Russia, Ukraine, Lithuania, Poland, Romania, and other regions where there had not been full emancipation. Since most of the native population in their home countries had viewed these Jews as an alien presence, they came to America from an insular Jewish background. As a consequence, few joined the Reform movement. The immigrants did not like the Reform service, which they found lacking in traditional Jewish elements. Many Reform Jews maintained a haughty attitude toward the newcomers, preferring not to remember that their own parents or grandparents had arrived in the United States one or two generations earlier under similar circumstances. Indeed, a mythology developed that had the "German" Jews descended from aristocrats. Historically inaccurate, it reflected a widely held perception.

Nevertheless, over the course of time increasing numbers of eastern Europeans joined Reform congregations. Under their influence, the Reform movement inched back toward a more traditional approach to Jewish thought and practice, hastened by world events. By the 1920s and especially the 1930s, with the worldwide rise of antisemitism, this direction became clear. Even though the 1885 *Declaration of Principles* had argued that Jews should remain together solely as a religious group to fulfill their mission of bringing ethical monotheism to the world, the rise in antisemitism threatened Jewish physical survival, a concern that far outweighed theology or ideology. Policies that had seemed levelheaded just a few decades earlier now appeared naïve and foolhardy. As a result, the CCAR adopted the Columbus Platform in 1937, officially named *The Guiding Principles of Reform Judaism*. This new platform embraced Jewish peoplehood and leaned toward support of political Zionism. The culmination of a revolutionary shift in the ideology of the American Reform movement, it encouraged a greater diversity of opinion and a multiplicity of approaches.

By 1945 the Reform movement was well on its way to accepting Zionism and the soon-to-be-created State of Israel. The interwar period saw the rise of two strongly Zionistic Reform rabbis, Stephen S. *Wise and Abba Hillel *Silver. Wise (no relation to Isaac Mayer Wise) began his rabbinic career in Portland, Oregon, then moved to New York, where he established his own congregation after Temple Emanuel refused to promise him freedom of the pulpit. In 1922, he established the Jewish Institute of Religion (JIR) in New York City to provide a Zionist alternative to Hebrew Union College. Wise believed in both the importance of social justice and the centrality of Jewish peoplehood. Like him, Abba Hillel Silver was a prominent leader in American and world Jewish affairs as well as a congregational rabbi. After serving as a rabbi in Wheeling, West Virginia, he became rabbi of the temple in Cleveland, Ohio. From this pulpit he worked tirelessly to build up the American Zionist movement in the hope of establishing a Jewish state. With Wise, Silver formed the American Zionist Emergency Council, which lobbied the U.S. Congress on behalf of the Zionist movement. Silver was the leader who announced to the United Nations that Israel had declared itself an independent state. Both men were Classical Reformers devoted to Jewish nationalism, a synthesis that would have been incongruous just a few decades earlier.

Post–World War II Developments

The aftermath of World War II brought a massive suburban construction boom that within American Judaism benefited the Conservative branch most. Conservative Judaism appealed to the now Americanized Eastern European immigrants and their children, because it appeared substantially more traditional than Reform but allowed far greater flexibility than Orthodoxy. Nevertheless, Reform Judaism benefited from this suburbanization trend as well. The 265 congregations in 1940, with 59,000 members in the UAHC, grew by 1955 to 520 congregations and 255,000 members.

Many suburban Jews who joined Reform congregations saw the temple mainly as an extracurricular activity for their children. Congregations that moved most rapidly to meet the needs of these new suburbanites thrived. The temple became a social center that substituted to some degree for the loss of the old Jewish neighborhoods, such as those once clustered on the Lower East Side or Brownsville in New York and its equivalences in other major urban settings. The Reform leadership faced the challenge of conveying a religious message to congregants who had not joined their synagogues primarily to share a religious vision. Yet the leaders needed to captivate and motivate them to care and to feel that the congregation was helping them fulfill themselves as ethically concerned people.

The Reform movement grew in large part because it benefited from strong leadership. While much of this strength was more perception than reality, it nevertheless inspired many in the rank-and-file. A tremendous amount of private infighting remained largely hidden from public view. Maurice N. *Eisendrath, who became UAHC executive director in 1943 and president in 1946, moved the national headquarters from Cincinnati to New York – and thus geographically separate from Hebrew Union College – where he constructed an entire building for the organization on Fifth Avenue across the street from Central Park and next to Congregation Emanu-El. He called the new headquarters the "House of Living Judaism," and it remained the operating center of the Reform movement until it was sold under the presidency of Eric H. Yoffie in 1998. Unlike the Conservative Movement, where the titular leadership of the movement is the chancellor of the Jewish Theological Seminary, the president of the Union is the titular and actual head of the Reform Movement.

Nelson Glueck, a world-famous archeologist who had appeared on the cover of *Time*, became president of HUC in 1947. While many viewed him as more interested in his archaeological pursuits than in his administrative responsibilities, his fame brought a great deal of attention to the movement. He oversaw the 1950 merger of HUC with JIR, and under his leadership HUC-JIR established a third U.S. branch in Los Angeles in 1954 and a fourth campus in Jerusalem in 1963. Although this growth may have owed more to the burgeoning of the American Jewish community than to Glueck, the perception grew that the Reform movement had competent and visionary leadership.

The leaders could project this image of a strong, unified movement partly because of the number of pressing causes that could galvanize members of Reform congregations. In the 1960s many Reform Jews became involved in the U.S. civil rights struggle as well as in the movement opposing the war in Vietnam. The Six-Day War of 1967 dramatically increased American Jews' emotional connection and commitment to the State of Israel. As they worried about its ability to survive in the face of Arab promises to destroy the country during the tense three weeks preceding the war, many came to realize how important the State of Israel had become to them. This fear resurfaced in 1973 when Israel's physical survival was in doubt during the early stages of the Yom Kippur War. The cumulative effect was to increase dramatically the Zionist fervor of most American Jews, a sea change felt throughout the movement.

Interest in liturgical issues also increased. Many began to feel that *The Union Prayer Book,* used in Reform congregations since the 1890s, had become outdated; new prayers would better express how people felt in response to the volatile 1960s. Joseph Glaser, executive vice president of the CCAR, initiated a campaign in 1971 to write and publish new forms of liturgy. A thick blue prayer book, *The Gates of Prayer,* replaced *The Union Prayer Book* in 1975 to a mixed response – great excitement at the numerous options offered, along with horror at the drastic changes. This publication was joined in 1978 by a completely reworked High Holy Day prayer book, *The Gates of Repentance*. Both new prayer books contained a great deal more Hebrew than their predecessors and reintroduced many traditionalist elements deleted from *The Union Prayer Book*. There were 10 different Friday night services offered, most of which presented a specific theological approach, as well as services that catered specifically to children or those preparing for bar mitzvah. Synagogues introduced new ceremonies and experimented with various types of innovations. While many congregants embraced these changes, others resisted – some who had ideological objections, some who missed the liturgy they had been using their entire lives. To this day, some congregations, such as Congregation Emanu-El in New York, continue to use *The Union Prayer Book*. Others, such as Temple Sinai in New Orleans, have a Friday-night service once a month that uses *The Union Prayer Book* instead of the more recent liturgical works. The Reform movement's boldness in its liturgical publications matches its brave leadership in the realm of social justice, as well as its willingness to break with traditional belief and practice.

New Approaches to Changing Social Trends

Alexander M. *Schindler, who became president of the UAHC in 1973, gained renown for his assertive support of the social action agenda of the Reform movement of the 1970s and 1980s, including civil rights, world peace, nuclear disarmament, a "Marshall Plan" for the poor, feminism, and gay rights, as well as his opposition to the death penalty. Although this advocacy landed Schindler frequently in the pages of the *New York Times*, he got along with traditional Jews and Israeli leaders better than had any of his predecessors. His command of Yiddish and his sense of humor and of fairness helped enormously. He played a central role as chairman of the Conference of Presidents' of Major American Jewish Organization in smoothing the way for Likud leader Menachem Begin, with whom he disagreed ideologically but with whom he established a warm and trusting personal relationship, to be accepted by American Jewish leaders who had long thought of Israel leadership as synonymous with Labor Israel. Despite a disinterest in administrative issues, Schindler and his German accent became synonymous with Reform Judaism. His leadership inspired not only individuals, but also entire temples, to join the movement. During his presidency, the UAHC grew from 400 congregations in 1973 to about 875 in 1995. Of course, the continuing move to suburbia made much of this growth possible, but Schindler's inspirational leadership on issues meaningful to American Jews disconnected from traditional belief or practice played an important role.

Schindler is perhaps best remembered for two issues, his outreach to intermarried couples and his advocacy of patrilineal descent. Intermarriage had long been a taboo in the Jewish community, and many parents ostracized children who "married out." Some would even sit *shiva* for children about to intermarry, as if the child had died. Schindler, who felt strongly that this taboo was counterproductive as well as inappropriate, came to believe that a bold gesture was in order. At a meeting of the UAHC's Board of Trustees in Houston in December

1978, he issued a public call to the Reform movement to reach out to the non-Jewish spouses in interfaith marriages. Even more surprising, he urged making the Jewish religion available to unchurched gentiles. This controversial call to proselytize those with no connections of blood or marriage to the Jewish community appeared to be a dramatic departure from two thousand years of Jewish religious policy against proselytization. His critics argued that such a move would encourage certain Christian groups to launch opposing campaigns against the Jewish community, using Schindler's call as an excuse for proselytizing unaffiliated Jews. Despite the attention that this suggestion created, little proselytizing of unchurched gentiles has occurred in the succeeding years, whereas many outreach programs to interfaith couples have been developed.

During the Schindler years the Reform movement adopted the patrilineal descent resolution, which stated that the child of one Jewish partner is "under the presumption of Jewish descent." While the document's vague wording led to some difficulties, the patrilineal descent policy insured that if one's father was Jewish and one's mother was not, one would still be regarded as Jewish, *provided that one was raised as a Jew.* This requirement of raising a child as a Jew was more stringent than *halakhah*. This would supplement rather than replace the traditional matrilineal descent policy, which established that the children of a Jewish mother would be Jewish regardless of their father's faith or even how they were raised.

Also during Schindler's presidency, the Reform movement allowed women to assume a more central role in the synagogue, a direct consequence of the feminist movement that influenced every aspect of American life. As American women in the 1960s and 1970s took on a far greater role in religious life than those of previous generations, the Reform movement responded quickly and actively to the changing sex-role expectations. Increasing numbers of congregations allowed women to assume responsibility for all aspects of religious and communal life, even the rabbinate. In 1972, Sally J. Priesand became the first woman ordained a Reform rabbi at HUC-JIR, a revolutionary breakthrough. Since 1972, hundreds of women have enrolled in HUC. As the changes in the Reform movement paralleled social changes, its character as an American religious denomination made it popular with an increasingly Americanized Jewish community.

Contemporary Trends

Reform practice today, especially in the synagogue itself, is characterized by the partial restoration of a number of formerly abrogated rites and rituals. Ritual items eliminated by the Classical Reformers, such as the *yarmulke*, *tallit*, and even *tefillin*, have been brought back. But because of the concept of religious autonomy, individual congregations cannot and do not require congregants to wear any of these traditional prayer items. Rather, they are offered to those who find them religiously meaningful or who prefer to wear them as an expression of traditionalist nostalgia. This generates some incongruous and perhaps amusing situations. For example, it is not uncommon to find congregations where many of the women wear *yarmulkes* and *tallitot*, while most of the men sit bareheaded and bare shouldered. This is the converse of the norm in traditional synagogues, where all men wear *yarmulkes*, *tallitot*, and on weekday mornings *tefillin*, and women rarely do. The Orthodox Jew who wanders into a Reform sanctuary by mistake would either break out laughing or withdraw in shock and horror.

Another dramatic trend has been the move away from a formal style of worship and music toward more jubilant and enthusiastic prayer. Certain particularly progressive congregations, such as the independent Congregation B'nai Jeshurun on the Upper West Side of New York, have served as models for most congregations that have been slowly evolving toward this more informal, exuberant style. The formalized Classical Reform service, which could uncharitably be called sterile, no longer impresses many with its dignity and majesty. Younger people have grown up with a different aesthetic. New types of music incorporate simple Israeli, ḥasidic, and folk styles, a style of worship developed at the UAHC summer camps under the rubric of the North American Federation of Temple Youth (NFTY) programs.

In a remarkably smooth transition of leadership, Eric H. *Yoffie, the president of the UAHC since 1996, inherited a movement that had grown substantially in numbers yet was perceived as having fundamental problems. Yoffie moved quickly and boldly to address these challenges, taking advantage of the new enthusiasm for spirituality and launching a systematic campaign to rebuild the entire Reform movement. He initiated a Jewish literacy campaign, which encouraged every Reform Jew to read at least four books with Jewish content every year. Recognizing that the NFTY, the movement's youth organization, had dwindled in effectiveness, Yoffie proposed a system that would include the appointment of full-time youth coordinators in each of the UAHC's thirteen regions.

Yoffie has only begun the process of reorienting the movement to meet the sociological challenges that Reform Judaism faces in contemporary America. At the same time, the rabbinic leadership has proposed a number of interesting initiatives, most notably Richard Levy's new Pittsburgh Platform. This restating of Reform religious beliefs generated a firestorm of controversy in 1998 and 1999. Although the CCAR at its annual conference in Pittsburgh in May 1999 eventually passed a revised version called *A Statement of Principles for Reform Judaism*, supporters found it severely watered down, while Classical Reformers viewed it as a betrayal of the Reform legacy in America. Despite a year-and-a-half of conflict over this issue, the values that inspired people to join the Reform movement have kept them from splitting off or leaving altogether. Although many remain persuaded that Reform Jews have no strong religious beliefs, the movement has created and propagated a religious vision that remains compelling after 200 years. It owes its success to its ability and willingness to respond theologically to changing times.

REJECTION OF JEWISH LAW. Traditional Judaism had focused on the observance of the *mitzvot*, the commandments given by God and incumbent on every adult Jew. The Reformers argued that if the Sages developed specific laws as a response to historical conditions, then *halakhah* could be changed or even abrogated. The Reform movement thus viewed *halakhah*, Jewish law, as no longer obligatory.

Yet there was never complete agreement over how to relate to ritual observance. By the middle of 19th century, a wide spectrum of opinion existed on the issue. The historical school, which developed into the Conservative movement, argued that although *halakhah* might develop over time, it nevertheless remained binding. The historical school developed innovative religious approaches as well. The main difference – a significant one – is that the historical school attempted to show that *halakhah* evolved in order to justify ritual change on the basis of contemporary needs. The Conservative movement viewed itself as faithful to the halakhic process.

But Reform thinkers understood the historical changes within Judaism as far more radical. According to a Reform understanding of the history of Judaism, the religion has evolved in a revolutionary fashion at several key points in its history. These changes were not simply adaptations of a minor nature, but dramatic developments that marked huge jumps in both belief and practice. Reform theologians believed that generations in different time periods fashioned a Judaism that suited their contemporary religious sensibilities.

But if Jewish law was not obligatory, then what was the purpose of Judaism? Many 19th-century rationalists believed that human beings possessed an autonomous sense of ethics and morals.

The rationalist philosophers argued that religion imposed an externally derived legal system on individuals that prevented them from exercising their autonomous will. Such reasoning could lead one to conclude that the essence of Judaism is ethics rather than law. That explains why so much of the early Reform literature stressed abstract ethical lessons and avoided describing ritual acts. Religious law, the Reformists believed, was inferior to ethics; Judaism's challenge was to develop along Kantian lines. Revelation became a bit tricky, because one needed autonomy to choose the ethical path. If God made all the decisions and issued all the commands, then the individual would not have autonomous choice. Therefore, Reform thinkers developed the notion of man and God as partners in an unfolding process of continuing revelation.

The rejection of *halakhah* as a legal system meant that every individual practice had to be justified on its own merits, which produced widespread inconsistencies and contradictions. For example, the *halakhah* requires all Jews to fast not only on Yom Kippur, but also on Tisha be-Av, a fast day commemorating the destruction of the First and Second Temples and other catastrophic events, and four additional minor fast days. But if *halakhah* no longer bound Reform Jews, then they no longer had to abstain from eating even on the holiest fast day of the year. Most pulpit rabbis seem to have chosen to ignore the glaring problem of ritual inconsistency, particularly in the private sphere. While Reform synagogues developed a standard liturgy and a formalized ritual, no corresponding code detailed how Reform Jews should live their lives outside the synagogue; each person had to decide what rituals, if any, remained meaningful. Perhaps the rabbis preferred not to interfere with the private habits of their congregants. Some theologians, however tried to provide an ethical justification for specific observance. In recent years, many Reform Jews have come to a new appreciation of the importance of ritual in religious life, which some Orthodox observers misinterpret as a return to halakhic observance. Rather, these Reformists find that specific traditional practices provide spiritual meaning for the individual. And that is, at heart, what the Reform movement stands for.

DIFFERENTIATING BETWEEN BIBLICAL AND TALMUDIC LAWS. From the beginning, lay leaders who wanted specific practical changes implemented pushed Reform forward. Innovation developed in response to local needs and took into account no overarching theological system or broad religious blueprint. Nevertheless, Reform thinkers had to develop a system for interpreting the tradition. One of their most important concepts was to differentiate between biblical and talmudic laws.

In traditional Judaism, the Sages differentiated laws that were *de-oraita*, from the Torah, from laws that were *de-rabbanan*, from the rabbis. But both types of laws were obligatory to the same degree, and one could not justify nonobservance by pointing out that a given law was "only" *de-rabbanan* rather than *de-oraita*. What was important to the Reformers was to develop a religious system that synchronized Jewish belief with contemporary trends yet retained enough particularistic elements to distinguish their religion as a form of Judaism. To this end, they wanted to eliminate laws and practices that would prevent or restrict their social and economic integration into the host society.

Writing in the 1960s and 1970s, American Jewish sociologist Marshall Sklare argued that the Jewish rituals most likely to endure were those capable of being redefined in modern, universal terms. A ritual would command widespread observance only if it did not bring with it social isolation or the adoption of a unique lifestyle. The message of the ritual had both to accord with the religious culture of the larger community and to provide a Jewish alternative to it. These usually focused on children and were performed infrequently so as not to be overly burdensome. Passover and Ḥanukkah, two holidays that met people's needs well, were therefore widely observed.

Reform Jews were quick to abandon practices such as *kashrut* that did not meet Sklare's criteria. Although it could be redefined in modern terms, for instance, keeping kosher would still demand a relatively high degree of social isolation as well as the adoption of a unique lifestyle. Nevertheless, some Reform Jews remained observant of the kosher laws, at least to some degree.

Reformers emphasized the prophetic ideals of justice and righteousness, arguing that these universalistic values formed the essence of Judaism. The 1885 Pittsburgh Platform, which differentiated moral and ritual laws and became the "principle of faith" for Classical Reform Judaism, stressed that most of the ancient laws were not to be observed.

Classical Reform was not only a system of beliefs, but also an aesthetic approach to religious practice. Although as immigrant Jews Americanized, they wanted their synagogues to reflect American norms, even in Europe many had seen the Orthodox way of worship as disruptive and undignified.

Many of the central European Jews not only believed that houses of worship should be places of propriety but also wanted their synagogue worship to reflect American norms and standards; they borrowed structural and stylistic features from local Protestant churches, copying their architecture, seating arraignments, musical styles, and so forth. Reform Jews also made a number of ritual changes solely on the basis of what they considered the most dignified approach. A Classical Reform aesthetic slowly developed into a compulsory system of ritual that replaced the halakhic system.

THE CHALLENGE OF UNRESTRICTED AUTONOMY. While Reform Judaism stood for the autonomy of the individual and against the belief that *halakhah* was binding in its entirety, in the post–World War II period, Reformers took a variety of positions on religious authority and how it can be reconciled with individual autonomy. While some argued against all boundaries, others tried to develop a post-halakhic justification for some form of Jewish legal authority. Reform thinkers understood that the freedom of action they advocated could result in unintended consequences. If individuals could make their own decisions over what to observe, then what would stop those individuals from observing nothing at all? Indeed, there were those who used the Reform movement to justify apathy and even apostasy. But no obvious solution presented itself.

In 1965, W. Gunther Plaut recommended to the Central Conference of American Rabbis (CCAR) that a Sabbath manual be written as a beginning toward a comprehensive guide for the Reform Jew. Plaut edited the result, *A Shabbat Manual*, published by the CCAR Press in 1972. The manual went much further than any previous CCAR publication in urging Reform Jews to perform certain *mitzvot* – to light Shabbat candles, to recite or chant the **kiddush*, and to avoid working or performing housework on the Sabbath. This watershed publication led to additional efforts to "return to tradition."

Yet a return to tradition should not be misunderstood as an acceptance of *halakhah* as a binding system. Most Reform Jews believe that religion in general, and Judaism specifically, is very much a human institution. They believe that it is impossible to know with absolute certitude what God wants from us. Certainly, behaving ethically is necessary for people of all faiths. But we cannot know what ritual behavior God expects from us. Eugene B. Borowitz, HUC-JIR theologian, has suggested that "when it comes to ritual, they [Reform thinkers] admit we are dealing largely with what people have wanted to do for God… ceremonial [behavior] discloses more of human need and imagination than it does of God's commands." The traditional belief that the *mitzvot* are binding because they are God-given is reinterpreted to acknowledge God's indirect inspiration in what is essentially a process of human spiritual expression.

THE QUESTION OF THEOLOGICAL BOUNDARIES. The question of whether the movement has theological boundaries was tested in the early 1990s when Congregation Beth Adam of Cincinnati applied to join the URJ. Its founder, Robert Barr, had graduated from HUC-JIR; many if not most of its congregants came from Reform backgrounds, including three current or former members of the HUC-JIR Board of Governors. An adherent of Sherwin T. Wine's Humanistic Judaism, Barr had founded Beth Adam in 1981. Arguing that it was possible to follow Judaism without believing in God and certainly without a traditional conception of God, Wine had established the small movement in 1963, along with the first Humanistic Jewish congregation, the Birmingham Temple, in Michigan. Beth Adam had grown unhappy with the organization, in particular, as Barr explained, because the group had begun ordaining its own leaders. After about 10 years of belonging to no national organization Barr and the congregation felt the need to be in closer touch "with the issues and concerns of the wider Jewish community." The board of Beth Adam decided to apply to join the URJ.

URJ president Alexander Schindler encouraged Beth Adam's application but took no public stand on what the Union should do, stating at the 1991 URJ biennial only that the controversy would "generate a boon to our community" by opening a debate on what a Reform congregation must accept, if anything. The debate centered on the congregation's exclusion of God from its liturgy. Neither the *Shema* nor the *kaddish* was recited, the group's literature explained, because prayers "which presume a God who intervenes or manipulates the affairs of this world" would be inconsistent with its religious message.

While some supported Beth Adam's application, the response was largely negative and even hostile, and in 1990 a majority of the CCAR Responsa Committee voted against accepting the group. Chairperson W. Gunther Plaut wrote that its "elision of God" means the congregation "does not admit of Covenant or commandments"; while the Reform movement can accept individuals who may be agnostic or even atheist, it cannot accept congregations whose declared principals contradict the religious beliefs of Reform Judaism. Three rabbis on the Responsa Committee disagreed with the majority view, arguing that to accept Beth Adam into the URJ would not necessarily imply that the Reform movement accepts its theological views. The debate continued through the early 1990s.

In June the URJ Board of Trustees spent an entire day deliberating the matter in Washington, DC. At the end of its deliberations, the board voted 115 to 13 with four abstentions to reject the application.

The Beth Adam decision meant that while congregations still had the right to adopt the prayer book of their choice or write one of their own, there were theological limits on what could legitimately be regarded as Reform liturgy. The vote also reaffirmed that the drive for inclusion did not obligate the Reform movement to accept every group from every background espousing every ideology.

THE MOVE TOWARDS RETRADITIONALIZATION. Rabbi Eric H. Yoffie, a Reform rabbi and the president of the URJ, is leading the restructuring and revitalization of the Reform movement. When Yoffie took office the Reform movement had to either make dramatic changes or watch its fortunes fade rapidly. Large numbers in the movement have been receptive to his proposals. New approaches to study, worship, and ritual practice are being implemented.

Yoffie then outlined a plan to reform Reform. "I propose, therefore, that at this biennial assembly we proclaim a new Reform revolution. Like the original Reform revolution, it will be rooted in the conviction that Judaism is a tradition of rebellion, revival, and redefinition; and like the original too, this new initiative will make synagogue worship our Movement's foremost concern." Yoffie urged that this "worship revolution" be built on a partnership among rabbis, cantors, and lay people.

The URJ leadership has prepared a series of initiatives that taken together constitute "a Reform revolution." Many insiders are very hopeful that the coming years will see radical changes that excite Reform Jews and get them involved in concrete religious activities. To bring the synagogue back as a central Jewish institution, Reformers are developing programs that appeal to a much broader range of individuals and client groups.

Much of the success of this effort relies upon how deeply it can touch people's emotions. In his Orlando address Yoffie asked, "What will be the single most important key to the success or failure of our revolution?" And then he answered his own question: "Music." "Ritual music is a deeply sensual experience that touches people in a way that words cannot. Music converts the ordinary into the miraculous, and individuals into a community of prayer. And music enables overly-intellectual Jews to rest their minds and open their hearts."

The new programming has occurred not only within the movement itself, but also in related efforts such as the Synagogue 2000 transformation project led by Rabbis Ron Wolfson and Lawrence Hoffman. As Wolfson put it, "What defines great, spiritual davening experiences is music, music, music." Some cutting-edge congregations like B'nai Jeshurun in Manhattan and Temple Sinai in Los Angeles have become nationally known for implementing vibrant music programs that draw hundreds to their Friday night and Saturday morning services. That neither congregation is affiliated with the Reform movement may not be a coincidence. A vibrant musical experience requires the congregants to actively participate, to sing the songs with passion as well as confidence, and most Reform Jews do not know the words well enough to sing along. Their Hebrew may be poor, and not enough congregants have so far expressed the willingness to put in the time and effort necessary to acquire more advanced Hebraic skills.

The URJ has inaugurated a number of programs specifically to address this issue, among them a Hebrew literacy campaign called "Aleph Isn't Tough: An Introduction to Hebrew for Adults" launched to "open the gates of prayer" to the average Jew. The URJ's new Hebrew primers will focus not only on phonetic reading but also on the comprehension of basic prayers and text. The hope is that more and more synagogues will use these or other texts to offer a variety of adult Hebrew classes. The more Hebrew that Reform Jews know, the more accessible is the textual tradition.

Yoffie argues that in the current religious climate, concrete programming designed to get people doing *mitzvot* must precede theological formulations.

YOUTH EDUCATION PROGRAMS. Temple youth groups are the entry points for many young people into congregational life, and over the last several years, the Reform movement has set out aggressively to nurture the development of teen leaders not only for youth groups but also for congregations as a whole.

Once a dynamic and successful organization, NFTY failed to keep up as society changed in the 1980s and the 1990s. As a consequence, more and more youth found NFTY no longer as nifty as it had once been, and they voted with their feet, particularly after their bar and bat mitzvahs. Other youth organizations that had experienced similar problems had taken steps to remake their images and reformat their activity offerings, including the Girl Scouts, as Fox News reported in November 2000. "We're no longer about baking cookies and toasting marshmallows around the fire," one Girl Scout leader told a news crew. "We now offer young women the chance to get advanced computer training, learn marketing skills, and network widely."

Yoffie himself called the teen dropout rate in the Reform movement "appallingly high." While many Reform teenagers appear to be uninterested in Reform Judaism and drop out for that reason, others claim that they would love to continue to be involved but are simply not the youth-group type. In response, Yoffie suggested revamping NFTY. To build a structure that could more effectively keep youth involved throughout their high school years, he announced that each URJ region would hire a full-time professional to organize and develop youth programming in that region. The hope was that this decentralization would allow the URJ regional directors to have more impact on youth programming, a far more effective approach than trying to run everything out of New York. Yoffie has further committed the entire movement to developing a range of new programs for teenagers who want alternatives to the standard youth group activities. His ideas include a summer travel program focusing on social action projects and a summer study program that combines SAT preparation and college visits with Judaica.

NFTY's own summer programs in Israel have proved remarkably popular, although registration dropped off precipitously as a consequence of the renewed tensions between Palestinians and Israelis. Eric Yoffie set off a controversy when he cancelled Reform youth trips to Israel at the height of the violence, arguing that it was not fair to use other people's children to make political points. In any case, the movement quickly reestablished its Zionist credentials. New trips were publicized, but it remains difficult to recruit teenagers willing to go or parents willing to allow their children to go. At its height, the summer program sent more than a dozen groups for six-week trips that incorporated touring, educational programs, and leadership training. The Israel trips were inspirational because they immersed the participant not only in the NFTY experience 24 hours a day, but also in the Israeli context. Most participants came back transformed, although it remains unclear how much of that "transformation" endured. But rabbis and educators feel convinced that a trip to Israel is one of the most significant experiences a family can give teenagers. An entirely different style of informal education is available at the Reform movement's summer camps, where generations of youngsters have had some of their most positive Jewish experiences. These regional camps provide "a joyous, invigorating and uplifting few weeks of total immersion in Judaism, with memories powerful enough to last the entire year."

The camps combine a rich Jewish atmosphere, positive development experiences, and a natural setting. As Lee Bycel explained in a temple bulletin: "No matter how much we do here at Fairmount Temple, it is hard to convey the depth and feeling of Judaism in just a few hours each week. At a Jewish summer camp, our young people are immersed in a total Jewish environment. Shabbat is a natural part of the week, which emerges from all they have learned and experienced during camp. For many years, I have spent time in our movement's summer camps. I love watching the faces on our young people as they gather for Shabbat – eager, joyful, immersed in the moment, understanding of the beauty of Shabbat, truly a sight to be seen."

Further, "Jewish summer camps can play an important role in building self-esteem. It is important for our young people to be in a healthy and safe environment, away from parents, where they can learn more about themselves and their own abilities and skills. They gain a lot by having to be responsible for themselves – and it is amazing what they can manage to do without our help." Finally, "hiking, sleeping out under the stars, having the time to see the beauty around them without a car or movies, or video games – teaches some of the most important lessons in life."

The first URJ camp in North America, was Olin-Sang-Ruby Union Institute (OSRUI) in Oconomowoc, Wisconsin. When OSRUI began, the music consisted largely of folk songs and, later, of civil rights movement chants "considered to have religious significance in that they embodied Reform principles." The folk music was slowly supplemented by traditional Jewish music and a new American Jewish folk music. OSRUI hired Debbie Friedman as a song leader in 1970 as "a new genre of music was coming to the fore. It was a Reform Jewish genre of music, songs that were mainly liturgical, written by [camp] song leaders. She brought her tunes and her compositions to the camp and helped to empower a whole generation in this region." This music continues to inspire many Reform Jews.

Friedman began song leading for her synagogue youth group in 1968, then attended a song leader workshop at the Kutz Camp Institute in Warwick, New York, and soon began writing her own music. "I taught it to a group of kids who were doing a creative service with James Taylor, Joan Baez, and Judy Collins music. Not only did they sing the *Ve-Ahavta*, they stood arm in arm. They were moved; they were crying. Here was something in a genre to which they could relate." In 1972 she recorded *Sing unto God,* an album of Sabbath songs that featured a high school choir. "I had planned [only] to make a demo tape, but when I found out it would cost only $500 more to make 1,000 LPs, I thought, why not? They sold like hot cakes at camp. That's how it started. It was a fluke." Friedman moved to Chicago, where she began leading services and continued her youth work. Later she took a position as a cantorial soloist in California, began performing more frequently, and recorded additional albums. Soon people began using her melodies in their synagogue services.

Perhaps her most famous creation is "*Mi-she-Berakh*," composed for a *simchat ḥokhmah*, a celebration of wisdom, to honor a friend on her 60th birthday. The prayer offers the hope of healing for those suffering. "My friend was having a very difficult time in her life and a number of her friends were also struggling. Yet she had arrived at this age and was determined to embrace it." Introduced at the URJ biennial in San Francisco in 1993, the tune has become the most popular adopted liturgical melody in recent decades.

A NEW COMMITMENT TO ADULT EDUCATION. Because study is not solely a youth concern, the URJ leadership has committed itself to creating a "synagogue of the future" that will provide a place of serious learning for all ages. In traditional Jewish thought, God spoke to individuals through their study of sacred texts. But few in the Reform movement could read Hebrew well enough to study the texts in the original, and most of the few English translations were not suitable for adult education programs.

One indication of the URJ's commitment is a resolution on Torah study adopted at the 1997 biennial conference in Dallas:

> We recognize that North American Jews face a Jewish literacy crisis. While we are the best-educated generation of Jews that has ever lived, we are often woefully ignorant of our own Jewish heritage. At the same time, we are witnessing a renewed enthusiasm for Jewish learning throughout the Reform movement. Those of us who have had the opportunity to study and taste the richness of Torah have discovered that learning is a source of inspiration and great adventure.

Adults throughout the Jewish community are finding their way back to serious textual study. Kenneth Cohen, a founding executive of the software giant Oracle, became involved in Lehrhaus, a Berkeley, California, adult education program named after Freies JüdischesLehrhaus (Free Jewish study center), the pioneer program developed by Martin Buber, Franz Rosenzweig, and a number of other German Jewish intellectuals in Frankfurt during the interwar period. Featured in 1998 in a widely distributed report from the Jewish telegraphic agency, Cohen spoke of his motivation for studying: "It's just inevitable that you say to yourself, 'What do I want to pass on to this kid [his child] other than my stock certificates?' I had to have a higher goal." He found that "doing and receiving Jewish education is a remarkable, rewarding thing. It's passing on not the latest hot computer chip, which will be obsolete next year, but taking the accumulated knowledge of humankind and perpetuating that, passing it on to new generations and pass it on [further]."

In almost every major city today, nondenominational independent institutions offer intensive Jewish adult education. The Florence Melton Adult Mini-School Program offers a two-year, 120-hour course of study to several groups of students at a time in 34 cities. Most students in all of these programs are middle-aged baby boomers searching for meaning. "It's an awakening," says Paul Flexner of the Jewish Education Services of North America. Many had stopped their Jewish education immediately after their bar or bat mitzvah two, three, or four decades earlier. They now feel an acute awareness of how much they have missed and how much they don't know. Many feel their textual illiteracy prevents them from passing on to their children a meaningful Judaism that goes beyond superficial ethnic foods and accents.

Along with the URJ, individual synagogues are developing new approaches to attract the many congregants who do not attend Jewish study sessions. When Congregation Beth Am in Los Altos Hills, California, hired Josh Zweiback in 1998 as adult educator, he took the first full-time position in a Reform congregation in the United States intended to "develop new frontiers of education in synagogue life," according to Richard Block, the congregation's senior rabbi. Funded by the Koret Foundation of San Francisco, Zweiback interpreted his mandate as spanning a very broad spectrum, from Torah study to "all sorts of experiences including praying and giving Tzedakah." He pointed out that "distinctions between mind and body were not made in classical times: living Torah and learning Torah went hand in hand." Zweiback has tried a number of interesting ideas. On the congregation's Tikkun Olam Day, he distributed a tape about the role of social action in Judaism that included mock interviews with famous Jews throughout history, a number of Hebrew concepts relating to the subject, and the senior rabbi teaching a blessing that should be recited before performing a mitzvah.

Among new paradigms being explored are family education, where the entire family – adults and children – study and experience Judaism together, and an intensive immersion program. Peter Knobel of Beth Emet, the Free Synagogue of Evanston, Illinois, takes about 50 members of his congregation to Jerusalem for one week every other year. "They stay in the dormitory of Hebrew Union College, and I get some of the best Jewish scholars in the world to teach them. They have been required to read a serious book on Judaism by a major scholar – they all have read it and have come prepared – and for a week they study with the scholars. We do no touring; when they are not in class they are free in Jerusalem. The success of this program indicates to me that many Jews really want to learn about the faith in a serious way." Unlike a special interest program for people from all over the country, Knobel's group comes from one temple in a Chicago suburb. The study trip's congregational nature accounts for its success, allowing the intense experience to include both extensive preparation and substantial follow-up.

New Definitions of Jewish Identity

The patrilineal descent resolution was thus less a significant departure from previous Reform policy than a public declaration of inclusivity, a logical step in the open society of the United States. To move in the direction of exclusion would severely limit the pool of potential recruits, just when the Reform movement was looking for new members. The acceptance of patrilineal descent sent a clear message that the children of intermarried couples – even those who were not halakhically Jewish – were welcome in the synagogue.

FEMINISM AND THE REFORM MOVEMENT. Despite the Reform movement's never having opposed equal rights for women, the male hierarchical structure remained in place until the 1960s. The push for egalitarianism was not a high priority for the 19th-century Reformers, who were far more concerned with reforming the liturgy and adapting Judaism's religious beliefs to the surrounding cultural environment.

Yet until the 1960s, most Reform congregations were run by men, and their dominance was accepted without question. Fitting in was important, and congregational social mores reflected the society's. Whether immigrant or native born, American Jews adjusted to American values and wanted to see those values reflected in their congregational structure and activities. This meant that women in the typical Reform congregation were relegated to the traditional woman's role, a situation accepted by almost all parties without dissent. Sisterhoods served central functions in temple life; without them, many if not most activities would have been impossible. Whether they were baking cakes for fundraising purposes, preparing the confirmation dinner, or simply attending services, women constituted the backbone of Reform religious and social life.

But in the 1960s, the feminist movement began to challenge the traditional roles assigned to women. Through the 1970s and 1980s, its impact on the synagogue was immense. As women began to move into roles of responsibility traditionally assigned to men, there was a great deal of dissonance. Rachel Adler, an early Jewish feminist and then a lecturer at

HUC-JIR in Los Angeles, in 1983 summarized the feeling of many women: "Being a Jewish woman is very much like being Alice at the Hatter's tea party. We did not participate in making the rules, nor were we there at the beginning of the party. At best, a jumble of crockery is being shoved aside to clear a place for us. At worst, we are only tantalized with the tea and bread-and-butter, while being confused, shamed and reproached for our ignorance." Women in the Reform movement studied for the rabbinate, the cantorate, and other professional positions, while others became synagogue presidents rather than sisterhood presidents. What had been seen as an oddity became an accepted phenomenon, then so commonplace as to be unworthy of note.

Many of the leading feminists were Jewish, and some of them took an interest in Jewish affairs. Other women admired the feminist leaders and specifically wanted to apply their perspective in a Jewish context. The Reform movement provided an ideal setting for this synthesis because of its non-halakhic nature, allowing a much greater flexibility than could have developed in Orthodox or even Conservative Judaism. Women wanted to be treated on an equal basis with men, both in the synagogue power structure and in their portrayal in the myths of the tradition.

The Struggle for the Ordination of Women as Rabbis

While the issue of women's ordination is only one aspect of the struggle for gender equality in the Reform synagogue, it is important not only for its symbolic value, but also for opening the way for women to increase in their influence dramatically. The ordination of Sally *Priesand in 1972 was an extraordinary event, because HUC-JIR was the first major rabbinical program in the history of Judaism to ordain a woman rabbi.

By the time Sally Priesand had finished her studies at HUC-JIR, the impact of feminism had transformed the Reform movement to a degree unimaginable just a few decades earlier. Nelson Glueck supported her petition – there was little basis upon which to deny her the certificate of ordination. Unfortunately, Glueck died before he could actually ordain Priesand, and new HUC-JIR president Alfred Gottschalk conducted the ordination ceremony. After a stint as an assistant rabbi and then as a chaplain, Priesand joined Monmouth Reform Temple in Tinton Falls, New Jersey, where she continued as the rabbi.

THE IMPACT OF FEMINISM ON REFORM LITURGY. Many modern American women found the language of the traditional prayer book restrictive and even sexist. Based on biblical models that portrayed God solely in masculine terms, the prayers assume that public worship is an obligation primarily for men. For example, the prayer that began "Praise be our God, God of our Fathers, God of Abraham, God of Isaac and God of Jacob" now seemed exclusionary. Where were the matriarchs? In 1972, a task force on equality, arguing that such language misleads worshipers about the true nature of both human beings and God, recommended altering masculine references in prayer. In the resulting effort to rewrite the prayers to reflect the growing egalitarian nature of American Jewish thinking, the names of the matriarchs were added in a series of gender-sensitive prayer books published in the early 1990s. The same prayer now reads, "Praised be our God, the God of our Fathers and our Mothers: God of Abraham, God of Isaac and God of Jacob; God of Sarah, God of Rebekah, God of Leah, and God of Rachel."

Dealing with the names of God framed in the masculine form was more difficult. In English, Reform prayer books had referred to God as "He" and "Him" and called God "the Lord." These references could be changed, but the practical problem of replacing prayer books in use for only a short time was daunting. Some congregations developed a list of gender-sensitive words that could be substituted for masculine references to God. Thus, the word "God" might be used to replace "the Lord" each time that phrase appeared in the prayer book. But this could confuse congregants, who had to be exceptionally alert to make all the correct substitutions in the right places and at the right times. In the mid-1990s a series of soft-cover experimental gender-sensitive prayer books, then a hard-cover gender-sensitive version intended to be semi-permanent, gradually supplanted the original Sabbath prayer book *Gates of Prayer*. A new gender-sensitive edition is under way.

Congregations did not want to replace the new edition of the High Holy Day prayer book, *Gates of Repentance*, so soon. The solution was a gender-sensitive version that matched the original, page for page. Unfortunately, many found the mix of the two High Holy Day prayer books in the same service confusing, as their neighbors seemed to be reading from a different text than they were. But the production of new prayer books would eventually resolve such issues. Most Reform Jews adjusted to the new liturgy and accepted the gender-sensitive wording without a murmur. Many women found it empowering and exhilarating.

Priesand's ordination opened the door for many other women interested in careers to which rabbinical ordination could provide them access. Large numbers applied to cantorial as well as rabbinical programs at HUC-JIR. The Rabbi Sally J. Priesand Visiting Professorship was launched in the fall of 1999 at HUC-JIR in New York. By May 2001, 373 women were ordained. At HUC-JIR in Los Angeles, the very first group of female ordainees in May of 2002 includes five women out of eight rabbinical graduates. Six women have been ordained in the Israeli program on the Jerusalem campus.

The increasingly active role that women are playing in the Reform congregation has fueled concerns that an increasing number of men may walk away from active leadership involvement. This phenomenon is not new; many-19th century Reform rabbis complained that their congregations on Shabbat morning were composed primarily of women, children, and the elderly. But if the new trends increase the alienation of Jewish men from the temple, the yoke of Jewish communal leadership may fall more and more on female shoulders. Others worry that Jewish professional work is starting to be seen as more suitable for women than men. There is a persistent rumor that HUC-JIR deliberately admits fewer women than men to avoid the "feminization" of the rabbinate. Some older male rabbis have grumbled that the rabbinate is becoming a "woman's profession" and, like grammar-school teaching and nursing, will decline in professional status and in salary range. They cite studies suggesting that when women enter certain professions in large numbers, those fields undergo profound and – from their perspective – negative changes.

Many women rabbis complain that their career path has been blocked. In Sylvia Barack Fishman's terminology, they had to break through "Jewish ceilings." Only a handful have been appointed as senior rabbis of large congregations in recent years. Paula Reimers, a rabbi in Arizona, said in 1992: "It's the same old story. Everyone is in favor of women rabbis – until it comes time to hire one. A congregation would rather take an incompetent man than a woman. Women are picked last." Such complaints, frequent in the early years, seem to have diminished, if not disappeared. Although a shortage of rabbis may explain the change in part, an increasing willingness to accept women in the rabbinate is apparent. Many congregations have had positive experiences with women rabbis; many boards may have found that female rabbis are more likely to deliver the type of service their congregation needs. In the face of this pragmatic reality, any residual resistance quickly melts away. Women cantors in the Reform movement have had an easier path in the years since Barbara Ostfield Horowitz was invested in 1975 as the first female cantor. An almost continuous shortage of ordained Reform cantors has guaranteed enough pulpits for all graduates of the School of Sacred Music at HUC-JIR in New York. Furthermore, it is easier for many of the old-fashioned congregants to accept a woman cantor than a woman rabbi, perhaps because cantors are perceived as subordinate to the rabbi. The fine voices of many of the women may also have dissipated potential opposition, as congregants discovered the new cantor's leading of the service to be a pleasant experience.

An increasing number of congregations simply take the equality of men and women for granted.

Laura Geller, the senior rabbi at Temple Emanuel in Beverly Hills since 1994, believes that she exemplifies a feminine approach to the rabbinate. "My style is one of shared leadership – I would argue that's a feminine model of leadership. Our congregation is not a hierarchy, but a series of concentric circles. One of my very clear goals is to empower lay people to mentor young people, lead services, teach, and really take responsibility for their own Jewish life." Credited with shattering the "stained-glass ceiling" by becoming the first female senior rabbi at a major metropolitan synagogue, Geller has been followed by senior rabbis Marcia Zimmerman at Temple Israel in Minneapolis and Amy Schwartzman at Temple Rodeph Sholom in Falls Church, Virginia. Geller wonders: "Are there so few of us in senior rabbi positions because we're not choosing them, or because we're not given a shot at it? The answer is a bit of both."

"I have come to discover, through my involvement over the years, that when women's voices are heard, a tradition changes," Geller says. "What happens when women become engaged in creating and reforming Jewish experience [is that] our experience becomes central and not marginal, and deserving of blessing and ceremony."

THE ISSUE OF HOMOSEXUALITY. The issue of *homosexuality cuts to the heart of how the Reform movement deals with the conflicting demands of tradition and modernity. Here is a case where the tradition could not be clearer – homosexuality was prohibited in the strongest terms. Yet liberal American Jews felt they had to find a way to reconcile this condemnation with their contemporary values. How the Reform rabbinate handled this sensitive question is worth a close look.

The CCAR first dealt with the issue of homosexuality in the mid-1970s and soon after was supporting human rights as well as civil liberties for gays and lesbians. Most Reform rabbis took liberal positions across the board and so were quick to embrace what many saw as another liberal social cause. One issue that concerned still closeted gay and lesbian rabbis was the impact on their career trajectory should they declare themselves publicly. HUC-JIR did not officially admit openly gay students, and the CCAR did not guarantee to support gay rabbis looking for congregational employment. In 1986, Margaret Moers Wenig and Margaret Holub proposed a CCAR resolution that recommended a nondiscriminatory admissions policy for HUC-JIR and a nondiscriminatory placement policy for the Rabbinical Placement Commission (RPC). The motion was not voted on but referred to the newly created Ad Hoc Committee on Homosexuality and the Rabbinate chaired by Selig Salkowitz.

The 17-member committee – eight congregational rabbis and representatives of HUC-JIR, UAHC, and the RPC – met regularly for study and deliberation for more than four years. They talked often with leaders of other Jewish denominations as well as with the Progressive movement in Israel. Consulting with Reform leaders in Israel was particularly important because any American resolution favoring gay rights would be used as a political weapon by the Orthodox in Israel, who opposed religious pluralism in the Jewish State. Israeli Reform rabbis told the Americans that any such resolution would make their already difficult position even more so, but this information had little impact.

In the belief that gays and lesbians were entitled to equal religious as well as civil rights, many Reform rabbis felt it was important to push ahead. Whereas the Orthodox saw homosexuals as violating an explicit commandment of the Torah, most Reformers saw them as people who needed and wanted the same spiritual sustenance available to heterosexuals. Alexander Schindler, well known for confronting controversial issues head-on, gave a public address in November 1989 adding his voice to those already supporting gay rights. "If those who have studied these matters are correct, one half million of our fellow Jews, no less than one hundred thousand Reform Jews, are gay. They are our fellow congregants, our friends and committee members and, yes, our leaders both professional and lay."

In June of that year at a CCAR meeting in Seattle, there was a debate on a widely publicized report issued by the CCAR's Ad Hoc Committee on Homosexuality and the Rabbinate. As a part of the educational process, the committee invited four Reform rabbis to prepare and submit papers on the topic of "Homosexuality, the Rabbinate, and Liberal Judaism." Despite the appearance of an active debate, it was clear that the movement as a whole would support greater rights for gays and lesbians. It was less clear exactly what the CCAR would decide concerning some of the technical questions.

In 1990 the committee issued a report noting that the Bible uses the harshest terms to condemn male homosexual behavior, referring to it repeatedly as a *to'evah,* an abomination. The Talmud and Codes reinforce the position that any male or female homosexual activity was strictly prohibited. Nevertheless, the committee rejected this position as untenable and stated that "all Jews are religiously equal, regardless of their sexual orientation." While the committee recognized that, in the Jewish tradition, heterosexual monogamous procreative marriage is the ideal, "there are other human relationships which possess ethical and spiritual value, and… there are some people for whom heterosexual, monogamous, procreative marriage is not a viable option or possibility." Thus the committee took the position that a homosexual relationship could possess spiritual value for those who could not form a heterosexual union.

One of the most pressing questions was how HUC-JIR should deal with gay and lesbian applicants to the rabbinical program, for although the two are separate organizations, it was expected that all rabbinic graduates of HUC-JIR would become Reform rabbis and join the CCAR. Gary Zola, HUC-JIR's national dean of admissions, showed the committee a written policy statement issued by HUC-JIR president Alfred Gottschalk on February 8, 1990. Gottschalk wrote, "The College will consider any qualified candidate in terms of an applicant's overall suitability for the rabbinate, his/her qualifications to serve the Jewish community effectively, and to find personal fulfillment within the rabbinate." The HUC-JIR Dean's Council felt that sexual orientation should not be a consideration in a candidate's decision to apply for admission; "I underline, however, that this does not commit us to the acceptance or rejection of any single student. Each applicant is judged as an individual on the basis of his total profile."

THE CONTEMPORARY REALITY. In the early 21st century, Reform Judaism is a pluralistic American religious denomination. No one could possibly argue that one must accept a specific set of theological principles in order to be a Reform Jew in good standing. Yet the movement is thriving. New congregations are joining the URJ and existing ones are increasing their membership. This popularity has little to do with Reform's specific theological formulations. Rather, the flexibility that has emerged from its theological pluralism has allowed the movement to draw strength from new types of adherents while creating new enthusiasm among substantial numbers of longtime members.

The Reform movement has come a long way from the theological uniformity of the 1885 Pittsburgh Platform. By the 1970s, there was such full acceptance of a wide range of traditions, customs, and practices that it would have been ridiculous to suggest that one official standard was uniformly accepted and required for a Reform service of any type. Behind this diversity of ritual expression lay the acceptance of the idea that there was no one Reform theology, that Reform Judaism represented many different ways of thinking about God and the relationship between God and the Jewish people.

Eugene Borowitz acknowledges this pluralism explicitly in his book *Liberal Judaism*, published by the URJ in 1984. He asks, "Who is a good Jew?" And he answers, "I consider nothing more fundamental to being a good Jew than belief in God." But he goes on to suggest that there are many different ways of looking at God, and that many of them can be religiously authentic for a believing Jew. "With our religious and communal authority largely replaced by the insistence of modern Jews on thinking for themselves, no one can easily claim the authority to overrule competing views." In discussing how Jews may legitimately view God, Borowitz admits: "With our new appreciation of pluralism, we have also gained greater appreciation of the extraordinary openness with which Judaism has allowed people to talk of God. 'My' good Jew believes in God but not necessarily in my view of God. We have numerous differing interpretations of what God might mean for a contemporary Jew.… I am saying that we Jews have been and remain fundamentally a religion, not that we are very dogmatic about it." From a theological point of view, the acceptance of such a broad spectrum of beliefs makes it impossible to present a clear and compelling religious vision that could motivate followers to sacrifice for the sake of God. There are simply too many images of God for the group to agree on any one. On the other hand, this theological diversity allows the Reform movement to reach out to a broad spectrum of people who differ not only in their lifestyles, but also in their religious convictions.

The pluralistic nature of American religion has mushroomed over the past 25 years. "Spiritual individualism" has become an important force as congregants became less willing to sit quietly listening to the choir sing and the rabbi sermonize. They expect to participate actively in a common spiritual quest. More and more Americans seek inspiration from their personal life experiences rather than from a doctrine handed down through creedal statements or religious hierarchies. "Spirituality" is becoming more and more detached from traditional religion. In an increasingly therapeutic age, religion will be viewed as just another means of solving or at least coping with emotional and even medical problems.

Despite these trends, the Reform movement would again urge Reform Jews to embrace traditional rituals and to this end would debate and pass yet another theological statement, the 1999 Pittsburgh Platform. But in spite of arguments over its substance among the Classical Reformers and the neo-Reformers, the movement has continued to grow, further proof that Reform thrives because of, not despite, its pluralism.

Problems Facing the Reform Movement in Israel

With such a diverse population expressing such a multiplicity of views and practicing religion in so many different ways, one might expect the Reform movement to find a ready niche in Israeli religious life. This has not proven to be the case. Since Israel's rabbinate controls all issues of personal status, non-Orthodox rabbis in that country are not able to perform legally binding marriage ceremonies, divorces, or even most burials. Reform and Conservative conversions are accepted by the Jewish Agency, thus allowing such individuals to immigrate to Israel under the Law of Return. Such converts, however, will not be recognized as Jews by the chief rabbinate and may therefore have problems once they settle in the country.

Complex and multifaceted problems face the Reform movement in Israel. The early Jewish settlers came from countries that lacked the pluralistic religious environment that would have allowed alternative forms of religious expression to develop. The settlers arrived in a Palestine ruled by the Turks, who likewise did not encourage Western liberal cultural or intellectual developments. The early Zionist pioneers included few Western immigrants, and most of those who did settle in Israel adapted themselves to the prevailing social and religious norms. While Maurice Eisendrath had argued in favor of the creation of an Israeli Reform movement as early as 1953, not until the late 1960s did the World Union for Progressive Judaism develop an Israeli movement, and not until 1968 did the group hold a biennial conference in that country.

Over the past three decades, the World Union has devoted much effort to building up the Israel Movement for Progressive Judaism (IMPJ), which was incorporated under Israeli law in 1971. The Israeli leaders chose to refer to themselves as the movement for Yahadut Mitkademet, Progressive Judaism, avoiding the use of the term "reform." By doing so they hoped to minimize the negative associations that many Israelis have of the American Reform movement. Particularly damaging was a video replayed on Israeli TV a number of years ago of an American Reform rabbi and a priest co-officiating at a wedding ceremony, a sight many Israelis, including many secularists, found shocking and offensive. The 2000 Greensboro, North Carolina, CCAR resolution sanctioning same-sex unions has attracted a great deal of attention and criticism. Israeli Orthodox leaders, including politicians, argue that the Reform movement has encouraged assimilation and has proven itself a destructive force. Periodically, well-known Israeli Orthodox rabbis have attacked Reform Judaism and its adherents, sometimes in the vilest of terms. Nevertheless, Israeli-born Reform leaders such as Uri Regev, founder of the Israel Religious Action Center and now executive director of the WUPJ, have become well-known personalities interviewed frequently by TV news crews. Regev has made a great deal of progress in pushing for greater rights through the court system. Each time he has petitioned the Israeli Supreme Court, news media interviewed him on the importance of his petition and his understanding of why it was necessary to change the religious status quo, further positive publicity for the Progressive movement.

Many non-Orthodox Israelis have been positively impressed. A few years ago, a number of leading Israeli writers and intellectuals called on the Israeli public to join the Reform movement to protest the Orthodox monopoly on life-cycle ceremonies. The Orthodox in turn renewed their attacks on the Reform movement. Orthodox spokesmen continued to lambaste Reform Judaism, and unknown individuals suspected to be from the ultra-Orthodox community vandalized buildings associated with Reform institutions.

But Orthodox hostility, only one facet of the problem, could work in the Progressive movement's favor, since many secular Israelis harbor resentment toward what they see as the religious coercion of the Orthodox. But the coalition agreements between the Labor and Likud Parties and one or more Orthodox parties have insured that the status quo is maintained in religious matters. As a consequence, an Orthodox rabbi must certify weddings between Jews, for example, although a few sympathetic Orthodox rabbis have signed for a Reform or Conservative rabbi who is the actual officiant. But the Orthodox rabbinate has worked vigorously to clamp down on those who helped circumvent the system. Most Jews who marry in a Reform ceremony in Israel then go to Cyprus to receive a civil marriage license, as the Israeli Ministry of Interior will accept any marriage certificate issued by an official government. Thus, the Israeli government recognizes a marriage certificate signed by a Cypriot judge but not one signed by an Israeli Reform rabbi.

There have been some encouraging developments. As part of a series of public relations campaigns, the IMPJ launched a $350,000 media blitz right before the High Holy Days of 1999, to encourage Israelis to attend a Progressive or Masorti (Conservative) synagogue. Billboards, posters on buses, and newspaper supplements featured the slogan, "There is more than one way to be Jewish." The accompanying radio campaign became immersed in controversy after the government-owned Israeli state radio tried to cancel the advertisements, claiming the wording would offend Orthodox Jews. The Supreme Court issued a show-cause order, and the campaign was allowed to proceed after IMPJ and Masorti leaders agreed to change the slogan on the radio to, "This is our way – you just have to choose." The IMPJ reported that an estimated 20,000 Israelis filled 27 synagogues and additional facilities rented for the High Holy Days. Many congregations doubled the number of attendees from just a year earlier. The IMPJ received many phone inquiries about membership and even a few requests for information on how to form congregations.

In March 2000, the IMPJ worked together with Israel's Masorti movement to promote non-Orthodox marriage ceremonies. The campaign ran full-page advertisements in the weekend editions of the major Israeli newspapers and four hundred radio ads featuring couples who had been married in either Progressive or Masorti ceremonies. The ads emphasized the egalitarian nature of the non-Orthodox wedding ceremony, as well as the lack of the intrusive questions Orthodox rabbis usually ask. The campaign also stated clearly that under current Israeli law, the couple would need to marry a second time in a civil ceremony abroad for their marriage to be recognized by the Interior Ministry.

The IMPJ is also continuing efforts to reach Russian-speaking immigrants. In February 2000, Michael Brodsky and a number of other Russian speakers published their first edition of the revised *Rodnik* (The source). Originally geared toward Jews in the Former Soviet Union (FSU), the magazine had shifted its focus to the emerging local movements. Now the editors refocused it on issues of interest to Israeli immigrants from the FSU. Brodsky, previously spokesperson for the Yisrael ba-Aliyah political party, now serves as the IMPJ's liaison with Russian-language media outlets. The IMPJ is also working with a number of Russian-language groups in Haifa, Nahariyyah, Netanyah, and Ra'ananna h. In August 2000, a congregation for immigrants from the FSU was founded in Ashdod. The group began meeting for *havdalah* services on Saturday nights and expanded to Friday night services led by HUC rabbinical students from the Jerusalem campus. The IMPJ hired a paraprofessional community organizer for the group and has hired similar community workers for the other Russian-language groups in Israel.

The IMPJ has recently formed a number of new congregations. Yozma in Modi'in, between Tel Aviv and Jerusalem, already has established four kindergarten classes as well as a first grade. Sulam Ya'akov was established in Zichron Ya'akov, between Tel Aviv and Haifa. Gusti Yehoshua-Braverman, the director of community development for the Israeli Progressive movement, states: "We must establish new congregations. However, we must also rejuvenate those that already exist but are struggling because they lack a rabbi or are in the periphery." Some long-standing congregations have expanded their programming, including Aḥvat Yisrael in Rishon le-Zion near Tel Aviv, which has also recently hired a community coordinator. The congregation has a growing Jewish study group that regularly brings in well-known guest lecturers and was recently given a city-owned building for its exclusive use. The structure is a former kindergarten in a quiet leafy neighborhood in the city. According to congregational chairperson Shai Eitan, it will need to be extensively renovated but offers "tremendous potential." In Nahariyyah, Emet Ve'shalom offers a lecture and field trip program for about 150 new immigrants. The IMPJ also caters to those with special needs. The movement offers special Shabbat activities for the residents of Kishor, a community of about 70 people with learning, functioning, and adaptive disabilities – a candle-lighting ceremony, *kiddush*, *Kabbalat Shabbat*, and other religious programming three times a month. Joint activities with the IMPJ-affiliated Harhalutz and the IMPJ's Young Adult Leadership Forum are also undertaken.

The Reform movement has built an impressive complex on King David Street in Jerusalem; it includes the Israeli campus of Hebrew Union College and Mercaz Shimshon, the WUPJ's cultural center, which opened in October 2000. Designed by world-famous architect Moshe Safdie, the $15 million facility was built adjacent to Beit Shmuel, WUPJ headquarters. Both centers offer panoramic views of Jaffa Gate, David's Citadel, and the walls of the Old City.

While the movement faced a great deal of resistance, land has been designated for Progressive congregational building projects in a number of municipalities. Affluent families in the area are enthusiastic about holding their sons' bar mitzvah ceremonies in the beautiful new Beit Daniel in North Tel Aviv. At services, the families seem to adjust without any problem to the mixed seating and the use of *Ha-Avodah she-Balev* (The service of the heart), the Israeli Progressive prayer book. There are now approximately 30 Progressive congregations in the country. Those with their own buildings and full-time rabbis have tended to attract a clientele looking for bar mitzvah celebrations, High Holy Day services, and so forth.

The Reform movement has poured effort and money into building up the Progressive presence in the State of Israel, yet the fear remains that the government would move quickly to pass new laws to bypass any legal gains achieved through future rulings by the High Court of Justice, the Israeli supreme court. Shas and other ultra-Orthodox political parties have already indicated their intention to do just that, if the need should arise. Until the movement can achieve official recognition and equal legal status with the Orthodox, it will remain a small, struggling, barely tolerated denomination on the fringes of Israeli life. The marginalization of the Israeli Progressive movement threatens to undermine the legitimacy of the Reform movement in the United States and throughout the world.

BIBLIOGRAPHY: J.L. Blau (ed.), *Reform Judaism: a Historical Perspective* (1973); E.B. Borowitz, *Choices in Modern Jewish Thought: a Partisan Guide* (1983); idem, *Liberal Judaism* (1984); idem, *Reform Judaism Today* (1983); E.B. Borowitz (ed.), *Reform Jewish Ethics and the Halakhah: an Experiment in Decision Making* (1994); S.B. Freehof, *Reform Responsa* (1960); idem, *Recent Reform Responsa* (1963); *Reform Jewish Practice and its Rabbinic Background* (1963); *Current Reform Responsa* (1969); A. Hirt-Manheimer (ed.),*The Jewish Condition: Essays on Contemporary Judaism Honoring Alexander M. Schindler.* (1995); L.A. Hoffman, *The Journey Home: Discovering the Deep Spiritual Wisdom of the Jewish Tradition* (2002); W. Jacob and M. Zemer (eds.), *Progressive Halakha: Essence and Application* (1991); D.E. Kaplan, *American Reform Judaism: An Introduction* (2003); D.E. Kaplan *Contemporary Debates in American Reform Judaism* (2001); idem, *Platforms and Prayer Books* (2002); idem, *American Reform Judaism: An Introduction* (2003); M.N. Kertzer, *What is a Jew?* (1993); T. Lenn, *Rabbi and Synagogue in Reform Judaism* (1972); M.A. Meyer, *Jewish Identity in the Modern World* (1990); idem, *Response to Modernity: A History of the Reform Movement in Judaism* (1988); K.M. Olitzky, L.J. Sussman, and M.H. Stern, *Reform Judaism in America: a Biographical Dictionary and Sourcebook* (1993); J. Petuchowski, *Prayerbook Reform in Europe* (1968); D. Philipson, *Reform Movement in Judaism* (1967[3]); W.G. Plaut, *Rise of Reform Judaism* (1963); idem, *Growth of Reform*

Judaism (1965); C. Seligmann, *Geschichte der juedischen Reformbewegung* (1922); A. Silverstein, *Alternatives to Assimilation* (1994); E.M. Lily Umansky, *Lily Montagu and the Advancement of Liberal Judaism: From Vision to Vocation* (1983); A. Vorspan and D. Saperstein, *Tough Choices: Jewish Perspectives on Social Justice* (1992); M. Washofsky, *Jewish Living: A Guide to Contemporary Reform Practice* (2001); M. Wiener, *Juedische Religion im Zeitalter der Emanzipation* (1933).

[Dana Evan Kaplan (2nd ed.)]

REFUGEES (1933–1949). When the Nazis came to power, many Jews believed that this chapter in German history would soon pass, that Germany would come to its senses, and that Hitler could not last long. Over time, however, the ranks of the pessimists swelled. After **Kristallnacht* (the November 1938 pogroms) for most German Jews the question was not whether to leave but where to go. Could a place of refuge be found? Would some country – any country – be willing to receive Jews? By the beginning of the war, the quest for refuge became a matter of life and death.

The first wave of German Jews seeking refuge began in 1933 when according to Reichsvertretung der Deutschen Juden records, 52,000 Jews left and 37,000 who were abroad remained there. In 1934 the pace of emigration slowed down as conditions stabilized and after the Nuremberg laws of 1935, it once again intensified. Most Jews went to neighboring countries presuming that they were leaving Germany for a time and not for good and never imagining that Germany would conquer the lands in which they had found refuge. By 1938 approximately one in four Jews had left. Some countries were willing to receive some Jews but never in the numbers that would resolve the problem; Turkey imported professors, architects, musicians, physicians, and lawyers to Westernize their country.

The quest for refuge was related to the perception of the viability of Jewish life in Germany. The calmer things remained the more Jews stayed and after periods of turmoil the pace of Jewish emigration quickened. By early 1938 the process of Aryanization had impoverished many Jews, making their lives within Germany ever more difficult and making them even less desirable to potential countries of refuge. In March, Germany entered Austria and as 200,000 more Jews became part of the expanded Reich, the Anschluss reversed, seemingly overnight, the "progress" that Germany had made during the previous years to be rid of its Jews. Efforts were made to speed up the emigration of Jews and Adolf *Eichmann was dispatched to Vienna to organize the departure of its Jews. His success there propelled his career. The *Evian Conference of July 1938, convened ostensibly to solve the refugee crisis, proved that countries were unwilling to receive the Jews, at least not in sufficient numbers to handle the crisis. Only the Dominican Republic was willing to receive a large number of refugees, the comfortable euphemism for Jews.

In October 1938, things went from bad to worse. Jews of Polish origin living in Germany were expelled, and in November *Kristallnacht* made matters all the more urgent.

At the beginning of the Jewish quest for refuge, Jews could leave with their possessions and could dispose of what they had in an orderly fashion. Year after year, this became less possible. Economic restrictions on the Jews undermined their basic ability to earn a living and Aryanization deprived them of businesses and resources. By the late 1930s many were impoverished and appeared desperate. The *Haavara agreement of 1933, which permitted Jews to dispose of their property in Germany and receive a percentage of their capital in Palestine, was not augmented by any other agreements.

[Aryeh Tartakower / Michael Berenbaum (2nd ed.)]

High Commissioner for Refugees from Germany

When Hitler came to power in Germany in 1933, thousands of Jews, together with many non-Jewish anti-Nazis, were compelled to take refuge in adjacent countries. Democratic governments and large Jewish organizations exerted pressure on the League of Nations to deal with the refugee problem. On Oct. 26, 1933, the League appointed James G. *McDonald as high commissioner for refugees from Germany, with the task of negotiating for international collaboration for solving the economic, financial, and social problems of the refugees. In order to avoid offense to Germany, at that time still a member of the League, the high commissioner worked independently and did not report to the League Council but to its own governing body. Its budget was mainly provided by Jewish organizations. The high commissioner achieved little except for conventions on political and legal protection (in 1933 and 1938), and, convinced that without the authority of the League his efforts were useless, he resigned on Dec. 27, 1935. In February 1936, after Germany left the League, Sir Neill Malcolm (1869–1953) succeeded McDonald as high commissioner, this time with direct responsibility to the League. In May 1938 his office was extended to help refugees from Austria, but it was limited to legal and political protection for refugees and intervention with the governments of the countries of asylum in order to provide residence and work permits. On Sept. 30, 1938, the Assembly of the League decided to merge the existing Nansen Office for Refugees of the League with the Office of the High Commissioner for Refugees from Germany and on Jan. 1, 1939, it appointed Sir Herbert Emerson (1881–1962) as high commissioner for all refugees for a period of five years. Despite the League's efforts to ease the situation of the refugees, the practical results were not encouraging. However, the Office of the High Commissioner for Refugees from Germany was marginally useful both in securing legal status for stateless refugees and in coordinating the work of the numerous Jewish voluntary and philanthropic organizations.

In 1939 the situation became ever more desperate. Jews were willing to go anywhere. Seventeen thousand Jews arrived in Shanghai. Jews from Eastern Europe were later to join them in Japanese-occupied China. But there were few places to go. The United States operated on a quota system. A British White Paper limited the number of Jews immigrating to Palestine. Cuba and the United States turned away the ship **St. Louis* carrying affluent Jewish refugees. With nowhere to go, they were forced to return to Europe.

When the Germans invaded Poland in September 1939, some Polish Jews faced a critical decision. History had taught them that refuge was in the West. During World War I, the Germans had been relatively benign during occupation. Did one go west or east to the land of Czar and of the pogroms, a land from which Jews had been fleeing for decades? Those who went against the grain of history and of collective wisdom suffered but were not killed. It is estimated that about half a million Jews left for the Soviet Union in the wake of the German advance. Many of these people were later engulfed by the German conquest of the Soviet-held territories, as were their counterparts, Jews who had left for France and Denmark, Belgium and Holland and other West European countries.

Neutral countries were reluctant to be overrun by Jews. Switzerland received 21,500 but thousands more were turned away. And in the fall of 1938, the Swiss Foreign Ministry requested that the Germans stamp Jewish passports with the letter *J* so that non-Jewish Germans could enter Switzerland freely. Spain received some Jews. Those who made it over the Pyrenees were not turned back; they were sent on to Portugal, from where many managed to leave for the United States. Some German allies, notably Italy and Hungary, received some Jews. Sweden provided a sanctuary for Scandinavian Jews fleeing Denmark, but that was in 1943 when it was understood that Germany would lose the war.

Clandestine passage to Palestine remained an option but the sinking of a stricken ship, the *Struma*, just outside Turkish waters in 1941 by a Soviet submarine, killing all but one of its passengers, underscored the difficulties of such dangerous routes. The Emergency Rescue Committee had a program for the cultural elite of Central Europe, but that was of little use to others. Among the great figures who fled were Jean Arp, Andre Breton, Marc *Chagall, Marcel Duchamp, Max *Ernst, Jacques *Lipshitz, Andre Masson, and Henri Matisse. Eminent musicians included George *Szell and Bruno *Walter. Many established writers came to the United States, among them Franz *Werfel, the novelist whose work, *Forty Days At Musa Dagh*, conveyed the tragedy of the Armenians and was invoked by Jewish resistance fighters in Bialystok and Warsaw. Lion *Feuchtwanger and Max *Brod, the friend and biographer of Franz *Kafka, were forced to flee. Feuchtwanger came to the United States and Brod reached Palestine. Sigmund *Freud dispatched his disciples around the globe before he left Vienna for London.

The Jewish refugee movement during the 12 years of Nazi rule (1933–45) differed in its structure from the usual population migrations, including Jewish migrations in previous generations. Among the German-Jewish immigrants to Palestine in the years 1933–37, practically all of whom were refugees, 52.2% were males and 47% females (0.8% were not recorded). The Jewish immigration to the U.S. in 1939–43, all of whom were refugees, showed a ratio of 46.3% males as against 53.7% females. The percentage of women refugees was much higher in comparison with general migration figures (in 1899–1914, out of every 100 immigrants to the U.S., 68.29% were males and 31.71% females), and even compared with general Jewish migration figures, where the percentage of women was always much higher (55.97% males as against 44.03% females). The refugee movement was thus mostly a family migration. This is also confirmed by the age structure of the movement and particularly by the considerable number of children (21% of the refugee migration to the U.S. in 1939–43; in the German-Jewish migration to Palestine in 1933–39, the age group of 1–20 was 32.5% – considerably more than within the Jewish population in Germany itself (21.5%) due to the fact that children were often sent out alone while the parents stayed behind in Germany) and old people, whereas people of working age were considerably less represented.

There were also differences in the occupational structure. Jewish mass migrations in the 19th and 20th centuries had consisted mostly of artisans and small traders, with no means of their own, who went abroad in search of a living. However, figures relating to German Jews coming to Palestine in 1933–39 showed 25.6% in the liberal professions and 27.7% as merchants, while industrialists and artisans accounted for 24.1%. Figures on Jewish immigration to the U.S. in 1932–43 showed nearly one-fifth (19.8%) in the liberal professions and 41.9% merchants. They brought with them rather considerable amounts of money, when some property could still be taken out of Germany. The estimate of such transfers to the U.S. up to the outbreak of World War II reached $650,000,000 while for Great Britain up to mid-1938 the figure was £12,000,000 (prewar parity $48,000,000). The *Haavara transferred the equivalent of £P 8,000,000 ($32,000,000) in the first years of Nazi rule into Palestine, while capital imported into the country in 1937–41 reached about £14,000,000. These possibilities of transfer gradually disappeared, until the refugees were forbidden to take with them any funds whatsoever and those who departed had less money because of years of economic harassment. Then the family character of the refugee movement and its occupational structure added to the difficulties of admission and absorption. Large numbers of people with commercial or free professions could not easily find employment in the prospective countries of immigration. The few refugees admitted as immigrants not infrequently had to switch over to other, mostly manual, work. For many refugees the abandonment of their occupation or profession and the changeover to physical work meant extreme hardship or even degradation. Only in Palestine was labor, and especially farming, socially favored, as part of the Zionist pioneer effort.

The Nansen Office, established in the early 1920s, when millions fled revolutionary Russia without any travel documents, continued to function up to the end of 1938 and assisted "stateless" Jewish refugees from Germany by issuing them the so-called "Nansen passports," which established their identity and enabled them to travel. Among the German-Jewish refugees (after 1933) only those from the territory of the Saar took advantage of its assistance. For the rest a special agency was created by the Assembly of the League of Nations, in October 1933, called the High Commissioner for Refugees (Jewish and Other) coming from Germany (see below). The intergovernmental *Evian Conference convened by President Roosevelt in July 1938, in which 32 governments and representatives of 39 private organizations, among them 21 Jewish bodies, participated, set up a permanent Intergovernmental Committee for Refugees with headquarters in London. In February 1939 it merged with the office of the High Commissioner for German Refugees, but it hardly fulfilled the aims for which it was established. Apart from a few unsuccessful attempts at negotiations with the German authorities, very little was done before and during the war to help the refugees and deportees. The failure was due to the general atmosphere of helplessness during those years and a lack of real understanding for the tragedy of the refugees. Even later, when the German policy of the total extermination of European Jewry was known all over the world, the *Bermuda Conference of Great Britain and the U.S. in April 1943 proved completely fruitless. Its task was to manage a domestic problem, not to solve a refugee problem. Only in January 1944, an election year, after facing enormous pressure from his Secretary of the Treasury Henry Morgenthau Jr. did President Roosevelt establish the War Refugee Board and open a temporary asylum in the United States.

A great deal more was accomplished by private, especially Jewish, relief agencies, which tried to mobilize public opinion, find countries willing to admit refugees, and rescue victims in the occupied territories. But even the accomplishments of bodies like the *Jewish Agency for Palestine, the American Jewish *Joint Distribution Committee, the *World Jewish Congress, and the Rescue Committee (Va'ad Haẓẓalah) of Orthodox Jewry were also pitifully small compared with the proportions of the disaster. In 1944, under considerable pressure of public opinion, the U.S. government established a special agency, the *War Refugee Board, which succeeded in saving small groups of Jews from German-occupied countries. The only intergovernmental body whose activities proved of some significance was the United Nations Relief and Rehabilitation Administration (*UNRRA), set up by 44 Allied countries in November 1943. UNRRA took care of the *Displaced Persons after the end of the war in the countries of their temporary residence as well as aiding them to return to their countries of origin. However, all attempts to induce UNRRA to extend the scope of its activities to include resettlement of non-repatriable Displaced Persons – as, e.g., the overwhelming majority of the Jews among them who refused to go back to Poland, the U.S.S.R., Hungary, etc. – failed. In this field much more was done in the following years by the International Refugee Organization (IRO), established in 1946 (see below).

[Shalom Adler-Rudel / Michael Berenbaum (2nd ed.)]

The Refugee Movement and its Proportions

An exact evaluation of the size of the Jewish refugee movement in the Nazi period and immediately after World War II presents considerable difficulties due to a lack of reliable statistics, especially during the last years of the war. An additional difficulty is how to define who is a refugee. Two attempts to produce accurate statistics were made at the end of 1943, one by the Institute of Jewish Affairs of the World Jewish Congress in New York and the other by the International Labor Organization (ILO). The Institute estimated the number of Jewish refugees at 2,391,000, the number of people deported from one country to another at 665,000, and those displaced within the same country at 2,205,000. These figures totaled over 5,000,000 – more than half of European Jewry. The ILO in a study of the war period proper estimated the number of Jewish war refugees at 2,200,000 and the number of deportees outside their country at 1,080,000, while Displaced Persons within their own country were estimated at 1,000,000. The total of this study was 4,150,000 and including Jewish refugees before 1939, the estimate comes to about 4,500,000. A deduction from the overall number of refugees of persons who found temporary admission in the interior of the U.S.S.R. during the war brings the figure to more than 800,000 distributed as seen in Table 1: Countries of Reception for Jewish Refugees 1933–1943. (For emigration of Jews from Germany in the period April 1933 to May 1939, including areas occupied by Germany by May 1939, see Table 2.)

Compared with the overall figure of 5,000,000 Jewish refugees and deportees in this period, those admitted to different countries (most of whom survived), came to no more than one-sixth. The number was everywhere severely limited; only the U.S., Palestine, and to a certain degree England admitted larger numbers than the others. The overall figures of refugees and deportees rose considerably in the remaining years of the war, as the Hungarian Jews were included in deportation in 1944 and the remnants of Jews in several countries of occupied Europe were rounded up and transported to other areas. The grand total may therefore have reached 7,000,000 and perhaps even more, but the great majority of them perished, some during the process of deportation itself (German official sources estimated that 30% of those deported died on the way), and the others in ghettos and in labor and extermination camps. No more than one-fourth survived the war period.

As to the definition of a refugee, two attempts deserve mention. In 1936 the Institute of International Law defined refugees as persons who have left or been forced to leave their country for political reasons, who have been deprived of its diplomatic protection, and who have not acquired the nationality or diplomatic protection of any other state (*Sommaire de l'Institut du Droit International*, vol. 1 (1936), 294). The second definition, in 1951, went much further, considering as a refugee any person forced to leave his place of residence for reasons independent of his will (*The Refugee in the Post-War World.* Preliminary Report of a Survey of the Refugee Problem. Published by the United Nations, Geneva, 1951. Part One, Chapter One. The Concept of "Refugee," pp. 3ff.). From the point of view of Jewish experiences, both definitions are unsatisfactory. The first neglects to take into consideration persons displaced within their own country whose number

Table 1: Countries of Reception for Jewish Refugees 1933–1943

Country	Number admitted (thousands)	Percent
United States	190	23.5
Palestine	120	14.8
England	65	8.1
France	55	6.8
Belgium	30	3.7
Holland	35	4.3
Switzerland	16	1.9
Spain	12	1.4
Other European countries	70	8.8
Argentina	50	6.2
Brazil	25	3.1
Uruguay	7	0.8
Bolivia	12	1.4
Chile	14	1.7
Other Latin American countries	20	2.4
China	25	3.1
South Africa	8	1.0
Australia	9	1.1
Canada	8	1.0
Other countries	40	4.9
Total	811	100.0

Table 2: Emigration of Jews from Germany in the Period April 1933 to May 1939, including Areas Occupied by Germany by May 1939[1]

Country of Reception	No. of German immigrants
United States	63,000
Palestine	55,000
Great Britain	40,000
France	30,000
Argentina	25,000
Brazil	13,000
South Africa	5,500
Italy	5,000
Other European countries	25,000
Other South American countries	20,000
Far Eastern countries	15,000
Other	8,000
Total	304,500

1 Estimated figures.

grew into the millions during the years of mass deportations, whereas the second definition is too broad because it includes victims of natural catastrophes, and only man-made events should be taken into consideration. A general definition, based mainly but not exclusively on Jewish experience in the 1930s and 1940s, would consider as refugees persons forced to leave their places of residence because of political or other man-made reasons, independent of their will or their individual character, mostly because of their race, religion, nationality, or political convictions.

[Aryeh Tartakower / Michael Berenbaum (2nd ed.)]

International Refugee Organization (IRO)

The IRO was created by the General Assembly of the United Nations on Feb. 12, 1946, as a specialized agency for refugees and stateless persons to assist in the repatriation, protection, and resettlement of refugees and Displaced Persons after World War II. A special Committee on Refugees and Displaced Persons was then set up to work out a draft constitution for a nonpermanent organization to replace existing refugee organizations (such as UNRRA and the Intergovernmental Committee for Refugees (IGCR)). The Economic and Social Council ratified the draft constitution on Sept. 30, 1946, and the General Assembly gave its final approval on December 15 that year. The IRO constitution determined the criterion for "eligibility" of a refugee or Displaced Person. The signatures of 15 member states who would contribute 75% of the operational budget were required before the organization could function effectively. By Dec. 31, 1946, eight governments had signed the constitution, thereby making it possible to establish a preparatory commission for the IRO (PCIRO) which would immediately assume certain functions and become fully operative. On June 30, 1947, this commission went into effect and the responsibilities of UNRRA and IGCR were transferred to it; but the organization did not formally come into existence until Aug. 20, 1948, when the 15th member ratified the constitution. When the PCIRO began operations there were over 1,000,000 refugees, 20% of whom were Jews, in the liberated countries of Europe. At the peak of its operations in 1948, the IRO was working in about 30 countries and employed an international staff of 2,800. Between 1947 and 1951, it maintained about 1,500,000 refugees, repatriated 75,000, and resettled 1,040,000. These results were achieved at a cost of $430,000,000 which was contributed by 18 countries. About 20 countries offered to resettle refugees. Three of these countries accepted nearly two-thirds of all the refugees for resettlement: the United States, 330,000; Australia, 182,000; Israel, 132,000. The IRO was helped by many governments and 25 voluntary societies which included six Jewish organizations, the American Jewish Joint Distribution Committee (JDC), the Jewish Agency for Palestine, *United HIAS Service, *ORT, *OZE, and the Jewish Committee for Relief Abroad.

The government of Israel in cooperation with the JDC and the Jewish Agency for Palestine undertook final responsibility for the resettlement and care of 8,700 hard-core cases toward which the IRO provided assistance amounting to $6,500,000. It contributed over $10,000,000 for transportation costs toward resettling refugees in Israel. The IRO succeeded the IGCR as trustee for international reparations (amounting to $25,000,000) for the resettlement of Jewish refugees. The IRO was dissolved in February 1952 when some of its functions were taken over by governments and voluntary agencies; others were handed over to the United Nations High Commissioner for Refugees and to the Provisional Intergovernmental Committee for the Movement of Migrants from Europe.

[Shalom Adler-Rudel]

BIBLIOGRAPHY: A. Tartakower and K.R. Grossmann, *Jewish Refugee* (1944); J.H. Simpson, *The Refugee Problem* (1939); Z. Warhaftig, *Uprooted: Jewish Refugees and Displaced Persons After Liberation* (1946); M. Wischnitzer, *To Dwell in Safety* (1948); J. Vernant, *The Refugee in the Post-War World* (1951); E.M. Kulischer, *The Displacement of Population in Europe* (1943); E. Dekel, *Bi-Netivei ha-"Beriḥah,"* 2 vols. (1958); Bauer, in: *Yalkut Moreshet*, 2, no. 4 (1965), 93–117; P. Frings, *Das internationale Fluechtlingsproblem 1919–1950* (1952). INTERNATIONAL REFUGEE ORGANIZATION (IRO): L.W. Holborn, *International Refugee Organization* (1956), incl. bibl. HIGH COMMISSIONER FOR REFUGEES FROM GERMANY: A.D. Morse, *While Six Million Died* (1968), index; J.G. Macdonald, *Letter of Resignation* (1935); J.H. Simpson, *Refugee Problem* (1939), 214–18. **ADD. BIBLIOGRAPHY:** D. Wyman, *Paper Walls: America and the Refugee Crisis 1938–1941* (1968), idem, *The Abandonment of the Jews* (1985); M. Marrus, *The Unwanted: European Refugees in the Twentieth Century* (1985).

REFUSENIKS, Jews who wished to leave the U.S.S.R. but were refused permission to do so. Some were allowed to leave in 1977, and under the policy of *glasnost* declared by Soviet leader Mikhail Gorbachev, most of the long-standing refuseniks were allowed to leave in 1988-89. For a full discussion of the subject see *Russia.

REGAVIM (Heb. רְגָבִים; "Earth Clods"), kibbutz in the Menasheh Hills, 6 mi. (10 km.) E. of Binyaminah, affiliated with Ha-Kibbutz ha-Me'uḥad. Regavim was founded during the War of Independence by pioneers from Tunisia, Algeria, and Italy. Its farming was based on field crops, fruit orchards, and dairy cattle. The kibbutz also produced building materials. In 1969 Regavim had 288 inhabitants; in 2002, 256.

[Efraim Orni]

REGBAH (Heb. רֶגְבָּה), moshav shittufi in N. Israel 2½ mi. (4 km.) S. of Nahariyyah, affiliated with Tenu'at ha-Moshavim. Regbah was founded by veteran soldiers of World War II, some of them Israel-born and some from Central Europe and other countries (1946). The village had highly intensive and fully irrigated farming (field crops, citrus groves, avocado plantations, poultry, cattle) and two factories, for kitchen cabinets and closets and for plastics. In 1969 Regbah had 311 inhabitants; in 2002, 548. Its name is derived from *regev* which means "clod of earth."

[Efraim Orni / Shaked Gilboa (2nd ed.)

REGELSON, ABRAHAM (1896–1981), Hebrew poet. Born near Minsk, Regelson arrived in the United States as a boy of nine. Though his formal education was not extensive, he read voluminously and acquired substantial knowledge in poetry and philosophy. He began to publish poems immediately after World War I. Although mainly a poet, he also wrote philosophical essays and satirical sketches, and translated from English into Hebrew, and from Hebrew and Yiddish into English. During his stay in Ereẓ Israel in 1933–36, he wrote a regular column for *Davar* and contributed occasionally to *Davar li-Yladim*. The latter contributions were published in a book of children's stories *Massa ha-Bubbot le-Ereẓ Yisrael* (1936; 1954). *Ein ha-Sus* (1967), another book for children, is a paraphrase of Greek legends. When he settled permanently in Israel in 1949, he worked for various newspapers and, sporadically, at the publishing house Am Oved. All of his collections of poetry are assembled in *Ḥakukot Otiyyotayikh* (1964) which includes translations of American, English, and Yiddish poetry. Influenced by Robert Browning, Regelson developed his own form of dramatic monologue in poetry. His philosophical aperçus were often given expression in longer poems in the form of poetic Midrashim. His most ambitious poem, "Cain and Abel," depicts struggling opposites: the man of action and the thinker who is poisoned by a sense of vanity of all things. The title poem of his collected works, "*Ḥakukot Otiyyotayikh*" (*Ha-Tekufah*, 30/31 (1945/46), 271–86), is an ecstatic hymn to the Hebrew language.

Regelson's prose appeared in three volumes: *Melo ha-Tallit Alim* (1941), *Sham ha-Bedolaḥ* (1942), and *Erelei ha-Maḥashavah* (1969). The last and most important of the three is both a critical evaluation of some contemporary philosophies and past philosophers and a repository of Regelson's own thought. His translations into Hebrew include stories by Kipling (1935), Melville's *Billy Budd* (1950); into English Glanz' Yiddish poems, M. Maisels' philosophical work *Maḥashavah ve-Emet* (in an abridged version, under the title *Thought and Truth* (1956),) and Jacob Klatzkin's philosophical essays, *In Praise of Wisdom* (1943). While in New York, he also edited a small literary and philosophical review, *Rivon Katan* (1944), of which only two issues appeared.

BIBLIOGRAPHY: A. Epstein, *Soferim Ivrim ba-Amerikah*, 1 (1952), 142–71; S.Y. Penueli, *Ḥulyot ba-Sifrut ha-Ivrit ha-Ḥadashah* (1953), 54–60; M. Ribalow, *Ketavim u-Megillot* (1942), 217–21; *Hemshekh* (Yid., 1945), 412–9 (biographical list); E. Silberschlag, in: O.I. Janowsky (ed.), *The American Jew: A Reappraisal* (1964). **ADD. BIBLIOGRAPHY:** Etiemble, "Le sonnet des voyelles en hébreu moderne," in: *Humanisme actif*, 1 (1968), 137–42; D. Rudavsky, "A. Regelson: A Reflective Hebrew Poet," in: *Hebrew Studies*, 18 (1977), 91–104; A.J. Band, "Regelson, Pagis, Wallach: Three Poems on the Hebrew Language," in: Z. Zevit, S. Gitlin (eds.), *Solving Riddles and Untying Knots* (1995), 505–22.

[Eisig Silberschlag]

REGEM-MELECH (Heb. רֶגֶם מֶלֶךְ), a name of uncertain meaning and origin, occurring in Zechariah 7:1ff. (cf. Regem in I Chron. 2:47). Regem-Melech is reproduced by the versions as a title: "*rab-mag* of the king" (Peshitta), and in a form that scholars consider to be a transliteration of a title: *arbeseer* (LXX A), a transliteration of the Hebrew *rav saris*, "chief eunuch [of] the king," and *arbeser* (LXX B), a transliteration of *rav sar ha-Melekh*, "chief officer [of] the king." The difficult passage in which the name occurs may mean that Bethel-Sarezer (see *Sharezer), Regem-Melech, and their men wrote (from Babylonia?) to the prophets and Temple priests in 518 B.C.E., when the reconstruction of the Temple was nearing completion, asking whether they should continue to wail and fast in the fifth month to commemorate the Temple's destruction.

[Bezalel Porten]

REGENSBURG (Ratisbon), city in Bavaria, Germany. Its Jewish quarter was the oldest in Germany (1020). During the First *Crusade (1096) the whole community was forcibly converted but a year later was allowed to return to Judaism by *Henry IV. In 1182 Emperor Frederick I Barbarossa, apparently renewing a charter originally granted to the Regensburg community by Henry IV, stated the principles of his attitude, as emperor, toward the Jews and added in the preamble: "We concede to our Ratisbon Jews and confirm with our imperial authority their good customs which their ancestors secured through the grace and favor of our predecessors until our time." The economic clauses of this charter relate to the functions of Regensburg Jews in trade with Slav countries, detailing that "they be allowed to sell gold, silver, and any other kinds of metals and merchandise of any sort, and also to buy them, according to their ancient custom" (Aronius, Regesten, no. 314d, pp. 139ff.). Thus at this time Regensburg Jewry was regarded as a community of traders continuing the traditions of its founders. When this privilege was renewed by King Henry in 1230, a further provision stipulated that they might be brought before judges of their own choosing only. In the 12th and early 13th centuries, Christians also lived in the Jewish quarter and owned homes there. Between 1210 and 1217 a synagogue was built and a plot for a cemetery acquired in 1210. By the end of the 12th century Regensburg had become a religious and cultural center for German Jewry. Among its rabbis were *Baruch b. Isaac, *Ephraim b. Isaac, and *Isaac b. Moses of Vienna (the author of *Or Zaru'a*). *Judah b. Samuel he-Ḥasid made the city the cradle and center of the *Ḥasidei Ashkenaz. Even in the 15th century, a time of economic decline and trouble, Regensburg attracted such luminaries as Israel *Bruna. At this time Regensburg yeshivot developed a *pilpul* and *ḥillukim* style of their own contrasted in the Ashkenazi yeshivot with that of Nuremberg. The economic importance of the community enabled it to weather the *Rindfleisch (1289), *Deggendorf (1338), and *Black Death persecutions (1348/49) and to reach new heights of prosperity by offering asylum to rich refugees. *Moneylending to secular and ecclesiastic princes, in addition to the merchants of the city, was conducted on a large scale.

In the 14th century the community suffered from heavy taxes and was hit by the annulments of debts to Jews decreed by Emperor Wenceslaus II in 1385 and 1390. After the time of the Black Death the municipality's aspirations to "ownership" of the Jews grew; its fiscal extortions were as severe as those of the Jews' other "owners" – the emperor, the duke of Bavaria, and the local bishop. Gradually the Jews were forced to rely mainly on moneylending, and their freedom of movement was severely curtailed. The general decline and impoverishment of Regensburg, combined with growing social tension between the upper and lower classes of the citizenry, made the years 1475–1519 a period of increased bitterness against the Jews, a struggle that ended in their total expulsion. The violent anti-Jewish sermons of Peter *Schwarz (Nigri) resulted in the confiscation of the property of the whole community (1476); following the accusation by one of the defendants in the *Trent ritual murder trial 17 Jews from Regensburg were imprisoned. After four years, under unremitting pressure from Frederick III, the city was forced to free them. Frederick exacted a heavy fine from the city and also a pledge that it would not expel its Jewry. Balthasar Hubmeier (1485–1528), later the Anabaptist leader, was the most virulent of many preachers who accused the Jews of usury and blasphemy and repeatedly demanded that the synagogue be converted into a church; the guilds insisted on expulsion. In 1498 the community was led by ten elders; its *takkanot* were enacted by majority vote in a council of 31. At this critical period of its history, the community's ordinances dealt with the preservation of internal peace (R. Straus, *Urkunden…* (1960), no. 676, pp. 228–30). When Emperor Maximilian died in January 1519, the interregnum was made the occasion for the immediate expulsion of the Jews, about 800 in all. The synagogue was razed and a chapel, which became the center of mass pilgrimages, was erected on the site. About 5,000 gravestones were wrenched out of the cemetery and used for building. Trophies of the "victory against the Jews" were prominently displayed on walls of houses in Regensburg and other cities. Most of the refugees settled in nearby Stadtamhof, on Bavarian territory, but were later expelled from there too (1551).

In 1545 the city received the privilege of *non recipiendis Judaeis* from *Charles V and guarded it jealously in the future. Nevertheless, Jewish *shtadlanim*, *Court Jews, and physicians continued to be present at the meetings of the Reichstag of the Holy Roman Empire, which were occasionally held in Regensburg. From 1669 the Reichstag convened regularly in Regensburg, and a Jewish settlement affiliated to the assembly sprang up under the protection of the hereditary dukes von Pappenheim. The number of *Schutzjuden* was bitterly contested between the dukes and the city and was finally fixed at three to four families (60–80 persons) throughout most of the 17th and 18th centuries. In the latter half of the 18th century Isaac Alexander gained temporary fame as the first rabbi to write on contemporary philosophical subjects in Germany. Philip Reichenberger (1750–1818), court agent of Ansbach and Brandenburg, and Wolf *Breidenbach led the fight for the abolition of the *leibzoll* ("body tax"). In 1805 the three richest families were granted the right to own land. Reichenberger unsuccessfully requested full citizenship in 1808. Regensburg passed to Bavaria in 1810. A cemetery was consecrated in 1822 and a synagogue in 1841. The community grew from 180 persons in 1810 to 635 in 1880 (1.96%); after this it declined gradually.

Under the Nazi regime the number of Jews decreased from 427 in 1933 to 226 in 1939. On Nov. 9, 1938, the synagogue was burned down, shops and homes were pillaged, and almost all the men arrested. About 230 Jews (including some from the countryside) were deported in 1942 to Theresienstadt, Auschwitz, and Lublin. After World War II a new community was organized, with 140 persons in 1970 (two-thirds over the age of 40) and its own rabbi and *shoḥet*.

The history of Regensburg's medieval Jewish community

became one of the outstanding instances of Nazi historiography when it was falsified by the Nazi historian Wilhelm Grau in his *Anti-semitismus im spaeten Mittelalter* (1934). He used the sources collected by the Jew Raphael Straus (published posthumously in 1960), which had been confiscated by the Gestapo. A new community center was consecrated in 1969. The Jewish community numbered 117 in 1989 and about 1,000 in 2005. The increase is explained by the immigration of Jews from the former Soviet Union.

BIBLIOGRAPHY: A Freimann, in: *Festschrift Martin Philippson* (1916), 79–95; U. Stern, in: JJLG, 18 (1927), 363–86; 20 (1929), 157–79; 22 (1932), 1–123; R. Straus, *Die Judengemeinde Regensburg im ausgehenden Mittelalter* (1932); idem, *Regensburg und Augsburg* (1939); idem (ed.), *Urkunden und Augsburg* (1939); idem (ed.), *Urkunden und Aktenstuecke zur Geschichte der Juden in Regensburg 1453–1738* (1960); Germ Jud, 1 (1963), 285–305; 2 (1968), 679–90; B. Altmann, in: PAAJR, 10 (1940), 5–68; G. Kisch, in: *Zeitschrift der Savigny Stiftung fuer Rechtsgeschichte*, 78 (1961), 389–93; H.H. Ben-Sasson, *Toledot Am Yisrael*, 2 (1969), 185–7. **ADD. BIBLIOGRAPHY:** *Germania Judaica*, vol. 3, 1350–1514 (1987), 1178–1230; K. Hoffmann, *Die Verdraengung der Juden aus oeffentlichen Dienst und selbstaendigen Berufen in Regensburg 1933 – 1939* (Rechtshistorische Reihe, vol. 110) (1993); S. Wittmer, *Regensburger Juden. Juedisches Leben von 1519 bis 1990* (Regensburger Studien und Quellen zur Kulturgeschichte, vol. 6) (1996); H. Brekle, *Das Regensburger Ghetto. Fotoimpressionen von den Ausgrabungen* (1997); U. Moosburger and H. Wanner, *Schabbat Schalom. Juden in Regensburg – Gesichter einer lebendigen Gemeinde* (1998); S. Wittmer, *Juedisches Leben in Regensburg. Vom fruehen Mittelalter bis 1519* (2001). CD-ROM: S. Codreanu-Windauer, *Das mittelalterliche Judenviertel. Eine multimediale Praesentation zu einem Projekt von europaeischem Rang* (Document Neupfarrplatz) (2002).

[Henry Wasserman]

REGGIO, ABRAHAM BEN EZRIEL (1755–1846), Italian rabbi and kabbalist. Born in Ferrara, Reggio was a pupil of Isaac *Lampronti and his son Solomon. He went to Gorizia where he studied under Moses Ḥefeẓ (Gentili), the local rabbi, and taught in the *talmud torah*. After the death of his teacher, Reggio was appointed to succeed him as rabbi of the town (c. 1796), and he held this office until his death. Reggio was considered an important *posek* in his time. Leading scholars of that period, including Mordecai *Baneth, addressed halakhic problems to him.

His only published work is *Tiglaḥat ha-Ma'amar* (Leghorn, 1844), a reply to the pamphlet *Ma'amar ha-Tiglaḥat* (Vienna, 1835) by his son, Isacco Samuel *Reggio, on the permission to shave during the intermediate days of a festival. His most important works, *Eshel Avraham*, on general principles and themes in the Bible, Mishnah, Talmud, prayer book and Kabbalah; *Mazkeret ha-Limmud*, novellae; and *Mashal u-Meliẓah*, letters, poems, and elegies, remain in manuscript.

BIBLIOGRAPHY: Benjacob, Oẓar, 55 no. 1041; Fuenn, Keneset, 63–64.

[Abraham David]

REGGIO, ISACCO SAMUEL (Ia-Sha-R; 1784–1855), Italian rabbi; one of the founders of the *Collegio Rabbinico Italiano. He published an Italian translation of the Pentateuch, with a Hebrew commentary (Vienna, 1821), and wrote *Ma'amar Torah min ha-Shamayim* ("The Torah as Divinely Revealed," Vienna, 1818) to prove the divine authority of the Pentateuch. Among his other biblical works are a poetic version in Italian of the Book of Isaiah (Udine, 1831); a Hebrew introduction to the Scroll of Esther (Vienna, 1841); and Italian translations of the books of Joshua, Ruth, and Lamentations, and of *Pirkei Avot*. In *Ha-Torah ve-ha-Filosfyah* (Vienna, 1827), written under the influence of Mendelssohn, Reggio tried to show that reason and philosophy were compatible with the Torah. His *Iggerot Yashar* (1834–36) are exegetic, historical, and philosophical notes in the form of letters to friends. He also edited some of the writings of Leone di Modena and wrote *Beḥinat ha-Kabbalah* (Gorizia, 1852). Reggio published other works on Kabbalah and philosophy in *Bikkurei ha-Ittim ha-Ḥadashim* under the pseudonym Iashar. His autobiography, *Mazkeret Yashar*, appeared in Vienna (1849). His Hebrew correspondence with S.D. *Luzzatto was collected by V. Castiglione (1902); it shows their mutual esteem and friendship. Reggio also wrote some halakhic and pedagogical works, one of which appeared in English: *A Guide for the Religious Instruction of Jewish Youth* (London, 1855). His views on Judaism did not always conform to tradition and led to polemics with German rabbis as well as his own father, Abraham *Reggio.

BIBLIOGRAPHY: E.S. Artom, in: *Settimana Israelitica*, 2 (1911), 1, 2–2; Milano, Bibl, 194; Milano, Italia, index; O. Lattes, in: RMI, 30 (1964), 107–12; I. Colombo, *ibid.*, 32 (1966), 130; 35 (1969), 270.

[Alfredo Mordechai Rabello]

REGGIO DI CALABRIA, city in S. Italy. The first Jewish settlement in Reggio can probably be traced back to the fourth century, but the earliest documents mentioning its presence date from 1127. The Jewish colony's main occupations were dyeing and dealing in wool and silk. On Feb. 17, 1475, the first dated Hebrew printed book (see *Incunabula), Rashi's commentary on the Pentateuch, was issued there by Abraham b. Garton b. *Isaac. In 1492–93 many Jewish refugees from Sicily, Sardinia, and Spain, including the whole Syracuse community, took refuge in Reggio. After Calabria had passed under Spanish rule, the Jews were banished from the town (July 25, 1511), leaving the sale of their property to trustees.

BIBLIOGRAPHY: Milano, Bibliotheca, index; Spanò-Bolani, in: *Archivio storico per le provincie napoletane*, 6 (1881), 336–46; Cotroneo, in: *Rivista storica calabrese*, 11 (1903), 390–418; N. Ferorelli, *Ebrei nell' Italia meridionale…* (1915), passim.

[Ariel Toaff]

REGGIO EMILIA, city in central Italy. The first Jewish settlement of Jewish loan bankers in Reggio Emilia, a fief of the House of Este, dates from the year 1413. For a long time they benefited from the favorable attitude of the ducal house to the Jewish settlements, which sometimes protected them from the persecutions instigated by Franciscan friars. When the papacy secured possession of the duchy of Ferrara in 1598, the duchy of Modena and Reggio was left in the hands of the House of Este. In the succeeding two centuries the duchy continued to welcome considerable groups of Jews, who engaged in moneylending and commercial activities. The ghetto was instituted in Reggio Emilia in 1669 and the Jews were able to carry on freely their business activities and exercise a variety of entrepreneurial, commercial, and cultural activities, including the production, manufacture, and trading of silk, silver, and diamonds. In 1652–53 the duke of Modena issued charters inviting foreign Jews to settle, proclaiming them "wealthy people and very likely to introduce traffic and commerce" and 60 Sephardi families settled in the duchy, mainly in Reggio Emilia. The majority of these were former Marranos from Spain who had recently reverted to Judaism, usually in Tuscany, and nine of them had migrated from Amsterdam and Hamburg. They were able to build an autonomous Portuguese community.

There was a renowned yeshivah in Reggio Emilia with learned rabbis such as *Benjamin b. Eliezer ha-Kohen Vitale and Isaiah *Bassano. A Jew of Reggio, Moses Benjamin *Foà, was book purveyor to the ducal library in Modena, participated in the Comizi of Lion, and worked actively with Moses Formiggini of Modena for the emancipation of the Italian Jews in the Napoleonic era, when the French occupation of 1796 temporarily brought the right to live outside the ghetto and to participate in public. In 1806–1807 Jacob Israel Carmi was one of the Italian rabbis who went to Paris for the Assembly of Notables and the Napoleonic *Sanhedrin; he gave a penetrating account of his experiences in his letters. In this period a number of Jews began to move to cities affording greater cultural and economic opportunities and at the beginning of the 19th century Reggio Emilia had a population of fewer than 800 Jews. During the Holocaust 18 Jews were deported to the death camps from the province of Reggio Emilia. In the early 21st century few Jews lived in Reggio Emilia and the community was affiliated to the community of Modena; the City Hall and the Italian State Ministry of Culture completed the restoration of the main synagogue in 2005.

BIBLIOGRAPHY: A. Balletti, *Gli ebrei e gli Estensi* (1930^2), passim; idem, *Il tempio maggiore israelitico di Reggio nell' Emilia…* (1908); Roth, Italy, index; Milano, Italia, index; Milano, Bibliotheca, index; Shulvass, in: *Reshumot*, 4 (1947), 98–130; Servi, in: *Corriere israelitico*, 5 (1866–67), 51–53. **ADD. BIBLIOGRAPHY:** S. Bondoni and G. Busi, *Cultura ebraica in Emilia-Romagna* (1987); A. Leoni, *La nazione ebraica spagnola e portoghese negli stati estensi* (1990).

[Ariel Toaff / Federica Francesconi (2nd ed.)]

REGHIN (also **Reghinul Săsesc**; Hung. **Szászrégen**; Ger. **Saechsisch-Regen**), town in northwestern Romania, Transylvania. The inhabitants of Reghin included Romanians, German-Saxons, and Hungarians. The city was founded in the 13th century by German (Saxon) and Romanian settlers. Although Jews began to settle there at the close of the 18th century, an organized community was established only during the middle of the 19th century, probably in 1849. The majority of the Jews came from Bukovina and Galicia. As a result of the battles during the Revolution of 1848 against Austria and the riots in Transylvania, Reghin and its Jewish population suffered severely. The first Jewish settlers, who arrived mainly from Bukovina and Galicia, were Orthodox, and the community remained Orthodox throughout its existence. Ḥasidic influence was also felt. Besides the synagogue, there were two prayerhouses (*kloyz*) where the Ḥasidim used to pray and had their own rabbis. A prominent figure in the community during its early years was the Orthodox rabbi Hillel Pollak (who was spiritually close to the extreme Orthodox rabbi Hillel *Lichtenstein).

A Jewish elementary school was founded in 1874. (Later it ceased its activities but was reestablished in 1910 and functioned until 1940.) The language of instruction in the school was Hungarian until 1918 after which it was Romanian. In 1885 the community became the administrative center for all the Jews of the district. The community numbered 282 in 1866, about 40 families in 1889, and 394 persons (about 7% of the total population) in 1891. Jews engaged in commerce, industry, and crafts. Their trade and industry were mainly connected with timber and some of them owned sawmills; there were also unskilled Jewish workers employed in the timber industry. The institutions of the community assisted the poor. Some of the *Ḥadarim* established by the community translated the Pentateuch into German instead of Yiddish in order to facilitate study of this language by the children. From 1919 there was considerable Zionist activity in Reghin, and many members of the youth organizations emigrated to Ereẓ Israel. The community numbered 1,587 (about 16% of the total population) in 1930, and 1,653 (about 10% of the total) in 1941.

Between the two world wars the Jews suffered from the nationalist and antisemitic activities of members of the Iron Guard, and from the official antisemitic policies of most of the Romanian governments. The change of rule in 1940 (from Romanian to Hungarian) did not bring with it any improvement, as was hoped by the Jews, who remembered their legal emancipation in 1867 by the Austro-Hungarian authorities.

Holocaust Period and After

In the summer of 1944 the local Jews were concentrated into a ghetto set up in a brick factory. Jews from the surrounding area were also brought there. From this ghetto about 6,000 Jews were deported to *Auschwitz by the Hungarian Horthiite authorities, at the request of the Nazi occupiers.

After World War II, in 1947 a community numbering about 820 was formed mostly by survivors of the death camps and other Jews who had arrived in Reghin from places in different parts of Romania. The community gradually declined as a result of immigration to Israel and elsewhere. In 1971 there were still some 20 to 25 families living in Reghin and even fewer in the early 21st century.

[Yehuda Marton / Paul Schveiger (2nd ed.)]

REGNER, SIDNEY L. (1903–1993), U.S. Reform rabbi and organizational executive. Regner was born in New York City and received his B.A. from the University of Cincinnati in 1924. In 1927, he was ordained at *Hebrew Union College, which also awarded him an honorary doctor of divinity degree in 1954. His career in the congregational rabbinate (1927–54) was spent at Temple Oheb Sholom in Reading, Pennsylvania, where he also served on the executive committees of the Jewish Community Council (1935–54) and the Central Atlantic States Region of the Council of Jewish Federations and Welfare Funds (1943–47); on the Governor's Committee on Children and Youth (1953–54); and as president of the Council of Social Agencies (1942–44). Long active in the *Central Conference of American Rabbis – as financial secretary (1939–52), executive board member, and chairman of its Committee on Publication (1952–54) – he became the CCAR's first executive vice president when the position was created in 1954. In this capacity, he represented the Reform movement's rabbinical association on the governing body of the *World Union for Progressive Judaism, the executive committee of the *Synagogue Council of America, and in meetings with heads of other national Jewish organizations. He also supervised the CCAR's publications, edited the yearbook and served ex-officio on joint commissions with the *Union of American Hebrew Congregations. Under his leadership, the CCAR became a recognized professional association with annual regional *kallot* (study retreats) in addition to its annual convention. He retired in 1971, becoming executive vice president emeritus (1971–93). A lifelong peace activist, he was elected vice president of the Jewish Peace Fellowship in 1980.

[Bezalel Gordon (2nd ed.)]

REHFISCH, HANS JOSE (1891–1960), German playwright. The son of a Berlin physician, Rehfisch was a successful lawyer who turned to literature, publishing many of his works under the pseudonyms Rene Kestner, Sydney Phillips, and Georg Turner. A free-lance writer until 1933, he escaped from the Nazi regime first to Vienna and then to London where he worked in industry. After World War II he taught at the New School for Social Research in New York (1947–49). He returned to Germany in 1950 and settled in Hamburg. Rehfisch wrote many successful plays mostly dealing with contemporary politics and society. He began his career as an expressionist with the drama *Die goldenen Waffen* (1913), but soon changed to realistic subject matter. His comedy, *Nickel und die 36 Gerechten* (1925), was inspired by the Jewish legend of the 36 (*Lamed Vav) Righteous Men.

Among his works most frequently staged were the tragicomedy *Wer weint um Juckenack?* (1924) and *Die Affaire Dreyfus* (1929), a historical drama written in collaboration with Wilhelm Herzog. Rehfisch's play *Quell der Verheissung* (1946) deals with German Jews who settled in Palestine. *Oberst Chabert* (1955) was a tragedy based on the novel by Balzac. In 1944, he edited the symposium *In Tyrranos: 4 Centuries of Struggle against Tyranny in Germany*, published by the Emigre 1943 Club. He was twice president of the Union of German Stage Writers and Composers (1931–33; 1951–53). In 1967 his selected works appeared in four volumes, edited by the Eastern German Academy of Arts in Berlin.

BIBLIOGRAPHY: F. Lennartz, *Deutsche Dichter und Schriftsteller unserer Zeit* (19598), 605–9. **ADD. BIBLIOGRAPHY:** H. Ritchie, "Rehfisch in Exile," In: *Aliens – Uneingebuergerte* (1994), 207–22; J.M. Ritchie, "The Exile Plays of Hans José Rehfisch," in: idem, *German Exiles* (1997), 146–60.

[Rudolf Kayser]

REHINE, ZALMA (1757–1843), merchant and Baltimore communal leader. Rehine was born in Prussia. After his arrival in America, he settled in Richmond, Virginia, and became a storekeeper. In 1793 he helped found the Richmond Light Infantry and served in it until 1800. When Isaac *Leeser went to the U.S. in 1824, he was employed by Rehine who was his uncle. In 1829 Rehine left Richmond for Baltimore, where he organized a *minyan* and, according to tradition, the first communal religious service by Baltimore Jews took place during High Holy Days in Rehine's home. The first Baltimore congregation grew out of this nucleus.

BIBLIOGRAPHY: *Occident*, 7 (1849), 226–7; 21 (1863), 143–4; H. Ezekiel and G. Lichtenstein, *History of the Jews of Richmond* (1917), 37–40.

[Isaac M. Fein]

REHOB (Heb. רְחוֹב, רְחֹב; "a wide place, square");

(1) Town allocated to the tribe of Asher, mentioned together with Hammon and Kana (Josh. 19:28), but apparently not conquered by the tribe (Judg. 1:31). It may be identical with the Rehob mentioned in the Egyptian Execration texts of the late 19th century B.C.E. and in the list of Thutmosis III (no. 87). It is variously identified both with Tell al-Balāṭ, southeast of Tyre, and with Khirbat al-ʿAmrī, northeast of Achzib.

(2) A second Rehob in the territory of Asher, mentioned together with Aphek (Josh. 19:30). It was one of the levitical cities (Josh. 21:31; I Chron. 6:60). A suggested identification is with Tell al-Birwa al-Gharbī where remains of the Middle and Late Bronze Ages and the Early Iron Age have been found. Some scholars consider it identical with (1) above.

(3) The Roobot of Eusebius (Onom. 142:11) and the Rehob known from various Egyptian inscriptions are identified with the large tell of al-Ṣārim, south of Beth-Shean, near the present-day al-Sheikh al-Riḥāb. This is the most important mound in the Beth-Shean Valley and the remains found there date from the third millennium B.C.E. to about the tenth century B.C.E. It may be identical with the Rehob mentioned in the Egyptian Execration texts of the 20th–19th centuries B.C.E. According to one of the Beth-Shean stelae of Seti I, it was attacked by forces from Pehel and Hamath, but was eventually relieved by the pharaoh's army. The name appears as Rahabu in the Taanach letters (15th century) and in Papyrus Anastasi I (13th century), where it is listed before Beth-Shean. The last mention of the place occurs in the list of towns conquered by Shishak (no. 26) and, therefore, the town must have ex-

isted until at least 925 B.C.E., although it is not mentioned in the Bible.

BIBLIOGRAPHY: Y. Aharoni, *Hitnaḥalut Shivtei Yisrael ba-Galil ha-Elyon* (1967), 51–52; Aharoni, Land, index; Bergman and Bransteter, in: BJPES, 8 (1941), 88; Albright, in: BASOR, 83 (1941), 33; 94 (1944), 23.

[Michael Avi-Yonah]

REHOBOAM (Heb. רְחַבְעָם; "the [divine] kinsman has been generous" or "the people has expanded"), king of Judah for 17 years (c. 928–911 B.C.E.); son of Solomon by Naamah the Ammonitess (I Kings 14:21; II Chron. 12:13). Rehoboam's name is connected with one of the most important events in the early history of Israel, namely, the division of David's united monarchy into two separate kingdoms (see *Israel; *Jeroboam son of Nebat). On Solomon's death, Rehoboam went to Shechem, "for all Israel had come to Shechem to acclaim him as king" (I Kings 12:1; II Chron. 10:1). The words "all Israel" here evidently refer to only the northern tribes, since Rehoboam seems to have been accepted by Judah as a matter of course (I Kings 11:43; II Chron. 9:31). As a precondition for accepting him as king, the representatives of Israel made the following demand of Rehoboam: "Lighten the hard service of your father and his heavy yoke upon us, and we will serve you" (I Kings 12:4; II Chron. 10:4; see *Solomon). Rehoboam asked the people to wait three days for his reply, and first consulted "the old men, who had served his father Solomon while he was alive" (I Kings 12:6). They advised him to accede to the people's request, thereby ensuring himself their loyalty "for ever" (12:7). But the king rejected the elders' counsel, preferring to be guided by the "young men who had grown up with him" (12:8); who counseled a hard line. He is reported to have used the words: "Whereas my father laid upon you a heavy yoke, I will add to your yoke; my father chastised you with whips, but I will chastise you with scorpions" (12:8–14). He also was swayed by the vulgarism of his advisers, who told him to tell the people, "My little one [i.e., my penis] is thicker than my father's loins." The people replied: "What portion have we in David? We have no inheritance in the son of Jesse. To your tents, O Israel! Look now to your own house, David" (12:16). The Israelites chose as their king Jeroboam son of Nebat, who had previously returned from Egypt (12:3, 20).

Naturally, Rehoboam did not recognize the legality of the split and provocatively sent *Adoram "who was taskmaster over the *corvee" in order to assert his rule, but the people stoned Adoram to death (I Kings 12:18). Rehoboam was forced to flee to Jerusalem and then to wage a prolonged war against Jeroboam, in a vain effort to reunite Israel with Judah (I Kings 12:21; 15:6; I Chron. 11:1; 12:15). The split in the kingdom and the prolonged fighting between Rehoboam and Jeroboam weakened the Israelites, and at the same time encouraged their neighbors not only to throw off Israelite rule and proclaim their absolute independence (see *Aram, *Ammon, *Moab, *Edom, and *Philistines), but even to attempt to enlarge their own territories at the expense of Israel and Judah. As a defensive measure, Rehoboam ringed his kingdom with a system of forts (II Chron. 11:5–12). On the west he fortified Aijalon, Zorah, Azekah, Soco, Gath, Mareshah, and Lachish; on the south, Lachish, Adoraim, and Ziph; and on the east, Ziph, Hebron, Beth-Zur, Tekoa, Etam, and Beth-Lehem. Possibly Rehoboam refrained from fortifying his border with the kingdom of Israel as an expression of his refusal to accept the split. Although the list of the fortified cities built by Rehoboam appears in the Bible before the account of Pharaoh *Shishak's invasion of Palestine, most scholars are of the opinion that Rehoboam carried out the work of fortification only after the Egyptian campaign. According to the two versions found in the Bible, the campaign took place in the fifth year of Rehoboam's reign (I Kings 14:25; II Chron. 12:2). The Egyptian king advanced into Judah with a large army, took the fortified cities "and came as far as Jerusalem" (II Chron. 12:3–4). Shishak carried off the Temple treasures, including the gold shields, and the treasures of the king's house. From the Egyptian list of places and cities captured by Shishak, it is clear that the campaign was not only directed against Judah but also, and mainly, against the kingdom of Israel (see *Jeroboam son of Nebat). Jerusalem is not mentioned in the list (at least, not in the extant sections of it), from which it may be deduced that Shishak did not conquer the city, but only passed threateningly close to it (cf. 12:7–8). Rehoboam went out to the north of Jerusalem to meet Shishak and paid tribute to him, thereby saving the city from conquest. Shishak's campaign led to the destruction of many of the cities of Judah, particularly those in the Negev, including Ezion-Geber on the coast of the Red Sea. Fortunately for Judah and Israel and the other little states of the region, however, Egypt lacked the unity and strength to maintain a permanent suzerainty over them.

See *Abijah.

[Bustanay Oded]

In the Aggadah

David praised God for having permitted Ammonite and Moabite women in marriage, since this allowed him (a descendant of Ruth, a Moabite woman) and Rehoboam (the son of Naamah, an Ammonite woman) to enter into the assembly of Israel (Yev. 77a). The treasures which the Jews removed from Egypt (Ex. 12:36) were retained, until Shishak, the king of Egypt, took them away from Rehoboam (Pes. 119a). All the curses with which David cursed Joab (II Sam. 3:29) were fulfilled in David's own descendants, Rehoboam being afflicted with a gonorrheal flux (Sanh. 48b). The rabbis, emphasizing the message to be derived from Rehoboam's failure, declared that the king is the servant of the people and not their ruler (Hor. 10a–b).

BIBLIOGRAPHY: Bright, Hist, 209–14; Malamat, in: JNES, 22 (1963), 247–53; Evans, in: JNES, 25 (1966), 273–9; Tadmor, in: *Journal of World History*, 9 (1968), 12–17. **ADD. BIBLIOGRAPHY:** C. Evans, in: ABD, 5:661–64; N. Na'aman, in: L. Handy (ed.), *The Age of Solomon* (1997), 57–61; M. Cogan, *I Kings* (AB; 2001), 345–56; A. Rainey and R. Notley, *The Sacred Bridge* (2006), 185–89. IN THE AGGADAH: Ginzberg, Legends, s.v. index.

REHOBOTH (Heb. רְחֹבוֹת).

(1) Rehoboth-in-the-Negev. Rehoboth is the etiological name of a well dug by Isaac in the Negev in order to escape from quarrels with the people of Gerar (Gen. 26:22). Some scholars locate it in the region around al-Ruḥayba, approximately 20½ mi. (33 km.) southwest of Beersheba. Near the tell, an Iron Age fortress was discovered. *Nabatean remains, including a building (caravanserai?) and a bilingual Nabatean and Greek inscription, suggest that the site was a stopping place for traders on the secondary road extending to the Sinai via Rhinocorura. The main remains at the site date to the Byzantine period. After Haluza, ancient Elusa, Rehoboth (22 acres) is the second largest town in the Negev. The ancient town contained a large central church, apparently built in the late fourth or fifth centuries C.E., and two additional churches on the northern and southern edges of the settlement. Found in the north church were small glass plaques decorated with images of saints. On the site are the remains of one of the best-preserved bathhouses in the Negev. Numerous Greek inscriptions were found on tombstones in the cemetery, the earliest from 488 C.E. and the latest from 555 C.E. A kufic inscription was also found at the site referring to Amr ibn-al-As, conqueror of Byzantine Palestine in the seventh century. Excavations were conducted at the site by Y. Tsafrir and R. Rosenthal-Higgenbottom between 1975 and 1979, with further excavations by Tsafrir and K. Holum in 1986.

(2) Rehoboth ha-Nahar (Heb. רְחֹבוֹת הַנָּהָר; "Rehoboth by the River"), the residence of Shaul, king of Edom (Gen. 36:37; I Chron. 1:48). Roman sources (*Notitia Dignitatum* 73:27), the Beersheba edict, and Eusebius (Onom. 142:13–14) mention it as a garrison in the Gebalene. In the Babylonian Talmud (Yoma 10a) it is located on the Euphrates, usually called *nahar* ("river") in the Bible. It is perhaps to be identified with Khirbat al-Riḥāb on the Sayl al-Riḥāb, a confluent of the river Zered (Wadi al-Ḥasaʾ). Remains on the site date to the Nabatean and Roman periods.

BIBLIOGRAPHY: T.E. Lawrence and C.L. Wooley, *The Wilderness of Zin* (1915), 117ff.; A. Musil, *Arabia Petraea*, 2 (1907), 79ff.; T. Wiegand, *Sinai* (1920), 57–61; N. Glueck, in: AASOR, 18–19 (1939), 59; A. Alt, in: ZDPV, 58 (1935), 30; Press, Ereẓ, s.v. **ADD. BIBLIOGRAPHY:** Y. Tsafrir, *Excavations at Rehovot-in-the-Negev 1: The Northern Church* (1988; cf. C. Dauphin, in: AJA 95 (1991), 186–88); Y. Tsafrir, L. Di Segni, and J. Green, *Tabula Imperii Romani. Iudaea – Palaestina. Maps and Gazetteer* (1994), 88, s.v. "Betomolachon."

[Michael Avi-Yonah / Shimon Gibson (2nd ed.)]

REḤOV, TEL (often spelled **Reḥob**; Arabic: **Tell eṣ-Ṣarem**; Israel map reference 197.207; UTM Grid 873.594), the largest mound in the alluvial Beth-Shean Valley, extending over 26 acres (10.4 hectares); its summit at an elevation of 116 m below sea level. Located between the Jordan River and the Gilboa ridge and 5 km south of Tel Beth-Shean, the mound dominates the north–south road through the Jordan Valley. It is located near plenty of water sources and fertile land. The site comprises an upper mound and a lower mound to its north, each covering about 13 acres.

Tel Reḥov was identified since the 1920s with Reḥob of Egyptian texts, based on the preservation of the name in the Byzantine Jewish town Roḥob and the Islamic tomb of esh-Sheikh er-Riḥab, both located nearby. Surveys conducted by W.F. Albright, A. Bergman [Biran], and N. Zori indicated occupation at the site throughout the entire Bronze and Iron ages.

Reḥov (the Hebrew word for "piazza" and "street") was the name of several cities mentioned in the Bible and Egyptian sources. Two cities by that name in the western Galilee are referred to in the city lists of Asher (Josh. 19:28–30). An Aramean city and state of that name are mentioned in Syria, mainly in relation to David's conquests (II Sam 10:6, 8).

Reḥov in the Beth-Shean valley is mentioned as Raḥabu in an Akkadian letter from Taanach (15th century B.C.E.). In the stele of Seti I found at Beth-Shean (c. 1300 B.C.E.), it is mentioned as remaining loyal to the Egyptian imperial rule at a time of local revolts. In Papyrus Anastasi I from the 13th century B.C.E., the city is mentioned in relation to Beth-Shean and the crossing of the Jordan. Pharaoh Shishak's list of conquered cities (c. 925 B.C.E.) mentions Reḥov (No. 17) after "The Valley" and before Beth-Shean. Several additional Egyptian sources refer to either the city in the Beth-Shean Valley or to that in the Western Galilee. These include the Execration Texts (19–18th Dynasties), Tuthmosis III's topographic list (No. 87), a 20th-dynasty papyrus in Torino, and a notation concerning the production of chariots parts in Papyrus Anastasi IV. Reḥov in the Beth-Shean Valley is not mentioned in the Old Testament.

Seven excavation seasons were conducted at the site between 1997 and 2005, directed by Amihai Mazar on behalf of the Institute of Archaeology of the Hebrew University and sponsored by John Camp. Four excavation areas (A, B, H, J) were excavated on the upper mound, and five (C, D, E, F, G) on the lower mound.

Third Millennium B.C.E.

A fortification system dating to the Early Bronze Age II–III was revealed in a narrow trench on the slope of the higher mound (Area H). It includes a 9.5-m-wide mud brick wall preserved to a maximum height of 6.5 m, abutted on its outer side by an earthen glacis preserved to 13 m wide and 3.5 m high. This impressive fortification, which apparently surrounded the upper mound, suggests that Tel Reḥov was the site of a major city during this period.

Evidence for an Intermediate Bronze Age (*ebiv/mbi*) settlement and cemetery was revealed in surveys of the alluvial plain west of the mound. Several burial caves from this period were excavated close to the southwestern corner of the mound, containing pottery vessels, metal weapons, and beads.

Second Millennium B.C.E.

The excavations did not reveal any remains from the first half of the second millennium B.C.E. (Middle Bronze Age). An

Old Babylonian seal found on the mound, and few Middle Bronze graves near the mound hint for a possible occupation level which was not yet exposed.

The occupation history during the second half of the second millennium B.C.E. (Late Bronze and Iron Age I periods) was explored in Area D, a 10-m-wide trench on the western slope of the lower mound. At the bottom of the trench (Phase D-11), a layer of dark silt and ash located 1.2 m below the present-day alluvial field west of the mound indicates a significant rise in the level of the plain during historical periods. This layer contained few pottery sherds dated to the 16th–15th centuries B.C.E. This layer was covered by a 2-m-thick layer of travertine (D-10), probably an evidence of a small lake or pond at the foot of the mound during part of the Late Bronze Age. From the 14th century onwards, a continuous urban settlement was detected. The earliest (Phase D-9) included the remains of a substantial building dated to the 14th–13th centuries B.C.E. In the next phase (D-8), still in the 13th century B.C.E., a thick plaster floor covered the remains of the earlier building. Two occupation layers are dated to the 12th century B.C.E.; the earlier (D-7) includes remains of several rooms in a large architectural complex and the later (D-6) includes flimsy walls, plastered industrial installations, and beaten earth floors which were mended several times. Phases D-5 and D-4 represent two architectural phases of an 11th century B.C.E. city, of which a north–south street and parts of houses on either side were excavated. The destruction of stratum D-4 was followed by a total change in the function of this area. In Phase D-3 an open area covered the previous buildings, and more than 40 pits were recovered in a rather small area, used for storage or refuse. The material culture in all phases D-9 to D-3 is Canaanite in nature; painted pottery continued to be utilized until the end of the Iron Age I. Area D thus revealed a continuous development of the Canaanite city from the 13th to the end of the 11th centuries B.C.E., in spite of at least three destructions. No evidence of fortifications was discerned in any of these strata.

The Iron Age IIA: 10–9th centuries B.C.E.

The term Iron Age IIA is used here to define a period of about 150 years, from c. 980 B.C.E. to ca. 830 B.C.E., the time of the Israelite United Monarchy and of the Omride Dynasty. This is the main period studied at Tel Reḥov, and the rich finds contributed much to the study of this debated period in northern Israel. Three strata were defined: VI, V and IV, based on correlation between local phases in various excavation areas. During this period the city was densely built according to a well-ordered town plan, with parallel blocks of buildings. However, no fortifications were found. Both the building technique as well as the buildings' plans are exceptional in the Iron-Age architecture of Israel: the houses were constructed of unbaked mud bricks without stone foundations; wood foundations were constructed for both walls and floors and the buildings lack the pillars which are common in Israelite architecture. An open air sanctuary was found next to one of the dwelling quarters, perhaps serving the local neighborhood and used for ancestors cult. In another area, beehives were found in a building of Stratum V, the first of their kind to be uncovered in the Levant.

The second of these three Iron IIA cities was partly destroyed by fire, and partly continued to survive in Stratum IV. The third (Stratum IV) was violently destroyed by fire, resulting in the abandonment of the lower city. A large number of 14C dates of grain and olive stones as well as conventional archaeological considerations indicate that Strata VI and V belong to the 10th century B.C.E., and Stratum IV to the 9th century B.C.E. The destruction of V occurred during the last third of the 10th century, perhaps during Shoshenq I raid; Stratum IV was destroyed during the 9th century, perhaps during the Arameans attacks in the days of Hazael.

The destruction layers yielded rich assemblage of finds representing a specific regional aspect of the Iron Age IIA material culture in northern Israel. The pottery is characterized by the appearance of red slip and hand burnish, though in Stratum VI Canaanite tradition of painted pottery was still abundant. The painting diminishes in the following strata, and the red slip and hand burnished pottery become dominant.

International trade is detected in the form of Phoenician, Cypriot, and Greek pottery. Of special interest are several Greek Proto-Geometric, Sub-Proto-Geometric, and Middle Geometric sherds, which are rare imports in the Levant and are of special importance for the study of the Greek Iron Age chronology and international connections.

Objects related to a local cult include a group of ceramic horned altars, some with naked female figurines attached to their fronts. These altars retain traditions known from Syria at the end of the Late Bronze Age. A ceramic model shrine was decorated with unique molding on its roof, depicting a crouching animal with its front paws on two grotesquely-shaped human heads. A variety of clay figurines belong to the Canaanite/Phoenician artistic tradition, others are typical of northern Israel, such as several examples of the "drum player" woman. A unique figurine in a crude local style depicts a naked female crouching on her knees.

A variety of seals and seal impressions represent animals (antelopes, ostriches, crabs, birds), while one example depicts two human figures on either side of a palm tree. A unique type of seal impression on jar handles, known so far only from Tel Reḥov and Tel Beth-Shean, shows schematic human figures (or deities?) striding on mountaintops (?). A unique ivory object shows an enthroned human figure dressed in a long garment. The object is hollow, the head, hands and legs were made separately and attached to the main body.

Three alphabetic inscriptions incised on pottery jars were found. One from Stratum VI reads lnḥ[ ], perhaps to be reconstructed "belonging to Nach[um]." A second inscription reads: lšq[?] nmš – "belonging to Shky (?) [son of?] Nimshi." The name Nimshi is known from a contemporary inscription at nearby Tel Amal, and in the Bible as the name of Jehu's father or grandfather. The third inscription was broken, only the letters m'.'m were preserved and the meaning remains elusive.

Reḥov, though not mentioned in the Bible, must have been one of the most important cities in the Northern Kingdom of Israel. The specific material culture found in the 10th–9th centuries levels may indicate that much of its population could have been descendants of the previous Iron Age I Canaanite inhabitants, though now the city was part of the Israelite geopolitical entity.

The Iron Age IIb

During the Iron Age IIB (c. 830–732 B.C.E.) the city was reduced to half its former size and limited to the upper mound. The city was now surrounded by a 9.5-m-wide mudbrick wall, probably intended to stand against the Assyrian threat. Several occupation phases were detected (Stratum III) ending with dramatic destruction, including evidence of people slaughtered in their houses, most probably during the Assyrian conquest in the year 732 B.C.E.

Two graves with Assyrian pottery, as well as scant occupational remains (Stratum II), are evidence of a short period of activity after the Assyrian conquest, but the site was soon abandoned.

The Early Islamic to Medieval Periods

After a gap of about 1,000 years, a small village was founded on the summit of the mound in the 8th century C.E., and it survived until the 12th century C.E. Only the edges of this settlement were excavated.

BIBLIOGRAPHY: H. Bruins, J. van der Plicht, and A. Mazar, "14C Dates from Tel Reḥov: Iron Age Chronology, Pharaohs, and Hebrew Kings," in: *Science*, vol. 300, no. 5617:11 (2003), 315–18; N. Coldstream and A. Mazar, "Greek Pottery from Tel Reḥov and Iron Age Chronology," in: IEJ 53 (2003), 29–48; A. Mazar, "The 1997–1998 Excavations at Tel Reḥov: Preliminary Report," in: IEJ, 49 (1999), 1–42; idem, "Three Tenth–Ninth Century B.C.E. Inscriptions from Tel Reḥov," in: C.G. den Hertog, U. Hübner, and S. Münger (eds.), *Saxa loquentur: Studien zur Archaeologie Palästinas/Israels. Festschrift für Volkmar Fritz zum 65. Geburtstag* (Alter Orient und Altes Testament 302) (2003), 171–84; idem, "Greek and Levantine Iron Age Chronology: A Rejoinder," in: IEJ, 54 (2004), 24–36; idem, Tel Reḥov: The Contribution of the Excavations to the Study of the Iron Age in Northern Israel," in: *2 ICAANE Proceedings Winnona Lake 2004* (2006); A. Mazar, H. Bruins, K. and van der Plicht, "Fine Tuning Iron Age Chronology: Radiocarbon Dates from Tel Reḥov, Israel," in: Bietak (ed.), "The Synchronisation of Civilization in the Eastern Mediterranean in Second Millennium B.C." in: *II: Proceedings of the SCIEM 2003 – EuroConference. Vienna* (2006); A. Mazar, "The Excavations at Tel Rehov and their Significance for the Study of the Iron Age in Israel," in: *Eretz Israel* 27 (2003), 143–60 (Heb.); A. Mazar, H. Bruins, N. Panitz-Cohen, and J. van der Plicht, "Ladder of Time at Tel Rehov: Stratigraphy, Archaeological Context, Pottery and Radiocarbon Dates," in: T. Levy and T. Higham (eds.), *Radiocarbon dating and the Iron Age of the Southern Levant. Proceedings of a Conference at Yarntom Manor* (2005).

[Amihai Mazar (2nd ed.)]

REḤOVOT (Heb. רְחוֹבוֹת; "Wide Expanses," a name based on Gen. 26:22), city in central Israel, in the Coastal Plain, 14 mi. (22 km.) S. of Tel Aviv-Jaffa. Reḥovot was founded in 1890, by First *Aliyah immigrants from Poland. The land had been bought from a wealthy Christian Arab owner through the efforts of Yehudah *Goor (Grasovski), Yehoshua *Hankin, and A. *Eisenberg. The founding group, Menuḥah ve-Naḥalah, was intent on establishing a moshavah independent of Baron Edmond de *Rothschild's aid and tutelage. Reḥovot was then the only Jewish village to achieve this status. Although the moshavah was based on private initiative and property, the settlers showed civic spirit and strove toward cooperation. Initially, they had to overcome many obstacles – the Arab neighbors' enmity, agricultural failures due to plant diseases and the like, and marketing difficulties of their grape and almond produce. Citriculture was introduced in the first decade of the 20th century and the population increased, particularly after 1906, with the settlement of immigrants from Yemen in the suburbs, e.g., Sha'arayim founded in 1912. In 1914 Reḥovot had 955 inhabitants and 2,750 acres (11,000 dunams) of vineyards and almond orchards as well as over 130 acres (530 dunams) of citrus groves. After the hardships of World War I, Reḥovot entered a phase of quick expansion. In 1922 the village received municipal council status. In 1932 the Agricultural Research Station of the Jewish Agency (since statehood under the authority of the Ministry of Agriculture) was transferred from Tel Aviv to Reḥovot. In 1934 Chaim Weizmann founded the Sieff Institute in Reḥovot and built a home in the moshavah in 1936. While throughout the 1930s and 1940s the citrus crop continued to constitute the mainstay of Reḥovot's economy, industrial enterprises, particularly citrus preserve plants, were opened. In 1949, the Sieff Institute was enlarged and became the *Weizmann Institute. In 1952 the Agricultural Research Station became the Faculty of Agriculture of the *Hebrew University. In 1948 Reḥovot had 9,000 inhabitants and became a city two years later. The population increased rapidly in the first years of statehood, reaching 23,000 in 1953. Later, its growth continued at a slower pace with 29,000 inhabitants in 1958 and 36,600 in 1968. Citrus and mixed farming still constituted an important element in the local economy, and Reḥovot became one of Israel's principal centers for citrus packing, particularly after the opening of *Ashdod port. Industry was diversified and included the production of artificial leather and chemicals, along with additional food-processing plants. In the late 1960s, a number of scientific enterprises connected with the Weizmann Institute added yet another element to the city's economy. The Kaplan Hospital is included in Reḥovot's municipal boundaries. In the mid-1990s the population was approximately 83,200, rising to 98,800 in 2002, on an area of 8.5 sq. mi. (22 sq. km.). A third of the population was religious, 21% had an academic education. The economy continued to be based on packing, food processing, and chemicals, services, commerce, and the science and research institutes.

BIBLIOGRAPHY: M. Smilansky, *Reḥovot – Shishim Shenot Ḥayyeha* (1950); Z. Gluskin, *Zikhronot* (1946); E.Z. Lewin-Epstein, *Zikhronot* (1932); Y. Harari, *Bein ha-Keramim* (1947). **WEBSITE:** www.rehovot.muni.il.

[Efraim Orni / Shaked Gilboa (2nd ed.)]

REHUM (Heb. רְחֻם; probably רְחוּם, an Aramaic hypocoristic of רחמאל, cf. רחמיאל in *Murashu tablets), a popular name borne by Jews and Arameans during the Persian period. Written in the Aramaic script, it has been confused by ancient scribes (cf. Ezra 2:2 with Neh. 7:7) and modern scholars (Kraeling, *The Brooklyn Museum Aramaic Papyri* (1953), 10:19, 11:14, 12:34) with the graphically similar Nehum.

(1) One of the 12 leaders joining Zerubbabel in the return from Babylonia (Ezra 2:2).

(2) As chancellor of the province Samaria or the satrapy Trans-Euphrates, Rehum and the scribe Shimshai succeeded in blocking construction of the Jerusalem wall during the reign of Artaxerxes I (Ezra 4:8–23).

(3) One of the levites who aided Nehemiah in the reconstruction of the Jerusalem wall (Neh. 3:17).

(4) A lay family name affixed to the agreement to observe the Torah (Neh. 10:26).

(5) As the name of a priestly family (Neh. 12:3) it may be a scribal corruption of Harim (cf. Neh. 10:6; 12:15; I Chron. 24:8).

[Bezalel Porten]

REḤUMEI, name of three Babylonian *amoraim*. REḤUMEI (I), *amora* of the mid-fourth century and a pupil of Rava and Abbaye (Pes. 39a; Naz. 13a). It is told that he died prematurely on the eve of the Day of Atonement, the circumstances of his death being given as follows: Reḥumei studied with Rava at Maḥoza and returned home to his wife only once a year on the eve of the Day of Atonement. One year he was so involved in his studies that he forgot to return. When he did not arrive, his anxious wife burst into tears. At that moment the roof collapsed and he was killed (Ket. 62b). REḤUMEI (II), *amora* of the mid-fifth century. He was a pupil of Ravina I, before whom he expounded a saying of Huna b. Taḥlifa (Zev. 77a). He also transmitted the customs of Ravina (Yoma 78a). Reḥumei succeeded Rafram II as the head of the academy of Pumbedita from 443 to 456. He died during the persecution of the Jews by Yazdegerd II. He may have also been called Naḥumai (*Iggeret R. Sherira Ga'on*, ed. B.M. Lewin, p. 96; *Seder ha-Qabbalah*, ed. Cohen, p. 34). REḤUMEI (III), *amora*, is also considered one of the early *savoraim*, although his teachings are still included in the Talmud. He differs with his contemporary Joseph on certain topics (Er. 11a; Men. 33b). He died in 505 C.E.

BIBLIOGRAPHY: Hyman, Toledot; S. Albeck, in: *Sinai Sefer Yovel* (1958), 65–67; H. Albeck, *Mavo la-Talmudim* (1969), 310, 379, 450.

REICH, ASHER (1937–), Hebrew writer. Reich was born in Jerusalem, grew up in the ultra-Orthodox milieu of Me'ah She'arim and was educated in religious schools. At 18 he defied the norms of his surroundings and joined the army, and later studied philosophy and literature at the Hebrew University. His first collection of poems, *Ha-Shanah ha-Shevi'it* ("The Seventh Year") appeared in 1963. It was followed by a dozen collections, including *Mareh Makom* (1978), *Seder Shirim* ("Collection of Poems," 1986), *Uvdot Bidyoniyyot* ("Fictional Evidence," 1993) and *Penei ha-Areẓ* ("A View of the Land," 1999). Reich's protest poems set up a mirror to the changes in Israeli society and mentality. Other poems are of a personal nature, contemplating love and loss and relating with poignant, sensual images to nature and landscape in Israel and in Europe. Particularly striking is his rich language, a poetic idiom which interweaves the language of the Scriptures and various Jewish sources with modern, colloquial Hebrew. Reich, who was for eight years co-editor of *Moznayim*, the magazine of the Hebrew Writers Association, participated in the International Writing Program at Iowa University and received several awards, including The Bernstein Prize. His autobiographical novel *Zikhronot shel Ḥoleh Shikheḥah* ("Reminiscences of an Amnesiac," 1993) tells the story of poet Yeshayahu Sonnenfeld, against the background of Berlin after the Unification and Tel Aviv under the threat of Saddam Hussein's SCUDS. The oxymoronic title points to the complex theme which underlies the novel, namely the power of past experiences and the inability to suppress painful memories. A collection of stories *Ish im Kelev* ("Man with Dog") appeared in 1999. Individual poems have been translated into various languages. Three of his collections as well as the novel were published in German. For further information see the ITHL website at www.ithl.org.il.

BIBLIOGRAPHY: Z. Shamir, in: *Maariv* (August 1, 1980); Sh. Levo, "*Al Seder ve-al Dimyon*," in: *Yedioth Aḥaronoth* (January 2, 1981); Sh. Avneri, in: *Al ha-Mishmar* (January 16, 1981); idem, "*He'arot le-Shirato shel A. Reich*," in: *Moznayim*, 51:6 (1981), 445–448; J. Hessing, in: *Frankfurter Allgemeine Zeitung* (May 2, 2001); N. Carmel-Yonatan, *Ha-Shir hu Zikkaron*, in: *Yedioth Aḥaronoth* (March 9, 1984); B. Sporri, in: *Juedische Allgemeine*, 15 (July 17, 2003).

[Anat Feinberg (2nd ed.)]

REICH, IGNÁC (1821–1887), teacher and historian. Born in Zsámbek, Hungary, Reich worked from 1851 as a teacher at the Jewish Community School of Budapest, where he proposed that religious subjects be taught in Hungarian. He wrote newspaper articles in favor of the emancipation of Hungarian Jewry and their assimilation as Hungarians. During the 1848 Revolution, Reich voiced his sentiments in patriotic poems. He was a frequent contributor to the Hungarian Jewish press, and translated Genesis and the *Haggadah* into Hungarian for use in schools (1879, 1878).

His main works included a collection of biographies of Hungarian Jews under the title *Beth El: Ehrentempel verdienter ungarischer Israeliten* (5 vols., 1856–65, 1878^2), an important source book for Hungarian Jewish history; and *Bet Lehem: Jahrbuch zur Befoerderung des Ackerbaues, des Handwerks und der Industrie unter den Israeliten Ungarns*, a yearbook for the advancement of agriculture, trade, and industry among Hungarian Jews (2 vols., 1872–73).

BIBLIOGRAPHY: *Magyar Zsidó Lexikon* (1929), 737.

REICH, KOPPEL (**Jacob**; 1838–1929), Hungarian rabbi. Born in Verbó into a rabbinical family, he studied under his father

Abraham Ezekiel Reich, rabbi of Bannewitz, and Abraham Samuel Benjamin *Sofer, rabbi of Pressburg. He married the daughter of Israel ha-Ro'eh, disciple of Moses *Sofer and rabbi of Szobotiszt, whom he succeeded in 1860. Twenty years later he became rabbi of Verbó where his grandfather had previously held office and was elected chief rabbi of the Orthodox community of Budapest in 1889. Reich possessed a wide general education and was active in Hungarian Orthodox communal affairs. In 1905 he presided over the convention of Orthodox rabbis and community leaders who drew up the regulations of Orthodox Jewry in Hungary. He delivered the opening speech in Hebrew – an unusual event in Hungary. These regulations were later ratified by the government and became the legal framework for the organization of Orthodoxy in Hungary. In the school which he established and directed, Torat Emet, both religious and secular subjects were taught. In 1927, although he was almost 90 years old, he took his seat in the upper house of the Hungarian parliament. Reich left no works, but he is quoted by rabbis of his generation. All his sons and sons-in-law held rabbinical office in Hungary.

BIBLIOGRAPHY: P.Z. Schwartz, *Shem ha-Gedolim me-Ereẓ Hagar* (1959²), pt. 2, 35.

[Itzhak Alfassi]

REICH, LEON (1879–1929), Zionist leader in eastern Galicia and a leader of Polish Jewry. Born in Lemberg, Reich joined the Zionist Movement in his youth and founded the first Zionist students' association in Galicia, called Emunah. By that time he was already known as an able lecturer and writer. After studying political science in Paris for two years, Reich returned to Galicia and became head of the Zionist Movement. He was also active in the political struggle for the civil rights of the Jews. In 1911 he was a candidate for the Austrian parliament, and, in spite of his failure to be elected, his influence increased in all Jewish circles. He was the editor of the Zionist Polish-language weekly *Wschód* and also edited a Polish Zionist almanac in 1910. During the political unrest in Galicia at the end of World War I (1918), he was arrested by the Polish government, accused of treason, and placed in a detention camp. He was released, however, on the intervention of West European leaders. He moved to Paris and became a leading member in the *Comité des Délégations Juives to the Versailles Peace Conference, on whose behalf he edited a book concerning the national rights of East European Jews, *Les Droits nationaux des Juifs en Europe Orientale* (1919). Back in Poland, he was elected a member of the Polish Sejm for the Lvov district, an office which he retained until his death.

In 1924 Reich was made chairman of the Jewish Club in the Sejm and Senate (Kolo Zydowskie) In this capacity he and O. *Thon negotiated an agreement with the Polish government according to which the Jewish members of the Sejm were to support the government, provided that certain concessions be given to the Jews. The agreement (known under its Polish name *Ugoda) met with wide opposition in the Jewish public and became void later, when, after a coup, a new regime was established in Poland. Reich was forced to resign from the chairmanship of the Jewish Club in the Sejm, but retained his influence, especially in eastern Galicia, where he was reelected to the Sejm in spite of pressures exerted by the Polish authorities in favor of their own candidates. At the same time, he carried on his Zionist work as president of the Zionist Organization in eastern Galicia and deputy chairman of the Zionist General Council. He took part in all Zionist congresses as a leading delegate of the *General Zionists. In order to increase his influence throughout Poland, he founded a second Zionist Polish-language daily in Warsaw, *Dziennik Warszawski*, in addition to *Chwila*, published in Lvov. The new paper was on a high level, but had to be closed because of financial difficulties. Reich's remains were brought to Tel Aviv in 1934.

BIBLIOGRAPHY: N.M. Gelber, *Toledot ha-Tenu'ah ha-Ẓiyyonit be-Galizyah*, 2 vols. (1958), 833–4 and index; I. Zineman, *In Gerangel* (1952), 94–105. **ADD. BIBLIOGRAPHY:** J. Majchrowski et al., *Kto byl kim w drugiej Rzeczypospolitej* (1994), 412.

[Aryeh Tartakower]

REICH, ROBERT BERNARD (1946–), U.S. political economist, educator, and government official. Born in Scranton, Pennsylvania, Reich was raised in Westchester County, N.Y., and educated at Dartmouth College (B.A. 1968), Oxford (Rhodes Scholar, M.A. 1970), and Yale Law School (J.D. 1973). He was an intern in the office of Senator Robert F. Kennedy in 1967, and worked for the presidential campaign of Eugene McCarthy in 1968. He was an assistant solicitor general in the Department of Justice, 1974–76; director of policy planning, Federal Trade Commission, 1976–81; and lecturer at the Kennedy School of Government, 1981–93. Reich was a contributing editor of the *New Republic*, 1982–93, and a cofounder of the journal *American Prospect* in 1990. An advisor to Democratic presidential candidates Walter Mondale in 1984, Michael Dukakis in 1988, and John Kerry in 2004, he was secretary of labor during the first term (1993–97) of the administration of President Bill Clinton, a friend Reich had known as a student at Oxford and Yale. Small in stature, he quipped that he always knew that he was on Clinton's short list. Reich was professor of social and economic policy at Brandeis University, 1997–2005. In 2002 he ran unsuccessfully in the Democratic primary for governor of Massachusetts. He became a professor at the Goldman School of Public Policy at the University of California, Berkeley.

From the early 1980s Reich was a prominent public "policy entrepreneur," an enthusiastic advocate and popularizer of economic policy ideas through public appearances, articles, and books, focusing on jobs, the global economy, and related issues. He was associated with the tendency known as neoliberalism, which combines a fundamental reliance on markets and free trade to achieve economic growth with a belief in government regulation and at least minimal social provision. Once an advocate of a comprehensive state industrial policy that would direct investment to certain industries, by the time he became secretary of labor he had abandoned that approach for one that favored education and retraining as a way of adapting the American workforce to a changing global economy whose conditions are determined by essentially unrestrained multinational corporate activities. He did implement generally liberal policies, however, having to do with sweatshops, child labor, minimum wages, worker safety, and pensions, and attempted to get the administration to address seriously the issues of economic insecurity on which it had been elected, but lost influence as Clinton moved politically to the center/right after the 1994 congressional elections. Reich argued against any attempt to keep American manufacturing jobs from being outsourced overseas, believing that such jobs are being lost everywhere because of automation, and that the benefits of cheaper products will generate more American jobs in the long run.

Among Reich's books are *Minding America's Business* (1982, with Ira Magaziner); *The Resurgent Liberal and Other Unfashionable Prophecies* (1989); *Public Management in a Democratic Society* (1990); *The Work of Nations: Preparing Ourselves for 21st Century Capitalism* (1991); *Locked in the Cabinet* (1997); *The Future of Success: Working and Living in the New Economy* (2000); and *Reason: Why Liberals Will Win the Battle for America* (2004).

[Drew Silver (2nd ed.)]

REICH, STEVE (1936–), U.S. composer and performer. Reich was born in New York and began studying drumming with Roland Kohloff at the age of 14. At Cornell University (1953–57) he devoted himself mainly to philosophy but also attended lectures of William Austin in music history. After returning to New York he began his composition studies, first privately with Hall Overton (1957–58) and later at the Juilliard School with Bergsma and Persichetti (1958–61). He received his master's degree under Berio (Mills College, California).

In the middle of the 1960s the idea of "phasing" captured his imagination; he composed some pieces where identical sound elements move out of synchrony with each other, i.e., in and out of phase (*It's Gonna Rain*, for tape, 1965, *Piano Phase*, 2 pianos, 1967, etc.). In this way, Reich became one of the founders of minimalism, or repetitive music. This music demanded a new type of reception, characterized by Reich as follows: "Some critics […] thought I was intending to create some kind of 'hypnotic' or 'trance' music. […] But I actually prefer the music to be heard by somebody who's totally wide awake, hearing more than he or she usually does, rather than by someone who's just spaced-out and receiving a lot of ephemeral impressions."

In the late 1960s Reich began giving concerts in New York galleries, where other minimalists (musicians, film artists, and visual artists) were also active. At the same time he and his own ensemble began making records of his music. He studied drumming with teachers from Africa and Asia, and often included percussion in his scores (*Music for 18 Musicians*, 1974–76; *Eight Lines*, 1979). *Music for 18 Musicians* became a new stage in his composition technique: within a context of many constantly recycling musical figures, each of them gradually changes.

In 1976–77 Reich devoted his time to Hebrew, Torah, and cantillation studies, visited Israel, and heard singers from Eastern Sephardi communities. Following this experience, he composed *Tehillim* for choir and instrumental ensemble (1981). His next opus, *The Desert Music* (1982–84) for choir and orchestra on the lines from William Carlos Williams, refer to the possible destruction of the planet. K.R. Schwarz characterized the opening of the finale as "[…] a solitary human running across a vast desolate plain – a desert at once intimidating and exhilarating."

In his most famous piece, *Different Trains*, 1988, Reich combines his childhood recollections of frequent train journeys between New York and California and his divorced parents with the memory of the different trains taking Jewish children to the death camps. Reich used recordings of train sounds and spoken testimonies of his governess, a retired Pullman porter, and Holocaust survivors, to be played as short melodies by live and recorded string quartets. *The New York Times* hailed *Different Trains* as an "astonishing work of such originality that breakthrough seems the only possible description … possesses an absolutely harrowing emotional impact." *The Cave*, Steve Reich and Beryl Korot's theater piece (1990–93), was also highly appreciated by the critics. The title is metaphoric: *The Cave* is about the cave at Hebron that is by tradition the burial place of Abraham and Sarah. Exploring the biblical story of Abraham, Sarah, Hagar, Ishmael, and Isaac, the 18-musician production consists of edited documentary video footage timed with live and sampled music. After *The Cave*, Reich and his wife, the video maker Beryl Korot, continued their collaboration in *Three Tales*, a full-evening music-theater piece on the topic of technology and its consequences. Noted choreographers often interpreted Reich's music, including Laura Dean, who commissioned *Sextet* (1984). The ballet, entitled *Impact*, earned Steve Reich and Laura Dean a Bessie Award in 1986. In 1994 Reich was elected to the American Academy of Arts and Letters.

BIBLIOGRAPHY: NG²; E. Strickland, *Minimalism: Origins* (1993); R. Kostelanetz (ed.), *Writings on Glass: Essays, Interviews, Criticism* (1996, incl. writings by Glass); K.R. Schwarz, *Minimalists* (1996); K. Potter: *Four Musical Minimalists: La Monte Young, Terry Riley, Steve Reich, Philip Glass* (2000).

[Yulia Kreinin (2nd ed.)]

REICH, WILHELM (1897–1957), Austrian psychoanalyst. In his earlier years Reich made significant contributions to psychoanalytic theory. He broke away from the orthodox Freudian approach, believing that neurosis is due to undischarged sexual energy and that any blocking of sexual discharge causes actual physiological disturbance of sexuality (*Die Funktion des Orgasmus*, 1927). According to Reich, mental health is the ability to achieve full orgasm. The sexually satisfied person would have already released his aggressions and thus behave in a socialized manner. He related these ideas to the prognosis of treatment in his paper "Concerning genitality from the standpoint of psychoanalytic prognosis and therapy" (1924, Eng., 1925). Another important contribution was Reich's focus on character and character formation. Previously psychoanalyses dealt mainly with the interpretations of unconscious material. In his study of character resistances he concentrated on the whole person, his habits, tensions, and mannerisms. He went to the U.S. in the 1930s.

He died in prison after he was convicted of fraud. He had sold "orgone boxes" which according to Reich attracted "orgone," a material found in the air that had therapeutic powers. His books which deal with character are *Der triebhafte Charakter* (1925) and *Charakteranalyse* (1933, Eng., 1945²), his most important work.

BIBLIOGRAPHY: *Wilhelm Reich Biographical Material* (1953); IESS, 13 (1968), 396–8; W. Briehl, in: F. Alexander et al. (eds.), *Psychoanalytic Pioneers* (1966), 430–8, incl. bibl.; C. Rycroft, *Reich* (1971).

[Miriam Gay]

REICHARD, PIROSKA (1884–1943), Hungarian poet, critic, and translator. Piroska Reichard's verses, which are outstanding for their great delicacy and were collected in *Az életen kivül* ("Out of Life," 1911) and *Oszi üdvözlet* ("Autumn Greetings," 1922), reflect the fate of the lonely woman. She was a noted translator from English and French as well as being an important essayist and critic of the *Nyugat* school. She committed suicide during the Nazi era.

REICHENBACH, HANS (1891–1953), philosopher. Reichenbach, who was born in Hamburg, is considered one of the most distinguished philosophers of science of the 20th century. He taught at the Technische Hochschule in Stuttgart (1920–26), and at the University of Berlin (1926–33). When Hitler came to power, he left Germany and obtained a teaching position at the University of Istanbul. From 1938 he was professor of philosophy at the University of California at Los Angeles. Reichenbach belonged to that group of scientifically minded philosophers whose conceptual ideals were embodied in the philosophy of logical positivism, a doctrine that was a blend of the new logic developed by Frege and Russell and of traditional British empiricism, modified by the phenomenalism of Ernst Mach. Though never a member of the Vienna circle in a formal sense, Reichenbach worked closely with its main representatives, especially Rudolf Carnap and Herbert *Feigl, and the spirit of their joint endeavors is well expressed in his *The Rise of Scientific Philosophy* (1951). Reichenbach's main contributions to philosophy fall into four main categories: (1) his analysis of the relativity theory; (2) his attempt to solve Hume's classical problem of induction; (3) his development and defense of a frequency theory of probability; (4) his highly original work on nomological statements in the field of inductive logic.

A prolific writer, Reichenbach was the author of 19 books, some of which were published posthumously. His masterpiece is generally considered to be his *Axiomatik der relativistischen Raum-Zeit-Lehre*, originally published in Germany in 1924, but translated into English as *The Philosophy of Space and Time* (1958).

REICHER, EMANUEL (1849–1924), one of the most famous actors of the naturalist movement in Germany. Born in Bochnia, Galicia, Austria, Reicher played first in Hungary, then in Munich, and came in the 1880s to Berlin, where he was promoted by Otto Brahm; he became a leading actor of the Freie Buehne, the Lessing Theater (1892), and the Deutsches Theater (1895, under O. Brahm). In 1902–04 he joined the Kleines Theater of Max Reinhardt, then returned to Brahm. He was a pioneer of the naturalistic play and an actor famous for roles in plays of H. Ibsen and G. Hauptmann. From 1915 to 1921 he lived in New York as an actor, and later as the manager of the Garden Theater. He also directed plays at Maurice Schwartz's Jewish Art Theater (1918) and later for the Theater Guild. He returned to Germany in 1923 and died in Berlin.

[Archiv Bibliographia Judaica (2nd ed.)]

REICHERSON, MOSES (1827–1903), Hebrew author and grammarian. Reicherson was born in Vilna where he earned his living as a part-time teacher of Hebrew and as a proofreader and editor for publishing houses. He was a childhood friend of J.L. *Gordon. He produced the first Hebrew translation of the proverbs of the Russian author I.A. Krylov (1860), and published a three-part Hebrew grammar, *Dikduk li-Sefat Ever* (1864, 1873, 1884). In 1890 he immigrated to New York where he translated Lessing's proverbs and stories in *Mishlei Lessing ve-Sippurav* (1902). He also wrote many essays on linguistics for American and European Hebrew journals.

BIBLIOGRAPHY: R. Brainin, *Fun Mayn Lebns-Bukh* (1941), 203–13; H. Hapgood, *The Spirit of the Ghetto* (1902), 40–51; Kressel, Leksikon, 2 (1967), 864.

[Yehuda Slutsky]

REICHERT, ISRAEL (1891–1975), Israeli botanist and agricultural scientist. Born in Ozorkow, Russian Poland, into a well-to-do Orthodox family, Reichert went to Palestine in 1908 and worked first as a laborer and then as a natural history teacher. He went back to Europe to study biology and plant pathology, returning to Palestine in 1921 to organize the plant pathology department at the newly formed Agricultural Experiment Station. In the 29 years he directed the department, it became a renowned research center in plant pathology, vegetable storage problems, disease control, mycology, bacteriology, virology, and lichenology. In 1942 Reichert joined the Hebrew University's new School of Agriculture at Reḥovot as a lecturer. From 1949 to 1959 he was professor of mycology and plant pathology. In 1938 he was a co-founder of the *Palestine Journal of Botany*. In 1955 he received the Israel Prize for natural sciences.

Reichert's early investigations were on cereal diseases such as rusts and smuts. He went on to diseases of vegetables and plantation crops – grapevines, citrus fruits, and bananas –

and did the earliest pioneering work on the mushrooms of Ereẓ Israel. He created the Hebrew terminology for his field of work, and coined the term "pathogeography" to describe the application of eco-geographical principles to plant pathology and to disease control. He was a world authority on the fungi and lichens of the Near East, which he classified according to these principles. His main contribution was to bridge the gap between plant-physiography and plant-geography.

BIBLIOGRAPHY: H.R. Oppenheimer, in: *Israel Journal of Botany*, 15 (1966), 83–85.

[Julian Louis Meltzer]

REICHINSTEIN, DAVID (1882–1955), physical chemist, born Mogilev, Russia. Reichinstein was professor physical chemistry at the University of Nizhni Novgorod (1918); the Ukrainian Agricultural Academy, (1924); Polytechnicum, Berlin-Charlottenburg (1928–33); and in Prague (1933–38). He was a private consultant in Zurich (1938–55). He wrote *Bestimmung von Geschwindigkeiten von Elektrodenreaktionen* (1913); *Eigenschaften des Adsorptionvolumens* (1916); *Der elektrolytische Stromverstaerkungseffekt* (1920–22); and *Grenzflaechenvorgaenge in der unbelebten and belebten Natur* (1930).

REICHMANN, family of international real estate developers, philanthropists. SAMUEL REICHMANN (1898–1975), a wealthy egg merchant from the small Hungarian town of Beled, and his wife, RENÉE (1898–1990), moved to Vienna in 1923. Deeply observant Jews, they eventually had six children. The family was visiting Samuel's sick father in Hungary when **Kristallnacht* took place and Nazi-inspired gangs attacked Jews and Jewish property in German and Austria. The Reichmann's did not return to Vienna. Instead, Samuel took his family first to London and then to Paris. When France fell to the Nazis in 1940, the family escaped to the international city of Tangier in then-Spanish-controlled Morocco. In the wide-open business atmosphere of wartime Tangier the family prospered as Samuel became a major currency trader. Renée, with the help of her daughter EVA (1923–1986), used the family's wealth and influence to pressure Franco's officials into issuing visas to Jews in Nazi-controlled Budapest, helping to save several thousand lives. Through the Spanish Red Cross, Renée also packed and shipped many thousands of food parcels to the inmates of Auschwitz and other concentration camps.

After the war, Samuel's son PAUL (1930–) left Tangier to study in yeshivot in Britain and Israel. He returned to Morocco as a rabbi in 1953 and began working to modernize Jewish religious education in Morocco. But like most Jews in Morocco, the Reichmann family would soon pack up and leave. Despite their financial success, the family joined an exodus of Moroccan Jews hoping to avoid turbulence looming in the wake of Morocco independence. Eva settled in London and EDWARD (1925–2005) went to Montreal with its already large Jewish community. In 1955 Edward founded Olympia Flooring and Tile to import and sell tiles from Europe. The rest of the family soon followed him to Canada. LOUIS (1927–) joined Edward in Montreal but ALBERT (1929–), PAUL (1930–), and RALPH (1933–) settled in Toronto, where they first extended Edward's tile business but eventually, under the corporate name of Olympia & York, branched out into construction and property development. Edward would later suffer business reversals and, aided by his younger brothers in Toronto, moved to Israel where he became successful in property development.

In Toronto the Reichmann brothers – soon known for their integrity, religious observance, protection of their privacy, and modest lifestyle – first built and operated warehouses and other commercial developments in the bourgeoning city's rapidly growing suburbs. With Paul at the helm, the Toronto company gained a reputation for building structures faster and more cheaply than any other developer. Building success on success, they expanded into the international property development and management business. Among the company's larger projects were First Canadian Place in Toronto, manor property development projects in Tokyo, and the successful New York City Battery Park development known as the World Financial Center. By the 1980s Olympia & York had grown to be the largest property development firms in the world and, in an effort at diversification, the Reichhmann company purchased Abitibi Price, a major pulp and paper firm, and in 1985 bought the Gulf Canada oil company. By the late 1980s the Reichmanns were reportedly among the ten wealthiest families in the world.

In the late 1980s the Reichmanns took a huge gamble when Olympia & York agreed to develop the 83- acre Canary Wharf site in remote east London, the largest development project in the world. They lost. As Britain slid into recession and property values tumbled, the project suffered enormous financial setbacks. With office space at Canary Wharf largely empty, Olympia & York ran out of money. In 1992 the company filed for bankruptcy and was dismembered in February 1993. The Reichmanns were left with only a small property management company known as Olympia & York Properties Corporation. During the decade that followed this new company rebounded to become a multibillion dollar firm, reclaiming a stake in the now prosperous Canary Wharf project, as well as First Canadian Place in Toronto. It also has begun to revitalize its stake in property development in major centers around the world. Today, the family's business interests are moving to the next generation.

The members of the Reichmann family in Toronto remained steadfast in their adherence to Orthodox religious tradition. At cost to themselves, the Reichmanns closed down their construction sites for the Sabbath and for Jewish holidays. Much honored in Toronto and international Jewish world, they were also generous in supporting an international infrastructure of Orthodox schools, yeshivot, *kolelim*, synagogues, and other institutions. The family was also very active in Soviet Jewry campaigns and in support of other charitable and educational causes in Canada, Israel, and around the world.

BIBLIOGRAPHY: A. Bianco, *The Reichmanns: Family, Faith, Fortune, and The Empire of Olympia & York* (1997).

[Harold Troper (2nd ed.)]

REICH-RANICKI, MARCEL (1920–), German journalist and literary critic. Born in Wloclawek, Poland, the son of a merchant, Reich-Ranicki moved with his family to Berlin in 1929, where he was able to finish high school in 1938 but – as a Polish Jew – was not permitted to study at the university afterwards. Soon he was arrested and deported to Poland, where he lived in Warsaw, from 1940 in the ghetto working as translator for the *Judenrat. In 1943 he and his wife hid in the underground, while most of his family was murdered by the Nazis. After liberation by the Soviet army, he joined the Communist Party of Poland, working as consul for the Foreign Ministry and also for the secret service of Poland in London from 1947 to 1949. Resigning from these posts, he returned to Warsaw, where he was excluded from the party and arrested because of "ideological alienation." This termination of Reich-Ranicki's diplomatic career was also the beginning of his career as a critic. Working as a publisher and journalist, he mediated between German literature and the Polish reader. He translated Kafka's *Das Schloss* and published a history of German literature from 1871 to 1954 (1955) and a book on Anna Seghers (1957). In 1958, he did not return from a trip to West Germany, remaining in Frankfurt/Main and from 1959 to 1973 in Hamburg, where he worked – supported by his friends Heinrich Boell and Siegfried Lenz – as a critic for several newspapers, such as the *Frankfurter Allgemeine Zeitung*, *Die Welt*, and *Die Zeit*. As a participant in "Gruppe 47" he soon became the most famous and influential as well as the most controversial critic in West Germany. In 1973, he took over the editorship of the literary section of the *Frankfurter Allgemeine Zeitung*, retaining the position until 1988, also editing from 1974 the *Frankfurter Anthologie*. His most influential activity as a critic, however, was to host the television program *Das literarische Quartett* (1988–2001), which was followed by *Reich-Ranicki – Solo*. Beside his many books on major German writers (e.g., Thomas Mann, Heinrich Heine, Heinrich Boell, Thomas Bernhard), he also wrote about the auxiliary streams of the German literary canon, e.g., in his essays *Die Ungeliebten – Sieben Emigranten* (1968) and *Ueber Ruhestoerer. Juden in der deutschen Literatur* (1973, 1989^2), where he represents Jewish writers as "outcasts" and "provocateurs," i.e., as critical voices. In 1999 he published his autobiography *Mein Leben* (*The Author of Himself*), which is not only a powerful account of his life as a Jewish intellectual during and after World War II but is also representative of Jewish history in 20th-century Europe as well as the intellectual and literary history of Germany, particularly after 1945.

BIBLIOGRAPHY: W. Jens (ed.), *Literatur und Kritik; aus Anlass des 60. Geburtstages von Marcel Reich-Ranicki* (1980); J. Jessen (ed.), *Ueber Marcel Reich-Ranicki* (1985); V. Hage and M. Schreiber, *Marcel Reich-Ranicki: Ein biographisches Portraet* (1997); H. Spiegel (ed.), *Welch ein Leben. Marcel Reich-Ranickis Erinnerungen* (2000); P. Demetz: in: *German Literature, Jewish Critiques* (2002), 289–302.

[Andreas Kilcher (2nd ed.)]

REICHSBUND JUEDISCHER FRONTSOLDATEN (RJF), organization of Jewish war veterans in Germany. Founded in February 1919 in Berlin (and simultaneously in other major cities) by Captain Leo Loewenstein (1877–1956), a scientist who had played an important role in the German war effort, the Reichsbund was formed to counteract the widespread anti-Jewish feeling prevalent after the post-World War I breakdown. These feelings were nurtured by the commonly held prejudice that Jews had either evaded conscription or had held safe office jobs in the army. A further impetus to its formation was offered by the exclusion of Jews from the Stahlhelm, the right-wing paramilitary veterans' organization. During the chaotic days of 1923–24 some Reichsbund members participated in street fights and guarded the Berlin Fasanenstrasse synagogue. Slighter activities were to discourage Jewish actors from telling vulgar Jewish jokes and persuading Jews not to wear ostentatious clothing and jewelry during the High Holy Days. The Reichsbund grew rapidly and by 1933 had more than 30,000 members in about 400 branches and published a periodical, *Der Schild*. Special stress was put on physical education (after 1933 judo and boxing in particular) and agricultural training. After the Nazi rise to power the Reichsbund tried to obtain preferred treatment for war veterans and for long-settled Jewish families. These demands, acknowledged by President Hindenburg, were ignored by the Nazis. The Reichsbund originally refused to join the Reichsvertretung der Juden in Deutschland (see *Reichsvereinigung) because of Zionist participation, and protested, with official approval, at the outcry abroad against Nazi anti-Jewish excesses. The Reichsbund eventually joined the Reichsvertretung and, with other Jewish organizations, was dissolved after 1938.

BIBLIOGRAPHY: K.J. Herrmann, *Das dritte Reich und die deutsch-juedischen Organisationen 1933–1934* (1969); A. Asch, in: *AJR Information*, 16 (Aug., 1961); M. Kreutzberger (ed.), *Bibliothek und Archiv* (1970) index s.v. *RJF*.

REICHSTEIN, TADEUS (1897–1996), Swiss organic chemist, endocrinologist, and 1950 Nobel laureate. Reichstein was born in Wloclawek, Poland, and his family moved to Zurich in 1908. He became professor of organic chemistry at Zurich in 1934 and in 1938 joined Basle University as head of the Institute of Pharmacy. In 1933 he succeeded in the synthesis of ascorbic acid (Vitamin C), the first total synthesis of a vitamin. He worked on other aspects of organic chemistry, and in 1934 began the isolation of the hormones of the adrenal cortex. He separated and characterized some 30 different steroids from adrenal glands, the most outstandingly important being corticosterone, cortisone, and cortisol, which are among the therapeutics used for sufferers from arthritis. In 1950 he, together with the Americans E.C. Kendall and P. Hench, was awarded the Nobel Prize in physiology and medicine "for their discoveries relating to the hormones of the adrenal cortex, their structure and biological effects." Reichstein used his Nobel prize money for other research work at the University of Basle.

BIBLIOGRAPHY: T.N. Levitan, *Laureates: Jewish Winners of the Nobel Prize* (1960), 161–3; L.G. Stevenson; *Nobel Prize Winners in Medicine and Physiology, 1901–1950* (1953), 272–83; *Chimia*, 11 (1957), 205; *Chemiker Zeitung*, 81 (1957), 506.

[Samuel Aaron Miller]

REICHSVEREINIGUNG (Reichsvereinigung der Juden in Deutschland – Ger. **Reich Association of the Jews in Germany**), compulsory organization of all Jews in Nazi Germany (excepting Austria and the Protectorate of Bohemia-Moravia), established on July 4, 1939, by the tenth executive ordinance (*10. Verordnung*) appended to the Reich's citizenship law (*Reichsbuergergesetz*) of 1935. The Reichsvereinigung replaced the previous framework called the Reichsvertretung der Juden in Deutschland ("Reich Representation of the Jews in Germany"), which in turn replaced the Reichsvereugbgung der Deutschen Juden (Reich Representation of German Jews). The name changes are significant, representing a worsening of the situation of the Jews in Germany, who were no longer considered by the regime as German Jews. There were several distinctions between the two organizations. From the Jewish communal perspective, the Reichsvereinigung was imposed upon the Jewish community rather than formed by a consensus of Jewish organizations. More importantly, the Reichsvereinigung included all Jewish subjects of the Nazi Reich as defined by the *Nuremberg Laws (1935), not only Jews by religion, it included those who had converted or even those whose parents had converted. The Reichsvereinigung was supervised by the Ministry of the Interior, i.e., by the security police. Its duties, as fixed by law, were to promote Jewish emigration from Germany – still possible and still desired by both the regime and the Jews in Germany – and to support the Jewish school system and Jewish welfare. A special provision empowered the minister of the interior to assign additional tasks to the Reichsvereinigung. To the Germans, the Reichsvereinigung was an instrumentality of its control much like the Jewish Councils which were later formed in the ghettos. It is clear that the Germans regarded it as useful to have the appearance of continuity of Jewish leadership rather than install their own puppets. This policy was also followed with regard to the Jewish Councils. The centralization of Jewish communal representations into one body was a matter of convenience and effectiveness; instead of dealing with many organizations, the Germans imposed unity on the Jews at least with regard to their dealings with the state. The existence of the Reichsvereinigung enabled the Nazis to implement many of their deadliest orders without much publicity and to play off the Jewish leadership against the Jewish population, who naturally blamed their own leaders, and thus responsibility and guilt was shifted onto a leadership that had few resources and even fewer options. Jewish leadership perceived itself to be struggling under difficult and soon to become impossible conditions for Jewish survival. Emigration was deemed essential, a matter of life and death. The prior leadership of the Reichsvertretung now filled the leadership positions in the Reichsvereinigung. Rabbi Leo *Baeck, Otto *Hirsch, Paul *Eppstein, and their colleagues continued at their posts until their arrest and deportation. There was no need to set up new departments because all the functions assigned by law to the Reichsvereinigung had already been carried out by its predecessor. The local activities of the Reichsvereinigung were executed by the Jewish communities, called Juedische Kultusvereinigung ("Jewish Synagogue Association") and its own *Bezirkstellen* ("district offices"). The latter dealt with small communities or with single Jewish families. In the course of time the Jewish communities were dissolved and their property transferred to the Reichsvereinigung. Under the leadership of the Rechsvereinigung Jewish education continued until June 1942. It undertook vocational training to teach Jews basic skills for survival and earning a living abroad and it attempted to provide welfare for the needy. All Jewish publications were suspended and only the publication of the bulletin of the Reichsvereinigung, *Juedisches Nachrichtenblatt*, was permitted. It served as a channel for the Gestapo to inform the Jews of new restrictions and confiscations without stirring up too much dissent from the outside.

From the start of World War II the activities of the Reichsvereinigung were slowed down. In the planning of the "Final Solution" (see *Holocaust, General Survey), the Gestapo used the statistical material prepared by the Reichsvereinigung and even utilized the activity of its statistical section for its own purposes. Its leadership protested the deportations in 1940 and from 1941 onward the central leadership was not involved in the deportations, but various branches were forced to cooperate. In the deportations the Gestapo used the services of the Reichsvereinigung: the organization cared for the deportees in the roundups, with the notion that they could alleviate their suffering – they did not perceive themselves to be an instrumentality of destruction – while the Reichsvereinigung leaders and staff served as hostages against the exact delivery of fixed batches of deportees. Several hostages were deported in place of Jews who escaped. Others were shot in retaliation for sabotage. Under orders of the *RSHA, the Reichsvereinigung concluded the "home buying agreements" (*Heimeinkaufsvertraege*) for *Theresienstadt, i.e., in which Jews were forced to sign away their money to the German government in return for an "alleged" apartment in Theresienstadt to which they were deported. On June 10, 1943, the remaining staff was arrested and the Reichsvereinigung in its original form dissolved. Only two of its leaders, Leo Baeck, who had refused offers to leave Germany and offers of personal safety, and Moritz Henschel, survived the Holocaust. In assessing their behavior one must see the dual function of Jewish leadership as instrumentalities – however unwilling – of the Germans and as representatives, however powerless and ultimately ineffective, of the Jews. The tightrope they walked was the result of their impossible situation. Integrity and wisdom could not compensate for the absolute lack of power and the murderous intent of those in power.

BIBLIOGRAPHY: S. Esh, in: *Yad Vashem Studies*, 7 (1968), 1–38, includes bibliography; R. Hilberg, *Destruction of the European Jews* (1961, 1985, 2003), index; K.J. Ball-Kaduri, *Vor der Katastrophe: Juden in Deutschland 1933–1939* (1967); Fabian, in: *Festschrift… L. Baeck* (1953), 85–93; K.J. Herrmann (ed.) *Das dritte Reich und die deutschjuedischen Organisationen* (1969). **ADD. BIBLIOGRAPHY:** O.D. Kulka, "The Reichsvereingigung and the Fate of German Jews 1938/1939–1943. Continuity or Discontinuity?" in: A. Paucker (ed.), *The Jews in Nazi Germany 1933–1943* (1986).

[Yehuda Reshef / Michael Berenbaum (2nd ed.)]

REICHSZENTRALE FUER JUEDISCHE AUSWANDERUNG (Center for Jewish Emigration), Nazi central agency for Jewish emigration matters, set up in the Ministry of the Interior by *Heydrich on *Goering's order (Jan. 24, 1939). Its principal aim was to increase and accelerate emigration, giving preferential exit to poor Jews, and speeding up individual cases. Heydrich appointed Heinrich *Mueller *Geschaeftsfuehrer* ("manager") of the Zentralstelle, which was run by a policy committee composed of representatives from different agencies and an executive which was, in practice, Department II of the *Gestapo. The Zentralstelle was modeled on *Eichmann's successful Zentralstelle fuer juedische Auswanderung set up in 1938 in Vienna. Employing Eichmann's methods, the Zentralstelle unified the various emigration authorities and coerced the wealthier Jews in Germany and abroad to pay for the exit of the poor Jews, using pressure and even imprisonment to gain its ends. The chief of the Zentralstelle on behalf of Mueller was Kurt Lischka, who was replaced by Eichmann after the establishment of *RSHA. The Zentralstelle set up its office in Berlin, and later others in Prague (July 15, 1939) and in Amsterdam (April 1941), but functioned in all other cities through the local Gestapo branches. This organization furthered Nazi policy, which prior to 1941 was to get rid of the Jews and to expropriate their property and possessions; it also ironically furthered Jewish interests, as leaving the Reich by whatever means possible was imperative. It literally was life saving. In 1940 the Zentralstelle joined up with the Gestapo section for evacuation but ceased its original functions when the order to stop emigration was issued in October 1941. Its personnel afterward organized deportations in the framework of the "Final Solution" (see *Holocaust, General Survey).

BIBLIOGRAPHY: *International Law Reports*, 6 (1968), 63–67; *Documents on German Foreign Policy 1918–45*, Series D. vol. 5 (1953), 933–6.

[Yehuda Reshef / Michael Berenbaum (2nd ed.)]

REIFENBERG, ADOLF (1899–1953), Israeli expert in soil chemistry, archaeologist, and numismatist. Reifenberg, who was born in Berlin, studied agricultural chemistry and graduated from Giessen University. A Zionist from his youth, he was among the first *ḥalutzim* who arrived in Ereẓ Israel from Germany after World War I. After working as an agricultural laborer at Kinneret for two years, he joined (1922) the laboratory for agricultural chemistry of the mandatory government. In 1924 he became a member of the staff of the Institute of Chemistry of the newly founded Hebrew University. He later founded and was head of its department of soil science. In 1947 he was appointed professor at the university. Reifenberg also served as dean of the faculty of agriculture and of the faculty of mathematics and science. In World War II Reifenberg, although overage for military service, volunteered for a Palestinian unit of the British Army, was torpedoed off Malta, but was rescued after a long time in the sea.

Reifenberg's contributions to agricultural chemistry were mainly in the field of soil research. Through his familiarity with the peculiar climatic and topographical conditions of the Mediterranean countries and his knowledge of chemistry and physiology, he was able to formulate a theory of the red soil (terra rossa) formations in the Mediterranean (*Karka Ereẓ Yisrael* (1938); *The Soil of Palestine*, 1947²). He investigated one of the major problems of Erez Israel: soil erosion and its prevention (*Milḥemet ha-Mizra ve-ha-Shimmamon* (1950); *The Struggle Between the Desert and the Sown*, 1955). Reifenberg also dealt with various practical problems connected with the use of the few raw materials provided by Ereẓ Israel, such as the Ḥuleh peat, potash, phosphate, and citrus peel.

Reifenberg was also an archaeologist and numismatist. He built up one of the finest collections of Palestinian and ancient Jewish coins (presented after his death to the State of Israel), and in 1951 became the first president of the Israel Numismatic Society. Together with L.A. *Mayer, he examined several ancient synagogues such as the one at Eshtemo'a (Samoa), south of Hebron, and that of Naveh in Hauran.

His main archaeological publications are *Architektur und Kunstgewerbe im alten Israel* (1925); *Palaestinensische Kleinkunst* (1927); *Denkmaeler der juedischen Antike* (1937); *Ancient Jewish Coins* (1947²); *Ancient Hebrew Seals; Ancient Hebrew Arts* (both 1950); and *Israel's History in Coins…* (1953). In 1950 he founded the *Israel Exploration Journal*, which he edited until his death.

BIBLIOGRAPHY: IEJ, 3 (1953), 213–6; M. Cassuto-Salzmann, *ibid.*, 4 (1954), 143–9 (bibl.); AJR *Information* (Oct. 1953), 4; *Jerusalem Post* (Aug. 28, 1953).

REIFMANN, JACOB (1818–1895), scholar and writer. Reifmann, born in the Lagow district of Radom, Poland, was raised in Apta and subsequently lived in Lublin, Zamosc, and Szczebrzeszyn. Growing estranged from Ḥasidim, who were then dominant where he lived, Reifmann turned more to the Haskalah. His field was criticism of the Bible and the Talmud. Highly respected in scholarly circles for his erudition and critical mind, Reifmann also caused antagonism, especially because he was outspoken. His life was spent in great poverty, and he did not receive any official position or recognition. The conflicts in his attempt to merge his traditional East European background with modern Western scholarship are apparent in his writing, and probably also contributed to his difficulties in adjusting to his environment.

Reifmann contributed hundreds of articles to the Hebrew periodicals of his time, and wrote 17 books. He covered a wide variety of areas, including Bible, Talmud, rabbinic literature, Aramaic translations of the Bible, liturgy, Jewish philosophy, and biography. He corresponded with such leading scholars of his time as S.J.L. Rapoport, L. Geiger, H. Graetz, M. Steinschneider, and S.D. Luzzatto. His correspondence and some of his unpublished writings are at the library of the Jewish Theological Seminary of America.

Among Reifmann's works are *Tavnit ha-Bayit* (1844) and *Pesher Davar* (1845), critical studies on talmudic matters; *Toledot Rabbenu Zeraḥyah ha-Levi* (1853), a biography; *Ḥut ha-Meshullash* (1859), on the familiarity of talmudic rabbis with foreign languages, on the history of fables among the Jews, and notes to the book **Mivḥar ha-Peninim; Beit ha-Talmud* (vol. 3), on the problems concerning the geonic work, *She'iltot; Sedeh Aram* (1875), on Targum Onkelos; and *Or Boker* (1879), on talmudic criticism. Some of his works were published by M. Herskovics in *Hadarom* (1964–69) and by N. Ben-Menahem, *Iggeret Bikkoret al Seder ha-Haggadah shel Pesaḥ* (1969) and *Iyyunim be-Mishnat Avraham ibn Ezra* (1962).

BIBLIOGRAPHY: Zeitlin, Bibliotheca, index; Kressel, Leksikon, 2 (1967), 867; Y.A. Klausner, *I.L. Peretz ve-Ya'akov Reifmann* (1969).

REIK, ḤAVIVAH (**Emma**; 1914–1944), one of four *Haganah envoys from Palestine parachuted into Slovakia during World War II. Ḥavivah Reik was born into a working-class family in a small Slovak village near *Banská Bystrica. She settled in Palestine in 1939, joining the Ha-Shomer ha-Ẓa'ir kibbutz Ma'anit. During the critical days of the war she volunteered to be parachuted into Slovakia. She was to reach Bratislava and establish contact with the "Working Group" (see Gisi *Fleischmann) but arrived too late. In mid-September 1944, she reached Banská Bystrica, where she assisted the Jewish remnant that had gathered there. On October 28, when Banská Bystrica (the center of the Slovak uprising) fell, she retreated into the mountains along with a group of Jewish fighters. Captured by Germans a week later, she was imprisoned and executed on November 20, 1944, in Kremnička. Kibbutz Lahavot Ḥavivah, the Israel freighter *Ḥavivah Reik*, and the research and educational center Givat Ḥavivah in Israel were named in her memory.

BIBLIOGRAPHY: D. and P. Bar-Adon, *Seven who Fell* (1947), 141–9.

[Livia Rothkirchen]

REIK, THEODOR (1888–1970), psychoanalyst. Reik, who was born in Vienna, met *Freud in 1910 and received his training analysis from Karl *Abraham in Berlin. After World War I he worked as an analyst first in Vienna, and then in Berlin until he moved to The Hague in 1934. In 1938 he immigrated to the United States. In 1946 he was elected president of the National Association for Psychoanalytic Psychology.

Reik wrote many psychoanalytic articles on literary and musical figures such as Flaubert and *Mahler, on clinical and anthropological themes, and on psychological theory. Four of his best-known papers of the 1920s were collected in *Das Ritual, psychoanalytische Studien* (1928^2; *Ritual, Psychoanalytic Studies*, 1931). The first paper dealt with "couvade," the primitive custom in which the father of a newborn child lies in bed, the last two papers with *Kol Nidrei and the *shofar*. A series of papers on problems of crime – including the compulsion to confess, and Freud's view of capital punishment – were developed in *Der unbekannte Moerder* (1932; *The Unknown Murderer*, 1936), in which he sets forth as a major concept that unconscious guilt motivates the crime itself and also the criminal's need to be caught and punished. Reik held that an analyst's theoretical assumptions may interfere with treatment and that the therapeutic relationship should be an "unconscious duet" between patient and analyst in which surprises to both parties provide important insights. He wrote about his new technique in *Der Ueberraschte Psychologe* (1935; *Surprise and the Psychoanalyst*, 1936), and *Listening with the Third Ear* (1948). In *Aus Leiden Freuden* (1940; *Masochism in Modern Man*, 1941) Reik stated his theory that masochistic suffering is basically a search for pleasure and, as in the case of the Christian martyrs, for final victory. He therefore regarded masochism and the associated death instinct as secondary rather than primary as seen by Freud.

Some of Reik's thought was iconoclastic. In *Psychology of Sex Relations* (1945) he rejected the classical psychoanalytic theory of the libido and some of the sexual concepts that go with it. Among his more than 50 books are the autobiographical *From Thirty Years with Freud* (1940), *Fragment of a Great Confession* (1949), and *The Search Within* (1956). His biblical tetralogy included *The Creation of Woman* (1960), and in 1962 he published *Jewish Wit*. In *Pagan Rites in Judaism* (1964) he endeavors to show that much of the pagan and prehistoric survives in the rites of Judaism as professed today.

BIBLIOGRAPHY: R. Lindner (ed.), *Explorations in Psychoanalysis* (1953), essays in his honor (incl. bibl.); J.M. Natterson, in: F.G. Alexander, et al. (eds.), *Psychoanalytic Pioneers* (1966), 249–64, incl. bibl.; D.M. Kaplan, in: *American Imago*, 25 (Spring 1968) 52–58; A. Grinstein, *Index of Psychoanalytic Writings*, 3 (1958), 1620–32; 7 (1965), 3940–41 (bibl. of his works).

[Louis Miller]

REINACH, family of French scholars and politicians. JOSEPH REINACH (1856–1921), political leader, journalist, and historian, was born in Paris. He graduated from the University of Paris and became a lawyer, also writing several works on European politics. Reinach's articles on foreign policy in the *Revue Bleue* were noticed by Leon Gambetta, who, when he became premier in 1881, made Reinach his *chef du cabinet*. After Gambetta's death, Reinach became political editor of the *Republique Française*. He was elected to the Chamber of Deputies in 1889 and reelected in 1893. One of the first to demand a new trial for Captain *Dreyfus, Reinach was subject to bitter attacks from the anti-Dreyfusards, lost his seat in the elections of 1898, and was dismissed from the army in which he was a reserve captain. Following Dreyfus' rehabilitation, Reinach was reinstated and reelected to parliament, where he served until his retirement in 1914. Reinach's historical works include a seven-volume history of the Dreyfus Affair, *Histoire de l'Affaire Dreyfus* (1901–11). While campaigning for the Dreyfus cause, he wrote a history of the case of Raphael Levy who was executed in 1670 on a ritual murder charge (*Raphael Levy*, 1898). Reinach published many works on general history and politics.

Solomon (1858–1932), archaeologist, philologist, and historian, was a brother of Joseph. As a member of the Ecole Française d'Athènes he took part in several excavations in Greece. He taught archaeology at the Ecole de Louvre and from 1886 served as curator of the Musee d'Antiquites Nationales at his native St. Germain-en-Laye. In 1893 he was appointed assistant keeper of the Musees Nationales, becoming keeper in 1902. He was a member of the Institut Français and of the Conseil Superieur des Beaux Arts. Reinach's scholarly work was devoted primarily to French archaeology and Gallic civilization. He also made numerous contributions to classical and French philology, the history of art, and the history of religion. His major work in the latter field, *Orpheus; histoire generale des religions* (1909, 1926[2]; Eng. 1909, 1930[2]; repr. 1942; Ger. 1910), is written in the Voltairean tradition of radical rationalism. It classifies Judaism and Christianity as "barbaric," and accepting the conclusions of contemporary Bible criticism, termed many biblical figures as mythical. Reinach has nothing but disdain for the Talmud and "for those backward Jews who follow its rules." Nevertheless, he took an active part in Jewish affairs. A confirmed Dreyfusard, like his brothers, he published a French translation of H.C. Lea's *History of the Inquisition* (3 vols., 1901–03) at the height of the Dreyfus Affair as a weapon in the fight against religious intolerance. He published various articles in the **Revue des Etudes Juives* and served as president of the Societe des Etudes Juives. He was vice president of the Alliance Israélite Universelle and helped in the establishment of the *Jewish Colonization Association. Anti-Zionist in principle, Reinach nevertheless gave assistance to colonization in Palestine.

Theodore (1860–1928), younger brother of Joseph and Solomon, was a scholar and politician. His studies extended to law, archaeology, mathematics, numismatics, and history of music and of religion. Reinach was appointed professor at the Ecole des Hautes Etudes where he taught the history of religions. He was also editor of the *Revue des Etudes Grecques*. A member of the Institut de France, Reinach presented a musical interpretation of a Delphic paean and himself played this resurrection of ancient music. He served in the Chamber of Deputies of Savoy during 1906–14. Active in the rather ineffective movement of French Reform Judaism (Union Liberale Israelite) and a confirmed assimilationist, he strongly opposed Zionism, believing that since the French Revolution Jews no longer were a nation but only a religious community. He presented these views in his widely read *Histoire des Israelites* (1884, 1910[4]). He also wrote a *Histoire sommaire de l'affaire Dreyfus* (1904, 1924). In the field of Jewish scholarship Reinach was important as a student of Jewish numismatics (*Les monnaies juives*, 1887) and as the editor of an important reference book, *Textes d'auteurs grecs et romains relatifs au Judaisme* (1895; repr. 1963). He was the general editor of a French translation of the works of Josephus (7 vols., 1900–32), completed after his death by his brother Solomon. Reinach also contributed to the *Revue des Etudes Juives*, and various French encyclopedias.

BIBLIOGRAPHY: H. Rigault, *M. Joseph Reinach* (Fr., 1889); S. Reinach, *Bibliographie de Salomon Reinach* (1936), incl. biographical notes; S. de Ricci, *Salomon Reinach* (Fr., 1933), 2ff., incl. bibl.; E. Pottier, in: *Revue Archéologique*, 36 (1932), 386ff.; M.J. Lagrange, *Quelques remarques sur l'Orpheus de M. Salomon Reinach* (1910); R. Cagnat, in: *Comptes Rendus des Séances de l'Académie des Inscriptions et Belles Lettres* (1931), 372ff.; S. de Ricci, in: REJ, 86 (1928)., 113ff, incl. bibl. (on Theodore); H. Dutrait-Crozon, *Joseph Reinach historien* (1905); J. Bernard, *La vie de Paris* (1921), 157–69.

[Gerard Nahon]

REINACH, ADOLF (1883–1917), German philosopher. Reinach, who was born in Mayence, was a student of *Husserl and taught at Goettingen with him. Through his lectures, articles, and personal discussions he had considerable influence on Husserl and on the early phenomenologists. Reinach's version of phenomenology was simpler and clearer than Husserl's and more concrete. He stressed the intuiting of the essential core of phenomena and developed a theory of the phenomenological *a priori*, a property of states of affairs rather than of acts of judging. He applied phenomenology to the philosophy of law, and tried to construct an *a priori* theory of law, contending that there are essential elements of law that have an absolute validity, independent of the mind that thinks of them and of temporal conditions. Reinach tried to explore the relationships of these elements. He was killed during World War I. His writings were collected and published by his students in *Gesammelte Schriften* (1921).

BIBLIOGRAPHY: Husserl, in: *Kantstudien*, 23 (1919); J.M. Oesterreicher, *Walls are Crumbling* (1952), 99–134: H. Spiegelberg, *Phenomenological Movement* (1960), 195–205.

[Richard H. Popkin]

REINER, CARL (1922–), writer, actor, and director. Born in the Bronx, New York, Reiner first came to prominence as an actor and writer for two seminal TV programs, Sid Caesar's *Your Show of Shows* (1950–54) and *The Dick Van Dyke Show* (1961–66), for which Reiner won several Emmy Awards. Moving to feature films, Reiner began his career by directing a filmed version of his 1958 semiautobiographical novel *Enter Laughing* (1967). He went on to direct and sometimes cowrite such comedies as *The Comic* (1969), *Where's Poppa?* (1970), *Oh God!* (1977), *The One and Only* (1978), *The Jerk* (1979), *Dead Men Don't Wear Plaid* (1982), *The Man with Two Brains* (1983), *All of Me* (1984), *Summer Rental* (1985), *Summer School* (1987), *Bert Rigby, You're a Fool* (1989), *Sibling Rivalry* (1990), *Fatal Instinct* (1993), and *That Old Feeling* (1997).

A familiar figure on both the small and the silver screen, Reiner appeared in such films as *The Gazebo* (1959), *The Thrill of It All* (1963), *The Art of Love* (1965), *The Russians Are Com-*

ing... (1966), *Generation* (1969), *The Spirit of '76* (1990), and *Slums of Beverly Hills* (1998). On TV, from 1954 he was a guest on dozens of programs, from *The Dinah Shore Chevy Show, The Tonight Show Starring Johnny Carson,* and *The Carol Burnett Show* to *Ally McBeal, Life with Bonnie, Ellen,* and *Boston Legal.* He also appeared many times on television and in a series of record albums (first released in 1960) as straight man to Mel Brooks in their comedy routine "The 2000-Year-Old Man."

Among his many honors and awards, including 12 Emmys and a Grammy, Reiner won the American Comedy Award for Lifetime Achievement in 1992; he was inducted into the Television Academy Hall of Fame in 1999; and in 2000 he was awarded the Mark Twain Prize for Comedy by the Kennedy Center for the Performing Arts.

Reiner wrote *All Kinds of Love* (1993), *Continue Laughing* (1995), *The 2000-Year-Old Man in the Year 2000* (with Mel Brooks, 1997), *How Paul Robeson Saved My Life and Other Mostly Happy Stories* (1999), *Tell Me a Scary Story ...but Not Too Scary* (2003), and *My Anecdotal Life: A Memoir* (2003).

His son is film director Rob *Reiner.

[Jonathan Licht and Ruth Beloff (2nd ed.)]

REINER, FRITZ (1888–1963), conductor. Born in Budapest, Reiner was a student at the Liszt Academy, Budapest, where he studied the piano with Bartók. He worked as répétiteur at the Vigopera, where he made his conducting début in *Carmen* at the age of 19. He became conductor at the Budapest People's Opera (1911–14) and musical director of the Dresden Opera (1914–21). In the United States, he was conductor in Cincinnati (1922–31), in Pittsburgh (1938–48), at the Chicago Symphony Orchestra (1953–63), and at the Metropolitan Opera, New York (1949–53). He taught conducting at the Curtis Institute of Music in Philadelphia (1931–41) where his pupils included *Bernstein and Lukas *Foss. Reiner also was guest conductor of the opera in Halle (1921), Rome (1921), Barcelona (1922), Buenos Aires and Budapest (1926), Philadelphia (1931–2), Covent Garden (1936–7), San Francisco (1936–8), and Vienna (1955). He embraced a wide orchestral and operatic repertory, ranging from Bach, Haydn, and Mozart to Bartók, Stravinsky, and Webern. Between 1954 and 1963 he made series of recordings including his famous interpretations of Bartók's Concerto for Orchestra and Music for Strings, Percussion and Celesta, Rimsky-Korsakov's *Sheherazade*, and Ravel's orchestration of *Pictures at an Exhibition.* He was regarded as a "conductor's conductor," and showed great technical mastery with breadth of interpretation.

BIBLIOGRAPHY: Grove Music Online; R.R. Potter, "Fritz Reiner, Conductor, Teacher, Musical Innovator" (Diss., Northwestern Univ., 1980); P. Hart, *Fritz Reiner: a Biography* (1994; repr. with rev. discography, 1997).

[Israela Stein (2nd ed.)]

REINER, MARKUS (1886–1976), Israeli engineer. Born in Czernovtsy, Reiner served as an officer in the Austrian army during World War I. He emigrated to Ereẓ Israel in 1922, first working as an agricultural laborer. He then became chief construction engineer of the public works department in Jerusalem, where he remained for 25 years, engaged in road, bridge, and housing construction and the restoration of ancient and historical sites, such as Herod's irrigation channels in Jericho. In 1926 Reiner published a paper on his research in the flow of elastic liquid in a capillary. His research was independently and simultaneously duplicated by E. Buckingham of the U.S. National Bureau of Standards, and their findings are thus known as the "Buckingham-Reiner equation." Their work resulted in a new branch of physics and mechanics known as rheology. From 1932 Reiner spent two years at Lafayette College, in Eaton, Pennsylvania, as a research professor, working with Professor E.C. Bingham, whom he joined as coeditor of the *Journal of Rheology.* Reiner's research covered a wide selection of subjects in mechanics, including investigation of rheological phenomena in the body. In 1948 he joined the Technion – Israel Institute of Technology – in Haifa as professor of practical mechanics.

Apart from nearly 200 articles and papers, Reiner published three standard works which have been translated into several languages: *Ten Lectures on Theoretical Rheology* (1943), *Deformation Strain and Flow* (1949), and *Agricultural Rheology* (1957), written together with G.W. Scott Blair of England. Reiner was awarded the Israel prize in 1958. He was a member of the Israel Academy of Science from its inception and of the Israel government's Research Council.

[Carl Alpert]

REINER, ROB (1945–), U.S. director and actor. Born in New York, the son of actor/writer/director Carl *Reiner, Rob Reiner began as a sketch writer for television's *Smothers Brothers Comedy Hour.* Reiner's breakthrough as an actor came in 1971 when he was chosen for the part of Mike Stivic ("Meathead," 1971–78) on the popular TV comedy series *All in the Family,* for which he won two Emmy Awards. Finding only limited movement in his acting career, Reiner turned to directing, and his feature film mock-documentary *This Is Spinal Tap* (1984), which he cowrote, was a surprise hit. Reiner followed this success with a series of well-reputed films: *The Sure Thing* (1985), *Stand by Me* (1986), *The Princess Bride* (1987), *When Harry Met Sally* (1989), *Misery* (1990), *A Few Good Men* (Oscar nomination for Best Picture, 1992), *North* (1994), *The American President* (1995), *Ghosts of Mississippi* (1996), *Spinal Tap: The Final Tour* (1998), *The Story of Us* (1999), *Alex & Emma* (2003), and *Rumor Has It* (2005).

As an actor, Reiner has appeared in such films as the TV movie *More Than Friends* (1979), *This Is Spinal Tap* (1984), *Throw Momma from the Train* (1987), *Postcards from the Edge* (1990), *The Spirit of '76* (directed and cowritten with his brother, Lucas, 1990), *Bullets over Broadway* (1994), *Mixed Nuts* (1994), *Bye Bye, Love* (1995), *For Better or Worse* (1996), *Spinal Tap: The Final Tour* (1998), *Ed TV* (1999), *The Story of Us* (1999), and *Alex & Emma* (2003).

A principal in Castle Rock Productions, Reiner also had a hand in producing a variety of films and TV series. From 1971 to 1979, Reiner was married to actress/director Penny Marshall.

ADD. BIBLIOGRAPHY: J. Ferry, *Rob Reiner (Behind the Camera)* (2002).

[Jonathan Licht / Ruth Beloff (2nd ed.)]

REINES, ALVIN JAY (1926–2004), scholar of Jewish philosophy. Born in Paterson, New Jersey, his early education was entirely Orthodox. He graduated from the Rabbi Jacob Joseph School in Manhattan and the Talmudical Academy of New York. He then entered Yeshiva University, where he earned his B.A. in 1947. From YU, he went to New York University Law School and left before completing his degree. In a rare move for Orthodox-educated Jews of his generation who when they left the Orthodox world moved over to the Jewish Theological Seminary, Reines went to Hebrew Union College and earned his MHL and ordination in 1952. He received the Mrs. Henry Morgenthau, Jr. Fellowship at Harvard where he earned a Ph.D. in 1958 studying with Harry Austryn Wolfson, and then joined the faculty of HUC-JIR as a professor of Jewish Philosophy and retired in 2003.

His field of specialization was medieval philosophy, particularly the work of Moses *Maimonides, and he struggled both to understand Maimonides as a halakhic and philosophical thinker and to deal with revelation as a source of absolute authority. Rejecting the notion of absolute authority led to his own original philosophical innovation. He developed the concept of polydoxy, meaning a religion of many opinions, in which the notion of absolute knowledge is abandoned and diversity and individual autonomy is not only respected but welcomed. This concept has had significant influence on liberal religious thought in the United States and elsewhere as well as within the Reform movement. He helped create the Institute for Creative Judaism and chaired its board, which was formed to develop religious and educational and liturgical material for free Judaism. It has evolved into The Polydox Institute, which is "committed to serving all polydoxians, be they of Jewish, Christian or other origin, and whether or not they view themselves as belonging to any historic religious group, or as being presently affiliated with any organized religious body." His work has thus had influence far beyond the Jewish community. For religious communities that reject the existence of infallible knowledge, Reines argued that the only morally justifiable position was to affirm individual autonomy. Such communities should be prepared, Reines maintained, to accommodate diverse and even unconventional beliefs, rituals, and practices.

The Reform Movement's *Gates of Prayer* (1975), included an edited version of the polydox Sabbath worship service written by Reines. His seminal work is *Polydoxy: Explorations in a Philosophy of Liberal Religion*, (1987). Among his other works are *Elements in a Philosophy of Reform Judaism* (1968), *Maimonides and Abarbanel on Prophecy* (1970), and *Reform Judaism as Polydoxy* (1970–1973). His work on the Institute includes services for Hanukah and Rosh Hashanah as well as a Passover *Haggadah*.

BIBLIOGRAPHY: K.M. Olitzsky, L.J. Sussman, and M.H. Stern, *Reform Judaism in America: A Biographical Dictionary and Sourcebook* (1993).

[Michael Berenbaum (2nd ed.)]

REINES, FREDERICK (1918–1998), physicist and Nobel Prize winner. Reines obtained his M.E. and M.S. degrees from Stevens Institute of Technology in Hoboken, New Jersey, and his Ph.D. from New York University in 1944. He was a member and then group leader of the theoretical division of the Los Alamos Scientific Laboratory (1944–59). He was professor and head of the Physics Department at Case Institute of Technology (1959–66) and professor and founding dean of Physical Sciences at UCI.

Reines, the great-nephew of the founder of the Mizrachi movement, Rabbi Isaac Jacob *Reines, was joint winner with Dr. Martin Perl of the 1995 Nobel Prize in physics for their discovery of two fundamental particles of matter, the tau and the neutrino. The existence of the neutrino was first postulated by Wolfgang Pauli in 1930 to account for apparent loss of energy when an atomic nucleus decays, releasing an electron, but it was Reines who first proved that the elusive particle, which has no mass and no charge, exists. The discovery started the new field of neutrino physics. Reines was honored with membership in the National Academy of Sciences and many other awards, including the National Medal of Science.

REINES, ISAAC JACOB (1839–1915), rabbi, one of the founders and first head of the *Mizrachi movement. Born in Karolin, Belorussia, Reines studied at the Eishishok (Eisiskes) and Volozhin yeshivot and was ordained by leading rabbis. He served in the rabbinate in Shavkyany (Saukenai), Lithuania, from 1867; in Sventsyany (Svencionys), Vilna district, from 1869; and in Lida from 1885 until his death. Reines made a distinct contribution to rabbinic scholarship, introducing a new and almost modern methodology which was in contrast to the current system of **pilpul*. It was based upon a purely logical approach and was influenced by Maimonides' *Millot ha-Higgayyon*; it is actually called "*Higgayon*" ("Logic"). In the introduction to his first major halakhic work, *Ḥotam Tokhnit* (2 parts, 1880–81) he emphasized this new approach, as he did in his later works (e.g., *Urim Gedolim*, 1887). The *Ḥotam Tokhnit* made a great impression, especially in Western Europe where Jews were not accustomed to works on *halakhah* with a strictly logical approach that had been written by Eastern European scholars. He also applied his new approach in his homiletical books (*Nod shel Dema'ot*, 1891), which, like others of his works, went through a number of editions. Reines tried to introduce the spirit of the times in his public activities, without breaking with tradition, and founded a yeshivah in Sventsyany. Because its curriculum included secular studies, he aroused the anger of some religious fanatics and was forced to close the school after a few months.

Reines joined the *Ḥibbat Zion movement from its creation. His attachment to Ereẓ Israel was due principally to the influence of his father, who stayed in Ereẓ Israel in the 1830s. Reines cooperated with Samuel *Mohilewer and proposed settlement programs for Ereẓ Israel that combined Torah study with physical labor. He was among the first rabbis to answer Theodor Herzl's call, and his joining the Zionist movement served as a great encouragement to Herzl in face of the opposition of most of the East and West European rabbis. He devoted much energy to propaganda for political Zionism among rabbis and Orthodox circles. Toward this end he published in 1902 the book *Or Ḥadash al Ẓiyyon* ("A New Light on Zion") in which he countered all the claims of those in the rabbinical circles opposed to Zionism. He participated in the first Zionist Congresses and was very close to Herzl, but he opposed the cultural work of the Zionist movement for fear that it would encroach on the status of religion. In 1902 he convened a large conference of rabbis and Orthodox people in Vilna and as a result the Religious Zionist movement, Mizrachi, was formed. Reines was the recognized leader of the movement and the outstanding personality at its founding convention in Pressburg (Bratislava; 1904). Many Orthodox rabbis, especially from Hungary, protested the convening of the founding conference and were against Mizrachi altogether. Reines answered them very sharply, sparing not even the greatest among them. He also founded the first journal of Mizrachi, entitled *Ha-Mizraḥ* (published in 1903 under the editorship of Ze'ev *Jawitz). His great attachment to Herzl found expression during the controversy over the *Uganda Scheme, when he proved to be an enthusiastic supporter of the plan.

Despite all his public activities, Reines continued to write. Only a small portion of his works were published, and the rest remain in manuscript (in about 100 volumes). In Lida, he realized his greatest personal dream – the establishment of a modern yeshivah in which secular studies were taught side by side with traditional studies, all within the framework of the meticulous observation of tradition. The yeshivah was established in 1905 and achieved a distinguished reputation. Reines developed the educational principles of the yeshivah in the booklets *Kol Ya'akov* (1908), *Mishkenot Ya'akov* (1910), and others. Although the Mizrachi movement viewed the yeshivah as its own project, its maintenance rested on Reines' shoulders. While the institution was developing, World War I broke out and the suffering that it brought affected Reines' health. In the past few years some of his works have come out in new editions and in facsimile editions.

BIBLIOGRAPHY: J.L. Fishman, *Zekhor Zot le-Ya'akov* (1934); M. Kohen, in: J.L. Fishman (ed.), *Sefer ha-Mizrachi* (1946), 83–101 (2nd pagination); Z.A. Rabiner, *Talelei Orot* (1955), 7–18; Y. Raphael, in: *Ba-Mishor*, 1 no. 34 (1940), 14; idem, *Madrikh Bibliografi le-Sifrut Ẓiyyonit Datit* (1960), 74–5; I.J. Reines, *Nod shel Dema'ot*, ed. by J.L. Fishman (1934); L. Jung (ed.), *Jewish Leaders* (1953), 273–93.

[Getzel Kressel]

REINHARDT (Goldmann), MAX (1873–1943), stage producer and director. Reinhardt, a leading force in the theater during the first part of the 20th century, was born in Baden, near Vienna. At 17 he became an actor and assistant director at the Salzburg State Theater. Otto *Brahm, director of the Deutsches Theater in Berlin, noted Reinhardt's work and brought him to the German capital in 1894. After succeeding Brahm as director of the theater in 1905, Reinhardt sought to integrate the two main theatrical traditions, the baroque, which he had learned in Vienna, and the literary and intellectual tradition then dominant in Berlin. "Our standard," he declared, "must not be to act a play as it was acted in the days of its author. How to make a play live in our time, that is decisive for us." Reinhardt offered the public a cosmopolitan repertory – revivals of the classics: Shakespeare, Goethe, Schiller, and Molière; and modern playwrights such as Wilde, Synge, Shaw, Ibsen, Gorki, and Strindberg.

Reinhardt's methods were experimental and spectacular. He used massive crowds and a projecting rostrum. For *A Midsummer Night's Dream* in 1905 he introduced a revolving stage; and for *Hamlet*, which he staged in 1909, he used modern dress. These technical innovations accompanied a revitalized concept of the theater that distinguished Reinhardt's productions and deeply influenced European stagecraft. Avoiding the star system, he was able to use leading performers in either major or minor roles, and he trained actors in his methods at a school which he established at the Deutsches Theater. Reinhardt created a furore in London with his productions of the wordless spectacle *The Miracle* at Olympia (1911) and of *Oedipus Rex* at Covent Garden (1912). In 1920 he produced *Jedermann* ("Everyman") at Salzburg, where until the 1930s it became an annual event at the festival he founded there.

In 1924 Reinhardt returned briefly to Berlin to present Shaw's *Saint Joan* with Elisabeth *Bergner and Pirandello's *Six Characters in Search of an Author.* When the Nazis came to power in 1933, Reinhardt was deprived of all connections with the German state theater. He immigrated to the United States in the following year and staged *A Midsummer Night's Dream* in the Hollywood Bowl, playing to 12,000 people nightly. He made a film version of the play with the same type of massive settings that he used in his stage productions. During his last years Reinhardt ran a school for actors on the West Coast.

BIBLIOGRAPHY: G. Adler, *Max Reinhardt, sein Leben* (1964); H. Carter, *The Theatre of Max Reinhardt* (1964); O.M. Sayler (ed.), *Max Reinhardt and His Theatre* (1924); H. Braulich, *Max Reinhardt, Theater zwischen Traum und Wirklichkeit* (1966), W. Haas, *Die literarische Welt* (1958), index.

[Stewart Kampel]

REINHARDT, STEPHEN R. (1931–), U.S. federal judge. Born in New York City, he received his bachelor's degree from Pomona College in 1951 and he graduated from Yale Law School in 1954. Reinhardt served in the U.S. Air Force General Counsel's Office from 1954 to 1956. He was law clerk to Judge Luther W. Youngdahl of the U.S. District Court in the District of Columbia from 1956 to 1957, then entered private practice in Los Angeles with the firm O'Melveny and Myers until 1958. He was a partner in the firm Fogel, Julber, Reinhardt, Rothschild, and Feldman from 1959 until 1980, when he was appointed a judge in the U.S. Court of Appeals in the Ninth Circuit, Los Angeles.

Judge Reinhardt ruled in several controversial cases, gaining a reputation as a liberal jurist. In *Phinpathya v. Immigration and Naturalization Service* (1981), he reversed and remanded the Board of Immigration Appeals' denial of an application for suspension of deportation, concluding that the Board erred in its finding that the petitioner had failed to meet the "continuous physical presence" requirement because of a three-month visit to Thailand to aid her sick mother. The Supreme Court reversed the decision, holding that the three-month visit did not fall within the exceptions to the requirement of continuous presence. In *Orhorhaghe v. Immigration and Naturalization Service* (1994), Reinhardt, writing for the panel, ruled that the Immigration and Naturalization Service's seizure of an alien based solely on a foreign-sounding name was a violation of the Fourth Amendment that warranted the suppression of the evidence of illegal status acquired in the course of the seizure.

Other controversial cases involved the right to die and restrictions on assault weapons. In *Compassion in Dying v. Washington* (1996), Judge Reinhardt, writing for the court, ruled that a Washington statute that imposed a criminal penalty on persons assisting in an attempted suicide violated the Fourth Amendment's due process clause. The Supreme Court reversed the decision in 1997. In *Silveira v. Lockyer*, which challenged California's restrictions on assault weapons, he ruled that the Second Amendment guarantees a collective right to bear arms but does not guarantee an individual's right to do so.

Reinhardt served in numerous professional organizations. He served on the California Advisory Committee to the U.S. Commission on Civil Rights from 1962 to 1974, and as its vice chairman from 1969 to 1974. A member of the American Bar Association, he was cochairman of the Committee on Labor Arbitration and Law of Collective Bargaining Agreements from 1967 to 1973. He was a member of the Committee on Legislation of the California Bar Association from 1973 to 1977 and of the Labor Law Section of the Los Angeles Bar Association from 1974 to 1980. In 1998 Judge Reinhardt received the Champion of Justice Award from the Association of Criminal Defense Lawyers.

[Dorothy Bauhoff (2nd ed.)]

REINHARZ, JEHUDA (1944–), Israeli-American scholar. Born in Haifa, he emigrated to Germany in 1958 and the United States in 1961 (naturalized 1966). He was educated at Columbia University (B.S. 1967), Jewish Theological Seminary of America (B.R.E. 1967), Harvard University (M.A. 1968), and Brandeis University (Ph.D. 1972). Reinharz taught at Hebrew College, Brookline, Mass. (1969–70); Brandeis University; Hiatt Institute, Jerusalem (1970); the University of Michigan, where he was the first professor of Judaic studies (1972–82); and from 1982 at Brandeis, where he became the Richard Koret Professor of Modern Jewish History and was president of the university from 1994. He had fellowships from the Woodrow Wilson National Fellowship Foundation, the American Council of Learned Societies, the Leo Baeck Institute, the Royal Historical Society (U.K.), and other organizations. He was a member of the Association for Jewish Studies, the Leo Baeck Institute, the World Union of Jewish Studies, the National Foundation for Jewish Culture, the Institute for Polish Jewish Studies, and a number of other professional and scholarly bodies. He was also is a member of the Council on Foreign Relations, the International Council of Yad Vashem, and the boards of the United Israel Appeal/Jewish Agency and the American Joint Distribution Committee as well as the Presidential Advisory Committee to the president of Israel.

Reinharz is a leading scholar of modern Jewish history as well as a leading public advocate for Israel. His *The Jew in the Modern World* (written with Paul R. Mendes Flohr) is a widely adopted college text, and his two-volume biography of Chaim Weizmann has won many awards. His appointment to the presidency of Brandeis, a private Jewish-sponsored university, after one of his predecessors tried to distance it from its Jewish roots, was widely heralded as a choice to return to its Jewish heritage, and Reinharz did not disappoint. As president of Brandeis, Reinharz presided over a great expansion of its programs and physical plant as well as a significant increase in its endowment. Under his leadership the university flourished, its student body improving and its faculty and course offerings growing in scope and depth. In 2005 he established the "nonpartisan" Crown Center for Middle East Studies, believing that existing academic centers are "infused with ideology" and "third-rate." Among Reinharz's books are *Fatherland or Promised Land? The Dilemma of the German Jew* (1975), *Chaim Weizmann: The Making of a Zionist Leader* (1985), *Chaim Weizmann: The Making of a Statesman* (1993), and *Zionism and the Creation of a New Society* (with Ben Halpern (1998; 20002), and a number of edited volumes, including volume 9 of *The Letters and Papers of Chaim Weizmann* (1977), *The Jew In the Modern World: A Documentary History* (with Paul R. Mendes Flohr, 1980; 1995²), *The Jewish Response to German Culture: From the Enlightenment to World War II* (with Walter Schatzberg, 1985), and *Essential Papers on Zionism* (with Anita Shapira, 1996). He also published many journal articles and contributed to yearbooks and collections of essays.

[Drew Silver (2nd ed.)]

REINMANN, SALOMON (c. 1815–c. 1880), traveler. A native of Galicia, he left his home country in the 1840s and traveled to Burma, where he supplied food to the British army. He amassed a great fortune but soon lost it, and was wounded when involved in battle, losing one eye and part of his left hand. Later he wandered around the Orient as a merchant, then settled in Cochin. Finally he returned to Europe, homeless and without hope, and died in Vienna. While in Austria, he was urged by Peretz *Smolenskin to write down the impressions and observations gained during his many years of travel. His *Masot Shelomo be-Ereẓ Hodu, Birman ve-Sinim* was edited and annotated after his death by Wolf *Schur of Warsaw and appeared in 1884. Though a rather uncritical account of countries and people, Jews and others, with many inaccuracies, the book is an important source of information on Jewish life in *Bombay (especially on the *Bene Israel), *Cochin, *Calcutta, *Burma, and other communities.

BIBLIOGRAPHY: S. Reinmann, *Masot Shelomo*, ed. by W. Schur (1884), 3–4; Sassoon, in: *Jewish Tribune* (Bombay, Oct. 1933), 10–11.

[Walter Joseph Fischel]

REINSDORF, JERRY (1936–), U.S. baseball and basketball owner, the third owner in the history of North American sports to win a championship in two different sports. Born in Brooklyn, New York, the son of a sewing machine peddler, Reinsdorf graduated from George Washington University in Washington, DC, and went on to receive his law degree from Northwestern University after moving to Chicago in 1957. His first job was as a tax attorney for the IRS, and then he went into private tax law practice. He made his fortune in Chicago real estate, heading up the multi-billion-dollar Balcor Corporation. Reinsdorf headed the partnership that purchased the Chicago White Sox and Comiskey Park from Bill Veeck for $19 million on January 29, 1981. He was a member of Major League Baseball's Executive Council, served as chairman of baseball's Ownership Committee, and was a member of the Long Range Planning, Restructuring, Expansion, Equal Opportunity, Strategic Planning, Legislative and Player Relations committees. Reinsdorf assumed the position of chairman of the Chicago Bulls on March 13, 1985, when he led the group that purchased controlling interest in the franchise for $16 million. During his tenure as chairman of the Bulls, the team captured six World Championships for Chicago (1991–93, 1996–98). Reinsdorf was also responsible for the construction of two new sports facilities in Chicago, Comiskey Park (1991), now U.S. Cellular Field, and the United Center (1994). Reinsdorf was the 1997 recipient of the Order of Lincoln Award, and his many contributions to the community have been recognized by such organizations as Keshet, the Interfaith Organizing Project, the American Academy of Achievement, the Cystic Fibrosis Foundation, and the Trial Lawyers Club of Chicago. In addition, he is the recipient of the Chicago Park District's 1990 Chicagoan of the Year Award, the 1992 PUSH Bridgebuilder Award, the National Italian-American Friendship Award, Northwestern University's Award of Merit, the U.S. Air Force American Spirit Award and a honorary degree in humane letters from Illinois College. Reinsdorf was awarded the Ellis Island Medal of Honor in 1993 and the 1997 Mayor's Medal of Honor.

[Elli Wohlgelernter (2nd ed.)]

REISCHER, JACOB BEN JOSEPH (also known as **Jacob Backofen**; c. 1670–1733), rabbi, halakhic authority, and author. Born in Prague, Reischer studied under Aaron Simeon Spira, rabbi of Prague, and was known as a prodigy in his early youth. Afterward he studied under Spira's son, Benjamin Wolf Spira, *av bet din* of the Prague community and rabbi of Bohemia, whose son-in-law he subsequently became. His brothers-in-law were Elijah Spira and David *Oppenheim. Reischer's surname, borne by his grandfather and uncles (see introduction to his *Minḥat Ya'akov*), derives from the fact that his family came from Rzeszow, Poland, and not, as has been erroneously stated, because he served as rabbi of that town.

While still young, he became *dayyan* of the "great *bet din* of *Prague." He was appointed *av bet din* of Ansbach, capital of Bavaria, and head of its yeshivah in 1709, and in 1715 *av bet din* of Worms. There, students flocked to him from all parts of Europe. He had, however, opponents who persecuted him. About 1718, he was appointed *av bet din* and head of the yeshivah of the important community of Metz. There, too, he did not find peace. He related that in 1728 "malicious men, as hard as iron, who hated me without cause, set upon me with intent to destroy me by a false libel, to have me imprisoned." His first work, *Minḥat Ya'akov*, was published, while he was still young, in Prague in 1689. In the course of time he was accepted by contemporary rabbis as a final authority (*Shevut Ya'akov*, vol. 1, no. 28; vol. 3, no. 61), and problems were addressed to him from the whole Diaspora, e.g., Italy, and also from Ereẓ Israel (*ibid.*, vol. 1, nos. 93 and 99). He made a point of defending the **rishonim* from the criticism of later writers, and endeavored to justify the Shulḥan Arukh against its critics. But there were also those, particularly among the Sephardi rabbis of Jerusalem, who openly censured his habit of criticizing *rishonim* and **aḥaronim* (*ibid.*, vol. 1, no. 22), and criticized him in their works. His replies to these criticisms were not always couched in moderate language (see *Lo Hibbit Aven be-Ya'akov*). The main target of his criticism was Joseph b. David of Breslau, author of *Ḥok Yosef* (Amsterdam, 1730). Jacob's only remaining son, Simeon, *av bet din* of Danzig, died in 1715.

Reischer was the author of the following works: (1) *Minḥat Ya'akov* (Prague, 1689) – part 1 is an exposition of the *Torat ha-Ḥattat* of Moses *Isserles, and part 2, entitled *Torat ha-Shelamim*, is an exposition of *Hilkhot Niddah* of the Shulḥan Arukh together with expositions and supplements to the *Kunteres ha-Sefekot* of *Shabbetai b. Meir ha-Kohen and responsa; a second edition, entitled *Solet le-Minḥah ve-Shemen le-Minḥah* (Dessau, 1696), contained the glosses of his son, Simeon; (2) *Ḥok le-Ya'akov*, novellae and expositions on *Hilkhot Pesaḥ* of the Shulḥan Arukh, subsequently included in the large edition of the Shulḥan Arukh; (3) *Shevut Ya'akov*, responsa in three parts – part 1 (Halle, 1710) also contains "*Pe'er Ya'akov*," the residue of his novellae on the Talmud which were destroyed by fire in 1689, part 2 (Offenbach, 1711) contains a revised edition of the laws of *migo* and *sefek sefeka* ("double doubt"), which had been published separately in Prague in 1689, and part 3 (Metz, 1789) contains his "*Lo Hibbit Aven be-Ya'akov*," a reply to the attacks on his first works; (4) *Iyyun*

Ya'akov (Wilhelmsdorf, 1729) is a commentary on the *aggadot* in *Ein Ya'akov* of Jacob *Ibn Ḥabib, and on *Avot.*

BIBLIOGRAPHY: A. Cahen, in: REJ, 8 (1884), 271–3; Fuenn, Keneset, 575f.; A. Marx, in: JQR, 8 (1917/18), 271f.; C. Tchernowitz, *Toledot ha-Posekim*, 3 (1947), 65, 164, 187–90.

[Ephraim Kupfer]

REISEN, ABRAHAM (Avrom Reyzn; 1876–1953), Yiddish poet, short-story writer, playwright, and editor. Born in Koidanovo, Russia (now Dzyarzhynsk, Belarus), Reisen was the son of the Hebrew and Yiddish poet Kalman Reisen (1848–1921) and the brother of the poet, short-story writer, and translator Sarah (Sore) Reisen (1884–1974) and the celebrated philologist Zalman *Rejzen (1887–1941). While he was still a teenager, his talent was recognized by *Shalom Aleichem and I.L. *Peretz, who arranged for the publication of his earliest poems. After some years in Minsk, Warsaw, Cracow, and Berlin, he settled permanently in New York in 1914. Influenced by Heinrich *Heine, whom he translated into Yiddish, he was one of the first Yiddish poets to make use of folksong material. His poetry, though mostly written in conventional quatrains, is suffused by a refined sensibility that adumbrates the writing of Di *Yunge. In contrast to the verse of the "sweatshop" generation, such as Morris *Vinchevsky or Morris *Rosenfeld, his work is characterized by a certain understated Romanticism and melancholy irony. Reisen shared the preoccupation with poverty and social problems manifested by his predecessors, but he entirely eschews their propagandistic rhetoric. Nonetheless, while most of his poetry is softly lyrical, a proportion has sufficiently social-critical implications to have been sung at clandestine workers' meetings in the forests. Many of his poems were set to music and became a standard part of Yiddish folk culture.

In hundreds of short stories, often written at a pace of one a week for the many newspapers to which he was a regular contributor, he reflected with transparent honesty the lives of simple Jews whether in the *shtetl* or as immigrants. His style completely lacked didacticism and the mediating narrators of earlier Yiddish fiction. Though set in a Jewish environment, the stories are animated by wider values. His characters are overwhelmingly Jewish, but they are beset by universal human problems. The narration is restrained, with minimal action and is often reminiscent of Anton Chekhov, another writer whom he translated into Yiddish. His stories are masterpieces of concision and evince his particular gift for catching the essential psychological traits of a character or a situation in a few strokes. His characters are ill-adjusted to their environment and suffer all manner of petty tragedies. He is particularly effective in his unsentimental, quietly realistic depiction of the miseries caused by poverty and the daily struggle to survive. Stories such as "Ayzn" (1912; "Iron," 1974) often constitute brilliant essays in unspoken psychopathology. He wrote with particular effectiveness on a wide variety of themes incorporating characterizations of hungry dreamers, prostitutes, workers, mothers and children, parvenus, and factory girls, all treated with equal lack of censoriousness. Though Reisen adopts a seemingly distanced, objective voice, the reader's sympathy is nonetheless all the more poignantly evoked. Reisen was immensely popular with the general reader and his public appearances were attended by thousands, yet, perhaps on account of his deceptive simplicity, it was only from the 1930s onwards that he began to receive due recognition by intellectual critics.

His valuable autobiography, *Epizodn fun Mayn Lebn* ("Episodes from My Life," 1929–35) covers events in his varied life up to his participation in the epoch-making *Czernowitz Yiddish Language Conference of 1908. Subsequent episodes were never published in book-form. He was also an indefatigable editor and publisher and brought out many important anthologies and a dozen or so journals of which most were fairly ephemeral. He had a deep interest in European literature, and was eager to disseminate acquaintance with the European writers in Yiddish translation as to promote Yiddish literature as an equal within the broader European context.

BIBLIOGRAPHY: Rejzen, *Leksikon* 4 (1929), 349–64; Sh. Slutsky, *Avrom Reyzn-Bibliografye* (1956, 1960); J. Glatstein, *In Tokh Genumen* (1947), 48–63, 514–44; S. Liptzin, *Flowering of Yiddish Literature* (1963), 118–22; C. Madison, *Yiddish Literature* (1968), 197–220. **ADD. BIBLIOGRAPHY:** LNYL 8 (1981), 458–78; Y. Yeshurin, in: A. Reisen, *Lider, Dertseylungen un Zikhroynes* (1966), 307–16; idem, *Gezamlte Shriftn*, 14 vols. (1928–33); Sh. Niger, *Yidishe Shrayber fun Tsvantsikstn Yorhundert* 1 (1946, 1972), 107–41; C. Leviant, in: A. Reisen, *The Heart-Stirring Sermon and Other Stories* (1992), xi–xxiv; D. Kay, *Jewish Writers of the Twentieth Century* (2003), 451–2.

[Hugh Denman (2nd ed.)]

REISENBERG, NADIA (1904–1983), U.S. concert pianist and piano teacher. Born in Vilna, Lithuania, Reisenberg moved with her family to St. Petersburg in 1915, where she studied piano at the Conservatory under Leonid Nikolaiev. After the Russian revolution, the family moved, eventually arriving in America in 1922. Under the helpful largesse of Isaac Sherman, Nadia gave private recitals and began to build a reputation. She gave her American debut concert to strong reviews in late 1922 and in 1924 began touring.

Reisenberg possessed a brilliant technique and her audiences were won over by the depth of her musicianship, diverse repertoire, strength and agility, and convincing and serious interpretations.

She married Isaac Sherman, an economist, in 1924, and they had two sons; Reisenberg credited the successful balancing of her concert career and raising a family to having "complete cooperation and understanding" from her husband. In 1930, she began studies with Josef Hoffman at the Curtis Institute, receiving a diploma in 1935 and teaching there from 1934 to 1938. She also taught at Mannes College, Queens College, CUNY, and the Juilliard School; in the 1960s she gave master classes at the Rubin Academy in Israel. Reisenberg focused significant attention on chamber music, which she considered "her first and real love in this world." She often concertized with the Budapest Quartet, or soloists such as cellist Joseph Schuster and violinists William Kroll and Erick Friedman.

In 1939–40, Reisenberg amazed radio listeners by performing the complete Mozart Piano Concertos in a cycle of weekly broadcasts, which she called "the most rewarding experience of my career, my private year with Mozart." Arthur Rubinstein said of this series, "She played brilliantly and I admired her very greatly."

Reisenberg toured with orchestras, including the New York Philharmonic under John Barbirolli, and was the first soloist to play twice in one season with that orchestra, in 1941. Nadia often played premieres of Russian composers, and frequently included newer compositions on her programs, although she did not like "ultra-modern" 20th century music. She also recorded for commercial labels. Reisenberg's last solo recital was at Carnegie Hall on November 21, 1947, though she still gave some concerts, such as a benefit for Israeli children at Carnegie Hall in 1948. In general, after 1950, she focused on teaching, becoming a beloved, sympathetic instructor with deep personal interest in all her students.

[Judith S. Pinnolis (2nd ed.)]

REISER, PAUL (1957–), U.S. actor and writer. Born in New York to a health food distributor, Reiser studied classical piano and composition at the State University of New York-Binghamton. He began performing stand-up comedy at New York comedy clubs, such as the Improv and Comic Strip. His big break came in Barry Levinson's *Diner* (1982). Reiser went on to appear in *Beverly Hills Cop* (1984), *Aliens* (1986), and *Beverly Hills Cop II* (1987). He also appeared on television specials, award shows, and pilots, including a *Diner* pilot in 1983. He starred on the NBC sitcom *My Two Dads* (1987–90). After the show ended, Reiser returned to feature films with roles in *Crazy People* (1990) and *The Marrying Man* (1991). Toward the end of *Dads*, Reiser developed a new show based on his own marriage. *Mad About You* debuted in 1992, featuring Reiser and Helen Hunt as a recently married couple dealing with life after the honeymoon, and ran successfully until 1999. The show's theme song, *The Final Frontier*, was written by Reiser and musician Don Was. In 1994, Reiser published his first book, *Couplehood*, a bestseller that featured unused material from his sitcom. That same year, Reiser received an Emmy nomination as a lead actor in a comedy series. In 1997, he released his second book, *Babyhood*. He continued to appear in movies, including *The Thing about My Folks* (2005), which he wrote.

[Adam Wills (2nd ed.)]

REISMAN, HEATHER (1948–), Canadian entrepreneur and philanthropist. Reisman was born in Montreal and went to McGill University where she studied social work. Later she moved to Toronto. Drawn to business, she co-founded Paradigm Consulting, a strategy and change management firm in 1979. She left Paradigm in 1992 to become president of Cott Corporation, the regional bottler which she helped grow into the world's largest retailer-branded beverage supplier. Harvard University developed two case studies focusing on the company's growth and development during Reisman's time as president. Reisman left Cott and in 1996 founded and became chief executive officer of Indigo Books, Music and More. The launch of Indigo was the culmination of a lifelong passion for books and music. After a merger with Chapters Books, Indigo became Canada's largest book retailer.

Reisman was recognized for her many contributions to the Jewish and larger community. In 2005, she was awarded the Canada Council of Christians and Jews (CCCJ) Human Relations Award for her contribution to a variety of initiatives that span social, religious, racial, and ethnic communities. She served as governor of McGill University and of the Toronto Stock Exchange, In addition to being the CEO of Indigo Books she was also an officer of Mount Sinai Hospital and a board member and adviser to many organizations, including World Literacy of Canada and Toronto's Holy Blossom Temple, where she and her husband established the Gerald Schwartz/Heather Reisman Centre for Jewish Learning, which sponsors lectures and study classes on a wide range of Jewish-interest subjects. Reisman and her husband were also active in support of the Liberal Party of Canada. Her husband, Gerald *Schwartz, served as chair and CEO of Onex Corporation.

[Mindy Avrich-Skapinker (2nd ed.)]

REISS, LIONEL (1894–1986), U.S. painter, printmaker, watercolorist. Born in Jaroslav, Galicia, a four-year-old Reiss and his family immigrated to New York in 1898. Reiss attended the Art Students League and then worked as a commercial artist for newspapers, publishers, and a motion picture company. Reiss was art director for Paramount Studios and the creator of the now famous MGM lion. In 1930, Reiss made a decision to leave New York to travel to Europe, North Africa, and the Near East, accumulating material for art with Jewish subject matter, often focusing on Jewish life in Eastern Europe. Reiss published some of the fruits of his travels in a limited edition folio titled *My Models Were Jews* in 1938. In part, this work attempted to negate Hitler's assertion of a distinctive "Jewish type" with images of a wide range of different Jews in varying milieus, including the Venice ghetto, the Jewish cemetery in Prague, and an array of shops, synagogues, streets, and marketplaces. All of his depictions are infused with a great sensitivity to details of dress, hair, facial features, and expression often suggested with an economy of line which still manages to retain a powerful descriptive quality. Reiss' subject matter was wide-ranging, from the gritty realism of a group of near-derelicts escaping the heat on a tenement rooftop in *New York Summer Night* (c. 1946) to more brilliantly colored images such as the watercolor and gouache *Spring Promenade* (c. 1946), which depicts a bevy of well-dressed New Yorkers parading through Central Park. Reiss also completed paintings lighter in hue and spirit which reflect the artist's observation of life in Israel, such as *Tel Aviv Balconies, Boy from Safed*, and *Yeminite Girl*. He published and illustrated *New Lights and Old Shad-*

ows (1954) and *A World at Twilight,* two books featuring text by I.B. Singer. He illustrated many other books including the English edition of Ḥayyim Naḥman *Bialik's poem *Hamatmid*, published in 1947, for which he created the etching *The Talmud Student*, a somewhat expressionistically rendered depiction of a reader, his weary but engrossed expression illuminated by vibrant candlelight. Reiss' work has been exhibited at the Art Institute of Chicago, the Carnegie Institute, and the Whitney Museum. His art has been collected by many institutions, including, among others, the Jewish Theological Seminary, the Smithsonian Institution, and the Tel Aviv Museum.

BIBLIOGRAPHY: L.S. Reiss, *My Models Were Jews: a Painter's Pilgrimage to Many Lands: a Selection of One Hundred and Seventy-Eight Paintings, Watercolors, Drawings, and Etchings* (1938); O.Z. Soltes, *Fixing the World: Jewish American Painters in the Twentieth Century* (2003).

[Nancy Buchwald (2nd ed.)]

REISZ, KAREL (1926–2002), British film director. Born in Ostrava, Czechoslavakia, Reisz came to Britain on a *Kindertransport* in 1938; his family perished in the Holocaust. Reisz served in the Royal Air Force and studied natural sciences at Cambridge. Initially a film critic, from 1959 Reisz became an influential film director, responsible for many hard-hitting and realistic dramas and comedies such as *Saturday Night and Sunday Morning* (1960), *Night Must Fall* (1964), *Morgan: A Suitable Case For Treatment* (1966), and, later, *The French Lieutenant's Woman* (1981). He was often compared to such contemporary dramatists as Harold *Pinter and Samuel Beckett.

BIBLIOGRAPHY: G. Gaston, *Karel Reisz* (1980).

[William D. Rubinstein (2nd ed.)]

REITLINGER, GERALD (1900–1978), British historian. Born in London and educated at Westminster School and Oxford, Reitlinger worked as an art dealer and critic while writing important pioneering works on the Nazi era. His *The Final Solution* (1953; revised edition, 1967) was one of the first comprehensive histories of the Holocaust and is still valuable. Reitlinger's *The SS: Alibi of a Nation* (1956) was one of the earliest serious accounts of the Nazis' agents of genocide. Reitlinger also wrote a three-volume history of art sales down the ages, *The Economics of Taste* (1961–70) and exhibited his own paintings.

[William D. Rubinstein (2nd ed.)]

REIZENSTEIN, FRANZ (1911–1968), composer and pianist. Reizenstein was born in Nuremberg, and studied the piano at the Berlin State Academy with Leonid Kreutzer and composition with Hindemith. He settled in London in 1934, undergoing a further period of study-of composition with Vaughan Williams and the piano with Solomon. He was a prolific composer in a lucid, neo-classical style, his works always showing clarity of thought and neatness of design. They include: two radio operas – *Men Against the Sea* (1949) and *Anna Kraus* (1952); the cantata *Voices of Night* (1939), for soprano, baritone, chorus, and orchestra; concerto for cello, violin, and piano (the first performance of the *Second Piano Concerto* was in June 1961, with Reizenstein as soloist); much chamber music; and pieces for solo piano, songs, etc. Reizenstein taught composition at the Guildhall School of Music, London.

[Max Loppert (2nd ed.)]

REIẒES (also **Reiẓeles**; in Heb. רייצ׳יס), **ḤAYYIM BEN ISAAC HA-LEVI** (1687–1728), and his brother **JOSHUA** (1697–1728), rabbis and Jewish martyrs in Poland. Ḥayyim was a wealthy and learned man who held the position of *av bet din* in *Lvov (Lemberg) and was rabbi of *Kamenka-Bugskaya. He was also a member of the provincial committee. Joshua headed a yeshivah in Lvov. In the spring of 1728 the bishop of Lvov accused the two brothers and other Jewish personalities of the town of having attempted to induce the Jewish apostate, Jan Filipowicz, to return to Judaism, and of having profaned the symbols of Christianity which he carried with him. The Reiẓes brothers were arrested, interrogated, tortured by the Inquisition tribunal, and condemned to death by burning at the stake. Information on the tragedy of the Reiẓes brothers stems from Jewish and Catholic sources. According to the Jesuit source, Joshua committed suicide in prison after which his body was abused, and burned at the stake. It is also related that on the day that Ḥayyim was to be burned at the stake a Jesuit priest attempted to convert him in exchange for a pardon, "but he could not convince his obstinate soul" ("*Sed nihil evicit in obstinato pectore*"). The property of the Reiẓes brothers was confiscated and set aside for financing a project to strengthen the town walls. Regularly, on the eve of Shavuot, the anniversary of the death of the martyred Reiẓes brothers, a special memorial service was held in the Naḥmanovich synagogue of Lvov for the repose of their souls.

BIBLIOGRAPHY: M. Balaban, *Dzielnica żydowska, jej dzieje i zabytki* (1909), 34–37; J. Caro, *Geschichte der Juden in Lemberg* (1894), 103–4, 174–7; *Paris Gazette* (1728), 302–3.

[Arthur Cygielman]

REJZEN (Reyzn), ZALMAN (1887–1940?), Yiddish lexicographer, literary historian, and editor. Born in Koidanovo, Minsk province (now Dzerzhinsk, Belorus), Rejzen, together with his elder brother, the poet and short story writer Abraham *Reisen, prepared the Yiddish textbook *Muter-Shprakh* ("Mother Language," 1908). That year he also published a widely used Yiddish grammar, which he expanded to the more definitive *Gramatik fun der Yidisher Shprakh* ("Grammar of the Yiddish Language," 1920), thus helping to standardize Yiddish grammar. He also helped to bring greater uniformity to Yiddish spelling by editing a book on Yiddish orthography prepared by a group of Yiddish teachers in 1913. But his most important contributions were in literary history. His *Leksikon fun der Yidisher Literatur un Prese* ("Lexicon of Yiddish Literature and Press") appeared in a single volume in 1914 under the editorship of S. *Niger and became the basis for his monumental bibliographic *Leksikon fun der Yidisher Literatur, Prese, un Filologi* ("Lexicon of Yiddish Literature, Press, and Philology"), published in four volumes in Vilna (1926–29), where he had settled in 1915 and assumed a leading role as journalist, editor, scholar, and stimulator of cultural life. When he became the editor of the Yiddish daily *Vilner Tog* in 1920, he fought for Jewish cultural autonomy and fostered new literary talents. In 1928 he was imprisoned for two months because of his opposition to the Polish government's attempt to compel Jews to accept Sunday as their day of rest. He also edited the linguistic journal *Yidishe Filologi* and several books, including the handbook for the history of Haskalah literature, *Fun Mendelssohn biz Mendele* ("From Mendelssohn to Mendele," 1923). With A. Fridkin he coauthored a study on Abraham *Gottlober and wrote on the life and works of I.L. *Peretz (*I.L. Peretz – Zayn Lebn un Zayne Verk*, "I.L. Peretz – His Life and His Works," 1931). He translated European classics into Yiddish. In 1925 he helped found the *YIVO Institute for Jewish Research, edited several of its important scholarly publications, and was especially active in its sections on philology and literature. The posthumous essay collection, *Yidishe Literatur un Yidishe Shprakh* ("Yiddish Literature and Yiddish Language," 1965) includes a full bibliography. When Soviet troops occupied Vilna in 1939, he was arrested, and when Vilna was handed over to the Lithuanian Republic, he was taken to Russia, where he was shot in June 1941. No reason was ever given for his imprisonment or execution.

BIBLIOGRAPHY: M. Ravitch, *Mayn Leksikon*, 2 (1947), 81–3; H. Abramowitch, *Farshvundene Geshtaltn* (1958), 171–81; Ch. Gininger, in: *Zamlbikher*, 8 (1952), 185–94; J. Glatstein, *In Tokh Genumen* (1960), 188–91. **ADD. BIBLIOGRAPHY:** A. Reisen, *Epizodn fun Mayn Lebn*, 1 (1938), 17–68; E. Schulman, *Yung Vilne* (1946), 8–12; Sh. Katsherginski, *Tsvishn Hamer un Serp* (1949), 16–20; LNYL, 8 (1981), 478–82.

[Moshe Starkman]

REKHASIM (Heb. רְכָסִים, "Ridges"), semiurban settlement in the Tivon Hills of Israel, 10 mi. (16 km.) S.E. of Haifa. Rekhasim, founded in 1951 as *Kefar Ḥasidim (*ma'barot* "A" and "B"), became a permanent settlement and received local council status in 1959. The population, numbering 1,500 in 1951, grew to 2,550 in 1970 as immigrants from Romania and North Africa were absorbed. Most of the inhabitants found employment in the Zebulun Valley. In the mid-1990s the population was approximately 4,970, increasing to 7,750 in 2002 and occupying an area of 1.2 sq. mi. (3 sq. km.). The majority of Rekhasim's population was ultra-Orthodox, with family income considerably below the national average.

[Efraim Orni / Shaked Gilboa (2nd ed.)]

°**RELAND, ADRIAN** (**Hadrian**; 1676–1718), Dutch Orientalist and theologian. Reland studied at Utrecht, was appointed professor of philosophy at Harderwijk in 1699, and professor of Oriental languages and antiquities at Utrecht in 1701.

He published *Antiquitates sacrae veterum Hebraeorum* (1708) and *De spoliis templi Hierosolymitani in arcu Titiaco Romae conspicuis liber singularis* (Utrecht, 1716). Reland's major work was *Palaestina ex monumentis veteribus illustrata* (2 vols., 1714), in which he collected all the knowledge then available on the historical geography of Ereẓ Israel and its ancient sites, arranging the latter alphabetically. His sources included not only the writings of classical authors, but also those of the church historians, the *Lives of the Saints*, and talmudic literature which he quotes in the original. Reland also recorded Nabatean and Palmyrene inscriptions, though he was unable to decipher them. All later Orientalists made use of his monumental compilation which is of value even today.

RELGIS (**Sigler**), **EUGEN** (1895–), Romanian author and journalist. Born in Jassy, Relgis showed an early inclination toward humanitarianism and pacifism. He wrote his first book, *Triumful Neființei* (1913), before embarking on his main journalistic and literary career. He contributed to leading Romanian periodicals and to the Jewish journals *Adam*, the official Zionist *Știri din lumea evreească, Renașterea Noastră.* For a time, he was on the editorial staff of the Zionist periodical *Mântuirea*. After 1920, he edited *Umanitatea* and *Cugetul liber* ("Free Thinking").

During the 1920s, Relgis was mainly concerned with his idealistic conception of humanitarianism – ultimately, the struggle to improve the human soul. His fundamental work was *Principiile umanitariste* ("Humanitarian Principles", 1922), which was translated into 17 languages and made Relgis one of the best-known figures in the intellectual world between the world wars. He developed his ideas in *Umanitarismul și internaționala intelectualilor* ("Humanitarianism and the Intellectuals' Internationale", 1922), *Umanitarismul și socialismul* ("Humanitarianism and Socialism", 1925), *Umanitarismul biblic* ("Biblical Humanitarianism", 1926) and similar works. Some of his books contained prefaces by such celebrities as Albert Einstein and Romain Rolland who declared Relgis to be his most worthy successor. During this period he wrote *Petre Arbore* (3 vols., 1924), *Glasuri în Surdin* ("Voices in a Low Key", 1927), and *Prieteniile lui Miron* ("The Friendships of Miron", 1934).

In the years immediately preceding World War II Relgis was active in the Jewish cultural institute attached to the Bucharest Choral Temple. In 1947, he left Romania and settled in Montevideo, Uruguay, lecturing at universities there and in Argentina and Brazil. He then republished his main works in Spanish. His articles on the values of Judaism, which he identified with modern humanitarianism, originally published in Romania as *Esseuri despre judaism* ("Essays on Judaism", 1936), appeared in an elaborated form in the volumes *Profetas y Poetas* (1955) and *Testigo de mi tiempo* (1961). Another collection of articles and lectures on Romanian-Jewish subjects, *Mărturii de ieri și de azi* ("Testimonies of Yesterday and Today"), was published in Israel in 1962.

BIBLIOGRAPHY: E. Lovinescu, *Istoria literaturii române contemporane*, 3 (1927), 207–9; G. Călinescu, *Istoria literaturii romîne…* (1941), 851; *Quaderni degli amici di Eugen Relgis* (1962–); *Homenaje a Eugen Relgis en su 60.° aniversario* (1955).

[Dora Litani-Littman andAbraham Feller]

REMAK, German family of neurologists. ROBERT REMAK (1815–1865) was born in the province of Posen and was one of the first Jews to become lecturer (*Dozent*) at the University of Berlin, by special permission of Emperor Frederick William IV. In 1859 he was appointed associate professor of medicine. He made important contributions in the fields of anatomy, histology, neurology, and electrotherapy. He discovered the nonmedullated nerve fibers (Remak fibers), and a sympathetic ganglion in the heart tissue (Remak's ganglion). In opposition to accepted theories, he stated that cell growth to form tissue is achieved by cell division. He also proved that the double middle embryological germ layer is a single structure. His contributions in the field of electrotherapy include substitution of galvanic for induced current and the introduction of galvanic therapy for certain nerve and muscle diseases.

His son, ERNST JULIUS REMAK (1849–1911), continued the work of his father in neurology and his contributions to medicine were mainly in electrodiagnosis and electrotherapeutics. He described the so-called Remak's reflex of the first three toes as an indication of disturbances in the spinal cord, and described a form of paralysis of the extensor muscles of fingers and wrists. His publications include *Grundriss zur Elektrodiagnostik und Elektrotherapie* (1909) and *Neuritis und Polyneuritis* (1899). Born in Berlin, he became an assistant in the clinic for nervous diseases at the Charité Hospital of that city. In 1902 he was appointed associate professor of neurology at Berlin University.

BIBLIOGRAPHY: S.R. Kagan, *Jewish Medicine* (1952), 153–4, 379–80.

[Suessmann Muntner]

°**REMBRANDT VAN RIJN** (1606–1669), Dutch painter and engraver, considered Holland's national cultural hero. Born in Leiden, he was probably reared in Calvinism, the official religion of Holland. There has been some speculation that Rembrandt became a Mennonite later in life. Rembrandt has always been associated with the Jews of Amsterdam. His religious-cultural background naturally brought him nearer to the Hebraic than the Hellenistic heritage and, like his fellow Dutchmen, he was well versed in the Old and New Testaments. The new Dutch Republic at that time was celebrating its liberation from Spain, and regarded itself as the chosen people, the "New Israel," and its land as a "New Jerusalem," while the Spanish oppressor was likened to Pharaoh or Haman of biblical times. Like other Dutch artists of the time Rembrandt painted Old Testament subjects and created many wonderful drawings and etchings. His pupils continued this trend, often using his drawings as the basis for their work. For these Old Testament depictions Rembrandt may have used Jewish models, which were portrayed in a sympathetic and, above all, human manner. Rembrandt learned his first lessons in giving form to biblical texts from his teacher Pieter Lastman (1583–1633), and from 16th-century prints. An early work by Rembrandt is *Balaam and the Ass* (1626; Paris), similar to and inspired by Lastman's work on the same subject (1622; Jerusalem). In certain instances his treatment of the themes deviates from the traditional and has led scholars to speculate that Rembrandt may have derived his novel interpretations from conversations with rabbinical authorities, who provided him with details from post-biblical Jewish literature. It has been shown that Rembrandt and other artists consulted the *Antiquities* of *Josephus Flavius to enrich their biblical iconography. In his New Testament depictions the Jews, especially when he depicts the Pharisees, are sometimes shown as "suspicious of the Christian Miracle."

Rembrandt lived in the Jewish Quarter in Amsterdam on the Breestraat from 1633 to 1635 and from 1639 to 1658. It has been suggested that his choice of a home in Amsterdam's Breestraat was motivated by its proximity to the city's growing Jewish community. In actual fact quite a few artists resided in this quarter. Rembrandt was friendly with two Sephardi Jews, one of whom was the physician Ephraim Hezekiah *Bueno (Bonus). The Rijksmuseum in Amsterdam owns a small Rembrandt oil portrait of Ephraim Bueno, a preliminary study for the etching of 1647. In World War II this portrait was "bought" by the Nazis for Hitler's museum, from the dealer Mannheimer. Rembrandt's other Jewish friend was *Manasseh ben Israel; Rembrandt's etching of him in 1636 is supposed to have been based on a painted portrait that has disappeared. It is doubtful, though, whether it is in fact a portrait of Manasseh ben Israel, but, on the other hand, there is no doubt that Rembrandt and Manasseh knew each other. In Rembrandt's 1635 *Balthazar's Feast* (National Gallery, London), a mysterious hand writes the words: *Mene Mene Tekel Upharsin* in Hebrew letters on the wall. Rembrandt may have consulted Manasseh about the script and in what manner the writing should be arranged. He wrote the words from top to bottom, according to an old Jewish tradition, which was later quoted in Manasseh's book *De Termino Vitae*. For Manasseh's book *Piedra Gloriosa, o de la Estatua de Nebuchadnesar* ("The Glorious Stone, or Nebuchadnezzar's Statue," 1655) Rembrandt made four etchings, one of which was the *David and Goliath*. His plates were not found acceptable on religious rather than aesthetic grounds, and a new commission was accordingly given to another artist – possibly the Jewish copper engraver Shalom *Italia.

The painting and the four etchings are based on the book of Daniel, and are related to messianic ideas common in Holland at that time. Manasseh was, in many respects, a mediator between Jews and Christians. He, like the philo-Semites, was fostering millenarian hopes for messianic salvation.

There has been much speculation as to whether Rembrandt and Baruch *Spinoza knew each other. The assertion that Rembrandt was Spinoza's drawing teacher has been rejected. Many scholars have claimed to see a likeness of Spinoza in paintings by Rembrandt, yet alleged identifications have remained highly debatable. There is a possibility that the two may have met at the home of Manasseh ben Israel, who was one of Spinoza's teachers, or at the home of Spinoza's Latin teacher, Dr. Frans van den Emden, where one of Rembrandt's pupils was a lodger, or at meetings of Collegiants and Mennonites which the philosopher occasionally attended.

Much of what we think about Rembrandt and the Jews derives from ideas formulated in the 19th century. E. Kolloff wrote in 1854 about Rembrandt's depictions of the biblical past as bearing a "strong touch of the Judaic." Rembrandt's financial problems, which eventually led to his bankruptcy in 1656, were believed to be the result of his relations with Jewish patrons, especially Manasseh ben Israel, who had allegedly influenced him to spend time and money on kabbalistic ideas.

Evidence of Rembrandt's artistic interest in the Jews he encountered in Amsterdam is provided by his numerous drawings, in pen and bistre, or brown or black chalk, of bearded old Jews in long coats. His early depictions of beggars in high hats are not of Jews, but probably based on J. Callot's prints of vagabonds. His etching known as *Jews in the Synagogue* (1648) shows nine Jews and not a *minyan* (quorum) as has been stated. Nor is it any longer agreed that the setting is a synagogue, and it has been suggested that the picture should be titled, *A Scene in the Jewish Quarter of Amsterdam*. *The Jewish Bride* (Rijksmuseum; painted after 1665) may not be a portrait of Jews at all, though one scholar maintains that the sitters are the Jewish poet Miguel de *Barrios, and his much younger wife, Abigail de Pinna. The title was given to the painting in 1825, and therefore lacks historical justification. It is now believed to be a biblical painting, most probably of Isaac and Rebecca. Already in the 18th century art collectors cataloguing their collections gave Jewish "Romantic" names to some of the artist's works, as for instance two etchings, labeled the *Great Jewish Bride* and the *Small Jewish Bride* by Valerius Rover, but which are not what they are called.

A number of portraits assigned to Rembrandt, including some that may be works by his pupils, are believed to be of Jews, though the titles alone, often supplied by dealers, are not sufficient proof. The sole documentary evidence that Rembrandt found patrons among the well-to-do Sephardim of Amsterdam is a deposition concerning a disagreement between the artist and a certain Diego d'Andrade over a portrait of a young woman (perhaps Diego's daughter) which the patron had found unsatisfactory. This painting has, very tentatively, been identified as one in a private collection in Toronto. All identifications of portraits of unknown Jews based on "racial" features are tentative, though in certain cases the physiognomy and style of clothing appear to be more persuasive than in others. Jewish sitters have thus been claimed for as many as 40 oils, but the number is open to challenge. A painting in Rembrandt's inventory of 1656 which is listed as "a Head of Christ, a study from life" and related works were probably painted after a Jewish model. According to S. Schama some of the types of people dressed in heavy coats and fur hats (*kolpaks*) are actually Polish noblemen from Gdansk, and not Jewish. It is assumed that quite often Jewish beggars, who were poverty-stricken Ashkenazi refugees from Poland, served as paid models.

Among Rembrandt's most celebrated oils on Old Testament themes in major public collections the following may be named: *Samson and Delilah* (1628; Berlin), *Jeremiah Lamenting the Destruction of Jerusalem* (1630; Amsterdam); *Saul and David* (1631; Frankfurt); *Sacrifice of Abraham* (1635; St. Petersburg); *Samson Threatening his Father-in-law* (1635; Berlin); *Blinding of Samson* (1636; Frankfurt); *The Angel Leaving the Family of Tobias* (1637; Paris); *Samson's Wedding Feast* (1638; Dresden); *David's Farewell to Jonathan* (1642; St. Petersburg); *Bathsheba at her Toilet* (1643; New York); *Susanna and the Elders* (1647; Berlin); *Bathsheba with David's Letter* (1654; Paris); *Joseph Accused by Potiphar's Wife* (1655; Berlin); *Saul and David* (c. 1655; The Hague); *Jacob Blessing the Sons of Joseph* (1656; Kassel); *Jacob Wrestling with the Angel* (c. 1659; Berlin); *Moses Holding the Tablets of the Law* (1659; Berlin). In this last-mentioned painting the tablets are inscribed in beautiful Hebrew lettering in accordance with the Amsterdam Sephardi manner.

Rembrandt made numerous drawings and prints of Old Testament subjects. Often he seeks to analyze the human motives and the psychological turning points of the episodes. Many are depictions of the stories of Genesis, such as *Joseph's Coat Brought to Jacob* (1633); *Abraham Casting Hagar and Ishmael* (1637); *Joseph Telling his Dreams* (1638); *Adam and Eve*, (1638); *Abraham's Sacrifice* (1655). The story of Tobias also held his fascination throughout his life. In 1651 he made the print of *The Blindness of Tobit*.

In his famous etching *The Triumph of Mordecai* of c. 1641 Rembrandt shows the Temple of Jerusalem through an arch, which is an allusion to the building of the Third Temple. The print is close in conception and composition to the *Nightwatch*, Rembrandt's great masterpiece.

Jewish artists after the Emancipation considered Rembrandt and his "Jewish" creations as proof of the fact that Jewish art was possible.

BIBLIOGRAPHY: J. Bab, *Rembrandt und Spinoza* (1934); W.R. Valentiner, *Rembrandt and Spinoza* (1957); L. Balet, *Rembrandt and Spinoza* (1962); J. Rosenberg, *Rembrandt* (1964); F. Landsberger, *Rembrandt, the Jews and the Bible* (1972²); C. Tuempel, *Rembrandt* (1992); M. Weyl and R. Weiss-Blok (eds.), *Rembrandt's Holland* (1993); S. Schama, *Rembrandt's Eyes* (1999); M. Zell, in: *Simiolus* 28 (2000–1), 181–97; S. Perlove, in: *Dutch Crossing*, 25 (2001), 2, 243ff.; M. Zell, *Reframing Rembrandt's Jews and the Christian Images* (2002); S. Nadler, *Rembrandt's Jews* (2003).

[Alfred Werner / Rivka Weiss-Blok (2nd ed.)]

REMÉNYI (Hoffmann), EDUARD (1830–1898), violinist. Born in Heves, Hungary, Reményi studied in Vienna, became involved in the Hungarian insurrection (1848), and after its failure fled to the United States and later toured in England. Pardoned in 1860, he was appointed solo violinist to the emperor of Austria. He was noted for his brilliant technique and intensely individual style. On one of his concert tours his accompanist was the 20-year-old Brahms, and Reményi's playing of Hungarian gypsy tunes became the inspiration for Brahms'

Hungarian Dances. Reményi made violin transcriptions of the piano works of Chopin and Field and wrote a violin concerto. He died in San Francisco, California, while on tour.

REMEZ (Drabkin), MOSHE DAVID (1886–1951), labor leader in the Jewish *yishuv* and Israeli politician, member of the First Knesset. Born in Kopys in the Mohilev district in Belorussia, Remez attended a *ḥeder*, and then studied at a gymnasium in the town of Yeltz. He was a member of *Po'alei Zion in his youth, and published Hebrew poems in *Ha-Shilo'aḥ*, then edited by Ḥayyim Naḥman *Bialik. He also served for a while as a teacher. After studying law in Constantinople, Remez settled in Palestine in 1913, where he worked as an agricultural laborer for five years in Ben-Shemen, Be'er Toviyyah, Karkur, and Zikhron Ya'akov. After World War I, he became one of the leaders of *Aḥdut ha-Avodah, and later of *Mapai, and was a key figure in the organizational and economic activities of the *Histadrut. In the years 1921–29 he headed the Public Works Office of the Histadrut, which later became *Solel Boneh, and served as secretary general of the Histadrut in the years 1935–44. Remez was chairman of the Va'ad Le'ummi from 1944 to 1948 and was one of the Jewish leaders arrested by the British authorities on June 29, 1946 ("Black Saturday"), spending several months in the Latrun detention camp. In 1948 he was appointed minister of transportation in the provisional government, and served in this position also in the first government formed by David *Ben-Gurion. In the second government he was appointed minister of education and culture, but he passed away in May 1951.

A linguist and writer, Remez introduced several new words into the Hebrew language, such as וֶתֶק (seniority); דַחְפּוֹר (bulldozer); רַמְזוֹר (traffic light). The housing complex of Ramat Remez in Haifa was named in his memory.

His only son, AHARON (1919–1994), served in the British Royal Air Force from 1942 to 1947 and from 1948 to 1951 was the first commander of the Israeli Air Force. He was a member of the Third Knesset. In 1965 he was appointed Israeli ambassador to Great Britain. In the years 1970–77 he was the head of the Israel Ports Authority, and in 1977–81 he served as chairman of the Airport Authority.

BIBLIOGRAPHY: S. Erez, *Tekufah Aḥat be-Ḥayyei David Remez 1934–45* (1977).

[Susan Hattis Rolef (2nd ed.)]

REMNANT OF ISRAEL (Heb. שְׁאֵרִית יִשְׂרָאֵל), a term denoting the belief that the future of Israel would be assured by the faithful remnant surviving the calamities that would befall the people as a result of their departing from the way of God. On the one hand the prophets foretold the forthcoming exile and destruction of Israel, and on the other they held forth the hope and promise of its survival and eternity. The doctrine of the Surviving Remnant resolved this contradiction. The doctrine is referred to by most of the prophets. Thus Micah (2:12) states, "I will surely gather the remnant of Israel"; Jeremiah (23:3) "and I will gather the remnant of my flock out of all the countries whither I have driven them and will bring them back to their folds, and they shall be fruitful and multiply." Joel promises, "For in Mount Zion and in Jerusalem there shall be those that escape and among the remnant those whom the Lord shall call" (3:5), and the first half of the verse is repeated almost literally by Obadiah (v. 17).

It is in Isaiah, however, that the doctrine is found in its most developed form which greatly affected Israel's thoughts about the future. He gives his son the symbolic name Shear-Jashub ("a remnant shall return," 7:3) and in 10:22 the phrase is repeated as a statement of fact "a remnant shall return, even the remnant of Jacob." The most detailed description of the doctrine appears in 6:13. The land shall be utterly destroyed, the children of Israel will be "removed far away," only a tenth will remain – even that tenth "shall again be eaten up" but "the holy seed" shall remain. Isaiah's concept of the remnant may have included both the faithful minority and those who would accept God's message, under the impact of the forthcoming disaster. Paul applied Isaiah's teaching to the Church (Rom. 9:27).

In the daily prayers there are included the prayers "Guardian of Israel, Guard the Remnant of Israel, and suffer not Israel to perish."

After World War II the phrase the "remnant which survives" (*she'erit ha-peletah*) was applied to the survivors of the Holocaust.

BIBLIOGRAPHY: E. Jenni, in: IDB, 4 (1962), 32–33, incl. bibl.

REMNICK, DAVID (1958–), U.S. editor, author. A native of Hillsdale, NJ, and a graduate of Princeton University with a degree in comparative literature, Remnick became the fifth editor of *The New Yorker* magazine in 1998 after an award-winning career as a reporter and foreign correspondent for *The Washington Post*. Starting in 1982 as an intern in the *Post's* Style section, he worked the night police beat and covered tennis and professional basketball for the Sports section and *The Post's* Magazine before going to Moscow for a four-year tour in 1988. Remnick chronicled the politics and personalities of the upheaval in the Soviet Union, which was soon to disappear as a national entity. He wrote *Lenin's Tomb: The Last Days of the Soviet Empire*, and it won the Pulitzer Prize in 1994. *The Wall Street Journal* compared the reportage with John Reed's influential eyewitness account of the formation of the Soviet Union, *Ten Days That Shook the World* (1919). After a stint as a visiting fellow of the Council on Foreign Relations, Remnick became a staff writer for *The New Yorker* and a frequent contributor to *The New York Review of Books* and other publications. His book, *King of the World: Muhammad Ali and the Rise of an American Hero* (1998), chronicles the early career of the heavyweight champion and placed Ali's career in a wider cultural context. In 1998, after a stellar career at the magazine, publishing more than 100 articles on an array of subjects, everything from Boris Yeltsin's political travails to Luciano Pavarotti's opera career to Mike Tyson's rise and fall, Remnick was named editor of *The New Yorker*, succeeding Tina Brown. Remnick brought a more serious tone to the magazine, which published major exposes, included articles by Seymour *Hirsch exposing degrading treatment of Iraqi prisoners by American military personnel at the Abu Ghraib prison. In addition to editing the magazine, and writing introductions to various collections of articles, Remnick continued to report and write his own lengthy articles for the magazine, some from the Middle East. In New York, he was on the Board of Overseers of *YIVO, which seeks to preserve the foremost resources for the study of the history and culture of East European Jews. His wife, Esther Fein, was a correspondent for *The New York Times.*

[Stewart Kampel (2nd ed.)]

REMOS, MOSES BEN ISAAC (c. 1406–c. 1430), physician, philosopher, and poet. Born in Majorca, he traveled widely, and eventually came to Palermo, where he was condemned to death after having been accused of poisoning a Christian patient. His judges offered to quash the sentence if he would convert (it seems that his grandfather, also named Moses Remos, had done this in Palma, Majorca, in 1391). Remos's reply was laconic: "Better that my body die than my soul. My portion is the Living Rock and the dead shall be His." Thus when only 24 years old he was put to death, his remains being buried outside Palermo, beside the city wall. The few poems which he left are of a philosophical nature, written in a careless, prosaic style.

The only one of his poems in print is an elegy on his forthcoming death: "Who would have thought that a villain's death.... " At the beginning of it he wrote: "I lament on this first day of the week, for they have told me that tomorrow they will kill me. Woe unto me! May it be God's Will that my death be the pardon for my sins. Bitterly weeping, without thinking or looking, I have taken my pen and have cried and written. In the name of the Lord, the God of Israel, I conjure the person into whose hands this falls, to read it, copy it, and send it to others until it reaches my unfortunate relatives." This elegy begins by describing a procession of worldly and natural forces, together with the arts which he had mastered during his lifetime, come to bewail the poet's death. In the latter part of the poem, the personal feelings of the author are clearly brought out. He confesses his sins, accepts his fate, and is thus prepared for his last journey.

BIBLIOGRAPHY: Steinschneider, in: *He-Ḥalutz*, 4 (1858–59), 67–70; D. Kahana (ed.), *Kinah le-Moshe Remos* (1892); Kaufmann, in: *Festschrift... Steinschneider* (1896), 225–32; Slouschz, in: *Centenario... Michele Amari*, 2 (1926), 186–204; Chajes, in: ZHB, 14 (1910), 168–70; I. Abrahams (ed.), *Hebrew Ethical Wills*, 2 (1926), 234–48; Schirmann, Sefarad, 2 (1956), 645–7.

[Yonah David]

°**RENAN, ERNEST** (1823–1892), French philosopher and Orientalist. Renan, born in Brittany, was one of the foremost French savants and authors of the 19th century. Educated for the priesthood, Renan rebelled against the oppressive Catholic intellectual atmosphere, and in 1846 abandoned his religious studies, dedicating himself to independent research. In 1847 he was awarded the Prix Volney for *L'Histoire Generale et Système Compare des Langues Semitiques*, in which his thesis was that monotheistic tendencies are inherent in the character of Semitic peoples. While working at the Bibliothèque Nationale in the department of Hebrew and Semitic manuscripts, Renan published an essay on Averroes and Averroism in 1852, a work of great erudition and insight into the world of medieval Arab philosophy. His real inclination toward biblical studies and historical research on the Jewish people and origins of Christianity soon became evident. His translations and commentaries on the Book of Job (1859), the Song of Songs (1860), and Ecclesiastes (1882) were widely appreciated at the time. When in 1860 he was barred from an appointment to the chair of Hebrew and Chaldaic at the Collège de France due to Catholic pressure, Napoleon III appointed him head of a French archaeological mission to Syria and Palestine. There Renan wrote the first draft of his famous *Vie de Jesus* (published in 1863). During this voyage he also conceived the project of a *Corpus Inscriptionum Semiticarum* (1881–92). In 1862 his appointment to the Collège de France was confirmed, but he was suspended due to the furore created by his inaugural lecture.

Vie de Jesus was the first volume of a monumental *Histoire des Origines du Christianisme*, of which the subsequent volumes were *Les Apôtres*; *Saint Paul*; *L'Antechrist* (1873), a portrayal of Nero's empire; *Les Evangiles et la Seconde Generation Chretienne*; and *Marc-Aurèle et la fin du monde antique* (1881). Renan made erudite use of rabbinic sources; see his *Le Judaïsme et le Christianisme – identite originale et separation graduelle* (1883). In the later part of his scholarly career, Renan turned to the history of the Jewish people. His five-volume *Histoire du Peuple d'Israël des origines à l'epoque romaine* was published during 1887 to 1893. As in an earlier article (*Le Judaïsme comme race et comme religion*, 1883), he declared himself an enthusiastic admirer of the great biblical prophets, who were socialists before their time. Renan collaborated with A. *Neubauer in *Les Rabbins français du 14me siècle* (1877) and *Les ecrivains Juifs français du 14me siècle* (1893), thus integrating these rabbinic writers into the literary history of France. Renan's work has been analyzed by René Dussaud in *L'Oeuvre Scientifique de Renan* (1951). A bibliography is given in H. Girard and H. Moncel, *Bibliographie des oeuvres d'Ernest Renan* (1923).

BIBLIOGRAPHY: A. Sulzbach, *Renan und der Judaismus* (1867).

[Yohanan (J.-G.) Cohen-Yashar (Kahn)]

RENASSIA, YOSSEF (1879–1962), Algerian rabbi. Renassia was a *dayyan* (rabbinical judge) in *Constantine, *Algeria, the chief rabbi of the community, and a primary force behind all types of Jewish education in that community. He was a significant figure in the entire Algerian Jewish community.

He wrote some 130 works covering the entire spectrum of Torah literature. His major efforts were devoted to translating into Judeo-Arabic and writing biblical commentaries.

Among his translations were the entire Mishnah (*Nishmat Kol Ḥai*), *Maimonides' *Mishneh Torah* (*Orah ve-Simḥah – Sefer ha-Rambam*, for which he received the Zadok Kahn award in 1961), and Isaac *Alfasi's commentary on the Talmud (*Sefer ha-Rif*).

Renassia also wrote works on history and belles lettres and edited the legends of the Talmud (*Ben-David*, 1923), translating them into Judeo-Arabic. He was the author of commentaries on biblical topics and responsa literature. He edited dictionaries as learning aids for students of Talmud and Arabic, French, and Hebrew and popularized basic works from the realm of Jewish philosophy and Kabbalah.

His educational approach was non-elitist seeking to reach everyone, from the uneducated to the advanced scholar. With that in mind he translated into the most commonly used dialect and into the *derush*, which was the sermonic style used in most synagogues.

Renassia's educational philosophy was based on the idea that one must develop students who become familiar with a wide range of subjects at an elementary level so that they continue on to specialization in those to which they are attracted. A direct result of this was that the Ez Ḥayyim *yeshivah* which he headed was home to a large number of students.

He had a unique attitude to modernity, not rejecting it but applying a selective openness. Renassia knew French very well, served in the French army, and was well acquainted with the basics of French culture, even though he absorbed only those elements he considered positive or worthy of being adopted. His main thrust was on Jewish cultural content which he felt was necessary for the maintenance of Jewish life in the Diaspora.

Upon Algeria's independence in 1962 he emigrated to Israel and at no time linked his destiny to the French people or to Jewish bodies loyal to France, such as the Consistoire or the Alliance, although he did not dissociate or alienate himself from them.

His approach to family, conversion, and observance of the commandments is rooted in his general attitude towards modernity. He felt that the solution to the processes of erosion wearing away the Algerian Jewish communities was in proper Jewish education which should be aimed at emigration to Israel. He acted tolerantly towards the problems of Jewish society as he understood – but did not condone – that it was going through gradual processes of secularization and abandonment of traditional values.

He favored a streamlined, convenient process of conversion, more so than the other Algerian rabbis, particularly after World War II. He thought that the phenomenon of conversion after the Holocaust was akin to a miracle and should be encouraged.

Renassia's correspondence with President Izhak Ben-Zvi was crucial to the saving of his works, since he used to send a dedicated copy of each to the president. If it had not been for that, it is doubtful whether it would have been possible to collect his writings, which were in threat of being lost after 1962.

All of his works are available in Jerusalem at the Jewish National and University Library, the Yad Izhak *Ben-Zvi Institute, and the Gei Yinnasei Institute, established in Jerusalem in his name and memory.

BIBLIOGRAPHY: J.L. Allouche and Laloum, *Les Juifs d'Algérie* (1968); *Y. Charvit, Un Voyage sur un Rocher – Constantine* (1990); idem, *"Ha-Ḥinnukh ha-Yehudi be-Konstantin (Algeria) be-Idan Temurot* 1837–1939," M.A. thesis (1986); J. Fraenkel, "L'Imprimerie Hébraïque à Djerba (étude bibliographiques)," Ph.D. thesis (1982); E. Tirosh Beker, *"Fonologia u-Ferakim be-morfologiyyah shel tirgum le-sefer tehilim be-Aravit Yehudit mi Konstantin (Algeria),"* M.A. thesis (1988).

[Yosef Chavit]

RENDELL, EDWARD GENE (1944–), U.S. Democratic politician. Born in New York City and educated at the University of Pennsylvania (B.A. 1965) and Villanova University Law School (J.D. 1968), Rendell was an assistant district attorney in Philadelphia from 1968 to 1977. After entering electoral politics, he was district attorney, 1978–85 (elected 1977 and 1981; he was the youngest DA in the city's history when he took office); ran unsuccessfully for governor of Pennsylvania, 1986; ran unsuccessfully for mayor of Philadelphia, 1987; was mayor, 1992–99 (elected 1991 and 1995); chairman of the Democratic National Committee, 1999–2000; and governor of Pennsylvania (elected 2002). Rendell was briefly in private law practice, 1987–91 and 2000–02. He also lectured on government and politics at the University of Pennsylvania.

Ed Rendell, a Clintonian Democrat, "stocky, balding, gravel-voiced, yet still oddly charismatic," as one journalist has put it, is known as a blunt, outspoken politician with a big personality, an effective campaigner and fundraiser. He was regarded as a law-and-order district attorney. When he became mayor of Philadelphia during a national economic recession, the city was deep in debt, and Rendell managed to balance the city's budget by imposing spending cuts, eliminating jobs, conducting competitive bidding for municipal contracts, privatizing some services, and forcing favorable wage settlements on municipal unions, establishing a national reputation as an effective manager. Legally barred from running for a third term, he was chosen to lead the Democratic National Committee during the 2000 election, but his tenure as chairman alienated him from some in the Gore presidential campaign, who felt that his public statements were frequently "off-message." Elected governor of Pennsylvania on the strength of his performance as mayor, Rendell has managed to get some parts of his legislative program enacted, but in general has had less success than he had in Philadelphia, since the state legislature is controlled by very conservative Republicans. As a Democrat able to win in a large, electorally important state, Rendell has been mentioned as a potential Democratic presidential candidate in 2008.

[Drew Silver (2nd ed.)]

RENE, ROY (known by his stage name, "**Mo**"; 1891–1954), Australian comedian. Born Henry Vande Sluice in Adelaide,

South Australia, the son of a Dutch-born Jewish cigar maker, Rene (the name he adopted from about 1910) became one of the best-known Australian comedians of his day. He originally worked as part of a vaudeville duo, "Stiffy and Mo," which toured the Australian theatrical circuit from about 1916 until 1933. Universally known as Mo, he continued on the stage alone thereafter and became a star on Australian radio in the 1940s and early 1950s in a famous series, *MacCackie Mansions.* He also starred in a film, *Strike Me Lucky* (1934).

Probably the most popular Australian comedian of his time, Mo spoke in an exaggerated "Jewish" lisp and was famous for his risqué material which often sailed close to the wind of Australia's strict laws. Many visiting celebrities, including Jack *Benny, said that he was among the best comedians they had ever seen, and urged Mo to try his luck in Hollywood, but he never left Australia. In private life, plagued by ill health, he was often a sad figure. He wrote an autobiography, *Mo's Memoirs* (1945).

BIBLIOGRAPHY: F.H. Parsons, *A Man Called Mo* (1973); ADB, 11, 360–61.

[William D. Rubinstein (2nd ed.)]

REPARATIONS, GERMAN. On Sept. 20, 1945, three months after the end of World War II, Chaim *Weizmann, on behalf of the *Jewish Agency, submitted to the governments of the U.S., the U.S.S.R., Britain, and France, a memorandum demanding reparations, restitution, and indemnification due to the Jewish people from Germany. He appealed to the Allied Powers to include this claim in their negotiations for reparations with Germany, in view of the "mass murder, the human suffering, the annihilation of spiritual, intellectual, and creative forces, which are without parallel in the history of mankind." Due to the deadlock and later interruption of the Allies' negotiations for reparations, no further development took place until March 12, 1951, when the Israel foreign minister, Moshe *Sharett, submitted a note to the four Allied governments which claimed global recompense to the State of Israel of $1,500,000,000 from the German Federal Republic (FRG, i.e., West Germany). This claim was based on the financial cost involved in the rehabilitation in Israel of those who escaped or survived the Nazi regime. The financial expense incurred by Israel in the absorption of 500,000 Nazi victims could be covered at $3,000 per capita. As a result of unofficial preliminary contacts, Chancellor Konrad *Adenauer declared on Sept. 27, 1951, the FRG's readiness to compensate Israel for material damage and losses and to negotiate with her and with representatives of Diaspora Jewry. The latter established a *Conference on Jewish Material Claims against Germany (Claims Conference) in New York (October 1951) presided over by Nahum *Goldmann.

After a resolution to enter into direct negotiations with the FRG was passed in the Knesset by a small majority after stormy street demonstrations staged by the *Ḥerut opposition and a heated three-day debate (Jan. 7–9, 1952), the FRG delegation, headed by Prof. Franz Boehm (d. 1977), first met with the Israel delegation, headed jointly by Giora *Josephthal and Felix Eliezer Shinnar (d. 1985), at The Hague on March 21, 1952. The delegation of the Claims Conference, headed by Moses *Leavitt, was in charge of the negotiations on individual claims for indemnification. Israel reduced her claim of $1,500,000,000 against the whole of Germany to $1,000,000,000 against the FRG alone. She reserved her right to claim the balance from East Germany (German Democratic Republic), which did not respond. On Sept. 10, 1952, after six months of negotiations, an agreement between Israel and the FRG was signed at Luxembourg by Moshe Sharett and Konrad Adenauer. The agreement was ratified and came into effect on March 21, 1953, after a delay caused by the Arab states' efforts to prevent ratification.

The FRG undertook to pay an amount of DM3,450,000,000 ($845,000,000) in goods, of which DM450,000,000 ($110,000,000) was earmarked for allocation by the Claims Conference. This $845,000,000 was to be paid in annual installments over a period of 14 years (between April 1, 1953, and March 31, 1966). Thirty percent was to pay for Israel's crude oil purchases in the United Kingdom. With the balance of 70%, Israel was to buy ferrous and nonferrous metals, steel, chemical, industrial, and agricultural products. The agreement was carried out by the FRG both in letter and in spirit. The reparations agreement was implemented by the government-owned Shilumim Corporation in Tel Aviv – *Shilumim* refers to recompense for material damage ("For the Lord hath a day of vengeance, a year of recompense for the controversy of Zion" (Isa. 34:8)) – which accepted orders from prospective buyers under the agreement, and by the Israel Purchasing Mission in Cologne, to place these orders with the German suppliers. Goods bought and imported under the agreement represented 12–14% of Israel's annual imports and thus made an important contribution to Israel's economy.

In 1988, the German government allocated another $125 million, enabling remaining Holocaust survivors to receive monthly payments of $290 for the rest of their lives. In February 1990, before its unification with West Germany, East Germany admitted for the first time that it was also responsible for war crimes committed by the German people during World War II and agreed to pay reparations.

In 1999, German government and German industry agreed, in response to the filing of numerous class action lawsuits in American courts, to compensate Jews and non-Jews specifically for slave and forced labor they performed for German industry during the war. In return for the dismissal of all such lawsuits and guaranteeing Germany and its industry "legal peace" from any such further litigation, the German government and German industry created a foundation, "Remembrance, Responsibility and the Future," with assets of 10 billion German marks (approximately US $5 billion). Slave and forced laborers still alive at the time of the settlement could apply to receive a lump sum payment of between $2,500–$7,500 from the German foundation. Over 140,000 Jewish survivors in over 25 countries received such payments, and the compensation program to the Jewish survivors was administered by the Claims Conference. Final payments from the Foundation were to be made by September 2006.

BIBLIOGRAPHY: Israel Ministry of Foreign Affairs, *Documents Relating to the Agreement between the Government of Israel and the Federal Republic of Germany, Signed on 10 September 1952 at Luxembourg* (1953); N. Robinson, *Ten Years Indemnification* (1964); F.E. Shinnar, *Be-Ol Koraḥ u-Regashot bi-Sheliḥut ha-Medinah: Yaḥasei Yisrael-Germanyah 1951–1966* (1967); Bank of Israel, *Ha-Shillumim ve-Hashpa'atam al ha-Meshek ha-Yisre'eli* (1965); *The Autobiography of Nahum Goldmann* (1969), 249–82; I. Deutschkron, *Bonn and Jerusalem* (1970).

[Felix Eliezer Shinnar / Michael Bazyler (2nd ed.)]

REPENTANCE. Repentance is a prerequisite for divine forgiveness: God will not pardon man unconditionally but waits for him to repent. In repentance man must experience genuine remorse for the wrong he has committed and then convert his penitential energy into concrete acts. Two substages are discernible in the latter process: first, the negative one of ceasing to do evil (Isa. 33:15; Ps. 15; 24:4), and second, the positive step of doing good (Isa. 1:17; 58:5ff.; Jer. 7:3; 26:13; Amos 5:14–15; Ps. 34:15–16; 37:27). The Bible is rich in idioms describing man's active role in the process of repentance e.g., "incline the heart to the Lord" (Josh. 24:23), "make oneself a new heart" (Ezek. 18:31), "circumcise the heart" (Jer. 4:4), "wash the heart" (Jer. 4:14), and "break one's fallow ground" (Hos. 10:12). However, all these expressions of man's penitential activity are subsumed and summarized by one verb which dominates the Bible, שוב (*shwb*, "to return") which develops ultimately into the rabbinic concept of *teshuvah*, repentance. This root combines in itself both requisites of repentance: to turn from the evil and to turn to the good. The motion of turning implies that sin is not an ineradicable stain but a straying from the right path, and that by the effort of turning, a power God has given to all men, the sinner can redirect his destiny. That this concept of turning back (to YHWH) is not a prophetic innovation but goes back to Israel's ancient traditions is clear from Amos, who uses it without bothering to explain its meaning (Amos 4:6–11). Neither he nor Isaiah stresses repentance, except in his earliest prophecy (1:16–18 – to which the prophet adds 19–20 by way of interpretation – and 27), not because they believe it is insignificant, but because in their time the people had sinned to such an extent, that they had overstepped the limits of divine forbearance and the gates of repentance were closed (Amos 7; Isa. 6). For Isaiah, the need to turn back indeed continues to play a role, but only for the few who will survive God's purge. This surviving remnant will itself actively engage in a program of repentence to qualify for residence in the New Zion (e.g., Isa. 10:20–23; 17:7–8; 27:9; 29:18ff.; 30:18–26; 31:6–7; 32:1–8, 15ff.; 33:5–6). Indeed, the name of this prophet's firstborn was imprinted with this message: "[Only] a remnant will return" (Shear-Jashub; Isa. 7:3).

In the teaching of both Hosea and Jeremiah, on the other hand, the call to turn back is never abandoned. When Jeremiah despairs of man's capability of self-renewal, he postulates that God will provide a "new heart" that will overcome sin and merit eternal forgiveness (31:32–33; 32:39–40; cf. Deut. 30:6; Ezek. 36:26–27).

[Jacob Milgrom]

Rabbinic Views

The rabbis are eloquent in describing the significance of repentance. It is one of the things created before the world itself (Pes. 54a); it reaches to the very Throne of Glory (Yoma 86a); it prolongs a man's life and brings on the Redemption (Yoma 86b). God urges Israel to repent and not be ashamed to do so because a son is not ashamed to return to the father who loves him (Deut. R. 2:24). God says to Israel: My sons, open for Me an aperture of repentance as narrow as the eye of a needle, and I will open for you gates through which wagons and coaches can pass (Song R. 5:2 no. 2). On public fast-days the elder of the congregation would declare: "Brethren, it is not said of the men of Nineveh: 'And God saw their sackcloth and their fasting' but: 'And God saw their works, that they had turned from their evil way' [Jonah 3:10]" (Ta'an. 2:1).

The rabbis were not unaware of the theological difficulties in the whole concept of repentance. Once the wrong has been done how can it be put right? The general rabbinic answer is that it is a matter of Divine Grace, as in the following passage, in which it is incidentally implied, too, that the concept of *teshuvah* has only reached its full emphasis as a result of a long development from biblical times: "They asked of wisdom? 'What is the punishment of the sinner?' Wisdom replied: 'Evil pursueth sinners' [Prov. 13:21]. They asked of prophecy: 'What is the punishment of the sinner?' Prophecy replied: 'The soul that sinneth it shall die' [Ezek. 18:4]. Then they asked of the Holy One, blessed be He: 'What is the punishment of the sinner?' He replied: 'Let him repent and he will find atonement'" (TJ, Mak. 2:7, 31d). The third-century Palestinian teachers debate whether the repentant sinner is greater than the wholly righteous man who has not sinned, R. Johanan holding the opinion that the latter is the greater, R. Abbahu that the repentant sinner is greater (Ber. 34b). R. Simeon b. Lakish said, according to one version, that when the sinner repents his sins are accounted as if he had committed them unintentionally, but, in another version, his sins are accounted as virtues. The talmudic reconciliation of the two versions is that one refers to repentance out of fear, the other to repentance out of love (Yoma 86b). Even a man who has been wicked all his days who repents at the end of his life is pardoned for all his sins (Kid. 40b). The ideal, is for man to spend all his days in repentance. When R. Eliezer said: "Repent one day before your death," he explained that since no man can know when he will die he should spend all his days in repentance (Shab. 153a).

The Day of *Atonement brings pardon for sin if there is repentance (Yoma 8:8), but Judah ha-Nasi holds that the Day of Atonement brings pardon even without repentance except in cases of very serious sin (Yoma 85b). The Day of Atonement is ineffective if a man says: "I will sin and the Day of Atonement will effect atonement." If a man says: "I will sin and repent, and sin again and repent" he will be given no chance to repent (Yoma 8:9). The second-century teacher R. Ishmael is reported as saying (Yoma 86a): "If a man transgressed a positive precept, and repented, he is forgiven right away. If he has transgressed a negative commandment and repented, then repentance suspends punishment and the Day of Atonement procures atonement. If he has committed a sin to be punished with extirpation (*karet*), or death at the hands of the court, and repented, then repentance and the Day of Atonement suspend the punishment, and suffering cleanses him from the sin. But if he has been guilty of the profanation of the Name, then penitence has no power to suspend punishment, nor the Day of Atonement to procure atonement, nor suffering to finish it, but all of them together suspend the punishment and only death finishes it." This scheme contains all the tensions resulting from the different aspects of atonement mentioned in the Bible.

Repentance involves sincere remorse for having committed the sin. The third-century Babylonian teacher, R. Judah, defined a true penitent as one who twice more encountered the object which caused his original transgression and he kept away from it. R. Judah indicated: "With the same woman, at the same time, in the same place" (Yoma 86b). The penitent sinner must confess his sins. According to R. Judah b. Bava a general confession is insufficient; the details of each sin must be stated explicitly. But R. Akiva holds that a general confession is enough (Yoma 86b). Public confession of sin was frowned upon as displaying a lack of shame except when the transgressions were committed publicly, or, according to others, in the case of offenses against other human beings (Yoma 86b). Confession without repentance is of no avail. The ancient parable, as old as Ben Sira (34:25–26), is recounted of a man who immerses himself in purifying waters while still holding in his hand a defiling reptile (Ta'an. 16a).

The sinner must be given every encouragement to repent. It is forbidden to say to a penitent: "Remember your former deeds" (BM 4:10). If a man stole a beam and built it into his house, he was freed from the obligation of demolishing the house and was allowed to pay for his theft in cash, in order to encourage him to repent (Git. 5:5). It was even said that if robbers or usurers repent and wish to restore their ill-gotten gains, the spirit of the sages is displeased with the victims if they accept the restitution, for this may discourage potential penitents from relinquishing their evil way of life (BK 94b).

[Louis Jacobs]

In Jewish Philosophy

Repentance was a favorite subject in medieval Jewish ethical and philosophical literature. *Saadiah discusses repentance in section five of his *Emunot ve-De'ot*. Baḥya ibn *Paquda devotes the seventh "gate" of his "Duties of the Heart," and *Maimonides, the last section of *Sefer ha-Madda*, "*Hilkhot Teshuvah*." to repentance.

Saadiah, Baḥya, and Maimonides agree that the essential constituents of repentance are regret and remorse for the sin committed, renunciation of the sin, confession and a request for forgiveness, and a pledge not to repeat the offense (*Emunot ve-De'ot*, 5:5; *Ḥovot ha-Levavot*, 7:4; Yad, Teshuvah, 2:2). In the case of sins perpetrated against other people it is necessary to beg forgiveness from the person one has wronged before one can receive divine forgiveness (*Emunot ve-De'ot*, 5:6; *Ḥovot ha-Levavot*, 7:9; Maim. Yad, Teshuvah, 2:9). Maimonides in particular, emphasizes the importance of verbal confession, or *viddui* (Yad, Teshuvah, 1:1), maintaining that one should publicly confess those sins that one has committed against one's fellow men. Of course, a verbal confession without inner conviction is worthless (*ibid.*, 13:3).

The conditions necessary for repentance, according to Baḥya, are:

(1) recognition of the evil nature of one's sin;

(2) realization that punishment for one's sin is inevitable, and that repentance is the only means of averting punishment;

(3) reflection on the favors previously bestowed by God; and

(4) renunciation of the evil act.

There are different gradations of repentance. The highest level of repentance, according to Saadiah, is the repentance which takes place immediately after one has sinned, while the details of one's sin are still before one. A lower level of repentance is that which takes place when one is threatened by disaster, and the lowest, that which takes place just before death. According to Baḥya, the highest level of repentance is the repentance of one, who, while still capable of sinning has conquered his evil inclination entirely. The next level of repentance is the repentance of one who, while managing to refrain from sin, is nevertheless constantly drawn toward sin by his evil inclination. The lowest form of repentance is the repentance of one who no longer has the power or opportunity to sin. Maimonides maintains that he has achieved perfect repentance (*teshuvah gemurah*) who, upon finding himself in the position of repeating his sin, is able to refrain from doing so (Yad, Teshuvah, 2:1).

Among the many other medieval works on repentance are *Iggeret ha-Teshuvah* ("Letter on Repentance," Constantinople, 1548) and *Sha'arei Teshuvah* ("Gates of Repentance," Fano, 1583) by Jonah b. Abraham Gerondi (c. 1200–1263), and *Menorat ha-Ma'or* ("The Candlestick of Light," Constantinople, 1514) by Isaac *Aboab (14th century).

[Samuel Rosenblatt]

Post-Medieval Period

The idea of repentance continued to play a central role in the life of the Jew in the postmedieval period, reinforced as it was by both the penitential liturgy and the rituals of the High Holidays. External stress, pogroms, and expulsions turned the Jew in on himself and led him to ask forgiveness of God for the sins which he assumed were at the root of his suffering. Messianic movements, often largely a consequence of the tribulations which beset Jewish communities, gave further incentive to renewed religious fervor and "re-turning" to God. Pietist movements, such as that of Ḥasidei Ashkenaz, practiced ascetic penitential techniques to scourge the sinful flesh.

Against this background kabbalistic speculation, which associated repentance not merely with the salvation of the individual soul but with the cosmic drama of redemption, gained ground. This doctrine reached its climax in Lurianic Kabbalah, where repentance was one step, but a most essential one, in the process of *tikkun*, or rectification. Through repentance, the Jew was able to assist God in the elevation of the holy sparks entrapped in the shells and thus usher in the messianic age – the work of creation having been completed and perfected.

The 18th and 19th centuries saw the rise of two important movements in Eastern European Jewry in which the idea of repentance played somewhat different theological roles. In Ḥasidism, where the highly personal and anthropomorphic relation to the Deity, either on the part of the ḥasid himself or at least on that of the *ẓaddik*, was emphasized, the severity of the doctrine of repentance was toned down. Confidence in the loving response of God and His forgiveness helped lessen the sense of overburdening sin. By contrast the Musar movement, which may be regarded as the response of the *Mitnaggedim* to the challenge that Ḥasidism presented to traditional Judaism, played up the factor of sin, and thus repentance became the persistent task of the Jew, day after day, year after year. The turning inward to scrutinize one's deeds and motives – in essence the heart of the Musar movement – gave the follower of this movement an awareness of sin of which the average Jew or the ḥasid would be totally oblivious. This process of self-scrutiny and repentance reached its pinnacle for the follower of the Musar movement in the month of Elul, preceding the High Holidays. This month was wholly given over to soul-searching, and there are well attested cases of great exponents of the Musar movement who inflicted discomfort and even suffering on themselves as part of the self-punishment involved in genuine repentance.

Modern Developments

In the modern period, marked by a drift of Jews away from traditional forms of religion and belief in God, the idea of repentance appears in two guises. On the one hand, there is the traditionalist interpretation which still sees repentance as something of which the believing, as well as the unbelieving, Jew is in need. On the other, there is the re-interpretation of repentance as the way back to God for those who have weak roots in Judaism, or have at some stage abandoned whatever roots they had.

The traditionalist interpretation takes its most original form in the writing of A.I. *Kook who devoted a whole work to the subject of repentance (*Orot ha-Teshuvah*, 1970[5]). Kook weaves together three themes in his concept of repentance: the kabbalistic idea that repentance is not merely something on the personal level, but partakes of cosmic proportions; messianic Zionism; the "re-turning" of the individual to God. By sinning, man isolates himself from the Deity and disrupts the potential unity and harmony of all existence. Repentance is the overcoming of this isolation, and communion with God, the ideal point of man's striving. In repentance, the harmony of the world is reestablished, for the repentance of one man helps to bring the whole world back to God. Israel's return to its ancestral land is seen by Kook as repentance (returning) on the national level and a further step in the reestablishment of the unity of the creative process. The repentance of the individual Jew strengthens national repentance and return, for righteousness is the very soul of Israel.

The importance of Franz *Rosenzweig for the modern reinterpretation of the idea of repentance is first and foremost the example of his own life. Rosenzweig's personal experience of finding his way back to Judaism has come to be the paradigm of the modern *ba'al teshuvah* ("one who repents"). In 1913, he was on the verge of converting to Christianity, but while attending a Day of Atonement service in an orthodox synagogue he changed his mind and ultimately his whole life. From then on his mode of life and his writings represent the struggles and ideas of a man on the way back ("re-turning") to Judaism. Rosenzweig gradually took upon himself the yoke of the *mitzvot* and tried to find means, mainly educational, to bring other assimilated Jews to an awareness of the "inner fire of the Jewish star of redemption." Rosenzweig's conception of repentance turns on his portrayal of existential man facing God and the dialectical tension between man's anticipation of the call of God and God's love which is ultimately at the basis of such a call. Having been called by God, the man of faith enters into dialogue with Him. The turning to God is not simply this dialogic openness to Him, it also involves the attempt to fulfill the *mitzvot* as far as one can, in the hope and belief that one's ability to fulfill *mitzvot* will widen. Rosenzweig's attitude to those *mitzvot* he did not keep was "not yet," i.e., although he was at the moment not ready to observe these commandments, he hoped that at some future time he would be.

Unlike Kook, who dealt with the subject of repentance in relation to Israel's return to God and nationhood, Rosenzweig was concerned with the turning away of the individual from Western culture, specifically Christianity, back to Judaism. This feature of his thought, typical of existentialism where biographical experience and philosophy meet, colors his whole discussion of the subject. Whereas Kook is concerned with the repentance of the Jew, orthodox or otherwise, Rosenzweig speaks only to the "hyphenated" Jew, i.e., one who has been strongly influenced by non-Jewish cultural values.

In the thought of Martin *Buber the idea of repentance is essentially the turning of the whole man to God, the Eternal Thou. Though God is revealed to man in his dialogic relationships to other men and the natural world, these relationships continually move from the plane of the "I-Thou" to that of the "I-It." The relationship with God is always, and necessarily, that of "I Thou" since God is the Eternal Thou who can never become It. Yet in order to maintain this relationship with God, a total response is called for from man, a response which is often only partially forthcoming. Repentance, "returning" to God, is thus the renewed total response of "I-Thou." The influence of ḥasidic thought on Buber is apparent both in the highly personalistic approach to the Deity and in the idea that turning to God involves a relationship with him not merely in religiously separated times and places, but even in the most mundane of situations. Unlike both Kook and Rosenzweig, Buber is addressing man as man, not qua committed or even uncommitted Jew but qua "I." This is true despite his attempt to locate his philosophy within a distinctly Jewish framework – rejecting the Christian framework of an already achieved redemption.

[Alan Unterman]

BIBLIOGRAPHY: C.R. Smith, *The Biblical Doctrine of Sin* (1953); E.F. Sutcliffe, *Providence and Suffering in the Old and New Testaments* (1955); W. Eichrodt, *Theology of the Old Testament*, 2 (1967), 380–495; J. Milgrom, in: VT, 14 (1964), 169–72. RABBINIC VIEWS: S. Schechter, *Aspects of Rabbinic Theology* (1909), 293–343; G.F. Moore, *Judaism* (1958), 507–552; A. Buechler, *Studies in Sin and Atonement* (1928); A. Cohen, *Everyman's Talmud* (1949), 104–10; E.E. Urbach, *Ḥazal* (1970), 408–15; C.G. Montefiore and H. Loewe, *Rabbinic Authority* (1938), 315–33. JEWISH PHILOSOPHY: C. Nussbaum, *The Essence of Teshuvah: a Path to Repentance*, (1993); C.G. Montefiore, in: JQR, 16 (1904), 209–57; A. Rubin, in: JJSO, 16 (1965), 161–76; J.J. Petuchowski, in: *Judaism*, 17 (1968), 175–85; S.H. Bergman, *Faith and Reason* (1961), 55–141; M. Buber, *I and Thou* (1958[2]); A.I. Kook, *Orot ha-Teshuvah* (1970[5]; Eng. tr. *Rabbi Kook's Philosophy of Repentance*, 1968); N.N. Glatzer (ed.), *Franz Rosenzweig: His Life and Thought* (1953, 1961[2]); idem (ed.), *On Jewish Learning* (1955); F. Rosenzweig, *Star of Redemption* (1971), N. Rotenstreich, *Jewish Philosophy in Modern Times* (1968), 175–238; S. Schwarzschild, *Franz Rosenzweig: Guide of Reversioners* (1960).

REPHAIM (Heb. רְפָאִים). The Rephaim are known from biblical, Ugaritic, and Phoenician sources. In the Bible two uses of the term are discernible. The first is as a gentilic (e.g., Gen. 14:5; 15:20; Deut. 2:11) referring to a people distinguished by their enormous stature. Especially singled out are Og king of Bashan (Deut. 3:11) and the powerful adversaries of David's heroes (II Sam. 21:16, 18, 20). The biblical authors trace their designation to an apparently human eponym Rapha(h) (e.g., II Sam. 21:16, 18, 20; I Chron. 20:8). The Bible's emphasis on the size and might of the Rephaim is responsible for the Septuagint's renderings *gigantes* and *titanes* as well as for *gabbārē* of the Peshitta and *gibbarāyyā* of the Targums. The *Genesis Apocryphon* (21:28) on the other hand prefers the noncommital *rephāʾayyā*.

In its second use Rephaim designates "shades" or "spirits" and serves as a poetic synonym for *metim* (מֵתִים; Isa. 26:14; Ps. 88:11). It thus refers to the inhabitants of the netherworld (Prov. 9:18). This second meaning is also found in Phoenician sources. King Tabnit of Sidon curses any prospective despoiler of his tomb: "May there be no resting-place for you with the Rephaim" (H. Donner and W. Roellig, *Kanaanäische und aramäische Inschriften* (KAI, 1962), 13, lines 7–8; COS II, 182), King Eshmunazar (*ibid.*, 14, line 8; COS II, 183) employs the same formula in the plural, adding "… and may they not be buried in a grave." The chthonic aspect of the Phoenician Rephaim is made even more explicit in a neo-Punic bilingual which equates the לעל [נם] אראפאם with *dis manibus sacrum* KAI (*ibid.*, 117, line 1).

The Ugaritic material is most problematic because the relevant texts referring to the *rpum* are fragmentary and difficult to interpret. These *rpum*, like their Phoenician counterparts, are divine in nature, being referred to as *ilnym* (I AB 6:46 ff.; Pritchard, Texts, 141; COS I, 357–58), literally "divine ones?" (cf. Heb. *eʾlohim*, "ghost[s]," literally "divine being[s]" (I Sam. 28:13; Isa. 8:19, 21). There is, however, no clear indication that the *rpum* are chthonic deities. Moreover, they seem to have a military function. One of their number is referred to as a *mhr*, the Ugaritic term for soldier, and the *rpum* are described as riding in chariots. The nonliterary Ugaritic texts mention a guild of *bn rpiym* who presumably were a group under the patronage of the divine *rpum*, as has been pointed out by B. Margulies (Margalit). In addition, the Ugaritic hero Dnil is described as *mt rpi* which may indicate his membership in such a group. (Marguiles errs in equating this last epithet with the alleged *ṣābe bilaṭi* which should be read *tillati* and which is not restricted to Canaan.) Another Ugaritic hero, Keret, is described as belonging to the *rpi arṣ* – the Rephaim of the land – a term which is paralleled by the *qbṣ dtn*, the group associated with Ditanu.

The existence of a god named *Rpu* has long been indicated by personal names such as *Abrpu* (C.H. Gordon, *Ugaritic Textbook* (1965), 311, line 10; Ditriech and Loretz, 2). This is now corroborated by the publication of a text (Ras Shamra 24. 252) that mentions *rpu mlk ʿlm*, "Rpu the eternal king" (Dietrich and Loretz, 187), described appropriately as *gṯr*, "mighty" (cf. Akk. *gašru*). Though this text is not free of difficulties, *Rpu* seems to be mentioned along with the *r[pi] arṣ* possibly as their patron. If the admittedly hypothetical interpretation of the Ugaritic material is correct, the biblical tradition of Rephaim as mighty warriors can be understood. Their huge stature would contribute to their military prowess. Furthermore, the biblical eponym Rapha(h) can be considered as an undeified god *Rpu*, more in keeping with biblical thought.

The Hebrew and Phoenician use of *Rephaim* as "shade, spirit," however, remains problematic. Various attempts have been made to discover an underlying etymology which would account for the development. The presence of an eponym in both Hebrew and Ugaritic, however, suggests that the ancients were unaware of the connection between Rephaim and any verbal root. It should further be noted that the verb *rpʾ* is unknown in Ugaritic outside of the onomastica. Notions such as "heal" and "gather" or "unite" attested in other Semitic languages for the root *rpʾ* were often adduced to explain Rephaim, but in Ugaritic these words are not connected with the root *rpʾ*. In Ugaritic the word for "heal" is *bny* while that for "gather" is *ʾsp, ḥpš* and *ʿdn*, in reference to plants, straw, and troops respectively.

BIBLIOGRAPHY: H.L. Ginsberg, *Legend of Keret* (1941), 23, 41; J. Gray, in: PEQ, 81 (1949), 127–39; 84 (1952), 39–41; A. Jirku, in: ZAW,

77 (1965), 82–83; J.C. de Moor, in: *Ugarit Forschungen*, 1 (1969); H. Mueller, *ibid.* **ADD. BIBLIOGRAPHY:** B. Margulies (Margalit), in: JBL, 89 (1970), 292–304; D. Pardee, in: *Ugarit Forschungen*, 15 (1983), 127–40; K. van der Toorn, CBQ, 52 (1990), 203–22; idem, in: BiOr, 48 (1991), 40–66; H. Rouillard, DDD, 692–700; M. Dietrich and O. Loretz, *Wordlist of the Cuneiform Alphabetic Texts from Ugarit…* (1996); W. Pitard, in: W. Watson and N. Wyatt (eds.), *Handbook of Ugaritic Studies* (1999), 259–86.

[S. David Sperling]

REPHIDIM (Heb. רְפִידִם, רְפִידִים), a stopping place of the Israelites on their way from Egypt, situated between the Wilderness of Sin and the Wilderness of Sinai (Ex. 17:1; 19:2; Num. 33:14–15). In Rephidim the lack of water caused the people to find fault with Moses and to challenge his position of leadership. Moses struck "a rock at Horeb" and water gushed forth. The place came to be known as Massah and Meribah (Ex. 17:1–7). In a parallel account (Num. 20) the place where this occurred is said to be *Kadesh. The defeat of the *Amalekites which later took place at Rephidim was effected by virtue of the force mustered by Joshua and Moses who kept his hands raised during the whole course of the battle. God's oath to wipe out Amalek was commemorated by an altar, named "YHWH is my ensign" (Heb. ה׳ נִסִּי; Ex. 17:8–16), erected at the spot.

No definite evidence has been forwarded for the exact site of Rephidim, which depends on the location of Mt. *Sinai. Most scholars who identify Mt. Sinai with Jebel Musa locate Rephidim in Wadi Fīrān, or, according to Abel, at Wadi Rafayd or Jebel Rafayd, about 22 mi. (36 km.) southeast of el-Arish.

BIBLIOGRAPHY: Abel, Géog, 2 (1938), 213; C.H. Cornill, in: ZAW, 11 (1891), 20ff.; H. Gressmann, *Mose und seine Zeit* (1913), 150ff.; C.J. Jarvis, *Yesterday and To-Day in Sinai* (1933), 174–5: S. Lehming, in: ZAW, 73 (1961), 71–77; C.L. Woolley and T.E. Lawrence, in: *Annual of the Palestine Exploration Fund*, 3 (1914–15), 62ff.

REPUBLICAN JEWISH COALITION. Formerly known as the National Jewish Coalition, the RJC began in 1985 as an effort by senior Jewish leaders to craft positive and productive relationships with Republican Party officials, decision-makers, and opinion leaders, and to serve as a bridge between the Republican Party and the Jewish community. RJC leaders worked on the first significant efforts to promote the GOP as a community that should and would welcome Americans Jews. Across a range of foreign and domestic issues, and over time, the national Jewish political conversation has, indeed, broadened.

In 2005 RJC was at the forefront of efforts within the Jewish community to work closely with a GOP White House and U.S. Congress, through its legislative affairs committee, and its continuing grassroots, media and public affairs outreach efforts. As well, the RJC (and its sister non-profit educational organization, the Jewish Policy Center) worked to communicate the GOP message to the Jewish community, with special focus on Israel, national security, and economic growth issues.

The national Jewish vote for Republican presidential candidates grew from 11 percent in 1992, to 16 percent in 1996, to 19 percent in 2000, to over 25 percent in 2004. Significant pockets of Jewish Republican support had begun to appear in the Orthodox, Persian, and Russian Jewish communities, and future growth was expected among younger Jews, many of whom have experienced sharp antisemitism from the Left on campuses.

Beyond this vote trend, however, lay a story of successful political fundraising. Many of the top donors to the presidential and congressional candidacies of the Jewish community's best friends in Washington, D.C., were affiliated with the RJC and the RJC PAC (Political Action Committee). Interestingly, many credited the 1998 RJC governors trip to Israel, wherein then-Texas governor George W. Bush and General Ariel Sharon shared a famous helicopter tour over the tiny Jewish state, as a signal moment in the formation of the political and ideological bond between the two individuals that would be critical during the very difficult and dangerous period of the second Intifada in Israel, rising antisemitism in Europe, and the War on Terror.

Early in the Bush Administration, the RJC national board embarked on an ambitious plan to grow its grassroots base. From six chapters in 2000, the RJC opened regional offices in California, Florida, New York, and Pennsylvania, and had over 21,000 members in 41 chapters by 2005.

With the appearance of President Bush at the RJC 20th anniversary luncheon on September 21, 2005, which honored Bernard Marcus, a founder of Home Depot; Sheldon Adelson, the Las Vegas hotel magnate; and Ken Mehlman, chairman of the Republican National Committee, the RJC had secured itself as an important and effective voice in both Washington and within the American Jewish community. It has assured visibility for Jews – a constituency, which in the last two thirds of the 20th century had been traditionally identified with the Democratic Party – within Republican circles.

[Larry Greenfield (2nd ed.)]

RESEN (Heb. רֶסֶן), according to Genesis 10:12, one of the cities (?) which Nimrod built "between Nineveh and Calah, the latter is the great[er] city." The verse describes the situation of the cities in the "Assyrian triangle" (inner Assyria) in the latter part of the second millennium, when Calah was still a more important city than Nineveh (cf. the differences of opinion between Rashi and Ibn Ezra). While the traditional interpretation of the verse takes Resen to be the name of a city like Calah and Nineveh, other interpretations have been advanced.

According to one possibility, Resen is related to the Akkadian stem *rsn* and is derived from the verb *rasānu or resēnu*, "to wash, to irrigate (?)," whence the noun *risnu*, "washing, cleansing." A second, more fruitful possibility is that Resen was part of a waterwork (standing between Nineveh and Calah). This suggestion is advanced by D. Dossin and E.A. Speiser, who interpreted Resen as a sandhi of the original *rēš īnī* or the Assyrian *rēš ēne* (Heb. ראש העין) meaning, especially in Assyrian, "source of water, spring." The term exists not only as a common noun (see *Chicago Assyrian Dictionary*, 7 (1960),

158) but also as an actual place-name, URU ("city") *Re-eš-e-ne* (see D.D. Luckenbill, *The Annals of Sennacherib* (1924), 79:91), near Nineveh, which was a station of the aqueduct to Nineveh reconstructed by Sennacherib.

BIBLIOGRAPHY: Th. Jacobsen and S. Lloyd, *Sennacherib's Aqueduct at Jerwan* (1935); E.A. Speiser, *Genesis* (1964), 68; S. Parpola, *Neo-Assyrian Toponyms* (1970), 293.

[Pinhas Artzi]

RESH (Heb. ר; רֵישׁ), the twentieth letter of the Hebrew alphabet; its numerical value is 200. The initial form of this letter – in the early Proto-Canaanite and Proto-Sinaitic inscriptions – is a pictograph of a human head. The Greek *rho* seems to indicate that the Canaanite name of the letter was *rosh*, while *resh* = "head" in Aramaic.

In the late Proto-Canaanite script the pictograph developed into a linear form 𐤓, which was preserved in the Greek P. Another Archaic Greek variant was the ancestor of the Latin R.

While the ancient Hebrew script preserved the closed top of the *resh* (hence Samaritan ࠓ), the Phoenician cursive opened the circular head at its lower part and the Aramaic script opened the top of the letter (compare with Aramaic *bet, dalet,* and *'ayin*) already in the late eighth century B.C.E. Later there was a tendency to curve the shoulder and thus the Jewish *resh* ר was developed.

As *resh* and *dalet* resemble each other, in some scripts both were often written in the same way. In Syriac only diaritic marks distinguish between them: ܕ = *dalet;* ܪ = *resh.* In the Nabatean cursive and, hence, in the Arabic script, the *resh* has been assimilated with the *zayin.* Therefore a diacritic point above the *za* (ز) distinguishes it from the *ra* (ر). See *Alphabet, Hebrew.

[Joseph Naveh]

RESHEPH (Heb. רֶשֶׁף), Canaanite "netherworld" god of the pest (appearing as an element in Mari and Sargonic personal names; see Huffmon, in bibl.). As a god, Resheph did not have a significant place in the pantheon of Ugarit, since his name was semantically assimilated in the word *ršp*, "pestilence" (see "The Legend of Keret," trans. by H.L. Ginsberg, in: Pritchard, Texts, 143, line 19, where *ršp* is rendered by "pestilence"). In addition, the name occurs as an element in Ugaritic personal names. In the Ugaritic-Akkadian god list (see *Ugaritica*, 5 (1965), 45:26) Resheph is identified with Nergal, the Akkadian god of the netherworld and pestilence (for further data cf. *ibid.*, p. 57). One mythological fragment from Ugarit reads: *b'l ḥṣ ršp*, "Resheph, the lord of arrow."

In late bilingual inscriptions from the Phoenician-Hellenic cult of Cyprus, Resheph is identified with Apollo (cf. also the place-name Arsuf = Apollonia). In one of the Amarna letters (EA 35:13) the logogram *MAŠ.MAŠ* (= Nergal, the pest god) can be read "Resheph" (cf. also *Ugaritica*, 5 (1965), 667; AFO, 21 (1966), 59). Like the above-mentioned fragment from Ugarit, Phoenician inscriptions from Cyprus also read *ršp ḥṣ* ("Resheph at the arrow").

Resheph was an important god in the Aramaic pantheon of the eighth century B.C.E. (see, e.g., the inscription of Panammu I; H. Donner and W. Roellig, *Kanaanaeische und aramaeische Inschriften*, 1 (1967), p. 38 no. 214: 1, where the divine names Hadad and El are followed by Resheph). A Hittite-Phoenician bilingual inscription from Karatepe carries the words *ršp ṣprm*, "Resheph of the birds" (like "arrow," a figure of speech for swiftness). An orthostat found at Karatepe features a god with a bird in his hands.

In Egypt, from the 18th Dynasty on, Resheph was known as the god of war (see Pritchard, Pictures, no. 473, where Resheph appears together with Qadeš and 'Anat; see also no. 474, no. 476; cf. further in bibl.) and the Pharaoh as a warrior is compared to him. The god Mikal of Beth-Shean, whom inscriptions from Cyprus connect with Resheph, is portrayed with similar characteristics (see Pritchard, Pictures, no. 487).

In the Bible

While Resheph is not mentioned in the Bible as a god, the word *reshef* appears in various uses:

(a) Resheph as a personal name in I Chronicles 7:25 (some scholars assume that there is some confusion here, questioning the probability of a Canaanite theophoric personal name in an Ephraimite family; but the name may not necessarily mean the Canaanite god; see below);

(b) in the general meanings of: "flame" (of true love, jealousy; Song 8:6); "arrow," i.e., "'flame' of the bow" (*rishpe qeshet*, Ps. 76:4);

(c) a synonym of *dever*, "pestilence" (Deut. 32:24; LXX "bird," thus also the traditional interpretation, Ex. R. 12:4; Hab. 3:5; cf. Ps. 78:48);

(d) "bird"

(?) (Job 5:7; cf. Ber. 5a: *reshef* means demons (?) and (burning) pains).

BIBLIOGRAPHY: J. Leibovitch, in: *Annales du service des antiquités de l'Égypte*, 48 (1948), 435–44; A. Caquot, in: *Semitica*, 6 (1956), 53–68; M. Dahood, in: *Studi Semitici*, 1 (1958), 83–86; H.B. Huffmon, *Amorite Personal Names in the Mari Texts* (1965), 263 (incl. bibl.); W. Helck, *Geschichte des alten Aegypten* (1968), 161.

[Pinḥas Artzi]

RESHEVSKY, SAMUEL HERMAN (1911–1992), U.S. chess master. Born in Poland, Reshevsky was a child prodigy. In 1919–20 he gave successful simultaneous displays against large numbers of strong opponents in Europe and America. During the same period he fared well in individual games, drawing against David Janowski. After settling in America he gave up chess during his adolescence in order to continue his education. He returned to the game in the 1930s and won the championship of the United States several times against opposition which included Reuben *Fine and Isaac Kashdan. He also won many of the famous tournaments in the United States, Latin America, and Britain. Against the very strongest opposition Reshevsky did well, but not as well as his great ability would suggest. Though a player of genius, in tournament play he would lose games "on the clock" because of the long spells of concentration demanded by his perfectionism. This explains his failure to win several candidates tournaments, including the world championship tourney in 1948 in which he was defeated by Mikhail Botvinnik.

Reshevsky's published collection of his own games, *Reshevsky's Best Games of Chess* (1960), is usefully annotated. He also wrote *How Chess Games are Won* (1962) and *The Art of Positional Play* (1978). An Orthodox Jew, Reshevsky always subordinated his chess life to his religious observances.

[Gerald Abrahams]

RESH KALLAH (Heb. רֵישׁ כַּלָּה), title that was awarded to the leading sages in Babylonian academies during the talmudic and geonic periods. R. Nathan b. Isaac *ha-Bavli (Neubauer Chronicles, 2 (1895), 87–88), in his description of the seating order of the *ḥakhamim* observed in the Babylonian academies, also discusses the status of the *resh kallah*. In Babylonian academies the 70 outstanding *ḥakhamim* were seated in the first seven rows, ten to a row, in order of their importance; the first and most important row was occupied by seven *reshei kallah*, each of whom was in charge of one row of *ḥakhamim*. The specific duty of the *reshei kallah* was to preach publicly in the academy. The Babylonian Talmud mentions by name only two *ḥakhamim* who were *reshei kallah*: R. Naḥman b. *Isaac (BB 22a) and R. *Abbahu (Ḥul. 49a). In talmudic times the *reshei kallah* were accustomed to preach only during the *kallah months, whereas in the geonic period the *reshei kallah* were accustomed to give sermons also on the rest of the Sabbaths. In the geonic period the *resh kallah* also bore the title of *alluf. In this period the title was awarded also to *ḥakhamim* who excelled in their studies in the academy, as well as *ḥakhamim* who resided in places other than Babylonia, such as Kairouan and Spain (e.g., Ḥisdai ibn *Shaprut). In the prayer *Yekum Purkan*, composed in the geonic period, the *reshei kallah* are mentioned before the exilarchs, the academy heads, and the *dayyanim*, although the latter were superior to the *reshei kallah* in rank; the reason for the *reshei kallah's* precedence here is not known.

BIBLIOGRAPHY: S.A. Poznański, in: *Ha-Kedem*, 2 (1908), 91–113 (Heb. pt.); J.Z. Lauterbach, in: *Hebrew Union College Jubilee Volume* (1925), 218ff.; A. Hildesheimer, in: *Festschrift... Jakob Freimann* (1937), 65–67 (Heb. pt.); S. Krauss, in: *Tarbiz*, 20 (1950), 131ff.; *She'iltot de-Rav Aḥai Ga'on* ed. by S.K. Mirsky, 1 (1959), 9–10 (introd.).

[Abraham David]

RESHUT (Heb. רְשׁוּת), a word found extensively in rabbinic literature and having three distinct and different connotations: authority, domain, and a duty which is optional or voluntary, in contrast to an obligatory duty, called *ḥovah*.

Reshut as Authority

The term *reshut* is used in rabbinic literature in the sense of power and authority, such as "Seek not acquaintance with the *reshut*," i.e., ruling power (Avot 1:10), or "Six things serve man; over three he has *reshut* and over three he has no *reshut*; over the eye, the ear, and the nose he has no *reshut*; over the mouth, the hand, the foot he has *reshut*" (Gen. R. 67:3).

Reshut as Domain

From this stems the concept of *reshut ha-yaḥid* to designate an area over which the individual has authority, i.e., a private domain, in contrast to *reshut ha-rabbim*, a public domain. The distinction is found mainly in the laws of Sabbath, with regard to the permissibility of transferring objects from one domain to another, and in connection with torts. Thus the Tosefta (Shab. 1:1) states: "Four domains are to be distinguished in connection with the Sabbath: the private domain [*reshut hayaḥid*], the public domain [*reshut ha-rabbim*], the semipublic domain [*karmelit*], and the exempted domain [*mekom petor*]" (also Maim. Yad, Shabbat, 14: 1). Similarly, in connection with torts, a differentiation is made between private and public domains. For instance the owner of an animal is liable for the damage done by it in the private domain of another. If, however, the damage is done in a public domain, to which everyone has the right of access, such as an open field or a marketplace, the owner is liable only if the animal gores or bites, since it has no right to cause damage to the people in the locality; but he is exempt from damage caused by the animal grazing or treading (cf. Maim. Yad, Nizkei Mamon, 1:7–8).

Reshut in the Sense of an Optional or Voluntary Duty

In the Talmud there is a difference of opinion between R. Joshua and Rabban Gamaliel as to whether the evening prayer is optional (*reshut*) or obligatory (*ḥovah*; Ber. 27b). A similar distinction is made between an optional war (to enlarge the borders of Israel) in contrast to an obligatory war, like that against *Amalek or Joshua's conquest of the land (Sot. 8:7). The word *reshut* is also used in medieval liturgical poetry (**piyyut*) for the introductory poem by the cantor who begs "permission" (*reshut*) despite his personal unworthiness to represent, and intercede for, the congregation.

[Abraham Arzi]

RESNICK, SALOMON (1894–1946), writer, journalist, lecturer, translator from Yiddish into Spanish, and community leader. Born in Russia, he immigrated to Argentina in 1902 as his father, Rabbi Moses Resnick, was hired by the JCA (Jewish Colonization Association) to serve the religious needs of the agricultural colonies. There, Salomon Resnick became a Spanish teacher. In 1914, he moved to Buenos Aires, where he started his literary career in the journal *Juventud*; in 1917 he joined the magazine *Vida Nuestra* publishing essays, articles, and translations from Yiddish writers. In 1918 he joined the founders of the daily Yiddish *Di Presse* as a journalist and editor; and from 1923 to 1933 he established and edited with Leon Kibrick the Spanish weekly *Mundo Israelita*, still appearing in the early 21st century. In 1923 Resnick launched the monthly Spanish journal *Judaica*, editing it until his death; this was his most outstanding project devoted to the promotion of Jewish culture through the publication of scholarly articles from all lines of thought, both Jewish and non-Jewish. As a community leader in 1923, Salomon Resnick participated in the foundation of the Sociedad Hebraica Argentina, a cultural and sport center oriented to Spanish-speaking Jews. He was named director of its newly created library. In 1924 Resnick was appointed director of public information of JCA; in 1938 he took part in the foundation of the Argentinean branch of YIVO – Yiddishn Wisnshaftlechn Institute (Jewish Research Institute) and was elected its first president; and from 1944 until his death he held the position of local director of the JDC – Joint Distribution Committee, Public Relations Office. He wrote four books: *Dos formas de nacionalismo espiritual judío: Ajad Haam y Dubnow* (1931), *La literatura de la post-guerra* (1931), *Esquema de la literatura judía* (1933), and *Cinco ensayos sobre temas judíos* (1943). His translations include the writings of most important Yiddish writers, such as Sholem *Asch, *Shalom Aleichem, Sholem Yankev *Abramovitsh (Mendele Mokher Seforim), and I.L. *Peretz. Resnick has been recognized as the preeminent expert in the Spanish version and interpretation of Yiddish literature. Over the years, he received many posthumous tributes in Latin America and Israel. His personal library was donated to Tel Aviv University by his family.

BIBLIOGRAPHY: *Judaica* (1933–1946); *Noaj* (1997).

[Rosa Perla Resnick (2nd ed.)]

RESNICK, ZVI (Hirsh) YOSEF HAKOHEN (1841–1912), Russian rabbi and *rosh yeshivah* also known as "Rebbe Hirsh Meitshitzer" (apparently from Molczada, the birthplace of his wife). Resnick taught in Slonim for many years, where his reputation grew to such an extent that he was popularly referred to as "The Slonimer" and in 1894 he was appointed head of the famous Suwalki yeshivah. Ohel Yiẓhak, established by Rabbi Isaac Eisik *Wildmann, holding the position until his death.

Resnick rejected urgent requests to publish his teachings and commentaries on the grounds that the time involved would detract from his study. Many of his teachings, however, are to be found in the works of his son, Rabbi Menahem Hakohen *Risikoff.

BIBLIOGRAPHY: B. Kaplinski, *Pinkas Zetel* (1957); B. Ayalon (ed.), *Yizkor Book Meitshet* (1973), 119–20; S. Gottlieb, *Ohelei Shem* (Pinsk, 1912); *Yizker Bukh Suvalk* (1961); M. Risikoff, *Mitorath Zvi Joseph* (1939), intro.

RESNIK, JUDITH ARLENE (1949–1986), U.S. scientist and astronaut and the second American woman to travel in space. Born in Akron, Ohio, to Marvin and Sarah Polens Resnik, she was an outstanding student and a talented classical pianist who received a doctorate in electrical engineering from the University of Maryland in 1977. An early marriage to Michael Oldak, a fellow student, ended in divorce in 1975. Resnik was recruited by the National Aeronautics and Space Administration for astronaut training in 1978. At NASA she worked on a number of projects in support of Orbiter development, including experiment software, the Remote Manipulator System (RMS), and training techniques. In 1984 Resnik served on the crew of the Orbitor *Discovery*, logging just short of 145 hours in space. The crew earned the name "Icebusters" in successfully removing hazardous ice particles from the Orbiter using the Remote Manipulator System. Resnik was killed with her six fellow crew members when the space shuttle *Challenger* exploded shortly after launch on January 28, 1986. She was posthumously awarded the Congressional Space Medal of Honor.

[Judith R. Baskin (2nd ed.)]

RESNIK, REGINA (1923–), U.S. mezzo-soprano singer. Born in New York City to Ukrainian parents, Resnik graduated from Hunter College, where she sang in Gilbert and Sullivan operettas. She studied as a soprano with Rosalie Miller, who introduced her to the conductor Fritz Busch, under whom she sang the part of Lady Macbeth in Verdi's opera (1942). In 1943, she reached the finals of the Metropolitan Opera Company's Auditions of the Air, but instead of finishing the competition, chose to sing the leading soprano parts in *Fidelio* and *Der Fliegende Hollaender* in Mexico City. In 1944, as the only woman finalist in the same competition, she received a contract for the 1944–45 season from the Metropolitan, where she made her debut as Leonora in *Il Trovatore.* For the next 30 years, she sang many soprano parts at the Metropolitan, including Ellen Orford in the New York premiére of Britten's *Peter Grimes*, Alice Ford in *Falstaff* under Beecham, and Sieglinde in *Die Walkuere* (she also sang this part at Bayreuth in 1953 and Fricka in 1961). Between 1953 and 1955 she took on several mezzo-soprano roles such as Azucena, Eboli and Herodias (*Salome*); and at the end of this period she decided to adapt her repertory to that of a mezzo-soprano. Her second debut took place at the Metropolitan Opera as Marina in *Boris Gudonov.* In 1957, she first appeared at Covent Garden as Carmen, and was hailed – as she was to be all over Europe and America – as one of the finest living exponents of the part; from then on she sang in almost every major operatic capital in the world. Admired as much for the gripping theatricality of her acting as for the warmth of her voice, Resnik was also acclaimed as Clytemnestra in Strauss's *Elektra*, Mistress Quickly in *Falstaff*, and Amneris in *Aida*. In later years, she turned to producing opera, such as *Elektra* at the Teatro la Fenice in Venice (1971). A third facet of her career was as stage director, with her husband Arbit Blatas as scenic and costume designer. She directed *Carmen* in Hamburg in 1971 and other works, such as *Salome*, *Falstaff*, and *The Bear and the Medium*. Among her many recordings are the parts written for the characters Sieglinde (1953, Bayreuth), Carmen, Clytemnestra and Mistress Quickly. She also acted in films.

BIBLIOGRAPHY: Grove Music Online.

[Max Loppert / Israela Stein (2nd ed.)]

RESPONSA (Heb. שְׁאֵלוֹת וּתְשׁוּבוֹת; lit. "queries and replies"), a rabbinic term denoting an exchange of letters in which one party consults another on a halakhic matter. Such responsa are already mentioned in the Talmud, which tells of an inquiry touching upon halakhic practice that had been sent to the father of *Samuel (Yev. 105a). It relates of Samuel that he sent to Johanan "13 camels" (some Mss. read גְּוָלִם "parchments" for גְּמַלִּים "camels") laden with questions concerning *terefot* (Ḥul. 95b). The same passage speaks of a ramified halakhic correspondence that took place between Johanan in Ereẓ Israel and Rav and Samuel in Babylon. Such "letters," of which the *amora* *Avin wrote many, constituted a general exchange of opinion in *halakhah* and did not necessarily bear the exact character of "query" and "reply" in the classical sense; they may be considered the inception of the responsa literature. The major novelty lay in the committing of halakhic subjects to writing, the prohibition against committing to writing words transmitted orally (Git. 60b) still being in force at the time. The Talmud (Sanh. 29a) speaks of a litigant who claimed that he could bring a letter from Ereẓ Israel which would support his view, the allusion being to a written "responsum" obtained on presentation of the facts of the case before the respondent in a distant locality.

The Geonic Period

The beginning of responsa literature as a literary and historical phenomenon of important dimensions, however, took place in the middle of the geonic period, when it played a decisive part in the process of disseminating the Oral Law and establishing the Babylonian Talmud as the sole authority in the life of the Jewish people, who were becoming ever more widely dispersed as a result of the Islamic conquests. The Jews of the Diaspora outside Babylon, already strangers to the language and format of the Talmud, turned to the scholars of the Babylonian academies, whom they had always regarded as their spiritual leaders, asking them to send them "such and such a tractate or chapter" together with "its explanation." They also turned to them for decisions on the many disputes which arose continually between different local scholars and on new halakhic problems for which they could find no precedent. Nor were problems wanting on scriptural subjects, traditions, beliefs, and opinions. Accordingly geonic responsa are divisible into: very short responsa, sometimes consisting of only one or two words, such as the earliest surviving responsa, those by *Yehudai Gaon; and responsa containing the exposition of an entire book, chapter, or topic. There was also, understandably, an intermediate group – the most common – of responsa of average scope, but most of these, too, tended toward extreme brevity. The second group mentioned, the "monographic," becomes more prominent toward the end of the geonic period, from *Saadiah Gaon onward, a classical example of this group (not on a halakhic topic) being the *Iggeret de-Rav *Sherira Ga'on*, written in response to an inquiry by *Jacob b. Nissim of Kairouan.

Of the tens of thousands of geonic responsa, only a small portion has been published in the various collections of geonic responsa. The major portion remains in the Cairo *Genizah* fragments and scholars are still engaged in publishing them. More than half the total of the known geonic responsa was written during the last generations of the geonic period, the most prolific writers being Sherira and his son *Hai. During this period of 300 years (750–1050), responsa literature embraced almost every aspect of Jewish life. Apart from issues of practical *halakhah*, they included explanations of verses and of talmudic themes, theological and ideological discourses, and various chronographic, medical, and scientific discussions, all written at the request of individuals or communities who desired this knowledge, either for the needs of the community or for their polemics with the *Karaites and with their Muslim neighbors. Generally speaking, the queries were assembled by the representatives of the yeshivot from the various Jewish centers of Spain, the countries of North Africa, and those surrounding Ereẓ Israel, to as far as Yemen in the south. These then transmitted them, along with the monetary donation of the communities for the financing and maintenance of the yeshivot, by way of the ramified routes of the postal caravan which passed through Egypt on its way to Babylonia. The representatives, who were usually outstanding scholars, sifted the queries, improved and corrected their language, and as far as possible refrained from answering questions to which answers had already been received on a previous occasion. The answers were copied by the representatives, several copies being preserved in anticipation of similar queries in the future. The yeshivah archives were often drawn upon by later *geonim* for their own decisions. That a large part of this material has been preserved in the Cairo *Genizah* is due to the fact that Egypt served as the postal junction of that time.

The yeshivot followed a set procedure for dealing with queries. In general hundreds of such questions were read and discussed at the yeshivah during each of the two months of **kallah* in the presence of the full forum of its scholars and pupils. At the conclusion of the discussion the yeshivah scribe wrote the decision of the head of the yeshivah at his dictation, and all the senior members of the yeshivah signed it. Urgent queries which could not be delayed were discussed and decided by the *gaon* as soon as they were received. In view of the fact that the questioners generally sent groups of queries, sometimes unrelated to one another, the reply of the *gaon* usually consisted of many sections. The scant mention of previous *geonim* and their rulings in the responsa stems from a desire to give them the character of impersonal finality, representative of the view of the yeshivah as a whole. The geonic responsa, which in themselves and in their many copies had begun to pile up by their thousands in the different centers of the postal route and outside it, were already collected in early times by various individuals into *kovaẓim* ("collections") or *kunteresim* ("booklets"), according to differing criteria: subject matter, the names of the respondents, order of tractates, etc. As a result, responsa which had comprised a single entity when written were divided up by the copyists and attached to different booklets piecemeal. The great number of such secondary booklets and the utter confusion in the names of the respondents, which they carelessly transcribed as a result of the arbitrary order prevailing in them and among their copyists, has rendered the problem of determining the authorship of various responsa one of the most difficult problems in present-day research into geonic responsa. In addition, the habit of most copyists of omitting those opening lines of the questions and answers which had no halakhic significance has increased the problem of identification. Much help is obtained, however, from the lists of responsa (without the responsa themselves) prepared by these copyists for themselves and preserved in the *Genizah*, in which the opening words of the responsa and the name of the author are noted.

Responsa of the Rishonim

Responsa literature acquired a different character during the period of the **rishonim*. Their contents became more and more confined to talmudic *halakhah*; the responsa became by degrees more and more detailed and lengthy, and the discussion of the parallel talmudic themes, whether closely or distantly related to the topic, grew correspondingly longer and all within the context of a definitive dependence upon the rulings of the *geonim* which had already become part of binding *halakhah*, almost like the Talmud itself, especially in the regions of Spain and North Africa. The responsa of the *rishonim* contain for the first time such expressions of humility as "in my humble opinion," "may the Merciful One save us from the abyss of judgment," and the like, and such admissions as that the understanding of a certain theme, or the determination of a correct reading, "requires further thought." One also encounters for the first time, in the middle of this period, an exchange of responsa between rabbis in different countries, for the purpose of clarifying and reinforcing their rulings and in order to diminish their responsibility in the event of their erring (cf. Hor. 3b). This correspondence also had great value in strengthening the ties between different localities. In contrast to geonic responsa, in which the mention of inter-geonic disputes is very slight (a factor to a certain extent attributable to the insistence of the *geonim* that their questioners were not to address the same query to more than one yeshivah), the responsa of the *rishonim* are filled with differences of opinion – another sign of the dwindling authority of the rabbis from the close of the geonic period.

A substantial number of responsa or remnants thereof from the period of the *rishonim* – some among the earliest – have already been published. Many of the numerous responsa of *Ḥanokh b. Moses and *Moses b. Ḥanokh, of the first generation of Spanish rabbis, for instance, have been published in various collections, especially in the compilation *Teshuvot Ge'onei Mizraḥ u-Ma'arav* (1888). Some of the responsa of *Gershom b. Judah, "the Light of the Exile," were published by S. Eidelberg (1955). Similarly most of Rashi's extant responsa and remnants of others were collected by I. Elfenbein (1943). Other responsa of the early *rishonim* of France and Germany were published in the *Teshuvot Ḥakhmei Ẓarefat ve-Loter* (1881). The situation is different with respect to North Africa, the responsa of whose scholars from the middle of the tenth century and for a considerable time afterward not being preserved in collected form or in great numbers. There are scattered specimens of these, especially in J. Hildesheimer's edition of the *Halakhot Gedolot* (1886–92) and in various *Genizah* fragments. The responsa of Isaac *Alfasi (the Rif) are chiefly from his last years in Spain.

The *rishonim* of France and Germany did not, in general, make collections of their responsa and such collections in our possession represent the work of their pupils and pupils' pupils, who assembled and edited the comprehensive literary legacy of their teachers. This is the case, for example, with the responsa of Jacob *Tam, which were incorporated by his pupils into his *Sefer ha-Yashar*, together with his novellae, rulings, glosses, etc.; with those of *Eliezer b. Nathan of Mainz; and also, in fact, with the various volumes of responsa which contain the complete literary heritage of *Meir b. Baruch (MaHaRaM) of Rothenburg. In contrast to the geonic responsa, specific collections of the responsa of *rishonim* have not been collected or arranged. This task was first undertaken by modern scholarship, and the work is still being pursued. The situation was slightly different in the countries of Spain and in the later period in North Africa, where many of the scholars, or their children, or pupils made collections of their responsa. To this can be attributed the large collections of responsa of Solomon b. Abraham *Adret (Rashba) and *Asher b. Jehiel (Rosh or Asheri), among Spanish scholars, and of *Isaac b. Sheshet (Ribash), Simeon b. Ẓemaḥ (Rashbaẓ), and Solomon b. Simeon (Rashbash) *Duran of North Africa, which were well preserved and frequently republished. Of the responsa of other Spanish scholars, however, such as *Naḥmanides (Ramban), Meir *Abulafia (Ramah), *Yom Tov b. Abraham Ishbili (Ritba), and others, only a minute portion has remained, and no additional manuscripts have been discovered.

Only a modicum of the responsa of *rishonim* has been published in scholarly editions, especially noteworthy among which are the numerous editions of the responsa of Maimonides (Rambam), the most recent and best being that of J. Blau (1957–61); and that of his son, *Abraham b. Moses b. Maimon (by A.H. Freimann, 1937). The fate of the Provençal scholars was completely different. Until very recent years hardly a single book of responsa by one of their outstanding scholars had been published. Only recently have relatively limited collections been published of the responsa of *Abraham b. David of Posquières (Rabad) and Abraham b. Isaac of Narbonne (Rabi [ראב״י]).

Until about the 16th century no self-inspired questions are found in rabbinic literature (with the single exception of the *She'iltot* of *Aḥa (Aḥai), which was also the first Hebrew book to be composed after the completion of the Talmud). They began to reach respectable proportions, however, in the middle of the 17th century, when the correspondence style became the accepted fashion among *maskilim*. For an analysis of this phenomenon see below.

Historical Significance of the Responsa

A special importance attaches to responsa as a primary source for knowledge of the history of the Jews in the various countries. Responsa literature has one advantage over such other accepted historical sources as chronographies, official documents, biographies, etc., since the evidence it affords is undesigned, without any specific historical purpose or intention. Moreover, while in general the accepted sources preserve only important events, the responsa echo the humdrum daily life of the ordinary person, his folkways, beliefs, dialects, and, of particular importance, details about the lives of villagers and townsmen whose identity is completely blurred in the usual sources. Since the beginning of modern Jewish *historiography the responsa literature has been drawn upon for this purpose. However, it is only during recent decades that monographs have been devoted both to individual collections of responsa which have been analyzed from the standpoint of their contents as books, and from the point of view of the study of a particular subject. Generally speaking, connected with this research is a study of the biography of the author of the responsa, and as a result, the history of the rabbinate has also benefited. The following works are examples: I. Epstein, *The Responsa of Rabbi Solomon ben Adreth of Barcelona… as a Source of the History of Spain* (1925); idem, *The Responsa of Rabbi Simon ben Ẓemaḥ of Duran as a Source of the History of the Jews of North Africa* (1930); A.M. Hershman, *Rabbi Isaac ben Sheshet Perfet and his Times* (1943); S. Eidelberg, *Jewish Life in Austria in the XVth century as Reflected in the Legal Writings of Rabbi Israel Isserlein and his contemporaries* (1962). This genre of literature is of additional importance for knowledge of the history of the *halakhah*, since in it is reflected the first reactions of the halakhic authorities of the various ages to new scientific inventions and discoveries which have increased considerably during recent centuries. It is no longer possible to recognize this immediate reaction of the *halakhah* in the codes, since the decisions of the respondents underwent many processes of modification and limitation before being summarized in the classical works of the *halakhah*. In this field a great deal of work was done by Isaak *Kahane, who wrote many monographs on the development of halakhic (but also historical) topics in the responsa literature throughout the ages. (See also **Ma'aseh*.)

Boaz Cohen's *Kunteres ha-Teshuvot* (1930), an annotated bibliography of the rabbinic responsa of the Middle Ages, which was one of the first attemps to classify and describe the responsa literature, became a standard reference work. There was, however, no list of individual responsa scattered in works devoted to other themes. The publication of Shmuel Glick's *Kuntress ha-Teshuvot he-Ḥadash: Bibliographic Thesaurus of Responsa Literature Published from ca. 1470-2000*, vol. 1: *aleph-lamed* (2005) is a major contribution toward accessing all types of responsa. In addition to the classic corpus of responsa, the work includes rare responsa found in other works focusing on spheres other than responsa. The *Kuntress ha-Teshuvot he-Ḥadash*, which has a bibliographical description of over 2,000 books of responsa, provides, among other features, authors' biographical details, a list of the editions of each work and their pagination, the original annotations of Boaz Cohen, and much updated scholarly information.

In 1963 the Institute for Research in Jewish Law attached to the faculty of law and the Institute of Jewish Studies in the Hebrew University of Jerusalem began to index the responsa literature. The index is made up of three parts: the first part gives in great detail all the legal material (*Ḥoshen Mishpat* and *Even ha-Ezer*) found in the responsa literature, classified alphabetically according to legal topics in modern scientific terminology; the second part cites all the halakhic sources mentioned in the responsa (from the Bible onward) while the third part gives all the historical material found in the responsa literature, divided according to subjects. Work has started on *rishonim* literature.

In its final form the project was to analyze the whole of the responsa literature according to a systematic legal index, rendering it possible to find any desired topic discussed in the literature.

[Israel Moses Ta-Shma]

From the Beginning of the 16th Century

After the expulsion from Spain, at the end of the 15th century, the exiles found their way to various countries, but chiefly to North Africa, the Balkans, Ereẓ Israel, and Egypt, where they either formed new centers, or new congregations in addition to those already there. As a result new problems arose. There were disputes about different customs, about the powers of the communities, including communal taxation and the apportionment between the original inhabitants and the newcomers, and about suffrage. Problems also arose in commercial matters regarding contracts and business dealings executed in accordance with the conditions obtaining in the locality from which the exiles hailed and their validity in their new localities, as well as in social and cultural relations. All these had to be given practical solutions in accordance with the principles of the *halakhah*.

In Germany changes also took place. In the wake of persecutions and expulsions German Jewry turned eastward, and new Jewish centers came into existence in Poland and Lithuania, where specific problems of a different type arose. The rivalries between communities with regard to settlement and trading, the apportionment of the taxes within the community itself and between the various communities, communal organization, relations between employee and employer in small industry – all of these had to be solved by means of **takkanot*, bans, and rulings, based on the *halakhah*. The communal leaders thereupon addressed themselves to the great contemporary scholars for solutions to these complex problems. There were in addition problems of **issur ve-hetter*, matters pertaining to marriage and divorce, and civil law. As a result a vast literature of responsa relating to different places and different customs was created. This literature, in addition to resolving the problems in accordance with the *halakhah*, serves as a source of knowledge for all aspects of life in these centers, their formation and their customs, the internal organization of the communities and relationship between them, and social, cultural, economic, and communal and private life.

Outwardly, this responsa literature was a continuation of that of the previous centuries – arranging the facts, clarifying the problem in all its aspects, and finally coming to the appropriate conclusion. Internally, however, changes took place in the content of the responsum. Discussions on matters of faith and belief and on philosophical views decreased, and were replaced by practical problems. There was also an increase in questions on the exposition of talmudic topics and on theoretical problems raised by the commentators, and on contradictions between halakhic rulings. It is from this century that the "responders" are referred to as **aḥaronim*, and they generally accept as binding the conclusions of the earlier *rishonim*. In matters already discussed by the *rishonim*, the main discussion was whether the data of the *aḥaronim* accorded with those of the *rishonim*, since only if there was such a correspondence was the conclusion of the *rishonim* binding. As a result of the examination of cases for this purpose, and because of the need to seek new solutions not given by the *rishonim*, the responsa became longer by the addition of novellae and complicated argumentation which could be followed only by a scholar, and they lost much of the simplicity and clarity that characterized the early responsa. The large number of new centers, the great number of problems, the lack of one central authority for Jewry as had formerly existed in Ereẓ Israel and Babylon, the extension of national and international trade, and the closely guarded principle of not resorting "to gentile courts" resulted in a broadening, deepening, and extension of the responsa literature to such huge dimensions that to date it numbers no less than some 250,000 responsa.

The list which follows, though it gives only the most outstanding and the most famous authors of responsa in the various centers from the 16th century, nevertheless numbers some hundreds. In some cases it notes unusual responsa.

The Turn of the 16th Century

COUNTRIES UNDER TURKISH RULE. While the oldest authors of responsa in the 16th century belonged to the previous century, their main responsa activity belongs to the 16th century. Among them are Elijah *Mizraḥi (Re'em), rabbi in Constantinople; Moses b. Isaac *Alashkar, *dayyan* in Cairo and then in Jerusalem; Jacob b. Moses Berab II (Ri-Berav; 1475–1546) in Safed; *Levi b. Jacob b. Ḥabib in Jerusalem; *David b. Solomon ibn Abi Zimra (Radbaz) in Egypt; and Joseph *Caro in Safed.

ITALY. To this generation belong Meir b. Isaac *Katzenellenbogen (Maharam) of Padua and Isaac Joshua b. Emanuel *Lattes, a contemporary of Joseph Caro, rabbi of Bologna and Ferrara, whose responsa were published in 1860 in Vienna. The end of the volume (pp. 139–140) gives the text of the authorizations given to two young women in Mantua in 1556 to practice *sheḥitah*, and states that "Jewish women are accustomed to study the laws of *sheḥitah*."

The 16th Century

COUNTRIES UNDER TURKISH RULE, THE BALKANS, AND NORTH AFRICA. There were Moses b. Joseph of *Trani (the Mabit) in Safed; Joseph b. David ibn *Lev (Maharival, Mahari b. Lev) in Constantinople (four volumes, 1–3 in Constantinople 1573, and 4 in Venice 1606), who, urged by his patron Gracia *Nasi, issued a ban against business dealings with the merchants of Ancona as a reaction against the cruelty of Pope Paul IV to the Jews and the burning of the Talmud in 1556 (no. 115); Samuel b. Moses de *Medina (Maharashdam) in Salonika; *Elijah b. Ḥayyim (Ranaḥ) in Constantinople; Solomon b. Abraham Cohen (Maharshakh), in Salonika; and Moses *Alshekh, in Safed; *David b. Ḥayyim of Corfu (Redakh); *Benjamin Ze'ev b. Mattathias of Arta; Simeon b. Ẓemaḥ *Duran in Algiers; Isaac b. Samuel *Adarbi in Salonika; Abraham b. Moses Di *Boton in Salonika; Baruch b. Solomon Kalai (see *Kalai, Mordecai; d. 1597) in Turkey; Yom Tov b. Akiva Ẓahalon Maharitaẓ (see *Ẓahalon Family), in Safed; and Aaron b. Joseph *Sasson in Salonika.

EGYPT. Jacob b. Abraham *Castro (Maharikash) was important.

ITALY. There were Azriel b. Solomon *Dienna in Sabbioneta and Menahem Azariah de *Fano (Rama [רמ"ע]), who deals with the question of whether it is permitted to sway while praying (no. 113).

POLAND. The study of Torah in Poland began to flourish with Jacob *Pollack and *Shalom Shakhna b. Joseph of Lublin. Their pupils were among the greatest talmudists in Poland and other countries, as well as the greatest responders. Henceforth Poland became an important source of responsa. Responders included Solomon b. Jehiel *Luria (Maharshal), who in one of his responsa (no. 72) deals with the permissibility of going bareheaded; Moses b. Israel *Isserles of *Cracow (Rema), three of whose responsa (5–7) are a dispute with Luria as to whether the study of philosophy, grammar, and Kabbalah are permitted; Meir b. Gedaliah (Maharam) of Lublin (see *Codification of Law); Benjamin Aaron b. Abraham *Slonik (Responsa *Masat Binyamin*, Cracow 1633), who was a pupil of the previous two, and among whose responsa are a number by Joshua *Falk.

The 17th Century

This period was characterized by the spread of Joseph Caro's Shulḥan Arukh with the glosses of Moses Isserles, and their acceptance as authoritative *halakhah*. As a result the responders henceforth relied upon the Shulḥan Arukh, and from this point of view were neither original nor independent in their responsa except on topics not mentioned in the Shulḥan Arukh.

GERMANY (INCLUDING BOHEMIA AND MORAVIA) AND POLAND. Among the outstanding responders of this generation were Joel *Sirkes (Baḥ); Menahem Mendel *Krochmal, rabbi of Holesov and Mikulov, who in one of his responsa banned the purchase of fish for some months to counter the excessive prices charged by the fishmonger (no. 28); Aaron Samuel b. Israel *Koidonover, rabbi of Brest-Litovsk and Frankfurt; Jacob b. Aaron *Sasportas of Amsterdam and Hamburg; Ẓevi Hirsch b. Jacob *Ashkenazi (the Ḥakham Ẓevi); Jacob b. Joseph *Reischer of Prague and Metz; Ezekiel b. Abraham Katzenellenbogen (1668?–1749; see *Katzenellenbogen Family) of Koidanov (Dzerzhinsk) and the joint communities of Altona, Hamburg, and Wandsbeck and author of the responsa *Keneset Yeḥezkiel* (Altona, 1733); and Jonah b. Elijah *Landsofer of Prague.

ITALY. There were Issachar Baer b. Israel Leiser Parnas Eilenburg of Gorizia; Leone (Judah Aryeh) *Modena; Moses b. Mordecai *Zacuto of Venice and Mantua; and Samuel b. Abraham *Aboab of Verona and Venice.

EREẒ ISRAEL, THE BALKANS, AND NORTH AFRICA. Responders included Jehiel b. Ḥayyim Basan (1550–1625), author of the responsa *Mahari Basan* (Constantinople, 1737); Jacob b. Israel ha-Levi of Salonika and Xanthe; Joseph b. Moses *Trani (Maharit), Moses b. Nissim Benveniste, and Abraham b. Solomon *Alegre – all in Constantinople; Jacob b. Ḥayyim *Alfandari; Joseph b. Saul *Escapa (responsa *Ri Escapa*, Frankfurt on the Oder, 1709), Ḥayyim b. Israel *Benveniste, and Aaron b. Isaac *Lapapa – all in Smyrna; Jacob (Israel) b. Samuel *Ḥagiz, Moses b. Solomon ibn *Ḥabib, and Abraham b. David *Yiẓhaki, Rishon le-Zion and author of the *Zera Avraham* (Pt. 1, Constantinople, 1732; Pt. 2, Smyrna, 1733) – all in Jerusalem.

EGYPT. There were, all in Cairo, *Mordecai b. Judah ha-Levi; *Abraham b. Mordecai ha-Levi; and Joseph b. Moses ha-Levi Nazir (see Moses ha-Levi *Nazir), author of responsa *Matteh Yosef* (Pt. 1, Constantinople, 1717; Pt. 2, 1726).

SALONIKA. There were Ḥayyim *Shabbetai (the MaHaRḤaSH), who wrote responsa on *Even ha-Ezer* with a *Kunteres Agunot* (Salonika, 1651) and also responsa *Torat Ḥayyim* on the other three parts of the Shulḥan Arukh (*ibid.*, 1713–22); Daniel *Estrosa; Solomon b. Aaron Ḥason (1605–1667), called "the younger" to distinguish him from his grandfather of the same name), who was author of the responsa *Beit Shelomo* (Salonika, 1720), and some of whose responsa were published in the collection *Mishpatim Yesharim* (*ibid.*, 1732) together with those of *Samuel b. Ali Gaon; Shabbetai Jonah (*Shai la-Mora*, Salonika, 1653); Baruch *Angel; Aaron b. Ḥayyim Abraham ha-Kohen *Peraḥyah; Ḥasdai b. Samuel ha-Kohen *Peraḥyah; Elijah b. Judah Covo (d. 1689; see *Covo Family); Ḥayyim b. Benjamin *Asael; Solomon b. Joseph *Amarillo; and Joseph b. Shemaiah Covo (c. 1660–1721; see *Covo Family).

The 18th Century

GERMANY (INCLUDING BOHEMIA AND MORAVIA). Among the responders were Meir b. Isaac *Eisenstadt; Jacob b. Ẓevi *Emden; Joseph b. Menahem *Steinhardt of Alsace and *Fuerth; Ezekiel b. Judah *Landau in Prague; and Israel b. Eliezer *Lipschuetz of Cleves.

ITALY. There were Samson b. Joshua Moses *Morpurgo of Ancona; Raphael *Meldola of Pisa and Leghorn; David b. Jacob *Pardo of Spoleto; and Isaiah ben Israel Hezekiah Bassano (see *Bassano Family) in Reggio Emilia.

EREẒ ISRAEL. Responders were Ḥayyim Joseph David *Azulai (the Ḥida), who included the writing of responsa in his manifold literary activities; Moses b. Jacob *Ḥagiz; Jonah b. Ḥanun *Navon; Moses Israel and his son Elijah *Mizraḥi (d. 1749), Rishon le-Zion and author of the responsa *Admat Kodesh* (Pt. 1, Constantinople, 1742; Pt. 2, Salonika, 1758) – all in Jerusalem; and Ḥayyim *Modai of Safed and Smyrna.

NORTH AFRICA, TURKEY, AND THE BALKANS. Responders included Yom Tov *Algazi; Judah b. Isaac *Ayash of Algiers, Leghorn, and Jerusalem; Ephraim b. Aaron *Navon of Constantinople; Zedekiah b. Saadiah Huẓin of Baghdad, author of the responsa *Zedakah u-Mishpat* (Pt. 1, Jerusalem, 1926); Isaac Bekhor David (1690–1755) of Constantinople, and Isaac b. Judah ha-Kohen *Rappaport of Jerusalem and Smyrna. In Salonika there were Asher b. Emanuel Shalem (turn of the 17th and 18th centuries), author of the *Matteh Asher* (Salonika, 1748); Moses b. Solomon Amarillo (see Solomon b. Joseph *Amarillo; beginning of the 18th century); *Joseph David; and Joseph Raphael b. Ḥayyim *Ḥazzan, in Smyrna, Hebron, and Jerusalem.

YEMEN. Yaḥya b. Joseph Ẓalaḥ (second half of 18th and first half of 19th century), rabbi and *av bet din* in San'a wrote responsa *Pe'ullat Ẓaddik* (Tel Aviv, 1946) dealing with problems of the Jews in Yemen such as: whether a leper could act as communal *shoḥet* (no. 71); and whether those going from one town to another on the Sabbath for prayer or for other religious duties or for a festivity, were permitted to carry walking sticks (no. 123). David b. Shalom *Mizraḥi (Misraki; c. 1696–1771) and his son Yaḥya (1734–1809) in San'a wrote responsa *Revid ha-Zahav* (Tel Aviv, 1955), on the Shulḥan Arukh (*Oraḥ Ḥayyim* and *Yoreh De'ah*) reflecting the customs of the Jews of Yemen.

The 19th Century

The new age ushered in by the 19th century, the era of *Emancipation effected by the French Revolution and the advances made in every sphere of life, brought with it a change in responsa literature. A distinction must be made between the literature created in Europe, the focal point of the upheaval, and that created in Turkey and the Balkans. In the latter countries, where autonomous Jewish jurisdiction continued to exist, no change in the responsa literature is noticeable. A substantial part of the responsa is devoted to the *Ḥoshen Mishpat* section of the Shulḥan Arukh, which deals with civil law and financial matters. In Europe it was otherwise; here the responsa literature bore the marks of the Berlin *Haskalah trend, the emancipation in Germany and Austria (including Galicia, Hungary, and parts of Poland under German or Austrian rule), the *Reform movement, the national movements, and the discoveries of technology. All are reflected in the responsa of this century.

theater was a forum for "the discussion of problems… that affect the lives and happiness of millions," but that did not prevent him from writing appealing little plays like *The Left Bank* (1931) and *Two on an Island* (1940). *Not for Children* (1935) was a satire on the theater.

His other plays include *See Naples and Die* (1929), *A New Life* (1944), *The Grand Tour* (1951), and *Love Among the Ruins* (1963). Two of his novels were *Imperial City* (1937) and *The Show Must Go On* (1949). Rice published an autobiography, *Minority Report*, in 1963.

BIBLIOGRAPHY: R. Hogan, *Independence of Elmer Rice* (1965); J. Meersand, *Traditions in American Literature, A Study of Jewish Characters and Authors* (1939), 25–32, index; B. Mantle, *Contemporary American Playwrights* (1941), 54–61; S.J. Kunitz, *Twentieth Century Authors, first supplement* (1955), incl. bibl.

[Joseph Mersand]

RICE, ISAAC LEOPOLD (1850–1915), U.S. lawyer and promoter. Rice was born in Wachenheim, Bavaria, and taken as a child to Philadelphia. He abandoned a career in music to study law, graduating in 1880 from Columbia Law School where he taught from 1882 to 1886. He devoted himself to railroad law, and was instrumental in reorganizing several southern railroads, which later constituted the Southern Railway, and the Philadelphia and Reading Railroad. In the 1890s Rice turned to electrical inventions, working on the electric storage battery, electric automobiles, and electric boat industries. He was president of the Electric Boat Co., the National Torpedo Co., the Electric Storage Battery Co., the American Casein Co., and numerous other firms manufacturing railway and marine vehicles and rubber tires. A prominent chess player, Rice invented the "Rice Gambit" opening and received the silver trophy for the International Universities Chess Match. Rice wrote *What Is Music?* (1875) and contributed to several periodicals, including *The Forum*, which he founded.

BIBLIOGRAPHY: AJYB, 6 (1904/05), 167–8; AJHSP, 25 (1917), 175–6; *New York Times* (Nov. 3, 1915), 15.

[Edward L. Greenstein]

RICE, JAMES P. (1913–1997), U.S. organization executive. Born in Cleveland, Ohio, Rice graduated from Case Western University and received a master's degree in social administration from Adelbert College. From 1936 to 1945 he served as a caseworker and later as an administrator in Cleveland, Chicago, and New York. At the end of World War II he was appointed by the *American Jewish Joint Distribution Committee to supervise its program for the resettlement of Jewish refugees in Italy, France, Switzerland, and Austria, where he oversaw programs that helped more than 500,000 Holocaust survivors. From 1955 to 1966 he served as executive director of *United HIAS Service, in which capacity he worked to strengthen the organization's ties with other international Jewish bodies. During this period he also served as representative to the United Nations on behalf of the International Council on Jewish Social and Welfare Services, working with government officials to codify a new immigration law that would ease entry restrictions for refugees. Rice then served as executive vice president of the Jewish Federation/Jewish United Fund of Metropolitan Chicago (1966–79). He helped the federation form a merger and structured a reorganization plan that expanded its services to people in need. After his retirement, Rice served as a consultant to several organizations, such as the United Jewish Appeal and Chicago's Council for Jewish Elderly.

[Hillel Halkin / Ruth Beloff (2nd ed.)]

RICE, JOSEPH MAYER (1857–1934), U.S. physician, editor, and educator. Rice, who was born in Philadelphia, Pennsylvania, was a pediatrician. Interested in problems of prophylaxis, he became increasingly concerned with school programs, and from 1888 to 1890 studied pedagogy at Jena and Leipzig. When he returned to the United States, he launched a journalistic crusade to reform the schools along progressive German lines. He first published his criticisms and recommendations in *The Forum and Century*, and then in a book entitled *The Public-School System of the United States* (1893). Later, while serving as editor of *The Forum and Century*, he undertook some of the first scientific investigations into teaching, beginning with a study of the effects of systematic instruction on achievement in spelling. Rice's studies and conclusions were collected in *Scientific Management in Education* (1913).

[Lawrence A. Cremin]

RICH, U.S. department store owners. The Rich family came from Kaschau (Hungary), from where Morris Rich (1847–1928) and his brother William moved to the United States in 1860; they became peddlers in Cleveland (Ohio). In 1865 Morris moved to Atlanta (Georgia) where in 1867 he opened a retail store which was the first of a leading chain of department stores in the South. His brothers Emanuel (1849–1897) and Daniel (1843–1920) who had come to the United States in 1862, and later Walter Henry (1880–1947), joined him in his successful business. Rich's of Atlanta was the first major retail store in the area to introduce liberal credit terms and homespun ways of merchandising, which popularized the store among the large black population. The firm's credit policy was a major factor in its rehabilitation after a disastrous fire swept Atlanta in 1917. The company also simplified internal administration and became famous for its excellent labor relations. Its owners and senior officers were prominent in many local and national civic organizations and charities which included the Rich Foundation, a major endower of Emory University's School of Business Administration.

BIBLIOGRAPHY: H.G. Baker, *Rich's of Atlanta: the Story of a Store Since 1867* (1953).

[Joachim O. Ronall]

RICH, ADRIENNE (1929–), U.S. poet. Rich was the daughter of a Jewish father who distanced himself from Judaism, and a gentile mother. Her Jewishness, and her response to it, inform much of the poignancy of her poems about claiming a heritage. No less importantly, her poetry is often bound up with her father, patriarchal authority, and her lesbianism. A revolt against, as well as a feminist reading of, a Judaism that is male-dominated, gives Rich's poetry a characteristic strength, compassion, and large embrace. In "Yom Kippur 1984," she reflects: "Am I writing merely about privilege/ about drifting from the center, drawn to edges...." Rich, often writing about the shared experiences of females and about historical women, began her career with tightly controlled poetry which brought her early recognition by critics and other poets. Her first book of verse, *A Change of World* (1951), was chosen by W.H. Auden for the Yale Younger Poets Award; a Guggenheim Fellowship followed (1952–53). *The Diamond Cutters and Other Poems* (1955) won the Ridgely Torrence Memorial Award of the Poetry Society of America. She was also awarded the National Institute of Arts and Letters Award for poetry (1960); another Guggenheim Fellowship (1961–62); and a Bollingen Foundation grant for translation of Dutch poetry (1962). In 1994, she was awarded a MacArthur Fellowship.

Rich married an economist, had three sons, and served as Phi Beta Kappa poet at William and Mary College, at Swarthmore College, and at Harvard College. After Rich and her family moved to New York City in 1966, she grew active in protests against the war in Vietnam. Rich's poetry became radicalized as well, moving away from the precise blank verse that had been her trademark to freer meters. *Leaflets* (1969) expressed her new conviction that the goal of poetry should be to illuminate the moment, rather than to be worked over for posterity.

In 1970 Rich's husband died and she became increasingly involved in the radical feminist movement. She won the Shelley Memorial Award of the Poetry Society of America in 1971 and served as the Fanny Hurst Visiting Professor of Creative Literature at Brandeis University in 1972–73. When she was awarded a National Book Award for her 1973 book of verse, *Diving into the Wreck*, she refused to accept the award as an individual, and instead accepted it in the name of all women. Her books of poetry include *Poems: Selected and New* (1975) and *A Wild Patience Has Taken Me This Far* (1981). Of special interest is Rich's volume of poetry *Your Native Land, Your Life* (1986) which speaks about her Jewish identity. Her *An Atlas of the Difficult World: Poems 1988–1991* was published in 1991; her *Collected Early Poems, 1950–1970* in 1993; *The School Among the Ruins: Poems, 2000–2004* in 2004. She has written several volumes of essays, among them *On Lies, Secrets, and Silence: Selected Prose, 1996–1978* (1979); *Blood, Bread, and Poetry: Selected Prose, 1979–1985* (1986); and *What Is Found There: Notebooks on Poetry and Politics* (1993).

ADD. BIBLIOGRAPHY: J.R. Cooper (ed.), *Reading Adrienne Rich: Reviews and Re-visions, 1951–81* (1984), J. Perrault, *Writing Selves: Contemporary Feminist Autobiography* (1995); A. Templeton, *The Dream and the Dialogue: Adrienne Rich's Feminist Poetics* (1994).

[Sylvia Barack Fishman / Lewis Fried (2nd ed.)]

RICH, BUDDY (Bernard; 1917–1987); U.S. drummer, bandleader, tap dancer. The son of a vaudeville team (Wilson and Rich), he was on stage at the age of 18 months, or so the legend goes. He was definitely a professional entertainer by age four, playing drums and tap dancing in the Broadway show *Pinwheel* in 1921, and by the time he was 11, Rich had formed his own band. As soon as he looked old enough, he was sneaking into clubs and sitting in on the drums whenever he could. In 1937, Rich was hired by Joe Marsala, and he then moved on to gigs with Bunny Berigan, Artie *Shaw, and Tommy Dorsey. His musical career was interrupted by military service during World War II, but he picked up where he had left off when he returned, rejoining Dorsey. According to a contemporary source, Rich was "cocky, rashly outspoken and brutally sarcastic." With a temper as explosive as his all-out playing style, he was also quick with his fists, fighting nearly everyone in the Dorsey band, including star singer Frank Sinatra. Yet when Rich left Dorsey to form his own band, Sinatra was one of his financial backers, so completely did he believe in the tempestuous drummer's talents.

Although his sense of rhythm was exquisite, Rich's timing as an entrepreneur was less sterling; he blossomed as a big-band drummer just as the economic foundations of the Big Bands collapsed. He toured with Norman Granz's Jazz at the Philharmonic troupe, worked as a vocalist after a heart attack in the mid-1950s, then came roaring back with a new Big Band in 1966. That fire-breathing group stayed intact in one form or another for about a dozen years. A second heart attack in the mid-1970s forced Rich to pare the band down to a sextet, but he remained musically active and a frequent guest on such TV staples as *The Tonight Show* almost up to his death from a brain tumor.

BIBLIOGRAPHY: "Buddy Rich," in: *MusicWeb Encyclopaedia of Popular Music*, at: www.musicweb.uk.net; B. Case and S. Britt, "Buddy Rich," in: *The Illustrated Encylopedia of Jazz* (1978); H. Siders, "Buddy Rich," in: *Down Beat Magazine* archives, at: www.downbeat.com; G.T. Simon, *The Big Bands* (1981).

[George Robinson (2nd ed.)]

RICH, MARC (1934–), international commodities trader. Born Marc David Reich in Antwerp, Belgium, he and his family emigrated to the United States in 1942. He attended New York University, but did not graduate, and worked as a commodities trader for his father, who was a successful producer of burlap sacks. Rich then worked with Philipp Brothers, a dealer in raw metals, learning about the international trading of raw materials with Third World nations. He later focused on trading with dictatorial regimes and embargoed nations such as Iran. In 1983 Rich and his partner, Pincus Green, were indicted on charges of tax evasion and illegal trading with Iran. According to the indictment, Rich set up a scam to have his company's oil relabeled by a reseller, and thus seemingly exempted from price controls. Rich's lawyers sought a deal to end the prosecution and spare him jail time. They offered $100 million if all charges were dropped. This was on top of $50,000 a day Rich was paying in contempt-of-court fines. During this period, Rich and Green were in Europe. When the deal was finally rejected, Rich and Green became fugitives when they decided to stay abroad. The resellers who were the main co-conspirators in the fraud were convicted and served 12 months in jail. Rich's companies pleaded guilty to 78 counts and paid over $150 million while he and Green remained fugitives.

Rich was joined in Switzerland by his wife, DENISE EISENBERG RICH (1944–), the daughter of Holocaust survivors who fled Germany for Worcester, Massachusetts. Her father made millions in a shoe factory while Denise went to Boston University, where she taught herself to play the guitar and began a songwriting career. They married in 1966 and she stayed with her husband in Europe. After about 10 years, she returned to New York City with their three daughters and reportedly received a large divorce settlement. Denise began pursuing her songwriting career in earnest, contributed heavily to the Democratic Party and the campaign of Bill Clinton, whom she met in 1993, and became famous for large parties in New York City. Over the years, her songs were nominated for Grammys and Oscars and she wrote songs for pop stars like Celine Dion, Aretha Franklin, and Patti LaBelle. The songs and parties continued until 1996 when the Riches' middle daughter, Gabrielle, died of leukemia at the age of 27. Denise then created the G & P Charitable Foundation (G for Gabrielle, P for Philip, her daughter's husband) to finance cancer research. Since its formation in 1998 the foundation raised millions, aided by an appearance at the first gala by then-President Clinton.

While in exile, Rich continued his questionable business practices. In 1988, the Defense Logistics Agency lifted its bar on contracting with a Rich company and between 1989 and 1992, the U.S. Mint issued at least 21 separate contracts for nickel, zinc, and copper to the company.

Over the years, Rich kept trying to win a pardon, his lawyers arguing that he was the victim of overly zealous prosecutors. Many of those who wrote letters of support for a presidential pardon were leaders of Jewish philanthropy in the United States and Israel. Rich had given to a variety of major institutions in Israel, including Shaare Zedek Medical Center, Ben-Gurion University, the Israel Museum, and the Jerusalem Foundation. He also helped bring dozens of Jews from Ethiopia and Yemen to Israel and was one of 14 people who pledged five million dollars to Birthright Israel, a program that sends young, primarily North American, Jews on free trips to Israel. On January 20, 2001, only hours before leaving office, Clinton granted Rich a pardon. Clinton explained his decision by noting that similar situations were settled in civil, not criminal, court, and cited clemency pleas from Israeli government officials, including Prime Minister Ehud Barak.

After his pardon, Rich began lucrative business dealings with Saddam Hussein of Iraq, which were disclosed in 2005 in connection with the United Nations oil-for-food scandals.

[Stewart Kampel (2nd ed.)]

RICHARDS, BERNARD GERSON (1877–1971), U.S. journalist, widely active in Jewish affairs. Richards was born in Keidan (Kedziniai), Lithuania, and was taken to the U.S. in 1886. He began his journalistic career as a reporter on the *Boston Post*, and wrote for several Boston and New York papers, as well as for Yiddish and other Jewish journals, including the *American Hebrew* and *The New Palestine*. He also edited the magazine *New Era*. From 1906 to 1911 Richards served as secretary of the Jewish Community of New York City, an organization designed to further the cause of Judaism, and in 1915 helped found the *American Jewish Congress, of which he was executive director until 1932. At the end of World War I he was a member of the American Jewish delegation to the Versailles Peace Conference. He also founded the Jewish Information Bureau of Greater New York (1932), and the American Jewish Institute, New York (1942) to further adult education. He was director of both these institutions. He was also a member of the Zionist Organization of America, and his revised edition of I. Cohen's *The Zionist Movement* (1946) included a supplementary chapter of his own on Zionism in the U.S. His other books were *The Discourses of Keidansky* (1903), and *Organizing American Jewry* (1947). His papers are in the library of the Jewish Theological Seminary, New York.

[Irving Rosenthal]

RICHARDS, MARTIN (**Morton Richard Klein**; 1932–), U.S. stage and film producer. Morton Richard Klein grew up in the Bronx and got his first job at the age of 10 as a newsboy in the Broadway show *Mexican Hayride* with June Havoc. He did other shows and commercials until his voice changed. At 17, a baritone, he began performing in nightclubs under his new name. He spent two years at New York University studying architecture, his grandfather's profession, while singing at night, but quit to pursue show business full-time. Realizing he would never make it big as a singer, Richards landed jobs as a casting director. He found actors for small roles in Manhattan-location movies like *The Seven Year Itch, Sweet Charity, The Boston Strangler,* and *Sweet Smell of Success.* He then raised funds to stage an Off-Broadway show, *Dylan,* which proved a success, and his producing career was born. Richards was determined to stage the dark musical *Chicago,* and he spent 27 years before it had its premiere on Broadway in 1975. The show, a smashing success, ran for more than 900 performances. That same year, Richards met Mary Lea Johnson, one of several children who were heirs to the Johnson & Johnson medical supply fortune. Johnson, a former actress and a woman who had two failed marriages, and Richards, an acknowledged homosexual, married. In 1976, with one million dollars from his wife, they established the Producers Circle, with Robert Fryer and James Cresson. The partnership produced such Broadway musical hits as *On the Twentieth Century* (1978), *Sweeney Todd* (1979), *La Cage aux Folles* (1983), *The Will Rogers Follies* (1991), and *Grand Hotel* (1989) among others. Their shows won more than 36 Tony Awards. *Crimes of the Heart* won a Pulitzer Prize. Off Broadway, the Circle produced *March of the Falsettos* and *Mayor.* Among their films were *The Boys from Brazil* (1978), *The Shining* (1980), *Fort Apache, the Bronx* (1981), and *Chicago*, which won an Oscar for best film of the year in 2003, along with five other Oscars. Five years after the death of her father, Mary Lea Richards and her brothers and sisters challenged their father's last will, which disinherited five of his six children and left the vast bulk of the $350 million estate to his third wife, his former maid. The case was the largest inheritance contest in the history of New York before it was settled out of court with the children dividing about 12 percent of the total. Legal challenges continued for Richards into the early years of the 21st century, years after the death of his wife. Richards spent millions establishing the Mary Lea Johnson Richards Institute at NYU and the Children's Advocacy Center of Manhattan.

[Stewart Kampel (2nd ed.)]

RICHIETTI, JOSEPH SHALLIT BEN ELIEZER (17th century), rabbi and emissary of the Holy Land. Richietti apparently came from Mantua and settled in Safed some time after 1659. From 1674 to 1676 he was an emissary of Safed in Italy. Moses *Zacuto welcomed him with great honor upon his arrival in Mantua in 1674. He was a Shabbatean of Zacuto's circle. During his mission he published his *Ḥokhmat ha-Mishkan* (Mantua, 1676) on the erection of the Tabernacle, at the end of which he republished the *Iggeret Mesapperet Yaḥasuta de-Ẓaddikei de-Ara de-Yisrael* ("A genealogical table of the righteous men of Ereẓ Israel"). In the introduction to the work he speaks of having drawn up a map of Ereẓ Israel. He appears also to have spent some time in Verona. According to documents of the Mantua community, he lent a sum of money to the community during a time of need. He possessed important manuscripts, among them a copy of the **Midrash ha-Gadol*, and was the first European scholar to make use of it.

BIBLIOGRAPHY: Yaari, Sheluḥei, 39, 57, 81, 84, 414; S. Simonsohn, *Toledot ha-Yehudim be-Dukkasut Mantovah*, 2 (1964), 291–2; I. Tishby, *Netivei Emunah u-Minut* (1964), 81–83.

[Abraham David]

RICHLER, MORDECAI (1931–2001), Canadian author. Richler's satiric portrayal of Montreal's Jewish Main gained both prominence and notoriety in 1955 with the publication of his second novel, *Son of a Smaller Hero.* Published in Britain, this slim, young man's novel of leaving one's community caused a stir in Canada, with its depiction of working-class Jews coming to terms with the breakdown of tradition and the speed with which a prosperous postwar Canada allowed middle-class Jews to assimilate and suburbanize themselves. These themes recur – more fully fleshed out and with greater humor – in Richler's breakthrough 1959 novel *The Apprenticeship of Duddy Kravitz.*

Richler's career would prove to be a writing away from and back to his childhood experiences in the neighborhood around Montreal's St Lawrence Boulevard, which existed as a Jewish enclave, with English Montreal to the west and French Montreal to the east. Between the middle 1950s and the early 1970s Richler made his home in London, England, raising a family and supporting himself by writing screenplays. Upon returning to Montreal to stay, Richler told friends that he worried that being too long away from his home turf might weaken his relationship with his richest material. The major novels that best reflect his ability to weave Montreal Jewish themes into a larger fictional tableau are *St. Urbain's Horseman* (1971), *Joshua Then and Now* (1980), and *Solomon Gursky Was Here* (1989). In the first of the three, Montreal plays the slightest role, and Richler addresses the Holocaust with deft, dark humor and moral outrage. *Joshua Then and Now* presents a loving portrait of a St. Urbain Street childhood. And in *Solomon Gursky Was Here*, Richler's most ambitious book, he takes liberties with the Bronfman liquor dynasty, the role of Jewish wealth and power in Canada, alongside a fanciful consideration of Jews in the Arctic. These major books confirmed Richler's place at the forefront of Canadian letters.

Richler's output also included three children's books featuring a character named Jacob Two-Two, as well as an excellent memoiristic collection, *The Street* (1969). Among his many literary awards are two Governor General's Awards, the Giller Prize, and the Commonwealth Writers Prize.

Alongside his fiction and memoir, Richler embraced freelance journalism and published regularly in Canada and abroad on subjects as varied as Israel and the sporting life. His willingness to editorialize aggressively and acerbically placed him at the center of the political and cultural debate concerning Quebec's national aspirations. Richler dismissed the *indépendantiste* movement as destructive, incoherent, and self-serving, insisting that its roots could be found in the xenophobic right-wing ideologies of 1940s Quebec. His influential, as well as provocative contributions to this discussion include a long essay, which appeared in *The New Yorker* in 1991, and his full-scale study and memoir *Oh Canada! Oh Quebec: Requiem for a Divided Country* (1992). With the latter's publication Richler found the Montreal Jewish community fully behind him – possibly for the first time in his career – as they applauded his criticism of Quebec nationalism. In the French-speaking community, Richler solidified his position as the Anglophone bête noir of French cultural life in the province.

In his last years, Richler was elevated to the role of cultural icon in Canada, a development that propelled his final novel, *Barney's Version* (1997), to bestseller status. The novel also became an unlikely success in Italy, where readers embraced Richler's characteristic brand of political incorrectness.

BIBLIOGRAPHY: J. Yanofsky, *Mordecai & Me: An Appreciation of a Kind* (2003).

[Norman Ravvin (2nd ed.)]

RICHMAN, JULIA (1855–1912), U.S. educator; the first woman district superintendent of schools in her native New York. She prepared for her teaching career at the Female Normal School (now Hunter College) and at New York University.

First serving as teacher and vice principal of Public School 77, she became the principal of its girls' department in 1884. In 1903 she was appointed district superintendent of schools, a post which she held until her death. Julia Richman helped immigrant children to adjust to American life, combated truancy and juvenile delinquency, and advocated educational programs for mentally retarded children. She organized an employment agency for school dropouts and provided medical and social services for pupils. She also pioneered in organizing the Parent-Teacher Association. She directed the Hebrew Free School Association and, as first president of the Young Women's Hebrew Association, 1886–90, influenced adult Jewish education. From 1895 to 1899 she was chairman of the committee on religious school work of the Council of Jewish Women. As educator and author of *Good Citizenship* (1908), with Isabel Richman Wallach, *The Pupils' Arithmetic* (1911–17), and *Methods of Teaching Jewish Ethics* (1914), she stressed the development and welfare of every child. A girls' high school in Manhattan was named after her.

BIBLIOGRAPHY: R. Proskauer and A.R. Altman, *Julia Richman* (1916).

[William W. Brickman]

RICHMOND, state capital of Virginia, U.S, and commercial center on the James River; 2001 population of metropolitan region 1,138,000 and within the city itself 192,000; Jewish population, 12,500.

There is evidence of Jews residing in Richmond as early as 1769. Revolutionary war veterans and business partners, Jacob I. Cohen and Isaiah Isaacs, the city's earliest known Jewish residents, were instrumental in the establishment of the state's first Jewish congregation in 1789. Kahal Kadosh Beth Shalome was the sixth and westernmost congregation in the colonies, and one of the six that congratulated George Washington upon his inauguration as first president. The 1790 census shows Richmond with the fourth largest Jewish population, following only New York, Charleston and Philadelphia. The first Jewish burial ground in the state was established on Franklin Street in 1791 and, the first synagogue was dedicated on Mayo Street in 1822.

The early Richmond Jews appear to have integrated easily into the city's life, holding a number of elective and civic positions. Jacob Cohen was elected to the City Council in 1793 and served as a Master of his Masonic Lodge; Samuel Myers became alderman in 1800; Benjamin Wolfe and Joseph Darmstadt were elected to the City Council in 1816; and Solomon Jacobs was elected recorder, the second highest municipal office after that of the mayor, in 1815 and again in 1818. Gustavus A. Myers (1801–1869), known as the most prominent Jew of the city in his day, served on the City Council for nearly 30 years, 12 of which as its president. Judah P. *Benjamin, former U.S. Senator from Louisiana, lived in Richmond while serving as secretary of state for the Confederacy.

In 1841 the German Jewish community broke from Beth Shalome to establish Beth Ahabah, a new synagogue in the Ashkenazic tradition. In 1898 the two congregations merged as Beth Ahabah, which continues as Richmond's largest Reform congregation. A Polish congregation, Keneseth Israel, was organized in 1856, while an influx of Russian Jews beginning in 1880 led to the establishment of the Sir Moses Montefiore Congregation. By the 20th century such ethnic distinctions had faded away and the latter two synagogues joined with the Aitz Chaim Congregation in forming the Orthodox Temple Beth Israel.

Jews played a vital role in reviving the city's economy after the U.S. Civil War (1861–65) left the capital of the Confederacy in shambles. Philip Whitlock, a Confederate veteran, and his tobacco firm, P. Whitlock, helped establish the city as a major tobacco center. Gustavus A. Myers and Edward Cohen established the Merchants and Savings Bank in 1867, and Charles Hutzler and William H. Schwarzschild Sr. founded the Central National Bank in 1911.

A number of early Jewish firms were still owned and managed by the same families for over a century after their inception, such as the Thalhimer Brothers department store, established in 1842 and the Binswanger Glass Works. Schwarzschild Jewelers, established in 1897, remains the last of Richmond's carriage trade stores.

Richmond's first public school was founded by the Beth Ahabah Congregation. Sir Moses Jacob *Ezekiel, an internationally known 19th-century sculptor, was born in Richmond and attended the Virginia Military Institute. Gustavus Millhiser (1850–1915) of the Millhiser Bay Company and Richmond Cedar Works was greatly respected in his time. William B. Thalhimer Sr. helped to convince President Franklin D. Roosevelt to legalize the deduction of charitable gifts from income tax returns. He was active on behalf of Richmond's Byrd Airport, group hospitalization, the conservation of wildlife in Virginia, and the settlement of refugees from Germany in the 1930s. Samuel Z. Troy and his wife were also active for refugees. At the end of World War II, a group of Jewish businessmen from Richmond, including Israel November and H.J. Bernstein partnered with friends from Virginia Beach to purchase and retrofit the former Chesapeake Bay ferry boat that became known to the world as the *Exodus* ship.

In 2006 the Jewish community continued to be heavily concentrated in various branches of manufacturing, merchandising, banking, medicine, law, real estate, and the wholesale and retail trade.

As of 2006 eight congregations continued to function: two reform – Beth Ahabah and Or Ami; three Conservative – Or Atid, Beth El, and Beth Shalom; and three Orthodox – Young Israel, Keneseth Beth Israel, and the Chabad Community Shul.

The social welfare structure of the Jewish community centers around the Jewish Community Federation of Richmond, formed in 1935 to galvanize the Jewish community in raising funds to assist co-religionists seeking refuge from the Nazi regime. In 2006, member agencies include the Beth Sholom Home of Virginia, which has a nursing home, assisted living, senior living apartments, and a rehabilitation clinic; the Carole and Marcus Weinstein Jewish Community Center; Jewish Family Services, the oldest family welfare agency in Virginia, established in 1849; two days schools – Rudlin Torah Academy (K-12) and the Solomon Schechter School; and two high schools for the Orthodox community – Shaarei Torah, a high school for girls, and Yeshiva of Virginia, a high school for boys. There are four summer camps and a religious school for children with special needs. The department of religion at the University of Richmond teaches Judaism and holds the endowed Weinstein-Rosenthal Chair. Virginia Commonwealth University has a Center for Judaic Studies headed by Rabbi Jack Spiro, rabbi emeritus for Beth Ahabah. There are four *mikva'ot* and a Kosher Conference and Retreat Center.

Richmond is the home of two Jewish museums, the Beth Ahabah Museum and Archives that chronicles over 300 years of Richmond Jewish History, and the Virginia Holocaust Museum that teaches tolerance through the experiences of local survivors. Spearheaded by Jay Ipson, the Holocaust Museum recently relocated to a 19th-century tobacco warehouse deeded to the museum by the State of Virginia. In 1997, "Commonwealth and Community: The Jewish Experience in Virginia" opened at the Virginia Historical Society and traveled through the state to The Chrysler Museum in Virginia Beach and Roanoke. Saul Viener and the Jewish Federation of Richmond partnered with the Historical Society to develop the exhibit that remains on view at the Beth Ahabah Museum & Archives. The Jewish Experience is also part of a permanent exhibition on Virginia history at the Virginia Historical Society. In 2001 a Virginia Historical Marker was installed on South 14th street marking the site of the first Beth Shalome synagogue.

Throughout the late 19th and the 20th century Richmond Jews continued to serve in a variety of elected offices and civic positions. William Lovenstein, served in the Richmond Light Infantry Blues during the Civil War and later as president *pro tem* of the Virginia State Senate. Alfred Moses, Julius Straus, A.H. Kaufman, Clifford Weil, Joseph Wallerstein, Lee A. Whitlock, and Nathan Forb were elected to City Council. Sol L. Bloomberg was a council president. Dr. Edward N. Calisch, the rabbi of Congregation Beth Ahabah from 1891 until 1946, was an important leader in the community. Norman Sisisky was elected as the delegate representing Petersburg in the Virginia General Assembly in 1973 and to nine terms as U.S. Representative for Virginia's Fourth Congressional District. Eric Cantor served as the chief deputy majority whip, U.S. House of Representatives, as the U.S. Representative for Virginia's Seventh Congressional District (2000); and as Henrico County delegate in the Virginia House of Delegates from 1992 to 2000. Michael Schewel served as Virginia's secretary of commerce and trade under Governor Mark Warner.

Jewish-Christian relations in the Richmond area were characterized for many years by the indifferent Christian response to Jewish efforts to establish a meaningful religious dialogue. In the late 1990s, Congregation Beth Ahabah forged new ties with its neighbor St. James Church when it was severely damaged by lightning. St. James held worship services at Beth Ahabah for two years during the restoration, and later partnered to build shared parking facilities for the two congregations.

BIBLIOGRAPHY: H.T. Ezekiel and G. Lichtenstein, *The History of the Jews of Richmond 1769–1917* (1917); *Richmond Jewish Community Council* (1955); *Through the Years, A Study of the Richmond Jewish Community. Generations*, vol. 2, no. 1 (Commemorative Issue, 2005).

[Susan Morgan (2nd ed.)]

RICHTER, BURTON (1931–), U.S. physicist and Nobel prize winner. Born in New York, Richter received his doctorate from the Massachusetts Institute of Technology in 1956. In the same year he joined Stanford University as a research associate, becoming assistant professor (1960). He moved to the Stanford Linear Accelerator Center as an associate professor (1963) and full professor (1967). In 1979 he was appointed the Paul Pigott Professor of Physical Science. He was director of the Center from 1984 to 1999. He served as president of the American Physical Society (1994), and the International Union of Pure and Applied Physics (1999–2002). He was a member of the National Academy of Sciences, the American Academy of Arts and Sciences, and the American Philosophical Society. Richter shared the 1976 Nobel Prize in physics with Samuel Ting of MIT for their discovery in 1974 – each working independently – of a new subatomic particle, called "psi" by Richter and "J" by Ting, three times heavier than the proton and with a life-span some 10,000 times longer than anticipated by theory at that time. This significant contribution in the field of elementary particles provided evidence for a fourth quark.

BIBLIOGRAPHY: *Science*, 194 (1976), 825; *Current Biography* (1977), 359–62.

[Bracha Rager (2nd ed.)]

RICHTER, ELISE (1865–1943), Austrian professor of Romance languages. Born and raised in Vienna, Elise Richter was among early matriculants when the University of Vienna opened its doors to female students in 1897. Richter passed her doctoral orals in comparative linguistics summa cum laude in 1901, and her post-doctoral dissertation defense for her university teaching credential (*Habilitation*) in Romance philology in 1905. It took two more years before she received her official appointment as the very first *Privatdozentin*, or female unsalaried lecturer, in Austria. In 1921, she was promoted to the rank of untenured associate professor, another first for an Austrian woman. She taught a wide range of courses on various Romance languages and published extensively, especially in the field of historical grammar. Only in 1923, however, did she finally receive a paid university teaching contract, which guaranteed her financial independence. She continued to teach phonetics courses at the University of Vienna until she was seventy-three years old, several years past the normal age of retirement.

Elise Richter participated actively in Austrian political life during the interwar years as a member of the small liberal

Bourgeois-Democratic Workers' Party. Despite her personal reticence, she helped to establish and then chaired the Federation of University Women of Austria from 1922 to 1930. This organization aimed at assisting women to break into previously inaccessible fields within academia.

After the *Anschluss* in March 1938, Elise Richter suffered many humiliations due to her Jewish descent. Not only was she dismissed from her teaching position, but she was also banned from using the university library and prevented from visiting museums and theaters. Her property, including her library, was confiscated and, although she continued her scholarly work until 1941, she could no longer publish in Germany. In October 1942, together with her sister, the English literary specialist Helene Richter, Elise Richter, was deported to Theresienstadt on the last large transport from Vienna; both elderly women became Holocaust victims.

Richter's students and disciples did not forget her, but continued to publish her work posthumously. The Austrian government erected a plaque in her memory as the first woman professor at the University of Vienna.

BIBLIOGRAPHY: H.H. Christmann, *Frau und "Jüdin" an der Universitaet: Die Romanistin Elise Richter* (1980). H.P. Freidenreich, *Female, Jewish, and Educated* (2002); L. Spitzer and H. Adolf, "In Memoriam Elise Richter," in: *Romance Philology*, 1 (1947–48): 329–41; B.M. Woodbridge, Jr., "A Bibliography of the Writings of Elise Richter," in: *Romance Philology*, 26 (1972): 342–360.

[Harriet Pass Freidenreich (2nd ed.)]

RICHTER, HANS (1888–1976), German artist and film maker. Born in Berlin, Richter was one of the first to make abstract feature films. He studied art in Paris and was attracted by the cubist and surrealist schools. In Zurich in 1916 he participated in the Dada movement and later joined Viking Eggeling, a Swedish painter, in making abstract films. His "scroll paintings," inspired by a desire to express Bach's fugues visually, was the forerunner of *Rhythm 21* (1921), which consisted of squares hypnotically regrouping themselves into evolving sets. Later films employed surrealistic glass eyes and bowler hats flying through the air. Richter was forced to flee from Germany, while he was making an anti-Nazi film, and he settled in the United States, where he produced *Dreams that Money Can Buy* (1946), a surrealistic fantasy. Among his other well-known experimental films were *"8 × 8"* (1947) involving squares on a chess board, and *Dadascope* (1961). His book *Dada – Kunst und Antikunst*, published in 1964, became a classic which was followed two years later by an exhibition that toured internationally, *Dada 1916–1966: Documents of the International Dada Movement*. Richter served as head of the Institute of Film Technique at the City College of New York (1943–56) and then specialized in teaching documentary film making.

BIBLIOGRAPHY: G. Habasque, in: *Quadrum*, 13 (Fr. 1962), 61–74; D. Hasenfratz, in: *Werk*, 50 (June, 1963), supplement, 126–7; S.C. Foster, *Hans Richter. Activism, Modernism, and the Avant-Garde* (1998); J. Goergen, *Hans Richter. Film ist Rhythmus* (2003); H. Hoffmann and W. Schobert (eds.), *Hans Richter. Malerei und Film*. Exh. cat. Deutsches Filmmuseums (1989); G. Hoßmann, *Hans Richter 1888–1976. Das bildnerische Werk* (1985).

[Jihan Radjai-Ordoubadi (2nd ed.)]

RICHTER, RAOUL (1871–1912), German philosopher. Richter, who was born in Berlin, was the son of the non-Jewish painter, Gustav Richter, and Carola, the daughter of the composer Giacomo *Meyerbeer. He grew up in the rich artistic and cultural atmosphere of his parents' circle. He became a teacher at Leipzig, and in 1905 a professor. His first writing was *Zur Loesung des Faustproblems* (1892).

In 1903 he published his important biographical study of Nietzsche, *Friedrich Nietzsche, sein Leben und sein Werk*. His *Der Skeptizismus in der Philosophie und seine Ueberwindung* (2 vols., 1904–08) is a historical and philosophical study of skepticism from ancient times up to Nietzsche. His last book, *Religionsphilosophie* (1912), contains his critique of positive religion, his opposition to theism and atheism, and his advocacy of pantheism. Richter believed God was neither personal nor impersonal, but rather a suprapersonal organism. In 1913 a volume of his *Essays* was published containing works on Faust, Nietzsche, and Pascal.

[Richard H. Popkin]

RICHTMANN, MÓZES (1880–1972), Hungarian scholar, teacher, and Zionist. Richtmann was born in Homonna (now in Slovakia). He completed his studies at the rabbinical seminary and University of Budapest, where he obtained a doctorate in philosophy (1904) and rabbinical diploma (1906). A gifted teacher, Richtmann taught at the Jewish Teachers' Seminary in Budapest over a period of 40 years, starting in 1907; from 1950 he lectured at the rabbinical seminary. Richtmann first attracted attention in Hungarian Jewish academic circles as a philosophy disciple of D. *Kaufmann. His doctoral thesis was "Az arab zsidó neoplatonikusok etikai nézetei" ("The Ethical Views of Arab-Jewish Neoplatonists," 1904). Richtmann also published works in Jewish history: *Landau Ezékiel prágai rabbi és a magyar zsidók* ("Ezekiel Landau Rabbi of Prague and the Jews of Hungary," 1905), and *A régi Magyarorszag zsidósága* ("The Jews of Ancient Hungary," in: *Magyar Zsidó Szemle*, vol. 29, 1912).

Principally, however, Richtmann devoted himself to work on behalf of Zionism, which he considered to be the solution for the spiritual crisis within Hungarian Jewry, especially among its intellectuals, and which would assure the continuity of Jewish vitality. He contributed to the official Zionist organ *Zsidó Szemle* and was its editor for a period during World War I. He was a frequent contributor to the general Jewish press, especially *Zsidó Ujság* (1925–38) and the Orthodox *Zsidó Ujság* (1939–44). After World War I and the ensuing revolutions, Richtmann's assimilationist rivals denounced him before the disciplinary tribunal of government teachers for the crime of "lack of patriotism," i.e., Zionism, but the minister of education annulled the proceedings against him. From then onward he published his articles anonymously. During the fascist regime in Hungary, he was among the few who were active in the resistance, and he published a number of anti-regime pamphlets illegally. Richtmann was elected member of the Pest *bet din* after World War II, and he devoted himself exclusively to research. The works *Orthodoxia és cionizmus* ("Orthodoxy and Zionism," 1920) and *Szombat Almanach* ("Saturday Almanac," 1927) were published under his editorship. In 1955, on the occasion of his 75th birthday, a tribute was published which includes a bibliography of his writings.

BIBLIOGRAPHY: *Magyar Zsidó Lexikon* (1929), 746; A. Scheiber, in: *új Élet* no. 38 (1950); Shunami, Bibl, 734 no. 4181.

[Baruch Yaron / Alexander Scheiber]

RICIUS, PAULUS (**Rici, Rizzi**, also known as *Paulus Israelita*; d. 1541), humanist, translator, and apostate. Probably born in Germany, Ricius was baptized in Italy about 1505 and in the following year met Erasmus at Pavia, where he became professor of philosophy and medicine. Ricius was one of the very few converted Jews of the age who made a serious contribution to Christian Hebraism, although he also wrote a series of works (*Sal Foederis*, 1507, 15142) designed to confirm his new faith and refute Jewish arguments by means of the Kabbalah. From 1514 he was body physician to the Emperor Maximilian in Augsburg; he was elected to the chair of Hebrew at Pavia in 1521; and the favor which he enjoyed at the imperial court led to his being ennobled as Baron von Sparzenstein in 1530. The works which Ricius published include translations of Jewish and Muslim texts and some original writings, mainly on mystical themes. The translations are: part of Joseph *Gikatilla's *Sha'arei Orah*; the sole surviving Latin edition of a medical treatise by the 12th-century Spanish scholar Albucasis; and works by Averroes.

It is, above all, as one of the architects of the Christian Kabbalah that Ricius is now mainly remembered. The *Sha'arei Orah* translation – *Portae lucis* (Augsburg, 1516) – was consulted by Conrad *Pellicanus while it was still in manuscript and inspired many later scholars to tackle similar projects (e.g., the Zohar translations of G. *Postel). Ricius helped to popularize the "prophecy of Elijah" (based on Sanh. 97a) and, like *Pico della Mirandola (whose knowledge of Kabbalah Ricius disparaged), he was able to "discover" the Trinity and other Christian doctrines in Jewish mystical works, which he defended against the attacks of Jacob *Hoogstraaten in his *Apologeticus sermo* (in Pistorius, *Artis Cabbalisticae … Tomus I*, 1587).

Other works by Ricius include the treatises *De anima coeli* (1519) and *Responsio ad interrogationem de nomine Tetragrammato* (1519), and *Statera prudentium* (c. 1532), which led to a controversy with the humanist Girolamo Aleandro because of the author's evident toleration of Protestantism. *De coelesti agricultura libri quattuor* (1541), a collection of Ricius' major works which appeared shortly before his death, contained a preface by his former teacher, the philosopher Pietro Pomponazzi.

BIBLIOGRAPHY: F. Secret, *Les Kabbalistes chrétiens de la Renaissance* (1964), 87–99 and index; idem, in: *Convivium*, 5 (1956), 550; idem, in: *Rinascimento*, 11 (1960), 169–92; Steinschneider, Cat Bod, 2141–43; C. Singer, in: E.R. Bevan and C. Singer (eds.), *The Legacy of Israel* (1927), 240; C. Roth, *Jews in the Renaissance* (1959), 80, 145.

[Godfrey Edmond Silverman]

RICKLES, DON (1926–), U.S. comedian and actor. Born in New York, New York, the comedian started out as a shy child, but by the time he attended Newton High School in Elmhurst, Long Island, Rickles was performing in school plays. During World War II, Rickles served with the U.S. Navy aboard the USS *Cyrene*. Rickles studied drama after his discharge in 1946, and two years later he started working stand-up routines in small clubs. His impressions and jokes were nothing remarkable, but the audience instantly connected with the off-the-cuff remarks he threw back at hecklers, which gave rise to his insult style of comedy. In 1957, Frank Sinatra walked into a Hollywood nightclub where Rickles was performing when the comedian famously told the crooner, "Make yourself at home Frank. Hit somebody." Sinatra found the comic hilarious, and by 1959 Rickles had signed to his first performance at the Sahara in Las Vegas; Rickles continued to headline in the city at different hotels for decades. In 1958, Rickles made his feature film debut with *Run Silent Run Deep* (1958), followed by such films as *The Rat Race* (1960) and *Beach Blanket Bingo*. On October 7, 1965, Rickles made his first of many appearances on Johnny Carson's *Tonight Show*. He recorded his bestselling first album, titled *Hello Dummy!*, for 7 Arts Records in 1967; his follow-up album was titled *Don Rickles Speaks*. Rickles and actor Ernest Borgnine starred in West Coast performances of *The Odd Couple* in 1967, and in 1968 ABC debuted the short-lived variety program *The Don Rickles Show*. Rickles had a starring turn in the World War II feature *Kelly's Heroes* (1970), and from 1971 to 1972 CBS ran a sitcom, the *Don Rickles Show*, which featured the comedian as an advertising executive. From 1977 to 1978 Rickles starred as a Navy chief petty officer in the NBC comedy *C.P.O. Sharkey*. On February 7, 1982, Sinai Temple in West Los Angeles, California, dedicated the Barbara and Don Rickles Gymnasium. In the 1990s, Rickles enjoyed a film comeback with parts in *Innocent Blood* (1992) and *Casino* (1995), and as the voice for Mr. Potato Head in the Disney/Pixar features *Toy Story* (1995) and *Toy Story 2* (1999).

BIBLIOGRAPHY: "Rickles, Don," in: *Contemporary Theatre, Film and Television*, vol. 42 (Gale, 2002). **WEBSITE:** www.imdb.com/name/nm0725543; www.thehockeypuck.com/bio.html.

[Adam Wills (2nd ed.)]

RICKOVER, HYMAN GEORGE (1900–1986), U.S. naval officer; "father" of the atomic-powered submarine. Rickover, born in Russian Poland, was taken by his family to Chicago in 1906, where his father became a tailor. He graduated from the United States Naval Academy in 1922 and was commissioned an ensign in the U.S. Navy.

After sea duty, Rickover studied electrical engineering at the U.S. Naval Academy at Annapolis and Columbia University. He served aboard submarines for three years and then held increasingly important staff and command positions. During World War II Rickover headed the Electrical Section, Bureau of Ships in the Navy Department, and was decorated for his effectiveness in obtaining men and materials to produce electric power and equipment necessary for naval shipbuilding and maintenance. Serving at Oak Ridge in 1946, site of the development of the atomic bomb, and visiting other nuclear research installations, Rickover became convinced of the feasibility of constructing nuclear-powered submarines. Almost alone against considerable opposition, he persuaded the navy to undertake the effort in late 1947. Rickover was soon placed in charge of the project, working with the Atomic Energy Commission, which designed and built the reactors. The "Nautilus," the first atomic-powered submarine in the world, was launched in January 1954. Despite his success, Rickover would have been forced to retire in 1953 if Congressional intervention had not kept him on duty and ensured his subsequent promotions to rear admiral and vice admiral. He made other contributions to nuclear-power developments, was active in the field of education, and received many decorations. In 1973 Rickover was promoted full admiral. In 1979 he was awarded the Harry S. Truman Good Neighbor Award and in the following year the Medal of Freedom by President Carter.

BIBLIOGRAPHY: C. Blair, *The Atomic Submarine and Admiral Rickover* (1954).

[Stanley L. Falk]

RIE, DAME LUCIE (1902–1995), British potter. Born in Vienna, the daughter of Benjamin Gomperz, a professor of medicine and a friend of Freud, Lucie Rie became a potter in the mid-1920s. She came to Britain with her husband, Hans Rie, in 1938, but after their divorce lived alone in London and worked at a studio in Bayswater. Her high standards made her one of the most famous potters in Britain and she was created a dame in 1990. Originally specializing in earthenware and jewelry, she later worked in stoneware and porcelain. Much of her later work was done in collaboration with her student and fellow refugee Hans Coper (1920–1981), a leading potter in his own right.

BIBLIOGRAPHY: ODNB online; T. Birks, *Lucie Rie* (1987); M. Coatts (ed.), *Lucie Rie and Hans Coper: Potters in Parallel* (1987); J. Houston (ed.), *Lucie Rie: A Survey of Her Life and Work* (1981); T. Birks, *Hans Coper* (1983).

[William D. Rubinstein (2nd ed.)]

RIEGELMAN, HAROLD (1892–1982), U.S. lawyer and public official. Riegelman, who was born in Des Moines, Iowa, entered private law practice after service in World War I. His public posts included: New York State veteran relief commissioner (1922–32); special assistant New York State attorney general (1929–30); special counsel to the U.S. Treasury Department (1935); delegate to the New York State Constitutional Convention (1938); and special counsel to the New York State Department of Taxation and Finance (1947–48). Riegelman was a pioneer in drafting housing legislation, first in New York and later of the 1937 National Housing Law. In 1953, at President Eisenhower's request, Riegelman served briefly as acting postmaster of New York City and in the same year he was the unsuccessful Republican mayoral candidate. He later served as one of the members of the U.S. delegation to the UN.

Active in Jewish affairs, Riegelman was vice president of the American Jewish Committee (1949–52), a member of its executive committee from 1951, and finance chairman of the American Friends of the Hebrew University. Riegelman, who served in the U.S. Army with the rank of colonel from 1942 to 1945 and was decorated for bravery, wrote three books about his experiences in the two world wars. These are: *War Notes of a Casual* (1931); *There's a Nip in the Air* (1946); and *Caves of Biak* (1955).

RIEGER, ELIEZER (1896–1954), Hebrew educationalist. Born in Gribov, Galicia, Rieger settled in Palestine in 1920. He made notable contributions to methods of instruction in Hebrew, Jewish history, and modern Arabic in Ereẓ Israel and pioneered in the teaching of civics and the social sciences. He was supervisor of Jewish secondary schools in Palestine (1937–38) and professor of education at the Hebrew University (1939–50). He compiled the first Hebrew frequency word list (1935), which served as a basic guide for educators in Israel and the Diaspora. His textbooks on modern Jewish history were widely used, and he wrote comprehensive surveys on Jewish education in Palestine (1940 and 1945). Rieger was among the founders of the Hebrew University's teacher training department and its secondary school. He was one of the chief opponents of the "trend" school system (see Israel, State of: *Education), and as director general of the Ministry of Education and Culture (1951–54) was in charge of its replacement by a system of state education.

[Alexander M. Dushkin]

RIEGER, PAUL (1870–1939), German rabbi, scholar, and historian. Rieger, who was born in Dresden, served as rabbi to the Reform congregations at Potsdam (1896–1902), Hamburg (1902–19), Brunswick, and Stuttgart (1922–39) where he died. He published works on the terminology and technology of handicrafts in the Mishnah, *Versuch einer Technologie und Terminologie der Handwerke in der Mischnah* (1894), and on various aspects of contemporary German-Jewish history. His major work was his participation, in collaboration with his friend Hermann Vogelstein, in a massive work on the history of the Jews in Rome (*Geschichte der Juden in Rom*), as the result of a prize competition sponsored by the Moritz Rapoport Foundation in Vienna in 1890. Rieger wrote the entire second volume (1895), dealing with the period from 1420 to 1870, as well as some parts of the first volume (1896). Notwithstanding the somewhat arid treatment and heavy style, it remains the standard work on the subject and is the basis of the work

Rome, a history of the Jews in Rome, published in English by Vogelstein in 1940.

BIBLIOGRAPHY: H. Liebeschuetz, in: YLBI, 8 (1963), 252–3.

[Cecil Roth]

RIEGNER, GERHART (1911–2002), Jewish public figure. Born in Berlin and trained as a lawyer, from 1936 Riegner was associated with the World Jewish Congress: first as legal officer and then as director of the Geneva office (1939–48), as a member of the World Executive and as director of coordination (1959–64), as secretary-general (1965–83), and as cochairman of the Governing Board from 1983. He was directly involved in virtually all major Jewish problems from the middle 1930s on. As international chairman of the World University Service (1949–55) and as president of the conference of nongovernmental organizations in consultative status with the UN (1953–1955) and with UNESCO (1956–1958), he established a wide network of international relations among the international leadership and became a leading specialist in this field. The main features of his activities in the service of the Jewish people include protection of Jewish rights in the League of Nations under the minorities treaties; decisive information and rescue activities during and after World War II, when he was the first to uncover the plan of systematic extermination of the Jews by the Nazi government in August 1942; active involvement in important international conferences, such as the Paris Peace Conference and UN meetings, where he was influential in the shaping of the UN Universal Declaration of Human Rights; a pioneering role in interreligious consultations with the Catholic Church (before, during, and after Vatican Council II), the World Council of Churches, the Lutheran World Federation, the Orthodox churches, and the Anglican Communion; and participation in the foundation of and, from 1982 to 1984, chairmanship of, the International Jewish Committee for Interreligious Consultations (IJCIC), which was created in 1969 as a representative platform of the Jewish community in its relations with official church bodies. In 1992, the Vatican conferred on him a papal knighthood of the Order of St. Gregory.

BIBLIOGRAPHY: *Christian Jewish Relations*, vol. 24:1–2 (1991). **ADD. BIBLIOGRAPHY:** J. Picard, *Die Schweiz und die Juden* (1992), index; G. Riegner, *Ne jamais déséspérer: soixante ans au service du peuple juif et des droits de l'homme* (autobiography) (1998; German trans. 2001).

[J. Halperin]

RIESMAN, DAVID (1909–2002), U.S. sociologist. Born of Jewish parents in Philadelphia, Riesman became a Unitarian. Graduating from Harvard Law School in 1934, he served as a law clerk to U.S. Supreme Court judge Louis D. *Brandeis (1935–36) and taught at the University of Buffalo Law School (1937–41). He then served as deputy assistant district attorney for New York County (Manhattan) (1942–43).

After World War II Riesman turned to sociology and became a professor at the University of Chicago in 1946. In 1958 he was appointed professor of social sciences at Harvard, where he taught until his retirement in 1980, when he assumed emeritus status.

He became widely known as the principal author (the others were N. Glazer and R. Denney) of *The Lonely Crowd: A Study of the Changing American Character* (1950; 1962[10]). His description of human types as "tradition-directed," "inner-directed," and "other-directed" have become part of the general vocabulary.

Among his numerous other publications are *Faces in the Crowd* (1952, 1960[2]); *Constraint and Variety in American Education* (1956, 1965[3]); *Thorstein Veblen: A Critical Evaluation* (1960); *Abundance for What?* (1964); and a collection of his social-critical essays, *Individualism Reconsidered* (1954, 1966[2]). Riesman was an active pacifist. In 1958 he published, together with Lazarsfeld and Thielens, *The Academic Mind: Social Scientists in a Time of Crisis*, an analysis of academic attitudes under the impact of the witch-hunt of liberals in the period dominated by Senator Joseph McCarthy. In 1960 he became one of the founders of the Committees of Correspondence, an organization under the auspices of the American Friends Service Committee, which explored moral and political issues regarding nuclear weapons.

Other works by Riesman include *Conversations in Japan* (with E. Riesman, 1967), *The Academic Revolution* (with Christopher Jencks, 1968), *Academic Values and Mass Education* (with J. Gusfield and Z. Gamson, 1971), *Academic Transformation* (1973), *The Perpetual Dream* (with G. Grant, 1978), *On Higher Education* (1980), and *Is My Armor Straight?* (with R. Berendzen, 1986).

BIBLIOGRAPHY: D.M. Rogers, *Riesman's 'The Lonely Crowd'* (1966); S.M. Lipset (ed.), *Culture and Social Character: The Work of David Riesman Reviewed* (1961). **ADD. BIBLIOGRAPHY:** O. Patterson, "The Last Sociologist," in: *New York Times* (May 19, 2002); H. Gans et al., *On the Making of Americans: Essays in Honor of David Riesman* (1979).

[Werner J. Cahnman / Ruth Beloff (2nd ed.)]

RIESS, LUDWIG (1861–1928), German historian. Born in Thuringia, Riess studied at the University of Berlin. Although his doctorate *Geschichte des Wahl rechts zum englischen Parlament* (1885; abridged translation *History of the English Electoral Law in the Middle Ages*; 1940) was widely hailed for its brilliant scholarship, Riess was unable to obtain a university position because he was a Jew. He therefore accepted an appointment at Tokyo Imperial University in 1887, and during the following 15 years was instrumental in furthering the spread of western historical methods, particularly of his mentor, Leopold von Ranke, in Japan. In 1902 he returned to Germany where he served as lecturer, later associate professor, at the University of Berlin.

A prolific writer, he produced many works on European history and a number of studies on Japanese topics. Best known are his *Lectures on English Constitutional History* (1891); *Allerlei aus Japan* (1904); and *Historik* (1912).

[Hyman Kublin]

RIESSER, GABRIEL (1806–1863), pioneer of Jewish emancipation in Germany. Born in Hamburg, Riesser studied law at the universities of Kiel and Heidelberg. After trying in vain to become lecturer in one of the universities, and after being refused permission to practice as a notary in Hamburg because of his faith (1830), Riesser decided to devote his life to the struggle of the Jews to achieve *emancipation. He published in 1831 a pamphlet, *Ueber die Stellung der Bekenner des Mosaischen Glaubens in Deutschland.* Addressed to Germans of all religious persuasions, it marked a turning point in the struggle for emancipation. Riesser demanded emancipation for the Jews in the name of honor and justice. In his view the claim that the Jews must convert in order to obtain full civil rights was evidence of contempt for religion. The Jews themselves must fight for their own rights, and for that purpose they must organize themselves in special associations, since only by a common effort and not as individuals do they have a chance of success. His call struck a responsive chord and the pamphlet soon had to be reprinted.

Riesser and his ideas were severely criticized, especially by the rationalist theologian and professor, H.E.G. Paulus from Heidelberg. Paulus maintained that the adherence of the Jews to their religion made them a different – Jewish – nation, and therefore they did not have the right to be citizens (*Staatsbuerger*). In the controversy with Paulus, Riesser tried to prove that the Jews had ceased to be a nation. He held that their religion was a religious denomination and therefore they were equal to all other Germans, Protestants or Catholics, in a country in which they had lived for many generations. Riesser vigorously rejected Paulus' claim that the Jewish identification with Germany would be delusive. He argued that the long-awaited political union of Germany could be achieved only in a state built on the principles of justice, liberty, and equality, and these principles also necessitated the granting of emancipation to the Jews. He propagated his views in comprehensive essays about the problem of Jewish emancipation in the constitutional debates of his time, which he published in his periodical *Der Jude, Periodische Blaetter fuer Religion und Gewissensfreiheit* (1831–1833). Its very name indicated Riesser's self-consciousness at a time when German Jewry was seeking to substitute the word "Jewish" with "Mosaic." He published in 1838 *Einige Worte ueber Lessing's Denkmal, an die Juden Deutschlands gerichtet.* Riesser expressed the hope, in messianic vein, that the struggle for the sake of human values would be crowned with success, and that love of mankind and tolerance would defeat religious hatred and the suppression of free conscience. At the same time Riesser tried in vain to be naturalized in Hessen and to take part in forming its constitutional regime. In 1840 he was permitted to open a notary's office in Hamburg. In the years preceding the 1848 Revolution, ideological and political strife in Germany intensified and this found expression in his work, *Juedische Briefe, Zur Abwehr und Verstaendigung* (1840–42), in which he entered into polemics with Bruno *Bauer and Wolfgang Menzel, who was a rabid opponent of Heinrich *Heine and Ludwig *Boerne. Riesser had already defended Boerne in 1831 when the latter was attacked because of his *Briefe aus Paris.*

Riesser's aspiration to function simultaneously as a German statesman and as an advocate of Jewish emancipation materialized during the Frankfurter Vorparlament und National Versammlung in 1848–49. Distinguishing himself in the National Assembly as a powerful speaker, he was vice president (for two months) and a member of the constitutional committee. He belonged to the right wing of the center in the National Assembly, expressing his views on "a free, united, great, and strong" Germany in his article, *Ein Wort ueber die Zukunft Deutschlands* (1848). The climax of his activity was the "*Kaiserrede*" (March 29, 1849), which was considered one of the most brilliant speeches delivered in the National Assembly. It contained the summary of the debate on the proposed constitution, and in it Riesser sought to provide justification for offering the imperial German crown to the king of Prussia; he was later one of the members of the delegation to the king, who declined the offer. Riesser proudly fought in the National Assembly for the acknowledgment of the Jews' right to full civil rights. His very status in the National Assembly was a partial expression of emancipation, which was given further expression in his later years. In 1849 not only was he naturalized in Hamburg but he became its representative in the Erfurt parliament (1850). With the formation of a citizens' council (*Buergerschaft*) in Hamburg, Riesser was elected to it and became its vice president (1859), and in 1860 he was appointed a member of the Hamburg High Court, the first German Jew to receive this title. Among his many travels outside Germany, Riesser visited the United States in 1856. He returned from this trip disappointed and shocked by the status of the American Blacks, which he regarded as a grave blow to the principle of equality and freedom, especially in a country whose democracy was theoretically the model for the rest of the world.

Riesser abandoned the observance of all Jewish tradition in his private life, but he insisted that those who wished to observe these traditions should do so of right and not on sufferance. Riesser was one of the leading members of the Hamburg Temple and associated himself generally with the moderate wing of the *Reform movement. He opposed giving up a special Jewish character in order to achieve emancipation. Only from the religious point of view were the Jews a minority, according to Riesser, a minority whose rights should be recognized by the ruling Christian majority.

The Jewish struggle for emancipation was identified with the figure of Riesser, whose sharp intellect and upright personality won him much reverence. Medals were struck in his honor and declarations of gratitude were presented to him during his lifetime. After he died a special association to perpetuate his memory was formed; M. Isler published Riesser's biography and writings under the auspices of this society (*Gabriel Riesser's Gesammelte Schriften*, 1867–68; repr. with an epilogue by J.H. Schoeps, 2001).

[Leni Yahil / Archiv Bibliographia Judaica (2nd ed.)]

His father LAZARUS JACOB (1763–1828) was born in the Bavarian village of Oettingen im Ries (hence his name) to a distinguished rabbinical family (*Katzenellenbogen) and studied Talmud under R. Raphael *Kohen, chief rabbi of *Altona. He subsequently married the latter's daughter, and served as secretary of the *bet din*; he also wrote his father-in-law's biography *Zekher Ẓaddik* (Altona, 1805) in fluent Hebrew. He lost his post in 1799, but later returned to Hamburg (after 1819).

BIBLIOGRAPHY: M. Rinott, in: YLBI, 7 (1962), 11–38; J. Weil, *Sendschreiben an Dr. Gabriel Riesser* (1832); B. Auerbach, in: *Gallerie der ausgezeichneten Israeliten aller Jahrhunderte*, 4 (1836), 5–42; N. Frankfurter, *Denkrede auf Gabriel Riesser* (1863); E. Lehmann, *Gabriel Riesser, ein Rechtsanwalt* (1870); M. Isler, *Gabriel Riesser's Leben* (1871); M. Silberstein, *Gabriel Riesser's Leben und Wirken* (1911); S. Bernfeld, *Gavriel Riesser* (Heb., 1901); F. Friedlaender, *Das Leben Gabriel Riessers. Ein Beitrag zur inneren Geschichte Deutschlands im 19. Jahrhundert* (1926); J. Seifensieder, *Gabriel Riesser* (1920), 3–14. **ADD. BIBLIOGRAPHY:** E. Lueth, *Gabriel Riesser, ein grosser Jude, Hamburger und deutscher Patriot* (1963); M. Zimmermann, in: *Zeitschrift des Vereins fuer Hamburgische Geschichte*, 61 (1975), 59–84; U. Barschel, *Gabriel Riesser als Abgeordneter…* (1987); G. Arnsberg, *Gavriel Riser* (Heb., 1990); R. Postel and H. Stubbe-da Luz, *Die Notare: J.H. Hübbe, E. Schramm, G. Riesser…* (2001).

RIESSER, JACOB (1853–1932), German jurist and banker. A nephew of Gabriel *Riesser, Jacob Riesser was born in Frankfurt. He was baptized in his youth. In 1880 he opened a lawyer's office in his home town. In 1888 he moved to Berlin and served as a director of the Darmstaedter Bank fuer Handel und Gewerbe until 1905, when he became a professor of law at the University of Berlin. His writings on legal aspects of the German capital market decisively influenced stock exchange and banking legislation. It was on his initiative that the Zentralverband des deutschen Bank- und Bankiergewerbes was formed in 1901, and in 1905 he became the editor of *Bankarchiv*, the profession's leading periodical. In 1909 he was a cofounder of the Hansabund, an industrial-commercial organization designed to oppose the government's pro-agricultural policies and attitudes. During 1916–28 he served as deputy in the Reischstag, first with the National Liberals, and from 1918 with the Volkspartei, and as vice president of the German parliament from 1921 to 1928. He was also a member of the 1919 Weimar Constituent Assembly.

His many publications include the standard work *Die deutschen Grossbanken und ihre Konzentration im Zusammenhang mit der Entwicklung der Gesamtwirtschaft in Deutschland* (1905; *The German Great Banks and Their Concentration in Connection with the Economic Development of Germany*, 1911), and *Finanzielle Kriegsbereitschaft und Kriegsfuehrung* ("Financial Preparation for War and for Making War," 1913^2).

BIBLIOGRAPHY: E. Hamburger, *Juden im oeffentlichen Leben Deutschlands*, 19 (1968), 361–3; J. Riesser, *Erinnerung an meine geliebte Mutter Pauline Riesser* (1895).

[Joachim O. Ronall]

RIETI (da Rieti, Rietti, Arieti (?)), family of bankers in Italy originating from the town of Rieti, located in the Latium region. First mentioned in the 14th century, some of the family moved from their town of origin to Rome, Florence, Siena, Bologna, and Mantua. One of its leading members was ISAAC RIETI (Maestro Gaio) father of Moses b. Isaac *Rieti. From 1469 to 1473, the physician MICHAEL BEN JUDAH DA RIETI lived in Terni; the family is found in the 15th century in Mantua, Rieti, Perugia, Rome, and Cesena. Around 1480, Moses ben Elchanan da Rieti established himself in Siena as a loan banker; his son LAUDADIO ISHMAEL continued his father's activity, while his brothers went to Bologna. This branch of the Da Rieti had strong family ties with another important family of Jewish bankers, the Da *Pisa. He also founded a small yeshivah, headed by Joseph d'Arles from 1537, followed by Isaac Lattes in 1552; Ismael also hosted Johanan b. Joseph *Treves. He established other loan banks in Tuscany, and probably exercised a certain degree of authority over the other Jewish bankers of the region. Due to the difficult situation in Siena after a popular insurrection, the family obtained the authorization to found a bank in Pisa (1547), until then forbidden to the Jews as in all the Duchy of Florence. Ishmael was on friendly terms with Duke Cosimo Medici and in high favor with Donna Benvenida Abrabanel. He gave hospitality to the pseudo-messiah David *Reuveni (1526), but did not show any enthusiasm for Reuveni's programs and refused to give him financial assistance. He undertook various philanthropic activities, followed in this by his son MOSES DA RIETI. When a hostile movement broke out against the Jews in Empoli (Tuscany), as a result of the prohibition by the Church against Christians engaging in trade with Jews and doing work for them on their Sabbath, Moses gave the money necessary to send a Jewish delegation to Rome and obtain from the pope a bull in favor of the Jews of Empoli. With his brothers, SIMONE and ANGELO, Moses used his influence with Cosimo to prevent the seizure of the Talmud ordered by Paul IV. At that time, SOLOMON MOSES DA RIETI was practicing in Rome as a physician.

An important branch of the family moved from Siena to Bologna where, in 1546, ELHANAN BEN ISAAC ELIAKIM DA RIETI was buried; his tombstone is preserved at the University of Bologna. In this town lived also, in 1556, Moses' nephew, son of Isaac, ASAEL RAPHAEL RIETI, father of ELIJAH ISAAC and HANANIAH ELIAKIM (1561–1623) the pupil of Judah b. Joseph Moscato. He served as rabbi of Mantua (1589) and Luzzara (1604) and was active in establishing the Shomerim la-Boker society in Mantua. Also a *ḥazzan*, he composed prayers and liturgical poems, many of which are included in the *Ayyelet ha-Shaḥar* (Mantua, 1612); others, especially for the morning of Hoshana Rabbah, form the *Mekiẓ Redumim* (Mantua, 1648), published, with an autobiographical foreword, by his son DAVID NAPHTALI; other liturgical poems have been collected in the *Minḥat Ḥananyah*, still in manuscript (Bibl. Oxford). In his compositions Hananiah harmoniously blended the elements from earlier **piyyutim* with those of his time. Other talmudic and ritualistic works (*Peri Megadim; Sedeh Levanon; Seder Tappuḥim*) have not yet been published. His wife Malkah studied the laws of *sheḥitah* with R. Solomon ben Samson Basilea who allowed her to practice (1581): as is recorded in various responsa.

The heirs of MORDECAI BEN ISAAC DA RIETI opened one of the five loan banks authorized by the duke of Mantua; other members of the family were in Scandiano, under the house of Este. SIMONE DA RIETI was a member, in 1590, of the Jewish delegation which discussed the placing of the Talmud on the papal index of prohibited books. In the 17th century there lived in Siena JOSEPH BEN SHABBETAI ELHANAN, rabbi and copyist. ELIEZER BEN ISAAC RIETI, a pupil of the yeshivah of *Conegliano, published in Venice in 1612 a *Lu'ah Ma'amarei Ein Yisrael* ("alphabetical index of Ein Yisrael"); another of his works was on the *Kelalei ha-Talmud*. Still in Venice HEZEKIAH BEN GABRIEL RIETI published in the "*Lingua Tosca*" ("Tuscan Language") an Italian translation of the Book of Proverbs dedicated partly to SERENA RIETI of Mantua; the book is preceded by a letter dedicated to Ria and Isaiah Massarani. In this period members of the Rieti family lived also in Padua, where in 1706 AARON VITA DI ANGELO, from the region of Veneto, received a doctorate in medicine and philosophy. In the 19th century, the painter ARTURO RIETI of Trieste was noteworthy. VITTORIO RIETI (1898–1994) was an important composer of ballet scores (*The Ball*, 1929, produced by S. Diaghilev, choreography by G. Balanchine, scenery and costumes by G. De Chirico), opera, and a variety of instrumental combinations in the tonal and neo-classical style; from 1948 to 1964 he was a teacher in American music academies and conservatories. His son FABIO RIETI (1925–) painted murals in Paris and other French cities ("Les piétons des Halles"; Les fenêtres de Beaubourg"). FABIO's son NICKY RIETI (1947–) worked as a stage designer for the major French and Italian theaters (Opéra Bastille; La Scala).

The genealogy of the family, reconstructed by M. Vogelstein and P. Rieger (Vogelstein-Rieger, 74), was completed by U. Cassuto (*Gli Ebrei a Firenze* … (1918), 349, n. 6), S. Simonsohn (*Toledot ha-Yehudim be-Dukkasut Mantovah*; 1964, 544 n. 305), and Y. Boksenboim (*Iggerot Beit Rieti*, 1988).

BIBLIOGRAPHY: Milano, Bibliotheca, index; Milano, Italia, index; D. Kaufmann, in: REJ, 26 (1893), 90–91; S.H. Margulies, in: RI, 3 (1903), 104–5, 154; Mortara, Indice, 54; I. Levy, in: *Vessillo Israelitico*, 53 (1905), 507ff.; U. Cassuto, *Gli Ebrei a Firenze*… (1918), index; idem, in: *Ha-Ẓofeh*, 7 (1924), 36–43; C. Roth, in: RMI, 5 (1930/31), 297; idem, *Jews in the Renaissance* (1959), index; E. Loevinsohn, in: *Annuario di studi ebraici*, 2 (1937), 125ff.; E. Castelli, *I Banchi feneratizi ebraici nel mantovano* (1959), index; A. Modena and E. Morpurgo, *Medici e chirurghi ebrei dottorati e licenziati nell'Università di Padova*… (1967), 69; Vogelstein-Rieger, index; G. Bedarida, *Ebrei d'Italia* (1948), index; S. Simonsohn, *Toledot ha-Yehudim be-Dukkasut Mantovah*, 2 vols. (1962–64), index. HANANIAH: M. Steinschneider, *Jewish Literature*… (1965²); C. Dushinsky, in: *Occident and Orient*… *Gaster Anniversary Volume* (1936), 96f. **ADD. BIBLIOGRAPHY:** M. Steinschneider, in: RMI, 38 (1972), 406–23, 487–99; A. Marx, in *Kovez Mada'i le-Zekher Moshe Shur* (1945), 271ff.; M. Cassandro, *Gli ebrei e il prestito ebraico a Siena nel Cinquecento* (1979); Y. Boksenboim, *Iggerot Beit Rieti* (1988); R. Crevier (ed.), *Fabio Rieti. Peinture textes et errances* (1992).

[Alfredo Mordechai Rabello / Alessandro Guetta (2nd ed.)]

RIETI, MOSES BEN ISAAC DA (1388–after 1460), Italian scholar, physician, and poet. He was born in Rieti. He devoted himself to medicine and philosophy, practicing as a physician in his home town until the death of his father (1422). Under the papacy of Eugene IV, he went to Rome where he held the position of chief rabbi to the local community, and later became private physician to Pope Pius II. His first literary work is the poem *Iggeret Ya'ar ha-Levanon*, an epic describing the decorations and vessels in the Temple (Parma, de Rossi Ms. 1394/2).

At the age of 24, Rieti wrote his most important work, *Mikdash Me'at*, after the fashion of Dante's *Divine Comedy*, and influenced by the philosophical work of Solomon ibn *Gabirol. Written in a rhetorical rather than poetic style, it is in many ways comparable to Dante's *Paradise*. The work consists of two parts. The first, *Ḥelek ha-Ulam*. is subdivided into five chapters and contains 435 strophes. It opens with the author's prayer resembling Dante's "Invocation", in which he introduces himself and his work. Then, in the form of a parody, he reviews Maimonides' 13 Principles of Faith, and the number of sciences and their ramifications according to Averroes, Avicenna, Ghazali, Alfarabi, and Maimonides, the Isagoge of Porfirio, and the commentary of Averroes, as well as Aristotle's *Book of Categories* with the commentaries of Averroes and Levi b. Gershom. The second part, *Ḥelek ha-Heikhal*, consisting of eight chapters containing 615 strophes, gives a description of the Celestial Court, where the patriarchs, the prophets, and the nation's saints occupy places of honor. In *Me'on ha-Sho'alim* he addresses a personal prayer to Moses, begging for a speedy redemption. *Ir Elohim* ("The City of God") reviews all the biblical figures, while *Oniyyot ha-Nefesh* presents the Mishnah and the Talmud, omitting not a single one of the *tanna'im, amoraim, geonim*, and their pupils' pupils, down to the rabbis of his own time. The thematic variety and harmonious poetic form made these works a treasure of Hebrew literature. The author himself was referred to as the "Hebrew Dante" and "Master of Poets", titles which suited neither the author nor his work. The complete text of *Mikdash Me'at* was published in 1851 by J. Goldenthal, with an introduction in Italian and Hebrew. Rieti lived to see parts of his poetic work sung in the synagogues of Italy. Some parts of *Mikdash Me'at* were even translated into Italian, while *Me'on ha-Sho'alim* was translated by Eliezer Maẓli'aḥ b. Abraham Kohen (Venice, c. 1585), Deborah Ascarelli (Venice, 1601–02), and Samuel de Castel Nuovo (Venice, 1609). At the end of his life, Moses abandoned poetry and devoted himself entirely to philosophy and apologetics. His last poetic work was an elegy in memory of his wife.

BIBLIOGRAPHY: Zunz, in: WZJT, 2 (1836), 321–6; L. Dukes: *Ehrensaeulen und Denksteine*… (1837), 50; Carmoly, in: *Israelitische Annalen*, 1 (1839), 55, 63; idem, in: *Literaturblatt des Orients*, 2 (1841), 234–5; Steinschneider, Cat Bod, no. 6548; Steinschneider, Uebersetzungen, 28–29, 76–77, 462, 660; A. Berliner, *Geschichte der Juden in Rom*, 2 (1893), 121; Guedemann, Gesch Erz, 2 (1884), 127; Vogelstein-Rieger, 2 (1895), 68–74ff.; Rhine, in: JQR, 1 (1910/11), 348–50; Milano,

Italia, 657–8; Davidson, Oẓar, 4 (1933), 450; J. Goldenthal, *Il Dante Ebreo* (1851); G. Karpeles, *Geschichte der juedischen Literatur*, 2 (1921³), 745ff.; I. Reggio, in: *Bikkurei ha-Ittim*, 9 (1829), 14; M.A. Shulwass, *Hayyei ha-Yehudim be-Italyah…* (1956), index.

[Yonah David]

RIETI, VITTORIO (1898–1994), composer. Born in Alexandria, Egypt, Rieti studied with Giuseppe Frugatta in Milan and later in Rome with Ottorino Respighi. During the 1920s and 1930s he was part of a group of French composers known as "Les Six" and spent most of his time in Paris, where he composed ballet and theater music in a neoclassical style. After moving to the United States in 1940, he became an instructor at various colleges and concentrated on symphonic and chamber music. Among his compositions are the music for Balanchine's ballets *Barabau* (1925) and *Le Bal* (1929) presented by Diaghilev, the ballet *David Triomphant* (1926), the operas *L'Arca di Noe* (1922), *Orfeo tragedia* (1928–29), *Teresa nel bosco* (1934), *Don Perlimplin* (1952), *Viaggio di Europa* (1954), *The Pet Shop* (1958), *The Clock* (1959–60), *Maryam the Harlot* (1966), oratorios, symphonies, orchestral works, chamber music, songs, and piano pieces.

BIBLIOGRAPHY: Grove online, s.v.; C. Ricci, *Vittorio Rieti* (1987).

[Israela Stein (2nd ed.)]

RIFKIND, SIR MALCOLM (1946–), British Conservative politician. Rifkind was born in Edinburgh, the son of a credit draper of Lithuanian origin. He was educated locally and graduated with a degree in law from Edinburgh University, where he was involved in politics, becoming chairman of the university Conservative Association in 1967. Called to the Bar in 1970 (he was later a Queen's Counsel), in the same year he was elected to Edinburgh Council and unsuccessfully contested the Parliamentary seat of Edinburgh Central. Elected to Parliament for Pentlands in 1974, he was appointed opposition front bench spokesman on Scottish Affairs in 1975. Having served on the Parliamentary committees dealing with foreign affairs, following the Conservative election victory in 1979 he served as minister for home affairs and the environment at the Scottish Office from 1979 to 1982 and Parliamentary undersecretary of state, Foreign and Commonwealth Office, 1983–86. In January 1986 he became the youngest member of the Cabinet and first Jewish secretary of state for Scotland. He held this office until he was appointed secretary of state for transport in 1990. In 1992–95 he was the first postwar Jewish secretary of state for defense since Emanuel *Shinwell. From 1995 to 1997 he served as foreign secretary, the first Jew to hold this post since 1931. Rifkind lost his seat in Parliament in the Labour landslide of 1997 and received a knighthood the same year. Subsequently he worked for the BHP oil company and, in 2004, was selected as the Tory candidate for the safe seat of Kensington and Chelsea. In public life he consistently maintained an interest in the affairs of Israel. He opposed the visit of PLO officials to London in 1975 and was honorary secretary of the Parliamentary group of Conservative Friends of Israel 1976–79. He was also an opponent of the 2003 Iraq war.

[David Cesarani / William D. Rubinstein (2nd ed.)]

RIFKIND, SIMON HIRSCH (1901–1995), U.S. attorney and jurist. Rifkind, who was born in Meretz, Russia, was taken to the United States in 1910. He graduated from the City College of New York in 1922 and received his LL.B. from Columbia Law School in 1925. He worked with Senator Robert F. Wagner as legislative secretary from 1927 to 1933, and from 1930 to 1941 practiced law as a partner in Wagner's law firm, Wagner, Quillinan & Rifkind. In 1941 Rifkind was appointed U.S. district judge of the Southern District of New York, holding this position until 1950, when he resigned to return to private practice with Paul, Weiss, Rifkind, Wharton & Garrison. In 1957 the firm opened a Chicago office with Adlai Stevenson as senior partner. Rifkind returned to judicial service as special master for the U.S. Supreme Court in the Colorado River case during 1955–61.

He served on administrative commissions and on quasi-judicial fact-finding bodies involving sociopolitical questions. He served New York City on the Board of Higher Education (1954–66); as a member of a state commission on city governmental operations (1959–61); in the 1963 teachers strike mediation; and on the commission that investigated the 1968 Columbia University turmoil. He served as chairman of John F. Kennedy's Presidential Railroad Commission in 1961–62. Rifkind represented New York State Democrats in reapportionment litigation in 1965–66, and was cochairman of the Presidential Commission on the Patent System in 1966–67. In the pamphlet *Reflections on Civil Liberties* (1954), Rifkind emphasized the constitution's circumscription of the status and function of congressional committees as lawmaking bodies.

Rifkind served as temporary special adviser on Jewish affairs in the European Theater to General Dwight D. Eisenhower in 1945–46, and in 1946 he testified before the Anglo-American Commission of Inquiry on Palestine that the only resolution of the plight of displaced persons was the opening of Palestine to settlement. He served as vice chairman of the board of directors of the Jewish Theological Seminary from 1947; as chairman of the "committee of five" on United Jewish Appeal allocations from 1949; and as chairman of the administrative board (1953–56) and of the executive board (1956–59) of the American Jewish Committee.

Some of his later landmark cases include the defense of Jacqueline Kennedy Onassis against paparazzi, and Pennzoil Company in its successful fight against Texaco in 1986. His many awards include the Medal of Freedom, presented to him by President Harry S. Truman.

In 1986 the City College of New York established the Simon H. Rifkind Center for the Humanities and the Arts, whose primary goal is to promote cultural activities in the humanities.

Rifkind wrote *The Basic Equities of the Palestine Problem* (1972), *One Man's Word: Selected Works of Simon H. Rifkind* (3 vols., ed. A. Bellow and W. Keens, 1986, 1989), and *At 90, on the 90s: The Journal of Simon H. Rifkind* (1992).

RIGA (Lettish **Rīga**), Baltic port, capital of Latvia; under Russian rule from 1710 to 1917, capital of Livonia (Livland); 1944–1991 in the Latvian S.S.R. The first documentary evidence of Jews in Riga – the record of a sale of merchandise to a Jew named Jacob – is dated 1536. During Polish and Swedish rule in Livonia (1561–1621 and 1621–1710, respectively) restrictions were imposed on Jewish residence, but in the course of time a number of Jewish merchants arrived there. By 1645 there was a special Jewish inn in the city where visiting Jewish merchants had to stay. In 1710 the Livonia region was incorporated into Russia and, according to reports by English merchants dating to 1714, Jews and Catholics then enjoyed religious freedom. In 1725 a few privileged Jews were given the right to reside outside the Jewish inn. In that same year they were permitted to bury their dead in Riga, whereas previously they had to be taken to *Courland for burial. Despite requests from the city authorities and the provincial governor, Empress Elizabeth Petrovna's decree of 1742, ordering the expulsion of Jews from *Russia, was also applied to the Jews in Riga. It was not until 1766, under Catherine II, that Jewish merchants were allowed into Riga, although they were restricted to a visit of six weeks and to residence at the Jewish inn; a few privileged Jews were given special permission to stay elsewhere.

Permission was granted for Jews to reside at Sloka (Ger. Schlock), a nearby town, in 1785, where in 1792 they were permitted to open a prayer room. A few managed to settle in Riga, although the official ban was still in force. In 1798 there were seven Jewish families living in Riga, and by 1811, 736 Jews in the city and suburbs including over half in Sloka. As Riga was outside the *Pale of Settlement, it continued to be difficult for Jews to enter the city. However, in 1813 the Jews of Sloka were given the right to settle there. The same year a community is mentioned. In 1822 Jews were permitted to engage in crafts. The "Jewish statute" of 1835 (see *Russia) confirmed the permanent residence rights of part of the population. In 1840 Sloka Jews were allowed to open a school in Riga which became one of the few modern institutions in Russia at that time. Max *Lilienthal was invited to Riga to become principal of the school and rabbi of the "German" synagogue. After he left there, Reuben *Wunderbar became principal of the school.

In 1841 Jews were allowed to register officially as inhabitants of the city, and later were permitted to build synagogues, own real property, and engage in commerce and trade; an organized community was officially founded in 1842 and continued to function until 1893. In 1850 the community asked for permission to buy land for a synagogue, on which building commenced in 1868. The number of Jews increased from 5,254 in 1869 to 22,115 (8 percent of the population) in 1897 and 33,651 (6.5 percent) in 1913. They played an important role in commerce, the export of goods (especially grain, timber, and flax), in industry, banking, and the various crafts. Jews owned timber mills, tanneries, and engaged in clothing and shoe manufacture. Before the outbreak of World War I the majority of dentists and 20 percent of the physicians were Jews, while only a few practiced as lawyers. There were a number of synagogues and ḥasidic prayer rooms, schools, *ḥadarim* both of the traditional and the reformed type, a library, charitable institutions, and various clubs and societies. Zionist activities were organized at the end of the 19th century and a delegate from Riga attended the First Zionist Congress. In 1898 the third branch of the *Society for the Promotion of Culture among the Jews in Russia (after St. Petersburg and Odessa) was formed in Riga. Among the official rabbis (see **kazyonny ravvin*) were two Hebrew authors, A.A. Pomiansky (1873–93) and J.L. *Kantor (1909–15). During the war, in 1915, Riga Jews gave refuge to the Jews from Courland, who had been driven out of their homes by the czarist authorities. During the war and the subsequent changes of regime in the area the Jewish population in Riga decreased.

After the establishment of the independent Latvian Republic, Riga became the capital of the new state; its Jewish population grew from 24,721 (13.6 percent of the total) in 1920 to 39,459 (11.68 percent) in 1925, 42,328 (11.20 percent) in 1930, and 43,672 (11.34 percent) in 1935. In 1935 Riga Jews formed approximately 47 percent of the total of Latvian Jewry. The increase was largely the result of internal migration, especially from the province of Latgale. Riga was the economic, political, cultural, and social center of Latvian Jewry.

Under the democratic regime of the country (1918–34), an autonomous Jewish school system was administered from Riga. A manifold network of Hebrew and Yiddish elementary and secondary schools was established. These included around 12 Hebrew and Yiddish schools, mainly supported by the city council; private secondary schools whose language of instruction was Russian or German; two vocational schools, one of *ORT and one of the Society for the Promotion of Culture among the Jews in Russia; a pedagogical institute; and a Froebel institute for kindergarten teachers where a large number of students were from Lithuania who returned to teach there. There was also a "Jewish university." The yeshivah in Riga was headed by its chief rabbi Menahem Mendel Sack, who was also active in the general communal affairs of Latvian Jewry; he perished in the Holocaust.

Chairman of the community was Mordecai *Dubin, leader of Agudat Israel and its representative in parliament. For a short time Riga was the center of the Lubavitch Ḥasidim where their leader Joseph Isaac *Schneersohn stayed for several years after leaving the Soviet Union. Several charitable institutions, among them Jewish hospitals, were established by contributions of philanthropists. The Yiddish theater of Riga was known even outside the borders of Latvia for its high level of artistic performance. There were also several sports clubs, headed by Maccabi. Two or three Yiddish daily newspapers were published, and newspapers and various periodicals in other languages were published by Jews: the best known was *Frimorgn* (1925–34), edited by J.Z.W. *Latzky-Bertholdi and Jacob *Hellman. The general Russian newspaper *Sevodnya*, which was known among Russian readers outside Latvia, was owned by Jews and devoted considerable space to Jewish affairs. There were a number of Karaites in Riga, among them owners of two cigarette factories. The Jewish share in the commercial, industrial, and banking activities of the city was substantial; the central office of the Association of Latvian Jewish Credit Cooperatives was situated in Riga. Jews sat on the city council, and there were Jews on the teaching staff of Riga University and the state music conservatory.

Holocaust Period

During the first period of Soviet regime in Latvia (from June 1940 to June 1941), Communist rule was introduced: Jewish, especially Zionist, public activity ceased, and Jewish commerce and industry were nationalized. After war broke out between the U.S.S.R. and Germany, Riga was occupied on July 1, 1941, and persecution began of the 40,000 Jews there. Anti-Jewish attacks were organized by the *Einsatzgruppen*, aided by Latvian fascists, resulting in the death of 400 persons; mass arrests of Jews took place and the synagogues were set on fire. In the period September–October 1941 a walled ghetto was established in the Moscow quarter to which 30,000 Jews were confined. On Nov. 30, 1941 (10 Kislev, 5702), approximately 10,600 Jews were shot in a nearby forest by *Einsatzgruppe* A; later similar *Aktionen* took place on December 7–9; a total of 25,000 Jews were killed, about 80 percent of the ghetto population (one of the victims was the historian Simon *Dubnow). The first ghetto (also known as the "large ghetto") was then liquidated, and the 4,000 remaining male Jews were put into a forced labor camp (the "little ghetto"). Women were imprisoned in a separate camp.

At the end of 1941 and the beginning of 1942, Jews deported from Germany, Austria, and Czechoslovakia began arriving in Latvia; most of them were murdered in the forests. About 15,000 of the deportees were put into a special camp in Riga (the "German ghetto") under a special Judenrat whose authority was later imposed on the whole ghetto. Several Jewish labor camps were also established in Riga and the vicinity. On Nov. 2, 1943, an *Aktion* took place in the Riga ghetto, in which the old, the very young, and the sick were murdered. Afterward the ghetto was liquidated, and the surviving Jews taken to the Kaiserwald concentration camp, near Riga. Latvian and other local inhabitants collaborated with the Nazis in the persecution and murder of Jews. In the summer of 1944, as a result of the Soviet offensive in the Baltic area, the Kaiserwald concentration camp was liquidated, and the remaining Jews deported to various camps in Germany; few of them survived. After the war the survivors chose to stay in the camps for *Displaced Persons rather than return to Riga (which was occupied by the Soviet Army on Oct. 13, 1944). Eventually most of them settled in Israel, and some in the United States and other countries.

[Joseph Gar]

Contemporary Period

The 1959 census indicated a Jewish population of 30,267 (out of 600,000 inhabitants of Riga), 14,526 of whom designated Yiddish as their mother tongue. Unofficially the number of Jews in Riga was estimated in the late 1960s at about 38,000, most of whom were originally not Latvian Jews, but had settled there from the Soviet interior after World War II. The Riga Jewish community contained about 80 percent of the Jews in the Latvian S.S.R. Only one synagogue was left in Riga, in the old city. In the 1950s bar mitzvah ceremonies continued to be held in synagogue and religious marriage ceremonies were performed there; but the number of these considerably diminished in the 1960s. After the last rabbi died, he was not replaced. In 1960 the congregation was fined 115,000 rubles for "overcharging" the price of *matzah* baked under its supervision. The following year *matzah* baking was prohibited, and a local paper reported in 1963 that *matzah* were being "smuggled" in from Vilna. Later, *matzah* baking by the congregation was again permitted. In 1964 the Jewish cemetery was declared a "general" cemetery, and non-Jews were subsequently buried there also. A Jewish choir performing Jewish songs was formed in Riga in 1957 within the trade union of commercial employees. In 1960–63 an amateur Jewish drama circle was formed which also performed in Vilna.

As young Jews in Riga began to display increasing and almost open interest in Jewish affairs and their identification with Israel, the town was considered by the Soviet authorities as a "hotbed of Zionism." In the Rumbuli forest, near Riga, where about 130,000 Jews had been massacred during the German occupation, young Jews organized rallies from 1962, and in 1964 collected the scattered remains of the victims, buried them in a mass grave and erected a monument to them. The authorities did not interfere with this action then, but ultimately insisted that a different "official" memorial should be erected there for the "victims of fascism," without mentioning that they were Jews. Eventually, through the efforts of the young Jewish initiators, a decision was reached that the inscription should read not only in Latvian and Russian but also in Yiddish. Mass gatherings in memory of the victims continued to be held there every year. Young Jews demonstrated their pro-Israel feelings on several occasions, as when Israel sports teams visited Riga to compete with local teams, and when the popular singer from Israel, Geulah Gil, performed in Riga. On the last occasion there were clashes between Jewish youth and the police near the concert hall (1965). In 1969–70 scores of Jews and Jewish families in Riga protested against the refusal of the authorities to grant them exit permits to Israel, addressing their protests not only to the Soviet government but also to the United Nations, the Israeli government, Western Communist parties, etc. In December 1970 a group of young Jews from Riga was tried in *Leningrad, and sentenced to severe terms of imprisonment for allegedly planning to hijack a Soviet plane in order to land abroad and eventually reach Israel.

With the mass exodus of Jews of the former Soviet Union in the 1990s, the Jewish population of Riga dropped to around 8,000 in the early years of the 21st century. At the same time Jewish life revived in independent Latvia. Two Jewish day schools, a community center, matzah factory, Jewish newspaper, and Jewish hospital were all in operation in Riga.

BIBLIOGRAPHY: Dubnow, Hist Russ, 3 vols. (1916–18), index; A. Bucholtz, *Geschichte der Juden in Riga* (1899); YE, vol. 13, pp. 478–87; L. Ovchinski, *Toledot Yeshivat ha-Yehudim be-Kurland* (1908); M. Schatz-Anin, *Yidn in Letland* (1924); idem, in: *Sovetish Heymland*, 11 (1971), issue 4, 164–71; *Yahadut Latvia*, ed. by B. Eliav et al. (1953); J. Gar, in: *Algemeyne Entsiklopedye, Yidn*, 6 (1963), 330–74; M. Bobe, *Perakim be-Toledot Yahadut Latvia* (1965); M. Kaufmann, *Vernichtung der Juden Lettlands* (1947); G. Movshovich, *25 Yor Yidishe Prese in Letland* (1933), 60–66. **ADD. BIBLIOGRAPHY:** D. Levin (ed.), *Pinkas ha-Kehillot – Latvia and Estonia* (1988).

RIGHT AND LEFT (right: Heb. יָמִין; Akk. *imnu, imittu*; Ugaritic, *ymn*; left: Heb. שְׂמֹאל; Akk. *šumēlu*; Ugaritic, *(u)šm'al*; and common Semitic). The biblical usages of "right" and "left" are basically fourfold: right as opposed to left; directions (cardinal points); strength and weakness; merism. As is the case in many cultures, right is favored over left in various contexts. Examples for each of these usages will be presented below, as well as Ancient Near Eastern parallels wherever appropriate.

Right as Opposed to Left

Right and left play an important role in Jacob's final blessing to his grandsons, Ephraim and Manasseh (Gen. 48: 12–20), whom Joseph places at the left and right sides of Jacob, respectively (verse 13), expecting his father to place his right hand on Manasseh (the firstborn) and his left on Ephraim, and then bless them. But Jacob crosses his hands, placing his right hand on Ephraim (verse 14) and his left on Manasseh, despite Joseph's objections (verse 18). Jacob explains his actions by stating that Ephraim will be greater than Manasseh (verse 19). Right and left parts of the body also play an important role in sacrifices as may be seen from the following phrases which occur many times in the Book of Leviticus and elsewhere: "the right thigh" (Ex. 29:22; Lev. 7:32, 33; 8:25, 26; Num. 18:18, etc.); "the right ear and the right thumb [or big toe]" (Ex. 29:20; Lev. 8:23, 24; 14:14, 17, 25, 28, etc.). Two Ancient Near Eastern parallels to this usage in sacrifice have been found at Ugarit. In one (RŠ 24.253; *Ugaritica*, 5 (1955), no. 13), in a sacrificial context, the phrase *žṣb šm'al dalpm* appears which may be provisionally translated: "the left protuberances [?] of two bulls." In another (RŠ 261.247; not yet published but quoted by C.H. Gordon, *Ugaritic Textbook* (1965), Glossary, nos. 1107, 2393a), the phrase *šq ymn* occurs, which is the same as the Hebrew *shoq ha-yamin*, שׁוֹק הַיָּמִין, "right thigh," quoted above. Finally, the right side (of the throne) is usually the side on which the king's or God's associates sit (I Kings 2:19, the queen; Zech. 3:1, Satan; Ps. 109:6, Satan, etc.). This is paralleled in Ugaritic literature by the following passage: *tʿdb ksu wyṯṯb lymn aliyn Bʿl*, "A throne is placed and he is seated to the right of Puissant Ba'al" (II AB 5:108–10; Pritchard, Texts, 134).

Direction (Cardinal Points)

Because the Hebrews – like others – oriented themselves by the place where the sun rises, in many biblical passages "right" means "south" and "left" means "north." In Abraham's separation from Lot (Gen. 13:9ff.), Abraham says (according to one interpretation): "If [you go] north [הַשְּׂמֹאל], I will go south [וְאֵימְנָה]; And if you go south [הַיָּמִין], I will go north [וְאַשְׂמְאִילָה]." The southern border of Manasseh is described in the Book of Joshua as *ha-gevul 'el ha-yamin* (הַגְּבוּל אֶל־הַיָּמִין, Josh. 17:7) "the boundary of the right," while "north of Damascus" is expressed as *mi-semo'l le-Dammeseq* (מִשְּׂמֹאל לְדַמָּשֶׂק), "to the left of Damascus" (Gen. 14:15). Perhaps the most instructive passages for this usage are those which use right and left together with the regular words for the other directions: "North and south [צָפוֹן וְיָמִין] You [God] have created them" (Ps. 89:13); "Then it [the border] turns eastward [מִזְרַח הַשֶּׁמֶשׁ]... and touches... northward [צָפוֹנָה], then it continues northward [מִשְּׂמֹאל; lit. "left"]..." Josh. 19:27). Finally, the tribe *Benjamin (*ben-yamin*, "son of the right") was the most southern tribe in "the House of Joseph" (II Sam. 19:17–21), and this usage has a direct parallel in the Mari letters where both the DUMU-*Iamīna*, "southern tribe," and the DUMU-*Simal*, "northern tribe," are often mentioned (e.g., *Archives royales de Mari*, 1 (1950), 60:9, p. 116). Semantically, DUMU-*Iamīna* (probably to read *mārē-yamīna*) is exactly parallel to Benjamin, though there is no valid evidence for any historical connection between the two.

Strength and Weakness

It is clear from several biblical verses that "right [hand]" was often a symbol for strength. The "right hand of God" was that which overcame Israel's enemies (Ex. 15:6, 12; Isa. 62:8; Ps. 17:7; 44:4, etc.) and which was worthy of the Psalmists' praises (Ps. 98:1; 118:15, 16, etc.). The "right eye" was considered the more valuable (Zech. 11:17) and it was the putting out of "every right eye" which Nahash the Ammonite demanded in return for making a nonaggresion pact with the inhabitants of Jabesh-Gilead (I Sam. 11:2). Conversely, that left-handedness was conceived of as a weakness, even a malady, is seen from the description of Ehud (Judg. 3:15), where the latter is called *'ish 'iṭṭer yad yemino* (אִישׁ אִטֵּר יַד יְמִינוֹ), "a man obstructed [in the use of] his right hand." The word used for "obstructed" is of the nominal construction that is usually utilized for physical defects – e.g., "blind" (עִוֵּר), "dumb" (אִלֵּם), and "deaf" (חֵרֵשׁ). Left-handed men are mentioned elsewhere in Judges 20:16, where it is stated that (despite their left-handedness) they never missed the target, and in I Chronicles 12:2, where both right-handed and left-handed men are mentioned. The right side of a man is the side on which God "marches" when assisting him in battle (Isa. 63:12; Ps. 109:31; 110:1, 5) and it is the right hand which God grasps as a symbol of election (Isa. 41:13; 45:1; Ps. 73:23). Finally, the pair "hand//right hand" is often used in synonymous parallelism to evoke the image of the might of God (Ps. 21:9; 74:11; 89:14; 91:7 (emended); 138:7; 139:10), the brave deeds of Israel's war heroes (Judg. 5:26), or God's power of creation (Isa. 48:13). In extra-biblical sources, the Ugaritic parallel pair *yd//ymn*, "hand//right hand," is often found conjuring up the same image of power as its biblical counterpart (e.g., II 76:6–7): *qšthn aḥd bydh wqṣʿth bm ymḥ*,

"His bow he has taken in his hand, also his darts in his right hand." The Akkadian creation epic, *Enūma eliš*, yields an interesting parallel to the use of "the right hand of God": *iššīma miṭṭa imnašu ušāḫiz*, "He [Marduk] lifted the mace, grasped it in his right hand" (*Enūma eliš* 4:37; Pritchard, Texts, 66). Finally, the Epilogue of the Code of Hammurapi has a parallel to God's proceeding on the right side when helping someone in battle: *Zababa... āliku imniya ašar tamḫārim kakkīšu lišbir*, "May Zababa ... who goes at my right side break his weapons on the battlefield" (27:81–87; Pritchard, Texts, 179; cf. Isa. 63:12). Related to the opposition strengthweakness is the opposition good luck-bad luck, which seems to be represented in Ecclesiastes 10:2; as interpreted in the (Hebrew) commentary of H.L. Ginsberg: "The wise man's mind (tends) to his right (i.e., to what brings him good luck), and the fool's to his left." The belief that omens that appear on the right side are lucky and such as appear on the left unlucky is implied by Ezekiel 21:27. Parallels from other cultures are very numerous. In Arabic, for example, *šimāl* means both "left hand" and "bad omen" (see also the Arabic dictionary on the verbs *šaʿama* and *yamana* and their derivatives).

Merism

Perhaps the most common usage of right and left in the Bible is as a merism meaning "everywhere, in any direction." The phrase "to deviate from the path in any direction" (Num. 20:17; 22:26; Deut. 2:27; 5:29; 17:11; I Sam. 6:12, etc.) is so common that it had probably reached the level of a cliché in early biblical times. Aside from "path," "instructions" (e.g., Josh. 1:7; 23:6), "commandment" (e.g., Deut. 17:20), and "commandments" (e.g., Deut. 28:14) may also be the object of deviation. In the same way, the verbal forms "to go right" and "to go left" are used together meaning "to depart from in any way" (II Sam. 14:19; Isa. 30:21). The meaning "everywhere" is also very common for this merism (I Kings 22:19; Isa. 9:19; Zech. 12:6, etc.). In extra-biblical sources, right and left are often used as a merism which may be seen from the following Akkadian and Ugaritic passages: *panukki Šēdu arkātuk Lamassu imnuk mešrû(!) šumēlukki dumqu*, "Before you is the protective spirit, behind you is the protective goddess, at your right riches, at your left prosperity" (E. Ebeling, *Die akkadische Gebetsserie Šu-ilu "Handerhebung"*... (1953), 60:16–17); *yʿdb uymn ušmal bphm* "[things] are placed in their mouths 'on right and on left'" (C.H. Gordon, *Ugaritic Textbook* (1965), 52:63–64; cf. Isa. 9:19).

[Chayim Cohen]

In Talmudic Literature

Although there does exist some evidence that the left was regarded as "sinister" in the Talmud, the general opinion, both in *halakhah* and *aggadah*, is merely that the right is more important and significant than the left. The word *yad* ("hand"), without qualification, was taken to refer always to the right hand, as the word *eẓba* ("finger") to the index finger of the right hand (Zev. 24a). All religious duties had normally to be performed with the right hand (or foot, see below). The only exception is the laying of *tefillin* which are laid (except in the case of a left-handed person) on the left hand. The reasons given are, firstly, that the plene spelling ידכה ("thy hand") in Exodus 13:16 is taken to indicate יד כהה ("the feeble hand"), and also that since the injunction is "and ye shall bind" (Deut. 6:8) and not "and ye shall place," the essential commandment is the binding, which must therefore be done with the right hand (Men. 36b, 37a). Thus it is stated, "the right hand controls all the precepts except for the *tefillin*" (Mid. Ps. 17). As a result, particularly because "one uses the right hand to point to the cantillation of the Torah," it was not to be used for unclean or unseemly purposes (Ber. 62a). Added to that was the statement, based on Deuteronomy 33:2, that the Torah was given with the right hand of God.

The right was the position of honor. All the turns of the high priest in the Temple as he encircled the altar to perform the sprinkling of the blood had to be to the right (Yoma 15b). It was regarded as a boorish lack of etiquette to walk on the right of one's teacher; but when he was accompanied by two, he walked in the middle and the greater of his companions walked on the right (Yoma 37a).

Left-handedness was not regarded as a disability, but it was naturally assumed that a person was right-handed. Nevertheless, it was regarded as so essential that *ḥaliẓah* be performed on the right foot of the *levir* (Yev. 12:2) it was stated that in the case of a left-footed person the ceremony had to be performed twice, once on each foot, and there is even one opinion that it cannot be performed at all (Sh. Ar., EH 169:25).

Since the *etrog* was regarded as the most important element of the *Four Species, it had to be taken in the right hand and the *lulav* and the other two in the left. Nevertheless, there is one statement to the effect that it is the *lulav* which is to be taken in the right (Yal. Ps. 670).

In rabbinic theology, God's right hand represents the Attribute of Mercy, his left hand, the Attribute of Judgment (MRY, p. 134). Similarly the question of the Midrash on the verse I Kings 22:19, "I saw the Lord sitting on his throne, and all the Host of Heaven standing by him on his right hand and on his left," namely, "Is there then a left on high? Is it not all right there?... (Song. R. to 1:9, no. 1) indicates that in the upper realm there is only mercy, and no judgment. This reflects an abstraction of the identification of right with mercy, even where there is no spatial or physical opposition to any "left." To give more encouragement than discouragement was expressed in the words, "Let thy left hand repulse and thy right attract" (Sot. 47a). Solomon ibn Gabirol says: "A man without a companion is like the left without the right" (*Mivḥar ha-Peninim* 20:11; cf. Meiri to Prov. 17:17).

[Louis Isaac Rabinowitz / Stephen G. Wald (2nd ed.)]

BIBLIOGRAPHY: U. Cassuto, in: *Tarbiz*, 14 (1943), 420; Y. Kaufmann, *Shofetim* (1962), 107; CH Gordon, *Ugaritic Textbook* (1965); J.C. de Moor, *Ugarit-Forschungen*, 2 (1970), 323–25. IN TALMUDIC LITERATURE: M. Plessner, in: *Folklore Research Center Studies* (1970), 259–74. **ADD. BIBLIOGRAPHY:** S. Wald, *The Doctrine of the Divine Name* (1988), 66–67.

RIGHTEOUS AMONG THE NATIONS (Heb. חֲסִידֵי אֻמּוֹת הָעוֹלָם, *ḥasidei ummot ha-olam*), term applied to non-Jews who saved Jews from their Nazi persecutors by endangering their own lives. (For earlier use of the term see *Ḥasidei Ummot ha-Olam.) In 1953 the Israeli parliament (Knesset) enacted the "Martyrs' and Heroes' Remembrance (Yad Vashem) Law." By authority of this law, *Yad Vashem was established in Jerusalem, to conduct research into the Holocaust and to document it in every possible aspect. The law also specifically charged Yad Vashem with carrying out the task of perpetuating the names of the Righteous Among the Nations "who risked their lives to save Jews." In the course of the formation and organization of Yad Vashem, a special public committee (Commission for the Designation of the Righteous) was established in 1962, to specify the criteria for the awarding of the Righteous title. Israel Supreme Court justice Moshe *Landau, who presided over the Eichmann trial, was appointed chairman of the commission, which comprised lawyers and jurists, Holocaust historians, public figures, representatives of organizations of former partisans, and Holocaust survivors. At Yad Vashem, a special department was set up to assist the commission in the gathering of material for its deliberations and for carrying out its decisions. In 1970, Moshe Bejski, also a Supreme Court Justice, and a Holocaust survivor thanks to Oskar *Schindler, replaced Justice Landau as chairman of the commission, and in 1995, he was followed by retired Supreme Court Justice Yaakov Maltz. Owing to the large number of applications three sub-committees were organized in 1978, which meet at fixed intervals in Jerusalem, Tel Aviv, and Haifa, each holding separate sessions. The three sub-committees meet together as a plenary commission to decide on problematic cases. Every request for the recognition of a person with the Righteous title is carefully scrutinized on an individual basis. The fundamental criteria established include: personal involvement in help to at least one Jewish person; risk to the safety of the person when extending such aid; no material or other compensation or reward to the rescuer as a precondition for his/her help; the availability of testimony from the side of the rescued person, or other valid documentary material. Although the basic principle of granting individual recognition, whether the rescuer saved one or many persons, has been adhered to in general, the Commission for the Designation of the Righteous has seen fit in certain instances to avoid an overly rigid interpretation of the criteria and has granted recognition in exceptional cases to persons who either risked their life to speak out against the persecution of Jews (such as church bishops) or bent the rules to allow many Jews to emigrate out of Nazi-controlled countries (such as diplomats).

Up to January 1, 2005, some 20,750 persons had been awarded the Righteous title, including men and women from all European countries, as well as persons from other countries who acted to save Jews in Europe during the Holocaust. A person honored with the title of "Righteous Among the Nations," whether living or dead, is entitled to a medal and certificate of honor, as well as inscription of the person's name on honor walls in the Garden of the Righteous Among the Nations. The planting of trees in honor of the Righteous was discontinued in 1989, due to the lack of space, after close to 2,000 trees had been planted representing some 3,000 persons (some trees were for couples and in some cases also their eldest children). The medal was designed by the Jerusalem artist Nathan Karp; depicted on it are two hands holding onto a rescue line woven out of barbed wire. The rescue line is wound around the globe and there is a feeling of movement in its rotation. The globe is surrounded by the rabbinic saying, "Whosoever saves a single life, it is as if he has saved an entire world." The reverse of the medallion has a schematic drawing of the memorial site of Yad Vashem in Jerusalem and the inscription of the honoree's name. The ceremonies at which the title of Righteous Among the Nations is bestowed – at Israeli embassies, or at Yad Vashem – are held with wide media coverage. Of equal importance, Righteous persons in need of financial and medical assistance are helped by two voluntary organizations in the United States and Switzerland. The Jewish Foundation for the Righteous, in New York, assists some 1,700 Righteous, mostly in Eastern Europe, with monthly stipends. The Anne Frank Fonds, in Basel, assists several hundred Righteous with hard-to-get medicine in the Righteous person's country of residence. Finally, at Yad Vashem, the current multivolume *Encyclopaedia of the Righteous Among the Nations* gives a summary of the deeds of the rescuers, who are listed alphabetically and by country.

Forms of Aid

There were four principal types of aid for which the Righteous title may be awarded to rescuers of Jews. These are: sheltering, dissimulating, moving, and help to children.

SHELTERING. This represents the principal form of aid. It consists of finding a secure hiding place for the fleeing Jew, either in the house of the rescuer, or nearby; of a remote and well-hidden space, unobservable to a visitor's eyes; a place where no one would suspect that a living human being was in hiding. Hiding places varied in size and personal comfort. It could be a dark corner in the attic, a space under the rescuer's home, with only mice and insects as close companions, or worse, a pit under the barn or pigsty, with its terrible stench. In several isolated cases, people hid in tombs, after removing the coffins, such as in the Manko Szwierczszak story, where three people lay huddled in a tomb in Buczacz, Poland, for over one-and-a-half years. In less unpalatable circumstances, it could be a dark corner in the rescuer's home, hidden from outside view by a piece of furniture; an unused section of a commercial storeroom, such as was the case with the Anne Frank family in Amsterdam, Holland; or within a large double wall or ceiling; or, again, as in the case of Reverend Gerrit Brillenburg, in Utrecht, Holland, in the garret of a church. All this, for as long as it might take: from a temporary arrangement lasting only days or weeks, to perhaps several months, and in some cases for as long as two-and-a-half years – that is, until the danger had passed and a particular area had been liberated from the Germans. In all these instances, the helpless hidden Jew was at the mercy of his rescuer for basic needs, such as food, washing, and the removal of bodily wastes. All these needs were now the responsibility of the rescuer and his family. In the Netherlands, Victor Kugler and Miep Gies, former business associates of Otto Frank, cared for his and another family, and saw to their daily needs while they remained hidden for two years in an annex of their former business premises. In Warsaw, Poland, the Wolski family hid several dozen Jews, including the famed Polish-Jewish historian Emanuel *Ringelblum, in an underground garden shelter near their home, on the non-Jewish side of the city. Outside Kaunas, Lithuania, Jonas Paulavicius hid a dozen Jews in several shelters outside his home, so that in the event that one was uncovered, the captured persons would not, even under torture, know and disclose the presence of the other hidden persons.

DISSIMULATING. Another major form of aid was helping a fleeing Jew disguise his real identity; that is, assist him in assuming a new and fictional non-Jewish-sounding name, together with a new biography, and help in learning local customs, especially the prevalent religious rites. This implied getting new documents for the rescued person, including birth or baptismal certificates, and a new place of residence. This was easier said than done, for one had to first carefully ascertain whether the Jew had what was considered a Jewish-looking appearance. This was not something one could take lightly, for the slightest error could be fatal. It was, moreover, not sufficient that the Jew did not have pronounced Jewish features, such as curly hair or inquisitive and sad-looking eyes, but he had to be well acquainted with the local customs, proper language inflection, folk mannerism, jokes, and religious beliefs; in short, everything needed to disguise otherness as well as to assume a type of behavior that would not make him or her immediately stand out in a crowd. Anyone wishing to try passing as a non-Jew, and there were thousands of such persons all over Europe, needed other persons to assist him, first in obtaining proper papers, then in moving to a new location, arranging living quarters and a place of work – requirements which were not necessarily accomplished by a single person. Another form of dissimulation was registration as an essential worker in a war-related industry under German supervision. Berthold Beitz employed over 1,000 generally unqualified Jews through the ruse that they were needed to run the oil refinery installations in Drohobycz, Poland. Julius Madritsch and Alfred Rossner did likewise for their many Jewish workers in the military uniform firms in Cracow and Bendin, and Hermann Graebe for his Jewish workers in railroad installations in Zdolbunov, Ukraine. The most celebrated case in this category is of Oskar Schindler, who claimed that his 1,200 Jewish workers were doing vital work in producing ammunition, in his factory in Brunnlitz, Moravia, when in fact very little of military value was produced during the whole eight months of the firm's operation. A third form of deception was that adopted by certain diplomats who claimed that certain groups of people were nationals of a foreign country with which Germany maintained friendly relations, and should therefore not be harmed. Numerous such "protective letters" were issued by the ambassadors of neutral countries in Budapest, in 1944, which were thus able to prevent the deportation of thousands of Jews. Included in this group one may mention Raoul *Wallenberg, of Sweden; Giorgio Perlasca, an Italian who masqueraded as the Spanish charge d'affaires; Carl Lutz, on behalf of Sweden, and Monsignor Angelo Rotta, the papal nuncio. All these diplomats utilized the "protective pass" ruse to try to save in combination tens of thousands of Jews in the Hungarian capital during the most critical phase of the Holocaust in that country.

MOVING. An additional principal form of help was to assist Jews who wished to flee from an endangered place to another location; either within German-controlled areas, or across frontiers to countries not embroiled in the war, such as Switzerland, Sweden, Spain, and Turkey. Even in areas under German spheres of influence, conditions for Jews varied. In France, for instance, it was somewhat easier to survive in the southern Vichy, so-called "free" zone, where antisemitic measures were applied with less severity than in the German-occupied north (including Paris). Conditions were even more favorable in southeastern France, in the provinces under Italian administration, where Jews were not mistreated. Similar conditions prevailed in other regions under Italian rule, up to September 1943, in western Yugoslavia, Albania, and the Italian zone in Greece, which included Athens. In Poland, conditions were bad and dangerous everywhere. At the same time, for people trying to pass as non-Jews it was safer to do so far away from one's own hometown, so as not to be recognized on the streets. Some persons also wished to flee from one to another ghetto, where it was felt life was relatively more tolerable, such as the Warsaw ghetto up to summer 1942, as compared with the Lvov (Lwów) ghetto. In Ukraine, persons close to the Romanian zone of occupation wished to flee there; again, because of the less severe conditions prevailing for Jews after the initial period of widespread pogroms by the Romanian military. In Ukraine and Belarus, one could also try fleeing into the deep forests, to join up with friendly partisans fighting the Nazis. In Greece, after the whole country came under Nazi rule in September 1943, Jews sought to escape into the hills, to enlist with the partisans, or by boat to neutral Turkey, where they were permitted to land. Similarly, in Norway and Denmark, thousands of Jews escaped, either by boat or by negotiating tortuous paths through the hills, to Sweden, where they were welcomed. In France, after the whole country, including the Italian zone, came under direct Nazi control, after September 1943, Jews sought to flee either to Switzerland or to Spain. In all these endeavors, to travel over long distances and tortuous trails and negotiate well-guarded border crossings without being apprehended, help was needed from non-Jews since the use of public transportation and public accommodations was forbidden to Jews by law. Of the many examples in this category, only a few may be mentioned. Tadeusz Soroka helped a group of nine Jews flee from the Grodno ghetto, in Poland, which was about to be liquidated in March 1944, aboard a German military train on its way to the front. Himself a railroad worker, Soroka accompanied them for a long night ride, as they lay huddled on the roofs of the cars. After Vilna, they jumped off, hoping to reach the partisans known to be operating in the vicinity. In Italy, Father Beniamino Schivo constantly moved a Jewish family from one location to another, and past German lines; in one instance hiding them in a monastery dressed as nuns, until he had seen them to safety with the arrival of the allied army. In the Netherlands, Joop *Westerweel arranged and led groups of Jewish youth on a long trek through occupied Belgium and France and up to the Spanish border, high in the Pyrenees. Several diplomats also facilitated the flight of many Jews from German hands. Such as Aristides de Sousa *Mendes, the Portuguese consul-general in Bordeaux, France, who freely issued thousands of Portuguese transit visas to Jewish refugees in the city, on the eve of its surrender to the Germans; Jan Zwartendijk and *Sempo Sugihara, the Dutch and Japanese consuls, respectively, in Kaunas, Lithuania, who likewise issued transit visas to thousands of Jews stranded in that country; finally, Paul Grueninger, the Swiss police border officer in St. Gallen, Switzerland, who issued false entry permits to several thousand fleeing Jews who appeared at his border outpost. Some of these senior government officials disobeyed instructions from their superiors that forbade the issuing of visas to fleeing Jews, or their entry into the country. Such open defiance by senior public servants on a moral issue, which led to the saving of at least several thousand lives, merited them the Righteous honor.

CHILDREN. The fourth and final major category pertains to the rescue of children. One need not belabor the point that saving children presented a special problem. For in most cases, where adult Jewish persons had to fend for themselves, such as in hiding places where silence and strict discipline were of the utmost importance, or circulating freely under an assumed identity, children could hardly be part of this conspiracy of subterfuge. If both parents and especially their children were to have a chance to survive, the two sides had to separate, and perhaps never to see each other again. This meant turning over one's child for an indefinite period for safekeeping and adoption in either a children's home or with a private family. Children old enough to distinguish between their natural and adopted parents had to be "reprogrammed," that is, to erase from their minds the remembrance of their true parents and their own earlier names, forget their Jewish affiliation and religious customs – all this for reasons not fully, if at all, understood by these tender minds – and readapt to totally new filial and group relationships, and new cultural and religious environments. Persons involved in this rescue operation included those who traveled long distances to make the proper arrangements, escorted the children to their new homes, and made routine inspection visits to make sure the children were well cared for. Nor should we overlook the host families who took the frightened children into their homes and showered them with love and affection, and patience, while fabricating stories to neighbors to explain the sudden appearance of a strange child in their household. Rough estimates place the number of children saved through the help of non-Jewish rescuers at several tens of thousands. Also included under this category are persons who led children across great distances and difficult terrain to cross well-guarded frontiers, such as into Switzerland. Of the many examples, one may mention Yvonne *Nevejean, who as head of Belgian's national child care agency opened the agency's doors for hundreds of Jewish children on their way to host families. In the Netherlands, the NV group is the most noteworthy of the several clandestine cells dedicated to rescuing Jewish children by dispersing them with various host families in distant locations. In France, Dr. Rita Breton dispersed several hundred children in the Normandy countryside, while Denise Bergon sheltered children in religious institutions. Rolande Birgy, who worked on behalf of a Catholic youth organization, and the Quaker-affiliated Helga Holbek and Alice Synnestvedt spirited many children across the Swiss border. In Poland, Irena *Sendler spirited children out of the Warsaw ghetto, and with the help of trustworthy aides helped disperse them in private homes and religious institutions. Still in Poland, Sister Matylda Getter is one of several nuns awarded the Righteous title for sheltering many Jewish girls in her religious orphanage.

Risks to the Rescuer

The Nazis, although they did not reveal the exact nature of their murderous intent with regard to the Jews, made it clear that they consigned them to a bitter fate. It also soon became clear to the local population that the Nazis intended to deal harshly with anyone who would place obstacles in their way by offering aid to Jews. To remove any doubts, the Nazis warned the local population of dire punishment, including the death penalty, for any violation of regulations forbidding aid to Jews in distress. In Poland, for instance, large posters appeared on bulletin boards in the major cities threatening the death penalty for various forms of aid to Jews on the run, including sheltering them in one's home, selling them provisions, and moving them from one place to another. Such was the following public warning, one of many, posted in Przemysl, on November 19, 1942, which stated in no unclear terms that: "(1) Every Pole or Ukrainian who admits a Jew in his home, or affords him hospitality, provisions and refuge, will be shot. (2) Every Pole or Ukrainian who assists in whatever way a Jew who is found outside the Jewish quarter, will be shot. (3) Every Pole or Ukrainian who even attempts to carry out items 1 and 2 will be shot." Similar dire warnings were repeated in Warsaw and other major cities in Poland. Some rescuers indeed paid with their lives for helping Jews. Such was the case with the rescuers of the noted Polish-Jewish historian Emmanuel Ringelblum, who was hidden together with a large group of

Jews in an underground shelter on the Aryan side of Warsaw. When the place was discovered, the Germans shot all the bunker's inhabitants, including their rescuers – the Polish Wolski family. Rescuers in other countries fared no less well. In Germany, the farmer Heinrich List was sent to the Dachau camp in 1942, where he died the same year, after being apprehended for sheltering a Jewish acquaintance on his farm. In Italy, Giovanni Palatucci was also sent to Dachau, where he perished, for aiding Jews and other persons sought by the Nazis, in Fiume. In Denmark, Henry Thomsen was arrested and sent to the Neuengamme camp, where he died, for his involvement in ferrying Jews across to Sweden. In France, Father Jacques (Lucien Bunel) was arrested in his Catholic seminary, in Avon, after it was discovered that he was sheltering three Jewish boys. He was sent to a concentration camp, where he died. Suzanne Spaak, deeply immersed in the rescue of Jewish children in the Paris region, was executed by the Nazis on the eve of the liberation of the city, in August 1944. In the Netherlands, Joop Westerweel, Jaap Musch, Joop Woortman, and Albertus Zefat, were executed on Dutch soil for their involvement in the rescue of Jews. Sometimes, not directly aiding but merely showing sympathy with Jews could land the person in a concentration camp. Adelaide Hautval, who complained of the treatment of Jews in a French prison, was dubbed a "Friend of the Jews," and deported to Auschwitz, which she luckily survived. These are but a few of many examples of rescuers who suffered martyrdom, or severe physical damage to their health, for their attempt to help Jews elude the Nazi dragnet. Much as the rescuers feared the Germans, the danger did not only stem from them but also from other quarters as well, such as local collaborators, anti-German partisans units who also attacked Jews and their protectors (especially in Eastern Europe), various antisemitic elements (pro- or anti-Nazi), and plain blackmailers holding to no particular political agenda.

Problematic Issues

Most rescue stories placed before the Commission for the Designation of the Righteous do not present problems, and do not therefore occasion serious divisions of opinion among commission members, insofar as the Righteous title is concerned. However, as with all issues dealing with human behavior during times of extreme stress and tension, from time to time cases of a special and unique character come to the fore which may not accord in all its aspects and contours with the criteria for the Righteous title. Such cases, due to their special and unique character, may require a different approach and judgment. Over the years, the Commission has acted in such specific cases, as follows:

1. The testimony of a rescued person who was an infant at the time is acceptable but not sufficient for the Righteous title, as it may be assumed that it is based on hearsay. What is required is an additional corroborative statement from someone who was at the age of understanding, or supporting documentary material in lieu of eyewitness testimony.

2. The rescuer saved one or more Jews, at the risk of his life, but at the same time was involved in reprehensible acts, inflicting harm on other Jews or members of other nationalities. He is not recognized. Such is the case with police officers who rounded up Jews for deportation but spared some out of personal friendship. A person having antisemitic sentiments is not automatically disqualified, if no acts followed upon such personal feelings. The noted Polish author Zofia Kossak-Szuczka, who made no secret of her antisemitic views, in 1942 issued a manifesto to her underground colleagues to step forward and save Jews from annihilation. She inspired the creation of *Zegota*, the sole Polish clandestine organization dedicated to the rescue of Jews, and herself sheltered a Jewish woman in her home. She was recognized.

3. A person who rescued but also collaborated with the enemy, or belonged to a Nazi or Fascist political movement – this requires a careful study of the person, his standing and influence in the community and the measure of the collaboration. Simply belonging to the Nazi Party does not, as in the case of Oskar Schindler, disqualify the person, if such membership was not coupled with the authority to delineate anti-Jewish policies, and the rescuer otherwise saved Jews at the risk of his life. At the same time, membership in the SS militia has so far automatically disqualified a person from bearing the Righteous title.

4. The rescuer carried out his operation at the behest of a clandestine, or partisan organization. In general, if he did not go beyond merely following orders, he would not be recognized. But if he went above and beyond instructions, and increased the risks to his person in affording aid to Jews, as was for instance the case of the Polish underground leader Henryk Wolinski, he would be recognized.

5. Persons who did not rescue but undertook great risks to themselves to try to stop the Holocaust. The German industrialist Eduard Schulte and the Polish underground courier Jan *Karski were awarded the Righteous title for trying to alert the world to the Final Solution, hoping that the free world would intervene to stop it.

6. Diplomats who saved – if they acted in contravention of instructions from above, coupled with a sizable number of Jews saved – would be awarded the Righteous title. This ruling has allowed the Portuguese diplomat Aristides de Sousa Mendes and the Japanese diplomat Sempo Sugihara – two of a larger group – to earn the Righteous title.

7. Rescue inside monasteries and convents – in general the Father or Mother Superior, in other words, the person with ultimate authority and responsible before the authorities, is recognized and not monks and nuns inside these houses, unless they acted in a special and unique way to save their Jewish wards.

8. The rescuer of his, or her, Jewish spouse would not earn the Righteous title, unless the rescue act also included family members of the Jewish spouse.

9. Baptized Jews who acted either as rescuers or rescued. In general, a Jew who freely and out of inner conviction and

persuasion converted out of Judaism before the advent of Nazism and anti-Jewish laws in his country is considered to have willingly left the Jewish fold, and his, or her, case (be it as rescuer or rescued) is not considered with the framework of the Righteous program. Such a ruling would not apply if the conversion was done to avoid persecution by the Nazis and their allies.

Motivations and Lessons

Several studies have been made to try to explain the motivations of the rescuers. Nechama Tec, in her research on Polish rescuers, concluded that most rescuers in her sample stood out from their immediate surroundings, since they did not identify with the behavioral norms of their neighbors. In short, rescuers tended to be nonconformists and individualists who preferred to draw their own conclusion as to the proper responses to various human issues confronting them. Samuel and Pearl Oliner researched rescuers from many European countries, and found, as opposed to Tec, that most rescuers had so completely internalized the social norms of their society, such as compassion and aid to the less favored, that whereas most others only paid lip service to the values taught in their society, rescuers in fact had taken these teachings so seriously that they became behavioral codes in their day-to-day lives – to a greater degree than non-rescuers and bystanders. Whatever the ultimate reasons for this unique kind of behavior (risking one's life to help strangers), the example of the Righteous Among the Nations suggests that man, left to his own devices, while not a saint – is not necessarily prone solely to evil deeds. When confronted and challenged, ordinary people have the capacity to perform acts of goodness for their own sake. The lessons to be drawn include the following: (a) That it was possible to save Jews at the individual level, even in spite of the risks involved; that the individual, left to his own devices, can decide to act right morally and can make a difference, and thereby serve as an example and role model for the behavior of others. (b) That helping others in distress may be a natural, not coerced, human behavioral mode, and represents man at his best. The French Jewish philosopher Emmanuel *Levinas has stated that a true ethic begins with a turning towards and responding to the Other, since such an encounter makes possible a true dialogue with one's own conscience – the questioning of oneself in light of the Other, who is somehow also present in ourselves, in our consciousness, yet is not of it. (c) An added dimension to the uniqueness of the behavior of the rescuers comes to the fore when one compares their responses with that of the perpetrators. Perpetrators usually say: "I did not do it exactly as described. Besides, I was forced into it, for orders have to be obeyed. Personally, I have nothing against Jews, and I am not responsible for my deeds. I am passing the buck." Rescuers, in contrast, generally say: "Of course I did it, and I would do it again, if called upon. I take full personal responsibility for my deed. I was not coaxed into it, and no one forced me to do it. Besides, it was the most natural thing." Herein lies the abyss separating these two types of moral conduct. (d) The example of the thousands of Righteous who risked their lives to save Jews from the Nazis is testimony to the human spirit as a potent creative force. Primo *Levi has stated this idea best when he reflected on the significance of his rescue by the Italian Lorenzo Perrone in the hell on earth that was Auschwitz: "However little sense there may be in trying to specify why I, rather than thousands of others, managed to survive the test, I believe that it was really due to Lorenzo that I am alive today; and not so much for his material aid, as for his having constantly reminded me by his presence, by his natural and plain manner of being good, that there still existed a just world outside our own, something and someone still pure and whole, not corrupt, not savage, extraneous to hatred and terror; something difficult to define, a remote possibility of good, but for which it was worth surviving… Thanks to Lorenzo, I managed not to forget that I myself was a man." In conclusion, the importance of the saving of even one life is an important Jewish moral principle; again, as it is stated in the Talmud (and etched on the Righteous medal): "Whosoever saves one life is as though he has saved an entire world."

BIBLIOGRAPHY: I. Gutman (ed.), *Encyclopaedia of the Righteous Among the Nations*, 6 vols. (2002–6); M. Paldiel, *Path of the Righteous* (1994); idem, *Sheltering the Jews* (1995); idem, *Saving the Jews* (2000); M. Gilbert, *The Righteous* (2003); M. Halter, *Stories of Deliverance* (1997); D. Gushee, *Righteous Gentiles of the Holocaust* (2003²); E. Silver, *The Book of the Just* (1992); A. Bauminger, *The Righteous* (1983).

[Mordecai Paldiel (2nd ed.)]

RIGHTEOUSNESS, the fulfillment of all legal and moral obligations. Righteousness is not an abstract notion but rather consists in doing what is just and right in all relationships; "…keep justice and do righteousness at all times" (Ps. 106:3; cf. Isa. 64:4; Jer. 22:3; Ezek. 18:19–27; Ps. 15:2). Righteous action results in social stability and ultimately in peace: And the work of righteousness shall be peace (Isa. 32:17; cf. Hos. 10:12; Avot 2:7).

In the Bible righteousness bears a distinctly legal character; the righteous man is the innocent party, while the wicked man is the guilty one: "And the judges judge them by justifying the righteous and condemning the wicked" (Deut. 25:1; cf. Ex. 23:7; II Sam. 15:4; Isa. 5:23). Righteousness requires not merely abstention from evil, but a constant pursuit of justice and the performance of positive deeds (Deut. 16:20; Jer. 22:3; cf. Prov. 16:17; Gen. R. 30:9; Jub. 7:20; Tob. 3:2; Kid. 40a). The meaning of righteousness is broadened to include actions beyond the letter of the law in the realms of ethics and ritual (Ezek. 8:5; Tob. 1:10–12; Eccles. 7; Lev. R. 27:1). Paralleling the concept of righteousness is that of wickedness (see *Ẓedaqah and *Rishʿah). Failure to perform obligations leads indirectly to the upsetting of social stability and, ultimately, to the deliberate undermining of the social structure (Isa. 5:23; Hos. 10:13; Amos 5:12; Avot 5:18; Sanh. 101b; RH 17a).

Against the juridical background of righteousness, the paradox of divine justice comes into prominence. A doctrine of exactly balanced rewards and punishments contradicts the reality in which the just man suffers in consequence of his very righteousness (Eccles. 7:15; cf. Gen. 18:23; Jer. 12:1; Hab. 1:13; Mal. 3:15; Ps. 32:10; Job, passim; Wisd. 2–3; Lev. R. 27; Ber. 7a; Shab. 55b; Hor. 10b). This individual problem takes on a national character in Jewish history, throughout which an innocent nation is constantly being persecuted (Wisd. 10:15; IV Ezra 10:22). The paradox becomes even more striking in view of the legal character of the covenant between God and His people: "And I will betroth thee unto Me in righteousness and in justice" (Hos. 2:21).

Attempts to come to grips with this paradox account for the notion that the righteous man suffers for and with his generation, and that his death expiates for their sins (MK 28a; Ex. R. 43:1; cf. Gen R. 34:2; Sanh. 108a). Often, however, man's anger and righteous indignation in the face of overwhelming injustice causes him to invoke that absolute righteousness which rests only with God: "for Thou art righteous" (Neh. 9:8; cf. II Chron. 12:6; lsa. 5:16; 45:22–25; Ps. 89: 16; II Macc. 12:6; Ḥag. 12b).

Because righteousness is not an inherent human characteristic, but rather a learned trait resulting from sustained performance of obligations, man can never attain the peak of righteous perfection: "For there is not a righteous man upon earth that doeth good and sinneth not" (Eccles. 7:20; cf. Ps. 143:2; Job 4:17; 15:14; Dan. 9:18). The impossibility of achieving absolute righteousness, however, does not preclude the constant striving toward this end. The Jew emulates the Patriarchs, conscious that God evaluates even their righteousness in relative terms (Gen. R. 30:9; Shab. 55a; Sanh. 107a; cf. Hab. 2:4; Yoma 38b; RH 16b; Sanh. 93a; Num. R. 3:1; Song R. 3:3; Zohar, Gen. 9). Judaism holds in contempt those who assume a pretense of piety and righteousness: "Be not righteous overmuch neither make thyself overwise" (Eccles. 7:16; cf. Eccles. 7:5; Nid. 30b), while, on the other hand, it exalts the *ẓaddikim nistarim* ("the hidden righteous") of each generation (Suk. 45b; Hul. 92a; Gen. R. 35:2).

The prophets conceive of the ideal society in terms of righteousness (Isa. 28:17; 60:21; Jer. 23:5–7; Hos. 10:12; Zech. 8:8; Ps. 7:10; 18:25; Dan. 9:24). Subsequent attempts to formulate a code for an ideal society rest heavily on practical principles of daily righteous conduct (En. 10:21; 13:10; Ps. of Sol. 17:27; Meg. 17b; cf. the teachings of the "Teacher of Righteousness" in the Dead Sea Scrolls). Eschatologically, righteous action within a righteous society will restore peace in the world and will reestablish Jerusalem as the citadel of righteousness: "And I will restore thy judges… afterward thou shalt be called the city of righteousness" (Isa. 1:26–27; Jer. 31:22).

[Zvi H. Szubin]

In rabbinic literature the term *ẓedakah* means "charity," "almsgiving," "practical benevolence," but does not refer to righteousness in general for which there is no special term. However, the name *ẓaddik*, "righteous man" (pl. *ẓaddikim*), is found throughout rabbinic literature denoting the good man, the man free from sin, the one who carries out his obligation to God and to man by obeying the precepts of the Torah. Occasionally in the literature the term *ẓaddik* denotes the specially pious, the man of extraordinary goodness, the holy man or saint, as when it is said that there are never less than 36 *ẓaddikim* in the world who see the Divine Presence each day (Suk. 45b). But in general the term *ẓaddik* does not necessarily suggest unusual piety, but simply the carrying out of God's will. This can be seen from the division of men (RH 16b) into the thoroughly righteous (*ẓaddikim gemurim*), the thoroughly wicked (*resha'im gemurim*), and the average persons (*beinonim*). In one passage (Ber. 61b) the distinction is made that the *ẓaddikim* are governed by the good inclination, the wicked by the evil inclination, and the average by both inclinations. When *Rabbah commented that he was an average person *Abbaye objected that this would mean that most people are wicked. The term "righteous" is used of women as well as of men (Song. R. 1:17; Sot. 11b). The *ẓaddikim* among the gentiles have a share in the world to come (Tos. Sanh. 13:2).

The *ẓaddikim*, in their humility, promise to do only a little for others but in reality do much (BM 87a). The *ẓaddikim* are so scrupulous in avoiding the slightest taint of theft that their honestly acquired property becomes dearer to them than their own person and they risk their lives to preserve it (Ḥul. 91a). They have a strong social conscience. They rise up early in the morning to attend to the needs of the community (Yalkut, Ex. 264). Even at the time of their death they worry not about their own affairs but about their communal responsibilities (Sifrei, Num. 138).

Even when they are dead the *ẓaddikim* are called "living," unlike the wicked who are called "dead" even while they are still alive (Ber. 18a). When a *ẓaddik* resides in a city, he adorns that city so that when he departs its glory departs with him (Gen. R. 68:6). The very stones of a place quarrel among themselves for the privilege of serving as a pillow for the *ẓaddik* who is obliged to sleep out of doors (Ḥul. 91b). Beauty, strength, riches, honor, wisdom, old age, gray hairs, and children are comely to the *ẓaddikim* and comely to the world (Avot 6:8). But the *ẓaddikim* suffer in this life. Whenever they wish to have a life of comfort Satan complains that they ought to be satisfied with the reward stored up for them in the hereafter and not wish to enjoy, too, the ease of this world (Gen. R. 84:3). God causes the *ẓaddikim* to suffer in this world to purge them of the few sins of which they are guilty, just as when a tree stands in a clean place with its branches overlapping an unclean place the branches are lopped off so that the whole tree can stand in a clean place (Kid. 40b). In another passage, however, it is said that Moses received no answer when he asked God why it is that one *ẓaddik* meets with good fortune in this world while another meets with evil (Ber. 7a).

A man can repent sincerely in his heart of the sins he has committed and by so doing change his status from that of *rasha* ("wicked") to that of *ẓaddik*. Thus if a man who is thoroughly wicked betroths a woman on the understanding that he is a *ẓaddik* the act is valid. Conversely, if a known *ẓaddik* betrothed a woman on the understanding that he is a *rasha* the act is also valid because he may have been guilty of an acceptance of idolatry in his heart and this would change his status (Kid. 49b). A man who has been a perfect *ẓaddik* all his life and is sorry for the good deeds he has done thereby cancels out all those good deeds. Conversely, a complete *rasha* who repents of his evil deeds at the end of his life cancels out thereby all those evil deeds (Kid. 40b). Nevertheless, a good deed is not disqualified by any self-seeking motive. For example, a man who gives charity so that his children may live or that he may have reward for it in the hereafter can still be considered a perfect *ẓaddik* (Pes. 8a–b).

In medieval Jewish thought a definite tendency can be observed to extend the scope of righteousness. Not only is greater inwardness demanded of the *ẓaddik*, but he is expected to observe as the norm rules of conduct which in rabbinic literature are set down as the ideal for the especially pious. The medieval moralistic literature consists mainly of such demands classified and codified as standards to which all should aspire. A typical example is the anonymous work with the revealing title of *Orḥot Ẓaddikim, "The Ways of the Righteous" (tr. S. Cohen (1969)). Thus the saying of R. Yose, who is described (Avot 2:8) as a *ḥasid* ("saint"), that all man's deeds should be for the sake of heaven (Avot 2:12), is formulated in the Codes (Tur, OḤ 231) as the rule for all men. When a man eats and drinks, for example, it should not be in order to enjoy his food and drink but to have strength for God's service. The same applies to his working, sleeping, marital relations, and conversing with others. All should be done for the sake of heaven and not for personal gratification.

In Maimonides' writings, the life of righteousness is made to embrace the Greek ideal of harmony and balance in choosing the middle way. The good man should be neither too prone to anger nor as indifferent to insult as a corpse; neither too ambitious nor too lazy; neither frivolous nor melancholic; neither greedy nor a spendthrift (Yad, Deot 1:4–5). Man is free to choose the way he wishes to follow. It is given to every man to be as great a *ẓaddik* as Moses or as great a *rasha* as Jeroboam (Yad, Teshuvah 5:2). Maimonides defines the *ẓaddik* as the man with more good deeds to his credit than bad. The *rasha* has more bad deeds than good ones, while the average man (*beinoni*) has his good and bad deeds equally balanced. The same assessment is made by God of a country and of the world as a whole. But it is not the mere quantity of the deeds which counts in this assessment. A good deed can be of such quality that it can succeed in outweighing many bad deeds, and the converse is also true (Yad, Teshuvah 3:1–2).

Among the kabbalists the term *ẓaddik* is given, as in a few instances in rabbinic literature, the meaning of "saint." The *ẓaddik* is no longer simply the ordinary good man but a holy man of elevated degree. In the Zohar, *ẓaddik* is the name of one of the **Sefirot* – *Yesod*, "foundation." This is the creative principle and is symbolized by the phallus. Consequently, the *ẓaddik* on earth is especially careful to avoid any flaw in the "sign of the covenant," i.e., he keeps himself free from all forms of sexual impurity. "One who does not guard the sign of the Covenant as he should cannot be called a *ẓaddik*" (Zohar, Gen. 94a). Among the biblical heroes, the counterpart of *Yesod* is Joseph who refused to yield to the blandishments of Potiphar's wife and who, as a result, is called "Joseph the *ẓaddik*" (Zohar, Ex. 23a). In Ḥasidism, too, the *Ẓaddik* is the miracle-working saint and holy man, the hasidic master. The term *ḥasid* could not have been applied to him since this was the name given to his followers, the ḥasidim. Once the term had been used in this sense the rabbinic references to the *ẓaddik* were interpreted in the Hasidic literature as referring to the holy man. In *Ḥabad* theory the terms *ẓaddik* and *rasha* are acknowledged to be used in the rabbinic literature, in some instances in the loose sense of one who is acquitted in judgment by God and one who is declared guilty. But the true definition of the *ẓaddik* is that he is the man "who has no evil inclination because he has killed it by fasting" (*Likkutei Amarim*, I, 1). The prescriptions for leading the good life found in the classical sources are not for such rare souls who do not need them, but for the "average men" (*beinonim*). The *beinoni* is now, in fact, not "average" at all but the righteous man who struggles against the evil within him in order to do God's will.

The pursuit of righteousness was the aim of the Lithuanian Musar movement but the approach was decidedly non-mystical. In response to the claim of Ḥasidism that the *ẓaddik* is invested with the power to cause harm by his curse, Israel Salanter, the founder of the movement, is said to have retorted that if that were so, the *ẓaddik* can be a danger to others and should be obliged to pay for any harm he may do in this way. The followers of Israel Meir ha-Kohen (the Ḥafeẓ Ḥayyim) used to say that while it was the boast of the *ḥasidim* that their *ẓaddik* decrees and God fulfills, of the Ḥafeẓ Ḥayyim it was rather true that God decrees and the *ẓaddik* fulfills. The righteous man, according to the Musarists, is other-worldly, ascetic, profoundly concerned with his ethical obligations, and devoted to the study of the Torah and the practice of the precepts. The Musar leaders and teachers were frequently referred to as *ha-rav ha-ẓaddik*, "The rabbi, the *ẓaddik*…"

In modern writings on Jewish religious thought, especially those in Western languages, the emphasis is chiefly on the ethical and moral content of righteousness and on its universal application.

[Louis Jacobs]

BIBLIOGRAPHY: S. Schechter, *Some Aspects of Rabbinic Theology* (1909); R. Mach, *Der Ẓaddik in Talmud und Midrasch* (1957); I. Tishby, *Mishnat ha-Zohar*, 2 (1961), 655–733; E.E. Urbach, *Ḥazal; Pirkei Emmunot ve-De'ot* (1969), 428–54.

RIGHTS, HUMAN. The following article deals with the subject of human rights, their essence and the contents of various fundamental rights as reflected in the sources of Jewish Law. The interpretation of Israel's Basic Laws concerning human rights in accordance with the principles of a Jewish and democratic state, and the principles of the Israeli Declaration of Independence, and the disputes over the method of finding a synthesis between these values are discussed at length in the entries: *Values of a Jewish a Democratic State; *Law and Morality; *Human Dignity and Freedom.

Rights and Obligations

Rights play a central role in contemporary legal systems in general, and in the field of public law in particular. A substantial part of constitutional law deals with various human rights, such as the right to equality, the right to freedom of expression, freedom of occupation, freedom of movement and so forth. This approach is anchored in various philosophical, humanist and liberal theories, such as those of J.S. Mill, Locke, Hobbes and others, which emphasize the central place of man and his right to freedom. The existence of and respect for human rights are also a fundamental principle of democracy, and therefore any discussion of the combination of Judaism and democracy or of the "Jewish and democratic state" (see *Values of a Jewish and Democratic State, and M. Elon, *Kevod ha-Adam ve-Ḥeruto be-Darkei ha-Hoẓa'ah le-Po'al – Arakheha shel Medinah Yehudit ve-Democratit* (Jerusalem 2000); M. Elon, *Ma'amad ha-Ishah –Mishpat ve-Shipput, Masoret u-Temurah, Arakheha shel Medinah Yehudit ve-Democratit* (Tel Aviv 2005); idem, *Ha-Mishpat ha-Ivri* (1988); idem, *Jewish Law* (1994)) must also take into consideration the place of human rights in Jewish law, their origin, their scope and the principles that accompany them.

The basic approach taken by religious legal systems, and in particular of Jewish law to the issues dealt with in the realm of human rights place *God*, rather than *man*, at the center. As a result, man is perceived first and foremost as having *obligations* and not *rights*. It is true that in contemporary legal theory, obligations are accompanied by parallel rights (thus, for example, the prohibition "you shall not kill" as applying to one individual consequently results in the right of another individual to life; the obligation "you shall not steal" implies the right of the other to property; the obligation to return what has been lost [see *Lost Property] implies the property rights of the one who has sustained a loss; and so forth). Nevertheless, the point of departure being from obligations rather than from rights creates a completely different legal system than that existing in modern constitutional law, and the point of balance between rights and obligations changes accordingly (M. Elon, *ibid.;* Rabbi Yitzhak Breuer, *Ẓiyyunei Derekh* (Jerusalem 1982), 57–86; M. Silberg, *Kakh Darko shel Talmud* (Jerusalem 1982), 66; R.M. Cover, "A Jewish Jurisprudence," in: *Journal of Law and Religion,* 5 (1987) 65; H.H. Cohn, *Zekhuyot ha-Adam ba-Mikra u-va-Talmud* (Tel Aviv, 1988); idem, *Ha-Mishpat* (Jerusalem 1992), 512–13; M. Vigoda, "*Bein Zekhuyot Ḥevratiyyot le-Ḥovot Ḥevratiyyot ba-Mishpat ha-Ivri,*" in: *Zekhuyot Kalkaliot ve-Tarbutiyyot be-Yisrael* (2005), 233–96).

An expression of Jewish law's basic approach to man's obligations can already be found in the first book of the Bible, in which Adam is placed in the Garden of Eden and commanded "to tend it and to keep it." Man is first and foremost "commanded," obligated, given duties rather than rights. Under this basic approach of Jewish law, as noted earlier, human rights are often formulated by way of negation, that is, by proscribing infringement of the various rights. Thus, for example, the Torah says "you shall not go around as a talebearer among your people" (Lev. 19:17) as an expression of the right to a good name; "you shall not rule over him with rigor" (Lev. 25:43) as an expression of man's dignity; "you shall not go into his house to fetch his pledge" (Deut. 24:10) as an expression of his liberty and right to privacy (see *Imprisonment for Debt), and so on, with "you shall" implicit in "you shall not."

Together with this, there are cases in which man is required, as a positive commandment, to respect various rights. Thus, regarding the obligation to maintain human dignity and physical integrity: "therefore take good heed unto yourselves" (lit., "your souls," interpreted as "your lives"; Deut 4:15) and, regarding freedom of movement: "proclaim liberty throughout the land unto all the inhabitants thereof" (see below).

Man's right to "self-fulfillment," or self-realization so extolled in the Western, humanist and liberal culture of our times as a central foundation of various rights, is by no means self-evident from the standpoint of Jewish law, because this conception places man in the center, whereas the Jewish religion, like other religions, places God at the center (A. Lichtenstein, "'*Im ke-Vanim, im ka-Avadim*' – *Zekhuyot ha-Perat le-Or ha-Halahhah,*" in: *Alon Shevut Bogrim,* 12 (1997), 103–110; idem, "'*Aseh Reẓono, Batel Reẓonkha*' – *Hirhurim al ha-Mifgash bein Halakhah u-Moderniyyut,*" in: *Alon Shevut Bogrim,* 13 (1999), 125–33; and see the ruling of Justice Y. Englard, HC 2458/01 *New Family v. The Committee for Approving Agreements to Carry Fetuses,* 57 (1) PD 419).

This basic distinction between "human rights" and "human obligations" is not merely a semantic difference, but also carries moral significance and consequences with regard to the desired balance between conflicting values. Whereas contemporary constitutional law speaks of the realization of *interests*, Jewish law stresses human *responsibility*. Thus, while contemporary theories emphasize man's "self-fulfillment," in Jewish law, notwithstanding that this value exists to a certain degree (see comments below on "Freedom of Expression and Creation"), the focus is on man's obligations and responsibilities towards others.

Another substantive difference between the approach of Jewish law and the basic premises of modern law, relates to the essential nature of human rights and their practical implications. In contemporary legal systems, the various rights afforded to human beings are of significance mainly in relation to other people. The modern theory of human rights holds that society (whether the state or individuals in society) must allow individuals to realize their right to freedom of expression, freedom of occupation and movement, and so forth. The rights are "theirs" – although they are, of course, entitled to waive them. This is not the attitude of Jewish law, where the emphasis is on man's obligations. According to this approach, in many cases people are not allowed to waive their rights, which are in fact obligations. Thus, they may not waive the "right to life" and commit suicide (see *Suicide), nor waive their "human dignity" and remove their clothes in public, even if no one else sees them.

This approach was uniquely expressed in a ruling of the Israel Supreme Court concerning a person who wished to waive his right to dignity and insisted that a police officer carry out a search of his person in the streets of the town. Justice Elon, on the basis of Jewish law, denied the request, stating that the preservation of "human dignity," which results from man being created in God's image, is not only a right but also an obligation imposed on human beings; hence, one is not entitled to waive it (see at length under *Human Dignity and Freedom, Cr. App. 2145/92 *State of Israel v. Guetta*, 46 (5) PD 704).

Terminology: "Right," "Liberty," "Freedom"

Like many other legal terms – such as **ḥazakah* (possession, ownership, acquiring or proving, presumption); **kinyan* (legal rights, act of acquisition); *ones* (Elon, *Ha-Mishpat ha-Ivri*, 71–72; *Jewish Law* (1994), 79) – the various terms used in the theory of human rights in Jewish law also have multiple meanings. Thus, for example, the term *zekhut* as used in Jewish law carries various different meanings depending on the context. At times it is used in the sense of a "right," as in modern legal terminology (thus, for example, M. Ketubbot 4:4: "The father has a right to receive his daughter's betrothal [money]"; Yad, Sekhirut 6:9 "You have no greater right in this house than I do"), but it frequently bears other meanings, whether those related to the world of law or those outside it. Thus, for example, the word *zekhut* may be used in the sense of "permission" (as in the legal term, *zekhut yoẓerim*, "copyright"), or in the sense of "merits" or "good deeds" chalked up to man's credit. The term *zekhut avot* – "ancestral merit" – is used to denote the special treatment a person enjoys because of his parents or his lineage (M. Avot 2:2) Similarly, "Every person has merits (*zekhuyyot*) and sins: one whose merits outweigh his sins is a righteous man; and one whose sins outweigh his merits is evil; half and half – mediocre" (Maim., Yad, Hilkhot Teshuvah 3:1). Another aspect of the term *zekhut* in the legal context relates to arguing on behalf of a person and defending his actions: "All are allowed to argue for acquittal, and not all may argue for conviction" (M. Sanhedrin 4:1); "Always judge a person leniently" (M. Avot 1:6). In yet other sources, the term is used to denote an advantage or benefit: "A slave benefits from gaining his freedom" (BM 19a).

In like fashion, the terms *ḥerut* (liberty) and *ḥofesh* (freedom) bear a number of different meanings in different contexts, which in any case are not identical to the modern term "freedom." On the contrary: according to different sources in Jewish law, man's "freedom" does not express the fact that he is free of all obligations and responsibilities, but rather that he is subject to a system of obligations and precepts. This is clearly evident in the Mishnah, which states that "No one is free but one who studies Torah." In like fashion, Rabbi Judah Halevi, one of the great Jewish poets of medieval Spain, writes in one of his poems that "Slaves of time are under the greatest servitude; only the servant of God alone is free." An echo of this approach is found in the rabbinic dictum that man is not at all free in this world, because he is subject to commandments of "you shall" and "you shall not," and that only in death one becomes free, because when a person is dead, he is free, in the sense of being exempt of the obligation of the commandments (Shab. 30a).

Consideration should be given to the fact that in the Bible itself the word *ḥofesh* does not appear in its modern sense of freedom, except in the phrase *bigdei ḥofesh* ("precious clothes," Ezek. 27:20, where its meaning is not altogether clear), or in the sense of an action or result (e.g., Exod. 21:5, "I will not go out free"; Deut. 15:12–13, 18: "you shall let him go free from you"; Exod. 21:2, 25–27: "He shall go out free… he shall let him go free"). In later sources, the term appears as an expression of freedom and liberty. Thus, for example, in the ancient book of Ben Sira it says: "Treasure an educated slave, do not keep him from freedom" (Sira 7:22).

The term *ḥerut* likewise does not appear at all in the Bible, and is mentioned for the first time in the words of the Sages (thus, for example in the Passover blessing: "You have brought us out from slavery to liberty," *Pesaḥim* 10:5, and from there in the Passover *Hagaddah*). At the same time, another term, *deror*, which in later generations was seen as standing for liberty and freedom, does appear in the Bible. Its first appearance relates to the commandment of the jubilee year, in a verse also inscribed on the Liberty Bell of the United States, commanding Israel: "And you shall hallow the fiftieth year, and proclaim liberty throughout the land unto all the inhabitants thereof" (Lev. 25:10). The Sages noted the special use of the word *deror*, which appears only once in the Torah, here and nowhere else. (In the words of the prophets Isaiah, Jeremiah, and Ezekiel, this expression appears another six times, expressing the freedom of one who is liberated from slavery. See, for example, Isaiah 61:1: "to proclaim liberty to the captives"; Jeremiah 34:8: "to proclaim liberty unto them"; and *ibid.* 15: "proclaiming liberty every man to his neighbor"; *ibid.* 17: "to proclaim liberty, every man to his brother, and every man to his neighbor; behold I proclaim for you a liberty"; in Ezekiel 46:17: a "year of liberty" is mentioned as a synonym for the jubilee year. It should be noted that the word *deror* as the name of a bird already appears in the book of Psalms (84:4): "Yea, the sparrow hath found a house and the swallow [*deror*] a nest for herself"). According to the Sages, the word *deror* here signifies freedom of movement and the right to live anywhere (with regard to freedom of movement, see below).

Classification of Rights

There is a tendency in contemporary law to distinguish among different kinds of rights. One distinction made is between "human rights," afforded to all human beings as such (as broadly manifested in the Universal Declaration of Human Rights adopted by the General Assembly of the United Nations in 1948), and "civil rights," only granted to the citizens of a state per se (such as the right to vote and to stand for election). There is a similar tendency to distinguish between "primary rights," such as a person's right to life, and "political rights" (freedom of expression, freedom of association, freedom to demonstrate, assemble and march, freedom of movement, etc.; see below), whose power and scope is wider, and secondary rights (such as some of the social rights), whose scope is more limited.

A similar, though not identical, distinction exists in Jewish law. Notwithstanding that it is a universal legal system, applying and operating throughout the world and not only within the borders of particular country (as is the case with modern "territorial" legal systems, which only apply within the territory of a given country, within defined borders), Jewish law also recognizes the distinction between what are known today as "human rights," applicable to all human beings as such, and rights with less force and scope, afforded to a more limited group. Thus, for example, the right to vote and stand for election (see below) is not afforded to all residents, but only to those who meet certain conditions of competency.

The Source of the Rights

In Jewish law, man's rights and liberty stem from the fact that he was created in God's image, as described in the book of Genesis (Gen. 1:27). From Adam on, this theory developed and was also introduced into the laws of nations.

Man's uniqueness, and his resultant obligations, are emphasized in the Talmud (Sanhedrin 38a): "Accordingly man was created as an individual, to teach us that whoever destroys a single soul, is as if he destroyed an entire world; and to ensure peace among men, so that no person can say to another, '[My] father is greater than your father!'... and to praise the greatness of the Holy One blessed be He, for when a man mints a number of coins from the same material, they are all identical to one another, whereas the King of Kings, the Holy One blessed be he, created all men in the image of the first man and yet not one of them is identical to another. Therefore each and every one must say 'the world was created for me.'"

Another source of great importance for human rights and the liberty that goes with them is the Exodus from Egypt, which served as the basis for the formation of Jewish culture and Jewish law, particularly with regard to man's freedom (see *Imprisonment; *Imprisonment for Debt, and see R. Hirsch's Commentary on Exodus 22:20, Gateshead (1973), vol. 2, p. 373).

Alongside those rights explicitly mentioned in the Bible, over the centuries, a theory of human rights developed in Jewish law. Scholars of the Mishnah and Talmud, followed by the *geonim* and the earlier and later authorities in all of Israel's Diasporas, developed and cultivated a defense of the different rights, and by means of various legal tools (such as regulation and custom, explication and rulebooks) created a broad system of rules and norms intended to protect human rights. In the sub-sections below examples are given from different places and times, expressing the wonderful creativity of Jewish law in developing a theory of human rights in all its shades.

The law courts in Israel and throughout the world acknowledge that Jewish law is one of the potential sources of human rights. An eloquent expression of this can be seen in the ruling of the Supreme Court, as given by Justice M. Elon: "Our sages taught us 'Beloved is man in that he was created in [God's] image' (Avot 3:14). This fundamental value in the world of Judaism serves as the infrastructure, the very heart of the principle of man's liberty (Justice M. Elon: M. App. 1/87 *Denenashvili et al. v. State of Israel*, 41 (2) PD 289, and Cr. App. 2145/92 *State of Israel v. Guetta*, 46 (5) PD 710–711. See also: M. Elon, "*Le-Zikhro shel Moshe Silberg*," in: *Shenaton ha-Mishpat ha-Ivri* 2 (5735), p. 4; ALA 184/87 *Attorney General v. Anon. et al.*, 42 (2) PD 676. And cf. the ruling of Justice Elon, CA 506/88 *Yael Shefer, minor, v. State of Israel*, 38 (1) PD 116, under *Medicine and Law). Similarly, the Supreme Court represented by Justice Orr based itself on the principle of the sanctity of life inferred from the creation of man, ruling that dialysis treatment should be given to a minor patient even in contradiction to the parents' wishes (ALA 5587/97 *Attorney General v. Anon*, 51 (4) PD 838–839).

The Supreme Court also invoked the idea of man's creation in the image of God in disqualifying a Knesset election list whose platform contained racist motifs. Sharply criticizing the temerity and sham involved in this list claiming to speak in the name of the Torah of Israel, Justice Elon said, among other things: "A basic foundation of Judaism is the idea that man is created in God's image (Gen. 1:27). This is how the Torah of Israel begins, and it is from this that *halakhah* derives fundamental principles regarding the value of man – all men – their equality and their being beloved [of God]. 'He [i.e., Rabbi Akiva] used to say: Beloved is man, who was created in [God's] image. Even more beloved is he, that it was made known to him that he was created in the Image, as it says (Gen. 9:6) "In the image of God He made man" (Avot 3:18). And thus, in this last verse, the prohibition against the spilling of blood by the sons of Noah is explained, even before the Torah was given" (EA 2/84 *Moshe Naiman v. Chairmen of the Central Elections Committee for the Eleventh Knesset*, 39 (2) PD 298. See also his comments in CA 294/91 *Ḥevra Kadisha Kehillat Yerushalyim v. Kastenbaum*, 46 (2) PD 512; and the comments of Justice M. Cheshin in FH 7325/95 *Yediot Aḥaronot Ltd. et al. v. Kraus* 52 (3) PD 1).

On a number of occasions, the Supreme Court relied on the biblical concept of man being created in God's image, as well as its stringent approach towards murderers who have taken the life of any human being. Thus, in a ruling dealing with the case of a Jew who murdered innocent Arabs, Justice Cheshin wrote:

> A person – any person – is a world in himself. A person – any person – is one, individual and unique. No one is like any other. One who was will not be again, and one who has gone will not return. And our teacher, the Rambam, taught regarding the uniqueness of man (Yad, Sanhedrin 12:3): "Man was created

alone in the world, to teach us that one who destroys a single soul in the world, is as if he has destroyed the whole world, and one who saves a single soul in the world is as if he has saved the whole world. For all those who come into the world are created in the form of Adam, and the face of no man is the same as that of any other. Accordingly, each and every one can say: the world was created for me." This is man, and this is his uniqueness. Who can dare say such a thing about a book or about a safe? (Cr.A. 1742/91 *Ami Popper v. State of Israel*, 51 (5) PD 305; and cf. Cr.A. 6841/01 *Yosef Biton v. State of Israel*, 56 (6) PD 800; CR.A. 6535/01 *Kusirov v. State of Israel*, 57 (3) PD 565; CR.A. 9804/02 *S.S. v. State of Israel*, 58 (4) PD 462; FTA (Tel Aviv-Jaffa) 1137/02 *State of Israel v. Nasser Mahmoud*, unpublished).

The creation of man in God's image also served as the foundation for a National Labor Court ruling (NLC 265–56/04 *Shimon Ḥassid v. The National Insurance Institute*, unpublished), in which the court accepted the claim of a homeless person that the National Insurance Institute should give positive consideration to awarding an income allowance to him and others like him, giving a broad interpretation to the law intended to ensure that the indigent have the right to live in dignity (see below). Similarly, the biblical description of the creation of man, both male and female, served as the basis by which the Supreme Court, represented by Justice Cheshin, anchored, among other things, the obligation to provide equal opportunities to both sexes when entering the workforce (HC 2671/98 *The Israel Women's Lobby v. Minister of Labor and Social Affairs*, 52 (3) PD the 36), as well as with regard to the terms of retirement from it (HC 6845/00 *Itana Niv et al. v. National Labor Court*, 57 (6) PD 663).

The Various Rights

THE RIGHT TO LIFE. The right to life is a value of prime importance, set down at the beginning of the various bills of rights. As the fundamental approach of Jewish law speaks, not only of man's *rights*, but first and foremost of his *obligations*, it imposes upon the human being an obligation to guard his/her own body, its most important expression being the commandment "Therefore take good heed to yourselves" (Deut. 4:15). Apart from exceptional cases (e.g., the prohibitions of bloodshed, idolatry and adultery), when cardinal values enter into the balance, the obligation to preserve life outweighs all other duties. A person is therefore commanded to desecrate the Sabbath in order to save a life, "for nothing stands in the way of saving life." The Sages expounded the verse "He shall live in them" (Lev. 18:5) – "and not die in them," (Yoma 85b) as meaning that the Torah's commandments have been given to live by and not to die by. According to some of the Sages, even with respect to those transgressions about which it was said that a person must allow himself to be killed rather than commit the transgression, this law only applies in public, in the presence of ten or more people. In private, however, a person must commit the transgression rather than allow himself to be killed. A special problem exists when a balance must be struck between two rights of the same type (see EA 84/2 *Naiman v. Chairman, Central Elections Committee*, PD 39(2) 225, per Justice Elon, and see *Euthanasia in *Medicine and Law). The definition of the State of Israel as a "Jewish and democratic state" finds expression in various ways related to human dignity and freedom. Thus, for example, with the exception of certain crimes of exceptional severity (e.g., crimes against humanity and the Jewish people, and the Nazis and Nazi Collaborators Punishment Law) the Israeli legislator abolished the death penalty that had been administered during the mandatory period. Similarly, corporal punishment was abolished by the Punishment of Whipping (Abolition) Law 5710 – 1950 (see *Values of a Jewish and Democratic State; *Human Dignity and Freedom; *Punishment).

THE RIGHT TO DIGNITY. Unlike contemporary law, Jewish Law views human dignity not only as a *right*, but as an *obligation* imposed upon man, stemming from the fact that he was created in the image of God. For this reason, he is neither permitted nor able to waive his dignity, even if he so desires (see *Human Dignity and Freedom).

THE RIGHT TO EQUALITY AND THE PROHIBITION OF DISCRIMINATION. The right to equality derives from the creation of man, as described in the Torah, as a solitary individual and a free man, from whom all of mankind has descended, such that no man can say to his fellow, "My father is greater than yours" (see above). An echo of this is found in the preamble to the United Nations' Universal Declaration of Human Rights, which recognizes "the inherent dignity and of the equal and inalienable rights of all members of the human family." Various expressions of the value of equality already appear in Scripture. Thus, for example, the Torah commands: "One law shall be to him that is homeborn, and to the stranger that sojourns among you" (Ex. 12:49; and see below, in the section dealing with the equality of nations). Many expressions of the value of equality are to be found in rabbinic literature. Thus, for example, the *tanna* Ben Azzai, maintains that the value of the equality of the sexes – embodied in the verse, "male and female He created them" (Gen. 1:27) – is "the greatest principle in the Torah," as opposed to the position of his colleague Rabbi Akiva, who sees the verse, "you shall love your neighbor as yourself" (Lev. 19:18) as the Torah's greatest principle (TJ Ned. 9:4 (41c)).

The value of equality also finds expression in the words of certain Sages with respect to specific issues. Thus, for example, two contradictory approaches are found in rabbinic literature regarding Torah study. The one is patently non-egalitarian, awarding the right to education exclusively to the children of the intellectual and economic elite (see below, sub-section dealing with the right to education). In contrast, there is an egalitarian approach that opens the gates of the study hall to all: "You might say that only the children of the elders, the children of the distinguished, should study. Therefore, the verse states: 'For if you shall diligently keep' (Deut. 11:22) – teaching that all are equal in Torah. Similarly it says: 'Moses commanded us a Torah, the inheritance of the congregation of Jacob' (Deut. 33:4). It is not written there: 'Priests,

Levites and Israelites,' but rather 'Jacob.' Similarly it says: 'You stand this day all of you' (Deut. 22:9)" (*Sifrei*, sec. 48 (ed. Finkelstein, p. 112)).

The obligation of equality applies likewise to legislation enacted by the king, which must be fitting and non-discriminating: "Any law promulgated by the king to apply to everyone and not to one person alone is not deemed robbery. But wherever he takes from one particular person only, not in accordance with a law known to everyone but by doing violence to this person, it is deemed robbery" (Maim., Yad, Gezelah va-Avedah 5:14).

Alongside such statements, Jewish Law contains no small number of laws that appear to violate the principle of equality and seriously discriminate on the basis of sex, race, nationality, age, or some other factor. In many, but not all such cases, the discrimination can be explained as a "permissible distinction" based on the principle that there are no absolute rights, and that even the value of equality is set aside by other values, and that the discrimination is for an "appropriate purpose and to an extent no greater than is required" (Section 8, Basic Law: Human Dignity and Freedom). Thus, for example, the preferred status of the priests and Levites is explained by historical reasons (their non-participation in the sin of the Golden Calf), or by their unique role as officiants in the Temple. Similarly, the disqualification of women for positions of public authority, and the absence in Scripture of their right to inherit (see *Inheritance) can be explained as stemming from the different social role they play from that of men (see at length the entry *Woman). Nevertheless, alongside the attempts, some clearly apologetic, to justify laws that appear to be discriminatory, the Sages of Israel have over the course of the generations made courageous attempts to mitigate the severity of these cases of discrimination to the point of their total abolition. For example, the ruling that prevents a non-Jew from serving in the Israeli Knesset or government, based on the biblical prohibition, "You may not set a stranger over you, who is not your brother" (Deut. 17:15), has effectively been abolished in the State of Israel. Similarly, the prohibition preventing woman serving in the Knesset or in any other public role (see *Woman: The Judicial Perspective) has in practice been abolished. Mechanisms have been established allowing a woman to receive an equal share of an inheritance (see *Inheritance, and see: R. Isaac Herzog, *Teḥukah le-Yisra'el al pi ha-Torah*).

The obligation of equality has ramifications in various circumstances and contexts. Thus for example, it is stated that a master/employer must provide his servant/worker with living conditions similar to his own: "'He shall be with you' – with you in food, with you in drink, with you in clean clothing: you [= the master, employer] may not eat fine bread while he eats coarse bread; you may not drink old wine while he drinks new wine; you may not sleep on cotton-wool while he sleeps on straw" (*Sifra*, *Behar*, sec. 5). Special emphasis was placed on the equal treatment of litigants in court (see *Bet Din), this being a fundamental principle of natural justice. Similarly, the rabbinic authorities have stressed not only the equality of rights, but also the equality of obligations and responsibilities.

In ancient legal systems, the "other" – the blind, the deaf, the crippled, the leper, and the like – was often rejected and subjected to unfavorable discrimination. Some viewed his condition as "a heavenly decree," a punishment for his sins, and hence as a reason to distance him from society. Thus, for example, during the Middle Ages, the term "leper" was applied to all of society's outcasts. Various popular beliefs that adhered to lepers contributed to their being cut off from community life. Testimony to this phenomenon is found in various sources of Jewish Law: for example, in the words of R. *Moses of Coucy, a 13th-century French Tosafist, who wrote in his *Sefer Miẓvot ha-Gadol* that a leper who wishes to enter a synagogue must "construct for himself a high partition four cubits wide, and enter first and exit last" – all this in order not to come into contact with the other members of the community.

As opposed to this approach, some authorities of Jewish Law viewed physical deformities as a "force majeure," which does not constitute grounds for denial of the "other"'s rights or discrimination against him. An example of the caution that must be practiced in this matter may be found in a responsum authored by Rashi (*Resp. Ḥakhmei Ẓarefat ve-Loter*, no. 40; see also A. Grossman, *Ḥakhmei Ẓarefat ha-Rishonim* (Jerusalem 1995), p. 140). In this responsum, Rashi rejects the argument of a man who wished to divorce his wife because she had been stricken with leprosy, and sharply reproaches him for his conduct.

PLURALISM, FREEDOM OF EXPRESSION, AND THE PUBLIC'S RIGHT TO KNOW. In modern constitutional law, pluralism – the multiplicity of views and the freedom to express them – has a most important place among human rights; some see it as the "queen of rights." This finds expression in various constitutions (such as the United Nations' Universal Declaration of Human Rights and the U.S. Constitution) that have established this principle and ascribed it supreme importance. Freedom of expression includes not only the right to express opinions, but also the right to hear them or, as it is usually called, "the public's right to know." The world of Jewish Law contains many expressions of praise for pluralism and multiplicity of views (see *Majority Rule; and see below Pluralism in the World of *Halakhah*). The great principle in this matter is mentioned already in the words of the Sages with respect to the controversy between the school of Shammai and the school of Hillel, who "disagreed for three years, these saying: The law is in accordance with us, and these saying: The law is in accordance with us. A heavenly voice issued forth and said: Both are the words of the living God" (Eruv. 13b). Nevertheless, on the practical level the matter was eventually decided: "And the law is like the school of Hillel" (*ibid.*).

As part of the recognition of pluralism and its importance as a value in its own right, Jewish Law assigns a place of honor to speech and to free speech, speech representing man's preeminence over the beast. This was given pointed expression in Onkelos's translation of the verse in the biblical account of Creation: "And man became a living soul" (Gen. 2:7) – *le-ru'aḥ memalela*, "a talking spirit." Man is speech, and the freedom to speak is the breath of life. However, even though man was given this freedom, he is commanded to use it wisely, for "in the multitude of words, sin is not lacking" (Prov. 10:19), and "too much talk brings sin." If this is true regarding neutral speech, all the more so regarding talk that involves slander and gossip, about which it is stated: "Guard your tongue from evil, your lips from deceitful speech. Depart from evil, and do good" (Ps. 34:14–15; and see above regarding man's right to a good name).

Despite the great similarity in certain matters, Jewish Law's conceptual starting point regarding freedom of speech is different from that generally accepted in our day, and thus its normative ramifications are also different. Modern law tends to justify this right with various principles inherent in it, including: clarifying the truth; strengthening democracy; "letting off steam," which in the absence of freedom of speech is liable to burst out in violent and undesirable channels; and self-realization. An examination of these principles teaches that most if not all of them are compatible with the principles – if not necessarily the particulars – of freedom of expression in Jewish Law. Nevertheless, it should not be inferred from this that the normative rights stemming from them, and especially its scope and application, are identical to those of Jewish Law.

Whereas modern law is occasionally ready to retreat from the truth in order to actualize freedom of expression and allow "freedom of false expression" (HC 6126/94, *Senesh v. Broadcast Authority*, PD 53(3) 817; HC 316/03, *Bakri v. Film Censorship Board*, PD 58(1) 249), Jewish law has sharp reservations about such an approach, and commands a person to distance himself even from that which contains the "dust" of falsehood. The sole allowance for veering from the truth is "for the sake of peace," and even this is strictly limited (Yev. 65b; Maim., Yad, Gezelah va-Avedah 14:13).

In contrast to modern law, which sees freedom of expression as an important component of man's autonomy and ability to achieve self-realization, various approaches in Jewish Law see speech as a necessity that should be limited. It is against this background that one needs to understand the dicta of the Sages in praise of silence (e.g., "a protection of wisdom is silence" (M. Avot 3:13); "a word for a *sela* (Talmudic measure of value), silence for two") (Meg. 18a).

Freedom of expression finds an anchor in Jewish Law in the sharp criticism of the prophets of Israel, who severely reproached both the authorities and private individuals. For example, "Your princes are rebellious, and companions of thieves; everyone loves bribes, and follows after rewards; they judge not the fatherless neither does the cause of the widow reach them" (Isa. 1:26; and see H. Cohn, *Zekhuyot Adam ba-Mikra u-ba-Talmud*; and the words of Justice Elon, EA 2/84 *Naiman v. Chairman, Central Elections Committee*, PD 39(2) 294; *idem, Ha-Mishpat ha-Ivri*, 1553–1557; *Jewish Law* (1994), 1846–1850; *Jewish Law (Cases and Materials)* (1999), 523–38. Indeed, the words of the prophets frequently stirred up the wrath of the ruling power, which did not always limit itself to a sharp verbal response, but at times adopted severe measures to forcibly suppress this freedom (see, for example, I Kings 18). According to one tradition, King Manasseh killed the prophet Isaiah and the people stoned the prophet Jeremiah for the opinions they voiced, and echoes of this tradition are found in the Talmud (Yev. 49b). It should also be remembered that the words of a prophet do not express full freedom of speech, for he is not free to say what is on his heart, but rather he is obligated to impart the word of God as he received it, without adding or detracting anything. This is exemplified by the attempts of Moses, "father of the prophets" (Exod. 3:11–12; 4:10–17), and the prophet Jeremiah (1:4–9) to avoid fulfilling the mission cast upon them, and their forced compliance. The obligation to proclaim God's word is so severe that the Sages asserted that a prophet who suppresses his prophecy is liable for death at the hand of Heaven. Moreover, the obligation to prophesy is conveyed exclusively to the prophet, and even he is not permitted to realize it whenever he wants, to the point that sometimes he "prophesies without knowing what he is prophesying" (see BB 119b). The prophet is thus frequently limited in his prophecy, and does not enjoy full freedom of expression, as is accepted in modern law. A prophet is also not permitted to say things that contradict the words of the Torah (Deut. 18:20; Shab. 104a).

Many testimonies are found in the responsa literature of attempts to reduce to a minimum infringement upon freedom of expression, even when committed for an "appropriate purpose" cause. This is sometimes accomplished through narrow interpretation of a rabbinic or communal enactment that clashes with freedom of expression, and at times even through the assertion that the enactment is null and void owing to its clash with this freedom. Thus, for example, Maimonides narrowly interpreted a communal enactment that attempted to prevent individuals from mentioning the name of the head of the Babylonian yeshivah (*Resp. Rambam*, no. 329 (ed. Blau, p. 596)). Similarly, R. Samuel de Medina narrowly interpreted a communal enactment that prevented members of the community from hearing the words of a sage who had fallen out of favor in the eyes of those who made the enactment (*Resp. Maharashdam*, vol. 1, no. 16; this responsum only appears in the first edition, and was omitted from later editions). These attempts to limit the freedom of expression of certain sages and silence them lest they compete with the community's leadership are known to us from other places and were not always successful (see, e.g., *Resp. Avkat Rokhel*, nos. 179–181).

Attention should also be paid to the fact that in contrast to the approach of contemporary constitutional law, according to which freedom of expression ensures the right of every individual to say anything, provided that he does not harm the interests of others, Scripture sometimes reflects a different approach, as exemplified by the attempt of Joshua bin Nun, servant of Moses, to silence Eldad and Medad who were "prophesying in the camp" (Num. 11:27) and his request of Moses to restrain them. In contrast, Moses' cold response, "Would that all the Lord's people were prophets" (Num. 11:29), expressed pluralism in "the marketplace of prophecy," and prevented their punishment, though *halakhah* has laid down that even when prophecy existed in Israel, not everyone who so desired was permitted to take the crown of prophecy for himself.

IN ISRAELI COURTS. The issue of freedom of expression in Jewish Law has been raised by the Israeli courts in various contexts, both in connection with libel suits (see *Slander) and in connection with constitutional issues, such as the right to run for office in the Knesset, which is part of the freedom of political expression (see below, subsection dealing with the right to vote and be elected), freedom of expression on gravestones, and other matters.

Two court rulings relate to the issue of freedom of expression on gravestones. The Israeli Supreme Court (per Justice Elon) discussed the issue of freedom of expression in Jewish Law at length, noting that, like other rights, this right is also not absolute and can be set aside if its realization clashes with other values, e.g., *human dignity and the sensitivities of other people (CA 92/1482, *Hager v. Hager*, PD 47(2) 793; CA 294/91. *Ḥevra Kadisha Kehillat Yerushalayim v. Kastenbaum*, PD 46(2) 464). The Supreme Court discussed this issue in another case dealing with the inscription of a date according to the Gregorian calendar on a gravestone. Justice Englard based his minority opinion on sources in Jewish law that ban such inscriptions, and in such circumstances prefer to set aside freedom of expression in favor of other values that conflict with it [CA 97/6024, *Fredrika Shavit v. Ḥevra Kadisha Rishon Le-Zion*, PD 53(3)600]. Another ruling discussed the broadcasting of a film on the Sabbath, where the main figures in the film, who were religiously observant, objected to its broadcasting owing to the Sabbath desecration profanation involved. Justice Dorner (in a minority opinion) sided with the plaintiffs, basing her opinion upon the views of those halakhic authorities who set aside the principles of freedom of expression and the public's right to know because of the Sabbath desecration that the realization of these rights would involve (HC 1514/01 *Ya'akov Gur Aryeh v. Television's and Second Television Authority*, PD 55(4) 282). She reviewed the various opinions on the matter in Jewish Law, and referred to the lenient approach that allows an observant film producer to sell his films to the Broadcasting Authority even when he knows that they will be broadcast on the Sabbath (M. Elon R. David Setav, "*Ẓulam be-Yom Ḥol, Shudar be-Shabbat*," in: *Nekudah*, 211 (1998), 52; and see R. Shlomo Zalman Auerbach, "*Shiddur Radyo Ḥozer be-Shabbat*," in: *Teḥumin*, 17 (1997), 13).

FREEDOM OF CONSCIENCE. Another important aspect of the modern idea of freedom is freedom of conscience, allowing a person to believe whatever his heart desires – not limited to matters of religious faith (see below, sub-section on the freedom of religion and ritual) – and to act in accordance with the demands of his conscience. This freedom is anchored in article 18 of the Universal Declaration of Human Rights and in the Declaration of the Establishment of the State of Israel, which promises "freedom of religion and conscience" to all its citizens and inhabitants.

As with other rights, Jewish Law does not speak of freedom of conscience, but of duty of conscience: i.e., that a person is not exempt from fulfilling his civic responsibilities because of the call of his conscience. Jewish Law deals with this issue at length in relation to the question of releasing people from their obligation to share the burden of community troubles owing to reasons of conscience. The issue is discussed in particular in the context of the question of the exemption granted to full-time yeshivah students from service in the Israeli army, and the question of conscientious objectors to military service. Many of the halakhic authorities who addressed this issue emphasized the duty falling upon every individual to share the burden of an "obligatory war," which overrides the duty of studying Torah.

Some have relied on the sharp call of Moses to the members of the tribes of Gad and Reuben: "Shall your brothers go to war, and you sit here?" (Num. 32:6; and see Judges 5:23). Others based their view on the biting Talmudic statement: "Who shall say that your blood is redder; perhaps the blood of the other is redder" – i.e., just as you ask your neighbor to risk his life to defend you, so are you obligated to risk your life on his behalf (Pes. 28b).

This issue of conscientious objection and Jewish Law was discussed in the Israeli Supreme Court, with respect to the refusal of a conscientious objector to serve in the Israeli army during the Lebanese war (HC 734/83, *Shein v. Minister of Defense*, PD 38(3) 404). Justice Elon denied the petitioner an exemption from military service, basing his ruling on numerous sources of Jewish law dealing with those seeking an exemption from army duty (e.g., Deut. 20:1–9; Judges 7:3; 1 Macc 3:55; M. Sotah 8:2–7; Tosefta (ed. Zuckermandel), Sot. 7:18–24; *Sifrei, Devarim*, secs. 192–197; Yad, Melakhim, 7; *Sefer ha-Ḥinnukh*, Aseh #502; and others). (See *Military Law.)

THE RIGHT TO VOTE AND TO BE ELECTED. The right to vote and to stand for election is one of the most important of all civil rights, as a clear expression of the democratic process. Because of its importance, in various legal systems, such as American law and Israeli law, this right has been established as an "entrenched section of the law," which can only be changed by a special majority of members of the House of Representatives (the Knesset).

Study of the sources of Jewish law shows that, notwithstanding that the system of governance reflected in many of them is very different from the democratic system in use today, there are many principles to be found in them that are equally valid and applicable today. (See in greater detail: M. Elon, "*Demokratyah, Zekhuyot Yesod u-Minhal Takin be-Pesikatam shel Ḥakhmei ha-Mizraḥ be-Moẓa'ei Gerush*

Sefarad," in: *Shenaton ha-Mishpat ha-Ivri*, 18–19 (5762), 9–63.)

A study of the Bible and of early rabbinic sources reveals that actual "election" processes are hardly to be found, and that the majority of "elected representatives" mentioned there are actually appointed and not elected to their position in a democratic process – nor did the biblical king receive his office through any actual process of election. Despite the fact that from the literal meaning of the verse, "you shall surely set him as king over you" (Deut. 17:15) it might be concluded that there was indeed a democratic process here of election by the people, the rest of the verse – "whom the Lord your God shall choose" – shows that this is not the case. This passage also shows us that the right to be elected was not given to everyone, but was limited only to the children of Israel: "from among your brethren shall you set a king over yourselves, you may not put a foreigner over thee, who is not your brother" (*ibid.*, and see above with regard to equality). Alongside this limitation, a further restriction was added at a later stage, by which "no king may be raised first other than in accordance with a court of 70 elders, and according to a prophet" (Maim., Yad, Melakhim 1:3). This restriction ensured a kind of "judicial review" of the selection process.

Restrictions relating to the right to vote may also be found in the sources of Jewish law. Thus, for example, it states in the Frankfurt Rulebook from 1774 that anyone has who has not paid his taxes that year may not take part in the elections, and the same is true of one regarding whom "at least two years have not passed since his wedding" (Rabbi R.D. Dessler, *Shenot Dor ve-Dor* (Jerusalem 2000), p. 413). A similar restriction existed in the Mantua community in Italy, where only people who had paid all their dues to the congregation and had lived within the city for a long time, at least 25 years, could participate in elections (S. Simonson, *Toledot ha-Yehudim be-Dukhasut Mantova* (Jerusalem 5723), p. 240).

Various restrictions were also placed on the right to stand for election, clearly reflected in the **Takkanot ha-Kahal* (communal enactments). Thus, for example, in a number of towns of Europe there was a regulation preventing a doctor or a broker from standing for election as "trustee" of the congregation, because these occupations were considered to be of low rank and were likely to undermine the public's faith in its leadership (Y. Baer, *Toledot ha-Yehudim be-Sefarad ha-Noẓerit* (Tel Aviv 1965), 256). The regulations of the Frankfurt congregation included a rule stating that a person standing for appointment as a community leader must have been married for at least nine years; for the position of "community dignitary" – at least six years; and for the position of *gabbai* (manager of synagogue affairs)– at least three years (Dessler, *ibid.*, p. 413). Another community rule enacted in Frankfurt states that only a person with considerable financial capital may be elected to the community committee (Y. Heilperin, *Zion*, 21 (1956), 64). This requirement apparently arose from the need to ensure the financial independence of the elected representative: in the absence of a salary for public positions, representatives needed to be of independent means in order to be able to devote their time to the position and to be free of extraneous pressures and considerations. In a number of communities in Christian Spain, a minimum tax payment was set as a condition for realization of the right to stand for election (Y.T. Assis, *Ha-Yehudim be-Malkhut Aragonya ve-Ezorei Ḥasutah*, in *Moreshet Sefarad*, H. Beinart, ed., Jerusalem 1992, p. 62 and note 115).

Restrictions of a different kind were applied to the expenditure permitted in an election campaign. Thus, for example, a rule was enacted in one of the Polish towns under which election expenses were limited to no more than six gold pieces, to prevent the waste of public money on the elections (S. Idelberg, "*Pinkas Schnadau*," in: *Galed*, 3 (1976) 304 #30). A similar provision was introduced in Israeli law, in the Parties Law 5752 – 1992, and the Party Financing Law, 5733 – 1973, which imposed a ceiling on the expenses permitted in an election campaign.

Another form of disqualification from election applied to individuals with a criminal past. In modern legal systems such as the Israeli system, criminals do not lose the right to vote, and a certain time after they complete their sentence they are entitled to stand for election, even if the crime they committed carries moral turpitude. On the other hand, in some Jewish congregations the right to vote and stand for election was taken away permanently from criminals (I.Z. Kahane, "*Sheloshah Kheruzim mi-Pinkas de-Kehillah Kedoshah Tribitsh*," in: *Kovez Al Yad* 14 (1948), p. 187). A case came before the Ḥatam Sofer regarding one of the leaders of a congregation whose other community leaders wanted to take away his right to vote or to stand for election for a period of ten years because of a crime he had committed. The Ḥatam Sofer fiercely denounced the faulty procedure they had followed, insisting that disqualifying a person from realizing his right to vote and stand for election only be done after review by the *bet din* and the local rabbi. In this regard, he added that, even if there had been defects in the election procedure, there was no reason to rush to invalidate it if these defects were only discovered after the election was over (Resp. Ḥatam Sofer, Likkutim, YD no.38).

IN THE COURTS. The issue of a criminal's right to vote recently came up in the Israeli Supreme Court regarding the matter of a prisoner who wanted to realize his right to vote. Justice Elon, sitting in judgment, based his decision giving the prisoner the right to vote on the basic principle of Jewish law "once he has been flogged – he is like your brother" (M. Makkot 3:15) (HC 337/84 *Hokama v. Minister of Interior*, 38 (2) PD 826; and see *Imprisonment). The question of the right of women to vote and stand for election was also discussed in depth in the ruling of Justice Elon in the Shakdiel affair (HC 153/87 *Shakdiel v. Minister of Religious Affairs*, 22 (2) PD 221, and see under *Woman: The Judicial Perspective).

Freedom of Demonstration, Assembly, and Procession

Freedom to demonstrate, assemble and march is an aspect of freedom of expression. In a modern, democratic country this freedom is one of the most important expressions of freedom of political expression, which differentiates a totalitarian regime from a democratic regime. A considerable portion of rules of Jewish law originated in entirely different political realities, which did not necessarily operate according to the democratic rules accepted today. But notwithstanding the differences, many democratic principles can be found which are similar, if not always identical, to the generally accepted rules today. Thus, for example, Jewish law provided a real possibility for those in disagreement with the leadership to express their opinions, and even to make use of the public domain for this purpose. Nevertheless, attempts can be seen on several occasions in the sources of Jewish law to silence these protesting voices – attempts which are not always successful. An early manifestation of this can be seen in the figure of the biblical prophet, crying out in public against various injustices, such as the strong words of the prophet Isaiah (1:21–23): "How is the faithful city become a harlot! She that was full of justice, righteousness lodged in her, but now murderers. Your silver is become dross, your wine mixed with water. Your princes are rebellious, and companions of thieves; everyone loves bribes, and followed after rewards; they judge not the fatherless, neither does the cause of the widow come before them."

One of the wonderful expressions of the right of the individual to "demonstrate" and protest against an injustice that has been done is the custom of "delaying [prayer] services" (alternatively referred to as: "canceling prayers," "cancellation of regular prayers," "delaying the public reading of the Torah"). This custom originated in the Jewish congregations of the Middle Ages, and it is used even today as a demonstrative sanction by a person who wishes to protest against an injustice he has suffered. The "delayer" is given permission to stop the prayers or the Torah reading, and will not allow the congregation to continue until his complaint has been heard. The responsa literature has preserved fascinating answers illustrating the considerable power of protest of this custom, often leading to a solution of the dispute that was the cause of the protest. (*Teshuvot Maimuniyyot,* Nashim #25; Maharam of Prague, 249; *Or Zarua*, 1 no.52; and see also: A Grossman, "*Reshito ve-Sodotav shel Minhag Ikuv ha-Tefillah*," in: *Millet*, 1 (1983), 199–219; M. Ben-Sasson, *Ha-Ẓa'akah le-Ẓibbur be-Beit ha-Knesset be-Araẓot ha-Islam bi-Ymei ha-Beinayim*, in: S. Elitzur et al. (eds.), *Knesset Ezra* (Jerusalem, 1994), 327–350; Y. Ta-Shma, *Minhag Ashkenazi ha-Kadum*, 303 and note 13; S. Golden, *Ha-Yiḥud ve-ha-Yaḥad*, 157–61).

FREEDOM OF ASSOCIATION. In contemporary discussion of human rights, the right of association constitutes a fundamental right. Some view it as an independent right, while others see it as a sub-category of freedom of expression. In light of the different legal reality, association in Jewish Law is not established in a formal manner as is common today (by means of the establishment of a corporation, non-profit association, cooperative society, or the like (see *Partnership; *Legal Person), but principles relating to the right of association are already found in various contexts within Jewish Law. Thus, for example, already in the tannaitic period (first and second centuries C.E.) enactments were made recognizing the right of members of a particular profession to join together to organize work relations between them – enactments reminiscent of those ordained by the members of the medieval guilds: "The wool dealers and dyers may declare: 'We shall be partners in all merchandise that comes into the town.'… The donkey drivers may declare: 'We will provide another donkey to anyone whose donkey dies.'… The boatmen may declare: 'We will provide another boat whenever anyone's boat is lost" (Tosefta, BM, 11:24–26). Similar ordinances were established in the modern period. Thus, for example, R. Moses Feinstein ruled that workers are permitted to organize in trade unions and to enact ordinances that are binding upon all of their members (*Resp. Iggerot Moshe*, vol. 2, ḤM, no. 58).

Responsa literature contains many testimonies to attempts to reduce infringement upon the freedom of association. This is sometimes accomplished through narrow interpretation of a rabbinic or communal enactment that clashes with freedom of association, and at times even through the nullification of the enactment owing to its clash with that freedom. Thus, for example, communal enactments that attempted to prevent individuals from establishing their own synagogues, that would give expression to their special customs, were reduced to a minimum. Such enactments were particularly common in the lands of the Ottoman Empire, following the expulsion of Jews from Spain and Portugal, when they established new "congregations" in many cities. The native residents saw the expansion of these "congregations" as posing a threat of the establishment of unbridled opposition and a breakdown of the social structure that had enormous economic importance. On the other hand, sweeping prohibitions limiting the right of association violated the freedom of the residents, and therefore they were interpreted narrowly, out of a desire to prevent such violation to the extent possible, unless it was done for "a worthy cause." Thus, for example, R. Samuel de Medina narrowly interpreted a communal enactment that indiscriminately prohibited the establishment of new synagogues in Salonika (*Resp. Maharashdam*, YD, no. 152).

FREEDOM OF MOVEMENT: In modern law, freedom of movement is perceived as among the most basic of all human rights. Man's liberty is manifested, among other things, in his ability to move freely from place to place, to live wherever he chooses, to leave the country and to enter it. In the modern discussion of rights, this right is an additional expression of the autonomy and liberty of the individual. Like other rights, this right is not absolute and must be balanced against such other fundamental rights as security of the state, public order, property rights etc.

Limitations on freedom of movement are divided into many stages: the most severe restriction of freedom of movement and the right to liberty is locking a man in prison, under an arrest warrant or detention order, and restricting him to movement within the prison walls. Of lesser severity is restricting freedom of movement to a particular place of residence, an alternative to imprisonment making the accused's release contingent upon his remaining at a particular address, known as "house arrest." A less severe measure is the restriction of his movement to a particular city, and even less severe is the restriction of freedom of movement by prohibiting a person from leaving the country, or prohibiting an accused from leaving the country, or curtailing the freedom of movement of a debtor which conflicts with the desire of society and the legislator to protect the property rights of his creditor and to enable him to collect the debt. An even less severe measure is a prohibition against a person from entering a certain country, such as prohibiting visits to an enemy state. In addition to the general restrictions mentioned above, there may at times be restrictions on freedom of movement in specific cases, both by force of legislation or by force of a court decision. Thus, for example, in the case of a demonstration or visit by a state personage, there may be restrictions on movement in certain areas for a limited time period in order to maintain public order and ensure the safety of the participants. Needless to say, the freedom of movement of an individual in the public domain is restricted by virtue of the wish to maintain public order and security. In certain cases (such as closing roads to traffic on the Sabbath), freedom of movement is set aside in favor of freedom of religion or the wish to avoid harming "religious sensibilities."

Jewish law rejects limiting freedom of movement and justifies it only for an appropriate purpose and insofar as it does not exceed the minimum required. The emphasis on freedom of movement as a significant component and basic principle of human freedom is expressed in the verse relating to the precept of the Jubilee year (also inscribed on the American Liberty Bell): "And you shall hallow the fiftieth year, and proclaim liberty throughout the land unto all the inhabitants thereof" (Lev. 25:10). The Sages took note of the special use of the word *deror* (liberty), which only appears this one time in the Torah and not in other places, where the word used is usually *ḥofesh* [freedom]. They interpreted this as referring specifically to freedom of movement and the right to live anywhere, and said that "liberty [*deror*] is the language of freedom [*ḥerut*]… like a person who lives everywhere and carries his merchandise to every country" (Rosh Hashanah 9b). Rashi adds (*ad loc.*) "one who lives wherever he wants, and is not subject to others."

On the other hand, even in the Bible there are already a number of restrictions on freedom of movement of a person or a group of people in various circumstances. Thus, for example, freedom of movement in or around holy places was restricted. At the time the Torah was given, the children of Israel were forbidden to even approach Mount Sinai (Exod. 19:12). There were special commandments with regard to the Tabernacle (and later, the Temple), whereby people who were unclean for various reasons, lepers, those with gonorrhea and those contaminated by the dead were not allowed to come near. On the other hand, the High Priest was proscribed from leaving the confines of the Temple during mourning: "neither shall he go out of the sanctuary, nor profane the sanctuary of his God" (Lev. 21:12). Another restriction on freedom of movement is given with regard to the tribes of Israel on the Sabbath: "see that the Lord has given you the Sabbath; therefore he gives you on the sixth day bread for two days; abide ye every man in his place, let no man go out of his place on the seventh day" (Exod. 16:29). This restriction was the source for the prohibition against going beyond "the Sabbath boundary," a concept developed in the Oral Law. Further restriction on freedom of movement is found in the institution of cities of refuge. A person who has committed murder by mistake or mishap is commanded to flee to one of the cities of refuge, and is forbidden to leave "until the death of the High Priest." (Num. 35:25) This restriction, however, is voluntary and not mandatory, and is intended to protect the killer from being avenged by the "blood avenger."

An extensive review of the limitations on freedom of movement can be found in the literature of the Sages and in post-talmudic halakhic literature. Thus, for example, a person is prohibited from leaving the land of Israel and going abroad unnecessarily. Similarly, there is mention of a prohibition against Jews traveling to Egypt or living there, based on the verse: "You shall not see them again any more forever" (Exod. 14:13; TJ Sukkah 5:1 (55b)). In later generations, there were those who sought to impose a similar "boycott of movement" on Jews returning to Spain (following the expulsion from Spain) or to Germany (following the Holocaust), but these prohibitions never took root in practice.

In different communities, where the number of Jewish residents was very limited, members of the congregation were prohibited from leaving the area because it was likely to result in it being impossible to find a *minyan* (prayer quorum of ten) for prayer on the Sabbath and festivals. An echo of this already appears in early responsa from Ashkenaz (Franco-Germany), as well as in the later period. Another regulation found in the sources of Jewish law restricts the freedom of movement of young people of the congregation to travel outside the town, lest this lead to "acts of immorality" (R. Joseph Caro, *Resp. Avkat Rokhel,* no. 206). Other examples of restrictions on freedom of movement imposed for "an appropriate purpose" appear in the community rulebooks. Thus, for example, the Lithuanian rulebook (p. 9 #39) mentions a prohibition against the leaders of the congregation going to Warsaw without the authorization of the State Council, lest they participate in the Polish Sejm assembly and contribute to decisions taken against the interests of the community as a whole. The regulation ends with the imposition of severe sanctions against anyone breaching this prohibition, stating that the infringer will be punished with "corporal punishment and financial punishment." Another restriction was imposed in Lithuania on the freedom of movement of wandering beggars. As it appears from this regulation, the increasing number of itinerant beggars wandering from town to town harmed the local poor and opened the way to acts of fraud. Accordingly, the Lithuanian rulebook (p. 17, #88) states that it is prohibited to allow indigents from other cities "to set foot in the towns / cities of Lithuania and Russia" unless they have relatives in town. Similarly, a woman can prevent her husband leaving for another country if there is a suspicion that he will not return and will leave her as an abandoned woman (see *Agunah). In such a case, the "appropriate purpose" of preventing a woman's abandonment takes precedence over his freedom of movement. This restriction is also anchored in Regulation 96(d) of the Rules of Procedure for the Rabbinical Courts: "the Court may discuss an application to prevent a man from leaving the country on the grounds of fear of abandonment." At the same time, if the man deposits a *get* (religious divorce papers), or even a conditional *get* (one that comes into force only if he does not return within the stated period of time), the appropriate purpose of preventing the woman's abandonment is achieved, and in this case the man may realize his freedom of movement (Sh. Ar., EH 154:8). The same holds true if there is a ruling that does not impose the obligation of a *get* on the man: in that case, the woman is not "entitled" to a divorce and the man's freedom of movement takes precedence. Consequently, if the man deposits a guarantee ensuring his return, there is no reason for denying him the freedom of movement. The Supreme Court in Israel has adopted this, among its other considerations, as a possible basis for refusing to extradite a criminal abroad if this is likely to leave his wife in a state of abandonment (see *Extradition).

A prohibition in principle against denying a woman's freedom of movement, alongside a recommendation severely limiting her freedom for reasons of modesty (apparently under the influence of Islam) is mentioned by Maimonides (Yad, Ishut 13:11):

> Every woman is allowed to go out to visit her father, or to go to the house of mourning or to a house of celebration to do kindness to her friends and relatives, so that they will also visit her. For she is not in prison, so that she can never come and go. Nevertheless, it is a disgrace if a woman is constantly going about, at times outside and at times in the street. And her husband is to prevent this, and not let her go out more than once or twice a month as is needed. For there is nothing more fitting for a woman than to sit in the corner of her home, as is written, "All the glory of the king's daughter is within" (Psalms 45:14).

At the same time, as we can see from contemporary historical sources, as well as in later periods, this "suggestion" to restrict women's freedom of movement was almost certainly influenced by what was customary in the surrounding Muslim society, and was not upheld in practice: "One who imposes a vow upon his wife that she not go to the house of mourning or to the house of feasting, must give her a divorce and pay her *ketubbah* money, for he locks her in; but if he does so because of 'another reason' he may do so." That is, restricting the woman's freedom of movement, so to speak "locking her in," is grounds for divorce, unless he claims "another reason" – e.g., that it is known that where she is going there are unruly and licentious people. According to Maimonides, a person who has made a vow denying his wife's freedom of movement must either retract his vow or divorce her, "since it is as if he has imprisoned her and locked her in."

Yet, notwithstanding the restrictions imposed on freedom of movement in certain cases, the halakhic sages imposed strict conditions on their use, limiting it to cases where the "appropriate purpose" was of greater value than denying the person's liberty – and even then they tended to reduce the restriction to the minimum necessary. For that reason, the use of imprisonment in Jewish law was considerably limited. Recognition of man's freedom of movement was also often manifested in rejecting the validity of a stipulation or other charge in an agreement that sought to deny a person this right.

In the State of Israel. The courts in the State of Israel often based freedom of movement on the principles and sources of Jewish law. Thus, for example, in a number of cases applications were made to prevent a husband from leaving the country lest he make his wife an *agunah*. In one case the Supreme Court discussed the case of a criminal suspected of committing a murder in France where extradition was requested. In connection with the question of extradition, Justice Elon discussed the source of Jewish law on this subject (see in greater detail *Extradition).

FREEDOM OF OCCUPATION. In modern law, freedom of occupation means man's *right* "to engage in any occupation, profession or trade" (Section. 3, Basic Law: Freedom of Occupation). According to the democratic understanding, this right is intended to allow a person autonomy in choosing his occupation, and assist him in fulfilling himself, but it does not obligate him to engage in any particular occupation, nor indeed to work at all, but leaves the decision to his individual judgment.

Following from Jewish Law's fundamental approach (see above), occupation is understood by Jewish Law not only as a right or a freedom, but also as an *obligation and duty*. Whereas modern law allows a person to engage in any profession, but does not obligate or command him to do so, Jewish Law commands a person to work and toil in some occupation that contributes to the promotion of civilization. Like any other right in law in general, and in Jewish Law in particular, freedom of occupation is not an absolute right. Over the course of the generations, various limitations were imposed upon it, some of which stemming from religious laws, others from public interests, and yet others from private interests. The various limitations set upon freedom of occupation may be divided into sub-groups: absolute limitations on certain occupations (e.g., commerce in articles connected to idolatry, lending at interest); conditional limitations that restricted the right to engage in a particular occupation to those who had received a license or authorization (e.g., ritual slaughter); limitations imposed upon members of a certain class (e.g., limitations imposed upon a Torah scholar or a judge not to engage in occupations deemed demeaning in the eyes of the public (or in order to free to study Torah and fulfill the commandment, "And you shall meditate therein day and night" (Josh. 1:7)); limitations on the times of certain occupations (e.g., on the Sabbath and festivals, during the *sabbatical and *jubilee years, and during a period of mourning); and limitations dependent upon time, place, and circumstances (e.g., the prohibition of monopolies and encroachment).

Some of these limitations were imposed through **takkanot* (enactments) or **takkanot ha-kahal* (communal enactments). Thus, for example, the Talmud records "enactments legislated by Joshua and his court," one of which relates to freedom of occupation with respect to fishing in "the lake of Tiberias." Anyone may catch fish in that lake, provided he uses "only a fish-hook," so as not to interfere with the movement of boats. But only members of the tribe of Naphtali, in whose territory the lake is located, may catch fish by spreading a net or keep a boat there (BK 80b; Maim., Yad, Nizkei Mammon 5:3; and cf. M. Elon, *Ha-Mishpat ha-Ivri*, 1452; *Jewish Law*, vol. 2, p. 552). Similarly, limitations were imposed upon merchants who wished to compete unfairly with their colleagues or in cases where they were liable to deprive them of their livelihood (see *Hassagat Gevul). So too, a prohibition was imposed upon the formation of a *ma'arufyah* (a form of private monopoly), cartel, or monopoly that would be injurious to the public interest (*Or Zaru'a*, BM 10a, no. 28; *Resp. Ge'onim Kadmonim*, and elsewhere). Limitations were also placed on freedom of occupation for the purpose of preventing profiteering (see *Hafka'at She'arim).

Various testimonies may be found in the sources of Jewish Law regarding agreements that were reached to limit the freedom of occupation of members of a particular group of people, such as those who engaged in a particular occupation. Thus, for example, the Talmud tells of an arrangement made by an association of butchers, dividing the work days among its members, and imposing a penalty upon those who violated the agreement (BB 9a; and see M. Elon, *Ha-Mishpat ha-Ivri,* 1:608; *Jewish Law*, vol. 2, p. 752). In the case under discussion, the agreement had been reached by way of an enactment of all "the townspeople," and nothing may be inferred from it regarding the law applicable to parties who reach a similar arrangement as individuals. Various testimonies regarding similar arrangements that were made as part of an agreement between individuals are found in the responsa literature, where the arrangements are called "restraints of trade" (*ketav issur*). The halakhic authorities issued various rulings regarding the validity of such arrangements (see, for example, *Resp. Divrei Malki'el*, vol. 3, no. 153; *Resp. Maharsham*, vol. 2, no. 22; *Resp. Ḥavalim ba-Ne'imim*, vol. 3, YD, no. 38). Such stipulations were prevalent in employment contracts, where the employer wished to prevent his employee from exploiting knowledge gained during his employ for his own future advantage or for the advantage of some other employer. The validity of such a stipulation is in doubt, because according to Jewish Law there is a difficulty entailed in acquiring ownership of something not yet in existence or having no substance (see *Acquisition). The problem was resolved, however, by way of an *obligation* that a person accepted upon himself to perform a certain act in the future, which is valid (*Haggahot Maimuniyyot*, *Shutafin* 4:2; *Ḥiddushei Ramban* to BB 9a; *Resp. Rashba*, vol. 3, no. 65; *Sefer ha-Terumot*, Section 64, Sect. 2:1; Tur, ḤM 60:10).

Alongside the problem of creating the obligation, a doubt exists as to the validity of a stipulation that seeks to violate a person's freedom of occupation. In this regard, it was established that when a limitation benefits none of the parties, but is intended only to restrain one of them, it reflects the trait of Sodom. This term was interpreted by most of the *Rishonim* as "inordinate privatism, that leaves one preoccupied with personal concerns to the neglect of others, or a degree of selfishness so intense that it denies the others at no expense to oneself." (See A. Lichtenstein, "Does Jewish Tradition Recognize an Ethic Independent of Halakhah?" in: M. Fox (ed.), *Modern Jewish Ethics*, 1975.) As such there are grounds for the nullification of stipulation reflecting those traits. On the other hand, when the stipulation is intended to prevent economic damage or is based on some other relevant consideration, it is not to be disqualified (*Ateret Ḥakhamim*, *Hashmatot*, *Resp.* ḤM, no. 21; *Resp. Imrei Yosher*, vol. 1, no. 169).

There is extensive evidence in the responsa literature of attempts to restrict infringement upon the freedom of occupation by narrowly interpreting laws and communal enactments that infringe upon that freedom. Echoes of this tendency are found already in the tannaitic literature. Thus, for example, the command regarding a Hebrew *slave: "And he shall remain his slave for life (*le'olam*, lit. 'forever'" Exod 21:6), was not interpreted in accordance with the plain sense of the text. Since the verse limits the slave's freedom and deprives him of the possibility of emancipation and choosing where to work, the Sages interpreted the term *le-olam*, not as "for life," but "until the jubilee" (i.e., until the next jubilee year) (*Mekhilta*, *Mishpatim*, sec. 2, ed. Horowitz-Rabin, p. 254; *Kiddushin* 21b; Josephus Flavius, *Antiquities of the Jews*, 4, 8:28; and see Elon, *Jewish Law*, vol. 3, p. 1031). In another case, a stipulation limiting freedom of occupation was interpreted narrowly (R. Abraham of Botosani, *Resp. Ḥesed le-Avraham*, second series, YD, no. 7). Another case in which one may void or restrict a stipulation that infringes upon freedom of occupation is when it infringes upon a public interest, leading to reduced competition and inflated prices (Naḥmanides, BB 9a; *Resp. Maharsham*, vol. 2, no. 22).

THE RIGHT OF PROPERTY. The right of property is anchored in various constitutions, its purpose being the protection of a person's property. The Basic Law of Israel states that this value must be interpreted in accordance with "the values of the State of Israel as a Jewish and democratic state" (secs. 1A, 3 of Basic Law: Human Dignity and Freedom).

As with regard to other rights (see above) Jewish Law defines this not as a right, but as an obligation: an obligation is incumbent upon the individual and upon society not to violate the property or proprietary rights of another person. The most striking command on this matter already appears in the Ten Commandments, "You shall not steal" (Exod. 19:13) (see *Theft), alongside of which there are dozens of other rules and commandments, e.g., the prohibition of theft applying to all of mankind (see *Noachide Laws), the prohibition of unlawful encroachment (see *Hassagat Gevul), and many others. Theft and robbery that violate the property rights of an individual are severely forbidden even when the offender intends to restore the property to its lawful owner (Maim., Yad, Genevah 1:2; see also *Theft and Robbery).

Based on the obligation to protect the property of another person, Jewish Law set down an important principle, according to which, in certain situations, even public interest may be set aside by the property rights of an individual. This principle is already anchored in the Talmud, which asks the rhetorical question, "Is the community a band of robbers?" and forbids the community to encroach upon the property of an individual in order to build a road (BB 100a).

Like other human rights, the right of possession is not absolute. In certain situations, permission is granted to violate the property of an individual in punishment for an offense that he had committed, for which purpose it was stated "property declared ownerless by the court is ownerless" (Git. 59b; Git. 36b; TJ Pe'ah 5:1; and see *Hefker). It was similarly established that the king is vested with the power to violate the property of individuals and to expropriate fields and their produce for the needs of his kingdom. This authority is based on the "king's law" found in Scripture (1 Sam. 8:11), echoes of which are heard in the story of Naboth and King Ahab (1 Kings 21). It is similarly established in the Mishnah that a king may "breach a fence" for the purpose of road-building, even when such action violates the property rights of an individual, and even to build "the king's road that has no measure" (M. Sanh. 2:4). The medieval halakhic authorities disagreed about the scope of this authority. Some, such as Rashi, greatly expanded it, explaining that the king is vested with this authority even in times of peace, and that he may violate the property rights of an individual even for the purpose of his own convenience (e.g., to provide himself with a shorter path to his fields; Rashi, at Yev. 76b). Other commentators severely restricted this authority, limiting it to "an appropriate purpose," where the king has no alternative, and only as "an emergency measure." In addition, an obligation was placed upon the king to compensate the individual for damage caused to his property (*Yad Ramah*, Sanh. 20b; Maim., Yad, Melakhim 4:6).

Regarding the expropriation of private property for public purposes, an obligation was imposed upon the ruling authority (the king, the community) to compensate the title-holder with money or alternative property (see 1 Kings 21:2). Similarly, the tendency was to limit the cases in which private property may be expropriated (*Tosafot*, Sanh. 20b, s.v *melekh*). These principles served as the basis for the attempts made by later generations of Sages to restrict the authority to violate the property rights of an individual by way of communal enactments or arguments of public interest (*Resp. Ramaz*, no. 37). To illustrate this idea, mention was made of the purchase of the cave of Machpelah by the patriarch Abraham, who paid for the property in full despite the promise that he would inherit the entire land, and the purchase of the Temple Mount by King David from Ornan the Jebusite for the purpose of building the Temple.

In Israeli courts. The principles of Jewish Law forbidding the violation of the property rights of an individual served as guidelines for various laws and judicial rulings in Israel. Thus, emphasis was placed on the obligation falling upon the public authority to compensate the owner of property expropriated for public purposes. The courts interpreted the expropriatory power of the public authority and, based upon the principles of Jewish Law, the courts obligated the public authority to compensate the owners for property expropriated for public purposes. In one case, the Supreme Court ruled that, if the public purpose that served as the basis for the expropriation ceased to exist, the expropriation is liable to be nullified. Justice Cheshin based his ruling, among other things, upon the scriptural account relating to Naboth and the talmudic principle, according to which "the community is not a band of robbers" (HC 96/2390, *Kerasik et al v. the State of Israel*, PD 55(2) 644. See also CA 119/01 *Akunas et al v. the State of Israel*, (unpublished) (Justice M. Naor) AA Tel Aviv-Yafo) 1146/02 *Eitan et al v. National Planning and Building Board* (unpublished) (Justice S. Dotan)). In another case, the Supreme Court, per Justice E. Rubinstein, cited sources of Jewish Law prohibiting the violation of an individual's property rights through expropriation, when it is possible to reduce the violation, whether by desisting from such expropriation, or by offering fitting compensation to that individual (AA 0989/04 *Local Planning and Building Committee of Petah Tikvah et al v. N.M. Zitman and Sons, Inc.* (unpublished)).

SOCIAL RIGHTS. As in the case with respect to other rights, so too regarding social rights, Jewish Law speaks of social obligations, rather than social rights. Thus, Jewish Law obligates almsgiving in order to help another person – every person – to live in dignity; it similarly imposes an obligation upon the individual and upon society to provide children with an education. Jewish Law also recognizes the workers' right to strike in certain situations, though it places greater restrictions on that right than are found in modern law (see *Labor Law). Similarly, Jewish law recognizes a person's right to education, to basic health care (see *Human Dignity and Freedom), to quality of life, to live in dignity, to strike.

Balancing the Various Rights

One of the most important principles regarding human rights is that all of the various rights are *relative*, rather than *absolute*, and that every right must be balanced against other rights and values. Thus, for example, sec. 13 of the Secret Monitoring Law states that, while evidence attained through secret monitoring is generally inadmissible in court owing to the infringement upon privacy that is involved, in exceptional cases, for example, "in a criminal proceeding regarding a serious felony," the court is authorized to rule that the evidence is admissible after having been persuaded, for the special reasons that it spells out, that in the circumstances in question, the need to arrive at a clarification of the truth outweighs the need to protect privacy.

This approach of balancing among the various values is firmly rooted in the world of Jewish Law. Thus, despite the extreme caution that Jewish Law takes regarding a person's right to privacy, this is set aside by the right to protect the health and welfare of the community. For that reason, a physician is permitted to publicly disclose that a certain person is suffering from an infectious illness, when the disease is liable to spread and endanger the health of the community. Similarly, despite a person's right to life and the wholeness of his body, Jewish Law did not refrain from administering corporal punishment and judicial execution. A person's right of property is also set aside by the various monetary penalties that may be imposed upon him (see *Punishment, *Capital Punishment), Similarly, a person's right to freedom of movement does not preclude the use of arrest or imprisonment, provided that these steps are taken for appropriate cause and not in excess of what is necessary (see *Imprisonment). So, too, the right of property may be set aside by the right of the public authority, in certain cases, to expropriate private property for purposes of the public needs.

On the basic level, this balance of interests is evident in all legal systems, but the method of balancing and its operation in specific cases differs from one system to the next. Inasmuch as it is a religious legal system, Jewish Law establishes a balance different from that found in modern legal systems. Thus, for example, in contrast to American and Israeli constitutional law, Jewish law assigns priority to the value of life over that of personal autonomy (Shefer ruling; see also *Medicine and Law; Euthanasia), and in certain cases prefers a person's right to a good name and his right to privacy over the public's right to know and freedom of expression.

[Aviad Hacohen (2nd ed.)]

The Right to Privacy

PROTECTION OF PRIVACY UNDER ISRAELI LAW. The right to privacy is one of the most important human rights (see: Cr.A. 1302/92 *The State of Israel v. Nahmias*, 49(3) PD 309, 353; Cr.M. 2145/92 *The State of Israel v. Viktor Guetta*, 46(5) PD 704; S.D. Warren & L.D. Brandeis, "The Right to Privacy," 4 Harv. L. Rev. (1890) p. 193) a right that extends to "those matters of the individual that, according to social consensus, the individual is entitled to keep to himself without someone else giving them public expression without his consent" (Introduction to the draft bill for the Protection of Privacy Law, 5740 – 1980, *Sefer ha-Ḥukkim* 1453, p. 206). The constitutional right of a person to privacy is derived from his dignity as a human being and from the nature of the State of Israel as a Jewish and democratic state. This right is also an integral part of international law and is anchored in several major international treaties (see, e.g., section 12 of the Universal Declaration of Human Rights from 1948; section 17 of the International Covenant on Civil and Political Rights; section 8(1) of the European Convention on Human Rights from 1950). The right to privacy embodies the individual's right not to have his private life disturbed by others, and includes the individual's interest to keep a degree of anonymity and intimacy for himself, such that his private affairs will be protected from another's view. The scope of the right to privacy includes the individual's right to manage his life within his own home without interference. Over the years, the right to privacy has become rooted in the decisions of the Supreme Court of the State of Israel as a basic legal right and has a considerable, although not absolute, degree of force. Its status as a supra-legal constitutional right was established in the Basic Law: Human Dignity and Freedom (*Sefer ha-Ḥukkim* 5792 – 1992, 150), Section 7 of which provides as follows:

7. (a) All persons have the right to privacy and to intimacy.

(b) There shall be no entry into the private premises of a person who has not consented thereto.

(c) No search shall be conducted on the private premises of a person, nor in the body or personal effects.

(d) There shall be no violation of the confidentiality of conversation, or of the writings or records of a person.

The court accorded quasi-constitutional status to the right to privacy even before it was anchored in the Basic Law: Human Dignity and Freedom. Because of its standing as a basic legal right, the governmental authorities ordered that it be respected, and it may not be infringed without express authority from the legislature; however, after being entrenched in the Basic Law, it received additional weight. The right to privacy already received express legal anchoring prior to the enactment of the Basic Law. The technological developments that facilitate invasion of the individual's domain with relative ease while concealing the fact of the invasion, and the apprehension regarding the transformation of personal affairs into public property and the harm that will be caused thereby to the individual's quality of life, to his personal security and to his autonomy, led the legislature to adopt the Secret Monitoring Law 5739 – 1979 (*Sefer ha-Ḥukkim* 5739 – 1979, 118) and the Protection of Privacy Law, 5740 – 1980. Both laws share largely similar goals and means for achieving them: defining actions that constitute an unauthorized intrusion into the private domain as criminal offenses; establishing rules defining those limited circumstances under which infringement of privacy will be permitted, whether in advance or retroactively; and determining that material gathered as a result of an invasion of privacy is inadmissible as evidence in legal proceedings. The exclusionary rule in the Secret Monitoring law may only be deviated from under certain, limited statutory conditions, in those cases where the goal is the thwarting of a serious felony or the promotion of the direct goal of the law – the eradication of secret monitoring by the prosecution of those who engage in it. The Protection of Privacy Law allows the deviation from the exclusionary rule at the request of the injured party or at the discretion of the court.

Protection of Privacy in Jewish Law

Based on the consecutive placement of two verses in the Torah, the Midrash derives the teaching that "…a person shall not enter another's home unless [the other] says to him: 'enter'" (*Midrash Lekaḥ Tov* (*Pesikta Zutra*), *Vayikra*, 1). The Talmud (Pesaḥim 112a) relates that Rabbi Akiva instructed his son Rabbi Joshua as follows: "My son… do not enter your own home suddenly, and all the more so another's home." In other words, there is a moral obligation to safeguard privacy, not only with respect to another person and his domain, but even in one's own home shared with one's own family. This respect of privacy became a binding norm during the period of the Talmud. Regulations were promulgated and prohibitions established to protect a person from the invasion of his privacy by others, with the goal of creating an orderly society in which people would be able to live together (see in detail, Menachem Elon, *Human Dignity and Freedom in the Execution of Court Decisions: The State of Israel's Values as a Jewish and Democratic State* (2000), p. 32 n. 88). We will present examples below of protection of privacy in Jewish Law, which served as a basis for the decisions of the Israel Supreme Court in general, and of the Deputy President, Justice Menachem Elon, in particular.

THE LACK OF SUPERVISION OF THE INDIVIDUAL WITHIN HIS OWN DOMAIN. According to Jewish Law, a person's private deeds and thoughts were not subject to supervision. This area was left to the accounting a person was required to render to his Maker – and to Him alone. In support of this approach, Rabbi Emanuel Rackman cites the words of the Talmud (Ket. 72a): "Rabbi Hinena b. Kahane said, in the name of Samuel: Whence do we learn that a *niddah* [a menstruant woman, who is ritually impure] counts for herself? It is said: 'And she shall count for her' – 'for herself.'" According to the *halakhah*, both men and women may become impure as a result of certain bodily secretions, and are subsequently required to immerse themselves in water; but before doing so they must count seven "clean days." In noting this obligation, the Torah states "and he shall count *for himself*" for a man and "and she shall count *for herself*" for a woman: that is, the counting is personal. There is no supervision or examination of this process to ensure that they do not cheat and thereby expedite the process of "purification." Jewish Law prefers trusting the individual over intrusion into his privacy. Refraining from supervision in these cases does not only stem from pragmatic concerns, such as the difficulties of supervising and absence of resources; the rabbinical courts could have encouraged informants or used inducements to entrap those who did not act as required. Jewish Law recognized such tactics, but only permitted them in one situation: regarding a person who instigated and led others astray to perform idolatry. What characterizes this exceptional situation is the threat to the integrity of Jewish society inextricably entwined in this offense. The inducement is designed, not to reveal the opinions of the criminal for their own sake, but rather to prevent him from leading others astray to follow his path and thereby damage the character of Jewish society (see below).

SLANDER. The duty to protect the individual's rights to dignity, a good name and privacy, are expressed in the legal realm in the laws of slander and gossip. Rabbi S.R. Hirsch (*Horeb* (1965), 253–59) explains the rationale and principles underlying of these laws. He claims that the prohibitions against slander and gossip are meant to protect the image that a person creates for himself in society, an image that is important for his happiness and self-fulfillment. According to Rabbi Hirsch, a society in which there is no protection of the values of human dignity and privacy is one that will bring upon itself "an eternal destruction of human life, and a bane of justice and integrity, happiness and peace" (see above on the right to a good name). In a case involving slander, Jewish Law gives the court authority to order, in addition to the punishment, destruction of the slanderous material or a prohibition on its distribution (see Resp. *Devar Moshe*, Pt, 2, no. 91, and see at length *Slander).

GOSSIP AND THE BAN OF RABBENU GERSHOM. One who reveals another's secret has committed an offense comparable to one who bears tales (Yoma, 4b). The prohibition on revealing secrets gave rise to the rule that "there is a prohibition on asking and searching in the private affairs of another" (Rabbi Jacob Ḥagiz, Resp. *Halakhot Ketannot,* vol. 1. no. 276). An important regulation based on this principle was enacted by Rabbenu Gershom, Me'or ha-Golah, cited in the responsa of Maharam of Rottenburg as follows: "Seeing a letter that one has sent to another without his knowledge is forbidden, and if he threw it away it is permitted" (*Takkanot Rabbenu Gershom Me'or ha-Golah*, as quoted in Resp. Maharam b. Rabbi Baruch, printed in Prague, at the end). A number of reasons are given for this regulation in the responsa literature (See: U. Ḥagiz, *Sefer Halakhot Ketannot,* pt. 1, no. 276; Rabbi Ḥayyim Palaggi Resp. *Ḥikekei Lev*, YD. Pt. 1. no. 49; Maharhash, *Torat Ḥayyim*, Pt. 3, no. 47). One reason is rooted in the overarching principles applying to all interpersonal behavior: "You should love your neighbor as yourself" and "That which is hateful to you, do not do to your fellow man." The second factor involved is the transgression of the rule "do not go bearing tales among your people" – in other words, there is a prohibition on searching among the hidden things of another. The third is because of theft, insofar as a person owns his personal information and another does not have the right to take it contrary to his wishes and without his knowledge. Regarding the sanction for this prohibition, it is written that "because there has been an increase among those who secretly open letters belonging to others, the court should establish a boundary and punish those who transgress as it sees fit" (Maharhash, *Torat Ḥayyim,* Pt. 3, no. 47, and Resp. Beit David, YD, no. 158). On this basis, Rabbi Sherman, a *dayyan* of the Rabbinical Court of Appeals of the State of Israel concluded that "it is clear that there is a halakhic prohibition on secret monitoring and a boundary must be established and those who transgress should be punished."

MEANS OF COLLECTING A DEBT. The fashioning of means for debt collection in Judaism was influenced by the right to privacy (see in detail *Imprisonment for Debt; *Execution, Civil; and the opinion of Justice M. Elon in HC 5304/92 *Peraḥ 1992 Siu'aḥ le-Nifga'ei Ḥukim ve-Takkanot le-Ma'an Yisrael Aḥeret – Amuta v. The Minister of Justice,* 47(4) PD 715, pp. 734–43; M. Elon, *Kevod ha-Adam ve-Ḥeruto be-Darkhei ha-Hoẓa'ah le-Po'al* (2000). Regarding the relationship between creditor and debtor, Jewish Law establishes a clear and unambiguous position (Deut. 24:10–11): "When you lend your brother anything, you shall not go into his house to fetch his pledge. You shall stand outside, and the man to whom you lent shall bring out the pledge to you." These verses embody the halakhic ideal – honoring the fundamental right of the debtor to privacy and personal freedom. The creditor's right to receive his money and to take the law into his own hands was limited, in that he was prohibited from entering the debtor's house. However, this arrangement did not stand the test of reality in the face of the socio-economic necessity to guarantee the payment of debts. Jewish Law takes the stand that a person's privacy in his own home is a right which deserves to be defended by law; however, it may not be exploited to impinge upon the rights of others and to obstruct the execution of the law. Thus, from the talmudic era, there is a balancing of the biblical injunctions while preserving privacy by means of transferring the authority and discretion to the judicial authority, so that only an emissary of the court may impinge upon an individual's privacy.

VISUAL TRESPASS. The Babylonian Talmud praises the people of Israel for protecting and guarding the privacy of the individual (Baba Batra 60a; for more detail on the subject see under "*Hezek Re'iyah,*" in: *Encylopedia Talmudit,* 8:659): "Rabbi Johanan said …'And Bilam lifted up his eyes, and he saw Israel abiding according to their tribes' (Num. 24:2). What did he see? He saw that the openings of their tents were not facing one another. He said: These [people] are worthy of having the *Shekhinah* dwell among them." This custom constituted the moral basis for enactment of the regulation regarding protection from *hezek re'iyah* ("visual trespass"; see *Nuisance) that constitutes an important element in the protection of personal privacy in Jewish Law. According to the Torah law, a person is only liable for compensation to another for damage if he performed a positive action. However, the Sages included within the prohibition of causing injury even that which stems from impingement on one's privacy –"visual trespass"; i.e., the damage caused by one person looking to another person's property. This damage is derived both from common sense and from the tradition, and was renewed by way of the regulation of the Sages. The broadening of the protection of privacy beyond the physical invasion of another's domain to include a prohibition even against looking at it from a distance, even from the property of the one looking, stems from the rule that "you shall do the upright and the good." Various reasons are given in the literature of the *rishonim* for the "visual trespass"; among others, there were those who viewed it as a kind of "*giri dilei*" (lit: throwing arrows). This concept relates to a situation in which a person commits an act on his own property (throwing arrows), as a result of which harm is caused to someone in a different place. From this, some of the *rishonim* argued that visual trespass is damage caused directly from one person observing another. A person is not interested in being exposed to the gaze of another while on his own property, nor in his personal details being known to others. The infringement of a person's privacy occurs, not only when his personal space is physically violated, but also when he is observed on his own property from outside. Moreover, the principle of the "visual trespass" also includes the obligation to avoid the very possibility of such observation which infringes upon the other's right to privacy, inasmuch as the very existence of such a possibility disturbs a person from acting in his home and in the surrounding property as he desires. Hence, one whose privacy has been infringed by the fact that his neighbor has opened a window facing his home and property is entitled, not only to receive an injunction against his neighbor prohibiting him from standing at his window and looking into his property, but the injured party is also entitled to demand that the situation be returned to its original state, in such a way that he will not suffer further injury. (See *Nuisance)

INFRINGEMENT OF PRIVACY IN MARITAL RELATIONS. Jewish law preserves the autonomy and privacy of each spouse in a marital relationship. This is true in the personal as well as in the monetary sphere. Jewish Law recognizes that the wife is entitled to respect, privacy and to autonomy over her body. These rights of the wife are at the basis of the *halakhah*'s prohibition of coerced cohabitation. The Talmud (Eruvin 100b) states: "Rami bar Ḥama said in the name of Rav Assi: "A man may not force his wife to perform a *mitzvah*…" This opinion is the authoritative position, accepted by all Talmudic authorities as well as by the later halakhic codifiers. From this we learn that, despite the fact that a wife is obligated in the marriage agreement to cohabit with her husband, and despite the fact that non-fulfillment of the obligation may constitute grounds for the husband to breach the agreement and to declare the wife a *moredet* (rebellious wife), none of this serves as license for the husband to perform an act that infringes upon her body, her dignity, her freedom, and her privacy. There is no doubt that married couples are expected to behave openly with one another and to live together with love, harmony and fellowship, but the obligation of openness in the couple's relationship does not allow one party to infringe upon the privacy of the other, even when the obligation of fellowship is breached (see: N. Rakover, "*Yaḥasei Ishut bi-Kefiyyah bein Baal le-Ishto,*" in: *Shenaton Ha-Mishpat ha-Ivri*, 6–7 (1979–1980), 295).

The status of the obligation "and they will not hide them …from one another," contained in the prenuptial agreement (*tenaim*) (*Naḥalat Shiva*, no. 10) is a point of disagreement among the halakhic decisors. According to Rabbi Joseph Colon (Resp. Maharik no. 57), this portion of the prenuptial agreement has a normative binding status. On the other hand, Rabbi Shlomo Kluger (Resp. *Tuv Ta'am ve-Da'at* (3rd ed.), No. 181) is of the opinion that this portion of the agreement does not have the status of a normative binding provision, but is rather considered as part of the opening comments. Rabbi Dikhovsky of the Rabbinical Court of Appeals of the State of Israel (S. Dikhovsky, "*Ha'azanot Seter,*" in: *Teḥumin*, 11 (1990), 299ff., at 303) expands the applicability of this condition to personal obligations and not just to monetary obligations.

SEARCHING A PERSON'S BODY. The question of conducting a search on a person's body arose in Jewish Law in the context of one who entered the Temple chambers to contribute his *shekalim*. According to one opinion (Tosef. Shekalim 2:2), it was customary to search the body and clothing of one entering the chamber, in order to preempt a claim, in the event that money was found in his possession on his way out, that he had brought his own money with him. According to another opinion (M. Shekalim 3:2), one who enters should not be humiliated by a search of his clothing and his body, and it is sufficient that he take care not to enter the chamber with clothing or possessions that would be likely to cast suspicion upon him. The Tosefta, *supra*, explains this difference of opinion as follows: The opinion that no search of a person's clothing should be made is the opinion of Rabbi Akiva, who states: "'And you shall do that which is right and good in the sight of the Lord' (Deut. 6:18) – good in the eyes of Heaven and right in the eyes of man." In other words, indeed a person has to do what is good in the sight of the Lord and to be clean in the eyes of Israel as well, that is, not to bring suspicion upon himself, but he must also take care to do what is right in the sight of man, and therefore not to be humiliated by a search, because conducting a search on a person's body is not right in the sight of man. (See M. Elon, *Ha-Mishpat ha-Ivri* (1988^3), pp. 512–15; *Jewish Law*, (1994), 624–28, and the notations there.) On the other hand, Rabbi Ishmael follows the first opinion, that "doing what is right refers to what is right in the sight of the Heavens" (Tosefta, *supra*) – in other words, that both the good and the right refer to the good and the right in the sight of Heaven, and what is good and right in the sight of Heaven will be so in any event in the sight of man – and therefore a search should be conducted in order to ascertain that he did not embezzle money belonging to the Chamber. The law was decided according to Rabbi Akiva, that a search not be conducted (Yad., Shekalim, 2. 10; and see *Ha-Mishpat ha-Ivri, supra*, 512–13; *Jewish Law*, 624–25).

The preservation of human dignity and the prohibition against humiliating people is applicable, not only to innocent members of society, but even to those suspected of having committed a crime. Where the Jerusalem Talmud (Sanhedrin 7:8) states that a suspicion based on an unsubstantiated charge that a certain person killed someone is sufficient to arrest the suspect until the charges are clarified, Rabbi Yose questions that statement: Do they apprehend someone in the marketplace and humiliate him? Rather, only where there is *prima facie* evidence regarding the commission of a crime by the suspect may he be placed in detention until his witnesses come (see the decision of Justice Menachem Elon in Cr.M. 71/78, *The State of Israel v. Rivka Abukasis*, 32(2) PD 240, pp. 248–49). The arrest of a person in the marketplace is a humiliation, and it is only permitted in the event that there is a suspicion regarding a serious crime, such as murder, in which case public safety is endangered if the suspect continues to walks about freely.

Jewish law also dealt with searches on and in a person's body. According to the teachings of the Sages, a person's dress is regarded as his dignity and his privacy: "For a person's dignity is his clothing" (Exodus Rabbah 18. 5).

Regarding Rabbi Johanan it was told that he called his clothing "my dignity," because "they dignify their owner" (Shabbat 113a, and Rashi ad loc; Bava Kamma 91b; Sanhedrin 94a). In addition, walking about naked is considered impure and an abomination: "There is nothing more impure and abominable to God than one who walks about naked in the marketplace" (Yevamot 63b). Against this background, Jewish Law specifically discusses the injury to human dignity caused by a person removing his clothes in public.

The Torah states: "You shall not wear a garment of diverse kinds, of wool and linen together" (Deut. 22:11; Yad., Kila'im, 10:1). In the Talmud (Berakhot 19b), the question is asked whether one who discovers mixed wool and linen fabric (*sha'atnez*) in his clothes while walking in the marketplace is required to remove the garment immediately so as not to transgress this prohibition, or only after he arrives home, because disrobing in the marketplace harms his dignity and humiliates him. In this context, the principle is cited: "Great is human dignity for it supersedes a prohibition written in the Torah." According to this principle, one may postpone removing the garment until arriving home. The Babylonian Talmud rules that a distinction must be made between the case in which the garment is of the kind of mixture that is forbidden according to the Torah and that forbidden by rabbinic law alone. In the latter case, the person need not remove the garment in the marketplace, for his dignity takes precedence over a transgression which is not of biblical force (*d'oraitah*); but in the case of *sha'atnez* that is forbidden according to the Torah, it is preferable not to transgress the prohibition, based on another principle: "There is no wisdom or understanding or counsel against the Lord" (Prov. 21:30). According to the passage in the Jerusalem Talmud (Kila'im 9:1), the principle of human dignity even overrides a negative commandment of *de-oraita* force, and not only one of rabbinic force (*de-rabbanan*). The simple reading of this passage is that there is a disagreement between the Jerusalem Talmud and the Babylonian Talmud, as set forth in the commentary of R. Elijah of London, according to which one of the *amoraim* is of the opinion that human dignity supersedes even a prohibition of the Torah (*Perush Rabbenu Eliyahu mi-Londrish*, ed. M.J.L. Zaks (1956), p. 2). A brilliant explication of this is given in the rulings of the Rosh, where it is stated: "Regarding *kilaim* (mixtures) that are prohibited by the Torah – clearly if one finds *kilaim* in his clothes, there is no wisdom or understanding against the Lord and he must remove the garment even in the marketplace. But if a person sees *kilaim* in another's garment, and the one wearing it is unaware, he should not be told in the marketplace until he arrives at his home, and he should be silent for the sake of his dignity and not require him [immediately] to cast off an inadvertent transgression."

PLANTING CONCEALED WITNESSES – ENTRAPMENT. In the view of the *halakhah*, enticing others to idolatry is an extremely serious offense. One who entices others to alien worship (Deut. 13:7–12) subverts the character of the Jewish society. His deed is particularly dangerous, inasmuch as it is done secretly and he entices his friends who are loyal to him and will not be quick to turn him over to the authorities or testify against him in court. Therefore, the rules of procedure regarding one who entices others to idolatry are more lenient in several aspects, one of which is relevant for our purposes. Ordinarily, it is prohibited to conceal witnesses or to use detective devices with the goal of following one who commits an offense and to gather evidence regarding such commission; however, this prohibition does not apply regarding one suspected of enticing others to idolatry. Because the enticer carries out his deeds in the utmost privacy and his offense strikes at the very foundations of the society, the *halakhah* is forced to use extraordinary means to expose him, by creating an artificial situation in order to trap him. In an article dealing with the subject of secret monitoring, Rabbis Dikhovsky and Dasberg disagree as to whether such concealment of witnesses is permitted regarding other offenses as well (see Dikhovsky, "*Ha'azanat Seter*," in: *Teḥumin* 11 (1990), 299, and Dasberg's response at the end of the article). Relying on the Rambam, Rabbi Dikhovsky argues that "…the difference between an enticer and others who commit capital crimes is only that with regard to an enticer there is an *obligation* (*mitzvah*) to entrap him, whereas with regard to others who have committed capital crimes, it is *permitted* to do so." Rabbi Dasberg, on the other hand, argues that "such entrapment is only permitted with regard to an enticer, and only when he cannot be dissuaded from commission of the offense by warnings and by opening a door to repentance. However, concealment of witnesses is forbidden with regard to any other offense, because the one who puts the entrapment in place violates the injunction 'do not place an obstacle before the blind' and disregards the *mitzvah* of reproaching another for his waywardness." The deputy president of the Supreme Court, Justice Menachem Elon, is also of the opinion that it is permissible to carry out entrapment in other exceptional cases, and he argues that under special circumstances secret monitoring is a *mitzvah*, such as in order to create evidence in a case of serious crime (incitement and enticement), and that it is permitted in order to create evidence regarding any criminal activity whatsoever (see Rabbi Joseph Babad, *Minḥat Ḥinukh*, on the *Sefer ha-Ḥinukh* §462). Justice Elon also relies on the *halakhah* that permits opening another person's letter where there is basis for suspecting that the one who wrote the letter intends to defraud the addressee of his money, and that the situation may be clarified by opening and reading the letter (see Rabbi Ḥayyim Palaggi, *Resp. Ḥikekei Lev*, Pt. 1, YD 49; Rabbi Joseph Colon, Resp. Maharik, no.110; *Haggahot Rema* to YD 228.33; cf. Justice Menachem Elon's opinion in FH 9/83 *Military Appeals Tribunal v. Vaknin*, 42(3) PD 837, para. 9.).

PROTECTION OF PRIVACY IN DECISIONS OF THE ISRAEL SUPREME COURT. The Israeli Supreme Court dealt with the question of privacy in a number of decisions. These decisions were based *inter alia* on sources in Jewish Law. One of the questions discussed in the *Afangar* case (Cr.A. 360/80, *The State of Israel v. Ya'akov Afangar*, 35(1) PD 228) was the question of the criminal liability of one who was enticed to commit a crime. Justice Elon based the rule set forth in Israeli case law, according to which one who was enticed is not thereby absolved of his criminal liability, on the above-cited sources of Jewish Law. The *Vaknin* case (FH 9/83, *Military Court of Appeals v. Vaknin*, 42 (3) PD 837) involved an incident in which military policemen forced a soldier to drink salt water against his will in order to determine whether he had swallowed a bag containing illegal drugs. The Court again reiterated that the Israeli law did not adopt the American doctrine of "fruit of the poisoned tree" even after the enactment of the Protection of Privacy Law and the Covert Listening Law. Considerations of educating those in positions of authority and protection of a defendant's dignity and his freedom are not sufficient to justify ignoring objective facts when the court must make a ruling regarding the legal truth. In that decision, Justice Elon elaborated on the position of Jewish Law regarding the question of the protection of privacy. He issued a call to the judges that "the material found in Jewish Law regarding protection of privacy, as well as many additional sources, should be used as a source to resolve various dilemmas regarding the protection of privacy." In another case (Cr.A. 2145/92 *The State of Israel v. Victor Goetta*, 46(5) PD 704), the police conducted a search on Victor Goetta, whom they suspected of possessing illegal drugs. It was alleged that the police stripped him and conducted a search of his body parts in order to ascertain if he was concealing drugs in his private parts. In that case, Justice Elon wrote a leading decision regarding body searches, based on sources in Jewish Law. The rules set forth there distinguish between permitted searches on the visible parts of a person's body, as opposed to a search in his internal organs, which is forbidden unless there is an explicit legal provision that permits it. In addition, even a permitted search must be conducted in such a manner that the person's dignity is respected, so that the image of God within him not be debased and humiliated.

The Attitude to Non-Jews

In the *Naiman* case (EA 3, 2/84, *Naiman v. Central Elections Committee, Chairman; Avneri v. Central Elections Committee, Chairman*, 39 (2) PD 225), the deputy president of the Israeli Supreme Court, Justice Menachem Elon, stated (at p. 298) that:

> One of the fundamental principles in the world of Judaism is the idea of man's creation in the Divine image (Gen 1:27). This is how the Torah begins, and from it the *halakhah* derives basic principles regarding the value of the human being – every human as such – and the right of every person to equal and loving treatment. "He [R. Akiva] would say: Beloved is man, for he was created in the image [of God]; it was an act of greater love that it was made known to him that he was created in the image [of God] in that it is stated 'In His image did God make man' [Gen. 9:6]" (M. Avot 3:18).
>
> There is a highly instructive dispute between two of the leading *tannaim* regarding the essence of the most fundamental principle in the realm of man's relation to his fellow man: "'You shall love your neighbor as yourself' [Lev 19:18]. Rabbi Akiva said: '*This* is a fundamental rule of the Torah.' Ben Azzai said: 'This is the book of the generations of man [in the day that God *created him in his image*]' [Gen. 5:6]. *This* is even more fundamental *than the former*" (*Sifra, Kedoshim* 4:10). According to R. Akiva, the highest value in inter-personal relations is the *love* of man and of one's fellow human being; while according to Ben Azzai, the greatest value is human *equality*, stemming from the creation of *every person* in the image of God.

Justice Elon continues:

> The two values taken together – human equality and love of humanity – became as one in the Hebrew nation, and together they constitute a fundamental principle of Judaism, throughout its generations and eras. The fundamental principle "you shall love your neighbor as yourself" is not only a matter of subjective feeling, an abstract love with no practical requirements, but a way of life in the practical world. It is this principle that is formulated in Hillel's words: "That which is hateful to you, do not do to your fellow man" (Shab. 31a).

Based on this approach, Rabbi Abraham Yitzhak Hacohen Kook wrote that,

> Love of humanity must be alive in one's heart and soul – love for each individual separately, and love for all nations [together with], desire for their advancement for their spiritual and material progress … An inner love from the depths of one's heart and soul, [a longing] to be beneficient to all nations to add to their material wealth, and increase their happiness. (*Middot ha-Re'iyyah, Ahavah*, sec. 5).

These basic and fundamental world-views also determined the attitude of Jewish sources to the national minority living under Jewish rule. A whole series of basic commandments of Judaism are explained in the Torah in terms of the historical memory of the people and its suffering as a minority under the rule of others: "for you were strangers in the land of Egypt" (Exod. 23:9; Lev. 19:30; 22:20; 23:9; and passim). Moreover: "You shall not abhor an Egyptian, for you were a stranger in his land" (Deut. 23:8). Racism, which has to this very day claimed so many victims over the course of human history, is unknown in the world of Judaism, and totally rejected thereby.

The Book of Leviticus (19:33–34) states, "and when a stranger dwells among you in your land, you shall not oppress him. Like a sojourner among you shall be the stranger who lives with you, and you shall love him like yourself, for you were strangers in the land of Egypt; I am the Lord your God." In the Book of Exodus (22:20), the prohibition is couched in somewhat different language: "You shall not wrong or oppress a stranger, for you were strangers in the land of Egypt." The prohibition against oppressing the stranger is addressed both to the individual in his relations with others and to governmental authorities and the general public. Rabbi Samson Raphael Hirsch saw the use of the singular as addressed to the state as a body, while those verses phrased in the plural were addressed "to the nation as a whole, also as an aggregate of individuals" (see Rabbi S.R. Hirsch, *Commentary to the Pentateuch*, on Exod. 22:20). The Torah emphasizes the prohibition against oppressing the stranger in order to express the value of equality in society, specifically with regard to members of other religions, and to warn man repeatedly not to surrender to the temptation of exploiting the weakness of those lacking in power or influence, as expressed well by Hirsch in his *Commentary* (*ibid.*, from the English translation of I. Levy (Gateshead, 1973), vol II, p. 373):

> It is not race, not descent, not birth or country or property, altogether nothing external or due to chance, but simply and purely the inner spiritual and moral worth of a human being, which gives him all the rights of a man and of a citizen. This basic principle is further ensured against neglect by the additional motive, [that you were strangers in the land of Egypt] …Your whole misfortune in Egypt was that you were *gerim*, "foreigners," "aliens" there; as such, according to the view of other nations, you had no *right* to be there, had no claims to rights of settlement, home, or property. Accordingly, you had no rights in appeal against unfair or unjust treatment. As aliens you were without any rights in Egypt, out of that grew all your.. slavery and wretchedness. Therefore beware, so runs the warning, from making rights in your own State conditional on anything other than on that simple humanity which every human being as such bears within him. With any limitation of these human rights the gate is opened to the whole horror of Egyptian mishandling of human beings.

Most of the halakhic sources interpreted the oppression of the stranger as referring specifically to the proselyte who was attached to the people of Israel in every respect – i.e., the *ger tzedek*, the righteous proselyte. Yet this interpretation presents a number of difficulties. The first of these is that the Torah prohibits oppressing any person from Israel, "You shall not oppress each man his fellow" (Deut. 25:124), so that the prohibition against the oppression of the proselyte seems superfluous, as they are in any event included within the totality of Israel. The second difficulty relates to the reason given for the prohibition, whether in Exodus, Leviticus, or Deuteronomy: "for you were strangers in the land of Egypt." The Israelites were certainly not "righteous proselytes" in Egypt, for they did not go there to settle permanently, but to reside their temporarily until the famine would pass, as confirmed by the fact that they did not assimilate within the Egyptian people. Hence, there were those who interpret the Torah as prohibiting the oppression of the stranger who lives among us, even if he did not accept Torah and *mitzvot*. And indeed, it was thus that Ibn Ezra interpreted it (in his shorter commentary, to Exod. 22:20): "And the phrase '*you shall not oppress the stranger*' refers to the resident stranger, because there is no one to help him from his own family, and any of the residents can deprive him of his wealth or of his home, and also bring pressure upon him by testimony, as Scripture says, '*you shall not oppress your neighbor*'" (Exod. 20:12).

Who then are these "resident strangers" (*gerei toshav*)? Rav Kook thought that the Muslims living in the Land of Israel fall under the rubric of *ger toshav* (see Resp. *Mishpat Kohen*, no.58), and Rabbi Isaac Halevi Herzog ruled similarly in his wake, emphasizing that "even though they were not formally accepted before a Jewish court, and even though we do not accept a person as a *ger toshav* in this era… an entire nation that took upon itself the seven [Noachide] mitzvot, even today, are subject to the rule of *ger toshav* (Resp. *Heikhal Yiẓḥak*, EH, Pt 1.12). This rule also applies to the Christian Arabs in Israel (see Rabbi I. Herzog, "Minority Rights According to the Halakhah," in: *Teḥumin*, 2 (1981), 172 (Heb.); on the issue of Christian faith and the seven Noachide commandments, see Rabbi Y. Harlap, "Idolatry through *Shituf* Among Noachides" (Hebrew), *Teḥumin*, 19 (1999), 148). Above and beyond the halakhic discussion regarding the status of the resident stranger – the attitude towards non-Jewish minorities and their freedom of religious practice is established by the principle in Jewish law of "ways of peace." As noted by the Talmud (Gittin 61a): "Our Rabbis taught: One provides sustenance to the poor among the non-Jews together with the poor among the Jews, and one visits the sick of the non-Jews together with the sick of Israel, and one buries the dead of non-Jews together with the dead of Israel, because of ways of peace" (see Rabbi Judah Gershuni, "Minorities and Their Rights in the State of Israel in Light of the Halakhah," in: *Teḥumin*, 2 (1981), 180, 192 (Heb.)). Hence, Jewish law recognizes the option of appointing a non-Jew to public office; this, because, despite the original prohibition against doing so was because of the dominion they might exert over the public. Today, when the power of office derives from the people, it does not present a problem (see Elisha Aviner, "The Status of the Ishmaelites in the State of Israel in Light of the *Halakhah*," in: *Teḥumin*, 8 (1987), 337, 358 (Heb.)).

One should note, vis-à-vis the freedom to practice their own religion on the part of the minorities living in the land, that the Hebrew nation does not engage in "missionizing" in order to add members of other peoples to its own ranks (see Micah 4:5; Yad., Melakhim 8:10). This fact expresses, among other things, the tolerance that Judaism affords to members of minority groups to live according to their own tradition and culture. The practice accepted in the ancient world – and in more recent times as well – was that the majority forcibly assimilates members of minority groups into the majority religion of the state – based on the accepted principle that "Cuius Regio Cuius Religio," i.e., he who rules is the master of religion. This practice led to the persecution of minorities to the extent of forcing them to accept the religion of the dominant majority. This practice was absolutely forbidden in the world of *halakhah*. For that reason, during those periods when Jewry enjoyed power, "the Court did not accept proselytes all the days of David and Solomon. In the days of David – lest they came out of fear; and in the days of Solomon – lest they came because of the kingship and greatness and material good which were then seen in Israel" (Yad, Issurei Bi'ah 13:15). These matters were summarized by Justice Elon in the *Naiman* case as follows (301–2):

> The national minority of a member of another people is defined in the *halakhah* as having the status of a resident alien (*ger toshav*), the only requisite demanded of him is to abide by the "Seven Noachide Laws" – the elementary rules of a legal order which the members of all civilized nations are commanded to observe, and which the Sages saw as a kind of universal natural law (Yad, Issurei Bi'ah 14:7 and cf. Melakhim 8:10–11; Sanhedrin 56a; Ramban, *Commentary on the Torah* to Gen. 34:13; and cf. M. Elon, op cit., 183ff.). The national minority is entitled to all of the civil and political rights of the other inhabitants of the country: "though he be a stranger, or a sojourner; that he may live with thee" (Lev. 25:35). "A *ger toshav* is to be treated with the same respect and kindness accorded a Jew, for we are commanded to let them live… and since one is obligated to let the *ger toshav* live – he must be given medical treatment without charge" (Yad, Melakhim 10:12; *ibid.*, Avodat Kokhavim 10:2). And the Sages further said: "One does not settle a *ger toshav* on the frontier, or in an undesirable dwelling, but in a desirable dwelling in the center of the Land of Israel, where he may practice his trade. As is said, 'He shall dwell in your midst, in a place which he shall choose in one of your gates [settlements] in your midst, wherever he pleases, you must not oppress him' [Deut 23:17]" (Masekhet Gerim 3:4) …Jewish rule and dominion – not in order to rule over the world, nor in order to dominate the Gentiles, but so that Israel will not be subject to any oppressor, but will engage in Torah and wisdom, and the land will be filled of knowledge. In these great words of the leading Sages of Israel are encapsulated the destiny and image of the Hebrew state."

ISRAELI LAW. The law does not explicitly mention the prohibition against oppressing the convert (*ger*), the foreigner or member of a minority group, but he does enjoy special protection under the provisions of a number of laws, such as the regulation that a work contract with a foreign worker must be in a language that is known to him and must include many of the details that are fixed in the law, including the employer's obligation to provide the foreign worker with medical insurance and suitable living accommodations (Section 1C of the Foreign Workers (Illegal Employment and Assuring Suitable Conditions) Law 5751 –1991. For the prohibition against withholding the passport of a foreign worker, see Section 376. of the Penal Law 5737 – 1977, and the remarks of Judge Arad in AA 1459/02, *Butcheman v. Best Yizum u-Benyah* (unpublished)). It also states that information about available positions in the State service, tenders of public bodies, and criteria for receiving subventions from the government budget must be made available to the Arab public, through their publication in Arabic (see: Amendment 15(b) to the Obligation of Tender Regulations 5753 – 1991, sec 6:1, for the procedure for submitting requests for support from the government budget in public institutions and discussion thereof, as amended in Official Publications (*Yalkut Pirsumim*) 5760, 3264). Similar rules were introduced in recent years requiring suitable representation in the government service and in the directorates of government companies and public corporations (sec 15a of State Service (Appointments) Law, 5719 – 1959, and Section 18 (a 1) of the Government Companies Law, 5735 – 1975).

The issue of oppression of the proselyte in Israeli law was discussed in a ruling, when Shoshanah (Susan) Miller, who had immigrated to Israel from the United States after converting to Judaism within the framework of the Reform Judaism, asked to be registered in the population registry as a Jewess. The Minister of the Interior, following legal consultation, ruled that there was no way of avoiding her request, but that hereon in, in similar cases, there would be a notation in the section for religion and nationality on the identity card: "Jew (converted)." The President of the Supreme Court, Justice Shamgar, ruled that the registration official had no power to add anything to the accepted form of registration in the sections of religion and nationality, and therefore accepted Miller's appeal and ordered that she be registered as a Jew without further addition. Justice Elon added the following to his words: (HC 230/86 Miller v. Interior Minister et al, PD 40(4), pp. 447–48):

> In my opinion, this "parenthetical" addition, intended as a completion or "description" in every case of conversion, following the word Jew, *also has absolutely no place or source in terms of the halakhah*. There is no person concerning whom the Torah warns us so frequently – in 36 separate places – as it does regarding the oppression of the proselyte, whether in speech, in action, or by way of halakhic-legal statements and notations… One does not mention to a proselyte his previous status and deeds, one does not treat lightly the respect due to him…. One of the recent halakhic sages said the following: "Every person whose behavior towards the proselyte differs from his behavior to any other Jewish person – violates this positive commandment, as is written: 'He shall be a sojourner among you… and you shall love him as yourself'" (Rabbi Jeroham Fischel Perla's *Commentary* to R. Saadiah Gaon's *Sefer ha-Mitzvot*, no. 82). And there is no doubt that, by adding the word "converted" in parentheses – which is not done regarding a "regular" Jew – we are not behaving in the same manner as we do regarding every other Jew; hence we are prohibited from doing so.

In the wake of the Six-Day War and the liberation of places holy to the three religions, the Israel Knesset passed the Protection of Holy Places Law, 5727 – 1967, Section 1 of which states that: "The holy places will be protected against all desecration and all other harm and anything that might impinge upon the freedom of access of members of all religions to those places holy to them, or their sentiments towards those places." Section 2 states: "One who desecrates the holy place or harms it in any other way is liable to imprisonment of seven years," and that "one who performs an action that is liable to harm the freedom of access of members of religions to places holy to them or their sentiments regarding those places, is subject to five years imprisonment." In view of the legislation of this law, it would appear that the purpose of the law was to ensure the freedom of access and worship in these historical, holy sites, that were just recently liberated, to each one of the religions.

In light of these provisions, Justice Elon ruled, regarding the controversy surrounding the *Kach party (ibid – *Naiman*, p. 302), that:

> The content of the Kach platform and the purpose of its promoters and leaders, as reflected in the material presented to us, stand in blatant contrast to the world of Judaism – its ways and perspectives, to the past of the Jewish nation and its future aspirations. They contradict absolutely the fundamental principles of human and national morality, the Declaration of Independence of the State of Israel, and the very foundations of present-day enlightened democracies. They come to transplant in the Jewish State notions and deeds of the most decadent of nations. This phenomenon should cause grave concern among the people who dwell in Zion. This court is charged with the preservation of the law and its interpretation, and the duty of inculcating the values of Judaism and civilization, of the dignity of man and the equality of all who are created in the divine image, rests primarily upon those whom the legislature and the executive branch have chosen for the task. When, however, such a seriously dangerous phenomenon is brought to our attention, we may not refrain from sounding the alarm against the ruinous effects of its possible spread upon the character, image and future of the Jewish State. The remedy lies, in the first place, in a reassessment of the ways of educators and pupils alike, in all walks of our society

In its judgment, the Court decided not to disqualify the Kach list, for reasons of *lack of judicial authority*, to do so. In relating to this matter, Justice Elon further wrote (*ibid*, 303):

> It was not, therefore, for lack of sensitivity to the gravity of the Kach list phenomenon that we refrained from endorsing its disqualification, but because the legislature has not empowered us or the Central Elections Committee to disqualify a list from participating in elections to the Knesset on ground of the content of its platform….
>
> The consequence of not disqualifying the Kach list is difficult and saddening, considering the content of its platform, but it is right and proper not only in terms of our respect for the rule of law but also because it precludes the drawing of undesirable conclusions in such an important and complex matter.

[Menachem Elon (2nd ed.)]

Pluralism in the World of Halakhah

As opposed to other religions, Judaism always attributed intrinsic importance to a multiplicity of opinions in the religious-halakhic-and philosophical dimension. We related to this phenomenon, to a certain extent in the entry *Majority Rule, and will devote some additional comments in the current context. There seems to be no more apposite expression of this than the statement made by the Sages regarding the controversy between the School of Shammai and the School of Hillel that "these and these are the words of the living God" (Eruvin 13b; TJ Berakhot 1:4; TJ Yevamot 1:6). Despite the fact that, in terms of practice and obligatory norms, the *halakhah* generally follows the School of Hillel, the opinions of the School of Shammai continue to constitute a legitimate and substantive opinion in the world of *halakhah*. This approach was one of the basic features of the *halakhah*. The "rebellious elder," even after the Sanhedrin – the High Court of the nation – had ruled against his opinion, was permitted to adhere to his own view "and to adhere to his own opinion," provided only that he did not rule thus for others in practice (M. Sanhedrin 11:2; TB Sanhedrin 86b). Moreover, the opinion of the minority, which is not followed in practical life, may at some future time have its day and become the accepted view according to which people will behave. R. Judah said: "The [dissenting] opinions of individuals are only mentioned among those of the majority, so that if some day they are needed, they may be relied upon" (Tosef., Eduyyot 1:4 (ed. Zuckermandel)). And the same teaching appears in M. Eduyyot 1:5; as stated in the commentary of R. Samson of Sens, ad loc: "Although the view of a single person is not accepted at first, and many disagree with him, at another time the majority may accept his reasoning and the law be decided accordingly, for the entire Torah was so given to Moses at times to forbid and at times to permit, and when he was asked: "until when shall we deliberate?" he answered: "follow the majority; however both are the living word of God" (cf. M. Elon, *Ha-Mishpat ha-Ivri* (1988), 870–878; *Jewish Law* (1994), 1061–1072). This plurality of views is not a negative phenomenon or defect, but is substantive to the world of the *halakhah*. "There is no instability or shortcoming, such as to say that he causes more than one law to exist, Heaven forbid! On the contrary – such is the way of the Torah, and both are the words of the living God" (R. Ḥayyim ben Bezalel, introduction to *Vikku'aḥ Mayim Ḥayyim* (Prague, 16th century); and see in detail Elon, *Ha-Mishpat ha-Ivri* at 1145–1149; *Jewish Law*, 1375–1379). Moreover, plurality of views and approaches has the power to create harmony and unity out of difference. As the last of the codifiers, R. Jehiel Michal Epstein, said at the beginning of the 20th century (*Arukh ha-Shulḥan, Ḥoshen Mishpat*, Introduction):

> All the disputes of the *tannaim* and the *amoraim*, of the *geonim* and the codifiers, are truly the words of the living God, and all are aspects of the *halakhah*. Indeed that is the glory of our pure and holy Torah, the entire *Torah* is a song, and the glory of a song is when it is sung in different voices. And this is the essence of its pleasantness.

Indeed this basic conception that "both are the words of the living God" has at all times exerted a decisive influence on the mode and substance of halakhic codification as well as decision. I have dealt elsewhere with the subject and need not expand upon it here (Elon, *Ha-Mishpat ha-Ivri* at 870, and the references in *Jewish Law*, 1061 n. 94).

In the *Naiman* case, Justice Elon noted that the plurality of views plays a material and fruitful role generally in the life of a just society. The rabbis even composed a special benediction to fit the secret encompassed in this notable phenomenon of a plurality of views in society: "If one sees a large crowd of people, one should say: Blessed is He who is wise in secrets; for neither their faces nor their thoughts are alike" (Tosefta (Zuckermandel), *Berakhot* 7:5; and see *Berakhot* 58a). This is a blessing for wisdom and creativity: "Just as the nature of creation still renders the countenances of all people different, so also are we to believe that wisdom is still shared by men each differing from the other" (*Vikku'aḥ Mayim Ḥayyim* (introduction)). Such a plurality of views should be respected by our leaders and government, as the following midrashic comments instructively indicate (Numbers Rabbah, *Pinḥas* 21:2; Tanhuma, *Pinḥas* 10):

> Just as the countenances (of people) are not alike, so also their views, and each person has his own opinion ...Thus on the point of death Moses begged of God: "Master of the Universe, the views of every one are well known to you and your children's views are not all alike. When I depart from them, I pray, appoint them a leader who will be tolerant of each person's view."

Justice Elon expressed this idea in the *Naiman* case: "That is the lesson of leadership and government in the heritage of Israel – tolerance for every individual and every group, according to their opinions and outlooks. And this is the great secret of tolerance and listening to the other, and the great potency of the right of every individual and every group to express their opinions, that they are not only essential to an orderly and enlightened regime but also vital to its creative power. For in the real world 'two opposing elements converge and fructify; how much more so in the spiritual world' (Rabbi A.I. Kook, *Ha-Nir* (Jerusalem, 1909) 47; *Eder ha-Yakar*, 13ff.)"

True, halakhic Judaism does not recognize the legitimacy of alternative streams that do not accept the binding yoke of *halakahah*. However, Deputy President of the Supreme Court Menachem Elon calls for tolerance in this area and attempts to find a balance between the practice that had developed within halakhic Jewry, the freedom of opinion that is a basic value in Judaism, and the avoidance of injury to the feelings of religious people.

An instructive example of this is his ruling in the matter of the Women of the Wall. In that incident, Justice Elon wrote:

> In the holy places there is no other option – where there is conflict between the freedom of worship of the various worshippers among themselves – but to attempt to find a common denominator among all worshippers, even if as a result the freedom to worship of one group may be realized at the expense of the freedom of worship of the other. The unique solemnity and dignity that adheres to the holy places and their sanctified character re-

> quires that worship be conducted in the holy places with quiet and dignity, without rancor and dispute, so that each person may serve his Creator without harming the worship of his fellow. There is no way of achieving this goal other than by finding the common denominator of all the worshippers.

Thus, regarding that issue, Justice Elon did not allow the Women of the Wall to worship at the Western Wall Plaza, and said the following: "It is obvious and self-evident that the petitioners are entitled to pray in their way in their own communities and synagogues, and no one will prevent them from doing so. The petitioners' freedom of worship remains as it always was. But due to the uniqueness of the Western Wall and the great sensitivity of this holiest place for the Jewish people, prayer must be conducted in this unique and special place according to a common denominator that allows the prayer of every Jew as such; and this means that the custom of the place as it has existed for generations – must be maintained."

[Menachem Elon (2nd ed.)]

BIBLIOGRAPHY: HUMAN RIGHTS: M. Elon, *Ha-Mishpat ha-Ivri*, 3:1391–92; idem, *Jewish Law* (1994), 1658–59, 1705, 1772–74, 1781, 1784; idem, *Jewish Law (Cases and Materials)* (1999), 539–43; S. Arieli, *Mishpat ha-Milḥamah* (1972), 35–36, 52–90; S. Goren, *Torat ha-Shabbat ve-ha-Mo'ed* (1982), 369–79; Y. Cohen, *Giyyus ka-Halakhah* (1993); A. Hacohen, *"Al Ḥovat ha-Shivyon be-Sherut ha-Ẓeva'i,"* in: *Daf Parashat ha-Shavu'a*, 74 (Iyyar 2002). RIGHTS AND FREEDOMS: M. Elon, *Ha-Mishpat ha-Ivri* (1988), 1319–1629; idem, *Jewish Law* (1994), 1575–1946; idem, *Jewish Law (Cases and Materials)* (1999), 429–537; idem, *Ma'amad ha-Ishah*, 53, 163–164, 173, 210, 213; A. Hacohen, *Parshanut Takkanot ha-Kahal*, 218–20; idem, *"Ha-Mishpat ha-Ivri ve-Ḥerut ha-Bittui,"* in: *Daf Parashat ha-Shavu'a*, 205 (2005); M. Vigoda, *"Ẓin'at ha-Perat ve-Ḥofesh ha-Bittui,"* in: *Daf Parashat ha-Shavu'a*, 129 (2003); idem, *"Bein Zekhuyot Ḥevratiyyot le-Ḥovot Ḥevratiyyot be-Mishpat ha-Ivri,"* in: Y. Rabin and Y. Shani (eds.), *Zekhuyot Kalkaliyyot, Ḥevratiyyot ve-Tarbutiyyot be-Yisra'el* (2004), 233; M.R. Konvitz (ed.), *Judaism and Human Rights* (2001^2). RIGHT TO PRIVACY: M. Elon, *Ha-Mishpat ha-Ivri* (1988^3); idem, *Jewish Law* (1994), 1856–60; idem, *Jewish Law: Cases and Materials* (1999), 545–66, §27; N. Lamm, "Privacy in Law and Theology," in: *Faith and Doubt* (1986), 290; E. Rackman, *"Zekhut ha-Peratiyyut u-Kefiah Datit be-Yahadut,"* in: G. Firshtik (ed.), *Zekhuyot Adam be-Yahadut* (1992), 255: N. Rakover, *"Ha-Haganah al Ẓinat ha-Perat,"* in: *Jewish Law*, 3 (1970); S. Dikhovsky, *"Ha'azanat Seter,"* in: *Teḥumin*, 11 (1990), 299; idem, *"Ha'azanat Seter,"* in: *Torah she-Be'al Peh*, 36 (1999), 58; *Du'aḥ ha-Va'adah le-Haganah bifnei Pegi'ah Ẓinat ha-Perat* (Jerusalem, 1978). THE ATTITUDE TO NON-JEWS: M. Elon, *Ha-Mishpat ha-Ivri* (1988), 1:9, 13f., 19, 23, 26, 32f., 46, 56, 86, 120, 416, 432ff., 516, 542f., 555, 575, 600, 602, 633ff., 641f., 646f., 649, 651, 654ff., 660, 663, 717, 885, 1223, 1247, 1256, 1322ff., 1374, 1606f.; idem, *Jewish Law* (1994), 55–57, 62–74, 786, 803, 806, 954–56, 959f., 971–72, 1688–90, 1914–17; idem, *"Ha-Aḥer" ba-Mishpat ha-Ivri u-be-Pesikat Bet ha-Mishpat ha-Elyon,"* in: *Mada'ei ha-Yahdut*, 42 (2004), 31–94; Y. Bar-Asher, "The Right of Muslims to dwell in the Land of Israel," in: *Zekhuyot ha-Adam be-Yahadut = Takdim* 3–4 (Winter 1992), 113 (Heb.); A. Hacohen, "Christianity and Christians in Rabbinic Eyes in the Modern Period: From Rabbi Kook to Rabbi Ovadiah Yosef" (unpublished). PLURALISM IN THE WORLD OF HALAKHAH: M. Elon, *Ha-Mishpat ha-Ivri* (1988), 227ff., 229ff., 870–72, 875–79f., 947ff., 965, 1016–18, 1212, 1465, 1553ff.; *Jewish Law* (1994), 1064–72, 1378–79, 1848–50; *Cases and Materials* (1999), 523–38, §25; H.H. Cohn, *Ha-Mishpat* (1992), 533–39; idem, *"Al Ḥofesh ha-De'ah ve-ha-Dibbur be-Masoret Yisrael,"* in: *Zekhuyot Adam be-Yehadut, Takdim*, 3–4 (1992), 179.

RIGLER, LEO GEORGE (1896–1979), U.S. physician and educator. Born in Minneapolis, Minnesota, Rigler was appointed professor of radiology at the University of Minnesota in 1927. From 1957 to 1963 he was executive director of Cedars of Lebanon and Sinai Hospitals, Los Angeles, and in 1963 was appointed professor of radiology at the University of California at Los Angeles, where in 1970 he founded the Leo G. Rigler research laboratory.

He was the first Jew to be president of the Radiological Society of North America. He was chairman of the Jewish Family Welfare Association, Minneapolis, Minnesota, and national vice president of the American Friends of the Hebrew University. Rigler's works include *Outline of Roentgen Diagnosis* (1938) and *The Chest* (1946). He arranged and edited the second U.S. edition of H.R. Schintz's *Lehrbuch der Roentgendiagnostik* (6 vols., 1928, 1965^6; *Roentgen Diagnosis*, 1968^2).

BIBLIOGRAPHY: J.R. Hodgson, in: *Radiology*, 95 (1970), 243; *Ha-Refu'ah*, 78 (1970), 409.

RĪHĀNIYYA, AL-, Circassian-Muslim village in northern Israel, on the Almah Plateau in Upper Galilee. It is one of the two Circassian villages west of the Jordan (the other is *Kafr Kāmā). It was founded by Circassians (Muslims from Caucasus) who left their homeland in the second half of the 19th century when it was annexed to Christian, czarist Russia. The houses of the picturesque village are laid out around a single, large, closed quadrangular courtyard. In 1969 Rīḥāniyya had 415 inhabitants; in 2002, 947.

[Efraim Orni]

RIJEKA (It. **Fiume**), Adriatic port in Croatia, until 1918 in Austro-Hungary; after World War I until 1945 in Italy. There were some Jews in Fiume during the 16th century under Austrian rule. Fiume was declared a free port in 1717 and attracted more Jews. When in 1776 it became attached to Hungary as its port, Jews from Hungary began to settle there, but until the mid-19th century the majority of Jews were Sephardim from *Split and *Dubrovnik, who followed the *minhag Ispalatto* (Spalato, "Split"). After 1848 with the influx of Hungarian, German, Bohemian, and Italian Jews, Italian and German rites were also used. A *ḥevra kaddisha* was founded in 1885; there were three cemeteries and a modern style synagogue was built in 1902. In 1900 there were 2,000 Jews in Rijeka. The congregation remained the only independent Orthodox one in Italy after the 1930 reforms. Children were sent to public schools – German, Hungarian, Italian, or Croatian ones – due to the heterogeneous composition of the population. The sermons were also delivered in German or Italian. In 1920 there were 1,300 Jews in Rijeka and in nearby Abbazia (Opatija), dropping to just 136 on the eve of the war.

Holocaust Period

In 1938 the racial laws of Fascist Italy were promulgated; Jews with Italian citizenship were subject to discrimination, and foreign Jews were to be interned in camps. Giovanni Palatucci, head of the foreigners' section of the Fiuman police, procured "Aryan" papers for Jews and sent many Jews to his uncle, a bishop in southern Italy, and later to institutions for people rendered mentally incompetent by the war. After the conquest of Yugoslavia by the Germans in April 1941, the Italian Second Army occupied Dalmatia and some other parts of the quisling "Independent Croatian State." Some Italian officers collaborated with Palatucci and his group, sending to him some 500 Jewish refugees from Croatia who were thus saved. When Italy capitulated to the Allies in September 1943 and Germans occupied all Italian territories, Palatucci remained at his post, destroyed his files, and warned the Jews of their imminent arrest. Most of them survived. Palatucci was arrested in September 1944 and died in Dachau in 1945.

Contemporary Period

When Rijeka became part of Yugoslavia in 1945, many Italian-speaking Jews left for Trieste and Italy; in 1947 there were some 170 Jews in Rijeka and the surrounding area. The community numbered 99 in 1969. Following the evacuation of Bosnian Jews from the war zone in 1992, around 60 families reconstituted the community, but many subsequently left for Zagreb and other localities in northern Croatia, leaving fewer than 100 Jews in 2004.

BIBLIOGRAPHY: Roth, Italy, 133, 176. **ADD. BIBLIOGRAPHY:** T. Morgani, *Ebrei in Fiume ed in Abbazia 1441–1945* (1979).

[Zvi Loker (2nd ed.)]

RIKLIS, MESHULAM (1923–), financier. Born in Istanbul, Turkey, Riklis was taken to Palestine as a child. He became a member of a kibbutz, and during World War II served in the British Army. After the war he emigrated to the United States, where he received an MBA from Ohio State University. To pay for his tuition, he worked full time as a teacher of Hebrew and Jewish history. He began his business career working for an investment house in Minneapolis, Minnesota. In 1954, backed by a group of Minneapolis investors, he began to amalgamate corporations into giant conglomerates. McCrory and Glen Alden Corporation, in which Riklis held large interests, belonged to the leading holding companies in the field of manufacturing and distributing consumer goods. Known as the father of the leveraged buyout, Riklis used borrowed money to purchase undervalued companies, then used those assets to provide the leverage for larger takeovers. In the early 1980s he became chairman and CEO of the Riklis Family Corporation, the successor to Rapid-American, a former public company that he had been made private in 1981. Riklis then became chairman of the privately held retail chain McCrory. His other holdings have included companies such as the Riviera Hotel and Casino in Las Vegas. He also owns a large shopping mall in Virginia.

Riklis was married to entertainer Pia Zadora from 1977 to 1993. In 1988 the couple purchased Pickfair, the former Beverly Hills estate of film legends Mary Pickford and Douglas Fairbanks. They generated a wave of criticism when they demolished the Hollywood landmark and rebuilt it to three times its size.

Riklis has been prominent in many Jewish institutions and active in the United Jewish Appeal. He was a generous supporter of the Jewish Theological Seminary of America, Brandeis University and of Martin Luther King's institutions as well as many public institutions in Israel.

BIBLIOGRAPHY: O. Schisgall, *The Magic of Mergers: The Saga of Meshulam Riklis* (1968). **ADD. BIBLIOGRAPHY:** I. Barmash, *For the Good of the Company: The History of the McCrory Corporation* (2003).

[Joachim O. Ronall / Ruth Beloff (2nd ed.)]

RIMINI (Heb. ארמיני), city on the Adriatic coast of Italy. There is evidence of the existence of a Jewish colony in Rimini from the beginning of the 12th century, which dealt in local commerce and in trade connected with the port. Under the benevolent rule of the Malatesta, Jewish moneylenders appeared there in the 14th century and carried on their business successfully, showing considerable initiative. Accounts of Jewish moneylending in and around the town mention names of bankers from Rimini: one of them, Menahem b. Nathan, left money in 1392 for the repair of the walls of Rome, his native city, and for improvements in the harbor of Rimini. Jewish bankers from Rimini were also active in moneylending in Modena in 1393 and subsequently in Padua. A century later the Franciscan Bernardino da *Siena visited the town and unsuccessfully tried to rouse anti-Jewish feeling there. Between 1521 and 1526 Gershom *Soncino worked in Rimini where he printed eight books. Jewish association with Rimini presumably ended with the expulsion from the Papal States in 1569. In 1587–89, 17 Jewish loan banks were authorized to be set up there in consequence of the tolerant policies of Pope Sixtus V, but the Jews were driven out again by the reactionary bull of 1593. In the first stages of the Italian war of independence, a platoon including about 20 Jewish volunteers fought the Austrians at Rimini (1831).

BIBLIOGRAPHY: Artom, in: *Miscellanea… H.P. Chajes* (1930), 1–9; Roth, Italy, index; Milano, Italia, index; Loevinson, in: REJ, 93 (1932), 176–7.

[Ariel Toaff]

RIMMON, apparently an epithet used in Damascus for the chief Aramean god, Baal-Hadad. Naaman and his master, the king of Syria, are said to have worshiped in the "Temple of Rimmon" (II Kings 5:18). Akkadian texts equate the Mesopotamian weather god, Adad, with the god Rammanu (perhaps derived from Akkadian *ramāmu*, "to thunder"), and it is thought that the Arameans may have transferred the latter name to their own chief god. The name Rimmon was used as a theophoric element in the names of both Tabrimmon (I Kings 15:18), and Hadadrimmon (Zech. 12:11).

BIBLIOGRAPHY: E. Schrader, *The Cuneiform Inscriptions and the Old Testament*, 1 (1885), 196–7; A. Deimel, *Pantheon Babylonicum*

(1914), 44–46; U. Cassuto, in: EM, 1 (1955), 322; B. Mazar, in: A. Malamat (ed.), *The Kingdoms of Israel and Judah* (1961), 143 (Heb.).

[Chayim Cohen]

RIMMON-PEREZ (Heb. רִמֹּן פֶּרֶץ), an encampment of the Israelites in the wilderness of Sinai, situated between Rithmah and Libnah (Num. 33:19–20). The location of the camp depends upon the view taken of the route of the *Exodus. Those following the traditional southern route locate Rithmah at Biʾr al-Ratama and Libnah at Biʾr al-Bayḍāʾ (Ar. Bayḍāʾ and Heb. Libnah (*livnah*) "white"). Rimmon-Perez would then be situated near a well in the Wadi Mayʾayn, close to the Naqb al-Biyār, one of the main passages through the eastern mountains of Sinai, about 19 mi. (30 km.) west of Akaba. On the other hand, those who see a northern route look for some site east of Hazeroth (ʿAyn Hasra?) near Jebel Halāl.

BIBLIOGRAPHY: Abel, Geog, 2 (1938), 214; Jarvis, in: PEQ, 70 (1938), 24ff.; Gray, in: VT, 4 (1954), 148–54.

[Michael Avi-Yonah]

RIMOCH, ASTRUC (14th–15th century), physician from Fraga, Aragon. Rimoch was close to the circle of poets under Solomon da *Piera. During the anti-Jewish riots of 1391, he was active in collecting funds to ransom the community from the rioters. A letter of encouragement and comfort which he sent to a Jew of Monzón, dating from the same period, is extant. It states that his father and brother converted to Christianity and reveals interesting details on the divisions within many Jewish families as a result of the riots – when some of their members abandoned their religion, while others remained faithful. During the *Tortosa disputation Rimoch converted to Christianity and changed his name to Franciscus de Sant Jordi. After his conversion, he wrote a letter to his friend Shealtiel Bonafos in order to persuade him to convert as well. The poet Solomon *Bonafed, a friend of Bonafos, replied to this sharply.

BIBLIOGRAPHY: Steinschneider, in: HB, 15 (1875), 108ff.; Baer, Urkunden, 1 (1929), index; Baer, Spain, 2 (1966), index s.v. *Astruc Rimoch.*

RIMON, JACOB (1902–1973), Hebrew writer. Born in Poland, he was taken to Palestine in 1908 by his family. From 1921 he worked for the communal council of Jaffa-Tel Aviv and later became secretary of the social welfare department. He was among the founding members of *Ha-Poʿel ha-Mizrachi and the *Torah va-Avodah movement. He published poetry, prose, and children's stories.

His books of poetry are *Hishtappekhut* (1926), *Arẓi* (1928), *Seneh* (1946), *Ke-Leket Shibbolim* (1966), and *Bi-Shevilei he-Amal* (1968). Rimon is one of the few Orthodox Hebrew poets, and his poetry is imbued with a deep religious faith. His novels include *Arẓenu ha-Kedoshah* (1935) and *Ḥulyot be-Sharsheret* (1957). Among his other works are *Yehudei Teiman be-Tel Aviv* ("Yemenite Jews in Tel Aviv," 1933) and *Asher Sipparti le-Nekhdi* (1969), stories for young people.

BIBLIOGRAPHY: Kressel, Leksikon, 2 (1967), 870.

[Getzel Kressel]

RIMON (Granat), JOSEPH ẒEVI (1889–1958), Hebrew poet. Born in Poland, he was educated in the yeshivot of Lida and Warsaw and came under the influence of Hillel *Zeitlin. He immigrated to Palestine in 1909, and served as secretary of Kolel Varsha ("the Warsaw community"). As a result of his association with members of the Second Aliyah, especially J.Ḥ. *Brenner and A.S. *Rabinovitz, he worked on the newspapers of the labor movement, Ha-Poʿel ha-Ẓaʿir and Ha-Aḥdut. He became a teacher in the religious school Taḥkemoni in Jaffa and worked as a librarian in Haifa. During World War I, he taught in Petaḥ Tikvah. In 1921, after being savagely mutilated by rioting Arabs, he secluded himself in the Ari Synagogue in Safed for many years, delving deeply into the study of the Kabbalah and of the Zohar. In 1939, he returned to Tel Aviv and his family. His first poem appeared in 1908 in *Ha-Peraḥim*, the weekly of Israel Benjamin *Levner. After his immigration to Palestine, he published his poems in most of the Palestinian newspapers. His volumes of poetry include: *Leket Shirim* (1910), *Devir* (1913), *Ba-Maḥazeh* (1916) and *Ketarim* (1944). Rimon's poetry is religious in quality and has established for itself a unique place in modern Hebrew literature. The sole ambition of the poet, apparently, was to know God by the aid of asceticism and abstinence from the world of the senses, and by immersing himself in the depths of his inner being. His book, *Aẓei Ḥayyim*, essays on outstanding Jewish leaders, appeared in two volumes in Jerusalem (1946, 1950).

BIBLIOGRAPHY: M. Farbridge, *English Literature and the Hebrew Renaissance* (1953), 90; R. Wallenrod, *Literature of Modern Israel* (1956), 199–201; S. Halkin, *Modern Hebrew Literature* (1950), 184, 190; Rabinowitz and Kariv, in: J. Rimon, *Ketarim* (1944), 730 (intro.); D. Sadan, *Avnei Boḥan* (1951), 116–29; idem, *Bein Din le-Ḥeshbon* (1963), 78–85; Rabbi Binyamin, *Mishpeḥot Soferim* (1960), 162–8. **ADD. BIBLIOGRAPHY:** Z. Luz, *"Iyyun bi-Ketarim le-Y.Z. Rimon,"* in: *Bikkoret u-Farshanut*, 2–3 (1973), 72–79; P.H. Peli, *"Y.Z. Rimon, Meshorer Dati be-Doro,"* in: *Moznayim*, 36 (1973), 327–336; D. Ider, *"Mitaḥat u-Meʿever li-Gderot: Iyyun bi-Yẓiratam shel Y.Z. Rimon ve-Admiel Kosman,"* in: *Tarbut Yehudit be-Ein ha-Seʿarah* (2002), 711–41; idem, *"Yeḥidi be-Derekh ha-Melekh shel Pardesim": Iyyun Sifruti-Kabbali ba-Poʾemot 'Eḥad' ve-'Ha-Levanah ha-Metah' le-Y.Z. Rimon,"* in: *Kabbalah*, 11 (2004), 301–68.

[Yonah David]

°**RINDFLEISCH**, German knight, instigator of the massacre of thousands of Jews in 146 localities in southern and central Germany in 1298. The background for the slaughter was a series of *blood libels in *Mainz (1281, 1283), *Munich (1285), Oberwesel (1287), and the accusation of Desecration of the *Host in Paris in 1290. On April 20, 1298, in the small Franconian town of Roettingen, 21 Jews were attacked and massacred by a mob led by Rindfleisch, who urged revenge for alleged Desecration of the Host. Rindfleisch subsequently went from town to town, followed by a plunder-hungry mob, exhorting the burghers to annihilate the Jews. A wave of massacres swept through Franconia, Swabia, *Hesse, *Thuringia, and finally Heilbronn (Oct. 19, 1298). The protector of the Jews, Emperor Albert I of Austria, was preoccupied with warfare, and only after vanquishing his rival, Adolf of Nassau, did he proclaim a *Landfriede* ("peace of the land"), warning against further attacks. This proclamation was barely heeded, and Jews continued to be massacred at *Gotha (1303), Renchen (1301) and Weissensee (1303). The Jewry of *Augsburg was saved through the steadfast protection of the municipality, as was that of *Regensburg. In *Nuremberg, 728 Jews were slaughtered when a mob stormed the castle in which they had sought to defend themselves with the aid of the garrison. Among the victims of Nuremberg were *Mordecai b. Hillel, his wife, and children. The council thereafter banished 20 persons in perpetuity. A number of *kinot* and *seliḥot* were composed in commemoration of the tragedy, which was most fully recorded in S. Salfeld's *Das Martyrologium des Nuernberger Memorbuchs* (1898).

BIBLIOGRAPHY: Graetz, Gesch, 7 (c. 1900^{4}), 232ff.; Graetz, Hist, 4 (1894), 35–37; Dubnow, Weltgesch, 5 (1927), 175–6; S. Bernfeld, *Sefer ha-Dema'ot*, 2 (1924), 33–39; Germ Jud, 2 (1968), index. **ADD. BIBLIOGRAPHY:** F. Lotter, in: *Zeitschrift fuer historische Forschung*, 15 (1988), 385–422.

[Reuven Michael]

RINGEL, MICHAEL (1880–?), Zionist leader in Galicia and Poland. Born in Borislav, Galicia, Ringel began his Zionist activity in high school. He practiced law in Vienna and several Galician towns. In 1908 he settled in Lemberg. Ringel worked on behalf of the Zionist Organization in the election campaigns to the Austrian parliament. He wrote pamphlets and hundreds of articles in Polish-language Zionist journals to foster Zionist ideas in Polish-speaking circles, Jewish and non-Jewish alike. His greatest contribution was to the Zionist daily *Nowy Dziennik* of which he was a founder. He also wrote in the Yiddish press in Galicia. After World War I he was, together with L. *Reich, among the leaders of the Zionist Organization and participated also in the *Comité des Délégations Juives at the peace conference in Paris. In 1922–27 he was a member of the Jewish Club (Kolo Zydowskie) in the Polish senate. A collection of his speeches in the senate concerning the Jewish problems in Poland was published in 1928. He was one of the attorneys for the young Jew who was accused of attempting to kill the president of Poland (see *Steiger Trial). During the Soviet occupation of Lvov in 1939–41, he was deported to the Soviet interior and nothing is known of him thereafter.

BIBLIOGRAPHY: N.M. Gelber, *Toledot ha-Tenu'ah ha-Ẓiyyonit be-Galiẓyah 1875–1918* (1958), index.

[Getzel Kressel]

RINGELBLUM, EMANUEL (Menahem; 1900–1944), historian of the Warsaw ghetto. Born in Buczacz, eastern Galicia, Ringelblum graduated from Warsaw University and subsequently taught history at a high school. He published a number of articles, mainly on the history of Warsaw Jewry, in which (influenced by the historian Ignacy Schiper) he stressed social and economic problems. He was a member of *YIVO, and in 1928 a founder of the "Circle of Young Historians" in Warsaw, which published the periodical *Der Yunger Historiker*. Throughout his life, Ringelblum combined public activity with his academic work. He was active in the left-wing Po'alei Zion and participated in the work of the Yiddish schools' association (*Tsentrale Yidishe Shul-Organizatsye*). From 1929 he was editor of *Folkshilf*, the publication of the Jewish cooperative funds. In 1938 the American Jewish *Joint Distribution Committee sent him to the frontier townlet of Zbaszyn, where 17,000 Jews who were Polish nationals living in Germany had been gathered and left destitute after being suddenly deported over the Polish border from their places of residence. They were caught in no man's land unable to enter Poland. Ringelblum directed relief work, collected testimonies from the deportees, and gathered information on events in Nazi Germany.

During the siege and air attacks on Warsaw, Ringelblum was a regular participant in the activities of the coordinating committee of Jewish-aid organizations. Later, when the Juedische Soziale Selbsthilfe (JSS) for self-help was formed out of this committee, Ringelblum headed the department to rally the Jewish population to mutual assistance, including help to the needy and shelter to the deportees and those whose homes had been destroyed. In the course of this work, Ringelblum kept in constant contact with active sources of information in the community at large, from whom he received reports and evidence on events in the capital and provincial towns at a time when there was no press other than the Nazi-approved and -controlled press.

Ringelblum understood that what was happening to Polish Jewry was without precedent and correctly perceived his efforts as providing the basic raw material for future histories of the ghetto and of Polish Jewry during the war. The work that Ringelblum directed is widely regarded as an essential manifestation of spiritual defiance, working against all Nazi efforts to eradicate memory and correctly believing against hope and against all odds that Jews somewhere, if not in Poland, would be able to write their own history of the killings and not rely on German documentation alone.

He recorded this information himself and directed his assistants, whose numbers steadily grew. Thus, a large and diversified enterprise was established for the collection of documents, reports, evidence, summaries, and even research work, memoirs, and literature produced during the period. The secretary of the underground archive reported that "every item, every article, be it long or short, had to pass through Dr. Ringelblum's hands." Most noteworthy is the collection of clandestine newspapers in various languages. The enterprise was given the code name Oneg Shabbat (literally "Enjoyment of the Sabbath") and employed dozens of workers directed and encouraged by Ringelblum. He also made efforts to have this material transmitted to London and through London to the West. His efforts led to the first word of the killings at Chelmno and the deportations of Warsaw Jewry. After the massive deportation of the summer of 1942, Ringelblum became a believer in armed resistance. After the great deportations, he worked with renewed urgency; no longer dealing in details, he sought to grapple with the larger issues of ghetto life in an attempt to comprehend what was happening. He created biographical notes on some of the great figures in the ghetto. Before the ghetto was destroyed, collections of material were put in containers and buried in three – or perhaps more – caches.

Ringelblum left the ghetto with his wife and young son and returned to the ghetto alone during the Uprising. What precisely happened to him is not known but he was arrested and found in the Trawniki camp. Two people arranged for his escape and he was brought to Warsaw, where he was hidden with other Jews.

He worked to the very end. This work even continued in the "Aryan" district after the destruction of the ghetto. In hiding he composed his master work on Polish-Jewish relations during World War II. The Gestapo discovered his hiding place in the "Aryan" district on March 7, 1944, and he and his family were arrested and murdered.

After the war, only two caches were recovered from the ruins, the third never coming to light. The material discovered became the property of the *Jewish Historical Institute in Warsaw (there are photocopies in *Yad Vashem, Jerusalem, and the United States Holocaust Memorial Museum). In the 1990s extensive efforts were made to preserve this documentation and to translate and publish this invaluable material. The Oneg Shabbat material is the main source for research into the history of Polish Jewry under German occupation.

Ringelblum's own notes, summaries, and essays, written during the occupation, were published after the war in *Ksovim fun Geto* (2 vols., 1961–63; *Notes from the Warsaw Ghetto*, ed. and tr. by J. Sloan, 1958). He also wrote *Kapitlen Geshikhte fun Amolikn Yidishn Lebn in Poyln* (1953) and *Di Poylishe Yidn in Oyfshtand fun Kościuszko 1794* (1937).

BIBLIOGRAPHY: Kermish, in: *Yad Vashem Studies*, 7 (1968), 173–83; idem, in: *Yad Vashem Bulletin*, 16 (1965), 16–25; Kozhen, *ibid.*, no. 6–7 (1960), 21–23; Eisenbach, in: E. Ringelblum, *Ksovim fun Geto*, 1 (1961), 13–60 (introd.); Eck, in: *Goldene Keyt*, 6, no. 24 (1955), 107–21. **ADD. BIBLIOGRAPHY:** E. Ringelblum, *Writings from the Warsaw Ghetto*, ed. J. Kermish and Y.L. Peretz (Yid., 1985); idem, *Polish-Jewish Relations during the Second World War*, ed. J. Kermish and S. Krakowski (1976); J. Kermish (ed.), *To Live with Honor and Die with Honor! Selected Documents from the Warsaw Ghetto Underground Archives* (1986).

[Nathan Eck / Michael Berenbaum (2nd ed.)]

RINGER, ALEXANDER L. (1921–2002), U.S. musicologist. Born in Berlin, Ringer was educated in Berlin and Amsterdam. Ringer was interned in the *Bergen-Belsen concentration camp in 1943–44. After World War II he emigrated to the U.S., where he received a Ph.D. from Columbia University in 1955. He held positions at various American universities until he joined the faculty of the University of Illinois, where he was made professor in 1963, and remained until his retirement. In 1964 he was invited by the Hebrew University of Jerusalem to lay the groundwork for the first Department of Musicology in Israel. He was a founder and honorary member of the International Kodaly Society and general editor (together with others) of the collected edition of Schoenberg's writings. Among his diverse research interests was his search for elements of "Jewishness" in the music of well-known Western Jewish musicians, such as *Mahler, *Mendelssohn, *Milhaud, E. *Bloch, *Kirchner, *Rochberg, and, in particular, Kurt *Weill and Arnold *Schoenberg, who received special attention in Ringer's writings. He was also a great believer in music education. The figure who had most influenced his thinking and attitude in this respect was the Hungarian composer Zoltán Kodály, the initiator of a special method of teaching music.

Ringer represented a higher type of intellectual with wide learning and command of major European languages, and a versatile musicologist who was distinguished by a strongly individual character which impressed itself on everything he wrote. His 167 works spanned an incredible range of subjects, including many synthetic studies on historically, culturally, and esthetically important trends and styles, and sociological issues affecting music. Among his major works are *The Early Romantic Era: Between Revolutions, 1789 and 1848* (1990); *A. Schoenberg – the Composer as Jew* (1990); *Musik als Geschichte*; and his last book, published posthumously: *Arnold Schoenberg: Das Leben im Werk* (2002).

BIBLIOGRAPHY: *New Grove*, s. v.; A. Shiloah, in: *Musica Judaica*, 16 (2001–02), 99–108.

[Amnon Shiloah (2nd ed.)]

RINGL+PIT, German-born photography team consisting of **Ellen Rosenberg Auerbach** (1906–2004) and **Grete Stern** (1904–1999), who achieved fame as an avant-garde pair in the Weimar Republic in the 1930s and later had individual careers of distinction in the United States and Argentina.

Rosenberg, better known by her married name, Auerbach, was born into a liberal Jewish family in Karlsruhe, Germany. After high school, she decided to become an artist and studied sculpture for three years at an art school in Karlsruhe and, in 1928, at the Academy of Art in Stuttgart. While studying there, her uncle gave her a camera and she abandoned sculpture, primarily because she thought she might earn a living as a photographer. She sought out Walter Peterhans, a member of the Bauhaus design movement, in Berlin where he maintained a successful commercial studio, and asked to be his student. He agreed, and for these lessons she was joined by another private student, Stern. The young women quickly became friends. When Peterhans decided to close the studio, they took over the premises and operated as Ringl + Pit, a name that combined their childhood nicknames. Stern was Ringl and Rosenberg was Pit. The name had the advantage of being ambiguous in terms of gender and ethnicity. It was probably the first photographic business of its type founded by women.

To have combined their surnames, Rosenberg said, would have "sounded too much like a firm of Jewish dressmakers."

At the time, the German advertising industry was booming and the team gained a reputation for innovative work. They also came to know – and photograph – leading cultural figures, such as Bertolt Brecht. Despite the commercial nature of their commissions, Ringl+Pit played with form and perspective to demonstrate the influence of Surrealism, as in their use in 1930 of a mannequin with a real hand to sell hair tonic. The firm was widely used by mainstream manufacturers to sell cigarettes and motor oil but in 1933, shortly after one of their still-life collages won first prize at an international photography exhibition in Brussels, they decided to leave Germany. Stern, who had a small inheritance, went to England and lent Auerbach money to go to Palestine. She was accompanied by her future husband, Walter Auerbach, a theater designer. They opened a children's portrait studio in Tel Aviv (a strong image of an Arab boy, snapped in the street in Jaffa, survives from 1934) and she took photographs for the Women's International Zionist Organization. Auerbach soon went to London and set up a studio but was unable to get a work permit. She then went to the United States and Stern to Buenos Aires, Argentina, in 1935. Relatively few examples of Ringl+Pit's work of the period have survived but they have become eagerly sought by museums and collectors. Politically, Walter Auerbach was an active leftist but his wife stayed out of politics, although she socialized with many left-wing artists. One of her more startling images shows Brecht at his typewriter with a light bulb sprouting from the back of his head. The Auerbachs, who had no children, divorced in 1945. Ringl+Pit were separated for ten years by World War II. They never worked together again but they remained lifelong friends.

In the United States, Ellen Auerbach took a number of powerful images of children but she never recaptured her professional status. Her growing interest in children led her to become a therapist, working with learning-disabled children, a career she pursued from 1965 until 1986, when she was 80. The rediscovery of her work was helped in part by the publication of two books of photographs, *Mexican Churches* (1987) and *Mexican Celebrations* (1990), which she had originally taken on a long journey in 1955 with a fellow photographer, Eliot Porter, brother of the artist Fairfield Porter.

In Argentina, Stern brought the idea of modernist photography to the country and was an important influence on the development of photography there. She made a long series of photomontages such as "Niño Flor" (Flower Child) in 1948 and "Made in England" in 1950 to illustrate a number of articles about psychoanalysis and dreams. She was also a portraitist, taking pictures of Brecht and Jorge Luis Borges, as well as documenting Argentine cities and regions.

In 1996 a documentary about Ringl+Pit won a number of awards and was shown in Berlin, Tel Aviv, London, and New York and on public television in the United States. Stern died in Buenos Aires, Auerbach in New York.

[Stewart Kampel (2nd ed.)]

RIO DE JANEIRO, state in the United States of Brazil; capital of the state and capital of the Republic until 1960 (when the capital was transferred to Brasilia); area of the state: 43.696 km^2; population: 14,391,282 (2000); population of the city: 6,094,183 (2005); estimated Jewish population: 30,000 (2000).

New Christians from Portugal immigrated to Rio de Janeiro from the 16th to the 18th centuries, and they played a significant role in the city's social and economic life. The Inquisition accused and prosecuted more than 300 New Christians in the city's region for practicing Judaism. With the proclamation of the independent Brazilian empire (1822) and the promulgation of the Constitution (1824), which espoused relative religious tolerance, some individual European Jewish dealers and immigrants began to appear in Rio de Janeiro, which was the capital and one of the most important harbors of the country. One of the prominent individuals among these first newcomers was Denis de Samuel (1782–1860), a young immigrant from England who gained great success and influence and earned the title of baron from the king of Portugal. Another prominent dealer who had business in Rio de Janeiro was Bernard Wallerstein.

The first attempt at communal organization was made in 1840–50 by Jews originating from Morocco who went to Rio de Janeiro from northern Brazil. The organization União Shel Guemilut Ḥassadim, which still exists, ascribes its origin to this attempt. In 1867 a council of the Alliance Israélite Universelle was established in the city. In 1873, Sociedade União Israelita do Brazil, a society for religious and welfare matters was registered; it continued its activities until 1893. Another institution of the imperial period was Sociedade Israelita do Rito Português (Jewish Society of the Portuguese Rite).

At the time of proclamation of the Republic (1889) the number of Jews in Rio de Janeiro was estimated at 200. In 1900 there were two synagogues, one formed by North African immigrants and the other by West European immigrants. In 1900 a new wave of Jewish immigration began, and by the end of World War I the city's Jewish population was estimated at 2,000.

A great wave of Jewish immigration to Rio de Janeiro occurred after World War I, and as the Jewish community grew, communal life became more diversified. The Jewish community established a well-organized institutional life and reached successful economic, social, and cultural integration into local culture and society.

In 1910 the Centro Israelita do Rio de Janeiro was founded; its principal objective was the establishment of a synagogue and a cemetery. The latter was founded in 1920 in Vila Rosali. The first philanthropic institution was established under the name Achiezer in 1912; its name was changed later (1920) to Sociedade Beneficente Israelita e Amparo aos Imigrantes (Hilfs-Ferein-Relief). The "Relief" was linked to ICA, HIAS, and Emigdirect, and in 1942 founded a Departamento de Seguro Mútuo Social (Department of Mutual Social Insurance), which in fact was a credit cooperative.

Other social institutions founded were: Sociedade das

Damas Israelitas (Jewish Women's Association – Froein Farein, 1923); Lar da Criança Israelita (Jewish Children's Home, 1923); Policlínica Israelita (1937, that later became a hospital); and Lar da Velhice (Old Age Home, 1963), created by Sociedade das Damas Israelitas). Jewish women prostitutes founded in Rio de Janeiro the Associação Beneficente Funerária e Religiosa Israelita (Beneficient, Funeral, and Religious Jewish Association) that functioned from 1906 to 1968.

During World War II the Jewish community was active and founded the Comitê Hebreu-Brasileiro para as Vítimas da Guerra (Jewish Brazilian Committee for War Victims) and the Comitê de Socorro aos Israelitas Vítimas de Guerra (Aid Committee for Jewish War Victims). The writer Stefan *Zweig immigrated to Brazil in 1936, joined the Jewish community, and wrote a famous book about the country: *Brasil, país do futuro.* His suicide in 1942 (together with his wife, Lotte), in the countryside city of Petrópolis, was a notable event in the life of the Jewish community and Brazilian history.

The community had its social and cultural center in the Praça Onze, close to the downtown area and the port, where an atmosphere of "*Yiddishkeit*" was present in daily life until the 1950s, when the Jews moved to other neighborhoods. The writer and Zionist leader Samuel Malamud is the main narrator of the memories from Praça Onze and of Jewish life in Rio de Janeiro. In Praça Onze, also the center of the local Carnaval and a cultural and social meeting point for black people, almost 3,000 Jews frequented the socialist club Cabiras, the parties of the Azul e Branco Club, and other local non-Jewish institutions.

The Zionist movement and the socialist groups were both very active in Rio de Janeiro. The First Zionist Congress in Brazil took place in 1922 with the participation of four different movements, including Tiferet Sion (1919). In 1921 a Brazilian delegate took part in the 12th Zionist Congress in Karlsbad. In 1929 a Brazilian delegate to the 16th Zionist Congress was elected by 1,260 votes. In 1934 the elections drew 2,647 voters. In 1927 the Central Committee of the Po'alei Zion Party was founded and later the Grêmio Hebreu-Brasileiro (Hebrew-Brazilian League).

Many Jewish leftist movements and parties were very active in Rio de Janeiro, among them socialists, communists, and the Bund, in the Biblioteca Israelita Brasileira Scholem Aleichem (Jewish Brazilian Sholem Aleichem Library, 1915), Colégio Israelita Brasileiro Scholem Aleichem (Jewish Brazilian Sholem Aleichem School, 1928), Sociedade Brasileira Pró-Colonização Judaica na União Soviética – Brazkor (Brazilian Society for the Jewish Colonization in the Soviet Union, 1928), and Centro Operário Morris Vinchevsky (Morris Vinchevsky Labor Center, 1928). The last two organizations founded a workers' school (*Arbeter Shule*) and edited the newspaper *Der Onheib.* Other leftist organizations were the União Cultural Israelita Brasileira Ikuf, Clube dos Cabiras (1941–50), the Associação Feminina Israelita Brasileira Vita Kempner, and the Associação Kinderland. In 2005 the Associação Scholem Aleichem (ASA) was an active political and cultural center and edited the *Boletim da ASA*, the sole Jewish leftist publication in Portuguese.

The Yiddish press was very active in Rio de Janeiro with the publication of a few newspapers: *Dos Yidishe Vochenblat, Yidishe Presse,* and *Brazilianer Yidishe Tzaytung.* Other important publications in Portuguese were the weekly magazine *Aonde Vamos?*, and *O Reflexo.* Adolf Eizen was a Brazilian pioneer of comics.

Later Developments

The Jewish community of Rio de Janeiro is the second largest Jewish community in Brazil, after São Paulo. The community has a solid network of institutions and a very active religious, social, political, and cultural life and is well integrated in the city's and the state's social and cultural life.

In 2005 there were 80 entities affiliated with the Federação Israelita do Estado do Rio de Janeiro (Jewish Federation of the State of Rio de Janeiro – FIERJ, founded in 1947), among them 30 synagogues, five schools, four other non-formal educational institutions and youth movements, Zionist women's organizations, beneficent and social assistance entities, sport and cultural associations. These institutions include: Organização Sionista, B'nai B'rith, Sociedade Beneficente das Damas, Lar da Criança Israelita, Sociedade Beneficente Israelita Hospital Albert Einstein, Hebraica, Monte Sinai, and Clube Israelita Brasileiro. In 1979 a Jewish industrialist, Israel Klabin, became the mayor of the city of Rio de Janeiro. FIERJ has a weekly TV program and is very active in political issues concerning the Jews in Brazil.

According to official numbers of FIERJ, 3,000 students attended the Jewish day schools: Eliezer Steinberg–Max Nordau, Colégio Israelita Brasileiro A. Liessin–Scholem Aleichem, Bar Ilan (Zionist religious), ORT, and the Machané Or Isreal and Beit Menachem (both non Zionist Orthodox).

Rio de Janeiro has a variety of synagogues, from ultra-Orthodox to Reform-Liberal, Ashkenazi and Sephardi, with imposing edifices and tiny *shtibels.* The Associação Religiosa Israelita (ARI) was founded by German Jewish immigrants in 1942 and follows a Liberal tradition. With a membership of 850 families, ARI supports Lar União – Associação Beneficente Israelita (founded in 1939) and the youth Zionist movement Chazit. ARI is the first synagogue in Brazil to have a woman as a rabbi and is very active in inter-religious dialogue and in cultural events in the city.

Congregação Judaica do Brasil (CJB) is a small Reform synagogue. Under the guidance of Rabbi Nilton Bonder, CJB was the most active Jewish presence at the NGO Global Forum during "Eco-92", the United Nations ecological conference held in Rio de Janeiro in June 1992. Bonder is the author of many books about Judaism that became bestsellers in Brazil. There are programs for Jewish studies and Hebrew in both the Federal University and the State University of Rio de Janeiro.

Jewish Organizations in the Interior of the State of Rio de Janeiro

Niterói has had an organized Jewish community since 1916. Its activities include religious services, with a synagogue and a cemetery, and it maintains a local school and organizes cultural and social activities. Petrópolis is a resort city for the residents of Rio de Janeiro. Its community is small, but it nevertheless established a yeshivah to train rabbinical students. In Nilópolis, situated on the route of the central railway of Brazil, a Jewish community was organized in the 1920s with a Centro Israelita (1936), the Sh. An-Ski complementary school, a synagogue, the Macabi club, Wizo, and a Yiddish theater group. In 1947, when Nilópolis became a city, there were 300 families, but later all the members moved to other cities. In Campos, the Sociedade União Israelita de Campos was established in 1929 by 40–50 families.

BIBLIOGRAPHY: A. Dines, *Morte no Paraíso. A tragédia de Stefan Zweig* (2004); A. Wiznitzer, *Os judeus no Brasil colonial* (1960); A. Milgram, *O 'milieu' judeu-comunista do Rio de Janeiro nos anos 30* (2001); B. Kushnir. *Baile de Máscaras: Mulheres Judias e Prostituição. As Polacas e suas Associações de Ajuda Mútua* (1996); E. and F. Wolff, *Campos. Ascensão e declínio de uma coletividade* (1986); E. London. *Vivência judaica em Nilópolis* (1999); S. Malamud, *Documentário. Contribuição judaica à memória da comunidade judaica brasileira* (1992).

[Roney Cytrynowicz (2nd ed.)]

RISCHIN, MOSES (1925–), U.S. historian. Born in New York City, Rischin received his Ph.D. from Harvard University in 1957. His work was centered on American, intellectual, Jewish, social, immigration, and urban history. He was appointed professor of history at San Francisco State College (later University) in 1964, and was also director of the Western Jewish History Center at Berkeley, California. He became professor emeritus at San Francisco State in 2002 upon his retirement.

Rischin's works include: *Inventory of American Jewish History* (1954); *Our Own Kind: Voting by Race, Creed, or National Origin* (1960); *The Promised City: New York's Jews, 1870–1914* (1962); *The American Gospel of Success* (1965); *Immigration and the American Tradition* (1976); and *Jewish Legacy and the German Conscience* (with R. Asher, 1991). He also edited Hutchins Hapgood's *Spirit of the Ghetto* (1967); Abraham Cahan's *Grandma Never Lived in America* (1985); *The Jews of North America* (1987); and *Jews of the American West* (with J. Livingston, 1991).

ADD. BIBLIOGRAPHY: J. Gorock and M. Raphael (eds.), *An Inventory of Promises: Essays on American Jewish History: In Honor of Moses Rischin* (1995).

[Samuel J. Hurwitz / Ruth Beloff (2nd ed.)]

RISHONIM (Heb. רִאשׁוֹנִים; lit. "the early authorities"), a term with many connotations – chronological, literary, ethical, and halakhic – serving to indicate the standing and authority of preceding scholars in relation to the scholars of the time in the domain of halakhic ruling and interpretation of the Torah. The distinction between "*rishonim*" and contemporaries is already found in the Talmud, which stresses the deterioration in worth of the generations as they progressively become further removed in time from Sinai; e.g., "If the *rishonim* were as angels, we are as men, and if the *rishonim* were as men, we are as donkeys" (Shab. 112b). The natural ambivalence involved in the practical use of this term was first raised in the later geonic literature, which set against this assessment the halakhic rule that "the law is in accordance with the later authority" (*Seder Tanna'im ve-Amora'im*, no. 25), the reason being either because these "were more painstaking than the *rishonim* in clarifying the *halakhah*" (Tos. to Kid. 45b), or because these had already seen and taken into consideration the reasoning of their predecessors and were therefore, in the words of the well-known proverb, like "a dwarf sitting on the back of a giant" (see Zedekiah b. Abraham, introd. to *Shibbolei ha-Leket*, in the name of Isaiah di Trani, S.K. Mirsky, ed. (1966), 107f.). Various limitations were made to this rule in order to reconcile these two contradictory statements (see Rabbinical *Authority). Moses *Alashkar (Responsa nos. 53–54) already grasped the full import of this ambivalence, attempted to draw all the conclusions from it, and limited the application of the rule that the law is in accordance with the later authority to the pre-geonic period, but his was a solitary opinion.

Nevertheless, it is clear that the actual division into "periods" stems from the profound and general recognition that there is indeed a progressive decline in importance and authority with the passage of time. Hence it was also laid down, at least formally, that it is altogether impossible to controvert the early scholars in general and the *geonim* (see *Gaon) in particular. In this matter, too, contradictory lines of approach have existed side by side throughout the generations. The term "*rishonim*" is now used to indicate a more or less well-defined period in the history of rabbinic literature; namely, the period between that of the *geonim* and the *rabbinate; the latter, called the period of the **aḥaronim*, continues to the present day. The exact dates establishing the limits to these periods are not precise and unchallenged, but neither are they of great practical importance. Historically the period of the *rishonim* commences with the eclipse of the Babylonian academies and the beginning of independent Torah centers throughout the Diaspora, and terminates shortly after the renewal of ordination (**semikhah*) by *Meir b. Baruch ha-Levi, which brought about a great change in Europe in the order of Torah study and its transmission from teacher to pupil. In general, the death of *Hai Gaon is accepted as the close of the geonic period. Accordingly, the period of *rishonim* begins in Spain with *Samuel ha-Nagid, in Germany with Gershom b. *Judah, and in North Africa with *Nissim b. Jacob and *Hananel b. Ḥushi'el. The last scholars who are regarded as *rishonim* are *Nissim b. Reuben and his pupil *Isaac b. Sheshet in Spain, the first members of the *Duran family in North Africa, and in Germany Jacob b. Moses *Moellin and Israel *Isserlein. The period of the *rishonim* thus extends from the middle of the 11th to the middle of the 15th centuries. Unlike the Middle Ages in general history, the intermediate period of the *rishonim* bears no implication of a transition from a period of cultural darkness to one of enlightenment. On the contrary, as stated, the generations are regarded as being on the decline, the spiritual stature of the early scholars being held as greater than that of their successors. The chief significance of the division into periods is psychological, its importance being methodological and chronological and valuable mainly as a conventional nomenclature.

From the point of view of literary history, the period of the *rishonim* is differentiated from that of the *geonim* by a process of subdivision into separate literary genres; i.e., the composition of books with distinctive contents in distinctive literary forms in accordance with their contents, such as *ethics and philosophy, and in the domain of *halakhah, *tosafot, pesakim, *hassagot, *haggahot*, *responsa, novellae (*Ḥiddushim*), biblical exegesis, etc. This process which reached the zenith of its efflorescence in the 11th century, brought in its wake an improvement in the means of expression. In consequence, works belonging to the period of the *rishonim* cover a much wider spectrum than was normal with the *geonim*. They contain more extended discussions, an explicit reliance upon previous scholars, and a marked desire to preserve local traditions and customs. Apart from these general literary aspects, there are no specific phenomena characteristic of the *rishonim*, since there existed great individual differences between the scholars of the east and the west, as well as between those of the west itself, even with regard to such primary problems as the right attitude toward the *geonim*, the degree of authority to be attributed to local regulations, and the authority of great scholars to intervene beyond the borders of their own country.

A list of all the published works of the *rishonim* up to 1959 with subsequent addenda (the last in the Internet journal *Jewish Studies*, vol. 1, 2002, pp. 129–80) was published in *Sarei ha-Elef* (see bibl.).

Additional Publications 1969–1972

From 1969 to 1972, no fewer than about 100 complete halakhic works belonging to the period designated as that of the *rishonim* were published from manuscripts, both critical and partly critical editions, as well as about half as many fragments, both large and small. This remarkable output, equivalent to the appearance of a new work every 10 days, is striking evidence of the flourishing literary activity in this department of rabbinical literature. A new and comprehensive list of all the works of the *rishonim* published since the invention of printing was due to appear in 1973 in a new edition of *Sarei ha-Elef* edited by M. *Kasher. Only the more important of these works and fragments will be surveyed here. Since almost all of them were published since 1970 in Israel (mainly Jerusalem, Tel Aviv, and Bene-Berak, though in many cases this refers only to the actual publishing, the works having been prepared in New York), with a few actually published in New York, the year and place of publication will generally not be given. In the case of fragments, reference is given to the periodicals in which they appeared.

Most of the halakhic works surveyed consist of commentaries on tractates of the Talmud (with a few on Maimonides' *Yad*); about a quarter belong to the field of responsa, biblical exegesis (in halakhic vein), halakhic rulings, halakhic monographs, and the like. This trend represents the publishers' desire to reach the tens of thousands of youths who study in the hundreds of yeshivot in Israel and the free world more than the aim of meeting the need for historical and literary research, in which field the number of scholars engaged is still very limited.

FRANCO-GERMAN SCHOOL. The *Tosafot ha-Rosh* (see *Asher b. Jehiel) to the Talmud has almost been completed with the printing of his commentaries to tractates *Shabbat* (published twice; see below), *Eruvin, Rosh Ha-Shanah, Gittin* (a complete critical text, based on three MSS), *Kiddushin*, and *Sanhedrin* (see also below). Much progress has been made with the *tosafot* of *Perez b. Elijah of Corbeil with the publication of his *tosafot* to *Berakhot, Pesaḥim, Beẓah*, and *Bava Meẓia*. The publication of the *tosafot* of English scholars (*Ḥakhmei Angliyyah*; see Tosafot, 15: 1281), have been virtually completed with the publication of these works on tractates *Pesaḥim, Beẓah, Megillah, Gittin, Kiddushin, Bava Kamma, Sanhedrin, Avodah Zarah*, and *Niddah*. The *tosafot* to the *halakhot* of Isaac *Alfasi by *Moses b. Yom Tov of London on *Kiddushin* have also appeared.

In addition to these actual *tosafot*, important works by the Franco-German tosafists have also appeared. Of great importance is "A Commentary from the School of Rashi on Tractate *Sukkah*" (*Sinai*, 63 (1970)). The *tosafot* of Sens (see *Samson b. Abraham of Sens) to *Makkot, Avodah Zarah* (printed in *Shittat ha-Kadmonim* to *Avodah Zarah*) and *Mishnah Shevi'it*, chapters 1–5 (by K. Cahana in *Ḥeker Ve-Iyyun*) completes the considerable number of these *tosafot* hitherto unpublished. The *Tosafot Yeshanim* to the first chapter of *Yevamot* has now appeared in full (HUCA, 40/41 (1970)) and also to *Rosh Ha-Shanah*. Although in effect they belong to the *tosafot* literature, they are not as comprehensive as the first group.

Among the works of the Franco-German scholars that do not belong to *tosafot* literature, the following may be mentioned: *Piskei R. *Jehiel of Paris* (in serial form, *Moriah* (1970/71)); *Piskei R. *Isaac of Corbeil (Sinai*, 67 (end of 1970)); a new responsum by *Ḥayyim b. Isaac, "Or Zaru'a" (*Sinai*, 66 (1970)); a series of compilations on regulations concerning the writing of Scrolls of the Law, *tefillin*, and *mezuzot* has been published in the important *Kovez Sifrei Setam*. This contains *Kitvei Otiyyot Tefillin* by R. *Judah he-Ḥasid, an amended edition of the *Barukh she-Amar* by Samson b. Eliezer, and a fine text of the *Tikkun Tefillin* by Abraham of Sinzheim and the *Alfa Beta* of Yom Tov Lipmann *Muelhausen. The unique project of re-editing the *Aguddah* of Alexander *Suslin from manuscripts continues, and the following have thus far appeared: tractate *Berakhot* and the Mishnah of the other tractates to the order *Zera'im*, all the tractates of *Mo'ed*, and *Bava Kamma* and *Bava Meẓia*. Of special importance are two anonymous early prayer books from the German school, published under the titles *Siddur Rabbenu Shelomo mi-Germeiza* and *Siddur Ḥasidei Ashkenaz*, which include Ashkenazi material that in some small part ante-date Rashi. In addition, the first complete edition from manuscripts and printed sources of *Jacob b. Asher's biblical commentary, *Ba'al ha-Turim*, has appeared. A large new collection of halakhic rulings and responsa by early Franco-German scholars of the 12th and 13th centuries is about to be issued by the *Mekize Nirdamim.

SPANISH SCHOOL. An important achievement is the reissuing of the halakhic works of great Spanish scholars. Although most of the works of *Naḥmanides have long been available, the existing edition is very defective, both as regards mistakes and omissions. About two years ago, Makhon ha-Talmud ha-Yisre'eli ha-Shalem began the comprehensive project of publishing a critical edition of all Naḥmanides' novellae to the Talmud, based on all extant manuscripts and printed editions. Those to the tractates *Makkot, Avodah Zarah*, and *Sanhedrin*, with a monograph on *Dinei de-Garme*, have already appeared. A similar project in respect of the works of *Yom Tov b. Abraham Ishbili, the *Ritba*, is being planned by Mosad ha-Rav Kook. A sample page of *Eruvin* was published in *Sinai*, 67 (1970). Of Naḥmanides' works, the following have been published for the first time: *Tashlum Derashat ha-Rambam "Torat ha-Shem Temimah*," the end of which was previously missing (*Tarbiz*, 40 (1971)); supplements to his commentary on the Torah (*Ha-Ma'yan*, 9 (1969)); the hitherto missing fragments from the first 11 pages of *Bava Mezia (Mattityahu*, Yeshivat Netanyah (1972)); *Kelalei ha-Ramban* by S. *Abramson, published by Mosad ha-Rav Kook, a collection gathered from the works of Naḥmanides, with some notes.

Works by other Spanish scholars published include a new and critical edition, based on an excellent manuscript, of the *Ḥukkot ha-Dayyanim* of Abraham b. Solomon ibn Tazarti, a pupil of Solomon *Adret, the previous edition of which was very faulty (two volumes, the Harry Fischel Institute); the completion of the *siddur* of *Judah b. Yakar, the teacher of Naḥmanides; the commentary of Rabbenu Perez ha-Kohen, the teacher of *Nissim b. Reuben, on the tractate *Nazir*, and to the same tractate by R. Todros b. Isaac of Gerona, early 14th century; the important commentaries of Nissim b. Reuben to tractates *Eruvin* and *Pesaḥim*; the commentary of *Aaron b. Joseph ha-Levi of Barcelona to tractate *Avodah Zarah* and the *Nimmukei Yosef* of Joseph *Ḥabiba to the same (in the *Shitah Mekubbezet* to that tractate); *Shitah le-Va'al ha-Zerurot* to tractate *Ta'anit* by *Ḥayyim b. Samuel b. David of Tudela; and fragments from the commentary by an anonymous pupil of Naḥmanides to tractates *Yoma* and *Sukkah* (S.K. Mirski Memorial Volume, New York (1971)); worthy of note are the anonymous commentary to *Kiddushin* published under the title *Shitah Kadmonit* and to *Middah*, by an anonymous scholar of the school of Naḥmanides, published under the title *Ḥiddushei ha-Ra*. Of the Bible exegetes from this school, worthy of note are the commentary to Genesis and Exodus attributed to a pupil of Nissim b. Reuben and the continuation of the commentary of Abraham b. Isaac *Tamakh on Proverbs 31 (in the Mirski Volume) and on Lamentations 3 (*Ha-Darom*, 28 (1929)).

PROVENÇAL SCHOOL. In contrast to former years, there has been a decrease in the publication of works from the Provençal school, which continues to be largely *terra incognita*. A great amount of effort has been squandered in the republication of the *Beit ha-Beḥirah* of Menahem b. Solomon *Meiri to about ten tractates based on "manuscripts." Despite the fulsome praise of their editors for the new light they provide, they constitute no improvement of any value over the previous editions printed during the past 30 years and still freely available. Their publication testifies only to the great demand for Meiri's works in yeshivah circles. This superfluous republication borders ethically on an encroachment upon the rights of the authors of the previous editions and is without any justification. An exception, and one of great value, is the publication for the first time of the *Ḥiddushei ha-Meiri* to *Eruvin* (up to the end of chapter 4; the remainder in print) by Mosad ha-Rav Kook. The existence of the manuscript had been known for many years and its publication fills a great need. The hitherto unpublished portion of *Hassagot* on Maimonides' *Yad* by Moses ha-Kohen of Lunel to *Nashim, Kedoshah*, and *Shoftim*, supplementing the previously published portion to *Madda, Ahavah*, and *Zemannim*, has now appeared, and the work is now complete. Of a planned complete and critical edition of the *Sefer ha-Menuḥah* by *Manoah of Narbonne, *Hilkhot Keri'at Shema, Tefillah*, and *Berakhot* have already appeared. Other works of Provençal scholars published are *Ezrat Nashim* by *Jacob b. Moses of Begnols; *Hilkhot Ḥamezu-Mazzah ve-Seder Leil Pesaḥ im Perush ha-Haggadah* by an anonymous Provençal scholar, these being published together with fragments of a sermon for Passover by *Abraham b. David of Posquières, which was not extant in manuscript, but has been collated from a number of sources. First published separately in *Ha-Darom* (1972), they have been published together in *Mi-Toratav shel Ḥakhmei Provens u-Sefarad be-Hilkhot u-ve-Minhagei Pesaḥ*. Important, too, is the recently published commentary by *Jonathan ha-Kohen of Lunel on Alfasi's commentary to *Kiddushin*. Two small fragments hitherto unknown are also worthy of note: a new letter by *Abraham b. Isaac of Narbonne, and the original letter of the scholars of Lunel to Maimonides, in which they asked him to send them "his other scholarly works" (*Tarbiz*, 39 (1970)). Finally, there is a criticism of the New Testament by Joseph b. Nathan *Official, which appeared in the Jubilee Volume for Isaac Kiev, New York (1972), after the *Sefer ha-Mekanne* was published.

ORIENTAL SCHOLARS. Of the works of Oriental scholars, note must first be taken of developments connected with *Maimonides. Seven new responsa have appeared (from a Parma MSS, not as stated from the *Genizah, Tarbiz, 39 (1970)), and a substantial part of his classical works, retranslated into Hebrew as part of a comprehensive project undertaken by Rabbi Y. *Kafah (who makes use of additional Arabic MSS), and most recently the *Sefer ha-Mitzvot* and the *Iggeret Teiman*. Kafaḥ has also published a small work containing a detailed index of all biblical verses in all the Maimonidean literature, titled

Ha-Mikra be-Rambam. It is of exceptional value, and is the first of its kind in comprehensiveness and quality. Of importance for textual research on the works of Maimonides is the reissue of *Ḥasifat Genuzim mi-Teiman* and the facsimile edition (by "Makor") of the unique and important Constantinople (1509) edition of the *Mishneh Torah.* Among the works of other Oriental scholars, note should be taken of the anonymous commentary to *Bava Batra – Perush Kadmon*; of the anonymous *Hilkhot Ereẓ Yisrael min ha-Genizah* (in *Koveẓ al Yad*, 7 (1968)), and of the small fragment of the commentary of *Peraḥyah b. Nissim to Alfasi's commentary on *Shabbat* (in *Seyata di-Shemaya* (1970)). Important is the commentary of *Hananel b. Samuel to the Alfasi on *Kiddushin*, printed in the *Shitat ha-Kadmonim* to this tractate. Ereẓ Israel *halakhot*, dating from the pre-Moslem period, from Genizah sources, which throw considerable light on the specific *halakhah* of Ereẓ Israel and clarify many hitherto obscure passages in the so-called *Sefer ha-Ma'asim* (see p. 330) and including new extracts from it – from the literary legacy of Prof. Mordecai Margaliot, collected by him over 20 years from all available sources – are now in the final stages of publication. Among Bible commentaries, mention may be made of the commentary to Job by Meyuḥas b. Elijah.

NORTH AFRICAN SCHOOL. The *editio princeps* of the *Rif* by Isaac Alfasi has now been published in facsimile by "Makor," with an introduction. Twelve responsa by Isaac Alfasi were published in *Or ha-Mizraḥ*, 20 (1971), and an amended and critical edition of the *Seder Rav Amram Ga'on* (see *Amram b. Sheshna), the first that can by usefully consulted, has appeared; a new edition of the **Halakhot Gedolot* based on very many MSS (Mekiẓe Nirdamim), and also a facsimile edition of the same work from the Paris MSS 1702 and a facsimile edition of the **Halakhot Pesukot*, from MSS Sassoon, both by "Makor." Belonging to a much later period is the commentary of Simeon b. Ẓemaḥ *Duran to *Berakhot*, published for the first time. Ch.D. Chavel has collated and published all extant fragments to the biblical commentary of R. Hananel ben Ḥushi'el.

ITALY. The great project of publishing the *Pesakim* of *Isaiah b. Mali (di) Trani and of his grandson, *Isaiah b. Elijah, continues. The following having been published recently: *Beẓah, Rosh Ha-Shanah, Ta'anit, Megillah, Ḥagigah, Mo'ed Katan*, and the *Halakhot Ketannot*. His Pentateuch commentary from a manuscript which belonged to R. Zedekiah *Anav was published lately with Anav's annotations; new responsa by Joseph *Colon as well as his commentary on the Passover laws of Maimonides and of the *Sefer Mitzvot Gadol*, as well as his commentary on the Pentateuch; the *Arugah ha-Shelishit* (Order of Blessings) of the *Shibbolei ha-Lekket* of Zedekiah Anav, published from the literary remains of S.K. Mirski in his Memorial Volume.

A work of unique value for the period of the *rishonim*, which includes new fragments from every sphere of Jewish culture, is *Ḥasifat Genuzim mi-Teiman*, the individual project of Judah Levi Nahum, an enthusiastic Yemenite who has for decades been collecting copies of Yemenite works from all periods and all subjects as well as pages of incunabula and fragments of old printed works extracted from the bindings of books originating in the Yemen. This work, of which only one part has been published thus far, contains among its 100 fragments very many from the works of *rishonim*, of which a considerable number deal with the work of Maimonides, which was especially popular in the Yemen. It is impossible to deal here with all the relevant fragments, but the commentary of David *Abudarham on *piyyutim* and *hoshanot* may be given as an example. The superiority of this work over the others mentioned above lies in the fact that it gives a facsimile of each fragment. This is especially important since lack of experience has caused a certain lack of precision in the reading of the fragments. It may be assumed that further volumes of this project, which is a kind of wandering *genizah* of Jewish literature, will make their appearance, and no doubt the copying of the fragments will be perfected.

Most of the books have been copied, edited, and published on the initiative and personal predilection of relatively young scholars, some of whom have had previous experience in this work, while others are new to it. Only a few have been published on the initiative of public Torah institutes, which have made long-term plans of great importance. As a result, together with the notable achievements there is a conspicuous and complete lack of coordination both among the editors themselves and between them and the organized institutions. At times, there is even open rivalry, with the result that sometimes the same work is published simultaneously more than once. The *Tosafot ha-Rosh* to *Sanhedrin* was published from the same unique manuscript simultaneously by B. Lipkin (posthumously; with supplements and notes by J. ha-Levi Lipschutz) in Jerusalem (1968) and by S. Ullman of Brooklyn in Tel Aviv (1969). The *Tosafot ha-Rosh* to *Shabbat* was also published twice: by I.S. Lange (of Zurich) in Jerusalem (1969) and by the same S. Ullman in Tel Aviv (1971), though in this case different MSS were used, the former using Parma and London MSS and the latter MSS in the New York Seminary and the Ginsberg collection. The *Tosafot ha-Rosh* to *Yoma* published in New York (1961; the main article in the EJ has 1965 – a typographical error) was republished from the same MSS by Ullman in Tel Aviv (1969), as though it were being published from the manuscript for the first time. Something similar has occurred with the publication of the Meiri (see above) and with the *Hashlamah* of Meshullam b. *Moses. More examples could be given.

Among institutes which have undertaken defined assignments in the period of the *rishonim* is the Makhon ha-Talmud ha-Yisraeli ha-Shalem, whose main projects are: the editing of the *Piskei Rid* and the *Riaz* (see above), following the order of the Talmud (thus far, *Berakhot* and all of *Mo'ed* have appeared); a series *Ginzei Rishonim*, within whose framework works of *rishonim* "that have never been published" are being printed, but there appears to be neither method nor system in the series, the printing of many of the works being interrupted and left uncompleted; a project to issue the complete novellae of Naḥmanides (see above). Mosad ha-Rav Kook has sponsored the main work of Rabbi Y. Kafaḥ, the issuing of new Hebrew translations of all Maimonides' Arabic works, and the editing of many works by *rishonim* of which he possesses single, or unique, manuscripts. It is also about to begin the printing of the series *Ha-Ritba ha-Shalem* on the Talmud (see above). Worthy of note is the project *Sanhedrei Gedolah* of the Harry Fischel Institute, which is reprinting all extant *rishonim* to tractate *Sanhedrin* or those whose subject matter refers mainly to that tractate. Hitherto four volumes have appeared and *Ḥukkot ha-Dayyanim* (see above). All the works published by these institutes have introductions, source references and notes by the editors.

The work of these individual scholars is of equal importance to the planned series. Quite a number of these scholars work according to their own private plan, e.g., Rabbi Ullman, who has published the remainder of the hitherto unpublished *Tosafot ha-Rosh* (without taking into consideration that some other person may be engaged in the identical task), and Rabbi Brizel, who has published the *Aguddah* with notes and source references. It is a cause for satisfaction that editors who were accustomed formerly to embellish their editions with an abundance of mostly superfluous notes have also recently begun to regard their principal work as simply the provision of a reliable text. As a result, the literature of *rishonim* is gradually returning to the original form in which it was always published in the past.

At present the editing of works by *rishonim* is wholly in the hands of yeshivah scholars and students of the Torah who are guided in their choice and in their work by the curriculum current in yeshivot. No work of any significance in this domain is being done in academic circles, although among them too are considerable numbers of rabbinical scholars. Any work needed for research into matters connected with rabbinical literature which does not fall within the curriculum of the yeshivot is still completely dependent on the possibilities (and the preferences) of the Mekiẓe Nirdamim society, and on the very few publications, too fragmentary to have permanent value, in a few periodicals. There exists a great need especially for facsimile editions (either with or without their parallel printed transcription), since these are the foundations of all exact scientific research, relieving the researcher from dependence upon the editors' reading of the photostat of the MSS. Because this task is not regarded as of significance for study in yeshivot, such works are well-nigh nonexistent. A praiseworthy exception is the Makor Publishing Company, which puts out excellent facsimile editions of those manuscripts (see above).

Among the chief workers in the field (of complete works) are: Rabbis Y. Kafaḥ, A. Sofer, M. Herschler, M.J. ha-Kohen Blau and Ch.D. Chavel who are veteran scholars of great experience; also S. Greenbaum, A.D. Pines, A.L. Feldman, I. ha-Levi Lipschutz and S. Ullman. Others, in alphabetical order, are: A. Brizel, S.Z. Broida, K. Cahana, J. Cohen, M. Glazer, M. Hildesheimer, D.Z. Hillman, W. Horowitz, H. Krauser, I.S. Lange, A. Liss, M.M. Meshizahav, I. Reinz, I. Rothstein, H. Segal, A. Shoshana, S. Sofer, and the *Seder Amram Ga'on* by Dr. Goldschmidt. Of publishers of fragments, particular mention may be made of A. Kupfer.

In contrast to the publication of texts, research has proceeded at a very slow pace. Nevertheless, many studies of value for the works of *rishonim* can be enumerated. It should first be noted that there has been a considerable general improvement in the standard of the introductions printed at the beginning of many of these books. Among studies of Maimonides, note must be taken of the *Ein Mitzvot*, a bio-bibliographical lexicon for the study of Maimonides' *Sefer ha-Mitzvot* and its commentators, by I.I. Dienstag (1969); also a list of all complete printed editions of the *Mishneh Torah* (in the Jubilee Volume for Kiev (1972), which, though not the first in this field, is a great improvement over its predecessors; the article "*Sefer Mishneh Torah*… Its Aims…," by I. Twerski, in *Israel National Academy of Sciences*, 5:1 (1972); and "*Mishneh Torah le-ha-Rambam* in the Possession of the Jews of the Yemen," by S.D. Pinḥasi, in the *Ḥasifat Genuzim mi-Teiman* (1971). S.Z. Havlin has published a valuable article on the printed editions of the *Mishneh Torah* (introduction to the above-mentioned Makor facsimile edition). Note should be taken of the article "The Literary Creation of Joseph Ibn Migas," printed in *Kiryat Sefer*, 45/47 (1970–72); the study by I. Spiegel of *Sefer Maggid Mishneh* on the *Mishneh Torah* (*Kiryat Sefer*, 46 (1971)); the article by I. Markus on Isaac ibn Ghayyat (*Sinai*, 67/8 (1970)); of great value is the article "*Tosafot Gornish*" (*Sinai*, 68 (1961)), where not only is the subject illuminated for the first time but the nature of *pilpul* and its developments clarified; finally, the unsatisfactory article by I. Shtzipanski on "Rabbenu Ephraim and the Rif" (*Tarbiz*, 41 (1972)), which is of little value. Not only does it not make use of all available data on the subject but it "reveals" a considerable amount of material long known and fully discussed by scholars. In addition to these articles, several introductions to books have been printed which give all the available biographical material and the authors of the work. Particular note should be taken of Horowitz's introduction to the *Sefer ha-Menuḥah* (see above) and the *Seridei Derashot ha-Rabad*, and to the introductions of I. Lipschutz and S. Feldman. Of particular importance is the article "*Ha-Siddur le-Va'al ha-Semak* with the commentary of the author of the *Maḥkim*," by S.D. Bergmann (in the Mirski Volume, see above), containing information about German scholars of the 13th and 14th centuries. Lastly, note should be made of the article "*Le-Ḥeker he-Arukh*," of *Nathan b. Jehiel of Rome, by S. Abramson in *Leshonenu*, 36 (1972), 100–22.

BIBLIOGRAPHY: M. Kasher and J.D. Mandelbaum, *Sarei ha-Elef*, (1959; a bibliographical list of the printed writings of the *rishonim*); addenda up to 1965, in: *Noah Braun Memorial Volume* (1970), 215–99; I. Ta-Shema, *Sifrei Rishonim* (1967); S. Poznański, *Babylonische Geonim im nachgaonaeischen Zeitalter*, (1914), 79–111.

[Israel Moses Ta-Shma]

RISHON LE-ZION (Heb. רִאשׁוֹן לְצִיּוֹן, "First in Zion"), city in central Israel, 7 mi. (12 km.) S.E. of Tel Aviv-Jaffa, founded in 1882 by ten pioneers from Russia headed by Z.D. *Levontin. The name Rishon le-Zion is based on Isaiah 41:27.

In acquiring the first 835 acres (3,340 dunams) of land for their village, the settlers were aided by Ḥayyim *Amzalak, then the British vice consul in Jaffa. It was the first settlement established by pioneers from outside Ereẓ Israel. In the first year of its existence, the population grew to 100 when *Bilu pioneers joined the village after receiving some agricultural training at *Mikveh Israel. Their experience, however, was still insufficient and their sparse means were almost totally spent on the cost of the land and on primary investments. They soon faced a grave crisis. A particular difficulty was the lack of water, as attempts to find water in shallow wells had failed and drinking water had to be hauled from Mikveh Israel in a camel-drawn carriage. As a last resource, the settlers in 1883 sent an emissary, Yosef *Feinberg, to enlist the aid of Jewish communities in Europe. He met Baron Edmond de *Rothschild, whose first contribution, F25,000 (francs), was utilized to drill a deep well. Subsequently, Baron Rothschild maintained the settler families and after a review of the village's farming program, introduced fruit growing, especially wine grapes, instead of grain cultivation. He sent agronomists and administrators to Rishon le-Zion, but a fresh crisis arose when the administrators regarded the settlers as hired workers and stifled their initiative. The vine strains brought from southern France proved unsuitable and the grapes had no market. Part of the vineyards were therefore replaced by almond plantations. The situation gradually improved after 1889, when the large Carmel Oriental wine cellars were installed by Baron Rothschild. The world's first Hebrew kindergarten and elementary school were opened here in the 1880s. The moshavah's holdings gradually expanded to 3,225 acres (12,900 dunams) in 1907 with a population of 500 in 1897, and 2,130 in 1917. Immigration from Eastern Europe and *Yemen brought additional Jewish laborers. Citrus groves became the principal farming branch. During World War I, the Turkish governor, in appreciation of the village's achievements in reclaiming formerly barren terrain, ordered an area of 5,000 acres (20,000 dunams) of sand dunes stretching from Rishon le-Zion west to the seashore to be annexed to its boundaries. This transfer was endorsed by the British administration in 1921. Aside from the dunes, the village area grew to 4,250 acres (17,000 dunams) in 1932. In 1922 the moshavah received municipal council status. In the 1930s, industrial enterprises (silicate bricks, beer, and razor blades) were set up. By 1948 Rishon le-Zion had 10,500 inhabitants. Considerable land reserves, a rich groundwater table and the nearby Tel Aviv conurbation favorably influenced Rishon le-Zion's further expansion. In 1950, it was given city status, and its population continued to increase rapidly, attaining 46,500 by 1970. By that time it had one of the country's largest municipal terrains with a total of 17 sq. mi. (44 sq. km.). Industry expanded while farming still played a role in the city's economy. By the mid-1990s, the population of Rishon le-Zion was approximately 154,300 and in 2002 it was 211,600, making it the fourth largest city in Israel, with its land area now increased to 23 sq. mi. (60 sq. km.) as the city expanded to the west and many business areas spread throughout. Most residents found work in the Tel Aviv conurbation. Rishon le-Zion is considered one of the most congested cities in Israel.

WEBSITE: www.rishonlezion.muni.il.

[Tsevi Atsmon / Shaked Gilboa (2nd ed.)]

RISHON LE-ZION (Heb. רִאשׁוֹן לְצִיּוֹן; "first of Zion"), a title given to the Sephardi head of the rabbis of Israel. His seat is in Jerusalem. The first scholar to be given the title was apparently Moses b. Jonathan *Galante (1620–89) when he and the other scholars of Jerusalem decided that their leader should bear the modest title of *rishon le-Zion*, mentioned in Isaiah (41:27), and not rabbi or *av bet din*. Until 1840 the authority of the **ḥakham bashi* ("chief rabbi") in Constantinople extended over all the communities of the Ottoman Empire, including Ereẓ Israel. From that year until 1920, the *rishon le-Zion* was granted the additional title of *ḥakham bashi* for Ereẓ Israel by the Ottoman government. The first to bear this double title was Ḥayyim Abraham *Gagin. However, the grant of this additional title was not always made immediately on appointment.

BIBLIOGRAPHY: Luncz, in: *Yerushalayim*, 4 (1892), 210–7: Frumkin-Rivlin, 2 (1928), 57f.; Gaon, in: *Mizraḥ u-Ma'arav*, 2 (1928), 29–36; Elmaleh, in: *Talpioth*, 9 (1964), 364–6; idem, *Ha-Rishonim le-Ẓiyyon* (1970); Hirschberg, in: *Yad Yosef Yiẓḥak Rivlin* (1964), 94–101.

RISHPON (Heb. רִשְׁפּוֹן), moshav in central Israel N. of *Herzliyyah. Rishpon was founded in 1936, in the framework of the Thousand Families Settlement Project (see *Israel, State of: Settlement), by immigrants from Eastern Europe. In 1970 Rishpon had 447 inhabitants, increasing to 540 in the mid-1990s and 794 in 2002 after expansion. Its economy was based on citrus groves, fruit plantations, flowers, vegetables, poultry and horse stables. The name is assumedly historical, and appears in the form "Rishponah" in an inscription of Tiglath Pileser III dating back to the year 732 B.C.E. It may be connected with the Canaanite deity Reshef.

[Efraim Orni]

RISIKOFF, MENAHEM (Mendel) HAKOHEN (1866–1960), rabbi and author. Risikoff, the son of Rabbi Zvi Yosef Hakohen *Resnick, was born in Zhetel (Dyatlovo) and studied in the yeshivot of Volozhin and Vilna, receiving *semikhah* at the age of 17 from some of the outstanding rabbis of the time.

Appointed rabbi of Kazan in 1895, he emigrated to the United States a few years later following pogroms in his community and served as rabbi in a number of Brooklyn synagogues, including Ohev Shalom and Williamsburg's Moore Street Congregation.

Among the many volumes published by him on *halakhah, aggadah*, biblical commentaries, sermons, and responsa may be mentioned: *Shaarei Zevaḥ* (1913), dealing with the laws of *sheḥitah* and *treifah*; *Shaarei Shamayim* (1937), a commentary on the Shulḥan Arukh; and *Torat ha-Kohanim* (1948), an exhaustive study of the laws pertaining to Kohanim.

BIBLIOGRAPHY: B. Ayalon (ed.), *Yizkor Book Meitshet* (1973), 119–20; S. Gottlieb, *Ohelei Shem* (1912).

RISKIN, SHLOMO (1940–), rabbi. Born in Brooklyn, New York, Riskin entered Yeshiva University in 1956. There he found a mentor in Rabbi Joseph B. *Soloveitchik (the Rav) and was impressed with his unique vision of Judaism, which proposed that *halakhah* (Jewish Law) actually deal with the most fundamental existential problems plaguing modern man.

Upon receiving his rabbinic ordination and graduating as valedictorian in 1960, Riskin was determined to open a new model of synagogue, one based on outreach and learning. This led to the opening of the renowned Lincoln Square Synagogue (LSS), established in a small apartment on the Upper West Side of Manhattan. Attendance grew and a permanent structure was established on Amsterdam Avenue. By the end of the 1970s, LSS had become one of the most vibrant centers for Judaism in New York and America. LSS as well as other educational institutions established by Riskin were the locus of Jewish life for thousands of Jews.

By 1983, however, Riskin decided to move to Israel. Criticized by some congregants for the move, Riskin explained his view that Israel was the only place where a Jew could live his/her life in a complete fashion. The Diaspora, he said, would always be a footnote in Jewish history, while Israel would be the nexus. He felt that the future of Jewish leadership would be based in Israel and he wanted to be a part of it, as well as to participate in what he called "the greatest expression of reclaiming our own destiny since the leaving of Egypt."

In 1983 he moved to the new garden city of *Efrat near Jerusalem, which he founded together with Moshe Moskovitz. Guided by the idea of an open urban community between *Gush Etzyon and Jerusalem, Efrat would serve as a bridge between the bloc of Jewish settlements and Israel's capital.

As chief rabbi of Efrat, Riskin established an educational institution called Ohr Torah Stone (OTS), comprised of yeshivah high schools and rabbinic and leadership training. OTS has grown into an all-encompassing educational organization. Its educational philosophy promotes Riskin's vision of Judaism that is based on the teachings of his childhood and Rabbi Soloveitchik's message of ethical monotheism that the Jew must impart to the world. For Riskin, Judaism presents the most fundamental notions of freedom, universal morality, and a code of ethics to the world. The importance of compassion and sensitivity in the practical application of a religious lifestyle is one of Riskin's major doctrines. God's law and its realization must express that love and compassion, within halakhic parameters.

Riskin was also a pioneer in the field of women's Torah learning and halakhic rights, as reflected both in his writings as well as the make-up of his educational institutions. He holds a master's in Jewish history and was awarded his Ph.D. from New York University's department of Near Eastern languages and literature.

He is also the author of five books: *The Rebellious Wife: Women and Jewish Divorce* (1989); *Yad L'isha* (2004); *The Passover Haggadah* (1983); *Around the Family Table* (2005); and *Torah Lights – Genesis Confronts Life, Love and Family* (2005).

His regular columns and articles appear weekly in the *Jerusalem Post* as well as in dozens of newspapers and magazines throughout the world.

[Edward Jacobs (2nd ed.)]

RITT, MARTIN (1914–1990), U.S. director, producer, actor. Born in Manhattan's Lower East Side, Ritt attended Elon College in North Carolina, where he played football and boxed. He was occasionally teased for being Jewish but had a good sense of humor and joked that the ham served on Fridays was actually turkey. Ritt left Elon after two years and went to St. John's University in Jamaica, N.Y., to study law. He soon befriended director Elia Kazan and left St. John's to act. After serving in World War II, where he acted and directed, Ritt worked in television. Between the 1940s and the early 1950s, Ritt appeared in more than 150 plays and directed 100 TV shows. Then, in the early 1950s, he was blacklisted for prior Communist Party involvement as part of the McCarthy-era "Red Scare." Unable to find television work, Ritt began teaching at the Actor's Workshop in Manhattan. In 1957, producer David *Susskind defied the blacklist and hired Ritt for his directorial debut, *Edge of the City*. Ritt went on to direct 25 more films. He directed and produced *Hud* (1963), starring Paul Newman, which earned Ritt a best director Academy Award nomination. One of Ritt's former Actor's Workshop students, Newman worked together with Ritt many times, including in *Paris Blues* (1961), *Hemingway's Adventures of a Young Man* (1962), and *Hombre* (1967), which Ritt also produced. In 1976, Ritt directed *The Front*, a fictional story of the McCarthy blacklist, that starred Woody Allen. Other Ritt films include *The Sound and the Fury* (1959), *The Molly Maguires* (1970), *Pete 'n' Tillie* (1972), *Norma Rae* (1979), and *Stanley and Iris* (1990).

[Susannah Howland (2nd ed.)]

RITTENBERG, DAVID (1906–1970), U.S. biochemist. Rittenberg, who was born in New York, was a member of the faculty of Columbia University from 1934 onward. He was professor of biochemistry at the university's College of Physicians and Surgeons until 1956 when he became executive officer of the department of biochemistry. In 1965 he was appointed chairman of the department. He was one of the pioneers in the use of isotopes to label molecules and so trace their movements and chemical transformation in metabolism. By this method, he and his co-workers showed that the constituents of the body, including its fat stores, are in a constant state of dynamic change. Rittenberg discovered, with the aid of isotopic labeling, that fatty acids and cholesterol originate in the body from small molecules such as acetate.

Rittenberg was associated with the U.S. Atomic Energy Commission and the Office of Research and Development. He was a member of the National Academy of Sciences and was a governor of the Weizmann Institute of Science in Israel.

[Mordecai L. Gabriel]

RITTER, IMMANUEL HEINRICH (1825–1890), German Reform rabbi. Ritter received an Orthodox education in Ratibor, Prussia, and studied history and philology at Breslau University. Unable to engage in an academic career in these fields, he became a teacher of religion in the Berlin Reform community and the successor of Samuel *Holdheim in his rabbinical post. Ritter established his reputation as defender of Jewish rights against the reactionary Prussian politician Wagener.

He wrote *Geschichte der juedischen Reformation* (4 parts, 1858, 1861, 1865, 1902), a history of the Reform movement which criticized Mendelssohn's lack of historical judgment (part 1, p. 53), as well as the first biographies of David *Friedlaender and Samuel Holdheim and the story of the Berlin Reform community.

RITZ BROTHERS (b. **Joachim**), AL (1903–1965), JIMMY (1905–1985), and HARRY (1908–1986), U.S. vaudeville comedy team. Born in Newark, New Jersey, the Ritz Brothers began public appearances as the Collegians. Their act, which remained fairly constant for decades, was comprised of precision dancing, tongue-twisting song parodies, ethnic humor, and physical comedy. Their slapstick succeeded in several Broadway revues, and their first film was *Sing, Baby, Sing* (1936). Other films were: *Life Begins in College* (1937), *One in a Million* (1937), *On the Avenue* (1937), *You Can't Have Everything* (1937), *The Goldwyn Follies* (1938), *Straight, Place and Show* (1938), *Kentucky Moonshine* (1938), *Pack Up Your Troubles* (1939), *The Gorilla* (1939), *The Three Musketeers* (1939), *Argentine Nights* (1940), *Behind the Eight Ball* (1942), *Never a Dull Moment* (1943), and *Hi 'Ya Chum* (1943). Their humor was better geared to a live audience, however, so they left the film industry and focused their attention on their nightclub appearances.

Harry and Jimmy were among the star-studded cast of *Won Ton Ton, the Dog Who Saved Hollywood* (1976). They all appeared on television.

BIBLIOGRAPHY: George Burns, *All My Best Friends* (1989); J. Robinson, *Teamwork: The Cinema's Greatest Comedy Teams* (1982).

[Ruth Beloff (2nd ed.)]

RIVA (di Trento), town on the Lake of Garda, N. Italy. A Jewish community existed there from the 14th century. Though expelled in 1520 as the result of the Simon of Trent blood libel, Jews returned to Riva soon after, but they were compelled to wear the *badge, pay a capitation tax, and were subject to other restrictions. There was a Hebrew printing press in Riva, which was active between 1558 and 1562 and produced about 35 titles.

The press owed its success to the cooperation of three men: Cardinal Cristoforo Madruzzo, bishop of Trent, who had jurisdiction over the town and whose coat-of-arms appears on many of the Riva publications; Joseph b. Nathan *Ottolenghi, rabbi and *rosh yeshivah* at Cremona; and Jacob Marcaria, *dayyan* and physician, also of Cremona, who was the printer and contributed learned prefaces to his productions. The first work issued was Isaac Alfasi's *Halakhot* (1558), followed by other halakhic works, including two editions of Jacob b. Asher's *Turim* (1560 and 1561). With the Talmud banned in Italy, there was a need for these substitutes. The press also produced philosophic works, notably the first printing of Levi b. Gershom's *Milḥamot Adonai* (1560), and ethical literature. The illiberal attitude of Cardinal Madruzzo's nephew and successor must have led to the abrupt end of Marcaria's venture. For about another year he continued to print non-Hebrew books, including some concerned with the Council of Trent (1545–64), though only one of them carried the printer's name. Joseph b. Jacob Shalit of Padua, who had been Marcaria's proofreader, took some of the unfinished works to Venice and had them printed there.

BIBLIOGRAPHY: D.W. Amram, *Makers of Hebrew Books in Italy* (1909), 296–305; J. Bloch, *Hebrew Printing in Riva di Trento* (1933).

RIVERA, JACOB RODRIGUEZ (1717–1789), U.S. merchant and a founder of Yeshuat Israel Congregation in Newport, Rhode Island. Born in Spain, Rivera was naturalized in New York in 1746, but soon moved to Newport. There during the two prerevolutionary decades, Rivera became a distinguished merchant shipper, trading in numerous commodities, including slaves, but his chief – and quite possibly pioneering – interest was the spermaceti candle industry. A charter member in 1761 of the United Company of Spermaceti Chandlers, he led its efforts to regulate competition. His colleagues, mostly non-Jews, esteemed him enough to forgo Saturday meetings on his account. Around 1760, he took as his partner the Newport cultural leader, Henry Collins, a founder of the Redwood Library, which Rivera also supported. Rivera is best known for his association with his enterprising son-in-law, Aaron *Lopez, and shared in many of Lopez' ventures. During the American Revolution, he accompanied Lopez to Leicester, Massachusetts and took up farming there but, following Lopez' untimely death in 1782, Rivera reestablished himself at Newport.

BIBLIOGRAPHY: AJHSP, 27 (1920), index; S.F. Chyet, *Lopez of Newport* (1969); M. Gutstein, *The Story of the Jews of Newport* (1936), index; J.R. Marcus, *Early American Jewry*, 2 (1953), index; idem, *American Jewry. Documents. Eighteenth Century* (1959), index; idem, *Colonial American Jews* (1969); *Commerce of Rhode Island*, 2 vols. (1914–15).

[Stanley F. Chyet]

RIVERS, JOAN (1933–), U.S. comedienne and actress. Born Joan Alexandra Molinsky in Brooklyn, New York, to Russian immigrants, Rivers acted in school productions at Barnard College, graduating Phi Betta Kappa with a bachelor's degree in English in 1954. Post-college jobs included working as a publicist for Lord and Taylor and as a fashion coordinator for Bond Clothing Stores, marrying the owner's son at 21; the marriage was annulled six months later. Rivers returned home and pursued her dream of becoming an actress, mostly working in off-Broadway plays. She soon shifted gears and tried stand-up comedy, at first using the name Pepper January and then performing as Joan Rivers. After working small East Coast clubs for seven years, she spent time in Greenwich Village coffeehouses developing an act that was sexually provocative and self-deprecating. Critics panned Rivers, but comedian Lenny *Bruce encouraged her. From 1961 to 1962, she was a member of the improvisational group Second City, and then wrote material for *Candid Camera* and Phyllis Diller. In 1965 she was booked on the *Tonight Show* and after a successful set was asked back. Rivers soon became a Las Vegas headliner, and was named Las Vegas comedienne of the year in 1976 and 1977. Rivers wrote and starred in the film *Rabbit Test* with Billy Crystal in 1978, and in 1983 she was named Woman of the Year by Hadassah. That same year, the woman known for her trademark line "Can we talk?" parlayed her frequent appearances on the *Tonight Show* into a regular guest host slot. After Carson left the *Tonight Show* in 1986, Rivers started her own talk show, *The Late Show Starring Joan Rivers* (1986–87) and published her first autobiography, *Enter Talking*. Her second husband was suffering from chemical depression due to heart medication at the time; he took the cancellation of his wife's program personally and committed suicide a few months later. Her husband's death tainted Rivers professionally, especially after her agent canceled her contract. Rivers started performing in small clubs again, appeared in Neil Simon's *Broadway Bound* (1986), and then took a regular spot as the center square on the television game show *Hollywood Squares*, which she held until 1989. She hosted her own syndicated talk show, *The Joan Rivers Show*, from 1989 to 1993, and won an Emmy for it in 1990. Rivers returned to Broadway with a play she wrote about Lenny Bruce's mother, *Sally Marr … and Her Escorts* (1994), which earned her a Tony nod for best actress. Rivers and her daughter starred as themselves in an NBC made-for-TV movie *Tears and Laughter: The Joan and Melissa Rivers Story* (1994), and the mother-daughter team has since become known for providing red-carpet commentary during the Oscars and other awards shows.

BIBLIOGRAPHY: "Rivers, Joan," in: *Newsmakers*, Issue 3 (2005); "Rivers, Joan," in: *Contemporary Authors* (Gale, 2005). **WEBSITE:** www.imdb.com/name/nm0001672.

[Adam Wills (2nd ed.)]

RIVERS, LARRY (1924–2002), U.S. painter, printmaker, sculptor, writer, and musician. Born Yitzroch Loiza Grossberg in the Bronx to immigrant parents from the Ukraine, Rivers initially made his reputation as a jazz saxophonist. After a brief stint in the U.S. Army during World War II (1942–43) he studied music theory and composition at the Juilliard School of Music (1944–45). Rivers started painting in 1945, and from 1947–48 he studied at the avant-garde Hans Hofmann School in New York. His initial work shows the influence of Abstract Expressionism.

In the early 1950s, Rivers began to paint autobiographical themes in pictures such as *The Burial* (1951, Fort Wayne Museum of Art, Indiana), a gesturally rendered canvas inspired by the memory of his grandmother's funeral, and *Europe I* (1956, Minneapolis Institute of Arts) and *Europe II* (1956, private collection, New York), the latter based on a formal portrait of Polish relatives. Parody enters his art in these years; in *Washington Crossing the Delaware* (1953, Museum of Modern Art, New York), for example, a canvas mocking the grand heroics of 19th-century American history painting, Rivers appropriates the imagery of Emanuel Leutze's iconic painting of the same name (1851, Metropolitan Museum of Art, New York) while also exploring paint application and other formal qualities. The Museum of Modern Art in New York acquired Rivers' version in 1951, his first painting to enter a major public collection.

This mode of parody also pervades *History of Matzah (The Story of the Jews)* (1982–84, private collection, New York), an ambitious project that attempts to tell the nearly four-millennium history of the Jews. Painted on commission, *History of Matzah* appears in a collage-like form with images and stories overlapping on three nine-by-fourteen-foot canvases in Part I, titled *Before the Diaspora*, Part II, *European Jewry*, and Part III, *Immigration to America*, all superimposed on a rendering of matzah. Other works influenced by Rivers' Jewish identity include a large mural, *Fall in the Forest at Birkenau* (1990), hanging in the United States Holocaust Memorial Museum; three posthumous portraits of the Holocaust memoirist Primo *Levi (1987–88, Collection La Stampa, Turin, Italy); and the illustrations for a Limited Editions Club publication of Isaac *Bashevis Singer's short story "The Magician of Lublin" (1984).

The multi-talented Rivers designed sets for the play *Try! Try!* (1951), written by Frank O'Hara, as well as a play by Le Roi Jones (1964) and Stravinsky's *Oedipus Rex* (1966). With O'Hara, Rivers also wrote the play *Kenneth Koch: A Tragedy* (1954). In 1957 he began making welded metal sculpture. Rivers wrote poetry, acted on stage, including a stint as Lyndon Johnson in Kenneth Koch's *The Election* (1960), and continued to perform in jazz bands throughout his life. His 1992 autobiography, titled *What Did I Do?*, chronicles his life in often lurid detail.

BIBLIOGRAPHY: L. Rivers with C. Brightman, *Drawings and Digressions* (1979); H.A. Harrison, *Larry Rivers* (1984); S. Hunter, *Larry Rivers* (1989); L. Rivers and A. Weinstein, *What Did I Do? The Unauthorized Autobiography* (1992); S. Baskind, "Effacing Difference: Larry Rivers' *History of Matzah (The Story of the Jews)*," in: *Athanor* (1999), 87–95; L. Rivers, *Larry Rivers: Art and the Artist* (2002).

[Samantha Baskind (2nd ed.)]

RIVISTA ISRAELITICA, Italian-Jewish scholarly periodical published in Florence between 1904 and 1915. *Rivista Israelitica: Periodico bimestrale per la scienza e la vita del Giudaismo* ("Bi-Monthly for the Science and the Life of Judaism") was founded by Samuel Hirsch *Margulies. It appeared regularly until 1913, and in 1915 a double number marked its last issue. The journal provided a forum for the emerging research on the history and culture of Italian Jewry, which in 1913 was marked by the foundation of a Florence-based Società per la storia degli ebrei in Italia ("Society for the History of the Jews of Italy") edited by Umberto Cassuto. The *Rivista Israelitica* separated, for the first time in the history of the Italian Jewish press, a scientific approach to Judaism from more general educational goals, which S.H. Margulies pursued instead in *La Settimana Israelitica* (published in Siena between 1910 and 1915). The two journals eventually merged with *Il Corriere Israelitico* of Trieste, resulting in the weekly *Israel* (1916–64), from which later stemmed both *Israel dei ragazzi* (1918–38), a monthly for the youth and *La Rassegna Mensile di Israel* (1925–). Many of the studies by the Italian and foreign contributors dealt with the history and culture of Italian Jewry. In 1904–06 an Italian translation of part of Abraham Berliner's *Geschichte der Juden in Rom* ("Storia degli Ebrei in Roma"; "History of the Jews of Rome") appeared in installments as an appendix. Contributors included: Moise Finzi (president of the Collegio Rabbinico Italiano and professor of statistics and political economy at the Istituto Tecnico of Florence), U. Cassuto, Elia Samuele Artom, Raffaele Ottolenghi, Samuele Colombo, G. Calò, G. Jaré, C. Castellani, Aldo Sorani, Edgardo Morpurgo, Giuseppe Levi, Israel Zoller and Aldo Cantone. The journal also attracted distinguished Jewish scholars from other countries. H.P. Chajes and I. Elbogen, who taught at the Collegio Rabbinico Italiano, contributed various studies.

[Tovia Preschel / Francesco Spagnolo (2nd ed.)]

RIVKES, MOSES BEN NAPHTALI HIRSCH (d. c. 1671/72), Lithuanian talmudist. It is not known when Rivkes went to Vilna, but he was one of those expelled from Vilna in 1655 (together with *Shabbetai b. Meir ha-Kohen, Ephraim Cohen, and Aaron Samuel *Koidonover) during the war between Poland and Russia. He reached the Prussian border but was prevented from proceeding further because of the Swedish army which was invading Russia. He then sailed for Amsterdam, where he was well received by the Sephardi community. Although most of the refugees were sent to Frankfurt, Rivkes, through the influence of Saul Levi *Morteira and Isaac *Aboab, remained in Amsterdam. He later returned to Vilna, where he died.

Rivkes' fame rests upon his *Be'er ha-Golah*. At the request of Ephraim *Bueno, "the distinguished doctor," and Jacob Castello, he corrected the edition of the Shulḥan Arukh printed in Amsterdam, adding to it the sources and clarifying the reasons for conflicting opinions. The work (first published in the Amsterdam (1661–66) edition of the Shulḥan Arukh) became an integral part of the Shulḥan Arukh, appearing in all editions. Rivkes also wrote additions to the Shulḥan Arukh and a commentary on the Mishnah, which were never published. In the sphere of Jew-gentile relations, Rivkes favored tolerance and mutual respect, condemning dishonesty toward non-Jews in commercial dealings and stressing the duty of Jews to respect Jews and gentiles alike, since Christians shared with Jews certain religious beliefs based upon the Bible. He was renowned for his personal piety and was called *he-Ḥasid* ("the pious"), an unusual appellation for that time. In his ethical testament he refers to his sons, Pethahiah, Joseph, and Judah, who died in his lifetime, and to his sister's son, David Lida, rabbi of Amsterdam. Rivkes was an ancestor of Elijah Gaon of Vilna, who was supported by a legacy established by him.

BIBLIOGRAPHY: S.J. Fuenn, *Kiryah Ne'emanah* (1912^5), 97–100; I. Klausner, *Toledot ha-Kehillah ha-Ivrit be-Vilna* (1938), 15; Ch. Tchernowitz, *Toledot ha-Posekim*, 3 (1947), 172–5; J. Katz, *Exclusiveness and Tolerance* (1961); *Yahadut Lita*, 1 (1959), 253, and index; 3 (1967), 71, and index.

[Itzhak Alfassi]

RIVKIN, BORUCH (pseudonym of **Boruch Abraham Weinrebe/Weinryb**; 1883–1945), Yiddish literary critic and essayist. Born in Jakobstadt, Courland (Jekabpils, Latvia), the son of a wagon driver, Rivkin became involved in the revolutionary activities of the *Bund, although he was more inclined toward philosophical anarchism. He suffered a year's imprisonment in 1904 and fled to Switzerland, where he was active in anarchist circles and published in Russian. Only after reaching London (1911) did he begin to write in Yiddish. A year later he settled in New York and was invited by the poet A. *Reisen to write for his newly-founded literary weekly *Dos Naye Land*. Rivkin became coeditor of its successor, *Di Literarishe Velt*, and also assisted A. *Liessin in editing *Tsukunft*. He was on the staff of the New York daily *Tog* (1917–19 and 1940–45). In the U.S., Rivkin was associated with Po'alei Zion. He suffered poverty and published only one booklet during his life. After his death, his second wife, Yiddish poet Mina Bordo-Rivkin, collected and published his essays in six volumes, which included: *A Gloybn far Umgloybike* ("A Religion for the Irreligious," 1947); *Yidishe Dikhter in Amerike* ("American Yiddish Poets," 1947); *Grunt-Tendentsn fun der Yidisher Literatur in Amerike* ("Main Trends in American Yiddish Literature," 1948); and *Undzere Prozaiker* ("Our Prose Writers," 1951). Rivkin is primarily a literary critic, who holds that religion and art are identical and that divine truth emanates from imaginative creation. Hence, Torah is art and Jewish holidays are theatrical embodiments of a drama of redemption. The Jewish man of letters can ennoble the Jewish people and direct its energies to messianic goals. Rivkin propagated the idea that Yiddish literature could serve as a spiritual territory for the Jewish people in the Diaspora. Messianism and spiritualism were two of Rivkin's main concerns. He was not a disciplined thinker but rather a passionate, dynamic critic who probed deeply into literary works, occasionally emerging with flashes of original insight.

BIBLIOGRAPHY: Rejzen, Leksikon, 4 (1929), 330–3; M. Bordo-Rivkin, *B. Rivkin: Lebn un Shafn* (1953), incl. bibl.; S.D. Singer, *Dikhter* *un Prozaiker* (1959), 291–4; A. Tabachnik, *Dikhter un Dikhtung* (1965), 455–73. **ADD. BIBLIOGRAPHY:** LNYL, 8 (1981), 448–51.

[Sol Liptzin / Eugene V. Orenstein (2nd ed.)]

RIVKIN, ELLIS (1918–), U.S. historian. Born in Baltimore, Maryland, Rivkin received a doctorate in history from Johns Hopkins University. He taught Jewish history at Gratz College before being appointed professor of Jewish history at the Hebrew Union College–Jewish Institute of Religion, Cincinnati, Ohio. He acquired renown as a perceptive analyst of the interrelationships between Jewish life and that of the surrounding culture as well as for his application of new methodologies to the problems of Jewish historiography. Best known among these approaches are his reconstruction of the problem of the Pharisees (e.g., "Defining the Pharisees: The Tannaitic Sources," in: HUCA, 40–41 (1969–70), 205–49) and his conception of the "unity principle," which he regards as the major constant in Jewish history. He feels that the Jewish people have confronted and comprehended cataclysmic changes and increasingly complex diversity through the ages without loss of their identity or ideals. After retiring from teaching, Rivkin was named professor emeritus of Jewish history at Hebrew Union College.

Rivkin's works include: *Leon da Modena and the Kol Sakhal* (1952); *Dynamics of Jewish History* (1970); *The Shaping of Jewish History: A Radical New Interpretation* (1971); *Hidden Revolution* (1978); and *What Crucified Jesus?* (1984).

ADD. BIBLIOGRAPHY: R. Seltzer (ed.), *Judaism: A People and Its History* (1989).

[Martin A. Cohen]

RIVKIND, ISAAC (1895–1968), librarian and scholar. Rivkind was born in Lodz, Poland, and studied at the yeshivot of Volozhin and Ponevezh. During World War I and after he helped organize the Mizrachi movement of Poland. In 1917 he founded the Ẓe'irei Mizrachi in Lodz and in 1919–20 was a member of the Jewish National Council of Poland. In 1920 he was a delegate to the London Zionist Conference and from there proceeded to the U.S. to work on behalf of Mizrachi. In 1923 he began to work in the library of the Jewish Theological Seminary of America, New York, eventually becoming chief of the Hebraica section. He was a co-founder of the U.S. branch of the Yiddish Scientific Institute (YIVO); on the executive of the Hebrew PEN Club of the U.S.A.; and a fellow of the American Academy for Jewish Research. During World War II and in the immediate postwar years he was the national chairman in the U.S. of the League for Religious Labor in Palestine.

Rivkind was the author of significant studies and essays in many fields, notably in Jewish bibliography, ethnography and folklore, Yiddish philology, and Zionism. He contributed to numerous periodicals and publications in Hebrew, Yiddish, and English, including *Kirjath Sepher, Reshumot*, and *Yidishe Shprakh*. He wrote the following works: *Le-Ot u-le-Zikkaron* ("For a Sign and a Reminder," 1942), a study on the history, development, and customs of bar mitzvah; *Der Kamf Kegn Azartshpilen bay Yidn* (1946), on the fight against gambling among Jews, with special reference to Old Yiddish poetry; and *Yidishe Gelt* ("Jewish Money," 1959), a Yiddish lexicological study on money in Jewish folkways, cultural history, and folklore. Other notable studies of his included *Ha-Naẓiv ve-Yiḥuso le-Ḥibbat Ẓiyyon* ("Rabbi Naphtali Ẓevi Yehuda Berlin and the Ḥibbat Zion Movement," 1919), *Elokei Bialik* ("The Religion of Bialik," in *Ein ha-Kor*, 1923), "Moses Provencal on Ball Playing" ("*Teshuvat*…," in *Tarbiz*, 4 (1932/33, 366–76), and "A Responsum of Leon of Modena on Uncovering the Head" (in *Sefer ha-Yovel… L. Ginzberg* (1946), 401–23). He assisted scores of scholars in their research.

BIBLIOGRAPHY: M. Kosover and A. Duker (eds.), *Minḥah le-Yiẓḥak* (1949), with bibl. of Rivkind's works; A. Zeitlin et al. in: *Hadoar*, 44 (1965), 351–8.

[Tovia Preschel]

RIVLIN, distinguished Jerusalem family. The Rivlin family claims descent from Moses *Rivkes (d. 1671), son of Naphtali Hirsch Sofer of the Prague Jewish community, son of Pethaḥiah Sofer of that community, son of the scholarly Joseph, and from Moses b. David *Kramer (d. 1688), who was *av bet din* and head of the yeshivah in Vilna. Elijah Ḥasid (d. 1710), son of Moses Kramer, married the daughter of Pethahiah, son of Moses Rivkes. The original family name, Riveles, derived according to the then prevalent custom from the feminine name Riva, or Rivka. Apparently the name Riveles (= Rivlin) was first used by Solomon Zalman, son of Ẓevi Hirsch, who was the rabbi and head of the community of *Shklov in Belorussia in the middle of the 18th century. He was a grandson of Elijah Ḥasid, son of Moses Kramer. Two of the sons of Solomon Zalman were Elijah and Benjamin Riveles, who were leading Jews in Shklov at the end of the 18th century and the beginning of the 19th. Benjamin was a second cousin and disciple of *Elijah b. Solomon Zalman, Gaon of Vilna, and his descendants formed the branches of the Rivlins who were *Perushim*, or *Mitnaggedim*, and observed the customs of Elijah, Gaon of Vilna. On the other hand, the sons of Elijah Riveles, also known as Elijah Platkes, were followers of *Shneur Zalman of Lyady, and they and their descendants were *Ḥabad Ḥasidim. The descendants of the brothers Elijah and Benjamin Riveles were among the leaders of Lithuanian and Belorussian Jewry, especially in the cities of Shklov, Mohilev and Vilna.

According to family tradition BENJAMIN RIVLIN (Riveles), founded an association called Ḥazon Zion, which had the aim of encouraging immigration to Ereẓ Israel. As a consequence, a group of the Gaon's disciples went to Ereẓ Israel, founded there the *kolel of the *Perushim* and renewed the Ashkenazi community in Jerusalem. Benjamin himself did not succeed in reaching the country, dying on the way in 1812. In addition to being a renowned Torah scholar, he also studied the natural sciences, particularly medicine and pharmacy, and traded in medicaments. Of his numerous works, only the small book *Gevi'i Gevi'a ha-Kesef* (Shklov, 1804) was published. His son HILLEL (1758–1838), born in Shklov, was active in the Ḥazon Zion association. In 1809 he immigrated to Ereẓ Israel at the head of a company of 70 people, among whom were disciples of the Vilna Gaon, and settled in Jerusalem. MOSES (1781–1846), son of Hillel, lived in Shklov, where he officiated as a *Maggid*. After his father immigrated to Ereẓ Israel, he headed the Ḥazon Zion association. He came to Ereẓ Israel himself in 1841 where he was appointed head of the Ashkenazi community in Jerusalem by the rabbis of Russia and Lithuania. Among his writings is *Beit Midrash*, published in Vilna in 1861 by his son ISAAC EISIK (?–1869). When Elijah Joseph Rivlin (1805–1865), grandson of Elijah Platkes, went to Jerusalem in 1847, the members of the Ḥabad branch of the family joined the family and Ḥabad Ḥasidim already in the country in such places as Jerusalem, Hebron, and Tiberias. Members of the family became heads of the *kolelim* and public institutions in Jerusalem and Hebron, such as *talmud torahs*, hospitals, and *gemilut ḥasadim* societies, and were among those who extended the limits of Jewish settlement in Jerusalem and other cities. Other members of the family traveled to Western Europe. There, too, branches of the family evolved, some of whose children moved to Jewish centers in America.

BIBLIOGRAPHY: H.H. Rivlin, *Ḥazon Ẓiyyon* (1947); M. Kasher, *Ha-Tekufah ha-Gedolah* (1969); A. Horowitz, *Mosad ha-Yesod* (1948); S.J. Fuenn, *Kiryah Ne'emanah* (1915); Frumkin-Rivlin, Toledot, 3 (1929), 175, 224, 227, 261; 263; S.Z. Rivlin, *Ha-Maggid Doresh Ẓiyyon* (1960).

[Benjamin Rivlin]

RIVLIN, ALICE (Mitchell; 1931–), U.S. economist and government official. Born in Philadelphia, Rivlin was raised in Bloomington, Ind., and educated at Bryn Mawr College (B.A. 1952) and Radcliffe College, Harvard University (M.A. 1955; Ph.D. 1958). She had a crowded resume, having served ably in many positions, including several professorships, and numerous leadership positions in various think tanks and in federal government offices.

Rivlin devoted her career to the analysis of public finance and social policy, and particularly to the federal budget. Based mainly at the Brookings Institution, a privately-funded centrist-liberal think tank, her government service began as a consultant to the House Education and Labor Committee in 1961. Rivlin was probably best known as the first director of the Congressional Budget Office (CBO), founded by Congress to provide it with economic information and analysis independent of the executive branch. There she established a tradition of nonpartisan analysis that later earned her criticism from the Reagan administration, but that enabled the CBO to withstand for many years pressures to become a political tool of a congressional majority. During the Clinton administration, as the director of the Office of Management and Budget, Rivlin concentrated largely, and successfully, on reducing the federal deficit. As vice chair of the board of governors at the Federal Reserve, she was involved in monetary policy, and encouraged greater use of electronic processing in the banking system.

Rivlin described her perspective as that of a "fanatical, card-carrying middle-of-the-roader." She articulated her ideas in many articles, mainly in professional journals but also in more popular publications; in the early 1970s she wrote a newspaper column for the *Washington Post*. Among her many books are: *The Role of the Federal Government in Financing Higher Education* (1961), *Microanalysis of Socioeconomic Systems: A Simulation Study* (1961, with Guy Orcutt et al.), *Measures of State and Local Fiscal Capacity and Tax Effort* (1962, with Selma J. Mushkin), *Systematic Thinking for Social Action* (1971), *Caring for the Disabled Elderly: Who Will Pay?* (1988, with Joshua M. Wiener), *Reviving the American Dream: The Economy, the States, and the Federal Government* (1992), and *Restoring Fiscal Sanity: How to Balance the Budget* (2004, with Isabel Sawhill).

[Drew Silver (2nd ed.)]

RIVLIN, ELIEZER (1889–1942), historian and journalist in Ereẓ Israel. Rivlin was born in Jerusalem into one of its old established families. He went into business and then became the secretary of the United Old Age Home in Jerusalem. As a young man, he became a correspondent for the New York Yiddish paper, *Morning Journal*, and also published studies on the history of Jewish settlement in Ereẓ Israel, Jerusalem in particular, and in neighboring countries. In this field, Rivlin's major achievement was his revised and enlarged edition of Aryeh Leib Frumkin's *Toledot Ḥakhmei Yerushalayim 1490–1870* ("History of Jerusalem Sages, 1490–1870," 3 vols., 1928–30), which he expanded into a history of all Jewish settlement in Ereẓ Israel.

Rivlin also published selections from the Pentateuch commentary by the 16th-century Jerusalem rabbi and physician Raphael Mordecai Malkhi, *Likkutim mi-Perush ha-Torah shel R.M. Malkhi* (2 parts, 1923–24); a biography of Joseph Sundel *Salant (Heb., 1927); a new edition of the 17th-century work on Jerusalem, *Ḥorvot Yerushalayim* (1928); and *Sefer ha-Yaḥas le-Mishpaḥat Rivlin u-Mishpaḥat ha-Gra mi-Vilna* (1935–40; "Genealogy of the Rivlin family and the family of Elijah of Vilna"). His collection of material on Ereẓ Israel in the responsa literature remained unpublished.

[Getzel Kressel]

RIVLIN, HARRY N. (1904–1991), U.S. educator. Born in New York, Rivlin was a schoolteacher before joining the department of education at the City College of New York. In 1939, he organized and headed the department of education at the newly-established Queens College. In 1957 he was appointed dean of teacher education for the newly-established City University of New York. In this post, he served as chief administrative officer of one of the largest teacher education programs in the country. As a coordinator for the Great Cities School Improvement Program, Rivlin studied the ways in which schools were dealing with the educationally and socially disadvantaged. When he was chairman of the Committee on Urban Teaching of the American Association of Colleges for Teacher Education, he was instrumental in setting up a national clearinghouse for research in urban education. He served as acting president of City College during 1961–62. One of America's foremost experts on the problems of education in urban ghettos, Rivlin was chiefly responsible for the plan for training teachers for schools in low socioeconomic areas, which was accepted by the New York City Board of Education in 1966.

He was one of the editors of the *Encyclopedia of Modern Education* (1943), and his published works include: *Educating for Adjustment* (1936); *Teaching Adolescents in Secondary Schools* (1948, 1961²) edited with Herman H. Remmers; *Growth and Learning* (1957); *New Teachers for New Immigrants* (1965); *Cultural Pluralism in Education* (with M. Stent and W. Hazard, 1973); *The Control of Urban Schools* (1974); *The College's Responsibility to Its Faculty* (1974); and *In Praise of Diversity* (with M. Gold and C. Grant, 1977).

BIBLIOGRAPHY: The City University of New York, Division of Teacher Education, *Teacher Education News and Notes*, 17 (March–April 1966).

[Ernest Schwarcz]

RIVLIN, JOSEPH JOEL (1889–1971), Israeli educator and scholar of Arabic language and literature. Born in *Jerusalem, Rivlin was the son of Reuven Rivlin, the last secretary of the general council of Keneset Yisrael. His mother, a sister of Avraham *Shapira, died when he was a week old. From 1910 to 1914, he taught at schools in Jerusalem. Rivlin was one of the main protagonists of spoken Hebrew, and he opposed the Hilfsverein and its domination of education in Ereẓ Israel. When the network of national schools was established, he became its secretary in Jerusalem.

At the beginning of World War I, Rivlin was compelled to leave Jerusalem and hide with his mother's relatives in Petaḥ Tikvah. In 1917 he volunteered to teach in Kefar Sava the children of those who had been expelled from Jaffa and Tel Aviv. He was taken prisoner there by the Turkish government and imprisoned in Jerusalem and then in *Damascus. Freed through the efforts of the engineer Gedaliah Wilbushewitz, who managed factories in Damascus for the Turkish army, Rivlin acted as his secretary until the end of the war. He remained there and taught in the Hebrew school for a time.

After the war, he took charge of the Damascus Hebrew girls' school established by the Zionist Organization. He was elected to the communal council of Damascus, together with Yehuda *Burla, who headed the boys' school; they represented the Zionist Organization in the city. In 1922 he returned to Ereẓ Israel, then went to study Arabic language and Islamic literature at the University of Frankfurt. On his return to Jerusalem in 1927, he was appointed to the Institute of Oriental Studies of the Hebrew University, and was eventually promoted to professor. In 1928 he was elected to the central organization of Ereẓ Israel Hebrew teachers and from 1930 to 1941 was its chairman. He was also a member of the Academy for the Hebrew Language. Rivlin participated actively in communal work, and was a founder and leader of many organizations, including the B'nai B'rith

At an early age, Rivlin began publishing stories, essays, criticisms, accounts of the settlement of Ereẓ Israel and its personalities, etc. He translated the *Koran and *A Thousand and One Nights* into Hebrew and wrote on the culture of the Kurdish Jews. He published many articles and various books on Jerusalem and its personalities.

[Benjamin Rivlin]

RIVLIN, SHELOMO ZALMAN (1886–1962), *ḥazzan*, composer, and rabbi, son of Yosef *Rivlin. Rivlin studied liturgical music with A.Z. Idelsohn. For 60 years, he was *ḥazzan* of the Shirat Israel Synagogue in Jerusalem, and founded and directed its school for *ḥazzanim* and Jewish music. He endeavored to produce a unified musical style based equally on the European and Oriental traditions, which he published in *Shirei Shelomo–ha-Shirah ha-Me'uḥedet* (1933). Rivlin's reputation as an outstanding teacher was spread by his students, many of whom became notable *ḥazzanim*. He also trained many of his pupils in homiletics and published the sermons he wrote for them to deliver in the Shirat Israel Synagogue in *Midrash Shelomo* (1953). His compositions and arrangements of traditional melodies were published in *Shirei Shelomo*, 3 vols. (1931–61). He also edited, together with J.C. Epstein, a Hebrew-English-Yiddish dictionary (1924).

BIBLIOGRAPHY: Tidhar, 4 (1950), 1743; E. Horowitz, in: *Yedi'ot ha-Makhon ha-Yisre'eli le-Musikah Datit*, 4 (1963/64), 354–60.

[David M.L. Olivestone]

RIVLIN, YOSEF YIẒḤAK (1837–1896), leader of the Jewish community in Jerusalem. Born in Jerusalem, Rivlin was a fourth-generation descendant of Hillel Rivlin (see *Rivlin family), the leader of the disciples of the Vilna Gaon who settled in Ereẓ Israel in the early 19th century. He entered public life at an early age, and from 1863 until his death was secretary – and, in fact, director – of Ha-Va'ad ha-Kelali Keneset Yisrael (General Committee of Keneset Yisrael), the central body of the Ashkenazi community in Jerusalem. As such he was instrumental in unifying the Ashkenazi community. Rivlin initiated the building of the first Jewish quarters in Jerusalem outside the Old City walls, e.g., Naḥalat Shiv'ah (1869), Me'ah She'arim (1874), and other housing centers in the west and northwest of the city. He took an active part in founding the first Jewish agricultural settlement, Petaḥ Tikvah. Rivlin's writings are mostly confined to publicistic commentary. His articles in Hebrew newspapers in Ereẓ Israel and abroad described Jewish life in the Holy Land. He argued with those who criticized the social and economic conditions of the old *yishuv* and especially the *Ḥalukkah* system, for he favored gradual reform, rather than major changes. Rivlin also wrote some poetry about the redemption of Israel and the upbuilding of Jerusalem. A selection of his articles and essays appeared in book form as *Megillat Yosef* (1966), edited with an introduction by N. Katzburg.

BIBLIOGRAPHY: P. Grajewski, *Ha-Rav Yosef Rivlin* (1926); Y. Rivlin, in: H.Z. Hirschberg (ed.), *Yad Yosef Yiẓḥak Rivlin* (1964).

[Nathaniel Katzburg]

RIZAIEH (until the 1930s called **Urmia**), town in N.W. Iran, on the Persian-Turkish frontier. There was a Jewish community in Urmia in early Islamic days; it first came to the fore in the 12th century with the appearance of the pseudo-messiah David *Alroy, who found many adherents in the town. Nothing more is heard of the community until 1828 when *David d'Beth Hillel visited it. In his *Travels* he mentions three synagogues in Urmia and gives a detailed account of the community's suffering as a result of a *blood libel. Further details are provided by Christian missionary sources. Letters published by I. Ben-Zvi and an account by Z. Shazar throw further light on the history of Jews in Urmia in the last century. As attested by a letter preserved in Chorny's *Sefer ha-Massa'ot* (1884; pp. 240–2), they had contacts with the Jews in the Caucasus. The community was severely affected by a famine in 1871. In 1902, about 350 Jewish families lived in 200 houses in Rizaieh, in four separate quarters with a synagogue in each. With the establishment of the State of Israel, most of the Jews in Rizaieh immigrated there and the rest left the town after the 1979 Islamic revolution.

BIBLIOGRAPHY: W.J. Fischel, in: *Sinai*, 5 (1939), 237ff.; idem, in: JSOS, 6 (1944), 195–226; A. Ben-Jacob, *Kehillot Yehudei Kurdistan* (1961), 22–25, 144; Z. Shazar, *Kokhevei Boker* (1961^{6}), 357–73; I. Ben-Zvi, *Meḥkarim u-Mekorot* (1966), index, s.v. *Urmi'ah*. **ADD. BILIOGRAPHY:** A. Netzer, "Jews of Urmia/Rezāiye," in: *Shofar* (Jan. 2001), 22 ff. (in Persian).

[Walter Joseph Fischel / Amnon Netzer (2nd ed.)]

RIZPAH (Heb. רִצְפָּה), daughter of Aiah and concubine of Saul. After Saul's death, Rizpah probably withdrew to the palace of her son *Ish-Bosheth (Ishbaal) at Mahanaim, where *Abner took possession of her (II Sam. 3:7). Abner was reprimanded for this by Ish-Bosheth, whose anger may be explained in light of the custom that the king's harem used to pass on to his successor (cf. II Sam. 16:21), and should have therefore passed on to Ish-Bosheth. Abner's action can also be seen against the background of the Near Eastern custom that the marriage of a former king's wife bestows legitimacy even on an aspirant to the throne who has no sufficient claim (cf. 16:21; I Kings 2:17–22). Abner's action was thus regarded as a step toward claiming the throne.

At a later period in David's reign, a three-year famine broke out which was thought to have been caused by Saul's guilt in slaying the Gibeonites. The Gibeonites demanded the blood of the guilty house of Saul, and David made expiation by handing over seven of Saul's sons, among them the two sons of Rizpah, Armoni and Mephibosheth, to be hanged (II Sam. 21:1–9). The Gibeonites hanged them in the first days of the barley harvest, and brought the bodies to Gibeon to be exposed. Rizpah displayed her devotion by keeping a constant vigil over the bodies to protect them from the birds of prey from the beginning of the barley harvest until the rain finally came (21:10). When David heard of Rizpah's fidelity, he brought her sons' bones to burial (21:13–14).

BIBLIOGRAPHY: Bright, Hist, 176; de Vaux, Anc Isr, 116; M. Tsevat, in: JJS, 9 (1958), 273–93.

ROBACK, ABRAHAM AARON (1890–1965), U.S. psychologist and Yiddish scholar. Born in Russia, Roback was taken to the U.S. as a child. He taught at several universities and was associated with the Massachusetts State Department of Education (1926–49). He served as chairman and professor of psychology at Emerson College (1949–1958). Roback's primary importance to psychology was as a historian and systematist. An early opponent of behaviorism, he believed in a broadly humanistic approach to psychology. He was the first to investigate the historical antecedents of American, as opposed to European, sources of psychology. He also stressed the Jewish contribution to the history of psychology. In addition, he devised tests for superior adult intelligence, scientific ingenuity, comprehension, and sense of humor. He wrote on personality and folklore and became interested in the study of linguistics, especially of Yiddish.

Roback was the first to introduce an academic course in Yiddish literature in the U.S., at the Massachusetts University Extension (1929) and organized the Yiddish collection (over 10,000 books) at Harvard University Library (1929). He was editor of *Der Keneder Odler* in Montreal (1908) and first editor of *Canadian Jewish Chronicle* (1914).

Roback's extensive research into the character and literary value of Yiddish also showed the cultural and spiritual impact which this language has made upon Western culture. He showed how Yiddish is permeated by the *folkgeist* of its Jewish speakers and *Weltanschauung* of the shtetl. Roback wrote the *Jewish Influence in Modern Thought* (1929) and *Psychology Through Yiddish Literature* (1931) in which he expressed his belief in the role of Jewish thought in the modern age. Roback was active in many communal and Jewish organizations.

Apart from Yiddish research, he was a prolific writer in his own field. He wrote many articles and over 20 books on psychology. Among the most important were: *The Psychology of Character* (1927, 1952^{4}); *Personality in Theory and Practice* (1949, 1957^{2}); *A History of American Psychology* (1952, 1964^{2}); *History of Psychology and Psychiatry* (1961, 1962^{2}); *Aspects of Applied Psychology and Crime* (1964).

BIBLIOGRAPHY: J. Berger, *The Destiny and Motivation of Dr. A.A. Roback* (1957).

[Menachem M. Brayer]

ROBACK, LEA (1903–2000), Canadian feminist, union organizer, communist, peace activist. Roback was known in the Jewish community but earned her fame among labor activists and feminists in Quebec Francophone society. Born in Montreal to Yiddish-speaking Polish parents, she was raised in Beauport, one of nine children. At home in French society, she went to the University of Grenoble for two years and then to the University of Berlin. Her association with the radical left began in Germany, where she witnessed the rise of Nazism and was herself beaten for her political activism. Returning to Montreal in 1932, she worked at the YWHA and then opened a Marxist bookstore. She became a labor organizer for the ILGWU and organized the Union of Electrical Workers. Given the anti-Marxist government of Duplessis, she continued her work underground when the bookstore was closed. Age did not diminish her enthusiasm or activism as she marched and spoke out for women's rights and against antisemitism, war, and the use of nuclear weapons. Even at age 92, she participated in the March of Bread and Roses. Friends and family set up an ongoing foundation in her honor that would raise money for education. Named to the Order of Quebec and honored by the YWCA and Temple Emanuel-Beth Sholom, Roback was listed as one of the 100 outstanding Quebecers of the 20th century in *L'Actualité*. She was the subject of a 1991 documentary film, *Des Lumières: Dans la grande noirceur*, by Sophie Bissonnette. Roback's papers are at the Jewish Public Library of Montreal. She never married but left a strong legacy that combined a fierce pride in being Jewish with a steadfast commitment to social justice, human rights, and peace. Her life stands as an example of Canadian multiculturalism at its best.

BIBLIOGRAPHY: A. Gottheil, *Les Juifs progressistes au Québec* (1988), 63–103; N. Joseph, "Jewish Women in Canada: An Evolving Role," in: R. Klein and F. Dimant (eds.), *From Immigration to Integration* (2001), 182–95; idem, "Jewish Women of Canada," in: H. Epstein (ed.), *Jewish Women 2000* (1999), 123–28.

[Norma Baumel Joseph (2nd ed.)]

ROBBINS, HAROLD (1916–1997), U.S. author. Born in New York City and listed as Francis Kane on his birth certificate but abandoned on the steps of a Roman Catholic orphanage, he was raised in a foster home by a Jewish family named Rubins. He dropped out of high school and worked in a succession of jobs, including inventory clerk in a grocery store. When he was 19, he borrowed $800 and started speculating on crop futures. He later said he was a millionaire by the time he turned 20 but lost it all gambling on the future price of sugar. In 1940, he got a job as a clerk in the New York warehouse of Universal Pictures and rose quickly. By 1942, he became executive director of budget and planning. He remained with Universal as an executive until 1957. He began writing at the age of 30. His first book, *Never Love a Stranger* (1948), drew on his own life as an orphan on the streets of New York and created controversy with its graphic sexuality. The book, later made into a film, was his first bestseller, and by his death he had sold more than 750 million books with more than 25 titles in 32 languages. *The Dream Merchants* (1949) was about Hollywood's film industry, from the first steps to the sound era. In it Robbins blended his own experiences, historical facts, melodrama, sex, and action into a fast-moving story. His 1952 novel, *A Stone for Danny Fisher*, about a sensitive boy growing to manhood while being victimized by circumstances, drew respect from some critics, unlike most of his other writings. The film version (1958) had the setting moved from Chicago to New Orleans; it was renamed *King Creole* and starred Elvis Presley. Among his best-known books was *The Carpetbaggers*, loosely based on the life of Howard Hughes. It took the reader from New York to California, from the aeronautical industry to the glamor of Hollywood. Robbins also wrote *Never Leave Me* (1953), *79 Park Avenue* (1955), *The Betsy* (1971) and *Dreams Die First* (1977). As his bankroll swelled, Robbins began living the sybaritic lifestyle of his characters, luxuriating on his yacht, maintaining villas on the French Riviera, Acapulco, and Beverly Hills, gambling at the world's casinos and marrying at least five times. Robbins said he had experienced all the vices he chronicled in his novels, many of which revolved around disguised versions of the rich and famous, including Aristotle Onassis, Porfirio Rubirosa and Lana Turner.

[Stewart Kampel (2nd ed.)]

ROBBINS (Rabinowitz), JEROME (1918–1998), U.S. dancer, choreographer, director, and producer considered by many the greatest American-born ballet choreographer and the best choreographer on Broadway. Moreover, his works embrace a wide range of styles and moods. Robbins was born in New York, studied ballet and modern dance, had violin and piano lessons, and was interested in marionettes. In 1940, he joined the Ballet Theatre (later the American Ballet Theater) and danced his first important role as Petrouchka in 1942. He subsequently proved an outstanding interpreter of comic and dramatic characters. His first choreographic work *Fancy Free* (1944), in a style based on contemporary movement, was an immediate success and was expanded into a musical, *On the Town*. Robbins choreographed *Interplay* (1945), *Facsimile* (1946), and other works for the Ballet Theatre. In 1948 he joined the New York City Ballet, where he was associate artistic director from 1949 to 1961, and created nine works for its company, including a reworking of Nijinsky's *Afternoon of a Faun* (1953) and *Concert Chopin* (1956). He later choreographed many works for the company, including Bach's *Goldberg Variations* (1971); Stravinsky's *Requiem Canticle*; and Philip Glass's *Glass Pieces* (1983). From 1944 onward, Robbins was also active in the Broadway theater, where his choreographic successes included *West Side Story*, in collaboration with composer Leonard *Bernstein (1957), which made him world famous. From 1958 to 1961, Robbins headed his own company, Ballets U.S.A., which played in Europe and America. In 1964, his direction of the musical *Fiddler on the Roof* was outstandingly successful. In 1952, Robbins assisted in the establishment of the *Inbal dance company in Israel. In 1966, he founded the American Theater Laboratory for the development of new forms in the musical theater.

Robbins was Chevalier de l'ordre des arts et lettres (France, 1964); was awarded an honorary doctorate from the City University of New York (1980); and received the Hans

Christian Andersen award (1988) and the Handel Medallion of the City of New York (1990).

BIBLIOGRAPHY: IED, vol. 5, 358b–368a; *International Dictionary of Ballet*, vol. 2, 1199–203.

[Marcia B. Siegel / Amnon Shiloah (2nd ed.)]

ROBERT (Levin), LUDWIG (1778–1832), German playwright. Born into a prosperous and "enlightened" Berlin family, Robert was the younger brother of Rahel *Varnhagen von Ense. Rejecting a business career to become a writer, he devoted himself mainly to the drama, and was the first Jew to have his plays performed on the German stage. Although he converted to Christianity, he was never allowed to forget his Jewish origin, and his lack of success was partly due to the prejudices of his contemporaries. Neither his adaptation of Molière's *Les Précieuses Ridicules* (staged in Berlin, 1804) nor his verse tragedy *Die Tochter Jephthas* (staged in Prague, 1813) aroused much enthusiasm. His staunch German patriotism during the Napoleonic era found expression in his verse collection, *Kaempfe der Zeit* (1817), whose technique influenced some of the poems of his young friend Heinrich *Heine. Robert's outstanding work, the tragedy *Die Macht der Verhaeltnisse* (1819), reflects the ambiguity of his position as a converted Jew. Based on the controversy between Achim von Arnim and Moritz Itzig that led to a duel in 1811, the play deals with class conflicts and the avenging of insults and was the forerunner of the great social dramas of Hebbel and Ibsen, but was not appreciated in its time. His correspondence with his sister Rahel Varnhagen appeared in 2001, edited by C. Vigliero.

BIBLIOGRAPHY: W. Haap, *Ludwig und Friederike Robert* (1895); S. Liptzin, *Germany's Stepchildren* (1948), 55–57; S. Kaznelson (ed.), *Juden im deutschen Kulturbereich* (1962^3), 16, 874. **ADD. BIBLIOGRAPHY:** L. Weissberg, "Das Drama eines preussischen Patrioten. Ludwig Roberts 'Jephthas Tochter,'" in: G. Biegel and M. Graetz (eds.), *Judentum zwischen Tradition und Moderne* (2002), 95–116.

[Sol Liptzin]

ROBERT OF READING (second half of 13th century), London Dominican friar, an excellent preacher, deeply skilled in Hebrew, who converted to Judaism, was circumcised, and, taking the name Haggai, married a Jewish woman. Summoned before the king and arguing boldly, he was handed to the archbishop of Canterbury for discipline. This entry for 1275 appears in the Worcester chronicle, derived with few additions from a lost Winchcombe chronicle. In his conversion Robert was not unique. Roth (see Bibliography) draws attention to Samuel Usque's reference in his *Consolaçam...* (Ferrara, 1553) to this episode.

BIBLIOGRAPHY: *Florence of Worcester: Chronicon ex chronicis* (ed. B. Thorpe), 2 (1849), 214; A. Gransden *Historical Writing in England c. 550–c. 1307* (1974), 421; C. Roth *History of the Jews in England* (1949^2) 273.

[Joe Hillaby (2nd ed.)]

ROBERTS, TONY (1939–), U.S. actor. Born in New York City, the son of a well-known radio announcer, Roberts studied acting at Northwestern University and then struck out for New York, working in commercials. He got a regular stint on the television soap opera *The Edge of Night* and then began a long-term friendship and professional relationship with the comedian-writer-director Woody *Allen when he was cast as Diane Keaton's husband in Allen's Broadway production *Play It Again, Sam* (1969). Roberts appeared in such Allen works as *Annie Hall* (1977), *Stardust Memories* (1980), *A Midsummer Night's Sex Comedy* (1982), and *Radio Days* (1987). In 1995 Roberts costarred on Broadway with Julie Andrews, playing a flamboyant homosexual cabaret entertainer in the musical version of Andrews' 1981 movie *Victor/Victoria*. He continued in film and on Broadway throughout the early years of the 21st century.

[Stewart Kampel (2nd ed.)]

ROBIN, RÉGINE (1939–), sociologist, essayist, and fiction writer. Robin was born in Paris, France, to working-class immigrants from Poland. Named Rivka Ajzersztejn, she was hidden with her mother in the Paris suburb of Belleville. Both survived the war, as did her father, a French soldier. But some 50 relatives in Poland were killed by the Nazis, as were others from France, following "la grande rafle" (roundup) of Parisian Jews on July 18, 1942. These events left an indelible imprint on the infant Rivka, and would become obsessions for the writer that Robin eventually became. Thus, at the end of her short-story collection, *L'Immense Fatigue des Pierres* (1995), she inserted photos of 50 empty picture-frames to represent her eradicated Polish family. In the same collection, her story "Gratok, langue de vie, langue de mort" depicts the little girl's hiding place and her French babysitter, Juliette, who fraternized with Nazis but never betrayed her. Robin grew up in a home where she imbibed radical ideas and a deep love for Yiddish. She completed a doctorate in history but switched to sociology. She was a university professor in France, then in Montréal after her father and mother died, respectively in 1975 and 1977. Her passion for Yiddish rekindled just as she began to divide her time between her new home and Paris. Nearly all of her writing, some 15 books, contains reflections on Yiddish language and culture. In 1984, she published *Pour l'amour du Yiddish: écriture juive et sentiment de la langue, 1830–1930*. In *Kafka* (1989), she discussed the fascination with Yiddish of the celebrated Czech writer. Her two novels, *Le Cheval Blanc de Lénine* (1979) and *La Québécoite* (1983), she labeled "autofiction," a combination of family history, imaginary elements and self-reflexive passages on writing. The much-discussed latter book treats imaginatively the narrator's complex search for identity between her Jewish roots, her French experiences and her efforts to integrate into Quebec society. This search resurfaces in *Cyberdémocraties: Traversées Fugitives* (2004). Among Robin's most important studies are *Berlin chantiers: Essai sur les passés fragiles* (2001; Prix littéraire de la Ville de Montréal) and *La Mémoire saturée* (2003). Both deal extensively with the Holocaust in German historiography and memorialization. She won the prestigious Governor-General's Award for

Le Réalisme socialiste: une esthétique impossible (1986). Robin is a fellow of the Royal Society of Canada.

BIBLIOGRAPHY: B.-Z. Shek, *"Pour l'amour du yiddish.* The Literary Itinerary of Régine Robin," in J. Sherman (ed.), *Yiddish After the Holocaust* (2004): 286–299.

[Ben-Zion Shek (2nd ed.)]

°ROBINSON, EDWARD (1794–1863), U.S. Orientalist. In 1830, he was appointed professor of theology at Andover, and later taught in Boston and at the New York Theological Seminary. His travels to Egypt and Palestine in 1837 and 1852 resulted in *Biblical Researches in Palestine* (3 vols., 1841); *Later Biblical Researches in Palestine* (1857); and *Physische Geographie des Heiligen Landes*, published posthumously in 1865 (*Physical Geography of the Holy Land*, 1865). Robinson's travels initiated a new period of biblical research. He went straight to the Arab inhabitants of Palestine, noting the names of places and ruins preserved by them, and was thus able to identify correctly hundreds of forgotten biblical locations. As his archaeological training was insufficient, he was unable to identify a site correctly if it lacked an Arabic name. By leaving the beaten track of the pilgrims and examining early traditions, he shed new light on biblical topography. He was also openly critical of the topographical studies of Jerusalem and discovered important remains of the Third Wall. He was greatly aided in his researches by his assistant Eli Smith, a local missionary who was thoroughly acquainted with Arabic. Robinson discovered five of the six ruined cities in the Negev, identified Masada and transformed knowledge of biblical Palestine.

BIBLIOGRAPHY: H.B. Smith and Hitchcock, *Life of E. Robinson* (1863); J.A. Bewer, in: JBL, 58 (1939), 355–63; F. Abel, *ibid.*, 365–72; A. Alt, *ibid.*, 373–7; W. Stinespring, *ibid.*, 379–87.

[Michael Avi-Yonah]

ROBINSON, EDWARD G. (Emanuel Goldenberg, 1893–1973), U.S. actor. Born in Bucharest, Romania, Robinson was taken to the U.S. in 1903. He made his first New York appearance in 1913 and came to prominence in the 1920s with the Theatre Guild, appearing on Broadway in such plays as *Samson and Delilah* (1921), *Peer Gynt* (1923), *The Adding Machine* (1923), *Androcles and the Lion* (1925), *The Firebrand* (1925), *The Brothers Karamazov* (1927), and *Kibitzer*, which he co-wrote with Jo Sterling (1929).

In his first starring film role, Robinson played a gangster in *The Racket* (1927), a portrayal that led to his being cast in the title role of *Little Caesar* (1931). His performance as a gang leader became a screen classic. He went on to play many such parts and was widely imitated. His film career continued through five decades. Among his more than 100 films are: *Kid Galahad* (1937), *Dr. Ehrlich's Magic Bullet* (1940), *The Sea Wolf* (1941), *Double Indemnity* (1944), *Our Vines Have Tender Grapes* (1945), *All My Sons* (1948), *Key Largo* (1948), *House of Strangers* (1949), *The Ten Commandments* (1956), *A Hole in the Head* (1959), *The Prize* (1963), *The Cincinnati Kid* (1965), and *Soylent Green* (1973).

Robinson returned to the stage on occasion, notably in *Darkness at Noon* (1951) and in Paddy Chayefsky's *Middle of the Night* (1956), for which he was nominated for a Tony Award.

In 1973 he was awarded, posthumously, an Honorary Academy Award, which is given for exceptional distinction in the making of motion pictures or for outstanding service to the Academy.

He was very active on behalf of various Jewish and Israeli causes. Robinson's autobiography, *All My Yesterdays*, was published in 1975.

BIBLIOGRAPHY: E.G. Robinson, Jr., *My Father My Son* (1958). **ADD. BIBLIOGRAPHY:** R. Beck, *The Edward G. Robinson Encyclopedia* (2001); A. Gansberg, *Little Caesar: A Biography of Edward G. Robinson* (1983); F. Hirsch, *Edward G. Robinson* (1975); J. Robinson, *Edward G. Robinson's World of Art* (1975); J Parish and A. Marill, *The Cinema of Edward G. Robinson* (1972).

[Frank Emblen and Stewart Kampel / Ruth Beloff (2nd ed.)]

ROBINSON, JACOB (1889–1977), jurist, diplomat, and historian. Born in Serijai (Lithuania – then Russia), Robinson graduated from the law school of the University of Warsaw (1914), served in the Russian army (from 1914), and was for a time in German captivity. He returned to what became independent Lithuania, entered into Jewish public life, and pioneered in the building of a Hebrew school system. For three years, he was director of the Hebrew Gymnasium in Verbalis. In 1922 he was admitted to the bar and in the same year was elected to the Lithuanian parliament, holding office as chairman of the Jewish faction and leader of the minorities bloc until its dissolution in 1926.

With the foundation of the Congress of Nationalities, he became (1925–31) one of the spokesmen for the Jewish cause at international gatherings. He was legal adviser to the Lithuanian Foreign Office (1931–33), and represented Lithuania in the Memel Case before the Permanent Court of International Justice at The Hague (1931), as well as the German-Lithuanian Conciliation Committee.

With the emergence of the Nazi threat to European Jewry, he organized a secret committee for the protection of Jewish rights and used his connections for admission of German Jews to Lithuania. He left Lithuania at the end of May 1940, and later reached New York, where, in 1941, he established the Institute of Jewish Affairs sponsored by the American and the World Jewish Congress. He headed the Institute for seven years, in the course of which he undertook a number of special assignments as special consultant for Jewish affairs to the U.S. chief of counsel, Robert H. Jackson, in the trial of the major war criminals in Nuremberg, and as consultant to the UN Secretariat in the establishment of the Human Rights Commission. When the Palestine question was submitted to the UN, he became legal adviser to the Jewish Agency and later legal adviser to the Israel mission to the UN (1948–57). In 1952, he was in charge of drafting Israel's Reparations Agreement with West Germany.

From 1957, he was adviser to the Conference on Jewish Material Claims Against Germany (subsequently the Memorial Foundation for Jewish Culture) and coordinator of research activities and publications on the Holocaust for *Yad Vashem and *Yivo. He was recognized as a leading authority in this field. Before and during the Eichmann trial, he was special consultant to the attorney general on problems of the history of the Holocaust and of international law.

Robinson was the author of numerous books and articles on international law and organization, and Jewish affairs. These include: *The Metamorphosis of the United Nations* (1958; a course given to the Hague Academy of International Law); *Guide to Jewish History under the Nazi Impact* (a bibliographical work with Philip Friedman, 1960); *And the Crooked Shall be Made Straight* (1965), which was a reply to Hannah *Arendt's *Eichmann in Jerusalem*; and *International Law and Organization* (1967). He also served as consultant editor and adviser to the Holocaust Department of the *Encyclopaedia Judaica*.

BIBLIOGRAPHY: *Académie de droit international, Recueil des Cours*, 94 (1958), 495–6; *Lithuanian Encyclopedia*, 25 (Boston, 1961), 372–3; *Yahadut Lita*, 3 (1967), 231.

[Maurice L. Perlzweig]

ROBINSON, NEHEMIAH (1898–1964), international lawyer. Born in Vištys, Lithuania, he studied law and political science at the University of Jena, Germany, and from 1927 practiced law in Kovno with his brother Jacob *Robinson. Soon after his arrival in New York (December 1940), he joined the Institute of Jewish Affairs and was appointed its director in 1947, in which post he continued until his death. He published a number of books and numerous articles on contemporary Jewish affairs, the United Nations, prosecution of war criminals, and indemnification of the victims of Nazi persecution. Robinson was International Law Adviser to the *World Jewish Congress. In the negotiations of the *Conference on Jewish Material Claims Against Germany with German authorities at The Hague, Robinson acted as chief adviser in formulating the agreement on indemnification, and later contributed to its legislative and judicial implementation. He also represented Jewish bodies in negotiating agreements on indemnification with the Austrian authorities.

Among his works are: *Indemnification, Reparations, Jewish Aspects* (1944); *Problems of European Reconstruction* (1945); *Ten Years of German Indemnification* (1964, includes biography and bibliography of his works on indemnification); *United Nations and the World Jewish Congress* (1956); *Genocide Convention* (1960); and *Universal Declaration of Human Rights* (1958).

BIBLIOGRAPHY: World Jewish Congress, *Dr. Nehemiah Robinson* (Eng. 1964); N. Goldmann in: *Ten Years of German Indemnification* (1964).

[Maurice L. Perlzweig]

ROBISON, SOPHIA (1888–1969), U.S. sociologist and criminologist. Born in New York, Sophia Robison was a professor at the New York School of Social Work from 1940 until her retirement in 1958. She did significant studies in the field of juvenile delinquency; her major publications in this field are *Can Delinquency Be Measured?* (1936) and *Juvenile Delinquency: Its Nature and Control* (1960). She also did pioneering work in the field of Jewish demography: her *Jewish Population Studies* (1943) present a thorough statistical analysis of a number of Jewish communities in the northeastern United States. Sophia Robison was a member of the Conference on Jewish Relations since its inception; she cooperated closely with the founder of the conference, Morris Raphael *Cohen.

[Werner J. Cahnman]

ROBLES, ANTONIO RODRIGUES (c. 1620–1690), Marrano merchant. Robles, who was born in Fundão, Portugal, of a family which had suffered at the hands of the Inquisition, settled in London as a merchant in the mid-17th century, but played no part in the crypto-Jewish community. When, however, his property was seized as that of an enemy alien after outbreak of war with Spain in 1656, he successfully obtained exemption on the grounds that although uncircumcised he was not a Spaniard but a Portuguese "of the Hebrew nation." The successful outcome of the "Robles Case" established the right of professing Jews to live in England without interference.

BIBLIOGRAPHY: Roth, England^3, 164f.; Wolf, in: JHSET, 1 (1893–94), 60–66, 77–86.

[Charles Reznikoff]

ROBSON, WILLIAM ALEXANDER (1895–1980), British political scientist. Born in London, Robson was the son of a pearl dealer and became the manager of one of Britain's first airports. There, he gave George Bernard Shaw his first ride in a plane in 1916, and, at Shaw's suggestion, went to the London School of Economics after he was demobilized from the Royal Air Force at the conclusion of World War I. Robson became a barrister in 1922 and lectured in administrative law at the London School of Economics from 1926 to 1947, when he was made professor of public administration. During World War II he held senior administrative positions in government service, becoming assistant secretary to the Air Ministry in 1943.

Robson's writings were principally concerned with the problem of modernizing English administrative law, the bureaucracy, and local government in the era of the welfare state. He strongly favored the coordination of the academic study of administration and government with the realities of practical politics and was founder and editor (from 1930 to 1975) of the *Political Quarterly*, which was designed to serve this purpose. He was also the author of over 25 books on public administration including *Justice and Administrative Law* (1951^3), *The Development of Local Government* (1954^3), *The Government and Misgovernment of London* (1948^2), *The Civil Service in Britain and France* (1956), and *Nationalized Industry and Public Ownership* (1962^2). From 1952 to 1955 he was president of the International Political Science Organization.

ADD. BIBLIOGRAPHY: ODNB online.

[Edwin Emanuel Gutmann]

ROCAMORA, ISAAC DE (1601–1684), Spanish Judaizer. Born into a Marrano family of Valencia, Rocamora became a Dominican friar, known as Vincente de Rocamora. His eloquence and reputation for piety led to his appointment as confessor to Princess Maria of Spain, subsequently the empress of Austria. In 1643, Rocamora disappeared from the Spanish peninsula. He made his way to Amsterdam and proclaimed himself a Jew, circumcising himself and adopting the name Isaac. In Amsterdam, Rocamora studied medicine and embarked on a successful career as a physician. He also played a significant role in the communal and cultural life of Amsterdam Jews. Designated an arbiter in the *Academia de los Sitibundos*, a literary society founded by Manuel de *Belmonte, Rocamora himself wrote Spanish and Latin verse. He provided administrative and medical services for Abi Yetomim, the community orphanage, and for the Maskil el Dal, the immigrant relief society. His son, SOLOMON, was also a physician in Amsterdam.

BIBLIOGRAPHY: C. Roth, *History of the Marranos* (1932), 246, 298, 337; Graetz, Gesch, 10 (1896), 179–80, 183; Graetz, Hist, 5 (1895), 109–10, 113; Kayserling, Bibl. 84; idem, *Sephardim* (Ger., 1859), 291–2.

ROCHBERG, GEORGE (1918–), U.S. composer. Born in Paterson, N.J., Rochberg studied composition with George *Szell, Leopold *Mannes, and Gian Carlo Menotti. In 1948 he joined the faculty of the Curtis Institute, where he remained until 1954. In 1960 he became chairman of the music department of the University of Pennsylvania and after resigning the chair in 1968, he remained at the university as professor of music. In 1979 he was named Annenberg Professor of the Humanities. In 1985 Rochberg was elected to the American Academy and Institute of Arts and Letters. His style evolved from Schoenbergian serialism of the 1950s to the blending of Modernist and Romantic elements in the 1980s and 1990s. Rochberg contributed many articles to professional periodicals; a collection of his writings, *The Aesthetics of Survival: A Composer's View of Twentieth Century Music*, was published in 1984. His compositions include symphonies, piano works, chamber music and songs.

BIBLIOGRAPHY: NG^2; J. Dixon, *George Rochberg: a Bio-Bibliographic Guide to his Life and Works* (1992).

[Yulia Kreinin (2nd ed.)]

ROCHELLE, LA, capital of the department of Charente-Maritime, W. France. The presence of Jews in La Rochelle is mentioned from the first half of the 13th century. The expulsion planned by *Alphonse of Poitiers in 1249 does not appear to have been carried out; in 1251 a Jew, Haquot, who had been banished for personal reasons, was recalled to La Rochelle from Bordeaux. The Jews were definitely expelled from La Rochelle in 1291. The medieval community occupied the Rue des Juifs, later known as Rue de l'Evêché. The apostate Nicholas *Donin, who instigated the campaign against the Talmud, originated from La Rochelle. It was here also that *Manasseh Ben Israel was born, his parents having stayed in the town after fleeing from Portugal. From the beginning of the 18th century, the Lameira family, originally from Portugal, lived in La Rochelle; it maintained connections with the Sephardi community of Bordeaux, whose *mohel* served La Rochelle. During World War II Jewish property was confiscated. The Jewish community in La Rochelle numbered approximately 200 in 1969.

BIBLIOGRAPHY: Gross, Gal Jud, 312f.; A. Barbot, *Histoire de La Rochelle*, 1 (1886), 107f.; L. Cardozo de Bethencourt, in: REJ, 20 (1890), 289ff.; Z. Szajkowski, *Analytical Franco-Jewish Gazetteer* (1966), 173.

[Bernhard Blumenkranz]

ROCHESTER, industrial city in New York State.

Early History

Established in 1812 as a mill town at the falls of the Genesee River in western New York, Rochester attracted its first Jewish residents some three decades later. The construction in the early 1820s of the Erie Canal, which crossed the Genesee at Rochester, opened a trade route west from the Hudson River and spurred migration to the area, including a number of Jewish merchants with packs on their backs. These young men, recently arrived from Germany, were located at first in the smaller canal towns of Brockport and Lockport, among others, but the booming settlement at the falls, which secured its first city charter in 1834, prompted several of these men to move there within the next decade.

Among four Jews listed in the city's 1844 directory was Meyer Greentree, generally regarded as Rochester's pioneer Jewish resident. Born in Bavaria in 1819, he had gone to Rochester as a peddler from New York in the early 1840s and soon married a local seamstress. They quickly combined their skills with those of three young newcomers, Joseph and Gabriel Wile and Hirsch Britenstool, in establishing Rochester's first ready-to-wear clothing firm.

As the number of Jewish residents increased, the need for religious services became more urgent, and twelve young men met in 1848 to organize Rochester's first congregation. The B'rith Kodesh Society eventually leased a former Baptist church, which it later purchased and remodeled as a temple. The number of Jews listed in the Rochester directories increased to 39 by 1850. Marcus Tuska became the first resident rabbi in 1851.

Increasing in numbers, the Jews of Rochester organized a Hebrew Benevolent Society which held its first public festival at Palmer's Hall in 1856. A half dozen of their most enterprising merchants had opened ready-to-wear men's clothing stores on the north side of Main Street bridge, a business that was rapidly becoming Rochester's second most important industry. A Hebrew, German and English Institute, also established in 1856, taught the increasing number of Jewish children until their parents decided, after the end of the Civil War, to rely on the public schools. A Harmony club, formed in 1868, assumed leadership in the social life of the Jewish community, which was now centered in the sixth ward on the city's northeast side. In 1865 the first Jewish alderman, Joseph Beir, was elected.

Modernizing tendencies at B'rith Kodesh prompted the withdrawal in the late 1860s of a conservative faction to form a second but short-lived synagogue. The original congregation brought Max Landsberg to Rochester as its rabbi. While Rabbi Landsberg progressively led his congregation, housed after 1876 in a new temple on the east side of town, into fuller conformity during the next decade with the Reform synagogues of Chicago and elsewhere, a group of newly arrived Polish Jews successfully established the more Orthodox Temple Beth Israel in 1879. A split in the old Harmony club produced the Phoenix club in the mid-seventies and the Eureka club a few years later, but while the German Jews who dominated these clubs hesitated to admit the newly arrived Polish and Russian Jews to membership, they quickly formed a committee in 1882 to raise funds for the relief of a new wave of destitute refugees from Eastern Europe. A move for the creation of the Western New York Jewish Orphan Asylum attracted its chief support at Rochester where it opened in 1885 on North St. Paul Street. Some of the sons of the first Jewish settlers joined two years later in establishing the Young Men's Jewish Association to assist newcomers in mastering the English language and adjusting to American ways.

East European Immigration

With the passage of years, as Beth Israel erected a new temple on Park Avenue on the city's more salubrious southeast side, where its members were moving, a new influx of Jews from Eastern Europe took their places in the old Jewish quarter and established several new Orthodox temples and institutions in that crowded district. The division between the several groups was aggravated after the turn of the century because of labor-management difficulties within the clothing industry. Many destitute newcomers, unable to find jobs except in the factories and sweatshops of their more fortunate predecessors, resented the proffered assistance of the United Jewish Charities and other German Jewish agencies and proceeded in 1908 to organize the Associated Hebrew Charities to maintain independent institutions of their own. The Jewish Sheltering Home they established gradually displaced the older Jewish Orphan Asylum and later, as the Jewish Children's Home, served the entire community until the growing demand for adoptions dispensed with the need for such shelters. A Jewish Home for the Aged, founded under Orthodox leadership in 1920, quickly expanded, and called the Jewish Home and Infirmary, maintains an enlarged and modern institution on St. Paul Street (1970). The rivalries among these and other Jewish welfare agencies were overcome and forgotten in 1924 with the establishment of the Rochester Council of Social Agencies, at which time the Community Chest assumed the fund-raising responsibility for all local welfare services.

Post-World War II

Jews of Rochester achieved a stronger unity in the mid-1940s as the struggle for the establishment of a Jewish homeland developed. All supported the State of Israel in 1948, and thereafter. Most Jewish residents were clustered in the southeastern city wards and in adjoining towns where they built many substantial homes and three new synagogues and schools in the sixties. In 1970, the Jewish population was 21,500 (3% of the total population).

Prominent Jews

Numerous Rochester Jews have played active roles in the broader community. In 1892 Max Brickner, a member of one of the city's leading clothing firms, which were nearly all controlled and staffed by Jews, was elected president of the Chamber of Commerce, the first of several Jews in Rochester and elsewhere in America to hold that position. Isaac L. Adler, a leader of the Good Government forces, became acting mayor of Rochester in 1930, and a decade later Samuel B. Dicker held that office for 16 years. Congressman Meyer Jacobstein and Louis Wiley (who left Rochester to become publisher of the New York Times) were Rochester Jews who attained national distinction. Rabbi Philip Bernstein, head of B'rith Kodesh from 1926, was prominent in national and international Jewish causes. He was deeply involved with the post-liberation care of survivors. Rabbi Abraham J. *Karp of Temple Beth-El was an American Jewish historian and bibliophile. Sol Linowitz was a native of Rochester and headed the Xerox Corporation before entering American diplomacy.

[Blake McKelvey]

The Rochester Jewish community of the new millennium continues to thrive. While stable in population – a demographic study sponsored by the Jewish Community Federation of Greater Rochester in 2000 records 22,850 Jewish residents – the community is characterized by a high degree of participation and affiliation in Jewish life.

The Federation, the modern center of Jewish philanthropy and community planning for the area, supports five beneficiary agencies in the Jewish community of Rochester: the Jewish Community Center, Jewish Family Service, the Jewish Home of Rochester, Hillel Community Day School, and Hillel of Rochester Area Colleges.

The JCC of the early 21st century is a modern facility in which a high percentage of Jews in the area hold membership, taking advantage of family programs, summer camps, senior activities, cultural arts, and athletic facilities. The old Jewish Home and Infirmary on St. Paul Street was a precursor to the Jewish Home of Rochester, a state-of-the-art nursing home with rehabilitation facilities, day treatment programs for seniors, and a separate complex for independent living.

There are a total of 12 synagogues in the Rochester area and a comparatively high number of residents (54%) belong to synagogues. This family-oriented community also has a high (20%) number of residents who are 65 or over. The Rochester Jewish community, which comprises about 3% of the Greater

Rochester area of over 1 million, is relatively affluent and gives generously to Jewish and other charitable causes.

The migration from city neighborhoods to Rochester's eastern suburb of Brighton that took place in the 1960s–1970s led to the significant presence of Jewish institutions and synagogues in that area. As of the year 2000, 48% of Jews lived in the community of Brighton, down from 55% in the late 1980s; Jews were dispersing to other eastern suburbs as well as communities in western Monroe county and areas of the city of Rochester.

The Rochester Federation, in addition to funding local Jewish agencies and social and humanitarian programs in Israel and around the world, houses the Center for Holocaust Awareness and Information (CHAI), which supports Holocaust education in the public schools. CHAI also sponsors educational workshops and events commemorating the Holocaust in the community. The Federation has a Jewish Education Services department that provides programming for families, teens, and Jewish adults; area synagogues also sponsor many programs in Jewish education. The Rochester Jewish community is heavily involved in Israel affairs and interfaith initiatives.

Professions among Jewish residents of Rochester are manifold. In addition to contributing to the high tech industries that have a foothold in Rochester (such as Xerox, Kodak, and Bausch & Lomb), Jews are counted among the faculty of several area colleges and universities. Jews in Rochester are well represented in the professions of medicine, law and finance, in addition to real estate.

A professorship at the University of Rochester was named after Rabbi Phillip Bernstein; William Scott Green was named the Phillip S. Bernstein Professor of Judaic Studies in 1991. Joel Seligman, a leading authority on securities law, took on the presidency of the University of Rochester in 2005. Dan Carp set Kodak onto the path of becoming a digital photography powerhouse as CEO of the company from 2000 to 2005.

[Margot Cohen (2nd ed.)]

BIBLIOGRAPHY: S. Rosenberg, *The Jewish Community in Rochester: 1843–1925* (1954); A. Wile, *The Jews of Rochester* (1912); A.J. Karp, *Jewish Experience in America* (1969), 316–34; B. McKelvey, in: ajhsp, 40 (1950/51), 57–73.

ROCHESTER, seaport in S.E. England. Jews are recorded here from 1187 onward and are mentioned as a group in 1231. At the entrance to the cathedral chapter house, there is a fine specimen of the conventional medieval statues representing Church and Synagogue, the latter as a dejected female bearing a broken staff and the Ten Commandments. In modern times, Rochester lost its primacy as a port to adjacent *Chatham. No organized Jewish community remains in Rochester today.

BIBLIOGRAPHY: J. Jacobs, *Jews of Angevin England* (1893), index; Rigg-Jenkinson, Exchequer, index; Edwards, in: JHSET, 18 (1958), 66f. **ADD. BIBLIOGRAPHY:** P. Skinner (ed.), *The Jews in Medieval Britain* (2003).

[Cecil Roth]

ROCHMAN, LEIB (1918–1978), Yiddish journalist and novelist. Born in Minsk Mazowiecki (Poland), he began his career writing for Warsaw's Yiddish daily, *Varshever Radio*. His diary of the perilous years 1943–44 was published in Paris as *Un in Dayn Blut Zolstu Lebn* ("And You Should Live in Your Blood," 1949). In 1950, he settled in Jerusalem, where he worked on the Yiddish broadcasts of Israel radio and as a correspondent for the New York daily, *Forverts*. His novel *Mit Blinde Trit Iber der Erd* ("With Blind Steps across the Earth," 1969) deals with the wanderings of Jews through Europe before reaching Israel.

BIBLIOGRAPHY: M. Ravitch, *Mayn Leksikon*, 3 (1958), 391f. **ADD. BIBLIOGRAPHY:** LNYL, 8 (1981), 374–76; Y. Rapoport, *Zoymen in Vint* (1961), 489–93; Y. Kahan, *Afn Tsesheydveg* (1971), 303–8; Y. Yanasovitch, *Penimer un Nemen*, 2 (1977), 296–303.

[Sol Liptzin]

ROCKEFELLER MUSEUM, name popularly given to the Palestine Archaeological Museum built in Jerusalem during the British Mandatory Administration from a gift of $1,000,000 by John D. Rockefeller, Jr., who also gave another $1,000,000 as an endowment fund. The building, designed by Austen St. B. Harrison, with stone plaques designed by Eric Gill around the central court, stands in about ten acres of land facing the northeast corner of the Old City walls. In addition to exhibition space, accommodation was provided for study galleries, record offices, a library, auditorium, photographic studio, workrooms, laboratories, storage rooms, and the offices of the Department of Antiquities. An ancient cemetery was discovered on the site, and a number of tombs were excavated, dating from the fifth century B.C.E. to the sixth century C.E. The museum was opened to the public in 1938.

During the Mandatory administration, the building and museum were administered by the Government Department of Antiquities. Before the termination of the mandate in 1948, the building was entrusted to an international board. In November 1966, however, the government of Jordan nationalized the museum and took possession of the building and its contents. After the Six-Day War (June 1967), the Israeli government entrusted the building and its contents to the Israel Department of Antiquities, which invited the Israel Museum to operate the exhibition galleries.

The exhibition is arranged chronologically, starting with the Stone Age, through the historical periods, to the year 1700 C.E. The exhibits include material from all the important excavations before 1948. Some of the highlights are the Galilee Skull, and prehistoric skeletons from the Mt. Carmel caves; the head of a statue in unbaked clay, painted and with inlaid shell eyes, from Jericho: a pottery mold for casting bronze implements and weapons from Sheḥem (Nablus); a decorated ewer with dedicatory inscriptions from a temple of Lachish; ivory carvings from Samaria and Megiddo; the *Lachish ostraca; Phoenician and Persian objects; Roman statues; Jewish ossuaries; and a representative collection of pottery and glass of all periods.

[Avraham Biran]

ROCKER, U.S. family in Cleveland. SAMUEL ROCKER (1864–1936), who was born in Goerlitz, Austria, emigrated to the United States in 1891. Five years later he founded the *Jewish Star*, a Yiddish newspaper, in Cleveland and in 1908 he founded the *Jewish Daily Press* (later *Jewish Daily World*, 1913), serving as editor and publisher of this first successful Yiddish newspaper in Cleveland. The *World*, published until 1943, became a spokesman for the East European Jews in the city. Samuel Rocker wrote *Divrei Ḥakhamim* ("Words of Our Sages," 1920), among other works.

His son, HENRY A. ROCKER (1883–1967), born in Hungary, practiced law with the firm Rocker, Zeller & Kleinman. He served as president of Park Synagogue congregation for more than 20 years beginning in 1929; president of the Jewish Welfare Federation of Cleveland; member of the board of directors, American Jewish Joint Distribution Committee from 1948 to his death; and member of the board of overseers of the Jewish Theological Seminary from 1951 to his death.

°**ROCKER, RUDOLF** (1873–1958), German-Christian anarchist, editor, writer, and translator. Rocker, who was born in Mainz, grew up in a Catholic orphanage, and became a disciple of Prince Peter Kropotkin, the Russian anarchist. In 1895 he went to Liverpool, where he founded and briefly edited the Yiddish monthly of social theory, *Germinal*. In 1898 he settled among the Jewish community of London's East End, and became both editor of the Yiddish anarchist newspaper *Der Arbeter Fraynd* and a leading figure in the Jewish anarchist movement. Rocker edited the paper until the outbreak of World War I, when he was interned as an enemy alien by the British. The paper was suppressed, and the anarchist club closed. After the war Rocker was deported to Germany. He was forced to flee when Hitler took power and subsequently went to the U.S. (1933).

Rocker translated works by Maxim Gorki, Jean Grave, Kropotkin, Friedrich Nietzsche, Fritz Lemmermayer, Johann Most, and Max Nordau into Yiddish for the benefit of his fellow anarchists. He also wrote a three-volume autobiography in Yiddish. A portion of this, dealing with his experiences in the Jewish anarchist movement, was translated into English and published as *The London Years* (1956).

BIBLIOGRAPHY: W.J. Fishman, *Jewish Radicals: From Czarist Stetl to London Ghetto* (1975); P. Wienand, *Der "geborene" Rebell…* (1981); H.M. Becker, in: *Schriften der Erich-Mühsam-Gesellschaft*, 7 (1995), 43–62; M. Graur, *An Anarchist "Rabbi"…* (1997).

ROCKET. The rocket mentioned in the Bible and in rabbinical literature is the garden rocket, *Eruca sativa*, a plant of the Cruciferae family which grows wild in Israel, but is also cultivated as a salad vegetable or for the extraction of a kind of mustard from its seeds. It is the *orot* ("herbs") mentioned in the Bible as the plant which one of Elisha's disciples went to gather during a year of famine; instead he found *pakku'ot* (colocynths) which were poisonous (II Kings 4:39). The Peshitta renders *orot* as *mallows, but the Targum explains that it refers to garden vegetables in general (cf. Kimḥi to Isa. 26:19). It seems R. Meir's identification of *orot* with *gargir*, the mishnaic (and also the Arabic) name for the garden rocket is correct, and Johanan explained that "they were so called because they enlighten the eyes" (*or*, "light"; Yoma 18b). This plant, particularly the species growing wild by the wayside, was considered to be a remedy for eye ailments, and R. Sheshet, who was blind, testified to its efficacy (Shab. 109a). Pliny too notes that eating rocket helps the sight (*Natural History* 20:125). Aphrodisiac qualities were also attributed to it (Yoma 18a–b). The plant is also mentioned by Josephus, who describes the shape of its leaves (Ant. 3:174).

BIBLIOGRAPHY: Loew, Flora, 1 (1926), 491–3; J. Feliks, *Olam ha-Ẓome'aḥ ha-Mikra'i* (1968^2), 190–1. **ADD. BIBLIOGRAPHY:** Feliks, Ha-Ẓome'aḥ, 44.

[Jehuda Feliks]

ROCKLAND COUNTY, New York State county on the Hudson River, 30 miles north of midtown New York City. Rockland County is 174 square miles in area. It has 35,670 acres of parkland and 60 lakes and ponds. The 2003 population projection was 292,989. There are five towns in Rockland: Clarkstown, Haverstraw, Ramapo, Orangetown, and Stony Point. The Jewish population of Rockland was estimated at 92,000. At 31% of the total population, the Jewish community has a major and significant presence in business, cultural, political, religious, and communal life.

Early Jewish settlers came in the late 1890s as peddlers and small retail shopkeepers. Congregation Sons of Israel was established in Nyack in 1891 and was the first synagogue in the county. Congregation Sons of Jacob in Haverstraw was established around the same time. During the 1930s and 1940s the Jewish population expanded as families who spent their summers in Rockland decided to relocate permanently to the suburbs. These people came predominantly from the five boroughs of New York City and Yonkers. A plurality came from the Bronx and kept moving north.

In December 1955, the Tappan Zee Bridge opened. Within the next 20 years, the general population increased from 90,000 people in 1950 to 229,903 in 1970 and approached 290,000 by the end of the 1990s. The Jewish population increased as well. Young families, many of them professionals, moved from the five boroughs of New York City northward to the suburbs. They came in search of affordable housing with large yards for their children, safety and security, and excellent schools.

This growth included Jews of all affiliations. The most significant growth occurred within the Orthodox Community, which expanded from a few hundred families in the early 1960s to over 5,000 families by 2005.

The Community Synagogue, under the leadership of Rabbi Dr. Moshe Tendler, firmly established the "Up the Hill" community of Monsey in the late 1950s. "Down the Hill Monsey" had also grown from its earlier roots in Spring Valley. Yeshiva of Spring Valley, Beth Jacobv of Spring Valley, Ashar, and

Bais Shraga provided private educational opportunities for the growing Orthodox community. By 1983 there were more than 3,000 Orthodox families in Spring Valley, Monsey and its northern neighborhoods. Twenty years later the Orthodox community had nearly tripled its size – from 15,000 people to close to 45,000, some of it attributable to a high birth rate and the rest to the attractiveness of the community for Orthodox Jews. Many new neighborhoods have developed with synagogues in walking distance to large neighborhood population centers. As one example, the Forshay neighborhood grew from 25 families and a single Orthodox synagogue in 1983 to close to 1,000 families and more than a dozen Orthodox houses of worship by 2005. The number of schools rose as well, since virtually all the Orthodox population attend yeshivot or Jewish day schools. In addition to the Modern Orthodox, Agudah, and Chabad Orthodox communities, several ḥasidic villages have been established. These include New Square and Kaiser (Vizhnitz).

The rise in the Orthodox population has created several political changes and challenges including the issue of density/down zoning and affordable housing, and the delicate situation in the East Ramapo school district, in which only 9,200 of the close to 25,000 students attend public schools.

Beyond Monsey's large Orthodox community, there are 14 established Conservative, Reform, and unaffiliated congregations. These exist primarily to the east of Route 45.

The trajectory of the Conservative Jewish population in Rockland reflects that in the country as a whole. During the 1950s, 1960s, and 1970s the movement was large and thriving, sustaining at least eight congregations. Today, there are five. New City Jewish Center, with 900 families, is the largest Conservative congregation in the county. Established in 1958, Rabbi Henry Sosland served the congregation for 43 years, becoming emeritus in 2005. Rabbi Craig Scheff who grew up in Rockland County leads Orangetown Jewish Center.

Reuben Gittelman Hebrew Day School was chartered in 1971 as the Solomon Schechter School of Rockland County. The school was housed in the Jewish Community Center of Spring Valley, a Conservative congregation that subsequently closed. In 1985, it moved to its present location on New Hempstead Road, where it was renamed. The school serves students in preschool through the eighth grade.

Camp Ramah in Nyack, is one of three day camps in the United States affiliated with the Jewish Theological Seminary, the Conservative movement's primary educational institution. The day camp serves children entering kindergarten through eighth grades from Rockland and surrounding counties.

The largest of the Reform congregations include Temple Beth Shalom, Temple Beth El, and Beth Torah Congregation. These synagogues have rich cultural, religious, educational, and social action programs for their congregants and the community at large. Several operate preschool programs in addition to their religious school programs.

The geographic makeup of the Rockland Jewish community has given rise to a new term called "this side, that side, or both sides of 45." Ninety percent of the Orthodox community resides on the west side of Route 45 and at least two-thirds of the non-Orthodox community lives east of Route 45.

At the geographic and philosophical center of the community are the Jewish Federation of Rockland County and its constellation of agencies – the JCC-Y and the Jewish Family Service. Established in 1984 the relatively young Jewish Federation – serves to support the UJC and Israel and overseas agencies nationally and internationally. Additionally the Federation has helped to establish and continues to support local communal agencies and programs. Beyond the JCC-Y and the Jewish Family Service, the Federation has focused locally to create and fund the Center for Jewish Education of Rockland, the Jewish Community Relations Council, and the *Jewish Reporter*, a monthly newspaper, which is distributed to over 15,000 households.

In late 2006, the Rockland Jewish Community Campus is scheduled to relocate to a larger facility in West Nyack. The 15-acre, 135,000-square-foot facility will house the JCC-Y, Jewish Family Service, Jewish Federation and its agencies and programs, Hadassah, and Huvpac.

The Jewish population is heavily represented in most professions in the county.

More than one-third of the physicians and dentists in the county are Jewish as are the attorneys and accountants. About 25% of the Jewish work force works within the county while the remainder of the professionals generally work either in New York City or in Northern New Jersey.

The Rockland Jewish Community prides itself on the concept of *unity* and has established several initiatives that address this subject. In the late 1990s almost 10,000 people participated in a "We Are One" Event at the Rockland Community College. The community comes together annually for a Yom ha-Shoah observance under the umbrella of the Rockland Holocaust Museum and Study Center. Rockland County proudly participates in the annual (June) New York Salute to Israel Parade with a consortium of more than a dozen synagogues and organizations.

By 2010 it is estimated that the Jewish population will surpass 100,000 people and represent 33% or more of the community. Rockland, a rural area before 1955, has now become a major Jewish population center with a large and extremely diverse Jewish population.

[Shimon Pepper (2nd ed.)]

RODAN, MENDI (1929–), Israeli conductor. Born in Romania, he studied the violin and conducting with Silvestri at the Bucharest Academy of Music (1945–7), then took a degree at the Arts Institute there (1947–9). He made his début when he conducted the Romanian Radio Orchestra in 1953. He immigrated to Israel in 1961. He has often conducted the Israel Philharmonic Orchestra and appeared in many countries abroad. From 1963 to 1972, Rodan was chief conductor of the Israeli Broadcasting Orchestra presenting new Israeli works. In 1965 he founded the Jerusalem Chamber Orchestra and, as its permanent conductor until 1969, toured with it in Europe, East Asia, Australia, South Africa, and the United States. In 1962 he began to teach at the Jerusalem Academy of Music and Dance, where he became pedagogic director (1973), and from 1984 to 1993 the head of the academy. From 1977 he took over the musical directorship of the Beersheba orchestra and served as chief conductor of the Belgian National Orchestra in Brussels (1983–89). Between 1993 and 1997, he was also co-conductor of the Israeli PO. Rodan was guest conductor of major orchestras, including Suisse-Romande Orchestra, Oslo Philharmonic, Vienna Symphony Orchestra, Brussels Radio Television Orchestra, Bergen Festival Orchestra, and Berlin Symphony Orchestra. He appeared with soloists such as *Rubinstein, *Barenboim, Rampal, *Perlman, and *du Prè and received the Musician of the Year award from the Israeli Ministry of Education and Culture (1997). He made a series of recordings with the Jerusalem Chamber Orchestra, including a collaboration with the harpsichordist Frank *Pelleg of music by Bach and his sons. In 2006 he won the Israel Prize.

BIBLIOGRAPHY: Grove Music Online.

[Israela Stein (2nd ed.)]

RODANIM (Heb. רוֹדָנִים; possibly Rhodians, inhabitants of the island of Rhodes), descendants of Javan (Gen. 10:4). In I Chronicles 1:7 and in the Samaritan, Syriac, and Septuagint versions of Genesis 10:4 they are called Rodanim, while in the Masoretic Text of Genesis 10:4 they are called Dodanim. It is likely that this is the result of an onomastic-ethnographic or epigraphic (between *r* and *d*) confusion. It is possible that the Rodanim should be equated with the Dananians (?) who are mentioned in the *El-Amarna letters (J.A. Knudtzon, *Die El-Amarna Tafeln*, 1 (1907), 151, lines 48–58, letter from Tyre) and in the Karatepe Inscriptions (see Donner and Roellig, in bibl.) or with *Yadnâna*, perhaps Cyprus (cf. *Elishah). However, the most plausible, although not entirely satisfactory, explanation remains that the Rodanim were inhabitants of Rhodes.

BIBLIOGRAPHY: H. Winckler, *Altorientalische Forschungen*, 2 (1900), 422; E. Dhorme, in: *Syria*, 13 (1932), 48; J.L. Myres, *Geographical History in Greek Lands* (1952), 308ff; R.O. Calaghan, in: *Orientalia*, 18 (1949), 193; W.F. Albright, in: *American Journal of Archeology*, 54 (1950), 170ff.; H. Donner and W. Roellig, *Kanaanaeische und aramaeische Inschriften*, 2 (1964), 39; U. Cassuto, *From Noah to Abraham* (1964), index.

[Pinhas Artzi]

RODA RODA, ALEXANDER (Sándor Friedrich Rosenfeld; 1872–1945), Austrian author and humorist. Born in Zdenci, Slavonia, he was the son of a Jewish landowner and of a non-Jewess. From 1892 Roda Roda was an officer in the Imperial Austrian army, but was dishonorably discharged 10 years later because of his unacceptable opinions. He then became a journalist and, as a roving foreign correspondent, traveled through Western Europe, serving on the Austrian front during World War I. He worked in the U.S.S.R. and other countries until 1933, when he severed his connection with the German-language press, and in 1939 emigrated to the U.S., where he remained until his death.

A prolific writer of comedies, satirical novels, and short stories, Roda Roda contributed to humorous magazines such as the *Simplizissimus* of Munich and was an outstanding exponent of the Viennese comic art. He excelled in lampooning the old Hapsburg *Kaiserreich* and is best remembered for *Der Feldherrnhuegel* (1910), a comedy about the Austrian officer caste written in collaboration with Carl *Roessler which was suppressed by government censors. His other works include *Der Schnaps, der Rauchtabak und die verfluchte Liebe* (1908), a best-selling novel; the autobiographical *Roda Rodas Roman* (1925, 1950²); *Die Panduren* (1935); and *Die rote Weste* (1945). He edited, in collaboration, a six-volume anthology of world humor (1910–11); and a collected edition of his works, in three volumes, appeared in 1932–34.

RODBELL, MARTIN (1925–1998), U.S. biochemist and Nobel laureate. Rodbell was born in Baltimore and received his B.A. at Johns Hopkins University (1949) after his studies were interrupted by Navy service in World War II, and his Ph.D. in biochemistry at the University of Washington, Seattle (1954). His first postdoctoral appointment was in the department of chemistry at the University of Illinois, Urbana. After research in Brussels and Leiden, Rodbell worked at the National Institutes of Health until 1985, apart from a period as professor at the University of Geneva (1981–83). In 1985 he was appointed scientific director of the National Institute of Environmental Health. His main research interest concerned transduction, the process by which cell membrane receptor binding by hormones and other stimuli is converted into an appropriate cell response. He received the Nobel Prize for medicine and physiology in 1994 (jointly with Alfred *Gilman) for delineating the contribution of guanine nucleotides (GTP) and magnesium ions to cell signaling. Rodbell had broad scientific and cultural interests, increased by his European connections.

[Michael Denman (2nd ed.)]

RODE (Rosenzweig), WALTHER (1876–1934), Austrian jurist. Born in Czernowitz (Chernovtsy), Rode was the son of Leon Rosenzweig, writer and deputy to the Austrian Reichsrat. He became a prominent criminal lawyer and was well known for his vehement attacks on the Austrian judiciary under the nom de plume Pamphilius.

In 1929 he published a collection of essays *Justiz*, and in 1931 *Knoepfe und Voegel*, a book of literary notes on crime, criminals, and penal courts. Rode worked as journalist in Geneva, and wrote *Frieden und Friedensleute* (1931), criticizing the League of Nations, and *Deutschland ist Caliban* (1934).

[Josef J. Lador-Lederer]

RODELL, FRED M. (1907–1980), U.S. legal scholar. Rodell, who was born in Philadelphia, served as a special legal adviser to Governor Gifford Pinchot of Pennsylvania until 1933. From then he taught at Yale Law School (professor, 1939–73) for 41 years. As a teacher, Rodell specialized in constitutional law, labor law, administrative law, federal taxation, and the legal profession.

Rodell is renowned for his cynical assessment of legal articles entitled "Goodbye to Law Reviews," published in 1936 in the *Virginia Law Review*. Not mincing words, he stated: "There are two things wrong with almost all legal writing. One is its style. The other is its content."

That article notwithstanding, Rodell was a prolific contributor to law reviews and general magazines. He also wrote *Fifty-Five Men: The Story of the Constitution* (1936); *Woe Unto You, Lawyers* (1939); and *Nine Men: A Political History of the Supreme Court, 1790–1955* (1955). Regarded as the "bad boy" of American legal academia, Rodell was noted for the ease and clarity of his writing, along with intemperate attacks on those with whom he disagreed. In his highly controversial *Nine Men*, Rodell developed as his central theme that the justices of the U.S. Supreme Court reach their decisions on the basis of essentially political considerations.

ADD. BIBLIOGRAPHY: K. Vinson, "Fred Rodell's Case against the Law," in: *Florida Law Review*, 24 (1996); L, Ghiglione, R. Newman, and M. Rodell (eds.), *Rodell Revisited: Selected Writings of Fred Rodell* (1994); "In Honor of Fred Rodell," in: *Yale Law Journal*, 84:1 (1974).

[Julius J. Marcke / Ruth Beloff (2nd ed.)]

RODENBERG (Levy), JULIUS (1831–1914), German author and editor. Born into a well-to-do family in Rodenberg, Hessen (a town that inspired his later change of name), he sought complete integration into German life. Rodenberg was educated at several German universities, and after spending a number of years in Paris, London, and Italy, settled in Berlin in 1862. In 1874, he founded the *Deutsche Rundschau* and succeeded in attracting to this literary monthly many distinguished writers. He wrote verse collections, novels, short stories, feuilletons and travel sketches.

A keen observer of city life, Rodenberg described Europe's great capitals in *Pariser Bilderbuch* (1856), *Alltagsleben in London* (1860), *Wiener Sommertage* (1875) and, above all, in the three volumes of *Bilder aus dem Berliner Leben* (1885–88). This last work reflects the early years he spent in Berlin, the disappearance of old landmarks, and Berlin's transformation into a noisy dynamic capital. His autobiographical works include *Erinnerungen aus der Jugendzeit* (2 vols., 1899–1901) and *Aus der Kindh* (1907). For his biblical drama, *Sulamit* (1899), based on the Song of Songs, Anton *Rubinstein wrote a musical setting. His correspondence with Conrad Ferdinand Meyer appeared in 1918, edited by A. Langmesser. His correspondence with Georg Brandes, edited by K. Bohnen, appeared in 1980.

BIBLIOGRAPHY: H. Spiero, *Julius Rodenberg* (Ger., 1921); H. Maync, *Julius Rodenberg* (Ger., 1925). **ADD. BIBLIOGRAPHY:** W. Haacke, *Julius Rodenberg und die Deutsche Rundschau* (1950); S. Neuhaus, "'Poesie der Sünde' – 'Triumph der Moral': Großbritannien in den Reiseberichten und Romanen des frühen Rodenberg," in: P. Alter and R. Muhs (eds.), *Exilanten und andere Deutsche in Fontanes London* (1996), 254–69; R. Berbig and J. Kitzbichler (eds.), *Die Rundschau-Debatte 1877. Paul Lindaus Zeitschrift "Nord und Süd" und Julius Rodenbergs "Deutsche Rundschau." Dokumentation* (1998); M. Günter, "'Dank und Dank: – ich wiederhole mich immer, nicht wahr?' Zum Briefwechsel zwischen Marie von Ebner-Eschenbach und Julius Rodenberg," in: R. Baasner, *Briefkultur im 19. Jahrhundert* (1999), 55–71; W. Hettche, "Nach alter Melodie, Die Gedichte von Julius Rodenberg, Wilhelm Jensen und Paul Heyse zum 70. Geburtstag Wilhelm Raabes," in: *Jahrbuch der Raabe-Gesellschaft* (1999), 144–56; P. Sprengel, "Zwischen Aesthetizismus und Volkstümlichkeit. Conrad Ferdinand Meyers Gedichte fuer Rodenbergs 'Deutsche Rundschau,'" in: M. Ritzer (ed.), *Conrad Ferdinand Meyer* (2001), 191–203.

[Sol Liptzin]

RODENSKY, SHEMUEL (1902–1989), Israeli actor. Born in Poland, Rodensky was an actor with Habimah and played a variety of roles, often Jewish folk types. After playing Tevya in *Fiddler on the Roof* in Israel, he did the same in West Germany to high praises. In 1984 he was awarded the Israel Prize for theater arts.

RODGERS, MARY, U.S. composer and author (1931–). Born in New York, the daughter of the composer Richard *Rodgers, she studied music at the Mannes College of Music in New York and at Wellesley College. She was married in 1951 and had three children before divorcing in 1957. Her 1959 stage musical, *Once Upon a Mattress*, was a huge hit in New York and helped launch the career of Carol Burnett, the comic actress. In 1961 Rodgers married a motion picture executive, Henry Guettel, and had two sons, one of whom, Adam, is a successful composer for the musical theater. Rodgers wrote for both the stage and the movies. Her children's book, *Freaky Friday*, was one of the most successful children's books from the 1950s through the beginning of the 21st century, and Rodgers wrote the screenplay for the film version, which was also a major success. Rodgers also wrote lyrics, music scores and playscripts. Her books for children frequently center on humorous and fantastic plots. Both *Freaky Friday* and *Billions for Boris*, a follow-up, involve adolescents and their relationships with adults. Often, the young people in her books assume more responsibility than the adults and the children have to cope with a parent's benign neglect. Rodgers also compiled the popular album *Free to Be You and Me*.

DOROTHY FEINER RODGERS (1909–1992), the wife of Richard Rodgers and the mother of Mary, came from an upper-middle-class Jewish background. A magazine writer and author of books on home decoration, Dorothy Rodgers had a background in the arts and conceived the permanent exhibition at the Jewish Museum in New York. She invented two basic household items. An avid seamstress, Rodgers sometimes sewed her husband's silk shirts. She found pattern stays made of tissue to be unsatisfactory. So she invented a pattern stay made of plastic that became a commercial success under the name Basic Try-On Dress Patterns. Her more famous invention was the Jonny Mop, a small mop to clean toilets with a disposable sponge at the "business end." Rodgers, considered the financial brains in the family, won a suit for patent infringement against

Johnson and Johnson, which tried to market a similar mop. Rodgers turned over the royalties to her daughters.

[Stewart Kampel (2nd ed.)]

RODGERS, RICHARD (1902–1979), U.S. composer. Born in New York, Rodgers studied at Columbia University and at the Institute of Musical Art. In collaboration with the lyricist Lorenz Hart, he wrote many musical comedies including: *The Girl Friend* (1926), *Babes in Arms* (1936), *The Boys from Syracuse* (1938), and *Pal Joey* (1940, revived 1957). When Hart died, Rodgers began his long-time partnership with Oscar *Hammerstein II, with whom he created, among others, the greatly successful musicals: *Oklahoma* (1943) which won a Pulitzer prize, *Carousel* (1945), *Annie Get Your Gun* (1946), *South Pacific* (1948), *The King and I* (1951), *The Flower Drum Song* (1958), and *The Sound of Music* (1959). The Rodgers and Hammerstein works established a style of music that proved highly influential and popular. Rodgers also composed *No Strings* (1962) and wrote the music for the television documentary for *Victory at Sea* (1952). Rodgers was one of the five recipients of the first award of the Kennedy Center Honors granted in December 1978.

BIBLIOGRAPHY: D. Taylor, *Some Enchanted Evenings: The Story of Rodgers and Hammerstein* (1953); D. Ewen, *Richard Rodgers* (Eng., 1957), incl. bibl.; Baker, Biog Dict (incl. supplement).

RODIN, ELISHA (1888–1946), Hebrew poet. Born in Mstislavl, Russia, Rodin became a bookkeeper. Between 1905 and 1907, he was active in the Jewish revolutionary movement in Lithuania and Poland. Excelling in Yiddish composition as a child, he published several collections of Yiddish poems in the Soviet Union in the early 1920s. His Hebrew poems and literary sketches began to appear in Ereẓ Israel in *Davar, Haaretz*, and *Gilyonot* (1929–38), which ultimately caused him to be imprisoned by the Soviet authorities. A book of poems and essays, *Bi-Fe'at Nekhar* ("In a Foreign Corner"), appeared in 1938 and expresses his devotion to the Hebrew language. The book includes "Prison Poems", a poem dedicated to Bialik (Rodin attributes his adoption of Hebrew in the late 1920s to Bialik's influence), and a poem on Elisha b. Avuyah. Rodin's son, to whom he was deeply attached, volunteered for the front in World War II and was killed in 1942. Poems to his son, written before and after his death, were collected in *La-Ben* ("To My Son"), and were published in Ereẓ Israel in 1942–43. After the war he worked briefly as a translator for the Jewish Anti-Fascist *Committee. In 1954 A.Y. *Kariv published all of Rodin's works (together with those of Ḥayyim *Lensky) in *He-Anaf ha-Gadu'a* ("The Severed Branch", 1954). Kariv prefaced the collection with a biographical sketch of Rodin, one of the last poets in the Soviet Union to write in Hebrew.

RODIN, JUDITH (1944–), U.S. psychologist, educator, and administrator. Born in Philadelphia, Rodin earned her bachelor's degree from the University of Pennsylvania in 1966 and her Ph.D. from Columbia University in 1970. She joined the faculty of New York University in 1970 as an assistant professor of psychology. In 1972 she began a 22-year career at Yale, becoming an associate professor in 1975. She was named full professor of psychology in 1979 and professor of medicine and psychiatry in 1985. She served as chair of the department of psychology and dean of the Graduate School of Arts and Sciences before becoming provost in 1992. Rodin's academic work concerns the relationship between psychological and biological processes in human health and behavior. The author of numerous articles for academic journals, she also published several books, including *Body Traps* (1992), which explores the role of physical appearance in women's psychological health.

In 1994 Rodin was appointed as the seventh president of the University of Pennsylvania, the first alumna to be named president. She also held faculty appointments as a professor of psychology in the School of Arts and Sciences and as a professor of medicine and psychiatry in the School of Medicine. As president, Rodin facilitated several international health initiatives, which included a collaboration with the government of Botswana to build a hospital, and projects in Saudi Arabia and India to address women's health issues. At the same time, she chaired an international research network studying health and behavior for the John D. and Catherine T. MacArthur Foundation. During her tenure, the University of Pennsylvania launched an extensive neighborhood revitalization program and established several interdisciplinary institutes as well as international educational programs and collaborations.

In 2005 Rodin was named president of the Rockefeller Foundation, where it was expected that she would guide extensive efforts to combat global disease and hunger through initiatives that promote economic development, education, and disease prevention. She previously served on President Bill Clinton's Committee of Advisors on Science and Technology, and she chaired the Council of Presidents of the Universities Research Association. She has served on the boards of Electronic Data Systems Corporation, the Brookings Institution, Catalyst, Air Products and Chemicals, and the Greater Philadelphia First Corporation. Rodin was elected to the American Academy of Arts and Sciences, the American Philosophical Society, and the Institute of Medicine of the National Academy of Sciences.

[Dorothy Bauhoff (2nd ed.)]

RODKER, JOHN (1894–1955), English writer and publisher. Rodker was born in Manchester to a recent immigrant who then moved to London's East End. In his youth, Rodker associated with other young Jewish intellectuals in London of similar background, including Isaac *Rosenberg, and, from 1922, became a professional writer. Rodker's poems appeared in *The Egoist, The New Age*, and other periodicals, and in a collection, *Poems* (1914), printed privately. Deeply influenced by the French poets of the late 18th and early 19th centuries, he translated much of their verse. He spent his later years in Paris as a publisher specializing in the avant-garde and then exporting these works to Britain. He became particularly interested in producing translations of works by Freud and his followers. The best known of many publishing houses with which he was associated was the Imago Press.

One of his novels, *Montagnes Russes*, was first published in a French translation in 1923, and his *Collected Poems 1912–1925* appeared in Paris in 1930. After World War I, he devoted himself largely to publishing and in 1920, at his Ovid Press, issued limited editions of poems by T.S. Eliot and Ezra Pound. Under the imprint of the Imago Press, he published the complete works of Sigmund Freud. Rodker's own writings include *The Future of Futurism* (1926). A new edition of his *Poems* and *Adolphe* (a novel he wrote in 1920), with an introduction by Andrew Crozier, was published in Manchester in 1996.

BIBLIOGRAPHY: *The Times*, London (Oct. 11, 1955).

[William D. Rubinstein (2nd ed.)]

RODKINSON, MICHAEL LEVI (Frumkin; 1845–1904), Hebrew writer and editor. Born in Dubrovno, Belorussia, his first books were tales of the Ḥasidim. After a short stay in St. Petersburg he moved to Koenigsberg, Germany, where he began publishing various Hebrew periodicals between 1876 and 1880, including *Ha-Kol* (1877–78), *Kol ha-Am* (in Yiddish), *Asefat Ḥakhamim* (1877–78), and *Ha-Me'assef.* He was a careless editor, but his collaborators, who included E.W. Rabinowitz and M. Vinchevsky, obtained contributions from such Haskalah Hebrew writers as Lilienblum, Kaminer, J.L. Gordon, and others. In 1879 *Ha-Kol* was banned in Russia and soon ceased publication. In the early 1880s Rodkinson published several books advocating religious reforms as a means of solving the "Jewish question." In 1889 he emigrated to the United States, where he attempted to revive his periodicals (*Ha-Kol* (1889) and *Ha-Sanegor* (1890)). In his later years he devoted himself to translating the Talmud into English. The value of this translation, printed in two editions, lies only in the fact that it is a pioneering effort. He was the brother of Israel Dov *Frumkin.

BIBLIOGRAPHY: M. Vinchevsky, in: *Ha-Toren*, 10 (Dec. 1923), 55–61; Rejzen, Leksikon, 4 (1929), 70–77; S.L. Zitron, in: *Haolam*, 15 (1927), index; I. Davidson, *Parody in Jewish Literature* (1907), index; Kressel, Leksikon, 2 (1967), 838–9.

[Yehuda Slutsky]

RODNEY, RED (Robert Chudnick; 1927–1994), U.S. jazz trumpeter. Rodney received his first trumpet as a bar mitzvah gift from an aunt and uncle. He became one of the premier bebop trumpeters, playing alongside Charlie Parker and other giants of the music, but he also was a heroin addict who spent seven years in prison and rehab centers.

The Philadelphia-born Rodney got his first musical training at Mastbaum High, where his classmates included John Coltrane and Buddy DeFranco. Rodney quickly mastered his instrument and was playing professionally with Jimmy Dorsey at age 15. He would be a featured trumpeter with many other dance bands of the 1940s, culminating in a stint with Woody Herman's bop-influenced Second Herd. Then Parker invited him to join his quintet in 1949. It was perhaps the most highly visible trumpet gig in jazz and, although the compulsively modest Rodney tried to turn Parker down, Bird insisted. When the band played the segregated South, Bird passed off the red-haired, freckle-faced Rodney as a "blues singer" named "Albino Red." Although Parker repeatedly warned his young trumpeter not to follow his lead into heroin, Rodney became a drug addict. Rodney supported his habit with steady musical work for a while before turning to non-violent crimes. When he kicked the drug, he enjoyed considerable financial success leading society bands out of Las Vegas, but the pleasure of banking regular checks was outweighed by the boredom of the musical drivel he was forced to play. In the late 1970s he reteamed with longtime collaborator Ira Sullivan, and the two were responsible for several brilliant albums of post-bop jazz in the 1980s.

BIBLIOGRAPHY: "Red Rodney," MusicWeb Encyclopaedia of Popular Music, at www.musicweb.uk.net; G. Robinson, "Red Rodney Hits the High Note," in: *Manhattan Jewish Sentinel* (July 7, 1993); P. Watrous, "Red Rodney, Jazz Trumpeter and Band Leader, Dies at 66," in: *New York Times* (May 28, 1994).

[George Robinson (2nd ed.)]

ROD OF AARON, Aaron's staff with which he used to perform signs before Pharaoh in order to convince him that he and Moses were sent by the Lord, the God of the Israelites (Ex. 7:8ff., 19–20; 8:1, 12). On another occasion, God caused a rod inscribed with Aaron's name to blossom and bear almonds in order to demonstrate his choice of Aaron for the priesthood and to quell the mutterings of the Israelites against God in the wilderness (Num 17:16–26).

[Shlomo Balter]

In the Aggadah

The Bible ascribes similar miraculous powers to the rods of Aaron and of Moses. One rabbinic opinion even regards the two as identical (Yal., Num. 763, Ps. 869). This staff bore the Ineffable Name (Num. R. 18:23).

The rod, with its blossoms and fruit, was created in the twilight between the sixth day and the Sabbath of creation (Pes. 54a). It was previously used by Jacob when crossing the Jordan, and it was also the staff which Judah gave to Tamar (Yal., loc. cit.).

Because it bore the Ineffable Name it blossomed overnight and yielded ripe almonds thus validating Aaron's claim to the priesthood (Num. R. 18:23). The almond, which is the first tree to blossom, indicated that God would quickly punish those who venture to usurp the priesthood (*ibid.*, Tanh. Aḥarei 8). This rod, which never lost its blossoms or almonds, was utilized by the kings of Judah until the destruction of the Temple when it disappeared. In the future, Elijah will reveal it and hand it over to the Messiah (Num. R. 18:23).

BIBLIOGRAPHY: Ginzberg, Legends, 7 (1938), 3.

ROD OF MOSES, Moses' wonder-working rod. When he drove Jethro's flock into the wilderness of Horeb (Ex. 3:1), the

Lord appeared to Moses and ordered him to cast his staff to the ground, and it became a serpent; then he was ordered to seize the serpent by the tail, and it became a rod again (4:1–5). Moses subsequently repeated this and other signs before the Israelites and then before Pharaoh to convince them that he was sent by the Lord. He manipulated the staff in the performance of various miracles in Egypt (Ex. 7:14ff.; 10:13), as well as the splitting of the Sea of Reeds (Red Sea; 14:16), and the producing of water from a rock in the wilderness (Num. 20:9ff.).

[Shlomo Balter]

In the Aggadah

The rod used by Moses in performing his miracles was created during the twilight of the eve of the first Sabbath of creation (Avot 5:6) from a branch of the tree of knowledge in the Garden of Eden (ARN, ed. Schechter, 157). On it were engraved the letters of the Ineffable Name (PdRK 19:140a, PdRK 42), the ten plagues inflicted upon the Egyptians, and the patriarchs, matriarchs, and twelve tribes (Targum to Ex. 14:21). The people originally thought that the staff could engender only destruction, since through its agency Moses had brought the plagues upon the Egyptians in Egypt and the Red Sea. When, however, Moses used it to smite the rock at Horeb, they learned that the rod could also produce the blessings of water (Ex. R. 26:2). With the rod, Moses smote and killed Sihon and Og (Deut. R. 11:10). He was also able to chastise the Angel of Death with it when the Angel came to take him (Deut. R. *ibid.*). In the next world, Moses was rewarded with the scepter which God had employed in the creation of the world. The rod which Moses used in this world was shaped and engraved in the image of this scepter (*Midrash Petirat Moshe*, in: A. Jellinek, *Beit ha-Midrash*, 1 (1938^2), 121).

One opinion identifies the Rod of Moses with the Rod of *Aaron (Yal., Num. 763, Ps. 869).

BIBLIOGRAPHY: Ginzberg, Legends, 7 (1938), 328, index s.v. *Moses, Rod of.*

RODRIGUES, BARTHOLOMEW (Jacob de Sequeira; d. 1692), Anglo-Indian merchant, son of the well-known merchant, Gomez Rodrigues (d. 1678). Bartholomew Rodrigues left London in 1683 for Fort St. George (Madras), the center of the diamond trade. Though originally an "interloper," he was admitted as freeman of the East India Company in 1684. His widespread commercial transactions in diamonds, precious stones, amber, and coral, and the extent of his trade with Manila, Pegu (Burma), Bengal, and China are documented in the records of the Madras Company up to 1692. As the representative of the "Hebrew merchant colony" in Madras, he served as alderman of the Madras Corporation in 1688. On his death, he was buried in the garden of his house in Mint Street, Madras. His brother Alphonso Rodrigues (d. 1716) was also a notable East India merchant and diamond importer in London.

BIBLIOGRAPHY: H.D. Love, *Vestiges of Old Madras*, 4 vols. (1913); W.J. Fischel, in: *Journal of the Economic and Social History of the Orient*, 3 (1960), 78–107, 175–95. **ADD. BIBLIOGRAPHY:** ODNB online for Alphonso Rodrigues; E. Samuel, "Diamonds and Pieces of Eight: How Stuart England Won the Rough Diamond Trade," in: idem, *At the Ends of the Earth: Essays on the History of the Jews in England and Portugal* (2004), 241–57.

[Walter Joseph Fischel]

RODRIGUES, DIONISIUS (Diniz; d. 1541), Marrano physician to the kings Emanuel and John III of Portugal. In 1518 he engaged in a once-famous controversy with the French physician Pierre Brissot on the rival systems of bloodletting of Galen and Hippocrates. Threatened as a Judaizer by the Inquisition (which subsequently burned him in effigy), he fled first to London where he was a member of the crypto-Jewish community under Henry VIII, then to Antwerp, and finally to Ferrara, where he died. He was the father of the eminent medical writer Manuel *Brudo.

BIBLIOGRAPHY: H. Friedenwald, in: *Bulletin of the History of Medicine*, 7 (1939), 460–7 (= idem, *Jews and Medicine*, 2 (1944), 460–7); L. Wolf, *Essays in Jewish History* (1934), 78.

[Cecil Roth]

RODZINSKY, ARTUR (1892–1958), conductor. Born in Split, Dalmatia (Yugoslavia), Rodzinsky first conducted the Warsaw Philharmonic and Opera Orchestra, and settled in the United States in 1925. In that year he became assistant conductor to Leopold Stokowski of the Philadelphia Orchestra, and in 1937 he organized the NBC Symphony Orchestra for Toscanini. He was appointed permanent conductor of the New York Philharmonic in 1943 but resigned in 1947. He conducted the Chicago Symphony Orchestra for a year, and after 1948 lived in Rome and toured in Europe and South America.

ROEDELHEIM, former town near Frankfurt on the Main. In 1290 Roedelheim received permission from Rudolf *II to accept six Jews, and in 1371 there is evidence of a Jewish settlement there. From that time until the middle of the 17th century, there is no record of the presence of Jews in the town. Before the end of the 17th century, however, services were conducted in a prayer room. In 1711 refugees from the conflagration at the *Frankfurt ghetto joined the Jews of Roedelheim, and in 1730 a synagogue was built; the community maintained a cemetery and an inn as well. About 1750 the Hebrew printer Karl Reich transferred his press from *Homburg to Roedelheim. In 1799 Wolf *Heidenheim established what was called an "Oriental and Occidental printing house," where he published, among other things, classical editions of liturgical texts. After his death in 1832, his partner Lehrberger printed S. *Baer's famous *Siddur, Avodat Yisrael* (1868) and other liturgical works. The clear Roedelheim texts were still being reproduced more than a hundred years later. In the years 1837–38, a new synagogue was erected in the town. About 400 Jews, mainly livestock merchants, lived there and constituted 33% of the total population. The community subsequently declined to 236 in 1880 (6% of the population) and to 100 in 1932, being later absorbed by the Frankfurt community.

BIBLIOGRAPHY: G. Faust, *Sozial-und wirtschaftliche Beitraege zur Judenfrage… in der ehemaligen Grafschaft Solms-Roedelheim* (1937); *Germania Judaica*, 2 (1968), 702; PK Germanyah. **PRINTING:** M. Steinschneider, *Juedische Typographie* (1938²), 61; A. Freimann, in: ZHB, 21 (1918), 18; L. Lewin, in: MGWJ, 44 (1900), 127ff.; 45 (1901), 422ff., 549ff; 53 (1909), 360ff.

°**ROEDERER, COUNT PIERRE LOUIS** (1754–1835), French politician and economist, born in Metz. When a member of the Constituent Assembly, Roederer sided with *Clermont-Tonnerre, Robespierre, and others in support of the Jewish claim for political equality (1789–91). He had become familiar with Jewish matters when, as a councilor in the parliament of Metz, he organized the contest sponsored by the Société Royale des Sciences et Arts of Metz, on the theme: "Are there means of rendering the Jews more useful and happier in France?" Roederer expressed his own views on the subject in a private memorandum written for the participants in the contest. "In calling an ancient and considerable people to the service of our society," he wrote, "we cannot flatter ourselves that we are calling it to virtues which are superior to their own." Nevertheless, he advised the participants to consider the "moral causes" of the negative social and political characteristics of the Jews, in order to correct them.

BIBLIOGRAPHY: *Nouvelle Biographie* Générale, 42 (1863), 492–5; A. Cahen, in: REJ, 1 (1880), 82–96; R. Mahler, *Divrei Yemei Yisrael, Dorot Aḥaronim*, (1952), index; A. Hertzberg, *The French Enlightenment and the Jews* (1968), 332–3; L. Berman, *Histoire des Juifs de France* (1937), 338–43.

[Emmanuel Beeri]

°**ROEHRICHT, REINHOLD** (1842–1905), German scholar, teacher, and researcher into the history of the Crusades. His publications include: *Deutsche Pilgerreisen nach dem heiligen Lande* (1880); *Bibliotheca Geographica Palaestinae* (1890), a standard bibliography of travelers' literature and cartographical sources; *Regesta Regni Hierosolymitani* (1893–1904; *Geschichte des Koenigreichs Jerusalem*, 1898), described on the basis of original documents.

[Michael Avi-Yonah]

ROESSLER, CARL (pseudonym of **Franz Ressner**; 1864–1948), Austrian playwright, author, and actor. Roessler was born in Vienna and joined the Elf Scharfrichter group, which created the "Ueberbrettl" satirical theater, of which the dramatist Frank Wedekind was also a member. For a short while he was a free-lance writer in Munich. Roessler wrote a number of successful plays but is mainly remembered for his comedy, *Die fuenf Frankfurter* (1912), set in the Frankfurt Judengasse. Roessler also wrote two novels, *Die drei Niemandskinder* (1926) and *Wellen des Eros* (1928). After the Austrian *Anschluss* in 1938, Roessler settled in London.

BIBLIOGRAPHY: J. Bab, *Theater der Gegenwart* (1928), 116. **ADD. BIBLIOGRAPHY:** P.-P. Schneider, "'Beinahe eine Inventaraufnahme.' Die Briefe Heinrich Manns an Carl Roessler 1939–1946," in: *Literaturmagazin*, 21 (1988) 39–55.

[Samuel L. Sumberg]

ROEST, MEIJER MARCUS (1821–1889), Amsterdam bibliographer and journalist. Having been trained as a religious teacher in the Haskalah-oriented Nederlandsch Israëlietisch Seminarium in Amsterdam, Roest became one of the first in the Netherlands to embrace the *Wissenschaft des Judentums*. From his early thirties he contributed numerous articles to Dutch and Jewish periodicals. From 1855 till 1870 he was employed by the auctioneer Frederik Muller, for whom he compiled catalogues of, inter alia, the Joseph Almanzi and Jacob Emden libraries (*Beth ha-Sefer*, 1868) and edited the Dutch journal *De Navorscher*. His magnum opus *Catalog der Hebraica und Judaica aus der L. Rosenthal'schen Bibliothek*, whose model of description closely resembled that of Joseph Zedner, was published in 1875. After the collection was presented to the Amsterdam municipality and incorporated in the university library, Roest became its first custodian, a position he continued to fill until his death.

In reaction to current Reformist tendencies, Roest founded (together with the seminary's rector and later chief rabbi J.H. *Dünner) the *Nieuw Israëlietisch Weekblad* (1865) and *Israëlietische Nieuwsbode* (1875), through which they hoped to promote a moderately conservative Judaism, supported by *Wissenschaft des Judentums*. In addition to these weeklies, Roest founded and edited the quarterly *De Israëlietische Letterbode* (1875–86), which served as a platform for international, historical as well as bibliographical, scholarship.

BIBLIOGRAPHY: J.M. Hillesum, "Voornaamste letterkundige producten van wijlen M. Roest Mizrachi," in: *Israëlietische Nieuwsbode*, 32, 34 (1890); J. Zwarts, NNBW, VII (1927), 1060–61; J. Lipschits, *Honderd jaar NIW: het Nieuw Israëlitisch Weekblad 1865–1965* (1966); L. Fuks, in: *Studia Rosenthaliana* 1 (1967), 4–22. **ADD. BIBLIOGRAPHY:** R. Cohen, in: *Studia Rosenthaliana*, 9 (1975), 90–102; L. Fuks, in: *Studia Rosenthaliana*, 13 (1979), 157–93; J. Meijer, *Meijer Marcus Roest (1821–1889). De biografie van een bibliograaf*, 2 vols (1980); A.K. Offenberg in: *Frederik Muller, leven en werken* (1996), 110–18.

[Frederik Jacob Hirsch / Irene E. Zwiep (2nd ed.)]

ROGACHEV, city in Gomel district, Belarus. The number of Jews counted as paying the poll tax in 1766 was 200. The community of Rogachev came under Russian domination in 1772. In 1797 there were 888 Jews in Rogachev (approximately 80 percent of the total population). The community was under the influence of *Chabad Ḥasidism. At the close of the 19th century and in the early 20th century, the community grew larger as the result of its commerce in wood. The number of Jews rose in 1897 to 5,047 (55 percent) and it was doubled by the eve of World War I. During the civil war years, the economic situation of Rogachev deteriorated so that by 1926 there were fewer Jews, 5,327 (47.5 percent), declining to 4,601 in 1939 (30.3 percent of the total population). Under the Soviet regime, the public and religious life of the Jews was stifled. A Jewish artisans' union with 150 members conducted its official activities in Yiddish. There were three Jewish kolkhozes. A Yiddish school with 320 pupils functioned there. Germans entered the town on July 3, 1941, and gathered the Jews into a ghetto, where they suffered from overcrowding, hunger, and disease. Between November 1941 and March 1942, 3,500 Jews were executed. The 1959 census gave no indication of Jews living in Rogachev, though their number was estimated at about 750. Rogachev was the native town of Joseph *Rozin, known as "the Rogachover." It was also the birthplace of the painter Tanhum Kaplan and the Yiddish poet Shmuel *Halkin; after Halkin's death in 1960 a street was named after him.

[Yehuda Slutsky / Shmuel Spector (2nd ed.)]

ROGATIN (Pol. **Rohatyn**), city in Ivano-Frankovsk (Stanislavov) district, Ukraine; formerly within Poland, it passed to Austria in 1772, and was incorporated within Stanislawow province, Poland, between the two world wars. One of Poland's oldest cities, Rogatin suffered severely from the depredations of the Tatars. A Jewish community apparently existed there from early times; in the 16th and 17th centuries, Jews from other parts of Poland attended fairs which took place in Rogatin. Within the framework of the Council of Four Lands (see *Councils of the Lands), Rogatin was within the "province of Russia." At the beginning of the 18th century, there were a number of Shabbateans in Rogatin. Jacob *Frank had many adherents there. The town was one of the three towns allocated to the Frankists by King Augustus III. A noted Frankist, Elisha Schoor (*Wolowski) lived in Rogatin. There were 797 Jews living in Rogatin in 1765 and the number increased during Austrian rule (1772–1919): the community numbered 3,192 (48.9 percent of the total population) in 1887; 3,217 (about 46 percent) in 1912; 1,294 (22.6 percent) in 1921; and 3,002 in 1931.

During World War I, the city was in the battle zone and did not recover during the period of the independent Polish republic. The Jews suffered from the discriminatory policy of the Polish government and the economic depression of the 1930s. Jews took part in the social and political life of the city, and their representatives were elected to the city council in 1927 and 1933. In the elections to the community council of 1933, the Zionists gained the most seats.

[Shimshon Leib Kirshenboim]

Holocaust Period

After the outbreak of World War II, during the period of Soviet rule (1939–41), Jewish community institutions were dissolved, political activity was banned, and restrictions were placed on private enterprise. Some Jews were deported to the Soviet interior. During the German campaign against the Soviet Union, Rogatin was captured by the Germans on July 2, 1941. On July 6 Ukrainian police attacked the Jews, and by the end of 1941 a ghetto was established. Its inhabitants suffered from hunger and from a typhus epidemic in which 30 to 40 persons died daily. Shlomo Amarant was head of the Judenrat. On March 20, 1942, 2,000 persons were murdered near the city. On Sept. 21, 1942, some 1,000 persons were deported to the *Belzec death camp. In October Jews from Bukaczowce, Bursztyn, and Bolszowce were brought to the Rogatin ghetto. On Dec. 8, 1942, an *Aktion* took place in which 1,250 persons, including the medical corps and patients from the Jewish hospital, were deported to Belzec. In January 1943 the ghetto area was reduced. The survivors in the community prepared bunkers and hideouts, and it was difficult for the Germans to search them out. On June 6, 1943, the Germans began to liquidate the ghetto. They surrounded it, set houses on fire and threw hand grenades into them. Some Jews were able to escape and reach the forests; the others were murdered and buried in mass graves near the new cemetery.

[Aharon Weiss]

BIBLIOGRAPHY: *Kehillat Rohatyn ve-ha-Sevivah* (Heb. and Yid., 1962), incl. Eng. summary. **ADD. BIBLIOGRAPHY:** *Pinkas ha-Kehillot Poland*, vol. 2, *Eastern Galicia* (1980).

ROGERS, BERNARD (1893–1968), U.S. composer. Born in New York, Rogers studied with Ernest *Bloch. His symphonic poem *To the Fallen* (1918) won him a Pulitzer traveling scholarship. He became an instructor at the Eastman School of Music, Rochester University, in 1929. Rogers wrote several operas, among them, *The Warrior* (1944), based on the story of *Samson and Delilah; choral works such as *The Exodus* (1932); an oratorio, *The Passion* (1942); and orchestral and film music. His *Art of Orchestration* appeared in 1951.

ROGERS, CLAUDE MAURICE (1907–1979), British painter. Rogers was born in London, the son of a dentist, and lived as a small child in Buenos Aires before returning to London, where he was educated at St. Paul's School and the Slade School of Art. Together with William Coldstream and Victor Pasmore, he founded an art school in London which gave rise to the "Euston Road Group" of painters, an English version of Sensitive Impressionism. After service in World War II, Rogers made a distinguished career as a teacher; from 1949 to 1956 at the Slade School and from 1963 to 1972 as professor of fine art at Reading University. A member of the London Group, of which he was president 1962–1965, he was also a member and vice chairman of the British Section of the UNESCO International Association of Artists. At different periods, he was a member of the Arts Panel of the Arts Council of Great Britain and of the National Council of Diplomas and Design. Rogers is represented in important public collections, including the Tate Gallery and the Victoria and Albert Museum.

ADD. BIBLIOGRAPHY: ODNB online; J. Pery, *The Affectionate Eye: The Life of Claude Rogers* (1995).

[Charles Samuel Spencer]

ROGERS, ERNESTO (1909–1969), Italian architect and critic. Rogers was born in Trieste. He belonged to BBPR, a partnership of four modern architects who became internationally known for their sanatorium at Legnano (1937–38). The group also designed housing, industrial buildings, and exhibition architecture. Their Torre Velasca, Milan (1957), created a stir by its apparent abandonment of functionalism. Rogers was editor of the architectural journals *Domus* and *Casabella*.

ROGINSKI, SIMON ZALMANOVICH (1900–1970), Russian physical chemist. Roginski taught at the Dnepropetrovsk University's Mining Institute from 1923 to 1928 and from 1925 was also attached to the Ukrainian Institute of Physical Chemistry. From 1928 to 1941, he was at the Leningrad Polytechnic and the Institute of Physical Chemistry of the U.S.S.R. Academy of Sciences in Leningrad, and from 1941 at the corresponding institute in Moscow.

His fields of research were catalysis, including the "theory of super-saturation," kinetics of explosions, isotopes, and free atoms of hydrogen, oxygen, and nitrogen. He wrote *Adsorbtsiya i kataliz na neodnorodnykh poverkhnostyakh* ("Adsorption and Catalysis on Heterogeneous Surfaces," 1948).

[Samuel Aaron Miller]

ROGOFF, HARRY (Hillel; 1883–1971), U.S. Yiddish journalist and editor. Born in Berezino, Belorussia, Rogoff immigrated to New York at the age of ten with his parents. In 1906 he became a reporter for the *Forverts*, and except for short absences, remained on its staff (as editor after the death of Abraham *Cahan) until his retirement in 1962. In his journalism and editorial writing, he interpreted and commented on political events and sociological trends in the U.S. His major books, *Civics: Vi Azoy Amerike Vert Regirt* ("Civics: How America Is Governed," 1918), and the highly regarded, five-volume *Geshikhte fun di Fareynigte Shtatn* ("History of the United States," 1928), helped to familiarize his largely immigrant readership with their adopted country. Rogoff wrote abundant literary criticism; a short-lived literary magazine, *East and West*, which he edited in 1915–16 was one of the earliest attempts at introducing Yiddish literature to American readers. His English publications, signed Harry Rogoff, include *An East Side Epic: The Life and Work of Meyer London* (1930), later rewritten in Yiddish, and *Nine Yiddish Writers* (1931), a collection of critical essays.

BIBLIOGRAPHY: Rejzen, Leksikon, 4 (1929), 58–60; E.H. Jeshurin, *Harry Rogoff Bibliography* (1958). **ADD. BIBLIOGRAPHY:** LNYL, 8 (1981), 303–4; A. Cahan, *Bleter fun Mayn Lebn*, 4 (1928), 466.

[Ruth Wisse]

ROHATYN, FELIX G. (1928–), U.S. financier. Born in Vienna, Austria, Rohatyn and his family fled Austria in 1935 for France and left in 1940, going to Casablanca, Lisbon, and in 1941, Rio de Janeiro, before arriving in the United States in 1942. He received a B.S. in physics from Middlebury College in 1949 and joined the New York office of the investment bank Lazard Freres under Andre Meyer. During the Korean War, he served in the U.S. Army in Germany, attaining the rank of sergeant and returned to Lazard, one of the most influential financial institutions in the world. He was made a partner in 1961 and rose to managing director, the top office in the firm, earning a reputation as a world authority on mergers and acquisitions. During that time he advised many notable financial figures, including Harold Geneen, then head of ITT, and Lew *Wasserman, head of the talent agency MCA. At the same time, from 1968 to 1972, he served on the board of governors of the New York Stock Exchange and on the boards of directors of a number of multinational corporations. He led the Stock Exchange's crisis committee through a period of great instability in the 1970s, working to find financing that kept tottering companies from collapse. New York City, where he lived, was suffering population decline during that period, like many urban centers, and saw an erosion of its industrial base. Race riots in the 1960s had also left their mark and by the 1970s the city had gained a reputation as a crime-ridden relic of history. In 1975, the city government was on the brink of financial collapse. The mayor, Abraham D. *Beame, asked Washington for assistance and was told, in a famous headline in *The Daily News*: "Ford to City: Drop Dead." Rohatyn was summoned to help the city. Through the Municipal Assistance Corporation, which he headed, Rohatyn forced the city to restructure its debt and the city had to accept increased scrutiny of its finances by an agency of New York State called the Financial Control Board. Rohatyn is credited with managing the negotiations with unions that put up their pension funds to back the city's debt as the city issued revenue and tax anticipation notes. The city survived, and the 1980s saw a rebirth of Wall Street with the city reclaiming its role at the center of the worldwide financial industry. Rohatyn headed the agency from 1975 to 1993. In 1997, when he retired from Lazard, Rohatyn was appointed United States ambassador to France by President Bill Clinton. He served until 2000 and was named commander of the French Legion of Honor. He was a member of the Council on Foreign Relations and the American Academy of Arts and Sciences. He also served as vice chairman of Carnegie Hall in New York and was a trustee of the Center for Strategic and International Studies in Washington. He established Rohatyn Associates in 2001 to provide financial advice to corporations. Among the boards he served on were those of LVMH Moet Hennessy Louis Vuitton, Publicis Group, Groupe Lardere, and Rothschild Continuation Holdings.

[Stewart Kampel (2nd ed.)]

RÓHEIM, GÉZA (1891–1953), U.S. psychoanalyst and anthropologist. Born in Budapest, he was for a time affiliated with the ethnological department of the Hungarian National Museum. In Berlin, he worked under F. von *Luschan and studied the theories of *Freud. In 1915, he underwent his first psychoanalysis at the hands of Sándor *Ferenczi and became the first ethnologist employing and advocating a psychoanalytic interpretation of culture, and during the next three years wrote a series of papers on his theories. About this time, he was appointed professor of anthropology at the University of Budapest. His treatise, *Nach dem Tode des Urvaters* (*Imago* (1923), 83–121), adjusted the Freudian theory in the light of anthropological data. In 1925 and 1926, he wrote two books on the psychoanalytic study of Australian totemism.

With Freud's encouragement and assistance, from 1928 to 1931 Róheim did fieldwork in Central Australia, Normanby

(Melanesia), on the Sipupu Island in Somaliland, and among the Yuma Indians in Arizona. On the basis of this research Róheim was enabled to produce a revision of psychoanalytic theory. Some of the products of this study appear in *Animism, Magic, and the Divine King* (1930) as well as various articles in the psychoanalytic journals of the early 1930s. His two books, *Riddle of the Sphinx* (1934) and *The Origin and Function of Culture* (1943), deal with folklore and the interpretation of myths. Between 1932 and 1938, he taught anthropology and psychoanalysis at the Budapest Institute of Psychoanalysis.

In 1938 he left for the United States and became affiliated with the Worcester State Hospital as an analyst. After 1940 he joined the New York Psychoanalytical Institute as a lecturer and engaged in private practice as a psychoanalyst.

In his studies of mythology and magic, he placed primary stress on sexuality but with some deviations from the Freudian doctrine. On the basis of both his fieldwork and his clinical experience, Róheim tended to reject Freud's theory of the primal family and the hypothesis of inherited racial memories as an explanation of totemism and other social data in religion and social structure. He moved toward an ontogenetic theory of culture explaining it on the basis of prolonged dependence of the human infant and child on the mother which results in emotional and social ties.

Róheim also developed a dream theory interpreting various phenomena of anxiety, ambivalence, and aggression as part of the human experience of mother separation. In 1949 he wrote "Technique of Dream Analysis and Field Work in Anthropology" and in 1950 *Psychoanalysis and Anthropology.* In *Magic and Schizophrenia* (1955), Roheim set out his belief that both individuals and societies evolve from a stage of magical symbolic thinking that he related to schizophrenia.

BIBLIOGRAPHY: G.B. Wilbur and W. Muensterberger (eds.), *Psychoanalysis and Culture; Essays in Honor of Géza Róheim* (1951), incl. bibl.; *American Anthropologist*, 55 (1953), 420; W. La Barre, in: F. Alexander et al. (eds.), *Psychoanalytic Pioneers* (1966), 272–81, incl. bibl; W. Muensterberger and B. Domhoff, in: IESS, 13 (1968), 543–6, incl. bibl.

[Ephraim Fischoff]

°**ROHLING, AUGUST** (1839–1931), antisemitic polemicist. A fanatical ultramontanist priest from the Rhineland, Rohling published in 1871 his *Der Talmudjude* (based on J.A. *Eisenmenger's *Entdecktes Judenthum*), a collection of deliberately corrupted quotations, imaginary statements, and forgeries against the Talmud. The book appeared in successive editions and became very popular. When Franz Holubek, a leader of the Viennese artisan movement, was sued for inciting a crowd against the Jews (April 4, 1882), he pleaded not guilty, claiming that he had obtained his information in good faith from the books of Rohling, a full professor at the German University of Prague. Rohling's academic appointments were obtained through the intercession of high Church dignitaries. Holubek's acquittal was a victory for the growing political antisemitism. Rohling and his works acquired further notoriety through the *Tiszaeszlar blood libel affair, when Rohling volunteered to testify that Jews required Christian blood for their ceremonies. After Franz *Delitzsch, the renowned Protestant Orientalist, had revealed Rohling's ignorance and baseness, Rohling accused Delitzsch of being a Jew and then castigated Adolf *Jellinek and Moritz *Guedemann as cunning knaves for denying Holubek's charges.

Rohling's challenger was Joseph Samuel *Bloch who, after repeated sorties against him, published a series of articles in July 1883 under the title, "An Offer to Commit Perjury," in which he branded Rohling a liar and perjurer. Forced by public opinion to sue Bloch for libel, Rohling enlisted the aid of two antisemites, Brimanus (a Romanian-Jewish renegade who had taught Rohling Hebrew and was author of the scurrilous *Der Judenspiegel* under the pseudonym "Justus") and Ecker (a convicted forger, priest, and professor at an obscure seminary in Paderborn). Neither could attend the trial. Bloch recruited the respected Orientalists Theodor Noeldeke and Karl August Wuensche, who completely demolished all Rohling's academic pretenses. Even Paul *Lagarde condemned Rohling's works. In 1885, shortly before the trial was due to open, Rohling withdrew his suit after Bloch had collected an immense amount of material against him. He paid the costs of the trial, lost his academic chair, and left the public scene, nevertheless continuing to publish antisemitic tracts. Rohling's *Talmudjude* was translated into several European languages; E. *Drumont wrote the introduction to the French edition. The work continued to be published for more than 50 years, and served as a source for Nazi antisemitic doctrines.

BIBLIOGRAPHY: J. Kopp, *Zur Judenfrage nach den Akten des Prozesses Rohling-Bloch* (1886); F. Delitzsch, *Was Rohling beschworen hat und beschwoeren will* (1883); idem, *Schachmatt den Blutluegnern Robling und Justus* (1883); *Akten und Gutachten in dem Prozesse Rohling contra Bloch* (1890–1901); J.S. Bloch, *My Reminiscences* (1923); M. Grunwald, *Vienna* (1936), 430–7; J.G. Pulzer, *The Rise of Political Anti-Semitism in Germany and Austria* (1964); D. van Arkel, Anti-semitism in Austria (Ph.D. thesis, Leiden University, 1966), 14–33.

ROITMAN, DAVID (1884–1943), **ḥazzan* and composer. Roitman was born in Dorozhinki, Russia, and studied with several *ḥazzanim*, notably Jacob Samuel *Morogowski (Zeidel Rovner). He was *ḥazzan* in Vilna (1909–12), St. Petersburg (1912–17), and Odessa, before emigrating to the U.S. in 1921. From 1924 until his death, he officiated at Congregation Shaare Zedek in New York. Roitman had a light, flexible, lyric tenor voice with an exceptional falsetto. He was noted for his clarity of rendition and his power of improvisation, while still maintaining an overall simplicity of expression. His compositions *Ashamnu mi-Kol Am* (in: G. Ephros (ed.), *Cantorial Anthology*, 2 (1940), 145–6) and *Raḥel Mevakah al Baneha*, both deeply moving liturgical laments, achieved widespread popularity. In 1961, L. Avery published *Selected Recitatives of Cantor David Roitman.*

ROJAS, FERNANDO DE (c. 1465–1541), Spanish Converso author. Rojas was born in Puebla de Montalbán near Toledo, studied in Salamanca and settled in Talavera de la Reina. In 1517 he was a witness in defense of a man accused of Judaizing and in 1525 the Inquisition objected to his serving as lawyer for his Converso father-in-law, Alvaro de Montalbán, because he was a New Christian. Acclaimed as the "father of the Spanish novel," Rojas is generally recognized as the author of all or most of one of Spain's greatest literary works and the earliest Spanish tragedy, *La Celestina* (first-known ed. Burgos, 1499). Though written completely in dialogue, this is more a novel than a play. The first edition was an anonymous 16-act *Comedia de Calisto y Melibea*. In the third-known edition (Seville, 1501), Rojas hesitantly reveals his authorship in a prefatory letter and in some acrostic verses, stating that he found a fragment of the first act and continued the work. The various editions dated 1502 (although printed later) contain a new prologue and five added acts, as well as numerous textual changes. The title was also changed to *Tragicomedia de Catisto y Melibea*. Rojas himself suggests that the first act may have been by Juan de Mena or Rodrigo de Cota de *Maguaque. He probably wished to obscure his own part in the writing because of the work's anticlericalism. From 1519 the play was known as *La Celestina*. The fact that Rojas was a Converso has been adduced to explain the pessimism of his work, unequaled in any contemporary production. The *Celestina* has probably inspired more studies than any other Spanish book with the exception of *Cervantes' *Don Quixote*, to which alone it is placed second. It has been translated many times into English (first by James Mabbe in 1631).

BIBLIOGRAPHY: S. Gilman, *The Art of La Celestina* (1956); J.M. Cohen, *A History of Western Literature* (1956), 130–2, 198; F. de Rojas, *The Spanish Bawd: La Celestina* (1964), translation and introduction by J.M. Cohen; M. Bataillon, *La Célestine selon Fernando de Rojas* (1961); L.G. Zelson, *The Celestina and Its Jewish Authorship* (1930), reprint from *Jewish Forum* (Dec. 1930); F.J. Norton, *Printing in Spain 1501–1520* (1966).

[Kenneth R. Scholberg]

ROKACH, ELEAZAR (1854–1914), Ereẓ Israel pioneer and writer. Rokach, the grandson of Israel *Bak, was born in Jerusalem. He also studied there, but moved to Safed after his marriage, whereupon he began contributing articles on Safed Jewry to the Hebrew press abroad (mainly anonymously) and later wrote for *Ḥavaẓẓelet on many issues. He advocated working the land and was among those who initiated the acquisition of the village Gei-Oni (later *Rosh-Pinnah), where he was one of the first settlers. Rokach went abroad in 1880 and lived first in Romania, and then in Galicia, calling upon the Jews to settle in Ereẓ Israel. He was an unusual mixture of romantic and realist – a dreamer yet a fighter for his beliefs – who was unappreciated in his time. From 1901 until the end of his life, he wandered all over Galicia, lecturing and writing. He died in Drohobycz.

Rokach wrote a pamphlet entitled *Maẓẓav ha-Ir ha-Kedoshah Ẓefat ve-Toshaveha ha-Ashkenazim* ("The Conditions of the Holy City of Safed and its Ashkenazi Inhabitants," Jerusalem, no date). He also published several Yiddish and Hebrew newspapers while abroad (*Yisrael*, Jassy-Piatra, 1881; *Talpiyyot*, Jassy, 1898–99; and *Ha-Yarden*, Buczacz, 1906, in which his coeditor was S.Y. Agnon).

BIBLIOGRAPHY: N. Sokolow, *Ḥibbath Zion* (Eng., 1935), 271–3; Y. Yaari-Poleskin, *Ḥolemim ve-Loḥamim* (1964[3]), 49–52; M. Smilansky, *Mishpahat ha-Adamah*, 2 (1954), 142–52; I. Klausner, *Ḥibbat Ẓiyyon be-Romanyah* (1958), index; idem, *Be-Hitorer Am* (1962), index; idem, *Mi-Katoviẓ ad Basel*, 2 (1965), index; G. Yardeni, in: *Aresheth*, 4 (1960), 296–321; idem, *Toledot ha-Ittonut be-Ereẓ Yisrael* (1968), index; S. Jawnieli, *Tekufat Ḥibbat Ẓiyyon*, 1 (1942), 7–9.

[Getzel Kressel]

ROKACH, SHIMON (1863–1922), leader of the Jaffa Jewish community. Born in Jerusalem, the grandson of Rabbi Israel *Bak, Rokach moved to Jaffa in 1884 to control the travel tax imposed upon travelers from Jaffa to Jerusalem, a post which he and his father had leased from the Turkish authorities. Together with his brother Eleazar *Rokach, he established the Ezrat Israel Society to assist immigrants passing through Jaffa. In 1887 he was founder of the first modern Jewish quarter in Jaffa, Neveh Ẓedek, and among those instrumental in unifying the city's Sephardi and Ashkenazi communities in 1890; he later served as president of the community. One of the pioneers of citriculture in Ereẓ Israel, in 1900 Rokach was a founder of the cooperative citrus-marketing company, Pardes, and served as its director. He utilized his extensive contacts with the Turkish authorities and with Arab notables for the good of the Jewish community. During World War I, he obtained a contract to supply wood for fueling Turkish army trains and employed many Jews to exempt them from Ottoman military service.

[Yehuda Slutsky]

His son, ISRAEL (1896–1959), Israeli public figure and mayor of Tel Aviv. Born in Jaffa, Rokach graduated in Lausanne, Switzerland, as an electrical engineer. He belonged to the non-labor camp of the *yishuv* and dedicated most of his years to the Tel Aviv municipality. He was elected to the first Tel Aviv municipal council in 1922 and served without interruption until 1953 (from 1929 as deputy mayor to *Dizengoff and in 1937–53 as mayor). Under his leadership, Tel Aviv grew from a garden suburb into the principal city of the country. In 1947, Rokach was held for several months in a British detention camp, together with the mayors of Ramat Gan and Netanyah and other *yishuv* leaders, for having aided underground activities against the Mandatory government. Politically he was a leading figure of the General Zionists (B) and from 1949 served as one of their members in the Knesset. In 1953–55 Rokach was minister of interior and in 1957–59 deputy speaker of the Knesset.

Another son, ISAAC (1894–1974), was active in business affairs connected with the citrus industry and was general manager of the Citrus Growers Cooperation society.

[Benjamin Jaffe]

BIBLIOGRAPHY: Shimon Rokach: *Ẓiyyun le-Nishmat S. Rokach* (1923); Tidhar, 1 (1947), 68–70; M. Smilansky, *Mishpaḥat ha-Adamah*, 2 (1947), 172–9. ISRAEL ROKACH: A. Remba, *Israel Rokach* (Eng. 1969), incl. bibl.

ROKEAḤ, DAVID (1916–1985), Hebrew poet. Born in Lvov, Rokeaḥ settled in Palestine in 1934, working as an engineer, and first published lyrical poems in 1935.

His books of poetry are: *Be-Gesher ha-Yi'ud* (1939), *Yamim Ashenim* (1941), *Mo'adei Ergah* (1954), *Arar alei Shaham* (1958), *Kinno shel Yam* (1963), *Mi-Kayiẓ el Kayiẓ* (1964), *Shaḥar le-Helekh* (1965), *Einayim la-Sela* (1967), and *Ve-Lo Ba Yom Aḥer* (1969). Many of his poems appeared in German translation by prominent poets such as Paul Celan and Erich Fried, and Rokeah was indeed one of the first Hebrew poets to be published in postwar Germany. For a full listing of Rokeaḥ's works in English translation, see Goell, Bibliography, 1191–207.

BIBLIOGRAPHY: M. Hamburger, in: *Ariel*, no. 12 (1965), 25–30. **ADD. BIBLIOGRAPHY:** H. Shoham, in: *Yedioth Aharonoth* (November 20, 1981); Z. Luz, "*Mar'ot ha-Zemannim: Motivim ve-Dimuyei-Yesod be-Shirato shel D. Rokeah*," in: *Bikkoret u-Farshanut*, 4–5 (1974), 64–69; J. Neusner, "On D. Rokeah's 'Jews, Pagans and Christians in Conflict,'" in: JQR, 74:3 (1984), 313–20; Y. Schwartz, "*Al D. Rokeah, 'Ha-Yahadut ve-ha-Naẓrut bi-Re'i ha-Pulmus ha-Pagani,'*" in: *Zion* 58:1 (1993), 115–19; A. Bodenheimer, "Das Wiedererkennen des Unbekannten: Zu P. Celans Uebersetzung des Gedichts '*Banechar*' von D. Rokeah," in: *Poetik der Transformationen* (1999), 129–136.

[Getzel Kressel]

ROKEAḤ or **ROKAḤ (Landau), ELAZAR BEN SHMELKE** (1665–1741), rabbi. Rokaḥ was born in Cracow, and after serving as rabbi in Rakov (1705) and Tarnow (1709), he was appointed *av bet din* (c. 1714) and subsequently rabbi of Brody. The Jewish community of Brody flourished greatly during this period. It possessed a *Klaus*, which was composed of kabbalists and talmudic scholars, and during his period of office, the first group of adherents of *Israel Ba'al Shem Tov was established in Brody. At this time also a considerable number of scholars from Brody and the neighborhood, such as R. *Abraham Gershon of Kutow and R. *Pereẓ b. Moses, immigrated to Ereẓ Israel.

In 1735 Rokaḥ accepted a call to Amsterdam, despite the violent controversy which had raged there since the death of the previous incumbent, R. Abraham Judah of Halberstadt. Rokaḥ was very well received, and a medallion was even struck in his honor, which roused the antagonism of R. Jacob *Emden. This was not the only dispute which surrounded him, and as a result, in 1740 he decided to immigrate to Ereẓ Israel. He settled in Safed, where he became the head of the small Ashkenazi community, applying himself to their immediate needs to such an extent that they accorded him the title "the Nasi of Ereẓ Israel," which was given to those who devoted themselves to the support of the *yishuv* in the country.

Rokaḥ was a determined and unwearying opponent of every sign of the Shabbatean heresy. While still in Brody, he violently attacked Moses Ḥayyim *Luzzatto, whom he accused of this heresy, and gave his approval to the banning of his works. In Safed he became so involved in a conflict with a group of Shabbateans there that he thought of emigrating from Ereẓ Israel, but he died suddenly exactly a year after his arrival here.

With his death the position of the Ashkenazi community deteriorated and they appealed for help to the *Council of Four Lands, mentioning the great help which Rokaḥ had obtained for them as a result of his contacts with Poland and Amsterdam.

Among Rokaḥ's works are *Ma'aseh Roke'aḥ* on the composition of the Mishnah (Amsterdam, 1740) and on the Pentateuch (Lemberg, 1850), and *Arba'ah Turei Even* (Lemberg, 1789).

[Jacob Barnai]

ROKISKIS (Heb. and Yid. **Rakishik**), city in Lithuania near the Latvian border. Situated on the Daugavpils-Liepaja railroad, it served as a commercial center for a large rural area and a point for the export of wood, grain, and flax. In 1847 there were 593 Jews in the town and in 1897 2,067 (75% of the total population). During World War I most of the Jews fled to the interior of Russia. The city was reestablished after the war. Jews numbered 2,013 in 1923, and although Rokiskis developed rapidly, its Jews had to contend with harsh competition from the Lithuanians, who were supported by the government. In 1939 there were 3,500 Jews in Rokiskis (40% of the total population). They were mostly *Ḥabad Ḥasidim. During the period of Lithuanian independence (1918–40), there were two Hebrew schools. When the Germans occupied the city in 1941, the Jews were deported to the ghetto of Joniskis and killed there. Rokiskis is the birthplace of the commander of the Soviet Air Force and Hero of the U.S.S.R., Yaakov *Shmushkevich.

[Yehuda Slutsky]

ROLAND-MANUEL (Roland Alexis Manuel Levy; 1891–1966), composer and writer. Born in Paris, Roland-Manuel studied with Roussel and Ravel, and in 1947 became professor of aesthetics at the Paris Conservatory. In 1947 he was elected vice president of the International Society for Contemporary Music, and in 1949 president of the International Music Council of UNESCO. His music is a blend of classicism and modernism, avoiding romantic tendencies. His writings include three books on Ravel, and the valuable popularization *Plaisir de la musique* (1947–55) in four volumes.

ROLL, MICHAEL (1946–), British pianist. Roll was born in Leeds to Viennese parents and studied the piano from the age of six with Fanny Waterman. At 12, he made his debut at the Royal Festival Hall, playing the Schumann concerto with Sir Malcolm Sargent. In 1963, the youngest of 88 competitors, Roll won the first Leeds International Piano Competition and thereafter performed with such conductors as Barbirolli, Boulez, Giulini, Gergiev, Haitink, Leinsdorf, Masur, *Previn, and Sawallisch, in many European cities and in Israel. His American debut occurred in 1974 with the Boston Symphony and Sir Colin Davis, appearing in Boston and New

York. He appeared at leading international festivals such as Aldeburgh, Bath, Edinburgh, Granada, Hong Kong, Vienna, and the Klavier-Festival Ruhr. He holds a professorship at the Folkwang Hochschule in Essen. His three CD recordings of the Beethoven Piano Concertos with the Royal Philharmonic Orchestra under Howard Shelley were highly praised by critics.

[Max Loppert / Israela Stein (2nd ed.)]

ROLNICK, JOSEPH (1879–1955), Yiddish poet. Born near Mir (Belorussia) into a miller's family, Rolnick was indelibly marked by the landscape of his youth. He emigrated to New York in 1899, debuted as a Yiddish poet in *Forverts* in 1900, and returned to Europe in 1901, re-emigrating to New York in 1907. Rolnick was one of the first American Yiddish poets to break with the dominant tradition of didactic social poetry, paving the way for impressionism and symbolism. The insurgent literary group Di *Yunge hailed him as a precursor of its ideals and poetic theory and welcomed him into the group. Rolnick avoided complex moods or complicated situations. In simple quatrains he conveyed a single mood or thought with maximum clarity and fidelity. As a mature lyric poet, his resignation was no longer the expression of despair but of a purer and deeper recognition and understanding. The creator of tranquil lyrics whose symbols emerge from village landscape and life, Rolnick has been compared to Robert Frost.

BIBLIOGRAPHY: Feygl Rolnick (ed.), *Yoysef Rolnik: Der Dikhter un Zayn Lid* (1961); S. Liptzin, *Flowering of Yiddish Literature* (1963), 202–5; J. Glatstein, *In Tokh Genumen* (1956), 136–44; S. Bickel, *Shrayber fun Mayn Dor* (1955), 29–34; A. Tabachnik, *Dikhter un Dikhtung* (1965), 101–32. **ADD. BIBLIOGRAPHY:** LNYL, 8 (1981), 376–8; Joseph Rolnick, *Zikhroynes* (1954).

[Sol Liptzin / Eugene V. Orenstein (2nd ed.)]

ROM, YOSEF (1932–1997), aeonautical engineer. Born in Poland, Rom immigrated with his parents to Ereẓ Israel in 1935. He studied aeronautic engineering and became dean of the Faculty of Aeronautic Engineering of the Technion in Haifa. He served as engineering consultant to many research and development institutions and to the defense industry in Israel, and developed supersonic wind tunnels. Rom was awarded the Israel Prize in 1976 for service to technology and applied engineering. He was elected to the Ninth Knesset in 1977, representing the Likud.

ROMAIN, JONATHAN A. (1954–), British rabbi and historian. A leading Progressive rabbi in Barkingside and in Maidenhead, Berkshire, and director of the Jewish Information and Media Service, Romain is also well-known for his publications on Jewish history and life, including (with Dr. Anne J. Kershen): *Tradition and Change: A History of Reform Judaism in Britain, 1840–1995* (1995), *Faith and Practice: A Guide to Reform Judaism Today* (1991), and *The Jews of England: A Portrait of Anglo-Jewry Through Original Sources and Illustrations* (1985).

[William D. Rubinstein (2nd ed.)]

ROMAN, town in Bacau province, Moldavia, N.E. Romania. According to a popular tradition, the first Jews settled in Roman in the second half of the 15th century. Another source attributes the beginning of the Jewish settlement there to the early 16th century. In 1579 the Jews were expelled, according to this source, by the prince of Moldavia. Jews in Roman are first mentioned in Romanian documents from the beginning of the 18th century, and the oldest Jewish tombstones there date from this period. In 1714 a case of blood *libel occurred in Roman. In 1825 priests demanded that the Jewish cemetery should be closed claiming that it was in the center of the town, but the Moldavian ruler rejected their request. The priests then brought several actions against the community, resulting in 1849 in compulsory closure of the cemetery which was subsequently also desecrated. In 1846 the community acquired land for a new cemetery. At first the "Jewish guild" assumed the community functions; subsequently some of them were taken over by the *ḥevra kaddisha* whose minute book is preserved from 1793. There were 16 prayerhouses, including the Great Synagogue (The Taylor's Synagogue). In 1875 the hostel for travelers (*hekdesh) was converted into a modern hospital and old-age home. The community bath (*mikveh*) also served as a public bath for Christians, being the only one in town.

The Jewish population numbered 288 in 1803, and 1,200 in 1831; it had increased to 6,432 by 1899 (39% of the total population). Persecutions led many Jews to emigrate in 1900 and the following years. The number of the Jews in Roman had decreased to 4,728 by 1910. In 1930 they numbered 5,963 (28% of the total population). At the beginning of the 19th century, the majority of the Jews were occupied in crafts; the number of those engaged in commerce increased by the early 20th century.

In 1865 Jewish educational institutions in Roman included a *talmud torah* and 20 *ḥadarim*, some belonging to the craftsmen, and others to the Ḥasidim. A modern Jewish elementary school, opened on directions of the authorities in 1860, was subsequently closed. In 1893, when Jews were expelled from the public schools, a new modern elementary school was opened with the aid of the Jewish Colonization *Association (ICA), and in 1899 a school for girls was founded. Among rabbis in Roman were David Isaacson, who officiated from 1839 to 1907, and his nephew, Solomon Isaacson (1910–47).

After World War I the community underwent reorganization. From 1926 its board was appointed by the government from among Jews who were members of the ruling party. Jews also served on the local council but as representatives of the Romanian parties. Antisemitism was strong in Roman especially between the two world wars, encouraged by the bishop, Lucian Triteanu, one of the leading antisemites in Romania. In 1910 A. *Cuza, the head of the antisemitic party, was elected deputy in this city, and in 1930 as representative of Roman in the Romanian parliament.

The community was not liquidated in the Holocaust. The Jewish population numbered 7,900 in 1947, and 4,500 in 1950.

Most of them left for Israel and by 1969 there were about 150 Jewish families. Two synagogues were in existence.

BIBLIOGRAPHY: PK Romanyah, 1 (1970), 246–53; J. Kaufman, in: *Revista israelită*, 1 (1886), 694–8, 759–65; 2 (1887), 27–28, 194, 221; 3 (1888), 111–37; Melchisedek (Bishop of Husi), *Cronica Romanului și a Episcopiei de Roman…* (1874), 36–39, 133; S. Wechsler, *Contribuție la monografia Comunității evreiești din Roman* (1929); S. Rivenzon, *Școala evreiască din tîrgul Romanului…* (1933); M. Schwarzfeld, in: *Anuar pentru israeliți*, 13 (1890/91), 1–29; A. Cramer, in: *Almanahul Ziarului Tribuna evreească*, 1 (1937/38), 239–41.

[Theodor Lavi]

ROMAN, JACOB BEN ISAAC (c. 1570–1650), bibliographer and writer; born in Constantinople of Spanish descent. While in Basle, Roman met Johannes *Buxtorf the Younger, who utilized the former's bibliographical knowledge for the appendix to his father's *Bibliotheca Rabbinica*, which he had edited. For a short while the two maintained correspondence, and the two extant letters by Roman were published in the *Revue des Etudes Juives* (8 (1844), 87–94). His plan to reestablish a Hebrew press in Constantinople did not reach fruition.

Roman compiled an Arabic-Turkish and an Arabic-Hebrew dictionary and composed a Hebrew prosody, *"Mozenei Mishkal."* He also translated some of Jonah ibn Janah's works from Arabic into Hebrew: none, however, was published.

BIBLIOGRAPHY: Zunz, Gesch, 233–4; Steinschneider, Cat. Bod, 1254 no. 5008; Steinschneider, Uebersetzungen, 377; idem, in: ZDMG, 9 (1855), 840.

[Victor A. Mirelman]

ROMANELLI, SAMUEL AARON (1757–1817), Italian Hebrew poet and traveler. Born in Mantua, he acquired a knowledge of ten languages including English, French and Spanish. He began his journeys through Europe at an early age. By his late 20s, he reached London where he wrote a Hebrew translation of Pope's *Essay on Man, Massah al ha-Adam*, and a lament on the death of Moses Mendelssohn (1786). On his way back to Italy in 1787, he decided to tour Morocco. While there he took up employment wherever he could find it and at the same time wrote his travelogue, *Massa ba-Arav* (Berlin, 1792; repr. with introd. by H. Schirmann in *Romanelli, Ketavim Nivḥarim*, 1968; Eng. trans. by Schiller-Szinessy, *Romanelli's Travels in Morocco*, 1887). It is for this attractive description of Jewish life in Morocco written in a biblical Hebrew style that he is best known. In 1790 he left for Europe where he eventually settled in Germany. There he befriended the principal *"me'assefim"* (see *Me'assef), e.g., I. *Euchel and D. *Friedlaender. While there he composed an allegorical play in three acts, *Ha-Kolot Yeḥdalun* (Berlin, 1791), for the marriage of one of the Jaffe Itzig family. The same year, he published his philosophical poem *Ru'aḥ Nakhon*, concerning the existence of the soul and God. In 1793 he worked as a proofreader in Vienna, where he published a play for the marriage of Charlotte Arnstein, *Alot ha-Minḥah*, which appeared with an Italian translation. After the French conquest of northern Italy, Romanelli returned to his homeland and settled in Mantua in 1807. The same year, and in Napoleon's honor, he published *Zimrat Ariẓim, Raccolta di inni ed odi*, Italian translations of poems and prayers composed by members of the Sanhedrin. In 1808 he published *Maḥazeh Shaddai… Illusione felice ossia visione sentimentale*, a metaphysical poem with an Italian translation (Turin, 1808). His latter years he spent in wandering through northern Italy, finally settling in Casale Monferrato where he died. Many of his works are still in manuscript, including his Hebrew translation of the Italian playwright Metastasio's play *Temistocle* under the title *Talmon*.

BIBLIOGRAPHY: Waxman, Literature, 3 (1960), 135–9; A.B. Rhine, in: JQR, 2 (1911), 49–52; S. Schiller-Szinessy, *Romanelli's Travels in Morocco* (1887), introd.; H. Schirmann, *Samuel Romanelli, Ketavim Nivḥarim* (1968), 7–12, incl. bibl.; R. Fahn, in: *Mizraḥ u-Ma'arav*, 5 (1932), 345–6. **ADD. BIBLIOGRAPHY:** N.A. Stillman, "Samuel Romanelli and his *Massa ba'rab*," in: *Hebrew Annual Review*, 9 (1985), 343–54; idem, "The Jewish Courtier Class in late 18th Century Morocco as Seen through the Eyes of Samuel Romanelli," in: *The Islamic World from Classical to Modern Times* (1989), 845–54; M. Pelli, "The Literary Genre of the Travelogue in Hebrew Haskalah Literature: Shmuel Romanelli's *Masa Ba'rav*," in: *Modern Judaism*, 11:2 (1991), 241–60; idem, "On the Role of the Melitzah in the Literature of the Hebrew Enlightenment," in: *Hebrew in Ashkenaz* (1993), 99–110; H. Schirmann, *"Sh.Romanelli, Ha-Meshorer ha-Noded,"* in: *Le-Toledot ha-Shirah ve-ha-Dramah ha-Ivrit* (rpt. 2003).

ROMAN EMPERORS. It is impossible to make generalizations about the attitude of the Roman emperors toward the Jews. Different attitudes were adopted by different emperors and even the same emperor would change his views, sometimes dependent upon whether it was directed to the Jews in Ereẓ Israel or in other parts of the empire. On the other hand, it is possible to make a sufficiently clear distinction between the attitude of the pagan emperors on the one hand and the Christian on the other.

In general, the pagan emperors were tolerant toward the various foreign religions and even Cicero stated: *"Sua cuique civitati religio est, nostra nobis"* (*Pro Flacco*, 28). Augustus (27 B.C.E.–14 C.E.) continued the favorable policy toward the Jews initiated by *Julius Caesar. Under Tiberius (14–37), as a result of the influence of the powerful Sejanus, the young Jews of Rome were deported to Sardinia to fight brigandage, and a large number of them died there. The Senate decreed that all Jews who would not abjure their faith be banished from Italy and that their articles of religious worship be confiscated. The decree, however, was not put into effect, and in 31, after the death of Sejanus, the protective edicts of Caesar and *Augustus were reconfirmed. Under *Caligula (37–41), Jewish insurrections took place in Ereẓ Israel and Egypt, after the emperor, who desired to be worshiped as a god, had his statue erected in the Temple. The danger was averted due to the efforts of the delegation from the Jews of Alexandria, headed by Philo, and more by the sympathetic legate to Syria, Petronius *Publius. *Claudius (41–54), who did not claim divinity, restored the edict of tolerance to the Jews and extended it to the whole Roman Empire. In 49–50, he decided to expel from Rome the Jews who, perhaps because of conflicts with the Christians, had disturbed the public order (*Iudaeos impulsore Chresto assidue tumultuantis Roma expulit*; Suetonius, *De vita Caesarum*, Claudius, 25); the expulsion, however, was applied to a few individuals only. In 66, during the reign of *Nero (54–68), the disturbances in Palestine became a full-scale war which ended with the destruction of the Temple (70). Nevertheless, according to Josephus, when *Titus became emperor (79–81), he wished to show a benevolent attitude toward the Jews; in Jewish tradition, however, he remains "Titus the Wicked." Vespasian instituted the *fiscus judaicus. It was collected with particular harshness by Domitian (81–96), under whose reign the Jews suffered both in life and property. The meek *Nerva (96–98) started to protect the Jews again, and abolished the stringency of the collection of the *fiscus*. *Trajan (98–117) harshly repressed the Jewish revolt in Palestine, Egypt and Cyrenaica.

The attitude of *Hadrian (117–138) has been the subject of much controversy. Under his reign the *Bar Kokhba Revolt broke out. According to *Dio Cassius, the immediate cause of the revolt was the decision of Hadrian to transform Jerusalem into a Greek city and the Temple into a temple of Jupiter, but, according to Spartianus, it was caused by the prohibition against circumcision. The Midrash (Gen. R. 64:10) attributes it to the breach of promise to reconstruct the Temple, as a result of Samaritan pressure. According to Eusebius, however, the Jews were regarded as responsible for the outbreak of the war, and in consequence anti-Jewish measures were taken. The agitation of the Jews continued also under *Antoninus Pius (138–161), despite his conciliatory attitude which included the repeal of the prohibition against circumcision; as non-Jews were severely punished for circumcision, this signified, in practice, the prohibition of conversion. In fact, conversions were looked upon with disfavor by the emperors and punished with different penalties (for example, the edict of Septimius *Severus in 204). In 212, with the *Constitutio Antoniniana* of Caracalla (211–217), the Jews of the empire also became Roman citizens. Alexander *Severus (222–235) was so favorable in his attitude toward the Jews that a synagogue in Rome was named after him and he was nicknamed the *archisynagogus*. *Diocletian (284–305), the harsh adversary of Christians, Manicheans, and Samaritans, was in contrast friendly toward the Jews, as is affirmed by the Talmud.

With the triumph of Christianity in 313, the empire became ever more intolerant; religious liberty declined. A period of persecutions and juridical and political restrictions began toward the Jews, who were regarded as of a lower degree than pagans and heretics. Theoretically, for example, the destruction of a synagogue was still considered a crime, but in practice the penalties laid down were only partially observed and numerous offenses were perpetrated by the Church. There was an interval of tranquility and a restoration of religious liberty with *Julian the Apostate (361–363), who entertained the idea of rebuilding Jerusalem and the Temple, but with his death there was a religious reaction. In 399 *Honorius tried in vain to sever the bond between the Jews of the Roman Empire in the West and their brethren in Palestine. In vain did *Theodosius I (379–395) declare that it "could not be ascertained that the sect of the Jews was prohibited by any law"; the Church Fathers rebelled against him and the emperor was forced to retract his declaration. As a result of Theodosius' *Novella*, 3 (Jan. 31, 438), ascribed to the emperors Theodosius II and Valentinian, the juridical capacity of the Jews in the public sector was completely exhausted. In their codices, Theodosius II (in 438) and Justinian (between 529 and 533) assembled the decrees of the various Christian emperors with regard to the Jews: Justinian even attempted to intervene in the very internal life of the Jewish community. To a greater or lesser degree, every Christian emperor followed, henceforth, the program of an empire become confessionist, endeavoring to impose the Christian faith on its subjects and repressing all which did not conform to it.

See also individual entries on the emperors and their bibliographies.

[Alfredo Mordechai Rabello]

ROMANIA, country in East-Central and South-East Europe, in the Carpatho-Danubian region, north of the Balkan Peninsula, partly on the littoral of the Black Sea. The territory comprising Romania was known as Dacia in antiquity; Jewish tombstones, other inscriptions with Jewish and Palmyrean names written in Greek or Latin from the Roman period (1st–3rd centuries C.E.) and a coin from the period of Bar Kochba's revolt with an inscription in Hebrew were discovered in the counties of Transylvania and Oltenia. Jewish and Palmyrean names are also present in some Greek inscriptions discovered in the county of Dobrogea, known in antiquity as the Roman province Moesia Inferior. Early Christian missionary activity in Dacia and the Hellenistic towns of Moesia may have been due to the existence of Jewish groups there. Later, the Carpatho-Danubian territory was mentioned in some Hebrew sources from the 10th to 12th centuries. A Jewish presence is attested in the 14th century in the port towns of the Southern Bessarabia county on the Black Sea. In the 15th century, there were Karaite communities in the same towns, one of them, Akkerman (in Romanian: Cetatea Albă; in Russian: Belgorod Dnestrovskij) called in Hebrew *Ha-Ir ha-Levanah* ("the white city"). The Karaite Jews continued to live there until the middle of the 18th century. Occasional temporary presence of Ashkenazi Jewish merchants in Moldavia (called in Romanian: Moldova, principality located in the North-East, between the Oriental Carpathians and the Dniester and the Black Sea, founded at the beginning of the 14th century) occurred in the second half of the 15th century and in the beginning of the 16th century. In the second half of the 16th century, some Sephardi Jews from the Ottoman Empire visited Wallachia (called in Romanian: Ţara Românească, the second Romanian principality, located in the South, between the Southern Carpathians and the Danube, founded at the beginning of the 14th century) as exporters of cattle to the Ottoman Empire, dealers of wine, importers of textiles, and moneylenders. Some of them settled in Bucharest, the capital of Wallachia. Jewish creditors from Constantinople loaned money to candidates to the thrones of the principalities: they needed the money to pay the amount demanded by the Turkish sultan to obtain the princely function, since the principalities had become vassals to the Ottoman Empire in the first half of the 15th century. Some of those Jewish creditors accompanied the new princes to the principalities to make sure that they would repay their debt. Other Sephardi Jews from Turkey and from Italian states served as physicians or diplomats at princes' courts. In 1594–1595 the princes Mihai Viteazul (Michael the Brave) of Wallachia and Aron Tiranul (Aron the Tyran) of Moldavia killed their Jewish and Muslim creditors to avoid paying their debts to them.

As Moldavia was on the trade routes between Poland-Lithuania and the Ottoman Empire many Jewish merchants traveled through it. Some settled there. In the 16th century there were Jewish communities in several Moldavian towns. More intensive waves of Jewish immigration resulted from the Chmielnicki massacres (1648–49). Beginning in the 17th century Moldavian princes granted special charters to Jews; known is a charter given to Jews from Jassy in 1666. The Great Synagogue of Jassy was built about 1670.

In the last decades of the 18th century, more Jews from Galicia began to settle in Moldavia as a result of demographic changes, the partition of Poland, Austrian emperor Joseph II's toleration edicts, and the economic growth of the Romanian principalities after the Kücük-Kainargi Russian-Turkish peace treaty (1774). It was the beginning of a new wave of immigration. Many of them were Ḥasidim. These Jewish craftsmen and merchants obtained special charters. They helped to re-establish war-ravaged towns or to enlarge others. Some of them settled at crossroads and founded commercial centers, the so-called burgs; in this activity they were encouraged by landowners. Many Jews were occupied in buying and selling agricultural products from neighboring villages to towns, and bringing and selling industrial products to peasants. The burgs were founded as a part of the economic development toward a commercial economy and the urbanization process. After the settlement of the Jews, landowners gave them charters including advantages, such as exemption from taxes, land for prayer houses, ritual baths, and cemeteries. When two counties of Moldavia were annexed by their neighbors (Bukovina by Austria in 1775 and Bessarabia by Russia in 1812), some Jews from these counties preferred to move to Romanian Moldavia, where they were not harassed by the authorities and had both family and business connections. Among the Jews occupied in commerce (in towns, but especially in burgs), there were also many craftsmen, such as furriers, tailors, boot makers, tinsmiths, and watchmakers; they settled mainly in the towns. There were also Jewish exporters of agricultural products and importers of industrial and luxury products, and Jewish moneylenders, who later on became bankers. In villages, Jews leased inns and brandy distilleries. The process of urbanization and the immigration of Jews continued in the first half of the 19th century. Many immigrants also arrived from Russia, partly as a result of the forced conscription in the period of Czar Nicholas I. The number of Jews grew in Moldavia as did the number of the so-called "Jewish burgs"; later part of them became insignificant. Jewish immigration into Wallachia was from Moldavia only (a re-emigration) and some Sephardi Jewish immigration from the Ottoman Empire as a result of the political and economic changes in the Balkan part of that empire.

Among the rabbis and Torah scholars present in Moldavia and Wallachia in the period from the 17th to the beginning of the 19th centuries may be mentioned Solomon ibn Aroyo, a kabbalist and also a physicist (Jassy, at the beginning of the 17th century); Nathan Hanover (Jassy, second half of the 17th century); Haim Thierer (present in some towns of Moldavia, second half of the 18th century); Eliezer Papo (Bucharest and Silistra, beginning of the 19th century).

From early on commercial competition was one of the main reasons for anti-Jewish hatred in Romania. In 1579 the sovereign of Moldavia, Petru Schiopul (Peter the Lame), ordered the banishment of the Jews on the grounds that they were ruining the merchants. In the Danube harbors it was the Greek and Bulgarian merchants who incited riots against the Jews, especially during Easter. Anti-Jewish excesses in the neighboring countries often extended to the Romanian principalities. In 1652 and 1653 Cossacks invaded Moldavia, attacking many Jews from Jassy. In 1714, there was a small pogrom in Bucharest and the synagogue (built of stones) was destroyed on the order of the sovereign of Wallachia, Stefan Cantacuzino. Greek Orthodox Christianity also preached intolerance toward Jews and shaped the first code of law: the Church laws of Moldavia and Wallachia in 1640, of Byzantine inspiration. Both proclaimed the Jews as heretics and forbade any relations with them. The state and the Church encouraged the conversion of Jews to Orthodox Christianity and offered economic and social advantages to the converts. With the exception of physicians, Jews were not accepted as witnesses in trials. In the codes of 1746 and 1780 the Jews are scarcely mentioned. On the other hand, the first books of anti-Jewish incitement of a religious character appeared around this time: *Alcatuirea aurita a lui Samuil rabbi jidovul* (The Golden Order of Rabbi Samuel the Jew) and "A Challenge to Jews" (Jassy, 1803). The image of the Jew in Romanian folklore includes satanic aspects: the Jews were satanized under the influence of the church. In the course of the rebellion against the Turks (1821), Greek volunteers crossed Moldavia on their way to the Danube, plundering and slaying Jews as they went (in Jassy, Herta (now Gertsa), Odobesti, Vaslui, Roman, etc.).

The judicial status of the Jews in the principalities was of an ethnical-religious guild (in Romanian: *breasla*, called *breasla jidovilor* in Moldavia, and *breasla ovreiasca* in Wallachia). There were guilds set up according to nationality and religion (e.g., Armenians, Catholic-Kiprovitchian Bulgarians, Jews) and others organized according profession (which included Moldavian or Wallachian Christian-Orthodox craftsmen or merchants from towns). The system was based on the Ottoman system of "isnafs" (in Turkish: *isnaf*). The guild took care of tax collection proportionate to the number of persons organized in it; the Jews (i.e., the Jewish Guild) were obliged to pay a poll-tax for the right to settle. This system, known from 1666 in Jassy (the right to settle was granted by the sovereign through a gold-charter, in Romanian: *hrisov*) may have existed some decades previously in Moldavia. The head of the guild was the "senior" (in Romanian: *staroste*; in Hebrew: *rosh medinah*). The "senior" was responsible for tax collection. The system was based on that existing in Poland: the Ashkenazi Jews, of Polish origin, maintained their tradition. The "senior" was exempted from payment and had some advantages, granted by the sovereign through a special charter. Later the abuses began: the "seniors" were elected from among members of the same family. In the 1830s the tax paid in Moldavia was called – in Romanian – the *crupca* (also a system of Polish origin; in Polish: *korowka*). The sovereigns preferred to put the rabbi in charge of collecting the tax, with him exempted from paying. Later (last decades of the 18th century) his administrative function was called in Turkish *hakham-bashe* and he was named *ḥakham-bashi* (the rabbi, who was the chief of the Jewish guild). Every rabbi, however, had to pay bribes (officially) to be recognized in his function. In Moldavia, the rabbis were from the same family: descendents of Rabbi Naphtali ha-Kohen of Posen, whose son, Bezalel was appointed as rabbi of Jassy community in 1719. In Wallachia the "senior" maintained his administrative and fiscal function, but consulted the rabbi of Jassy for halakhic problems and became his representative in Bucharest. The collective tax, set by the guild in agreement with the tax-collector, was paid from the tax on kosher meat, taxes on religious ceremonies, and contributions from every family head. The expenses of the institutions (*talmud torah, hekdesh*, cemetery) were covered by the remainder. The rabbi's salary was set according to the number of slaughtered cattle, of religious ceremonies, and of boys learning in the *talmud torah*.

The situation changed once again at the end of the 18th–first decades of the 19th centuries. Owing to the competition among the rabbis for this function and to the fact that many Jews considered the *ḥakham bashi* as insufficiently learned in Torah, his prestige was low, and learned rabbis were considered by the Jews as their real spiritual leaders. The growing number of immigrants from Galicia and Russia at the beginning of the 19th century opposed the *ḥakham bashi*, since such an institution was unknown to them and many of them were followers of Ḥasidism and led by *ẓaddikim*. As they were foreign subjects they asked their consuls to intercede, and in 1819 the prince of Moldavia decided that the *ḥakham bashi* should have jurisdiction only over "native" Jews. The Ḥasidim did not buy meat slaughtered by a non-Ḥasidic slaughterer, because his knife was not polished. So, they bought meat from "illegal" slaughterers and did not pay the tax on kosher meat. The collective tax paid by the Jewish guild to the state was smaller. Finally, after agreements with the representatives of the immigrant Jews (Ḥasidim), because of permanent strife among the diverse groups of Jews and their complaints to the authorities, the latter decided in 1834 to abolish the *ḥakham bashi* system and institution in Moldavia. In Wallachia, although the *ḥakham bashi* institution was not abolished, it remained inactive. Jewish communal life and organization were changed. The Ottoman system was changed to the Russian system. The Jewish guild became the Jewish community, called "the Jewish nation" (in Romanian: *natia ovreeasca*). Since the fiscal system could not be changed radically, the method of collective taxation on kosher meat remained in use but was carried out by representatives of the government for a relatively short period. After around a decade it was changed, proving impractical: only the wealthy Jews bought meat, while the poor consumed mainly vegetables. The functions of the community devolved on to the various prayer houses and the artisans' guilds and sometimes on the *ḥevra kaddisha* or the Jewish hospital.

(For the early history of the other regions which later made up Romania see *Bessarabia, *Bukovina, and *Transylvania).

Emerging Romania

The Russian-Turkish peace treaty of Adrianopol (1829) canceled the interdiction of the export of some Moldavian and Wallachian agricultural products from the Ottoman Empire and decreed freedom of commerce. Between 1829 and 1834 Moldavia and Wallachia were occupied by Russia. A nearly similar constitution (the so-called Organic Law) was prepared for both principalities during that period and promulgated in 1832. The constitution was similar to the one already existing in Wallachia and Moldavia. From 1832 to 1856 the two principalities were protectorates of Russia. The Organic Law of Moldavia (together with additions promulgated between 1834 and 1856) also dealt with the position of the Jews. Their communal organization was on the Russian model (*kahal*). Jews were forbidden to own property in the villages. Additions to the laws promulgated in 1839 and 1843 gave the authorities the right to determine which Jews were useful to the country, the others being declared vagrants and expelled. However, the Organic Law of Moldavia stipulated that Jewish children could attend public schools if they dressed like the Christian children. Jews were exempted from military service. The number of Jews increased owing to emigration from Galicia and Russia. The number of Jewish burgs in Moldavia also grew. In Bucharest (Wallachia) the community was fragmented. In the early 1840s the Sephardi Jews of Bucharest left the community and founded their own community with their own traditions. The Ashkenazi Jews of Bucharest who were Austrian and Prussian subjects also left the community and founded a community supported by the Austrian and Prussian consuls, in order not to pay taxes. The "native" and Polish (Russian) Jewish subjects remained as the Ashkenazi community. Later on, these two Ashkenazi communities reunited.

In the 1848 revolutions of Moldavia and Wallachia, directed against the Russian protectorate and against absolutism and serfdom, the revolutionaries appealed to the Jews to participate. They distinguished, however, between useful and non-useful Jews (the latter being nominated for expulsion) and proposed the "emancipation of the Israelites and transformation into useful citizens," proclaiming their civic equality. Some Jews took part in the 1848 revolution of Wallachia (see Davicion *Bally), but the majority of Jews did not participate in the revolutions. However, under the influence of revolution, some "progressive" Jews revolted against the leadership of the Ashkenazi community and took over for a short period. The revolutions were suppressed (in Moldavia immediately by the sovereign, in Wallachia after three months by the Russian and Ottoman armies).

Independent Romania

The peace treaty of Paris (1856), which concluded the Crimean War and granted the principalities a certain autonomy under the suzerainty of the seven European powers, proclaimed inter alia that in the two Danubian principalities all the inhabitants, irrespective of religion, should enjoy religious and civil liberties (the right to own property and to trade) and might occupy political posts. Only those who had foreign citizenship were excluded from political rights. The leaders of the Moldavian and Wallachian Jews addressed themselves both to the Romanian authorities and to the great powers, asking for the abolition of the discriminations against them. However, the opposition of Russia and of the Romanian political leaders hindered this: the special assembly decided that only Christians would obtain citizenship. The two principalities united in 1859; Bucharest became the capital of the new state (United Principalities, and from 1862 Romania); Alexandru Ioan Cuza, who was a member of the 1848 revolutionaries' group and not antisemitic, became their sovereign. The number of Jews was then 130,000 (3% of the total population). In 1864 native Jews were granted suffrage in the local councils ("little naturalization"); but Jews who were foreign subjects still could not acquire landed property. Political rights were granted to non-Christians but only parliament could vote on the naturalization of individual Jews – but not a single Jew was naturalized.

In 1866 Alexandru Ioan Cuza was ousted by anti-liberal forces. A new sovereign, Carol of Hohenzollern-Sigmaringen, was elected and a new constitution adopted. Under the pressure of demonstrations organized by the police (during which the Choir Temple in Bucharest was demolished and the Jewish quarter plundered), the seventh article of the constitution, restricting citizenship to the Christian population, was adopted. Even the visit to Bucharest of Adolphe Crémieux, president of the Alliance Israélite Universelle, who delivered a speech in the Romanian parliament, had no effect. In the spring of 1867 the minister of interior, Ion Bratianu, started to expel Jews from the villages and banish noncitizens from the country. In the summer of the same year Sir Moses Montefiore arrived in Bucharest and demanded that Prince Carol put a stop to the persecutions. But these continued in spite of the promises given. Hundreds of families, harassed by humiliating regulations (e.g., a prohibition on building *sukkot*), were forced to leave the villages. Local officials regarded such persecution as an effective method of extorting bribes. Neither the repeated interventions of Great Britain and France nor the condemnatory resolutions in the parliaments of Holland and Germany had any effect. The Romanian government reiterated that the Jewish problem was an internal one, and the great powers limited themselves to protests.

At the Congress of Berlin (1878), which finalized Romanian independence, the great powers made the grant of civil rights to the Jews a condition of that independence in spite of opposition by the Romanian delegates. The Romanian representatives threatened the delegates of the Jewish world organizations, as well as the representatives of the Jews of Romania, by hinting at a worsening of their situation. Indeed, after the Congress of Berlin other antisemitic measures were introduced, and there was incitement in the press and public demonstrations organized by the authorities on the Russian model, in order to prove to the great powers that the people were against Jewish emancipation. Their aim was also to create an antisemitic atmosphere on the eve of the session of parliament which was to decide on the modification of the article in the 1866 constitution concerning Jewish naturalization. Prince Carol, opening parliament, declared that the Jews had a harmful influence on economic life and especially on the peasants. After stormy debates parliament modified the article of the constitution which made citizenship conditional on Christianity, but stated that the naturalization of Jews would be carried out individually, by vote of both chambers of parliament. During the following 38 years 2,000 Jews in all were naturalized by this oppressive procedure; of those, 883 were voted in en bloc, having taken part in the 1877 war against Turkey.

This caused the great powers to refuse for a time to recognize independent Romania. However, they finally followed the example of Germany, which took the first step after having received pecuniary compensation from the Romanian government through the redemption of railway shares belonging to Silesian Junkers and members of the German imperial court – at six times their quoted value. The situation of the Jews continued to grow worse. Up to then they had been considered Romanian subjects but now they were declared to be foreigners. The Romanian government persuaded Austria and Germany to withdraw their citizenship from Jews living in Romania. The Jews were forbidden to be lawyers, teachers in public schools, chemists, stockbrokers, or to sell commodities which were a government monopoly (tobacco, salt, alcohol). They were not accepted as railway officials, in state hospitals, or as officers. Jewish pupils were later expelled from the public schools (1893). Meanwhile political intimidation continued. In 1885 some of the Jewish leaders and journalists who had participated in the struggle for emancipation, among them Moses Gaster and Elias Schwarzfeld, were expelled from Romania. Both major political parties in Romania – the Liberals and the Conservatives – were antisemitic, with only slight differences. In 1910 the first specifically antisemitic party, the National Democratic Party, was founded, under the leadership of the university professors A.C. Cuza and Nicolae Iorga.

Ḥasidism, Haskalah, Religious Reform

The majority of the Jews of Moldavia were Ḥasidim. Most of them followed the *admor* of Ruzhin, Rabbi Israel *Ruzhin Friedmann. Others, especially those of Russian origin, were Ḥasidim of the Chabad movement. In 1809, Rabbi *Abraham Joshua Heshel of Opatow settled in Jassy, having been invited by the local leader and moneylender Rabbi Michel ben Daniel; he left the town in 1813. The next year another Ḥasidic rabbi, Joseph David Ha-Kohen from Zwolew (1750–1828) settled in Jassy. In 1834, at the suggestion of the *admor* Rabbi Israel of Ruzhin, the Ḥasidic Rabbi Joseph Landau was invited to Jassy, where he became the town's rabbi until his death (1853). Owing to the large number of appeals to the rabbinical tribunal, another Ḥasidic rabbi, Aharon Moses *Taubes, was invited to Jassy and settled there; he died in Jassy in 1852. In 1852 the *admor* Menahem Nahum Friedman settled in Stefanesti and founded the Ḥasidic dynasty and "court" of Stefanesti. In 1866, the *admor* Isaac ben Shalom Friedman settled in Buhusi and founded the Ḥasidic dynasty and "court" of the same name, which became the central Ḥasidic court in Romania. Later, *admorim* from the same family founded other Ḥasidic dynasties and "courts" in Romania, such as Pascani, Adjud, and Focsani. Other *admorim* and Ḥasidic rabbis from the Gutman, Halpern, Derbaremdige, Landman, Zilberfarb, Wahrman, Teumim, Drimer, Frenkel, and Sulitzer-Moscovici families also settled in Romania in the 19th–first half of the 20th centuries.

The presence of *maskilim*, many of them having emigrated from Galicia, is also attested from the 1830s. Later they became more active and began to organize. One of them was Michel Alter Finkelstein of Jassy, fighter for cultural integration, modernization, and changing of Jewish East-European manner of dress. An important *maskil* from Bucharest was Judah ben Mordechai (Julius) *Barasch, a physicist and also a writer in the Hebrew, German, and Romanian languages. The first Jewish school functioning with a Haskalah movement curriculum was founded in Bucharest in 1851, in the Jewish community holding Austrian and Prussian citizenship, with Julius Barasch as its principal; in 1852 in Bucharest (in the community of "native" and Polish Jews) Naftaly K. Popper became a Hebrew teacher; in Jassy (1853) Benjamin Schwarzfeld became the principal. A "Society for Israelite Culture" was founded in 1862 in Bucharest, functioning for only one year. At the end of the 1850s and in the 1860s some *maskil* Hebrew writers were active in Moldavia: Matitiahu Simha Rabener (editor of the Hebrew review *Zimrat Ha'aretz*; Mordechai Streslisker (Marvad Sat); Hillel Kahane; Hirsh Mendel Pineles (Ha-Shalash) and others.

Some *maskilim* adopted the idea of also reforming religious worship. They advanced their proposals in the 1850s in Bucharest. After a conflict with *Malbim, the rabbi of Bucharest from 1858, they succeeded in influencing the Romanian government to expel him, maintaining that he was against progress (1864). However the majority of the Jews were Orthodox and remained loyal to him. In 1866, the reformists opened the "Choral Temple" in Bucharest; its first preacher was Antoine Levy. In the same period the Choral Temple "Beth Ya'aqov" was opened in Jassy, founded by the baron Jacob Neuschatz. In 1889 the Sephardi reform temple (Cahal Grande) was founded in Bucharest. However the trend was only of moderate reform: most of the reform rabbis were graduates of the Breslau seminary. This trend continued after World War I in the period of the first chief rabbi, Dr. Jacob Isaac *Niemirower.

At the end of the 19th century, the currents of radical Haskalah, Jewish socialism, and Jewish nationalism also appeared in Romania. Activists for Jewish nationalism were Karpel Lippe, a Hebrew writer; Samuel Pineles; Menahem-Mendel Braunstein (Mibashan), also a Hebrew writer, who later immigrated to Palestine; and Israel Teller. At the end of December–beginning of January 1882, a conference of Ishuv Eretz Israel organizations in Romania took place in the town of Focsani.

Internal Organization

Because of conflicts between Ḥasidim and *maskilim*, and also due to the integrationist trend, Jewish communities ceased to exist or became inactive at the beginning of the 1870s. A new form of organization became necessary. The first general Jewish representative body, after the dissolution of the Jews' Guild and the internal strife in the communities, was the Brotherhood of Zion society, the forerunner of the B'nai B'rith, created in 1872 under the influence of Benjamin Franklin Peixotto, the first American diplomat in Romania. He thus succeeded in shaping a cadre of leaders for the Jewish institutions, but did not see any solution for the masses but emigration. For that purpose he initiated a conference of world Jewish organizations which convened in Brussels (Oct. 29–30, 1872). Under the influence of assimilationist circles, emigration – considered to be unpatriotic – was rejected as a solution of the Jewish problem. The conference suggested to the Jews of Romania that they should fight to acquire political equality. After some years, however, a mass movement started for immigration to Ereẓ Israel.

The political organization founded in 1890, under the name The General Association of Native Israelites, tended to assimilation and strident patriotism, claiming citizenship only for those Jews who had served in the army. Under pressure by a group of Jewish socialists it extended its demands, claiming political rights for all Jews born in the country. In 1897 antisemitic students attacked members of the congress of the association and caused riots in Bucharest. The association ceased its activity, and an attempt at reorganization in 1903 failed. Under the pressure of increasing persecution accompanied by an internal economic crisis, in 1900 a mass emigration of Jews began; they traveled on foot as far as Ham-

Map 1. Jewish communities in Romania on the eve of World War I. Based on Pinkas ha-Kehillot: Rumanyah, *Vol. 1, Jerusalem, 1969. Courtesy Yad Vashem Archives, Jerusalem.*

burg and from there went to the United States, Canada, and Great Britain. Up to World War I about 70,000 Jews left Romania. From 266,652 (4.5% of the total population) in 1899 the Jewish population declined to 239,967 (3.3%) in 1912. The 1907 revolt of the peasants, who at first vented their wrath on the Jews, also contributed to this tendency to emigrate; Jewish houses and shops were pillaged in many villages and cities of Moldavia, 2,280 families being affected. At the same time the persecution of the Jews increased. Their expulsion from the villages assumed such proportions that in some counties of Moldavia (Dorohoi, Jassy, Bacau) none remained except veterans of the 1877 war.

In 1910 the political organization called Uniunea Evreilor Pamanteni (The Union of Native Jews), UEP, was founded to combat anti-Jewish measures and to achieve emancipation. Its first head was Adolphe Stern, former secretary of B.F. Peixotto. The UEP tended toward integration in Romanian society. It operated by intercession with politicians, through petitions to parliament, and by printed propaganda against antisemitism. In a single case it was successful through direct intercession with King Carol I, who held up the passage of a bill discriminating against Jewish craftsmen (1912).

At the end of the 19th century there began the organization of Jewish communities, together with the creation of a Jewish school system as a result of the expulsion of Jews from the public schools (1893). The impoverishment of the Jewish population also created a need for social assistance which could not be provided by the various existing associations. To achieve the legalization of the communities, several congresses of their representatives were organized (April 1896 in Galati, 1902 in Jassy, and 1905 in Focsani), but they could not agree on the proper nature of a community. Some claimed that it should have an exclusively religious character; others wanted a lay organization dealing only with social welfare, hospitals, and schools. The different Jewish institutions (synagogues, religious associations, hospitals) endeavored to preserve their autonomy. There was a struggle for the tax on meat, too, each demanding this income for itself. At the same time assimilationist groups of students and intellectuals launched a drive against the community, which they defined as an isolationist instrument; in this move they were joined by antisemites who called the community a "state within a state," a Jewish conspiracy aiming to establish supremacy over the Romanians. Some proposed putting the communities under the Ministry of the Interior. An attempt in 1897 to introduce into parliament a bill on the Jewish communities, its purpose being defined by the proposer as "to defend the Jewish population against its ignorant religious fanatics," failed because of the opposition of the liberal government of the day. Later the principle of autonomy prevailed at Jewish community congresses, owing to the influence of the Zionists, especially Rabbis J. [Jacob] Nacht and J. Niemirover. Protests were lodged against the interference of the local authorities (mayors, chief commissioners of police, etc.) as well as against the oath *more judaico*. The principle of autonomy finally triumphed, owing to the young Zionists who penetrated the local communities, especially in the country.

The Struggle for Naturalization

Following World War I Romania enlarged her territory with the provinces of Bukovina, Bessarabia, and Transylvania. In each of these the Jews were already citizens, either of long standing like those who had lived in the Austro-Hungarian Empire, or more recent like those from Bessarabia who achieved equality only in 1917. Indeed, the naturalization of the Jews of Romania was under way in accordance with the separate peace treaty concluded with Germany in the spring of 1918. In August 1918 the Romanian parliament passed an act concerning naturalization with many very complicated procedures, the latter being, moreover, sabotaged when they had to be applied by the local authorities. After the defeat of Germany, Prime Minister Ionel Bratianu realized that at the peace conference the naturalization of the Jews would be brought up again, so he tried to resolve the problem in good time by issuing a decree of naturalization on Dec. 28, 1918, proclaiming individual naturalization on the lines adopted after the Congress of Berlin. The decision had to be made by the law courts instead of parliament, on the basis of certain certificates which were very difficult to obtain. Though threatened by the government the Jewish leaders rejected the law, and, following their warning, the Jewish population abstained from putting in applications to the court. Their demand was for citizenship to be granted en bloc by one procedure – after a declaration by every candidate at his municipality that he was born in the country and held no foreign citizenship, the municipality would have to make out the certificate of citizenship.

Although the Romanian government continued to assert that the Jewish problem was an internal one, of national sovereignty, when the delegation led by Ionel Bratianu appeared at the peace conference in Paris (May 1919) Georges Clemenceau reminded him that after the Congress of Berlin Romania had not implemented the provisions concerning the political rights of the Jews. This time the great powers decided to include guarantees in the peace treaty. A Jewish delegation from Romania, composed of UEP, Zionist and Jewish socialist representatives, arrived in Paris. They joined the Jewish delegations participating in the peace conference and claimed that the peace treaty should lay down the kind of obligatory laws concerning naturalization which Romania should pass. To prevent the conference's imposition of naturalization of Jews, Ionel Bratianu wired to Bucharest the text of a law (promulgated as a decree on May 22, 1919), according to which citizenship could now be obtained by a declaration of intent in writing to the law court, the latter being obliged to make out a certificate of confirmation which conferred the exercise of political rights. Those who did not possess foreign citizenship, those who satisfied the requirements of the enlistment law, and those who had served in the war were declared citizens, together with their families.

The peace conference did not, however, fail to include in the treaty the obligation of Romania to legislate the political emancipation of the Jews, which no other measure should abrogate. Bratianu resigned in protest, and only after an ultimatum sent by the peace conference did the new Romanian government led by Alexandru Vaida-Voevod sign the peace treaty. In Bukovina 40,000 Jews were threatened with remaining stateless, on the pretext of their being refugees who had only recently entered the country. A professor of the faculty of law at Jassy published a study in 1921 asserting that this naturalization was anti-constitutional. In 1923 there began a new struggle for the enactment of naturalization in the new constitution. Adolphe Stern, the president of the UEP, was elected as a deputy to parliament and had to fight the law proposed by the Bratianu government which in effect canceled most of the naturalizations already acquired. After hard bargaining, not without renewed threats on the part of the government, the naturalization of the Jews was introduced into the constitution on March 29, 1923, thus also confirming the naturalization of those from the newly annexed territories who would otherwise have been threatened with expulsion. Nevertheless there was a great difference between the laws and the way in which they were implemented. In a regulation published two months after the passing of the constitution, many procedural restrictions on the Jews living in the new provinces were introduced. In practice, the civil service, the magistracy, university chairs, and officers' corps remained closed to Jews. UEP became the Union of Romanian Jews (Uniunea Evreilor Români – UER) and Wilhelm *Filderman became its president.

Increasing Antisemitism

Growing social and political tensions in Romania in the 1920s and 1930s led to a constant increase in antisemitism and in the violence which accompanied it. Antisemitic excesses and demonstrations expressed both popular and student antisemitism and cruelty; they also served to divert social unrest to the Jews and show Western public opinion that intervention on their behalf was bound to miscarry. In December 1922 Christian students at the four universities proclaimed *numerus clausus* as their program; riots followed at the universities and against the Jewish population. As was later revealed in parliament, the student movements were organized and financed by the Ministry of the Interior. The leader of the student movements was Corneliu Zelea Codreanu, the secretary of the League of National Christian Defense which was headed by A.C. Cuza. The students formed terrorist groups on the Fascist model and committed several murders. In 1926 the Jewish student Falic was murdered at Chernovtsy. The assassin was acquitted. In 1927 Codreanu broke away from A.C. Cuza and founded the Archangel Michael League, which in 1929 became the Iron Guard, a paramilitary organization with an extreme antisemitic program.

On Dec. 9, 1927, the students of Codreanu's League carried out a pogrom in Oradea Mare (Transylvania), where they were holding a congress, for which they received a subsidy from the Ministry of the Interior: they were conveyed there in special trains put at their disposal free of charge by the government. Five synagogues were wrecked and the Torah scrolls burned in the public squares. After that the riots spread all over the country: in Cluj eight prayer houses were plundered, and on their way home the participants in the congress continued their excesses against the Jews in the cities of Huedin, Targu-Ocna, and Jassy. At the end of 1933 the liberal prime minister I.G. Duca, one of the opponents of King Carol's dictatorial tendencies, dissolved the Iron Guard and after three weeks was assassinated by its men. The guard was reformed under the slogan, "Everything for the Country." Codreanu's ties with the Nazis in Germany dated from that time. Carol II later aided other political bodies with an antisemitic program in an attempt to curb the Iron Guard. From 1935 Al. Vaida-Voevod led the Romanian Front, and made use in his speeches of such slogans as the blood libel, the parasitism of the Jews, their defrauding the country, their international solidarity, and the Judaization of the press and national literature.

After Hitler came to power in Germany (1933), the large Romanian parties also adopted antisemitic programs. In 1935 the new National Christian Party announced that its program included "the Romanization of the staff of firms and the protection of national labor through preference for [our] ethnic element" – that is to say, the removal of Jews from private firms. Gheorghe Bratianu, leading a dissident liberal party, demanded "nationalization of the cities, proportional representation in public and private posts, in schools and universities, and revocation of Jewish citizenship." In July 1934 the "Law for Employment of Romanian Workers in [Private] Firms" was enacted, and in fact established a *numerus clausus*. The Ministry of Industry and Trade sent all firms special questionnaires which included a clause on "ethnic origin." In 1935 the board of Christian Lawyers' Association, founded that year by members of the bar from Ilfov (Bucharest) gave an impetus to antisemitic professional associations. The movement spread all over the country. Its program was the *numerus nullus*, i.e., revoking the licenses of Jewish lawyers who were already members of the bar and not accepting new registrations. At the universities students of the Iron Guard forcibly prevented their Jewish colleagues from attending lectures and the academic authorities supported the *numerus clausus* program, introducing entrance examinations; in 1935–36 this led to a perceptible decrease in the number of Jewish students, in certain faculties reaching the *numerus nullus*. In other professional corporations no Jews were elected to the board; they were prevented by force from participating in the elections. The great Romanian banks began to reject requests for credits from Jewish banks as well as from Jewish industrial and commercial firms, and the Jewish enterprises were burdened by heavy taxes, imposed with the aim of ruining them. Jewish firms were not granted import quotas for raw materials and goods. Meanwhile Germany financed a series of publications and newspapers aimed at fastening an alliance between the two countries and removing Jews from all branches of the professions and the economy. Many a Jewish merchant and industrialist was compelled to sell his firm at a loss when it became unprofitable under these oppressive measures.

Jewish Political Life

Despite the attempts of the older assimilationist and established Jewish groups, the inclination of Romanian Jewry – thanks largely to the trends among Jews of the newly annexed provinces and to the impact of Zionism – was toward a clear-cut Jewish stance in politics. In 1919 the Union of Romanian Jews, led by W. Filderman, recommended that the Jews vote for those Romanian parties which would be favorable to them. As none of the parties formulated an attitude toward the Jewish problem, the Union decided that the Jews should withhold their votes. In the 1920 elections the Union joined the Zionists to form a list which conducted its election campaign under the symbol of the *menorah*. As the elections were rigged, not a single candidate succeeded in entering parliament. The Union managed to send Adolphe Stern to parliament in 1922 through joining with the Peasants' Party. From 1923 the Zionists pressed for a policy of a national minority

Campaign poster for the Romanian League of National Defense, exhorting Christian citizens to vote for A.C. Cuza, a candidate for the post of minister for Jewish affairs. Cuza is described as a "strong man," who will "fight against infiltration of Jews, who are destroying Romania" (1930). Courtesy Yad Vashem Archives, Jerusalem.

status for the Jews. Their proposal was not accepted by the Union.

In 1926 the first National Jewish deputies and senators were elected from Bukovina, Transylvania, and Bessarabia. As a consequence of these successes the National Jewish Club, in which representatives of the Zionist parties also participated, was founded in Bucharest. Such clubs were established in all the cities of the Old Kingdom. In 1928 four National Jewish deputies were returned to parliament (two from Transylvania, one from Bukovina, and one from Bessarabia). They formed a Jewish parliamentary club. In 1930 the Jewish Party (Partidul Evreesc) was established in the Old Kingdom and on May 4, 1931, it held its general congress. Adolphe Stern joined this party. In the elections to parliament, a month later, the Jewish Party gained five seats, and in the 1932 elections it again obtained five. The situation of the Jewish parliamentarians was far from easy, because they were not only interrupted during their speeches but were often physically attacked by the deputies of the antisemitic parties. After 1933 there were no more Jewish members of parliament, except for J. Niemirower, who in his capacity of chief rabbi was officially a senator.

In 1913, the Ashkenazi Jewish community of Bucharest was founded as a modern association open to all the Ashkenazi Jews in the capital. Similar communities were founded in other towns of the Old Kingdom. In 1921 the Union of the Jewish Communities of the Old Kingdom was founded. Yet the undefined legal status of the Jewish communities in Romania tempted local authorities to meddle more and more in their affairs. A rabbi from Bucharest, Hayyim Schor, proclaimed himself chief rabbi. He demanded recognition of a separate Orthodox community everywhere in Romania, and was willing to be satisfied with the status of a private association for the Jewish community, thus abandoning the demand for its recognition as a public body. The Union and the Zionists opposed him. On May 19, 1921, the congress of Jews from the Old Kingdom met in Bucharest and elected Dr. Jacob Itzhak Niemirower as chief rabbi. In 1922 Jewish representatives demanded that two communities be recognized: the Ashkenazi and the Sephardi (and for Transylvania an Orthodox community too, as was traditional there). Only in 1928 did parliament pass the Law of Religions applying the provisions of the constitution, which recognized Judaism as one of the eight historical religions and the community as a juridical person in public law. On the basis of this law all the property of the religious institutions was transferred to the ownership of the communities. In January 1929 the minister of religions limited the application of this law, instructing that communities become juridical persons only after the approval of their statutes by the ministry; he also permitted communities of "diverse rites," and not only the Ashkenazi or Sephardi, and in Transylvania the Orthodox type, thus accepting the program of Rabbi Schor. Mayors and police commissioners thought that this gave them a legal cover to dissolve the elected boards of the communities and to appoint others to their liking, although the Ministry of Religions issued a circular prohibiting interference by local authorities. Only in 1932 did the communities gain general recognition as juridical persons in public law. In 1936, the unions of Jewish communities from all the provinces of Romania (also the Orthodox and Sephardi unions of communities) founded a representative organization for all the Jews of Romania: the Federation of the Unions of Jewish Communities of Greater Romania.

The certificates of Jewish schools were not recognized and their pupils had to pass state examinations, paying a fee (which was a charge on community budgets as they covered this fee for the poor) until 1925, when the certificates of Jewish schools were recognized if the language of tuition was Romanian. (Although Romania had signed the Minorities Treaty in Paris, it had never implemented it.) All Jewish schools were maintained by the communities; in Bessarabia, Tarbut maintained Hebrew schools. The Ministry of Education contributed only a token subvention. The Jews of annexed Transylvania used the Hungarian language in the Zionist press, even under Romanian rule, those of Bukovina German, while in Bessarabia the language of the Jewish press was Yiddish. Each province kept its traditions, autonomous structure, and cultural life, within the framework of the all-Romanian Federation of Jewish Communities. Culturally, the deeply rooted Jewish life of Bessarabia, with its Hebrew teachers, writers, and journalists, had a great influence, especially in the Old Kingdom.

In 1924 there were 796,056 Jews in enlarged Romania (5% of the total population): 230,000 in the Old Kingdom, 238,000 in Bessarabia, 128,056 in Bukovina, and 200,000 in Transylvania. In 1930 their number was 756,930 (4.2% of the total population): 263,192 in the Old Kingdom, 206,958 in Bessarabia, 92,988 in Bukovina, and 193,000 in Transylvania.

Social Structure

The Jewish population of Old Romania was for the most part an urban one. According to the 1899 census, 79.73% of the Jews lived in cities, forming 32.10% of the whole urban population of the country. Only 20.27% lived in villages, forming 1.1% of the whole rural population. This phenomenon was a result of the ban on Jews dwelling in a rural area. In the Moldavia province, where the Jews were most heavily concentrated, they formed a majority in several towns. In Falticeni they were 57% of the total population; in Dorohoi, 53.6%; in Botosani, 51.8%; in Jassy, 50.8%. In several smaller towns of that region their proportion was greater: in Gertsa, 66.2%; in Mihaileni, 65.6%; in Harlau, 59.6%; in Panciu, 52.4%. The Romanian population was 84.06% farmers, the Jews constituting the middle class. According to 1904 statistics, 21.1% of the total number of merchants were Jews, but in some cities of Moldavia they were a definite majority, such as in Jassy, 75.3%; Botosani, 75.2%; Dorohoi, 72.9%; Tecuci, 65.9%, etc. Jews represented 20.07% of all artisans, and in several branches they were a majority: 81.3% of engravers, 76% of tinsmiths; 75.9% of watchmakers; 74.6% of bookbinders; 64.9% of hatmakers; 64.3% of upholsterers, etc. Industry was not advanced in Romania before World War I. There were 625 industrial firms altogether, 19.5% of them owned by Jews. Jews were 5.3% of the officials and workers in these industrial enterprises. In several branches of industry there were Jewish factory owners: 52.8% of the glass industry; 32.4% of the wood and furniture industry; 32.4% of the clothing industry; 26.5% of the textile industry. Of the liberal professions only medicine was permitted to Jews. They constituted 38% of the total number of doctors. The occupational distribution of the Jews was as follows; agriculture, 2.5%; industry and crafts, 42.5%; trade and banking, 37.9%; liberal professions, 3.2%; various occupations, 13.7%.

There are no detailed statistics of the period between the two world wars. The provinces of Bessarabia, Transylvania, and Bukovina were annexed to Old Romania, increasing the Jewish population threefold. In every province their occupational structure was different as the result of historical development. In the two annexed provinces, Transylvania and Bukovina, the Jews had enjoyed civil rights from the days of the Austro-Hungarian Empire, and were also represented in the liberal professions. On the other hand, their situation in Bessarabia in czarist times was worse than in Old Romania – a fact which also influenced their occupational structure. The few known figures refer to Greater Romania, with all the annexed territories. The only census taken in Bessarabia was in 1930, and according to those figures the occupational distribution of the Jewish population was as follows: industry and crafts, 24.8%; trade and banking, 51.5%; liberal professions, 2.9%; miscellaneous, 8.2%. It should be noted that Jewish bankers (such as the bank of "Marmorosh-Blank") invested money in the developing industry of Greater Romania. Some industrial enterprises, comprising several factories such as the sugar, metal, and textile works, etc., were owned by Jews. In the late 1930s, under the influence of Nazi Germany in Romania, the whole occupational structure of the Jews collapsed because of persecution on the economic level, which preceded political persecution and murder.

Cultural Life

Since most Romanian Jews were of Polish or Russian extraction, their religious and cultural traditions were similar to those of the Jews of Eastern Europe. Their rabbis and teachers, as well as their religious trends came from there. The spoken language of the Ashkenazi Jewish population was Yiddish; Judeo-Spanish was used by Sephardi Jews; Romanian became more widely used among them only in the second half of the 19th century, at the time when the first Romanian universities were established (Jassy in 1860 and Bucharest in 1864). In that period, too, the development of modern Romanian literature began. In 1857 Julius Barasch published the first newspaper in Romanian and French – *Israelitul Român* – whose function was to fight for equal civil rights for Romanian Jewry. In 1854 another two newspapers – *Timpul* (*Di Tsayt*; Bucharest) and *Gazeta Româno-Evreească* (Jassy) – appeared in Romanian and Yiddish, but all three papers ceased publication before the end of a year. Other such attempts met the same fate. Only in 1879 did the weekly *Fraternitatea* begin to appear, lasting until 1885, when it ceased publication upon the expulsion from Romania of its chief editors, Isaac Auerbach and Elias Schwarzfeld, for their stand against persecutions. This paper, which represented the assimilationist trend, was opposed to the incipient pre-Zionist movement which sponsored the establishment of the colonies of Zikhron Ya'akov and Rosh Pinnah in Ereẓ Israel. Then two papers in Romanian also appeared, supporting *aliyah: Apărătorul*, which was published in Bucharest from 1881 to 1884 with A.S. Gold as editor, and the weekly *Stindardul*, which was published in Focsani from 1882 to 1883. The Yiddish paper *Ha-Yo'eẓ* which appeared in Bucharest from 1874 to 1896 also supported *aliyah*. Eleazar Rokeah, an emissary from Erez Israel, published as special organs of the pre-Zionist movement the Hebrew paper *Emek Yizre'el* in Jassy (1882), and the Yiddish *Di Hofnung* in Piatra-Neamt (1882), and *Der Emigrant* in Galati (1882). Of the Jewish press in Romania the weekly *Egalitatea*, edited by Moses Schwarzfeld, survived for half a century. The weekly *Curierul Israelit*, edited by M. Schweig, began to appear in 1906 and continued up to 1948, becoming the mouthpiece of the Uniunea Evreilor Români (Union of Romanian Jews) after World War I. In the time of Herzl several Zionist papers appeared in Romania but did not last long. In 1913 the monthly *Hatikva* in Romanian was issued in Galati under the editorship of Leon Gold who gathered round him the outstanding Jewish authors in Romanian. Apart from original articles they also published translations of a high literary standard from modern Hebrew poetry and classical Yiddish literature. After World War I, from 1919 to 1923, there was published in Bucharest a daily newspaper in Romanian with a Zionist national tendency, *Mântuirea*, edited by A.L. Zissu, with Abraham Feller as chief editor. This paper stood for the idea of a Jewish political party and sharply attacked the tendencies of assimilationist circles. The weekly *Renasterea Noastră* (1923–42, 1944–48), edited by Samuel I. Stern, continued in this direction subsequently. The Zionist Federation published the weekly *Ştiri din Lumea Evreească*, edited by I. Ludo and later by Theoder Loewenstein. Between the two world wars the Zionist students' association published the monthly *Hasmonaea*. The number of Jewish journalists grew between the two wars, some of them even becoming chief editors of the great democratic papers. They included Constantin Graur, B. Branisteanu, Em. Fagure, G. Milian (Bucharest); A. Hefter (Jassy), and S. Schaferman-Pastoresu (Braila). After they had acquired a knowledge of Romanian, several Jewish scholars at the end of the 19th century became distinguished in the field of philology and folklore: Lazar Saineanu (Sainéan), compiler of the first practical dictionary of Romanian (1896); M. Gaster, who did research on early Romanian folklore; Hayman Tiktin, author of a scientific grammar of Romanian in two volumes (1893–94). This tradition continued down to later times. I.A. Candrea also compiled a Romanian dictionary (1931), as did J. Byk and Al. Graur after World War II. A number of these scholars also devoted time to research on the history of Romanian Jewry. The pioneer in this field was J. Psantir, whose two Yiddish volumes contained Hebrew headings: *Divrei ha-Yamim le-Arẓot Rumanye* (Jassy, 1871) and *Korot ha-Yehudim be-Rumanye* (Lemberg, 1877). A society for research into the history of Romanian Jewry was established in 1886 and named for Julius Barasch. Among its active members were J. Psantir, M. Gaster, Lazar Saineanu, Isac David Bally, Elias Schwarzfeld, Moses Schwarzfeld, and others. In the three publications of their bulletin they published source material, memoirs, and bibliographical notes, as well as some combined research and monographs of Jewish communities. Although the society ceased activities after four years the scholars continued their researches. Part of their works appeared in the 19 volumes of the annual *Anuarul pentru Israeliţi* and in the weekly *Egalitatea* published by M. Schwarzfeld. Frequently, the articles are apologetic or polemic, their authors being interested in demonstrating the length of the Jewish presence in Romania as an element justifying Emancipation. Between the two world wars Meir A. Halevy published several monographs on the history of the Jews of Romania. The Templul Coral ("Choir Synagogue") then erected in Bucharest a museum, library, and archives for the history of Romanian Jewry. In some bulletins of these institutions and in the annual *Sinai* (1926–32), edited by Meir A. Halevy, there also appeared researches on the history of Romanian Jewry.

The Jewish theater also developed in Romania. The first Judeo-Spanish play written by Moshe Kofinu was presented in Giurgiu and published in Bucharest in 1862. The Yiddish theater was founded in Jassy in 1876, by Avrum Goldfaden, writer, producer and actor.

Holocaust Period

German penetration into the Romanian economy increased as the Nazis moved eastward with the *Anschluss* of Austria (1938), the annexation of Czechoslovakia (1939), and the occupation of western Poland at the outbreak of World War II. A considerable number of Romanian politicians agreed to serve German interests in exchange for directorships in German-Romanian enterprises, and German trade agreements with Romania always demanded the removal of Jews in the branch involved. In this way, Jews were expelled from wood commerce and industry.

In the summer of 1940 Romania succumbed to German and Soviet pressure (after the Molotov-Ribbentrop treaty) and transferred Bessarabia and part of Bukovina to the Soviet Union. Following the Hitler-Mussolini agreement, in September 1940 northern Transylvania was transferred to Hungary, and southern Dobrudja to Bulgaria. On June 30, 1940, 52 Jews were murdered in Dorohoi by a retreating Romanian regiment. Hoping to ensure its borders after the concessions, Romania, which had not been invaded by the German army, became a satellite of Nazi Germany. The first result of this move was the cancellation of Romanian citizenship for Jews, a measure taken by the government, which included members of the Iron Guard, under German pressure in August 1940. On September 6, when King Carol abdicated, Ion Antonescu, who had been minister of defense in the Goga government, came to power. His government included ministers from the ranks of the Iron Guard, and Romania was declared a National-Legionary State (the members of the Iron Guard styled themselves "legionnaires"). There followed a period of antisemitic terrorism that lasted for five months. It began with the confiscation of Jewish-owned shops, together with the posting of signs "Jewish shop" and picketing by the green-shirted "legionary police." The reign of terror reached its height when Jewish industrial and commercial enterprises were handed over to the members of the "Legion" under pressure from the Iron Guard. The owners of the enterprises were arrested and tortured by the "legionary police" until they agreed to sign certificates of transfer. Bands of "legionnaires" entered Jewish homes and "confiscated" any sums of money they found. This resulted in a mortal blow to the Romanian economy and chaos that frightened even the German diplomats. Antonescu tried on several occasions to arrest the wave of terrorism, during which a number of Romanian statesmen opposed to the Iron Guard were killed.

On Jan. 21, 1941, the Iron Guard revolted against Antonescu and attempted to seize power and carry out its antise-

Map 2. Jewish communities in Romania showing areas (shaded in) taken away from Romania and ceded to neighboring countries. Based on Pinkas ha-Kehillot: Rumanyah, *Vol. 1, Jerusalem, 1969. Courtesy Yad Vashem Archives, Jerusalem.*

mitic program in full. While part of the "Legion" was fighting the Romanian army for control of government offices and strategic points in the city, the rest carried out a pogrom on Bucharest Jews, aided by local hooligans. Jewish homes were looted, shops burned, and many synagogues desecrated, including two that were razed to the ground (the Great Sephardi Synagogue and the old *bet ha-midrash*). Some of the leaders of the Bucharest community were imprisoned in the community council building, worshipers were ejected from synagogues, the Palestine Office of the Zionist Organization was attacked and its director murdered, and wealthy Bucharest Jews were arrested, according to a previously prepared list. Those arrested were taken to centers of the Iron Guard movement: some were then taken into the forests near Bucharest and shot; others were murdered and their bodies hung on meat hooks in the municipal slaughterhouse, bearing the legend "kosher meat." The pogrom claimed at least 125 Jewish lives. There were no acts of violence in the provinces because the army was in firm control and fully supported Antonescu. This was also Hitler's reason for supporting Antonescu. Romania held an important role in the war contemplated against the Soviet Union, not only as a supply and jumping-off base, but as an active partner in the war.

A period of relative calm followed the Bucharest pogrom and permitted Romanian Jews to gather strength after the shock of the violence. Antonescu, however, was thereafter under constant German pressure, for when their revolt failed, members of the Iron Guard found refuge in Germany, where they constituted a permanent threat to his position, as he now lacked his own party to serve as a counterbalance. In January 1941 Manfred von Killinger, a veteran Nazi known for his antisemitic activities, was appointed German ambassador to Romania. In April he was joined by Gustav Richter, an adviser on Jewish affairs who was attached to Adolf Eichmann's department. Richter's special task was to bring Romanian anti-Jewish legislation into line with its counterpart in Germany.

During the War

On June 22, 1941, when war broke out with the Soviet Union, the Romanian and German armies were scattered along the banks of the Prut River in order to penetrate into Bukovina and Bessarabia. Romania, under the government of Marshal

Antonescu, was an ally of Germany and fought with the Nazi army in the war against the Soviet Union. The declared purpose of Romania's involvement in the war was to retrieve the Romanian territories (Bukovina and Bessarabia). One week after the war started, on June 29 and 30, 1941, the large Jewish community in Jassy was shattered by a pogrom unprecedented in all of Europe. Over 14,000 Jews lost their lives during the massacres in the city, massacres initiated and supervised by the army and the local police. In addition, many perished in the subhuman conditions of the death trains that transported Jews who had been arrested.

The Jewish population of Bessarabia (approximately 200,000) and Bukovina (93,000) was considered hostile, foreign, and destined for "elimination" in the program of "cleansing the land" conceived by Antonescu. This intensely antisemitic propaganda campaign, conducted on all levels of the state hierarchy and especially in the army, portrayed this population – and, by extension, all Jews – as the embodiment of the "Bolshevik danger." The Jews in the reacquired territories were held responsible for mistreating, humiliating, and even killing many Romanian soldiers during the retreat in the summer of 1940.

A completely different fate, though no better, befell the Jews in Transylvania (approximately 200,000, including those in Banat). In northern Transylvania, under Hungarian rule, the Jews shared the fate of Hungary's Jews during the war, most of them being deported and exterminated at Auschwitz. Of the 200,000 Transylvanian Jews, 160,000 (mostly Orthodox) were in the northern part. Until close to the end of the war, the fate of the Jews in southern Transylvania, which was still part of Romania, was similar to that in the other Romanian regions – Moldavia and Wallachia, known as the Regat.

The armies' combined advance through Bessarabia, Bukovina, and the Dorohoi district was accompanied by massacres of the local Jewish population. At the beginning of August 1941 the Romanians began to send deportees from Bukovina and Bessarabia over the Dniester River into a German-occupied area of the U.S.S.R. (later to be known as Transnistria). The Germans refused to accept the deportees, shooting some and returning the rest. Some of these Jews drowned in the river and others were shot by the Romanian gendarmerie on the western bank; of the 25,000 persons who crossed the Dniester near Sampol, only 16,500 were returned by the Germans. Some of these survivors were killed by the Romanians, and some died of weakness and starvation on the way to camps in Bukovina and Bessarabia. Half of the 320,000 Jews living in Bessarabia, Bukovina, and the Dorohoi district (which was in Old Romania) were murdered during the first few months of Romania's involvement in the war, i.e., up to Sept. 1, 1941.

After this period the Jews were concentrated in ghettos (if they lived in cities), in special camps (if they lived in the countryside, or townlets such as Secureni, Yedintsy, Vertyuzhani, etc.). German killing squads or Romanian gendarmes, copying the Germans, habitually entered the ghettos and camps, removing Jews and murdering them. Jews living in villages and townlets in Old Romania (Moldavia, Wallachia, and southern Transylvania) were concentrated into the nearest large town. The Jews of northern Moldavia, which bordered on the battle area, were sent to the west of Romania: men under 60 were sent to the Targu-Jiu camp and the women, children, and aged were sent to towns where the local Jewish population was ordered to care for the deportees (who owned nothing more than the clothing on their backs). The homes and property of these deportees were looted by the local population immediately after they were deported.

On Sept. 16, 1941, those in camps in Bessarabia began to be deported to the region between the Dniester and the Bug rivers called Transnistria, from which the Germans had withdrawn, handing control over to the Romanians under the Tighina agreement (Aug. 30, 1941). The deportations included 118,847 Jews from Bessarabia, Bukovina, and the Dorohoi district. At the intervention of the Union of Jewish Communities in Romania, an order was given to stop the deportations on October 14; they continued however until November 15, leaving all the Jews of Bessarabia and Bukovina (with the exception of 20,000 from Chernovtsy) and 2,316 of the 14,847 Jews from the Dorohoi district concentrated in Transnistria. In two months of deportations 22,000 Jews died: some because they could walk no further, some from disease, but the majority were murdered by the gendarmerie that accompanied them on their journey. All money and valuables were confiscated by representatives of the Romanian National Bank. The Jews then remaining in Old Romania and in southern Transylvania were compelled into forced labor and were subjected to various special taxes. The prohibition against Jews working in certain professions and the "Rumanization of the economy" continued and caused the worsening of the economic situation of the Jewish population.

According to the statistical table on the potential victims of the "Final Solution" introduced at the Wannsee Conference, 342,000 Romanian Jews were destined for this end. The German embassy in Bucharest conducted an intensive propaganda campaign through its journal, *Bukarester Tageblatt*, which announced "an overall European solution to the Jewish problem" and the deportation of Jews from Romania. On July 22, 1942, Richter obtained Vice Premier Mihai Antonescu's agreement to begin the deportation of Jews to the Belzec extermination camp in September. From November 1942, however, it was obvious that the Romanian authorities were delaying this plan. Eventually they abandoned it entirely, owing to pressure both from Allied forces and the Romanian opposition, which was summoned especially by W. *Filderman, the most respected leader of the Romanian Jews. Pressure was also exerted by diplomats from neutral countries, as well as by the papal nuncio, Andreas Cassulo. Nevertheless, Eichmann's Bucharest office, working through the local authorities, succeeded in contriving the deportation of 7,000 Jews from Chernovtsy and Dorohoi and groups from other parts of Romania to Transnistria because they were "suspected of Communism" (they were of

Bessarabian origin and had asked to return to the Soviet Union in 1940), had "broken forced-labor laws," etc.

At the beginning of December 1942 the Romanian government informed the Jewish leadership of a change in its policy toward Jews. Defeat at Stalingrad (where the Romanians had lost 18 divisions) was already anticipated. In 1942–43 the Romanian government began tentatively to consider signing a separate peace treaty with the Allies. Although a plan for large-scale emigration failed because of German opposition and lack of facilities, both small and large boats left Romania carrying "illegal" immigrants to Palestine, some of whom were refugees from Bukovina, Poland, Hungary, and Slovakia. Between 1939 and August 1944 (when Romania withdrew from the war) 13 boats left Romania, carrying 13,000 refugees, and even this limited activity was about to cease, as a result of German pressure exerted through diplomatic missions in Romania, Bulgaria, and Turkey. Two of the boats sank: the *Struma* (on Feb. 23, 1944 with 769 passengers) and the *Mefkure* (on Aug. 5, 1944 with 394 passengers).

Despite German efforts, the Romanian government refused to deport its Jews to the "east." At the beginning of 1943, however, there was a return to the traditional economic pressures against the Jews in order to reduce the Jewish population. This was achieved by forbidding Jews to work in the civilian economy and through the most severe measure of all, forced labor (from which the wealthy managed to obtain an exemption by paying a considerable sum). In addition, various taxes were imposed on the Jewish population in the form of cash, clothing, shoes, or hospital equipment. These measures, particularly the taxes to be remitted in cash – of which the largest was a levy of 4 billion lei (about $27,000,000) imposed in March 1943 – severely pressed Romanian Jewry. The tax collection was made by the "Jewish Center." W. Filderman, chairman of the Council of the Union of Jewish Communities, who opposed the tax and proved that it could never be paid, was deported to Transnistria for two months.

At the end of 1943, as the Red Army drew nearer to Romania, the local Jewish leadership succeeded in obtaining the gradual return of those deported to Transnistria. The Germans tried several times to stop the return and even succeeded in bringing about the arrest of the leadership of the clandestine Zionist pioneering movements in January and February 1944; however, these leaders were released through the intervention of the International Red Cross and the Swiss ambassador in Bucharest, who contended that they were indispensable for organizing the emigration of those returning from Transnistria and refugees who had found temporary shelter in Romania. In March 1944 contacts were made in Ankara between Ira Hirschmann, representative of the U.S. War Refugee Board, and the Romanian ambassador, A. Cretzianu, at which Hirschmann demanded the return of all those deported to Transnistria and the cessation of the persecution of Jews. At the time, the Red Army was defeating the Germans in Transnistria, and there was a danger that the retreating Germans might slaughter the remaining Jews. Salvation came at the last moment, when Antonescu warned the Germans to avoid killing Jews while retreating. Concurrently, negotiations over Romania's withdrawal from the war were being held in Cairo and Stockholm, and thus Antonescu was eager to show goodwill toward the Jews for the sake of his own future. In the spring Soviet forces also conquered part of Old Romania (Moldavia), and they made an all-out attack on August 20. On August 23 King Michael arrested Antonescu and his chief ministers and declared a cease-fire. The Germans could no longer control Romania, for they were dependent on the support of the Romanian army, which had been withdrawn. Eichmann, who had been sent to western Romania to organize the liquidation of Jews in the region, did not reach Romania.

The question of the number of Romanian Jews and of those in the territories under Romania's control who were murdered during the Holocaust is a complex issue, requiring more research. An International Commission on the Holocaust in Romania concluded in 2004 that between 280,000 and 380,000 Romanian and Ukrainian Jews were murdered or died during the Holocaust in Romania and the territories under its control. The Israeli historian Jean Ancel, author of essential studies on the topic, disagreed with this evaluation, and based on his extensive research, estimated that the number is considerably higher, at least 420,000 Jewish victims. These statistics of the Report include more than 45,000 Jews – probably closer to 60,000 – who were killed in Bessarabia and Bukovina by Romanian and German troops in 1941. At least 105,000 – other findings state as many as 120,000 – of the deported Romanian Jews died as a result of the expulsions to Transnistria. At least 130,000 indigenous Jews – or according to other statistics as many as 180,000 – were liquidated in Transnistria (especially in Odessa and the districts of Golta and Berezovka). Sometimes Romanian officials worked with German help, but more often they required no outside guidance. Nazi Germany was also responsible for killing Romanian Jews in Bessarabia, Bukovina, and mass killings in Ukraine and later in Transnistria. The Romanian authorities were accomplices in varying degrees to these murders. The documents do record numerous instances of Romanians – both civilian and military – rescuing Jews. But these initiatives were isolated cases, and in the final analysis were exceptions to the general rule. Of the 150,000 Jews of Northern Transylvania, 135,000 were killed in Nazi concentration camps after being deported by the Hungarian gendarmerie; no Romanian authority was involved in this operation.

Jewish Resistance

PREPARATORY STEPS. As soon as Hitler assumed power in Germany (1933), Jewish leaders in Bucharest decided not to remain passive. In November the congress of the Jewish Party in Romania decided to join the anti-Nazi boycott movement, disregarding the protest raised by the Romanian press and antisemitic groups, but the Union of the Romanian Jews (UER) did not participate in the campaign. The necessity for a united political, as well as economic, struggle soon became obvious. On Jan. 29, 1936, the Central Council of Jews in Romania, composed of representatives of both Jewish trends – the UER and the Jewish Party – was established for "the defense of all Jewish rights and liberties against the organizations and newspapers that openly proclaimed the introduction of the racial regime." At the end of the year the Council succeeded in averting a bill proposed in the parliament by the antisemitic circles suggesting that citizenship be revoked from the Jews. During the same period the Romanian government attempted to suppress the state subvention for Jewish religious needs, as well as the exemption from taxes accorded to Jewish community institutions. The Council could not obtain the maintenance of the subvention, and it was finally reduced to one-sixth of its allotment.

When Goga's antisemitic government came to power, the Council began a struggle against it, gaining support and attention outside Romania. Filderman, president of the Council, left at once for Paris, where he mobilized the world Jewish organizations with headquarters in France and England and informed local political circles and the League of Nations of events in Romania. At the same time the Jews in Romania began an expanded economic boycott, refraining from commercial transactions, withdrawing their deposits from the banks, and delaying tax payments. The outcome was "large-scale paralysis of the economic life," as the German minister of foreign affairs stated in his circular of March 9, 1938. Thus the dismissal of the Goga government after only 40 days was motivated not only by external pressure, but by the effects of the Jewish economic boycott.

THE UNION OF THE JEWISH COMMUNITIES. Following the downfall of the Goga government, King Carol's royal dictatorship abolished all the political parties in Romania, including the Jewish Party and the Union of Romanian Jews. The single body of the Jews in Romania was the Union of the Jewish Communities, whose board was composed of the leaders of both Jewish currents. The Union assumed the task of fighting against the increasing number of anti-Jewish measures promulgated by the Romanian authorities under pressure from local antisemitic circles and the German government. In some cases its interventions were successful; for example, it achieved the nullification of the prohibition against collecting contributions to Zionist funds, and, as a result of its protests, the restrictions against the Jewish physicians and the Jewish industrial schools were abrogated. In the summer of 1940, after Romania ceded Bukovina and Bessarabia to the Soviet Union, the Romanian police tried to eject Jewish refugees from those two provinces. The Union's board succeeded in moving the Ministry of the Interior to annul the measure. When the interdiction of ritual slaughter was decreed, the board obtained an authorization for ritual slaughtering of poultry. The cancellation of the prohibition against Jews peddling in certain cities was also achieved. When the antisemitic newspapers incited against the leaders of the Union, the police began to search their homes.

Ion Antonescu's government, with the participation of the Iron Guard, closed several synagogues (those with less than 400 worshipers in cities and 200 in villages) and transferred the property to Christian churches. The disposition was canceled after three days, however, as a result of an audience between the Union's president, Filderman, and Antonescu; simultaneously the minister of religion, who ordered the measure, was forced to resign. These acts took place during the first period of the new regime, dominated by the Iron Guard, when trespasses were committed against the Jews daily. The Union's board constantly informed Antonescu and the diverse ministries of these acts, pointing out their illegality and arbitrariness. The argument that constantly recurred in the memoranda presented by the Union's board was that the confiscation of Jewish shops and industrial companies caused the disorganization of the country's economic life. Antonescu used the information provided by the board to support his stand against the trespasses. The Iron Guard responded with a terror campaign against the Jewish leaders; some were arrested and tortured by the "legionary police," others were murdered during the revolt against Antonescu.

The Zionist leadership negotiated with Antonescu about organizing the emigration of Romanian Jews (see Zionism in Romania). The minister of finance proposed that the emigration be financed by Romanian assets, which had been frozen in the United States, because Romania had joined the Axis. The transaction had to be accomplished through the American Jewish Joint Distribution Committee (JDC), whose representative in Romania was also the president of the Union. In every city the Jewish community had to register those who wanted to emigrate and were able to pay the amount demanded by the government. The Union's board utilized this agreement as a leverage for achieving certain concessions, especially after Romania joined Germany in the war against the Soviet Union (June 1941). For example, when the evacuation of Jews from villages and towns began, the Union secured the government's agreement not to send these Jews to concentration camps (as had previously been ordered), but rather to lodge them in the big cities, where they were to be cared for by the local Jewish communities. Another achievement (on Aug. 14, 1941) was the liberation of the rabbis, leaders of communities, and teachers employed in Jewish schools, who had been arrested after the outbreak of war with the U.S.S.R., from the Targu-Jiu concentration camp. The Union raised the argument that the plans concerning the release of the Romanian properties in the United States were dependent upon those local leaders. On Aug. 2, 1941, the board achieved the cancellation of the order that Jews wear the yellow badge and other measures, including the creation of ghettos in the cities and mobilizing women for forced labor, in which Jewish men were already engaged. Richter insisted on the reintroduction of repressive measures, and on September 3 the order to wear the yellow badge was re-endorsed. This time, in addition to intervention by the Union's leaders, Chief Rabbi Alexander Safran appealed to the head of the Christian Orthodox Church, Patriarch Nicodem, and on September 8 Antonescu annulled the order. Nevertheless, the yellow badge was maintained in a number of Moldavian cities, as well as in Chernovtsy (Cernauti), the capital of Bukovina, where the German influence was strong.

During this period, when Romania suffered great losses on the front and Germany called for an increase in Romanian participation, the Union's board employed the argument that Romania, being an ally of the Third Reich, and thus a sovereign state, did not have to accept anti-Jewish laws that were applied only to German satellite countries. Hungary and Italy, allies that did not apply such measures at that time, were presented as examples. It is known from von Killinger's reports that Antonescu raised these objections in his dealings with the Nazi government.

After Jews began to be deported from Bessarabia and Bukovina to Transnistria, the board delegated Chief Rabbi Safran to intervene with the queen mother, Patriarch Nicodem, and the archbishop of Bukovina and induce them to intercede with Antonescu to halt the deportations and permit aid to those who had already been transported over the Dniester. Until a decision could be achieved through their intervention, and against the opposition of von Killinger, the 17,000 Jews who remained in Chernovtsy were not deported. However, the steps taken, with permission to provide assistance to those who had already been deported to Transnistria were sabotaged by difficulties raised by lower authorities. The Union also endeavored to gain the support of the U.S. ambassador, who interceded with the Romanian government. Nevertheless, when the ambassadors of Brazil, Switzerland, and Portugal proposed to the U.S. ambassador the initiation of an international protest against the Romanian anti-Jewish excesses, the latter reported to Washington that he did not possess enough exact information. Later on, however, in another report (Nov. 4, 1941), he described in detail the massacres committed in Bessarabia and in Bukovina and the cruelties that were committed during the deportations to Transnistria. The description was based on the information received from the Union. (It was only at the end of 1941 that Romania broke off relations with the United States, under German pressure.) The antisemitic press – financed and inspired by the German embassy – including the German-language *Bukarester Tageblatt*, then intensified the incitement against the Jewish leaders and their constant interventions against anti-Jewish measures.

At the end of 1941 the Union of the Communities was dissolved under pressure from Richter, and the Centrala evreilor (Central Board of the Jews) was set up at his suggestion in January 1942. Its leaders were appointed by Radu Lecca, who was responsible for Jewish affairs in the Romanian government, but they were actually subordinate to Richter. Nearly all of the new leaders were unknown to the Jewish public, with the exception of A. Willman, who shortly before his appointment had published a number of pamphlets proposing a kind of neo-territorialist plan to be accomplished with the aid of Nazi Germany. From the outset, the Jewish population expressed its distrust of the new organ. The former leaders of the Jewish institutions formed a clandestine Jewish Council with Chief Rabbi Alexander Safran as its president. The Council leaders handed memoranda personally to, or interceded individually with, Antonescu or his ministers, who went on to deal with them because the government did not trust the Central Board either.

In the spring of 1942 changes were made in the framework of the Central Board. Willman and some of his followers were removed and replaced by others appointed from among the leadership of the Zionist movement and the Union of the Romanian Jews (UER). Thus the Central Board was prevented from taking any harmful initiatives against the Jewish population. In the summer the Zionist Organization was dissolved at the request of the Germans, and this was a sign that the Germans disagreed with the Romanian policy, which aided Jewish emigration. In order to avoid the Nazi plan of deportation to Belzec, the queen mother was convinced by Safran to intercede with Ion Antonescu. Others were also requested to intercede on behalf of the Jews, such as the papal nuncio, Andreas Cassulo; the Swiss ambassador, René de Weck; and even Antonescu's personal physician. The nuncio's efforts were supported by the Swedish and Turkish ambassadors, and by the delegates of the International Red Cross. At the same time the Jewish Council achieved the annulment of the order to deport to Transnistria 12,000 Jews accused of having committed crimes or breaches of discipline.

THE STRUGGLE TO REPATRIATE DEPORTED JEWS. After overcoming the danger of deportation to the extermination camps in Poland, the Jewish leaders began to request the return of those who had survived the deportations to Transnistria. The dealings with the Romanian government began in November 1942 over the question of a ransom to be paid by Zionist groups outside Romania. Eichmann's unceasing interventions prevented a clear-cut decision until, on April 23, Antonescu – under German pressure – issued the order that not a single deportee should return. The Jewish leaders then initiated the struggle for a "step by step" resolution to the problem, asserting that a series of categories had been deported arbitrarily, without previous investigation. The Romanian government ordered a detailed registration of categories. At the beginning of 1943 an official commission was appointed to classify the deportees. In July Antonescu authorized the return of certain cases (aged persons, widows, World War I invalids, former officers of the Romanian army, etc.). Implementation of the order, however, encountered difficulties raised by the governor of Transnistria, who was under the influence of German advisers. Only at the beginning of December did the deportees begin to return, according to categories: yet it was a struggle against time, as meanwhile the front had reached Transnistria.

From the beginning of 1944 the clandestine Zionist Executive dealt separately with Antonescu on the question of emigration. Its efforts had an influence on the general situation, as the Romanian authorities made the return of the deportees conditional upon their immediate emigration.

THE COMMITTEE OF ASSISTANCE. Whole strata of Romanian Jewry were pauperized because of the anti-Jewish economic measures. The former committee of the JDC continued its activity clandestinely under the control of the Union of the Jewish Communities and afterward of the Jewish Council. In October 1943 it was officially recognized within the framework of the "Jewish Central Board" as the Autonomous Committee of Assistance. Assistance was thus provided to the Jews evacuated from towns and villages who could not be maintained by the local communities. The most important accomplishment, however, was the aid in the form of money, medicines, utensils for craftsmen, coal, oil heaters, window glass, clothing, etc. transmitted to Transnistria. In order to cover the budget, money and clothing were collected in the regions not affected by deportations. These means, however, were far from adequate. Only owing to the important amounts acquired from the JDC, the Jewish Agency, and other world Jewish organizations was the Autonomous Committee of Assistance able to continue its activity.

In addition to all the official difficulties raised by the Romanian central authorities (the compulsory transfer of money through the National Bank at an unfavorable exchange rate, and the obligation of paying customs for the objects sent), the transports were frequently plundered on the way or confiscated by the local authorities in Transnistria. The assistance, however, was in itself an element of resistance. The mere fact that the deportees knew that they had not been abandoned, at least by their fellow Jews, contributed to the maintenance of their morale. The aid in its various forms saved thousands of lives. Through clandestine correspondence, carried by non-Jewish messengers, reports were received concerning the situation of the refugees. This means of providing information was insufficient, however, and the Autonomous Committee of Assistance therefore wanted to review the situation directly on the spot.

As early as January 1942 authorization was obtained from the Ministry of the Interior for a delegation of the committee to go to Transnistria; nevertheless, due to the opposition of the governor of Transnistria, the representatives could not get there until Dec. 31, 1942. The governor received them in audience at Odessa and tried to intimidate them by means of threat, telling them that their behavior would determine whether or not they would return to Romania. He gave them permission to visit only three of the camps in which deported Jews were concentrated. The delegates of the committee responded by requesting a regional conference with representatives of all the camps. During the railway journey to Mogilev, the delegates visited the Zhmerinka camp and received information about the surrounding camps. Upon their arrival at Mogilev (Jan. 8–9, 1943), a regional conference took place with the participation of about 70 delegates. Before the conference opened, the prefect and the commander of the gendarmes warned the delegates not to complain about their situation, adding the threat that complaints might endanger the further receipt of aid. However, the delegates clandestinely submitted a written report concerning the real situation to the representatives of the committee. From Mogilev the delegation left for Balta, where it did not receive a license for a regional conference, but each delegate from the ghettos or camps of the area was authorized to report individually about the situation. Back in Bucharest, after this two-week tour in Transnistria, the delegates presented their report, which was also sent to Jewish organizations abroad.

In December 1943 representatives of the Autonomous Committee of Assistance again left for Transnistria to organize the return of the deportees, taking with them wagons of clothing. One group of representatives left for the north, to Mogilev and its surroundings; another for the south, to Tiraspol. The central administration of Transnistria did not display any goodwill, but the local authorities provided wagons for the transport. On Feb. 15, 1944, two delegations started out to aid the return of the orphans. On March 17, 1944, another two delegations set out for Transnistria, but they could not reach their destination as the area had already become a front area, the northern part occupied by the Red Army.

The delegates installed themselves in Tighina (Bessarabia), whence they made contact with Tiraspol on the eastern bank of the Dniester River and succeeded in saving almost all those concentrated there. The Germans still had the time to organize a last massacre, murdering 1,000 Jews who were in detention in the Tiraspol jail. When Transnistria and Bessarabia were reconquered by the Soviets, the deportees who followed the armies were the last to succeed in returning to Romania, for afterward, at the end of June 1944, the Soviets closed the frontier. It was reopened only in May 1945 for a last group of 7,000 deportees, after prolonged dealings in Bucharest between the Jewish leaders and General Vinogradov, the head of the Soviet armistice commission.

[Theodor Lavi / Lucian-Zeev Herscovici and Leon Volovici (2nd ed.)]

The Early Post-Holocaust Years

When Romania broke with Nazi Germany and entered the war on the side of the Allies (Aug. 23, 1944), Romanian Jewry had been considerably decreased as a result of the Holocaust and it was about to decrease even further through emigration. The struggle for Jewish independence in Palestine influenced Romanian Jews, and the goal of *aliyah*, which had been deep-seated in the community in the past, became a powerful force. The decisive factor in the life of Romanian Jews after World War II, however, was the political regime in Romania, which exercised its authority over the community life of Romanian Jewry, determined the structure of its organization, and limited its aspirations. Government control was prevalent during the first period – from Aug. 23, 1944, until the abolition of the monarchy (Dec. 30, 1947) – and even more so in succeeding periods, through all the internal changes that altered the regime in Romania.

The Communist Period

For a few years after the abolition of the monarchy, Romania closely followed the line dictated from Moscow. This situation continued until the end of the 1950s, when the first signs of an independent Romanian policy began to appear. Until 1965 the pattern of this policy gradually solidified, and from then, with the personal changes after the death of the general secretary Gheorghe Gheorghiu-Dej, Romania entered with a more independent policy. All the changes in government and policy also left their on Jewish community life. The situation of Romanian Jewry always had a special character. Even in the days of complete dependence on Moscow, when the tools and institutions of national Jewish identity were destroyed and expression of Jewish aspirations was repressed, Romanian Jewry was not compelled to be as alienated from its national and religious identity as were the Jews of the Soviet Union. At the end of the 1960s the Jewish community in Romania found itself in an intermediate position. Its activities displayed indications of free community life as well as the limitations imposed by the government. Variations in the government's policy also reflected the connection between the status of Romanian Jewry and the official attitude of Romania toward Israel. This mutual influence was expressed in all the areas of Jewish life and especially through the central issue of the right to leave the country and settle in Israel.

POPULATION. The characterizing factor of the demography of Romanian Jewry during this period was the constant decrease in the community's size. The only source on the size of the Romanian Jewish community at the end of World War II is a registration (the results of which were published in 1947) that was carried out on the initiative of the World Jewish Congress. According to the registration, there were 428,312 Jews in Romania at the time. This number was the balance after the losses caused by the Holocaust, the annexation of Bessarabia and North Bukovina by the U.S.S.R., and the migration to Palestine during the war. The professional composition of the community at that time (1945) was as follows: 49,000 artisans, 35,000 employees, 34,000 merchants and industrialists, and 9,500 in the free professions. Ten years later the Jewish population had been reduced to about a third. According to the census taken on Feb. 21, 1956, there were 144,236 Jews in Romania, of whom 34,263 spoke Yiddish. But these figures are probably lower than the true numbers, as it is known that in the above-mentioned census members of minority groups were not allowed to identify freely with their national group. The drastic reduction in the size of the Romanian Jewish community was largely a result of mass emigration, especially during the years 1944–47. The means of emigration were dictated by the conditions of the war and its aftermath. At the end of the war thousands of Jews, terrified by the Holocaust, fled Romania through its western border, which was still open, and reached the West by their own means. In addition to this spontaneous migration, 14 refugee boats left Romanian ports carrying 24,000 "illegal" immigrants to Palestine. A portion of Romanian Jewry, including thousands who left Romania of their own volition immediately after the war, was also among those who boarded refugee boats to Palestine in other European ports. From the establishment of the State of Israel (1948) until the end of the 1960s, over 200,000 Romanian Jews settled in the new state. In addition, it should be noted that not all the Jews who emigrated from Romania went to Israel; about 80,000 others were scattered throughout other countries. At the end of the 1960s the Romanian Jewish community numbered no more than 100,000.

THE LIQUIDATION OF JEWISH ORGANIZATIONS. On Aug. 23, 1944, when Romania joined the Allies, the Zionist movement came up from underground to operate legally and openly through all its currents and institutions. The same was true of the Jewish Party, which was reorganized as the representative body of Romanian Jewry and headed by the Zionist leader A.L. Zissu. In 1945 an extension of the Communist Party was established among the Jewish population under the name the Jewish Democratic Committee (Comitetul Democrat Evreesc). For about four years the Zionist movement maintained regular activities in the fields of organization, education, training farms, and Zionist funds, as well as through international ties. In 1948 there were 100,000 members in the movement and 4,000 in He-Halutz, with 95 branches and 12 training farms. The Zionist Organization in Romania participated in the world Zionist Congress in Basle in 1946. A general representation of Romanian Jewry (including delegates from the Jewish Democratic Committee) was present at the Montreux conference (1948) of the World Jewish Congress. These were the last regular contacts of Romanian Jewry with Jewish organizations abroad; afterward the ties were severed for an extended period.

The more the Communist Party strengthened its power, the more Zionist activity in Romania turned from "permitted" to "tolerated," until it was finally outlawed completely. The instrument of this process was the Jewish Democratic Committee, which never succeeded in striking roots among the Jewish population, in spite of the support it received from the authorities. The cue to abolish Zionist activities was given in the decision of the central committee of the Communist Party on June 10–11, 1948, in the midst of Israel's War of Independence. The decision stated that "the party must take a stand on every question concerning the Jews of Romania and fight vigorously against reactionary nationalist Jewish currents." As early as the summer of 1948 the liquidation of Zionist training farms was begun, and the process was completed in the spring of 1949. In November 1948 the activities of the Zionist funds were forbidden. On Nov. 29, 1948, a violent attack on the branch of the Zionist Organization in Bucharest was organized by the Jewish Communists. On Dec. 12, 1948, the party decision was again publicized, including a clear denunciation of Zionism, "which, in all its manifestations, is a reactionary nationalist movement of the Jewish bourgeoisie, supported by American imperialism, that attempts to isolate the masses of Jewish workers from the people among whom they live." This statement was published in the wake of a bitter press campaign against Zionism during November and December 1948.

The persecution of the Zionist movement was also expressed by the imprisonment of *sheliḥim* from Ereẓ Israel. On Dec. 23, 1948, a general consultation of Zionists was held and resulted in the decision to dissolve "voluntarily" the Zionist organizations. Following this decision, the Zionist parties began to halt their activities, with the exception of Mapam, the youth movements, and He-Halutz. The World Jewish Congress also ceased to operate in Romania. Those organizations that did not close down at the time continued to operate formally until the spring of the following year. On March 3, 1949, however, the Ministry of Interior issued an order to liquidate all remnants of the Zionist movement, including youth movements and training farms. With this order the Jewish community in Romania was given over completely to the dominance of the government alone – at first by means of the Jewish Democratic Committee, until it too was gradually dissolved. In April 1949 the youth movement of the Jewish Democratic Committee was disbanded just as the Communist Party Youth (UTM) was organized, and the committee itself was disbanded in March 1953, together with all other national minorities' organizations in Romania. In 1949–50 the activity of the American Jewish Joint Distribution Committee in Romania was discontinued by order of the government. The hostile attitude toward the Zionist movement was also expressed in Romania's attitude toward Israel, which gradually hardened and led to the frequent imprisonment of previously active Zionists. The periods of time when emigration was ceased (April 1952 until 1956) were led by violent anti-Zionist campaigns. Zionist organizations were banned as of 1949. Yet the new Communist regime brought about a radical change: a significant number of Jews became prominent in the political and administrative hierarchy of the new regime, among them the long-time Communist militant Ana *Pauker.

There were ups and downs, however, especially in the area of propaganda, until the situation in general began to improve at the beginning of 1967.

COMMUNITY LIFE. With the liquidation of the Zionist Movement and the dissolution of the Jewish Democratic Committee, the religious communities (*kehillot*) were the only organized bodies left in Romanian Jewry. The legal foundations for their activities were laid down even before other Jewish frameworks were destroyed. In 1945 the "Regulations on Nationalities" were passed and declared the formal equality of members of all national minority groups before the law. Regulations of the activities of the recognized religions, including Judaism, were set down in the Aug. 4, 1948, order of the presidium of the Grand National Assembly (which also served as the presidency of the state). The regulations of the Federation of Communities of the Mosaic Religion, which were approved by the Assembly's presidium on June 1, 1949, were based upon this order. Dr. Moshe Rosen became chief rabbi in 1948. He was instrumental in organizing massive Jewish emigration from Romania as well as in establishing a satisfactory community life even within the Communist regime and the threat of fast diminution of Jewish communities.

The Federation's scope of activity was limited to the area of religious worship alone. In the first years of the Communist regime and its complete dependence upon Moscow, Jewish Communists infiltrated into the Federation, but afterward their participation in Jewish religious bodies decreased, although it did not cease altogether. The Federation of Communities was responsible for maintaining synagogues and cemeteries and supplying religious objects, unleavened bread for Passover, kosher food, and the like. It was not authorized to deal in matters of Jewish education, however, although it did have the right (according to a decision of the department of religions on Nov. 13, 1948) to set up seminaries for training rabbis, and for a few years it maintained a yeshivah in Arad (Transylvania). According to the registration of 1960, there were 153 communities throughout Romania that maintained 841 synagogues and *battei midrash* (56 of which were no longer in use), 67 ritual baths, 86 slaughterhouses, and one factory for unleavened bread (in Cluj). From 1956 the Federation also published a tri-language biweekly (in Romanian, Yiddish, and Hebrew) entitled *Revista Cultului Mozaic din R.P.R.* ("Journal of (Romanian) Religious Jewry"). From 1964 the chief rabbi Rosen officiated as the chairman of the Federation and was also a member of the National Assembly. Thus the Federation became the general Jewish representative in the country.

EDUCATION. With the renewal of Jewish life after the war, Jewish education also began to operate again. In 1946 the total number of Jewish schools was 190 with 41,000 students. In 1948 five yeshivot, 50 *talmud torah* schools, 10 Bet Jacob schools, one elementary school of Tarbut, five dormitories for students, 14 dormitories for apprentices, the agricultural training institute (Cultura AgricolD), three vocational schools in Bucharest, and three vocational schools in provincial cities (Huși, Sibiu, Radauti) were supported by the American Jewish Joint Distribution Committee. A substantial number of educational institutions were maintained by the various Jewish communities without outside support. The network of Jewish education was destroyed in the autumn of 1948, when all schools in Romania were nationalized. At that time a small number of schools in which the language of instruction was Yiddish were established (in Bucharest and in Jassy) and remained open until the 1960/61 school year. After the nationalization Jewish education remained in the hands of *melammedim*, whose activities were tolerated by the authorities. In 1960 there were 54 *talmud torah* schools, in addition to the yeshivah that was established in Arad in 1956. By the end of the 1960s the number of educational institutions had very considerably decreased.

CULTURE. At the beginning of the period under discussion, the language of Jewish writers and poets, including those who wrote about Jewish subjects, was Romanian. During the first years after World War II the Jewish press was fairly large. The most important newspaper was *Mântuirea*, which began to reappear after Romania joined the Allies and continued to be published until the Zionist movement ceased to exist. In 1945 the press of the pro-Communist "Jewish Democratic Committee" began to appear, and its major newspaper was *Unirea*, in Bucharest, which lasted until 1953. As long as Zionist activity was permitted, the Zionist publishing house Bikkurim and the He-Halutz publishing house, as well as the Yavneh Company for the distribution of books on Jewish history and Hebrew literature, continued to operate. In Jewish contributions to Romanian literature, art, and music, the influence of the memories of the Jewish milieu was sometimes felt. The writers and poets A. Toma, Maria Banus, Veronica Porumbacu, Barbu Lazareanu, and others belonged to this group. Among the writers who wrote in Yiddish were Jacob Groper, Alfred Margul Sperber, and Ludovic Brukstein. The most outstanding Jewish artists were Josif Iser, M.H. Maxy, and Jules Perachim. Well-known Jewish musicians were Matei Socor, Alfred Mendelsohn, and Max Eisikovits. The only Jewish cultural institution was the Jewish theater in Bucharest. It was established as a state institution in 1948. The Jewish theater in Jassy, which was established at the same time, closed down in 1968. During the 20 years of its existence, the theater produced 107 plays including works by A. Goldfaden, Shalom Aleichem, Yiddish playwrights, and others. In 1968 the Bucharest Jewish theater performed on tour in Israel.

Israel-Romania Relations to the End of the 1960s

In September 1948 the first Israel representative to Romania, the painter Reuven Rubin, arrived in Bucharest, but neither he nor his successors succeeded in substantially developing the relations between the two countries for a number of years. Until 1965 the relations were regular but cool, especially because of the attitude of the Soviet Union toward Israel, which was strictly followed by Romanian foreign policy. Every so often the relations between the two countries were shaken by crises that were felt on the level of diplomatic representation (the extended absence of a minister at the head of the mission) or were expressed by the expulsion of Israel diplomats. Cultural ties were not developed during the period, and trade also remained static at a modest level (in the climax year, the mutual trade balance between Israel and Romania reached $4.5 million). These relations improved considerably, however, as Romania grew more independent of the U.S.S.R. in international affairs. From February 1966 a Romanian minister again headed the Romanian mission in Israel. In March 1967 a high-level Romanian economic delegation visited Israel for the first time, and afterward an Israel economic delegation, headed by the finance minister, went to Bucharest; full trade agreements were signed. In 1968 the trade balance between the two countries reached $20,000,000, and subsequently trade increased. Cultural relations also expanded (Israeli musicians, choirs, etc. visited Romania and the countries exchanged art exhibitions), as did tourism from each country to the other. The Six-Day War (1967) served as a decisive test in the relations between Israel and Romania. On June 10, 1967, a consultation of all East European nations, including Yugoslavia, was held in Moscow and resulted in a denunciation of Israel's "aggression." The participating states also decided to sever diplomatic relations with the State of Israel. Romania, however, refused to sign the denunciation and also refused to carry out the conference's decisions. She did not sever diplomatic relations with Israel and refrained from taking part in the anti-Israel Soviet propaganda campaign. Romania repeatedly expressed her stand that the Arab-Israel dispute must be settled by political means, taking into consideration the just rights of both sides. In August 1969 Romania and Israel elevated their diplomatic missions to the rank of embassies.

[Eliezer Palmor]

Contemporary Period

The official census published in June 1977 gave the Jewish population as only 25,600; despite the fact that according to the statistics given by the Federation of Jewish Communities, which based itself on a registry of those in need of the community's services, the number was approximately 45,000, and its files did not include those Jews who had no connection with the communities. If these Jews are included, it would bring the total Jewish population to approximately 70,000. The Jewish community of Romania is an aging one; 25.51% of all Jews in Romania belong to the age category 41–60 and 46.2% to the age category 60–80. The majority of the Jews of Romania are professionals.

The institutions of the community, both local and central, have continued to function. The Federation of Jewish Communities, on which all the communities throughout Romania are represented, was recognized by the authorities and headed by Chief Rabbi Dr. Moshe Rosen who was a member of the Romanian Parliament.

Romania continued to be until the late 1980s the only country within the Soviet sphere of influence whose Jewish community maintained contact with international Jewish organizations and with communities outside Romania; close ties existed with the World Jewish Congress, the Joint Distribution Committee and others, as well as with Jewish communities throughout the world. Representatives of Romanian Jewry participated in the conference of the European branch of the World Jewish Congress which took place in Madrid (Dec. 4–6, 1976), and a delegation of the Federation of Communities, headed by Rabbi Rosen, participated in the Synagogue Federation Conference held in Jerusalem in February 1978. The Jewish State Theater in Bucharest continued to produce plays in Yiddish despite the dwindling of the potential audience. Several books in Yiddish have also been published.

In an earthquake which struck Bucharest on May 4, 1977, the Choral Temple and Malbim synagogue were damaged. During his official visit to Romania on Aug. 1, 1977 (see below), Prime Minister Menahem Begin participated in the Sabbath services in the Choral Temple and addressed the large congregation.

RELIGION AND CULTURE. Synagogues throughout the country (about 150) continued to function. In addition to the chief rabbi, there were two other rabbis, Rabbi Yitzhak Meir Marilus in Bucharest and Dr. Ernest Neumann in Timisoara. Kosher meat was provided by ritual slaughterers who visited the various communities weekly.

In the latter part of December 1977 the Museum for the History of the Jews in Romania was opened in Bucharest, along with a center for documentation and research. In the same year the centenary of the founding of the Jewish theater in Romania was celebrated by a gala performance at which *Tevye der Milchiger* by Shalom Aleichem, *The Dybbuk* by Anski, and Lessing's *Nathan the Wise* were presented. A history of the Yiddish theater in Romania by Israil Bercovici was published in Yiddish and in Romanian (1976, 1981).

In September 1981 Romania was the site of the convention of the European Rabbinical Conference, the first time a major Jewish gathering had been held in an East European country since World War II. The chief rabbis of England, France, Italy, and Holland were among the participants. The 25th anniversary of the publication of *Revista Cultului Mozaic* was celebrated in September 1981. The state publishing house has published a bibliographical work on the Jewish press in Romania, *Yiddishe Presse in Rumenye* by Wolf Vladimir Tamburu. An annual in Yiddish, *Bukarester Shriftn*, including Yiddish literature and studies on the history of Romanian Jews, was published between 1978 and 1988.

Research in the history of the Jews of Romania has been undertaken by a group of Jewish historians. Their activities center on the Federation of Communities' biweekly and deal especially with the role of the Jews in Romanian history. They also conduct research in municipal archives and the Jewish archives of the Federation. Several significant historical papers and collections of documents were published, edited by experienced historians (Itzik Şvarţ-Kara, Lya Benjamin, Victor Eskenasy).

RELATIONS WITH ISRAEL. Political relations between Israel and Romania were strengthened with statesmen exchanging visits, and particularly visits by Israelis. Romania consistently campaigned for a political settlement of the Near East conflict, for the implementation of the November 1967 Security Council resolution, and for a solution that will guarantee the territorial integrity and independence of all states in the region and lead to the withdrawal of Israeli forces from territories occupied after the Six-Day War. Romania also underscored the need to solve the problem of the Palestinian Arabs in conformity with their national interests. The fact that the Romanian government adopted a policy quite different from that of the U.S.S.R. and the other East European governments and did not brand Israel as an "aggressor" permitted Romania and Israel to maintain normal relations.

In August 1977 Prime Minister Begin paid an official visit to Romania. He held wide-ranging talks with his counterpart Manea Manescu, with Foreign Minister Macovescu, and held two lengthy political talks with the President of Romania, Nicolae Ceausescu. The Begin-Ceausescu meeting played an important role in the decision of the president of Egypt to visit Jerusalem in November 1977, and Romania was the only East European country which expressed open support for the Israeli-Egyptian peace initiative. Two unscheduled meetings were held between the Romanian President and Moshe Dayan, Israeli foreign minister, in April 1978. Economic and trade agreements and an agreement for technical and agricultural cooperation was signed by both countries. The latter agreement, which was renewed in February 1977, is designed particularly to train experts in various agriculture-related fields or to supplement their knowledge. In 1980 Israeli exports to Romania amounted to $35 million, while Israel imported from Romania goods worth $48.5 million.

Post-Communist Period

The central development in Romanian life and especially in the life of the ever-dwindling Jewish community was the overthrow of the Communist regime and the attempts at introducing democracy into the country along Western lines. The change of rule did not bring in its wake any real changes in the life of the few Jews left in the country. Until his death in May 1994, the dominating figure in Jewish life continued to be Chief Rabbi Moses Rosen. The remnants of the Romanian Jewish community welcomed the overthrow of Ceausescu and the community journal published a special issue expressing joy at the change.

In the new spirit of freedom Rabbi Rosen was the object of personal attacks by antisemitic groups, which accused him of close cooperation with the communist regime. Two antisemitic newspapers waged this campaign, which the chief rabbi saw as an attack on the entire community. *Romania Mare* ("Great Romania") and *Europa,* weeklies publishing virulent antisemitic material, aimed their barbs personally at Rabbi Rosen. In order to quash the harsh complaints about active antisemitism, President Ion Iliescu invested effort, internally and externally, to placate Chief Rabbi Rosen. In 1993 he took the rabbi with him to the opening of the Holocaust Museum in Washington, DC, and before that participated in a memorial service for Holocaust victims held in the Bucharest Choral Synagogue, where Iliescu spoke and condemned antisemitism.

Upon the immigration to Israel of Rabbi Pinhas Wasserman of Dorohoi (1989), the home for the aged and the *kasher* restaurant there were closed. Otherwise, all the institutions, restaurants, and homes for the aged were still in operation – 10 restaurants and four homes (two in Bucharest, and two smaller ones in Arad and Timisoara). Needy Jews receive packages of food and clothing. All this activity is financed by the JDC, fighting a rearguard action to maintain the few remaining Romanian Jews. The situation of the elderly has worsened considerably as their pension's value has eroded to nothing because of inflation, and without the Joint's help they would be starving.

Despite the declining number of Jews, the communities run smoothly and without assistance from the Federation, whose central place has been taken under the prevailing circumstances by the Joint. In addition to the Bucharest community, there are organized communities in the Transylvania region, in Cluj, Oradea, Arad, Timisoara. and in eastern Romania in Piatre-Neamt, Botosani, Jassy, Braila, Galati, Constanta, Ploesti, Brasov, Sighet, Satu-Mare, and a number of small communities. 10 *kasher* canteens were still operated by the communities and *kasher* meat was provided by three ritual slaughterers.

Romania lost its special status regarding relations with Israel, since it was no longer the only Eastern bloc country to have diplomatic relations with the Jewish state. Relations continued to be normal and friendly, with efforts at increasing bilateral trade. From the late 1990s Jewish life throughout Romania continued to revolve around the synagogues and the *kasher* restaurants, operated by the Federation of Romanian Jewish Communities and funded by the Joint Distribution Committee.

Since the establishment of the State of Israel some 300,000 Romanian Jews have emigrated there. The more the number of Jews in Romania shrinks, the more difficult it is to obtain reliable current Jewish population figures. The Federation of Communities, whose numbers are used by the Joint, estimate that there is a total of 15,000 Jews, 8,000 of whom are in Bucharest, the capital. Timisoara (in Transylvania) and Jassy each has a community of some 900 people; all the others are scattered among a Romanian populace of 22 million people. The official 1992 government yearbook, citing statistical data from a kind of census, states that there are 9,000 Jews. It may be that not all Jews were counted or admitted to being Jewish, particularly those in mixed marriages. Even though the total number of Jews is small, emigration to Israel continues.

The death of Rabbi Moses Rosen in May 1994 significantly affected the remaining Jews of Romania. The passing at age 83 of the man who for over 40 years had served as chief rabbi and head of the federation of Romanian Jewish communities signified the end of an era which included the collapse of the Communist regime in the country.

The feeling of stagnation which followed the death of the Rabbi Rosen prompted the representatives in Romania of the AJDC, which essentially administers to Jewish life there, to find a new chief rabbi quickly. Among the five candidates, all from Israel, they chose in May 1995 the Romanian-born professor Yehezkel Marek, a lecturer in literature at Bar-Ilan University. After his return to Israel in 1999, Menahem Hacohen became chief rabbi.

Rabbi Rosen's death also put an end to the concentrated centrality of the Federation of communities and allowed for greater freedom to the individual communities. The Federation was no longer headed by the rabbi but by Prof. Nicolae Cajal, a well-known scholar and member of Romanian Academy. After his death in 2004, Dr. Aurel Veiner, an economist, was elected as president of the community.

The community biweekly was revamped and changed its names to *Realitatea evreiască* ("Jewish Reality"). Yiddish is no longer used, and the paper now appears in Romanian, English, and one page in Hebrew, for a total of 12 pages presenting information on the Jewish world with emphasis on Jewish culture and many quotations from Israeli newspapers translated into Romanian. The editor is Dorel Dorian, while the veteran editor, Chaim Riemer, who immigrated to Israel some years ago and then returned to Romania as an emissary of the Joint, was appointed "Honorary Director" and writes the Hebrew page. The Hasefer publishing house, sponsored by the Jewish Federation, is dedicated to topics connected to Judaism, Jewish culture and history, as well as to the study of the Holocaust.

In recent years antisemitism in Romania has been on a back burner, mainly in intellectual circles and, with few exceptions, is not accompanied by violent acts. Its most prominent spokesman was Corneliu Vadim Tudor, editor of the weekly *Romania Mare*. Especially during the 1990s, the journal and the political party of the same name incited against the Jews, against Israel, and also against the democratic forces in post-Ceausescu Romania. The Romanian president Ion Iliescu worked to block any rising antisemitism, especially when considering America's decision regarding the granting of economic concessions as a most favored nation. The Jewish community's attitude, as expressed by Cajal, differs from that held in the past by Rabbi Rosen. Cajal did not declare a general, vocal war on antisemitism, but focuses on providing information to convince the Romanians of the great contribution the Jews made to the Romanian people and to the country. The main important universities (Bucharest, Cluj, Iaşi, Craiova) set up special departments and centers for the study of Judaism, Jewish history, and for teaching Hebrew. However, public discourse was constantly fed by numerous antisemitic publications, which placed a special emphasis on denying crimes committed by the Antonescu regime against the Jewish population. An international commission of historians to study the Holocaust in Romania was set up in 2003 and chaired by Elie Wiesel. The conclusions of the Report issued by the commission were accepted by President Ion Iliescu as well as by his successor, Traian Băsescu. A National Institute for the Study of Holocaust in Romania was inaugurated on October 10, 2005, as one of the first significant implementations of the commission's recommendations. Several expressions of Holocaust commemoration were officially initiated in Romania, especially on October 9, established as official date for commemorating the Holocaust (on which date in 1941 the deportations to Transnistria began).

[Naftali Kraus / Lucian-Zeev Herscovici and Leon Volovici (2nd ed.)]

BIBLIOGRAPHY: S. Baron, *The Jews in Roumania* (1930); J. Berkowitz, *La Question des Israélites en Roumanie* (1923); I. Cohen, *The Jews in Romania* (1938); W. Filderman, *Adevarul asupra problemei evreesti din Romania* (1925); M.A. Halevy, in: *Anuarul evreilor din Romania* (1937); A. Ruppin, *Die Juden in Rumaenien* (1908); E. Schwarzfeld, in: AJYB, 3 (1901/02), 25–87; idem, in REJ, 13 (1886), 127ff.; idem, *Impopularea re-impopularea si intemeierea targurilor si targusoarelor in Moldova* (1914); M. Schwarzfeld, *Ochire asupra istoriei evreilor in Romania* (1887); idem, *Momente din istoria evreilor in Romania* (1889); idem, *Excursiuni critice asupra istoriei evreilor in Romania* (1888); idem, in: *Annuar pentru Israeliți*, 10 (1887/88); 18 (1896); PK Romanyah (1970), 141–209, 219–224 (first pagin.), introduction and comprehensive bibl.; T. Lavi, in: *Yad Vashem Studies*, 4 (1960), 261–315; 5 (1963), 405–18; idem, *Yahadut Romanyah be-Ma'avak al Hazzalatah* (1965); M. Carp, *Cartea Neagra*, 1 (1946); I. Hirschmann, *Caution to the Winds* (1962). **ADD. BIBLIOGRAPHY:** E. Aczél, *Publicațiile periodice evreiești din România*, vol. 1 (2004); J. Ancel, *Toledot ha-Sho'ah: Romanyah*, 2 vols. (2002); L. Benjamin, *Evreii din România în texte istoriografice* (2002); I. Bercovici, *Pirkei Romanyah* (Tel Aviv, 1975); S. Bickel, *Yahadut Romanyah: Historyah, Bikkoret Sifrutit, Zikhronot* (Tel Aviv, 1978); N. Cajal and H. Kuller (eds.), *Contribuția evreilor din România la cultură și civilizație* (1996); W. Filderman, *Memoirs and Diaries*, ed. J. Ancel (2004/05); C. Iancu, *Jews in Romania, 1866–1919* (1996); idem, *Les juifs en Roumanie, 1919–1938* (1996); E. Mendelsohn, *The Jews of East Central Europe between the World Wars* (1983); A. Stern, *Din viața unui evreu-român*, vols. 1–3 (2001); L. Rotman and R. Vago (eds.), *Toledot ha-Yehudim be-Romanyah*, vols. 1–4 (1996–2003); L. Volovici, *Nationalist Ideology & Antisemitism: The Case of Romanian Intellectuals in the 1930s* (1991).

ROMANIAN LITERATURE.

Biblical and Hebraic Influences

Unlike the languages of surrounding peoples and cultures in the area, Romanian is of Latin or Romance origin, dating back to Roman colonization of Dacia (present-day Romania and Bessarabia). Although Romania's national movement could not discard the dominant Orthodox Christianity, which was a legacy of Slavic influence in the Balkans, Calvinism was a significant religious factor in the 16th century (as also in neighboring Hungary and the disputed territory of Transylvania), and this had interesting literary repercussions. Under the impact of the Hussite movement and the Reformation, attempts were made to replace Church Slavonic (see *Bulgarian Literature) with services in the vernacular and to translate the Bible into Romanian. Thus some of the earliest extant texts in Romanian are of a religious character. They include two versions of the Psalter: *Psaltirea Scheiana* (1482) and *Psaltirea Voronețeană* (1580), so named after the monasteries in which the manuscripts were discovered.

Early Writings

Of all the books of the Bible the Psalms were especially favored and inspired numerous translations. The first extant Romanian printed texts are the "Psalters of Coresi" (1568, 1578), published by Coresi, a friar-printer of Brașov. The Psalms were generally translated as *Psaltirea Sfîntului Prooroc și Impărat David* ("The Psalter of the Holy Prophet and Emperor David"). Two of the best-known translations were a versified rendering by the Moldavian metropolitan Dosoftei (Uniev 1673) and a version by the erudite metropolitan Antim-Ivireanu (1694). During the 18th century alone, some 30 editions of the Psalter appeared in Transylvania, Moldavia, and Muntenia (Greater Walachia). The *Carte a Profeților* ("Book of the Prophets") was also printed in 1673. The first complete translation of the Bible, *Biblia lui Șerban*, named in honor of its patron, Prince Șerban Cantacuzino, was published in Bucharest in 1688. Written in the Muntenian dialect, this work was based on the Septuagint and not only inspired all subsequent Romanian Bibles, but was also a formative influence on the Romanian language. In this, the Șerban Bible may be compared with the German version of Martin *Luther, the English Authorized Version, and Reformist texts in other lands. Later Romanian Bibles were published by the historian Samuil Micu (1795) and by Ion Eliade Rădulescu (1858). Gala *Galaction and Vasile Radu produced an excellent 20th-century translation (1938).

In the sphere of religious literature there were also several widely distributed works on biblical history and exegesis, such as Veniamin Costache's *Istoria Scripturii Vechiului Testament* ("History of Old Testament Scripture," 1824) and Filaret Scriban's *Istoria Sfîntă a Vechiului Testament* ("Sacred History of the Old Testament," 1872[3]). The Bible, particularly the Psalms, was the foundation of Romanian poetry, Dosoftei's verse translation of Psalms being considered its earliest monument, mainly because of the numerous lyrical variations on the original text.

A version of Genesis and Exodus, embellished with legends and known as the *Palia* (Paloea), was published in Romanian translation in 1882. The great Romanian-Jewish folklorist, Moses *Gaster, traced this to the Jewish legends of the *Sefer ha-Yashar* and the *Pirkei Rabbi Eliezer*. In view of the large number of translations, biblical influences on Romanian literature may well have been much stronger. In the earlier, preliterary period, this influence was mainly one of style. The chroniclers of the 17th and 18th centuries often used biblical expressions, drew many of their similes from the Bible, and also quoted biblical maxims. Dimitrie Cantemir (1673–1723), the humanist prince of Moldavia, a brilliant linguist who became a member of the Berlin Academy of Sciences, made constant use of biblical quotations in his philosophical treatise, *Divanul sau gâlceava înțeleptului cu lŭmea* (1698).

Later Influences

Modern Romanian literature came into existence toward the middle of the 19th century, in the era of Romanian national resurgence. Ion Eliade Raˇdulescu (1802–1872), one of the first great literary figures in modern Romania, published a version of the Bible, translated *Byron's *Hebrew Melodies* (in 1834), and

Tasso's *Jerusalem Delivered* (in 1847). He also wrote many religious, philosophical, and political commentaries on biblical texts (*Biblice...*, 1858). Following his example, other writers also turned to the Bible. They include G.G. Filipescu, who published a novel about the *Wandering Jew (1835); J.A. Vaillant, a French professor who settled in Romania, author of *Legenda lui Aman și Mardoheu* ("The Legend of Haman and Mordecai," 1868); and G. Gârbea, who wrote a dramatic poem about Job (1898). Job also inspired Nicolae Davidescu (1888–1954) to produce a verse play (1915), his other works including the poem *Judeea* (1927). Alexandru Macedonski (1854–1920) and Cincinat Pavelescu (1872–1934) collaborated in the tragedy *Saul* (1893), based on the Hebrew king's dramatic conflict with the prophet Samuel. Other works of note on biblical themes are *Eliezer* (1908), a biblical one-act play by Eugen Lovinescu (1881–1943), and reworkings of the Song of Songs by Corneliu Moldovanu (1908) and Marcel Romanescu (1925). The evocation of Divine majesty in the numerous psalms of Tudor Arghezi (1880–1967) elevated Romanian poetry to new artistic heights. The poems of George Caˇlinescu (1899–1965) abound in references to biblical characters and incidents, as well as to the landscape and flora of Canaan, which he described in many poems of great artistry. Another eminent writer, Gala Galaction, was steeped in the Bible, which inspired his mystical prose and several biblical novels, including *Roxana* (1930).

Romanian-Jewish writers did not particularly distinguish themselves in the field of biblical literature. The Zionist poet Enric *Furtuna (1881–1965) wrote the dramatic poem *Abișag* (1963) and other biblical verse, while Camil *Baltazar (1902–1977) published *Biblice* ("Poems from the Bible," 1926), a collection notable for its sensual treatment of figures such as Ruth, Tamar, Esther, and the Shulammite. Two poets inspired by the Songs of Songș were Marcel Breslașu (1903–1966), whose *Cîntarea Cîntărilor* (1938) was staged as an oratorio, and Maria *Banuș.

The Image of the Jew

While Romanian writers presented a positive image of the Hebrews or Jews of Bible times, their treatment of the contemporary Jew was often less favorable and even undisguisedly hostile. In the words of Queen Elizabeth of Romania (1843–1916), known to literature as Carmen Sylva, "all draw from the Bible and persecute the people that gave it." The popular conception of the Jew originated in religious and other works translated from Greek, Latin, and Church Slavonic and disseminated from the second half of the 18th century. In popular tales and anecdotes the Jew was said to be damned for having rejected the Christian savior, and Romanian folklore added antisemitism to theological antipathies by describing Jews as agents of the Devil, covetous of Christian blood, money-grubbing, cowardly, and villainous. Jewish intelligence and inventiveness were acknowledged with an invariable sneer. The roots of Romanian antisemitism were basically those found elsewhere: religious prejudice and intolerance, economic competition, and chauvinistic xenophobia. Only the pretexts varied according to circumstance. Thus it was alleged that the "invasion of Russian and Polish Jews would place Romanian commerce in their hands"; there was resentment of Jewish appeals to Western countries for the ending of persecution; and indignation over the insistence of these nations on the extension of civil and political liberties to the Jews of Romania following the peace treaties of 1878 and 1919. Such "injustices" intensified native antisemitism, which was especially fostered by certain writers. Ironically enough, the most violent anti-Jewish fanatics were often those whose own ethnic origin was least reliably Romanian.

THE CLASSIC STEREOTYPE. For literary antisemites the Jew was responsible for all the ills of the Romanian people. In the case of the eminent nationalist writer Vasile Alecsandri (1821–1890), the titles of some of his plays are significant – *Lipitorile satelor* ("The Village Leeches"), *Herșcu Boccegiul* ("Hershel the Peddler"), and *Năvălirea Jidanilor* ("The Invasion of the Yids"). The poet Mihail Eminescu (1850–1889) viciously attacked the Jews' "anti-national" character; the scholarly Bogdan Petriceicu Hașdeu (1838–1907), who was himself of partly Jewish descent, considered Jews a plague within society; and Costache Negruzzi (1808–1868) even resented their alleged dislike of nature and flowers.

Both before and after World War I the Romanian intelligentsia was poisoned by such anti-Jewish sentiments. Three university professors – A.C. Cuza (1857–1946), Bogdan-Duică (1865–1934), and Nicolae Iorga (1871–1940) – also spread the idea that the Jews of Romania were descendants of the *Khazars, who had once dominated parts of Eastern Europe.

During the 1930s, under the growing influence of Nazism, Romanian antisemitic movements (which included many students) increased their strength. Other writers who succumbed to the doctrines of racism included Nael Ionescu (1890–1940), once a friend of the Jews, and Nicolae Davidescu, the poet steeped in the Song of Songs, who became the antisemitic theoretician of *Vremea*, a review which had formerly published many works by Jewish writers. Ion Alexandru Brătescu-Voinești (1868–1946), who abandoned pacifism for xenophobic nationalism, concluded that all Jewish writings were pornographic and aimed at the destruction of family life. The poet Octavian Goga (1881–1938), who was also prime minister of Romania, injected his anti-Jewish venom into *Mustul care fierbe* ("The Boiling Must," 1927), and another writer, Nichifor Crainic (1889–1972), who was Romania's minister of propaganda during World War II, expressed his hatred of the Jews in religious terms as editor of the review *Gândirea* (1926–44). In his novel *1907* (1937), Cezar Petrescu (1892–1961) blamed the Jews for the peasants' rebellion of that year, while another novelist, Ionel Teodoreanu (1897–1954), created amoral Jews who speak a mutilated Romanian. Even the Socialist Panait Istrati (1884–1935), a disciple of the humanitarian Romain Rolland, who wrote mainly in French, predicted the downfall of the Jews because of their supposed identification with the Communism he had rejected.

OBJECTIVE ATTITUDES. Literary societies did not, however, adopt antisemitism as a policy. Although *Semănătorul*, the review of Nicolae Iorga, received contributions from many antisemites, it remained impartial. So did *Viata Românească*, which reflected the popular-democratic views of writers such as Constantin Stere (1865–1936), Mihail Sadoveanu (1880–1961), and G. Ibraileanu (1861–1936). Political issues were also excluded from *Flacăra, Convorbiri literare, Viaţa Nová*, and *Sburătorul Literar*, which were only concerned with aesthetic problems.

Among Romanian writers who showed understanding for the Jew's position were the democratic historian Nicolae Bălcescu (1819–1852), Alexandru Odobescu (1834–1895), and the revolutionary hero Aleco Russo (1819–1859), who wrote in his *Cugetări* ("Reflections," 1856) that "it is not wise to oppress the Children of Israel." *Junimea*, the literary society that created the "New Direction" in modern Romanian literature, did not espouse antisemitism, although most of its members toed the anti-Jewish line. This was due to the firm control of the founder, Titu Liviu Maiorescu (1840–1917), a conservative prime minister and Romania's first great literary critic. He was supported by Petre P. Carp (1837–1918), a translator of Shakespeare, who admired Jewish talent. Ion Luca Caragiale (1852–1912), who scorned antisemitism as a bestial aberration, was the first great Romanian writer to present a Jew's state of mind in a work of literary importance. His masterly short novel, *O făclie de Paşti* ("An Easter Candle," 1889), is a psychological study of a Jewish innkeeper, Leiba Zibal, terrorized by his would-be murderer one Easter night.

SYMPATHETIC PORTRAYALS. The outstanding prose writer Mihail Sadoveanu (1880–1961), who was a prominent figure in Romanian cultural life, actively opposed the antisemites. His attitude led to the burning of his works by bands of hooligans who nicknamed him "Jidoveanu" (i.e., the Jew-lover, Sadoveanu). Whole passages of his works deal with the life of Jews whom he had come to know in his native townlet. One of his best stories, "Haia Sanis" (1909), explores the painful state of mind of a Jewish girl in love with a gentile.

Liviu Rebreanu (1885–1944), one of the great Romanian novelists, published the impressive novella *Iţic Strul dezertor* ("Itzik Shtrul the Deserter," 1921), the tale of a Jewish soldier who is driven to commit suicide when his superior officer involves him in a fictitious desertion. However, in 1938, Rebreanu succumbed to Fascist influence and published the novel, *Gorila* ("The Gorilla"), in which one character presents antisemitic prejudice in a very favorable light. On the other hand, the religious writer Gala Galaction published many books and articles about Judaism and in support of Zionism and often described poverty-stricken Jews, endowing them with moral distinction. In his best novel, *Papucii lui Mahmud* ("Mohammed's Slippers," 1932), Galaction was optimistic about the peaceful coexistence in the future of Christians, Muslims, and Jews. This was also the case with Victor Ion Popa (1895–1946) in his play, *Take, Ianke, şi Kadír* (1933), Another leading opponent of antisemitism was the critic Eugen Lovinescu, leader of the review and literary group entitled *Sburătorul literar.* Many distinguished Jewish writers received their literary training under this exponent of French culture and modernism.

A particularly courageous stand was taken by George Călinescu (1899–1965), one of the most eminent of modern Romanian writers. In 1939, when antisemitism was reaching its peak, he expressed his opposition in a famous article entitled "Evreii" ("The Jews"), which appeared in his Jassy review, *Jurnalul literar*. Călinescu's vast *Istorie a Literaturii Roâmne* ("History of Romanian Literature," 1941) included details of all the Jewish writers officially removed from the annals of Romanian literature by the fascist Antonescu regime and dealt with their works in an objective spirit. His attitude led to violent demonstrations by antisemitic students and to the public burning of his books. In 1941 a notorious anti-Jewish journalist, Pamfil Şeicaru, denounced his opus as "a national scandal." The Jewish characters in Călinescu's fiction – novels such as *Enigma Otiliei* ("Otilia's Enigma," 1938) and *Scrinul negru* ("The Black Chest," 1960) – have the virtues and vices of people despised and rejected by their host society.

Treatment by Jewish Writers

Apart from their output of polemics against antisemitism, Romania's Jewish writers were also concerned with projecting a favorable image of Jews and Jewish life in works of fiction. Among the poets, Avram Axelrad and Alexandru Dominic stressed the melancholy situation of their people in an alien and hostile environment, a theme especially elaborated by Adolf Rodion *Steuerman, whose volume of collected Jewish verse, *Spini* ("Thorns," 1915), highlighted the spiritual conflicts of the Jewish intellectual. The question of Jewish survival assumed major importance in prose. The most significant work by Moïse *Roman-Ronetti was his play *Manasse* (1900), which dealt with the conflict between the old and the new Jewish generations and between Jews and gentiles. Its performance gave rise to antisemitic student disorders, and moved Adrian Verea to write a sequel to Roman-Ronetti's drama (1915). Henric *Sanielevici used his literary and scientific gifts to combat Nazi race theories with *In slujba Satanei* ("In the Service of the Devil," 1930–35); while Isac Iacovitz *Ludo, a veteran Jewish publicist who made his peace with the Communists after World War II, fiercely satirized leading Romanian antisemites and demolished their portrayal of Jewish types. A positive image was presented by the novelists Ion *Călugăru, whose works constitute a vast fresco of Romanian Jewry, and Isac *Peltz, who wrote pioneering and successful novels about Jewish ghetto life in Bucharest. A few of the latter's works, such as *Calea Vacaresti* (1933) and *Foc în Hanul cu Tei* ("Fire at the Khan Inn," 1934), went through several editions. *De două mii de ani* ("For the Past 2,000 Years," 1934), by Mihail *Sebastian, was a moving description of a Jewish intellectual's antisemitic ordeals and spiritual torment. Although its hero is unable to accept either Zionism or Communism, the book contains some excellent description of pre-World War II Jewish life in Romania. A rare instance of Jewish self-hatred was the novelist Ury Benador (1895–1971), whose Marxist convictions led him to portray Romanian Jewry, in works written after the Holocaust, in a generally hostile manner. On the other hand, Iulia Soare, a writer of the postwar generation, produced an objective study of a middle-class Jewish family during the second decade of the 20th century.

Jewish Contribution to Romanian Literature

In so culturally backward a land as Romania, Jews naturally played an important literary role from the late 19th century, despite the prejudices and restrictions that operated against them. In philology, folklore, and bibliography they were acknowledged pioneers, and many Romanian Jews who later gained distinction as poets, playwrights, and novelists, began their career in journalism. By common admission, Romanian philology was largely the creation of Jewish scholars. Heinrich *Tiktin and Lazăr *Săineanu (L. Săinéan) were experts of international renown, the former producing the first – and to date the most scientific – Romanian grammar, the latter publishing the first comprehensive dictionary of the Romanian language. Denied Romanian citizenship, Tiktin moved to Berlin and Săinéanu to Paris, both men broadening their work to include general philological research. I.A. Candrea Hecht (1872–1950) was also a lexicographer of the first rank. In folklore two outstanding figures were Moses Gaster and Moses *Schwarzfeld. Gaster's many learned works include the pioneering *Literatura populară română* (1883) and *Chrestomația română* (1891). A staunch Jewish nationalist, he antagonized the Romanian government with his protests against antisemitism and in 1885 was expelled and settled in England. E. Schwarzfeld, an eminent historian of Romanian Jewry, was also expelled and settled in Paris. Two other great philologists and linguists were A. Grauer (Brauer; 1900–?) and J. Byck (1897–1964).

LITERARY PIONEERS. Curiously enough, the first significant Jewish contribution to Romanian literature was made by a semiliterate peddler, Moïse *Cilibi (Ephraim Moses b. Sender), whose annual books of folk wisdom, dictated to the printer, enjoyed an extraordinary success from 1858 until his death. Although objective critics stressed the important role of emerging Jewish writers as apostles of avant-garde ideas and techniques, those less sympathetic to Jewish literary aspirations could always find fault with their work. Some claimed that the Jews dealt with Romanian national themes that they could not possibly appreciate, while others maintained that they unjustifiably neglected specifically Jewish questions. While it is undeniable that many Romanian-Jewish writers showed greater concern for Romanian than for Jewish issues, it is worth recalling that Roman-Ronetti's dramatic masterpiece, *Manasse*, which did investigate the problems of Romanian Jewry, was driven off the stage of the Romanian National Theater by antisemitic nationalist demonstrators. During the years preceding World War I, when Titu Maiorescu's aesthetic theories were dominant, Constantin *Gherea-Dobrogeanu, a literary critic and Socialist writer, introduced his own social and materialist conception of art, inaugurating a new school of scientific criticism. The same period saw the emergence of other Jewish literary scholars and critics, notably Ion Trivale, whose brilliant career was cut short by World War I, and Henric Sanielevici, one of Romania's most erudite and incisive polemical critics.

POETS. Among creative writers, Barbu *Nemțeanu introduced a Heinesque note into the poetry of his time, while D. Iacobescu ushered in French symbolism. The few poems printed at that time by Tristan *Tzara and his review, *Simbolul*, already foreshadowed the future rebel and creator of Dadaism; while the verse of Felix *Aderca proclaimed the poetic innovator, though not the great novelist that he was to become between the two world wars. Another remarkable poet of the time was Eugen *Relgis who later inaugurated the intellectual current of humanitarianism in Romania. Other leading poets were Leon Feraru, Enric Furtună, A. Toma, and the versatile Samson Lazar, who settled in Israel. Jewish suffering especially preoccupied two other poets, Avram Axelrad and Adolf Rodion Steuerman.

Immediately after World War I, the economic prosperity which followed Romania's annexation of Transylvania, Bukovina, and Bessarabia was accompanied by an unusual literary boom. The euphoria of a hard-won emancipation also contributed to the increasing activity of Jewish writers. Benjamin *Fondane, known in his earlier Romanian years as Beniamin (Wechsler) Fundoianu, wrote poems about the countryside, but his works were suffused with Jewish inspiration. Even after his emigration to France in 1923, Fondane occasionally published Romanian verse. The collection *Priveliști* ("Landscapes"), one section of which describes life in the Moldavian *shtetl*, was published in 1930. The new lyrical themes and imagery introduced by Camil Baltazar during the 1920s led him to be acknowledged as one of the most gifted poets of his time. He was closely followed by Ilarie *Voronca, whose review, *75 HP*, inaugurated the new integralist trend in 1924. Another avant-garde poet was Sașa *Pană (1902–1981); his highly nonconformist verse appeared in the review *Unu*, whose guiding spirit he was during the years 1928–32. Marcel Breslașu wrote biblical poetry, while Maria Banuș with her verse collection *Tara fetelor* ("The Maidens' Land," 1937) revealed herself to be Romania's outstanding poetess. By contrast, a forerunner of the absurd in poetry was Alexandru Robot (Alter Rotman, 1916–1943). Classical verse was published during the 1920s and 1930s by Andrei Tudor (1907–1959), and by Virgiliu Monda and Emil *Dorian, both of whom became better known as novelists, as well as by Leon Feraru and Alexandru Dominic, whose poem "Israel" (1920) was hailed by the critics as a masterpiece.

PLAYWRIGHTS AND NOVELISTS. Writers of the period between the world wars include the playwrights B. Luca and Adrian Verea, who also published verse. Isaia Răcăciuni (1900–?) wrote social novels such as *Mâl* ("Swamp," 1934) and *Dați-ni-l înapoi pe Isus* ("Give Us Back Jesus," 1936) and *Paradis uitat* ("Forgotten Paradise," 1937), as did Sergiu *Dan and Cella Serghi. Mihail Sebastian, one of the most prolific and versatile prose writers in Romania, wrote essays, criticism, novels, and plays. His drama *Steaua fără nume* ("The Nameless Star," 1943) was the only work by a Jew staged (albeit under an assumed name) during the era of Nazi persecution. With his novels and poems Marcel *Blecher was a pioneer of surrealism and existentialism, while Ion Călugăru and Isac Peltz portrayed Jewish life in Romania's towns and villages. Abraham Leib *Zissu, a leading Zionist, wrote novels and sketches exclusively on Jewish themes.

THE NAZI ERA AND ITS AFTERMATH. Although Jewish writers in Romania suffered less from the Nazi "Final Solution" than Jews in most other lands under Hitler's domination, their works were suppressed and they had to spend the war years (1941–44) in hiding or anonymous seclusion. The restrictive atmosphere so prevalent in the country already led many Jewish writers to emigrate after World War I and a remarkable number of talented Jewish writers made their way to France, notably Benjamin Fondane, Isidore Isou (1925–), Adolphe Orna (1882–1925), Claude Sernet (1902–1968), Tristan Tzara, and Ilarie Voronca. Fondane, who was murdered in the Birkenau death camp, was the most consciously Jewish among them. Two other Romanian-Jewish writers who emigrated to France were the talented novelist Sorana *Gurian and the critic Aureliu Weiss. Enric Furtună ended his life in Brazil and Eugen Relgis settled in Montevideo in 1947. Three who moved to Israel were Samson Lazar, A.L. Zissu, and the poet Mayer *Rudich (1913–), who resumed his literary and journalistic career in Tel Aviv in 1959.

Several Jewish writers who had risen to eminence before World War II, including Baltazar, Ludo, and Peltz, dutifully conformed to the requirements of Romania's postwar Communist regime. Ludo's attacks on the former royal family and the hostile accounts of the Jewish bourgeoisie published by Ury Benador were devoid of literary value. On the other hand, Maria Banuș and Marcel Breslașu, though faithful to the party line, maintained a higher ethical and artistic standard in their works, as did Samuel Gregore with his fantastic novel *Dincolo* ("Beyond," 1944). The new writers of the post-World War II era did not, in general, pay much attention to Jewish questions. Many adopted Romanian names, obscuring their Jewish origin. As authors and critics, they made an important contribution to the development of neo-realistic literature. Among the literary historians and critics who held leading posts on the editorial boards of various reviews were Vera Câlin, Paul (Cohn) Cornea (1924–), Ovid Crohmâlniceanu, Samuil (Druckman) Damian (1930–), B. (Bernstein) Elvin (1927–), Silvian Iosifescu, Mihail Petroveanu (1923–), Lucian (Leibovici) Raicu (1934–), Nicolae Tertulian, and Henri Zalis (1932–). Elvin published books on Sebastian (1956), Anatole France (1957), and Chekhov (1961) and studies of Ionesco and Camus; Petroveanu in his *Studii literare* (1966) wrote on Fondane; while Zalis wrote on Flaubert (1968). In drama, Aurel *Baranga (1913–1979), Alexandru Mirodan, and Dorel Dorian wrote plays that were highly praised and often performed on the Romanian stage.

Representative prose writers of the period were Radu Cosașu, Sorana Gurian, Norman Manea (1936–), Ieronim Șerbu, Cella Serghi, Alexandru Sever, Iulia Soare, and Vladimir Colin (1921–1991), a state prize winner, whose stories for children and adolescents were widely appreciated. When the Communist regime relaxed its stringent demands in the 1960s, several Romanian-Jewish poets were able to tackle themes about human relationships with skill and sensitivity. Such writers included Veronica *Porumbacu, Nina Cassian, George Toma Maiorescu, Petre Solomon (1923–1991), Stefan Jures (1931–), and Florin Mugur, who was awarded an international poetry prize at Sarajevo, Yugoslavia, in 1969.

Literature of the Holocaust

In Romania, as in other lands once under Nazi control, a special literature arose reflecting the era of the European Holocaust. Non-Jewish novelists who dealt with this theme included Eusebiu Camilar (1910–1965), who described the mass murder of Jews in *Negura* (1949), and George Calinescu, whose *Scrinul Negru* (1960) dealt with Jewish deportation to and life in the camps of Transnistria. The latter work also contains a powerful description of the massacre of the Jews from Odessa. After their visits to former death camps in Poland, George Bogza (1908–1993) and Eugen Jebeleanu (1911–1991) wrote moving poems about the Nazi atrocities, while Ion Grigorescu's novel, *Obsesia* ("Obsession," 1960), concludes with the suggestion that a new Wailing Wall be erected at Auschwitz.

The Holocaust was the one Jewish theme that inspired a significant number of Jewish writers in postwar Romania. Documentary works were published by Filip Brunea-Fox (1898–1977) who disclosed details of the Bucharest pogrom organized by Romanian Nazi legionaries in his *Orașul Măcelului* ("City of Slaughter," 1944); by M. Rudich in *La braț cu moartea* ("Hand in Hand with Death," 1945), which described the deportations from Bukovina and Bessarabia; and by Aurel Baranga, who collected data on the most significant acts of terror perpetrated by Romania Nazis in *Ninge peste Ucraina* ("Snow falls over the Ukraine," 1945[1], 1946[2]). Other Jewish writers wrote novels and shorter prose works on Nazi war crimes. Emil Dorian's novel *Otrava* ("Poison," 1946) described the early antisemitic outbreaks in Bucharest; while Sergiu Dan in *Unde începe noaptea* ("Where the Night Begins," 1945) and *Roza și ceilalți* ("Rosa and the Others," 1947), Ieronim Serbu in *Nunta în stepă* ("Wedding on the Steppe," 1955), and Isac Peltz in *Israel îns-îngerat* ("Bloodstained Israel," 1946) reach a climax with detailed descriptions of life in the

Transnistrian camps. Matei Gall's novel *Masacrul* (1957) described the murder of a group of Jewish communists by an SS unit and Arnold Dagani's diary of the deportation, *Groapa este în livada de vişini* (1947), was one of the most impressive accounts of its type. Another survivor, Oliver Lustig, wrote two novels on his experiences in Auschwitz, while Maria Arsene (Arthur Leibowici, 1909–1975) published various works about the Nazi terror in Romania, including the novels *Hotel Ambasador* (1967) and *Los* (1968). Other works on the Holocaust were written by Cella Serghi, G.T. Maiorescu, and Alexandru Jar (1912–1988), whose novel, *Trădarea lunii* ("The Moon's Treason," 1968), is set in Nazi-occupied Vilna. Finally, poems on Jewish suffering at the hands of the Nazis were written by Camil Baltazar, Maria Banuş, Saşa Pană, Veronica Porumbacu, and Mayer Rudich.

Consciously or unconsciously, Jewish writers in Romania revealed their spiritual heritage in such characteristics as their interest in research, their spirit of innovation, their predilection for philosophical reflection, and their ability to grasp the torments of the human soul. Even their inclination toward social revolt has its ethical roots in the Bible. Although they may have drifted far from religious tradition, only a very few Romanian-Jewish writers advocated total assimilation. Most of the non-Zionists merely submerged themselves in the themes and ideals of their era without renouncing their ties with the Jewish people. This is also true of the more recent writers whose lack of specifically Jewish appeal is attributable to the limitations imposed by Romania's Marxist theoreticians rather than to their own free choice and mode of expression. It is significant that, after 1967, Romania's friendly relations with Israel – unique among communist states of Eastern Europe – brought about an upsurge of Jewish consciousness among the country's younger writers.

BIBLIOGRAPHY: M. Gaster, *Ilchester Lectures on Greco-Slavonic Literature* (1887); M. Schwarzfeld, in: *Anuar pentru Israeliţi* 5652 (1891); O. Densusianu, *Studii de filologie română: Psaltirea Voroneţeană* (1898); idem, *Literatura română modernă*, 2 vols. (1929); G. Panu, *Amintiri de la "Junimea" din Iasi* (1908); E. Lovinescu, *Istoria civilizaţiei române moderne* (1924); idem, *Istoria literaturii române contemporane* (1927); L. Feraru, *Development of Romanian Poetry* (1929); G. Călinescu, *Istoria literaturii române* (1941); D. Murarasu, *Nationalismul lui Eminescu* (1955); Perpessicius, *Mentiuni de istoriografie literară si folclor* (1957); E. Turdeanu, in: *Revue des Etudes Roumaines* (1960), nos. 5–7.

[Dora Litani-Littman]

ROMANIN, SAMUELE (1808–1861), Italian historian. Born in Trieste, Romanin went to live in Venice at age 12, living there for the rest of his life. He became famous as the author of *La Storia dei Popoli Europei dalla Decadenza dell'Impero Romano*, and especially *Storia Documentata di Venezia*, a work in 10 volumes written between 1853 and 1861.

BIBLIOGRAPHY: G. Pavanello, "Gli studi sulla più antica storia veneziana dal Romanin ai nostri giorni," in: *Teneo Veneto* (1903), 265–5.

[Massimo Longo Adorno (2nd ed.)]

ROMANIN JACUR, LEONE (1867–1928), Italian politician. He was a leading light of Paduan Jewry. Romanin Jacur was senator of the Kingdom of Italy from 1880 to 1913. He became famous for the attention he paid to the issues related to the modernization of the countryside. He opposed Zionism and on the occasion of Theodor Herzl's visit to Italy refused to arrange for him an audience with Pope Pius X, which had been asked for by Felice Ravenna. Romanin Jacur was on good terms of friendship with Pius X dating back to the times when the future pope was a parish priest in the Padua countryside. Romanin Jacur also held the office of minister of public works from 1894 to 1896 and was undersecretary at the Ministry of the Interior in 1899.

BIBLIOGRAPHY: Claudia De Benedetti (ed.), *Il Cammino della Speranza: gli Ebrei e Padova*, vol. 2 (1998), 97–99.

[Massimo Longo Adorno (2nd ed.)]

ROMANIOTS. The name Romaniots is employed to define the original Jewish population of the territories of the Byzantine Empire, Constantinople, the Balkans, and Asia Minor, and their descendants in all matters relating to their customs, language, and tradition. The family names of the Romaniots were Greek, their synagogues were known by Greek names, and they were considerably influenced by Greek culture and especially the Greek language, which had also been adopted in their synagogue services. In 1547 a translation of the Torah in Greek and Ladino was published in Constantinople. The Greek translation was printed in square characters (see *Judeo-Greek). The customs and special versions of the Romaniots' prayers were collected in the "*Maḥzor Romania*" which includes the New Moon prayer given in Judeo-Greek. For many years, they read the Book of Jonah on the Day of Atonement in Hebrew and in Greek. It was also the custom to read Ruth, Lamentations, the tractate *Avot*, and a commentary to the Song of Songs in Greek. From the 16th century, the Romaniots were on the defensive culturally and socially against the waves of immigrants who arrived from the European countries, notably from *Spain and *Portugal, and who gradually imposed their way of life and customs on the existing population. The number of their synagogues decreased and their Greek dialect became limited to the Greek Jews in the towns of Kastoria, Ioannina, and Chalcis and to the *Karaites of the Haskoy district of Constantinople. The synagogue of the "Gregos Community" continued to exist in Constantinople until 1660, that of *Sofia until 1898, and that of *Adrianople until it was burnt down in 1905. Among the customs and traditions of the Romaniots may be mentioned the seven wedding blessings that are recited at the betrothal (*erusin*) ceremony, whereas the usual custom is to recite it at the actual marriage ceremony. Originally, the husband did not inherit from the wife but later the marriage contract was amended according to which the husband shared the wife's inheritance with her offspring.

BIBLIOGRAPHY: Rosanes, Togarmah, 1 (1930^2); Assaf, in: *Sefer ha-Yovel le… S. Krauss* (1937), 169–77; D. Goldschmidt, in: *Sefunot*, 8 (1964), 205–36; J. Starr, *The Jews in the Byzantine Empire*

(1939), passim; idem, *Romania* (1949), passim; A. Galanté, *Les Juifs de Constantinople sous Byzance* (1940), 55–58; idem, *Histoire des Juifs d'Istanbul*, 2 (1942), 171–6; S. Marcus, *The Judeo-Spanish Language* (1965), 144–7.

[Simon Marcus]

ROMAN LITERATURE. Although there is information concerning the Jews in Rome as early as 139 B.C.E., the first Latin writers to mention the Jews or Judaism in their writings are *Cicero and Varro, who lived at the end of the republic. It is significant that Cicero does not mention the Jews or Judaism in his philosophical works, but only in his orations – in his speech in defense of Flaccus (*Pro Flacco*) of 59 B.C.E., and in his *De Provinciis Consularibus* of 56 B.C.E. – in both instances his remarks are derogatory. The Jewish religion he defines as a *superstitio*, and the Jews themselves are described as a people born to slavery, but there is no need to draw far-reaching conclusions from his polemical thrusts since they arose from the fact that the Jews were to be found in the opposite camp from the one Cicero was representing. In similar situations, other nations received no more sympathetic treatment at the hands of the great orator. The stereotyped antisemitic complaints of the Hellenistic period are, at any rate, not mentioned by him. In contrast to Cicero, Varro, the foremost scholar in the period of the late republic, treats the Jewish way of life with respect. He praises Jewish religious worship which opposed all pictorial and plastic representation, and compares it with the early Roman practice which similarly rejected them in their worship of the gods.

The growth of the Jewish population in Rome in the time of Augustus is reflected in the mainstream of contemporary Roman literature. The poet Tibullus alludes to the Jewish Sabbath; Horace refers to the missionary fervor of the Jews and to their gullibility; the historian Livy speaks of the Temple of the Jews in Jerusalem and stresses that the worship therein is unique in that it contains no representation or any idol whatsoever of the godhead. Ovid was familiar with the Jewish Sabbath, and Augustus himself mentions it in a letter to Tiberius, although – like many of the Greeks and Romans of those days – he was under the impression that it was customary for the Jews to fast on the Sabbath.

The longest description of Judaism extant from the writers of the age of Augustus is that found in the epitome of *Pompeius Trogus' "Universal History." He relates the history of the Jews, the origin of their religion and their commonwealth, as well as a description of the physical properties of their land, in his description of the Seleucid Empire. He deals with the origin of the nation at length, but only cursorily with its later history. The treaty between Judea and Rome (161 B.C.E.) is considered to have been a decisive step toward the achievement of independence from the Seleucid yoke on the part of the Jews. His description of the beginnings of the Jewish people is a potpourri of information gleaned from the Bible, from a Damascene source, and from the well-known Greco-Egyptian tradition concerning their origin. Trogus, without doubt, utilized sources written in Greek.

Roman literature of the Augustan age does not yet contain ideological antisemitism. This enmity begins to develop somewhat later, and *Seneca would seem to be its first representative. Other protagonists are such famous writers as Quintilian, *Tacitus and *Juvenal. They belong to the period (the end of the first and beginning of the second centuries C.E.) in which the attraction toward Judaism among the gentiles reached its height. At this time, there were many Romans – both men and women – who accepted to a greater or a lesser extent the practices and the beliefs of Judaism. In the eyes of many representatives of the Roman aristocracy, Judaism and its offshoot, Christianity, were undermining the very foundations of Roman society. Most of the Roman writers who attacked Judaism also expressed dissatisfaction with the spread of the Eastern cults and their penetration into Roman society.

Seneca looked upon the Jews as a wicked people, whose customs had spread throughout the entire world and thus "turned the vanquished into the vanquishers." He inveighs against the Jewish Sabbath and against the lighting of lights in honor of the godhead on the Sabbath day, since the gods are in no need of this light. Seneca's younger contemporary, the satirist Persius, saw the practices of Judaism as one of the expressions of the superstition reflected in other rites originating from the East, such as those in Phrygia and in Egypt.

A frontal attack upon Judaism and those who believe in it, and particularly upon its followers and sympathizers among the Romans, may be found in Tacitus' famous description of the Jews at the beginning of Book 5 of his *Historiae*. Tacitus there brings six different explanations concerning the origin of the Jews, but relates at inordinate length the tradition which originated in the rabidly antisemitic Hellenistic circles in Egypt (see *Greek Literature, Ancient). Tacitus does not hide his extremely negative attitude toward Judaism. He describes the Jews as outstanding in their hatred of other peoples while at the same time equally notable for their solidarity among themselves. Those who become proselytes learn the ways of the Jews and become similarly disdainful of the gods and indifferent to the welfare of their former country and families. Tacitus notes the Jewish conception of monotheism, and its opposition to the fashioning of any statue or pictorial representation of God, but does not indicate his reaction to this. He is familiar with the identification of the Jewish religion with the Dionysic rites but rejects it out of hand. Tacitus' geographical description contains nothing very specific and concentrates upon a description of the Dead Sea, its balsam and bitumen. The historical description ignores the early period of independence and pictures the Jews as a people who have usually been subject to foreign domination. According to Tacitus, Antiochus was prevented from extirpating the Jewish superstition because of his involvement in a war with Parthia, and it was the international political constellation which was instrumental in enabling the Jews to found their own polity.

This was of a priestly nature and it nurtured their superstition. He concludes that Judea eventually acquired all the negative characteristics of an Oriental monarchy. However, it should be noted that in his description of Roman rule in Judea, Tacitus does not attribute a particularly rebellious character to the Jews; he blames corrupt Roman procurators, such as Felix and Florus, for the outbreak of the Jewish War (66–70 C.E.), rather than Jewish insubordination.

Tacitus' antipathy – like that of his contemporary, Juvenal – does not confine itself to Judaism but rather encompasses other Eastern religions as well, such as that of Egypt. What does particularly disturb him is the success of the proselytizing movement, which to his eyes was a serious menace to Roman society. He looked upon the threat to the Roman social fabric posed by Jewish religious propaganda as being incomparably more serious than the political or military danger posed by Jewish arms. A similar attitude toward Jews and Judaism is reflected in the works of the Roman satirist Juvenal. In his satires is reflected the impression which the Jewish beggars in Rome made upon him, but they also include the most impressive description found anywhere in Roman literature of the "downward path" toward Judaism taken by the Roman populace, which began with the observance of the Sabbath on the part of the father and ended with the complete proselytizing of the son. The events of Trajan and Hadrian's reigns and the widespread diffusion of Christianity weakened both the proselytizing movement and the sympathy for Judaism. Hence Jewish religious propaganda ceased to be a burning issue, anti-Christian polemic taking its place. Nevertheless, Roman writers still continued to take an interest in Judaism. Some of them persisted in the anti-Jewish attitude of the preceding period, but a more moderate approach can also be discerned. Disdain for Judaism is clearly the stand of the African-born Latin writer Apuleius (d. 160 C.E.), in contrast to the respect which he shows toward other Eastern religions, particularly the Egyptian rites in honor of Isis.

A negative attitude toward the figure of the Jew as such, as well as echoes of Seneca's approach, are also reflected in the works of the representative of the pagan Roman aristocracy of the early fifth century C.E., *Rutilius Namatianus. However, in the *Historia Augusta*, the reaction to the Jewish phenomenon is quite different. This is a historiographical work produced in the Roman aristocratic circles of the very end of the classical period. The ideal emperor described therein – Alexander Severus – is represented as treating the patriarch Abraham with respect and positively emphasizing Jewish sayings and customs. For further details, see the respective individual articles.

BIBLIOGRAPHY: Reinach, Textes; M. Radin, *The Jews among the Greeks and Romans* (1915), 97 ff. I. Heinemann, in: Pauly-Wissowa, suppl. 5 (1931), 3–43; J. Lewy, in: *Zion*, 8 (1942/43), 1–34, 61–84; idem, *Olamot Nifgashim* (1960), 79–203; J.C. Rolfe (trans.), *Ammianus Marcellinus*, 3 (1939; Loeb Classical Library), 558–61; J. Parkes, *The Conflict of the Church and the Synagogue* (1934), 207 f.; N. Bentwich, in: JQR, 23 (1932/33), 344; J. Bernays, *Ueber die Chronik des Sulpicius Severus* (1861). **ADD. BIBLIOGRAPHY:** M. Stern, *Greek and Latin Authors on Jews and Judaism*, 3 vols. (1976, 1980, 1984).

[Menahem Stern]

ROMANO, JUDAH BEN MOSES BEN DANIEL (It. **Leone de Ser Daniel**; 14th century), Italian philosopher and translator. Judah's contemporary, Immanuel of *Rome, wrote a poem and a composition in rhymed prose in his honor (*Maḥbarot*, vol. 1 (1957), no. 12, pp. 217 ff.), and also praised him elsewhere in his *maqāmāt* and his biblical commentaries. According to information contained in manuscripts (Paris, Bibliothèque Nationale, Cod. Héb. 1079, and Budapest, Kaufmann Ms. 281), Judah prepared translations for Robert II of Anjou, king of Naples, though this is not altogether certain. Moses *Rieti, who lived in the 15th century, reports that the king studied the Bible in the original Hebrew under Judah's guidance. Judah took pains to spread a knowledge of philosophy among the Jews, and to acquaint them in particular with the works of Christian scholars. He was the first to compare the language of Isaiah with that of Cicero. The Latin works, some of which were translations of Arabic originals, were translated by him into Hebrew for the purpose of making them known to the Jews.

As far as is known, they include the following: Pseudo – Aristotle's *Liber de causis* (*Sefer ha-Illot*; in some manuscripts also entitled *Ha-Tov ha-Gamur* or *Pirkei ha-Elohut*); Averroes' *De substantia orbis* (*Ma'amar be-Ezem ha-Shamayim*); Thomas Aquinas' *De ideologia* (*Ma'amar ha-Hemshelim*); the treatise ascribed to Boethius, *De unitate et uno* (*Ma'amar ha-Eḥad ve-ha-Aḥdut*); some shorter works of Albertus Magnus, Thomas Aquinas, Aegidius Colonna, Alexander of Alexandria and Angelo of Camerino. Judah often added his own observations and comments to his translations. He also wrote:

(1) a philosophical commentary on the story of creation in Genesis;

(2) explanatory notes on the *Kaddish* and *Kedushah*;

(3) an introduction to the prophetical books, written in a philosophic vein;

(4) *Ben Porat*, a commentary on the first four chapters of Maimonides' *Sefer ha-Madda*;

(5) a Hebrew-Italian glossary of philosophic terms;

(6) explanatory notes to various passages in the Bible. It is possible that he also wrote a commentary on the *Ma'arekhet ha-Elohut* of Perez ha-Kohen b. Isaac. Except for some fragments, none of Judah's translations or original works has been published.

BIBLIOGRAPHY: J.B. Sermoneta, *La dottrina dell'intelletto e la "fede filosofica" di Jehudàh e Immanuel Romano* (1965); Zunz, Schr, 3 (1876), 155 ff.; Perreau in: *Jeschurun*, 6 (1868), 50 ff.; Steinschneider, *ibid.*, 104; idem, *Giuda Romano* (1870), 3 ff.; idem, *Al-Farabi* (1869), 114, 249; idem, *Letteratura Italiana del Giudei* (1876), 36; Kauffmann, Schr, 3 (1915), 427 ff.; Guedemann, Gesch Erz, 2 (1884), 115, 151, 157; Vogelstein-Rieger, 1 (1896), 440–20. For bibliography of manuscripts, see catalogs of De' Rossi, Assemani, Biscioni, Neubauer, Perreau, Zotenberg, Steinschneider, Weisz, Hirschfeld, Bernheimer, and Margoliouth.

[Umberto (Moses David) Cassuto]

ROMANO, MARCO (1872–1942), Bulgarian Zionist leader and lawyer. Born in Plovdiv (Philippopolis), he participated in the first Zionist convention in Plovdiv (1898) and contested the *Alliance Israélite Universelle concerning the Jewish national character of schools. The controversy resulted in the dismissal of teachers and their replacement by Hebrew teachers. Romano was the representative of Bulgaria's Jews at the Zionist Congresses, even when he lived in Italy. He established and edited the official Zionist weekly in Bulgaria, *Shofar,* which existed intermittently until 1940. In 1927 and 1938, Romano wrote several essays on the political problems of Zionism, Arab-Jewish relations, and the Mandatory government in Palestine (in French). He settled in Palestine in 1937.

BIBLIOGRAPHY: A. Romano et al., *Yahadut Bulgaryah* (1967), 613 and index.

[Getzel Kressel]

ROMANO, SAMUEL (1906–1941), Yugoslav author, editor, and translator. Born in Sarajevo and raised in an observant Sephardi family, Romano studied at the Hochschule fuer die Wissenschaft des Judentums in Berlin. He later became a teacher of religion in the high schools of Zagreb and remained active in the profession until his death, which coincided with the Nazi invasion of Yugoslavia. As a writer and educator, Romano did much to widen the scope of Jewish knowledge and culture, and much of his literary work is concerned with Jewish national themes.

In his youth, he wrote lyric poetry in Serbo-Croatian and hundreds of children's poems, some of which were collected in *Bajke, priče, slike Šemuela čike* ("Tales, Stories, and Pictures of Uncle Samuel," 1938). During the 1920s and 1930s, he also edited the Zagreb children's monthly *Ha-Aviv* and the literary supplement of the Jewish weekly *Židov,* in which many of his outstanding translations of modern Hebrew prose and poetry appeared. His translations of stories by Burla and Hameiri also appeared in book form. Romano was the first to collect and publish the proverbs of the Bosnian Sephardim, and his study of Solomon ibn Gabirol appeared in 1930. He also helped to translate an anthology of modern Hebrew literature by Rabinson and Bistritski (*Antologija novohebrejske književnosti,* 1933).

[Cvi Rotem]

ROMANOS MELODOS (first half of sixth century), hymnographer and composer. Romanos was born of a Jewish family in Emesa (the present Homs), Syria. It is not known whether his parents had already converted to Christianity or whether he did so himself in youth. He became a deacon at Berytus (Beirut) and during the reign of Anastasius I (491–518) went to Constantinople, where he joined the clergy of the Theotokos church. According to legend, he was inspired by a vision of Mary to write, and immediately sing, the work which became his most famous one – "the First Kontakion on the Nativity," thus also creating the poetical-musical form which was to remain the foremost vehicle of Byzantine liturgical poetry until the seventh century. The kontakion (essay) is a long strophic poem, often of 24 equistructural stanzas prefaced by an introduction, the *koukoullion* (lit. "hood"), which furnishes the refrain. About 85 of the hundreds of kontakia ascribed to Romanos have been proved to be by him but his authorship of the most famous hymn of the Byzantine Church, "*Akathistos,*" is still in doubt, nor can it be ascertained whether any of his original melodies have survived in manuscripts or in the traditional repertoire. Romanos' kontakia are elaborately constructed "poetical sermons" on subjects from the New and Old Testament, and were greatly influenced by the forms established by St. Ephraem the Syrian. Links with the contemporary rise of the synagogal *piyyut may well be possible but need further investigation. Romanos, considered by tradition and scholarship alike as the "father of Byzantine hymnology," was canonized and his feast day is October 1st.

BIBLIOGRAPHY: P. Maas and C.A. Trypanis (eds.), Saint Melolodos Romanos, *Sancti Romani Melodi Cantica* (1963); J. Grosdidier de Matons (ed.), *Romanos le Melode*, 3 vols. (1964–65); E. Wellesz, *A History of Byzantine Music and Hymnography* (1961^2), 179–97; M. Stoer, in: MGG, 11 (1963), 784f.

[Bathja Bayer]

ROMAN-RONETTI, MOÏSE (originally **Aharon Blumenfeld**; 1847–1908), Romanian author. Born in Oziran, East Galicia, Roman-Ronetti emigrated to Romania in 1867 (using the identity papers of a dead Romanian peasant named Roman). He earned his living by teaching Hebrew and Jewish studies, but in 1869 some friends helped him to get to Germany, where he was given a scholarship by the Alliance Israélite *Universelle. He studied a variety of subjects, including medicine and philology, before returning to Bucharest in 1874. For a time he was a schoolteacher and then became a translator at the foreign ministry, but in 1882 he left the city and became a farmer. During the peasants' revolt of 1907, he fled with his family to Jassy, where he learned that the peasants had burned his home and destroyed all his property. He never recovered from the shock. Roman-Ronetti had already begun publishing articles on Judaism and Talmud in Hebrew periodicals before he left Oziran, and he continued to contribute to such periodicals as *Ivri Anokhi* (Brody, Ukraine) and *Ha-Maggid* (Lyck, Poland), signing himself Moshe Roman.

His first published work in Romanian was a poem, "Russia," which appeared in the newspaper *Reforma* in 1877. In the same year he put out a pamphlet, *Domnul Kanitverstan* ("Mr. Kanitverstan"), attacking the notorious antisemitic writer V.A. Ureche, in whose school he had been a teacher. In 1898 he attacked the antisemitic policy of the government in the widely read newspaper *Adevarul.* Discussing Jewish survival, he opposed official Romanian policy toward the Jews who, in his opinion, were entitled to a national life of their own. These essays were later collected in *Două măsuri* ("Two Measures", 1898). Roman-Ronetti's most important work was the play *Manasse* (1900), which had a dual theme: the conflict between three generations of Jews and the antagonism between gentiles and Jews. Performed before the Romanian royal family, the play had a warm reception by leading critics, but it provoked serious unrest among antisemitic students, who were opposed to its production at the Bucharest National Theater. *Manasse* was translated into several languages, including Hebrew and Yiddish, and was staged in many countries. The English version is entitled *New Lamps for Old* (1913).

BIBLIOGRAPHY: E. Lovinescu, *Istoria Literaturii Române Contemporane*, 1 (1926), 60–70; G. Calinescu, *Istoria Literaturii Romîne…* (1941), 488–9; Sadoveanu, in: *Foi de Toamnă* (1916); JC (Jan. 28, 1910); Jaffe, in: *Me'assef*, 5–6 (1965/66), 445–59.

[Dora Litani-Littman]

°**ROMANUS I LECAPENUS**, Byzantine emperor, 920–944, and co-ruler with *Constantine VII Porphyrogenitus. Romanus decreed that the Jews in the realm should be forcibly baptized, partly to demonstrate that, although he had come to the throne by usurpation, he was following the traditions set by the emperors *Basil I and *Leo VI. Romanus was also exhorted to take this step by the patriarch of Jerusalem in 932. The communities of Otranto and Oria in southern Italy were severely affected by the decree, although it is not mentioned in the Hebrew chronicle *Megillat *Aḥimaʿaz*. This may be because further consequences of Romanus' decree were prevented by the intervention of *Ḥisdai ibn Shaprut, to whom a letter addressed to Helena, wife of the co-emperor Constantine VII, has been attributed. The Arab chronicler al-Masudi states that in 943–944 Jews from all parts of the empire fled to Khazaria whose Jewish king "slew many of the uncircumcised" in a vain attempt to force Romanus to stop the persecution. The statement in the Vision of Daniel (see *Daniel, Vision of) relating that Romanus troubled the Jews by expulsion "not by destruction but mercifully" remains a problem for clarification.

BIBLIOGRAPHY: J. Starr, *Jews in the Byzantine Empire* (1939), 7–8, 151–3; S. Runciman, *Emperor Romanus Lecapenus and His Reign* (1963), 77, 231; Dunlop, Khazars, 89; S. Schechter, in: JQR, 3 (1912/13), 208, 217; A. Sharf, *Byzantine Jewry* (1971), index; idem, in: *Bar-Ilan Sefer ha-Shanah*, 4–5 (1967), 203–7 (and Eng. summary); Baron, Social², 3 (1957), 182–3; A.A. Vasiliev, *Byzance et les Arabes*, 2 (1950), 31–32; Mann, Texts, 1 (1931), 10–16; 23–25; A.N. Poliak, *Kazariyyah* (Heb., 1951), index.

[Andrew Sharf]

ROMBERG, MORITZ HEINRICH (1795–1873), German neurologist, born in Meiningen. He made fundamental contributions in the field of neuropathology.

His *Lehrbuch der Nervenkrankheiten des Menschen* (1846) is considered to be the first systematic textbook in the field of neurology (English translation, *A Manual of the Nervous Diseases of Man*, 2 vols., 1853). He discovered a pathognomonic sign of locomotor ataxia: the inability of ataxics to stand firm or reach the destination of the intended movement when their eyes are closed (Rombergism). He described facial hemiatrophy or trophoneurosis called "Romberg's disease," and a complex of symptoms caused by dilatation of blood vessels in the splanchnic area. He was the first to describe ciliary neuralgia. In 1838 he became associate professor of internal medicine at the University of Berlin.

BIBLIOGRAPHY: S.R. Kagan, *Jewish Medicine* (1952), 373.

[Suessmann Muntner]

ROMBERG, SIGMUND (1887–1951), composer. Born in Nagykanizsa, Hungary, Romberg began his musical career as a child prodigy. He was commissioned a lieutenant in the Austrian army, and then studied music in Vienna with Victor Heuberger. In 1909 he went to the United States and worked in various restaurant and theater orchestras. In 1911 he wrote his first successful song, "Memories," and then began to compose musical shows and operettas. Romberg composed over 70 operettas, in a tuneful vein indebted equally to the Viennese tradition and to Victor Herbert, the founder of the genre in the U.S. His best-known works include *The Student Prince* (1924), *The Desert Song* (1926), *The New Moon* (1928), and *Up in Central Park* (1945). Many of his operettas were filmed, and Romberg himself also adapted other composers' operettas and even operas for the film. He was president of the Song Writers' Protective Association. A fictionalized biography of Romberg, *Deep in My Heart*, was written by E. Arnold (1949).

BIBLIOGRAPHY: Baker, Biog Dict.

ROME, capital of Italy.

The Classical Period

THE MIDDLE AND LATE REPUBLIC. The earliest record of contact between Jews and the Roman Republic is the embassy sent by *Judah the Maccabee to Rome, headed by Eupolemos ben Joḥanan, and Jason ben Eleazar. The two ambassadors arrived in Rome, and there concluded an alliance with the Roman Republic (I Macc. 7:23–29, Jos., Ant. 12:417–19 and War 1:38). Successive Hasmoneans rulers renewed the treaty. Jonathan sent two envoys to Rome, Numenius son of Antiochos and Antipater son of Jason, to renew the treaty with Rome (I Macc. 12:1–23, and Jos., Ant. 13:164–170). Simon sent another embassy, perhaps headed by the same Numenios, envoy of Jonathan (I Macc. 14:24, Jos., Ant. 13:227). Also John Hyrcanus renewed the alliance in 132 B.C.E. (Jos., Ant. 13:259–66). In the treaty mentioned by Josephus, the Roman Republic recognized the conquests of Simon the Maccabee.

These treaties, however, are not evidence for the presence of Jews and even less so a Jewish community in Rome. However, Valerius Flaccus (I, 3:3) mentions that in 139 B.C.E. the praetor peregrinus G.C. Hispanus expelled Chaldeans, astrologers, and Jews who "attempted to contaminate the morals of the Romans with the worship of Jupiter Sabatius." It is thus clear that according to the Roman author there was a presence of Jews other than the Hasmonean envoys, trying to proselytize.

The first nucleus of a Jewish community probably consisted of Jews arriving at the end of the second century B.C.E. and early first century B.C.E. These were joined by the Jewish prisoners brought in 61 B.C.E. by Pompey after his campaigns in Judea against the Hasmonean state (Philo, *Legatio* 23:155). Aristobulos II, who precipitated the war against Pompey, embellished the Roman warlord's triumph (Plutarch, *Life of Pompey* XLV). When L.V. Flaccus, propraetor of the Province of Asia in 62 B.C.E., was accused of the embezzlement of funds, which included the half-shekel sent by the Jews of Asia to the Temple of Jerusalem, Cicero took his defense. In the oration (*Pro Flacco* 67–68), Cicero mentions that "Jews sent gold also from Italy" to Jerusalem and also notes the "aggressiveness of the Jewish mobs at political gathering." It is probable that by then there existed an organized Jewish community in Rome, which included Jews who had arrived before 63 B.C.E. and of course the Jewish prisoners of Pompey who had been freed. The legal status of the Jews living in Late Republican Rome thus varies from that of citizens, *liberti* (freed slaves possessing Roman citizenship), *peregrines* or foreigners, and of course slaves. The community was organized as a collegium, with a special status. Moreover this community regularly sent the half-shekel tax to the Temple in Jerusalem, like all the other organized Jewish communities in the Diaspora. Last but not least, it is possible that some of the Jews living in Rome took the side of the "*populares*," at least according to Cicero. It seems that Rome's Jews supported Julius Caesar. This is quite possible, as the latter restored in part the glories of the Hasmonean state tarnished by Pompey. In addition, Caesar exempted the Jewish synagogues from the laws he enacted to curb the power of the Roman collegia. It is no surprise then that according to Suetonius (*Julius Caesar* LXXXIV), Jews as a group mourned at Caesar's funeral in the middle of the Roman Forum.

The Early Empire

Only with Augustus is there clear-cut evidence of an organized Jewish community in Rome. By then Judea was firmly under the rule of King Herod, a staunch ally of Rome. Thus Augustus recognized the Jewish community as a *collegium licitum*, with privileges. Jews could send to Jerusalem both the half-shekel and the first fruits. The Roman state assisted poor Jews with the *annona* (free distribution of money or grain). If the distribution was made on the Sabbath, Jews were entitled to get the money or grain the next day (Philo, *Legatio* 156–58). Most of the Jews lived in an area across the Tiber, the Transtiberinum. At least three synagogues can be dated to the Augustan period, the congregations of the Augustienses, of the Agrippienses, and of the Herodians. Jews were quite conspicuous in Augustan Rome. The proselytizing activity of the Jews aroused the interest of the poet Horace (*Saturae* I, 4:140–43).

Under the rule of the Julio-Claudians (14 C.E.–68 C.E.) a number of incidents connected with the Jewish community in Rome are worthy of mention. Thus, under Tiberius, it seems that Sejanus, the *praefectus praetorius* tried to expel the Jews from Rome. The occasion arose when a Roman matrona, Fulvia, wife of the senator Saturninus (Jos., Ant. 18:81–84) was victimized by four Jews. Consequently Tiberius ordered the banishment of the Jews from Rome in 19 C.E., and around 4,000, were to be sent to Sardinia to fight against the bandits (Tacitus, *Annales* II, 85:4). However, it seems that Jews who were Roman citizens were not affected. Thus only foreign Jews were expelled. On the other hand the Jews who were sent to Sardinia had the status of freedmen. With Sejan's execution the ban was probably revoked. Under Claudius, Suetonius records that Claudius expelled "Judaeos impulsore Chraesto" (*Claudius* 25:4). This sentence had been the subject of various interpretations. It seems that only Judeo-Christians were expelled, or those Jews who took part in brawls with Christians. Josephus mentions that under Nero, as member of an embassy from Judea, he was graciously received by the empress Poppaea under the protection of the Jewish actor Alityros, a favorite of Nero (Josephus, *Life* 3).

The Jewish War of 66–70 C.E. deeply affected the Jewish community in Rome. First a great number of Jews arrived in Rome as prisoners. These prisoners, some of them later freed, significantly augmented the Jewish population of Rome. The Jewish leaders *Simon bar Giora and *John of Giscala walked in chains during Titus' triumph (Jos., *War* 7:118–57). Moreover, the gold from the Temple in Jerusalem was used to finance various building projects, the most important being the Flavian amphitheater known as the Colosseum. The new ruler, Vespasian, enacted a law that obliged the Jews living in the Roman Empire to pay a new poll tax, the *fiscus Judaicus*, to the Temple of Jupiter Capitolinus, instead of the half-shekel paid to the Temple in Jerusalem, now destroyed. The handling of the tax was administered by an official whose title was *procurator ad capitularia Judaeorum*. Vespasian did not enact any other discriminatory law against the Jews, nor did any anti-Jewish rioting occur following the war in Rome, as in other cities of the empire, most notably in Alexandria and Damascus. Domitian the last Flavian ruler, is remembered for his strict and harsh enforcement of the *fiscus Judaicus* (Suetonius, *Domitianus* 12:2). When the emperor discovered in 95 C.E. that Flavius Clemens and his wife, Flavia Domitilla, both members of the imperial family, were probably proselytes to Judaism, he had Flavius executed and his wife exiled. It is not clear if this was a measure directed against Jewish proselytism, or only an episode connected to members of the Imperial family. During Domitian's reign the poet Martial was active in Rome. In his poetry the degraded social condition of some of the Jews then living in Rome is reflected. Martial thus remarks that Jews are begging (XII, 57:13) and writes about his Jewish slave (VII, 35:3–4). It is in this period that the Jewish patriarch Rabban *Gamaliel II, with three scholars, *Joshua ben Ḥananiah, *Eleazar ben Azariah and Rabbi *Akiva visited Rome (Mish., Ma'as. Sh. 5:9, Er. 4:1; TB, Suk. 23a, 41b, Mak. 24a; Sifrei Deut. 43; TJ Er. 1, 19b, Suk. 2:4, 52d; Avot de Rabbi Nathan 1:14, 32a).

After Domitian's murder the new emperor, Cocceius Nerva, abolished all abuse connected with the enforcement of the Jewish tax. Coins bearing the legend *Calumnia Judaica sublata* were minted. Trajan, although he repressed a revolt in Judea, and in the last year of his rule had to face the huge Diaspora revolt of Cyrenaica, Cyprus, and Egypt, did not modify the legal situation of the Jews living in Rome. On the contrary he appears in a positive light as the protagonist of various Midrashim. Hadrian, Trajan's successor, enacted around 131 C.E. a law banning circumcision. Although there is no other data, it is probable that this law also affected the Jewish community living in Rome. During the reigns of Trajan and Hadrian the Roman poet Juvenal was active. His *saturae* reflects the prejudices of the Romans towards the Jews. Thus once again Juvenal gives a picture of Jewish beggars camping near the Egeria grove (3:12–16), asking for alms near synagogues (3:296), or telling fortunes to passersby (6:542–47). Juvenal also despises the Roman proselytes who fear the Sabbath, represented as a day of idleness (14:96–106). However, Juvenal's poetry does not reflect any special anti-Jewish feeling. Like most Romans, Juvenal despised foreigners. His invectives against other ethnic groups coming from the provinces, like Egyptians and Orientals, are even stronger than those against Jews.

THE LATE EMPIRE. For Late Antiquity, classic texts are supplemented by epigraphic and archaeological evidence. Antoninus Pius, the first ruler of the Antonine dynasty, abolished Hadrian's ban on circumcision. However, he enacted harsh decrees forbidding the Jews to proselytize. It seems that Marcus Aurelius and Commodus opened public offices to Jews. According to Callistus, the future pope, he broke into a synagogue to disrupt the Sabbath service. The Roman authorities reacted swiftly, and Callistus was sentenced by the praetor to forced labor in the mines of Sardinia. Under Septimius Severus and his dynasty the government attitude towards the Jews continued to be positive. Thus Septimius Severus renewed Marcus Aurelius' decree to allow Jews to be eligible for public office, and he exempted them from such duties as might interfere with their religious practice (*Digesta* 27, 1.15.6; 50, 2.3.3). However, Septimius Severus once more forbade Jewish proselytism (Spartianus, *Severus* 17:1). His son Antoninus is remembered for his "Constitutio Antoniniana," which granted Roman citizenship to all the free inhabitants of the Roman Empire, including Jews. The Jewish community in Rome was probably affected, because Jews living in Rome under the status of *peregrine* now became Roman citizens. According to Lampridius (*Antoninus Heliogabalus* 3:4–5), Heliogabalus wished to observe both Judaism and Christianity. Alexander Severus was known as the "Syrian archisynagogus" by his enemies (Lampridius, *Alexander Severus* 28:7), stressing a tie, true or imagined, with the Jews. Moreover he had a high regard for both Judaism and Christianity. Rome's Jews probably suffered from the anarchy and the economic situation of the third century C.E. following Alexander Severus' murder. But that affected the other peoples of the Roman Empire as well. In 284 Diocletian became emperor. His reorganization of the Roman Empire did not affect the Jewish community of Rome legally. However, with Constantine, who emerged as the Roman emperor in the West in 313 C.E., the legal situation of the Jews began to change for the worse.

In Late Antiquity there were various synagogues in Rome. To the synagogues of the Augustienses, the Agrippienses, and the Herodians, new synagogues were added, such as the synagogue of the Calcarensians, the Campensians, Elaea, Hebrews, Secenians, Siburensians, Tripolitans, Vernaclensians, Volumnesians, and perhaps of Severus. Synagogue membership thus united the congregations according to various criteria. Hence some congregations were created by clients or liberti of a Roman personality (like the synagogues of the Augustienses, the Agrippienses, the Volumnesians, and of Severus), other congregations were composed of members coming from the same place (like the synagogue of the Tripolitans), and still others perhaps took their names from the profession of most of the congregation's members (like the synagogue of the Calcarensians or lime burners) or from its location in Rome (Campensis from the Campus Martius quarter, Siburensians from the Subura quarter). Other synagogues' names indicated a social group, such as the synagogue of the Vernaclensians, or of Roman-born Jews. The synagogue of the Hebrews probably took its name from the fact that its members were Hebrew-speaking.

It is not certain that the Roman Jewish community had a central body as did, for example, the Jewish community of Alexandria. Most of the scholars do not believe they did. Each synagogue was headed by an *archisynagogus*, assisted by *archontes*. It is possible that some congregations had a *gerousia*, or council of elders. Then the *gerousia* was headed by the gerousiarches. The *grammateus*' office was probably that of secretary of the congregation. The titles Pater Synagogae and Mater Synagogae were honorary and these were given to some of the members of the congregation.

The Roman Jewish community was on the whole Greek-speaking. Very few inscriptions are in Latin, or in Hebrew. The names of Ancient Rome's Jews reflect this situation. Most of the names are characteristic Greek names used by Jews, such as Alexander, Theodoros, Theodothos, and Zosimos. Latin names are translations of Jewish names like Benedicta and Vitalis as well as genuine Roman names like Aurelius and Julius. Sometimes double names are used. Few names are Jewish, like Isaac, Judas, or Sarah. The professions of the Roman Jews are unknown for the more wealthy members. The more humble were painters, actors, lime burners, and even a soldier, a certain Rufinus. In all probably about 10,000 Jews lived in Late Imperial Rome.

Epigraphy also throws light on the existence of spiritual life in Ancient Rome. Thus through epitaphs some "Teachers of the Law" as well as "Students of the Sages" are known. The Talmud indeed mentions a Jewish sage from Rome called Josa Todros (probably *Theodosius). He introduced the *minhag* of including in the meal on Passover eve a roast lamb in commemoration of the paschal lamb sacrificed in Jerusalem (TJ, Pes. 7:1, TB, Ber. 19a). The sages grudgingly accepted the practice.

Roman Jews used *catacombs to bury their dead. Six Jewish catacombs have been excavated around Rome. The Monteverde Catacombs situated between the ancient Via Aurelia and the Via Portuense, the Catacombs of Vigna Cimarra, Vigna Rondanini, and Via Appia Pignatelli (although research shows that it was used by non-Jews), all situated near the Via Appia, the Labicana Catacombs situated near Via Labicana, and the Catacombs of Villa Torlonia situated near the ancient Via Nomentina. These catacombs together contain about 100,000 graves. Approximately 600 inscriptions have been found in Greek, many more in Latin, and formulae in Hebrew. The catacombs consist of a complex of subterranean corridors and chambers with loculi and arcosolia. Some of the catacombs (Vigna Rondanini and Villa Torlonia) are decorated with ceiling paintings combining pagan (Nike, peacocks, dolphins) as well as Jewish symbols (*menorah*). The inscriptions are sometimes decorated with the *menorah*, the Torah ark, the *etrog* and the *lulav*. Some sarcophagi have been found. Again pagan iconography such as the Four Seasons and theater masks are blended with obviously Jewish *menorot*. Clay lamps as well as glass objects decorated with Jewish symbols have been excavated.

The Jews of ancient Rome lived in an environment that even today could be characterized quite open and friendly. Imperial law protected them, although with some limitations (the ban on proselytism). Moreover, with the exception of the *fiscus Judaicus* Jews were not discriminated against. Even in times of tension, such as during the 66–70 war, the imperial government did not revoke any of their privileges. The local population was never physically hostile (as for example in Alexandria), even if sometimes the Jews were seen in a negative light, but only because some of them were foreigners or poor and not because they were Jews. Rome's Jews were thus successful in assimilating many elements of the surrounding Roman-Italic society, both in the organization of the community and in their material culture, but they still held clearly to a separate cultural identity.

[Samuele Rocca (2nd ed.)]

In Talmudic Literature

The relationship between Rome and the Jews living in the Land of Israel was often characterized by periods of strain and war. Thus Pompey's campaigns in the East ended with the conquest of the Hasmonean kingdom. The Roman administration of Judea between 6 C.E. and 66 C.E. was often characterized by cruel and corrupt officials. Moreover the Great Revolt against the Romans (66–74 C.E.), which ended in the destruction of the Temple and Jerusalem, and the Bar Kokhba War (132–135 C.E.), which ended in the destruction of almost all the Jewish settlements in Judea, could only contribute to a totally negative image of Rome. It is not surprising then that Rome is referred to in rabbinic literature by various negative designations – *Edom, Esau (see *Esau, In the *Aggadah*), *Amalek, Seir, *Tyre; the guilty kingdom; the wanton government; the fourth kingdom; and other epithets, mostly denigratory. It is compared, among other things, to the pig and the eagle, both impure animals (both animals appeared on the Vexilla (standards) of the Roman legions based in the Land of Israel).

The first sages, however, who lived between the destruction of the Temple and the Bar Kokhba War, were already divided in their attitude towards Rome. Scholars like *Zechariah b. Avkilus and activists like Akiva as well as R. *Simeon bar Yoḥai took a totally negative view. The attitude of the moderates found expression in *Joḥanan b. Zakkai's dictum not to be hasty "to demolish the high places of gentiles lest they be rebuilt by your hands" (Tanḥ. ed. Hoffman, p. 58; ARN[2] 31, 66).

While in the time of the *tannaim*, in the second century, a time of prosperity for the Roman Empire, there were those who argued: "The government takes in abundance and gives in abundance" (Sif. Deut. 354), in the period of the *amoraim*, in the third and fourth centuries, a time of distress for the Roman Empire, they came to deride the hypocrisy of Rome which robs and puts on an appearance of innocence and compassion to the poor (Ex. R. 31:11; Tanḥ. Mishpatim 14; PdRK 95b; Mid. Ps. to 10:6). They were well aware in former times of the extortion practiced by provincial government officials (ARN[11] 11, 46, 47).

The rabbis were aware of the great wealth of Rome (ARN[1] 28, p. 85; Git. 58a) but also of its arrogance and pride (Sif. Num. 131). They said that the Romans' claim that they were brothers to Israel was mere hypocrisy (Pes. 118b).

The Roman emperor, the ruler of the empire, has a place apart in talmudic literature. Many Roman emperors are mentioned, such as *Nero, *Vespasian, *Titus, *Trajan, *Hadrian, *Antoninus, Septimius *Severus, and *Diocletian. Though many of the statements about them are legendary, it is not always so (cf. the story that Trajan's wife gave birth to a son on the Ninth of Av – TJ, Suk. 5:1, 55b – with the statement that his daughter was born on the day the Temple was destroyed – Suetonius, Titus, 5). It is interesting that most emperors, with the obvious exception of Titus and Hadrian, are depicted often in a neutral and even positive way.

It is important to stress that most of the sages lived in a period of quite friendly relations between Rome and the Jews living in the Land of Israel, mainly Galilee, symbolized by the relationship between *Judah ha-Nasi and the legendary Antoniunus. Thus, beginning with the end of the second century C.E., the sages began to enjoin not to anticipate "the end of days," which is concealed (Sanh. 97b; DE, ed. Higger, p. 313); they also said that there was an oath extracted from the Jews not to rebel against the government and that one must even honor the government (Mekh. Pisḥa 13). There were also scholars who actively called for prayers for the welfare of Rome, "since but for the fear of it, men would swallow each other up alive" (Avot 3:2; cf. Av. Zar. 4a). On the other hand stringent criticism was also heard against the *Pax Romana* of "this guilty kingdom," "which is engaged in war the whole time" (Mekh. Be-Shallaḥ 1 (89), Amalek 1 (181)) and which "levies recruits from every nation" (PdRK, Ha-Kodesh ha-Zeh, 7–89–90). These criticisms were leveled against Rome in general and not because of a specific problem between the Roman government and the Jews. In a bold homily, either of praise or of delicate ironic sarcasm, Simeon b. (Resh) Lakish praises the government of the country, saying that it is very good, better than the kingdom of heaven, because it exacts justice for men (Gen. R. 9:13). The criticism of the government of Rome as inferior to that of heaven (cf. Ber. 28b) is probably connected with the fact that from the close of the first century C.E. *emperor worship became official in Rome. They stressed that Israel was not subject to Rome but to the will of God. The sages were divided on the question of the political status of Rome. Some claimed that "this nation has been enthroned by Heaven" (Av. Zar. 18a) and that one should submit to it even at a time of religious persecution.

In everyday life, Rome as such was known to the Jews and the rabbis living in the Land of Israel through its provincial administration. Thus the Romans seen in the Land of Israel were more often than not the governor and the various magistrates responsible for the application of Roman law, officials responsible for taxation, and of course the omnipresent Roman soldiers. For example, Roman court procedure, including methods of investigation, tortures, and punishments, are described at length in rabbinic literature, which also recognizes that in general the Empire was indeed administered according to the law (with its defects) but that in times of persecution the protection of the law was completely removed (Mekh. Shirata 7; cf. Sif. Deut. 24 and 323). Many descriptions have been preserved of the deeds of tyrannical and cruel Roman officials, who on behalf of the government confiscated Jewish lands after the destruction of the Temple and after the Bar Kokhba Revolt (see, e.g., Kil. 7:6; BK 117a; Sif. Deut. 317; 357; BM 101a; Lam. R. 5:4).

Roman taxation, mainly in the difficult third century, is treated at length in talmudic literature. The sources speak of the *baleshet* ("inspectorate") and *balashim* ("inspectors"), who came chiefly in connection with the payment of tolls and taxes (see *Taxation), and of collectors and tax collectors, who were suspected of misappropriating the property of the inhabitants (Tosef., Beẓah 2:6; Toh. 7:6; Tosef., Toh. 8:5). For this reason most *tannaim* held it permissible to avoid payment of tolls and even to swear falsely to the tax collectors (Ned. 3:4; Tosef., Shevu. 2:14; TJ, Ned. 3:4–5, 38a; BK 113a); only on rare occasions during a period of good relations with Rome, is the reverse opinion heard (Pes. 112b). In a still later period the *halakhah* was laid down, out of fear of harsh persecutions, that he who cheats the tax is as though "shedding blood… as if worshiping idols, acting immorally, and desecrating the Sabbath" (Sem. 2:9; cf. Lev. R. 33:6). Instructive descriptions have also been preserved of the methods both of the tax collectors and of those who avoided the tax (see, e.g., Tosef., Kel. 1:1, BM 3:9, BM 7:12, 8:25), and special halakhic arrangements were also made to facilitate the orderly collection of taxes (TJ, Ket. 10:5, 34a, 13:2, 35d). Jewish publicans and inspectors who cooperated with the government were regarded as guilty of grave transgressions and were reckoned as robbers whose repentance was exceptionally difficult.

On the other hand there were different and conflicting views with regard to Jews, including scholars, serving in the Roman service, whether perforce or of choice (see *Eleazar b. Simeon, *Ishmael b. Yose b. Ḥalafta, *Joshua b, Korḥa). Another problem was whether it was permitted to hand over Jews wanted by the Roman authorities (see *Joshua b. Levi; cf. Tosef., Ter. 7:20). Nevertheless, *informers who acted willingly were regarded as exceptionally degenerate and compared with heretics and apostates (Tosef., BM 2:33, Sanh. 13:5).

The influence of the Roman Law is discernible to a considerable degree in the *halakhah* and is reflected in many various and unusual spheres, such as the disqualification of a bill of divorce that has not the proper Roman date (Git. 8:5; cf. Tosef., BB 11:2 and Git. 8 (6):3; Yad. 4:8) "because of peril" (TJ, Git. 8:5, 49c), originally introduced for good relations with the state; or the disqualification of "coin of the revolt" as a substitute for the second tithe (**ma'aser sheni*; Tosef., Ma'as. Sh. 1:5–6: "Coins of Bar Kokhba and coins of Jerusalem may not be substituted…"). Although in these cases the halakhic possibilities were limited by the existence of the Roman government, the reverse is also true.

The Roman legions are viewed sometimes with open admiration, as in a homily in the Pesikta of Rabbi Kahana, where the Ten Plagues are compared to a Roman Legion besieging a city (Pesikta of Rabbi Kahana 7:11). However the deterioration in the quality of the Roman soldiers at the end of the second and the beginning of the third century C.E. was observed. Thus even in the view of *Judah ha-Nasi, the friend of Rome, the Roman legion was of no value (Tanḥ. Va-Yeshev 3).

Roman culture in the Hellenistic East and of course the Land of Israel was not as widespread as in the Latin West.

The Latin language was seldom used in the East, where Greek was commonly used also by the Roman administration. It is significant that Latin words are much less frequent in rabbinic literature than Greek (the proportion being approximately 1 to 8). Most of the sages could not even speak Latin and were naturally ignorant of its literature. In their view the Latin language was good for "war" (i.e., it was merely the language of the army; TJ, Meg. 1:11, 71b; see also S. Krauss, *Lehnwoerter*, 1, xix, xxi).

Characteristic Roman buildings adopted in the Greek East were the bathhouse, the theater (inherited by the Greeks), and the amphitheater. In principle Roman bathhouses were permitted. Thus it was permitted to bathe in a small gentile bathhouse immediately after the Sabbath if there was "a local authority" in the town, since it could be assumed that the heating of the water, was done for the non-Jews (Makhsh. 2:5). However, if the bathhouse served a pagan temple it was forbidden (*avodah zarah*). The sages forbade the Jews to go to the theater or the amphitheater, the former because it was considered a waste of time, the latter because the sages were averse to bloodshed in every form and gladiatorial games were not considered at all in a positive light. However, attending both the theater and amphitheater was permitted for reasons of state or the saving of lives.

After the Constitutio Antoniniana of 212 C.E., the Jewish

ruling class in the Land of Israel received Roman citizenship. One of the symbols of this new status was the wearing of the toga. The sages warns against assimilating to the Roman costume: "that thou say not: since they wear the toga, I too will wear it" (Sif. Dent. 81 and cf. *ibid.* 234). It was also forbidden to adopt the Roman tonsure, except for scholars who were "in contact with the government," and for the same reason (Sot. 49b), they were permitted to learn Greek and "to look into a mirror" (TJ, Shab. 6:1, 7d).

The sages particularly warned against the excessive esteem in certain circles toward Roman law and culture: "Perhaps you will say: They have statutes and we do not have statutes?… there is yet place for the evil inclination to reflect and say: Theirs are more suitable than ours!…" (Sifra to Aḥarei Mot 13:9).

In conclusion the sages were divided in their evaluation of Rome and its activities. Judah said "How becoming are the deeds of these people: they built markets, they built bridges, they built bathhouses"; however, Simeon b. Yoḥai replied: "Whatever they built they merely did for themselves; they built markets to settle harlots in, bath houses to delight themselves in, bridges to take tolls" (Shab. 33b; cf. the *aggadah* on Rome in judgment before the Holy One in the time to come – Av. Zar. 2b). In the opinion of Reuben b. Strobilus: "the public buildings and baths and streets which this wicked kingdom makes, were their intentions for the sake of heaven, they would have been worthy to possess the world, but their sole intention is for their own needs" (Mid. Hag. to Gen. 44:24); and according to Gamaliel: "the kingdom feeds on four things – tolls, baths, theaters, and taxes" (ARN[1] 28, 85).

Joshua b. Levi, who visited Rome, there saw "pillars covered with tapestry so that in winter they should not contract and in summer they should not split, but in the market he saw a poor man wrapped in a single mat – others say in half an ass' pack saddle" (Gen. R. 33:1).

In the diversity of their views on Rome the rabbis are no different from their contemporaries, as can be seen by comparison with the evaluations of the Greeks, the Church Fathers, and even the Romans themselves. The dialogues between the sages and eminent Romans preserved in rabbinic literature are instructive since these conversations have an actual historical, political, social, or ideological background. It is immaterial whether they actually took place; what is important is that the subjects of these conversations are not accidental but characteristic of the time and of the speakers.

[Moshe David Herr / Samuele Rocca (2nd ed.)]

The Christian Empire

With the adoption of Christianity by the Roman emperors the position of the Jews changed immediately for the worse. While Judaism remained officially a tolerated religion as before, its actual status deteriorated, and every pressure was brought on the Jews to adopt the now-dominant faith. In 387–388, a Christian mob, after systematically destroying heathen temples, turned its attention to the synagogues and burned one of them to the ground. The same took place later under Theodoric (493–526) when, in consequence of the punishment of some Christian slaves for the murder of their Jewish master, the Jews were attacked, their synagogue burned, and that of the Samaritans confiscated. When Rome was captured by the Vandals in 455, the Jerusalem Temple spoils preserved as trophies in the Temple of Jupiter were carried off to Africa. Thereafter the city ceased to be regarded as capital of the empire, and it lost greatly in importance, prosperity, and population. There is no detailed information of the lot of the Roman Jews at this period, but it must be imagined that they suffered and declined economically with the rest of the inhabitants.

Following the fall of the Roman Empire in the West, the Christian bishop of Rome, the pope, became the dominant force in the former imperial city and the immediate neighborhood, with moral authority recognized, to a greater or lesser degree, over the whole of western Christendom. Hence, over a period of some 1,400 years, the history of the Jews in Rome is in great part the reflection of the papal policies toward the Jews. However, down to the period of the Counter-Reformation in the 16th century, there was a tendency for the papal anti-Jewish pronouncements to be applied less strictly in Rome than by zealous rulers and ecclesiastics abroad, while on the other hand the papal protective policies were on the whole followed more faithfully in Rome itself than elsewhere. The keynote to papal policy was set by *Gregory I (the Great; 590–604), who firmly proclaimed that while the Jews should not be allowed to presume to more than was allowed them by law, the minimal rights accorded them of maintaining their synagogues and performing their religious rites should in no circumstances be infringed. The Roman Jews (who apparently at this time were engaged in foreign trade extending to the south of France) were in a position to approach the pope on behalf of their brethren abroad in case of emergency and to secure his intervention. His policies were presumably followed by succeeding popes.

Scholarship and Literary Activities

It was about this period that the revival of Hebrew studies took place in Italy. The scholars of Rome begin to figure in tenth-century rabbinic sources, which mention with respect talmudic scholarship centered on a local yeshivah Metivta de Mata Romi. The first scholar of note was R. *Kalonymus b. Moses, father of R. *Meshullam b. Kalonymus the Great (second half of the tenth century) who apparently taught in Rome before settling in Lucca; then came R. Jacob "Gaon" of Rome, who headed the yeshivah. Hebrew poetry, following the tradition established in Ereẓ Israel, found one of its principal exponents in *Solomon b. Judah "the Babylonian." Italian-Hebrew learning reached its climax with R. *Nathan b. Jehiel of Rome whose great talmudic dictionary, the *Arukh*, bears testimony to the wide rabbinic learning and linguistic range of educated Roman Jewry at this time. The Roman Jews received their traditions mainly from Ereẓ Israel, passing them on in turn to France and Germany. This was the case, in particular, with the liturgical tradition (see *Liturgy) originally called the *Minhag Romi*, later the Italian rite, which with the expansion of Roman Jewry became widely established in Italy and in one or two places overseas and was the parent of the Ashkenazi rite. The formulation of this is associated with the name of R. *Menaḥem b. Solomon b. Isaac, author of the popular *Midrash Sekhel Tov*.

Learning continued to flourish in Rome in the succeeding centuries, mainly being centered in the ancient Anau (Anav) family, including Zedekiah b. Abraham *Anav (13th century), author of the *Shibbolei ha-Leket*; his brother Benjamin b. Abraham *Anav, physician and talmudist, author of the *Massa Gei Ḥizzayyon*; Jehiel b. Jekuthiel *Anav author of the *Ma'alot ha-Middot*; and several others. *Immanuel of Rome (1260–c. 1328) introduced the complexities of the Spanish tradition of Hebrew poetry to Italy, and was also a prolific writer of verse in Italian – probably by no means the only one.

In 1020 the Jews were said to have caused an earthquake in Rome by mocking a crucifix, and a number were savagely punished, but the details are vague and the story may be legendary. On the other hand, from 1130 to 1138 *Anacletus II, a grandson of the converted Roman Jewish capitalist *Pierleoni, was able to maintain his authority for some time as antipope because of the support of the Roman populace. *Benjamin of Tudela, who spent some time in Rome c. 1159, found there a community of about 200 whom he described as being of high status and paying no special taxes, some of them being in the papal service; he singled out Jehiel, grandson of the author of the *Arukh*, and mentioned, in addition, half a dozen other scholars whom he considered outstanding. Since Benjamin specifically mentioned that one of them lived in Trastevere, it appears that the Jews now resided on both sides of the river. A building still standing on the right bank of the Tiber is believed to be one of the synagogues in use at this period.

Papal Legislation

The anti-Jewish legislation of the Fourth *Lateran Council (1215) inspired by Pope *Innocent III does not seem to have been strictly enforced in the papal capital. Nevertheless, the record of the community was checkered. There is some evidence that copies of the Talmud were burned here after its condemnation in Paris in 1245 (see *Talmud, Burning of). In 1270 the cemetery was desecrated. The wearing of the Jewish *badge was imposed in 1257 and the city statutes of 1360 ordered male Jews to wear a red tabard, and the women a red petticoat. There was brutal horseplay against the Jews in the carnival period, in the Circo Agonale and Monte Testaccio; this abuse was ended in 1312 when the community agreed to make an annual payment, thereby constituting an unfortunate precedent for special humiliatory taxation. In 1295 Pope Boniface VIII set the example abusing the Jewish delegation which went to congratulate him on his accession. In 1298, R. Elijah de' Pomi[s] was judicially murdered by the Holy Office on a trivial charge. From 1305 to 1378 the papacy was transferred to Avignon and Rome was left for a time to its own devices. When Emperor Henry VII came to Rome in 1312, the Jews went to greet him bearing the Scrolls of the Law, thereby setting a precedent which was long followed. In 1320 orders were sent from Avignon for the expulsion of the Jews from Rome, and although a deputation headed by the prolific poet and translator *Kalonymus b. Kalonymus secured the withdrawal of the decree, it appears that before the news was received Roman Jewry en masse was driven temporarily into exile. In 1322 the Talmud was again burned in Rome in obedience to a papal order.

Pope *Boniface IX (1389–1404), who tried to restore papal authority in the Italian possessions of the Holy See, was on the whole exceptionally tolerant. He favored a succession of Jewish physicians, and in 1402 granted a charter of protection to the Roman community in which their rights as citizens were specifically recognized. His immediate successors, exposed to the legislation of the *Church Councils of Constance and Basle and to the pressure of the *Franciscan friars, were ambivalent in their attitudes. *Martin V (1417–31) authorized the Roman community to distribute part of its financial burden among the other communities of the Papal States, employed Elijah b. Shabbetai as his personal physician, and tried to restore peace in the Roman community by appointing the surgeon Leuccio as its responsible head. *Eugenius IV (1431–47) embodied the anti-Jewish legislation of the 19th session of the Council of Constance in a bull of such severity that there seems to have been an exodus of Roman Jews to the marquisate of Mantua. At the moment of crisis the Italian Jewish communities decided to raise an emergency fund in order to back up their efforts to have the bull withdrawn; the community of Rome, however, was ultimately left to shoulder the whole burden, notwithstanding the efforts of its rabbi, the poet-physician Moses da *Rieti. *Nicholas V (1447–55) renewed the former anti-Jewish legislation, and patronized the anti-Jewish activities of John of *Capistrano. In 1450, Capistrano staged a religious disputation in Rome against one Gamaliel, and boasted so overwhelming a victory that he offered the pope a ship in which to transport the remnants of the community overseas. This did not eventualize; but on the accession of Capistrano's pupil *Calixtus III in 1455, a riot took place against the Jewish delegation who, according to custom, came to congratulate him.

The Renaissance Community

The period of the High Renaissance witnessed the heyday of Roman Jewry. The popes were strong enough to resist pressure and more influenced by political motives or cultural interests than by religious preconceptions. Every pope had a Jewish physician in his employment in Rome: outstanding were Samuel Sarfati at the court of Sixtus IV and Bonet de

*Lattes as that of *Leo x. Whereas elsewhere in Italy Jewish loan-bankers were admitted only on a contractual basis, in Rome the number was not limited. However, the majority of the community consisted of craftsmen. A professional census taken in 1527 reveals that 44 Jewish householders out of the 104 whose callings were indicated engaged in various branches of the clothing industry. In 1541 the Jewish and non-Jewish tailors' guilds came to an agreement for the regulation of their activities, so as to avoid competition.

David *Reuveni was magnificently greeted and received when he came to Rome in 1524, even by Pope Clement vii, who was greatly impressed also by Solomon *Molcho and extended barely credible protection to him. In 1524, under the auspices of the same pope, Daniel da *Pisa, a member of the famous Tuscan banking family then living in Rome, drew up a new intercongregational constitution for the Roman Jewish community at large.

Cardinal *Egidio da Viterbo (c. 1465–1532) had a profound interest in the Kabbalah, a considerable knowledge of Hebrew, and maintained Elijah *Levita in his home as his Hebrew tutor. Jacob *Mantino, personal physician to Paul iii, was nominated lecturer in medicine in the Sapienza in Rome in 1539 – one of the very few authenticated instances of a Jew holding an academic appointment before the age of Emancipation.

The expulsion from the Spanish dominions in 1492 brought a large body of refugees to Rome who were reluctantly received by the native community, nervous for their own position. Henceforth, by the side of the communities following the indigenous Roman liturgy, there were also synagogues according to the Aragonese, Castilian, Catalonian, and Sicilian liturgical traditions, and for a time also French and Ashkenazi synagogues.

The Counter-Reformation and the Ghetto Period

The entire tenor of Roman Jewish life suddenly changed for the worse with the Counter-Reformation. In 1542 a tribunal of the Holy Office on the Spanish model was set up in Rome and in 1553 Cornelio da Montalcino, a Franciscan friar who had embraced Judaism, was burned alive on the Campo dei Fiori. In 1543 a home for converted Jews (House of *Catechumens), later to be the scene of many tragic episodes, was established, a good part of the burden of upkeep being imposed on the Jews themselves.

On Rosh Ha-Shanah (September 4) 1553 the Talmud with many more Hebrew books was committed to the flames after official condemnation. From now on, notwithstanding occasional periods of relaxation at the outset, talmudic literature as a whole was banned in Rome, with disastrous consequences on Roman Jewish intellectual life. Most of this anti-Jewish action was inspired by Cardinal Caraffa, the embodiment of the spirit of the Counter-Reformation, who became Pope *Paul iv on May 23, 1555. Shortly afterward, he issued his bull *Cum nimis absurdum* (July 12, 1555) which reenacted remorselessly against the Jews all the restrictive ecclesiastical legislation hitherto only intermittently enforced. This comprised the segregation of the Jews in a special quarter, henceforth called the *ghetto; the wearing of the Jewish badge, now specified as a yellow hat in the case of the men, a yellow kerchief in the case of the women; prohibitions on owning real estate, on being called by any title of respect such as signor, on the employment by Christians of Jewish physicians, and on dealing in corn or other necessities of life; and virtual restriction to dealing in old clothes and second-hand goods. This initiated the ghetto period in Rome, and continued to govern the life of Roman Jewry for more than 300 years.

There were periods of relaxation e.g., in the pontificate of Pius iv (1559–65) and of Sixtus v (1585–90). On the other hand, Pius v (1566–72) not only renewed the severity of the system, but by his bull *Hebraeorum gens* of 1569 excluded the Jews from the cities of the Papal States, except Rome and Ancona; a good part of their population took refuge in Rome, where Di Capua, Di Segni, Tivoli, Terracina, Tagliacozzo, Recanati, and so on, commemorating their former places of residence, became characteristic surnames. Similarly, *Gregory xiii (1572–85) renewed and regulated the iniquitous system of the conversionist sermon, henceforth usual in Rome for many generations (see *Sermons to Jews). Whereas before the mid-16th century the Roman Jewish community had probably enjoyed more favorable circumstances than that of almost any other city in Italy and perhaps in Europe, from now on, in the age of the ghetto, the reverse was the case.

The area chosen for the Roman ghetto was a low-lying dank site on the left bank of the Tiber, subject to intermittent flooding and therefore highly insalubrious. The total Jewish population, which at its peak probably exceeded 5,000 – the highest in any city in Italy – was crowded in this circumscribed area. The rapacity of gentile landlords was, however, to some extent mitigated by the development among the Jews of the *jus gazaga* or proprietary right on houses, recognized also by the non-Jewish authorities. Originally the ghetto was supposed to have only a single entrance, but this was found impracticable and ultimately there were several. However, at night, on major Christian holidays, and in the Easter period, from Holy Thursday to the Saturday, the gates were closed and no Jew was allowed out of the quarter. The bull of 1555 permitted the Jews only one synagogue: this was, however, evaded by having five synagogues (or *Scuole*) according to the different rites under a single roof.

Among themselves the Jews, as elsewhere in Italy, spoke a *Judeo-Italian dialect, retaining old local forms and incorporating Hebrew or Spanish terms and written generally in Hebrew characters. The Jewish loan banks were finally suppressed in 1682; henceforth the occupation of the vast majority of Roman Jews was dealing in old clothes and second-hand goods, for which purpose they perambulated amid insults and contempt in all the quarters of the city. There were also a few tailors and petty shop-

Jewish population of Rome

Year/Period	Population
Late Roman	10,000
1159	200
16th cent.	5,000
1682	1,750
18th cent.	6,000
1873	4,880
1886	5,600
1910	10,000
1936	13,000
1943	10,000
1948	11,000
1965	12,928
2005	18,000

keepers and a very small number of better-established merchants.

Occasional raids were made as late as the 18th century on the ghetto to ensure that the Jews did not possess any "forbidden" books – that is, in effect, any literature other than the Bible, liturgy, and carefully expurgated ritual codes. Each Saturday selected members of the community were compelled to go to a neighboring church to listen to conversionist sermons, running the gauntlet of the insults of the populace. In some reactionary interludes, the yellow Jewish hat had to be worn even inside the ghetto. Pressure was placed on the Jews to become converted, and it was forbidden for a Jew to pass under the windows of the House of Catechumens lest he should attempt to communicate with any of the occupants. Kidnapping children for the purpose of baptism was retroactively endorsed as valid, and thereby encouraged. At the carnival season Jews had to participate in a foot race down the Corso, amid the jeering of the crowd. Each new pope was humbly greeted near the Arch of Titus by a delegation of the elders of the community who presented him with a *Sefer Torah*, which he returned to them with contumely. The Jews were not allowed to sing psalms or dirges when they escorted their dead to the traditional burial place on the Aventine hill nor to erect tombstones over their graves. It is not remarkable that in the age of the ghetto there were few scholars or communal leaders of any distinction, the case of the courageous and erudite Tranquillo Vita *Corcos (1660–1730) being exceptional.

The popes, in accordance with their former humane tradition, still indeed protected the Jews against such accusations as the *blood libel, which was virtually unknown in Rome; but in other respects the lot of the Roman Jews was increasingly pitiable. The *Editto sopra gli Ebrei* (1775) of Pope Pius VI reiterated all of the previous restrictions with accumulated humiliations, down to the last detail. When in 1783 two orphans were kidnapped for baptism on the demand of a remote relative who had been converted, there was a veritable revolt in the ghetto, followed by widespread arrests. A petition presented to the pope imploring for some alleviation in conditions, supported by a memorandum presented by 12 courageous Christian advocates, proved fruitless. The leaders of the community now canvassed the possibility of organizing systematic emigration to some less bigoted land such as England.

Freedom, Reaction, and Eventual Emancipation

When the reactions of the French Revolution reached Rome, there were widespread arrests among the Jews, and in January 1793 the ghetto narrowly escaped total sack – a providential deliverance thereafter commemorated by an annual celebration. On Feb. 21, 1798 the occupying French forces proclaimed equality for the Jews, but with the subsequent changes of regime, conditions remained precarious until 1809, when Rome was annexed to the Napoleonic Empire, and a *consistory on the French model was set up in 1811. However, in 1814 the rule of the popes was reestablished and from then on the ghetto and the restrictive practices of the ghetto period were once again enforced, excepting only the enforcement of the wearing of the Jewish badge. With the election of Pope Leo XII in 1823, conditions became grimmer still. Jews who had opened shops outside the ghetto had to close them, attendance at conversionist sermons again became compulsory, Jews were forbidden to employ Christians even to light fires for them on the Sabbath, and enforced baptisms again became common. On the accession of Pius IX in 1846, the gates and walls of the ghetto were removed, but thereafter the once-kindly pope turned reactionary and relentlessly enforced anti-Jewish restrictions until the end. During the Roman Republic of 1849, under Mazzini, Jews participated in public life, and three were elected to the short-lived Constituent Assembly; but within five months the papal reactionary rule was reestablished to last, without any perceptible liberalization, until the capture of Rome by the forces of united Italy in 1870. On October 13 a royal decree abolished all religious disabilities from which citizens of the new capital had formerly suffered, and the Jews of Rome were henceforth on the same legal footing as their fellow Romans.

Released prisoners obviously could not recover overnight from the legacy of the long centuries of ghetto humiliation. Some of the more gifted naturally were now able to find a proper outlet for their talents, and, in addition, the capital of united Italy attracted ambitious Jews from other cities who entered into government service, commerce, and industry. Many of the erstwhile peddlers became shopkeepers and even antique dealers. Thus a new sort of society began to be formed at the apex of the Jewish community, strongly affected, however, as in other cases, by assimilation and indifference. But still the bulk of the Roman Jewish community remained street merchants, familiar figures in the thoroughfares and on the steps of the ancient monuments, as they had been ever since classical times. Hence demographically the Roman Jewish community remained the healthiest in Italy. While other historic Jewish centers diminished through emigration, and

Tashlikh—a ceremony held near a sea or a running stream on the first day of Rosh Ha-Shannah—the name deriving from "You wilt cast [*tashlikh*] all their sins into the depths of the sea" (Micah 7:19). *Photo: Ya'acov Sa'ar, Israel Government Press Office.*

The Jewish holy days and festivals fall into two categories: those commanded by the Pentateuch, such as Sabbath, Rosh Ha-Shanah, Day of Atonement (Yom Kippur), and the Pilgrim Festivals (Passover, Shavuot, and Sukkot), and those added later, such as Purim (1st–2nd century C.E.) and Ḥanukkah (2nd century). All these are observed in various ways by Jews around the world.

SABBATH AND FESTIVALS

The "*ḥalakah*"—first haircut for a three-year-old boy on the Lag Ba-Omer festival at Meron near Zefat. *Photo: Hanan Isachar.*

Bonfire on the Lag Ba-Omer festival in Jerusalem. *Photo: Moshe Milner, Israel Government Press Office.*

The North African Purim custom of cutting off a girl's curl and throwing it into a well, so the girl will become as pretty as Queen Esther. *Photo: Z. Radovan, Jerusalem.*

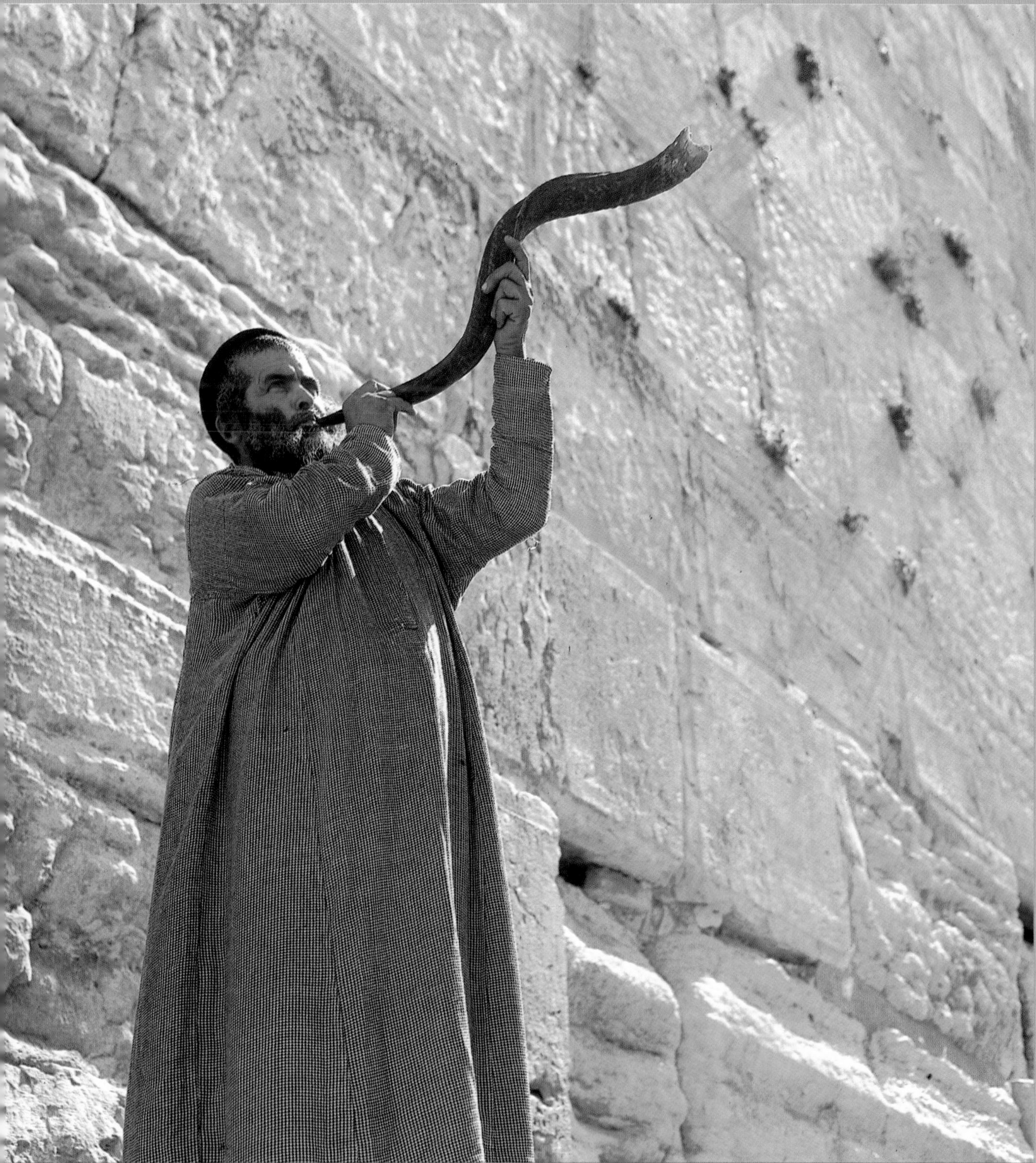

A Yemenite Jew blowing a *shofar* at the Western Wall. *Photo: Werner Braun, Jerusalem.*

Priestly blessing during the Sukkot festival. In the days when the Temple stood in Jerusalem, it was a pilgrimage site, where people used to come to receive the blessings of the priests (kohanim). Today the ceremony is held at the Western Wall. The men with the white prayer shawls, *tallitot*, are the kohanim blessing the assembled. *Photo: Z. Radovan, Jerusalem.*

A man sits on a mattress and reads from a prayer book late in the evening on Tishah Be-Av, which marks the destruction of the Temple, 2000. *© Reuters/Corbis.*

A young girl pours water into Miriam's cup as her mother and another woman look on during a women's *seder* in New York City, 2001. Traditional *seders* place a cup of wine on the table for the prophet Elijah, but women's *seders* also add a cup of water in honor of Miriam, who was associated with a well of water that miraculously followed the Jews as they wandered in the desert. *AP Images.*

A clown in a *dreidel* costume entertains children at a Ḥanukkah party at the Jewish Museum in New York City, 2005. © *Richard Levine/Alamy.*

Moroccan Jewish women in traditional dress bless the Sabbath candles, Jerusalem. *Photo: Z. Radovan, Jerusalem.*

Lighting the Hanukkah candles in a Jerusalem synagogue. *Photo: Z. Radovan, Jerusalem.*

those who remained barely maintained their numbers, Rome was increased both by immigration and by the vigorous state of its Jewish proletariat – the only one remaining in Italian Jewry which could be so designated.

Yet in other respects the progress of Roman Jewry was slow, notwithstanding all efforts. The city corporation took the lead in destroying the old ghetto quarter, a magnificent new synagogue with an organ being built on the site in 1900–04 to replace the old *Cinque Scuole* ("Five Synagogues") which were accidentally burned around this time. After a succession of rabbis brought from the Levant (Judah de Leon (Leoni di Leone), 1796–1830; Israel Moses *Ḥazzan, 1847–52) and even vacancies in the office, the Italian-trained Moses Ehrenreich was appointed in 1890; he was succeeded by Ḥayyim *Castiglioni (1903–11), one of the last of the Italian school of Hebrew poets, and he in turn by the courageous Angelo *Sacerdoti (1912–34). In 1887–1904 an unsuccessful attempt was made to reestablish in Rome the once-distinguished rabbinical seminary of Padua (see *Collegio Rabbinico Italiano); it was to return to Rome definitely on a more secure basis in 1930 after a brilliant interlude in Florence. But it was only during the period after World War I, with the remarkable, development of Rome itself, that Roman Jewry may be said to have regained the primacy in Italian Jewish life which it had enjoyed in the remote past.

[Cecil Roth]

Hebrew Printing

In the opinion of most scholars nine or ten *incunabula printed in square type without date or place-name, probably before 1480, should be ascribed to Rome. Among them are the Pentateuch commentaries of Rashi and Naḥmanides, Maimonides' Code *Mishneh Torah* and *Guide of the Perplexed*; Nathan b. Jehiel's *Arukh*, Moses b. Jacob of Coucy's *Sefer Mitzvot Gadol*, Solomon b. Abraham Adret's responsa, Levi b. Gershom's commentary to Daniel, and David Kimḥi's *Shorashim*. Only one Hebrew Press was licensed in Rome in the 16th century, and few Hebrew books were brought out by non-Jewish printing houses. The one Jewish press was run by Elijah Levita who, with the help of the three sons of his kinsman Avigdor Ashkenazi Kaẓav and under a papal privilege, printed here in 1518 three of his grammatical works. Around 1508 a prayer book was produced by J. Mazzochi and perhaps a Hebrew grammar a few years later. Between 1540 and 1547 Samuel Sarfati, Isaac b. Immanuel de Lattes in partnership with Benjamin b. Joseph d'Arignano, and Solomon b. Isaac of Lisbon printed a number of works with Antonio Bladao. Among them were Hebrew grammars by David ibn Yaḥya, then rabbi in Naples, and David Kimḥi: the *Mahalakh*; responsa by Nissim b. Reuben Gerondi, and smaller works. Between 1578 and 1581, Francesco Zanetti, with the help of Levita's baptized grandson Giovanni Battista *Eliano, printed editions of Genesis, the Five Scrolls, and Psalms. Owing to the reactionary atmosphere which henceforth prevailed in Rome in the 17th century, only some missionary tracts in Hebrew were printed in Rome, and in 1773 a Psalter for non-Jewish use with an Italian translation by Ceruti.

Holocaust Period

A few days after the Germans occupied Rome on September 9–10, 1943, SS Chief Heinrich *Himmler ordered immediate preparations for the arrest and deportation of all Jews in Rome and the vicinity – more than 10,000 persons. As a first step, SS Major (soon to be Lieutenant Colonel) Herbert Kappler, the SS commanding officer in Rome, demanded 50 kilograms of gold from the Jewish community on September 26, to be paid within 36 hours. Otherwise, he informed the community, 200 Jews would be arrested and deported to Germany. The Jews collected the gold, with some help from sympathetic non-Jews, and delivered it on time. Nevertheless, a special German police force broke into the offices of the Jewish community on September 29 and looted the ancient and contemporary archives, seizing, among other things, lists of members and contributors. On October 13, the Germans returned to loot the priceless libraries of the community and the rabbinical college.

Most Roman Jews were still not alarmed enough to go into hiding. Many were confident that the presence of the pope in the city would protect them, since the Germans would not dare take anti-Jewish actions under his windows. Moreover, the Jews lacked any precise information about Nazi death camps. Although they listened illegally to the BBC, it did not broadcast any specific news on that subject. The Jews also believed that the ongoing diplomatic discussions of Rome's status as an open city would save them from hostile Nazi actions.

On October 16, 1943, German SS police under Kappler and SS Captain Theodor Dannecker launched a massive roundup of the Jews of Rome. Provided with carefully prepared lists of names and addresses, the police made house-to-house searches throughout the city and arrested all the Jews they could find. Some of the non-Jewish population helped Jews escape, but 1,259 men, women, and children were nevertheless caught and held for two days at the Collegio Militare in Lungara Street. About 252 of them were released because they were the children or spouses of mixed marriages, foreigners from neutral countries, or non-Jews arrested by mistake. The remaining 1,007 Jews were deported to Auschwitz on October 18. Only 17 of them survived.

On the morning of October 16, Pope *Pius XII received Princess Enza Pignatelli, who informed him of the ongoing roundup. He immediately asked the Vatican Secretary of State Cardinal Luigi Maglione to summon the German ambassador to the Holy See, Ernst von Weizsaecker. Maglione met with the ambassador that same day and asked him to stop the arrests of Jews in order that the pope not be obliged to protest. The ambassador replied that for the sake of good relations between Germany and the Holy See, he preferred not to convey Maglione and the pope's threat of a protest to Berlin. Maglione accepted this. Jews continued to be arrested and deported. Pius XII never protested publicly.

Between October 16, 1943, and June 4, 1944, the day of the liberation of Rome, the methodical roundup of Jews hiding in the homes of non-Jewish friends or in Catholic institutions continued. In this latter period, perhaps as many as 1,200 additional Jews were caught and deported to Auschwitz, where most of them died. Another 75 Jews were among the 335 prisoners executed in the Fosse Ardeatine, outside Rome, as a German reprisal measure for an Italian partisan action in the via Rasella on March 23, 1944, in which 33 German soldiers were killed.

Some 4,000 individual Jews are believed to have hidden in Catholic institutions in Rome, including Vatican properties. A small number were sheltered behind the walls of Vatican City itself. There is no evidence that Pius XII or his chief advisors gave instructions for this rescue effort, or even knew its extent.

[Daniel Carpi / Sergio Itzhak Minerbi (2nd ed.)]

Contemporary Period

When the Allies entered Rome on June 5, 1944, the Jewish population numbered 11,000. That same day a solemn prayer that united the Roman Jews who had survived a year of terror and the Jews serving in the U.S. 5th Army, was led by Rabbi David Panzieri in the small synagogue of the Tiberine Island, which had been used clandestinely during the German occupation. An unknown future faced the community. The chief rabbi, Italo *Zolli, who had abandoned his flock during the war to find a haven in the Vatican, converted to Catholicism. Only in 1946 did Rabbi David *Prato take the place of the apostate rabbi. Under his firm leadership the Jewish community of Rome could look to a better future. Moreover, Jewish units from Palestine assisted the community. Rabbi Prato sponsored a moving ceremony the day the State of Israel was proclaimed on May 14, 1948, under the Arch of Titus. From that moment on, for the Jews to pass under the arch that symbolized the Diaspora was no longer a humiliation. In the following years the community grew due mainly to the natural increase. In 1953 Elio Toaff succeeded Prato as chief rabbi of Rome and Italy. From 1956 to 1967, after the *Six-Day War, about 3,000 Jews arrived from Libya. Some of them subsequently immigrated to Israel but the majority was absorbed by the community. In 1965 the Jewish community reached a total of 12,928 (out of a total of 2,500,000 inhabitants).

The geographic distribution of the community is still influenced by the continued existence of the traditional ghetto in the S. Angelo district and adjoining parts of the city, although there is a growing movement to the outlying residential areas. The community of Rome is the only one in Italy that shows a demographic increase, with a fertility rate not far below that of the Italian population as a whole, a fairly high marriage rate, and a limited proportion of mixed marriages. Occupational changes from the traditional fields to new technical specializations and to the free professions were rather slow but by the year 2000 it could be considered accomplished. A very serious episode of antisemitism darkened the life of the community on October 19, 1982, when Palestinian terrorists opened fire on worshipers leaving the Great Synagogue. A child, Stefano Tache, was killed and others were wounded. On April 13, 1986, Pope *John Paul II visited the Great Synagogue, and was welcomed by Chief Rabbi Toaff.

In the early 21st century the community numbered about 18,000 Jews, still tied by strong bonds of affection to Jewish traditions. The chief rabbi of Rome and Italy was Riccardo Di Segni. Apart from the Great Synagogue of Italian rite, the Lungotevere Cenci houses a Sephardi synagogue and the Jewish Museum, and there are another two prayer houses of Italian rite, one on the Tiberine Island, the other, the Oratorio Di Castro, in Via Balbo. An Ashkenazi synagogue is located in the same building. Among the Jewish institutions there is a kindergarten, the Vittorio Polacco elementary school, and a high school. There are many relief organizations, the Pitigliani orphanage, a Jewish hospital, and a home for invalids. Rome is the seat of the chief rabbinate of the Union of the Italian Jewish Communities (UCEI), and of the Italian Rabbinical College. The following Jewish journals are published: *Israel, Shalom, Karnenu, Portico d'Ottavia.*

[Sergio DellaPergola / Samuele Rocca (2nd ed.)]

BIBLIOGRAPHY: The standard authority on the history of the Jews in Rome is H. Vogelstein and P. Rieger, *Geschichte der Juden in Rom*, 2 vols. (1895–96); on the classical period, H.J. Leon, *Jews of Ancient Rome* (1960). The catacomb inscriptions are scientifically edited in Frey, Corpus, 1 (1936). Several subsidiary studies by A. Milano on the ghetto period are reprinted in his *Il Ghetto di Roma* (1964), cf. also Gregorovius, *The Ghetto and the Jews of Rome* (1948). For the Roman Jewish dialect, see A. Milano, *Il Ghetto di Roma* and C. del Monte, *Sonetti guidaico-romaneschi* (1927). For the period 700–1100 the fullest authority is now Roth, Dark Ages. For the Jewish monuments of Rome, see E. Loevinson, *Roma israelitica* (1927); B. Postal, *Landmarks of a People* (1962). For the background of Italian Jewish history, Roth, Italy (also Heb. tr.), Milano, Italia, and L. Poliakov, *Les Banchieri juifs et le Saint-Siège du XIIIe au XVIIe siècle* (1965). For the full literature of Roman Jewish history, see Milano, Bibliotheca… and Supplements, index. Other works on the subject include: M. Lowenthal, *A World Passed by…* (1938); Geller, *Roma Ebraica – Jewish Rome* (1970); C. del Montè, *Nuovi sonetti giudaico-romaneschi* (1933); idem, *Sonetti postumi giudaico-romaneschi e romaneschi* (1955). IN TALMUDIC LITERATURE: M. Sachs, *Beitraege zur Sprach-und Altertumsforschung*, 2 (1854), 134ff.; W. Bacher, in: MGWJ, 20 (1871), 226f.; idem, in: REJ, 33 (1896), 187–96; H.L. Reich, *Zur Genesis des Talmud. Der Talmud und die Roemer; Culturhistorische Studie* (1893^2); M. Gruenbaum, *Gesammelte Aufsaetze zur Sprachund Sagenkunde* (1901), 169–74; A. Kurrein, *Judaea und Rom* (1901); T. Reinach, in: REJ, 47 (1903), 172–8; I. Ziegler, *Die Koenigsgleichnisse des Midrasch* (1903); L. Hahn, *Rom und Romanismus im griechisch-roemischen Osten* (1906); S. Krauss, *Monumenta Talmudica*, 5 pt. 1: *Greichen und Roemer* (1914); idem, *Paras ve-Romi ba-Talmud u-ba-Midrashim* (1948); R. Rieger, in: JQR, 16 (1925/26), 227–35; M. Hadas, in: *Philological Quarterly*, 8 (1929), 369–87; idem, in: *Classical Philology*, 24 (1929), 258ff.; N. Wasser, *Die Stellung der Juden gegenueber den Roemern* (1933); J. Bergman, in: *Sefer Klausner* (1937), 150–2; Ginzberg, Legends, index s.v. *Rome, Roman Empire, Romans*; H.M.J. Loewe, *Render unto Caesar* (1940); J.W. Swain, in: *Classical Philology*, 35 (1940), 1–21; S. Lieberman, *Greek in Jewish Palestine*

(1942), index; idem, *Hellenism in Jewish Palestine* (1950), index; idem, in: JQR, 35 (1944/45), 1–57; Allon, Toledot, index s.v. *Romi*; idem, in: *Scripta Hierosolymitana*, 7 (1961), 53–78; I. Heinemann, *Darkhei ha-Aggadah* (1954²), index; H. Fuchs, *Der geistige Widerstand gegen Rom in der antiken Welt* (1964²); N.N. Glatzer, in: *Politische Ordnung und menschliche Existenz; Festgabe E. Voegelin* (1962), 243–57; B. Cohen, *Jewish and Roman Law* (1966); E.E. Urbach, *Ḥazal; Pirkei Emunot ve-De'ot* (1963), index s.v. *Romi, Romiyyim*; A.H. Cutler, in: JSOS, 31 (1969), 275–85; M.D. Herr, in: *Scripta Hierosolymitana*, 21 (1971). HEBREW PRINTING: A. Freimann, in: *J. Freimann... Festschrift* (1937), 121ff.; H.D. Friedberg, *Toledot ha-Defus ha-Ivri be-Italyah* (1956²), 9ff.; Habermann, in: KS, 12 (1935/36), 125ff. HOLOCAUST PERIOD: R. Katz, *Death in Rome* (1967); S. Friedlaender, *Pius XII and the Third Reich; a Documentation* (1966); M. Tagliacozzo, in: *Yalkut Moreshet*, no. 10 (1969), 55–59, Eng. summ. and bibl.; A. Foa, *ibid.*, 60–71; R. Surano, *ibid.*, 72–78, Eng. summ.; Comunità Israelitica di Roma (ed.), *Ottobre 1943: Cronaca di una infamia* (pamphlet printed in 1961); A. Ascarelli, *Le fosse Ardeatine* (1945); G. Debenedetti, *16 ottobre 1943* (1945, 1961²); R. Leiber S.J., "Pio XII e gli ebrei di Roma, 1943–1944," in: *La Civiltà Cattolica*, anno 112 (1961), vol. 1, quad. 2657 (March 4, 1961), 449–58. **ADD. BIBLIOGRAPHY:** D. Di Castro (ed.), *Arte ebraica a Roma e nel Lazio* (1994); S. Frascati, Un'iscrizione giudaica dale catacombe di villa Torlonia, in: *Rivista di Archeologia Cristiana* 65 (1989), 135–142; P. Galterio and M. Vitale, "La presenza ebraica a Roma dalle origini all'impero," in: *Arte ebraica a Roma e nel Lazio* (1994), 15–48; J. Goodnick Westenholz (ed.), *The Jewish Presence in Ancient Rome*, (Bible Lands Museum Jerusalem, 1994); A. Konikoff, *Sarcophagi from the Jewish Catacombs of Ancient Rome* (1990); D. Noy, *Jewish Inscriptions of Western Europe 2, The City of Rome* (1995); P. Richardson, "Early Synagogues as Collegia in the Diaspora and Palestine," in: J.S. Kloppenborg and S.G. Wilson, *Voluntary Associations in the Graeco-Roman World* (1996), 90–109; L.V. Rutgers, "The Jewish Catacombs of Rome Reconsidered," in: WCJS, 10 (1990), 29–36; idem, *The Jews in Late Ancient Rome: Evidence of Cultural Interaction in the Roman Diaspora*, Religions in the Graeco-Roman World, vol. 126 (1995). F. Coen, *16 ottobre 1943: La grande razzia degli ebrei di Roma* (1993); R. Katz, *Black Sabbath: A Journey Through a Crime Against Humanity* (1969); M. Tagliacozzo, "La Comunità di Roma sotto l'incubo della svastica: La grande razzia del 16 ottobre 1943," in: *Gli Ebrei in Italia durante il fascismo: Quaderni del Centro di Documentazione Ebraica Contemporanea*, 3 (November 1963), 8–37; S. Zuccotti, *Under His Very Windows: The Vatican and the Holocaust in Italy* (2000).

ROME, DAVID (1910–1996), Canadian historian. Rome was born in Vilna, Lithuania. From his first experiences in Canada the 11-year-old was, in his words, "thrown into Canadian Jewish history" as, due to a sudden change in Canada's Immigration Law, boatloads of Jewish immigrants in the fall of 1921 were detained in the Halifax immigration sheds. The four members of the Rome family finally arrived in Vancouver in December 1921.

Rome obtained a B.A. in English literature at the University of British Columbia in 1936 while working as editor for the *Jewish Western Bulletin*. After studying literature at the University of Seattle in Washington between 1936 and 1938, he obtained a degree in library science from McGill University (1939) and in English literature from the Université de Montréal (1962).

Upon his initial arrival in Montreal, which he later made his home, Rome was the national director of the Labor Zionist organization from 1939 to 1940. Following a two-year stint in Toronto as editor of the *Daily Hebrew Journal*, Rome returned definitively to Montreal in 1942, joining the Canadian Jewish Congress as press officer and editor of the *Congress Bulletin*. He also served as secretary of the Committee for Jewish-French-Canadian Relations from 1942 to 1953, beginning what became an enduring commitment to English-French and Christian-Jewish dialogue. During his early years at CJC he worked with many of the shapers of the Canadian Jewish community: Samuel *Bronfman and Saul *Hayes, H.M. *Caiserman and Louis *Rosenberg. During those years he became something of a spokesman and representative for the Canadian Jewish community, even ghostwriting for CJC's general secretary H.M. Caiserman and other community figures.

From 1953 to 1972, Rome enjoyed a more public role, for which he is remembered by many, as director of the Montreal Jewish Public Library. During these years, he also lectured in the Department of Religion at the forerunner of the current Concordia University in Montreal. He then returned to CJC in 1973 to become the archivist and later historian of the organization. In his later years, he was officially honored on several occasions, receiving CJC's H.M. Caiserman Award in 1980, being invested as a Knight in the Order of Québec in 1987, followed by the Prix d'excellence award by Government of Quebec Ministry of Cultural Communities and Immigration in April 1991, and an Honorary Doctorate of Laws by Concordia University, in June 1991.

David Rome is the author of *Les Juifs du Québec, bibliographie rétrospective annotée*, with Judith Nefsky and P. Obermeir (1979), co-author with Jacques Langlais of *Les Juifs et les québécois français: 200 ans d'histoire commune* (1986) (Eng., 1991), and *The Stones that Speak/ Les pierres qui parlent* (1992). Between 1974 and 1994, he authored over 60 monographs on Canadian Jewish history, in the *Canadian Jewish Archives, New Series* and *Clouds in the Thirties, On Anti-Semitism in Canada (1929–1939)*. His last years were devoted to the compilation and translation of articles from Canadian Yiddish sources.

From his desk at the National Archives of CJC, David Rome continued until his 1994 retirement, and indeed, despite failing health, until the end of his days, to instruct and to absorb the experience of Canadian Jewish history in a changing society.

[Janice Rosen (2nd ed.)]

ROMM, family of printers and publishers in Vilna. In 1789 BARUCH B. JOSEPH (d. 1803) received permission to establish a press in Grodno. He opened a second plant in Vilna in 1799. After his death, his son MENAHEM MANNES (d. 1841), directed the operation and between 1835 and 1854 published an edition of the Babylonian Talmud. This caused a dispute with a press operated by the Shapiro family of Ḥasidic rabbis in Slavuta and more than a hundred rabbis were involved in the resulting litigation. In 1836 the Russian government closed all but two Jewish printing houses, the Romm plant being the only one left in all of Lithuania and Belorussia. In 1841 the plant burned down. JOSEPH REUBEN and his son DAVID headed the company from 1841 to 1862. After their deaths, David Romm's widow DEBORAH (d. 1903) headed the company, together with her two brothers-in-law. This is the origin of the name of the company, which came to be known as "Defus ha-Almanah ve-ha-Aḥim Romm" (The Press of the Widow and Romm Brothers). The firm prospered from 1867 to 1888 under the leadership of its literary director, the Hebrew writer Samuel Shraga Feiginsohn (known as שפ"ן הסופר). Modern presses were installed, rights to various manuscripts purchased, many reprints were published, and painstaking editorship prevailed. Most of the firm's income came from the publication of religious works in editions of tens of thousands of copies. Among the more important publications was the Babylonian Talmud with over a hundred commentaries and addenda ("The Vilna Shas," first ed., 1880–86). Romm also published popular works in Yiddish, such as the books of I.M. *Dick, *Shomer, and Haskalah works.

After the death of Deborah Romm, the firm declined. The heirs were not interested in running it and Feiginsohn was reinstated as director. He remained with the firm even after it was sold to Baron D. *Guenzburg in 1910 and resold several years later to the firm of Noah Gordon and Ḥaim Cohen. During this period, a complete edition of the Jerusalem Talmud was published. The Romm Press continued in Vilna until 1940. With the Soviet conquest, the plant was confiscated and turned into a Russian-Lithuanian printing house.

BIBLIOGRAPHY: Feiginsohn, in: *Yahadut Lita*, 1 (1959), 268–302; Kon, in: KS, 12 (1935/36), 109–15; Katz, in: *Davar* (Feb. 8, 1957).

[Yehuda Slutsky]

ROMNY, city in Sumy district, Ukraine. The beginnings of a Jewish community date from the 18th century. In 1803 there were 127 Jews in the town, and in 1847 the Jews numbered 759. The community developed rapidly after the opening of the Romny-Libava railway line (1874), which became one of the important trade arteries of western Russia. From 1863 to 1901, Eliezer Arlosoroff served as the local rabbi. Tensions arising from economic competition between Jews and Christians resulted in pogroms in 1881 and, most seriously, on October 19–20, 1905, when 8 Jews were killed and 30 injured. In 1897 there were 6,378 Jews in Romny (28.3 percent of the total population); on the eve of World War I the number was estimated at 13,400 (43 percent of the total population). During the war, thousands of refugees from the battle areas fled to Romny. In 1919 *Denikin's troops organized a pogrom with loss of Jewish life and property. Under the Soviet regime, Romny declined economically; many Jews went to work in textile factories and on the railway. By 1926 the number of Jews had declined to 8,593 (about 33 percent of the population) and dropped further to 3,834 in 1939 (15 percent of the total population). Jewish public life was stifled. Romny was occupied by the Germans on September 10, 1941. In early November they concentrated the Jews in army barracks, and on November 19 they murdered 3,000 Jews, and by January 1942 they had killed another 700. In 1959 there were about 1,100 Jews (about 3 percent of the total population) living in Romny. Romny was the native town of P. *Rutenberg and Ch. *Arlosoroff. During the Second *Aliyah period, the "Romny Group," associated with Trumpeldor, which figured in the early development of the kibbutz movement in Palestine, was organized in the city.

BIBLIOGRAPHY: *Die Judenpogrome in Russland*, 2 (1909), 257–62; B. Fishko, *Gilgulei Ḥayyim* (1948), 26–47; M. Peysyuk, *Bleter Zikhroynes*, 3 (1944), 62–81.

[Yehuda Slutsky / Shmuel Spector (2nd ed.)]

RONA, PETER (1871–1945), biochemist. Rona was born in Budapest, Hungary, and from 1906 worked at the City Hospital in Berlin. From 1922 until the coming of the Nazis in 1933, he was professor of medicinal chemistry at the University of Berlin and director of the chemical department of the Pathological Institute, and consultant to the Charité Hospital. In 1935 he went to Budapest. In 1944 he was under the protection of the Swedish Embassy there, but he died in early 1945, probably murdered by the Nazis.

He contributed papers to scientific journals, dealing with blood serum, alkaloids, adsorption, enzymes, poisons, and sugars. From 1920 to 1935 he was the editor of *Berichte ueber die gesamte Physiologie und experimentelle Pharmakologie*, and from 1923 to 1924 of a parallel *Jahresberichte*. He was author of *Praktikum der physiologischen Chemie*, 3 vols. (1929–31), and of *Praktikum der physikalischen Chemie insbesondere der Kolloidchemie fuer Mediziner und Biologen* (1930).

BIBLIOGRAPHY: *Arzneimittel-Forschung*, 10 (1960), 321–7, incl. bibl.

[Samuel Aaron Miller]

RÓNAI, JÁNOS (1849–1919), first head of the Zionist movement in Hungary. Born in Alba-Iulia, Transylvania, he worked as a lawyer in Fogaras and Balazsfalva. Rónai wrote a book against the antisemitic movement in Hungary, led by the member of parliament G. *Istóczy, entitled *Kosmopolitismus és Nationalismus különös tekintettel a zsidóság jelenkori állására* ("Cosmopolitanism and Nationalism with Special Consideration of the Jewish Situation in Our Time," 1875), in which he justified Jewish national consciousness and the need to preserve it. In 1897, before the First Zionist Congress convened in Basle, he published *Zion und Ungarn*, a polemical book against the opponents of Zionism. He took part in that Congress and spoke there on the situation of the Jews of Hungary, warning against the swelling reaction and antisemitism in spite of the existing liberal regime. He founded

Zionist associations in Hungary and Transylvania and was persecuted by the government, which sought the assimilation of the Jews for political reasons. In the Zionist Conference of Hungary held in 1902 in Pressburg (Bratislava) with Herzl as chairman, Rónai was chosen the first chairman of the Zionist Organization in Hungary and later became its honorary president. He published articles in Die *Welt and in the Hungarian press.

BIBLIOGRAPHY: *Magyar Zsidó Lexikon* (1929), 750; L. Marton, in: *Uj Kelet* (Aug. 31, 1948).

[Jekutiel-Zwi Zehawi]

RONLY-RIKLIS, SHALOM (1922–1994), Israeli conductor. Born in Tel Aviv, Ronly-Riklis studied piano under Vincze-Kraus at the Rubin Academy of Music at Tel Aviv University. He took conducting courses with Igor Markevich in Salzburg from 1953 to 1956. He played the horn in the orchestra of the Jewish Brigade during World War II and built up the Israel Defense Forces Orchestra which he conducted until 1960. From 1957, he conducted the Gadna Youth Orchestra, taking it on tour to Holland and both Americas. From 1961 to 1971, he was director of the Kol Israeli Orchestra, Jerusalem, and in 1971 became artistic coordinator of the Israel Philharmonic Orchestra. He was sent by the Foreign Ministry to Singapore to form a national symphony orchestra there. Ronly-Riklis conducted many Israeli orchestras as well as others abroad. He again conducted the Jerusalem Symphony Orchestra and the Israel Young Philharmonic Orchestra from 1984 to 1988. From 1970, he was head of the orchestra department at the Rubin Academy of Music at Tel Aviv University. Ronly-Riklis recorded with several orchestras, including the Israel Kibbutz Chamber Orchestra and the Tasmanian Symphony Orchestra.

[Uri (Erich) Toeplitz and Yohanan Boehm / Israela Stein (2nd ed.)]

°ROOSEVELT, FRANKLIN DELANO (1882–1945), 32nd president of the United States. As governor of New York (1928–32), Roosevelt's strong advocacy of old-age pensions endeared him to the Jewish community which shared with him an overriding commitment to the welfare state. His election to the presidency in 1932 was followed by a deluge of liberal New Deal legislation. His overwhelming victory in 1936 included the support of the vast majority of Jews. In the elections of 1940 and 1944 Roosevelt lost much of his earlier support from ethnic groups, but American Jews delivered over 90% of their votes to him. Jewish loyalty to the New Deal was reciprocated. Roosevelt maintained close liaison with Rabbi Stephen *Wise. An unprecedented number of Jews were appointed to high positions within his administration. The pejorative epithet "Jew Deal" became popular among antisemitic elements.

The verve characteristic of Roosevelt's early reform program was little in evidence in response to the foreign problems of the 1930s. In October 1937, he attempted to probe isolationist strength by delivering his "quarantine the aggressors" address, but adverse reaction may partly account for his subsequent reluctance to lead public opinion toward a firmer posture against the Axis. The Japanese attack on Pearl Harbor ultimately solved Roosevelt's dilemma. Roosevelt openly detested Nazism and recalled Ambassador Wilson from Germany in protest at the November 1938 pogroms. He felt unable, however, to admit more refugees being restricted by existing law and public opinion. In March 1938 he called a conference on refugees to meet at Evian les Bains (see *Evian Conference) to bring order into the chaos caused by Nazi policy and worldwide immigration restrictions, but he accepted British requests not to discuss Palestine as a haven there or later at the *Bermuda Conference of 1943. During World War II Roosevelt, as the ally of Great Britain which administered Palestine, would not act against British policy there, thus possibly also alienating Arab leaders, on whose neutrality the Allies counted. He unsuccessfully attempted to promote some settlement of the Palestine question favorable to Jews and acceptable to Arab leaders, principally King Ibn Saud of Saudi Arabia. Later he assured the Arabs that they would be consulted before any decision on Palestine was reached. The President also issued various pro-Zionist statements to American Jews, particularly before the 1944 elections.

Roosevelt's response to the Holocaust was similarly cautious, and he used the State Department as a foil against agitation directed toward himself on this subject. In January 1944, after Secretary of the Treasury Henry Morgenthau Jr. presented conclusive evidence that the State Department was sabotaging rescue efforts, he established the War Refugee Board with special powers to quicken rescue work. However, it came on the scene too late to save the major part of European Jewry.

[Henry L. Feingold]

His wife was ANNA ELEANOR (1884–1962), U.S. diplomat, humanitarian, and author. She became active in the Democratic Party in the 1920s and remained politically active until her death. A prominent international figure, Mrs. Roosevelt served as U.S. representative to the United Nations General Assembly from 1945 to 1952 and as a delegate in 1961. In 1946 she was elected chairman of the United Nations Commission on Human Rights, serving until 1953. She defended minority groups against discrimination and received numerous awards for her humanitarianism. An outspoken advocate of a Jewish state in Palestine, she opposed the U.S. embargo of arms shipped to Israel during the 1948 War of Independence and urged the U.S. to support Israel during the 1956 Sinai campaign with defensive arms and diplomatically. Mrs. Roosevelt was a patron of *Youth Aliyah. In her *India and the Awakening East* (1954), she recorded her visit to the Middle East, during which she was impressed with the Israel spirit of dedication and purpose.

[Edward L. Greenstein]

BIBLIOGRAPHY: W.E. Leuchtenburg, *Franklin Roosevelt and the New Deal 1932–1940* (1963); L. Fuchs, *Political Behavior of Amer-*

ican Jews (1956); S. Halperin, *Political World of American Zionism* (1961); idem and I. Oder, in: *Review of Politics*, 24 (1962), 320–41; A. Morse, *While Six Million Died* (1968); J.M. Bloom, *Roosevelt and Morgenthau* (1970); H.L. Feingold, *The Politics of Rescue* (1970). ANNA ELEANOR ROOSEVELT: *New York Times* (Nov. 8, 1962), 35 ff.; A. Steinberg, *Mrs. R.: The Life of Eleanor Roosevelt* (1958).

°**ROOSEVELT, THEODORE** (1858–1919), 26th president of the United States, 1901–09. During his early career, Roosevelt shared the disdain of his class for the Jewish mass immigration then arriving at Ellis Island. This bias gradually disappeared as Roosevelt came to understand the hardships of ghetto life during his political service in New York as Governor of New York State. His respect for Jewish valor was increased by the performance of 17 Jewish Rough Riders under his command during the Spanish-American War. The president's acquaintance with "uptown" Jews was an intimate one and many of these wealthy Republicans followed his progressive leadership even to the point of supporting Roosevelt's 1912 Bull Moose revolt. During the neutrality period of World War I, Roosevelt denounced "hyphenated Americans," but he understood that Jews retained fewer Old World loyalties than other ethnic groups.

Roosevelt had more personal contact with Jews than any previous president. He appointed the first Jew (Oscar S. *Straus) to the Cabinet, and William Loeb served as his private secretary. In his closing years he supported the *Balfour Declaration despite the fact that this stand aligned him with his political archfoe, President Wilson.

[Selig Adler]

ROPCZYCE (Yid. **Ropshits**), town in Rzeszow province, S.E. Poland; in the period between the two world wars in Cracow province, W. Galicia. Jews settled in the town soon after its foundation. King Sigismund III Vasa (1587–1632), complying with the demands of the townsmen who wanted to remove Jewish competition, prohibited Jews from residing in Ropczyce, excepting those who leased the crown taxes. The prohibition was annulled by King John II Casimir in 1662, and subsequently Jews again settled in Ropczyce, numbering 663 by 1765. During the 19th century the Jewish population increased, by 1909 numbering 1,054 (29.4% of the total population). It decreased during World War I and had dwindled to 311 (10%) in 1921. At the beginning of the 19th century, Ḥasidism had a strong influence in the community. The celebrated *Ẓaddik*, Naphtali Ẓevi (*Ropshitser), established his "court" in Ropczyce. A report of the head of the police in *Lvov (1827) mentions Rabbi Asher of Ropczyce, and also states that the influence of Ḥasidism had diminished.

[Shimshon Leib Kirshenboim]

Holocaust Period

On Sept. 7, 1939, Ropczyce was occupied by the Germans. They immediately set fire to the synagogues including their Torah scrolls, and proceeded to confiscate Jewish property, deny Jews the rights of citizens, and send them to forced labor. In the spring of 1942 some of the Jewish males were transferred to the Pustkow labor camp. On June 22, 1942, a ghetto was established in Ropczyce where the Jews suffered from overcrowding, hunger, and disease. On July 2, 1942, they were deported. The aged and sick were shot near the city, and the others sent to the *Belzec death camp.

[Aharon Weiss]

ROPSHITSER (of **Ropczyce**), **NAPHTALI ẒEVI** (1760–1827), Ḥasidic *Ẓaddik*, and founder of Ḥasidic dynasties. A participant in the "holy company" whose mentor was *Elimelech of Lyzhansk, Naphtali Ẓevi was one of the main leaders of Ḥasidism in Galicia after the death of *Jacob Isaac ha-Ḥozeh (the Seer) of Lublin (1815); he is also considered as a pupil of Israel, the *Maggid* of *Kozienice and Menahem Mendel *Rymanower. Recollections of him were preserved only in folktales and stories which drew as much on imagination as truth. His admirers perceived esoteric and symbolic allusions in his every word and deed. According to Ḥasidic tradition, Naphtali Ẓevi feared that the rise of Napoleon would have bad effects for the Jews of Poland, such as military service, attendance at gentile schools, and the spread of unbelief, while his teacher Menahem Mendel held that Napoleon's victory would bring them deliverance.

His works are *Ohel Naftali* (1910), a collection of his talks and stories about him; *Ayyalah Sheluḥah* (1862), a commentary on Genesis and Exodus; and *Zeta Kodesh* (1868), sermons on the Pentateuch and for the festivals.

His son ELIEZER OF DZIECKOWITZ (Dzikow; d 1861), his disciple and successor, was a colleague of Issachar Baer *Radoshitser and Hirsch *Rymanower. In his last days he cut himself off from almost all contact with his Ḥasidim. Naphtali Ẓevi's other son, JACOB OF MALITSCH (d. 1839), officiated as a rabbi in Kolbuszowa and Malitsch and from 1827 became a *Ẓaddik*. By virtue of the miracles ascribed to him, he was known as the "Little Ba'al Shem Tov."

BIBLIOGRAPHY: M. Buber, *Tales of the Hasidim*, 2 (1966[3]), 193–7; idem, *Gog u-Magog* (1967); L.I. Newman, *Hasidic Anthology* (1963), index s.v. Ropshitzer; Dubnow, Ḥasidut, index; Horodetzky, Ḥasidut, index; A. Burstein, *Ẓidkat Ḥakham* (1966).

[Esther (Zweig) Liebes]

ROSALES, JACOB (first half of 16th century), Portuguese merchant and shipowner who, after the expulsion of the Jews from *Portugal (1497), went to *Morocco. Rosales shipped imported textiles and resins from *India for varnish, mainly to Larache and *Salé-Rabat, the large port of the kingdom of *Fez. His commercial house in *Lisbon was well known. After the expulsion he probably lived in Fez. The court of Fez benefited from Rosales' commercial affairs and he maintained good relations with the court of John III of Portugal. When Moulay Ali ben-Hassan became sultan in May 1526, he invited Rosales to take up his residence in *Meknès. Rosales used his influence to protect his coreligionists and the Megorashim (exiles from the Iberian Peninsula) regarded him as their leader. When, in September 1526, Moulay Ahmad dethroned his uncle Moulay Ali ben-Hassan and assumed the sultanate at Fez, he chose Rosales as his confidant. From then onward, Rosales was entrusted almost exclusively with political relations with the Christian world and was sent officially to Portugal in 1529. Rosales appears to have been the initiator of diplomatic relations between Morocco and *France. Pierre de Piton, the French ambassador, arrived in Morocco with a shipment of Jewish books for the community (such consignments were absolutely prohibited by the Church and this breach was like providing the enemies of Christianity with weapons). In 1534 the sultan entrusted Rosales with opening important negotiations with John III; he was in charge of the negotiations in Portugal for two years; they led to the signing of a peace treaty on May 8, 1538, at Arzila. In the meantime Rosales died, probably in Portugal. His successor as counselor, ambassador, and foreign minister was Jacob (1) *Rote.

BIBLIOGRAPHY: D. Corcos, in: *Sefunot*, 10 (1966), 104ff. and the sources quoted; Bernardo Rodrigues, *Anais de Arzila*, ed. by D. Lopès, 2 (1919), 104, 191; J.D.M. Ford (ed.), *Letters of John III* (1931), nos. 126, 151; *Les Sources Inédites de l'Histoire du Maroc*, ser. 1 index (1926); Hirschberg, Afrikah, index.

[David Corcos]

ROSALES, JACOB HEBRAEUS (**Immanuel Bocarro Frances**; c. 1588–c. 1668), Portuguese physician, astronomer, astrologer and poet. Born in Lisbon, Rosales was the son of a Marrano physician (Ferdinand Bocarro) and member of a family that included the poets Jacob *Frances and Joseph Frances. He studied medicine, mathematics and classical languages at Montpellier, after which he returned to Lisbon, where he attained a considerable reputation as a physician. Among the many noble personages he attended was the Archbishop of Braga. In addition to a thriving medical practice, Rosales developed a serious interest in astronomy, publishing in 1619 *Tratado dos Cometas que aparecciao en Novembro de 1618*. Five years later, he published a far more influential astrological work, *Status Astrologicus sive Anacephalaeosis da Monarchia Lusitania* (Lisbon, 1624), written in verse. The work is dedicated to King Phillip III of Spain and praises Portugal's kings and nobility. In 1625, together with other Marranos, Rosales left Lisbon for Rome, possibly out of fear of the Inquisition. In Rome he cultivated a friendship with Galileo, who had a profound influence upon him and inspired him to write *Regnum Astrorum Reformation* (Hamburg, 1644). During the early 1630s, Rosales made his way to Hamburg, where there was a settlement of Marranos. On July 17, 1647, Emperor Ferdinand III bestowed upon him the title of count palatine in recognition of his scientific achievements. Later, in Leghorn, Rosales openly called himself a Jew, having assumed the name Jacob Hebraeus. As a consequence, he was denounced to the Inquisition in Lisbon in 1658 together with other notable Marranos.

Among his other works are *Poculum poeticum*, a poem in honor of his friend, Abraham *Zacuto, printed in the latter's treatise, *De medicorum principum historium* (Amsterdam, 1629–42); *Carmen intelectuale* and *Panegrycus in laudem eximii*, which appears in *Ẓeror ha-Ḥayyim; Menasseh ben Israel de Termino Vitae* (Amsterdam, 1639).

BIBLIOGRAPHY: R. Landau, *Geschichte der juedischen Aertzte* (1895), 113; Kayserling, Bibl, 95–96; idem, *Sephardim* (Ger., 1859), 209–11; idem, *Geschichte der Juden in Portugal* (1867), 298–300; H. Friedenwald, *Jews and Medicine*, 2 vols. (1944), 304, 311, 314, 756; Roth, Marranos, 219, 298.

ROSANES (**Rosales**), Spanish family originating in the town of Castallvi de Rosanes, near Barcelona. With the expulsion of the Jews from Spain, the members of this family emigrated to Portugal. There they were compelled to convert to Christianity, changing their family name to Rosales. The members of this family were then dispersed in the Oriental countries and those of Eastern and Western Europe. The most prominent members of this family included: JACOB *ROSALES (beginning of the 16th century) in Fez; JACOB HEBRAEUS *ROSALES (17th century); ẒEVI HIRSCH *ROSANES (18th century); and ABRAHAM ABELE ROSANES of Minsk. JACOB ROSANES (19th century), the German mathematician, also belonged to this family.

A large part of the family settled in *Turkey and the Balkan countries. ABRAHAM B. MEIR ROSANES (1635?–1720) was a leading rabbi in Constantinople. He was born there and studied under Yom Tov *Ẓahalon and Solomon ha-Levi ha-Zaken. Between 1659 and 1677, he was rabbi in Adrianople, where he was the leader of the rabbis who issued a *Ḥerem* ("ban") against *Shabbetai Ẓevi. His son-in-law was his nephew JUDAH B. SAMUEL *ROSANES, who mentioned some of the teachings of his father-in-law in his work *Mishneh la-Melekh* on Maimonides' *Mishneh Torah*. At the end of Abraham's life, he managed the press of his father-in-law, R. Samuel Franco, in Constantinople. He wrote notes and novellae as well as criticisms on *Giddulei Terumah* by Azariah *Figo. ISAAC B. DAVID ROSANES (1660?–1749) was a rabbi in Constantinople and settled in Jerusalem in 1733. A number of his responsa were published in the works of contemporary *Ḥakhamim*. ABRAHAM B. ḤAYYIM ROSANES (1665?–1744) was a rabbi and *posek*, the disciple of his uncle, R. Judah Rosanes. In 1718 he became chief rabbi of Constantinople. In 1743 he settled in Jerusalem, where he died. His responsa are scattered in the works of his contemporaries, such as the *Battei Kehunnah* by Isaac ha-Kohen *Rappaport. ABRAHAM B. JOSEPH ROSANES (1686–1757?) was a rabbi and *posek* in Constantinople and fought the Shabbatean movement. His responsa and novellae were published in the works of contemporary *Ḥakhamim*. ISAAC B. ḤAYYIM ROSANES was a wealthy merchant and purveyor to the Turkish army; he was assassinated in 1758 because of a debt which was owed to him by the vizier Valalodin Pasha.

ABRAHAM B. ISRAEL ROSANES also known as Ha-ABIR (from the acronym Ha-Rav Abraham ben Israel Rosanes; 1838–1879), was a *Ḥakham* and merchant. He was born in

Ruschuk (now Ruse), Bulgaria, where he engaged in commerce and established a yeshivah. In 1867 he emigrated to Ereẓ Israel. He sent letters on his impressions of Ereẓ Israel to his friend Menahem Farḥi, which were published in *Ha-Maggid* (11–12 (1867–68)) under the title *Masot he-Ḥakham Ha-Abir* and a second time by A.M. Habermann (see bibliography). In these letters, he describes the towns of Safed, Tiberias, Jerusalem, Hebron, and their surroundings. After a short while he returned to his native town. His brother, MORDECAI ROSANES, financed the paving of the Western Wall area in Jerusalem in 1874. Abraham's son SOLOMON *ROSANES was a scholar and historian of the Jews of the Oriental countries.

BIBLIOGRAPHY: Frumkin-Rivlin, 3 (1929), 19–20; *Recueil jubilaire en l'honneur de Salomon A. Rosanes* (1933), passim; M.D. Gaon, in: *Mizraḥ u-Ma'arav*, 5 (1930–32), 398–409; idem, *Yehudei ha-Mizraḥ be-Ereẓ-Yisrael*, 2 (1937), 635–43; Rosanes, Togarmah, 4 (1934–35), 107–13; 5 (1937–38), 17–19, 64–65, 90, 178; A.M. Habermann, in: *Sinai*, 33 (1953), 312–9, 373–82; 34 (1953–54), 241–64; Hirschberg, Afrikah, 2 (1965), 302–3, 305; Z. Harkavy, in: *Ḥokhmat Yisrael be-Ma'arav Eiropah*, 2 (1963), 249–56.

[Abraham David]

ROSANES, JUDAH BEN SAMUEL (1657–1727), Turkish rabbi, *posek* and preacher. Rosanes was born in Constantinople. He studied under R. Solomon ha-Levi the Elder and R. Joseph b. Isaiah Trani (grandson of Joseph b. Moses *Trani). In his youth, he worked in the business of Abraham Rosanes, his uncle and father-in-law, who had business connections with the Turkish army. After his uncle's death, Judah engaged in business with his two brothers, Ḥayyim and Aaron. Later he was appointed to the rabbinate of Constantinople, where he served until his death. He was regarded as one of the greatest Turkish rabbis of his time and was among the rabbis of Constantinople who persecuted the Shabbateans there. In 1714 he was one of the signatories to the ban of excommunication against Nehemiah Ḥiyya *Ḥayon that was circulated to the whole Diaspora. In 1725, however, three Constantinople rabbis, of whom Judah was one, released Ḥayon from the excommunication on condition that he abandon the study of Kabbalah and Shabbatean beliefs. The rescinding of the excommunication angered the other rabbis of the town. Apparently this was the reason for zealots' breaking into his house and destroying his writings. What remained of his writings was collected after his death and prepared for publication by his pupil, Jacob *Culi. His *Mishneh la-Melekh*, novellae and disquisitions on Maimonides' *Mishneh Torah*, was first published in Constantinople in 1731 and later reprinted together with the text and other commentaries. Since then his commentary has been published in most editions of the *Mishneh Torah*. Rosanes' fame rests upon this work, one of the most erudite and penetrating commentaries on the *Mishneh Torah*. Rosanes' second work, published by Culi, was *Parashat Derakhim* (Constantinople, 1728), containing 26 sermons on *halakhah* and *aggadah*, and appended to his *Derekh Mitzvotekha* on the 613 commandments of the Torah according to the enumerations of Maimonides, *Naḥmanides, and *Moses b. Jacob of Coucy. The book also contains his notes and glosses to *Sefer ha-Ḥinnukh*, attributed to Aaron ha-Levi of Barcelona. Excerpts from the *Parashat Derakhim* were published also in the *Mikhlal Yofi* (Frankfurt on the Oder, 1775) of Isaac b. Ben Zion of Apta. Some of his responsa are to be found in the works of his contemporaries. A definite trend toward leniency is discernible in his rulings and commentary. He even regarded apostates as having been compelled to change their religion by *force majeure*.

Rosanes is not to be confused with the Shabbatean Judah Rosanes who lived in the mid-17th century and was one of the Constantinople scholars who excommunicated the two Smyrna rabbis Aaron *Lapapa and *Solomon (Nissim) b. Abraham Algazi I in 1666, after they excommunicated *Shabbetai Ẓevi.

BIBLIOGRAPHY: Rosanes, Togarmah, 4 (1935), 200–9; A. Freimann, *Inyenei Shabbetai Ẓevi* (1912), 53–55; J. Sasportas, *Ẓiẓat Novel Ẓevi*, ed. by I. Tishby (1954), 133–5.

[Abraham David]

ROSANES, SOLOMON ABRAHAM (1862–1938), historian. He was born in Ruschuk (Ruse), Bulgaria. While still in his teens he began to engage in money changing, and in 1878 he was attacked by robbers and seriously injured. After his recovery, acting upon a vow he had taken, he devoted himself to writing, but had to combine his studies with business as his father died and he had to support his family. During his many business trips, he managed to pursue research in libraries and archives in various localities. During World War I, he settled in Sofia, where he served as librarian of the Jewish community and resided until his death. Rosanes contributed to Hebrew, Ladino, Romanian, and Bulgarian publications, writing chiefly on the history of the Jews in the Balkans. His works include a genealogy of the Rosanes family (French, 1885); *Shekel Yisrael*, a treatise on ancient Jewish coins; and a history of the Jewish community of Ruschuk (Ladino, 1914). His major work was *Korot ha-Yehudim be-Turkyah ve-Arẓot ha-Kedem* ("A History of the Jews in Turkey and in the Orient," 6 vols., 1930–45), of great importance because of the wealth of source material it contains. Part of it appeared under its original title, *Divrei Yemei Yisrael be-Togarmah* (1907–14). Rosanes, who knew many languages, also wrote *Safah Aḥat u-Devarim Aḥadim* (1928–29), a study on the beginnings of human speech, in which he propounded the view that all languages had developed from a pre-biblical Hebrew.

BIBLIOGRAPHY: M.D. Gaon, *Yehudei ha-Mizraḥ be-Ereẓ Yisrael*, 2 (1937), 638–42; Z. Harkavy, in: *Ḥokhmat Yisrael be-Ma'arav Eiropah*, 2 (1963), 249–56; E. Eškenazi, in: *Bulgarska akademiya na naukite*, 13 (1963), 113–21.

[Tovia Preschel]

ROSANES, ẒEVI HIRSCH BEN ISSACHAR BERISH (1733–1804), Polish rabbi; grandson of Jacob Joshua *Falk. He was rabbi of Bolechow and in 1787, on the death of Mordecai Ze'ev Ornstein, was appointed rabbi of Lemberg, as his grandfather had been. He was the only rabbi of Lemberg after

Mordecai Ze'ev Ornstein who was not a member of the Ornstein family. Rosanes' considerable influence is shown by the large number of authors who sought his approbation of their works. Of particular interest is his enthusiastic approbation of the *Ahavat David vi-Yhonatan* of David ha-Kohen (Lemberg, 1801). This work, as its title indicates, is a commentary on the novellae of Jonathan *Eybeschuetz, of whom his grandfather was one of the greatest opponents. His *Tesha Shitot* (*ibid.*, 1800), a work distinguished for its acumen and profundity, also contains his father's novellae, entitled *Ḥezkat Ahavati*. His wife Judith was a well-known personality and managed a printing works in Lemberg.

BIBLIOGRAPHY: H.N. Dembitzer, *Kelilat Yofi*, 1 (1888), 1496–506; S. Buber, *Anshei Shem* (1895), 198; Yaari, in: KS, 17 (1940), 95–108; Margalioth, in: *Sinai*, 31 (1952), 91.

[Itzhak Alfassi]

ROSARIO, second-largest city in Argentina, comprises the second-largest Jewish community in the country: according to data of Vaad Hakehilot, there were some 1,600 Jewish families out of a total population of about 1,012,000 (2000). The first Jewish families settled in Rosario in 1887. Several years later their number was increased by the arrival of immigrants who had failed to adapt to the conditions in the Jewish agricultural settlement Moiseville, as well as by new immigrants, both Ashkenazim and Sephardim. A group of 28 persons established the Asociación Israelita de Beneficencia on Sept. 6, 1903, to attend to religious and welfare needs. Acquiring the first Jewish cemetery in 1909, the Asociación Israelita gradually became the central organization for both Ashkenazim and Sephardim in Rosario. In 1909 the total number of Jews in Rosario was 3,059. By that time the community already had a Zionist center (founded 1904) as well as a *Talmud Torah* which served as the foundation for the large Ḥayyim Naḥman Bialik School. Both the Sephardim and the Ashkenazim established their own synagogues apart from the one belonging to the Asociación Israelita de Beneficencia. A socialist workers' organization, founded in 1909, opened the Yiddishe Arbeter Bibliotek in the same year. In 1919, during the pogroms in *Buenos Aires (the "Tragic Week," January 7–13; see also *Argentina), the Jews in Rosario were identified with "Russians" and "Bolsheviks," and popular incitement against them reached such intensity that only the timely intervention of the authorities averted serious damage and disorder.

Between the two world wars, Rosario's Jewish community increased in number; in 1943 its population was estimated at 10,000. As a consequence of this growth, new community organizations were formed and the older ones were enlarged; the Po'alei Zion party was founded (1919), as were WIZO (1926) and committees for Keren Hayesod and the Jewish National Fund, while the Zionist movement grew more influential. Welfare organizations and activities also became more diversified. The first women's welfare organization, founded in 1909, was augmented by Hakhnasat Orḥim and Bikkur Ḥolim, which assisted poor immigrants and organized medical services for the needy. In 1924 the library maintained by the left-wing workers, whose organization had become communist, was supplemented by the facilities of the Ateneo Juventud Israelita, an organization for Spanish-speaking youth, and by the athletic facilities of the Maccabi sports club. As a result of Aaron Schallman's initiative, the Yiddish weekly *Rosarier Lebn* began publication in 1924, and it continued to be published in Spanish and Yiddish at least until 1968. It was the only Jewish newspaper in all the cities of the Argentine interior which was published periodically.

During the inter-war period, the Jews were engaged principally as peddlers and businessmen. The Jewish community's tendency toward cooperative organization created important financial institutions, some of them continued to function until the end of 20th century, including the Banco Cooperativo (founded 1926); the Cooperativa Mutual Fraternal (founded 1927), a business cooperative for peddlers; and the Banco Comercial Israelita (founded 1921), which was owned by central community institutions and has become an authorized bank. Amid this institutional diversity, the Asociación Israelita de Beneficencia continued to serve as the central Jewish organization. Although the Sephardim established separately such communal institutions as Eẓ Ḥayyim (1916), for Spanish-speaking Jews from Turkey; Shevet Aḥim (1924), for Syrian Jews; and the Confraternidad Israelita Latina (1924), for Moroccan immigrants, they continued to share the cemetery and the educational facilities with the Asociación Israelita de Beneficencia. During the 1920s and 1930s, the Asociación expanded, built a large central building, and developed communal services with special emphasis on education, but refused to support leftist, anti-religious schools.

In 1971 the Asociación comprised 2,585 families of which only 168 were Sephardim. Its building houses both a large synagogue and the Bialik School. The latter contains a preschool class, a kindergarten, an elementary school, and a secondary school offering both the general curriculum and Hebrew courses. As part of its cultural program, the Asociación maintains a full schedule of conferences, concerts, plays, and celebrations of Jewish holidays. In addition, it supports the activities of youth groups, administers the cemetery, and takes part in such community matters as the fight against antisemitism. Like the *kehillah* in Buenos Aires (*AMIA), but on a much more modest scale, the Asociación Israelita de Beneficencia serves as the central organization of the Jews of Rosario. Nevertheless, there are various other social-cultural organizations such as the Círculo Sefaradí, Hebraica, political organizations, youth movements, and welfare organizations. Social life is also enriched by the Aḥad Ha-Am Library and the Sociedad Hebraica. Many Jewish students attend the Universidad Nacional del Litoral, whose main faculties are located in Rosario.

BIBLIOGRAPHY: Jewish Colonization Association, *Rapport* (1909); Boletín de la Asociación Israelita de Beneficencia, no. 49 (1966); *Idishe Tzaytung Spetsyeler Khanukas ha-Bayit* (Apr. 1928).
WEBSITE: http://www.kehilarosario.com.ar

[Lazaro Schallman]

ROSE (Heb. וֶרֶד, *vered*, mishnaic), the genus *Rosa*. Two species grow wild in Israel, the white rose, *Rosa phoenicea*, which grows on the banks of rivers, in swamps and woods, and the *vered ha-kelev* – *Rosa canina* – which has pink and sometimes white blossoms and grows close to water. These wild roses have five petals and are not particularly beautiful or fragrant. The fragrant rose arrived in Ereẓ Israel from Persia only during the Greco-Persian period. Its Persian name was *varda* whence its mishnaic name *vered* (Aramaic *varda*, Gr. ῥόδον). The rose is not mentioned in the Bible, even though according to tannaitic tradition Jerusalem possessed "a garden of roses [in which fruit trees also grew] that existed from the time of the early prophets" (Ma'as. 2:5; Tosef., Neg. 6:2; BK 82b), though it was otherwise forbidden to plant gardens in Jerusalem. The rose (*rodon*) is mentioned a number of times in the Greek translation of Ben Sira but, in the Hebrew fragments discovered in the *genizah* (Ecclus. 39:13; 50:8), the word *shoshan* ("lily") appears. This substitution of *shoshan* or *shoshannah* for *vered*, even though erroneous (see *Flowers, of the Bible, Lily), already occurs in the Midrash which speaks of "a red *shoshannah*" (i.e., a rose, since the lily is white) and even mentions a "*shoshannah* of a *vered*" (Lev. R. 23:3). The source of this mistaken identification lies chiefly in the explanation of "the *shoshannah* among the thorns" (Song 2:2), which was understood to refer to the thorns on the stalk of the rose. The red rose is mentioned in the Apocrypha (I En. 82:16; 106:2).

In rabbinic literature, the rose is frequently mentioned: the bridegroom wears a crown of roses (Meg. Ta'an. 327) and idolators decorate their shops with them (Av. Zar. 12b). There is an adage that "youth is like a crown of roses" (Shab. 152a). R. Johanan's beauty was compared to a crown of red roses encircling a silver cup containing pomegranate seeds (BM 84a). A white rose is also mentioned (Git. 68b). A handsome man is called *vardina'ah* ("roselike," Nid. 19b and cf. Git. 41a). The main use of roses was in the preparation of an aromatic oil made by soaking the petals in olive oil (Shev. 7:6, et al.). It was apparently also customary to soak rose blossoms in water. The Talmud describes a Persian noble's concept of enjoying life as "sitting up to his neck in roses surrounded by naked harlots" (Av. Zar. 65a; Rashi: "sitting in a bath of roses"). Medieval halakhic literature speaks of "rosewater" as a medicament. Jam made from rose petals was a favorite food (Sh. Ar., OḤ 204:11).

BIBLIOGRAPHY: Loew, Flora, 3 (1924), 193–211; J. Feliks, *Olam ha-Ẓome'aḥ ha-Mikra'i* (1968^2), 238–9; H.N. and A.L. Moldenke, *Plants of the Bible* (1952), index. **ADD. BIBLIOGRAPHY:** Feliks, Ha-Ẓome'aḥ, 146.

[Jehuda Feliks]

ROSE, ALEX (**Royz, Olesh**; 1898–1976), U.S. trade unionist and politician. Rose, who was born in Warsaw, Poland, was the son of a wealthy tanner. Arriving in the U.S. in 1913, Rose found employment as a millinery operator and became active in the labor union. During World War I, he enlisted in the Jewish Legion and saw service in the Middle East. In 1923, three years after his return, Rose became secretary-treasurer of the United Hat, Cap, and Millinery Workers Union, Local 24. He held this post until 1950, when he became the union's president. Here, he was instrumental in overcoming the incursions of communists and labor racketeers, and in combating the chaotic competition so destructive of labor standards in the garment industries. Rose also became prominent in the field of labor and liberal politics. As New York State secretary of the American Labor Party (1936–44), Rose helped to steer a course away from independent labor and ideological politics toward balance of power and pressure politics. The party provided the margin of victory for New Deal candidates in New York, including Franklin D. Roosevelt, Herbert Lehman and Fiorello La Guardia.

As chief strategist for the Liberal Party from its founding in 1944, Rose came to embody a politics of compromise. The Liberal Party became a minor satellite party, fearful of innovation and excess, despite its position as New York State's leading minor party. During the early 1960s, a period of decline set in but under Rose's leadership the Liberal Party reasserted its decisive position in New York politics by providing the balance of power for John Lindsay's election as New York City's mayor in 1965 and 1969.

BIBLIOGRAPHY: D. Robinson, *Spotlight on a Union* (1948), passim; B. Rosenberg, in: *Commentary*, 37 (Feb. 1964), 69–75; Zion, in: *New York Times* (June 28, 1965), 24:2.

[Kenneth Waltzer]

ROSÉ, ARNOLD JOSEF (**Rosenblum**; 1863–1946), violinist. Born in Jassy, Romania, Rosé became concertmaster of the Vienna Opera and the Vienna Philharmonic at the age of 18, after conversion to Catholicism, and held these posts until 1938. In 1882 he founded the Rosé String Quartet, which won fame in Europe and in the United States. He also taught at the Vienna State Academy of Music until 1924. When the Nazis invaded Austria in 1938 he fled to England. Rosé married Gustav *Mahler's sister, Justine. His brother EDWARD, a cellist, and his daughter ALMA, a violinist, died in a concentration camp.

ROSE, ARNOLD MARSHALL (1918–1968), U.S. sociologist. Born in Chicago, Rose taught at Bennington College and Washington University in St. Louis and from 1952 until his death was professor of sociology at the University of Minnesota. His interest was primarily in the field of social problems, especially those relating to the labor movement and race relations. In the latter field he was considered a leading authority. Rose first entered the complex area of race relations as an assistant to Gunnar Myrdal, the author and editor of *An American Dilemma* (1944). Rose published a condensed edition of this classic entitled *The Negro in America* (1948).

He also wrote *Studies in the Reduction of Prejudice* (1947, 1948^2); *The Negro's Morale* (1949); and *America Divided; Minority Group Relations in the United States* (with C. Rose, 1948, 1949^2). He edited *Race Prejudice and Discrimination* (1951) and *Human Behavior and Social Processes* (1962); and coedited *Minority Problems* (1965). His other works include: *Union Solidarity: The International Cohesion of a Labor Union* (1952); *Theory and Method in the Social Sciences* (1954); and a widely-used text, *Sociology: The Study of Human Relations* (1956, 1965^2). Rose was involved in a lawsuit in 1963–64 after having been denounced as a security risk because of his alleged communist activities. He won the case, which he described in *Libel and Academic Freedom, A Lawsuit against Political Extremists* (1968). One of his last works was *Power Structure; Political Process in American Society* (1967).

[Werner J. Cahnman]

ROSE, BILLY (**William Samuel Rosenberg**; 1899–1966), U.S. showman. Rose was born to a poor family in New York. He acquired an unusual mastery of speed at shorthand, which during World War I won him a job with Bernard *Baruch. After the war, Rose decided that songwriting was a lucrative field and, on studying successful lyrics, established that they either romanticized the commonplace or played on ordinary words. His "Ain't Nature Grand" (1920) became a "hit," and three years later, at 24, Rose was earning $100,000 a year as a songwriter. He wrote lyrics for nearly 400 songs, about 50 of which were popular successes. In 1924 he opened a small nightclub and began to pioneer nightclub-style entertainment for people of moderate means. He also owned the Diamond Horseshoe in New York. In 1929 he married Fanny Brice, the Broadway musical star, the first of his five wives. From 1930, Rose produced shows on Broadway, among them *Jumbo* (1935), *Carmen Jones* (1943), and *Seven Lively Arts* (1944). He bought the Ziegfeld Theater (1954) and the National Theater (1958), which was renamed The Billy Rose Theater. Investing in real estate and stocks after World War II, he became the largest single stockholder in the American Telephone and Telegraph Company. He collected art on a grand scale, and in 1965 donated his sculptures to the *Israel Museum in Jerusalem, including works by Rodin, Jacob Epstein and Daumier, to be housed in the Billy Rose Sculpture Garden. He also donated a collection of paintings that included a Gainsborough, a Reynolds, a Romney and a Turner. His sister, Polly Rose Gottlieb, wrote his biography, *The Nine Lives of Billy Rose* (1968).

BIBLIOGRAPHY: E. Conrad, *Billy Rose, Manhattan Primitive* (1968).

[Lee Healey]

ROSE, ERNESTINE POTOVSKY (1810–1892), U.S. feminist and social activist. Ernestine Potovsky was born in Piotrkow, Poland, the daughter of an Orthodox rabbi. Early in life she rebelled against her traditional upbringing and at the age of 17 she left home and traveled first to Europe and then to England in 1830. In 1832 she met the English social reformer Robert Owen, whose disciple she became; the same year she married another non-Jewish Owenite, William Rose, a jeweler and silversmith by trade. The couple moved to New York City in 1836 and Ernestine Rose traveled throughout the eastern United States giving Owenite lectures on the science of government, religion, free schools, abolition of slavery and women's rights. From 1843 to 1846, she and her husband lived in an Owenite commune near Syracuse, New York, while she continued to lecture. She campaigned especially for the passage of a married women's property rights bill in New York State, which finally passed the legislature in 1848. In 1850 Ernestine Rose helped organize the first National Woman's Rights Convention, which met in Massachusetts. An acquaintance and colleague of such abolitionists and feminists as Ralph Waldo Emerson, William Lloyd Garrison, Lucretia Mott, Elizabeth Stanton and Susan Anthony, she campaigned vigorously in the years to come all over the U.S. on behalf of women's property rights, women's suffrage and reform of divorce laws, especially in New York State. Together with Susan Anthony she was a leader of the more radical wing of the suffrage movement that refused to concede that other social issues, most notably abolition and rights of black Americans, had precedence over feminist questions, and as such she bitterly attacked the 14th and 15th amendments for constitutionally emancipating blacks but not women, and urged their rejection. Along with other militants, she helped found the Women's Suffrage Society in 1869. In the same year she and her husband returned to England where she lived a life of semi-retirement because of bad health, though continuing to speak out on feminist issues. Although she seemed to attach no particular significance to her Jewish background, she did engage in 1863 in a long-published debate with Horace Seaver, the abolitionist editor of the *Boston Investigator*, whom she accused of antisemitic opinions.

BIBLIOGRAPHY: Y. Suhl, *Ernestine P. Rose and the Battle for Human Rights* (1959).

[Hillel Halkin]

ROSE, FRED (**Rosenberg**; 1907–1983), Canadian communist activist, member of Parliament, spy. Rose was born in Lublin, Poland, and moved with his parents to Montreal in 1916. As a young man he found work in a factory and joined the Young Communist League and helped organize unions for the unemployed. Trained as an electrician, in 1929 Rose became national secretary of the Young Communist League and visited Moscow the following year. Back in Montreal, he was closely watched by the RCMP and in 1931 was arrested, charged with sedition, and sentenced to a year in prison. After his release, he became a member of the Communist Party of Canada's covert leadership group and was an active political pamphleteer. He unsuccessfully stood for public office several times, but in 1943, with the Soviet Union a World War II ally of Canada, Rose stood for election to the House of Commons for the Communist Labor Progressive Party from the heavily Jewish Montreal Cartier riding. He won, defeating both David *Lewis and Lazarus *Phillips. Canada's first and only communist Member of Parliament, Rose was reelected in the 1945 federal election. During this campaign, American singer Paul Robeson personally endorsed Rose and sang at his campaign headquarters. However, Rose's parliamentary career was cut short when he was accused by Soviet Embassy defector Igor Gouzenko of spying for the Soviet Union. Following a sensational trial, Rose was found guilty of espionage and served four and a half years of a six-year sentence. Released from prison in 1951, Rose when into exile in Poland. In 1957 the Canadian government revoked his Canadian citizenship. Rose died in Warsaw.

[Gerald Tulchinsky (2nd ed.)]

ROSE, HERMAN (1909–), U.S. painter, watercolorist, and educator. Born in Brooklyn, he studied at the Art Students League and the National Academy of Design and served in the WPA. Although Rose painted subjects in England, Israel, Spain, and Mexico, he is best known for depicting the architecture of New York City and Brooklyn in small cityscapes with a palette of sober colors. An oil painting like *Blake Avenue, Brooklyn* (1940) manages to evoke intimacy while also depicting the Brooklyn street of the title as a dynamic diagonal which plunges the viewer from foreground to background. Rose's work has a picturesque, quietly emotive quality which compares to that of the 18th-century English Romantics. The artist often utilized a painting technique which involved applying small spots of paint to the surface of his work, and then moving warm and cool tones over one another; this resulted in a low level relief in which the paint dabs retained their identity. For instance, the painting *Manhattan Tops*, which the artist painted from his New York rooftop studio, depicts the city skyline dominated by a thickly textured sky. Rose also painted portraits and still-lifes. He carried the nuances of his vision from pale tonal impastos to thinner, more luminous washes throughout the years. His work has been exhibited at many museums and galleries, including the "Fifteen Americans" exhibition of 1952, the Pennsylvania Academy of Art and the Rutgers University Art Gallery. He received a Lee Krasner award in recognition of lifetime achievement. Many major museums and galleries own examples of his work, including the Newark Museum, the Museum of Modern Art, the Norton Museum of Art, and the Whitney Museum.

BIBLIOGRAPHY: G. Berman and J. Wechsler, *Realism and Realities: the Other Side of American Painting, 1940–1960, January 17–March 26, 1982* (1981); L. Campbell, "Objects on Parade – Paintings by Herman Rose," in: *Art in America*, vol. 84 (Jan. 1996).

[Nancy Buchwald (2nd ed.)]

ROSE, IRWIN (Ernie) (1926–), U.S. biologist and Nobel laureate in chemistry. Born in New York, Rose grew up in Spokane, Washington, where he attended Washington State College before serving as a radio technician in the U.S. Navy in World War II. He graduated with a B.S. (1949) from the University of Chicago, where he also gained his Ph.D. after working on nucleic acid synthesis with Birgit Vennesland (1952). After fellowships at Western Reserve (now Case-Western Reserve) University and New York University, he became a member of the biochemistry faculty at Yale University (1954–63) before joining the division of basic science at the Fox Chase Cancer Center in Philadelphia (1963–95). Since 1997, he has been a researcher in the Department of Physiology and Biophysics at the University of California, Irvine College of Medicine. He was awarded the Nobel Prize in chemistry (2004) jointly with Avram *Hershko and Aaron *Ciechanover for his contributions to characterizing the ubiquitins, the series of enzymes which govern the breakdown of cellular proteins. This research has major implications for understanding cell growth and proliferation in health and disease and for developing novel anticancer drugs. Rose's current research concerns the role of proton transfer in enzyme recycling, especially in carbohydrate synthesis. Rose was elected to the U.S. Academy of Sciences (1979). He is married to the research biochemist Zelda Budenstein Rose.

[Michael Denman (2nd ed.)]

ROSE, LEONARD (1918–1984), U.S. cellist. Born in Washington, D.C., Rose began to study the cello with Walter Grossman at the age of ten. He was awarded a scholarship for further study with Felix Salmond at the Curtis Institute of Music, Philadelphia, where he remained until 1938 and where he was head of the cello department from 1951. At the age of 20, after only three weeks with the orchestra, he became first cellist of the NBC Symphony under Toscanini. He then went to the Cleveland Orchestra for a four-year period, and finally to the New York Philharmonic. He appeared as cello soloist with most of the major orchestras in Europe and America; and the trio which he formed with Isaac *Stern and pianist Eugene Istomin was similarly acclaimed in chamber music concerts. Rose was also on the teaching faculty of the Juilliard School of Music, New York.

[Max Loppert (2nd ed.)]

ROSE, MAURICE (1899–1945), U.S. Army officer. Rose, who was born in Middletown, Connecticut, and whose father was a rabbi, served with the AEF during World War I as a second lieutenant. He advanced through the ranks and was promoted to brigadier general in 1943. From 1942 to 1943, as chief of staff of the 2nd Armored Division, he fought through the North African campaign and negotiated the unconditional surrender of the German forces in Tunisia. He was then assigned to command the 3rd Armored Division and was subsequently given the rank of major general. Rose led the 3rd in fighting through France, Belgium, and into Germany, where he was killed in action. Rose Memorial Hospital in Denver, Colorado, was named for him.

ROSE, MAURICE ("**Mauri**"; 1906–1981), Jewish race car driver, three-time winner of the Indianapolis 500. Rose was born in Ohio and began his career in the late 1920s racing on dirt tracks before moving to California. He finished second in Indianapolis in 1934 in his second outing. Rose's first Indy victory came in 1941 at a speed of 115 mph (185 kph) in the last race run before World War II. His other victories came back-to-back in 1947 and 1948. After his retirement from racing, he invented a device allowing amputees to drive an automobile.

He was named to the International Motorsports Hall of Fame (1994) and the Motorsports Hall of Fame of America (1996).

[Alan D. Abbey (2nd ed.)]

ROSEN (formerly **Rosenzweig**), **ABRAHAM** (1889–1974), Hebrew poet. Born in a village near Dunayevtsy (Podolia province), Rosen taught in various Russian towns from 1908 on, and in Chernovtsy (Bukovina) from 1921 to 1925. Settling in Ereẓ Israel in 1925, he taught there until his retirement in 1957. From 1920, Rosen's poems appeared in Hebrew newspapers and periodicals, both in Israel and other countries.

His books of poetry are: *Im Loven Derakhim* (1933); *Yamim* (1937); *Le-Nir Avot* (1929); *Sheloshah ba-Moledet* (1941); *Shirim* (1950); *Shirim Ḥadashim* (1957); *Shivim va-Ḥamishah Shirim Ḥadashim* (1964). A book of his stories, *Temurot*, appeared in 1968. He was the editor of a volume commemorating the community of Kamenets-Podolski. He translated Pushkin's "Legends" into Hebrew (1947). A collection of poems (*Mivḥar Shirim*) appeared in 1993.

[Getzel Kressel]

ROSEN, ALBERT LEONARD (**Al**; "Flip"; 1924–), U.S. baseball player. Rosen was born to Louis and Rose in Spartanburg, S.C., where his grandfather, a Polish immigrant, ran a department store . The family moved to Miami, where Rosen and his brother, Jerry, were raised by their mother and grandmother after their parents divorced. Rosen learned boxing in order to fight off antisemites in the neighborhood, and despite having his nose broken 11 times, was good enough to win the middleweight championship in a Florida high school tournament. Rosen attended Florida Military Academy, and was a four-sport man, excelling at football, basketball, boxing, and baseball. At 16, he was given a tryout with the Cleveland Indians. He attended the University of Florida and later the University of Miami, where he was an all-round athlete. Rosen spent two years in the Navy during World War II, emerging in 1946 as a lieutenant. He debuted in the Major Leagues on September 10, 1947, and became the Indians' full-time third-baseman in 1950, having an outstanding rookie season: he hit 37 home runs, enough to set an American League rookie record and lead the AL in home runs in 1950, becoming the first AL rookie to win the home run title. Rosen also had 100 walks, 100 runs and 116 RBIs. His 37 HRs was a rookie record that stood until 1987. Rosen drove in 100 or more runs for five consecutive seasons (1950–54), and finished in the top seven in RBIs from 1950 to 1954 and the top seven in walks from 1950 to 1955. In 1953 Rosen failed to achieve by a whisker the exalted Triple Crown. He won the AL home run title with 43 and the RBI crown with 146, but his .336 batting average fell .0011 short of winning the American League batting title, which went to Mickey Vernon, whose teammates conspired to help him win. He was also first in runs (115), total bases (367), slugging (.613), OPS (1.034), runs created (153), extra base hit (75), and times on base (290). He was the first unanimous AL MVP in history. Rosen was elected to appear in the All Star Game from 1952 to 1955, winning MVP honors in 1954 when he hit two HRs and had five RBIs. Rosen's lifetime batting average was .285, with 192 HRs and 717 RBIs in 1,044 games. He also appeared on the cover of *Sports Illustrated* in 1955. "When I was up there in the majors," he once said, "I always knew how I wanted it to be. I wanted it to be, 'Here comes one Jewish kid that every Jew in the world can be proud of.'" Rosen suffered a broken finger in 1954 and had several other nagging injuries that forced him to retire in 1956. He later served as president of the New York Yankees (1978–79), Houston Astros (1980–85), and San Francisco Giants (1985–92), being named Major League Executive of the Year in 1987.

[Elli Wohlgelernter (2nd ed.)]

ROSEN, CARL (1918–1983), U.S. apparel manufacturer. Rosen, a native New Englander, joined a small regional dress firm owned by his father, Arthur, and built it into one of the most successful apparel businesses in the U.S. At the time of Rosen's death, Puritan Fashions Corporation – founded in Boston in the first decade of the 20th century – had become a $300 million-a-year business. Rosen, one of the garment industry's more colorful personalities, also owned thoroughbred horses and was a regular at tracks around the country. He was a benefactor of many institutions, including Brandeis University in Waltham, Mass., where he endowed the Arthur Rosen Chair in economics. He began his lifelong career at Puritan in 1936 when still a teenager, starting in the cutting room as a sweeper. He entered the U.S. Army as a private during World War II, emerging as an artillery captain. He returned to Puritan, became chairman and chief executive officer in 1953, and remained in those posts for the next 30 years. In the 1960s, Rosen foresaw the vast changes that U.S. social customs, dress codes, and retailing concepts were about to undergo. He was one of the first American apparel makers to realize the business potential of the Beatles, the rock group then taking England by storm but still relatively unknown in the U.S. Rosen secured a license to make Beatles T-shirts, knit shirts, and sweatshirts, then managed to sell them to the conservative J.C. Penney Co. chain. They were an instant hit. In 1965, Rosen opened Paraphernalia, a Madison Avenue store modeled after the boutiques then popular in London. Small and trendy, its mod fashions – vinyl miniskirts and neon bikinis, for example – helped launch the careers of such hip new designers as Betsey Johnson and Mary Quant. By 1968 there were 44 Paraphernalia franchises in the U.S., but the name had become diluted because of too-rapid expansion and the last one closed around 1976. In 1977, Rosen made perhaps his most astute move at Puritan, getting the license to produce Calvin *Klein jeans for men and women. Within three years, Puritan was shipping 500,000 pairs of jeans a week. When Rosen died, his son Andrew, then 26, became head of the company. Later that year, Klein and his partner, Barry Schwartz, acquired Puritan, subsequently changed its name and in 1989 Andrew Rosen left to join the Anne *Klein Apparel Group.

[Mort Sheinman (2nd ed.)]

ROSEN, CHARLES (1927–), pianist, author and musicologist. Rosen was born in New York City, where he studied the piano from the age of seven at the Juilliard School of Music, and later with the great virtuoso pianist Moriz Rosenthal. At Princeton University, he studied French literature (with special emphasis on the connections between music and poetry in 16th-century France), graduating with the highest honors. This led to his winning a two-year Fulbright scholarship to study medieval French music in Paris. On his return to the United States in 1953, simultaneously with teaching French literature at the Massachusetts Institute of Technology, he began his career as a concert pianist, the ultimate international success of which eventually reduced his teaching activities to a minimum. Rosen won an enviable reputation as a critic, regularly reviewing books on painting, literature and music for the *New York Review of Books*, and also as an author. His *The Classical Style* (1971), a study of the music of Haydn, Mozart, and Beethoven, received universal critical admiration and won the National Book Award for Arts and Letters in 1972. Rosen's deep understanding of the process of composition and personal insights in the music itself is also manifested in his study *Sonata Forms* (1980). His Harvard lectures on Romantic musical thought and composition were published under the title *The Romantic Generation* (1995). Rosen's wide range of musical sympathies as a pianist – from Bach and the classical composers through Liszt and the virtuoso school to the music of *Schoenberg and of modern composers such as Elliott Carter and Pierre Boulez – was complemented by a powerful technique and a profound intellectual grasp of the works he played. All these factors combined to make Rosen one of the most interesting and important performing musicians of his day.

BIBLIOGRAPHY: NG².

[Max Loppert / Yulia Kreinin (2nd ed.)]

ROSEN, FRED SAUL (1930–2005), U.S. pediatrician. He was born in Newark, New Jersey, and received his A.B. from Lafayette College (1951) and M.D. from Western Reserve University (1955). He was a member of the department of pediatrics of Harvard Medical School from 1966 where he was James L. Gamble Professor of Pediatrics from 1972 and head of the Boston Children's Hospital's division of immunology (1968–85). Rosen's main research concerned inherited immunodeficiency disorders in infancy and childhood on which he was an acknowledged international authority. He was chairman of WHO's committee on immunodeficiencies. He was an outstanding teacher and clinician. His honors included: the Mead Johnson award for pediatric research of the American Academy of Pediatrics (1970), election to the Institute of Medicine of U.S. National Academy of Sciences, and the American Academy of Arts and Sciences, and recipient of the inaugural Dana Foundation Award in Human Immunodeficiency Research (2005).

[Michael Denman (2nd ed.)]

ROSÉN, HAIIM B. (1922–1999), Israeli linguist. Born in Vienna, Rosén received his Ph.D. from the Hebrew University of Jerusalem in 1948; he taught from then at the university and became professor in 1968. His research interests cover a wide range from general and Indo-European linguistics and the linguistic and philological study of classical languages to the study of Israeli Hebrew. His *Ha-Ivrit Shellanu* (1956) was the first work to examine Israeli Hebrew as the object of modern linguistic analysis and stimulated much academic discussion. He was a member of the Israel Academy of Arts and Sciences and in 1978 was awarded the Israel Prize in the humanities.

BIBLIOGRAPHY: *Lezikhro shel Haiim Baruch Rosén – Devarim she-Ne'emru bi-Mlot Sheloshim le-Moto, 22 Tishrei 5761*, Ha-Akademyah ha-Le'ummit ha-Yisre'elit le-Madda'im; S. Sznol, "The Linguist as Historian – The Contribution of Haiim Rosén to the Study of Ancient and Medieval Jewish History," in: Y. Tobi (ed.), *Ha-Ḥug ha-Yisre'eli shel Ḥavrei ha-Ḥevrah ha-Eropit le-Balshanut – Proceedings of the 16th Annual Meeting, Divrei ha-Mifgash ha-Shenati ha-16* (2000), 5–12.

ROSEN, JOSEPH A. (1877–1949), agronomist and social worker. Rosen was born in Moscow. He studied agriculture in Russia and Germany and emigrated to the U.S. in 1903. His discovery, the "Rosen rye," was introduced all over the U.S. In 1921 Rosen went to Russia for the *American Jewish Joint Distribution Committee (JDC) on a relief mission for Jews. He initiated a land settlement project in the Ukraine and Crimea in 1924 for poor Jews who had been deprived of Soviet citizenship rights. Heading the Agro-Joint, which was sponsored by the JDC for colonizing activities, he obtained the agreement and financial participation of the Soviet government for the project (1928), through which some 14,000 families were settled on the land by 1934. Artisan cooperatives, trade schools, and health stations were also organized. By 1938 the Agro-Joint was dissolved and its Russian Jewish staff was arrested and disappeared; most of the settlers either left the colonies for urban occupations or were killed by the Germans during the war. In 1939 Rosen was sent by the JDC on an investigation of British Guiana as a place for Jewish settlement. Later he spent some time guiding a JDC-sponsored settlement in the Dominican Republic.

BIBLIOGRAPHY: H. Agar, *Saving Remnant* (1960), index; O. Handlin, *A Continuing Task* (1964), index; L. Jung (ed.), *Jewish Leaders* (1953), 393–403.

[Yehuda Bauer]

ROSEN, JOSEPH BEN ISAAC (d. 1885), Russian rabbi and author. Rosen was born in Gorodok, Belorussia. His father intended him for a business career, but he early displayed unusual scholarly abilities and studied for the rabbinate. His first position was in Gorodok near Vitebsk, and in 1864 he was appointed rabbi of Telz (Telsiai). In 1873 he was appointed rabbi of Slonim, succeeding the renowned Joshua Isaac *Shapira, known as "Eisel Ḥarif." The period of his rabbinate at Slonim was exceptionally difficult for him. The *maskilim* of Slonim had begun to organize themselves and made considerable progress. Nevertheless, as a result of his moderation and conciliatory ways, his rabbinic authority remained unimpaired, and he enjoyed the respect of both the Ḥasidim and the *maskilim*. In 1881 a fire broke out in the city, as a result of which about 75% of its Jewish inhabitants were left homeless. Rosen placed himself at the head of an organization to rehabilitate them, and through his organizational ability and moral influence he succeeded in effecting the rebuilding of the homes and the erection of new and modern communal buildings. Rosen's daughter married Isaac Jacob *Reines.

All his works, which display his profound learning, include his name in their titles. They are: *Edut bi-Yhosef* (Vilna, 1866), novellae to the Shulḥan Arukh, *Yoreh De'ah; Porat Yosef* (Warsaw, 1884), responsa and novellae to the Shulḥan Arukh, *Ḥoshen Mishpat*; and *She'erit Yosef* (*ibid.*, 1914), responsa and halakhic clarification.

BIBLIOGRAPHY: *Pinkas Slonim*, 1 (1962), 72–73, 85; *Yahadut Lita*, 3 (1967), 94.

[Itzhak Alfassi]

ROSEN, MATHIAS (1804–1865), banker and member of the Polish Council of State. Rosen was born in Warsaw and took over his father's banking business there in 1846. Because of his financial status and close relations with the government, he was appointed head of the Warsaw community in the 1840s. In this capacity he established philanthropic institutions and fostered the influence of *Haskalah in religious education. As a result of the increase of the Jewish population in Warsaw, the leader of the community became the representative of all the Jews in the country. For his services, Rosen was elected a member of the Council of Warsaw in 1862, and in the following year of the Council of State. He was entrusted by Grand Duke Constantine with the commission to study the moral, industrial and agricultural conditions of the Alsatian Jews. Rosen collaborated with the *Encyklopedja Powszechna* of S. Orgelbrand and with the *Biblioteka Warszawska*, being a member of the editorial board from 1849.

BIBLIOGRAPHY: *Encyklopedja Powszechna*, 22 (1866), 275; R. Mahler, *Ha-Ḥasidut ve-ha-Haskalah* (1961), 231–51; S. Lastik, *Z. dziejów oświęcenia żydowskiego* (1961), 186–243; J. Shatzky, *Geshikhte fun Yidn in Varshe*, 2–3 (1948–53), indexes. **ADD. BIBLIOGRAPHY:** M. Fuks, *Zydzi w Warszawie* (1992), index.

ROSEN, MOSES (1912–1994), chief rabbi of Romania from 1948, when his predecessor, Rabbi Alexander *Safran, left the country, and chairman of the Federation of Jewish Communities of the Socialist Republic of Romania from 1964. Born in Moinesti, Moldavia, where his father, Rabbi Abraham Aryeh had served as rabbi, Rosen was ordained as a rabbi around the beginning of World War II. From 1957 he was a member of the Great National Assembly (the parliament) of Romania, his original constituency being a quarter of Bucharest that at one time had a large Jewish population. He was the editor of the *Journal of Romanian Religious Jewry*, the trilingual (Romanian, Hebrew, Yiddish) biweekly published by the Romanian Jewish community from 1956, the only Hebrew publication in Eastern Europe. Rosen's speeches and sermons were published in this periodical, which also contained items of Jewish news from abroad and articles on the contribution of Romanian Jews to Jewish culture. Rosen's main achievement was the creation of legal conditions for adequate Jewish religious life in Romania.

[Eliezer Palmor]

ROSEN, MOSHE (1933–1999), Israeli physicist. Rosen was born in Czernowitz (Chernovtsy) and immigrated to Israel in 1948. In 1969 he was appointed associate professor of physical metallurgy and head of the Materials Engineering Department of the newly founded University of the Negev (now the Ben-Gurion University of the Negev) and in 1973 full professor. In 1974, he was also appointed rector. From 1968 to 1973 he was scientific coordinator and project engineer at the Research and Development in Physics and Metallurgy, Nuclear Research Center – Negev, Beersheba. In 1971 he became a member of the Subcommittee for Research of the Israel Atomic Energy Commission, Office of the Prime Minister. In 1982 he joined the faculty of Johns Hopkins University. In addition to serving as a department head there (1988–92) he was editor in chief of the scientific journal *Ultrasonics* and president of the Maryland Institute of Metals. In his research Rosen examined phase transformations in solids, elasticity and anelasticity in metals, composites and ceramics, and nondestructive characterization of materials and processes.

ROSEN, NORMA (1925–), U.S. novelist. Born in Manhattan, Norma Rosen grew up in Brooklyn, N.Y. She received a B.A. from Mount Holyoke College in 1946, and an M.A. from Columbia in 1953. In her book *Accidents of Influence* (1992), an essay uniquely describes her family's situation in relation to Judaism. Neither devout nor assimilated, her family "… stood in a proud and terrible place outside the 'two cultures.'" In 1959, she began writing seriously. Her first novel, *Joy to Levine!*, was published in 1962. The book, dealing with parental authority, is slightly sardonic, since it is in part a satire on the American pastime of "getting ahead." Her next book, *Green* (1967), a novella and eight short stories, deals with maturity in relation to the "sellout" of an artist to commercial art in advertising. The novella, according to Stanley Kaufman, demonstrates Rosen's ability to realize men and plunge into sentiment, "confident that genuineness and distillation will keep her from sentimentality."

In the 1960s, Norma Rosen began to confront the psychological damage of the Holocaust. As she later explained in a 1987 essay, the novel deals "with the response of those not involved directly with the Holocaust except through imagination, and examines its impact on them." Rosen's American women of the novel, *Touching Evil* (1969), are obsessed with the testimony of eye witnesses to the Holocaust. As S. Lillian Kremer states in a 2002 article on Norma Rosen, *Touching Evil* "… is distinctive in its deliberation on American Holocaust reaction and a feminine perspective."

Rosen's next long novel, *At the Center* (1982), touches on the theme of abortion and assistance to pregnant women. Robert Miner's review states that although Norma Rosen never supports the "Right to Life" movement, hard questions about abortion still exist. And this is the book's moral strength.

Norma Rosen's novel, *John and Anzia: An American Romance* (1989), re-imagines a brief love affair between a Jewish immigrant, Anzia Yezierska, and the American John Dewey. Helen A. Weinberger reviewed the novel and felt that Norma Rosen wrote a magical novel, "… mixing fact and fiction in a kind of transcendental philosophical poem about the cross between a real early 20th-century America and an always wished-for land."

The author also published *Accidents of Influence: Writing as a Jew and a Woman in America* (1992), a volume of essays, and *Biblical Women Unbound* (1996), a re-staging of Old Testament stories.

[Mark Padnos (2nd ed.)]

ROSEN (Rosenblueth), PINḤAS (Felix) (1887–1978). Zionist and Israeli politician, member of the First to Sixth Knessets. Born in Berlin, Rosen studied Law at the Universities of Freiburg and Berlin, receiving his degree in 1908. In 1905 he became active in the Zionist students' movement *Bund Juedischer Corporationen*, which was later renamed *Kartell Juedischer Verbindungen*. In 1911 he was a cofounder of the Zionist youth movement *Blau-Weiss. Rosen served in the German army in World War I, and reached the rank of officer. In 1920–23 he served as chairman of the Zionist Organization of Germany. He emigrated to Palestine in 1923. In 1926 he became a member of the Zionist Executive in London, as head of the Organization Department, in which capacity he served until 1931, when he returned to Palestine. In Palestine he opened a private law practice and worked as a lawyer until 1948. In 1935 he was elected to the Tel Aviv Municipal Council in which he represented the immigrants from Central Europe, and continued to serve on the municipality until 1950. In 1940–48, he was chairman of the German and Austrian Immigrants' Association. Rosen was active in *General Zionists (A), and was close to *Weizmann in his approach to Zionism. In 1940–41, he was a member of a committee established by the League for Jewish-Arab Rapprochement and Cooperation, that prepared a report for the Jewish Agency on constitutional development in Palestine, better known as the Bentov Report (see Mordechai *Bentov). The Committee's report was based on the premise that Ereẓ Israel would become a binational state (see *Binationalism). In 1942 he was one of the founders of the Aliyah Ḥadashah Party. In the period of the struggle for statehood, he objected to Jewish terrorism, and supported the 1947 UN partition plan. Rosen was elected to Asefat ha-Nivḥarim in 1944, and after the establishment of the state was one of the founders of the Progressive Party. He was elected to the First Knesset in 1949, and remained a member of the Knesset through the Sixth Knesset, on the Progressive list, then on the *Israel Liberal Party list, and finally on the *Independent Liberal Party list, when it broke off from the Liberal Party in 1965. Rosen served as minister of justice from 1948 to 1961, and was instrumental in organizing the judicial and legal system of Israel. He was chairman of the Board of the Israel Philharmonic Orchestra until 1961, and published articles on Zionist themes in German, English, and Hebrew. A chair in constitutional law was established in Rosen's name at Tel Aviv University in 1972. In 1973 he was awarded the Israel Prize for law.

BIBLIOGRAPHY: H.H. Cohen, *Sefer Yovel le-Pinḥas Rosen* (1967); R. Bondy, *Felix: Pinḥas Rosen Uzmano* (1990).

[Susan Hattis Rolef (2nd ed.)]

ROSEN, SAMUEL (1897–1981), U.S. otologist. Rosen was born in Syracuse, New York, and originally studied law at the Syracuse Law School. He subsequently switched to medicine, however, graduating from the Syracuse Medical School in 1921. He specialized in otology at the Mount Sinai Hospital in New York, where he was consulting otologist and later emeritus clinical professor of otolaryngology.

In 1952 Rosen discovered a new method for restoring hearing to patients suffering from otosclerosis by an operation, the so-called Stapes-Mobilization procedure. As a result, thousands of patients regained their hearing, and Rosen demonstrated the method throughout the world, including Egypt, Israel, and the U.S.S.R. President *Nasser expressed his appreciation to him after he performed surgery at the Cairo Medical School. When Rosen expressed his surprise that Nasser had invited a Jew, he answered: "your work is above race and country." Rosen was also elected a member of the Soviet Medical Academy.

In 1957, he received the Hektoen-Gold Award for "original work in medicine" of the American Medical Association as well as an award by the University of Bologna. In 1964, he was awarded the George-Arents Pioneer Medal for Excellence in Medicine by Syracuse University. He made several trips, with his wife, to a remote area of the Sudan to investigate the remarkable hearing ability of the Mabaan tribe. He was also a member of the first medical team in a quarter of a century to visit China, and lectured extensively on Chinese medicine and acupuncture.

His autobiography, published in 1973, was widely acclaimed.

BIBLIOGRAPHY: *The Autobiography of Dr. Samuel Rosen* (1973); A.M. Sackler, in: *Medical Tribune* (June 6, 1973); J.M. Lawrence, in: *Syracuse University Alumni News* (Summer 1973); B.G. Rudolph, *From a Minyan to a Community. A History of the Jews of Syracuse* (c. 1970), 252–54.

[Heinz Hartman]

ROSEN, SHELOMO (1905–1985), Israeli politician. Rosen was born in Moravska-Ostrava, Czechoslovakia and immigrated to Ereẓ Israel in 1926. There, he was a founder of Kibbutz Sarid. While secretary of Ha-Kibbutz ha-Arẓi from 1944, and a member of Mapam's political committee, he was recognized as that movement's foremost economist expert. He maintained that a prosperous settlement cannot be based only on agriculture, and he fostered the development of kibbutz industry. In 1965 he was elected to the Sixth Knesset and was deputy speaker in the Seventh. Chairman of the Knesset's Social Services Committee, he became chairman of the subcommittee of the finance committee which dealt with state comptroller's reports. Appointed deputy minister of absorption in 1972, he became minister in March 1974, and sought to eliminate the confusing overlapping of functions between his ministry and the Jewish Agency. Subsequently he was named minister of housing. He continued to serve until the elections of May 1977.

ROSEN, YEHOSHUA (1918–2002), Israeli basketball coach. Known in Israel as "Mister Basketball" and considered one of the outstanding coaches in the country, Rosen came to Israel with his family from Egypt in the 1920s and immediately began to play basketball. At the age of 14 he was already playing on the Maccabi Tel Aviv senior team, continuing with them into the 1940s. In 1947 he was named coach of Israel's national basketball team and led it to three European tournament finals. In 1953 he became the coach of Maccabi Tel Aviv, running the team 18 years and winning 12 national championships and nine state cups. In 1984 he led Hapoel Tel Aviv to the state cup. Rosen coached for 40 years, until his retirement at the end of the 1980s, mentoring some of Israel's top homegrown players, such as Mickey *Berkowitz and Doron Jamchi. He was awarded the Israel Prize in 1989 for his contribution to Israeli basketball.

BIBLIOGRAPHY: E. Sahar, "Not just a coach, but also teacher and educator," in: *Ha'aretz* (Feb. 7, 2002).

[Shaked Gilboa (2nd ed.)]

ROSENAK, LEOPOLD (1869–1923/24), rabbi. Rosenak, who was born in Pozsonynadas, Hungary, was rabbi at Bremen, Germany, from 1896. Here he was especially active in aiding Russian and Polish Jewish refugees who passed through the port of Bremen on their way to the U.S. From 1915 to 1918 Rosenak was chaplain to the German army of occupation in Lithuania (Ober Ost), using his influence with the German authorities to alleviate the sufferings of the Jewish population. The yeshivah of *Slobodka, then in exile in the Ukraine, was reopened with his assistance, as was a Hebrew high school in Kovno. Rosenak died at sea on his return from a visit to the U.S., where he had sought aid for Ukrainian pogrom victims and for the new Bremen synagogue.

His thesis, *Fortschritt der hebraeischen Sprachwissenschaft vom 10.–13. Jahrhundert*, was published in 1898, and his talmudic novellae (*Ma'amar Mordekhai*) were printed in *Festschrift… S. Carlebach* (1915).

ROSENAU, WILLIAM (1865–1943), Reform rabbi. Born in Wollstein, Prussia, the son of a rabbi, he was educated in public school and came to the United States with his family in 1876, first to Boston and then to Philadelphia. Rosenau received his B.A. from the University of Cincinnati (1888) and was ordained a year later from HUC in Cincinnati. He served congregations in Omaha, Nebraska, for three years beginning in 1889 and then went to Baltimore as rabbi of Ohev Shalom where he served for almost half a century until his retirement in 1939. Concurrently he studied at Johns Hopkins University where he received his Ph.D. in 1900 in Semitics and then joined its faculty, where he served until 1932.

Religiously liberal he was also politically a non-Zionist and a member of the American Council for Judaism.

For a time he was expected to be the leading candidate for the presidency of the Hebrew Union College after the retirement of Kaufmann *Kohler in 1921 but that was not to be. He lost in a close vote to Julian *Morgenstein and elected to remain in Baltimore rather than lead a more prominent congregation. He was deeply active in his community, concentrating on areas of general and higher education. He was a member of the Baltimore Board of Education of the Governor's Commission on Higher Education for Negroes. In national Jewish life, he was active in the Central Conference of American Rabbis and served as its president from 1915 to 1917. He was a member of the Associated Jewish Charities, a member of Baltimore's Federation, a founder of the Jewish Welfare Board and the Jewish Chautauqua Society, and edited the revised *Union Prayer Book* and *Union Haggadah*. He was a contributor to the *Jewish Encyclopedia*.

Among his works are *The Rabbi in Action* (1937); *Hebraism in the Authorized Version of the Bible* (1902); and *Semitic Studies in American Colleges* (1906).

BIBLIOGRAPHY: W.F. Rosenblum, *The Life and Work of Rev. Dr. William Rosenau* (1946); K.M. Olitzsky, L.J. Sussman, and M.H. Stern, *Reform Judaism in America: A Biographical Dictionary and Sourcebook* (1993).

[Michael Berenbaum (2nd ed.)]

ROSENBACH, ABRAHAM SIMON WOLF (1876–1952), U.S. bibliophile and bookdealer. Rosenbach was born in Philadelphia. His parents, Isabella Polock, the descendant of a distinguished Philadelphia family, and Meier Rosenbach, an immigrant from Germany, were observant Jews. Rosenbach attended the University of Pennsylvania, from which he obtained a doctorate in English literature. In his college days, he became a passionate bibliophile, and when his bookdealer uncle, Moses Polock, died in 1903, he took over the latter's stock and launched the Rosenbach Company, a rare-book concern. Combining erudition with personal charm and the risk-taking instincts of a gambler, Rosenbach soon rose to national prominence in the rare-book field. Dealing primarily in first and early editions of Americana and English literature, he acquired among his steady customers such millionaire collectors as Henry Huntington, Pierpont Morgan, Carl Pforzheimer, Lessing Rosenwald, Harry Widener, Edward S. Harkness, and Henry Folger, to whom he sold a first quarto edition of Shakespeare's plays in 1919 for $128,000, reputedly one of the highest prices ever paid for a rare book up to that time. From the 1920s on, Rosenbach Company was the acknowledged leader in the rare-book trade in the U.S. and hardly a major auction took place in which it did not successfully and often spectacularly bid.

Rosenbach was a man of enigmatic contradictions. An astute businessman, he was also for much of his life a confirmed alcoholic; a person of deep Jewish interests, he lived in a permanent liaison with a Christian woman whom he reputedly refused to marry because she was not Jewish. He himself compiled a pioneer bibliographical study, *An American Jewish Bibliography* (1926), as well as a historical sketch of Congregation Mikveh Israel (1909), to which he and his parents belonged. For many years president of the American Jewish Historical Society, he was also a benefactor of Graetz College in Philadelphia and the Jewish Division of the New York Public Library, as well as a founder and first president of the American Friends of The Hebrew University. Among the several accounts he wrote of his adventures in the book trade were *A Book Hunter's Holiday* (1936) and *Books and Bidders* (1927). After his death, his private collection was installed in a library in Philadelphia under the auspices of the Rosenbach Foundation, which was established by his brother and junior partner Philip Rosenbach (1863–1953).

BIBLIOGRAPHY: E. Wolf and J.F. Fleming, *Rosenbach* (1960).

[Hillel Halkin]

ROSENBAUM, JONATHAN (1947–), U.S. scholar, administrator and rabbi; president of Gratz College from 1998. A graduate of the University of Michigan where he received his B.A. summa cum laude in 1968 and was elected to Phi Beta Kappa, Rosenbaum then earned rabbinical ordination and an M.A. at the Hebrew Union College-Jewish Institute-Jewish Institute of Religion in Cincinnati (1972) and a Ph.D. in Near Eastern Languages and Civilization from Harvard University working with Professor Frank M. Cross, Jr. on "A Typology of Aramaic Lapidary Script from the Seventh to the Fourth Centuries, B.C.E." (1978). He taught in the Department of Religious Studies at the University of Nebraska and then went to the University of Hartford, where he was the Maurice Greenberg Professor of Judaic Studies, professor of history, and director, Maurice Greenberg Center for Judaic Studies, University of Hartford, from 1986 to 1998. He conceived and helped guide the Henry Luce Forum in Abrahamic Religions, a national program jointly sponsored by the University of Hartford and Hartford Seminary that is devoted to advancing scholarship concerning and mutual understanding among American Jews, Christians, and Muslims. In addition, Rosenbaum conceived and oversaw an awards program that recognizes the best teachers of Holocaust studies in New England.

He also taught in the graduate school at the University of Connecticut and at its law school as well as the Hartford Theological Seminary.

A rarity in the contemporary Jewish world, he has served as a rabbi in Reform, Conservative, and Orthodox Congregations. During his student years at HUC, he held a student rabbi position at Congregation Israel (Reform), Galesburg, IL, from 1970 to 1972. While at Harvard he was assistant rabbi, Temple Israel (Conservative), Swampscott, MA, (1972–76), and then a part-time rabbi of Congregation Israel (Conservative), Danville, IL (1976–84). And finally as his commitment to Jewish law deepened he was rabbi (*mara' de-atra*) at Congregation Agudas Achim, a mainstream, century-old Orthodox congregation in West Hartford, CT, from 1994 to 1998.

Among the awards he received were doctor of divinity, *honoris causa*, by Hebrew Union College-Jewish Institute of Religion, in March 1997, and doctor of Hebrew Letters, *honoris causa*, from the Jewish Theological Seminary in November 1998.

Among his works are *Making a Life, Building a Community: A History of the Jews of Hartford* (co-authored with David G. Dalin, 1997) and a special issue of the *Journal of Jewish Communal Service* (78:4, 2002) devoted to Philadelphia Jewry that he co-edited with Dr. Ernest M. Kahn.

From 1995 to 1998 Rosenbaum served as a deputy director of the Ein Gedi Archaeological Expedition in Israel, an excavation co-sponsored by the Hebrew University of Jerusalem and the University of Hartford. At Ein Gedi he oversaw the excavation's academic program including two courses in archaeology and Near Eastern history. He also organized and chaired "Paleographical Studies in the Ancient Near East," a scholarly section of the national meeting sponsored by the Society of Biblical Literature.

An administrator-scholar, at Gratz he instituted new programs, expanded the faculty and staff, renovated the academic plant, and balanced the budget. He renewed a distinguished institute and refashioned its mission in a changing academic climate. Prior to that at the University of Hartford he initiated the Greenberg Center and established a major in Judaic Studies along with a minor. He also expanded the full-time faculty to six and three adjunct faculty. All the while, he continued with his teaching and writing.

[Michael Berenbaum (2nd ed.)]

ROSENBAUM, MORRIS (1871–1947), English rabbi and scholar. Rosenbaum, who was born in London, received his early education in the Jewish Orphanage, London. Later he studied at Jews' College and University College, London. After doing communal work in London, Rabbi Rosenbaum became minister of the Jewish congregation of Hanley (Staffordshire), and shortly afterward of the community in Newcastle-on-Tyne. In 1905 he returned to London to become minister-secretary of the Borough Synagogue, a post he held until his retirement 30 years later. Rosenbaum's wide interests included mathematics, and he was a recognized authority on the Jewish calendar and was responsible for the authorized Jewish almanac. His labors in the field of Anglo-Jewish genealogy brought him inquiries from prominent historians. He was also active in freemasonry and held offices in the brotherhood. Rosenbaum, together with A.M. *Silbermann, translated Rashi's commentaries on the Torah into English: *Pentateuch with Targum Onkelos, Haphtaroth and Prayers for Sabbath and Rashi's Commentary* (5 vols., 1929–34).

[Alexander Tobias]

ROSENBAUM, MOSES ḤAYYIM LITS (1864–1943), Hungarian rabbi. Rosenbaum was born in Pressburg, and was ordained by Simḥah Bunim Sofer (see *Sofer family). He served as rabbi of two large communities, in Szilágysomlyó (Simleul Silvaniei), Transylvania, from 1888 to 1897, and from 1898 until his death in Kleinwardein. On the death of R. Koppel Reich in 1929, he was asked to represent Orthodox Jewry in the upper house of the Hungarian parliament but refused, preferring to devote himself to his large community. He was an excellent preacher in Yiddish, German and Hungarian.

He published *Meshiv Devarim* (2 parts, 1900–02), responsa on *Oraḥ Ḥayyim* and *Yoreh De'ah* by his father Gershon, rabbi of Tallya, adding his own notes. He was also the author of *Leḥem Rav* (1921), on the prayer book. The bulk of his writings, however, which fill 15 large volumes, remained in manuscript; among them is a diary, one chapter of which was published by N. Ben-Menahem in *Aresheth*, 1 (1958), that is of considerable interest. Although an extremist in religious matters, Rosenbaum did not ignore the *Haskalah literature, and sent a message of congratulation to Leopold *Zunz, founder of *Wissenschaft, on his 90th birthday. Of his two sons, Samuel, who succeeded him in Kleinwardein, perished in the Holocaust in 1944, and his grandson, Pinḥas Rosenbaum, published his responsa *Elleh Divrei Shemu'el* (1961).

BIBLIOGRAPHY: N. Ben-Menahem, in: *Aresheth*, 1 (1958), 486–8; idem, *Be-Sha'arei Sefer* (1967), 126–8.

[Naphtali Ben-Menahem]

ROSENBAUM, SAMUEL (1919–1997), cantor and organizational executive. Rosenbaum was born in New York City and received his B.A. from New York University in 1940. Simultaneously, he studied music and liturgy privately under renowned Cantor Jacob *Beimel. He began his cantorial career at the Queens Jewish Center, Queens Village, New York (1940–42), which was interrupted by military service in the U.S. Army during World War II. In 1946, Rosenbaum became cantor of Temple Beth El in Rochester, New York, where his innovative work in musical programming won him national recognition in the form of awards from the Cantors Assembly and the *United Synagogue (1965). Upon his retirement, he was awarded an honorary doctor of music degree from the *Jewish Theological Seminary in 1985.

Rosenbaum was active in the Cantors Assembly from its founding in 1947, serving as the editor of its journal, *The Cantor's Voice* (1951–66), before being elected president of the association (1956–59). Following his term of office, Rosenbaum was appointed the organization's executive director (1959–97). Under his leadership, the assembly grew to become the world's largest association of cantors and spearheaded the expansion of its members' roles beyond performing at services to becoming involved in congregational and educational programming. Rosenbaum was also a fellow at the Cantors Institute of the *Jewish Theological Seminary (1960), where he assisted in placing graduates. In 1970, he became managing editor of the *Journal of Synagogue Music*, published by the Cantors Assembly.

A prolific composer, Rosenbaum was commissioned by Conservative and Reform congregations to write some 30 solo and choral works. In 1973, his oratorio *Yizkor: In Memory of the Six Million*, written with Sholom *Secunda, was performed on ABC-TV's *Directions* and nominated for an Emmy Award. Rosenbaum also wrote books and narrated several record albums. He developed a new method for teaching biblical cantillation, which he set forth in *A Guide to Haftarah Chanting* (1973). His other books are *Sabbath and Festival Songs for the Young Singer* (1959) and *To Live as a Jew* (1960). He released *Four Holiday Recordings* in 1981. Other major musical compositions include: *Sing a Song of Israel* (with Issachar Miron, 1962); *Oneg Shabbat* (with Sholom Secunda, 1964); *A Singing of Angels* (with Charles Davidson, 1967) and *The Last Judgment* (with Lazar Weiner, 1967).

[Bezalel Gordon (2nd ed.)]

ROSENBAUM, SEMYON (**Shimshon**; 1860–1934), jurist and Zionist. Born in Pinsk, Rosenbaum practiced law there and in Minsk. In 1880s he joined the *Ḥibbat Zion movement, and was a delegate to the Zionist Congresses until World War I. At the Fourth Congress in 1900, he was elected to the Zionist General Council and served as a delegate of the Zionist center to the Minsk district. He organized the *Minsk Conference of Russian Zionists in 1902. Rosenbaum's point of view was close to that of the *Democratic Fraction in the Zionist Organization, and he helped to organize the first *Po'alei Zion groups in the Minsk district in Lithuania. He was among the leaders of Ẓiyyonei Zion, who actively opposed the *Uganda Scheme. At the *Helsingfors Conference in 1906, he was made a member of the Zionist central committee of Russia.

Rosenbaum held a central position in the League for the Attainment of Legal Rights for the Jews in Russia. He was elected to the first Russian *Duma in 1906 and joined the liberal Constitutional-Democratic ("Kadet") faction. When the Duma was dissolved, he was among those Duma members who signed the manifesto calling for civil disobedience and nonpayment of taxes and was sentenced to prison. After his release, he engaged in providing legal assistance to pogrom victims and to Zionists persecuted by the Russian authorities. After the outbreak of World War I, Rosenbaum moved to Vilna and was elected head of the Zionist organization there. He participated in the negotiations with the Turkish government concerning the future of Palestine after the war (1918). He also took part in the establishment of independent Lithuania in 1919. He was deputy minister of foreign affairs in the first Lithuanian government and a member of its delegation to the Versailles Peace Conference. He signed the peace treaty with the Soviet Union on behalf of the Lithuanian Republic. He was a member of the commission that drafted the Lithuanian Republic's constitution, which granted the Jews wide national autonomy. Rosenbaum was the president of the National Council of the Jews in Lithuania and in 1923 became minister of Jewish affairs. In 1924, after the annulment of the Jewish autonomy, he went to Palestine, where he engaged in public activities in *General Zionist circles. He was chairman of the supreme Jewish peace court, and one of the founders of the Tel Aviv School of Law and Economics. He wrote many essays on Zionist and juridical subjects, including his research *Der Souveraenitaetsbegriff* (1932).

BIBLIOGRAPHY: M. Sudarsky and U. Katzenellenbogen (eds.) *Lite* (Yid., 1951), index; Ch. Leikowicz (ed.), *Lite*, 2 (Yid., 1965), index; Tidhar, 3 (1949), 1317–18.

[Yehuda Slutsky]

ROSENBERG, ABRAHAM (1870–1935), U.S. labor leader. Born in Russia, Rosenberg immigrated to the United States in 1883. He worked as a cloakmaker in New York's sweatshops and by 1885 was active in the immigrant labor movement. Because the American Federation of Labor (AFL) neglected semiskilled and unskilled immigrants, Rosenberg joined in organizing a dress and cloakmakers' union as part of the Knights of Labor. Its failure led Rosenberg to help create the International Ladies Garment Workers' Union (ILGWU), the first permanent labor organization in the women's garment industry.

In 1908 Rosenberg was elected president of the ILGWU. He assumed control at a crucial moment. The panic of 1907 and the ensuing depression spread unemployment and decimated the union's ranks. Within three years however, Rosenberg helped to guide the ILGWU to victory in two major strikes, those of the waistmakers in 1909 and the cloakmakers in the following year. The latter strike was settled on the basis of the famous Protocol of Peace – a concept which Rosenberg helped to spread of labor-management bargaining supervised by impartial arbitrators representing the public.

As president of the ILGWU, Rosenberg was overshadowed by his secretary-treasurer John *Dyche. Dyche came into conflict with New York's rank and file cloakmakers, who were anxious to break the protocol outlawing strikes. The 1914 ILGWU convention, dominated by the socialists, deposed both Rosenberg and Dyche for being union conservatives and antisocialist. In fact, while committed to peaceful collective bargaining and moderate union tactics, Rosenberg was a devoted socialist. He played no prominent role in union affairs after 1914. Rosenberg remained a general organizer of the union until his retirement in 1929. In 1920 he wrote his memoirs in Yiddish, *The Cloakmakers and their Union*, which show his direct, warm, and human approach to all the problems he had to deal with.

[Melvyn Dubofsky]

ROSENBERG, ABRAHAM ḤAYYIM (1838–1928), Hebrew writer. Born in Russia, he wrote articles for the Hebrew and Yiddish press. He emigrated to the U.S. in 1891, and operated a Hebrew printing shop.

Rosenberg's main achievement was the biblical encyclopedia in ten volumes, *Oẓar ha-Shemot* (1898–1922). For a brief period of time, in 1897, he coedited (with A.M. Radin) the Hebrew monthly *Ner ha-Ma'aravi*, and between 1900 and 1902 *Ha-Modi'a le-Ḥodashim*, a Hebrew monthly (first together with H. Rosenthal, and in 1902 alone).

BIBLIOGRAPHY: Kressel, Leksikon, 2 (1967), 841.

[Eisig Silberschlag]

°**ROSENBERG, ALFRED** (1893–1946), chief Nazi ideologist and head of the Nazi party's foreign policy department. Rosenberg was born in Reval (Tallin), Estonia. There is some doubt about the family's German origin though their name is German. Rosenberg studied architecture at Riga and Moscow and witnessed the Russian Revolution, which he believed to have been "engineered by Jewry." He fled to Germany and settled in Munich at the end of 1918, immediately became active in nationalist, antisemitic circles and published *Die Spur der Juden im Wandel der Zeiten* ("The Track of the Jews Through the Ages," 1920). When the German Workers Party (DAP), the precursor of the NSDAP (Nazi Party), was founded, he joined it even before *Hitler. Later, as a member of Hitler's inner circle, he became editor (1921) and later chief editor (1923) of the party's *Voelkischer Beobachter.* He impressed Hitler with his linkage of the Jews, the Bolsheviks, and the Masons as supposedly engaging in a conspiracy to destroy the foundations of German civilization. Rosenberg published antisemitic pamphlets and introduced the Protocols of the *Elders of Zion in Nazi propaganda. He participated in the 1923 beer hall putsch. In 1930 he published his main work, *Der Mythus des 20. Jahrhunderts*, which appeared in 24 editions by 1934, constituting a hodgepodge of ideas from Nietzsche and various racist theories. The book propounds the doctrine of an "Aryan race" as the creator of all values and culture. The protagonists of this "Aryan race" are the Germanic peoples, while the "Jewish race" had corrupted culture in different forms, one of them being Paulinic Christianity. Bolshevism, he claimed, was a new form of the Jewish quest for world rule, and, to rid themselves of Jewish corruption, the German people were obliged to replace Christianity by a new faith, based on "blood and race." With Hitler's advent to power, Rosenberg achieved renown, became head of all the party indoctrination organizations, and was later appointed by Hitler chief of the Nazi Party's foreign policy office (APA), where he ineffectually dabbled in diplomatic affairs. In fact, his office served only for disseminating antisemitic propaganda. In 1940 Hitler appointed Rosenberg head of the Hohe Schule, the future ideological University of Nazism. On its behalf Rosenberg's emissaries ransacked Jewish libraries all over Europe and concentrated their contents in Frankfurt. He headed a special staff which plundered objects of art and furniture belonging to Jews in occupied Western Europe and French art works from France, which were brought to Germany. At the outbreak of the war against Russia Rosenberg was appointed minister of occupied countries in the East and head of their civil administration (November 1941). He did not object to the annihilation of Jews, but came into conflict with the SS and their collaborators on the policy of murder, starvation, and repression of the non-Russian minorities in the occupied areas of the U.S.S.R., as it appears from correspondence in the so-called "Braune Mappe" (on the status of the local population in the Soviet territories occupied by the Germans, including correspondence with *Eichmann). He preferred more lenient methods in order to set the minority peoples against the Russians. Finally he accepted the harsher methods advocated by leading personalities of the Reich. Rosenberg, unrepentant and immovable at his trial, was hanged by sentence of the International Military Tribunal. *The Memoirs of Alfred Rosenberg* (ed. by S. Lang and E. Schenck) appeared in 1949, and Rosenberg's *Letzte Aufzeichnungen* was published in 1955.

BIBLIOGRAPHY: E. Davidson, *Trial of the Germans* (1966), 125–43; IMT, *Trial of the Major War Criminals*, 24 (1949), index; G.M. Gilbert, *Nuremberg Diary* (1947), index; L. Poliakov and J. Wulf (eds.), *Das dritte Reich und die Juden* (1955), index; idem, *Das dritte Reich und seine Denker* (1959), index; J. Billig, *Alfred Rosenberg dans l'action idéologique, politique et administrative du Reich hitlérien* (1963). **ADD. BIBLIOGRAPHY:** E. Cecil, *The Myth of the Master Race: Alfred Rosenberg and Nazi Ideology* (1972); F. Noca, *Alfred Rosenberg: Nazi Theorist of the Holocaust* (1986); J. Feist, *The Face of the Third Reich: Portraits of Nazi Leadership* (1970).

[Yehuda Reshef / Michael Berenbaum (2nd ed.)]

ROSENBERG, ANNA MARIE LEDERER (1902–1983), U.S. assistant secretary of defense; public relations and labor consultant. Born in Budapest, Hungary, the daughter of Albert Lederer and Charlotte Bacskai, Rosenberg moved with her family to New York City in 1912. She married Julius Rosenberg in 1919 and became a naturalized citizen the next year. As she became active in Democratic politics, then New York Governor Franklin Roosevelt sought her advice on labor matters. Rosenberg went on to serve in a number of capacities during the New Deal. She was an assistant to Nathan Straus, Jr., regional director of the National Recovery Administration (NRA) and succeeded him when Straus resigned. After Rosenberg served as New York regional director of the Social Security Board, President Roosevelt asked her to study industrial relations in both Great Britain and Sweden. Throughout her work on the Social Security Board, Rosenberg maintained a consulting firm. In 1942 the U.S. House Appropriations Committee investigated allegations of impropriety in holding two positions, but found Rosenberg to be innocent of any wrongdoing. Still, when she accepted the position of director of the War Manpower Commission for New York State that same year, she put her consulting practice in abeyance for the duration of the war. Her work on the War Manpower Commission included recruiting workers of all races to fill some 20,000 positions for the Pacific Coast Kaiser shipyards. As the war was winding down, Roosevelt sent Rosenberg to Europe to investigate what soldiers wanted after the war. Her report that they wanted to improve themselves through education helped lead to the GI Bill of Rights. President Harry S. Truman also called upon her expertise in evaluating the repatriation and demobilization of the troops. When Anna Rosenberg was appointed assistant secretary of defense, the first woman to hold that position, she had to survive a smear campaign claiming that she was a communist, an allegation that was proved false. Rosenberg worked on increasing the number and use of women in the military and she helped draft the Universal Military Service and Training Act. When President Eisenhower replaced her, she returned to decades of consulting work at Anna M. Rosenberg & Associates. Rosenberg received many honors, including the Medal of Freedom in 1945; in 1947 she became the first woman to receive the Medal for Merit. The Department of Defense recognized her with its Exceptional Civilian Award in 1953, and in 1966 she received the Medallion of the City of New York for her beautification efforts. As early as the 1930s, she was known for her philanthropic work, serving on the National Council of Jewish Women, the ORT Reconstruction fund, and the women's division of the Joint Distribution Committee of Jewish Charities.

BIBLIOGRAPHY: C.L. Thurston. *American National Biography* (1999); Columbia University houses her oral history.

[Sara Alpern (2nd ed.)]

ROSENBERG, ARTHUR (1889–1943), German communist leader and historian. Born in Berlin, Rosenberg lectured in history at Berlin University and joined the German Independent Social Democratic Party (USPD) in 1918. Two years later, he became attached to the German Communist Party (KPD), in which he achieved considerable prominence as communist City Councilor of Berlin, a member of the Party Central Committee, and a member of the Reichstag from 1924 to 1928. Rosenberg joined the extreme left-wing faction but in 1927 left the Communist movement altogether largely in protest at the failure of the Soviet Comintern to deal with the question of China. He withdrew from political life, and devoted himself to scholarly work. After Hitler's seizure of power, Rosenberg left Germany and lived in Liverpool, England, where he was granted a fellowship at the university. He went to New York in 1938 and taught history at Brooklyn College until his death. Rosenberg converted to Christianity in his youth but later was active in Jewish student and academic circles in Germany and England. The fact that he became adviser to the Avukah Zionist Students Federation of America testifies to the radical change in his religious views.

His many publications include: *Geschichte des Bolschewismus von Marx bis zur Gegenwart* (1932; *History of Bolshevism*, 1934); *Demokratie und Sozialismus* (1938; *Democracy and Socialism*, 1939); *Geschichte der deutschen Republik* (1935; *History of the German Republic*, 1936); and *Die Entstehung der deutschen Republik, 1871–1918* (1928; *Birth of the German Republic*, 1931).

ADD. BIBLIOGRAPHY: H. Schachenmayer, *Arthur Rosenberg* (1964); F.L. Carsten, in: *Historians in Politics* (1974), 315–27; R.W. Mueller, G. Schaefer (eds.), *"Klassische" Antike und moderne Demokratie: Arthur Rosenberg…* (1986); L. Riberi, *Arthur Rosenberg* (2001); M. Kessler, *Arthur Rosenberg* (2003).

[Noam Zadoff]

ROSENBERG, EUGENE (1907–1990), British architect. Rosenberg was born in Topolcany, Slovakia, went to England in 1939, and from 1944 practiced as an architect. He made an important contribution to postwar building in Britain with his designs for over 50 primary and secondary schools, and a number of university buildings at Warwick, Oxford, Liverpool, Leeds and Rochdale.

His public buildings include the United States Embassy in London (together with Eero Saarinen Associates) and a series of new airports. He also designed hospitals, industrial buildings, department stores, offices, and a number of housing schemes. He designed the new building for Jews' College London, the synagogue in Belfast, and the London offices of the Jewish Welfare Board.

ADD. BIBLIOGRAPHY: Obituary in *The Architect's Journal* 22 (1990), 12.

[Charles Samuel Spencer]

ROSENBERG, HAROLD (1906–1978), U.S. art critic and scholar. Born in New York City, Rosenberg was educated at the City College of New York, and he received an LL.B. degree from St. Lawrence University in 1927. From 1939 to 1942 he worked for the Works Progress Administration in Washington, D.C., as a writer and lecturer, authoring the *American Guide* series. Rosenberg was deputy chief of the domestic radio bureau of the Office of War Information from 1942 to 1945. He directed the Longview Foundation from 1944.

Rosenberg lectured extensively throughout the United States on art and literature. He joined the University of Chicago as a professor of social thought in 1966. From 1967 until his death in 1978 he was art critic for *The New Yorker*, and in that capacity he influenced the critical reception of many of the emerging artists of the time, including Jackson Pollock and Willem de Kooning. Called one of the most provocative critics of his time, Rosenberg rejected the formalistic approach of other leading art theorists, including Clement *Greenberg, placing the value of the work on the act of creation.

From the early 1950s Rosenberg had shown great interest in the work of a group of artists that included Pollock, de Kooning, and Arshile Gorky. Rosenberg coined the term "action painting," now widely used in art history and criticism, to describe their work, which he described as "not a picture but an event." His many reviews and essays were influential in the development of public awareness of the emerging Abstract Expressionist movement, and in the success of many of the Abstract Expressionists, including Mark *Rothko, Hans Hoffman, and Philip *Guston. At the same time, Rosenberg was a detractor of Pop Art and other art trends of the period and, while he rejected formalism, he was equally dismissive of the postmodern critique.

Rosenberg wrote several influential books, including *The Tradition of the New* (1959), *The Anxious Object: Art Today and Its Audience* (1964), *The De-Definition of Art* (1972), *Art on the Edge* (1975), and monographs on Willem de Kooning, Barnett Newman, Arshile Gorky, and Saul Steinberg. His articles appeared in numerous publications, including *Partisan Review, Art in America, Kenyon Review, Tempes Modernes*, and *Art News*.

Rosenberg received numerous awards and honors, including the Frank Jewett Mather Award from the College Art Association of America in 1964 and the Morton Dauwen Zabel Award from the National Institute of Arts and Letters in 1976. He was a member of the International Society of Art Critics and of the American Academy of Arts and Sciences.

[Dorothy Bauhoff (2nd ed.)]

ROSENBERG, ISAAC (1890–1918), English poet and painter, who died on active service during World War I. The son of a peddler, Rosenberg was born in Bristol and brought up in the East End of London, where he was apprenticed to an engraver. In 1911 he went to the Slade School of Fine Arts but he felt that he got, in his own words, "more depth" into writing than into painting. In 1912 he produced the first of three privately printed pamphlets of verse, *Night and Day*, following it with *Youth* (1915) and *Moses* (1916). Although he had weak lungs, Rosenberg enlisted in the British Army on his return from a year in South Africa in 1915, and it was while serving in France that he wrote his so-called "Trench Poems," several versions of his play *The Unicorn*, and many other poems and fragments.

Four years after his death, the first volume of Rosenberg's poems, with an introduction by the poet Laurence Binyon, appeared in print – his first publication apart from some scattered verse in anthologies. In 1937, his *Collected Works* were published with a brief, generous foreword by Siegfried *Sassoon, who wrote of Rosenberg's "fruitful fusion between English and Hebrew culture." Isaac Rosenberg was the first important poet to emerge from Anglo-Jewry and he remains a figure of major significance. Certain images and ideas, such as that of the root, recur throughout his work, giving coherence to his writing. Linguistically he is complex but the sense is controlled by his sensuous feeling. Rosenberg articulates the rootless condition of the Diaspora Jew most clearly in his poem "Chagrin." In his three "God" poems, he moves from the figure of an acceptable and benign Authority to that of a malignant God. "Dead Man's Dump," "Break of Day in the Trenches," and "Daughters of War" are among the most powerful and subtle poems of World War I. Rosenberg is, however, not merely a realist of the trenches: there is in his poetry a streak of romantic lyricism and a love of beauty more reminiscent of Blake than of any 20th-century poet.

Three books about Rosenberg appeared in the summer of 1975. They were *Journey to the Trenches: The Life of Isaac Rosenberg 1890–1918* by Joseph Cohen, *Isaac Rosenberg* by Jean Liddiard, and *Isaac Rosenberg* by Jean Moorcraft Wilson. Cohen's book excels on the literary background and the nature of his Jewishness; Liddiard's on his paintings and drawings; and Wilson uses letters and memoirs extensively. The book by Cohen contains a useful bibliography. Rosenberg's self-portrait is exhibited at the National Portrait Gallery, London, and another was hung in the Tate Gallery in London in 1972. Further biographies and studies of Rosenberg continue to appear.

In January 1978 the trustees of the Imperial War Museum in London accepted 15 of his paintings and some 200 manuscripts, and in 1979 there appeared *The Collected Works of Isaac Rosenberg: Prose, Letters, Paintings and Drawings* (Oxford) in which he is referred to as "the best Jewish poet writing in English that our century has given us." A plaque in Poets' Corner in Westminster Abbey, London, commemorating the notable British writers who died in World War I, includes the name of Isaac Rosenberg, surely the only British Jew officially honored in an Anglican church, and a tribute to his stature and fame.

BIBLIOGRAPHY: Bewley, in: *Commentary*, 7 (1949), 34–44; D.W. Harding, *Experience into Words* (1963), ch. 5; F. Grubb, *Vision of Reality* (1965), 85–94, index; Silk, in: *Judaism*, 14 (1965), 462–74; JC Lit. Suppl. (May 24, 1968), 3, 7. **ADD. BIBLIOGRAPHY:** ODNB online; D. Maccoby, *God Made Blind: Isaac Rosenberg, His Life and Poetry* (1999); P. Quinn (ed.), *British Poets of the Great War: Brooke, Rosenberg, Thomas: A Documentary Volume* (2000).

[Jon Silkin]

ROSENBERG, ISRAEL (1875–1956), U.S. Orthodox rabbi and communal leader. Rosenberg was born in Poland and attended the most prestigious *yeshivot* in Eastern Europe. Recognized as a prodigy, he was ordained in Russia in 1899 by Jehiel Michel *Epstein. He immigrated to the United States in 1902 and became the rabbi of a series of congregations: Poughkeepsie, N.Y. (1902–05); Bayonne, N.J. (1905–10); Burlington, Vermont (1910–12); Paterson, N.J. (1912–08); and Jersey City, N.J. (1919–20). In each community, he established a *talmud torah* school for young children. A leading authority on the laws of **kashrut*, he was appointed chief *kashrut* supervisor for several leading meat-packing companies.

Rosenberg was passionate about philanthropy. Under the auspices of the Agudat Harabbonim (*Union of Orthodox Rabbis of the United States Canada), he was instrumental in founding the Central Relief Committee (later absorbed by the American Jewish *Joint Distribution Committee) to help the poor. The following year (1915), he formed the Agudat Harabbonim's Ezras Torah Fund, which supports needy Torah scholars and their families throughout the world. He continually solicited contributions for major yeshivot in Europe and Ereẓ Israel (Palestine) and organized a high-level delegation, headed by Rabbi Abraham Isaac *Kook, comprising to conduct a fundraising campaign on their behalf in the United States in 1924.

Also concerned about the need to produce American-born Orthodox rabbis, Rosenberg was an active supporter of Yeshiva University's Rabbi Isaac Elchanan Seminary, serving as its first vice president (1910–12) and as acting dean during a leave of absence taken by Rabbi Bernard *Revel (1922–23).

Throughout his career, Rosenberg held the highest leadership positions in the Union of Orthodox Rabbis of the United States and Canada, serving as its vice president (1910, 1913); chairman of its executive committee (1911–12, 1914–15); a lifetime member of the presidium (1926–28, 1940–56); a two-term president (1928–30, 1940–43); and honorary president (1930–39). He traveled to Europe with a rabbinic delegation in 1919 to organize relief efforts for Jewish communities devastated by World War I and came to the rescue of Jewish refugees in Poland. He also headed the Talmud Publication Society of Agudat Harabbonim, which published a new edition of the Talmud to replace copies destroyed during the war. Years later, he represented Agudat Harabbonim as a member of a five-man commission that met with President Roosevelt in 1942 and received his assurance that Nazis guilty of perpetrating crimes against Jews would be punished.

Rosenberg was an ardent supporter of religious Zionism's aspirations to settle Ereẓ Israel and served as a *Mizrachi delegate to the World Zionist Congresses in London (1920) and Zurich (1929). He also contributed numerous articles on Jewish law to rabbinic journals, as well as essays to the Yiddish press.

[Bezalel Gordon (2nd ed.)]

ROSENBERG, JAMES NAUMBURG (1874–1970), U.S. lawyer, artist, philanthropist and author. Rosenberg, who was born in Allegheny City, Pennsylvania, engaged in private law practice until 1947; he then retired to pursue an art career; his paintings were subsequently hung in several major U.S. museums. Active in public and Jewish affairs, Rosenberg served as chairman of the Joint Distribution Committee in Europe (1921); founded the Society for Jewish Farm Settlements in Russia (1926), directing the population transfer of 30,000 Jews to Birobidzhan; helped found the Central Bank of Cooperative Institutions in Palestine; and founded the Agro-Joint. He was president of the Dominican Republic Settlement association formed to settle the 100,000 refugees that Trujillo's government offered to accept at the 1938 Evian Conference. Rosenberg led the U.S. delegation (1947) that sponsored the Genocide Convention adopted by the UN General Assembly in 1948. An art patron as well as a painter, Rosenberg founded New York's New Gallery which exhibited and sold the works of unknown artists. Rosenberg's written works include: *Corporate Reorganization and the Federal Court* (1924); *On the Steppes* (1972); *Painter's Self-Portrait* (1958); and *Unfinished Business* (1967), including personal papers.

ROSENBERG, LAZAR (1862–1936), painter. Rosenberg was born in Kaunas, Lithuania. At the age of 14, he entered the Vilna Art School, in 1879 he enrolled at the Koenigsberg Art Academy and in 1881 was admitted to the Academy in Berlin. There his painting of a copy of one of *Rembrandt's religious works won him a gold medal and brought him into prominence. In 1890 he moved to Paris and enrolled at the Académie Julian where he was influenced by the work of the Impressionists. An article on his work in the Zionist monthly *Ost und West*, February 1904, written by Julius Levin in Paris, reveals a series of studies of children and old Rembrandtesque Jewish heads. His admiration for the great Dutch painter may have inspired his move to Holland, where he lived from 1910 to 1935, paying annual visits to his family in Lithuania. He gained considerable prominence as a painter and draftsman in Holland, but working outside the main centers of modern art and being of a retiring nature, he has been unfairly neglected. Rosenberg's mature work is largely concerned with Dutch subjects – landscapes, the fishing village of Volendam, fishermen and their wives, interiors of Dutch houses, etc. The influence of Rembrandt remained constant, in the rich, expressive manner of his oil paint; but in the interiors with figures there is evidence of his admiration for older Dutch artists like Vermeer, as well as of Jozef *Israëls in his sympathetic treatment of simple people.

[Charles Samuel Spencer]

ROSENBERG, LOUIS (1893–1987), Canadian demographer, Jewish community worker. Rosenberg was the foremost demographer of Canadian Jewish life and a pioneer in the social scientific study of Canadian Jews. He was born in Poland and raised and educated in Leeds in the United Kingdom. He graduated with a bachelor of arts degree and a teachers certificate from Leeds University in 1914, and moved to Canada in 1915. Throughout his life, Rosenberg shared three strong passions: Zionism, socialism, and the social scientific study of Jewish life.

In Canada Rosenberg settled first in Saskatchewan, where from 1919 to 1940 he was the director of settlements of the Jewish Colonization Association. He believed in the Labor Zionist credo of personal and Jewish redemption through agricultural collective settlement. While in the Canadian west, he also became involved with the Canadian democratic left and the CCF. In 1935 he published the bestselling *Who Owns Canada?* under the pen name of Watt Hugh McCollum. A second edition was released in 1947. The tract critically analyzed Canada's Anglo-Protestant corporate power structure. It was while living in Saskatchewan that Rosenberg also began the research and writing of his classic and pioneering text, *Canada's Jews*, published in 1939 by the Canadian Jewish Congress. This book, in over 400 pages and with 273 tables, presented a comprehensive socio-demographic portrait of the Canadian Jewish community, based largely on data from the 1931 census and other sources, collected by the Dominion Bureau of Statistics, now Statistics Canada. Unmatched in either Jewish or Canadian ethnic demography in terms of its detailed, comprehensive nature, this study was reissued by McGill-Queen's University Press in 1993.

From 1940 to 1945, Rosenberg served as executive director of the western region of the Canadian Jewish Congress. In 1945 he moved to Montreal, where he became national research director of the Bureau of Social and Economic Research of the Canadian Jewish Congress. In fact, Rosenberg was the Bureau and produced a steady stream of research reports on Canadian Jewish demographic, sociological, and economic characteristics. A pioneer in Canadian and Jewish demography, during his lifetime Rosenberg's achievements and commitment to Jewish scientific research were either undervalued or unrecognized in both the Jewish communal world and in the general Canadian scholarly community.

[Morton Weinfeld (2nd ed.)]

ROSENBERG, LUDWIG (1903–1977), German trade union leader. Born in Berlin, Rosenberg was the son of a merchant, and received a commercial education. In 1925 he joined the Clerical Workers' Union and in 1928 became a full-time official of the union. After a course of study at the government school for economics and administration, Rosenberg was appointed head of the commercial section of the union. He went to Britain as a refugee in 1933, where he taught in the Workers' Educational Association and was a freelance journalist. During World War II, Rosenberg headed a section of the British Ministry of Labor. He continued to work for the revival of the German trade union movement and returned to Germany in 1946. In 1949, he became a member of the executive of the trade union movement, and was made the head of its foreign relations department in 1954. In 1959, he became vice president and, in 1962, president of the trade union movement. Rosenberg did much to bring the German trade union movement back into democratic politics, saying that it was not bad politics that affected character but bad character that corrupted politics. He enjoyed a high reputation in Germany and was the first president of the movement who did not come from the working classes. He visited Israel on several occasions and was instrumental in establishing friendly relations between the German trade union movement and the *Histadrut.

BIBLIOGRAPHY: F. Ahland, "Rosenberg. Der Buerger als Gewerkschafter" (Dissertation: Ruhr-Universitaet Bochum, 2002); D. Schuster *Ludwig Rosenberg. Ein Portrait* (1969).

[Monika Halbinger (2nd ed.)]

ROSENBERG, MOISHE (1904–1940). Mexican journalist and Yiddish writer. Born in Yablone, province of Warsaw in Poland. At age 18 he moved to Warsaw, where he took general studies. Together with a group of young people he published a journal in Yiddish. In 1929 Rosenberg immigrated to Mexico and in the next year published the first number of the journal *Der Veg*, which became one of the most important information channels of the Ashkenazi community in Mexico. In the middle of 1932 he failed to transform his weekly publication into a daily newspaper, though after 1937 he did succeed in publishing it three times a week.

In 1929 Rosenberg took part in the organization of the youth Zionist movement *Tzeirei Yehuda*. His Zionist position was very evident in *Der Veg*, but he avoided identification with any political party.

At the end of 1937 he started the translation and publication of *The History of the Jews* by Heinrich *Graetz, and until his death he succeeded to publish nine volumes.

[Efraim Zadoff (2nd ed.)]

ROSENBERG, STUART E. (1922–1990), Canadian rabbi. Arguably the most influential rabbi in Canada in the 1960s,

Rosenberg is remembered mostly for the bitter power struggle between him and the officers of Beth Tzedec Synagogue in Toronto, which claimed then to be the largest congregation in the world. It is a harsh fate for a man who inspired thousands and was the driving force behind the creation of several important Toronto Jewish institutions.

Born in Brooklyn, New York, Rosenberg was educated at the Flatbush Yeshiva elementary school, a public high school, Brooklyn College (B.A.), Columbia University (Ph.D. in Jewish history), and the Jewish Theological Seminary (M.H.L. and rabbi). In 1946, he took his first pulpit, Temple Beth El in Rochester, New York, where his dynamism and forceful manner of speaking made an impact in the synagogue and in the community at large. In 1956, he was called to the pulpit of Toronto's Beth Tzedec, formed through the merger of the two upscale inner-city synagogues founded by Jews of Eastern European origin. The new congregation had just erected a cathedral synagogue in a suburban setting, a short distance from the (Reform) Holy Blossom Temple, and its board sought a rabbi who would enable the new synagogue to outdistance its neighbor in prestige and influence. The new rabbi did not disappoint.

In his early years at Beth Tzedec, Rosenberg strengthened the congregational school, established the Prozdor education program for high school and university students, pushed for the establishment of a day school at a time when most Conservative Jews opposed all-day Jewish schools, and spearheaded the drive to bring the Ramah camping movement to Canada. At his prompting, Beth Tzedec established the first Jewish museum in Canada and sponsored an impressive array of adult education programs including hosting Elie *Wiesel and David *Ben-Gurion. On an average Sabbath morning, more than 1,000 people heard Rosenberg speak from the pulpit.

The rabbi also established himself as a community leader by becoming a force in charitable and professional organizations in the Jewish and general communities. In 1967 he became the first rabbi to head Toronto's annual UJA fund drive. Six years earlier, he had journeyed to the Soviet Union. Despite community pressure, he spoke out publicly against the oppression of Soviet Jews and succeeded in bringing the issue to the forefront of the community agenda. Rosenberg supported University of Toronto students in their campaign for a Jewish Studies program and, together with lay leaders, set up the Canadian Foundation for Jewish Culture in 1965 to promote teaching and research in Jewish Studies. He served as president. He wrote a regular column in the Toronto *Star*, published 17 books, and wrote dozens of articles on Judaism, Canadian Jews, theology, Quebec separation, and other topics.

Not all of Rosenberg's initiatives were successful. Notable failures were his attempt to establish a Canadian branch of the Jewish Theological Seminary and his campaign to obtain public funding for Jewish day schools. And, as might be expected, the successes often left hurt and resentful people in their wake.

By the late 1960s, Beth Tzedec congregants inspired by the *ḥavurah* movement and a young, new educational director, Rabbi Ben Hollander, began pressing for a more personal, more traditional, less rabbi-centered synagogue. Rosenberg resisted, and a bruising struggle between his supporters and opponents ensued, including lawsuits and accusations of both impropriety and criminal behavior. The suits were settled out of court. Rosenberg went on to Beth Torah, a small Toronto synagogue, but he never regained his former influence.

BIBLIOGRAPHY: S.E. Rosenberg, *The Real Jewish World: A Rabbi's Second Thoughts* (1984).

[Michael Brown (2nd ed.)]

ROSENBERG, YEHUDA YUDEL (1859–1935), Canadian rabbi and author. Rosenberg was born in Skaryszew, Poland, and acquired a thorough rabbinic and ḥasidic education. He also was exposed to maskilic literature and became fluent in Russian, earning an official permit to function as a rabbi in Poland. Having failed in business, he turned to rabbinic positions in Tarlow, Lublin, Warsaw and Lodz, where he attempted to create a ḥasidic following as the Tarler Rebbe (1909–13) before immigrating to North America. He arrived in North America in 1913, settling first in Toronto (1913–18), and then in Montreal (1919–35). In both cities he engaged in often heated disputes with other immigrant Orthodox rabbis over the supervision of kosher meat. In Montreal, he was instrumental in the creation of a united Orthodox rabbinate, and became vice president of the rabbinic council (Va'ad ha-Rabbanim) of Montreal's Jewish Community Council (Va'ad ha-'Ir) (1923–35).

Rosenberg was a prolific author in Hebrew and Yiddish in numerous genres. His rabbinic publications included a supercommentary on Tractate *Nedarim*, *Yaddot Nedarim* (1902), and *Me'or ha-Hashmal* (1924) on the halakhic issues surrounding electricity. He published several volumes of homilies, including *Ateret Tiferet* (1931), and *Peri Yehudah* (1935). A volume of responsa remains in page proof. He edited a short-lived rabbinic journal, *Kol Torah* (1908). He is best known for his re-edition and translation of the *Zohar* into Hebrew, entitled *Zohar Torah* (7 vols., 1924–30), and for his stories of the Maharal of Prague (*Nifla'ot Maharal im ha-Golem* (1909), and *Sefer Ḥoshen ha-Mishpat shel ha-Kohen ha-Gadol* (1913)), the first of which served to popularize the story of the Maharal and the Golem in the 20th century. In these works, he did not present himself as the author of the tales but rather as an editor of manuscripts emanating from a nonexistent "Royal Library of Metz." He further published tales of biblical heroes (*Sefer Eliyahu ha-Navi* (1910) and *Sefer Divrei ha-Yamim le-Shelomo ha-Melekh* (1914)) and of ḥasidic leaders (*Tiferet Mahar'el mi-Shpole* (1912); *Der Greiditzer* (1913?)), and a medical book (*Sefer Refa'el ha-Malakh* (1911)) which reflected in part his practice of homeopathic medicine.

BIBLIOGRAPHY: I. Robinson, in: *Canadian Jewish Studies* (1993), 41–58; I. Robinson, in: *Judaism* (1991), 61–78; S. Leiman, in: *Tradition* (2002), 26–58; E. Yassif (ed.), *Ha-Golem mi-Prag* (1991), 7–72.

[Ira Robinson (2nd ed.)]

ROSENBERG CASE, U.S. spy case involving Julius Rosenberg (1918–1953), his wife, Ethel (1920–1953), Morton Sobell (1918–), and others. They were charged and convicted of conspiracy to deliver U.S. atomic bomb secrets to Russia (1951). The case was tried in New York before Judge Irving R. *Kaufman, who declared he sought divine guidance before imposing sentence. The principal witnesses, judge, and chief prosecutor were Jews. The Rosenbergs were sentenced to death. There was a worldwide outcry: Some felt that the Rosenbergs were not guilty; others felt they should be permitted to live in case one day they might be persuaded to talk, and finally there were those who were against capital punishment in general or felt that peace-time spying should not be a capital offense. The case was carried to the U.S. Court of Appeals and then the Supreme Court. After executive clemency was denied by President Eisenhower, a further effort was made to secure a Supreme Court review. Justice Douglas granted a stay during the court's summer recess, but the court was summoned into extraordinary session and, by a narrow vote, set aside the stay and permitted the sentence to be carried out. Justice Felix *Frankfurter wrote a dissenting judgment, protesting the unseemly haste and lack of full review. The Rosenbergs were the first civilians convicted as spies to be executed in the U.S. Sobell was not charged with transmission of the bomb secrets but with having agreed to supply national defense data. He was sentenced to 30 years' imprisonment. His wife and mother worked tirelessly on his behalf and enlisted many distinguished persons in his cause. His wife raised and spent $1,000,000 on seven court appeals. Sobell was released by a United States Court of Appeals in 1969 after having served 17 and a half years. The case remained a highly controversial one, the subject of many books and articles by objective students as well as proponents of special causes. The Rosenbergs were executed on a Friday evening, which was regarded by some as evidence of antisemitism in the case; their children were raised under the name of their adoptive parents. Robert and Michael Meeropol have pressed for an opening of some secret records.

After the collapse of the Soviet Union and the opening of its archives, little doubt remains in the scholarly community over Julius' guilt, but the participation of Ethel is seen as marginal at most. Among those who switched positions was Smith College historian Allen Weinstein, who said that under today's circumstances Ethel would probably have not been indicted, let alone executed. She is listed in Soviet archives as Julius' wife but did not have a code name.

BIBLIOGRAPHY: *Rosenberg Letters* (1953); J. Root, *Betrayers: The Rosenberg Case* (1963); S.A. Fineberg, *Rosenberg Case* (1953); G. Flayfair and D. Sington, *Offenders* (1957), 186–213; J. Wexley, *Judgment of Julius and Ethel Rosenberg* (1955); W. and M. Schneir, *Invitation to an Inquest* (1965). **ADD. BIBLIOGRAPHY:** R. Meeropol, *An Execution in the Family: One Son's Journey* (2001); A. Weinstein and A. Vassilev, *The Haunted Wood: Soviet Espionage in America – The Stalin Era* (1999); R. Radosh and J. Milton, *The Rosenberg File: Second Edition* (1997); S. Roberts, *The Brother: The Untold Story of the Rosenberg Case* (2002). M. SOBELL: National Rosenberg-Sobell Committee, *Request for Senate Investigation* (1954); *International Herald Tribune* (Jan. 15, 1969).

[Elmer Gertz / Michael Berenbaum (2nd ed.)]

ROSENBLATT, BERNARD ABRAHAM (1886–1969), U.S. lawyer and Zionist. Rosenblatt, who was born in Gorodok, Galicia, was taken to the U.S. in 1892. Rosenblatt, as a Columbia University student, established in 1905 the first Zionist student organization, the Columbia University Zionist Organization, and was a founder of the Collegiate Zionist League at the end of 1906. From 1911, he served as the secretary of the American Zionist Federation. In 1916 he was an unsuccessful Democratic candidate for Congress and in 1921 he was appointed a New York City magistrate. As founder and first president of the American Zion Commonwealth (1915), a land development firm dedicated to facilitating Jewish settlement in Palestine, he supervised the land acquisition for, and subsequent establishment of, the towns of Herzliyyah, Afulah, Balfouria, and settlement in the Haifa Bay region. In his capacity as the first U.S. delegate to be appointed to the World Zionist Executive (1921), he was responsible for floating the first issue of Palestinian bonds in the U.S., setting the pattern for subsequent Israel bonds sales.

He was chairman of the board of Tiberias Hot Springs, Ltd. (1935–40), president of both the Jewish National Fund (1923–37) and the Keren Hayesod of America (1941–46), and vice president of the Zionist Organization of America (1927–48). Rosenblatt wrote: *Two Generations of Zionism* (1967), his autobiography; *Social Zionism* (1919); *Federated Palestine and the Jewish Commonwealth* (1941); and *The American Bridge to the Israel Commonwealth* (1959).

BIBLIOGRAPHY: A. Friesel, *Ha-Tenu'ah ha-Ẓiyyonit be-Arẓot ha-Berit ba-Shanim 1897–1914* (1970), 155–7 and index; S.S. Wise, *Challenging Years* (1949).

ROSENBLATT, H. (pseudonym of **Ḥayyim Royzenblit**; 1878–1956), U.S. Yiddish poet. Born in Rishoshe, Poland, he emigrated to the U.S. in 1892. From the age of 13, he worked in a sweatshop. Having tried 15 different professions, Rosenblatt turned to poetry, with which he had always been preoccupied. From 1900, he published his lyrics in Yiddish periodicals. At first he was under the influence of Morris *Rosenfeld and followed the realistic tradition of the "*Sweatshop Poets," but he also felt the impact of the Yiddish lyric masters S.S. *Frug, Abraham *Reisen, *Yehoash, and of English and American poets. He reproduced in Yiddish verse the rhythms, alliterations, and assonances of Edgar Allen Poe's "The Raven" and Oscar Wilde's "Ballad of Reading Gaol." In symbolism he discovered a more congenial style for his lyrics. The impressionistic literary movement, Di *Yunge, then hailed him as its precursor and ally. In 1916 he edited the Detroit literary weekly *Detroyter Vokhnblat*, obtaining contributions from poets and novelists of Di Yunge. In 1921 he settled in Los Angeles where for more than a third of a century he was a central figure in Yiddish cultural life. The collected poems of his pre-California period appeared in 1915, but his best lyrics, ballads, and contemplative verses were the later works included in the volumes *Odems Kinder* ("Adam's Children," 1944), *Mayn Likhtike Nesiye* ("My Illustrious Journey," 1944), *In Shenstn Tog fun Harbst* ("On the Nicest Day of Autumn," 1953), and *Far-Nakht* ("Evening," 1957). Rosenblatt discovered for Yiddish poetry the American West, especially California's deserts, mountains, and ocean, and versified legends of Native Americans. His poems, set to music by various composers, had a calm, optimistic attitude and a gentle humor.

BIBLIOGRAPHY: Rejzen, Leksikon, 4 (1929), 299–305; J. Glatstein, *In Tokh Genumen* (1956), 255–60; S.D. Singer, *Dikhter un Prozaiker* (1959), 14–18; E. Brownstone, *Fun Eygn Hoyz* (1963), 96–100; S. Liptzin, *Flowering of Yiddish Literature* (1963), 197–202; Shunami, Bibl, nos. 4195–96. **ADD. BIBLIOGRAPHY:** B. Rivkin, *Yidishe Dikhter in Amerike* (1947), 119–36; Y. Pat, *Shmuesn mit Yidishe Shrayber* (1954), 243–60; B. Grin, *Yidishe Shrayber in Amerike* (1963), 101–4; Sh. Niger, *Yidishe Shrayber fun Tsvantsikstn Yorhundert*, 1 (1972), 336–48; J. Glatstein, *In der Velt mit Yidish* (1972), 26–30; LNYL, 8 (1981), 430–33.

[Sol Liptzin]

ROSENBLATT, JOSEF (Yossele; 1882–1933), *ḥazzan* and composer. Born in Belaya Tserkov, Russia, Rosenblatt toured Eastern Europe as a child prodigy, conducting synagogue services together with his father. When he was 18 years old he was appointed *ḥazzan* in Mukachevo. He moved to Bratislava in 1901 and to Hamburg five years later. In 1912 he emigrated to the U.S. and became *ḥazzan* of the Ohab Zedek Congregation in New York. Rosenblatt became widely known in the U.S. and Europe through extensive concert tours. In 1918 he refused, on religious grounds, to appear with the Chicago Opera Company in Halevy's *La Juive* at $1,000 per performance, but in 1928 he did allow his voice to be heard in the first full sound film, Al *Jolson's *The Jazz Singer.* The most popular *ḥazzan* of his time, Rosenblatt earned huge salaries and concert fees. Nevertheless, he was almost continually in debt, giving much of his income to charity and to the support of members of his family. Naïve in business matters, he agreed to provide financial backing for a dubious Jewish newspaper venture. In 1925 he was forced to declare bankruptcy but undertook a rigorous schedule of appearances in vaudeville to pay off his debts. Rosenblatt's immense popularity with Jewish and gentile audiences never waned. He died in Jerusalem while working on a Yiddish film. Rosenblatt possessed a tenor voice with the exceptional range of two-and-a-half octaves of full voice combined with a remarkably agile falsetto. He constantly impressed his listeners with his brilliant coloratura coupled with the sweetness and control of his voice and his "sob" in devotional passages. He composed hundreds of liturgical melodies that reflect his Ḥasidic background in their tunefulness; many of these achieved great popularity and a permanent place in the repertoire of the synagogue. Some of his compositions, however, are of little melodic interest, while others demand a vocal range as wide as that of the composer and are therefore rarely sung by other *ḥazzanim*. Some of his best-known pieces appeared in the collection *Tefillot Yosef* (1907; 1927^2). The extent of his popular appeal and his influence on synagogue music may be gauged from the widespread distribution of his numerous recordings, which were repeatedly reissued even many years after his death.

BIBLIOGRAPHY: S. Rosenblatt, *Yossele Rosenblatt* (1954; Heb. trans., 1961); A. Holde, *Jews in Music* (1959), 33–35; Jewish Ministers Cantors' Association of America, *Geshikhte fun Khazones* (1924), 188–9; idem, *Goldene Yoyvl Zhurnal* (1947), 19–20; P. Szerman, in: *Di Khazonim Velt* (June 1934), 1–2; S. Kaufman, *ibid.*, 3–4; S. Mandel, in: *Morning Journal* (Jan. 20, 1948), 5; I. Goldfarb, in: *Proceedings of the Seventh Annual Conference-Convention of the Cantors' Assembly of America* (1954), 24–27; Sendrey, Music, indices.

[David M.L. Olivestone]

ROSENBLATT (Weizel), MORDECAI BEN MENAHEM (d. 1906), Lithuanian and Polish rabbi and author. Rosenblatt was born in Antopol, district of Grodno, and studied in the yeshivot of Semyatich and Pinsk. He occupied himself with Kabbalah and although unconnected with the Ḥasidic movement achieved renown as a *Ẓaddik whose blessings were effective. He served as rabbi in various cities – in Buthen, whence his designation as "the *Ẓaddik* of Buthen," in Korelitz from 1887, in Oshmyany from 1892, and from 1904 until his death in Slonim. Although he wrote many responsa and novellae to the Talmud, only one of his works, *Hadrat Mordekhai* (1899), containing responsa and novellae, has been published.

BIBLIOGRAPHY: A. Ben-Ezra, *R. Mordekhai mi-Slonim* (1958); Lichtenstein, in: *Pinkas Slonim*, 1 (c. 1962), 123–7.

ROSENBLATT, SAMUEL (1902–1983), U.S. rabbi and scholar. Rosenblatt, son of the famous *ḥazzan* Josef (Yossele) *Rosenblatt, was born in Bratislava and was taken to the United States in 1912. He was a *cum laude* graduate of City College (1921) and received a rabbinical degree from the Jewish Theological Seminary (1925); he studied in Jerusalem on a fellowship from the American Schools of Oriental Research; and received a Ph.D. from Columbia (1927). In 1926 he served as a rabbi in Trenton and then from 1927 onward Rabbi Rosenblatt served Congregation Beth Tefiloh in Baltimore, Maryland. He headed the Baltimore Board of Rabbis (1952); *Mizrachi (1938–42); and the American Jewish Congress (1942–47). He lectured at Columbia University from 1926 to 1928 and then was associated with Johns Hopkins University from 1930, Rosenblatt taught Jewish literature until 1947, and thereafter Oriental languages.

His writings include: *High Ways to Perfection of Abraham Maimonides* (2 vols., 1927–38); *Interpretation of the Bible in the Mishnah* (1935); a translation of Saadiah Gaon's *Book of Beliefs and Opinions* (1948); and *Yossele Rosenblatt* (1954), as well as volumes of sermons and occasional writings. His memoirs appeared as "The Days of My Years," published in weekly installments in *Baltimore Jewish Times*, 1974 onward, and he was also the author of a weekly column in *Baltimore News-American* (1960), and a contributor to *Jewish Quarterly Review.*

ROSENBLATT, SOL ARIEH (1900–1968), U.S. lawyer. Rosenblatt was born in Omaha, Nebraska. In 1935 he began a private law practice in New York, in the course of which he handled the litigation of many celebrities. In 1934 Rosenblatt was appointed administrator of the National Recovery Administration's division on amusement and transportation codes. Later that year he became national administrator of code compliance and was responsible for setting the first minimum wage for theater performers. In 1940 Rosenblatt was general counsel to the Democratic National Committee, and from 1942 to 1945 he was a colonel in the U.S. Army Air Force. From 1935 to 1940 and from 1947 to 1968, Rosenblatt was impartial chairman of the New York coat and suit industry, responsible for supervising labor conditions.

BIBLIOGRAPHY: *New York Times* (May 5, 1968), 87.

[Edward L. Greenstein]

ROSENBLOOM, CARROLL (1907–1979), businessman and U.S. National Football League team owner who ran some of the game's most successful teams from the 1950s to the 1970s, a friend of celebrities and known for gambling on football and horses. He worked in his father's shirt company in Baltimore after attending the University of Pennsylvania, where he was a member of Jewish fraternity ZBT. He was so successful he retired at 33. As World War II began, he returned to business and manufactured material for military work uniforms. In 1953, NFL commissioner Bert Bell, his football coach at Penn, convinced him to organize a group to rescue a failing franchise and create the Baltimore Colts. Rosenbloom's initial personal cash investment for 51 percent ownership was $13,000. Five years later the Colts defeated the New York Giants 23–17 in the NFL championship, an overtime contest sometimes called "The Greatest Game Ever Played." The Colts repeated as NFL champions in 1959, and remained an elite team through the 1960s. The Colts went into Super Bowl III in 1969 against the American Football League's New York Jets as heavy favorites, but were defeated in one of the greatest upsets in U.S. sports history when Joe Namath led the Jets to a 16–7 victory. Rosenbloom and fellow owners Art *Modell (Cleveland Browns), and Art Rooney (Pittsburgh Steelers) facilitated the NFL merger with the AFL by moving to the newly created AFC. The Colts won the first post-merger Super Bowl in 1971, and two years later Rosenbloom traded the Colts to Robert Irsay for the Los Angeles Rams, paying Rosenbloom a reported $3 million on the side to seal the deal. An active owner, Rosenbloom made the Rams a successful team in the 1970s that won six consecutive division titles. Rosenbloom died in a mysterious drowning in 1979. His widow, Georgia, whom he had met at the Palm Beach home of presidential father and businessman Joseph P. Kennedy, became the Rams' majority owner. Rosenbloom, with business associates Morris Mac Schwebel and Lou Chesler, also acquired the film libraries of Warner Brothers and Twentieth Century Fox, major U.S. movie studios launched by Jews. The deals came under U.S. Securities and Exchange Commission scrutiny.

[Alan D. Abbey (2nd ed.)]

ROSENBLOOM, MAX EVERITT (**"Slapsie Maxie"**; 1904–1976), U.S. boxer, light heavyweight champion 1930–34, member of Ring Boxing Hall of Fame and International Boxing Hall of Fame. Rosenbloom was born in Leonard's Bridge, Conn., the son of Russian-Jewish immigrants, His family moved in 1907 to New York's Lower East Side, where Rosenbloom's father worked as a shoemaker, and later to Harlem. He started boxing at the Union Settlement House in Harlem, influenced by an older brother who fought as Leonard Rose, and held various odd jobs, such as elevator operator, railroad laborer, and lifeguard while continuing to box. Rosenbloom first fought professionally at 19 on October 8, 1923, and thereafter he fought often: by the end of 1925 Rosenbloom had fought 48 professional fights with only six losses, and was ranked 10th in the middleweight division in the 1925 annual rankings by *Ring Magazine*. Rosenbloom began his career as a slugger, but because he was not a strong puncher he soon developed an unorthodox hit-and-run style of smacking opponents with open gloves, which led New York sportswriter Damon Runyon to tag Rosenbloom with the nickname "Slapsie."

On October 21, 1929, two months after the massacre of Jews in Hebron, Rosenbloom – along with Ruby *Goldstein and Jackie "Kid" *Berg – fought at a benefit at Madison Square Garden on behalf of the "Palestine Relief Fund." Nearly 20,000 contributors paid $101,000 to attend. On June 25, 1930, Rosenbloom beat Jimmy Slattery in 15 rounds to win the world light heavyweight championship, as recognized by the New York Athletic Commission. He was acclaimed the undisputed champion when he defeated Lou Scozza on July 14, 1932. Rosenbloom disliked training and was considered a playboy outside the ring. Nevertheless, he was the busiest titleholder in boxing history, fighting 109 times while champion – only seven were title defenses – the equivalent of one bout every 15 days. Rosenbloom lost the title on November 16, 1934, to Bob Olin, although many sportswriters at ringside believed Rosenbloom had won. It was the 10th and last title match ever between Jewish boxers. His final record in 299 bouts across 16 years was 210 wins (19 KOs), 38 losses, 26 draws, 23 no decisions, and two no contests. After his retirement from boxing, Rosenbloom parlayed his colorful reputation into a successful acting and night club career, often portraying a punch-drunk fighter. He also ran successful nightclubs, Slapsie Maxie's, in San Francisco and Los Angeles. Rosenbloom was inducted into the Ring Boxing Hall of Fame in 1972 and the International Boxing Hall of Fame in 1993.

[Elli Wohlgelernter (2nd ed.)]

ROSENBLOOM, SOLOMON (1866–1925), U.S. banker and philanthropist. Rosenbloom, born in Grodno, Russia, emigrated to the U.S. in 1889 and eventually settled in Pittsburgh.

Extremely active in Jewish affairs and a vigorous supporter of settlement in Palestine, he endowed Jewish studies at the Hebrew University (1922) and served as treasurer and board member of the Palestine Development Council. Rosenbloom was also a founder and president of the Hebrew Institute of Pittsburgh, as well as a trustee of the Jewish Theological Seminary of America and a member of the United Synagogue of America's executive council.

His wife, CELIA NEUMARK ROSENBLOOM, born in Lyck, Germany, was active with her husband in communal and philanthropic work. She donated the building of the Institute of Jewish Studies at the Hebrew University, on Mt. Scopus, Jerusalem, in her husband's memory. An executive board member of the American Friends of the Hebrew University, she was an organizer and honorary president of the Women's Division of the American Jewish Congress.

Their son CHARLES (1898–1973) was also a prominent financier and active in many Jewish causes. He was chairman of the United Jewish Appeal and president of the Jewish Federation of Charities in Pittsburgh. He was also chairman of commissioners of the housing authority in Pittsburgh.

ROSENBLUM, FRANK (1887–1973), U.S. labor leader. Born in New York, Rosenblum moved with his family to Philadelphia, Pennsylvania, where he learned the trade of cloth cutting and joined Local 110 of the United Garment Workers (UGW). In 1908 he settled in Chicago where, as a member of Cutters Local 61, he was active in organizing the clothing workers. During the 1910 general strike in the industry, Rosenblum was active as a strike leader, serving as secretary of the strike committee. The strike settlement, arrived at four months later, contained a provision for arbitration of disputes and an agreement not to discriminate against workers for union activities. In 1914, a split took place in the UGW and Rosenblum was elected vice president of one of the factions, the Amalgamated Clothing Workers of America (ACWA), and later director of its Western Organization Department.

During the 1930s, Rosenblum devoted his special organizing abilities to the new Committee for Industrial Organization. He served as a vice president of the Congress of Industrial Organizations (CIO) from 1940 until 1955, when it merged with the AFL. In 1940, when ACWA general-president Sidney *Hillman took up a position in a government agency, Rosenblum was elected general secretary-treasurer, a post which he held until his retirement in 1972.

Throughout his career, Rosenblum was active in the struggle for world peace. He was one of the first major U.S. labor leaders to speak out against U.S. involvement in the Vietnam War and was a founder of the Labor Leadership Assembly for Peace in 1967 and of Labor for Peace in June 1972, both formed with the aim of bringing the Vietnam -War to an end. In 1963, Rosenblum received the Clarence Darrow Humanitarian Award for services to the Chicago community. He was a staunch supporter of Israel and the *Histadrut.

ROSENBLUM, HERZL (1903–1991), Israeli journalist. Born in Latvia, Rosenblum studied law at the University of Vienna. An associate of Ze'ev *Jabotinsky, he made *aliyah* in 1935, after which he worked as a journalist on the Revisionist newspaper *Ha-Boker.* He was a leading member of the "Jewish State" Party, and as its representative signed the Declaration of Independence (signing with the Hebraized translation of his name, Herzl Vardi). Giving up a promising political career in the Knesset, Rosenblum was appointed editor of **Yedioth Aharonoth*, after the "putsch" in 1948 by its editor, Dr. Azriel *Carlebach, and the founding of the **Maariv* newspaper. With the newspaper's newsgathering carried out by Dov *Yudkovsky, Rosenblum's work comprised writing a signed editorial column which appeared daily until his retirement in 1983. Taking a Revisionist line, the widely read column, with its telegraphic style, also reflected popular Israeli opinion. In *Yedioth Aharonoth*'s tradition of being the "nation's newspaper," Rosenblum ensured that the newspaper's op-ed pages were open to a broad spectrum of political opinion. His son and grandson, Moshe *Vardi and Doron Rosenblum, were also journalists, Vardi becoming editor of *Yedioth.* His memoirs, *Tippot min Ha-Yam* ("Drops from the Ocean"), were published in 1988.

[Yoel Cohen (2nd ed.)]

ROSENBLUM, SIGMUND GEORGIEVICH (known as **Sidney Reilly** and often referred to as "**Reilly, Ace of Spies**"; 1874–1925?), British spy. Born in Bedzin, Russian Poland, as Shlomo ben Hirsh Rozenblum (and a descendant of the Vilna Gaon), Rosenblum came to London around 1895, and from 1899 was known as Sidney George Reilly. His first exploit occurred in 1895, while serving as cook for a party of three British officers, who were exploring the Amazon in Brazil. The officers were attacked by their bearers and guides, and Rosenblum came to their defense. Rosenblum returned with them to London, where he worked for the British Secret Service, especially in the Far East. He also earned a fortune as an armaments contractor. Before World War I, he played an important role in uncovering the secrets of the German armaments program. During the war (in which he received several medals), he was parachuted many times by the Allies into Germany, enlisted in the German Army, deserted when an assignment was completed, and reenlisted under another name. On one occasion, he murdered a German staff colonel for whom he served as a driver, dressed in the former's uniform, and took his place at a meeting where Kaiser William II and Generals Ludendorff and Hindenburg discussed war plans. Rosenblum was involved in an abortive plot to overthrow the Bolsheviks after the Russian Revolution. He also found time for philandering and in 1918 eight Russian women claimed him as their legal husband. His last mission to Russia took place in 1925. Rosenblum made contact with what he believed to be an anticommunist society, fell into a trap set by GPU (Russia's secret police), and was never heard of again. Reacting to a British television series, the Russians said he was executed in 1925. R.

Bruce Lockhart, however, a noted British agent, thought he was still alive in 1932 and cooperating with the Russians. The balance of evidence, however, suggests that he was executed by the Soviets in Moscow in November 1925. In the 1970s, a popular British television series, *Reilly, Ace of Spies*, was made about his life.

BIBLIOGRAPHY: R.B. Lockhart, *Ace of Spies* (1967). **ADD. BIBLIOGRAPHY:** ODNB online; M. Kettle, *Sidney Reilly* (1983).

[Morton Mayer Berman]

ROSENBUSCH, KARL HARRY FERDINAND (1836–1914), German geologist. Rosenbusch, who was born at Einbeck, was appointed professor of petrography at Strasbourg University in 1873 and in 1878 became professor of mineralogy and geology at Heidelberg, where he spent the rest of his life. From the 1870s, when he began to publish important works on the subject, until his death, he was one of the great pioneers of petrographic research, and these years were often referred to in the profession as the "Rosenbusch period."

His *Mikroskopische Physiographic der petrographisch wichtigen Mineralen* (1873; with E. Wuefling, 1904^4) identified rocks by studying the morphological, physical and chemical properties of their mineral components. It became a standard textbook on the microscopic investigation of rocks for many generations of students and scholars. No less important was his *Mikroskopische Physiographie der massigen Gesteine* (1877, 1896), which made a fundamental contribution to the development of systematic petrography. Combining microscopic and chemical research with field observations, this book gave a strong impulse to the discussion of genetic problems and the passive or active behavior of the magma in mountain building. Rosenbusch's most widely-used textbook was *Elemente der Gesteinslehre* (1898), which laid great emphasis on rock-chemistry and on the geodynamic processes in the formation of crystalline schists. In this field, he had made a classic contribution as early as 1877 through his study, *Steiger Schriefer und ihre Kontakt-Zone an den Graniten von Barr-Andlau uńd Hohwald.*

[Leo Picard]

ROSENCOF, MAURICIO (1933–), Uruguayan playwright, novelist, and poet. Born in Florida, Uruguay, he became one of the country's leading writers and journalists. He was a leader in the underground National Liberation Movement (Tupamaros), and in 1972 he was detained by the military government and held as a political prisoner in complete isolation for more than 11 years. His memoirs as a detainee are compiled in the three-volume *Memorias del calabozo* (1987–88). Rosencof is a major dramatist in Uruguay. His works *Las ranas* (1961), *La valija* (1965), *El saco de Antonio* (1985), and *... y nuestros caballos serán blancos* (1985) are classics of 20th century Uruguayan theater. His early works almost exclusively consisted of a critical view of Uruguayan society and political processes with particular emphasis on the struggle for social justice. Many of his post-incarceration works may be classified as children's literature, such as *Canciones para alegrar a una niña* (1985), *Leyendas del abuelo de la tarde* (1990), and *Los trabajitos de Dios* (2001). The novel *Las cartas que no llegaron* (2000) represents the author's first effort to write a specifically Jewish-themed text. The novel is an intimate, personal memoir of his time spent imprisoned as a political detainee interwoven with his family's connection to the Holocaust. In doing so, Rosencof joins a number of Latin American Jewish authors who find common ground in the persecution of so-called subversives, tortured and killed in concentration camps by neo-fascist military governments, and Jews murdered under European Nazism.

[Darrell B. Lockhart (2nd ed.)]

ROSENDALE, SIMON WOLFE (1842–1937), U.S. lawyer and public servant. Rosendale, who was born in Albany, New York, received his early education at the school maintained by Rabbi I.M. *Wise. He was admitted to the bar in 1863 and practiced thereafter in his native city. He was recorder of Albany (1868–72) and attorney general of New York State (1892–94). Rosendale was an active worker for the Union of American Hebrew Congregations and B'nai B'rith. He was a founder of the Jewish Publication Society of America and of the American Jewish Historical Society. He served as a vice president of the latter and contributed to its proceedings.

BIBLIOGRAPHY: I. Lewi, in: AJHSP, 35 (1939), 320–2.

[Sefton D. Temkin]

ROSENFARB, CHAVA (1923–), Yiddish writer. Born in Lodz, Rosenfarb began writing at age eight and was educated at the Medem school and then at a Polish high school. In the Lodz ghetto, her poetry brought her to the attention of Simkha-Bunim *Shayevitsh, author of the epic poem "*Lekh Lekho*," who became her mentor and introduced her to the writers' group in the ghetto. Upon liquidation of the ghetto (August 1944), Rosenfarb was deported to Auschwitz, and thence to Sasel and Bergen-Belsen, where she was liberated. In 1950, she immigrated to Montreal. Her literary output after 1947 was prodigious, including four volumes of poetry: *Di Balade fun Nekhtikn Vald* ("The Ballad of Yesterday's Forest," 1947); *Dos Lid fun Yidishn Kelner Avrom* ("The Song of the Jewish Waiter Avrom," 1948); *Geto un Andere Lider* ("Ghetto and Other Poems," 1950), and *Aroys fun Gan-Eydn* ("Out of Paradise," 1965). Her play *Der Foygl fun Geto* ("The Bird of the Ghetto"), about the final days of Vilna Ghetto leader Isaac *Wittenberg, was performed in Hebrew in Israel by Habimah in 1966. Dissatisfied with both poetry and drama as means of expression for Holocaust experience, Rosenfarb turned to fiction, publishing the trilogy *Der Boym fun Lebn* (1972; *The Tree of Life*, 1985), chronicling the destruction of Jewish Lodz in 1939–44; it won the Manger Prize in 1979. It remains one of the very few novels – as opposed to memoirs or diaries – written about the Holocaust by an actual survivor. While Rosenfarb's next novel, *Botshani* (1982), is a prequel to *Der Boym fun Lebn*, the shadow of the Holocaust hovers proleptically over the novel, as is the case in all of Rosenfarb's work (Eng. tr. in 2 vols., *Bociany* and *Of Lodz and Love*, 2000). Rosenfarb's novel *Briv tsu Abrashn* ("Letters to Abrasha," 1992) describes the horrors of the concentration camps. Most of Rosenfarb's essays and stories appeared in *Di Goldene Keyt*; some of the stories appeared in a translated collection, *Survivors: Seven Short Stories* (2004). Rosenfarb also published non-fiction in English, notably "Feminism and Yiddish Literature: A Personal Approach," which problematizes the double marginalization of a woman writer who is also a Yiddish writer. In 1994, she published a pamphlet called *Yiddish Poets in Canada*. Rosenfarb was one of the foremost Yiddish writers of the second half of the 20th century.

BIBLIOGRAPHY: N. Ravvin, in: *A House of Words* (1997), 85–98. J. Sharlett, in: *Pakn Treger* (1997), 50–65; E. Naves, *Putting Down Roots: Montreal's Immigrant Writers* (1998); G. Morgentaler, in: *Holocaust Literature* (2003), with bibliography.

[Goldie Morgentaler (2nd ed.)]

ROSENFELD, ABRAHAM ISAAC JACOB (1914–1980s?), rabbi and *ḥazzan*. Rosenfeld was born in Jerusalem and studied at the Yeshivah Etz Ḥayyim and Merkaz ha-Rav there. He served as both rabbi and *ḥazzan* to the Finchley Synagogue in London (1941–70) and was appointed honorary president of the Cantors' Association of England. He served as an army chaplain and in 1971 was appointed rabbi of the Wellington, New Zealand, congregation, returning to Israel in 1978. His translation into English of the *Seliḥot* service (1956) and the *Kinot* for the Tishah be-Av (1965) received the approbation of the chief rabbi of England, Rabbi Sir Israel *Brodie. He composed a special memorial prayer for the victims of the Holocaust.

[Akiva Zimmerman]

ROSENFELD, AHARON (1846–1916), Hebrew writer. Born in Volhynia, Rosenfeld taught in various places and in his later years served as government rabbi of Bakhmut.

Rosenfeld, who usually signed his pieces "Avner," wrote poetry and stories and was chief assistant and stylist for the first Hebrew daily, *Ha-Yom*. He edited the popular children's reader *Gan Sha'ashu'im* (1880), which opened a new era in the field of children's literature in Hebrew. He also published an epic poem entitled *Hillel ha-Zaken* ("Hillel the Elder," 1881).

BIBLIOGRAPHY: Waxman, Literature, 4 (1960^2), 442.

[Getzel Kressel]

ROSENFELD, FANNY (1905–1969), track and field athlete, Olympic gold and silver medal winner, Canada's Female Athlete of the Half Century (1950), and sports journalist. Rosenfeld was born in Russia in 1905 and immigrated with her family to Canada as a child. She grew up in Barrie, Ontario, before moving to Toronto in 1922. By 1925 Rosenfeld, widely known as "Bobby," had won several Canadian titles and set a number of Canadian track and field records. In 1924 she won the Toronto Women's Tennis Championship and was also a member of several championship basketball, softball, and hockey teams, including some sponsored by the YMHA in Toronto.

Rosenfeld represented Canada at the 1928 Olympic Games in Amsterdam, the first time that women's track and field appeared on the Olympic program. She ran for Canada in three events, the 400-meter relay, the 100-meter dash, and the 800-meter race. She won a gold medal in the 400-meter relay and a silver in the 100-meter dash and took fifth place in the 800-meter race. Controversy arose over the finish in the 100-meter dash. Canadian fans were convinced that Rosenfeld actually won even though the medal went to American competitor Elizabeth Robinson. In the 800-meter race, she held back to run beside a faltering teammate in order to offer moral support. She came in fifth in that race when she could easily have won a gold or silver medal. Rosenfeld remains the only Jewish athlete to ever win a gold medal in track and field at the Olympics.

In 1929 Rosenfeld's sporting career was curtailed and finally ended in 1933 as a result of severe arthritis. In 1939 Rosenfeld began a 20-year career writing on sports for Canada's *Globe and Mail* newspaper. Her column, "Feminine Sports Reel," focused on women in sports and sport issues across Canada. In 1950, Rosenfeld was honored as Canada's Woman Athlete of the Half-Century. Public parks in Toronto and Barrie have been named in her honor, and in 1996, Canada Post issued a stamp in her memory. The annual Canadian Female Athlete of the Year awarded is also named in Fanny Rosenfeld's honor and in 2000 the Jewish Women's Archive in the United States named Rosenfeld one of their Women of Valor.

[Avi Hyman and Brenda Cappe (2nd ed.)]

ROSENFELD, ISAAC (1918–1956), U.S writer and critic. Isaac Rosenfeld enters literary history as a footnote to the life and career of Saul Bellow. In the early 1930s, Bellow and Rosenfeld were schoolmates at Tuley High School in the Humboldt Park neighborhood of Chicago. As young men they went to New York together to make their careers. Bellow would emerge as one of the superstars in the American firmament, while Rosenfeld would be recalled in a Jungian way as his shadow.

Rosenfeld began publishing short stories in *Partisan Review* as early as 1944, the year of Bellow's novel *Dangling Man*. His novel, *Passage from Home* appeared in 1946, a year before Bellow's *The Victim*. He was also making a name for himself as a book reviewer for the *New Republic* in 1942, where he would remain for over 10 years, while also writing for *Partisan Review*, *Commentary*, the *Nation*, *Kenyon Review*, and *Harper's*, the major journals of opinion of his day. Those reviews, slashing and acerbic in the New York intellectual manner of their day, belied the more tender and vulnerable spirits that found voice in his fiction, a fiction largely of what his generation referred to as "alienation."

He was the son of one of those embittered and distant Jewish fathers that turn up all over Jewish fiction of his generation. Sam Rosenfeld, whom Isaac referred to as "Ozymandias,"

Shelley's king of kings, was a severe, dictatorial figure. Since his mother had died when he was just 22 months old, Rosenfeld drew such emotional nourishment as he could from two spinster aunts, who were the mainstays of childhood.

Passage from Home was an auspicious debut for a young writer (just 28 in 1946). A postwar disenchantment novel, typical of its time, it was a public exhibition of his alienation, in which he wrote passionately about his childhood, as if by doing so he could stanch his wounds and cleanse his spirit. The hero, Bernard Miller, a name Americanized as though to universalize him, is Isaac Rosenfeld in all but name, and his struggles with his father are the very same that had driven Rosenfeld from the home of Ozymandias. The Jewish family in *Passage from Home* is a weakened institution, in which the father's tyranny has been divorced from any semblance of religious authority. An American, Chicago born, Bernard Miller has learned – to borrow a formula from Abraham Joshua Heschel – the danger and gloom of this world but not the infinite beauty of heaven or the holy mysteries of piety.

Rosenfeld's essays and some short stories possessed fair amounts of traction and thrust, and much that remains memorable in his career can be found in posthumous collections titled *An Age of Enormity* (essays) and *Alpha and Omega* (stories).

Despite a certain dishevelment that marked his fiction, Rosenfeld was a vivid individual well remembered for his playfulness and his capacity for mimicry and invention. Bellow recalled his prevailing sense of life as one of "hard-headed gemutlichkeit." His writing at its best was saturated with his trademark blend of passion and intelligence. In his stories, essays, and journals, he performed a sort of Reichian character analysis, looking beneath the skin of writing or writers for blockages, symptoms, armor, and open corridors to feeling. He wrote as a physician of the will, and as a result his book reviews tended to be pathograms, CAT scans of malignant tissues.

Rosenfeld died in 1956 of a heart attack at the age of 38. But his legacy was to be memorialized by others, in memoirs by Irving Howe, Alfred Kazin, and William Barrett, in the novel *To An Early Grave* by Wallace Markfield, and, most notably in Bellow's "Zetland" story. Indeed, the character of the ill-fated poet Von Humboldt Fleisher in Bellow's novel *Humboldt's Gift* is thought by some to owe as much to Rosenfeld as to Delmore Schwartz.

BIBLIOGRAPHY: I. Rosenfeld, *Preserving the Hunger: An Isaac Rosenfeld Reader*, ed. and intro. M. Shechner (1988); J. Atlas, "Golden Boy," in: *The New York Review of Books* (June 29, 1989); S.J. Zipperstein, "The First Loves of Isaac Rosenfeld," in: *Jewish Social Studies*, 5:1–2 (Fall 98/Winter 99); idem, "Isaac Rosenfeld's Dybbuk and Rethinking Literary Biography," in: *Partisan Review*, 69:1 (2002).

[Mark Shechner (2nd ed.)]

ROSENFELD, JONAH (1880–1944), Yiddish novelist and short story writer. Born in the Ukraine, he was orphaned at 13, when both parents died during a cholera epidemic. He then wandered from town to town before settling in Odessa, where his older brother arranged an apprenticeship for him with a turner. In 1904, encouraged by Ḥ.N. *Bialik and I.L. *Peretz, he wrote his first short story, *Der Lernyingl* ("The Apprentice"), based on his own experiences. His stories soon found an audience in Yiddish periodicals. After 1909, they were reprinted in book form, culminating in a six-volume edition of his *Gezamlte Shriftn* ("Collected Works," 1924), which also included descriptions of his experiences before he left Russia (1920). After his arrival in New York (1921), his story "*Konkurentn*" ("Competitors," in Howe/Greenberg) was dramatized and successfully staged (1922), followed by his comedy *Arayngefaln* ("Lapsed," 1924). His significant later works included *Er un Zi* ("He and She," 1927), "the diary of an ex-writer"; *Eyner Aleyn* ("All Alone," 1940; Heb. 1964), a vivid autobiographical depiction of Rosenfeld's early apprenticeship, highly praised in the Yiddish press. Rosenfeld was a perceptive portrayer of strange characters and their complex psychic states. He viewed himself as a Yiddish Maxim Gorky whose short stories and autobiographical fiction chronicled the inner life of the Jewish working class in Odessa and the Lower East Side tenements. He is one of the most original Yiddish prose writers of his generation.

BIBLIOGRAPHY: Rejzen, Leksikon, 3 (1929), 133–9; B. Rivkin, *Undzere Prosaiker* (1951), 140–56; G. Sapozhnikov, *Fun di Tifenishn* (1958), 15–123; Z. Zylbercweig, *Leksikon fun Yidishn Teater*, 4 (1963), 2808–11; I. Howe and E. Greenberg, *A Treasury of Yiddish Stories* (1953), 386–401. **ADD. BIBLIOGRAPHY:** Y. Varshavski [I.B. Singer], in: *Forverts* (July 5, 1964), 11/5; J. Schwarz, in: *Imagining Lives: Autobiographical Fiction of Yiddish Writers* (2005), 79–97.

[Moshe Starkman / Jan Schwarz (2nd ed.)]

ROSENFELD, MORRIS (1862–1923), Yiddish poet. Born in Suvalk, Poland, Rosenfeld survived a cholera epidemic that claimed the lives of 12 of his siblings. He learned the tailor's trade from his father, which he practiced until he could earn his living by his pen. After several abortive attempts at emigration to Amsterdam and London, he arrived in New York in 1886, where he resided until his death. There he worked in the city's burgeoning garment industry, and the sweatshop became his poetic muse. Rosenfeld lamented the punishing life of the immigrant worker and attracted a wide reading audience with his melodramatic-sentimental portraits of this existence, also composing a great many Zionist poems. Over the course of the next decade, he published: *Di Gloke* ("The Bell," 1888), *Di Blumenkete* ("The Flower Wreath," 1890), *Poeziyen un Lider* ("Poems and Songs," 1893), and *Lider Bukh* ("Book of Poems," 1897). It was this last volume that attracted the attention of Leo *Wiener. The following year Wiener published an English translation of the poet's works entitled *Songs from the Ghetto*, which aroused interest in Rosenfeld outside his already substantial Yiddish audience and catapulted him to international fame. In 1894 he co-edited a humorous, satirical weekly *Der Ashmeday*, and in 1905, the daily *New Yorker Morgenblat*. Rosenfeld's popularity continued to grow as his works were translated into a number of European languages. He contributed to many Yiddish publications, including regularly to the *Forverts* (1908–14). With the rise of Di *Yunge in the second decade of the 20th century, Rosenfeld was displaced from the canon of modern Yiddish poetry, his works dismissed as politically tendentious and sub-poetic. While this view may be accurate concerning his earliest poems, Rosenfeld's contribution to modern Yiddish literature was his engaging, emotional portrayal of the immigrant sweatshop worker, which eschewed politics and focused on the existential struggles of the community represented. Of his 20 published volumes, the most widely read were his collected works in six volumes, *Shriftn* ("Writings," 1908–10), *Gevelte Shriftn* ("Selected Writings," 1912), in three volumes, and *Dos Bukh fun Libe* ("The Book of Love," 1914). He also wrote biographies of Judah Halevi and Heinrich Heine, two poets who had exerted a great influence on his own lyrics. Like other Yiddish writers such as *Sholem Aleichem, Sholem *Asch, and Isaac *Bashevis Singer, Rosenfeld represented the world of the East European Jew to a wide international audience.

BIBLIOGRAPHY: L. Goldenthal, *Toil and Triumph* (1960); C. Madison, *Yiddish Literature* (1968), 151–64; S. Liptzin, *Flowering of Yiddish Literature* (1963), 138–43; Waxman, Literature, 4 (1960²), 1005–8; A.A. Roback, *Story of Yiddish Literature* (1940), 172–82; Bialostotzky, in: JBA, 20 (1962), 100–6; Reyzen, Leksikon, 4 (1929), 141–69; B. Rivkin, *Yidishe Dikhter in Amerike*, 2 (1947), 35–48. **ADD. BIBLIOGRAPHY:** E. Goldenthal, *Poet of the Ghetto* (1998); S. Liptzin, *A History of Yiddish Literature* (1972), 96–97; L. Wiener, *The History of Yiddish Literature in the Nineteenth Century* (1899),124–30; A. Tabachnik, *Dikhter Un Dikhtung* (1965), 7–32; N.B. Minkoff, *Yidishe Klasiker-Poetn* (1937), 67–98; I. Howe, *World of Our Fathers* (1976), 421–24.

[Moshe Starkman / Marc Miller (2nd ed.)]

ROSENFELD, PAUL (1890–1946), U.S. author and critic. A New Yorker, Rosenfeld was born into a prosperous family originating in Germany. He studied at Yale and Columbia, worked briefly as a reporter, and turned to writing. He became a critic and editor specializing in literature, art, and above all music and co-editing the magazine *Seven Arts* (1916–17). He was among the first to recognize the talents of Ernest *Bloch, Leo *Ornstein, Aaron *Copland, Waldo *Frank and Alfred *Stieglitz.

His first book, *Musical Portraits* (1920), was followed by *Musical Chronicle* (1923), *Port of New York* (1923), *Men Seen* (1925), and *By Way of Art* (1928). He embodied the story of his early life in an autobiographical novel, *The Boy in the Sun* (1928). From 1920 to 1927, he was musical critic for the monthly magazine *The Dial*. In 1927 he joined Alfred Kreymborg and Lewis Mumford in editing *The American Caravan* – a yearbook of American literature – on which he was active from 1927 to 1935. Rosenfeld regarded criticism in the arts, not as a means of displaying academic erudition, or of instructing the artist, but as a way of arousing in the audience an appropriate emotional empathy and discriminating appreciation. His essays on Waldo Frank and Van Wyck Brooks, both old friends, remain notable for their rigor of judgment, penetrating psychological analysis, and timely prophetic forebodings. Conscious of his own Jewish attachments, Rosenfeld was one of the earliest writers to react to the threat of Nazism. Though sometimes identified as a member of the Stieglitz circle, Rosenfeld was in fact, both as critic and patron, the center of a wide circle of his own, a group of varied talents. Although his last twelve years were undermined by the economic depression, the rise of Hitlerism, and World War II, some of his best work was done during this period, notably, *Discoveries of a Music Critic* (1936). Among the editors and critics of his day, it would be hard to pick out another figure who so consistently and selflessly found his own self-expression through serving his fellow writers and artists.

BIBLIOGRAPHY: J. Mellquist and L. Wiese (eds.), *Paul Rosenfeld, Voyager in the Arts* (1948); S.J. Kunitz (ed.), *Twentieth Century Authors*, first suppl. (1955), s.v.; *Current Biography Yearbook 1946* (1947), 520–1; *New York Times* (July 22, 1946), 21.

[Lewis Mumford]

ROSENFELD, SAMUEL (1869–1943), journalist. Born in Russia, he devoted himself to journalistic work on Zionism in Hebrew and in Yiddish. In 1900 Rosenfeld assumed responsibility for the Yiddish edition of the Zionist organ *Die Welt*.

He also published in Hebrew, *Ha-Congress ha-Bazilai ha-Shelishi* (1900), and *Ha-Congress ha-Ẓiyyoni ha-Sheneim Asar* (1922). He edited the Yiddish *Der Fraynd* and the Hebrew **Ha-Ẓefirah*. In 1923 he emigrated to the U.S. and joined the staff of the Yiddish daily The **Jewish Day*. His monograph on Israel Salanter appeared in Yiddish, Russian and Hebrew.

BIBLIOGRAPHY: *Kol Kitvei J.Ḥ. Brenner*, 2 (1960), 380–1; H. Tchernowitz, *Massekhet Zikhronot* (1945), 238–43.

[Eisig Silberschlag]

ROSENFELD, SHALOM (1914–), Israeli journalist. Rosenfeld was born in Poland and settled in Palestine in 1934. In 1948 he was one of the group of journalists who broke away from **Yedioth Aharonoth* following disagreements with its proprietor to found **Maariv* as a journalistic cooperative. He served as deputy editor (1960–74) and editor-in-chief (1974–79). He then headed the Journalism Studies Program at Tel Aviv University. In 1985 he founded and subsequently directed the Institute for the Study of Jewish Press and Communications, which later became part of the Andrea and Charles Bronfman Center for the Media of the Jewish People at Tel Aviv University. In 1987 he founded the Institute's journal, *Kesher*. In 1986 he received the Israel Prize for political journalism and essays.

ROSENHEAD, LOUIS (1906–1984), British mathematician. Born in Leeds, Rosenhead began his teaching career in 1931 as an assistant lecturer at the University College of Wales. In 1933 he was appointed professor of applied mathematics at Liverpool University, a position he returned to in 1946 after six years' war service at the Ministry of Supply. He was dean of the university's science faculty in 1945–47, a member of its council 1956–65, and pro-vice chancellor 1961–65. He spent the years 1956–60 at the Haifa Technion, Israel. Elected a fellow of the Royal Society in 1946, he was on its council from 1956 to 1958. Rosenhead is best known for his work in the field of fluid mechanics, especially the flow of fluids and the motion of the surface of the earth. He made a significant contribution to the theory of the stability of Karman vortex streams. He was part-author of *Index of Mathematical Tables* (1946) and *A Selection of Tables for Use in Calculations of Compressible Airflow* (1952), and edited *Laminar Boundary Layers* (1963).

[Julian Louis Meltzer]

ROSENHEIM, ARTHUR (1865–1942), German inorganic chemist. Rosenheim was born in New York. He was a professor at the University of Berlin (1921–32). His main fields of research were the complex acids and salts of metals, the complex compounds of phosphorus, and thiocyanates and organic acids containing sulfur.

ROSENHEIM, JACOB (1870–1965), Orthodox leader. Born in Frankfurt on the Main, Rosenheim acquired by his own efforts a wide Jewish and general culture. He was first apprenticed to a bank, and later founded the Hermon Publishing House, which produced a wide range of religious literature. In 1906 he transferred publication of the weekly **Israelit*, which he had recently acquired, from Mainz to Frankfurt. Under his direction, it became the influential organ of German Orthodoxy for 30 years. Apart from taking a leading part in the Israelitische Religionsgesellschaft, the independent Orthodox Frankfurt congregation, Rosenheim revived the Freie Vereinigung fuer die Interessen des orthodoxen Judentums, founded by S.R. *Hirsch in 1886, as a platform for the different elements in German Orthodoxy. In 1906 he founded the Deutsch-Hollaendische Palaestinaverwaltung, which established a network of schools in Palestine before World War I. Rosenheim was one of the founders, ideologists and leaders of *Agudat Israel (Katowice (Kattowitz), 1912), and became its president in 1929. Rosenheim was also instrumental in the setting up of the union of Orthodox communities in Germany, and Prussia in particular. From 1940, he lived in the U.S. and spent his last years in Israel. He was a master of German style and an outstanding orator. The guiding light of Rosenheim's life was the union and organization of world Orthodoxy in order to make it face its tasks in the modern world. Although there were many in the Agudah who opposed any recognition of or cooperation with secular Zionism at the establishment of the State of Israel, Rosenheim's influence was exercised in favor of the Agudah joining the provisional government and becoming one of the parties in the Knesset.

His collected addresses and articles were published in 1930 (*Ausgewaehlte Aufsaetze und Ansprachen*, 2 vols.). Some of his essays were translated into English: *Tent of Jacob* (1957) and *Samson Raphael Hirsch's Cultural Ideals…* (1951). Rosenheim's memoirs were published in Hebrew (*Zikhronot*, 1955), and a *Festschrift* was published on his 60th birthday in 1931. A collection of his memoirs, *Erinnerungen, 1870–1920*, arranged and brought to press by H. Eisenmann and H.N. Kruskal, was published in 1970.

BIBLIOGRAPHY: H. Schwab, *Jacob Rosenheim* (1925); idem, *History of Orthodox Jewry in Germany* (1950), index; I. Grunfeld, *Three Generations* (1959), index.

ROSENHEIM, MAX (Leonard), BARON (1908–1972), medical investigator and educator. Born in England, Rosenheim specialized in the research and treatment of kidney diseases and hypertension. He began his medical career in 1932, holding various hospital posts and traveling fellowships until joining the Royal Army Medical Corps in 1941. In 1950 he became professor of medicine at the University of London and director of the medical unit at University College Hospital Medical School. He was made a life peer in 1970.

Rosenheim became president of the Royal College of Physicians in 1966, and was a member of the World Health Organization's advisory committee on medical research, and of the Hebrew University's board of governors. He contributed articles to various medical journals.

[Julian Louis Meltzer]

ROSENHEIM, OTTO (1871–1955), British biochemist, born in Germany. In 1895 he went to teach at the University of Manchester and in 1901 moved to King's College, London, where he taught physiology. Later he was reader in biochemistry in the University of London until 1920. In 1925 he started 20 years' work at the National Institute for Medical Research in Hampstead.

His published studies deal with the constituents of the brain, spermine phosphate, uric acid, toxicity, putrefaction, the placenta, and particularly sterols (including ergosterol) and vitamins D and A. Tests for detecting vitamin A in cod liver oil and for the determination of total sulfates in urine are named after him.

BIBLIOGRAPHY: King, in: *Nature*, 175 (1955), 1019–20; idem, in: *Journal of the Chemical Society* (1956), 799–801.

[Samuel Aaron Miller]

ROSENMAN, SAMUEL IRVING (1896–1973), jurist and counsel to presidents Franklin D. *Roosevelt and Harry *Truman. Born in San Antonio, Texas, of Russian immigrant parents, he was admitted to the New York State bar in 1920, and established his legal and political career in New York City.

Serving in elective and appointive office with the New York State legislature, his liberal politics and exceptional legal competence led Governor Roosevelt to appoint him counsel and in 1932 to the State Supreme Court. Throughout Rosenman's 11-year judicial career, he continued to assist Roosevelt. Most noted as presidential speechwriter and originator of the political slogan "New Deal," he also organized Roosevelt's Brains Trust. During the U.S. mobilization for World War II, Rosenman was a major force in the creation of national defense agencies, helping mold a bureaucracy able to contend with war emergencies without extensive curtailment of New

Deal legislation. In 1943 he resigned judicial office to become counsel to the president. He edited the 13-volume *Public Papers and Addresses of Franklin D. Roosevelt* (1938–50) and described his years with the president in *Working with Roosevelt* (1952).

After Roosevelt's death, Rosenman was instrumental in assisting President Truman to formulate his domestic program and in preparations for the *War Crime Trials at Nuremberg. In 1946 he resigned as counsel but continued to serve as presidential adviser.

In 1943 Rosenman worked with Chaim *Weizmann in discussions with the State Department on the establishment of a Jewish state. One of Weizmann's voices in the Truman White House, Rosenman secretly brought Weizmann the news in April 1948 that Truman would recognize the Jewish state if partition was not abandoned by the UN General Assembly before establishment. His activities on behalf of Israel independence prompted Weizmann to write that it was "only proper" that the first letter he addressed as Israel's president be to Rosenman, who had "contributed so much of [his] effort and wisdom toward bringing about some of the happy results."

BIBLIOGRAPHY: Hand, in: *Journal of American History*, 55 (1968), 334–48.

[Samuel Hand]

ROSENMANN-TAUB, DAVID (1927–), Chilean poet, musician, and artist. Rosenmann-Taub's parents emigrated from Poland to South America in the early 1900s. From earliest childhood, he evinced gifts for both literature and music that were fostered by his parents. His mother began teaching him piano when he was two, and by nine he was giving lessons himself. From the age of seven, he had been sure of his vocation as a poet and had started to write daily. In his teens, he wrote *El Adolescente* (which would become his first published work), and began *Cortejo y epinicio*, the book that first made his name and in which such poems as "Schabat" and "Elegía y Kadisch" drew on his Jewish background.

He read broadly and thoroughly, acquiring the erudition that has always informed his poetry – especially the knowledge of physics that he considers fundamental to his work. He continued his musical education, studying piano and composition. In 1948 he graduated from the University of Chile with the title of professor of Spanish.

The next year, when he was 22, *Cortejo y epinicio* came out to wide acclaim, with a reputation-making review from the preeminent literary critic of Chile, Hernán Díaz Arrieta.

In the three decades that followed, Rosenmann-Taub published more than 10 volumes of poetry in Chile and Argentina, including *Los Surcos inundados* ("The Flooded Furrows"), for which he received the Premio Municipal de Poesía, one of Chile's highest literary honors. His poetry was admired by various critics and authors, among them Witold Gombrowicz, Victoria Ocampo, and Francis de Miomandre.

While working full time as a private tutor, he wrote each night into the small hours. In the first half of the 1970s, he suffered major blows: his parents' deaths; the theft of more than 5,000 pages of his poetry in manuscript; and the rise of a murderous dictatorship in Chile. During the latter half of the decade, he traveled on a grant in South America and Europe and gave lectures in New York City.

In 1985, he settled in the United States, embarking on a period of prodigious artistic activity. While producing hundreds of new poems and revising past work, he also assembled the drawings done over a lifetime, and continued to make music. Such compositions as *Abecechedario* ("Alphabet") and *Orbe* ("Orb") contain up to six different, precisely interlocking piano parts, played by the composer himself.

Given the fact that Rosenmann-Taub devoted every moment to his work, and none to self-promotion, it was not surprising that for many years his reputation lagged behind his achievement. In 2000, however, LOM Ediciones, in Chile, undertook to progressively issue all of Rosenmann-Taub's poetry. Since 2002, four books have been published: a new edition of *Cortejo y epincio*; *El Mensajero* ("The Messenger"); *El Cielo en la fuente/La Mañana eterna* ("The Sky in the fountain/the Eternal morning"); and *País más allá* ("Country beyond").

Rosenmann-Taub's poems have appeared in a number of Jewish anthologies, including *Voices within the Ark: The Modern Jewish Poets*, *Jüdische Literatur Lateinamerika*, and *El Gran libro de América Judía*.

[Fred Rosenbaum (2nd ed.)]

°ROSENMUELLER, ERNST FRIEDRICH KARL (1768–1835), Protestant German Bible exegete and Orientalist. His academic career centered at the University of Leipzig where he taught from 1792 (full professor of Semitics, 1813). His Bible commentaries and Arab lexical studies were significant scholarly achievements.

He wrote: *Scholia in Vetus Testamentum* (16 pts., 1788–1817; excerpted in 5 pts., 1828–35); *Handbuch fuer die Litteratur der biblischen Kritik und Exegese* (4 pts., Goettingen, 1797–1800); *Institutienes ad fundamenta linguae arabicae* (Leipzig, 1818), with an Arab-Latin glossary; *Das alte und neue Morgenland, oder Erlaeuterungen der heiligen Schrift aus der natuerlichen Beschaffenheit, den Sagen, Sitten und Gebraeuchen des Morgenlands* (6 vols., 1818–20); *Handbuch der biblischen Alterthumskunde* (4 vols., 1823–31), of which portions concerning the flora, fauna and mineralogy of the Holy Land were translated into English (*Biblical Geography of Asia Minor, Phoenicia, and Arabia*, 1836; *Biblical Geography of Central Asia*, 2 vols., 1836–37; and *Mineralogy and Botany of the Bible*, 1840); and *Analecta Arabica* (1824).

[Zev Garber]

ROSENSAFT, JOSEF (1911–1975), business executive. Rosensaft, who was born in Bedzin, Poland, was active in the Labor Zionist movement from his youth. In the years preceding World War II, he was a scrap metal dealer. In 1943 Rosensaft escaped from an Auschwitz-bound train by diving from it into the Vistula River. Although wounded in his escape, he managed to walk back to the Bendin Ghetto. Soon recaptured by the Germans and tortured in Auschwitz, he was shuttled to several concentration camps before being liberated at Bergen-Belsen in April 1945. Shortly afterward, Rosensaft was chosen by Bergen-Belsen survivors to become chairman of the camp committee representing them. He was also chairman of the Central Committee for Displaced Persons in the British Zone of Germany until the camps were terminated in 1950. In these capacities, he intrepidly furthered Jewish DP (displaced persons) rights and interests against the anti-Zionist British administration. During this period, Rosensaft actively aided the "illegal" movement of Jewish survivors out of Eastern Europe, and the attempt to smuggle Jews into Palestine.

Rosensaft lived in the U.S. and Switzerland after 1950 and was active in various Jewish organizations. He was president of the World Federation of Bergen-Belsen Survivors, a group dedicated to perpetuating the memory of the Holocaust and its victims. Rosensaft assembled a notable art collection.

His son, MENACHEM, who was born in the DP camp of Bergen-Belsen, was a lawyer and the founding chairman of the International Network of Children of Jewish Holocaust Survivors as well as a member of the United States Holocaust Memorial Council.

BIBLIOGRAPHY: S.J. Goldsmith, *Twenty 20th-Century Jews* (1962), 86–92. **ADD. BIBLIOGRAPHY:** M. Rosensaft, *Life Reborn: Jewish Displaced Persons, 1945–1951* (2001).

ROSENSOHN, ETTA LASKER (1885–1966), U.S. civic and Zionist leader. A member of the *Lasker family, she was born in Galveston, Texas, and began her career as a research worker for the New York Guild of the Jewish Blind. During World War I, Etta Rosensohn was district supervisor of the N.Y. Home Division of the Red Cross, and also began her 25-year career with the National Travelers Aid Society. She was a social and civic worker prominent in many organizations, including the National Council of Jewish Women, Conference of Jewish Relations, and Board of Governors of the Hebrew University. As a Hadassah leader, Etta Rosensohn held important offices for more than three decades, and played an outstanding role shaping Hadassah's health and social welfare program. After serving as Hadassah Medical Organization Chairman (1947–51), she became president of Hadassah (1952–53).

[Gladys Rosen]

ROSENSTOCK, JOSEPH (1895–1985), conductor. Born in Cracow, Rosenstock studied there, later in Vienna with *Schrecker. In 1922 he was appointed conductor, and in 1925 general music director, at the Darmstadt Opera; from 1927 to 1929 he held a similar position at Wiesbaden. He made his debut at the Metropolitan Opera, New York, during the 1929–30 season, and from 1930 to 1933 was music director at Mannheim until he was dismissed by the Nazis. He found work as the music director of the Juedische Kulturbund in Berlin (1933–36). From 1936 to 1941 he was honorary music director of the Nippon Philharmonic, Tokyo, returning there in 1945. He went to the United States in 1946, working with various orchestras until 1948 and conducting at the New York City Opera in 1952–56. After conducting in Cologne in 1958–59, he returned to the Metropolitan in New York in 1961–68, directing 175 performances of 16 operas, chiefly works of Mozart, Strauss, and Wagner.

[Max Loppert / Israela Stein (2nd ed.)]

ROSENSTOCK-HUESSY, EUGEN (1888–1973), German philosopher and theologian. Rosenstock was the son of a banker in Berlin, and grandson of Moritz Rosenstock, the principal of the Jewish school in Wolfenbuettel. At the age of 16 he converted to Christianity. In 1909 he finished his doctoral thesis and was one of the youngest teachers at a German university. In 1912–14 he was lecturer in medieval constitution at the University of Leipzig. In 1914 he married Margrit ("Gritli") Huessy (1893–1959) and added her name to his own. In World War I he served on the French front. After the war was over Rosenstock was asked to draft a constitution for the Republic but decided to devote his life to various projects on labor relations. In 1923 he accepted an appointment at the University of Breslau and in 1933 emigrated to the U.S. because of the Nazis. After a period at Harvard, he became professor at Dartmouth College.

He was a person of rare religious force and believed that the importance of language is in its relationship to authentic human experience and religious life. His importance to Jewish philosophy is his extraordinary influence on Franz *Rosenzweig, who came to him in Leipzig in 1913 when he was also considering conversion. After a memorable discussion in which Rosenzweig took the stand of a relativist and Rosenstock that of a religious thinker, Rosenzweig left Leipzig in July 1913 and promised to convert. However, instead of undergoing baptism he found his way back to Judaism.

In World War I both served in the German army, on different fronts, and an important correspondence developed between them. In these highly interesting letters of 1916 on Christianity and Judaism (*Judaism Despite Christianity*, 1969), Rosenstock attacked Judaism violently and Rosenzweig defended it. They also touched on many current problems. Studies of the correspondence were made by D. Emmet and A. Altmann (included in *Judaism Despite Christianity*).

Rosenzweig's major philosophical work, *Stern der Erloesung* ("The Star of Redemption," 1921), was written while he was still under the influence of Rosenstock. The relation between the two thinkers was existential. Rosenzweig accepted from Rosenstock: (a) the uncompromising necessity to take a religious stand on current questions, while abandoning the attitude of productivity for its own sake; (b) the idea of revelation as "orientation" in life; (c) the importance of language and time in terms of religious philosophy; and (d) the concept of cyclical time in terms of yearly religious events.

As an outcome of their relationship, Rosenzweig attempted to construct a philosophy of history that recognizes two true religions, Judaism and Christianity, which have their unity in Adam and separate historical configuration. After World War I Rosenstock, in the journal *Die Kreatur*, attempted to bring Catholics, Protestants, and Jews together for an exchange of views. On the other hand, he accepted from Rosenzweig the positive evaluation of the French Revolution as the Johanine Age. In his early writings he had a negative attitude to the age of emancipation (*Judaism Despite Christianity*, pp. 143–158).

The philosophy of language that Rosenstock developed in 1916 in a pamphlet for Rosenzweig later called *Angewandte Seelenkunde* (Darmstadt, 1924) was written to explain his theological language theory. In it he took his point of departure in the saying, "God called me therefore I am." Rosenstock's dialogue theory precedes that of Martin *Buber, and in contrast to the I-Thou of Buber, he emphasized the dynamism of the situation which changes from instant to instant. They agree on the fact that the Thou always precedes the I.

In his book *Out of Revolution* (1938) Rosenstock explained European history in accordance with a cyclical calendrical outlook, in which he considered the repetition of events as an important factor. This theory developed in the war letter of 1916 and was accepted by Rosenzweig not in terms of history but in terms of the yearly repetition of the holidays. Both thinkers gave up university careers after World War I in their attempt to reach the common people. Rosenstock became interested in labor camps and adult education, first in Germany and then in the U.S. President Roosevelt invited him to train leaders for the civilian Conservation Corps. Some of his disciples in Germany attempted a resistance movement against Hitler during the war, and died in concentration camps. The interest in his philosophy in Germany has grown considerably since 1945. Rosenstock's other works include: *The Multiformity of Man* (1949); *The Driving Power of Western Civilization* (1950); and the *Christian Future or the Modern Mind* (1966). Rosenstock tried time and again to convince Rosenzweig of the truth of Christianity. In 1913 he almost succeeded in bringing his friend to it but Rosenzweig decided to remain a Jew and with time slowly but enthusiastically discovered the deeper layers of his Jewish existence. In the intensive correspondence of 1916 Rosenzweig explained the relevance of his Jewish existence. Yet, also after this exchange of letters, in which Rosenzweig clearly elucidated his new viewpoint, Rosenstock did not stop his attempts to convert Rosenzweig. Of great importance in this context are Rosenzweig's numerous letters to Gritli Rosenstock-Huessy, whom he met in June of 1917. These "Gritli" letters are an example of the rare possibility of cross-cultural and transcultural understanding. Unfortunately, scholars do not have Gritli's letters to Rosenzweig. However, judging from Rosenzweig's letters to Gritli, with whom he developed a close relationship, Gritli was attentive to Franz's expressions of his Judaism. She accepted his otherness, making it possible for him to express himself freely. In contrast to Eugen, she did not wish to convert him, but was able to support him in his spiritual odyssey that led him to the discovery of important aspects of Jewish life and finally to the acceptance of the Law rooted in the experience of love.

BIBLIOGRAPHY: K. Ballerstedt, *E. Rosenstock-Huessy, Bibliography and Biography* (1959); P. Smith, *Historian and History* (1964); L. Sabine, in: *Universitas*, 8 (1965/66), pt. 3. **ADD. BIBLIOGRAPHY:** H. Stahmer, *"Speak that I May See Thee!" The Religious Significance of Language* (1968.); E. Rosenstock-Huessy (ed.), *Judaism Despite Christianity* (1969); L. van der Molen, *A Complete Bibliography of the Writings of Eugen Rosenstock-Huessy* (1989); W. Schmied-Kowarzik, *Franz Rosenzweig. Existentielles Denken und gelebte Bewährung* (1991), 121–73 (= *Franz Rosenzweig und Eugen Rosenstock. Ein juedisch-christlicher Dialog – und die Folgen von Auschwitz*); *F. Rosenzweig. Die "Gritli"-Briefe. Briefe an Margrit Rosenstock-Huessy*, R. Inken and R. Mayer (eds.) with a preface by R. Rosenzweig (2002); M. Brasser, "Rosenstock und Rosenzweig ueber Sprache. *Die Angewandte Seelenkunde* im *Stern der Erlösung*," in: idem (ed.), *Rosenweig als Leser. Kontextuelle Kommentare zum Stern der Erlösung* (2004), 173–207; E. Meir, *Letters of Love: Franz Rosenzweig's Spiritual Biography and Oeuvre in Light of the Gritli Letters* (2006).

[Richard Hirsch / Ephraim Meir (2nd ed.)]

ROSENTHAL, A.M. (1922–2006), U.S. journalist. Abraham Michael Rosenthal, who was born in Sault Ste. Marie, Ontario, Canada, went to New York as a child and was educated at the City College of New York. He became editor of a college newspaper, which led to a job as college correspondent for *The New York Times*. He became a reporter there in 1943 in his senior year, beginning a 56-year career at the paper, and quit college but got his degree six years later. In 1945 Rosenthal was assigned to cover the United Nations, where he developed an interest in foreign affairs. At the *Times*, he began to use the initials A.M. in what he described as an effort, common in those days, not to appear too Jewish, at least not to his superiors. In 1954 he was assigned to India, and also roamed about Pakistan, Nepal, Afghanistan and Ceylon. The next assignment was Poland, in 1958. There he produced a memorable article titled "There Is No News from Auschwitz," recounting his visit to the bleak remains of the infamous crematoria. Poland's Communist government at the time was in turmoil, and Rosenthal was expelled after a year and a half for "probing too deeply into the internal affairs" of the country and the Communist Party. In 1960 he won the Pulitzer Prize for his reporting from Poland. He also authored the famous phrase: "Forgive them not, Father, for they knew what they were doing," describing German behavior in the Holocaust.

The death of Orville Dryfoos, publisher of *The Times*, in 1963 ushered in a quiet revolution at the *Times* that led to a shift in power in the newspaper's newsroom. Rosenthal returned from a choice assignment in Tokyo to become metropolitan editor and quickly shifted the focus to more in-depth reporting, interpretation and analysis, and brighter writing. One of the first major stories under his watch involved the murder of a young woman in Kew Gardens, NY in Queens, who cried out for help against her assailant. A reporter found that 37 witnesses had heard her cries and offered no help. The story shook the city and led to a book by Rosenthal about the case. In 1967 Rosenthal moved up to assistant managing editor, beginning a climb to executive editor in 1977. Under one title or another, Rosenthal was in charge of daily news operations at the *Times* for 16 years and daily and Sunday operations for about 10 years. The most important story he oversaw during that period was the publication in 1971 of the Pentagon Papers, a hitherto secret history of the United States involvement in the war in Vietnam. Rosenthal championed publication of the stories on First Amendment grounds and the publisher, Arthur Ochs *Sulzerberger, sided with Rosenthal against the advice of several lawyers. The Nixon administration tried to prevent publication of the papers, which led to a major victory for the press in the United States Supreme Court. In a 6-to-3 ruling, the court said that the government could not stop the press from printing stories and analyses about the Pentagon Papers unless it could prove that national security was at stake. Rosenthal also commissioned a study of the *New York Times* coverage of the Holocaust, which he found woefully inadequate.

During Rosenthal's tenure, the *Times* went through major changes to preserve the character of the paper but also to make it more attractive to its readers. The two-part newspaper became a four-part paper, with a full news report, a magazine with a changing focus every day (Dining, Home, Science, Weekend) and Business Day, a full-fledged financial section. As Rosenthal famously said, "We had a choice to put more water in the soup or to put more tomatoes in. We chose the tomatoes." The venerable newspaper of record found new economic life with the introduction of the new sections. Rosenthal, who was conservative in his approach to changes in American society, resisted calling homosexuals "gays" in the pages of the paper and also resisted using the honorific "Ms," much to the consternation of homosexuals, feminists and others. The *Times* eventually allowed both terms. Rosenthal was also involved in two internal suits at the *Times*, to give women more opportunities in the newsroom, and to hire more black reporters and editors. *The Times* reached settlements with those groups without admitting wrongdoing.

After Rosenthal's retirement, mandatory at age 65, in 1988, he became a columnist for the *Times* and wrote "On My Mind" until 1999. Then he moved to other newspapers, where he championed such causes as the American invasion of Iraq in 2003. He also publicized the war on drugs and championed the rights of young African women against genital mutilation.

[Stewart Kampel (2nd ed.)]

ROSENTHAL, BENJAMIN STANLEY (1923–1983), U.S. politician. Born and raised in New York City, Rosenthal graduated from Stuyvesant High School in 1940, and later from Long Island University and City College. Following service in the U.S. Army during World War II, he attended Brooklyn Law School (LL.B., 1949) and New York University (LL.M., 1952). He was admitted to the New York bar in 1949 and the Supreme Court bar in 1954. On February 20, 1962, he won a special congressional election to succeed U.S. Rep. Lester Holtzman, who resigned. Rosenthal was subsequently elected to 11 succeeding congresses to represent Queens, and died of cancer in Washington, D.C., shortly after being sworn in for his 12th term.

As the senior Jewish member of the House Committee on Foreign Affairs, he was the person most of his colleagues turned to for leadership on issues involving Israel. He was the first in the House to challenge the sale of sophisticated weapons to Israel's Arab enemies. He was responsible for drafting and shepherding through the House generous aid programs for Israel. As chairman of the Foreign Affairs Subcommittee on Europe, he held the first congressional hearings on the plight of Soviet Jewry.

His outspoken opposition to the war in Vietnam was unpopular among constituents for many years as well as the leadership of his own party, but he did not waver. He incurred the wrath of President Lyndon B. Johnson in a 1969 House speech accusing the United States of being "virtually a puppet" of the Saigon government. But he stood firm on his principles, winning the respect – and votes – of those who disagreed with him.

Rosenthal was well known for his facile mind, quick wit, and devastating style of questioning – some critics called him abrasive – particularly when it came to deflating the stuffed shirts who appeared before his committees. He was compassionate and had a strong sense of justice but little tolerance for those he considered to be acting against the public interest. The Benjamin S. Rosenthal Library at City University of New York's Queens College was named in his memory as was a street in Queens and a senior center in Flushing.

[Douglas M. Bloomfield (2nd ed.)]

ROSENTHAL, ERICH (1912–1996), U.S. sociologist. Born in Wetzlar, Germany, Rosenthal studied in Germany and the United States. He received his M.A. in 1942 and his Ph.D. in 1948 from the University of Chicago. A student of Louis Wirth, he became a research associate at the University of Chicago; research consultant of Group Work agencies in Chicago; director of research at the Chicago Bureau of War Records; and professor of sociology at Roosevelt and Northwestern universities at Chicago and Evanston, Ill., at the University of Iowa, and from 1951 to 1978 at Queens College in New York.

Rosenthal was an expert in income distribution and acculturation. In particular, his reputation rests with his work in the demography of the Jews in America. Through his work on Jewish assimilation and group identity, he brought to national attention the high intermarriage and low fertility rates among American Jews. His works in this field include: "Acculturation without Assimilation? The Jewish Community of Chicago, Illinois" (*American Journal of Sociology*, 66 (Nov. 1960), 275–88); "Jewish Fertility in the United States" (AJYB,

62 (1961), 3–27); "Studies of Intermarriage in the United States" (AJYB, 64 (1963), 3–53); and "Jewish Intermarriage in Indiana" (AJYB, 68 (1967), 243–64).

[Werner J. Cahnman / Ruth Beloff (2nd ed.)]

ROSENTHAL, ERWIN (**Isaac Jacob**; 1904–1991), Orientalist. Rosenthal, born in Heilbronn, Germany, emigrated in 1933 to England, where he became lecturer in Hebrew at University College, London. From 1936 to 1944, he lectured on Semitic languages and literature at Manchester University, and during World War II carried out various educational tasks for the British army and foreign office. Rosenthal taught (from 1948) Oriental studies at Cambridge University. From 1961 to 1991, he was a fellow, and then emeritus fellow, of Pembroke College, Cambridge.

Rosenthal wrote the following works on Arabic political philosophy: his dissertation, *Ibn Khalduns Gedanken ueber den Staat* (1932), *Political Thought in Medieval Islam* (1958), and *Islam in the Modern National State* (1965), and he published a critical edition of Averroës' commentary on Plato's *Republic* (1956). He also wrote *Judaism and Islam* (1961) as well as works on Christian Hebraists. Rosenthal edited the third volume of *Judaism and Christianity* (*Law and Religion*, 1938, repr. 1969). His other works include: a biography, *Don Isaac Abravanel* (1937); *Griechisches Erbe in der juedischen Religionsphilosophie des Mittelalters*, the F. Delitzsch lectures which he gave in 1957; and *Studia Semitica* (2 vols., 1971). He also edited *Saadya Studies* (1943).

ROSENTHAL, FERDINAND (1838–1921), rabbi and scholar. Rosenthal, who was born in Kenese, Hungary, studied with E. Hildesheimer at the Eisenstadt Yeshivah and at Berlin and Leipzig universities. He served as rabbi at Beuthen, Silesia (from 1862) and Breslau (from 1878). He was the first Orthodox rabbi to join the Allgemeiner Deutscher Rabbinerverband, the majority of whose members were Reform. Rosenthal's scholarly interest lay chiefly in early talmudic history.

His published works include: *Erlaesse Caesars und die Senatsconsulte in Josephus* (1879) and *Vier apokryphische Buecher* (1885). Rosenthal edited the responsa of Jacob *Tam (from his *Sefer ha-Yashar*, 1898) and was coeditor of the D. *Kaufmann memorial volume (1900), to which he contributed Kaufmann's biography.

ROSENTHAL, FRANZ (1914–2003), Orientalist. Rosenthal was born in Berlin, where he obtained his doctorate for a thesis on *Die Sprache der palmyrenischen Inschriften* (1936). He was the first winner of the Lidzbarki Medal and Prize of the International Congress of Orientalists, for his book *Die aramaeistische Forschung seit Theodor Noeldekes Veroeffentlichungen* (1938). However, he was not granted the prize money because he was Jewish. In 1940 he became assistant professor at Hebrew Union College in Cincinnati and in 1948 professor at the University of Pennsylvania. In 1956 he was appointed the Louis M. Rabinowitz Professor of Semitic Languages at Yale and became a Sterling Professor in 1967. He resumed his Aramaic studies with his *Aramaic Handbook* (1967), in which such scholars as H. *Ritter and H.J. *Polotsky participated (1967). When he retired from teaching, he was named Sterling Professor Emeritus of Near Eastern Languages and Civilizations at Yale in 1985.

Rosenthal's main interest was the history of scholarship in *Islam. Apart from many papers and editions of smaller texts, he published: *The Technique and Approach of Muslim Scholarship* (1947); *A History of Muslim Historiography* (1952, 1968^2); a fully-annotated translation of Ibn Khaldun's *Muqaddimah (Bollingen Series*, 3 vols., 1958); *Gifts and Bribes: The Muslim View* (1964); and *Knowledge Triumphant* (1970). He also wrote a comprehensive paper of special Jewish interest on "Judeo-Arabic work under Sufic influence" (HUCA, 15, 1940). Together with R. *Walzer, he published and translated into Latin al-*Fārābī's *De Platonis philosophia*, the Arabic original of Shem Tov b. Joseph *Falaquera's account in *Reshit Ḥokhmah (Plato Arabus*, 2, 1943).

His later works include: *The Herb: Hashish vs Medieval Muslim Society* (1971); *Gambling in Islam* (1975); *Muslim Intellectual and Social History* (1990); *The Classical Heritage in Islam* (1994); and *Sweeter Than Hope* (1997).

Among the many organizations he belonged to and the numerous honors he received, Rosenthal served as president of the American Oriental Society and in 1994 was the first recipient of the AOS Medal of Merit.

[Martin Meir Plessner / Ruth Beloff (2nd ed.)]

ROSENTHAL, HAROLD (**David**; 1917–1987), English writer, music editor, critic, and historian. Born in London, Rosenthal began to teach after finishing his army service. While still a university student, he had written articles as an opera enthusiast and took the opportunity offered him of collaborating with the Earl of Harewood on the magazine *Ballet and Opera* (1948–49). With Lord Harewood, he launched the magazine *Opera* in 1950; he was the editor from 1953 to 1986 and under his guidance the journal became the most influential publication in the operatic world. Rosenthal was also an archivist at the Royal Opera House, London (1950–56), historian (*Two Centuries of Opera at Covent Garden*, 1958), lecturer, broadcaster, and the author of books such as: *Sopranos of Today* (1956), *A Concise Oxford History of Opera* (with John Warrack, 1964), *Great Singers of Today* (1956), *Covent Garden: A Short History* (1967), and *The Mapleson Memoirs* (annotated ed., 1966). He edited *The Opera Bedside Book* (London, 1965).

BIBLIOGRAPHY: Grove Music Online.

[Max Loppert / Israela Stein (2nd ed.)]

ROSENTHAL, HERMAN (1843–1917), writer and pioneer of Jewish settlement in the United States. He was born in Friedrichstadt (Jaunjelgava), in Courland (Latvia), and started to work as a printer in Kremenchug, Ukraine. During the Russo-Turkish War (1877–78), he served with the Red Cross and was decorated. As a result of the pogroms of 1881, Rosenthal reached the conclusion that the solution to the Jewish problem in Eastern Europe lay in emigration from Russia and in agricultural settlement. Organizing a group of 70 people in Yelizavetgrad, he set out for the United States to pave the way for their settlement there. In 1882 he established the first agricultural settlement for Russian Jews on Sicily Island, near New Orleans, Louisiana. After the destruction of the settlement by the Mississippi floods, he attempted to establish a new settlement, named Crémieux, in Dakota, but this was also short-lived. In later years, Rosenthal continued to foster the idea of Jewish settlement. He published the newspaper *Der Yidisher Farmer*, and in 1891 participated in the establishment of the ICA colony of Woodbine, New Jersey. In 1901, together with Abraham Ḥayyim *Rosenberg, he published the monthly *Ha-Modi'a le-Ḥodashim*. From 1898, Rosenthal headed the Slavonic department of the New York public library. He was the editor of the department of Russian Jewry in the *Jewish Encyclopedia* and made an important contribution to its high standard. Rosenthal wrote poems in his mother tongue, German, among them poetic translations of Song of Songs and Ecclesiastes (1893).

BIBLIOGRAPHY: *Ha-Meliẓ*, nos. 84 and 86 (1883); A. Menes, in: E. Tcherikower (ed.), *Geshikhte fun der Yidisher Arbeter Baveg-ung in di Fareynikte Shtatn*, 2 (1945), 223–7, 471; Z. Szajkowski, in: PAJHS, 40 (1951), 245–8.

[Yehuda Slutsky]

ROSENTHAL, IDA (1886–1973), businesswoman, dressmaker and inventor of the modern brassiere. Ida Kaganovich was born near Minsk, in Czarist Russia; her father was a Hebrew scholar and her mother ran a small general store. She emigrated to the United States in 1904 at the age of 18, following her boyfriend, William Rosenthal, whom she married in 1907. With a Singer sewing machine purchased on an installment plan, Ida made a living as a seamstress. In the early 1920s, the Rosenthals joined with Enid Bisset to open Enid Frocks, a small custom dress shop in Manhattan. Unhappy with the way their expensive dresses fit around the bosom, the partners designed a brassiere with cups that separated and supported the breasts; they called the bra a "Maiden form." The Enid Manufacturing Company they founded to meet the demand for their new product became the Maiden Form Brassiere Company in 1923 and Maidenform, Inc. in 1960. In 1925 they stopped making dresses and made Maiden Form bras exclusively. Ida Rosenthal managed the sales and traveled nationally and internationally to open new markets. By the end of the 1930s, Maiden Form products, eventually including other kinds of women's lingerie and swimsuits, were sold throughout the world. During World War II, the Rosenthals had no trouble getting rubber for elastic straps because studies showed that working women who wore the bra suffered less fatigue than women who did not wear this garment. The Rosenthals also helped the war effort by producing a "pigeon vest," a cup-shaped cloth that held a courier pigeon. A 1949 advertising campaign built their brand name with racy ads, featuring bra-clad women in various settings, starting with, "I dreamed I went shopping in my Maiden Form bra." The Rosenthals made many philanthropic contributions, including establishing the Ida and William Rosenthal Fellowship in Judaica and Hebraica at New York University. When William died in 1958, Ida Rosenthal became the chief executive officer of the company. In 1963 she was the only female member of an American apparel industry delegation that visited the Soviet Union. Rosenthal went to her office each day until her death from pneumonia at the age of 87; her daughter Beatrice Coleman succeeded her as chief executive.

[Sara Alpern (2nd ed.)]

ROSENTHAL, JUDAH (1904–1976), scholar. Born in Makov, Poland, Rosenthal went to the U.S. in 1939. He served as librarian (1944–65) and professor of biblical exegesis (1944–69) at the College of Jewish Studies, Chicago. In 1969 he settled in Jerusalem. A contributor to various periodicals, scholarly miscellanies and encyclopedias, Rosenthal was the author of numerous studies and essays in Jewish history, literature and religion.

His publications included *Hiwi Al-Balkhi* (1949); *The Talmud on Trial: The Disputation in Paris in the Year 1240* (1956); and *Meḥkarim u-Mekorot* ("Studies and Texts," 2 vols., 1967). On the subject of Jewish-Christian polemics, he published: "Anti-Christian Polemics from Its Beginnings to the End of the 18th Century" (*Aresheth*, 2, 1960) and editions from manuscripts of Jair b. Shabbetai's *Ḥerev Pifiyyot* (1958), Jacob ben Reuben's *Milḥamot ha-Shem* (1963), and Joseph Official's *Yosef ha-Mekanne* (1970).

[Tovia Preschel]

ROSENTHAL, LEON (**Judah Leib**; 1817–1887), Russian financier, *maskil* and philanthropist. Rosenthal was born into a wealthy family in Vilna. His father, Moses, one of the first *maskilim* in Vilna, educated him in the spirit of the *Haskalah. After his marriage, he went to live in Brest-Litovsk. When Moses *Montefiore visited Russia in 1846, Rosenthal submitted to him a memorandum claiming that education and modern schools would solve the problems of Russian Jewry. In the 1850s, Rosenthal settled in St. Petersburg, where he became associated with the *Guenzburg family and was one of the city's leading financiers and bankers. He corresponded with *maskilim* all over Russia, assisting them in their dealings with the government, distributing their literature, and also supporting them financially. In 1863 Rosenthal was among the founders of the *Society for the Promotion of Culture among the Jews of Russia; he served as the society's treasurer, contributed largely to its budget, and participated actively in its work. Advocating the spread of Hebrew language and literature and opposing assimilationist trends, he was influential in the society's support of Hebrew journals and books. In his later years, he began to write the history of the society, *Toledot Ḥevrat Marbei Haskalah be-Yisrael be-Ereẓ Rusyah* (2 vols., 1885–90), which also contains records and documents from the society's archives and is of great value for the history of the Haskalah in Russia. He was also one of the founders of the society for promotion of crafts and agriculture among Jews in Russia, ORT, and was one the main contributors to the society.

BIBLIOGRAPHY: J.L. Kantor, in: L. Rosenthal, *Toledot Ḥevrat Marbei Haskalah*, 2 (1890), introd.; E. Tcherikower, *Istoriya Obshchestva rasprostraneniya prosveshcheniya sredi yevreyev*, 1 (1913), passim.

[Yehuda Slutsky]

ROSENTHAL, LESER (**Eliezer**; 1794–1868), bibliophile and bibliographer. Rosenthal, born in Nasnelsk, Plock, Russia, served as teacher at Paderborn (Germany) and later as *Klausrabbiner* at Hanover. He began collecting Hebraica and Judaica by spending his entire dowry on books. At his death, Rosenthal's library contained 32 manuscripts and 6,000 printed volumes, including incunabula and rare books. He himself compiled a catalog of his collection titled *Yode'a Sefer* (Heb. and Ger.), which was edited by M. *Roest and published in 1875 (repr. 1966). Rosenthal's son, BARON GEORG ROSENTHAL, a banker, offered the collection to Bismarck for the Kaiserliche und Koenigliche Bibliothek (Preussische Staatsbibliothek) in Berlin, but the offer was refused. In 1880 descendants living in Holland presented the collection to the city of Amsterdam and it was incorporated in the university library there under the name of Bibliotheka Rosenthaliana (see *Libraries).

BIBLIOGRAPHY: Zunz, Gesch, 244; Steinschneider, in: HB, 15 (1875), 32; AZDJ, 32 (1868), no. 37; J. Berg, in: *Systematische Catalogus van de Judaica der Bibliotheca Rosenthaliana*, 1 (1936).

[Jacob H. Copenhagen]

ROSENTHAL, LUDWIG A. (1855–1928), German rabbi and scholar. Rosenthal, who was born in Putzig, Western Prussia, served as rabbi in Koethen, Rogasen, Preussisch Stargard, and Berlin, where he also lectured in the preparatory department of the Hochschule (Lehranstalt) fuer die Wissenschaft des Judentums.

Of importance are his Mishnah studies, in particular his *Ueber den Zusammenhang, Quellen und Entstehung der Mischna* (3 vols., 1918^2). Rosenthal took an active part in the controversy over Friedrich F. *Delitzsch's views (*Babel und Bible*, 1902; *Hammurabi Gesetz*, 1903), and wrote a comparative study on Joel, Nahum, and Habakkuk (1905). He acted as editor of *Rahmer's Juedisches Literaturblatt*, and edited the 10th edition of Kayserling's *Lehrbuch der juedischen Geschichte und Literatur* (1922). He also wrote a biography of Lazarus Geiger (1884). His other articles were published in *Gesammelte Schriften* (1926).

ROSENTHAL, MANUEL (**Emmanuel**; 1904–2003), conductor and composer. Born in Paris, he studied solfège with Mme. Marcou and the violin with Jules Boucherit at the Paris Conservatoire (1918–23). He was also Ravel's student and was among his master's closest disciples, a privileged interpreter and confidant. After conducting Parisian orchestras, he became leader of the National Radio Orchestra in 1934. During World War II, he was a prisoner in Germany and at the end the war he conducted, at the French Radio in Paris, the concert given to mark the liberation (September 28, 1944), which included the first performance of Messiaen's *Chant des déportés* for choir soprano, tenor and orchestra (published in 1945). He became instructor of composition at the College of Puget Sound in Tacoma, Washington, in 1948 and was the conductor of the Seattle Symphony Orchestra from 1949 to 1951. In April 1973, he conducted the first performance to mark the reopening of the Paris Opera. Rosenthal also appeared on many occasions at the Metropolitan Opera in New York, and in 1987 he conducted the Russian première of *Pelléas et Mélisande*. He was professor of conducting at the Paris Conservatoire (1962–74) and made recordings of the music of Debussy and Ravel. As a composer, he rejected the compartmentalized aesthetics of French music in the interwar period and put his individual language into his work. He wrote in almost every musical genre, including opera (such as *Rayon des soieries*, opéra-bouffe, 1926–28), ballet (such as *Un baiser pour rien*, 1928–29) chamber, and orchestral music, as well as choral and sacred music *Cantate pour le temps de la Nativité* (1943–44); and *Missa Deo gratias*, (1953).

BIBLIOGRAPHY: Grove Music Online; D. Saudinos, *Manuel Rosenthal* (1992); M. Marnat (ed.), *Ravel: souvenirs de Manuel Rosenthal* (1995).

[Israela Stein (2nd ed.)]

ROSENTHAL, MAX (1833–1918), painter, printmaker, and inventor. Born in Turck, Poland, Rosenthal was apprenticed to a Paris lithographer, Martin Thurwanger. When in 1849 his employer went to the U.S. to work for a lithographic firm in Philadelphia, Rosenthal accompanied him as his chief assistant, and studied at the Pennsylvania Academy of Fine Arts. The Rosenthal family, including Max's brothers Morris, Louis, and Simon, organized a lithography business in Philadelphia: Max was the principal artist. Rosenthal was a pioneer of chromolithography in the U.S. and made the plates for the first American book furnished with a set of chromo-illustrations, *Wild Scenes and Wild Hunters*. In 1854 he produced the largest chromolithograph yet made (22 × 25 inches) in the U.S., after his own drawing, *Interior of the Old Masonic Temple in Philadelphia*. During the Civil War, Rosenthal traveled with the Army of the Potomac as official illustrator for the United States Military Commission, and produced the color plates for a medical and surgical history of the war. He made detailed images of every camp until Gettysburg. Rosenthal's chromolithograph *Battle of Antietam* (1865) depicts the Union Army victorious against the forces of General Robert E. Lee. Until 1884, he made a living making lithographs of famous Americans; after that year, he concentrated on etchings of British and American military leaders, illustrations for the poems of Henry Wadsworth Longfellow, and original works such as *Jesus at Prayer*. This altar painting for a Protestant church in Baltimore was found objectionable due to the phylacteries which Rosenthal included on Jesus' forehead and right arm. A Catholic church then offered a substantial sum for the work if the artist would paint in a halo, but Rosenthal refused to do so. A versatile man, Rosenthal also became known for his technical achievements, among them his invention of the sandblast process of engraving glass. Rosenthal portraits are numerous. His mezzotint *Colonel George Washington* displays the future president as a young man, pensive but determined. Another mezzotint *Portrait of General Smallwood* depicts this military leader in dramatic illumination which imparts the sagging face of his sitter with flattering chiaroscuro. His son, ALBERT ROSENTHAL (1863–1939), was his collaborator on many projects. He was a painter and lithographer but was best known for his knowledge of 18th and 19th-century American art, and he often served as an expert both for American museums and for private collections. Rosenthal's works are in the collections of the Albright-Knox Art Gallery, Buffalo, New York; the Fine Arts Museum of San Francisco; the National Portrait Gallery; the Peabody Essex Museum, Salem, Massachusetts; the Smithsonian Institution; and the State Museum of Philadelphia, among other museums.

BIBLIOGRAPHY: C. Roth, *Jewish Art: An Illustrated History*. Revised ed., Bezalel Narkiss (1971); R. Tyler, *American Canvas: The Art, Eye, and Spirit of Pioneer Artists* (1990).

[Nancy Buchwald (2nd ed.)]

ROSENTHAL, MORIZ (Maurycy, 1862–1946), pianist. Rosenthal was born in Lvov (Lemberg, Galicia), the son of a professor at the Lvov Academy of Music. He began playing the piano at the age of eight, and in 1872 entered the Academy, where he studied with its director, Karol Mikuli, from 1872 to 1874. In the following year, Rosenthal's family moved to Vienna, where he continued his studies with Joseffy and he gave his first recital in 1876. He then began to tour, finishing his studies with Liszt at Weimar, and in Rome. For six years, he abandoned the concert platform, dedicating himself to a study of philosophy. Returning to the concert platform in 1886, he appeared as an artist in whom maturity of feeling and thought was matched by a virtuoso technique of the highest order; his reputation spread rapidly all over Europe and America, and was equaled only by that of *Godowsky. In 1903, he published (with Schytte) the manual, *Schule des hoeheren Klavierspiels*. In 1938, he took up residence in New York City, where one of his last pupils was the American pianist Charles Rosen, to whom he bequeathed the legacy of Liszt's teaching.

[Max Loppert (2nd ed.)]

ROSENTHAL, NAPHTALI (1727–1798), Hungarian talmudist, founder of the Jewish community of Mor. While studying in Berlin at the yeshivah of David Fraenkel, he made the acquaintance of Moses *Mendelssohn; they became friends and maintained the friendship by correspondence after Rosenthal had left Berlin. After staying in Prague, he later settled in Mor, where his house became a center of learning, hospitality and traditional Judaism. An atmosphere of religious study permeated his household: even his wife was acquainted with biblical and talmudic passages in the original. His son-in-law, F. Gomperz, assisted him in the management of the yeshivah of Mor. Rosenthal's public activities were not confined to his own community: he was also the spokesman of the whole of Hungarian Jewry at the court of Vienna under Joseph *II and the two subsequent monarchs.

His son ELIJAH (1758–1833) was a businessman and bibliophile. Between the ages of 13 and 18 he studied at the yeshivah of Pressburg (Bratislava) and became an accomplished talmudic scholar. From 1785 he lived in Komarom (Komarno), Hungary, where he kept an inn. His fellow-citizens wanted to give him the freedom of the town in recognition of his charitable acts and public service, but the authorities would not confirm this. Moving to Pest, he opened a shop for Hebrew books and stationery in 1804. He himself was a book collector and his library was praised by Leopold *Zunz. Following the French Revolution (1789), he became active in the struggle for Jewish civil rights, remembering his own humiliating experience in Komarom. He wrote various memoranda and petitions in pursuit of this aim.

BIBLIOGRAPHY: P. Buechler, *A móri Chevra Kadisa története (1791–1891)* (1891), 5, 8; M. Kayserling, *Die juedischen Frauen* (1879), 180; I. Reich, *Beth-El, Ehrentempel verdienter ungarischer Israeliten*, 2 (1868), 334–54; J.J.(L.) Greenwald (Grunwald), *Toledot Mishpaḥat Rosenthal* (1921).

[Jeno Zsoldos]

ROSENTHAL, PAVEL (Pinhas; pseudonyms: **Anman, P. Rol**; 1872–1924), physician and author, a leader of the *Bund. Rosenthal, who was born in Vilna, where his merchant father was both a *maskil* and a religious Jew, joined clandestine socialist circles when at secondary school and at the University of Kharkov, where he became a Marxist. At the university he organized socialist activity among the Jewish Lithuanian students, was arrested, and expelled. He did not complete his studies until 1898. Rosenthal joined the group of Jewish Social Democrats in Vilna. From 1895 he headed the "Jargon Committee" for the publication and propagation of popular scientific literature in Yiddish among the workers. From the autumn of 1899, he practiced medicine in Bialystok, acting also as leader of the local Bund, and as editor of its organ *Bialystoker Arbeter*. He attended the third convention of the Bund (1899) and from 1900 served on its central committee. In conjunction with J. *Portnoy at the Bund's fourth convention (Bialystok, 1901), Rosenthal drafted the resolution on the national question. He was the author of the "Manifesto to the Jewish Intelligentsia," which was published in the name of the Bund in three editions. Again imprisoned, Rosenthal was exiled to Siberia between 1902 and 1905. He played a prominent role in the revolt of the exiles in Yakutsk, the "Romanovka," which he described in his book of the same name (Rus., 1924). A member of the editorial board of *Veker*, the legally authorized organ of the Bund, Rosenthal shared all the vicissitudes of the Bund during the 1905 revolution. He was among the moderates regarding the Bund's return to the Russian Social Democratic Party. During the period of reaction following 1905, he turned his attention to the problems of promoting culture and education for adults. In World War I Rosenthal served at the front. After his discharge at the end of 1917, he was elected to the central committee of the Bund at its eighth convention. Resuming his professional and literary work in Moscow, Kiev, and Petrograd, Rosenthal was authorized to return to Vilna in 1921. Having previously identified with the internationalist wing of the Bund, in Poland he joined the short-lived Polish Social Democratic Bund.

A prolific author, Rosenthal had wide and varied interests. His work on revolutions in Western Europe, *Vi Zaynen Forgekumen Revolutsies in Mayrev Oyropa*, appeared in 1905. In his *Der Kampf far Velthershaft un Velt-Vegn* ("The Struggle for World Domination and World Routes," 1924, first published in Russian, 1923), he included a chapter on the general role of the Jews. His articles on the history of the Bund are included in *Royter Pinkes*, 1 (1921), 45–63; 2 (1924), 5–21.

Rosenthal's wife, ANNA, née Heller (1872–c. 1940), a dentist, was an early member of the Ḥovevei Zion group of Vilna and was later active in both the "Jargon Committee" and the Bund committee. With her husband, she took part in the revolt of the exiles in Yakutsk ("Romanovka"). She later resumed her Bundist activities. During World War I, Anna was active in the OSE and the Red Cross. Between the two world wars, she taught in Vilna in CYSHO institutions, and was active in YIVO. She was a Bundist delegate at the congress of the Socialist International (1931). Her memoirs were published in *YIVO Historishe Shriftn* (vol. 3, 1939). After the occupation of Vilna by the Soviets, she was arrested and died in prison.

BIBLIOGRAPHY: Rejzen, Leksikon, 4 (1929), 123–5; LNYL, 1 (1956), 128–31; J. Hertz et al. (eds.), *Doyres Bundistn*, 1 (1956), 157–92; G. Aronson et al. (eds.), *Geshikhte fun Bund*, 3 vols. (1960–66), indexes.

[Moshe Mishkinsky]

ROSENTHAL, PHILIPP (1855–1937), German industrialist and founder of the Rosenthal porcelain works. Born in Werb, Westphalia, Rosenthal entered the porcelain trade as a young man, and left Germany in 1872 to work in the same field in the United States. Upon his return in 1879, he established a porcelain factory in Asch, Bohemia, and subsequently a second in Selb. Together with his brother Max, he developed the enterprise into the largest of its kind in the world. "Rosenthal" became a hallmark for fine china and many of its pieces are regarded as art items. Rosenthal converted to Christianity. In 1933 he came into conflict with the Nazis due to his Jewish origins. Due to his company's reputation, the Nazis did not risk attacking Rosenthal directly; eventually, however, they were able to have him declared legally incapacitated by exploiting quarrels in his family, thus depriving him of his rights.

BIBLIOGRAPHY: Wininger, Biog; H. Schreiber, D. Hanisch, F. Simoneit, *Die Rosenthal-Story* (1980).

[Monika Halbinger (2nd ed.)]

ROSENTHAL, WILLIAM (1920–1974), U.S. sociologist. Rosenthal was born in Newark, New Jersey. He taught at Wagner College and was on the faculties of the Adelphi University School of Social Work and the Cornell University School of Labor and Industrial Relations and was also a field instructor for Wayne State University, New York University and Columbia University. He was associated with the Wurzweiler School of Social Work of Yeshiva University from its foundation in 1957 and was appointed dean in 1973.

Among his many activities in a lifetime devoted to general and Jewish social work and education, Rosenthal served as secretary of the Health and Hospital Division, Essex County Social Agencies; as supervising consultant to the Economic Opportunities Committee, New York City; and as consultant to the Department of Social Services, New York City. He was executive director of the Jewish Community Center, Utica, N.Y., and from 1954 to 1965 executive director of the Jewish Community Center in Staten Island, where he made his home.

Rosenthal edited the Group Work section of the *Journal of Jewish Communal Services*, and *News and Notes* for the National Association of Jewish Center Workers.

ROSENWALD, U.S. family. JULIUS ROSENWALD (1862–1932), merchant and philanthropist, was born in Springfield, Illinois, the son of German Jewish immigrants. From 1879 to 1885, he was in New York City, working first at an uncle's clothing store, then opening his own, and finally starting to manufacture lightweight summer clothing. He moved the business to Chicago in 1885, where, as Rosenwald and Weil, it was fairly successful. In 1895 he bought a one-quarter interest in the recently established mail-order firm of Sears, Roebuck and Company for $37,500 and became its vice president. He became company president in 1909. By 1925 his original investment was worth $150,000,000. Rosenwald was responsible for opening factories that produced much of the firm's merchandise; introduced the famous "money-back-if-not-satisfied" guarantee; and expanded distribution of the firm's mail-order catalog to 40,000,000 copies annually. Rosenwald, who was somewhat paternalistic in employee relationships, stressed recreational facilities and introduced a profit-sharing plan. In 1925 Rosenwald became chairman of the board, and remained in that post until his death.

In the area of philanthropy, Rosenwald heavily subsidized the erection of YMCA buildings for African Americans in 25 cities and the establishment of thousands of rural schools in the southern U.S. from 1910 on. He served continuously from 1912 as a trustee of Tuskegee Institute, and donated $2,700,000 for the construction of model housing for African Americans in Chicago. The Julius Rosenwald Fund, established in 1917 with a capital of $30,000,000, was Rosenwald's chief philanthropic instrument. He directed that the fund's capital and interest be expended within 25 years of his death.

Rosenwald was president of the Associated Jewish Charities of Chicago (1907); contributed substantially to Jewish war relief during World War I and the post-war period; pledged $6,000,000 to promote Jewish agricultural colonization in the Soviet Union; and gave $500,000 each to the Hebrew Union College and Jewish Theological Seminary. Rosenwald opposed Zionism but contributed modestly to educational and agricultural institutions in Palestine. He served for many years as vice president of the American Jewish Committee. Active in general civic affairs, Rosenwald was a trustee of the University of Chicago, to which he donated $5,000,000; he pledged $3,000,000 for the Chicago Museum of Science and Industry; and he served on the Advisory Commission of the Council of National Defense during World War I.

LESSING JULIUS ROSENWALD (1891–1979), the eldest son of Julius Rosenwald, was a merchant, book collector and philanthropist. Rosenwald, who was born in Chicago, Illinois, entered Sears, Roebuck and Company as a shipping clerk in 1911, and worked his way up through the company's ranks. After naval service in World War I, he took charge of the Sears plant in Philadelphia and, upon his father's death in 1932, succeeded him as chairman of the board until 1939. During World War II, Rosenwald served as director of the Bureau of Industrial Conservation. In 1943 he led the foundation of the *American Council for Judaism and was its first president. Rosenwald and the Council campaigned vigorously in the U.S. and before the UN against the establishment of a Jewish national state in Palestine. Rosenwald continued the philanthropic tradition of his family through service and contributions to Jewish and general civic causes. In addition, he was noted as a collector of rare books and prints and contributed generously to the National Gallery of Art and Library of Congress.

WILLIAM ROSENWALD (1903–1996), the second son of Julius Rosenwald, was a philanthropist and financier. Rosenwald, who was born in Chicago, Illinois, served briefly as a director of Sears, Roebuck and Company before concentrating on his own investments. These included the American Securities Corporation and Ametek, Inc. and Western Union. Rosenwald was one of the outstanding figures in American Jewish philanthropic activity from the 1930s. He served as chairman of the national United Jewish Appeal campaign, and vice chairman of the Joint Distribution Committee, American Jewish Committee and United HIAS Service. He also supported Tuskegee Institute, the Chicago Museum of Science and Industry and the New York Philharmonic Symphony Society.

BIBLIOGRAPHY: M.R. Werner, *Julius Rosenwald* (1939); Angell, in: AJYB (1932), 141–76; E.R. Embree and J. Waxman, *Investment in People: The Story of the Julius Rosenwald Fund* (1949); *Current Biography* (1947), 551–4; *Forbes*, 102 (Sept. 15, 1968), 74. **ADD. BIBLIOGRAPHY:** *Crisis and Response 1933–1983. Published in Honor of William Rosenwald's 50 Years of Leadership in Jewish Philanthropy* (1983).

[Morton Rosenstock]

ROSENWILLER (Rosenweiler), town in Alsace in the department of Bas-Rhin, E. France. There is evidence of Jews in Rosenwiller from the middle of the 16th century. Although an expulsion order was issued by the local lord in 1563, it does not seem to have been effectively carried out, but the number of Jews there remained small. The Rosenwiller community was important because its Jewish cemetery, dating from at least 1621, served some 20 Jewish communities in the area. In the second half of the 18th century, almost 100 burials a year took place there.

BIBLIOGRAPHY: M. Ginsburger, in: *Souvenir et science*, 1 (1930), 24–51.

[Bernhard Blumenkranz]

ROSENZWEIG, FRANZ (1886–1929), German Jewish philosopher and theologian. Rosenzweig was born in Kassel, Germany, the only son of well-to-do parents. His father Georg financially supported many charity institutions, including the Jewish community, but the family's adherence to Judaism was minimal. In his youth, Franz came under the influence of his great-uncle, Adam Rosenzweig, a bachelor, an artist and a learned Jew, who lived in the Rosenzweig home and spent many hours with Franz. Through him the young boy learned of the Jewish world in an otherwise assimilated milieu. Unlike the rest of his family, Rosenzweig fasted on *Yom Kippur* (the Day of Atonement) and also took private Hebrew lessons. In 1905, he enrolled at the university, where he initially studied medicine, as many a Jewish student did, but then turned to philosophy and history, concentrating on Hegel and German idealism. He wrote his Ph.D. dissertation on "Hegel and the State."

In 1909, Rosenzweig tended towards assimilation, and justified the conversion of his cousin Hans Ehrenberg to Christianity. He did not see the advantage that Judaism could have over Christianity, the dominant culture, which would also help him obtain a teaching position, almost impossible for a Jew to get. Another cousin and friend, Rudolf Ehrenberg was already born a Christian. Eugen *Rosenstock, a Jewish convert to Christianity, became Rosenzweig's closest friend. Rosenstock, who would become an important nonconformist Protestant theologian, repeatedly urged him to abandon what he considered Rosenzweig's merely nominal Judaism and to convert. After months of deep conversations, and especially the catastrophic conversation with Rosenstock during the night of July 7, 1913, Rosenzweig decided to convert. But he then made the condition, to convert not "as a pagan," but "as a Jew." All this led to a crisis and almost to suicide. He left his converted friends for a few years and refrained from having any contact with them. In the same year, on Yom Kippur of 1913, he attended in Berlin the synagogue of Rabbi Petuchowski and felt a profound identification with the praying Jewish community. After a few days he wrote his friends, "I shall remain a Jew." He then reshaped his life, rethought his identity, and devoted his further life to a sincere return to Judaism, moving from the periphery of Jewish life to its center.

He developed a very close relationship with the philosopher Hermann *Cohen, who had retired from the University of Marburg and now taught at the Hochschule fuer die Wissenschaft des Judentums, the institution for adult Jewish education in Berlin. Cohen was of enormous importance for the young returning Jew, who saw in his teacher a great philosopher and someone who represented a source of Jewish tradition. Only in 1916 did Rosenzweig resume his lengthy theological correspondence with Rosenstock, after he had strengthened his renewed Jewish roots; in this correspondence with his friend he explained his new existential position. Although he disliked Rosenstock's continued attempts to convert him, the two remained in close contact. Rosenzweig inherited from his friend the idea of revelation as "orientation" in life, and devoted his first Jewish theological essay (*Atheistische Theologie*) to the idea of revelation, which went beyond what Rosenstock wrote and debated with Buber.

In World War I Rosenzweig served in the German army, and, while stationed in the Balkans, planned the revival of Jewish education. He sent his plan to Hermann Cohen as an open letter called *Zeit ists* (*It is Time*, 1917), a letter that had an enormous influence. Towards the end of the war, in the trenches, with the retreat of the Balkan-troops and in the army hospital he wrote the first draft of his *Stern der Erloesung* (*Star of Redemption*), his main work. At a feverish pace he wrote his major philosophical work, which contains hundreds of pages. New light has now been shed on it by Rosenzweig's correspondence with Gritli Rosenstock, which will be discussed below. The *Star of Redemption* was written from August 23, 1918, to February 16, 1919, and published in 1921.

In his return to Judaism, Rosenzweig was supported primarily by Hermann Cohen, but also by people such as Rabbi Nehemiah Nobel, Martin Buber, Joseph Prager, and Eduard Strauss. In 1920 he married Edith Hahn, and progressively observed the Jewish laws. Their son Raphael was born in September 1922. Realizing that, as a returnee to Judaism, he could play a pivotal role in bringing Jews back to their roots, Rosenzweig became interested in Jewish education, and in 1920 was appointed director of the Freies Juedisches Lehrhaus, an institute of adult Jewish education in Frankfurt on the Main, in which the participants were invited to express their view on Jewish problems and to try to understand their identity. The same year, he turned down an offer by Friedrich Meinecke to become a professional historian. Instead, he desired to free himself from what he called "dead science" and from "mere cognition," so that he could enter into the flow of life, where real questions demand answers. In the Lehrhaus, he used his talents not to write books, but to provide living answers to questions from the public, who were increasingly interested after the war in the return to Jewish faith.

According to Rosenzweig, the uniqueness of the Lehrhaus was in that people took part in conversations through questions and counter-questions. "*Lernen*," which in German means to study, but which, according to Rosenzweig in a 1919 letter to Margrit Rosenstock, in a Jewish context means both to study and to teach, is possible wherever people come together and try to overcome their estrangement from Judaism. The Lehrhaus in Frankfurt was not dependent on rabbis or religious teachers, but on people who knew little, in Rosenzweig's words: "*am ha-arets*" (without Jewish education), but who brought with them a great enthusiasm in their return to Judaism. The teachers were Jews on the periphery who were assimilated and wanted to rediscover their identity. People would be willing to read Jewish texts, such as the Bible, Midrash, Talmud, the *siddur* or *maḥzor*, and discover and build a Jewish life. It was not the books in themselves but rather the actual living encounter with other Jews that would create the opportunity to build Judaism.

In Rosenzweig's day, the dialogical method of learning was something novel, and at the universities it was completely absent. Today this method is more accepted. Practically, teaching now means being in interaction with the audience, certainly in informal adult education. Yet, Rosenzweig rightly understood that when Jews study together, something else happens. *Lernen* is not merely interactive learning, it means creating a community of people who make ancient texts speak again to the present generation, in constant renewal.

Alfred Jospe criticized the Lehrhaus in Frankfurt as being over-intellectualized. In his view, the program addressed itself mainly to the intelligentsia and did not really reach the men and women who had questions but lacked a higher education. Secondly, he felt that the school's accent was more on the transmission of knowledge than on the experiencing and living of Jewish values and ideas. While this criticism may be correct from a certain point of view, Rosenzweig's concept of the Lehrhaus was important and functioned as a model for other houses of study in Europe and America. One of the great advantages of the Lehrhaus was that people, through participating in the programs and projects, could express the profound questions that dwelled within them and cultivate a sense of at-homeness with Judaism and the Jewish community. Rosenzweig had to realize his educational project within a public that was not used to interaction and, on his part, he had to abandon the attitudes that prevented him from being truly dialogical. However, the very concept of a new, permanent, dialogical learning style was revolutionary and remains so today.

In the 1920s, Rosenzweig published a translation of 92 poems by *Judah Halevi with a commentary. Together with Buber he began translating the Bible, reaching Isaiah 52. In their Bible translation, the two wanted to bring the reader into as much contact as possible with the oral origin of the Bible. The translation gained great popularity. They rendered the Tetragrammaton in the pronominal forms "I," "You," and "He," highlighting in this manner the divine presence today. Rosenzweig accepted higher Bible criticism, and believed that there can be no contradiction between Torah and science, but considered the abbreviation "R." not as referring to the final Redactor, but rather to "(*Moshe*) *Rabbenu*," Moses our teacher, and considered the unity of the biblical text as the source of the Jewish faith. Rosenzweig, in opposition to extreme rationalism, appreciated biblical anthropomorphisms as attesting to the living dialogue between God and man, and as a preeminent way of speaking of this relationship.

Rosenzweig's important essay *Die Bauleute* (*The Builders*, 1923) discusses the attitude of the Jew to the commandments. Unlike the orthodox Jew, Rosenzweig did not accept all of the commandments, but distinguished between the subjective "commandment" (*Gebot*), which addresses the individual in the present, and which he readily accepted, and objective Law (*Gesetz*), which he could "not yet" accept. His beautiful introduction to Hermann Cohen's Jewish writings and his other Jewish essays further testify to Rosenzweig's steadily growing interest in Jewish life.

Parallel to his religious evolution, Rosenzweig developed his existential philosophy and subsequently explicated it in a more popular way in *Das neue Denken* (*The New Thinking*, 1925). The essay shows his dissatisfaction with German idealism and describes his kind of "new thinking," which takes into account the importance of dialogue, pluriform reality, language, and time. Instead of a philosophy serving history and politics and knowing nothing about revelation, Rosenzweig posited revelation as leading to a life of community. Eternity (*Ewigkeit*) is to be realized in the everyday life in the community of believers.

In his magnum opus, Rosenzweig conceived of the All collapsing into three separate elements: God, man, and the world. In opposition to pantheism, materialism, and extreme anthropology, he rejected the philosophical attempt to reduce these elements to one, and pointed to their interaction with each other in the relationships of creation, revelation, and redemption. In revelation, God addresses man with the commandment "Thou shalt love," which is the basis of all laws. Judaism and Christianity as collective answers to revelation are two twin communities, which are different, complementary, and critical towards each other. They are partial truth in history, whereas God as the ultimate truth transcends them. Yet, as in Judah Halevi's *Kuzari*, Judaism is given clear priority in the *Star*.

In opposition to the idealistic attempts to find God in history and to make the world into a platform of the developing Absolute Spirit as did Hegel, Rosenzweig's *Star* did not put history in the center, but "revelation" and "eternity," which are a "rupture" of history. Jewish history has no epochs; it transcends time and is eternal. For Rosenzweig, there is a new form of interaction between philosophy and theology: theology talks about revelation as the objective breach of history, whereas philosophy approaches the same revelation from the subjective point of view.

With his revelation-centered philosophy, Rosenzweig criticized idealism, which was current in the German universities of that time and in which he was well versed. In 1917 he had published *Das aelteste Systemprogramm des deutschen Idealismus*, in which he identified as Schelling's a manuscript written in Hegel's hand on a unified system of idealism. (Pöggler now argues that the program fits Hegel and not the early Schelling; the subject is in debate.) In 1920 Rosenzweig published his *Hegel und der Staat* (1920).

However, it was the *Star* that interested Rosenzweig most. In it he developed his anti-idealistic thinking, and he expressed his existential philosophy in ancient Jewish terms. The *Star*, a compendium of Jewish insights, was first of all the result of his deep Jewish development: first through the crisis of 1913 and then through the friendship with Hermann Cohen. After the *Star* he led a Jewish life as a paralyzed, sick man, who worked on translations of Jewish texts and on matters of Jewish adult education. He contracted amyotrophic lateral sclerosis (ALS), a disease that gradually prevented him from performing any motor function except from moving his eyebrows. Rosenzweig died after 7 years of long suffering in 1929, at the age of 43.

Rosenzweig and Buber

Over the years, the possibility of a friendship between Buber and Rosenzweig prior to the publication of Buber's *I and Thou* in 1922 had been considered; surprisingly, through numerous manuscripts and letters it was possible to prove that Buber's theory of dialogue developed out of their dialogue. This research was undertaken by Rivka Horwitz in *Buber's Way to I and Thou* (1978), which throws new light on the intimate personal and intellectual relationship between the two. It shows that an early version of *I and Thou*, *"Religion als Gegenwart"* (*Religion as Presence*) was presented by Buber in Rosenzweig's Lehrhaus. Additional evidence is found in the correspondence between Rosenzweig and Martin Buber in 1922, while Buber was writing his monumental *Ich und Du*.

Rosenzweig criticized Buber's dialogical philosophy, because it is based not only on the I-You relation, but also on I-It, a notion which Rosenzweig rejected as idealistic. He thought the counterpart to I-You should be He-It, namely "as He said and it became": building it around the human I – the human mind – is an idealistic mistake. Therefore, Rosenzweig preferred concentrating on the divine He, whose world man is searching for. The world is God's world; He is the Creator of the world. There is ample proof that Buber accepted Rosenzweig's criticism with regard to *Ich und Du*, although not immediately, as it would have demanded a drastic change in the book, but in his later writing – not only in the Bible translation where the Tetragrammaton is translated *Er* ("He"), but also in his own philosophy in the coming years. Buber then wrote about the Creator next to the Eternal Thou. The archival evidence thus makes it increasingly clear that Rosenzweig's philosophy played a more important role in the development of Buber's philosophy of dialogue than previously recognized.

Rosenzweig and Margrit Rosenstock

Rosenzweig's voluminous and recently published correspondence with Margrit Rosenstock-Huessy, Eugen's wife, called Gritli, from mid-1917 until late-1925, casts unexpected and lively light on Rosenzweig's *New Thinking*, as well as on his Judaism, his Jewish identity, his problems with his parents, with his friends and cousins, his attachment to uncle Adam, and his attitudes toward Christianity and Germany. They contain numerous philosophical and theological remarks and offer valuable insights into the birth and development of Rosenzweig's masterpiece, the *Star of Redemption*. In June of 1917,

Rosenzweig met Gritli in Kassel and he became her lover for some time. Whereas Eugen and his other friends wanted to convert Franz, Franz appreciated the attitude of Gritli, who was tolerant of the expression of his Jewishness. She did not try to convert him, and rather said to him in times of crisis: "Franz ich suche dein jüdisches Herz" ("Franz, I search for your Jewish heart"). The Gritli letters give new impetus for scholarly research into Rosenzweig's philosophy and into the complexity of his life. Reading the Gritli letters, we see that the former tendency to write much about Hegel and Schelling as a source for Rosenzweig does not follow from these letters, whereas little has been written as yet on Eugen Rosenstock, Hans and Rudolf Ehrenberg, or Hermann Cohen's profound influence on Rosenzweig. In the letters, Rosenzweig gave Rosenstock a great deal of credit and he greatly appreciated Cohen, from whom he borrowed the idea of revelation as a new creation.

The documents reveal many details about the *Star*, making it clear that the *Star* led Rosenzweig from thoughts about the exteriority of death and suicide to the positive experience of the life-transforming exteriority of revelation, which nourishes life in the community. In writing the *Star* Rosenzweig freed himself from a paralyzing and dead thinking, as well as from suicidal thoughts. He emphasized that the *Star* only elucidates one concept: that of factuality "*Tatsächlichkeit*": the fact (*die Tatsache, das Faktum*) which stands free from the idea. In the letters Rosenzweig speaks about his anti-idealistic thoughts on language, time, and eternity. He discusses the importance of the name, explained why he appreciated anthropomorphisms and attributed a special place to paganism, namely as the truth in embryonic form, and elucidated his concept of the miracle (*Wunder*) of revelation as "sign" (*Zeichen*), i.e., as predicted in creation. He stressed the Jewish character of the *Star*, wanted a Jewish publisher for the book, and described the *Star* as counterpart of Rosenstock's chief work *Im Kreuz der Wirklichkeit* (*Cross of Reality*).

From these letters, we also learn about many existential problems, about his mother's suicidal tendencies and Eugen's continual attempts to convert him. Most importantly, the letters contain many remarks on Rosenzweig's progress on his way to Judaism. He wrote on the Lehrhaus, on his translations, and on his joy of being of Jew. Noteworthy are his thoughts on the "New Law" (*neues Gesetz*), which is based on the commandment of love, which pertains to the whole of life and is not restricted to religion. This "New Law," being linked to the divine imperative of love, is not characterized by coercive force, but by its possible subjectivization: the objective Law, *Gesetz*, may become a personal commandment, *Gebot*. Just as "New Thinking" was required for philosophy leading "into life" (*ins Leben*), so the "New Law" in Jewish life could make a person alive (*lebendig*), turning him into a lively, responsive, and responsible being.

Rosenzweig's thoughts on the complex relationship between religion and revelation remain crucial for any future Jewish-Christian dialogue. They are an eminent example of dialogue, showing its possibilities and its boundaries. However, the Gritli letters inform us that Rosenzweig changed his view on the relationship between Judaism and Christianity during the year 1919. Whereas in the *Star* he still viewed the twin religions as antipodal, he now became increasingly influenced by Gotthold Ephraim *Lessing's parable of toleration, *Nathan the Wise*, and developed a view of Judaism and Christianity that is less antithetical and more egalitarian than in the *Star*. The emphasis now was on human beings, not Judaism or Christianity. The institutions are not God's bride; they are homes for the children of God, for people. Although Rosenzweig, like Lessing, conceived the truth as still having to be realized, he also remained critical towards Lessing and thought that the view expressed in *Nathan the Wise* is too bloodless and abstract; all persons are essentially different.

Influence

The Gritli letters, which contain more than a thousand pages and were published to a large extent in recent years, aroused renewed interest in Rosenzweig's writings. Interest is also growing from another direction, as a result of the great scholarly interest in the work of French Jewish philosopher Emmanuel *Levinas, who clearly recognized and expressed his debt to Rosenzweig. In May 2005, the Internationale Rosenzweig-Gesellschaft was founded, which organizes scholarly activities in Europe, the U.S., and Israel. Rosenzweig's impact on Jewish-Christian dialogue has been profound. His combination of a dynamic interest in Jewish learning, of vast general culture, and of a non-parochial Judaism has attracted many Jewish intellectuals.

BIBLIOGRAPHY: Y. Amir, *Faith-Full Cognition – A Study in Rosenzweig's Star of Redemption* (Heb., 2004); L. Anckaert, M. Brasser, and N. Samuelson (eds.), *The Legacy of Franz Rosenzweig. Collected Essays* (2004); L. Batnitzky, *Idolatry and Representation. The Philosophy of Franz Rosenzweig Reconsidered* (2000); G. Bensussan, *Franz Rosenzweig – Existence et philosophie* (2000); M. Brasser (ed.), *Rosenzweig als Leser. Kontextuelle Kommentare zum "Stern der Erloesung"* (2004); R. Burkhardt-Riedmiller, *Franz Rosenzweigs Sprachdenken und seine Erneuerung humanistischer und jüdischer Lerntraditionen* (1995); H.M. Dober, *Die Zeit ernst nehmen. Studien zu Franz Rosenzweigs "Der Stern der Erloesung"* (Epistemata, Würzburger Wissenschaftliche Schriften, Reihe Philosophie, vol. 84 (1990)); P.W. Franks, M.L. Morgan (eds.), *Franz Rosenzweig. Philosophical and Theological Writings. Translated and Edited with Notes and Commentary* (2000); R. Freund, *Die Existenzphilosophie Franz Rosenzweigs – Ein Beitrag zur Analyse seines Werkes "Der Stern der Erloesung"* (1959); N.N. Glatzer (ed.), *Franz Rosenzweig: His Life and Thought* (1961); idem, *On Jewish Learning* (1955; paperback ed., 1989) Y. Greenberg Kornberg, *Better than Wine. Love, Poetry and Prayer in the Thought of Franz Rosenzweig* (1996); R. Horwitz, *Buber's Way to "I and Thou." The Development of Martin Buber's Thought and His "Religion as Presence" Lectures* (1988; first published in Heidelberg 1978); idem, *Franz Rosenzweig – A Selection of Letters and Diary Fragments* (Heb., 1987); W. Licharz – M. Keller (eds.), *Franz Rosenzweig und Hans Ehrenberg. Bericht einer Beziehung* (Arnoldshainer Texte, Band 42) (1986); E. Meir, *Star from Jacob – The Life and Work of Franz Rosenzweig* (Heb., 1994); idem, *Letters of Love: Franz Rosenzweig's Spiritual Biography and Oeuvre in Light of the Gritli Letters* (2005); P. Mendes-Flohr (ed.),

The Philosophy of Franz Rosenzweig (1988); I. Rühle, *Gott spricht die Sprache der Menschen. Franz Rosenzweig als jüdischer Theologe – eine Einführung* (2004); N. Samuelson, *A User's Guide to Franz Rosenzweig's Star of Redemption* (1999); E.L. Santner, *On the Psychotheology of Everyday Life. Reflections on Freud and Rosenzweig* (2001); R. Schaeffler, B. Casper, S. Talmon, and Y. Amir, *Offenbarung im Denken Franz Rosenzweigs* (1979); W. Schmied-Kowarzik (ed.), *Der Philosoph Franz Rosenzweig (1886–1929) Internationaler Kongress- Kassel 1986.* Bd.1: *Die Herausforderung juedischen Lernens.* Bd. 2: *Das neue Denken und seine Dimensionen* (1988); idem, *Franz Rosenzweig. Existentielles Denken und gelebte Bewährung* (1991); J. Turner, *Faith and Humanism – Reflections on the Religious Philosophy of Franz Rosenzweig* (Heb., 2001); R. Horwitz, "Hermann Cohen and Franz Rosenzweig on Creation and Revelation," in: *Archivio di Filosofia*, 71 (2003), 115–29; A. Jospe, "The Frankfurt Lehrhaus: A Model for American Jewish Education?" in: E. Jospe and R. Jospe (eds.), *To Leave Your Mark. Selections from the Writings of Alfred Jospe* (2000), 82–83; R. Jospe and E. Meir, "Franz Rosenzweig's Inexpressible Joy," in: E. Meir and H. Pedayah (eds.), *Festschrift for R. Horwitz*; E. Meir, "La presenza biblica nella cultura ebraica contemporanea: M. Buber – F. Rosenzweig – E. Levinas," in: S.J. Sierra (ed.), *La lettura ebraica delle Scritture* (1995), 465–95; idem, "Goethe's Place in Rosenzweig's *Star of Redemption*," in: *Daat – A Journal of Jewish Philosophy and Kabbalah*, 48 (2002), 97–107 (Heb.); idem, "The Unpublished Correspondence between Franz Rosenzweig and Gritli Rosenstock-Huessy in the *Star of Redemption*," in: *Jewish Studies Quarterly*, 9 (2002), 21–70; H. Putnam, Introduction to F. Rosenzweig, *Understanding the Sick and the Healthy. A View of World, Man and God*, tr. Nahum N. Glazer (1999), 1–20; M. Scwarcz, "The Place of Franz Rosenzweig in the Philosophy of Judaism," in: Introduction to the Hebrew translation of the *Star*, 9–42 (Heb.); H.M. Stahmer, "Franz Rosenzweig's Letters to Margrit Rosenstock-Huessy, 1917–1922," in: *Leo Baeck Institute Yearbook*, 34 (1989), 385–409.

[Ephraim Meir and Rivka G. Horwitz (2nd ed.)]

ROSENZWEIG, GERSON (1861–1914), U.S. Hebrew writer. Born in Lithuania, he taught Hebrew in Bialystok, and in 1888 he immigrated to the United States. Rosenzweig edited several Hebrew periodicals – *Ha-Ivri* (1891–1902), *Kadimah* (1899–1902), *Ha-Devorah* (1911–12) – they were short-lived and earned him neither fame nor a livelihood. He also edited Hebrew columns in the Yiddish press.

Though he was a versifier rather than a poet, he had a genuine flair for satire and he was known to his contemporaries as the "sweet satirist of Israel" and as a parodist he earned an honorable place in Hebrew literature. His *Talmud Yanka'i* ("Yankee Talmud", 1907, 1909) poured a stream of ill-humored sarcasm on the peddler, the teacher, the rabbi. The pages of that collection of satires resembled the pages of the Talmud: the text in large letters, wreathed by commentary in Rashi script, is divided into six tractates instead of the talmudic six orders. Rosenzweig also denounced the vulgarisms of the country, the worship of money, the religion of success. Epigrammatic neatness was his forte. Example: "What is the difference between a convert and an anarchist? A convert denies what he believes, an anarchist believes what he denies." Using a biblical phrase, he quipped sardonically about his impending death by cancer of the tongue: "Life and death are at the mercy of the tongue" (Prov. 18:21). He published two books of epigrams: *Shirim, Meshalim u-Mikhtamim* (1893) and *Ḥamishah ve-Elef Mikhtamim* (1903; reprinted in Russia).

In the English preface to his Hebrew translations of "America," "The Star-Spangled Banner," and "Columbia, the Gem of the Ocean" which appeared in the booklet *Mi-Zimrat ha-Areẓ* (1898), he ventured to suggest that "the youngest nation is the heir of the oldest, and all that was best in the Jewish nation is now in the possession of the American nation to be developed and cultivated for the benefit of all humanity."

BIBLIOGRAPHY: E.R. Malachi, *Massot u-Reshimot* (1937), 178–86; E. Silberschlag, in: JBA, 18 (1960/61), 62–66; J. Kabakoff, *Ḥaluẓei ha-Sifrut ha-Ivrit ba-Amerikah* (1966), 211–66; Kressel, Leksikon, 2 (1967), 845–6.

[Eisig Silberschlag]

ROSETTA (Rashid), town in Egypt, situated on the western bank of the western tributary of the Nile. The *Genizah documents point to the economic activity of the Jews in Rosetta, e.g., a letter dated February 16, 1000, from Fustat sent to Yeshua ben Ismail al-Maghrebi in Rosetta. Meshullam of Volterra mentioned the existence of a Jewish community in Rosetta in 1481. When, at the beginning of the 16th century, *Alexandria lost its commercial importance, Rosetta became the most important transit harbor for the maritime trade between *Egypt and *Turkey. Jews in Rosetta did business with Jews from Rhodes. There were Jews in the town during the late Middle Ages, but the Jewish population increased considerably during the 16th century with the arrival of Spanish refugees. Rosetta became a well-organized community headed by learned rabbis. These included: R. Moses ibn Abudraham, R. Judah Meshʿal, R. Abraham b. Sur, and R. Abraham Medina in the 16th century; the great *posek* R. Mordecai ha-Levi (born in Rosetta in 1620); in the first half of the 17th century the great *dayyan* R. David Gershon; R. Abraham b. Nathan (d. 1725); and R. Shabbetai Nauavi, his brother Isaac, and R. Judah Crispin in the 19th century. Abraham ben Ḥayyim Nathan (d. 1725) settled in Rosetta in 1695 and for 30 years dealt in international trade, employing agents in Turkey and *Italy in the 18th century. He contributed money to the Viga Yeshivah in *Jerusalem. Close to the year 1740, there was a debate about his inheritance, whose result was the foundation of the Ḥesed le-Avraham u-Binyan Shelomo Yeshivah in Jerusalem in 1747. In the 17th century Israel Crispin and David Re'uel served also as *dayyanim*. The *Karaite Samuel b. David, who visited Egypt in 1641, relates that there were then two synagogues in Rosetta. Israel Benjamin (*Benjamin II) found 50 families there in the middle of the 19th century. After the opening of the Mahmudiya Canal which connected the Nile with Alexandria, Rosetta lost its importance and the majority of its Jews left, so the community disappeared. The Jews lived earlier in their own quarter. The Jewish translator for the French vice consul in Rosetta at the beginning of the 18th century was Abraham Metinoly. In 1709 there was a Jewish dragoman (translator) who served the French merchants in Rosetta. The scholars of the community had good connections with the Jerusalem community. There were Ottoman Jews, like Joseph Mitinoly who were translators. There were also Jews in the city who were French subjects. Some were also customs officers in the Ottoman period.

BIBLIOGRAPHY: Neubauer, Chronicles, 1 (1887), 156; J.Saphir, *Even Sappir*, 1 (1866), 3a; A. Yaari, *Mas'ot Erez Yisrael* (1946), 230; Ashtor, Toledot, 1 (1944), 23–24; 2 (1951), 113, 423, 445, 486, 506, 537; J.M. Landau, *Jews in Nineteenth-Century Egypt* (1969), 31; E.N. Adler, *Jewish Travellers* (1930), 163–4, 223, 335–8. **ADD. BIBLIOGRAPHY:** N. Golb, in: *Journal of Near Eastern Studies* 33 (1974), 137; S.Z. Havlin, in: J.M. Landau (ed), *Toledot ha-Yehudim be-Mizraim ba-Tekufah ha-Otmanit, 1517–1914* (1988), 275, 301; M. Rozen, in: *ibid.*, 428, 431, 445, 468; E. Bashan, in: *ibid.*, 84–85; L. Bornstein-Makovetsky, in: *ibid.*, 149, 194; S.Z. Havlin, in: *Shalem*, 2 (1976), 152ff.; A. David, in: *Pe'amim*, 54 (1993), 117–32; M. Gil, *Be-Malkhut Ishmael*, I (1997), 683.

[Eliyahu Ashtor / Leah Bornstein-Makovetsky (2nd ed.)]

ROSEWATER, EDWARD (1841–1906), U.S. journalist, publisher, editor and politician. Rosewater, who was born in Bukoven, Bohemia, went to the U.S. with his family in 1854. He soon became a telegrapher, and as a member of the United States Military Telegraph Corps during the Civil War, he accompanied Union forces and was responsible for transmission of Lincoln's Emancipation Proclamation. Rosewater went to Omaha as manager of Edward Creighton's Pacific Telegraph Company and also worked as a newspaper correspondent. He was elected to the Nebraska State Legislature in 1871 and founded the Omaha *Daily Bee* in connection with a campaign to establish an Omaha Board of Education. The rights of the common man and public improvements were constantly championed in the pages of the *Bee*, and though Rosewater gained numerous enemies, he became one of Omaha's best known and most influential citizens. Active in politics, Rosewater served on the Republican National Committee and its advisory board, represented the United States at two Universal Postal Congresses, and served on the Mint Commission. Advocating direct election of U.S. senators, civil service and labor reforms, a postal telegraph system, and postal savings banks, and opposed to trusts and unequal taxation, Rosewater twice unsuccessfully ran for the United States Senate. His son VICTOR ROSEWATER (1871–1940) succeeded him as editor of the *Bee*. He was active in Republican Party politics, chaired Omaha's first home rule charter convention and served on the University of Nebraska Board of Regents, the Omaha Public Library Board, and other public bodies. He was also a founding member of the American Jewish Committee. Rosewater retired from newspaper work in 1920. He was director of publicity for the Sesquicentennial Exposition, and later devoted himself to writing and lecturing. His books include: *Liberty Bell* (1926) and *History of Cooperative News Gathering in the United States* (1930).

BIBLIOGRAPHY: C. Gendler, *Jews of Omaha* (thesis, University of Omaha, 1968); J.A. Micks, in: DAB (1935), 171–2; *New York Times* (July 13, 1940), 13.

[Carol Gendler]

ROSH HA-AYIN (Heb. רֹאשׁ הָעַיִן), urban settlement in the coastal plain of Israel, 3 mi. (5 km.) east of Petaḥ Tikvah, near the Yarkon, whence the name Rosh ha-Ayin ("Head of the Spring") is derived. Ancient place names of the vicinity, the Hebrew *Aphek and the Greek Pegai (πηγαί, "springs"), also point to the river sources. Since the Middle Bronze period, the site constituted a major road station on the Via Maris leading from Egypt to Mesopotamia. As the area also commands the commodious entrance to the northern Judean Hills, sites of the vicinity were repeatedly fortified in history (Aphek, *Antipatris). The springs (which today are important in Israel's national water planning), and adjacent pumping installations, which provided water to Jerusalem during the British Mandate, were occupied by Israeli forces in July 1948. A large British army camp erected during World War II was converted in 1950 into a *ma'barah* that provided shelter for immigrants from Yemen. In 1951, Rosh ha-Ayin was transformed into a permanent settlement, and in 1955 it received municipal council status. The town was Israel's only large Jewish agglomeration in which nearly all the inhabitants originated in a single country, i.e., Yemen. The population grew through natural increase from 5,880 persons in 1950 to 11,600 in 1970, although hardly any immigrants came after 1951 and a considerable number of inhabitants left for other places in Israel over the years. Most breadwinners were employed outside Rosh ha-Ayin in industrial and other enterprises in Petaḥ Tikvah and other towns in the outer ring of the Tel Aviv conurbation. In the mid-1990s, the population was approximately 17,800, doubling to 35,200 in 2002 as the city absorbed many residents from the Gush Dan area (the Tel Aviv conurbation). In 1994 Rosh ha-Ayin received city status in the presence of late Prime Minister Yitzḥak Rabin. Its municipal area was 11.5 sq. mi. (30 sq. km.), its population heterogeneous, and its new industrial area (Afek) based on high-tech industry, mainly communications.

WEBSITE: www.rosh-haayin.muni.il.

[Shlomo Hasson / Shaked Gilboa (2nd ed.)]

ROSH HA-SHANAH (Heb. רֹאשׁ הַשָּׁנָה), the Jewish New Year, the autumn festival celebrated on the first and second days of Tishri.

In the Bible

The name Rosh Ha-Shanah as it is used in the Bible (Ezek. 40:1) simply means the beginning of the year, and does not designate the festival. The months of the year were counted from the spring month (Ex. 12:2), later called by the Babylonian name Nisan. The month known by the Babylonian name Tishri is, therefore, called the "seventh month" in the Pentateuch. When the festival on the first of this month is recorded, it is referred to as the festival of the seventh month and as a day of "memorial proclaimed with the blast of horns," or "a day of blowing the horn" (Lev. 23:23–25; Num. 29:1–6). In the Bible, the festival lasts for one day only; the two-day festival arose out of the difficulty of determining when the *new moon actually appeared.

The Babylonian name Tishri seems to derive from the root *seru*, which means "to begin." The ancient Semitic peoples thought of the year as beginning in the autumn, at the time of the late harvest; cf. the expressions *be-ẓet ha-shanah* ("at the end of the year"), and *tekufat ha-shanah* ("(at) the turn of the year"), by which the Feast of Ingathering, or *Sukkot, which is in a sense the popular equivalent of the more priestly Day of Remembrance, is dated in Exodus 23:16 and 34:22 respectively. The *Gezer Calendar in fact begins with two Months of Ingathering. This was the beginning of the economic year, when crops began to be sold. It is plausible, therefore, that the biblical feast originally marked the beginning of the agricultural year. If this is correct, the rabbinic name Rosh Ha-Shanah only makes explicit that which had been implicit in the observance of the day from earliest times. It was on the first day of the seventh month that Ezra the Scribe read the book of the Law before the people (Neh. 8:1–8). The people, conscious of their shortcomings, were distressed to hear the words of the Law; but Nehemiah, Ezra's companion, said to them: "Go your way, eat rich viands, and drink the sweet beverages, and send portions to him who has none prepared; for this day is holy to our Lord; do not be sad; for joy in the Lord is your refuge" (Neh. 8:10). The psalmist is almost certainly referring to this festival when he proclaims: "Blow the horn at the new moon, at the full moon for our feast day. For it is a statute for Israel, an ordinance of the God of Jacob" (Ps. 81:4–5). In the critical view, the Pentateuchal legislation in which the festival appears belongs to the Priestly Code (P) and, therefore, to the post-Exilic period, when the Babylonian influences had become particularly pronounced. The older critical views consider the whole institution to be post-Exilic, pointing out, for instance, that there is no reference to it in the lists of the feasts in Deuteronomy (16:1–17). More recently, however, S. Mowinckel (*The Psalms in Israel's Worship*, 1 (1962), 120ff.) has advanced the suggestion that there existed in pre-Exilic Israel an autumnal New Year festival on which God was "enthroned" as King (analogous to the Babylonian enthronement of *Marduk). He claims to have found marked traces in many of the psalms to substantiate his assertion. Although Mowinckel's thesis has won wide acceptance, it is still the subject of debate.

In Rabbinic Literature

The Mishnah (RH 1:1) speaks of four periods of the year, each known as Rosh Ha-Shanah (see *New Year). One of these is the first of Tishri, and it is to this day that the name generally refers. It is a day when all mankind is judged (RH 1:2). R. Eliezer taught that the world was created in Tishri; R. Joshua that it was created in Nisan (RH 10b–11a). In the Rosh Ha-Shanah liturgy, the reference to the day as the day on which the world was created follows the opinion of R. Eliezer (RH 27a). The motif of Rosh Ha-Shanah as a day of judgment is independent of the theme of creation. R. Naḥman b. Isaac interprets "From the beginning of the year even unto the end of the year" (Deut. 11:12) to mean that God determines at the beginning of the year what is to be at the end of the year (RH 8a). Another opinion has it that on Rosh Ha-Shanah heaven assigns to a person how much he will earn during the coming year (Beẓah 16a). Confidence in God's mercy is expressed when it is said: "It is the custom of men who appear before a court of justice to wear black clothes, to let their beards grow long because the outcome is uncertain. But Israel does not do so. On the day of judgment (Rosh Ha-Shanah), they wear white garments and have their beards shaven and they eat, drink, and rejoice in the conviction that God will perform miracles for them" (TJ, RH 1:3, 57b). The theme of God as King is particularly stressed on Rosh Ha-Shanah because of the day's association with His judgment (Ber. 12b). During the prayers of the day, it is necessary to recite ten biblical texts which have the theme of God as King (*malkhuyyot); ten which have the theme of God as He Who remembers (*zikhronot); and ten which have reference to the *shofar (shofarot; RH 4:5–6). These are explained as God saying, "Recite before Me on Rosh Ha-Shanah *malkhuyyot, zikhronot* and *shofarot: Malkhuyyot* so that you may proclaim Me King over you; *zikhronot* so that your remembrance may rise favorably before Me; and through what? Through the *shofar*" (RH 16a). The four names of the festival in Jewish tradition, based on the above, are: Rosh Ha-Shanah, Yom Teru'ah ("Day of Blowing the Horn"), Yom ha-Din ("Judgment Day"), and Yom ha-Zikkaron ("Day of Remembrance").

R. Keruspedai said in the name of R. Johanan: "Three books are opened on Rosh Ha-Shanah, one for the completely righteous, one for the completely wicked and one for the average persons. The completely righteous are immediately inscribed in the book of life. The completely wicked are immediately inscribed in the book of death. The average persons are kept in suspension from Rosh Ha-Shanah to the Day of Atonement. If they deserve well, they are inscribed in the book of life, if they do not deserve well, they are inscribed in the book of death" (RH 16b). The theme of the books of life and death feature prominently in Rosh Ha-Shanah liturgy. The intellectual difficulties in the whole concept were much discussed in the Middle Ages (see e.g. Naḥmanides, "*Torat ha-Adam*," in: H.D. Chavel (ed.), *Kitvei Rabbenu Moshe ben Naḥman*, 2 (1964), 264ff.).

The Shofar

The essential ritual of Rosh Ha-Shanah is the sounding of the *shofar*. The Mishnah (RH 3:2) rules that the horn of any animal (e.g. sheep, goat, antelope), except the cow, may be used as a *shofar* on Rosh Ha-Shanah. One of the reasons why the horn of a cow is not used is its reference to the golden calf and "a prosecuting counsel cannot act for the defense" (RH 26a). At a later period, the ram's horn was preferred in order to recall the binding of Isaac for whom a ram was substituted (RH 16a; see Gen. 22:13). It is considered meritorious to use a curved *shofar*, symbolic of man bowing in submission to God's will (RH 26b). The silence of the Scriptures as to why the horn is blown on this day left room for a wide variety of interpretations among later teachers. There are ten frequently-quoted reasons, which scholars have attributed to *Saadiah Gaon (see *Abudraham ha-Shalem*, ed. S. Krauser (1959), 269–70): (1) Trumpets are sounded at a coronation and God is hailed as King on this day. (2) The *shofar* heralds the beginning of the penitential season (from Rosh Ha-Shanah to the Day of Atonement). (3) The Torah was given on Sinai accompanied by blasts of the *shofar*. (4) The prophets compare their message to the sound of the *shofar*. (5) The conquering armies that destroyed the Temple sounded trumpet blasts. (6) The ram was substituted for Isaac. (7) The prophet asks: "Shall the horn be blown in a city, and the people not tremble?" (Amos 3:6). (8) The prophet Zephaniah speaks of the great "day of the Lord" (Judgment Day) as a "day of the horn and alarm" (Zeph. 1:14, 16). (9) The prophet Isaiah speaks of the great *shofar* which will herald the messianic age (Isa. 27:13). (10) The *shofar* will be sounded at the resurrection.

Maimonides (Yad, Teshuvah 3:4) writes: "Although it is a divine decree that we blow the *shofar* on Rosh Ha-Shanah, a hint of the following idea is contained in the command. It is as if to say: 'Awake from your slumbers, ye who have fallen asleep in life, and reflect on your deeds. Remember your Creator. Be not of those who miss reality in the pursuit of shadows, and waste their years in seeking after vain things which neither profit nor save. Look well to your souls and improve your character. Forsake each of you his evil ways and thoughts.'"

The particular *shofar* sounds blown on Rosh Ha-Shanah have an extended development. "A day of blowing the horn" (Num. 29:1) is, in Hebrew, called *yom teru'ah*, and is rendered by the Targum as *yom yabbava*. The phrase concerning the mother of Sisera who is said to have "looked through the window" (*va-teyabbev*; Judg. 5:28) is interpreted by the Rabbis as "and she wept." Hence the *shofar* blast is said to be a weeping sound. According to rabbinic tradition, however, the *teru'ah-yabbava* sound must always be followed and preceded by an extended, unbroken note, *teki'ah*. Since there are three references to the *teru'ah-yabbava* sound (Lev. 23:24; 25:9; Num. 29:1), it follows that three *teru'ah-yabbava* sounds are required, each preceded and followed by a *teki'ah* (RH 33b, 34a). There are doubts as to whether the weeping sound means three groaning notes (*shevarim*) or a series of nine very short wailing notes (*teru'ah*). Is the biblical *teru'ah-yabbava*, then, a *shevarim* note, or a *teru'ah* note, or both together? In order to eliminate all doubt, the practice arose, and is still followed, of sounding all three notes. The order became:

teki'ah shevarim teru'ah teki'ah (3 times)
teki'ah shevarim teki'ah (3 times)
teki'ah teru'ah teki'ah (3 times).

The final *teki'ah* is especially long and drawnout, and is known as *teki'ah gedolah*, "the great *teki'ah*." This series of 30 notes, first sounded after the reading of the Torah, is again sounded during the repetition of the *Musaf Amidah* (in some rites in the silent *Amidah*), and in many congregations also at the end of the service with an additional ten notes, so as to make a total of 100. The sounding of the *shofar* in the synagogue is an occasion of great solemnity at which God is entreated to show mercy to His creatures. The Midrash remarks: "R. Josiah said: It is written: 'Happy is the people that know the sound of the trumpet' (Ps. 89:16). Do not the nations of the world know how to sound the trumpet? They have numerous horns, sirens and trumpets, and yet it is said: 'Happy is the people that know the sound of the trumpet.' This means that Israel is the people which knows how to win over their Creator with the blasts of the *shofar* so that He rises from His throne of judgment to His throne of mercy and is filled with compassion for them and turns His quality of judgment into the quality of compassion" (Lev. R. 29:4).

The Laws and Customs of Rosh Ha-Shanah

On the first night of Rosh Ha-Shanah it is customary to greet one's friends with: "May you be inscribed (in the book of life) for a good year." The Sephardi version of the greeting is: "May you be inscribed for a good year; may you be worthy of abundant years." At the festive meal, it is customary to dip the piece of bread, over which grace has been recited, into honey as a token of the sweet year it is hoped will come. For the same reason, a piece of apple is dipped in honey and before eating it, the prayer is recited: "May it be Thy will O Lord our God and God of our fathers, to renew unto us a good and sweet year." Nuts should not be eaten on Rosh Ha-Shanah because they produce phlegm, and make it more difficult to recite the prayers of the day; also because the numerical value of the Hebrew for "nut" (*egoz*) is the same as that of "sin" (*Ḥet*). In some communities, the loaves for the festival meal are baked in the form of ladders to symbolize the fortunes of men in the year ahead: some ascending, others descending life's ladder. The custom of sending greeting cards before Rosh Ha-Shanah finds no support in the Jewish tradition, though it is now a widespread practice.

The prophet Micah speaks of God casting the sins of Israel into the depths of the sea. "And Thou wilt cast (*ve-tashlikh*) all their sins into the depths of the sea" (Micah 7:19). On the basis of this verse, the **Tashlikh* ceremony arose in which Jews go to a place where there is running water, the sea, a river, or a well (if neither of the former two are within walking distance) to recite this and other scriptural verses as well as penitential hymns and prayers on the first afternoon of Rosh Ha-Shanah (on the second if the first day falls on a Sabbath). There is no reference to the *Tashlikh* rite in the Talmud. A pagan origin for the custom has been suggested (J.Z. Lauterbach, *Rabbinic Essays* (1951), 299–433); a traditional interpretation has it that the fish in the river, whose eyes never close, are a reminder of the ever-watchful eyes of God, open always to look down on His creatures in mercy.

The scriptural readings in the synagogue on Rosh Ha-Shanah are: On the first day, Genesis 21 and the *haftarah*, I Samuel 1:1–2:10; on the second day, Genesis 22 and the *haftarah*, Jeremiah 31:2–20. The *maftir* on both days is Numbers 29:1–6.

Although Rosh Ha-Shanah as a festival is not more important than the other festivals, greater solemnity has come to be attached to it since it is also considered a day of judgment. *Hallel is, therefore, not recited. The day is imbued with an aura of awe as expressed in the prayer: "Now, therefore, O Lord our God, impose Thine awe upon all Thy works, and Thy dread upon all that Thou hast created, that all works may revere Thee and all creatures prostrate themselves before Thee, that they may all form a single band to do Thy will with a perfect heart."

BIBLIOGRAPHY: N.H. Snaith, *Jewish New Year Festival* (1948); S.J. Zevin, *Ha-Mo'adim ba-Halakhah* (1942[9]), 26–56; L. Jacobs, *Guide to Rosh Ha-Shanah* (1959); M. Arzt, *Justice and Mercy* (1963); S.Y. Agnon, *Days of Awe* (1965); Ta-Shema, in: *Tarbiz*, 38 (1968/69), 398f.; P. Goodman, *Rosh Hashana Anthology* (1971).

[Louis Jacobs]

ROSH HA-SHANAH (Heb. רֹאשׁ הַשָּׁנָה; "New Year"), eighth tractate in the order of *Mo'ed*; in some earlier Mishnah and Talmud editions it is seventh, and in current Talmud editions it is placed fifth. Although Rosh Ha-Shanah is the rabbinic designation for one of the major festivals of the Jewish calendar, that which falls in "the seventh month, on the first day of the month" (Lev. 23:24), the tractate does not deal exclusively with this New Year. It opens with the statement that there are four days of the calendar, each of which is a New Year for its own specific purpose. Thus the first of Nisan is the New Year for kings and for festivals, and the 15th of Shevat (or the first) the New Year for trees. However, the first day of Tishri, the "New Year for years," i.e., the beginning of the calendar year, became known as the New Year par excellence, and the bulk of the tractate's discussion is elaboration of the laws concerning it, its religious significance, and the details of the sounding of the *shofar*. In mishnaic times, though the authorities were familiar with astronomical calculations, the New Moon was fixed on the basis of observation, which meant that, as a rule, the *bet din* formally proclaimed the New Month only after it had heard evidence of witnesses who had actually seen the new moon.

The tractate is divided into four chapters. Chapter 1 speaks of the various New Years and indicates Rosh Ha-Shanah as the day of judgment for all mankind. It then deals with regulations concerning the fixing of the New Moon, and especially with the qualification of the witnesses to it. Chapter 2 continues with the subject of the determination of the New Moon, and concludes with the dramatic account of how Rabban *Gamaliel asserted his patriarchal authority to make R. *Joshua yield to his ruling. Chapter 3 deals mainly with particulars of the *shofar*. The chapter includes a profound homily explaining that it is not the actual sound of the horn but its devotional effect which is important. Chapter 4 first discusses whether the *shofar* is blown on the Sabbath when Rosh Ha-Shanah falls on that day. Ordinances enacted by Johanan b. Zakkai concerning various subjects are recorded. It then deals with the order of benedictions for Rosh Ha-Shanah, which are arranged in the *Musaf* service. The tractate has Tosefta and *Gemara* in both the Babylonian and Jerusalem Talmuds. In the Babylonian *Gemara*, there is a discussion as to whether the world was created in Nisan or in Tishri (10b–12a); the latter view seems to have been accepted in later amoraic times, as reflected in the Rosh Ha-Shanah prayers of those days. Of particular interest is the elaboration on the idea of Rosh Ha-Shanah being the day of judgment for every individual as well as for mankind (16a–18a).

Tractate *Rosh Ha-Shanah* is characterized particularly by two topics. The first is the intercalation of the year and how and when and for what reasons intercalation is effected, and what are the considerations which normally influence the determination of the yearly *calendar. The second is a systematic, philosophical, speculative discussion on everything concerning providence, and reward and punishment in this world and in the next. These topics are much better arranged and edited than others and more systematically than in all other tractates. The talmudic tractate was translated into English by Maurice Simon in the Soncino edition (1938).

BIBLIOGRAPHY: Epstein, Tanna'im, 363–72; Ḥ. Albeck, *Shishah Sidrei Mishnah*, 2 (1958), 305–9.

[Arnost Zvi Ehrman]

ROSH PINNAH (Heb. רֹאשׁ פִּנָּה), moshavah in northern Israel, on the slope of Mt. Canaan south of the Ḥuleh Valley. Rosh Pinnah was first founded in 1878 by pious Jews from *Safed who wanted to live by their own means instead of by *Ḥalukkah. They named their settlement Gel Oni ("Valley of My Strength," an adaptation of the name of the nearby Arab village Jāʿūna). The settlers, lacking both funds and farm experience, and harassed by their Arab neighbors, gave up after just over two years. In 1882, however, the settlement was renewed by First *Aliyah pioneers from Romania. The symbolic name "Corner Stone" is taken from Psalms 118:22.

Although Baron Edmond de *Rothschild extended aid to the isolated moshavah, it did not make much headway. The farmers tried to grow tobacco, mulberry trees for silkworms, and other specialties in addition to grain crops. After short periods of apparent prosperity these branches had to be abandoned for lack of markets. The British Mandate authorities maintained a police station and customs office near Rosh Pinnah. In the 1936–39 Arab riots, the moshavah suffered from repeated attacks. During the late 1930s the *Betar movement established a collective group in Rosh Pinnah which maintained itself by working on the local farms. In 1938 three of its members who attacked an Arab bus in retaliation for Arab terrorist acts were caught and tried by a British court. One of them, Shelomo *Ben-Yosef, was hanged in Acre Prison and buried in Rosh Pinnah. A memorial stone was erected at the site near the highway where the episode occurred. After 1948, immigrants were absorbed in the village and in a nearby *ma'barah* (immigrant transit camp) so that Rosh Pinnah's population rose to 1,480 by 1953. Some of the newcomers, however, were later transferred to the nearby development town of *Hazor or elsewhere, with the result that the 1961 population droppped to 702 and in 1970 was just 805. In 1949 Rosh Pinnah received municipal council status.

Grain crops and deciduous fruit orchards were its characteristic farm branches. In the mid-1990s, the population was approximately 1,820, increasing to 2,210 in 2002 on an area of 7 sq. mi. (18 sq. km.). Many of Rosh Pinnah's residents earned their livelihoods in the tourist industry, mainly in the area's guest houses. Some still worked in agriculture.

[Efraim Orni / Shaked Gilboa (2nd ed.)]

ROSHEIM, small town in the Bas-Rhin department, E. France. The earliest explicit evidence of the presence of Jews dates from 1215, when the Jews of Rosheim are mentioned as being engaged in *moneylending (the pledges consisting of Church vessels). At the time of the *Armleder massacres of 1338 and of those which occurred in 1345 the town protected its Jewish residents On the other hand, during the Black *Death persecutions (1349) the community suffered extensively although it did not cease to exist. After 1447 there was a temporary expulsion of the Jews. During the 16th century the community enjoyed exceptional renown through Joseph b. Gershon of *Rosheim, leader and official representative of the Jews far beyond the boundaries of lower Alsace. At the close of the 17th century there were 18 Jewish families, comprising 94 persons, in Rosheim. Under French rule the town endeavored to obtain at least a partial expulsion of the Jews, but its numerous requests were refused by the royal agent. In 1784 there were 52 Jewish families (268 persons) in Rosheim. The number reached 500 (about 14% of the total population) at the close of the 19th century, but it declined sharply in the 20th century. During World War II, 35 of Rosheim's Jews were deported by the Nazis. In 1970 only a handful of Jews were living in the town.

BIBLIOGRAPHY: F. Blumstein, *Rosheim et son histoire* (1899), 34–45; Z. Szajkowski, *Analytical Franco-Jewish Gazetteer 1939–1945* (1966), 250; Germ Jud, 1 (1963²), 310f.; 2 (1968), 704.

[Bernhard Blumenkranz]

ROSIN, DAVID (1823–1894), German educator and scholar. Rosin was born in Rosenberg, Silesia. After having attended the yeshivot of Kempen, Myslowitz, and Prague (he was ordained by S.J. *Rapoport), he wished to receive a regular school education. He went to Breslau, where he entered the *Gymnasium*, and graduated in 1846. Then he studied at the universities of Berlin and Halle (Dr. phil. 1851) and passed his teacher's examination. Returning to Berlin, he taught in various private schools and was, on Michael Sachs' recommendation, appointed head of the newly founded religious school of the Berlin Jewish community in 1854. He also taught at the teachers seminary. In 1867 he succeeded Manuel *Joel as professor of Midrash, Bible exegesis, and homiletics at the Breslau Jewish Theological Seminary.

Rosin's main scholarly work was on *Samuel b. Meir (*R. Samuel b. Meir als Schrifterklaerer*, 1880), whose Pentateuch commentary he published from a complete manuscript (*Perush ha-Torah Asher Katav Rashbam*…, 1881, repr. 1949), which is the only scholarly edition of this work. He also published a volume of Abraham *Ibn Ezra's poetry, vocalized, with a German rhymed translation and with commentary (*Reime und Gedichte des Abraham Ibn Esra*…, 1885–94). Rosin's lectures on Ibn Ezra's philosophy were published by his pupil David *Kaufmann in the *Monatsschrift fuer Geschichte und Wissenschaft des Judentums*, 42–43 (1898–99), to which Rosin occasionally contributed. Among other subjects, Rosin dealt with the *Sefer ha-Ḥinnukh* ascribed to Aaron ha-Levi of Barcelona (*Ein Compendium der juedischen Gesetzeskunde aus dem vierzehnten Jahrhundert*, 1871), and the ethics of Maimonides (*Die Ethik des Maimonides*, 1876). He edited M. Sachs' sermons (*Predigten. Aus dessen schriftlichem Nachlass*, 2 vols., 1868–69). Rosin's son HEINRICH became professor of medicine at Berlin University; a nephew, also called HEINRICH, was a well-known professor of law at Freiburg-im-Breisgau.

BIBLIOGRAPHY: M. Brann, *Geschichte des juedisch-theologischen Seminars in Breslau* (1904), 97–99, 115, 128–9 (incl. bibl.); M. Grunwald, in: *Breslau Seminary Memorial Volume* (1963), 313–4; B. Drachman, *ibid.*, 322. **ADD. BIBLIOGRAPHY:** D. Kaufmann, in: *Monatsschrift*, 42 (1898), 17–18.

[Archiv Bibliographia Judaica (2nd ed.)]

ROSKIES, DAVID G. (1948–), author, editor, and scholar of Jewish studies. Born in Montreal, Canada, he attended Yiddish secular schools. He was educated at Brandeis University, receiving his bachelor's degree in 1969, his master's degree in 1971, and his doctorate in 1975. He joined the faculty of the Jewish Theological Seminary in 1975, as associate professor; he became the Sol and Evelyn Henkind Chair in Yiddish Literature and Culture and professor of Jewish Literature. An expert in the field of Eastern European Jewry, Roskies wrote and lectured extensively on the subject.

In 1971 Roskies received critical attention for his *Night Words: A Midrash on the Holocaust*, one of the first liturgies on the Holocaust. The work has been translated into Hebrew and has been issued as an audio cassette. In 1975 he coauthored, with Diane Roskies, *The Shtetl Book: An Introduction to East European Jewish Life and Lore*, which became a standard text.

His 1984 work, *Against the Apocalypse: Responses to Catastrophe in Modern Jewish Culture*, won the Ralph Waldo Emerson Prize from Phi Beta Kappa. In this work Roskies traces the evolution of Jewish literature from a passive acceptance of suffering to a stance of advocacy and a refusal to surrender. Awarded a Guggenheim fellowship in 1985, he began a study of the modern Jewish return to folklore and fantasy; he edited *The Dybbuk and Other Writings by S. Ansky* in 1992, and authored *A Bridge of Longing: The Lost Art of Yiddish Storytelling* in 1995. Roskies's 1999 work, *The Jewish Search for a Usable Past*, considers the modern Jewish community's self-image in relationship to the roles and values found in Jewish literature. Examining the promotion of modern goals, such as nationalism and secularism, by Jewish writers, he contends that contemporary Jewish memory has been shaped by literary convention rather than fact.

In 1981 Roskies cofounded, with Alan Mintz, *Prooftexts: A Journal of Jewish Literary History*, published by the University of Indiana Press. From 1998 he served as editor-in-chief of the New Yiddish Library, published by Yale University Press. He also served as a member of the editorial board of the Posen Library of Jewish Culture and Civilization, and he was a member of the Association for Jewish Studies.

[Dorothy Bauhoff (2nd ed.)]

ROSMARYN, HENRYK (1882–1955), lawyer, journalist and political leader in Poland. Rosmaryn, who was born into an assimilated family in eastern Galicia, joined the Zionist organization and while still a law student was elected a member of its central committee. Before World War I, he edited the Zionist weekly in Polish *Wschód*. In 1918 he founded, with G. *Zipper, the Zionist daily in Polish *Chwila, which was published in Lvov, heading the editorial board until 1939.

For many years, he was a member of the Zionist Actions Committee representing the Zionists of eastern Galicia, and president of the Maccabi organization of Poland. From 1922 Rosmaryn was elected three times to the Polish Sejm (parliament) in Warsaw and was an active parliamentarian. Rosmaryn was a member of the presidency of the Jewish Club ("*Kolo Zydowskie*") in the Sejm, and became known for his struggle against the antisemitic policy of the government during the 1930s. With the outbreak of World War II, he fled to Romania, from where he went to Palestine in 1940. Between 1941 and 1945, he represented the Polish government-in-exile of London in Tel Aviv in the capacity of consul-general.

BIBLIOGRAPHY: N.M. Gelber, *Toledot ha-Tenu'ah ha-Ẓiyyonit be-Galiẓyah*, 2 (1958), index; I. Schwartzbart, *Tsvishn Beyde Velt Milkhomes* (1958), index.

[Moshe Landau]

ROSOWSKY, SOLOMON (1878–1962), composer and musicologist. Born in Riga, the son of the noted cantor Baruch Leib Rosowsky, he studied at St. Petersburg under Rimsky-Korsakov, Glazunov and Liadov. He was a cofounder of the *Society for Jewish Folk Music in St. Petersburg (1908), where he also served as musical director of the Yiddish Art Theater. In 1920 he founded the first Jewish Conservatory of Music at Riga. Rosowsky immigrated to Ereẓ Israel in 1925, taught music there and did research on biblical cantillation. He attempted, in cooperation with Y.L. *Ne'eman, to present and analyze the "essence" of the East Ashkenazi (Poland-Lithuania) style. This resulted in the voluminous work, *The Cantillation of the Bible (The Five Books of Moses)*, published in New York in 1957. Rosowsky composed songs, chamber and orchestral music, and music for the Hebrew theater. In his quest for a modern Hebrew style based on traditional and Oriental elements, he was a pioneer. His latter years were spent in New York, where he taught at the Cantors' Institute of the Jewish Theological Seminary.

BIBLIOGRAPHY: L. Appleton (ed.), *The Music of... Solomon Rosowsky* (1963), 9ff., incl. bibl.; M. Bronzaft, *Ha-Askola ha-Musikalit ha-Yehudit* (1940), 68–75, index; *New York Times* (Aug. 1, 1962), 31.

[Mordechai Breuer]

ROSS, BARNEY (**Barnet**, **Dov Ber**, **David "Beryl" Rasofsky**, "The Pride of the Ghetto"; 1909–1967), U.S. boxer, three-time champion as lightweight (1933–35), junior welterweight (1933–35), and welterweight (1934, 1935–38), only Jewish fighter to win two different world championships, member of Boxing Hall of Fame and International Boxing Hall of Fame. Ross was born on the Lower East Side of New York to Sarah and Isadore, religious immigrants from Brest-Litovsk, Russia. The family moved to the Maxwell Street neighborhood of Chicago when Ross was two, where his father, who was also a rabbi, ran Rasofsky's Dairy store. A week before his 14th birthday in December 1924, Ross' father was shot to death during a store robbery. His mother suffered a nervous breakdown and had to be taken care of by relatives; Ross and his older brother, Morrie, moved in with a cousin, and the three younger siblings were placed in an orphanage. In his anger, Ross rejected his Orthodox lifestyle and became obsessed with reuniting his scattered family. He became a petty thief and numbers runner, and worked for Al Capone, who reportedly gave him $20 and advised him to go straight. He turned to the ring, changing his name to Barney Ross so that his mother would not know he was boxing, and fought as often as five times a week, pawning his winning medals for three dollars apiece. In 1929, Ross won the Western and Inter-City Golden Gloves featherweight titles. His first professional fight was on August 31, 1929, and his big break came on June 23, 1933, when he fought Tony Canzoneri in Chicago for the world lightweight and junior welterweight titles, winning by a split decision and becoming the first fighter in the modern era to win two titles simultaneously. "Winning the titles was almost an anti-climax," Ross said later. "My big thrill came a few weeks before the fight. That was when I was able to take the younger kids out of the orphanage asylum and reunite them with Mom." His most famous fights were three welterweight championship bouts against Jimmy McLarnin in 1934 and 1935 – Ross won the first and third, the latter despite breaking his left thumb in the sixth-round – which captured the nation's attention and drew huge gates. Ross became only the third boxer in history to win world titles in three divisions. His last fight was on May 31, 1938, against Henry Armstrong. Referee Arthur Donovan moved to stop the bout in the late rounds and award Armstrong the victory, but Ross pleaded to allow the fight to continue, saying, "I've got to go out like a champion. Let me finish." He lost the title in a 15-round decision and retired after the fight, having never been knocked out in over 300 professional and amateur fights. His record in 81 bouts was 74 wins including two newspaper wins (22 KOs), four losses, and three draws.

In World War II, Ross fought at Guadalcanal, and while on patrol on November 20, 1942, he and three comrades ran into an advance party of Japanese. With the others wounded,

Ross defended them through the night while reciting Hebrew prayers from memory. He was awarded a Silver Star and a Presidential Citation. At the military hospital where he was treated for shrapnel in his legs and sides, Ross became addicted to morphine. His habit cost him $500 a week until Ross sought admission to a federal drug treatment facility, where he kicked the habit.

Ross, who was tremendously popular among American Jews, became active in the Emergency Committee to Save the Jewish People of Europe, also known as the Bergson Group. He also was active in another Bergson committee, the American League for a Free Palestine, which sought to rally American support for the creation of a Jewish state. His autobiography, *No Man Stands Alone: The True Story of Barney Ross* (1957) was made into a Hollywood movie, *Monkey on My Back* (1957). He is also the subject of a biography, *Barney Ross*, by Douglas Century (2006). Ross was elected to the Boxing Hall of Fame in 1956 and to the International Boxing Hall of Fame in 1990.

[Elli Wohlgelernter (2nd ed.)]

ROSS, DENNIS (1948–), U.S. diplomat. Ross was born to a Jewish mother and a Catholic father and grew up in Marin County in Northern California. Trained as a political scientist at the University of California, Los Angeles, Ross worked on two presidential campaigns (Robert Kennedy and George McGovern) before settling into a career as a foreign policy professional. His first government assignments were working on U.S.-Soviet relations, arms control, and the Middle East during the presidencies of Jimmy Carter and Ronald Reagan. Ross eschewed dogma and confrontational positions in favor of engagement and problem-solving through intensive, interest-based negotiations. His close relationship with Vice President George H.W. Bush at the end of the Reagan presidency led to his promotion to the senior ranks of American diplomacy following Bush's victory in 1988.

As director of Policy Planning under Secretary of State James Baker, Ross had substantial influence in shaping American policy toward the Soviet Union as the Cold War ended. Ross advocated U.S.-Soviet cooperation in promoting Arab-Israeli peace and was instrumental in organizing the 1991 Madrid peace conference – which led to the first sustained, multilateral peace negotiations between Israel and its Arab neighbors.

Ross' behind-the-scenes approach, together with his widely regarded diplomatic skills, allowed him to make the transition to the Clinton Administration where he was named Special Middle East Coordinator. Following the signing of the 1993 Israeli-Palestinian "Declaration of Principles" (the Oslo agreement), which was reached without American mediation, Ross' stature grew as American involvement in Arab-Israeli peacemaking intensified during the ensuing seven years. Ross did not favor American arbitration, intrusive monitoring, or explicit conditionality between foreign aid and the negotiations, though he advocated a stronger American position at the end of the Oslo process.

When Israeli-Palestinian negotiations reached an impasse, or when violence threatened to derail the process, Ross' involvement often reached a fever pitch. He led marathon negotiations that led to the signing of the Interim Agreement (1995), the Hebron Accord (1997), and the Wye River Agreement (1998). Ross worked closely with President Clinton, who became much more personally involved in the negotiations at the end of his presidency.

Ross believed strongly in the strategic importance of an Israeli-Syrian peace agreement and devoted significant attention to these negotiations, though the talks ultimately collapsed in early 2000. In the last months of the Clinton administration, Ross led an intensive effort to reach an Israeli-Palestinian "final status" agreement. But this final push for peace, which included the abortive Camp David summit in mid-2000, ended in failure as large-scale, sustained Israeli-Palestinian violence displaced the negotiations.

In his best-selling memoir, *Missing Peace* (2004), Ross blamed Palestinian leader Yasser *Arafat for the collapse of the Oslo process. After leaving government service, Ross took a senior position at the Washington Institute for Near East Policy. Ross also became chairman of the Jerusalem-based Jewish People Policy Planning Institute.

Although American Jews had previously served at the highest ranks of the foreign policy and national security establishment, they had generally not been granted overriding authority to manage U.S. diplomacy toward Israel and its neighbors. He was the first to attain such a dominant position and remained at the helm of America's peace process diplomacy under both Republican and Democratic administrations.

BIBLIOGRAPHY: D. Ross, *The Missing Peace*, (2004); S. Lewis "The Receding Horizon: The Endless Quest for Arab-Israeli Peace," in: *Foreign Affairs* (September/October 2004); J. Heilbrun, "Dennis Ross and the Endless Peace Process," in: *New Republic* (July 8, 1996).

[Scott Lasensky (2nd ed.)]

ROSS, HERBERT (1925–2001), U.S. dancer, choreographer, and film director. Ross began his career as a dancer and choreographer but after 1969 he became known principally as a film director. He directed such films as *Play It Again, Sam* and *The Owl and Pussycat*, and the dance-oriented films *The Turning Point* (1977), collaborating in its making with his wife, the ballerina Nora *Kaye; *Nijinsky* (1980); *Footloose* (1984); *Pennies from Heaven* (1982); and *Dancers* (1987). Ross also became an active dance director in theater and television. With his wife, he founded a short-lived company, the Ballet of Two Worlds, for which he created a full-length dramatic ballet, the *Dybbuk*. Ross created the choreography for various Broadway productions and in Hollywood he directed the musical version of *Good-bye Mr. Chips*.

BIBLIOGRAPHY: IED, 5:408.

[Amnon Shiloah (2nd ed.)]

ROSS, LILLIAN (1928?–), U.S. writer. Born in Syracuse, N.Y., Ross moved to New York City in her youth and worked briefly for the newspaper *PM* before joining the staff of *The New Yorker* in 1945. Notoriously reticent about her age, she is listed in one literary reference work as having been born in 1928, which would have made her 17 when she went to work for the magazine. There she became one of the better-known practitioners of a style of fly-on-the-wall reporting in which the writer never directly imputes motivitation. Nevertheless, her portraits of people like Ernest Hemingway and Adlai Stevenson, among others, were considered to be succinct and revealing. In 1950, her first portrait of Hemingway was published in *The New Yorker.* It was an account of two days Hemingway spent in New York in 1949 on his way from Havana to Europe. Ross captures Hemingway shopping for an elephant gun at Abercrombie & Fitch, aiming an imaginary weapon at the sky while walking along Madison Avenue. To celebrate the centenary of Hemingway's birth, in 1999, Ross wrote a second portrait, detailing the friendship the two struck up after the completion of the first article. Together, the two works provide the definitive sketch of one of America's greatest writers. Ross stayed with the magazine until 1987 and returned in 1993. She was the author of 12 books, including her memoir *Here but Not Here: A Love Story,* about her 40-year relationship as the mistress of William Shawn, the longtime editor of *The New Yorker.*

[Stewart Kampel (2nd ed.)]

ROSS, STEPHEN (1942–), U.S. developer. A native of Detroit, Ross earned a bachelor's degree in accounting from the University of Michigan Business School and a law degree from Wayne State before obtaining a master's in tax law at New York University. He worked for two years as a tax lawyer at the Detroit office of Coopers & Lybrand, then a major accounting concern. He was influenced by the success of his uncle Max *Fisher, who built a business empire in oil and gas, and became one of the nation's leading philanthropists. Ross yearned to work in New York, and he picked up experience at two investment firms, as an assistant vice president in the real estate subsidiary of Laird, Inc. and in the corporate finance department of Bear, Stearns & Co. In 1971 he began to organize deals by which wealthy investors incurred risk-free tax losses in affordable housing to shelter other income. He combined the idea of tax losses for wealthy investors with the procurement of subsidies for affordable properties. In 1972 he founded Related Housing Companies with the goal of building or rehabilitating housing to blend into the community. Throughout the 1970s and 1980s, Ross and his team built on the success to expand into a wider range of developments, starting with Riverwalk, a large, planned mixed-use development along the East River in Manhattan, which was never built. Related built its first office complex, with 880,000 square feet, in Westchester. From these beginnings came diversification into retail, industrial, office and mixed use, and a name change to the Related Companies, which included New York Development, Related Urban Development, Related Lodging Group, Related Retail, Related Apartment Preservation, Related Management Company and Related Urban Management Company. There were offices in Miami, Chicago, and California in addition to New York, and the Related Group of Florida became the largest and most successful developer in the state. In New York, the Related Companies was the developer of the $1.7-billion, 2.8-million-square-foot Time Warner Center on Columbus Circle in Manhattan, which opened in 2004. The company's portfolio, valued in excess of $8 billion, made it one of the leading real-estate developers in the country. In 2004, Ross gave $100 million to the University of Michigan; it was the largest donation to any U.S. business school, and the university trustees promptly renamed the school the Stephen M. Ross School of Business. Ross was also involved in a number of philanthropies. He was active in planning for a major renovation of the Guggenheim Museum, designed by Frank Lloyd Wright, in New York. He was a trustee of the Juvenile Diabetes Research Foundation. Ross and his partners in the Time Warner Center contributed $60 million to build the core and shell of the 100,000-square-foot new home for Jazz at Lincoln Center. Ross was a long-time supporter of the United Jewish Appeal-Federation of New York and was honored by the Jewish Association of Services for the Aged, among other groups.

[Stewart Kampel (2nd ed.)]

ROSSELLI, Italian family distinguished for its patriotic activities in the 19th and 20th centuries. Settling in London in partnership with the *Nathan family, parents of Ernesto *Nathan, later mayor of Rome, they kept open house for Italian conspirators and patriots, especially Giuseppe Mazzini, who thanked God for the friendship of the family. Giannetta Nathan married Pellegrino Rosselli, and with him continued to follow the family tradition; it was in their house in Pisa (now a national monument) that Mazzini died, a fugitive, in 1872. Their descendants included CARLO ROSSELLI (1899–1937), socialist writer and economist, author of *Socialismo liberale* (1930, 1945) and of *Scritti politici ed autobiografici* (1944). Rosselli was one of the foremost opponents of Fascism, and founded for this purpose the movement Giustizia e Libertà with its own publication. He led an eventful life, including a daring escape by speedboat from Fascist confinement at Lipari in 1934 and various commands during the Civil War in Spain, where he served with the International Brigade and was wounded in 1936. His brother NELLO (1900–1937) wrote *Mazzini e Bakunin* (1927), *Carlo Pisacane nel Risorgimento Italiano* (1932), and other works. He shared his brother's views and fought with him in the underground against Fascism. At a Jewish youth movement convention in Leghorn in 1924, he propounded the thesis that Judaism is above all the religion of liberty. The two brothers were murdered in Bagnoles de l'Orne, France, by hired assassins of the Fascist government (June 1937).

BIBLIOGRAPHY: Levi, in: RMI, 5 (1930/31), 587–612; S. Trantin, *Dix aus de fascisme totalitaire en Italie…* (1937), 228–36; G. Salvemini, *Carlo and Nello Rosselli, A Memoir* (1937).

[Giorgio Romano]

ROSSEN, ROBERT (1908–1966), U.S. film writer, producer, director. Born in New York, Rossen was a prizefighter in his early years and worked on the stage before becoming a screenwriter in 1939. He wrote, produced, and directed: *All the King's Men* (Oscar winner for Best Picture and nominated for Best Director and Best Screenplay, 1949), *Alexander the Great* (1956), *The Hustler* (Oscar nominations for Best Picture, Best Director, and Best Screenplay, 1961), and *Lilith* (1964). He wrote and directed *Johnny O'Clock* (1947), *Mambo* (1954), and *They Came to Cordura* (1959). He produced and directed *The Brave Bulls* (1951) and directed *Body and Soul* (1947) and *Island in the Sun* (1957).

Other films for which he wrote and/or co-wrote the screenplay include: *Marked Woman* (1937), *They Won't Forget* (1937), *A Child Is Born* (1939), *The Roaring Twenties* (1939), *The Sea Wolf* (1941), *Out of the Fog* (1941), *Blues in the Night* (1941), *Edge of Darkness* (1943), *A Walk in the Sun* (1945), *The Strange Love of Martha Ivers* (1945), and *Desert Fury* (1947).

BIBLIOGRAPHY: A. Casty, *The Films of Robert Rossen* (1969).

[Ruth Beloff (2nd ed.)]

ROSSENA, DANIEL BEN SAMUEL OF (15th–16th century), Hebrew poet in N. Italy. His principal work (1506) is a Hebrew adaptation in rhymed prose of the Italian romance "*Bernabo e Luciana*," still unpublished (Mss. Bodl. and Turin). Some of his shorter compositions have been published, including his contribution to an interchange of poems in praise and blame of women by contemporary Italian Jewish poets. His first marriage proving barren, he received special authorization to take a second wife.

[Cecil Roth]

ROSSI, AZARIAH (Bonaiuto) BEN MOSES DEI (c. 1511–c. 1578), the greatest scholar of Hebrew letters during the Italian Renaissance. He was born in Mantua to the Min ha-Adummim family, one of the most eminent families in the history of Italian Jewry. According to a legend quoted by Rossi himself, the family was one of the few that the emperor Titus brought to Rome from Jerusalem after the destruction of the Second Temple. From the 13th century, the family produced a line of scholars, polemicists, rabbis, and artists, many of whom became famous in Jewish and Italian culture, especially during the Renaissance. At that time, the family was centered in the court of the Gonzaga princes in the city of Mantua, where the composers Anselmo de' Rossi and his relative Salamone de' *Rossi produced their work. Rossi received both his general and Jewish education in Mantua, but spent most of his life outside his native city. He studied medicine and apparently earned a meager living as a doctor throughout his life. He wandered to several cities in Italy, especially in the Papal States, and lived for some time in Ferrara, Ancona, Bologna, and Sabbioneta. When the pope expelled the Jews from his domains in 1569, Rossi settled again in Ferrara, where he wrote his major work. Toward the end of his life, he returned to Mantua, where he died after supervising the printing of his *Me'or Einayim* ("Enlightenment to the Eyes," 1573–75). Rossi did not publish anything until he was 60 years old. It seems that he did not even intend to publish, though a reading of his major work reveals that there is no doubt that he spent most of his time studying classical and medieval Latin and Italian literature as well as Jewish history and literature. An unusual event caused him to write an important book. In 1571, when he was living in Ferrara, the city was struck by a disastrous earthquake which lasted intermittently for about ten days. Rossi, along with the majority of the survivors, fled to the fields outside the city. The event seemed to him to be a direct intervention of God in the life of the city and in his own life, and in the first chapter of *Me'or Einayim* entitled "*Kol Elohim*" ("The Voice of God"), he describes the phenomenon in great detail, giving a vivid description of each phase of the earthquake and its effect upon the citizens, Jews and non-Jews. He added a learned discourse on the reasons for, and the significance of, earthquakes according to classical and medieval non-Jewish scholars, comparing the natural causes given by the non-Jewish writers with the statements concerning the divine origin of this phenomenon found in the Bible, the Talmud, and the writings of medieval Jewish scholars. While outside the city during the earthquake, Rossi met a Christian scholar who was then studying the Greek pseudepigraphical work, Letter of *Aristeas (see Apocrypha and *Pseudepigrapha). The scholar asked Rossi for the true meaning of some part of the work, assuming that he was familiar with the Hebrew original of the text. When Rossi told him that there was no Hebrew original, and that the work was unknown to the Jews, the Christian scholar was very much surprised. Since the Letter of Aristeas is important to the study of the text and development of the Old Testament (the book describes the translation of the Old Testament from Hebrew into Greek), Rossi decided to translate the work. He entitled his translation *Hadrat Zekenim* ("The Glory of the Elders"), which became the second part of *Me'or Einayim*. The two chapters comprising *Hadrat Zekenim* are quite short, the largest and most important part of *Me'or Einayim* being the third part, *Imrei Binah* ("Words of Wisdom"), which is divided into 60 chapters. This latter part is a revolutionary study of the development of the Bible and of Jewish history, chronology, poetry and culture.

The sources which Rossi used reveal unusual knowledge and erudition, unequaled by any previous Hebrew literary scholar and by few subsequent scholars. Knowing very little Greek, he used Latin and Italian translations of the writings of the Greek philosophers and writers. He was fluent both in classical and medieval Latin, and was a master of medieval and Renaissance Italian literature. More than a hundred non-Jewish scholars are quoted in his work (see the list in D. Cassel's edition of *Me'or Einayim*, 1866), not only the oft-quoted

Greek philosophers, Plato, Aristotle, and Pythagoras, but also Homer, Aesop and Euclid. Classical literature is represented by Virgil, Terence, Tibulus, Seneca, Cicero, Themistius, and others. Because of the nature of his study, he had special interest in classical historians, relying upon such writers as Herodotus, Xenophon, Livy, Suetonius, Plutarch, Caesar, Dionysius of Halicarnassus, Diodorus Siculus and Dio Cassius. In the fields of geography and natural history, he cites the works of Pliny and Strabo, and in medicine and law he also refers extensively to classical writers. Rossi paid special attention to the writings of Jewish scholars in the Hellenistic period, especially *Philo (whose name he translated as Jedidiah ha-Alexandroni). In fact, he was responsible for reviving the interest of Jewish writers in Philo after the philosopher had fallen into oblivion for 1,500 years. Intensively studying the works of the philosopher, he proved, among other things, that Philo did not use the Hebrew text of the Bible but the Greek Septuagint translation. He conducted a special search in Italian libraries for remnants of the works of Jewish writers contemporary with Philo who wrote in Greek. The most unexpected of Rossi's sources are the writings of prominent Church Fathers, among them Eusebius, Jerome, Augustine, Justin Martyr and Clement of Alexandria. Employing the works of such writers to solve problems in Jewish history and chronology was inconceivable to other contemporary Jewish scholars. Medieval Latin and Italian literature constitute a significant part of his sources. The works of Thomas Aquinas, Isidore of Seville and Hugo of St. Victor are frequently quoted, and Dante and Petrarch greatly impressed him. He was especially influenced by Pico della Mirandola, among Renaissance writers, not only by the content of his works but also by his methods of scholarly study. Thus Rossi was well equipped to fulfill the prodigious task that he set himself when he began to write *Imrei Binah*.

In *Imrei Binah*, he studied the ancient history of the Jews by comparing the Hebrew sources, especially the Talmud, with the classical sources, Jewish and non-Jewish. His methods, essentially those of the critical history which began to be written in the Renaissance, were not applied to all the Jewish texts. Rossi refrained from using the critical method in the study of the Bible, but he applied it to talmudic legends, which many previous scholars had not accepted as absolute religious truth. The novelty of his approach was that although he was a Jewish scholar, Rossi usually accepted the facts given in the non-Hebrew sources rather than those given in the Talmud. (Occasionally where he failed to use critical methods with Greek and Latin sources, he made errors.) In the study of ancient Jewish history, Rossi discovered a more accurate length of the Persian period, i.e., the period between Ezra and Nehemiah and the conquest by Alexander the Great. Talmudic chronology and its medieval followers considered this period to be very short; Rossi attempted to determine its actual span and its importance in Jewish history. He proved that the *Josippon, regarded by medieval Hebrew scholars and historians as an authoritative source on Jewish history, is a medieval compilation, which, although making use of writings of Josephus, falsified many historical facts and is therefore unreliable. This disclosure came as a shock to traditional scholars, who for many generations accepted the *Josippon* as the main authority on the history of the Jews during the Second Temple period. Another important aspect of *Imrei Binah* is its discussion of the revival of Jewish-Hellenistic literature written in Greek during the period of the Second Temple and after its destruction. Rossi was the first Jewish scholar to make use of these writings in the study of Jewish history, literature, religion and culture (though Christian scholars used them during the Middle Ages because they were included in Greek and Latin translations of the Bible).

Probably the most important part of *Imrei Binah* is that devoted to the study of Jewish chronology. In a very detailed study, Rossi proved that counting the years from the creation and basing a calendar on this count is a relatively recent Jewish usage; none of the ancient sages in the talmudic or geonic period, and certainly not in the Bible, used a calendar reckoned from the creation. Even in the early Middle Ages more ancient calendars were used, especially one based on the conquest of Palestine by Alexander. Thus he exposed the fact that the calendar accepted in his day was not of ancient origin. In addition, he tried to prove that the Bible and the other ancient sources are insufficient for reconstructing the chronology from the creation to the present time. He thereby indicated that the calendar was not only untraditional, but that it also made a false claim. These findings seemed heretical to his traditional contemporaries, and even his friends among the Italian Renaissance scholars could not accept such a radical point of view. In the same critical manner, Rossi dealt with countless other subjects – archaeology, Jewish coins, the development of the Hebrew language and the use of Aramaic by ancient Jews, Hebrew poetics and poetry, etc. Although modern scholarship does not accept many of his conclusions, some are scientifically sound, and, in any case, there is no doubt that Rossi's scholarship was more than 200 years ahead of its time.

The advanced critical spirit and method of *Me'or Einayim* made the work a subject of controversy for a long time. While it was being printed in Mantua, rabbis who heard about its contents raised objections, some of which Rossi answered in the work itself. When the work was published, the traditional rabbis in Italy were shocked, especially by Rossi's attitude toward talmudic and midrashic legends and his denial of the validity of the chronology claiming to date from the creation. Even his friend and associate, Moses b. Abraham *Provençal, fiercely criticized Rossi's attitude toward the calendar, as did Isaac Finzi of Pesaro. In 1574, even before the printing of *Me'or Einayim* was completed, the rabbis of Venice, headed by Samuel Judah *Katzenellenbogen, published a proclamation of *ḥerem* against possessing, reading, or using the book, unless one received special permission from the rabbis of his city. Rossi was not personally attacked, the impeccable conduct of his private life easily meeting Orthodox standards of behavior. The *ḥerem* was followed by similar declarations in such cities as Rome, Ferrara, Padua, Verona and Ancona, in which rabbis warned their congregations against reading the work. The controversy spread to other Jewish communities; in Safed a proclamation of *ḥerem* was prepared for the signature of Joseph b. Ephraim *Caro, the great halakhist, but Caro died before signing it, and the *ḥerem* was published by the other rabbis of Safed. Judah Loew b. *Bezalel of Prague, who defended the absolute truth of the talmudic legends and traditions, dedicated a major part of his work on the oral tradition, *Be'er ha-Golah* (Prague, 1598), to direct attacks against Rossi and his teachings. Even in Mantua, where the author was well known and where the book was printed, persons under 25 were forbidden to read it. Before his death, probably in 1578, Rossi wrote a reply to his critics, *Maẓref la-Kesef* (1845; "The Purification of Silver"), which deals especially with the problem of the calendar and chronology. Later, *Maẓref la-Kesef* was printed together with *Me'or Einayim*. The ban on *Me'or Einayim* persisted for more than a hundred years, during which time few scholars dared to use or even mention the work. Renewed interest in the book was aroused only with the beginning of the Haskalah period late in the 18th century, when *maskilim* found in Rossi's work ideas similar to their own. The first modern printing of the work (after the Mantua edition) was published by the *maskilim* of Berlin in 1794.

BIBLIOGRAPHY: Zinberg, Sifrut, 2 (1956), 290–5; C. Roth, *Ha-Yehudim be-Tarbut ha-Renaissance be-Italyah* (1962), passim; S. Simonsohn, *Toledot ha-Yehudim be-Dukkasut Mantovah*, 2 (1965), 462ff.; Introduction to *Me'or Einayim* (1863, ed. by J.L. Zunz); Introduction to *Me'or Einayim* (1866, ed. by D. Cassel); D. Kaufmann, in: REJ, 33 (1896), 77–84; S. Baron, *La Méthode historique d'Azaria de Rossi* (1929); Waxman, Literature, 2 (1970), 516–22.

[Joseph Dan]

ROSSI, MADAMA EUROPA DE', highly accomplished professional singer in the court of the Gonzaga family in late 16th and early 17th century Mantua. The sister of the composer and musician Salamone De' *Rossi, she was the daughter of Bonaiuto De' Rossi and the wife of the prominent Jewish community leader David ben Elisha, whose last name was also De' Rossi. Madama Europa had two sons, Bonaiuto (Azaria), who became a prominent Jewish leader and educator, and Angelo (Mordechai), who became a court lutanist in Turin and a banker. Madama Europa's grandsons also served as skilled court musicians and bankers in Turin.

Madama Europa's musical activities in Mantua are known through court salary records and letters from audience attendees. In one document of 1592–93 she is listed as "Europa di Rossi," along with a group of other musicians, including Claudio Monteverdi. The Christian community richly rewarded talented women singers who displayed high levels of skill. Female singing groups were also in fashion, and Europa apparently sang in some of those ensembles. In Renaissance Italy, singers were frequently instrumentalists, and Europa may have played a lute or *chitarrone*. Madama Europa may have derived her stage name from singing "The Rape of Europa," an intermedio written by Giovanni Gastoldi to the lyrics of Gabriello Chiabrera. One such performance took place in 1608 as part of the festivities for the nuptials of Francesco Gonzaga, the crown prince, to the *infanta* Margherita of Savoy. Federico Follino, who may have arranged these events, wrote that Madama Europa "reached the middle of the stage, then in her capacity as a woman most understanding of music, she sang to the listeners' great delight and their greater wonder, in most delicate and sweet voice, the madrigal.... While she sang, with the sweetest harmony, these tearful notes, the listeners were awakened, through pity, to shed tears."

[Judith Pinnolis (2nd ed.)]

ROSSI, SALAMONE DE' (Heb. **Shelomo Min-ha-Adummim**; fl. first third of 17th century), composer from Mantua. Salamone de' Rossi became the leading Jewish composer of the late Italian Renaissance, and a court musician of the Gonzaga rulers of Mantua. Very little is known about his life. He was apparently the son of a certain Bonaiuto (Azariah) de' Rossi; but this Azariah cannot be identical with the well-known philosopher of the same name who expressed regret that he had no sons to survive him. Rossi's published works ranging between the years 1589–1628 are the only direct documentation on his life and work. It has been assumed that he was born about 1570. He entered the service of Duke Vicenzo I in 1587 as a singer and viola player, and soon became the leader of the duke's musical establishment and of an instrumental ensemble composed most probably of Jewish musicians. This group achieved a high reputation and was occasionally loaned to neighboring courts, as in 1612 when Alessandro, duke of Mirandola, invited "the Jew Salamon and his company" to his court. Rossi's name as a violist appears on the ducal payrolls until the year 1622. The death of the last Gonzaga duke and the sack of Mantua by the Austrian (Hapsburg) army (1628–30) put an end to the golden age of Mantuan court music. In that year, many Jews fled to the Venetian ghetto where the Mantuan music circle found a certain measure of continuation in the Jewish musical Accademia degli Impediti under the leadership of Rossi's sponsor, the famed Leone *Modena, although it cannot be ascertained whether Rossi himself was still alive and active in the Accademia. With Salamone de' Rossi, a peak was reached in Jewish contributions to western art music (see *Music). He was perhaps the last, but certainly the most important, of a long and distinguished list of Jewish court musicians (instrumentalists, singers, dancers, players) who were active in Mantua throughout the 16th century, and included Abramo dall' *Arpa (c. 1542–c. 1577), a harpist, and the son of a distinguished harpist; Abramino, his nephew; Isacchino Massarano, flutist, dancer, and dancing master (1583–99); Davit da Civita, madrigalist (published work, 1616); and Allegro Porto, composer (works published 1619, 1625).

At the Mantuan court, Rossi developed his abilities through a constant exchange of views and techniques in composition with the well-known musicians of the court, who included M.A. Ingenieri (his teacher and that of his colleague C. Monteverdi), G.G. Gastoldi, J. de Wert and L. Viadana.

Like the other Mantuan court musicians, Rossi started as a madrigalist but soon tried his creative talents at the new style of ornamental monody, i.e., songs or instrumental pieces with one leading solo voice supported by a fundamental bass. He is considered the pioneer of these new baroque forms which include the trio sonata and suite. As a Jewish musician, his lasting contribution is his *Ha-Shirim Asher li-Shelomo* (published by Pietro and Lorenzo Bragadini, Venice, 1622/23), 33 settings for three to eight voices of Hebrew texts, comprising psalms, hymns, and other religious poems for festive synagogue services. The settings are composed in the then prevailing a cappella style of Palestrina and G. Gabrieli, with intent to regenerate traditional musical liturgy with polyphonic choral settings.

Other musicians of the Rossi family included his sister, known as "Madama *Europa," and her sons Anselmo, Angelo and Bonaiuto. Angelo and his sons Giuseppe and Bonaiuto were musicians at the court of Savoy in Turin between 1608 and 1649.

Rossi's other published works are: *Canzonette a tre voci* (vol. 1, 1589; vol. 2, 1592 (lost); reprint, Venice, 1596?); *Madrigali a cinque voci*, vol. 1 (1596?; Antwerp, 1598?; Venice, 1600; reprints, Venice, 1603, 1607; Antwerp, 1610?; Venice, 1612?; Antwerp, 1618); vol. 2 (Venice, 1599?; Venice, 1602; reprints, Venice, 1605, 1610); vol. 3 (Venice, 1603; reprints, Venice, 1609, 1620); vol. 4 (Venice, 1610; reprint, Venice, 1613); vol. 5 (Venice, 1622); *Madrigali a quattro voci* (vol. 1, Venice, 1610), *Madrigalleti a due voci* (Venice, 1628); "Balletto," in: *Musiche... composte per la Maddalena...*, (Venice, 1617). Instrumental music: *Sinfonie, gagliarde*, etc. (vol. Venice, 1622; reprint: Venice, 1636?; 1642). Modern editions 1, Venice, 1607; vol. 2, Venice, 1608; vol. 3, Venice, 1613; vol. 4, of Rossi's works include: S. *Naumbourg and V. d'Indy (eds.), *Cantiques de Salamon Rossi* (1877; 33 of the 35 pieces in *Ha-Shirim Asher li-Shelomo*, and a selection of madrigals); F. Rikko (ed.), *Ha-Shirim Asher li-Shelomo* (1967; 2 vols. of transcriptions; the 3rd, with facsimiles and translations of the prefatory matter, not yet published, 1971); F. Rikko and Joel Newman (eds.), *Salamon Rossi – Sinfonie, Gagliarde, Canzone 1607–1608*; E. Werner (ed.), Salomone de' Rossi, *Three Hebrew Compositions* (1956); others, including arrangements with organ accompaniment, see Sendrey, Music, index.

BIBLIOGRAPHY: MGG; Riemann-Gurlitt; Grove, Dict; Baker, Biogr Dict; Sendrey, Music, index; C. Roth, *Jews in the Renaissance* (1959), 274–304; S. Simonsohn, *Toledot ha-Yehudim be-Dukkasut Mantovah*, 2 (1964), ch. 7, and passim on other members of the Rossi family; A. Einstein, in: HUCA, 23 (1950–51), pt. 2, 383–96; E. Birnbaum, *Juedische Musiker am Hofe von Mantua* (1893), and an updated Italian edition by V. Colorni, in: *Civiltà Mantovana*, 2 (Mantova, May–June, 1967), 185–216; J. Newman, *The Madrigals of Salamon de Rossi* (unpubl. diss. Columbia, 1962), Ann Arbor University Microfilms 63-6121, incl. also a revised translation of A. Einstein's article in: HUCA, 23 (see above); Adler, Prat Mus, 55–64; I. Adler, in: *Jewish Mediaeval and Renaissance Studies* (1967), 331–2, 340–4.

[Edith Gerson-Kiwi]

ROSSIN, SAMUEL (1890–1941), Soviet Yiddish writer. Born in Shumyachi, Smolensk, Rossin began his career with *Bobe Mayses* ("Fairy Tales," 1919), versified fairy tales for children, which were specifically Jewish in atmosphere and imagery. There followed poetry, stories, and a drama. His love poems, *Farlibterhayt* ("In Love," 1938), expressions of individual longing and fulfillment, eschewed social protest. Upbraided for composing melancholy, individualistic works in a collectivist, progressive society, he replied that a poet could not compel his heart to march in step like a soldier. In his last lyrics, *Lider Vegn Tatn* ("Poems about Father," 1939), his father, who died when the poet was thirteen, becomes the symbol of all Jewish fathers: restless, joyless, careworn, wandering with a pack on his back, barely eking out a living. Although past fifty when the Germans invaded Russia, he enlisted in the Soviet army and was among the early war casualties.

BIBLIOGRAPHY: Rejzen, Leksikon, 4 (1929), 215f. **ADD. BIBLIOGRAPHY:** A. Kushnirov, in: *Heymland*, 2 (1947), 144–49; B. Mogilner (ed.), *Lirik* (1983).

[Sol Liptzin]

ROSTEN, LEO CALVIN (1908–1997), U.S. humorist. Born in Lodz, Poland, Rosten was taken to the U.S. as a child. He received a Ph.D. from the University of Chicago in 1937. He had a distinguished career in the U.S. government as a consultant to the secretary of war and as a social scientist but was best known as a writer. Under the pen name of Leonard Q. Ross, he was the creator of one of the most famous characters in modern American fiction, Hyman Kaplan, a pupil at a night school for immigrants. Kaplan's existence outside this setting is never described and he is nowhere identified specifically as a Jew, but the matter is never in doubt. In his struggles with the English language Kaplan expresses the Jewish immigrant's effort to integrate himself into American society and culture, his aspirations, and his sense of freedom and wonder in a new environment. Such matters are treated hilariously in both *The Education of H*Y*M*A*N K*A*P*L*A*N* (1937) and its sequel, *The Return of H*Y*M*A*N K*A*P*L*A*N* (1959), where Rosten deals with the interesting pupil-teacher relationship. Under his own name, Rosten wrote studies of journalism and Hollywood and a novel about an army psychiatrist, *Captain Newman, M.D.* (1962). In 1968 he published *The Joys of Yiddish*, an amusing and informative survey of the Yiddish language and its influence on everyday speech. In 1976, *O K*A*P*L*A*N! My K*A*P*L*A*N!* was published.

BIBLIOGRAPHY: R. Newquist, *Counterpoint* (1964), 522–36; S.J. Kunitz (ed.), *Twentieth Century Authors*, first suppl. (1955).

[Irving Fineman]

ROSTOV, capital city of the Rostov district, Russian Federation. The town was founded in the middle of the 18th century, and Jews started to settle there in the early 19th century; their population reached 5,000 in 1880, in a total population of 100,000. Rostov's development dates from the close of the 19th century, when Jews actively participated in the development of its commerce. In 1887 the town was transferred (together with the town of *Taganrog) to the region of the Don Cossacks and was thus excluded from the *Pale of Settlement. After the plans to expel the Jews (with the exception of merchants and owners of real estate) were nullified, only Jews who had lived there before 1887 were authorized to reside in the city. In 1897 there were 11,838 Jews (about 10 percent of the total population) in Rostov. Jews, particularly the Poliakov brothers, were an important factor in developing Rostov as a transport center. Some Jews were grain wholesalers, others operated banks, and about 80 percent of the city's doctors were Jews. Between 1899 and 1910, Moses Eleazar *Eisenstadt held the position of government-appointed rabbi (*kazyonny ravvin*) in Rostov. He was very active in the strengthening of Judaism and the propagation of Zionism within the community, after Russian assimilation had influenced its members.

In October 1905, pogroms accompanied by looting and the murder of about 150 Jews broke out in the town, lasting three days. During World War I, many refugees from the battle areas arrived in Rostov. These included the *ẓaddik* of Lubavich, R. Shalom Dov Schneersohn (see *Schneersohn family), the leader of Chabad Ḥasidism, who died in Rostov in 1920. Under the Soviet regime the Jewish public life of the town was suppressed, the Chabad followers were brought to trial, and many members of the He-Ḥalutz movement were arrested and tried. There existed a Yiddish elementary school and club, but they were closed in the mid-1930s. In 1926 there were 26,323 Jews (8.5 percent of the population) living there, and their numbers grew to 27,039 in 1939 (5.4 percent of the total population). The town was occupied twice by the Germans: November 21–29, 1941, and from July 24, 1942. On August 11, 1942 about 13,000 Jews were murdered by the Germans near the village of Zmiyevka three miles from town. All Jews discovered later were executed at the Jewish cemetery; altogether about 15,000–18,000 were killed in Rostov and its environs.

According to the 1959 census, about 21,500 Jews were again living in the Rostov oblast (district), 1,395 of them having declared Yiddish as their mother tongue; but the actual number of Jews was probably closer to 30,000. From 1959, *matzah* baking in the synagogue was stopped for reasons of "sanitation"; *matzah* is brought yearly from Tbilisi. In 1970 there was no synagogue, rabbi, or cantor in Rostov.

Though many Jews left during the 1990s, Jewish life already revived in the late 1980s and an active community center was inaugurated, as well as a Jewish day school, yeshivah, kindergarten, and Sunday school. Chief Rabbi Chaim Fridman conducts varied religious activities at the synagogue. In the early 21st century the Jewish population of the city was around 10,000.

BIBLIOGRAPHY: *Merder fun Felker* (1944); *Die Judenpogrome in Russland*, 1 (1909).

[Yehuda Slutsky / Shmuel Spector (2nd ed.)]

ROSTOW, EUGENE VICTOR DEBS (1913–2002), U.S. lawyer, economist, and government official; brother of Walt Whitman *Rostow. Born in New York City, Rostow graduated from Yale University in 1933. He began teaching law in 1938 at Yale, where in 1944 he was appointed professor of law. During World War II, he worked for the Lend Lease administration. After the war he helped develop the Marshall Plan, which offered U.S. financial aid to foster economic recovery in Europe. In 1964 Rostow became professor of law and public affairs and was dean of the Yale Law School from 1955 to 1965. During his teaching career (1944–84), Rostow served as adviser to the State Department (1942–1944) and was assistant executive secretary of the Economic Commission for Europe (1949–1950). He was also a member of the U.S. attorney general's national committee for the study of anti-trust laws (1954–55); a member of the advisory council of the Peace Corps; and consultant to the undersecretary of state from 1961 to 1966 and undersecretary of state from 1966 to 1969. He was one of President *Johnson's close advisers on U.S. policy toward the Arab-Israeli crisis, and was known in Washington for his firm support of the Israeli position during and after the Six-Day War. He was a leading supporter of U.S. military intervention in Vietnam. With the change in administration in 1969, Rostow returned to teach law at Yale. He returned to public office when he was appointed head of the Arms Control and Disarmament Agency (1981–83) by President Ronald Reagan. Rostow was the highest-ranking Democrat to serve in the administration.

Rostow's writings include: *A National Policy for the Oil Industry* (1948), *The Sovereign Prerogative* (1962), *Perspectives on the Court* (with M. Friedman and W.M. Beaney, 1967), *Law, Power, and the Pursuit of Peace* (1968), *Peace in the Balance* (1972), *Middle East: Critical Choices for the U.S.A.* (1977), *Toward Managed Peace* (1993), and *The Ideal in Law* (1995).

BIBLIOGRAPHY: *Current Biography Yearbook 1961* (1962), 393–5. **ADD. BIBLIOGRAPHY:** W. Whitworth, *Naïve Questions about War and Peace: Conversations with Eugene V. Rostow* (1970).

ROSTOW, WALT WHITMAN (1916–2003), U.S. economist; brother of Eugene *Rostow. Born in New York City, Rostow received a Ph.D. in economics from Yale University in 1940. That year, he taught economics at Columbia University. During World War II (1942–45), he served as a major in the Office of Strategic Services (OSS). After serving as assistant chief of the State Department's German-Austrian economic section (1945–46), he went to Oxford, England, as professor of American history (1946–47). In the latter year, he became assistant to the executive secretary of the Economic Commission for Europe, a post he held until 1950 when he was appointed professor of American history at Cambridge University. Later that year, Rostow returned to the United States to teach economic history at the Massachusetts Institute of Technology in Boston. In 1961 he moved to Washington to serve as deputy special assistant to President John F. *Kennedy, and in the same year became counselor of the policy-planning council of the State Department. In 1966 President Lyndon *Johnson named him his Special Assistant for National Security Affairs, and he became known as an advocate of United States military intervention in Vietnam. In the Middle East, Rostow urged a policy of U.S. diplomatic and military support for Israel, particularly after the 1967 Six-Day War. In 1969, with the change in the administration, he returned to teaching economics and history – at the University of Texas. When he retired from teaching, Rostow became the Rex G. Baker, Jr. Professor Emeritus of Political Economy. In 1992, he helped found the Austin Project and served as chairman of the board and task force director from 1992 to 1998.

Among his many honors, Rostow received the Order of the British Empire (honorary, military division, 1945); the Legion of Merit (1945); and the Presidential Medal of Freedom (with distinction, 1969).

Rostow's more than 30 publications include: *The Stages of Economic Growth* (1952), a widely influential work in which Rostow outlined five stages of economic growth through which societies pass; *Dynamics of Soviet Society* (1953); *The United States in the World Arena* (1960); *View from the Seventh Floor* (1964); *Politics and the Stages of Growth* (1971); *How It All Began* (1975); *Why the Poor Get Richer and the Rich Slow Down* (1980); *Theorists of Economic Growth from David Hume to the Present* (1990); *The Great Population Spike and After* (1998); and *Concept and Controversy* (2003).

BIBLIOGRAPHY: D. Wise, in: L. Tanzer (ed.), *Kennedy Circle* (1961), 29–57; P. Anderson, *Presidents' Men* (1968), 383–5; *Current Biography Yearbook 1961* (1962), 395–7. **ADD. BIBLIOGRAPHY:** C. Kindleberger and G. Di Tella (eds.), *Economics in the Long View: Essays in Honor of W.W. Rostow* (1982).

[Joachim O. Ronall / Ruth Beloff (2nd ed.)]

ROTBAUM, JACOB (1901–), Polish producer. Born in Warsaw, Rotbaum acted with experimental groups and traveled in Europe and in the U.S. Returning to Warsaw, he worked during the 1930s as a professional producer. His first important production was *Roar China* by the Soviet writer S.M. Tretyakov. This was followed by Itzik *Manger's *The Three Hotzmachs* (based on *Goldfaden) for the Yung Theater, and Shalom Aleichem's *Groser Gevins*. He also worked in the Polish theater and produced N.F. Pogodin's *Man with the Gun* (1938). After World War II he again produced on the Polish stage.

ADD. BIBLIOGRAPHY: *"Mayn Tsuzamenarbet mit'n Yiddishen Melukhe -Teater.in Poylen,"* in: *25 yor yiddisher Meluche teater in Folks-Poylen (1949–1974)*, 23–32 (Yiddish); 34–35 (English); 35–36 (Polish).

ROTBLAT, SIR JOSEPH (1911–2005), physicist and Nobel Peace Prize laureate. Rotblat was born in Warsaw, Poland, and became a U.K. citizen in 1945. He graduated with an M.A. in physics from the Free University of Poland (1932) and a doctorate in physics from the University of Warsaw (1938). He worked in the Warsaw Radiological Laboratory before joining James Chadwick as an Oliver Lodge Research Fellow at the University of Liverpool (1939). His work helped to establish, firstly, that a sustained fissile chain reaction could follow the bombardment of uranium with neutrons, and secondly, that this reaction produced the transuranic element later named plutonium. Subsequently in 1944, he joined the Manhattan Project in Los Alamos but returned to the U.K. the same year because of moral scruples about producing nuclear weapons once it was clear that the Germans could not do so. He was the only project member who left on moral grounds. He was director of research in nuclear physics at Liverpool University (1945–49) before becoming professor of physics at St. Bartholomew's Hospital Medical College, University of London, and chief physicist at St. Bartholomew's Hospital (1950–76), after which he became emeritus professor. During this period he pursued research on the biological effects of irradiation and the clinical applications of radioisotopes resulting in notable papers on subjects such as the diagnosis of thyroid disease and the deleterious effects of the bone-seeking isotope strontium-90. His concerns over the potential catastrophic effects of nuclear weapons were enhanced by his analysis of the radioactive fallout from hydrogen bomb tests at Bikini Atoll. This led him to sign the Russell-Einstein manifesto of 1955 warning about the consequences of war involving nuclear weapons. In 1957 Rotblat and Bertrand Russell founded the Pugwash Conference on Science and World Affairs, an international organization of scientists and others seeking solutions to global security threats and ultimately to eliminate nuclear weapons. In 1995 he and the Pugwash Conference shared the Nobel Peace Prize. He continued to express his concerns over nuclear and biological warfare after the Cold War ended and continually stressed the social responsibilities of scientists. His honors include the C.B.E. (1985), the Albert Einstein Peace Prize (1992), belated election to the Royal Society (1995), and a knighthood (1998). His wife, the former Tola Gryn, was unable to join him in 1939 and perished in the Nazi occupation of Poland.

[Michael Denman (2nd ed.)]

ROTE (Roti, ar-Reuti, Arrueti, Aruety, Aroti, al-Rueti, er-Routi, Rutty, Ruti, Rute), Spanish-Moroccan family which originated either in Rota on the Bay of Cadiz, or in Rueda (At. Rot'a), Aragon. The first person known by this name was R. ISAAC AROTI, a Spanish rabbi whose father settled in *Egypt together with *Maimonides. During the 14th century several members of the Rote family ranked among the leaders of various Jewish communities in Spain. Among them were JACOB BEN SAMUEL AL-RUETI of Pamplona and JUCE (JOSEPH) AR-RUETI (d. after 1367) of Saragossa, one of the favorites of King Pedro IV. During the 15th century, HABRAN (ABRAHAM) ARUETY of Pamplona was highly respected. ABRAHAM ROTE (d. after 1525), one of the Spanish-Portuguese refugees settled in Safi, traveled to Lisbon, where he sought a number of privileges from John III and met David *Reuveni.

His son JACOB (I) ROTE was appointed official interpreter of the Portuguese in *Safi in 1523. In 1536 he settled in *Fez, after supplying a considerable quantity of arms to the Wattasid ruler; he also became the latter's counselor. In this capacity he participated in the battle of Oued al-ʿAbid, where the army of the *Wattasids was defeated by the *Sadis. Rote was then called upon to get John III to support the Wattasids. Honors were heaped upon him after this mission and he was named *sheikh al-Yahūd*, or **nagid*, of the Jews of the kingdom of Fez and given extensive powers. The *takkanot* of the *megorashim* (expellees) were drawn up under his aegis. The Christian captives were also under him and he made great efforts to secure their redemption. The pope issued a special safe-conduct pass to enable him to travel in complete security through all the Christian countries.

With his brother MOSES ROTE, he established a powerful firm for maritime trade, particularly the export of cereals, at first in Arzila and later in Tangier. As a result of his economic activities Rote became one of the leading merchants in Morocco. His relations with the *Marranos in Portugal were largely facilitated by his position and he encouraged them to establish themselves in Morocco and return to Judaism. When he was appointed ambassador of Portugal in 1539, he devoted his time to financing the transportation of the Marranos and their establishment in Morocco, where they openly returned to Judaism. The Inquisition was informed of these activities, and as it also sought to promote the affairs of the Christian merchants who were involved in the maritime cereal trade at the Rotes' expense, it ordered Moses Rote's arrest in Tangiers. This incident aroused strong protests on the part of both the king of Fez and the Portuguese ambassador in Morocco; John III personally intervened in the affair and Moses Rote was released in 1542. As a result of the progressive decline of the Wattasids, Jacob Rote was unable to make the alliance with Portugal effective. After the occupation of Fez in 1549 by the Sadis, Rote remained at the head of the community of Fez. The last meeting he presided over took place in 1556.

His son ABRAHAM ROTE (d. after 1603) succeeded him as *nagid*, and several new *takkanot* were formulated under his aegis. His son JACOB(2) ROTE (d. after 1622) was the person through whom the famous Aḥmad al-Manṣur "ruled." He lived in *Marrakesh with this sultan, and in his capacity as "minister of foreign affairs" he favored the English. After the death of the sovereign in 1603, he returned to Fez where he presided over the community through a troubled period. R. ISAAC BEN JACOB ROTE (d. after 1706) headed his family's yeshivah in Fez. Some of his works are extant in manuscript. After the death of his sons ABRAHAM ROTE and JACOB ROTE (d. after 1730), the Rote family ceased to exist. In his epistle to Oliver Cromwell, which sought to obtain the admission of the Jews to England in 1655, Manasseh Ben Israel praised the merits of the "noble family" of the Rotes.

BIBLIOGRAPHY: Neubauer, Chronicles, 2 (1895, repr. 1965), 242; Baer, Urkunden, 2 (1936), 302, 379, 394, 729; D. Corcos, in: *Sefunot*, 10 (1966), 105ff.; Hirschberg, Afrikah, index.

[David Corcos]

ROTEM, CVI (**Zvi**; **Erich Rothmüller**; 1903–1981), journalist and editor. Born in Slavonia (Croatia), Rotem lived in Zagreb. He received his Ph.D. in philosophy from Wuerzburg, and he studied Judaism in Berlin at the Hochschule fuer Jüdische Wissenschaften; he also completed the Law School of Zagreb University. From his youth on, he occupied leading positions within the Zionist movement and was among the founders of the Radna Palestina (Labor Palestine) organization. He edited various publications, including the "Red Book" of Ha-Shomer ha-Ẓa'ir in 1935. That same year he immigrated to Ereẓ Israel. He first worked as the Haifa bureau chief of the Labor daily, *Davar*, later moving to Tel Aviv, becoming head of its economic section. He also edited *Omer*, a vocalized daily journal for new immigrants.

Rotem was among the leaders of Hitaḥdut Olei Yugoslavia (Association of Immigrants from Yugoslavia), editing its *Bilten* and other publications, including *Toledot Yehudei Yugoslavyah*. Simultaneously, he acted as correspondent of the Belgrade daily *Politika*.

Through his extensive writings, Rotem significantly contributed to Yugoslav-Israeli relations. He translated and edited the works of Hinko Gottlieb. He also contributed articles to the first edition of *Encyclopaedia Judaica*.

BIBLIOGRAPHY: C. Rothmüller, *Židovska kolonizacija Palestine* (1925); idem, *Bjalik* (1933); idem, *Jevrejska omladina Južne Srbije* (5692/1932); Y. Eventov, *Toledot Yehudei Yugoslavyah* (ed. C. Rotem) (1971); Hinko Gottlieb, *Works* (Heb.; tr. and ed. C. Rotem), 2 vols. (5740/1980).

[Zvi Loker (2nd ed.)]

ROTENBERG, MATTIE LEVI (1897–1989), first woman and first Jew to receive a Ph.D. in physics from the University of Toronto (1926); founder of Toronto's first Jewish day school; Canadian journalist and award-winning national radio commentator. Born in Toronto, the eldest of 10 children, Rotenberg was a brilliant student who also received a B.A. (1921) and M.A. (1922) from the University of Toronto and was the recipient of several National Research Council Scholarships. Her research focused on photo-electric properties of fluorescent crystals. In 1924, she married Meyer Rotenberg, with whom she had five children between 1925 and 1934. Rotenberg's doctoral thesis, "On the Characteristic X-Rays from Light Elements," was published in the *Transactions of the Royal Society of Canada* (1924). In 1941–42, she was appointed an assistant demonstrator in physics at the University of Toronto at a salary of $1.25 an hour. Rotenberg was a demonstrator from 1947 to 1962 and an instructor from 1962 to 1968. In 1929, committed to her children's being both observant and knowledgeable Jews, she founded Hillcrest Progressive School, despite community resistance from parents who protested against the "segregating" of Jewish children and the study of Hebrew. She was the school's director for several years and remained active until 1944, when her youngest child left the school. From 1930 to 1932, Rotenberg was editor of the women's section of *The Jewish Standard*, published in Toronto and edited by Meyer *Weisgal, the political representative of Chaim *Weizmann in North America. Rotenberg also wrote a weekly column, "As the Woman Sees It," for *The Standard*. From 1939 until 1966, she wrote and broadcast regularly her commentary on the Canadian Broadcasting Corporation (CBC), Canada's national radio, on a program devoted to women's issues called "Trans-

Canada Matinee." On April 12, 1943, she gave a detailed report about the Final Solution, condemning the Western nations, including Canada, for their indifference. "Asking themselves the question, 'Am I my brother's keeper?' the democratic nations of the world, our country among them, answered: 'No.'" She concluded her talk: "Some action must be taken at once. If it is not, within a few months six million people will have been murdered, and the nations of the world will not be able to escape the charge of being accomplices to the bleakest crime in history." In 1945, she won the Canadian Women's Press Club Memorial Award for a radio broadcast titled "The Post-War Woman." It was the first time in its 10-year history that the award was given in the field of radio writing. In February 1947, she covered the United Nations Status of Women Commission at the first formal session of the UN at Lake Success, New York. She attended the UN annually for several years, broadcasting for the CBC on the position of women around the world.

[Nessa Rapoport (2nd ed.)]

ROTENBURG, family in Cochin (*Kochi). Probably originating in Frankfurt, the Rotenburgs were one of the leading "White" Jewish families in Cochin throughout the 18th century. The first prominent member of the family was SIMON SAMSON ROTENBURG, whose business trip to Mocha on behalf of his relative Ezekiel *Rahabi became a cause célèbre (1733–40). From 1763 to 1772 JOSEPH ROTENBURG came to the attention of the Dutch East India Company and the rajah of Cochin because of his unauthorized departure from the state. His case led to an investigation of the legal status of the White Jews in relation to the company and the rajah. When Cochin was under British rule, NAPHTALI ROTENBURG was a leading figure in the community and his Hebrew signature is found on many communal documents. He saved the life of Colonel Macauley, British resident of Cochin and Travancore, during a rising of the population in 1808. As a token of gratitude, Colonel Macauley presented the Paradesi Synagogue with a gold and silver crown for the Torah scroll.

BIBLIOGRAPHY: Fischel, in: *Studia Rosenthaliana*, 1 no. 2 (1967), 32–44 (Eng.).

[Walter Joseph Fischel]

ROTENSTREICH, FISCHEL (1882–1938), Zionist leader. Born in Kolomyya, Galicia, Rotenstreich was active in the student Zionist movement in Galicia and later in Vienna. He taught at various government high schools in Galicia. With the collapse of the Austro-Hungarian monarchy at the end of World War I and the establishment of the "West Ukrainian State" (1918) in Galicia, Rotenstreich became the chairman of the Jewish National Council. When the district was returned to Polish rule, he was arrested by the Poles. From 1922 to 1927, he was a member of the Polish senate, and from 1927 to 1930 a member in the Polish Sejm. In both of these capacities, he took an interest mainly in economic affairs. At the 18th Zionist Congress (1935), he was elected to the Executive of the Jewish Agency by the *General Zionists (B). In the same year, he settled in Palestine, where he directed the agency's Department of Commerce and Industry until his death. He published many articles in Hebrew, Yiddish and Polish on economic and financial matters.

BIBLIOGRAPHY: Y. Gruenbaum, *Penei ha-Dor*, 1 (1957), 295–9; Tidhar, 3 (1949), 1442–43.

[Getzel Kressel]

ROTENSTREICH, NATHAN (1914–1993), Israeli philosopher and author. Born in Sambor, Poland, the second son of Fischel *Rotenstreich, a distinguished leader of Polish Jewry, Nathan Rotenstreich joined the Zionist movement in his early youth. He immigrated to Ereẓ Israel in 1932 and soon became known as an original thinker and prolific writer. In 1951 he joined the faculty of the Hebrew University of Jerusalem, where he taught philosophy for close to four decades. From 1958 to 1961 he was dean of the Humanities Faculty and in 1965–69 rector of the university. An academic philosopher, who was intensely engaged in the upbuilding of the Jewish community, the so-called Zionist *yishuv*, in Palestine, and then in the State of Israel, Rotenstreich was a public intellectual par excellence. A prolific scholar, who published some 30 books and 600 scholarly articles (in English, French, German, and Hebrew), he tirelessly wrote political and cultural feuilletons for the Israeli daily press, cultural journals, political forums, and educational bulletins, responding to issues of the day. His committed engagement in the public discourse of the State of Israel was borne by his conviction that philosophical culture has a direct bearing on the task of furthering human dignity in the realm of history and politics. Dedicated to systematic, "conceptual clarification" – a term that, indicatively, recurs frequently in his writings – philosophy should, he held, contribute decisively to heightening the rational understanding required if human beings are to act within history in a judicious and ethically responsible manner.

Accordingly, the historical dimension of human existence determined much of the thematic thrust of both his scholarship and popular writings. He contemplated history not as an account of the past, but as a way of explaining the present, more precisely, the object of his inquiry was historical knowledge as it is bears on the present. This focus took his work in two distinctive but related directions: the epistemology of historical knowledge and the cultural function of historical consciousness, especially within the context of the modern Jewish experience. As a modern historical consciousness took hold of the Jews, Rotenstreich argued, the structure of Jewish life and sensibility was radically transformed. Modern Jewish thought is thus straddled with the twin challenge of historicism – which pits the relativistic conclusions of critical historiography against traditional Jewish memory and self-understanding – and the "return of the Jews to history" as conscious actors in the shaping of their own political destiny. This process, which is one of the hallmarks of secularization, Rotenstreich observed, was set into motion by European Jewry's quest for civic emancipation, a protracted struggle whose dialectic ineluctably led to Zionism and the restoration of Jewish political sovereignty in the Land of Israel.

In contrast with many of the early Zionist thinkers, Rotenstreich deemed the mere renewal of Hebrew as the secular vernacular of the Jewish people to be in and of itself an insufficient basis to ensure that the emerging culture sponsored by Zionism would have the requisite "energy" to engage the minds and souls of contemporary Jews. Although Hebrew is a necessary condition for the development of an intellectually and spiritually compelling Jewish national, that is, secular culture, he argued, it must be supplemented by a well-informed knowledge of the sources of Jewish tradition. A sound grounding in the classical texts of Judaism would also facilitate a desired dialogue between secular Jews and those Jews still bound to the religious beliefs and practices of the tradition. This dialogue, Rotenstreich affirmed, will allow Judaism to remain, even for the secular Jew, the grammar of Jewish imagination and creativity.

In his political activity, Rotenstreich identified himself with *Mapai, the dominant party in the Zionist Labor movement, but in 1961 he joined the break away faction led by Pinḥas *Lavon, Min ha-Yesod, which strongly opposed to David Ben-Gurion's leadership. As a philosopher, he had a deep interest in German idealism and particularly in Kant and neo-Kantianism. Widely regarded as one of the leading contemporary Kantian scholars, Rotenstreich also emerged as a philosopher in his own right, initiating a series of systematic treatises on historical knowledge. He developed an original set of philosophical principles with which he sought to clarify the epistemological and phenomenological character of various human activities, such as, religious and secular faith. Rotenstreich was clearly influenced at this stage by *Husserl's phenomenology. His writings contain vigorous criticism of many philosophical trends, such as existentialism, Marxism, neo-positivism, linguistic philosophy, and even some specific approaches within the phenomenological movement. In 1963 he was awarded the Israel Prize in the humanities. At the time of his death he was the vice president of the Israel Academy of Sciences and Humanities and a foreign associate of the U.S. National Academy of Education.

His writings include *Between Past and Present: An Essay on History* (New Haven 1958); *Jewish Philosophy in Modern Times: From Mendelssohn to Rosenzweig* (New York 1968; 2nd ed., Detroit 1994); *Tradition and Reality. The Impact of History on Modern Jewish Thought* (New York 1972); *Essays on Zionism and the Contemporary Jewish Condition* (New York 1980); *Jews and German Philosophy* (New York 1984); *Essays in Jewish Philosophy in the Modern Era*, with an introduction by P. Mendes-Flohr, edited by R. Munk (Amsterdam 1996); *Wege zur Erkennbarkeit der Welt* (Freiburg 1983); *On Faith*, ed. P. Mendes-Flohr (Chicago 1998).

For a comprehensive intellectual biography of Rotenstreich, see A.Z. Bar-On, "Nathan Rotenstreich," in: *Interpreters of Judaism in the Late Twentieth Century*, ed. by Steven T. Katz (Washington, D.C., 1993), pp. 229–48.

[Paul Mendes-Flohr (2nd ed.)]

ROTH, AARON (1894–1944), founder of a ḥasidic dynasty. Born in Ungvar, in his youth Roth attended yeshivot in Galicia and Hungary. He was attracted to Ḥasidism at an early age, and studied under several *Ẓaddikim*, including Issachar Dov of Belz. His main teacher was Ẓevi Elimelech of Blazowa, who instructed him to establish a ḥasidic community, although Roth was not descended from *Ẓaddikim*. The ḥasidic community which gathered around him in *Satu Mare and Beregszász (*Beregovo) bore many of the characteristics of early Ḥasidism. The major points of his system were complete adherence to simple faith, and rejection of any compromise with modern views and ways of life. He demanded of his Ḥasidim that they support themselves by their own labor, and employ the ecstatic mode of praying.

At the end of his life Roth settled in Ereẓ Israel and, although ill, he succeeded in establishing there an enthusiastic and active, though small, ḥasidic community. He regarded the recent sufferings of the Jews, and especially the Holocaust, as a punishment for abandoning simple faith and the traditions of the ancients, and constantly called for repentance. Roth was succeeded by his son-in-law ABRAHAM ISAAC KAHAN, and by his son ABRAHAM ḤAYYIM ROTH.

His writings include *Shulḥan ha-Tahor*, on *kashrut* (1933); his main book *Shomer Emunim* (1942, published in several editions) consists of homilies concerning faith, confidence, individual providence, reward and punishment, and redemption, including at the end *Kunteres Ahavat ha-Bore*, expressing his longings and yearning for God, and songs of devotion and joy.

BIBLIOGRAPHY: A. Roth, *Uvda de-Aharon*, written and ed. by E. Kohen Steinberger (1948).

[Adin Steinsaltz]

ROTH, CECIL (Bezalel; 1899–1970), Jewish historian; editor in chief of the first edition of the *Encyclopaedia Judaica*. Roth, who was born in London, the son of a manufacturer of building supplies, saw active service in the British infantry in 1918 before being educated at the City of London School and at Merton College, Oxford, obtaining his doctorate in 1925. He was trained as a general historian, with a special interest in Italy, his first major work being *The Last Florentine Republic* (1925). A traditional, observant Jew who learned Hebrew from his father and under Jacob *Mann, he was from the first interested in Judaica: as an undergraduate in 1920, he produced a paper identifying the convert Duarte Brandao with the military adventurer Sir Edward Brampton. In that same year, under the influence of Herbert *Loewe, Roth also translated a number of the *Kinot* (liturgical poems for the Ninth of Av), foreshadowing a continuing interest in Jewish liturgy, especially of the more recondite rites. He subsequently devoted himself to Jewish subjects, first as freelance writer and lecturer, and from 1939 to 1964 as reader in Jewish Studies at Oxford.

Roth combined naturally English ways and loyalties with Jewish nationalism. When he retired from his Oxford appointment in 1964, he settled in Jerusalem, taking up a visiting professorship at Bar-Ilan University. Soon after his appointment he was accused of unorthodoxy by a pamphlet which quoted his citation (in the *Short History of the Jewish People*) of doubts expressed by others about the historicity of Moses but omitting Roth's refutations of these doubts. Although supported by the university authorities and other Orthodox spokesmen, Roth, who had suffered a heart attack, resigned from Bar-Ilan. For the rest of his life he divided his time between Jerusalem, where he edited the *Encyclopaedia Judaica*, and New York, where he lectured at Queens College, City University, and at Stern College.

Roth's remarkable facility as a writer is shown by an immense literary output. A bibliography compiled in 1966 by O.K. Rabinowitz lists 572 items, and his total output numbered at least 779 items, including translations into many languages. His lasting influence was as writer, lecturer, and collector, rather than as teacher, for conditions in Anglo-Jewry, where he spent most of his academic life, precluded cultivating disciples, though he was both an inspiring and painstaking teacher. Roth wrote the standard modern histories of: the Jews of England (1964^3) and Italy (1946); a history of the *Marranos (1959^2); a history of the Jews in the Renaissance (1964^2); *The House of Nasi* (2 vols., 1947–48); and popular works such as the *Short History of the Jewish People* (1936) and *The Jewish Contribution to Civilization* (1938). He edited the successful *Standard Jewish Encyclopaedia* (1959, and several later editions), and was from 1966 until his death editor-in-chief of the *Encyclopaedia Judaica*. He had a vivid literary style and a taste for picaresque characters, but this was combined with precise erudition, as in his bibliographical works, such as the *Magna Bibliotheca Anglo-Judaica* (1937); in his studies of Jewish printing; and in detailed monographs such as his *Intellectual Activities of Medieval Anglo-Jewry* (1949). Three volumes of his collected essays appeared: *Gleanings, Essays in Jewish History and Art* (1967), *Essays and Portraits in Anglo-Jewish History* (1962), and *Personalities and Events in Jewish History* (1953).

The *Dead Sea Scrolls controversy led Roth to contribute a historian's approach to the examination of the evidence. His identification, on historical evidence, of the Qumran Sect with the *Zealots, while not accepted by the supporters of the Essene theory, was cogently expounded (*Dead Sea Scrolls*, 1965^2) and, after initial doubts, won the support and collaboration of the Semitic philologist Godfrey *Driver.

Roth's artistic flair led him to Jewish art, including the scientific study of illuminated Passover *Haggadot*. He edited a record number of *Haggadot* and collaborated with the artist Arthur *Szyk on what was probably the most sumptuously illustrated *Haggadah* ever printed (1940). He assembled Jewish art objects, including a remarkable *menorah* collection and rare Hebrew books and manuscripts (of which he published a catalog, in *A. Marx Jubilee Volume*, 1950). His collection of *ketubbot* combined both his literary and artistic interests. These collections formed the setting of his Oxford home, which served as a center of hospitality both for local Jewish undergraduates and visiting scholars. Roth's extensive library and manuscripts were bequeathed to the University of Leeds, England, and his art collection now forms a museum attached to the Beth Tzedec Synagogue, Toronto, Canada.

During his life in Britain, Roth worked devotedly for Jewish culture in the Anglo-Jewish community, although he viewed its future with realistic pessimism. In spite of the warmth and friendship of some of Anglo-Jewry's leading figures, he did not receive the recognition in Britain which he achieved in other countries, where his brilliance as a lecturer won him an enthusiastic reception on several wide-ranging tours. His services to the *Jewish Historical Society of England, which he kept alive during the difficulties of World War II, were recognized by his reelection as president a number of times and the presentation of a festschrift (*Remember the Days*) in 1967. Elected a member of Italian learned societies before 1939, Roth resigned his membership as a protest against Mussolini's anti-Jewish legislation. After 1965 he was reelected a corresponding member of the Accademia Colombaria of Florence, and in 1969 he was appointed a commendatore of the Order of Merit of the Italian Republic for services to Italian culture.

Roth's "meliorist" view of Anglo-Jewish history, implicitly contrasting the liberal evolution of Jewish life in Britain with the horrors of the Continent, won wide acceptance at the time. Recently it has been challenged by younger Anglo-Jewish historians who see more hostility to the Jews than Roth admitted; this view has itself been challenged more recently still. Roth's greatest achievement was unquestionably his editing of the *Encyclopaedia Judaica*, an effort which would have taxed the abilities of a superhuman. That the *Judaica* has been the standard reference work of the entire Jewish world for more than a generation is fitting testimony to his ability.

He was a brother of Leon *Roth, the philosopher. Roth's widow, Irene Roth, wrote a biography, *Cecil Roth: Historian Without Tears* (1982).

BIBLIOGRAPHY: C. Raphael, in: *Commentary*, 50 no. 3 (Sept. 1970), 75–81. **ADD. BIBLIOGRAPHY:** ODNB online.

[Vivian David Lipman]

ROTH, DAVID LEE (1954–), flamboyant, cocky frontman and lyricist for hard rock giants Van Halen during their 1978–85 heyday, and successful solo artist in the late 1980s and 1990s. Born in Bloomington, Indiana, Roth spent several years in Massachusetts before moving to Pasadena, California, in 1963. Roth attended Hebrew school, and later said that singing during Sabbath services gave him a feeling of belonging and strengthening his self worth. After his bar mitzvah, his Jewish education took a back seat to a lifelong devotion to karate and to the verbal street poetry he was hearing from people like Wolfman Jack and Cassius Clay. He visited his Uncle Manny Roth in New York who owned the famed Cafe Wha?, which further exposed him to varieties of music. During his senior year of high school in 1972, he joined a covers band, and it was on the party circuit that he met the Van Halen brothers, Eddie and Alex. After briefly studying music theory at Pasadena

State College, Roth and the Van Halens joined forces in late 1974 along with bassist Michael Anthony, and at Roth's urging named the band Van Halen. They released their self-titled debut in 1978, and their metal-meets-melody style and the Jagger-Richards combination of Roth and Eddie Van Halen made their albums instant hard-rock classics. Wearing spandex and strutting around the stage like a rooster, Roth used his fast-talking huckster persona, self-deprecating smile, and athletic pyrotechnics to become one of the most riveting frontmen in rock. One critic wrote that Roth "simply updated vaudeville. He wrapped himself in Hollywood hype, plugged in, turned the volume to 11, and voila, created 'Diamond Dave,' a hedonistic rock & roll character." For Roth, it had more meaning: "Every step I took on that stage was smashing some Jew-hating, lousy punk even deeper in the deck ... if you were vaguely antisemitic, you were under my wheels." With tension between Roth and Van Halen mounting, Roth left the band in 1985, just after releasing a successful four-song EP *Crazy from the Heat*, featuring remakes of The Beach Boys' "California Girls" and the vaudeville medley of "Just a Gigolo/I Ain't Got Nobody." His solo career kept him in the limelight through the mid-1990s. In 2004, Roth disclosed that he had trained to become a paramedic and began working on an ambulance in the Bronx. He took over Howard *Stern's national radio talk show in January 2006, but was removed in April due to poor ratings. He is the author of a well-received autobiography, *Crazy from the Heat* (1997).

[David Brinn (2nd ed.)]

ROTH, HENRY (1906–1995), U.S. novelist. Roth was born in Austria-Hungary. When he was 18 months old, his mother brought him to New York, where his father had been working to save money for their passage. In New York, young Roth was close to his mother and alienated from his father. At first the family lived on New York's Lower East Side, where Roth felt a sense of belonging in the Jewish community of the neighborhood that he did not receive at home. Later, the family moved to Harlem, a diverse community with a large Irish population. There Roth suffered considerably because of his Jewish heritage, and began to adapt to his gentile neighborhood. In the mid-1920s, he studied biology at the City College of New York and developed an interest in writing. During this period, Roth also met Ida Lou Walton, a New York University professor, and the two began living together. By 1930, Roth began writing his first novel. Three and a half years later the novel, *Call It Sleep*, was completed. Walton left Roth and eventually married David Mandel, a partner in the Robert O. Ballou publishing company. In early 1935, Ballou published *Call It Sleep*, on Walton's recommendation. This autobiographical work describes a young Jewish immigrant boy's search for belonging in New York City, from age six to nine, in the 1930s. The protagonist, David Schearl, is disturbed by his father's doubts of his paternity, his gentile neighborhood, and the Jewish religion he does not understand. David feels close only to his mother and this Oedipal aspect causes David to pull away from her throughout the novel. Symbolism in the work points to the main theme – redemption. Roth's dialect and ethnic speech patterns reveal the extent of David's isolation. Finally, turning to myth and the Isaiah story for his transfiguration at the end of the novel, David touches a milk ladle to the third rail of the trolley tracks in an attempt at symbolic purification through electrocution. David's survival softens his father's feelings toward him, and there is hope that he will transcend his inner conflict.

The critical reception of Roth's *Call It Sleep* in 1935 was predominantly favorable. Fred T. Marsh believed the novel "... to be the most compelling and moving, the most accurate and profound study of an American slum childhood that has yet appeared in this day..." The reviewer reminds his readers "... that this novel would never have been published if *Ulysses* had not won the decision in our courts. And the law has enlightened public opinion." Roth's language in the novel is seen as "... nothing short of the highest talent. It moves from a kind of transmutation of picturesque, warm, emotional and gentle Yiddish, to the literal English argot of the Ghetto, an ugly, fascinating, and expressive speech." Undoubtedly, any first-novel author would be flattered by Marsh's final judgment: "To discerning readers, I believe, for its profound intensity, its rare virtuosity, its sensitive realism, its sheer weight, its power, circumference and depth, this first novel of this Mr. Roth will be remembered for some time to come. I should like to see *Call It Sleep* win the Pulitzer Prize – which it never will."

Joseph Gollomb, in contrast to Marsh, thought Roth magnified the foulness of life on the Lower East Side instead of accurately portraying it. Although initially praising Roth's "sensitive ear for speech," Gollomb passes final judgment on Roth's literary truthfulness: "... still let me repeat the book in part and as a whole does violence to the truth. Someone once wished that novels of the east side life did not have to be so 'excremental.' *Call It Sleep* is by far the foulest picture of the east side that has yet appeared, in conception and in language. Certainly there was and is foulness down there as in other places. But Mr. Roth treats it not with the discriminating eye of the artist but with a magnifying glass, and if not with a relish, certainly with an effort to see what Emerson saw, with 'even in the mud and scum of things, there always, always something sings.' Whoever omits that something in his picture of east side life omits the very things which kept that life so long a fertile field for the creative writer."

Call It Sleep was republished in the early 1960s. Thus, almost 30 years after its initial publication, Roth's novel was "rediscovered" by Harold Ribalow, who wrote: "It is no wonder, then, that the best novel ever written in the United States should have been 'rediscovered' in 1960. It is *Call It Sleep*, by Henry Roth." Leslie Fiedler and Alfred Kazin both called attention to Roth's novel in articles and lectures. Although the novel may have remained a fond memory in the minds of a few enthusiastic readers, Henry Roth disappeared from the literary scene. Ribalow's correspondence with Roth in 1959 was the beginning of the novel's comeback. Ribalow's view of

Roth's work after the correspondence is summed up in this quote: "If most of us, passing through only once, can leave behind us a work of art comparable to *Call It Sleep*, we would have every reason to be proud of ourselves."

It is crucial to mention here Roth's debt to the early modernists, T.S. Eliot and James Joyce. In one of his last novels, *From Bondage* (1996), Roth reveals this influence: "*Ulysses* … showed … how to address whole slagheaps of squalor, and make them available for … art … the sorcery of language … to fluoresce, to electrify the mood … the Chicago packing houses … used every part of the pig except the squeal. Joyce elucidated ways to use even the squeal."

The republication of *Call It Sleep* resulted in a financial windfall for Roth (the paperback edition in 1964 sold more than one million copies), and rejuvenated his artistic talent in the late 1970s. He began work on a four-volume novel entitled *Mercy of a Rude Stream* in 1979, picking up on the story of David Schearl, renamed Ira Stigman. This last literary project consisted of *A Star Shines Over Mt. Morris Park* (1994), where Ira encounters antisemitism; *A Diving Rock on the Hudson* (1995), which reveals tantalizing glimpses of the wholesome, idealized American boyhood of Ira's non-Jewish friends; and the posthumous volumes *From Bondage* (1996) and *Requiem for Harlem* (1998), where Ira's growing intimacy with Edith (Walton) helps him escape from domestic and sexual tensions.

Sexuality in Roth's fiction is discussed in detail in *Redemption*, Henry Roth's biography by Steven G. Kellman, and a *New Yorker* article by Jonathan Rosen. Both delve into Roth's psyche, revealing the sexual frustrations of Roth's protagonist and of Roth himself. According to Rosen, "Roth's characterization of his Harlem exile as a kind of hell makes more sense when considered alongside the revelation that it was there that he began an incestuous relationship with his sister, Rose." According to Kellman, Roth had been "groping his sister since he was 12 and she was 10; by the time Roth was 16 he was having intercourse with her. When he was 18, he also seduced his 14-year-old first cousin Sylvia, leading her into the basement at a *bris*." Rosen interprets Kellman's *Redemption* in regard to David Schearl's incest as a "dramatic magnification of immigrant insecurity, the newcomer's inability to invest their emotions in anything beyond the reassuring confines of the clan." As a matter of fact, Rosen feels that "… the guilt that Roth felt hung over him like a kind of Biblical curse."

BIBLIOGRAPHY: "Henry Roth (1906–1995)," in: *Contemporary Literary Criticism*, vol. 104 (1998), 236–332; F.T. Marsh, in: *New York Herald Tribune Books*, 2:24 (Feb. 17, 1935), 6; J. Gollomb, in: *Saturday Review of Literature*, 2:35 (March 16, 1935), 552; H. Ribalow, in: *Wisconsin Studies in Contemporary Literature*, 3:3 (Fall 1962), 5–14; F. Bloch, in: *Jewish Writers of the Twentieth Century* (2003), 468–70; S.G. Kellman, *Redemption* (2005); J. Rosen, in: *The New Yorker* (Aug. 1, 2005), 74–79.

[Mark Padnos (2nd ed.)]

ROTH, JOEL (1940–), Conservative rabbi. After completing undergraduate studies at Wayne State University in Detroit, Michigan, in 1961, Roth received a master's degree in Hebrew literature at the Jewish Theological Seminary, and in 1968, rabbinic ordination. After completing a Ph.D. in Talmud in 1973, he was appointed to the JTS faculty as associate professor of Talmud. Roth held both academic and administrative positions at JTS. In 1978 he was appointed to the Committee of Jewish Law and Standards, where he served as chairman from 1984 to 1992. Roth served as the dean of the Rabbinical School of JTS, from 1981 to 1984 and in 1992–93. In 1998 he was appointed the Louis Finkelstein Professor of Talmud and Jewish Law, and in 2000 he became the head of the Conservative yeshivah in Jerusalem, an institution founded by the Conservative movement in 1995 to enable men and women to learn traditional Jewish texts in an open, co-educational environment.

Throughout his rabbinic career, Roth has advocated for a Conservative movement ideology and practice rooted in the halakhic (legal) system, whose workings he elaborated upon in his 1986 book, *The Halakhic Process: A Systemic Analysis*. In writings on homosexuality and the ordination of women, among other topics, he has urged the movement to embrace the Conservative movement's doctrine of "tradition and change," but not by circumventing a strict process of legal precedent in service of social trends such as feminism. One of Roth's more prominent responsa has supported the rabbinic ordination of women, among the most important policy decisions of the Conservative movement, and has stated that a woman may exempt the community from its ritual obligations if she accepts upon herself ritual obligations commanded to men. He has also written an extensive series of responsa on the permissibility of organ donation, and on conversion and Sabbath observance, among other topics. Roth drew the ire of many members of the movement when, in 1992, he led the Committee on Law and Standards in its decision against ordaining homosexual rabbis or performing same-sex marriages, citing insurmountable halakhic objections to homosexuality. Roth has come to represent and to anchor the "right-wing" of the Conservative movement, a position that has at times placed him at odds both with the generally less traditionally observant laity of Conservative synagogues in the United States, on the one hand, and with many Orthodox leaders, on the other, who consider his rulings on egalitarianism and the ordination of women to be outside the bounds of *halakhah*.

[Liora R. Halperin (2nd ed.)]

ROTH, JOSEPH (1894–1939), Austrian novelist. Born near Brody in East Galicia, Roth volunteered for service in the Austrian army during World War I. He became an officer and was captured by the Russians. His subsequent career was in journalism and for a decade from 1923 he worked for the *Frankfurter Zeitung*. He fought for a new humanism and was a strenuous opponent of German militarism. Roth left his adopted country when Hitler came to power in 1933. Much of his restless life was spent abroad and he finally sought refuge in

Paris where in a fit of depression he tried to commit suicide and died in a hospital for the poor.

Apart from many newspaper articles and short stories, Roth wrote 14 novels, notable for their lucid style. At first a psychological realist in the tradition of Stendhal and Dostoevsky, Roth was later influenced by the Viennese impressionists such as H. von *Hofmannsthal and A. *Schnitzler. Always affected by the sufferings of others, Roth projected recollections of his own unhappy and impoverished youth into his best-known novel, *Hiob* (1930; *Job*, 1931), which describes the bitter life of an East European Jewish family. Other novels, such as *Die Flucht ohne Ende* (1927) and *Rechts und Links* (1929), depict the social consequences of war and the decomposition of the old order through revolution and inflation. His last novel, *Die Legende vom heiligen Trinker* (1939), is a kind of self-portrait and reflects some of the author's own disappointments. The essays of *Juden auf Wanderschaft* (1927) deal with the social position of East European Jewry. A different atmosphere prevails in Roth's historical novels. The best known of these, *Radetzkymarsch* (1932), nostalgically portrays Austria and the imperial army under Franz Joseph. Three other novels were *Die hundert Tage* (1936), *Die Geschichte von der 1002. Nacht* (1939), and *Der Leviathan* (1940). Years after his death, *Der stumme Prophet*, a work full of forebodings about totalitarianism, appeared in 1966. Roth's collected works were published with an introduction by Hermann *Kesten (3 vols., 1956). Roth gained belated recognition as one of Austria's outstanding novelists.

BIBLIOGRAPHY: H. Linden, *Joseph Roth, Leben und Werk* (1949); H. Kesten, *Meine Freunde die Poeten* (1953), 167–99; A. Werner, in: *Jewish Outlook* (Feb. 1942), 7–9; Kinn, in: *Tribune*, 5 (1966), 2063–66; H. Kesten (ed.), *Joseph Roth: Briefe 1911–1939* (1970).

[Rudolf Kayser]

ROTH, KLAUS FRIEDRICH (1925–), English mathematician. Born in Breslau, Germany (now Wroclaw, Poland), Roth came to England where he was educated at St. Paul's School, London, before graduating with a B.A. in mathematics from Cambridge University (1945). After teaching at Gordonstoun School in Scotland, he joined the mathematics department of University College, London (1946–66) where he gained his M.A. (1948), Ph.D. (1950) and became professor (1961). He moved to Imperial College of Science and Technology, London as professor of pure mathematics (1966–88) and visiting professor (1988–96) before returning to Scotland. Roth's main interest is the theory of numbers. He solved the major problem of approximating algebraic numbers by rationals (his solution is now known as "Roth's theorem") and published *Rational Approximations to Irrational Numbers* (1962). He made other important contributions to the theory of natural numbers. His achievements have been recognized by many honors including the Fields Medal (1958), election to the Royal Society of London (1960) and the award of the Royal Society's Sylvester Medal (1991).

[Michael Denman (2nd ed.)]

ROTH, LEON (**Ḥayyim Judah**; 1896–1963), philosopher; brother of Cecil *Roth. Roth – a pupil of Samuel *Alexander – devoted his early studies and publications to the rationalist tradition in European thought, especially in the 17th century. He held a lectureship in philosophy in Manchester University from 1923 to 1927, at which time he was named as the first incumbent of the newly-established chair of philosophy at the Hebrew University, Jerusalem. During his tenure of this professorship, Roth served as rector of the university, 1940–43, and as dean of the Faculty of Humanities, 1949–51. In the tensions and internal struggles within the university, Roth was closely allied with Judah L. *Magnes; his views on the direction of Palestinian political life were also close to those of Magnes. In 1948 the establishment of an independent Jewish state and the death of Magnes introduced a new era with which Roth was completely out of sympathy. Accordingly he resigned his professorship in 1951 and returned to England. There Roth concerned himself chiefly with studies of Jewish ethics and biblical subjects. He died suddenly, at Wellington, New Zealand, while on a visit to that country.

As an educator, Roth's major contribution was to establish the school of philosophy in the Hebrew University, a task that was shared by such colleagues as Julius *Guttmann and Samuel Hugo *Bergman. Important to this work was the program of translation of philosophic classics into Hebrew, a program that Roth began. As well as translating, he assumed considerable supervisory and editorial responsibility for the entire series of translations and edited a volume of selections illustrative of post-biblical Jewish ethical and religious thought.

Roth's early preoccupation with 17th-century rationalism, especially as represented by Descartes and Spinoza, remained a central interest of his philosophic studies throughout his later years. In addition, he studied carefully *Maimonides' *Guide of the Perplexed* as his guide to the original and systematic philosophy of Judaism toward which he worked during much of his life. Roth's desire was to explore and understand the inner cohesion of theology, ethics, and biblical hermeneutics in Judaism, and thus to be able to interpret Judaism as a unitary system. He approached this synthesizing statement in his last major work, *Judaism, a Portrait* (1960).

Roth was also a publicist of Judaism in the non-Jewish world. He contributed *Jewish Thought as a Factor in Civilization* to the UNESCO series, "The Race Question and Modern Thought" in 1954. He was elected a Fellow of the British Academy. Roth's major works include *Spinoza, Descartes, and Maimonides* (1924, repr. 1963); *The Science of Morals: An Essay in Method* (1928); and *Spinoza* (1929, repr. 1954).

BIBLIOGRAPHY: T.E. Jessop, in: *Proceedings of the British Academy*, 50 (1965), 317–29, incl. bibl.; R.J. Loewe (ed.), *Studies in Rationalism* (1966), 1–11, incl. bibl.; JC (April 5, 1963), 40.

[Joseph L. Blau]

ROTH, MARK (1951–), U.S. bowler, member of Pro Bowlers Association (PBA) Hall of Fame. Roth, a native of Brooklyn who lived most of his life in Wall Township, NJ, joined the PBA tour in 1970 as a 19-year-old phenom with an unusual, variegated 5-to-11 step approach, and an aggressive hook which stood out in an era of mostly conservative curve-ball throwers. Despite the raw talent, it took Roth five years to tally his first tournament victory. Thereafter Roth enjoyed a remarkable run of 14 years in which he won 34 PBA titles (third best all-time), was named PBA Bowler of the Year four times (1977–79, 1984), and led the PBA in average six times (1976–79, 1981, 1988). Roth's average for the 1979 season of 221.6 was the first time in PBA history that a player had maintained an average above 220. This record stood until 1993, when averages across the league jumped because of improved ball technology. His eight tournament victories in 1978 are a record that most bowling analysts concur is unlikely to ever be broken. He also shares the record for most consecutive tournament victories (3). Roth is one of only three bowlers in PBA history to have managed to place high enough to win a cash prize in every tournament entered for an entire season. And despite having played when cash prizes were approximately a quarter of the value of current tournament prizes, Roth is still one of the top career money-earners of all time, at over $1.6 million. Roth is considered to be the originator of the fast, sharp hook style which is prevalent throughout the PBA today. He retired from the PBA Tour in 1991, but decided 10 years later to join the Seniors Tour, and promptly won honors as the Senior Rookie of the Year in 2001, and then Senior Player of the Year in 2002, becoming the only bowler in PBA history to win Player of the Year Awards in both the regular and senior circuits. Roth then retired to concentrate on investing and running bowling alleys across the United States. He was Maccabi Union Jewish Athlete of the Year in 1985.

[Robert B. Klein (2nd ed.)]

ROTH, SIR MARTIN (1917–), British psychiatrist. Born in Budapest and educated at the University of London, Roth became professor of psychology at Newcastle University (1956–77) and was subsequently the first professor of psychology at Cambridge University, retiring in 1985. Roth served as the first president of the Royal College of Psychiatrists in 1971–75. His best-known work is probably *The Reality of Mental Illness* (1986), written with Jerome Kroll. Roth also wrote widely on Alzheimer's Disease. He was knighted in 1972.

[William D. Rubinstein (2nd ed.)]

ROTH, PHILIP MILTON (1933–), U.S. novelist. Born in Newark, New Jersey, Roth was educated at Rutgers, Bucknell, and Chicago universities, and taught English at the last from 1955 to 1958. He later took a teaching post in Iowa and was writer-in-residence at Princeton where he specialized in creative writing. He developed his own literary career, publishing stories in various magazines including *The New Yorker, Esquire* and *Commentary*. In the latter he published an essay "Writing about Jews" (36 (1963), 446–52). *Goodbye, Columbus* (1959), a collection of short stories, revealed the stylistic influence of F. Scott Fitzgerald and illustrated Roth's bent for a satirical and incisive portrayal of middle-class American Jews. In his first novel, *Letting Go* (1962), he transferred his attention to Jewish intellectual circles in U.S. universities. Roth's second novel, *When She Was Good* (1967), was not favorably received. It was followed by *Portnoy's Complaint* (1969), a bestseller written in the fashionable vein of "black humor." Here the novelist was brutally satirical in his dissection of the all-devouring Jewish mother. In telling the story of his sexual and other frustrations to his psychoanalyst, the 33-year-old Alexander Portnoy explodes in a cruel, obscene and comic fantasy. As Roth himself predicted, his book aroused a storm of protest in the U.S. but increased his reputation, both at home and abroad.

Roth's fiction also began to develop the character of the novelist Nathan Zuckerman, beginning with *The Ghost Writer* (1979) and continuing with *Zuckerman Unbound* (1981), *Anatomy Lesson* (1983), *Zuckerman Bound* (1985), *The Counterlife* (1987), *American Pastoral* (1997), *I Married A Communist* (1998), and *The Human Stain* (2000).

In the early Zuckerman novels, Nathan is a man of hyperbolic contradictions. He longs for success – but he does not wish to be recognized and hounded by fans once his novels are successful. He behaves as an archetypical good boy to his family, then disobeys his father's orders and publishes fiction which puts his family in a bad light. He craves excitement and he craves quietude; he marries intellectual, stable women and then rejects them because they are intellectual and stable. He pursues sexual adventure, but he bitterly resents critical response to his adventures. He writes ribald novels almost exclusively about Jews and cannot understand why the Jewish establishment reacts to him with vocal outrage.

In *The Counterlife*, Roth finally pulls his protagonist out of "the oepidal swamp" of preoccupation with sex and writing. Within the four parts of the novel, Roth plays with the alternative routes which life-and-art can follow. Areas which Roth has left fallow since the stories in *Goodbye Columbus* are picked up in *The Counterlife*, as Roth explores the meaning of contemporary Jewish experience. He articulates an updated argument between various forms of Diaspora and Israeli Judaism, makes them live and breathe and seem like counterlives indeed.

In the later novels, Zuckerman attains the repose that only pathos brings. He has witnessed the destruction of those he admires. He has been helpless to prevent the catastrophes that engulf them.

Roth's later writing, specifically *An American Pastoral*, *I Married a Communist*, and *The Human Stain* developed a narrative of Jewish acculturation to and recoil from American ideologies that either offered rationales to or promoted the violent self. Intriguingly, this trilogy is reminiscent of the achievement of 19th-century Russian realism, with its focus on the family endowing an individual with political choice and civic culture. In his extraordinary study of modern American life, Roth examined those who were caught up in, or witnesses to, the collision of American myths and a seeming autonomy. The novels move from anti-communist witch hunts to the deadly and childish violence of the 1960s to the rhetoric and power of destructive self-righteousness. Roth's trilogy allows the representatives of such movements to have their voice and, tragically, often to have their way. These works present protagonists whose uneasy lives suggest the compromises they have made – and shall have to make – with contemporary notions of justice, politics, and politically correct rhetoric.

These novels also offer a modern reading of American political tragedy. Roth's protagonists choose what they believe to be a life in the American grain – whether through communism, or through the means of a responsible life, or through adopting an identity that offers security. Nonetheless, their confidence in the achieved present is undermined, if not destroyed, by the consequences of the past. Within these novels, characters discover how Jewishness, the lived social inheritance of Judaism, comports with the American present. With his last novel in this series, *The Human Stain*, a meditation upon chosen identities that are central to America's understanding of itself (witness *The Great Gatsby*), Roth suggests that the Jewish intellectual has become a "type," a configuration of personality traits that can be imitated and lived within. Nonetheless, the comic pathos of Jewish neuroses, found for instance in *Portnoy's Complaint*, is transformed into the tragic destiny of yet another "type": the Jew who cannot elude a chosen self.

A study of contemporary America's affirmation of right-wing ideology retrojected into the past, *The Plot Against America* (2004) presents a study in alternative history. Roth painfully describes an America with Charles Lindbergh as president, and antisemitism as an official matter of state. The novel has its immediate ancestry in Sinclair Lewis' *It Can't Happen Here*. Although *The Plot Against America* ends with relief, Roth's warnings of an American fascism in the making add a dark note to American-Jewish existence.

Clearly, Roth is defining himself as a novelist concerned with the notion of a social good and the good itself. His works swell with implications about the chances for dignity, for compassion, and for justice in contemporary America. The early satire, for example, of *Our Gang*, is now replaced by novels that set the terms for an understanding of American political literature.

Roth's reflections on his own life can be found in *The Facts: A Novelist's Autobiography* (1988) and in his study of his father in *Patrimony: A True Story* (1991).

BIBLIOGRAPHY: A. Cooper, *Philip Roth and the Jews* (1996); D. Royal (ed.), *Philip Roth: New Perspectives on an American Author* (2005); D. Shostak, *Philip Roth: Countertexts, Counterlives* (2004).

[Milton Henry Hindus and Sylvia Barack Fishman / Lewis Fried (2nd ed.)]

ROTHBERG, SAMUEL (1910–), U.S. business executive and Jewish community leader. Rothberg, who was born in Belezekov (near Kiev), Russia, was director of both the American Distilling Co. and the Parvin Dormeyer Co. Rothberg retired in 1965 so that he could devote more time to Jewish affairs, in which he had previously been active. He served from 1955 as national campaign chairman of the Israel Bonds Organization (of which he was a founder); a member of the national campaign cabinet of the United Jewish Appeal; chairman of both the board of governors of the Hebrew University and the board of directors of the American Friends of the Hebrew University; vice president of the American Committee for the Weizmann Institute; and an honorary founder of the Harry S. Truman Institute for the Advancement of Peace. Rothberg was president of the Israel Investors Corp. and founder of Capital for Israel Corp. He was also president of Congregation Agudat Achim in his home city of Peoria, Illinois. In 1970 he was elected a non-party member of the executive of the World Zionist Organization and of the Jewish Agency.

In 1975, in honor of his 65th birthday, the Hebrew University established the annual Samuel Rothberg Prize for Jewish Education. At Bradley University in Peoria, the Samuel Rothberg Professional Excellence Award is presented for distinguished contributions to research or creative productions.

In 1981, the Hebrew University's school for pupils from abroad was officially named the Rothberg School for Overseas Students in honor of Rothberg, who was one of the major forces in the establishment and development of the school. In 1998 the name was changed to the Rothberg International School. He was chairman of the school's International Board of Overseers.

ROTHENBERG, MORRIS (1885–1950), U.S. jurist, communal leader and Zionist. Rothenberg, who was born in Dorpat, Estonia, was taken to the U.S. in 1893. He was admitted to the New York bar in 1905. An expert in labor law, Rothenberg served as an arbiter in numerous labor-management disputes. During World War I, he was a member of a federal bread price-fixing commission. In 1937 New York Mayor La Guardia appointed Rothenberg to a ten-year term as city magistrate, and he was reappointed by Mayor O'Dwyer in 1947.

Extremely active in Jewish affairs from his youth, Rothenberg was a founder and executive committee member of the Jewish Welfare Board, a founder of the Joint Distribution Committee, and an executive committee member of the Council for German Jewry. He was also president of the Zionist Organization of America (1932–35). A founder of the Jewish Agency for Palestine (1929), Rothenberg was cochairman of its international council (1933, 1935).

ROTHENBURG OB DER TAUBER, city in Bavaria, Germany. Individual Jews are mentioned there in 1180. A community is first recorded in 1241, when it paid the small sum of 10 silver marks in taxes. In the mid-13th century *Meir ben Baruch, the acknowledged scholarly authority of his era, settled in Rothenburg, attracting pupils by the score; the town thus became a center of Jewish religious life and the Rothenburg community grew. During the *Rindfleisch persecutions (1298), the community was almost totally annihilated. On June 25, 57 were murdered; on July 18, 32 were massacred and their corpses burned in the cemetery. The survivors (around 380) fled into the castle and after a three-day siege were slaughtered and burned.

A new community was established after a short time. A source of 1346 mentions an old synagogue, therefore a new synagogue must have been built. In 1323 Emperor Louis III of Bavaria assessed the taxes of the community at 200 Haller pounds; in 1342 he levied one gulden from each Jew in Rothenburg (see *Opferpfennig*) and obliged the city elders to swear that they would freely admit and protect the Jews, his subjects. During the *Black Death persecutions (1349), the community was annihilated, and afterward the burghers celebrated August 27 annually in commemoration of the city's salvation from "poisoning by the Jews." In 1352, *Charles IV pardoned the burghers for the extermination of the community and allowed the city to admit Jews. The new community, established under the protection and jurisdiction of the city, suffered heavily from the annulment of debts in 1385 and 1390. A short and partial banishment was decreed in 1397, caused by inflammatory sermons on Good Friday, but the Jews were readmitted to the town seven years later. The 15th-century community was probably not allowed to keep a cemetery, for no tombstones of this period have survived. In 1414 an onerous imperial tax was exacted from the Jewish community; some members attempted to flee, and all were put under arrest until it was arranged that the tax would be paid by 21 members of the community. The burghers of Rothenburg successfully resisted, in 1422, the bishop of Wuerzburg's demand that they imprison the Jews and expropriate their property, turning over to the bishop the debts they owed to the Jews. The city opposed any attempt to deprive it of its jurisdiction over the Jewish community, and the economic benefits it derived from them, but the bishop seems to have been successful in imposing a distinctive *badge on the Jews. Jews wishing to remain in Rothenburg were obliged to present annual declarations to the city, stating their names, occupations, and willingness to pay taxes and obey the laws; the city reciprocated by granting legal protection to individual Jews.

In the early 16th century expulsions of Jews from cities in southern Germany became common. The Rothenburg community in 1517 requested the protection of Emperor *Maximilian I against Claus Wolgemut, a robber baron who applied pressure on the city to extort money from the Jewish inhabitants or expel them. The expulsion, which took place three years later, was meticulously planned by the city council, which was advised by Caspar Mart, legal counselor of the empire, to exploit the death of Maximilian in 1519 by taking immediate steps. The preacher Johannes Teuschlein (an early exponent of the Reformation) agitated, with the approval of the council, for the expulsion of the Jews as a reformatory, "cleansing" measure. The council employed a lawyer to help the Jews liquidate their businesses; the last six Jews left on Feb. 2, 1520. Requests by the nobility for a stay of expulsion on behalf of their Jewish associates were not heeded. The expellees were obliged to state, in writing, that they had not been forced to leave and had no outstanding demands. Throughout these proceedings the word "expulsion" was avoided in official correspondence and replaced by *Beurlauben* ("leave of absence," "dismissal"); the illusion that the Jews had left voluntarily was maintained. Attempts by the refugees to return failed. In 1659 Jews were allowed to attend the city's fairs but not to display their wares in public.

A Jewish community was not reestablished until 1875, totaling 86 persons (1.32% of the total population) in 1880. Their number declined from 100 in 1910 to 44 in 1933, when the community possessed a cemetery and *mikveh*. No Jews returned to Rothenburg after World War II. The medieval Jewish wedding hall was rebuilt.

BIBLIOGRAPHY: H. Breslau, in: ZGJD, 3 (1889), 301–36; 4 (1890), 1–17; A. Schnizlein, in: MGWJ, 61 (1917), 263–84; M. Grunwald, *ibid.*, 72 (1928), 204–12; M. Schuetz, *Eine Reichsstadt wehrt sich. Rothenburg ob der Tauber im Kampfe gegen das Judentum* (1938); Germ Jud, 1 (1963), 311–2; 2 (1968), 707–8.

[Henry Wasserman]

ROTHENSTEIN, (William) MICHAEL (1908–1993), British printmaker. The son of Sir William *Rothenstein and brother of Sir John Rothenstein, he was educated at art schools in London and set up a private press outside London, becoming one of Britain's most distinguished printmakers, with a wide international reputation. Rothenstein is noted for the powerful imagery of his designs and for the constant search for new and often brilliant technical effects. He was a regular participant in all important international exhibitions of print-making. During World War II, he produced a famous series of watercolors of endangered sites, *Recording Britain*. He was awarded a Gold Medal for Engraving at the Buenos Aires Biennale. He wrote widely on his craft, particularly in two books, *Frontiers of Printmaking* (1966) and *Relief Printing* (1970). His work is to be found in all major public collections of graphic work, including the Tate Gallery, London, the Museum of Modern Art, New York, and the Library of Congress, Washington. Rothenstein was elected to the Royal Academy in 1984.

ADD. BIBLIOGRAPHY: ODNB online; M. Gooding, *Rothenstein's Boxes* (1992); Tessa S., *The Prints of Michael Rothenstein* (1993).

[Charles Samuel Spencer]

ROTHENSTEIN, SIR WILLIAM (1872–1945), British painter. Rothenstein was a distinguished English impressionist and an outstanding teacher. Born in Bradford, England, the son of a German-born businessman, Rothenstein was educated at Bradford Grammar School and the Slade School of Art, and then spent a year at a Paris art school, where he met Degas, Pissarro and Whistler. On his return, he spent some time in Oxford, where he produced the series of lithographs, *Oxford Characters* (1893–96). He became a leading personality of the fin de siècle, a friend of Max Beerbohm, Aubrey Beardsley, and Oscar Wilde, and a contributor to the *Yellow Book*.

During World War I, he served as an official war artist and, from 1917 to 1920, held the post of professor of civic art at the University of Sheffield. He attained his greatest prominence, however, as principal of the Royal College of Art, London (1920–35). During World War II, he was attached to the Royal Air Force as an artist. Rothenstein chiefly painted portraits, still lifes and landscapes. Among his work is a group of Jewish subjects and synagogue interiors, such as *The Talmud School* (1904) and *Carrying the Law* (1909). He wrote a number of books, mostly portraits of eminent contemporaries. His two autobiographical works, *Men and Memories* (1931–32) and *Since Fifty* (1934), offer vivid descriptions of artists and events he knew. He was knighted in 1934. Rothenstein helped many impoverished Jewish artists and other artists in need. Volumes of his correspondence with Max Beerbohm and Rabindrinath Tagore were published in 1972 and 1975.

His son SIR JOHN ROTHENSTEIN (1901–1992), who was educated at Bedales and Oxford, was director of the Tate Gallery, London (1938–64). He had no connection with the Jewish community and converted to Christianity. He wrote three volumes of autobiography, published in 1965–70.

A younger brother of William Rothenstein, ALBERT DANIEL (1881–1953), who changed his name to Rutherston during World War I, was also an artist and illustrator who designed an imaginative *Haggadah* (1930). Another son, Michael *Rothenstein (1908–1993), was a prominent printmaker.

BIBLIOGRAPHY: R. Speaight, William Rothenstein, *The Portrait of an Artist in his Time* (1962). **ADD. BIBLIOGRAPHY:** ODNB online for all three; I. Rogerson, *Albert Rutherston* (1998); M. Rutherston, *Albert Rutherston, 1881–1953* (1988).

[Charles Samuel Spencer]

ROTHKO, MARK (1903–1970), U.S. painter. Born Marcus Rothkowitz in Dvinsk, Russia, Rothko immigrated to the United States in 1913 with his family, settling in Portland, Oregon. He attended Yale University on a scholarship (1921–23), but after two years he moved to New York and briefly studied at the Art Students League, notably with Max *Weber. In 1928 the former yeshivah student was commissioned to draw maps for Rabbi Lewis Browne's book *The Graphic Bible*. Rothko also supported himself by teaching art to children at the Brooklyn Jewish Center, a position he held from 1929 until 1952. He found success early with expressionistic, painterly, representational canvases, shown in his first group exhibition at the Opportunity Galleries (1928) and his first one-man show at the Contemporary Arts Gallery (1933), both in New York. As a member of The Ten, an artist-group that he co-founded in 1935 with Adolph *Gottlieb and *Ben-Zion, and affiliated with for five years, Rothko exhibited imagery stimulated by aspects of mythology, and at times Christian iconography, such as the crucifixion. He worked as a Works Progress Administration artist from 1936 to 1937.

In the early 1940s Rothko fell under the influence of Surrealism, often making images comprised of organic forms. At the end of the decade Rothko painted fully abstract imagery with an oil technique that approximated his watercolor experimentations in the mid-1940s. Typical of Rothko's signature style is *Green and Tangerine on Red* (1956, Phillips Collection, Washington, D.C.), a large canvas consisting of two flat, rectangular shapes of thin color. Filling the canvas, the nearly translucent hues seem to float on the surface of the composition. Rothko exploited this formula with differing color variations, size of colorfields, and application of the paint to convey an array of sensations, ranging from meditative to ominous. By 1961 Rothko was a celebrated artist who enjoyed a retrospective at the Museum of Modern Art in New York City.

Rothko received several public commissions, including the artwork for an octagonal chapel in Houston, Texas. Decorated with 14 canvases in nuanced shades of black and maroon, the Rothko Chapel was dedicated in February 1971, a year after the artist committed suicide.

BIBLIOGRAPHY: D. Waldman, *Mark Rothko, 1903–1970: A Retrospective* (1978); B. Clearwater, *Mark Rothko: Works on Paper* (1984); A.C. Chave, *Mark Rothko: Subjects in Abstraction* (1989); J.E.B. Breslin, *Mark Rothko* (1993); D. Anfam, *Mark Rothko, The Works on Canvas: Catalogue Raisonné* (1998).

[Samantha Baskind (2nd ed.)]

ROTHMUELLER, AARON MARKO (1908–1993), baritone and composer. Born in Trnjani, Yugoslavia, Rothmueller studied composition with Alban Berg in Vienna. He sang opera in Europe. He lived in England but after World War II moved to the United States and in 1952 was appointed professor of music at the University of Indiana. His compositions include *Four Sephardic Folksongs, Three Palestinian Folksongs, Three Palestinian Love Songs*, a setting of Psalm 15, and *In Memory of C.N. Bialik* for violin, viola and cello. He wrote *Die Musik der Juden* (1951; *The Music of the Jews*, 1953).

ROTHSCHILD, family of financiers and philanthropists, patrons of the arts and sciences who greatly contributed to Jewish causes, particularly to the settlement of Ereẓ Israel and the State of Israel. (See charts: Rothschild Family).Over the years their name became a byword for opulence and munificence, serving both as a positive symbol of Jewish wealth, influence, and philanthropy, among the Jewish masses, particularly in Eastern Europe (see, e.g., in *Shalom Aleichem's stories) and as a negative, sinister symbol in antisemitic literature and propaganda, which used it as tangible "proof" for the existence of an international plutocracy.

The Founding Branch

The family name is derived from a red shield which once hung in front of the house of ISAAC ELHANAN (d. 1585), grandson of URI (d. c. 1500), first recorded member of the family, in Frankfurt; though the grandson of Isaac Elhanan left the house, his descendants continued to bear the surname. Until the birth of MAYER AMSCHEL (1744–1812), son of AMSCHEL MOSES ROTHSCHILD, the Rothschilds were undistinguished merchants and communal servants. Mayer Amschel began trading in antiques and old coins and in money changing and thus in 1764 began doing business with the future Landgrave William IX of Hesse-Kassel, an avid coin collector and heir

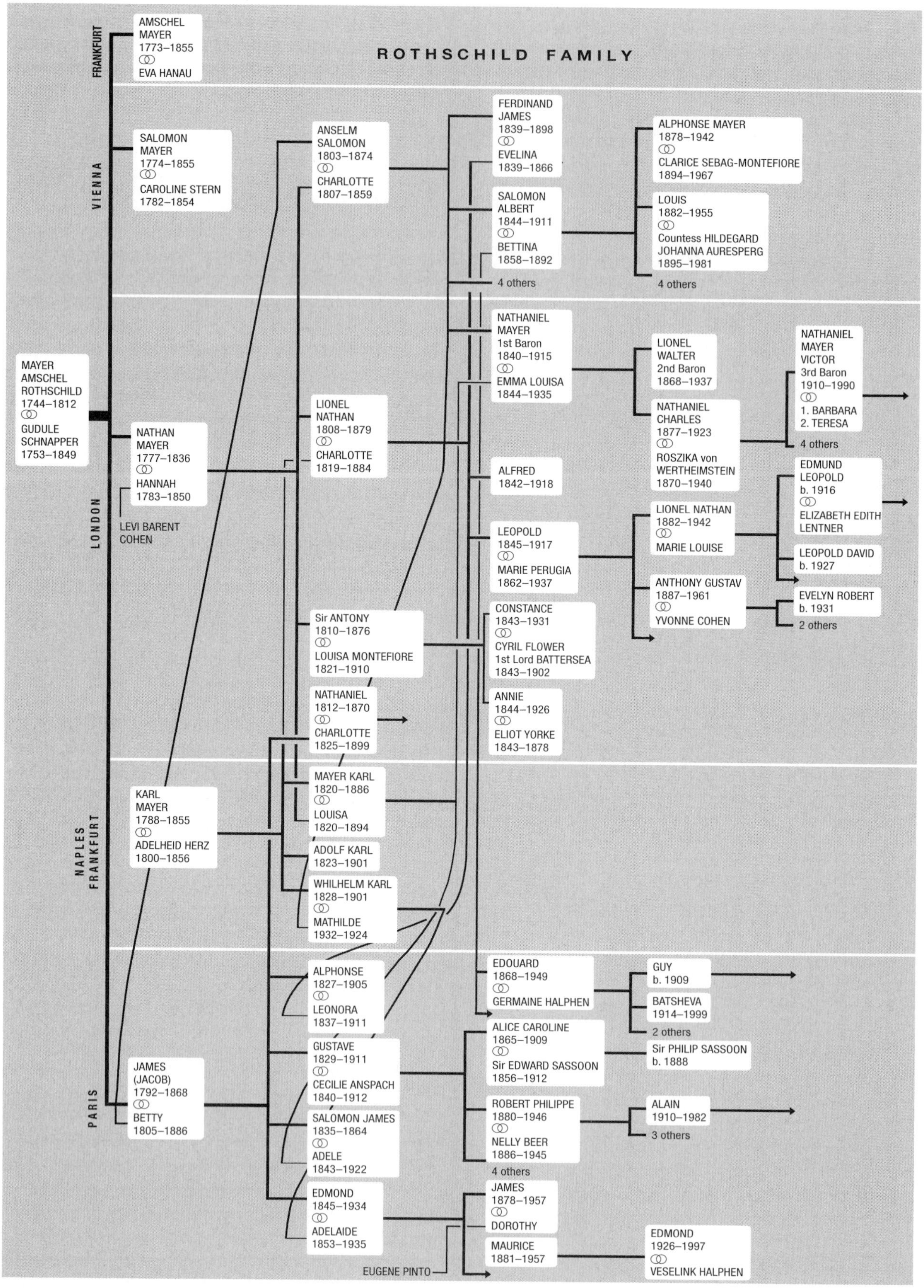

ROTHSCHILD FAMILY

FRANKFURT

AMSCHEL MAYER 1773–1855
⚭
EVA HANAU

VIENNA

SALOMON MAYER 1774–1855
⚭
CAROLINE STERN 1782–1854

ANSELM SALOMON 1803–1874
⚭
CHARLOTTE 1807–1859

FERDINAND JAMES 1839–1898
⚭
EVELINA 1839–1866

SALOMON ALBERT 1844–1911
⚭
BETTINA 1858–1892

4 others

ALPHONSE MAYER 1878–1942
⚭
CLARICE SEBAG-MONTEFIORE 1894–1967

LOUIS 1882–1955
⚭
Countess HILDEGARD JOHANNA AURESPERG 1895–1981

4 others

LONDON

MAYER AMSCHEL ROTHSCHILD 1744–1812
⚭
GUDULE SCHNAPPER 1753–1849

NATHAN MAYER 1777–1836
⚭
HANNAH 1783–1850

LEVI BARENT COHEN

LIONEL NATHAN 1808–1879
⚭
CHARLOTTE 1819–1884

NATHANIEL MAYER 1st Baron 1840–1915
⚭
EMMA LOUISA 1844–1935

ALFRED 1842–1918

LEOPOLD 1845–1917
⚭
MARIE PERUGIA 1862–1937

LIONEL WALTER 2nd Baron 1868–1937

NATHANIEL CHARLES 1877–1923
⚭
ROSZIKA von WERTHEIMSTEIN 1870–1940

LIONEL NATHAN 1882–1942
⚭
MARIE LOUISE

ANTHONY GUSTAV 1887–1961
⚭
YVONNE COHEN

2 others

NATHANIEL MAYER VICTOR 3rd Baron 1910–1990
⚭
1. BARBARA
2. TERESA

4 others

EDMUND LEOPOLD b. 1916
⚭
ELIZABETH EDITH LENTNER

LEOPOLD DAVID b. 1927

EVELYN ROBERT b. 1931

Sir ANTONY 1810–1876
⚭
LOUISA MONTEFIORE 1821–1910

NATHANIEL 1812–1870
⚭
CHARLOTTE 1825–1899

CONSTANCE 1843–1931
⚭
CYRIL FLOWER 1st Lord BATTERSEA 1843–1902

ANNIE 1844–1926
⚭
ELIOT YORKE 1843–1878

NAPLES FRANKFURT

KARL MAYER 1788–1855
⚭
ADELHEID HERZ 1800–1856

MAYER KARL 1820–1886
⚭
LOUISA 1820–1894

ADOLF KARL 1823–1901

WHILHELM KARL 1828–1901
⚭
MATHILDE 1932–1924

PARIS

JAMES (JACOB) 1792–1868
⚭
BETTY 1805–1886

ALPHONSE 1827–1905
⚭
LEONORA 1837–1911

GUSTAVE 1829–1911
⚭
CECILIE ANSPACH 1840–1912

SALOMON JAMES 1835–1864
⚭
ADELE 1843–1922

EDMOND 1845–1934
⚭
ADELAIDE 1853–1935

EDOUARD 1868–1949
⚭
GERMAINE HALPHEN

ALICE CAROLINE 1865–1909
⚭
Sir EDWARD SASSOON 1856–1912

ROBERT PHILIPPE 1880–1946
⚭
NELLY BEER 1886–1945

4 others

JAMES 1878–1957
⚭
DOROTHY

MAURICE 1881–1957

EUGENE PINTO

GUY b. 1909

BATSHEVA 1914–1999

2 others

Sir PHILIP SASSOON b. 1888

ALAIN 1910–1982

3 others

EDMOND 1926–1997
⚭
VESELINK HALPHEN

to the largest fortune in Europe. By c. 1769 Mayer Amschel had received the title of court agent and was supplying William with rare coins and printing his own coin catalogs. When William became landgrave in 1785, Mayer Amschel was only one of a dozen Jewish court agents competing for the favor of doing business for a landgrave who lent large sums to other rulers. Mayer Amschel managed to increase his share of financial transactions very gradually: his close connections with William IX's confidential financial adviser, C.F. Buderus (who eventually became his silent partner), were of inestimable importance in securing the confidence of the landgrave.

The major breakthrough occurred after the Battle of Jena (1806): exiled from his country, William IX entrusted NATHAN MAYER (1777–1836), Mayer Amschel's son in London, with the purchase of huge amounts of British securities. By discreet and brilliant speculation Nathan succeeded in amassing a fortune without damaging the landgrave's interests. Nathan Mayer had originally settled in Manchester in 1798, a commission agent dealing in cotton goods, but he moved to London in 1808. In 1806 he married Hannah, the daughter of Levi Barent *Cohen and sister of Moses *Montefiore's wife. He rapidly became the outstanding figure on the London Stock Exchange. His prime activity was that of helping the government cover the costs of Wellington's army in Spain, including transporting immense sums even through the heart of France. In this endeavor he was helped by his brother James (see below) in Paris, while the father and the elder son, Amschel Mayer (see below), remained in Frankfurt. Another major cooperative undertaking was transmitting the British bullion subsidy to the continental allies in the last stages of the Napoleonic wars. After the Congress of Vienna the Rothschilds were instrumental in transmitting the French war indemnity (£120,000,000) to the allies and participated in the many governmental reconstruction loans and bond issues. By the time of his death Nathan Rothschild was one of the very richest men in Britain, worth an estimated £5 million, and had become a legendary figure in British finance. In this period two Rothschild brothers established themselves in Vienna and Naples.

Carl Mayer (1788–1855), founded the Italian branch in Naples in 1821, in the aftermath of the suppression of an anti-Bourbon uprising by Austrian troops. He loaned large sums to Sardinia, Sicily, and Naples, the Papal States, and other lesser duchies. His four sons all married members of the Rothschild family. ADOLF CARL (1823–1901) succeeded him as head of the Italian branch but returned to Frankfurt upon the unification of Italy. Another son of Mayer Amschel, SALOMON MAYER (1774–1855), moved to Vienna in 1816, where he was soon on very friendly terms with *Metternich (during the 1848 Revolution he was accused of helping Metternich to escape) and was thus able to ignore or overcome the various discriminations to which Jews were subjected in Vienna and Austria (since a Jew was not allowed to purchase a house, he rented a whole hotel); in addition he had to contend with the rivalry of the established banking houses, foremost of which were the *Arnstein and *Eskeles firms. In 1822 he was ennobled. He was soon participating in the floating of government bonds. His main achievement was building Austria's first railroad and establishing the Oesterreichische Kreditanstalt, with which his descendants were closely connected and which later became Austria's state bank. Salomon was succeeded by ANSELM SALOMON (1803–1874), who was appointed to the Austrian House of Lords in 1861 and had married a daughter of Nathan Mayer Rothschild of London. He was succeeded by his son SALOMON ALBERT (1844–1911), noted for his philanthropic and artistic interests. His sons, ALPHONSE MAYER (1878–1942) and LOUIS (1882–1955), were forced to witness the decline of the firm in the political and economic upheavals of the post-World War I era. Two days after the *Anschluss*, Louis was arrested and held hostage for a year until he was finally released through a combination of ransom and informal financial pressure exerted by international banks. After his departure the Austrian Rothschild branch was liquidated. The Wittkowitz coal mines in Czechoslovakia, among the largest in Central Europe, were transferred to British and neutral holdings before the Munich agreement. The Nazis were thus unable to confiscate them, but were able to pressure the Rothschilds into selling the mines for one-third of their value. The sale did not go into effect because of the outbreak of World War II, and after the end of the war the Rothschilds were able to receive partial compensation from the Czech government.

Amschel Mayer (1773–1855), continued to head the paternal Frankfurt branch. He loaned large amounts to many German rulers and took steps to have the **Leibzoll* abolished in Bavaria and other German states. Very pious, he furnished the financial backing for the secessionist Orthodox community of S.R. *Hirsch in Frankfurt. The Frankfurt house was attacked during the *Hep! Hep! disturbances, and again during the 1848 Revolution, when anticapitalist, antisemitic, and democratic feelings coalesced against the Rothschilds. Amschel was succeeded by his nephew MAYER CARL (1820–1886) from Naples, who was elected to the North German Reichstag in 1867, and appointed to the Prussian Upper Chamber shortly thereafter, the first of the only two Jews ever to receive the honor. The conservative Mayer Carl had long been pro-Prussian and had recommended Gerson *Bleichroeder to *Bismarck as his private banker. The Bleichroeder bank continued to maintain close connections with the Rothschilds, often serving as their agents in Berlin. Amschel's other nephew, WILHELM KARL (1828–1901), was sole head after his brother's death. After his death the Frankfurt branch was discontinued.

[Henry Wasserman]

The French Branch

JAMES JACOB ROTHSCHILD (1792–1868), the youngest of the brothers, settled in Paris in 1812 as an agent of Nathan Mayer and founded there the firm of Rothschild Frères. From then on, apart from its banking activities, the Rothschild family took a great interest in the activities of the Jewish community in Paris and later in the whole of France. The Rothschilds were particularly active from 1840 in connection with the *Damascus affair and later in the work of the Jewish *Consistory of Paris, the Central Consistory of the Jews of France, and the Jewish Charity Committee of Paris which later became the Paris Jewish Committee for Social Work. James de Rothschild presented to the community of Paris the Rothschild Hospital, which is still in existence. James, who was financier to both the Bourbon and Orléans kings of France, weathered the 1848 Revolution to serve Napoleon III. A pioneer railroad entrepreneur, he feuded with the rival *Fould and *Pereire brothers for governmental railway concessions. A railway accident released a flood of antisemitic literature, popularizing the slogan "Rothschild Ier, Roi des Juifs." His wife Betty, a noted philanthropist, was friend and patron of Heinrich *Heine. James also maintained close business connections with Leopold I of Belgium. His son ALPHONSE (1827–1905) became head of the French house in 1854 and president of the board of directors of the family's *Chemin de Fer du Nord* in 1869. After the defeat of France in 1870/71 Alphonse led war indemnity negotiations with the Prussians and guaranteed their rapid payment. A syndicate of French bankers, partly motivated by antisemitic sentiments, unsuccessfully sought to challenge the French house in the 1870s. Alphonse's philanthropy, benefiting both Jews and gentiles, was on an immense scale. GUSTAVE (1829–1911), another of James's sons, was president of the Paris Consistory for over 40 years. A third son, Edmond de *Rothschild (1845–1934), gave crucial support to the early settlements in Ereẓ Israel, an expression of his lifelong devotion to Zion and the Jewish people. The son and grandson of Alphonse, EDOUARD (1868–1949) and GUY (b. 1909), and the son and grandson of Gustave, ROBERT PHILIPPE (1880–1946) and ALAIN (1910–1982), were presidents of the Central and Paris Consistories. Alain also became president of the Fonds Social Juif Unifié (FSJU). Guy was president of the Comité de Solidarité avec Israel (1956). Edouard's daughter BETHSABÉE (Batsheva, 1914–1999), founded the *Batsheva Dance Company in Tel Aviv in 1964. In addition to the Bathsheva Dance Company, Bathsheva de Rothschild founded the Bat-Dor Dance Company, which combines classical ballet and modern dance, in 1967. Among her other endeavors were the project to translate ancient literature into Hebrew, a music library in Tel Aviv, and a fund for loans and grants to students, outstanding young Israeli scholars, and immigrant scholars. She received the Israel Prize in 1989 for special contribution in national and social fields. Edmond's eldest son James de *Rothschild (1878–1957) left France to settle in England, where he continued his father's activities, which were later taken over by Dorothy de Rothschild (1895–1988), the widow of James de Rothschild. EDMOND (1926–1997), grandson of the first Edmond, was also president of the Comité de Solidarité avec Israel (1967). The Germans made efforts to capture members of the family in 1940, but all escaped and passed the war in England or the U.S. Guy joined the Free French and was an adjutant to De Gaulle's military governor of Paris at the end of the war.

[Simon R. Schwarzfuchs]

The English Branch

Nathan Mayer's son, LIONEL NATHAN (1808–1879), led the struggle for Jewish emancipation; after having first been elected to parliament in 1847 (as a Liberal), he finally took his seat as the first Jewish member in 1858 after the passing of the Jews' Disabilities Bill. He remained a member of Parliament (with a short break in 1868–69) until 1874. As head of the banking house at New Court, he was responsible for many government loans, including those for the relief of the Irish famine, the Crimean War, and the purchase of the Khedive's Suez Canal shares. The character of Sidonia in Benjamin Disraeli's *Coningsby* is an idealized portrait of him. His wife CHARLOTTE (1819–1884; daughter of Baron CARL MAYER VON ROTHSCHILD of Naples) collaborated in his philanthropic ventures, being particularly concerned with the Jews' Free School (a special interest of the family). He acquired a great mansion at Tring, Hertfordshire, and was a considerable landowner. He left a personal fortune of £2.7 million at his death. His brother SIR ANTHONY (1810–1876), an English baronet as well as an Austrian baron, lived as a country gentleman (all the Rothschilds of the second generation acquired estates on the Buckinghamshire-Bedfordshire borders) but was also active in the Jewish community: he was the first president of the *United Synagogue. He was granted an English baronetcy (a hereditary knighthood) in 1846. His daughters ANNIE (1844–1926) and CONSTANCE (1843–1931) respectively married (after his death) the Hon. Eliot Yorke and the politician Cyril Flower, later Lord Battersea.

Lionel Nathan's eldest son, NATHANIEL (Natty) MAYER, FIRST BARON ROTHSCHILD (1840–1915), succeeded as head of the firm and effective lay head of Anglo-Jewry, holding the presidency of the United Synagogue and many other offices. Created the first Jewish peer in 1885, he was lord-lieutenant of Buckinghamshire. A governor of the Bank of England and director of many companies, he was the only Jewish member of the Royal Commission on Aliens and firmly resisted attempts to limit immigration. He and his brothers, ALFRED (1842–1918), who was interested in the arts, and LEOPOLD (1845–1917), a sportsman and communal worker, were personal friends of the Prince of Wales, later Edward VII. Their cousin FERDINAND JAMES (1839–1898), of the Viennese branch but born in Paris, married the first Lord Rothschild's sister EVELINA (1839–1866), who died in childbirth and was commemorated by her husband in the Evelina Hospital for Sick Children in London and the Evelina de Rothschild School in Jerusalem. Ferdinand, who became a British subject and a member of parliament, was an art collector and connoisseur and builder of the fabulous Waddesdon Manor. He was the first Rothschild to be visited at his home by Queen Victoria. He was active in communal work, including service as a synagogue warden. While the first Lord Rothschild was not sympathetic to Zionism, though impressed by Theodor Herzl's personality, the second baron, LIONEL WALTER (1868–1937), a distinguished naturalist who owned a private zoo, was a Zionist and the recipient in 1917 of the *Balfour Declaration.

Leopold's sons were LIONEL NATHAN (1882–1942), president of the United Synagogue, and ANTHONY GUSTAV (1887–1961), who was prominent in hospital administration. In the next generation, EDMUND LEOPOLD (1916–), nephew of the second baron, succeeded Anthony Gustav as head of the firm and held high communal office. His cousin Nathaniel Mayer Victor *Rothschild (1910–1990), the third baron, was a distinguished biologist. In 1868 HANNAH ROTHSCHILD (1851–1890), the daughter of Baron Mayer de Rothschild, married Archibald Primrose, later fifth Earl of Rosebery (1847–1929), a leading Liberal politician who served as Britain's prime minister in 1894–95. The Jewish community was generally highly critical of the marriage of the leading Rothschild heiress to a prominent gentile. Their son, (ALBERT) HARRY MAYER ARCHIBALD PRIMROSE, sixth Earl of Rosebery (1882–1974) was a leading landowner and racehorse owner who served in the 1945 Conservative Cabinet as secretary of state for Scotland.

Between the world wars, the development of other major banking concerns and high taxation reduced the relative importance of the Rothschilds' financial power. So, too, did a series of political events – the loss of such traditional areas of endeavor as Russia (from 1917) and Germany (from 1933) – and changes in the nature of government finance, with individual merchant banks becoming less prominent than previously, as governments increasingly financed their own projects directly. Before and during World War II the Nazis set special value upon expropriating the Rothschilds. The ownership of their property had, however, often been legally transferred in time to holding companies in neutral or noncombatant countries, or secured by other means. After World War II, however, the Rothschilds adapted themselves to the new opportunities in merchant banking, building modern offices at New Court, running unit trusts, acquiring great interests in Canada, and investing in films and television. In America, where few Rothschild investments were made, their agent in the 1840s was August *Belmont, financier and politician. Belmont warned against any recognition of the Confederacy and the Frankfurt Rothschilds were active in the acquisition and sale of Northern bonds.

In charity and philanthropy, the Rothschilds continued to give unostentatiously to many causes, the third baron, for instance, financing educational television in Israel. James de *Rothschild, son of Baron Edmond de Rothschild, settled in England and became a Liberal MP. He inherited Waddesdon from Ferdinand and left the estate to the nation, as well as a fortune to various causes in Israel. However, members of the family have increasingly married non-Jews and their share in the management of the affairs of the British Jewish community has diminished.

[Vivian David Lipman]

BIBLIOGRAPHY: F. Morton, *The Rothschilds* (1962); C. Roth, *The Magnificent Rothschilds* (1938); E.C. Corti, *The Rise of the House of Rothschild* (1928); idem, *The Reign of the House of Rothschild* (1928); C.W. Berghoeffer, *Meyer Amschel Rothschild* (Ger., 1923); B. Gille, *Histoire de la Maison Rothschild*, 1 (1965); 2 (1967); H. Schnee, *Rothschild* (Ger., 1961); J. Bowier, *Les Rothschilds* (1967); R. Hilberg, *The Destruction of the European Jews* (1967), 66–72; R. Glanz, in: JSOS, 19 (1957), 3–28; V. Eichsaedt (ed.), *Bibliographie zur Geschichte der Judenfrage* (1938), 232f.; L. Kreutzberger (ed.), *Bibliothek und Archiv* (1970), index s.v. *Rothschild*; *Heine Bibliographie*, 2 (1958), index s.v. *Rothschild*; B. Brilling, in: BLBI, 7 (1964), 165–71; D.S. Lands, in: YLBI, 5 (1960), 206–17; K. Grunwald, *ibid.*, 12 (1967), 168ff.; Roth, Mag Bibl, 149, 150, 433; R.P. Lehmann, *Nova Bibliotheca Anglo-Judaica* (1961), 108, 113, 117; J. Picciotto, *Sketches of Anglo-Jewish History* (1956^2), index; Y. Toury, *Mehumah u-Mevukhah be-Mahpekhat 1848* (1968), index; W. Verity, in: *History Today*, 18 (April, 1968); A. Rubens, in: *Transactions*, 22 (1970), 76–87. **ADD. BIBLIOGRAPHY:** ODNB online; N.Ferguson, *The World's Banker* (1998); R. Davis, *The English Rothschilds* (1983); S.D. Chapman, *N.M. Rothschild, 1777–1836* (1977); Lord Rothschild [Nathaniel, Baron Rothschild], *The Shadow of a Great Man* (1982). C. Bermant, *The Cousinhood* (1961), index.

ROTHSCHILD, BARON EDMOND JAMES DE (1845–1934), philanthropist, patron of Jewish settlement in Ereẓ Israel, and art collector. Rothschild was born in Paris (see *Rothschild family). In contrast to his two older brothers, Edmond was not given to banking, and from his youth was devoted to humanist and cultural matters, especially art. His art collection, which occupied him throughout his life, brought him fame as an art expert, and he was elected to the Institut des Beaux Arts in Paris. He was close to both Jewish and non-Jewish intellectuals in France. In 1877 he married Adelaide the daughter of Wilhelm Carl Rothschild, who was known for his extreme religiosity and his unwillingness to become involved with matters concerning Ereẓ Israel.

"I have always been concerned with the future of Judaism," Rothschild wrote in an autobiographical letter dated 1928. He only began public activity in the Jewish sphere, however, after the pogroms in Russia in the 1880s. He was on the French Committee to Aid the Emigration of Refugees and became involved in affairs concerning Ereẓ Israel only after the founding of the first settlements and the first overtures from settlers and members of Ḥovevei Zion in Europe. It is known that as early as 1873 he was influenced by *La Femme de Claude*, a play by Alexandre Dumas *fils*, which advocated the return of the Jewish people to the Land of Israel; Dumas reiterated this idea in a letter to Rothschild (published in part by Nahum *Sokolow, without revealing the name of the recipient, in *History of Zionism*, 2 (1919), 263–5). When the first settlements in Ereẓ Israel faced a financial crisis serious enough to endanger their existence, the leaders of *Rishon le-Zion turned to Rothschild, together with Samuel *Mohilewer through the mediation of Chief Rabbi Zadoc *Kahn in Paris. The result of these appeals was Rothschild's support for the settlements Rishon le-Zion and Zikhron Ya'akov and afterward the founding of the settlement Ekron. During 1883–84, the first settlements began to be patronized by Rothschild. Due to his desire to remain anonymous in this venture, he was known by a cover name "Ha-Nadiv ha-Yadu'a" ("the Well-Known Benefactor"), and in Ereẓ Israel and the Ḥovevei Zion groups this name became better known than his real one. His aid to the first settlements saved them from collapse, as testified to by Peretz *Smolenskin and Moses *Lilienblum at the time.

Rothschild himself later defined his activities as "not merely philanthropy, but something entirely different." For decades, including the era of Theodor *Herzl's activity, Rothschild advocated "quiet" settlement work as the basis for a promising future, and only after World War I did he join the political activity of the Zionist Organization (aiding Chaim *Weizmann and Sokolow in particular).

Rothschild's patronage was of two types: the first was full (Rishon le-Zion, Zikhron Ya'akov, Rosh Pinnah, and Ekron) and the second was partial (Petaḥ Tikvah and others). He became the major address for all problems in the *yishuv*, large and small alike, to such a degree that he became known as the "Father of the *Yishuv*." All the agricultural experiments carried out in the settlements by French experts were covered by his funds. His support was implemented by a bureaucracy, mostly staffed by Frenchmen whose mentality was alien to that of the settlers. This caused sharp antagonism that even reached the level of revolt in several settlements. This type of bureaucratic patronage was the greatest problem of the Jewish settlements during a 20-year period and aroused sharp criticism. However, in retrospect it is recognized that Rothschild's bureaucracy also played a positive role. It introduced new plant species into Jewish agriculture and instructed the first settlers in the agriculture of the country.

Rothschild's first visits to Ereẓ Israel (1887, 1893, 1899) were devoted to tours of the settlements, investigating the rate of development, and demanding self-labor in the settlements, modest living standards, the speaking of Hebrew, and a concern for religious tradition. In addition, lands were purchased on his orders for new agricultural settlement (in the Golan and Hauran, among other places). In the 1890s Rothschild came into conflict with Herzl and with the Ḥovevei Zion in Russia. Herzl read his "Address to the Rothschild Family" to him, but no common denominator could be found between Rothschild's settlement methods and the notion of a charter, which symbolized Herzl's political Zionism. The second conflict was with the Russian Ḥovevei Zion, and particularly *Aḥad Ha-Am, over the patronage system. Aḥad Ha-Am denounced this system of settlement in his famous article "Ha-*Yishuv ve-Apotropsav*" (1902). Before the publication of this article, a delegation of Ḥovevei Zion from Russia, including Aḥad Ha-Am, and representatives of the settlements visited Rothschild (May 14, 1901) and demanded that the patronage system cease. The result of these conflicts was the transfer of Rothschild's settlements to the supervision of the *Jewish Colonization Association (ICA) in 1900, together with a grant of 14,000,000 francs. The transaction covered about 250,000 dunams (62,500 acres) and a network of 12 settlements, most of which, due to Rothschild's support, were ready to become self-supporting.

Under ICA the settlements expanded, to a large degree with Rothschild's direct and indirect support. In 1914, during Rothschild's fourth visit, he expressed satisfaction with his settlement activities, which had also influenced other settlements, especially those of the Zionist Organization. In addition to his agricultural settlement activity, Rothschild played a major role in the development of the wine industry in Ereẓ Israel (see *Israel, State of: Wine Industry), was a cosponsor of the Palestine Electric Corporation, the founder of smaller industries, and contributed funds to the establishment of the Hebrew University. Against the background of this practical work, Rothschild grew closer to the Zionist Organization after his return from this visit. He told Weizmann, "Without me, the Zionists could have done nothing; but without the Zionists, my work would have been dead" (Ch. Weizmann, *Trial and Error*, p. 165). In turn, Weizmann stated that Rothschild was "far-sighted in his political and national thought." The road to cooperation between Rothschild and the Zionists was paved during World War I and especially toward its end, with the preparatory work for the *Balfour Declaration. Rothschild softened the objections of the assimilationists in France to the political activity of the Zionist Organization.

Toward the end of World War I, Rothschild's son James arrived in Ereẓ Israel with the British army and was among the recruiters for the Jewish battalions in the *yishuv*. Rothschild expressed his joy at "seeing his heir carrying on his great work, to which he was completely devoted." Toward the end of 1923, his work was again reorganized. Rothschild founded the Palestine Jewish Colonization Association (*PICA) headed by his son James, which continued the settlement activity, particularly in Samaria. The first settlement founded in Samaria, Binyamina, bore Rothschild's Hebrew name (Avraham Binyamin). According to Rothschild's instructions, the main purpose of PICA was to found new settlements. He visited the country in 1924 and finally in 1925, when he gave a speech in Tel Aviv containing his credo about settlement activity over the decades. He combined economic foundations with cultural, spiritual, and political motivations. Rothschild won the admiration and appreciation of all sectors of the *yishuv* and the Zionist Organization, as expressed in Weizmann's comment: "In my opinion he was the leading political Zionist of our generation." David *Ben-Gurion said of him: "Until his appearance in the arena of settlement activity and until this very day [1954], there is no one whose personal role in cultivating and expanding settlement can match with his."

With the enlargement of the *Jewish Agency (1929), Rothschild was chosen its honorary president, and until his last days he maintained an avid interest in all activities, large and small, in the *yishuv*. Rothschild died in Paris, a year before his wife. He left nearly 500,000 dunams (125,000 acres) and almost 30 settlements in his wake. In 1954 his remains and those of his wife were reinterred in Ramat ha-Nadiv, near Zikhron Ya'akov.

BIBLIOGRAPHY: N. Sokolow, *History of Zionism*, 2 (1919), index; D. Druck, *Baron Edmond Rothschild* (Eng., 1928); C. Roth, *Magnificent Rothschilds* (1939); I. Naiditch, *Edmond de Rothschild* (Eng., 1945); G. Kressel, *Avi ha-Yishuv* (1954); I. Margalith, *Le Baron Edmond de Rothschild et la colonisation juive en Palestine* (1957), incl. bibl.; F. Morton, *The Rothschilds* (1964²), 174–84; B. Dinaburg, *Mefallesei Derekh* (1946), 69–89.

[Getzel Kressel]

ROTHSCHILD, FRIEDRICH SALOMON (Sally; 1899–1995), psychiatrist. Rothschild was born in Giessen near Frankfurt. In 1925 he joined Frieda *Fromm-Reichmann in her psychiatric sanatorium in Heidelberg, where he studied psychoanalysis and was analyzed by Erich *Fromm. From the beginning of his career, Rothschild was concerned with problems of mind-body relations, especially the relation between emotions, perceptions, and thought of man and his central nervous system.

His first paper, written at the age of 23 (published in 1924), was concerned with the dysfunction of the brain in psychotic and neurotic states ("Die primaere Insuffizienz der nervoesen Organe"). He became increasingly dissatisfied with contemporary concepts in psychiatry and neurology, as far as their usefulness to problems of mind-body relations were concerned. Under the influence of Ludwig Klages, creator of modern graphology, Rothschild's study extended to the fields of the science of expression: mime, pantomime, physiognomy and graphology. His book *Symbolik des Hirnbaus* (1935; "The Symbolism of Brain Structure") is built upon these ideas, and a later work, *Das Zentralnervensystem als Symbol des Erlebens* (1958), related these theories to developments in science such as cybernetics, neurophysiology, and communications theory.

Rothschild went to Palestine in 1936. In 1948 he became associated with Lipman *Halpern in the department of neurology at the Hebrew University. In 1955 he was appointed clinical associate professor of psychiatry.

[Louis Miller]

ROTHSCHILD, JACOB M. (1911–1973), U.S. rabbi and civil rights organizer. Rothschild was born in Pittsburgh, Pennsylvania, and earned his B.A. from the University of Cincinnati in 1932. He was ordained in 1936 at *Hebrew Union College, which also awarded him an honorary D.D. in 1960. His first pulpits were with Temple Emanuel of Davenport, Iowa (1936–67) and Rodef Shalom Congregation in Pittsburgh, Pennsylvania (1937–42). In 1942, he entered the United States Army as a chaplain, spending more than a year in the Pacific theatre and seeing infantry combat with the American Division on Guadalcanal. In 1946, he became rabbi of Hebrew Benevolent Congregation (The Temple) in Atlanta, Georgia, where he served until his death.

Rothschild was a courageous voice, championing civil rights during a turbulent era in the South. He and his family received threats of violence, and a bomb exploded at the Temple in 1958. He remained steadfast and was instrumental in convincing the city of Atlanta to honor Martin Luther King, Jr., when he won the Nobel Peace Prize in 1964. Rothschild was also an interfaith activist who served on the executive board of the National Conference of Christians and Jews, established an Institute for the Christian Clergy, and was a founding member of the Atlanta Community Relations Commission, in addition to serving as vice president of the Greater Atlanta Council on Human Relations (1962–26). In the Jewish community, Rothschild served terms as president of both the Atlanta Rabbinical Association and the Atlanta Federation for Jewish Social Services (1954–57). In the Reform movement, he served on the executive board of the *Central Conference of American Rabbis (1953–55) and as chairman of the CCAR's Commission on Justice and Peace (1954–56). Subsequently, he was named to the Board of Governors of Hebrew Union College–Jewish Institute of Religion (1962–64) and to the Board of Trustees of the *Union of American Hebrew Congregations (1966–8). A member of the Advisory Committee of the Religious Action Center of Reform Judaism and of the Advisory Board of the Southeast Region of the Anti-Defamation League, he was honored twice by the ADL, receiving the Citation of Merit Award in 1964 and the Abe Goldstein Human Relations Award in 1968, the same year he was the recipient of Clergyman of the Year Award by the National Conference of Christians and Jews.

[Bezalel Gordon (2nd ed.)]

ROTHSCHILD, JAMES ARMAND DE (1878–1957), British politician, Zionist and philanthropist. Born in Paris, the son of Baron Edmond de *Rothschild, he was taken to England at an early age and became a British subject. Rothschild served with distinction in France during World War I and was then transferred with the rank of major to General *Allenby's staff in the Middle East. He was sent to Palestine to recruit volunteers for the Palestinian battalion of the *Jewish Legion (the Royal Fusiliers). When the *Zionist Commission arrived in Palestine (1918), he was seconded to it as liaison officer, and from that time on his interest in Palestine never flagged. In 1924 he was appointed president for life of the newly-founded Palestine Jewish Colonization Association (*PICA), which was largely financed by his father. He also took an active interest in other enterprises in Palestine, including the Palestine Electric Corporation, the Hebrew University, and excavations at *Hazor, which he sponsored.

In 1929 Rothschild was elected to Parliament (as Liberal member for the Isle of Ely), and he held this seat until 1945. Although he generally did not take a very active part in parliamentary debates, he participated vigorously in the debates on both the Passfield and MacDonald White Papers (see *White Papers). On both occasions, he attacked British policy, accusing it of failing to fulfill the terms of the Mandate. In a speech on the MacDonald White Paper, Rothschild proposed that Palestine be made into a British colony, claiming that this was the only way to preserve the rights of both Jews and Arabs and prevent domination of one part of the population by the other. His effectiveness as a member of Parliament was probably hampered by the fact that he was a Liberal, the party having only a handful of members in Parliament. After his death, his widow informed the Israeli prime minister of the termination of the work of PICA (which was taken over by the Israel government). At the same time, the sum of IL6,000,000 was donated for the construction of a new Knesset building in Jerusalem.

BIBLIOGRAPHY: E. Corti, *Die Rothschilds* (1962), passim; *Exchange of Letters Between Mr. James A. de Rothschild, President of Pica, and Mr. David Ben-Gurion, Prime Minister of Israel* (1957). **ADD. BIBLIOGRAPHY:** C. Bermant, *The Cousinhood* (1961), index.

[Israel Philipp]

ROTHSCHILD, KURT (1920–), Canadian businessman and philanthropist. Rothschild was born into a prominent family in Cologne, Germany, where he attended Jewish schools. In 1938 he escaped Nazi Germany to England. In 1940 he became one of thousands of Germans and Austrians rounded up and detained in Britain after the fall of France as Britain feared a German invasion. Rothschild was transferred by ship to Canada, along with more than 2,200 mostly Jewish refugees, where, as an "enemy alien," he spent more than a year in Canadian internment camps. After his Canadian release, Rothschild attended Queen's University in Kingston, Ontario. He graduated in 1946 with a degree in electrical engineering.

Rothschild founded and was chairman of the State Group, a large multi-trade, construction and management company. Through its involvement in a number of commercial construction projects, the State Group helped reshape the Toronto, Winnipeg, Calgary and Vancouver skylines. The firm was also a major contractor to the automotive, steel and petrochemical industries.

Rothschild retired from business in 1987 to devote himself entirely to community service in Israel, Canada, the United States, South America, and Central and Eastern Europe. A fervent supporter of Jewish education, Rothschild was active on the Boards of Yeshiva University, Bar-Ilan University, Jerusalem College of Technology, Yeshivat Hakotel, and Toronto's Eitz Chaim School. He was also an active member of the Canada-Israel Committee and UJA Federation of Toronto. Rothschild's numerous communal leadership positions include chairman of World Mizrachi, president of Canadian Mizrachi, president of Canadian Zionist Federation, member of the Boards of Jerusalem's Sha'arei Zedek Hospital and Mount Sinai Hospital of Toronto.

[Paula Draper (2nd ed.)]

ROTHSCHILD, NATHANIEL CHARLES JACOB, FOURTH BARON ROTHSCHILD (1936–), banker and public figure. Born in London, Jacob Rothschild was educated at Eton and Oxford. He joined the family bank, N.M. Rothschild, in 1964 and by his dynamism revived its fortunes. He left, however, in 1980, after conflict with its head, his cousin Evelyn de Rothschild, over Jacob's conduct of Rothschild Investment Trust. A series of mergers which he subsequently masterminded led to the creation of the influential financial institution Charterhouse J. Rothschild. From 1971 he was chairman of St. James's Place Capital (formerly J. Rothschild Holdings plc) and from 1980, chairman of Five Arrows Ltd. His activity in public life focused on culture and the arts. From 1985 to 1991, he was chairman of the board of trustees of the National Gallery and in 1992–98 was chairman of the new board of trustees of the National Heritage Memorial Fund. In the House of Lords he sat as an independent. In 1992, the year of the opening of the Israeli Supreme Court building, a gift of Yad Hanadiv, the Rothschild family foundation, he was awarded an honorary Ph.D. from the Hebrew University of Jerusalem (1992) and was made an Honorary Fellow of the City of Jerusalem. In the same year he became president of the Institute of Jewish Affairs.

He succeeded his father as fourth Baron Rothschild in 1990. He was closely involved in the redevelopment of Somerset House, London, as an art gallery, and received several honorary degrees.

[David Cesarani]

ROTHSCHILD, NATHANIEL MAYER VICTOR, LORD (1910–1990), British biologist. A fellow of Trinity College, Cambridge (1935–39), he served in military intelligence during World War II and was awarded the George Medal (1944) and the U.S. Legion of Merit (1946). On his return to civilian life, he pursued research in embryology, particularly on the biochemistry and physiology of the egg and sperm cells. Investigating the reactions leading to fertilization in a series of research projects with M.M. Swann (1949–52), Lord Rothschild showed that fertilization brings about changes in the egg surface which protect the egg against the penetration of additional spermatozoa. His book *Fertilization* (1956) described the fertilization process in invertebrates, vertebrates, and plants. His other publications include *A Classification of Living Animals* (1961, 1965^2). From 1948 to 1958, Lord Rothschild was chairman of the British Agricultural Research Council and from 1950 he was assistant director of research in the department of zoology of Cambridge. In 1965 he became research coordinator of the Royal Dutch Shell Group. Rothschild served as director-general of the Central Policy Review Staff ("Think-Tank") of the British Cabinet Office from 1971 to 1974 and as chairman of the Royal Commission on Gambling from 1976. He was elected a fellow of the Royal Society. Keenly interested in Israel, he was appointed a governor of the Weizmann Institute of Science and of the Hebrew University of Jerusalem. He was appointed GBC Knight (Grand Cross of the Order of the British Empire) in 1975. His autobiography *Meditations of a Broomstick* was published in 1977.

See *Rothschild family.

[Mordecai L. Gabriel and Henry Wasserman]

ROTHSCHILD, ROBERT PHINEAS (1914–2000), Canadian soldier. Rothschild was born in the small town of Cochrane, Ontario. He received his secondary education in Montreal before entering the Royal Military College of Canada in Kingston in 1932. Fellow students nicknamed him "the baron" though he was unrelated to the European Rothschilds; he graduated in 1936, then earned a degree at McGill University in mining engineering. In 1938, with war threatening in Europe, he joined the Royal Canadian Horse Artillery as a lieutenant. In June 1940, Rothschild landed in France as part of the First Canadian division and helped cover the British retreat at Dunkirk. He was one of the last Canadian soldiers evacuated from France to Britain five days later. He underwent further training and was promoted to major with the 5th Canadian Armoured division. He landed with the Canadian forces on D-Day, June 6, 1944, and, engaging in heavy fighting, was wounded in action in late July 1944. He returned to the fighting three weeks later, promoted to lieutenant colonel, and participated in the Canadian offensives in northern Europe. Believed to be the highest-ranking Jew in the Canadian Army at the end of World War II, he was twice mentioned in dispatches and was made a Member of the Order of the British Empire; he also was made an Officer of the Order of Orange-Nassau with swords by the Dutch government in 1945.

After the war, Rothschild was appointed director of the Canadian Army Staff College in Kingston, then successfully moved through a series of major staff positions at Canadian military headquarters in Ottawa including quartermaster general of the Canadian Army. He also held several overseas postings. In 1954, he was promoted to the rank of brigadier and later to major general, the first Jewish general in the Canadian Army. He retired from the Army in 1970.

[Gerald Tulchinsky (2nd ed.)]

ROTHSCHILD, WALTER N. (1892–1960), U.S. department-store executive. Rothschild was born in New York City. He began working with his grandfather Abraham *Abraham, a founder of the Brooklyn department store Abraham and Straus. After serving in the Naval Reserve during World War I, he was made general manager of the department store (1925), and under his leadership the store expanded into one of the largest in sales in the city. In 1929 the store came under the holding company Federated Department Stores, Inc., along with *Lazarus of Columbus, Ohio, and Filene's of Boston. Remaining active in the management of Federated and of Abraham and Straus, Rothschild became president of that store in 1937, then chairman (1955), and at his death he was also chairman of Federated Department Stores.

During World War II, Rothschild served as chairman of the Army-Navy Commission of the National Jewish Welfare Board, overseeing activities in England for a time; he was also on the executive commission of the United Service Organization. He served as trustee of the Federation of Jewish Philanthropies, on the executive commission of the American Jewish Committee, and as trustee for several other organizations.

His son WALTER N. ROTHSCHILD JR. (1920–2003) graduated from Harvard in 1942 with a B.A. before enlisting in the U.S. Army in World War II. He served as an army officer in Europe in 1942–46. He joined Abraham and Straus in 1950 and rose to be president (1963–69); in the year he stepped down from that position to pursue a civic career, the store was accounted the third largest in New York City, with annual sales estimated at $250 million. During his presidency at A&S, Rothschild was active as liaison agent between the store and the Brooklyn community, in work for a cleaner urban environment, and in improving the quality of merchandise provided by manufacturers.

He served as trustee of the Federation of Jewish Philanthropies and on several hospital boards, and was a member of the Second Regional Planning Commission. In 1970 he was appointed New York chairman of the Urban Coalition, the national agency devoted to improving urban life (1970–73). He then served as chairman of the National Urban Coalition (1973–77). Rothschild's longstanding interest in providing vocational opportunities for minorities in America was instrumental in the creation of the Ventures Scholars Program, a national nonprofit program designed to promote access to higher learning for young adults interested in pursuing math- and science-based careers.

ROTH-SHACHAMOROV, ESTHER (1952–), Israeli track and field star. Roth was born in Tel Aviv and became the first Israeli athlete to reach an Olympic final. By the ninth grade she had already broken the Israeli hurdles record. At the 1970 Asian Games she won gold medals in the 100m hurdles and pentathlon and silver in the long jump. In 1971 she was sportswoman of the year in Israel and Asia. In 1972 she took part in the Olympic Games in Munich. After she reached the 100m semifinals, her coach, Amitzur Shapira, predicted she would win a medal, but the dream was shattered when he and another 10 Israeli sportsmen were kidnapped and murdered by Palestinian terrorists. Recovering from the tragedy she returned to competition a year later, winning three gold medals at the Ninth Maccabiah Games in 1973 though three months pregnant. Though recovering from a Caesarian delivery she won three more gold medals at the 1974 Asian Games, this time in the 200m dash, the 100m hurdles, and the 100m sprint. In 1976, at the Montreal Olympics, she reached the finals in the 100m hurdles, finishing sixth. This was her last major competition, as Israel was expelled from the Asian Federation for political reasons and then joined the boycott of the 1980 Moscow Olympics. Retiring officially in 1980, she became a track and field coach. In 1999 she was awarded the Israel Prize for her contribution to sports.

[Shaked Gilboa (2nd ed.)]

ROTHSTEIN, ARNOLD ("A.R.," "The Brain," "The Fixer"; 1882–1928), U.S. gangster and criminal mastermind, credited with developing the "numbers" racket, centralizing illegal racetrack bookmaking, fixing the 1919 baseball World Series, and developing 20th-century U.S. organized crime during the Prohibition Era. Rothstein was the second of five children born in Manhattan to Esther and Abraham. Abraham, known as "Abe the Just," was a board member of a major Jewish hospital, and was often asked to mediate community and business disputes. Rothstein was jealous of older brother Harry – a pious young man who wanted to become a rabbi – and rejected Jewish tradition in opposition to him. Rothstein began gambling, shooting pool, and lending money illegally at usurious interest rates ("loan-sharking") in his teens. When Rothstein married a Catholic showgirl in Saratoga, New York, his father sat *shiva* for him, and later forbade him to go to synagogue with his brothers to pray for their dying mother. Nonetheless, Rothstein was aware of his Jewishness, used it during his criminal career, and was buried in a Jewish cemetery. Rothstein was heavily involved as a financier or organizer of virtually every U.S. major criminal activity of the early 20th century: gambling, stock market swindles, "rum running" during Prohibition, and illegal drugs. He was a liaison between the crooked Tammany Hall organization that controlled New York City politics for more than a generation and the criminal community. He was a partner of the first generation of U.S. Jewish gangsters, including Irving Wexler (Waxey Gordon), and mentored a generation of future gangsters, including Meyer *Lansky, Charles Lucania (Lucky Luciano), and Louis (Lepke) *Buchalter. Rothstein was involved in but never convicted of fixing the results of the 1919 World Series, as was his alleged bag man, Abe *Attell. Rothstein died of a gunshot wound in 1928 in a shooting that may have been motivated by an unpaid gambling debt but has never been fully explained, and no one was ever convicted for the murder. Rothstein was the inspiration for Meyer Wolfsheim in *The Great Gatsby* and Nathan Detroit in *Guys and Dolls*.

[Alan D. Abbey (2nd ed.)]

ROTHSTEIN, IRMA (1906–1971), U.S. sculptor. Rothstein was born in Rostov, Russia, lived in Vienna, and immigrated to the United States in 1938. Her media included wood, cast stone, terracotta, and bronze. Her sculptures often featured expressive heads and torsos of women. Rothstein's style varied, from references to ancient Greek and Roman sculpture, to a compact, muscular terracotta of a sleeping nude evocative of Gauguin, to a bronze with an exaggerated, elongated neck and slightly tilted head, her haughty stare rendered with an Expressionist economy of means. Her well-known busts include George Bernard Shaw, Ernest Hemingway, and the conductor Dimitri Mitropoulos. She exhibited in New York art galleries, including the Galerie St. Etienne, as well as the American Artists Professional League, the Metropolitan Museum of Art, the Museum of Modern Art, the New School for Social Research, and the Pennsylvania Academy of Art. She belonged to the American Artists Professional League and the National Association of Women Artists. Her work is in the collections of the Beinecke Library, Yale University, the George Walter Smith Museum, Springfield, Massachusetts, and the Newark Museum, New Jersey, among other institutions.

[Nancy Buchwald (2nd ed.)]

ROTTEMBOURG, HENRI (1769–1836), French army officer. Born in Phalsbourg, Moselle, Rottembourg enlisted in the French army in 1784 and fought against Austria from 1792 to 1797. Rottembourg became an officer in Napoleon's Imperial Guard, and fought in Prussia and Poland. He was wounded at the battle of Wagram (1809) but later recovered to serve in Spain and was promoted to major general. He later became inspector general of infantry. After the fall of Napoleon in 1815, Rottembourg was appointed president of the Committee for Infantry by the Bourbon regime. He received numerous honors from both the Napoleonic and Bourbon governments and his name is engraved on the north side of the Arc de Triomphe in Paris.

ROTTOVÁ (Mirovská), INNA (1935–), Czech writer, publicist, and translator. Born in Leningrad (St. Petersburg), U.S.S.R., into a Polish-Czech-Jewish family, she grew up in the Soviet Union (she experienced the siege of Leningrad), where she completed her studies in engineering, although her main interest was music. She married a Czech, studied the Czech language in Prague, and began to write in 1974. She published many stories in numerous literary magazines. After 1989 at least 25 books, collections of stories, short stories, and non-fiction sketches appeared, some of them as detective stories. There are many Jewish themes, characters, and topics in her works, especially in the documentary report *A jiný glóbus nemáte?* ("Don't You Have Another Globe?" 1998) or in *Utajená svatba* ("A Secret Wedding," 2000) and *Tajemný cizinec a jiné židovské pověsti* (1999; French, *Legendes juives*, 1999; German, *Juedische Legenden*, 1999). She was awarded the František Langer Prize and the Society of Agatha Christie Prize. Rottová lived in Prague.

BIBLIOGRAPHY: "Literární encyklopedie Salonu," in: *Právo* (2004).

[Milos Pojar (2nd ed.)]

ROUDNICE NAD LABEM (Ger. **Raudnitz an der Elbe**), town in N. Central Bohemia, Czech Republic. The pogrom of 1541 is the earliest record of Jewish settlement in Roudnice. Twenty-three families lived there in 1570; 14 families in 1592. In 1595 the Jews were granted a charter and owned 16 houses. Thus the town belonged to the four oldest Jewish communities in Bohemia, known as Carvin. In 1610 both the houses and the cemetery had to be abandoned to make way for a monastery that was built there. (Tombstones from the cemetery dated 1610 still existed in 1970.) In 1631, 25 families (90 people) lived in Roudnice. That year, the Jewish community saved the town from being destroyed by the Saxons by paying a large sum of money. Nevertheless, the Saxon army burned down the ghetto. In 1651, there were 218 Jews living in 23 houses. One-third of the Jewish population died during the 1713 plague; but the following year's record stated that 100 Jewish families lived in the town. Yet four years later, another record noted 51 houses. In connection with the expulsion of the Prague community (1744), Roudnice was the scene of the murder of a number of Jews. The eastern part of the ghetto was abolished in 1727–28. Only 45 houses are recorded in 1785 and 63 in 1840. Until 1872 Roudnice was the seat of the district rabbinate. A new synagogue was built in 1853, and the third cemetery was established in 1896. It was closed down in 1885. In the mid-19th century, 176 families lived in the city. In 1893 the community numbered 79 families, according to one source;

according to another, in 1902 the community numbered 448 in 17 localities. In 1910 there were 320 Jews in Roudnice (3.5% of the total population); in 1921 there were 194 (2.2%); and in 1930, 166 (1.7%). When the community was liquidated by the Nazis in 1942, the contents of the synagogue were sent to the Central Jewish Museum in Prague (see *Museums). No congregation was reestablished after World War II. Richard *Feder served as rabbi of Roudnice. In 1953 the 17th-century synagogue was converted into a boarding house.

BIBLIOGRAPHY: Loewy, in: H. Gold, *Juden und Judengemeinden Boehmens…* (1934), 522–8; Pešák, in: JGGJČ, 7 (1935), 1–35; JE, 10 (1906), 332; Feder in: *československý kalendář*, 40 (1920/21), 19f.; 41 (1921/22), 106; 42 (1922/23), 43; 43 (1923/24), 125; 44 (1924/25), 180; 45 (1925/26), 176; 46 (1926/27), 182; Boleslav, in: *Schweizerische Israelitische Gemeindezeitung* (1968), 46–50, 74–75, 79–81, 107–11. **ADD. BIBLIOGRAPHY:** J. Fiedler, *Jewish Sights of Bohemia and Moravia* (1991), 161–62.

[Jan Herman / Yeshayahu Jelinek (2nd ed.)]

ROUEN, former capital of Normandy, capital of the department of Seine-Maritime, northern France. The presence of Jews in Rouen goes back to at least the early 11th century. Under Richard, duke of Normandy, Rouen Jewry suffered from the persecutions that affected the Jews of France in general beginning in 1007 or 1009. A notable of the town, Jacob b. Jekuthiel, interceded with Pope John XVIII, who called for a cessation of the persecutions throughout France. With the exception of Metz, Rouen was the only locality in what is today France where several Jews were put to death and others forced to accept baptism at the time of the First Crusade. At that time, Rouen, like the rest of Normandy, was under the dominion of the English crown. It was probably to these Jews that the English king William II (*Rufus*) granted the legal right to practice their faith. Archaeological discoveries in the 1970s and the study of manuscripts have revealed that, owing to the wrong identification of places mentioned in these manuscripts, many of them relating to Rouen (the capital of Normandy in the Middle Ages) were ascribed to other cities. The ancient Latin name Rothomagus was shortened in the Middle Ages to Rothoma or Rodom and the latter name was then variously transcribed as רודם, רדום and רודום; those names were thereafter often wrongly copied as דרום ("south"), רודם, and דרוס. As a result, many documents and scholars belonging to Rouen were associated with such places as Rhodez in Languedoc and *Dreux, southwest of Paris. Thus, for example, Solomon b. Judah "the Saint" mentioned in the first edition of the Judaica as being at Dreux was actually of Rouen. As a result, Rouen is now known to have been the seat of a much more important Jewish community than was previously assumed. During the 12th century, the Jews of Rouen were placed under the authority of a local bailiff rather than under the commissioner of the Jews of Normandy, who may have been *Peter of Cluny mentioned in a number of documents as the "Jewish king of Rouen." A number of Jews from London owned houses in the Jewish quarter of Rouen, while some Jews of Rouen had debtors in England. Nevertheless, Rouen's Jews were engaged in moneylending to a lesser extent than the Jews of England. The Jewish quarter, the "Rue as Gyeus," became the modern Rue des Juifs. One house at the beginning of the street is said to have served as a synagogue and another as the school. The cemetery, situated outside the town, was referred to as Mont-aux-Juifs.

Rouen's return to French sovereignty in the 12th century appears to have been followed by a decline in the Jewish community, as evidenced by its modest contribution to the poll tax levied on the Jews of Normandy. A new and even smaller community was reestablished in Rouen after 1359. (Its existence is confirmed at the latest in about 1380.) After the "final" expulsion of Jews from France in 1394, there were no Jews in the city until the arrival of some *Marranos at the close of the 16th century. The fate of the community remained uncertain throughout the 17th and 18th centuries. In 1605, 40 *Marrano Jews were living in Rouen, but by 1609 they had dispersed. A few years later a new wave of Marranos followed them. In the new community the family of Gonçalo Pinto Delgado (father of the poet Joâo Pinto *Delgado) played a principal role. In addition to merchants, the community also included several physicians. Although outwardly practicing Christian observances, the Jewish community of Rouen owned its own cemetery. From 1632, however, the so-called "Portuguese merchants" were accused of "Judaizing." In spite of several severe judgments against them, other Marranos continued to arrive in Rouen. In 1648 alone 20 new families settled in the city. Few Jews arriving in Rouen in the 17th century remained there, however. Those who came at the beginning of the 17th century eventually emigrated to Amsterdam, Antwerp, and Hamburg; while those arriving in the second half of the century left to join the new Jewish community in London. By the early 18th century the Marrano community had all but disappeared. In its place, a new Jewish community was established in mid-century, composed almost entirely of Alsatian Jews, who owned a cemetery from at least 1786. Another community was formed immediately after the French Revolution.

[Bernhard Blumenkranz and Norman Golb / David Weinberg (2nd ed.)]

The Rouen synagogue, destroyed during the bombardment in 1940, was rebuilt by the small community in 1950. The community grew to 500 members in 1960 and, after the influx of Jews from North Africa, numbered around 1,000 in 1971. In 1987, it was estimated that there were 1,200 Jews in the city. Rouen is the seat of a rabbinate.

[Georges Levitte]

BIBLIOGRAPHY: Gross, Gal Jud, 622ff.; B. Blumenkranz, *Juifs et Chrétiens* (1960), 136; H.G. Richardson, *English Jewry under Angevin Kings* (1960), index; C. de Beaurepaire, in: *Bulletin de la commission des antiquités de la Seine-Inférieure*, 9 (1891/3), 196–200; 12 (1900/2), 89; I.S. Revah, in: *Mélanges Isidore Lévy* (1953), 539–52; C. Roth, in: REJ, 88 (1929), 113–55; Z. Szajkowski, *Analytical Franco-Jewish Gazetteer* (1966), 266; N. Golb, *Toldot ha-Yahudim be-Ir Rouen bimei ha-Beinayim* (History and Culture of the Jews of Medieval Rouen, 1976); idem, in: *Archaeology*, 30 (1977), 314–5; idem, in: *Pro-*

ceedings of the American Academy for Jewish Research (1980), 100–1; B. Blumenkranz, *Comptes Rendus de l'Academie des Inscriptions et Belles Lettres* (1976), 663–7. **ADD. BIBLIOGRAPHY:** *Guide du judaïsme français* (1987), 39.

ROUFFACH (Ger. **Rufach**), town in the Haut-Rhin department, E. France. The earliest indication of the presence of Jews in Rouffach dates from 1288. Accused by the townsmen of having expressed support for Emperor Adolf of Nassau, against whom they were at war, the Jews were massacred at the beginning of 1298. By 1308 Jews were again living in the town. Many lost their lives in the *Armleder persecutions of 1338. Having returned to the town at the latest in 1340, they were all massacred at the time of the *Black Death (1349). Since then, there has been neither a Jewish community nor even individual Jews in Rouffach. The *Judenhof* ("Jewish courtyard") mentioned in 1338 possibly refers to the area of the synagogue, which was built in about 1300 and was still in existence in 1970, after having been rediscovered in 1905. The former Judengasse (Jewish Street) is now known as the Hassengasse.

BIBLIOGRAPHY: M. Ginsburger and C. Winkler, in: *Schriften der Gesellschaft fuer die Geschichte der Israeliten in Elsass-Lothringen*, 22 (1906); S. Dietler, in: *Die Gebweiler Chronik*, ed. by J. v. Schlumberger (1898), 22: Th. Walter, *Rouffach…* (1958); Germ Jud, 2 (1968), 723f.

[Bernhard Blumenkranz]

ROULEAU, ERIC (**Elie Rafoul**; 1926–), journalist and diplomat. Rouleau was born in Cairo. From 1953 to 1960 he was an editor for the Middle East service of the Agence France Presse and from 1956 a reporter for *Le Monde*, writing a column on the Near and Middle East from 1960. In the 1970s he spent some time in the United States; in 1974 he was a research associate at the University of California and in 1978–79 a research associate for the Council of Foreign Affairs in New York and a lecturer at Princeton University. In 1983 he became an adviser to the Television Française 1.

Rouleau is a noted journalist whose recognized expertise is in the areas of the Arab world and Middle Eastern subjects. He has links to excellent sources in Arab countries, particularly in the radical ones. During the course of his career he has interviewed almost all leaders in the Middle East since the 1950s. In 1985 French president Mitterrand appointed him ambassador to Tunisia, but he was forced to resign after a little over a year's service because of opposition to him by the Tunisian government, which considered him to be associated with the opposition and the PLO. In 1988–92 he was ambassador to Turkey and from 1994 Middle East correspondent of *Le Monde*. He published: *Le Troisième combat* (1967), in collaboration with J. Lacouture and O.F. Held, *Biographie de Kurt Waldheim* (1977), *Entretien avec Abu Iyad* (1979), and *Etude sur les Palestiniens* (1984).

[Gideon Kouts]

°**ROUSSEAU, JEAN JACQUES** (1712–1778), French author and philosopher, born in Geneva. The international influence that Rousseau exerted on his contemporaries and on posterity was unequaled in European history until the impact of Karl Marx a century later.

The political ideas of Jean Jacques Rousseau have contributed in large measure to the emancipation of the Jews, at first in France and later in other Western European countries. His educational theories had a direct effect on the *Haskalah movement which developed in Jewish circles during the following century. Rousseau not only demanded equal civic rights for the Jews; he also, uniquely among French writers of the Enlightenment, expressed the hope that they would be restored to a country of their own: "I do not think I have ever heard the arguments of the Jews as to why they should not have a free state, schools, and universities where they can speak and argue without danger. Then alone can we know what they have to say" (*Emile*, Book 4, tr. B. Foxely (1911; repr. 1966), 268). In a page unpublished in his lifetime, Rousseau expressed his admiration for the national qualities of the "eternal people":

"The Jews present us with an outstanding spectacle: the laws of Numa, Lycurgus, and Solon are dead; the far more ancient ones of Moses are still alive. Athens, Sparta, and Rome have perished and all their people have vanished from the earth; though destroyed, Zion has not lost her children. They mingle with all nations but are never lost among them; they no longer have leaders, yet they are still a nation; they no longer have a country and yet they are still citizens…"

BIBLIOGRAPHY: L. Poliakov, *Histoire de l'antisémitisme*, 3 (1968), 118–26; P.M. Masson, *La Réligion de Rousseau* (1916).

[Leon Poliakov]

ROUSSILLON, region and former province in S. France, corresponding to the present department of Pyrénées-Orientales. In 1172 the county of Roussillon passed to the kings of Aragon and did not become a French possession again until 1642. Names of places such as the Iudegas quarter (territory of Clayra, township of Rivesaltes) or a Villa Iudaicas (near Sainte-Hippolyte), whose existence is confirmed from the 11th century, indicate that there were at that time some Jews in Roussillon. The first documentary evidence of the presence of Jews there, however, dates only from 1185 and concerns a Jew in *Perpignan. Jews lived in Elne, Collioure, Arles-sur-Tech, Banyuls-sur-Mer, Thuir, Céret, Salces, Ille-sur-Tet, Prades, Millas, and *Villefranche-de-Conflent. In 1243 a Jewish quarter, the Call, was set aside in Perpignan, and from 1251 Jews were compelled to live there. The communities of Thuir, Ille, and Céret (perhaps others too) had their own cemeteries, like **aljama* of Perpignan. In 1276 the county of Roussillon was awarded to the king of Majorca, who exercised his authority over the Jews of Roussillon through the intermediary of the count. Subsequently the royal procurator was responsible for civil and criminal jurisdiction over the Jews of Roussillon. Until 1314, when the wearing of the *badge was imposed, the Jews wore a cape as a distinctive garment. Pedro IV of Aragon, who annexed the kingdom of Majorca (1344), authorized the

Jews of Roussillon to travel to France for business purposes. In addition to engaging in such occupations as commerce (including peddling) and moneylending, Jews of Roussillon worked as bookbinders, tailors, goldsmiths, and especially as dyers. The anti-Jewish persecutions of 1391 in Spain reached the Jews of Roussillon in 1392. There was a similar delay of one year a century later at the time of the expulsion from Spain (1492), when a number of Jews from there sought refuge in Roussillon, only to be expelled in 1493, along with the Jews of Roussillon.

[Bernhard Blumenkranz]

Cultural History

The Jews of Roussillon produced scholars who distinguished themselves through their mastery of many different branches of learning, both secular and Jewish. Most notable were the Jewish physicians who served in the towns and villages of the province, such as Bernard de Jorena in Perpignan in 1226, Solomon Moses de Villemanŷa in Elne in 1327, and Jacob de Guanges in Elne in 1380. Jacob Bonjuhes functioned in a similar capacity in Ille in 1407 and Thuir in 1410. Many Jews of Roussillon studied science and medicine at the University of Montpellier in the 14th century, a period when Perpignan flourished as a center of learning. There was much literary interest as well; poets included Jehoseph *Ezobi and *Phinehas b. Joseph ha-Levi. The study of Bible flourished; an intense polemic developed at the beginning of the 14th century between the partisans and opponents of the study of philosophy. At the center of the controversy was Levi b. Abraham of Villefranche-de-Conflent, probably the grandfather of *Levi b. Gershom, who brought down upon himself the ire of the Orthodox of his time, including Solomon b. Abraham *Adret, for his support of philosophic studies; he also studied astronomy. By the end of the 14th century, Perpignan had become a center for the study of astronomy. Rabbinic studies also were not lacking. The most prominent scholars of Roussillon were Menahem b. Solomon *Meiri (1249–1306), Abraham b. Isaac *Bedersi, and Isaac b. Judah de Lattes. Prominent in an earlier generation was Abraham b. David de Roussillon, Meiri's grandfather. Among the Hebrew manuscripts at the University of Bologna is a *maḥzor* with glosses by a R. Judah Roussillon (REJ, 120, 124). Jews continued to pursue their intellectual and cultural interests until their expulsion in 1493.

[Alexander Shapiro]

BIBLIOGRAPHY: Gross, Gal Jud, 632f.; P. Vidal, in: REJ, 15 (1887), 19–55; 16 (1888), 1–23, 170–203; J.G. Gigot, in: *Cerca. Centre d'Etudes et de Recherches Catalanes des Archives*, 30 (1965), 253–7.

ROUTTENBERG, MAX JONAH (1909–1987), U.S. Conservative rabbi and organizational executive. Routtenberg was born in Montreal, Quebec, and received a B.S. from New York University in 1930. In 1932, he was ordained at the *Jewish Theological Seminary, where he earned a D.H.L. in 1949. He became rabbi of Kesher Zion Synagogue in Reading, Pennsylvania (1932–48), where he created an educational center that helped establish Conservative Judaism in eastern Pennsylvania. He took a leave of absence during World War II to serve as a senior chaplain in the U.S, Army in Europe.

In 1949, Routtenberg was appointed executive vice president of the *Rabbinical Assembly, where he worked to fill the growing demand for pulpit rabbis. From 1951 to 1954, he served as executive vice president of the Jewish Theological Seminary, as well as dean of the Cantors Institute and the Seminary College of Jewish Music. He also lectured on synagogue administration at the JTS Teachers Institute (1950–52). In 1954, Routtenberg returned to the congregational rabbinate to serve Temple B'nai Sholom of Rockville Center, Long Island, where he remained until his retirement in 1972. At the same time, he was appointed chairman of the National Academy of Adult Jewish Studies (1955–60). Under his leadership, B'nai Sholom became a model synagogue center, complete with its own Institute of Adult Jewish Studies, Women's Institute, Judaica library and Lecture Forum.

In 1964, Routtenberg was elected president of the Rabbinical Assembly and led the Conservative movement's rabbinical association into the *Conference of Presidents of Major Jewish Organizations. Following his term of office (1964–66), he chaired the RA's Committee on Chaplaincy during the turbulent years of the Vietnam War, when JTS students voted to reject the system of compulsory procurement of chaplains for the U.S. armed forces. In 1970, he was tapped to chair the Special Committee on Revitalization of the Law Committee, established in the wake of the resignation of most of the committee's members. Subsequently, he chaired the RA's Publications Committee (1972–82), the committee that revised the Rabbinical Assembly constitution in 1977 and the Liturgical Committee as it oversaw the issuance of a new *siddur* for Sabbath and Festivals, as well as Conservative Judaism's amended *ketubbah*. He was also program director for two television programs that depicted Judaism to the outside world: *The Eternal Light*, produced by the JTS for NBC, and ABC TV's *Directions*.

He also served on the Commission on the Jewish Chaplaincy of the *National Jewish Welfare Board, the Delegates Council of the *Synagogue Council of America, and the Internal Affairs Commission of the New York Board of Rabbis. Routtenberg wrote *Seedtime and Harvest* (1969), *Decades of Decision* (1973), and *One in a Minyan and Other Stories* (1977), a collection of short stories. His final work, undertaken with Max Gelb, was the English translation of Abraham Joshua Heschel's *Torah Min ha-Shamayim be-Aspeklarya shel ha-Dorot* (*Heavenly Torah As Refracted Through the Generation*) and was completed by Gordon Tucker and published in 2004.

[Bezalel Gordon (2nd ed.)]

ROVIGO, capital of Rovigo province, N. Italy, Veneto, and of Polesine, agricultural district coextensive with the province. The presence of Jews in Rovigo from the latter part of the 13th century is attested in the municipal statutes (1227–1429) against "fornicatione inter Judaeum et Christianam." Their numbers increased as the local agricultural economy developed commercial and industrial activity. In 1386 a group of

Jews are mentioned at Lendinara, who were placed in charge of collecting the municipal taxes. The Rovigo municipality invited Salomon, son of Musetto of Judaea, and the brothers Alvicio and Emanuele, sons of Musetto of Bologna to open a loan bank in the town in 1391 with the authorization of the Este, the Dukes of Ferrara. A Jew named Consiglio, possibly an ancestor of the prominent Consiglio family of Rovigo, is mentioned at Badia Polesine in 1425.

The position of the Jews did not change after Rovigo was annexed by Venice in 1484. The loan bank at Rovigo became the property of the Consiglio family with which the Venetian republic renewed the contract every five years. Other members of the community, who had at first been largely connected with the loan bank, later engaged in other activities. The bank, however, retained its supremacy in both the economic and communal spheres of community life. Even when in 1508 the first *Monte di Pieta' was opened, the banking activities continued. A celebrated controversy arose in Rovigo in 1594 in connection with the local *mikveh*. The rabbi was then Avtaylon Consiglio. In 1594 Jekuthiel Consiglio built a *mikveh* in his house the ritual validity of which was questioned. The problem was submitted to various rabbis both in Italy and abroad, entire volumes being devoted to their discussions. Officially, the Jews were restricted to dealing in secondhand clothing. A report by the mayor to the Venetian senate in 1572 indicates the impoverished state of the local Jews which had also led to a split in the community; the rich members were anxious to monopolize the leadership while the poor members wanted a representative system irrespective of economic status.

Orders to set up a ghetto in Rovigo were issued in 1612, and implemented in 1615, only the loan bankers and their families being permitted to reside outside it. There were 17 Jewish families living in Rovigo in 1617. The destruction of a synagogue was ordered in 1629 because it was situated in the vicinity of a church.

In the 18th century the Jews played an important part in developing the wool industry in the Polesine region. At least three Jewish firms were engaged in this industry in Rovigo in the middle of the 18th century, owned by Moise' Luzzatto, Marco Consigli, and Moise' D'Ancona. Frequent attempts to oust them were made by Christian competitors, mainly from Padua. There were about 230 Jewish residents in 1785. The congregation celebrated a local Purim (Purim Katan), or Purim of the Fire, in memory of escape from fire in the 18th century and a fast to commemorate the desecration of the synagogue and pillaging of Jewish houses by hooligans in 1809.

With the French occupation in 1797, the Jews received equal civil rights. However, under French and Austrian rule the economic situation throughout the Polesine was poor. The Jewish population of Rovigo increased in 1823, when Jews immigrated to Rovigo from the Papal States, after Leo XIII's new restrictions. Reactionary tendencies persisted and in 1857 a *blood libel charge was brought against a Jew, Calimano Ravenna at Badia Polesine. Rovigo Jews took an important part in the Italian Risorgimento's wars. From 1848 to 1849 six Jews volunteered. In 1859 22 Jews volunteered to serve in the Piedmontese Army, the largest number from all the Italian communities, including the Kingdom of Sardinia! Giacomo Levi Civita fought with Garibaldi in 1866, and later he was appointed senator in the Italian Parliament. The Jewish population reached its peak in 1870, when 430 Jews lived in Rovigo. Around 450 Jews lived in Rovigo and Polesine together in 1886. The community had four charitable associations: Gemilut Ḥasadim, Shomer la-Boker, Malbish Arumim, and Le-Hasi Betulah.

By 1930, the numbers had dwindled to 100 and it was amalgamated with the *Padua community. The same year, in a rebuilding project for the town center, work was begun on demolition of the ghetto and the synagogue, which had been restored in 1858. The Ark, the floors, and marble were used for a new synagogue. With the German occupation in 1943, most of the members of the Jewish community managed to find safe haven; however two community members were deported.

BIBLIOGRAPHY: C. Roth, *Venice* (1930), index; Roth, Italy, index; Milano, Italia, index; Milano, Bibliotheca, index; idem, in: RMI, 33 (1967), 211–2, and 8 illustrations; F. Luzzatto, *ibid.*, 6 (1932), 509–25; G. Bachi, *ibid.*, 12 (1938), 218–9, 300; R. Cessi, *Gli ebrei el il commercio della lana in Rovigo nel secolo 18* (1906); M.A. Shulvass, in: *Sinai*, 20 (1947), 198–205; A. Yaari, *ibid.*, 34 (1954), 367–74; S.J. Sierra, in: *Scritti Bedarida* (1966), 271–81; J. Pinkerfeld, *Battei Keneset be-Italyah* (1954), 21, and tables 24–26. **ADD. BIBLIOGRAPHY:** F. Brandes, *Veneto Jewish Itineraries*, Venice (1996), 92–97.

[Alfredo Mordechai Rabello / Samuele Rocca (2nd ed.)]

ROVIGO, ABRAHAM BEN MICHAEL (c. 1650–1713), Italian kabbalist and Shabbatean. Born in Modena, Rovigo studied in Venice, where he became one of the leading pupils of Moses *Zacuto in Kabbalah and formed a lifelong close friendship with *Benjamin b. Eliezer ha-Kohen Vitale, who shared his inclinations and convictions. Since he belonged to a wealthy family, Rovigo was able to devote himself exclusively to his studies; he became widely known as a supporter of pious enterprises and later also of Shabbatean activities. As a young man, he was swept up in the wave of messianic enthusiasm and retained his belief in the messianic mission of *Shabbetai Ẓevi for many decades, probably until his death. Becoming one of the main supporters of the moderate wing of Shabbateanism, he gathered around him many secret followers of the movement who used to visit him when they were in Italy. Thus he invited to Modena Issacher Behr *Perlhefter and *Mordecai (Mokhi'aḥ) ben Ḥayyim (between 1677 and 1682) and Mordecai Ashkenazi (1695–1702). He corresponded with many of the movement's leaders, beginning as early as 1675 with an enthusiastic letter to *Nathan of Gaza (then in Kastoria), accepting him as a true prophet. As well as collecting information about Shabbetai Ẓevi and others active in the movement and assembling their writings, he encouraged or invited claimants to heavenly revelations. But he kept all these activities a closely guarded secret and cross-examined people carefully before he divulged his Shabbatean convictions. At times in association with his friend Benjamin b. Eliezer ha-Kohen, he prepared to emigrate to Jerusalem, but he was always held up in the final stages. In 1700–01 he spent a whole year seeing through the press the Zoharic commentaries of Mordecai Ashkenazi, in Fuerth, a place that seemed more sympathetic to secret Shabbateans than Mantua or Venice. Finally, in 1702 he traveled to the Holy Land, accompanied by his family and a group of scholars, and founded a yeshivah in Jerusalem, most of whose members were supporters of Shabbateanism. A description of this journey by one of his company has been published by Jacob Mann (see bibl.). Considered a man of great influence and independent means, he was prevailed upon by the rabbis of Jerusalem to serve as an emissary to Europe, first in 1704–07, and a second (and perhaps third) time in 1710–13. He traveled through many countries – Poland, Germany, Holland, and Italy – and died on his last mission while passing through Mantua. Important sections of his extant papers remained unknown to collectors and libraries until the 1920s; these have proved very valuable sources for the history of Shabbateanism.

BIBLIOGRAPHY: Moses Zacuto, *Iggeret ha-Remaz* (Leghorn, 1780), passim; J. Mann, in: *Zion*, 6 (1934), 59–84; G. Scholem, *Ḥalomotav shel ha-Shabbetai R. Mordekhai Ashkenazi* (1938); I. Sonne, in: *Sefer ha-Yovel … A. Marx* (1943), 89–103; idem, in: *Sefunot*, 3–4 (1960), 39–69; 5 (1961), 275–95; A. Yaari, *Iggerot Ereẓ Yisrael* (1943), 223–42; Yaari, Sheluḥei, 347–51; S. Assaf, in: *Zion*, 6 (1941), 156f.; J. Leveen, in: *Semitic Studies in Memory of I. Loew* (1947), 324–33, I. Tishby, *Netivei Emunah u-Minut* (1964), index s.v. *Rovigo*.

[Gershom Scholem]

ROVINA, HANNA (1889–1980), Israeli actress. She was born in Berezino, Minsk district, Russia, and trained as a kindergarten teacher. During World War I, she took charge of an institute for refugee children at Saratov. In 1917 she joined the Hebrew theatrical studio being organized by Nahum *Zemach in Moscow and became one of the founder-members of the *Habimah Theater Company. She achieved success and fame with her portrayal of Leah in the Hebrew translation of Anski's *Dybbuk*, the Habimah's first important production (1922), and as the mother of the Messiah in David Pinsky's *The Eternal Jew*. She played both these parts in Leningrad in 1925, in Riga in 1926, and on Habimah's subsequent tours in Western Europe and the U.S. Arriving with the company in Palestine in 1928, she was soon acknowledged as the country's leading actress and henceforth her career was identified with Habimah. Endowed with beauty and dignity, she was able to give authority and distinction to such varied heroines as Gordin's *Mirele Efros*, Euripides' *Medea*, and Shakespeare's *Cordelia*, later excelling in mother types, as in Capek's *The Mother* and Brecht's *Mother Courage*.

BIBLIOGRAPHY: I. Gur, *Actors in the Hebrew Theatre* (1958), 21–37; M. Kohansky, *Hebrew Theatre* (1969), index.

[Mendel Kohansky]

ROVINSKY, SAMUEL (1932–), Costa Rican playwright and author. The son of Polish Jewish immigrants, Rovinsky is a central figure in his country's theater and also involved in experimental dramatic innovations; his works have been included in school curriculies. Together with his main interest in Central American reality, Rovinsky contributed Jewish themes to the national and regional scene. His dramas also contain social satire, parody, and humor. His plays include *Las fisgonas de Paso Ancho* ("The Busybodies of Paso Ancho," 1971); *Un modelo para Rosaura* ("A Model for Rosaura," 1974); *El martirio del pastor* ("The Martyrdom of the Pastor," 1983); *La víspera del sábado* ("Sabbath Eve," 1985); *El laberinto* ("The Labyrinth," 1985); *Gulliver dormido* ("Sleeping Gulliver," 1985); *Los pregoneros* ("The Town Criers," 1990). He published the short story volumes *Cuentos judíos de mi tierra* ("Jewish Tales from My Land," 1982) and *El embudo de Pandora* ("Pandora's Funnel," 1991); and the novel *Ceremonia de Casta* ("Caste Ceremony," 1979). Rovinsky also wrote essays on theater, play writing, and Costa Rican culture.

BIBLIOGRAPHY: R. Di Antonio and N. Glickman, *Tradition and Innovation: Reflection on Latin American Jewish Writing* (1993); M.A. Giella and P. Roster, *Reflexiones sobre teatro latinoamericano del siglo XX* (1989); D.B. Lockhart, *Jewish Writers of Latin America. A Dictionary* (1997).

[Florinda F. Goldberg (2nd ed.)]

ROVNO (Pol. **Równe**), capital of Rovno district, Ukraine; under Poland until the First Partition (1793) and between the world wars. A Jew is first mentioned as hailing from Rovno in 1566, and Jewish creditors from the town are recorded in 1571. When the town passed to the princes of the house of Lubomirski in 1723, they tried to develop it by various means, including attempts to attract Jews there. On July 13, 1749, Prince Stanislaw Lubomirski granted a charter establishing a full-fledged community with all institutions. Prince Józef Lubomirski confirmed and renewed these rights on April 21, 1789. The *kahal* of Rovno is mentioned in 1739–40 in a decision at *Radom on the distribution of Jewish taxes in the Volhynia region of the *Council of the Lands. In 1765 there were 1,186 Jews in Rovno community (890 in the town itself and 296 in villages subject to the *kahal*); there were 2,147 Jews in the town in 1801; 3,788 in 1847; 13,780 (56 percent of the total population) in 1897; 21,702 (71 percent) in 1921; 22,737 in 1931; and about 28,000 in 1939. Under czarist Russia, Rovno became a border town not far from the frontier of Austria (at Brody), and developed into a commercial center dealing in military supplies. With the completion of the Kiev-Warsaw railroad and later with the Vilna-Rovno line (1885) it also became an important railroad center for all eastern Volhynia. Since it had become a supply center, various local light industries were also set up in the area under Polish rule.

The short-lived period of Ukrainian independence (1918–20) was a time of trepidation for Rovno Jewry. In the spring of 1919, the soldiers of *Petlyura carried out several *pogroms; later the town was conquered by the Red Army, and in the spring of 1920 it returned to Polish rule, which lasted until 1939.

A *Ḥibbat Zion group was formed in Rovno in 1884. Later various Zionist parties were established, with members participating in all the Zionist congresses. During Ukrainian rule Rovno's central Zionist office coordinated activities throughout Volhynia and Podolia. A *Bund group was formed in 1903. As in all Jewish communities in Poland, the *Haskalah was the forerunner of modern Jewish education in Rovno, and Zionism brought with it a revival of Hebrew. At first it was taught in the *ḥeder metukkan* (see *Education) and in private Hebrew schools. In 1911 a branch of the Ḥovevei Sefat Ever ("Lovers of the Hebrew Language") was formed. A branch of the *Tarbut organization, established in 1919, soon became the central branch for all Volhynia. That same year the Tarbut secondary school was established, and shortly after, three Tarbut elementary schools, several Hebrew kindergartens, a Tarbut Polish-language high school and a business high school. There was also a *talmud torah*, and for a short period (until 1921) there were two Yiddish schools. The Tarbut secondary school attracted Jewish pupils from all the villages of Volhynia. From 1924 to 1939 the Yiddish weekly, *Vohliner Lebn* ("Volhynian Life"), was published in Rovno.

[Shmuel Spector]

Holocaust Period

Under Soviet rule (1939–41), Jewish organizations ceased to function, Bund and Zionist leaders were imprisoned, Jewish businessmen were discriminated against, and Hebrew schools were closed down. Many Jewish refugees from western Poland found shelter in Rovno, which soon became one of the important centers of underground Zionist activity, helping Jews to escape to *Vilna and southward to the Romanian and Hungarian borders. With the outbreak of the Soviet-German war (June 22, 1941), young Jews joined the Soviet army. Rovno fell to the Germans on June 29, and on the same day 300 Jews were slaughtered. Murder and torture were rampant. Between October and November 1941, the number of Jews killed exceeded 1,000. A Judenrat was set up by the former director of one of the Jewish secondary schools, Dr. Bergman. With the introduction of the German policy of extermination, a Judenrat member, Leon Sucharczuk, committed suicide. Murder on the largest scale was committed on Nov. 6, 1941, when some 18,000 Jews from Rovno were machine-gunned in a pine grove in Sosenki. After this *Aktion*, a ghetto was established for the remaining Jews. Starvation and disease claimed many victims despite mutual help and attempts to reduce epidemics. On July 12, 1942 the 5,000 surviving Jews were brought to the vicinity of Kostopol and murdered there in a forest. Rovno Jews joined the partisan groups operating in the district and helped to liberate Rovno from the Nazis in February 1944.

Contemporary Period

After the war about 1,200 Jews were living in an area around the Great Synagogue. Only 100 were survivors from the original Rovno community. A search was made to find Jewish children among the peasants in the nearby villages and to mark the sites of the mass graves of Jews murdered by the Nazis. Gradually, like many others, the Rovno community dissolved through emigration. In 1957 the Jewish cemetery was divided into two sites, for a park and a grazing ground. The last remaining synagogue, consisting of only one room, was closed down by authorities in 1959, and Torah scrolls were confiscated. The former large synagogue was converted into a sports gymnasium. There was no monument on the mass graves of Jews murdered by the Nazis. In the late 1960s the Jewish population in Rovno was estimated at about 600. Only in the 1990s was a memorial erected in Sosenki for the Jews murdered by the Nazis.

[Aharon Weiss]

BIBLIOGRAPHY: *Rovnah: Sefer Zikkaron* (1956); *Słownik geograficzny Królestwa polskiego*, 9 (1888), 818–23; *Regesty i nadpisi*, 1 (1899), no. 569; 3 (1913), no. 2321; Avatiḥi-Hadari, in: *Yalkut Vohlin*, 1 no. 8 (1947), 8–21. **ADD. BIBLIOGRAPHY:** Sh. Spector (ed.), *Pinkas ha-Kehillot Poland*, vol. 5 (1990).

ROWE, LEO STANTON (1871–1946), U.S. political scientist. Rowe grew up in Philadelphia and from 1895 taught political science at the University of Pennsylvania, becoming professor in 1904. Appointed to a commission to revise the laws of Puerto Rico in 1900, Rowe became interested in Latin American affairs, to which he devoted almost his whole life's work. In 1917 he became the assistant secretary of the U.S. Treasury, and in 1919–20 he headed the Latin American section of the State Department. Rowe was president of the American Academy of Political and Social Sciences (1902–30) and wrote many works including: *The United States and Puerto Rico* (1904); *Problems of City Government* (1908); and *The Federal Systems of the Argentine Republic* (1921).

°**ROWLEY, HAROLD HENRY** (1890–1969), English Protestant theologian and Bible scholar. Rowley was associate professor of biblical literature at the Shantung Christian University (1924–29); assistant lecturer in Semitic languages at University College of South Wales and Monmouthshire, Cardiff (1930–34); professor of Semitic languages, University College of North Wales, Bangor (1935–45), and lecturer in the history of religions (1940–45); vice principal (1940–45) and dean of Bangor School of Theology (1936–45); and professor of Semitic languages and literatures at the University of Manchester (from 1945). He was, among other things, president of the Baptist Union of Great Britain and Ireland (1957–58).

Rowley wrote a number of works on the unity, importance, and relevance of the Bible. He argued that the pure monotheism of the prophets is rooted in the Mosaic period. He maintained that Deutero-*Isaiah's understanding of the Servant of the *Lord underwent a development from the symbolic suffering of the people of Israel to the vicarious death of an individual. He staunchly maintained that the Book of *Daniel, apart from secondary additions, was the work of a single author writing in the years of Antiochus *Epiphanes' persecution of Judaism, and held that the reform of Josiah rooted in Deuteronomy was at first welcomed by Jeremiah and then rejected by the prophet because of its dangerous implications. He commented upon every major problem of biblical history from Moses to Qumran, including the problems of the Exodus, the Samaritans, sacrifice, and the Qumran sectarians. His only full-length biblical commentary was on Job, and was published posthumously.

In addition to semi-popular dictionaries on biblical names and themes (1968), he wrote: *From Joseph to Joshua* (1950); *The Servant of the Lord* (1952); *Prophecy and Religion in Ancient China and Israel* (1956; Jordan Lectures, 1954); *The Faith of Israel* (1956); *The Zadokite Documents and the Dead Sea Scrolls* (1952); *The Aramaic of the Old Testament* (1929); *Darius the Mede and the Four World Empires in the Book of Daniel* (1935, 1959²); *Teach Yourself Bible Atlas* (1960); and *Men of God* (1963). He was also editor of: *Studies in Old Testament Prophecy* (*T.H. Robinson Festschrift*, 1950); *The Old Testament and Modern Study* (1951, 1961⁵); *Journal of Semitic Studies* (1956–1960); *Peake's Commentary on the Bible* (with Martin Black, 1962); M.A. Beek's *Atlas of Mesopotamia* (1962); *Hastings' Dictionary of the Bible* (1963² with F.C. Grant); *Companion to the Bible* (1963); *The Century Bible* (1967); and the series "Recent Foreign Theology," in: *Expository Times*, 58–81 (1946–70).

BIBLIOGRAPHY: For a select bibliography of the works of Rowley until 1954, see M. Noth and B.W. Thomas (ed.), *Wisdom in Israel and in the Ancient Near East* (1955).

[Zev Garber]

ROZDOL (Pol. **Rozdół**; in Jewish sources ראזלו), town in E. Drogobych district, Ukraine; formerly in E. Galicia within Austria and independent Poland. For many years the owner of the town, Rzewuski, waged a struggle against the province of Bratslav, which claimed the right to collect taxes from the Jews of Rozdol. In 1751 the tax tribunal in Radom decided in favor of Rzewuski and the Jews were ordered to pay their taxes to him. In the 17th century, a large number of the Jews in the town became followers of Shabbateanism (see *Shabbetai *Zevi), influenced by Rabbi Fishel, who claimed he was the *Messiah descended from Joseph, and that Jonathan *Eybeschuetz was the Messiah descended from David. After appeals to the civic authorities, R. Fishel was expelled on the ground that he was insane. According to an inadequately based theory, the founder of Ḥasidism, *Israel b. Eliezer Ba'al Shem Tov, was the rabbi of Rozdol who participated in the disputation against the *Frankists held in *Lvov in 1759.

On the eve of the partition of Poland and its incorporation into Austria in 1772, there were 639 Jews in Rozdol (1765). The Jewish population increased during the 19th century and by 1912 numbered 2,262 (about 50 percent of the total population). During World War I it declined, and in 1921 numbered 1,725 (about 45 percent). After World War I Jewish public activity expanded in the town which was known for its party conflicts, mostly between Ḥasidim and Zionists. The Germans occupied Rozdol on June 23, 1941. Most of the community was deported to Belzec death camp on September 4–5, 1942. The remaining Jews, who worked for German enterprises, were sent on September 30 to Stryi, where they were probably killed with others on February 3, 1943.

BIBLIOGRAPHY: *Pinkas ha-Kehillot Poland*, vol. 2 – *Eastern Galicia* (1980).

[Shimshon Leib Kirshenboim]

ROZENMACHER, GERMÁN (1936–1971), Argentine playwright and short-story writer. He was born to a religious family in Buenos Aires, where his father was a *ḥazzan* and *mohel*. He graduated from the University of Buenos Aires and went on to work as a teacher of Hebrew, a journalist, a theater critic, and a playwright for television. Rozenmacher was considered to be one of the foremost Argentine writers to emerge in the 1960s, first earning recognition for his short stories and later for his plays. He was killed in an automobile accident in August 1971.

Rozenmacher achieved fame with his collection of stories *Cabecita negra* (1962), which examines the influence of Peronism on Argentine society in a variety of innovative and interesting settings. While the majority of the stories speak to the general Argentine population by depicting the solitude, despair, poverty, and frustration occasioned by social injustice, three of the stories deal specifically with the often difficult Jewish experience in Buenos Aires.

Rozenmacher gained permanent renown for his four dramatic works, which have become classics of Argentine theater. His first play, *Requiem para un viernes a la noche* was presented in 1964 at the *Yiddishes Folks Teater* IFT (Jewish Popular Theater) in Buenos Aires. It played for two years and continues to be produced. It has been studied mainly as a play about generational conflict, cultural identity, and assimilation. It is clear that the play reflects many aspects of his own life: he married a Catholic woman, and he dedicated the play to both his parents and his wife. Rozenmacher offers no solution to the problems presented in the play. Indeed, the work seems to signal the fact that there is no reconciliation possible between the opposing stances represented by father and son in the play and therein lays the tragedy. His play *El Lazarillo de Tormes* presented in 1971 was based on the 16th-century Spanish picaresque novel of the same title. Jewish themes are present only obliquely in the play, mainly when the topic of the Inquisition arises. *Simón Brumelstein, el caballero de Indias* was written in 1971, but not performed until 1982 and finally published in 1987. It is often considered to be his most ambitious and accomplished play. Simón, the main character, lives in a fantasy world and struggles with his deep desire to assimilate wholly into Argentine society and shed his Jewishness. However, he is constantly reminded that he will never be permitted to be completely Argentine. Ultimately, *Simón Brumelstein* is about the clash of cultures, assimilation, antisemitism, and crises of identity. His works have stood the test of time and found their place in the Argentine literary canon of the 20th century.

[Darrell B. Lockhart (2nd ed.)]

RÓŻEWICZ, TADEUSZ (1921–), Polish poet and dramatist. Born in Radomsko, Różewicz studied art history at the

Jagiellonian University in Cracow. The terrors of the Nazi occupation dominate Różewicz' earlier verse collections, such as *Niepokój* ("Anxiety," 1947). Influenced by Ionesco and Beckett as a dramatist, he also produced 15 highly acclaimed plays along with a dozen books of poetry in the modernist manner as well as stories and satires. Among his works translated into English are *The Card Index, & Other Plays* (1969), *Faces of Anxiety: Poems* (1969); *The Witnesses & Other Plays* (1970), *The Survivor and Other Poems* (1976), *Conversation with the Prince: and Other Poems* (1982); *Mariage Blanc and the Hunger Artist Departs: Two Plays* (1983), *Forms in Relief and Other Works* (1994), *Reading the Apocalypse in Bed: Selected Plays and Short Pieces* (1998), and *Recycling* (2001).

ROZIN (Rosen), JOSEPH (1858–1936), Polish talmudic genius, called "the Rogachover" after his birthplace (Rogachov). His erudition and profundity were phenomenal. It is said that when he was eight years old, the local scholars felt incompetent to teach him, for he knew the whole of the talmudic order of *Nezikin* with its commentaries. When he was 13, his father took him to Slutsk where J.B. *Soloveichik taught him together with his own son Ḥayyim. From there he went to Shklov, where he frequented the court of the ḥasidic rabbi of Kapost, of the Chabad sect. He spent the next eight years studying in Warsaw. In 1889 he was appointed rabbi of the ḥasidic community of Dvinsk. During World War I, as the German army drew near, he fled to St. Petersburg [later Leningrad], where he remained as rabbi of the ḥasidic community for ten years, thereafter returning to Dvinsk.

A man of penetrating intelligence, Rozin possessed a phenomenal encyclopedic knowledge and great powers of industry. He knew the Babylonian and the Jerusalem Talmuds, all the known tannaitic and amoraic literature, and most early books without needing to consult them. He visited Rogachov each year on the anniversary of his father's death, on one occasion remarking that he had studied half of the Talmud during his journey there and would finish it on the return journey. He saw a subject as a whole and in its detail, analyzing it carefully and getting to the core of the *halakhah*. He would show by comparison with other passages which basic concepts were involved, give relevant rules and definitions, and make the subject clear. He frequently explained the Talmud in a way fundamentally different from that of the standard commentators. This is especially noticeable in his treatment of the Jerusalem Talmud which has no early commentary: Rozin's work contains thousands of new explanations. In speaking he was fluent and lucid; his writing, however, is obscure. He refers to his sources by a mere "*vide* so and so," making tens of references but neither quoting the passage nor explaining its relevance. Despite his difficult style, he was a prolific correspondent who enjoyed writing, and he encouraged correspondents to send him their problems. He answered without any effort all who wrote to him on any topic, and thousands of his letters are to be found throughout the world. His ability to find sources in the Talmud was extraordinary. He often quoted a passage from a subject apparently completely unrelated to the matter under discussion, and inferred from it a persuasive proposition which answered the question. For Rozin, the Talmud was decisive. When he found a source for a custom in the Talmud he practiced it, but not otherwise. He traced to the Talmud the philosophical ideas of Maimonides and the latest discoveries of science. Because of this, great scientists enjoyed conversing with him. His remarkable knowledge of philosophy and science is revealed in his commentary on the Pentateuch. He possessed a keen critical sense and when what purported to be the lost text of the Jerusalem Talmud on *Kodashim* appeared, his insight recognized it for the forgery it proved to be.

Rozin's imposing and majestic appearance made a deep impression on all who saw him. Though one of the greatest scholars of any age, he was essentially a humble man. He was courteous, striving to see things from the other man's point of view. He bore the physical pain of his closing years stoically, though grudging the time it took him from learning, and continued to answer all who consulted him, whether in writing or in person.

During his lifetime, Rozin published a commentary on Maimonides' *Mishneh Torah* in five volumes (1903–08) and two volumes of responsa. Four further volumes of responsa were published in 1935–38. During World War II, one of his students, I.A. Sufran-Fuchs, photographed all the manuscripts he could collect and sent the films to a relative in the U.S. There they remained in a box until they were shown to R. Menaḥem *Kasher in the 1950s. He appreciated their true value, and they have subsequently been in the process of publication. All his works appear under the title *Ẓafenat Pa'ne'aḥ*. A number of volumes of the novellae and the commentary on the Pentateuch have appeared (5 vols., 1960–65). Rozin died in Vienna and his remains were buried in Dvinsk.

BIBLIOGRAPHY: O. Feuchtwanger, *Righteous Lives* (1965), 75–78; M. Grossberg, *Ẓefunot ha-Rogachovi* (1958); M.S. Kasher, *Ha-Ga'on ha-Rogachovi ve-Talmudo* (1958); A. Shurin, *Keshet Gibborim* (1964), 249–53; S.J. Zevin, *Ishim ve-Shittot* (1966[3]), 87–153.

[Ernest Hamburger]

ROZOVSKI, PINḤAS (1843–1904), rabbi and Zionist. Born in the Minsk district, Rozovski studied at the Yeshivah of Volozhin. From 1867 he was rabbi of Lipkany, near Slonim, until he succeeded Isaac J. *Reines as the rabbi of Svencioneliai (Yid. Shventsian), Lithuania, in 1887. He knew a number of languages, ancient and modern, including Arabic, and was learned in ancient and modern history and philosophy. Yet he lived meagerly, devoting his attention entirely to literature and the Torah. He wrote many books on biblical, philological, talmudic, and midrashic issues, as well as responsa and commentaries. Since Rozovski had no financial means, none of these books was published. Some of his articles, however, were published in various periodicals. He was attracted to Zionism and sought to give the national renaissance movement a religious ideology. He took part in the founding conference of

Ha-*Mizrachi in Vilna (1902), as well as in the Second and Sixth Zionist Congresses, and the *Minsk Conference of Russian Zionists (1902). In the educational controversy between religious and secular Zionists, he supported the proposal to establish two separate educational communities within the Zionist Organization, so as to enable each to conduct its own policy in matters of culture and education.

BIBLIOGRAPHY: H.H. Markon, in: *Ha-Mizraḥ*, 1 (1903), 380–2.

[Yitzchak Raphael]

RÓZSAVÖLGYI, MÁRK (Mark Mordecai Rosenthal; 1789–1848), composer and violinist. Born in Balassagyarmat, Hungary, Rózsavölgyi studied the violin in Prague and became a violinist in various theatrical ensembles. After 1813 he lived for some time in Baja, but undertook numerous concert tours, and from 1833 to his death lived in Pest. He began to publish his works in 1817 – from 1824 onward mostly under the name of Rózsavölgyi, although the official change of name was granted to him only in 1846.

Rózsavölgyi composed over 100 pieces in the popular style of the Hungarian *Verbunkós* ("Recruiter's dance") and czardas, some suite-like collections of Hungarian dances, and two stage works. His works, especially the czardas pieces and the dance suites, are of major importance for the development of the form. Three of Franz Liszt's Hungarian rhapsodies are indebted to compositions by Rózsavölgyi: the allegretto of the 8th, the introduction of the 12th, and the vivace of the 13th. The authorship of the "Rakoczi March" was erroneously attributed to Rózsavölgyi by the musicologist Fetis, and in spite of later research this has been persistently repeated in a number of books. Rózsavölgyi's autobiography, written in 1834, has been preserved in manuscript in the Ráday Library in Budapest.

His son GYULA (1822–1861), together with Norbert Grinzweil, founded the important music publisher's firm of Rózsavölgyi és Társa in 1850. The firm existed, with various changes of proprietorship, until 1949, when it was nationalized.

[Bathja Bayer]

ROZWADOW, town in Rzeszow province, S.E. Poland. In 1727 there were a synagogue and 30 houses owned by Jews in Rozwadow. According to the 1765 census, there were 333 Jewish poll-tax payers and a further 35 in the surrounding villages. The Jewish population increased rapidly during the second half of the 19th century following the construction of the railway which linked the town with Cracow and Lemberg. In 1880, 1,628 Jews (76% of the total population) lived in the town. The wealthiest among them (known as the Danzig merchants) exported timber by raft to Germany and mobilized peasants of the district for agricultural work in Prussia. The majority of the Jews of Rozwadow earned their livelihood in small trade and crafts such as carpentry, tailoring, shoemaking, the manufacture of soap, and the making of shirts for the peasants. From the middle of the 19th century the rabbis of Rozwadow were descendants of the *Ẓaddik* Naphtali Hurowic of Ropczyce. In 1910 there were 2,372 Jews (70%) in the town. The president of the Jewish community, Dov Ber Reich, also held the office of mayor (1907–40). From 1900 to 1914, a school founded by the *Baron de Hirsch functioned in the town. On the eve of Shavuot 1915, the Russian army expelled the Jews who had remained in the town and many of them were exiled to Siberia. In the fall of 1918, a Jewish national council headed by Jacob Schreiber was formed in Rozwadow. During the transition period and the first weeks of Polish rule, a Jewish youth group was organized to protect the Jews from rioters. In 1921 the Jewish community numbered 1,790 (66% of the total population). Between the two worlds wars the Zionist movement in Rozwadow gained in strength, and a Hebrew school, a Hebrew library, and the sport clubs "Maccabi," "Judah," and "Trumpeldor" were established.

[Arthur Cygielman]

Holocaust Period

In 1939 the Jewish population of Rozwadow numbered more than 2,000. On Sept. 24, 1939, the town was captured by the Germans and on October 2 they ordered it to be evacuated within 24 hours. The Jews were deported across the San River into the Soviet-held area of Poland. The deportees dispersed in the Soviet-occupied zone. In the summer of 1940, many were exiled to the Soviet interior. Later Jews were permitted to return to Rozwadow. In September 1940, 400 Jews lived there legally. The first head of the Judenrat was Eliezer Perlman, the second was B. Gorfinkiel. In the summer of 1941, the community had to provide workers for the labor camp at Pustkow.

The final expulsion took place on July 21, 1942. All the Jews in Rozwadow were assembled in the market square; many were killed on the spot, others were placed into railroad cars and taken to Debica, where Jews from the entire vicinity were concentrated. Some were killed in a nearby forest; others were deported to camps at Tarnobrzeg, Pustkow, Rzeszow, Mielec, Stalowa Wola, and other localities. A labor camp was established in Rozwadow. On Sept. 1, 1942, 80 Jews were brought there from Sieniawa, Lezajsk, and the vicinity. As the rate of expulsion of Jews from the vicinity grew, 600 male Jews, mostly from Wieliczka, were brought to the camp. On Sept. 15, 1942, 450 Jews from Wolbrom arrived. Late in 1942, there were more than 1,200 prisoners, including Jews from Przemysl and Rzeszow. The prisoners worked in the steel factories of Stalowa Wola. Working conditions were hard and anyone who could not withstand the physical strain was shot. More than 1,000 Jews died in the camp.

[Aharon Weiss]

BIBLIOGRAPHY: M. Baliński and T. Lipiński, *Starożytna Polska* (1845), 482; B. Wasiutyński, *Ludność żydowska w Polsce w wiekach XIX i XX* (1930), 118; R. Mahler, *Yidn in Amolikn Poyln in Likht fun Tsifern* (1958), index; N. Blumenthal (ed.), *Sefer Yizkor Rozvadov ve-ha-Sevivah* (Heb. and Yid., 1968), incl. Eng. introd.

ROZWÓJ, antisemitic Polish nationalist organization. Rozwój was founded in 1913 as the propaganda wing of the Polish National-Democratic Party (*Endecja), bearing the official name "Organization for the Support of Polish Trade and Industry." Its rise was due to Polish-Jewish tensions in Warsaw after the elections to the Fourth *Duma in 1912, which reached a climax in the announcement of an anti-Jewish boycott (see Róman *Dmowski). The goal of Rozwój was to assure the nationalists' influence on the Polish petite bourgeoisie by means of demagogical propaganda slogans, emphasizing the liberation of the Polish homeland from Jewish and other foreign influences. Apart from the economic areas, the organization was active in publishing tendentious literature and propaganda, such as *Rozwój* (1918–19) and *Gazeta Niedzielna* (1924–25). Party membership increased markedly after 1917, and in 1923 reached 80,000. Since it was believed that the assassination of G. Narutowicz, Poland's first president, was partly due to anti-Jewish agitation and popular demonstrations, the government of W. Sikorski ordered a temporary ban on Rozwój's activities at the beginning of 1923. As a result, the party's influence declined somewhat but eventually Rozwój was successful in constantly assuming new forms and remaining a pressure group, largely through urging an anti-Jewish boycott.

BIBLIOGRAPHY: I. Schiper et al. (eds.), *Żydzi w Polsce odrodzonej*, 2 vols. (1932/33).

[Moshe Landau]

RSHA (abbr. of Ger. **Reichssicherheitshauptamt**, i.e., Reich Security Main Office). The precursors of the RSHA were the SD and the *SS surveillance and intelligence units, which were established by Himmler before the Nazis came to power and became state functions. The second element of the RSHA was the *Gestapo, originally the political police of Prussia. By 1936 all the political police of the German states were unified and the Gestapo became the core of Nazi control employing surveillance, denunciation, and torture, and having the power to imprison. The third element was the Criminal Police (Kripo). In 1936 Kripo and the Gestapo were reorganized as SIPO under Heydrich's control. On September 22, 1939, the RSHA became one of the 12 main offices of the SS as the umbrella authority over the different Nazi secret police and intelligence organizations, with the exception of military intelligence (*Abwehr*). It was set up under *Himmler's orders to unify the *Sipo* (*Sicherheitspolizei* – "security police") and SD (*Sicherheitsdienst* – "security service"). Reinhard *Heydrich, who had been head of both services, continued as chief of the RSHA. The RSHA was originally divided into six offices (*Aemter*), later into seven, which were subdivided into departments (*Abteilungen* – later *Gruppen*), the latter further broken down into sections (*Referate*). Among the heads of the various divisions were Dr. Otto Ohlendorf, who dealt with economic matters, culture, and ethnic Germans. He commanded *Einsatzgruppe D*. Heinrich *Mueller was the head of the Gestapo. Werner Best and Dr. Neckmann were in charge of organization and law. In April 1944 the *Abwehr*, which was suspect, was taken over and became the *Amt Mil* ("military office") of the RSHA, headed by Walter *Schellenberg.

With the German conquests, the RSHA sent representatives to all the occupied countries to run foreign branches on the model of the headquarters in Berlin. But neither in Germany nor abroad were services fused on a local level. Abroad the RSHA acted through *Einsatzgruppen* ("mobile killing units"), which functioned in the rear of the army. With the end of combat operations the *Einsatzgruppen* became local branches of the RSHA. Heydrich remained chief of the RSHA even after he was appointed protector of Bohemia and Moravia. Following Heydrich's death, Himmler provisionally headed the RSHA, but the actual direction was left to Heinrich Mueller and Schellenberg. Ernst *Kaltenbrunner was appointed chief in January 1943, and served until the end of the war.

The RSHA assumed the powers of its parent organization over the Jews, became the supervising authority over the *Reichsvereinigung, and took over the *Zentralstelle* ("emigration center"). At its outset, the RSHA handled "Jewish affairs," its Section IIB4 dealt with research, and Section IVB3 dealt with "Jewish enemies." Section IVB4 was set up at the end of 1939 under Adolf *Eichmann, who was already head of the *Zentralstelle* and had achieved notable success in the forced emigration of Jews from Vienna. With the onset of the War, Eichmann's section organized evacuations following the decision to drive the Jews and Poles out of the western provinces of Poland. At the same time, the *Einsatzgruppen* killed tens of thousands of Jews and Poles. The RSHA helped in the ghettoization of Jews in the East and was instrumental in the promulgation of anti-Jewish legislation. RSHA delegations in the occupied countries had Jewish sections and dispatched special commandos, e.g., to *Salonika (1943) and to *Hungary (1944). The *Einsatzgruppen* murdered more than 1,000,000 Jews in Russia. Under Heydrich the RSHA became the instrument of the "Final Solution," i.e., the murder of European Jewry. The headquarters of the "Final Solution" was Section IVB4, which later became IVA4b. The local branches of the RSHA rounded up the Jews, confiscated their property, and deported them to death camps. The RSHA sought more efficient killing methods. It invented the gas vans and serviced them in its own vehicle section. Through its *Zentralstelle* in Prague, the RSHA ran the *Theresienstadt ghetto. It decided the fate of every transport, which was dispatched to the East. After the war the International Military Tribunal declared the *Gestapo and the SD components of the RSHA criminal organizations.

BIBLIOGRAPHY: H. Krausnick et al., *Anatomy of the SS State* (1968), 172–87 and index; R. Hilberg, *Destruction of the European Jews* (1961), 181–7 and index; G. Reitlinger, SS, *Alibi of a Nation* (1956), index; E. Crankshaw, *Gestapo: Instrument of Tyranny* (1956), index. See also bibliographies for *Gestapo, *SS, and *SD.

[Yehuda Reshef / Michael Berenbaum (2nd ed.)]

RU'AḤ HA-KODESH (Heb. רוּחַ הַקֹּדֶשׁ; lit. "the Holy Spirit"). Although the phrase *Ru'aḥ ha-Kodesh* occurs in the Bible (cf. Ps. 51:13; Isa 63:10), its specific connotation as divine inspiration is wholly post-biblical. In rabbinic thought it is the spirit of prophecy which comes from God, a divine inspiration giving man an insight into the future and into the will of God. Traditionally the Pentateuch was given directly by God to Moses, but the other canonical writings were all produced under the inspiration of *Ru'aḥ ha-Kodesh*. Thus the determination of what should be included as canonical scripture turns on whether or not a given work was composed with the aid of the Holy Spirit (see Tosef., Yad. 2:14; Song R. 1:1, no. 5). This power of the spirit was given to the prophets in unequal measure (Lev. R. 15:2), and could be passed on to a disciple, Joshua inheriting it from Moses, and Elisha from Elijah (Deut. 34:9; II Kings 2:9–10). There are a number of references to the cessation of the *Ru'ah ha-Kodesh* from Israel, some dating it from the end of the First, some from the end of the Second Temple (cf. Yoma 21b). The most significant passage for the central use of the term as prophetic inspiration is "When the last of the prophets, Haggai, Zechariah, and Malachi, died, the Holy Spirit ceased from Israel" (Yoma 9b).

Apart from its function as prophetic inspiration the Holy Spirit also rests on charismatic or exceptionally holy individuals, who are not prophets in the accepted sense (cf. SER, 10:48). They are thus possessed of an ability to divine the future (Er. 64b). When the rabbis were gathered in Jericho a divine voice announced to them that there were two among them who were worthy of *Ru'aḥ ha-Kodesh* (TJ, Hor. 3:7; 48c). The Holy Spirit is also promised to other categories, e.g., those who teach Torah in public (Song R. 1:1 no. 8), those who study from pure motives (*li-shemah*; SEZ, 1), and those who perform even one *mitzvah* in complete faith (Mekh. Be-Shallaḥ, 2:6). The Midrash says: "All that the righteous do, they do with the power of *Ru'aḥ ha-Kodesh*" (Tanḥ. Va-Yeḥi 13). *Ru'ah ha-Kodesh* may be attained by the saintly man, and the spiritual stages toward its attainment are found in the Mishnah: "Phinehas b. Jair says: 'Heedfulness leads to cleanliness, and cleanliness leads to purity, and purity leads to abstinence, and abstinence leads to holiness, and holiness leads to humility, and humility leads to the fear of sin, and the fear of sin leads to saintliness, and saintliness leads to [the gift of] *Ru'aḥ ha-Kodesh*'" (Sot. 9:15 end; see also Av. Zar. 20b and TJ, Shab. 1:3, 3c for different versions).

A connection between the possession of *Ru'aḥ ha-Kodesh* and ecstasy, or religious joy, is found in the ceremony of water drawing, Simḥat Bet ha-Sho'evah, on the festival of Sukkot. The Mishnah said that he who had never seen this ceremony, which was accompanied by dancing, singing, and music (Suk. 5:4), had never seen true joy (Suk. 5:1). Yet this was also considered a ceremony in which the participants, as it were, drew inspiration from the Holy Spirit itself, which can only be possessed by those whose hearts are full of religious joy (TJ, Suk. 5:1, 55a). The people of Israel as a whole were in some way guided by the power of *Ru'aḥ ha-Kodesh*. Thus when the problem arose among the rabbis as to whether the paschal offering should be brought on the Sabbath, it was to how the ordinary people would act concerning the Sabbath restrictions that the rabbis turned for a decision. Hillel declared: "Leave it to them, for the Holy Spirit is on them. If they are not in themselves prophets, they are the sons of prophets" (Tosef., Pes. 4:2).

A more problematical use of the term *Ru'aḥ ha-Kodesh* is when it is in some way hypostatized, or used as a synonym for God. This tendency toward hypostatization is already apparent in such expressions as "*Ru'aḥ ha-Kodesh* resting" on a person or a place, or someone "receiving *Ru'aḥ ha-Kodesh*." But it is pronounced in descriptions of the *Ru'aḥ ha-Kodesh* speaking (Pes. 117a), or acting as defense counsel on Israel's behalf (Lev. R. 6:1), or leaving Israel and returning to God (Eccles. R. 12:7). This hypostatization is essentially the product of free play of imagery, and does not have the connotations of *Ru'aḥ ha-Kodesh* as an entity separate from God. Neither are there any overtones of the *Ru'aḥ ha-Kodesh* somehow forming part of the Godhead, as is found in the Christian concept of the Holy Ghost, which was a translation of *Ru'aḥ ha-Kodesh*. The problems centering on this use of the term *Ru'aḥ ha-Kodesh* are the product of its different uses shading into one another. Sometimes it is used merely as a synonym for God, and at others it refers to the power of prophecy through divine inspiration. In order to maintain a perspective on the matter, the monotheistic background and the image character of rabbinic thinking must always be kept in mind.

There are a number of texts in which the two terms *Ru'aḥ ha-Kodesh* and **Shekhinah* are found interchanged in different versions (cf. Pes. 117b; Shab. 30b; and TJ, Suk. 5:1, 55a; see also Tosef., Sot. 13:3f.; Sot. 48b; Sanh. 11a). This interchange may be due to the fact that though *Ru'aḥ ha-Kodesh* and *Shekhinah* are conceptually distinct, they are identical over a certain range and are both sometimes used as straight synonyms for God. G.F. Moore, however, considers the exchange of terms to be mainly the result of copyists' errors (*Judaism*, 1 (1927), 437). *Ru'aḥ ha-Kodesh* must also be distinguished from the **bat kol*, or heavenly voice. Both are, in some sense, a revelation of the divine, but their mode of action and relative importance differ. The *bat kol* is an artificial element, pictured literally as a heavenly voice, and not always accepted as halakhically determinative (see BM 59a, where the pronouncements of a *bat kol* are rejected). *Ru'aḥ ha-Kodesh*, on the other hand, works through man as divine inspiration, and is theologically incontrovertible.

[Alan Unterman]

In Jewish Philosophy

PHILO. To *Philo also the Divine Spirit is that which inspires the prophet to prophecy. In *De Specialibus Legibus* (4:49) he writes that: "no pronouncement of a prophet is ever his own; he is an interpreter prompted by Another in all his utterances, when knowing not what he does he is filled with inspiration, as the reason withdraws and surrenders the citadel of the soul to a new visitor and tenant, the Divine Spirit (τοῦ θείου πνεύματος) which plays upon the vocal organism and dictates words which clearly impress its prophetic message." Influenced by Plato's notion of divine inspiration or frenzy, Philo interprets Abraham's "deep sleep" (Gen. 15:12) as a form of ecstasy which the prophet experiences: "This is what regularly befalls the prophets. The mind is evicted at the arrival of the Divine Spirit, but when that departs the mind returns to its tenancy" (Her. 265). According to Philo, the Divine Spirit "comes upon" man, "fills" him, visits him, or speaks to him only occasionally. But in an exceptional case, such as that of Moses, the Divine Spirit remains continuously in man's soul.

Philo maintains that the Divine Spirit is a separate spiritual entity – a "unique corporeal soul" whose function is to act as an "intermediary of divine communications to man" (H.A. Wolfson, *Philo*, 2 (1948), 32). While unique, it is of the same nature as the incorporeal soul of man or as the angels, which are unembodied souls. Although Philo does not apply the term *Logos to the Divine Spirit, he does refer to it as Wisdom, which he identifies with the Logos.

Philo however uses the term Divine Spirit in several other senses as well: in the sense of the rational soul, as in *De Specialibus Legibus* (4:123), where he identifies the Divine Spirit with the "breath of life breathed upon the first man" – which is the rational soul (see H.A. Wolfson, *Philo*, 1 (1948), 395); in the sense of air, the third element, as in Genesis 1:2: "the spirit of God was moving above the water" (Gig. 22); and in the sense of the "pure knowledge in which every wise man naturally shares." Philo bases this last sense of the term on Exodus 31:2 in which Bezalel is said to have been filled by God "...with the Divine Spirit, with wisdom, understanding, and knowledge to devise in every work" (Gig. 23).

The concept of the Divine Spirit in the Dead Sea Scrolls is similar to that of Philo, insofar as it is regarded as a spirit that "comes upon" man or "speaks" to him. In the scrolls, man, as a result of purification from carnal pollution (connected with baptism) is reborn and receives a new spirit. While there are many Platonic and Gnostic elements in the conception of Divine Spirit found in the Dead Sea Scrolls, D. Flusser maintains that the origin of the concept is Jewish (*Scripta Hierosolymitana*, (1958), 252ff.). The influence that the Dead Sea Scrolls exercised upon the Christian concept of the Holy Ghost is well known.

[Rivka G. Horwitz]

Medieval Jewish Philosophy

The concept of Holy Spirit (*Ruaḥ Ha-Kodesh*) is intrinsically connected to medieval Jewish philosophical approaches to prophecy. Essentially one can find two different yet related usages of this concept, as can already be seen by Philo. It may refer to a separate entity which is the source of prophecy, as well as other forms of divine providence; it also may refer to that which is received by choice individuals. In the latter case, some thinkers distinguished this reception from prophecy proper.

SAADIAH GAON. *Saadiah Gaon deals with the Holy Spirit in his *Commentary on the Book of Creation*. In this treatise he insists that it is not a hypostasis or divine intermediary, as it is conceived by the Christians. At the same time he ascribes to it many of the characteristics that are reminiscent of the *Logos, particularly as this notion was conceived in the Arabic-speaking world. The author of the *Book of Creation* terms the first of the *Sefirot* "the Spirit of the Living God" [*Ru'aḥ Elohim Ḥayyim*] which he also identifies as the Holy Spirit (4:1). Saadiah interprets the Holy Spirit as a reference to the divine will, but goes on to maintain that God's will is not a distinct entity. Rather it signifies that God creates everything without engaging in physical activity. He offers an analogy of God's relation to the world, comparing it to the relation of the animate force to living creatures. God is, figuratively speaking, the animate force of the world, or better yet, the intellect of the world: "The volition of the Creator – that is, His power – spreads in the air, which is simple and subtle. It exists in it [the world] and moves it, as the animate force moves the body. The Creator is found in all of this and governs it, just as the intellect is found in the animate force and governs it" (J. Kafih (ed.), *Sefer Yeẓirah im Perush ha-Gaon Rabbenu Sa'adya b. R. Yosef Fayyumi* [1972], 106). The continuation of Saadiah's remarks, however, suggests a different picture. He describes the Spirit as the most subtle entity created by God and it fills the entire world. This entity is known also as the "Glory" (*kavod*) and the "Indwelling" (*shekhinah*); in it is produced the speech heard by the prophets. Moreover, not only the visible and audible manifestations of prophecy originate in this entity, but also exceptional wisdom and the power of valor that God bestows upon choice individuals (108–9). The rabbinic *bat kol* is treated by Saadiah as yet another manifestation of the Holy Spirit.

In his subsequent treatise, *Book of Beliefs and Opinions*, Saadiah attacks the Christians for treating both the Spirit of God and the Word of God as divine beings (2:5–6). While he does not deal explicitly with the notion of Holy Spirit, he describes the Glory or *Shekhinah* as possessing the purest substance of God's created entities. The only task, however, that he ascribes to it is to provide visible proof to the prophet of the truth of the divine communication (2:10; 3:5). The Speech heard by the prophets is treated simply as sounds created by God and conveyed through the air (2:12). In Saadiah's *Haggadah* for Passover there is an explicit and unique reference the notion that God did not redeem Israel from Egypt by means of the Speech (*Dibber*), a clear rejection of the *Logos* idea. One can detect in his approach a desire to counter the danger posed to strict monotheism by ascribing to the Holy Spirit too active a role in the divine governance of the affairs of the world.

JUDAH HALEVI. The early 12th-century philosopher *Judah Halevi refers to the Holy Spirit in several passages of the *Kuzari*. He presents in the name of the Aristotelian philosophers the view that the Holy Spirit is identical to the Active Intellect, the source of the emanation of prophecy. Halevi rejects this approach, maintaining that prophecy comes directly from God and not any intermediary (1:87). In explaining the visible manifestations of prophecy Halevi utilizes Saadiah's discussion in the *Commentary to the Book of Creation*, though he draws a distinction between the Holy Spirit and the Glory. Halevi writes: "The air and all the bodies act by His will ... From the subtle spiritual body called the Holy Spirit were shaped the spiritual forms called the Holy Glory, figuratively called God" (2:4). The Holy Spirit and Glory assume here the role of passive intermediaries. As in the case of Saadiah, Halevi at times speaks also of non-visible manifestations of the Holy Spirit. In a passage in which Halevi presents his own commentary on the *Book of Creation* he adds that the angels are created from the Holy Spirit and souls conjoin with it (4:25). The Spirit is also described by him as "enwrapping the prophet" (4:15) resulting in the individual's reception of prophecy, or in his being aided and strengthened in a given matter. The same phenomenon occurs during the anointing of a nazirite, the anointing of the king, and when the High Priest consults the *Urim and Thummim in order to divine the future. One passage in the *Kuzari* alludes to a strong connection between the Holy Spirit and the *Amr Ilahi* (Divine Matter or Command), a notion whose definition has been a source of controversy among scholars. Halevi illustrates divine speech by "the speech of the prophets when they are enwrapped by the Holy Spirit. The Divine Matter directs all their words. The prophet exercises absolutely no volition in his speech (5:20)." Visible and non-visible manifestations also are true of the *Shekhinah* (2:62; 3:19; 5:23), which Halevi at times treats interchangeably with the Holy Spirit.

One may also interpret the notion of being "enwrapped by the Holy Spirit" in a less literal manner and see in it a figurative image for the reception of a special type of knowledge or ability. In the presentation of the philosophers' worldview in the last part of the *Kuzari*, based on a short treatise by Avicenna, Halevi writes: "In some individuals, the rational faculty succeeds in conjoining with the Universal Intellect. It is thereby elevated above the use of syllogism and deliberation, or the toil of learning, by means of inspiration (*ilham*) and revelation (*wahy*). Its special trait is termed "sanctity" and the "holy spirit" (512)." In 4:15 Halevi indicates that the prophet is enwrapped by the Holy Spirit after his soul "conjoins with the angels."

MAIMONIDES. *Maimonides does not use the Holy Spirit to refer to a spiritual entity but confines his usage to the emanation received by the prophets or other special individuals, such as the High Priest when he consults the Urim and Thummim. In *Eight Chapters* 7 and in *Laws of the Principles of the Torah* 7:1, 6 he appears to use the term as synonymous with prophecy (though in 7:1 the term may refer to the acquired intellect). In his discussion of the levels of prophecy in the *Guide of the Perplexed* (2:45), on the other hand, he counts the reception of the Holy Spirit as the two lowest degrees of prophecy and distinguishes them from prophecy proper. The first of these degrees consists of divine help that moves an individual to perform a great and righteous action. The next degree consists of a situation in which "an individual finds that a certain thing has descended upon him and that another force has come upon him and has made him speak; so that he talks in wise sayings, in words of praise, in useful admonitory dicta, or concerning governmental or divine matter – and all this while he is awake and his senses function as usual." Saadiah in his *Commentary on the Book of Creation* also speaks of these two manifestations of the Holy Spirit as discrete from prophecy proper, though he is less interested than Maimonides in drawing a sharp distinction between the two phenomena. By means of this distinction Maimonides ascribes an inferior standing to the books of the Bible that belong to the Hagiographa, treating their authors as non-prophets. The distinction also enables Maimonides to ascribe a non-prophetic status to Balaam, who received the Holy Spirit but did not possess the requisite perfection to attain prophecy in his view. The same is true of the High Priest when consulting the Urim and Thummim

Maimonides' distinction between prophecy and the Holy Spirit, as well as his confining the use of Holy Spirit to refer to a certain type of reception and not to a spiritual entity, influenced subsequent Jewish philosophers. Even Ḥasdai *Crescas and Joseph *Albo who broke with Maimonides on many points of his philosophy continued to accept his approach on this issue.

[Howard Kreisel (2nd ed.)]

The Modern Period

The concept of the Holy Spirit is of central importance in Hermann *Cohen's last book *Die Religion der Vernunft aus den Quellen des Judentums* (1929, pp. 116–30). Objecting to Philo's conception of the Logos as an independent being intermediate between God and man, he maintains that the Holy Spirit characterizes the correlation between God and man. He relates the Holy Spirit to ethical purification on the basis of Leviticus 22:32, and claims that it finds expression in active ethical behavior rather than the passive receptivity of grace. Through ethical purification man attains a new spirit. The Holy Spirit can neither be alone with God nor alone with man, but is present only in correlation.

For the liberal thinker K. Kohler the Holy Spirit is the gift of reason given by God to man (*Jewish Theology* (1918), 200ff.). While the rabbis believed that the first man was endowed with the most perfected reason and was familiar with "every branch of knowledge," in the modern period it is believed that man's knowledge has increased through the ages. Thus Kohler believed that the Holy Spirit should be seen as dynamic. It is the spirit that manifests itself most clearly in the development and evolution of all areas of life – social, intellectual, moral, and spiritual – "toward the highest of goals" (*ibid.*, 230).

[Rivka G. Horwitz]

BIBLIOGRAPHY: G.F. Moore, *Judaism*, 3 vols. (1927–30), index, s.v. *Holy Spirit*; A. Marmorstein, *Studies in Jewish Theology* (1950), 122–44; A.J. Heschel, *Torah min ha-Shamayim be-Aspaklaryah shel ha-Dorot*, 2 vols. (1962–65). **ADD. BIBLIOGRAPHY:** A. Altmann, *Studies in Religious Philosophy and Mysticism* (1969), 140–60; H. Kreisel, *Prophecy: The History of an Idea in Medieval Jewish Philosophy* (2001), index, s.v. Holy Spirit; *Shekhinah*.

RUBENOVITZ, HERMAN H. (1883–1966), U.S. rabbi and Zionist. Rubenovitz, born in Kovno, Lithuania, was taken to the United States in about 1890 and lived in Pittsburgh. In 1908, he graduated from the Jewish Theological Seminary and took his first pulpit in Louisville, Kentucky. There Rubenovitz initiated the idea of an association of Conservative synagogues, which eventually took the form of the *United Synagogue of America. In 1910 he became rabbi of Congregation Mishkan Tefila, Boston, which, over the years, he succeeded in making Conservative in outlook and in style of worship. Rubenovitz was among the rabbis who, with Mordecai *Kaplan, developed the Society of the Jewish Renascence in 1920, which later became the *Reconstructionist movement.

He also was among the founders of the Boston Rabbinical Association, serving as its president for 15 years. He was active in Jewish education in the Boston area and initiated the plan for a training school for Jewish teachers. Rubenovitz presided over the Zionist Council in Boston and was chairman of the New England Board of the Jewish National Fund for four years. His wife, MIGNON RUBENOVITZ, was an active leader in Hadassah Women's Organization, in the National Council of Jewish Women, and in the National Women's League of the United Synagogue of America. They published memoirs and letters in *The Waking Heart* (1967), and Mignon Rubenovitz published other works under her own name.

RUBENS, ALFRED (1903–1998), English collector and historian. A London surveyor and estate agent by profession, he began early in life to collect engravings of Jewish interest and his *Anglo-Jewish Portraits* (1935) was based on his collections. This was followed by a similar work of wider scope, *A Jewish Iconography* (1954; rev. ed. 1981) extending to engravings of scenes of Jewish life and to continental engraved portraits. A logical outcome was his *History of Jewish Costume* (1967). Rubens was chairman of the London Jewish Museum for many years and was president of the Jewish Historical Society of England (1956–58).

ADD. BIBLIOGRAPHY: "In Memoriam Alfred Rubens (1903–1998)," in: JHSET, 35 (1996/98).

[Cecil Roth]

RUBENS, BERNICE (1927–2004), British novelist, film writer and director. Born in Cardiff, Rubens was educated at University College, South Wales. She taught English and from 1950 worked as a documentary film writer and director. Her first novel, *Set on Edge*, was published in 1960. She also published two plays, *Third Party* (1972) and *I Sent a Letter to My Love* (1979), which is based on her novel of the same title.

Rubens' first novels, *Set on Edge* (1960), *Madame Sousatzka* (1962), *Mate in Three* (1965), and *The Elected Member* (1969), are all extreme fictional versions of the author's Cardiff Jewish childhood. She has been described as a "chronicler of the frayed edge of middle-class Jewish life." In particular, the question of destructive familial expectations is a central motif in Rubens' early fiction. *Spring Sonata* (1979) addresses this theme from the startling viewpoint of an unborn child and *I Sent a Letter to My Love* (1975) is a Welsh version of this theme.

Rubens' fiction is concerned with marginal characters whose personality is often on the point of breakdown. Representative examples of this preoccupation are *The Elected Member*, her Booker Prize-winning novel; *A Five Year Sentence* (1978); *Sunday Best* (1980), the journal of a transvestite; and *Mr. Wakefield's Crusade* (1985). For the most part, Rubens avoids a gloomy pessimism – inherent in her subject matter – by dotting her fiction with welcome black humor. In later years, she reverted to an exclusively Jewish environment with the publication of *Brothers* (1983), an ambitious Jewish family saga. Above all, Rubens' fiction evoked with considerable power the dark underside of what passes for normal human behavior. In this way, she has challenged the cozy reality of mainstream Anglo-Jewish fiction.

BIBLIOGRAPHY: J. Vinson (ed.), *Contemporary Novelists* (1982), 566; *The Jewish Quarterly*, 21, 1–2 (1973).

[Bryan Cheyette]

RUBENS, PAUL ALFRED (1875–1917), playwright and composer. Born in London, the son of a stockbroker, Rubens was educated at Winchester and Oxford. He wrote lyrics and librettos, for which he often composed musical settings. His stage successes, mainly written in collaboration, include *Lady Madcap* (1904), *Miss Hook of Holland* (1907), *The Balkan Princess* (1910), and *The Girl from Utah* (1913). From 1912 until his death, he was the principal composer for London's Gaiety Theatre. He died of tuberculosis at the age of only 41.

ADD. BIBLIOGRAPHY: ODNB online.

RUBENSON, ROBERT (1829–1902), Swedish meteorologist. Born in Stockholm, he attended the University of Uppsala, where he taught mathematics until 1859. For three years, Rubenson carried out meteorological research work in Germany, France and Italy. In Rome he completed an extensive investigation on the polarization of the atmosphere, which he published in book form (Uppsala, 1864). In 1873 he organized at Uppsala a network of meteorological observations. He was appointed director of the Swedish Central Meteorological Institute, a professor at the University of Stockholm, and a member of the Swedish Academy of Sciences. He is considered the founder of modern Swedish meteorology.

[Arthur Beer]

RUBENSTEIN, LOUIS (1861–1931), Canadian ice-skating champion, community activist and municipal politician. Rubenstein was born in Montreal in 1861. Widely regarded the father of figure skating in North America, at various times between 1882 and 1891 he was figure skating champion of Canada, the United States, North America and the world. Rubenstein won his first title, the Montreal Championship, in 1878. In 1885 he captured the North American title and defended it successfully for the next four years. In 1890 Rubenstein also won at the world figure skating championships in St. Petersburg, Russia, the first North American figure skater to compete abroad. The championships in St. Petersburg proved to be very problematic for Rubenstein. Due to widespread Russian antisemitism of the day, the Canadian Jewish skater expected he would be unwelcome to compete and came forearmed with a letter of introduction from Canada's governor-general Lord Stanley. In spite of police harassment, Rubenstein was allowed to remain in Russia for the competition, and his performance was so outstanding that not even obviously biased judging could deny him the gold medal.

In 1891, at the top of his career, Rubenstein retired from skating. He remained, however, active in the sports world. He founded the Canadian Figure Skating Association with the objective of standardizing judging in skating competitions. He also served as president of several different Canadian sports organizations including bowling, lifesaving, skating, tobogganing, bicycling and curling.

Rubenstein was also active in the larger community. While active in his family's silver plating business, he was elected a Montreal alderman, a position he held for 17 years until his death. For many years he was also president of the Montreal YMHA. In 1981 Rubenstein joined Fanny Rosenfeld as the first Canadians inducted into the International Jewish Sports Hall of Fame in Israel and in 2004 Rubenstein became the subject of a film produced by the National Film Board of Canada.

[Avi Hyman and Brenda Cappe (2nd ed.)]

RUBENSTEIN, RICHARD LOWELL (1924–), U.S. rabbi and theologian. Rubenstein was born in New York City; his parents were non-observant Jews and he did not have a bar-mitzvah. He was tempted to enter the ministry but was told that he would have to change his name. Instead, he embraced his own tradition. He entered Hebrew Union College to study for the rabbinate, simultaneously attending the University of Cincinnati (BA 1946). He was at HUC during the Holocaust years when the reality of Jewish life clashed with the optimistic liberalism of Reform Judaism. Becoming more observant, he switched to JTS when Abraham Joshua Heschel left HUC to join the Seminary faculty. He also studied at Yeshiva Torah Vodaath. He was ordained at the Seminary and received his MHL in 1952. While serving as rabbi in Brockton (1952–54) and in Natick (1954–56), Massachusetts, and as interim director of the Hillel Foundation at Harvard (1956–58), he studied at Harvard Divinity School where he received his STM (1955) and at the graduate school where he received his Ph.D. in 1960.

In 1958 he became director of Hillel and chaplain to Jewish students at the University of Pittsburgh (1958). In 1969 he was appointed adjunct professor of humanities at the University of Pittsburgh. Given the controversy of his writings and what he defined as "bureaucratic excommunication," Rubenstein's career in the rabbinate was stymied but academic positions in religion were becoming open to Jewish scholars. From 1971 to 1995, he was a professor of religion at Florida State University. In February 2001 the university created a professorship in his name. In 1987 the JTS conferred the degree of Doctor of Hebrew Letters, *honoris causa*, upon him. Many years later, Rubenstein became president of the University of Bridgeport.

There is general agreement among theologians that Rubenstein's first book, *After Auschwitz* (1966), initiated the contemporary debate on the meaning of the Holocaust in religious thought, both Jewish and Christian. In it he argued that after Auschwitz the belief in a redeeming God who is active in history and who will redeem mankind from its vicissitudes is no longer possible. Belief in such a God and an allegiance to the rabbinic theodicy that attempted to justify Him would imply that Hitler was part of a divine plan and that Israel was being punished for her sins. His rejection of God, however, does not entail an end to religion or an end to Judaism, for in a meaningless world human community becomes all the more important. Consequently, Rubenstein emphasizes the importance of rituals, rites of passage, and religious community over doctrine and ethics.

Rubenstein's next work was *The Religious Imagination,* a psychological study of Midrash, which was followed by an autobiography, *Power Struggle.* In 1972 he published a slim but influential work entitled *The Cunning of History*, which argued that the Holocaust is an expression in the extreme of what was common to the mainstream of Western civilization. Rubenstein viewed the Holocaust as manifestation of major political, demographic, economic, and bureaucratic trends in contemporary civilization and therefore of importance far beyond the Jewish community. Rubenstein's later book, *La Perfidie de l'Histoire* (2005), deals with the challenge of Islamic extremism to Western civilization.

Among his other books are *The Age of Triage* (1983), and *Approaches to Auschwitz* (2003), co-authored with John K. Roth. Always a strong supporter of Israel, a life-long student of genocide and of antisemitism, Rubenstein spent the opening years of the 2000s seeking to understand the phenomenon of Islamic antisemitism as manifested particularly in Europe.

BIBLIOGRAPHY: M. Berenbaum and B.R. Rubenstein (eds.), *What Kind of God?: Essays in Honor of Richard L. Rubenstein* (1995).

[Michael Berenbaum (2nd ed.)]

RUBIN, EDGAR (1886–1951), Danish psychologist. He was professor of psychology at the university of his native Copenhagen. When the Germans overran Denmark during World War II Rubin sought refuge in Sweden. He returned to Denmark after the war, but died after protracted illness, brought on, in part, by the hardships suffered in his flight to Sweden. Rubin's work ranged widely and included studies of perceived movement, tactual and auditory senses, temperature, and gustation. He discovered paradoxical cold – the fact that cool stimuli 0.1–1.5° C below skin temperature arouse faint sensations of warmth. His best known discovery involved the finding that visual perception is normally divided into two parts, figure and ground.

Rubin's laws governing the selection of the figure were phenomenological in the tradition of *Husserl. They did not explain why a figure was selected but merely stated the conditions under which one structure among possible alternatives was selected. Although not a Gestalt psychologist himself, Rubin's ideas were quickly incorporated into Gestalt theory. Rubin did not approve of theories and schools of psychology. His position, as stated in his address to the Ninth International Congress of Psychology at New Haven, Connecticut, in 1929, was to let the facts speak for themselves.

BIBLIOGRAPHY: W.C.H. Prentice, in: *American Journal of Psychology*, 64 (1951), 608–9; D. Katz, in: *Psychological Review*, 58 (1951), 387–8.

[Helmut E. Adler]

RUBIN, GAIL (1939–1978), U.S. photographer. The only child of a prominent New York family, Rubin graduated from Finch College and worked as a photographer in advertising and as an editor at several publishing houses before moving to Israel in 1971. She began her photographic career in Israel as a press photographer and served as a war photographer. She was one of the first civilians to cross into Egypt with Israeli troops during the 1973 war.

Rubin turned her attention to nature photography and a collection of her wildlife photographs was exhibited at the Jewish Museum in New York in 1977. In March of 1978, Rubin was shooting the nesting habits of storks and pelicans in a bird sanctuary when she was shot to death by Palestinian terrorists who had infiltrated a remote beach north of Tel Aviv.

Her legacy is a book called *Psalmist with a Camera*, published in 1979. Rubin's descriptions and photographs are rooted in biblical phrases; she had resolved to show the birds, beasts, and other aspects of nature mentioned in the Bible. In the Ḥuleh Nature Reserve, for example, she photographed water buffalo, pelicans, and doves. The book also contains impressionistic images of the bark of eucalyptus trees at different seasons.

[Stewart Kampel (2nd ed.)]

RUBIN, HADASSAH (1912–2003), Yiddish poet. Born in Yampol, Ukraine, Rubin moved with her family to Zbarazh, Galicia (now Ukraine) at the age of nine, and later to Kremenets (Krzemieniec). She graduated from a Polish secondary school. From 1935 she was a member of the illegal Polish Communist Party and was arrested several times. After spending World War II in Kyrgyzstan, she returned to Poland and became chairman of the *Yidisher Kultur-Gezelshaftlekher Farband* in Stettin (Szczecin) from 1948 to 1952, and a staff member of the magazine *Yidishe Shriftn* in Warsaw from 1956 to 1959. In 1960 she immigrated to Israel. Her poems were first published in 1931 in the *Kremenitser Shtime* and the *Vilner Tog*, then in various other Yiddish publications. Her poetry, which is characterized by original imagery, deals with social problems, the Holocaust, the joys of love and motherhood, the lost illusions and life in Israel. It was collected in the volumes: *Mayn Gas iz in Fener* ("My Street Is Full with Banners," 1953); *Veytik un Freyd* ("Pain and Joy," 1955); *Trit in der Nakht* ("Steps in the Night," 1957); *Fun Mentsh tsu Mentsh* ("From Person to Person," 1964); *In Tsugvint* ("In a Whirlwind," 1981); *Eyder Tog* ("Before Dawn," 1988); and *Rays Nisht op di Blum* ("Don't Pluck the Flower," 1995).

BIBLIOGRAPHY: R. Katznelson-Shazar, *Al Admat ha-Ivrit* (1966), 225–7. **ADD. BIBLIOGRAPHY:** LNYL, 8 (1981), 410–11; D. Sfard, *Shtudies un Skitsn* (1955), 101–5; D. Sadan, *Avnei Miftan*, 2 (1970), 194–8; G. Mayzel, in: *Di Goldene Keyt*, 51 (1965), 211–13; K. Molodowsky, *Sevive*, 19 (1966), 17–19.

[Arieh Pilowsky]

RUBIN, MORTON JOSEPH (1917–1972), U.S. meteorologist. Born in Philadelphia, Rubin was supervising meteorologist of Pan American Airlines (1942–49) before joining the Federal Weather Bureau. In 1952 he was one of the heads of a project for weather forecast charts of the southern hemisphere and did research on circulation in that area. During the Third International Geophysical Year (1955), Rubin was appointed to the Antarctic Weather Research Center and was entrusted with the development of analysis methods for its project. During 1957–59, he was special assistant to Harry Wexler, and liaison meteorologist with the Soviet Mirnyy station in the Antarctic on problems concerning research into and analysis of the upper strata of the atmosphere. Rubin later directed the polar meteorology research project of the Federal Weather Bureau (1959–62) and combined research projects on meteorological, oceanographical and glaciological problems of the Antarctic. From 1965 he was a senior scientist in the Environmental Science Services Administration (ESSA) and shared responsibility for research planning.

[Dov Ashbel]

RUBIN, REUVEN (1893–1974), Israeli painter. Born in Galats, Romania, the son of Feiga and Joel Zelicovici, Rubin drew from the time he was a young *ḥeder* pupil. At 14 he had already published his drawings in local illustrated journals and books. In 1912 Rubin traveled to Jerusalem intending to study in the Bezalel School of Art and Design. A year later he moved to Paris to study at the Ecole des Beaux Arts and at the Academie Colarossi. Rubin returned to Tel Aviv only in 1923 but continued to travel and to exhibit all over the world. Pictures by Rubin were acquired by the world's main museums, such as the Musée National d'Art Modern in Paris (*Goldfish Vendor*, 1955) and the Museum of Modern Art in New York (*The Flute Player*, 1940). In Israel his art works appeared in national institutes, such as the painting *The Glory of Galilee* (1965–66) located in the Knesset in Jerusalem and the stained glass windows in the Residence of the President of Israel in Jerusalem (1969). Rubin participated in the Venice Biennale more than once. He was the first Israeli minister plenipotentiary to Romania (1949–50).

Rubin was awarded the Israel Prize in 1973. In 1974 Rubin signed a contract with Tel Aviv's mayor in which he turned his house over to the city. This building, which stands on Bialik

Street near the Bialik House as well as close to the old municipality building, became the Rubin House Museum.

Most of Rubin's pictures expressed the local environment of Ereẓ Israel. The views reflect the landscapes, the flora, the fauna, and the variety of types of people he saw in the country, all painted in a unique way combining naïve and simplified styles.

The naïve image was created mainly by the distortion of proportions. The lack of shadows, the existence of contour lines, and the strange perspective were part of the naïve style of the 1930s and expressed Rubin's impression regarding the significance of the location. In a self-portrait he showed himself as a dark-skinned person with a half-open shirt, seated on a simple stool. The view that appeared through the window was mostly a view of Jaffa with Arabic figures and houses (*Self Portrait*, 1925, Paris).

During the 1940s he described the olive fields of the Galilee. The figures he dealt with were the biblical figures that he had felt especially close to since he had been a child and even more so when he was situated in Israel. His picture series *Jerusalem the Golden* combined the real landscape of the Judean Mountains and the imaginary temple set in its supposed original place. Later in the windows of the President's Residence he combined fragments from his art works with the biblical scenes of *Jacob Wrestling with the Angel, King David Enters Jerusalem* and *Elijah Ascending to Heaven*. Although it was a huge project using a new technique, Rubin, then approaching his 76th year, accepted the assignment with delight. He declared the windows his gift to the nation.

BIBLIOGRAPHY: S. Wilkinson, *Reuven Rubin* (1975); Tel Aviv, Rubin museum, *Catalogue of the Permanent Collection*, 1993.

[Ronit Steinberg (2nd ed.)]

RUBIN, ROBERT E. (1938–), U.S. financier, 70th secretary of the U.S. Treasury. Born in New York City, Rubin graduated summa cum laude from Harvard in 1960. He attended the London School of Economics and received an LL.B. from Yale Law School in 1964. He entered private practice with the law firm of Cleary, Gottlieb, Steen, and Hamilton in New York. In 1966 he joined Goldman Sachs as an associate in the risk arbitrage division, and his brilliance there earned him a general partnership in 1971. In 1980 Rubin became a member of the management committee, then vice chairman and co-chief operating officer in 1987. He served as co-senior partner and co-chairman at Goldman Sachs from 1990 to 1992.

When Bill Clinton took office as U.S. president in January 1993, Rubin joined the White House as assistant to the president for economic policy, directing Clinton's newly created National Economic Council. The passage of the North American Free Trade Agreement (NAFTA) in 1993, an early success for Clinton, was also considered a victory for Rubin and an endorsement of the new "Rubinomics." In 1995 Rubin succeeded Lloyd Bentsen as Treasury secretary, serving until 1999. This period saw one of the highest levels of economic growth in U.S. history, for which Rubin is generally credited. It was also the first time when virtually every leading position in the Clinton economic team was held by a Jew.

As Treasury secretary, Rubin's economic policies included measures for a steep deficit reduction, which ultimately resulted in a federal budget surplus; at the same time, the U.S. economy experienced both vigorous growth and very low levels of national unemployment. Internationally, Rubin urged the support of developing economies, including Mexico and Argentina, orchestrating a substantial loan guarantee for Mexico. With his deputy secretary Lawrence Summers (Rubin's eventual successor) and Alan Greenspan, Rubin coordinated the U.S. response to the Asian financial crisis of the late 1990s.

In 1999 Rubin resigned as secretary and joined Citigroup, where he served as chairman of the executive committee. He has served on the board of trustees of the Carnegie Corporation of New York, Mt. Sinai Hospital and Medical School, the Securities and Exchange Commission Market Oversight and Financial Services Advisory Committee, the Mayor of New York's Council of Economic Advisors, and the Governor's Council on Fiscal and Economic Priorities for the State of New York. He has written, with journalist Jacob Weisberg, *In an Uncertain World: Tough Choices from Wall Street to Washington* (2003), a memoir documenting his years in the Clinton administration.

[Dorothy Bauhoff (2nd ed.)]

RUBIN, RUTH (1906–2000), singer, folk-music collector, and author. Born in Khotin, Bessarabia, she was taken to Canada at the age of four, and was educated in English, French, and Yiddish. At an early age she showed a deep love for music and studied Yiddish folksong. She recorded Yiddish songs in Montreal and Toronto, Canada, and New York City between 1947 and 1964, as well as in London, Tel Aviv, and elsewhere. She published the songs she collected and learned, performed, and recorded them. Her research was published in *A Treasury of Jewish Folksong* (1950), *Voices of a People* (1963), and *Jewish Folk Songs* (1965); in these collections, the songs are discussed in their historical settings. She also recorded herself singing these songs and her records were published. A selection of her recordings was donated to the Haifa Music Museum and Library (approx. 20 hrs); the majority of her recordings were donated to the Archive of Folk Cultures of the Library of Congress in Washington (approx. 66 hrs.). Some of her papers and recordings were donated to YIVO archives for Yiddish research and culture in New York.

[Gila Flam (2nd ed.)]

RUBIN, SAMUEL (1901–1978), U.S. philanthrophist. Rubin was born in Bialystok, Poland, but was brought to the U.S. by his parents at the age of four. He studied at the City College of New York, but entered business and in 1937 founded the firm of Faberge, importers of French perfumes, which he sold in 1963 for $25 million.

Rubin was an outstanding philanthropist for both United States and Israeli causes. He was one of the founders of the

New York Bellevue Medical Center, and the Fordham University Medical Library, and endowed the chair of anthropology at Brandeis University, in addition to supporting numerous other medical and cultural institutions. In 1955 he donated $250,000 for the establishment of a chain of community cultural centers in Israeli development areas; he founded a cancer detection clinic at the Rambam Hospital, Haifa. In 1957 the Rubin Foundation, which he founded, provided the funds to acquire a building to house the Jerusalem Conservatoire of Music, to which he donated $325,000 through the American-Israel Cultural Foundation, and it was given the name of the Rubin Academy of Music.

On the 20th anniversary of the Rubin Academy of Music in 1977, he donated a laboratory for electronic music.

RUBIN, SOLOMON (1823–1910), Hebrew writer. Born in Dolina, Galicia, Rubin was one of the most prolific writers of the Haskalah period; his main subjects were general and Jewish folklore, customs, superstitions, and the like. Rubin's work was for the most part devoted to the study of thought and of popular beliefs accepted as sacred. His sympathy for the victims of intellectual censorship induced him to translate K. Gutzkow's *Uriel Acosta* (1857; see Uriel da *Costa) from German to Hebrew, and this led him to an interest in Spinoza, whose writings preoccupied him for an extended period.

He published *Moreh Nevukhim he-Ḥadash* (2 vols., 1857), a synopsis of Spinoza's two books on the basis of the French adaptation of Emile Laisset, and, when this resulted in attacks upon him and Spinoza by Samuel David *Luzzatto, he countered with *Teshuvah Nizzaḥat* (1859). A book on Spinoza and Maimonides (in German, 1869) earned him his doctorate at the University of Goettingen. He also wrote on Spinoza in *Ha-Shaḥar,* and published two additional works on the philosopher: *Hegyonei Spinoza* (1897), on divinity, the universe, and the soul of man, and *Barukh Spinoza* (1910). He also translated Spinoza's "Ethics" into Hebrew (*Ḥeker Eloha im Torat ha-Adam*; 1885) and his grammar (*Dikduk Sefat Ever*; 1905), in the introduction to which Rubin discusses the Sephardi pronunciation, which formed the basis of Spinoza's Hebrew grammar. Rubin also wrote *Tehillat ha-Kesilim* (1888), a parody in the style of Erasmus' *In Praise of Folly,* the only book of its kind in Hebrew.

[Getzel Kressel]

RUBINER, LUDWIG (1881–1920), German poet and essayist. Rubiner, a native of Berlin, was a social revolutionary who campaigned passionately for peace and social justice. A member of no political party, he expounded his ideology in a series of essays collected in the volume *Der Mensch in der Mitte* (1917). In his poetry, as in his prose, he was an expressionist.

His own verse included *Die indischen Opale* (1911) and *Das himmlische Licht* (1916). He also edited an anthology, *Kameraden der Menschheit, Dichtungen zur Weltrevolution* (1919). This was a collection of manifestos "for the fight against the old world and for the advancement toward a true humanity," and in it he called on the poets to side with the rebellious masses. For a short time, Rubiner edited the expressionist journal *Zeit-Echo* (1918). He edited a selection of Tolstoy's diaries, *Tagebuch 1895–1899* (1918), and also translated some of the works of Voltaire, *Die Romane und Erzaehlungen*, 2 vols. (1919).

ADD. BIBLIOGRAPHY: K. Petersen, *Ludwig Rubiner. Eine Einf. m. Textausw. u. Bibliogr.* 1980; B. Choluj, "Vom Abstrakten zum konkreten Enthusiasmus. Dargestellt an Ludwig Rubiner, Erich Muehsam und Leonhard Frank," in: K. Sauerland (ed.), *Melancholie und Enthusiasmus,* (1988), 181–94; V. Belentschikow, "Rußlands 'Neuer Mensch' in der Deutung der deutschen Expressionisten. Der Kreis um Pfemfert und Rubiner," in: *Die Welt der Slaven,* 38:2 (1993), 201–213; A. Trevisani, "Lo spazio anelato. Corpo e parola nel 'Tänzer Nijinski' di Ludwig Rubiner," in: *Studi germanici,* 37:1 (1999), 153–162.

[Rudolf Kayser]

RUBINGER, DAVID (1924–), Israeli photojournalist. Born in 1924 in Vienna, Rubinger emigrated to Palestine in 1939, where he later joined the British Army. He worked as a photographer for *Ha-Olam ha-Zeh* (1951–53), and *Yedioth Aharonoth* (1953–54). In 1954 he covered the *Kasztner trial for *Time,* and in 1956 the Suez Campaign for *Life*. In addition to working for *The Jerusalem Post,* including as its picture editor, most of his work since was for *Time* magazine, where he became a contracted photographer. He covered the early story of *aliyah* and Israel's wars. His approach was the human angle such as the *ma'barot* (shanty camps) for immigrants. Rubinger is most remembered for the photograph, shot lying on his back, of three paratroopers at the Western Wall immediately after its capture in the Six-Day War of 1967. Another famous photograph was of the IDF chief military chaplain, Rabbi Shlomo *Goren, blowing the *shofar* at the liberated wall. Informal shots of political leaders like David *Ben-Gurion, Golda *Meir, Menaḥem *Begin, and Yitzchak *Rabin showed the subject's human and informal side. In 1997 he was awarded the Israel Prize in photography.

[Yoel Cohen (2nd ed.)]

RUBINOW, ISAAC MAX (1875–1936), U.S. economist and social worker. Rubinow was born in Grodno, Russia and arrived in New York City in 1893. He qualified at New York Medical College in 1898 but abandoned medical practice in favor of statistics and social work. During service with several U.S. government agencies, Rubinow concentrated on social insurance. Rubinow's efforts on behalf of social insurance brought about his appointment as executive secretary of the Social Insurance Commission of the American Medical Association (AMA) in 1916. However, his efforts to commit the AMA to state health insurance failed.

Rubinow believed that social insurance, national in scope, covering health, unemployment, accidents, and old age, and providing adequate benefits, should replace charity and other forms of voluntary relief. He held that it should provide assistance as a right and thus take care of human needs "without injury to the man's ego and self-respect and that of his fam-

graphic survey of "anti-Zionist" literature in the previous two decades, was published. Its author, Alexander Romanenko, denied the very existence of the Jewish nation, of any Jewish language (either Hebrew or Yiddish), and of Jewish culture. He justified the prerevolutionary pogroms as a manifestation of the class struggle against the Jewish bourgeoisie. The Zionists were also blamed for the Holocaust! According to Romanenko, the Zionists were more dangerous than the Nazis since they had succeeded in defeating the latter and then proceeded, by blackmail and threats, in totally bankrupting the Federal Republic of Germany by forcing it to pay reparations to Israel. This fantastic ideology was regularly foisted off on the Soviet population at Party and trade union meetings, on television, and in the press.

The Jews were also being assigned a demonic role in Russian history, for example, in the vulgar historical novels of Valentin Pikul. A special place in this demonology was reserved for Leon Trotsky, who was depicted (for example, in the novel *Petrograd-Brest* [-Litovsk] by I. Shamiakin) as a symbol of Russia's enemies and described in terms of an anti-Jewish caricature.

One of the aims of the anti-Zionist campaign was to discredit the idea of emigration and to intimidate activists in the growing Jewish national movement in the country. However, despite the jamming of foreign radio stations, a relatively realistic picture of life beyond the "iron curtain" reached Soviet Jews via letters from the thousands of relatives and friends who had already emigrated. This encouraged them to continue the struggle to emigrate.

In an effort to put an end to the refusenik phenomenon, the authorities initially allowed some of the leaders to emigrate. This tactic backfired by increasing the number of activists. Then repression became the order of the day. Special KGB groups were assigned to monitor Jewish activity. They bugged telephone conversations, opened letters, infiltrated informers among the refuseniks, intimidated activists and their families, arranged for some people to be fired from their jobs and for others to be beaten up, and so on. All forms of independent Jewish cultural and public activity were persecuted, including the teaching of Hebrew, the publishing of *samizdat* journals, the organization of kindergartens, the performance of *purim-shpils* (often satirical Purim plays) in private apartments, or public meetings to commemorate the Holocaust. There were frequent searches of apartments and jailings of activists on fabricated charges of anti-Soviet activity and propaganda, slander of the Soviet state, and on trumped-up criminal charges, such as possession of narcotics. Sometimes the people arrested were beaten. Occasionally, activists were placed in special psychiatric hospitals. Yet there was a limit to the persecution: mass arrests were not resorted to. The number of Jewish activists imprisoned at any one time between 1983 and 1986 amounted to about 15, probably representing the quota decided upon by the central authorities. It appeared that the government wanted to maintain a certain low level of Jewish activity with an eye toward negotiations with the West while the KGB was interested in the continuity of such activity in order to justify the existence of their "anti-Zionist" cadres.

In response to the continued accusations from abroad that they were persecuting Jewish culture in the U.S.S.R., the Soviet authorities did sponsor some Jewish cultural enterprises of their choice. A number of these took place far from the large Jewish population centers, in the so-called Jewish autonomous Oblast (province) of Birobidzhan, the 50th anniversary of which was celebrated in 1984. In 1982 a Yiddish textbook was published there in a minuscule print run and permission was granted for an optional course in Yiddish at one of the schools in the province. At the same time, several propaganda booklets were published describing the alleged flourishing of Jewish culture in Birobidzhan. In Lithuania several prose works of Grigorii Kanovich were published on Jewish themes. In 1984 a Russian-Jewish [Yiddish] dictionary was published in Moscow and an evening celebrating the 125th anniversary of the birth of Shalom Aleichem was held at the Union of Soviet Writers.

In March 1985, General Secretary of the Central Committee of the Communist Party of the Soviet Union Mikhail Gorbachev proclaimed *perestroika*, which originally did not envision any change in official Jewish policy. As late as October 1986 Soviet jails still held 13 Jewish activists, five of whom (Roald Zelichenok, Leonid [Arye] Volvovskii, Evgenii Koifman, Vladimir Lifshits, and Aleksei Magarik) were arrested under Gorbachev. However, to succeed in their intended reforms, the Soviet leadership came to realize that they desperately needed foreign policy successes and economic aid from the West, which increasingly were seen to depend on a liberalization of their policy toward Soviet Jewry.

The Refusenik Community. From the early 1980s, Soviet Jews found themselves in a hopeless situation. Their social status continued to decline; antisemitism prevented them from fully assimilating; almost all expressions of Jewish life were banned; and at the same time permission to emigrate was denied. The response to this situation was the growth of illegal, independent Jewish cultural activity, which was almost completely centered around the refuseniks. The first stirrings of public and cultural activity were felt among the *aliyah* activists in the 1970s. However, only the long period of hiatus in emigration allowed the Jewish movement the opportunity to attain an unprecedented breadth, stability, and continuity of leadership. Often, the veteran refuseniks best known in the West, particularly those who had been imprisoned, ceased playing a leading role but became symbols of the struggle and spokesmen of the movement to the foreign media. New less-known enthusiasts assumed an active role in the organizational, political, and cultural spheres. Veteran leaders, who returned to an active role after being released from prison, could be rearrested. Thus, in November 1982, Iosif Begun was imprisoned for the third time.

During their years of "refusal," activists gained experience and knowledge, proved their mettle in confrontations with the authorities, and established contacts with comrades in other communities. They also amassed an unprecedented amount of Jewish cultural material such as books, textbooks, and religious objects. Interested Jews were able to attend underground classes in Hebrew, Jewish culture, history, and religion, and to enjoy Jewish dramatic productions in private homes. There were activities for children as well. Channels were established for exchanges of information with Israel and the organizations for the rights of Soviet Jewry operating in the West. Thus, any persecution of refuseniks soon became known throughout the world. Those who were arrested (and their families) gained effective legal, medical, and material aid, as well as moral support. Jailed *aliyah* activists, referred to as "prisoners of Zion," knew that they were not abandoned; this often gave them the strength to avoid mental breakdowns and public recantations. Their sense of community helped refuseniks to compensate for the infringement of their rights and their pariah status.

Hebrew teaching occupied a key role in the Jewish movement. Moscow was the center of Hebrew instruction where long-range programs were elaborated, accelerated teacher training organized for teachers from other locations, and teaching materials reproduced and disseminated. Iulii Kosharovskii was one of the main organizers of the teaching network. Teachers of Hebrew, who received special support for their efforts from Israel, became a main target for persecution; they constituted about half the prisoners of Zion. In Moscow alone, the Hebrew teachers Alexander Kholmianskii, Iulii Edelshtein, Leonid Volvovskii, and Aleksei Magarik were arrested between 1984 and 1986.

In Leningrad, starting in late 1979, the center for the Jewish movement was the historical and cultural seminars headed by Grigorii Kanovich (not to be confused with the Lithuanian writer) and Lev Utevskii. In an attempt to halt the seminars, the authorities gave permission for both leaders to emigrate. At the same time a series of roundups of participants in the seminars took place. Activist Evgenii Lein was arrested in May 1981. After a year-long struggle to maintain the seminars, which had been open to all interested parties, the seminars succumbed. However, a group made up of amateur Jewish historians survived for five more years. Works by members of this group were published in *Leningradskii evreiskii almanakh* (see "The Jewish Press"). An attempt in 1985 to renew popular lectures on Jewish culture in Leningrad ended with the arrest of the organizers, Roald Zelichenok and Vladimir Lifshits.

In contrast to Leningrad, where Jewish history was practically exclusively the domain of refuseniks, Moscow was the site of some permitted Jewish scholarship headed by the professional ethnographers Mikhail Chlenov and Igor Krupnik. In January 1982 there was an announcement of the formation, in conjunction with the journal *Sovetish Heymland*, of a Jewish Historical and Ethnographic Commission. The members of the commission hoped to be able to publish their research without interference. However, the ban on almost everything Jewish often compelled the scholars to restrict themselves to peripheral topics of little social relevance, such as the derivation of Jewish family names and descriptions of small subethnic Jewish groups in the Soviet Union.

The celebration of traditional Jewish holidays and Israel's Independence Day became a widespread expression of national solidarity. In a number of cities, Purim was the occasion for the private performance of *purimshpils*, where sharp criticism of the authorities was often presented in disguised form. It is not surprising that the latter activity was particularly subject to government repression.

Another indicator of the growth of national consciousness among Soviet Jews was the public meetings commemorating the mass murder of Jews during World War II. Such meetings were held in Riga at Rumbula forest, in Vilnius at Ponari, in Kiev at Babi Yar, and in Leningrad at the Jewish Preobrazhenskii Cemetery.

The 1980s saw an increased interest in Orthodox Judaism, which had been among the most slandered and persecuted of all the religions in the U.S.S.R. In the course of previous decades, Jewish religious education had suffered particularly. There was only a handful of rabbis, *mohalim* (circumcisors), and *shoḥetim* (ritual slaughterers who provided *kasher* meat) in the whole U.S.S.R. There was no way, either legally or practically, that such knowledgeable Jews could be replaced. Simple Jews who know how to pray were a dying breed. Often Jewish intellectuals who were God-seekers turned to the Russian Orthodox religion due to their lack of familiarity with their own roots.

In the 1980s in Moscow, Leningrad, and subsequently in other places, informal groups of young people who wanted to study Torah and Jewish tradition were established. Some of the participants became *ḥozrim bi-teshuvah* or "returners to religion." The original impetus for this religious revival was Zionist activity among the refuseniks, which first brought Jews together and provided them with basic knowledge, particularly of Hebrew, without which a mastery of the tradition is hardly possible. The Jewish religious awakening was made possible materially due to the fact that some of the aid from abroad to refuseniks included religious literature, religious objects, and *kasher* food. In the mid-1980s, there were up to 2,000 newly-observant Orthodox Jews, half of whom resided in Moscow and one fifth in Leningrad. Despite its relatively small core, the religious community had some impact on a broader range of Jews and even led to the conversion to Judaism of some non-Jews, a unique phenomenon in Soviet history. The religious stream within the total Jewish movement among Soviet Jewry was diminished in 1986–1987 with the emigration of a large segment of the newly religious Jews, including their young leadership.

The religious groups were basically divided into Chabad, Agudat Israel, and religious Zionists. In Moscow religious activity originally centered around Vladimir Shakhnovskii, Mikhail Nudler, and Eliahu Essas (Agudat Israel), Mikhail Shnaider and Grigorii Rozenshtein (Chabad), and Vladislav Dasheskii, Pinkhas Polonskii, Mikhail Karaevano, and Kholmianskii (the religious Zionists). Leningrad with the religious leaders Itzhak Kogan (Chabad) and Grigorii Vasserman (Agudat Israel) lacked the religious Zionist orientation.

Although the Jewish movement in the 1980s included in its ranks only several thousand people, in the atmosphere of fear that dominated the Soviet Union at that time, it was virtually the only mass opposition movement in the country. It was not exclusively Zionist. Participation in illegal Jewish activity during their years of refusal, however, increased activists' national consciousness and instilled in many the desire to go straight to Israel as soon as they were free to leave. Many activists after their emigration joined Jewish organizations in Israel and the West (especially in the U.S.), and continued to study and teach Jewish history, Hebrew, and the Jewish religion. A number of books written in refusal have now been published (mostly in Israel). Among them are *Ivrit* ("Hebrew") by Leonid Zeilinger; *Sinagoga-razgromlennaia no nepokorennaia* ("The Synagogue – shattered but unconquered") by Semen Iantovskii (book appeared under the pseudonym of Israel Taiar); *Evrei v Peterburge* (*The Jews of St. Petersburg* [published in Russian and in English]) by Mikhail Beizer; *Delo Dreifusa* ("The Dreyfus Case") by Leonid Praisman; and *Ani Maamin* (*Ia veriu*) ("I Believe") by Mikhail Shnaider and Grigorii Rozenshtein.

Soviet Jewry and the West. The Soviet Jewry movement would never have become an international issue had it not been for support from abroad. The following factors were involved in the struggle in the West: Israel's interest in mass immigration, which reflected both Zionist ideology and Israel's demographic problem; the desire of Western, especially American, Jewish leaders to rally Diaspora Jewry around a goal of importance for the whole Jewish people; the tendency of the American administration to utilize "human rights" and, particularly, the struggle of Soviet Jews for the right to emigrate, as a basic weapon in its ideological confrontation with Communism.

Special organizations were established in the West for the struggle for Soviet Jewry. These included the National Conference on Soviet Jewry, the Student Struggle for Soviet Jewry, the Union of Councils for Soviet Jewry, in the United States, and in Britain the Committee of 35. The organizing center in Israel was the Liaison Bureau for Soviet Jewry of the Foreign Ministry. The Bureau collected information about Soviet Jews, sent them literature and material aid, organized support from the Jewish and international press, and, on occasion, coordinated international protest campaigns in defense of prisoners of Zion and the right of emigration for Soviet Jews. Most aid from the Bureau was given to those refuseniks, especially teachers of Hebrew, who aspired to *aliyah*. Israel regularly provided up-to-date information about emigration statistics, the level of state antisemitism, persecution of Hebrew, and the suffering of prisoners of Zion to both Jewish and non-Jewish organizations active in the struggle, as well as to political and social figures. Hundreds of foreign tourists who visited Moscow, Leningrad, and other open cities in the U.S.S.R. were in fact voluntary emissaries of international Jewish organizations or, sometimes, Israeli citizens with dual nationality sent by the Liaison Bureau, to bring in books, *kasher* food, clothing, and other goods, to provide moral support, to give lectures on Jewish history, to share Sabbaths and holidays with their fellow Jews, and to bring back to the West fresh information, texts of protests and appeals, along with various requests for the refuseniks.

The tourists who made contact with Soviet Jewry were often halted by the authorities, searched, subjected to harassment and intimidation, and expelled from the country before the end of their visit; sometimes they were beaten by KGB agents. The Soviet authorities prevented former Israel president Ephraim Katzir, who was visiting the U.S.S.R. as part of a scientific delegation, from meeting with refuseniks. However, even during the most difficult times, the flow of visitors did not cease.

The Public Council for Soviet Jewry (headed by Avraham Harman) supported by the Israeli government was founded in 1970. In the 1980s, a kind of rival to the council, the Soviet Jewry Education and Information Center (headed by the former refusenik and prisoner of Zion Yosef Mendelevich), was established in affiliation with the American Union of Councils. It favored a strategy of public protest while the more moderate National Conference and the Israeli Liaison Bureau pursued a policy of quiet diplomacy.

Due to the efforts of Jewish organizations, the question of the rights of Soviet Jewry gained exposure in parliamentary discussions and in election campaigns in Western democracies. The issue was increasingly raised during intergovernmental contacts with the Soviet government and in the mid-1980s became a focus of demands made on the Soviet Union. In the American congress speeches were often to be heard about refuseniks and prisoners of Zion such as Anatoly Shcharansky, Iosif Begun, and Ida Nudel. When visiting the U.S.S.R., many senators and congressmen met with Jewish activists. U.S. president Reagan and British prime minister Thatcher spoke out in support of the struggle for Soviet Jewry and the issue was also raised in the European Parliament. The International Association of Lawyers encouraged legal experts to provide aid to persecuted and arrested Jews. The situation of individual Soviet Jews was taken up by professional associations in the West, particularly the international scientists' committee which took up the cause of refusenik scientists, including Victor Brailovskii, Alexander Paritskii, and Yurii Tarnopolskii. In New York mass marches and public meetings, which attracted up to 100,000 people, began in 1982.

The well-known British historian Martin Gilbert visited Moscow and Leningrad in 1983 and interviewed a number of leading refuseniks. Although some of the material he collected was confiscated by customs authorities when he was leaving, one year later he published The *Jews of Hope*, which due to his fresh eyewitness point of view and the author's reputation, had considerable influence in mobilizing public support for Soviet Jewry in English-speaking countries and Israel (where the book appeared in Hebrew).

A key event in the struggle was the Third World Conference for Soviet Jewry held in March 1983. The preceding conferences were held in Brussels in 1971 and 1976. The choice of Jerusalem as the location for the third one signified the central role of Israel in the struggle.

Originally the Israeli government had preferred to remain in the background so that the issue of Soviet Jewry would be seen not as a parochial problem but as a universal issue of the violation of human rights. Not wishing to complicate the already difficult position of Jewish activists in the U.S.S.R., Israel avoided criticizing the Soviet Union on issues unconnected with Jewish concerns. Tourists sent to the U.S.S.R. by the Liaison Bureau were forbidden to say that they were from Israel and told to travel on second passports. Although following these instructions made the visits less dangerous for the emissaries, this practice gave some Soviet Jewish activists the false impression that they were of more concern to their Western brothers than to the Israelis.

The inclusion of the issue of Soviet Jewry in the agenda of the American-Soviet summit conference in Reykjavik in October 1986 was a considerable achievement. The Soviet delegation there was presented with a list, compiled in Israel, of the names, addresses, and dates of refusal of the many members of the Jewish refusenik community in the U.S.S.R.

The continuing struggle harmed the international reputation of the U.S.S.R., especially after it signed the Helsinki Accords on human rights. On the other hand, the Soviet Union did gain from the international furor. It allowed the Soviets to raise the price on its "merchandise" of Jewish hostages, for example allowing them to exchange individual Jews for Soviet spies caught by the West (as it happened with Anatoly Shcharansky in February 1986) and to use the issue of Soviet Jewry – in terms of a possible concession on the Soviet side in return for American concessions – in its negotiations with the U.S. on limiting strategic and nuclear weapons.

PERESTROIKA AND GLASNOST. *Changes in Official Policy and in the Social Status of Soviet Jewry.* The primary goal of the policy of *perestroika* was originally to help the Soviet Union emerge from its economic crisis by allowing a degree of democratization, permitting the holding of small private and cooperative property, the weakening of centralization and Party control in the periphery, and the broad encouragement of initiative on the part of the Soviet population. The latter were to be mobilized by granting them a number of civil rights entailing freedom of speech, public organization, and freedom of cultural life (*glasnost*). Owing to the difficulties of overcoming social inertia and to the opposition of the entrenched bureaucracy, *perestroika* only began to be felt by the public in early 1987. By late 1989 the changes assumed a character unforeseen by the architects of the policy.

Despite the authorities' intentions, *glasnost* was utilized by the peoples of the U.S.S.R. to promote their national aspirations. With the unprecedented burgeoning of national movements that threatened the Soviet Union itself, the issue of the right of Soviet Jews to free emigration and national cultural expression – which had been a major concern of Western public opinion in the 1980s – was no longer so major. At this time of domestic turmoil the Soviet government decided to make concessions on Soviet Jews within the framework of the broadening of civil rights and in exchange for political and economic support from the West.

In January 1987 a new government decree came into effect that regulated entrance into and exit from the U.S.S.R. The decree granted the right to emigrate only for family reunification with close relatives abroad. Still it was an advance, since Soviet emigration procedures were now embodied in law rather than secret government directives. The number of exit visas granted increased each month and in May OVIR began accepting applications to emigrate from people who did not have close relatives abroad. The same year saw applications also accepted for reunification with relatives in countries other than Israel. This change in policy raised the problem of "dropouts" or those Jewish emigrants who, from the Israeli perspective, denied their tie to the Jewish homeland and chose other destinations.

An indication of a new policy toward emigration was the uncharacteristically mild reaction to the March 1987 demonstration of seven refuseniks in Leningrad. As a result of the demonstration one participant received permission to emigrate while a photograph of the whole group appeared in a local Leningrad newspaper.

Early in the same year several Jewish activists were released from prison before serving their full terms.

The curtailment of the Party's anti-Zionist campaign, a major turnabout, was first signaled by criticism in the journal *Voprosy istorii KPSS* (No. 1, 1987) of Romanenko's *On the Class Essence of Zionism* (see above).

The end came to the ban on importation of Jewish religious literature, Hebrew textbooks, and books on Judaism. The long-standing Soviet domestic policy of proscribing national cultural activity outside the borders of officially designated national regions was rejected in July 1988 when the 19th CPSU Congress passed a resolution granting ethnic groups the right to satisfy their cultural and religious needs throughout the Soviet Union. This change of policy was particularly important for the Jews, almost all of whom live outside their supposed national region, the so-called Jewish Autonomous Oblast in Birobidzhan. One consequence of this new policy was the appearance of many independent Jewish culture associations in all parts of the country. With the simultaneous removal of the ban on discussion in the media of all issues relating to Jews, the number of publications and broadcasts on Jewish topics increased astronomically. The majority of them dealt with domestic concerns rather than the previously common condemnations of Israel. Furthermore, events in the Middle East began to be treated by Soviet journalists in a more objective manner, with Soviet coverage occasionally appearing to be more pro-Israeli than that in the West.

In 1988–1989 almost all remaining veteran refuseniks were given permission to emigrate and the emigration process itself was considerably simplified. The authorities practically ceased persecuting, or even condemning, those who wished to emigrate. Former Soviet citizens living in Israel and the United States, including former Jewish activists, were allowed the possibility of visiting their former homeland without hindrance. Previously minuscule, permitted tourism of Soviet Jews abroad, including to Israel, began to develop. The 1991 law on entrance to and exit from the U.S.S.R. not only guaranteed the right of all Soviet citizens to travel abroad but also allowed people to emigrate permanently without losing their Soviet passports (as was previously the case with emigrants who "repatriated" to Israel). It also specified timetables and procedures for handling emigration documents so that Soviet emigration legislation finally corresponded with international norms.

Cultural ties between the Soviet Union and Israel began to flourish and, soon thereafter, economic cooperation as well. A series of bilateral diplomatic contacts led in December 1990 to the exchange of consular delegations and one year later to the establishment of full diplomatic relations. The Soviet ambassador to Israel, Alexander Bovin, was the last emissary named by Gorbachev before the formal liquidation of the U.S.S.R. and he remained as the Russian ambassador.

Changes occurred also in the social status and employment profile of Soviet Jewry. Secret restrictions on the acceptance of Jews into institutions of higher education, graduate study, prestigious work, and so on were withdrawn. Jews increasingly appeared among Soviet scientists and cultural figures visiting the West and Israel. Although their numbers hardly increased in the top echelons of Soviet power – the Central Committee of the Communist Party, the government, the army high command, and the diplomatic corps – the number of Jews in secondary positions rose, for example, among government advisers.

There was a perceptible increase in the activity of Jews in social and political life, where a majority of such activists belonged to the liberal democratic forces. Fifteen Jews were elected to the national congress of People's Deputies of the U.S.S.R. in 1989. The following year 15 Jews passed the first round of elections in the RSFSR, and 9 of them actually became deputies to the Russian Congress of People's Deputies. Some Jews, especially in the Russian hinterland, were elected to local city and all-Russian government councils. Jews actively participated in the fights for the general democratization of the Soviet Union, the rights of national minorities, liberalization of the economy, and protection of the environment. There were many Jews among the radically oriented journalists. However, in rare cases, Jews such as the secretary of the board of the Writers' Union of Russia, Anatolii Salutskii, supported Russian nationalist trends.

Jewish Life. During the period of *glasnost,* Jewish social and cultural life came to involve many people throughout Russia and the other Soviet republics. This activity was influenced both by the increase of national consciousness among other peoples in the U.S.S.R. and by the growing contacts between Soviet Jews and Israel.

On May 21–22, 1989, a meeting of 120 people representing approximately 50 Jewish social and cultural organizations from 34 Soviet cities took place in Riga. The final document adopted by participants expressed their determination to defend the rights of Soviet Jews to free emigration to Israel and to cultural autonomy within the Soviet Union. The delegates called for the establishment of diplomatic relations between the U.S.S.R. and Israel and the repeal of UN Resolution 3379 which equated Zionism with racism. In the same year 490 delegates took part in a congress of Lithuanian Jews, which elected a Council of Jewish Communities of the republic.

A congress of Jewish community organizations from all over the country took place in Moscow in December 1989. Delegates from approximately 200 bodies and many guests from abroad, including the chairman of the Jewish Agency, Simcha Dinitz, were present. A national umbrella organization – the Council of Jewish Culture Associations of the U.S.S.R. (Vaad) – was established with three co-chairmen, Mikhail Chlenov (Moscow), Yosef Zisels (Chernovtsy), and Samuil Zilberg (Riga). After the dissolution of the U.S.S.R., a Russian Vaad was established at a congress in Nizhni Novgorod in April 1992.

Official, i.e., state-promoted, Jewish figures who, before *perestroika*, had exercised a legal monopoly in representing Soviet Jewry found themselves forced to compete with independent Jewish organizations. One example of the ill-fated effort by these court Jews to sustain their influence took place in early 1989 when a group of people close to the editor of *Sovetish Heymland* founded the short-lived Association of Activists and Friends of Jewish Culture.

Both the leaders of Vaad and the "official" Jewish spokesmen became involved in efforts to resolve the Middle East conflict. With this aim in April 1990 Mikhail Chlenov met with PLO executive committee member, Abu Mazen, while in July former members of the Soviet Public Anti-Zionist Committee announced the establishment of a Peace Today committee (ostensibly on the model of the Israeli Peace Now organization), with its stated goal of facilitating Jewish-Arab dialogue. The second congress of Vaad in January 1991 condemned contacts between the Soviet government and the PLO.

During the August 1991 crisis, Vaad chairman Chlenov did not openly criticize the coup leaders but restricted himself to an expression of concern about the future of Jewish organizations, the possible curtailment of emigration, and the danger of antisemitism.

In contrast to Vaad, the opposing wing of Jewish public life is composed of those who consider any Jewish activity in the country either unnecessary or actually harmful unless it is directed toward preparing Soviet Jewry for immigration to Israel. In August 1989 the Hebrew teacher Lev Gorodetskii announced the founding in Moscow of the Zionist Organization in the Soviet Union, which soon opened branches in Leningrad, Riga, Vilnius, Kiev, and Kharkov. Many Zionist youths groups, such as Ha-Shomer ha-Ẓa'ir, Dror, Betar, Maccabi, and Rabim, also began functioning.

A significant feature in Jewish life was the commemoration of the Jewish victims of the Holocaust on the territory of the Soviet Union. This involved groups of Jewish veterans of World War II and concentration camp survivors. In Riga, Vilnius, Leningrad, Minsk, and many other sites, on the anniversaries of mass executions of Jews there, and even in cities which the Nazis did not occupy, increasing numbers of Soviet Jews had been gathering for memorial meetings on Holocaust and Heroism Day (the anniversary of the Warsaw Ghetto uprising). In September 1989 official permission was granted for the first time for such a meeting at *Babi Yar, organized by the Kiev Jewish community. Among the participants were local Party and government officials, leaders of the Ukrainian national movement, and the Church. Finally, after many years, an inscription was placed on the monument indicating, in Russian and in Yiddish, that Jews were the main victims at Babi Yar.

By late 1989, there were almost 200 Jewish associations, clubs, and culture centers in, among other places: Tallinn, Riga, Vilnius, Leningrad, Cheliabinsk, Tashkent, Donetsk, Baku, Kharkov, Lvov, Chernovtsy, Kiev, Kishinev, Odessa, Minsk, Bobruisk, and Krasnoyarsk. Kiev in late 1989 had 12 different Jewish organizations, including cultural, religious, and even musical groups. In Kishinev the Menora cooperative was established in April 1989; there hundreds of people have studied Hebrew and the fundamentals of Judaism. Tbilisi even granted official recognition to the Aviv association whose goal was to prepare Jews for *aliyah*. Riga Jews have (since July 1988) a culture association, a Yiddish school, and a society for Latvian-Israeli friendship while Vilnius has its own culture association and branches of Betar, B'nai B'rith, and Maccabi.

The greatest number of Jewish culture organizations were concentrated in Moscow. These included: *Iggud morim* (the Association of Teachers of Hebrew, founded 1988), the Association for Friendship and Cultural Ties with Israel (abbreviated ODISKI, summer 1988), the Moscow Jewish Culture and Education Association (MEKPO, September 1987), the Jewish Culture Association, the Gesher youth association, and the Youth Center for Studying and Developing Jewish Culture (abbreviated MTS-IRK, 1988). Early 1988 saw the opening of the Solomon Mikhoels Jewish Culture Center and the Shalom Jewish Culture Center.

Efforts were undertaken to encourage the teaching and study of Jewish studies in the Soviet Union and, after 1991, in its successor, the Commonwealth of Independent States (CIS). Seminars and conferences on Jewish history with the participation of foreign scholars were inaugurated in Moscow and elsewhere.

Jewish religious life ceased to be persecuted. In February 1989, at the initiative of the Israeli rabbi and scholar Adin Steinsaltz, a yeshivah, under the official name of the Center for the Study of Judaism, was established with the Academy of Sciences of the U.S.S.R. Other yeshivot and Torah-study groups sprang up in a number of cities. Among the teachers were a number of Lubavitch Ḥasidim from Israel, who had formerly been Soviet citizens.

Owing to the lack of trained rabbis, except in Moscow and Leningrad/St. Petersburg, some American rabbis began serving as the spiritual leaders of the main republic synagogues. The national-religious stream in Judaism was represented by Maḥanaim (Hebrew for "two camps"), which had centers in Moscow and Jerusalem. The Bnei Akiva Orthodox Jewish youth movement became active in several localities, and in April 1990, for the first time, a progressive (Reform) group, Ineni (Hebrew *Hineni* or "here I am") was registered in Moscow. Camp Ramah, of the Conservative movement, also began to operate. In 1990–1991 Jewish religious holidays were celebrated in public places, including the Palace of Congresses in the Kremlin! Starting in 1992, Russian television began broadcasting programs on basic tenets of Judaism. A number of synagogues confiscated under Stalin were returned to their communities. Nonetheless, it would still be premature to speak of a real religious revival. The majority of newly-observant Jews have been emigrating and the Jewish communities do not have the means to either refurbish or maintain their recently regained synagogues.

In connection with the emigration of many nationally oriented Jews, by early 1990 there had been a decline of interest in Jewish culture in the U.S.S.R. A number of Jewish periodicals had ceased appearing and fewer people attended lectures on Jewish history. Interest not only waned in the recently established libraries of the culture centers and synagogues, but those books in demand were increasingly limited to Hebrew study guides and material on *aliyah* and absorption in Israel. The growth in the number of Jewish organizations was accompanied by a decrease in the membership of each of them. At the same time the Jewish elite intelligentsia remained uninvolved in Jewish life.

Israeli and Western Jewish organizations initiated and supported local Jewish institutions and associations. Consequently, the period of amateurs passed – to be replaced by the growth of a significant group of professional Jewish activists directly or indirectly subsidized from abroad. In this environment of support from abroad organizations proliferated, sometimes duplicating existing ones and occasionally being even basically fictitious. In Moscow alone, in 1992 there were several hundred groups. Soviet Jewry, which lacked the experience of autonomous and self-supporting community life, was not able to support its own institutions on the basis of voluntary contributions. This factor lent a somewhat unstable character to the considerable activity that was indeed taking place.

At the same time, some Jewish organizations in Russia and the republics, first of all Vaad, were attempting to chart an independent course while simultaneously trying to gain influence in the international Jewish bodies which provide some of their financing. In May 1991 Vaad became a member of the World Jewish Congress and also had representatives at the Memorial Foundation for Jewish Culture based in New York. In June 1992 at the 32nd World Zionist Congress in Jerusalem, a Vaad delegation and the Zionist Federation of Russia demanded to be represented in all key bodies of the World Zionist Organization, which did not agree. There was also a conflict between Vaad and the Jewish Agency since the latter's goal for Soviet Jewry is maximum *aliyah*; Vaad was mainly interested in Jewish revival in Russia and would also have liked Jews who emigrate to be viewed as part of a Russian-Jewish cultural community rather than have them seen only as part of their new host communities, e.g., Israel and American Jewry.

EMIGRATION AND ALIYAH. The number of emigrants fell from 51,300 in 1979 to 1,320 in 1983. Then until 1986 the annual number of exit visas granted hovered around 1,000. Already in the banner year 1979 it was obvious that approximately two thirds of the emigrants preferred the United States to Israel as their destination. America automatically granted them the status of refugees persecuted on ethnic or religious grounds. The greater part of those who went directly to the U.S. without trying Israel came from the more assimilated regions of the RSFSR and the Ukraine; a small proportion came from the territories annexed by the Soviet Union during World War II and from non-Ashkenazi Jewish communities. Between 1983 and 1986 the proportion of those who went to the U.S. rather than Israel fluctuated between 59 and 78 percent. This situation was viewed with alarm by those Jewish activists within the Soviet Union who had fought for emigration under the banner of "repatriation" to Israel. The refusenik circles in Moscow and Leningrad then succeeded in somewhat lowering these two cities' proportion of "dropouts," as they were called by Israelis and Israel-oriented activists, in contrast to other centers of assimilation where pressure to consider *aliyah* was less effective.

In 1987 the number of Soviet Jews emigrating was nine times that of the previous year. In 1988 almost 17,000 Soviet Jews took advantage of the increased opportunity to emigrate directly to the U.S., Canada, Australia, and elsewhere rather than Israel.

Processes that increased under *perestroika*, such as the lack of basic commodities, environmental dangers, and the increase of overt antisemitism, encouraged almost everyone to consider emigration. The fact that the gates of emigration were open, combined with the fear that they might close again at any time, moved thousands of Jews from all over the country to leave. The number who emigrated between 1988 and 1990 rose dramatically. The vast majority chose to make their new homes elsewhere than in Israel. In this situation Israel demanded that those Jews who were leaving the Soviet Union on Israeli invitations go only to Israel and that the American government cease granting the status of refugees to Jews who were leaving the U.S.S.R. under the status of repatriates to Israel. After long negotiations on this issue, in October 1989 the American government introduced a quota on immigrants from the U.S.S.R. and ceased automatically granting refugee status to Israeli invitation holders. One result was the closing of the Italian transit camp at Ladispoli, the way station to the U.S. of a large number of Jews from the U.S.S.R. Another was the fundamental redirection of Soviet Jewish emigration. A more objective picture of Israel in the Soviet media and enthusiastic reports about Israel from Soviet tourists who visited that country also led to a sharp increase in the number of Jews emigrating to Israel. In 1990 over 185,000 Soviet Jewish emigrants went to Israel, establishing a record annual rate for immigration to Israel from a single country.

In late 1989 the rate of emigration had been limited by the capacity of Soviet OVIR offices, customs, and transportation facilities and by the rate of dispatch of visas from Israel. Bucharest and Budapest served as transit points. By the summer of 1990, the pressure somewhat declined as the process of sending Israeli visas was speeded up and additional routes to Israel were established via Poland, Czechoslovakia, Finland, and other European countries. These emergency measures considerably increased the flow despite attempts by the Palestine Liberation Organization to sabotage the Hungarian and Polish airlines and the refusal of the Soviet Union to allow direct flights to Israel. However, this last obstacle was removed with the normalization of diplomatic relations between Israel and the U.S.S.R. Direct flights were then inaugurated from Moscow, Leningrad, and some republic capitals to Israel.

In 1991–1992 word of the difficulties of absorption into Israeli life and the growing percentage of non-Jews included in the Jewish emigration as parts of mixed families once again turned a not insignificant proportion of the emigration toward the U.S., Germany, and other countries.

Among the immigrants to Israel, the median age increased annually while the number of children per family decreased. The percentage of non-Jews also increased. These features reflect demographic processes in the country of emigration. Serious problems in the absorption of these immigrants in Israel stem from two basic problems: the gap between their professional profiles and the needs of the Israel economy; the lack of Jewish traditions and knowledge among most of the immigrants.

[Michael Beizer]

In the Russian Federation

Russian Jewry faced a new reality after the breakup of the U.S.S.R. at the end of 1991 and the creation of the Russian Federation, where most of the Jews who remained in the former Soviet Union after the years of mass emigration would continue to live. From the outset, the policy of the Russian government became even more liberal. Direct flights were begun from Moscow and St. Petersburg (the former Leningrad) to Israel. The Russian government even agreed to allow the Jewish Agency to operate in the Soviet Union. In 1992 the vice president of Russia, Alexander Rutskoi, the chairman of the Russian parliament, Ruslan Khasbulatov, and former president of the Soviet Union, Mikhail Gorbachev, all visited Israel.

The 1993–94 period in Russia was characterized by a protracted economic crisis, rampant inflation, decreasing living standards, rising crime rate and political instability. The growing confrontation between the presidency and the conservative legislature led in October 1993 to President Yeltsin's order to dissolve parliament. The armed rebellion by supporters of the parliament was suppressed by forces loyal to the president; about 150 people were killed in the clashes. In the wake of the Parliament insurrection, 15 conservative and radical-right press organs were temporarily suspended by Yeltsin's order.

The parliamentary elections which were held in December 1993 unexpectedly brought an impressive victory to V. Zhirinovsky's Liberal Democratic Party of Russia. In 1991, Zhirinovsky, an aggressive nationalist and chauvinist, who had not been conspicuous before, obtained several million votes and finished third in the presidential election in which Yeltsin triumphed. In 1993 his LDPR captured the second-largest number of seats in the Duma, the lower house. The other big faction in the Duma comprised the Communists and the pro-Communist Agrarian Party. The victory of the hardliners marked a turn to a more conservative approach in government policy, both domestic and foreign.

In December 1994 Russian troops launched an offensive against rebel forces in the breakaway autonomous republic of Chechnya, in the northern Caucasus.

RELATIONS BETWEEN RUSSIA AND ISRAEL. After the dissolution of the U.S.S.R., Russia succeeded the Soviet Union in many matters concerning the Middle East. The former embassy of the U.S.S.R. in Israel, with Alexandr Bovin as ambassador, became the embassy of the Russian Federation.

Normal relations continued between the two countries during the 1992–93 period. Russian authorities did not hinder activities of Israeli organizations, nor of the Jewish Agency in Russia. Economic and scientific cooperation developed between Russia and Israel. Israeli Aircraft Industries and the Aerospace Design Office of Russia launched the joint project of the Galaxy plane. In December 1994, the first meeting of the Joint Russian-Israeli Commission on Scientific and Technical Cooperation took place in Moscow; a number of other joint projects were discussed, e.g., in such areas as telecommunication systems, medical technology, and environment protection.

In April 1994, Israel Prime Minister Yiẓḥak Rabin visited Moscow officially, and in the following years relations between the two countries remained friendly, with Prime Minister Ehud Barak visiting Moscow in 2000 and President Vladimir Putin visiting Israel in 2005. With Russia embroiled in largely Muslim Chechnya, its standing in the Arab world declined and it found itself aligned with Israel in the war against Arab terrorism. At the same time, Russian missile sales to Syria and aid to Iran's nuclear program were sources of friction between the two countries. Not insignificant in the close relations between the two countries was the existence of a kind of Russian diaspora of a million Russian Jews in Israel. Israeli exports to the Russian Federation were $319 million in 2004 while imports stood at $688 million (two thirds of this was in diamonds).

DEMOGRAPHY. The mass emigration begun in 1989 continued throughout the 1990s, only tailing off in 2002. Estimates based on the last three census returns for the area of the Russian Federation (see Tolts, 2004) show a decline in the "core" (self-declared) Jewish population from 570,000 in 1989 to 409,000 in 1994, and 254,000 in 2002. The figure further dropped to around 243,000 in 2004 (out of a total 395,000 for the former Soviet Union as a whole). In 2002, about half lived in the provinces, a third in Moscow, and a sixth in St. Petersburg. The overwhelming majority of Jews emigrating from the Russian Federation, as well as from the former Soviet Union as a whole, arrived in Israel, though the proportion of actual Jews among Russian emigrants to Israel dropped from 82 percent in 1992 to 43 percent in 2002, largely reflecting mixed marriages. By 2004 about half the "core" Jewish population of the former Soviet Union was living in Israel, a quarter in the FSU, and a quarter in other countries, mostly the United States and Germany.

THE REVIVAL OF JEWISH LIFE. For the Jews who remained behind, in the Russian Federation as well as in the former Soviet Union as a whole, the post-Communist period was one of organizational growth and diversification of Jewish life. The conception of Jewish life broadened; in a legal form, it started in 1989–91 as a cluster of "Jewish Culture Associations" and "Societies for Jewish Culture" in various cities throughout the U.S.S.R.; their aim was limited to the study and preservation of Jewish culture and history. By 1993–94 the network of the primary Jewish organizations in Russia included such bodies as: religious communities, social relief organizations, educational institutes, unions of Jewish war veterans and of the survivors of the Holocaust, research groups, Zionist organizations, branches of the Maccabi organizations, etc. There were, for example, 60 Jewish organizations in St. Petersburg alone in 1994, including: three religious communities – mainstream Orthodox, Chabad and Reform; the Jewish Association of St. Petersburg (JASP, playing the role of an umbrella organization); the Holocaust Research Group, affiliated to the JASP; the Ḥesed Avraham Welfare Center for the elderly; the Eva charity fund; the Children's Fund; local branches of Bnei Akiva, Maccabi and the International Association of Jewish businessmen; the Union of Jewish War Veterans; five day schools, four Sunday schools, four kindergartens and a Jewish university. The question of coordinating their activities was urgent.

There continued to be a cleavage between the organizations aiming to revive diversified Jewish community life in Russia, and the *aliyah*-oriented organizations, which regarded reviving the non-Zionist community as useless and even harmful. The first type of organization was supported by the Joint Distribution Committee (JDC) and, organizationally, by the World Jewish Congress (WJC); the latter by the World Zionist Organization (WZO). The majority of the Jewish organizations set up in Russia in the 1990s have been nonreligious. The head of the Moscow Jewish Religious Community, Vladimir Fedorovsky, complained in an interview to *Mezhdunarodnaia evreiskaia gazeta* in 1993 that the synagogue had ceased to be the center of Jewish life; Jews of Moscow preferred organizations oriented toward Israel and *aliyah*.

The leading body of Russian Jewry was the Council of Jewish Cultural Organizations (Vaad), which was established in April 1992, after the dissolution of the Soviet Union, to succeed the Vaad of the U.S.S.R. Mikhail Chlenov, the former head of the all-Union Vaad, became its chairman, with Roman Spektor as deputy. The Vaad was recognized by the World Jewish Congress; in 1993 its delegation participated in the meeting of the Congress in Washington, together with the representatives of the Ukraine, Belarus, Moldova, Georgia and Uzbekistan; it was the first case in which Russian Jewry and the Jewries of other former Soviet republics were represented at such an assembly. The Eurasian section of the WJC, embracing the Jewish organizations of the CIS, was formed, and Chlenov became its chairman.

Another umbrella organization was set up in February 1993 at the first Congress of Jewish Communities and Organizations in Russia whose purpose was to unite communities of different directions, both Orthodox and liberal. The newly formed body was named the Congress of Jewish Religious Communities and Organizations in Russia (KEROOR; in 1994 its name was shortened to the Congress of Jewish Communities in Russia) and Vladimir Fedorovsky became its president.

An internal split in the Vaad emerged in 1993 and became open in 1994. The conflict flared up over the issue of the structure of the Vaad – whether it should be a federation of Jewish organizations throughout Russia, or of regional federations of Jewish organizations which should be set up, whose supreme coordinating organ would be the Vaad. The roots of the conflict were in fact much deeper; it marked a discontent between the old leadership which depended financially and organizationally on the support of Israel and Western Jewish organizations, and new leaders, businessmen, who partially subsidized Jewish activities in Russia and wanted to influence the Vaad. Besides, unlike the old leaders, who had been political dissidents in the Soviet period and based the Vaad on the pre-1990s underground Jewish network, some of these new leaders had had some administrative experience, and some had even been nominees of the Soviet authorities of 1989–91, and hence had better relations with the authorities in 1993–94.

At the beginning of 1993, there were 32 Jewish communities in Russia. Restitution of synagogues confiscated by the authorities in the Soviet period continued. The network of Jewish education in Russia also grew; seminars and courses for teachers were conducted in Moscow, St. Petersburg, and elsewhere. By the early 21st century, Russia had 17 Jewish day schools, 11 preschools, and 81 supplementary schools with about 7,000 students, as well as four Jewish universities (see below). Chabad had stepped up its presence and made a significant contribution to rebuilding Jewish religious life. In 1998 Russia became part of the newly established Federation of Jewish Communities uniting 15 countries of the former Soviet Union and aiming to revitalize Jewish life, culture, and religion. Berel Lazar of Chabad was chief rabbi of Russia and chairman of the Rabbinical Alliance, founded in 1992 to spearhead religious life in the former Soviet Union. Chabad also founded the Association of Jewish Public Organizations in 2002 as a rival to the Conference of Leaders of Jewish Organizations, affiliated with the Russian Jewish Congress.

THE JEWISH PRESS. At the beginning of the 1980s, the total legal Jewish press in the U.S.S.R. amounted to two publications in Yiddish: the Moscow Jewish monthly journal *Sovetish Heymland* and the Birobidzhan newspaper *Birobidzhaner Shtern*, plus an annual in the Judeo-Tat language, *Vata Sovetimu*. Issued in languages not understood by the majority of Soviet Jews and consisting largely of propaganda, the existence of these publications was intended to demonstrate that "Jewish culture" was permitted in the Soviet Union.

Attempts in refusenik circles to establish illegal publications were strictly repressed and led to the gradual curtailment of all Jewish *samizdat* publishing. *Evrei v SSSR* ("Jews in the U.S.S.R.," Moscow) ceased publication in 1979, *Nash ivrit* ("Our Hebrew," Moscow) in 1980, *Din umetsiiut* ("Justice and Reality," Riga) in 1980, *Evrei sovremennon mire* ("Jews in the Contemporary World," Moscow) in 1981. The Riga journal *Chaim*, which appeared irregularly starting in 1979, could not fill the vacuum due to its minuscule print run and its distance from the main Jewish centers. An exception was *Leningradskii evreiskii almanakh* ("Leningrad Jewish Almanac," abbreviated LEA) which first came out in late 1982, at the height of the repressions, and succeeded in appearing regularly from 1984 to 1989. This publication focused on cultural and historical articles written by Leningrad refuseniks. Due to the size of its print run (up to 200, which was large for a *samizdat* publication) and its effective system of distribution, LEA succeeded in reaching distant corners of the country and in demonstrating the need for an independent Jewish press.

Change came with the beginning of the general liberalization in the country. In 1987–1988 several Moscow *samizdat* journals appeared. There were *Evreiskii istoricheskii almankah* ("Jewish Historical Almanac") and *Shalom* with their cultural orientation, and several publications dealing with such topics as *aliyah* and absorption in Israel: *Informatsionnyi biulleten po problemam repatriatsii i evreiskoi kultury* ("Information Bulletin of Problems of Repatriation and Jewish Culture"), *Paneninu le-Israel* ("Looking towards Israel"), and *Problemy otkaza v vyezde iz strany* ("Problems of Refusal Regarding Exit from the Country").

There was also a revolution in terms of the technology of publication. While the first illegal publications were typed in multiple copies (occasionally copies were made via photography), the *samizdat* publications of the transitional period were produced on personal computers from abroad and photocopied so that print runs were dramatically increased. Several publications were printed in Israel and sent back to the Soviet Union for distribution. In December 1988 the first legally permitted independent Jewish newspaper, *Khash-akhar*, was issued in Tallinn by the local Jewish culture association. This publication was typeset and appeared not only in Estonian, but also in Russian, which made it accessible to almost all of Soviet Jewry. Its print run was over 1,000 and it soon gained a reputation throughout the country.

In Moscow in April 1989 the authorities launched the semiofficial *Vestnkik evreiskoi sovetskoi kultury* ("Herald of Soviet Jewish Culture," abbreviated VESK) in an attempt to compete with the independent Jewish press. After a year which saw a change of editor and of name – to *Evreiskaia gazeta* ("Jewish Newspaper") – this publication gained more of an independent status.

In Riga in March 1990, there appeared *Vestnik evreiskoi kultury* ("Herald of Jewish Culture," VEK). In 1990 Jewish newspapers in Russian with real Jewish content began to appear in Kiev (*Vozrozhdenie*, "Revival"), Leningrad (*Narod moi*, "My People"), Kishinev (*Nash golos*, "Our Voice"), Tashkent (*Mizrakh*, "Orient"), Moscow (*Menora*), Vilnius (*Litovskii Ierusalim*, "Jerusalem of Lithuania"), and elsewhere. These newspapers all gained legal status while those which were issued without permission ceased being persecuted. Thus the distinction between *samizdat* and permitted publications was erased.

Sovetish Heymland softened its hard-line policy and began to publish more cultural and historical material. In 1990–1991 the former editor of *Birobidzhaner Shtern*, Leonid Shkolnik, began the independent newspaper *Vzgliad* ("View"), which included many items of Jewish interest.

The geographical distribution and sharply increased print runs, the increased scope of topics treated, and the widely understood Russian language of the majority of publications have made the new Jewish press a significant factor in the formation of Jewish national consciousness and a source of elementary Jewish knowledge for many thousands of people. The press has also become a source of information about emigration and *aliyah*, and both a mirror and monitor of Jewish life in the country. The very fact of the legalization of the Jewish press has made a deep impression on the average Jews who saw that it was no longer necessary to fear public expression of Jewish life.

However, there is also a negative side to the picture. A number of Jewish periodicals ceased publication after their first issues. Few managed to appear more frequently than once a month and the promised periodicity was often not maintained. The professional level of the Jewish press was frequently low. Articles on Jewish culture and history were often reprints or translations from abroad. Factual errors reflecting a lack of basic knowledge of Jewish traditions, Jewish history, and Hebrew among both authors and editors appeared in many articles. These problems stemmed from the lack of publishing experience of those involved, the lack of qualified authors with some Jewish expertise, the difficulties of publication in the Soviet Union, and the considerable turnover of staff as active members of Jewish culture associations often emigrated.

In 1989 the Jewish press consisted of at least 30 publications; more than half of these appeared in Russia, the majority of them in Moscow. Over the following three years, due to the growing role of the Jewish press in the Ukraine, the undisputed dominance of Russia declined while Moscow continued to dominate the scene in Russia. Late 1991 saw the demise of *Sovetish Heymland*. In the same year, at least 50 Jewish newspapers and journals appeared, with at least one in practically every republic and some in cities in the hinterland. The Jewish press of the CIS represents a whole range of religious and political orientations, with Israeli and Western organizations sometimes supporting publications which favor their policies. This latter factor suggests some doubts not only about the spontaneity of the Jewish publication boom as well as its actual scope but also about its future.

By 1990–91 there were 47 periodicals published in Russia (among them, 26 in Moscow). In 1992–93 their number shrank to 28 (17 in Moscow). This decline may be attributed to the large-scale emigration of Russian Jews, and to growing economic hardships accompanied by a sharp rise in publishing costs. Only those publications had a chance to survive which received financial support from abroad – either from Israel, or from Diaspora, mainly North American, Jewish organizations.

The most influential and widely circulating Jewish newspaper in Russia was *Mezhdunarodnaia evreiskaia gazeta* ("The International Jewish Newspaper"), the successor of VESK (see above), which made efforts to mirror not only Russian-Jewish life, but also Jewish life in the entire area of the former Soviet Union. The paper was published in Moscow, twice a month, by Tankred Golenpolskii and Eliezer Feldman. The most popular Jewish newspaper in St. Petersburg continued to be *Narod moi – Ami*, published by the Jewish Association of St. Petersburg, also twice a month. In the northern Caucasus region, the most conspicuous newspaper was *Vatan-Rodina* ("The Homeland"), published twice a week by Mikhail Gavrielov in Derbent, Daghestan, in Judeo-Tat (the language of the Mountain Jews) and Russian. Among other relatively widely circulating newspapers were: *Tarbut* ("Culture," in Samara, formerly Kuibyshev), *Stern-Zvezda* ("The Star," in Ekaterinburg, formerly Sverdlovsk), and from July 1993 on, *Gazeta evreev Severnovo Kavkaza* ("The Newspaper of the Jews in the North Caucasus," Nalchik, Karbardino-Balkaria). The *Birobidzhaner Shtern* ("The Birobidzhan Star") continued to be published in Yiddish and Russian in the Jewish Autonomous Region. The magazine *Sovetish Heymland* in 1993 changed its title to *Di Yiddishe Gass* ("The Jewish Street") and continued to appear in Russian and Yiddish. Papers were published by Jewish organizations abroad e.g., *Rodnik* ("The

Spring," or "Source," by the World Union of Progressive Judaism), *Lekhaim* ("To Life," by the international Jewish organization Chabad-Lubavitch), and several papers, by the Jewish Agency. Jewish newspapers were also issued in Briansk, Novosibirsk, and Perm. Two academic Jewish journals were published: *Vestnik Evreiskovo Universiteta v Moskve* ("Herald of the Moscow Jewish University"), from 1992 on, and *Vreiskaia Shkola* ("Jewish School"), issued by the St. Petersburg University, both supported by the JDC.

ACADEMIC LIFE. One of the most remarkable developments in Russia (as well as in some other countries of the CIS) in the field of Jewish life was the emerging and broadening of Jewish higher education and Jewish studies.The Moscow Jewish University has been functioning since 1991; in 1993 it gained official status, i.e., the right to give officially recognized university degrees to its graduates. In 1990, the St. Petersburg Jewish University was established; in 1994 it gained the right to give degrees in philology. Departments of Jewish Studies were opened in some old established universities: courses in Judaic studies were established at Moscow State University in 1993; the School for the Comparative Study of Religions, including Judaism, was set up in the Russian State Humanitarian University in Moscow.

ANTISEMITISM AND THE JEWISH QUESTION. During the years of *perestroika,* covert but effective state and bureaucratic antisemitism gradually declined while there was a rise in grass-roots anti-Jewish trends. The protracted economic crisis and weakening of the central authority produced populist spokesmen who found it easier to cast blame for all the failures of the country, past and present, on various ethnic groups, especially the Jews, than to offer practical solutions for the dire straits of the country. One factor feeding antisemitism was envy stemming from the reality that Jews could emigrate while for Russians this way out was basically barred. Further oil on the flame was the fact that Jews could now visit relatives abroad and receive material aid from them.

With *glasnost* Soviet Jewry began encountering overt antisemitism in the press and on television, in the pamphlets of political parties, in conversations at work places, on the street and on public transport. Antisemitic parties and organizations sprang up like mushrooms. These included: Pamiat (Memory), Rossy (the [Original] Russians), Patriot, Rodina (Homeland), Otechestvo (Fatherland), Nationalnodemokraticheskaia partiia (National Democratic Party), Russkii nationalno-patrioticheskii tsentr (the Russian National Patriotic Center), Soius russikh ofitserov (the Union of Russian Officers), and Republikanskaia narodnaia partiia Rossii (the Republic People's Party of Russia). The year 1989 saw the establishment of the neo-Communist movement Obediennyi front trudiashchikhsia R.S.F.S.R. (the United Front of the Workers of the R.S.F.S.R.) and in 1991 its spinoff, Rossiiskaia kommunisticheskaia rabochaia partiia (the Russian Communist Workers' Party), which espoused antisemitism as an organic part of their ideology. About this time Vladimir Zhirinovskii became leader of the rightist populist group which called itself Liberalno-demokraticheskaia partiia Rossii (the Liberal Democratic Party of Russia).

The Pamiat Association, originally a conservative movement concerned about the preservation of Russia's past and its environment, became more nationalistic in 1984 when its leadership was taken over by photographer Dmitrii Vasilev. The movement gained notoriety when it blamed Jews for the destruction of Russian churches, and for the serious problem of alcoholism in the country. Originally the authorities did not object to Pamiat's activities and even supported them. In May 1987 Boris Yeltsin, then first secretary of the Moscow city committee of the CPSU, received representatives of Pamiat after a demonstration it staged on Manezh Square. On May 31, 1988, Vasilev announced the transformation of the association into Nationalno-patrioticheskii front "Pamiat" (Pamiat: the National Patriotic Front), i.e., a political organization in opposition to the Communist Party. Between 1989 and the early 1990s, Pamiat split into several groups, the most extreme of which, Pravoslavnyi nationalnopatrioticheskii front "Pamiat" (Pamiat Orthodox National Patriotic Front), headed by A. Kulakov, espoused restoration of the monarchy while simultaneously expounding the necessity of continuing Stalin's antisemitic policy.

Antisemitism has not been confined to words. Acts of vandalism have been directed against Jewish targets. In April 1987 the Leningrad Jewish cemetery was desecrated and in the following two years approximately 30 such incidents were recorded in the U.S.S.R. In Moscow attacks were carried out against a Jewish cafe and the editorial offices of *Sovetish Heymland* and arson was committed at the synagogue by the cemetery in Malakhovka. In 1992 a swastika was painted on the Moscow Lubavitch Ḥasidic synagogue and a firebomb was thrown into the building.

Leningrad, the home of a number of antisemitic organizations, became the center of antisemitism in 1988–1990. It was a teacher at the Leningrad Technological Institute, Nina Andreeva who, evidently on orders from the central Committee of the CPSU, on March 13, 1988, published a letter, "I Can Not Yield My Principles," calling for the rehabilitation of Stalin and the restoration of the kind of law and order that existed before *perestroika.* In her letter Andreeva attacked the Jews as "cosmopolitans" and a "counterrevolutionary people," who were pushing the Russian people toward a rejection of socialism. In the summer of 1988 Leningrad's Ruminatsev Park was the daily site of Pamiat rallies. The city also regularly heard calls to expel Jews from Russian scientific, cultural, and educational institutions.

In nationalist journals such as *Molodaia gvardiia* ("Young Guard") and *Nash sovremennik* ("Our Contemporary"), a group of Moscow writers and journalists, the neo-Slavophiles Valentin Rasputin, Vasillii Belov, Victor Astafev, and Vadim Kozhinov, utilized the traditionally high status of the writer in Russian society to protest ostensibly harmful Jewish influence on Russian culture. For example, they condemned the 1989 publication in the journal *Oktober* of the novella *Vse techet* ("All Is Flowing") by the late writer of Jewish origin Vasili *Grossman, in which the Russian people is allegedly described as having a slave mentality. The January 1990 issue of *Molodaia gvardiia* contained praise of a painting, *The Warning* by Igor Borodin, which the journal claims shows an image of the biblical queen Esther who "after gaining power of the king in his bedroom, and also by clever machinations...urged [King] Artarxerxes to commit the bloody slaughter of 75,000 totally innocent people when there was no threat at all to the Jewish people." The painting (reproduced in the journal) shows Esther on her knees before the czar while under the throne are visible bloodied heads of famous figures of Russian and world culture and history. In 1992 *Evreiskaia gazaeta* reported the existence of 47 antisemitic newspapers and 9 such journals in Russia alone.

Some scientists also denigrated the Jews. Writing appeared denying Jewish contributions to science. A particular target was Albert Einstein, whose discoveries were consistently attributed to others, as in the 1988 monograph of Prof. A. Logunov about Henri Poincaré. The mathematician Igor Shafarevich published a book *Rusofobia* ("Russophobia"), in which a "small people" (for which read "the Jews") was blamed for all the troubles of a "great people," the Russians. In 1992 antisemitism among scientists was revealed in elections to the Russian Academy of Sciences. None of the Jews nominated to become members of the academy was elected, in contrast to the election of a number of Jews during the pre-Gorbachev "period of stagnation."

A significant indication of antisemitic attitudes between 1988 and 1990 was the repeated circulation of rumors about impending pogroms. The first such large-scale pogrom was predicted for June 1988 to coincide with the thousandth anniversary of the baptism of Russia. There were similar rumors in Dnepropetrovsk and other cities in the Ukraine before Easter 1989 and in Leningrad on the eve of elections to local and republic soviets on February 25, 1990. There were rumors of another pogrom set for May 5, 1990, the day of St. George, the patron saint for many nationalists. In that same month a Muslim mob burned and looted dozens of Armenian and Jewish homes in the Uzbek city of Andizhan. Although no exclusively Jewish pogrom took place, the number of reported attacks on individual Jews grew. Soviet Jews lacked confidence in the ability of the authorities to defend them in the face of failures to prevent or halt interethnic conflict in the republics or to halt the rise in crime in Russia itself.

At the same time that the Jewish population of the country was decreasing due to emigration, the Jewish question increasingly became an issue in the internal Soviet power struggle. In pre-election campaigns, the democratic press often indicated its sympathy for the Jews and stressed the antisemitism of their political opponents while Russian nationalists often branded as "Jews" anyone who advocated radical reform, the introduction of a market economy, or civil rights. These "Jews" in fact included such non-Jews as Politburo member Alexander Yakovlev; radical opposition leader in the Supreme Soviet of the U.S.S.R., Yurii Afanasev; editor of the *perestroika-oriented* journal *Ogonek*, Vitalii Korotych; and even Boris Yeltsin.

Lithuanian, Ukrainian, and other nationalists saw the Jews in their republics as possible allies in their fight for self-determination against the central authorities and their local Jewish culture movements as forces opposing Russification. On May 28, 1989, a conference of the national movements of Lithuania, Latvia, and Estonia adopted a resolution condemning Soviet antisemitism in the past and present and calling for opposition to it. A similar resolution was adopted at its founding meeting in September 1989 by Rukh, the democratic national movement in the Ukraine.

The growing antisemitism disturbed the liberal part of the Russian intelligentsia, which saw in it a threat to the overall process of democratization in the country. The "pogromlike" atmosphere was first protested in an open letter by a group of Moscow intellectuals led by the philologist Sergei Lyosov and the physicist Sergei Tishchenko. Almost simultaneously (on June 7) the Leningrad historian Natalia Iukhneva spoke out in public about increasing antisemitism in Russian society. She associated this growth with the unequal position of Jews and Jewish culture in the U.S.S.R. and rejected as false and unjust the attempt to condemn Zionism along with antisemitism. Gradually articles against antisemitism began to be featured in many *perestroika-oriented* journals and newspapers. Some publications even took a positive rather than defensive approach to Jewish topics. For example, the Moscow journal *Znamia* in 1990–1991 published a whole series of articles on Jewish topics, including a translation of the story "Unto Death" by the Israeli writer Amos Oz. Public opinion also had the opportunity to be influenced by the first objective film on Israel shot *in situ* by Evgenii Kiselev and shown on Soviet television between August and October 1989. Due to the cessation of government funding for "anti-Zionist" works, a number of their authors, such as Dadiani, Vladimir Nosenko, Victor Magidson, and Adolf Eidelman, switched camps and became opponents of antisemitism, perhaps with the hope of support from Israeli and Western Jewish institutions.

The victory of democratic forces in the elections of local soviets in March 1990 led to the mobilization of law enforcement agencies against antisemitic agitation. For the first time in decades, the state prosecutor's office prosecuted antisemitic actions under article 174 of the Criminal Court of the RFSFR, which deals with the incitement of ethnic strife. The sentencing to a jail term of Pamiat leader Smirnov-Ostashvili (who committed suicide in prison) was viewed as a victory for democracy in the country. Public opinion was favorably influenced toward the Jews in August 1991 when one of the three victims killed defending democracy against the attempted coup turned out to be the young Jew Ilya Krichevskii. The fall 1991 repeal (supported by the Soviet Union) of the UN resolution equating Zionism with racism also was a factor in deflating antisemitic propaganda.

In November 1992, almost a year after the dissolution of the Soviet Union, the committee on human rights of the Supreme Soviet of the Russian Federation inaugurated hearings on the problem of antisemitism in Russia. The committee concluded that there was a decline in antisemitic attitudes in Russian society in 1991–1992 and that antisemitic activity was basically restricted to extremist groups and parties. At the same time, legislative measures were discussed which, without infringing upon freedom of speech and the press, would stipulate punishment for arousing ethnic hatred. Antisemitism was increasingly being treated in Russia as not only a Jewish problem.

Though official, state antisemitism had virtually disappeared in post-Soviet Russia, it was adopted by numerous radical right parties and organizations, the greatest and most influential of which had now become the LDPR. Its leader, Vladimir Zhirinovsky, who allegedly had a Jewish father and in 1989, for a short time, was a legal advisor of the Jewish Cultural Association Shalom (allegations he denied in the 1990s), claimed he was not an antisemite. Nevertheless, after the December election of 1993 he made a number of harshly antisemitic statements, some of them in a characteristically anti-Zionist guise. On March 4, 1994, he told *Die Zeit*: "Why are the Zionists so bad? … Because they weaken Russia. The American Jews make America strong but the Russian Jews make Russia weak. They do this so that they can leave for Israel … Our greatest problems are the Americans and the Zionists." In November, during a visit to the United States, Zhirinovsky told the UN Correspondents' Association that "the majority of journalists who welcomed the [collapse of the Soviet Union] joyously are of Jewish nationality"and that new businesses in Russia were "headed by Jews and a lot of the population understand that most of the money in these banks and structures is dirty money." On October 21 he said in a speech to the parliament: "I tell the whole world: It is you from Tel Aviv and Washington who are doing everything bad that is happening to us."

Besides this big party, there are many small antisemitic parties and movements filling a spectrum between Russian-Orthodox conservative to neopagan, and from National Communist groups to Nazis. According to various estimates, there were c. 80–100 such organizations at the end of 1993. Some of them, e.g., the neo-Nazi Russian National Unity led by Aleksandr Barkashov (its members wear black uniforms with the swastika emblem), sought contacts and cooperation with similar neo-Nazi groups in Germany and other western countries. The specter of a "red-brown" alliance, i.e., between hardline communists and neo-Nazis, with viciously antisemitic slogans and aims, began to appear.

The most conspicuous antisemitic parties and organizations, apart from the LDPR and Barkashov's RNU, continued to be Pamiat, led by Dmitrii Vasiliev (see above), the imperialist National Salvation Front, the Russian National Council, led by the former KGB general Alexandr Sterligov, the St. Petersburg-based National Republican Party of Russia, led by Nikolai Lysenko, the neo-Communist Working Russia, led by Viktor Anpilov, and the quasi-Communist National Bolshevik Union, led by the writer Eduard Limonov.

The radical right and conservative press thrived. Some of the former Soviet official newspapers, such as *Pravda, Sovetskaia Rossiia* and *Literaturnaia Rossiia*, turned into conservative nationalist papers; the latter two devote considerable place to antisemitic articles, including the so-called "Zionist conspiracy against Russia." However, in May 1993, *Pravda* also published an article entitled "The satanic tribe – who is hiding behind the murder of novices?" which claimed that a Russian Orthodox priest and two novices who were killed during the Easter holiday had been the victims of a ritual murder. The article was denounced by the pro-Yeltsin newspaper *Izvestiia* and condemned by both the Russian and the U.S. governments; *Pravda* published an apology blaming the author of the article for inaccuracies.

In addition to these old established, relatively mass-circulation newspapers, numerous fringe newspapers, small with small circulations, but some with considerable ones, appeared. They are more openly antisemitic. Among the most prominent, *Den/Zavtra* may be mentioned. The paper was founded in 1992 under the title *Den* and edited by the novelist Aleksandr Prokhanov, one of the leaders of the National Salvation Front; in 1993, after it was banned by Yeltsin, in the wake of the Parliament insurrection, it changed its name to *Zavtra*. The second conspicuous antisemitic paper was *Al-Quds*, established in 1992 by a Palestinian businessman and self-proclaimed head of the "Palestinian Government in Exile," Shaaban Khafez Shaaban. *Al-Quds* specialized in publishing materials alleging a Zionist conspiracy against Russia and the Palestinian people. In late 1994 the paper was closed down by the authorities.

Following the Parliament insurrection in 1993, there were a number of anti-Yeltsin demonstrations and rallies, many of them with overtly antisemitic slogans. On November 7, 1994, in Moscow, on the 77th anniversary of the Russian October Revolution, a 15,000-strong rally of Communists was held in Lubyanka Square; some of the anti-government banners contained slogans attacking Jews, Zionists and the "Kike-Masonic conspiracy." On October 3, on the anniversary of the events of 1993, there was also a demonstration in St. Petersburg, at which anti-Jewish banners were displayed.

Russian antisemites did not limit themselves to rallies and demonstrations. There were numerous antisemitic incidents; e.g., in May 1993 Jewish cemeteries in St. Petersburg and Nizhni Novgorod were desecrated; in June, windows were broken and swastikas and anti-Jewish slogans daubed on the Moscow Choral Synagogue; in July the attack on the synagogue was repeated. In December the synagogue in Marina Roshcha district in Moscow was badly damaged in a fire. In 1994, Jewish cemeteries were desecrated in St. Petersburg (where 160 gravestones were desecrated), in Novosibirsk, Krasnoyarsk, Smolensk, Kazan, Klintsy, Briansk region, and Nizhni Novgorod. Several cases of racially motivated attacks on Jews were registered. On February 16, 1994, a firebomb was thrown into the office of the Committee for Repatriation to Israel in Novosibirsk; the office and adjoining library were badly damaged in the ensuing fire. In February, following the massacre of Muslims by a Jewish settler in a Hebron mosque, threats were made against the Jewish community and against the Derbent synagogue, in Daghestan. Also, there was street violence in Makhachkala, and on the local television the sheikh of Daghestan called for a jihad against the Jews. Numerous books of antisemitic content were published and an opinion survey of 1993 carried out by Robert Brym with the assistance of the All-Russian Center for Public Opinion Research (VTSIOM), and covering also Ukraine and Belarus, revealed antisemitic perceptions, strong by North American standards. In Moscow, negative attitudes toward Jews were more widespread among older people, low-income earners and non-Russians. Eighteen percent of Muscovites believed that there existed a global "Zionist conspiracy" against Russia, and another 20 percent were undecided.

An added ingredient in the continued antisemitism that remained part of Russian life was the emergence of the so-called oligarchs, who divided up Russia's wealth and gained control of its media after the breakup of the Soviet Union. The Jews among them, most prominently Mikhail *Khodorkovsky, Roman *Abramovitch, Vladimir *Gusinsky, Boris *Berezovsky, and Leonid *Nevzlin, are perceived as having been targeted by the Russian authorities for prosecution for various economic crimes against the background of their Jewish origins.

[Michael Beizer / Daniel Romanowski (2nd ed.)]

For information on the countries of the Former Soviet Union, see entries for individual countries.

BIBLIOGRAPHY: G.D. Hundert and G.C. Bacon, *The Jews in Poland and Russia: Bibliographical Essays* (1984). GENERAL WORKS: Institute of Jewish Affairs, London, *Soviet Jewry* (1971), an extensive bibliography; L. Greenberg, *The Jews in Russia*, 2 vols. (1951); S.W. Baron, *The Russian Jew under Tsars and Soviets* (1964).

1772–1917: J.S. Raisin, *The Haskalah Movement in Russia* (1915); Dubnow, Hist Russ; J. Kunitz, *Russian Literature and the Jew* (1929); I. Levitats, *The Jewish Community in Russia, 1772–1844* (1943); J. Frumkin et al. (eds.), *Russian Jewry 1860–1917* (1966); V. Nikitin, *Yevrei zemledeltsy* (1887); M.L. Usov, *Yevrei v armii* (1911); L. Zinberg, *Yevreyskaya periodicheskaya pechat v Rossii* (1915); Yu. Gessen, *Istoriya yevreyskogo naroda v Rossii*, 2 vols. (1925–26); S.Y. Borovoy, *Yevreyskaya zemledelcheskaya kolonizatsiya v staroy Rossi* (1928); N. Buchbinder, *Geshikhte fun der Yidisher Arbeter Bavegung in Rusland* (1931); A. Levin, *Kantonistn... 1827–1856* (1934); S. Ginzburg, *Historishe Verk*, 3 vols. (1937–38); B. Dinur, *Bi-Ymei Milḥamah u-Mahpekhah* (1960).

1917–1970: International Military Tribunal, *Trials of the Major War Criminals*, 4 (1950), 3–596; S.M. Schwarz, *The Jews in the Soviet Union* (1951); idem, *Yevrei v Sovietskom Soyuze s nachala vtoroy mirovoy voyny* (1966); L. Kochan (ed.), *The Jews in Soviet Russia Since 1917* (1978); N. Levin, *The Jews in the Soviet Union Since 1917: Paradox of Survival*, 2 vols. (1988); J. Tenenbaum, *Race and Reich* (1956), 347–70; B. West (ed.), *Struggle of a Generation: The Jews under Soviet Rule* (1959); idem, *Hem Hayu Rabbim* (1968); L. Lénéman, *La Tragédie des Juifs en U.R.S.S.* (1959); J.B. Shechtman, *Star in Eclipse: Russian Jewry Revisited* (1961); B.Z. Goldberg, *The Jewish Problem in the Soviet Union* (1961); E. Schulman, *A History of Jewish Education in the Soviet Union* (1971); E. Wiesel, *The Jews of Silence* (1966); *Gli ebrei nel' U.R.S.S.* (1966); Ben-Ami (A. Eliav), *Between Hammer and Sickle* (19672); S. Rabinovich, *Jews in the Soviet Union* (Moscow, 1967); L. Kochan (ed.), *The Jews in Soviet Russia since 1917* (1970); A. Dagan, *Moscow and Jerusalem* (1971); *Jews in Eastern Europe* (1958–); S. Agursky, *Di Yidishe Komisariatn un di Yidishe Komunistishe Sektsies* (1928); N. Gergel, *Di Lage fun Yidn in Rusland* (1929); A. Rafaeli (Zenziper), *Eser Shenot Redifot* (1930); S. Dimanstein (ed.), *Yidn in FSSR.* (1935); L. Zinger, *Dos Banayte Folk* (1941); J. Lestschinsky, *Dos Sovetishe Idntum* (1941; *Ha-Yehudim be-Rusyah ha-Sovyetit*, 1943); T. Belsk, *Yehudei Ya'ar* (1946); M. Kahanovitch, *Milḥemet ha-Partizanim ha-Yehudim be-Mizraḥ Eiropah* (1954); Y.A. Gilboa, *Al Ḥorvot ha-Tarbut ha-Yehudit bi-Verit ha-Mo'aẓot* (1959); idem, *The Black Years of Soviet Jewry* (1971); Ch. Shmeruk (ed.), *Pirsumim Yehudiyyim bi-Verit ha-Mo'aẓot* (1961); idem (ed.), *A Shpigl oyf a Shteyn* (1964); A. Pomeranz, *Di Sovetishe Harugey Malkhes* (1962); J. Levavi *Ha-Hityashevut ha-Yehudit be-Birobidzhan* (1965); A.A. Gershuni, *Ha-Yahadut be-Rusyah ha-Sovyetit* (1965); J. Litvak, in: *Gesher*, 12, nos. 2–3 (1966), 186–217; M. Guri et al. (eds.), *Ḥayyalim Yehudim be-Ẓivot Eiropah* (1967), 135–57; S. Nishmit, in: *Dappim le-Ḥeker ha-Sho'ah ve-ha-Mered*, Series B, Collection A (1969), 152–77; S. Redlich, in: *Beḥinot*, 1 (1970), 70–79; *He-Avar* (1952–). ARCHIVAL MATERIAL: Yad Vashem Archives, Jerusalem: Unit 0-53/Ludwigsburg/, files nos. 1–10, 13–14, 15–17, 22–33, 36, 44–45, 57, 83, 86, 88–91, 93. Unit 0-53/F (JM-2996)/ Ludwigsburg/; "*Čhornaya Kniga.*" PUBLICATIONS: *The Black Book, the Nazi Crimes against the Jewish People* (1946); I. Ehrenburg, V. Grossman, *The Complete Black Book of Russia* (2002); R. Hilberg, *The Destruction of the European Jews* (1961); G. Reitlinger, *The Final Solution* (1968^2); S. Schwartz, *Yevrei v Sovetskom Soyuze s. nachala vtoroy mirovoy voyny* (1966); *Prestupleniya nemetskofashistskikh okupantov v Belorussii 1941–1944* (Minsk, 1965); *Rozprawa sadowa w sprawie o bestialstwa popelnione przez niemieckich najeźdźiców faszystowskich i ich slugusów na terytorium miasta Krasnodaru i kraju krasnodarskiego w okresie przejściowej ich okupacji/July 14–17, 1943/* (Moscow, 1943).

1970– : Y. Ro'i, in: EJYB 83–85:405–10; Y. Litvak, in: EJYB 86–87:363–70; R. Vago, in: EJYB 88–89:405–5; M. Beizer, in; EJYB 90–91:388–95; idem, in: *The Shorter Encyclopaedia Judaica in Russian*, Suppl. 1, (1992), 31–41; idem, in: *Jews and Jewish Topics in the Soviet Union and Eastern Europe* (hereafter *Jews and Jewish Topics*), 2:12 (1990), 69–77; idem, in: *Jews and Jewish Topics*, 3:19 (1992) 62–77; T. Friedgut, in: *Soviet Jewry in the 1980s* (1989), 3–25; M. Altshuler, in: *Jews and Jewish Topics*, 2:9 (1989), 5–29; idem, in: *Jews and Jewish Topics*, 3:16 (1991), 224–40; Z. Gitelman, in: *Soviet Jewish Affairs*, 19:2 (1989), 3–4; Y. Florsheim, in: *Jews and Jewish Topics*, 2:15 (1991), 5–14; idem, in: *Jews and Jewish Topics*, 3:19 (1992), 5–15; M. Tolts, in: *Jews and Jewish Topics*, 2:18 (1991), 13–26; idem, in: *East European Jewish Affairs*, 22:2 (1992), 3–19; A. Greenbaum, in: EJYB 90–91:179–83; I. Dymerskaya-Tsigelman, in: *Jews and Jewish Topics*, 3:10 (1989), 49–61; B. Pinkus, in: *Jews and Jewish Topics*, 2:15 (1991), 15–30; M. Gilbert, *The Jews of Hope* (1984); idem, *Ukrainian Diary, September–October, 1991*, manuscript; D. Prital (ed.), *Yehudei Berit ha-Mo'atsot* ("The Jews of the Soviet Union"), vols. 8–15 (1985–1992); "The Seeond Congress of Vaad," in: *Jews and Jewish Topics*, 3:16 (1991), 224–40; Z. Gitelman, in: *Soviet Jewish Affairs*, 19:2 (1989), 3–4; Y. Florsheim, in: *Jews and Jewish Topics*, 2:15 (1991), 5–14; idem, in: *Jews and Jewish Topics*, 3:19 (1992), 5–15; M. Tolts, in: *Jews and Jewish Topics*, 1:14 (1991), 31–59. **ADD. BIBLIOGRAPHY:** U. Schmelz and S. DellaPergola, in: AJYB, 1995, 478; *Supplement to the Monthly Bulletin of Statistics*, 2, 1995, Jerusalem; Y. Florsheim, in: *Jews in Eastern Europe*, 1 (26) 1995, 25–33; M. Beizer and I. Klimenko, in: *Jews in Eastern Europe*, 1:24 (1995), 25–33; *Antisemitism World Re-*

port 1994, London: Institute of Jewish Affairs, 143–153; *Antisemitism World Report 1995*, London: Institute of Jewish Affairs, 196–206; D. Prital (ed.), *Yehudei Berit ha-Moazot be-ma'avar*, 16:1 and 17:2; *Mezhdunarodnaia Evreiskaia Gazeta* (MEG), 1993–1994; M. Tolts, "The Post-Soviet Jewish Population in Russia and the World," in: *Jews in Russia and Eastern Europe*, 1, 52 (2004), 37–63. **WEBSITE:** www.fjc.ru.

RUSSIAN LITERATURE.

Biblical and Hebraic Influences

The Jewish impact on Russian literature may be traced back 900 years to the period when that body of writing was still the common patrimony of a people that was to emerge later as three distinct East Slavic ethnic groups: the Russians, the Ukrainians, and the Belorussians, each with its separate language and, ultimately, its own literature. The 11th-century "Primary Chronicle," of which 13th-century transcriptions are extant, begins with an account of the biblical story of the Tower of Babel. Equally ancient is the 11th-century translation of *Josephus' *Jewish War* into East Slavic, although the original translation was later supplemented by newer versions. Not only was Josephus' work extremely popular in Russia throughout the Middle Ages, but for several centuries his style and imagery continued to exert a powerful influence on original Russian literary works, particularly martial tales. In 1106–08 the abbot Daniel made a pilgrimage to the Holy Land, and his account of the journey, extant in 15th-century transcriptions, contains a number of interesting descriptions of Jerusalem and its surroundings.

Polemical attacks on Judaism as a creed antedate the appearance in Russia of any sizable Jewish population. Thus the metropolitan Ilarion, in his *Slovo o zakone i blagodati* ("Sermon on Law and Grace," written 1037–50), attacks Judaism for its alleged lack of Divine grace, a stock claim of Christian theologians over the centuries. It is likely that the metropolitan's attack was prompted by fear of the *Khazars, then Kiev's neighbors and rivals, among whose ruling class Judaism was widely professed. In a popular 12th-century tale, "The Virgin's Road Through Torments," Mary intercedes on behalf of various sinners whom she encounters on her journey through Hell. Only for the Jews can she find no compassion, since they are the alleged murderers of her son. In this doctrine, too, Russian Orthodoxy did not differ from Western European Christianity.

Judaism's theological threat to Russian Christianity became somewhat more real in the 15th century, with the appearance in the cities of Novgorod and Moscow of a heresy whose adherents were dubbed "*Judaizers" (*Zhidovstvuyushchiye*). Because most of their works were destroyed by the Church, little is known about these heretics other than their skepticism with regard to several articles of Christian faith, including the Trinity and Virgin Birth, and their high regard for the Old Testament, the importance of which Russian Orthodoxy has traditionally minimized. Russia's "Judaizers" translated anew from Hebrew sources (and not, as had been customary, from existing Greek translations) a number of biblical texts, particularly the Psalms and the books of Daniel and Esther. They were also the first to translate a treatise on logic by *Maimonides. Some Russian church historians maintain rather unconvincingly that these translations were made by Jews such as Feodor the Jew for coreligionists who no longer knew Hebrew. Among the best-known works of apocryphal literature was the "Tale of the Centaur," extant in a 15th-century text, which was based on an ancient Jewish story about Solomon building the Temple without recourse to iron.

During the 16th century certain Western European anti-Jewish philippics were translated from Latin into Russian, notably works by *Nicholas de Lyre and by an apostate known as Samuel the Jew. In the following century Old Testament authority and biblical imagery were frequently invoked by opponents of the official Church. An outstanding example was the archpriest Avvakuma (1621–1682), founder of the Old Believers' sect, whose autobiography, *Zhitiye protopopa Avvakuma* (written 1672–75) is a milestone in the development of the modern Russian literary language.

BIBLICAL DRAMA AND POETRY. The first Russian theatrical performance, which took place in Moscow in 1672, was a German stage adaptation of the Book of Esther. Early plays on biblical themes for the Moscow repertories were written by Semyon Polotski and a German Lutheran pastor, Johann Gottfried Grigori, the author of a morality play on Adam and Eve, and there were also adaptations of the stories of Judith, Daniel, and David and Goliath. Conventional imagery and allusions drawn from the Bible are as characteristic of later Russian literature as they are of other literatures, and biblical motifs regularly occurred in the works of Russian authors of the 19th century. Such was the case with the magnificent statement of the poet's mission in "Prorok" ("The Prophet," 1826) by Alexander Pushkin (1799–1837). Among later, prerevolutionary writers, Leonid Nikolayevich Andreyev (1871–1919) wrote a drama about Samson (*Samson v okovakh*, 1925; *Samson in Chains*, 1923), and Alexander Ivanovich Kuprin (1870–1938) published *Sulamif* (1908; Eng. tr. *Sulamith*, 1923), a stylized romance about Solomon. Their Jewish contemporary, Akim Lvovich *Volynski, wrote a critical study of the Bible in Russian poetry.

The last prerevolutionary decade was marked by an upsurge of interest in both biblical and modern Hebrew literature. Interest in the latter was heightened by the fact that many of the founding fathers of the new Hebrew writing, preeminently *Bialik, were Russian Jews then still living in Russia. V. *Jabotinsky translated Bialik into Russian, and Bialik thus gained wide appreciation both among writers (e.g., Gorki) and among the public. Among the translators and popularizers of modern Hebrew verse at the turn of the century were such eminent Russian symbolist poets as Valeri Bryusov (1873–1924) and Feodor Sologub (1863–1927); of a slightly later vintage was the émigré poet, the half-Jew Vladislav *Khodasevich. A journey to Palestine inspired some poetry by another émigré, Ivan Bunin (1870–1953).

After the Bolshevik Revolution biblical works naturally fell into disfavor, but it is significant that two Jewish writers of the post-Stalin era turned to the Bible for themes expressive of their spirit of protest. Semyon Isaakovich *Kirsanov, who had published a poem entitled *"Edem"* ("Paradise") in the late 1940s, wrote *"Sem dney nedeli"* ("Seven Days of the Week," 1957), an anti-materialist narrative poem based on the Creation story; while Yosif *Brodski, a prime target of Soviet antisemitism, also wrote a long narrative poem entitled *"Isaak i Avraam"* ("Isaac and Abraham"), which, like his other original works, had to be published in the West (in *Stikhotvoreniya i poemy*, 1965).

The Image of the Jew

Although one of the stock characters of the *Vertep* puppet show – Russia's oldest form of theater – was a grotesque caricature of a greedy and cowardly Jew, there were very few Jewish motifs in Russian literature during the 18th century. One reason for this may be the fact that the Jews lived in areas to the west with which Russian writers, mostly from central Russia, were unfamiliar. Another is that Russian writing of the period rarely featured anyone who was not an aristocrat. To a lesser extent this was also true of Russian literature of the first half of the 19th century, despite the sudden increase in Russia's Jewish population after the annexation of former Polish territories following that country's partitions at the end of the 18th century.

THE ANTISEMITIC STEREOTYPE. Biblical portraits gradually gave way to a stylized, romantic portrayal of the Jew reminiscent of the Jews in Sir Walter Scott's *Ivanhoe*, but familiar since *Shakespeare's *Merchant of Venice*. An antisemitic stereotype tempered by courtly gallantry, the Russian figure was normally an incongruous combination of an ugly and repugnant Jewish father (more often than not a greedy usurer and hater of Christians) and his beautiful daughter. A noteworthy example may be found in *Ispantsy* ("The Spaniards," 1830), an early drama by Russia's foremost Byronic poet, Mikhail Lermontov (1814–1841), which portrays hapless lovers against the background of the Inquisition. Ivan Turgenev (1818–1883) was no romantic, but his realistic short story *Zhid* (1847; *The Jew…*, 1899) exudes the familiar blend of human compassion and aristocratic disgust with a Jew about to be executed on suspicion of espionage. Turgenev's portrayal of the Jew, which sharply contrasts with his humane understanding of the plight of the Russian peasant, is not unlike that found in *Taras Bulba* (1842), a novella by Nikolai Gogol (1809–1852), who both as a man and a writer was otherwise very different from the Westernized and liberal Turgenev. In Gogol's short novel, set during the 17th-century Polish-Cossack wars, a Jewish innkeeper, also suspected of espionage, is described as shifty, mercenary, and treacherous, in many respects far more despicable than the Polish enemy. Curiously enough, this motif of a Jew suspected of spying for the Poles (who are themselves shown to be antisemitic) reappeared nearly a century later in a short story by the Soviet-Jewish writer Isaac *Babel ("Berestechko," in *Red Cavalry*, 1926), in which a Communist soldier calmly slits the throat of an old Jew.

Hostile portrayals of Jews are scattered throughout the writings of Fyodor Dostoyevski (1821–1881). A noteworthy instance is the criminal who remains faithful to the practices of Judaism in *Zapiski iz mertvogo doma* ("Memoirs from the House of the Dead," 1861–62). The works of Leo Tolstoy (1828–1910) display an ambivalence characteristic of his attitude toward other ethnic minorities, such as the Poles. On the one hand Tolstoy, particularly in his later years, condemned antisemitism as inconsistent with the commandment to love one's neighbor; on the other, he showed in his own few literary references to Jews the disdainful attitude of a haughty seigneur toward pitiful but despicable creatures.

In the mid-19th century the unfriendly depiction of the Jew underwent yet another shift. Aristocratic contempt for the Jew had largely disappeared, but it was replaced by the hostile references of plebeian writers. Some of these, driven by chauvinism and religious intolerance, accused the Jews of plotting against Russia's traditional values and institutions, identifying them with revolutionary terrorists. Representative of this tendency were Vsevolod Krestovski's (1840–1895) *Tma Yegipetskaya* ("Egyptian Darkness," 1889) and the "anti-Nihilist" writings of Alexey Pisemski (1821–1881). Simultaneously, however, anti-Jewish notes could be discerned in the works of such Populists and radical sympathizers as the poet Nikolai Nekrasov (1821–1878), the novelist Feodor Reshetnikov (1841–1871), and Russia's foremost satirist, Mikhail Saltykov-Shchedrin (1826–1889). The latter's attitude toward the Jews was, however, like Tolstoy's, inconsistent and contradictory. In the works of these writers (as in the pronouncements of some revolutionary parties of the period, notably Narodnaya Volya) the Jew was often abused as the merciless exploiter of Russia's downtrodden and impoverished masses.

OBJECTIVE PORTRAYALS. During the second half of the 19th century other writers began to defend the Jews from their numerous enemies and to attack all forms of antisemitic persecution and discrimination. Some of these champions of the Jews were politically and religiously moderate conservatives. Outstanding among these was Nikolay *Leskov, some of whose tales contain traditional antisemitic stereotypes, but whose overall output constitutes a clever attack on Russian antisemitism. Leskov, a prolific writer on the Jewish question, also published anonymously a pamphlet entitled *Yevrei v Rossii* ("The Jews in Russia," 1884), undoubtedly the most impassioned defense of Russian Jews ever written by a Russian author. Most of their defenders were, however, moderates, liberals, and leftists. There are sympathetic portrayals in works by Anton Chekhov (1860–1904), such as in the short story *Skripka Rotshilda* ("Rothschild's Violin," 1894), and *Ivanov* (1887), one of his early serious plays. In this, a Jewish woman forsakes her faith and her family in order to marry the man she loves, but he ultimately insults her by calling her a despicable Jewess. Chekhov also distinguished himself as an ardent defender of Alfred *Dreyfus, losing many of his friends as a result. Alexander Kuprin portrayed a Jewish fiddler in his short story *Gambrinus* (1907, Eng. tr., 1925) while in his whimsical tale *Obida* (1906; "An Insult," in *The Bracelet of Garnets...*, 1917), a delegation of thieves indignantly protests the "slanderous" insinuations of a newspaper that anti-Jewish pogroms are the work of underworld elements. Yevgeni Chirikov's (1864–1936) play *Yevrei* (1904; *Die Juden*, 1904) was also an attack on antisemitism, as were the numerous short stories and newspaper articles by Vladimir *Korolenko and Maxim *Gorki, who warmly championed Russia's Jews, particularly the poor ones.

During the latter part of the 19th century Jews themselves began to write on Jewish themes. Before 1917, however, they were never fully accepted as Russian writers and none of them achieved literary stature. Russian Jewry was, in any case, only superficially secularized and its artistic energies were canalized into the literary realms of Hebrew and Yiddish. Three pioneer authors were Osip *Rabinovich, Grigori Bogrov, and Lev *Levanda, whose descriptions of Jewish life were intended to demonstrate the brutal oppression of an inoffensive minority, and to gain the sympathy of all decent and fair-minded Russian Christians. A more militant note was sounded in the poetry of Shimon Shmuel (Semyon) *Frug, who at first linked his hopes for the salvation of Russia's Jews with the triumph of the revolutionary cause, but who later became more attracted to Zionism. Two writers whose reputation has proved more lasting were Andrey *Sobol and Semyon *Yushkevich. In his novel *Pyl* ("Dust," 1915), Sobol expressed the Jewish revolutionary's disenchantment with socialism as a solution of the Jewish problem, a feeling reflected in another semi-autobiographical work, *Oblomki* ("The Wreckage," 1923), a collection of stories published after the Bolshevik triumph.

The Soviet Position

The distinction between portrayals of Jews in Russian literature by writers who were themselves Jews and those who were not loses much of its validity during the Soviet period. In the first place, Jewish writers in the U.S.S.R. were, for the most part, culturally assimilated; many of them wrote under Slavic-sounding names which concealed their origin. Secondly, the everpresent threat of an accusation of "Jewish nationalism" caused many of them – either out of genuine Communist conviction or from ordinary fear – to shy away from excessive preoccupation with Jewish subjects. And last but not least, the many levels of ideological control over Soviet literature, operative from the early days of the regime, have to a greater or lesser extent – depending on the period – prevented the appearance of works too much at variance with the official party position on the subject; and these controls have been roughly applicable to all Soviet writers, regardless of their ethnic background. The periodical shifts in the portrayal of Jews in Soviet literature have thus been more closely tied to fluctuations in official policy and to the stringency of literary censorship than to the preferences of the authors themselves or, more important still, to the social conditions which their works purported to reflect in a realistic manner.

The official Soviet position may be reduced to the following essentials. The Jews, like all other ethnic groups, are really divided, as Lenin stated, into two warring nations in one – the exploiters and the exploited. The exploited and the poor of all nations are natural allies, as are the rich exploiters of the various ethnic groups. The former are to be portrayed with compassion and sympathy, and the latter are to be shown as their villainous foes. There can be no recognition of an ethnic group that might transcend class antagonisms. This article of faith was to be observed with particular stringency in Soviet literature's treatment of Jewish themes, and it has resulted in some grotesque descriptions of manifestations of antisemitism and other phenomena which, in one way or another, affect all Jews, regardless of their religious ties, economic status, or political allegiance.

In the distorting mirror of Soviet literature, where ideology takes precedence over historical or artistic truth, there are few exceptions to the rule that only the Jewish poor are shown to be victims of antisemitism, whereas the bourgeoisie are somehow unaffected by it. In fact, Jewish capitalists – who, as a rule, are also portrayed as the only Jews infected with the dual poison of religious faith and Zionism – are shown making common cause with antisemites, provided that the latter are their class allies – fellow capitalists and enemies of the working class. This tendency can be discerned in Soviet literature from the earliest years of the Soviet regime and is not, as is commonly thought, a phenomenon of Stalin's last years. However, since antisemitism as such was condemned during the early years of Soviet rule, and because antisemitic policies were in the 1920s associated with the *ancien régime*, Soviet books describing poor Jews in czarist Russia portrayed them in a sympathetic light as victims of persecution.

A documentary of unusual interest and importance that was unearthed some 45 years after its publication is the poem "*Yevrey*" ("The Jew") by the otherwise conformist Soviet writer Vladimir Mayakovski, a leader of the Futurist movement. Here Mayakovski, a friend of Bialik (to whom he dedicated another of his poems), vigorously attacked Russian antisemitism and championed the victims of its constant slanders. The poem, first read to a meeting in favor of Jewish economic rehabilitation which he had himself helped to organize in November 1926, subsequently appeared in *Izvestiya*; but it has been carefully omitted from Mayakovski's collected works. Another poem, "*Zhid*" ("Jew"), written in May 1928 as a protest against the resurgence of antisemitism, appeared in *Komsomolskaya Pravda* (June 15, 1928).

Subsequently, in the 1930s, as glorification of Russia's past became more fashionable, czarist antisemitism tended to be avoided, although the familiar attitude continued to be maintained in works describing Jews still living in capitalist countries. This, too, became muted in the early 1940s and was almost entirely suppressed after World War II, perhaps in order to avoid undesirable parallels with the Soviet Union's own brand of antisemitism, which began in the late 1940s with Stalin's virulently antisemitic purges of *"cosmopolitans." These culminated in the closure of all Soviet Yiddish cultural institutions in 1948 and the execution of Soviet Yiddish writers in 1952. By then, nearly all discussion of antisemitism, past and present, Russian or foreign, or of any other Jewish themes, had become practically taboo. The worldwide sensation created by the appearance in 1961 of a brief poem, "Babi Yar," by Yevgeni *Yevtushenko, condemning Nazi and prerevolutionary antisemitism, and the mutilation by Soviet censorship of *Babi Yar* (1966; Eng. 1967, revised 1970), a documentary novel by Anatoli Kuznetsov (1929–1979) about the Nazi massacre of Soviet Jews in a ravine near Kiev, demonstrate that, in contrast to other areas of Soviet life, there was no real thaw in Soviet literature's treatment of Jewish themes.

THE JEW THROUGH SOVIET EYES. Early Soviet literature portrayed two types of "sympathetic" Jews: the victims of prerevolutionary persecution, and the fighters for the Communist cause and, occasionally, the passive victims who were transformed into active fighters. It is interesting that the victims were usually endowed with various ethnic traits, such as observance of Jewish tradition, attachment to Jewish culture, and even loyalty to the Yiddish language; but these they would discard in the process of transformation into good Communists. At the same time, Jewish villains, usually "class enemies" from the past such as rich merchants and rabbis, were depicted as "socially alien elements" who had somehow succeeded in worming their way into the Communist Party. The fact that Jewish heroes outnumbered Jewish villains in early Soviet fiction reflects Soviet literature's general predilection for "positive" characters as well as the undeniable fact that the impoverished Jewish masses were sympathetic to the Bolshevik cause, many Jews having fought in the civil war on the Communist side.

The most celebrated portraits of "positive" fighting Jews are to be found in works such as Alexander Fadeyev's (1901–1956) novel *Razgrom* (1927; *The Nineteen*, 1929) and Eduard *Bagritski's *Duma pro Opanasa* ("The Lay of Opanas," 1926). A middle-class Jew who hates the Soviet regime is depicted in Yuri *Libedinski's *Nedelya* (1923; *A Week*, 1923), while an obnoxious, pushy young Jew nicknamed "little Trotsky" appears in Sergey Malashkin's (1890–?) collection of stories *Luna s pravoy storony* ("The Moon on the Right," 1927). Small-town Jews, reminiscent of those found in Yiddish literature, were portrayed in scores of works, including Ilya *Ehrenburg's *Burnaya zhizn Lazika Roytshvantsa* (1928; *The Stormy Life of Lasik Roitschwantz*, 1960). Joseph *Utkin described the sudden metamorphosis of a humble tailor steeped in Jewish tradition into an emancipated and internationalist Bolshevik in his *Povest o ryzhem Motele…* ("The Tale of Motele the Redhead…," 1926). The fullest and most sophisticated portrait of Russian Jewry during the last decade of czarist Russia, at the time of the Revolution and the civil war, and in its first years under Soviet rule is found in the works of Isaac *Babel.

During the 1930s the manner in which Jews were portrayed in Soviet fiction, poetry, and drama underwent a significant change. Not only heroes, but also villains and even marginal characters were no longer, as a rule, described as Jews – persons with specifically Jewish problems, hopes, and aspirations – but rather as Soviet men and women whose Jewish origin could only be guessed from their names, or from fleeting references to their family backgrounds. This can only partly reflect the changes that actually took place in Soviet Jewry. Much of the explanation must be sought in the already stringent political controls imposed on Soviet literature. Two examples of such literary characterization are the enthusiastic engineer Margulis in Valentin Katayev's (1897–1986) "production novel" *Vremya, vperyod!* ("Time, Forward!," 1932), and Davydov, the organizer of a collective farm, in *Podnyataya tselina* ("Virgin Soil Upturned," 1932–59) by the Nobel Prize-winning novelist Mikhail Sholokhov (1905–1984). The latter case is particularly noteworthy in view of the fact that, in the novel, Davydov's Jewish background is almost imperceptible, despite the fact that he was partly modeled on a real-life Jewish Communist.

The artificiality and insincerity in Soviet literature's portrayal of Jews during the 1940s is particularly striking in works dealing with World War II. At a time when the Nazi extermination of Jewish civilians and prisoners of war must already have been common knowledge, these continued to portray Soviet people of Jewish birth as almost completely unaware of their Jewishness. This fact, and the enforced tendency to avoid Jewish subjects altogether, is corroborated by the memoirs of Ehrenburg, which were published during the relatively liberal years following Stalin's death. The contrived nature of the portrayal of Jews in Soviet literature during the late 1940s and early 1950s is further evident from the fact that the few "positive" Jewish heroes found in Soviet writings of the period – such as the engineers Liberman and Zalkind in Vasili Azhayev's (1915–1968) novel *Daleko ot Moskvy* ("Far from Moscow," 1948) – display no awareness of the existence of antisemitism in the U.S.S.R. itself. Confirmation of this assumption may again be found in the memoirs of Soviet writers, notably Ehrenburg and Samuel *Marshak.

The most important distortion, however, took the innocuous form of silence. At a time when Jewish and non-Jewish writers throughout the world were shaken and inspired by the two most important events in the past 2,000 years of Jewish history – the Nazi massacre of 6,000,000 Jews and the reestablishment of an independent Jewish state – Soviet literature affected a pose of indifference and apathy. Nor, understandably, was there any reaction in Soviet literature to the wave of officially inspired antisemitism then sweeping the U.S.S.R. Very muted echoes of this can be found in Soviet writing of the post-Stalin era, such as Ehrenburg's novella *Ottepel* (1954; *The Thaw*, 1955) and Yevtushenko's poetry. By 1970, problems such as Soviet antisemitism and Jewish identity were dealt with only in underground literature circulating illegally in the U.S.S.R., much of it actually published in the West. The most notable writer in this category was the non-Jew Andrey Sinyavski (1915–1997), whose works appeared under the Jewish-sounding pseudonym Abram Tertz. Particularly interesting are his *Fantasticheskiye povesti* (1961; *Fantastic Stories*, 1967), and the novels *Sud idyot* ("The Trial Begins," 1959) and *Lyubimov* (1964; Eng. tr., *The Makepeace Experiment*, 1965). Other "underground" writers included Yuli *Daniel, whose works appeared under the pseudonym Nikolay Arzhak, and Yosif *Brodski. Sinyavski, Daniel, and Brodski were all sentenced to varying terms of forced labor.

The Jewish Contribution

Since the late 19th century, hundreds of Jews have played an active, and often major role in Russian literary affairs. As in Germany, there was at first a tendency for Russian Jewish writers to accelerate their assimilation through baptism: the poet and essayist Nikolai *Minski and his brother-in-law, the literary scholar Semyon *Wengeroff, were two such converts. The feuilletonist Miron (Meyer) Davidovich Ryvkin (1869–1915), who wrote for Jewish and liberal journals, successfully conveyed the atmosphere of the *shtetl. His historical novel *Navet* (1912; Yid. tr., *Der Velizher Blut-Bilbl*, 1913) dealt with a blood libel. After the Bolshevik Revolution a number of Jewish writers left Russia. They included the critic Yuli *Aikhenvald (who was expelled in 1922); the novelist Mark *Aldanov; the poets Sasha *Cherni and V.F. Khodasevich; and the playwright Lev Natanovich *Lunts. Another émigré, Mikhail Osipovich Zetlin (1882–1945), was the author of *Dekabristy – Sudba odnogo pokoleniya* (1933; *The Decembrists*, 1958) on the 1825 insurrection. Among those who remained in the U.S.S.R. were David *Aizman; Mikhail *Gershenzon, who promoted Hebrew culture but fought Zionism; and Ilya Ehrenburg.

Despite the pressures of Soviet life, Russian Jewish writers were as active in the "liberal" camp as among the conformists. Rejection of or indifference to the Jewish heritage characterized the first post-revolutionary generation of Jewish authors, which included the Komsomol poet Alexander Bezymenski (1898–1973); the humorist Ilya *Ilf; the eminent poet Osip *Mandelshtam, who had an obsessive dislike of everything Jewish; the Nobel Prize-winning poet and novelist Boris *Pasternak, author of *Doctor Zhivago* (1957; Eng, tr., 1959); the half-Jewish author and critic Victor Shklovski (1893–1984); and the novelist and literary scholar Yuri *Tynyanov. The critic Abram Zakharovich Lezhnev (1893–1938) wrote *Sovremenniki* ("Contemporaries," 1927), which contains three chapters on Babel, Pasternak, Selvinski, and Utkin, and *Proza Pushkina* (1937). The philosophy of Jewish assimilation under the Soviet regime suffered a setback with the great purges of the 1930s, when Leopold *Averbach and Vladimir *Kirshon disappeared, and many other Jewish writers, notably the poet Joseph Utkin, were exposed to severe criticism. The problem of reconciling their Jewish identity with their Soviet allegiances preoccupied Isaac Babel (who was liquidated by the regime), Ilya Ehrenburg, Ilya Selvinski, and Mikhail *Svetlov. Like Ehrenburg, Emmanuil *Kazakevich, a former Yiddish writer from Birobidzhan, escaped the antisemitic excesses of the Stalin era and was a prominent "liberal" during the post-Stalin thaw; while Samuel Marshak, the poet and translator, also survived, despite his evident "cosmopolitanism." A decade or more after Stalin's death many Jewish writers in the U.S.S.R. still felt the weight of Soviet oppression. Vladimir *Admoni was a defense witness at the 1964 Brodski trial; Vasili *Grossman courageously attempted to document Nazi crimes against the Jews in the face of official displeasure; Lev Kopelev (1912–1997), an ally of Alexander Solzhenitsyn (1918–), was a dissident literary scholar.

There are relatively few translations from Hebrew literature into Russian, although translations from Yiddish literature are quite numerous, some of them – above all those of *Shalom Aleichem – among the most effective in any language. This is due partly to the traditional excellence of the art of literary translation in Russia, and partly to the fact that the Yiddish language lends itself well to translation into Russian, since both have two distinct lexical components: the lofty with religious overtones (Hebraisms in Yiddish and Church Slavonicisms in Russian), and the informal vernacular (Germanic in Yiddish, and common speech in Russian). There are numerous successful translations of Russian literature into Hebrew. The most noteworthy are *Shlonsky's poetic version of Pushkin's *Eugene Onegin* (1937, 1953[4]) and Lea *Goldberg's translations from several Russian authors.

BIBLIOGRAPHY: V. Aleksandrova, in: Ya. G. Frumkin et al. (eds.), *Kniga o russkom yevreystve 1917–1967*, 2 (1968); E.J. Brown, *Russian Literature since the Revolution* (1969); B.J. Chaseed, in: E.J. Simmons (ed.), *Through the Glass of Soviet Literature: Views of Russian Society* (1953), 110–58; D.I. Čiževskij, *History of Russian Literature from the Eleventh Century to the End of the Baroque* (1962); J. Kunitz, *Russian Literature and the Jew: a Sociological Inquiry…* (1929); D.S. Mirsky, *A History of Russian Literature* (1949), incl. bibl.; G.P. Struve, *Russkaya literatura v izgnanii* (1956); idem, *Soviet Russian Literature 1917–1950* (1951).

[Maurice Friedberg]

RUTENBERG, PINḤAS (**Piotr**; 1879–1942), prominent figure in the revolutionary movement in Russia, *yishuv* leader, and pioneer of modern industry in Ereẓ Israel. Born in Romny, Ukraine, Rutenberg graduated from St. Petersburg Technological Institute and was first employed at the large Putilov metallurgical works. As a student he became active in the revolutionary movement (first as a Social Democrat and then a Social Revolutionary) and was imprisoned several times. He marched with Father Gapon on "Bloody Sunday," which ushered in the 1905 Revolution, and helped Gapon flee from Russia. A year later, when the Social Revolutionaries came to the conclusion that the priest was serving as a police agent, Rutenberg was instructed by the party to organize Gapon's execution. He spent the years 1907–15 in Italy, working as an engineer and specializing in irrigation. During the latter part of this period, he became interested in Jewish affairs, and after the outbreak of World War I he went to London to urge Zionist leaders to raise Jewish military units for the liberation of Palestine. When he learned of Vladimir *Jabotinsky's interest in the matter, Rutenberg contacted him to assure joint action and went to the U.S. in 1915 to propagate the idea. There Rutenberg became involved in the campaign for the creation of the first American Jewish Congress, which was to formulate Jewish proposals to be brought before the Peace Conference at the conclusion of war. While in America, he drew up a comprehensive irrigation plan for Palestine. He also published a Yiddish translation of a pamphlet he had written in Italy under the title *The National Revival of the Jewish People* and signed "Pinḥas Ben-Ammi."

With the overthrow of czarist rule in Russia at the beginning of 1917, Rutenberg left the U.S. for Petrograd, where Kerensky appointed him deputy governor of the capital in charge of civilian affairs. During the Bolshevik coup, on Nov. 7, Rutenberg, was among the last defenders of the site of the provisional government in the Petrograd Winter Palace. Some six months of imprisonment followed, after which he went to Moscow to work for the Center of the Russian Cooperative Organizations, and soon escaped to Kiev, capital of the temporarily independent Ukraine. At the end of 1918, he left for Odessa, where he joined a French-sponsored "White" Russian government that did not last long. By the middle of 1919, Rutenburg left Russia forever. When he came to the conclusion that there was antisemitism even in revolutionary movements, he went to Palestine (November 1919).

With some aid from the Zionist Organization, Rutenberg organized a survey of the country's water resources, mainly of the Jordan River, as a prerequisite to obtaining a government concession to develop the potential of these resources and supply the country with power. For practical reasons, stress was laid on the hydroelectric aspects of his planning, and the proposal was then brought before the first postwar Zionist Conference in London (1920). Together with Jabotinsky, Rutenberg organized the self-defense in Jerusalem at the time of the Arab riots in 1920; in 1921 he became head of Haganah in Tel Aviv and also served as adviser to the Anglo-French commission for the delimitation of Palestine's northern boundaries.

After he overcame great financial and political difficulties, Rutenberg established the Palestine Electric Company (1923), which was subsequently granted a concession to use the waters of the Jordan and Yarmuk rivers for the supply of energy (see Israel, State of: *Economic Affairs (Energy Sources). Initial successes enabled him to secure the services of outstanding personalities as heads of the company's board: Lord Melchett, Lord Hirst, Lord *Samuel, and Lord *Reading. Preoccupied with company affairs, Rutenberg could no more than follow, and indirectly influence, internal affairs of the *yishuv*, but in the crisis year 1929 he was called upon to head the Va'ad Le'ummi and use his considerable influence with the Mandatory administration. He left the Va'ad Le'ummi after the crisis had passed, but joined it again in 1939. In the 1930s he cooperated with a number of other Jewish personalities (including Judah L. *Magnes, M. *Novomeysky, Moshe *Smilansky, G. *Frumkin) in search of a program for Arab-Jewish understanding. Though he had the ear of King *Abdullah of Transjordan, nothing came of his efforts. Domestically, Rutenberg sought to remove the acute friction between the *Histadrut and the *Revisionists. Through his good offices, David *Ben-Gurion and Jabotinsky negotiated an agreement in 1934 which failed, however, to be ratified by the Histadrut. At the beginning of World War II, he again became president of the Va'ad Le'ummi but his health soon failed, and he died in Jerusalem. Before his death, Rutenberg addressed a special call for national unity to Jewish youth and willed his possessions to the Rutenberg Foundation for youth activities; his house on Mount Carmel subsequently became a large and active youth center.

BIBLIOGRAPHY: Y. Yaari-Poleskin, *Pinḥas Rutenberg, ha-Ish u-Fo'olo* (1939); L. Lipsky, *Gallery of Zionist Profiles* (1956), 124–8; H. Sacher, *Zionist Portraits and Other Essays* (1959), 99–101; M. Sharett, *Yoman Medini 1936* (1968), index.

[Moshe Medzini]

RUTH, BOOK OF (Heb. מְגִלַּת רוּת), one of the five scrolls incorporated in the *Ketuvim* (Hagiographa) section of the traditional Hebrew Bible. In the Septuagint, followed by Christian Bibles, Ruth is found immediately after Judges.

Contents

In the days of the Judges, Elimelech, of Beth-Lehem in Judah, immigrated with his wife Naomi and his two sons Mahlon and Chilion to Moab on account of famine. He died there and so did his two sons, who had married Moabite women, Orpah and Ruth. Left without either husband or sons, and having no grandchildren, Naomi decided to return to Beth-Lehem. The two daughters-in-law wanted to move to Judah with her, but she bade them stay in their homeland. Orpah obeyed but Ruth vowed that she would share the fortunes of her mother-in-law. Arriving in Beth-Lehem at the beginning of the grain harvest, Ruth took advantage of the privilege of gleaning which custom accorded the poor. The field she came to glean in belonged to a prosperous farmer by the name of Boaz. When Naomi learned that Boaz had shown Ruth special kindness out of appreciation for her devotion to her mother-in-law, she was doubly delighted because Boaz was a kinsman of Elimelech, and hence of Ruth's dead husband Mahlon, and the old woman could see a prospect of a levirate marriage for Ruth. The levirate marriage with Ruth involved the redemption of the land of the dead husband, which Naomi had sold. Boaz consented to marry Ruth and to redeem the land. Thus he fulfilled the ancient patriarchal duty of "establishing the name of the dead upon his inheritance" (Ruth 4:5; cf. Deut. 25:6). Through this marriage Boaz became the ancestor of King David.

Aim of the Book

The book concludes with the genealogy of David (4:17–22), which was highly significant to the author. One aim of his was to present in an idyllic way the origin of the great king David. A similar, though less idyllic, account is found in the story about Judah and Tamar (Gen. 38), the parents of Perez, an even earlier ancestor within the Davidic genealogy. The circumstances of the birth of Perez in that story are similar to those of the birth of Obed, the grandfather of David, in the story of Ruth. Perez was born by a levirate marriage and so was Obed; in both cases it was not the proper levir – Latin for "brother-in-law," or the nearest relative (Ruth 3:12) – who performed his duty of levirate marriage (cf. Deut. 25:1–10), but another kinsman. Both stories concern a woman of foreign stock (Tamar – Canaanite; Ruth – Moabite) and in both of them the woman waiting for levirate espousal resorts to a stratagem in order to obtain it. Tamar sits on the crossroads disguised as a prostitute in order to allure Judah (Gen. 38:14), while Ruth, at night, lies down at the feet of Boaz who is sleeping on the threshing floor (3:1ff.). The author of the story of Ruth bears this analogy in mind and finds an opportunity to recall the older story by having the people and the elders of the town bless Boaz: "Let your house be like the house of Perez whom Tamar bore to Judah" (4:12). The provenance of the house of Perez and of the House of David is thus recounted in a similar way.

Furthermore, from the literary point of view the stories of Judah and Boaz contain the motif that also underlies the stories of the Patriarchs: the obstacles put in the way of the emergence of an important family in the history of the nation. The stories of the Patriarchs especially reflect the difficulties that lay in the way of the continuation of the line of the chosen people. The stories about the births of Isaac and Jacob exemplify how much was at stake when the national heroes were about to be born. One cannot avoid mentioning in this context the similarity in circumstance between the birth of Jacob and Esau on one hand and Perez and Zerah on the other. In both instances the favored son, Jacob in one case and Perez in the other, was actually not the first born, but attained his primogeniture through force or cunning. The rejected sons, Esau and Zerah, are both affiliated with Edom (for Zerah cf. Gen. 36:17; I Chron. 1:37), the harsh enemy of David (I Kings 11:15–16). Both stories have certain identical stylistic formulations (cf. Gen. 25:24 with 38:27).

The connection between the Davidic and the patriarchal genealogies becomes more salient when the two following facts are taken into account: (1) The superscription of the genealogical line *toledot* (תולדות), outside of the Pentateuch (the Priestly strand), is found only in Ruth 4:18. (2) Malamat (JAOS, 88 (1968), 163ff.) has shown that royal genealogies in the Ancient Near East were constructed according to the following lines: (a) the genealogical stock, whose formulation is mostly artificial, referring to some common ancestors of various ethnic groups, which is parallel to the genealogical list in Genesis 11:10–26; (b) the determinative line which delineates the specific descent of the dynasty or the people, as Abraham, Isaac, and Jacob in Israel; (c) the actual pedigree of the king involved (as Ruth 4:18–22). The first and third listings usually comprise ten generations, whereas the second is a short list usually of two or three generations. The linkage of the third to the second list in this case has been shown above, and in the light of the fact that the Pentateuchal sources were certainly not crystallized before David, it stands to reason that, as in Mesopotamia, so also in Israel the genealogy of the first type is also to be considered an organic part of the royal genealogy ending with David. Thus there is no justification for the view that the genealogy does not form an integral part of the book and that it is an addition to the book.

The Davidic genealogy is especially significant because it bolsters the book's subtle but forceful protest against the Ezra-Nehemiah attitude toward foreign women (Ezra 9–10; Neh. 13:23–29); had Boaz not married the Moabite woman Ruth, the line of Perez would have ended and David would never have been born.

Theology

As is true in some of the stories of Genesis and the succession narratives of David, so also in the Book of Ruth the events occur in the human realm. Miracles and angelic figures are absent, and God works behind the scenes. The occurrences, which look like a chain of natural happenings evolving one from the other, reveal themselves in the end as the outcome of God's plan. So, for example, in the story of Joseph the events are moved and motivated by purely human impulses. However, the narrator reveals in two brief sentences (Gen. 45:7; 50:20) that all these complex events are none other than the realization of God's plan. There is no chance happening in this world; whatever happens is caused by God (cf. II Sam. 16:10–11). The events in David's court also seem to be caused by purely human motivation: Conflicts in connection with the struggle for the crown. However, for the author these stories come to demonstrate the way of the realization of God's plan to establish David's throne through the enthronement of Solomon.

The Book of Ruth, which also recounts a natural story in which everything moves by human agents and, as it were, without divine interference, actually serves as a testimony to the wondrous ways in which God leads human destiny. Ruth "happens" to choose, as if at random, the field of Boaz (2:3) but that choice turns out to be the decisive act for the birth of David, the illustrious king of Israel. Naomi indeed attributes her success in this coincidence to God, "who did not withhold His kindness from the living and the dead" (2:20). This is reminiscent of Abraham's servant who asks God "to make it happen today" (Gen. 24:12), i.e., to enable a proper choice, and indeed after it becomes clear to him that his wish has been realized, he proclaims: "Blessed be the Lord who has not withheld His steadfast kindness from my master. For I have been guided on my way by the Lord" (24:27). The phrase "[God] who did not withhold His kindness" is found in the Bible only in these two instances, which is not without significance.

Date of Composition

The Book of Ruth was written not before the period of the Monarchy, which is clear from the genealogy at the end of the book, terminating with David. The opening verse of the book, "In the days when the judges ruled," also attests to the fact that the book was written at a time when the period of the

Judges belonged to the historical past. From one statement in the book one may even get the impression that at least a few generations have passed since the occurrence of the events: "This was formerly done in Israel in cases of redemption and exchange: to validate any transaction one man would take off his sandal and hand it to the other" (4:7). Temporal distance made it necessary for the author to explain this forgotten practice to the audience.

The atmosphere of the Book of Ruth, set in the period of the judges, is idyllic. The good characters, Orpah and the anonymous kinsman, are contrasted with the superlative characters, Ruth, Boaz, and Naomi. Judges, although set in the same period, is full of violence, murder, pillage, and rape. Nevertheless, Judges and Ruth have in common their depiction of women who manage to get what they want within the limitations of an ancient society dominated by men. Given the dominance of female characters in Ruth and the presence (at least attempted) of a female point of view, and the fact that there were literate women in the ancient world, a female author for Ruth is not an impossibility.

STYLISTIC-LITERARY EVIDENCE. The late author of Ruth was familiar with many of the earlier writings that make up the Hebrew Bible, and used them in the construction of his own book. Sometimes the references are direct, at other times allusive. The love of Naomi and Ruth is reminiscent of the love of David and Jonathan. As Jonathan pledges love and loyalty to David (I Sam. 18:1–3; 20:12–13, 17) so does Ruth to Naomi (1:16–17), and in both cases a common formula of imprecation is used: "Thus and more may the Lord do to me" (1:17; cf. I Sam. 20:13), which is found only in the Books of Samuel and in the North-Israelite narratives of the Books of Kings. The contents of the imprecation, "if (even) death part me from you" (Ruth and Naomi will be buried in the same place), are reminiscent of the words of David in his elegy over Saul and Jonathan that they were not parted in life or death (II Sam. 1:23).

The book provides an archaic flavor by using expressions of gracious manners characteristic of the patriarchal narratives and the Books of Samuel. The meeting of Boaz and Ruth concludes with the prostration of Ruth (2:10) and words of praise and appreciation by Boaz (2:11–12), which is similar to the encounter of David with Abigail in I Samuel 25:23ff. Abigail "prostrates with her face to the ground," like Ruth, and David, like Boaz, praises Abigail for her courage and good qualities. At the second meeting with Ruth, Boaz exclaims: "Be blessed to the Lord" (3:10), a formula also found at the meeting of David and Abigail (I Sam. 25:32–33) and in the narratives of the Book of Genesis (24:31; 14:19), and elsewhere in the Books of Samuel (I Sam. 15:23; II Sam. 2:5). The manner in which thankfulness is expressed in the Book of Ruth is also very instructive. Reacting to the praise of Boaz, Ruth says: "I am grateful to you [אמצא חן בעיניך] my lord, for comforting me and speaking kindly to your maidservant" (2:13). The usage of אמצא חן בעיניך for expressing gratitude is common in the books of Genesis and Samuel (Gen. 33:9; 47:25; I Sam. 1:18; II Sam. 16:4). Bidding farewell in Ruth is expressed by "kissing" (and also "weeping," 1:9, 14) which is similar to farewell expressions found in Genesis (31:28; 32:1; 50:1), Samuel (II Sam. 19:40), and the North-Israelite narratives of Kings (I Kings 19:20).

Other clichés in the Book of Ruth that draw on earlier Israelite literature worthy of mention are: 1:1: "he and his wife" (cf. Gen. 13:1); 1:2: "The man's name… his wife's name" (cf. I Sam. 25:3); 1:4: "The name of the one… and the name of the other" (cf. Gen. 4:19; I Sam. 1:2); 1:9, 14: "to lift up the voice and weep" (i.e., to weep aloud; cf. Gen. 21:16; 27:38; 29:11; cf. 45:2; I Sam. 24:17; 30:4; II Sam. 3:32; 13:36; Job 2:12 – on the patriarchal atmosphere of Job cf. Sarna, in JBL, 76 (1957), 13–25); 1:16–17 (cf. Judges 17:8–9); 1:19: "The whole city buzzed with excitement" (cf. I Kings 1:41); 2:5: "Whose" (למי; cf. Gen. 32:18; I Sam. 30:13); 2:8: "here" (כה; cf. Gen. 22:5; 31:37; Ex. 2:12; Num. 11:31; 23:15; II Sam. 18:30); 2:12: "reward" (משכרתך; cf. Gen. 29:15; 31:7, 41); 2:14: "come here" (גשי הלם; cf. I Sam. 14:38); 2:20: "who did not withhold his kindness" (cf. Gen. 24:7); 2:21: "until they finish" (עד אם כלו; cf. Gen. 24:19); 3:7: "eat and drink and be in cheerful mood" (cf. Judg. 19:6 [9]; I Kings 21:7); 3:7: "come in stealthily" (cf. Judg. 4:21); 3:8:"[it was] in the middle of the night" (cf. Ex. 12:29); 3:16: "How is it with you?" (מי את; cf. Judg. 18:8; and see S. Loewenstamm, in: *Leshonenu*, 23 (1959), 74); 4:1:"so and so" (פלוני אלמוני; cf. I Sam. 21:3; II Kings 6:8 as against Dan. 8:13); 4:4: "tell" (גלה אזן; cf. I Sam. 9:15; 20:2, 12, 13; 22:8, 17; II Sam 2:27); 4:7: "formerly done in Israel" (לפנים בישראל; cf. I Sam. 9:9); 4:9: "You are witnesses today" (cf. Josh. 24:22); 4:15: "better to you than seven sons" (cf. I Sam. 1:8). All these phrases and expressions are found in settings no later than the ninth or early eighth century B.C.E. But setting must be distinguished from time of composition. There are numerous Aramaisms and late linguistic traits in Ruth, such as: לקים דבר (4:7) instead of להקים דבר ("to confirm a promise/pact/deal"; cf. Num. 23:19; Deut. 9:5; I Sam. 3:12; *ʿgn*, (Ruth 1:13) not known elsewhere in the Bible, but well-known in rabbinic *agunah*, "bound woman"; *qnh l'šh*, "take as wife," is very close to Mishnaic Hebrew usage. Most important though for purposes of dating is the fact that the author knows most of the Bible, including late sources such as Leviticus and Job, and makes use of it for his own purposes. (For examples of borrowings see Zakovitch, 24–32.) During the Persian period of Jewish history (539–331) when Ruth was written, the question of personal status had become acute. Late books of the Bible that stem from this period reflect differing attitudes about the possibility of a non-Jew becoming a Jew. In contrast to Ezra-Nehemiah, according to which there are no means for those not born to the "holy seed" (Ezra 9:3, legal midrash on Isa. 6:13) to become Jews, the author of Ruth makes it possible for a foreigner to find protection under the wings of YHWH (Ruth 2:12). Ruth's author effectively repeals the exclusion of Moabites (Deut 23:4) enforced in Nehemiah 13:23–27, which appeals to the precedent of how Solomon strayed by taking foreign wives. Instead, the Book of Ruth points to the precedent of the ancient worthies who built up the house of Israel by ignoring the letter of the law when the growth of the house of Israel was at stake. Thus, Jacob's marriage to the two sisters Rachel and Leah (Ruth 4:11) violated Leviticus 18:18, and Tamar's union with Judah (Ruth 4:12) violated Leviticus 18:15. As such, one need not worry about the restriction of Deuteronomy 23:4. The qualities of a foreigner are more important than her origins. Ruth, whose foreign origin is repeatedly emphasized (1:22; 2:2, 6, 8, 21; 4:5, 10), is an *eshet ḥayil* (Ruth 3:11) "virtuous woman," worthy of Boaz the *gibbor ḥayil* "virtuous hero" (Ruth 2:1). Incidentally, the author of Ruth may have been influenced by the fact that the *eshet ḥayil* of Proverbs 31 has a husband "known in the gates when he sits among the elders" (Prov. 31:23; cf. Ruth 4:1–13).

The Place of the Book in the Canon

Talmudic tradition ascribes the book to the Hagiographa (BB 14b), but this is based on the opinion that the Canon contains 24 books. A variant tradition (Jos., Apion, 1:39) speaks only of 22 books in the Bible. According to this system, Ruth is attached to the Book of Judges and Lamentations to Jeremiah, an arrangement adopted by the Septuagint. According to the order of the Five *Scrolls in modern Hebrew Bibles, Ruth is the second scroll after Song of Songs, because the latter is to be recited on Passover whereas Ruth is to be read on Shavuot. The order in the talmudic source quoted above is different: Ruth opens the Hagiographa preceding the Psalms. Here the sequence is a historical one. Ruth relates to the period of the Judges while Psalms is attributed to David, who is later.

The Book of Ruth was one of the first biblical books to be examined through the lenses of "the Bible as literature" approach (Rauber).

[Moshe Weinfeld / S. David Sperling (2nd ed.)]

In the Aggadah

Ruth was a daughter of the king of Moab (Ruth R. 2:9). After the death of Mahlon, Naomi attempted to dissuade her from returning to Ereẓ Israel lest she be treated contemptuously as a foreigner (*Midrash Zuta* to Ruth 1:8). Ruth is regarded as the prototype of the righteous convert. Naomi could not discourage her from taking this step although she told her of the stringencies of Jewish law and that its transgression would entail corporal and capital punishments from which she was hitherto exempt (Ruth R. 2:24). When Naomi told her that Jewish daughters do not frequent theaters and circuses, she replied, "Whither thou goest, I will go"; when informed that Jewish daughters only dwell in houses sanctified by *mezuzot*, she responded: "where thou lodgest, I will lodge"; "thy people will be my people" implied "I will destroy all idolatry within me"; and "thy God shall be my God" to repay me the reward of my deeds (Ruth 1:16; Ruth R. 2:22, 23). They arrived on the day that the wife of *Boaz was buried (BB 91a). Ruth's piety impressed Boaz when he noticed that she did not glean the fields if the reapers let more than two ears fall since the gleanings assigned to the poor by the law refer only to two ears inadvertently dropped at one time. He also admired her grace, decorum, and modest demeanor (Ruth R. 4:6; *Midrash Zuta* to Ruth 2:3). After Naomi made her a party to her plan to force Boaz into a decisive step, Ruth strictly adhered to her directions except that she did not wash, anoint, and finely clothe herself until after she reached her destination, since she feared to attract the attention of the lustful (Shab. 113b). The next day she was taken in marriage by Boaz, who was 80 years of age. Ruth herself was barren and 40 years old at the time, and it was against all expectations that this union should be blessed with issue (Ruth R. 7:14). Possibly because she retained her original name even after her conversion, it is interpreted as meaning that she was the ancestress of *David, "who saturated ("רוה") the Holy One, blessed be He, with songs and hymns" (Ber. 7b). Another explanation is that she considered well (*ra'atah*) the words of her mother-in-law (Ruth R. 2:9).

See also *David and *Ammonites and *Moabites in *halakhah*.

[Aaron Rothkoff]

In the Arts

Despite the grandeur of Ruth's story and the romantic appeal of her religious identification and the dynastic link with King David, she has inspired surprisingly few important works in the arts. The subject was muted in literature of the Middle Ages, first appearing significantly in the 17th century with three works in Spanish: João Pinto *Delgado's poem *Ruth* (1627), Tirso de Molina's drama, *La mejor espigadera* (1634), and an *auto sacramentale* by Pedro Calderón de la Barca. The new literary movements of the 19th century directed fresh attention to the potentialities of the subject. Karl Streckfuss wrote the German epic *Ruth* (1805) and there were a number of dramas, including two in French, both entitled *La Moabite*, by Henri Bornier (1880) and the patriotic writer Paul Déroulede (1881). One of the most memorable evocations of the theme occurs in the English poet John Keat's "Ode to a Nightingale" (1819) with the lines: "Perhaps the self-same song that found a path/Through the sad heart of Ruth, when, sick for home,/She stood in tears amid the alien corn…" Perhaps the outstanding 19th-century treatment was, however, "Booz endormi," one of the "petites épopées" included in Victor Hugo's *La Légende des siècles* (1859), which is generally regarded as among Hugo's finest poems. The theme was not neglected by Jewish writers of the period: In Germany Isaac Jojade Cohn published a three-act Hebrew play, *Bo'az ve-Rut* (1834); Emanuel Baumgarten wrote the poem, *Rut, MeliẒah…* (1885); and Solomon Rosenzweig was the author of another Hebrew play, *Rut Torat Ḥesed* (1893).

Twentieth-century works about Ruth have covered a wider range of languages, beginning with Siegmund Werner's *Ruth, und andere Gedichte* (1903). Many appeared between the world wars, such as Pilar Millán Astray's three-act Spanish play *Ruth la Israelita* (1923); and Emanuil Pop Dimitrov's Bulgarian *Rut*; and *Boass un Rute* (1926), a Lettish play by Aspazija (Elza Rozenberga). The subject also attracted the attention of Yiddish writers: Victor Spritzer's *Rut; Dramatishe Poeme* appeared at Buenos Aires in 1933, and Saul Saphire wrote *Rut; Biblisher Roman fun der Tsayt fun di Shoftim* (1936). Modern interest in and reinterpretation of the Ruth theme acquired new significance both during and after the Nazi era. Poems were written by Else *Lasker-Schueler ("Boas") and Yvan *Goll ("Noémi"); and the works which appeared after World War II included a novel, *Ruth*, by the U.S. author Irving *Fineman (1949) and Frank G. Slaughter's *The Song of Ruth. A Love Story from the Old Testament* (1954).

In art, Ruth appears in medieval manuscripts from the 12th century onward, including the 12th-century *Admont Bible* (State Library, Vienna), a late 13th-century Franco-German **maḥzor* (British Museum, additional 22413), in which a harvesting scene depicting Ruth and the gleaners illustrates the prayers for Shavuot; and the 14th-century *Queen Mary Psalter* (British Museum) and *Bible of Jean de Papeleu* (Arsenal Library, Paris). The subjects treated are Ruth gleaning and, more rarely, Boaz taking Ruth to wife. In the 17th century, the magnificent painting of Summer by Nicolas Poussin in the Louvre, one of four illustrating the seasons, also shows Ruth among the gleaners. This study of the abundance of nature is full of memories of the classical world. The English poet and painter William *Blake executed a stark watercolor painting (Victoria and Albert Museum, London) of Naomi, Ruth, and Orpah in the land of Moab. The modern Israel artist Jakob *Steinhardt illustrated the Book of Ruth with woodcuts (1957).

BIBLIOGRAPHY: H. Gunkel, *Reden und Aufsätze* (1913), 65–92; H.H. Rowley, in: HTR, 40 (1947), 77–99; J.L. Myers, *The Linguistic and Literary Form of the Book of Ruth* (1955); S.R. Driver, *An Introduction to the Literature of the Old Testament* (1956), 453–6; O. Loretz, in: CBQ, 22 (1960), 391–9; M. Weinfeld, in: *Ture Yeshurun* (1966), 10–15; H.L. Ginsberg, *The Five Megilloth and the Book of Jonah* (1969). IN THE AGGADAH: Ginzberg; Legends, index. **ADD. BIBLIOGRAPHY:** D. Rauber: in, JBL, 89 (1970), 27–37; B. Levine, in: H. Huffmon (ed.), *The Quest for the Kingdom of God Studies ... Mendenhall* (1983), 95–106; J. Sasson, Ruth ... (1979); P. Trible, in: ABD, 5:843–47, incl. bibl.; Y. Zakovitch, *Ruth* (1990), incl. bibl.

RUTH RABBAH (Heb. רוּת רַבָּה), aggadic Midrash on the Book of *Ruth, the product of Palestinian *amoraim*.

The Name

The *editio princeps* was called *Midrash Ruth*, the title *Ruth Rabbah* being derived from later editions (from that published in Venice, 1545, and onward) in which the work was printed together with Midrashim on the other Scrolls (Song of Songs, Lamentations, Ecclesiastes, Esther) and with five on the Pentateuch, the whole commencing with Genesis *Rabbah. Hence, the general designation of *Rabbah* applied to all these Midrashim (see *Midrash).

The Structure

Ruth Rabbah is an exegetical Midrash which expounds the Book of Ruth chapter by chapter, verse by verse, and, sometimes, word by word. It is a compilation, made by the redactor, of various expositions. In the printed versions, the Midrash is divided into eight sections with introductory poems. Actually there are only four sections, each introduced by a poem or poems, the division being as follows:

(a) from the beginning of the proems to the end of section 3;

(b) sections 4–5;

(c) sections 5–7;

(d) section 8.

The work has apparently a total of ten proems, these being of the classical type found in amoraic Midrashim, in that they commence with an extraneous verse, taken usually from the Hagiographa, which is expounded and then connected with the one treated at the beginning of the section. While some of the proems are anonymous, others are stated in the name of a sage. The first original section concludes with an assurance and consolation (in the printed versions, at the end of section 3).

The Language

Ruth Rabbah is written mainly in mishnaic Hebrew, and, to a certain extent (particularly the narrative parts), in Galilean *Aramaic, like the Jerusalem Talmud. It also contains many Greek words.

The Redaction

The redaction drew upon tannaitic literature, the Jerusalem Talmud, *Genesis Rabbah, Leviticus *Rabbah, Lamentations *Rabbah*, and Pesikta de-Rav *Kahana. Zunz's assertion that the Babylonian Talmud was used as well has been disproved by *Albeck. The sages mentioned in the Midrash flourished not later than the end of the fourth century C.E. It seems, therefore, that the work was redacted in Ereẓ Israel and belongs to the early amoraic aggadic Midrashim. Since, however, it drew on *Pesikta de-Rav Kahana*, it is difficult to assign the compilation of *Ruth Rabbah* to a date prior to the sixth century C.E.

Editions

Ruth Rabbah, first published at Pesaro in 1519 together with the four Midrashim on the other Scrolls (to which it bears no relation), has often been reprinted on the basis of this *editio princeps*. The printed versions are quite defective.

BIBLIOGRAPHY: Zunz-Albeck, Derashot, 128, 130; H.L. Strack, *Introduction to the Talmud and Midrash* (1931), 220; D. Hartmann, *Das Buch Ruth in der Midrasch-Litteratur* (1901).

[Moshe David Herr]

°RUTILIUS NAMATIANUS, holder of a civic post in Rome in 416 C.E. In a poem commemorating his return to his native Gaul, he describes how, at Faleria (Falesia) on the Tyrrhenian coast (near present-day Piombino), his party met the Jewish keeper of a fishpond. The inhospitality of the Jew prompted Rutilius to condemn the Jews as a disgusting and overly influential race whose presence in Rome was to be regretted. He speaks contemptuously of their dietary laws, circumcision and Sabbath, and voices the familiar Roman anti-Jewish sentiments.

BIBLIOGRAPHY: J.W. and A.M. Duff (eds.), *Minor Latin Poets* (1935), 796–9 (text and Eng. tr.); Pauly-Wissowa, 1 (1914), 1249–54, no. 13.

[Jacob Petroff]

°**RUTLAND, SUZANNE** (1946–), Australian historian. Probably the first academic historian to write on Australian Jewish history, Sydney-born Suzanne Rutland was the author of one of the first modern accounts of the Jews in Australia, *Edge of the Diaspora* (1988), and a history of the Jewish press in Australia, *Pages of History* (1970; 1995^2), as well as other works in this field. She taught at the University of New South Wales and was the editor of the Sydney edition of *The Australian Jewish Historical Society Journal.*

[William D. Rubinstein (2nd ed.)]

RUWANDIZ (**Rawanduz, Rowanduz**), district town in the province of Irbil in Iraqi *Kurdistan. In Ruwandiz there was an ancient Jewish community which suffered a great deal at the hands of cruel governors. During the 17th century the two *paytanim*, R. Isaac b. Moses Ḥariri and his son R. Phinehas (Pinḥas), who wrote several *piyyutim* and kabbalistic works, lived there. The situation of the Jews improved to some extent at the beginning of the 19th century with the Turkish occupation. In 1848 *Benjamin II found a number of wealthy Jews led by the *nasi* Muʿallim Nissim, who owned fields and vineyards. The Jews were engaged in agriculture and they spoke Jebel ("mountain") Aramaic. In 1881 there were about 50 to 60 Jewish families; from 1884 to 1906, 120 Jews; in 1910, 40 families; and in 1914, 100 Jews. The penetration of the Russians into Kurdistan in 1915 liquidated this community. The synagogue was destroyed together with its *Sifrei Torah*. The community was renewed after World War I. According to the official census of 1930, there were 17,787 inhabitants in the whole district of Ruwandiz, of whom 250 were Jews. In 1932 there were 20 Jewish families with a synagogue. All emigrated to the State of Israel.

[Abraham Ben-Yaacob]

RUZHANY (Pol. **Różana**; Yid. **Rozhanoy** or **Rozhinoy**), town in Brest district, Belarus; within Poland-Lithuania until the partitions of Poland and between the two world wars. The community of Ruzhany, which was placed under the jurisdiction of the community of Brest-Litovsk by the Lithuanian Council in 1623 (see *Councils of the Lands), existed before that date. From 1662 it is mentioned as an independent community. Following a *blood libel in Ruzhany in 1657, attacks on the Jews by the Christian populace were prevented by the owner of the town. However, agitators demanded that two of the community's notables be handed over to them, and as a result R. Israel b. Shalom and R. Tobias b. Joseph were executed on the second day of Rosh Ha-Shanah. A special *seliḥah* in their memory was written by the son of R. Israel, and it was read every year during the *ne'ilah* prayer of the Day of Atonement.

The Jews of Ruzhany suffered during the Polish civil war and the Russian-Swedish War (1700–10). In 1721 the Ruzhany community paid 1,100 zlotys in poll tax, the same amount as the Vilna community and only slightly less than Minsk. However, by 1766 their number had declined to 326 in the town and district (c. 154 in the town itself). By 1847 the Jewish population of the town had risen to 1,467; it numbered 3,599 (71.7% of the total population) in 1897; and 3,718 (66.2%) in 1921. Jews earned their livelihood from trade and crafts, mainly connected with the local fairs, industry and agriculture. Industries were established in Ruzhany from the beginning of the 19th century: there were six textile mills and a number of spinning mills employing about 2,000 Jewish workers, tanneries, and flour mills. Many families engaged in vegetable growing and cultivating orchards which they leased. In 1850 two Jewish agricultural villages were established near Ruzhany; some of their inhabitants were later among the founders of the moshavah *Ekron in Ereẓ Israel. Jews from Ruzhany were among the first to join the Ḥovevei Zion, sending a delegate to the *Kattowitz conference in 1884. In 1904 a Jewish *self-defense group was organized which prevented pogroms. In 1905 revolutionary activities were organized by members of various parties.

During World War I Jewish-owned factories in Ruzhany were burned down and the Jews were robbed by the retreating Cossacks. In 1918, after the withdrawal of the German occupation forces, Polish "legionaries," with the help of the local population, attacked the Jews; several died and many houses were looted. After the war Jewish trade and crafts were severely affected by the Polish government's antisemitic restrictions. The local Gemilut Ḥasidim society was expanded into a cooperative people's bank. In this period many Jews left.

In 1923 a Yiddish secular school was established (later directed by the Central Yiddish School Organization, CYSHO). There were also a Hebrew *Tarbut school, a private elementary school, a Hebrew and Yiddish public library named after Peretz, and a theatrical company. Zionist groups were active.

Ruzhany was a center of Jewish learning. There existed a *ḥeder*, a *talmud torah*, and a yeshivah. Notable rabbis of Ruzhany included R. Jonathan b. Joseph, author of *Yeshu'ah be-Yisrael* (Frankfurt, 1720), a work on astronomy; Avigdor b. Samuel ("Ḥarif") in the 18th century; R. Isaac Ḥaver, a leading Lithuanian rabbi (officiated 1819–1833); and Moredecai-Gimpel *Jaffe. Other Ruzhany personalities included the Zionist pioneer and author Jehiel Michael *Pines; I.T. Eisenstadt (d. 1893), author of *Da'at Kedoshim* (1897–98); A. *Luboshitzki (1874–1942), Hebrew author and poet; J. Krinski, pedagogue and author of educational textbooks; and Zelig Sher (Shereshevski), journalist active in the Jewish labor party in the United States.

[Dov Rabin]

Holocaust Period

There were about 3,500 Jews living in Ruzhany in 1939. During the period of Soviet rule (1939–41), Jewish community activities ceased. In April 1940 Jewish youth were drafted into the Red Army, and when the German-Soviet war broke out (June 1941) fought against Nazi Germany. Ruzhany was captured by the Germans on June 24, 1941. Twelve of the Jewish intelligentsia in Ruzhany were executed on July 12, and on July 14 another 18 Jews suspected of being Communists were killed.

An open ghetto was established in August of 1941. On Nov. 2, 1942, the entire Jewish population of Ruzhany was deported to Volkovysk; about 500 stragglers were shot by guards on the way. There they were concentrated in a camp of underground bunkers for the Jewish population of the entire area. On November 28, 1942 they were deported to the *Treblinka death camp. Jewish life in Ruzhany was not reconstituted after the war.

[Aharon Weiss]

BIBLIOGRAPHY: *Rozhinoi-Sefer Zikkaron la-Kehillah ve-li-Sevivatah* (1957); S. Dubnow, in: *Voskhod*, 13 no. 7 (1893); idem, *Pinkas ha-Medinah* (1925), 152, 164; G. Aronson et al. (eds.), *Geshikhte fun Bund*, 1 (1956); *Yahadut Lita*, 1 (1960), 696.

RUZHIN, ISRAEL (Friedmann; 1797–1850), ḥasidic leader. Israel was a great-grandson of Dov Baer, the Maggid of *Mezhirech. Ḥasidim claimed to recognize his outstanding qualities almost from birth. His uncle Mordecai of Chernobyl declared that the baby had the soul of the Ba'al Shem Tov. At the age of six Israel lost his father. At the age of 13 he married and moved to Botosani.

When Israel was 16 years old his brother Abraham died, and he was appointed to succeed him as the leader of the Ḥasidim. Possessed of great organizing ability, he rapidly established a large Ḥasidic center attracting thousands of followers. He then moved to Ruzhin where he set up a splendid "court" and like his father, Shalom Shakhna, lived in great luxury and unusual splendor. His dwelling place was that of a noble with all its opulence. He rode in a splendid carriage with silver handles, harnessed to four galloping horses, and surrounded by many servants. The ideological explanation given by Israel himself for his mode of behavior was that Satan is already involved in all the behavior of the Ḥasidic *Ẓaddikim*, although he is unaware that within the external extravagance and wealth a precious stone is concealed.

In 1838 Israel was accused of having given the order to put to death two Jewish informers – Isaac Ochsman and Samuel Schwartzman – who had been engaging in illegal exploitation and informing. When their activities began to endanger the Jews and their communities, the lay communal leaders decided to put them to death. One was put into the boiler of the ritual bath and the other was drowned. For a long time the Ḥasidim and members of the community succeeded in hiding the affair, and even after the body was found in the river the cause of death remained a secret until revealed by a third informer. An extensive investigation was then initiated, and the case was transferred to a higher authority. Hundreds of persons were imprisoned and subjected to severe tortures. Eighty of them were brought before a military court in a trial that lasted a year and a half. Six lay leaders were sentenced to hard labor for life and flogging, from which most of them died. Israel was imprisoned for 22 months, during the whole period of the investigation. He was placed in solitary confinement in prison in Kiev, but was permitted to receive food in his own utensils.

On the conclusion of the investigation in 1840, in which the defendants did everything in their power to exonerate Israel from the accusation leveled against him, he was released, but was placed under continual surveillance as he was also suspected of an ambition to become ruler of the Jews. Policemen went in and out of his room while he was praying. He moved to Kishinev where the provincial governor was better disposed toward the Jews. However, when his followers learned that their leader was to be exiled to a distant place, they speedily obtained a travel permit to Moldavia for him, promising that he would return if required to do so. He then settled in Jassy in Romania. The Russian governor who provided the permit, in fear of his superiors, hastened to send emissaries in secret to Jassy to have Israel extradited. However, the Ḥasidim anticipated this and removed him to Shatsk in Bukovina, which belonged to Austria. He moved from town to town including Kompling, and Skola, until after many efforts, described in numerous Ḥasidic legends, he was authorized by the Austrian emperor Ferdinand I (Dec. 20, 1845) to live in Sadgora in Bukovina. Israel's Ḥasidim purchased an estate for their leader called Zolotoi-Potok near Sadgora.

At Sadgora thousands of Ḥasidim streamed to him, and he built himself a splendid palace there, continuing the same life of opulence that he had led in Ruzhin. Israel had a great influence upon the numerous Ḥasidim and *Ẓaddikim*, especially the Romanian Ḥasidim.

On the death of the rabbi of *Apta, Israel was also appointed head of the Volhynia Kolel in Ereẓ Israel, and did much on behalf of the Jews in Ereẓ Israel. The splendid synagogue Tiferet Yisrael in Jerusalem (destroyed by the Jordanians after 1948), also called the Nisan Bak synagogue, was named after Israel of Ruzhin because he provided the funds for buying the ground and building the synagogue.

The impressions of contemporaries who knew him are interesting. Dr. S. Rubin describes him as follows "He spoke little, confining his remarks to the absolute essential. All his movements were deliberate… He sat upon his throne dressed in immaculate and expensive garments, like one of the Russian nobles, and on his head a hat embroidered in gold. From the tips of his toes to his head, there was an elegance about his expensive clothes." Dr. Mayer, who visited him in 1826, was filled with enthusiasm for Israel's personality: "When I visited him in his home, I found there Field-Marshal Witgenstein who honored him in every possible manner and wanted to present him with one of the most beautiful of his palaces, in a neighboring town, so that he should take up residence there… in truth he deserves all this honor. Although not particularly educated, he has a preeminently naturally keen mind. With his sharp eye and keen intellect he immediately penetrates to the heart of any difficulty brought to him, however obscure and complicated, and arrives at a decision. His imposing presence and his stature make a pleasing impression upon the onlooker. He is noble and refined: He has no beard, only a moustache. His eyes exercise a hypnotic charm so that even his greatest opponent is compelled to submit to him."

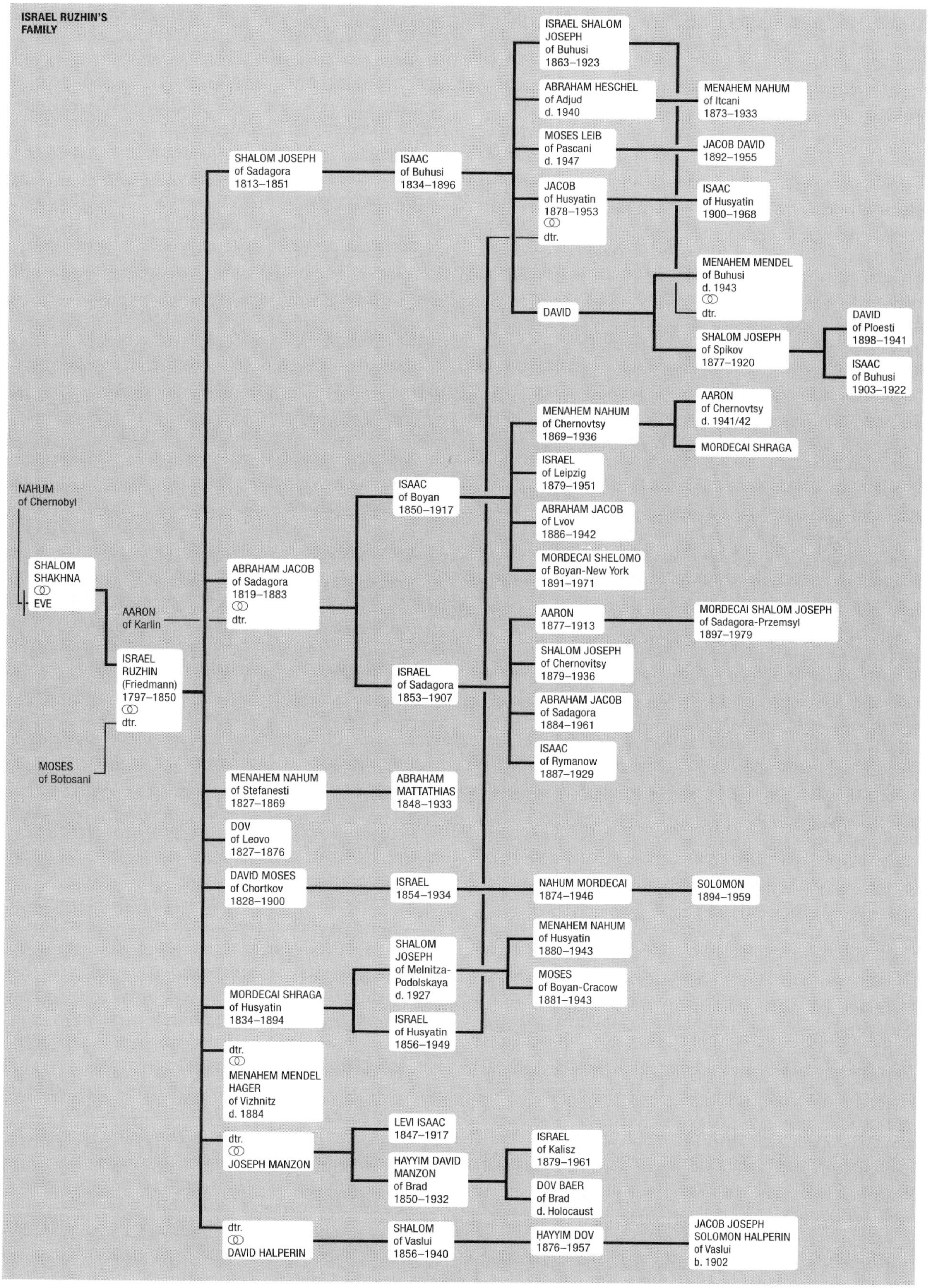
ISRAEL RUZHIN'S FAMILY
NAHUM of Chernobyl
SHALOM SHAKHNA ⚭ EVE
AARON of Karlin
ISRAEL RUZHIN (Friedmann) 1797–1850 ⚭ dtr.
MOSES of Botosani
SHALOM JOSEPH of Sadagora 1813–1851
ISAAC of Buhusi 1834–1896
ISRAEL SHALOM JOSEPH of Buhusi 1863–1923
ABRAHAM HESCHEL of Adjud d. 1940
MOSES LEIB of Pascani d. 1947
JACOB of Husyatin 1878–1953 ⚭ dtr.
DAVID
MENAHEM NAHUM of Itcani 1873–1933
JACOB DAVID 1892–1955
ISAAC of Husyatin 1900–1968
MENAHEM MENDEL of Buhusi d. 1943 ⚭ dtr.
SHALOM JOSEPH of Spikov 1877–1920
DAVID of Ploesti 1898–1941
ISAAC of Buhusi 1903–1922
ABRAHAM JACOB of Sadagora 1819–1883 ⚭ dtr.
ISAAC of Boyan 1850–1917
MENAHEM NAHUM of Chernovtsy 1869–1936
AARON of Chernovtsy d. 1941/42
MORDECAI SHRAGA
ISRAEL of Leipzig 1879–1951
ABRAHAM JACOB of Lvov 1886–1942
MORDECAI SHELOMO of Boyan-New York 1891–1971
ISRAEL of Sadagora 1853–1907
AARON 1877–1913
MORDECAI SHALOM JOSEPH of Sadagora-Przemsyl 1897–1979
SHALOM JOSEPH of Chernovitsy 1879–1936
ABRAHAM JACOB of Sadagora 1884–1961
ISAAC of Rymanow 1887–1929
MENAHEM NAHUM of Stefanesti 1827–1869
ABRAHAM MATTATHIAS 1848–1933
DOV of Leovo 1827–1876
DAVID MOSES of Chortkov 1828–1900
ISRAEL 1854–1934
NAHUM MORDECAI 1874–1946
SOLOMON 1894–1959
MORDECAI SHRAGA of Husyatin 1834–1894
SHALOM JOSEPH of Melnitza-Podolskaya d. 1927
MENAHEM NAHUM of Husyatin 1880–1943
MOSES of Boyan-Cracow 1881–1943
ISRAEL of Husyatin 1856–1949
dtr. ⚭ MENAHEM MENDEL HAGER of Vizhnitz d. 1884
dtr. ⚭ JOSEPH MANZON
LEVI ISAAC 1847–1917
HAYYIM DAVID MANZON of Brad 1850–1932
ISRAEL of Kalisz 1879–1961
DOV BAER of Brad d. Holocaust
dtr. ⚭ DAVID HALPERIN
SHALOM of Vaslui 1856–1940
HAYYIM DOV 1876–1957
JACOB JOSEPH SOLOMON HALPERIN of Vaslui b. 1902

Israel of Ruzhin wrote no books. His teachings are collected in *Irin Kedishin, Beit Yisrael, Tiferet Yisrael, Keneset Yisrael, Pe'er Yisrael*, etc.

Six sons of Israel of Ruzhin established Ḥasidic dynasties which attracted large numbers of followers.

The eldest SHALOM JOSEPH (1813–1851) made Sadagora his center, and died in Leipzig ten months after the death of his father. His son ISAAC (1834–1896) was the founder of the Buhusi dynasty and was the main propagator of Ḥasidism in Romania. Isaac's sons dispersed throughout the country, ISRAEL SHALOM JOSEPH (1863–1923) in Buhusi, and ABRAHAM HESCHEL (d. 1940) in Adjud, MOSES LEIB (d. 1947) in Pascani, while the fourth son, JACOB (1878–1953), was appointed to succeed his father-in-law Israel of Husyatin, the author of *Oholei Ya'akov*. Other descendants were his grandson SHALOM JOSEPH OF MELNITSA-PODOLSKAYA (d. 1927), who also made Lemberg (Lvov) his center. MENAHEM NAHUM OF ITCANI (1873–1933), the son of Abraham Heschel of Adjud, was a scholar and kabbalist who wrote works on philosophy. ISAAC B. JACOB OF HUSYATIN, the last head of this dynasty (1900–1968), was chosen as leader in Ereẓ Israel. David, the son of Isaac of Buhusi, had two sons, MENAHEM MENDEL OF BUHUSI (d. 1943) who was the son-in-law of Israel Shalom Joseph, and SHALOM JOSEPH OF SPIKOV (1877–1920). JACOB DAVID (1892–1955), the son of Moses Leib of Pascani, died in Jaffa.

The last survivor of this dynasty, ISAAC OF BUHUSI (1903–1992), the son of Shalom Joseph of Spikov, settled in Tel Aviv. A devoted Zionist, he was active on behalf of the Jews in Romania during the Holocaust. His brother, DAVID OF PLOESTI (1898–1941), perished in the Holocaust.

The second son of Israel of Ruzhin, ABRAHAM JACOB (1819–1883), was the principal successor of his father and retained his residence in Sadagora. He married the daughter of Aaron of *Karlin. As a result of calumny, he was arrested in 1856 and remained in prison for 15 months. He was succeeded as head of the dynasty of Sadagora by his son ISRAEL (1853–1907), whose elder brother ISAAC (1850–1917) founded the important dynasty of Boyan in Bukovina.

Of the sons of Israel of Sadagora, AARON (1877–1913), the author of *Kedushat Aharon*, had considerable musical accomplishment; SHALOM JOSEPH (1879–1936) was head of the dynasty of Chernovtsy (Czernowitz); ABRAHAM JACOB (1884–1961) of Sadagora, a leader of the Agudat *Israel, settled in Ereẓ Israel in 1938; and ISAAC OF RYMANOW (1887–1929). The last head of the Sadagora dynasty was MORDECAI SHALOM JOSEPH (1897–1979) who, after serving as *admor* in Sadagora and Przemzyl, settled in Tel Aviv in 1939. He was the author of *Keneset Mordekhai*.

The Boyan dynasty spread to an even greater extent. Of the sons of Isaac, the founder of this dynasty, MENAHEM NAHUM (1869–1936), the author of *Devarim Niḥumim* and *Zeh Yenaḥamenu*, had his seat in Chernovtsy. ISRAEL (1879–1951) lived in Leipzig, but settled in Ereẓ Israel in 1939. ABRAHAM JACOB (1886–1942) lived in Lemberg (Lvov) and perished in the Holocaust. MORDECAI SHELOMO (1891–1971) was the last head of the dynasty. After residing in Vienna for 20 years he emigrated to New York. His remains were interred in Ereẓ Israel. The dynasty was continued by the sons of Menahem Nahum; AARON OF CHERNOVTSY, who perished in the Holocaust in 1941–42, and MORDECAI SHRAGA.

The third son of Israel of Ruzhin, MENAHEM NAHUM OF STEFAN-ESTI in Romania (1827–1869), left an only son ABRAHAM MAT-TATHIAS (1848–1933). With his death the Stefanesti dynasty came to the end.

The fourth son of Israel of Ruzhin, DOV OF LEOVO (1827–1876), was a tragic figure. An *admor* in Husi in Romania, he was successively in Seuleni, in Ukraine, and lastly in Leovo in Romania. In 1869 he published a manifesto attacking Ḥasidism, left his home, and moved to Chernovtsy, where he took up residence with one of the local *maskilim*. The incident caused a storm in the Jewish world, and gave rise to a particularly fierce controversy between the Ḥasidic dynasty of Zanz (see *Halberstamm) and that of Sadagora, which led to a burning hatred between them, bringing in its wake excommunications and recriminations. This controversy, known as the Zanz-Sadagora conflict, produced a vast polemical literature. Dov later repented and returned to Sadagora, but he no longer received any of his followers. This did not, however, put an end to the controversy, which continued until the death of Ḥayyim Halberstamm, the *admor* of Zanz. Dov left no children.

The fifth son of Israel of Ruzhin, DAVID MOSES (1828–1900), author of *Divrei David*, was one of the greatest *Ẓaddikim* of his time. His center was first in Potek, but in 1859 he moved to Chortkov. His followers were the aristocracy of the Ḥasidim of Poland. He was succeeded by his son ISRAEL (1854–1934), the author of *Tiferet Yisrael*, an outstanding leader of the Agudat Israel. After World War I he moved to Vienna. Israel was succeeded in his turn by his son NAHUM MORDECAI (1874–1946) who settled in Ereẓ Israel in 1939 where he became a member of the Mo'eẓet Gedolei ha-Torah of the Agudat Israel. The last leader of the dynasty was his son SOLOMON (1894–1959).

The sixth and last son of Israel of Ruzhin was MORDECAI SHRAGA OF HUSYATIN (1834–1894). His followers were the outstanding Ḥasidim of Galicia. He was succeeded by his son ISRAEL (1856–1949). A noble character, he was one of the first members of the Ḥovevei Zion movement. After World War I he moved to Vienna, and in 1937 emigrated to Ereẓ Israel. Both MOSES OF CRACOW (1881–1943), author of *Darkhei Moshe*, the spiritual head of the Yeshivat Ḥakhmei Lublin, and his brother MENAHEM NAHUM OF HUSYATIN (1880–1943), who had his center in Lemberg (Lvov), were the grandsons of Mordecai Shraga, the sons of his son Shalom Joseph, and both perished in the Holocaust. There was no successor to this dynasty.

Israel of Ruzhin had three sons-in-law: MENAHEM MENDEL HAGER OF *VIZHNITZ, a noted Ḥasidic leader, and Joseph Manzon and David Halperin, who belonged to wealthy families. Joseph Manzon's son ḤAYYIM DAVID (1850–1932), the *admor* of Brod, was severely persecuted by the local *maskilim*, while another son, LEVI ISAAC (1847–1917), author of *Bekha Yevorakh Yisrael*, had his center in Vienna. Two sons of Ḥayyim David acted as *admorim*, DOV BAER in Brad, who perished in the Holocaust, and ISRAEL (1879–1961) in Kalisz, who emigrated to the United States in 1939. SHALOM (1856–1940) the son of David Halperin was *admor* in Vaslui in Romania; he had a phenomenal memory, and had an extensive knowledge of secular subjects. He was succeeded by his son ḤAYYIM DOV (1876–1957), who after residing in Vaslui and Bucharest emigrated to Ereẓ Israel in 1956. The last leader of the Vaslui dynasty was JACOB JOSEPH SOLOMON (b. 1902), who settled in Tel Aviv.

BIBLIOGRAPHY: H.M. Hillmann, *Beit Yisrael* (1907); A.D. Twersky, *Sefer ha-YaḤas mi-Tchernobil ve-Ruzhyn* (1938); E.E. Dorf, *Ateret Tiferet Yisrael* (1969); L.H. Grosman, *Shem u-She'erit* (1943); Horodezky, Ḥasidut, index; A.J. Bromberg, *Mi-Gedolei ha-Ḥasidut*, 6 (1967^3); *Yeshu'ot Yisrael* (1955^2).

[Itzhak Alfassi]

RYBACK, ISSACHAR (1897–1935), Russian-French artist. Ryback was born in the Ukrainian town of Elisavetgrad (now Kirovo) and studied at the Academy in Kiev. After the Revolution of 1917, the central committee of the Jewish Cultural League in Kiev appointed him as drawing teacher. Ryback visited the Jewish farm colonies that had sprung up in the Ukraine under the new regime. The fruit of this journey was a portfolio, *On the Jewish Fields of the Ukraine* (1926), with reproductions of drawings and paintings. He showed strong sunburned men and women as opposed to the pale and wan Jews he had known in Kirovo. In 1926 he went to Paris, where he became a success, and in 1935, Wildenstein, the art dealer, planned a large retrospective exhibition of his work. On the eve of the opening Ryback died suddenly.

Ryback learned a great deal from the French cubists as well as from the German expressionists. Most of his work, however, is devoted to themes remembered from his youth. The murder of his father by Cossack bands in a pogrom became a kind of obsession. Ryback drew and painted much the same subjects favored by Chagall, with whom his talent bears comparison. His manner, however, was more somber and more tragic. In addition to drawings, paintings, and prints, he left a series of delightful small ceramic figures, representing folk types of the *shtetl*. Ryback House, displaying the finest examples of the artist's work, was opened in 1962 at Ramat Yosef in Israel. The collection was donated by his widow, Sonia, who became the director of this small, but important, museum.

BIBLIOGRAPHY: R. Cogniat, *J. Ryback* (Fr., 1934).

[Alfred Werner]

RYDER, WINONA (Winona Horowitz, 1971–), U.S. film actress. Born in Winona, Minnesota, Ryder grew up on a commune in California. When she was 10, her parents enrolled her in acting classes at the American Conservatory Theater in San Francisco. She appeared in such popular films as: *Beetlejuice* (1988), *Heathers* (1989), *Edward Scissorhands* (1990), *Mermaids* (1990), and *Night on Earth* (1991). At age 22, Ryder achieved the status of one of Hollywood's most sought-after actresses, with starring roles in Francis Ford Coppola's *Dracula* (1992) and Martin Scorsese's *Age of Innocence* (1993), for which she received an Oscar nomination for Best Supporting Actress. Ryder went on to act in such films as: *The House of Spirits* (1993), *Reality Bites* (1994), *Little Women* (Oscar nomination for Best Actress, 1994), *How to Make an American Quilt.* (1995), *The Crucible* (1996), *Alien: Resurrection* (1997), *Celebrity* (1998), *Girl, Interrupted* (1999), *Autumn in New York* (2000), *Mr. Deeds* (2002), *S1mone* (2002), and *The Darwin Awards* (2005). She also produced and narrated the 2003 documentary *The Day My God Died* about the child sex slave trade in India.

In 1996 she was nominated for a Grammy for her reading of the audio book of *The Diary of Anne Frank*. In 1997 Ryder was named one of the 50 Most Beautiful People in the World by *People* magazine.

ADD. BIBLIOGRAPHY: N. Goodall, *Winona Ryder: The Biography* (1998); D. Thompson, *Winona Ryder* (1996).

[Jonathan Licht / Ruth Beloff (2nd ed.)]

RYMANOW, town in Rzeszow province, S.E. Poland. It is assumed that the town developed out of a colony of prisoners of war who settled there in the 15th century. The Jewish community was formed soon after the town was founded. Most of the Jews were merchants of wines imported from Hungary. About 1594 the Council of Four Lands (see *Councils of the Lands) debated the matter, and as a result, the community was warned by Meir b. Gedaliah of *Lublin to be careful about libation wine. At first the council intended to forbid the Jews entirely to deal in such wine, but since it was their main occupation a decision was made finally to issue just a warning. In connection with their commerce the Jews of Rymanow had to visit Krasno, a town in the same province, which had the privilege of excluding Jews (*de non tolerandis Judaeis*). This led to tensions between them and the townsmen of Krasno. In the 17th and 18th centuries the municipality of Krasno allowed its townsmen to rob and even put to death any Jew from Rymanow who attended the fair at Krasno. At the beginning of the 17th century, the Jews of Rymanow were prosecuted by the bishop of Przemysl for the alleged profaning of Christian festivals; the bishop won the suit. In 1765 there were 1,015 Jews in Rymanow (42.8% of the total population). At the beginning of the 19th century, as a result of the activity of R. Hirsch Mesharet, mentioned in 1838 by the head of the police in Lvov as having great influence on the Jews of Galicia, Rymanow became an important Ḥasidic center. It was the seat of the *Ẓaddikim* Menahem Mendel *Rymanower and his disciple Ẓevi Hirsch *Rymanower. The dwelling of the Ḥasidic rabbi, and the synagogue, erected in the 16th or 17th century, were the finest buildings in the town. At the end of the 19th century, Jewish communal life in Rymanow expanded.

This continued when Rymanow reverted to independent Poland after World War I. Controversies arose, however, especially between *Agudat Israel and the Zionists. In the 1930s Agudat Israel gained the majority within the community council, whereas in the elections to the municipal council in early 1939 the Zionists won three out of the five places reserved for Jews. Because of the anti-Jewish *boycott in the 1930s, the Jews suffered economically; in 1938 Jews were not permitted to deal in tobacco, a state-owned monopoly in Poland. The Jewish population numbered 1,391 (42.8% of the total) in 1865, and 1,412 (39.9%) in 1921.

[Shimshon Leib Kirshenboim]

Holocaust Period

After the outbreak of World War II, when the Germans occupied Rymanow at the end of September 1939, they issued an order for almost all the Jews in Rymanow to move within 24 hours to the Soviet-occupied area on the east bank of the River San. Only a small number were permitted to remain in the city. Many of those who went to the Soviet area were deported in the summer of 1940 to the Soviet interior. Those remaining in Rymanow were compelled by the Germans to pay fines, and subjected to confiscation of property and forced labor. On Aug. 1, 1942, all Jewish males aged 14 to 35 were deported to the Plaszow labor camp, where many met their deaths. On Aug. 13, 1942, the remainder of the Jewish community was deported to the *Belzec death camp.

[Aharon Weiss]

BIBLIOGRAPHY: Yad Vashem Archives.

RYMANOWER (of Rymanow), MENAHEM MENDEL (d. 1815), *ḥasidic ẓaddik*. A pupil of *Elimelech of Lyzhansk, he was born in Przytyk but spent most of his life in Rymanow. Ḥasidic tradition relates that in his youth he attended various yeshivot, finally settling at that of Shmelke of Nikolsburg (Mikulov). Legends about Menahem Mendel are included in stories concerning his pupil, Naphtali Ẓevi *Ropshitser. An ascetic, he became known for his regulations dealing with women's dress; he also instituted regulations concerning weights and measures. According to legend, he saw the Napoleonic wars as the battles of Gog and Magog which will precede redemption and the coming of the Messiah and he prayed for Napoleon's victory. Menahem Mendel appears in *David of Makow's list (1798–1800) of the cursed *ẓaddikim* of the generation (*Shever Poshe'im*, in M. Wilensky's *Ḥasidim u-Mitnaggedim*, 2 (1970), 102).

Menahem Mendel's works are *Ilana de-Ḥayyei* (1908), a commentary on the Pentateuch; *Menaḥem Ẓiyyon* (1851), sermons for Sabbath and festivals, collected by his pupil Ezekiel *Panet; *Divrei Menaḥem* (1863), sermons for Sabbath; *Ateret Menaḥem* (1910), practical talks and interpretations of the law; and *Torat Menaḥem* (1876), sermons on the weekly portions.

BIBLIOGRAPHY: M. Buber, *Tales of the Hasidim*, 2 (1966[3]) 123–38; idem, *Gog u-Magog* (1967[2]); L.I. Newman, *Ḥasidic Anthology* (1963), index s.v. *Rimanover The Menachem Mendel*; Dubnov, Ḥasidut, 318–9, 458; Horodezky, Ḥasidut, index; M.E. Gutman, *R. Mendel mi-Rymanow* (1953); idem, *Mi-Gedolei ha-Ḥasidut*, 3–4 (1931); L.H. Grosman, *Shem u-Sherit* (1943), 101.

[Esther (Zweig) Liebes]

RYMANOWER, ẒEVI HIRSH (1778–1847), Ḥasidic leader known as "Hirsh Mesharet" ("Hirsh the Attendant"). He was born in Dombrowa and learned tailoring as a boy. Under the influence of Moses of Przeworsk he became a Ḥasid and disciple of Mendel Rymanower. After the latter's death he stayed with Naphtali Ẓevi *Ropshitser for about 12 years, was recognized as his successor in 1827, and became known as a miracle-worker. His only son, Joseph ha-Kohen Rymanower (d. 1913), was his successor. *Be'erot ha-Mayim* (1894), edited by A.A. Kanarvogel, contains Ẓevi Hirsh's sermons on the daily portions of the Torah and those for Sabbath and festivals. Between the sermons, the editor included tales about Ẓevi Hirsh, adding at the end of the book a collection of sermons called *Yikkavu ha-Mayim* by Ẓevi Hirsh and some other Ḥasidic leaders.

BIBLIOGRAPHY: G. Kamelhaar, *Sefer Mevasser Tov* (1900); M. Buber, *Tales of the Hasidim*, 2 (1966[3]), 738–47; L.I. Newman, *Ḥasidic Anthology* (1963), index s.v. *Rimanover Hirsch*; Horodezky, Ḥasidut, 4 (1951), 112; L.H. Grosman, *Shem u-She'erit* (1943), 101.

[Esther (Zweig) Liebes]

RYPIN, town in Budgoszcz province, N. central Poland; from 1815 until World War I within Russia. In 1799 the Jews of Rypin were granted civic rights and freedoms by the municipal council, which sought to improve the economic situation of the town with their assistance. Henceforward the Jewish population increased, numbering 517 (35% of the total population) in 1827; 1,024 (47.8%) in 1856; 1,706 (38.6%) in 1897; and 2,791 (38.6%) in 1921. The Jews developed commerce and crafts in the town. After World War I, 300 Jewish families (about 60% of the total Jewish population) were engaged in commerce, and 25% in the crafts. In the 1930s their economic situation was undermined, however, as a result of a campaign launched by antisemites.

The community was organized on democratic principles after World War I. In the first elections to the council held in 1924, as well as in those of 1931 and 1936, the Zionists obtained a majority, although the Ḥasidim had considerable influence within the Jewish population. Noteworthy of the community's rabbis were Nahum Manasseh Guttentag-Tavyomi, who appears to have participated in the Polish uprising of 1863, and Asher Gershon Luria, rabbi of the town for 40 years (d. 1932). There was a network of Jewish schools and cultural institutions of various kinds. Modern social and cultural activity began under the German occupation of World War I.

[Shimshon Leib Kirshenboim]

Holocaust Period

During the Nazi occupation, Rypin was part of Reichsgau Danzig-Westpreussen by Hitler's decree of Oct. 26, 1939. Before the outbreak of World War II, Rypin had nearly 2,500 Jews. Before the Germans entered on September 8, many Jews escaped, but trickled back afterward. Some 100–150 refugees who returned were probably shot on the outskirts of town. In September and October 1939, several Jews were arrested and some leading persons were murdered. The Germans set the main synagogue and *bet midrash* on fire. The Germans arrested the president of the community, Shimeon Kron (or Kran), for starting the fire, and the community was obliged to pay a high "contribution" (or fine). A large number of Jews, especially youth, escaped to the Soviet-occupied territories. The remaining Jews, ordered by the German authorities to leave the town in the middle of November 1939, became dispersed in various towns – *Mlawa, *Ciechanow, *Plonsk, Szrensk, and others. Some went to Warsaw. After this exodus, the Germans destroyed the two Jewish cemeteries. About 280 Jews from Rypin survived the Holocaust, including 180 who eventually returned from the Soviet Union, and 65 who survived in labor and concentration camps. The remainder had "Aryan" documents or were hidden by Christians. A number of the survivors returned to Rypin in 1945–46 but remained only a short time. Most of them emigrated.

[Danuta Dombrowska]

BIBLIOGRAPHY: *Sefer Rypin* (Heb., Yid., Eng., 1962), a memorial book; S. Huberband, *Kiddush ha-Shem* (1969), 294.

RYSHKANY (formerly **Ryshkanovca**, Rom. **Râşcani**), town in N. Moldova. Ryshkany developed into an urban community during the 19th century as a result of the large Jewish settlement in Bessarabia at that time. In 1897 there were 2,247 Jews (69% of the total population) in the town, and in 1930 there were 2,055 (66% of the total). In the 1930s the communal institutions included a kindergarten and an elementary school, both maintained by the *Tarbut organization. The community was destroyed when the Germans and Romanians entered Bessarabia in July 1941. In 1970 the Jewish population was estimated at about 150 families.

[Eliyahu Feldman]

°**RYSSEL, VICTOR** (1849–1905), German Protestant Bible critic who taught at the University of Leipzig. The fruit of his activity as teacher appeared in writings on exegesis, hermeneutics, theology, and particularly in commentaries on the Bible and the Apocrypha.

For "*Kurzgefasstes exegetisches Handbuch zum Alten Testament*," he revised A. *Dillmann's *Exodus-Leviticus* (1897^3) and E. Bertheau's *Esra, Nechemia und Esther* (1887^2). His studies of the Prayer of Manasseh, the Additions to Esther, Ecclesiasticus, the Syriac Apocalypse of Baruch, and the Greek Apocalypse of Baruch, all of which appear in E. Kautzsch, *Die Apokryphen und Pseudepigraphen des Alten Testaments* (1900; 1921), represent the classic German investigation of this literature.

[Zev Garber]

RYVEL (pseudonym of **Raphael Lévy**; 1898–1972), Tunisian author and educator. He was born in *Tunis and received pedagogical training at the Ecole Normale Israélite Orientale (ENIO), the teachers' school of the *Alliance Israélite Universelle (AIU). After completing his training, Ryvel returned to *Tunisia where he taught at the AIU primary school in Sousse. He was later recruited to teach at the AIU boys' schools in *Casablanca and Tunis. In the latter city, he served as the school's principal. Ryvel belonged to a small nucleus of AIU teachers that often opposed that organization's hostility or indifference to Zionism. He was instrumental in promoting aspects of modern Hebrew studies at the Tunis school. During this time he published more than a dozen books of stories, poems, and plays on Tunisian daily Jewish life, many of which were performed. His most representative works are *La hara conte* (1920), a compilation of essays dealing with life in the Jewish ghetto, *Terre d'Israël* (1927), and *L'enfant de l'Oukala,* also on Jewish quarter folklore, for which he received the important *Prix de Carthage* in 1931.

BIBLIOGRAPHY: A. Elmaleh in: *Mahberet*, 14:5–7 (1965); A. Alcalay, "Intellectual Life," in: R.S. Simon, M.M. Laskier, S. Reguer (eds.), *The Jews of the Middle East and North Africa in Modern Times* (2003), 107; H. Saadoun, "Tunisia," in: *ibid.*, 450.

[Michael M. Laskier (2nd ed.)]

RZESZOW (Pol. **Rzeszow**; Heb. **Risha**), capital of Rzeszow province, S.E. Poland. Until the 18th century Rzeszow was a private city; its last owners, the Lubomirsky family, ruled the city until the Austrian annexation in 1772. The Jewish community of Rzeszow dates back to the 15th century. Jewish settlement there was authorized by King Stephen Bathory. The community was heavily taxed and was subject to various restrictions on commerce and crafts. In the 17th century, a synagogue was erected (later known as the "old" synagogue) and a cemetery was opened. Within the framework of the *Councils of the Lands, Rzeszow belonged to the Land of "Russia." At the beginning of the 18th century, a controversy broke out between the Rzeszow and *Przemysl communities over R. Ezekiel Joshua Feivel Fraenkel-Teomim, who was first rabbi of Przemysl and subsequently moved to Rzeszow. The Przemysl community then deprived him of his office as rabbi of the province (*galil*) and elected Samuel Mendelowicz of Lvov rabbi of the Przemysl community and the province. The controversy was debated at a convention of the provincial council of Przemysl in 1715 and at a convention of the Land of "Russia" at Jaroslav. Following the dispute, the Rzeszow community broke away from the provincial council and constituted itself an independent entity in relation to the Council of the Four Lands. The amount of tax which the Rzeszow community paid the Council in 1715–19 shows that it was then a large community. In the middle of the 18th century, the budget of the community amounted to 17,000 zlotys. At that time most of the city's shops were Jewish-owned. Cloth trade and goldsmithing were exclusively Jewish occupations, and the high quality of their products was known throughout Europe. "Rzeszow gold" was noted at fairs. The Jewish seal engravers there also became celebrated and they supplied the courts at Stockholm and St. Petersburg. A non-Jewish traveler in Rzeszow in the middle of the 19th century referred to Rzeszow as the "little Jerusalem." Various economic and political restrictions remained in force until the Austrian revolution in 1848. By the end of the 19th and beginning of the 20th centuries, the Jews of Rzeszow enjoyed equal rights and participated in municipal and parliamentary elections.

The Jewish population numbered 1,202 in 1765; 3,375 (c. 75% of the total) in 1800; 7,000 (38.2%) in 1900; 8,000 (36.3%) in 1910; and 11,228 in 1931.

The *Haskalah movement was particularly influential there. Its early *maskilim* included Wilhelm Turteltaub. Prominent in Hebrew literature were Moses David Geschwind (1846–1905), a translator of the Polish poet J. Slowacki into Hebrew, and Abraham Abba Appelbaum (1861–1933), an early member of the Ḥovevei Zion in Galicia and founder of the first Hebrew school in the city, who wrote historical essays in the field of Jewish history in Italy.

Ḥasidism began to spread in Rzeszow in the 19th century. A large synagogue was built in the 19th century, as well as a hospital, old age home, and charitable and cultural institutions. The rabbis of the community included Samuel Ha-Levi (d. 1729), son-in-law of R. *Isaac b. Eliakim of Poznan (Posen), and Jacob *Reischer, head of the yeshivah and author of *Shevut Ya'akov*, who also served as rabbi in *Worms. The later rabbis include Aaron b. Nathan *Lewin, who was a representative of *Agudat Israel in the Polish Sejm. In the 20th century there was large-scale Zionist activity and Zionists were members of the community council, replacing the assimilationists. Hebrew was taught in the kindergartens, and a Hebrew school established in the Bet ha-Am. The latter became a center for young Zionist pioneers. Zionist organizations were established, such as Shulamit, a Zionist women's organization.

[Klara Maayan]

Holocaust Period

On the outbreak of World War II, there were about 14,000 Jews in Rzeszow. The German army entered the city on Sept. 10, 1939, and the anti-Jewish reign of terror began. In December 1941 a closed ghetto was established in Rzeszow. On July 7–13, 1942, the first mass deportation took place: about 14,000 Jews from the entire district of Rzeszow were concentrated in the ghetto and immediately deported together with some 8,000 Jews from the city to the *Belzec death camp. At the time of the deportation, 238 Jews were shot for offering passive resistance, while another 1,000 were taken to the nearby Rudna Forest and executed there. On Aug. 8, 1942, about 1,000 women and children were deported from the ghetto to the Peikinia concentration camp, where all of them were exterminated shortly afterward. In November 1942 only about 3,000 Jews still remained in the ghetto, which was transformed into a forced-labor camp and divided into two isolated parts: "A" for slave laborers, and "B" for members of their families. In September 1943 part A was transferred to the forced-labor camp of Szebnia, where the majority of the inmates met their death; part B was liquidated in November 1943, when all the inmates were deported to *Auschwitz and exterminated. Only about 600 Jews remained in a local forced-labor camp until July 1944. Some of them succeeded in escaping and hiding themselves in the nearby forests; others were deported to Germany. Jewish life was not reconstituted in Rzeszow after the war.

[Stefan Krakowski]

BIBLIOGRAPHY: Moshe Yaari-Wald (ed.), *Sefer Zikkaron li-Kehillat Risha* (Heb., some Yid. and Eng., 1967).

Illuminated initial letter "S" of the word Salvus *at the opening of Psalm 68 (Vulgate; 69 according to the Masoretic text) in the* Bohun Psalter, *14*th *century. The four scenes from the story of David are, top left, the Ark being carried up to Jerusalem (II Sam. 6:1–15); right, Michal watches David dancing before the Ark (*ibid., *16); bottom left, David reproves Michal for her criticism of him (*ibid., *20–23); right, the prophet Nathan assures David of the endurance of his kingdom (II Sam. 16). London, British Museum, EG 3277, fol. 46v.*

SAA-SAM

SA'AD (Heb. סַעַד; "Buttress"), kibbutz in southern Israel, on the border of the Negev, 4 mi. (6 km.) southeast of Gaza, affiliated with Ha-Kibbutz ha-Dati. Sa'ad was founded in 1947 by *Youth Aliyah graduates from Germany and Austria. The settlers were joined by Israeli-born youth and immigrants from various countries. In the *War of Independence Sa'ad was completely leveled in long and bitter battles with the invading Egyptian army. The settlers held out in underground dugouts. After the war they built the village anew about 1 mi. (2 km.) further east. Sa'ad then developed intensive farming with irrigation from the Yarkon-Negev line and, later, from the National Water Carrier. The economy was based on livestock, field crops, citrus and other fruit, poultry, and dairy cattle. The kibbutz also had plants manufacturing plastic shrinkwrap film for packaging, as well as popcorn products and pet food. Other enterprises were a fashion outlet, a handmade jewelry workshop, and an auto service center. In 1970 there were 530 inhabitants; in 2002, 582.

WEBSITE: www.saad.org.il.

[Efraim Orni / Shaked Gilboa (2nd ed.)]

ṢA'ADĪ, JUDAH BEN SOLOMON (c. 1665–1740), *av bet din* in *San'a after the return of the Jews from exile in *Mawza'. During Ṣa'adī's lifetime the dispute over the version of prayers to be adopted in *Yemen broke out. He and R. Yaḥyā Ṣāliḥ (Maharis) fought for the original Yemenite version (*baladī*), and against the Sephardi version (*shāmī*), which had spread with the introduction of printed *siddurim*. Some opinions have attributed to him the work *Dofi ha-Zeman* ("Fault of the Times"), a history of Yemenite Jewry during the years 1717–26 (see *Saadi, Said b. Solomon).

BIBLIOGRAPHY: *Tikhlal, Eẓ Ḥayyim*, 1 (1894), introd.

[Yehuda Ratzaby]

SAADIAH (**Sa'id**; c. 16th century), poet. Saadiah ranks among the group of early Yemenite poets. His poetry is distinguished for its motifs, style, and form, which later, during the Mashtā period (17th century), became the principal elements of Yemenite poetry.

The subjects of his poetry are the Sabbath, the festivals, exile and redemption, friendship, and *Kabbalah. His poetry is mostly written in Hebrew. His poem *La-Ner ve-li-Vesamim*, a *Havdalah* for the conclusion of the Sabbath, is still recited in the homes of Yemenite Jews.

BIBLIOGRAPHY: A.Z. Idelsohn and H. Torczyner (eds.), *Shirei Teiman* (1930), 34–41.

[Yehuda Ratzaby]

SAADIAH BEN JOSEPH HA-LEVI (16th century), Yemenite rabbi, poet, and *paytan*. Saadiah was one of the leading scholars of his time in *San'a (and later in Jiblah). He composed *piyyutim* and poems.

Several of his *piyyutim*, including one on the *Akedah* (the binding of Isaac), were published or mentioned by H. Brody, D. Sassoon, and A.Z. Idelsohn (see bibliography). *Zechariah al-Dahiri composed a panegyric in his honor, published in the *Sefer ha-Musar*, in which he notes that Saadiah lived in San'a at the time of the persecutions of 1568 and describes the latter's greatness in Torah. He may possibly be the Saadiah b. Joseph whose *piyyut* was published in the *Aleppo prayer book of 1527.

BIBLIOGRAPHY: H. Brody, in: *Kobez al Jad*, 6 (1894), 12–14, 27–29; D. Sassoon, in: KS, 2 (1925/26), 258–64; 3 (1926/27), 168–71; A.Z. Idelsohn and H. Torczyner (eds.), *Shirei Teiman* (1930), 256–62; Zechariah al-Ḍāhirī, *Sefer ha-Musar*, ed. by Y. Ratzaby (1965), index.

SAADIAH (Ben Joseph) GAON (882–942), greatest scholar and author of the geonic period and important leader of Babylonian Jewry. Saadiah was born in Pithom (Abu Suweir), in the Faiyum district in Egypt. Little is known about his family except that his opponents slandered his father because he was not a scholar and earned his living from manual labor. Perhaps there is some truth to his opponents' claim that his father was banished from Egypt and died in Jaffa, but no reason for this expulsion is given. It is noteworthy that Sherira Gaon refers to Saadiah's father with respect (*Iggeret Rav Sherira Ga'on*, ed. by B.M. Lewin (1921), 112). The information given on the members of his family, apart from his wife and children, is mere speculation. While there is no doubt that in his youth he already displayed outstanding talents both as an author and in communal activity, there is scant information about his teachers, whether in Jewish studies or in Greco-Arabic philosophy. The Arab writer Mas'udi states that when Saadiah was in Ereẓ Israel, he studied under Abu Kathir Yaḥya b. Zechariah al-Katib of Tiberias. However, earlier than that, when he still lived in Egypt, he had already written two books (see below) and corresponded with R. Isaac b. Solomon *Israeli of Kairouan. It is therefore certain that when he left Egypt he was already a learned scholar of Torah and secular sciences, and had left behind many disciples. There is no information about him between the years 905, when he wrote his responsum to Anan (see below), and 921; nor are the reasons for his departure from Egypt clear. From a fragment of a letter written in the summer of that year it is known that he was then in Aleppo, from where he proceeded to Baghdad, and, as stated above, it is known that he had been in Ereẓ Israel.

From 921 Saadiah appears as the leading protagonist in an ongoing bitter struggle between Aaron *Ben Meir, head of the Jerusalem academy, and the leaders of the Jewish communities in Babylonia. In 922 (4682) Ben Meir announced that Passover that year would fall on Sunday, and not on Tuesday as accepted according to the Babylonian calendar, and therefore that Rosh Ha-Shanah would fall on Tuesday and not Thursday. These changes would also affect the fixing of the days of the other holidays during the year 923/4 (see *Calendar). Ben Meir also deviated from accepted practice of midday as the deciding line for the declaration of the new moon. Scholars agree that the head of the Jerusalem academy did not deviate from the norm willingly. It is not clear on what or whose authority he based this deviation and he upheld a tradition that recognized the sole right of Ereẓ Israel to declare new moons and holidays. Ben Meir sincerely believed in the halakhic rightness of his acts. In his demand that the Babylonian authorities accept his view, he claimed the prerogative both of *halakhah* and of Ereẓ Israel; perhaps he hoped to magnify the importance of the academy which he headed. Saadiah and his followers, however, denied the validity of Ben Meir's arguments. Possibly while he was still in Ereẓ Israel, Saadiah became aware that he and Ben Meir differed with regard to the calendar and he consequently wrote to Yehudai b. Naḥman Gaon regarding the fixing of the calendar.

While Saadiah was still in Aleppo, he was informed by some students who came from Baghdad of Ben Meir's intentions, and he attempted to dissuade him from implementing it. Ben Meir, however, did not heed his advice. He considered his intended act as being of supreme importance and refused to heed demands that he abandon it. On the contrary, he felt obliged at all costs to defend the sole right of Jerusalem to establish the new moon and fix the calendar; he thus demanded that Babylonian Jewry act in accordance with his instructions, as all previous generations had depended on Jerusalem for the necessary information on this matter. The Babylonian authorities had in fact acknowledged the authority of the Jerusalem academy in this matter in 855 (Mann, Egypt, 1 (1920), 52–53; 2 (1922), 41–47). On his instructions his son declared from the Mount of Olives that in 4682 (921) Rosh Ha-Shanah would fall on Thursday, and Passover on Sunday. The leaders of the Jewish community in Babylonia were shaken by the danger of an impending schism in the Jewish community. In spite of their previous differences, the exilarch and the *geonim* agreed that Ben Meir must be prevented from carrying out his plan. Saadiah, who had returned to Babylonia, sent letters to Ben Meir and his colleagues, which at first were couched in conciliatory language, but to no avail. In a letter full of bitterness Ben Meir accused his former supporters of abandoning him to submit to the Babylonian authorities, and stated that under no circumstances would he change his mind. The controversy continued and the schism materialized. From a statement by the Karaite *Sahl b. Maẓli'aḥ, who gleefully recorded the occasion, and by a Christian who mentions it in passing, it is known that the Jews in Ereẓ Israel observed Rosh Ha-Shanah in 4683 (922) on Tuesday, and the Jews in Babylonia, on Thursday, and it can be assumed that in both countries there were those who adhered to different days. The controversy grew in bitterness and invective and Ben Meir lost ground. The action of the Babylonian scholars in defending their tradition prevented people from following the head of the Palestinian academy, and caused some who had previously followed him to desert him. Saadiah was requested to compose a detailed account on the event which would serve as a reminder to Jews, and accordingly wrote *Sefer ha-Zikkaron*, which was read in public in Elul 922. The duration of the schism after 923 and the manner in which it was resolved cannot be determined. Ben Meir continued as head of the academy but Saadiah and the Babylonian leaders had achieved victory, and he was considered one of the greatest authorities in the field of fixing the calendar. He wrote *Sefer ha-Mo'adim*, which gives a complete account of the dispute.

It would appear that immediately on his arrival in Babylonia in 922, Saadiah was appointed to the yeshivah of Pumbedita, as from that year his letters bear his signature along with the title **resh* ("head of") *kallah* or **alluf*. After the Ben Meir controversy had subsided, Saadiah found time for literary work and several of his works were written in the 920s. His talents and personality attracted many, and some of the important leaders in Baghdad were his colleagues and aides, among them Sahl b. Netira, a wealthy merchant esteemed by the authorities. When the question of the continuation of the academy of Sura was under discussion, Saadiah's name was proposed. The famous academy had been through a difficult period. The honor in which it had been held had declined. His predecessor, R. Yom Tov Kahana b. Mar Rav Jacob, who headed it for ten years, was a weaver by calling, and after his death it was suggested that the academy be closed down completely and the students transferred to Pumbedita. The exilarch *David b. Zakkai, however, decided to maintain the Sura academy. At first, however, R. Nathan the son of Yehudai Gaon was appointed *alluf*, but he died before he could take up the office (*Iggeret Ray Sherira Ga'on*, 112). The exilarch then wished to appoint Saadiah. According to *Nathan ha-Bavli, there were other candidates, and perhaps there is a historical basis to the report that the exilarch had to decide whether to appoint R. Ẓemaḥ b. Shahin ("because he was wellborn and learned") or Saadiah (Neubauer, Chronicles, 2 (1895), 80). The family connections of the former certainly were taken into consideration. Most of the *geonim* came from a limited number of families and it was not easy to deviate from this tradition. Saadiah was a stranger, apparently not well connected. Although it was conceded that Saadiah was the greater scholar, it was difficult to ignore the characteristics enumerated by *Nissi b. Berechiah al-Nahrwani which appear in Nathan ha-Bavli's report: "Although he [Saadiah] is a great man and a profound scholar, he is not afraid of any man and does not show favor to anyone because of his great knowledge, eloquence, and piety" (*ibid.*). Saadiah's virtues, however, determined the exilarch's decision.

His conflict with Ben Meir and his writings against heretics such as *Ḥiwi al-Balkhi and against the Karaites had proved his fearlessness, his dedication to the Torah, and his loyalty to the exilarch. It could certainly be hoped that under Saadiah's leadership the academy of Sura would be revived. His standing and his firmness would counterbalance *Kohen Ẓedek b. Joseph, the *gaon* of Pumbedita. David b. Zakkai thereupon appointed Saadiah head of the Sura academy in the spring of 928. As a precaution, the exilarch administered the oath to the new *gaon* "that he do not disobey me, or plot against me, or regard anyone but me as exilarch, or associate with any of my opponents" (A.E. Harkavy, *Zikkaron la-Rishonim*, 1 pt. 5 (1832), 232).

Saadiah immediately embarked upon his administrative work with energy and dedication. He set himself two tasks: to increase the number of students in the academy, and to secure the financial needs of the institution. To achieve the latter, he employed the methods of his predecessors (and to an even greater extent of his successors), of requesting aid from the Jewish communities far and near. Abraham *Ibn Daud reports in the name of R. Meir ibn Bibas that Saadiah sent a letter to Spain, "to the communities of Cordoba, Elvira, Lucena… and all the Jewish communities in its vicinity" (*Sefer ha-Qabbalah* (G.D. Cohen, ed., 1967), 79). Of special significance are the two successive requests he sent to Egypt, "to the Jewish communities in the city of Fostat" (B.M. Lewin, in: *Ginzei Kedem*, 2 (1963) 34, 35), the first containing the greetings of the head of the academy, his son She'erit, and the *allufim*, as well as the rest of the scholars of the academy and the "important and esteemed burghers of Baghdad." He further says that the aforesaid "burghers," "the sons of Mar Rav Netira and Mar Rav Aaron," will help him in obtaining any request from the government. Saadiah also urged the Jews in Egypt to maintain contact with him, in order that he could regard himself as the acknowledged leader of all Jewry. The second letter refers with satisfaction to his early leadership of the academy; it is composed entirely of admonitions and moral instruction to the people (every verse begins with the phrase "the children of Israel") and is written in a tone of authority. Saadiah openly requested support for the academy in both letters. He also gathered the members of the academy who had left or had moved to Pumbedita during Sura's decline and restored it to its former glory. Saadiah's character aided him in his energetic fulfillment of his task. Whatever one thinks of the grave accusations against him leveled by David b. Zakkai, it must be conceded that while Saadiah was *Gaon* he was not intimidated by those in power and did not show favoritism.

His ways and deeds probably stimulated envy and complaints on the part of the exilarch. Only on the assumption that there already existed tension between Saadiah and the exilarch prior to their final quarrel is it possible to understand how a single incident could have provoked a bitter and difficult dispute. According to Nathan ha-Bavli (Neubauer, *ibid.*, 80–81), Saadiah refused to confirm the terms of settlement of a will which would greatly benefit the exilarch. At first Saadiah was evasive and requested that Kohen Ẓedek, the head of the Pumbedita academy, should first append his signature, anticipating that he would not sign. When, however, Kohen Ẓedek did sign, Saadiah announced his refusal to confirm the inheritance. There is no doubt that Saadiah acted in accordance with the law; his answer to the son of the exilarch, "ye shall not respect persons in judgment" (Deut. 1.17), showed that he was conscious of his high office as an impartial judge. On the other hand, from the fact that Kohen Ẓedek confirmed the decision, it may be assumed that there was no definite miscarriage of justice, but that it was a controversial issue, which was difficult to decide. David b. Zakkai's anger at Saadiah was boundless and the quarrel came out in the open. He deposed Saadiah, appointing *Joseph b. Jacob bar Satia as *Gaon*. Saadiah in his turn appointed another exilarch, Josiah Hasan, the brother of David b. Zakkai. Apparently, when the quarrel started, the *gaon* was certain of his victory. Close to the wealthy classes in the city, he hoped that with their influence he would prevail in his dispute with the exilarch. Nonetheless, it seems that those interested in the quarrel, i.e., the members of the academy and the elite of the community, were divided into two camps. Nathan ha-Bavli's statement that "all the wealthy in Babylonia, the academy students, and prominent members of the community were on Saadiah's side," assisting him financially in presenting his case to the caliph, his officers, and advisors (Neubauer, *ibid.*, 80) is probably exaggerated. He himself states earlier that Khalaf b. Sarjado (*Aaron b. Joseph Sargado; Sarjado) had assisted the exilarch and that the head of the Pumbedita academy supported him. Until 932, Saadiah was in a strong, if not a dominant, position. At that time he wrote the first version of *Sefer ha-Galui* in flowery Hebrew. The work exudes self-confidence. In a letter attacking Saadiah (Harkavy, *ibid.*, 227), the *gaon's* conduct during those years is criticized. However, when the caliph al-Kahir (932–934) assumed the throne, his fortune changed. The caliph needed money badly and Aaron Sarjado's contribution decided the issue. The sons of Netira and the sons of Aaron did not wish to become involved in the issue, as their influence had waned, especially after Aaron Sarjado appeared as the leading antagonist of the *gaon*. The reasons for his deep hatred of the *gaon* are not known. It is possible that it stemmed from his own ambitions to become *gaon*, which he did not attain until 943, or he was hurt by Saadiah's arrogance. In any case, he became Saadiah's inveterate enemy, and his invective and insults were harsher than those of David b. Zakkai and Kohen Ẓedek. Aaron Sarjado's open support of David b. Zakkai and the fact that the other wealthy members of the community were either unable or unwilling to become involved, resulted in Josiah Hasan's banishment to Khurasan, where, apparently, he died shortly afterward. Saadiah was forced to relinquish the gaonate and take refuge from the wrath of his opponents. It was a blessing in disguise, since as a result Saadiah was free to pursue his creative work. During this period he wrote his philosophic work, *Emunot ve-De'ot* ("Beliefs and Opinions"), and a second version of *Sefer ha-Galui*, with a long introduction in Arabic and an Arabic commentary on the original.

According to Nathan ha-Bavli (Neubauer, *ibid.*, 81–82), the opponents were reconciled in 937 when Bishr b. Aaron b. Amram, the father-in-law of Aaron Sarjado, was persuaded to intervene in this matter and make peace between the two sides. Bishr undoubtedly found the entire quarrel tiresome, and complied. He had supported Saadiah, as the *Gaon* testifies, and the differences between himself and his son-in-law did not please him. The disputants were also weary of the quarrel and were prepared for reconciliation. Saadiah again headed the academy in Sura, despite the fact that David b. Zakkai's candidate, Joseph b. Mar Rav Jacob, continued to receive a salary. Sarjado's stand regarding this change is not known. He apparently acquiesced in the face of a situation which he could not prevent. In the meantime he was busy with his own affairs. R. Kohen Ẓedek died early in 936; and Aaron Sarjado, to his dismay, was not appointed his successor. It was only in 943 that he succeeded to the position; according to Sherira Gaon, he took it by force. Saadiah's last years were peaceful. The exilarch died in 942, while he was on good terms with the *gaon*. It is exemplified by the fact that when David's son Judah died shortly after his father, Saadiah took Judah's son into his home and brought him up.

[Abraham Solomon Halkin]

As Halakhist

Saadiah's halakhic works are still largely in manuscript, particularly in thousands of scattered *Genizah* fragments, and although not even a small part has so far been assembled and investigated, the general picture nevertheless is gradually becoming clearer. From the little that has been published, as well as from the various evidences of Saadiah himself and of other *geonim*, the dimensions of his halakhic work can be reconstructed. It is clear that the largest and most important part of it consists of monographs on halakhic decisions, which covered most of what is at present included in the *Ḥoshen Mishpat* of the Shulḥan Arukh, as well as books on Ritual Purity and Impurity (*Niddah, Sheḥitah, Terefot*), Incest, Festivals, and the proclamation of the new month. Saadiah was one of the creators of rabbinic literature, if not the actual pioneer in this field, and the first to write "books" in the modern sense of the word. He was also the first to give his halakhic works the form of monographs, assigning a separate one to each topic of Hebrew law: a book on the Laws of Gifts, another on the Laws of Commercial Transactions, and so on. He was likewise the first to set a standard pattern for his books of halakhic decisions by dividing each one into sections and subsections. Every subject begins with a brief definition of the topic under discussion, followed by various details and talmudic proofs of them. Saadiah goes into the fullest details of every halakhic topic he touches on, but he frequently omits entire *halakhot* which have a direct bearing on the subject at issue, either because he thought of dealing with them within the context of some other halakhic monograph, or because he regarded them as too unimportant to be included in the discussion. Saadiah's halakhic books are thus distinguished by their systematic structure and logical order and by a lengthy detailed introduction which he prefaced to each book of halakhic decisions. One exception to all this is his Book of Inheritance, which omits the talmudic proofs of the *halakhot* mentioned in it. This gave rise to the conjecture among scholars that at first Saadiah's procedure was not to state the sources but that after complaints from rabbis he changed his method. There is, however, no support for this supposition. It is more probable that the extant Book of Inheritance is an abbreviated version of the original work, which contained the sources. Saadiah's books of halakhic decisions represent a complete revolution when compared to other similar lengthy works that preceded it, **Halakhot Gedolot* and **Halakhot Pesukot*, which, following the pattern of talmudic themes, lack the structure of a code. Saadiah was the first to write halakhic works in Arabic, which had in his days replaced Aramaic as the principal language spoken by the Jews in Babylonia. This constituted something of a revolution. Following him, various *geonim* also wrote extensively in this language. Saadiah's halakhic writings exercised a great influence on succeeding *geonim*, although this is not superficially apparent since the *geonim* seldom quoted the names of their geonic predecessors.

Several of Saadiah's halakhic works were collected and edited by J. Mueller and published in Paris in 1897. These consist of The Book of Inheritance; The Book of the 613 Commandments; An Interpretation of the Thirteen Hermeneutic Rules; collected responsa; and statements in his name collected from various sources. The Book of the 613 Commandments was republished with a very extensive commentary by Jeroham Fischel *Perla. The collected responsa ascribed to Saadiah require to be examined to authenticate their authorship. Extracts from *Sefer ha-Shetarot*, his book on documents and deeds, which had a unique structure and arrangement, were published by S. Assaf in: J.L. Fishman (ed.), *Rav Sa'adyah Gaon* (1957; see bibliography); further extracts appeared in *Tarbiz*, 9 (1938). The commentary on *Berakhot*, published by S.A. Wertheimer (1908) and attributed to Saadiah, is not by him. In addition, many of Saadiah's halakhic statements have been preserved in his *siddur* (see below). He also wrote on the methodology of the Talmud, apparently in a general introduction to it, of which a few extracts were quoted in a similar work of Bezalel *Ashkenazi that was published by A. Marx in *Festschrift… David Hoffmann* (1914) and in other writings of this scholar.

[Israel Moses Ta-Shma]

Saadiah's Philosophy

Although Saadiah was not the first medieval Jewish philosopher, in light of his public standing, the scope of his philosophical oeuvre, and the influence it had on subsequent generations, he can be considered the founding father of medieval Jewish philosophy.

Saadiah's major philosophic work, written in Arabic, *Kitāb al-Amānāt wa-al-Iʿtiqādāt* (ed. by S. Landauer, 1880; tr. by S. Rosenblatt, *The Book of Beliefs and Opinions*, 1948; abridged version, tr. by A. Altmann, in: *Three Jewish Philosophers*, 1965), is the earliest Jewish philosophic work from medieval times to have survived intact. It was translated into Hebrew by Judah ibn *Tibbon in 1186 under the title *Sefer ha-Emunot ve-ha-De'ot* (Constantinople, 1562), and in this version exercised a profound influence on Jewish thought. A new Hebrew translation was prepared by Y. Kafiḥ and published together with the Arabic original (1970).

There exist several manuscripts of an earlier anonymous Hebrew paraphrase of the work, *Pitron Sefer ha-Emunah*, which was probably written by an author who lived within the boundaries of Byzantine culture in the 11–12th century (critical edition: Hebrew paraphrase of Saadiah Gaon's *Kitāb al-Amānāt wa-al-Iʿtiqādāt*, ed. R.C. Kiener, Ph.D. thesis, University of Pennsylvania (1984); idem, in: *AJS Review*, 11:1 (1986), 1–25). Saadiah also wrote an Arabic commentary on the *Sefer Yeẓirah* ("The Book of Creation"), titled *Tafsīr Kitāb al-Mabādi* (ed. and tr. into French under the title *Commentaire sur le Sefer Yesira par le Gaon Saadya*, by M. Lambert, 1891), which was translated into Hebrew by Moses b. Joseph of Lucena, probably sometime during the 12th century (Ms. Munich, no. 92). A new Hebrew translation was prepared by Y. Kafiḥ and published together with the Arabic original (1972). References to other Hebrew translations of this work are found in the commentary on *Sefer Yeẓirah* by *Judah ben Barzillai al-Bargeloni (ed. by S.J. Halberstam, 1885), and in Berechiah ha-Nakdan's *Meẓaref* (ed. by Gollancz, 1902). Saadiah's philosophical views are also contained in some of his introductions to the Pentateuch (see Y. Kafiḥ, *Perushei Rabbenu Sa'adyah Ga'on al ha-Torah*, 1963). Exegetical works, especially introductions to commentaries, also served as a vehicle for Saadiah to expound his philosophical system, e.g., in the introduction to Job he discusses at length divine justice and the suffering of the righteous, in the introduction to Daniel he refutes the validity of divination in general, and astrology in particular, to forecast the future, as opposed to prophecy, which is the only true source for knowing future events (notably the ultimate redemption), because of its divine origin.

Saadiah was close to the school of the Muʿtazilites (see **Kalām*), but it is evident that he was also influenced by Aristotelianism, Platonism, and Stoicism. He, in turn, influenced Jewish Neoplatonists, such as *Baḥya ibn Paquda, Moses *Ibn Ezra, and *Abraham ibn Ezra. Jewish Aristotelians such as Abraham *Ibn Daud also borrowed some of his ideas. The influence of Saadiah declined with the appearance of the *Guide of the Perplexed*, in which Maimonides attacks *Kalām* philosophy, alluding to Saadiah, although never mentioning him by name. However, in the 14th and 15th centuries, Maimonides' philosophical opponents drew upon Saadiah's work, and *Sefer ha-Emunot ve-ha-De'ot* was influential until the *Haskalah period.

In line with Muʿtazilite thought, Saadiah in *Sefer ha-Emunot ve-ha-De'ot* did not attempt to establish a complete philosophical system resting upon an independent foundation, but rather set out to find a rational basis for the dogmas of the Oral and Written Law. Saadiah explains that he wrote this work in order to provide his fellow Jews with spiritual guidance in the face of the confusion which the multiple sects and religious disputes of the tenth century had created among the people, and to combat heretical views, such as those of Ḥiwi al-Balkhi. The *Emunot ve-De'ot* (as it is usually referred to) is a polemical work, in which Saadiah, in addition to clarifying and expounding his own views, devoted much space to disproving opposing theories. Saadiah believed that it was a religious obligation to provide a rational basis for the Law and the Jewish faith, in order to dispel doubts and refute views at variance with those which he accepts. Saadiah's importance lies in his being the first medieval Jewish philosopher to attempt to reconcile the Bible and rabbinic tradition with philosophy, reason with revelation and tradition. Unlike his predecessor *Al-Muqammis, Saadiah related his system of religious thought directly to the Jewish sources, and he did it with the authority of his position as *gaon*.

Saadiah was one of the earliest thinkers (though not the first) to establish a list of normative beliefs ("articles of faith," ten in number). Although he did not include this list in any halakhic work, and so did not give them any legally binding status, it seems that they had some influence, and may have paved the way for Maimonides in establishing his 13 articles of faith.

THEORY OF KNOWLEDGE. In the introduction to the *Emunot ve-De'ot*, in an attempt to refute the skeptics and to show that one can achieve a knowledge of the truth by means of speculation, Saadiah presents a psychological and epistemological account of the reasons for doubt, and explains why men in their search for the truth become involved in error. He identifies three sources of knowledge: (1) sense perception; (2) self-evident principles, such as the approval of telling the truth and the disapproval of lying, and (3) inferential knowledge gained by syllogistic reasoning.

He attacks the claim of the skeptics that these sources of knowledge are not to be relied upon, but at the same time discusses the errors that one may make in utilizing them, and the steps that one must take in order to insure their reliability. There is, in addition, a fourth source of knowledge, reliable tradition, i.e., confidence in the truth of the reports of others, which is indispensable for the functioning of human society. In Judaism reliable tradition has special significance in that it refers to the transmission, through Scripture and the oral tradition, of God's revelation to the prophets, and subsequently to the sages. Saadiah maintains that while one can arrive at a knowledge of the truth by means of speculation, revelation is necessary in order to impart the truth to those who are incapable of rational investigation, as well as to provide guidance for those who are involved in speculation. In the division between the three sources of rational knowledge and the reliable tradition Saadiah is part of the Muʿtazilite tradition. This division in turn is the basis for the distinction between rational laws and revealed ones. Even while engaged in speculation one must not set aside the doctrines contained in Scripture.

Saadiah believes that there is a correspondence between reason and revelation, and that one cannot refute the other. Therefore, one must reject the validity of any prophet whose teachings contradict reason, even if he accompanies his teachings with miracles. Those biblical statements which appear to contradict the results of rational investigation (e.g., anthropomorphic descriptions of God) must be interpreted metaphorically. The establishment of a systematic exegetical methodology is for Saadiah an essential means for the correct rational interpretation of the Bible. Saadiah points out that in interpreting anthropomorphic expressions metaphorically he is not subordinating revelation to reason, but is actually following revelation, which teaches that God is incorporeal.

CREATION. In typical Muʿtazilite fashion, Saadiah opens the body of his work with a discussion of creation. He maintains that the world was created in time, that its creator was other than itself, and that it was created *ex nihilo*. He presents four proofs for creation, the first based indirectly (probably through an Arabic version of the writings of John Philoponus) on Aristotelian premises, the other three drawn from the *Kalām*. In the first proof, invoking the principles that the world is finite in its dimension, and that a finite body cannot possess an infinite force, Saadiah concludes that the force preserving the world is finite and consequently that the world itself must be finite, i.e., must have a beginning and an end. In the second proof, on the basis of the fact that whatever is composed must have been put together at some point in time, Saadiah argues that the world, which is composed of various elements, must have been created at some point in time. In the third proof Saadiah argues that the world is composed of various substances all of which are the bearers of accidents. Since accidents originate in time, and since substances cannot exist actually without accidents, the world itself must have originated in time. The fourth argument is taken from the nature of time. Were the world uncreated, time would be infinite. But infinite time cannot be traversed, and hence the present (or any other finite) moment could never have come to be. But the present clearly exists, and hence time cannot be infinite. It follows that the world must have had a beginning.

Following these four proofs for creation, thus refuting the eternity of the world, Saadiah adduces three arguments that prove that the world did not create itself, i.e., that it has a creator who is other than the world itself. Another set of five (unnumbered) arguments is then brought forward by Saadiah to prove that the Creator of the world made it out of nothing (*ex nihilo*). This set establishes the important principle that while the Creator is eternal everything else is generated in time.

Having advanced these three sets of proofs for creation in time by the Creator, Saadiah proceeds to refute 12 other cosmogonic theories which differ from his own. These range from theories which, while accepting the principle that a creator created the world in time, deny that it was created out of nothing, through that which upholds the eternity of the world, to theories which are skeptical about the possibility of human knowledge and hence about demonstrating either the creation or eternity of the world (*Emunot ve-De'ot*, 1:3).

NATURE OF GOD. Saadiah's concept of the nature of God is based upon his view of God as creator. God is the cause of all corporeal existence, He cannot Himself be corporeal, for if He were corporeal, there would have to be something beyond Him which was the cause of His existence. Since God is incorporeal, He cannot be subject to the corporeal attributes of quantity and number (or any other property which may be defined by Aristotle's Categories, *Emunot ve-De'ot*, 2:9–12), and hence cannot be more than one. Turning to the question of divine attributes, Saadiah demonstrates that an analysis of the concept of God as creator leads to distinguishing three attributes of essence in Him: life, power, and wisdom. The attribution of these qualities to God does not imply a plurality in God. In reality all these qualities are united in Him, but we are forced to speak of them as separate because of the limitation of human language (*Emunot ve-De'ot*, ch. 2). Other scriptural descriptions of God have to be interpreted as referring to his actions, or otherwise to his revelations (*Shekhinah*) or messengers (notably angels). All Jewish thinkers who followed the system of Kalām accepted the distinction between attributes of the essence of God and attributes of His actions, which was typical of that system. Similarly to the Muʿtazilite position, the question thus turns into a linguistic-exegetical one rather than an ontological one. The creation of the world was not the result of a need or compulsion on the part of God, but an act of free will. In creating the world God wished to benefit His creatures by giving them the opportunity of serving Him through the observance of His commandments, by means of which they could attain true happiness (*Emunot ve-De'ot* 1:4).

CLASSIFICATION OF COMMANDMENTS. The laws given by God to Israel may be divided into two categories: the rational laws (*mitzvot sikhliyyot*), which have their basis in reason and which man would have discovered by means of reason even if they had not been revealed, because God planted them in the minds of human beings from their birth, and the traditional laws (*mitzvot shimiyyot*), ritual and ceremonial laws, such as the dietary laws, which do not have their basis in reason. This classification, which results from Saadiah's theory of knowledge (inspired by the Muʿtazila and which crystallized in Muʿtazilite thought about a generation before Saadiah), had a deep and enduring influence on Jewish philosophy in the Middle Ages. The acts to which the traditional laws refer are neither good nor evil from the point of view of reason, but are made so by the fact that they are commanded or prohibited by God. All the rational laws can be subsumed under three basic rational principles: First, reason demands that one express gratitude to one's benefactor. Hence, it is reasonable that God should demand that man render thanks to Him through worship. Second, reason demands that a wise person not permit himself to be insulted. Hence, it is reasonable that God should prohibit man from insulting Him, i.e., should prohibit man from taking His name in vain, or from describing Him in human terms. Third, reason demands that creatures should not harm one another. Hence, it is reasonable that God prohibit men from stealing, murdering, and committing adultery, and harming one another in various other ways. While the individual traditional laws do not have their basis in reason, these laws as a class can also be subsumed under a principle of reason. It is reasonable for a wise man to give unnecessary employment to a poor man merely in order to be able to pay him and thereby confer a benefit upon him. Thus, it is reasonable that God should present man with various ceremonial laws in order to be able to reward man for observing them. While the basis of the traditional laws is the fact that they are commanded by God, it is possible upon careful examination to discern even in these laws a certain intrinsic value and rationality, or rather usefulness, which is termed by Saadiah as God's wisdom (Ar. *ḥikma*). For example, the commandment to refrain from work on the Sabbath provides man with an opportunity to devote himself to spiritual matters. Revelation is obviously necessary in order for man to arrive at the knowledge of the traditional laws. It is also necessary in the case of the rational laws, for reason grasps only abstract principles and general norms. The details necessary for the concrete application of these principles are communicated by means of revelation (*Emunot ve-De'ot*, ch. 3).

NATURE OF MAN AND DIVINE JUSTICE. Saadiah views man as a composite of body and soul. The soul is made of very fine material (comparable to the material of which the celestial spheres are made, and even finer than they are), and has three essential faculties: appetite, which controls growth and reproduction; spirit, which controls the emotions; and reason, which controls knowledge, and is ideally supposed to govern the other two faculties. The soul cannot act on its own, and is therefore placed in the body, which serves as its instrument. By means of his actions, i.e., by means of the performance of the divine commandments, man can attain true happiness. One may ask why God does not reward man without his having to undergo hardship and suffering in this world. Saadiah explains that the only real reward is that which man wins for himself through actions for which he is responsible. It is precisely the quality of infinite goodness in God which demands that man be given the opportunity to win his own reward (*Emunot ve-De'ot* 6:4). It follows that man must have freedom of choice, for if he did not, he would not be responsible for his actions, and God's rewarding and punishing him would be unjust. A further indication that man possesses freedom of choice is the fact that he feels that he is free to act, and does not feel anything preventing him from acting. Saadiah attempts to reconcile the paradox of free choice with God's foreknowledge by stating simply that God's knowledge is not a cause of man's actions, and hence does not restrict his freedom of choice. God merely knows what the outcome of man's deliberation will be (*Emunot ve-De'ot* 4:3, 4). The problem which troubles Saadiah more is the question of theodicy – why the evil prosper and the good suffer. The solution, according to Saadiah, lies in the balance between suffering in this world and the reward in the next. The righteous who suffer in this world will be rewarded in the **olam ha-ba*. In the latter part of *Emunot ve-De'ot* Saadiah discusses extensively problems of Jewish eschatology such as resurrection of the dead, the Messiah, and redemption. He concludes with a long ethical treatise describing how man should conduct himself in this world in order to achieve true happiness. The Golden Mean is a leading principle in this treatise.

As Grammarian

Saadiah devoted much attention to the Hebrew language. In addition to many linguistic annotations in his biblical commentary he wrote three separate works on the subject. His first work on the Hebrew language was *Sefer ha-Agron* (ed. by N. Allony, 1969), which he wrote at the age of 20, in vocalized, accented, and flowery Hebrew. After several years he issued a second edition with an introduction in Arabic, as well as an Arabic translation of the Hebrew text. His purpose was to provide a dictionary of a large part of the Hebrew language and in particular to help poets in writing Hebrew poetry by giving a rhyming dictionary of word-endings. In his work he also sought to teach the principles of grammar. In its Hebrew preface, of which only a fragment has survived, he explained the differences between the root letters and the affixes, enumerating the letters used as the latter. In the second edition he added a discussion, with examples, of some of the characteristic features of a poem. In the Arabic introduction he explicitly stated that he was prompted to compose the work through the influence of an Arab writer, but following in his footsteps he aimed only at what would promote the Hebrew language, a brief historical survey of which he embodied in the Hebrew preface to the book. Only fragments have been published.

His second linguistic work, *Pitron Shiv'im Millim*, ed. by Dukes in ZKM, 5 (1844) 115–36 and subsequent editions, contains an incomplete list of the **hapax legomena* in the Bible, which are explained from the language of the Mishnah. The form of the work, as extant in manuscripts and in printed versions, gives the impression of being a fragment of a much larger book from which it was detached to constitute a separate treatise. The aim of the work was polemical, in that it set out to prove that the Oral Law is indispensable, since it is impossible to comprehend these biblical words without the help of the Mishnah. Saadiah explicitly said: "They [that is, the *Karaites] are unaware of the fact that they have come to know the sense of these words only from what I have adduced as proof and thus revealed their meaning from the Mishnah." For their part, the Karaites accused him of distorting the truth so as to invent proof of the indispensability of the Mishnah.

Saadiah's third work, *Sefer Ẓaḥut ha-Lashon ha-Ivrit*, deals with Hebrew grammar; only fragments of it were discovered in recent times. The work is divided into 12 sections, each of which treats of a grammatical problem. From these fragments it would appear that he replied to questions, and in doing so dealt with the letters and the vowels and their combinations, the inflection of the noun and of the verb, the formative letters, the *dagesh* and the *rafeh*, the rules of the *sheva*, and metathesis. He established the conjugation in Hebrew and illustrated it by *kal* and *hifil*. Like all his other writings, Saadiah's work on grammar attests to his extensive knowledge and the great vigor with which he applied himself to whatever task he undertook. His detailed knowledge of the Hebrew language as preserved in the masorah, extending even to the vowels, is astonishingly precise. It is still more astonishing to read his "*Shir shel ha-Otiyyot*," which he wrote on each letter of the Hebrew alphabet, including the final letters. On each he composed two couplets which, by words and biblical allusions, give the number of times that particular letter occurs in the Bible. Each poem, in addition to giving the precise figure, conveys an idea. The lines written on *alef* will serve as an illustration:

אהל מכון בניני ששם עלו זקני הקהל עשו קרבני ולזבח תודה באו בני

… the meaning of which is as follows: "The Temple, the foundation of all buildings, To which the elders of Israel went on pilgrimage, And where the people offered sacrifices, And the children of Israel came to sacrifice a thanksgiving offering." The number of times the letter *alef* (אֹהל) occurs in the Bible corresponds to the numerical value of the initial letters of the words following אהל, that is, מ״ב (אלף) שע״ז (= 42,377), the mnemonics for which are הקהל (Neh. 7:66, "The whole congregation [הקהל] together was forty and two thousand three hundred and three score") and ולזבח (Num. 7:17, "And for the sacrifice [ולזבח] of peace-offerings, two oxen, five rams, five he-goats, five he-lambs of the first year," making a total of 42,360+17.

[Abraham Solomon Halkin / Haggai Ben-Shammai (2nd ed.)]

Saadiah's Translation of the Bible

All Saadiah's grammatical work was ancillary to his activity as an exegete, and his most enduring and comprehensive work in the field of exegesis is his Arabic translation of, and partial commentary to, the Bible. This was the first translation of the Bible from Hebrew into Arabic, and has remained the standard Bible for Arabic-speaking Jews. He first prepared a translation, probably of all books of the Bible with an extensive commentary designed for learned readers, and then proceeded to write a popular translation which, as its name *Tafsir* (commentary) indicates, was both translation and commentary. In order to make it accessible and intelligible to the ordinary reader, he did not confine himself to a literal translation, but translated freely, sometimes disregarding syntax or paraphrasing the whole chapter. The *Tafsir* is rational, and Saadiah goes out of his way to eliminate all anthropomorphisms. One of the peculiarities is that he follows the Pseudo-Jonathan Targum (not, as would appear from Malter, the Targum Onkelos) in translating the proper names in the Bible, for which he was severely taken to task by Abraham ibn Ezra (to Gen. 2:21). Ibn Ezra, however, excuses him on the grounds that he probably did so in order to avoid criticism by those Muslims who might read the work that the Jews did not know the meaning of many words in their own Scriptures. Unlike many other Jewish scholars who wrote in Arabic, he used the Arabic and not the Hebrew alphabet (see also *Bible, Translations, Arabic).

As Liturgist and Paytan

Saadiah devoted considerable attention to all matters appertaining to liturgy. Since in his time there did not yet exist a methodically arranged prayer book, he made a systematic compilation in Arabic of the prayers for the whole year. Titled *Kitāb Jamʿī al-Ṣalawāt wa al-Tasabīh* ("Collection of All Prayers and Praises"), the book was very well known in Egypt and in other countries where Arabic was the vernacular. With the passage of time, however, it was forgotten and was published only in recent times by I. Davidson, S. Assaf, and B.I. Joel under the name of *Siddur Rav Sa'adyah Ga'on* (1941) in the Arabic original, with a Hebrew translation, and with many additional *piyyutim*.

Saddiah was a great innovator in the sphere of **piyyut*, in language, form, and content. His **bakkashot* received high praise from Abraham ibn Ezra; in his commentary to Ecclesiastes (5:1) he said of them "that no author had composed their like." Maimonides was asked whether it was necessary to stand when reciting the *bakkashot* of the *Gaon* (Responsa Maimonides, ed. by Blau, no. 14). Because of their importance and interest, they were translated into Arabic and circulated in many communities. In addition to the *bakkashot*, scholars through the generations also mention Saadiah's **azharot* and his **hoshanot*. (His "*Shir shel ha-Otiyyot*," "The Poems of the Letters," belongs rather to grammar than to liturgy, and is dealt with in the appropriate section above.) Many of his *piyyutim* were found in the Cairo **Genizah* and edited by Menahem *Zulay; they reveal Saadiah as a prolific writer of *piyyutim*, deft in the use of language and the devices of the *piyyut* form. Today it is known that besides the *piyyutim* already mentioned, Saadiah composed **kerovot*, **seliḥot*, **kinot* and philosophical poems. In his *tokheḥah* (poem of reproof) "*Im Lefi Beḥirkha*" ("If by your Choice"), Saadiah gave expression to many of the philosophical ideas which are also found in his *Emunot ve-De'ot*. There are similar ideas in some of his *bakkashot*, and also in his hymn for the Day of Atonement *Barekhi Nafshi* ("Let My Soul Bless") and there is no doubt that he was the first to compose philosophical *piyyutim*. These were later to serve as a model for such Spanish *paytanim* as Solomon ibn *Gabirol and *Judah Halevi.

[Abraham Meir Habermann]

Saadiah's Influence

Saadiah is one of the dominant figures in the development of Judaism and its literature. Although he had predecessors in some of the branches of that literature in which he engaged, he was the first to weld these numerous and diverse studies into a complete system. He provided a powerful impetus to all those who followed in his footsteps in the various branches of that literature, and there is hardly one of the outstanding figures in them who does not pay generous and laudatory tribute to his pioneering work. In philology, *Menahem b. Jacob ibn Saruq speaks of "the accuracy of his interpretations and the comprehensiveness of his linguistics"; the renowned grammarian Jonah *Ibn Janaḥ praises his great work in that field; the mathematician and astronomer Isaac b. Baruch ibn Abbatio states that "he was greater in science than I am"; to Abraham ibn Ezra in his biblical commentary he is "the *Gaon*" par excellence, and in his devastating criticism of the *paytanim* (to Eccles. 5:1), he singles out Saadiah as an exception. Maimonides disagreed with his philosophical views in many fundamental points, but states "were it not for Saadiah the Torah would have well-nigh disappeared from the midst of Israel" (*Iggeret Teiman*). His halakhic works penetrated to the Franco-German center and to the tosafists. He is the most authoritative geonic source, a fact which incidentally is evidence that his Arabic works were early translated into Hebrew, in versions which are no longer extant. "Taken all in all" says Malter, "Saadiah must be considered a remarkable milestone on the long road of Israel's development as a 'people of the book.'"

BIBLIOGRAPHY: J.L. Fishman (ed.), *Rav Sa'adyah Ga'on – Kovez̧ Torani Madda'i* (1924); *Saadiah Anniversary Volume* (1943), incl. bibl. compiled by A. Freimann; E.I.J. Rosenthal (ed.), *Saadya Studies* (1943); L. Finkelstein (ed.), *Rab Saadia Gaon, Studies in his Honor* (1944), incl. selected bibl. by Boaz Cohen; A. Marx, *ibid.*, 53–95; H. Malter, *Life and Works of Saadiah Gaon* (1921, 1970); S.W. Baron, in: *Saadiah Anniversary Volume* (1943), 9–74; N. Lamm, in: JQR, 55 (1964/65), 208–34; Z. Broshi, *Rav Sa'adyah Ga'on, Ḥayyav Mishnato u-Mifalav* (1942); S. Bernfeld, *Rabbenu Sa'adyah Ga'on* (1892); A. Hollaender, *Sa'adyah Ga'on ben Yosef Ge'on Sura* (1958); D. Kahana, *Sefer le-Toledot Rasag* (1892); S.K. Mirsky, *Rav Sa'adyah Ga'on* (1912); A. Marmorstein, *Le-Toledot Rav Sa'adyah Ga'on, Parashah bi-Tekufat ha-Ge'onim* (1951); M. Zuker, *Al Targum Rasag la-Torah* (1959, with Eng. summary); S.L. Skoss, *Saadia Gaon, the Earliest Hebrew Grammarian* (1955). As PHILOSOPHER: Guttman, Philosophies, 61–73; Husik, Philosophy, 23–41; Jacob Guttmann, *Die Religionsphilosophie des Saadiah* (1882); I. Efros, in: JQR, 33 (1942/43), 33–70; A. Heschel, *ibid.*, 265–313; H.A. Wolfson, in: *Saadiah Anniversary Volume* (1943), 197–245; G. Vajda, in: REJ, 126 (1967), 135–89, 375–397; M. Ventura, *La Philosophie de Saadia Gaon* (1934); A. Altmann, *Saadya's Conception of the Law* (1944); Z. Diesendruck, *Saadya's Formulation of the Time Argument for Creation* (1935); D. Druck, *Saadya Gaon, Scholar Philosopher, Champion of Judaism* (1942); L. Klaperman, *The Scholar-Fighter, The Story of Saadia Gaon* (1961); S.B. Urbach, *Ammudei ha-MaḤashavah ha-Yisre'elit*, 1 (1953). As LITURGIST AND PAYTAN: M. Zulay, *Ha-Askolah ha-Paytanit shel Rav Sa'adyah Ga'on* (1969); A. Firkowitsch, in: *Ha-Meliz̧* (1868); n. 26–27. **ADD. BIBLIOGRAPHY:** H. Ben-Shammai, in: *Pe'amim*, 54 (1993), 63–81 (Heb.); idem, in: *Da'at*, 37 (1996) 11–26 (Heb.); idem, in: D.H. Frank and O. Leaman (eds.), *History of Jewish Philosophy* (1997), 115–48; in: *Aleph*, 4 (2004), 11–87; H.A. Davidson, in A. Altmann (ed.), *Jewish Medieval and Renaissance Studies* (1967), 75–94; idem, in: S.D. Goitein (ed.), *Religion in a Religious Age* (1974), 53–68; idem, *Proofs for Eternity, Creation and the Existence of God in Medieval Islamic and Jewish Philosophy* (1987), *passim*; G. Freudenthal, in: *Arabic Sciences and Philosophy* 6,1 (1996) 113–36; L.E. Goodman (tr.), *The Book of Theodicy: Trans-*

lation and Commentary on the Book of Job by Saadiah ben Joseph al-Fayyumi (1988); Y.T. Langermann, in: *The Jews and the Sciences in the Middle Ages* (1999), ch. 2; S. Stroumsa, in: D.H. Frank and O. Leaman (eds.), *The Cambridge Companion to Medieval Jewish Philosophy* (2003) 71–90; H.A. Wolfson, *Repercussions of the Kalam in Jewish Philosophy* (1979), *passim*.

SAALSCHUETZ, JOSEPH LEWIN (1801–1863), German rabbi and archaeologist. Saalschuetz was born at Koenigsberg, where he served the Jewish community as preacher and teacher from 1835. In 1847 he was admitted to Koenigsberg University as lecturer in Hebrew archaeology, although he was denied a professorship, despite his undoubted capabilities, because of his Jewishness.

Among Saalschuetz's published works are *Von der Form der hebraeischen Poesie* (1825); *Archaeologie der Hebraeer* (2pts., 1855/56), a pioneering work describing the dress, science, customs, and government of the Jews, which includes the earlier *Geschichte und Wuerdigung der Musik bei den Hebraeern* (1829); and, of special importance, *Das mosaische Recht, mir Beruecksichtigung des spaeteren juedischen* (2 pts., 1846–48), *Das mosaische Recht, nebst den vervollstaendigenden thalmudisch-rabbinischen Bestimmungen* (1853^2). This work, dealing in its first part with public laws, and the second with private (civil) law, has retained its value as a source book for the study of Jewish law. Saalschuetz was among the contributors to the early volumes of the *Monatsschrift*.

His son, LOUIS SAALSCHUETZ (1835–1913), was a noted mathematician, who taught at Koenigsberg University.

BIBLIOGRAPHY: ADB, 30 (1890), 103–6.

[Max Wurmbrand]

SAARBRUECKEN, city in Germany, capital of the Saar. Jews were probably present in the city in 1321 when Duke John I granted the city its charter and reserved jurisdiction over the Jews. It is certain, however, that there were Jews in the adjacent villages of St. Wendel, Sarrebourg, and Sarreguemines at the time. There are no further sources mentioning the presence of Jews until 1732 when a *Judenordnung* ("Jewry regulation") was issued for the Saarbruecken community by the Count of Usingen-Nassau. During the French occupation (1792–1813) equality was granted and a Saarbruecken arrondissement was established with a Jewish population of 71. The Saarbruecken community grew from 10 families in 1837 to 376 persons in 1885 and 1,103 in 1910. Between 1920 and 1935 the Saar region was administered by the *League of Nations. The Saarbruecken community grew to 2,650, with another 1,700 Jews dispersed in 23 rural communities. At the time of the 1935 plebiscite on the future of the region, the Jews were accused of disloyalty and subjected to intensive harassment. Large numbers of Jews chose French and Belgian citizenship, and many emigrated with special "Nansen" passports. The Saarbruecken synagogue was burned down on Nov. 9/10, 1938, and by the summer of 1939 only 175 Jews were left. The Jews of the Saar were deported, together with Baden Jewry, to *Gurs in 1940. After the war a new community was founded, which grew from 180 in 1945/6 to 224 in 1948 and 350 in January 1970. A new synagogue was built in 1951. The Jewish community numbered 700 in 1960; 236 in 1989; and 1,110 in 2004. The increase is due to the immigration of Jews from the former Soviet Union.

BIBLIOGRAPHY: FJW, 260–1; H. Steinthal, in: *Nachrichtenblatt der Synagogen-Gemeinden des Saargebiets*, 7 (1934); S. Ruelf, *Stroeme im duerren Land* (1964), 64–70, 85–107, 249–62; *Germania Judaica*, 2 (1968), 726; M. Salomon, in: *Jewish Frontier*, 23 (Jan. 1956), 26–29. **ADD. BIBLIOGRAPHY:** M. Mueller-Knoblauch, *Der November-Pogrom 1938 in Saarbruecken. Zum Gedenken an die Opfer der antisemitischen Ausschreitungen vor 50 Jahren* (1988); A. Marx, *Die Geschichte der Juden im Saarland. Vom Ancien Régime bis zum Zweiten Weltkrieg* (1992); C. Kasper-Holtkotte, *Juden im Aufbruch. Zur Sozialgeschichte einer Minderheit im Saar-Mosel-Raum um 1800* (Forschungen zur Geschichte der Juden. Abteilung A Abhandlungen, vol. 3) (1996). **WEBSITE:** www.synagogengemeindesaar.de.

SAATCHI, CHARLES (1943–), British advertising agent and art collector. Born in Baghdad, the Saatchis fled to Britain in 1948 due to antisemitic pogroms by the Iraqis at the time of the creation of Israel. Charles Saatchi left school at 17 and founded the famous advertising agency Saatchi & Saatchi with his brother in the early 1970s. By the 1980s it had become one of the biggest advertising agencies in the world, and it is seen as an important factor in Margaret Thatcher's electoral victory in 1979, producing the famous poster "Labour Isn't Working." The Saatchis were ousted from their firm in a boardroom coup in 1994 and established a new agency, M & C Saatchi. Charles Saatchi is best known as one of the most important and controversial collectors and patrons of contemporary art in the world, giving a start to such artists as Damien Hirst. In 1985 he founded the Saatchi Gallery of Contemporary Art at the London County Hall site, and he has one of the most valuable private collections of contemporary art in the world. His brother BARON MAURICE SAATCHI (1946–) was also born in Baghdad and, following his career as an advertising agent, became an important force in the British Conservative Party. He was awarded a life peerage in 1996 and served as a Shadow spokesman in the House of Lords before becoming joint chairman of the Conservative Party in 2003.

BIBLIOGRAPHY: I. Fallon, *The Brothers: The Rise and Rise of Saatchi & Saatchi* (1988); R. Hatton and J.A. Walker, *Supercollector: A Critique of Charles Saatchi* (2000).

[William D. Rubinstein (2nd ed.)]

SABA, ABRAHAM BEN JACOB (d. c. 1508), Spanish exegete, preacher, and kabbalist. On the expulsion of the Jews from *Spain, Abraham settled in Oporto (Portugal), where he wrote commentaries on the Pentateuch, the Five Scrolls, and on *Avot*. When the forced conversion of the Jews was decreed in Portugal in 1497, his two young sons were baptized and his extensive library plundered. He left Oporto, taking his writings with him, but when near Lisbon he was warned by the local Jews of the danger of entering the city with Hebrew books in his possession, which was a capital offense. He thereupon buried his manuscripts under an olive tree. In Lisbon he was arrested and imprisoned together with other scholars, pressure being exerted on them to accept baptism. After nearly six months he succeeded in escaping to Fez in Morocco, where he fell ill. When he recovered, he began to rewrite his lost works from memory. He succeeded in completing only his commentaries on the Pentateuch, Ruth, and Esther. He remained in Fez for ten years, and in 1508 he was in Tlemcen in Algeria, and, it is thought, later in Italy.

Ḥ.J.D. Azulai tells an anecdote relating to Abraham. On a sea voyage to Verona, Saba became dangerously ill and, during a heavy storm, exacted a promise from his fellow travelers that, should he die, he would be given Jewish burial on dry land. As a result of his prayers the storm abated. He died on the eve of the Day of Atonement and the captain saw to it that the local Jews carried out his request. According to another account, however, he died in Fez. In Spain, Portugal, and Morocco Saba preached in the synagogues, urging the congregations to fulfill the principles of Judaism. He attributed their misfortunes to that, in their pride and arrogance, they had forgotten their ancestral land, building themselves palatial residences in alien countries, neglecting the Torah, and desecrating the Sabbath.

Abraham's works included *Ẓeror ha-Mor* (Venice, 1522), a commentary on the Pentateuch: a Latin translation of this by Conrad Pellicanus is extant in manuscript in the city library of Zurich; *Eshkol ha-Kofer*, commentaries on the Five Scrolls (the commentary on Esther published in 1904, on Ruth published in 1908); *Perush Eser Sefirot*, on the ten *Sefirot*, extant in manuscript, which he wrote in Tlemcen. His lost works include commentaries on Job; on the commandments, *Ẓeror ha-Kesef*, which he wrote in his youth; *Ẓeror ha-Ḥayyim*, on tractate *Avot*; on Psalms; and a kabbalistic commentary on the daily prayers.

BIBLIOGRAPHY: Michael, Or, no. 199; N.S. Leibowitz, *Rabbi Avraham Saba u-Sefarav …* (1936).

[Shmuel Ashkenazi]

SABA, UMBERTO (pseudonym of **Umberto Poli**; 1883–1957), Italian poet. Saba's mother, a niece of S.D. *Luzzatto, was abandoned by her Catholic husband before the birth of her son, and some scholars have argued that he adopted the Hebrew surname Saba ("grandfather") as a tribute to Luzzatto; but more likely the surname was chosen by him for its assonance to his Slovenian nurse's name, Saber. In his youth, Saba struggled with hardship and poverty and, after abandoning commercial studies, joined the mercantile marine and later the army, enlisting in an infantry regiment in 1908. His early *Versi militari* date back to those years and were later collected, with others, in *Coi miei occhi* (1912), the book which first brought him renown. Saba opened a secondhand bookshop in Trieste, his birthplace, which became a rendezvous for poets and writers. For almost 30 years he continued to publish poetry, but, despite its favorable reception by critics, he remained a literary outsider. Antisemitic persecution did not spare Saba: aware of the conflict between the two worlds to which he belonged, he chose to share the fate of the Jews. He immigrated to Paris, but returned to Italy in 1943, and remained in hiding until the end of World War II. Sick and exhausted, he then returned to Trieste.

Saba is considered one of the major contemporary Italian poets. His themes include Trieste, its sailors and people, his troubled youth, his wife, daughter, and friends, human suffering, animals, and nature. His verse is tinged with melancholy and pessimism, and enriched with a deep feeling for the world's misery, and eagerness for warm human contacts. With his lucid style, and a language that is almost prosaic in its use of everyday words and expressions, Saba achieves a musical and deeply poetic effect. His works include *Il Canzoniere* (1921), *Autobiografia* (1924), *Figure e canti* (1926), *Tre Composizioni* (1933), and *Parole* (1934). Poems of the years 1900–54 appear in a second *Canzoniere* (1963), while a complete edition of his poems has been published in a dozen volumes.

In order to explain the inner development of his poetry, Saba wrote a detailed self-critical and autobiographical essay in *Storia e cronistoria del Canzoniere* (1948). Autobiographic details also appear in two other prose works, *Scorciatoie e raccontini* (1946) and *Ricordi-Racconti* (1956). In the latter, some chapters collected under the title "Gli Ebrei" ("Jews," pp. 22–87, with a preamble by Carlo *Levi) give sketches of the life of the Jewish community of Trieste in the author's boyhood years. Among these sketches there is a description of an episode in the life of the young Luzzatto. Notes at the end of each narrative show that Saba had some knowledge of Hebrew and of the vernacular of Trieste's Jews. In his introduction to "Gli Ebrei" Saba emphasizes, somehow apologetically, that these tales, describing Jewish life in Trieste in an ironical and not always sympathetic way, were written at the beginning of the 20th century, far before the explosion of antisemitism in Europe and the tragedy of the Holocaust. Also in his poetry Saba shows ambivalence towards his Jewish roots, sometimes identifying himself with his Jewish ancestors and relatives, and sometimes criticizing them. Many of his poems have been translated into other languages.

BIBLIOGRAPHY: G. Debenedetti, *Saggi critici*, 1 (1929), 91ff.; idem, in: *Nuovi argomenti* (1958), 7–18; S. Solmi, *Scrittori…* (1963), 32–38, 72–77, 135–40; G. Ravegnani, *I Contemporanei* (1960^2), index; W. Binni, *Critici e poeti dal Cinquecento al Novecento* (1963^2), 223–36; G. Titta Rosa, *Poesia Italiana del Novecento* (1953); F. Portinari, *Umberto Saba* (It., 1963); E. Caccia, *Lettura e storia di Saba* (1967); G.G. Ferrero, *L'Opera poetica di Umberto Saba* (1958); N. Baldi, *Il paradiso di Saba* (1958). **ADD. BIBLIOGRAPHY:** G. Voghera, *Gli anni della psicanalisi* (1980), 53–102 and passim; H. Stuart Hughes, *Prisoners of Hope* (1983), 32–33; G. Lopez, "Umberto Saba e l'anima ebraica," in: M. Carla and L. De Angelis, *L'ebraismo nella letteratura italiana del Novecento* (1995), 87–99.

[Giorgio Romano]

SABAN, HAIM (1944–), American-Israeli media executive. A native of Alexandria, Egypt, Saban and his parents fled to

Tel Aviv following the Suez War of 1956. He attended agricultural school and served in the Israel Defense Forces. After establishing a leading tour business, he relocated to France in 1975 and built a record company that became a major European label, selling over 18 million albums in eight years. In 1983, Saban moved to Los Angeles, where he launched a chain of recording studios that became one of the leading suppliers of music for television. He formed Saban Entertainment in 1988, an international television, production, distribution, and merchandising company, best known for creating the Mighty Morphin Power Rangers, to this day the No. 1-selling toy for boys in the United States. In 1995, Saban merged his company with Rupert Murdoch's Fox Kids Network and acquired the Fox Family Channel (restructured as Fox Family Worldwide) in 1997. He sold it to the Walt Disney Co. in 2001 and became founder and CEO of Saban Capital Group, Inc. Saban supported many charities, including the Israel Cancer Research Fund, the John Wayne Cancer Institute, the Children's Hospital of Los Angeles, and the Milken Community High School. He also founded the Saban Institute for the Study of the American Political System at the University of Tel Aviv and the Saban Center for Middle East Policy at the Brookings Institute in Washington, D.C. In 2002, Governor Gray Davis appointed Saban to the University of California Board of Regents, the governing body of the University of California. Saban resigned from this post in 2004 after being publicly criticized for not attending meetings.

[Amy Handelsman (2nd ed.)]

SABATH, ADOLF JOACHIM (1866–1952), U.S. congressman. Sabath, who was born in Zabori, Bohemia, went to the U.S. at the age of 15 and settled in Chicago. He subsequently began practicing law in 1893 and became a justice of the peace in 1895. As a police magistrate from 1897 to 1907, Sabath was instrumental in the abolition of the fee system, the establishment of the juvenile court, and the implementation of a parole system. Elected to the U.S. Congress as a Democrat from Chicago's Fifth District in 1906, Sabath served in the House for 23 consecutive terms until his death, the second longest continuous service of any congressman. Representing a reform-minded immigrant constituency, he was a vigorous liberal who used his seniority and influence fully on behalf of New Deal and Fair Deal legislation.

In contrast to the prevailing climate of opinion during the 1930s, Sabath was a strong supporter of military preparedness and subsequently voted for the Lend-Lease Act. Sabath unsuccessfully sought the abolition of the House Un-American Activities Committee, which he considered detrimental to civil liberties in the U.S. From 1939 to 1947, and from 1949 to 1952, he was chairman of the powerful House Rules Committee.

SABBATH (Heb. שַׁבָּת; *Shabbat*; related to the verb *shavat*, "cease, desist, rest"), the seventh day of the week, the day of rest and abstention from work.

In the Bible

The etiology of the Sabbath is given in Genesis 1:1–2:3, although the name of the day does not appear there: God worked six days at creating the world; on the seventh he ceased working (*shavat mi-kol mela'khto*), blessed the day, and declared it holy (see 2:1–3). The special status of the seventh day and its name were disclosed to Israel in the episode of the manna. God supplied each day's need of manna for five days; on the sixth, a double portion was provided to last through the seventh day, on which no manna appeared. Correspondingly, the Israelites were commanded to go out, collect, and prepare each day's portion for the first five days; on the sixth, they were to prepare for two days; on the seventh they were not to go out at all but were to remain at home. Thus they learned that the seventh day was "a Sabbath of the Lord," which they must honor by desisting from their daily food-gathering labor (Ex. 16:22). The fourth "word" of the *Decalogue generalizes the lesson of the manna. All work (*mela'khah*) is banned on the Sabbath, which here for the first time is given a rationale, drawn directly from the formulation of Genesis 2:1–3 and expressly identifying the Sabbath with the seventh day of creation (Ex. 20:8–11). The meaning of the "blessedness" and "sanctity" of the day is inferrable from the manna experience.

According to Exodus 23:12 and 34:21, work is to cease on the seventh day in order to give slaves and draft animals rest; this must be observed even during the critical seasons of plowing and harvest. Deuteronomy's version of the Decalogue embodies this humanitarian motive in its divergent rationale of the Sabbath rest; Israel is to keep the Sabbath so that its slaves might rest, and because God, who liberated it from Egyptian bondage, so commanded (Deut. 5:14–15). God's instructions concerning the building of the Tabernacle end, and Moses' conveyance of them to the people begins, with an admonition to keep the Sabbath, indicating its precedence even over the duty of building the Sanctuary. The Sabbath is called a sign both of God's consecration of Israel, and of His six-day creation. The rulings are applied in the exemplary tale of Numbers 15:32ff. A man was found collecting wood (to make a fire) on the Sabbath. Apprehended by witnesses and brought before Moses, he was sentenced to death by stoning at the hands of the whole community. Besides the daily sacrificial offering, an additional one, amounting to the total offering of a weekday, was prescribed for the Sabbath (Num. 28:9–10; cf. Num. 28:3–8). Admonitions to observe the Sabbath are coupled once with reverence toward parents (Lev. 19:3; cf. the juxtaposition in the Decalogue), and twice with reverence toward the Sanctuary (Lev. 19:30; 26:2). As a time marker, the Sabbath terminated the week. Thus in the Tabernacle cult, the weekly replacement of shewbread occurred on the Sabbath (Lev. 24:8; I Chron. 9:32).

Only scraps of evidence are available concerning the nature of the Sabbath during the monarchy. In the Northern Kingdom during the ninth and eighth centuries, Sabbath and New Moon are mentioned together as days when business activity was halted (Amos 8:5), and people paid visits to men of God (II Kings 4:23). From Hosea 2:13 it appears that the Sabbath, like the New Moon and the festival mentioned before it, was among "all the joys" of the North that were under God's doom; this is a precious attestation of the joyous character of the day. In eighth-century Judah, too, Sabbath and New Moon were popularly celebrated in sacred convocations held in the Jerusalem Temple (Isa. 1:13; cf. Lam. 2:6 for later times). Again, as a time marker, the Sabbath was the day on which the palace guard was changed weekly (II Kings 11:5–9). Esteem of the Sabbath rose just before, during, and after the Exile. Jeremiah 17:19–27 berates the rulers and populace of Judah for condoning the hauling of burdens (market wares) into and within Jerusalem on the Sabbath. In an unprecedented prophecy, the fate of the dynasty and the city is made to depend upon the observance of the Sabbath. Ezekiel contains similar prophecies. Chapter 20:12ff. lays stress on the Sabbath as a sign of Israel's consecration to God; its significance is shown by juxtaposition with all the rest of the divine laws, the Sabbath alone being singled out by name. In catalogs of sins for which Jerusalem was doomed, desecration of the Sabbath occurs repeatedly. As part of his program for a reconstituted Israel, the prophet innovates the priestly duty of seeing that the Sabbath is kept holy (44:24). Noteworthy too is the increase in the number of animals prescribed for the Sabbath sacrifice from double that of the weekday to the befitting number seven (Ezek. 46:4). The Exilic "Isaiah" also singles out the observance of the Sabbath, juxtaposing it to all the rest of the covenant obligations as the precondition of individual and national restoration (56:2, 4, 6; 58:13: "If you call the Sabbath a delight/That which the Lord has sanctified – a day to be honored"). This prophet looks to an eventual universalization of the Sabbath among all nations (66: 23).

The prophets' estimate of the fateful importance of Sabbath observance was taken to heart in the fifth-century community of restored Jerusalem. The public confession of Nehemiah 9:14 once again singles out the Sabbath from all the "commandments, laws, and teachings" given to Israel through Moses. A special clause in the covenant subscribed to by the community's representatives forbids commerce with outsiders on Sabbaths and holy days (Neh. 10:32). Nehemiah enforced this clause rigorously as governor of Judah, reminding the indifferent aristocrats that for desecrating the Sabbath their ancestors had been visited with catastrophe (13:15–22).

HISTORICAL AND LITERARY-HISTORICAL CONSIDERATIONS. Evidence that in the period of the monarchy the Sabbath was a popular, joyous holy day, marked by cessation of business and celebrated publicly and by the individual, in the Sanctuary and outside it, accords with the pentateuchal traditions that it was among the chief stipulations of the Mosaic covenant. The antiquity and interrelation of the various rationales given in the Pentateuch for the Sabbath are, however, problematic. Such rationales appear in both versions of the Decalogue. That of Exodus, associating the Sabbath with the Creation, is theocentric and sacramental. The sanctity of the day is grounded in an event in the life of God – His cessation from work, His rest, His blessing and consecration. Israel's observance of the day is imitative and out of respect for God's authority. The revelation of the day's sanctity exclusively to Israel – with the attendant obligation to keep it – is a sign of Israel's consecration to God. This rationale is worked out in the creation story, the Exodus Decalogue, and the two admonitions connected with the building of the Tabernacle. Critical analysis assigns all these passages to the Priestly Source (P); their interrelation is, in any event, beyond dispute. The Deuteronomic version of the Decalogue grounds the Sabbath, ambiguously, on the liberation of Israel from slavery. On the one hand, the humane concern of Exodus 23 over the welfare of slaves is involved, on the other, the authority of God to give such laws by virtue of His having redeemed Israel. Since none of these rationales is reflected in the meager extra-pentateuchal passages on the Sabbath, speculation on their age and interrelationship can be based only on internal evidence. Even if conceptual or literary development can be shown, absolute dating is impossible – all the more so when it is borne in mind that presently interrelated ideas may have arisen independently and contemporaneously, and in either case, before their literary embodiment. The compassionate ground of Exodus 23:12 is conceptually simpler than the historical-humanistic one of Deuteronomy. On the other hand, Deuteronomy's is tangential to the essence of the Sabbath day – its holiness. That is accounted for only by the cosmic-sacramental rationale associated with the Exodus Decalogue. But if the rationale in Exodus is the best developed, it is not necessarily the latest. Deuteronomy's seems to have been substituted for it, as more in accord with the spirit of that work, in its version of the Sabbath commandment. Critics consider the sacramental (probably priestly) rationale an Exilic conception, since its esteem of the Sabbath as a sign of Israel's consecration agrees with the Exilic views of the importance of the day. But is a historical explanation really needed for the priestly esteem of a holy day whose centrality in Israel's life is vouched for by its inclusion in the Decalogue – the only holy day so honored? Distinctively Exilic is the appreciation of the Sabbath as a decisive factor in national destiny, and that is lacking in the priestly material as elsewhere in the Pentateuch. Warnings of doom for violation of the covenant laws single out idolatry (Ex. 23:24; Deut. 4:25ff.) as the fatal national sin; Leviticus 26:34–35, 43 – of priestly provenance – adds neglect of the Sabbatical (fallow) Year to the causes of national doom. But violation of the Sabbath day is nowhere held to be a factor in Israel's downfall, nor is its observance a warrant of national well-being – as in Jeremiah, Ezekiel, the Exilic Isaiah, and Nehemiah. This suggests that the age of Jeremiah is the *terminus ad quem* of the pentateuchal material on the Sabbath. The increased regard for the Sabbath from Jeremiah's time on is to be connected with the danger of assimilation to the gentiles that loomed since the reign of Manasseh (cf. Zeph. 1), and greatly troubled the religious leaders of the Exile (Ezek. 20:32ff). With the Temple destroyed and the Jews dispersed, the distinctively Israelite day of rest, which allowed for public and private expression and which was not essentially bound up with a sacrificial cult, became a chief vehicle of identification with the covenant community. To mark oneself off from the gentiles by observing the peculiar, weekly "sign" of God's consecration of Israel was an act of loyalty which might well be counted the equivalent of the rest of the covenant commandments, while disregard of the Sabbath might well be considered as serious a breach of faith with the God of Israel as the worship of alien gods. Such in fact was the view of Exilic and post-Exilic thinkers who put forward the idea that the breaking of the Sabbath was a cause of the nation's collapse.

Speculation on the origin of the Sabbath has centered on the apparent Babylonian cognate, *šapattu*, the mid-month day of the full moon, called "the day of calming [the god's] heart" – apparently an auspicious day. The biblical combination of "New Moon and Sabbath" has been thought, accordingly, to reflect what were originally two holy days, one at the start, the other in the middle of the month. Another partial analogy to the Sabbath has been found in the "evil days" of the Babylonian month (mostly at seven-day intervals) on which the king's activity was severely restricted. How the *šapattu* might have been combined with the entirely distinct "evil days," become dissociated from the lunar cycle, and finally emerge as the joyous, weekly "Sabbath of the Lord" has not been persuasively explained. Nonetheless an ultimate connection between the biblical and the Babylonian phenomena seems likely. If so, the history of the Sabbath began with a radical severance from the past. The particularity of the biblical day was its positive sanctity – so that abstention from work on it expressed piety, and that sanctity was a divine ordinance – not a matter of lucky and unlucky times. It was perhaps first grounded on God's compassion toward workers, later brought into relation with the Creation, and later still with the Exodus.

[Michael J. Graetz]

In the Apocrypha

According to the Book of Maccabees, the Sabbath was at one time observed so strictly that on one occasion during the Maccabean revolt, the Jews allowed themselves to be killed rather than resist on the Sabbath (I Macc. 2:31–38). Later, it was decided that the Sabbath may be transgressed in order to save life (I Macc. 2:40–41). The Book of Jubilees (2:17–32 and 50:6–13) is extremely severe on Sabbath desecration, death being the penalty even for such offenses as walking any distance, fasts, or traveling on a ship on the Sabbath. The Book of Jubilees (50:8) also forbids marital relations on the Sabbath, whereas in the rabbinic teaching it is considered meritorious to perform these on the Sabbath (BK 82a, Ket. 62b).

In Rabbinic Literature

The rabbis wax eloquent on the value of Sabbath observance. "If Israel keeps one Sabbath as it should be kept, the Messiah will come. The Sabbath is equal to all the other precepts of the Torah" (Ex. R. 25:12). "God said to Moses: 'Moses, I have a precious gift in My treasury whose name is the Sabbath and I want to give it to Israel. Go and tell them'" (Beẓah 16a). "The Sabbath is one sixtieth of the world to come" (Ber. 57b). "The Sabbath increases Israel's holiness. 'Why does so-and-so close his shop?' 'Because he keeps the Sabbath.' 'Why does so-and-so refrain from work?' 'Because he keeps the Sabbath.' Furthermore, whoever keeps the Sabbath testifies of Him at whose word the world came into being; that He created the world in six days and rested on the seventh" (Mekh. Sb-Y to Ex. 31:14). The juxtaposition of the instructions to build the Sanctuary and the prohibition of Sabbath work caused the rabbis to deduce that it was forbidden on the Sabbath to do any work that was required for the Sanctuary. The rabbinic definition of forbidden Sabbath work is, therefore, that which was needed for the Sanctuary (Mekh. Sb-Y. to Ex. 35:1; Shab. 49b). Any work analogous to those types used for the building of the Sanctuary is classified as being biblically forbidden. There are thus 39 main classes of work ("fathers of work," *avot*) used in the building of the Sanctuary, and many others derived from these ("offspring," *toledot*), with only slight technical differences between "father" and "offspring" (BK 2a). Watering of plants, for instance, is a *toledah* of sowing; weeding, of plowing; adding oil to a burning lamp, of lighting a fire. The Mishnah (Shab. 7:2) gives a list of the 39 main classes of work. (It has been noted that the number 39 is a standard number in rabbinic literature and that these types of work are all of a kind obtaining in the rabbinic period.) The Mishnah (Ḥag. 1:8) also states that the laws of forbidden work on the Sabbath are as mountains hanging by a hair, for there is little on the subject in the Scriptures yet the rules are many. In addition to the biblical prohibitions, there are various rabbinic prohibitions introduced as a "fence to the Torah" (Avot 1:1), such as the handling of tools or money (*mukẓeh*), riding a horse, instructing a gentile to do work. These rabbinic prohibitions are known as *shevut* ("rest"; Beẓah 5:2). One who profanes the Sabbath in public is treated as an idolator (Ḥul. 5a). Conversely, whoever observes the Sabbath as it should be, is forgiven his sins, even if he practiced idolatry (Shab. 118b).

The Sabbath is a festive day and three meals should be eaten on it (Shab. 118a). It was considered meritorious for a man to make some preparations for the Sabbath himself, even if he had servants to do it for him (Kid. 41a). R. Safra used to singe the head of an animal, R. Huna used to light the lamp, R. Papa to plait the wicks, R. Ḥisda to cut up the beets, Rabbah and R. Joseph to chop the wood, R. Zera to kindle the fire (Shab. 119a). R. Ḥanina would say on the eve of the Sabbath: "Come let us go out to meet the Bride, the Queen." R. Yannai used to adorn himself and say: "Come O Bride, come O Bride" (*ibid.*, BK 32a–b). Out of respect for the sacred day, it was forbidden to fast on the eve of the Sabbath (Ta'an. 27b). In a well-known passage (Shab. 119b), it is said that on the eve of the Sabbath two ministering angels accompany a man from the synagogue to his home. If, when he arrives home, he finds the lamp burning, the table laid, and the couch covered with a spread, the good angel declares, "May it be thus on another Sabbath too" and the evil angel is obliged to answer "Amen."

But if not, the evil angel declares, "May it be thus on another Sabbath too" and the good angel is obliged to answer "Amen." At the beginning of the Sabbath, the special sanctification (*Kiddush*) is recited (Pes. 106a), and after the termination of the Sabbath the *Havdalah* ("distinction") benediction (which signifies the separation of the Sabbath from the weekday) is recited (Ber. 33a), both over a cup of wine. A man should wear special garments in honor of the Sabbath; he should walk differently from the way he does on a weekday, and even his speech should be different (Shab. 11a–b).

In Jewish Thought

From an early period, the Sabbath became a day of spiritual refreshment. Philo (II Mos. 216) and Josephus (Apion, 2:175) refer to the practice of public discourses on the Torah on this day, as do the rabbis (Yal., Ex. 108). Philo (Decal. 96) sees the Sabbath as an opportunity for man to imitate his Creator who rested on the seventh day. Man, too, should rest from his weekday labors in order to devote himself to contemplation and to the improvement of his character. The Midrash (Mekh. Sb-Y to 20:11) similarly states that if God, who exerts no effort, "writes about Himself" that he rested, how much more should man rest of whom it is said that he was born to toil. The benediction for the Sabbath afternoon service sums up the rabbinic attitude to the Sabbath as a precious gift from God, and as a sacred day kept even by the Patriarchs: "Thou art One and Thy Name is One, and who is like Thy people a unique nation upon the earth? Glorious greatness and a crown of salvation, even the day of rest and holiness, Thou hast given unto Thy people – Abraham was glad, Isaac rejoiced, Jacob and his sons rested thereon – a rest granted in love, a true and faithful rest, a rest in peace and tranquility, in quietude and safety, a perfect rest wherein Thou delightest. Let Thy children perceive and know that this their rest is from Thee, and by their rest may they hallow Thy Name."

The medieval Jewish philosophers tend to dwell on the symbolic nature of the day. For Maimonides (*Guide*, 2, 31), the Sabbath has a twofold significance: It teaches the true opinion that God created the world, and it provides man with physical rest and refreshment. According to Isaac Arama (*Akedat Yiẓhak*, 55 ed. Bialystok (1849), 285–89), the Sabbath teaches the three fundamental principles of Judaism: belief in *creatio ex nihilo*, in revelation (because the Sabbath is a time when the Torah is studied), and in the world to come (of which the Sabbath is a foretaste). *Judah Halevi looks upon the Sabbath as a God-given opportunity for men to enjoy complete rest of body and soul for a sixth part of their lives, in a way denied even to kings, who know nothing of this precious boon of complete cessation from toil and distraction (*Kuzari*, 3, 10).

Samson Raphael *Hirsch (*Horeb*, section 2:21; tr. by I. Grunfeld, 1 (1962), 61–78) understands the prohibition of creative activity on the Sabbath (the types of forbidden work do not so much involve effort, as they are creative) to be a lesson for man to acknowledge his Creator as Creator of everything there is. Man is allowed to rule over the world for six days by God's will, but is forbidden on the seventh day to fashion anything for his own purpose. On each Sabbath man restores the world to God, as it were, and thus proclaims that he enjoys only a borrowed authority.

The Laws and Customs of the Sabbath

The mistress of the house kindles at least two candles before the advent of the Sabbath, one corresponding to "remember the Sabbath day" (Ex. 20:8), the other to "observe the Sabbath day" (Deut. 5:12). For each meal two whole loaves of bread are placed on the table, covered by a cloth, to correspond to the double portion of manna for the Sabbath (Ex. 16:22–26). Before the *Kiddush* is recited, the parents bless the children. During the festive meals of the day, special table hymns (*zemirot*) are chanted. Whenever possible, guests should be invited to participate in the Sabbath meals. There is a special order of service for Sabbath in the synagogue. Psalms are recited before the evening service on Friday night, and the morning service includes the weekly readings from the Torah, as well as a *Musaf Amidah*. The afternoon service also includes a Torah reading from the portion to be read on the following Sabbath. When the Sabbath is over, the *Havdalah* benediction is recited, together with a benediction over spices (to restore the soul saddened by the departure of the day), and over light (which could neither be lit nor blessed on the Sabbath). Where there is danger to life (*pikku'aḥ nefesh*), the Sabbath must be set aside and Sabbath profanation in such circumstances is meritorious in the extreme. Unlike the *Karaites, who took the verse "let no man go out of his place on the seventh day" (Ex. 16:29) literally, the rabbis placed no restrictions on freedom of movement within one's town, but they prohibited any walking outside the town beyond a distance of 2,000 cubits (a little more than half a mile). This boundary is known as the *teḥum shabbat* (Sabbath limit). It is, however, permitted to place, before the Sabbath, sufficient food for two meals at the limits of the 2,000 cubits; then, by a legal fiction known as *eruv*, this place becomes one's "abode" for the duration of the Sabbath, so that the 2,000 cubits may then be walked from there. It is forbidden to instruct a non-Jew to do any work on the Sabbath which is not permitted to a Jew, unless it is for the sake of health. In cold climes, the heating of the home by a non-Jew falls under the heading "for the sake of health."

Modern inventions have produced a host of new questions regarding Sabbath observance. Orthodox Judaism forbids travel by automobile on the Sabbath, Reform Judaism permits it. Conservative Judaism has differing views on this question, but generally permits travel by automobile on the Sabbath solely for the purpose of attending synagogue. The basic legal question regarding the switching on of electric lights is whether the noncombustive type of burning produced by electricity falls under the prohibition of making a fire or any of the other prohibitions listed above. Orthodox Jews refrain from the use of electrical appliances on the Sabbath, with the exception of the refrigerator, which may be opened and closed on the grounds that any electrical current produced in the process is incidental and without express intention. It has, however, become the practice for observant Jews to use electrical appliances on the Sabbath which are operated by time switches set before the Sabbath. In Israel, on religious kibbutzim, the same procedure is used to milk the cows on the Sabbath. Israel also has local bylaws forbidding certain activities on the Sabbath. There is, however, no comprehensive law covering the whole country. Thus, whereas public transportation does not operate on the Sabbath in Jerusalem and in Tel Aviv, it does in Haifa. Except for specifically non-Jewish sections of the country, the Sabbath is the official day of rest on which all business and stores must close, but there is some doubt as to what is a business for this law (see *Israel, State of: Religious Life).

[Louis Jacobs]

In Kabbalah

The seven days of the week, reflections of the seven primeval days of creation, symbolize in Kabbalah the seven lower *Sefirot*, from *Ḥesed* to *Malkhut*, which are known as the *Sefirot ha-Binyan* because of their part in "building" creation. According to the kabbalists, the Torah hints at the existence of the two Sabbaths in the system of the *Sefirot* when it says "Ye shall keep My Sabbaths" (Lev. 19:30). Even in the kabbalistic literature, which was influenced by the Zohar to a slight degree or not at all, and which generally avoids stressing erotic elements in divinity, the Sabbath was interpreted as the element of union in the system of the *Sefirot*. Interpreting "And God blessed the seventh day, and hallowed [*va-yekaddesh*] it" (Gen. 2:3), these kabbalists linked *va-yekaddesh* with *kiddushin* ("betrothal") since the "*atarah* [*Malkhut*] is betrothed to *Tiferet*" (*Ma'arekhet ha-Elohut* (Mantua, 1558), 185a). In the same way they interpreted the Sabbath eve prayer: "You hallowed [*kiddashta*] the seventh day" as meaning "you betrothed the seventh day, which is the basis to the *atarah*" (*ibid.*).

Inverting the story in *Genesis Rabbah* 11:8, in which the Sabbath complains to God: "You gave a mate to everyone, while I have none," and was given **Keneset Yisrael* as her mate, the kabbalists regarded *Keneset Yisrael* as the symbol of the *Sefirah Malkhut*, as the feminine mate of the Sabbath, which is the masculine principle in divinity (*Yesod* or *Tiferet*). Since according to the kabbalists the souls are the outcome of the union in the system of *Sefirot*, the idea of the holy union which takes place on the Sabbath is linked to the Sages' belief that on Sabbath additional souls are given. In the Sefer *ha-Bahir this word is expounded in connection with the *Sefirah Yesod*, which "maintains all the souls" and from which the souls fly. Many sayings of the Sages and the different customs they initiated are given a mystical meaning in Kabbalah. The concept of "family peace" (*shelom bayit*), which must be kept especially on the Sabbath, is interpreted in Kabbalah as "peace, which is the *Sefirah Yesod*, is at home [*bayit*] in the *Sefirah Malkhut*" (*ibid.*). The Sabbath candles lit by the wife are symbols of the additional souls emanating from the *Sefirah Malkhut*, which is called *sukkat shalom* ("canopy of peace"). The Zohar treats at length of the Sabbath, the time when the entire arrangement of the order of the worlds is changed. Lights descend like dew from the upper to the lower *Sefirot*, and from there the divine abundance flows to all creatures. The additional souls that descend through the medium of the divine harmony illuminate the faces of the people who enjoy the holiness of the Sabbath. Many passages in the Zohar are poetical descriptions of the position of the worlds on the Sabbath. A typical passage is to be found in the second part of the Zohar, 135a–b. This passage is reproduced in Ḥasidic prayer books and is recited ecstatically on Sabbath eve.

The author of the Zohar and other kabbalists who followed him decided not to recite the part of the *Ma'ariv* prayer beginning "and He is compassionate" on Sabbath eve, for they feared that the mention of sins in the prayer might awaken the forces of the *sitra aḥra*, which, according to the Zohar, do not have any power on the Sabbath.

During the renaissance of Kabbalah in 16th-century Safed, new customs were established which spread to the Diaspora. Two of the main ones were the order of *Kabbalat Shabbat* ("the reception of the Sabbath") and matters concerning the Sabbath meal. It is said that Isaac *Luria and his disciples used to go out of Safed on Friday afternoon to meet the Sabbath, a practice which is described in the *Shulḥan Arukh shel ha-Ari*: "The Sabbath is received in the field: you must stand facing west, preferably in a high place, and there must be an open space behind you." While singing Psalm 92 during the reception of the Sabbath, the kabbalists used to close their eyes to identify themselves with the *Shekhinah, who lost her sight by weeping incessantly for the exile of Israel. There are signs that in Safed itself there was some opposition to this custom of going out into the fields, which is expressed in Moses *Cordovero's commentary on the prayers and in the writings of Isaiah *Horowitz (the Shelah). Some of the kabbalists used to go out into the garden or the courtyard, but eventually the custom of turning westward was adopted. The author of *Ḥemdat Yamim* notes with resentment that he is not able to go out into the fields as was formerly done and states that in his own day (c. 1700?) this was still the custom in Jerusalem. Moses Cordovero's circle adopted the custom of reciting during this service six psalms for the six days of the week, along with Psalm 92 for the Sabbath. This order of the *Kabbalat Shabbat* service, including the hymns *Lekhah Dodi*, written by Solomon Alkabeẓ, and *Bar Yoḥai*, written by Simeon *Labi, is to be found in the books of *Tikkunei Shabbat* which were printed at the beginning of the 17th century.

Concerning the Sabbath meal, these books state that it was the custom to recite *Shalom Aleikhem* and *Eshet Ḥayil* (Prov. 31:10–31), the latter being introduced since it is expounded by the Zohar and various kabbalists as referring to the *Shekhinah*. These books also contain hymns which Isaac Luria wrote for each of the Sabbath meals and the invocation of the divine powers in accordance with one of the ways instituted by the Zohar. Among some kabbalists great importance was attached to the fourth Sabbath meal which takes place at the end of the Sabbath. In the same way as the first three Sabbath meals were related to the Patriarchs, this fourth one was identified with David, the King Messiah. It therefore became particularly significant for the Shabbateans (see *Shabbetai Ẓevi), who often continued it until midnight. The third meal was of special importance for the Ḥasidim; it took place at a "favorable hour," which, according to the kabbalists, was the time of the *Minḥah* prayer on Sabbath.

[Efraim Gottlieb]

In Art

THE SABBATH LIGHT. The commandment of kindling the Sabbath lights has been fulfilled in a myriad of ways over the generations. Rabbinic texts from the Mishnah onwards are concerned with the types of fuel used to light and the material of the wicks, but not with the type of implements that contain the sources of light. Both local custom and the need to provide light throughout the day no doubt influenced the design of lamps for the Sabbath. In the ancient period clay lamps with one or more spouts were used. Later versions were probably made of metal. Archaeological evidence from the Land of Israel after the destruction of the Second Temple shows that ceramic lamps in use by the Jews were decorated with Jewish symbols to distinguish them from the lamps used by the local non-Jewish populace.

European Sabbath Lamps. Hanging Sabbath lamps of the Middle Ages consist of nozzles arranged in a circle at the periphery of an open, flat saucer filled with oil, thus creating their characteristic star shape. These lamps, usually made out of bronze or silver, often were hung at the end of a ratcheted hook which enabled raising and lowering. Certain lamps had bowls underneath for the collection of oil drips, some connected the nozzles to this bowl with attached metal ducts, others had various tools attached to them for trimming and cleaning. More elaborate lamps, made by non-Jewish craftsman, are embellished with figurines, narrative reliefs or other decorations. The Italians deepened the central saucer into a bowl, provided a silver drip pan to catch the excess oil, and hung the lamp by chains which converged at the top in a finial. In central and eastern Europe the central bowl was kept small and the spouts enlarged, the result being a star-shaped lamp called the *Judenstern.* While the form of the lamp was influenced by local design, the term *Judenstern* has been found in a record book of a silversmith from the 16th century, showing the association of this item with Jewish practice. Depictions of such lamps appear in Jewish manuscripts from both Spain and Ashkenaz of the 14th and 15th centuries (for example, the *Sarajevo Haggadah* (Sarajevo, National Museum of Bosnia and Herzegovina, fol. 31v), the *Second Nuremburg Haggadah* (Jerusalem, Schocken Ms. 24087, fol. 4v), and the *Ashkenazi Haggadah* (London, British Library, Ms. 14762, fol. 6r)). The Italian rabbi, Leone *Modena (1571–1648), mentions in his *Historia de riti Hebraici* that women would light anywhere from four to six lights, congruent to the six pointed lamps depicted in manuscripts and printed books.

Candles were also used for lighting in the medieval period in Europe, as revealed by both halakhic texts and illuminated manuscripts. The candlesticks depicted in the Rothschild Miscellany (Jerusalem, Israel Museum Ms. 180/51), late 15th century Italy (fols. 55v, 156v), show striking similarity with candlesticks in use in private homes in Europe. Candles in Europe were often made from animal fat and thus not permissible for Jewish use. The 19th-century development of synthetic materials for candles led to their greater diffusion among the Jews. Concomitantly, advances in indoor illumination technology gave the lighting of the Sabbath candles a more symbolic and less practical function, also prompting the move away from oil lamps. In Poland, brass candlesticks with anywhere from three to seven candles, decorated with lions and eagles, often inscribed in Hebrew "to kindle the Sabbath lights," were common in Jewish homes, besides pairs of candlesticks.

North African and Oriental Jewish Communities. The use of oil as the main form of fuel among the North African and Oriental Jewish communities continued until the contemporary era. In Morocco, sheet brass rectangular vessels with wicks in the four corners were traditionally used for lighting. In Persia and Afghanistan, the silver vessel used for lighting resembled the shape of the ancient clay oil lamp, with a deep bowl for the oil and two wick-nozzles. Sometimes there were two separate bowls, one for each light. The base was often decorated with birds or floral motifs and engraved with the woman's name. In Yemen, a simple hanging round stone lamp with notches for multiple wicks was used.

KIDDUSH CUPS. There is speculation that the gold glasses found in the catacombs of Italy were originally used for the blessing on wine. Jewish illuminated *Haggadot* from the late Middle Ages show elaborate goblets, sometimes with lids, sometimes double goblets, such as those depicted in the *Ashkenazi Haggadah* (London, British Library, Ms. 14762, fol.2v) and the *Cincinnati Haggadah* (Cincinnati, Hebrew Union College, Ms. 444, fol. 2v). As with Sabbath candlesticks, these cups were often copies of local types, generally made by non-Jewish craftsmen, and often decorated with vegetal motifs or geometric designs. In certain Oriental Jewish communities, the tradition of the lidded kiddush cup continues to the present time, often decorated with a small bird on the lid.

ḤALLAH COVERS AND KNIVES. Other ritual objects for use on the Sabbath include a special cover for the **ḥallah* and a special knife for cutting the *ḥallah*. Leone Modena mentions a long cloth used to cover the *ḥallah*, as depicted in both the *Ashkenazi* (fol. 6r) and the *Cincinnati* Haggadot (fol. 2v). Extant examples of embroidered *ḥallah* covers from the 19th century from various European communities have survived, as well as such knives.

CONTEMPORARY RITUAL ART. Twentieth-century Jewish artists, such as Ludwig Wolpert and Moshe Zabari, applied their skills to making modern versions of all the Sabbath implements, and contemporary Judaica artists such as Zelig Segal continue this trend for a growing market. The blossoming of contemporary Jewish art makes the list of artists working in this field too numerous to mention.

THE SABBATH IN PAINTING. The earliest printed depiction of a Jewish woman lighting a six-pointed *Judenstern* appears in the *Sefer ha-Minhagim* of Venice from the year 1593. Christian works on the Jews, such as Johann Christoph Georg Bodenschatz' *Kirchliche Verfassung der heutigen Juden sonderlich derer in Deutschland* (Frankfurt and Leipzig: Johannes Friedrich Becker, 1748–49) also show women lighting Sabbath lamps. Sabbath candlesticks as an attribute of the Jewish women appear on Jewish carved gravestones from the 19th century. Moritz *Oppenheim in Germany in his *Bilder aus dem altjüdischen Familienleben* ("Scenes rom Traditional Jewish Family Life," 1866), shows a woman lighting a traditional oil lamp, and devotes several works in the series to the subject of the Sabbath. Jewish artists of the late 19th and early 20th centuries, such as Isidor *Kaufmann, show traditional Jewish women on Sabbath eve with two lit candlesticks on the table. The Scandinavian Jewish artist, Geskel Saloman, shows two women lighting from a four-branched Polish-style candlestick. The subject of the Sabbath appears in the works of Samuel Hirszenberg, Boris *Schatz, Hermann *Struck, Jacob *Steinhardt, Josef *Budko, and Max *Band, among others. The use of the candlesticks to symbolize Jewish tradition and the home can be found in the works of Marc *Chagall, and Naftali *Bezem, while Yossl *Bergner uses the spice box (see **Havdalah*). The subject of the Sabbath in the life of the pioneers was dealt with by Israel artists Yohanan Simon and Joseph Kossonogi.

[Susan Nashman Fraiman (2nd ed.)]

BIBLIOGRAPHY: E. Millgram, *Sabbath: The Day of Delight* (1944, incl. full bibl.); U. Cassuto, *From Adam to Noah* (1961), 165–9; de Vaux, Anc Isr, 475–83 (incl. bibl.); H.J. Kraus, *Worship in Israel* (1966), 78–88; see also Maim. Yad, Shabbat; Sh. Ar., OḤ, 242–344; J.Z. Lauterbach, *Rabbinic Essays* (1951), 437–70; H. Biberfeld, *Menuḥah Nekhonah* (1965³); A.J. Heschel, *The Sabbath* (1951); S. Goldman, *Guide to the Sabbath* (1961); Y.L. Baruch, *Sefer ha-Shabbat* (1956). ADD. BIBLIOGRAPHY: Y.L. Bialer, "Shabbat Implements in Art," in: *Mahanaim*, 85–86 (1964), 138–43 (Heb.); H. Friedberg, "The Contemporary Design of Ritual Art," in: *Mahanaim*, (new series) 11, part 2, (1995), 230–39 (Heb.); F. Landsberger, "The Origin of the Ritual Implements for the Sabbath," in: HUCA, 27 (1956; repr. in J. Gutmann (ed.), *Beauty in Holiness: Studies in Jewish Customs and Ceremonial Art* (1970), 167–203; V. Mann, "New Examples of Jewish Ceremonial Art from Medieval Ashkenaz," in: *Artibus et Historiae*, no. 17 (1988), 13–24; K. Schwartz, "Shabbat in Art," in: Ya'akov Nacht et al. (eds.), *Sefer HaShabbat* (1958), 551–64 (Heb.); I. Shachar, *Jewish Tradition in Art: The Feuchtwanger Collection of Judaica* (1981); V. Sussman, *Ornamented Jewish Oil Lamps from the Fall of the Second Temple Through the Revolt of Bar Kochba* (Heb., 1972); R. Wischnitzer-Bernstein, "The Sabbath in Art," in: A.E. Millgram, *Sabbath The Day of Delight* (1965), 319–33; B. Yaniv and Z. HaNegbi, Zohar, *Shabbat Shalom* (1998); E. Zoref, "Shabbat in Jewish Painting," in: *Mahanaim*, 85–86 (1964), 152–57 (Heb).

SABBATHS, SPECIAL, those Sabbaths on which special events are commemorated. They are distinguished from the regular Sabbaths through variations in the liturgy and special customs. Two such Sabbaths, which recur on several occasions throughout the year, are numbers 1 and 2 below.

1) Shabbat Mevorekhin

(Heb. שַׁבַּת מְבָרְכִין), the Sabbath that immediately precedes a new month. In the later Ashkenazi rite a special petition, composed by *Rav "to renew unto us this coming month for good and for blessing," etc. (Bet. 16b), is recited in the synagogue after the reading of the law. The older Ashkenazi rite, and that of Ḥabad, begins with "He who wrought miracles…." The name of the new month and the day on which Rosh Ḥodesh occurs are then announced. In many communities, where women did not usually attend Sabbath services, they went on *Shabbat Mevarekhin* because of the new month petition (see *New Moon, Announcement of).

2) Shabbat Rosh Ḥodesh

(Heb. שַׁבַּת רֹאשׁ חֹדֶשׁ), a Sabbath which coincides with Rosh Ḥodesh. The reading of the Torah for the New Moon is added, and a special *haftarah (Isa. 66:1–24) is read.

The other Sabbaths (listed here chronologically according to the Jewish calendar) are:

3) Shabbat Shuvah

(Heb. שַׁבַּת שׁוּבָה; "Sabbath of Repentance"), also called (erroneosly) *Shabbat Teshuvah* (תְּשׁוּבָה), the Sabbath which occurs during the *Ten Days of Penitence (between Rosh Ha-Shanah and the Day of Atonement). The name is derived from the initial word of the *haftarah* "Return [שׁוּבָה], O Israel, unto the Lord" (Hos. 14:2) read on that Sabbath. One main feature of *Shabbat Shuvah* is the sermons on repentance delivered by the congregational rabbis.

4) Shabbat Ḥol ha-Mo'ed

(Heb. שַׁבַּת חוֹל הַמּוֹעֵד), the Sabbath of the *Passover and *Sukkot intermediary days. The liturgy includes *piyyutim appropriate to the festivals and special Torah readings, instead of the regular weekly Torah portion. *Song of Songs during Passover and *Ecclesiastes during Sukkot are also recited.

5) Shabbat Ḥanukkah

(Heb. שַׁבַּת חֲנֻכָּה), the Sabbath (sometimes two) during *Ḥanukkah. It is marked by an added Torah reading for the festival and, if it coincides with Rosh Ḥodesh *Tevet, also for the New Moon (see above).

6) Shabbat Shirah

(Heb. שַׁבַּת שִׁירָה; "The Sabbath of the Song"), the Sabbath on which the Torah reading is Exodus 14–17. The name is derived from Exodus 15, which includes "The song of Moses and of the children of Israel" at the Red Sea. In some rituals special *piyyutim* are also recited. This Sabbath does not occur on a specific date but depends on when the Torah portion is read.

7) Shabbat Shekalim

(Heb. שַׁבַּת שְׁקָלִים), the first of four special Sabbaths, which are also called *Arba Parashiyyot* ("the four pericopes"), and which occur in spring. *Shabbat Shekalim* is observed on the Sabbath immediately preceding the month of *Adar (in a leap year, the second month of Adar). In addition to the weekly Torah portion, Exodus 30:11–16, whose theme is the duty of donating half a *shekel toward the upkeep of the Temple, is also read. It commemorates the custom according to which on the first of Adar special messengers were dispatched to all Jewish communities to collect these donations (Shek. 1:1). Special *piyyutim* are included in the ritual of the Sabbath.

8) Shabbat Zakhor
(Heb. שַׁבַּת זָכוֹר; "Sabbath of Remembrance"), the second of the four special Sabbaths. It is the Sabbath before Purim. The name derives from the additional Torah portion read from Deuteronomy 25:17–19 whose theme is the duty "to remember" what *Amalek did to Israel. The traditional belief is that *Haman the Agagite was a direct descendant of Agag, the king of the Amalekites (e.g., 1 Sam. 15:9ff.). In some rites special *piyyutim* are recited.

9) Shabbat Parah
(Heb. שַׁבַּת פָּרָה; "Sabbath of the Red Heifer"), the third of the four special Sabbaths. It is the Sabbath preceding *Shabbat ha-Ḥodesh*. An additional portion is read from the Torah (Num. 19:1–22) whose theme is the ritual purification with the ashes of the red heifer. The purification was compulsory in Temple times for all those who had been defiled by contact with a corpse. *Shabbat Parah* commemorates the custom of everyone who would participate in the Passover pilgrimage to Jerusalem having to cleanse himself in due time. Special *piyyutim* are also added to the liturgy in some rites.

10) Shabbat ha-Ḥodesh
(Heb. שַׁבַּת הַחֹדֶשׁ), the last of the four special Sabbaths. It precedes, or falls on the first day of, the month of *Nisan. On it, in addition to the weekly Torah portion, Exodus 12:1–20 is also read. It states that the month of Nisan "shall be the beginning of the months [of the Jewish year]" and includes many details on the ritual laws concerning the Passover sacrifice and the interdiction to eat leavened bread (**ḥamez̤*) on the festival. Special *piyyutim* are also recited in some communities.

11) *Shabbat ha-Gadol

12) Shabbat Ḥazon
(Heb. שַׁבַּת חֲזוֹן; "Sabbath of Vision"), the Sabbath that precedes the Ninth of *Av. The name is derived from the initial word of its *haftarah*. "The vision of Isaiah" (Isa. 1:1–27), in which the afflictions which God will visit on Israel in punishment of its sins are prophesied. The Yemenites call this Sabbath "*Shabbat Eikhah*," and read Isaiah 1:21ff. for the *haftarah* portion. *Shabbat Ḥazon* occurs during the period of mourning (see *Nine Days) for the destruction of the Temple, and the *haftarah* is therefore appropriate since its theme is destruction and possible redemption. The destruction is understood as a punishment for the sins of Israel, and repentance is a prerequisite for the restoration of the Temple. It was customary not to dress in festive garments during that period, including (in a few communities) the Sabbath.

13) Shabbat Nahamu
(Heb. שַׁבַּת נַחֲמוּ), the Sabbath immediately following the Ninth of Av. It is so called after the first word of the *haftarah* "Comfort ye [Naḥamu], Comfort ye My people" (Isa. 40:1).

On most of these special Sabbaths the memorial prayer for the deceased (see *Av ha-Raḥamim) as well as the prayer *Z̤idkatkha* in the *Minḥah service are omitted. In the Reform ritual some of these Sabbaths (e.g., *Zakhor, Parah*) are not observed. On the other hand, other special Sabbaths (e.g., "Brotherhood Sabbath," "Sisterhood Sabbath," "United Nations Sabbath") have been innovated.

BIBLIOGRAPHY: Elbogen, Gottesdienst, 156, 159, 163; E. Levi, *Yesodot ha-Tefillah* (1952^2), 308, 244.

SABBATICAL YEAR AND JUBILEE (Heb. שְׁמִטָּה, *shemittah*; יוֹבֵל, *yovel*). According to the Bible, during the seventh year all land had to be fallow and debts were to be remitted (Ex. 23:10–11; Lev. 25:1–7, 18–22; Deut. 15:1–11). The close of seven sabbatical cycles instituted the Jubilee (Lev. 27:16–25; Num. 36:4; whether the Jubilee Year was the 49th or the 50th see below).

A brief statement in the Book of Nehemiah (10:32) records the post-Exilic community's firm agreement to suspend all agricultural work during the seventh year and to forgo all debts as commanded in the "Law of God." The reference is to these three passages in the Torah, each of which dwells on a different aspect of the seventh-year release. The earliest, found in the Book of the Covenant (Ex. 23:10–11), calls on the Israelites to let the land lie fallow and the vineyards and olive groves untouched that the poor people may eat of them, as well as the wild beasts. The second passage (Lev. 25:1–7, 18–22) refers to the fallow year as a "Sabbath of the Lord" and a year of complete rest for the land, promising the divine blessing on the crop of the sixth year to those who suspend their work on the seventh (cf. the double portion of manna on the sixth day; Ex. 16:22ff.). The Deuteronomist (Deut. 15:1–11) commands the Israelites to observe every seventh year as a "year of release," when debts contracted by fellow countrymen are to be remitted. At the same time, they are cautioned not to let the recurrence of the seventh-year release harden their hearts against the distressed who seek loans in the hour of their need. While Deuteronomy does not mention the fallow, the passage is clearly connected with that of Exodus by the use of the common verb *šmṭ* (שמט). D. Hoffmann argued that the remission of debts is entailed by the fallow – that it is precisely because the debtor cannot work his fields during the seventh year that he is unable to make his payments, and the creditor is enjoined not to dun him for them. The same reasoning, according to Hoffmann, explains why the debts of aliens are not remitted – i.e., the fact that their income is not affected by the Sabbatical Year.

Ever since J. Wellhausen, a number of scholars have seen a connection between the surrender of the produce of the seventh year to the poor (Ex. 23:11) and the liberation of the Hebrew slave following the sixth year of his purchase (Ex. 21:2–6; cf. Deut. 15:12–18). Accordingly, they maintain that the Book of the Covenant did not intend the seventh-year fallow to be observed throughout the land on a fixed date any more than the manumission of all of the Hebrew slaves. Each field, vineyard, and olive grove, then, had its own fallow cycle, just as each slave had his own release date. Otherwise, the practice could not possibly have been observed, for there would not have been enough food for all of the inhabitants of the land. Hence, the Deuteronomist, who had to operate within the framework of a fixed, universal, seventh-year release (cf. Deut. 15:9), disregarded the agricultural fallow and called for the remission of debts instead, as well as the release of debtors who had been enslaved (15:12–18). This is why, according to A. Menes, the Deuteronomist also commanded that the Torah be read aloud every year of remission in the hearing of all Israel (31:10ff.). Such an assembly could take place then, after all the Israelite debtors had been set free and were able to appear as equals among their people. The Sabbatical Year, a fixed, universal, seventh-year fallow, as opposed to the year of remission, then, was a later construction of the priestly writers which was never observed in the pre-Exilic period (cf. Lev. 26:34–35, 43; II Chron. 36:21), and is attested for the first time during the Second Temple period, and then only in certain parts of the land (cf. I Macc. 6:49, 53).

Plausible as it has seemed to many scholars, the theory is not supported by the evidence. In the first place, there is no necessary connection between the manumission of the Hebrew slave and the fallow year other than the fact that both involve a seven-year period. Secondly, Wellhausen failed to see that not only the Priestly Code but also the Covenant Code connect the seventh-year fallow with the weekly Sabbath (cf. Ex. 23:12 with 23:10–11). As M. Noth correctly observes, both commandments require that the animals benefit in some way from their observance – a concern that derives not merely from compassion for dumb beasts but from the recognition that they are part of the nature which man must cease to dominate on the Sabbath. Finally, since Wellhausen claims that the demands of the Deuteronomist were utopian in character, the argument that a universally fixed date for the fallow year is impossible because of its impracticality is inapplicable. It is true that, outside the legislative texts of the Bible, there is no reference to the Sabbatical Year in the pre-Exilic sources. But an *argumentum ex silentio* is of dubious value, especially when dealing with ancient historical materials.

A similar problem exists with regard to the Jubilee Year, which is described in detail in Leviticus 25:8–17, 23–55. Among its provisions are: the dating of the recurrent Jubilee Year, the proclamation of its start with the sounding of the *shofar* on the Day of Atonement, the return of all Israelites to their ancestral lands and families, the observance of the fallow, the fixing of prices for the sale of land (except for houses in cities) in relation to the occurrence of the Jubilee, the redemption of the land of next of kin, special land regulations for levites, and the freeing of defaulting debtors and all Israelite slaves. The text justifies these prescriptions in terms of two basic principles: God's ownership of the land (25:23) and His undisputed possession of all Israelites as His slaves (25:55).

Two other passages in the Priestly Code refer to the Jubilee Year (Lev. 27:16–25; Num. 36:4), as does possibly Ezekiel (46:16ff.), but it is not mentioned in any historical texts, not even in post-Exilic ones. Evidently, it was not observed in Second Temple times, as is attested by the conditions in the time of Nehemiah (cf. 5:1–13, where there is no mention of the institution), the obscure description of it in Josephus (Ant. 3:280ff.), and the explicit comment of one of the *tannaim* (Sifra 8:2).

Though the Priestly Code clearly distinguishes between the Jubilee and the Sabbatical Years, many scholars consider the former a post-Exilic theoretical reworking of the latter. Thus, they suggest that the manumission of slaves on the Jubilee replaces the one on the Sabbatical Year, and that the notion of the divine ownership of the land is an extension of the claim that all Israelites belong to God. They concede that the Jubilee law does not require the remission of debts. Still, Leviticus 25:24 may be interpreted, they maintain, as a form of debt release, with the alienated property comparable to a foreclosed mortgage. The Jubilee, then, is "an artificial institution superimposed upon the years of fallow regarded as harvest Sabbaths after the analogy of Pentecost" (Wellhausen). In this way, one can explain the impossible demand for a two-year fallow created by the Jubilee following the Sabbatical Year, as well as the directions for the manumission of slaves, which were inconsistent with the earlier ones of the Covenant Code.

That the matter is not so simple is evidenced by the appearance of ancient terms in Leviticus 25 as well as pre-Israelite usages (see next section).

The etymology of *yovel* (יוֹבֵל) is not clear, with some suggesting that it is derived from the root (יבל) meaning "to bear along [in procession]," hence *yevul* (יבול) signifying "produce" or "that which is borne," and *yuval* (יוּבַל), "transfer" (of properties; cf. Ibn Ezra on Lev. 25:10). More likely, the basic meaning of *yovel* is "ram's horn" (cf. Ex. 19:13; Josh. 6:5; cf. also Phoenician *ybl*, "ram," and the comment of R. Akiva quoted by Bertinoro on RH 3:2). The Jubilee, then, is "the year that is inaugurated by the blowing of the ram's horn" (W.R. Smith). If this is so, then serious consideration must be given to R. North's suggestion that this is an ancient Near Eastern legal requirement for a public proclamation (*Šûdûtu*) "as a sort of registration-formality prerequisite to the exchange of property administration."

Closer inspection of the biblical text, too, proves the arguments of the Wellhausen school to be far from convincing. The assumption that Hebrew slaves were to be released in the Sabbatical Year is, as seen, unwarranted. The Jubilee laws do not refer to mortgaged properties but to those that have actually been sold. And, finally, it is highly doubtful that the belief in the divine ownership of the land arose at a late period in Israel's history. On the contrary, the evidence seems to point in the opposite direction, i.e., both the Sabbatical and Jubilee Years are rooted in ancient traditions, although some of the prescriptions connected with them, such as the restrictions on the redemption of houses in a city (Lev. 25:29ff.) and the remission of debts (Deut. 15:1ff.), were added later. Moreover, the elements basic to both institutions go back to early Israelite, and even pre-Israelite, times. They are the seven- and 50-year cycles, the fallow, the inalienability of ancestral lands (see below), and the maintenance of the integrity of the clan.

As far as the seven-year cycle is concerned, there is reference to it in the Joseph stories (Gen. 41:25ff.) and in the earlier Near Eastern texts. Thus, the land is blighted for a seven-year period because of the death of Aqhat (Pritchard, Texts 153), just as it flourishes for seven years after Baal defeats Mot (*Poems about Baal and Anath*, 5; Pritchard, Texts, 141). Similarly, Anu warns Ishtar that a seven-year drought would follow the slaying of Gilgamesh (*Gilgamesh Epic*, 6, lines 101–106; Pritchard, Texts, 84–85). As for the existence of a 50-year cycle, this is not as clearly attested, though J. Lewy claims to have discovered a primitive agricultural "pentecontad" calendar among the Amorites of Assyria, Babylonia, Syria, and Palestine near the end of the third millennium B.C.E. His interpretation of the relevant texts is, however, open to question, and note should be taken of a recent suggestion that the Jubilee occurred not in the 50th but in the 49th year, coinciding with the seventh Sabbatical Year (cf. Lev. 25:8–9 and M. Noth on 25:10).

The fallow, as described in the Torah, has nothing to do with crop rotation and does not seem to have had any agricultural value, such as that of replenishing the soil; no other crop was planted that year nor were the fields worked, as this was strictly forbidden during the Sabbatical Year. C.H. Gordon suggests that it was originally connected with Canaanite fertility rites. However, even if this is not so, Noth is undoubtedly correct in considering it an example of *restitutio in integrum*, when the land was permitted to return to its undisturbed rest. G. Dalman makes a similar observation with regard to the release of alienated lands during the Jubilee, seeing in it a recognition by the Israelites that they had no right permanently to set aside the lands allotted by God to the tribes and clans at the time of the conquest of Canaan. The release of Israelite slaves, then, and their return to their ancestral lands may also be considered a *restitutio in integrum*, the restoration of the structure of Israelite society as it had been divinely ordained in ancient days.

Accordingly, A. Jirku concludes that the concept of both the Sabbatical and the Jubilee Years originated under simple economic and social conditions, possibly when agriculture was not yet the major source of the food supply of the Israelites. This relates to a time not long after the conquest, which also provides a proper setting for the idea of the Jubilee. At this early date, tribal solidarity was still strong, the consciousness of the common possession of the ground and soil fresh in their minds, and the memory of the patriarchal relationships in the desert vivid.

These arguments, however, are not conclusive, since the ideals of the desert period lived on among the people for many centuries, especially outside the large centers. At any rate, neither the Sabbatical nor the Jubilee Year appears in the Bible as a nascent institution. While they drew on earlier Semitic practice for some of their ideas, in their present form they represent a unique Israelite attempt to combat the social evils that had infected Israelite society and to return to the idyllic period of the desert union when social equality and fraternal concern had prevailed.

[David L. Lieber]

Ancient Near Eastern Legal Background

The background of the legal conceptions embodied in the Sabbatical and Jubilee Years is illuminated by ancient Near Eastern evidence of (a) resistance in principle to the alienation of patrimonial lands; and (b) the institution of periodic royal releases from certain kinds of debt and obligation, in connection with which cognates to terms found in Leviticus 25 appear.

(a) Hurrian custom attested in the *Nuzi tablets banned the sale of patrimonial land. The prohibition seems to have been grounded on a feudal system, in which all land belonged to the king, and was held only as a grant or fief by his subjects. They had possession, but not ownership, of the property entrusted to them. In return, each subject owed some service to the king, but he had no right to dispose of or transfer his property to any person other than a male relative of his immediate family (cf. Laws of Hammurapi 36–39; Pritchard, Texts, 167–8). In order to transfer real estate out of the family, the fiction of adoption was resorted to, by which the seller "adopted" the buyer as his "son," in consideration of the latter's "gift" – the purchase price (Steele, in bibl., 14–15). The conception of possession without ownership, with its concomitant ban on alienation of property, evokes the biblical notion that the land of Israel is God's, and that Israel are merely His tenants ("you are but strangers resident with Me," Lev. 25:23). The time of the Nuzi tablets (mid-second millennium), and the chief region of Hurrian influence (the Khabur River Valley) coincide with the period, and pre-Canaan location, of Israel's ancestors. This is but one of several indications that Hurrian culture left a mark on Israelite ideas and institutions (see bibl.).

Old Babylonian legal writings contain a law (Eshnunna 39; Pritchard, Texts, 163) and a number of contracts showing the right of an owner of real property to redeem it after he had been forced by financial need to sell it. One of the contracts suggests that the right may have existed even when the property was not up for sale (as in Lev. 25:25–32).

(b) In their first full regnal year, Old Babylonian kings were accustomed to issue an edict of "justice" (*mīšarum*) throughout their realm, referred to in date formulas and inscriptions as "establishing the freedom" (*andurarum*, cognate with Heb. *deror* (Lev. 25:10, etc.)) of their subjects. The one extant exemplar – attributed to Ammi-ṣaduqa (second half of the 17th century B.C.E.) – consists mainly of remissions (for a limited period) of specific kinds of debts and obligations, including the release of persons held in debt-bondage. Such edicts were demonstrably enforced, and were issued at intervals of seven or more years – the periodicity being as yet unknown (Finkelstein). Property (real and human) for which the full price had been paid, however, was not subject to the *andurarum*-release (Levy); such property is described in a Ras Shamra (Ugarit) document as *ṣamit ana... ana dariti*, "finally transferred [lit. yoked] to... forever" – compare Leviticus 25:30, *liẓmitut le-X le-dorotaw*. Y. Muffs has suggested that the theory of Leviticus 25 is that the full price of land was never paid: only crop years are bought (25:15–16), hence land could never be finally transferred but was always subject to the release. Similarly, in the case of self-sale of persons, no sale could be final since title to every Israelite is vested solely in God (25:42).

The Sabbatical and Jubilee Years thus adapt, elaborate, and synthesize pre-Israelite elements. In the new creation, the Divine King, having liberated His people and made them free men in His land, provides for the preservation of their liberty through periodic corrections of the economic imbalances that, sundering men from the land, would turn them into slaves again. His authority flows from His ownership of both people and land, and is, in turn, brought to mind through the execution of His decrees.

[Moshe Greenberg]

Post-Biblical

Whereas the Sabbatical Year was in force during the Second Temple period (and is applicable, in theory, to the present day), the Jubilee was no longer observed. The two subjects are therefore treated separately.

Jubilee in the Second Temple Period

HALAKHAH AND DEVELOPMENT. The relevant laws in the literature of the Second Temple period are primarily the interpretation of the biblical precepts of the Sabbatical Year and the Jubilee, and of the law of emancipation of the Hebrew slave whose ear was pierced, since *le-olam* ("forever"; Ex. 21:6) was interpreted to mean "until the Jubilee" (Mekh., Nezikin 2). The laws of the Jubilee were not in practice in the time of the Second Temple (see below), but since the laws of the Jubilee and the calculation of the years of the *shemittah* are linked with the laws of the Sabbatical Year, which were in force, one can find in these *halakhot* something of the life and customs of that period. According to the *halakhah*, all rules applicable to the Sabbatical Year, with regard to the prohibition of land cultivation, the renunciation of ownership of produce, and the obligation of the householder to remove all produce gathered for his needs when that species is not found in the field, apply also to the Jubilee: "What applies to the Sabbatical Year applies equally to the Jubilee" (Sifra, Be-Har 3:2). From the verse, "For it is a Jubilee, it shall be holy to you" (Lev. 25:12), the tannaim derived that the sanctity of the produce of the Sabbatical Year was such that, if the householder sold it and bought meat with the proceeds, the stringencies of the Sabbatical Year applied both to the produce itself and to the meat, i.e., they deduced the laws of the Sabbatical Year from verses dealing with the Jubilee and vice versa. Thus, in the verse applying to the Jubilee, "Ye shall eat the increase cleared out of the field" (*ibid.*), they taught, "As long as you eat from the field you may eat from your house. If what is in the field has been consumed, then you must clear out what is in the house" (Sifra, Be-Har 3:4), applying it to the Sabbatical Year. The *halakhah* also combined the Jubilee with the Sabbatical Year with regard to their applicability during the Second Temple period; the opinion was even expressed that, since the Jubilee does not apply "at the present day," so also the observance of the Sabbatical Year is not a biblical precept, but merely rabbinic (TJ, Shev. 10:3, 39c). This conception probably served Judah II (Nesiah) as a theoretical basis for many of the relaxations in the law which he inaugurated in respect of the Sabbatical Year (TJ, Shev. 6:4; Ḥul. 6b and parallel texts).

Only the law on the remission of debts which comes into force at the end of the Sabbatical Year (Sif. Deut. 111) does not apply to the Jubilee; against this, however, there are, according to the *halakhah*, two precepts of the Jubilee which do not apply to the Sabbatical Year – that land sold returns to its owners during the Jubilee Years (Lev. 25:23, 24) and that slaves go free (Sifra, Be-Har 3:6). The verse, "And in the seventh he shall go out free for nothing" (Ex. 21:2), was interpreted as referring not to the seventh year, which was the Sabbatical Year, but to the seventh year from the date on which he was sold (TJ, Kid. 1:2, 59a); if the Jubilee came in the middle of his six-year term, however, the slave went free then (Kid. 1:2). This law was also applied to the Hebrew bondsmaid, although it is not explicitly mentioned in the Torah, and was apparently an innovation of the *tannaim*. A Hebrew slave sold to a gentile did not go free in the seventh year but only in the Jubilee (Sifra, Be-Har 8:4). In addition, the Hebrew slave who refused to go free in his seventh year went free on the Jubilee (Mekh., Nezikin 2; cf. Jos., Ant. 4:273).

THE CALCULATION OF THE JUBILEE. Both in the tannaitic literature and in the Apocrypha two different systems of calculation for the Jubilee and the Sabbatical Year are found. A *baraita* declares that the Jubilee year is the 50th year, after the completion of the seven sabbatical cycles, the following year being the first of the ensuing *shemittah* (Ned. 61a; TJ, Kid. 1:2, 59a). This cyclical system also occurs in the *Seder Olam in respect of the First Temple period. Judah, however, holds that "the Jubilee year enters into the calculation of the heptad," i.e., the Jubilee Year is the 50th year after the previous Jubilee and thus also the first of the ensuing *shemittah* and Jubilee (Ned. 61a). According to Judah's view there was a widespread tannaitic tradition that, with the exile of the tribes of Reuben, Gad, and the half-tribe of Manasseh, the laws of the Jubilee fell into desuetude. According to the *geonim*, not only were the laws of the Jubilee not in force from the time of the exile of these tribes (see later), but after the destruction of the First Temple the Jubilee Years were not even calculated; only those of the *shemittot* (A. Harkavy, *Teshuvot ha-Ge'onim*, in: *Zikkaron la-Rishonim ve-la-Aḥaronim*, 14 (1887) 20 no. 45; Responsa of Maimonides, ed. J. Blau, 2 (1960), 666 no. 389). Whether in accordance with the view of Judah or with the tradition that the Jubilee was not calculated in the period of the Second Temple, the fact is that only Sabbatical Years were counted from the Second Temple period onward. Whether to chronicle the years or to determine the Sabbatical Year, the author of the Book of Jubilees, which gives the chronology from the creation by Jubilees, counts a Jubilee period as 49 years only; the 127 years of Sarah's life are specifically referred to as "two Jubilees, four heptads, and one year" (19:7), and this applies throughout the book. According to the Book of Maccabees, Simeon the Hasmonean was murdered in the month of Shevat, in the year 177 of the Seleucid era, corresponding to 135 B.C.E. John Hyrcanus sought to avenge his father's murder and besieged the fortress of Dagon in which Ptolemy, the murderer, had shut himself. The siege dragged on, but as a result of famine due to the fact that it was a Sabbatical Year, he was compelled to raise the siege (I Macc. 16: 14ff; Jos., Ant. 13:228–35). The Sabbatical Year nearest to that date was in the year 3724 of the creation, i.e., 37 B.C.E., since Josephus tells that in Herod's conquest of Jerusalem in the summer of that year, the besieged in the city suffered from a food shortage because of the Sabbatical Year (Jos., Ant. 14:475). That the 98 years between those two dates are equivalent to 14 *shemittot* without an intervening Jubilee Year is confirmed from other references. The Samaritans also reckoned only according to *shemittot*, and even where they divided periods into Jubilees, it was a Jubilee of 49 years (see A. Neubauer, *Chronique Samaritaine* (1873), 3, 8ff.).

According to the Talmud, the Jubilee Year did not come into effect automatically, with the advent of the 50th year, but the *bet din* had to see to its implementation and officially proclaim it by sounding the *shofar* (cf. Lev. 25:9). It was the duty of the *bet din* to count the years of the *shemittah* as one counts the days of the *Omer, but whereas the latter was the duty of every individual Jew, the Jubilee Years were counted only by the *bet din* (Sifra, Be-Har 2, 106c). According to the majority of the sages, if land was not returned to its owner, slaves not freed, and the *shofar* not sounded, the sanctity of the Jubilee Year did not obtain. Judah, however, made the sanctity of the Jubilee dependent solely on the emancipation of the slaves, while Yose made it dependent only on the sounding of the *shofar* (TJ, RH 3:5, 58d; RH 9b; Sifra, Be-Har 2, 107a). The *shofar* had to be sounded by every individual, even on the Sabbath (Sifra, Be-Har 106d). Although, according to the Bible (Lev. 25:9), the release of slaves and the return of land took effect on the Day of Atonement, the Jubilee was regarded as starting on Rosh Ha-Shanah (Sifra, *ibid.*). At the beginning of the Jubilee Year, in addition to the sounding of the *shofar*, a special prayer was recited which included **Malkhuyyot*, **Zikhronot*, and **Shofarot*, as on Rosh Ha-Shanah (RH 29a).

THE JUBILEE IN HISTORY. That the Jubilee did not apply during the period of the Second Temple was deduced from the verse "unto all the inhabitants thereof" (Lev. 25:10), with the corollary that "from the time that the tribes of Reuben and Gad and the half-tribe of Manasseh were exiled the Jubilees were discontinued" (Sifra, Be-Har 2:3). The Talmuds, also, in discussing the various problems relating to the observance of the precepts of the Sabbatical Year in the Second Temple period (such as the laws of walled cities and of the Hebrew slave), assume it as a fact that the Jubilee did not apply at that time (TJ, Git. 4:3, 45d; Kid. 69a). It is difficult to determine when this conception had its origin, since a number of precepts which according to tradition depend on the observance of the Jubilee (such as the laws appertaining to the Sabbatical Year, the canceling of debts (TJ, Git. 4:3, 45d), or walled cities), continued to apply throughout the Second Temple period (Ar. 29a). According to this view, all the precepts bound up with the Sabbatical Year and the Jubilee are regarded as a whole, with the result that, where the precepts of the Jubilee cannot be observed, the other precepts do not apply; nevertheless, it is certain that the precepts of the Sabbatical Year, such as the remission of debts at the close of the Sabbatical Year and the redemption of houses, were practiced, as is shown by numerous references in both tannaitic and other sources. However, while there is evidence of the observance of the other precepts and of various regulations made to modify their severity, there is no evidence throughout the whole Temple period of the actual observance of the Jubilee, reflecting the difficulties involved in observing it. The *halakhah* provides, for instance, that only the Sabbatical Year is not to be made a leap year, etc.

From Alexander's conquest and during the period of Roman rule, there is evidence that foreign rulers took into account the problem of tax payments on agricultural produce in the Sabbatical Year, when the Jews did not cultivate their fields. Either they freed them from taxes, as did Alexander the Great and Julius Caesar, or insisted on payment, as did Hadrian after the Bar Kokhba war. There is, however, no echo of the complex problems which would have been raised by the Jubilee in this regard either in the Talmud or in other contemporary documents. Nevertheless, although the Jubilee was not in force for as long as the *shemittah*, the problems which it raised were of greater gravity than those of the Sabbatical Year. The commandment of the Jubilee brought in its train complicated questions concerning the commercial laws of the sale and hiring of land; yet there is hardly an echo of the existence of the Jubilee either in the *halakhah* which deals with it or in any reference in the various passages dealing with practical life, whether in the talmudic literature or in documents revealed by archaeology. Despite this fact the ideas contained in the precepts of the Jubilee were of considerable influence, both on the *halakhah* and on events of the Second Temple period.

In the *halakhah* and in various traditions reflecting ancient custom, there is evidence of the concern over keeping the patrimonial estate in the family, the farmer's concern to safeguard the ownership of his plot of land, and the obligation to redeem land that had been sold. Although the *halakhah* did not forbid the absolute sale of land, it viewed it unfavorably: "One is not permitted to sell his property… unless he become impoverished. If he does sell it, however, the sale is valid" (Tosef., Ar. 5:6). A public ceremony even took place in order to shame a person who sold his patrimony, and he was praised when he redeemed it: "When a man sold his field, his relatives would take jugs filled with roasted grains and nuts and smash them in front of the children, who would gather them and say, 'So and so has cut himself off from his possession.' And when the field returned to him they should do the same and say, 'So and so has returned to his possession'" (TJ, Ket. 2:10, 26d; see *Keẓaẓah). Similarly the *halakhah* laid down that when a man inherited land from his wife, her relatives paid him for it in order to get it back from him (Tosef., Bek. 6:19). In contrast to the situation prevalent in the Orient, where extensive land belonged to the temples, the Jewish Temple possessed no landed property of its own. Even if one consecrated his land, it would be sold, and it was the duty of the former owner to be first in its redemption (Ar. 8:1). These *halakhot* and practices exercised a decisive influence, which accounts for the fact that in the last generations of the Temple period and for a considerable period afterward, most of the land in the country was not in the hands of large landowners but remained in the possession of smallholders.

THE JUBILEE IN THE AGGADAH. Mention has already been made of the link which the sages saw between the precepts of the Jubilee and those of the Sabbatical Year. It is certain that in every period they saw a link between the laws of the emancipation of slaves, remission of debts, and prohibition of land cultivation in the Sabbatical Year, which are the capstone of these laws, and the precepts of the Jubilee, since the Jubilee involves them all. The sages emphasized the practical and social connections between the various precepts of the Jubilee, as well as the religious and metaphysical connection between them. They reckoned the historical order and the end of time by Sabbatical Years and Jubilees: "Israel counted 17 Jubilees from the time they entered the land to the time they left it" (Ar. 12b). Elijah told Judah, the brother of Sala Ḥasida, "The world will endure not less than 85 Jubilees, and on the last Jubilee the Son of David will come" (Sanh. 97b). The precept of the Jubilee is often regarded as one of the basic precepts of the Torah. "And its seven lamps thereon" (Zech. 4:2) is interpreted as referring to the seven precepts – "offerings, tithes, *shemittot*, Jubilees, circumcision, honor of father and mother, and study of the Torah, which excels them all" (PR 8:4). The continued dwelling in the land was dependent upon the observance of the *shemittah* and the Jubilee (Shab. 33a).

[Shmuel Safrai]

Sabbatical Year in Post-Biblical Times

According to the exposition of the Talmud, the precept of the Sabbatical Year includes three positive commandments and six prohibitions (see *Commandments, The 613). The three positive commands are that in "the seventh year thou shalt let it rest and lie fallow" (Ex. 23:11); "the seventh year shall be a Sabbath of solemn rest for the land" (Lev. 25:4); and "At the end of every seven years thou shalt make a release. And this is the manner of the release: every creditor shall release that which he hath lent unto his neighbor" (Deut. 15:1–2). The six negative precepts are "[1] Thou shalt neither sow thy field [2] nor prune thy vineyard. [3] That which groweth of itself of thy harvest thou shalt not reap, [4] and the grapes of thy undressed vine thou shalt not gather" (Lev. 25:4–5). [5] "He shall not exact it [the loan] of his neighbor" (Deut. 15:2). [6] "Beware that there be not a base thought in thy heart, saying: 'The seventh year, the year of release, is at hand'; and thine eye be evil against thy needy brother, and thou give him nought" (Deut. 15:9).

The laws of the sabbatical remittance of debts are applicable both in Ereẓ Israel and in the Diaspora. However, the obligation to let the land lie fallow is limited to the boundaries of Ereẓ Israel in accordance with the verse that these laws begin only "When ye come into the land which I give you" (Lev. 25:2). Whether the sabbatical laws are still biblically relevant after the destruction of the First Temple, when the Jubilee Year is no longer operative, is disputed in the Talmud. According to Judah II, it is only observed today because of rabbinic enactment to "perpetuate the memory of the Sabbatical Year." However, the rabbis held the operation of the Sabbatical Year nowadays still to be biblical (MK 2b; Git. 36a–b). Later commentaries and codes remained divided on this issue; Maimonides seemingly ruled in accordance with the viewpoint of Judah (Maim. Yad, Shemittah 9:2, 3 and Kesef Mishneh ad loc.; cf. Kesef Mishneh to Shemittah 4:29).

At the time of the Temple, it was also biblically forbidden to work the land during the 30 days prior to the start of the Sabbatical Year. The rabbis extended this pre-sabbatical prohibition until the preceding Shavuot for orchards, and Passover for grain fields. After the destruction of the Temple these additional restrictions were no longer in force, and today it is permissible to work the land until Rosh Ha-Shanah of the Sabbatical Year (MK 3b–4a).

Produce which grows of itself during the Sabbatical Year is considered holy and its usage is restricted. It is forbidden to harvest this growth solely for commercial purposes (Shev. 7:3) or to remove it from Ereẓ Israel (Shev. 6:5). It may only be eaten or utilized in its usual fashion, so that items such as wine and vinegar may only be used for nourishment and not for anointing purposes (Shev. 8:2). The sabbatical produce may only be eaten as long as similar produce is still available in the field for the consumption of animals (Shev. 9:4). Once such produce has been consumed, all remaining sabbatical products of the same species must also be destroyed (Shev. 9:8).

The sabbatical money release was intended to free the poor from their debts and to enable them to attempt again to achieve financial stability. However, when *Hillel later saw that people refrained from lending money before the Sabbatical Year, he instituted the *prosbul (Git. 36a). The following are excluded from cancellation by the Sabbatical Year: wages, merchandise on credit, loans on pledges, a note guaranteed by mortgage, a note turned over to the *bet din* for collection, and the debtor's waiving the cancelation of his debt (Git. 36a–b, 37a–b).

Observance

POST-BIBLICAL PERIOD. Among the commitments which the Jews took upon themselves at the famous assembly described in Nehemiah was a promise to observe the Sabbatical Year (Neh. 10:32). There is evidence that during the whole of the Second Temple period they rigidly adhered to this commitment. When *Alexander the Great reached Jerusalem during his march through Ereẓ Israel, he acceded to the high priest's request that the Jews be exempted from paying tribute during the Sabbatical Year, when they did not work their land (Jos., Ant. 11:338). During the Hasmonean War, the fall of Beth Zur to the forces under Lysias and Eupator was attributed to a famine within the city since it was a Sabbatical Year (I Macc. 6:49, 53–54). Julius Caesar later reaffirmed this privilege of tax exemption during the Sabbatical Year since "they neither take fruit from the trees nor do they sow" (Jos., Ant. 14:202).

Following the destruction of the Temple (70 C.E.), the observance of the sabbatical prohibitions imposed ever-increasing economic hardships upon the agrarian society of ancient Israel. It became a constant source of challenge to the religious tenacity of the farmers. The rabbis constantly exhorted the masses to continue to observe properly the sabbatical restrictions, declaring that exile (Shab. 33a), poverty (Suk. 40b), and pestilence (Avot 5:9) result from the transgression of these laws. Immediately following the destruction, most of the land was left in Jewish hands and the Sabbatical Year was observed. Permissible organized distribution of sabbatical produce was arranged by the rabbis in order to ease the burden of the farmers, although there was some opposition to this procedure (Shev. 4:2; and see S. Safrai in bibl., 312–18). However, after the unsuccessful *Bar Kokhba Revolt (132–135 C.E.), the Roman government abrogated its previous tax exemption (Safrai, 320f.). Many Jews now compromised their observances due to the new economic pressures engendered by the demand for taxes during this year (Mekh., Shabbata 1). Some gathered sabbatical crops in order to pay these taxes, while others even traded in the produce (Sanh. 3:3, 26a). An entire city was described in which all the residents transgressed the sabbatical laws (Tosef., Dem. 3:17). An instance was even recorded where a proselyte retorted to the reproaches of a native Jew by exclaiming, "I will merit divine reward since I have not eaten the fruits of the Sabbatical Year like you" (Bek. 30a; Git. 54a). Nevertheless, even during this period, there were individuals who resolutely observed the sabbatical restrictions. R. Eleazar b. Zadok remarked about such a person, "I have never seen a man walking in the paths of righteousness as this man" (Suk. 44b).

As a consequence of the hardships now encountered in sabbatical observances, the rabbis relaxed many of the prohibitions. Their actions were probably also prompted by the viewpoint of *Judah II that the institution of the Sabbatical Year was only rabbinic during the Second Temple period when the Jubilee was not operative because the land was not fully occupied by Israel (Git. 36a–b; Rashi and Tos. ad loc.; S.J. Zevin, in bibl., 105–12). Areas such as Ashkelon (Tosef., Oho. 18:4), Beth-Shean, Caesarea, Bet Guvrin, and Kefar Ẓemaḥ (TJ, Dem. 2:1, 22c) were exempted from the restrictions of the Sabbatical Year. Judah ha-Nasi also permitted the buying of vegetables immediately after the close of the Sabbatical Year (Shev. 6:4) and the importing of produce from the Diaspora during the Sabbatical Year (TJ, Shev. 6:4, 37a; 7:2, 37b), both transactions which were previously forbidden. Many Jews still transgressed the sabbatical prohibitions which remained in force since they knew that their institution was only rabbinic (TJ, Dem. 2:1, 22d). It was related that an individual disobeyed the sabbatical laws but carefully observed the **ḥallah* rules, since the latter was still a biblical commandment (TJ, Shev. 9:8, 39a).

Rabban *Gamaliel, the son of Judah ha-Nasi, continued his father's policies, and also relaxed sabbatical restrictions. He permitted the previously forbidden actions of tilling the fields until the actual start – Rosh Ha-Shanah – of the Sabbatical Year (MK 3b; Tosef., Shev. 1:1), and the preparation of olives with an olive-crusher during this year (Shev. 8:6; Tosef., Shev. 6:27). During the third century, conditions worsened for the Jewish farmers. Taxes were increased, so that the constantly changing Roman rulers could support their armies and military expeditions. The rabbis therefore permitted the actual sowing of the seeds that produced the necessary food for the foreign armies (Sanh. 26a; TJ, Sanh. 3:6, 21b; Maim. Yad, Shemittah, 1:11). They also extended the time that fruits could be harvested and eaten during the Sabbatical Year (Shev. 9:3; Pes. 53a). Even during this difficult period, individuals continued to be meticulous in their observances. It was related that R. Safra investigated the rules governing his removing a barrel of Ereẓ Israel sabbatical wine to the Diaspora before he did so (Pes. 52b). The rabbis declared that the verse "Ye mighty in strength, that fulfill His word" (Ps. 103:20) refers to those who leave their fields and vineyards untilled for a full year and still do not complain when they pay their taxes to the Roman government (Lev. R. 1:1). The observance of these laws remained sufficiently widespread so that the gentile nations were able to mock the Jews by stating, "The Jews observe the law of the Sabbatical Year and therefore have no vegetables. Consequently, the Jews sadden camels by eating the thorns which otherwise would have been consumed by the camels" (Lam. R., Proem 17).

MODERN PERIOD. For centuries, *shemittah* remained a theoretical problem, discussed solely by talmudic scholars. However, with the dawn of modern Zionism and the subsequent settlement of Ereẓ Israel, it became a practical problem for the settlers. Before the *shemittah* of 1889, the leading rabbis of the generation debated whether it was permissible to enact a formal sale of all the Jewish-owned fields and vineyards to non-Jews in order to permit the working of the land during the Sabbatical Year. R. Isaac Elhanan *Spektor of Kovno issued the following statement permitting this transaction:

> I was asked several months ago to express my opinion concerning Jewish colonists, who live on the produce of the fields and vineyards of our Holy Land, as the *shemittah* year is approaching in 1889. If we do not find a *hetter* it is possible that the land will become desolate and the colonies will turn into wasteland, God forbid. Hundreds of souls will be affected by it. Although I am very much preoccupied and very weak, yet I find it necessary to deal with this important problem and permit the work in the fields, by selling them to the Muslims for a period of two years only. After that period, the vineyard and the fields go back to the owners; and the sale must be to Muslims only and may take place during the coming summer. I prepared, with the help of God, a special brochure dealing with this subject, but in practice I never came out with a *hetter* because I did not want to be the only one in this new matter, as is always my practice in such things.
>
> But now that I received a letter informing me that my good friends, the rabbis: R. Israel Joshua of Kutna, R. Samuel Mohilewer of Bialystok, and R. Samuel Zanwil of Warsaw gave due consideration to this problem and came out with a *hetter,* and wait for my approval, I am greatly pleased to find that I am not alone in this great issue. My opinion is, therefore, to follow my above mentioned suggestion [sell the land to non-Jews]. Furthermore, the work in the fields and vineyards is to be done by non-Jews, but in the case of poor people who cannot afford to engage non-Jewish labor, let them consult the aforementioned honored rabbis; and may the Lord grant us the privilege to come joyously to our land, and observe the mitzvah of *shemittah* as it was originally ordained for us and in accordance with all its rules and regulations.
>
> It must be explicitly stated that this *hetter* is only for the year 5649 (1889) but not for future *shemittot*. Then further meditation will be necessary, and a new *hetter* will he required; and may the Lord help His people so that they should not need any *hetter* and should observe *shemittah* in accordance with the Law, as I have fully explained it in the special brochure, with the help of God (E. Shimoff, Rabbi Isaac Elchanan Spektor (1959), 134f.).

Spektor's lenient decision was opposed by the Ashkenazi *kehillah* of Jerusalem and its rabbis, Moses Joshua Judah Leib *Diskin and Samuel *Salant. Many of the colonists originally refrained from work during the Sabbatical Year in accordance with the stringent ruling. However, with the continued growth of the new settlements, many more farmers abided by the lenient decision during the next *shemittah* of 1896.

Before the Sabbatical Year of 1910, the controversy regarding the sale of the land to Muslims revived. Rabbi Abraham Isaac *Kook, then the chief rabbi of Jaffa, was the leading proponent of the sale, while Rabbi Jacob David *Willowsky of Safed opposed it. During the ensuing *shemittah* years, the chief rabbinate of Ereẓ Israel continued to abide by the lenient ruling, although there was always opposition to its decisions. Most prominent among the opponents has been Rabbi Abraham Isaiah *Karelitz of Bene-Berak. In Kibbutz Ḥafeẓ Ḥayyim attempts to grow vegetables in water (hydroponics) have met with some success as a method of observing the restrictions of the Sabbatical Year. Various Israel institutes devoted to studying agriculture in light of *halakhah* also experiment with methods suitable to growing fruits and vegetables during Sabbatical years.

Sabbatical Years during the second half of the 20th century fell during 5712 (1951/52); 5719 (1958/59); 5726 (1965/66); 5733 (1972/73); 5740 (1979/80); 5747 (1986/87); and 5754 (1993/94).

[Aaron Rothkoff]

BIBLIOGRAPHY: Wellhausen, Proleg, 116–20; S.R. Driver, *Deuteronomy* (ICC, 1902), 174–81; D. Hoffmann, *Sefer Va-Yikra*, 2 (1954), 217–23, 228–9; idem, *Sefer Devarim*, 1 (1959), 232–48; W.R. Smith and G.H. Box, in: EB, 15 (1911[11]), 532–3; W.R. Smith and S.A. Cook, *ibid.*, 23 (1911[11]), 962; Pedersen, Israel, 1–2 (1926), 86–89, 510; A. Menes, in: BZAW, 50 (1928), 79–83; N.M. Nicolskij, in: ZAW, 50 (1932), 216; E. Ginzberg, in: JQR, 22 (1931–32), 343–408; Dalman, Arbeit, 3 (1933), 183–5; C.H. Gordon, in: *Orientalia*, 22 (1953), 79–81; R. North, in: *Biblica*, 34 (1953), 501–15; idem, in: VT, 4 (1954), 196–9; idem, in: VT, 4 (1954), 196–99; idem, *Sociology of the Biblical Jubilee* (1954), 245; U. Cassuto, *Perush al Sefer Shemot* (1953), 209–10; J. Morgenstern, in: VT, 5 (1955), 34–76; H. Cazelles, *ibid.*, 322–4; N.H. Tur-Sinai, *Ha-Lashon ve-ha-Sefer,* 3 (1956), 205–8; E. Neufeld, in: RSO, 33 (1958), 53–124; M. Noth, *Exodus* (1959), 153–4; idem, *Leviticus* (1959), 157–69; de Vaux, Anc Isr, 173–7; K. Elliger, *Leviticus* (1966), 349–54; H. van Oyen, *Ethik des Alten Testaments* (1967), 80–82. ANCIENT NEAR EASTERN LEGAL BACKGROUND: F.R. Steele, *Nuzi Real Estate Transactions* (1943), 13ff.; F.R. Kraus, *Ein Edikt des Koenigs Ammi-ṣaduqa von Babylon* (1958); J. Lewy, in: *Eretz-Israel*, 5 (1958), 21ff.; E.A. Speiser, in: EM, 3 (1958), 61; idem, in: *Y. Kaufmann Jubilee Volume* (1960), 29ff.; J.J. Finkelstein, in: JCS, 15 (1961), 91ff.; idem, in: AS, 16 (1965), 233ff.; idem, in: Pritchard, Texts[3], 526ff.; Y. Muffs, *Studies/Readings in Biblical Law*, 4 (1965, unpublished lectures); idem, *Studies in the Aramaic Legal Papyri from Elephantine* (1969), 20. JUBILEE IN THE SECOND TEMPLE PERIOD: Maim. Yad, Shemittah ve-Yovel, 10–12; Maimonides Responsa, ed. by J. Blau, 2 (1960), 666 no. 389; J. Bornstein, in: *Ha-Tekufah*, 11 (1921), 230–60; A. Gulak, *Le-Ḥeker Toledot ha-Mishpat ha-Ivri bi-Tekufat ha-Talmud* (1929), 35–42; Kahana, in: *Sinai*, 56 (1965), 197–202; S. Safrai, in: *Tarbiz*, 35 (1965/66), 304–28; 36 (1966/67), 1–21. SABBATICAL YEAR, POST-BIBLICAL PERIOD: S.J. Zevin, *Le-Or ha-Halakhah* (1957[2]), 85–134; Wander, in: *Ha-Ma'yan*, 6 no. 2 (1966), 26–72 (contains bibliographical list).

SABBIONETA, town in Lombardy, Italy, in the former duchy of *Mantua. Jewish settlement in Sabbioneta dates from the 15th century. In 1436 the brothers Azariah and Meshullam, the sons of Joab of Pisa, arrived there to found the third bank of the duchy of Mantua. On Feb. 10, 1530, the adventurer David *Reuveni visited the town and stayed in the home of Eleazar *Portaleone. From the 16th century, the Jewish population of Sabbioneta constantly increased. In 1746 the town came under Austrian rule. In 1779, in the reign of Maria *Theresa, the first attempt was made to abolish the judicial autonomy of the Mantuan communities, including Sabbioneta. Rabbis and scholars of Sabbioneta including Azriel b. Solomon *Dienna, Johanan b. Joseph *Treves, and Joseph b. Jacob Padua Ashkenazi.

Printing

Sabbioneta is best known, however, for its Hebrew press, which was founded in 1551 by Joseph b. Jacob Shalit of Padua and Jacob b. Naphtali of Gazzuala, in the house of Tobias b. Eliezer *Foa. In 1553 Foa became sole owner of the press, with Cornelio *Adelkind as the printing expert, and Joshua Boaz Baruch as corrector and setter. After Adelkind converted to Christianity, Foa's sons, Eliezer and Mordecai, took his place; 26 books were issued, including the first printed edition of Isaac Abrabanel's *Mirkevet ha-Mishneh* (1551), before the press was compelled to close down in 1559. A proposed edition of the Talmud did not go beyond one tractate (*Kiddushin*, 1553), and a Mishnah edition with Maimonides' and Bertinoro's commentaries was not printed beyond the order *Zera'im* and part of *Mo'ed* (1558); the rest appeared in Mantua.

In 1567 Vicenzo Conti, the gentile printer of *Cremona, who had served his apprenticeship with Foa at Sabbioneta, left Cremona and in that year printed a number of works at Sabbioneta.

BIBLIOGRAPHY: S. Simonsohn, *Toledot ha-Yehudim be-Dukkasut Mantovah*, 2 vols. (1962–64), index. HEBREW PRINTING. D.W. Amram, *Makers of Hebrew Books in Italy* (1909), 288ff., 316; H.D. Friedberg, *Ha-Defus ha-Ivri be-Italyah...* (1956[2]), 76ff.; A. Ya'ari, *Meḥkerei Sefer* (1958), 345ff.; idem, in: KS, 17 (1940/41), 393ff.; Sonne, *ibid.*, 4 (1927/28), 269ff.; 7 (1930/31), 275f.; 8 (1931/32), 513, 519.

SABEA (Heb. סְבָא, שְׁבָא – *S(h)eva'*; Ass. *Saba'ai* (Tiglath-Pileser III); Sum. *Sabum/Sabu*? (see Montgomery in bibl.)), state in S. Arabia in the region exposed to the monsoon from Hadhramaut to Yemen, contemporary with the Israelite monarchy. Explorations and excavations conducted by the University of Louvain (1951–52) and the American Foundation for the Study of Man (1950–53) uncovered epigraphic evidence in the area, dating from the beginning of the second millennium B.C.E. to the sixth century C.E., which reflects political development from theocracy, through secular monarchy, to oligarchy.

Sabea, roughly coinciding with Yemen, displayed the greatest durability in the various shifts of power between the Sabean, Minean, and Qatabanian states. Radiocarbon dating indicates that Sabea flourished from around 900 to 450 B.C.E. (for beginnings, see Grohmann in bibl.). Besides engaging in agriculture, which utilized seasonal rainfall and advanced irrigation, these kingdoms, exploiting their proximity to Africa across the Straits of Bab el Mandeb, were essentially trading empires, serving as entrépôts of maritime trade from India and East Africa, and transporting foreign luxuries and their home-produced incense (Jer. 6:20; Ps. 72:15) by camel caravans (Isa. 60:6; Job 6:19 [?]) to Mesopotamia, Syria, and Egypt. A South Arabian clay seal from the ninth century found in debris at Beth-El possibly attests to such trade with the early Israelite monarchy.

The visit of the Queen of *Sheba (I Kings 10) is one of the earliest examples of a trade mission. It was occasioned by Solomon's occupation of the head of the Gulf of Akaba and his enterprise in the Red Sea, which was a threat to South Arabian monopoly of the caravan trade. The alphabetic inscriptions from South Arabia furnish no evidence for women rulers, but Assyrian inscriptions repeatedly mention Arab queens in the north, so that the Queen of Sheba may have been one of these; Northern Sabeans were also doubtless those mentioned in Job 1:15 (cf. Gen. 25:3; I Chron. 1:32) and their name may have survived in the Wadi Shaba northeast of Medina. Both southern and northern Sheba are to be distinguished from Seba (Heb. סְבָא), north Sudan (Isa. 43:3; Ps. 72:10).

By the end of the first century B.C.E. the Sabean state had absorbed the Minean kingdom to the south and Qataban to the north, and soon also the Hadhramaut. This aggrandizement eventually involved Sabea in war with the Abyssinians, but its final decline was due to internal dissensions between Jews and Christians, the latter sponsored by Abyssinia, then a Christian state, and the former identified with Arab nationalism. The last king of Sabea, Yusuf *Dhû-Nuwâs, adopted the Jewish faith. His persecution of the Christians provoked an Abyssinian invasion in 525 C.E. and occupation of the land and the oases on the caravan route to the north. This, together with the development of the Red Sea trade route, brought about the end of the state of Sabea, conventionally associated with the bursting of the great dam at Ma'rib in 542 which is symptomatic of the general neglect of the vital irrigation works after the collapse of the native government. The Abyssinian rule ended by 575 and was succeeded by Persian dominion for just over half a century, whereafter the native Sabeans were finally absorbed in the politico-religious empire of Islam.

The religion of Sabea was as well organized as that of any Semitic state in the Ancient Near East. Temples were well built and endowed with a large and well-organized staff. Inscriptions attest to native polytheism, including many unnamed gods of families and divine local lords (Baals). The chief gods were the moon-god, called A'lmaqah in Sabea; the sun-goddess; and ʿAthtar, the god of the planet Venus, the brightest star in those latitudes, who was the guide of caravans. Unlike the Mesopotamian Venus deity Ishtar, the South Arabian ʿAthtar was not worshipped as a goddess but as a god.

BIBLIOGRAPHY: T.W. Rosmarin, in: *Journal of the Society of Semitic Studies*, 16 (1932), 1–2; J.A. Montgomery, *Arabia and the Bible* (1934); A. Grohmann, *Arabia* (Ger., 1936), 24, index s.v. *Saba' (Reich)*; J. Ryckmans, *L'institution monarchique en Arabie méridionale...* (1951[2]); W. Phillips, *Qataban and Sheba* (1955); A. Jamme, in: M. Brillant and R. Aigrain (eds.), *Histoire des Religions*, 4 (1956), 239–307; H.W. Haussig (ed.), *Woerterbuch der Mythologie*, 1 (1965), 485ff.

[John Gray]

SABIN, ALBERT BRUCE (1906–1993), U.S. virologist. Sabin was born in Bialystok, Poland, and emigrated to Paterson, New Jersey, with his family in 1921. He graduated in medicine from New York University and thereafter worked on polio viruses and other infectious agents at the Rockefeller Institute in 1935–39. He joined the University of Cincinnati College of Medicine, where he progressed to professor of research pediatrics and distinguished service professor (1939–69), a period interrupted by World War II service in the U.S. Army Medical Corps, where he studied viral infections such as dengue fever threatening U.S. troops. He developed a live "attenuated" polio virus, which did not cause disease but induced immunity to polio virus infections and was given orally. Its safety and efficacy were established in 1960 after European trials, and it was used extensively in the U.S. between 1962 and 1964, supplanting the *Salk intramuscular killed viral vaccine at least temporarily. The respective merits of the two vaccines caused great general and personal controversy. He also worked on the genetics of antiviral resistance and on a simple test for antibodies to the toxoplasma parasite. After 1969 his services were in great demand as a visiting professor and as a member of expert committees in the U.S. and abroad; he was president of the Weizmann Institute of Science (1970–72). He was elected to the U.S. National Academy of Sciences (1951) and the U.S.S.R. Academy of Medical Sciences, and received the U.S. National Medal of Science in 1970. His contributions were broadly humanitarian as well as scientific. He is buried in the Arlington National Cemetery.

[Michael Denman (2nd ed.)]

SABINUS (end of first century B.C.E.), Roman official. Sabinus, then Augustus' treasurer in Syria, was sent to Judea after Herod's death in 4 B.C.E., to take charge of the latter's estate as procurator. On his arrival he acceded to the request of Varus, governor of Syria, to hand over the custody of the citadels and treasures to Herod's son *Archelaus, pending Caesar's decision concerning Herod's will. However, immediately after the departure of Varus and Archelaus for Antioch and Rome, respectively, he took possession of the royal palace and demanded from the custodians particulars regarding Herod's treasure. Sabinus' conduct caused a revolt on the festival of Shavuot, when many pilgrims had assembled in Jerusalem. Sabinus seized the Tower of Phasael, from which he gave the signal to attack the rebels. As the battle developed, the Romans set fire to the Temple chambers, capturing and plundering the Temple treasury. These acts further enraged the people, and they besieged the royal palace where Sabinus and his followers had fortified themselves. The Jews demanded that the Romans leave the city, offering to spare their lives, but Sabinus would not trust them. Riots continued throughout Judea until Varus hurried back to suppress them. When he reached Jerusalem, Sabinus fled.

BIBLIOGRAPHY: Jos., Ant., 17:221–94; Jos., Wars, 2:16–74; Schuerer, Hist, 161f.; Klausner, Bayit Sheni, 4 (1950^2), 173–7; Pauly-Wissowa, 2nd series. 2 (1920), 1595f., no. 4; A.H.M. Jones, *The Herods of Judea* (1938), 159, 161–2, 165.

[Lea Roth]

SABSOVICH, H.L. (Hirsch Loeb; 1861–1915), U.S. agronomist and a leader of the Am Olam movement. Sabsovich was born in Berdiansk, Russia. As a law student at Odessa University during the 1881 pogroms, he helped to organize Jewish self-defense. After advanced agronomy studies in Switzerland, Sabsovich became manager of an estate in the Rostov region. Immigrating to the United States in 1887, Sabsovich obtained a post as assistant director of the Agricultural Experiment Station in Fort Collins, Colorado. He was then called upon by the Baron de Hirsch Fund to direct the founding of Woodbine, New Jersey (1891), a Jewish farming-industrial community, where he was superintendent for 15 years, followed by another decade as the Fund's general agent in New York. Among his achievements was the pioneering Baron de Hirsch Agricultural School (1894–1919). Sabsovich worked closely with the Jewish Agricultural Society, the Federation of Jewish Farmers, and the Society of Jewish Social Workers of Greater New York (as president).

BIBLIOGRAPHY: J. Brandes, *Immigrants to Freedom* (1971), index.

[Joseph Brandes]

SACERDOTE, DAVID (1550–1625), composer and banker. He came from Rovré or Rovere in the duchy of Piedmont (today Roreto Chisone in the province of Turin) and is known as the author of a single work written in his youth, *Il primo libro di madrigali a sei voci*, published in Venice in 1575. Only one copy, and that of the part-book *quinto* (fifth voice), has been found so far and is in the British Museum. Sacerdote, who at that time lived in Casale Monferrato, dedicated the work to the Marquis Alfonso del Vasto, the son of Isabella Gonzaga, who was governor of the marquisate of Monferrato on behalf of her brother Guglielmo Gonzaga, duke of Mantua.

Sacerdote was also a banker, first at Casale, together with his brother Leone (1576–80), then at Acqui (1580–85), and finally at Cortemilia in Piedmont (from 1585 onward), together with his relative Ventura Bacchi. He was also then the holder of a moneylender's concession at Bologna (from 1587 onward), at the Marchese Del Carreto fiefs in Calizzano and Carcare (1591–1611), and finally, from 1618 onward, at Cengio, which then belonged to another branch of the Del Carretto family.

The musical value and stylistic relationships of the *Madrigali* cannot be discerned from the surviving *quinto* part; neither has it been possible as yet to connect it definitely with the circle of Jewish musicians around Salamone de' *Rossi. The combination of the banker's profession with a musical education is typical of his time and social circumstances.

BIBLIOGRAPHY: S. Foa, *Gli ebrei nel Monferrato nei secoli XVI e XVII* (1914, repr. 1967), 47 n. 62; 73 n. 17; 74 n. 18; 75 n. 19; 77 n. 20; E. Loevinsohn, in: REJ, 93 (1932), 49, 159, 163, 168 (correct: David instead of Daniele Sacerdote di Rovere); A. Einstein, in: J. Newman, *Madrigals of Salamon De Rossi* (1962), 321 (Diss. Colum. Univ. N.Y.).

[Vittore Colorni]

SACERDOTI, ANGELO-RAPHAEL CHAIM (1886–1935), chief rabbi of Rome and Zionist leader in Italy. Born and educated in Florence, he officiated as the rabbi of Reggio Emilia until 1912, when he was invited to take up the post of chief rabbi of Rome, which he retained until his death. While he was preoccupied with the reorganization of the Rome community, World War I broke out. He volunteered to serve as an army chaplain and organized Jewish chaplains to serve on all the fronts. After the war he began an active campaign to revitalize Italian Jewry, of which he was a leading guide and teacher. When Mussolini assumed power, Sacerdoti held a series of meetings with him in an attempt to protect Jewish interests and ensure that the Jews of Italy would not be harmed by the Fascist regime. He was instrumental in obtaining the passage of a law that required all Italian Jews to belong to one of the 26 united communities, unless they specifically renounced their Judaism. This led to increased participation in Jewish community life. He also transferred the Rabbinical Seminary from Florence to Rome. Sacerdoti was active in the Zionist field, participating in the opening of The Hebrew University (1925) as the representative of the Rome community and the Italian government. Due to his efforts, a political office of the Zionist Organization was established in Rome.

BIBLIOGRAPHY: R.R. Cohen, in: *Hed ha-Mizraḥ*, no. 34–35 (March 28, 1945), 18–19.

[Getzel Kressel]

SACHAR, ABRAM LEON (1899–1993), U.S. educator and historian; founding president of *Brandeis University. Sachar was born in New York and brought up in Saint Louis. In 1929 he began to teach history at the University of Illinois. Sachar was one of the organizers of the B'nai B'rith Hillel Foundation and played an important role in its development, establishing Hillel Houses for Jewish students on the campuses of American universities. He himself directed the University of Illinois unit from 1929 to 1933 and then served as national director of the Hillel Foundations from 1933 to 1948. In 1948 he was appointed the first president of Brandeis University and was largely responsible for its rapid development, guiding its academic progress and raising the requisite funds for the construction of its extensive campus. In 1968 Sachar was appointed chancellor of the university and a fellow of the American Academy of Arts and Sciences. His writings include a popular one-volume *A History of the Jews* (1965[5]); a history of Jewish life between the two world wars, *Sufferance Is the Badge* (1939); *The Course of Our Times* (1972); *Brandeis University: A Host at Last* (1976); and *The Redemption of the Unwanted: From the Liberation of the Death Camps to the Founding of Israel* (1983).

His son HOWARD MORLEY SACHAR (1928–), historian, was born in St. Louis, Missouri. He taught history at the University of Massachusetts in 1953 and later directed Hillel Foundations at UCLA and Stanford University. In 1961 he became founder-director of Brandeis University's Jacob Hiatt Institute in Israel. From 1965 he taught modern and Middle Eastern history at George Washington University, Washington, D.C. In 2004 he became professor emeritus at the university. Sachar's works include *The Course of Modern Jewish History* (1958); *Aliyah: The Peoples of Israel* (1961); *From the Ends of the Earth: The Peoples of Israel* (1964); *Emergence of the Middle East, 1914–1924* (1969); *Europe Leaves the Middle East, 1936–1954* (1972); a novel, *The Man on the Camel* (1980); *Egypt and Israel* (1983); *Diaspora: An Inquiry into the Contemporary Jewish World* (1985); and *A History of Israel: From the Aftermath of the Yom Kippur War* (1987).

[David Rudavsky / Ruth Beloff (2nd ed.)]

SACHER, HARRY (1881–1971), British Zionist and lawyer. Born in London, the son of a tailor, Sacher was educated at London and Oxford Universities (winning a scholarship) and in Europe. He was called to the bar but did not practice. During 1905–09 and 1915–19 he was a member of the editorial board of the *Manchester Guardian* and achieved prominence in the field of political analysis. He belonged to the Manchester Zionist Circle headed by Chaim *Weizmann and was instrumental in winning the *Manchester Guardian* to the Zionist cause during the political efforts preceding the *Balfour Declaration. Sacher was married to the sister of Simon *Marks (later Lord Marks of Broughton), one of the founders of Marks & Spencer and an ardent Zionist and patron of Zionist causes. In 1920 Sacher settled in Palestine, where he practiced law.

At the 15th Zionist Congress (Basle, 1927) Sacher was elected to the Zionist Executive and was reelected to it in 1929 at the 16th Congress (Zurich), serving until 1931. His term began during the days of an economic crisis in the *yishuv*, following the height of the Fourth Aliyah. He channeled the economic policy of the Zionist Organization with a firm hand in an effort to balance its budget, encountering strong opposition on the part of the labor movement. The "Sacher regime" became synonymous with economic efficiency, in contrast to various other – daring – programs, which lacked the means of implementation. The second part of Sacher's term coincided with the Arab riots of 1929, when he defended Zionism against its detractors among Arabs and the British authorities. In his testimony before the Shaw Commission, which set out from London to investigate the causes of the riots, he defined the Zionist aims for Jewish-Arab relations: "We do not wish to rule over others, but we do not wish others to rule over us."

Sacher returned to England in 1930 and became a director of Marks and Spencer, serving until 1962. Throughout the years he remained active in the Zionist movement and, after 1948, in pro-Israel affairs. He edited Anglo-Jewish Zionist journals, such as *The Jewish Review*. His books include *Israel, The Establishment of a State* (1952) and *Zionist Portraits and Other Essays* (1959); he edited the anthology, *Zionism and the Jewish Future* (1916). He also donated the Sacher Building to New College, Oxford, and was one of the greatest benefactors of the college in its history.

His wife, MIRIAM (neé Marks, a sister of Baron *Marks, 1892–1975), was one of the leaders of *WIZO. His son, MICHAEL (1917–1986), was active in fund-raising for Israel in Britain and a governor of the Weizmann Institute of Science. In 1971 he was elected to the Jewish Agency Executive.

BIBLIOGRAPHY: Ch. Weizmann, *Trial and Error* (1949), index; R. Weltsch, in: *Haaretz* (Sept. 14, 1961). **ADD. BIBLIOGRAPHY:** ODNB online.

[Getzel Kressel]

SACHS, family of U.S. educators, physicians, and bankers. JOSEPH SACHS, who immigrated to the United States in 1848, was briefly a rabbi in Baltimore and Boston. His oldest son, Julius *Sachs, was an educator and philologist. Another son, Bernard *Sachs, was a noted neurologist. Two other sons of Joseph Sachs, SAMUEL and HARRY SACHS, were founding members of the banking house of *Goldman, Sachs and Company. Samuel Sachs' son, WALTER EDWARD SACHS (1884–1980), and Harry Sachs' son, HOWARD JOSEPH SACHS (1891–1969), succeeded their fathers as partners in the firm. Julius Sachs' son, ERNEST SACHS (1879–1958), became a prominent neurosurgeon in St. Louis, Missouri, and Samuel Sachs' son, PAUL J. SACHS (1878–1965), was professor of fine arts at Harvard and director of the Fogg Art Museum.

BIBLIOGRAPHY: L. Endlich, *Goldman Sachs: The Culture of Success* (1999).

SACHS, ANDREW (1930–), British actor. Born in Berlin, Sachs came to Britain as a child, following his father, who had been arrested and released by the Gestapo a few days before **Kristallnacht.* Sachs was an actor from 1948 and appeared in supporting roles in dozens of films, as well as on television and radio. He became internationally renowned for playing "Manuel," the hapless Spanish waiter, in the BBC's *Fawlty Towers,* produced in two series in 1975 and 1979 and often regarded as the greatest British television comedy ever made. In 2004 Sachs produced a series for BBC radio on the history of the Jews of Britain, *The Jewish Tapestry.*

BIBLIOGRAPHY: M. Bright and R. Ross, *Fawlty Towers: Fully Booked* (2001).

[William D. Rubinstein (2nd ed.)]

SACHS, BERNARD (1858–1944), U.S. neurologist. Sachs, who was born in Baltimore, belonged to the *Sachs family of scholars. He studied medicine in Europe and, when he returned to the U.S., became professor of nervous and mental diseases at the New York Polyclinic and professor of clinical neurology at Columbia University. He was president of the First International Neurological Congress which was held in 1931. Sachs, a pioneer in the field of child neurology, is best known for his description of the Tay-Sachs disease in children – a progressive impairment of mental functions, muscles, and vision ending in blindness. He made various studies on nervous disorders in children and published several books on the subject, among them: *A Treatise on the Nervous Diseases of Children* (1895, 1905^2); *The Normal* (1925); and *Puberty and Adolescence* (1936).

BIBLIOGRAPHY: S.R. Kagan, *Jewish Medicine* (1952), 384.

[Suessmann Muntner]

SACHS, CURT (1881–1959), German musicologist. Born in Berlin, Sachs became director of the Berlin state collection of instruments in 1919. The same year he began to lecture at the University of Berlin, and from 1933 to 1937 was adviser to the museum of musical instruments at the Musée de Trocadéro in Paris. He supervised the production of two series of historical recordings, *2,000 Jahre Musik* (Berlin) and *L'Anthologie Sonore* (Paris). In 1937 he emigrated to the U.S., where he lectured at New York University until 1957 and at Columbia from 1953. The wide scope of his research included an inquiry into the creative origins and evolution of musical instruments which led him, with E.M. von Hornbostel, to compose a classification system which bears their names. Sachs was a pioneer in the comparative study of musical instruments and embodied his researches on this subject in his *History of Musical Instruments* (1940).

He published *Eine Weltgeschichte des Tanzes* (1933; *A World History of the Dance*, 1937, 1963^2); *The Rise of Music in the Ancient World – East and West* (1943); and *Rhythm and Tempo* (1953), on the relationship of rhythmic expression and musical styles. In *The Commonwealth of Art* (1946) Sachs gave expression to his personal philosophy of the unity of the arts. His other works include *Our Musical Heritage* (1948, 1955^2), a short history of music; and *The Wellsprings of Music* (1962, ed. posthumously by Jaap Kunst).

BIBLIOGRAPHY: G. Reese and R. Brandel (eds.), *The Commonwealth of Music: in Honor of Curt Sachs* (1965), 1–25; E. Hertzmann, in: *Musical Quarterly*, 27 (1941), 263–9, 275–7; K. Hahn, in: *Acta Musicologica*, 29 (1957), 94–106, a bibliography of Sachs's writings; E. Gerson-Kiwi, in: *Tazlil*, no. 5 (1965), 96–98 (Heb.), incl. bibl.

[Edith Gerson-Kiwi]

SACHS, HANNS (1881–1947), non-medical psychoanalyst. Sachs was born in Vienna and studied law. In 1904 he read Freud's *Interpretation of Dreams* and in 1909 joined Freud's group, becoming a member of its executive the following year. Sachs was one of the six men closest to Freud, "The Committee," and in 1912 he was appointed coeditor of *Imago* with Otto *Rank. In 1918 he abandoned law and opened a psychoanalytic practice in Zurich. In 1920 he was invited to become a training analyst in Berlin. In 1932 Sachs left Berlin for Boston, where he continued as a training analyst and lectured. He received one of the few non-medical appointments as an instructor at the Harvard Medical School. Sachs was an indefatigable editor and teacher. His early writings are essentially devoted to questions of dream interpretation and everyday terrors. His later works mainly concern the application of psychoanalysis to literature and art.

Together with Karl *Abraham he advised Pabst, the film director of *Secrets of the Soul.* Sachs kept in touch with Pabst and in 1925 wrote *Notes About the Psychology of the Film.* His first major publication, written with Otto Rank, was *The Significance of Psychoanalysis for the Mental Sciences* (1915), which deals with the application of psychoanalysis to civilization, myth, religion, art, and philosophy. Other books include *Psychotherapy and the Pursuit of Happiness* (1941), *The Creative Unconscious* (1942), and *Freud, Master and Friend* (1944). Sachs's literary research was far-reaching. He thought that in writing *The Tempest*, Shakespeare freed himself from guilt at having left his daughter when she was a child (*Der Sturm,*

1912). Sachs wrote three books in his search to understand human beings and how clearly they may know themselves: *Caligula* (1931), *Notes About the Knowledge of Human Beings* (1936; not translated), and his last book, published posthumously and given the title by A.A. Roback, *Masks of Love and Life* (1948); it contains a sketch of Julius Caesar's personality and a chapter about the apostle Paul.

BIBLIOGRAPHY: F. Moellenhoff, in: F. Alexander et al. (eds.), *Psychoanalytic Pioneers* (1966), 180–99; J. Rickman, *Index Psychoanalyticus 1892–1926* (1928), 225–6.

[Louis Miller]

SACHS, JULIUS (1832–1897), German botanist. Born in Breslau of a poor family, he was encouraged in his studies by the Czech physiologist Johannes Evangelista Purkinje (1787–1869), then at the University of Breslau. When Sachs was 18, Purkinje moved to Prague, and he invited Sachs to come to his institute as an assistant. After obtaining his degree at the University of Prague, Sachs went to Tharandt, where first he taught botany at the forestry school; in 1861 he was appointed professor at the agricultural school at Poppelsdorf, near Bonn. In 1867 Sachs became professor of botany at Wuerzburg, remaining for nearly 30 years.

Sachs held an important place in the history of biology, both as a teacher and as a researcher. His textbooks, *Handbuch der Experimentalphysiologie der Pflanzen* (1865) and the *Lehrbuch der Botanik* (1868; *Textbook of Botany*, 1875), widely influenced the teaching of botany. Sachs's personal influence as a teacher was equally great. Under his genial and enthusiastic leadership, Wuerzburg became an international center for plant physiology, where some of Europe's most eminent botanists were trained.

Sachs has been called the creator of experimental botany. Among Sachs's noteworthy contributions were his demonstration that starch is the first perceptible product of photosynthesis and that it is translocated from the leaf in the form of sugar. Sachs was the first to demonstrate that the chloroplasts are the site of photosynthesis, and it was he who showed that light is necessary for the synthesis of chlorophyll. Sachs also pioneered in studies of the nutritional requirements of plants; he published the first formula for a standard culture solution, a necessary basis for identifying the mineral elements essential for growth. Sachs introduced the auxanometer, an instrument for quantitatively studying plant growth, and the clinostat, a rotating apparatus by means of which he investigated the plant's response to gravity.

BIBLIOGRAPHY: E.G. Pringsheim, *Julius Sachs* (Ger., 1932).

[Mordecai L. Gabriel]

SACHS, JULIUS (1849–1934), U.S. educator. Sachs, who was born in Baltimore, Maryland, was founder and headmaster of the Sachs Collegiate Institute School of Boys in New York City (1871–1904), a school considerably attended by the German-Jewish upper class of that city; and professor of secondary education at Columbia Teachers College (1902–17). Sachs gained national recognition for leadership in raising the standards of secondary school education and improving teacher training. He served as president of the Schoolmasters' Association of New York (1889) and the Headmasters' Association of the United States (1899). In addition to activities and publications concerned with education, Sachs produced several studies in the field of philology and archaeology. He was president of the American Philological Association in 1891. He belonged to the *Sachs family of educators.

[Frederick M. Binder]

SACHS, LEO (1924–), Israeli geneticist. Sachs was born in Leipzig, Germany, and in 1933 immigrated to England with his parents following Hitler's accession to power. He received his doctorate from Cambridge in 1951 and in 1952 came to Israel as a research scientist at the Weizmann Institute of Science, Rehovot. He initiated research on various aspects of biomedical sciences and established the Department of Genetics and Virology. He was appointed associate professor in 1960 and full professor in 1962. His research pioneered new approaches to basic and medically applied aspects of stem cell biology, development, hematology, and oncology, and led to new therapies. His honors include the Israel Prize for natural sciences (1972), the Rothschild Prize in biological sciences (1977), the Wolf Prize in medicine (1980), and the EMET Prize for life sciences, medicine, and genetics (2002). He is a member of the Israel Academy of Sciences and Humanities, a foreign associate of the U.S. National Academy of Sciences, and a fellow of the Royal Society, London, since 1997.

[Bracha Rager (2nd ed.)]

SACHS, LEONARD (1909–1990), British actor. Sachs went to England from South Africa in 1930 and acted with repertory companies. In 1936 he and Peter Ridgeway founded the Players' Theatre in London, and apart from three years in the army, Sachs continued to direct there until 1947. In 1951 he launched *Mr. Sachs's Song Saloon* at the Battersea Festival Gardens and took it on tour through Britain. Sachs appeared, generally in supporting roles, in numerous British films and television plays between 1936 and 1976.

SACHS, MAURICE (originally **Jean-Maurice Ettinghausen**; 1906–1945?), French author, critic, and translator. Born in Paris, Sachs was abandoned by his parents and fell prey to alcoholism, homosexuality, and kleptomania. Vainly trying to free himself from moral depravity, he became a Catholic and entered a seminary, but left it and went to the U.S., where he married a Protestant minister's daughter. Returning to France, he became a Nazi collaborator and black marketeer. He is believed to have died in a prison fight in Hamburg toward the end of World War II. Sachs' literary talent revealed itself in novels, essays, and a number of picaresque stories.

These include *La Décade de l'Illusion* (1950), published first in English as *The Decade of Illusion* (1933); *André Gide* (1936); and *Au temps du Boeuf sur le Toit* (1939). *Le Sabbat* (*The*

Day of Wrath, 1953), written in 1939 and published in 1946, is the brutal confession of a lost soul, a brilliantly written, penetrating analysis of bohemian life in Paris. Most of Sachs' works are autobiographical. Those published posthumously include *La Chasse à courre* (1948), *Chronique joyeuse et scandaleuse* (1948), *Tableau des moeurs de ce temps* (1951), *Abracadabra* (1952), and *Le Voile de Véronique* (1958).

BIBLIOGRAPHY: P. Monceau, *Le Dernier Sabbat de M. Sachs* (1950); Catane, in: *Ma'ariv* (Dec. 2, 1960).

[Moshe Catane]

SACHS, MICHAEL (1808–1864), German rabbi and scholar. Sachs, who was born in Glogau, Silesia, became a preacher in Prague in 1836, succeeding L. Zunz, and from 1844 was a preacher in Berlin, where he also served as *dayyan* at the *bet din*. He declined an invitation to become rabbi to the small but growing Orthodox congregation in Frankfurt, which eventually chose S.R. *Hirsch. A strong traditionalist, Sachs opposed the introduction of the organ – more for historical than halakhic reasons – although he consented to the omission of *piyyutim* from the synagogue service. His middle-of-the-road position earned him the suspicion and antagonism of the old-time Orthodox, while he disappointed the hopes of the Reformers (he threatened to resign when in 1860 the Berlin Jewish community planned to bury the Reform leader S. *Holdheim in the "Rabbis' Row" of the cemetery).

Sachs possessed a wide Jewish and general education, and was familiar with classics and Semitics and their modern philological-historical methodology no less than with Bible, Talmud, and particularly Midrash, as shown by his commentaries on the *piyyutim*. As a scholar, he was one of the leaders in the emerging *Wissenschaft des Judentums. He worked on a German Bible translation with Zunz, contributing 15 books, including Psalms (1835), which appealed to his lyric-poetical nature. Sachs' major work was *Religioese Poesie der Juden in Spanien* (1845, 1901^2), which consisted of renderings of the poetry of the great medieval Spanish-Hebrew poets, as well as a historical survey. This influential work probably inspired Heinrich Heine's *Hebraeische Melodien*.

Of a more philological nature were Sachs' *Beitraege zur Sprach- und Altertumsforschung* (2 vols., 1852–54), in which he treated the relationship between the classical world and that of the Talmud and Midrash. His *Stimmen von Jordan und Euphrat* (2 vols., 1853, 1891^2) is an anthology of *aggadah*. Sachs' edition of the *maḥzor* in both the German and East German (Polish) rites, with translation and notes (9 vols., 1855 and many subsequent editions), was highly popular with German Jewry, as was his edition and translation of the *siddur* (1858 ff.). In an appendix to the *maḥzor* (*Be'er Mikhael*, published posthumously by A.A. Ehrlich), Sachs occasionally expressed criticism of W. *Heidenheim, his great predecessor in this field. Sachs was an outstanding preacher, and two volumes of his sermons were published posthumously, *Predigten* (1867–69). A memorial volume was published on the 100th anniversary of his birth.

BIBLIOGRAPHY: S. Bernfeld, in: M. Sachs, *Religioese Poesie ...* (1901^2); idem, *Michael Sachs ...* (Heb., 1900); J. Eschelbacher, *Michael Sachs* (Ger., 1908); L. Geiger (ed.), *Michael Sachs und Moritz Veit, Briefwechsel ...* (1897).

[Ernst Daniel Goldschmidt]

SACHS, NELLY (**Leonie**; 1891–1970), German poet and Nobel Prize winner. The daughter of a Berlin industrialist, Nelly Sachs grew up in an artistic home where she early imbibed a love of literature. At 17 she began writing neoromantic poetry in traditional, rhymed forms and puppet plays with a fairy-tale flavor. Her first work, *Legenden und Erzaehlungen* (1921), reflected a Christian intellectual world tinged with mysticism. The poet was then rooted in the world of German Romanticism, the Catholic Middle Ages, and the mysticism of Jacob Boehme. After 1933, when Nelly Sachs, like so many other assimilated German Jews, discovered her Jewish heritage, she found ideas akin to Boehme's in the Zohar. Her early work remained largely unknown, and she refused to allow it to be republished. Her reputation is largely based on her output after the end of World War II. In 1940 Nelly Sachs emigrated to Sweden through the good offices of the writer Selma Lagerlöf and the Swedish royal family. At first she made a modest living in Stockholm by translating Swedish poetry into German, but eventually published several successful volumes of her translations.

Throughout the war years, however, Nelly Sachs wrote some of the poetry that was to bring her fame. The motif of flight and pursuit, the symbol of the hunter and his quarry, are at the center of her poetic thought. Her poetry is ecstatic, mystical, and visionary. It is also very much in the German romantic tradition and, as such, has been criticized by some as disingenuous and incompatible with her subject matter. Although her poems were mostly composed in free verse, she wrote with careful craftsmanship, using an exquisite German flavored with the Psalms and filled with mystical imagery of Ḥasidic origin. "If I could not have written, I could not have survived," Nelly Sachs wrote. "Death was my teacher... my metaphors are my sounds." *In den Wohnungen des Todes* (1946), dedicated "to my dead brothers and sisters," includes cycles titled "Prayers for the Dead Fiancé," "Epitaphs Written On Air," and "Choruses After Midnight." *Sternverdunkelung* (1949) contains poems expressing unquenchable faith in the indestructibility of the people of Israel and the importance of its mission. Three subsequent collections were *Und niemand weiss weiter* (1957), *Flucht und Verwandlung* (1958), and *Die Suchende* (1966). On the occasion of her 70th birthday, her collected poetry was issued as *Fahrt ins Staublose* (1961). Her *Spaete Gedichte* (1965) contains the extended poetic sequence "Gluehende Raetsel" (1964) and suggests a mystical border whose language touches silence.

The 14 collected plays of *Zeichen im Sand* (1962) include *Eli, ein Mysterienspiel vom Leiden Israels* (1951). Written in 1943, this deals with the cosmic aftermath of the Holocaust. In 17 loosely connected scenes, the tragedy of an eight-year old Polish shepherd boy, who raises his flute heavenward in anguish and is murdered by a German soldier, is interwoven with the old Jewish legend of the *Lamed Vav Ẓaddikim* (36 Hidden Saints). *Eli* was later presented as a radio play and as an opera. *O the Chimneys*, an English version of selected poems and of *Eli* by Michael Hamburger and other translators, was published in 1967. The 1966 Nobel Prize for literature, which Nelly Sachs shared with S.Y. *Agnon ("Agnon represents the State of Israel. I represent the tragedy of the Jewish people"), was the culmination of several awards honoring her work.

BIBLIOGRAPHY: *Nelly Sachs zu Ehren: zum 75. Geburstag…* (1966), incl. bibl.; O, Lagercrantz, *Versuch ueber die Lyrik der Nelly Sachs* (1967); S. Rappaport, *Tribute to Nobel Prize Winners*, 1966 (1967); D. Bronsen, in: *Judaism*, 16 (1967), 120–8.

[Harry Zohn]

SACHS, SENIOR (1815–1892), Hebrew scholar. Born near Kovno, Lithuania, Sachs lived for two years in Brody (1839–40), studying Hebrew scholarly and philosophic literature, and specializing in German and other ancient and modern languages. For two years he taught in Raseiniai, where he befriended the novelist Abraham *Mapu. In 1856, Baron J. *Guenzburg took him to Paris to teach his son and grandson; Sachs remained there until the end of his life. His studies encompassed several aspects of medieval Jewish literature, especially religio-philosophical thought and the Hebrew poetry of Spain. From ancient manuscripts he published many selections, concentrating especially on Solomon ibn *Gabirol. His articles and studies, written only in Hebrew, were published in the Hebrew periodicals from the 1840s on.

Among the pamphlets and journals which he edited were *Kanfei Yonah* (1848); *Ha-Palit* (1850); *Ha-Teḥiyyah* (2 vols., 1850–57), a journal that published old manuscripts with notes; and *Kikayon Yonah* (1860). He also compiled a list of books and manuscripts in the Guenzburg library (unpublished), *Reshimot Sefarim Kitvei Yad* (1866); and *Shir ha-Shirim Asher li-Shelomo Gevirol* (1868). He edited *Kerem Ḥemed from 1854 to 1856.

BIBLIOGRAPHY: Kressel, Leksikon, 1 (1965), 761–2.

[Getzel Kressel]

SACHSENHAUSEN-ORANIENBURG, Nazi concentration camp near Berlin, opened in 1936. It served as the chief concentration camp for Berlin. The first German-Jewish prisoners arrived in Sachsenhausen-Oranienburg in June 1938. The camp was built in the area of the Inspectorate of Concentration Camps on the outskirts of Oranienburg. After the November pogroms known as **Kristallnacht*, *Himmler ordered the deportation of Jewish men age 16–60 to concentration camps and 10,000 Jews from Berlin, Hamburg, Mecklenburg, and Pomerania were interned there. Subsequently, the majority of them were released if they could prove that they were able to leave Germany (i.e., if they possessed emigration papers). At that point the forced emigration of Jews was German policy. At the outbreak of World War II, thousands of political suspects and stateless or Polish Jews were imprisoned in the camp. Conditions worsened. Disease, starvation, exhaustion, exposure, and abuse claimed many lives. During the war prisoners arrived from all over Europe. Twelve hundred Polish prisoners were sent to Sachsenhausen in 1940 from Pawiak prison in Warsaw, among them 60 Polish priests, as an essential part of the German plan to destroy the elite of Polish non-Jewish society and to make the Poles a subservient people. In the fall of 1941, 1,800 Soviet prisoners of war were shot there; afterwards thousands more were either shot or killed by phenol injection. Some 13,000 Soviet POWs were killed in all. A Nazi-directed counterfeiting operation was set up in the camp by an SS man, Bernhard Krueger. He employed 140 Jews in forging British currency as well as stamps, passports, identity documents, secret credentials, false code books, etc. Nearly all these Jews survived, in part because of their unique skills. In October 1942 all the Jewish prisoners, except those employed in the counterfeit operation, were transferred to *Auschwitz. Jewish prisoners were sent back beginning in the summer of 1944. The camp supplied slave labor for the German armament industry and housed several factories. In 1944 after the Warsaw Uprising (not to be confused with the 1943 Warsaw Ghetto Uprising) 3,500 Poles were sent to Sachsenhausen. There was a gas chamber in Sachsenhausen but it was used only under special circumstances. As in other camps, the prisoners also served as human guinea pigs for pseudo-medical experiments. In mid-January 1945 there were 65,000 prisoners, including 13,000 women, in the overpopulated camp. In the latter half of April 1945, the SS evacuated the bulk of the inmates on a death march. Those who endured the march were liberated by the Red Army near Schwerin, Germany. Of the total of 140,000 inmates who were sent to this camp, at least 30,000 died there. The number may actually have been much larger.

A Soviet Military Tribunal tried 16 former SS guards from Sachsenhausen in late October 1947. One year later all were convicted. Fourteen were sentenced to life imprisonment and two received 15-year sentences.

In postwar East Germany, the camp became a hodgepodge of would-be memorials, a virtual lesson in how not to preserve an authentic site. Since the reunification of Germany, efforts have been made to rectify the situation. The task is ongoing and Herculean.

BIBLIOGRAPHY: L. Grosser (ed.), *K.Z. Sachsenhausen* (Ger., 1945); A. Weiss-Ruethel, *Nacht und Nebel* (1946); F. Sige (ed.), *Todeslager Sachsenhausen* (1948); O. Nansen, *Day after Day* (1949), 399–571; *Urteil gegen Sorge und Schubert* (Akt 8 ks 1/58 des Landgerichtes Bonn, 6.2.1959).

[Yehuda Reshef / Michael Berenbaum (2nd ed.)]

SACK, BENJAMIN G. (1889–1967), Canadian journalist and historian. Born in the Kovno region of Lithuania, in 1905 Sack and members of his family joined his father, already in Montreal. Sack received some traditional education, but was for the most part an autodidact who overcame poverty and muscular dystrophy to learn Russian and English while still in Europe, and French and various secular subjects in Canada. With the encouragement of his older brother, Sack began writing poetry and drama in Hebrew and Yiddish. In 1907 Sack began a 50-year relationship with the Montreal Yiddish daily the *Keneder Adler*. He served as editor-in-chief in 1914–16, and again in 1922–28, and as associate editor from 1929 until his retirement. Sack wrote some 5,000 articles on subjects ranging from local news to literature, published for the most part in the *Adler*, although some of his articles also appeared elsewhere in the Yiddish and English press.

From his early days on the *Adler*, Sack was drawn to Canadian Jewish history, an area that was virtually untouched and in which he would become a pioneer. Drawing on material in archives, discussions and correspondence with informants, occasionally using sources in private hands that no longer survive, as well as consulting the Jewish and non-Jewish press, Sack produced a substantial survey of Canadian Jewish history in A.D. Hart's *The Jew in Canada* (1926). Another noteworthy achievement was the publication of the first volume of what was to be a two-volume study of Canadian Jewish history. It was published first in English in 1945 as *History of the Jews in Canada: From the Earliest Beginnings to the Present Day* and in Yiddish in 1948 as *Geshikhte fun Yidn in Kanade*. He never completed volume two, but the English translation of his unfinished manuscript has been published as *Canadian Jews – Early in this Century* (Montreal, 1975). Sack also served as a contributing editor for the *Universal Jewish Encyclopedia*. In his *History* and other historical writings, Sack could be overenthusiastic in his celebration of certain Jewish heroes, and he certainly wanted to demonstrate to Jews and non-Jews alike the positive contributions of Jews to Canadian history, even reaching back to New France when no Jews lived there. For all their shortcomings, Sack's publications, both his journalism and historical efforts, rank among the most important bodies of work in Canadian Jewish nonfiction.

BIBLIOGRAPHY: C.L. Fuks (ed.), *Hundert yor yidishe un hebreyishe literatur in Kanade* (1982), 118–21; R. Menkis, *Canadian Ethnic Studies*, 23:2 (1991), 24–38; R. Margolis, *B.G. Sack Articles in the Keneder Adler, 1910–1955*, manuscript in National Archives of Canadian Jewish Congress, Montreal; S. Hayes, Preface to *Canadian Jews-Early in this Century* (1975).

[Rebecca Margolis and Richard Menkis (2nd ed.)]

SACKLER, HARRY (1883–1974), U.S. Hebrew and Yiddish author. Born in Bohorodczany (Bogorodchany), Galicia, Sackler emigrated to the United States in 1902. An attorney by profession, he served as secretary of the *Kehillah* in New York City (1917–18); member of the staff of the Zionist Organization of America (1918–23); administrative secretary of the Jewish Education Association (1923–26); executive secretary of the Brooklyn Jewish Community Council (1940–44); and member of the executive staff of the Joint Distribution Committee (1945–55) in whose public relations office he later served. After his retirement in 1955 he devoted himself entirely to his writing.

The most eminent exponent of historicism in Hebrew letters in the United States, Sackler, a prolific writer, endeavored to fathom the mystery of Jewish existence. In story, novel, play, and essay he recreated a panorama of Jewry throughout the ages, and asserted, above all, the strength and the innocence of Judaism's spiritual leaders. His themes are drawn from remote times, e.g., the patriarchal period and the conquest of Jericho, and from recent times, e.g., the lot of the immigrant in the United States. Messianic and Ḥasidic innovations intrigued his imagination. He wrote mainly in Hebrew and Yiddish. *Festival at Meron* (1935), however, his best novel, was published in English. It depicts the period of the *Bar Kokhba revolt and is almost pure fiction, since the primary sources are sparse. Its central figure is the paradoxical and fascinating *Simeon b. Yoḥai.

Sackler's other works include the novels *U-Sefor ha-Kokhavim* (1961), about the patriarch Abraham; *Bein Ereẓ ve-Shamayim* (1964); *Sefer ha-Maḥazot* (1943), and *Masakh u-Masekhot*, various plays (1964); the autobiographical *Sof Pasuk* (1966); and, in Yiddish, *Dramen fun H. Sackler* (4 vols., 1925–28).

BIBLIOGRAPHY: E. Silberschlag, in: *Bitzaron*, 9 (1944), 249–56; A. Epstein, *Soferim Ivrim ba-Amerikah*, 2 (1952), 273–90; M. Ribalow, *Im ha-Kad el ha-Mabbu'a* (1950), 221–30. **ADD. BIBLIOGRAPHY:** Y. Kabakoff, "H. Sackler," in: *Biẓaron*, 65 (1974), 168–171; E. Silberschlag, "Harry Sackler – Mystical Rationalist on the Centenary of his Birth," in: *Jewish Book Annual*, 40 (1982), 105–199.

[Eisig Silberschlag]

SACKS, JONATHAN HENRY (1948–), chief rabbi of the British Commonwealth, from 1991. Born in London, Sacks combined brilliant success in secular studies with his Jewish education. He obtained a doctorate in moral philosophy at London University in 1981 and was ordained from both Jews' College and Yeshivat Etz Ḥayyim in London, in 1976. After lecturing in moral philosophy at Middlesex Polytechnic, he taught Jewish philosophy and Talmud at Jews' College from 1973 to 1982 and served as the college's principal from 1984 to 1990. Simultaneously he was rabbi of Golders Green Synagogue, 1978–82, and Marble Arch Synagogue, 1983–90. He edited *Tradition and Transition* (1986) and *Traditional Alternatives* (1989), which stemmed from a major conference on contemporary Judaism that he convened in 1989. It was followed in 1990 by a gathering focused on women in Judaism.

A frequent radio broadcaster, Rabbi Dr. Sacks delivered the prestigious Reith Lectures in 1990, subsequently published to wide acclaim as *The Persistence of Faith* (1991). He also published *Tradition in an Untraditional Age* (1991) and *Covenant and Crisis: Jewish Thought after the Holocaust* (1992). His broadcasts and publications established the new chief rabbi as a popular representative of Judaism, although this has not been matched by uniform acceptance among British Jews. He created controversy in 1985 with a pamphlet on Jewish attitudes to wealth and poverty, issued by the right-wing Social Affairs Unit.

His scope for initiative in office was limited by a financial crisis in the United Synagogue and the polarization of Anglo-

Jewry. He disappointed Progressive Jews by declining to participate in a radio discussion if a Reform rabbi was included. He inaugurated an unprecedented review of the position of women in the United Synagogue, but his decision to permit women's prayer groups only outside the synagogue, and without use of a Scroll of the Law, was considered a conservative compromise. Popular hostility to the recognition of homosexuals within communal life led him to sanction their exclusion from a fund-raising event, dismaying liberal opinion. These controversies overshadowed his achievements in promoting Jewish learning under the banner "Decade of Renewal."

[David Cesarani]

SACKUR, OTTO (1880–1914), German physical chemist, born Breslau. Sackur was professor of physical chemistry, University of Breslau (1911), and departmental head in the Kaiser Wilhelm Institute for Physical Chemistry, Berlin-Dahlem (1914). He died as a result of an explosion in his laboratory. He wrote *Die chemische Affinitaet und ihre Messung* (1908) and *Lehrbuch der Thermochemie und der Thermodynamik* (1912; *Text of Thermochemistry and Thermodynamics*, 1917).

SACRAMENTO, capital of California, 90 miles N.E. of San Francisco in the Central Valley; Jewish population (2005) 25,000. Jewish settlement in Sacramento began in 1849 with the arrival of merchants who catered to the local trade and supplied goods for resale during the Gold Rush. One such merchant, David Lubin, opened a clothing store with his half brother, Harris Weinstock, in 1874, which became the Weinstock-Lubin department store (now all Macy's). By 1851, Orthodox Congregation B'nai Israel, composed of Germans and Poles, owned and occupied the first synagogue building in the state. The early rabbis of the congregation conducted services locally and in interior mining towns. The members of the community founded men's and ladies' Hebrew benevolent societies. The B'nai B'rith Lodge, organized in 1859, is the second oldest in California. In 1895 Congregation B'nai Israel became Reform. In 1916, 150 Jewish families lived in Sacramento. About 1912 East European Jews organized the Mosaic Law Congregation, which became Conservative in about 1947. In 2005 Jews were engaged in all occupations and professions, well integrated into the social, cultural, and political activities in the city. The State Legislature meets annually and has a number of Jewish members; many Jews are employed in the state civil service. The existence of many high tech companies provides jobs for both local Jewry and itinerant Israelis.

Jewish life is organized around the synagogues, which include Reform, Conservative and Orthodox. Each congregation has a religious school, although the Jewish community high school, Yachad, is run by the Jewish Federation of the Sacramento Region. There is one Jewish day school, Shalom School; a Jewish social service agency, Jewish Family Service; and a Hillel for California State University, Sacramento, and the University of California, Davis. For the observant, there is a *mikveh*, a kosher store, and a number of kosher caterers. There is a Jewish cemetery, Home of Peace, in addition to designated areas in other cemeteries. In terms of cultural events, there is a Jewish film festival, Jewish food fair, and community-wide observances of Yom ha-Sho'ah, Hanukkah, Israel Independence Day, and other Jewish holidays. In addition to the Jewish Federation, there are local chapters of many national Jewish organizations.

In 1998, the Sacramento Jewish community experienced a major antisemitic attack when three area synagogues were firebombed in one night. As is customary in the United States, the general community turned out in full force and supported the Jewish community as more than 4,500 people attended a memorial gathering. The perpetrators were convicted and sentenced for their crimes, which included murdering a gay couple in addition to the arsons.

Prominent Jewish elected officials include former Sacramento Mayor Anne Rudin, former Assemblyman Darrell Steinberg, Sacramento City Councilman Steve Cohn, and Sacramento Municipal Utility District members Peter Keat and Bill Slaton.

[Robert E. Levinson / Kathleen Kahrl (2nd ed.)]

SACRIFICE.

IN THE BIBLE

In the Bible various verbs are used to designate the act of sacrifice. Two of them, שחט and טבח, are used for the slaughter of animals for both secular (cf. Gen. 43:16; Num. 11:22) and sacred purposes, while the verbs זבח (hence the name of the talmudic treatise *Zevaḥim*, dealing only with the slaughter of animals for sacrifice, as distinct from *Ḥullin*, which deals with slaughter for food), העלה and הקריב are only used for sacrifice. The last word, as does its cognate noun *korban*, expresses the idea "to bring near."

Although libation of wine and meal offerings played a prominent role in the rituals, the most important sacrifices were those of animals. The surrender of a living thing was a major factor in nearly every kind of sacrificial ritual; that life was being forfeited was signified by the extraction of an animal's blood: "For the life of the flesh is in the blood; and I have given it for you upon the altar to make atonement for your souls; for it is the blood that makes atonement, by reason of the life [that is in it]" (Lev. 17:11). The people were therefore forbidden to eat the blood (Lev. 17:10; also Gen. 9:4; Lev. 3:17; 7:26; Deut. 12:16, 23; 15:23), since life belonged only to God. The offering had to be the property of the person making the sacrifice (Lev. 1:2). Only domesticated animals raised for the purpose of providing food were acceptable, thus excluding both wild animals and work animals (contrast the allusions to slaying an ass at Mari, ARM II No. 37. 11.5–124). The sacrificial animal had to be without physical blemishes, which are defined and summarized in Leviticus 22:17–25 (see *Blemish). An animal could not be offered before it was eight days old (Lev. 22:26–30).

The sacrifices can be divided into various categories: propitiatory and dedicatory offerings, meal offerings, libation offerings, fellowship offerings, thanksgiving offerings, freewill offerings, and ordination offerings.

Propitiatory Offerings

Two sacrifices belong to this category, the sin offering (חַטָּאת, *ḥaṭṭa't*) and the guilt offering (אָשָׁם, *'asham*).

SIN OFFERINGS. The sin offering was suited to the rank and circumstance of the person offering it. The high priest brought a young bull (Lev. 4:3) as did the congregation (4:14), except, apparently, when a ritual infraction was involved (Num. 15:24). A *nasi* ("ruler") brought a male goat (Lev. 4:23), and a commoner a female goat (Lev. 4:28; Num. 15:27) or a lamb (Lev. 4:32). If he was poor, he could bring two turtledoves or two young pigeons (one of the pair served as a burnt offering; Lev. 5:7), or, in extreme cases, even merely a tenth of an *ephah* of fine flour (Lev. 5:11–13; cf. Heb. 9:22).

The offerer executed the symbolic act of laying his hand on the offering (Lev. 4:4, and passim), thus identifying it with himself. The animal was slain on the north side of the altar (Lev. 4:24, 29; 1:11). The high priest collected the blood of his own, or of the congregation's sacrifice, in order to sprinkle some before the veil and some on the horns of the incense altar there (Lev. 4:5–7, 16–18). On the Day of Atonement he took his and the people's sacrificial blood into the Holy of Holies (Lev. 16:14–15). From all the other animals the blood was applied to the horns of the altar of burnt offering (Lev. 4:18, et al.); that of the birds was sprinkled on the side of the altar (Lev. 5:9). The remaining blood was poured or drained out at the base of the altar (Lev. 4:7, and passim). The choice parts of the entrails – the fatty tissue (חֵלֶב, *ḥelev*) over and on the entrails, the two kidneys and their fat, and the appendage to the liver – were all consumed on the altar (Lev. 4:8–10, and passim). In the case of a bull for the priest or the people, the carcass and the remaining entrails were disposed of by burning outside the camp (Lev. 4:11–12, 21). This rule prevailed for the bull in the ordination rites of Aaron and his sons (Ex. 29:10–14; Lev. 8:14–17). Otherwise the priest received the edible flesh for food; it was to be eaten within the sacred precincts, and very strict rules of ritual purity governed its handling (Lev. 6:25–30; cf. 10:16–20).

A sin offering of one male goat was required at each of the sacred festivals: the New Moon (Num. 28:15), each day of Passover (Num. 25:22–24), Shavuot (Num. 28:30), Rosh Ha-Shanah (Num. 29:5), the Day of Atonement (Num. 29:11; besides the special sin offerings for that day), and each day of Sukkot (29:16, 19, and passim). The high priest brought a bull for himself and then offered one of the two goats on the *Day of Atonement. Rites of purification called for lesser sin offerings, lambs or birds, after childbirth (Lev. 12:6–8), leprosy (Lev. 14:12–14, 19, 22, 31), unclean issues and hemorrhages (Lev. 15:15, 30), or defilement during the period of a Nazirite vow (Num. 6:10–11; for the strictly individual cases requiring sin offerings see below).

GUILT OFFERINGS. The guilt offering (Lev. 5:14; 7:1–7) was a special kind of sin offering (cf. Lev. 5:7) required when someone had been denied his rightful due; in addition to the reparation of the amount defrauded, plus a fine of 20% (Lev. 5:16–24), the guilty person had to bring a guilt offering. The animal prescribed was usually a ram (Lev. 5:15, 18; 19:21); the leper after cleansing and the defiled Nazirite brought a male lamb (Lev. 14:12, 21; Num. 6:12). The offerer's part in the ritual was probably identical to his part in the sin offering, but the priest sprinkled the blood around the altar (Lev. 7:2). The choice entrails were consumed on the altar as usual (Lev. 7:3–5). In the case of the cleansed leper, some of the blood was then applied to the tip of his (the leper's) right ear, thumb, and big toe (Lev. 14:14). As with the sin offering, the animal went to the priest as food (Lev. 7:6–7; 14:13). Ritual infractions, such as eating unlawfully of the "holy things" (Lev. 5:14–19; 22:14), required payment of the sum (or commodity) that had rightfully belonged to God, plus one-fifth of the amount concerned, and the fine was given to the priest (Lev. 5:16; II Kings 12:17). The case of the leper can be assigned to this category, in that the Lord was deprived of the service due from the infected person so long as his disease kept him outside the pale of the ritually clean society (Lev. 14:12–18). Likewise, the Nazirite who became defiled during the course of his period of Nazirite separation had to bring a guilt offering in reparation for what he had pledged and not fulfilled (Num. 6:12).

On the social plane, swearing falsely with regard to violation of property rights through fraud could be atoned for only by the guilt offering and a 20% fine. Such acts included cheating in matters of deposit or security, robbery or oppression, denying the finding of lost property, or failing to testify (Lev. 5:20–25). Seduction of a betrothed slave girl (Lev. 19:20–22) was also a violation of property rights. In every case the guilty party had to confess his sin, make full restitution plus the fine of one-fifth, and offer the guilt offering. If the offended party was no longer alive and there were no surviving kinsmen, the payment went to the priests (Num. 5:5–10).

Dedicatory Offerings

The offerings in this category reflect the more universal idea of offering. The emphasis is on surrender of the gift to God (though only a handful of the meal offering was consumed on the altar). They represented the act of committal that should follow the repentance expressed by the sin and guilt offerings, thus opening the way to the fellowship or communal sacrifices that could follow.

Burnt Offerings

Burnt offerings (Heb. עוֹלָה *'olah*, "that which goes up") are referred to in Lev. 1:3–17; 6:1–6). The burnt offering consisted of a bull (Lev. 1:3–5), a sheep or goat (Lev. 1:10), or a bird (Lev. 1:14). The offerer brought the animal, laid his hand on it, and slaughtered it on the north side of the altar (Lev. 1:3–5, 11); the bird was then handed over to the priest (Lev. 1:15). The priest collected the blood, presented it before the Lord, and sprinkled it around the altar (Lev. 4:5, 11). In the case of a bird, he killed it by pinching the back of its neck and drained the blood out on the side of the altar (Lev. 1:15). There was emphasis on the flaying and dissection of the animal, the washing of its unclean parts, and the careful arrangement of all the pieces (except the crop and feathers of the bird) on the altar (Lev. 1:6–9, 12–13). The consumption of the whole was meant as *re'aḥ niḥo'aḥ* ("a pleasing odor") to the Lord. Only the hide was given to the priest (Lev. 7:8). The main administrative concern was for constant maintenance of the fire (thus the need for an uninterrupted supply of fuel) and the proper attire of the officiating priest during the ritual of renewing the fire each morning (Lev. 6:1–6). The burnt offerings were by far the most frequent sacrifices at the Israelite sanctuary.

The continual burnt offering (עוֹלָה, עוֹלַת תָּמִיד, *ʿolah, ʿolat (ha-) tamid*, or simply *ha-tamid*) was made twice daily – a male lamb morning and evening (Ex. 29:38–42; Num. 28:18, and passim). The entire procedure for the morning sacrifice is vividly described in the Mishnah (*Tamid*; see sacrifices during the Second Temple period below). Two additional lambs were offered each Sabbath (Num.28:9–10). No sin offerings accompanied these sacrifices. On the other hand, a sin offering of one goat was required along with the burnt offerings on the other holy days. On the New Moon, two young bulls, one ram, and seven male lambs were sacrificed (Num. 28:11–14). The same number of animals was required for each day of the Passover (Num. 28:19–24) and again on Shavuot (Num. 28:26–29). For Rosh Ha-Shanah and the Day of Atonement the standard was one bull, one ram, and seven lambs (Num. 29:2–4, 8), besides the special burnt offerings for the atonement ritual itself, which consisted of one ram for the high priest and one for the people (Lev. 16:3, 5, 24). The last of the annual festivals, Sukkot, was marked by a series of elaborate burnt offerings (plus one goat per day as a sin offering). On the first day the regulations called for 13 young bulls, two rams, and 14 male lambs (Num. 29:12–16). Each day thereafter the number of bulls was decreased by one until on the seventh day there were only seven (the number of rams and lambs remained the same; Num. 29:17–34). The eighth day saw a return to the amounts designated for Rosh Ha-Shanah and the Day of Atonement, i.e., one bull, one ram, and seven lambs (Num. 29:35–38; for the associated meal and drink offerings, cf. below). Various purification rituals also called for burnt offerings as well as sin offerings: after childbirth (Lev. 12:6–8), unclean issues (Lev. 15:14–15) and hemorrhages (Lev. 15:29–30), or after defilement during a Nazirite vow (Num. 6:10–11). Meal offerings were offered only for the cleansing from leprosy (Lev. 14:10, 19–20, 22, 31) and the completion of a Nazirite vow (Num. 6:14, 16). The burnt offerings, signifying complete surrender to God, were therefore associated with sin offerings in the process of atonement (as in the purification rites above; cf. also II Chron.).

Meal Offerings (Lev. 2; 6:7–16).

A regular concomitant of the animal sacrifices was the meal offering (מִנְחָה, *minḥah*). Outside the ritual codes the term *minḥah* could refer to any gift or offering, including animals (Gen. 4:3–5; Judg. 6:18; I Sam 2:17), but in prescriptive texts it signifies a concoction of fine flour (*solet*), oil (*shemen*), and frankincense (*levonah*). Its form could be baked loaves (*ḥallot*), wafers (*rekikim*), or morsels (*pittim*); the offerings of firstfruits (*bikkurim*) were to be "crushed new grain from fresh ears" (Lev. 2:14). No leaven or honey was permitted (Lev. 2:11) on the cakes being offered, though those commodities were acceptable as a firstfruits offering (Lev. 2:12), in which case they went to the priests. The offerer was responsible for bringing the prepared loaves or wafers, etc. to the sanctuary. The priest burned one handful on the altar as its "invocation" (*azkarah*; Lev. 2:2 et al.), and the rest was his to eat (Lev. 6:9; 7:9). When the priest offered a meal offering for himself, it was wholly burnt on the altar (Lev. 46:15–16).

The meal offering normally accompanied every burnt offering, especially those in the sacred calendar (Num. 28–29, passim). The quantities were fixed according to the animal being sacrificed: three-tenths of an *ephah* and one-half *hin* of oil for a bull, two-tenths *ephah* and one-third *hin* for a ram, and one-tenth *ephah* plus one-fourth *hin* for a lamb (Num. 15:2–10). Other joyous occasions included the cleansing of a leper (Lev. 14:10, 20, 21, 31) and the successful consummation of a Nazirite vow (Num. 6:15, 19). That no meal offering accompanied the rites for cleansing after childbirth (Lev. 12:6–8), unclean issues (Lev. 15:14–15), or hemorrhages (Lev. 15:29, 30) may be accounted for by the fact that sacrifices of a more somber nature were intentionally made without a meal offering. On the other hand, peace offerings were always accompanied by such offerings (Lev. 7:12–14; Num. 15:4). One of each from the cakes and wafers went to the priest. The rest was to be eaten with the flesh of the sacrificial animal. Wheat flour was used for the meal offering, the only exception being the one-tenth of an *ephah* of barley meal required in the jealousy ritual; it was to have no oil or frankincense (Num. 5:15, 18, 25–26). A very poor person could bring one-tenth of an *ephah* of fine flour, also without oil or frankincense, as a sin offering (Lev. 5:11–13).

Libation Offerings (נֶסֶךְ, nesekh)

A libation normally accompanied burnt and peace offerings (Num. 15:1–10); the standard was one-fourth of a *hin* of wine for a lamb, one-third for a ram, and one-half for a bull. The expression "strong drink" (שֵׁכָר; *shekhar*), used with reference to the drink offering (Num. 28:7), is apparently only a synonym for wine (Ex. 29:40). The libation was considered an additional "pleasing odor" offering (Num. 15:7). As with the burnt offering, all was expended and nothing was given to the priest; the entire libation was poured out in the sanctuary (Num. 28:7). Drink offerings are specifically mentioned with the daily offering (Ex. 29:40–41; Num. 28:7) and with the offerings for the Sabbath (Num. 28:9) and the New Moon (Num. 28:14). Likewise, reference is made to them in connection with the days following Shavuot (Num. 29:18, 21, 24, 27, 30, 33, 37). The same may hold true for the Passover, firstfruits, and Rosh Ha-Shanah rituals (Num. 28:16–29: 11; cf. Ezek. 45:17). A libation was specified for the Nazirite's concluding rites (Num. 6:17), but not for the cleansing of the leper (Lev. 14:10–20). It never accompanied a sin or guilt offering alone.

Fellowship Offerings

This category consists of those offerings that expressed a voluntary desire on the part of the offerer. They were not required (except in the case of the Nazirite – Num. 6:17 – and Shavuot – Lev. 23:19–20) by explicit regulations, but were permitted on condition that the offerer had met with the requirements of expiation and consecration. Burnt offerings could accompany these sacrifices as an additional expression of devotion (cf. above).

Peace Offerings

The term "peace offerings" (the singular שֶׁלֶם, *shelem*, occurs only in Amos 5:22, otherwise pl. שְׁלָמִים, *shelamim*; Lev. 3; 7:11–36). This is the basic sacrifice of all communal offerings; the others are simply different types of the peace offering. In terms of "holiness," i.e., restrictedness, they were not so strictly defined as those discussed above. Any domesticated animal from the herd or flock, male or female (Lev. 3:1, 6, 12), was permissible. The usual rules of freedom from blemishes were in force. Unleavened cakes were also stipulated, at least for the thanksgiving (Lev. 7:12–13) and Nazirite offerings (Num. 6:15, 17, 19; see below). The presentation and laying on of the hand were the same as for other offerings, but instead of the animal being slaughtered on the north side of the altar, it was done at the door of the sanctuary, i.e., to the outer court (Lev. 3:1–2, 7–8, 12–13). The priest collected the blood and threw it against the altar as with the burnt offering (Lev. 3:2, 8, 13). The choice entrails were burnt for a "pleasing odor" (Lev. 3:3–5, 6–11 (including the fat tail of the sheep), 14–16 (cf. Lev. 7:22–25); 7:30–31). Certain portions of the offering were allotted to the priest; he was permitted to eat it in any ritually clean place and to share it with his family (Lev. 7:14 and 30–36), whereas the other sacrifices had to be eaten in the sanctuary compound (Num. 18:10–11). He received one of the cakes and the breast as a wave offering (cf. below), and the right thigh as a "contribution" from the offerer. This latter is the so-called heave offering; the technical term used, *terumah* (תְּרוּמָה), though developed from the root signifying "to be high" and meaning "that which is lifted up," did not represent a special type of presentation ceremony (in contrast to the wave offering, below).

Every peace offering culminated in a communal meal. Except for the portions burned on the altar or assigned to the priest, the sacrificial animal was given to the offerer. He used it as food for a communal meal for himself, his family, and also the levite in his community (Deut. 12:12, 18–19). This had to take place at the divinely appointed sanctuary (Deut. 12:6–7, 11–12, 15–19, 26; cf. I Sam 1:3–4), and very strict rules of purity had to be observed by the participants (Lev. 7:19–21). The meat of a thanksgiving offering had to be eaten on the same day as the sacrifice (Lev. 7:15), while that of the votive or freewill offerings could be finished off on the next day (Lev. 7:16–18). Whatever was left over from either kind had to be burned within a specific time. The peace offering was only specified in three instances, i.e., in the celebration of Shavuot (Lev. 23:19–20), in the ritual for completion of a Nazirite vow (Num. 6:17–20), and at the installation of the priesthood (cf. the ordination offering, below). Other public ritual occasions included the inauguration of the Tent of Meeting (Lev. 9:8–21) and of the Temple (I Kings 8:63; II Chron. 7:7). National events that called forth the peace offering were: successful conclusion of a military campaign (I Sam 11:15), cessation of famine or pestilence (II Sam 24:25), acclamation of a candidate for kingship (I Kings 1:9, 19), or a time of national spiritual renewal (II Chron. 29:31–36). At the local level, they were sacrificed for the annual family reunion (I Sam 20:6) or other festive events, such as the harvesting of the firstfruits (I Sam. 9:11–13, 22–24; 16:4–5).

THANKSGIVING OFFERINGS (זֶבַח (הַ)תּוֹדָה, ZEVAḤ (HA-) TODAH). The most frequently mentioned type of peace offering was the thanksgiving offering (Lev. 7:12–13, 15; 22:29) for blessings already bestowed (Ps. 56:13–14; 107:22; 116:17; Jer. 33:11). In many contexts the term thanksgiving offering is used as the virtual synonym for peace offering (e.g., II Chron. 29:31; Jer. 17:26; cf. II Chron. 33:16).

Wave Offerings (תְּנוּפָה, tenufah)

The priest's portion of the peace offering (cf. above) was "waved" before the Lord as a special act signifying that it was His. Then it went to the officiant as his personal share. This is reminiscent of the presentation of the ceremonial food to the Mesopotamian deity, after which it was given to the king. The basic difference seems to be that there the deity was considered to have partaken of the food and added his "radiance" to it, while in Israel the priest ate the divine portion as God's representative, thus showing that the offerer's food was being shared by Him. The same technical term was applied to offerings other than the communal sacrifices: the precious metals given for construction of the sacred artifacts (Ex. 35:22; 38:29), the guilt offering of the cleansed leper (Lev. 14:12, 21, 24), the sheaf of firstfruits (Lev. 23:15), the two loaves at Shavuot (Lev. 23:17, 20), and the levites themselves (Num. 8:11, 13, 15, 21).

Votive Offerings (נֶדֶר, neder)

This was usually a peace offering, and the flesh could be eaten on the second day but not the third (Lev. 7:16–17); but it could also be a burnt offering (Lev. 22:17–20). A specific example was the vow of a Nazirite which was consummated by a peace offering (Num. 6:17–20). In the broadest sense the vow included any kind of offerings or gifts promised to the Lord (Num. 30, passim).

Freewill Offerings (נְדָבָה, nedavah)

The minimum offering that one could bring to the holy convocations that took place on the three Pilgrim Festivals (II Chron. 35:8; Ezra 3:5) was the freewill offering (Lev. 7:16; 22:18, 21, 23; Num. 15:3; 29:39; Deut. 12:6, 17). Like the votive offering, it could be a burnt as well as a peace offering (Lev.

22:17–24; Ezek. 46:12), and if it were the latter, the flesh could be consumed on the second day but had to be burned before the third (Lev. 7:16–17).

Ordination Offerings (מִלּוּאִים, millu'im)

The Septuagint interprets this sacrifice as one of "completion," or "perfection"; however, the same Hebrew term is used with regard to the "settings" of precious stones (Ex. 25:7; 35:9, 27; I Chron. 29:2), so perhaps the modern expression "installation" is more suitable. The ordination offering was intimately related to the concept of "filling the hand" (מִלֵּא יָד; *mille' yad*), which meant consecrating someone, or oneself, to divine service (Ex. 28:41; 29 passim; cf. Ex. 32:29, et al.), and it required a state of ritual purity and spiritual devotion (II Chron. 29:31). The details of the ritual are spelled out in a prescriptive (Ex. 29:19–34) and a narrative-descriptive (Lev. 8:22–32) text. Moses appears in the role of the officiant, since Aaron and his sons were obviously not qualified to serve in their own ordination. He brought the ram of consecration and the priests laid their hands on it. Then Moses slew it and handled the blood in a special manner. It was applied by him to the tip of the right ear, thumb, and big toe of Aaron and of each of his sons; then the rest was thrown about the altar. The waving of this offering was also unique in its execution: the choice entrails, three of the accompanying cakes, and the right thigh were all placed in the hands of the candidates for priesthood and waved before the Lord; then they were all consumed together on the altar as a "pleasing odor." Though Moses did not receive the thigh, he was granted the breast, which he waved himself and took as his portion. Finally, the anointing oil mixed with blood from the altar was sprinkled upon the candidates and their garments. They were thus prepared to eat the remaining flesh of the ordination offering, which they had to boil at the entrance to the sanctuary. Like the votive offering, none was allowed to remain to the following day.

IN BIBLICAL TRADITION AND HISTORY

Age of the Patriarchs

The terminology used with regard to the patriarchal age is that of the Torah as a whole; it is unlikely that the same words in Genesis mean something different in the other Books of Moses. Thus, Cain and Abel each brought a "gift" (*minḥah*; Gen. 4:4f.), which was usually of a cereal nature, as brought by Cain (Lev. 2, et al.), but could also refer to an animal offering (I Sam. 2:17; 26:19). Noah offered up a burnt offering (*'olah*; Gen. 8:20ff.) and the pleasing odor of the sacrifice is stressed. Job is also depicted as making burnt offerings periodically (Job 1:5) and for specific purposes (Job 42:7–9). The Patriarchs normally are said to have "called on the name of the Lord," e.g., Abraham (Gen. 12:8, 13–4; 21:33) and Isaac (Gen. 26:25). The association of this phrase with the building of an altar shows that it refers to the approach to God through sacrifice. With Jacob the naming of the specific altar is stressed (Gen. 33:20; 35:7). Once Abraham is said to have offered an *'olah* (Gen. 22:13), but Jacob (Gen. 31:54; 46:1) offered *zevaḥim*. The most unusual sacrifices described in Genesis are the covenant ritual with the divided carcasses (Gen. 15:4ff.) and the almost consummated sacrifice of Isaac (Gen. 22; see **Akedah*).

From Moses to Samuel

The covenant sacrifice inaugurating the relationship between the Lord and His people (Ex. 24:3–8) is not paralleled by specific rituals in the Mosaic liturgy. Burnt and peace offerings were first offered, and then the blood from them (not from a sin offering) was thrown half against the altar and half upon the people. In the land of Canaan the Israelites made sacrifices at various places, e.g., at Bochim (Judg. 2:1–5) and Ophrah (Judg. 6:24–26). The human sacrifice of Jephthah's daughter (Judg. 11:30–40) was hardly normative; instead it is pointed out as evidence of Israel's sad spiritual state at that time. The main center for sacrificial ritual was at Shiloh (I Sam 1:3ff.), where faithful Israelites came for an annual festive offering. That the ritual there was highly developed and detailed is proven by the explicit description of malpractice on the part of Eli's sons (I Sam 2:13–17) in taking their portion of the meat before the entrails were burned. However, Shiloh was not the only legitimate place of sacrifice; others included Beth-Shemesh (I Sam 6:14–15), Mizpah (I Sam 7:9), Ramah (I Sam. 7:17; 9:11–24), and Gilgal (I Sam. 10:8; 11:15; 13:9). Family and clan sacrifices were commonplace (I Sam. 16:2–5).

THE MONARCHY. Under Saul the main center of worship was evidently Nob (I Sam. 21:1ff.), though private offerings were made at Shiloh (II Sam. 15:12). Saul and David's families made peace offerings and held family feasts at the time of the New Moon (I Sam. 20:5, 24–25). David inaugurated a new cult center in Jerusalem at the threshing floor of Araunah (Ornan; I Chron. 21:23–26), to which he moved the Ark (II Sam. 6:17–18; I Chron. 16:2, 40). The horned altar had been located at Gibeon (II Chron. 1:3; I Chron. 21:29) but was soon moved to Jerusalem (I Chron. 22:1). David is credited with a complete reorganization of the ritual and the attendant personnel (I Chron. 23:28–31).

With the dedication of Solomon's Temple, Jerusalem became the main focus of sacrificial ritual (I Kings 8:5, 62–65; II Chron. 5:6; 7:4–8). Nevertheless, high places continued in use locally (I Kings 13:2ff.; 18:30–32; II Kings 14:4; 15:4, 35; et al.). Jeroboam I of the northern kingdom established shrines at Dan and Bethel (I Kings 12:28–29); besides these famous sites in Israel, Beer-Sheba may have enjoyed a similar status in Judah (Amos 5:5). Various references show that sacrifices were offered regularly at Jerusalem (II Chron. 13:10–11; 23:18; 24:14; II Kings 12:5–17; 16:13–15). Sacrificing on the high places was also tolerated in Judah (II Chron. 15:17; 20:33); Hezekiah abolished many of them (II Kings 18:4) and seems to have reconstituted the Temple as a sacrificial center (II Chron. 29:21–35; 32:12; cf. above). The high places returned under Manasseh (II Chron. 33:3–4) and were again removed by Josiah (II Chron. 34:3–13).

The Return to Zion

Offerings were reconstituted soon after the return (Ezra 3:2–7), and when Darius authorized the building of the Temple, he ordered that provisions be furnished for the cultus (Ezra 6:9–10). Henceforth, the Second Temple became the sole center for Judean sacrificial ritual (Ezra 6:17; 7:17; 8:35; 10:19; Neh. 10:33–37; 13:5, 9). At Elephantine in Egypt, a colony of Jewish mercenaries had maintained their own temple replete with meal offerings, incense, and burnt offerings. It had been standing long before 525 B.C.E., when Cambyses invaded Egypt, and was destroyed by jealous opponents in 410. In 407 the priest and his colleagues wrote to Bagohi, the governor of Judah, as well as to Helaiah and Shelemiah, the sons of Sanballat, governor of Samaria, asking them to exert their influence toward having the ruined temple rebuilt. Though they yearn for restoration of the entire sacrificial cultus, the reply suggests that they apply to Arsames for resumption of the meal offerings and the incense, which they did (Pritchard, Texts, 492). This tendency to permit worship at local shrines, but without animal sacrifice, may be reflected in the fact that the Jewish temple at Lachish (so-called Solar Shrine) had no altar for burnt offerings, while its pre-Exilic counterpart at Arad did. The Lachish temple was evidently built in the post-Exilic period and refurbished in the Hellenistic period (probably under John Hyrcanus, late second century B.C.E.; see also Temple of *Onias).

The Prophetic and Wisdom Literature

The prophets of the First Temple period often spoke out against sacrificial ritual (Amos 5:21–27; Hos. 6:6; Micah 6:6–8; Isa. 1:11–17; Jer. 6:20; 7:21–22). Righteous and just behavior, along with obedience to the Lord, is contrasted with the conduct of rituals unaccompanied by proper ethical and moral attitudes (Amos 5:24; Micah 6:8; Isa. 1:16–17; Jer. 7:23). It has thus been assumed by many scholars that the prophets condemned all sacrificial rituals. De Vaux has shown the absurdity of such a conclusion since Isaiah 1:15 also condemns prayer. No one holds that the prophets rejected prayer; it was prayer offered without the proper moral commitment that was being denounced; the same holds true for the oracles against formal rituals. Similar allusions in the Psalms, which might be taken as a complete rejection of sacrifice (e.g., 40:7–8; 50:8–15), actually express the same concern for inner attitude as the prophets. The wisdom literature sometimes reflects the same concern for moral and ethical values over empty sacerdotal acts (Prov. 15:8; 21:3, 27).

Certain other statements by Amos (5:25) and Jeremiah (7:22) have been taken to mean that the prophets knew nothing of a ritual practice followed in the wilderness experience of Israel. De Vaux has noted that Jeremiah clearly knew Deuteronomy 12:6–14 and regarded it as the Law of Moses. The prophetic oracles against sacrifice in the desert are really saying that the original Israelite sacrificial system was not meant to be the empty, hypocritical formalism practiced by their contemporaries. The demand by Hosea for "mercy and not sacrifice… knowledge of God more than burnt offerings" (Hos. 6:6; cf. Matt. 9:13; 12:7) is surely to be taken as relative, a statement of priorities (cf. also 1 Sam. 15:22). The inner attitude was prerequisite to any valid ritual expression (Isa. 29:13). Foreign elements that had penetrated the Israelite sacrificial system were, of course, roundly condemned by the prophets. Such was especially the case with Israel (Amos 4:5; Hos. 2:13–15; 4:11–13; 13:2) but also in Judah (Jer. 7:17–18; Ezek. 8; et al.).

[Anson Rainey]

SECOND TEMPLE PERIOD

During the Second Temple period sacrifices were offered only in the Temple in Jerusalem, with the sole exception of the Temple of Onias in Egypt. The order of the sacrificial service in general followed that of the Bible. The only rigidly significant addition to the sacrificial order given in the Bible was the water libation on Sukkot (see below). After the sacrificial system came to an end with the destruction of the Temple, the rabbis saw in the theoretical study of the sacrifices a substitute for the actual offerings (Ta'an. 27b; Men. 110a) and devoted themselves to that study. Most of the discussion in the Mishnah and Talmud is post-Temple and is therefore largely academic. However, in the Talmud, particularly in tractate *Tamid*, full details of the sacrificial service are preserved. The fifth chapter of tractate *Zevaḥim* gives every detail of the places where the various sacrifices were slaughtered and eaten and the time allotted for their consumption. The rabbis divided the sacrifices into two categories: one was: *kodshei kodashim* (the "most holy"), which are so termed in the Bible (Ex. 30:10); for the others they coined the term *kodashim kalim* ("those of lesser sanctity").

The following is a detailed account of the sacrificial system and order of service. The high points of the sacrificial service were the two daily offerings, the *tamid*, one at daybreak and the other in the afternoon, which began and concluded each day's sacrifices. All other individual and public sacrifices were brought in between them. Although the Pentateuch does not mention any prayers which accompanied the sacrifices, liturgical additions were made during the Second Temple period. These included petitions, blessings, and readings from the Pentateuch. After the incense was offered, the priests recited the *priestly blessing as a single sentence (Tam. 7:2). Daily, the priests recited the **Shema* and its blessings, the Ten Commandments, and the *Avodah* and *Sim Shalom* blessings from the **Amidah*. On the Sabbath they added a blessing for the incoming watch of priests, the outgoing saying to the incoming, "May He who has caused His name to dwell in this house cause to dwell among you love, brotherhood, peace, and friendship" (Tam. 5:1; Ber. 12a). The levites played musical instruments and recited the daily psalm during the service (Tam. 7:4; Maim. Yad, Keli ha-Mikdash, 3:4–5). After the sacrifices, the representative *ma'amad* of Israelites prayed and read from the Pentateuch (see *Mishmarot and Ma'amadot). On the Day of Atonement, the high priest read from the Torah, concluding with eight benedictions (Yoma 7:1). On the Sabbath, festivals, and the New Moon, the additional **Musaf* sacrifice was also offered. There were also specific services for the various holidays such as the **omer* on Passover, the two wave-loaves of Shavuot, and the water-drawing ceremony of Sukkot.

Daily Service

The service began immediately after dawn, when the herald announced that "The priests should prepare for the service, the levites for song, and the Israelites for the *ma'amad*" (TJ, Shek. 5:2, 48d). The first part of the service was the removal of ashes from the altar, since sacrificial meat was consumed on it all night. Those priests desiring to do this rose early and immersed themselves before the superintendent came. He usually came around dawn, and lots were then drawn to choose the priest to remove the ashes (see *Lots). The superintendent then took the key, opened the small door, and went from the Fire Chamber into the Temple court. The priests went in after him, carrying two lighted torches. They divided into two groups, one of which went along the portico to the east, while the other went along it to the west. They made an inspection to see whether all the vessels were in order, finally arriving at the place where the griddle cakes (Lev. 6:12–15) were made. There the two groups met and verified that all was in place. They then appointed the griddle cake maker to make the cakes, and instructed the priest who had won the lottery exactly how he was to clear away the ashes. When he had completed this task, the other priests hastened to wash their hands and feet in the laver. They then went up to the top of the altar, where they rearranged the unconsumed limbs and pieces of fat on special large blocks of wood which were brought up to the altar for that purpose. They then kindled the fire, and descended and went to the Chamber of Hewn Stone (Tam. 1:2–4; 2:1–5).

Lots were then cast to decide which of them should carry out the various duties associated with the sacrifice. A priest stationed on a roof would announce that the first light of dawn had illumined the whole of the sky as far as Hebron. The silver and gold vessels for the day's service were then arranged, and the sacrificial lamb which had been examined on the previous evening was again inspected by torchlight. They to whom it fell to clear the inner incense altar of ashes and to trim the candlesticks now proceeded toward the porch. The priest selected for slaughtering the *tamid* did not commence his duties before he heard the great gate that led to the sanctuary being opened. The priest who cleared the inner altar scooped up the ash in his fists and deposited it inside the ash-bin. He then swept up what was left and departed. The priest who cleaned the candlesticks entered, and if he found the two western lights burning, he trimmed the rest, leaving these two burning. If he found that they had been extinguished, he trimmed them and kindled them from those that were still alight, and then trimmed the rest (but see Maim. Yad, Temidin u-Musafin 3:13 and Rabad ad loc.). Meanwhile the lamb was slaughtered and its blood sprinkled against the altar. The portions of the sacrifice were then prepared for the altar and left on the lower half of the ascent of the altar, together with the fine flour for the meal offering, the griddle cake offering of the high priest, and the wine for the drink offering. The priests then came down to the Chamber of Hewn Stone to recite prayers (Tam. 3:1–9; 4:1–3).

At this point the superintendent told them to pronounce one blessing, either the blessing for light or the *Ahavah Rabbah* (Ber. 11b). It was followed by the Ten Commandments, the three portions of the *Shema*, and three benedictions. These were: "True and Firm," *Avodah*, and the concluding *Sim Shalom* blessing of the *Amidah* (Tam. 5:1). On the Sabbath a fourth blessing was added for the incoming watch of priests. On the completion of the prayers, those who had never yet offered the incense cast lots for this privilege. All the priests were, however, permitted to cast lots for the right to take the sacrificial portions from the ramp (*kevesh*) to the altar. The incense was then placed in the sanctuary by the designated priest, assisted by another priest who brought glowing coals from the outer altar to the inner altar for this offering. Afterward they struck with the *magrefah*, a gong shaped like a shovel, between the porch and the altar. It caused a reverberation so loud "that it drowned conversation in Jerusalem." Priests would thus know that their colleagues were about to prostrate themselves and would rush to join them. Similarly, levites would hasten to join their fellow levites in the singing. All ritually unclean priests were made to stand at the eastern gate to show that it was not out of idleness that they were not serving in the Temple (Tam. 5:1–6; Rosh to 5:6).

Those who had been chosen to clear the inner altar and the candlestick led the procession back to the sanctuary. The ash-bin was removed, and only the westernmost lamp of the candlestick was left burning for the day, since from it all the lights were later kindled in the evening. The coals were then spread on the inner altar and the incense was scattered and burned by the designated priests. As each priest finished his duty, he prostrated himself and left the sanctuary. The high priest next went in and prostrated himself, followed by the other priests (Tam. 6:1–3; 7:1). While the incense was being offered, the *ma'amad* of Israelites present in the Temple also gathered together to pray. Apparently Jews outside the Temple also prayed at this time (cf. Judith 9:1).

All the priests who had completed their allotted tasks came and stood on the steps of the porch. They then pronounced the priestly blessing over the people as a single benediction, enunciating the ineffable Name of God. All apart from the high priest raised their hands above their heads during the blessing. The high priest did not raise his hands above the plate (*ẓiẓ*) on his forehead, since the Name of God was inscribed on it (Tam. 7:2; Sot. 7:6). When those assembled in the Temple heard the Divine Name pronounced, they prostrated themselves (Ecclus. 50:21; for the practice of praying daily in the Temple see Lam. R. to 3:9, no. 3). After this benediction, the limbs were lifted up to the top of the altar and thrown onto its fire, the meal offering was sacrificed, and the wine offering was poured out upon the appropriate places of the altar. Before the libation of the wine, a *teki'ah*, *teru'ah*, and *teki'ah* (see *Shofar*) were sounded on the trumpets. During the libation, the cymbals were struck, and the levites chanted the daily psalm. At stated intervals in the psalm, a *teki'ah* was sounded and the public prostrated themselves. With the conclusion of the psalm, the service of the morning *tamid* was completed (Tam. 7:3–4; Suk. 5:5).

The offering of individual sacrifices was completed by half past the eighth hour of daylight, and the sacrifice of the concluding afternoon *tamid* then took place. It was slaughtered and offered up an hour later (Pes. 5:1). The ritual of the afternoon *tamid* resembled that of the morning lamb, except that the wood on the altar was not rearranged and the priestly blessing was not recited. Two new logs of wood were brought up by two priests to reinforce the flames (Yoma 26b). Oil was also added to the candlestick, and all seven lamps were kindled. Following the sacrifice of the afternoon *tamid*, the gates to the sanctuary and to the priestly court were closed. Nonetheless, a few priests still entered the court during the night, so that they could place the limbs from the day's sacrifices on the altar and continue to add wood to its fire (cf. Zev. 9:6; Ber. 1:1).

Sabbath Service

The sacrifices of private individuals were not offered on the Sabbath, but all work connected with the public offerings was permitted. In addition to the two *tamid* offerings, a *Musaf* sacrifice was also brought and the *shewbread set in order. After the *Musaf*, the watches of the priests were changed, although the new watch was already present for the morning *tamid* when it was blessed by the outgoing group of priests (Tosef., Suk. 4:24–25). A section of the Song of *Ha'azinu* (Deut. 32:1–43), which was divided into six portions, was recited while the *Musaf* was brought (RH 31a). The service of the new group of priests began with their arranging the new shewbread. Eight priests entered the sanctuary, two carrying the two rows of shewbread and two the two dishes of frankincense which accompanied the loaves. The other four removed the shewbread and frankincense of the previous week. Those who brought them in stood at the north side facing the south, and those who removed them stood at the south side facing north. They removed them in such a way that always one handbreadth of one overlay a handbreadth of the other, thus fulfilling "Before me always" (Ex. 25:30; Men. 11:7).

The Pilgrim Festivals

On the Pilgrim Festivals, the order of the Temple service was changed to accommodate the vast number of sacrifices which were brought. In addition to the festival's *Musaf* offering, there were also the festival peace offerings and whole offerings of those who made the pilgrimage to Jerusalem (Beẓah 2:4). In contrast to the daily practice of removing the ashes from the outer altar after dawn, this altar was already cleaned before midnight. The gates to the Temple court were opened at midnight, and by dawn the courtyard was filled with Israelites (Yoma 1:8; Jos., Ant., 18:29). The gates and curtains leading to the sanctuary were also left open, so that the pilgrims could see the Temple vessels (Yoma 54a; Jos., Ant., 3:128). For these festivals, priests from all parts of Ereẓ Israel came to the Temple, and they all shared equally in the holiday's sacrifices and in the division of the shewbread (Suk. 5:7).

PASSOVER. The paschal lamb was unique in that it was offered by groups of Israelites rather than individuals. Between ten and twenty persons jointly brought one lamb (Pes. 64b; Jos., Wars, 6:425). To accommodate the large number of paschal sacrifices, the daily afternoon *tamid* on the eve of Passover was slaughtered at half after the seventh hour and offered up an hour later. After this, the Passover offering was brought (Pes. 5:1), and it was slaughtered in three groups. When the first group entered and filled the Temple court, its gates were closed and the *shofar* was sounded. The priests stood in rows and in their hands were basins of silver and gold. The basins were not mixed, each row being wholly silver or wholly gold. The Israelites slaughtered their own offerings and the priests caught the blood. The priest passed the basins filled with blood to fellow priests, each receiving a full basin and giving back an empty one. The priest nearest to the altar tossed the blood in one motion against the base of the altar. When the first group left, the second group came in; and when the second group was finished the third group came in. The rite was repeated for each group, and during the entire time *Hallel* was chanted by the levites (Pes. 5:5–7). After the lamb was roasted, it was eaten after nightfall by the company which brought it as part of the Passover *seder* (Pes. 10:1–9). The size of the throng that participated in this ritual is emphasized by the Talmud, which relates that King Agrippa once took a census of the Jewish people. At his request, the high priest took a kidney from each paschal lamb, and 600,000 pairs of kidneys were counted, despite the fact that those who were unclean and on a distant journey were excluded from participating. Since there was not a single paschal lamb for which a minimum of ten people had not registered, they called it "the Passover of the dense throngs" (Pes. 64b). Josephus estimated from the number of lambs offered on the Passover before the outbreak of the Jewish War (65 C.E.) that more than 3,000,000 Jews gathered in Jerusalem for that Passover festival (Jos., Wars 2:280; cf. Wars 6:425).

The evening after the first day of Passover, preparations began for the bringing of the *Omer* on the next day. This was in accordance with the view of the Pharisees that "from the morrow after the day of rest" (Lev. 23:15) means after the first day of Passover, and not after the Sabbath that falls during Passover as the Sadducees advocated (Men. 65b–66a). The rabbis therefore insisted that the *omer* be reaped with much display to indicate that the Sadducees were mistaken in their interpretation (Men. 10:3). After the barley was reaped that evening, it was placed in baskets and brought to the Temple court. There it was prepared as fine flour, and the next day it was mixed together with oil and frankincense. A handful was removed by the officiating priest and burned on the altar, and the remainder was eaten by the priests. Soon after the *omer* was offered, the markets of Jerusalem were full of meal and parched corn of the new produce, though the sages disapproved (Men. 10:4–5).

SHAVUOT. The two leavened wave-loaves which were brought on Shavuot (Lev. 23:16–20) were divided among all the priests present in the Temple and not confined to those of the weekly watch. The rabbis added six days to the Shavuot celebration during which the Jewish pilgrims could offer their holiday sacrifices (Ḥag. 17a–b). Beginning with this holiday, *first fruits (*bikkurim*) were brought to the Temple. The *bikkurim* procession was led by an ox which was later sacrificed as a peace offering (Bik. 3:3).

SUKKOT. Due to the large number of the Sukkot sacrifices (Num. 29:12–35), this holiday comprised eight of the 12 annual days on which the entire *Hallel* was recited and the flute played before the altar (Ar. 2:3; TJ, Suk. 5:1, 55a). On each of the seven days of the festival, a libation of water was made together with the libation of wine at the morning service (Suk. 4:1). The water was drawn in a golden flagon holding three *logs* from the pool of Siloam. It was carried to the water gate of the Temple where a *teki'ah*, *teru'ah*, and *teki'ah* were sounded on the *shofar*. The officiating priest then took it up the ramp of the altar and turned to his left, where there were two silver bowls. One was for water and the other was for wine, and both libations were poured out simultaneously (Suk. 4:9). Since this water libation is not mentioned in the Bible, the rabbis declared that it was a Mosaic law from Sinai (Zev. 110b) or an institution of the prophets (TJ, Suk. 4:1, 54b), and found homiletical justification for it in the Pentateuch itself (Shab. 103b). The water libation was offered at this time of the year "in order that the new rainy season would be blessed" (RH 16a). The Sadducees strongly opposed this innovation and totally denied its validity. The refusal of King Alexander *Yannai, Sadducean high priest (107–76 B.C.E.), to make the libation caused a bloody riot in the Temple. When he contemptuously poured the water on his feet, all those present in the Temple area pelted him with their *etrogim* (Suk. 48b; Jos., Ant., 13:372). Subsequently, the rabbis required the officiating priest to raise his hand when he poured out the water at the libation, so that it could be observed that he was properly discharging the precept (Suk. 4:9).

The New Year

The sacrifices offered on New Year followed the biblical description (Num. 29:2–6). The special New Year sacrifices were offered in addition to those of the New Moon and the two daily *tamid* sacrifices.

The Day of Atonement

For the Temple ritual on the Day of Atonement, see **Avodah*.

Sacrifices from Non-Jews

Sacrifices could be accepted from gentiles (Lev. 22:25; I Kings 8:41–43), and this became common during the Second Temple period. The rabbis established as the rule that "what is vowed or freely offered is accepted of them, but what is not vowed or freely offered is not accepted of them" (Shek. 1:5). It was also ordained that, if a gentile sent a whole offering from a distant region without sending the accompanying drink offering, the latter was offered at the expense of communal funds (Shek. 7:6). Josephus records numerous instances of non-Jews sacrificing upon the altar (e.g., Jos., Ant., 13:242; 16:14), and declared that this sacred spot was "reverenced by all mankind" (Jos., Wars, 5:17). In addition to the sacrifices sent by gentiles, offerings were also made for the well-being of the non-Jewish rulers (e.g., Ezra 6:10; I Macc. 7:33). Sacrifices were later offered daily for the Roman emperor (Jos., Wars, 2:197), and at times the emperor himself contributed toward the cost of these sacrifices (Philo, *On the Embassy to Gaius*, 157). The destruction of Jerusalem was attributed to the refusal of the rabbis to accept an offering which contained a slight blemish, although it had been sent by the Roman emperor (Git. 56a). The revolt against Rome was signaled by the refusal of those who officiated in the Temple to sacrifice on behalf of the emperor (Jos., Wars, 2:409).

Cessation of Sacrifice

The importance which the Jews attached to sacrifice is evidenced by the fact that they continued to offer the daily *tamid* sacrifice throughout almost the entire period of the siege of Jerusalem. Despite the hardship and privations of this period and the famine which raged, the Temple service continued until the walls of the city were breached by the Romans on the 17th of Tammuz. The *tamid* sacrifice then had to be discontinued due to the lack of lambs and qualified priests within the Temple precincts (Ta'an. 4:6; Jos., Wars, 6:94). Three weeks later, on the Ninth of *Av, the Temple was destroyed by the Romans and the sacrificial system came to an end. (With regard to the question of the possibility of the reintroduction of sacrifice, and particularly the offering of the paschal lamb even after the destruction of the Temple, see *Temple Mount.)

LATER INTERPRETATIONS

Throughout the ages attempts have been made to find a spiritual meaning for the sacrificial system. The proposed explanations can be divided into three categories: the symbolic, juridical, and rational.

Symbolic

Philo devoted a treatise to the subject (De Victimis; see Spec. 1:112–256). He pointed out that only domesticated animals and the most gentle birds were suitable for sacrifice and that they had to be free of blemish, which he took as a symbol that the offerers must also be wholesome in body and soul. The Jew had to approach the altar with his soul purged of its passions and viciousness if the sacrifice was to be acceptable (Spec. 1:166/167, 257). The wicked would be rejected, even if they offered hundreds of sacrifices (Spec. 1:271). The rabbis stated that the sacrificial statutes indicated that God is with the persecuted. The ox is pursued by the lion, the goat by the leopard, and the lamb by the wolf. Therefore God commanded, "Do not offer those that persecute, but rather those that are persecuted" (Lev. R. 27:5). The requirement that fowl be offered with their feathers symbolized that a poor man was not to be despised. Therefore his offering was placed on the altar in its full adornment, despite the nauseating odor normally arising from the burning of feathers (Lev. R. 3:5). Salt, an indispensable ingredient of sacrifice, was symbolic of the moral effect of suffering, which purifies man and causes sins to be forgiven (Ber. 5a). Judah Halevi declared that the fire on the altar was kindled by the will of God, as a sign that the people found favor in His sight and that He was accepting their hospitality and offerings (Kuzari 2:26). Samson Raphael Hirsch explained that the Pentateuch required the person to lay his hands upon the head of the sacrifice to indicate that the "hands" that have become morally weakened "support" themselves on the resolution of the future betterment that is expressed by the offering (his commentary to Lev. 1:4). David Hoffmann declared that sacrifices are symbols of man's gratitude to God and his dependence on Him, of the absolute devotion man owes to God, as well as of man's confidence in Him (Introd. to commentary on Lev. (Heb. ed.), 64–67).

Juridical

The juridical approach is put forward by Ibn Ezra (commentary to Lev. 1:1) and to some extent by Naḥmanides (commentary to Lev. 1:9). According to them, the sinner's life is forfeit to God, but by a gracious provision he is permitted to substitute a faultless victim. His guilt is transferred to the offering by the symbolic act of placing his hands on the victim. When observing the pouring out of the blood and the burning of the sacrifice, the person should acknowledge that, were it not for divine grace, he should be the victim, expiating his sin with his own blood and limbs (Naḥmanides to Lev. 1:9). Many Christian exegetes adopted this explanation and on it built the whole theological foundation of their Church.

Rational

Quite different is the rational view of sacrifice advocated by Maimonides. He rejected the symbolist position which discovered reasons for the details of the various sacrifices. Those who trouble themselves to discover why one offering should be a lamb, while another is a ram, are "void of sense; they do not remove any difficulties, but rather increase them" (Guide, 3:26). Maimonides held that the sacrificial service was not really of Jewish origin. It was the universal custom among all peoples at the time of Moses to worship by means of sacrifices. Since the Israelites had been brought up in this atmosphere, God realized that they could not immediately completely abandon sacrifice. He therefore limited its application by confining it to one place in the world, with the ultimate intention of weaning them from the debased religious rituals of their idolatrous neighbors. The new service stressed the existence and unity of God, "without deterring or confusing the minds of the people by the abolition of the service to which they were accustomed and which alone was familiar to them." Maimonides cited the experience of Israel, led not by the shorter way, but by the circuitous route through the land of the Philistines (Ex. 13:17). Likewise, through a circuitous road, Israel was to be led gradually and slowly to a deeper perception of religion and divine worship (Guide, 3:32). He gives the added remarkable parallel that it would be equally incomprehensible for anyone in his generation to suggest that prayer could be offered in thought alone, without the recitation of words.

Abrabanel strengthened the arguments for Maimonides' viewpoint. He explained that only within this framework can it be understood why the Torah limited the sacrificial service to one locality, while prayers may be recited in all places (Introd. to his commentary on Lev., 2d). Abrabanel cites a Midrash which states that the Hebrews had become accustomed to idolatrous sacrifices while in Egypt. To wean them from these idolatrous practices, God commanded, while tolerating the sacrifices, that they be offered in one central sanctuary. This was illustrated by the parable of a king who observed that his son loved to eat forbidden foods. The king then decided to serve him these foods daily, so that he would ultimately lose his desire for them and forego his evil habits (Lev. R. 22:8). D. Hoffmann later proposed a different explanation for this Midrash, declaring that the king insisted that the son was to eat exclusively at his table, so that he would only be served proper food and thus curb his appetite for forbidden foodstuffs (Introd. to commentary on Lev., p. 61).

With the destruction of the Temple and the automatic cessation of the sacrificial system, it was laid down that prayer took the place of the sacrifices. The *Shaḥarit* service was regarded as taking the place of the morning *tamid* and the *Minḥah* service, the afternoon *tamid*. On all occasions when an additional offering was brought, the *Musaf* prayer was introduced (Ber. 4:1, 7; 26b). One of the rabbis later declared that prayer was even more efficacious than offerings (Ber. 32b). Nevertheless, the rabbis never ceased to look forward to the rebuilding of the Temple and the reinstitution of sacrifice during the messianic era. An additional supplication was introduced at the end of the *Amidah* requesting "that the Temple be speedily rebuilt in our days... And there we will serve Thee with awe... Then shall the offering of Judah and Jerusalem be pleasant unto the Lord, as in the days of old, and as in ancient years" (Hertz Prayer Book, 157).

The Reform movement entirely abolished or modified the *Musaf* service and other liturgical references to sacrifice, since Reform Judaism no longer anticipated the restoration of this service. Some Conservative congregations also have rephrased references to the sacrifices, so that they indicate solely past events without implying any hope for the future restoration of sacrifice. Orthodox Jews nevertheless continue to pray for its reinstitution. Joseph *Hertz declared:

> Moderns do not always realize the genuine hold that the sacrificial service had upon the affections of the people in ancient Israel. The Central Sanctuary was the axis round which the national life revolved. The people loved the Temple, its pomp and ceremony, the music and song of the levites and the ministrations of the priests, the high priest as he stood and blessed the

> prostrate worshippers amid profound silence on the Atonement Day (Hertz Prayer Book, 33–34).

The position of Orthodoxy was thus stated by Michael *Friedlaender:

> The revival of the sacrificial service must, likewise, be sanctioned by the divine voice of a prophet. The mere acquisition of the Temple mount or Palestine by Jews, whether by war or political combinations, could not justify the revival. It is only the return of the Jews to Palestine, and the rebuilding of the Temple by divine command and by divine intervention, that will be followed by the restoration of the sacrificial service (*The Jewish Religion* (1913), 417; cf. Maim. Yad, Melakhim, 11:4).

[Aaron Rothkoff]

In the Kabbalah

The kabbalistic interpretation of the sacrifices is usually associated with the esoteric exposition of the tabernacle and the Temple, whose every detail has symbolic significance in the realm of the *Sefirot*, and with the connection between the individual Jew and the Jewish people as a whole and the divine world, both the good powers and the evil. In the Sefer ha-*Bahir, the earliest text of the Kabbalah, the sacrifices are explained as the process which symbolically unites the priest performing the sacrifices with the divine world. The Hebrew term for sacrifice, *korban*, is interpreted as coming from the root *karev* – to bring together, to unite. The ideas of the *Bahir* were explained and details added by *Isaac the Blind and developed by his pupil *Ezra b. Solomon and by *Azriel of Gerona. The mystical conception of the nature and purpose of sacrifice explains the act as a process which brings about the dynamic union of the divine powers, the *Sefirot*, and restores the soul of man and other created elements to their place of origin, that is to the *Sefirah* of which they had formed a part. The most detailed exposition of the symbolic meaning of the sacrifices is to be found in the *Zohar and in the writings of the subsequent kabbalists. It is possible that their detailed treatment of this subject had a polemical purpose – to oppose Maimonides' conception of sacrifice, which denied its intrinsic value and held that the practice originated in pagan customs which God conceded to the Jews after the exodus from Egypt, because they had not reached a high enough religious level to enable them to worship Him in a spiritual manner. The kabbalists, from the *Bahir* to the Zohar and onward, interpreted the sacrifices as spiritual worship of God in which material means are employed as symbols.

In the Zohar the unifying effect of the sacrifice is explained in three ways: it joins the upper and lower worlds, bringing together the believer and God Himself; it unites the *Sefirot Ḥokhmah* and *Binah* (the "father" and "mother"); and, most important, it brings about the union of masculine and feminine principles in the divine world – the *Shekhinah*, that is the *Sefirah Malkhut*, and her husband, the *Sefirah Tiferet*. This symbolic process is interpreted in great detail in the Zohar, especially regarding the sacrifices on the Day of Atonement. The material nature of the sacrifice, the use and slaughter of animals, is explained as a symbolic atonement for material sins. Because the evil powers in man are embedded in his flesh and blood, flesh and blood have to be sacrificed. More than that, the sacrifice frees the spirit of the animal, enabling it to rise to its divine root; the animals are symbolically connected with the animals described by Ezekiel in the throne-chariot, the *Merkabah. According to the Zohar and later kabbalists, the sacrifices are also significant in the cosmic fight between good and evil in the divine world. In one place it is stated that the flesh of the sacrifice is, in fact, intended for Satan, and God receives only the *kavvanah*, the religious intention of the person who gives the sacrifice. Most kabbalists consider that at least part of the sacrifice is given to the evil power, the *sitra aḥra*, to placate it. Other sacrifices are intended solely for the *sitra aḥra*, especially the scapegoat on the Day of Atonement. Its purpose is to drive the evil powers away from the holy union between Israel and God which is achieved on this day; it may also turn the Satan's enmity toward Israel into a more positive attitude and thus help achieve this union.

[Joseph Dan]

BIBLIOGRAPHY: IN THE BIBLE: J.H. Kurtz, *Sacrificial Worship of the Old Testament* (1863); C.F. Keil, *Manual of Biblical Archaeology*, 1 (1887), 246–482; 2 (1887), 1–101; A. Cave, *The Scriptural Doctrine of Sacrifice* (1890); G.B. Gray, *Sacrifice in the Old Testament* (1924); W.T. Mc-Cree, in: JBL, 45 (1926), 120–8; W.R. Smith, *The Religion of the Semites* (1927^3); E.O. James, *The Origins of Sacrifice* (1933); W.O.E. Oesterley, *Sacrifices in Ancient Israel* (1938); T.H. Gaster, in: *Mélanges Syriens offerts à M.R. Dussaud*, 2 (1939), 577–82; J.E. Coleran, in: CBQ, 2 (1940), 130–44; P. Saydon, *ibid.*, 8 (1946), 393–9; H.W. Robinson, in: JTS, 48 (1942), 129–39; D.M.L. Urie, in: PEQ, (1949), 67–82; H.H. Rowley, in: BJRL, 33 (1950), 74–110; G.R. Driver, in: JSS, 1 (1956), 97–105; N.H. Snaith, in: VT, 7 (1957), 308–17; M. Haran, *ibid.*, 10 (1960), 113–29; de Vaux, Anc Isr (1961), 415–510; B.A. Levine, in: JCS, 17 (1963), 105–11; idem, in: JAOS, 75 (1965), 309–18; idem, in: *Leshonenu*, 30 (1966), 3–11; idem, in: *Eretz-Israel*, 9 (1969), 88–95; idem and W. Hallo, in: HUCA, 38 (1967), 17–58; Y. Aharoni, in: IEJ, 18 (1968), 157–69; A.F. Rainey, in: *Biblica*, 51 (1970), 485–98. SECOND TEMPLE PERIOD: S.R. Hirsch, commentary to Leviticus; M.L. Malbim, commentary to Leviticus; D. Hoffmann, *Das Buch Leviticus* (1905); J.H. Hertz, *The Pentateuch and Haftorahs; Leviticus* (1932), 42–49; E. Levy, *Yesodot ha-Tefillah* (1952^2), 26–29, 37–59, 95–101; S. Schaffer, *Ḥukkei ha-Korbanot* (1968^3). IN KABBALAH: G. Scholem, *Reshit ha-Kabbalah* (1948), 141f.; I. Tishby, *Mishnat ha-Zohar*, 2 (1961), 194–215.

SACRILEGE, the deliberate or inadvertent violation of sacred things. The Torah ordains the punishment of *karet for anyone who deliberately flouts the sanctity of the Temple precincts or deviates in the slightest from any of the rules or rituals connected with its service. Under this heading comes slaughtering, offering, or partaking of the sacrifices outside their appointed time or place, entering the sanctuary, officiating, or eating holy things while ritually unclean or when disqualified by reason of non-priestly status (Lev. 17:1–9; 19:5–8; 22:1–16). The priest profaned his sacred office by officiating, when suffering from a *blemish, when in mourning, or by contracting a forbidden union, such as marrying a divorcée, which disqualified his offspring from the priesthood and from marrying a priest (Lev. 21). To make a replica of any of the utensils or ingredients, such as the incense used in the Temple, is also regarded as sacrilege (Ex. 30:32). The seriousness of the sin of sacrilege is underlined by the biblical stories of Nadab and Abihu, burnt to death for offering "strange fire," and the stoning of Achan for taking the spoils of war dedicated to the sanctuary (Lev. 10:1–2; Josh. 7). The inadvertent use of sacred things, termed *me'ilah*, is also penalized in the Pentateuch (Lev. 5:14ff.). The offender is required to bring a guilt offering and reimburse the Temple treasury to the value of the theft plus one-fifth.

A whole tractate of the Talmud (see *Me'ilah) is devoted to the offense which became obsolete with the destruction of the Temple. But the principle involved lived on to safeguard the remaining sancta of Jewish life, in a carefully graded order of holiness: the *Sefer Torah*, religious articles such as *tefillin* and *ẓiẓit*, printed holy books, and the synagogue and its appurtenances. The rabbis adopted the formula of *ma'alin bekodesh ve-ein moridin* – "holiness may be increased but not decreased." The Mishnah in *Megillah* (3:1, 2) forbids the sale of a synagogue for a public bath or tannery, a *Sefer Torah* for books of lesser sanctity such as the Prophets. Even a disused synagogue may not be used as a shortcut or for spreading nets or drying fruit. Printed pages of holy books must be buried (see *Genizah) out of respect for the name of God inscribed therein (see *Shemot). No benefit may be derived from the dead, including the shroud or the corpse itself, except for the purpose of saving life (see *Autopsies). Cemeteries must be treated with the utmost reverence, and it is not permitted to walk over the graves or pasture cattle there (Sh. Ar., YD 368). The scholar who adopted an irreverent approach to difficult passages in the Torah was guilty of sacrilege too (Maimonides, *Hilkhot Me'ilah*, end).

Under a law promulgated by the State of Israel for safeguarding the holy sites of Judaism and other faiths (1967), there is a penalty of seven years' imprisonment for "profaning a holy place or violating it in any manner" (see *Holy Places). Detailed regulations have been gazetted by the Ministry of Religious Affairs prohibiting sacrilegious behavior at Jewish holy sites (Protection of Holy Places Law, 5727 – 1967, in: *Laws of the State of Israel*, 21 (1966/67), 76). These prohibit ritual slaughter, eating and drinking, smoking, sleeping, hawking, profanation of the Sabbath and festivals, and immodest dress. These regulations have been applied to Jewish holy sites in Jerusalem and other parts of Ereẓ Israel. After the Six-Day War the Israel Chief Rabbinate proclaimed it sacrilegious for a Jew to enter the Temple Mount because of ritual defilement.

[Aryeh Newman]

°SACY, ANTOINE ISAAC SILVESTRE DE (1758–1838), French Orientalist and Hebraist of the Romantic-Catholic school. In 1817, he published a pamphlet entitled *Lettre à M. Le Conseiller de S.M. le Roi de Saxe…* opposing the integration of the Jews within Christian society, written in criticism of C. *Bail's *Des Juifs au 19e siècle* (1816). In the opinion of Sacy, integration of the Jews would be equivalent to a unification of religions or abolition of the specific characteristics of the various religions. This he considered an impossibility:

> The believing Jew cannot doubt that he is a member of the Chosen People of God which has been separated from all other peoples; or that its autonomy, its political existence, its ritual, and its national glory must one day be reestablished. On the other hand, the Christian knows that the Bible has taught him that this people, still awaiting a Messiah who has already come, has been preserved among the nations by Divine Providence as a living witness of heavenly retribution, but at the same time is a precious offspring of promised regeneration.

Sacy's work aroused lively polemics in France and Germany which continued until around 1825.

BIBLIOGRAPHY: A.T. D'Esquirons de St. Agnon, *Considérations sur l'existence civile et politique des Israélites* (1817); L. Bendavid, in: *Zeitschrift fuer Wissenschaft der Juden* (1822), 197–230.

[Baruch Mevorah]

SADAGORA (Rom. **Sadagura**; Ger. **Sadagora**), town in Chernovtsy district, Ukraine. From 1775 until World War I Sadagora passed to Austria and between the two world wars was within Romania. The first Jews settled there during the 17th century. In 1775, 45 Jewish families (186 persons) were enumerated among 180 families in the town. There were 100 Jewish families in 1808, and 3,888 Jews (80.3% of the total population) according to the census of 1880. Once the community developed, 16 smaller Jewish communities were affiliated to it. Communal institutions developed from the 18th century. The central synagogue was apparently built about 1770, but there were also numerous additional synagogues and prayer houses. The community had a yeshivah and a Jewish school, established under Austrian rule. The Jews of Sadagora mainly engaged in commerce and crafts, while among the Jews of the vicinity, who in practice belonged to the community of Sadagora, there were also lessees and wealthy landowners. A special occupation of the local Jewish poor was the haulage of water in barrels from distant wells to houses in the town. Between 1883 and 1914, a Jew was town mayor.

In 1914, before the outbreak of World War I, there were 5,060 Jews living in Sadagora and a further 3,000 in the 16 communities affiliated to it. During World War I the town and its surroundings suffered extensively from the fighting there, and many of its Jewish inhabitants left, and the number of Jews had declined to 900 in 1919. After the war a number returned and continued to live there under Romanian rule. There were 1,459 in 1930, declining to 654 in 1941. Zionist organizations were early established in Sadagora and were particularly active in the interwar period under the Romanian rule. Jews also took part in the municipal life, and their parties were well represented in the municipal administration. In June 1940 the town was annexed to the U.S.S.R., and the Soviets exiled many Jewish merchants and artisans to Siberia.

Sadagora was an important center of Hasidism, from the period of Austrian rule over Bukovina until the liquidation of the community. Most of the Jewish inhabitants of the town belonged to the *Ruzhin Ḥasidim. R. Israel Friedmann of Ruzhin arrived in Sadagora after he was released from prison in Russia and established a magnificent "court" there. His royal style of living aroused opposition from the Ḥasidim of Zanz (see *Halberstam). After World War II the center of the Sadagora dynasty was transferred to Ereẓ Israel.

Holocaust and Contemporary Periods

In 1941 the town was restored to Romanian administration, which collaborated with the Germans. During this period 186 Jews lost their lives in attacks made against the Jews. In 1941 almost all of the 1,488 Jews remaining in Sadagora were deported by the Romanian and German authorities to death camps in *Transnistria. A few Jews returned to Sadagora in 1944, but community life was not reorganized after the war.

BIBLIOGRAPHY: H. Gold, *Geschichte der Juden in der Bukowina*, 2 (1962), 96–105.

[Yehouda Marton]

ṢA'DAH, walled city, capital of north *Yemen. Ṣa'dah was once an iron mining and tanning center and an important station along the Ḥimyar *San'ā-Mecca trade route. Later, Ṣa'dah was chosen as the capital of the Zaydi state and became the center of Zaydi learning in the al-Hādī Mosque. It is still an important institution for education in Zaydism. It is built on a 2,300 m high plateau about 250 km north of San'ā. Evidence for the existence of a Jewish settlement in Ṣa'dah in the first half of the Middle Ages is found in fragments from the Cairo *Genizah. A *gaon*, whose name is unknown, rebukes Amram b. Johanan of Ṣa'dah for having abandoned the custom of his forefathers by not sending the pledges and contributions from himself and from his town to the yeshivah, sending them instead to another yeshivah. Indeed, many letters from the people of Yemen and Yamāmah to the yeshivah also describe 'Amram's evil deeds. At the end of his *iggeret* ("letter") the *gaon* demands that all pledges and contributions be sent immediately to him by way of the *sar* ("minister") Nethanel in Ṣa'dah. A different document speaks of a Jew from Ṣa'dah who visited Fustat (in 1134) and, when called upon to lead the prayers, added to the *kaddish* a prayer for the head of the academy in *Egypt. The representative of the Babylonian academy was insulted by this, for according to the usual custom only the head of the Babylonian academy was entitled to this honor. In the 14th century one of the rabbis of Ṣa'dah wrote an allegorical commentary on the Pentateuch. He was severely criticized by the rabbis of San'ā, but the rabbis of Ṣa'dah supported him and rejected the criticism.

According to tradition, when the Zaydi imam conquered Ṣa'dah (c. 1200), he destroyed all synagogues because the Jews sold wine to the Muslims. In general, however, the conditions in northern Yemen were more favorable for the Jews, and the restrictions and ordinances of the Covenant of *Omar were not strictly enforced. For example, the Jews' houses were as high as those of the Muslims, and they were permitted to carry daggers and even live ammunition. There is no definite information, however, about the size of the Jewish population. A. Tabib recounts heavy losses suffered by the Jews of the area in the upheavals of 1906. In addition to their traditional livelihoods, the Jews of Ṣa'dah also engaged in wholesale trading. Prior to the immigration to Israel the community numbered about 60 families (280 souls) with three synagogues; most of the Jews were silversmiths, coppersmiths and cobblers.

BIBLIOGRAPHY: B.M. Lewin, in: *Ginzei Kedem*, 3 (1925), 20–21; S.D. Goitein, in: *Sinai*, 33 (1953), 225–37; idem, in: *Tarbiz*, 31 (1961/62), 357–70; idem, in: *Harel, Koveẓ Zikkaron la-Rav Refa'el Alsheikh* (1962), 133–48; Y. Qāfih, *Ketavim* (1999), 1. 341–363; idem., in Y. Tobi (ed.), *Le-Rosh Yosef* (1995), 11–67.

[Yosef Tobi (2nd ed.)]

SADAI, YIZḤAK (1935–), Israeli composer and music theorist. Born in Sofia, Bulgaria, Sadai came to Israel at the age of 14 (in 1949). In 1956 he graduated from the Tel Aviv Academy of Music under A.A. *Boskovich and also studied composition with Joseph *Tal (1954) and *Haubenstock-Ramati (1959). His works consist of orchestral and chamber music as well as electronic music, and they have been performed at four international festivals of contemporary music. Sadai founded the electronic music studio at Tel Aviv Univeristy (1974), and from 1960 he was a lecturer at the Rubin Academy of Music in Jerusalem and at the Rubin Academy of Music at Tel Aviv University (since 1966), where in 1980 he was appointed professor. His special interest lies in interdisciplinary research. His early works as a composer show an integration of *maqāmāt* with Bergian expressionism (in the chamber cantata *Ecclesiastes* and in the *Ricercare symphonique*). From 1965 Sadai embarked on a post-Webern Impressionist style (*Interpopulation* for strings and harpsichord; *Nuances* for orchestra; and *Prelude à Jerusalem* for choir, orchestra, and electronic tape). Among his other compositions are three canatatas – *Kohelet, Ha-Ẓevi Yisrael*, and *Psikoanalisah; Serenade* for woodwinds; and *Anamorphoses* (1981–82) for orchestra and electronic tape.

He published a book on methodology of musical theory (1960) as well as *Harmony in Its Systemic and Its Phenomenological Aspects* (1980).

BIBLIOGRAPHY: Grove Music Online; A.L. Ringer, "Musical Composition in Modern Israel," in: *Music Quarterly* (1965), 282–87.

[Yohanan Boehm and Uri (Erich) Toeplitz / Israela Stein (2nd ed.)]

SA'D AL-DAWLA AL-ṢAFĪ IBN HIBBATALLAH (d. 1291), court physician and vizier in Mongol *Persia. He came from Abhar in the province of Jibāl. The sources refer to him by the honorific title "Sa'd al-Dawla" ("support of the State") or "the Jewish vizier," etc.

In two devastating attacks, the *Mongols succeeded in crushing three important Persian centers of power, namely in Khwārazm, in Alamut, and, finally in *Baghdad, the capital of the Abbasid Caliphate. Thus, in the middle of the 13th century, a new era began in Persia which continued until the end of the Ilkhanid in 1335. Significant changes were introduced in the social, economic, legal, and governmental structures of Persia during this period. These changes influenced numerous intellectual activities, especially those related to art, historiography, prose, and poetry. Because of the religious attitude of the *Mongols, especially that of the first rulers, the Muslims lost some of their privileges as the rulers and governors in the Islamic lands. This change allowed members of religious minorities to occupy high positions under those Mongol rulers who had not yet accepted Islam as their religion. Saʿd al Dawla was a product of this change.

His Hebrew name is unknown. Saʿd al-Dawla is first mentioned in *Mosul. He subsequently moved to Baghdad where he practiced in 1284 as a physician. There he acquired expert knowledge of the financial administration and in 1285 was appointed a member of the *diwan*. His abilities and promotion evidently aroused the enmity of his colleagues, who in 1288 obtained his transfer as physician to the court of Arghūn Khān, in *Tabriz, Azerbaijan. A brilliant scholar and linguist, speaking Persian, Arabic, Turkish, and Mongolian, Saʿd al-Dawla soon won favor with the Mongol ruler, and in 1289 was appointed vizier of the whole Īl-Khān kingdom. According to custom, he immediately removed his opponents and filled the key posts in the administration with dependable Mongols, Christians, or Jews, primarily with members of his own family. He appointed one brother, Fakhr al-Dawla, governor of Baghdad; another brother, Amīn al-Dawla, was put in charge of the districts of Mosul and Diyār Bakr, Diyār Rabīʿa, and Mardin. The Persian and Arabic sources credit him with the establishment of the administration on the basis of law and justice. But the rule of these Jewish officials caused much resentment among the Muslim population. Moreover, Saʿd al-Dawla had personal enemies among Mongol leaders, who were jealous of Arghūn's unlimited confidence in him. When Arghūn became dangerously ill, court circles accused the vizier of having poisoned his benefactor. At a banquet, Saʿd al-Dawla and the majority of his supporters were arrested, a large number were slain at once, and Saʿd al-Dawla was executed the following day. A large-scale persecution of Jews in Tabriz, Baghdad, and other Jewish communities ensued. All his brethren and relatives subsequently met a violent death, described in the Arabic writings of Ibn al-Fūṭi, *Bar-Hebraeus, and others.

ADD. BIBLIOGRAPHY: Bar Hebraeus, *Chronography*, ed. and tr. E.A., Wallis Budge, 1 (1932), 484–91; W.J. Fischel, *Jews in the Economic and Political Life of Mediaeval Islam* (1969), 90–117; Ibn al-Fuwati, al-*Hawādith al-Jāmiʿa fi al-mia al-sābiʿa*, ed. Mustafa Jawād (1922), 457–65; D. Krawulsky, "Saʿd al-Dawla," in: EIS^2, 8 (1995), 702–3; W. Shirāzi, in: *Tārikh*, 2 (1852), 235–45.

[Walter J. Fischel / Amnon Netzer (2nd ed.)]

SADAN (Stock), DOV (1902–1989), Yiddish and Hebrew writer and scholar. Born in Brody, Eastern Galicia, from his youth Sadan was an ardent Zionist and active in the propagation of the Hebrew language and culture. In the early 1920s he was a leader of the He-Ḥalutz movement in Poland.

After immigrating to Ereẓ Israel in 1925, Sadan worked as an agricultural laborer until 1927, when Berl Katznelson offered him a position on the staff of the newspaper *Davar*. In 1928 he went to Germany on behalf of the He-Ḥalutz movement. There he came in close contact with modern Germanic culture, especially with the new trends of culture history and psychoanalysis. Upon his return he taught in schools in Lower Galilee and in Jerusalem, but in 1933 he resumed his work on *Davar*, where he remained for the next ten years. In 1944 he joined the staff of Am Oved, the publishing house of the Histadrut. Sadan became a faculty member of The Hebrew University, teaching Hebrew composition, and was appointed chairman of the Yiddish department in 1952. From 1965 to 1970 he also taught Hebrew literature at Tel Aviv University. Elected to the Knesset as a member of Mapai in 1965, he resigned before the end of his term. He was an active member on the boards of many literary and cultural institutions, such as the Academy of the Hebrew Language and the board of directors of Mosad Bialik.

Sadan began his prolific literary career at an early age; his more than 50 volumes represent less than half his total output. Although his initial literary efforts were in poetry, he abandoned this medium and, turning to prose, became one of the great masters of modern Hebrew prose. He developed a highly individual style, complex, very "literary," rooted in Jewish sources, and yet graceful and flexible. Throughout his career he experimented with various modes of fiction, ranging from the memoir story (he published two volumes of childhood memories) to the modern surrealistic story (Sadan was the first to translate Kafka into Hebrew). The bulk of his work, however, comprises nonfiction, especially essays and literary and scholarly articles in Judaic studies. His essays cover a wide variety of subjects, such as current events, memoirs, portraits of famous personalities, and essays on problems of Jewish culture. He pursued research in such areas as folklore, humor, idioms, and the Hebrew and Yiddish languages, etc. His literary and scholarly creativity, however, reached its zenith in his studies of Hebrew and Yiddish literature.

Sadan's critical approach to literature and other Jewish studies is based on a broad and novel view of modern Jewish history. He rejects the view which identifies modern Jewish literature only with those Hebrew and Yiddish literary trends that grew out of the modern "secular" Jewish culture, beginning with the Haskalah (18th and 19th centuries) and continuing in the nationalistic literature (end of the 19th and the beginning of the 20th centuries). He argues that modern Jewish literature was a major reaction to the crisis in traditional Jewish culture in Central, and especially Eastern, Europe at the end of the long Jewish "Middle Ages" in the 18th century. It developed in three principal directions, and not one, as claimed by the *maskilim*: (1) the new "rabbinic" movement, centered mainly around the Lithuanian Mitnaggedic movement, which was a revitalized continuation of halakhic literature; (2) the mystic-ḥasidic trend which developed a versatile literature consisting of many genres (sermons, parables, allegory, legend, hagiography, mystic-philosophic writings);

(3) the Haskalah trend which aimed at creating a European humanistic literature.

This vast, complex, and intricate body of literary writings, written in several languages (Hebrew, neo-biblical, as well as late Hebrew, Yiddish and European languages), with its different spiritual trends, Sadan sees as one literature, which he terms "the Israel literature," and defines it all as literature written by Jews for a Jewish readership. In this giant network Hebrew literature must be the foundation and principal axis, yet the scholar or the critic should not concentrate exclusively on it. Sadan demands that the literary historian and critic: (1) see modern Jewish literature ("Israel literature") as one multi-faceted unified body and accept the different languages in which it was written; (2) study each of the above areas individually but at the same time try to find ideational, thematic, and linguistic links between them. For instance, it is impossible to give a profound, objective, and critical evaluation of the biting, at times virulent, satirical-parodic anti-ḥasidic Haskalah literature without studying it in relation to ḥasidic literature's "mixed" Hebrew, which was the butt of the Haskalah parody; (3) study the dialectical essence of the relationship between the different areas of the literature. According to Sadan, the antithetical tension between these areas will, in time, be resolved into a harmonious synthesis.

Central to Sadan's Jewish world view is the belief that the modern "secular" Jewish culture which broke away from traditional Judaism is only an antithetical transient ("episodic") stage in the history of Jewish culture. The emerging Jewish culture, however, will not return to its ancient traditional form but, deriving its inspiration from the source of all Jewish culture – religious faith – will be molded into a new cultural synthesis in which the experience gained by the Jewish culture in its temporary secular stage will play a significant role. Sadan finds the first signs of this synthesis in modern Jewish literature at climactic points of development where the Jewish culture reaches the zenith of artistic and aesthetic accomplishment. In Hebrew literature he points to two artistic peaks: Bialik's poetry and Agnon's fiction.

Sadan uses different critical methods to establish the connecting links between the different areas of Jewish culture, which are often contradictory in their literary expression. He most frequently resorts to the study of motifs, idioms, and linguistic combinations, a method founded on Freud's theory of the psychic. The psychoanalytical approach is particularly apparent in his early critical works (especially in his articles on J.Ḥ. Brenner and Ḥ.N. Bialik); later, however, this method is used only indirectly. (Sadan introduced the psychoanalytic approach into Hebrew literary criticism.) He continued, however, to employ freely the method of "investigation" which requires of the critic keen perception and a phenomenal amount of knowledge in all the facets of literature. This method lends a "technical" character to some of his scholarly writings, and Sadan therefore often resorts to the graceful short essay form which gives him an all-embracing and original view of the world of an author and the whole body of his works. Sadan's literary criticism is always sensitive to the canons of good taste.

Sadan translated many volumes from Yiddish, German, and Polish and two large volumes of Jewish jokes (*Ka'arat Egozim*, 1953; *Ka'arat Ẓimmukim*, 1950) which he compiled.

His main collections of Hebrew literary criticism are *Avnei Boḥan* (1951), *Al S.Y. Agnon* (1959), *Avnei Bedek* (1962), *Bein Din le-Ḥeshbon* (1963), *Bein She'ilah le-Kinyan* (1968), and *Avnei Gader* (1970). Late works include *Avnei Sha'ashu'a* (1983) and a collection of essays on Hebrew and Yiddish literature entitled *Ḥadashim Gam Yeshanim* (1987). A bibliography of his works was prepared by Y. Galron-Goldschlager (1987; 1994). His main collection of Yiddish literary criticism is *Avnei Miftan* (vols. 1 and 2 (1961, 1970)).

BIBLIOGRAPHY: S. Halkin, *Derakhim ve-Ẓiddei Derakhim ba-Sifrut*, 2 (1969), 241–9; I. Kohen, *Aspaklaryot* (1968), 111–36; S.Y. Penueli, *Sifrut ki-Feshutah* (1963), 362–76; D. Sadan, in: *Moznayim*, 29 (1969–70), 3–9. **ADD. BIBLIOGRAPHY:** G. Shaked, "*Bein Lashon le-Ḥevrah*," in: *Masa*, 13 (1972), 1, 5; E. Schweid, "*Haguto shel Sadan*," in: *Molad*, 7 (1976), 405–7; A.B. Jaffe, in: *Al ha-Mishmar* (March 4, 1977); S. Halperin, "*Otobiografiyyah shel Shefa: Al D. Sadan*," in: *Moznayim:* 54:3–4 (1982), 23–25; H. Hever, "*Ha-Ma'agal ha-Shelishi*," in: *Siman Keriah*, 16/17 (1983), 574–77; D. Miron, "*D. Sadan, Ba-Derekh el ha-Kiliyut*," in: *Molad*, 42 (1985/86), 129–35; Sh. Werses, "*Weygen di Yidishe Ketavim fun D. Sadan*," in: *Di Goldene Keyt*, 122 (1987), 5–16; D. Weinfeld, *Iyyunim ba-Sifrut: Devarim she-Ne'emru be-Erev li-Khvod Dov Sadan* (1988); Sh. Werses, "*D. Sadan be-Olamah shel ha-Sifrut ha-Ivrit ha-Ḥadashah*," in: *Moznayim*, 64:3–4 (1990), 18–24; Y. Szeintuch, "*Shemesh ha-Or*," in: *Shenaton ha-Sefer ha-Yehudi* (1992), 175–84; N. Govrin, "*Dov Sadan – Av ha-Binyan*," in: *Yerushalayim*, 19 (2002), 215–20.

[Dan Miron]

SADAT, MUHAMMAD ANWAR AL- (1918–1981), president of the Arab Republic of Egypt, Oct. 1970–Oct. 1981. Sadat was born to poor parents in the Egyptian village of Mit Abu-Kom. He joined the army and during World War II was active in an anti-British underground group (and was arrested in consequence). After the war, still in the army, he joined the "Free Officers" group, led by *Nasser, which carried out the July 1952 Revolution. Overshadowed by Nasser, Sadat managed the new regime's daily, *al-Gumhuriyyah*, served as a cabinet minister for one year and then as speaker of the parliament. Appointed as Nasser's vice president after the 1967 defeat, Sadat was elected president after Nasser's death on September 28, 1970.

Gradually, Sadat asserted himself increasingly as president and introduced a growing measure of economic and political liberalization, which bolstered his increasing popularity. Eager to overcome Egypt's military inferiority versus Israel, he signed a treaty of friendship with the Soviets which, however, failed to deliver the needed hardware for war. Consequently, he expelled them from Egypt in 1972 and started to prepare for war on his own, all the while attempting a political rapprochement with certain European states and the U.S. in order to secure their sympathy for his military moves against Israel.

The October 1973 attack in Sinai, while not leading to an Egyptian victory, gave Egypt the pretext to coopt the U.S. as an honest broker instead of a partisan of Israel. Thus, the Disengagement Treaties of May 1974 and September 1975 with Israel increased Sadat's prestige and started the process towards a settlement with Israel. Sadat's main argument was that such a peace should be achieved in parallel with Israel's renunciation of the so-called "conquered territories." This was the ideological basis of Sadat's visit to Jerusalem in November 1977 and of the Camp David negotiations, sponsored by Jimmy Carter, in September 1978. Israel's agreement to recognize the autonomy of the Palestinians paved the way for the signing of the peace treaty between Egypt and Israel on the lawn of the White House in March 1979. This was the peak of Sadat's achievement, for which he was awarded, together with *Begin, the Nobel Peace Prize.

In subsequent years, Sadat's international prestige grew, but in Egypt, owing to the increasing poverty and unemployment, social criticism of Sadat increased, exploiting the very openness he had encouraged. Some of this nurtured Islamic fundamentalism. Sadat, an orthodox Muslim himself, first attempted to persuade the Islamic leaders to tone down their zeal, then started to arrest them in the thousands during the last months of his life. His assassination, during a festive military review on the eighth anniversary of the Yom Kippur War, ended the plans he had for Egypt.

In his later years, Sadat openly expressed his disappointment with Israel's policies, especially the June 1981 Israeli attack on the Iraqi nuclear reactor and what he considered as Israel's dragging its feet over the granting of Palestinian autonomy. He argued that the return of Sinai was a "natural" act, since this had been Egyptian territory, and he perceived Israel as "ungrateful." U.S. economic assistance, too, could not solve Egypt's numerous social problems, nor appease popular criticism of his regime.

Sadat's assassination was welcomed by many, in contrast with the bitter national mourning following Nasser's death. Nevertheless, Sadat's legacy was both revolutionary and original, the likes of which have not yet been seen in Arab countries. His colorful and dynamic personality, aiming at radical solutions, was expressed in the heat of war and the challenges of peace. His talent for changing direction and undertaking new initiatives was unique. He was criticized by several Arab states for signing a peace with Israel which enabled it – they claimed – to oppress the Palestinians and attack Lebanon. However, Arab and Muslim states which had ostracized him found themselves following his example some 20 years later. Although relations between Egypt and Israel since 1977 have had their ups and downs, the treaty has served as a model for others.

BIBLIOGRAPHY: R. Israeli, *The Public Diary of President Sadat*, 1-2-3 (1978–79); idem, *Man of Defiance: The Political Biography of President Sadat* (1985); idem, "Sadat: The Calculus of War and Peace," in: Craig and Loewenheim (eds.), *The Diplomats 1939–79* (1994), 435–58.

[Raphael Israeli (2nd ed.)]

SADDUCEES (Heb. צְדוּקִים, *Ẓedukim*), sect of the latter half of the Second Temple period, formed about 200 B.C.E. Active in political and economic life, the Sadducean party was composed largely of the wealthier elements of the population – priests, merchants, and aristocrats. They dominated the Temple worship and its rites and many of them were members of the Sanhedrin (the supreme Jewish council and tribunal of the Second Temple period).

Origin of the Name

According to a talmudic tradition (ARN1[5]), the name derives from Zadok, a disciple of Antigonus of *Sokho who, misunderstanding his teacher's maxim, denied afterlife and resurrection and formed a sect in accordance with those views (see *Boethusians). The most probable explanation of the name, however, is that it is derived from Zadok, the high priest in the days of David (II Sam. 8:17 and 15:24) and Solomon (cf. I Kings 1:34ff. and I Chron. 12:29). Ezekiel (40:46, 43:19 and 44:10–15) selected this family as worthy of being entrusted with the control of the Temple. Descendants of this family constituted the Temple hierarchy down to the second century B.C.E., though not all priests were Sadducees. Hence the name "Sadducees" may best be taken to mean anyone who was a sympathizer with the Zadokites, the priestly descendants of Zadok. In the talmudic literature, the designations Boethusians and Sadducees are used interchangeably to designate the same party or sect. Some scholars believe, however, that the Boethusians were a branch of the Sadducees, deriving their name from their leader Boethus. (See L. Ginzberg, in: JE, 3 (1902), 284–5, and Schuerer, Gesch, 2 (1907[4]), 478–9.)

Beliefs and Doctrines

The Sadducees were the conservative priestly group, holding to the older doctrines, and cherishing the highest regard for the sacrificial cult of the Temple. The party was opposed to the *Pharisees down to the time of the destruction of Jerusalem in 70 C.E. The main difference between the Pharisees and the Sadducees concerned their attitudes toward the Torah. The supremacy of the Torah was acknowledged by both parties. However, the Pharisees assigned to the Oral Law a place of authority side by side with the written Torah, and determined its interpretation accordingly, whereas the Sadducees refused to accept any precept as binding unless it was based directly on the Torah. The theological struggle between the two parties, as J.Z. Lauterbach puts it (*Rabbinic Essays*, 23–162), was actually a struggle between two concepts of God. The Sadducees sought to bring God down to man. Their God was anthropomorphic and the worship offered him was like homage paid a human king or ruler. The Pharisees, on the other hand, sought to raise man to divine heights and to bring him nearer to a spiritual and transcendent God.

The Sadducees therefore rejected the Pharisaic supernatural beliefs, claiming that they had no basis in Mosaic Law. They denied the doctrine of the resurrection of the body (Matt. 22:23; Mark 22:18; Luke 20:27; Acts 23:8), denied the immortality of the soul (Jos., Wars, 2:162f. and Ant., 18:16), and rejected the Pharisaic doctrine regarding the existence of angels and ministering spirits (Acts 23:8). Because of the strict adherence to the letter of the law, the Sadducees acted severely in cases involving the death penalty. The Mosaic principle of *Lex talionis*, for instance (Ex. 21:24), was interpreted literally rather than construed as monetary compensation – the view adopted by the Pharisees. They were opposed to changes and innovations and refused to accept the oral traditions with which the Pharisees supplemented the Written Law. It was never a question of whether certain laws were derived from tradition, but whether those laws that were admittedly derived from tradition were obligatory. Apart from differences between the Pharisees and the Sadducees as to the oral tradition and supernatural beliefs, there were numerous legal ritualistic details upon which these two parties differed, especially those connected with the Temple. On the whole, it can be said that while the Pharisees claimed the authority of piety and learning, the Sadducees claimed that of genealogy and position.

The rivalry between the Pharisees and the Sadducees was, in a sense, the renewal of a conflict between the prophets and priests of pre-Exilic times. Following the restoration of the Temple and its sacrificial cult, the priests were also restored to their former position as religious leaders. Priestly authority was, however, weakened by two factors: the rise of laymen and "scribes" who possessed a knowledge of the law; and the advent of Greek rule – since among the Greeks themselves priests were the servants not the leaders of the community.

Attitude Toward Prayer and Sacrifice

Josephus and the Talmud say little about the Sadducean position on prayer, but the Sadducees would naturally not favor a religious service consisting of prayer and study alone, as would the Pharisees. This would tend to lessen the importance of the sacrificial cult and thereby weaken their own position as priests.

Fate

On the problem of human conduct and activities, the Sadducees seemed to have believed that God is not concerned with man's affairs. As Josephus puts it: "As for the Sadducees they take away fate and say there is no such thing, and that the events of human affairs are not at its disposal, but they suppose that all our actions are in our own power, so that we ourselves are the cause of what is good and receive what is evil from our own folly" (Ant., 13:173). Unfortunately no statement has survived from the Sadducean side on their beliefs and principles. There are controversial references in rabbinical literature with regard to the Sadducean interpretation of the law. The Sadducees have been represented as lax and worldly-minded aristocrats, primarily interested in maintaining their own privileged position, and favoring Greco-Roman culture.

The Sadducees and the New Testament

In the New Testament, John the Baptist jointly condemned the Pharisees and the Sadducees, calling them a "generation of vipers" and challenging them both to "bring forth fruits meet for repentance" (Matt. 3:7ff.). In his denunciation of their doctrines, Jesus, too, grouped Sadducees and Pharisees together (Matt. 16:6ff.) and both parties were said to have posed questions designed to perplex Jesus (Matt. 15:1). According to Acts (4:1ff., 5:17), Peter and John were imprisoned by them. Since many Christian doctrines have more in common with those of the Pharisees than with those of the Sadducees, it is clear why the Apostolic Church, in the first years of its existence, had most to fear from the Sadducees (Acts 4 and 5).

Historically the Sadducees came under the influence of Hellenism and later were in good standing with the Roman rulers, though unpopular with the common people, from whom they kept aloof. The Sadducean hierarchy had its stronghold in the Temple, and it was only during the last two decades of the Temple's existence that the Pharisees finally gained control. Since the whole power and *raison d'être* of the Sadducees were bound up with the Temple cult, the group ceased to exist after the destruction of the Temple in 70 C.E.

BIBLIOGRAPHY: E. Baneth, in: MWJ, 9 (1882), 1–37, 61–95; V. Eppstein, in: JBL, 85 (1966), 213–24. For further bibliography see *Pharisees.

[Menahem Mansoor]

ṢADE (**Ẓadi;** Heb. צ, ץ; צָדִי, צָדִי), the eighteenth letter of the Hebrew alphabet; its numerical value is 90. It is assumed that the earliest form of the *ṣade* was a pictograph of a blossom. In the late second and early first millennia B.C.E., the *ṣade* became. In the Hebrew script, from the eighth century B.C.E. onward, the downstroke was shortened and a hook was added on the letter's right side, which has been preserved in the Samaritan. The Phoenician and Aramaic scripts lengthened the downstroke and thus in the fifth century B.C.E. Aramaic script three forms developed:. While from the first form, through the Nabatean, the Arabic *ṣad* evolved, the Jewish script adopted the third form, which was the ancestor of the medial צ and final *ṣade* ץ. See *Alphabet, Hebrew.

[Joseph Naveh]

SADEH, PINḤAS (1929–1994), Israeli writer. Born in Lvov, Sadeh was taken to Palestine in 1934 and lived for a while in Tel Aviv. A radical individualist and autodidact, he then worked as a shepherd in the Jezreel valley, and later as a night watchman in Jerusalem. His first publications were a story in *Ba-Ma'aleh* (1945) and a poem in *Ittim* (1946). The first collection of poems, *Massa Dumah* ("Vision of Dumah"), positioned him in the tradition of Hebrew Expressionistsm and his first novel, *Ha-Ḥayyim ke-Mashal* (1958, 1968; *Life as a Parable*, 1966), foreshadows Expressionistic principles, mainly, the work of art as a cry of protest and an expression of the self. In confessional style, interweaving reflections and meditations on human existence and nature with personal experiences, Sadeh's autobiographical novel rejected the ubiquitous collective experience in favor of far-reaching individualism. The novel echoes perceptions and views which are closer to Christianity and to marginal religious sects in Jewish history (such as Shabbateanism and to the Frankists) than to the norms dear to Zionist society in Israel of the 1950s. With his work distinguished by images taken from his own life, Sadeh writes about love, erotic excitement, and loneliness, contemplates sin and grace, alludes to the New Testament and to Kierkegaard's and Dostoyevsky's oeuvre. Following the success of this unusual novel, Sadeh became, both on account of his writing and his sequestered, self-dramatized way of life, an idol for young Israelis and would-be artists. In 1967 he published *Al Mazzavo shel ha-Adam* ("Notes on Man's Condition") followed by the novella *Mot Avimelekh* ("The Death of Avimelech," 1969). Sadeh published further collections of poetry, in which he extols feminine beauty and women's self-sacrifice and reflects on nature, transience, and mortality. Among these are *Sefer ha-Shirim* ("Book of Poems"), *El Shetei Ne'arot Nikhbadot* ("To Two Honorable Young Ladies," 1977), and *Sefer ha-Agasim ha-Ẓehubim* (1985). He also wrote essays on Bialik (1985) and books for children (*Ha-Ganav*, "The Thief," 1988), edited a selection of European stories, *Mivḥar ha-Sippur ha-Eiropi* (1959), and anthologized ḥasidic legends (English translation as *Jewish Folktales*, 1989; 1990). Sadeh's *Collected Poems* appeared in 2005. Sadeh, who lived in his later life in Ramat Gan, received the Bialik Prize in 1990. For translations of his work see the ITHL website at www.ithl.org.il.

BIBLIOGRAPHY: J. Mundi, *Siḥot ba-Ḥaẓot-Laylah im Pinḥas Sadeh* (1969); A. Cohen, "*Ha-Sipporet shel P. Sadeh*," in: *Hadoar*, 50 (1971), 84; S. Lindenbaum, "Vision or Poetry? P. Sadeh's Poems," in: *Modern Hebrew Literature*, 4, 1 (1978), 43–46; T. Reshef, "*Keri'at Ma'amakim*," in: *Prozah*, 101–102 (1988), 7–9; O. Bartana, "*Min ha-Pesikhologiyah el ha- Nevu'ah*," in: *Moznayim*, 64:9–10 (1990), 13–16; A. Navot, "*Ha-Maẓav ha-Revi'i*," in: *Mozanyim*, 65:6 (1991), 4–9; M. Forcano, "Pinkhas Sadeh, o de la memoria ferida," in: *Anuari de Filologia*, 17, E4 (1994), 105–116; Y. Barezl, "*Pirkei P. Sadeh*," in: *Hadoar* 76:6 (1997), 15–17; Z. Luz, *Ha-Meẓiut ha-Aḥeret: Al Shirat P. Sadeh* (2000); E. Ben Ezer, *Le-Hasbir la-Dagim: Edut al Pinchas Sadeh* (2002); Y. Laor, in: *Haaretz* (July 1, 2005); M. Harel, in: *Haaretz, Sefarim* (July 13, 2005).

[Anat Feinberg (2nd ed.)]

SADEH (Landsberg), YIẒḤAK (1890–1952), creator of the *Palmaḥ and its first commander. Born in Lublin, Poland, Sadeh served in the Russian army in World War I and was decorated for bravery. He continued to serve in the Red Army, where he commanded the first company of the first battalion. After the war he enrolled at the University of Simferopol, Crimea, studying philology and philosophy, and became a champion wrestler and weight-lifter. A meeting with Joseph *Trumpeldor, which took place in 1917, had a profound influence on the course of Sadeh's life. In 1920, when news reached him of Trumpeldor's death in action at Tel Ḥai, Sadeh left for Ereẓ Israel, where he became one of the founders of *Gedud ha-Avodah (the Joseph Trumpeldor Labor Battalion) and was elected its head. As such, he divided his time between working as a skilled laborer (he was an expert stone quarrier) and providing the men of the Gedud ha-Avodah with military training. When the Gedud ha-Avodah disintegrated, Sadeh retired for a while from public service, but presented himself again to the *Haganah at the outbreak of the 1936 riots. He was the first to propose to the Haganah the policy of "breaking out of the perimeter," i.e., not to confine itself to static defense behind the barbed wire fence of the settlement, but to attack the Arab terrorist bands in the open. This policy resulted in the formation of the Haganah field companies (*peluggot sadeh*, abbr. "Fosh"), which Sadeh commanded until 1938, when they were replaced by the field corps (*ḥeil sadeh*, abbr. "Ḥish"). Sadeh also became the commander of the new formation and within its framework founded a special commando unit (*peluggah li-fe'ullot meyuḥadot*, abbr. "Pom"), which incorporated a naval platoon and was trained for fighting on land and at sea. Sadeh commanded the operations of this unit in defending the establishment of the strategically placed new settlement *Ḥanitah in western Galilee. In 1941, when the Palmaḥ was founded – largely on Sadeh's initiative – he became staff officer for Palmaḥ affairs at Haganah headquarters and after a short while was appointed commanding officer of the Palmaḥ, which now had become a countrywide formation. He remained at this post until 1945, when he was promoted to acting chief of the Haganah general staff, and as such coordinated the combined resistance activities of the Haganah and the *Irgun Ẓeva'i Le'ummi and *Loḥamei Ḥerut Israel against the government in the final years of the Mandatory regime.

During the *War of Independence, Sadeh took part in a series of significant operations, the battle for Jerusalem among them. It was he who commanded the successful defense of Mishmar ha-Emek, which turned into a rout of the Arab Liberation Army. Upon his initiative, the Israel army formed its first armored brigade (which eventually became the Eighth Brigade); Sadeh became its commander, with the rank of *alluf*, and as such took part in "Operation Dani," capturing Lydda Airport and other points of strategic importance in the central sector of the front. One of the brigade battalions played a key role in the capture of the town of Lydda. In October 1948 the brigade was transferred to the Southern Command and in "Operation Yo'av" captured the Egyptian-held police fortress of Iraq-Suwaydān. In "Operation Ḥorev" (December 1948–January 1949) he took Niẓẓanah on the Sinai border and took part in the fighting around Rafi'aḥ (Rafah).

At the end of the war Sadeh retired from the Israel Defense Forces (IDF). Throughout his military career he had had a profound influence on the training, tactics, and strategy employed by the Haganah and the IDF and was both teacher and commander of most of Israel's senior military officers. Reconnaissance, field engineering, naval, and air operations were all innovations first introduced by him.

Sadeh was also a prolific writer of articles, short stories, and particularly plays, only a part of which were published. In the last years of his life, he worked on his memoirs, of which he completed the part dealing with his childhood and adolescence (*Ha-Pinkas Patu'aḥ*, 1952). He also wrote *Mi-Saviv la-*

Medurah (1946) and *Mah Ḥiddesh ha-Palmaḥ* (1950). He was buried at kibbutz Givat Brenner.

BIBLIOGRAPHY: N. Lorch, *The Edge of the Sword* (1962⁸), index; Z. Gil'ad (ed.), *Sefer ha-Palmaḥ*, 2 vols. (1953), index; Dinur, Haganah, index; M. Braslavsky, *Tenu'at ha-Po'alim ha-Ereẓ Yisre'elit*, 4 (1962), index; Mifleget ha-Po'alim ha-Me'uḥedet, *Le-Zikhro shel Yiẓḥak Sadeh* (1952); D. Lazar, *Rashim be-Yisrael*, 1 (1953), 16–19.

[Yigal Allon]

SA'DĪ, SA'ĪD BEN SHELOMO (late 17th early–18th centuries), Yemenite historian who lived in *San'ā, the author of *Dofi ha-Zeman* ("Fault of the Times"), a chronicle on the history of the Jews in *Yemen between 1717 and 1726. It was the first historical work to be written by a Yemenite scholar, followed by many others into the 20th century. It reflects the severe moral deterioration of the Jewish community of San'ā as a result of the destruction of the communal system after Yemenite Jews returned from their exile in *Mawza'. The authority of the religious and temporal authorities was almost completely lost – there were even Jewish prostitutes in San'ā. So the principal objective of this work, like that of his contemporary R. Yiḥye Ṣaliḥ in his *Peri Ẓaddik*, was to show the moral to be drawn from the misfortunes which befell Yemenite Jewry. It is therefore not surprising that the *tokhaḥot* of the author hold an important place in the work. The above events also left a deep impression on the author himself, because he lost three of his sons at that time.

BIBLIOGRAPHY: S. Geridi, *Mi-Teman le-Ẓiyyon* (1938), 119–22; Y. Qāfiḥ in: *Sefunot*, 1 (1956), 185–242. **ADD. BIBLIOGRAPHY:** Y. Tobi, *Iyyunim bi-Megillat Teman* (1986), 17–18.

[Yosef Tob (2nd ed.)]

SADIE, STANLEY (John, 1930–), British music critic, musicologist, author, and editor. Sadie was born in London, where he received his education, as well as at Gonville and Caius College, Cambridge. His dissertation was on "British Chamber Music, 1720–1790" (U. of Cambridge, 1958). He was a teacher at the Trinity College of Music, London (1957–65), a music critic of the London *Times* from 1964 to 1981, and a reviewer for *Gramophone* (1965–). He took over the editorship of the *Musical Times* in 1967 and was the editor in chief of the *New Grove's Dictionary of Music and Musicians* (1980) as well as its second edition (London 2000). Sadie served as president of the councils of the Royal Musical Association (1989–94) and The International Musicological Society (1992–97) and on the boards of several journals, including *Music and Letters*, from 1989, and *Journal of Musicology*, from 1982. His publications include *Handel* (1962), *Mozart* (1966, 1981), *Beethoven* (1967), *The Pan Book of Opera/ The Opera Guide* (with Arthur Jacobs, 1964, 1969), and *Handel Organ Concertos* (1972). A frequent contributor to musical journals, Sadie edited much 18th-century music, on which – as on Mozart and Handel – he was considered an expert. Along with his writings Sadie and his wife, the cellist, bass viol player, and musicologist Julie Anne Vertrees, initiated the foundation of the Handel House Museum in London; they are authors of a guide to European composer museums, *Calling on the Composer* (London 2000).

ADD. BIBLIOGRAPHY: Grove Music Online.

[Max Loppert / Israela Stein (2nd ed.)]

SA'DIS (Banū Sa'd), Arab dynasty of *sharīf*s (descendants of the Prophet *Muhammad) who penetrated *Morocco and ruled it from the mid-16th century to the 1660s. They succeeded the *Wattasids, retained *Fez as their capital, and fought relentlessly against the Spanish and Portuguese occupation of parts of Morocco. At first the Sa'dis appeared to be fanatical religious zealots who were intolerant of non-Muslims. They imposed heavy taxes on the local Jewish community. As they consolidated their authority in the country, however, they gradually evinced greater toleration toward the Jewish minority. Like their Wattasid predecessors, the Sa'di sultans now employed Jews as physicians, diplomatic emissaries, and interpreters. Beginning in 1603, Abraham bin Wach and later Judah Levi served as ministers of the treasury. Members of the Jewish aristocratic Cabessa and Palache families were recruited by the sultan's court as agents and negotiators with European merchants who entered the country. Whereas the authorities increasingly proved to be friendly toward the Jews, the same could hardly be said of the Muslim masses as well as local urban and rural chieftains and governors – the Arabs more than the *Berbers – who from time to time subjected them to harsh humiliations. The Sa'dis were succeeded in 1666 by another branch of their family, the *Alawid dynasty, whose sultans and kings ruled Morocco continuously. The current king of Morocco, Muhammad VI, is a member of this dynasty.

BIBLIOGRAPHY: E. Bashan, *Yahadut Marokko* (2000); D. Corcos, *Studies in the History of the Jews of Morocco* (1976); H.Z. Hirschberg, *A History of the Jews in North Africa*, vols. 1–2 (1974); D.J. Schroeter, *The Sultan's Jews: Morocco and the Sephardi World* (2002); N.A. Stillman, *Jews of Arab Lands* (1979).

[Michael M. Laskier (2nd ed.)]

SAFDIE, MOSHE (1938–), architect and urban designer. Safdie was born in Haifa. A youthful Zionist and socialist, he was dismayed when his family relocated to Montreal when he was 15. He graduated in architecture at McGill University in 1961 before moving to Philadelphia, where he apprenticed for two years under Louis I. *Kahn. Safdie returned to Montreal to open his own architectural office. He took charge of the master plan for Expo '67 in Montreal and was able to realize his graduate thesis as "Habitat 67," a cellular housing scheme. Like LEGO, this prefabricated residence complex could be transported and resituated. This innovative design brought Safdie immediate international recognition and project commissions in Puerto Rico and New York.

In 1967 Safdie returned to Israel and a Jerusalem reunified after the Six-Day War. He opened a Jerusalem office in 1970 and contributed significantly to the restoration of the Old City of Jerusalem and to connecting the New and Old Cities of Jerusalem. He also was engaged in developing the city of

Modi'in, the Yad Vashem Holocaust Museum, the Rabin Memorial Center, and the new Ben-Gurion International Airport in Israel.

In 1978, Safdie was appointed Ian Woodner Professor of Architecture and Urban Design at the Harvard Graduate School of Design and established his firm's main office in Somerville, Massachusetts. However, he continued to have a strong Canadian presence. He designed major Canadian public institutions, including the Vancouver Public Library, the Quebec Museum of Civilization, and the National Gallery of Canada. Safdie's institutional, cultural, and educational commissions are also found across the United States, in Israel, and around the world, with projects in Singapore, Iran, Senegal, India, and the Canadian arctic. Many of his commissions have been honored with major national and international awards.

In addition to his headquarters in Somerville, Safdie maintains offices in Toronto and Jerusalem. In 1986 Safdie was made an Officer of the Order of Canada. He is the brother of the artist Sylvia *Safdie.

[Aliza Craimer (2nd ed.)]

SAFDIE, SYLVIA (1942–), artist. The daughter of Leon and Rachel (Essen) Safdie, Sylvia Safdie was born in Aley ('Aleih), near *Beirut, Lebanon, into an artistic and literary family. Her brother Moshe *Safdie (1938–) is a renowned architect. Her brother GABRIEL SAFDIE (1940–) is a poet and teacher of literature. Sylvia Safdie spent her early years in Haifa but immigrated to Montreal with her family in 1953. After graduating from Concordia University in Fine Arts, Safdie earned a national and international reputation as a visual and conceptual artist, with numerous solo and group shows to her credit. She employed a wide variety of media, from traditional drawing, painting, and sculpture to inventories of found objects, installation art, and video. Her work is in permanent collections in Canada, Brazil, Denmark, Switzerland, and the United States. With her trip to Israel in 1978, when she visited desert areas as well as older parts of Haifa, Jaffa, and Jerusalem, Safdie's art embraced her Israeli roots. Other significant art trips took her to Morocco in 1981, Mexico in 1985, and more recently to India. Her pieces are usually developed in specific series, sometimes over many years, often carrying simple Hebrew words as titles: *Be'er* (well), *Ever* (other side), *Glimot* (cloaks), *Keren* (light ray), *Kever* (grave), *Lehav* (eternal flame), *Sefer* (book), *Tzel* (shadow), *Zakhor* (memory). Other series titles include: Bronze/Stone, Earth Marks, Earth Notes, Conjunctions, Feet, Head, Journals, Notations, Source, Steel/Stone, Threshhold. Safdie seems to find her strongest inspiration in natural organic forms, including the human figure, and in cultural artifacts. One of her most interesting pieces is Earth (1977), an ongoing collection and installation of small vessels filled with earth of various colors and textures collected from some 500 places around the world.

BIBLIOGRAPHY: J.D. Campbell, *Sylvia Safdie* (1987); A. Lamarre, "Sylvia Safdie," in: *Parachute*, 62 (April-June 1991), 37–39; (1995); R. Daskalova, "Mindful Movement: Rossitza Daskalova Contemplates the Work of Sylvia Safdie," in: *C: International Contemporary Art*, 66 (Summer 2000), 22–26; G. Wajcman, *Autres Territoires/Other Places* (2000); I. Zantovska Murray and S. Reid, *Sylvia Safdie: The Inventories of Invention* (2003).

[Bernard Katz (2nd ed.)]

SAFED (Heb. צְפַת), principal town of Upper Galilee, situated on a mountain 2,780 ft. (850 m.) high, 30 mi. (48 km.) east of Acre, 25 mi. (40 km.) north of Tiberias. Not mentioned in the Bible, Safed has sometimes been identified with Sepph (Gr. Σεπφ), the city fortified by Josephus in the Upper Galilee at the time of an expected Roman attack in 66 C.E. (Wars, 2:573); the name is missing in a parallel list (Life, 187–8). In the Jerusalem Talmud (RH 2:1, 58a) Safed is mentioned as one of the mountaintop points from which fire signals were given to announce the New Moon and festivals during the Second Temple period. Two liturgical poems for the Ninth of Av by Eleazar *Kallir, *Eikhah Yashevah* and *Zekhor Eikhah*, refer to Safed as a place where priestly families (Jakim and Pashhur) settled after the destruction of the Temple. The name is repeated in the various *kerovot* (hymns recited before the *Amidah*) by poets who wrote in the sixth, seventh, and eighth centuries.

Between the talmudic period and the Crusades the history of Safed is not known. The town reappears in 1140 under the name Saphet, a "fortress of very great strength between Acre and the Sea of Galilee" built by King Fulk of Anjou. Amalric I, the king of Jerusalem, handed it over in 1168 to the Knights Templar. Twenty years later, after his victory at Ḥittin, *Saladin took Safed (December 1188). His successors, the *Ayyubids, ordered the dismantling of the fortress in 1220; however, in 1240 Safed was recaptured and rebuilt by the Knights Templar. In 1266 it passed from the crusaders to the Mamluk sultan Baybars, who continued to strengthen its fortifications. In Safed, the *Mamluks established the headquarters of a "Mamlakah," a province which extended over Galilee and the Lebanon.

Jewish settlement in Safed is attested by *genizah* documents from the first half of the 11th century. However, Benjamin of Tudela, who visited the city in 1170/71, stated that no Jews lived there. Fifty years later the settlement was revived under Mamluk protection; R. Zadok, head of an academy of the *gaon* Jacob, was its most prominent member. **Genizah* documents confirm that there was a community at Safed in the 13th century; it continued to exist in the time of R. *Estori ha-Parḥi (early 14th century). In 1481 the Jewish community of Safed and of the villages in its vicinity numbered 300 families; it flourished under the protection of the Mamluk governors. Toward the end of Mamluk rule the community was greatly strengthened by an influx of refugees from Spain (1492). In 1495 the Jews of Safed were reported as trading in spices, cheese, oil, vegetables, and fruits. The Sephardi element further increased after the Ottoman conquest in 1516. In 1522 R. Moses *Basola found 300 Jewish families in Safed, composed of Sephardim, Moriscos, and Jews from the Maghreb. Later, three groups emerged among the Jews of Safed: Sephardim, Ashkenazim, and Italians. Among the prominent leaders of the community in the 16th century was R. Jacob (I) *Berab, who tried to reestablish the Sanhedrin and renew rabbinical ordination (*semikhah*). Other prominent rabbis included R. Joseph *Caro, the author of the Shulḥan Arukh, and his contemporary R. Moses *Trani. The leading kabbalist R. Isaac *Luria lived in Safed and his important disciple R. Ḥayyim *Vital resided there for some time. In the 16th century Safed was the center of Jewish mysticism (see *Kabbalah). The spiritual flowering of the town was accompanied by material prosperity. The newcomers established looms, whose products competed with those of *Venice. In addition the Jews of Safed traded in the local produce of Galilee: oil, honey, silk, and spices. They also received both Jewish and gentile pilgrims in their homes.

Turkish statistics of 1548 show Safed as the center of a district of 282 villages. Approximately 1,900 families of taxpayers lived in the town (716 of them Jewish), as well as 251 single taxpayers (only 56 of them Jewish). In 1563 the brothers Ashkenazi set up the first printing press in the town (see below); it was not only the first one in Ereẓ Israel but also the first in the Orient. The Jews of Safed had eight synagogues; they numbered their town among the Four Sacred Cities of the Holy Land, calling it also Beth-El. In addition to the Jewish community, Samaritans also lived there during the 16th century. With the gradual decline in the quality of Turkish rule in the 17th century, the prosperity of the Jewish community also began to drop off. The material decline did not immediately influence the spiritual level of the community. In spite of high taxes and 1,200 poor living on charity, there were 300 rabbinical scholars, 18 schools, 21 synagogues and a large yeshivah with 100 pupils, and 20 teachers at the beginning of the 17th century. The Jewish community at that time split into four congregations: Ashkenazim, Portuguese Jews, Provençal Jews, and Italians. Toward the end of the 17th century the community declined rapidly – in 1695/96 only 20 Jews paid the poll tax. An epidemic decimated the community in 1747 and an earthquake in 1759 killed 2,000, among them 190 Jews. After the disaster the survivors began to leave the town; by 1764 there were only 50 Sephardi families in Safed.

Toward the end of the 18th century the establishment of a more stable government in Galilee (first by the sheikh Dhāhir al Omar and then by Jazzr Pasha) led to an improvement in the position of the community. Moreover, immigration was renewed, with settlers coming from East European countries. In 1778 over 300 Ḥasidim, disciples of R. *Israel b. Eliezer Ba'al Shem Tov, settled in Safed; they were led by R. *Menahem Mendel of Vitebsk. The disciples of Elijah, the Gaon of Vilna, who were opponents of the Ḥasidim, came in 1810, led by R. *Israel b. Samuel of Shklov. Renewed warfare between the Bedouins, and epidemics in 1812–14, caused an exodus of Jews, mainly to Jerusalem and the villages in Galilee.

[Michael Avi-Yonah]

Modern Period

Under the benevolent rule of *Ibrahim Pasha (1831–40) the town at first progressed and became Galilee's commercial center, but toward the end of his rule it suffered from the strife between Arabs and Druzes and the Arab revolt against Ibrahim Pasha. It was particularly stricken in a violent earthquake (1837) which destroyed most of its houses and reportedly caused the death of 5,000 persons, 4,000 of whom were Jews. Many of the surviving rabbinical scholars went to Hebron. The Hebrew printing press of Israel *Bak, which had been founded in 1831, was transferred after the earthquake to Kefar Jarmaq (Mount Meron) and later to *Jerusalem (see below). The Jewish community, which in 1839 had dwindled to 1,500 persons, further decreased to a mere 400 in 1845. However, the country's administration stabilized under the Turkish sultan ʿAbdul Majīd and Safed's situation improved. The former Jewish inhabitants returned and new immigrants settled, bringing the Jewish community to 2,100 persons in 1856, and to 6,620 in 1895 (comprising 4,500 Ashkenazim and 2,120 Sephardim), who then constituted the majority of a total population of 12,820. The Jewish community increased further to 8,000 persons in 1908, and to 11,000 (out of a total population of 25,000) in 1913.

At the end of the 19th century Rabbi M. Taubenhaus founded a weaving shop at Safed to provide employment for Jewish workers, and opened a soup kitchen for the poor. The first Jewish kindergarten was opened on his initiative in 1906 with the support of B'nai B'rith; in 1910 it was enlarged to become a modern elementary school. The initiative for the changeover to productive work in this community influenced groups of Jews from Safed to attempt agricultural settlement at Gei Oni (later *Rosh Pinnah) and at Benei Yehudah on the Golan. Workshops, mostly for local consumption (e.g., bakeries), were opened in the Jewish quarter, but the majority of the community remained dependent on *ḥalukkah* from abroad. In World War I the Safed community was cut off from its sources of support in Europe, and its Jewish population was decimated by hunger and disease. The city's Arab population, whose economy was based on trade, commerce, and auxiliary farming, was less affected. On Sept. 28, 1918, the town was occupied by the British forces under Allenby. In 1922 Safed's population of 8,760 was composed of 5,431 Muslims, 2,986 Jews, and 343 Christians. While good relations between Arabs and Jews had previously been the rule, the Arab population, instigated by the nationalists, assaulted the Jewish quarter in the 1929 riots and killed several of the inhabitants. By 1935 the number of Jews decreased to 2,475, and their percentage in the total population fell to 27%. It shrank further in the 1930s and 1940s when local educational and economic opportunities for the community's youth were limited. In Israel's *War of Independence (1948), less than 2,000 of the 12,000 inhabitants were Jews, living in the narrow quarter on the northern and northwestern slope of Safed Hill. When the British evacuated the town they permitted Arab forces (estimated at 4,000–4,500 men, including detachments of the Iraqi and

Lebanese armies) to occupy the two large police buildings in key positions, thereby sealing off the Jewish quarter. On May 1, 1948, a *Palmaḥ force advanced from positions on Mount Canaan and *Biriyyah, occupied the Arab villages of Biriyyah and Ein Zeitun, and from there entered the Jewish quarter by hidden paths, bringing the number of its defenders from about 60 to 222. On May 10–11, 1948, the defenders launched attacks on the Arab positions and captured them as well as the Meẓudah ("fortress") on top of Safed Hill. The entire Arab population and armed forces fled. Safed became a Jewish town.

After 1948 mainly new immigrants from different countries settled in Safed. Its population numbered 7,900 in 1953 and 13,100 in 1970. The town's economy was based principally on branches of tourism, recreation, and industry. Some of the hotels operated mainly in the summer months. The dry mountain air in summer is noted for its curative quality for respiratory ailments. The hotels were situated both in the town proper and on Mt. Canaan (3,000 ft., 920m., above sea level). A regional hospital with 500 beds was built in 1970. Industry included metal factories (for sewing machines), textile weaving and apparel, food products (notably instant coffee), tobacco, and diamond polishing.

In 2002 the population of Safed was 26,400, occupying an area of 15 sq. mi. (40 sq. km.). Residents were employed in industry, services, and commerce. The picturesque artists' quarter, where scores of painters and sculptors live permanently or seasonally, continued to constitute a tourist attraction. In addition to the individual artists' galleries there was a communal exhibit in the quarter. There were also Bible and Kabbalah museums and a flourishing *ba'alei teshuvah* community as well as thousands of Russian and Ethiopian immigrants. Every summer the city hosts a klezmer festival and pilgrims flock to the graves of Jewish saints on the outskirts of the city, the most famous being the grave of R. *Simeon Bar Yoḥai, where tens of thousands congregate on *Lag ba-Omer.

[Efraim Orni / Shaked Gilboa (2nd ed.)]

Historic Buildings and Archaeological Restorations

Safed still contains six old synagogues, including the famous Ari synagogue (of R. Isaac Luria) dating from the 16th century, which belongs to the Sephardi community and consists of two vaulted rooms with a courtyard. Another synagogue of Luria belongs to the Ashkenazim and was renewed after the earthquake of 1837. Other famous synagogues are named after R. Yose ha-Bannai, R. Joseph *Caro, and R. Isaac *Aboab.

Muslim rule in Safed has left numerous monuments, mostly of the Mamluks. These include: the so-called Zāwiyat Banāt Hamīd (built in 1372 with additions in 1449); the Red Mosque (el-Jamiʾ el-Aḥmar; built in 1275–76); the Jamiʾ el-Jukandār (named after a Mamluk ruler of 1309–11, though the building actually is from a later date); the "Cave of the Daughters of Jacob" (*Magharat Banī Yaʿqūb*) and its adjoining mosque (both repaired in 1412); and the Main Mosque (Jamiʾ as-Sūq) of 1901 and another of 1913. Excavations were started under Israeli auspices in the citadel by M. Dothan in 1950 on behalf of the Department of Antiquities. Crusader and Mamluk walls and foundations were uncovered (most of the walls visible above the surface had been dismantled by the Arabs) as were a complicated system of wells and channels underground.

[Michael Avi-Yonah]

Hebrew Printing

In 1573 the well-known Hebrew printer Eliezer b. Isaac Ashkenazi and his son, Isaac of Prague, left Lublin for Ereẓ Israel, taking with them their printing tools, type, and decorations. After three years in *Constantinople, where they printed some books, they proceeded to Safed. There they set up as printers in partnership with Abraham b. Isaac Ashkenazi, a resident of Safed who provided the funds necessary for the enterprise. Between 1577 and 1580 they issued three books. Then Abraham left for *Yemen as an emissary of the Tiberias yeshivah, selling his books at the same time. In 1587 Eliezer printed three more books; like the first three, they were all by Safed authors.

In 1832 the printer Israel Bak of Berdichev settled in Safed and issued four books up to 1834, the year the community was pillaged by Arab villagers. In 1836 printing was resumed with the publication of *Pe'at ha-Shulḥan* by Israel of Shklov. As a result of the earthquake of 1837 Bak went on to Jerusalem. Between 1863 and 1866 Dober b. Samuel Kara, of Skole (Galicia), printed some eight books in Safed. Ten years later Abraham Ẓevi Spiegelmann and his partners began printing, but only three works are known to have appeared up to 1885. In 1913 Barukh Barzel and his partners opened a Hebrew press called "Defus ha-Galil," with some 20 books being printed up to 1926. This press served Hebrew writers who found refuge in Safed during World War I. Later, A. Friedmann took over the press, which printed the Haganah paper *Kol Ẓefat* during the War of Independence.

[Avraham Yaari]

BIBLIOGRAPHY: Avi-Yonah, Geog; Neubauer, Géogr, 227; Conder-Kitchener, 1 (1881), 248ff., 255–6; S. Klein, *Beitraege zur Geographie und Geschichte Galilaeas* (1909), 58; V. Guérin, *Description géographique…*, 2 pt. 3 (1880), 419, 426; J. Braslavski, *Le-Ḥeker Arẓenu* (1954), index; idem, in: BJPES, 9 (1941–42), 55–56; Abel, in: RB, 40 (1931), 602; Israel, Misrad ha-Ḥinnukh ve-ha-Tarbut, *Alon Maḥleket ha-Attikot*, 3 (1951), 13; I. Ben-Zvi and M. Benayahu (eds.), *Sefer Ẓefat*, 2 vols. (= *Sefunot*, vols. 6–7, 1962–63), incl. bibl.; M. Ish-Shalom, *Masei Noẓerim le-Ereẓ Yisrael* (1965), index; E. Rey, *Les Colonies franques de Syrie…* (1883), 445; I. Ben-Zvi, *Sefer ha-Shomronim* (1935), 76; idem, *Ereẓ Yisrael ve-Yishuvah* (1967^2), index; S. Schechter, *Studies in Judaism*, 2 (1908), 202–306; M. Benayahu, in: *Sefer Assaf* (1953), 109–25; idem, in: *Sefer ha-Yovel le-Yiẓḥak Baer* (1960), 248–69; idem, in: *Sinai*, 43 (1958), 35–113; J. Kena'ani, in: *Zion*, 6 (1934), 172–217; J. Katz, *ibid.*, 16 (1951), 28–45 (second pagination); B. Lewis, *Notes and Documents from the Turkish Archives* (1952), index; idem, in: *Yerushalayim*, 4 (1953), 134–7; U. Heyd, *ibid.*, 5 (1955), 128–35; idem, *Ottoman Documents on Palestine* (1960), index; idem, in: *Press Festschrift* (1954), 184; B. Lewis, *ibid.*, 134–5; *Sefer ha-Yishuv*, 1 (1939), 142; 2 (1944), 54; D. Tamar, in: *Divrei ha-Congress ha-Olami ha-Revi'i le-Madda'ei ha-Yahadut*, 2 (1968), 181–7 (Heb. sec.); idem, in: Y. Raphael (ed.), *Rabbi Yosef Caro* (1969), 7–18; J. Pinkerfeld, *Battei Kenesiyyot be-Ereẓ Yisrael* (1946), 38–44, pts. 21–24; idem, L.A. Mayer, and J.W. Hirschberg (eds.), *Some Principal Muslim Religious Buildings in Israel* (1950), 41–48; A.M. Habermann, *Toledot ha-Defus ha-Ivri bi-Ẓefat* (1962); Yaari, Sheluḥei, index; idem, *Ha-Defus ha-Ivri be-Arẓot ha-Mizraḥ*, 1 (1936), 9–28; idem, in: KS, 24 (1947/48), 66. **ADD. BIBLIOGRAPHY:** Y. Tsafrir, L. Di Segni, and J. Green, *Tabula Imperii Romani. Iudaea – Palaestina. Maps and Gazetteer.* (1994), 226–27, s.v. "Sephoris." **WEBSITE:** www. sefad.co.il.

SAFFRON (Heb. כַּרְכֹּם, *karkom*), the *Crocus sativus*; an aromatic golden dye was extracted from the stigmas of its golden blossoms. It was also dried and used for flavoring foods. In the Bible *karkọm* is mentioned once among the various spices that grew in the imaginary spice garden to which the charms of the beloved are compared (Song 4:14). Most of them are enumerated in an early *baraita* as ingredients of the incense used in the Temple (Ker. 6a; v. *Pittum ha-Ketoret*). Since both passages refer to tropical spices brought from distant lands, Immanuel Loew was of the opinion that the *karkom* is a tropical incense plant, the *Curcuma longa*, called by the ancients "Indian saffron," *Crocus indicus*. This belongs to the family of Zingiberaceae from whose rhizome a golden yellow material called Curcumin is extracted and used for dyeing and flavoring food, as well as for dyeing clothes. This identification is doubtful, however, because the substance is not especially aromatic, nor is there any reason to doubt the traditional explanation that biblical *karkom* is indeed identical with saffron (Sanskrit *kurkuma*, Gr. and Lat. *krokos*). It is a tuber which apparently originated in the mountains of the Caspian Sea region. Its name in Aramaic and Arabic is *zafrana*, from which the word saffron is derived. During the mishnaic and talmudic period saffron was widely used in Ereẓ Israel and Babylon. It was planted in fields, and a "field full of saffron" was considered very precious. According to tradition, Joshua the son of Nun had already made regulations with regard to this plant (BK 81a). The verb *nitkarkem* (i.e., "turned yellow," pale) derives from the yellow color of the *karkom* (Gen. R. 99:9 et al.). In the Talmud, Abbaye describes the structure of the stigma from which the saffron was extracted (Nid. 20a). In medieval times saffron was a valuable commodity and Jews traded extensively in it. Since some adulterated saffron by adding fibers of horse meat to it, Solomon b. Abraham *Adret of Barcelona in the 13th century forbade its use in food. The yellow *badge the Jews were compelled to wear – according to the first papal decree instituting it – had to be dyed with saffron (see Singermann in bibl.). The importance of saffron has diminished, although Oriental Jews occasionally use it to color and flavor their food. It is hardly grown at all in Israel. Seven species of crocus, some with very beautiful flowers, grow wild in Israel.

BIBLIOGRAPHY: F. Singermann, *Ueber Juden-Abzeichen* (1915); Loew, Flora, 2 (1924), 7–25; H.N. and A.L. Moldenke, *Plants of the Bible* (1952), index; J. Feliks, *Olam ha-Ẓome'aḥ ha-Mikra'i* (1968^2), 249–51.

[Jehuda Feliks]

SAFI, formerly **Asfi**, Atlantic seaport, provincial capital, and province, Tansift region, western *Morocco. It was originally settled by the Canaanites and absorbed such groups as the Carthaginians, who named the city Asfi, Romans, Jews who arrived from Palestine, Goths, and, after 640 C.E., the invading Arab Muslims. The Portuguese conquered and occupied Safi at the beginning of the 16th century and held on to it until 1541, building a citadel around it. Since then Safi was dominated by the Sharifian dynasties – the Sa'dis and Alawites. Safi became a prosperous port serving as a link between vital commercial arteries for parts of southern and western Morocco, and as the port for the export goods of important inland cities like *Marrakesh. The city's prosperity reached its zenith in the first half of the 17th century. Nevertheless, this port is still blessed to this day with burgeoning textile and chemical (phosphate-based) industries. It also conducts major fishing and sardine canning activities.

Safi's Jewish community maintained vital trade relations with Majorca and Portugal during the 14th and 15th centuries. Its Jews were entrusted with overseeing business affairs in the trade conduits between Morocco, Portugal, and Guinea. Numerous exiles (*megorashim*) from the Iberian Peninsula settled there in 1492 and 1497. Even though Portugal expelled its Jews, in Safi and other parts of Morocco, the occupiers – the Portuguese – collaborated with the expellees – the Jewish refugees – in commercial activity.

Under the rule of the Portuguese, the Jews were assured that they would neither be exiled from Safi nor be compelled to accept Christianity. The Portuguese monarchy elevated a number of Jews to prominence, such as interpreters, officials, counselors, and trade negotiators. After the retreat of Portugal and the ascendance of the *Sa'dis (the 1540s), the position of the Jews improved markedly. Moreover, with the penetration of British trade and political influence into Moroccan towns along the Atlantic coast, among them Essaouira (*Mogador) and Safi, beginning in the 17th century, the port of Safi was often leased to Jewish merchants, who gradually cultivated a monopoly of the commercial transactions with Europe and the Americas. Among the noted Jewish families engaged in trade were the *Palaches, Xérès, Corcos, and *Chriqui-Delevante.

On the eve of World War I there were approximately 2,500 Jews in Safi out of no more than 25,000 inhabitants. The community managed to remain large (over 3,600 in 1936 and 4,500 in 1951) throughout the French protectorate era. After Moroccan independence in 1956, its numbers dwindled to 1,434 in 1960 and fewer than 700 in 1968. This was attributed to migration to parts of Europe, Canada, and *aliyah* to Israel.

BIBLIOGRAPHY: D. Corcos, "Safi," in: *Sefunot*, 10 (1964); H.Z. Hirschberg, *A History of the Jews in North Africa*, 1–2 (1974); M.M. Laskier, *The Alliance Israélite Universelle and the Jewish Communities of Morocco 1862–1962* (1983); J.-L. Miège, *Le Maroc et l'Europe 1830–1894*, 1–4 (1961–63); J.M. Toledano, *Ner ha-Ma'arav* (1911).

[Michael M. Laskier (2nd ed.)]

SAFIRE, WILLIAM (1929–), columnist. Born in New York, he studied at Syracuse University but left after only two years, in 1949. His first job was as a researcher for Tex McCracy, who had a gossip column in the *New York Herald Tribune*. After serving as a correspondent in Europe and the Middle East for WNBC radio and TV, he joined the U.S. Army in 1952, working for the Armed Forces Radio Network for the next two years.

On leaving the service, Safire returned to New York, where he worked for Tex McCracy's public relations firm and helped to produce McCracy's syndicated radio show. In 1959 Safire opened his own public relations firm and traveled to Moscow that year for the American National Exhibition. While there, he met Vice President Richard Nixon and helped to set up the famous "kitchen debate" between Nixon and Soviet Premier Nikita Khrushchev, in which each leader argued the merits of his country's particular system of government.

During the 1960 presidential campaign, Safire was in charge of special projects for the Nixon-Lodge candidacy and wrote much of the campaign literature. In 1961 he established Safire Public Relations Inc., which handled the campaigns of a number of New York Republican leaders, including Nelson Rockefeller, Jacob Javits, and John Lindsay. His first two books appeared during this period, *The Relations Explosion* (1963) and *Plunging into Politics* (1964).

From 1965 on Safire was immersed in Richard Nixon's campaign for the presidency. He ghostwrote Nixon's syndicated column and, in 1968, authored Nixon's election victory speech. His third book appeared that year entitled *The New Language of Politics*. As a special assistant to President Nixon, Safire wrote major speeches for the president on the Vietnam War and economic policies. On loan to Spiro Agnew in 1972, Safire coined the oft-quoted alliterative phrases "nattering nabobs of negativism" and "hopeless hysterical hypochondriacs of history." His articles for the *New York Times* and *Washington Post* during the campaign ultimately led to the invitation for him to write a regular column in the *New York Times*, which he began in 1974.

Safire wrote his White House memoirs in a non-fiction volume entitled *Before the Fall* (1975) and in a political novel, *Full Disclosure* (1977). He combined the talents of columnist and investigative reporter when in 1977 he broke the story on the financial affairs of Bert Lance, President Jimmy Carter's special assistant and key fundraiser. That investigation led to Safire's winning a Pulitzer Prize in 1978 for "distinguished commentary."

In 1979 he began a regular Sunday column in *The New York Times Magazine* entitled "On Language," which focuses on grammar, usage, and etymology.

An avowed "hawk" on foreign policy, Safire also strongly supported Israel. He especially championed the government of Menachem Begin and Begin's bombing of the nuclear reactor in Iraq.

His other books include *On Language* (1980), *Safire's Washington* (1980), *Leadership* (1991), *Fumblerulers* (1991), *Safire's New Political Dictionary* (1993), *The First Dissident: The Book of Job in Today's Politics* (1992), *No Uncertain Terms* (2003), and the novels *Freedom* (1987), *Sleeper Spy* (1995), and *Scandalmonger* (2000). He also edited *Good Advice* (with L. Safire, 1993) and *Lend Me Your Ears: Great Speeches in History* (1997).

Safire's grandfather was the publisher of one of New York's daily Yiddish newspapers.

[David Geffen / Ruth Beloff (2nd ed.)]

SAFRA (first half of fourth century C.E.), Babylonian *amora*. In Babylon, Safra studied under *Abba (Pes. 51b). He paid several visits to Ereẓ Israel but never received permission to teach there. His decisions are not quoted in Palestinian sources, although he is known to have discussed *halakhah* with such Palestinian authorities as *Abbahu (Av. Zar. 4a; Git. 29b). As a result he transmitted to Babylon some of the early traditions followed in Ereẓ Israel (Kid. 30a). *Abbaye states that Safra's reports were often quoted in the Babylonian academies (MK 25a), and Safra also asked Zerika specific questions on Abbaye's behalf (Ḥul. 110b). Among his Babylonian colleagues were *Ḥanina b. Papa (Git. 29b) and Huna b. Ḥanina (Shab. 124a). Like most Babylonian scholars, Safra was more versed in the *halakhah* than in *aggadah*. On one occasion, when the authorities of Caesarea doubted Safra's right to exemption from the payment of tax (a concession to scholars), Abbahu pointed out "He is a scholar of the Talmud, not of the Bible" (Av. Zar. 4a).

Safra was a businessman (BB 144a), a partner of *Issur Giora (BM 31b), and his business honesty was legendary (Mak. 24a). It is related that once, while praying, he was approached by a prospective buyer for his ass. The buyer, interpreting Safra's refusal to interrupt his prayers as a sign of disapproval of the price offered, successively raised his bids. However, when Safra had completed his prayers, he insisted on taking the price first offered (*She'iltot, Parshat Va-Yeḥi*, ed. Minsky, 252). He was also highly praised for his piety and modesty (Pes. 113a–b), and for his courtesy toward his colleagues (Suk. 39a; cf. Ḥul. 94b). Little is known of Safra's private life. His wife died soon after their marriage, and he never remarried (Pes. 113a). His brother Dimi was also a scholar. When Safra died, in Pumbedita, Abbaye instructed his pupils to accord him the highest honors due to a deceased scholar (MK 25a).

BIBLIOGRAPHY: Hyman, Toledot, 966–9.

SAFRA, family of bankers. The family's roots in banking go back to the early 19th century, in *Aleppo, Syria. From there the Safra family financed trade and exchanged currencies from several different countries in Asia, Europe, and Africa, as well as precious metals such as silver and gold. In the mid-19th century, the family founded Safra Frères et Cie, the first bank bearing the family's name. The reputation acquired by the bank enabled its expansion to Istanbul, Alexandria, and Beirut, and in the 20th century also to Europe and America.

In the early 20th century, JACOB SAFRA (1891–1963) founded the Jacob Safra Bank in *Beirut. He laid the foundation for modern banking based on improved communication and the growing demand for trade between the Middle

East and North America. In 1951 the Safra family moved beyond the Middle East, first to Italy and then, in 1952, to Brazil. Since then the family banking business has expanded to Europe, the United States, and throughout selected markets in Latin America.

Under the direction of Jacob's sons – ELIE (1922–), EDMOND (1932–1999), MOISE, and JOSEPH (1938–) – the Safra's business expanded. Edmond and Joseph focused primarily on furthering the family's prominence in banking worldwide, particularly private banking.

Edmond Safra founded with his father the Trade Development Bank in 1956, which was sold to American Express in 1983. In 1966, Edmond founded the Republic National Bank of New York, which became one of the most respected banks worldwide. In 1988, he established Safra Republic Holdings S.A., a wealth management firm catering to the European marketplace. Both companies were sold to HSBC in 1999.

Joseph built the Safra Brazilian banking and investment businesses, the most prominent of which were Banco Safra Brazil in 1957; Safra National Bank of New York in 1980; Banque Safra Luxembourg in 1985; Banque Jacob Safra Suisse in 2000. Among other successful global investments are Aracruz in 1985 (pulp factory) and Cellcom Israel (cellular phone company) in 1994, which was sold in 2005.

The Safra family is distinguished for its prolific philanthropy and is particularly generous to Jewish causes. They have undertaken numerous donations to hospitals, schools, universities, and synagogues throughout the world.

[Rachel Mizrahi (2nd ed.)]

SAFRAI, SHMUEL (1919–2003), scholar in the fields of Jewish history, Talmud, and Bible. Safrai was born in Warsaw and arrived in Palestine with his parents in 1922. From 1931 to 1939 he studied at the Merkaz ha-Rav Yeshivah, being ordained there as a rabbi at the age of 20. In 1952 and 1957 he received his M.A. and Ph.D. degrees from The Hebrew University of Jerusalem, becoming a professor there in 1978. With his colleagues David *Flusser and Robert Lindsey, he founded the Jerusalem School of Synoptic Research, dedicated to the historical, linguistic, and critical study of the synoptic gospels. He was also a frequent contributor to *Jerusalem Perspective* magazine. Safrai received the Jerusalem Prize in 1986 and the Israel Prize in 2002 for "his great expertise in the Mishnah and Talmud, in Greek and Latin sources, and in the formation of nascent Christianity." He wrote over 80 articles and 12 books, including *Pilgrimage in the Period of the Second Temple* and *Rabbi Akiva ben Yosef: His Life and Teachings.*

[Shaked Gilboa (2nd ed.)]

SAFRAN, ALEXANDER (1910–2006), rabbi. Born in Bacău, Romania, he was elected chief rabbi of Romania in 1940, thereby becoming the only representative of the Jewish community in the Romanian Senate. The Fascist government made Safran their first Jewish hostage, but this did not prevent him from making his home the center of the Jewish underground movement. He repeatedly intervened with Romanian government officials, the Church, diplomatic representatives of neutral countries, and other international bodies to alleviate anti-Jewish measures and in 1942 was able to bring pressure on the government to resist the Nazi demand that the Romanian Jews be deported. On the advent of Communism in 1948, he moved to Switzerland and was appointed chief rabbi of Geneva and lecturer in Jewish thought at Geneva University. Safran was active in many international Jewish organizations and wrote books on Jewish subjects.

SAFRAN, BEZALEL ZE'EV (1866–1930), Romanian rabbi. Safran studied under his grandfather Hanoch Henikh Safran of Pomeran, Galicia, Isaac Aaron Ittinga of Lemberg and Jacob Wiedenfeld of Grimailov. He served as rabbi of the Romanian towns of Secueni from 1887, and of Ştefaneşti from 1899. From 1905 until his death he was rabbi of the Romanian oil town Bacău and district. He was regarded as the most important halakhic authority in Romania and virtually every Romanian rabbi addressed problems to him. In his responsa he discusses topical problems, such as mixed dancing at weddings, and the heating of food in an electric oven activated on the Sabbath by a time switch. In his responsa he makes wide use of the Jerusalem Talmud, which was generally ignored as a source by the authors of responsa. J.J. Weinberg described him as "one of the most erudite scholars of our generation," and "a living library of the vast rabbinic literature."

He wrote *Responsa Rabaz* on the Shulḥan Arukh *Oraḥ Ḥayyim* and *Yoreh De'ah* (1930), and on *Even ha-Ezer* (1962); *Yalkut ha-Ḥinnukhi*, responsa on aggadic matters – an appendix to Part 1 of the *Responsa Rabaz; Doresh le-Ẓiyyon*, on the religious duty of settling in Ereẓ Israel (about which he expresses enthusiasm), also included in the *Minḥat Azkarah* (1933), which contains his biography, and letters appraising his *Responsa Rabaz*; and *Yevakkesh Da'at*, glosses and notes to the *She'elot u-Teshuvot Maharsham* of Shalom Mordecai of Brzeziny. *Yevakkesh Da'at* was originally lost but was recovered among the various works saved from the Holocaust.

Safran left a ramified family, many of whom served in the Romanian rabbinate and were later dispersed throughout the world. They included Hanoch Henikh Safran, rabbi of Bucharest and publisher of his books; Dr. Alexander *Safran, chief rabbi of Romania and then rabbi of Geneva; Dr. Joseph Safran, chief rabbi of Jassy; and Dr. Menahem Safran, rabbi of Ploeşti.

BIBLIOGRAPHY: J.J. Weinberg, in: *Oẓar ha-Ḥayyim*, 8 (1932), 173–5; idem, in: *Kibbuẓei Efrayim*, 11 (1932), 19f.; H.H. Safran, *Minḥat Azkarah* (1933); A. Stern, *Meliẓei Esh al Ḥodshei Kislev... Adar* (1962), 32 no. 103; L. Jung (ed.), *Men of the Spirit* (1969), 437–55.

[Itzhak Alfassi]

SAFRAN, JOSEPH (1911–), rabbi and educator. Safran, the son of Rabbi Bezalel Ze'ev Safran, was born in Bacău, Romania. He studied at the Jewish Theological Seminary in Vienna where, among his teachers were Samuel *Krauss and A. Aptowitzer, receiving his rabbinical diploma from the Seminary in 1936 and his doctorate from the University of Vienna in 1937.

In 1938 he was appointed chief rabbi of Jassy, Romania, where he developed a remarkable educational network which strengthened the Jewish educational system of the community, especially after the mass pogrom of 1941.

In 1944 he immigrated to Ereẓ Israel and served as head of the Marriage Bureau of the Chief Rabbinate of Tel Aviv until 1957, when he emigrated to the United States. In the following year he was appointed to the teaching staff at the Yeshiva University in New York and then professor of Jewish Education at the Ferkauf Graduate School of Humanities and Social Sciences at Yeshiva University.

SAFRIN, ISAAC JUDAH JEHIEL (1806–1874), ḥasidic leader. Safrin was the son of Alexander Sender (d. 1818), author of *Zikhron Devarim* (1871), who served as rabbi in Zhidachov, Zhuravno, and Komarno, and founded the Komarno branch of the *Zhidachov dynasty. Isaac Safrin made his living at various times as a stonecutter and bookkeeper, renting a tavern in a village and collecting tolls. His teachers in Ḥasidism were his father, his uncle Moses of Sambor, his father-in-law Abraham Mordecai of Pinczow, and Isaac Eizik of Zhidachov.

Safrin left a diary, *Megillat Setarim* (1944), a book of visions (*ḥezyonot*) similar to Ḥayyim *Vital's *Sefer ha-Ḥezyonot* (1954). It relates dreams, revelations, and his search for "the root" of individual souls. In it Safrin hints that he is the *Messiah the son of Joseph, using the numerical value of the date of his birth תקס״ו (1806) in a Hebrew letter equation of משיח בן יוסף *Meshi'aḥ Ben Yosef* ("Messiah son of Joseph"), though he considered that his soul was the reincarnation of Simeon bar *Yoḥai, Isaac *Luria, and Israel b. Eliezer Ba'al Shem *Tov. Central to his thought was the necessity to bring about the restoration of the world order (*tikkun olam*), considering himself as one who would bring about the imminent End of Days and the Redemption. Thus his attitude toward Shabbateanism combined both attraction and antagonism. Safrin relates in his diary that "from the age of two until I became five years old, I had marvelous visions. A holy spirit filled me and I spoke words of prophecy… and I indeed saw from one end of the world to the other"(*Megillat Setarim*). He tells about his poverty and asceticism; he ate little and slept only two hours daily. He maintained the idea of constant *devekut* ("devotion to God") which is integrated into the pattern of man's life even in acts performed merely for his survival. According to Safrin, *devekut* is a state of constant dialectic tension between the ego (*Ani*) and the divine mystic nothingness (*Ayin*). While aiming at self-denial and lack of consciousness, at the same time one remains conscious of one's own identity and self. "Every man must be in the aspect of *Ayin*… and there [in the aspect of *Ayin*] at every moment the aspects of *Ayin* and *Ani* become one" (*Noẓer Ḥesed*, 2 (1856)).

Safrin reaches radical conclusions in his doctrine of the sublimation of impure or foreign thoughts (*maḥashavot zarot*). The attempt to banish such thoughts entirely from the consciousness he considers heresy, being the denial of the presence of God at every level of existence. Man is obliged to elevate impure thoughts and abolish the evil that is in them by confronting them without utter rejection, despite the possible moral danger resulting from this involvement with the *sitra aḥra* ("other side"; "evil"; see *Kabbalah). To dismiss impure thoughts means putting out the divine spark (*niẓoẓ*) present in evil. According to this theory, many of the disciples of Dov Baer the Maggid of *Mezhirich and other ḥasidic leaders were heretics.

Safrin's works include *Oẓar Ḥayyim* (1858), a kabbalist commentary on the 613 precepts; *Zohar Ḥai*, on the *Zohar (pt. 1, 1875; pt. 3, 1881); *Noẓer Ḥesed* (1856), on *Avot*, including *Sefer Adam Yashar*, remedies against the plague, according to Lurianic Kabbalah; and *Shulḥan ha-Tahor* (ed. A.A. Zis, 1963–65) on *Oraḥ Ḥayyim* of the Shulḥan Arukh.

BIBLIOGRAPHY: B. Yashar (Shlikhter), in: *Sinai*, 53 (1963), 167–73, 346–9; idem, *Beit Komarna* (1965); A.A. Zis (ed.), "*Shoshelet ha-Kodesh – Toledot Zidachov Komarna*," in: *Shulḥan ha-Tahor*, 2 (1965); idem, in: *Sinai*, 59 (1966), 283–6; H.J. Berl, *Yiẓḥak Eizik mi-Komarna* (1943); L.H. Grosman, *Shem u-She'erit* (1943), 28–30; N. Ben-Menahem, in: *Sinai*, 54 (1964), 264–76.

[Esther (Zweig) Liebes]

SAGALOWITZ, BENJAMIN (1901–1970), journalist and historian. Born in Vitebsk, Russia, he graduated in law in Zurich, Switzerland. He wrote for Jewish and non-Jewish papers and from 1938 to 1964 was in charge of the JUNA (Juedische Nachrichtenagentur), the news agency of the representative body of the Jewish communities, the SIG (Schweizerischer Israelitischer Gemeindebund).

In July 1942, a German industrialist, Edward Schulte, approached Sagalowitz about the Nazi plan to exterminate European Jewry. Sagalowitz transmitted this information to Gerhard Riegner, the representative of the WJC in Geneva, who informed the free world. However, the U.S. delayed the official publication for months.

After 1945 he was a correspondent for the influential paper *Neue Zuercher Zeitung* and reported from the Nuremberg Trials and later Nazi trials, and also from the Eichmann trial in Jerusalem.

He built a comprehensive archive about antisemitism and the rise of the Nazi system, but also about Jewish-Christian dialog. He was an active Zionist and supporter of Social Democracy. He received Swiss citizenship after living 39 years in Switzerland.

BIBLIOGRAPHY: J. Picard, *Die Schweiz und die Juden 1933–1945* (1994), 130–35.

[Rafi Siano (2nd ed.)]

SAGAN, CARL EDWARD (1934–1996), astronomer. Sagan was born in New York. He graduated from the University of Chicago in 1954, received his doctorate in 1960, and was appointed astrophysicist at the Smithsonian Astrophysical Observatory in Cambridge, Mass. (1962–68), during which period he was also assistant professor at Harvard. In 1968 he was appointed a member of the faculty of Cornell University, where he was David Duncan Professor of Astronomy and Space Sciences and Director of the Laboratory for Planetary Studies. He played a leading role in the Mariner, Viking and Voyager unmanned missions to the planets, and was from 1968 to 1980 editor-in-chief of *Icarus: The International Journal of Solar System Studies.* Sagan served as chairman of the Division for Planetary Sciences of the American Astronomical Society, as president of the Planetology Section of the American Geophysical Union, and was responsible for the Pioneer 10 and 11 and Voyager 1 and 2 interstellar messages.

He wrote *The Atmospheres of Mars and Venus* (1961), *Planets* (1966), *Intelligent Life in the Universe* (1966), *Planetary Exploration* (1970), *Mars and the Mind of Man* (1973), *The Cosmic Connection* (1973), *Other Worlds* (1975), *The Dragons of Eden* (1977), *Murmurs of Earth: The Voyager Interstellar Record* (1979), *Broca's Brain* (1979), and *Cosmos* (1980).

Sagan was the recipient of numerous awards, including the NASA Medals for Exceptional Scientific Achievement (1972), and for Distinguished Public Service (1977), the Prix Galabert (1973), and the Pulitzer Prize for Literature (1978).

SAGIS, family originally from Spain who settled in Brusa, Turkey. Among its members were:

(1) JOSEPH SAGIS (d. 1572), an eminent Safed rabbi and head of a yeshivah there. According to a tradition, which is not accepted, however, he was one of the four rabbis ordained by *Jacob Berab I. In Safed he was the main teacher of Eleazar *Azikri in Talmud, and his influence is clearly discernible in his works. He was associated with Joseph *Caro and Moses *Trani (the Mabit), and his signature appears together with theirs on many rulings. In 1570 he founded in Safed an association of Yirei Adonai ve-Ḥasidim ("God-fearing pious men") who met in the synagogue every Friday to give an account of their actions during the week.

(2) SOLOMON BEN MOSES SAGIS (d. between 1587 and 1589), Safed rabbi. According to one source he was the son-in-law of Isaac *Luria. Among his pupils were Joseph b. Moses *Trani, Ḥiyya *Rofe, and Tovijah b. Abraham ha-Levi, who quotes some of his teacher's novellae in his *Ḥen Tov* (Venice, 1605).

(3) JONATHAN SAGIS (16th century) was one of the important pupils of Isaac Luria and an associate of Ḥayyim Vital. His son-in-law was Moses *Galante I.

BIBLIOGRAPHY: Conforte, Kore, index; Horodezky, in: *Ẓiyyunim… le-Zikhrono shel Y.N. Simḥoni* (1929), 149; Frumkin-Rivlin, 1 (1929), 107; Rosanes, Togarmah, 3 (1938), 280; Scholem, in: *Zion*, 5 (1940), 134, 144f.; Benayahu, in: *Sinai*, 35 (1954), 60f.; idem, in: *Aresheth*, 2 (1960), 109, 121; idem, in: *Sefer Yovel… Y. Baer* (1961), 249; idem, in: *Sefunot*, 6 (1962), 17, 24f., 28f.; idem, in: *Sefer Toledot ha-Ari* (1967), index.

[Abraham David]

SAHAGÚN, town in Leon province, N.W. Spain. Jewish settlement there originated near the monastery, at the beginning of the tenth century. Jews filled the roles of purveyors and craftsmen for the monastery. Subsequently the Jewish quarter was situated in a locality called Santa Cruz. In 1126 the town's 30 Jewish heads of families were handed over by King Alfonso *VII to the jurisdiction of the superior of the monastery. In 1171, the superior gave the Jews of Sahagún land for a cemetery situated in a district of vines outside the town. In the 13th century Sahagún was one of the thriving communities in the north. In 1255 Alfonso X formulated several of the regulations of the Sahagún community, which was granted the *fuero* (charter) of the community of Carrión de los Condes, and he made the community dependent for its internal affairs on *Burgos, a day's journey distant. Among other matters, the amount of ransom for the killing of a Jew was fixed at a total of 500 solidos payable to the head of the monastery, and in 1268 the king further prescribed a special *oath for the Jews of Sahagún. Few details are known about the Jews of Sahagún during the 14th century, but at its close it contained 30 heads of families occupied in agriculture and work for the monastery, around which the life of the town was concentrated. In 1401 Henry III yielded to the request of the community representatives and ordered the head of the monastery to take no steps against the community and to respect its rights. Despite this, Sahagún did not escape the impoverishment which befell the communities of Castile toward the middle of the 15th century. The last information available about the Jews of Sahagún dates from June 7, 1492, a few weeks after the edict of expulsion. This is an appeal from the Jews of Sahagún to the crown to ensure that debts be reimbursed to them, and that they not be imprisoned for nonpayment of debts. Comparison with other communities shows that in Sahagún, too, the Christian inhabitants declined to discharge their debts to the Jews compelled to leave the kingdom.

BIBLIOGRAPHY: Baer, Spain, index; Baer, Urkunden, 2 (1936), index; J. Rodríguez, in: *Archivos Leoneses*, 7 (1953), 5–78; F. Cantera, *Sinagogas españolas* (1955), 271; J. González, *El Reino de Castilla en la época de Alfonso VIII* (1960), 132; Suárez Fernández, Documentos, index; L. Pilar Tello, *Los judíos de Palencia* (1967), docs. 13, 22, 45, 232.

[Haim Beinart]

SAHL, MORT (Lyon, Morton Sahl; 1927–), U.S. comedian and satirist. Born in Montreal, Canada, Sahl worked in experimental theaters, but his success in a San Francisco nightclub in 1953 led to engagements in nightclubs throughout the U.S., and on radio and television. He excelled in monologue, directing his satire mostly at political figures, appealing to young, liberal, well-educated audiences. He prided himself in speaking his truth and "offending everyone." Once close to the Kennedys, he fell out of favor with the family when he made the new president the target of his wit. With Lenny *Bruce, he represented a new kind of stand-up comic, deflating icons and attacking sacred cows. In 1966 he opened his own nightclub in Los Angeles.

He appeared in the Broadway revue *The Next President* (1958) and in *Mort Sahl on Broadway* (1987) and *Comedy To-*

night (1994). On screen, he appeared in the films *In Love and War* (1958), *All The Young Men* (1960), *Johnny Cool* (1963), *Doctor, You've Got to Be Kidding* (1967), *Don't Make Waves* (1967), the documentary *Lenny Bruce without Tears* (1972), *Nothing Lasts Forever* (1984), and the TV documentaries *The Great Stand-ups* (1984), *Jonathan Winters: On the Ledge* (1987), *Sam Peckinpah: Man of Iron* (1992), and *Inside the Playboy Mansion* (2002). He was the subject of the TV documentary *Mort Sahl: The Loyal Opposition* (1989). Sahl was #40 in the film *Comedy Central Presents: 100 Greatest Stand-Ups of All Time* (2004). His book *Heartland* was published in 1976.

[Ruth Beloff (2nd ed.)]

SAHLĀN BEN ABRAHAM (11th cent.), leader of the Iraqi community in *Cairo. Sahlān was a member of an ancient Egyptian family which originated in the town of *Sunbāṭ. He inherited his position from his father Abraham (Barhūn in Arabic), a spice merchant who had become the leader of the Iraqi community. Sahlān was learned, wealthy, and had good relations with the government. He maintained a regular correspondence with the *gaon* *Solomon b. Judah, the head of the *Jerusalem academy, and supported the Jewish population in Palestine. In times of misfortune, the Jerusalem *gaon* appealed to him to intervene in favor of the scholars of the academy. However, as the community leader of the Jews of Iraqi origin, Sahlān recognized the authority of the *geonim* of Iraq and was referred to by the Iraqi title of **alluf*. R. *Hai Gaon, as well as the exilarch *Hezekiah b. David II, supported him when a controversy broke out within his community in the 1030s. He also wrote some religious poems.

BIBLIOGRAPHY: Mann, Egypt, index; Mann, Texts, index; idem, in: *Tarbiz*, 5 (1934), 277–9; Chapira, in: REJ, 82 (1926), 317–31; Assaf, in: *Tarbiz*, 9 (1936/37), 30–32; Davidson, Oẓar, index; H. Schirmann, *Shirim Ḥadashim Min ha-Genizah* (1965), 75–78.

[Eliyahu Ashtor]

SAHL BEN MAẒLI'AḤ HA-KOHEN ABU AL-SURRĪ (second half of the 10th century), *Karaite propagandist and author. Sahl ben Maẓli'aḥ was a resident, and possibly a native, of Jerusalem, whence he appears to have undertaken periodical missionary journeys abroad in search of converts to Karaism from among the local Rabbanite communities. During one such journey, he came into conflict, presumably in Cairo, with an influential Rabbanite elder, Jacob ben Samuel, who was a zealous follower of *Saadiah Gaon and therefore hostile toward the Karaites. When he heard of Sahl's missionary activity before Rabbanite audiences, Jacob addressed a letter to him in Arabic, accusing him of having come to a peaceful community in order to stir up controversy, and then fish in the troubled waters in order to obtain converts to his cause. In reply to this charge, Sahl indited a series of ten short responsa, followed by a long Epistle, both in Hebrew, in which he not only repudiated Jacob's accusations, but also appealed over his head to the Rabbanite community at large to accept his message.

The Hebrew text of Sahl's Epistle (Sahl himself states that "he may write an Ishmaelite (Arabic) version of this Epistle so that he who does not know the Jewish (Hebrew) language may read it." It is not known whether he did so, no copy of it having been discovered so far.) was edited by a 17th-century Karaite scholar, Elijah b. Baruch "Yerushalmi," who added a short foreword citing two (originally three?) of the responsa. The Epistle is prefaced by a Hebrew poem by Sahl criticizing the main Rabbanite doctrines. The work itself appears to be a composite of two original works, a polemical blast at Jacob ben Samuel personally and a Hebrew version of the standard missionary sermon delivered by Sahl, no doubt in Arabic, before Rabbanite audiences. The contrasting tone of these two components reveals Sahl's consummate skill as a propagandist: when addressing Jacob ben Samuel, his language is harsh and his discourse full of angry and contemptuous denunciations; when addressing the Rabbanite public, he assumes a humble and compassionate pose, commiserating with his audience and shrewdly appealing to them to cast off what he characterizes as the heavy yoke of their rapacious and hypocritical leaders, and to go back to the original and pure Mosaic faith, meaning of course Karaism.

The Epistle is of considerable historical value. It is the earliest preserved complete specimen of practical Karaite propaganda, addressed not to the Rabbanite upper class, from which Sahl could expect no sympathy, but to the ordinary Rabbanite man in the street. It describes a number of popular customs and superstitions prevalent at that time among the lower classes, as well as some of the reprehensible practices indulged in by some representatives of Rabbanite officialdom, and it gives some historical details about early Karaite scholars and their works. Sahl's statements are obviously not free from deliberate exaggeration and bias, however, and must be approached with some caution.

In addition to his Epistle, Sahl also wrote (in Arabic) a code of law (*Sefer ha-Mitzvot* and *Sefer Dinim*, presumably two parts of the same work), of which only the Hebrew introduction has been published (by A. Harkavy. *Me'assef Niddahim*, I, no. 13). A tract against Saadiah, mentioned in the Epistle, has not yet been discovered. Fragments of a commentary on the Pentateuch, in Arabic, are also tentatively ascribed to him.

The Epistle was published by S. Pinsker, in *Likkutei Kadmoniyyot*, 2 (Vienna, 1860), 24–43; an abridged English translation appears in L. Nemoy, *Karaite Anthology* (New Haven, 1952), 109–22, 349–52.

BIBLIOGRAPHY: S. Poznański, *Karaite Literary Opponents of Saadia Gaon* (1908), 30–41; Mann, Texts, 2 (1935), 22–29; L. Nemoy, in: PAAJR, 38/39 (1972), 145–77 (including corrections and emendations to Pinsker's text).

[Leon Nemoy]

SAHL IBN FAḌL (**al-Tustarī**; Heb. **Yashar b. Ḥesed**; late 11th century), *Karaite scholar of Tustar, or Shustar, in *Persia. Of his numerous Arabic writings, fragments have been preserved of a commentary on the Pentateuch; a theologico-philosophical treatise entitled *Al-Talwīḥ alā al-Tawḥīd wa-al-ʿAdl*; a disquisition on the *Metaphysics* of Aristotle; and a treatise on incest. Other works by him are known only by title.

BIBLIOGRAPHY: Steinschneider, Arab Lit, 113, 342; S. Poznański, *The Karaite Literary Opponents of Saadiah Gaon* (1908), 53–55; Mann, Texts, 2 (1935), 39f., 99f.; L. Nemoy, *Karaite Anthology* (1952), 235, 377.

[Leon Nemoy]

SAHLINS, MARSHALL (1930–), U.S. anthropologist. A native of Chicago, he was educated at the University of Michigan, where he received his bachelor's degree in 1951, and at Columbia University, where he received his Ph.D. in 1954. From 1955 to 1957 Sahlins was a lecturer in anthropology at Columbia University. He then taught at the University of Michigan at Ann Arbor, in 1957 as an assistant professor, and later as a full professor. In 1974 he left Ann Arbor to join the faculty of the University of Chicago as a professor of anthropology; he was later named the Charles F. Grey Distinguished Professor of Anthropology Emeritus.

Considered one of the most prominent American anthropologists of his era, Sahlins is known as an ethnographer and historian of Polynesia. His theories about European contact in Polynesia have sparked major debates, and his long-running scholarly debate with anthropologist Gananath Obeyesekere of Princeton University has apparently fueled several works by both authors. Much of this debate has involved differing interpretations of the reception of Captain James Cook by native Hawaiians in 1779. Sahlins in early works argued that Cook had been initially welcomed as the god Lono; on his return a week later, Cook was killed by the natives because of a cycle of worship that emphasized the warlike god Ku. Obeyesekere responded in his *Apotheosis of Captain Cook* (1992), emphasizing what he considered the erroneous influence of European myth models, and arguing that Sahlins's theory implied a condescending view of the native Hawaiians.

Sahlins's 1995 work, *How "Natives" Think: About Captain Cook, for Example*, continued the debate by challenging Obeyesekere's insistence on a practical rationality, which suggests that he is captive to Western concepts. Sahlins questions whether Western scholars (including Obeyesekere, as a Sri Lankan who works within a Western tradition) can ever really speak for non-Western peoples. Called an "analytical masterpiece," the work was said to challenge the definitions and practices of the postcolonial academic world.

Sahlins was a Guggenheim fellow in 1967–1968. He was a fellow of the British Academy and an honorary fellow of the Royal Anthropological Institute of Great Britain and Ireland and of the Association of Social Anthropologists of Oceania. He was awarded the Laing Prize by the University of Chicago in 1978 and 1996, and he received the Staley Prize from the School of American Research in 1998.

[Dorothy Bauhoff (2nd ed.)]

SAHULA, ISAAC BEN SOLOMON ABI (b. 1244), Hebrew poet, scholar, physician and kabbalist. Sahula, who had relatives in Burgos and in the town of Guadalajara in Castile, was a disciple of the kabbalist Moses of Burgos and was acquainted with *Moses b. Shem-Tov de Leon, his fellow townsman. He was also trained in traditional rabbinic studies and in medicine. He lived during the reign of Alfonso the Wise of Castile, and traveled from one place to another practicing medicine and avowing not to be dependent upon his patrons. In 1281 he was in Egypt, when he decided to consecrate his life to writing with a clearly moral purpose. His major work, *Meshal ha-Kadmoni* (between 1281 and 1284), was a book of fables expressly written to displace, with an original Hebrew work, such light literature as *Kalila and Dimna* and the *Voyages of Sinbad the Sailor*, which were read extensively by Jews in the Middle Ages in Hebrew translations. Hence Ibn Sahula introduced in his book a similar structure and mode of presentation, and even added illustrations to his book, as was prevalent in non-Jewish literature. The manuscripts and all the printed editions of the work are embellished with extremely interesting miniatures or woodcuts. Divided into five chapters, *Meshal ha-Kadmoni* contains a large collection of parables, stories, and tales, all written in *maqāma*-like form with pedagogical purpose. He declares his sorrow for the way his contemporaries use Hebrew. The author's mastery of language and exceptional talent as a storyteller are revealed in this work, obscured, however, by the large amount of popular scientific material woven into the narrative. Each section starts with the words of a Cynic against one of the main virtues (wisdom, penitence, sound counsel, humility) that are conveniently refuted by the Moralist; the fifth section, on "reverence," is a diatribe against astrology and determinism. The book contains three quotations of one of the oldest components of the *Zohar*, the *Midrash ha-Ne'lam*, but it is closer to Maimonides than to the doctrines of the Kabbalah. The *Meshal ha-Kadmoni* enjoyed a wide circulation in the Middle Ages. Some fragments of another *maqāma*, discovered and commented upon by Schirmann, in which the author calls himself "Isaac," could also be by Ibn Sahula.

Meshal ha-Kadmoni was reprinted eight times, first by Soncino in Brescia (c. 1491); in 1953 I. Zamora published it in Tel Aviv with a fully vocalized text and with the woodcut illustrations from the Venice edition (c. 1547); in 2004 Raphael Lowe published it with an English translation. Its Yiddish version (1st, Frankfurt on the Oder, 1693), the editions of which outnumbered the Hebrew (nine are known), also appeared with woodcuts. M. Steinschneider and M.Y. Bin Gorion translated some of the stories into German. In addition, Sahula wrote a commentary on the Song of Songs (still in manuscript) in a kabbalistic vein, and a commentary to some Psalms.

BIBLIOGRAPHY: G. Scholem, *Perakim be-Toledot Sifrut ha-Kabbalah* (1931), 59–68; M. Marx, in: *Sefer ha-Yovel… A. Marx* (1943), i–viii (Eng. pt.); A.M. Habermann, in: *YIVO Bleter*, 13 (1938), 95–101; idem, in: KS, 29 (1953/54), 199–203; idem, in: *Aresheth*, 3 (1961), 106 n. 12; Waxmann, Literature, 2 (1960), 596–7. **ADD. BIBLIOGRAPHY:** Schirmann-Fleischer, *The History of Hebrew Poetry in Christian*

Spain and Southern France (Hebrew; 1997), 345–65; P.F. Fumagalli, in: *Rassegna Mensile di Israel,* 69:1 (2003), 31–48; R. Loewe, *Meshal Haqadmoni: Fables from the Distant Past; A Parallel Hebrew-English Text* (2004).

[Abraham Meir Habermann / Angel Sáenz-Badillos (2nd ed.)]

SAHULA, MEIR BEN SOLOMON ABI (1260?, perhaps 1251–after 1335), Spanish kabbalist, younger brother of Isaac Abi *Sahula. During the 1280s and 1290s, and possibly for a longer period, Sahula lived in *Guadalajara, the center of a group of kabbalists. Halakhic responsa were addressed to him in this city by Solomon b. Abraham Adret (Responsa 1: nos. 270–6, 280–92). His teacher in *Kabbalah was Joshua *Ibn Shuaib, a senior disciple of Solomon b. Abraham Adret. Sahula only began to write kabbalistic works in his later years. It is not clear whether Sahula's commentary (1875) on the esoteric material in *Nahmanides' commentary on the Bible is his own or that of his teacher. Sahula himself re-edited one of the commentaries on the kabbalistic allusions of Naḥmanides, taking to task its author and supplanting the original comments with his own. The book that served as the subject of his criticism was not the commentary of Shuaib, but that of another scholar who was not his teacher. He began writing this commentary in 1320, but by 1325 he had only completed the part on Genesis. During that year he began a commentary on Sefer *Yeẓirah which he completed in 1331, after a delay of some years. The preface to this commentary is a lengthy commentary on *Midrash Shimon ha-Ẓaddik*, a kabbalistic book of the circle of *Sefer ha-Iyyun*. The commentary on *Sefer Yeẓirah* is a severe criticism of Naḥmanides' comments on the first chapter of *Sefer Yeẓirah*. It also contains a long passage on the mystical account of creation.

His approach to Kabbalah differs from that of Naḥmanides, Solomon b. Abraham Adret, and the *Zohar, and is based on his own speculations, which he ascribed to *Midrash Shimon ha-Ẓaddik*. In addition, he concentrated on the sayings of the kabbalists of Gerona and of *Asher b. David. When his commentary on *Sefer Yeẓirah* was completed, he began one on *Sefer ha-*Bahir*; apparently he completed this commentary in 1335, and it was published anonymously in the 1883 edition of *Sefer ha-Bahir* under the title *Or ha-Ganuz*. Perhaps the entire manuscript, or at least a major part of his commentary on *Sefer Yeẓirah* in the Angelica Library of Rome (De Capua 53), is in the author's own handwriting. Sahula also wrote a kabbalistic commentary on *Pirkei de-R. Eli'ezer*, which is lost. His comments on *Sefer Yeẓirah* and *Sefer ha-Bahir* are highly arbitrary, and he attributes views to Naḥmanides which contradict the latter's real opinions. The kabbalists of Salonika in the early 16th century were acquainted with his books. Thus, Solomon *Alkabeẓ accused Sahula of "not aiming at the truth." On the other hand, Meir *Poppers praised his commentary on the *Yeẓirah* and made it a basis for his own commentary, *Or Bahir* (G. Scholem, *Kitvei Yad be-Kabbalah*, (1930), 147).

[Gershom Scholem]

SAʿĪD IBN HASAN (13th–14th cent.), Alexandrian Jew who converted to *Islam in 1298, became a fanatical Muslim, and oppressed his former coreligionists and the Christians. Saʿīd relates that the cause for his apostasy was a severe illness during which, in a dream, he heard a voice which ordered him to convert. After his conversion, he requested that a public disputation be held between him and the Jewish and Christian scholars in the presence of the sultan. He prided himself that he would prove from the Bible the veracity of the Muslim claims against Judaism. Saʿīd did not succeed in holding this disputation and therefore wrote a polemical book in which he presented his opinions. This book, *Maṣāliḥ al-Naẓar fī Nubuwwat Sayyid al-Bashar* ("Methods of Study into the Prophecy of the Lord of All Men"), was written in 1320 in the Great Mosque of *Damascus, where Saʿīd lived at that time. In this book he set out to prove that certain verses of the Bible are allusions to the coming of *Muhammad, and that it is forbidden to tolerate the adoration of the icons in the churches; he also means to reveal the real nature of the philosophers. However, Saʿīd's knowledge of the Bible, Jewish history, and other branches of literature was scanty and his book is of low standard. Generally, Saʿīd condemns the Christians more than the Jews. According to him, they are the worst disbelievers because they deify Jesus. The philosophers are the enemies of God and of the prophets, his messengers, and were the inventors of idol worship. Their greatest sin is their belief in the eternity of the world, which he tries to refute in a special chapter of his book.

BIBLIOGRAPHY: Goldziher, in: REJ, 30 (1845), 1–23; Weston, in: JAOS, 24 (1903), 312–83; Ashtor, Toledot, 1 (1944), 283–8.

[Eliyahu Ashtor]

ŞAINEANU, LAZAR (Lazar Schein; 1859–1934) philologian and folklorist. Born in Ploieşti, Romania, Şaineanu was appointed without salary to teach Romanian language and literature at the University of Bucharest and made a living teaching Latin in a high school. In spite of becoming well known and respected for his contribution to Romanian studies, as a Jew he always encountered general antagonism. He won prizes from the Romanian Academy and was the most prominent Romanian philologist, but was continuously denied Romanian citizenship even after he embraced Christianity. He finally left the country in 1901, taking up residence in Paris, where he taught Romanian folklore at the Ecole des Hautes Etudes at the Sorbonne. There he took the French form Sainéan as his name. While in Romania he contributed to Jewish publications under pseudonyms, writing Romanian Jewish history as well as Yiddish philology. He compiled a Romanian dictionary in four volumes (1895) which went through 84 editions. He also wrote several linguistic and folkloristic studies, his monumental work being a study on Oriental influences in Romanian culture and language (3 vols., 1900). As both a folklorist and linguist, he was interested in the popular elements of language which, in turn, led to his interest in slang. After settling in France he gained considerable notoriety for his studies on French slang and on Rabelais.

He published many books in these fields including: *L'Argot Ancien 1455–1850* (1907); *Les Sources de l'Argot Ancien* (1912, 2 vols.); *L'Argot des Tranchées (1915); Le Language Parisien au XIXe Siècle* (1920); *La Langue de Rabelais* (1922–23, 2 vols.); *L'Influence et la Réputation de Rabelais* (1930). He collaborated on the great edition of Rabelais by Abel Lefranc (1912–22). His opus magnum on French etymology is his *Les Sources Indigènes de l'Etymologie Française* (3 vols., 1925–30) and *Autour des Sources Indigènes* (1935).

BIBLIOGRAPHY: *Lettres de L. Sainéan...* (1936), preface by C. Şaineanu.

[Abraham Feller]

SAINT-DENIS (Heb. דיאוניזאן), a suburb N. of Paris. In 1111 King Louis VI granted the abbot of Saint-Denis jurisdiction over the five Jewish families who lived there. Jews played a considerable role in the economy of the abbey and contributed toward the development of its estates. A special officer, the "provost of the Jews," was in charge of all Jewish affairs. The tax paid by Jews amounted to 40 pounds in 1302. On the eve of World War II several hundred Jewish families lived in Saint-Denis, and in 1941, 325 Jews were still accounted for. A community was reestablished after the war, and its size increased, especially with the arrival of Jews from North Africa. In 1971 there were about 2,000 Jews in Saint-Denis. In the early 2000s it was the scene of a number of antisemitic attacks.

BIBLIOGRAPHY: A. Grabois, in: *Zion*, 30 (1965), 115–9; G. Lebel, *Histoire... de l'abbaye de Saint-Denis* (1935), 212; Z. Szajkowski, *Analytical Franco-Jewish Gazetteer* (1966), 265; Gross, Gal Jud, 151.

[Bernhard Blumenkranz]

SAINTES, town in the Charente-Maritime department, W. France. The presence of Jews in Saintes is explicitly confirmed from 961. A charter of that date even mentions that they all lived together, probably in the street subsequently called Rue Juive, a name it retained until at least 1629 (it was later known as Rue des Jacobins). In 1236, when the Jews of the whole province of Saintonge, or perhaps only those of Saintes, were attacked by crusaders, Pope Gregory IX called on the bishop of the town to protect them. Although threatened with expulsion by *Alphonse of Poitiers in 1239, Jews were still living in Saintes in 1266. The only scholar of Saintes whose name has survived is a certain R. Isaac who ratified a decision of *Samuel of Evreux. Before 1735 Jewish merchants from *Bordeaux and *Comtat Venaissin were trading in Saintes, with the connivance of an important local personality whose house they used as a warehouse and shop. A few Jews lived in Saintes on the eve of World War II, but in 1970 there was no Jewish community.

BIBLIOGRAPHY: Gross, Gal Jud, 659f.; H. See, in: REJ, 80 (1925), 179–81; *Bulletin de la Société des arch, de le Saintonge et de l'Aunis*, 17 (1897), 456f.; P.F. Fournier and P. Guébin (eds.), *Enquêtes Administratives d'Alphonse de Poitiers* (1959), 197f.

[Bernhard Blumenkranz]

SAINT GALL, canton and its capital city in N.E. Switzerland. The first document mentioning Jews in St. Gall is dated in 1268; in 1292 two houses in the town were inhabited by Jews. On Feb. 23, 1349, during the *Black Death, the Jewish inhabitants were burned or driven out. Jews were not allowed to settle in St. Gall again until the 19th century.

The mother community of St. Gall was Hohenems in nearby Vorarlberg. From 1617 Jewish businessmen were present in St. Gall on weekdays. After 1810 there seems to have been a de facto presence in the city, against all official rules. Since the government tried to curb the economic activity of the Jews by introducing costly "patents for Hebrews," the Jews successfully boycotted the city and the fees were reduced.

The first synagogue, in a private home, was founded in 1866, and a permanent Moorish-style synagogue built in 1881, serving as the model for the synagogue of Zurich. In 1870 the Jewish population was 158. St. Gall had a distinctly liberal religious orientation until after the engagement of Rabbi Lothar Rothschild (1943–68). The rabbi of St. Gall also serves the Jewish community of Kreuzlingen (near Constance). Jews played a prominent role in the St. Gall textile industry until 1912, especially in the famous embroidery branch. In 1919 refugees from Eastern Europe settled in St. Gall, forming a separate community. German and Austrian Jewish refugees began crossing the border into the canton in 1938, and a refugee care organization was set up there. From 1939 to 1944 the town was the center for preparing Jewish refugee children for *Youth Aliyah to Palestine. In 1944, 1,350 Jews (mostly Hungarian) from *Bergen-Belsen concentration camp were brought to St. Gall (on the "Kasztner transport"), and a year later 1,200 Jews from *Theresienstadt camp arrived there. Police officer Paul Grueninger, later designated as *Righteous among the Gentiles, helped Jewish refugees after 1938. He was ousted from office, lost his pension, and died in misery. Years after his death, citizens fought successfully for his posthumous rehabilitation. A square in St. Gall is named after him.

In 1952 the two Jewish communities united. In 2004 the community had about 153 members. Its future is uncertain, since many young couples have moved to bigger cities. In 1994 the community received state recognition. For many years, Rabbi Hermann Schmelzer (active from 1968), taught Jewish Studies at the St. Gall University.

The community takes care of the Jewish cemetery in nearby Hohenems (Austria/Vorarlberg). Hohenems is home to a well-organized Jewish museum that displays the history of the region, including eastern Switzerland.

BIBLIOGRAPHY: A. Weldler-Steinberg, *Geschichte der Juden in der Schweiz* (1966/70), vol. 1, 72–75, 209, vol. 2, 210–214, v. index; L. Brandt, *Chronik... der Israelitischen Kultusgemeinde St. Gallen zu ihrem 50 jaehrigen Jubilaeum* (1913); L. Rothschild, *Im Strom der Zeit; Jubilaeumsschrift zum hundertjaehrigen Bestehen der israelitischen Gemeinde St. Gallen* (1963); Germ Jud, (1968), 733–4; H.I. Ziegler, Schmelzer, *Zeugnis und Perspektive. Die Israelitische Gemeinde St. Gallen in den Jahren 1963 bis 1988* (1988).

[Uri Kaufmann (2nd ed.)]

SAINT-GILES, small town W. of Arles, France. The earliest implicit evidence of the presence of Jews in Saint-Giles dates from the beginning of the 12th century, with the polemic representation of an allegorical *Synagoga* on the abbey church (western face, southern door). About 1165 *Benjamin of Tudela found there 100 Jews (or heads of families). The community paid the abbot an annual tenure of 100 sols. In the autumn of 1215, Saint-Giles was the site of a meeting of delegates from communities between *Marseilles and *Narbonne who sought to forestall certain anti-Jewish canons which were being prepared for the Fourth *Lateran Council. After the expulsion of 1306, Jews of the locality took refuge in *Provence, and particularly in Marseilles. Scholars mentioned in Saint-Giles by Benjamin of Tudela are unknown from other sources.

BIBLIOGRAPHY: Gross, Gal Jud, 650ff.; S. Kahn, in: *Mémoires de l'Académie de Nîmes*, 35 (1912), 1–23; B. Blumenkranz, in: *Mélanges… R. Crozet* (1966), 1155.

[Bernhard Blumenkranz]

SAINT JAMES'S CONFERENCE (known also as the London Conference), a round-table conference with Jewish and Arab leaders convened by the British government in February–March 1939. After rejecting the partition plan of the Royal Commission (see *Palestine Partition Plans and *White Papers), the British government decided on a drastic change of policy toward Palestine. The round-table conference with Jewish and Arab leaders was to discuss the entire problem. Jewish leaders and representatives of the Palestinian Arabs and, for the first time, the Arab states were invited and convened on Feb. 7, 1939, in the Palace of St. James. Representatives of Iraq, Saudi Arabia, Egypt, and Transjordan attended the conference, together with the Arab delegation from Palestine, headed by Jamal al-Husseini, the lieutenant and kinsman of Amīn al-Husseini, the fugitive leader of the Arab rebellion of 1936–39. The Jewish delegation consisted of the leaders of the Jewish Agency, the Va'ad Le'ummi, Agudat Israel, and some leaders of the Jewish community in Britain. It was headed by Chaim *Weizmann, David *Ben-Gurion, Moshe *Sharett, and Stephen S. *Wise. The Arabs refused to attend joint meetings with the Jews, and the British conferred with each side separately.

The new British policy was based on the assumption that war with Nazi Germany and Fascist Italy was imminent and that the enmity of the Arab world would be a serious threat to British interests in the Middle East, whereas the Jewish side would have no choice in a conflict with the Nazis. The British thus asked that the Jewish leaders "of their own free will dispose of their rights by offering terms of conciliation," as Lord Halifax, the foreign secretary, put it at a conference meeting on February 14. On March 15 the British government offered its proposals, according to which the "ultimate objective" of the government was "the establishment of an independent Palestine State possibly of a federal nature." The new state would be neither Jewish nor Arab, but both nations would "share in government in such a way as to ensure that the essential interests of each be safeguarded." Both the Jewish and Arab delegations rejected the proposals, and the conference ended in failure on March 17, 1939. Two months later, on May 17, 1939, the British government published its statement of policy known as the White Paper 1939 or the MacDonald White Paper.

BIBLIOGRAPHY: Ch. Weizmann, *Trial and Error* (1949), index; D. Ben-Gurion, *Pegishot Im Manhigim Aravim* (1967), 214–69; Y. Bauer, *From Diplomacy to Resistance* (1970), 16–51.

[Daniel Efron]

SAINT-JEAN-DE-LUZ, town in the Basses-Pyrenées department, S.W. France. There is no record of the presence of Jews in Saint-Jean during the Middle Ages; it was only from the 16th century that a number of Marranos settled there. In 1612 an official submitted a report to the Conseil d'Etat, notifying it of the presence of a large colony of Marranos. In 1619 Catherine de Fernandés, a woman who had recently arrived from Portugal, was accused of having spat at the Host when she went to receive communion. In spite of the criminal investigation conducted by the royal prosecutor, the populace seized the accused and burned her at the stake in the town square. At the same time a priest of Portuguese origin was also accused of being a crypto-Jew and of having been chosen as priest by a large number of Portuguese New Christians who, in fact, conducted themselves more like Jews than Christians. All the Portuguese New Christians were expelled from Saint-Jean, apparently fleeing to Biarritz.

BIBLIOGRAPHY: M. Philippson, in: *Archives Israélites*, 29 (1868), 1115–17; H. Prague, in: *Annuaire des Archives Israélites 5663*, 19 (1902), 37–52.

[Bernhard Blumenkranz]

SAINT-LÉON, ARTHUR MICHEL (1815?–1870), dancer and choreographer; creator of famous 19th-century ballets. Saint-Léon came of a theatrical family and in the 1830s toured Europe, appearing from 1840–42 at the Vienna Opera. He married the celebrated ballerina Fanny Cerrito, and, until they separated in 1850, choreographed many ballets for her, including his first ballet, *La Vivandière*, in London in 1844. Among the many ballets and divertissements he did for the Paris Opera were *La Fille de Marbre* (1847), *Le Violon du Diable* (1849), in which he displayed his accomplishments as a violinist, and *Stella or The Smugglers* (1850), in which he introduced a group of Jewish merchants. In 1859 Saint-Léon became ballet master of the Imperial Theatre in St. Petersburg and there staged the first ballet on a Russian theme, *The Humpbacked Horse* (1864). Touring the European capitals as a guest choreographer, he restaged many of his own works under different titles, which made his output seem larger than it actually was. After the failure of his ballet *The Goldfish* (1867), he returned to the Paris Opera and was part author of the ballet *Coppélia*, staged in 1870 shortly before his death. In 1852 Saint-Léon published *La Sténochorégraphie ou l'art d'écrire promptement la danse*, an attempt at a workable system of dance notation.

BIBLIOGRAPHY: C.W. Beaumont, *Complete Book of Ballets* (1937).

[Marcia B. Siegel]

SAINT LOUIS, principal city in the state of Missouri, founded in 1764 as a French outpost in the Louisiana Territory. The area became part of the United States under the Louisiana Purchase in 1804. In 1876, the City of St. Louis formally split from St. Louis County, which itself contains numerous incorporated communities. The Jewish community of Greater St. Louis refers to the combined population of the City of St. Louis and St. Louis County. The professional Jewish Demographic Study, conducted in 1995 by Gary A. Tobin, found that the Jewish population in Greater St. Louis (City and County combined) was 59,400 Jews and related non-Jews living in 24,600 households. The *American Jewish Year Book* (2004) estimates the Jewish population of Greater St. Louis at 54,500. Through the years, formal surveys and *American Jewish Year Book* estimates have been remarkably stable, estimating the Jewish population as between 45,000 and 60,000, with most estimates closer to 55,000. The 2004 United States Census lists the population of the City of St. Louis at 343,279, down from its 1950 peak of 575,238. St. Louis County in 2004 had an overall population of 1,009,235. It is estimated that the Jewish population of Greater St. Louis is roughly 2.1 percent of the total.

Pierre Laclede, a French fur trader, founded St. Louis in 1764. In the 18th century, as in other French territories at the time, no non-Catholics were permitted to settle in St. Louis, a situation which would continue until after the Louisiana Purchase. Jews did make trips during this period in the 1760s from New Orleans and across into the English Illinois country.

According to research by St. Louis Jewish historian Donald I. Makovsky, and follow-up work by historian Dr. Walter Ehrlich, the first Jew definitively known to settle in the city was Joseph Philipson, a Jew of either Polish or German origins, who opened a store in St. Louis in 1807. He had immigrated to Philadelphia around 1800 at the age of 34, with his two brothers; they became involved in merchandising and the lead and fur businesses.

Philipson brought $10,000 worth of goods from Baltimore to St. Louis, where he gradually expanded his enterprises to include ownership of a brewery (later one of the major industries of St. Louis), a distillery, a sawmill, large stockholdings in the city's second bank and substantial real estate. Philipson was active in cultural and community affairs, but there is no hard evidence that he helped start the local Jewish community. Cincinnati, a rival city, had its first Jewish congregation within a few years after the arrival of its first Jew in 1817, while St. Louis had to wait 30 years after Philipson's arrival, for the founding of a fledgling congregation.

Early Jewish Activities

During the late 1830s and early 1840s, St. Louis was on its way to becoming the fourth largest city in the United States by 1900. From 1835 to 1840, the city population jumped from 8,316 to 16,349, including fewer than 100 Jews. This small Jewish community formed numerous institutions between 1837 and 1842. Starting in 1837, High Holy Day *minyanim* were held, starting with services on the Mississippi River front. In 1840, 33 Jews contributed funds to establish the first Jewish cemetery. United Hebrew Congregation, originally Orthodox, and now Reform, was started officially in 1841 by 12 men from Posen (Prussia), Bohemia, and England. In 1842, the Hebrew Benevolent Society was formed to care for needy Jews.

In 1843–44, various religious practices were initiated by the United Hebrew Congregation. Regular Ashkenazi services in the Polish tradition were conducted in a rented room.

By 1850, when the city's total population was 77,680, about 700 Jews comprised the community. Most were merchants; only two physicians and one lawyer are known to have been among the Jewish community during this period. Factors which limited the growth of the St. Louis Jewish community included the St. Louis Fire of May 17, 1849, a cholera epidemic, and the Gold Rush, which lured many to California.

Civil War Period

Nearly the entire Jewish community in St. Louis supported the North during the Civil War. Isidore Bush (1822–1898), a member of the City Council and Board of Education, and an early congregational leader, strongly supported emancipation. Only one St. Louis Jew was known to be a slaveholder. When General Ulysses S. Grant issued his infamous antisemitic Order 11 in 1862, against Jews in Union-occupied territory, Mayer Friede (1821–1888), a jeweler and a B'nai El founder, serving as Missouri's first Jewish representative in the state legislature, denounced the order on the floor of the House. He was one of many influential Jews who persuaded President Lincoln to repudiate the order and the antisemitic sentiments it expressed.

Congregational Growth

A group of United Hebrew members desiring a less traditional ritual observance, founded Congregation Emanu El in 1847, made up largely of German Jews. In 1849, a similar group of Bohemian Jews formed Congregation B'nai B'rith. They merged in 1852 to form B'nai El Congregation. A proposed merger with United Hebrew fell through when B'nai El received a windfall gift of $3,000 for a building from the estate of Jewish philanthropist Judah Touro. Competed in 1855 at Sixth and Cerre Streets, the B'nai El building was the first synagogue structure west of the Mississippi.

REFORM MOVEMENT TAKES ROOT. The 1860s was a period of continued growth of Reform Jewish congregations and institutions in St. Louis. The St. Louis Temple Association was founded in 1865, made up of dissident members of B'nai El. By 1867–68, the group was functioning as a nascent congregation, which was formally chartered in 1869, as Congregation Shaare Emeth, the first Reform synagogue in St. Louis, founded as such and part of the national movement. Dr. Solomon Sonneschein (1839–1908) was Shaare Emeth's first rabbi, but in 1866, the congregation's board split over his radical religious views, which resulted in his termination. Rabbi Sonneschein's supporters went with him to found Temple Israel. B'nai El, Shaare Emeth, and United Hebrew, which became

Reform, continue in the 21st century. Other Reform congregations include Temple Emanuel, Central Reform Congregation, Kol Am, and Kol Hanishama.

ORTHODOX AND CONSERVATIVE MOVEMENTS. In the 1870s, at least three Orthodox synagogues were formed, of which Beth Hamedrosh Hagodol (1879) survives. Other Orthodox congregations as of 2006 include Agudas Israel of St. Louis; Bais Abraham Congregation, Bais Menachem-Chabad, Nusach Ari B'nai Zion, Tpheris Israel, Traditional Congregation and Young Israel of St. Louis. B'nai Amoona was founded in 1881 as an Orthodox synagogue but later became Conservative. Shaare Zedek and Brith Sholom Kneseth Israel also serve the Conservative Jewish community of St. Louis.

RECONSTRUCTIONIST AND JEWISH RENEWAL MOVEMENTS. St. Louis is served by two Reconstructionist congregations, the Reconstructionist Minyan of St. Louis and Shir Hadash Reconstructionist Community. There is one local congregation associated with the Jewish Renewal movement, Neve Shalom.

Philanthropic Institutions

In the mid-to-late 19th century, various institutions were created to coordinate fund-raising to serve the entire Jewish community regardless of denomination. These included the Hebrew Benevolent Association (1842), B'nai B'rith Missouri Lodge 22 (1855), which continues to function; and Ebn Ezra Lodge 47, which later merged into the Missouri Lodge. The Hebrew Relief Association was formed in 1871 in the aftermath of the devastating Chicago Fire, which brought many Jewish refugees to St. Louis who were in desperate need of direct relief support. By 1898, various similar organizations merged into the United Jewish Educational and Charitable Associations, which evolved into the present-day Jewish Family and Children's Service. Other groups came together in 1901 to create the Jewish Educational and Charitable Union in order to better coordinate all Jewish philanthropic campaigns. The JECU later changed its name to the Jewish Federation of St. Louis, which continues to serve as the "central address" for all community-wide fund-raising, planning and budgeting for a family of local, national and overseas beneficiary agencies. The Jewish Federation's annual campaign typically raises in excess of $10 million in its annual campaigns, and has also developed a substantial group of major endowment funds.

Eastern European Immigration

The large waves of Jews from Eastern Europe who came to America's shores from the 1880s through the 1920s, included many who chose St. Louis as their new home. The still-famous 1904 St. Louis World's Fair, formally called the Louisiana Purchase Exposition, celebrated modernism and the status of St. Louis as the fourth largest city in the United States. There was considerable work available for the immigrants in building, maintaining, and later dismantling the elaborate infrastructure for the World's Fair, which took place in the city's Forest Park, a facility larger than New York City's Central Park.

In 1880, the St. Louis Jewish community numbered 10,000 in a city of 350,000. The community was solidly "German," part of the larger wave of German immigrants who came to St. Louis after the Revolution of 1848. These largely acculturated and Reform German Jews, often openly expressed distaste and discomfort over their East European co-religionists, but the very institutions the German Jews helped establish – the Jewish Federation, the Jewish Hospital, the Jewish Family Service, etc. helped the East European Jews adjust to life in the New World. Local Jewish historian Walter Ehrlich, author of the two-volume history of the community, *Zion in the Valley: The Jewish Community of St. Louis*, credits the public school experience of young second-generation Jews at high schools like Soldan and University City High School, for having broken down the barriers between the "German" and "Russian" communities through social contact, dating, and eventual marriage.

Another point of positive contact between the German and Russian communities, which had founded rival country clubs – Westwood for the Germans and Meadowbrook for the Russians – was the Young Men's Hebrew Association (YMHA), founded locally in 1896. The YMHA, which later evolved into the present-day Jewish Community Center (JCC), was initially alien to the East European Orthodox Jewish community. The 1902 YMHA banquet featured an appetizer of Blue Point Oysters. Later, the JCC and other major Jewish organizations would accommodate the *kashrut* needs of the traditional Jewish community.

Other communal institutions were established during this period, which served both the "German" and "Russian" Jewish communities, including the Jewish Hospital (1902), now Barnes-Jewish Hospital. The needs of the elderly were served for many years by two separate institutions, the Jewish Orthodox Old Folks Home and the (Reform) Home for Aged and Infirm Israelites, which were later to merge into the Jewish Center for Aged, now the Cedars at the JCA.

World War I Period

The St. Louis Jewish community strongly supported the American war effort during World War I. The local German population, both Jewish and non-Jewish was especially eager to be seen as being pro-American and not in sympathy with Germany and its war aims. Several prominent members of the Jewish community had leadership roles during this period. Louis Aloe, a member of the Board of Freeholders and later of the Board of Aldermen, became acting mayor of St. Louis, when Mayor Henry Kiel fell ill in 1917. Rachel Stix Michael chaired the instruction committee of the Missouri Women's Committee of National Defense, which trained women to fill jobs vacated by men called to military service. Edwin B. Meissner, Sr. (1884–1956), vice president and later president for 19 years of Congregation Shaare Emeth, and president of the St. Louis Car Company, was commissioned a lieutenant colonel in the Ordinance Reserve in 1918. In addition to railroad and streetcar equipment and cars, his plant produced aircraft, artillery carts and munitions vital to the war effort.

Residential and Occupational Patterns
In 1900, the Jewish population of St. Louis was about 40,000, among the total city population of 575,288. The German segment, now a minority, was English-speaking, upwardly mobile, middle class, Reform in its orientation, and moving west from the city into new suburbs, including University City and Clayton, and in later decades, Ladue, Olivette, Creve Coeur, Chesterfield and throughout the metropolitan region, including St. Charles County, which is served by B'nai Torah, an interdenominational synagogue. Initially, the Eastern Europeans, Orthodox, and largely Yiddish speaking in the first generation, remained in the immigrant sections of the city.

In 1920, when the total city population was 772,897, some 20,000 Jews had moved into the Central West End of the City and into St. Louis County suburbs in increasing numbers. The 30,000 Eastern Europeans were now moving west into the suburbs. Congregations which had been located in the city, which split from St. Louis County in 1876, began to move to suburban locations, starting with Temple Israel. By the 1970s, beginning with the formation of Central Reform Congregation and its Rabbi Susan Talve, the Jewish community in the city has made a dramatic comeback, although the overwhelming majority of St. Louis Jewry continues to reside in St. Louis County.

Other Local Institutions
The Orthodox and Conservative communities in 1924 established the Vaad Hoeir to oversee *kashrut* and personal status issues. The Vaad Hoeir was one of the few North American communities to employ a chief rabbi of the Orthodox Jewish Community, starting with Rabbi Hayim Fischel Epstein (1874–1942). He was succeeded by Rabbi Menachem Zvi Eichenstein (1911–1981), who in turn was succeeded by Rabbi Sholom Rivkin (b. 1926), who served from 1981 until his retirement as chief rabbi emeritus in 2005.

Day Schools
The Rabbi H.F. Epstein Hebrew Academy, formed in 1945, was the first Jewish day school in St. Louis. In addition, the community is also served by the Block Yeshiva High School and Torah Prep (Orthodox), the Solomon Schechter Day School (Conservative) and the Saul Mirowitz–Reform Jewish Day School (Reform). There is also a Central Agency for Jewish Education, formed in 1969, which works with the various congregational schools and day schools, and which sponsors a number of adult educational programs as well as the Jewish Community High School among others.

Community Relations
In 1938, following the infamous *Kristallnacht* in Nazi Germany, the local Jewish Community Relations Council was formed, bringing together under one umbrella a current total of 19 Jewish community relations, defense, and communal groups. Among its founding members were the Jewish Federation, B'nai B'rith, and the local chapters of the American Jewish Committee, the American Jewish Congress, the Anti-Defamation League and Hadassah, among others.

Zionism
Chronicled in detail in the book *The Struggle for Zion's Rebirth* by Zionist leader Moses Joshua Slonim, organized Zionism took root in St. Louis by 1898. The first time the Zionist flag flew over an official building was at the Palace of Nations at the 1904 World's Fair. In 1911, several local Jews, led by Simon Goldman, sponsored a settlement in Palestine near Lake Kinneret, called Poriah. The project fell victim by 1916 to a series of misfortunes, but the village *Poriyyah took form on the site of the ruins of the original St. Louis Zionist enclave.

Over the years, a thriving chapter of the Zionist Organization of America, along with Hadassah and other Zionist groups, including the Pioneer Women (now Na'amat), took root and flourished over the decades. Jewish Federation-sponsored "Missions to Israel" and events sponsored by the local chapters of the American Israel Public Affairs Committee and other groups have also contributed to strong local Jewish support of the Jewish community in Israel. During the 1940s, there was an active chapter of the anti-Zionist American Council for Judaism, but the overwhelming majority of the local Jewish community is strongly pro-Israel.

Writers and Chroniclers
St. Louis Jewry has produced locally and nationally noted writers, novelists and poets through the decades, including Howard Schwartz, author of numerous books of poetry, stories, fables and a major work on Jewish mythology published in 2005. Schwartz and Barbara Raznick, director of the Saul Brodsky Jewish Community Library, have also co-edited several editions of *The Sagarin Review, First Harvest,* and *New Harvest,* collections of literary contributions, short stories, poems and life stories by St. Louis Jewish writers. Other writers of note include Louis Daniel Brodsky, a noted poet; historian Max I. Dimont (*Jews, God and History*), Fannie *Hurst, Stanley *Elkin, Harold Brodkey, Howard *Nemerov, poet Michael Castro, Stephen Schwarzchild, A.E. Hotchner, and Glenn Savan. Mystery writer Michael Kahn has also developed a national following, and Ellen Harris has published two acclaimed "true crime" books, including *Guarding the Secrets,* about a local cell of the Abu Nidal Palestinian terrorist organization.

Local Jewish historians include, notably, Dr. Walter Ehrlich, author of the definitive two-volume *Zion in the Valley: The Jewish Community of St. Louis*; Burton I. Boxerman; Murray Darrish, a leading expert on Jewish genealogy and local Jewish history; and Donald I. Makovsky, author of the definitive monograph on Joseph Philipson and his family, the first known Jews from St. Louis.

The back files of the *St. Louis Jewish Light* (first published in 1947; reorganized in 1963), the local Jewish community weekly newspaper, is also an excellent repository of information about St. Louis Jewry, as is the St. Louis Jewish Archives, located in the Saul Brodsky Jewish Community Library.

BIBLIOGRAPHY: W. Ehrlich, *The Struggle for Zion's Rebirth: the Jewish Community of St. Louis*, vol. I, 1807–1907; vol. II, The Twentieth Century (1997 and 2002); D.I. Makovsky, *The Philipsons: The First Known Jewish Settlers in St. Louis, 1807–1858* (1958); idem, "Origin and Early History of the United Hebrew Congregation of St. Louis, 1841–1859" (unpub. master's degree thesis, Washington University, 1958); M.J. Slonim, *The Struggle for Zion's Rebirth: A History of Zionism in St. Louis*, serialized in the *St. Louis Jewish Light* (1972); A. Bondi, *Autobiography* (1910); B.A. Boxerman, "Reactions of the St. Louis Jewish Community to Anti-Semitism, 1933–45" (unpub. master's degree thesis, St. Louis University, Washington University 1954); idem, "A History of the Jewish Hospital of St. Louis," in: *Missouri Historical Society Review* (2004); R. Fischlowitz (Marget), *The Y Story* (history of the Jewish Community Center; 1964); G.A. Tobin, "Jewish Population Movements in St. Louis," in *Gateway Heritage Magazine* (Spring 1986); Jewish Demographic Study for St. Louis, 1981 and 1995; *Guide to Jewish Life*, published annually by the *St. Louis Jewish Light*, since 1988, an annual profile of the local Jewish community; *St. Louis Jewish Light* back files and issues, 1947–2006.

[Robert A. Cohn (2nd ed.)]

SAINT-PAUL-TROIS-CHÂTEAUX, town in the Drôme department, S.E. France. The first evidence of Jews in the town dates from 1206, when a Jew named Benicrescas is mentioned in a document. In 1239 a "Tour des Juifs" is recorded. Using the *blood libel of *Valréas as a pretext, in 1247 the bishop of Saint-Paul had the Jews of his diocese thrown into prison after he had stripped them of their belongings; Pope Innocent IV firmly protested against his action. Even after the Dauphiné – in which Saint-Paul-Trois-Châteaux was situated – had come under the authority of the king of France, Jews continued to live in Saint-Paul. However, in 1486 only three families remained there, and there is no further mention of the Jewish community after that date. A Hebrew inscription in the presbytery hall could still be seen at the close of the 19th century.

BIBLIOGRAPHY: Gross, Gal Jud, 640–2; M. Schwab, *Inscriptions hébraiques en France du VIIe au XVe siècles* (1898), 38f.; J. de Font-Reaulx, *Cartulaire de l'Evêché de Saint-Paul-Trois-Châteaux* (1946), 172; S. Grayzel, *Church and the Jews* (1966^2), 266f.

[Bernhard Blumenkranz]

SAINT PETERSBURG, Pinellas County, Florida. Florida's fourth largest city, with 61 square miles, is located on the west coast of Florida in Pinellas County (St. Petersburg, Clearwater, Palm Harbor, Largo, Gulfport and Tarpon Springs). It has 234 miles of coastline, mostly on the Gulf of Mexico, and is known as the "Sunshine City." The first-known Jews were Mr. and Mrs. Henry Schutz, who arrived from Germany in 1901 and opened a dry goods store, the only Jewish merchants for seven years. Their store on Central Avenue, which had a basket on a pulley to carry money to a balcony to make change, later served as a temporary home for St. Petersburg High School. Olga and Leon Manket opened a dry good store in 1908; their daughter Anne was the first-known Jewish child born there. The first-known boy was Julius Lovitz in 1909; the Lovitz family were the first-known Jews in Tarpon Springs, a Greek sponge fishing village. Sam Lovitz was known as "Mr. Jew Sam." That family moved to Clearwater, and another relative, Abe Tarapani, had a store in St. Petersburg in 1911, before also moving to Tarpon Springs. The Ben Haliczers had a gas station and tire store from 1910 and had four children in Florida – two in St. Petersburg. Ben's brother Leon arrived in 1921 and had a watch repair store.

In 1920 St. Petersburg had 14,000 people, streetcars, daily band concerts in the park, unpaved streets, and people who went to the Beach to open businesses were thought "crazy." The pioneer Jewish families' names, in addition to those already mentioned, included Jacobs, Davis, Goldman, Sierkese, Cohen, Katz, Heller, Benjamin, Wittner, Rothblatt, Argintar, Lew, Solomon, and Gilbert. Some of these early families had come from Europe first to Key West, Florida, then migrated to other areas of Florida, including St. Petersburg. The Jews faced the "gentlemen's agreement" and antisemitic signs, lived near Central Avenue and had bicycle, jewelry, and grocery stores. On Sundays and holidays, Jewish families would drive through Pinellas County to pick oranges at the groves for 50 cents a bushel or drive to the waterfront and swim, filling jugs with the water that supposedly had health-giving properties – an early spa. In the evenings, the families would congregate in each other's homes to play poker and pinochle while their children played. They ordered kosher meat from Finman's in Tampa, which was delivered by boat across Tampa Bay; often it arrived spoiled, which discouraged many from keeping kosher. By 1925 a bridge was built and the meat came by bus – a big improvement!

The Jews also went to Tampa for religious services until 1923, when Congregation B'nai Israel was chartered and Conservative services were held in a rented store. The first president was Hymen Jacobs, and daughter Goldie Schuster recalls, "The discrimination and the schools were worse than her native Chicago." The first Jewish women's organization, the Ladies Auxiliary, was organized by Dora Goldberg to help the needy. In 1928 Reform Jews founded Temple Beth-El. The membership outgrew its original small home in downtown St. Petersburg, moving to its present location in 1955, and completing the Religious School addition in 2002 to meet the needs of its 600 member families.

During World War II, many Jewish servicemen enjoyed the hospitality of the small Jewish community for Sabbath dinners and the Passover *seder.* Bunny Rothblatt Katz collected scrap metal for the war effort in 1941 with her slogan "Your scrap will whip the Japs." Her father, David, was a legless veteran who owned Southern Grocery and was active in both civic and Jewish affairs. After the war, the Jewish population grew rapidly to about 1,500 families, and the first Jewish nursery school was opened in 1959. Since 1960 Gulf Coast Jewish Family Services has been helping infants, children, families and elders in serious physical, medical, mental, social and financial crisis, enabling them to remain free and independent with families and loved ones. In 1970 Menorah Manor was built to serve the Jewish aged; it includes a nursing home and assisted living facility. Philip Benjamin Tower is an apartment complex adjacent to Menorah Manor. In the early 21st century plans were being made to build a $16 million North County Campus of Menorah Manor. In 1986 the Jewish Federation of Pinellas County approached Jim Dawkins and Karen Wolfson Dawkins to start and publish their own Jewish community newspaper for Pinellas County, *Jewish Press,* which continues bi-weekly.

Opened in 1992 on the grounds of the former Jewish Community Center of Pinellas County in Madeira Beach, The Florida Holocaust Museum (www.flholocaustmuseum.org) – the fourth largest Holocaust museum in the U.S. – moved in 1998 to the heart of St. Petersburg's museum district. The permanent exhibit includes an original boxcar from Poland once used to transport prisoners during the Holocaust. Traveling art and historical exhibitions change regularly, and the museum is currently the only one of its kind in the country to house a permanent art collection related to the Holocaust. The museum was begun as the vision of St. Petersburg philanthropist and businessman Walter Loebenberg, who escaped Nazi Germany in 1939, together with a group of other business and community leaders.

The Jewish Federation of Pinellas County has the following beneficiary agencies: Gulf Coast Jewish Family Services, Pinellas County Jewish Day School, Golda Meir/Kent Jewish Center in Clearwater, and TOP Jewish Foundation. A Jewish demographic study in Pinellas County in 1993 showed 24,200 Jews who live there year round. Most have come from Michigan, Ohio, New Jersey, New York, and Pennsylvania. The congregational roster for Pinellas County includes five Reform, three Conservative, two Orthodox, and one independent.

BIBLIOGRAPHY: Archives of the Jewish Museum of Florida – much of the early history written by Goldie Jacobs Schuster, who settled in St. Petersburg with her family in 1920.

[Marcia Jo Zerivitz (2nd ed.)]

SAINT PETERSBURG (**Petrograd** from 1914 to 1924; **Leningrad** from 1924 to 1992), capital of Russia until 1918, now in the Russian Federation; industrial city and major port on the Baltic Sea. Some apostates or Marranos appeared in St. Petersburg soon after its foundation in 1703. Anton Divier, who was of Portuguese Jewish origin, was appointed the first police minister of the new capital in 1718. "The Portuguese Jew," Jan Dacosta, was one of the jesters at the royal court during the first half of the 18th century. Jewish physicians and financiers held various positions in the city during the 18th century: Lippmann was financial agent of the court during the 1720s. In 1738 the proselyte officer Alexander *Voznitsyn and Baruch Leibov of Dubrovna, who had introduced him to Judaism, were burnt at the stake in St. Petersburg. Because of the intolerant attitude of Czarina Elizabeth (1741–62) the few Jews who lived in St. Petersburg left. *Catherine II, on the other hand, was interested in attracting Jewish contractors, industrialists, and physicians to the city, and issued instructions to the authorities to overlook the presence of those "useful" Jews who lived there with their families and clerks and had the protection of court officials. Toward the end of Catherine's reign, there was a large community in the town; most prominent was the contractor Abraham *Peretz, whose household included Mendel of Satanov and J.L. *Nevakhovich. The latter published the first work of Russian Jewish literature, *Vopl dshcheri iudeyskoy*, in St. Petersburg in 1803.

From the end of the 18th century, when St. Petersburg had become the government center for millions of Jews who were incorporated into the Russian Empire after the partition of Poland, communal workers and *shtadlanim* streamed into the city. Many others arrived as a result of their business activities or in search of a livelihood in the prosperous city. During the years 1798 and 1800–01, Shneur Zalman of Lyady, the leader of the *Chabad* Ḥasidim, was imprisoned in St. Petersburg. In 1802 a group of Jews leased a plot of land in the Lutheran cemetery, thus laying the foundations of a permanent community in the city. The situation of the Jews worsened with the accession of Czar Nicholas I. He ordered that all Jews living in the city "without doing anything" be expelled. According to the official estimate, there were 370 Jews living in the city at that time. These included craftsmen, merchants, and various *shtadlanim*; most of them were ordered to leave. Regulations were issued authorizing Jews to stay in St. Petersburg on business for a maximum period of six weeks; by a special permit from the local authorities this could be extended to between six and ten months. Right of residence was granted to a number of physicians (including the czar's dentist and the midwife of the royal court). After 1827 many *Cantonists went to St. Petersburg and some of them brought their families to the city. They maintained a prayer house, and those Jews who had to come to St. Petersburg on business found refuge in their homes. The prohibition on Jewish residence was stringently applied; anyone found living in the city without a permit was liable to be pressed into the army. From time to time the police hunted down Jews living in the city illegally. There was a large and increasing number of apostates, most of whom changed their names and disappeared among the general population.

The situation changed once more with the beginning of the reign of Alexander II, especially after the publication of the laws granting right of residence outside the *Pale of Settlement to merchants of the first guild, intellectuals, and craftsmen. Wealthy Jewish merchants and financiers (the families *Guenzburg, *Polyakov, A. *Varshavski, Friedland, L. *Rosenthal, and others), physicians, advocates, and scientists soon settled in the city. Many Jewish students registered at the university and the other higher schools of the city (326 in 1886 and 848 in 1911). The influence of the wealthy and the *maskilim* was decisive within the community. Jews and apostates played an important role in the life of the city as journalists, publishers, advocates, scientists, artists, and physicians. In 1881 there were 17,253 Jews (c. 2% of the total population) in St. Petersburg. Ten years later, after a period of strict supervision of residence rights under Police Minister Greser, there were 15,331 Jews (1.6%). According to the 1897 census there were 17,254 (including 310 Karaites), forming 1.4% of the population. In fact, the number of Jews in the city was greater at all periods, because many, whose right to reside there was dubious, evaded the census officers.

Despite its small numbers, the St. Petersburg community played an important role in Russian Jewish life, thanks to the riches of individual members and their proximity to and influence at the court. The barons of the Guenzburg family, as well as other rich Jews, were considered as the spokesmen of the whole of Russian Jewry before the central government. From time to time gatherings of rabbis and community representatives were called to St. Petersburg for official and semiofficial meetings, at which vital problems were discussed. From the 1860s an organized community existed in the city. The right of a communal vote depended on payment of 25 rubles tax, thus assuring that the wealthy had control of the community. Several leading personalities held the position of **kazyonny ravvin* ("government appointed rabbi") in St. Petersburg, including A. Neumann, A. *Drabkin, and M. *Eisenstadt. Among the traditional rabbis was Isaac *Blaser, who held office from 1864 to 1878; the last rabbi of the community was David Tevel *Katzenellenbogen (1907–30). The poet J.L. *Gordon was the community secretary from 1872 to 1879. After many endeavors and numerous refusals, a magnificent central synagogue, containing 1,200 seats and built in the Moorish style, was completed in 1893. In spite of prohibitions and unremitting police persecutions, the community continued to grow, numbering 35,000 (1.8% of the population) in 1914. Severe *censorship regulations caused the Jewish press (Hebrew, Russian, and Yiddish) to be centered in St. Petersburg from the 1870s until the 1905 revolution. The newspapers *Ha-Meliz* (1871–73 and 1878–1904), *Ha-Yom* (1886–88), *Dos Yudishes Folksblat* (1881–90), and the first Russian daily newspaper in Yiddish, *Der Fraynd* (1903–08), were all published there. Above all, the city was the center of Russian-Jewish journalism and literature. The periodicals *Yevreyskaya Biblioteka* (1871–80), *Razsvet* (1879–83), and *Voskhod* (1881–1906), the Zionist organ *Razsvet* (1907–18), and many other newspapers, were also published in St. Petersburg. One of the outstanding publications was the Russian-Jewish encyclopedia, *Yevreyskaya Entsiklopediya*.

In addition to local cultural and charitable institutions (such as the Society for the Support of Poor Jews, which was established in 1907 to coordinate the activities of the various charitable societies and was recognized as a legal institution under whose aegis their work could be carried out), many nationwide Jewish organizations had their headquarters in St. Petersburg. Oldest of these organizations was the Society for the Promotion of Culture among the Jews of Russia (founded in 1863). Others included *ORT; the Jewish Colonization Association (ICA); the Hovevei Sefat Ever (called *Tarbut after the 1917 Revolution); the Historical-Ethnographic Society, which published the historical quarterly *Yevreyskaya Starina*; and the Society for Jewish Folk Music. The city's Asian museum housed a valuable Hebrew department, based on the library of the wealthy M. Friedland. The Imperial Public Library (now the State M.E. Saltykov-Shchedrin Public Library) contains one of the world's oldest and most important collections of Hebrew manuscripts. Under the initiative of Baron D. *Guenzburg, courses in Oriental studies were opened in St. Petersburg in 1907. It was intended to develop these into a higher institute of Jewish studies. The concentration of public and cultural institutions in the town attracted Jewish authors and intellectuals (these included A.A. *Harkavy, J.L. *Katzenelson, S. *Dubnow, and M. *Kulisher).

With the outbreak of World War I, *YEKOPO ("Jewish Committee for the Relief of War Victims") was established to concentrate all the relief activities on behalf of hundreds of thousands of Jews who were refugees from the battle regions. After the February Revolution in 1917, all residence restrictions affecting the Jews of Petrograd were abolished, and the city became a center of the organizational activities of all the parties and factions of Russian Jewry. In June 1917, the seventh conference of the Zionist Organization of Russia was held in the town. Large numbers attended, demonstrating the strength of the movement and the loyalty of Russian Jews to the Zionist ideal even after they had been granted full civic emancipation. Preparations were also made to convene a general Jewish assembly in Petrograd. During the troubled days in the latter part of 1917 a Jewish battalion under the command of J. *Trumpeldor was formed, made up of Jewish soldiers of the local garrison. Around this battalion a self-defense unit was organized, which protected Jewish lives and property during the revolution of October 1917. The transfer of the seat of government from Petrograd to Moscow (1918) and the shortages and famine reigning in the city during the Russian civil war severely affected the Jewish community. Many Jews returned to their families in provincial towns. In 1920 there were 25,453 Jews (3.5% of the total population) in Petrograd. With the consolidation of the Soviet regime, the number of Jews rapidly increased, to 52,373 (4.9%) in 1923 and 84,505 (5.2%) in 1926. The 1926 census listed their occupations as: clerks (40.2%), craftsmen (14%), laborers (13.5%), government and municipal employees (10.2%), and liberal professions (2.5%); the remainder was unemployed. Organized Jewish life was liquidated in Leningrad as in all places throughout the Soviet Union. A small group of Russian-Jewish intellectuals attempted to continue its literary-scientific work under the new regime. They maintained their former cultural societies and continued to publish scientific and literary periodicals in Russian. By the end of the 1920s, these projects were also liquidated by the Soviet regime. Some intellectuals then left Russia (including S. *Dubnow and S. *Ginzburg), and others were integrated in Soviet life (I. *Zinberg, Yu. Hessen). In a poem, the Hebrew poet H. *Lenski described the atmosphere of the city during the Soviet period. According to the January 1939 census, there were 201,542 Jews (6.32% of the total population). The percentage of academicians among Jews was much higher than in the general population: 123 vs. 31 per 1,000 persons. Many thousands of Jews were drafted into the Red Army, and tens of thousands evacuated. The city was under German siege for 900 days (September 8, 1941–late January 1944), and about 900,000 inhabitants died from fighting activities and starvation, among them tens of thousands of Jews. Also remaining in the besieged city were Jewish writers such as A. Chakovski and Vera Inber, who documented the time. After the war, during the "Cosmopolitan" hunt, many intellectual Jews suffered.

[Yehuda Slutsky]

In the census of 1959, 162,344 Jews were registered in Leningrad but the real number was probably closer to 200,000; 13,728 of them declared Yiddish as their mother tongue. The city had one large, imposing synagogue, from the prerevolutionary period, a wedding room, a poultry slaughterhouse, and a *mazzah* bakery. Thousands of Jews congregated in the synagogue and its vicinity on the High Holidays. The congregation published a Jewish calendar on the eve of Rosh Ha-Shanah in the 1950s and 1960s. In the 1950s the city's synagogue board had a dynamic chairman, Gedaliah Pecherski, who was not only devoted to the religious needs of his congregation, but also initiated petitions to the Soviet government and the municipal authorities asking to be allowed to organize courses in such subjects as Hebrew and Jewish history. One petition was also signed by scholars, among them the non-Jewish authority on ancient and medieval Hebrew literature, K.B. Starkova. The petitions were rejected out of hand, and Pecherski was arrested in 1961 and sentenced to seven years' imprisonment, ostensibly for having "maintained contact with a foreign [Israel] embassy." The rabbi of the synagogue, Rabbi Lubanov, who had been imprisoned in a forced labor camp during the Stalin era, returned to office and was venerated by the congregation as a scholar and spiritual leader.

The department of Oriental and Hebrew studies at Leningrad University was run mostly by scholars, Jewish and non-Jewish, who studied there before the Revolution and who tried to continue the tradition of independent research and scholarly publication in the field of Jewish history, archaeology, etc. Joseph Davidovich Amusin published a book on the Dead Sea Scrolls which became popular with the Soviet public at large. The Saltykov-Shchedrin Library contains a rich section of Hebrew and Yiddish books (about 40,000 volumes) and also displays a number of Hebrew and Yiddish periodicals from abroad, including Israel. Jews and non-Jews frequented this section, though it was generally assumed that "excessive interest" in Hebrew language and literature was viewed with suspicion by the security officials. In 1962 a Jewish drama circle was established, but it soon stopped functioning because of lack of funds.

In 1962–64, as in other parts of the U.S.S.R., the baking of *mazzah* in the Leningrad synagogue was discontinued by the authorities. In 1962, with the intensification of the antireligious drive, directed mainly against Judaism, several Jews were arrested, some of them charged with "illegally" baking *mazzah*. The same year, on the eve of Simḥat Torah, 25 Jewish youths were arrested while dancing in the street near the synagogue. The local newspaper, *Vecherniy Leningrad*, carried an article (Oct. 27, 1962) condemning the synagogue's activity. In 1963 flour for *mazzah* baking was confiscated in private Jewish homes. From 1963 the authorities prohibited the use of the Jewish cemetery, which was finally closed down in 1969. Jews buried their dead in a section allotted to them in the general cemetery. In 1964, when thousands of Jewish youths danced and sang near the synagogue on Simḥat Torah eve, several of them were arrested. Later the militia put up barriers in the street opposite the synagogue to prevent Jewish youth from congregating and dancing on Simḥat Torah.

After the Six-Day War (1967), Jewish youth displayed more openly its identification with Israel in spite of the official anti-Israel campaign. Many started to study Hebrew in private groups; others protested publicly against the refusal to grant them exit permits for Israel and their protests were published abroad. In June 1970 some of them were arrested in their homes and places of work and their trial has not yet taken place (January 1971). Another group of young Jews, mostly from Riga, together with two non-Jews, were tried in Leningrad in December 1970 for allegedly planning to hijack a Soviet plane in order to land abroad and ultimately to reach Israel. Two were sentenced to death and the others to prison terms of 4–15 years. A worldwide storm of protests, including by Communist parties and newspapers in the West, preceded the appeal of the condemned in the Supreme Court of the Russian Republic in Moscow 1971; the death sentences were commuted to 15 years' hard labor and some of the other sentences were reduced.

Though mass emigration reduced its Jewish population from 107,000 in 1989 to 40,000 in 2002, Saint Petersburg reemerged as a vibrant Jewish community after the fall of Communism, with a full range of religious and educational facilities, including a yeshivah and a Chabad House. Most cultural activities were centered in the Grand Choral Synagogue, which included a home for the poor and an orphanage.

BIBLIOGRAPHY: S. Ginzburg, *Amolike Peterburg* (1944); idem, *Meshumodim in Tsarishn Rusland* (1946), 11–53, 194–206, 279–308; Feinberg, in: *Heawar*, 4 (1956), 21–36; B. Dinur, *Bi-Ymei Milhamah u-Mahpekhah* (1960), 44–304; L. Gordon, in: *Voskhod*, nos. 1–2 (1881); O.S. Grusenberg, *ibid.*, no. 1 (1891); H.A. Soloveychik, *ibid.*, no. 5 (1892); S. Dneproveki (Dubnow), in: *Nedelnaya Khronika Voskhoda*, nos. 35–36 (1893); L. Klyachko, in: *Yevreyskaya Letopis*, 2 (1923), 114–22.

SAINT-RÉMY-DE-PROVENCE, town in the Bouches-du-Rhône department, S.E. France. The presence of Jews in Saint-Rémy is confirmed from 1305 at the latest; at that time all the metal dealers were Jews. The community increased rapidly, augmented by refugees from the kingdom of France. That the community was important is indicated by the fact that it owned several synagogues, a bakery, a market, a butchery, and a cemetery (the last is still in existence). Until 1339 Jews supplied all the meat sold in Saint-Rémy, and the townsmen complained that the ritually slaughtered meat was tasteless. The community continued to exist until 1501 when the Jews were expelled from Provence. At that time several local Jews accepted baptism. There was no subsequent settlement.

BIBLIOGRAPHY: E. Leroy, *Les Archives Communales de Saint-Rémy-de-Provence* (1950 ff.), passim (includes the art. published in: REJ, 47 (1903), 301–7); B. Blumenkranz, in: *Bulletin Philologique et Historique* (1965), 615, 618, 622.

[Bernhard Blumenkranz]

SAINT-SIMONISM, a 19th-century social reform philosophy and movement, inspired by Claude-Henri de Rouvroy, Comte de Saint-Simon (1760–1825). It had prominent disciples of Jewish descent. Its ultimate goal was a technologically oriented industrial society, under a dictatorship of competent scientist-technicians and property-owning businessmen and bankers, inspired by the bizarre ideology of a "New Christianity" shorn of other-worldliness and asceticism. In a nonviolent fashion, caste privileges would be surrendered, work provided for all, rewards allocated according to merit, inheritance abolished, and equality of both sexes established. Saint-Simonism displayed an elective affinity toward the compassionate social messianism of the Hebraic prophets. Revivalist exaltation – upon which the sect eventually foundered – included the expectation of the woman-messiah "Mother," a Jewess from the Orient, who would formulate the new morality and whom the disciples must go out and find. Saint-Simon's earliest apostle was Benjamin Olinde Rodrigues (1795–1851), who was of Jewish origin. He nominated the two "supreme fathers" of the Saint-Simonian temple, Bazard (1791–1832) and Erefantin (1796–1864), and published Saint-Simon's and the disciples' collected writings. Among those Rodrigues introduced into the fold were his brother, Eugene, and his cousins, Emile and Isaac *Péreire with whom, later, he promoted French railway construction and corporate banking. Other eminent Saint-Simonians were Léon *Halévy, Gustave d'*Eichthal, and Jules *Carvallo. The active presence of the Jewish element sparked the violent reaction of both the Socialist Fourier and Catholic Church spokesmen, who denounced Saint-Simonism as a Jewish plot to subvert civilization. After due consideration it was rejected by Marx and Engels, together with all other pre-Marxist doctrines. However, among the contemporaries who were impressed by the doctrine were the historians Carlyle and Michelet, the sociologist Comte, the composers Berlioz and Liszt, and the author George Sand, in addition to such German Jewish intellectuals as Eduard *Gans, Heinrich *Heine, Rahel *Varnhagen, and Moritz *Veit.

BIBLIOGRAPHY: C.H. de R. Saint-Simon, *Oeuvres de Saint-Simon et d'Enfantin*, 47 vols. (1865–78; repr. 1963–); G. Weill, in: REJ, 31 (1895), 261–73; Z. Szajkowski, in: JSOS, 9 (1947), 33–60; F.M.H. Markham (ed.), *Selected Writings of Saint-Simon* (1952); J. Talmon, in: *Commentary*, 26 (1958), 158–72.

[Hanns G. Reissner]

SAINT-SYMPHORIEN-D'OZON, village in the Isère department, S.E. France. When the village was ceded to *Dauphiné by *Savoy, there was already an important Jewish community there, which in 1355 was granted advantageous privileges: freedom to bequeath both movable and immovable property; permission to engage in commerce and moneylending; exemption from various tolls; liberty of movement; and protection of the community against judicial irregularities. The numerical and economic importance of the community can be gauged from the fact that it paid almost half of the taxes imposed on the Jews of Dauphiné. In 1408 the municipality asked the dauphin to reduce the rate of interest of Jewish moneylenders from 50% to 25%. In the course of the 15th century the Jewish community ceased to exist.

BIBLIOGRAPHY: A. Prudhomme, in: *Bulletin de l'Académie Delphinale*, 3rd series, 17 (1881/82), 164 ff.; idem, in: REJ, 9 (1884), 260 f.; Gross, Gal Jud, 663.

[Bernhard Blumenkranz]

SAITOWITZ, STANLEY (1949–), U.S. architect. Saitowitz was born in Johannesburg, South Africa, and became professor of architecture at the University of California. Known in California for a variety of buildings, especially lofts, and home design, as well as the award-winning New England Holocaust Memorial (1995) in Boston, Saitowitz's wide-ranging works also include schools, synagogues, skate parks, a house for the drummer of Metallica, and the San Francisco Embarcadero Promenade. He experimented with fusing elements of modernism with classicism. He was cautious in his use of computer-assisted designs, preferring to maintain the conceptual integrity of his designs. Speaking at Yale University in 2004, Saitowitz described his theory of "expanded architecture" to mean that he tends to focus on air rather than substance in his designs, in order to create a world of what he called "constructed emptiness." His buildings are constructions of bars and rectangles characterized by wide, empty expanses and light. From his early houses in the Transvaal to his recent urban loft structures in the Bay area, he has focused on bringing light into his interiors. His loft buildings seem to squeeze remarkable spaces into densely crowded urban spaces. The Yerba Buena Lofts, south of Market Street in San Francisco, is a 300,000 square foot building containing 196 loft and live-work units, plus ground floor commercial space. His work has been described by Robert A.M. Stern, dean of the Art and Architecture School at Yale, as a "free-wheeling modernism." He is conscious of the environmental effect of his buildings. For example he designed a house in Napa Valley, CA, whose rusted walls were meant to reflect the seasonal changing of the colors of the landscape. Such characteristics suffuse the New England Holocaust Memorial in Boston, which depends on air and light, and their opposite, darkness and shadow, for their dramatic effects. Situated in the very heart of downtown Boston, the Memorial has an open and airy feeling that contrasts sharply with its underground component and its fiery pit. The design features six 54″ high glass towers lit from within. Their sides are etched with six million numbers suggesting the tattoos on the arms of murdered Jews. A black granite path passes under the towers. At the base of each tower, there is a stainless steel grate that covers a six foot deep chamber where the names of the primary Nazi death camps are inscribed. Smoldering coals at the base of each pit illuminate these names. Saitowitz hoped to convey the ungraspable nature of the Holocaust, as well as survival and hope.

BIBLIOGRAPHY: G. Wagner (ed.), *Stanley Saitowitz: A House in the Transvaal* (1995); M. Bell (ed.), *Stanley Saitowitz* (1995).

[Betty R. Rubenstein (2nd ed.)]

SAJAROFF, MIGUEL (1873–1958), pioneer of agrarian cooperativism in Argentina. Born in Mariupol, the Crimea (Russia), he earned a degree in agronomical engineering in Wittenberg, Germany. Under the influence of Tolstoyan thought, he aspired to become a farmer and live close to nature. Acquiescing to the request of his brother-in-law, Noah *Yarcho, he went to Argentina in 1899 and settled in the Colonia Leven, Entre Ríos, as an "independent settler," on land granted him by the *Jewish Colonization Association (ICA). He hoped to improve the economy and the cultural life of the settlement by participating in the establishment of the cooperative Fondo Communal in Domínguez in 1904. After assuming its presidency in 1908, he advocated and promoted the development of agricultural cooperatives not only in all the Jewish settlements but also throughout Argentinean life. After his death a town in the province of Entre Ríos was named Ingeniero Miguel Sajaroff.

[Lazaro Schallman]

SAKEL, MANFRED JOSHUA (1900–1957), Austrian psychiatrist. Born in Nadvorna, Galicia (then Austria), Sakel went to Berlin, where he specialized in treating addicts. On an accidental overdosage of the then newly discovered insulin, given to an addict who was diabetic, he observed that the patient lost her craving for narcotics. Sakel then started his experiments with the insulin cure for therapeutic purposes in schizophrenic patients. After the rise of Hitler, Sakel returned to Vienna and continued his work at the University Clinic, the birthplace of Wagner-Jareggs' experimental malaria treatment and a center of therapeutic initiative. It was here that Sakel developed the details of the insulin coma treatment, which for many years was the standard therapy in schizophrenia, especially in its early stages. In 1935 he published his dissertation on insulin therapy; *Neue Behandlungsmethode der Schizophrenie*. In 1936 Sakel emigrated to the U.S. and continued his work at the New York State Mental Health Department. He refused many offers of academic appointments, preferring to remain independent. He died in New York. His two principal works, *Epilepsy* (1958) and *Schizophrenia* (1958), were published posthumously. A Sakel Foundation was established, which arranged two international congresses, one in 1959 and one in 1962, that dealt with the topic of biological therapy and, especially, insulin cure.

Sakel was a fervent Zionist and politically supported the *Irgun Ẓeva'i Le'ummi movement.

BIBLIOGRAPHY: *Current Biography Yearbook 1957* (1958), 375.

[Heinrich Zwi Winnik]

SAKIAI (**Shakyai** or **Shakyay**; Heb. **Saki**; Ger. **Schaken**; Pol. **Szaki**; Rus. **Shaki**), city in S.W. Lithuania. The first Jewish settlement was in the 18th century, and in 1897 there were 1,678 Jews (74% of the total population) in the town. In 1915 the Russian retreat during World War I brought pogroms against the Jews, who soon emigrated from Sakiai. When the war ended, some Jews returned, and in 1923 there were 1,276 Jews (62% of the total population) in the town. When the town became a district capital, the economic condition of the Jews began to deteriorate. Many immigrated abroad or to the large cities; a 1936 census showed that only 600 (20% of the total population) had remained in Sakiai. With the German invasion of 1941 the community was destroyed. Sakiai was the birthplace of the brothers Dov (Boris) and Isaac Leib *Goldberg.

BIBLIOGRAPHY: *Yahadut Lita*, 3 (1967), 396.

[Yehuda Slutksy]

SAKOWITZ, BERNARD (1907–1981), U.S. retailer. Sakowitz was born in Galveston, Texas, five years after his father, Tobias, and his uncle Simon co-founded the specialty store that carried the family name in nearby Houston. Under Bernard Sakowitz's leadership, Sakowitz Brothers would not only become a Houston institution but would enjoy national prominence. It would never go public but remained the last of the family-owned major specialty chains in the U.S. Sakowitz left Texas to attend the Wharton School of Commerce at the University of Pennsylvania, earning a B.S. in 1929. Almost immediately, he began his retail career at R.H. Macy & Co. in New York City, but before the year was out he returned to Houston to join the family business. He married the former Ann Baum in 1933. They had two children, ROBERT (1938–), who would eventually head the store, and LYNN, who would marry Oscar Wyatt, a controversial energy tycoon, and become an internationally distinguished hostess. In 1937, Sakowitz was named vice president in charge of merchandising. He served as a captain with the U.S. Army Air Force during World War II, then rejoined the store. In 1957, he was appointed president of the company, which by then had opened four stores in Houston. Two years later, Sakowitz expanded to the suburbs, building a store on Westheimer Road. The move turned that location into a robust retail destination. Neiman-Marcus soon joined Sakowitz there, as did the Galleria shopping mall, and the area became known as Uptown Houston. In the 1960s, Sakowitz opened branches in other cities, including Dallas and Midland, Texas, and Phoenix, Arizona. By the 1970s, the chain had 17 specialty stores in Texas, Arizona, and Oklahoma. Sakowitz, who was named Retailer of the Year by *Esquire* magazine in 1972, became chairman in 1975. He was succeeded as president by his son, who had joined the business in 1963 after graduating from Harvard University. When Sakowitz died in 1981, Robert added the titles of chairman and chief executive officer. Bernard Sakowitz was a prominent member of the Houston community. His interests ranged from the Houston Farm and Ranch Club to the city's Contemporary Music Society. He was on the board of Congregation Beth Israel and was a director of the Texas Medical Center and St. Luke's Episcopal Hospital, leading many fundraising campaigns for cancer research. Within four years after his death, a recession in the oil industry, upon which the Houston area was so dependent, had taken its toll and the store declared Chapter 11 bankruptcy. Hooker Corporation of Australia funded the Chapter 11 petition and took majority control, but to no avail. Sakowitz was put up for sale, but liquidated in 1990 after failing to find a buyer.

[Mort Sheinman (2nd ed.)]

SAKS, GENE (1921–), U.S. director, actor. Trained as an actor at the Dramatic Workshop of the New School for Social Research, a precursor of the Actors Studio, Saks was a cofounder of an acting troupe in the late 1940s. He made his Broadway acting debut in *Juno and the Paycock* (1947). He began directing on Broadway in 1963 with Carl *Reiner's play *Enter Laughing*, and went on to excel in staging comedies and musicals, including *Mame* (1966), which featured his then wife, Beatrice Arthur, and *Same Time, Next Year* (1975). But he became best known for his deft touch with comedic plays by Neil *Simon. He directed Simon's autobiographical trilogy *Brighton Beach Memoirs* (1983), *Biloxi Blues* (1985), and *Broadway Bound* (1986). He also directed several Simon movies, including *Barefoot in the Park* (1967), with Robert Redford and Jane Fonda, *The Odd Couple* (1968), with Jack Lemmon and Walter *Matthau, and *Last of the Red Hot Lovers* (1986). He made his film acting debut in 1965, recreating his stage role as a paranoid kiddie-show host, Chuckles the Chipmunk, in *A Thousand Clowns*.

[Stewart Kampel (2nd ed.)]

°SALADIN (Salah al-Dīn, Yūsuf ibn Ayyūb; 1138–1193), founder of the dynasty of *Ayyubid sultans, of Kurdish origin. In 1169 he was elevated to the rank of vizier in Egypt, which was then still under the weak dominion of the *Fatimids.

In 1171 he removed the last Fatimid sultan, al-ʿĀḍid, from his throne, thus returning Egypt to the nominal rule of the *Abbasid caliphs by mentioning the name of al-Mustaḍī, the caliph who then ruled in Baghdad, in the Khuṭba (the sermon of the festive Friday prayer), and on coins. For a while, Saladin considered himself to be a vassal of Nūr al-Dīn, the Seljuqid *atabek* (maior domus) and ruler of Syria who lived in Damascus and had established the state which was a serious challenge to the crusaders in Ereẓ Israel and Syria. Immediately after the death of Nūr al-Dīn in 1174, however, Saladin seized control of Syria. In a brilliant and rapid campaign, in 1187, at the head of 12,000 horsemen, Saladin conquered Tiberias, Hattin, and Jerusalem, and almost the whole of Ereẓ Israel fell into his hands. These victories prompted Christian Europe to organize the Third Crusade (1189–92). In the meantime, Saladin's treasury had become empty and his troops were halted before Tyre, where some of them deserted him. The crusaders succeeded in occupying Acre after a siege which lasted two years (1189–91), and Saladin was compelled to sign a peace treaty with the king of England, Richard the Lionhearted, according to which the Ereẓ Israel coastal region from Jaffa to Tyre remained in the hands of the crusaders. Saladin died a short while later.

The attitude of Saladin toward the Jews, the Christians, and even the defeated Christians who lived under his rule, was most tolerant. According to Judah *Al-Ḥarizi, he issued a manifesto in 1190 in which he called upon the Jews to settle in Jerusalem (their presence in the town had been prohibited during its occupation by the Crusaders). Indeed, when Al-Ḥarizi visited Jerusalem in 1216, he found an important community which was composed of immigrants from France, the Maghreb, and former inhabitants of Ashkelon. Ibn Abi Uṣaybiʿa, a friend of *Abraham ben Moses b. Maimon, relates that *Maimonides was the court physician of Saladin and of his son al-Malik al-Afḍal, and that both greatly honored the Jewish physician and scholar. It appears, however, that there is no historical basis to this information.

BIBLIOGRAPHY: Ashtor, in: HUCA, 27 (1956), 305–26; Lewis, in: *Eretz Israel*, 7 (1964), 70–75 (Eng. pt.); Prawer, Ẓalbanim, index. **ADD. BIBLIOGRAPHY:** EIS[2]; M.C. Lyons and D.E.P. Jackson, *Saladin the Politics of the Holy War* (1982); Y. Lev, *Saladin in Egypt* (1999), ch. 6.

[Haïm Z'ew Hirschberg]

SALAMAN, English family. CHARLES KENSINGTON SALAMAN (1814–1901), pianist and composer, was elected a member of the Royal Academy of Music at the age of ten, and made his debut on the concert platform in 1828. After completing his music studies in Paris, he returned to London in 1831 and, besides composing, teaching, and giving recitals, devoted much time to promoting the musical life of the capital. He inaugurated an annual series of orchestral concerts (1833), founded London's first amateur choral society (1849), helped to establish chamber concerts (1853), and was one of the founders of the Musical Society of London (1858).

In 70 years of composing, Charles Salaman produced many works for piano, organ, and orchestra, and a comic opera, *Pickwick* (1889). He was especially prolific as a writer of songs in English, Italian, and Hebrew and of devotional music for the synagogue. An early advocate of Reform Judaism, he composed more than a hundred settings for the service of the West London Synagogue, as well as anthems and settings of psalms. Several of his anthems were used by Anglicans, and his setting of the 84th Psalm was sung at the reopening of Worcester Cathedral. He wrote *Jews as they Are* (1882, 1885[2]). Four of Charles Salaman's sisters rose to prominence in art and literature. JULIA SALAMAN (1812–1906), who married Louis Goodman, was a well-known portrait artist who exhibited at the Royal Academy from 1838–1901. Her younger sister KATE SALAMAN (1821–1856) was noted for her miniature portraits. RACHEL SALAMAN married Sir John *Simon in 1843, and wrote *Records and Reflections*, selected from her writings during half a century (1894). ANNETTE SALAMAN (d. 1879) assisted in compiling a second edition of *Footsteps in the Way of Life* (1874[2]), an illustrated guide to the Bible, and the children's story book *Aunt Annette's Stories to Ada* (1876[1]; 1879[5]).

Charles Salaman's oldest son, MALCOLM CHARLES SALAMAN (1855–1940), was a drama and art critic. From 1883 to 1894 he was a drama and art critic of the *Sunday Times* and, from 1890 to 1899, was also on the staff of the *Daily Graphic*. In the art world he was regarded as England's outstanding authority on color prints and woodcuts.

His numerous books on prints included *The Old Engravers of England* (1906), *Old English Colour-Prints* (1909), *The Great Painter-Etchers from Rembrandt to Whistler* (1913), and the series *Modern Masters of Etching and Masters of the Colour Print*. From 1923 to 1938 he published an annual review, *Fine Prints of the Year*. He edited the published plays of Sir Arthur Wing Pinero (1891–1900). Three of his own plays were staged – *Deceivers Ever* (1883), *Dimity's Dilemma* (1894), and *A Modern Eve* (1894). He also wrote a large number of song lyrics.

BIBLIOGRAPHY: Grove, Dict; MGG; DNB.

[George H. Fried]

SALAMAN, REDCLIFFE NATHAN (1874–1955), pathologist and geneticist. He was director of the Pathological Institute of the London Hospital from 1901 to 1904. His later scientific investigations were devoted chiefly to the genetics and diseases of the potato, and in 1926 he was appointed director of the potato virus research station in Cambridge. One of his major achievements was the initiation of stocks of virus-free seed potatoes. He wrote *Jewish Achievements in Medicine* (1911) and *Racial Origins of Jewish Types* (1922). Two books on his specialty were *Potato Varieties* (1926) and *The History and Social Influence of the Potato* (1949). In 1935 he was elected a Fellow of the Royal Society.

During World War I Redcliffe Salaman served in Palestine and in 1920 published *Palestine Reclaimed*. He had a lifelong commitment to the Jewish community and to Zionism, was a trustee of Jews' College, London, and a governor of the Hebrew University of Jerusalem. He also served as president of the Jewish Historical Society of England, the Jewish Health Organization of Great Britain, and the Jewish Commission for Relief Abroad. His first wife, NINA RUTH SALAMAN (née Davis; 1877–1925), was well known as a poet and translator of medieval Hebrew poetry. Her own verse included *Apples and Honey* (1921) and she translated *Judah Halevi's poems (1924). Their son, MYER HEAD SALAMAN (1902–1994), was a bacteriologist and doctor. Engaged in cancer research and pathology in World War II, he joined the Department of Cancer Research, London Hospital Medical College, in 1946, where he became director in 1948.

BIBLIOGRAPHY: JC (June 17, 1955), 12; K.M. Smith, in: Royal Society of London, *Biographical Memoirs of Fellows of the Royal Society*, 1 (1955), 239–45; J.W. Parkes, in: JHSET, 18 (1953–55), 296–8.

[George H. Fried]

SALAMANCA, city in western Spain. The Jewish settlement of Salamanca seems to have been one of the oldest in the kingdom. From its start at the time of Christian rule, the Jewish quarter was close to the old citadel. The first documents mentioning Jews in Salamanca date back to the end of the 12th century. In the *Fuero* granted to the city by Fernando II, the Jews enjoyed judicial equality with the Christians. Following the death of Alfonso IX of León, the Jews of Salamanca were severely attacked but soon recovered, and the community became one of the strongest and most prosperous in the area. In the middle of the 13th century a *barrio de iudeis* is mentioned. Later the quarter was called *iuderia*. In the second half of the 13th century three synagogues are mentioned: the *vieja* (old), the *menor* (small), and the *nueva* (new). At that time many of the streets in the Jewish quarter were well known; one of the synagogues was situated in that leading down to Calle Postigo Ciego, where the Jewish shops and workshops of the Jews were located. At the beginning of the 13th century the city was granted a charter (*fuero*) which included important sections relevant to the local Jews, and full rights of protection and justice equal to those of the other natives of Salamanca, Christians and Moors. At each feast of the nativity the Jews of Salamanca had to pay 15 gold pieces to the crown. The charter also regulated several matters regarding the slaughter of *kasher* meat and its sale in the town and Jewish quarter. In 1285 the community was made to pay 1,800 maravedis as a special war tax. At that time there were some 300 to 500 Jews in Salamanca. The Jews were merchants, moneylenders, physicians, shoemakers, and parchment makers.

From the 14th century several resolutions of the town council regarding the affairs of its Jews are known. In 1335 the council forbade Christians to receive medical aid from Jew or Moor; it was forbidden for Jewish or Moorish wet nurses to tend Christian children; Christians were forbidden to serve in Jewish houses; Jews and Moors were forbidden to rent houses in the neighborhood of the Christian churches and cemeteries. Four years later (1339) *Alfonso XI confirmed the privilege of the Jews of the town, dispensing them from appearing before Christian judges, lay or ecclesiastic, in matters concerning the collection of debts owed them by Christians, though, in principle, they had to be judged by Christian judges in mixed lawsuits. Toward the end of the 14th century R. Menahem b. Ḥayyim he-Arukh (d. 1425) was active as rabbi of the community. He approached *Isaac b. Sheshet Perfet (Responsum 251) in regard to the sentencing of two murderers who attacked a member of the community under orders from the *alcalde* (mayor) of the town. Isaac b. Sheshet permitted him to sentence them to death and execute them, but at the same time pointed out that the whole affair belonged to the jurisdiction of the king. In 1389 the Jews requested permission to erect a new synagogue, as one of their synagogues had been confiscated.

The sparing of the community of Salamanca during the persecutions in 1391 was accomplished by Vicente *Ferrer, who came to the town and preached in its synagogues in 1411–12. He succeeded in persuading many to convert, and one of the synagogues was turned into a school named "The True Cross." In 1413 Juan II conferred upon the University of Salamanca the *bet midrash* with its courts and all that belonged to it, most of the community having left Judaism by then. In place of the *bet midrash*, a hostel for pupils of the university was set up.

It would appear that the community recovered in the course of the 15th century. Yet instead of the yearly tax of 14,740 maravedis in the old coinage, it only paid the sum of 1,200 maravedis in 1439. In 1456 the community was accused of murdering a Christian child (Joseph ha-Kohen, *Emek ha-Bakha* (1895), 93). However, Henry v intervened in time, and the Jews of the town were saved from the danger. Abraham b. Samuel *Zacuto, who was born there, was engaged in 1480 in astronomical work by the bishop of Salamanca. His *Sefer Yuḥasin* is the most important chronicle written by a Jew from Sefarad.

In 1490 the community participated in the sum of 208,600 maravedis toward the redemption of the Jewish captives of *Málaga. When preparing to fulfill the order of expulsion, the community sold its synagogues and cemeteries. But on June 25 the crown forbade the sale or purchase of all congregational property. On July 30 the old synagogue was handed over to the head of the Church in the town, and he converted it into a residence. Abraham *Seneor, together with Luis de Alcalá, received the right to collect the debts which the Jews left behind. There were many Conversos in Salamanca, and there is also knowledge of Conversos who went there in order to revert to Judaism. On Oct. 25, 1490, theologians and jurists gathered there at the instigation of the monk Fernando de Santo Domingo to hold a *consulta de fé* in the matter of the child *La Guardia. Upon the expulsion, the Jews of Salamanca crossed the border to Portugal near Ciudad Real. Even after the expulsion the University of Salamanca continued to be a center for Hebrew studies, and in the 16th century some of the best intellects of Spain were concentrated in it.

The Jewish quarter in Salamanca, which was in the southwest of the city, was not exclusively inhabited by Jews, some of whom lived outside it.

BIBLIOGRAPHY: Baer, *Spain*, index; Baer, *Urkunden*, index; L. Serrano y Sanz, *Origenes de la dominación española en América*, 1 (1918), 68; M. de la Pinta Llorente, *Proceso criminal contra el hebraista salmantino Martin Martinez de Cantalapiedra* (1946); F. Cantera, *El Judio salmantino Abraham Zacut* (1931); idem, *Abraham Zacut* (1935); idem, *Sinagogas españolas* (1955), 271–82 and bibliography; Cantera-Millás, *Inscripciones*, 331–2; Suárez Fernández, index. **ADD. BIBLIOGRAPHY:** C. Carrete Parrondo, *Fontes iudaeorum regni Castilla*, I, *Provincia d Salamanca*, (1981); idem, *Hebraístas judeoconversos en la Universidad de Salamanca (siglos XV–XVI)*, (1983); F. Ferrero, in: *El pasado histórico de castilla y León, Actas del I Congreso de Historia de Castilla y León*, 1 (1983), 401–18; M.F. García Casar, *El pasado judío de Salamanca*, (1987); idem, in: *Las tres culturas en la Corona de Castilla y los Sefardíes*, (1990), 59–64.

[Haim Beinart / Yom Tov Assis (2nd ed.)]

SALAMON, ERNO (1912–1943), Hungarian poet. Born in Gyergyószentmiklós, Transylvania (now Gheorghieni, Romania), Salamon joined the clandestine Communist Party at Cluj. As a journalist of the left, he was persecuted for his political activities, first by the Romanians and, after 1940, when northern Transylvania was annexed to Hungary, by the Hungarians. He was also imprisoned several times. In 1942, Salamon was mobilized into a forced labor unit of the Hungarian army and sent to the eastern front. During the Hungarian retreat, he caught spotted typhus and, delirious with fever, ran amok and was shot to death by Italian soldiers. Salamon is considered one of the outstanding modern Hungarian poets. Although his chief subject was the suffering of the exploited workers, Salamon also wrote daringly expressive love poems.

During his lifetime, he published two collections of verse, *Gyönyörű sors* ("A Wonderful Fate," 1937), and *Szegények küszöbén* ("On the Threshold of the Poor," 1938). Others appeared in an anthology published by a group of young Jewish intellectuals, with the support of the Cluj B'nai B'rith, entitled *Kelet és Nyugat között. Zsidó fiatalok antológiája* ("Between East and West – An Anthology of Young Jews," 1937). Salamon contributed verse to the left-wing press, wrote plays, and translated poems from the Romanian. After World War II some of his works appeared in an anthology which also contained poems by two other Transylvanian-Jewish poets who died in the Holocaust, Sándor Korvin and Viktor Brassai; and volumes of Salamon's selected poems were published in Bucharest, *"Dal utódoknak"* (1961, 1967²); *Összegyüjtött versek* (1966); and in Budapest, *Mindmáig békétlenül* (1966). On the occasion of the 25th anniversary of his death, a statue of Salamon was erected in his birthplace.

BIBLIOGRAPHY: P. Pándi, *Elsüllyedt irodalom*, 2 (1963); *Ararát évkönyv*, 1 (1939), 119.

[Yehouda Marton]

SALANT, JOSEPH SUNDEL BEN BENJAMIN BENISH (1786–1866), spiritual father of the *Musar movement. A pupil of Ḥayyim *Volozhiner and of R. Akiva *Eger, he lived in Salant in Lithuania. Despite his great learning, he refused to accept a position as rabbi and barely earned a living as a small merchant, working only a few hours a day and for the rest of the day studying Torah. He conducted himself with extreme modesty, dressing as a humble peasant and never indicating his knowledge of the Torah. In 1831, during the Polish revolution, he was suspected of spying and miraculously saved from hanging. The First of Kislev, the day of his deliverance, was observed by his descendants as a holiday. In 1837 he went to Ereẓ Israel, settling in Jerusalem. While he was still in Vilna, the heads of the Vilna *kolel* in Jerusalem appointed him to be their rabbi. However, when his son-in-law, R. Samuel *Salant, went to Ereẓ Israel he vacated the office in his favor. Nevertheless, many continued to turn to R. Joseph Sundel. He established several institutions in Jerusalem, but occupied no official position in them. In Jerusalem too he refused to support himself from public funds and opened a vinegar factory. His humility and good-heartedness, which became legendary, greatly influenced his student R. Israel *Lipkin (Salanter), founder of the Musar movement, who held up Joseph Sundel as the ideal ethical man. In his will he requested no title of honor. He had two additional distinguished sons-in-law, Uri Shabbetai, a member of the Jerusalem *bet din*, and Nathan Nata Natkin, one of the emissaries of the Holy Land.

BIBLIOGRAPHY: E. Rivlin, *Ha-Ẓaddik Rabbi Yosef Zundel mi-Salant ve-Rabbotav* (1927); Frumkin-Rivlin, 3 (1929), 220f.; Malachi, in: *Hadoar*, 32 (1953/54), 273–5; D. Katz, *Tenu'at ha-Musar*, 1 (1958[3]), 93–136.

[Itzhak Alfassi]

SALANT, SAMUEL (1816–1909), chief rabbi of *Jerusalem and one of the foremost 19th-century rabbis in Jerusalem. Born near Bialystok (Russia, now Poland), Salant studied at yeshivot in Vilna, Salant, and Volozhin. His second wife was the daughter of Joseph Sundel *Salant, who had inspired the Musar movement, and he continued studying at his father-in-law's house. He set out for Ereẓ Israel in 1840, but was delayed for a few months in Constantinople, where he first met Sir Moses *Montefiore, with whom he established a firm friendship. In 1841 he reached Jerusalem, where the heads of the *kolel Lita* appointed him rabbi of the Ashkenazi community. A leading figure in Jerusalem, he became Ashkenazi chief rabbi in 1878, holding the position until his death. Salant strove to develop the institutions of the Ashkenazi community, which increased from 500 members at his arrival to 30,000 at the time of his death, and succeeded in obtaining for the Ashkenazim the official status previously enjoyed only by the Sephardi community. Between 1848 and 1851, and in 1860, he traveled to several European countries to collect money for religious institutions in Jerusalem. Salant was a founder of the Eẓ Ḥayyim Talmud Torah and Yeshivah, the Bikkur Ḥolim Hospital, and the Keneset Israel General Committee, which united all the *kolelim* under a single administration. He also encouraged the establishment of the Jewish quarters, such as Me'ah She'arim, Keneset Israel, and others, outside the Old City walls. His only son, BEINUSH, was one of the seven founders of the Naḥalat Shivah quarter. Salant's attitude to the Haskalah movement and Zionism was moderate. He favored the introduction of Hebrew and Arabic into the curriculum of the Talmud Torah schools and opposed the excommunications pronounced by zealots on "modernists." He also tried to lessen the friction between the veteran settlement and the new *yishuv*, combated the activities of the mission schools and ameliorated the relations between the Ashkenazi and Sephardi communities.

Salant lived an exemplary life of the utmost frugality. He devoted himself without stint to the needs of his community, even in the last years of his long life when his eyesight was affected. In his method of study he tended toward the plain meaning, eschewing *pilpul*, and followed the *minhag* of *Elijah b. Solomon Zalman, the Gaon of Vilna. He was an outstanding *posek*, distinguishing himself by his power of decision, and showed a definite tendency toward leniency in his decisions.

Some of his novellae have been published in the talmudic journals *Torat Ẓiyyon* and *Torah Or*, and in the *Ha-Tevunah* of Israel Lipkin *(Salanter). They are also found in the works of contemporary rabbis. On his 90th birthday, in 1906, the Keren Shemu'el Fund was launched in Jerusalem.

BIBLIOGRAPHY: Frumkin-Rivlin; Yaari, Sheluḥei, index; idem, *Zikhronot Ereẓ Israel*, 2 vols. (1947), index; E. Cohen-Reiss, *Mi-Zikhronot Ish Yerushalayim* (1967), index; J. Rimon, *Shemu'el be-Doro* (1961); Y. Gelis, *Shivim Shanah bi-Yrushalayim, Toledot Ḥayyav shel Rabbenu Shemu'el Salant* (1960).

[Geulah Bat Yehuda (Raphael)]

SALCHAH (Heb. סַלְכָה), town in Bashan, which marked the farthest limit of the territory of Og, king of Bashan, who was defeated and dispossessed by the Israelites (Deut. 3:10; Josh. 12:5; 13:11). According to I Chronicles 5:11, the tribe of Gad settled there. It is usually identified with modern Salkhad, but some question this identification, as it is doubtful if the area of Gad extended that far to the northeast.

In postbiblical times, the place is mentioned in several Nabatean inscriptions (as Salḥad) and was apparently part of the Nabatean kingdom in the first century C.E. Jewish sources identify it with Seleucia. In Roman times it was called Tricomias and was garrisoned by the Equites promoti Illyriciani (*Notitia Dignitatum* 81:15); it is mentioned as an independent locality in Georgius Cyprius (*Descriptia Orbis Romani*, line 1024). Salchah was an important town in Arab times, and in the 14th century contained a Jewish community. The modern town of Salkhad numbered approximately 15,000 inhabitants in the early 2000s, mainly Druze.

BIBLIOGRAPHY: Pauly-Wissowa, 2nd series, 13 (1939), 101, s.v. *Tricomia*; Avi-Yonah, Geog, 174; R. Dussaud, *Topographie historique de la Syrie*… (1927), 324, 366; Abel, Geog, 2 (1938), 440–1; Press, Ereẓ, 3 (1952), 66f.; Aharoni, Land, index.

[Michael Avi-Yonah]

SALE (Heb. מְכִירָה, *mekhirah*). Sale may be defined as the permanent transfer for consideration of existing legal rights from one person to another. The consideration may be in money or in kind. By extension the term "sale" is also used to denote a transfer of rights for a lengthy (but predetermined) period, such as the sale of land for a period of many years (BM 79a; BB 136b; cf. Yad, She'elah, 1:5). When sale is mentioned, however, it primarily refers to the transfer of real or proprietary rights and not to mere personal rights, i.e., obligations or debts, since it was at first legally impossible to transfer such rights (see *Assignment). The *geonim* already laid down that rights in rem applied only to corporeal or tangible things (Hai Gaon, *Sefer ha-Mikkaḥ ve-ha-Mimkar*, ch. 2, introd. i; cf. Resp. Maharashdam, ḤM 271), and therefore anything having neither length, breadth, nor depth – such as the smell of an apple or the taste of honey or the glitter of a precious stone – was incapable of being conveyed (Yad, Mekhirah, 12:14; cf. also TJ, BB 3:1, 13d and *Ha-Ittur*, vol. 1, introd., ch. 2, "*Kinyan*"). This is probably the reason why it is impossible to convey title in something which is not yet in existence – since, being intangible, it cannot be the subject matter of a real right – as also it is impossible to convey to someone who has not yet been born (see below).

In the biblical period the sale of real property was restricted. Thus, fields could only be sold until the Jubilee, in which year they would automatically revert to their owners (Lev. 25:13 ff.), whereas dwelling houses in walled cities – if not redeemed within a year of their sale – would rest irrevocably with their purchasers regardless of the Jubilee (*ibid.*). In Jewish law the term sale does not mean an agreement to sell in the future, but an immediately effective transfer of ownership. Sale, nevertheless, raises many of the problems relating to the creation, interpretation, and execution of contractual obligations. In the Talmud, *mekhirah* is an example used for clarifying these problems, since the laws of sale are an application of the wider principles of property and contract. The transaction of a sale is concluded with the *gemirat ha-da'at* ("firm decision") of the parties to transfer the relevant rights irrevocably from one to the other – at which point neither may resile from the bargain. The parties rely on the sale if there has been a manifestation of their *gemirat ha-da'at* by such a way of speech or conduct as will be understood by most people as an agreement to conclude the transaction – whether or not this is in accordance with the subjective intention of either of the parties. Undisclosed thoughts are of no consequence, and the test of the conclusion of the sale is purely objective; if in the particular circumstances most people would express their intention to conclude the transaction in that particular and manifest manner, the transaction will accordingly be effective, and it is immaterial that either party did not really intend to conclude the transaction in that particular way, or that there was no *consensus ad idem* between one party and the other. A corollary of this test is the principle that the parties need not make up their minds to the identical thing, and there may sometimes be no actual consensus between the parties even if outwardly their conduct is so interpreted. Moreover, when it is manifest that one of the parties had not properly made up his mind to the transaction, he may withdraw from it but not the other party who had done so – as may happen in the case where one party is mistaken as to the quality of the subject sold (Yad, Mekhirah, 17:1), or he has been overcharged in respect of the price (*ibid.*, 12:4).

The Decision of the Parties

The decision of the parties to conclude a sale is finalized by the performance of one of the appropriate acts of *kinyan* ("acquisition") by one of the parties – generally the purchaser – after the other parties have expressed their agreement that this be done (Ned. 44a; BB 54b; see *Acquisition (*Kinyan*)). Ownership thereupon passes, regardless of the question of possession, since possession sometimes accompanies the passing of ownership and sometimes not (see, e.g., BM 46a–b). If the consideration for the sale is a monetary payment, the purchaser, upon the passing of ownership, undertakes to pay the purchase price and it becomes a debt for which he is liable (BM 45b, 78b).

Furthermore, if an act is performed that brings about the *gemirat ha-da'at* of one or all of the parties but is not concluded by one of the customary acts of *kinyan*, any of the parties may withdraw; ownership will not have passed and the seller will remain responsible for the object. Nevertheless, since some of the parties rely upon such a sale and believe that all have made up their minds not to resile from it, any party who does retract is subject to the curse of "He who exacted vengeance from the generation of the flood and the generation of the dispersion will find redress from one who does not stand by his word" (BM 4:2). Hence, if the purchaser pays the consideration money to the seller but does not obtain possession of the object sold (i.e., *meshikhah*), the party who retracts will be subject to the said curse, since the payment of money is not a method of concluding a transaction in movables (BM 44a). Similarly, the fact that the seller has marked the object sold so as to distinguish it as his own will suffice to submit a retracting party to the curse – even though it is not local custom to conclude a transaction by making such a mark (BM 74a) – since there is a presumption that in affixing his mark the party concerned made up his mind to the bargain. Wherever the affixing of a mark is the customary manner of concluding a transaction, however, the sale will be effective and the parties will no longer be able to retract (BM 74a; see **Minhag*). The sages disapprove of a party who retracts, even where the transaction is only concluded verbally, without the performance of any act by any party. If, however, there was a verbal promise which was not relied upon, the promisor may withdraw (BM 49a).

When it is clear that one of the parties has not made his decision to conclude the transaction – i.e., when most people would not do so in the circumstances – he may retract even if it has been agreed that title be effected and the act of *kinyan* performed. This is illustrated in the case of overreaching (see **Ona'ah*), *mistake, certain cases of duress (see **Ones*), the nonfulfillment of a condition of the sale, or when one of the parties lacks understanding, and whenever people for any other reason would not normally rely on the transaction. If a person under duress sells a part of his property, the sale will be effective, since he makes up his mind and agrees to the sale simply to rid himself of the duress. Some scholars, however, express the opinion that if he is under duress to sell a specific field the sale will be void (BB 48a). If, prior to the sale, the seller made a statement before witnesses to the effect that he was selling only because of duress – whether of a physical or monetary nature – and the witnesses know of the duress, it will be manifest that the seller had not made up his mind to the sale and the transaction will be void (BB 40a–b).

This is also the law in the case of mistake as to price, whether due to deceit and intentional or inadvertent, or whether the object was sold for more than its true value and the purchaser overcharged, or sold for less than its true value and the seller thus deceived (BM 51a). If the mistake as to price is within a discrepancy of less than one-sixth, the sale will still be effective, since such comparatively small margins are usually overlooked; if the rate is one-sixth exactly, the sale will be effective, but the difference must be refunded; if the rate exceeds one-sixth, the sale is voidable, and the party standing to lose may retract, since such a large mistake would not usually be tolerated. Refunding the difference or avoiding the transaction is only permitted within a specified period, during which the party at disadvantage could have become aware of his mistake; thereafter it is presumed that he has waived the rights arising from the mistake in favor of the other party and made up his mind to uphold the transaction as it stands (BM 49b; Rashi on the Mishnah, *ibid.*). The rules of mistake as to price apply equally to mistake in respect of any other aspect of the sale. Whenever the property sold or any of the conditions of the sale vary from that which the purchaser relied upon – and the variation is so great that people in similar circumstances would normally be particular enough to look upon the transaction as being something other than the one upon which they relied – it will be a case of a purchase in error (*mikkaḥ ta'ut*) which voids the transaction (see Sh. Ar., ḤM 232:6 and glosses thereto). Generally, if as a result of a variation in the property sold it is unsuited for the use for which the purchaser wanted it, it will be a case of *mikkaḥ ta'ut* (see, e.g., Yad, Mekhirah, 15:12, 13).

If the parties conclude the transaction of a sale and perform an act of *kinyan*, but have failed to determine the price, the purchaser will not have acquired title since there was no reliance on the transaction by the parties, and both of them may retract; if, however, the purchase price was fixed and known, the sale will be effective (Yad, Mekhirah, 4:11–12). Maimonides also expressed the opinion that a person cannot acquire from another something that is undetermined even as to species (Yad, Mekhirah, 21:1–3). Thus a purchaser cannot acquire title to "everything that is in this house, or box or sack, which the owner is selling for so much," even if he has performed an act of *kinyan*, since he does not rely on this transaction; however, when the species is known, e.g., "this heap of wheat or cellar of wine at such and such a price," the sale will be effective even if the actual measure and weight are unknown at that moment.

A sale by a person lacking legal capacity – such as a deaf-mute, idiot, or minor – is void, since he lacks understanding and hence the absence of the element of *gemirat ha-da'at*. The sages prescribed, however, that certain sales by such parties would be valid "for the sake of his sustenance" (Git. 59a), i.e., in order to procure the necessities of life. It was laid down that the minimum required age in the case of a minor would depend on the degree of his understanding (*ibid.*) and this was detailed as follows: a minor aged six years and over, having sufficient understanding to appreciate the nature of the transaction, could sell and purchase movable property; from the age of 13, his sale or purchase would be effective in respect of movables, even if he could not appreciate the nature of the transaction, but ineffective in respect of land unless he could appreciate the nature of the transaction; a minor could not sell land inherited from his ancestors until he reached the age of 20 (Yad, Mekhirah, 29:6ff.). In the post-talmudic period, too, the age of majority was varyingly determined in respect of different legal transactions, depending upon the social and economic circumstances of the time (see Elon, in bibliography).

Sale of a Thing Not Yet in Existence

The Talmud records conflicting opinions as to whether or not a person can transfer title in respect of something not yet in existence. Some scholars answer in the negative, on the ground that the purchaser does not rely on the transaction, or for the reason that there is nothing to which ownership can apply and so ownership cannot be transferred. Another opinion in the Talmud is that a thing not yet in existence may be assigned and that the acquisition will take effect upon the thing's coming into existence, with the result that the parties may not retract. Even according to this opinion, however, only that which will come into existence in the ordinary course of events – such as the fruit of a tree – can be assigned; otherwise all the scholars agree that no transaction can be effected (BM 33b). The scholars who answer this point in the negative expressed the further opinion that a person could not transfer a thing which was not yet his, e.g., if he should say "let this field be acquired by you as of the moment that I shall have taken it for myself" and thus was the *halakhah* decided (Yad, Mekhirah, 22:5). The sages, however, prescribed that the sale by a poor hunter (lacking the necessities of life) of "everything that my hunt will produce to-day," would be effective, as would similar acquisitions in keeping with this rule (Yad, Mekhirah, 22:6). On the other hand, a person can undertake an obligation to transfer a thing not yet in existence (Sh. Ar., ḤM 60:6; see Law of *Obligations; *Contract). He can furthermore transfer a real right in property which is in existence, e.g., by transferring "the body for its fruits," and thereby confer title to a thing not yet in existence, such as a "tree for its fruit" or an "animal for its young" (Yad, Mekhirah, 23:1–2). An opinion is also expressed that if the thing which is sold is available on the market, the sale will be effective even though it is not yet the seller's, and the latter is obliged to deliver it to the purchaser (Yad, Mekhirah, 22:3 and *Kesef Mishneh* thereto).

With regard to a sale to a person as yet unborn, one opinion is that even if a person may transfer something that is not yet in existence, he cannot do so to a person as yet unborn; another opinion is that one can confer title in favor of a person as yet unborn even if he cannot do so with regard to a thing not yet in existence (Git. 13b and Tos. thereto). The *halakhah* was decided to the effect that a person could not confer title on a person as yet unborn, in the same way that he could not do so in respect of a thing not yet in existence (Sh. Ar., ḤM 210:1).

It is the accepted view that a person can neither consecrate nor confer title in respect of a thing which is not in his possession, even though it is his property (BK 70a and Tos. thereto); hence a person cannot do so in respect of property stolen from him, since the thief gains possession thereof (*ibid.*). However, another opinion is that one may consecrate, renounce (see *Hefker*), and confer title even in respect to property which is not in one's possession (BK 68b).

The Conditions of the Sale

The decision of the parties to conclude a transaction is often made subject to various conditions, which must be fulfilled if the transaction is to be effective (see *Conditions). Thus if a person sells a house to another on condition that the latter perform some specific act on a specified day, the purchaser acquires the house if and when he performs the act in the specified manner, but not otherwise; the same applies if property is sold to the purchaser on condition that the latter give it to a third party, or if the seller has stipulated that the property is to be returned after a specified period – in which event the transaction is effective and the property must be returned (Yad, Mekhirah, 11:1). Likewise, the sale will be effective where a person stipulates that if he sells his field, the purchaser shall acquire it as of that moment, at a price to be determined later by three valuers (Yad, Mekhirah, 8:8).

The seller's decision to impose a condition on the sale must be manifest and made clear to all, including the purchaser, in the manner in which people would normally do so. Failing this, the sale may be effective but not the condition, since it will be seen from the seller's conduct that he did not intend to impose a material condition capable of voiding the transaction but a mere condition at large, not seriously intended. Hence, he must phrase his statements in the form of a double condition, i.e., specify what will be if the condition is fulfilled and what if not – since Hebrew-language usage requires both the affirmative and the negative to be specified, and if he does not follow the manner in which Hebrew is spoken, he is apparently not particular about fulfillment of the condition. Some scholars expressed the opinion that the requirement of a double condition applies only in the cases of *marriage and *divorce but not of sale, where a condition is effective whether a double one or not (*Hassagot Rabad*, Zekhiyyah, 3:8). Moreover, the phraseology of the condition requires the affirmative sentence to be included before the negative one, as only thus is it manifest that the party seriously intends to be particular about the fulfillment of the condition (*Beit ha-Beḥirah*, Kid, 61a); he must first state the condition and thereafter the act which is contingent on it, and not vice versa, and the condition must be one which is capable of being fulfilled by the purchaser, lest it appear that it was not seriously intended and the sale be effective without the condition (BM 94a; Kid. 61a).

At times, when it is manifest from the circumstances that the fulfillment of a condition has been relied upon, such condition will be effective even if the above-mentioned phraseology has not been adopted. Moreover, if it is manifest from the circumstances that the seller has relied on a certain condition, the condition will be effective even if he has not given any verbal expression thereto, since everything is dependent upon what people normally imply from the circumstances (Tos. to Kid. 49b). Often the parties do not specify any conditions and may not even be thinking of any, but the presumption is that they intend to sell and purchase in accordance with local custom. Hence local customs relating to purchase and sale are superimposed to supplement the decision of the parties; furthermore, statements of conditions which are not clearly expressed are construed in accordance with local custom (Yad, Mekhirah, 17:6; 26:7–8; 27:11; also *Hassagot Rabad*, Mekhirah 24:12). If the parties wish to exclude the conditions of local custom, they must make express provisions to this effect. Thus a person who transfers ownership to another generally intends it to pass upon the performance of the *kinyan* by the transferee; however, if for example, he says, "perform the *kinyan* and acquire 30 days hereafter," the acquisition will only be complete after 30 days (Ket. 82a).

Of the customary conditions, the most important one is the warranty of authority. Thus, one who purchases something which is later taken from him for reasons connected with the seller – for instance, that the land was not his or that it was mortgaged to his creditor – may hold the seller liable and recover the cost of it from him. This warranty of ownership by the seller is implied in every sale, even if not expressly formulated (Yad, Mekhirah, 19:3). If the seller wishes to be absolved from all or any part of such responsibility, he must do so by express stipulation (*ibid.*, 19:8). Another opinion (BM 14a) is that in an ordinary sale the seller takes no responsibility upon himself unless a specific provision to the contrary is made.

The Mishnah, in listing various categories of sale, clarifies the different (implied) conditions that will be included unless otherwise provided for by the parties and if not contrary to local custom. Thus one who sells a field sells also the stones which serve the land, the unreaped grain, the watchman's booth, and the trees which have no intrinsic value, but not the stones that are not necessary to the land, or the grain that has been severed from the ground, and the like (BB 4:8). So too, one who sells a field for sowing does not include rifts in it or rocks which are more than ten handbreadths high (BB 7:1); one who buys two trees in another's field does not buy any land with them, but one who buys three trees, buys also the land on which they are growing (BB 5:4); one who has sold a wagon has not sold the mules, and if he has sold the mules he has not sold the wagon (BB 5:1); one who has sold the head of a large animal, has not sold its feet also, but in the case of sheep the feet are included in the sale of the head (BB 5:5). Similarly, the Mishnah enumerates that which is included or excluded in the sale of numerous items of property ranging from houses, buildings, and trees to slaves and animals (BB 4–7). Implied conditions also apply with regard to the price. Thus one who has sold wheat to another for a fixed amount of money without specifying the quantity, must deliver wheat according to the market price at the time of the sale (Yad, Mekhirah, 21:4).

In cases where there is difficulty in construing the parties' intention, their ultimate purpose may be arrived at with the aid of the rule that "he who sells, sells in a liberal spirit," i.e., a liberal interpretation of the agreement is made. Thus, one who sells a house but does not include the cistern in the sale must purchase from the buyer a right of way to it, since the terms of the sale are to be interpreted liberally and he did not retain a right of way (BB 64a–b). However, a person who has sold a field but retained two trees for himself will also retain the soil in which they grow, even though the purchaser of only two trees acquires no soil with them (BB 71a). There are conflicting views on the matter, some scholars stating that a restrictive interpretation is also possible, i.e., "one who sells, sells in an illiberal spirit." However, all scholars accept that the maxim of a liberal interpretation is applicable in the case of *gifts (BB 65a).

In the State of Israel

The rules of sale are set out in the Sales Law, 5828/1968, which in general adopts the draft uniform law relating to international sales, submitted at The Hague International Conference in 1964. In certain matters this law takes cognizance of the attitude of Jewish law (see Elon, in bibliography).

BIBLIOGRAPHY: J.S. Zuri, *Mishpat ha-Talmud*, 5 (1921), 60–88; Gulak, Yesodei, 1 (1922), 55–93; 2 (1922), 152–9; Gulak, Oẓar, 159–82, 238–42, 306–8, 345f.; idem, *Le-Ḥeker Toledot ha-Mishpat ha-Ivri bi-Tekufat ha-Talmud*, 1 (*Dinei Karka'ot*, 1929), passim; idem, *Toledot ha-Mishpat be-Yisrael bi-Tekufat ha-Talmud*, 1 (*Ha-Ḥiyyuv ve-Shi'budav*, 1939), 10, 33 n. 12, 62–65, 74, 100–4, 106; Herzog, Instit, 2 (1939), 61–71, 107–39; ET, 1 (1951^3), 153–60, 216–8; 6 (1954), 616–24, 625–31, 661–83; 7 (1956), 30–67; B. Rabinowitz-Te'omim, *Ḥukkat Mishpat* (1957); M. Elon, in: ILR, 4 (1969), 91 n. 49, 122. **ADD. BIBLIOGRAPHY:** M. Elon, *Ha-Mishpat ha-Ivri* (1988), 1:69, 106, 179, 327ff., 571ff., 581, 595, 741ff.; 2:1284, 1290, index; idem, *Jewish Law* (1994), 1:77, 120, 200, 392ff.; 2:703ff., 716, 735, 913; 3:1533, 1540; 4; index; M. Elon and B. Lifshitz, *Mafte'aḥ ha-She'elot ve-ha-Teshuvot shel Ḥakhmei Sefarad u-Ẓefon Afrikah* (legal digest) (1986), 78–80, 213–27; B. Lifshitz and E. Shochetman, *Mafte'aḥ ha-She'elot ve-ha-Teshuvot shel Ḥakhmei Ashkenaz, Ẓarefat ve-Italyah* (legal digest) (1997), 51, 160–65; *Enẓiklopedyah Talmudit*, vol. 7, s.v. *"davar shelo ba le-olam,"* 30ff.; index.

[Shalom Albeck]

SALEM, EMMANUEL RAPHAEL (1859–1940), Greek lawyer. Born in *Salonika, Salem specialized in international law and the law of capitulations, and became legal adviser to foreign consulates in *Turkey. He published several studies on the capitulations and on the conditions of foreign subjects in Turkey in international law periodicals in Paris and Brussels (1888–1900). In 1889 Pope Leo XIII awarded him the knighthood of the order of the Holy See. He served as the legal advisor to La Banque de Salonique (The Bank of Salonika), founded in 1888, which was Jewish run and owned, and the first bank established in Salonika.

Salem was active in the general communal life of Salonika. He donated an orphanage to the Jewish community, and assisted in the modernization of its hospital. With the revolution of the Young Turks of 1908, he went to *Istanbul to play an active part in the work of the Council for Legislative Reforms, which established the legal system of the Turkish republic. He solved many legal problems between the Ottoman and other governments. He also mediated between Turkey and the Vatican. He was frequently called by different governments in connection with diplomatic issues in the Near East. Salem was a member of the Ottoman delegation to the Lausanne Conference of 1922, where he played a considerable part in elaborating those sections dealing with the status of the Dardanelles and with the capitulations regime. In gratitude for his legal services and efforts, he received recognition and honors from the Ottoman sultans Abdul Hamid and Rashid, and the governments of Austria, Italy, France, Greece, Belgium, Bulgaria, and the Vatican. His wife, like wives of other Salonikan Jewish benefactors, dignitaries, and community leaders, received the Ottoman honor Şafakat Level II or III. During the last years of his life, Salem lived in Paris, where he was the president of the Sephardi congregation and a member of the central committee of the Alliance Israélite Universelle.

His son RAPHAEL (1898–1963) was a noted mathematician. He worked in the Bank of Paris until World War II, when he escaped to the U.S. There he taught at Harvard University and the Massachusetts Institute of Technology. In 1955 he became professor of mathematics at the Sorbonne in Paris. His works include *Theorie générale des Séries trigonométriques*; *Séries trigonométriques lacunaires et aléatoires*; *Ensembles parfaits et séries trigonométriques*; and *Algebraic Numbers and Fourier Analysis*. His collected works were published in 1967.

ADD. BIBLIOGRAPHY: D.A. Recanati, *Zikhron Saloniki* I (1972), 196; E. Carasso, *Les Juifs de Salonique 1492–1943, L'Echelle de Jacob* V (2000), 132.

[Joseph Nehama / Yitzchak Kerem (2nd ed.)]

SALÉ-RABAT, twin towns on the Atlantic coast of *Morocco, separated by the Bou-Regreg River and situated on the site including the Merinid necropolis of Chella. Ancient Sala, ruins of which still exist in Chella, was an important Roman town known as a center for buying gold dust. The existence of a Jewish colony there during the second century C.E. is confirmed in an inscription on the tombstone of a hellenized Jew. The region was subject to Jewish influence over a long period, and the conversion of the country's inhabitants to *Islam in the eighth century gave rise to the heresy of the Berghwata, who were inclined to Judaism. The *Almohads, who liquidated the Berghwata in the 12th century, built the town of Rabat, which did not lose its position of importance to the more ancient town of Salé until the fall of the dynasty in 1269. Abraham ibn Daud mentions the Jewish community of Salé (Sala) in his *Sefer ha-Kabbalah*. The merchant shipowners of the western Mediterranean conducted an active trade in Salé, especially the Jews of Majorca during the 13th–14th centuries. Later, the Genoese gained the monopoly over trade in Salé, and in 1492 the Jewish exiles from *Spain were badly received by them. After 1550 the Jews of Salé were wealthy and numerous. They lived among the Muslims, who were mainly of Andalusian origin. A few Jews settled in Rabat, which at that time was only known by the name New Salé, in contrast to the neighboring town which was Old Salé; the twin towns became one of Morocco's most important trading centers. In Rabat the

Hornacheros, Muslims who had arrived from Spain in 1610, had little sympathy for the Jews; nevertheless, they welcomed them as soon as the privateering against Christendom, especially Spain, gained in intensity, calling for supplies of European arms and rigging, and pouring into the town goods and Christian captives, which the Christian nations hastily redeemed. At that time Rabat and Salé finally constituted themselves into independent republics.

Although the Jews conducted their affairs in Rabat, the majority lived in Salé, where Dutch Jews also settled. Between 1620 and 1660 the leading merchants in the two towns were Samuel b. Sofat, R. Aaron *Siboni, and the Dutchmen Benjamin Cohen and Aaron Querido. Moses Santiago was the counselor of the governor of Rabat, negotiating the truce with the king of *France in 1630. The peace treaty of 1683 with The Netherlands was negotiated by Isaac and Joseph Bueno de *Mesquita, merchants in Salé, the place of residence of Gideon *Mendes, the Dutch consul in 1699. Moreover, until the 1850s several Jews of Salé-Rabat acted as consuls for the European powers. The Shabbatean movement won many followers in the towns, where the *dayyan* of that period, R. Jacob *Sasportas, successfully overcame the resulting unrest. The yeshivot of Salé and Rabat were very active, and graduates included talmudists and legal authorities such as R. Ḥayyim b. Moses *Attar, author of the famous Pentateuch commentary, *Or ha-Ḥayyim*, who after many wanderings immigrated in 1741 to Ereẓ Israel; R. Shem-Tov Attar, R. Samuel de *Avila and his son R. Eliezer, R. Abraham Rodriguez, R. Samuel Caro, R. Solomon Tapiero, R. Judah Anahory, and R. Joseph *Elmaleh. The Jews of Rabat were among the founders of the Jewish communities of *Gibraltar in 1705, *Mogador in 1767, *Lisbon in 1773, and Mazagan in 1825, as well as the community of the Azores which they founded in 1820. A short while later some of their distinguished families – Amzallag, Aburbi, Amiel, Ben-Tobo, and Moyal – settled in *Haifa, *Jaffa, and *Jerusalem, having transferred their assets to these places.

After 1750 the community of Salé was absorbed mainly by that of Rabat, which numbered over 6,000 persons. This population, a very active one, enjoyed considerable affluence, and its wealthiest elements obtained leases on the collection of customs duties, both in Rabat and other ports, later adding numerous other monopolies. In 1790 Governor Bargash saved the Jews of Salé-Rabat from the persecutions of the sultan Moulay Yazīd, but they were nevertheless compelled to pay the large sum of 600,000 gold mithkals to the sovereign. More than one half of the Jewish population of Salé-Rabat perished in the plague of 1799. In 1807 they were confined to two mellahs for the first time. This measure, which was painfully felt, initiated a wave of emigration, especially to South America, while a large number of families whose wealth was of recent acquisition converted to Islam. New elements, mainly from Tlemcen, established themselves in the mellah of Rabat in 1830. Both the old and the new communities were impoverished by the isolationist policy of the sultan Moulay Sliman. The *dahīr*, which Sir Moses *Montefiore obtained in 1864 on behalf of the Jews of Morocco, caused some of the Jews of Rabat to exceed their rights, thus setting off severe disturbances. The rabbis and the authorities only succeeded with difficulty in allaying the agitation. There were massive departures for *Casablanca, where the Zagury, Hayot, Lasry, Benchaya, and Marrache families, as well as others from Rabat, were the most influential in the new community for a long time. Under the French Protectorate (since 1912), various Jewish institutions were established in Rabat, notably the Supreme Rabbinical Tribunal (abolished by the government in 1965) which was headed by Rabbis Raphael Encaoua and Joseph Benatar over a long period.

In 1947 there were 20,000 Jews in the region of Salé-Rabat. Of these, 12,350 lived in Rabat and 3,150 in Salé. Until the mid-1950s there were also branches of the *Jewish National Fund and *WIZO in Rabat. In 1970 Salé had not a single Jewish inhabitant, while about 4,000 Jews still lived in Rabat. The majority of the Jews of Rabat had immigrated to France, the *United States, and *Canada, those of Salé going almost exclusively to Israel. By 2005, only several hundred Jews remained in Rabat. Ya'akov Mellul, chief rabbi of Rabat, noted at the end of the 20th century that, with the exception of the larger community of Casablanca, most other Moroccan Jewries, Rabat included, had no prospects for Jewish continuity. Most of the Jewish schools in Rabat were closed, including the wide network of the *Alliance Israélite Universelle and Oẓar ha-Torah schools and a rabbinical seminary, founded in 1951. There were no rabbis, no infrastructure for community life, and the young left their homes for the West in pursuance of their higher education. Their parents followed the children to the West to preserve the close-knit nature of the family, as well as to protect them from marrying non-Jews.

BIBLIOGRAPHY: J. Goulven, in: *Bulletin de la Société Géographique du Maroc* (1922), 11–41; idem, *Les Mellahs de Rabat-Salé* (1927); Miège, Maroc, passim; J. Caillé, *La Ville de Rabat jusqu'au Protectorat Français* (1949), passim; D. Corcos, in: *Sefunot*, 10 (1966), 98f.; idem, *Les Juifs du Maroc et leurs Mellahs* (1971); Hirschberg, Afrikah, index; A.N. Chouraqui, *Between East and West* (1968), index s.v. *Rabat, Salé*. **ADD. BIBLIOGRAPHY:** K.L. Brown, *People of Salé: Tradition and Change in a Modern City, 1830–1930* (1976); M.M. Laskier, *The Alliance Israélite Universelle and the Jewish Communities of Morocco: 1862–1962* (1983); idem, *North African Jewry in the Twentieth Century: The Jews of Morocco, Tunisia, and Algeria* (1994).

[Haim J. Cohen / Michael M. Laskier (2nd ed.)]

SALERNO, city in Campania, S. Italy. A Latin tombstone of the daughter of a rabbi called Abundantius shows that a Jewish settlement existed in Salerno as early as the 3rd or 4th century. In the Middle Ages the town was the seat of a famous medical school founded in about 800. According to tradition, its founders included not only an Arab, a Greek, and a Latin, but also a Jewish teacher. Jews are mentioned in the town from 872, and the Jewish quarter (Judaica) of Salerno in a document of 1005. *Benjamin of Tudela, who visited Salerno around 1159, found there about 600 Jews, including several scholars. As a result of the persecutions in south Italy around 1290–94, 150

Jewish families were converted, but many continued secret allegiance to Judaism. In 1485 R. Obadiah of *Bertinoro was for some months in Salerno and apparently frequented the medical school. With the expulsion of the Jews from the Kingdom of *Naples in 1510, the much-reduced Jewish community of Salerno also ceased to exist.

BIBLIOGRAPHY: Milano, Bibliotheca, index; Milano, Italia, index; Roth, Italy, index; Roth, Dark Ages, index; N. Ferorelli, *Ebrei nell' Italia meridionale…* (1915), passim; Carucci, in: *Archivio storico della provincia di Salerno*, 1 (1921), 74–79; Cerone, in: *Studi… Michelangelo Schipa* (1926), 59–73; Marongia, in: *Archivio storico per le provincie napoletane*, 62 (1937), 238–63; Frey, Corpus, no. 568. **ADD. BIBLIOGRAPHY:** C. Gambardella, "Gli ebrei a Salerno," in: *Architettura Giudaica in Italia. Ebraismo, sito, memoria dei luogh* (1994), 269–83; N. Pavoncello, "Epigrafia ebraica nel Museo Duomo di Salerno," in: *Istituto Universitario Orientale: Annali*, 18 (1968) 198–203; M. Galante, "Tre nuovi documenti sui cristiani novelli a Salerno nei secoli XIII–XIV," in: *Sefer Yuhasin*, 9:1–3 (1993), 3–14; D. Abulafia, "Il mezzogiorno peninsulare dai bizantini all'espulsione," in: *Storia d'Italia. Annali 11, Gli ebrei in Italia. Dall'alto Medioevo all'età dei ghetti* (ed. Corrao Vivanti) (1996), 5–44.

[Ariel Toaff / Nadia Zeldes (2nd ed.)]

SALFELD, SIEGMUND (1843–1926), German rabbi and historian. Salfeld, who was born in Stadthagen, Germany, served as rabbi in Dessau from 1870, and in Mainz from 1880. Salfeld received the title professor from the grand duke of Hesse in 1912. His scholarly interest was devoted to the history of German Jewry, and especially of the Mainz community. He described the political and social conditions of German Jews in the Middle Ages, based on research into source material, and his major work in this area was *Bilder aus der Vergangenheit der juedischen Gemeinde Mainz* (1903).

Salfeld's most important work was *Das Martyrologium des Nuernberger Memorbuches* (1898), which connected the *Memorbuch found in Mainz with Nuremberg, a contention disputed by M. Weinberg who assigned it to Mainz (*Die Memorbuecher der juedischen Gemeinden in Bayern* (1937–38), 3–4). Many of Salfeld's studies appeared in learned periodicals and *Festschriften*. In 1879 he published *Das Hohelied Salomo's bei den juedischen Erklaerern des Mittelalters*.

BIBLIOGRAPHY: *Gedenkreden beim Heimgang des Altrabbiners S. Salfeld* (1926).

[Jacob Rothschild]

ṢĀLIḤ, ABRAHAM (c. 1825–1905), *dayyan* and preacher in *Yemen. Ṣāliḥ was the great-grandson of Yaḥya b. Joseph *Ṣāliḥ (Mahriṣ). He acted as *ḥazzan* and communal leader in the synagogue of the Ṣāliḥ family. He held the position of *dayyan* for 38 years. Of an emotional nature, his sermons and *tokhaḥot* deeply moved his audiences. He was referred to as "the prophet Jeremiah," because of the tears to which his listeners were moved.

BIBLIOGRAPHY: A. Koraḥ, *Sa'arat Teiman* (1954), 65; J.L. Nahum, *Mi-Ẓefunot Yehudei Teiman* (1962), 228f.

[Yehuda Ratzaby]

ṢALIḤ, YAḤYA (Yihye) BEN JOSEPH (Maharis; c. 1715), Yemenite scholar; *av bet din* and rabbi of *Sanʿa. His authority was recognized by all the Yemenite Jewish communities and even by the distant community of *India. Many halakhic questions were addressed to him from all parts of *Yemen. They all received clear and complete replies, the fruits of his meditation and casuistry, in which the legal point was clarified. He would not accept a salary from his rabbinate, and he earned his livelihood with difficulty as a Torah scribe. His work was artistic, and some of it is extant in various manuscripts. J. *Saphir, who visited Yemen in 1859, mentions the esteem and love which Yemenite Jewry accorded him: "his name is renowned throughout Yemen and his decisions are accepted as the law given by Moses at Sinai" (*Ḥadrei Teiman*, Lyell 1866, 101b).

He wrote *Zevaḥ Todah*, novellae and explanations on Shulḥan Arukh *Yoreh De'ah*, the laws of ritual slaughter (1851); *Sha'arei Kedushah*, a summary of *Zevaḥ Todah* in the form of legal decisions which was written to facilitate its study by *shoḥatim* and pupils (1841); *Ḥelek ha-Dikduk* (or *Toẓe'ot Ḥayyim*), biblical masorah, with punctuation and musical cantillation (published in full length by C.D. Ginsberg, *Ha-Masorah*, 3 (1885), 53–105); the section on the Pentateuch and *haftarot* was published in the editions of the Yemenite *Taj* (from 1889), *Sha'arei Tohorah*, the laws of *niddah* – written in Arabic, the prevalent tongue among women and the masses (1894); *Ez Ḥayyim*, a commentary on the *Tiklāl* (*siddur* of the prayers of the whole year), according to the plain and esoteric meaning (1894); *Pe'ullat Ẓaddik*, responsa and legal novellae on the four *Turim* (3 vols., 1946–45) – the most important collection of Yemenite Jewry's responsa literature, containing 762 responsa which he dealt with during a period of about 40 years (1764–1803); *Me'il Katan*, a commentary on the *Shenei Luḥot ha-Berit* of R. Isaiah *Horowitz; and *Oraḥ la-Ḥayyim*, a collection of Midrashim and explanations on three *megillot*, in symbolic and esoteric style (in manuscript). He wrote a chronicle of Yemenite Jewry (published by David Sassoon, see bibliography).

BIBLIOGRAPHY: Bacher, in: JQR, 14 (1901/02), 581–621, 240; Sassoon, in: HḤY, 7 (1923), 1–14; A. Koraḥ, *Sa'arat Teiman* (1954), 19–23; S. Geridi, *Mi-Teiman le-Ẓiyyon* (1938), 134–8; Y. Ratzaby, in: *Shevut-Teiman* (1945), 100–17; idem, *Bo'i Teiman* (1967), 248–73; idem, in: *Afikim*, 5 (July 7, 1965).

[Yehuda Ratzaby]

ṢALIḤ IBN YAḤYA (Yihye) IBN JOSEPH (17th century), San'a scholar and *paytan*. Ṣāliḥ was the grandfather of R. Yaḥyā ibn Joseph *Ṣāliḥ, who, in his works, makes considerable mention of his grandfather. Two works of his have been preserved: they deal with the laws of ritual slaughter (extant in Ms.). The *piyyutim* which he wrote deal with exile and redemption and echo the cruel exile from *Mawzaʿ which took place during his lifetime (his grandson R. Yaḥyā Ṣāliḥ included ten of these in the Yemenite *maḥzor, Ez Ḥayyim*, 3 (1894) 158–65). In two of his *tokhaḥot* which have been preserved, he calls upon his generation to repent. He had a reputation as a miracle worker.

BIBLIOGRAPHY: A. Koraḥ, *Sa'arat Teiman* (1954), 16; Ratzaby, in: KS, 28 (1952/53), 270, nos. 93–94.

[Yehuda Ratzaby]

SALINGER, JEROME DAVID (1919–), U.S. author. Born in New York City, Salinger attended the Valley Forge Military Academy, a preparatory school which resembled the one attended by the hero of his first celebrated novel, *Catcher in the Rye* (1951). After serving in the U.S. Army during World War II, Salinger published *Catcher in the Rye*, which established his reputation as a writer. The novel's hero, Holden Caulfield, has been described as a kind of latter-day Tom Sawyer or Huckleberry Finn. A fashionable as well as a popular author, Salinger contributed stories to leading magazines, including *The Saturday Evening Post, Esquire, Cosmopolitan*, and *The New Yorker*. He wrote *Nine Stories* (1953), *Franny and Zooey* (1961), and *Raise High the Roof Beam, Carpenters* and *Seymour: an Introduction* (both 1963). All of these deal with the adventures of the Glass family of New York, a family of mixed Irish-Jewish origin.

Salinger gave a new and dramatic presentation of estrangement and crises of faith through such characters as Holden and Franny and Seymour Glass. Moreover, he was one of the first American-Jewish writers to draw upon the themes of Zen Buddhism. Salinger had a great impact on the mores of his youthful readers with *The Catcher in the Rye* (the word "prince" became part of a signature vocabulary just as Holden's cap also became part of a younger reader's costume – as far afield as East Germany), and a welcome reception among an older public. Nonetheless, his works had little discernible influence on the major traditions of American-Jewish literature as Jewish writing within America. Although the Glass family is notable, given its mixed heritage and brilliance, crises of faith are often anguishingly felt problems about a transcendent guarantee for meaning. In this sense, the Glass "fictions" make a common front with Isaac *Rosenfeld's *Passage from Home* (1946) and Edgar Lewis *Wallant's *The Pawnbroker* (1961) which weld Christianity, *Yidishkeit*, and American culture together. What is at stake in these works is the capacity to have faith within, and often against, a secularizing, pluralistic America. These works look forward to Hortense *Calisher's sweeping panorama of intermarriage and the commingling of faiths in *Sunday Jews* (2002).

Salinger's deeply reclusive life and decision not to publish further writings have led to various, if not contentious, biographical speculation.

ADD. BIBLIOGRAPHY: P. Alexander, *Salinger: A Biography* (1999); H. Bloom (ed.), *J.D. Salinger* (2002); I. Hamilton, *In Search of J.D. Salinger* (1988); K. Kotzen and T. Beller (eds.), *With Love and Squalor: 14 Writers Respond to the Work of J.D. Salinger* (2001); J. Maynard, *At Home in the World: A Memoir* (1998); M. Salinger, *Dream-Catcher: A Memoir* (2000).

[Milton Henry Hindus / Lewis Fried (2nd ed.)]

SALISBURY, former capital of Rhodesia (renamed **Harare** and now capital of *Zimbabwe). Organized Jewish life in Salisbury dates from June 2, 1895, when, under the chairmanship of Joseph van Praagh (Salisbury's first Jewish mayor), a meeting of 20 men and two women founded the Salisbury Hebrew Congregation. The first synagogue was built in 1901 and the present one in 1920. The first minister was appointed in 1909. The first Sephardi arrived in Salisbury in 1895, and from 1905 there was a large influx into Rhodesia of Sephardim, mainly from the Aegean island of *Rhodes. They were scattered in all parts of the country, and it was not until 1931 that a separate Sephardi Hebrew Congregation was founded in Salisbury. Its first rabbi was appointed in 1944. There were a few Sephardim in centers outside Salisbury, but most have gravitated to the capital. The Ashkenazi and Sephardi congregations built imposing communal centers, comprising synagogues, schools, halls, and youth centers. A Reform Congregation was started in 1960. Both the Sephardi and Ashkenazi congregations maintained an afternoon Hebrew and religious school with a total enrollment of 220 pupils. A Jewish primary day school opened in 1960. In the decade between 1958 and 1968 the Salisbury Jewish community grew rapidly and eventually outstripped the one in *Bulawayo. Jews have played an active role in the developing Salisbury and the city has had a number of Jewish mayors: J. van Praagh (1900–01), H.L. Lexard (1914–17), H. Pichanick (1955–57), I. Pitch (1961–62, 1967–68), and B. Ponter (1964–65). In 1968 the Jewish population of Salisbury was about 2,500, two-thirds of them Ashkenazim and the rest Sephardim. With the outbreak of civil war in Rhodesia and the transfer of power to the black majority at the end of the 1970s, the Jewish population of the city dropped sharply, reaching barely 350 in 2003.

BIBLIOGRAPHY: M. Konviser, *Golden Jubilee of the Salisbury Hebrew Congregation* (1945); idem, in: *Rhodesian Jewish Times* (Sept. 1950), 5–9; M. Gitlin, *The Vision Amazing* (1950), index.

[Maurice Wagner]

SALIT, NORMAN (1896–1960), U.S. lawyer, rabbi, and communal leader. Born in Brooklyn, New York, Salit was admitted to the bar in 1920. The previous year he had received his rabbinical degree from the Jewish Theological Seminary of America. Salit became rabbi of Temple Israel in the Bronx in 1920 and served as rabbi of Shaaray Tefila synagogue in Far Rockaway, Queens, from 1924 to 1929. Salit combined his legal and rabbinical professions. He headed the Queens County Bar Association committee on legislation from 1933 to 1937, and in 1947 and 1949 ran, unsuccessfully, as a Democrat for the positions of presiding supervisor of Nassau County and of Children's Court judge, respectively.

During World War II he was executive director of the Wartime Emergency Commission for Conservative Judaism, which aided congregations whose rabbis had entered military service. In 1935–54 he was president of the Synagogue Council. Salit was an active member of many Jewish organizations. He was on the board of overseers of the Jewish Theological Seminary of America and the executive committee of the Zionist Organization of America. *The World of Norman Salit* (1966), edited by Abraham Burstein, contains sermons, essays, reports, comments on the weekly Torah portion, and miscellaneous material written by Salit.

SALITA, DMITRIY ("Star Of David," "The Kosher Knockout"; 1982–), U.S. boxer, NABA junior welterweight champion. Born in Odessa, Ukraine, Dmitriy moved with his family to Brooklyn at the age of nine. He originally started out with karate, but his older brother Michael introduced him to boxing, and he started boxing at 13 at the Starrett City Boxing Club. When his mother, Lyudmila, was diagnosed with breast cancer and then died when Salita was a teenager, he underwent a religious transformation with the help of a Lubavitch rabbi who comforted him through his ordeal. As a result, Salita is a strictly observant Jew who keeps kosher, will not fight on the Sabbath or holidays, and studies daily with a rabbi. He won the 2000 U.S. National Under-19 amateur championship, and on April 5, 2001, won the New York Golden Gloves championship, earning the Sugar Ray Robinson Award as the outstanding boxer in the tournament. He won his first professional fight on June 24, 2001, and claimed the NABA junior welterweight championship August 26, 2005. "He looks Russian, prays Jewish, fights black" said his trainer, Jimmy O'Pharrow. At the end of 2005, Salita was 24–0, with 14 KOs.

[Elli Wohlgelernter (2nd ed.)]

SALITERNIK, ZVI (1897–1993), Israeli physician. Saliternik was born in Proskurov, Ukraine, where he graduated in medicine (1918) and worked in local hospitals before emigrating to Palestine (1920). He specialized in clinical care and research in malaria as inspector at Hadassah Hospital, Jerusalem, from 1921, and as director of the anti-malaria department at the Ministry of Health from 1962, where his efforts led to the eradication of the disease in Israel. He also directed the eradication of the parasitic disease schistosomiasis from the country. He was awarded the Israel Prize for medicine (1962).

[Michael Denman (2nd ed.)]

SALK, JONAS (1914–1995), U.S. virologist. Salk was born in New York City, graduating in medicine from New York University Medical School (1939). Pursuing his commitment as a student to killed antiviral vaccination, he worked on influenza virus vaccines at the University of Michigan with Thomas Francis before moving to the University of Pittsburgh in 1947, where he became director of viral research. Exploiting Enders' 1949 discovery of methods for growing poliomyelitis virus in tissue culture, Salk developed an inactivated anti-polio virus vaccine given by intramuscular injection. Clinical trials of the vaccine in the U.S. and Canada showed a dramatic fall of over 90% in the incidence of the polio virus-induced disease, paralytic poliomyelitis, by 1955. Initial problems of infectious virus persistence in one commercial vaccine preparation were overcome, and vaccination with Salk vaccine was adopted routinely in the U.S. and other countries. Salk refused to profit financially from his vaccine. The efficacy of a killed virus vaccine led to the development of similar vaccines against other viruses. Albert *Sabin's alternative oral live-virus antipolio vaccine, with the prospect of conferring lifelong immunity, supplanted the Salk vaccine in the U.S. and other countries, at least temporarily. The different approaches to antipolio vaccination in 1963 led to intense personal and general controversy. Salk founded the Institute for Biological Sciences named for him in La Jolla, California, where he continued his research, including attempts to develop an anti-HIV virus. His honors included the Lasker award for clinical medical research (1956), the U.S. Order of Merit, and a Congressional Gold Medal.

[Michael Denman (2nd ed.)]

SALKIND, JACOB MEIR (Zalkind, Yankev-Meyer; 1875–1937), Hebrew and Yiddish writer. Born in Kobrin (Belorussia), Salkind studied at the Volozhin yeshiva and at German and Swiss universities. After the *Kishinev pogroms in 1903, he organized a self-defense group in Bern. Moving to England around 1904, he organized in London a Zionist group, Aḥuzah ("Estate"), on behalf of whose members he went to Palestine in 1913 and obtained land at Karkur, on which they were able to settle in 1921. During World War I, he led the anti-war agitation among the Russian Jews in England and opposed *Jabotinsky's efforts to form a Jewish Legion. For this purpose, he founded and edited *Di Yidishe Shtime* (1916), first as a weekly, then as a daily. After becoming an anarchist, he edited, along with Rudolf *Rocker, the anarchist organ, *Der Arbayter Fraynd* (1920–23). Salkind's literary contributions began in *Ha-Tsefira* in 1900; he knew and published in many languages, chiefly Hebrew and Yiddish. His Hebrew plays for children (1903–22) were often staged in Jewish schools. He translated four tractates of the Talmud into Yiddish: *Berakhot* ("Blessings") from the Babylonian Talmud; *Pe'ah* ("[Field]-Corner"), *Demai* ("Doubtfully Tithed Crops") and *Kilayim* ("Hybrid") from the Jerusalem Talmud (1922–32). He died in Haifa.

BIBLIOGRAPHY: Rejzen, Leksikon, 1 (1926), 1030–4; LNYL, 3 (1960), 535–40; M. Goldwasser, in: *Studies in the Cultural Life of the Jews in England* 5 (1975), 61–75; L. Prager, *Yiddish Culture in Britain* (1980), 717.

[Jerucham Tolkes / Leonard Prager (2nd ed.)]

SALKINSON, ISAAC EDWARD (Eliezer; 1820–1883), Hebrew translator who converted to Christianity and became a missionary. Raised in Belorussia, he trained as a teacher, then studied grammar, Bible, and German, and translated the first act of Schiller's *Kabale und Liebe* into Hebrew. While living in London he converted to Christianity (1849). He became a Presbyterian pastor in 1856, and in 1876 was sent as a missionary to Vienna, where he spent the rest of his life. Despite his conversion Salkinson regarded himself as a Jew. Emotionally and intellectually he had strong ties to the Hebrew language, which he believed should replace Latin as the sacred language of Christianity. His translations reflect his dual motives and fall into two categories: some were intended to bring Jews closer to Christianity; others were done for purely artistic reasons. The first type included *Va-Yegaresh et ha-Adam* (1871), a translation of Milton's *Paradise Lost*; and *Ha-Berit ha-Ḥadashah* (The New Testament), published posthumously in 1883. The second type included translations of *Othello (Ithiel ha-Kushi)* and *Romeo and Juliet (Ram ve-Ya'el*; Vienna, 1874 and 1875). A conscientious craftsman who wrote in lucid, neobiblical style, Salkinson was one of the finest translators of the Haskalah period.

BIBLIOGRAPHY: I. Cohen, *Isaac Edward Salkinson* (Heb., 1942); Kressel, Leksikon, 1 (1965), 751–3.

[Elieser Kagan]

SALMON, family of English caterers. ALFRED SALMON (1868–1928) was the eldest son of Barnett Salmon (1829–1897), partner in the firm of retail tobacconists, Salmon and *Gluckstein. With Joseph *Lyons and the brothers Isidore and Montague Gluckstein, he was a founder of the famous catering establishment, J. Lyons and Company. Alfred Salmon began by selling cigars in his father's concern at the age of 13. After learning the catering business, he started his career in Lyons as manager of the refreshment room at the Imperial Institute, and in 1922 succeeded Montague Gluckstein as chairman of the company, retaining the position until his death. He was also interested in hospital work and closely connected with the development of the London Hospital. His brother, SIR ISIDOR SALMON (1876–1941), began his career as a kitchen apprentice and later served at Olympia, London's great exhibition and entertainments center, where J. Lyons and Company were the catering contractors. He was active in the development of the company and followed his brother as its chairman. In World War I he organized the Army and Navy Canteen Board and revolutionized army catering. He also founded the Westminster Technical School for the training of waiters and cooks. From 1924 to 1941 he was Conservative member of parliament for Harrow and sat on numerous parliamentary committees. He also played an active part in the municipal administration of London and in Jewish communal affairs, being president of the South London Jewish Schools, vice president of the Board of Deputies of British Jews and of the Jewish orphanage, and closely connected with the United Synagogue. Isidore Salmon was knighted in 1933. Another brother, HENRY SALMON (1881–1950), was instrumental in developing the modern wholesale tea industry in Britain. Other members of the family were SIR SAMUEL (ISIDORE) SALMON (1900–1980), chairman of J. Lyons and Company from 1965 to 1968 and an active member of the London County Council; SIR JULIAN SALMON (1903–1978), deputy chairman of Lyons and catering adviser to the Royal Air Force; GEOFFREY ISIDORE HAMILTON SALMON (1908–1990), chairman of Lyons from 1968 and catering adviser to the British Army; and BRIAN SALMON (1921–2000), chairman of the firm from 1972 and the author of the Salmon Report on senior nursing staff structures.

BIBLIOGRAPHY: P.H. Emden, *Jews of Britain* (1943), 486–91. **ADD. BIBLIOGRAPHY:** "Henry Salmon," in: DBB, 5, 20–22.

SALMON, ALEXANDER (1822–1866), English traveler. Salmon was the son of a London banker, and while serving in the South Seas on a whaler, met and married Arii Tamai, 20-year-old chieftainess of the Teva clan on the island of Tahiti. He then became chief adviser to the rulers of Tahiti. Salmon, who was considered by the natives to be impartial, managed to persuade them not to resist the French when they established their rule over the island. In the late 1850s he went to Paris to see Napoleon III with a list of grievances from the natives which had been ignored by the French governor of Tahiti. He was not received and went off to London where, in 1858, he published his letter of complaint, *Lettre concernant l'état actuel de Tahiti*. His wife's memoirs, edited in part by Henry Adams, appeared in 1901. Their daughter Joanna married Maran Taroa, the last king of Tahiti, and their son Tati became an intimate friend of Robert Louis Stevenson.

BIBLIOGRAPHY: Ramsden, in: *Australian Jewish Historical Society Journal*, 1 (1949), 57–71 (includes bibliography).

SALMON, CYRIL BARNET, BARON (1903–1991), English judge. Born in London, the son of a member of the *Salmon family who co-owned J. Lyon & Co., and educated at Mill Hill school and Cambridge, Salmon was admitted to the Bar in 1929 and became a King's Counsel in 1945. His first judicial appointment in 1947 was as recorder of Gravesend, and in 1957 he was made a high court judge and knighted. In 1964 Salmon was promoted to lord justice of appeal and two years later he became chairman of the Royal Commission on Tribunals of Inquiry. In 1972 Salmon was appointed a Lord of Appeal in Ordinary in succession to Lord Donovan, and made a life peer as Baron Salmon. From 1974 to 1976 he was chairman of the Royal Commission of Conduct in Public Life. In 1967 he lectured at The Hebrew University on this subject, and his lecture was published as *Tribunals of Inquiry* (1967). Salmon was noted for consistently upholding liberal values.

ADD. BIBLIOGRAPHY: ODNB online.

[Israel Finestein]

SALMON, KAREL (**Karl Salomon**; 1897–1974), Israeli composer. Born in Heidelberg, Salmon studied composition with Max Reger and in Richard Strauss's "master class." From 1919 to 1933 he was active in Germany as conductor and singer (bass), and in 1933 he settled in Palestine. With the establishment of the Palestine Broadcasting Service (later Kol Israel), he became its musical director and remained at this post until 1958. He then was director of Kol Israel's transcription-exchange service for four years. Salmon also taught at the Academy of Music in Jerusalem and appeared as conductor and singer. Many of his works belong to the "Mediterranean style" period of Israel music and attempt a blending of his European heritage with Near Eastern and Jewish folklore material.

They include *Ali Be'er – Variations on a Hebrew Folksong* for orchestra (1937, the theme song is by Sara Levi-Tannai); four Greek folk dances, for orchestra (c. 1942, ending with a "Horah Stellenica"); *Israel Lives* ("*Am Yisrael Ḥai*"), variation for piano solo or string trio or string orchestra (1947); the "puppet opera" *David and Goliath* in which the composer often sang the part of Goliath; an *Israeli Youth Symphony*, and many other vocal, choral, and instrumental works.

BIBLIOGRAPHY: I. Shalita, *Enziklopedyah le-Musikah…* (1959). 732 3; P. Gradenwitz, *Music and Musicians in Israel* (1959), 42–44, 154; *Who is Who in ACUM* (1965), s.v.

[Bathja Bayer]

SALMON BEN JEROHAM (**Sulaym ibn Ruhaym**; tenth century), Karaite polemicist and writer, a fervent spokesman for the Mourners of Zion (*Avlei Zion), a native of Ereẓ Israel or Iraq. According to Karaite tradition, he was the teacher of *Saadiah Gaon, an impossibility since Salmon was much the younger man of the two. However, the tradition may possibly reflect some actual personal conflict between them, which could partially explain Salmon's extreme hatred of Saadiah. Salmon's principal work, *Milḥamot Adonai*, written in Hebrew, is a rhymed attack on the Rabbanites and on Saadiah. Even for an age characterized by abusive polemics, the language of the book is unusually vehement, and the author treats Saadiah more as a personal enemy than a theological adversary. In his subject matter, Salmon merely repeats the arguments of older Karaite polemicists, but the violent language and quasi-poetic form are all his own. If the hypothesis that Salmon is the same person as Ibn al-Sākawayh is correct, Saadiah refuted his attacks in a special work, only fragments of which remain. In the 950s Salmon wrote a series of commentaries on the Bible. Complete mss, fragments and quotations identified so far include commentaries on Psalms, the Song of Songs, Lamentations, Ecclesiastes, and Isaiah. Though less violent in tone, they still contain many attacks on Saadiah's views, and on the Rabbanites in general. The commentary on Lamentations is especially interesting because it apparently constitutes the mourning rites and sessions of the Karaite Mourners of Zion. In his commentary on Ecclesiastes he expounds his ethical and intellectual views. Some scholars cast doubts on the authenticity of these two commentaries, because they contain much less anti-rabbinic bias. Salmon condemned all secular studies as ungodly and forbidden.

BIBLIOGRAPHY: I. Davidson (ed.), *Book of the Wars of the Lord* (1934), introd.; Steinschneider, Arab Lit., 76–78; S. Poznański, *Karaite Literary Opponents of Saadiah Gaon* (1908), 12–14; Mann, Texts, 2 (1935), index s.v. *Salmon b. Yeruham*; L. Nemoy, *Karaite Anthology* (1952), 69–82; Z. Ankori, *Karaites in Byzantium* (1959), index s.v. *Salmon b. Yeruham*. **ADD. BIBLIOGRAPHY:** L. Marwick (ed.), *The Arabic Commentary of Salmon ben Yeruham the Karaite on the Book of Psalms, Chapters 42–72* (1956); G. Vajda, *Deux commentaires karaïtes sur l'Ecclésiastes* (1971); M. Gil, *Palestine during the First Muslim Period (634–1099)* (1992), index; H. Ben-Shammai, in: S. Elizur et al. (eds.), *Knesset Ezra: Literature and Life in the Synagogue: Studies Presented to Ezra Fleischer* (Heb., 1994), 191–234; M. Polliack (ed.), *Karaite Judaism: A Guide to Its History and Literary Sources*, (2003), index; N. Wieder, *The Judean Scrolls and Karaism* (2005), index

[Leon Nemoy / Golda Akhiezer (2nd ed.)]

SALOME. A figure unnamed in the New Testament, but called Salome by Josephus. She was the daughter of Herodias and, through the latter's remarriage, stepdaughter of the tetrarch Herod *Antipas, youngest son of Herod the Great (Jos., Ant., 18, 136). According to Mark (6:17–18): "For Herod [Antipas] himself had sent forth and laid hold upon John [the Baptist], and bound him in prison for the sake of Herodias, his brother Philip's wife: he had married her. For John said unto Herod: It is unlawful for thee to have thy brother's wife" (cf. Matt. 14:3–4; Luke 3:18–20). There is some confusion in Josephus as to when exactly the marriage between Herodias and Herod Antipas occurred and whether it was before or after John's death. The problem was in Herodias having married her two uncles, while both were still alive, a union forbidden by Jewish law. Salome was the child of the first marriage. The point John would have made in his teaching is that such a union was not in keeping with Leviticus (18:6). The Gospels seem to suggest that Antipas had no plans to kill John, but that a set of circumstances led to his execution at the behest of Herodias, who suggested that Salome ask for his head. This occurred on the occasion of a banquet to celebrate Herod's birthday in which he promised Salome anything that she desired because of her exquisite dancing. There are two passages dealing with the story (Matt. 14:1–12; Mark 6:14–29) and a comparison of the two is quite instructive. While the passage in Matthew is very factual in presentation, Mark's account is much more colorful. While in Matthew Salome was "instructed" by her mother beforehand (i.e., Herodias planned the beheading in a premeditated fashion), the story in Mark is that it was the result of a whim, with Salome having to leave the banquet hall to consult her mother: "What shall I ask?"

Salome was a popular name in the Second Temple period: there are 52 recorded instances of the name and its variants (Heb. Shelomit, Shalom) in inscriptions and written sources. In the Gospels she is not mentioned directly by name and she is simply referred to there as "Daughter of Herodias" (Mark 6:22). It is Josephus who provides us with her exact name (Ant., 18:136). The Greek word associated with her in Mark indicates she was a very young girl, perhaps only 12, when she danced in front of Herod. Hence, she was probably born at the earliest in 16 C.E. Later, she is believed to have married Aristobulus, King of Lesser Armenia, but there have been some doubts about this. Jacobus de Voragine (c. 1230–1298) has preserved an apocryphal story about Salome's death, perhaps reflecting the wishful thinking of Christian writers who could not accept the possibility that Salome might have gotten away with it, i.e., there had to be some retribution for her act (*Leg. Aur. Sanct.*). According to the story, she was walking across an icy pond when the ice gave way and she drowned. Another chronicler says that "the earth swallowed her alive."

[Shimon Gibson (2nd ed.)]

In the Arts

In literature, the theme was not popular before the mid-19th century, and most writers have considerably embroidered the stark tale to heighten its dramatic effect. One of the very few Jewish writers attracted by the theme was Judah L. *Landau, whose Hebrew drama, *Dam Taḥat Dam*, appeared in 1897. The outstanding work on the subject was Oscar Wilde's tragedy, *Salomé*, which had a *succès de scandale* following its publication in French in 1893. Wilde made Salome a depraved personality driven on by her baffled lust for the Baptist, a treatment well calculated to outrage contemporary English opinion. An English translation by Lord Alfred Douglas appeared in 1894 and was subsequently published as *Salomé; La sainte courtisane; A Florentine tragedy* (1911). The play, first performed in Paris in 1896, only reached the English stage in 1931 when tastes had changed and censorship requirements had relaxed. Wilde provided an original dénouement by having the tetrarch order Salome's own execution amid her dreadful triumph. Another late 19th-century treatment of the subject was the German dramatist Hermann Sudermann's five-act tragedy, *Johannes* (1898²; *John the Baptist*, 1909). The theme retained its popularity in the 20th century, beginning with *Salome* (1908), a Swiss-German tragedy by Richard Zwez. Salome also inspired a poem by the French surrealist Guillaume Apollinaire and a Croatian drama by Miroslav Krleža. Her mother, Herodias, was the heroine of two French works of the 19th century on closely related themes: *Hérodiade* (1869), a verse drama by Stéphane Mallarmé, and "Hérodias," the third of Gustave Flaubert's *Trois Contes* (1877), which imaginatively recreates the atmosphere of Roman-occupied Judea.

In art, there were from the 11th century a number of representations of the feast at which Salome danced. In these Herod presides, wearing a crown or a medieval Jewish conical hat. On a capital from the cloister of St. Etienne (Musée des Augustins, Toulouse) he is shown in the act of tenderly chucking Salome under the chin. In the oldest representations, Salome dances in an upright position with movements of the hips, but in those produced after the 12th century she turns somersaults and stands on her hands in the manner of medieval acrobats. She was known in medieval France as "la danserelle" or "la sauterelle" (the grasshopper) and an acrobatic dance was named after her. In art she is shown performing dances which vary according to the fashion of the period. The dance of Salome appears in medieval carvings, stained-glass windows, the 12th-century bronze doors at St. Zeno, Verona, and in 12th- and 13th-century mosaics at the Florence Baptistery and St. Mark's Cathedral, Venice. It was also a popular subject in the early Italian Renaissance, when it was treated by Giotto (1266/67–1337) in his fresco at St. Croce, Florence; by Donatello (1386–1466) in a bronze bas-relief in the Baptistery of St. Giovanni, Siena; and by Fra Filippo Lippi (1406–1469) in a fresco at Prato Cathedral. The subject later appears in 17th-century Russian frescoes and in a drypoint etching by Picasso in which Salome dances before Herod in the nude. The scene where Salome receives John's head on a charger is usually shown together with that of his prior beheading. Salome's mother, Herodias, who is seated with Herod at the feast, is sometimes shown cutting a slit down the Baptist's forehead or piercing his tongue. Often, however, Herod and his wife cover their faces in horror, whereupon Salome faints. This scene is represented in a number of the sources already mentioned, and in paintings by Luini (Prado) and Lucas Cranach (1472–1553; Wadworth Athenaeum, Hartford, U.S.). In the 19th century, the French symbolist painter Gustave Moreau (1826–1896) painted *The Apparition* (now in the Louvre) – an opulent study of the dancing Salome who sees the head of John the Baptist in a vision. A portfolio of the English artist Aubrey Beardsley's drawings to illustrate Oscar Wilde's play was published in 1920.

In Music

In music, the story has inspired general works, which the fancy of the librettists elaborated far beyond anything that can be found in the sources. Jules Massenet's *Hérodiade* (text by Paul Milliet and Georges Hartmann under the pseudonym of Henri Grémont) was first performed in Brussels in 1881 and has remained in the repertoire. Here, Salome loves John and does not know that she is the daughter of Herodias; Herod falls in love with her and in the final dénouement, Salome kills herself. The most famous universal treatment of the theme is Richard Strauss's opera, *Salome*, written in 1904–05 to a libretto by Hedwig Lachmann based on Oscar Wilde's play. The opera's gruesome theme and the horrors it contained aroused strong opposition wherever it was performed, the sensuousness of the text being faithfully paralleled by the music. The "Dance of the Seven Veils" which forms *Salome's* climax is sometimes performed as a concert piece and, in the early 1920s, it was often presented as a vaudeville attraction. A setting of Wilde's play in the original French version was composed by Antoine Mariotte before 1905, but had its première only in 1908 (at Lyons), and this involved the composer in difficulties with Richard Strauss. Three works on the same subject followed almost immediately. Florent Schmitt's ballet, *La Tragédie de Salomé* (1907), included many Oriental themes which he had collected in 1900 on his travels in the Near East, especially in Palestine ("heard near the Dead Sea"). The same year saw the appearance of Karol Szymanowski's *Salome*, a circle of songs with orchestra (text by J. Kasprovicz; revised orchestration 1912), and Granville Bantock's opera, *The Daughter of Herodias*. Bantock also wrote incidental music for the Wilde play in 1918. Paul Hindemith's *Hérodiade* (1944), for chamber orchestra, was based on the verse drama by Mallarmé; it has also served for a ballet. Among compositions of incidental music for the play is that by Leonard Bernstein (1955).

[Bathja Bayer]

BIBLIOGRAPHY: H. Daffner, *Salome, Ihre Gestalt in Geschichte und Kunst* (1912); R. Cansinos-Assens, *Salome en la Literatura. Flaubert, Wilde, Mallarmé, Eugenio de Castro, Apollinaire* (1919), includes translations; H.G. Zagona, *The Legend of Salome and the Principle of Art for Art's Sake* (1960); M. Roston, *Biblical Drama in England*

(1968), index. **ADD. BIBLIOGRAPHY:** C. Haldeman, "The Feverish Head on the Disk of the Sun: Salome Through the Ages," in: *International History Magazine,* 10 (1973), 64–79; N. Kokkinos, "Which Salome did Aristobulus Marry?" in: PEQ, 118 (1986), 33–50; S. Gibson, *The Cave of John the Baptist* (2004), 242–44; T. Ilan, *Lexicon of Jewish Names in Late Antiquity. Part I: Palestine 330 B.C.E.–200 C.E.* (2002), 249–53.

SALOME ALEXANDRA (Heb. שְׁלוֹמְצִיּוֹן, *Shelomziyyon*; Gr. **Salina, Salampsio**; 139–67 B.C.E.), queen of Judea and wife of *Aristobulus I and *Alexander Yannai, upon whose death she ascended the throne to reign as sole Jewish monarch during the years 76–67. Josephus first mentions her as an accomplice in the plot to assassinate Antigonus, brother of her husband Aristobulus I, but most historians attribute this accusation to the animosity toward the Hasmonean rulers of those historians whom Josephus saw as his source. Upon the death of Aristobulus (103 B.C.E.), it seems that the widow of the presumably childless king was required to marry his brother Yannai, in accordance with the Jewish law of *levirate marriage. However, Josephus nowhere mentions this explicitly, and this has led some scholars to believe that Yannai in fact married another woman of the same name. It is probable that the first assumption is the more correct. On Aristobulus' death she released his three brothers (including Yannai), who had been imprisoned for some time. There are no reports of Alexandra's political influence during the reign of Yannai, although she seems to have opposed the king's persecution of the Pharisees. It is certain, however, that she won the affection of the Judean populace, thereby convincing her husband before his death that the Jews would bow to her authority as they would to no other. Alexandra's accession in 76 B.C.E. was considered a moral and political victory for the Pharisees, and the close relations between that sect and the queen are referred to in rabbinic traditions. Simeon b. Shetaḥ, leader of the Pharisees (see Ber. 48a; Gen. R. 91:3), was reportedly received by Salome at the palace at the period of her husband's dispute with the Pharisees. After her accession he was recalled from Egypt and appointed joint judicial and religious head of the Sanhedrin with *Judah ben Tabbai. The Pharisees immediately demanded that the Temple ritual be reformed in accordance with their practices, and that the fixing of the calendar and judicial leadership be under their control. Josephus, while admitting that the Pharisees may have used the queen's favor to assume the practical administration of the state, nevertheless stresses that she retained the reins of government with regard to larger matters. The queen was a strict observer of religious traditions, and dismissed any violator of religious law. The Pharisees used their privileged position to settle old scores. In one instance they brought about the execution of Diogenes, one of the advisers of Yannai, who was accused of having incited the king to crucify 800 Pharisees. Alexandra took no reprisals, however, against the Sadducees who had fought under her husband and were at the mercy of their enemies.

Alexandra's foreign connections were extensive, and her influence was felt and respected by neighboring monarchs. By continual recruiting, and by collecting foreign troops, she doubled the size of her army. However, the Pharisees were sufficiently powerful to prevent her from continuing the traditional Hasmonean wars abroad, although a military expedition to Damascus was led by her son Aristobulus. It proved ineffectual, and by means of treaties and gifts she warded off the occupation of her kingdom by Tigranes, king of Armenia, who had invaded Syria and was marching toward Judea (c. 70 B.C.E.). Shortly after this success the queen fell ill, and internal dissension again threw Judea into bitter turmoil. Of the queen's two sons by Yannai, the elder, *Hyrcanus, had been appointed high priest, and was considered sole heir to the throne. His younger brother, *Aristobulus, not content with the secondary role accorded him, courted the support of those elements whose power had diminished under the rule of the Pharisees. Gathering a large mercenary force, Aristobulus took possession of numerous fortresses throughout the country and proclaimed himself king. Before the queen could move against him, she died, leaving the incompetent Hyrcanus to agree to the terms dictated by Aristobulus. Josephus praises Alexandra for keeping the nation at peace. The rabbis relate how Ereẓ Israel was so fertile in her reign that the grains of wheat, oats, and lentils grew to extraordinary sizes and were kept to show to future generations what piety could achieve.

BIBLIOGRAPHY: Jos., Wars, 1:76–77, 85, 107–19; Jos., Ant., 13:320, 405–32; 20:242; Pauly-Wissowa, 1 (1894), 1376, no. 2; Schuerer, Gesch, 1 (1901⁴), 286–90; Halevy, Dorot, 1 pt. 3 (1923), 455–6, 459–60, 503–46; Klausner, Bayit Sheni, 3 (1950²), 142–5, 165–78; Zeitlin, in: JQR, 51 (1960/61), 1–33; L. Finkelstein, *The Pharisees*, 1 (1962³), 275–6; 2 (1962³), 612–3.

[Isaiah Gafni]

SALOMON, ALBERT (1891–1966), sociologist. Born in Berlin, Salomon was professor of political sociology at the Deutsche Hochschule fuer Politik in Berlin from 1926 to 1931 and at the Berufspaedagogisches Institut in Cologne from 1931 to 1933. For some years he edited *Gesellschaft*, the journal of the Social-Democratic Party. Forced to emigrate after Hitler's advent to power, Salomon went to New York, where he was a professor of sociology at the graduate faculty of the New School for Social Research from 1935 until his death. Salomon followed the historical and philosophical traditions of French and German classical sociology. He paid attention to the importance of literature in a developing theory of society. His major books were *Autoritaet und Freiheit* (1936) and *Tyranny of Progress* (1955; *Fortschritt als Schicksal und Verhaengnis*, 1957).

BIBLIOGRAPHY: C. Mayer, in: *Social Research*, 34 (1967), 213–25.

[Werner J. Cahnman]

SALOMON, ALICE (1872–1948), German economist and educator. Born in Berlin of a merchant family that had settled in north Germany in the 18th century, Alice Salomon converted to Protestantism at the beginning of World War I. She was active mainly in the training of women for professional social work and their inclusion in that field. In 1908 she founded in Berlin a school for that purpose, which she directed until 1924. Expelled from Germany in 1937, she went to England and from there to the U.S., where until her death she continued her literary activity in the field of the social education of the woman and the protection of the working woman. Although she was not a suffragette in the political sense, she was active in the women's international movement. She founded and directed the Konferenz sozialer Frauenschulen Deutschlands, the Deutsche Akademie fuer soziale und paedagogische Frauenarbeit, and the Internationales Komitte sozialer Schulen. She was vice president of the International League of Women.

She wrote many books which became classics of social work: *Die Ursachen der ungleichen Entlohnung von Maenner- und Frauenarbeit* (1906); *Einfuehrung in die Volkswirtschaftslehre* (1909, 1921[5]); *Die Ausbildung zum sozialen Beruf* (1927); *Leitfaden der Wohlfahrtspflege* (1921, 1928[3]). Her autobiography was published many years after her death, first in German translation as *Charakter ist Schicksal* (1983, 1984), and later in the English original, *Character is Destiny* (2004). Salomon's collected works were published in three volumes under the title *Frauenemanzipation und soziale Verantwortung* (1997–2003).

BIBLIOGRAPHY: H. Muthesius (ed.), *Alice Salomon: die Begruenderin des sozialen Frauenberufes in Deutschland* (1958), includes bibliography of her writings. **ADD. BIBLIOGRAPHY:** J. Wieler, *Erinnerung eines zerstoerten Lebensabends* (1987); R. Orywa and A. Droege (eds.), *Alice Salomon in ihren Schriften* (1989); M. Berger, *Alice Salomon* (1998); A. Feustel, in: *Frauen Erinnern* (2000), 111–27; C. Kuhlmann, *Alice Salomon* (2000); A. Schueler, *Frauenbewegung und soziale Reform* (2004).

[Shalom Adler-Rudel / Noam Zadoff (2nd ed.)]

SALOMON, CHARLOTTE (1917–1943), German painter. The daughter of a Berlin physician, Salomon was sixteen when the Nazis came to power. She refused to continue her schooling because of the humiliations to which she was subjected, but in 1935 she was still able to attend the local Academy of Fine Arts. In 1939 she emigrated to France, where she married another refugee, Alexander Nagler. They lived in relative security until the Germans occupied the Riviera in September 1943, five months after their marriage. Then the Gestapo conducted one of the most brutal mass roundups in Western Europe, during which the young couple were dragged out of their home by the Gestapo, and both died in the gas chambers of Auschwitz. While a refugee from Nazi Germany, during 1941 and 1942, Salomon portrayed her life in an autobiography titled *Leben oder Theater? Ein Singspiel* ("Life or Theater? An Operetta"). It takes the unprecedented form of a musical drama in 1,325 gouaches of astonishing vividness and force, painted in flat, cool colors, with an unusual perspective and a great deal of purely decorative detail. "Life or Theater?" is peopled by characters based on her family and friends, ordered by acts and scenes, narrated by dialogues and commentaries, and accompanied by musical cues.

The autobiography makes one family emblematic of its era. Salomon records the creative milieu of Berlin through the experiences of her stepmother, Paula Salomon-Lindberg, a well-known opera singer, and of her mentor and lover, Alfred Wolfsohn, a philosopher of music. The autobiography also registers the impact of Nazism on an assimilated Jewish family: first Charlotte Salomon's grandparents emigrated from Germany, then her stepmother was restricted to performing for Jewish audiences; her father, Dr. Albert Salomon, was deprived of his professorship at the Berlin University Medical School, then imprisoned in Sachsenhausen. Charlotte Salomon was among the handful of Jewish students admitted to the Berlin Academy of Fine Arts, but was expelled in 1938, and left Germany in 1939.

Joining her grandparents in Villefranche on the French Riviera, Salomon witnessed her grandmother's suicide in 1940 and only then learned that her mother's death years earlier was also a suicide. The menace of suicide and the duress of exile forced her to decide, she said, "whether to take her own life or undertake something unheard of and mad" – an autobiography in art. After working more than a year on *Leben oder Theater?*, she gave its paintings and texts to a friend in Villefranche, saying: "Keep this safe. It is my whole life." The paintings often have explanatory captions: one reads, "I cannot bear this life, I cannot bear these times." When a collection of these gouaches was published in 1963 as *Charlotte, A Diary of Pictures*, Charlotte Salomon came to be regarded as the Anne *Frank of painting.

After the war, her father and stepmother brought Life or Theater? to Amsterdam, where it now resides in the Jewish Historical Museum. Exhibitions in Europe, the U.S., and Israel (Beth Hatefutsoth, 1985), as well as published reproductions, a film, and plays, have given Life or Theater? international standing as an artwork, autobiography, and historical document.

BIBLIOGRAPHY: *Charlotte: Life or Theater? An Autobiographical Play*, intro. by J. Belinfante, G. Schwartz, and J. Herzberg (1981); *Charlotte:A Diary in Pictures*, intro. by E. Straus (1963); "Charlotte" (film) by J. Herzberg and F. Weisz (1981); *Charlotte Salomon – "Leben oder Theater?" Das 'Lebensbild' einer jüdischen Malerin aus Berlin*, ed. C. Fiseher-Defoy (for 1986 exhibition, Berlin Fine Arts Academy). **ADD. BIBLIOGRAPHY:** J.C.E. Belinfante (ed.), *Charlotte Salomon – Leben? Oder Theater?* (1994; with catalogue raisonné); M. Lowenthal Felstiner, *To Paint Her Life. Charlotte Salomon in the Nazi Era* (1994); E. van Voolen, J.C.E. Belinfante, *Charlotte Salomon – Leben? Oder Theater?* (Anlaesslich der Ausstellung Charlotte Salomon: Leben? Oder Theater?, Staedelsches Kunstinstitut und Städtische Galerie, Frankfurt am Main) (2004).

[Alfred Werner and Mary Felsteiner]

SALOMON, ERICH (1886–1944), German photographer. Trained as a lawyer in Berlin, Salomon took up photography as a full-time profession when the 35-millimeter camera appeared in 1925. This small camera allowed a candidness and instantaneousness which had been the aim of documentary photographers since the invention of the camera. Salomon first used this camera for behind-the-scenes glimpses of internationally famous political personalities at League of Nations conferences in the late 1920s. An audacious, ingenious cameraman, his many subterfuges included cutting a hole in his derby hat for a concealed lens; wearing an armsling which hid both camera and the little glass slides he first used; and carrying an impressive leather-bound volume hollowed out to serve the same purpose. Another of his famous tricks was to place the camera in a flowerpot, window sill, or desk, and trigger the shutter by a cable release hidden in flowers, carpet, or wall. Salomon was one of the world's first photo-historians. He covered the League of Nations, diplomatic and other meetings in Geneva, Paris, London, and Washington. Erich Salomon died with his family in the gas chambers of Auschwitz. A son, Peter Hunter-Salomon, survived the Holocaust and published a book on his father, *Portraet einer Epoche* (1963).

[Peter Pollack]

SALOMON, GAVRIEL (1938–), specialist in educational psychology. Salomon was born in Tel Aviv. In 1966 he received his M.A. degree in education and psychology from The Hebrew University of Jerusalem, and in 1968 he received his Ph.D. in educational psychology and communication from Stanford University. From 1969 until 1974 he was a lecturer at The Hebrew University, and in 1975–77 he was head of the educational psychology program there. From 1984 to 1987 he served as head of the computer and education program at Tel Aviv University. He served as editor of *Educational Psychologist* (1991–95) and as president of the Educational, Instructional and School Psychology Division of the International Association of Applied Psychology (IAAP) in 1990–94. Subsequently he became co-director of the Center for Research on Peace Education. In 1992 Salomon became a professor at Haifa University and in 1993–98 was the dean of the Faculty of Education there. His work covers a range of topics: the cognitive effects of media's symbol systems, the expenditure of mental effort, mindfulness and mindlessness, organizational change, the design of intelligent computer tools, the design and systemic study of technology-afforded learning environments, and education for peace. His books include *Interaction of Media, Cognition and Learning Communication and Education* (1981) and *Technology and Education in the Information Age* (Heb.). He also edited *Distributed Cognition* (1993) and *Peace Education: The Concept, Principles, and Practices Around the World* (2002). In addition he published more than 100 empirical, theoretical, and methodological articles. In 2001 he was awarded the Israel Prize for education.

[Shaked Gilboa (2nd ed.)]

SALOMON, GESKEL (1821–1901), Swedish artist and art historian. Born and educated in Denmark, he settled in Sweden in 1850 and became professor at the Stockholm Art Academy. Among his books on art history were *Die Statue des Venus von Milo* and *Die Statue des Belvederischen und Vatikanischen Apollo*. He painted historical events, portraits, and genre subjects. These last include Jewish scenes which illustrate religious observances in 19th-century Scandinavia. *Lighting the Sabbath Candles* was painted when the artist was almost 80 years old.

SALOMON (Salomon de la Tour), GOTTFRIED (1892–1964), German sociologist. Salomon's father was Jewish and his mother was of French Protestant descent. Born in Frankfurt, he studied under Georg *Simmel, but later became assistant to Franz *Oppenheimer, an adherent of politico-historical sociology. In 1933 Salomon emigrated to France and in 1941 fled to the U.S., where he taught at the New School for Social Research, Columbia University, Hunter College, and Yeshiva University. In 1958 he returned to Frankfurt.

Salomon's publications (such as *Allgemeine Staatslehre*, 1930) are chiefly concerned with political ideology and the history of sociology and socialism. He became widely known as editor of the *Jahrbuecher fuer Soziologie* and of the works of Ludwig *Gumplowicz, Lorenz von Stein, and Giambattista Vico. His first publication was *Proudhon und der Sozialismus* (1920) and his last *Moderne Staatslehren* (1965).

BIBLIOGRAPHY: W. Bernsdorff (ed.), *Internationales Soziologenlexikon* (1959), s.v., incl. bibl. of his writings.

[Werner J. Cahnman]

SALOMON, GOTTHOLD (1784–1862), German preacher and reformer. After receiving a thoroughly Orthodox education, at the age of 16 Salomon was sent to Dessau, where he was influenced by modern trends. He then became a teacher and preached his first sermon there in 1806. A frequent contributor to **Sulamith*, he also vigorously answered the antisemitic writings of the professors C.F. *Ruehs and J.F. *Fries in 1817 (in 1843 he answered Bruno *Bauer). Two years later he was called to the pulpit of the Hamburg Reform temple, where he collaborated with E. *Kley. His reputation as a preacher had been established by a collection of sermons (*Auswahl mehrerer Predigten*, 1816), the first of a voluminous series. Salomon's sermons, modeled, like those of other preachers, on Protestant examples, were praised by his contemporaries, notably H. *Heine. When in 1841 Isaac *Bernays banned the prayer book he had composed, Salomon defended his position in the subsequent fierce controversy (*Das neue Gebetbuch…*, 1841). He vigorously supported the rabbinical assemblies of the mid-1840s in Brunswick, Frankfurt, and Breslau.

BIBLIOGRAPHY: G. Salomon, *Selbst-Biographie* (1863); P. Philippson, *Biographische Skizzen*, 2 (1866); B. Italiener, in: *Festschrift zum 120.... Bestehen des israelitischen Tempels in Hamburg* (1937), 17–24; A. Altmann, in: *Studies in Nineteenth-Century Jewish Intellectual History* (1964), index.

SALOMON (Solomon), HAYM (1740–1785), early American merchant and Revolutionary War patriot. Salomon, who was born in Lissa, Poland, arrived in New York about 1775 after wandering in Europe and became one of the most prominent 18th-century American Jews. During the Revolutionary War he was a distiller and sutler to the American army, and was captured as a spy by the British. His life was spared, and he served as an interpreter in their commissary department. Continuing to give information to the Americans, he assisted their prisoners to escape British captivity while operating a profitable victualing business in New York City under British occupation. Married to Rachel Franks in 1777, he had to flee a year later to Philadelphia, where he began a brokerage and commission business. In 1781 he became an assistant to Robert Morris, superintendent of the Office of Finance, after serving in a similar capacity as broker and treasurer for the huge expenses of the French army stationed in America. Morris characterized him as "useful to the public interest." Salomon also lent money without charge to impecunious members of the Continental Congress, among them James Madison, who recommended him as "our little friend in Front Street." In 1784 Salomon expanded his business activities to New York, opening a brokerage and auctioneering house there with Jacob Mordecai. A mason, Salomon was a major contributor in 1782 to the Congregation Mikveh Israel building, Philadelphia. He argued against a New Testament oath taken by officeholders in Pennsylvania and worked for political rights of Jews. Though a successful merchant, Salomon invested most of his money in Continental stocks and bonds, and his accounts showed a deficit at the time of his death. The newspaper obituary referred to him as "an eminent broker of this city… remarkable for his skill and integrity in his profession, and for his generous and human deportment." He left four children and a widow, who later married David Hilborn. By 1799 she was living in the Batavian Republic. Benjamin Gomez was appointed guardian of Salomon's son HAYM M. (1785–1858), and Joseph Andrews of his daughter DEBORAH (1783–1808). Exaggerated claims were made for Salomon's services to the American Revolution, largely as a point of Jewish apologetics. Without question, however, he was a vigorous patriot at great personal risk, and a competent financial servant of American independence and of some of its leaders.

[Leo Hershkowitz]

SALOMON, JOEL MOSES (1838–1912), Ereẓ Israel pioneer and founder of Petah Tikvah. Born in Jerusalem, Salomon was a descendant of a pupil of *Elijah the Vilna Gaon and settled in Ereẓ Israel in 1808. His grandfather, Solomon Zalman *Ẓoref, and his father, R. Mordecai Salomon, were leaders of the early Ashkenazi community in Jerusalem. Salomon was educated at yeshivot in Jerusalem and Lithuania. He studied printing at Koenigsberg, East Prussia, and, on his return to Jerusalem, he and several partners established a printing press. In March 1863, they printed the first issues of the first Ereẓ Israel periodical, *Ha-Levanon (spelled by them *Halbanon*), edited by Jehiel *Brill, to which Salomon contributed.

Salomon was active in the Ashkenazi community and strove to obtain for it a status equal to that of the Sephardi community and to make peace between its factions. He joined a group of young community leaders who wished to extend the scope of Jewish settlement in Jerusalem and even engage in agricultural work. Salomon was one of the founders of Jerusalem's Naḥalat Shivah quarter (1869), one of the first to be built outside the walls of the Old City, and participated in the establishment of Me'ah She'arim and other quarters. He took active part in the Yishuv Ereẓ Israel Association, which endeavored to purchase agricultural land for settlement. In 1877–78 he published the paper *Yehudah vi-Yrushalayim* ("Judea and Jerusalem"), in which he advocated plans for agricultural settlement and called for "action and deed." In the autumn of 1878 he was among the founders of Petaḥ Tikvah; after the first settlers were severely affected by malaria, he helped establish the nearby settlement of Yahud and to attract to it scholars, in order to establish a yeshivah there. After living there for seven years, he returned to Jerusalem and took up his public work for the institutions of the old *yishuv*.

BIBLIOGRAPHY: A. Yaari, *Goodly Heritage* (1958), index; M. Salomon, *Sheloshah Dorot ba-Yishuv* (1960[2]); *Sefer ha-Yovel le-Petaḥ Tikvah* (1929), 81–96; Y. Trivaks and E. Steinman, *Sefer Me'ah Shanah* (1938), 151–62; M. Smilansky, *Mishpaḥat ha-Adamah*, 1 (1954), 58–62; G. Kressel (ed.), *Yehudah vi-Yrushalayim* (1955), 13–39; B. Gat, *Ha-Yishuv ha-Yehudi be-Ereẓ-Yisrael 1840–1881* (1963), index.

[Yehuda Slutsky]

SALOMON, JULIUS (1853–1922), Danish archivist and historian of 19th-century Danish Jewry. Appointed librarian of Copenhagen's newly established municipal library in 1897, Salomon assembled an outstanding collection of material for scholarly research. From 1907 to 1917 he was assistant secretary to the upper house of the Danish Parliament.

In 1914, to celebrate the centenary of the royal decree which granted Danish Jewry full civil liberties, he published *Mindeskift i Anleding of Hundredaarsdagen for Anordningen of 29 Marts 1814*. Together with J. Fischer, he wrote *Bidrag til dansk-jødisk Historie 1820–1845* ("Contribution to Danish-Jewish History 1820–1845," 1918). He was a cofounder and editor of the Jewish journal *Tidsskrift for Jodisk Historie og Literature*, in which many of his studies of Danish-Jewish history appeared between 1917 and 1922.

[Herbert A. Strauss]

SALOMON-CALVI, WILHELM (1868–1941), German geologist. Salomon-Calvi was a member of the faculty of Heidelberg University from 1897, being appointed professor of geology in 1908. In 1934, despite the fact that he was a convert to Christianity, he left Germany and went to Turkey, where he became head of the geology department of the agriculture faculty at Ankara University.

His main work was connected with the Adamello-Marmolata and Gotthard massifs of the Alps, the tectonics of the rift valley of the Rhine, and the influence of magmatic upheavals on mountain building. Salomon-Calvi discovered thermal springs near Heidelberg and played a part in the groundwater exploration of Turkey. He was for many years editor of the *Geologische Rundschau* and an active member of the Heidelberg Academy.

[Leo Picard]

SALOMONS, SIR DAVID (1797–1873), first Jewish lord mayor of London. David Salomons was born in London, the son of Levi Salomons, a prominent Ashkenazi stockbroker. He became a member of the Stock Exchange in 1823 and a Lloyds underwriter in 1834. As a founder of the London and Westminster Bank in 1832, he was one of the few Jews to participate in the development of joint stock banking in Britain. An ardent fighter for Jewish emancipation, national and municipal, Salomons played a prominent part in the campaign to abolish the last Jewish disabilities. In 1835 he was elected a sheriff of London; after being twice refused, he was finally elected alderman in 1847; on both occasions special legislation was carried through to enable him to take the oath in a form acceptable to him. He became lord mayor of London in 1855 without any attempt being made to debar him. Elected to parliament in 1851, he took his seat in the House of Commons, but was forced to withdraw because he refused to recite the conclusion of the oath, "on the true faith of a Christian." After the amendments to the oath brought about the bill of 1858, he sat in parliament as a Liberal from 1859 until his death. His particular interests were social problems and Jewish welfare.

Salomons was active on the Jewish Board of Deputies (twice replacing Sir Moses *Montefiore temporarily as president) and took an interest in the Westminister Jews' Free School, Jews' Hospital, and the Society for Hebrew Literature. In 1869 he was made a baronet, being succeeded by his nephew SIR DAVID LIONEL SALOMONS (1851–1925), a pioneer of electrical engineering and automobiles.

BIBLIOGRAPHY: A.M. Hyamson, *David Salomons* (1939); Roth, England, 253–5, 262–3; J. Picciotto, *Sketches of Anglo-Jewish History* (1956^2), index; DNB, s.v. **ADD. BIBLIOGRAPHY:** ODNB online; C. Bermant, *The Cousinhood* (1971), index; G. Alderman, *The Jewish Community in British Politics* (1983), index.

[Vivian David Lipman]

SALOMONS, SIR JULIAN EMANUEL (1836–1909), Australian politician and jurist. Born in Birmingham, England, Salomons, the son of a merchant, emigrated to New South Wales in 1853 and worked first for a bookseller and then for a stock jobber. His mother's sister married Sir Saul *Samuel. Salomons became secretary of the Sydney Great Synagogue, and his ability as a public speaker led the synagogue to send him to England in 1858 to study law. In 1861 he returned to Sydney and was admitted to the bar. His keen powers of analysis and gift for submitting evidence rapidly led him to outstanding success. In 1868, he defended the Irish nationalist O'Farrell on a charge of shooting at the Duke of Edinburgh, a son of Queen Victoria. In 1869 Salomons was nominated a member of the New South Wales Legislative Council and in the same year became solicitor-general, representing the government in the Upper House. He resigned in 1870. Salomons was made chief justice of New South Wales in 1886, but resigned before even being sworn in because of the hostility of some members of the court. He was reappointed to the legislative council in 1887 and was vice president of the cabinet until 1889. He served as agent-general for the colony in London from 1889 to 1890 and again from 1899 to 1900. Originally opposing the campaign for federation of the Australian colonies, after the passage of the 1900 Constitution Act he became a strong supporter and took part in working out the compromise federation agreement which was embodied in the Imperial Decree of July 1900. He was knighted in 1891. Salomons always outspokenly defended his Jewish background.

ADD. BIBLIOGRAPHY: ADB, 6, 81–83; H.L. Rubinstein, Australia I, 377–79.

[Isidor Solomon / William D. Rubinstein (2nd ed.)]

SALOMONSEN, CARL JULIUS (1849–1924), Danish physician and bacteriologist. Born in Copenhagen, Salomonsen began his bacteriological investigations in 1873 as an assistant at the Copenhagen Municipal Hospital. He studied with Julius Friedrich Cohnheim (1839–84), Robert Koch (1843–1910), and Louis Pasteur (1822–95), and then introduced bacteriology as a scientific discipline into Denmark and was appointed lecturer on bacteriology at the University of Copenhagen. Salomonsen was professor of pathology from 1893 to 1920 and rector magnificus (1919–20). With the introduction of serotherapy and the discovery of diphtheria antitoxin, Salomonsen established a serotherapeutic laboratory in 1895 which became the foundation of the well-known Danish State's Serum Institute. Salomonsen was known as the last polyhistor at the University of Copenhagen. A great number of monographs on various branches of science afford evidence of his extensive knowledge and interests.

BIBLIOGRAPHY: *Dansk biografisk leksikon*, 20 (1941), 516–9.

[Julius Margolinsky]

SALONIKA (Thessaloniki), port located in N.E. Greece. Although historical evidence is scarce, it is believed that the Alexandrian Jews who arrived in ca. 140 B.C.E. were among the first Jews to settle in Salonika. Several sources give evidence of the existence and growth of the Jewish community during the Hellenistic and Roman periods. It is known that the apostle Paul preached for three consecutive Sabbaths in the synagogue of Salonika and that afterward he was forced to leave the town. The Romans granted autonomy to the community, whose members lived in a neighborhood near the port; therefore, the Jews had the opportunity to develop strong commercial ties with many parts of the world. The Jews of Salonika during the Roman and Byzantine periods had Greek names and spoke Greek.

Byzantine Period

After the splitting up of the Roman empire in 395 C.E., Salonika became the second most important city – after Constantinople – in the *Byzantine Empire. The Byzantine emperors in their efforts to "Christianize" their subjects were hostile to the Jewish communities in their territory and especially to the Jews of Salonika. Constantine the Great (306–37) and Theodosius II (408–50) enforced anti-Jewish laws. Justinian I

(527–65) and Heraclius (610–42) prohibited public fulfillment of the *mitzvot*. Basil I (866–86), the Macedonian, and Leo III (717–41), the Philosopher, forced the Jews to convert or leave the country. One of the very few emperors who acted favorably toward the Jews was Alexius I Comnenus, who during the First Crusade alleviated the taxes imposed upon them. During the same period, in 1096, the messianic movement that had started in Germany as a result of the persecutions in Mainz and had spread throughout Europe also reached Salonika. In 1169 Benjamin of Tudela visited Salonika and mentions that at that time there were about 500 Jews in the city. The sufferings of the Jews continued during the Latin Empire, which was established by the Crusaders (1204–61), as well as under Theodore Ducas Angelus, the despot of Epirus, who ruled the kingdom of Salonika from 1223 or 1224 to 1230.

During the second half of the 14th century Salonika attracted Jews, among the first being Hungarian Jews in 1376. Refugees from the 1391 riots in the Iberian Peninsula, mostly from Catalonia, found refuge in Salonika. In 1394, Jews migrated to the city from Provence. Like the Ashkenazim, the immigrants from the latter two regions formed their own synagogues. In 1423, Andromachos, the governor of Salonika, sold the city to the Venetians. The Venetians imposed heavy taxes on the Jews, who sent a special delegation to Venice to convince them to alleviate the burden. In spite of the hardships they suffered during the Byzantine period, the Jewish community of Salonika flourished: most of the Jews were merchants, engaging especially in the silk trade. Jews from Sicily, Venice, and other Italian cities migrated to Salonika and formed the synagogues Sicilia Yashan and Italia Yashan. There was also a veteran Romaniot community in the city. It is to be noted that the oldest synagogues of Salonika – Etz ha-Hayyim (which existed until the 1917 fire) and Etz ha-Da'at – date as early as 142 B.C.E., and until the arrival of the Iberian expulsees in 1492, they observed the Romaniot prayer rite and customs. Nevertheless, it is impossible to affirm the continuity of the community.

Turkish Conquest – Sephardi Immigration (15th–16th Centuries)

In 1430 Salonika was occupied by the Turks. At approximately the same time waves of Jewish immigrants started arriving in the town. In 1470 Bavarian Jews arrived in Salonika and formed the Ashkenazi community near the existing Romaniot community. The two communities differed in every aspect: clothing, eating habits, religious rites, prayer books, etc. The Ashkenazi community continued to exist until the beginning of the 20th century and the members were not assimilated into the other Jewish groups in Salonika. During the 15th and 16th centuries many Jewish expellees from Spain, Portugal, Italy, Sicily, and France, and refugees from North Africa, settled in Salonika. The largest numbers came in 1492–3 and 1536. Once in Salonika they founded separate synagogues ("congregations," *kahal kadosh*). These synagogues were named after their native countries or towns: Sicily, Calabria, Majorca, Lisbon, etc. Salonika also received Marranos who were expelled from Portugal. In 1514 the rabbinical triumvirate of Salonika issued a special *haskamah* regarding the Marranos as Jews as far as marriage and divorce were concerned, i.e., they practically regarded the Marranos as Jews in every respect. Additionally, in 1555, when the Marranos from Ancona were persecuted by Pope Paul IV, the Jewish merchants of Salonika decided to boycott Ancona and incited the Jewish merchants all over the *Ottoman Empire to follow them in their act. Nevertheless, as a result of political and economic reasons, the boycott did not succeed. There was some emigration from Salonika, but not to a great extent. The reasons for the emigration were plagues and fires that ravaged the town in 1543, 1545, and 1548. It is estimated that by 1553 there were 20,000 Jews in Salonika: the location of the city and the fact of being a port – constituting a key point on the international trade route between the East and the West – helped attract settlers. Merchandise from the East came to Salonika and from there was transferred to the West and vice versa. The Jewish immigrants maintained their relations with their coreligionists and colleagues in their countries of origin – France, Flanders, Egypt, and especially with the Italian ports, above all Venice. They therefore had a relative advantage in international trade, Salonika's location helping to exploit this advantage to the maximum. Troubles, of course, were not lacking, coming in the form of pirates and highwaymen. The Jews of Salonika also engaged in the crafts, and the city was famous for its Jewish weavers and silk and wool dyers. Nearby there were gold and silver mines in Siderokastro and many of the miners were Jews. Another craft was the manufacture of jewelry.

There were three main concentrations of Jews in Salonika: a quarter next to the city wall at the port, i.e., very close to the main artery of trade; the Francomahalla, i.e., the quarter of the "Francos" (foreigners from Europe), which presumably consisted of the elite of the Jewish inhabitants; and the quarter near the hippodrome, which was primarily Greek. Thus, the Jews did not live near the Turks, the rulers of the town. The organization of Jewish life in Salonika was of a special character. There were about 30 independent congregations who sometimes associated themselves as a voluntary body that took care of the common interests of the congregations. The *takkanot* issued by this body had to be accepted by every congregation to be valid for it. They included women's rights, ethical matters, religious matters, etc. These *takkanot* were based on the *takkanot* of Toledo (1305), Aragon (1335), and Castile (1432). The heads of each community were called *parnasim, memunim, nivrarim*, and *anshei ma'amad*, and were elected by all the members of each congregation. A committee elected by the *parnasim* of each congregation decided what proportion of taxes each congregation had to pay to the Turkish authorities, according to the number of members and their financial state. Women, orphans, and the poor were exempt from taxes. Each congregation had the following communal organizations: *Ḥevra kaddisha*, which was also called *Ḥevrat kevarim; gemilut ḥasadim* ("philanthropic organization"); *bikkur ḥolim* (sick wards); yeshivah; and *bet din*. The religious head of each *kahal kadosh* was the *marbiẓ torah* or *ḥakham shalem*, who was elected for a limited period of time and usually came from the town or country of origin of the *kahal kadosh*. The *marbiẓ torah* taught at the yeshivah of the congregation, was usually also the *dayyan* of the congregation, and delivered sermons on Sabbaths and holidays. Jews were forbidden by the *halakhah* to go to the Turkish authorities for matters pertaining to inheritance and *ketubbot*. The Talmud Torah Hagadol was formed in 1520 as a communal solution to education, since maintaining a school for each of the more than 30 *kahalim* became an insurmountable burden. It was a very large institution of 200 teachers, serving more than 10,000 students, and was not only a school but also had a communal treasury, library, printing press, a fabric industry, and its own prayer congregation. Salonika became a center of Torah learning and attracted many students from abroad. During the 16th century there were numerous important rabbis whose influence spread beyond the borders of Salonika and even the Ottoman Empire. Among the most prominent were: Joseph *Caro, the famous rabbinic decisor who lived in Salonika during the years 1532–34 and continued to work there on his monumental *Bet Yosef*; Solomon *Alkabetz, the author of *Lekhah Dodi*; Isaac *Adarbi, the author of *Divrei Rivot* and *Divrei Shalom*; Moses *Almosnino, the author of many important works including *Regimiento de la Vide* and inventor of an astrolabe; Moses de Boton (d. 1570) and his son Abraham de *Boton (d. 1592), the author of the responsa *Leḥem Rav* and *Leḥem Mishneh*, a commentary on Moses *Maimonides' 12th-century code of Jewish law, *Mishneh Torah*; and Samuel di *Medina ("RaSHdaM"), who left over 1,000 responsa and is considered among those halakhic authorities whose decisions both in *halakhah* and in practice can be relied upon. Salonika was also renowned as a center of Kabbalah. In addition to the rabbinical schools in Salonika in the 16th century, there was a *bet midrash* for *piyyutim* and singing, as well as a *bet midrash* for secular studies where medicine, natural sciences, astronomy, and other subjects were taught. Saadia Longo was a noted local poet, and Israel *Najara of Damascus, who was of Salonikan familial origin, spent time there. The physician *Amatus Lusitanus, who wrote treatises on circulation, taught in that above school of medicine when he settled in Salonika in 1558.

From 1515 the Jewish weavers of Salonika provided the Ottomans with cloth for army uniforms. Later the community could pay the mandatory poll tax (the jizya) as a protected minority religious group through this service. Thus, the Jewish community was recognized as "Musselemlik," recipient of "a freedom letter" which exempted it from other taxes and made it an autonomous administrative body directly under the Sublime Porte.

17th Century

At the beginning of the 17th century the city once again suffered from plagues and fires (1604, 1609, 1610, 1618, 1620, 1630, 1636, 1640, 1648), causing emigration; nevertheless, by the middle of the century there were about 30,000 Jews, or half of the total population of the town. Trade continued to flourish in spite of the drop in Venetian trade, which resulted from the loss of Crete to the Turks in 1669 and the riots caused by the janissaries at the same time. The Jews continued to export grain, cotton, wool, silk, and textiles. Many Jewish women worked in growing tobacco and its industry. At the same time fewer and fewer Jews worked in the crafts. Toward the end of the century a decline in commercial activities took place as a result of the decline of the Ottoman Empire, which had entered a state of continuous war with various countries and peoples. In spite of all these troubles Salonika remained a center of religious studies and *halakhah*. The famous halakhic authority R. Hayyim Shabbetai (1556–1647), author of the *Torat ha-Hayyim* and *Teshuvot Rav Ḥayyim Shabbetai*, lived in the city during the first half of the 17th century; other important religious authorities included Aaron Cohen Perahiyah, the author of *Parah Matteh Aharon*, David *Conforte, author of *Kore ha-Dorot.*, Eliya Judah Kovo, *av bet din* from 1670 and author of *Shenei Me'orot ha-Gedolim*, and the great talmudic scholar Aaron Ḥayyim ha-Kohen (1648–1698), author of the two-volume *Matteh Aharon*.

While in theory, the 1568 edict provided Salonikan Jewry protection from the whims of the local authorities, in practice local governors and government officials in the capital often ignored it. Dozens of firmans provide testimony as to how local authorities extorted additional sums from Salonikan Jewry for the poll tax. In 1636 the sultan ordered the execution of Rabbi Judah Covo when he underestimated the amount and quality of the cloth transmitted for tax payment from the Jews of Salonika to the authorities. Frequently, the Jews had to finance the sultan's wars by paying a special tax (avarish), and in 1646 a firman was issued for the rabbinical court judges of Salonika to issue a special tax to finance the war against Crete. The Jews, like other non-Muslims, were also frequently tormented by the Janissaries serving in the city.

The most influential event for the Jewish community in the 17th century was the appearance of the pseudo-messiah *Shabbetai Ẓevi. Expelled from *Izmir ca. 1651–54, he arrived in Salonika sometime afterward. In the beginning he was very well treated, and he preached in the Shalom synagogue; but later, when he married a Torah scroll, he was expelled after a decision made by the most important rabbis of the town. In 1666, after it was declared that he was the true messiah, he was arrested and given the choice by the sultan between death or conversion, he converted to Islam, and seven years after his death, in 1683, a group of believers – some 300 Jewish families – also converted to Islam. This sect was called the *Doenmeh (in Turkish "apostates") and their religious center was in Salonika, from which they spread to Constantinople and other places. *Shabbetai Ẓevi's passage from Salonika and the conversion in 1666 that ensued caused turmoil among the Jews in Salonika; the community consequently felt the need to unite. In 1680 the 30 congregations merged into one, with a supreme council composed of three rabbis and seven dignitaries. The three rabbis were elected for life and could not be replaced unless all three died. The first triumvirate was composed of Moses b. Hayyim Shabbetai, Abraham di Boton, and Elijah Kovo. Another important step was the reorganization of all the rabbinical courts into three bodies along the following lines: matrimonial; rents, possessions (*Ḥazakot*); and ritual matters (*issur ve-hetter*). Each *bet din* was composed of three rabbis who were elected by the triumvirate; they were known for their justness, and many Muslims and Greeks preferred to try the cases they had with Jews in these courts instead of the Turkish ones.

18th–19th Centuries

As the Ottoman Empire declined, the community's financial situation in Salonika worsened, and French merchants began to gain control of business interests. In 1720–30, Portuguese Marranos, called "Francos," immigrated to Salonika. Most of them were well-educated, and among them were merchants and bankers, who had been established in Italy and in particular in Livorno.

They did not pay taxes to the sultan since they were considered as interpreters of the consuls. In the beginning they also refused to pay the relevant taxes to the Jewish community, but after a decision by the central committee of the community, they acceded to the community's demands. The Jewish population at that time was between 25,000 and 30,000. Nevertheless, both religious and secular studies declined, and only study of the *Kabbalah still flourished.

Leading rabbis of the 18th century were Asher Ben Emanuel Salem, author of *Responsa Asher* (1748), Moses ben Solomon Amararillo, who wrote the 3-vol. *Responsa Devar Moshe* (1742, 1743, 1750), and Joseph ben David, author of *Responsa Bet David* (1740).

End of 19th–Beginning of 20th Centuries

Toward the second half of the 19th century the Turkish governors of the city initiated a further expansion of the town. A new port was built in 1889, which helped to develop trade. European culture and technology also began to flow into Salonika, and signs of this "Westernization" became apparent among the Jewish inhabitants as well. In 1873 the *Alliance Israélite Universelle established a school, and additional schools along Western standards were also built. By the end of the 19th century, the Alliance educational system in Salonika and other locations had produced a new generation of European-educated entrepreneurs; prepared students to learn medicine, pharmacy, law, and education; created secular literacy; and enticed its graduates to pursue journalism, theatrical performance, and even the publication of novels, historical works, and short stories. Physicians who had studied in Europe helped to eliminate epidemics.

In 1864, Juda Nehama printed *El Lunar*, the first Judeo-Spanish newspaper in Salonika. Though it was short-lived, it was a new format of communication. He brought to the attention of the public items about science, translations from noted rabbinic works, stories, historical pieces, folkloric stories, commercial issues, and the like.

The main Judeo-Spanish newspaper of Salonika, *La Epoca*, was founded in 1875 by Saadi Halevi Ashkenazi, who was an active publisher in Salonika and was a scion of a family that published many exegeses from Sephardi ḥakhamim in Salonika and elsewhere in the Ottoman Empire. This commercial and literary newspaper appeared twice a week until the summer of 1898, when it appeared also every Friday. The Halevis struggled financially to print the newspaper and keep it running, and it closed in 1912.

Parallel to Yiddish theater in the Ashkenazi world, the Sephardim of the Balkans had an active Judeo-Spanish theater. The Judeo-Spanish theater was the most active in Istanbul in the last quarter of the 19th century, but by the end of the 19th century it would be surpassed by the Salonikan stage. The first plays took place at the time of the opening of the local Alliance schools. The play *Saul* by Vittorio Alfieri was adapted into Judeo-Spanish by Joseph Errera, a local poet and train station manager who coordinated the dramatic productions of the organization. In 1882, *El Tiempo*, a translation of Racine's *Esther*, was also performed in Salonika, and in 1884, David Hassid adapted *L'Avare* of Molière into Judeo-Spanish for the local Salonikan stage. In the 20th century in Salonika, ideological movements like the Socialist Labor Federation, which essentially was a Jewish movement with 6,000 Sephardi Judeo-Spanish speaking members Jews, or Zionist movements and organizations like Betar, B'nai Mizrachi, Maccabi, Tiferet Israel, B'nai Zion, Cercle Max Nordau, and Po'alei Zion organized Judeo-Spanish theatrical productions. In 1914, the drama group of the Socialist Federation produced both Molière's *Garonudo* and the comedy *El hastron*. In 1919 the above group performed Tolstoy's *Resureccion*.

Some of the Judeo-Spanish plays performed by the religious Westernization helped in the development of trade. In Istanbul and Izmir, the Jews could not compete against the Greek-Orthodox and Armenian merchants, as the latter were much more numerous and powerful, but in Salonika, where the Jews were a majority, they attained great wealth, developed the city industrially, and controlled the port, the commerce, banking, the tobacco trade, and the artisan professions. As a result of their European education, Salonikan Jews represented big European firms as maritime, commercial, insurance, and tobacco agents. As Salonika became connected to Mitrovitsa (1871), Belgrade (1880), Vienna (1888), Monastir (1893), and Istanbul (1895) by rail, exports from the city increased greatly, but the local Jews also developed industrial infrastructures, with small factories supplying Macedonia and Ottoman markets with flannel, knitted goods, and wool and cotton products. Nevertheless, the export of cotton, hides, silkworms, and wool continued to represent an important part of its activity. The volume of the Salonikan port rose from one to two million tons between the years 1880 and 1912.

As a result of this Westernization, liberalism became paramount among the Jews of Salonika. Nevertheless, this did not undermine the traditional ways of the community, and many new yeshivot were established. The Ḥevrat Kadimah – for the spreading of the Hebrew language – was founded in 1899, and the well-known teacher Isaac *Epstein was brought to Salonika to teach Hebrew. In 1887 the rabbinical triumvirate was dismissed, and Jacob Kovo was appointed to the post of **ḥakham bashi* (chief rabbi). In 1900 there were approximately 80,000 Jews in Salonika (out of a total population of 173,000). In 1908, when the Young Turks rose against the Ottoman sultan Abdul Hamid II, Jews were among their numbers. One of the first actions of the Young Turks when they came to power was the recruiting of all non-Muslims into the Turkish army. As a result, many young Jews left Salonika and emigrated to the U.S. in order to avoid serving in the Turkish army.

The Jews and the Doenmeh in Salonika, in particular, and Jews in other parts of the Ottoman Empire were active in the Young Turk Movement, the Committee for Union and Progress. The religious minorities led by Muslim reformists united, and were optimistic that they could induce change and play a more integral part in the political life of the Ottoman Empire. Some Salonikan Jews like Emmanuel Carasso, Moise Cohen (who was born in Serres and later changed his name to Tekinalp to assert his patriotism to Turkey), the attorney Emmanuel Salem, Nissim Mazliah (initially from Izmir), and Sam Levy were active and were somewhat prominent in CUP, but their influence has been questioned by scholars. During the demonstration in Salonika at Freedom Square ushering in the Young Turk Revolution and declaring a constitution, Carasso was one of the four speakers. In 1908 Carasso was one of four Ottoman Jews elected to the Ottoman Parliament. He refused the appointment of minister of public works in 1910, but was elected to the Senate in 1912 (along with two other Jews).

Since the Jews believed that the new government was more liberal and tolerant than the former one, they openly organized socialist and syndicalist movements. Avraham Benaroya of Plovdiv, an active Bulgarian socialist and former student of Bochor Azaria, moved to Salonika in 1907 to try the challenge of organizing a socialist movement. The Socialist Labor Federation of Salonika became primarily a Jewish socialist movement of some 6,000 workers. Benaroya was ultimately exiled and imprisoned by both the Young Turk government and the Greek authorities after Salonika became part of Greece in 1912.

At the same time, the first Zionist organizations, Agudath Bnei Zion and Maccabee, appeared in Salonika. By the eve of World War II there were more than 20 Zionist organizations. The Young Turk revolution marked a new "golden" era for the Jews of Salonika, and they could be found in every profession: merchants, tobacco workers, lawyers, physicians, teachers, while the Jewish stevedores of Salonika were famous. On Sabbaths the town and the port came to a standstill since the Jews did not work.

When the Greek army entered the town in 1912, King George declared that Jews and all other minorities were to have the same rights as the Greek population. After the Balkan Wars (1912–13), Salonika could no longer be used as the port for the Balkan states. Nevertheless, trade continued to flourish during World War I since Salonika became a center for Allied soldiers. In 1917 a great fire destroyed most of the town, leaving some 55,000 Jews homeless. The Greek government, which followed a policy of Hellenizing the town, was ready to compensate the Jews whose houses had been destroyed, but it refused to let the Jews return to certain parts of the town, causing many of them to leave the country and emigrate to the U.S., France, Italy, and Alexandria. In 1923, a separate electoral college was set up for the Jews of Salonika (as well as for the Muslims in Thrace). While this enabled several Jews to be elected to parliament, they could not participate in national elections for the prime minister. This discriminatory system, which the Salonikan Jews unsuccessfully tried to fight internationally, continued until after the 1933 elections. In 1924 a law (no. 236) was enacted which forced all the inhabitants of Salonika to refrain from working on Sundays, thus causing another wave of emigration. Some went to Palestine, while most immigrated to Paris, where they founded an important community. In the 1931 Campbell riots, which accompanied the elections and were antisemitic in tone, an entire Jewish neighborhood was burned to the ground by hooligans of the EEE (Greek National Front) student movement and Asia Minor refugees, and most of the Jews who lived in the Campbell neighborhood emigrated afterward to Palestine. In the 1930s, 15,000–18,000 Salonikan Jews immigrated to Ereẓ Israel, and some 15,000 emigrated to France, mostly to Paris, but also to Marseilles and Lyons. In 1935 there were nearly 60,000 Jews in Salonika, and in spite of the drop in Jewish population from the turn of the century and all the riots and fires, the Jews continued to maintain their status in the economic activity of the town. The coup d'etat of Metaxas (1936) brought a change for the better in the lives of the Jews of Salonika.

[Jacov Ben-Mayor / Yitzchak Kerem (2nd ed.)]

Holocaust Period

The Salonikan Jewish community, which was the most prolific Sephardi cultural and religious center in the world and which dominated the city as a plurality or majority throughout most of 450 years since the Spanish expulsion, suffered greatly in the Holocaust. Its pre-World War II population of 56,000 was almost totally annihilated in the Holocaust – 98 percent of its Jewish community, 54,000 Sephardi Jews, died in Auschwitz-Birkenau, or during the long, exhausting Death March from January to May 1945. Salonika, the heart of the Sephardi world, was thus destroyed, and everyday Sephardi life in a natural setting would never return. By the time of the Holocaust, whether in Turkey, Jerusalem, the Americas, or elsewhere, Sephardi communities had assimilated into local cultures to such an extent that Judeo-Spanish Sephardi culture had nearly vanished as a vital and dominant force. Only in Salonika, where the community had an active Judeo-Spanish theater, a thriving Judeo-Spanish press, a vast secular and religious literature, and a wide array of Sephardi musical performers, ensembles, and choirs, was the Sephardi Judeo-Spanish culture an all-inclusive and self-perpetuating phenomenon.

World War II began for Greece and Greek Jewry on October 28, 1940, when Greek dictator Metaxas refused to surrender to Mussolini, and Italy attacked Greece from Albania. Greece fought valiantly to push back the Italians but finally capitulated on April 26, 1941. The Jews had a very active role in fighting for the Greek army, with 12,898 Jews conscripted for this special war effort. Four-thousand Jews fought on the front line in the Albanian campaign and in Macedonia, and 513 fought against the Germans. A total of 613 Jews were killed on both fronts, and at least 174 were from Salonika. Other Jewish casualties included 3,743 wounded, 1,412 of them severely. The Greek Macedonian Brigade 50 that fought in Albania was nicknamed the "Cohen Battalion," as it included many Jews from Salonika and other parts of Macedonia.

At first the German rule in Salonika was relatively quiet. The Jewish newspapers were closed, including *El Mesagero*, the last Judeo-Spanish newspaper to be published in traditional script. New pro-Nazi Greek newspapers, *Nea Evropi* and *Apoyevmatini*, appeared and spread vehement antisemitic sentiment. Jews were forced to guard train lines against sabotage by the resistance, and Jews had to give rooms in their homes to German soldiers. There was little terror against the Jews and very few restrictions. As the Germans neglected the Greek economy, there was mass starvation in 1941–42, with as many as 60 Jews dying each day in Salonika. The Rosenberg Commission entered Salonika in mid-June 1941 and confiscated massive amounts of Jewish books, documents, Torah scrolls, and religious artifacts, taking them back to the Nazi Institute for Jewish Research in Frankfurt. In the early 1990s, some of the communal documents from Salonika and Athens appeared as part of confiscated German documents in the Osobyi Archives in Moscow.

On July 11, 1942, the Germans assembled 9,000 Jewish males between the ages of 18 and 45 for forced labor. Waiting on the Sabbath in their holiday clothes, they were compelled to do humiliating calisthenics and many were beaten. Some 4,000 Jews were recruited for grueling road work from August to December 1942. The Jews were released from forced labor after paying an exorbitant ransom, but the Germans ordered the destruction of the 500-year-old Sephardi cemetery with its half-million graves.

From the beginning of German occupation in Salonika on April 9, 1941, until the end of the deportations of Salonikan Jewry to Birkenau from March 15, 1943, to August 1943, as many as 3,000–5,000 Jews fled Salonika, mostly by train, to the temporarily "safe" Italian zone below the Platona line (below Katerini and to the north of Larisa in the Thessaly region) and sought refuge in Athens. While most Salonikan Jewish families hesitated to leave their familiar surroundings and appear not to have known what was happening under German occupation in northern Europe, there were many Jews who were politically astute and succeeded in finding a way to flee.

At least 800 Salonikan Jews went to the mountains of Macedonia in early 1943 to join the ELAS Communist- leaning resistance movement. Some were organized Communists, but most just went to save themselves and became motivated to fight against the Germans. More would have gone if the large nuclear traditional Salonikan Sephardi families would have agreed to split up, and others were hesitant due to the rugged life in the mountains or due to the association of ELAS with the militant Communist movement. While ELAS opened its ranks to Jewish men and women as fighting soldiers or in the services, and harbored entire Jewish families in its village and mountain strongholds, the rightist royalist movement generally did not admit Jews, and there were only four known cases of Jews serving in that movement, which was most active in western Greece in Epirus. The Italian diplomats were lenient in consenting to protect Italian Jewish nationals, those of Italian descent, or others whom they could save by registering their applications to begin the citizenship process. They actively saved some 800 Jews in such a manner and transported them by car or Italian military train to the free Italian zone. They arrived in Athens and remained safe there until the Germans replaced Italian rule in September 1943. The local Spanish diplomats with their status of a neutral country tried to delay deportation for their nationals, but on August 2, 1943, a group of 367 Jews was deported to Bergen-Belsen. They stayed there under preferential conditions until they were transferred in February 1944 to Barcelona, and then on to Morocco and to Ereẓ Israel. Some 144 Jewish Spanish nationals had escaped to Athens.

At the end of January 1943, the Nazis created three distinct neighborhood ghettos where there were large concentrations of Jews: Kalamaria (encompassing almost half the city to the east and where most of the Jews lived), Singrou (west of the White Tower) in the central area of the city, and Vardar/Agia Paraskevi (near the old train station in the western part of the city). Jews living outside these neighborhood ghettos were transferred in, and several families had to occupy a given residence. From these ghettos, Jews were transferred to the Baron Hirsch transit camp, where they arrived at least a day before deportation and often several weeks before, and waited for the transport which took them mainly to Birkenau (Auschwitz II). The crowded and dark cattle cars departing every few days took on anywhere from 1,000 to 4,000 Jews at a time, but most of the trains carried 2,200 to 2,800 Jews. The Salonikan Jewish population was so large that the deportations took several months. One deportation was sent to Treblinka, and there might have been one to Sobibor in view of the presence of a group of Salonikan Jews there.

At least 37,000 Salonikan Jews were gassed upon their arrival in Auschwitz-Birkenau, but the figure may be several thousand higher. There was a large Salonikan contingent of some 2,000 men in Buna (Auschwitz III) who worked in the I.G. Farben factory laying cables and digging. The Salonikan middleweight boxing champion Jacko *Razon organized boxing matches in the camp for Sunday's half-rest day entertainment, and as a boxer worked in the kitchen and daily smuggled out a 25-liter soup barrel, which served as an extra ration at night for fellow Salonikans and other Jewish inmates. In Auschwitz, the Salonikan Jews were a main part of the work force throughout 1943 and 1944 since they numbered some 11,000. Jacko *Maestro, a crafty young Salonikan Sephardi youth who spoke German, became *Arbeitsdienst* coordinator in Auschwitz, assigning the daily work schedule to some 16,000 camp inmates and saving numerous lives by finding easier work places for the weak and the sick.

As a large part of the work force in Birkenau, the Salonikan Jews were also a large part of the **Sonderkommando*, the work group that labored by the gas chambers and pulled out the dead bodies and burned them in the crematorium. Since the prisoners in this *kommando* were witnesses to the German death process, they were executed after working three months in the gas chambers. When a general camp revolt was canceled, the Greek *Sonderkommando* Jews decided to revolt themselves, joined by the French and Hungarian Jews as well as by 19 Russian Jewish soldiers. Isaac Kabelli estimated that 135 Greek Jews participated in the revolt in Crematoria III and IV, which started at about 2:15–2:20 P.M. on October 7, 1944. After attacking two German guards in Crematorium IV and taking their weapons, a group of 25 Greek prisoners ran to Crematorium III. During the furious battle there, numerous German guards were killed when the Germans from outside shot at the prisoners inside. Historian Steven Bowman noted that some 20 guards were killed. Isaac Baruch, a Salonikan Jew of Skopjian familial descent, placed a bomb in the furnace of Crematorium III. The explosion demolished the building. Before the Germans killed all of the prisoners in the crematorium, the prisoners sang a tune from the Greek partisans and finally the Greek national anthem. The *Sonderkommando* in Crematorium II did not revolt, since at the beginning of the uprising the Germans acted quickly and locked up all of them in a crowded room for the day.

Auschwitz Salonikan Jewish prisoners, as foreigners who were unfamiliar with Polish Jewry and Warsaw, were sent to clean up the destroyed Warsaw Ghetto and establish a forced labor camp there. The Salonikan Jews were the first group sent from Auschwitz to Warsaw in August 1943 and physically built the camp. A second group of Salonikans was sent in October 1943. Together, the Salonikan Jews numbered over 1,000, and they were the largest group of any origin in the Genshovka camp. A Salonikan Jew, Shaul Senor, who had previously made aliyah to Ereẓ Israel and returned to Salonika to organize further immigration under the pioneering Heḥalutz movement, tried to escape from Warsaw, was caught, and executed a month later on June 25, 1944, in front of all the Salonikan and other Jewish prisoners. His death inspired his Sephardi brethren not to give up hope and continue their struggle to survive despite the typhus, meager food, and terrible conditions. Most of the Salonikan and other Jewish prisoners were cleared out of Warsaw by foot at the end of July 1944 and headed toward Germany.

The Greek Jews – particularly the Salonikans but not exclusively – were victims of medical experiments in Auschwitz-Birkenau. Of 400 known experiments, the Greek Jews constituted about a quarter of the victims. Pregnant and single women had cancers implanted in their uterus, men had testicles removed, most twins did not survive, and others were frozen or victims of other heinous Nazi war crimes. The pregnant Salonikan Aliza Sarfati Baruch survived her two operations, was assisted in the infamous Auschwitz Bloc 10 by a Jewish doctor named Dr. Shmuel who later mysteriously disappeared, and miraculously bore children in Israel after the war; but most women, if they survived, never were able to conceive.

The deportations in Salonika, protested by Greek Archbishop Damaskinos and heads of national professional unions, signaled to most other Greek Jewish communities that the same terrible fate awaited them.

[Yitzchak Kerem (2nd ed.)]

Contemporary Period

After the war, survivors of the Salonikan community, together with remnants of smaller communities, concentrated in Salonika. As the Jews of the other communities spoke Greek, Ladino has all but disappeared as a spoken language in the community. The number of Jews fell from about 2,000 in 1946 to about 1,500 in 1971 as a result of emigration to Israel and, to a lesser degree, other countries. In 1971 there was an organized community, but only two synagogues were in use. Religious services took place on festivals, and there was a *minyan* for Sabbath services only. The children of the community studied in Greek schools, but provisions were made for Jewish education, which was handled mostly by teachers from Israel. In addition, there was a youth club and the *Maccabi organization. In the 1980s, the population of the community was around 800, but by the early 21st century it had grown to 1,100 due to increased family size. In the 1980s, the synagogue on Irakleon Street was renovated, and a Jewish study center and library was set up on an upper floor of the same office building. In the mid-1990s, Andreas Sephiha became community president and placed emphasis on cultural proliferation, Jewish religious continuity, and education. Rabbi Dayan was brought over from Israel and later replaced by the Athenian-born and Israeli-educated Mordechai Frizis. In 2005 the Jewish community had an active youth center and pedagogical resource staff and center, and employed two full-time rabbis. The elderly were cared for at the Modiano Old Age Home, and the community also ran a nursery school, elementary school with six grades, and a summer camp for all the Jewish youth of Greece. A new Jewish museum was founded at the turn of the century.

The major collections of archival material on the community of Salonika are located in Jerusalem, at the Central Archives of the Jewish People and Ben-Zvi Institute, and in the Instituto Arias Montano in Madrid. Until Greece took over the city in 1912, the great majority of the community's documents were written in Ladino in Oriental script; later, Greek became the language of use.

The Jews of Salonika constituted an important source of *aliyah*, particularly after World War I. They were active among the Sephardi community in Palestine, and played an important role in the construction of Tel Aviv. Among the notable families from Salonika were the Florentin, *Recanati, Molcho, and Uzziel families. Leon Recanati founded the Israel Discount Bank, which later developed into one of the most important banks in the country, and the Florentin quarter of Tel Aviv is a manifestation of the initiative of immigrants from Salonika.

Salonikan Jews made a unique contribution to the penetration of Jews into seamanship in Erez Israel. As early as 1914, Izhak *Ben-Zvi was sent to Salonika to encourage Jewish seamen to settle in Erez Israel, but the outbreak of World War I destroyed the plan. In 1924 a group of more than 40 fishermen immigrated to Palestine. They initially settled in Acre, but the group dispersed after the Arab riots in 1929, principally in Haifa and Tel Aviv. As a result of Abba *Khoushi's visit to Salonika in 1933, 300 seamen, stevedores, and porters and their families immigrated to Palestine and settled in Haifa. It was thanks to them that Jewish labor penetrated into the port of Haifa. Over the years other families from Salonika joined them. In 1936 some of them moved to Tel Aviv and laid the foundations of the port there. A moshav ovedim of Greek settlers, some of them from Salonika, was established at Zur Moshe in the Sharon Plain in 1937.

[Chaim Yahil / Yitzchak Kerem (2nd ed.)]

Hebrew Printing

Early in the 16th century (c. 1512), Don Judah *Gedaliah and his son (Moses) and daughter arrived in Salonika after fleeing from Portugal. Gedaliah had previously managed the printing press of Eliezer Toledano in *Lisbon; he brought at least some of the latter's typographical material with him, and later he had some new types cut. Many of his productions, in the main liturgical works, have been lost, but some important items have survived: a Pentateuch with Onkelos and Rashi (1513); the first edition of Jacob ibn Ḥabib's *Ein Ya'akov* (1515–23); parts of Hagiographa with Rashi (1515); the tractate *Yoma*; Tur, *Orah Ḥayyim*; a Pentateuch with Rashi's and Nahmanides' commentaries (1520); *Yalkut Shimoni* on Prophets and Hagiographa (1521); and Solomon *Molcho's sermons (1529). In 1525, Moses *Soncino left Rimini (Italy) for Salonika, and in 1526 he issued the *Yalkut* on the Pentateuch and a *maḥzor* of the Catalonian rite in 1527. His kinsmen Gershom and Eliezer arrived – also from Rimini – in 1526 and printed David Kimhi's *Sefer ha-Shorashim*, together with Abraham Bedersi's dictionary of biblical synonyms, *Ḥotam Tokhnit* (1527), and a *maḥzor* of the Aragonian rite (1529), before moving on to Constantinople.

The Italian Soncino printing house of Rabbi Gershon Soncino established a branch in Salonika in 1527 and later in Istanbul in 1530. The famous dictionary *Sefer Shoreshim* of Rabbi David Kimḥi was published in Salonika, but due to epidemics and fires, the printing house closed.

Beginning in 1543 with Spanish refugees Solomon and Joseph *Jabez, a great variety of Hebrew books were printed in Salonika, among them a *maḥzor* of the Ashkenazi rite (1551–55). For a time, the enterprise had to be transferred to *Adrianople (1555). Eventually Solomon Jabez went to Constantinople, whereas Joseph returned to Salonika in about 1560 and until about 1572 printed many works, notably a series of Talmud tractates based on the Bomberg and Giustiniani editions; works by Moses *Almosnino; and translations into Judeo-Spanish and Provencal of parts of the Bible and prayer books. When he left, his typographical material was bought by David b. Abraham Azubib, who was active in printing from 1578 to 1588.

Shabbethai Mattathias *Basevi (d. 1601) acquired the Jabez press, and he and his son issued various works until 1605, including a *Midrash Rabbah* (1594), an *Ein Ya'akov*, and a *Shulḥan Arukh Oraḥ Ḥayyim* (1595). The Salonika *talmud torah* administration printed a *maḥzor* of the Catalonian rite in 1695, and some Talmud tractates in 1707. This press passed through various hands in the 18th century when many works were printed. During the time of Sultan Mustafa, the printing house of Raphael Yehuda Kalay and Mordecai Naḥman printed Rabbi David Pardo's *Le-Menaẓe'aḥ le-David* and *Minḥah le-David*, as well as Rabbi Eliyahu Mizraḥi and Rabbi Eliyahu Ben Ḥayyim's *Mayim Amukim* (1805), and more. Between 1814 and 1941, eight more Hebrew printers worked in Salonika, among them the presses of Isaac Jahon; the Gemilut Hasadim Society, which was founded about 1870 and printed selections from the Zohar; and the Etz ha-Ḥayyim Society, which was founded about 1875 and printed *maḥzorim*.

Bezalel Halevi Ashkenazi came from Amsterdam to Salonika (ca. 1738) and continued his family's tradition of printing. In his printing press, he published many books of responsa, derushim, and exegeses in Hebrew and Ladino. His descendants continued his printing activities. Saadi Halevi Ashkenazi (1820–1903) published the Judeo-Spanish newspaper *La Epoca* (1876–1912) in Judeo-Spanish Rashi script, but also coplas (a type of Judeo-Spanish balladry for holidays), and other ballads and *piyyutim* in Judeo-Spanish and Hebrew. The printing house existed until it was destroyed in the 1917 fire.

Leah Bornstein Makovetski noted the existence of 31 works of rabbinic *derashot* published in Salonika between 1750 and 1900. The last known publication of Hebrew rabbinic exegesis in Salonika was Rabbi Jacob Hanania Kovo's *Kokhav me-Ya'akov* in 1935.

BIBLIOGRAPHY: J. Nehama, *Histoire des Israélites de Salonique*, 5 vols. (1935–59); M. Molho and J. Nehama, *In Memoriam; Hommage aux victimes Juives des Nazis en Grèce*, 3 vols. (1948–53); idem, *Sho'at Yehudei Yavan 1941–1944* (1965); T.B. Ashkenazi, *Saloniki ha-Yehudit, Ḥissulah shel Ir va-Em be-Yisrael*, 1 (1960); *Saloniki Ir va-Em be-Yisrael* (1967); I.S. Emmanuel, *Histoire des Israélites de Salonique* (1936); idem, *Gedolei Saloniki le-Dorotam* (1936); idem, *His-*

toire de l'Industrie des Tissus des Israélites de Salonique (1935); idem, *Matzevot Saloniki*, 2 vols. (1936–68); Rosanes, Togarmah; F. Doelger, in: *Joshua Starr Memorial Volume* (1953), 129–33; C. Roth, in: *Yalkut ha-Mizraḥ ha-Tikhon*, 2 (1950), 114–8; idem, in: *Commentary*, 10 (1950), 49–55; M. Molho, in: *Sefarad*, 9 (1949), 107–30; idem, in: *Sinai*, 28 (1951), 296–314; idem, in: *Homenaje a Millás-Vallicrosa*, 2 (1956), 73–107; I.R. Molho, *Tor ha-Zahav be-Toledot Saloniki ba-Dorot ha-Aḥaronim* (1948); idem, in: *Zion*, 11 (1946), 150ff.; I.R. Molho and A. Amarijlio, in: *Sefunot*, 2 (1958), 26–60; Scholem, Shabbetai Sevi, index; idem, in: D.J. Silver (ed.), *In the Time of Harvest* (1963), 368–86; R. Hilberg, *Destruction of the European Jews* (1961), 442–8; A.E. Bakalopoulos, *History of Thessalonika* (1963); David ben Avraham Pipano, *Hagor ha-Efod* (1925). HEBREW PRINTING: Ḥ.D. Friedberg, *Toledot ha-Defus ha-Ivri be-Italyah…* (1956^2), 130–42; A. Elmaleh, in: *Ha-Tor*, 4 (1923–4), nos. 12ff; also as: *Le-Toledot ha-Yehudim be-Saloniki* (1924); M.J. Covo, *Etudes Saloniciennes* (1928); J. Rivkind, in: KS, 1 (1924), 294–302; 3 (1926), 171–3; 6 (1930), 383–5; A. Yaari, *ibid.*, 7 (1931), 290–308; 16 (1940), 374–81. **ADD. BIBLIOGRAPHY:** D. Benvenisti, *Yehudei Salonika be-Dorot ha-Aḥaronim* (1973); R. Atal, *Yahadut Yavan, mi-Gerush Sefarad ve-ad Yameinu, Bibliografiyah* (1984), with later supplement; Y. Kerem and B. Rivlin, "Salonika," in: *Pinkas ha-Kehillot Yavan* (1999), 217–299; A. Matkovski, *A History of the Jews in Macedonia* (1982), 58; M. Ben-Sasson et al. (eds.), *Studies in a Rabbinic Family, the de Botons* (1998); A. Nar, "Social Organization and Activity of the Jewish Community in Thessaloniki," in: I.K. Hassiotis (ed.), *Queen of the Worthy, Thessaloniki, History, and Culture* (1997), 266–295; Y. Kerem, "The Deunme: From Catholicism to Judaism to Islam," in: C. Meyers and N. Simms (eds.), *Troubled Souls, Conversos, Crypto-Jews, and Other Confused Jewish Intellectuals from the Fourteenth through the Eighteenth Century* (2001), 150–63; A. Nar, "The Jews of Thessaloniki March through Time," in: *Justice* (Spring 1999), 9–13; E. Benbassa and A. Rodrigue, *Sephardi Jewry, A History of the Judeo-Spanish Community, 14th–20th Centuries*, 81; S. Salem, "Portraits of Famous Jewish Lawyers and Jurists in Greece," in: *Justice* (Spring 1999), 14–21; Y. Kerem, "The Talmud Tora of Salonika; A Multi-faceted Changing Institution from the 16th Century Traditionalism until Modern Political Zionism," in: Aviva Doron (ed.), *The Culture of Spanish Jewry, Proceedings of the First International Congress, Tel Aviv, 1–4 July 1991* (1994), 159–68; L. Bornstein-Makovestky, "Halakhic Literature in Salonika between 1750–1900," in: *Ladinar* II (2001), 15–35 (Hebrew); Y. Kerem, "Forgotten Heroes: Greek Jewry in the Holocaust," in: M. Mor (ed.), *Crisis and Reaction: The Hero in Jewish History* (1995), 229–38; J.M. Landau, *Tekinalp, Turkish Patriot* (1984), index; M. Mazower, *Salonica… 1430–1950* (2004); R.Lewkowicz, *The Jewish Community of Salonika* (2006).

SALONS. For almost two centuries, salons hosted by Jewish women were important sites for cultural performances and discussion of music, art, literature, philosophy, and politics. Until recently, such social gatherings had seemed an isolated moment in Jewish history: Emerging in Berlin in the last decades of the 18th century, they had reached their peak around 1800. The Prussian capital saw at least 17 Jewish homes that consistently welcomed guests to open houses, usually for tea. After the Prussian defeat at the hands of Napoleon in 1806, the importance of these informal institutions was believed to have diminished. But in fact this was not the end of the story. This model of artistic and intellectual conviviality, persistently arising at a site in urban society connected with the feminine and the Semitic and bringing together individuals of diverse ethnic, religious, and social backgrounds, reappeared after 1815 and continued to be influential throughout the 1820s. Its reverberations survived into the late 19th and early 20th centuries with the emergence of comparable Jewish salons in Paris, London, and Rome. Versions of the salons survived World War II in cities as far away from Berlin as New York City and Los Angeles.

A 2005 exhibition at the Jewish Museum in New York City, entitled "Jewish Women and their Salons: The Power of Conversation," represented the entire history of this social and communicative experiment. To the well-known names of early salonnières such as Rahel Levin *Varnhagen and Henriette *Herz of Berlin, Fanny von Arnstein and Caecilie von Eskeles of Vienna, historians now add Geneviève Straus, a friend of Marcel Proust in Paris; Ada Leverson, Oscar Wilde's friend in London; Berta Zuckerkandel of Vienna along with her sister Sophie Clemenceau in Paris; Margherita Sarfatti in Rome; and the American writer Gertrude *Stein who resided most of the time in Paris. In New York City, Florine Stettheimer opened her house to regular cultural gatherings, while in Los Angeles Salka Viertel provided her co-emigrants from Germany and Austria with an environment in which to discuss ideas, creative achievements, and the events of the day. The intellectual, social, artistic, as well as political achievements of these women cannot be overestimated.

BIBLIOGRAPHY: M. Susman, *Frauen der Romantik* (1929; 1996); I. Drewitz, *Berliner* (1979); D. Hertz, *Jewish High Society in Old Regime Berlin (1988);* P. Wilhelmy, *Der Berliner Salon im 19. Jahrhundert (1989);* P. Seibert, *Der literarische Salon* (1993); H. Schultz (ed.), *Salons der Romantik* (1997); B. Hahn, *The Jewess Pallas Athena. This Too a Theory of Modernity* (2005); E. Bilski and E. Braun (eds.), *Jewish Women and their Salons* (2005).

[Barbara Hahn (2nd ed.)]

SALONTA (Hung. **Nagyszalonta**), town in W. Romania: within Hungary until the end of World War I and between 1940 and 1944. The first Jews settled there around 1840, but it was only after the abolition of residence restrictions in 1848 that the Jewish population increased. An organized community was established in 1850, when the first synagogue was also erected. A *ḥevra kaddisha* was established in 1859. A large and magnificent synagogue (still standing) was opened in 1886. The community school functioned between 1869 and 1936; until the end of World War I, the language of instruction was Hungarian. The cultural character and the everyday language of the local Jews was mostly Hungarian, with very little Yiddish being spoken. From 1882 the rabbis of the Great Synagogue preached exclusively in this language, even after Salonta passed to Romania. After the schism within Hungarian Jewry of 1868–69 (see *Hungary), the community joined the Neologist organization. In 1927 a few members founded an Orthodox community. Prominent among the rabbis of Salonta was Abraham Isaac Nébel (1887–1967; d. in Jerusalem), who was appointed rabbi of the town in 1925. The small Orthodox community was headed by Nathan Brisk, who perished in the

Holocaust From 1885 the community also served as the official center for the Jews living in 15 villages in the vicinity. The Jewish-Zionist cultural activity initiated by R. Nébel caused some agitation in this assimilated community; but though it gave rise to ramified Zionist activities, it did not diminish the Jews' Hungarian acculturation and sense of belonging.

The Jewish population numbered 534 (42% of the total) in 1891; 843 in 1910; 740 (4.8%) in 1930; 593 (3.7%) in 1941.

The Jews of Salonta were involved in the processing of the agricultural produce of the entire region, which was then sold throughout the country and even exported. Many Jews were landlords and also involved in agricultural production.

After 1919 the majority of the Jewish population continued to support the Hungarians, even in the face of the conflict between the former rulers, the Hungarians, and the new ones, the Romanians.

Holocaust and Contemporary Periods

Under Hungarian rule, Jewish men were drafted into labor battalions in 1942–43, most of them perishing. In the summer of 1944, the Jews in Salonta were deported via Oradea to *Auschwitz. After the war the survivors returned to the town and reorganized the community. They numbered 190 in 1947. Monuments in memory of those who had perished were erected opposite the synagogue and in the cemetery. The number of Jews in Salonta dwindled to ten families in 1971, as a result of emigration to Israel and other countries, and was further reduced by the turn of the century.

BIBLIOGRAPHY: A. Nébel (ed.), *Jubileumi emlékkönyr* (1936); *Magyar Zsidó Lexikon* (1929), 634–5.

[Yehouda Marton / Paul Schveiger (2nd ed.)]

SALSBERG, JOSEPH B. (1903–1998), Canadian labor leader, politician, journalist. Born in Lagev, Poland, Salsberg was 11 years old when he arrived in Toronto with his parents in 1913. He had only a few years of elementary education before he left school to help support his family. As a youth, he was associated with the Po'alei Zion movement, but, angered at the working conditions in the clothing manufacturing industry in Toronto, he joined the Communist Party in 1926 and was active in the trade union movement as Canadian vice president of the Hatters' International Union. During the 1930s he was a labor organizer for the Communist-affiliated Workers' Unity League. A skilled orator in both English and Yiddish, in 1938 he was elected alderman in a heavily Jewish inner-city Toronto neighborhood and in 1943 to the Ontario legislature for the Communist Labor Progressive Party. Salsberg was outspoken in his support for human rights and helped pass breakthrough anti-discrimination legislation He was defeated by Conservative Alan *Grossman in the 1955 elections.

In 1956 Salsberg visited the Soviet Union to undertake an investigation of the condition of the Jews in the U.S.S.R. He interviewed major Soviet leaders, including Nikita Khrushchev, and became convinced that there was little hope of recognition of the cultural rights of Soviet Jewry, and that antisemitic views were deeply entrenched through all layers of Soviet leadership. On his return to Canada, he wrote a long series of articles on his Russian visit in the left-wing Canadian Jewish Weekly, *Vokhenblat*. In 1957 Salsberg left the Communist Party and the United Jewish People's Order, which was Communist-inspired, taking a block of former Jewish Communist supporters. He went on to help to set up the left-leaning New Fraternal Jewish Association. A reborn Zionist, Salsberg was active on behalf of Israel and in fostering the Yiddish language. For many years Salsberg wrote a popular column for the weekly *Canadian Jewish News*.

[Ben Kayfetz (2nd ed.)]

SALT. Considered the most common and essential of all condiments, salt plays an essential role in Jewish life, ritual, and symbolism. It was plentiful in Ereẓ Israel, with inexhaustible quantities being found in the area of the Dead Sea. Its first mention in the Bible is in reference to Lot's wife turning into a pillar of salt (Gen. 19: 26).

Salt was an essential requisite for all sacrifices. The possibility that the verse "with all thy sacrifices shalt thou offer salt" (Lev. 2:13) may, in fact, refer only to the meal-offering mentioned in the context, is denied by the Talmud (Men. 20a) which lays it down that the statement applies to all sacrifices. The significance of this injunction seems evident from the prohibition, in the same context, of honey and leaven to be used in sacrifices. Honey and leaven symbolize fermentation and subsequent decay and decomposition; salt is a preservative. The idea of permanence is the basis of the "covenant of salt" mentioned on various occasions in the Bible. The rights of the priests to their share of the offerings is "a due for ever, an everlasting covenant of salt" (Num. 18:19), and Abijah, king of Judah, assures Jeroboam, who had seceded from the House of David, that God has given the kingdom to the House of David by "a covenant of salt" (II Chron. 13: 5). It is in this sense that the passage in Ezra (4:14), in which the enemies of the returned exiles protest their loyalty to the king of Persia "because we eat of the salt of the palace" is to be understood as an expression of abiding loyalty to the palace, and not as the Authorised Version's "maintenance of the palace." The extent to which salt was used in the sacrifices may be seen in the statement in Josephus (Ant. 12: 140) that Antiochus the Great made a gift of 375 medimni (bushels) of salt to the Jews for the Temple service, and there was a special Salt Chamber in the Temple (Mid. 5:3).

The cleansing and hygienic power of salt is reflected in Elisha's act of purifying the bad waters of Jericho by casting salt into the springs (II Kings 2:20, 21), and in the custom of rubbing newly born infants with salt (Ezek. 16:4). On the other hand, it was known that salinity in soil caused aridity (Deut. 29:22; Job 39:6), and when Abimelech captured and destroyed Shechem, he "sowed it with salt" as a sign that it should not be rebuilt (Judg. 9:45).

The importance of salt as a condiment is also stressed in the Bible. Job asks rhetorically whether "that which hath no savor be eaten without salt" (6:6), and Ben Sira includes salt among the nine essentials of life (Ecclus. 39:26). Salt was an essential element of the Jewish table, and it became customary to put salt on the bread over which grace before meals was recited. A Yiddish proverb has it that "no Jewish table should be without salt" which is in accordance with the homily that makes one's table "an altar before the Lord" (cf. Avot 3:4). The ability of salt to absorb blood (Ḥul. 113a) is the basis of the important laws of kashering meat so that all blood be removed (see *Dietary Laws). Salt of Sodom (*Melaḥ Sedomit*) was particularly potent, having an admixture probably of the acrid potassium chloride of the Dead Sea. Its presence in common salt ("one grain in a *kor* of salt"), and the harmful effect it might have on the eyes, caused the custom of *mayim aḥaronim*, the washing of one's hands after a meal, to be instituted, in addition to the statutory washing before meals (Ḥul. 105b). There is a difference of opinion as to whether this washing of the hands is obligatory or merely advisable. *Tosafot* (loc. cit.) lays it down that, since salt of Sodom does not exist in France, the custom of *mayim aḥaronim* did not obtain there. Despite this ruling, the retention of the custom is widespread today. Salt of Sodom was also an ingredient of the incense used in the Temple during the period of the Second Temple (Ker. 6a).

In modern Israel the custom has developed for the mayor of Jerusalem or the elders of the city to greet distinguished visitors with an offering of bread and salt at the entrance of the city, and not with bread and wine as Melchizedek, king of Salem (Jerusalem), greeted Abraham (Gen. 14:18). There is no rabbinic authority for this practice. Philo (Jos. 35: 210), however, states that Joseph invited his brethren to a meal of "bread and salt" (cf. Gen. 43: 16, 31), and among the ancient Arabs it was the custom to seal a covenant with bread and salt.

BIBLIOGRAPHY: Loew, in: *Jewish Studies G.A. Kohut* (1935), 429–62 (inc. bibl.); EM, 4 (1962), 1053.

[Louis Isaac Rabinowitz]

SALTEN, FELIX (originally **Siegmund Salzmann**; 1869–1945), Austrian novelist, playwright, and critic, creator of "Bambi." Born in Budapest, Salten studied in Vienna, where he became a writer of feuilletons for the *Neue Freie Presse*, continuing the high standard of his friend and predecessor, Theodor *Herzl. As a dramatic critic, he made and unmade literary and stage reputations and his best essays on the theater were collected in *Schauen und Spielen* (1921). However, his own plays, from the anti-militarist *Der Gemeine* (1899) and the comedy *Das staerkere Band* (1912), to *Louise von Koburg* (1932), had no lasting success. Salten's novels were notable for their humor, satire, and eroticism. He also wrote novellas and essays such as *Wiener Adel* (1905), *Das Burgtheater* (1922), and *Geister der Zeit* (1924). His international fame rests on his best-known animal story, *Bambi* (1923), about a deer's life in the forest. This became a juvenile classic and was filmed by Walt Disney. Salten's Jewish interests came to the fore in his novel *Simson* (1928), and in essays about his visit to Palestine, *Neue Menschen auf alter Erde* (1925). In 1938 Salten left Austria for Hollywood but after World War II settled in Zurich, Switzerland.

BIBLIOGRAPHY: S.J. Kunitz (ed.), *Twentieth Century Authors* (1944), 1224; *ibid.*, first supplement (1955), 860 (both incl. bibl.).

[Sol Liptzin]

SALT TRADE AND INDUSTRY. Jews took a considerable part, from at least the tenth century, in the salt trade and its extraction – which were generally state monopolies – in a number of European countries, principally as lessees of the mines. In the main areas of salt extraction on the coast of the Bay of Biscay, for example, as well as in Germany, Poland, and Spain, Jews played a prominent role. Some surmise that in Muslim countries, too, Jews took part in the production and distribution of this commodity. The leasing of a salt mine required technical knowledge as well as financial resources, and was a large-scale enterprise undertaken mostly by wealthy and influential Jews as part of their overall activity. In some places, especially Poland, Jewish lessees were granted jurisdiction over their non-Jewish employees.

The Jewish traveler and geographer of the tenth century, *Ibrahim ibn Yaʿqūb, noted a salt mine operated by Jews near *Halle in Germany, and a little later in the same vicinity one Tidericus Judeus is mentioned as a partner in a salt-producing company. In 1132 Alfonso VII of Castile conferred the locality of Otos, next to the salt-rich Tagus, on the Ibn Zadok brothers (see Solomon *Ibn Zadok). In the 13th century a member of the same family, Isaac ibn Zadok, was known as Don Çag de la Maleha, evidently in reference to the large number of salt concessions he held. Also prominent among Jewish salt contractors in Spain was Judah de Cavalleria, bailiff of Saragossa, who was granted the total crown revenues from salt by the king of Aragon in 1264. In 1280 Abraham of Medinaceli obtained the rights to exploit the extensive salt deposits in the area of Velasco for four years.

In the 14th century the wealthy Cracow Jew, *Lewko, operated a large number of salt mines in *Wieliczka and Bochnia. The number of Jews in the Polish salt trade rose steeply during the 15th century, and a number of salt mines in *Drohobych, Jasienica, *Kolomyya, *Dolina, and *Zhidachow were leased to Jews by the king during this period. At the beginning of the 16th century the minor nobility of Poland embarked on a century-long struggle to wrest this rich source of revenue from the Jews. The nobles succeeded in intimidating the heads of the *Councils of the Lands, who in 1580 prohibited, *inter alia*, the leasing of any "*zupa*" (Pol. "salt mine") from the king or the nobility. The wars which afflicted Poland at the end of the 18th century and led to its partition put an end to the leasing of salt mines to Jews; salt trade by Jews on a lower level continued in the partitioned regions: 3,651 of the 5,450 salt traders in Polish towns in 1823 were Jews. In 1824 local authorities were prohibited from granting any new salt concessions to Jews until the number of Christian salt traders equaled that of the Jewish. The decree was repealed in 1830, though in Warsaw, for example, in 1840 there were 151 Jewish and only 64 Christian salt traders.

Dutch Jews in the 17th century played a prominent part in importing salt to their country. The firm of Curiel, for example, imported salt from Tripoli. Jeronimo Nuñez da Costa imported salt from Portugal where there was a big salt production at *Setubal, and exported it to *Gdansk. In Germany the *Court Jews, purveyors to kings and princes, played an important part in the leasing of salt mines-granted sometimes in lieu of paying their debts, or sometimes for services rendered – from the middle of the 17th and throughout the 18th centuries. Noah Samuel Isaac of Sulzbach, in the 17th century, having furnished the crown prince of Bavaria with one million talers for his wedding celebrations, received the revenues of three Bavarian salt mines. In the same century the Bavarian salt monopoly was leased to Nathan Moyses, the Schwabach Court Jew. He and his partners were known as the "salt Jews." In 1698 the Court Jew of Palatinate, Lemle Moses Reinganum, advanced 120,000 florins for the exclusive rights to trade in salt. Samson *Wertheimer, who was responsible for the prosperity of the salt industry in Transylvania, also organized the salt trade monopoly in Poland, both advancing the necessary capital and supervising the transportation of salt from Wieliczka to Silesia and Hungary. At the end of the 18th and beginning of the 19th century, David Seligman signed a series of contracts for salt production in Bavaria. The part played by Jews in the German salt trade came to an end with the disappearance of the Court Jews from the stage of history.

BIBLIOGRAPHY: Baer, Urkunden, 2 (1936), 12, 16, 70ff.; J. Jacobs, *An Inquiry into the Sources of the History of the Jews in Spain* (1894), 14,21,23,24; Régné, Cat, nos. 893, 2341; I. Schiper, *Di Virtshafts-geshikhte fun di Yidn in Poyln besyn Mitlalter* (1924); Ph. Friedmann, in: *Jewish Studies... G.A. Kohut* (1935), 195ff.; S. Stern. *The Court Jew* (1950), index; Baron, Social, 4 (1957), 169; H. Schnee, *Die Hoffinanz und der moderne Staat*, 4 (1963), 58ff., 190ff., 215ff., 222.

[Jacob Kaplan]

SALTZMAN, HARRY (1915–1994), film producer. Harry Saltzman was born in Saint John, New Brunswick. While a child, he moved to the United States but is said by one biographer to have returned to Canada to serve in the Canadian military during World War II. He did not see overseas duty but was attached to a Canadian Air Force supply unit. In the late 1940s he was back in the United States, where he spent several years working in early American and British television. In the 1950s he emerged as one of the pioneers in London's New Wave/Angry Young Man movement. His first major film work was with Woodfall, the company that produced Saltzman's well-received and money-making social dramas *Look Back in Anger* (1959), *Saturday Night and Sunday Morning* (1960), and *The Entertainer* (1960). In the later 1950s he became interested in the James Bond series of novels, and paid writer Ian Fleming $50,000 for a six-month option, but could not interest a major film company until he teamed up with Albert R. "Cubby" Broccoli. They founded EON (Everything Or Nothing) Films and Danjaq, S.A. (an amalgam of their wives' first names, Dana and Jacqueline). After agreeing to a film deal with United Artists in 1961, they jointly produced the Bond thrillers *Dr. No* (1962), *From Russia with Love* (1963), *Goldfinger* (1964), *You Only Live Twice* (1967), *On Her Majesty's Secret Service* (1969), *Diamonds Are Forever* (1971), *Live and Let Die* (1973), and *The Man with the Golden Gun* (1974). Saltzman made other films on his own, including the Harry Palmer spy series (with Michael Caine as Harry Palmer, "the thinking man's James Bond"). In 1975 Saltzman sold his interest in Bond to United Artists. He produced one more film, *Nijinsky* (1980), before he suffered a stroke at the age of 65 and was forced to retire.

[Joel Greenberg (2nd ed.)]

SALTZMAN, MAURICE (1918–1990), U.S. apparel manufacturer, philanthropist. Saltzman was born in Cleveland, Ohio, one of 10 children. Having lost both parents by the time he was four, he was raised in a local orphanage, but went on to become a preeminent maker of moderate-price women's sportswear and a leading philanthropist in the Cleveland area. His company, Bobbie Brooks Inc., was one of the first U.S. clothing manufacturers to reach an annual volume of more than $100 million. Following his graduation from Cleveland Heights High School at the age of 16, Saltzman went to work in the shipping room of Lampl Fashions, a local dress manufacturer. Five years later, in 1939, he and Max Reiter borrowed a couple of thousand dollars and launched Ritmore Manufacturing Co., producing dresses with a label that said Barbara Brooks. A year later, they changed the label to Bobbie Brooks and switched from dresses to junior sportswear, then a relatively new clothing category. In 1953, when Reiter left to go into his own business, Ritmore became Bobbie Brooks Inc., with Saltzman as chairman and chief executive officer. Its concept of coordinated sportswear – pieces that could be purchased separately and worn in various combinations – was highly successful, and the company went public in 1960. In the 1970s, Bobbie Brooks reached $100 million in volume, a mark attained by few apparel firms up to that time, but over-expansion was a problem. By 1977, the company initiated a restructuring program to sell or liquidate its marginal or losing units. It filed for Chapter 11 bankruptcy in 1982 and emerged a year later. In 1986, the company began licensing the Bobbie Brooks label to other manufacturers. After suffering a stroke in 1987, Saltzman retired. He was one of Cleveland's leading philanthropists, donating millions to such institutions as the Jewish Community Federation, Mt. Sinai Medical Center, and Bellefaire/Jewish Children's Home, formerly the Jewish Orphans Home, where he spent 11 years as a child. The campus of that home is now called the Saltzman Campus for Child Care. Saltzman, who was vice president of Cleveland's Temple Emanu-El, also founded the Saltzman-Wuliger Senior Citizens Center in Tel Aviv and a library and museum at the Children's Village of Gan Yavneh in Israel. He received a Humanitarian Medal from B'nai B'rith and a National Human Relations Award from the National Conference of Christians and Jews.

[Mort Sheinman (2nd ed.)]

SALUS, HUGO (1866–1929), Prague poet who wrote in German. A native of Česká Lípa, Salus was a gynecologist by profession, practicing in Prague. Between 1898 and 1928 he published volumes of impressionistic verse and was considered by contemporary critics as the foremost German lyricist.

Outstanding among his works are *Ehefruehling* (1900), *Trostbuechlein fuer Kinderlose* (1909), and *Die Harfe Gottes* (1928). Salus was a militant protagonist of German liberalism and Jewish assimilation. His views on the Jewish question are quoted in J. Moses' *Die Loesung der Judenfrage* (1907). Jewish themes appear in his poems "Ahnenlied" (about his grandfather, a peddler), "Der hohe Rabbi Loew," "Ahasver," "Sulamith," "Simson," and "Talmudische Legende," and in a short story, *Die Beschau* (1920). Salus was influenced by Rainer Maria Rilke and Hugo von *Hofmannsthal and, in his turn, influenced Max *Brod.

BIBLIOGRAPHY: *Jews of Czechoslovakia*, 1 (1968), 477–8; F.R. Tichy, in: *Zeitschrift fuer die Geschichte der Juden*, 3 (1966), 230–2; M. Brod, *Streitbares Leben* (1969), index; idem, *Der Prager Kreis* (1966), index.

SALUZZO, town in Piedmont, N.W. Italy. From 1142 to 1548 Saluzzo was the capital of the marquisate of the same name, long a bone of contention between France and the house of Savoy. Jews are first mentioned there in the 15th century; they ran 16 loan-banks in 1588, four at Saluzzo, two at Carmagnola, and the others in minor centers like Venesco, Verzuolo, and Piasco. In 1589 Duke Charles Emmanuel I of Savoy confirmed the existing privileges granted to the Jews by the French kings. In 1616 he gave the monopoly of Jewish loan-banking in Saluzzo to Leon Segre, who was murdered a few years later, though it is not known whether his death was caused by Christian reaction or the vengeance of his Jewish competitors. The Jews at Saluzzo formed a community in 1724 and were confined to a ghetto in September of the same year, in spite of attempts by the governor, Count Rovero, and the bishop, Giuseppe Morazzo to prevent this. The Jews in the ghetto, who were required to wear a yellow armband, were excluded from military service and the magistrature, funerary honors were denied them, and they were forbidden to keep Christian servants. Vittorio Amedeo of Sardinia forbade the Jews to pawn at the local loan-bank (*Monte di *Pietà*). A new ghetto was established in a more salubrious area in 1795. In that year the community founded a *talmud torah* and mutual aid institution aimed at propagating the Torah and providing assistance; special care was devoted to Jewish education. There were three Jewish burial grounds; the synagogue, located in the ghetto courtyard, was rebuilt in 1832. When in 1848 the Jews in the independent kingdom of Sardinia were granted a statute by King Charles Albert, those of Saluzzo also became full citizens. The community set up three important communal institutions, the Gemilut Ḥasadim (1865), Ḥevrat Baḥurim, and Ḥevrat Nashim. By a royal decree of September 1931, the community of Saluzzo became part of the larger one in *Turin. Some Jews from Saluzzo distinguished themselves as magistrates or politicians, such as Consul David Segre and Emanuel *Segre, an attorney general in Turin. Noteworthy rabbis included Marco Tedeschi, B. Artom, E.D. Bachi, and R. *Segre. About 100 Jews lived in the marquisate in the middle of the 16th century. There were nine in 1759, 90 in 1767, 210 in 1807, 320 in 1860, and 59 in 1931: 29 of these were victims of the Nazis. There were five Jews in Saluzzo in 1970.

BIBLIOGRAPHY: Roth, Italy, 136–7, 341, 512; Milano, Italia, 13, 257; F. Servi, in: *Corriero Israelitico*, 6 (1867–68), 278–80; R. Bachi, in: RMI, 12 (1938), 197–201; S. Foa, *ibid.*, 21 (1955), 331–3; 520–1, includes map of the Marquisate.

[Alfredo Mordechai Rabello]

SALVADOR, Sephardi London family that settled in colonial America. JOSEPH (1716–1786) was a wealthy London merchant who immigrated to America. Known in the Sephardi community of London as Joseph Jessurun Rodrigues, he was born into a wealthy family which had gone to England from Holland in the early 17th century. In 1738 he married Rachel, daughter of Isaac Lopes, third Baron Suasso. Salvador enhanced his wealth between 1738 and 1749 in the Spanish and Portuguese trade, working with his father, Francis. He also served as a liaison for the English merchants of Cadiz. Later he imported and exported coral and gems from India. Salvador was the first Jew to be made a director of the Dutch East India Company. He also was a financial adviser to the British government. Active in synagogue and philanthropic affairs, Salvador served as *parnas* of the Bevis Marks Spanish and Portuguese congregation in London. In his later years, Salvador suffered financial setbacks, notably with the failure of the Dutch East India Company. He sold part of a 100,000-acre holding in South Carolina's backcountry to his nephew and son-in-law, Francis (see below), who set up an indigo plantation in an effort to recoup the family losses. Later, Salvador sold most of his land, and in 1784 emigrated to South Carolina, presumably to support himself from remaining lands. He died in Charleston. FRANCIS (1747–1776), Revolutionary patriot; first Jew to serve in a legislative body in America. Francis was born in London and traveled extensively. When the family wealth was lost, young Salvador purchased some 7,000 acres of South Carolina land from Joseph. He emigrated there in 1773, on the eve of the American Revolution. Salvador early identified himself with the Colonial cause, and Carolina leaders, impressed with his education and ability, took him into their councils, despite his being a Jew. He was made a delegate to the Revolutionary Provincial Congresses of South Carolina (1775–76), which rejected British rule and constituted itself as the legislature of the newly independent state of South Carolina. Salvador thus became the first Jew to represent the people in a legislative body in America, and possibly the first Jew in the modern world to hold such public office. When the British attacked Charleston in 1776, Salvador quickly joined the patriot forces defending the frontier where his plantation lay. His detachment was ambushed by Indians near Keowee, S.C., and Salvador was shot and scalped. He was the first Jew to give his life in the struggle for American independence.

BIBLIOGRAPHY: J. Picciotto, *Sketches of Anglo-Jewish History* (1956), 109–12, 114–5, 153–6, and passim; B.A. Elzas, *Jews of South Carolina* (1905), 68–77, 108–18; L. Huehner, *Francis Salvador*, in: *The Jewish Experience in America* (ed. Karp) 11 (1969), 276–91; C. Reznikoff, *Jews of Charleston* (1950), 34–40; Rosenbloom, Biogr Dict; 151; M. Woolf, in: JHSET, 21 (1962–67), 104–37.

[Thomas J. Tobias]

SALVADOR, JOSEPH (1796–1873), French scholar. Salvador, the descendant of Spanish Jews, was born in Montpellier. He studied medicine there and graduated at the age of 20. His thesis dealt with the "Application of Physiology to Pathology" (1816). Shortly afterward he settled in Paris, where he became known mainly for his scholarly interest in the history of religions. To the study of religion in general and Jesus in particular, he applied the methods of historical criticism and might thus be considered in some respects in advance of German scholarship. His *Jésus-Christ et sa doctrine* (1838) was violently criticized by the *Gazette de France* when it was published, but was favorably reviewed by A.I.S. de *Sacy in the *Journal des Débats* of the same year and by J.E. *Renan in his *Études d'histoire réligieuse* (1857). In *Paris, Rome, Jérusalem, ou la Question réligieuse au 19e Siècle* (1859), Salvador attempted to outline a universal creed, founded on a kind of reformed Judaism, or on the fusion of Judaism and Christianity into one single doctrine of progress. Salvador imagined that the center of the syncretistic religion of which he dreamed would be in Jerusalem, and he saw this ultimate faith as the lineal outgrowth of what he imagined classic Judaism to have been. This emphasis on Jerusalem has led a number of historians of Zionism, beginning with Nahum Sokolow, to regard Salvador as one of the precursors of Zionism, but the Jerusalem of his dreams was a "heavenly Jerusalem," and the society of which it was to be the center was a universal culture and not that of a restored Jewish people. In his search for a general religious synthesis, Salvador might also have been motivated by the urge to solve his own spiritual dilemma, as his mother was a Catholic. Moreover, Salvador's outlook comes close to that of the Saint-Simonians; Benjamin Olinde Rodrigues, one of Saint-Simon's foremost Jewish disciples, seems to have been influenced by Salvador's writings (see *Saint Simonism).

He also wrote *La Loi de Moïse, ou, Système réligieux et politique des Hébreux* (1822); *De quelques faits relatifs au système historique des Evangiles* (1839); and *Histoire de la domination romaine en Judée et de la ruine de Jérusalem* (1846). The Catholic Church put two of Salvador's works, *Jésus-Christ et sa doctrine* and *Paris, Rome, Jérusalem…*, on its official index of forbidden books.

BIBLIOGRAPHY: G. Salvador, *J. Salvador; sa vie, ses oeuvres et ses critiques* (1881); H. Reinhold, in: *Zion*, 9 (1944), 109–41.

SALVENDI, ADOLF (1837–1914), rabbi, early adherent of Ḥovevei Zion, and organizer of charitable projects. Born in Waag-Neustadt, Slovakia, Salvendi officiated as a rabbi in Berent, Prussia (from 1864), and from 1865 acted as the district rabbi of more than 30 communities in Frankenthal, Bavaria, while living in Duerkheim. He continued in this capacity until 1910, when he went to live with his daughter in Karlsruhe. He resisted the influence of the extreme Reform movement (whose leaders persecuted him throughout his life) in the communities under his control and did much to further traditional religious education. At the same time Salvendi became well known as an organizer of relief projects for needy Jews. At first he collected money for the Jews of Russia, Persia, and other countries, and from 1877 for Ereẓ Israel. He published the names of donors and the sums collected in special lists, adding information about events in Ereẓ Israel, especially in the new settlements. Over 1,100 such lists were published over a period of 30 years, and this contributed substantially to the strengthening of Ḥibbat Zion in Western Europe, especially in Germany. The articles accompanying the lists were also of outstanding value as informative and propaganda material for Ḥibbat Zion. As a result of these activities, Salvendi was made an honorary member of the central committee of Ḥovevei Zion at the *Kattowitz Conference.

BIBLIOGRAPHY: A.B. Posner, in: A. Elmaleḥ (ed.), *Ḥemdat Yisrael* (1946), 136–46.

[Getzel Kressel]

SALZ, ABRAHAM ADOLPH (1864–1941), Zionist leader in Galicia. Born in Tarnow, Salz studied in Vienna and in 1884 joined the Zionist student society *Kadimah there. After he completed his studies, he returned to Tarnow (1887) and began diversified Zionist activities. He succeeded in acquiring the support of the ḥasidic *rebbe* of Czortkow for the Jewish national idea and plans of settlement in Ereẓ Israel. At the first conference of the Zionist societies in Galicia, which took place in Lemberg in 1893, he was elected president of the executive committee and was among the founders of the Polish-Zionist newspaper *Przyszlosc* ("The Future"). Salz successfully combated assimilationist trends among Polish Jews. He also was among the founders of the Ahavat Zion society for the establishment of a settlement of Galician Jews in Ereẓ Israel. Immediately after the appearance of Theodor *Herzl, he joined the Zionist movement, participated in the First Zionist Congress (1897), and was elected its vice president. He participated in all Zionist Congresses until the 11th in 1913. After World War I he concentrated his Zionist activities in Tarnow, where he published his memoirs on his activities from 1884 to 1914 in the Jubilee Book in honor of 50 years of the Zionist movement in Tarnow (Polish, 1934).

BIBLIOGRAPHY: N.M. Gelber, *Toledot ha-Tenu'ah ha-Ẓiyyonit be-Galiẓyah*, 2 vols. (1958), index; L. Jaffe, *Sefer ha-Congress* (1950²), 317–8.

[Max Wurmbrand]

SALZBURG, city and province in W. Austria, formerly archbishopric and duchy. The first mention of Jews in the archbishopric occurred as early as 803 in a letter from Archbishop

Arno (798–821) asking for the settlement of a Jewish physician in his district. A customs list from 905 contains references to Jewish salt merchants, and the term "Judendorf" occurs in sources dating from 1074, 1107, and 1197. The first clear reference to Jewish settlement occurred, however, during the tenure of Archbishop Conrad I (1106–47), who utilized Jews as financial advisers. A Judenstrasse in the market town of Admont is mentioned in a source dating from 1124. The oldest gravestone in the archbishopric, dating from 1240, was discovered in Friesach; 13th–century settlements were noted in Muehldorf, Hallein, and Pettau (Ptuj). The first references to Jews in the city of Salzburg itself dates from 1282. In 1267 the district council prescribed for Jewish males the wearing of a horn-shaped hat (*cornutus pileus*), and forbade their visiting Christian baths and employing Christian domestics. Jews functioned as *moneylenders in the city of Salzburg, including among their customers members of the city administration; in 1285 a Jewish banker, Isaac, is noted among those who lent money to the treasury of the archbishop. Sources early in the 14th century indicate widespread Jewish commercial ventures with the investment of considerable capital. In the city a Jewish gate, Judenstrasse, and synagogue date from the period.

During the course of the *Black Death persecutions of 1349, some 1,200 Jews in the archbishopric lost their lives, despite two unsuccessful efforts on the part of Pope *Clement IV to intervene. Although the city councils prohibited the return of converted Jews to the faith they abandoned during the persecutions, Jews are found again in the archbishopric in 1352. Their return was facilitated by the liberality of Archbishop Ortolph (1344–65). Jews began to appear in large numbers in the city of Salzburg only in the 1370s, partly as a result of the bold economic policies of Archbishop Pilgrim II (1365–96). In 1377 a new place for worship was leased to the community to replace the one formerly used (in 1400 it was bought by three Jewish representatives of the community), and in the same year a cemetery was consecrated. Beginning in 1382 the archbishop began to call Jews to military service. The archbishopric in this period served as a sanctuary for Jews fleeing persecution elsewhere; in 1397, for example, a severe persecution of Jews in *Styria and *Carinthia brought a considerable number of refugees into Salzburg. A Salzburg scholar named Judah wrote a code on *sheḥitah* in this period. Despite the liberality of Salzburg's administration, however, an accusation of desecrating the *Host (1404) was directed against the Jews of Hallein and Salzburg. In Salzburg many Jews were burned at the stake; the rest were driven out of the city and their property confiscated. By 1418 a relatively large number of Jews had once more settled in the city. In the same year the provincial council extended its regulation on the wearing of a distinctive hat for Jewish males to Jewish women as well, ordering that bells also be attached to their garments. From 1429 Archbishop John II followed a particularly enlightened policy toward the Jews, inviting Jewish refugees from Speyer, Zurich, Mainz, and Augsburg. Jews were given considerable freedom, e.g., they were allowed to acquire houses and other real estate. In 1439 a new synagogue was constructed in the city; in 1448 a *mikveh* was built in Hallein, where a synagogue also was in existence. In 1498 Jews were, however, accused of having stolen a sacred object of the church; as a result, the synagogues of both Hallein and Salzburg were destroyed and the Jews were banished in perpetuity from the archbishopric. At that same time, a wooden image of a sow with Jewish children nursing from it was set up in the town hall. Later reproduced in marble, the figures were not removed until 1785. Jewish traveling merchants traded in Salzburg during the 17th and 18th centuries. The **Leibzoll* was repealed in 1790 and two *Court Jews were established in Salzburg by 1800. Nevertheless, until 1867 there was no permanent Jewish settlement in what had been the Austrian duchy of Salzburg for 350 years; in 1867 full equality was granted to the Jews. By 1869 there were 42 Jews in Salzburg, and by 1882 there were 115. In the 1890s an organization was set up to coordinate the religious and cultural needs of the Jews living in the duchy. In 1893 a new synagogue was dedicated in Salzburg and a *ḥevra kaddisha* was formed. For a while, Theodor *Herzl practiced law in Salzburg, leaving the city in 1884. In 1894 a cemetery was consecrated in Aigen.

Adolf Altmann, who acted as rabbi in the community from 1907 to 1914, wrote extensively on the history of Salzburg's Jews. Between the world wars, Salzburg's Jews contributed significantly to the rich musical and literary life of the city. Both Stefan *Zweig and Bruno *Walter were among the many renowned Jewish personalities of the period. After the *Anschluss* almost all Jews were deported; in November 1938 the synagogue was destroyed and the cemetery desecrated; several Jewish enterprises were destroyed and 70 Jews arrested. After World War II Salzburg served as a center for some 200,000 Jewish displaced persons. In 1953 a community was reestablished, and in 1968 the newly rebuilt synagogue was rededicated. The Salzburg university library houses a significant collection of Hebrew manuscripts. Around 100 Jews lived there in 2005.

BIBLIOGRAPHY: Aronius, Regesten, 29–30, paragraphs 69, 80; Germ Jud, 1 (1963), 318–19 incl. bibl.; 2 pt. 2 (1968), 728–31, incl. bibl.; M. Karin-Karger and E. Landau (eds.), *Salzburgs wiederaufgebaute Synagoge* (1968); A. Altmann, *Geschichte der Juden in Stadt und Land Salzburg*, 2 vols. (1913–30); idem, in: JJLG, 19 (1928), 69–83; 20 (1929), 99–179; G. Wolf, *Zur Salzburger Chronik* (1873); idem, in: MGWJ, 25 (1876), 284–5; R. Glanz, in: JSOS, 4 (1942), 100–2, incl. bibl. notes; E. Isaac, *ibid.*, 19 (1957), 65–68; E. Scheuer, *Zu den Rechtsverhaeltnissen der Juden in den deutsch-oesterreichischen Laendern* (1901), 543–71; H. Rosenkranz, *Reichskristallnacht* (1968), 53ff.; Y. Bauer, *Flight and Rescue: Bricha* (1970), index.

[Alexander Shapiro]

SALZMAN, PNINA (1924–), Israeli pianist. Born in Tel Aviv, Salzman began her music studies at the Shulamit Conservatory with Lina Hopenko. Alfred Cortot, on tour in Israel, heard her and immediately recommended that she study in Paris at the Ecole Normale de Musique under his supervision, where she graduated at the age of 12. She then studied at the Conservatoire National de Musique in Paris, and at 14 won a *premier prix*. At 15 she made her concert debut. Bronislaw *Huberman attended one of her concerts and wrote to the Israel Philharmonic Orchestra to engage the brilliant young pianist. Salzman played three concertos with the IPO in one evening and was greatly acclaimed. From then on, she regularly performed with the orchestra in Israel and toured other countries. Salzman is an artist of great versatility, known for her brilliant virtuosity as an orchestral soloist, a recital pianist, and an enthusiastic performer of chamber music. She was considered the first Israeli-born pianist to attain international artistic rank. In 1963 she was the first Israeli invited to perform in the U.S.S.R. Again, in 1994, she was the first Israeli pianist invited to play in China. Professor Salzman was head of the piano department of the Rubin Academy of Music at Tel Aviv University and was constantly invited to give master classes at important music centers abroad. She was frequently requested to act as a jury member at international piano competitions. In 2006 she received the Israel Prize.

BIBLIOGRAPHY: NG²; B.I. Meir, "Pnina Salzman: Her Career and Interpretive Art" (DMA Diss., 2000).

[Naama Ramot (2nd ed.)]

SALZMAN, WILLIAM (1883–1970), U.S. businessman and educator. Born in the Ukraine, Salzman emigrated in 1908 to New York City, where he founded the Standard Bag Corporation. He served as president and later chairman of the board until its merger with another company in 1966.

An amateur scholar of rabbinic and modern Hebrew literature, Salzman helped to found, finance, and maintain a number of important Hebrew educational institutions in New York City, among them the Herzliah Hebrew Teachers College, of which he served for many years as president, and the Institute of Hebrew Studies of New York University. He was an active member of Mordecai *Kaplan's Society for the Advancement of Judaism and chairman of the Israel Matz Foundation, which supports Hebrew writers in the United States and Israel. His Hebrew autobiography, *Netiv Ḥayyai* ("The Path of My Life") was published posthumously (1970).

SAMAEL, from the amoraic period onward the major name of Satan in Judaism. The name first appears in the account of the theory of angels in the Ethiopic Book of Enoch 6, which includes the name, although not in the most important place, in the list of the leaders of the angels who rebelled against God. The Greek versions of the lost Hebrew text contain the forms Σαμμανή (Sammane) and Σεμιέλ (Semiel). The latter form takes the place of the name Samael in the Greek work of the Church Father Irenaeus in his account of the Gnostic sect of the Ophites (see below; ed. Harvey, 1, 236). According to Irenaeus the Ophites gave the snake a double name: *Michael and Samael, which in the Greek work of the Church Father Theodoretus appears as Σαμμανή (Sammane). The Greek version of Enoch used by the Byzantine Syncellus retained the form Σαμιέλ (Samiel). This form still retains the original meaning derived from the word *sami* (סמי), meaning blind, an etymology which was preserved in various Jewish and non-Jewish sources until the Middle Ages. In addition to Samiel, the forms Samael and Sammuel date from antiquity. This third version is preserved in the Greek Apocalypse of Baruch 4:9 (from the tannaitic period), which states that the angel Sammuel planted the vine that caused the fall of Adam, and therefore Sammuel was cursed and became *Satan. The same source relates in chapter 9, in an ancient version of the legend of the shrinking of the moon, that Samael took the form of a snake in order to tempt Adam, an idea which was omitted in later talmudic versions of the legend.

In the apocalyptic work "The Ascension of Isaiah," which contains a mixture of Jewish and early Christian elements, the names Beliar (i.e., Belial) and Samael occur side by side as names or synonyms for Satan. What is recounted of Samael in one passage is stated in another about Beliar. For example, Samael dominated King Manasseh and "embraced him," thus taking on the form of Manasseh (ch. 2). In chapter 7, Samael and his forces are stated to be under the first firmament, a view that does not accord with his position as the chief of the devils. Samael is mentioned among the "angels of judgment" in the Sibylline Oracles 2:215. In the tannaitic and amoraic period, Samael is mentioned as being outside the alignment of the hosts of the *Merkabah. Drawing from Jewish tradition, several Gnostic works refer to Samael as "the blind god" and as identical with Jaldabaoth, who occupied an important place in Gnostic speculations as one of, or the leader of, the forces of evil. This tradition apparently came down through the Ophites ("the worshipers of the snake"), a Jewish syncretistic sect (Theodore Bar Konai, Pagnon ed., 213). Partially ecclesiastical traditions of this period, such as the pseudepigraphic versions of Acts of the Apostles, Acts of Andrew, and Matthew 24, retain the name Samael for Satan, acknowledging his blindness. He is mentioned as head of the devils in the magical Testament of Solomon (*Testamentum Salomonis*), which is essentially a superficial Christian adaptation of a demonological Jewish text from this period (ed. Chester Charlton McCown (1922), 96). Undoubtedly Simyael, "the demon in charge of blindness" mentioned in Mandean works (Ginzā, trans. M. Lidzbarski (1925), 200, and *The Canonical Prayer Book of the Mandaeans*, ed. E.S. Drower (1959), 246), is simply a variant of Samael.

In rabbinic tradition the name first occurs in the statements of Yose (perhaps b. Halafta or the *amora* Yose) that during the exodus from Egypt "Michael and Samael stood before the *Shekhinah*" apparently as prosecutor and defender (Ex. R. 18:5). Their task is similar to that of Samael and *Gabriel in the story of Tamar (Sot. 10b), in the statement of Eleazar b. Pedat. Samael retains the role of prosecutor in the account of Ḥama b. Ḥanina (c. 260 C.E.; Ex. R. 21:7), who was apparently the first to identify Samael with Esau's guardian angel during the struggle between Jacob and the angel. His name, however, does not appear in *Genesis Rabbah* (Theodor ed. (1965), 912), but he is mentioned in the old version of the *Tanḥuma, Va-Yishlaḥ* 8. In the parallel version in *Songs of Songs Rabbah* 3:6, the *amora* has Jacob saying to Esau: "your countenance resembles that of your guardian angel," according to the version of the *Sefer Mattenot Kehunnah* (Theodor ed.). Surprisingly, in the section of the *Midrash Yelammedenu* on Exodus 14:25, Samael fulfills a positive function during the dividing of the Red Sea, pushing back the wheels of the chariots of the Egyptians. In *gematria*, Samael is the numerical equivalent of the word *ofan* ("wheel"; in Ms. British Museum, 752, 136b; and in the *Midrash Ha-Ḥefeẓ ha-Teimani*, which is cited in *Torah Shelemah*, 14 (1941) to this verse).

Mention of Samael as the angel of death first occurs in Targum Jonathan on Genesis 3:6, and this identification frequently appears in late *aggadot*, especially in the legends on the death of Moses at the end of *Deuteronomy Rabbah*, at the end of *Avot de-Rabbi Nathan* (ed. Schecter (1945), 156). In *Deuteronomy Rabbah* 11, Samael is called "Samael the wicked, the head of all the devils." The name "Samael the wicked" is repeated consistently in *Heikhalot Rabbati* (1948), chapter 5, an apocalyptic source. The Hebrew Enoch 14:2, acknowledges him as "chief of the tempters" "greater than all the heavenly kingdoms." This text differentiates between Satan and Samael, the latter being none other than the guardian angel of Rome (*ibid.* 6:26). In traditions concerning the rebellion of the angels in heaven (PdRE 13–14 (1852)), he is the leader of the rebel armies. Prior to his defeat he had 12 wings, and his place was higher than the *ḥayyot* ("holy heavenly creatures") and the seraphim. Several tasks are attributed to him: Samael is in charge of all the nations but has no power over Israel except on the Day of Atonement, when the scapegoat serves as bribe for him (*ibid.* 46). It is he who rode on the snake in the course of the fall of Adam and hid in the golden calf (*ibid.* 45). In *Midrash Avkir* (see *Midrashim, Smaller), Samael and Michael were active at the time of the birth of Jacob and Esau, and even on the way to the **Akedah* of Isaac, Samael intervened as a prosecutor (Gen. R. 56:4). The war between him and Michael, the guardian angel of Israel, will not be completed until the end of days, when Samael will be handed over to Israel in iron shackles (Gen. R., ed. Albeck, 166, following Mak. 12a, and similarly in the messianic chapters (*pirkei mashi'aḥ*) in A. Jellinek, *Beit ha-Midrash* 3 (1938), 66f.).

Particular motifs on Samael in later *aggadah* include the following: Samael does not know the path to the tree of life, even though he flies through the air (Targ. Job 28:7); he has one long hair in his navel, and as long as this remains intact his reign will continue. In the messianic era, however, the hair will bend as a result of the great sound of the *shofar*, and then Samael will also fall (*Midrash Piyyutim*, quoted in a commentary on Ms. Munich 346, 91b). In Jewish astrological sources, which in time influenced those of other groups, Samael was considered the angel in charge of Mars. This idea recurs at first among the Sabans in Haran, who called him Mara Samia (D. Chwolson, *Die Ssabier und der Ssabismus*, 2 (1856); *Picatrix*, ed. H. Ritter (1933), 226) and later in medieval Christian astrological magic literature. He appears as the angel in charge of Tuesday in Sefer *Razi'el (Amsterdam, 1701), 34b; in *Ḥokhmat ha-Kasdim* (ed. M. Gaster, *Studies and Texts*, 1 (1925), 350; in *Judah b. Barzillai's commentary on Sefer *Yeẓirah (1885), 247, and in many other works. In demonological sources known to the brothers *Isaac and *Jacob b. Jacob ha-Kohen, Spanish kabbalists of the mid-13th century, an echo of the ancient etymology is still retained and Samael is called Sar Suma ("blind angel").

In later literature, Samael often appears as the angel who brought the poison of death into the world. These same demonological sources contain the earliest references to Samael and *Lilith as a couple in the kingdom of impurity (Isaac ha-Kohen's essay on *aẓilut, Madda'ei ha-Yahadut*, 2 (1927), 251, 260, 262). These sources are full of contradictory traditions concerning the roles of Samael and the war against *Asmodeus, then regarded as guardian angel of Ishmael. Different systems were constructed of the hierarchy of the leaders of the demons and their consorts (*Tarbiz*, 4 (1932/33), 72). According to one view, Samael had two brides (resp., *Sidrei de-Shimmusha Rabbah, Tarbiz*, 16 (1945), 198–9), an idea which also appears in *Tikkunei Zohar* (Mantua, 1558). The couple Samael and Lilith are mentioned many times in the *Zohar, mostly without specifically mentioning the name Lilith (e.g., "Samael and his spouse"), as the leaders of the *sitra aḥra* ("the other side"; i.e., evil). In *Ammud ha-Semali* by *Moses b. Solomon b. Simeon of Burgos, a contemporary of the author of the Zohar, Samuel and Lilith constitute only the eighth and tenth *Sefirah* of the left (evil) emanation (*Tarbiz*, 4 (1932–33), 217f.). In the Zohar, the snake has become the symbol of Lilith, and Samael rides on her and has sexual intercourse with her. Samael is cross-eyed and dark (*Zohar Ḥadash* 31, 4) and has horns (*Tikkunei Zohar* in *Zohar Ḥadash* 101, 3), perhaps influenced by the Christian idea about the horns of Satan. However, the image of Satan is linked with the goat in Targum Jonathan to Leviticus 9:3. The party, hosts, and chariots of Samael are mentioned in Zohar part 2, 111b; part 3, 29a. Different classes of demons, all called Samael, were known by the writer of *Tikkunei Zohar* (published in the main body of the Zohar 1, 29a). "There is Samael and there is Samael, and they are not all the same."

The conjurations of Samael often appear in magical literature and in practical Kabbalah. In 15th-century Spain a system was developed in which the heads of the demons were Samael, the representative of Edom, and his assistant Amon of No, representing Ishmael. A legend telling of their downfall at the hands of *Joseph della Reina appears in several sources (G. Scholem, in *Zion*, 5 (1933), 124f.). After Isaac *Luria had introduced the practice of not pronouncing the name of Satan, the custom of calling him *Samekh Mem* became widespread (*Sha'ar ha-Mitzvot* (Salonica, 1852), Exodus; *Sha'ar ha-Kavvanot* (Salonica, 1852), *Derushei ha-Laylah* 1).

BIBLIOGRAPHY: R. Margulies, *Malakhei Elyon* (1945), 248–70; M. Schwab, *Vocabulaire de l'angélologie* (1897), 199; H.L. Strack and P. Billerbeck, *Kommentar zum Neuen Testament aus Talmud und Midrasch* (1922), 136–49; E. Peterson, in: *Rheinisches Museum*, 75 (1926), 413–5; J. Doresse, *The Secret Books of the Egyptian Gnostics* (1960), index; G. Scholem, *Origines de la Kabbale* (1966), 311–4.

[Gershom Scholem]

SAMAMA (Shemama?), NESSIM (1805–1873), Tunisian *qāʾid*; born in *Tunis and died in Leghorn. After a long career as a textile merchant, Samama entered the service of the general Ben Ayad as a paymaster; in 1853 he went on to serve the prime minister Mustafa Khaznadar, quickly taking control of the functions of treasurer and controller of finances. In October 1859 he was appointed *qāʾid* of Tunisian Jewry, and the following year he became director and chief revenue collector for the state. He was raised to the rank of brigadier general. In 1864 Samama left for *Paris on an official mission to negotiate a loan for *Tunisia. He carried 20 million gold francs with him and, without any intention of returning, he settled at first in Paris and then, in 1871, in Leghorn. As a result of the conduct of the Prime Minister Khaznadar, the bey of Tunis was compelled to file a suit challenging the rights of inheritance of Samama's considerable estate. The subsequent suits for and against the validity of the inheritance of the estate gave rise to numerous articles which were published in Arabic, Italian, French, and Hebrew. During his lifetime Samama contributed to the publication of several works of Tunisian and other rabbis, and also to the maintenance of a yeshivah in *Jerusalem which bore his name.

His nephew SALOMON SAMAMA (d. 1886) was also a *qāʾid*, and was chief collector of Tunisian revenues from 1864 to 1866 and 1869 to 1873. When the estate of his uncle was disputed, Samama fled to Corfu, escaping with several million gold francs; a large part of the money was successfully recovered by the Tunisian government. He died in Paris.

BIBLIOGRAPHY: J. Brill, in: *Ha-Levanon*, 9 (1872–73), 224; AZDJ, 37 (1873), 143–4; *Mosé*, 8 (1885), 35–36; I. Loeb, in: REJ, 18 (1889), 156–7; M.S. Mzali and J. Pignon, in: *Revue Tunisienne*, 8 (1937), 209ff.; J. Ganiage, *Origines du Protectorat Français en Tunisie: 1861–1881* (1959), index; R. Attal, in: *Sefunot*, 5 (1961), 507 (index).

[Robert Attal]

SAMANDAR, *Khazar town N. of the Caucasus, four days from Bāb al-Abwāb and seven or eight days from *Atil on the Volga. As in the case of *Balanjar, Samandar originally seems to have been the group name of the inhabitants. The Zabender (apparently = Samandar) are mentioned by the Greek writer Theophylact Simocatta as emigrating from Asia to Europe in about 598 C.E., while a town M-s-n-d-r (vowels uncertain) in the land of the Huns, north of Darband (Bāb al-Abwāb), occurs in the Armenian geography attributed to Moses of Chorene. According to Masʿūdī (*Murūj*, 2 (1877), 7), in the earliest Arab period Samandar was the Khazar capital; subsequently *Atil on the Volga was made the capital, evidently to be out of reach of Arab attacks. Samandar figures regularly in accounts of the fighting in the second Arab-Khazar war. Al-Iṣṭakhrī, the tenth-century geographer, describes the town as possessing many gardens and thousands of vineyards. There was a considerable Muslim population, but the king was a Jew and related to the king of the Khazars. According to the geographer Ibn Ḥawqal (tenth century, later than Al-Iṣṭakhrī), Samandar was destroyed by the Russians in 968 C.E. (358 A.H.). The exact site of ancient Samandar is unknown, but it is generally agreed to have been somewhere in the region of present-day Qizlar on the Terek, which, like Samandar, is noted for its vineyards. Remains of a large town which may be Samandar have been found deep in the woods along the lower Terek (communication of M.I. Artamonov to D.M. Dunlop, November 1964).

BIBLIOGRAPHY: Dunlop, Khazars, index; A.N. Poliak, *Kazariyyah* (1951), index; M.I. Artamonov, *Istoriya Khazar* (1962), 392ff., 399.

[Douglas Morton Dunlop]

SAMARIA (Heb. **Shomron**, modern **Sebaste**), city established as the capital of the northern kingdom of Israel during the reign of Omri c. 884 B.C.E. Prior to the Omride period the site appears to have been the center of an extensive wine and oil production area, which may have accounted for its choice as the new capital. Apparently the origin of the name of the site was from Shemer, the eponymous owner of the land that Omri purchased for two talents of silver (I Kings 16:23–24).

The site has been excavated by two archaeological expeditions. The first was the Harvard Expedition, initially directed by G. Schumacher in 1908 and then by G.A. Reisner in 1909 and 1910 with the assistance of architect C.S. Fisher and D.G. Lyon. The second expedition was known as the "Joint Expedition," a consortium of five institutions directed by J.W. Crowfoot between 1931 and 1935, with the assistance of K. Kenyon, E.L. Sukenik, and G.M. Crowfoot. The leading institutions were the British School of Archaeology in Jerusalem, the Palestine Exploration Fund, and the Hebrew University. In the 1960s small-scale excavations directed by F. Zayadine were carried out on behalf of the Department of Antiquities of Jordan.

The city is built on the summit of a rocky hill, and the foundations of the monumental buildings from later periods often plowed down through the earlier strata to the bedrock, which was never far below. In modern times the site has been used as farmland by the villagers of neighboring Sebaste; this meant that most of the excavated areas had to be back-filled and returned to agricultural use. These two developments hindered excavation and later analysis of the remains. The earliest remains consist of extensive rock-cut installations, initially thought to date to the Early Bronze Age by Kenyon. These were reevaluated, first by Stager and then by Franklin, and are now recognized to be the remains of an extensive early Iron Age oil and wine industry (designated Building Period 0).

Only the acropolis of Samaria has been extensively excavated down to the bedrock. The palace was excavated solely by the Harvard Expedition and recognized by it as the Palace of Omri (designated Building Period I). The Omride palace was located on an elevated 4-meter-high rock-cut platform that isolated it from its immediate surroundings. Immediately below the palace, cut into the face of the bedrock platform, there are two rock-cut tomb chambers that have only

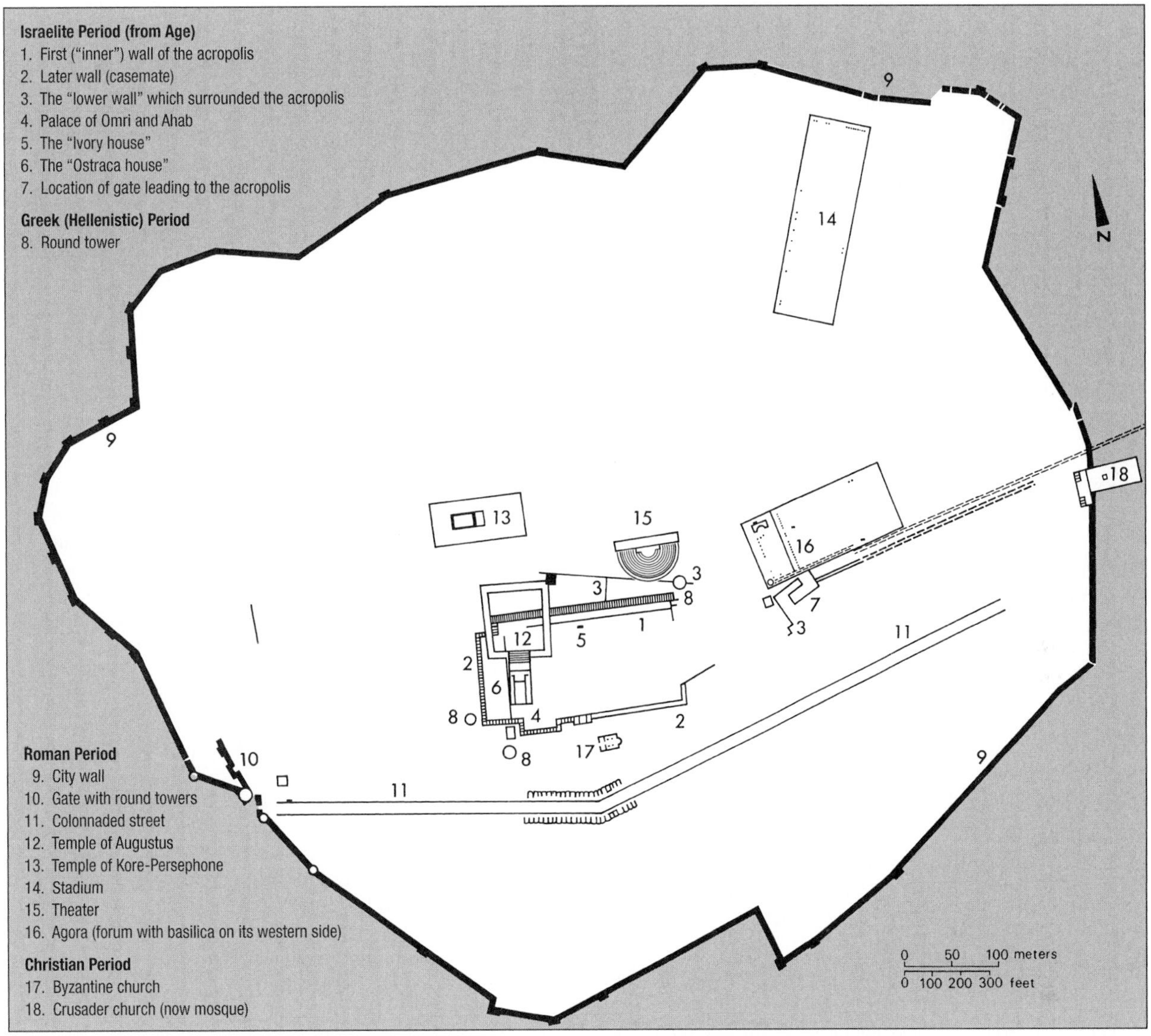

Plan of the site of Samaria. Based on Encyclopedia of Archaeological Excavations in the Holy Land, *Jerusalem, 1970.*

recently been recognized and attributed to Omri and Ahab. West of the palace there are meager remains of other Building Period I buildings, but much of the rock surface has been severely damaged by later buildings. The Omride palace continued in use during the next building phase (designated Building Period II), but it was no longer isolated on an elevated platform. The acropolis area was extended in all directions by the addition of a massive perimeter wall built in the casemate style; the new enlarged rectangular acropolis measured c. 290 ft. (90 m.) from north to south and at least c. 585 ft. (180 m.) from west to east, and the surface was now raised to a uniform elevation by the addition of a massive fill. This phase (Building Period II) was traditionally attributed to Ahab due to the misallocation of Wall 161 that runs parallel to the northern casemates and the identification of a large rock-cut pool near the northern casemate wall as the biblical "Pool of Samaria"; the wall (Wall 161) is now recognized to belong to Building Period II and the "pool" is a rock-cut grape-treading area that originated in Building Period 0 and continued in a reduced form in Building Period I. Consequently the onset of Building Period II can only be relatively fixed. There is neither a biblical anchor nor securely dated pottery to establish the chronological affiliation of Building Period II. The Omride Palace was still in use and the royal tombs were still accessible (now via subterranean rooms) and there was an administrative building, the "Ostraca House" (named for the 63 ostraca retrieved from the floor's make-up) built west of the palace on the newly extended acropolis. The ostraca provide a wealth of data concerning oil and wine supplies, and can possibly be attributed to the period of Jeroboam II c. 785–749, thus providing a probable date for Building Period II. North of the palace a rich cache of Phoenician ivories (furniture ornamentation) was retrieved. This was mixed with later debris, but it was presumed by the excavators (the Joint) that it was in this area that the "Ivory House" that Ahab built for Jezebel (I Kings 22:39) stood. Northeast and below the acropolis a number of Iron Age tombs were found and their location probably delimits the area of the city in that direction. In essence only the acropolis was excavated down to the Iron Age, but it is presumed by the excavators (the Joint) that the city extended down over the northern and southern slopes of the hill. During the reign of the last king of the northern kingdom, Hosea (II Kings 10), the Assyrians invaded in 722/721 B.C.E. (initially under Shalmaneser V and finally under Sargon II), when they established complete control over the capital city and the remainder of the northern kingdom. The fragment of a stela with an Assyrian inscription attributed to Sargon II was found on the eastern slope of the acropolis testifying to their presence. In addition, according to inscriptions from Sargon's palace at Khorsabad, the inhabitants of Samaria were deported to Assyria. The remains of a wall relief in Room 5 of Sargon's palace are thought to depict Samaria and its defeated defenders. New inhabitants were brought in (from Arabia and the Syro-Mesopotamian area, II Kings 17:24) and, together with the remnant not deported, they formed a new Samaritan population. The city together with the neighboring highland area became known as Samerina and was ruled by an Assyrian governor. There are only meager remains from the succeeding Babylonian period and it was only in the Persian period, in the mid-fifth century, that the city reemerged in importance. The tensions between the ruling family of Sanballat and Jerusalem under the governorship of Nehemiah are documented in the Bible (Ezra 4:10, Neh. 2:1–8). Samaria became a Hellenistic town in 332 B.C.E. and thousands of Macedonian soldiers were settled there following a revolt by the Samaritans. Three 13-m.-diameter round towers dating to that period have been excavated (the first two by Harvard, which attributed them to the Israelite period) and a later, massive, fortification wall with square towers. These fortifications were breached during the destruction of the city by John Hyrcanus in 108 B.C.E. Traces of the destruction wrought by *Hyrcanus were found by the excavators, but the city was apparently resettled under *Yannai. In 63 B.C.E. Samaria was annexed to the Roman province of Syria. In 30 B.C.E. the emperor Augustus awarded the city to *Herod, who renamed it Sebaste in honor of Augustus (Gr. Sebastos = Augustus). The outstanding remains from this period are: the Augusteum, consisting of a temple and a large forecourt built over the Omride palace at the summit of the acropolis; a city gate and an east-west colonnaded street; a theater on the northeast slope of the acropolis; a Temple to Kore on a terrace north of the acropolis; and a stadium to the northeast in the valley below. East of the acropolis and in an area that today links the ancient city with the modern village of Sebaste lies the forum, flanked on the west by a partially excavated basilica. Water for Roman Sebaste was provided by an underground aqueduct that led into the area of the forum from springs in the east. The city was encompassed by a city wall 2½ mi. (4 km.) long, with imposing towers that linked the gateways in the west and north. A number of mausoleums with ornate sarcophagi were excavated in the area of the modern village and adjoining fields.

The city was rebuilt without any major changes in the second century C.E. by Septimius Severus, when the city was established as a colony. Samaria has been associated with the burial place of John the Baptist and his tomb, reached by a steep flight of steps, is situated beneath the Crusader cathedral in the village. A small basilica church, first founded in the fifth century, was excavated on the southern slope of the acropolis. The church is traditionally the place of the invention of the head of John the Baptist. A monastery was added to it at a later date. In the 12th century C.E. a Latin cathedral dedicated to John the Baptist and marking the spot of his tomb, was built east of the Roman forum and combined elements of the Roman period city wall. It later became the Sebaste village mosque.

ADD. BIBLIOGRAPHY: G.A. Reisner, C.S. Fisher, and D.G. Lyon, *Harvard Excavations at Samaria (1908–1910)*, 1–2 (1924); J.W. Crowfoot and G.M. Crowfoot, *Early Ivories from Samaria* (Samaria-Sebaste 2) (1938); J.W. Crowfoot, K.M. Kenyon, and E.L. Sukenik, *The Building at Samaria* (Samaria-Sebaste 1) (1942); J.W. Crowfoot, K.M. Kenyon, and G.M. Crowfoot, *The Objects of Samaria* (Samaria-Sebaste 3) (1957); F. Zayadine, "Samaria-Sebaste: Clearance and Excavations (October 1965–June 1967)," in: ADAJ, 12:77–80 (1966); A.F. Rainey, "Toward a Precise Date for the Samaria Ostraca," in: BASOR, 272:69–74 (1988); L.E. Stager, "Shemer's Estate," in: *Bulletin of the American Schools of Oriental Research* 277/278:93–107 (1990); B. Becking, *The Fall of Samaria: An Historical and Archaeological Study* (1992); R. Tappy, *The Archaeology of Israelite Samaria. Early Iron Age through the Ninth Century B.C.E.*, vol. 1, Harvard Semitic Studies 44 (1992); R. Tappy, *The Archaeology of Israelite Samaria. The Eighth Century B.C.*, vol. 2, Harvard Semitic Studies 50 (2001); N. Franklin, "The Tombs of the Kings of Israel," in: ZDVP, 119 (2003), 1–11; idem, "Samaria: from the Bedrock to the Omride Palace," in: Levant, 36:189–202 (2004); S. Gibson, *The Cave of John the Baptist* (2004).

[Norma Franklin (2nd ed.)]

SAMARITANS. This article is arranged according to the following outline:

HISTORY

- **Samaritan Origins**
- **The Samaritans in the Time of Nehemiah**
- **The Samaritans in the Second Temple Period**
- **Samaritans in the Graeco-Roman Diaspora**
- **Excavations on Mt. Gerizim**
- **Late Roman to Crusader Period**
- **Later History**
- **Statistics**

RELIGION AND CUSTOMS

- **Holidays and Festivals**
  - THE SABBATH
  - THE FESTIVALS
- **Religious Ceremonies**
  - CIRCUMCISION
  - THE LAWS OF RITUAL IMPURITY AND PURITY
  - COMPLETION OF THE TORAH

HISTORY

Samaritanism is related to Judaism in that it accepts the Torah as its holy book. Samaritans consider themselves to be the true followers of the ancient Israelite religious line. The Samaritan temple was on Mt. Gerizim near Shechem (modern Nablus), where dwindling numbers of Samaritans still live and worship today.

Passages in the Hebrew Bible indicate that Mt. Gerizim has a legitimate (albeit obscure) claim to sanctity through its association with those who visited it. Abraham and Joseph both visited Shechem (Gen. 12:6–7, 13:18–20), as did Joseph (Gen. 37:12–14 and Josh. 24:32). In Deuteronomy (11:29 and 27:12), Moses commanded the Israelites to bless Mt. Gerizim when they entered the land of Canaan. When the Israelites crossed the Jordan they built an altar on Mt. Ebal (opposite Mt. Gerizim), and six of the tribes faced Mt. Gerizim while blessing the people of Israel as Moses commanded (Josh.8:30–33). Throughout Samaritan history, Samaritans have lived near Mt. Gerizim (Pummer 1968, 8).

After the fall of Samaria (724 B.C.E.), the Assyrian conquerors sent much of the population into exile to be resettled in various parts in the Assyrian empire. Towards the end of the seventh century B.C.E., Josiah tried to reform the cult in Jerusalem and, from then on, the stories and laws of the five first books of the Bible (the Torah, or Pentateuch) were at the heart of Jewish monotheism.

The Samaritan tradition maintains that its Torah (the *Samaritikon*) dates to the time of Moses and that it was copied by Abiša ben Phineas shortly after the Israelite entered the land of Canaan. However, modern literary analysis and criticism does not support this position. In fact, there are two main versions of the Torah: the Jewish version and the Samaritan version, and they are almost the same, which can only mean that both derive from the same original. While the Torah is a composite of traditions from both northern and southern Israel, the center of literary activity was Judaean, starting with the work of the Yahwists and ending with the editorial work of the Judaean diaspora (Pummer 1968: 93).

Samaritan Origins

There are a number of theories about the origins of the Samaritans, all of which have in common a tradition that originally the cult of YHWH was widespread through the land of Israel. Even so, the origins and early history of the Samaritans are quite problematic because the sources are far removed from the events and because the non-Samaritan sources tend to be hostile.

One tradition is that the Samaritans originated with the northern tribes of Israel because only a small proportion of these tribes was deported during the Assyrian conquests of the late eighth century B.C.E. and that those who remained on the land formed what later became the Samaritans (Mor 1989, 1).

Another Samaritan tradition claims Samaritan origins lie in the pre-exilic period, at the very beginnings of Israelite history, and that the split between Samaritanism and Judaism only arose when the heretical priest Eli stole the Ark of the Covenant and established a rival cult.

Until that time, the Ark of the Covenant had been kept at the sanctuary of YHWH on Mt. Gerizim. According to this tradition, the priest Eli was prevented from rising to the high priesthood because he was of the family of Itamar, not the high priestly family of Eleazar. Nevertheless, he took the Ark of the Covenant from Mt. Gerizim to Shiloh and established a rival cult there. As a result of this, two centers of the priesthood arose. One center was on Mt. Gerizim, at whose head stood the legitimate high priest, Uzzi (a descendant of Phineas and of the family Eleazar). The second (heretical) priesthood was at Shiloh, and the priest Eli, a descendant of Itamar, was at its head.

Thus, according to Samaritan tradition, Samaritanism is a perpetuation of the true Israelite faith, and Judaism only the continuation of Eli's heresy. This is the case, the Samaritan tradition claims, all the way through Samuel, Saul, David, and the Judaean monarchy, with the rival cult of Eli eventually shifting from Shiloh to Jerusalem and continuing up to this day.

A non-Samaritan tradition from the same period claims that the Samaritans originated in the Assyrian post-conquest settlement of populations from Babylon, Cuthah, Avva, Hamath, and Sepharvaim in northern Israel (II Kings 17:24–41), and that they were forced to worship the god of Israel by the native peoples. These immigrant groups brought with them the idols of their native cities, whom they continued to worship in conjunction with the deity of their new home. (II Kings 17:24–41; Ezra 4:2, 10; Mor 1989, 1): "Even while these people were worshipping the Lord, they were serving their idols. To this day their children and grandchildren continue to do as their fathers did" (II Kings 17:41).

Another non-Samaritan tradition is that the Assyrian conquest of Israel was far from total, that significant numbers of Israelites remained on the land, and that the Assyrians settled a separate group of exiles in what used to be the Israelite northern kingdom. These populations eventually intermingled, in time becoming a discrete group of people who later came to be referred to as Cutheans and Samaritans (Jos., Ant. 9:288–391; Mor 1989, 1).

But, unfortunately, even Samaritan historical traditions are not in agreement on either the time or the circumstances of their return. The Samaritan text Chronicle Adler relates the story of two returns, one under the high priest Seraiah in the early seventh century B.C.E. and another under the high priest Abdiel in the late sixth century B.C.E.!

Samaritans in the Time of Nehemiah

The first direct references we have to the Samaritans come from the book of Nehemiah. In 445 B.C.E., when the person we know as the biblical Nehemiah was appointed by the Persian king Artaxerxes I (464–424 B.C.E.) to rebuild the temple at Jerusalem and later (during a second "tour of duty") to be the governor of the province of *Yehud*. During some internecine rivalry surrounding the building of a wall around Jerusalem, Nehemiah named his enemies as Tobiah (the "Ammonite servant"), Geshem (the "Arab"), and *Sanballat (the "Horonite"). Tobiah was a member of an established Jewish family (see *Tobiads) from Transjordan (Neh. 2:10; 2:19; 4:7; 6:1). Geshem led the Arab tribes in the southern part of Judea. Sanballat the Horonite was a Samaritan who was coincidentally the Persian-appointed governor of Samaria, and therefore a direct rival of Nehemiah and a person with whom Nehemiah refused to have any contact (Mor 1989, 2–3).

Sanballat, as the Persian-appointed governor of Samaria, may indeed have been in direct competition with Nehemiah, since Jerusalem was to be refortified, whilst Samaria, a provincial center, was not. Urban wall systems of the mid-fifth century are found only at Lachish and Tel en-Nasbeh and at Jerusalem during the time of Nehemiah (Hoglund 1992, 211).

Another reason for Nehemiah's rejection of the Samarian contingent may have been that Judah had previously been part of the province of Samaria and that the Persian province of Yehud only came into being with the arrival of Nehemiah. This might explain why Sanballat wanted to be involved in the building project. If Samaria had controlled Judah up to this point (and there is a hint of this in the earlier attempts to stop the building program of Ezra), then the hostility towards Nehemiah may have been real. In the same vein, Nehemiah may have felt threatened by Sanballat, feeling that he might be trying to promote integration of Yehud back into the province of Samaria. In either case, there is no proof; only supposition and guesswork.

Nehemiah's program of wall-building can also be seen as an indicator of a reversal in the Persian attitude towards Jerusalem by reference to an earlier and failed attempt to rebuild the fortifications (Ezra 4:7–23). During that earlier attempt, officials in Samaria reported it to the Persian court, and Artaxerxes I ordered that the work be stopped. Samarian officials used imperial military forces to make sure his order was enforced. This lends some support to the idea expressed above that Judea might once have been part of the province of Samaria, hence the rivalry between Sanballat and Nehemiah, both Persian officials.

One of Sanballat's daughters married a son of the Jerusalem high priest Joiadah (Neh. 13:28; Jos, Ant. 11:306–12). Since Nehemiah believed in the "purity" ideology of the returnees, his reaction was to expel the couple from Jerusalem (Mor 1989, 4; Smith-Christopher 1994, 259).

The Samaritans in the Second Temple Period

Until the arrival of Alexander the Great in the near east in 332 B.C.E., there is little information about the Samaritans. Then, at least according to Josephus, they once more come into view in Judea, where Manasseh, the brother of the high priest Jaddus, married Nikaso, a daughter of Sanballat III (a descendant of the Sanballat of the time of Nehemiah) (Jos., Ant 11:302–3; Mor 1989, 4). Josephus reports that this Sanballat, like his ancestor a governor of Samaria, hoped that through the marriage of his daughter to the high priest's brother he could establish ties with the Jewish community in Jerusalem. However, Manasseh was offered two choices by the Jerusalem hierarchy: to stay in Jerusalem and divorce his wife, or to leave the city and take his Samaritan wife with him. Manasseh chose the second option, whereupon his father-in-law promised to build a temple on Mt. Gerizim where Manasseh would be high priest and that, in addition, he would take over civic leadership of Samaria on the death of his father-in-law. According to Josephus, many priests left Jerusalem and followed Manasseh to Samaria (Ant. 11:306–12; Mor 1989, 5).

Sanballat III sent 8,000 soldiers to support Alexander's campaigns and also convinced him that it would be to his advantage to allow the Samaritans to build a temple on Mt. Gerizim, where his son-in-law would be high priest. During this period when the Macedonians were consolidating their hold on the region and the Persians were not yet fully vanquished, the Samaritans quickly built their temple (it took less than nine months). The founding of a temple was not unusual; however, this temple was not far from its Jerusalem rival, and from the establishment of this temple the Samaritans and the Jews grew further apart, and it is from this period onwards that much of the anti-Samaritan polemic in the Hebrew Bible and extra-biblical texts (such as Josephus) originates.

The temple was completed around 332 B.C.E., at the time that Alexander finally took control of Gaza (Mor 1989, 7), and was also contemporary with the establishment of a Macedonian colony in the city of Samaria and the rebuilding and resettling of Shechem (Purvis 1968, 105).

However, Sanballat III died just two months into Alexander's siege of Gaza (Jos., Ant. 11:325) and, according to the historian Quintus Curtius, after the siege of Gaza Alexander left a Greek official named Andromachus in charge of the region. Despite Sanballat III's promise to his son-in-law, and for the first time since the Persian conquest, a Samaritan was not in charge of Samaria (Mor 1989, 9). The Samaritan leadership reacted strongly to this, rebelled against the Macedonians, captured and burned Andromachus alive, and then fled from Shechem to a cave in the Wadi Daliyeh just north of Jericho (Cross 1985, 7–17). The Macedonians retaliated immediately, with Alexander himself said to have left Jerusalem to punish the Samaritans. All of the rebels were killed, all Samaritans were banished from Samaria, and the city of Samaria was settled with Macedonian veterans (Mor 1989, 10).

According to Josephus (Jos., Apion, 2:43), following the post-rebellion massacre, administrative control of the district of Samaria was given to the Jews because of their loyalty to Alexander. The Samaritans who survived the Macedonian massacre, and who had heretofore exercised control and political authority and cultural leadership in Samaria, were now wholly disenfranchised and they could not turn to Jerusalem for help.

From the death of Alexander the Great, nothing much is known about the Samaritans until the rise of the Seleucid empire in around 200 B.C.E. From Josephus (Ant. 12:5–10) we know that a number of Samaritans and Jews settled in Egypt and that relations between them were very strained, with each side demanding that sacrifices be directed to their respective sanctuaries. Any grace or favor to one side was seen as detrimental to the other, and so a tit-for-tat hostility developed.

In Palestine, the first report of open hostility between Shechemites and Jews in Jerusalem is dated to the time of Ptolemy V (Epiphanes) and Antiochus III in around 200 B.C.E. (Jos., Ant. 12:154–56). According to Josephus, the Jews were being harassed by Samaritans through raids on Jewish land and the capture and sale of Jews into slavery, and the Samaritans found themselves under pressure from Antiochus III, because they had allied themselves with pro-Ptolemaic policy, thinking that they would prevail against the Syrians. This was nothing new. This loyalty dated back to the Persian period when Sanballat the Horonite and Tobiah the Ammonite had allied against Nehemiah, the governor of the province of Judaea.

In 168 B.C.E. the two groups grew still further apart when the Seleucid king (Antiochus IV Epiphanes) ordered the Jews and the Samaritans to rededicate their temples to Zeus. In Judea, *Judah Maccabee organized a rebellion which culminated in the ousting of Zeus from the temple and its subsequent repurification. During this period, both Samaritans and Jews were subject to the persecutions of Antiochus IV Epiphanes (175–164 B.C.E.), as is seen in II Maccabees (5:23; 6:2), even though Samaria did not rebel against Antiochus IV.

What had been a religious division now became a political conflict as well. Judea, having fought for its freedom from Seleucid rule, became an independent state, ruled by a line of high priests derived from the Hasmonean dynasty. One of them was John *Hyrcanus (134–104 B.C.E.), whose political program included the expansion of the state along with a campaign of propaganda to advertise itself and, as part of this campaign, Hyrcanus utilized a policy of forced conversion to Judaism. While Antiochus VII (Sidetes) was in the east, John Hyrcanus invaded northern Palestine and Syria.

Among the places he captured were Shechem and Mt. Gerizim. Later in his reign, Hyrcanus laid siege to Samaria and after a year's campaign took it (Jos., Wars 1:64ff; Ant. 13:275ff.). The bustling, cosmopolitan, and mainly non-Israelite city of Samaria was utterly destroyed by Hyrcanus (Isser 1999, 571), and in around 128 B.C.E., the sanctuary and temple on Mt. Gerizim were destroyed (Jos., Wars 1:62f.; Ant. 13:254ff.).

While the Jewish priesthood ceased to function after 70 C.E., the Samaritans continued to have an active priesthood with a high priest even after the temple on Mt. Gerizim was destroyed (Pummer 1998, 26–27), and whereas the inevitable dispersal of the Samaritans had not yet happened, the process was underway, not least because the Samaritans were now under the economic and political control of Jerusalem. However, a core group of Samaritans stayed near Mt. Gerizim in the town of Sychar (which may have replaced Shechem as the center of Samaritan religious authority).

There are very few sources other than Josephus to help outline the history of the Samaritans in the early Roman period, and those that do exist are often very hostile to their subject. Josephus, for instance, did not even consider the Samaritans to be Jews (Ant. 11:341).

Pompey's conquest of Palestine in 63 B.C.E. ended Jewish domination of Samaria (Jos., Wars 1:166). The cities that had been captured by the Hasmoneans were restored to their previous inhabitants. Samaria and other regions were joined to the Roman province of Syria and protected by two full Roman legions. Because so many of the people of Samaria had been killed or were too scattered to bring back together, the Romans repopulated the newly built town of Samaria with new colonists (Jos., Wars 1:169f.; Ant. 14:90f.; Isser 1999, 572).

The proconsul of Syria, Aulus Gabinius (57–54 B.C.E.) had to quell an uprising by another Hasmonean, Alexander, son of Aristobulus, during which Roman soldiers sought refuge and came under siege on Mt. Gerizim. (Jos., Wars 1:175ff.; Ant. 14:100). In 43 B.C.E., with Roman backing, *Herod the Great restored order in Samaria (Jos., Wars 1:229; Ant. 14:284; Isser 1999, 572). At the end of the Roman civil war, Herod declared his loyalty to Octavian, who confirmed him as the Jewish king and conferred on him new territories (Jos., Wars 1:396ff.; Ant. 14:217); among these new territories was Samaria. Herod rebuilt and extended the city of Samaria and added a further 6,000 colonists to its population. He renamed the city Sebaste in honor of Octavian (Jos., Wars 1:403; Ant. 14:295ff.; Isser 1999, 573).

There are numerous reports of acts of hostility against the Jews by Samaritans. How true these are is unknown, but there does seem to be a prevailing tradition of antagonism between the groups. As an example of the sort of thing reported, Josephus records that during the procuratorship of Coponius (6–9 C.E.) it had been the practice to keep the gates of the Jerusalem temple open after midnight at Passover. On one such occasion, a number of Samaritans are said to have secretly entered and scattered human bones throughout the grounds, rendering them unclean (Ant. 18:29 f.).

There is another account in Josephus (Ant. 18:85–89) about a massacre of Samaritans during the Procuratorship of Pilate (26–36 C.E.). Josephus reports that a man whom he describes as a rabble-rouser promised to show the Samaritans the sacred vessels of the *mishkan* (the ancient tabernacle) which, according to Samaritan tradition, Moses had buried in a secret place on Mt. Gerizim. This discovery would signal the Age of Divine Favor (the fulfillment of Samaritan eschatological belief involving Moses, the *mishkan* and a person (the "rabble-rouser") who was a sort of messianic figure – the "restorer"). A large group gathered in a nearby village with the intention of climbing Mt. Gerizim, but Pilate interpreted this as the prelude to revolt and so the gathered Samaritans were intercepted by Roman troops and killed or captured. The leaders were executed at Pilate's orders. This was too much for the Samaritan council, who complained to Vitellius, the governor of Syria, who accepted their accusations against Pilate and sent Marcellus to take over in Judea and ordered Pilate to return to Rome for trial before the emperor Tiberius. This Pilate did, but Tiberius had died, and we know nothing further about this episode (Grabbe 1994, 424; Isser 1999, 576).

An even more serious event occurred during the Procuratorship of Cumanus (48–52 C.E.) at a village named Gema (between Samaria and the Plain of Esdraelon to the north). Josephus reports that some Samaritans attacked a group of Galileans who were on their way to Jerusalem for a festival and killed either many or one (War 2:12:3, 232; Ant. 20, 6:1, 118; Tacitus, *Annals* XII, 54). When the Jews appealed to Cumanus he did nothing (allegedly because he had been bribed by the Samaritans). A mob of Jews took matters into their own hands and attacked some Samaritan villages. Cumanus then intervened, and both Jews and Samaritans appealed to the Syrian governor, Quadratus. After a preliminary investigation, Quadratus sent Cumanus, the military tribune Celer, some of the Samaritan notables, the high priests Jonathan and Ananias, and other Jewish leaders to Rome for trial before Claudius. Agrippa II petitioned Claudius on behalf of the Jews and Claudius found in their favor, executing the Samaritan delegation and exiling Cumanus. The tribune Celer was taken back to Jerusalem and executed publicly there (Isser 1999, 574–75).

Acts 8:4ff. reports a successful mission of the preacher Philip among the Samaritans. He performed healings, exorcisms, and baptized many in the name of Jesus. After this, Peter and John came from Jerusalem and bestowed on the new converts the Holy Spirit. Nothing more is mentioned about the Samaritan converts (Isser 1999, 576). In general, however, the Samaritans (as with the Jews) regarded Jesus as a false prophet (Isser 1981, 166ff).

It is clear from Josephus at least that the relation between Samaritanism and Judaism was tense, as is presupposed in the story about the good Samaritan. However, Jesus, especially in the Gospel of Luke, contrasts Samaritan openness with Jewish rigidity (Luke 10:30–37; 17:16; John 4; Acts 8:25).

While Josephus does not say that the Samaritans fought with the Jews during the war of 66–73 C.E., he does note that large numbers of them collected on Mt. Gerizim, ready for war. Even though the Romans faced a steep ascent to join battle with the Samaritans, thirst and desertion among the Samaritans made their work easier and quicker. Despite this, those Samaritans who remained would not surrender and died fighting (Josephus, Wars 3:307–15).

In the wake of the Jewish and Samaritan rebellion, the Emperor Vespasian founded the new town of Flavia Neapolis (Jos., Wars IV, 449; Pliny, *Natural History* V, 13:69) which later came to be called Nablus by the Arabs. This settlement became the new center for the Samaritans and remains so to this day (Isser 1999, 577).

Samaritans in the Graeco-Roman Diaspora

In the Diaspora, when Jews and Samaritans lived in the same communities, they would have had to explain their allegiances to the authorities from whom they requested privileges, and Josephus records difficulties between Jews and Samaritans in Egypt (Ant. 12:10, 74–79). Thus, while Jerusalem exerted its influence on Diaspora Jews, so Gerizim influenced the Diaspora Samaritans (Purvis 1968, 110).

In 1979, two inscriptions were found near the stadium on *Delos by Philippe Fraisse of the Ecole française d'Athènes. Both were found in an unexcavated area just beneath current ground level near the shoreline of the east of the island. Both are dedicated by the "Israelites who offer to Holy Argarizein." The term *Argarizein* is the Greek rendering of the Hebrew *Har Gerizim*, that is, Mt. Gerizim, and these two inscriptions certainly provide evidence of a hitherto unknown community of Samaritans on the island (Matassa 2006; White 1987, 141–42).

The first inscription reads "The Israelites on Delos who make first-fruit offerings to Holy Argarizin crown with a golden crown Sarapion son of Jason of Knossos for his benefactions on their behalf," and has been dated to between 150 and 50 B.C.E. (Bruneau 1982, 469–74; Matassa 2006). It is not clear whether the honoree is himself a Samaritan, Jew, pagan, resident of or visitor to Delos. It does, however, identify the dedicators as "the Israelites on Delos," and there seems little doubt that this refers to a Samaritan community of some sort on this tiny island.

The second inscription reads, "[The] Israelites who make first-fruit offerings to holy Argarizin honor Menippos, son of Artemidoros of Heraclea, himself as well as his descendants to have established and dedicated its expenses, for an offering/prayer [to God], [- - - - - - -] and [- - - - -] and crowned it with a golden crown and [- - -]," and is dated to around 250–175 B.C.E. (Bruneau 1982, 469–74; Matassa 2006).

The inscriptions show that the dedicators (on Delos or elsewhere) were connected to Mt. Gerizim, and it could be that offerings were sent to Mt. Gerizim while the Samaritan temple still stood there or that offerings continued to be made and sent to Samaria after the destruction of the temple. Or, indeed, it could be that the offerings were made on Delos, perhaps in the form of votives, and were dedicated by Samaritan visitors to the island, Samaritan residents of the island, or even friends or business partners of Samaritans elsewhere on their behalf – as the two inscriptions are the only evidence of Samaritans on the island, it is impossible to know. There is certainly no evidence of a synagogue (either Jewish or Samaritan) on the island, but the inscriptions do at least indicate there was a permanent colony of Samaritans on Delos in the Second Temple period (Matassa 2006).

Excavations on Mt. Gerizim

Yitzhak Magen's excavations on Mt. Gerizim uncovered some 480 marble inscriptions and around 13,000 coins. About 90% of the inscriptions were written in ancient Aramaic script, and the remainder in either Hebrew or Greek. The inscriptions were votive offerings brought to the sanctuary and dedicated there. According to Magen, those inscriptions indicate that the sanctuary was there as early as the end of the sixth century B.C.E. (Magen, Tsafania and Misgav 2000(c), 125–32).

The excavations on the top of Mt. Gerizim began in 1983, but only as late as 1998 did the profile of the temple begin to emerge. The temple was found under the remains of a fifth-century Byzantine church (the Church of Mary the Theodokos built by the Emperor Zeno in 484 C.E.). The excavation team uncovered six-foot-thick walls, gates, and altars, and it is thought that the totality of this find could provide the first real indication of what the Jewish temple, destroyed by the Romans in 70 C.E., might have looked like (Magen 2000(a), 74–118; Magen 2000(b), 133).

The Mt. Gerizim excavations show that the temple was surrounded by residential quarters, such as those in Jerusalem. Some 15,000 people lived in a city spread out over 100 acres, which the excavators have taken to indicate that Josephus was correct in saying that the Mt. Gerizim temple was a replica of the temple in Jerusalem. While the exact dimensions of the Jerusalem temple are not known, the foundation of the temple on Mount Gerizim appears to be about 400 × 560 feet (Magen 2000(a), 74–118; Magen 2000(b), 133).

[Lidia Domenica Matassa (2nd ed.)]

Late Roman to Crusader Period

After brief reports of the building of Tiberias and Caesaria in the reigns of Tiberius and Vespasian, the Samaritan Chronicle II narrates the events of Hadrian's time. Both Jews and Samaritans suffered under this emperor (117–38), according to one part of the chronicles, but a later addition tells of the success of the Samaritans in gaining Hadrian's favor by helping him to overcome the defenders of Jerusalem during his siege of the city. This version states that Hadrian was allowed to build a place of worship on Mt. Gerizim and that all Jews living in the area were forcibly removed. Samaritan guards were placed at the emperor's *beit kinshah*, as it was called (see Montgomery, 91, for further details from other sources), but while Hadrian was away in Rome his priests defiled the *beit kinshah* by burning corpses there. The defilement, in Samaritan eyes, resulted in a gathering of people destroying the building and then purifying the place ritually. The outcome was that Hadrian sent an army which attacked and killed many of the Samaritans. At last one clever Samaritan managed to put the blame on the Jews and managed to persuade Hadrian of the Samaritans' innocence, so that the emperor attacked the Jews instead. Throughout the chronicles, statements are made about the loss of Samaritan literature during times of persecution. The worst of these periods seems to have been during the rule of Hadrian (and later of Commodus and Severus), when most of the literature kept in Shechem was destroyed. The high priest lists, however, were probably preserved.

Both Samaritan and Jewish sources tell of the friendship of Antoninus Pius (138–61) for their respective peoples. For the Samaritans, the worst of all persecutions was that of Commodus (180–92). They were forbidden to read the Torah or teach it to their children, synagogues were closed, and many Samaritans suffered crucifixion for minor offenses. The reason for Commodus' persecutions given in Abu-al-Fatḥ and Chronicle II was a dispute between *Alexander of Aphrodisias and a Samaritan called Levi. A philosophical discussion, which was the starting point, led to the anger of the emperor and severe repression of Levi's compatriots, with the consequent destruction of their written documents and scrolls (some of which were hidden and saved). Claudius Gelenus (who died c. 200) is brought into the story, and it is claimed that he persuaded Commodus to force the Samaritans to eat the meat of pigs. Subsequent trials compelled many Samaritans to flee to other regions. At the end of Commodus' reign, 300,000 Samaritans were reported living in the Shechem area.

Nothing is reported of Septimius Severus (193–211), but Alexander Severus (222–35) is reported to have persecuted the Samaritans almost as severely as had Commodus. He enforced the worship of Roman gods, thus bringing about a series of rebellions against his rule, which he put down mercilessly. His reign was also a time of famine and pestilence. Since the Samaritans' great hero *Baba Rabbah is recorded as having lived during Alexander Severus' rule, it may be assumed that there is some confusion in the account (see Montgomery, 96, for an alternative view). Severus' successors are correctly stated to have been Gordianus (238–44), Philip (244–49), and Decius (249–51). This period seems to have been a difficult one for Samaria on the whole, but little more is heard from Samaritan sources until the advent of Muhammad. From the evidence of external sources, it is confirmed that Samaria suffered from the many political and military maneuverings of the era. The next source of trouble and change for Samaria was the Christianization of the empire. The edict of Constantius, which prohibited the marriage of Christian women to Jews (Montgomery, 100), led to social intolerance throughout Palestine. Circumcision, prohibited by Hadrian, seems to have been prohibited again in the time of Bishop Germanus, whose jurisdiction included Nablus.

The story of Baba Rabbah may properly be related to the period of Bishop Germanus. The chief importance of this Samaritan hero was that he revived the Samarian hopes of freedom. He organized Samaria into districts, built synagogues, encouraged literature, and raised a standing army. The Baba Rabbah story, despite some legendary accretions, is not as absurd as Montgomery claims (103), for a great change in Samaritanism undoubtedly took place at about this time (witness the work of *Markah and his family, who gave new shape to religious thinking and gave Samaritan religion a firm base).

During a long period of gradual Christianization in Palestine, the Samaritans fared badly; there were continual attacks by Samaritans on Christians and Christians on Jews and Samaritans, and the holy places of Israel were taken over by the Christians. Under certain rulers, a measure of protection was accorded to both Jews and Samaritans, but the long reign of Theodosius II (408–50) brought in its wake many deprivations, and both Jews and Samaritans became in effect second-class citizens with minimal rights. It was not until the latter part of the fifth century that the full fury of the new order was felt in Samaria, for under Zeno (474–91) Jews and Samaritans suffered terrible massacres, and the Samaritan chronicles tell of many incidents during this period which resulted in increasing repression. For the period of Anastasius (491–518) and Justinian I (527–65), the chronicles have little information, but external sources (see Montgomery, 113ff.) reveal further devastations of the dwindling Samaritan community. Many small-scale uprisings had taken place almost annually throughout the Christian period, but the greatest seems to have occurred soon after Justinian I became emperor. This was in the year 529, and there are many sources of information about it (Montgomery, 114–6). It is clear that thousands of Samaritans died in the fighting and that they tried to establish their own state. Jews and Samaritans seem to have been treated alike by the Christian victors; sources speak of 50,000 Jewish and Samaritan soldiers being offered by the Samaritans to the Persian king if he would take over Palestine. This attempt, which was foiled, was symptomatic of the state of affairs in Samaria. The people of Samaria became increasingly desperate, and things were to become even worse as more repressive laws were promulgated by Justinian, for a rising number of Samaritans relinquished their faith and embraced Christianity, thus further reducing the number adhering to the ancient faith. Indeed the Samaritans, as a recognizable religious group, had all but been outlawed by Christianity. They lived in territory sacred to the Christians; they were regarded, with the Jews, as eternal enemies of the new faith; and even when they converted, they were not accorded the full rights of other Christians.

According to the chronicles, many Samaritans fled eastward after 634, when the Muslims were victorious at Yarmuk. Throughout the account of Samaritan history, from earliest times, there were frequent emigrations eastward, and contact between the émigrés and *Nablus seems to have been lost frequently until the 13th century, when migrations back to Nablus began. The story of life under the caliphs is one of revolt and suppression. Little information on the basic cause of the troubles is available because Muslim and Samaritan historians hardly refer to the Samaritans in historical terms. During the early part of the reign of Hārūn al-Rashīd (d. 809), plague and famine blighted Samaria, but after these calamities the Samaritans enjoyed peace in his time. The reign of Ma'mūn (813–33) was a period of respite, on the whole, but the reign of his successor, Muʿtaṣim (833–42), brought considerable calamity to Samaria when certain Muslim fanatics demolished many synagogues and all but destroyed Nablus.

As time went on, religious bitterness increased and the Muslims imposed prohibitions on religious practices, especially pilgrimages to Mt. Gerizim. During the tenth century, however, matters improved under the Fatimid caliphs. Samaritan, Islamic, or Christian sources tell little about the period of the Crusades. The Samarian capital was the center of political intrigue and ecclesiastical debate during the early part of the 12th century. In 1137 Nablus seems to have undergone the catastrophe of further devastation and decimation of its inhabitants when the Saracens attacked it. Thereafter, until 1244, Muslims assumed rule of the Samarian capital.

[John Macdonald]

Later History

The final destruction of crusader rule in Palestine by the Mamluks (1291), who established their own hegemony over the country, did not bring about an improvement in the situation of the Samaritans. Instead of the Christian rule that unceasingly pressured the thousands of Samaritans who remained true to their ways came the rule of the Mamluks, who were even more cruel and fanatic about their religion: and in place of forced conversion to Christianity came the conversion out of fear of entire Samaritan families. At the very beginning of their rule, the Mamluks plundered the Samaritan religious center in Shechem (Nablus) and turned it into a mosque, in addition to destroying all the other buildings there.

Muslim pressure created substantial opposition on the part of the Samaritans. It was expressed in the figure of the high priest, Phinehas b. Yūsuf (1308–63), who, together with his sons and other members of the family of high priests, established a religious movement among the Samaritans to reinforce their faith and stand up against the pressure to convert to Islam. In addition to their foremost center in Shechem, the Samaritans also had an important center in Damascus from the 11th century. In the course of the 14th century the two centers achieved the height of their social and religious development, and the contact between them, which sometimes reached the dimension of competition, brought about the strengthening and crystallization of the Samaritan life by the renewed writing of books on religious law, history, and the order of rituals. By the beginning of the Ottoman conquest, however, this movement was no longer intact.

During the same period the Samaritans had centers of secondary importance in Cairo and Gaza. Both these centers, as well as the one in Damascus, observed annual pilgrimages to Mt. Gerizim and the community centered in Shechem. The family of the high priests in Shechem functioned as the supreme institution for all the Samaritan centers. The center in Cairo was influential in the Mamluk court. Its wealth aided the Mamluk authorities in their conquests, but was also a burden to the Samaritans themselves. Of the three sects in Egypt at the end of the 15th century – the Jews, the Karaites, and the Samaritans – the last were forced to pay half the royal taxes that were imposed on the three sects as a whole. The center in Damascus reached the height of its development in the 13th and 14th centuries, and a family of high priests, which was subordinate to that in Shechem and was a scion of Aaron's descendants, was even established there. The community produced important writers, poets, commentators, and grammarians, as well as physicians, some of whom became viziers in Mamluk courts.

With the beginning of the Ottoman conquest, the persecutions suffered by the Samaritans at the hands of their Muslim neighbors and local governors grew in strength and frequency. The beginning of the collapse of the Samaritan center in Damascus is recorded by Samaritan historians as taking place in the middle of the 16th century, with the transfer of the Damascus family of high priests, together with important members of the Damascus community, to Shechem to strengthen the community there. In 1625 the remaining Samaritans in Damascus were massacred, and their spiritual centers were transferred to Muslim hands.

The Samaritans in Egypt were, likewise, plagued by persecutions. The community there, which had been in existence since the age of Alexander the Great, reached the height of its development and wealth at the end of the 16th century, when their affairs with the Mamluks were under the control of the Jewish *nagid*. The Samaritans nonetheless frequently incited the Mamluks against the Jews. With the penetration of Ottoman rule into Egypt, the Samaritans were accused of supporting the Mamluks, and many of them were imprisoned and converted to Islam. The small Samaritan community remained in existence until the beginning of the 18th century, when the surviving members joined the community in Shechem and Samaritan settlement in Egypt came to an end.

The most important event relating to the decrease in the size of the Samaritan community was the disappearance of the line of high priests descending from Aaron. The last high priest of this line, Shalmiah b. Phinehas (1613–24), did not father any sons, and with his death the priesthood passed to the family of levites, the sons of Uzziel b. Kehat, which has filled this office until the present. After the death of Shalmiah, the persecutions by local Muslims against the Samaritans increased: houses and fields were plundered and many families were forced to convert to Islam for fear of their lives. Access to Mt. Gerizim was forbidden to the Samaritans by the Arabs, and they were forced to hold the Passover sacrifice on the eastern slope of the mountain. Beginning with the middle of the 17th century, there was a community of Samaritans in Shechem, a small but strong one in Gaza, and an even smaller one in Jaffa. The levite family descended from Uzziel the uncle of Aaron was also about to die out as a result of internal conflicts, but at the last moment it was saved, due to a compromise when a Samaritan woman from Jaffa was married to the last offspring of the family, Tabia b. Isaac (1751–86).

At the beginning of the 19th century the Samaritans lived in a certain degree of comfort in Shechem, but once again the Muslims interfered and prevented them from ascending to the top of Mt. Gerizim for the Passover sacrifice. This prohibition was in effect until 1820, when the Samaritans were again allowed to go up the mountain due to the intervention of the British consulate with the Turks. During the same period, however, the community in Gaza came to an end as the result of its expulsion by the Muslims.

By the third decade of the 19th century, only the small community of Samaritans in Shechem remained. This community was also on the verge of extinction in 1842. The Arabs of Shechem, incited by their religious teachers, cruelly persecuted the Samaritans and threatened to murder the entire community, claiming that the Samaritans were atheists because the script in which the Samaritan Pentateuch was written was not recognized by the Muslims. After the Samaritans turned to the Jewish community in Jerusalem, they received an authorization from the chief rabbi, Abraham Ḥayyim, that "the Samaritan people is a branch of the Jewish people that confesses to the truth of the Torah." In the same year the Samaritans were again forbidden to sacrifice on the top of Mt. Gerizim, and the prohibition lasted until 1849, when it was again rescinded through the influence of the British consulate.

It can be seen with certainty that the replenishment of the Samaritan community in Shechem by the survivors of other Samaritan centers was the factor that allowed the Samaritans to survive the 400 years of Ottoman rule. The surviving community was led by the high priest Jacob b. Aaron (Hārūn; 1874–1916), who reinforced the religious framework of Samaritan life in the hope of reviving the Samaritans, although scholars and writers of the end of the 19th century had begun to envision certain annihilation for the Samaritans. All the community's lands, riches, and property were taken from it, and the Samaritans remained in a dark ghetto, as it were, on the northern slope of Mt. Gerizim. Their situation deteriorated, both from a personal and economic point of view. The state of their industry and finances was expressed by the fact that most of the Samaritans engaged in copying documents for scholars and tourists who visited Shechem at the beginning of the 20th century. These books were sold for pennies, as it were, and the profit, in many cases, saved the Samaritans from starvation. The number of men was greater than the number of women, at a ratio of about two to one.

The Turkish administration tended to deal with the Samaritans harshly, and the latter were subject to the whims of the Arab families in Shechem, who competed for the local position of leadership at the office of the Turkish pasha in Acre. The Samaritans were often punished on accusations that they had cooperated with the party that lost the competition for the ruling position. A number of Samaritan youth were even forced to join the Turkish army. The plague that broke out in Shechem at the time of the withdrawal of the Turkish army left the community with the smallest population in its history, 146 souls.

With the beginning of the British Mandatory administration in Palestine, the situation of the Samaritans improved. The family of Tsedaka from Shechem had moved to Jaffa and become acquainted with Izhak *Ben-Zvi already in 1907. Throughout his career in Palestine and the State of Israel, Ben-Zvi devoted attention to improving the situation of the Samaritans, from every possible point of view. He convinced the Samaritans, for lack of a viable choice, to cancel their prohibition against marrying women from outside the community, and as a result a number of Samaritans have done so over the decades (beginning in 1923). Ben-Zvi also established friendship leagues between Samaritans and Jews that helped the Samaritans culturally and economically (e.g., a school for Jewish studies was established in Shechem with their aid). He used his position and personal influence to contact important and influential institutions (e.g., the *American Jewish Joint Distribution Committee) and procure aid for the Samaritans.

The Samaritan population doubled within a span of 30 years. With the establishment of the State of Israel (1948), the Samaritan community split into two centers: the first was in Shechem, under the government of the Hashemite Kingdom of Jordan; the second was in Israel, under the leadership of Japheth b. Abraham Tsedaka. As a result of Tsedaka's activities and Ben-Zvi's influence, in 1949 the Samaritans were recognized as citizens under the Law of Return, a fact that contributed to the reunification of Samaritan families from Shechem and the growth of the Samaritan community scattered throughout Israel. In 1953 the Samaritans were allowed, for the first time, to cross the border to celebrate Passover with their brethren on Mt. Gerizim, and this privilege, attained through an agreement by the Israel-Jordan Mixed Armistice Commission, remained in effect until the Six-Day War (1967), when Shechem came under Israeli rule. In the same year the obligation of Samaritans in Israel to serve in the Israel Defense Forces was officially recognized, although Samaritans had been serving in the IDF since its establishment. In 1954 all the Samaritans scattered throughout the State of Israel relocated in permanent living quarters in Ḥolon, and a unified Samaritan center was created in Israel. In 1963 President Ben-Zvi dedicated the first Samaritan synagogue in Israel.

The center in Shechem continued to exist in complete isolation under Jordanian rule. During the 19 years of Jordanian administration of the area, the Samaritans enjoyed the toleration and even support of the government. On the other hand, this sympathetic attitude also led to blind hatred of the Samaritans on the part of the Muslim inhabitants of Shechem, and every Arab demonstration in Shechem against Hashemite rule found its way into the small Samaritan quarter. Under the leadership of the high priests Abishua b. Phinehas (1941–60) and Amram b. Isaac (1960–1980), however, the Samaritans were able to find a middle road between these two forces. The Six-Day War ended the isolation of the two branches of the Samaritan community.

By 1977 the Samaritan population of Israel, including both Shechem and Holon, had risen to 500, a level that was maintained into the 21st century. A study undertaken by the Samaritan journal *A.B.* in 1977 revealed that the community had been transformed from an aging and dwindling one, numbering only 150 at the end of the 1920s, to the youngest community in the world, 21% being within the age group 1–10 and the same percentage in the age group 11–20; the disproportion between the ratio of females to males is, however, 5:3. The average number of marriages per year increased from 1.23 between 1910 and 1948 to 4.53 during 1967–1974. The attempts of the four clans of the Samaritans, Kohen, Tsedaka, Danfi and Marchiv, to keep their females within their clans was causing genetic problems arising from interbreeding. A study undertaken by an anthropologist, Dr. Joseph Ginat, in 1975 revealed that 58% of the 128 marriages contracted between 1910 and 1974 were within the same clan, and in the same year Dr. Bat-Sheva Bonne, the head of the faculty of genetics of Tel Aviv University, pointed to the frequency of color blindness and to the considerable number who are in need of genetic guidance before marriage in order to avoid the birth of physically handicapped children. The percentage of marriages with Jewesses had increased to 5%.

[Benyamim Tsedaka]

Statistics

An inscription from the period of Sargon II describing the destruction of Samaria tells that 27,290 Samaritans were exiled (721 B.C.E.). It is clear, however, that this number is only a minority of the inhabitants of the northern Kingdom of Israel, which, in the days of Menahem b. Gadi (743 B.C.E.), numbered 60,000 landowners who each paid 50 shekels tax to Tiglath-Pileser III (II Kings 15:19–20). It can therefore be assumed that the Israelite majority, which included an alien minority that was brought by the Assyrian kings, numbered more than 100,000 people at the beginning of the seventh century B.C.E. This community developed and spread into the Assyrian provinces in the center of the country. It is possible to learn of the large number of Samaritans during the period from the expansion of their settlement from Samaria into Gaza and Egypt in the south, and Beth-Shean, Acre, and Sidon in the north.

Clearer figures are known for the first centuries of the Common Era. In the three uprisings against the Byzantines (484, 529, and 579), the Samaritans lost tens of thousands of soldiers. In the largest uprising (in 529), which was a reaction to the Justinian persecutions, the Samaritans lost 100,000 soldiers, according to Procopius, or 20,000, according to the version of Malalas. Theophanes and Malalas related that the Samaritans sent emissaries to the king of Persia suggesting that he conquer the country from the Byzantines and agreeing to place 50,000 Samaritans and Jews at his disposal for this purpose. These sources imply that there were hundreds of thousands of Samaritans in the country. The decisive decrease in this number was a result of the frequent uprisings against the Byzantines.

The massacre of Samaritans continued even after the collapse of Byzantine rule. Tens of thousands were massacred or taken captive at the time of the Arab conquest, which led to the flight of the Samaritans eastward. In 1163 *Benjamin of Tudela found some 1,000 Samaritans outside of Shechem. It is therefore possible to surmise that the total Samaritan population of the country was about 2,000. The Arab writers a-Bīrūnī (1048), Idrīsī (1173), Yāqūt al-Ḥamawī (1125), al-Dimashqī (1300), and others relate that there was a large number of Samaritans in Shechem, and some of them estimated the population at more than 1,000.

In 1480 Meshullam of Volterra found 50 Samaritan clans in Egypt and 700 other Samaritans outside Shechem. According to the testimony of all the above-mentioned writers, and if one takes into account that the census was restricted to adults only, it can be assumed that in Palestine alone there were 5,000–6,000 Samaritans before the beginning of Mamluk rule, and 2,000–2,500 remained by the beginning of Ottoman rule.

The *Defters* (land records of Palestine kept in Constantinople which were published by Bernard Lewis) determined that in 1525–26 there were 25 Samaritan families in Gaza; in 1533 there were 15 families in Gaza and 29 in Shechem; and in 1548 there were 18 families in Gaza and 34 in Shechem. The high priest Shalma b. Tabia notes in his letter to Europe in 1820 that "we number less than 500 souls," and even then he was exaggerating the size of the Samaritan population, which stood at less than 200 people, as Shechem was the only center that remained. According to a letter of the British consul James Finn in 1851, there were 35 tax-paying Samaritans in Shechem, a fact which raises the number of Samaritans to over 150. The traveler M.E. Rogers related, on the basis of testimony from the high priest Amram b. Shalma, that in 1855–59 there were 196 Samaritans in Shechem. According to the census of the British consulate, there were 160 Samaritans in 1881; 196 in 1902; and 162 in 1904. M. Gaster counted 103 in 1905, and P. Kahle 173 in 1909.

With the end of Ottoman rule, a total of 146 Samaritans remained in Shechem, but suddenly their numbers began to grow. One of the causes for this was marriages to Jewish women, so that in 1934 the community numbered 206 (according to the testimony of the high priest published in that year). In 1948 there were 58 Samaritans in the State of Israel and 250 in Shechem. As a result of the unification of families (from Shechem to Ḥolon), in 1954 there were 87 in the State of Israel and 200 in Shechem; in 1963 there were 350 Samaritans in all, and in 1970 there were 430. In 2005 the two communities numbered around 500.

[Benyamim Tsedaka]

RELIGION AND CUSTOMS

The sources of knowledge of the Samaritan religion are the Samaritan Pentateuch and Targum, *Memar Markah*, the liturgy, and various expositions of law and commentaries on the books of the Pentateuch (see Language and Literature). Aside from the Pentateuch, the sources span a period of about 1,400 years. In terms of religious development these may be divided into three broad periods: (1) from the completion of the Pentateuch (date uncertain) to the Roman period, the period of formulation; (2) the third to fourth centuries C.E., the period of consolidation; (3) the 13th–14th centuries, the period of expansion. Religious writing in other centuries, though important in several respects, did not radically change the general nature of Samaritan religion.

It is likely that the Samaritan creed in its earliest form was a simple statement of belief in God and in the Pentateuch. Belief in Moses as the sole prophet of God, so prominent a feature of Samaritanism, probably developed long before the Roman conquest of Palestine, and almost certainly belief in Mt. Gerizim as the one true sanctuary chosen by Israel's God was well established before Alexander the Great (witness the large sacred area on Mt. Gerizim dated to his time). Belief in the resurrection, which is stated in many of the religious writings, certainly was in existence before the fourth century C.E., as it is to be found, but in a less developed form, in *Memar Markah*. As basis for this belief the Samaritan exegetes of all periods provide the "proof-text," Gen. 3:19 (see below), but it seems certain that such "proof-texts" were pegs on which to hang beliefs that came into Samaritan religion at a later time. Belief in the *taheb*, i.e., restorer (or according to some "returner"), as one who would restore all things prior to the last day, the cataclysm, the judgment, and finally paradise, is undoubtedly the latest of the creedal tenets. This tenet probably took hold in Samaritan soil during the time of religious ferment in Palestine around the destruction of Jerusalem in 70 C.E.

The doctrine of God is clear, simple, and mainly biblical. The absolute oneness of God is expressed on every hand. He is wholly "other" in substance and essence, present in all things, all-powerful, without peer, and beyond attribution. His purposes for mankind, especially Israel, were once and for all communicated to the world through Moses. The six beliefs can only be understood in terms of Moses. He was God's "Man," "the son of His house (= world)," almost His vice regent on earth; he it was who "wrote" the five books of the Pentateuch; it was he who authorized Mt. Gerizim as "the place which God chose" (not "will choose" as in Deut. 12:5 in the MT). There is some uncertainty about how Moses came to be associated with the *taheb*. It is in the didactic hymns of the 13th–14th-century part of the liturgy (many of which are to be found in manuscripts in various libraries, but see the long festival hymns in Cowley, *The Samaritan Liturgy*, vol. 2) that Moses is associated with the resurrection and judgment and with the restorer. Samaritan religious development did not quite formalize this association in the way that the other tenets were formalized, but in general it may be said that Samaritanism attributes to Moses every word and action, both for this world and beyond, which relates to the divine will for mankind.

The problem of belief in the resurrection in sectarian Samaritanism is fraught with difficulties. *Dositheanism may or may not have been one large sect. It may have comprised two or more sects stemming from an initial "heresy." Whether or not Dositheanism as a whole, or originally, believed in the resurrection as distinct from the priestly authority, there is no lack of evidence in the mainstream of Samaritan religious writing for such a belief. It is hardly likely that all such literature is "heretical."

The best view of essential Samaritan religion may be gained from a study of what the religious literature claims about Moses in relation to God and Israel. "Lord of all worlds," "the word of living truth," Moses is preeminent in all things; as the word in creation, the light shining on and in men, men's intercessor before God, lawgiver, teacher, priest, savior. All these and many other attributes, which are commonplace from the *Memar Markah* onward, indicate how far Samaritanism is "Mosaism." Almost a christological position is reached when Markah writes: "He who believes in him [= Moses] believes in his Lord" (*Memar Markah*, 4:7). Gnostic elements are prominent in the religious literature. These are elements found in common with the early Jewish and Christian literatures, but their influence on Samaritanism is often terminological rather than doctrinal. However, the emphasis on Moses as the word and the light seems to be best explained by reference to Gnosticism.

A typical Samaritan feature is the prominence of their priesthood in the life of the community. The priests are the interpreters of the law and the keepers of the secret of the calendar, upon which the true observation of their festivals depends. The famous *Baba Rabbah was the firstborn of a high priest.

Since the Samaritans possessed only the Pentateuch as against the threefold Bible of Judaism and had no codified second law corresponding to the Mishnah, the outlines of their beliefs were easier to delineate. Moses was "the prophet" to the Samaritans, and Joshua alone of all the other biblical prophets is held in high esteem, even called king, because he is mentioned in the Pentateuch as the servant of Moses, who was initiated by him to fill his place. This last remark gives the clue to the development of Samaritan doctrine, namely that no concept which had no warrant in the Pentateuch could be regarded as valid. So the resurrection doctrine is bound up with the Samaritan text of Gen. 3:19, "to your dust you shall return." There are many instances of Samaritan and masoretic textual disagreements, mostly insignificant, but a few are of the significance of the example just quoted, where a doctrine is at stake. The Ten Commandments of the masoretic Bible are regarded as nine by the Samaritans, who have a tenth of their own (of considerable length) stipulating the prime sanctity of Mt. Gerizim.

Some of the differentiae of Samaritan and Judaic religion are explained in this way. Other doctrines developed during certain eras, such as the belief in the judgment day. Belief in a day of vengeance and recompense, as it is called, could well have sprung from or given rise to Deuteronomy 32:35, where the Samaritan text reads "on the day of" against the masoretic text's "mine," a difference of two Hebrew letters.

Most of the beliefs about paradise are set in Islamic-type terms, and no doubt many details of the pictures of "the garden" were supplied during the long Islamic period, but as early as the *Memar Markah* there is sufficient evidence of such beliefs. The parallelism with early Jewish and Christian teachings on the subject is often striking, but not surprising if one takes into account the influence of Gnosticism on them.

There is no sign in Samaritan writings of the religious malpractices of which the Samaritan syncretists were condemned in II Kings 17:29ff.; indeed, the religion which emerges from the sources is remarkably pure and free from pagan influences. There is no indication anywhere of dove worship (R. Naḥman ben Isaac, Ḥul. 6a) or the adoration of a "god" called Ashima (Ibn Ezra, introduction, *Commentary on Esther*). This last accusation was based on a misunderstanding, as Ibn Ezra was not cognizant of the Samaritan usage to evade pronunciation of the Tetragrammaton by applying a surname "*Shema*" or "*Ashema*" instead (like *ha-Shem* in Jewish religious practice).

On the practical side of religion, the Samaritans have developed their code of religious practice by direct interpretation of biblical laws. A *halakhah* came into being, though not in the same way as in Judaism. It often differs from the rabbinical *halakhah* by its stricter adherence to the letter of the law, as in the laws of Sabbath and festivals or marriage between close relatives. In other cases it is based on different interpretation, as in the law concerning the levirate marriage (Deut. 25:5–10) or fixing the date of Pentecost, etc. There was no systematic codification of the law, and the few extant Samaritan halakhic compendia are arranged very loosely. Jewish, Karaite and Rabbanite, influence on their legal literature is evident in *Kitāb al-Mīrāth* ("Book of Inheritance"), probably belonging to the 12th century C.E., and in the classification of the 613 commandments of the Pentateuch. Mention of the number 613 is found even earlier in *Kitāb al-Kāfi* (1042 C.E.), but a systematic enumeration and classification is found first in a liturgical poem by Aaron b. Manīr of the 13th–14th century. His system shows striking dependence upon that of Maimonides. These influences are not surprising, as large Samaritan communities in Damascus and Cairo lived close to Jews, Rabbanites and Karaites.

Continuation of the festivals prescribed in the Torah was contingent on the political circumstances of the times, but throughout the vicissitudes of all these, the celebration of the Passover according to the strict regulations of the Torah was and is continued, whenever possible on Mt. Gerizim itself. Two other festivals, Pentecost and Tabernacles, were like Passover, regarded as pilgrimages, according to the Pentateuch (Ex. 23:17; 34:24; Lev. 23; Deut. 16), and to this day these pilgrimages are carried out as such (see M. Gaster, *The Samaritans*, pp. 168, 178 for details).

[John Macdonald]

Holidays and Festivals

THE SABBATH. The seventh day of the week serves as the basic rite for all Samaritan holidays and festivals. On the Sabbath the Samaritans hold four prayers. The first, which is held on the Sabbath eve, lasts for about an hour until the setting of the sun. The second is the Sabbath morning service, which begins, on regular Sabbaths, between three and four o'clock. The third is the afternoon prayer, which is held only on regular Sabbaths and those that fall during the counting of the Omer; it begins at noon and continues for about two hours. The fourth prayer is held at the end of the Sabbath and continues for about half an hour until the setting of the sun.

On Sabbaths and holidays the Samaritans dress in special clothing consisting of a long-sleeved, striped robe. During the prayers a long-sleeved white *tallit* made out of simple cloth is worn over the robe. The Samaritan synagogue is always oriented toward Mt. Gerizim. The worshipers stand on rugs spread out on the floor, and before one enters the synagogue he must remove his shoes. In addition, the worshipers must have a head covering while praying. The portion of the week is read at home by the head of the family, after the service, from *siddurim*.

The Samaritans do not light fires on the Sabbath or travel. They eat hot meals prepared beforehand only on the Sabbath eve, when they also kindle the lights that will remain on throughout the Sabbath; neither do they leave the vicinity of their community. The priests wear white miters on the Sabbath, to distinguish from the red ones worn during the week. They also lead the services and religious rites and open the reading of the weekly portion.

THE FESTIVALS. The Samaritans celebrate seven *mo'adim*, four of which are called *mo'adim* and three *ḥaggim*. The *ḥaggim* are the pilgrimages ordered in the Torah, e.g., Ex. 23:14–19. This special designation seems to have arisen under the influence of the Arabic *hajj*, which means "pilgrimage." The first *mo'ed* is Passover, which falls on the 15th day of the first month. On the eve of the festival, the Samaritans carry out the ceremony of the sacrifice on Mt. Gerizim. The second *mo'ed* is the Festival of the Seventh Month, which is celebrated on the first day of the seventh month and is parallel to the Jewish holiday of Rosh Ha-Shanah, except that it is celebrated for one day only. The third *mo'ed* is the Day of Atonement, which is celebrated on the tenth day of the seventh month from evening to evening. The fourth *mo'ed* is Shemini Aẓeret, which is celebrated on the 22nd day of the seventh month.

The first *ḥag* is Ḥag ha-Maẓẓot ("Feast of Unleavened Bread"), which is celebrated on the 21st day of the first month. The Samaritans make a pilgrimage to the top of Mt. Gerizim for the first time (in their cycle of ḥaggim). The second *ḥag* is the Festival of the Pentecost, which takes place on the day after the seventh Sabbath counted from the first Sabbath following Passover. As a result, it is traditional to celebrate this holiday on a Sunday. At this time the Samaritans make a pilgrimage for the second time. The third *ḥag* is Sukkot, which takes place on the 15th day of the seventh month, and the Samaritans make their third pilgrimage of the annual cycle. The Samaritans do not celebrate Purim or Ḥanukkah, because these holidays are not mentioned in the Pentateuch and were declared after the split between the Samaritans and the Jews. On the other hand, they celebrate the Independence Day of the State of Israel.

It should be noted that the Jews and the Samaritans rarely celebrate their holidays and festivals on the same days, as the determination of the beginning of the month and the intercalation of the years are made according to different calendar systems. Therefore, the differences of time between the Jewish and Samaritan holidays sometimes reach an entire month.

Passover. Passover is the time when the Samaritans celebrate the sacrifice of the paschal lamb on Mt. Gerizim. The ceremony is held 800 meters from the summit of the mountain, near the Samaritan center of 70 homes. At twilight on the 14th day of the first month all the members of the community gather at the site of the altar in two groups: the first carries out the sacrifice and the second, composed of community dignitaries and priests, participate in prayer. The high priest climbs upon a large stone and gives the signal to prepare to slaughter the sheep, while reading the story of the Exodus from Egypt (beginning with Exodus 12). The Samaritans have brought to the spot a number of sheep, corresponding to the number of families in the community, and, following the order of the high priest, the sheep are slaughtered as the congregation raises its voice in prayer. Immediately after the *kashrut* of the slaughter has been checked, the wool of the sheep is plucked with the aid of boiling water from two barrels placed upon the altar. Afterward, the sheep are hung from hooks and their intestines are cleaned and burned on the altar (together with those parts which are forbidden as food, according to the Samaritan Pentateuch).

At the end of cleaning and rinsing, the sheep are salted and laid aside for two hours, until the blood is absorbed by the salt. At about eight o'clock in the evening the sheep are carried on spits and placed into ovens for more than six hours. These ovens are dug into the earth and are sealed by means of shrubs and wet earth. At midnight the Samaritans return with bowls, open the ovens, remove the sheep, and divide the meat into the bowls. Each family takes its portion home, where it quickly eats the sacrifice together with *maẓẓot* and bitter herbs; any remains are returned to the altar and burned. Throughout the entire ceremony, the Samaritans continually sing, pray, and retell the story of the Exodus.

Festival of Pentecost (Shavuot). On this festival, as on Ḥag ha-Mazzot, the Samaritans make a pilgrimage to Mt. Gerizim. The holiday is celebrated on the 50th day of *sefirat ha-Omer*, which is on a Sunday. The Samaritans divide the period of the *sefirah* into seven weeks, and on each of the Sabbaths during the period they devote the service to one of the seven stations the Children of Israel passed on their Exodus from Egypt until they arrived at Mt. Sinai: the (Red) Sea (Exodus 14:26–15:21); the second Sabbath is called *Shabbat Marah* (Exodus 15:22–26); the third Sabbath is called *Shabbat Elim* (Exodus 15:27–16:3); the fourth Sabbath is *Shabbat ha-Man* (Ex. 16:4–36); the fifth is *Shabbat ha-Ẓur ba-Ḥorev* (Ex. 17:1–7); and the seventh *Shabbat Amalek* (Ex. 17:8–17).

On the fourth day after the sixth Sabbath of *sefirat ha-Omer*, the Samaritans celebrate the day of standing at Mt. Sinai. According to their tradition, the Pentateuch was given to the Children of Israel from above Mt. Sinai on this day. They pray and read from the Pentateuch from the middle of the night until the following evening. The seventh Sabbath during *sefirat ha-Omer*, the 49th day of the period, is called the Sabbath of the Ten Commandments (Ex. 19:120:14).

The pilgrimage on the Festival of Pentecost begins early in the morning, and during the processional all the places holy to the Samaritans that are situated on the peak are visited: Givat Olam, on which Moses' tabernacle stood; Isaac's altar, the spot where Abraham bound his son; and the site of the 12 rocks that Joshua placed before erecting Moses' tabernacle, according to Samaritan tradition.

The Festival of the Seventh Month. The Samaritan calendar begins with this festival each year, and it is the beginning of the Days of Awe for the Samaritans. The festival is celebrated one day only, the first day of the seventh month. At the close of this day begin the prayers of the Ten Days of Repentance each evening and each morning until the Day of Atonement.

Day of Atonement. This holiday begins during the late afternoon and the fast continues for 25–26 hours of prayer and continuous reading of the Pentateuch and *piyyutim*. Every member of the community over the age of one year must fast.

Sukkot and Shemini Azeret. On the eve of Sukkot, the Samaritans place palm branches on the net roof of the *sukkah*, put interwoven twigs on the palm branches, hang citrus fruit on string from the net roof of the *sukkah*, and hang willow branches from the roof, which is supported by four poles. The *sukkah* is erected inside the house. The Arab riots that plagued the Samaritans during various periods forced them to build their *sukkot* in their houses, and over hundreds of years this has become a tradition. The eve of Sukkot is devoted to building the *sukkah*, and on the morning of the holiday the Samaritans make the third pilgrimage to the top of Mt. Gerizim.

The periods are of *ḥol ha-mo'ed* Sukkot and also of Passover are devoted to special prayers each morning and evening. The Samaritans sit in the *sukkah* but do not sleep there.

Shemini Aẓeret begins on the 22nd day of the seventh month and is also called Simḥat Torah. After prayers, which begin shortly after midnight and continue for more than ten hours, like the prayers of all holidays and festivals, the priest carries the Torah around the synagogue for one round, while the worshipers clap hands.

Religious Ceremonies

CIRCUMCISION. The Samaritans are obligated to circumcise their sons at the age of eight days, for any male who is not circumcised eight days after birth is not considered an "Israel Samaritan" (Genesis 17:14). Because of the limited number of Samaritans who can perform the circumcision ceremony, this act has been handed over to non-Samaritans. The high priest officiates at the circumcision ceremony, which must take place immediately after morning prayers, at dawn. At the end of the ceremony, the high priest gives his blessing by reciting a poem on the subject ascribed to Markah (fourth century). The father of the infant then honors his guests and pays the high priest.

THE LAWS OF RITUAL IMPURITY AND PURITY. These laws are completely binding within the Samaritan community. During her menstrual period, for seven days, the woman is obliged to remain separated from her family, who must wait upon her and supply all her needs. She is forbidden to touch any household vessels, and anything upon which she sits must be rinsed with water. On the seventh day she bathes in water and becomes clean at sundown. A man who has had a nocturnal emission must wash his body in water and is unclean until nightfall. He sits during prayers in a special place outside the worshipers' hall, is forbidden to raise his voice, and is forbidden to touch holy articles until evening comes. A woman giving birth to a son is unclean for 40 days, and if the child is a daughter she is unclean for 80 days, after which she purifies herself (Lev. 12 and 15). The redemption of the circumcised firstborn son takes place only after the mother is cleansed of impurity of her childbirth. The high priest collects the redemption money.

COMPLETION OF THE TORAH. The completion of the Torah sets the official seal upon the beginning of the Samaritan's way of life in his tradition. In content it is reminiscent of the Jewish *bar mitzvah ceremony, but the difference is fundamental. The Jewish bar mitzvah takes place at the age of 13, while the Samaritan's bar mitzvah is dependent upon his education and ability. Only after he has learned the whole Pentateuch can the ceremony of completing the Pentateuch be arranged for a boy by his father. At the age of four or five, the father takes his son or daughter to the *ḥakham* (scholar) of the community, or to one of the priests, to have them taught Samaritan traditions and the principles of their faith. In an emergency, the father himself teaches his children. The child reads the Pentateuch in the ancient Hebrew script and in the special Samaritan pronunciation, as transmitted from generation to generation, and also learns writing. Able children complete the reading of the Pentateuch at the age of six, but some take as long as until the age of ten. On completing the reading, the child learns the blessing of Moses (Deut. 33–34) by heart. The father gathers all the Samaritans to the place of the rejoicing and the high priest gives the signal. The child, standing in the center upon a high chair, clothed in his best outfit, recites the blessing of Moses, following it by a speech (by heart) prepared for him by his teacher. He then descends from the chair, kisses the hands of the priests and other dignitaries, and receives gifts from them. He is now regarded as one of the quorum needed for community prayers. On the following Sabbath after the prayers he reads a portion of the Pentateuch immediately after the high priest. The Samaritans are then invited to a feast prepared by the parents of the child. The ceremony takes place to the accompaniment of liturgical hymns and poems written by Samaritan *paytanim* of all eras.

KIDDUSHIN. The proposal is the first of three stages in Samaritan marriage: *kiddushin, erusin, nissu'in*. They express the status of the girl in family life. When a Samaritan girl is certain of her choice, she urges him to request his parents to ask her parents for her hand. Occasionally, when a young man is in love he may request his parents to approach the girl's parents even without telling her of it. On being asked, the girl's parents reply: "We will call the damsel and inquire at her mouth" (Gen. 24:57). The girl's wish is now tested. If she desires the man, though her parents are opposed, she may reply affirmatively. She then appoints a guardian to perform the *erusin* (betrothal) ceremony on her behalf. The *kiddushin* ceremony takes place in the girl's home, and even a minor priest can sustain the bond and bless it by "recital of the *Shema*" and similar verses from the Pentateuch. The breaking of the *kiddushin* does not require divorce. Whenever conditions do not permit the continuation of the attachment, the man informs the girl's parents of it in writing or by word of mouth, and he is not liable for damages.

ERUSIN. The betrothal usually takes place a short time after the *kiddushin*. Release from *erusin* requires a divorce. The girl is herself not present, but her representative, her father or her uncle, or, in the event of her father not consenting to the betrothal, the guardian, sits opposite the young man. They clasp right hands together as a sign of the bond. The high priest sitting opposite, places his right hand upon their clasped hands and pronounces the *erusin* blessings over the bond. The high priest then receives a tied handkerchief containing six silver shekels from the young man and hands them to the girl's representative as a symbol of the dowry. When the priest finishes reading, "It is not good that the man should be alone; I will make him a helpmeet for him" (Gen. 2:18–25), the fiancé kisses the hand of the priest and of the notables. The fiancé and his fiancé are now regarded as husband and wife.

NISSU'IN. Marriage is the final stage, the formal act whose purpose is to complete the betrothal. Rejoicing on these occasions is greater than at any joyful Samaritan ceremony. The bridegroom's family proclaims a week of rejoicing to begin the Sabbath before the wedding. This is called the *Shabbat ha-Petiḥah* ("the Opening Sabbath" of the rejoicing). On this Sabbath the weekly portion of the law is read in the house of the groom's father. When the afternoon service is completed, the groom's relatives walk in procession from house to house and invite the guests to take part in the week of rejoicing. On the termination of the Sabbath, the men have a great feast in the house of the groom's father and sing wedding songs. The father of the groom bestows gifts upon the honored guests. On Sunday evening the women arrange their feast in the house of the bride's mother and they, too, indulge in much singing and music. On Monday evening one of the groom's relatives invites the men to a feast prepared in his house, and they again indulge in hymn singing and praises. In the center of the party sit the men, who sing, verse by verse, the account of Rebekah's marriage to Isaac (Gen. 24), each man taking a turn, with the bridegroom completing the reading. The evening of the third day is called "the red night," the night of the rejoicing of the bride. She is clothed in red garments symbolizing the purity of her virginity. The women prepare a splendid feast for her, the high point of which is the dance of the bridegroom's mother holding a parcel decorated with flowers containing the garments of the groom. The wedding takes place on the fourth day when the luminaries, symbolized by the bridegroom and bride, were created. During the day the bridegroom takes a piece of parchment to one of the scholars among the priests and asks him to write the marriage contract (*ketubbah*). He also rewards him for his trouble. In the evening the men assemble in the house of the groom, where they partake of the marriage feast. Afterward the groom's father invites the high priest to the place of rejoicing where the marriage is to take place. The high priest, the bridegroom, and the guests await the coming of the bride. She is accompanied by her relatives, who sing the Song of the Red Sea (the song of the prophetess Miriam) to the music of tambourines and with dancing. On the bride's arrival the priests break out in poetic song and marriage psalms. When the singing is finished, the groom rises, hands the marriage contract to the high priest, and kisses his right hand. The priest reads it slowly, and then details the virtues and rank of the families of the bridegroom and bride and the conditions upon which their marriage is taking place. When the reading ends the contract is handed to the bride's representative, her father, uncle, or guardian, for safekeeping. The groom kisses the hands of the high priest, gives him his fee and receives a wedding gift from him. The groom then turns to the bride, lifts the veil from her head, kisses her, and places a ring upon the finger of her right or left hand (a new custom). Sometimes they strengthen the bond by both drinking wine from the same cup (there is no canopy or breaking of a glass). During the following Sabbath prayers, songs signifying the joy of marriage are added. These are sung by the priest except when the groom is of a priestly family, in which case a lay Samaritan sings them. The groom reads the weekly portion of the law. The meal that takes place after the reading of the portion concludes the week of marriage.

INTERMARRIAGE. Samaritan *halakhah* permits intermarriage with the Jewish community on authorization by the high priest, after he is convinced that the convert will be fit to bear the brunt of observing Samaritan tradition. The attitude of the Samaritans toward Jews is expressed as: the Jews are children of the Jewish people who have deviated from the right path but will return to it "on the day of vengeance and recompense." A Samaritan may marry a Jewess only if she declares herself ready to observe Samaritan tradition. In such cases the Jewess lives in the bridegroom's house for at least six months and learns the customs of the community. The high priest tests her knowledge of what is required of her and only then gives his authorization. A Samaritan girl can be married to a Jew only if he declares his willingness to become a Samaritan.

Such marriages, which Samaritans regard as a sign of a renewed tie between the two sectors of Israel – the Samaritan and the Jewish – are recognized by the Ministry of the Interior, and the marriage certificates are official forms of the ministry, which recognizes the high priest's right to register the marriage. Up to 1970 six such cases had occurred, and in each case Samaritan men married Jewesses. The first case took place in 1923 and the last in 1969, despite the opposition in all cases of the Jewish chief rabbinate, which is not recognized by the Samaritan high priesthood.

DIVORCE. Divorce is very rare in the Samaritan community. In the 20th century, up to 1970, only three cases had taken place, the last being in 1962. Divorce releases from betrothal or marriage. Three causes are recognized by Samaritan *halakhah*:

(1) abominable practices committed by either party, or by both together;

(2) quarreling that makes the life of either party unbearable;

(3) immorality, i.e., rumors or proofs that either party maintains extramarital relations. In each case the cause must be confirmed by two or three witnesses. The high priest imposes upon the applicants a period for appeasement of at least a year, and when all efforts have failed, the man and woman go to the house of the high priest together with a limited number of their relatives. The high priest reads the bill of divorce in the hearing of the couple, tears the marriage contract, and removes the rings from their fingers. The divorced woman may not remarry her husband if either she or he marries another after the divorce. The guilty party must pay damages, as fixed by the high priest.

MOURNING. Samaritans bury their dead in their cemetery on Mount Gerizim. They place the corpse in a coffin with its head pointing in the direction opposite to the peak of Mt. Gerizim in order that his face should be toward the mountain. After the death, they read the Pentateuch all night long. On next morning they wash the corpse. Anyone touching it becomes unclean and is obliged to bathe. They place the body in the coffin and carry it to the cemetery. The high priest eulogizes the person but does not make himself ritually unclean by touching the body (Lev. 21:10–15). When the party returns from the burial, a family unrelated to the dead invites those who were at the funeral to a meal of comfort. Samaritans mourn their dead seven days, as did Joseph his father. They do not stay indoors seven days as do Jews, but satisfy themselves by visiting the grave and delivering memorial addresses every morning and evening. On the seventh day the mourning is over. At the end of 30 days the relatives of the dead invite the Samaritans to a memorial meal, and this officially concludes the mourning ceremonies. They display no external signs of mourning for the dead (Deut. 14:1), they tear no garment nor do they place earth upon the head. On the Sabbath the whole of the Pentateuch is read in the home of the relatives of the dead. This is repeated daily in order to purify the soul of the deceased. For a year after the death, no festivity takes place in the house of the deceased. At the recital of the *piyyutim* of the festivals, special stanzas are said in his memory. On each festival, when the prayers are finished, the high priest recites **Kaddish* for the exaltation of souls of all "the community of Israel who prostrate themselves before the holiest of mountains, Mt. Gerizim."

[Benyamim Tsedaka]

SAMARITAN CHRONOLOGY

No extant Samaritan work explains the Samaritan chronology, and the facts relating to this topic must therefore be gleaned from their writings.

The Samaritan Calendar

Based on a lunisolar system, the Samaritan calendar year (lunar year) has 354 days, divided into 12 months of 29 or 30 days each. The first day of the month is fixed by the conjunction (*ẓimmut* or *kibbuẓ*) of the moon with the sun (not by the appearance of the new moon). If the conjunction occurs at night or in the morning, not later than six hours before noon, that day is considered the first of the new month, which has 30 days; if it occurs later, the first of the new month is counted from the following and the month has 29 days. The civil year and the counting of the *shemittot* begin in the seventh month, Tishri; the religious year begins in Nisan (in their present-day calendars and in their astronomical tables the Samaritans count the *shemittot* from Nisan). In accordance with the Pentateuch, the months had no special names, but were counted as the first, the second, etc., starting with the month of Aviv (Ex. 12:2; Deut 16:1). This system is still practiced. In their historical and halakhic writings, however, one also encounters the later, non-pentateuchal names of Nisan, etc.

In the Pentateuch, Nisan is called "the month of Aviv" (Deut. 16:1), which is explained as the "month of ears of corn," when the barleycorn begins to ripen. This description means that Nisan must always occur in the same season, which is impossible in a strict lunar year. Therefore, the Samaritans (like the Jews) had to bind their lunar year to a solar year and thus arrived at a lunisolar year. This solar year is a mixture of the Persian and the older Julian (or Syrian) year, as evident from the Samaritans' astronomical tables. It has 365¼ days. In order to keep the lunar months in the solar seasons, it was necessary to intercalate one month in each second or third year, seven times in the 19-year moon cycle. In contradistinction to the Jewish calendar, the Samaritan leap years are not bound to a fixed year in this cycle but are decided upon according to need. The intercalated month comes before Nisan. The Samaritan rule for intercalating is as follows: they calculate whether the conjunction of the first month will occur before or after the 12th of Adar (one of the Syrian solar months; March of the Julian calendar). In the latter case, the day of the conjunction is fixed as the first of Nisan; if it occurred on or before the 12th of Adar, the month is intercalated and the new year is a leap year.

The religious duty of intercalation is alluded to in the poems of the fourth-century Samaritan writers Amram Darah, and Markah: "...He [God] gave them feasts that do not shift and bound their names to the [celestial] lights" (Darah, Song 16, Ben-Ḥayyim, III. 2 p. 74). According to Samaritan tradition, the calendar was always based on calculation, not on observation of the new moon. This system, much venerated by them, is called *Ḥeshbān Kishṭah* (True Reckoning) or *Maḥshav Ayyamim* (Reckoning of the Days). The oldest description of it is found in the *Abu-al-Ḥasan of Tyre's compendium of law, *al-Ṭabbākh* (11th century), in which he explains why the Samaritan rite of fixing the first of each month according to the conjunction is the only way of arriving at the true beginning of the new month, as the conjunction signifies a real new occurrence each month, whereas the new moon differs only in degree from its later phases during the month.

A detailed account is given in the *Tolidah* (earliest part, 12th century). The origin of this "True Reckoning" is there attributed to Adam, who received the system from God through the angels and from whom it was passed on to Shem, Eber, Noah, Abraham, Isaac, Jacob, and finally Moses, who fixed the month of Nisan as the first month of spring and who taught the system to Phinehas, Aaron's grandson. When the Israelites entered the Promised Land, Phinehas applied this reckoning to the latitude of Mt. Gerizim. This passage explaining the principles of his system is written in Aramaic, showing that it was composed when this language was still used by Samaritan scholars, i.e., around the tenth century. The fixation of this date for the existence of the Samaritan calendar, more or less in its present form, can be corroborated by the external evidence of the tenth-century Karaite scholar Kirkisānī, who polemized vehemently against the Samaritan system of fixing the first of the month by conjunction and reckoning, instead of by observation of the new moon. From Phinehas onward, the duty and privilege of fixing the calendar remained a heritage of the family of high priests. To this day, they issue the calendar twice a year (in the months of Av and Shevat). It is binding on the entire community, and each of its male members is obliged to buy a copy. The principles underlying its calculation are a secret of the family.

At the end of the 16th century, when European scholars came in contact with the Samaritans, they were interested in learning the secret of the calendar, but their questions remained unanswered. Finally, in 1831, S. de Sacy was able to obtain astronomical tables from Nablus and published a specimen, and in 1896 M. Heidenheim followed suit; however, neither could explain the use of the table to compute the calendar. That was accomplished in 1939 by E. Robertson (in BJRI), whose work was supplemented by A.A. Akavyah in 1950 (in *Melilah*), who translated Robertson's paper into Hebrew, annotating it, and adding a short article of his own. Thanks to the efforts of all these scholars, it has become possible to understand a great deal about the calculation of the Samaritan calendar. About 600 tables were composed by Murjān al-Danfi and his two sons, Muslim and Abdallah. They were calculated for 200 Muslim years (1101–1300 A.H. = 1689–1883 C.E.) and their copying was finished in 1712.

The specimen published by Robertson comprises the tables relating to 1101 A.H. They bear the caption: "The year 6128 [after Creation], 3328 [after the settlement of the Israelites in Canaan], the 21st in the [solar] cycle of 28 [years] and the 9th in the [lunar] cycle of 19 [years], excerpt for the Hebrew [= Samaritan] solar year 1058 according to the era of Jezdegerd." The inscription implies that the calculations are based on a solar year, which is counted according to the era of Jezdegerd, the last Persian king of the Sassanid dynasty, who lost his empire to the Arabs. The era, named after him, begins in 632 C.E., the year he ascended the throne. The Persian solar year differs from the older Julian one and was used by the Arabian scholars for their astronomical calculations, which reached greatest perfection in the eighth–ninth centuries. Together with the Arabic astronomical tables, the Samaritans adopted the counting of the solar years according to this era. They did not take over its exact system, however, but kept to the solar year of the older Julian calendar, which they had probably learned (like the Jews) from the Byzantines. This last fact allows the inference to be made that the Samaritan system of calculating the calendar was developed during the time of Byzantine rule and revised later by the advanced system of their Arab overlords.

An interesting feature in the tables is the designation of the Samaritan lunar months by their Muslim names, in addition to their old names, the first, second, etc; the two designations are still applied in their present-day calendar. However, as the Muslim year, being strictly lunar, revolves through all the seasons, there are permanent changes in the coincidence of the Muslim with the original Samaritan names.

Historical Chronology

In the Pentateuch, which is also regarded by the Samaritans as a historical book for Samaritans, no fixed date era is given as the starting point from which years are counted successively; instead, the time of a certain event is given in relation to one preceding or following it. Nonetheless, several eras are mentioned in the Samaritan chronicles and datings of their manuscripts. The main era, to which all the others are related, after the Creation of the World or from Adam, is based on the lifespan of each of the Patriarchs in the Pentateuch, from

Adam to the death of Moses, i.e., until the entry of the Israelites into Canaan. According to the Samaritan Pentateuch, this era extended for 2,794 years. The continuation of this calculation is founded on the lists of Samaritan high priests in their chronicles, especially the *Salsalah* and *Tolidah* (see below, Samaritan Language and Literature), and several other eras are mentioned. The Table: Beginning of Eras in Six Samaritan Chronicles, shows the beginning of some of the more important eras in six Samaritan chronicles.

The date of the entry into Canaan is identical in all six chronicles, except for a slight deviation of two years in the oldest, the *Asatir*. This conformity is a result of computations based upon figures mentioned in the Samaritan Pentateuch. From then on, one must rely on the other five Chronicles – one begun in the 12th century C.E., two from the 14th century, and two from the beginning of the 20th century. The date of the beginning of the divine disfavor is alike in all of them; it is reached by adding 260 years, the reign of six high priests, to the date of the entry into Canaan. The disappearance of the holy Tabernacle, which was the beginning of the divine disfavor, occurred one year before the death of Uzzi, the sixth high priest, when Eli b. Jafni usurped the functions of the high priest. The *Tolidah* and the chronicle from 1908 (edited partly by J. Mac-Donald) postpone this event to the year of Uzzi's death. There are wide discrepancies in dates given for the start of three of the last eras. One of the reasons for the differences is omissions or additions in the lists on which they are based.

Some scholars surmise that all the numbers in the Samaritan chronicles are founded on the theological concept that the world, in its present state, was meant to exist for 6,000 years – 3,000 years of divine favor (*Rahutah*) followed by 3,000 years of divine disfavor (*Fanutah*), after which the Messiah (*Taheb*) would appear, and return the holy Tabernacle and bring redemption and peace to all the world. The date 3054 after creation fits approximately into that theory as marking the end of the period of the divine favor. From then to the appearance of Alexander the Great, about 1,000 years elapsed, i.e., one third of the period of divine disfavor. The date 4600 A.C. for *Baba Rabbah places the salvation he brought his people in the middle of this period of hardship and distress. Another 500 years from then to the rise of Muhammad fix the end of the divine disfavor and the advent of the *Taheb* at around 1,000 years after Muhammad.

Like their Muslim surroundings, the Samaritans began to reckon their dates according to the Muslim era, which they denoted as according to the Kingdom of Ismāʿīl, Ismāʿīliyya (= of Ismāʿīl) or Hijriyya (= of the Flight). The use of this era became dominant and even more widespread than the appellation "after the Creation," which kept its place in the chronicles but served to a lesser degree for dating documents. All dated Samaritan inscriptions mentioned in *Sefer ha-Shomronim* are dated by the Muslim era only. Even in the Samaritan calendar, issued twice a year by the high priest, the dating is by the Muhammadan year, sometimes synchronized to other systems, in addition to the counting of the years of *shemittah*, probably the oldest Samaritan way of dating events by starting from a fixed point.

In the Pentateuch (Lev. 25:8 ff.) the Children of Israel are ordered to count Sabbatical (*shemittah*) Years (every seventh year) and Jubilees (every 50th year) after their entry into Canaan. The Samaritan tradition understood this to mean that the first year of their entry into Canaan was a Sabbatical Year, as it was the seventh year after their arrival in Transjordan. The second redactor of the *Tolidah* states that he finished his work in the year 747 A.C., which was the fourth year of the fifth Sabbatical in the 61st Jubilee since the entry of the Israelites into Canaan, the 5778th year A.H. and the 714th of Jezdegerd. Synchronization of several eras was widespread in Muslim writings, its aim being to exclude dating errors by later copyists, after that the writer of the *Tolidah* proceeds to outline the Samaritan system of counting the Jubilees. The first is counted 50 years, after which 49 are added for each following till the end of the fifth (= 246 years). This total is doubled to get the 10th Jubilee (= 492 years). He proceeds in this fashion to the 40th Jubilee (= 1968 years). After that he skips to the 55th (= 2706 years). From then on he adds only one or two at a time until he comes to the 65th Jubilee (= 3196 years), which is more than

Beginning of Eras in Six Samaritan Chronicles

	Asatir c. 11th century C.E.	Tolidah first part 544 A.H.; 1149 C.E.	Samaritan Book of Josua 1362 C.E.	Abu al-Fatḥ 756 A.H.; 1354 C.E.	Chronicle edited by Adler-Seligs 1307 A.H.; 1900 C.E.	Chronicle edited by J. MacDonald 1326 A.H.; 1908 C.E.
Death of Moses; Entry into Canaan	2796*	2794	2794	2794	2794	2794
Disappearance of Holy Tabernacle. Beginning of Divine Disfavor; First Schism between Samaritans and Jews		3055	3054	3054	3054	3055
Alexander the Great, Era of Contracts			3930	4100	3944	3945
Birth of Jesus				4350	c. 4321	4292
Baba Rabbah		4600			c. 4600	4600
Advent of Muhammad. Era of the Flight				5047	4921	4893

* All the years in this table are counted After Creation of the World (A.C.).

four Jubilees after the time of the composition of that part of the *Tolidah* and ten years short of the year 6000 A.C., the time of the expected advent of the *Taheb*.

The antiquity of the system of counting according to Jubilees is borne out by the apocryphal Book of Jubilees (second century B.C.E). It seems to have been used by the Samaritans throughout the ages, alongside younger and more convenient systems. Today they count only the Sabbatical Years, dispensing with the Jubilees. It remains, however, undecided whether this system or the Era of the Contracts was the oldest used by them. It is not known when the Samaritans started to count by their main era, i.e., after Creation, as their oldest extant manuscripts are from the 12th century. As example for its use at that time serves the colophon of one fragmentary manuscript of the Pentateuch: "[Written by]… son of Abraham son of Joseph Zarfataah in the year 5579 A.C., which is the year 544 A.H." Dating by this system was common throughout the Byzantine Empire, in Christian and Jewish circles alike, for documents, tombstones, and manuscripts from the seventh century C.E., and the same probably applies to the Samaritans. The system is first known from fragments of a "Book of Kings," whose author was Demetrius (third century B.C.E.), a Hellenic Jew from Alexandria. Byzantine sources from the seventh century cite fragments of Christian, Syrian, and Alexandrian chronologers from the third and fifth centuries C.E. who built their systems on the era "After the Creation of the World." In Jewish sources, the system is first mentioned in the fifth century C.E. (Av. Zar. 9b). The length of this era differs in Jewish, Samaritan, and Christian tradition, being the longest in the Christian (5492 or 5501 years until the beginning of the Common Era) and the shortest in the Jewish (3761 years), the Samaritans occupying a position in between.

The colophon of the Samaritan chronicle completed in 1900 C.E. (ed. by Adler-Seligsohn) includes the era after Creation (6179 years), that from the Entry into Canaan (3385 years), the Common Era (1900 years), the Muslim era (1317 years), and mention of the Era of Diocletian (1616 years). The latter, also called Era of the Martyrs, was inaugurated in Alexandria in 284 C.E., the year Diocletian ascended the throne. Its importance lay in the introduction of the 19-year moon cycle, which enabled the Christian Church Fathers to calculate more exactly than by their former 8-year cycle the date of Easter, which must fall on a Sunday after the first full moon in the month of spring. The 19-year moon cycle is used by the Samaritans to the present, although it is not known when they began to employ it or when they first dated by the Diocletian era.

LANGUAGE AND LITERATURE

Language

Throughout their history the Samaritans have used four languages: Hebrew, Greek, Aramaic, and Arabic. Apart from the Pentateuch (see Samaritan *Pentateuch), Hebrew was retained as the language of liturgy, revived from the 14th century on. This later Hebrew was mixed with Aramaic words and grammatical forms and developed under the influence of the Samaritan Arabic vernacular. Likewise, Hebrew translations of Aramaic and Arabic works done by 19th- and 20th-century writers for European scholars, notably Moses Gaster, show clear Arabic influence in words, grammar, and syntax. A peculiarity of post-biblical Hebrew is the confusion of the gutturals.

Only scanty literary fragments have survived from the Hellenistic era and they testify to the use of the Greek language among the Samaritans. They are all excerpts from Alexander Polyhistor, a Roman historian (c. 80–40 B.C.E.), which were transmitted by Eusebius in his *Praeparatio Evangelica* (third to fourth century C.E.; for further information see Montgomery, op. cit., pp. 283–6). Fragments of a Greek translation of the Samaritan Pentateuch have been found in Egypt. Origen refers in his Hexapla to a "Samareitikon," which is understood by most scholars to mean a Greek translation of the Samaritan Pentateuch. In 1953 a Greek archaeologist found a Samaritan synagogue inscription in Greek in Thessalonika which might belong to the fourth century C.E. (Kippenberg, p. 148). Samaritan Aramaic, a dialect of Western Aramaic, has been preserved in compositions dating from the early Roman period to the 11th century C.E. (see *Aramaic). Arabic has been used by the Samaritans as a spoken language for many centuries. It is not known exactly when Aramaic fell into disuse, but it seems to have died out as a written language in about the 11th century, and most of the non-Hebrew writings from that time on are in Middle Arabic.

Many manuscripts in Western libraries and in the Samaritan community set out a text in three parallel columns: Hebrew, Aramaic, and Arabic. These include the Pentateuch, *Memar Markah*, and some later exegetical works. There is also a glossary to the Pentateuch called *Ha-Meliẓ*, meaning "dictionary," which sets out in parallel columns the Aramaic and Arabic equivalents of the Hebrew words of the Pentateuch. It was edited for the first time by Z. Ben-Ḥayyim (I, II no. XI). Ben-Ḥayyim showed that it was composed in two stages, the first part being the Hebrew-Aramaic from the 10th to the 11th centuries. Later, when Aramaic began to fall into disuse, another author added the Arabic column, very often translating not the Hebrew word but its Aramaic translation, which he no longer understood properly. This part was added to between the second half of the 11th to the 14th century. The only extant manuscript was copied in 1476. This glossary is today the most important source for knowledge of Samaritan Aramaic.

Literature

Extant Samaritan literature is relatively rare. The earliest work is the Pentateuch, which is the center of Samaritan life. To this day, the Samaritans jealously guard their most precious scroll, known as the Abisha Scroll, which they believe to be the actual copy of the Pentateuch made by Abisha, grandson of Eleazar, in the 13th year of the settlement of the Israelites in Canaan. All scholars agree that it belongs to a later period, but there is no agreement as to the exact time, and opinions vary between the first (M. Gaster) and the 14th century C.E. (P. Kahle). Perez Castro reached the conclusion that the scroll consists of one older part, which belongs to the 12th or 13th century C.E., and of more recent additions from the 14th century. *Abu al-Fatḥ ends his account on *Sefer Avisha* with the encouraging message that after having been lost it had reappeared in his days, "this being a sign of the approaching return of the Divine Favor" (p. 35). Next in order comes the Targum written in the Aramaic type similar to that of the *Defter* and *Memar Markah* (see *Markah). It is a fairly literal translation, but manuscripts exist with interpretive additions. The presence of a number of Greek words suggests a date between the first and fourth centuries C.E., as Greek was probably still in use as a literary medium alongside Aramaic during the early part of that period in Samaria. Apart from some fragments, the oldest manuscript is the Barberini Triglot of 1226 C.E.

The *Defter* (Gr. *diphtera*, book) constitutes the oldest part of the liturgy and was probably composed in the fourth century C.E. (for the text, see A.E. Cowley, I, pp. 1–92; Z. Ben-Ḥayyim, III, 2, pp. 41–274). Additions were made in later times in Aramaic and Hebrew. This part of the liturgy contains some early hymns (e.g., the Hymn of the Angels, the Hymn of Joshua), and these, together with the hymns of Amram Darah, Markah, and Nanah, the son of Markah, may be described as the basic prayer book of the Samaritan community. The *Memar Markah* is of prime importance for the study of Samaritan Aramaic and for the history of Samaritan concepts.

LITURGISTS. Liturgists of a later period who still wrote in Aramaic were Taviya ben Darta of the 10th–11th century C.E., Abu al-Ḥasan al-Ṣurī of the 11th century, al-Dustān before the 13th century, and Av Gillugah of the 12th century. Aaron b. Manīr of Damascus from the 13th to 14th centuries, and Mattanah Hamazri from the Samaritan community in Egypt, wrote in Hebrew, like the high priest of Shechem, Phinehas b. Yusuf, the reviver of the Samaritan *piyyut* in Hebrew (1308–1367 C.E.), and his sons Eleazar and Avisha. Phinehas himself and his son Eleazar occasionally still used Aramaic in attempting to write "verses of Markah," i.e., to imitate the style of "the Samaritan Poet." Avisha, who received the epithet *baʿal ha-mēmar* (i.e., "the writer") and, after Markah, perhaps the most famous and beloved liturgist in the Samaritan community, wrote in the Samaritan Hebrew that began to emerge by then and consisted of a mixture of classical Hebrew and Aramaic forms and words. He was a very prolific writer and his poems were included to a large extent in the Samaritan liturgy. Another famous liturgist was the scholar Ibrāhim b. Yaʿqūb al-Ayya of the 18th century. In the 19th century the outstanding Samaritan scholar Phinehas b. Isaac (d. 1898), who was surnamed Fard Zavnēh ("unique in his time"), composed liturgical poems of great beauty.

CHRONICLES. A number of chronicles are extant.

(1) The earliest is the *Asāṭīr* (see *al-Asāṭīr), a midrashic work written in late Aramaic and probably composed in the tenth or 11th century C.E.

(2) *Al-Tolidah* ("genealogy"), written in Hebrew, except for one Aramaic section dealing with the meridian of Mt. Gerizim, contains mainly genealogical lists from Adam to the entry into Canaan, and from then on lists of the high priestly and other important Samaritan families, interspersed at places by short historical accounts. The chronicle begins with a description of the Samaritan system in fixing their calendar, counting the Jubilees, etc. (see Historical Chronology). This work was composed by Jacob b. Ishmael, himself of high priestly origin, in 1346 C.E. He testifies that he copies the main part from an earlier work written by his ancestor Eleazar b. Amram in 1149 C.E. From then on it was added to by each generation.

(3) The Samaritan *Book of Joshua* (in Arabic) recounts the history of the Samaritan people from the initiation of Joshua by Moses to the days of Baba Rabbah. It contains much legendary material, and the place of origin and name of its author are not mentioned. In the opening sentences the writer states that he translated his work from a Hebrew source, which has not yet been discovered. The Hebrew *Book of Joshua*, which M. Gaster claimed to have found, is actually only one part of another Samaritan chronicle, a late compilation composed in about 1900 by Jacob b. Hārūn, as shown by P. Kahle, D. Yellin, and S. Yahuda. An Arabic *Book of Joshua* is enumerated by Abu al-Fatḥ as one of the sources which he used for the composition of his *Annals*. The oldest manuscript (in the Leiden Library) consists of two parts: the first from 1362 C.E. (chs. 1–46); the second from 1513. The manuscript was sold to J. Scaliger in 1584 by the Samaritan community in Cairo (Juynboll, p. 340).

(4) The *Annals* (*Kitāb al-Taʾrīkh*) by Abu al-Fatḥ were composed in Arabic in 1355 C.E.

(5) *Shalshalah* ("chain") is a genealogy of high priests ascribed to Eleazar b. Phinehas of the 14th century C.E. and added to up to Jacob b. Hārūn (19th–20th century C.E.).

(6) The *New Chronicle* or *Chronicle Adler* (one of the editors) was written in Samaritan Hebrew by Av-Sakhva b. Asad ha-Danfi. It relates from Adam to 1900 C.E., the year of its composition, uses the earlier chronicles, and shows acquaintance with historical books of the Bible.

(7) Another *New Chronicle* in Samaritan Hebrew was written by Taviah b. Phinehas in 1908 (see review to MacDonald's edition of Chronicle II by Z. Ben-Ḥayyim in *Leshonenu*, 30 (1971), 293–302). M. Gaster refers to this chronicle in *The Samaritans* (p. 157), saying that it was first ascribed to Taviah and then to Phinehas. The writer used the earlier Samaritan chronicles, mainly the *Annals* of Abu al-Fatḥ and great parts of the historical books of the Bible. The chronicle ends with the narration of the events in the writer's own time.

HALAKHIC LITERATURE. Several halakhic works have survived, all in Middle Arabic:

(1) *Al-Kāfi* ("the [all] sufficient") composed by Yūsuf al-ʿAskarī in 1042 C.E.

(2) *Kitāb al-Ṭabbākh* of the same period by *Abu al-Ḥasan of Tyre. Abu al-Ḥasan is also said to be the translator of the

Samaritan Pentateuch into Arabic. His translation, however, fell into disuse, because of the many interpolations, which had crept into it from the Rabbanite Arabic translation of Saadiah. It was revised in the 13th century by the Samaritan scholar Abū Saʿid (B.H. I, pp. xxxiv, xxxv).

(3) *Masāʾil al-Khilāf* (the differences between the Samaritan and Jewish communities, Rabbanites and Karaites alike) of the 12th century by Munajja b. Ṣadaqa, the physician of Damascus. He is also said to be the author of a treatise on forbidden degrees of marriage, *Sefer ha-Ervah*; others ascribe this treatise to a certain Baraka of Shechem from the 14th century. The John Rylands Library contains a bilingual manuscript in Arabic and modern Samaritan Hebrew, translated and copied in 1930 by Avisha b. Phinehas from an old Arabic manuscript owned by his father (no. 250). Munajja polemicized against the Jewish scholar Saadiah and the Karaite al-Kirkisānī.

(4) *Kitāb al-Mīrāth* or *Sefer ha-Yerushot* ("The Book of Inheritance") is ascribed to Ibrāhīm b. Isḥāq b. Mārūth, surnamed "The Sun of the Learned" (*Shams al-Ḥukamāʾ*) physician to Ṣāliḥ al-Dīn, who lived in Damascus (or Baalbek?) in the 12th century.

(5) *Kitāb al-Farāʾiḍ* ("Book of Laws"), composed by Abu al-Faraj Nafīs al-Dīn-al-Kathār of the 13th or 14th century, is an important halakhic work. In this compendium of religious usage, the author mentions 613 commandments divided into 365 prohibitions (like the days of the year) and 248 orders (like the parts of the human body). The 613 commandments are referred to earlier in *Kitāb al-Kāfi*, but without such division or enumeration.

(6) *Shirat ha-Mitzvot*, a long poem by the 13th–14th-century liturgical poet Aaron b. Manīr of Damascus, enumerates the 613 commandments in accordance with the above-mentioned division. His system shows striking resemblance to that of Maimonides.

(7) The *Ḥillūk* or *Khilāf al-Irshād* ("Differences in Teaching"), a late Samaritan halakhic work, is ascribed by the sons of Phinehas b. Isaac ha-Kohen and of Jacob b. Hārūn to their fathers, respectively. It is divided into ten chapters and contains differences between Jews and Samaritans, based on readings in the Pentateuch. It ends with a section on death, divine punishment, and resurrection. The first chapter contains a brief sketch on Samaritan history, and Samaritan communities such as Aleppo, Damascus, Cairo, and Gaza are mentioned as places where Samaritans continue to live, although these communities disappeared long ago. This shows that the book was compiled from old materials.

None of these works presents a systematic codification of Samaritan oral law; the nearest to attain this aim is *Kitāb al-Farāʾiḍ*. All contain polemics against Karaite and Rabbanite Jews, and even against certain Muslim philosophical teachings and Christian beliefs (e.g., in *Kitāb al-Tabbākh*). Vast sections are commentaries to passages of the Pentateuch.

PENTATEUCH COMMENTARIES. Like the halakhic writings, the Samaritan commentaries to the Pentateuch, still extant, are all from the Arabic period and are written in Middle Arabic. Apart from lexicographical and grammatical material contained in them, they show familiarity with medieval philosophy, astrology, astronomy, and even medicine, as famous Samaritan physicians were among the commentators. The influence of Karaite or Rabbanite writings is discernible in some commentaries.

(1) A commentary on Genesis 1–28:10 by an unknown author (composed in 1053 C.E.), a specimen of which has been published by Neubauer, is of Karaite provenance. It was adapted to the Samaritan pentateuchal text in an external and very perfunctory manner prior to the year 1348, when the single extant manuscript was copied (Loewenstamm, *Perush Kara'i al ha-Torah bi-Levush Shomroni*).

(2) Ṣadaqa b. Munajja al-Ḥakīm (d. 1223 in Haran), physician to Malik al-Ashraf, composed a philosophical treatise *Kitāb al-Tawḥīd* ("Book of [God's] Oneness"), in which he adduces proofs for the absolute oneness of God from verses of the Pentateuch. A commentary to Genesis is ascribed to him (M. Steinschneider, ALJ, 331).

(3) Abu al-Faraj Nafīs al-Dīn (author of *Kitāb al-Farāʾid*) wrote a commentary on Leviticus 26 called *Sharḥ* ("interpretation") *"im be-Ḥukkotai."* In it he cites from a lost Aramaic commentary of al-Dustān, well known as a liturgical poet in the Aramaic language.

(4) Several treatises are ascribed to Ghazzāl or Tabiah b. alDoweik of the 13th–14th century: (a) the Story of Balaam, (b) the Affirmation of the Second Kingdom (Rylands' Catalogue, p. 110, Cod. VIII), and (c) an unfinished commentary to Exodus.

(5) Ibrāhim al-Kabāṣi, noted scholar and liturgist of Damascus (16th century), wrote a book *Sair al-Qalb* ("Conducts of the Heart"), wherein he expounds the need to conduct a life in accordance with divine teachings. He, too, enumerates 613 commandments. His system, like that of Aaron b. Manīr, shows striking resemblance to that of Maimonides. His second book, a commentary to Deuteronomy 32:3, 4 called "Sharḥ Efshem" or "al-Fātiḥa," deals with the power of the divine name. Deuteronomy 32:3, 4, like the first Sura of the Koran, became the basic verses in the Samaritan prayers. This book is of special interest as it shows influence of esoteric teachings.

(6) An important midrashic work from 1537 C.E., *Molad Moshe*, a panegyric to Moses, was composed in Arabic by Yishmael Haramḥi (Ismāʿīl al-Rumyḥī) of Damascus, a disciple of Ibrāhīm al-Kabāṣī, who honored him by writing the introduction to his pupil's work (edited by S.J. Miller, New York, 1949, together with a Samaritan Hebrew version by Phinehas b. Isaac ha-Kohen).

(7) the most comprehensive commentary to Genesis, Exodus, Leviticus, and Numbers was composed in the 18th century. Begun by Meshalma or Muslim b. Murjān, of the Danafite family, renowned for its scholars and scribes, it was continued and partly rewritten by his nephew and disciple Ibrāhīm b. Yaʿqūb al-ʿAyya from Genesis 46:28 to the end. Ibrāhīm al-ʿAyya, commentator, liturgist, grammarian, chro-

nologer, and scribe, was one of the most famous Samaritan scholars. He took part in the correspondence between Samaritans and European scholars. Parts of his commentary have been edited as doctoral dissertations.

(8) At about the same time (1753/54), Ghazzāl ibn Abu al-Sarūr al-Ghāzi composed an aggadic commentary called *Kāshifal-Ghayāhib* or *Megalleh Temirin* ("Revealer of Hidden Things").

GRAMMATICAL WORKS. Although the Samaritan Pentateuch is not bound by a masorah, like that of the Jews, there is a fixed pronunciation of the Torah, which is transmitted very carefully by oral teaching from generation to generation. An extant work from the end of the 10th–11th century by the poet Taviya ibn Dartah called "A Canon on the Rules of Reading" deals with the accents used in reading the text of the Pentateuch. The treatise was composed in Arabic, but the Aramaic names of the accents and the Aramaic verse at its close testify to the antiquity of the sources from which it was gleaned. Dealing with the same topic is the "Treatise Concerning the Reading" by Ibrāhīm al-ʿAyya, who wrote several other grammatical treatises, one about the vowel signs, another concerning the articulation of the 22 letters of the Hebrew-Samaritan alphabet, and a third on "Words Similar in Pronunciation." The works of Ibn Dartah and of al-ʿAyya were edited for the first time by Z. Ben-Ḥayyim in *Ivrit ve-Aramit Nosaḥ Shomron* (I, II), together with other Samaritan grammatical and lexicographical writings. Here it may suffice to refer to the earliest Samaritan grammar (Sect. 1), *Kitāb al Tawṭiʿa* ("Book of Introduction") by the physician Abu Isḥāq b. Ibrāhīm b. Faraj. b. Mārūth of Damascus (or Baalbek?) from the 12th century (supposed composer of *Kitāb al-Mīrāth*). Abu Isḥāq does not mention any predecessor, and his work is in accordance with that of Jewish and Arabic grammarians of his time. Like them he accepts the assumption of the three-radical stem of the word (in contradistinction to that adduced in the commentary of the unknown author from 1053 and in the dictionary "*Ha-Meliẓ*)." On this basis, he succeeds in creating his own grammatical system of the Hebrew language according to the pronunciation typical of the Samaritan community. His treatise shows that, from his time until today, only a few minor changes occurred in this pronunciation. His work, however, seems not to have been very popular in the Samaritan community, as shown by the single extant manuscript and by a later abridgment called *Mukhtaṣar al-Tawṭiʿ a* by Eleazar b. Phinehas b. Joseph, high priest of the Samaritan community from 1363 to 1387. This work seems to have enjoyed great popularity, as shown by the many extant manuscripts and the number of different names given to it (Ben-Ḥayyim I, Sect. III).

Some minor grammatical treatises were written by Phinehas b. Isaac Ha-kohen (d. 1898): on the *hifil* perfect and imperfect of hollow verbs (Ben-Ḥayyim I, Sect. VI, a.b.g.). Phinehas stood in high esteem as scholar and liturgist and, in addition to "Fard Zavnēh" ("Unique of his Time"), was surnamed Ḥashov Ḥeshbān Kishṭah" ("Reckoner of the True Reckoning") because of his proficiency in Samaritan chronology and fixing of the calendar. He is said to have encouraged Av-Sakhva to compile his chronicle (i.e., the *New Chronicle*), as the high priest Phinehas b. Yūsuf of the 14th century asked Abu al-Fatḥ to compose his *Annals* (B.Ḥ. I pp. xlvii, xlviii). Another modern chronicle is ascribed to him. Like many contemporaries, among them the high priest Jacob b. Hārūn, he translated Samaritan manuscripts from Arabic into Samaritan Hebrew.

Samaritan literature, only part of which has been dealt with here, is wholly centered around the Pentateuch and the religious life of the community. The liturgical, halakhic, midrashic, grammatical, lexicographical, philosophical, and chronological literature all developed with the same aim: to guide the community to understand the very meaning and intention of the divine book and to teach them to fulfill its commandments. Even the historical literature fits into this system, as it sets out to show that man's welfare depends on his obedience to the laws of "The Book."

[Ayala Loewenstamm]

IN ISLAM

In the Koran, al-Sāmirī is a strange figure. He incited the people of Israel to make the Golden Calf and Aaron's warnings were of no avail. Al-Sāmirī succeeded by using sorcery and was punished by having to proclaim forever: *lā misāsa* ("touch me not!," Sura 20:85–97). The name al-Sāmirī is difficult to explain and usually is interpreted as an allusion to the Samaritans, who according to Muhammad bore some of the responsibility for calf worship in Samaria. Speyer, however, believes that it alludes to the act of Zimri b. Salu, who was killed by Phinehas for his misconduct with a Midianite woman (Num. 25:1–15). This assumption appears to be forced and the tale of the Sāmirī remains a mystery.

[Haïm Z'ew Hirschberg]

MUSICAL TRADITION

The musical tradition of the Samaritans, which is closely linked to their linguistic tradition, is completely devoid of instrumental music; in fact, the Samaritans do not even sound the *shofar*. Moreover, the Samaritans have no formal theoretical system of tones, meter, or rhythm. The two main styles of the Samaritan *melos* are the *kal* ("light") and the *kaved* ("heavy") style. The *kal* style is mainly syllabic. Its rhythm is linked to that of the text and its range is extremely limited. The center tone generally serves as the axis of the melody, with seconds on either side, and only occasional extensions to a third, fourth, and fifth. The *kaved* style is basically nonsyllabic and rich in embellishments. The melodic axis in this style consists of the center tone with the embellishments adjacent to it, but at times the melody projects over larger intervals such as the fifth, sixth, seventh, or even the octave, and then returns to its center. The manner of rendering Samaritan songs is chiefly characterized, in almost every melodic texture and prominently so in the *kaved* style, by strong vibrato, by glissando to the degree that it is difficult to fix the duration of the tone, and especially by the *zaʿak* – the sforzato ejaculation, which is extremely loud and often precedes or succeeds the vibrato or appears on either side of the glissando.

In the vibrating *kaved* style, the pronunciation of the text is often extended by filler-syllables, which stretch and support the melodic line. A word such as *ʾat* may be transformed in the *kaved* cantillation to *ʿa-ta-wa-nu-wa*. An intermediate style called *ḥazi kaved* ("half-heavy") is also recognized. The Samaritan Bible cantillation is not based upon a system of *masoretic accents. The present usage is regulated by just four cadential formulas: the half-*rakza* and *rakza* which mark the hemistichs; the *waqfa* at the end of the verse; and the *nāhwa*, placed at the end of the *qiṣṣa* does the melodic impetus quicken and the melodic curve becomes more pronounced. There are distinct melodic schemes for cantillation on various occasions – for certain Sabbaths and feasts, readings by the priests, private study, etc. An old and obscure tradition utilizes a different system: the ten *sidrei mikreta* (pronounced *sedari maqrata*), i.e., "rules" or "principles of reading," effected by signs placed after words or phrases. The signs seem to have had a combined exegetical-syntactical-musical function similar, in principle, to the Jewish accentual system and its cognates in the Near East (especially the Syriac). The signs and their Aramaic names are as follows (pronunciation bracketed):

('enged or 'nēged).. נגד
(ʾfāsaq or ʿafsaʾ): פסק
(ānʾāʾʾū)° אנחו
(erʾkānu) / ארכנו
(sīyʾyāla) ¨< שאילה
(zāʿeīqa). – זעיקה
(etʾmāʾu) <: אתמחו
(ʿbāʾu) <. בעו
(zāʾʿif):= זעפ
(ʿtūru) |: תורו

The signs are no longer used either in the Samaritan scrolls of the Law or the prayer books, and their precise meaning and application were apparently lost many centuries ago.

The most interesting rendition of the *piyyutim* is the antiphonal performance which the Samaritans call "lower and upper" or "right and left." The congregation divides itself into two groups on either side of the *parokhet*, and simultaneously recite different parts of the hymn, each with its own melody. A polyphony, which is extremely dissonant to the Western ear, is thus created, although the Samaritans execute it most naturally and each member of the congregation is habituated to his "half" of the performance.

The Samaritans do not seem to possess any truly secular songs. However, on special occasions, such as weddings and circumcisions, they sing *piyyutim* in an easy and metrical "light" style.

On the periphery of the Samaritan tradition there are light songs, usually Arabic ditties with overtly secular themes, bearing the imprint of the Arab *melos* and poetical form. But for the Samaritans, a song such as *Sir binā siḥrā nadīmī* is an allegorical song and not one merely of love and desire.

These elements, however, have become an integral part of the musical tradition of the Samaritan community. Some manuscripts of religious poems have headings which indicate, in Arabic, the melody or style in which the poems are to be sung.

A feature often apparent in all genres of Samaritan singing-songs, hymns, and prayers is the phenomenon designated by the musicological-historical term *parallel organum*: the rendition of one melody by a group of singers, adults and/or children, in which each individual or subgroup proceeds on an independent tonal level, thus creating a polyphony of strictly parallel strands. The procedure is entirely unconscious and spontaneous, and the Samaritans themselves do not have a term for it (a very similar usage is also found among the Yemenite Jews and in a few other cultures in various parts of the world).

The characteristics of Samaritan song (which has only begun to be subjected to a thorough musicological analysis) give it a peculiarity which is apparent at first hearing. All the elements – vibrato, glissando, *zaʿaq*, the melodic curve itself, "right and left," and *organum* – combine to make a strongly original style, which has no parallel either in the musical traditions of the Jewish communities or those of any present Near Eastern culture. Samaritan music evinces the survival of archaic elements whose import has yet to be explored.

[Shlomo Hofman]

BIBLIOGRAPHY: BIBLIOGRAPHY: A.D. Crown, *A Bibliography of the Samaritans* (1984); UNTIL 1300: E. Vilmar, *Abulfatḥi; Annales Samaritani* (1865); A. Neubauer, *Chronique Samaritaine* (1873), = JA, 14 (1869), 385–470; T.W.J. Juynboll, *Chronicon Samaritanum* (1848); E.N. Adler and M. Seligsohn, in: REJ, 44 (1902), 188–222; 45 (1902), 70–98, 160, 223–54; 46 (1903), 123–46; J. Macdonald, *The Samaritan Chronicle no. 2 (or Sefer ha-Yamim). From Joshua to Nebuchadnezzar* (1969), = BZAW, 107 (1969); C.D. Mantel, in: *Bar Ilan, Sefer ha-Shanah*, 7–8 (1970), 162–77; G.E. Wright, in: HTR, 55 (1962), 357–66; idem, *Shechem* (1965); F.M. Cross, in: BA, 26 (1963), 110–21; idem, in: HTR, 59 (1966), 201–11; J.A. Montgomery, *The Samaritans* (1907, 1968); I. Ben-Zvi, *Sefer ha-Shomronim* (1970^2). 1300–1970: J.A. Montgomery, *The Samaritans* (1907, 1968), 13–45, 125–42; A.E. Cowley, *The Samaritan Liturgy* (1909); S. de Sacy, *Correspondance des Samaritains de Naplouse* (1831); R. Tsedaka, *Samaritan Legends (Aggadot Am Shomroniyyot)* (1965), 33–56, 86–88; E.T. Rogers, *Notices of the Modern Samaritans* (1855); Ben-Zvi, Ereẓ Yisrael, 419–30; R. Kirchheim, *Karmei Shomron* (1851, 1970), 1–54; M. Ish-Shalom, *Masei ha-Noẓerim le-Ereẓ Yisrael* (1966), index s.v. *Shomronim*; I. Ben-Hanania, in: *Yediʿot ha-Ḥevrah la-Ḥakirot Ereẓ Yisrael va-Attikoteha*, 11 no. 3–4 (1945), 57–63; B. Tsedaka, in: *Ba-Maʿarakhah* (1969). STATISTICS: E. Robertson, *Catalogue of the Samaritan Manuscripts in the John Rylands Library*, 2 (1962), 275 ff.; P. Kahle, in: PJB, 26 (1930), 89–103. RELIGION AND CUSTOMS: J.A. Montgomery, *The Samaritans* (1907, 1968), ch. 12 and 13; M. Gaster, *The Samaritans* (1925), second lecture; J. Macdonald, *The Theology of the Samaritans* (1964); M. Haran, in: *Eretz Israel*, 4 (1956), 160–9; A.S. Halkin, in: *Goldziher Memorial Volume* (1958), 86–100. NEW YEAR AND DAY OF ATONEMENT: B. Tsedaka, in: *Ba-Maʿarakhah*, 101 (1969); R. Tsedaka, *Siddurei Tefillot Moʿed ha-Ḥodesh ha-Sheviʿi, Shabbat Aseret Yemei ha-Seliḥot u-Moʿed Yom ha-Kippur* (1963) (in Samaritan-Hebrew letters). THE FEAST OF TABERNACLES AND SHEMINI AZERET: B. Tsedaka, in: *Ba-Maʿarakahah*,

97 (1969); 102 (1969); I. Tsedaka, *Siddur Teffilat Ḥag ha-Sukkot ve-Shabbat Mo'ed Ḥag ha-Sukkot* (1963); D.J. Boys, London *Quarterly and Wolborn Review* (1961); 32–37; R. Tsedaka, *The Prayer of the Ten Commandments* (in Samaritan Hebrew letters; 1962). PASSOVER: R. Tsedaka, *Samaritan Legends* (1965), 73–76 (bibl.); *Pesach on Hargrizim. The Samaritans*; special edition of the Samaritan newspaper "*A–B – The Samaritan News*" (n.d.). SHAVUOT: B. Tsedaka, in: *Ba-Ma'arakhah*, 98 (1969). SAMARITAN CHRONOLOGY: *Chronique Samaritaine*, ed. by A. Neubauer (1873), 6–12; Abu-al-Ḥassan al-Ṣuri, al-Tabbaḥ, Ms. Huntingdon 24 (= Nicholl, Sam. Arab. V), pp. 17, 42, 5, 58–59, J. Al-Kirkisānī, *Kitāb al-Anwār wa-al-Marāqib*, ed. by L. Nemoy (1942), 40; 185–6; 800–1; Z. Ben-Ḥayyim, *Ivrit ve-Aramit Nosaḥ Shomron*, 3 pt. 2 (1967), 74, 80, 212, 240; E. Robertson, in: BJRL, 23, 2 (1939), 458–86; A.A. Akavyah, in: *Melilah*, 3–4 (1950), 328–44; H.J. Bornstein, in: *Ha-Tekufah*, 8 (Warsaw, 1921), 287ff.; 9 (1921), 202–58; I. Ben-Zvi, *Sefer ha-Shomronim* (1970), 163–226; S. de Sacy, *Notices et extraits des manuscrits de la bibliothèque du roi*, 12 (1831), 153; M. Heidenheim, *Bibliotheca Samaritana*, 3 (1896), 119–22; Pauly-Wissowa, s.v. *Demetrios*; A. von Gall, *Der hebraeische Pentateuch der Samaritaner*, 1 (1914), li; L. Ideler, *Handbuch der mathematischen und technischen Chronologie*, 2 (1826), 231–7; 444–53; F.K. Ginzel, *Handbuch der mathematischen und technischen Chronologie*, 1 (1906), 263–5; 2 (1911), 80–82. LANGUAGE AND LITERATURE: J.A. Montgomery, *The Samaritans* (1907, 1968); A.E. Cowley, *The Samaritan Liturgy* (1909); Z. Ben-Ḥayyim, *Ivrit ve-Aramit Nosaḥ Shomron*, 4 vols. (1957–67); I. Ben-Zvi, *Sefer Ha-Shomronim* (1970^2); F. Pérez Castro, in: *Sefarad*, 13 (1953), 119–29; J. Macdonald, *Memar Marqah*, in: BZAW, 84 (1963); A.S. Halkin, *The Relation of the Samaritans to Saadia Gaon*, in: *Saadia Anniversary Volume* (1943), 271–92; L. Goldberg, *Das samaritanische Pentateuch Targum* (1935); M. Gaster, *The Samaritans* (1925); idem, *The Samaritan Literature* in: EI, 4 (1925; supplement to the author's article *The Samaritans*); Steinschneider, Arab Lit, 319–34; E. Vilmar, *Abu-al-Fatḥ, Annales Samaritani* (1865); A. Neubauer (ed.), *Chronique Samaritaine* (1873); J. Bowman, *Transcript of the Original Text of the Samaritan Chronicle Tolidah* (1954); T.W.J. Juynboll, *Chronicon Samaritanum... Liber Josuae* (1848); M. Gaster, in: JRAS, 31 (1909), 115–27, 149–53; E.N. Adler and M. Seligsohn, *Une nouvelle Chronique Samaritaine* (1903); A. Loewenstamm, in: *Sefunot*, 8 (1964), 165–204; M. Haran, in: *Eretz-Israel*, 4 (1956), 252–68; A.S. Halkin, in: *Memorial Volume I. Goldziher* (1958), 86–100; S.J. Miller, *Molad Moshe* (Ar. with translation in Samaritan Hebrew by Phinehas b. Isaac ha-Kohen; 1949); M. Klumel, *Mishpâtim, ein samaritanisch-arabischer Commentar zu 21–22:15 von Ibrahim ibn Jacub* (1902); G. Levin-Rosen, The Joseph Cycle (*Genesis 37–45) in the Samaritan-Arabic Commentary of Meshalma ibn Murjan* (1951); H.G. Kippenberg, *Garizim und Synagoge* (1971). M. Gaster in: *Festschrift zum 75-jaehrigen Bestehen des Juedisch-theologischen Seminars* (1929), 393–404; L.A. Mayer, *Bibliography of the Samaritans* (1964); R. Weiss (ed.), *Leket Bibliografi al ha-Shomronim* (1970). IN ISLAM: Tabarī, *Tavzxrikh*, 1 (1357 A.H.), 296–7; Tha'rlabi, *Qiṣaṣ* (1356 A.H.), 175–7; Kis'ăi, *Qisas* (1956 A.H.), 219–21; H. Speyer, *Die biblischen Erzaehlungen im Qoran* (1961), 323–33; J.A. Montgomery, *The Samaritans* (1907, 1968), 151–2, no. 39. MUSICAL TRADITION: A.Z. Idelsohn, *Toledot ha-Neginah ha-Ivrit* (1924), 53–58; idem, in: *Yerushalayim*, 11–12 (1916), 335–73; idem, in: MGWJ, 61 (1917), 117–26: Z. Ben-Ḥayyim, *Ivrit ve-Aramit Nosah Shomron*, 1 (1957), 53–57; 2 (1957), 304–403; D. Cohen and R. Torgovnik Katz, in: *Ethnomusicology*, 4 (1960), 67–74; J. Macdonald, in: *Islamic Quarterly*, 6 (1961), 4754; M. Ravina, *Organum and the Samaritans* (1963); C. Sachs, *Wellsprings of Music*, ed. by J. Kunst (1965), 64f., 169f.; E. Gerson-Kiwi, in: *Yuval*, 1 (1968). 169–93 (Eng. section); S. Hofman. *ibid.*, 36–51 (Heb. section); idem, in; *Divrei ha-Congress ha-Olami ha-Revi'i le-Madda'ei ha-Yahadut*, 2 (1968), 385–94 (Eng. abstract, 208f.); J. Spector, *ibid.*, 153–6 (Eng.); R.T. Hassafarey, *Kitāb al-Tasābich* (Heb., 1970). **ADD. BIBLIOGRAPHY:** J. Bowman (ed.), *Samaritan Documents Relating To Their History, Religion and Life* (1977); P. Bruneau, "Les Israélites de Délos et la juiverie délienne," in: *Bulletin de Correspondence Hellénique*, 106 (1982), 465–504; R.J. Coggins, *Samaritans and Jews. The Origins of Samaritanism Reconsidered* (1975); S.J.D. Cohen, *The Beginnings of Jewishness. Boundaries, Varieties, Uncertainties* (1999); M.F. Collins, "The Hidden Vessels in Samaritan Tradition," in: *Journal for the Study of Judaism*, 3 (1972), 97–116; F.M. Cross, "Samaria Papyrus 1: An Aramaic Slave Conveyance of 335 B.C.E. Found in the Wadi el-Dâliyeh," in: *Eretz Israel* (EI), 18 (1985), 7–17; A.D. Crown (ed.), *The Samaritans* (1989); A.D. Crown, *A Bibliography of the Samaritans* (19932); idem, "New Light on the Interrelationships of Samaritan Chronicles from Some Manuscripts in the John Rylands Library," in; *Bulletin of the John Rylands University Library of Manchester* (BJRL), 54 (1971/72), 283–313; 55 (1972/73), 86–111; F. Dexinger and R. Pummer (eds.), "Einführung in den Stand der Samaritanerforschung," in: *Die Samaritaner* (1992), 1–66; L. Grabbe, *Judaism from Cyrus to Hadrian* (1994); C. Hezser, *Jewish Literacy in Roman Palestine* (2001); I. Hjelm, *The Samaritans and Early Judaism* (2000); K.G. Hoglund, *Achmaemenid Imperial Administration in Syria-Palestine and the Missions of Ezra and Nehemiah* (1992); S. Isser, "Jesus in the Samaritan Chronicles," in: *Journal of Jewish Studies* (JJS), 32 (1981); idem, "The Samaritans and Their Sects," in: W. Horbury, W.D. Davies, and J. Sturdy (eds.), *The Cambridge History of Judaism*, vol. 3 (1999); A.T. Kraabel, "New Evidence of the Samaritan Diaspora Has Been Found on Delos," in: *Biblical Archaeologist* (March 1984); Y. Magen, "Mt. Gerizim – A Temple City," in: *Qadmoniot*, 33:2 (120) (2000(a)), 74–118; idem, "Mt. Gerizim During the Roman and Byzantine Periods," in: *Qadmoniot*, 33:2 (120) (2000(b)), 133; Y. Magen, L. Tsafania, and H. Misgav, "The Hebrew and Aramaic Inscriptions from Mt. Gerizim," in: *Qadmoniot*, 33:2 (120) (2000(c)); 125–32; L.D. Matassa, "The Myth of the Synagogue on Delos," in: *Symposium on Mediterranean Archaeology 2004*, Trinity College, Dublin, *British Archaeological Reports* (2006); M. Mor, "Samaritan History," in: A. Crown (ed.), *The Samaritans* (1989); R. Pummer, *The Samaritans* (1987); idem, "Samaritan Material Remains and Archaeology," in: A.D. Crown (ed.), *The Samaritans* (1989); idem, "The Samaritans – A Jewish Offshoot or a Pagan Cult?" in: *Bible Review*, 7:5 (1991), 22–29, 40; idem, "How To Tell a Samaritan Synagogue from a Jewish Synagogue," in: BAR, 24:3 (May/June 1998), 24–35; J.D. Purvis, *The Samaritan Pentateuch and the Origin of the Samaritan Sect* (1968); idem, "The Samaritans," in: W.D. Davies and L. Finkelstein (eds.), *The Cambridge History of Judaism*, vol. 2 (1989); L.Y. Rahmani, "Stone Synagogue Chairs: Their Identification, Use and Significance," in: IEJ, 40:2–3 (1990), 192–214; D.L. Smith-Christopher, "The Mixed Marriage Crisis in Ezra 9–10 and Nehemiah 13: A Study of the Sociology of the Post-Exilic Judaean Community," in: T.C. Eskenazi and K.H. Richards (eds.), *Second Temple Studies, 2. Temple and Community in the Persian Period*, in: *Journal for the Study of the Old Testament*, Supplement Series 175 (1994); E. Stern and Y. Magen, "The First Phase of the Samaritan Temple on Mt. Gerizim – New Archaeological Evidence," in: *Qadmoniot*, 33:2 (120) 2000, 119–124; T. Shemaryahu, "A Masada Fragment of Samaritan Origin," in: IEJ, 47 (1997), 220–32; L.M. White, "The Delos Synagogue Revisited: Recent Fieldwork in the Graeco-Roman Diaspora," in: *Harvard Theological Review* (1987), 135–54.

SAMARKAND, capital of Samarkand district, Uzbekistan. Jews are mentioned there from hearsay for the first time by *Benjamin of Tudela (12th century) as a large community. It was apparently destroyed when the town was captured by Bab Mehmet Khan in 1598. The Jews later suffered from Muslim oppression. In 1843, at the request of the Jews, a special area was allocated to them for the construction of a Jewish quarter: they were led by a *nasi*, named Kulantur, approved by the emir of *Bukhara. The situation of the Jews improved after the Russian conquest (1868), and in 1887 there were 3,792 Jews in Samarkand, the overwhelming majority of them of the Bukharan community.

Settlement of Ashkenazi Jews from *Russia began with the construction of the railroad to Samarkand in 1888; they played an important role in the commercial development of the city. In 1897 there were 4,307 Jews (c. 8% of the total population). Their number subsequently increased with Jewish immigration from the emirate of Bukhara and from Russia. The Russian authorities were opposed to this immigration, and, in contrast to the local Jews, the "foreign" Jews (from Bukhara) and the Jews of European Russia were subjected to persecutions. In 1907 the Jewish population numbered 5,266.

With the outbreak of the Revolution of 1917, the Zionist movement in Samarkand gained in strength and served as a factor unifying the various communities there. A communal center and Hebrew secondary school were established. Under the Soviet regime a Jewish-Bukharan branch of the Communist Party was formed in Samarkand; for a number of years it carried on a struggle with the *Yevsektsiya over the right of the local Jews to maintain a Hebrew school. The Yevsektsiya took steps to oppose the national and religious traditions of the Jews. By 1933 15 of the synagogues in the Jewish quarter had been closed down. In 1935 "sovietization" of the Jewish Museum (founded in 1922) expurgated its national-religious character and the evidence of the close ties existing between the Jews of Samarkand and Ereẓ Israel. The Jews of the Bukharan community numbered 7,740 in 1926, and 9,832 in 1935 (8% of the total population); of those 8,898 lived in the Jewish quarter, whose name was changed in 1926 to "Eastern Quarter," while 95% of the inhabitants were Jews. According to the census of January 1939 there were 7,593 Jews – 5.57% of the total. The Jewish school, whose language of instruction was Tajiki (or Judeo-Tajiki; the language spoken by the Bukharan Jews), was attended by over 1,400 children. During World War II many Jewish refugees from the western part of the Soviet Union arrived in Samarkand.

Contemporary Period

In the late 1960s the Jewish population was estimated at 15,000 (mainly Bukharan Jews), most of whom resided in the former Jewish quarter. There remained one synagogue in the old part of the city, where the Jewish quarter is located; it included a separate section for the Ashkenazi Jews. Samarkand retained a Jewish cemetery. In 1951 the rabbi Ḥakham Ezekiel was sentenced to 25 years imprisonment for "religious activity," but was released in 1957, having served six years. In March 1964 the community was compelled by the authorities to protest against the sending of matzot from Israel and the baking of matzot was carried on at home. Since Uzbekistan attained independence in 1991 there has been a steady exodus of Jews to Israel and the West (mainly the United States), with around 2,000 remaining in Samarkand in 2005. One of the city's two synagogues is still in use, but often there is no *minyan* for Sabbath services.

BIBLIOGRAPHY: Z.L. Amitin-Shapiro, *Ocherk: Sotsialisticheskogo stroitelstva sred: sredne-aziaskikh Yevreyev* (Tashkent, 1933); I. Ben-Zvi, in: *He-Avar*, 1 (1953), 67–73; A. Ben Ami, *Between Hammer and Sickle* (1967), 191ff., 198 and passim.

[Yehuda Slutsky]

SAMAU'AL BEN JUDAH IBN 'ABBĀS AL-MAGHRIBĪ, convert to Islam, mathematician, physician, and author of an anti-Jewish manual. He converted to Islam in 1163 and died ca. 1170. He left a polemical attack on the Jews and on Judaism, composed following his conversion, as well as an autobiographical account of his conversion, besides other works on scientific, especially mathematical, subjects. The name "al-Maghribī" indicates a connection with the Islamic west, and he may have been born there, but he spent most of his life in the east, converting to Islam in the city of Maragha (now in Azerbaijan). The son of a well-known father (Judah b. 'Abbās was a poet and a friend of *Judah Halevi), Samau'al refrained from converting for a long time out of respect for his father, but he eventually became a Muslim shortly before his father's death.

The reasons behind his conversion were of two kinds. The Prophet *Muhammad appeared to him in a dream, which he recounts in his work. However, while dreams are known quite often to lead to conversion, Samau'al did not accept religious experience as a legitimate argument for conversion. Only rational argument was acceptable to him. Thus, in his autobiography he describes his conversion as the product of a process of study and intellectual analysis which took place over a considerable period of time (an exchange of letters with an anonymous correspondent, published together with the autobiography, attempting to justify the conversion, wears the appearance of a literary construct).

Samau'al's main surviving work is his *Ifḥām al-Yahud* (*Silencing the Jews*). In this work Samau'al claims that the Bible is merely an invention by Ezra, that its transmission was unreliable, and that it cannot be regarded as authentic divine revelation. Nonetheless, like many a polemicist before and after (e.g., *'Abd al-Ḥaqq al-Islāmī), Samau'al is prepared to recognize the biblical text as authentic when it suits his case: he identifies several examples of biblical texts prophesying the advent of Muhammad (in particular Gen. 17:20 and Deut. 18:15–18) and uses *gematria* to show that Muhammad is referred to in the Bible (in the phrase *bi-me'od me'od*, Gen. 17:20, referring to the descendants of Ishmael, the sum of the numerical values of the letters of the Hebrew words equals the sum of the values of the letters in the name "Muhammad"). Above all, though, Samau'al claims that Judaism is to be rejected because the same arguments that can be made for Moses can also be made for Jesus and Muhammad – either all are to be accepted or all are to be rejected.

The argument of the equivalence of faiths might have led to atheism or to retention of Judaism, but Samau'al uses it to justify acceptance of Islam, on the ground that that faith includes all of the faiths that have preceded it. Acceptance of the faith of the majority thus has an intellectually respectable, as well as a socially pragmatic, aspect.

Samau'al's conversion was one of several at the time: besides Samau'al, we know also of the doctor and philosopher Abū al-Barakāt Ḥibbat Allāh, who converted at the end of his life, and of Isaac the son of Abraham b. Ezra. As all three were acquainted, there have been suggestions that Ḥibbat Allāh may have acted to influence the other two to convert, or that all these converts were part of a circle of intellectuals with shared interests and paths to Islam, but Stroumsa argues persuasively that this supposition is unfounded and that the conversions were independent.

BIBLIOGRAPHY: M. Perlmann (ed. and trans.), Samau'al al-Maghribī, *Ifḥam al-Yahūd Silencing the Jews* (= *Proceedings of the American Academy for Jewish Research*, vol. 32) (1964); F. Rosenthal, "Al-Asturlabi and as-Samaw'al on Scientific Progress," in: *Osiris*, 9 (1950), 555–64; H. Lazarus-Yafeh, *Intertwined Worlds. Medieval Islam and Bible Criticism* (1992), index; S. Stroumsa, "On Jewish Intellectuals Who Converted in the Early Middle Ages," in: *The Jews of Medieval Islam* (1995), 179–97.

[David J. Wasserstein (2nd ed.)]

SAMBARI, JOSEPH BEN ISAAC (known by the name **Qātāya**), Egyptian chronicler, who lived in the 17th century, and was apparently a member of the Cairene, Musta'rib congregation (see *Musta'ribs). Sambari wrote two Hebrew chronicles: *Divrei Ḥakhamim*, a historical account from Adam to Rabbanan Savorai (see *Savora), that is not extant, and *Divrei Yosef*, which was completed on January 23, 1673 and is extant in five different manuscripts (= mss.). Two of the mss. contain most of the original written by Sambari, i.e., that of the Alliance Israélite Universelle library (AIU H130A), Paris, and that of the Bodleian (Neubauer Cat., No. 2410), Oxford. An annotated edition of the chronicle was published by Sh. Shtober on the basis of the corpus of the mss. (See *Sefer Divrei Yosef* [= SDY], Jerusalem: the Ben-Zvi Institute, 1994.) Another book written by Sambari is the *Porat Yosef*, in which he deals exclusively with the topics of Massorah and biblical cantillation. This work is extant in a unique manuscript in the Alliance Israélite Universelle library (AIU H41A).

There is no information about Sambari's life in any of the sources, and what is known about him is found in *Divrei Yosef*. He was a pupil of R. Hananiah Barhun, the pupil of R. Abraham Iskandari, and may have been one of the latter's young disciples in *Cairo. According to Sambari's own testimony, Iskandari's rich library aroused in him an intense curiosity in history, and later on he made extensive use of it in writing his works. In the 1660s he earned his livelihood as a clerk or a scribe working for Raphael Joseph, the minister of finance (*sarrafbashi*) of the governor of Ottoman Egypt. Owing to the close contacts of his patron with *Shabbetai Ẓevi, it is most likely that Sambari himself also became one of the adherents of that messianic movement. The collapse of Shabbateanism after the apostasy of the false messiah had made Sambari disillusioned, and this was one of the main drives that brought about the accomplishment of the SDY in 1673. Sambari began this historical work with the emergence of Islam, presenting the figure of *Muhammad, as seen through Jewish eyes. Henceforth he included the history of the Jewish people in the history of the Islamic nations. The full scope of the eastern Islamic dynasties from the earliest, the *Ummayads to the Ottomans, served him as backdrop to the Jewish historical materials. Sambari's uniqueness lies in the fact that he successfully integrated these two histories, connecting them through the chain of cause and effect. His access to the Arabic material enabled him to enrich the Islamic chapters of his book with the essentials found in the Islamic biographical literature (Sira), in *Hadith traditions, and in Muslim historiography. In dealing with the Muslim kingdoms he mainly relied on al-Maqrizi, Ibn Taghri-birdi, and Ibn Zunbul.

The centrality of Egypt in the SDY made Sambari enter into great detail in describing the Jewish settlements that existed in the Nile Valley during the 10th–16th centuries; portraits of their leaders, foremost among them *Maimonides, his descendants and other *negidim* (i.e., heads of the Jews); the persecutions they had undergone there; and even the hydrological regime of the Nile. Indispensable for an understanding of Jewish life in *Fatimid and *Mamluk Egypt are Sambari's details about the various synagogues in Fustat, Cairo, Jizeh, and other places in the region of the Delta.

Sambari's main sources for his history of the Jews were *Yuḥasin* by Abraham Zacuto; *Shevet Yehudah* by Solomon Ibn Virga; *Divrei ha-Yamim* by Joseph ha-Kohen; *Shalshelet ha-Kabbalah* by Gedaliah Ibn Yahya, and *Seder Eliyahu Zuta* by Elijah Capsali, *Kore ha-Dorot* by David Conforti. He also integrated into his work archival documents, excerpts of Responsa (of Maimonides and R. David Ibn Abi Zimra) and bio-bibliographical notes about prominent sages living in Spain and later on in the Eastern provinces of the Ottoman Empire.

As Sambari was imbued with Jewish mysticism, he was fascinated by *Kabbalah, and therefore he depicted outstanding kabbalists who were active in *Safed during the 16th and 17th centuries. Moreover, he includes in his work the complete, most precise, and earliest version of the hagiography of R. Isaac Luria, *Sefer Toledot ha-Ari*. In the wake of his personal involvement in the messianic experience of his generation, Shabbateanism, Sambari incorporated in the SDY the stories of eight messianic and prophetic figures, beginning with David Alroy and concluding with ha-Ari and Shabbetai Ẓevi. It is especially significant that Sambari wrote down "the story of *Nathan of Gaza who prophesied concerning Shabbetai Ẓevi, his prophet," but unfortunately this has been torn out from the manuscripts of the work.

The circulation of the holograph of Sambari's historical work was very limited in the 17th–19th centuries, and only small sections dealing with the Ottoman sultans, messianic figures and kabbalists were published in *Sippur Devarim* (Constantinople, 1728) and in *Me'ora'ot Olam* (Smyrna, 1756). The *editio princeps* of 1728 was translated into Ladino (Constantinople, 1767), named *Sippur Malkhey Otmanlis es declare del Reyno di Otmanjik.*

BIBLIOGRAPHY: Ashtor, Toledot, index; A. Berliner, *Quellenschriften zur juedischen Geschichte und Literatur*, 1 (1896), index; idem, in: MWJ, 17 (1890), 50–58; W. Fischel, in: *Zion*, 5 (1939), 204–13; Z H B, 10 (1906), 154; M. Schreiner, in: ZDMG, 45 (1891), 295–300; M. Brann, in: MGWJ, 44 (1900), 14–24; 138–40; M. Benayahu, *Sefer Toledot ha-Ari* (1967), 15–18; 123–6; R.A. Ibn Simeon, *Tuv Miẓrayim* (1908), 19; H.Z. Hirschberg, in: *Eretz Israel*, 10 (1971); Sh. Shtober (ed.), *Sefer Divrei Yosef: Eleven Hundred Years of Jewish History under Muslim Rule* (1994); idem, "Muhammad and the Beginnings of Islam in the Chronicle Sefer Divrey Yosef," in: *D. Ayalon Festschrift* (1986), 319–52; idem., "Divrei ha-Yamim shel ha-Mamlakhot ha-Muslimiyyot be-Sefer Divrei Yosef," in: *H. Beinart Festschrift* (1988), 415–27; idem, *"Mi-Bet ha-Din ha-Yehudi el Bet ha-Din ha-Shari': Ha-Sikhsukh bein ha- Musta'ribim ve-ha-Maghribim be-Kahir ba-Mea'h ha-Shesh-Esreh,"* in: *Meḥkarim be-Aravit ve-Tarbut ha-Islam*, 2 (2001), 107–28; H.Z. Hirschberg, "The Agreement between the Musta'ribs and the Maghribis in Cairo 1527," in: *S.W. Baron's Jubilee Volume* (1974), 577–90; A. Gross, *R. Yosef ben Avraham Hayun: Manhig Kehilat Lisbon* (1993), 25–27; M. Winter, "Historyon Yehudi ben ha-Me'ah ha-Sheva'-'Esreh," in: *Pe'amim*, 65 (1995), 154–56.

[Shimon Shtober (2nd ed.)]

SAMBATYON (also **Sanbatyon** and **Sabbatyon**), a legendary river across which part of the ten tribes were exiled by the Assyrian king, Shalmaneser, and which rested on the Sabbath. The river is mentioned in the Targum Pseudo-Jonathan (Ex. 34:10): "I will take them from there and place them on the other side of the Sambatyon River." The rabbis declared that the ten tribes were exiled three times: once beyond the Sambatyon River, once to Daphne of Antioch, and once when the divine cloud descended upon them and covered them (TJ, Sanh. 10:6, 29c; Lam. R. 2:9; cf. Gen. R. 73:6). The first ascription of miraculous qualities to this river is found in the Talmud. When *Tinneius Rufus asked R. Akiva how he could prove that the Sabbath was divinely ordained as the day of rest, he replied, "Let the River Sambatyon prove it" (Sanh. 65b). It was unnavigable on weekdays because it flowed with strong currents carrying along stones with tremendous force, but it rested on the Sabbath (Gen. R. 11:5). These passages give no indication as to the supposed location of the river or of the origin of its name. The only inference that can be drawn from them is that it was located in Media. The most extensive description of both its name and locality is given by Naḥmanides (to Deut. 32:26). He identified the river with the River Gozan of the Bible (e.g., II Kings 17:6), explaining the name (on the basis of Num. 11:31) as meaning "removed," i.e., the ten tribes were "removed" from the rest of their people. Naḥmanides also held that its name derived from its Sabbath rest, since *Sabbat* was the local word for the Sabbath.

Pliny the Elder (24–79 C.E.) described the river in his *Natural History*, and his observations agree with the rabbinic sources. He also claimed that the river ran rapidly for six days in the week and rested on the Sabbath (31:24). This characteristic of the Sambatyon prevented the ten tribes from leaving their place of exile, since they could not cross the river during the six days of the week, and though it rested on the seventh day, the restrictions on travel on the Sabbath rendered the crossing equally impossible (see *Ten Lost Tribes). Josephus, however, described the periodicity of this river in a different fashion, claiming that it was quiescent on weekdays and flowed only on the Sabbath. He related that when Titus marched from Beirut to the other Syrian cities, displaying the Jewish captives, he observed a unique river. It ran between Arce, at the northern extremity of the Lebanon range, and Raphanea. Josephus adds: "It has an astonishing peculiarity. For, when it flows, it is a copious stream with a current far from sluggish; then all at once its sources fail, and for the space of six days it presents the spectacle of a dry bed; again, as though no change had occurred, it pours forth on the seventh day just as before. And it has always been observed to keep strictly to this order; whence they have called it the Sabbatical river, so naming it after the sacred seventh day of the Jews" (Jos., Wars, 7:96–99). According to this description there is no explanation for the inability of the ten tribes to cross the Sambatyon during the weekdays.

In the post-talmudic period, especially in the apocryphal literature, legends about the Sambatyon increased. The exact date that the ten tribes were to return from their places of exile during the messianic period was recorded in the *Sefer Eliyahu*. Tishrei 25 was designated for the return of those beyond the Sambatyon. Although 17,000 men and women would leave this area, 20 men and 15 women would be killed on the way to the Holy Land (Judah ibn Samuel, *Midreshei Ge'ullah* (1954^2) 31f., 43; cf. Num. R. 16:25). *Eldad ha-Dani claimed that the Sambatyon did not surround the land of the ten tribes but rather that of the children of Moses. These people originated as a result of God's promise to Moses that "I will make of thee a great nation" (Ex. 32:10). Eldad depicted the river as consisting entirely of sand and stones. His description was as follows:

"The children of Moses are surrounded by a river resembling a fortress, which contains no water but rather rolls sand and stones with great force. If it encountered a mountain of iron it could undoubtedly grind it into powder. On Friday, at sunset, a cloud surrounds the river, so that no man is able to cross it. At the close of the Sabbath the river resumes its normal torrent of stones and sand. The general width of the river is 200 ells, but in certain places it is only 60 ells wide, so that we may talk to them, but neither of us can cross to the other one's side" (A. Epstein 5f.).

*Pethahiah of Regensburg, the 12th-century Jewish traveler, claimed that in Jabneh there was a spring which ran six days a week, but ceased to flow on the Sabbath (*Travels of Rabbi Petachia*, ed. by A. Benisch (1865), 56f.). Interest in the Sambatyon legend was revived in the 17th century through the fantastic stories of Gershon b. Eliezer ha-Levi in his *Gelilot Ereẓ Yisrael* and by *Manasseh Ben Israel in his *Mikveh Yisrael*. The former related that, in his journey through India in 1630, he heard the clattering noise of the Sambatyon River, which was a distance of two days' journey from where he was staying. He claimed that the Sambatyon was 17 miles wide and threw stones as high as a house. On the Sabbath it was dry and resembled a lake of snow or of white sand. The river ceased to flow on Friday, two hours before sunset, and during this interval before the start of the Sabbath, the Jews beyond the river raided the neighboring lands. Manasseh Ben Israel, while attempting to prove the existence of the river, claimed that even when its sand is kept in a glass, it is agitated during six days of the week and rests on the Sabbath (*Mikveh Yisrael*, ch. 10, Lemberg, 1847 ed., p. 10a–b). The Sambatyon also figured in kabbalistic works. In 1260 the kabbalist Abraham *Abulafia traveled to Ereẓ Israel, where he started to search for the Sambatyon. He was trying to contact the Ten Lost Tribes. Sambatyon was also associated with *Shabbetai Ẓevi. The students of *Nathan of Gaza circulated a story after Shabbetai Ẓevi's death that he had gone to the Ten Lost Tribes that live on the other side of the Sambatyon. There he married the daughter of Moses. For a similar tale, see the Letter of Nathan of Gaza to Raphael Joseph (1665; published in *Ẓiẓat Novel Ẓevi*, ed. Tishby (1954), 11–12). The students were to wait for Shabbetai Ẓevi to return after the seven-day wedding celebration and to redeem them – if they were worthy of it. If they were not worthy, he would stay beyond the Sambatyon and great troubles would befall Israel (*Zikkaron li-Venei Yisrael* (1676), 68).

BIBLIOGRAPHY: E.N. Adler, Jewish Travellers (1930), index; J.D. Eisenstein, *Oẓar Massa'ot* (1926), 84, 122, 184f.; M. Gruenbaum, in: ZDMG, 23 (1869), 627–30; D. Kaufmann, in: REJ, 22 (1891), 285–7; A. Epstein (ed.), *Eldad ha-Dani* (1891), introd. 13–16; S. Krauss, *Griechische und lateinische Lehnwoerter*, 2 (1899), 369f.; J. Theodor and H. Albeck (eds.), *Midrash Bereshit Rabba*, 1 (1965^2), 93 n. 3. **ADD. BIBLIOGRAPHY:** H. Halkin, *Across the Sabbath River: In Search of a Lost Tribe of Israel* (2002).

[A.Ro.]

SAMBERG, ISAAC (Aizik; 1889–1943), Polish Yiddish actor. Samberg helped to organize the Warsaw Central Theater in 1920 and acted in Sholem Asch's *Motke the Thief* and Gogol's *Inspector-General*. Joining the Vilna Troupe in 1923, he appeared with them in various productions. A relative of the Kaminskis, he also acted with their company in Shalom Aleichem, Peretz, and Shakespeare. He visited the U.S. in 1932, London in 1934, and played in the film version of *Der Dybbuk*, 1937. He and his wife Regina Zukor perished in Maidanek, or possibly in Dachau.

SAMBOR, town in Lvov oblast, Ukraine; annexed by Poland in 1349; from 1772 to 1918 under Austrian rule (eastern Galicia); and from 1918 until 1939 once more under Polish rule. Jews came as settlers to the recently acquired land in the 15th century. Some engaged in trading salt, which was mined in the region of the town, while others were tax-farmers. In 1542 the townsmen of Sambor obtained a royal privilege *de non tolerandis Judaeis* which was ratified by Queen Bona in 1551, and Jews were moved to the suburb of Blich. In the middle of the 17th century the municipal authorities of Sambor prevented Jewish merchants and craftsmen from entering the town and endeavored to expel the Jews from Blich, where there was an organized community under the jurisdiction of that of *Przemysl, but they were allowed to remain on payment of an indemnity, guaranteed by the Przemsyl community (1682). A privilege granted by King Augustus II in 1725 authorized the Jews to reside in the area controlled by the fortress of Sambor and placed them under the jurisdiction of the royal governor. The king also permitted them to trade freely and to maintain a synagogue, a cemetery, and one slaughterhouse. This privilege was ratified by King Augustus III in 1740. Permission to build a synagogue was officially granted in 1763; this magnificent building, which took a number of years to complete, remained standing until World War II. In 1764 the Jewish community numbered 513 persons. At the close of the 18th century there was a Jewish press in Sambor which specialized in printing calendars. In the 1790s the Austrian authorities ordered a reduction in the size of the Jewish quarter. Throughout the 19th century Ḥasidism exerted a powerful influence on the community.

The Jewish population of Sambor numbered 2,129 (42% of the total population) in 1880, rose to 3,072 (48%) in 1900, and 4,073 (38%) in 1910, decreasing slightly to 4,067 (42%) in 1921. The majority earned a livelihood as small craftsmen and shopkeepers, while the wealthy families engaged in the wholesale trade of wood and cereals. At the beginning of the 20th century the municipal council was headed by a Jewish delegate, Dr. Steierman. A Jewish commercial school, which received government recognition, was founded at that time. There was also a Jewish hospital and a hostel for Jewish students of the local high school, where 150 Jewish youths studied in 1910. At the end of 1918, a Jewish national council was established. Between the two world wars *Tarbut and Beth Jacob schools functioned in the town. Zionist parties and organizations played a considerable role in the Jewish public life of Sambor. According to the 1931 census, there were 6,068 Jews in Sambor. Estimates for 1939 put the number of Jews at about 8,000.

[Meir Balaban and Arthur Cygielman]

Holocaust Period

When war broke out, a wave of refugees from further west came to Sambor. During the period of Soviet occupation, which lasted from the end of September 1939 until the end of June 1941, Jewish communal activities were banned, the only exception being the synagogues, which continued to function while paying heavy taxes. In the summer of 1940 hundreds of Jews were deported to the Soviet Union. When war with Germany broke out in June 1941, many young Jews from Sambor joined the Soviet Army. When the city fell to the Germans (July 1, 1941), about 100 Jews were immediately killed by the Ukrainians, with German support. In the winter of 1941–42 the able-bodied Jewish men were sent to labor camps to work on road constructions. Many of them succumbed to the harsh conditions. In March 1942 an open ghetto was established in the suburb of Blich, into which Jews from Sambor district and the vicinity were brought. The Judenrat was headed by Dr. Schneitscher.

The first mass *Aktion* took place on Aug. 4, 1942, when 4,000 Jews were "selected" and sent to *Belzec death camp. On September 4 about 100 aged persons were executed; 2,000 Jews were sent to Belzec, followed by 3,000 on October 17, and more on October 22. On Dec. 1, 1942, the ghetto was closed down. A small number of remaining Jews were sent to the labor camp of Janowska, in Lvov. At the beginning of 1943 there was an attempt to organize a Jewish underground. A group of young Jews, one of whose most active members was Artur Sandauer (d. 1989), acquired firearms, and began training in the area of the Jewish cemetery. A series of *Aktionen* carried out by the Nazis interfered with the preparations for active resistance: on March 14, 1943, the remnants of the Jewish community were brought to the Jewish cemetery. Mothers were ordered to put their children in a central open space, where they were forced to watch them being shot. Nine hundred persons were killed on this day. Two months later 1,200 Jews were murdered. An attempt by some Jews to leave the ghetto through sewage canals was thwarted. By July 1943 the Jewish community of Sambor ceased to exist, and the city was declared "*judenrein*." The last remaining Jews were executed in a forest near Radlowice. In the summer of 1944, 165 Jews in hiding were found and executed. When the Russians occupied the city in August 1944, a handful of Jews were still alive. No Jewish community was reestablished.

[Aharon Weiss]

BIBLIOGRAPHY: Halpern, Pinkas, 282, 285, 286, 288; Warsaw, Archiwum Główne Akt Dawnych, *Ksiegi kanclerskie*, no. 26, *Przywilej Augusta IIIIII* (= CAHJP, ḤM 2703/1); A. Eisenbach et al., *Żydzi a powstanie styczniowe, matreriały i dokumenty* (1963), index; B. Wasiutyński, *Ludność żydowska w Polsce w wiekach XIX i XX* (1930), 118, 128, 147, 152, 157; I. Schiper, *Studya nad stosunkami gaspodarczymi Żydów w Polsce podczas średniowiecza* (1911), index; M. Balaban, *Dzieje Żydów w Galicji i Rzeczypospolitej Krakowskiej 1772–1868* (1916), index; Brustin-Bernstein, in: *Bleter far Geshikhte*, 6 no. 3 (1953), 45–100.

SAMBURSKY, DANIEL (1909–1977), composer. Born in Koenigsberg, brother of Samuel *Sambursky, he studied at the Danzig Conservatory and at the University of Berlin, went to Palestine in 1932, and settled in Tel Aviv. In Berlin he had written the music for Shaul (Sally) Levin's Zionist play *Die einzige Loesung* (1931), and in 1933 composed the songs for the Keren *Hayesod film *The Promised Land*. He worked as a music teacher in schools and at teachers' seminaries, and from 1935 to 1950 also led the weekly singing meetings *(shirah be-ẓibbur)* at the Histadrut's Brenner House, and in radio broadcasts. In 1947, together with M. Bronzaft (later Gorali), he edited the three-volume anthology *Sefer Shirim u-Manginot*, one of the standard collections of Israel songs, which went into several editions.

Many of Sambursky's own songs have entered the folk repertoire, such as: *Ba'ah Menuḥah la-Yage'a, Hakh Pattish, Be-Harim Kevar ha-Shemesh Melahetet* (all to works by Nathan *Alterman), for the film *The Promised Land*; the latter taken over from *Die einzige Loesung* and given new words; *Zemer ha-Peluggot* (N. Alterman), for O. Wingate's Special Night Squads (1938); *Ner Dakkik*, children's Ḥanukkah song (Levin *Kipnis; 1935, *Paneinu el ha-Shemesh ha-Olah* (I. Shenhar), also taken over from *Die einzige Loesung* and given new words. *Sisu ve-Simḥu be-Simḥat Ḥag*, which appears in most collections as an anonymous folk melody, and in some as by "Galinka" (an erroneous transliteration from the Hebrew), is actually an adaptation by Sambursky of a polka by Glinka. Sambursky published a short autobiography in *Taẓlil*, 9 (1969), 180–2.

BIBLIOGRAPHY: M. Shalita, *Enẓiklopedyah le-Musikah*, 1 (1959²), s.v.; *Who is Who in* ACUM (1965).

[Bathja Bayer]

SAMBURSKY, SAMUEL (1900–1990), Israeli scientist and historian. Born in Koenigsberg, Germany, Sambursky studied physics before going to Palestine in 1924. Four years later he joined the physics department of the Hebrew University of Jerusalem. His sense of history and his humor made him a particularly successful lecturer. In 1945, in order to harness the country's scientific potential to the development of Palestine, the Mandatory government set up the Board of Scientific and Industrial Research, with Sambursky as its executive secretary. This board was the forerunner of the Research Council of Israel established in 1949, with Sambursky as its architect and first director (1949–56). He remained vice chairman when, in 1957, he returned to full-time academic life as dean of the Hebrew University's faculty of science. In 1959 he became professor of the history and philosophy of science in a new department he helped to create. Sambursky was active in UNESCO, serving for some years as vice chairman of Israel's national committee for the organization. In 1968 he received the Israel Prize for Humanities.

His works include *Ha-Kosmos shel ha-Yevanim* (1954; *The Physical World of the Greeks*, 1956); *Physics of the Stoics* (1959); and *Physical World of Late Antiquity* (1962). A revised edition of these three works appeared in 1965 in one volume under the title *Das Physikalische Weltbild der Antike*. His brother was the composer Daniel *Sambursky.

[Paul G. Werskey]

SAMEGAH, JOSEPH BEN BENJAMIN (d. 1629), Italian rabbi and author. Samegah was born in Salonika where he later became rabbi. Compelled to leave, seemingly because of persecution by his community, he went to Venice, where he served as rabbi and head of a yeshivah. According to Isaac Ḥayyim *Cantarini in his *Paḥad Yiẓḥak*, Samegah headed a yeshivah in Padua. Among his pupils were Ḥayyim *Benveniste and Joseph Solomon *Delmedigo.

Joseph was the author of *Mikra'ei Kodesh* (2 pts., Venice 1586), on the meaning of the precepts of the Torah; *Porat*

Yosef (Pt. 1, Venice, 1590), novellae on the works of Isaac *Alfasi and *Nissim b. Reuben Gerondi to *Ketubbot*, *Ḥullin*, and *Beẓah*, and a few novellae on other tractates of the Talmud; *Perush Derekh Yemin* (*ibid.*, 1606), a criticism of the *Yemin Adonai Romemah* of Menahem Azariah Da *Fano. Joseph's responsum, permitting the use of the *mikveh* of *Rovigo, about the ritual fitness of which arose a great controversy involving many scholars, was published in the *Mashbit Milḥamot* (*ibid.*, 1606). In the introduction to *Mikra'ei Kodesh* he refers to two other works he wrote: *Binyan Olam*, homilies, and *Kevod Elohim*.

BIBLIOGRAPHY: Conforte, Kore, 43b, 44a, 50a; Ghirondi-Neppi, 136; Fuehn, Keneset, 488–9; S. Simonsohn (ed.), in: Yehudah Aryeh of Modena, *Ziknei Yehudah* (1956), 50 (introd.).

[Abraham David]

SAMEKH, the fifteenth letter of the Hebrew alphabet; its numerical value is 60. The early Proto-Canaanite form of this letter has not yet been attested, but in the tenth century B.C.E. it consisted of three horizontal strokes crossed by a vertical downstroke ≢. Later there was a tendency to draw the various strokes continuously; thus in the Hebrew script 𐤎, in the Phoenician 𐤎, while in the Aramaic the *samekh* developed as follows: 𐡎 → 𐡎 → 𐡎 → 𐡎 → 𐡎. Hence the Jewish ס and Nabataen *samekh*, 𐢖, evolved. In the Arabic script the *samekh* has been replaced by س (*sin*), which developed from the Aramaic *shin* (Arabic *shin* = ش). See*Alphabet, Hebrew.

[Joseph Naveh]

SAMFIELD, MAX (1844–1915), Reform rabbi. Samfield was born in Marksteft, Bavaria. His father was a rabbi. He completed his rabbinical studies and his secular education in Germany before coming to the United States as part of the great migration from Central Europe in 1867.

In the United States he first served as a rabbi of B'nai Zion Congregation, Shreveport, Louisiana, and then went to Temple Israel in 1871 (when it was called Congregation Children of Israel), Memphis, TN, where he served until his death. The advertisement of his position read: "Wanted: A Minister and reader at a salary of $2500 who can preach in English and German." His initial sermon pledged "the vigor of my youth, the faculties of my soul, the energies of my mind, nay my very life, I consecrate to your moral welfare and to the welfare of Judaism and humanity." He was true to his word. By the time he came the synagogue had ceased being Orthodox and affiliated with the nascent Reform movement. Samfield moved it more so toward the Reform camp, asking and receiving permission to remove his hat. From 1875 on worship was hatless during his rabbinate. In 1871 the synagogue was one of 28 congregations that formed the *Union of American Hebrew Congregations and contributed toward the establishment of *Hebrew Union College

Rabbi Samfield was recalled with admiration for his courage during the yellow fever epidemics that afflicted Memphis three times during the 1870s, in 1873, 1878, and 1879. He remained in Memphis and ministered to the sick, helping the orphans and burying the dead regardless of race or conditions. In 1878, 20,000 people fled the city, cutting the population by more than half. Eight in ten of those who remained contracted yellow fever and 5,150 people died, more than one in four. In seven weeks 51 Jews were buried in the synagogue cemetery; nearly twice as many as had died the entire year before. Samfield served all the citizens of the community. He also adopted three orphans whose parents had died during the epidemic, in addition to his four natural children. He was recognized as a scholar and as a leader in public affairs, also taking on public school work. The times required that he be a man of action as well as a visionary in his performance as a speaker relating to matters of public utility.

Samfield's marriage registries show he converted individuals prior to officiating at their marriage. He was also the editor of the *Jewish Spectator*, a weekly newspaper, from October 1885 to his death. By the time he died, the newspaper was being published in New Orleans. It started as the only Jewish weekly in the South since the Jews had first settled in this region of the United States.

Locally, he was one of the founders of The Tennessee Society for the Prevention of Cruelty to Animals and Children, The United Charities of Memphis, The Hebrew Relief Association, and The Young Men's Hebrew Association, Memphis. He was one of the organizers and a member of Board of Memphis Howard Association for the promulgation of Prison Reforms, a group of Memphis doctors and prominent businessmen. He was also a trustee of the New Orleans Orphan Asylum Home and a member of the board of governors of the Hebrew Union College.

Under his leadership the congregation welcomed new immigrants and began construction of its new, prominent downtown building.

He was widely respected throughout the community. At his death local businesses closed their doors; the Memphis Railway Company cut its power and brought every street car to a halt for one full minute.

BIBLIOGRAPHY: J.G. Ringel, *Children of Israel: The Story of Temple Israel, Memphis, Tennessee, 1854–2004* (2004); 30th Anniversary Issue of *Jewish Spectator* (October 1915).

[Margerie Kerstine (2nd ed.)]

SAMINSKY, LAZARE (1882–1959), composer. He studied mathematics and philosophy at the University of St. Petersburg, and simultaneously composition with Rimsky-Korsakov at the Conservatory there. In 1908 he was among the founders of the *Society for Jewish Folk Music. In 1913 he went to the Caucasus as a member of Baron *Guenzburg's ethnological expedition In 1923 Saminsky settled in New York. There he was appointed music director of Temple Emanu-El and held the position until his death.

He wrote five symphonies (the last, with chorus, subtitled *Jerusalem, City of Solomon and Christ* (1929–30)), liturgical choruses, and services to Hebrew words. He was active as choral conductor and lecturer. He published several books: *Music of Our Day* (1939^2), *Music of the Ghetto and the Bible* (1934), and *Living Music of the Americas* (1949).

BIBLIOGRAPHY: D. de Paoli et al., *Lazare Saminsky, Composer and Civic Worker* (1930), incl. bibl., 62–65; G. Saleski, *Famous Musicians of Jewish Origin* (1949), 151–4; Petit, in: *Revue Musicale*, 10 (Jan. 1929), 222–6; Baker, Biog Dict; Grove, Dict; Sendrey, Music, indexes.

[Nicolas Slonimsky]

SAMOGITIA (Yid. and Heb. **Zamet** or **Zamut**; Lith. **Žemaitisa**; Pol. **Źmudź**; Rus. **Zhmud**), historical region of W. Lithuania. Jewish settlement in the area dates from the 14th century, and it gained in importance under the grand duke Witold of Lithuania, who granted the Jews a number of significant privileges. In the 16th century, especially after the union of Poland and Lithuania (1569), several Jewish communities were established. The Jews acted as government tax collectors, exporters of raw materials to Germany (timber, grain, etc.), and importers of silver and gold objects and manufactured goods.

Samogitia played an important role in the second half of the 17th century, when Lithuanian Jewry had a semiautonomous organization. This came about because of the growth of the already established communities and the creation of many new ones. The area attracted immigrants from other parts of Lithuania and Poland, and in particular refugees from the *Chmielnicki massacres, from which Samogitia itself had been spared. In the early period of the Lithuanian Council (see *Councils of the Lands; which lasted officially from 1623 to 1764) most of the communities of the Samogitia region belonged to the province of Brest-Litovsk, except for those in the vicinity of the Niemen River, which belonged to the Grodno district. In the third quarter of the 17th century Samogitia became a separate administrative unit, named *Medinat Zamet*, and consisted of three districts: *Kedainiai (in the southwest), *Birzai (in the northwest), and Vyžuonis in the east. At its beginning, the entire Samogitia unit had a single rabbinical court, but in the course of time several of the larger communities appointed their own rabbis.

The Kedainiai district, which was the largest, comprised the communities of *Jurbarkas, *Plunge, *Siauliai, *Raseiniai, *Palanga, *Kelme, Kraziai, *Skuodas, and *Telsiai, the spiritual leaders of the district being the rabbis of the *Katzenellenbogen family. The Birzai district consisted of the communities of Salantai, Pasvalys, Seta, Pumpenai, and Pakrojus. The Vyžuonis district comprised the communities of *Braslav, *Druya, *Kraslava, *Utena, and Anyksciai, and its spiritual leaders were the rabbis of the Ginsburg family. Samogitia continued to maintain administrative links with Brest-Litovsk, and the rabbi of Brest-Litovsk attended the Samogitia district meetings and affixed his signature to their minutes. Samogitia was one of the 11 central districts which came under the jurisdiction of the Lithuanian Council, and its name is frequently mentioned in the protocols of the early meetings of the Council which listed the communities paying the poll tax. (The "Council" was abolished in 1764, but the communal organizations that had been established in Samogitia continued to function for another two decades.) The first census of Lithuanian Jewry, conducted in 1764 and the beginning of 1765, showed a total of 157,250 taxpayers, Samogitia accounting for 15,759, or 10% of the total. In the Third Partition of Poland (1795), Samogitia became a part of the Russian Empire and remained so until 1915, when Lithuania was occupied by German troops. After World War I it became a part of independent Lithuania. At first the main center of the district was Raseiniai and later, Telsiai. During the Nazi occupation (1941–44), Samogitia was a part of Generalbezirk Litauen, and its Jews shared the tragic fate of the rest of Lithuanian Jewry.

As a center of Lithuanian Jewry, Samogitia was also famous as a center of Jewish religious life and learning. There were a number of world-renowned yeshivot in the area, and some of the communities were headed by great rabbis, whose authority extended far beyond their constituencies. When the *Haskalah movement spread in Lithuania, it also found adherents in Samogitia; the influence of German Haskalah was especially strong, due to the geographic proximity of the region to its sources.

BIBLIOGRAPHY: S.A. Bershadski, *Litovskye vevrei* (1883); D.M. Lipman, *Le-Toledot ha-Yehudim be-Lita-Zamut* (1934); *Lite*, 1 (1951), 2 (1965); *Yahadut Lita*, 1 (1959), 3 (1967); E.E. Friedman, *Sefer ha-Zikhronot* (1926), 8–90.

[Joseph Gar]

SAMOILOVICH, RUDOLPH (Reuben) LAZAREVICH (1881–1939), Soviet mining engineer and Arctic explorer. Born in Azov-on-Don, Samoilovich qualified as a mining engineer at Freiberg, Germany, and studied law in St. Petersburg. Twice convicted of revolutionary activities, he was exiled to Archangel in 1908 and to Pinega two years later. During the years 1910–15 he joined three expeditions to Spitsbergen, where he discovered high-quality anthracite, and also worked on the Kola peninsula immediately before the Bolshevik Revolution. In 1918 Samoilovich was a founder of what was to become the Leningrad Institute for Arctic Research, which he later headed. His research work took him to the Arctic islands of Novaya Zemlya in 1925–26. He became an international celebrity, however, when he led a Soviet expedition in 1928 to rescue the survivors of General Umberto Nobile's ill-fated Arctic flight in the dirigible *Italia*. After a voyage of seven weeks Samoilovich, on his icebreaker *Krassin*, managed to rescue Nobile and eight other members of the original Italian crew of 15, who by then were facing certain death on a rapidly melting iceberg. The operation made headlines throughout the world and Samoilovich was awarded the Soviet Red Banner of Labor. His account of the expedition, *S.O.S. v Arktike*, was published in 1930, a year after he became a professor at the University of Leningrad. He later explored Franz Josef Land and in 1931 made a flight over the North Pole in a Soviet airship.

BIBLIOGRAPHY: H.P. Smolka, *40,000 Against the Arctic* (1937).

SAMOKOV, town in Bulgaria. During the 18th century, the Jews of Samokov were not listed in the tax registers and did not pay taxes. They therefore objected to the arrival of coreligionists from other countries, lest this would prejudice their position. Toward the end of the Ottoman rule (which lasted until 1877), the Jews owned mines, muslin factories, and tanneries. In 1874 the Alliance Israélite opened a mixed school from which many *maskilim* graduated; they later played an important role in banking and commerce. In 1873 there were about 600 Jews in the town; in 1919, 1,000; and in 1943, 374. After the establishment of the State of Israel, the Jews of Samokov immigrated there, together with most of the rest of Bulgarian Jewry.

BIBLIOGRAPHY: Rosanes, Togarmah, 5 (1938–39), 165; BAIU (1873, 1874, 1876, 1878, 1910); N. Greenberg, *Dokumenti* (Bul., 1945), 179.

[Simon Marcus]

SAMOKOVLIJA, ISAK (1889–1955), Yugoslav author. Samokovlija, who was born in Goražde, Bosnia, was a practicing physician. He published his first story in 1927 and wrote nine volumes of short stories, beginning with *Od proljeća do proljeća* ("From Spring to Spring," 1929) and including post-World War II books such as *Nosač Samuel* ("Samuel the Porter," 1946), *Solomunovo slovo* ("Solomon's Letter," 1949), and *Djerdan* ("The Necklace," 1952). Three volumes of Samokovlija's collected tales appeared in 1951–56.

Samokovlija wrote entirely about Jewish life in Bosnia. Although many of his stories deal with the isolated Jewish existence of the Bosnian Sephardim during the 19th century, a few relate the tragic events of the Holocaust era. Samokovlija generally presents the picture of a Sephardi community in some small town, where the Jews live in self-imposed isolation, having much in common with their non-Jewish fellows, but refusing to assimilate. Between the world wars, Samokovlija also wrote plays: *Hanka* (1931), *Plava Jevrejka* ("The Blonde Jewess," 1932), *On je lud* ("He is Crazy," 1935), and *Fuzija* ("Fusion," 1939).

BIBLIOGRAPHY: E. Finci, in: *Zapisi*, 4 (1929); I. Andrić, in: Život, 6 (1955), 97–99; S. Vinaver, in: *Republika* (Jan. 25, 1955); B. Novaković, in: *Letopis Matice srpske*, 1 (1957); M. Marković, in: *Književne novine* (Jan., 1957); M. Begić, in: *Izraz*, 4 (1958), 240–50. **ADD. BIBLIOGRAPHY:** Z. Loker, *"Sureti s Isakom Samakovlijom,"* in: *Novi Omanut* (Zagreb), No. 26 (1998).

[Ana Shomlo-Ninic]

SAMPRAS, PETE ("Pistol Pete," "The King of Swing"; 1971–), U.S. tennis player, 1997 U.S. Olympic Committee "Sportsman of the Year." Sampras is considered by many tennis analysts to be the greatest tennis player of all time. He was born in Washington, DC, to a Greek family, though his paternal grandmother was a Sephardi Jew. At the age of seven he began playing tennis, and by the age of 11 was spotted by a tennis enthusiast who correctly identified his talent and arranged for personalized formal training. Sampras turned professional at age 17 and within two years won his first titles, including the 1990 U.S. Open, where he defeated Andre Agassi to become the youngest player ever to win that tournament. Ironically, Sampras' final match before retirement would be another defeat of Agassi for the U.S. Open title, this time making Sampras the oldest player ever to win the Open. As a professional from 1988 to 2002, he won 762 of 984 matches, capturing 64 singles titles, including a record 14 Grand Slam victories, with eight of them won in straight sets. Throughout his career, Sampras was known for his intense concentration, and especially for his highly accurate 130 mph (209 kph) serve – in 1993, he became the first player to serve over 1,000 aces in a season. Amongst Sampras' other records are his six consecutive years finishing as the Association of Tennis Professionals (ATP) No. 1 ranked player in the world (1993–98), 286 consecutive weeks at No. 1 in the ATP, and seven Wimbledon titles (tied with Willie Renshaw).

[Robert Klein (2nd ed.)]

SAMPTER, JESSIE ETHEL (1883–1938), U.S. poet and Zionist writer. Although she grew up in a highly assimilated home, her father being one of the pioneers of *Ethical Culture, Jessie Sampter became a staunch Jewess, partly under the influence of an elder sister of the poet Emma *Lazarus and of Henrietta *Szold. Her first book, *The Great Adventurer* (1908), was dedicated to Josephine Lazarus. Henrietta Szold, whom she first met in about 1912, persuaded her to write educational material for *Hadassah, notably the popular manual, the first edition of which was entitled *A Course in Zionism* (1915, reissued as *A Guide to Zionism*, 1920, and *Modern Palestine*, 1933). Although a childhood attack of infantile paralysis had left her a semi-invalid, Jessie Sampter emigrated to Palestine in 1919 and at first lived in Jerusalem, where she established evening classes for Yemenite working girls, one of whom she adopted. In 1920 she helped to organize the country's first camp for Jewish scouts at Reḥovot. Four years later she herself moved to Reḥovot and continued to do social work among the Yemenite Jews there. Her tour of the Jewish pioneering settlements in the Jezreel Valley inspired a series of 15 prose poems, published in 1927 as *The Emek*. These vivid sketches of kibbutz life had an important influence on U.S. Zionist circles before World War II. In 1933 she joined kibbutz Givat Brenner and used the proceeds of the sale of her Reḥovot house to build a convalescent home at the kibbutz.

Jessie Sampter's writing – which she sometimes published under the pen name Hashunamit – include *Brand Plucked from the Fire* (1937), a collection of poems on her attitude to Judaism and Zionism, which was translated into Hebrew by Pinḥas Lander in a specially vocalized text (*Ud Muẓal me-Esh*, 1944–45). Like *The Emek*, her last poem, "Palestinian Portrait," described the harsh realities of Jewish immigrant life in her day. Her prose works include *The Seekers* (1910); *The Book of the Nations* (1917); and "Testimony," a documentary account of the Arab riots and Hebron massacre of 1929 (published in *The New Palestine*, Sept. 27 / Oct. 4, 1929). She also wrote a volume of poems entitled *The Coming of Peace* (1919); *Around the Year in Rhymes for the Jewish Child* (1920); *Far Over the Sea* (1939), translations of *Bialik's poems for children; and two essays on Ecclesiastes, which appeared posthumously in Hebrew and English. *The Speaking Heart* and *In the Beginning*, two works of autobiography, were not published.

BIBLIOGRAPHY: B. Badt-Strauss, *White Fire* (1956).

[Harry Zohn]

SAMRA, DAVID (d. 1960), Iraqi jurist. After practicing law, he was appointed a judge to the *Mosul court of appeals in 1908. The following year he was appointed to a similar post in *Syria. Returning to *Baghdad, he resumed his legal practice, maintaining it until after the British conquest of *Iraq, when he was reappointed to the bench. In 1919 he became a judge on the Baghdad court of appeals and in 1923 deputy president of the court, the highest rank held by an Iraqi (the president of the court being British). From 1921 until his death he also served as a lecturer at the law school in Baghdad.

[Haim J. Cohen]

SAMSON (Heb. שִׁמְשׁוֹן; from *shemesh*, "sun"), son of Manoah, a Danite living in Zorah, a judge in Israel. Samson's heroic exploits are recounted in Judges 13–16.

His father was married to a woman who long remained childless. An angel of the Lord appeared to her to announce that she would give birth and that since the son whom she was carrying was to be a Nazirite from the womb, she herself was forbidden to partake of wine or strong drink or to eat anything unclean; it is possible that her husband was under the same restriction. Once the child was born, she was not to allow his hair to be cut (cf. Num. 6; see also 4Q Sam. 1:23 where Samuel is similarly described as a Nazirite from birth). The angel also announced that this child was destined to "begin to save Israel from the hand of the Philistines." In a second appearance, this time before Manoah as well as his wife, the angel substantially repeated his earlier message and then rose to heaven in the flames of Manoah's burnt offering, to the awe-struck wonder of the couple (Jud. 13:2–25).

All of the incidents recorded from the life of Samson stem from his involvement with three women. The first was a Philistine woman from Timnah (not to be confused with the Judahite town of that name). Samson demanded that his parents arrange his marriage to her. They were reluctant to have their son marry a woman from among the "uncircumcised" Philistines, but they were unaware that this was part of the Lord's plan by means of which an excuse to attack the Philistines would be obtained (14:1–4).

Samson's first heroic adventure took place on his way to Timnah to arrange the marriage. About to be attacked by a lion, he was seized by the spirit of the Lord, and he slew the beast barehanded. He later returned to the scene of this adventure and, finding that a swarm of bees had collected in the carcass of the lion, lustily partook of their honey, even bringing some to his parents, whom he did not inform of its origin (14:5–9).

Arriving at Timnah, Samson held a wedding feast at which he posed a riddle based on his adventure with the lion, and bet with the guests that they would not be able to solve it. The Philistines, unable to solve the riddle, enlisted the help of Samson's bride, who cajoled him into telling her the answer. When the Philistines responded correctly, Samson realized that his secret had been betrayed. He was again infused with the spirit of the Lord and rushed to Ashkelon, where he singlehandedly slew 30 men in revenge and then angrily returned to his parents' home, leaving his wife behind to be given to a companion (14:10–20).

When Samson returned to discover the fate of his wife, he vented his rage on the Philistines by tying 300 foxes in pairs by their tails with firebrands inserted between them and letting them run loose through the fields of the Philistines. When the latter took revenge on the family of his Timnaite wife, Samson in turn wreaked terrible vengeance upon them and then withdrew to the rock of Etam in Judah (15:1–8).

When the Philistines then encamped at Lehi, the Judahites, fearful of attack, sent a 3,000-strong delegation to Samson demanding that he surrender himself to the enemy. Samson agreed on a Judahite promise of safe-conduct. He was bound with two new ropes and brought to the Philistine camp where the spirit of the Lord came upon him, enabling him to snap the ropes and to kill 1,000 Philistines with the jawbone (*leḥi*) of an ass. This story is an etiology for the place name. A second etiology explains the name of a spring at Leḥi. This spring is said to have appeared after Samson called upon the Lord to provide water with which to quench his great thirst after the battle. Accordingly the spring was called En-Hakkore, "the spring of him who called" (15:9–20).

The second Philistine woman with whom Samson became involved was a prostitute from Gaza. The Philistines surrounded her house in the hope of seizing Samson when he emerged in the morning, but the plan was foiled when he arose in the middle of the night, uprooted the city gate, and carried it off to a hill in the vicinity of Hebron, about 40 miles away (16:1–3).

The third woman, who caused Samson's ultimate downfall, was *Delilah. Although not specifically identified as a Philistine, she conspired, for a price, with the Philistine rulers to ascertain the source of Samson's strength. After three unsuccessful attempts, she finally induced him to divulge that the secret lay in his unshorn locks of hair. Thereupon, she (see Sasson) shaved off his seven locks while he slept. Deprived of his strength, Samson was seized by the Philistines, who blinded and incarcerated him (16:4–21).

Some time later, the Philistines gathered in their temple for a religious festival and had Samson entertain them there. Samson, whose hair had meanwhile grown again, had his guide place his hands on the temple pillars. Then, uttering a final prayer to the Lord for vengeance, he seized them and brought the building toppling down, killing himself and the

3,000 worshipers (16:22–30). The final note of Samson's burial in his ancestral tomb between Zorah and Eshtaol closes the narrative (16:31).

The Samson stories are significant in that although their present form contains late linguistic features, they paint a picture of life in the Shephelah on the border between Judah, Dan, and Philistia during the late 12th or early 11th century B.C.E., before the Danite migration to the north. At this time, although Philistine pressure was beginning to be felt, as is reflected in the narrative, there was still open intercourse and trade between the Philistine and Israelite populations, a fact attested by the numerous Philistine artifacts found in the excavations of the Israelite settlement at Beth-Shemesh from this period. Since Israel at this time was not engaged in full-scale hostilities with the Philistines, Samson, unlike all the other judges, is never depicted as leading an army in battle or as having "saved" Israel from the Philistines. Rather it is told that he "began to save Israel" from them (13:5). He is the only judge who fell into enemy hands and who died in captivity. He is said to have "judged" Israel for 20 years (15:20; 16:31).

Elaborate theories about the possible mythical nature of the Samson narratives have been widespread, inspired particularly by the fact that the name Samson obviously contains the word for sun (*shemesh*) and that Samson's home was in Zorah which was situated on a mountain ridge north of the Wadi Sorek, directly opposite Beth-Shemesh, a place whose very name means "Temple of the Sun." Further evidence of mythology has been sought in the name Delilah, in which the Hebrew word for night (*laylah*) may be construed to appear. However, although some elements in these narratives may have been inspired by mythological heroic tales, their overall nature with their exuberant earthiness seems to point overwhelmingly to their folk origins as tales of the daring adventures of a superhuman hero against the foreign oppressor.

[Myra J. Siff]

In the Aggadah

Samson's birth is a striking example of the shortsightedness of humans. The judge Ibzan (identified as Boaz) had not invited Samson's parents to any of the 120 feasts in honor of the marriages of his 60 children because he thought that "the sterile she-mule" would never be able to repay his courtesy. However, Samson's parents were blessed with an extraordinary son, while Ibzan's 60 children died during his lifetime (BB 91a).

Samson's strength was superhuman and the dimensions of his body were gigantic. He measured 60 ells between his shoulders, but was maimed in both legs (Sot. 10a). He uprooted two great mountains and rubbed them against each other as though they were pebbles. Whenever the Holy Spirit rested on him he emitted a bell-like sound which could be heard from afar. While the spirit remained with him he could cover the distance between Zorah and Eshtaol in one stride (Lev. R. 8:2; Sot. 9b–10a). Samson's supernatural strength made Jacob think that he would be the Messiah (Gen. R. 98:14). Abraham's covenant of peace with the Philistines was only valid for three generations (Gen. R. 54:2), and for this reason Samson was permitted to wage war with them.

Samson was not without virtues. He was totally unselfish and never asked for the smallest service for himself. When Samson told Delilah that he was a "Nazirite unto God," she was certain that he had divulged the true secret of his strength since she could not imagine that Samson would couple the name of God with an untruth. But he allowed sensual pleasures to dominate him, with the result that "he who went astray after his eyes, lost his eyes" (Sot. 9b). He continued his profligate life in prison, and the Philistine women set aside all consideration of marital bonds in the hopes of gaining offspring who would inherit his strength and stature (Sot. 9b–10a).

Before his death, he entreated God to realize in him the blessing of Jacob (Gen. 27:28) and to endow him with divine strength (Gen. R. 66:3). He expired with these words upon his lips: "O Master of the Universe, vouchsafe unto me in this life recompense for the loss of one eye. For the loss of the other I will wait to be rewarded in the future." So great was the fear he inspired that the Philistines did not attack the Israelites for 20 years after his death (TJ, Sot. 1:8, 17b). Identified with Bedan (I Sam. 12:11), and so called because he belonged to the tribe of Dan, he is regarded as one of the most unworthy of leaders. Nevertheless "Bedan in his generation is as Aaron in his" (RH 25a–b).

[Aaron Rothkoff]

In the Arts

Samson, as one of the classic heroes of the Jewish people, has inspired innumerable writers, artists, and musicians. In the early literature of the Church he was generally seen as a prefiguration of Jesus and this interpretation was particularly evident in Christian works of the Middle Ages, although he was sometimes also equated with Hercules in classical legend. However, Samson was not given special prominence in the medieval mystery plays and only began to figure prominently in the works of Renaissance writers. Among these were Alessandro Roselli's Italian miracle play, *La Rappresentatione di Sansone* (Florence, 1551); the German *Meistersinger* Hans Sachs's tragedy, *Simson* (1556); a Hungarian verse play by Péter Kákonyi (1550–60); and *Samson* (1599), a Danish play by H.J. Ranch of Vibourg. The theme became increasingly popular in the 17th century, particularly among Protestant writers who tended to regard Samson as a symbol of the Reformation's struggle with the tyranny of Rome. In England, *Sam(p)son*, a biblical drama by the writers Rowley and Jewby, was staged in 1602 and in one scene Samson appeared carrying the town gates on his neck, to the delight of the Elizabethan audience. In Germany the baroque writer Philipp von Zesen turned to a new literary genre with his novel, *Simson* (1679). Interest in the subject was not, however, confined to Protestants. The English Catholic *Stonyhurst Pageants* (c. 1625) include one about Samson, and in Holland Joost van den Vondel, a Protestant convert to Catholicism, published the five-act tragedy

Samson (1660). The Converso writer Juan Pérez de Montalván (1602–1638) wrote *El divino nazareno Sanson* (published in Seville, c. 1720) and, in the Marrano diaspora, the playwright Antonio Enriquez *Gómez published a biblical epic, *El Sansón nazareno* (Rouen, 1656). The outstanding 17th-century treatment of the theme – and, perhaps, the loftiest interpretation in Western literature – was John *Milton's *Samson Agonistes* (1671), a drama in the strict Greek classical tradition that has been more studied than performed. In the blind Hebrew judge Milton clearly saw a representation of his own plight, and echoes of the story reverberate throughout his writings. Milton's Samson is, by comparison with the figure portrayed in the Bible, highly idealized; and his drama has been acclaimed as the zenith of biblical playwrighting in the Protestant tradition, the English of the Puritan Commonwealth representing the "New Israel." In the late 19th century a Hebrew translation of *Samson Agonistes* was published by the Manchester writer J. Massel (*Shimshon ha-Gibbor*, 1890).

Apart from oratorios, a five-act opera by Voltaire (1733) that never reached the stage, some Spanish *Relaciones burlescas* of the 1760s, and a poem by William *Blake (in *Poetical Sketches*, 1783), the only significant treatment of the 18th century was Moses Ḥayyim *Luzzatto's early verse play, *Shimshon ve-ha-Pelishtim*, best known as *Ma'aseh Shimshon* (1724), a product of the Italian Hebrew revival written in a colorful style. However, the political and literary conflicts of the 19th century revived serious interest in the theme. A. Carino's Italian poem, *Nascita, vita, e morte di Sansone* (Naples, c. 1820), was followed by S.S. Raschkow's Hebrew poem, *Ḥayyei Shimshon* (1824) and by another in Hungarian by Mihály Tompa (1863). An unusual interpretation of the biblical story was the French poet Alfred de Vigny's "La Colère de Samson" (in *Les Destinées*, 1864). Here the betrayed and outraged Hebrew expresses Vigny's own stoicism and violent misogyny. There have been many treatments of the subject by writers of the 20th century, notably dramas such as Frank Wedekind's *Simson oder Scham und Eifersucht* (1914); the Albanian Fan S. Noli's *Israilite dhe Filstine* (1907); Sven Lange's Danish *Samson og Dalila* (1909); and a five-act tragedy by the Russian dramatist Leonid Nikolayevich Andreyev (translated by Herman Bernstein as *Samson in Chains*, 1923).

Predictably, the theme has proved especially attractive to modern Jewish writers, who have laid varying interpretations on the character of Samson. Two early 20th-century works, Jaroslav *Vrchlický's dramatic Czech *Trilogie o Simsonovi* (1901) and Hugo *Salus' German biblical poem, "Simson," led the way, to be followed by Samson Zuckermandel's four-act Hebrew drama, *Gevurat Shimshon* (1906), and the more original *Samson* (1907), a French drama by Henri-Leon *Bernstein, in which Delilah, a gold digger, is typical of the writer's unattractive anti-heroines. Most of the later literary treatments by Jews have been in the form of the novel. These include *Simson de Godgewijde* (1927–29) by the Dutch writer Israël *Querido; Vladimir *Jabotinsky's *Samson nazorey* (1927; *Samson the Nazarite*, 1930); Felix *Salten's *Simson, das Schicksal eines Erwaehlten* (1928; *Samson and Delilah*, 1931); and Saul Saphire's Hebrew novel, *Shimshon ha-Gibbor* (1935). Two works on the theme by writers of the post-World War II era were Kazimierz Brandys' Polish novel, *Samson* (1948), which forms part of a tetralogy (*Między wojnami*, 1948–51), and *Ahavat Shimshon* (1951–52) by the Israeli poet Lea *Goldberg.

In art, too, the Samson theme has enjoyed an enduring popularity. The story of Samson is represented in five fourth-century bas-reliefs in marble from the Santa Restitute chapel in Naples Cathedral. It is later found in many manuscripts including scenes in Hebrew manuscripts such as the 13th-century French *British Museum Miscellany* (add. 11639) and the 15th-century *Second Nuremberg Haggadah* (Schocken Collection, Jerusalem). The story was also illustrated in stained glass and in the round. Later the subject held a particular fascination for *Rembrandt, who painted many pictures of Samson. Early works by Rembrandt are his Samson's wedding (Judg. 14:10; Dresden), in which the sprawling giant propounds the riddle to his guests, and Samson threatening his father-in-law (Judg. 15:3; Berlin Museum). In the Middle Ages, Samson was regarded as one of the many prototypes of Jesus. The most popular episode in medieval art was therefore Samson rending the lion (Judg. 14:5–6) because it was understood to represent Jesus triumphing over Satan and breaking the jaws of Hell. It was very common in 12th-century sculpture and enamelwork throughout Western and Central Europe.

Samson and Delilah (Judg. 16:4–20) has been a favorite subject of artists in recent centuries. There is a grisaille painting by Mantegna (1431–1506; National Gallery, London) and a painting by Tintoretto in the collection of the Duke of Devonshire. The subject was particularly popular in northern Europe. In a painting now in the Augsburg Museum, Lucas Cranach showed Samson asleep on Delilah's lap against a mountainous landscape. There are paintings by Rubens (private collection), Van Dyck (1599–1661; Dulwich Gallery, London), and Rembrandt (Berlin Museum). Max *Liebermann painted a violent, sensual, and strangely modern study of Samson and Delilah, with both characters in the nude, and Jacob *Steinhardt made a similarly erotic woodcut of the subject. The capture and the binding of Samson (Judg. 16:21) and the final scene of the story, Samson tearing down the temple of Dagon (Judg. 16:29–30), were often favorite subjects for artists.

A musical dialogue between Samson and Delilah, *Samson dux fortissime*, appears in the Harleian Ms. 978 (13th century) and is something of a historical enigma (cf. G. Reese, *Music in the Middle Ages* (1940), 244). In the second half of the 17th century there were stock Italian oratorios, including *La caduta de' Filistei* by Veracini (1695; libretto only survived) and *Samson vindicatus* by Alessandro Scarlatti (1696; music lost). Voltaire's *Samson* was set by Rameau (1732), but not performed; another setting was made at the beginning of the 19th century by Stanislas Champein, and a third in 1890 by Wekerlin. Milton's *Samson Agonistes* was the basis of Newburgh Hamilton's libretto for Handel's oratorio, *Samson*, which had its première at the Covent Garden Theatre, London, in 1744. Works on the subject composed at the end of the 18th and beginning of 19th century are notable only for the fact that they mark the transfer of the subject to the stage. Camille Saint-Saëns' opera, *Samson et Dalila* (text by Fernand Lemaire), had its first performance at Weimar, in a German translation, in 1877. Delilah's aria, "Softly awakes my heart…" has remained a standby for every mezzo-soprano. Rubin *Goldmark was the composer of a symphonic poem, *Samson* (1913); Nicholas Nabokov wrote incidental music to Milton's *Samson Agonistes* (1938); and Bernard *Rogers devoted a one-act opera, *The Warrior*, to the Samson and Delilah story (1947). At the beginning of the Israel War of Independence Marc *Lavry wrote his *Ẓe'ad Shimshon* (text by Avigdor *Hameiri) for tenor solo, three-part men's choir, and orchestra ("March, Samson, towards Philistia… march, thou regiment of a desperate nation…") as a topical choral piece.

[Bathja Bayer]

BIBLIOGRAPHY: G.F. Moore, *Judges* (ICC, 1895), 312–65; P. Haupt, in: JBL, 33 (1914), 296–8; C.F. Burney, *Judges* (1930), 335–408; Pedersen, Israel, 1–2 (1926), 72, 102, 222–4, 380–2; 3–4 (1940), 35–37, 205–6, 264–5, 487–8, 493; A. van Selms, in: JNES, 9 (1950), 65–75; Albright, Arch Rel, 111–2; Albright, Stone, 283–4. IN THE AGGADAH: Ginzberg, Legends, index. IN THE ARTS: K. Gerlach, *Der Simsonstoff im Drama* (1929); W. Kirkconnell, *Invincible Samson* (1964), deals with the theme in world literature; M. Roston, *Biblical Drama in England* (1968), index. **ADD. BIBLIOGRAPHY:** N.H. Tur-Sinai, *Ha-Lashon ve-ha-Sefer*, 2 (1959), 58–93; E. Greenstein, in: *Prooftexts*, 1(1981), 237–60; J. Sasson, in: *Prooftexts*, 8 (1988), 333–46; J. Crenshaw, in: ABD, 5:950–54; A. Bellis, *Helpmates, Harlots, and Heroes, Women's Stories in the Hebrew Bible* (1994), 112–39 (incl. bibl.); Y. Amit, *Judges* (1999), 218–56.

SAMSON, BENJAMIN ABRAHAM (1916–), Indian naval officer. Samson, a member of the *Bene Israel community, was born in Poona. He received a direct commission as lieutenant to the Royal Indian Navy in 1939. After serving in the Royal Navy in the Mediterranean, the Red Sea, and the Bay of Bengal, his was the last vessel out of Rangoon, the capital of Burma, when it fell to Japanese forces. He was commissioned in the Indian Navy when India gained its independence and, in 1948, was appointed naval adviser on the staff of the High Commissioner for India in the United Kingdom. In 1951 he was promoted to rear-admiral, the youngest to hold this rank in the Indian Navy. He served as commandant of the Indian National Defence College and was appointed flag officer of the fleet in 1965. In the following year he received the Vishisht Seva (Distinguished Service) Medal, Class I, for "distinguished service of a most exceptional order." On his retirement in 1968 he became superintendent of the Magazon Naval Dock Yards in Bombay, and in 1972 was promoted to the honorary rank of vice admiral by the president of India, for "loyal and dedicated" service.

SAMSON BEN ABRAHAM OF SENS (late 12th–early 13th century), one of the great French tosafists, known also as *Ha-Sar* ("the prince") of Sens. He was the brother of *Isaac b. Abraham (Riẓba) and grandson of *Samson b. Joseph of Falaise, brother-in-law of Jacob *Tam. In his youth he studied under Tam and Ḥayyim *ha-Kohen, but his main teacher was *Isaac b. Samuel of Dampierre. His authority was widely recognized, even beyond France. During the first *Maimonidean controversy (1202), the French rabbis were requested to express their views in the dispute between Meir *Abulafia, who attacked Maimonides, and *Aaron b. Meshullam of Lunel, who defended him. Samson replied on behalf of the French rabbis in lengthy letters. He sharply criticized the *Mishneh Torah*, describing its defects, and even advising against its study. He particularly opposed Maimonides' view on resurrection. On the other hand, he expressed profound esteem for Maimonides himself, concluding "that the gates of understanding were opened to him, enabling him to see wonders in the divine Torah." However, his attitude did not satisfy the opponents of Maimonides. On a much later occasion (1235), Abraham, the son of Maimonides, referring to an unconfirmed report that Samson had disagreed with his father, vigorously denied that he had excommunicated him.

The extent of Samson's ties with Germany is not known. However, his works circulated and were accepted there. Isaac of Vienna (see *Or Zaru'a*, 3 (1887); BK, no. 436) writes of him, "he was unique in his knowledge and his wisdom." He composed *tosafot*, known as *Tosafot Sens*, on almost the whole of the Talmud (see Urbach, Tosafot, p. 232ff. for detailed list).

Some of those printed in the standard editions of the Talmud are actually from his pen (RH, Suk., Men., Bek.), while others are the work of his disciples and their disciples (Shab., Er., Yev., Ket., BM, BB). Other collections of *tosafot*, such as those of Touques and of Asher b. Jehiel, are based on them. His *tosafot* on *Pesaḥim* were published (1956), others are still in manuscript. His commentary on the *mishnayot* of *Zera'im* (excluding *Berakhot*) and *Tohorot* (excluding *Niddah*) is the most important commentary on these orders, and it was made use of by all later commentators, such as Asher b. Jehiel and Obadiah of Bertinoro. He is known to have written a commentary on *Shekalim*, *Eduyyot*, and *Kinnim*, which has not come down to us. The one printed as *Tosafot Sens* on *Eduyyot*, *Makkot*, and *Sotah*, as well as the commentary on the *Sifra*, have been erroneously attributed to him. Jacob of Courson, one of his disciples, collected his responsa and halakhic decisions in a work which has not been preserved. Urbach gives a list of his responsa which are scattered among the works of the halakhic authorities (*Tosafot*, 264).

At the beginning of the 13th century Samson migrated to Ereẓ Israel (Graetz' view that he went with the 300 French rabbis in 1211 is unsupported), and he is therefore sometimes referred to as "of Ereẓ Israel" or "of Jerusalem." Maimonides' son Abraham states that they did not meet because Samson did not pass through Egypt; he would therefore appear to have sailed directly to Acre. He lived in Jerusalem and Acre, where he died, and was buried at the foot of Mount Carmel.

Urbach gives the date of his death as before 1216, but others date it c. 1230.

BIBLIOGRAPHY: Frankel, Mishnah, 352–5; Gross, Gal Jud, 165, 168f.; 622; V. Aptowitzer, *Mavo le-Sefer Ravyah* (1938), 24f.; 418–20; Urbach, Tosafot, 226–65, 534; S.H. Kook, *Iyyunim u-Meḥkarim*, 2 (1963), 128f.

[Shlomoh Zalman Havlin]

SAMSON BEN ELIEZER (b.c. 1330), German scribe and authority in his vocation. Samson was born in Saxony. When still a child he was taken to Prague by his parents, who died there when he was eight years old. The community thereupon apparently apprenticed him to a Torah scribe called Issachar. Issachar passed on to Samson many oral traditions and much professional lore, and also gave him an ancient *Tikkun* ("compendium on the laws of writing *tefillin*") compiled by the scribe Abraham b. Moses of Sinzheim, who had been a pupil of Meir b. Baruch of Rothenburg and who had devoted his life to clarifying the regulations concerning the writing of scrolls of the Pentateuch, *tefillin*, and *mezuzot*, in which all the pertinent material was carefully collated. Samson eventually became so proficient in this craft, particularly in the writing of *tefillin*, that his fame spread throughout Germany. He revised Abraham's work and added his own notes, the resulting work being known as *Sefer Barukh she-Amar*. Samson was also known as *Barukh she-Amar* from the melodious manner in which he rendered the prayer beginning with these words whenever he functioned as *ḥazzan*. Samson achieved great importance as a preserver of the German tradition in the sphere of *halakhah*, based as it was primarily upon the authority of Meir of Rothenburg. Samson's work was written after he had emigrated to Ereẓ Israel and had seen the great neglect of his profession in that country. He succeeded in introducing there many improvements in the writing of *tefillin* and was instrumental in the disqualification of scribes whose writing he found unacceptable. Samson is known to have traveled in various places, and to have examined and invalidated *tefillin* with the approval of the local scholars in the district of Lausitz and in Erfurt, Germany.

An incomplete version of *Sefer Barukh she-Amar* was published in Dubnow in 1796, under the title *Dinei Ketivat Tefillin*. The complete version was apparently first published in Shklov in 1804. The published work contains the notes of Yom Tov Lipmann Muelhausen – which can possibly be distinguished from the text of the book since they are devoted exclusively to the laws of the *Sefer Torah*. The *Perush... Al Ẓurot Otiyyot ha-Alef Bet*, which is the second part of the book, is entirely the work of Yom Tov Lipmann – based upon Samson's work. The text in our possession is in a state of considerable disorder, text and notes by many hands being so intermingled as to be practically indistinguishable, though later additions can sometimes be recognized. Similar disorder is to be found in the many manuscripts of the book still in existence. The book was known to all the great *posekim*, among them Jacob *Moellin, Joshua *Soncino, David Blumes, who lived in Ereẓ Israel (cf. Responsa Maharshal, no. 37), and Elijah *Shapira.

BIBLIOGRAPHY: J. Kaufmann, *Yom Tov Lipmann Muelhausen* (1927), 12, 71–75.

[Israel Moses Ta-Shma]

SAMSON BEN ISAAC OF CHINON (14th century), one of the last French tosafists. Samson was nevertheless the first tosafist to write a work on talmudic methodology, *Sefer Keritut*. In it he incorporated the whole of the methodological material embodied in the *tosafot* literature. The first four parts of the book deal with the *hermeneutical rules, with the chronology of the *tannaim* and *amoraim*, and with the principles on which the *halakhah* is decided in cases of difference of opinion. The fifth part, *Leshon Limmudim*, which is also the most comprehensive, deals with the methods of talmudic hermeneutics, and with the methods of the Mishnah, *baraita*, and Talmud. In the course of his presentation Samson enters into detailed discussion, in the manner of the tosafists, maintaining that from such discussion there emerge more principles and methodological rules. Early methodological works, such as *Seder Tanna'im ve-Amora'im* and the letter of Sherira Gaon, served Samson chiefly for the first four chapters, the last chapter, his main work, being based entirely on the tosafists. The work shows little originality, but its main importance lies in the systematic assembly of the material and the manner in which he clarifies it. The *Sefer Keritut* was first published in Constantinople in 1515 and has been frequently republished, together with commentaries by various scholars, among them Jacob *Ḥagiz. In his work Samson speaks of having written *tosafot* on the Talmud, but none of these is extant. In the responsa of *Isaac b. Sheshet (no. 157) Samson is reported, in the name of Perez b. Isaac ha-Kohen, to have opposed Kabbalah and the doctrine of the *Sefirot, saying: "I pray childlike." Isaac b. Sheshet referred to him as the "greatest rabbi of his generation."

BIBLIOGRAPHY: Urbach, Tosafot, index; Renan, Rabbins, 461–4; Samson ben Isaac of Chinon, *Sefer Keritut*, ed. by Y.Z. Roth (1961), 8–10.

[Israel Moses Ta-Shma]

SAMSON BEN JOSEPH OF FALAISE (12th century), French tosafist. Samson was an older contemporary of Jacob Tam, with whom he corresponded and who addressed him with exceptional humility (see *Sefer ha-Yashar*, responsa, nos. 3 and 4). He may have been a pupil of Rashi. His sister Miriam was the second wife of Tam, and after his death she was consulted by scholars as to her husband's customs and observances. Some of Samson's teachings are included in the novellae section of the *Sefer ha-Yashar*, and he is mentioned in the printed *tosafot* to several tractates. The *rishonim* quote from an extensive halakhic work by him which is no longer extant. Samson apparently met a martyr's death and his remains were handed over for burial only six months after his death. The two renowned tosafists, *Isaac b. Abraham and his brother Samson of Sens, were his grandsons. The Eliezer of

Falera mentioned in the *tosafot* to *Bava Batra* (79b) may have been his son-in-law.

BIBLIOGRAPHY: Gross, Gal Jud, 477–8; Urbach, Tosafot, index.

[Israel Moses Ta-Shma]

SAMSON BEN SAMSON OF COUCY (called **ha-sar mi-Coucy**; 13th century), French tosafist. Samson, a descendant of Joseph *Bonfils, belonged to a distinguished family of French scholars. Judah of Corbeil was his uncle and *Moses of Coucy his brother-in-law. He was one of the younger pupils of *Isaac b. Samuel of Dampierre, but his main teacher was *Judah b. Isaac, Judah Sir Leon of Paris. His words are quoted frequently in the standard *tosafot* on several tractates, and many citations from his rulings and responsa, as well as remnants of his *tosafot*, have been preserved in the works of *rishonim*. Samson was a teacher of *Isaac b. Moses Or Zaru'a, and also, apparently, of *Hezekiah b. Jacob of Magdeburg.

BIBLIOGRAPHY: Gross, Gal Jud, 554–6; Urbach, Tosafot, index.

[Israel Moses Ta-Shma]

SAMSON HA-NAKDAN (13th century), Hebrew grammarian and vocalizer, who lived in Germany. It may be conjectured that Samson lived in Xanten, and he was apparently the grandfather and teacher of *Joseph b. Kalonymus ha-Nakdan of Xanten. He was the author of *Mafte'aḥ ha-Dikduk* (Cat. de-Rossi No. 3891) which Steinschneider believed to be identical with the *Sefer Kelalei ha-Dikduk* (Cat. Berlin no. 29; Vatican No. 296). He also wrote the *Ḥibbur ha-Konim*, which is also called *Sefer ha-Shimshoni*, on the *masorah. In his book he quotes the main medieval grammarians.

BIBLIOGRAPHY: Zunz, Gesch, 113–4; Freimann, in: *Festschrift... Simon Dubnow* (1930), 169; Germ Jud, 1 (1963), 499–500. **ADD. BIBLIOGRAPHY:** I. Eldan, "*Mi-Kitvei Askolat ha-Dikduk ha-Ashkenazit–ha-Shimshoni*," in: *Leshonenu*, 43 (1979), 100–111; 201–210; D. Ben-Menahem, *Ḥibbur ha-Konim le-Rabbi Shimshon ha-Nakdan* (1987)

SAMTER, ERNST (1868–1926), German historian of ancient religions. Samter, who was born in Posen, taught in Danzig and Berlin before being appointed professor at the Berlin Gymnasium zum Grauen Kloster in 1925. In 1913 he founded the Institute for the Study of Religions, bringing together theologians, philologists, philosophers, ethnologists, and folklorists for the comparative study of religion.

His works include *Familienfeste der Griechen und Roemer* (1901); *Geburt, Hochzeit und Tod, Beitraege zur vergleichenden Volkskunde* (1911); *Die Religion der Griechen* (1914); *Griechische Sagen* (1925); and *Die Goetter der Griechen* (1926). His interest in education is indicated by several books, including his work on folklore in the teaching of classical languages, *Volkskunde im altsprachlichen Unterricht*, 1 (1923). He also contributed to Jewish history, including studies on antisemitism in ancient Greece and Rome.

[Irwin L. Merker]

SAMUDA, JOSEPH D'AGUILAR (1813–1885), British shipbuilder and railway pioneer. Born in London to Sephardi parents – his father was a broker and overseas merchant – Samuda became an engineer in partnership with his brother JACOB (1811–1844). From 1832 to 1848 Samuda Brothers, their firm, were leading builders of marine engines and, from the early 1840s, leading iron shipbuilders, especially for the Royal Navy, responsible for many engineering innovations. Samuda was vice president of the Institution of Naval Architects and, from 1865 to 1880, served as a Liberal member of Parliament. He is best remembered, however, as a pioneer with his brother of "atmospheric railways," engineless trains propelled by creating a vacuum in front of the train in a pneumatic tube adjacent to the track. The Samuda brothers patented this invention in 1839. Although some examples of "atmospheric railways" were built by the Samudas and others, especially a route they constructed in south Devon in the early 1840s, the technology simply did not exist at the time for these to work on a regular basis, and steam-driven trains remained unchallenged for many decades.

BIBLIOGRAPHY: ODNB online.

[William D. Rubinstein (2nd ed.)]

SAMUEL (Heb. שְׁמוּאֵל), Israelite judge and prophet who lived in the 11th century B.C.E. His name is very close to that of the ancient Babylonian royal ancestor of Hammurapi, Sūmû-la-il, and similar in form to other *Amorite names such as Sūmû-Abum, Sūmû-Samas, and others (HALOT, 1438). Standing at the close of one era and the beginning of another, Samuel was instrumental in the painful, but necessary, transition from a loose confederation of Hebrew tribes to a centralized monarchy. He played a part in events which eventually saw his people completely freed from subjection to the Philistines and from the threat of the utter loss of national life.

The Biblical Account

The record of Samuel's career in I Samuel 1–16, which is intricately interwoven with that of Saul, the first king, involves many baffling questions. It tells a story about the birth of a "child of prayer" to Hannah and Elkanah in an Ephraimite home in Ramathaim-Zophim (1:1) or Ramah (1:19). His mother dedicated him to a Nazirite life in the important sanctuary of Shiloh (1:11, 28; 2:11; 3:1). Here the aged priest *Eli, whose sons were lewd and impious good-for-nothings, officiated (2:12–17, 22–25). A rare divine revelation came to the boy in the night, involving terrible judgment on the house of Eli; and this was the beginning of a career that marked Samuel as a "prophet of YHWH" (3:20). Chapters 4–6 recount the shattering defeat of the Hebrews by the well-equipped Philistines; worst of all, the ark of YHWH was captured, the immediate house of Eli wiped out, and, probably (Jer. 7:12, 14), the vital Shiloh sanctuary was permanently razed.

Samuel is next depicted as a "judge" (I Sam. 7), first in the sense of a charismatic deliverer in a battle of miraculous proportions (verse 13 seems to be highly idealized) and then as an arbiter of disputes, traveling over a considerable area covering Bethel, Gilgal, Mizpah, and Ramah (7:16–17). Samuel was married and had two sons, Joel and Abijah, who acted as judges in Beer-Sheba (8:2; cf. 1 Chron. 6:13).

Two or more divergent accounts of the founding of the monarchy follow. One (9:1–10:16) is favorable to the kingship regarding it as the answer to the desperate needs of the hour. Another (7:3–8:22; 10:17–19; 12:1–25) reacts, sometimes violently, against such a move. Some think there is a third account (10:20–11:15; see *Samuel, Book of; see below, Critical Evaluation). One cannot be completely certain about Samuel's attitude toward the people's request for a king (cf. 10:1 with 10:19). It is clear, however, that the political crisis demanded a much more closely knit government if the Hebrews were to survive as an entity.

One account has an Ammonite attack on Jabesh-Gilead pushing the handsome Benjaminite Saul into a position where, after an impressive victory, he was publicly acclaimed as king (chapter 11). Another shows Samuel's gift of clairvoyance aiding Saul in locating his father's lost donkeys. Samuel then acted as priest at the local hill shrine and by divine revelation he anointed, the next morning, the surprised Saul as leader or prince (*nāgid*) of Israel to rescue her from her pressing foes. Shortly thereafter, in a public conclave at Mizpah, Samuel cast the sacred lot and Saul was chosen; then the older man delivered an address explaining the rights and responsibilities of a king, and a written record was made. An immediate clash with the Philistines followed; first a small-scale outpost skirmish, then a significant victory. However, in 7:3–8:22; 10:17–19; and 12:1–25, Samuel denounces the idea of monarchy as apostasy, since the Lord has always been the king and savior of Israel. Yet by divine revelation Samuel is directed to give grudging consent (8:22).

Chapter 15, a later account evidently based on earlier tradition, portrays a heartrending break between Samuel and Saul, a permanent and devastating rejection of the king (15:34–35; but cf. 19:24). This had already been foretold (e.g., 13:13–14). It is not clear whether the issue was simply the king's failure to obey the provisions of the **ḥerem* of the holy war, or whether it was that Samuel surmised that Saul was aspiring not only to political but also to religious prerogatives. At any rate, except for his mention as head of a band of ecstatic prophets in 19:18–20, his death notice in 25:1, and a séance in which his ghost was brought back in chapter 28, Samuel permanently leaves the stage.

Critical Evaluation

Scholars (e.g., A. Weiser) have moved somewhat away from seeing completely mutually exclusive (pro-monarchical and anti-monarchical) accounts in 1 Samuel 1–16. The alternative is a series of varying concepts that developed in different circles, and existed side by side. Such traditions were finally strung together somewhat loosely without an attempt at reconciling them. Moreover I. Mendelsohn showed that the Israelites would have been quite aware of the dangers of oppressive monarchical government from what they saw around them in their own century. Thus Samuel 8:11–17 does not need to be a late reminiscence, as was once claimed. Nonetheless, one must allow for idealization in certain of the traditions. While many questions cannot be answered with certainty, it is clear that Samuel played a powerful part in the formation of the monarchy, and the titles of seer, prophet, judge, and priest are indicative of his influence, perhaps in different circles. As is true of Moses, so many roles are assigned to him that it is difficult to define the historical nucleus of the Samuel traditions. He was later claimed as a levite (1 Chron. 6:12–13), as one of the founders, with David, of the system of gatekeepers of the Tent of Meeting (1 Chron. 9:22), as a great intercessor comparable to Moses (Jer. 15:1), and as ranking with Moses and Aaron. According to Ps. 99:6, God spoke to Samuel along with Moses and Aaron in the Cloud Pillar. The Bible portrays Samuel as an incorruptible leader (1 Sam. 12:3–5), and as the Lord's spokesman in guiding Israel, in critical days, from the old era into the new, and her greatest leader since Moses.

[John H. Scammon / S. David Sperling (2nd ed.)]

In the Aggadah

Even before his birth, "a heavenly voice went forth" and proclaimed the imminent delivery of a righteous man. When people observed his deeds, they were certain that he was this righteous individual (Mid. Sam. 3:4). Shortly before Samuel's novitiate in the sanctuary, Eli succeeded to the three highest offices in the land, those of high priest, president of the Sanhedrin, and ruler over Israel (Tanḥ. Shemini, 2). However, Eli's sons were not worthy to succeed him, but "Before the sun of Eli set, the sun of Samuel rose" (Gen. R. 58:2). The greatness bestowed on Samuel was not granted to any other king or prophet. No one ever challenged his authority and five terms of praise were applied to him: faithful, honored, prophet, seer, and man of God (*Mishnat R. Eliezer*, p. 151). He rebuked the people shortly before his death, refraining from doing so earlier lest people be embarrassed upon meeting their censurer (Sif. Deut. 2). Samuel was an incorruptible judge, who refused compensation even when he was legitimately entitled to it (Ned. 38a). He went on circuit to judge the people in order to spare them the trouble of coming to him. Accordingly, God spoke directly to Samuel, unlike Moses who first had to go into the tabernacle to receive the divine message (Ex. R. 16:4). He refused to enjoy hospitality at public expense, taking his personal requirements with him on his journeys (Ber. 10b). Despite the fact that his sons did not follow in his way, Samuel did have the satisfaction of seeing one of them mend his ways and become the prophet Joel (Mid. Sam. 1:6).

Samuel did not object to the appointment of a king in principle, since it was commanded in the Bible (Deut. 17:15). His objection was to the fact that the people demanded a king "that we may be like other nations" (Sanh. 20b). Samuel's failure to recognize David until he was revealed to him was a punishment for his arrogance in saying to Saul "I am the seer"

(1 Sam. 9:19; Sif. Deut. 17). Although Saul should have died immediately after his sin during the Amalekite war, Samuel interceded for him. He prayed that his life be spared at least for the duration of his own life, pleading that his action in anointing Saul be not destroyed before his eyes. God was hesitant to grant this request since the time of David's succession was rapidly approaching. In order to fulfill Samuel's request and to prevent the people from ascribing Samuel's death to his sins, Samuel was made to age rapidly, and though he was only 52 when he died, the people were under the impression that he died as an old man (Mid. Sam. 25:2; Ta'an. 5b). Samuel wrote only part of the book which bears his name. It was completed by Gad the seer and Nathan. He also wrote the books of Judges and Ruth (BB 15a).

[Aaron Rothkoff]

In Islam

In Sura 2:247–9 it is related that the people of Israel requested that the prophet appoint a king to rule them. However, when the prophet informed them that Allah had chosen Ṭālūt (Saul), they refused to crown him as their king. In post-Koranic literature it is said that this reference is to the prophet Samuel (Shamwīl); details are also related about his life and deeds, which are interwoven in the tales of Saul and David. It is noteworthy that the name Shamwīl is no longer used in the Arabic language and only the name of al-Samaw'al is to be found.

[H.Z. Hirschberg]

In the Arts

Treatment of the prophet Samuel in the arts generally involves the two kings of Israel whom he anointed, Saul and David, although Samuel himself does figure independently in some works, particularly in art. Literary interest in the subject has been somewhat restricted. In the English verse epic *Davideis* (1656) by Abraham Cowley, Samuel expresses the writer's own antagonism toward the concept of monarchy during Oliver Cromwell's republican Commonwealth. The theme later inspired Pieter t'Hoen's Dutch novella, *Samuël de Profeet; of De Joodsche regeering hoe langer hoe erger* (1796), but interest thereafter lapsed until the 20th century. Samuel then makes a dramatic appearance in D.H. Lawrence's play *David* (1926), and is denigrated in *Samuel the Kingmaker* (1944), one of the English writer Laurence Housman's fiercely anti-biblical *Old Testament Plays* (1950), which makes the prophet a spiteful, jealous impostor. This treatment finds a contrast in the respectful approach of *Abraham l'hébreu et Samuel le voyant* (1946), a biblical verse epic by the French Jewish writer Emmanuel *Eydoux. A related subject is treated in two 20th-century plays about Eli, Samuel's priestly guardian and mentor: *Beit Eli; o Aron ha-Elohim Nilkeḥah* (1902), a Hebrew drama by Meir Foner, and *Silo is krank…* (1956), a drama in Afrikaans by the South African writer Daniel François Malherbe.

In Christian art, Samuel's attributes are the lamb he offered in sacrifice (1 Sam. 7:9) and his horn of unction. Figures of Samuel with the lamb are found on the Gothic cathedrals of Chartres and Rheims; at Chartres he is placed between Moses and David. The presentation of Samuel to Eli by his mother Hannah, who dedicated him to God (1 Sam. 1:24–28) is a subject found in the third-century C.E. murals of the synagogue at *Dura-Europos. It also occurs in medieval wall painting and manuscripts, including the 13th-century *St. Louis Psalter*, the 14th-century *Queen Mary Psalter*, and the 15th-century German *Second Nuremberg *Haggadah* (Schocken Library, Jerusalem). There are a number of examples from the 17th-century Dutch school, including a painting by *Rembrandt (Bridgewater Collection, London) and one by his pupil, Barent Fabritius (Art Institute, Chicago). A touching study of Samuel and Eli was painted by the U.S. portraitist John Singleton Copley (Wadsworth Atheneum, Hartford, Connecticut) whose painting of Samuel denouncing Saul is in the Boston Museum of Fine Arts. The English artist Sir Joshua Reynolds painted studies of Samuel as a child and the infant Samuel in prayer (1 Sam. 3:4); these are at Dulwich College and in the National Gallery, London. Samuel's slaying of Agag, whom Saul had failed to kill (1 Sam. 15:32–33), appears in a 13th-century Hebrew manuscript from France (British Museum Miscellany, add. 11639) and in a mural in the Basle town hall by Hans Holbein (1497?–1543). The anointing of David by Samuel (1 Sam. 16:13) appears in the murals of Dura-Europos. This subject has also been popular in Christian art, where David is regarded as the "anointed one" par excellence, the type and ancestor of Jesus. The scene appears in medieval frescoes, carvings from the Gothic cathedrals, and in Byzantine and Western manuscript illumination. Samuel's posthumous appearance before Saul on the latter's visit to the witch of Endor (1 Sam. 28:8ff.) was a rare subject in the Middle Ages. It later received melodramatic treatment from the 17th-century painter Salvator Rosa (Louvre); and there is a watercolor by William *Blake in the National Gallery of Art, Washington.

Musical works in which Samuel is the main figure are few; they include Andreas Hammerschmidt's songs to a play by Keimann, *Samuel* (1646); Anton Cajeta Adlgasser's oratorio, *Samuel und Heli* (= Eli; 1763); a Spanish oratorio by José Duran, *Samuel presentado al Templo* (1765); Simon Mayr's oratorio, *Samuele* (1821); an early American oratorio, *Samuel*, by Homer Newton Bartlett (1845–1920); and *Die Jugend Samuel's*, an oratorio by Victor *Hollaender (1866–1940). A recent work is the *Inbal troupe's *The Boy Samuel.*

Tomb of Samuel

Traditionally sited on al-Nabī-Samwīl, the highest mountain overlooking Jerusalem. Theodorus Lector records that the Byzantine emperor, Arcadius, in 406 removed the bones of Samuel to Constantinople where he built a church next to the Hebdomon (Eccles. Hist., 2:63). The 10th-century geographer, al-Muqadasi, mentions a monastery at al-Nabī-Samwīl. Ramah of the Bible was later identified with *Ramleh and consequently Samuel's grave was located there (cf. 1 Sam. 25:1; 28:3). The Karaites had a synagogue at Ramleh in 1013. Benjamin of Tudela records in 1173 that the crusaders had removed Samuel's remains from there to al-Nabī-

Samwīl (A. Asher, *The Itinerary of Rabbi Benjamin of Tudela* (1927), p. 42).

In 1099 the site was named by the crusaders Montjoie (Mons Gaudii) because it was from there that they caught their first sight of Jerusalem; among the Jews and the Latins al-Nabī-Samwīl was generally called *Shiloh (Silo) through mistaken identity. Baldwin II (1118–31) gave the hill and surrounding land to the Premonstratensian order who built a church on the site in 1157 on the hill al-Burj, south of al-Nabī-Samwīl. In 1187 the church was captured and ruined by Saladin. Muslims and Jews turned the ruins into prayer houses. Jewish pilgrims also identified the site with the graves of Hannah, Elkanah, and his two sons as well as with the *mikveh* of Hannah. On the 28th of Iyyar (the traditional date of Samuel's death) thousands of Jews gathered in medieval times at the shrine from all over the Diaspora and Ereẓ Israel to light lamps there, offer charity, and pray. It was so usual for them to drink wine at these festivities, that owing to excesses a *takkanah* was passed by the Jerusalem rabbi forbidding "those under the influence of drink from going to al-Nabī-Samwīl" (*Zikhron bi-Yrushalayim*, 503). Pantaléo de Aveiro reports that in 1560 Jews went to the grave every eight days to light candles and had obtained the right of residence on the site from the sultan (*Itinerario da Terra Sancta* (1927), 424) and an English traveler in 1601 reported that the Jews cut their hair there (*The Travels of John Sanderson* (1931), 100). From other sources it appears that fathers took their sons there to trim their hair as an offering. The Karaites also spent two days of Passover on the site singing special hymns to Samuel.

In the 18th century Jews used to bring money, clothes, and jewelry there and burn them there as an offering, but about 1730 the Turks closed up the cave, built a mosque and prayer house there, and forbade the Jews to enter. After this few Jews went, and they had to pay for entrance. The land around the shrine was acquired by the group Naḥalat Israel Ramah in 1887 but attempts to settle there failed. The mosque and tower were almost completely destroyed in World War I and later rebuilt. Few Jews pray there now owing to the doubtfulness of the site's authenticity.

BIBLIOGRAPHY: Noth, Hist Isr, 168, 175; Bright, Hist, 165–6; W.F. Albright, *Samuel and the Beginning of the Prophetic Movement* (1961); G. Von Rad, *Old Testament Theology*, 1 (1962), 324–7. IN THE AGGADAH: Ginzberg, Legends, 4 (1913), 65–70; 6 (1928), 215–37. IN ISLAM: Ṭabarī, *Ta'rīkh*, 1 (1357 A.H.), 329–30; idem, *Tafsīr*, 2 (1323 A.H.), 378–9; ʿUmāra, Ms. fol. 39r–39v; Thaʿlabī, *Qiṣaṣ* (1356 A.H.), 227–9; Kisā'ī, *Qiṣaṣ* (1356 A.H.), 250–8. In the Arts: R. Wischnitzer, *Samuel Cycle in the Wall Decoration of the Synagogue at Dura-Europos* (1941; repr. PAAJR, 11 (1941), 85–103); M. Roston, *Biblical Drama in England* (1968), index. TOMB OF SAMUEL: M. Benveniste, *The Crusaders in the Holy Land* (1970), index; Z. Vilnay, *Maẓẓevot Kodesh be-Ereẓ Yisrael* (1951), 153–62. **ADD. BIBLIOGRAPHY:** B. Birch, *The Rise of the Israelite Monarchy: The Growth and Development of 1 Samuel 7–15* (1976); J. van Seters, *In Search of History* (1983); idem, EncRel, 12 (2005), 8099–8100; G. Ramsey, ABD, 5:954–57; A. Brenner (ed.), *Feminist Companion to Samuel and Kings* (2000). See also bibliography to *Samuel, Book of.

SAMUEL (**Mar** or **Samuel Yarhina'ah**; end of second century to mid-third century), Babylonian *amora*. Samuel was born at Nehardea and studied with his father, *Abba b. Abba ha-Kohen (Zev. 26a) and also with Levi b. Sisi (Shab. 108b), who had emigrated to Babylonia from Ereẓ Israel. His principal teachers, however, are unknown. From the story that Samuel cured Judah ha-Nasi of an eye ailment (BM 85b) some scholars infer that he attended the latter's *bet midrash* in Ereẓ Israel, and that Judah ha-Nasi was his main teacher. This is not conclusive evidence; Samuel could have sent the medicine to Judah ha-Nasi by a messenger. In any event, Samuel quotes no *halakhot* which, it may be asserted, he would have heard from Judah ha-Nasi, nor does he report any custom he saw in the latter's home, although this was a practice of the scholars of both the Babylonian and Jerusalem Talmuds. D. Hoffmann contends that Samuel studied in Ereẓ Israel under Ḥanina b. Ḥama, inasmuch as both used the drawing of a palm branch as their signatures (TJ, Git. 9:9, 50d) and prescribed identical cures. However, there is no conclusive evidence for this assertion, as the same was true of different people living in widely separated areas.

Samuel's sons died in their youth (Shab. 108a; MK 18a), two of his daughters were taken captive and later ransomed in Ereẓ Israel (Ket. 23a), and another daughter married a non-Jew (who was subsequently converted to Judaism: see Rashi, Ber. 16a). His economic circumstances were extremely good, his father having left him fields (Ḥul. 105a) and plantations which were cultivated by tenant-farmers and laborers (BK 92a), and the household chores were attended to by maidservants (Nid. 47a).

Samuel was the head of an important *bet midrash-bet din* at Nehardea in the middle of the third century (Git. 36b). He was the outstanding authority of his day in civil law (Bek. 49b), in which sphere later generations accepted his pronouncements as decisive (*ibid.*). Samuel was the author of the momentous principle that in civil matters "the law of the state is the law [for its Jews]" (BK 113b), which has influenced the entire Diaspora. Other principles of his are: "The obligation of producing proof rests on the claimant" (*ibid.* 46a) and "In pecuniary cases we do not follow the majority" (*ibid.* 46b). His concern for orphans led him to rule that their money may be lent out on interest (contrary to the rule that money was not to be lent to Jews on interest; BM 70a). As a *dayyan* he was on his guard against even the slightest taint of bribery. Thus, he refused to act as a judge in the case of a man who had put out his hand to assist him in fording a river on a board (Ket. 105b). His integrity is revealed in other instances. He refused to take advantage of a seasonal scarcity to obtain higher prices for his products (BB 90b), and he vigorously opposed those who arbitrarily raised prices. When after Passover the merchants, reacting to an increased demand, raised the prices of pots (the Babylonian Jews not using those in which leaven had been cooked before the festival), Samuel warned that, unless they took fair prices, he would permit the use of the old pots (Pes. 30a). Similarly, when those who sold myrtle branches (for the

Four Species in the Festival of Tabernacles) charged exorbitant prices, Samuel warned that, unless they asked a reasonable price, he would declare permissible even such myrtle branches whose tips were broken off (Suk. 34b). The great authority enjoyed by his *bet din* was entirely owing to his prestige; only his *bet din* and that of Rav at Sura were allowed to write a prosbul (a declaration, made in a *bet din*, that the limitation of the Sabbatical Year shall not apply to the loan about to be made; Git. 36b). He held that in certain cases *dayyanim* were entitled to use their discretion in judging (BB 35a, and Tos. to *ibid.*), and he would order lashes (Er. 44b), as well as arrest and detention in prison (Nid. 25b), indicating his great authority.

Samuel had many contacts with his distinguished colleague, Rav, who appreciated his erudition (Ḥul. 59a), showed him every respect (Meg. 22a), and, when on a visit to Nehardea, observed the customs instituted by Samuel (Er. 94a). After Rav's death in 247 C.E., Samuel became the preeminent authority and was recognized as such by all the Babylonian sages (*Iggeret Rav Sherira Ga'on*, ed. by B.M. Lewin (1921), 81), whereas during Rav's lifetime the Jews of Sura and its neighborhood had adopted the usages laid down by Rav, while the Jews of Nehardea and its neighborhood adopted those of Samuel (Ket. 54a).

Samuel was close to the exilarch and his officials (TJ, Ta'an. 4:2, 68a) and would sit in front of Mar Ukva, the exilarch, when the latter judged a case (MK 16b). He was also personally acquainted with Sapor, the king. Samuel's extensive knowledge of medicine and astronomy assisted him in the establishment of various *halakhot*. He discovered a salve, known as "*killurin de-Mar Shemu'el*," for curing eye ailments (Shab. 108b), and asserted that he could cure all maladies except three (BM 113b). He was known as Samuel Yarḥina'ah ("Samuel the Astronomer": BM 85b), and such was his knowledge of *astronomy that he declared: "The paths of heaven are as familiar to me as the streets of Nehardea" (Ber. 58b). Though his knowledge of this science enabled him to fix and draw up a calendar (RH 20b), according to his own testimony he did not devote much time to its study (Deut. R. 8:6). It may have been his knowledge of astronomy which brought him into contact with non-Jewish Babylonian scholars, with one of whom, Avlet, he dined (Av. Zar. 30a) and discussed nature (Shab. 129a, 156b). Samuel also met non-Jewish scholars in the Bei-Avidan (*ibid.* 116a, and Rashi *ibid.*). But because his chief activity centered on his industrious acquisition and dissemination of the knowledge of the Torah, he was called *shoked* (TJ, Ket. 4:2, 28b) or *shakud* (TB, *ibid.* 43b), that is, "the industrious Torah scholar."

He ruled that it was forbidden to deceive non-Jews as well as Jews (Ḥul. 94a), and that whoever puts a slave to shame must compensate him accordingly (Nid. 47a). Samuel made some interesting observations on the past and future of the Jewish people. He traced the ascendancy of Rome and the subsequent destruction of the Temple to Solomon's marriage with Pharaoh's daughter, who introduced idolatry into Jerusalem (Shab. 56b). In his view the Messiah will come only after the Jewish people will have suffered cruel persecutions (Ket. 112b), and he maintained that the only difference between present and messianic times will be freedom from oppression by foreign powers in the latter period (Ber. 34b). Samuel was opposed to a life of mortification (Ta'an. 11a) and declared even those who imposed restrictions upon themselves in fulfillment of a vow to be wicked (Ned. 22a). He favored the enjoyment of the things of this world (Er. 54a), provided that it is preceded by the appropriate blessing (Ber. 35a).

Rav and Samuel were accorded the honorable title of "our rabbis in Babylonia" (Sanh. 17b) or "our rabbis in the Diaspora" (TJ, Shab. 5:4, 7c).

BIBLIOGRAPHY: G. Bader, *Jewish Spiritual Heroes*, 3 (1940), 78–90; D. Hoffmann, *Mar Samuel* (Ger., 1873); Bacher, Bab Amor, 37–45; Halevy, Dorot, 2 (1923), passim; Graetz-Rabbinowitz, 2 (1893), 354–61; Hyman, Toledot, 1120–31; Weiss, Dor, 3 (19044), 146–56.

[Moshe Beer]

SAMUEL, BOOK OF, the eighth book of the Hebrew Bible and the third in the subdivision known as the Former Prophets. Originally a single unit, the Septuagint and the Vulgate divide the book in two, titling the resulting parts First and Second Kingdoms (I and II Samuel), followed by Third and Fourth Kingdoms (I and II Kings). In the later Vulgate tradition "Kingdoms" becomes "Kings." Hebrew manuscripts continued to treat Samuel as one book until the introduction of the printed Bible in the 15th century, when the division into I and II Samuel was accepted. English Bibles follow the same division, I and II Samuel appearing in ninth and tenth positions (Ruth intruding after Judges as in LXX).

Title, Authorship and Text

The title of the book (or books) in the Hebrew canon is Samuel, no doubt because Samuel is the first major personality to appear in it rather than because of any theories of authorship such as we encounter in I Chronicles 29:29 and *Bava Batra* 14b–15a (cf. I Samuel 10:25). In fact, the title of the book has no serious bearing on authorship. It is now generally agreed that the finished form of the book comes from the hand of a Deuteronomic compiler in the sixth century B.C.E. It has often been surmised that one or more of the sources in Samuel were written by a high official(s) in the court of David or Solomon, such as *Abiathar the priest, or *Jehoshaphat the *mazkir*, or Ahimaaz son of Zadok the priest (for Ahimaaz was himself one of Solomon's provincial governors; I Kings 4:15). That a royal official was responsible for the archival materials is certain, and it is plausible that such an official wrote some of the extended narrative sources; but no exact identification is compelling.

The text of Samuel has been badly preserved in the Masoretic Text, apparently because the book fell into neglect in some circles once a more idealized version of the same period was provided by Chronicles. Fortunately the Masoretic Text of Samuel can be frequently corrected with the help of Chronicles and of the Septuagint. The discovery at Qumran of portions of Samuel in a Hebrew text that closely corresponds to the Septuagint enhances the value of the Greek version for textual criticism of Samuel, in that the Septuagint now appears to have relied upon a generally more accurate Hebrew text tradition than has been preserved in the Masoretic Text.

Contents and Major Themes

The narrative of Samuel, chiefly concerned with the rise and succession of rulers in the early united monarchy of Israel, falls into divisions determined by the succession of principals who provide the central action. Complexity is introduced by the fact that the protagonists (Samuel, Saul, David) are involved in intricate relationships or interdependence and rivalry. When David emerges triumphant, the dynamics shift toward the king's relations with his sons. A division based on the principals may be schematized as follows:

(1) I Samuel 1–7 – Samuel.

(2) I Samuel 8–15 – Samuel and Saul.

(3) I Samuel 16–31 – Saul and David.

(4) II Samuel 1–8 – David's rise to power.

(5) II Samuel 9–20 and I Kings 1–2 – Court history or succession story of David.

(6) II Samuel 21–24 – Appendix concerning the reign of David.

Number (6) was inserted before the end of (5) as a dramatic summary of the rule of David. This had the effect of making the deathbed deliberations of David (now I Kings 1–2) an introduction to the reign of Solomon, and the division of the Deuteronomic history into separate books recognized this fact by beginning a new book with it.

The basic narrative tells how the monarchy arose and how the line of kings was maintained in early Israel (see *History). The thematic stresses make it abundantly clear, however, that the chief interest is not in giving an account for future historical reference. Annalistic materials are included in the narrative but the overriding concern of the book is to establish the national-religious significance of the monarchy for Israel. The shaping of the materials themselves and the location of the book within the vast Deuteronomic history as the record of one phase in the history of Israel from Moses to the Exile, indicate that the intent is to assess the national-religious benefits and perils in monarchy, under the curse and blessing of Israel's God. The narrative is finally shaped by a later historical context in which Israel has lost the independent monarchy and, therefore, reads the record of the rise of the monarchy with critical questions in mind: In what way was the monarchy a gift of God? In what way was the monarchy a rejection of God? Can we identify the junctures at which the divinely granted monarchy became an occasion for apostasy? How does God overrule human sin? If Israel is to survive and be renewed as a people, what must be learned from the ambivalent experience of monarchical government?

Within the overarching set of questions posed by the Deuteronomic final stage of Samuel, many proximate thematic emphases emerge in complex sequences and patterns. Among the teeming monarchic sub-themes are the following: the triumph of David's dynastic line over Saul's; the triumph of one of David's sons over his brothers (Solomon over Absalom and Adonijah); the subduing of the enemies of Israel by Saul and David (Philistines, Amalekites, Transjordanian peoples, Arameans); the reward of Jonathan's loyalty to David (in his treatment of Mephibosheth); the giving way of the institution of judgeship to that of monarchy (Samuel both prepares for and loses out to Saul and David); prophecy as support for, and critique of, the king (Nathan and Gad); the securing of the unity of north and south by the establishment of the capital in Jerusalem; the installation of the ark in Jerusalem and the preparation for building of the Temple; the replacement of the line of Eli by the Zadokite priesthood and its immediate rival Abiathar; the expiation of the sins of kings (and of their sons and officials): as punishment for Saul's murder of Gibeonites, famine and the death of seven of his sons; as punishment for David's murder of Uriah, the death of Bath-Sheba's firstborn, the rebellion of Absalom, and the king's passive acceptance of the curse of Shimei; for Amnon's rape of Tamar, his death; for Absalom's rebellion, his death; for David's census, a plague and the building of an altar on the site of the future temple; for Joab's murder of Abner and Amasa, his death.

These sub-themes are joined, on the one hand, in the Deuteronomic Exilic context with its searching existential theological questions about the survival of Israel. They are anchored, on the other, in the immediate historical contexts in which the various single units and sub-blocs of the book emerge. The materials in Samuel, therefore, require examination in the light of the whole range of their traditional-historical development, in terms of the reasons for the preservation and compilation of the traditions and their meaning at each stage of development. They must be seen as the product of the history of Israel's ideas, as a series of widening reflections on the history of this people – particularly of its royal leaders and institutions – extended over more than five centuries from approximately 1000 to 550 B.C.E.

The Basic Building Units

Samuel is not a simple homogeneous composition by a single author, although a single hand shaped its final form. In order to understand the composition of the book, it is necessary to characterize the main kinds of primary literary units employed in it.

NARRATIVES. The majority of the basic units in Samuel are narratives which typically display unity of character, time, and place and a number of compositional features such as fondness for dialogue (sometimes expanded into lengthy disquisitions), repetition of formulas (keywords and refrains), framing by means of similar beginnings and endings (so-called "envelope" or "ring" composition), foreshadowing and retrospection, retardation of action, stylized descriptions of scene and action, and a predilection for certain numbers (notably three and seven).

For the most part, the separate narratives can be distinguished by their highly circumstantial treatment of events. At times, however, the narrative is compressed and abstract, serving to sum up a series of actions of one type or to point forward to subsequent events. The more compressed and abstract narratives are usually signs of an attempt to link up the more episodic narratives. The extent to which the distinguishable narratives form coherent sequences is a critical consideration for determining the existence of pre-Deuteronomic sources in Samuel.

POEMS. Samuel contains poetic compositions which have been introduced into narratives as words attributed to characters in the story (I Sam. 2:1–10; 15:22–23; II Sam. 1:17–27; 3:33–34; 20:1; 22:1–51; 23:1–7). The fact that some of these same poetic pieces appear in other contexts (II Sam. 20:1 in I Kings 12:16; II Sam. 22 in Ps. 18) and are often very general in their references, raises the question in each instance as to whether the composition should indeed be attributed to the speaker or even to his period or circle. The laments over Saul and Jonathan and over Abner are usually attributed by modern scholars to David; the Song of Hannah is usually not attributed to Hannah. The Song of David and David's "last words" probably stem from royal psalmic circles but whether from the time of David, or from David himself, is in doubt. The source of the lament over Saul and Jonathan is said to have been the Book of Jashar (II Sam. 1:18).

ORACLES. Speeches from God in the form of instructions or pronouncements are fairly common in Samuel, sometimes addressed directly to a person (I Sam. 3:11–14; 8:7–9; 9:15–16; 15:10–11; II Sam. 7:4–7; 21:1; 24:11–12), but more often as a prophetic or cultic speech delivered to the addressee by a spokesman for God (I Sam. 2:27–36; 6:3–9; 8:10–18; 10:17–19; 12:6–17, 20–25; 17:45–47; II Sam. 7:3, 8–16; 12:7–14; 24:13). The private and public forms of the oracle are complexly related in some contexts in typical messenger style, the private oracle instructing God's spokesman concerning what he is to say publicly. For the most part the oracles appear as elements within narratives, but, on occasion, they constitute virtually the entire literary unit (e.g., I Sam. 12; II Sam. 7).

LISTS AND ANNALS. Frequently the narrative flow is broken by lists of persons, such as sons and officials of the king, or of foreign peoples and districts and cities in Israel. There are annals or annalistic summaries which catalog military or administrative actions. In their sharpest form the lists and annals stand as separate units (I Sam. 7:13–17; 14:47–52; II Sam. 3:2–5; 5:13–16; 8:15–18; 20:23–26; 21:15–22; 23:20–39). More often they are subordinated stylistically to the narrative or are themselves expanded by narrative detail (I Sam. 13:1–3; 22:2; 30:26–31; II Sam. 2:8–11; 5:4–5, 9, 17–25; 8:1–14; 12:26–31; 23:8–19; 24:5–9). The lists and annals read like materials drawn from official archives, sometimes expanded in a more popular narrative style. Literary devices for working the lists and annals into the narratives are numerous and intricate, as illustrated in II Samuel 23 where a list of the three mighty men of David and a list of the 30 mighty men of David have been worked together with annalistic expansions concerning the three and concerning two of the 30. An inaccurate total of mighty men for the present form of the text is given as 37 (II Sam. 23:39).

MISCELLANEOUS. Other types of basic literary units may be noted. A prayer by David occurs at a climactic point in II Samuel 7:18–29. On two occasions, accounts of alleged crimes requiring adjudication by the king are presented to David in order to serve as quasi-parables by which the king is tricked into condemning himself (II Sam. 12:1–6; 14:4–17). Popular proverbs or rulings are frequent on the lips of figures in the narratives (I Sam. 10:12; 18:7; 19:24; 21:11; 24:13; 29:5; 30:24–25; II Sam. 11:21; 20:18). Occasional explanatory remarks provide background information for understanding terms, situations, or practices which might otherwise be obscure to the reader (I Sam. 2:13–14; 9:9; 13:19–22; 28:3b; II Sam. 13:18; 18:18).

Pre-Deuteronomic Sources

It is widely agreed that the Book of Samuel received its finished form at the hands of the Deuteronomist, who constructed the great sequence of tradition down to Kings. However, the scope and details of the final composition and its relation to the preceding development of the contents are much disputed.

The question is whether the Deuteronomist simply compiled the separate units described above, supplying the necessary arrangement and links, or whether he made use of definite preexistent sub-blocs, or sources, so that his major contribution consisted in the articulation of the sources. Given that such sources existed, the question remains whether they can be delineated and whether they are at all related to the narrative sources which have been identified in Genesis through Numbers and perhaps also in Joshua and Judges (i.e., J and E sources). Another question is whether there was a pre-Deuteronomic edition of Samuel which the D compiler employed, expanding and deleting it in accordance with his purposes. In short, the problem is that of clarifying the process by which the distinguishable units of Samuel were linked up, either in stages or all at once, to form the extant edition.

At one extreme is the claim that the final compiler simply gathered totally separate narratives, poems, oracles, and other units and constructed his book. At the other extreme is the contention that the final compiler used a number of sources, each covering different parts of the story he wanted to tell. By arranging the sources consecutively or interweaving them, the impression of a continuous account was created.

The evidence for sizable pre-existent sources is cumulatively impressive. To be sure, the criteria for distinguishing these sources by their literary, historical, and ideological features cannot be applied with equally convincing results in all cases. Yet it is evident that Samuel is not simply a single compilation of random fragments. The materials cluster together in groupings and the constant features which link the units in the various clusters are not demonstrably Deuteronomic in origin.

Among the pre-Deuteronomic clusters which can be discerned in Samuel are the following:

(1) A story of the boyhood of Samuel (I Sam. 1–3) recites the birth and call of Samuel and the venality and prophesied doom of the priesthood of Eli.

(2) A story of the ark (I Sam. 4:1–7:2) recounts the capture of the ark, the deaths of Hophni, Phinehas, and Eli, the destruction which the captured ark visited on the Philistines, and the return of the ark, first to Beth-Shemesh and then to Kiriath-Jearim. II Samuel 6:1–15 is the logical continuation of this story which the compiler moved to its present position because 20 years had elapsed between the placing of the ark in Kiriath-Jearim and its transfer to Jerusalem by David. Possibly, the original nucleus of II Samuel, which seems to have anticipated how the ark would be placed in a temple, also belonged to the ark source.

(3) A story of Samuel and Saul and the rise of the monarchy associated with Mizpah and Ramah (I Sam. 7:3–12; 8:1–22; 10:17–27; 12:1–25; 15:1–35) is composed of units in which the oracles are dominant and in some cases almost crowd out narrative altogether. Samuel is the deliverer of the people from the Philistines, but, in his old age, the people call for a king rather than face the prospect of his corrupt sons becoming his successors. The kingship is condemned as contrary to God's will, and a description of the oppressive nature of kingship is supplied. Nevertheless, Saul is chosen as king by lot. Samuel gives a "farewell speech" affirming his just leadership, reviews the saving deeds of God in the past, and warns the people not to continue in the rebellion they have exhibited in demanding a king. Finally, when Saul fails to destroy all the Amalekites and their booty in accord with the sacred ban, his rejection by God is announced by Samuel. The farewell speech of chapter 12 is worked and expanded by the D compiler, but its essential structure belongs to the older source. The units 7:3–12 and 15:1–35 are not so clearly of the same source as the other units but there are substantial if not conclusive reasons for including them.

(4) A story of Samuel and Saul and the rise of the monarchy associated with Gilgal (I Sam. 9:1–10:16; 13:1–14:46) is composed of narratives in which the oracular elements are more terse and more effectively subordinated to the narrative than in the Mizpah-Ramah source. Saul is selected by Samuel to be king at the direct initiative of God, the sign of his efficacy as king being his inspired participation in the prophesying of a band of prophets. Samuel sends Saul to Gilgal where he is to wait for seven days for further directions. At Gilgal the Philistine threat mounts, and Saul offers the sacrifices to initiate the war. Samuel arrives to condemn him for this independent sacral action and to announce Saul's rejection as king. Saul's and Jonathan's successes against the Philistines are then related. I Samuel 31 may also belong to this source since it describes the death of Saul with dignity and compassion. Less certain is the inclusion of I Samuel 28 in which Saul's recourse to a medium at En-Dor to raise up the spirit of Samuel is sympathetically presented. The problem in the present form of the story is that it is linked with the Amalek story of I Samuel 15, which may be the compiler's editorial adjustment.

I Samuel 11 is frequently assigned to the Gilgal story, but it is an erratic bloc that does not fit smoothly into either story of the rise of the monarchy. Conceivably, 11:1–11 belonged to the Gilgal source and had as its aim the demonstration of Saul's inspired military prowess against the Ammonites preparatory to his attacks on the more powerful Philistines. However, 11:12–15 can only be understood as yet another version of how Saul was made king, this time at Gilgal. The disruption of the story line is only imperfectly dealt with by the harmonizing reference, "Let us go to Gilgal, and there renew the kingdom" (11:14).

The remaining materials in Samuel may best be approached by demarcating the most obvious source first and then working backward to the less easily demarcated sections.

(5) An expiatory court history or succession story of David (II Sam. 9–20; I Kings 1–2) consists of a series of beautifully proportioned episodes, expertly linked in a virtual novella (comparable to the Joseph story in Genesis), which focuses on the relation between David and his sons and specifically on the issue of which of David's sons will succeed him on the throne. The whole sequence is profoundly affected by the problem of David's expiation for his sin in murdering Uriah in order to possess Bath-Sheba. The death of Bath-Sheba's firstborn, the rape of Tamar and the death of Amnon, and the rebellion of Absalom and his death are connected with the initial sin of David. Joab's sin in killing Abner and Amasa is expiated by his death. The final sign that all David's wrongdoing has been adequately expiated is given in the raising of Solomon, his favorite son by Bath-Sheba, to the throne.

It is curious, however, that this superbly molded source lacks a clear beginning. II Samuel 9 is usually assigned as the start because it introduced Mephibosheth who is integral to the story later on, and II Samuel 10 is included because it accounts for the wars against Ammon in which Uriah perishes. However, II Samuel 9 is not an adequate starting point for the source. Either the beginning has been lost or it is to be found somewhere between I Samuel 16 and II Samuel 8. There are some clues in the court history that it may indeed have begun at an earlier point in David's life. In I Kings 2:5, David urges the death of Joab because he killed Abner, and Shimei's curse of David in II Samuel 16:8 says, "YHWH has avenged on you all the blood of the house of Saul," which seems to make David responsible in his eyes for either the deaths of Saul and Jonathan or the death of Ishbaal, or both. These references may be construed to demonstrate that the court history went back at least to the story of Ishbaal and Abner (II Sam. 3–4). Moreover, the common theme of making a claim to royal power by lying with the king's concubine appears not only in II Samuel 16:20–22 and I Kings 2:13–25 but also in II Samuel 3:6–11.

That parts of the court history may be present in sections of I Samuel 16–31 is hinted at by the way in which David's decision "to show kindness for the sake of Jonathan" to Mephibosheth alludes back to the covenant of David with Jonathan in I Samuel 18:1–4; 20:8, 14–17, 42. The story of David's acquisition of Abigail, wife of Nabal (I Sam. 25), is told in such a way as to constitute a dramatic foil to the manner in which he later acquired Bath-Sheba, wife of Uriah. So the possibility must be entertained that what is known as the court history is the culmination of a larger account of the public life of David which may have begun as early as II Samuel 2 and perhaps even as early as I Samuel 16. If this is the case, the early parts have been excerpted and lack the tight cohesion of II Samuel 9–20 and I Kings 1–2.

At this point it is necessary to consider the remaining materials in Samuel, extending from I Samuel 16 to II Samuel 8. The segment in I Samuel gives an account of the anointing of David as king, by Samuel, his introduction to the court of Saul, his victories over the Philistines, Saul's growing jealousy, David's flight and exile in the Negev both as a freebooter and as a client of Achish of Gath, his marriage to Abigail, and the stroke of fortune by which he was saved having to fight with the Philistines against Saul in the latter's mortal defeat. Typical of these stories is a large number of doublets which repeatedly disturb the continuity: two versions of David's coming to Saul's court, two accounts of David's escape from Saul, two descriptions of David's desertion to the Philistines, two episodes concerning David's sparing of the life of Saul, and two explanations of the death of Saul.

These doublets are commonly seen as reflections of two parallel sources which are in turn linked with the two accounts of the rise of the monarchy and frequently regarded as segments of the J and E sources of the Pentateuch. The case for seeing two continuous sources in I Samuel 16 through all or part of II Samuel is very insecure. The doublets when separated do not form two sources with anything like the cohesion of the two stories of the rise of the monarchy. If these materials were drawn from two continuous sources, they must have been drastically excerpted, and, if they formed the continuations of J and E, their reworking has been so extensive that their original forms are no longer discernible. It is possible, as noted above, that the court history did in fact once begin with the public emergence of David, but its unity prior to II Samuel 9 has been shattered by the D compiler in two primary ways: for the period prior to David's enthronement the court history version of events was extracted and worked in with many other accounts of the same events (largely drawn from the various locales where the actions took place), and for the period of the early reign of David it was worked in with lists and annals, as well as with the end of the ark story transferred to II Samuel 6–7.

The Deuteronomic Compiler

From the foregoing it may be concluded that the D compiler of Samuel had in hand the following major blocs of material: the story of the boyhood of Samuel, the story of the ark, the Mizpah-Ramah story of the rise of the monarchy, the Gilgal story of the rise of the monarchy, and the court history or succession story of David. In addition, he had access to court archives with lists and annals, some unattached poems and oracles, and a number of single (or paired) narratives concerning David which had not been drawn into any of the larger blocs.

There is no firm evidence that these preexistent materials had been arranged in parallel sources analogous to or a continuation of the pentateuchal sources. There is also no need to posit a pre-Deuteronomic linkage of the separate blocs in a larger composition. All the signs of editorial linkage can be explained either as the work of those who shaped each of the original blocs or as the work of the Deuteronomic compiler. Similarly, there is no basis for the claim that II Samuel 21–24 was added by a post-Deuteronomic editor.

The essential method of composition of the compiler was to arrange the blocs in approximate chronological order and then to make adjustments where necessary by transferring units from one place to another in order to produce a better chronology or to associate themes, or by interweaving two accounts of the same chain of events. Thus the conclusion of the ark story in II Samuel 6 (and perhaps the original II Sam. 7) was moved to the proper chronological spot at the beginning of David's reign in Jerusalem. The section of the Mizpah story of the rise of the monarchy that told of Samuel's military exploits (I Sam. 7:3–12) was separated from the rest of the source by a summary of the work of Samuel (I Sam. 7:13–17), and the Mizpah version of the rejection of Saul (I Sam. 15) was placed after a summary of the work of Saul (I Sam. 14:47–52). The two stories of the rise of the monarchy were joined by splicing the Gilgal version into the Mizpah version in an effort to make them continuous. Portions of the Gilgal story were put at later points in the account since they told of the latter days of Saul (I Sam. 28:1–25; 31:1–13).

Into the resulting basic framework composed of the joined, interwoven, and readjusted blocs, the compiler introduced lists, annals, poems, and single or paired narratives at appropriate points. I Samuel 11:12–15 supplied yet a third version of the enthronement of Saul. Several duplicate accounts concerning the early fortunes of David (including some from the probable beginning of the court history) were introduced into an account of David's rise to power, from I Samuel 16 on. Lists of David's officials and sons and annalistic accounts of his wars were inserted into the materials that told of his early reign at Hebron and Jerusalem (II Sam. 2–8).

An impression of unity was given to the resulting account by inserting annalistic summaries of the external and internal accomplishments of the chief leaders at crucial junctures in the overall story: of Samuel, in I Samuel 7:13–17; of Saul, in I Samuel 14:47–52; of David, in II Samuel 8 and again in II Samuel 20:23–26; 21:15–22; 23:8–39. It is noteworthy that in each instance the summary comes long before the leader described actually disappears from the story. These summaries are in fact alerting devices which indicate to the reader that a new phase of the story has been reached in which a different balance in the relationships among the principals is to be expected. After Samuel's "summary," he is important only as the one who prepares for Saul and David. After Saul's "summary," he is important only as the one who decreases as David increases in importance. After David's initial "summary," he is secure on his throne in Jerusalem, and the interest shifts to which of his sons will gain the succession; after David's final "summary," the stage is set for the entrance of Solomon as the new monarch.

Apart from these annalistic summaries, there are a few framework-like notes (in the manner of Judges and Kings) and a few harmonizing additions. By and large, the D compiler refrains from rewriting or inserting extensive interpretations of his own. I Samuel 12 and II Samuel 7 display the fullest rewriting or expansion on the part of D, and even there the extent of the D work is debated. The compiler was largely content to let the edited story speak for itself once it was placed within the comprehensive framework of Deuteronomy through Kings. The materials in II Samuel 21–24 which separate the end of the succession story (I Kings 1–2) from the main body (II Sam. 9–20) are arranged in a chiastic structure as follows:

A. Narrative of the expiation of Saul's murder of Gibeonites.

B. Annalistic report of the battles of David's heroes with Philistines.

C. Song of David.

C¹. Last words of David.

B¹. Annalistic report of battles with Philistines and lists of David's heroes.

A¹. Narrative of the expiation of David's census-taking.

The appendix should be read with the three pairs arranged in the order: C–C¹; B–B¹; A–A¹. The center of the supplement is the innermost pair of poems which extol the virtues of the king as military and judicial leader and which are grouped on formal analogy with the Song of Moses (Deut. 32) and the Blessing of Moses (Deut. 33). From this center the lines radiate outward, both forward and backward, through two paired layers of tradition: exploits of David's heroes, which portrays the king as military leader; and successful expiations of guilt, in one of which David satisfies God by delivering up members of the guilty family and in the other he himself submits humbly to the judgment of God. The resulting thematically radiating chiasm is an impressive dramatic summation which brings the story of David to its effective climax.

Historical and Religious Value

Samuel is a source of incalculable importance for the understanding of the circumstances of the rise and establishment of the monarchy in Israel and for a grasp of the various ethical-religious valuations placed upon that institution by ancient Israel. Clearly there is no simple homogeneous historical account in Samuel nor is there a single undifferentiated religious perspective. Yet there is ample evidence of a firsthand nature to reconstruct the main stages in the evolution from the tribal league to the monarchy and to discern the domestic and foreign policies through which Saul and David established and consolidated power. There is also ample indication of the struggle to understand the monarchy in terms of the religious ideology of Israel. The Mizpah and Gilgal stories of the rise of the monarchy and the oracle of II Samuel 7 are classical texts for this inquiry. The former assumption of scholars that all the pro-monarchical materials in Samuel are early and all the anti-monarchical materials are late (i.e., at least post-Solomonic) is now generally discarded. It is recognized that divergent attitudes toward the monarchy were present from earliest times and that, if anything, the anti-monarchical religious sentiments were more persuasive in the time of Saul than were the pro-monarchical religious sentiments.

Likewise, the D compiler is seen to entertain a highly ambivalent stance toward the monarchy. In fact he reads the whole history of Israel from Saul to the Exile in terms of the paradoxical reality that the God-given monarchs again and again violated the will of God but, thanks to the divine grace, the line of David was continued. D's reading of Israel's history in terms of the divine curse and the divine blessing incorporates the disparate blocs of material in Samuel in such a way that even the apparently "profane" court history of David appears as an instance of the conflict between disobedience and obedience and their active consequences in curse and blessing. The D compiler was able to give this effect largely by periodizing the separate blocs within the total framework of his ethical-theological interpretation of history (notably expressed in the programmatic prospectus of Deuteronomy and in the framework of Judges and Kings). While the developed schematic form of his evaluation can be distinguished from the earlier more naive or one-sided interpretations in his sources, it is evident that the early sources and the circles they stemmed from were already shaped by a troubling mixture of gratitude and praise for the kingship, on the one hand, and of misgiving and tormented conscience toward that same institution, on the other hand. To one degree or another, the historical and religious origins of the monarchy as preserved in Samuel attest the compiler's judgment: Israel's king is both the anointed of God and a man of bloodguilt.

BIBLIOGRAPHY: COMMENTARIES: K. Budde (Ger., 1890, Eng., 1894); H.P. Smith (Eng., 1899, ICC); A.R.S. Kennedy (Eng., 1904); H. Gressmann (Ger., 1921²); G.B. Caird et al. (Eng., 1953); H.W. Hertzberg (Ger., 1960², Eng., 1964). GENERAL STUDIES: S.R. Driver, *Notes on the Hebrew Text of the Books of Samuel* (1913²); O. Eissfeldt, *Die Komposition der Samuelsbuecher* (1931); L. Rost, *Die Ueberlieferung von der Thronnachfolge Davids* (1926); I. Hylander, *Der literarische Samuel-Saul-Komplex* (1932); M. Noth, *Ueberlieferungsgeschichtliche Studien* (1957); R.R.A. Carlson, *David the Chosen King. A Traditio-Historical Approach to the Second Book of Samuel* (1964); M.H. Segal, *The Pentateuch, Its Composition and Its Authorship…* (1967), 173–220. **ADD. BIBLIOGRAPHY:** S. Gevirtz, *Patterns in the Early Poetry of Israel* (1973); P.K. McCarter, *I Samuel* (AB; 1980); idem, *II Samuel* (AB; 1984); R. Klein, *I Samuel* (Word; 1983); idem, in: DBI, 2:431–35; A. Anderson, *2 Samuel* (Word; 1989); J. Fokkelmann, *Narrative Art and Poetry in the Books of Samuel*, 4 vols. (1981–83); A. Brenner (ed.), *A Feminist Companion to Samuel and Kings*; S. Bar-Efrat, *I Samuel* (1996); idem, *II Samuel* (1996); G. Keys, *The Wages of Sin: A Reappraisal of the Succession Narrative* (1996). MEDIEVAL JEWISH COMMENTARIES: M. Cohen, (ed.), *Mikra'ot Gedolot "Haketer" Sefer Shemuel* (1993).

[Norman K. Gottwald]

SAMUEL, EDWIN, Second Viscount (1898–1978), public administrator and writer. Samuel served in the British army in Palestine in World War I and on the staff of the Zionist Commission headed by Chaim Weizmann. He joined the British Colonial Service and was appointed a district officer in Palestine, where he was director of broadcasting during the last three years of the Mandate. In 1945 he established the nucleus of what later became Israel's Institute of Public Administration, of which he was principal. He divided his time between Britain and Israel, where he lectured on British institutions and political theory. He was the *Encyclopaedia Judaica* departmental editor for the State of Israel. He published a number of books, among them *Problems of Government in the State of Israel* (1956), *The Theory of Administration* (1947), and *The Social Structure of Israel* (1969). His memoirs, *A Life Time in Jerusalem*, were published in 1970. He also wrote short stories.

BIBLIOGRAPHY: R.J. D'Arcy Hart (ed.), *The Samuel Family of Liverpool and London from 1755 Onwards…* (1958). **ADD. BIBLIOGRAPHY:** C. Bermant, *The Cousinhood* (1971), index.

[Vivian David Lipman and Daniel Efron]

SAMUEL, HAROLD (1879–1937), pianist and composer. Born in London, Samuel began his studies at the Royal College of Music at the age of 17, where he later became a professor. The course of his concert career was changed dramatically in 1921 when he appeared before the public in a series of six brilliant recitals, given within one week, in which he played all Bach's keyboard works from memory. He became most famous as an interpreter of J.S. Bach. Samuel frequently toured in the United States and other countries. Samuel's few compositions include music for *As You Like It* (1907), a comic opera, *The Hon'ble Phil*, songs, and piano pieces.

BIBLIOGRAPHY: NG, s.v.

[Israela Stein (2nd ed.)]

SAMUEL, HAROLD, Baron Samuel of Wych Cross (1912–1987), British property developer and art collector. A qualified property surveyor who was educated at Mill Hill school and at the College of Estate Management, in 1944 Samuel became chairman of Land Securities, which took over City Centre Properties and other companies, becoming the largest property company in the world. Samuel served as a member of the Covent Garden Market Authority from 1961 to 1974, which had the complex task of relocating the Central London fruit and vegetable market from its Covent Garden site to a new building at Nine Elms. He was active in other public work, including the presidency of the Central London Housing Trust for the Aged and vice presidency of the British Heart Foundation. He was knighted in 1963 and created a life peer in 1972. He was active in support for university education. He was also a noted art collector, bequeathing his collection, and his country house, Wych Cross Place in Sussex, to the Corporation of London. He was a cousin of the property developer and publisher Howard *Samuel.

BIBLIOGRAPHY: H. Pollins, *Economic History of the Jews in England* (1982), 229. **ADD. BIBLIOGRAPHY:** O. Marriott, *The Property Boom* (1967), 62–64.

[Vivian David Lipman]

SAMUEL, HERBERT LOUIS, First Viscount (1870–1963), British statesman and philosopher. Born in Liverpool, the son of Edwin Samuel (elder brother of Samuel *Montagu, the first Lord Swaything), Samuel was raised in London, where his father, who died in 1876, became senior partner in the firm of Samuel and Montagu (later Samuel Montagu and Company), bullion brokers. He was educated at University College School and Balliol College, Oxford, of which he later became visitor. His Jewish background was Orthodox, but he was not a practicing Orthodox Jew, although he retained his membership in the New West End Synagogue in London throughout his life and in later years attended services on festivals and formal occasions. Although raised in a politically conservative home, by the age of 18 Samuel had become an active Liberal, standing for Parliament unsuccessfully in 1895 and 1900. Between graduation and becoming a member of Parliament, he played an active role in the transformation of the Liberals into a party with a program of constructive social reform.

Samuel entered Parliament in 1902 and, after the Liberal victory of 1906, held his first junior ministerial office in the Home Office, promoting the new Workmen's Compensation for Accidents Bill, the establishment of a probation system in England, and the Children's Act, popularly known as the "Children's Charter." Appointed a privy councilor in 1908, he became chancellor of the duchy of Lancaster, with a seat in the cabinet (the first held by a professing Jew) in 1909, postmaster general in 1910, and president of the local government board in 1914. In 1914 he was responsible for the absorption of 250,000 Belgian refugees, most of whom returned to Belgium at the end of the war. In 1915, when Prime Minister Herbert Asquith formed his coalition government, Samuel became postmaster general again, temporarily losing his seat in the cabinet; but early in 1916 he was promoted to home secretary. When Lloyd George succeeded Asquith as prime minister in 1916, however, Samuel remained loyal to Asquith and refused to serve in the new government.

Before 1914 Samuel had taken no part in Zionist activities because he did not regard them as practicable. On the day Great Britain declared war on Turkey, however, he broached the subject of Zionism and the establishment of a Jewish state in Palestine, first with D. *Lloyd George and later with the foreign secretary, Sir E. Grey, and found them most enthusiastic. Later he prepared a special memorandum on the subject, which he circulated among the members of the cabinet in January and March 1915. In his memorandum he advocated a British protectorate under which "facilities would be given to Jewish organizations to purchase land, to found colonies, to establish educational and religious institutions, and to cooperate in the economic development of the country, and that Jewish immigration, carefully regulated, would be given preference, so that in course of time the Jewish inhabitants, grown into a majority and settled in the land, may be conceded such degree of self-government as the conditions might justify." Palestine was a small country "the size of Wales" and, as such, it could not absorb all the Jews, but it could absorb some 3,000,000 people and thus bring some relief to Jews in Russia and elsewhere. But what was more important was the effect upon the Jewish people throughout the world. Therefore, "let a Jewish center be established in Palestine, let it achieve, as it may well achieve, some measure of spiritual and intellectual greatness, and insensibly the character of the individual Jew, wherever he might be, would be raised." Nothing came out of this proposal because of the opposition of Prime Minister Asquith. But in the field of practical politics, Samuel helped Chaim Weizmann, whom he first met in December 1914, in the work that ultimately led to the *Balfour Declaration.

As a result of his close connection with the policy of a Jewish National Home, Samuel was appointed the first high commissioner of Palestine (1920–25), thus being the first Jew to rule the Land of Israel in 2,000 years. His term of office can be roughly divided into two parts: from 1920 to 1922 when British policy was crystallized, and from 1922 to 1925. In the first period Transjordan was excluded from the area destined to become the Jewish National Home, and a new concept about immigration to the country was formulated, namely that of the "economic absorptive capacity." An advisory council consisting of ten British officials, four Muslims, three Christians, and three Jews was established, but it ceased functioning after two years because of Arab refusal to cooperate. As a capable administrator, Samuel laid the foundations of the country's civil administration. During his term of office the Jewish population doubled (from 55,000 in 1919 to 108,000 in 1925), extensive Jewish settlement was carried out, and the number of settlements rose from 44 to 100. Official recognition was given to Jewish representative bodies, local councils were organized, and the chief rabbinate was established. Great improvements were carried through in the legal and judicial system, and education, sanitation, and communications were much improved. The Hebrew language was recognized as one of the three official languages of the country. However, Samuel's efforts to appease Arab anti-Zionism by appointing the young extremist Hajj Amin al-*Husseini as Mufti of Jerusalem, thus investing him with the highest Muslim authority in Palestine, and by stopping, and later restricting, Jewish immigration under Arab pressure, were severely criticized by many Zionists. The sharpest critic of Samuel's policy was Vladimir *Jabotinsky, but also in the Zionist labor movement, and the *yishuv* in general, Samuel's policy eventually caused deep disappointment.

Samuel's interest in the National Home and the development in the Jewish community never diminished. In 1936 he became the chairman of the board of the Palestine Electric Corporation. He was also a constant supporter of The Hebrew University and member of its board of governors. He fought against the anti-Zionist policy adopted in the 1939 White Paper, and after World War II he also attacked the anti-Zionist policy of the British foreign secretary, Ernest *Bevin.

Samuel returned to Liberal politics in England and reentered the House of Commons in 1928. By this time, however, the Liberals were no longer one of the two major parties, having been superseded by the Labour Party. During the government crisis of 1931 he was one of those who advised the king to form a national government to be led by Ramsay MacDonald. In this government he was home secretary, until he resigned over policy differences in 1932. He never held office again, though Neville Chamberlain did invite him to join his government in 1938. He had been knighted in 1920 and in 1937 was made a viscount. He led the Liberal Party in the House of Lords from 1944 to 1955. In 1958 he received the distinction of the Order of Merit to mark 50 years as a privy councilor.

Samuel also wrote considerably on philosophy, succeeding Lord Balfour as president of the British Institute of Philosophy. In his works he mainly developed the ideas of the liberal philosophy. Among his philosophical works are *Liberalism* (1902), *Practical Ethics* (1935), *Belief and Action, an Everyday Philosophy* (1937, 1953[3]), *Creative Man* (1949), *Essays in Physics* (1951), and *In Search of Reality* (1957). He played a leading role in the movement to aid German refugees, visiting the United States and various European countries to raise funds and working for the admission of German Jewish children to Britain before World War II broke out. He also played a leading role on important Anglo-Jewish occasions, presiding in 1956 over the Tercentenary of Jewish Resettlement in England. As a minister Samuel was immensely diligent, lucid, and competent, rather than a brilliant front-rank politician. In later life his clarity of expression, aided by his superbly mellow voice, won him wide popularity as a broadcaster. In his last years his integrity and balanced judgment made him perhaps the most respected of British elder statesmen. In 1945 Samuel published his *Memoirs*. Samuel's career lasted for an extraordinarily long period of time. As an undergraduate he met William E. Gladstone; the last entry in his diary concerns the Cuban missile crisis of 1962. He was possibly the leading example of the spirit of "meliorism," the widespread belief long held by many acculturated British Jews that they lived in a country inevitably evolving towards liberalism and tolerance, although Samuel, unlike many of his background, was also a leading Zionist. Bermard Wasserstein's *Herbert Samuel: A Political Life* (1992) is the standard biography. His son was Edwin, Second Viscount *Samuel.

BIBLIOGRAPHY: J. Bowle, *Viscount Samuel* (1957); L. Stein, *Herbert Samuel* (1963); idem, *The Balfour Declaration* (1961), 103–16 and index; Ch. Weizmann, *Trial and Error* (1949), index; E. Kedourie, *The Chatham House Version...* (1970), 52–81; R.J. D'Arcy Hart (ed.), *The Samuel Family of Liverpool and London from 1755 Onwards...* (1958). **ADD. BIBLIOGRAPHY:** ODNB online; C. Bermant, *The Cousinhood* (1971), index.

[Vivian David Lipman and Daniel Efron]

SAMUEL, HOWARD (1914–1961), British property developer and Labour publisher. Born in London, the son of a prominent jeweler, Howard Samuel was the cousin of the property developer Harold *Samuel, Baron Samuel of Wych Cross. Howard Samuel was educated at St. Paul's School and founded his own estate agency with his brother Basil. After 1945 Samuel's firm, Land Securities, emerged as Britain's largest property developer and estate agent. The holding company Samuel formed, Great Portland Estates Ltd., also became nationally known. Although one of the richest men in the country, Samuel was a strong supporter of the Labour Party and was actively involved in financing the left-wing periodicals *Tribune* and the *New Statesman*. He was also a close friend of the radical Labour leader Aneurin Bevan. Samuel died in Greece of a heart attack at the age of only 48, leaving a fortune of £3.8 million, making him probably one of the twenty richest men in Britain at the time.

BIBLIOGRAPHY: ODNB online; O. Marriott, *The Property Boom* (1967).

[William D. Rubinstein (2nd ed.)]

SAMUEL, MAURICE (1895–1972), U.S. author and translator. Born in Macin, *Romania, Samuel spent his boyhood in Manchester, England, migrating to the U.S. in 1914. At home in both Jewish and Anglo-American culture, he tried to maintain an equilibrium between them, but before long saw dangers in this bicultural experience. In provocative volumes beginning with *You Gentiles* (1924) and *I, the Jew* (1927), and continuing with *Jews on Approval* (1931), *The Great Hatred* (1941), and *The Gentleman and the Jew* (1950), he came to the conclusion that Jewish and gentile approaches to ultimate questions were antithetical. Antisemitism was not a Jewish problem, but an affliction of the gentiles to which Jews had to accustom themselves. It was "the great hatred" in the amoral pagan soul in Western man for the Jewish-Christian jailer who had bound it with fetters of moral law. Samuel also contrasted the Jewish with the gentile ideal of man. During the years between the Balfour Declaration of 1917 and the establishment of the Jewish state in 1948, Samuel was a most influential and popular exponent of Zionist ideology. Having spent ten years in Ereẓ Israel, he believed that the Jews would succeed in building a moral commonwealth and gave expression to his faith in *Harvest in the Desert* (1944), calling upon American Jews to assist this venture on their ancient soil. In *Level Sunlight* (1953) Samuel reiterated his faith in the messianic aspects of Zionism, maintaining that the objective of classical Zionism went beyond the mere building of a state. It included the regeneration of the Jewish people in all lands with the help of the Jewish center in Israel, and in this process American Jewry had a vital part to play. Samuel also wrote fiction, including the novels, *Beyond Woman* (1934); *Web of Lucifer* (1947); *The Devil That Failed* (1952); and *The Second Crucifixion* (1960), the story of a Jewish girl in Hadrian's Rome. Among other works of Jewish interest are *On the Rim of the Wilderness* (1931), a study of the Palestine Arabs and the Zionist movement; *The World of Sholom Aleichem* (1943); *Prince of the Ghetto* (1948), on I.L. *Peretz; *Certain People of the Book* (1955), studies of biblical figures and biblical morality; *Little Did I Know* (1963), recollections and reflections on the worthwhileness of being a Jew; *Blood Accusation* (1966), a reexamination of the notorious *Beilis trial; *Light on Israel* (1968); and *In Praise of Yiddish*. Samuel translated novels by Sholem *Asch and Isaac Bashevis *Singer; *Bialik's *Selected Poems* (1926); the Passover *Haggadah* (1942); and works by Peretz and Shemaryahu *Levin. In *The Professor and the Fossil* (1956) he wittily and effectively answered Arnold J. Toynbee's treatment of the Jews in his *Study of History* (1934–54). A brilliant orator and conversationalist, he reached a wide audience through his broadcast discussions on biblical topics with the poet and critic Mark van Doren.

BIBLIOGRAPHY: S. Liptzin, *Generation of Decision* (1958), 249–54; idem, *Jew in American Literature* (1966), 176–9, 221–2; S.J. Kunitz, *Twentieth Century Authors – First Supplement* (1955), index; A. Lelyveld, in: JBA, 22 (1964), 109–14; R. Alter, in: *Commentary*, 37 (1964), 50–54.

[Sol Liptzin]

SAMUEL, RALPH E. (1892–1967), U.S. investment banker. Born in Rochester, New York, Samuel joined the family business and served as president of this retail chain until 1932. He then became a partner in a Wall Street brokerage firm, and in 1938 organized and headed his own firm. In 1954 he started one of the first mutual funds in the United States. From the beginning of his career he took an interest in Jewish and general community work. He was a voluntary fund raiser for the Federation of Jewish Philanthropies and served as its president from 1948 to 1951. He was a vice president and chairman of the board of the American Jewish Committee and instrumental in founding its publication, *Commentary*. His other activities included the chairmanship of the American-Jewish Tercentenary Committee (1954–55), and the vice chairmanship of the Board of Trustees of the New York School of Social Work at Columbia University. Despite his conservative financial views and approaches toward business, he supported liberal Democrats such as Franklin D. Roosevelt and Adlai E. Stevenson. He died during a visit to Israel.

[Joachim O. Ronall]

SAMUEL, RAPHAEL (1934–1996), British historian. Samuel was born in London. His father was a solicitor and his mother, Minna (Nerenstein, 1909–1999), was both a left-wing activist and a composer of note, who wrote under the name of Minna Keal. Samuel's interest in history was aroused by his uncle, the well-known historian of Jewish socialism CHIMEN ABRAMSKY (1917–), who was professor of Jewish studies at University College, London. Samuel was educated at Oxford, where he became a dedicated Communist, abandoning his party membership after Khrushchev's famous speech of 1956 detailing Stalin's crimes. Samuel was one of the founders of the *Universities and Left Review*, which, after 1960, became known as the *New Left Review* and was one of the main organs of Britain's intellectual "new left." His academic career was rather unorthodox: he spent almost all of his career as a tutor at Ruskin College, Oxford, a working-man's institution funded by the trade unions, although he was briefly a professor at the University of East London shortly before his death. Samuel originated the "history workshops," and, in 1976, was one of the founders of *History Workshop Journal.* His best-known works include *Village Life and Labour* (1975), an edited three-volume work, *Patriotism* (1989), and *Theatres of Memory* (1996). Samuel's theatrical style of lecturing made him a charismatic figure on the British left and added greatly to his important impact. His autobiographical essay, "The Lost World of British Communism" (*New Left Review,* 154 (1985) and 156 (1987)) sheds much light on the appeal of Communism to some British Jews.

BIBLIOGRAPHY: ODNB online.

[William D. Rubinstein (2nd ed.)]

SAMUEL, SIR SAUL (1820–1900), Australian politician and communal figure. Born in London, Samuel emigrated to Australia with his widowed mother in 1832 to join her brother, a successful Sydney merchant. Samuel became a leading merchant in Sydney and Bathurst and a large-scale pastoralist on the Macquarie River. In 1846 he became the first Jew to be appointed a justice of the peace in Australia. From 1851 he was involved in the search for gold in Victoria. In 1854 he was appointed a member of the Legislative Council of New South Wales, and in 1859 became New South Wales' first elected Jewish member of Parliament. When first taking his seat, he stated that he was happy that no difficulties existed in New South Wales regarding his taking the oath, since it was only one of allegiance and not based, as in England, "upon an exclusive and sectarian prejudice." Samuel sat in Parliament for over 20 years and held numerous ministerial posts. He was three times colonial treasurer and was responsible for the financial arrangements for separating Queensland from the parent colony of New South Wales. As postmaster general he negotiated a postal service to Great Britain in 1872, and as agent-general of New South Wales in London from 1880 was responsible for loans running into millions of pounds. He was knighted in 1882 and created a baronet in 1898. Samuel was a director of numerous companies, especially in mining and insurance. He was prominent in Jewish communal affairs as president of the Sydney Great Synagogue and was active in Jewish education. After 1880 he lived chiefly in London, dying at his South Kensington home.

ADD. BIBLIOGRAPHY: ADB, 6, 84–85; H.L. Rubinstein, Australia I, 375–76.

[Israel Porush / William D. Rubinstein (2nd ed.)]

SAMUEL, SIGMUND (1867–1962), Canadian industrialist, philanthropist, patron of the arts. Samuel was born in Toronto to Lewis and Bavarian-born Kate, who emigrated to Canada from England in 1855. Sigmund's father, Lewis, and his brother Mark began a successful hardware and scrap metal business that grew into a major steel production enterprise, raising the Samuel family to the first rank of Canada's early industrialists. Unlike some other early Canadian industrialists of Jewish heritage, the Samuel family retained a connection to their traditional roots. Members of the family were founding members of the then Orthodox Holy Blossom Congregation in its new quarters on Richmond Street, where Sigmund was first called to the Torah. Sigmund attended the elite Upper Canada College and the Toronto Model School. Reflecting the Toronto of his day, he notes in his autobiography that, even as a wealthy and acculturated industrialist with entrée to the best social circles, he was subject to antisemitism.

As a young man Samuel entered the family business and helped expand its operations, including the purchase of Algoma Steel in Sault St. Marie, Ontario. In 1930, with Samuel at the helm, the firm was a major producer of hardware items of every type, including steel tubing, pig iron, and flat sheets of steel. Samuel continued to lead the firm until his death, when it was taken over by his grandson, Ernest L. Samuel.

Samuel's legacy is enshrined in two key Toronto institutions. A keen supporter of the arts, he bequeathed money to the Royal Ontario Museum for its Canadiana Gallery of Art (formerly the Sigmund Samuel Collection). In 1954 he also gave the University of Toronto money to build a library for the humanities. Dubbed "Sig Sam" by subsequent generations of University of Toronto students, the library remains a fixture on the university's King's College Circle.

BIBLIOGRAPHY: S. Samuel, *In Return: The Autobiography of Sigmund Samuel* (1963).

[Frank Bialystok (2nd ed.)]

SAMUEL, SYDNEY MONTAGU (1848–1884), British journalist. Born in London and educated at London University, a nephew of the first Baron Swaythling, Samuel was active in Jewish social welfare work. A prolific writer, he ranged from poetry to finance and wrote an annual financial survey for the *Times.* In 1878 he acquired part ownership of the *Jewish Chronicle* and wrote for that paper on many subjects. His series of travel articles was published as a book, *Jewish Life in the East* (1881). He was also active in the theater and wrote a comedy, *A Quiet Pipe* (1880). Samuel was a merchant banker in the City of London, dying, it is said, of overwork, at the age of 36.

SAMUEL, WILFRED SAMPSON (1886–1958), British businessman and historian. Born in London, the son of a steel pen manufacturer who died soon after his birth, Samuel was educated in Belgium and Germany. In 1904, with several of his cousins who had been piano manufacturers, he founded the Decca gramophone and record company in London. Samuel served as an officer in World War I. He and his cousins developed Decca into one of the largest recording companies in the world. He then engaged in research on the history of the Sephardi community in London, which resulted in his *The First*

London Synagogue of the Resettlement (1924), placing the story of the beginnings of the London community on a new basis. He subsequently published many papers on the period, and on the history of the Jews in the West Indies, mainly in the *Transactions of the Jewish Historical Society of England*. With Cecil *Roth he founded the Jewish Museum in London in 1932, of which he was chairman until his death. His cousin FRANK SAMUEL (1889–1954), the son of a piano manufacturer, was educated at Clifton and was also one of the founders of Decca. In 1928 he sold his interest in the company at the peak of the boom and, a few years later, became managing director of the United Africa Company, a commodity trading subsidiary of Unilever. Although generally very successful in this venture, he is best remembered for the ill-considered Tanganyika "groundnuts scheme" of 1946–51. Samuel was, nevertheless, a leading figure in the economic development of east Africa. Wilfred's son EDGAR SAMUEL (1929–), who was educated at Clifton and London University, is one of the best-known historians of the early modern period of Jewish, especially Sephardi, settlement in England. He served as director of the Jewish Museum in 1993–95 and was president of the Jewish Historical Society of England in 1988–90. Many of his essays were collected in his *At the Ends of the Earth: Essays on the History of the Jews in England and Portugal* (2004).

BIBLIOGRAPHY: C. Roth, in: JHSET, 19 (1960), 210–3. **ADD. BIBLIOGRAPHY:** Frank Samuel in ODNB online; DBB, 5, 37–43; E. Samuel, "Decca Days: The Career of Wilfred Sampson Samuel (1886–1958)," in idem, *At the Ends of the Earth* (2004), 385–426.

[Cecil Roth / William D. Rubinstein (2nd ed.)]

SAMUEL BEN ALI (Samuel ha-Levi ben al-Dastur – "the Aristocrat"; d. 1194), one of the *geonim* of the post-geonic period (which lasted for about 200 years after the geonic period proper). He was the most prominent and important of the 12th-century Babylonian scholars, and the only one of the neo-geonic period whose written work has survived. Samuel was head of the academy in Baghdad for about 30 years. He was also the recognized leader of the neighboring countries, according to the statement of the traveler, Pethahiah of Regensburg: "In the whole of Assyria, in Damascus, in the towns of Persia and Media and in Babylon, they have no *dayyan* except one assigned by Samuel, head of the academy, and he appoints judges and teachers in every town" (ed. by L. Greenhut (1905), 10). Both Benjamin of Tudela and Pethahiah describe in the diaries of their travels the manner of Samuel's influence and his conduct of the academy, which resembled to a certain degree the customs of both the *geonim* and of the exilarchs. Samuel is chiefly known for his polemics with Maimonides both on halakhic matters and on Maimonides' attitude to the resurrection of the dead (*Ma'amar TeḤiyyat ha-Metim*, in: *Kovez Teshuvot ha-Rambam* (1859) pt. 2, 8dff.). Samuel wrote glosses to the *Mishneh Torah* of Maimonides, who replied in a letter to his pupil in Baghdad, Joseph b. Judah (*She'elot u-Teshuvot ha-Rambam*, ed. by J. Blau, 3 (1961), 142 no. 464). In addition to his well-known responsum on the subject of traveling on rivers on the Sabbath (*ibid.*, 2 (1960), 570 no. 309), several of his responsa have been published by Poznański (responsum to Moses of Kiev, a pupil of Jacob Tam; see bibl., 53–56), Aptowitzer (on the minutest quantum of *Ḥamez*), and Mann (a responsum of 1166; HḤY, 6 (1922), 104ff. A large and important collection of letters by Samuel and his contemporaries was published by Assaf in *Tarbiz*, Year 1 (1930).

Samuel had one daughter who was well versed in the Bible and the Talmud, and she taught Bible through a window of the building in which she sat, the pupils outside below unable to see her (Pethahiah, p. 9f.). There is also a reference to his two sons-in-law, Zechariah b. Berachel of Aleppo, "the *av bet din* of the yeshivah" (letter of Samuel, in: *Tarbiz* 1, no. 2 (1930), 61), who was greatly praised by his father-in-law, and "his beloved son-in-law and pupil… head of the academy, Azariah (Eleazar ha-Bavli, *Diwan*, ed. by H. Brody (1935), no. 10, p. 13). Some (S. Assaf) think that Azariah is a copyist's error (though it occurs twice) for Zechariah, while others hold that Samuel had two daughters married to these two scholars. A third view is that his only daughter was betrothed to Azariah, who died before the marriage, and that she subsequently married Zechariah. There is no sufficient basis to the statement that the daughter died the same day as her father, although it is possible that Azariah died the same day as Samuel.

BIBLIOGRAPHY: S. Poznański, *Babylonische Geonim in nachgeonaeischem Zeitalter* (1914), 15ff., and index; V. Aptowitzer, in: ZHB, 19 (1916), 36f.; J. Mann, in: HḤY, 6 (1922), 106–22; idem, in: HUCA, 3 (1926), 294f.; Mann, Texts, index; S. Assaf, in: *Tarbiz*, 1 (1930), no. 1, 102–30, no. 2, 43–84, no. 3, 15–80; idem, *Tekufat ha-Ge'onim ve-Sifrutah* (1955), 127–9; A.H. Freimann, in: *Sefer ha-Yovel… B.M. Lewin* (1940), 27–41; D.H. Baneth (ed.), *Iggerot ha-Rambam* (1946), 31–90; Dinur, Golah, 2 vol. 3 (1968), 115–26, 332–4.

[Samuel Abba Horodezky]

SAMUEL BEN AVIGDOR (1720–1793), Lithuanian rabbi. Samuel b. Avigdor was Vilna's last official rabbi. His father, Avigdor b. Samuel (d. 1771) was nicknamed *Ḥarif* ("the sharp one"). Between 1719 and 1746 he served as rabbi of Pruzhany, Zelwa, Volkovysk, and Ruzhany. His approbations are found in many works. He is mentioned in responsa in *Mekom Shemu'el* (Altona, 1738) and *Givat Sha'ul* (Zolkiew, 1774). In his old age he lived with his son.

Samuel was at first a merchant who contracted several business agreements with the Vilna community (1745), but was appointed rabbi of Vilna in 1750, succeeding his influential father-in-law, Judah b. Eliezer (known as *Yesod*). Later Samuel was also appointed rabbi of *Smorgon. As a result of complaints against him that he intended to dominate the community by the infiltration of members of his family into the communal organizations of Vilna, in 1777 the community decided to oust him from the rabbinate. The civil government also intervened in the ensuing battle. That year a temporary compromise was reached whereby the rabbi obtained several posts for the members of his family, he in his turn relinquishing several of his financial demands, but the furore broke out again in 1782. The dispute was brought before several courts, both Jewish and gentile. The resolution of the community on the dismissal of the rabbi from his post that was finally adopted in 1785 was endorsed by the civil court in 1787. In the second stage of the dispute (1782–91), Samuel was supported by merchants and artisans in the town, who represented a new power in the community and demanded that the community alleviate their situation and associate them in the conduct of its affairs. One of the chief opponents of the domination of Vilna by the wealthy was Simeon b. Ze'ev Wolf, who did not refrain even from false allegations and calumny. Although all the reforms were not achieved, some of them were implemented. In the end neither side won a clear victory, but, as a result of the controversy, no one was thereafter officially appointed rabbi of Vilna. Samuel was an opponent of Ḥasidism and was among the first signatories of the Vilna excommunication of Ḥasidim in 1772. Samuel published no writings (his novellae, in pilpulistic style, and *Hadrat Zekenim*, his novellae on the entire Talmud, are still in manuscript), but he is mentioned with great reverence in rabbinic literature.

BIBLIOGRAPHY: Ḥ.N. Maggid-Steinschneider, *Ir Vilna* (1900), 17f.; S.J. Fuenn, *Kiryah Ne'emanah* (1915^2), 138–44, 171; Y. Zinberg, in: *He-Avar*, 2 (1918), 45–74, idem, in: *YIVO Historishe Shriftn*, 2 (1937), 291–321; I. Klausner, *Toledot ha-Kehillah ha-Ivrit be-Vilna* (1935), 127–31; idem, *Vilna bi-Tekufat ha-Ga'on* (1942), 141–50, 285–7, 293; H. Lunski, in: *Reshumot*, 2 (1946), 62–68; I. Halpern, *Yehudim ve-Yahadut be-Mizraḥ Eiropah* (1968), 159–62; M. Wilensky, *Ḥasidim u-Mitnaggedim* (1970), 1 pt. 1, 60f., 64f.;1 pt. 2, 73, 114, 132f.

[Yehoshua Horowitz]

SAMUEL BEN AZARIAH (13th century), *exilarch in *Baghdad. Samuel b. Azariah was the grandson of *Samuel, the exilarch of Baghdad, and the last exilarch under the *Abbasid dynasty. During the period of his office the *Mongols conquered Baghdad (1258). He retained his position under their rule and was even appointed as adviser to Īl-Khan Hulagu, the Mongolian ruler who conquered Baghdad. It is not known until when Samuel remained in office.

BIBLIOGRAPHY: Kobak, in: *Jeschurun*, 6 (1868), 29–34; Mann, in: *Sefer Zikkaron … S.A. Poznański* (1927), 24–25; Goode, in: JQR, 31 (1940/41), 167–8.

[Abraham David]

SAMUEL BEN DANIEL ABU RABĪ'A HA-KOHEN (13th century), last *gaon* of *Baghdad, succeeding his father R. Daniel Abu Rabīa. Samuel wrote two letters in 1288 on the controversy over the ban (*ḥerem*) on *Maimonides' *Moreh Nevukhim*. In one of the letters, sent to R. *David Maimuni ha-Nagid and the rabbis of Acre, Samuel states that he has issued a ban against R. Solomon b. Samuel Petit, Maimonides' bitter opponent.

BIBLIOGRAPHY: Halberstamm, in: *Jeschurun*, 7 (1871), 76–80; H. Brody (ed.), *Divan Elazar ben Ya'akov ha-Bavli* (1935), no. 173; S. Poznański, *Babylonische Geonim im nachgaonaeischen Zeitalter* (1914), 52–53, 70–71; Mann, in: HHY, 6 (1922), 121–2; Mann, Texts, 1 (1931), 227–8, 273; A. Ben-Jacob, in: *Zion*, 15 (1949/50), 69; idem, *Yehudei Bavel* (1965), 34.

SAMUEL BEN DAVID (known from his acronym as **Rashbad**; 12th century), Provençal commentator, *posek*, and preacher. Samuel was born in Narbonne and studied under Moses b. Joseph, head of its yeshivah. He later moved to Lunel where he became a member of the group of scholars known as *Ḥavurat Lunel* ("company of Lunel"). He then went to Montpellier where he served as rabbi. Samuel wrote a commentary to the Talmud, but only fragmentary quotations from the orders *Mo'ed*, *Nashim*, and *Nezikin*, and the tractate *Berakhot*, have survived in the works of Provençal scholars. It therefore seems that his commentary embraced at least these three orders, together with those tractates whose laws are of practical application. In his commentary Samuel mostly follows the Provençal traditions, and, like his teacher, aimed at arriving at the definitive *halakhah*. Samuel was also the author of a book of sermons mentioned by Judah *Lattes. Among his pupils was *Asher of Lunel, author of *Sefer ha-Minhagot*. The high esteem his contemporaries held him in is demonstrated by *Abraham b. David of Posquières. Samuel doubted the ritual fitness of the *mikveh* of the head of the Montpellier community that had been constructed according to the *mikveh* built by Abraham b. David for himself. Abraham b. David adduced a number of arguments to prove the correctness of his views, and he ended his responsum with the words: "and now tell the scholar [Samuel] not to be angry, nor to be jealous because his view has been challenged and his reasoning confuted, for this is one of the matters left to us [by heaven] whereby we may distinguish ourselves." Samuel's influence prevailed in Provence for many generations.

BIBLIOGRAPHY: B.Z. Benedikt, in: KS, 27 (1951), 237–48; idem, *R. Samuel, Rabbi of Montpellier* (Ms.); I. Sonne, in: KS, 28 (1952), 416; J. Twersky, *Rabad of Posquières* (1962), index.

[Binyamin Zeev Benedikt]

SAMUEL BEN DAVID (d. 1673), *Karaite traveler. Samuel set out in 1641 from *Yevpatoriya in the Crimea, journeyed via *Istanbul and *Egypt to Ereẓ Israel, and returned home through *Syria. The account he left of his travels contains valuable information on the Karaite communities in the Near East, as well as his own impressions of the countries and peoples visited. Samuel's account was published by J. Gurland in his *Ginzei Yisrael* (1865) and in A. Yaari's *Masot Ereẓ Yisrael* (1946), 221ff.

BIBLIOGRAPHY: Mann, Texts, 2 (1935), 721.

[Leon Nemoy]

SAMUEL BEN DAVID MOSES HA-LEVI (1625?–1681), Polish rabbi. Samuel was born in Poland and studied under *David b. Samuel ha-Levi and Shabbetai *Horowitz. He lived at first in Mezhirech in the district of Poznan. When Mezhirech was destroyed by Czarniecki in 1656, Samuel escaped to Halberstadt, where for three years he lived in great poverty and was assisted by a number of friends he made there. From Halberstadt he went to another town (whose name he refrained from mentioning because of the suffering caused him by its inhabitants), and remained there for a year and a half. In 1660 he was appointed regional chief rabbi of Bamberg, but since the authorities would not permit the rabbi of Bamberg to live in the town itself, his seat was at Zeckendorf, a village about two hours' journey from Bamberg. Samuel based his rulings almost exclusively upon the *halakhah*, without regard to the local customs which originated with the scholars of Germany. As a result, he aroused the opposition of the rabbis and laymen of the district and was compelled to leave Bamberg in 1665. For a time he was without a post, until he was appointed rabbi of Kleinsteinbach, where he remained until his death.

Samuel's fame rests upon his *Naḥalat Shivah*, which he finished in 1664 and the publication of which he personally supervised (Amsterdam, 1667). In 49 sections he deals with the formula of legal deeds of every kind, both in matrimonial and civil law, and clarifies all the relevant laws in accordance with the earlier and later *posekim*. Toward the end of his life Samuel succeeded in publishing the *Mahadura Batra* ["second edition"] *le-Sefer NaḤalat Shivah* (Frankfurt, 1681), which includes corrections and additions, as well as replies to the strictures upon it which appeared after its first publication, especially those of Jair Ḥayyim *Bacharach in his *Ḥut ha-Shani* and those of Aaron Samuel *Koidanover. *Naḥalat Shivah* became very popular among rabbis because of its practical value in the drawing up of documents, particularly *gittin, ketubbot*, and the like. After Samuel's death, his son Abraham republished the book in Fuerth in 1692, adding a second part containing 85 of his own responsa as well as others, including those of Aaron Samuel Koidanover. The importance of the work is evidenced by its frequent reprinting: Frankfurt, 1694; Fuerth, 1724, 1739, 1784: Russia, 1818; Lemberg, 1874, et al.; and as late as 1962 in Jerusalem.

BIBLIOGRAPHY: Aaron Samuel Koidanover, *Emunat Shemu'el* (Frankfurt, 1683); Jair Ḥayyim Bacharach, *Ḥut ha-Shani* (*ibid.*, 1679); idem, *Ḥavvot Ya'ir* (*ibid.*, 1699), introduction and section no. 1; Ḥ.N. Dembitzer, *Kelilat Yofi* (1888), 58b; A. Eckstein, *Geschichte der Juden im ehemaligen Fuerstbistum Bamberg* (1898), 160.

[Shlomo Tal]

SAMUEL BEN ELIEZER OF KALWARIA (mid-18th century), preacher and kabbalist. His only extant book is a homiletical work, *Darkhei No'am*, printed in Koenigsberg in 1764 and probably written before 1760. Among the *haskamot* (recommendations) in the foreword to the work is one by the Gaon of Vilna. It is a homiletical exposition of Lurianic Kabbalah, in the form of an interpretation of the *aggadot* of Rabbah b. Bar Ḥana in the Talmud, which he explains by the four methods of *pardes. The book contains some calculations as to the time of the redemption, and it appears that Samuel expected it to begin in the year 1781. Some of his moralistic admonitions seem to be directed against the early groups of the Ḥasidim, which proves that such ḥasidic groups existed in Lithuania before the death of *Israel b. Eliezer Ba'al Shem Tov in 1760.

BIBLIOGRAPHY: I. Tishby, in: *Zion*, 32 (1967), 16–24.

SAMUEL BEN HANANIAH (12th century), *nagid* of Egyptian Jewry. Samuel, who was known by the Arabs as Abu Manṣūr, was descended from a family of scholars. He himself was well versed in Jewish learning. Like his father, he was a physician and was one of the physicians in the court of the *Fatimid caliphs. In 1134, when Caliph al-Ḥāfiẓ requested that he prepare a poison for his son Ḥasan, he refused; a Christian physician agreed to do so. Later, the caliph regretted his action, the Christian physician was put to death, and Samuel was appointed chief court physician. The documents found in the Cairo *Genizah* which mention Samuel as *nagid* are dated between 1142 and 1159. When the poet *Judah Halevi arrived in *Alexandria, Samuel invited him to *Cairo. Judah Halevi then became friendly with him and praised him in several poems. Samuel was supplanted for a short time by *Zuta.

BIBLIOGRAPHY: Mann, Egypt, index; Mann, Texts, index; Abramson, in: KS, 29 (1953/54), 133–44; M. Margalioth, *Hilkhot ha-Nagid* (1962), 68–73; Scheiber, in: *Tarbiz*, 36 (1966/67), 156–7.

[Eliyahu Ashtor]

SAMUEL BEN HOPHNI (d. 1013), *gaon* of *Sura; he was a descendant of scholars of the *Pumbedita academy, his grandfather *Kohen Ẓedek was *gaon* of Pumbedita, as was his uncle Nehemiah. His father held the post of *av bet din* at the same academy. Samuel was not appointed to the Pumbedita academy, but became the *gaon* of the Sura academy about the year 997. *Hai, the noted *gaon* of Pumbedita, was his son-in-law.

Samuel was one of the most prolific writers of the geonic period. The scope and pattern of his literary activity followed closely the creations of *Saadiah, his great predecessor in office. His literary works, however, did not share the good fortune of Saadiah's; the greater part of his works is no longer extant and is known mainly through book lists, quotations by subsequent scholars, and other indirect references. But significant fragments are slowly coming to light out of the *Genizah. The works of Samuel range over the following central themes: responsa and talmudic treatises, biblical exegesis, philosophy, theology, and polemical writings.

Samuel possessed an orderly, analytical mind which is reflected in both his talmudic and exegetical works. He shows a special predilection for systematic, numbered classification of subjects under discussion. He was the first to write an introduction to the Talmud, summarizing and classifying its basic principles. This work is mentioned by early scholars and is currently being recovered from the *Genizah*. *Samuel ha-Nagid made use of this work in his *Mavo la-Talmud*. He also wrote a book of precepts – on the commandments. Some 15 other works on various subjects are known; fragments of some of them have been published. Samuel translated and wrote a commentary on the Pentateuch in Arabic. Scholars differ as to whether it covered the whole Pentateuch or merely completed the work begun by Saadiah and *Aaron ibn Sargado (*Gaon* of Pumbedita). The translation and commentary of the last three portions of Genesis (ch. 41–50) were published in Arabic by I. Israelsohn (1886). Other scattered verses of the commentary have been published in various periodicals. His commentary was used widely by authors of note such as Abraham *Ibn Ezra, *Abraham b. Moses b. Maimon and *Baḥya b. Asher. The author of the *Midrash ha-Gadol also made use of his work.

In the Bible commentary he employs the above-mentioned method of classification in elaborating on concepts, on meaning of individual words, and on implied talmudic principles. This frequently led him to digressions far from the subject under immediate discussion. His commentary is basically rooted in talmudic-midrashic tradition. At times he offers explanations different from those mentioned in the above sources. Grammatical treatment of words is infrequent, nor does he show acquaintance with the triliteral theory of Hebrew stems advanced by his contemporary Judah ibn Ḥayyuj. Jonah *Ibn Janaḥ in the 11th century refers to him as a commentator of *peshat* ("literal exegesis").

Of his philosophical works, one is known through references by later authors. He was apparently well acquainted with the classical philosophic writings, and was basically a rationalist. In one connection, his son-in-law Hai speaks disparagingly of him for this reason. Maimonides and his son Abraham refer to his philosophic concepts in support of their own ideas. Samuel makes use of the ideas of the philosophers in his Bible commentary, though he does not quote them directly. There is some uncertainty as to whether Samuel wrote a specific polemical work against the heretics of his time. His books, however, contain direct and indirect refutation of the arguments advanced by numerous skeptical or atheistic groups.

According to revised opinions based on *Genizah* sources, Samuel died in the year 1013. He was not the last *Gaon* of Sura, as has been assumed, being succeeded by Dosa son of Saadiah. Following Dosa's death in 1017, Samuel's own son Israel succeeded to the gaonate, and even after his death in 1034, the Sura academy continued to function. The bibliography of his published works and letters was edited by A. David in the preface to the book *Me'assef Nidaḥim* by A.E. Harkavy (1970), a great part of which was dedicated to Samuel b. Hophni.

BIBLIOGRAPHY: A. Harkavy, *Zikkaron la-Rishonim*, 1 pt. 3 (1880); Mann, Texts, index, s.v.; idem, in: *HUCA Jubilee Volume* (1925), 233–4; S. Assaf, *Tekufat ha-Ge'onim ve-Sifrutah* (1955), 194–7; idem, in: *Tarbiz*, 18 (1946/47), 28–33; A. Greenbaum, in: *L. Jung Jubilee Volume* (1962), 215–39 (Heb. pt.); Bacher, in: REJ, 15 (1887), 277–88; 16 (1888), 106–23; Abramson, in: *Tarbiz*, 17 (1945/46), 138–64; 18 (1946/47), 34–45; M. Zucker, *Al Targum Rav Saadiah Gaon la-Torah* (1959), 22–29; idem, in: *Abraham Weiss Jubilee Volume* (1964), 461–81 (Heb. section); Ibn Daud, Tradition, 60.

[Aaron Greenbaum]

SAMUEL BEN JACOB OF KELMY (1797–1867), rabbi. Samuel came from Neustadt (district of Kovno) and lived in Kelmy (Lithuania). In 1858 he immigrated to Ereẓ Israel, associating in Jerusalem with Meir *Auerbach of Kalisch and Sundel *Salant. In 1860 he went back to Europe but returned to Jerusalem in 1866. Samuel was a brother of Elijah Rogoler.

In 1870 after Samuel's death his son, A.L. *Frumkin, went to Israel, and he called the first edition of his *Toledot Ḥakhmei Yerushalayim, Even Shemu'el* (1874) after his father. At the end of Part I of this edition he incorporated *Naḥalat Ya'akov*, containing responsa and Torah novellae by his father and uncle (145–55). Many of Samuel's responsa, his novellae to tractates of the Talmud, and glosses to the *Sha'agot Aryeh* are still in manuscript.

BIBLIOGRAPHY: A.L. Frumkin (ed.), *Seder Rav Amram ha-Shalem* (1912), 478; idem, *Toledot Eliyahu* (1937²), 5, 65–82; Frumkin-Rivlin, introd. 12, 3 (1929), 249–51.

[Yehoshua Horowitz]

SAMUEL BEN KALONYMUS HE-ḤASID ("The Pious") OF SPEYER (12th century), one of the first leaders of the *Ḥasidei Ashkenaz movement and a member of the most important Jewish family in medieval Germany. His father moved from Mainz to Speyer after the persecutions of 1096 and Samuel was born there. Nothing is known of his life, and very few of his writings have survived. It seems that he wrote some exegetical works on the Torah and the Midrash. However, only a few quotations in later works have survived. He undoubtedly studied esoteric theology, and probably even wrote in this field. The titles, "the Pious, the Saint, and the Prophet" by which he was known to later generations, seem to indicate that he was regarded as a mystic. He contributed to the authorship of *Sefer Ḥasidim*. It has been proved that he wrote the first part of the book (in the Parma Ms. version), which deals with the fear of God and the subject of repentance. It is probable that some other sections of that book are his, and were included in it by its main author, his son *Judah he-Ḥasid. Hebrew and Yiddish collections of stories of the 15th and 16th centuries incorporate many tales of his magical powers. According to these, he competed against gentile magicians and used his powers to save Jews from their oppressors. Such stories were also told about his son Judah. Though knowledge of Samuel's work is extremely limited, there is no doubt that he served as a creative link between the oral traditions of the Kalonymus family in the fields of ethics, theology, and mysticism, and the literature of the Ḥasidei Ashkenaz movement which developed in the late 12th and the 13th centuries. The Ḥasidim regarded Samuel as their earliest leader and the movement reached its peak under the leadership of his son Judah he-Ḥasid. Another son, Abraham, was one of the leading halakhic scholars of his generation.

BIBLIOGRAPHY: A. Epstein, in: *Ha-Goren*, 4 (1903), 81–101 (reprinted in his collected writings, part 1 (1950), 247–68); I.A. Kamelhar, *Ḥasidim ha-Rishonim* (1917), 27–32; Y. Dan, *Torat ha-Sod shel Ḥasidei Ashkenaz* (1968), 47–50.

[Joseph Dan]

SAMUEL BEN MEIR (Rashbam; c. 1080–85–c. 1174), commentator on Bible and Talmud. Born in Ramerupt in northern France, Samuel was the son of Meir, one of the first tosafists and a prominent disciple of *Rashi, whose daughter, Jochebed, Meir married. Samuel was the elder brother of Jacob

*Tam and was a colleague of Joseph Kara. In his early youth he studied under his father, but mainly under his grandfather, Rashi, in Troyes. He entered into discussions with Rashi on biblical and talmudic subjects. In some instances Rashi accepted his grandson's opinion and amended his own commentary accordingly.

Samuel b. Meir earned his livelihood from sheep-farming and viticulture. He led a life of extreme piety and modesty, but resolutely holding to his own opinion when he felt it necessary. He used to pray that he might be privileged to know the truth and to love peace. He was well versed in worldly matters and may have had a knowledge of Latin. He participated in disputations with Christians. His scholarly activity was comprehensive. In addition to his commentaries on the Bible and Talmud he devoted himself to *piyyutim* and wrote a grammatical work, *Sefer Daikut*.

Bible Commentary

He apparently wrote a commentary on all the books of the Bible; only his commentary on the Pentateuch, however, has come down almost in its entirety. It was well edited from a manuscript by David Rosin (1881) who also wrote a comprehensive treatise on Samuel as Bible commentator. The edition by A.I. Bromberg (1965) is inaccurate. Of the remainder of Samuel's commentaries only fragments have survived in the works of later commentators, notably in the *Arugat ha-Bosem* of Abraham b. *Azriel (ed. by E.E. Urbach, 4 (1963), index, s.v. Shemuel (Samuel) b. Meir). A. Jellinek published part of the commentary on Esther, Ruth, and Lamentations (1855); he wrongly attributed to Rashbam the commentary on Ecclesiastes and Song of Songs, which he also published (see detailed discussion in Rosin's edition, xviii–xxii).

Samuel's biblical commentaries are characterized by his extreme devotion to the literal meaning (*peshat*). He constantly refers to "the profound literal meaning of the text." He strongly condemns earlier commentaries, including those of his grandfather, Rashi, even referring to some as "nonsense," "lies," and "crooked explanations," without naming their authors; in point of fact he generally refrains from mentioning other commentators by name. This method of literal interpretation he adopted in his youth, and he relates how he argued on the subject with his grandfather, who conceded that "if he had the time, he would have had to write another commentary, more in accordance with the literal approach, then daily gaining ground" (Rashbam, on Gen. 37:2).

On rare occasions he bases his interpretation on halakhic or midrashic interpretations if these seem to him to agree with the literal meaning. At times he even interprets a verse against the *halakhah* (e.g., Gen. 1:5; Ex. 21:6, 10), despite the fact that he considered the *halakhah* as authoritative and "every word and interpretation of our sages are correct and true" (on Gen. 1:1). His uncomplicated faith and spiritual wholeness prevented him and those who followed his method from any feeling of tension or contradiction. In his opinion *peshat* and *derash* belong to different categories. While the former explains Scripture according to the laws of language and logic, the latter bases itself on redundancies in language employing the hermeneutical rules by which the Torah is expounded. He states: "Let every sensible person know and understand that, although they are of primary importance, I have not come to explain the *halakhot* ... derived as they are from textual redundancies. They can partly be found in the commentaries of Rabbi Solomon, my maternal grandfather. My aim is to interpret the literal meaning of Scripture" (preface to section "*Mishpatim*").

Samuel was greatly influenced by Rashi, and to a considerable extent regarded his commentary as complementing that of Rashi, especially in those cases where Rashi did not follow the *peshat*. He sometimes remarks that, since Rashi had already commented on a certain matter, there is no need to repeat what he had said. Some of his explanations, however, are completely identical with those of his grandfather.

His exposition is concise and lucid and confined to explanation of the subject matter and language. He does not usually state the difficulties explicitly; but these may be inferred from their solutions in the commentary. Unlike Rashi, he gives one explanation only. In his commentary he takes *cantillation into consideration. Like Rashi he often uses French glosses to explain words, and he often interprets verses in accordance with contemporary custom and usage (e.g., Gen. 49:24). Samuel enters deeply into grammatical questions, generally relying upon Menahem b. *Saruk and Dunash b. *Labrat. In some cases he disagrees with them, demonstrating his own superior scholarship. In contrast to Rashi he insists that biblical Hebrew differs from mishnaic, and the meaning of a biblical word cannot therefore be determined by its meaning in mishnaic Hebrew (on Ex. 12:7). Occasionally, however, when he cannot find a biblical parallel, he deviates from this rule (on Ex. 1:13).

He took pains to find accurate texts of the Bible, especially from Spain, according to them – and sometimes even according to his own opinion – amending the Bible texts before him (Ex. 23:24). Sometimes he quotes biblical verses different from the accepted text (e.g., Gen. l:5, 21; Deut. 32:11). This seems in some cases to be the result of adjusting the text in accordance with his explanation, but in others it is due to the fact that he had a different text before him. He laid down an important rule with regard to biblical poetry (cf. on Ex. 15:6) which was accepted by his grandfather who, accordingly, amended his own commentary. Another principle widely applied by Rashbam is that the details which appear to be redundant are necessary, however, for the elucidation of the events that follow. Targum *Onkelos on the Pentateuch is one of his major sources. He also quotes the Palestine Targum on the Pentateuch once and the Targum to the Hagiographa twice. Twice he quotes the Vulgate but rejects its readings (Gen. 49:10; Ex. 20:13). He was the first Bible commentator to incorporate in his commentaries attacks on christological exposition. In this connection he gives reasons for certain laws, especially those whose validity was challenged by Christians. In some cases his extreme adherence to the literal meaning of the text may be attributed to those controversies with Christians. This emerges from the oft-repeated expression "according to the literal meaning of the text and in answer to sectarians."

His self-confidence in his ability as a commentator emerges clearly from his commentary. That self-confidence may explain his vigorous criticism of other commentators, his limiting himself to single explanations, the complete absence of the admission "I do not understand" (often found in Rashi), and his preparedness to make textual amendments. S.Z. Ashkenazi wrote a supercommentary *Keren Shemu'el* (Frankfurt on the Oder, 1727) on Samuel b. Meir's commentary.

[Avraham Grossman]

As Tosafist

In addition to his importance as a biblical commentator, Samuel b. Meir is also one of the first, and the most important, of the *tosafists. Only part of his halakhic writings have come down to us. The most significant and important are his supplements to Rashi's commentary on the Talmud where Rashi did not manage to complete his final version. Two of these were published instead of Rashi's missing commentary – one on chapter 10 of *Pesaḥim*, and the other on most of *Bava Batra*, from folio 29a. The commentary on *Bava Batra* was written after Rashi's death. Two versions of the commentary which differ considerably exist: that of the Bomberg edition (Venice, 1521), and that of the Pesaro edition (1510). Some scholars ascribe to him the anonymous commentaries on a few of the small tractates of the Talmud, but there is no evidence for this. The commentary to *Bava Batra* was in the hands of Abraham b. Isaac of *Narbonne during Samuel b. Meir's lifetime. His commentaries are characterized by their excessive prolixity, so that at times one of his comments is as long as a whole passage of *tosafot*. In addition to explaining the text, he propounds and answers difficulties, proposes alternative explanations, weighing one against the other, and all within the framework of a running commentary on the Talmud. He also wrote *tosafot* to various tractates; only a number of quotations and a greater number of references have been preserved in the standard *tosafot* and in the works of other *rishonim*. A larger number of fragments occur in the *tosafot* to the third chapter of *Makkot*, from folio 20 onward, which are introduced with the words *perush ha-kunteres*. The commentary to *Alfasi's compendium there ascribed to Rashi is also his. Large sections of his commentary to *Avodah Zarah* have come down in the works of other *rishonim*, when they discuss the themes of this tractate. Many quotations from his commentary to *Avot* are preserved in the anonymous commentary to this tractate in the Maḥzor *Vitry and in that of Isaac b. Solomon of Toledo. Samuel b. Meir was also the first scholar of northern France to make frequent use of Alfasi's compendium, to which he even wrote a kind of *tosafot*. Various manuscripts refer to his commentary on *piyyutim*.

[Israel Moses Ta-Shma]

BIBLIOGRAPHY: D. Rosin, *R. Samuel ben Meir (Rašbam) als Schrifterklaerer* (1880); S. Poznański (ed.), *Perush al Yeḥezkel ve-Terei-Asar le-R. Eliezer mi-Belganẓi* (1913), xxix–l (introd.); Margalioth, in: *Sefer Assaf* (1953), 357–69; Moses b. Isaac, *Sefer ha-Shoham*, ed. by B. Klar (1946), vii (foreword); Gross, Gal Jud, 229, 542, 637; A.I. Bromberg (ed.), *Perush ha-Torch la-Rashbam* (1965), 7–19 (introd.); Kasher, in: *De'ot*, 30 (1966), 269–74; Esh, in: *Textus*, 5 (1966), 84–92. AS TOSAFIST: E.E. Urbach (ed.), *Arugat ha-Bosem*, 4 vols. (1939–63), index; Urbach, Tosafot, index; Dienemann, in: *Festschrift… Israel Lewy* (1911), 259–69 (Ger. section); Epstein, in: *Tarbiz*, 4 (1932/33), 185–6; Ta-Shema, in: KS, 42 (1966/67), 507–8.

SAMUEL BEN MOSES AL-MAGHRIBĪ (ha-Ma'aravi; 15th century), *Karaite physician and author living in *Cairo. In 1434 Samuel completed a code of Karaite law in Arabic entitled *al-Murshid* ("The Guide"), divided into 12 sections. His exposition is orderly and lucid, with infrequent polemics against the *Rabbanites, and he readily adopted Rabbanite customs that seemed to him unobjectionable. Samuel's work is apparently the last Karaite legal code to have been written in Arabic; all the later codes were, so far as is known, written in Hebrew. Although soon superseded by the code of *Bashyaẓi, Hebrew translations of "The Guide" were still current in the 18th century.

BIBLIOGRAPHY: Steinschneider, Arab Lit, 250 f.; S. Poznański, *Karaite Literary Opponents of Saadiah Gaon* (1908), 81 f.; Mann, Texts, 2 (1935), index; L. Nemoy, *Karaite Anthology* (1952), 196–229.

[Leon Nemoy]

SAMUEL BEN NAḤMAN (Naḥamani; late third and early fourth centuries C.E.), Palestinian *amora*. He was one of the most renowned aggadists of his time (TJ, Ber. 9:1, 12d). A native of Lydda in Ereẓ Israel (Lev. R. 35:12), Samuel apparently paid a short visit to Babylon in his youth. On his return, he studied under *Joshua b. Levi (TJ, RH 4:4, 59b) and *Jonathan b. Eleazar (Pes. 24a), in whose name he quotes several sayings (Yoma 9b). Samuel, who may have come into contact with *Judah ha-Nasi in his youth, was on intimate terms with *Judah II. The two went to Tiberias on Diocletian's order (c. 286), and bathed in the hot springs there (TJ, Ter. 8, 110, 46b; Gen. R. 63:8). Among his other colleagues were *Simeon b. Jehoẓadak, *Ammi, Ḥanina b. Papa, and *Ḥelbo. Samuel is known to have made two official visits to Babylon. The first was to determine the intercalation of the calendar, a function which, for political reasons, he could not perform in Ereẓ Israel (TJ, Ber. 2:1, 2d). The second was in his old age, when he petitioned the empress *Zenobia (267–73) to pardon an orphaned youth who had committed a grave political crime (TJ, Ter. 8:10, 46b). His halakhic decisions are recorded in the Babylonian (e.g., Meg. 2a) and Jerusalem Talmuds, and his authority is illustrated by his refusal to allow Ammi to lift a ban on a certain colleague (MK, 17a).

Samuel was considered an authority on the *aggadah* (Pes. 15b). Among his sayings was, "Whoever associates the name of Heaven with his suffering [by blessing God for the evil, or by prayer], his sustenance shall fly to him like a bird, as it says, in Job 22:25, 'And silver shall fly to thee'" (Bet. 63a, JPS "And precious silver unto thee"). His vivid description of the grief of Abraham, Isaac, Jacob, and Rachel over the destruction of the Temple, written in Hebrew and accompanied by dirges in Aramaic (Lam. R. Proem 24), reveals his poetic mind. Among those who transmitted his sayings were Ḥelbo, Levi, and Abbahu (Lev. R. 35:12), and Eleazar b. Pedat.

He was survived by two sons, Naḥman and Hillel; sayings have been preserved from both of them (Gen. R. 10:5, TJ; King. 1:9, 61c).

BIBLIOGRAPHY: Bacher, Pal Amor; Hyman, Toledot; Ḥ. Albeck, *Mavo la-Talmudim* (1969), 266–7.

SAMUEL BEN NATRONAI (between 1100 and 1110–before 1175), German scholar. Samuel was the brother-in-law and teacher of *Joel b. Isaac ha-Levi and married the daughter of *Eliezer b. Nathan some time before 1133. His birthplace and the names of his teachers are unknown, but it is known that he studied in Regensburg and that on various occasions he was in Bonn, Mainz, and Cologne. Many of his teachings, which are conspicuous for the sharpness of his style, are contained in the *Sefer Raban* (Prague, 1610) of his father-in-law and in the *Sefer Ravyah* of *Eliezer b. Joel ha-Levi of Bonn, the son of his brother-in-law. His rulings were highly regarded by the great scholars of the time. Samuel is known to have written *tosafot* to several tractates, and a book of his halakhic decisions is quoted by the *rishonim*; he also wrote a *seliḥah* for the Day of Atonement that has survived.

BIBLIOGRAPHY: V. Aptowitzer, *Mavo le-Sefer Ravyah* (1938), 69–75; Urbach, Tosafot, index.

[Israel Moses Ta-Shma]

SAMUEL BEN SAMSON (13th century), Ereẓ Israel settler, who emigrated from France to Ereẓ Israel in 1210 and described his journey in an extant letter. Samuel was one of a large group that emigrated from France and England; he entered the country by way of Egypt together with Jonathan b. David ha-Kohen of Lunel, a Provençal scholar. Samuel then traveled throughout the country with two of the company of immigrants, Saadiah and Tobiah, as well as the exilarch from Mosul who had come to pray at the holy places and the graves of the pious. In his letter to the Diaspora Samuel described his arrival in Jerusalem and its holy places. From there he went to the cave of Machpelah, entering with the help of a dyer of wool, the only Jew there. From Hebron he returned to Jerusalem and went by way of Bethel, Shiloh, and Shechem to Beth-Shean and Tiberias, describing the tombs of the pious in the latter's vicinity. Traveling from there to Safed, he toured its environs. His descriptions include not only the graves of the pious in the Upper Galilee, but also ruins of ancient synagogues he saw, and which he believed to be some of the 24 synagogues erected by Simeon b. Yoḥai. He also visited Kefar Biram, Kefar Nivrata, Gush Ḥalav, Meron, and Almah, and testified that "in all these places there are communities of more than eight *minyanim*" (A. Yaari, *Iggerot*…, (1943), 80, 81), i.e., in each village of Upper Galilee mentioned he found more than 80 Jewish families. This pointed to the remnants of an agricultural settlement in Upper Galilee, even after the conquest of the country by the crusaders. From there he went to Dan and Damascus, later visiting Naveh in Transjordan, where he saw the ruins of the ancient synagogue which has been rediscovered in modern times.

BIBLIOGRAPHY: E. Carmoly, *Itinéraires de la Terre Sainte* (1847), 115–68; A. Berliner, in: MWJ, 3 (1876), 157–60; Heb. section: 35–38; A.M. Luncz, in: *Ha-Me'ammer*, 3 (1920), 26–35; J.D. Eisenstein, *Oẓar ha-Massa'ot* (1926), 62–65; S. Schultz, in: *Ha-Ẓofeh le-Ḥokhmat Yisrael*, 14 (1930), 69–81, 375–8; A.L. Sukenik, in: *Zion Me'assef*, 2 (1927), 108–11; S. Krauss, in: REJ, 82 (1926), 333–52; E.N. Adler, *ibid.*, 85 (1928), 70–71; A. Yaari, *Iggerot Ereẓ-Yisrael* (1943), 75–83, 540–1.

[Avraham Yaari]

SAMUEL BEN SHILAT (first half of third century C.E.), Babylonian *amora*. Samuel was a pupil of Rav, whose sayings he transmitted. He is distinguished in the Talmud, however, as an outstanding pedagogue, utterly devoted to teaching children. Rav recognized his devotion and sincere dedication to his disciples and held him in high esteem, considering Samuel the ideal instructor of the young. Once Rav found him standing in his own garden during school hours and asked him whether he had forsaken his calling. Samuel answered, "For 13 years I have not seen my garden, and even now my thoughts are of pupils." Whereupon Rav applied to him the verse (Dan. 12:3), "they that turn the many to righteousness [shall shine] as the stars for ever and ever" (BB 8b).

BIBLIOGRAPHY: Hyman, Toledot, s.v.

SAMUEL BEN SOLOMON OF FALAISE (**Sir Morel**; 13th century), tosafist. All that is known of Samuel's father is that he was a scholar, as was his father-in-law Abraham b. Ḥayyim ha-Kohen, possibly the son of the tosafist *Ḥayyim ha-Kohen. His teachers included *Judah Sir Leon, Solomon of Dreux, and *Baruch b. Isaac of Worms. He wrote a commentary on the **kerovah El Elohei ha-Ruḥot le-Khol Basar* in which he explains all the Passover laws in the *piyyut* according to the traditions of the elders of Falaise and Dreux. Samuel's teachings are incorporated in the *Or Zaru'a* of his colleague, *Isaac b. Moses of Vienna. Samuel was patently apprehensive about rendering halakhic decisions and hesitated to permit what it had been customary to forbid, even when he was certain that the custom was an erroneous one and not a definite tradition. The most eminent of his pupils was *Meir b. Baruch of Rothenburg. The standard *tosafot* mention Samuel only in the *tosafot* to the tractates *Pesaḥim* and *Yoma*, but the standard *tosafot* to *Avodah Zarah* are simply adaptations of his *tosafot* and often quote him verbatim. His biblical exegesis is included in the various collections of the biblical commentaries of the tosafists. He was a participant in the *disputation in Paris with Nicholas *Donin.

BIBLIOGRAPHY: Gross, Gal Jud, 478–80; J. Jacobs, *Jews of Angevin England* (1893), 53, 146, 421; Urbach, Tosafot, index.

[Israel Moses Ta-Shma]

SAMUEL BEN URI SHRAGA PHOEBUS (second half of 17th century), Polish rabbi and author of a well-known commentary on the Shulḥan Arukh *Even ha-Ezer* called *Beit Shemu'el.* In his youth, he studied with R. *Joshua Heshel in Cracow. Upon his teacher's death, he continued his studies under R. Heshel's successor, R. Leib Fischeles, whose daughter he married. Samuel first officiated as rabbi in Szydlowiec, Poland, where he wrote the first version of his commentary. In his introduction he states that he was isolated in Szydlowiec and could not benefit from the counsel of students and colleagues. The work was published in 1689 in Dyhernfurth, with the text of the *Even ha-Ezer,* and was the first Hebrew book printed there. In 1691 Samuel was called to the important and lucrative rabbinate of Fuerth, Germany, where he displayed great activity. Together with the students who gathered around him in Fuerth, he reviewed and revised his work, and the second and final version was published there in 1694. This clear and comprehensive work is regarded as one of the best commentaries of its kind and was accepted in all scholarly circles as the standard and authoritative commentary to *Even ha-Ezer.* It has frequently been reprinted, together with the text. Despite his achievements in Fuerth, he was not happy there and longed for his former, smaller rabbinate. In 1694 he received a call to return to Szydlowiec. It appears that he accepted the invitation, since he is mentioned as the rabbi of that town in the approbation to *Ir Binyamin* which appeared in Frankfurt on the Oder in 1698. He also wrote responsa, one of which is published in *Ḥinnukh Beit Yehudah* of R. Enoch b. Judah of Schneitach (Frankfurt, 1708) no. 131.

BIBLIOGRAPHY: Ḥ.N. Dembitzer, *Kelilat Yofi*, 1 (1888), 81a–b; 2 (1893), 586f., Ch. Tchernowitz, *Toledot ha-Posekim*, 3 (1947), 161–3; Maimon, in: *Kovez R. Yosef Caro* (1969), 60–62.

SAMUEL COMMISSION, inquiry commission sent in 1919 by the British government to Poland to examine the causes of antisemitic tension and disturbances which had aroused sharp criticism in the West. The Commission arrived after the *Morgenthau Commission had already completed its inquiries there and remained in Poland from September until December 1919. Sir Stuart Samuel, who headed the Commission, was president of the *Board of Deputies of British Jews between 1917 and 1922 (he was a brother of Herbert *Samuel). Also prominent on the Commission was Capt. Peter Wright, who had been influenced by the preconceived ideas prevalent in Poland concerning Jews.

The Commission visited many areas, especially those with evenly mixed populations, such as eastern *Galicia, and gathered reliable testimonies on recent incidents of violence. Meetings were held with the Polish premier I. Paderewski and government ministers. At the conclusion of their journey, Samuel and Wright did not share the same opinions, and the subsequent published report comprised Samuel's account only, a fact which weakened its influence on public opinion. In an effort to ameliorate the tensions between Poles and Jews, Samuel advanced the following 12 proposals:

(1) Implementation of the clauses of the agreement concerning rights of Jewish citizens in Poland
(2) The practice of true equality
(3) Prosecution of criminal acts to persons or property committed out of motives of racism or religious bigotry
(4) Restoration of Jewish civil servants in Galicia to their former posts
(5) Restoration of Jewish railway workers to their positions throughout Poland
(6) Abolition of the *numerus clausus for Jewish university students
(7) Prohibition of discriminatory trade practices
(8) Immediate judicial examination of all those being held in detention camps
(9) Facilitation of the founding of new industries
(10) The guarantee of British government aid in Jewish migration overseas (to Palestine, Canada, South Africa, etc.)
(11) Aid for the establishment of banks in which the Jewish public would have confidence
(12) Attachment of a Yiddish-speaking secretary to the British embassy in Warsaw

Samuel himself intended to establish a bakelite factory in Poland to employ thousands of Jewish workers, but the government disapproved when he requested that Jewish workers be allowed to work on Sunday instead of Saturday. His book, *Mission to Poland*, was published in 1920.

BIBLIOGRAPHY: H.M. Rabinowicz, *Legacy of Polish Jewry* (1965), 41–44. **ADD. BIBLIOGRAPHY:** S. Samuel, "Report on a Mission to Poland," in: *Bulletin du Comité des Délégation Juives,* No. 16 (Aug. 18, 1920).

[Moshe Landau]

SAMUEL HA-KATAN (early second century C.E.), *tanna.* Some explain that the name *ha-Katan* ("the small") was given him because of his extreme modesty, while others maintain that he was so called because he was only a little inferior to the prophet Samuel (TJ, Sot. 9:13). His modesty and greatness are best illustrated by the following incidents. When the patriarch *Gamaliel II called a conference of seven scholars and eight appeared, he asked the outsider to withdraw. Samuel, not wanting the intruder to be embarrassed, rose and said, "I am the one without invitation." Nevertheless, Gamaliel understood that it could not be he and ordered him to sit, praising him in very high terms (Sanh. 11a). On another occasion, when a heavenly voice proclaimed at an assembly of scholars that "there is one here who is worthy that the *Ru'aḥ ha-Kodesh* [Holy Spirit] should descend upon him," everyone understood that the reference was to Samuel (*ibid.*). Samuel is best known for *Birkat ha-Minim*, which expressed anathema against Judeo-Christians, sectarians, and informers. It was composed at the request of Gamaliel II and incorporated into the daily *Amidah* (Ber. 28b). He explained the verse, "There is a righteous man that perisheth in his righteousness" (Eccles. 7:15) as meaning that the Creator of the world knows that the pious sometimes sin, therefore God says, "I will take him away in his righteousness before he has the opportunity to err" (Eccles. R. 7:15). Samuel was childless, and at his funeral Gamaliel II and Eliezer b. Azariah eulogized him: "For Samuel it is proper to cry and mourn. Kings die and leave their crowns to their sons, wealthy men their riches to their children. Samuel died and took his treasures with him" (Sem. 8). It is told that before his death he prophesied the persecutions of Trajan and the killing of the Ten Martyrs (Sanh. 11a).

BIBLIOGRAPHY: Hyman, Toledot; Bacher, Tann; I. Konovitz, *Ma'arekhot Tanna'im*, pt. 4 (1969), 115.

[Elliott Hillel Medlov]

SAMUEL HA-NAGID (Ismail ibn Nagrelʿa; 993–1055 or 1056), vizier of *Granada, statesman, poet, scholar, and military commander. The meteoric rise and political and military career of Samuel ha-Nagid marks the highest achievement of a Jew in medieval Muslim Spain. Samuel was born in Córdoba to a prominent family which originally came from Merida. He received an excellent Jewish and general education, including training in Arabic and the Koran, and studied *halakhah* under *Ḥanokh b. Moses of Cordoba. While a young man, he made his first allusions to his Davidic descent, a belief which inspired his confidence in his rise to power and his career. In 1013 Samuel was among those forced to flee Cordoba in the wake of the Berber conquest. According to the 12th-century historian, Abraham *Ibn Daud, he opened a spice shop in Malaga, and shortly afterward, was approached by a maidservant of Ibn al-ʿArīf, *kātib* (secretary) to the vizier of Granada, who asked him to write letters to her master. The vizier was so favorably impressed by Samuel's Arabic style that he advised King Ḥabbūs, the Berber ruler of Granada, to appoint Samuel to his staff (Ibn Daud, Tradition, 72–73). Samuel advanced from tax collector to *kātib* (after Ibn al-ʿArīf's death) to assistant to the vizier Abu al-ʿAbbas in 1020. Later he himself became vizier. In 1027 the Jews conferred upon him the title *nagid* of Spanish Jewry. In 1038, after Ḥabbūs' death, a struggle for succession between his sons Bādis and Bullugin took place. With Samuel's aid, Bādis eventually won the throne. As a result of this steadfast loyalty, Samuel became the leading influence on Bādis.

Much of Samuel's work as vizier entailed leading the army of Granada, which was occupied in constant warfare with Arab Seville. It was indeed remarkable that a Jew stood at the helm of a Muslim army, which from 1038 to 1056 (the span of Samuel's command) knew only two years of respite from fighting. A major source of information on Samuel's campaigns is his poetry in the *Diwan*, some of which is addressed to his son *Jehoseph ha-Nagid. Samuel is credited as having introduced poetry of war and battle into Hebrew literature. In 1038–39 Samuel fought his first major battle, against the army of Almeria, ruled by Zuhayr, a Slav, and his fanatic Arab vizier Ibn ʿAbbās. Both were killed and Samuel's victory elicited the celebration of a special "Purim" by Granada's Jews. In 1039 a heroic victory over Seville – celebrated in a poem – took place around Carmona; the latter was finally taken in 1043. In 1042 Samuel successfully came to the aid of Lorca in eastern Spain. His difficult campaigns against Abu Nūr of Ronda in 1045 and against Malaga in 1049 resulted in narrow escapes from death. In the 1050s Samuel was constantly on the move throughout Andalusia, fighting against Seville and her allies. His triumphs were viewed by the Jews as national victories. The constant travel weakened him considerably and in 1055–56 he died on a campaign. His position was inherited by his ill-fated son Jehoseph.

In addition to being a poet (see below) Samuel was a halakhist and communal leader. His major work in *halakhah*, *Sefer Hilkheta Gavrata* (published as *Hilkhot ha-Nagid*, ed. by M. Margaliot, 1962), is a compilation and explanation of *halakhah* based on both Talmuds, the decisions of the *geonim* (sometimes criticized), Midrash, and the *She'iltot* of *Aḥai of Shabḥa. To judge from the surviving fragments, it was written in Aramaic and Hebrew and possibly partly in Arabic. *Hilkheta Gavrata* apparently was completed in 1049, though parts appeared earlier, and directly influenced later Spanish halakhists such as Isaac *Ibn Ghayyat, Isaac *Alfasi, and *Judah al-Bargeloni. Its appearance was viewed by some, including the poet Solomon ibn *Gabirol, as the victory of the Spanish grandee over *Hai Gaon of Pumbedita. Accused of insulting the gaonate, Samuel wrote a poetic apology acknowledging its supremacy. Abraham ibn Daud, however, cites Samuel as one of "the first of the generation of the rabbinate" (Ibn Daud, Tradition, 78) who marked the end of the geonic predominance in talmudic and halakhic scholarship. The Nagid was also the author of criticism of the Koran, which was cited by a contemporary Muslim author. After reading the latter's version of Samuel's critique, the Arab historian-philosopher, Ibn Ḥazm, wrote a bitter polemic against it.

As leader of Spanish Jewry Samuel corresponded with the important contemporary scholars, including R. *Ḥushi'el, R. *Hananel, and R. Nissim of Kairouan, whose daughter married Samuel's son Jehoseph. His relations with the Babylonian gaonate were generally good. While no correspondence between Hai Gaon and the Nagid has been discovered, Hai's successor, the exilarch *Hezekiah b. David, was a friend of Samuel. He also maintained friendly relations with the Palestinian communities, supplying the synagogues in Jerusalem with olive oil (*ibid.*, 75). Samuel was one of the patrons of Solomon ibn Gabirol, who addressed the Nagid as "my father, my rider, my chariot," and dedicated several poems to him.

As Poet

Samuel's poems have come down in three works: *Ben Tehillim, Ben Mishlei*, and *Ben Kohelet*. The poems are refined and reflect profound worldly wisdom, as well as the many facets of his life as Jew, father, intellectual, *nagid*, vizier, and military commander. Samuel's poetry is more developed and diversified than that of his contemporaries, the first generation of Hebrew poets in Spain. His war poems, which evince great skill in creating epics, are unique in Hebrew poetry. The pleasures and vanities of life, which he knew well, stimulated his poetic inspiration. Besides poems devoted to love and wine, he composed poems of praise and glory, friendship and polemic, mourning and holiness, wisdom, morality, and meditation. Just as he wrote of wine and victory, he wrote of the illnesses of his children, and of the death of his brother Isaac. A literary artist of high order, his sure command of language is demonstrated by the great variety of subjects he chose for poetic expression. Despite the success he attained through his poetry, worldly wisdom, and pleasant manners, he was never content: the canker of melancholy continually gnawed at him. Even in his poems of love and wine a note of pessimism is sounded. He saw in the suffering of the Jews in exile his own personal suffering, and the poems reveal his yearning for Zion. At the royal court many secretly envied him and others were openly hostile. In their quest for royal favor these courtiers often acted treacherously, shifting or betraying loyalties without hesitation.

Just as he influenced the poets of his day so too they influenced him. He translated poems from Arabic and also composed in that language. The boasting and self-exaltation traditional to medieval Arabic and Hebrew poetry are recognizable in Samuel's poems, but to a more limited degree than in the work of other poets, such as Solomon ibn Gabirol. As was usual in those times, Samuel's poems were read at gatherings of poets, some of whom found them faulty in grammar and style, while others praised their novelty and inventiveness. Samuel bestowed gifts on his favorite poets, who then praised him in their poems; those from whom he withheld his generosity deprecated his poetry.

In 11th-century Granada no one was considered educated unless he could compose poetry. Children copying the poems of their father also characterized Arabic culture at that time. For these and other reasons Samuel educated his children to value and study poetry. He charged his sons with the copying and arranging of his poems and paid them for each completed work. When they performed their task well he praised them. Samuel had three sons and one daughter. Of the daughter and the son, Judah, nothing is known, but both probably died during their father's lifetime. The most beloved of his children was the first born, Jehoseph, regarded by Samuel as his successor. Jehoseph began to copy his father's poems (*Ben Tehillim*) at the age of eight and a half. Another son, Eliasaf, also copied his father's poems (*Ben Kohelet*), beginning when he was only slightly more than six years old. The children added captions descriptive of the poetry's contents and origins. *Ben-Mishlei*, a book of poems, was dedicated by Samuel to Jehoseph and Eliasaf.

The poems were copied many times during the Middle Ages, and it appears that Samuel himself took pains to ensure that they were circulated among knowledgeable people. The first author to refer to his poems was Moses *Ibn Ezra in *Shirat Yisrael* (66). Samuel's non-sacred poetry, however, came to be known only in the 19th century. The first to publish a substantial number of the poems was A.E. Harkavy (St. Petersburg, 1879). The three volumes of his poetry were published by David S. Sassoon (Oxford, 1934). Only in later editions did these works appear with vocalization and commentaries, as in the *diwan* containing *Ben Tehillim* (1947) published by A.M. Habermann, and in *Ben Mishlei* (1948) and *Ben Kohelet* (1953) issued by S. Abramson. New editions of the "*Shirei ha-Milḥamah*" (1963) and the *diwan* (1966) were published by A.M. Habermann and Dov Yarden respectively.

BIBLIOGRAPHY: A. Harkavy, in: *Me'assef*, 1 (1902), 1–56; R. Dozy, *Spanish Islam* (1913), 607–53; idem, *Histoire des Musulmans d'Espagne*, 3 (1932), 18–20; Lévi Provençal, in: *Al-Andalus*, 3 (1835), 233ff.; Schirmann, Sefarad, 1 (1954), 79–168; 2 (1956), 678; idem, in: *Zion*, 1 (1935), 761–83, 357–76; idem, in: *Hesperis*, 35 (1948), 163–88; idem, in: JSOS, 13 (195l), 99–126; Stern, in: *Zion*, 15 (1950), 135–45; D. Jarden, *Divan Shemu'el ha-Nagid* (1966), with complete bibliography; Ratzaby, in: *Bar Ilan*, 4–5 (1967), 160–80; E.I. Weinberger, *Jewish Prince in Modern Spain: Selected Poems of Samuel ibn Nagrela* (1973). **ADD. BIBLIOGRAPHY:** R. Ayoun, in: D. Tollet (ed.), *Politique et religion dans le judaïsme anciens et médiéval*, (1989), 209–24.

[Abraham Meir Habermann]

SAMUEL HA-SHELISHI BEN HOSHANA (d. after 1012), Palestinian liturgical poet. His name is mentioned in many documents of the Cairo *Genizah*, from which it appears that he was a member of the Ereẓ Israel academy in Jerusalem. He progressively rose in importance until he was awarded the title of *Ha-Shelishi* ("third of the company"), that is, the third man in the seating order at the side of the *Gaon* in the academy. For unknown reasons, he went to Egypt and settled in Fostat, where he became friendly with *Shemariah b. Elhanan. His disciples included R. *Nathan b. Abraham (I). On Shevat 3, 4772, at the time of the funeral of Putiel ha-Ḥazzan, he was a witness to and also a victim of the three-day riots perpetrated by the Muslims against the Jews of Fostat. He commemorated these events in a special scroll entitled *Megillat Miẓrayim* ("The Scroll of Egypt"), which has become an important historical source. He also wrote *kerovot* and *seliḥot* in memory of these events. Upon his death in Egypt *Sahlan b. Abraham eulogized him, mentioning among other achievements his erudition in Torah and his wide knowledge of talmudic and midrashic literature.

Samuel was one of the most prominent liturgical poets of his century, but only some of the hundreds of his extant *piyyutim* have been published, by various scholars. Samuel composed many *yoẓerot*, of every category, on all the weekly portions of the Pentateuch. Some of his *piyyutim* are written in a concentrated style and are filled with allusions, while others are written in an easy and colorful style. A few were signed *Shemu'el Yizkeh* or *Shemu'el he-Ḥaver Yizkeh*.

BIBLIOGRAPHY: Davidson, *Oẓar*, 4 (1933), 479, s.v. *Samuel he-Ḥaver*, Mann, Egypt, 1–2 (1920–22), index; idem, in: HUCA, 3 (1926), 258–62; Weiss, in: HḤY, 8 (1924), 154–202; Zulay, in: YMḤSI, 3 (1936), 163–75; Assaf, in: *Sefer Magnes* (1938), 2–4; M. Wallenstein, *Some Unpublished Piyyutim from the Cairo Genizah* (1956); Mirsky, in: KS, 33 (1957/58), 80–88; J. Schirmann, *Shirim Ḥadashim min ha-Genizah* (1965), 63–69; E. Fleischer, in: *Sinai*, 66 (1970), 237–8.

[Abraham David]

SAMUEL IBN ʿĀDIYĀ (**al-Samawal b. Ghārid Ablaq**; mid-sixth century), poet in *Tayma, Hejaz, N. Arabia. Samuel b. Ādiyā's Arabic poetry ranks with the finest heroic traditional Arabic battle poetry of the pre-Islamic period and shows little trace of Jewish origins and themes. For a time he resided in the citadel of Ablaq near Tayma and was called "King of Tayma" by the local Arabs. His mother was an Arab of the Ghassan tribe. He was Jewish, although Shaikho, the Jesuit who published his diwan, attempted to prove that he was a Christian, or at least belonged to a Judaeo-Christian sect. He lived to be an old man and was known for his loyalty and fulfillment of pledges. When the noble Imruʾal-Qays deposited his arms in Samuel's home, and the castle was besieged by his enemies after he left for Byzantium, Samuel allowed his own son to be killed rather than surrender Imru's arms to the invader. This act earned him lasting fame among Arabs, and he is the subject of several poems by later authors. A popular proverb on the extent of one's loyalty was coined, "more loyal than Samuel" (Ar. *Awfā min al-Samawʾal*). His descendants were landowners in the region of Taima during the Umayyad dynasty and later converted to Islam. Moses Ibn Ezra in his book *Shirat Israel* (Helper edition, 49) notes Samuel as a Jewish poet. One of his sons and a grandson are said to have been poets, too.

Poetry

Nine poems and fragments attributed to Samuel were collected by the philologist Nifṭawayh (d. 935). Most scholars agree that these poems were composed by a Jew but doubt that all were written by Samuel. The first poem is considered an example of classical Arabic poetry. Called *Lāmiyyat al-Samawʾal*, it expounds the virtues of purity of blood, generosity, honor, and strength. The battles of his people and their deaths on the battlefield are extolled, indicating the extent of the cultural assimilation of the Jews to Arab society. The second poem, however, expresses his belief in resurrection and glorifies the kings and prophets of Israel, also mentioning the splitting of the Red Sea. Its philological importance lies in the rhyming of certain stanzas as an aid to exegesis of the *Koran and in the traces of the Arabic dialect of the Jewish tribes. Poem number 6 exalts the fortress of Samuel's father and his loyalty to Imruʾal-Qays. A 26-line poem attributed to Samuel appears in the collection edited by Sheikho, who interpreted the phrase "our prophet came and brought peace to all men" as evidence of the poet's Christian origin. His opinion has been contested, as the poem possesses a koranic style and hence indicates its later composition by a Jew refuting Muslim claims. A fragment from the Cairo **Genizah*, signed Samuel of the *Qurayẓa (al-Quraẓi) tribe, had previously been attributed to Samuel ibn ʿĀdiyā. H.Z. Hirschberg, however, presumes that the author wrote this poem during the period of struggle between the Jews and *Muhammad, and therefore is not Samuel ibn ʿĀdiyā. Hirschberg sees the influence of the Jewish *aggadah* and Midrash in Samuel's poetry, rather than their Koranic adaptations. Schwartzbaum perceives these verses as poetic examples of the *Israiʾliyyāt* and *Qiṣaṣ al-Anbiyāʾ* literature. The Muslim–Arab legends are literature which draws upon Jewish aggadic and midrashic sources, and especially upon the Jewish elements in the Koran.

BIBLIOGRAPHY: H. Hirschfeld, in: JQR, o.s. 15 (1903), 167–179; H.Z. Hirschberg, *Yisrael ba-ʿArav* (1946), 242ff.; idem, *Diwan des As-Samauʾal Ibn ʿAdyāʾ* (1931); Baron, Social², 3 (1957), 72f.; I. Lichtenstaedter, in: PAAJR, 10 (1939), 192. **ADD. BIBLIOGRAPHY:** H. Schwartzbaum-Ben-Yaacov, in: *Horev*, 5 (1939), 169–89; A. Goren, in: *Ariel*, 42 (1976), 55–65.

[Shmuel Moreh / Leah Bornstein-Makovetsky (2nd ed.)]

SAMUEL OF EVREUX (also called **Ha-Sar mi-Evreux**, "the prince from Evreux," first half of 13th century), talmudist and tosafist of Normandy. He was apparently a pupil of *Isaac b. Abraham and was also in contact with *Jehiel of Paris and *Nethanel of Chinon, to whom he addressed halakhic problems. The sources (see *Orḥot Ḥayyim and *Kol Bo) speak of his pious customs. Samuel, together with his brothers *Moses and *Isaac, headed the yeshivah of Evreux where, except for a brief stay in Chateau-Thierry, he dwelt most of his life. His halakhic methods are incorporated in the works written jointly with his brothers that were known as *Shitat Evreux* ("the school of Evreux"), and the particular contributions of each brother are not always distinguishable. Samuel's pupils included *Jonah Gerondi, *Isaac of Corbeil, *Perez b. Elijah, and *Meir b. Baruch of Rothenburg.

BIBLIOGRAPHY: Gross, Gal Jud, 39–41, 258; Urbach, Tosafot, index, s.v. *Shemuʾel ben Sheneʾur mi-Evreux*; Y.H. Lipshitz, *Tosafot Evreux* (1969), 29–32.

[Israel Moses Ta-Shma]

SAMUELSON, SIR BERNHARD (1820–1905), British ironmaster and promoter of technical education. Samuelson was born in Hamburg and taken by his father, a merchant, to Hull in England's northeast soon afterwards. By the 1840s he had become a merchant engaged in selling British locomotives and engines in Europe and had acquired considerable engineering knowledge. From 1848 Samuelson was an agricultural implements manufacturer and, after 1853, an ironmaster at Middlesbrough, also in England's northeast. By the end of the 19th century he was one of the largest ironmasters in Britain, and one of the few Jewish entrepreneurs in Britain directly engaged in running a successful heavy industry. Samuelson served as a Liberal member of Parliament in 1859 and from 1865 to 1895. In Parliament he served on many committees and commissions concerned with technical education and did much to advance it in Britain. He was made a baronet (a hereditary knight) in 1884.

BIBLIOGRAPHY: ODNB online; DBB, 5, 46–51.

[William D. Rubinstein (2nd ed.)]

SAMUELSON, PAUL ANTHONY (1915–), U.S. economist. Born in Gary, Indiana, Samuelson received his B.A. from Chicago University in 1935 and his M.A. (1936) and Ph.D. (1941) from Harvard University. He first taught at Harvard (1937) and from 1940 at the Massachusetts Institute of Technology, where he was appointed professor in 1960. From 1941 to 1943 he served as consultant to the National Resources Board, from 1945 to the War Production Board, and from 1945 to 1952 to the U.S. Treasury. In 1948 and 1949 he was chairman of the U.S. President's Task Force for Maintaining American Prosperity. His major interests were economic theory, statistics, business cycles, mathematical programming and econometrics.

In 1970 he was the first American to be awarded the Nobel Prize for Economics for his efforts to "raise the level of scientific analysis in economic theory." From 1966 to 1981 he wrote a regular column in *Newsweek*.

After retiring from teaching, he became professor emeritus at MIT.

Among his many published and widely translated works are *Foundations of Economic Analysis* (1947); *Economics – An Introductory Analysis* (1948, 18th edition 2004), the bestselling economics textbook of all time; *Readings in Economics* (1952, third edition 1958); *Linear Programming and Economic Analysis* (with R. Dorfman and R.M. Solow, 1958); *Stability and Growth in the American Economy* (Stockholm, 1963); *International Economic Relations* (1969); *Economics from the Heart* (1983); and *The Collected Scientific Papers of Paul A. Samuelson* (five volumes, 1966–86).

BIBLIOGRAPHY: *Current Biography Yearbook 1965* (1965), 356–9. **ADD. BIBLIOGRAPHY:** M. Linder and J. Sensat, *The Anti-Samuelson* (2005).

[Joachim O. Ronall / Ruth Beloff (2nd ed.)]

ABBREVIATIONS

GENERAL ABBREVIATIONS

This list contains abbreviations used in the Encyclopaedia (apart from the standard ones, such as geographical abbreviations, points of compass, etc.). For names of organizations, institutions, etc., in abbreviation, see Index. For bibliographical abbreviations of books and authors in Rabbinical literature, see following lists.

*	Cross reference; i.e., an article is to be found under the word(s) immediately following the asterisk (*).
°	Before the title of an entry, indicates a non-Jew (post-biblical times).
‡	Indicates reconstructed forms.
>	The word following this sign is derived from the preceding one.
<	The word preceding this sign is derived from the following one.

ad loc.	*ad locum*, "at the place"; used in quotations of commentaries.
A.H.	*Anno Hegirae*, "in the year of Hegira," i.e., according to the Muslim calendar.
Akk.	Addadian.
A.M.	*anno mundi*, "in the year (from the creation) of the world."
anon.	anonymous.
Ar.	Arabic.
Aram.	Aramaic.
Ass.	Assyrian.
b.	born; *ben, bar.*
Bab.	Babylonian.
B.C.E.	Before Common Era (= B.C.).
bibl.	bibliography.
Bul.	Bulgarian.
c., ca.	Circa.
C.E.	Common Era (= A.D.).
cf.	*confer*, "compare."
ch., chs.	chapter, chapters.
comp.	compiler, compiled by.
Cz.	Czech.
D	according to the documentary theory, the Deuteronomy document.
d.	died.
Dan.	Danish.
diss., dissert,	dissertation, thesis.
Du.	Dutch.
E.	according to the documentary theory, the Elohist document (i.e., using Elohim as the name of God) of the first five (or six) books of the Bible.
ed.	editor, edited, edition.
eds.	editors.
e.g.	*exempli gratia*, "for example."
Eng.	English.
et al.	*et alibi*, "and elsewhere"; or *et alii*, "and others"; "others."
f., ff.	and following page(s).
fig.	figure.
fl.	flourished.
fol., fols	folio(s).
Fr.	French.
Ger.	German.
Gr.	Greek.
Heb.	Hebrew.
Hg., Hung	Hungarian.
ibid	*Ibidem*, "in the same place."
incl. bibl.	includes bibliography.
introd.	introduction.
It.	Italian.
J	according to the documentary theory, the Jahwist document (i.e., using YHWH as the name of God) of the first five (or six) books of the Bible.
Lat.	Latin.
lit.	literally.
Lith.	Lithuanian.
loc. cit.	*loco citato*, "in the [already] cited place."
Ms., Mss.	Manuscript(s).
n.	note.
n.d.	no date (of publication).
no., nos	number(s).
Nov.	Novellae (Heb. *Ḥiddushim*).
n.p.	place of publication unknown.
op. cit.	*opere citato*, "in the previously mentioned work."
P.	according to the documentary theory, the Priestly document of the first five (or six) books of the Bible.
p., pp.	page(s).
Pers.	Persian.
pl., pls.	plate(s).
Pol.	Polish.
Port.	Potuguese.
pt., pts.	part(s).
publ.	published.
R.	Rabbi or Rav (before names); in Midrash (after an abbreviation) – *Rabbah*.
r.	recto, the first side of a manuscript page.
Resp.	Responsa (Latin "answers," Hebrew *She'elot u-Teshuvot* or *Teshuvot*), collections of rabbinic decisions.
rev.	revised.

Rom.	Romanian.
Rus(s).	Russian.
Slov.	Slovak.
Sp.	Spanish.
s.v.	*sub verbo, sub voce*, "under the (key) word."
Sum	Sumerian.
summ.	Summary.
suppl.	supplement.
Swed.	Swedish.
tr., trans(l).	translator, translated, translation.
Turk.	Turkish.
Ukr.	Ukrainian.
v., vv.	*verso*. The second side of a manuscript page; also verse(s).
Yid.	Yiddish.

ABBREVIATIONS USED IN RABBINICAL LITERATURE

Adderet Eliyahu, Karaite treatise by Elijah b. Moses *Bashyazi.
Admat Kodesh, Resp. by Nissim Ḥayyim Moses b. Joseph |Mizraḥi.
Aguddah, Sefer ha-, Nov. by *Alexander Suslin ha-Kohen.
Ahavat Ḥesed, compilation by *Israel Meir ha-Kohen.
Aliyyot de-Rabbenu Yonah, Nov. by *Jonah b. Avraham Gerondi.
Arukh ha-Shulḥan, codification by Jehiel Michel *Epstein.
Asayin (= positive precepts), subdivision of: (1) *Maimonides, *Sefer ha-Mitzvot;* (2) *Moses b. Jacob of Coucy, *Semag.*
Asefat Dinim, subdivision of *Sedei Ḥemed* by Ḥayyim Hezekiah *Medini, an encyclopaedia of precepts and responsa.
Asheri = *Asher b. Jehiel.
Aeret Ḥakhamim, by Baruch *Frankel-Teomim; pt, 1: Resp. to Sh. Ar.; pt2: Nov. to Talmud.
Ateret Zahav, subdivision of the *Levush*, a codification by Mordecai b. Abraham (Levush) *Jaffe; *Ateret Zahav* parallels Tur. YD.
Ateret Ẓevi, Comm. To Sh. Ar. by Ẓevi Hirsch b. Azriel.
Avir Ya'akov, Resp. by Jacob Avigdor.
Avkat Rokhel, Resp. by Joseph b. Ephraim *Caro.
Avnei Millu'im, Comm. to Sh. Ar., EH, by *Aryeh Loeb b. Joseph ha-Kohen.
Avnei Nezer, Resp. on Sh. Ar. by Abraham b. Ze'ev Nahum Bornstein of *Sochaczew.
Avodat Massa, Compilation of Tax Law by Yoasha Abraham Judah.
Azei ha-Levanon, Resp. by Judah Leib *Zirelson.

Ba'al ha-Tanya – *Shneur Zalman of Lyady.
Ba'ei Ḥayyei, Resp. by Ḥayyim b. Israel *Benveniste.
Ba'er Heitev, Comm. To Sh. Ar. The parts on OḤ and EH are by Judah b. Simeon *Ashkenazi, the parts on YD AND ḤM by *Zechariah Mendel b. Aryeh Leib. Printed in most editions of Sh. Ar.
Baḥ = Joel *Sirkes.
Baḥ, usual abbreviation for *Bayit Ḥadash*, a commentary on Tur by Joel *Sirkes; printed in most editions of Tur.
Bayit Ḥadash, see *Baḥ*.
Berab = Jacob Berab, also called Ri Berav.
Bedek ha-Bayit, by Joseph b. Ephraim *Caro, additions to his *Beit Yosef* (a comm. to Tur). Printed sometimes inside *Beit Yosef*, in smaller type. Appears in most editions of Tur.
Be'er ha-Golah, Commentary to Sh. Ar. By Moses b. Naphtali Hirsch *Rivkes; printed in most editions of Sh. Ar.
Be'er Mayim, Resp. by Raphael b. Abraham Manasseh Jacob.
Be'er Mayim Ḥayyim, Resp. by Samuel b. Ḥayyim *Vital.
Be'er Yiẓḥak, Resp. by Isaac Elhanan *Spector.
Beit ha-Beḥirah, Comm. to Talmud by Menahem b. Solomon *Meiri.
Beit Me'ir, Nov. on Sh. Ar. by Meir b. Judah Leib Posner.
Beit Shelomo, Resp. by Solomon b. Aaron Ḥason (the younger).
Beit Shemu'el, Comm. to Sh. Ar., EH, by *Samuel b. Uri Shraga Phoebus.
Beit Ya'akov, by Jacob b. Jacob Moses *Lorberbaum; pt.1: Nov. to Ket.; pt.2: Comm. to EH.
Beit Yisrael, collective name for the commentaries *Derishah, Perishah,* and *Be'urim* by Joshua b. Alexander ha-Kohen *Falk. See under the names of the commentaries.
Beit Yiẓḥak, Resp. by Isaac *Schmelkes.
Beit Yosef: (1) Comm. on Tur by Joseph b. Ephraim *Caro; printed in most editions of Tur; (2) Resp. by the same.
Ben Yehudah, Resp. by Abraham b. Judah Litsch (ליטש) Rosenbaum.
Bertinoro, Standard commentary to Mishnah by Obadiah *Bertinoro. Printed in most editions of the Mishnah.
[Be'urei] Ha-Gra, Comm. to Bible, Talmud, and Sh. Ar. By *Elijah b. Solomon Zalmon (Gaon of Vilna); printed in major editions of the mentioned works.
Be'urim, Glosses to Isserles *Darkhei Moshe* (a comm. on Tur) by Joshua b. Alexander ha-Kohen *Falk; printed in many editions of Tur.
Binyamin Ze'ev, Resp. by *Benjamin Ze'ev b. Mattathias of Arta.
Birkei Yosef, Nov. by Ḥayyim Joseph David *Azulai.
Ha-Buẓ ve-ha-Argaman, subdivision of the *Levush* (a codification by Mordecai b. Abraham (Levush) *Jaffe); *Ha-Buẓ ve-ha-Argaman* parallels Tur, EH.

Comm. = Commentary

Da'at Kohen, Resp. by Abraham Isaac ha-Kohen. *Kook.
Darkhei Moshe, Comm. on Tur Moses b. Israel *Isserles; printed in most editions of Tur.
Darkhei No'am, Resp. by *Mordecai b. Judah ha-Levi.
Darkhei Teshuvah, Nov. by Ẓevi *Shapiro; printed in the major editions of Sh. Ar.
De'ah ve-Haskel, Resp. by Obadiah Hadaya (see *Yaskil Avdi).*

Derashot Ran, Sermons by *Nissim b. Reuben Gerondi.
Derekh Ḥayyim, Comm. to *Avot* by *Judah Loew (Lob., Liwa) b. Bezalel (Maharal) of Prague.
Derishah, by Joshua b. Alexander ha-Kohen *Falk; additions to his *Perishah* (comm. on Tur); printed in many editions of Tur.
Derushei ha-Ẓelaḥ, Sermons, by Ezekiel b. Judah Halevi *Landau.
Devar Avraham, Resp. by Abraham *Shapira.
Devar Shemu'el, Resp. by Samuel *Aboab.
Devar Yehoshu'a, Resp. by Joshua Menahem b. Isaac Aryeh Ehrenberg.
Dikdukei Soferim, variae lections of the talmudic text by Raphael Nathan*Rabbinowicz.
Divrei Emet, Resp. by Isaac Bekhor David.
Divrei Ge'onim, Digest of responsa by Ḥayyim Aryeh b. Jeḥiel Ẓevi *Kahana.
Divrei Ḥamudot, Comm. on *Piskei ha-Rosh* by Yom Tov Lipmann b. Nathan ha-Levi *Heller; printed in major editions of the Talmud.
Divrei Ḥayyim several works by Ḥayyim *Halberstamm; if quoted alone refers to his Responsa.
Divrei Malkhi'el, Resp. by Malchiel Tenebaum.
Divrei Rivot, Resp. by Isaac b. Samuel *Adarbi.
Divrei Shemu'el, Resp. by Samuel Raphael Arditi.

Edut be-Ya'akov, Resp. by Jacob b. Abraham *Boton.
Edut bi-Yhosef, Resp. by Joseph b. Isaac *Almosnino.
Ein Ya'akov, Digest of talmudic *aggadot* by Jacob (Ibn) *Habib.
Ein Yiẓḥak, Resp. by Isaac Elhanan *Spector.
Ephraim of Lentshitz = Solomon *Luntschitz.
Erekh Leḥem, Nov. and glosses to Sh. Ar. by Jacob b. Abraham *Castro.
Eshkol, Sefer ha-, Digest of *halakhot* by *Abraham b. Isaac of Narbonne.
Et Sofer, Treatise on Law Court documents by Abraham b. Mordecai *Ankawa, in the 2nd vol. of his Resp. *Kerem Ḥamar.*
Etan ha-Ezraḥi, Resp. by Abraham b. Israel Jehiel (Shrenzl) *Rapaport.
Even ha-Ezel, Nov. to Maimonides' *Yad Ḥazakah* by Isser Zalman *Meltzer.
Even ha-Ezer, also called *Raban* of *Ẓafenat Pa'ne'aḥ,* rabbinical work with varied contents by *Eliezer b. Nathan of Mainz; not identical with the subdivision of Tur, Shulḥan Arukh, etc.
Ezrat Yehudah, Resp. by *Isaar Judah b. Nechemiah of Brisk.

Gan Eden, Karaite treatise by *Aaron b. Elijah of Nicomedia.
Gersonides = *Levi b. Gershom, also called Leo Hebraecus, or Ralbag.
Ginnat Veradim, Resp. by *Abraham b. Mordecai ha-Levi.

Haggahot, another name for *Rema.*
Haggahot Asheri, glosses to *Piskei ha-Rosh* by *Israel of Krems; printed in most Talmud editions.
Haggahot Maimuniyyot, Comm,. to Maimonides' Yad Ḥazakah by *Meir ha-Kohen; printed in most eds. of Yad.
Haggahot Mordekhai, glosses to *Mordekhai* by Samuel *Schlettstadt; printed in most editions of the Talmud after *Mordekhai.*
Haggahot ha-Rashash on Tosafot, annotations of Samuel *Strashun on the Tosafot (printed in major editions of the Talmud).
Ha-Gra = *Elijah b. Solomon Zalman (Gaon of Vilna).
Ha-Gra, Commentaries on Bible, Talmud, and Sh. Ar. respectively, by *Elijah b. Solomon Zalman (Gaon of Vilna); printed in major editions of the mentioned works.
Hai Gaon, Comm. = his comm. on Mishnah.
Ḥakham Ẓevi, Resp. by Ẓevi Hirsch b. Jacob *Ashkenazi.
Halakhot = Rif, *Halakhot.* Compilation and abstract of the Talmud by Isaac b. Jacob ha-Kohen *Alfasi; printed in most editions of the Talmud.
Halakhot Gedolot, compilation of *halakhot* from the Geonic period, arranged acc. to the Talmud. Here cited acc. to ed. Warsaw (1874). Author probably *Simeon Kayyara of Basra.
Halakhot Pesukot le-Rav Yehudai Ga'on compilation of *halakhot.*
Halakhot Pesukot min ha-Ge'onim, compilation of *halakhot* from the geonic period by different authors.
Ḥananel, Comm. to Talmud by *Hananel b. Ḥushi'el; printed in some editions of the Talmud.
Harei Besamim, Resp. by Aryeh Leib b. Isaac *Horowitz.
Ḥassidim, Sefer, Ethical maxims by *Judah b. Samuel he-Ḥasid.
Hassagot Rabad on Rif, Glosses on Rif, *Halakhot,* by *Abraham b. David of Posquières.
Hassagot Rabad [on Yad], Glosses on Maimonides, *Yad Ḥazakah,* by *Abraham b. David of Posquières.
Hassagot Ramban, Glosses by Naḥmanides on Maimonides' *Sefer ha-Mitzvot;* usually printed together with *Sefer ha-Mitzvot.*
Ḥatam Sofer = Moses *Sofer.
Ḥavvot Ya'ir, Resp. and varia by Jair Ḥayyim *Bacharach
Ḥayyim Or Zaru'a = *Ḥayyim (Eliezer) b. Isaac.
Ḥazon Ish = Abraham Isaiah *Karelitz.
Ḥazon Ish, Nov. by Abraham Isaiah *Karelitz
Ḥedvat Ya'akov, Resp. by Aryeh Judah Jacob b. David Dov Meisels (article under his father's name).
Heikhal Yiẓḥak, Resp. by Isaac ha-Levi *Herzog.
Ḥelkat Meḥokek, Comm. to Sh. Ar., by Moses b. Isaac Judah *Lima.
Ḥelkat Ya'akov, Resp. by Mordecai Jacob Breisch.
Ḥemdah Genuzah, , Resp. from the geonic period by different authors.
Ḥemdat Shelomo, Resp. by Solomon Zalman *Lipschitz.
Ḥida = Ḥayyim Joseph David *Azulai.
Ḥiddushei Halakhot ve-Aggadot, Nov. by Samuel Eliezer b. Judah ha-Levi *Edels.
Ḥikekei Lev, Resp. by Ḥayyim *Palaggi.
Ḥikrei Lev, Nov. to Sh. Ar. by Joseph Raphael b. Ḥayyim Joseph Ḥazzan (see article *Ḥazzan Family).
Hil. = Hilkhot … (e.g. *Hilkhot Shabbat).*
Ḥinnukh, Sefer ha-, List and explanation of precepts attributed (probably erroneously) to Aaron ha-Levi of Barcelona (see article **Ha-Ḥinnukh*).
Ḥok Ya'akov, Comm. to Hil. Pesaḥ in Sh. Ar., OḤ, by Jacob b. Joseph *Reicher.
Ḥokhmat Sehlomo (1), Glosses to Talmud, *Rashi* and Tosafot by Solomon b. Jehiel "Maharshal") *Luria; printed in many editions of the Talmud.
Ḥokhmat Sehlomo (2), Glosses and Nov. to Sh. Ar. by Solomon b. Judah Aaron *Kluger printed in many editions of Sh. Ar.
Ḥur, subdivision of the *Levush,* a codification by Mordecai b. Abraham (Levush) *Jaffe; *Hur* (or *Levush ha-Hur)* parallels Tur, OḤ, 242–697.
Ḥut ha-Meshullash, fourth part of the *Tashbeẓ* (Resp.), by Simeon b. Zemaḥ *Duran.

Ibn Ezra, Comm. to the Bible by Abraham *Ibn Ezra; printed in the major editions of the Bible *("Mikra'ot Gedolot").*
Imrei Yosher, Resp. by Meir b. Aaron Judah *Arik.
Ir Shushan, Subdivision of the *Levush,* a codification by Mordecai b. Abraham (Levush) *Jaffe; *Ir Shushan* parallels Tur, ḤM.
Israel of Bruna = Israel b. Ḥayyim *Bruna.
Ittur. Treatise on precepts by *Isaac b. Abba Mari of Marseilles.

Jacob Be Rab = *Be Rab.
Jacob b. Jacob Moses of Lissa = Jacob b. Jacob Moses *Lorberbaum.
Judah B. Simeon = Judah b. Simeon *Ashkenazi.
Judah Minz = Judah b. Eliezer ha-Levi *Minz.

Kappei Aharon, Resp. by Aaron Azriel.
Kehillat Ya'akov, Talmudic methodology, definitions etc. by Israel Jacob b. Yom Tov *Algazi.
Kelei Ḥemdah, Nov. and *pilpulim* by Meir Dan *Plotzki of Ostrova, arranged acc. to the Torah.
Keli Yakar, Annotations to the Torah by Solomon *Luntschitz.
Keneh Ḥokhmah, Sermons by Judah Loeb *Pochwitzer.
Keneset ha-Gedolah, Digest of *halakhot* by Ḥayyim b. Israel *Benveniste; subdivided into annotations to *Beit Yosef* and annotations to Tur.
Keneset Yisrael, Resp. by Ezekiel b. Abraham Katzenellenbogen (see article *Katzenellenbogen Family).
Kerem Ḥamar, Resp. and varia by Abraham b. Mordecai *Ankawa.
Kerem Shelmo. Resp. by Solomon b. Joseph *Amarillo.
Keritut, [Sefer], Methodology of the Talmud by *Samson b. Isaac of Chinon.
Kesef ha-Kedoshim, Comm. to Sh. Ar., ḤM, by Abraham *Wahrmann; printed in major editions of Sh. Ar.
Kesef Mishneh, Comm. to Maimonides, *Yad Ḥazakah,* by Joseph b. Ephraim *Caro; printed in most editions of *Yad Ḥazakah.*
Keẓot ha-Ḥoshen, Comm. to Sh. Ar., ḤM, by *Aryeh Loeb b. Joseph ha-Kohen; printed in major editions of Sh. Ar.
Kol Bo [*Sefer*], Anonymous collection of ritual rules; also called *Sefer ha-Likkutim.*
Kol Mevasser, Resp. by Meshullam *Rath.
Korban Aharon, Comm. to *Sifra* by Aaron b. Abraham *Ibn Ḥayyim; pt. 1 is called: *Middot Aharon.*
Korban Edah, Comm. to Jer. Talmud by David *Fraenkel; with additions: *Shiyyurei Korban;* printed in most editions of Jer. Talmud.
Kunteres ha-Kelalim, subdivision of *Sedei Ḥemed,* an encyclopaedia of precepts and responsa by Ḥayyim Hezekiah *Medini.
Kunteres ha-Semikhah, a treatise by *Levi b. Ḥabib; printed at the end of his responsa.
Kunteres Tikkun Olam, part of *Mispat Shalom* (Nov. by Shalom Mordecai b. Moses *Schwadron).

Lavin (negative precepts), subdivision of: (1) *Maimonides, *Sefer ha-Mitzvot;* (2) *Moses b. Jacob of Coucy, *Semag.*
Leḥem Mishneh, Comm. to Maimonides, *Yad Ḥazakah,* by Abraham [Ḥiyya] b. Moses *Boton; printed in most editions of *Yad Ḥazakah.*
Leḥem Rav, Resp. by Abraham [Ḥiyya] b. Moses *Boton.
Leket Yosher, Resp and varia by Israel b. Pethahiah *Isserlein, collected by *Joseph (Joselein) b. Moses.
Leo Hebraeus = *Levi b. Gershom, also called Ralbag or Gersonides.
Levush = Mordecai b. Abraham *Jaffe.
Levush [Malkhut], Codification by Mordecai b. Abraham (Levush) *Jaffe, with subdivisions: *[Levush ha-] Tekhelet* (parallels Tur OḤ 1–241); *[Levush ha-] Ḥur* (parallels Tur OḤ 242–697); *[Levush] Ateret Zahav* (parallels Tur YD); *[Levush ha-Buẓ ve-ha-Argaman* (parallels Tur EH); *[Levush] Ir Shushan* (parallels Tur ḤM); under the name *Levush* the author wrote also other works.
Li-Leshonot ha-Rambam, fifth part (nos. 1374–1700) of Resp. by *David b. Solomon ibn Abi Zimra (Radbaz).
Likkutim, Sefer ha-, another name for *[Sefer] Kol Bo.*

Ma'adanei Yom Tov, Comm. on *Piskei ha-Rosh* by Yom Tov Lipmann b. Nathan ha-Levi *Heller; printed in many editions of the Talmud.
Mabit = Moses b. Joseph *Trani.
Magen Avot, Comm. to *Avot* by Simeon b. Ẓemaḥ *Duran.
Magen Avraham, Comm. to Sh. Ar., OḤ, by Abraham Abele b. Ḥayyim ha-Levi *Gombiner; printed in many editions of Sh. Ar., OḤ.
Maggid Mishneh, Comm. to Maimonides, *Yad Ḥazakah,* by *Vidal Yom Tov of Tolosa; printed in most editions of the *Yad Ḥazakah.*
Maḥaneh Efrayim, Resp. and Nov., arranged acc. to Maimonides' *Yad Ḥazakah* , by Ephraim b. Aaron *Navon.
Maharai = Israel b. Pethahiah *Isserlein.
Maharal of Prague = *Judah Loew (Lob, Liwa), b. Bezalel.
Maharalbaḥ = *Levi b. Ḥabib.
Maharam Alashkar = Moses b. Isaac *Alashkar.
Maharam Alshekh = Moses b. Ḥayyim *Alashekh.
Maharam Mintz = Moses *Mintz.
Maharam of Lublin = *Meir b. Gedaliah of Lublin.
Maharam of Padua = Meir *Katzenellenbogen.
Maharam of Rothenburg = *Meir b. Baruch of Rothenburg.
Maharam Shik = Moses b. Joseph Schick.
Maharash Engel = Samuel b. Ze'ev Wolf Engel.
Maharashdam = Samuel b. Moses *Medina.
Maharḥash = Ḥayyim (ben) Shabbetai.
Mahari Basan = Jehiel b. Ḥayyim Basan.
Mahari b. Lev = Joseph ibn Lev.
Mahari'az = Jekuthiel Asher Zalman Ensil Zusmir.
Maharibal = *Joseph ibn Lev.
Mahariḥ = Jacob (Israel) *Ḥagiz.
Maharik = Joseph b. Solomon *Colon.
Maharikash = Jacob b. Abraham *Castro.
Maharil = Jacob b. Moses *Moellin.
Maharimat = Joseph b. Moses di Trani (not identical with the Maharit).
Maharit = Joseph b. Moses *Trani.
Maharitaẓ = Yom Tov b. Akiva Ẓahalon. (See article *Ẓahalon Family).
Maharsha = Samuel Eliezer b. Judah ha-Levi *Edels.
Maharshag = Simeon b. Judah Gruenfeld.
Maharshak = Samson b. Isaac of Chinon.
Maharshakh = *Solomon b. Abraham.
Maharshal = Solomon b. Jeḥiel *Luria.
Mahasham = Shalom Mordecai b. Moses *Sschwadron.
Maharyu = Jacob b. Judah *Weil.
Maḥazeh Avraham, Resp. by Abraham Nebagen v. Meir ha-Levi Steinberg.
Maḥazik Berakhah, Nov. by Ḥayyim Joseph David *Azulai.

*Maimonides = Moses b. Maimon, or Rambam.
*Malbim = Meir Loeb b. Jehiel Michael.
Malbim = Malbim's comm. to the Bible; printed in the major editions.
Malbushei Yom Tov, Nov. on *Levush*, OḤ, by Yom Tov Lipmann b. Nathan ha-Levi *Heller.
Mappah, another name for *Rema.*
Mareh ha-Panim, Comm. to Jer. Talmud by Moses b. Simeon *Margolies; printed in most editions of Jer. Talmud.
Margaliyyot ha-Yam, Nov. by Reuben *Margoliot.
Masat Binyamin, Resp. by Benjamin Aaron b. Abraham *Slonik
Mashbir, Ha- = *Joseph Samuel b. Isaac Rodi.
Massa Ḥayyim, Tax *halakhot* by Ḥayyim *Palaggi, with the subdivisions *Missim ve-Arnomiyyot* and *Torat ha-Minhagot.*
Massa Melekh, Compilation of Tax Law by Joseph b. Isaac *Ibn Ezra with concluding part *Ne'ilat She'arim.*
Matteh Asher, Resp. by Asher b. Emanuel Shalem.
Matteh Shimon, Digest of Resp. and Nov. to Tur and *Beit Yosef,* ḤM, by Mordecai Simeon b. Solomon.
Matteh Yosef, Resp. by Joseph b. Moses ha-Levi Nazir (see article under his father's name).
Mayim Amukkim, Resp. by Elijah b. Abraham *Mizraḥi.
Mayim Ḥayyim, Resp. by Ḥayyim b. Dov Beresh Rapaport.
Mayim Rabbim, , Resp. by Raphael *Meldola.
Me-Emek ha-Bakha, , Resp. by Simeon b. Jekuthiel Ephrati.
Me'irat Einayim, usual abbreviation: *Sma* (from: *Sefer Me'irat Einayim*); comm. to Sh. Ar. By Joshua b. Alexander ha-Kohen *Falk; printed in most editions of the Sh. Ar.
Melammed le-Ho'il, Resp. by David Ẓevi *Hoffmann.
Meisharim, [*Sefer*], Rabbinical treatise by *Jeroham b. Meshullam.
Meshiv Davar, Resp. by Naphtali Ẓevi Judah *Berlin.
Mi-Gei ha-Haregah, Resp. by Simeon b. Jekuthiel Ephrati.
Mi-Ma'amakim, Resp. by Ephraim Oshry.
Middot Aharon, first part of *Korban Aharon,* a comm. to *Sifra* by Aaron b. Abraham *Ibn Ḥayyim.
Migdal Oz, Comm. to Maimonides, *Yad Ḥazakah,* by *Ibn Gaon Shem Tov b. Abraham; printed in most editions of the *Yad Ḥazakah.*
Mikhtam le-David, Resp. by David Samuel b. Jacob *Pardo.
Mikkaḥ ve-ha-Mimkar, Sefer ha-, Rabbinical treatise by *Hai Gaon.
Milḥamot ha-Shem, Glosses to Rif, *Halakhot,* by *Naḥmanides.
Minḥat Ḥinnukh, Comm. to *Sefer ha-Ḥinnukh,* by Joseph b. Moses *Babad.
Minḥat Yiẓḥak, Resp. by Isaac Jacob b. Joseph Judah Weiss.
Misgeret ha-Shulḥan, Comm. to Sh. Ar., ḤM, by Benjamin Ze'ev Wolf b. Shabbetai; printed in most editions of Sh. Ar.
Mishkenot ha-Ro'im, Halakhot in alphabetical order by Uzziel Alshekh.
Mishnah Berurah, Comm. to Sh. Ar., OḤ, by *Israel Meir ha-Kohen.
Mishneh le-Melekh, Comm. to Maimonides, *Yad Ḥazakah,* by Judah *Rosanes; printed in most editions of *Yad Ḥazakah.*
Mishpat ha-Kohanim, Nov. to Sh. Ar., ḤM, by Jacob Moses *Lorberbaum, part of his *Netivot ha-Mishpat;* printed in major editions of Sh. Ar.
Mishpat Kohen, Resp. by Abraham Isaac ha-Kohen *Kook.
Mishpat Shalom, Nov. by Shalom Mordecai b. Moses *Schwadron; contains: *Kunteres Tikkun Olam.*
Mishpat u-Ẓedakah be-Ya'akov, Resp. by Jacob b. Reuben *Ibn Ẓur.
Mishpat ha-Urim, Comm. to Sh. Ar., ḤM by Jacob b. Jacob Moses *Lorberbaum, part of his *Netivot ha-Mishpat;* printed in major editons of Sh. Ar.
Mishpat Ẓedek, Resp. by *Melammed Meir b. Shem Tov.
Mishpatim Yesharim, Resp. by Raphael b. Mordecai *Berdugo.
Mishpetei Shemu'el, Resp. by Samuel b. Moses *Kalai (Kal'i).
Mishpetei ha-Tanna'im, Kunteres, Nov on *Levush,* OḤ by Yom Tov Lipmann b. Nathan ha-Levi *Heller.
Mishpetei Uzzi'el (Uziel), Resp. by Ben-Zion Meir Hai *Ouziel.
Missim ve-Arnoniyyot, Tax *halakhot* by Ḥayyim *Palaggi, a subdivision of his work *Massa Ḥayyim* on the same subject.
Mitzvot, Sefer ha-, Elucidation of precepts by *Maimonides; subdivided into *Lavin* (negative precepts) and *Asayin* (positive precepts).
Mitzvot Gadol, Sefer, Elucidation of precepts by *Moses b. Jacob of Coucy, subdivided into *Lavin* (negative precepts) and *Asayin* (positive precepts); the usual abbreviation is *Semag.*
Mitzvot Katan, Sefer, Elucidation of precepts by *Isaac b. Joseph of Corbeil; the usual, abbreviation is *Semak.*
Mo'adim u-Zemannim, Rabbinical treatises by Moses Sternbuch.
Modigliano, Joseph Samuel = *Joseph Samuel b. Isaac, Rodi (Ha-Mashbir).
Mordekhai (Mordecai), halakhic compilation by *Mordecai b. Hillel; printed in most editions of the Talmud after the texts.
Moses b. Maimon = *Maimonides, also called Rambam.
Moses b. Naḥman = Naḥmanides, also called Ramban.
Muram = Isaiah Menahem b. Isaac (from: Morenu R. Mendel).

Naḥal Yiẓḥak, Comm. on Sh. Ar., ḤM, by Isaac Elhanan *Spector.
Naḥalah li-Yhoshu'a, Resp. by Joshua Ẓunẓin.
Naḥalat Shivah, collection of legal forms by *Samuel b. David Moses ha-Levi.
*Naḥmanides = Moses b. Naḥman, also called Ramban.
Naẓiv = Naphtali Ẓevi Judah *Berlin.
Ne'eman Shemu'el, Resp. by Samuel Isaac *Modigilano.
Ne'ilat She'arim, concluding part of *Massa Melekh* (a work on Tax Law) by Joseph b. Isaac *Ibn Ezra, containing an exposition of customary law and subdivided into *Minhagei Issur* and *Minhagei Mamon.*
Ner Ma'aravi, Resp. by Jacob b. Malka.
Netivot ha-Mishpat, by Jacob b. Jacob Moses *Lorberbaum; subdivided into *Mishpat ha-Kohanim,* Nov. to Sh. Ar., ḤM, and *Mishpat ha-Urim,* a comm. on the same; printed in major editions of Sh. Ar.
Netivot Olam, Saying of the Sages by *Judah Loew (Lob, Liwa) b. Bezalel.
Nimmukei Menaḥem of Merseburg, Tax *halakhot* by the same, printed at the end of Resp. Maharyu.
Nimmukei Yosef, Comm. to Rif. *Halakhot,* by Joseph *Ḥabib (Ḥabiba); printed in many editions of the Talmud.
Noda bi-Yhudah, Resp. by Ezekiel b. Judah ha-Levi *Landau; there is a first collection *(Mahadura Kamma)* and a second collection *(Mahadura Tinyana).*
Nov. = Novellae, Ḥiddushim.

Ohel Moshe (1), Notes to Talmud, *Midrash Rabbah,* Yad, *Sifrei* and to several Resp., by Eleazar *Horowitz.

Ohel Moshe (2), Resp. by Moses Jonah Zweig.
Oholei Tam. Resp. by *Tam ibn Yaḥya Jacob b. David; printed in the rabbinical collection *Tummat Yesharim.*
Oholei Ya'akov, Resp. by Jacob de *Castro.
Or ha-Me'ir Resp by Judah Meir b. Jacob Samson Shapiro.
Or Same'aḥ, Comm. to Maimonides, *Yad Ḥazakah,* by *Meir Simḥah ha-Kohen of Dvinsk; printed in many editions of the *Yad Ḥazakah.*
Or Zaru'a [the father] = *Isaac b. Moses of Vienna.
Or Zaru'a [the son] = *Ḥayyim (Eliezer) b. Isaac.
Or Zaru'a, Nov. by *Isaac b. Moses of Vienna.
Orah, Sefer ha-, Compilation of ritual precepts by *Rashi.
Oraḥ la-Ẓaddik, Resp. by Abraham Ḥayyim Rodrigues.
Oẓar ha-Posekim, Digest of Responsa.

Paḥad Yiẓḥak, Rabbinical encyclopaedia by Isaac *Lampronti.
Panim Me'irot, Resp. by Meir b. Isaac *Eisenstadt.
Parashat Mordekhai, Resp. by Mordecai b. Abraham Naphtali *Banet.
Pe'at ha-Sadeh la-Dinim and Pe'at ha-Sadeh la-Kelalim, subdivisions of the *Sedei Ḥemed,* an encyclopaedia of precepts and responsa, by Ḥayyim Hezekaih *Medini.
Penei Moshe (1), Resp. by Moses *Benveniste.
Penei Moshe (2), Comm. to Jer. Talmud by Moses b. Simeon *Margolies; printed in most editions of the Jer. Talmud.
Penei Moshe (3), Comm. on the aggadic passages of 18 treatises of the Bab. and Jer. Talmud, by Moses b. Isaiah Katz.
Penei Yehoshu'a, Nov. by Jacob Joshua b. Ẓevi Hirsch *Falk.
Peri Ḥadash, Comm. on Sh. Ar. By Hezekiah da *Silva.
Perishah, Comm. on Tur by Joshua b. Alexander ha-Kohen *Falk; printed in major edition of Tur; forms together with *Derishah* and *Be'urim* (by the same author) the *Beit Yisrael.*
Pesakim u-Khetavim, 2nd part of the *Terumat ha-Deshen* by Israel b. Pethahiah *Isserlein' also called *Piskei Maharai.*
Pilpula Ḥarifta, Comm. to *Piskei ha-Rosh, Seder Nezikin,* by Yom Tov Lipmann b. Nathan ha-Levi *Heller; printed in major editions of the Talmud.
Piskei Maharai, see *Terumat ha-Deshen,* 2nd part; also called *Pesakim u-Khetavim.*
Piskei ha-Rosh, a compilation of *halakhot,* arranged on the Talmud, by *Asher b. Jehiel (Rosh); printed in major Talmud editions.
Pitḥei Teshuvah, Comm. to Sh. Ar. by Abraham Hirsch b. Jacob *Eisenstadt; printed in major editions of the Sh. Ar.

Rabad = *Abraham b. David of Posquières (Rabad III.).
Raban = *Eliezer b. Nathan of Mainz.
Raban, also called *Ẓafenat Pa'ne'aḥ* or *Even ha-Ezer,* see under the last name.
Rabi Abad = *Abraham b. Isaac of Narbonne.
Radad = David Dov. b. Aryeh Judah Jacob *Meisels.
Radam = Dov Berush b. Isaac Meisels.
Radbaz = *David b Solomon ibn Abi Ziumra.
Radbaz, Comm. to Maimonides, *Yad Ḥazakah,* by *David b. Solomon ibn Abi Zimra.
Ralbag = *Levi b. Gershom, also called Gersonides, or Leo Hebraeus.
Ralbag, Bible comm. by *Levi b. Gershon.
Rama [da Fano] = Menaḥem Azariah *Fano.
Ramah = Meir b. Todros [ha-Levi] *Abulafia.
Ramam = *Menaham of Merseburg.
Rambam = *Maimonides; real name: Moses b. Maimon.
Ramban = *Naḥmanides; real name Moses b. Naḥman.
Ramban, Comm. to Torah by *Naḥmanides; printed in major editions. ("Mikra'ot Gedolot").
Ran = *Nissim b. Reuben Gerondi.
Ran of Rif, Comm. on Rif, *Halakhot,* by Nissim b. Reuben Gerondi.
Ranaḥ = *Elijah b. Ḥayyim.
Rash = *Samson b. Abraham of Sens.
Rash, Comm. to Mishnah, by *Samson b. Abraham of Sens; printed in major Talmud editions.
Rashash = Samuel *Strashun.
Rashba = Solomon b. Abraham *Adret.
Rashba, Resp., see also; *Sefer Teshuvot ha-Rashba ha-Meyuḥasot le-ha-Ramban,* by Solomon b. Abraham *Adret.
Rashbad = Samuel b. David.
Rashbam = *Samuel b. Meir.
Rashbam = Comm. on Bible and Talmud by *Samuel b. Meir; printed in major editions of Bible and most editions of Talmud.
Rashbash = Solomon b. Simeon *Duran.
*Rashi = Solomon b. Isaac of Troyes.
Rashi, Comm. on Bible and Talmud by *Rashi; printed in almost all Bible and Talmud editions.
Raviah = Eliezer b. Joel ha-Levi.
Redak = David *Kimḥi.
Redak, Comm. to Bible by David *Kimḥi.
Redakh = *David b. Ḥayyim ha-Kohen of Corfu.
Re'em = Elijah b. Abraham *Mizraḥi.
Rema = Moses b. Israel *Isserles.
Rema, Glosses to Sh. Ar. by Moses b. Israel *Isserles; printed in almost all editions of the Sh. Ar. inside the text in Rashi type; also called *Mappah* or *Haggahot.*
Remek = Moses Kimḥi.
Remakh = Moses ha-Kohen mi-Lunel.
Reshakh = *Solomon b. Abraham; also called Maharshakh.
Resp. = Responsa, *She'elot u-Teshuvot.*
Ri Berav = *Berab.
Ri Escapa = Joseph b. Saul *Escapa.
Ri Migash = Joseph b. Meir ha-Levi *Ibn Migash.
Riba = Isaac b. Asher ha-Levi; Riba II (Riba ha-Baḥur) = his grandson with the same name.
Ribam = Isaac b. Mordecai (or: Isaac b. Meir).
Ribash = *Isaac b. Sheshet Perfet (or: Barfat).
Rid= *Isaiah b. Mali di Trani the Elder.
Ridbaz = Jacob David b. Ze'ev *Willowski.
Rif = Isaac b. Jacob ha-Kohen *Alfasi.
Rif, *Halakhot,* Compilation and abstract of the Talmud by Isaac b. Jacob ha-Kohen *Alfasi.
Ritba = Yom Tov b. Abraham *Ishbili.
Riẓbam = Isaac b. Mordecai.
Rosh = *Asher b. Jehiel, also called Asheri.
Rosh Mashbir, Resp. by *Joseph Samuel b. Isaac, Rodi.

Sedei Ḥemed, Encyclopaedia of precepts and responsa by Ḥayyim Ḥezekiah *Medini; subdivisions: *Asefat Dinim, Kunteres ha-Kelalim, Pe'at ha-Sadeh la-Dinim, Pe'at ha-Sadeh la-Kelalim.*
Semag, Usual abbreviation of *Sefer Mitzvot Gadol,* elucidation of precepts by *Moses b. Jacob of Coucy; subdivided into *Lavin* (negative precepts) *Asayin* (positive precepts).
Semak, Usual abbreviation of *Sefer Mitzvot Katan,* elucidation of precepts by *Isaac b. Joseph of Corbeil.

Sh. Ar. = *Shulḥan Arukh,* code by Joseph b. Ephraim *Caro.
Sha'ar Mishpat, Comm. to Sh. Ar., ḤM. By Israel Isser b. Ze'ev Wolf.
Sha'arei Shevu'ot, Treatise on the law of oaths by *David b. Saadiah; usually printed together with Rif, *Halakhot;* also called: *She'arim of R. Alfasi.*
Sha'arei Teshuvah, Collection of resp. from Geonic period, by different authors.
Sha'arei Uzzi'el, Rabbinical treatise by Ben-Zion Meir Ha *Ouziel.
Sha'arei Ẓedek, Collection of resp. from Geonic period, by different authors.
Shadal [or Shedal] = Samuel David *Luzzatto.
Shai la-Moreh, Resp. by Shabbetai Jonah.
Shakh, Usual abbreviation of *Siftei Kohen,* a comm. to Sh. Ar., YD and ḤM by *Shabbetai b. Meir ha-Kohen; printed in most editions of Sh. Ar.
Sha'ot-de-Rabbanan, Resp. by *Solomon b. Judah ha-Kohen.
She'arim of R. Alfasi see *Sha'arei Shevu'ot.*
Shedal, see Shadal.
She'elot u-Teshuvot ha-Ge'onim, Collection of resp. by different authors.
She'erit Yisrael, Resp. by Israel Ze'ev Mintzberg.
She'erit Yosef, Resp. by *Joseph b. Mordecai Gershon ha-Kohen.
She'ilat Yavez, Resp. by Jacob *Emden (Yaveẓ).
She'iltot, Compilation arranged acc. to the Torah by *Aḥa (Aḥai) of Shabḥa.
Shem Aryeh, Resp. by Aryeh Leib *Lipschutz.
Shemesh Ẓedakah, Resp. by Samson *Morpurgo.
Shenei ha-Me'orot ha-Gedolim, Resp. by Elijah *Covo.
Shetarot, Sefer ha-, Collection of legal forms by *Judah b. Barzillai al-Bargeloni.
Shevut Ya'akov, Resp. by Jacob b. Joseph Reicher.
Shibbolei ha-Leket Compilation on ritual by Zedekiah b. Avraham *Anav.
Shiltei Gibborim, Comm. to Rif, *Halakhot,* by *Joshua Boaz b. Simeon; printed in major editions of the Talmud.
Shittah Mekubbeẓet, Compilation of talmudical commentaries by Bezalel *Ashkenazi.
Shivat Ẓiyyon, Resp. by Samuel b. Ezekiel *Landau.
Shiyyurei Korban, by David *Fraenkel; additions to his comm. to Jer. Talmud *Korban Edah;* both printed in most editions of Jer. Talmud.
Sho'el u-Meshiv, Resp. by Joseph Saul ha-Levi *Nathanson.
Sh[ulḥan] Ar[ukh] [of Ba'al ha-Tanyal], Code by *Shneur Zalman of Lyady; not identical with the code by Joseph Caro.
Siftei Kohen, Comm. to Sh. Ar., YD and ḤM by *Shabbetai b. Meir ha-Kohen; printed in most editions of Sh. Ar.; usual abbreviation: *Shakh.*
Simḥat Yom Tov, Resp. by Tom Tov b. Jacob *Algazi.
Simlah Ḥadashah, Treatise on *Sheḥitah* by Alexander Sender b. Ephraim Zalman *Schor; see also *Tevu'ot Shor.*
Simeon b. Ẓemaḥ = Simeon b. Ẓemaḥ *Duran.
Sma, Comm. to Sh. Ar. by Joshua b. Alexander ha-Kohen *Falk; the full title is: *Sefer Me'irat Einayim;* printed in most editions of Sh. Ar.
Solomon b. Isaac ha-Levi = Solomon b. Isaac *Levy.
Solomon b. Isaac of Troyes = *Rashi.

Tal Orot, Rabbinical work with various contents, by Joseph ibn Gioia.
Tam, Rabbenu = *Tam Jacob b. Meir.
Tashbaẓ = Samson b. Zadok.
Tashbeẓ = Simeon b. Zemaḥ *Duran, sometimes also abbreviation for Samson b. Zadok, usually known as Tashbaẓ.
Tashbeẓ [Sefer ha-], Resp. by Simeon b. Ẓemaḥ *Duran; the fourth part of this work is called: *Ḥut ha-Meshullash.*
Taz, Usual abbreviation of *Turei Zahav,* comm., to Sh. Ar. by *David b. Samnuel ha-Levi; printed in most editions of Sh. Ar.
(Ha)-Tekhelet, subdivision of the *Levush* (a codification by Mordecai b. Abraham (Levush) *Jaffe); *Ha-Tekhelet* parallels Tur, OḤ 1-241.
Terumat ha-Deshen, by Israel b. Pethahiah *Isserlein; subdivided into a part containing responsa, and a second part called *Pesakim u-Khetavim* or *Piskei Maharai.*
Terumot, Sefer ha-, Compilation of *halakhot* by Samuel b. Isaac *Sardi.
Teshuvot Ba'alei ha-Tosafot, Collection of responsa by the Tosafists.
Teshjvot Ge'onei Mizraḥ u-Ma'aav, Collection of responsa.
Teshuvot ha-Geonim, Collection of responsa from Geonic period.
Teshuvot Ḥakhmei Provinẓyah, Collection of responsa by different Provencal authors.
Teshuvot Ḥakhmei Ẓarefat ve-Loter, Collection of responsa by different French authors.
Teshuvot Maimuniyyot, Resp. pertaining to Maimonides' *Yad Ḥazakah;* printed in major editions of this work after the text; authorship uncertain.
Tevu'ot Shor, by Alexander Sender b. Ephraim Zalman *Schor, a comm. to his *Simlah Ḥadashah,* a work on *Sheḥitah.*
Tiferet Ẓevi, Resp. by Ẓevi Hirsch of the "AHW" Communities (Altona, Hamburg, Wandsbeck).
Tiktin, Judah b. Simeon = Judah b. Simeon *Ashkenazi.
Toledot Adam ve-Ḥavvah, Codification by *Jeroham b. Meshullam.
Torat Emet, Resp. by Aaron b. Joseph *Sasson.
Torat Ḥayyim, , Resp. by Ḥayyim (ben) Shabbetai.
Torat ha-Minhagot, subdivision of the *Massa Ḥayyim* (a work on tax law) by Ḥayyim *Palaggi, containing an exposition of customary law.
Tosafot Rid, Explanations to the Talmud and decisions by *Isaiah b. Mali di Trani the Elder.
Tosefot Yom Tov, comm. to Mishnah by Yom Tov Lipmann b. Nathan ha-Levi *Heller; printed in most editions of the Mishnah.
Tummim, subdivision of the comm. to Sh. Ar., ḤM, *Urim ve-Tummim* by Jonathan *Eybeschuetz; printed in the major editions of Sh. Ar.
Tur, usual abbreviation for the *Arba'ah Turim* of *Jacob b. Asher.
Turei Zahav, Comm. to Sh. Ar. by *David b. Samuel ha-Levi; printed in most editions of Sh. Ar.; usual abbreviation: *Taz.*

Urim, subdivision of the following.
Urim ve-Tummim, Comm. to Sh. Ar., ḤM, by Jonathan *Eybeschuetz; printed in the major editions of Sh. Ar.; subdivided in places into *Urim* and *Tummim.*

Vikku'aḥ Mayim Ḥayyim, Polemics against Isserles and Caro by Ḥayyim b. Bezalel.

Yad Malakhi, Methodological treatise by *Malachi b. Jacob ha-Kohen.

Yad Ramah, Nov. by Meir b. Todros [ha-Levi] *Abulafia.
Yakhin u-Vo'az, Resp. by Ẓemaḥ b. Solomon *Duran.
Yam ha-Gadol, Resp. by Jacob Moses *Toledano.
Yam shel Shelomo, Compilation arranged acc. to Talmud by Solomon b. Jehiel (Maharshal) *Luria.
Yashar, Sefer ha-, by *Tam, Jacob b. Meir (Rabbenu Tam); 1st pt.: Resp.; 2nd pt.: Nov.
Yaskil Avdi, Resp. by Obadiah Hadaya (printed together with his Resp. *De'ah ve-Haskel).*
Yaveẓ = Jacob *Emden.
Yehudah Ya'aleh, Resp. by Judah b. Israel *Aszod.
Yekar Tiferet, Comm. to Maimonides' *Yad Ḥazakah,*by David b. Solomon ibn Zimra, printed in most editions of *Yad Ḥazakah.*
Yere'im [*ha-Shalem*], [*Sefer*], Treatise on precepts by *Eliezer b. Samuel of Metz.
Yeshu'ot Ya'akov, Resp. by Jacob Meshullam b. Mordecai Ze'ev *Ornstein.
Yiẓhak Rei'aḥ, Resp. by Isaac b. Samuel Abendanan (see article *Abendanam Family).
Ẓafenat Pa'ne'aḥ (1), also called *Raban* or *Even ha-Ezer,* see under the last name.
Ẓafenat Pa'ne'aḥ (2), Resp. by Joseph *Rozin.
Zayit Ra'anan, Resp. by Moses Judah Leib b. Benjamin Auerbach.
Ẓeidah la-Derekh, Codification by *Menahem b. Aaron ibn Zerah.
Ẓedakah u-Mishpat, Resp. by Ẓedakah b. Saadiah Huẓin.
Zekan Aharon, Resp. by Elijah b. Benjamin ha-Levi.
Zekher Ẓaddik, Sermons by Eliezer *Katzenellenbogen.
Ẓemaḥ Ẓedek (1) Resp. by Menaham Mendel Shneersohn (see under *Shneersohn Family).
Zera Avraham, Resp. by Abraham b. David *Yiẓḥaki.
Zera Emet Resp. by *Ishmael b. Abaham Isaac ha-Kohen.
Ẓevi la-Ẓaddik, Resp. by Ẓevi Elimelech b. David Shapira.
Zikhron Yehudah, Resp. by *Judah b. Asher
Zikhron Yosef, Resp. by Joseph b. Menahem *Steinhardt.
Zikhronot, Sefer ha-, Sermons on several precepts by Samuel *Aboab.
Zikkaron la-Rishonim . . ., by Albert (Abraham Elijah) *Harkavy; contains in vol. 1 pt. 4 (1887) a collection of Geonic responsa.
Ẓiẓ Eliezer, Resp. by Eliezer Judah b. Jacob Gedaliah Waldenberg.

BIBLIOGRAPHICAL ABBREVIATIONS

Bibliographies in English and other languages have been extensively updated, with English translations cited where available. In order to help the reader, the language of books or articles is given where not obvious from titles of books or names of periodicals. Titles of books and periodicals in languages with alphabets other than Latin, are given in transliteration, even where there is a title page in English. Titles of articles in periodicals are not given. Names of Hebrew and Yiddish periodicals well known in English-speaking countries or in Israel under their masthead in Latin characters are given in this form, even when contrary to transliteration rules. Names of authors writing in languages with non-Latin alphabets are given in their Latin alphabet form wherever known; otherwise the names are transliterated. Initials are generally not given for authors of articles in periodicals, except to avoid confusion. Non-abbreviated book titles and names of periodicals are printed in *italics.* Abbreviations are given in the list below.

AASOR	*Annual of the American School of Oriental Research* (1919ff.).
AB	*Analecta Biblica* (1952ff.).
Abel, Géog	F.-M. Abel, *Géographie de la Palestine,* 2 vols. (1933-38).
ABR	*Australian Biblical Review* (1951ff.).
Abr.	Philo, *De Abrahamo.*
Abrahams, Companion	I. Abrahams, *Companion to the Authorised Daily Prayer Book* (rev. ed. 1922).
Abramson, Merkazim	S. Abramson, *Ba-Merkazim u-va-Tefuẓot bi-Tekufat ha-Ge'onim* (1965).
Acts	Acts of the Apostles (New Testament).
ACUM	*Who is who in ACUM [Aguddat Kompozitorim u-Meḥabbrim].*
ADAJ	*Annual of the Department of Antiquities, Jordan* (1951ff.).
Adam	Adam and Eve (Pseudepigrapha).
ADB	*Allgemeine Deutsche Biographie,* 56 vols. (1875–1912).
Add. Esth.	The Addition to Esther (Apocrypha).
Adler, Prat Mus	1. Adler, *La pratique musicale savante dans quelques communautés juives en Europe au XVIIe et XVIIIe siècles,* 2 vols. (1966).
Adler-Davis	H.M. Adler and A. Davis (ed. and tr.), *Service of the Synagogue, a New Edition of the Festival Prayers with an English Translation in Prose and Verse,* 6 vols. (1905–06).
Aet.	Philo, *De Aeternitate Mundi.*
AFO	*Archiv fuer Orientforschung* (first two volumes under the name *Archiv fuer Keilschriftforschung)* (1923ff.).
Ag. Ber	*Aggadat Bereshit* (ed. Buber, 1902*).*
Agr.	Philo, *De Agricultura.*
Ag. Sam.	*Aggadat Samuel.*
Ag. Song	*Aggadat Shir ha-Shirim* (Schechter ed., 1896).
Aharoni, Ereẓ	Y. Aharoni, *Ereẓ Yisrael bi-Tekufat ha-Mikra: Geografyah Historit* (1962).
Aharoni, Land	Y. Aharoni, *Land of the Bible* (1966).

Ahikar	Ahikar (Pseudepigrapha).
AI	*Archives Israélites de France* (1840–1936).
AJA	*American Jewish Archives* (1948ff.).
AJHSP	*American Jewish Historical Society – Publications* (after vol. 50 = AJHSQ).
AJHSQ	*American Jewish Historical (Society) Quarterly* (before vol. 50 =AJHSP).
AJSLL	*American Journal of Semitic Languages and Literature* (1884–95 under the title *Hebraica*, since 1942 JNES).
AJYB	*American Jewish Year Book* (1899ff.).
AKM	Abhandlungen fuer die Kunde des Morgenlandes (series).
Albright, Arch	W.F. Albright, *Archaeology of Palestine* (rev. ed. 1960).
Albright, Arch Bib	W.F. Albright, *Archaeology of Palestine and the Bible* (1935^{3}).
Albright, Arch Rel	W.F. Albright, *Archaeology and the Religion of Israel* (1953^{3}).
Albright, Stone	W.F. Albright, *From the Stone Age to Christianity* (1957^{2}).
Alon, Meḥkarim	G. Alon, *Meḥkarim be-Toledot Yisrael bi-Ymei Bayit Sheni u-vi-Tekufat ha-Mishnah ve-ha Talmud,* 2 vols. (1957–58).
Alon, Toledot	G. Alon, *Toledot ha-Yehudim be-Ereẓ Yisrael bi-Tekufat ha-Mishnah ve-ha-Talmud,* I (1958^{3}), (1961^{2}).
ALOR	Alter Orient (series).
Alt, Kl Schr	A. Alt, *Kleine Schriften zur Geschichte des Volkes Israel,* 3 vols. (1953–59).
Alt, Landnahme	A. Alt, *Landnahme der Israeliten in Palaestina* (1925); also in Alt, Kl Schr, 1 (1953), 89–125.
Ant.	Josephus, *Jewish Antiquities* (Loeb Classics ed.).
AO	*Acta Orientalia* (1922ff.).
AOR	*Analecta Orientalia* (1931ff.).
AOS	American Oriental Series.
Apion	Josephus, *Against Apion* (Loeb Classics ed.).
Aq.	Aquila's Greek translation of the Bible.
Ar.	*Arakhin* (talmudic tractate).
Artist.	Letter of Aristeas (Pseudepigrapha).
ARN[1]	*Avot de-Rabbi Nathan,* version (1) ed. Schechter, 1887.
ARN[2]	*Avot de-Rabbi Nathan,* version (2) ed. Schechter, 1945^{2}.
Aronius, Regesten	I. Aronius, *Regesten zur Geschichte der Juden im fraenkischen und deutschen Reiche bis zum Jahre 1273* (1902).
ARW	*Archiv fuer Religionswissenschaft* (1898–1941/42).
AS	*Assyrological Studies* (1931ff.).
Ashtor, Korot	E. Ashtor (Strauss), *Korot ha-Yehudim bi-Sefarad ha-Muslemit,* 1(1966^{2}), 2(1966).
Ashtor, Toledot	E. Ashtor (Strauss), *Toledot ha-Yehudim be-Miẓrayim ve-Suryah Taḥat Shilton ha-Mamlukim,* 3 vols. (1944–70).
Assaf, Ge'onim	S. Assaf, *Tekufat ha-Ge'onim ve-Sifrutah* (1955).
Assaf, Mekorot	S. Assaf, *Mekorot le-Toledot ha-Ḥinnukh be-Yisrael,* 4 vols. (1925–43).
Ass. Mos.	Assumption of Moses (Pseudepigrapha).
ATA	Alttestamentliche Abhandlungen (series).
ATANT	Abhandlungen zur Theologie des Alten und Neuen Testaments (series).
AUJW	*Allgemeine unabhaengige juedische Wochenzeitung* (till 1966 = AWJD).
AV	Authorized Version of the Bible.
Avad.	*Avadim* (post-talmudic tractate).
Avi-Yonah, Geog	M. Avi-Yonah, *Geografyah Historit shel Ereẓ Yisrael* (1962^{3}).
Avi-Yonah, Land	M. Avi-Yonah, *The Holy Land from the Persian to the Arab conquest (536 B.C. to A.D. 640)* (1960).
Avot	*Avot* (talmudic tractate).
Av. Zar.	*Avodah Zarah* (talmudic tractate).
AWJD	*Allgemeine Wochenzeitung der Juden in Deutschland* (since 1967 = AUJW).
AZDJ	*Allgemeine Zeitung des Judentums.*
Azulai	Ḥ.Y.D. Azulai, *Shem ha-Gedolim,* ed. by I.E. Benjacob, 2 pts. (1852) (and other editions).
BA	*Biblical Archaeologist* (1938ff.).
Bacher, Bab Amor	W. Bacher, *Agada der babylonischen Amoraeer* (1913^{2}).
Bacher, Pal Amor	W. Bacher, *Agada der palaestinensischen Amoraeer* (Heb. ed. *Aggadat Amora'ei Ereẓ Yisrael),* 2 vols. (1892–99).
Bacher, Tann	W. Bacher, *Agada der Tannaiten* (Heb. ed. *Aggadot ha-Tanna'im,* vol. 1, pt. 1 and 2 (1903); vol. 2 (1890).
Bacher, Trad	W. Bacher, *Tradition und Tradenten in den Schulen Palaestinas und Babyloniens* (1914).
Baer, Spain	Yitzhak (Fritz) Baer, *History of the Jews in Christian Spain,* 2 vols. (1961–66).
Baer, Studien	Yitzhak (Fritz) Baer, *Studien zur Geschichte der Juden im Koenigreich Aragonien waehrend des 13. und 14. Jahrhunderts* (1913).
Baer, Toledot	Yitzhak (Fritz) Baer, *Toledot ha-Yehudim bi-Sefarad ha-Noẓerit mi-Teḥillatan shel ha-Kehillot ad ha-Gerush,* 2 vols. (1959^{2}).
Baer, Urkunden	Yitzhak (Fritz) Baer, *Die Juden im christlichen Spanien,* 2 vols. (1929–36).
Baer S., Seder	S.I. Baer, *Seder Avodat Yisrael* (1868 and reprints).
BAIU	*Bulletin de l'Alliance Israélite Universelle* (1861–1913).
Baker, Biog Dict	*Baker's Biographical Dictionary of Musicians,* revised by N. Slonimsky (1958^{5}; with Supplement 1965).
I Bar.	I Baruch (Apocrypha).
II Bar.	II Baruch (Pseudepigrapha).
III Bar.	III Baruch (Pseudepigrapha).
BAR	*Biblical Archaeology Review.*
Baron, Community	S.W. Baron, *The Jewish Community, its History and Structure to the American Revolution,* 3 vols. (1942).

Baron, Social	S.W. Baron, *Social and Religious History of the Jews*, 3 vols. (1937); enlarged, 1-2(1952²), 3-14 (1957–69).
Barthélemy-Milik	D. Barthélemy and J.T. Milik, *Dead Sea Scrolls: Discoveries in the Judean Desert*, vol. 1 *Qumram Cave* I (1955).
BASOR	*Bulletin of the American School of Oriental Research.*
Bauer-Leander	H. Bauer and P. Leander, *Grammatik des Biblisch-Aramaeischen* (1927; repr. 1962).
BB	(1) *Bava Batra* (talmudic tractate). (2) *Biblische Beitraege* (1943ff.).
BBB	Bonner biblische Beitraege (series).
BBLA	*Beitraege zur biblischen Landes- und Altertumskunde* (until 1949–ZDPV).
BBSAJ	*Bulletin*, British School of Archaeology, Jerusalem (1922–25; after 1927 included in PEFQS).
BDASI	*Alon* (since 1948) or *Hadashot Arkhe'ologiyyot* (since 1961), bulletin of the Department of Antiquities of the State of Israel.
Begrich, Chronologie	J. Begrich, *Chronologie der Koenige von Israel und Juda* (1929).
Bek.	*Bekhorot* (talmudic tractate).
Bel	Bel and the Dragon (Apocrypha).
Benjacob, Oẓar	I.E. Benjacob, *Oẓar ha-Sefarim* (1880; repr. 1956).
Ben Sira	see Ecclus.
Ben-Yehuda, Millon	E. Ben-Yedhuda, *Millon ha-Lashon ha-Ivrit*, 16 vols (1908–59; repr. in 8 vols., 1959).
Benzinger, Archaeologie	I. Benzinger, *Hebraeische Archaeologie* (1927³).
Ben Zvi, Eretz Israel	I. Ben-Zvi, *Eretz Israel under Ottoman Rule* (1960; offprint from L. Finkelstein (ed.), *The Jews, their History, Culture and Religion* (vol. 1).
Ben Zvi, Ereẓ Israel	I. Ben-Zvi, *Ereẓ Israel bi-Ymei ha-Shilton ha-Ottomani* (1955).
Ber.	*Berakhot* (talmudic tractate).
Beẓah	*Beẓah* (talmudic tractate).
BIES	Bulletin of the Israel Exploration Society, see below BJPES.
Bik.	*Bikkurim* (talmudic tractate).
BJCE	Bibliography of Jewish Communities in Europe, catalog at General Archives for the History of the Jewish People, Jerusalem.
BJPES	Bulletin of the Jewish Palestine Exploration Society – English name of the Hebrew periodical known as: 1. *Yedi'ot ha-Ḥevrah ha-Ivrit la-Ḥakirat Ereẓ Yisrael va-Attikoteha* (1933–1954); 2. *Yedi'ot ha-Ḥevrah la-Ḥakirat Ereẓ Yisrael va-Attikoteha* (1954–1962); 3. *Yedi'ot ba-Ḥakirat Ereẓ Yisrael va-Attikoteha* (1962ff.).
BJRL	*Bulletin of the John Rylands Library* (1914ff.).
BK	*Bava Kamma* (talmudic tractate).
BLBI	*Bulletin of the Leo Baeck Institute* (1957ff.).
BM	(1) *Bava Meẓia* (talmudic tractate). (2) *Beit Mikra* (1955/56ff.). (3) British Museum.
BO	*Bibbia e Oriente* (1959ff.).
Bondy-Dworský	G. Bondy and F. Dworský, *Regesten zur Geschichte der Juden in Boehmen, Maehren und Schlesien von 906 bis 1620*, 2 vols. (1906).
BOR	*Bibliotheca Orientalis* (1943ff.).
Borée, Ortsnamen	W. Borée *Die alten Ortsnamen Palaestinas* (1930).
Bousset, Religion	W. Bousset, *Die Religion des Judentums im neutestamentlichen Zeitalter* (1906²).
Bousset-Gressmann	W. Bousset, *Die Religion des Judentums im spaethellenistischen Zeitalter* (1966³).
BR	*Biblical Review* (1916–25).
BRCI	*Bulletin of the Research Council of Israel* (1951/52–1954/55; then divided).
BRE	*Biblical Research* (1956ff.).
BRF	*Bulletin of the Rabinowitz Fund for the Exploration of Ancient Synagogues* (1949ff.).
Briggs, Psalms	Ch. A. and E.G. Briggs, *Critical and Exegetical Commentary on the Book of Psalms*, 2 vols. (ICC, 1906–07).
Bright, Hist	J. Bright, *A History of Israel* (1959).
Brockelmann, Arab Lit	K. Brockelmann, *Geschichte der arabischen Literatur*, 2 vols. 1898–1902), supplement, 3 vols. (1937–42).
Bruell, Jahrbuecher	*Jahrbuecher fuer juedische Geschichte und Litteratur*, ed. by N. Bruell, Frankfurt (1874–90).
Brugmans-Frank	H. Brugmans and A. Frank (eds.), *Geschiedenis der Joden in Nederland* (1940).
BTS	*Bible et Terre Sainte* (1958ff.).
Bull, Index	S. Bull, *Index to Biographies of Contemporary Composers* (1964).
BW	*Biblical World* (1882–1920).
BWANT	*Beitraege zur Wissenschaft vom Alten und Neuen Testament* (1926ff.).
BZ	*Biblische Zeitschrift* (1903ff.).
BZAW	*Beihefte zur Zeitschrift fuer die alttestamentliche Wissenschaft*, supplement to ZAW (1896ff.).
BŻIH	*Biuletyn Zydowskiego Instytutu Historycznego* (1950ff.).
CAB	*Cahiers d'archéologie biblique* (1953ff.).
CAD	*The [Chicago] Assyrian Dictionary* (1956ff.).
CAH	*Cambridge Ancient History*, 12 vols. (1923–39)
CAH²	*Cambridge Ancient History*, second edition, 14 vols. (1962–2005).
Calwer, Lexikon	*Calwer, Bibellexikon.*
Cant.	Canticles, usually given as Song (= Song of Songs).

Cantera-Millás, Inscripciones	F. Cantera and J.M. Millás, *Las Inscripciones Hebraicas de España* (1956).
CBQ	*Catholic Biblical Quarterly* (1939ff.).
CCARY	Central Conference of American Rabbis, *Yearbook* (1890/91ff.).
CD	*Damascus Document* from the Cairo *Genizah* (published by S. Schechter, *Fragments of a Zadokite Work*, 1910).
Charles, Apocrypha	R.H. Charles, *Apocrypha and Pseudepigrapha . . .*, 2 vols. (1913; repr. 1963–66).
Cher.	Philo, *De Cherubim.*
I (or II) Chron.	Chronicles, book I and II (Bible).
CIG	*Corpus Inscriptionum Graecarum.*
CIJ	*Corpus Inscriptionum Judaicarum,* 2 vols. (1936–52).
CIL	*Corpus Inscriptionum Latinarum.*
CIS	*Corpus Inscriptionum Semiticarum* (1881ff.).
C.J.	Codex Justinianus.
Clermont-Ganneau, Arch	Ch. Clermont-Ganneau, *Archaeological Researches in Palestine*, 2 vols. (1896–99).
CNFI	*Christian News from Israel* (1949ff.).
Cod. Just.	Codex Justinianus.
Cod. Theod.	Codex Theodosinanus.
Col.	Epistle to the Colosssians (New Testament).
Conder, Survey	Palestine Exploration Fund, *Survey of Eastern Palestine*, vol. 1, pt. I (1889) = C.R. Conder, *Memoirs of the . . . Survey.*
Conder-Kitchener	Palestine Exploration Fund, *Survey of Western Palestine*, vol. 1, pts. 1-3 (1881–83) = C.R. Conder and H.H. Kitchener, *Memoirs.*
Conf.	Philo, *De Confusione Linguarum.*
Conforte, Kore	D. Conforte, *Kore ha-Dorot* (1842^2).
Cong.	Philo, *De Congressu Quaerendae Eruditionis Gratia.*
Cont.	Philo, *De Vita Contemplativa.*
I (or II) Cor.	Epistles to the Corinthians (New Testament).
Cowley, Aramic	A. Cowley, *Aramaic Papyri of the Fifth Century B.C.* (1923).
Colwey, Cat	A.E. Cowley, *A Concise Catalogue of the Hebrew Printed Books in the Bodleian Library* (1929).
CRB	*Cahiers de la Revue Biblique* (1964ff.).
Crowfoot-Kenyon	J.W. Crowfoot, K.M. Kenyon and E.L. Sukenik, *Buildings of Samaria* (1942).
C.T.	Codex Theodosianus.
DAB	*Dictionary of American Biography* (1928–58).
Daiches, Jews	S. Daiches, *Jews in Babylonia* (1910).
Dalman, Arbeit	G. Dalman, *Arbeit und Sitte in Palaestina*, 7 vols.in 8 (1928–42 repr. 1964).
Dan	Daniel (Bible).
Davidson, Oẓar	I. Davidson, *Oẓar ha-Shirah ve-ha-Piyyut,* 4 vols. (1924–33); Supplement in: HUCA, 12–13 (1937/38), 715–823.
DB	J. Hastings, *Dictionary of the Bible,* 4 vols. (1963^2).
DBI	F.G. Vigoureaux et al. (eds.), *Dictionnaire de la Bible,* 5 vols. in 10 (1912); Supplement, 8 vols. (1928–66)
Decal.	Philo, *De Decalogo.*
Dem.	*Demai* (talmudic tractate).
DER	*Derekh Ereẓ Rabbah* (post-talmudic tractate).
Derenbourg, Hist	J. Derenbourg *Essai sur l'histoire et la géographie de la Palestine* (1867).
Det.	Philo, *Quod deterius potiori insidiari solet.*
Deus	Philo, *Quod Deus immutabilis sit.*
Deut.	Deuteronomy (Bible).
Deut. R.	*Deuteronomy Rabbah.*
DEZ	*Derekh Ereẓ Zuta* (post-talmudic tractate).
DHGE	*Dictionnaire d'histoire et de géographie ecclésiastiques,* ed. by A. Baudrillart et al., 17 vols (1912–68).
Dik. Sof	*Dikdukei Soferim,* variae lections of the talmudic text by Raphael Nathan Rabbinovitz (16 vols., 1867–97).
Dinur, Golah	B. Dinur (Dinaburg), *Yisrael ba-Golah,* 2 vols. in 7 (1959–68) = vols. 5 and 6 of his *Toledot Yisrael,* second series.
Dinur, Haganah	B. Dinur (ed.), *Sefer Toledot ha-Haganah* (1954ff.).
Diringer, Iscr	D. Diringer, *Iscrizioni antico-ebraiche palestinesi* (1934).
Discoveries	*Discoveries in the Judean Desert* (1955ff.).
DNB	*Dictionary of National Biography,* 66 vols. (1921–222) with Supplements.
Dubnow, Divrei	S. Dubnow, *Divrei Yemei Am Olam,* 11 vols (1923–38 and further editions).
Dubnow, Ḥasidut	S. Dubnow, *Toledot ha-Ḥasidut* (1960^2).
Dubnow, Hist	S. Dubnow, *History of the Jews* (1967).
Dubnow, Hist Russ	S. Dubnow, *History of the Jews in Russia and Poland,* 3 vols. (1916 20).
Dubnow, Outline	S. Dubnow, *An Outline of Jewish History,* 3 vols. (1925–29).
Dubnow, Weltgesch	S. Dubnow, *Weltgeschichte des juedischen Volkes* 10 vols. (1925–29).
Dukes, Poesie	L. Dukes, *Zur Kenntnis der neuhebraeischen religioesen Poesie* (1842).
Dunlop, Khazars	D. H. Dunlop, *History of the Jewish Khazars* (1954).
EA	El Amarna Letters (edited by J.A. Knudtzon), *Die El-Amarna Tafel,* 2 vols. (1907 14).
EB	*Encyclopaedia Britannica.*
EBI	*Estudios biblicos* (1941ff.).
EBIB	T.K. Cheyne and J.S. Black, *Encyclopaedia Biblica,* 4 vols. (1899–1903).
Ebr.	Philo, *De Ebrietate.*
Eccles.	Ecclesiastes (Bible).
Eccles. R.	*Ecclesiastes Rabbah.*
Ecclus.	Ecclesiasticus or Wisdom of Ben Sira (or Sirach; Apocrypha).
Eduy.	*Eduyyot* (mishanic tractate).

EG	*Enziklopedyah shel Galuyyot* (1953ff.).
EH	*Even ha-Ezer.*
EHA	*Enziklopedyah la-Ḥafirot Arkheologiyyot be-Ereẓ Yisrael,* 2 vols. (1970).
EI	*Enzyklopaedie des Islams,* 4 vols. (1905–14). Supplement vol. (1938).
EIS	*Encyclopaedia of Islam,* 4 vols. (1913–36; repr. 1954–68).
EIS²	*Encyclopaedia of Islam, second edition (1960–2000).*
Eisenstein, Dinim	J.D. Eisenstein, *Oẓar Dinim u-Minhagim* (1917; several reprints).
Eisenstein, Yisrael	J.D. Eisenstein, *Oẓar Yisrael* (10 vols, 1907–13; repr. with several additions 1951).
EIV	*Enẓiklopedyah Ivrit* (1949ff.).
EJ	*Encyclopaedia Judaica* (German, A-L only), 10 vols. (1928–34).
EJC	*Enciclopedia Judaica Castellana,* 10 vols. (1948–51).
Elbogen, Century	I Elbogen, *A Century of Jewish Life* (1960²).
Elbogen, Gottesdienst	I Elbogen, *Der juedische Gottesdienst ...* (1931³, repr. 1962).
Elon, Mafte'aḥ	M. Elon (ed.), *Mafte'aḥ ha-She'elot ve-ha-Teshuvot ha-Rosh* (1965).
EM	*Enẓiklopedyah Mikra'it* (1950ff.).
I (or II) En.	I and II Enoch (Pseudepigrapha).
EncRel	*Encyclopedia of Religion*, 15 vols. (1987, 2005²).
Eph.	Epistle to the Ephesians (New Testament).
Ephros, Cant	G. Ephros, *Cantorial Anthology,* 5 vols. (1929–57).
Ep. Jer.	Epistle of Jeremy (Apocrypha).
Epstein, Amora'im	J N. Epstein, *Mevo'ot le-Sifrut ha-Amora'im* (1962).
Epstein, Marriage	L M. Epstein, *Marriage Laws in the Bible and the Talmud* (1942).
Epstein, Mishnah	J. N. Epstein, *Mavo le-Nusaḥ ha-Mishnah,* 2 vols. (1964²).
Epstein, Tanna'im	J. N. Epstein, *Mavo le-Sifruth ha-Tanna'im.* (1947).
ER	*Ecumenical Review.*
Er.	*Eruvin* (talmudic tractate).
ERE	*Encyclopaedia of Religion and Ethics,* 13 vols. (1908–26); reprinted.
ErIsr	*Eretz-Israel*, Israel Exploration Society.
I Esd.	I Esdras (Apocrypha) (= III Ezra).
II Esd.	II Esdras (Apocrypha) (= IV Ezra).
ESE	*Ephemeris fuer semitische Epigraphik*, ed. by M. Lidzbarski.
ESN	*Encyclopaedia Sefaradica Neerlandica,* 2 pts. (1949).
ESS	*Encyclopaedia of the Social Sciences,* 15 vols. (1930–35); reprinted in 8 vols. (1948–49).
Esth.	Esther (Bible).
Est. R.	*Esther Rabbah.*
ET	*Enẓiklopedyah Talmudit* (1947ff.).
Eusebius, Onom.	E. Klostermann (ed.), *Das Onomastikon* (1904), Greek with Hieronymus' Latin translation.
Ex.	Exodus (Bible).
Ex. R.	*Exodus Rabbah.*
Exs	Philo, *De Exsecrationibus.*
EẒD	*Enẓiklopeday shel ha-Ẓiyyonut ha-Datit* (1951ff.).
Ezek.	Ezekiel (Bible).
Ezra	Ezra (Bible).
III Ezra	III Ezra (Pseudepigrapha).
IV Ezra	IV Ezra (Pseudepigrapha).
Feliks, Ha-Ẓome'aḥ	*J. Feliks, Ha-Ẓome'aḥ ve-ha-Ḥai ba-Mishnah* (1983).
Finkelstein, Middle Ages	L. Finkelstein, *Jewish Self-Government in the Middle Ages* (1924).
Fischel, Islam	W.J. Fischel, *Jews in the Economic and Political Life of Mediaeval Islam* (1937; reprint with introduction "The Court Jew in the Islamic World," 1969).
FJW	*Fuehrer durch die juedische Gemeindeverwaltung und Wohlfahrtspflege in Deutschland* (1927/28).
Frankel, Mevo	Z. Frankel, *Mevo ha-Yerushalmi* (1870; reprint 1967).
Frankel, Mishnah	Z. Frankel, *Darkhei ha-Mishnah* (1959²; reprint 1959²).
Frazer, Folk-Lore	J.G. Frazer, *Folk-Lore in the Old Testament*, 3 vols. (1918–19).
Frey, Corpus	J.-B. Frey, *Corpus Inscriptionum Iudaicarum*, 2 vols. (1936–52).
Friedmann, Lebensbilder	A. Friedmann, *Lebensbilder beruehmter Kantoren*, 3 vols. (1918–27).
FRLT	*Forschungen zur Religion und Literatur des Alten und Neuen Testaments* (series) (1950ff.).
Frumkin-Rivlin	A.L. Frumkin and E. Rivlin, *Toledot Ḥakhmei Yerushalayim*, 3 vols. (1928–30), Supplement vol. (1930).
Fuenn, Keneset	S.J. Fuenn, *Keneset Yisrael,* 4 vols. (1887–90).
Fuerst, Bibliotheca	J. Fuerst, *Bibliotheca Judaica,* 2 vols. (1863; repr. 1960).
Fuerst, Karaeertum	J. Fuerst, *Geschichte des Karaeertums*, 3 vols. (1862–69).
Fug.	Philo, *De Fuga et Inventione.*
Gal.	Epistle to the Galatians (New Testament).
Galling, Reallexikon	K. Galling, *Biblisches Reallexikon* (1937).
Gardiner, Onomastica	A.H. Gardiner, *Ancient Egyptian Onomastica,* 3 vols. (1947).
Geiger, Mikra	A. Geiger, *Ha-Mikra ve-Targumav*, tr. by J.L. Baruch (1949).
Geiger, Urschrift	A. Geiger, *Urschrift und Uebersetzungen der Bibel* 1928²).
Gen.	Genesis (Bible).
Gen. R.	*Genesis Rabbah.*
Ger.	*Gerim* (post-talmudic tractate).
Germ Jud	M. Brann, I. Elbogen, A. Freimann, and H. Tykocinski (eds.), *Germania Judaica*, vol. 1 (1917; repr. 1934 and 1963); vol. 2, in 2 pts. (1917–68), ed. by Z. Avneri.

GHAT	*Goettinger Handkommentar zum Alten Testament* (1917–22).
Ghirondi-Neppi	M.S. Ghirondi and G.H. Neppi, *Toledot Gedolei Yisrael u-Ge'onei Italyah ... u-Ve'urim al Sefer Zekher Ẓaddikim li-Verakhah* . . .(1853), index in ZHB, 17 (1914), 171–83.
Gig.	Philo, *De Gigantibus.*
Ginzberg, Legends	L. Ginzberg, *Legends of the Jews,* 7 vols. (1909–38; and many reprints).
Git.	*Gittin* (talmudic tractate).
Glueck, Explorations	N. Glueck, *Explorations in Eastern Palestine,* 2 vols. (1951).
Goell, Bibliography	Y. Goell, *Bibliography of Modern Hebrew Literature in English Translation* (1968).
Goodenough, Symbols	E.R. Goodenough, *Jewish Symbols in the Greco-Roman Period,* 13 vols. (1953–68).
Gordon, Textbook	C.H. Gordon, *Ugaritic Textbook* (1965; repr. 1967).
Graetz, Gesch	H. Graetz, *Geschichte der Juden* (last edition 1874–1908).
Graetz, Hist	H. Graetz, *History of the Jews,* 6 vols. (1891–1902).
Graetz, Psalmen	H. Graetz, *Kritischer Commentar zu den Psalmen,* 2 vols. in 1 (1882–83).
Graetz, Rabbinowitz	H. Graetz, *Divrei Yemei Yisrael,* tr. by S.P. Rabbinowitz. (1928 1929^{2}).
Gray, Names	G.B. Gray, *Studies in Hebrew Proper Names* (1896).
Gressmann, Bilder	H. Gressmann, *Altorientalische Bilder zum Alten Testament* (1927^{2}).
Gressmann, Texte	H. Gressmann, *Altorientalische Texte zum Alten Testament* (1926^{2}).
Gross, Gal Jud	H. Gross, *Gallia Judaica* (1897; repr. with add. 1969).
Grove, Dict	*Grove's Dictionary of Music and Musicians,* ed. by E. Blum 9 vols. (1954^{5}) and suppl. (1961^{5}).
Guedemann, Gesch Erz	M. Guedemann, *Geschichte des Erziehungswesens und der Cultur der abendlaendischen Juden,* 3 vols. (1880–88).
Guedemann, Quellenschr	M. Guedemann, *Quellenschriften zur Geschichte des Unterrichts und der Erziehung bei den deutschen Juden* (1873, 1891).
Guide	Maimonides, *Guide of the Perplexed.*
Gulak, Oẓar	A. Gulak, *Oẓar ha-Shetarot ha-Nehugim be-Yisrael* (1926).
Gulak, Yesodei	A. Gulak, *Yesodei ha-Mishpat ha-Ivri, Seder Dinei Mamonot be-Yisrael, al pi Mekorot ha-Talmud ve-ha-Posekim,* 4 vols. (1922; repr. 1967).
Guttmann, Mafte'aḥ	M. Guttmann, *Mafte'aḥ ha-Talmud,* 3 vols. (1906–30).
Guttmann, Philosophies	J. Guttmann, *Philosophies of Judaism* (1964).
Hab.	*Habakkuk* (Bible).
Ḥag.	*Ḥagigah* (talmudic tractate).
Haggai	*Haggai* (Bible).
Ḥal.	*Ḥallah* (talmudic tractate).
Halevy, Dorot	I. Halevy, *Dorot ha-Rishonim,* 6 vols. (1897–1939).
Halpern, Pinkas	I. Halpern (Halperin), *Pinkas Va'ad Arba Araẓot* (1945).
Hananel-Eškenazi	A. Hananel and Eškenazi (eds.), *Fontes Hebraici ad res oeconomicas socialesque terrarum balcanicarum saeculo XVI pertinentes,* 2 vols, (1958–60; in Bulgarian).
HB	*Hebraeische Bibliographie* (1858–82).
Heb.	Epistle to the Hebrews (New Testament).
Heilprin, Dorot	J. Heilprin (Heilperin), *Seder ha-Dorot,* 3 vols. (1882; repr. 1956).
Her.	Philo, *Quis Rerum Divinarum Heres.*
Hertz, Prayer	J.H. Hertz (ed.), *Authorised Daily Prayer Book* (rev. ed. 1948; repr. 1963).
Herzog, Instit	I. Herzog, *The Main Institutions of Jewish Law,* 2 vols. (1936–39; repr. 1967).
Herzog-Hauck	J.J. Herzog and A. Hauch (eds.), *Real-encyklopaedie fuer protestantische Theologie* (1896–1913^{3}).
HḤY	*Ha-Ẓofeh le-Ḥokhmat Yisrael* (first four volumes under the title *Ha-Ẓofeh me-Ereẓ Hagar)* (1910/11–13).
Hirschberg, Afrikah	H.Z. Hirschberg, *Toledot ha-Yehudim be-Afrikah ha-Zofonit,* 2 vols. (1965).
HJ	*Historia Judaica* (1938–61).
HL	*Das Heilige Land* (1857ff.)
ḤM	*Ḥoshen Mishpat.*
Hommel, Ueberliefer.	F. Hommel, *Die altisraelitische Ueberlieferung in inschriftlicher Beleuchtung* (1897).
Hor.	*Horayot* (talmudic tractate).
Horodezky, Ḥasidut	S.A. Horodezky, *Ha-Ḥasidut ve-ha-Ḥasidim,* 4 vols. (1923).
Horowitz, Ereẓ Yis	I.W. Horowitz, *Ereẓ Yisrael u-Shekhenoteha* (1923).
Hos.	Hosea (Bible).
HTR	*Harvard Theological Review* (1908ff.).
HUCA	*Hebrew Union College Annual* (1904; 1924ff.)
Ḥul.	*Ḥullin* (talmudic tractate).
Husik, Philosophy	I. Husik, *History of Medieval Jewish Philosophy* (1932^{2}).
Hyman, Toledot	A. Hyman, *Toledot Tanna'im ve-Amora'im* (1910; repr. 1964).
Ibn Daud, Tradition	Abraham Ibn Daud, *Sefer ha-Qabbalah – The Book of Tradition,* ed. and tr. By G.D. Cohen (1967).
ICC	International Critical Commentary on the Holy Scriptures of the Old and New Testaments (series, 1908ff.).
IDB	*Interpreter's Dictionary of the Bible,* 4 vols. (1962).
Idelsohn, Litugy	A. Z. Idelsohn, *Jewish Liturgy and its Development* (1932; paperback repr. 1967)
Idelsohn, Melodien	A. Z. Idelsohn, *Hebraeisch-orientalischer Melodienschatz,* 10 vols. (1914 32).
Idelsohn, Music	A. Z. Idelsohn, *Jewish Music in its Historical Development* (1929; paperback repr. 1967).

IEJ	*Israel Exploration Journal* (1950ff.).
IESS	*International Encyclopedia of the Social Sciences* (various eds.).
IG	*Inscriptiones Graecae,* ed. by the Prussian Academy.
IGYB	*Israel Government Year Book* (1949/50ff.).
ILR	*Israel Law Review* (1966ff.).
IMIT	*Izraelita Magyar Irodalmi Társulat Évkönyv* (1895 1948).
IMT	International Military Tribunal.
INB	*Israel Numismatic Bulletin* (1962–63).
INJ	*Israel Numismatic Journal* (1963ff.).
Ios	Philo, *De Iosepho.*
Isa.	Isaiah (Bible).
ITHL	Institute for the Translation of Hebrew Literature.
IZBG	*Internationale Zeitschriftenschau fuer Bibelwissenschaft und Grenzgebiete* (1951ff.).
JA	*Journal asiatique* (1822ff.).
James	Epistle of James (New Testament).
JAOS	*Journal of the American Oriental Society* (c. 1850ff.)
Jastrow, Dict	M. Jastrow, *Dictionary of the Targumim, the Talmud Babli and Yerushalmi, and the Midrashic literature,* 2 vols. (1886 1902 and reprints).
JBA	*Jewish Book Annual* (19242ff.).
JBL	*Journal of Biblical Literature* (1881ff.).
JBR	*Journal of Bible and Religion* (1933ff.).
JC	*Jewish Chronicle* (1841ff.).
JCS	*Journal of Cuneiform Studies* (1947ff.).
JE	*Jewish Encyclopedia,* 12 vols. (1901–05 several reprints).
Jer.	Jeremiah (Bible).
Jeremias, Alte Test	A. Jeremias, *Das Alte Testament im Lichte des alten Orients* 1930^{4}).
JGGJČ	*Jahrbuch der Gesellschaft fuer Geschichte der Juden in der Čechoslovakischen Republik* (1929–38).
JHSEM	Jewish Historical Society of England, *Miscellanies* (1925ff.).
JHSET	Jewish Historical Society of England, *Transactions* (1893ff.).
JJGL	*Jahrbuch fuer juedische Geschichte und Literatur* (Berlin) (1898–1938).
JJLG	*Jahrbuch der juedische-literarischen Gesellschaft* (Frankfurt) (1903–32).
JJS	*Journal of Jewish Studies* (1948ff.).
JJSO	*Jewish Journal of Sociology* (1959ff.).
JJV	*Jahrbuch fuer juedische Volkskunde* (1898–1924).
JL	*Juedisches Lexikon,* 5 vols. (1927–30).
JMES	*Journal of the Middle East Society* (1947ff.).
JNES	*Journal of Near Eastern Studies* (continuation of AJSLL) (1942ff.).
J.N.U.L.	Jewish National and University Library.
Job	Job (Bible).
Joel	Joel (Bible).
John	Gospel according to John (New Testament).
I, II and III John	Epistles of John (New Testament).
Jos., Ant	Josephus, *Jewish Antiquities* (Loeb Classics ed.).
Jos. Apion	Josephus, *Against Apion* (Loeb Classics ed.).
Jos., index	*Josephus Works,* Loeb Classics ed., index of names.
Jos., Life	Josephus, *Life* (ed. Loeb Classics).
Jos, Wars	Josephus, *The Jewish Wars* (Loeb Classics ed.).
Josh.	Joshua (Bible).
JPESB	Jewish Palestine Exploration Society Bulletin, see BJPES.
JPESJ	Jewish Palestine Exploration Society Journal – Eng. Title of the Hebrew periodical *Kovez̩ ha-Ḥevrah ha-Ivrit la-Ḥakirat Erez̩ Yisrael va-Attikoteha.*
JPOS	*Journal of the Palestine Oriental Society* (1920–48).
JPS	Jewish Publication Society of America, *The Torah* (1962, 1967^{2}); *The Holy Scriptures* (1917).
JQR	*Jewish Quarterly Review* (1889ff.).
JR	*Journal of Religion* (1921ff.).
JRAS	*Journal of the Royal Asiatic Society* (1838ff.).
JHR	*Journal of Religious History* (1960/61ff.).
JSOS	*Jewish Social Studies* (1939ff.).
JSS	*Journal of Semitic Studies* (1956ff.).
JTS	*Journal of Theological Studies* (1900ff.).
JTSA	Jewish Theological Seminary of America (also abbreviated as JTS).
Jub.	Jubilees (Pseudepigrapha).
Judg.	Judges (Bible).
Judith	Book of Judith (Apocrypha).
Juster, Juifs	J. Juster, *Les Juifs dans l'Empire Romain,* 2 vols. (1914).
JYB	*Jewish Year Book* (1896ff.).
JZWL	*Juedische Zeitschift fuer Wissenschaft und Leben* (1862–75).
Kal.	*Kallah* (post-talmudic tractate).
Kal. R.	*Kallah Rabbati* (post-talmudic tractate).
Katz, England	*The Jews in the History of England, 1485-1850 (1994).*
Kaufmann, Schriften	D. Kaufmann, *Gesammelte Schriften,* 3 vols. (1908 15).
Kaufmann Y., Religion	Y. Kaufmann, *The Religion of Israel* (1960), abridged tr. of his *Toledot.*
Kaufmann Y., Toledot	Y. Kaufmann, *Toledot ha-Emunah ha-Yisre'elit,* 4 vols. (1937 57).
KAWJ	*Korrespondenzblatt des Vereins zur Gruendung und Erhaltung der Akademie fuer die Wissenschaft des Judentums* (1920 30).
Kayserling, Bibl	M. Kayserling, *Biblioteca Española-Portugueza-Judaica* (1880; repr. 1961).
Kelim	*Kelim* (mishnaic tractate).
Ker.	*Keritot* (talmudic tractate).
Ket.	*Ketubbot* (talmudic tractate).

Kid.	*Kiddushim* (talmudic tractate).
Kil.	*Kilayim* (talmudic tractate).
Kin.	*Kinnim* (mishnaic tractate).
Kisch, Germany	G. Kisch, *Jews in Medieval Germany* (1949).
Kittel, Gesch	R. Kittel, *Geschichte des Volkes Israel,* 3 vols. (1922–28).
Klausner, Bayit Sheni	J. Klausner, *Historyah shel ha-Bayit ha-Sheni,* 5 vols. (1950/512).
Klausner, Sifrut	J. Klausner, *Historyah shel haSifrut ha-Ivrit ha-Ḥadashah,* 6 vols. (1952–582).
Klein, corpus	S. Klein (ed.), *Juedisch-palaestinisches Corpus Inscriptionum* (1920).
Koehler-Baumgartner	L. Koehler and W. Baumgartner, *Lexicon in Veteris Testamenti libros* (1953).
Kohut, Arukh	H.J.A. Kohut (ed.), *Sefer he-Arukh ha-Shalem,* by Nathan b. Jehiel of Rome, 8 vols. (1876–92; Supplement by S. Krauss et al., 1936; repr. 1955).
Krauss, Tal Arch	S. Krauss, *Talmudische Archaeologie,* 3 vols. (1910–12; repr. 1966).
Kressel, Leksikon	G. Kressel, *Leksikon ha-Sifrut ha-Ivrit ba-Dorot ha-Aḥaronim,* 2 vols. (1965–67).
KS	*Kirjath Sepher* (1923/4ff.).
Kut.	*Kuttim* (post-talmudic tractate).
LA	Studium Biblicum Franciscanum, *Liber Annuus* (1951ff.).
L.A.	Philo, *Legum allegoriae.*
Lachower, Sifrut	F. Lachower, *Toledot ha-Sifrut ha-Ivrit ha-Ḥadashah,* 4 vols. (1947–48; several reprints).
Lam.	Lamentations (Bible).
Lam. R.	*Lamentations Rabbah.*
Landshuth, Ammudei	L. Landshuth, *Ammudei ha-Avodah* (1857–62; repr. with index, 1965).
Legat.	Philo, *De Legatione ad Caium.*
Lehmann, Nova Bibl	R.P. Lehmann, *Nova Bibliotheca Anglo-Judaica* (1961).
Lev.	Leviticus (Bible).
Lev. R.	*Leviticus Rabbah.*
Levy, Antologia	I. Levy, *Antologia de liturgia judeo-española* (1965ff.).
Levy J., Chald Targ	J. Levy, *Chaldaeisches Woerterbuch ueber die Targumim,* 2 vols. (1967–68; repr. 1959).
Levy J., Nuehebr Tal	J. Levy, *Neuhebraeisches und chaldaeisches Woerterbuch ueber die Talmudim . . .,* 4 vols. (1875–89; repr. 1963).
Lewin, Oẓar	Lewin, *Oẓar ha-Ge'onim,* 12 vols. (1928–43).
Lewysohn, Zool	L. Lewysohn, *Zoologie des Talmuds* (1858).
Lidzbarski, Handbuch	M. Lidzbarski, *Handbuch der nordsemitischen Epigraphik,* 2 vols (1898).
Life	Josephus, *Life* (Loeb Classis ed.).
LNYL	*Leksikon fun der Nayer Yidisher Literatur* (1956ff.).
Loew, Flora	I. Loew, *Die Flora der Juden,* 4 vols. (1924 34; repr. 1967).
LSI	*Laws of the State of Israel* (1948ff.).
Luckenbill, Records	D.D. Luckenbill, *Ancient Records of Assyria and Babylonia,* 2 vols. (1926).
Luke	Gospel according to Luke (New Testament)
LXX	Septuagint (Greek translation of the Bible).
Ma'as.	*Ma'aserot* (talmudic tractate).
Ma'as. Sh.	*Ma'ase Sheni* (talmudic tractate).
I, II, III, and IVMacc.	Maccabees, I, II, III (Apocrypha), IV (Pseudepigrapha).
Maimonides, Guide	Maimonides, *Guide of the Perplexed.*
Maim., Yad	Maimonides, *Mishneh Torah (Yad Ḥazakah).*
Maisler, Untersuchungen	B. Maisler (Mazar), *Untersuchungen zur alten Geschichte und Ethnographie Syriens und Palaestinas,* 1 (1930).
Mak.	*Makkot* (talmudic tractate).
Makhsh.	*Makhshrin* (mishnaic tractate).
Mal.	Malachi (Bible).
Mann, Egypt	J. Mann, *Jews in Egypt in Palestine under the Fatimid Caliphs,* 2 vols. (1920–22).
Mann, Texts	J. Mann, *Texts and Studies,* 2 vols (1931–35).
Mansi	G.D. Mansi, *Sacrorum Conciliorum nova et amplissima collectio,* 53 vols. in 60 (1901–27; repr. 1960).
Margalioth, Gedolei	M. Margalioth, *Enẓiklopedyah le-Toledot Gedolei Yisrael,* 4 vols. (1946–50).
Margalioth, Ḥakhmei	M. Margalioth, *Enẓiklopedyah le-Ḥakhmei ha-Talmud ve-ha-Ge'onim,* 2 vols. (1945).
Margalioth, Cat	G. Margalioth, *Catalogue of the Hebrew and Samaritan Manuscripts in the British Museum,* 4 vols. (1899–1935).
Mark	Gospel according to Mark (New Testament).
Mart. Isa.	Martyrdom of Isaiah (Pseudepigrapha).
Mas.	Masorah.
Matt.	Gospel according to Matthew (New Testament).
Mayer, Art	L.A. Mayer, *Bibliography of Jewish Art* (1967).
MB	*Wochenzeitung* (formerly *Mitteilungsblatt*) *des Irgun Olej Merkas Europa* (1933ff.).
MEAH	*Miscelánea de estudios drabes y hebraicos* (1952ff.).
Meg.	Megillah (talmudic tractate).
Meg. Ta'an.	*Megillat Ta'anit* (in HUCA, 8 9 (1931–32), 318–51).
Me'il	*Me'ilah* (mishnaic tractate).
MEJ	*Middle East Journal* (1947ff.).
Mehk.	*Mekhilta de-R. Ishmael.*
Mekh. SbY	*Mekhilta de-R. Simeon bar Yoḥai.*
Men.	*Menaḥot* (talmudic tractate).
MER	*Middle East Record* (1960ff.).
Meyer, Gesch	E. Meyer, *Geschichte des Alterums,* 5 vols. in 9 (1925–58).
Meyer, Ursp	E. Meyer, *Urspring und Anfaenge des Christentums* (1921).
Mez.	*Mezuzah* (post-talmudic tractate).
MGADJ	*Mitteilungen des Gesamtarchivs der deutschen Juden* (1909–12).
MGG	*Die Musik in Geschichte und Gegenwart,* 14 vols. (1949–68).

MGG² — *Die Musik in Geschichte und Gegenwart, 2nd edition (1994)*
MGH — *Monumenta Germaniae Historica* (1826ff.).
MGJV — *Mitteilungen der Gesellschaft fuer juedische Volkskunde* (1898–1929); title varies, see also JJV.
MGWJ — *Monatsschrift fuer Geschichte und Wissenschaft des Judentums* (1851–1939).
MHJ — *Monumenta Hungariae Judaica,* 11 vols. (1903–67).
Michael, Or — H.Ḥ. Michael, *Or ha-Ḥayyim: Ḥakhmei Yisrael ve-Sifreihem,* ed. by S.Z. Ḥ. Halberstam and N. Ben-Menahem (1965²).
Mid. — *Middot* (mishnaic tractate).
Mid. Ag. — *Midrash Aggadah.*
Mid. Hag. — *Midrash ha-Gadol.*
Mid. Job. — *Midrash Job.*
Mid. Jonah — *Midrash Jonah.*
Mid. Lek. Tov — *Midrash Lekaḥ Tov.*
Mid. Prov. — *Midrash Proverbs.*
Mid. Ps. — *Midrash Tehillim* (Eng tr. *The Midrash on Psalms* (JPS, 1959).
Mid. Sam. — *Midrash Samuel.*
Mid. Song — *Midrash Shir ha-Shirim.*
Mid. Tan. — *Midrash Tanna'im* on Deuteronomy.
Miége, Maroc — J.L. Miège, *Le Maroc et l'Europe,* 3 vols. (1961 62).
Mig. — Philo, *De Migratione Abrahami.*
Mik. — *Mikva'ot* (mishnaic tractate).
Milano, Bibliotheca — A. Milano, *Bibliotheca Historica Italo-Judaica* (1954); supplement for 1954–63 (1964); supplement for 1964–66 in RMI, 32 (1966).
Milano, Italia — A. Milano, *Storia degli Ebrei in Italia* (1963).
MIO — *Mitteilungen des Instituts fuer Orientforschung* 1953ff.).
Mish. — Mishnah.
MJ — *Le Monde Juif* (1946ff.).
MJC — see Neubauer, Chronicles.
MK — *Mo'ed Katan* (talmudic tractate).
MNDPV — *Mitteilungen und Nachrichten des deutschen Palaestinavereins* (1895–1912).
Mortara, Indice — M. Mortara, *Indice Alfabetico dei Rabbini e Scrittori Israeliti ... in Italia ...* (1886).
Mos — Philo, *De Vita Mosis.*
Moscati, Epig — S, Moscati, *Epigrafia ebraica antica* 1935–1950 (1951).
MT — Masoretic Text of the Bible.
Mueller, Musiker — [E.H. Mueller], *Deutisches Musiker-Lexikon* (1929)
Munk, Mélanges — S. Munk, *Mélanges de philosophie juive et arabe* (1859; repr. 1955).
Mut. — Philo, *De Mutatione Nominum.*
MWJ — *Magazin fuer die Wissenshaft des Judentums* (18745 93).

Nah. — Nahum (Bible).
Naz. — *Nazir* (talmudic tractate).
NDB — *Neue Deutsche Biographie* (1953ff.).
Ned. — *Nedarim* (talmudic tractate).
Neg. — *Nega'im* (mishnaic tractate).
Neh. — Nehemiah (Bible).
NG² — *New Grove Dictionary of Music and Musicians* (2001).
Nuebauer, Cat — A. Neubauer, *Catalogue of the Hebrew Manuscripts in the Bodleian Library ...,* 2 vols. (1886–1906).
Neubauer, Chronicles — A. Neubauer, *Mediaeval Jewish Chronicles,* 2 vols. (Heb., 1887–95; repr. 1965), Eng. title of *Seder ha-Ḥakhamim ve-Korot ha-Yamim.*
Neubauer, Géogr — A. Neubauer, *La géographie du Talmud* (1868).
Neuman, Spain — A.A. Neuman, *The Jews in Spain, their Social, Political, and Cultural Life During the Middle Ages,* 2 vols. (1942).
Neusner, Babylonia — J. Neusner, *History of the Jews in Babylonia,* 5 vols. 1965–70), 2nd revised printing 1969ff.).
Nid. — *Niddah* (talmudic tractate).
Noah — Fragment of Book of Noah (Pseudepigrapha).
Noth, Hist Isr — M. Noth, *History of Israel* (1958).
Noth, Personennamen — M. Noth, *Die israelitischen Personennamen. ...* (1928).
Noth, Ueberlief — M. Noth, *Ueberlieferungsgeschichte des Pentateuchs* (1949).
Noth, Welt — M. Noth, *Die Welt des Alten Testaments* (1957³).
Nowack, Lehrbuch — W. Nowack, *Lehrbuch der hebraeischen Archaeologie,* 2 vols (1894).
NT — New Testament.
Num. — Numbers (Bible).
Num R. — *Numbers Rabbah.*

Obad. — Obadiah (Bible).
ODNB online — *Oxford Dictionary of National Biography.*
OḤ — *Oraḥ Ḥayyim.*
Oho. — *Oholot* (mishnaic tractate).
Olmstead — H.T. Olmstead, *History of Palestine and Syria* (1931; repr. 1965).
OLZ — *Orientalistische Literaturzeitung* (1898ff.)
Onom. — Eusebius, *Onomasticon.*
Op. — Philo, *De Opificio Mundi.*
OPD — *Osef Piskei Din shel ha-Rabbanut ha-Rashit le-Ereẓ Yisrael, Bet ha-Din ha-Gadol le-Irurim* (1950).
Or. — *Orlah* (talmudic tractate).
Or. Sibyll. — Sibylline Oracles (Pseudepigrapha).
OS — *L'Orient Syrien* (1956ff.)
OTS — *Oudtestamentische Studien* (1942ff.).

PAAJR — *Proceedings of the American Academy for Jewish Research* (1930ff.)
Pap 4QS^e — A papyrus exemplar of IQS.
Par. — *Parah* (mishnaic tractate).
Pauly-Wissowa — A.F. Pauly, *Realencyklopaedie der klassichen Alertumswissenschaft,* ed. by G. Wissowa et al. (1864ff.)

PD	*Piskei Din shel Bet ha-Mishpat ha-Elyon le-Yisrael* (1948ff.)
PDR	*Piskei Din shel Battei ha-Din ha-Rabbaniyyim be-Yisrael.*
PdRE	*Pirkei de-R. Eliezer* (Eng. tr. 1916. (1965²).
PdRK	*Pesikta de-Rav Kahana.*
Pe'ah	*Pe'ah* (talmudic tractate).
Peake, Commentary	A.J. Peake (ed.), *Commentary on the Bible* (1919; rev. 1962).
Pedersen, Israel	J. Pedersen, *Israel, Its Life and Culture,* 4 vols. in 2 (1926–40).
PEFQS	*Palestine Exploration Fund Quarterly Statement* (1869–1937; since 1938–PEQ).
PEQ	*Palestine Exploration Quarterly* (until 1937 PEFQS; after 1927 includes BBSAJ).
Perles, Beitaege	J. Perles, *Beitraege zur rabbinischen Sprach- und Alterthumskunde* (1893).
Pes.	*Pesaḥim* (talmudic tractate).
Pesh.	Peshitta (Syriac translation of the Bible).
Pesher Hab.	Commentary to Habakkuk from Qumran; see 1Qp Hab.
I and II Pet.	Epistles of Peter (New Testament).
Pfeiffer, Introd	R.H. Pfeiffer, *Introduction to the Old Testament* (1948).
PG	J.P. Migne (ed.), *Patrologia Graeca,* 161 vols. (1866–86).
Phil.	Epistle to the Philippians (New Testament).
Philem.	Epistle to the Philemon (New Testament).
PIASH	*Proceedings of the Israel Academy of Sciences and Humanities* (1963/7ff.).
PJB	*Palaestinajahrbuch des deutschen evangelischen Institutes fuer Altertumswissenschaft,* Jerusalem (1905–1933).
PK	*Pinkas ha-Kehillot,* encyclopedia of Jewish communities, published in over 30 volumes by Yad Vashem from 1970 and arranged by countries, regions and localities. For 3-vol. English edition see Spector, *Jewish Life.*
PL	J.P. Migne (ed.), *Patrologia Latina* 221 vols. (1844–64).
Plant	Philo, *De Plantatione.*
PO	R. Graffin and F. Nau (eds.), *Patrologia Orientalis* (1903ff.)
Pool, Prayer	D. de Sola Pool, *Traditional Prayer Book for Sabbath and Festivals* (1960).
Post	Philo, *De Posteritate Caini.*
PR	*Pesikta Rabbati.*
Praem.	Philo, *De Praemiis et Poenis.*
Prawer, Ẓalbanim	J. Prawer, *Toledot Mamlekhet ha-Ẓalbanim be-Ereẓ Yisrael,* 2 vols. (1963).
Press, Ereẓ	I. Press, *Ereẓ-Yisrael, Enẓiklopedyah Topografit-Historit,* 4 vols. (1951–55).
Pritchard, Pictures	J.B. Pritchard (ed.), *Ancient Near East in Pictures* (1954, 1970).
Pritchard, Texts	J.B. Pritchard (ed.), *Ancient Near East Texts* ... (1970³).

Pr. Man.	Prayer of Manasses (Apocrypha).
Prob.	Philo, *Quod Omnis Probus Liber Sit.*
Prov.	Proverbs (Bible).
PS	*Palestinsky Sbornik* (Russ. (1881 1916, 1954ff).
Ps.	Psalms (Bible).
PSBA	*Proceedings of the Society of Biblical Archaeology* (1878–1918).
Ps. of Sol	Psalms of Solomon (Pseudepigrapha).
IQ Apoc	The *Genesis Apocryphon* from Qumran, cave one, ed. by N. Avigad and Y. Yadin (1956).
6QD	*Damascus Document* or *Sefer Berit Dammesk* from Qumran, cave six, ed. by M. Baillet, in RB, 63 (1956), 513–23 (see also CD).
QDAP	*Quarterly of the Department of Antiquities in Palestine* (1932ff.).
4QDeut. 32	Manuscript of Deuteronomy 32 from Qumran, cave four (ed. by P.W. Skehan, in BASOR, 136 (1954), 12–15).
4QEx^a	Exodus manuscript in Jewish script from Qumran, cave four.
4QEx^α	Exodus manuscript in Paleo-Hebrew script from Qumran, cave four (partially ed. by P.W. Skehan, in JBL, 74 (1955), 182–7).
4QFlor	*Florilegium,* a miscellany from Qumran, cave four (ed. by J.M. Allegro, in JBL, 75 (1956), 176–77 and 77 (1958), 350–54).).
QGJD	*Quellen zur Geschichte der Juden in Deutschland* 1888–98).
IQH	*Thanksgiving Psalms* of *Hodayot* from Qumran, cave one (ed. by E.L. Sukenik and N. Avigad, *Oẓar ha-Megillot ha-Genuzot* (1954).
IQIs^a	Scroll of Isaiah from Qumran, cave one (ed. by N. Burrows et al., *Dead Sea Scrolls* ..., 1 (1950).
IQIs^b	Scroll of Isaiah from Qumran, cave one (ed. E.L. Sukenik and N. Avigad, *Oẓar ha-Megillot ha-Genuzot* (1954).
IQM	The *War Scroll* or *Serekh ha-Milḥamah* (ed. by E.L. Sukenik and N. Avigad, *Oẓar ha-Megillot ha-Genuzot* (1954).
4QpNah	Commentary on Nahum from Qumran, cave four (partially ed. by J.M. Allegro, in JBL, 75 (1956), 89–95).
IQphyl	Phylacteries *(tefillin)* from Qumran, cave one (ed. by Y. Yadin, in *Eretz Israel,* 9 (1969), 60–85).
4Q Prayer of Nabonidus	A document from Qumran, cave four, belonging to a lost Daniel literature (ed. by J.T. Milik, in RB, 63 (1956), 407–15).
IQS	*Manual of Discipline* or *Serekh ha-Yaḥad* from Qumran, cave one (ed. by M. Burrows et al., *Dead Sea Scrolls* ..., 2, pt. 2 (1951).

IQS[a]	The *Rule of the Congregation or Serekh ha-Edah* from Qumran, cave one (ed. by Burrows et al., *Dead Sea Scrolls* ..., 1 (1950), under the abbreviation IQ28a).
IQS[b]	*Blessings* or *Divrei Berakhot* from Qumran, cave one (ed. by Burrows et al., *Dead Sea Scrolls* ..., 1 (1950), under the abbreviation IQ28b).
4QSam[a]	Manuscript of I and II Samuel from Qumran, cave four (partially ed. by F.M. Cross, in BASOR, 132 (1953), 15–26).
4QSam[b]	Manuscript of I and II Samuel from Qumran, cave four (partially ed. by F.M. Cross, in JBL, 74 (1955), 147–72).
4QTestimonia	Sheet of Testimony from Qumran, cave four (ed. by J.M. Allegro, in JBL, 75 (1956), 174–87).).
4QT.Levi	*Testament of Levi* from Qumran, cave four (partially ed. by J.T. Milik, in RB, 62 (1955), 398–406).
Rabinovitz, Dik Sof	See Dik Sof.
RB	*Revue biblique* (1892ff.)
RBI	*Recherches bibliques* (1954ff.)
RCB	*Revista de cultura biblica* (São Paulo) (1957ff.)
Régné, Cat	J. Régné, *Catalogue des actes . . . des rois d'Aragon, concernant les Juifs* (1213–1327), in: REJ, vols. 60 70, 73, 75–78 (1910–24).
Reinach, Textes	T. Reinach, *Textes d'auteurs Grecs et Romains relatifs au Judaïsme* (1895; repr. 1963).
REJ	*Revue des études juives* (1880ff.).
Rejzen, Leksikon	Z. Rejzen, *Leksikon fun der Yidisher Literature*, 4 vols. (1927–29).
Renan, Ecrivains	A. Neubauer and E. Renan, *Les écrivains juifs français* ... (1893).
Renan, Rabbins	A. Neubauer and E. Renan, *Les rabbins français* (1877).
RES	*Revue des étude sémitiques et Babyloniaca* (1934–45).
Rev.	Revelation (New Testament).
RGG[3]	*Die Religion in Geschichte und Gegenwart*, 7 vols. (1957–65[3]).
RH	*Rosh Ha-Shanah* (talmudic tractate).
RHJE	*Revue de l'histoire juive en Egypte* (1947ff.).
RHMH	*Revue d'histoire de la médecine hébraïque* (1948ff.).
RHPR	*Revue d'histoire et de philosophie religieuses* (1921ff.).
RHR	*Revue d'histoire des religions* (1880ff.).
RI	*Rivista Israelitica* (1904–12).
Riemann-Einstein	*Hugo Riemanns Musiklexikon*, ed. by A. Einstein (1929[11]).
Riemann-Gurlitt	*Hugo Riemanns Musiklexikon*, ed. by W. Gurlitt (1959–67[12]), Personenteil.
Rigg-Jenkinson, Exchequer	J.M. Rigg, H. Jenkinson and H.G. Richardson (eds.), *Calendar of the Pleas Rolls of the Exchequer of the Jews*, 4 vols. (1905–1970); cf. in each instance also J.M. Rigg (ed.), *Select Pleas* ... (1902).
RMI	*Rassegna Mensile di Israel* (1925ff.).
Rom.	Epistle to the Romans (New Testament).
Rosanes, Togarmah	S.A. Rosanes, *Divrei Yemei Yisrael be-Togarmah*, 6 vols. (1907–45), and in 3 vols. (1930–38[2]).
Rosenbloom, Biogr Dict	J.R. Rosenbloom, *Biographical Dictionary of Early American Jews* (1960).
Roth, Art	C. Roth, *Jewish Art* (1961).
Roth, Dark Ages	C. Roth (ed.), *World History of the Jewish People*, second series, vol. 2, *Dark Ages* (1966).
Roth, England	C. Roth, *History of the Jews in England* (1964[3]).
Roth, Italy	C. Roth, *History of the Jews in Italy* (1946).
Roth, Mag Bibl	C. Roth, *Magna Bibliotheca Anglo-Judaica* (1937).
Roth, Marranos	C. Roth, *History of the Marranos* (2nd rev. ed 1959; reprint 1966).
Rowley, Old Test	H.H. Rowley, *Old Testament and Modern Study* (1951; repr. 1961).
RS	*Revue sémitiques d'épigraphie et d'histoire ancienne* (1893/94ff.).
RSO	*Rivista degli studi orientali* (1907ff.).
RSV	Revised Standard Version of the Bible.
Rubinstein, Australia I	*H.L. Rubinstein, The Jews in Australia, A Thematic History, Vol. I (1991).*
Rubinstein, Australia II	*W.D. Rubinstein, The Jews in Australia, A Thematic History, Vol. II (1991).*
Ruth	Ruth (Bible).
Ruth R.	*Ruth Rabbah.*
RV	Revised Version of the Bible.
Sac.	Philo, *De Sacrificiis Abelis et Caini.*
Salfeld, Martyrol	S. Salfeld, *Martyrologium des Nuernberger Memorbuches* (1898).
I and II Sam.	Samuel, book I and II (Bible).
Sanh.	*Sanhedrin* (talmudic tractate).
SBA	Society of Biblical Archaeology.
SBB	*Studies in Bibliography and Booklore* (1953ff.).
SBE	*Semana Biblica Española.*
SBT	*Studies in Biblical Theology* (1951ff.).
SBU	*Svenkst Bibliskt Uppslogsvesk*, 2 vols. (1962–63[2]).
Schirmann, Italyah	J.Ḥ. Schirmann, *Ha-Shirah ha-Ivrit be-Italyah* (1934).
Schirmann, Sefarad	J.Ḥ. Schirmann, *Ha-Shirah ha-Ivrit bi-Sefarad u-vi-Provence*, 2 vols. (1954–56).
Scholem, Mysticism	G. Scholem, *Major Trends in Jewish Mysticism* (rev. ed. 1946; paperback ed. with additional bibliography 1961).
Scholem, Shabbetai Ẓevi	G. Scholem, *Shabbetai Ẓevi ve-ha-Tenu'ah ha-Shabbeta'it bi-Ymei Ḥayyav*, 2 vols. (1967).
Schrader, Keilinschr	E. Schrader, *Keilinschriften und das Alte Testament* (1903[3]).
Schuerer, Gesch	E. Schuerer, *Geschichte des juedischen Volkes im Zeitalter Jesu Christi*, 3 vols. and index-vol. (1901–11[4]).

Schuerer, Hist	E. Schuerer, *History of the Jewish People in the Time of Jesus,* ed. by N.N. Glatzer, abridged paperback edition (1961).
Set. T.	*Sefer Torah* (post-talmudic tractate).
Sem.	*Semaḥot* (post-talmudic tractate).
Sendrey, Music	A. Sendrey, *Bibliography of Jewish Music* (1951).
SER	*Seder Eliyahu Rabbah.*
SEZ	*Seder Eliyahu Zuta.*
Shab	*Shabbat* (talmudic tractate).
Sh. Ar.	J. Caro Shulḥan Arukh. OḤ – *Oraḥ Ḥayyim* YD – *Yoreh De'ah* EH – *Even ha-Ezer* ḤM – *Ḥoshen Mishpat.*
Shek.	*Shekalim* (talmudic tractate).
Shev.	*Shevi'it* (talmudic tractate).
Shevu.	*Shevu'ot* (talmudic tractate).
Shunami, Bibl	S. Shunami, *Bibliography of Jewish Bibliographies* (1965^{2}).
Sif.	*Sifrei Deuteronomy.*
Sif. Num.	*Sifrei Numbers.*
Sifra	*Sifra* on Leviticus.
Sif. Zut.	*Sifrei Zuta.*
SIHM	Sources inédites de l'histoire du Maroc (series).
Silverman, Prayer	M. Silverman (ed.), *Sabbath and Festival Prayer Book* (1946).
Singer, Prayer	S. Singer *Authorised Daily Prayer Book* (1943^{17}).
Sob.	Philo, *De Sobrietate.*
Sof.	*Soferim* (post-talmudic tractate).
Som.	Philo, *De Somniis.*
Song	Song of Songs (Bible).
Song. Ch.	Song of the Three Children (Apocrypha).
Song R.	*Song of Songs Rabbah.*
SOR	*Seder Olam Rabbah.*
Sot.	*Sotah* (talmudic tractate).
SOZ	*Seder Olam Zuta.*
Spec.	Philo, *De Specialibus Legibus.*
Spector, Jewish Life	*S. Spector (ed.), Encyclopedia of Jewish Life Before and After the Holocaust (2001).*
Steinschneider, Arab lit	M. Steinschneider, *Die arabische Literatur der Juden* (1902).
Steinschneider, Cat Bod	M. Steinschneider, *Catalogus Librorum Hebraeorum in Bibliotheca Bodleiana,* 3 vols. (1852–60; reprints 1931 and 1964).
Steinschneider, Hanbuch	M. Steinschneider, *Bibliographisches Handbuch ueber die . . . Literatur fuer hebraeische Sprachkunde* (1859; repr. with additions 1937).
Steinschneider, Uebersetzungen	M. Steinschneider, *Die hebraeischen Uebersetzungen des Mittelalters* (1893).
Stern, Americans	M.H. Stern, *Americans of Jewish Descent* (1960).
van Straalen, Cat	S. van Straalen, *Catalogue of Hebrew Books in the British Museum Acquired During the Years 1868–1892* (1894).
Suárez Fernández, Docmentos	L. Suárez Fernández, *Documentos acerca de la expulsion de los Judios de España* (1964).
Suk.	*Sukkah* (talmudic tractate).
Sus.	Susanna (Apocrypha).
SY	*Sefer Yeẓirah.*
Sym.	Symmachus' Greek translation of the Bible.
SZNG	*Studien zur neueren Geschichte.*
Ta'an.	*Ta'anit* (talmudic tractate).
Tam.	*Tamid* (mishnaic tractate).
Tanḥ.	*Tanḥuma.*
Tanḥ. B.	*Tanḥuma.* Buber ed (1885).
Targ. Jon	Targum Jonathan (Aramaic version of the Prophets).
Targ. Onk.	Targum Onkelos (Aramaic version of the Pentateuch).
Targ. Yer.	Targum Yerushalmi.
TB	Babylonian Talmud or Talmud Bavli.
Tcherikover, Corpus	V. Tcherikover, A. Fuks, and M. Stern, *Corpus Papyrorum Judaicorum,* 3 vols. (1957–60).
Tef.	*Tefillin* (post-talmudic tractate).
Tem.	*Temurah* (mishnaic tractate).
Ter.	*Terumah* (talmudic tractate).
Test. Patr.	Testament of the Twelve Patriarchs (Pseudepigrapha). Ash. – Asher Ben. – Benjamin Dan – Dan Gad – Gad Iss. – Issachar Joseph – Joseph Judah – Judah Levi – Levi Naph. – Naphtali Reu. – Reuben Sim. – Simeon Zeb. – Zebulun.
I and II	Epistle to the Thessalonians (New Testament).
Thieme-Becker	U. Thieme and F. Becker (eds.), *Allgemeines Lexikon der bildenden Kuenstler von der Antike bis zur Gegenwart,* 37 vols. (1907–50).
Tidhar	D. Tidhar (ed.), *Enẓiklopedyah la-Ḥalutẓei ha-Yishuv u-Vonav* (1947ff.).
I and II Timothy	Epistles to Timothy (New Testament).
Tit.	Epistle to Titus (New Testament).
TJ	Jerusalem Talmud or Talmud Yerushalmi.
Tob.	Tobit (Apocrypha).
Toh.	*Tohorot* (mishnaic tractate).
Torczyner, Bundeslade	H. Torczyner, *Die Bundeslade und die Anfaenge der Religion Israels* (1930^{3}).
Tos.	*Tosafot.*
Tosef.	Tosefta.
Tristram, Nat Hist	H.B. Tristram, *Natural History of the Bible* (1877^{5}).
Tristram, Survey	Palestine Exploration Fund, *Survey of Western Palestine,* vol. 4 (1884) = *Fauna and Flora* by H.B. Tristram.
TS	*Terra Santa* (1943ff.).

TSBA	*Transactions of the Society of Biblical Archaeology* (1872–93).
TY	*Tevul Yom* (mishnaic tractate).
UBSB	United Bible Society, *Bulletin*.
UJE	*Universal Jewish Encyclopedia*, 10 vols. (1939–43).
Uk.	*Ukẓin* (mishnaic tractate).
Urbach, Tosafot	E.E. Urbach, *Ba'alei ha-Tosafot* (1957^2).
de Vaux, Anc Isr	R. de Vaux, *Ancient Israel: its Life and Institutions* (1961; paperback 1965).
de Vaux, Instit	R. de Vaux, *Institutions de l'Ancien Testament*, 2 vols. (1958 60).
Virt.	Philo, *De Virtutibus*.
Vogelstein, Chronology	M. Volgelstein, *Biblical Chronology (1944)*.
Vogelstein-Rieger	H. Vogelstein and P. Rieger, *Geschichte der Juden in Rom*, 2 vols. (1895–96).
VT	*Vetus Testamentum* (1951ff.).
VTS	*Vetus Testamentum* Supplements (1953ff.).
Vulg.	Vulgate (Latin translation of the Bible).
Wars	Josephus, *The Jewish Wars*.
Watzinger, Denkmaeler	K. Watzinger, *Denkmaeler Palaestinas*, 2 vols. (1933–35).
Waxman, Literature	M. Waxman, *History of Jewish Literature*, 5 vols. (1960^2).
Weiss, Dor	I.H. Weiss, *Dor, Dor ve-Doreshav*, 5 vols. (1904^4).
Wellhausen, Proleg	J. Wellhausen, *Prolegomena zur Geschichte Israels* (1927^6).
WI	*Die Welt des Islams* (1913ff.).
Winniger, Biog	S. Wininger, *Grosse juedische National-Biographie ...*, 7 vols. (1925–36).
Wisd.	Wisdom of Solomon (Apocrypha)
WLB	*Wiener Library Bulletin* (1958ff.).
Wolf, Bibliotheca	J.C. Wolf, *Bibliotheca Hebraea*, 4 vols. (1715–33).
Wright, Bible	G.E. Wright, *Westminster Historical Atlas to the Bible* (1945).
Wright, Atlas	G.E. Wright, *The Bible and the Ancient Near East* (1961).
WWWJ	*Who's Who in the World Jewry* (New York, 1955, 1965^2).
WZJT	*Wissenschaftliche Zeitschrift fuer juedische Theologie* (1835–37).
WZKM	*Wiener Zeitschrift fuer die Kunde des Morgenlandes* (1887ff.).
Yaari, Sheluḥei	A. Yaari, *Sheluḥei Ereẓ Yisrael* (1951).
Yad	Maimonides, *Mishneh Torah (Yad Ḥazakah)*.
Yad	*Yadayim* (mishnaic tractate).
Yal.	*Yalkut Shimoni*.
Yal. Mak.	*Yalkut Makhiri*.
Yal. Reub.	*Yalkut Reubeni*.
YD	*Yoreh De'ah*.
YE	*Yevreyskaya Entsiklopediya*, 14 vols. (c. 1910).
Yev.	*Yevamot* (talmudic tractate).
YIVOA	*YIVO Annual of Jewish Social Studies* (1946ff.).
YLBI	*Year Book of the Leo Baeck Institute* (1956ff.).
YMḤEY	See BJPES.
YMḤSI	*Yedi'ot ha-Makhon le-Ḥeker ha-Shirah ha-Ivrit* (1935/36ff.).
YMMY	*Yedi'ot ha-Makhon le-Madda'ei ha-Yahadut* (1924/25ff.).
Yoma	*Yoma* (talmudic tractate).
ZA	*Zeitschrift fuer Assyriologie* (1886/87ff.).
Zav.	*Zavim* (mishnaic tractate).
ZAW	*Zeitschrift fuer die alttestamentliche Wissenschaft und die Kunde des nachbiblishchen Judentums* (1881ff.).
ZAWB	*Beihefte* (supplements) to ZAW.
ZDMG	*Zeitschrift der Deutschen Morgenlaendischen Gesellschaft* (1846ff.).
ZDPV	*Zeitschrift des Deutschen Palaestina-Vereins* (1878–1949; from 1949 = BBLA).
Zech.	Zechariah (Bible).
Zedner, Cat	J. Zedner, *Catalogue of Hebrew Books in the Library of the British Museum* (1867; repr. 1964).
Zeitlin, Bibliotheca	W. Zeitlin, *Bibliotheca Hebraica Post-Mendelssohniana* (1891–95).
Zeph.	Zephaniah (Bible).
Zev.	*Zevaḥim* (talmudic tractate).
ZGGJT	*Zeitschrift der Gesellschaft fuer die Geschichte der Juden in der Tschechoslowakei* (1930–38).
ZGJD	*Zeitschrift fuer die Geschichte der Juden in Deutschland* (1887–92).
ZHB	*Zeitschrift fuer hebraeische Bibliographie* (1896–1920).
Zinberg, Sifrut	I. Zinberg, *Toledot Sifrut Yisrael*, 6 vols. (1955–60).
Ẓiẓ.	*Ẓiẓit* (post-talmudic tractate).
ZNW	*Zeitschrift fuer die neutestamentliche Wissenschaft* (1901ff.).
ZS	*Zeitschrift fuer Semitistik und verwandte Gebiete* (1922ff.).
Zunz, Gesch	L. Zunz, *Zur Geschichte und Literatur* (1845).
Zunz, Gesch	L. Zunz, *Literaturgeschichte der synagogalen Poesie* (1865; Supplement, 1867; repr. 1966).
Zunz, Poesie	L. Zunz, *Synogogale Posie des Mittelalters*, ed. by Freimann (1920^2; repr. 1967).
Zunz, Ritus	L. Zunz, *Ritus des synagogalen Gottesdienstes* (1859; repr. 1967).
Zunz, Schr	L. Zunz, *Gesammelte Schriften*, 3 vols. (1875–76).
Zunz, Vortraege	L. Zunz, *Gottesdienstliche vortraege der Juden ...* 1892^2; repr. 1966).
Zunz-Albeck, Derashot	L. Zunz, *Ha-Derashot be-Yisrael*, Heb. Tr. of Zunz Vortraege by H. Albeck (1954^2).

TRANSLITERATION RULES

HEBREW AND SEMITIC LANGUAGES:

	General	Scientific
א	not transliterated[1]	ʾ
בּ	b	b
ב	v	v, b̲
גּ	g	g
ג		ḡ
דּ	d	d
ד		d̲
ה	h	h
ו	v – when not a vowel	w
ז	z	z
ח	ḥ	ḥ
ט	t	ṭ, t
י	y – when vowel and at end of words – i	y
כּ	k	k
כ, ך	kh	kh, k̲
ל	l	l̲
מ, ם	m	m
נ, ן	n	n
ס	s	s
ע	not transliterated[1]	ʿ
פּ	p	p
פ, ף	f	p, f, ph
צ, ץ	ẓ	ṣ, ẓ
ק	k	q, k
ר	r	r
שׁ	sh[2]	š
שׂ	s	ś, s
תּ	t	t
ת		t̲
ג׳	dzh, J	ğ
ז׳	zh, J	ž
צ׳	ch	č
◌ָ		å, o, ǒ (short) â, ā (long)
◌ַ	a	a
◌ֲ		a, ^{a}
◌ֵ		e, ẹ, ē
◌ֶ	e	æ, ä, ę
◌ֱ		œ, ě, ^{e}
◌ְ	only *sheva na* is transliterated	ə, ě, e; only *sheva na* transliterated
◌ִ ◌ִי	i	i
◌ֹ וֹ	o	o, o, o
◌ֻ וּ	u	u, ŭ û, ū
◌ֵי	ei; biblical e	
‡		reconstructed forms of words

1. The letters א and ע are not transliterated.
An apostrophe (') between vowels indicates that they do not form a diphthong and are to be pronounced separately.
2. *Dagesh ḥazak* (forte) is indicated by doubling of the letter, except for the letter שׁ.
3. Names. Biblical names and biblical place names are rendered according to the Bible translation of the Jewish Publication Society of America. Post-biblical Hebrew names are transliterated; contemporary names are transliterated or rendered as used by the person. Place names are transliterated or rendered by the accepted spelling. Names and some words with an accepted English form are usually not transliterated.

YIDDISH

א	not transliterated
אַ	a
אָ	o
בּ	b
בֿ	v
ג	g
ד	d
ה	h
ו, וּ	u
וו	v
וי	oy
ז	z
זש	zh
ח	kh
ט	t
טש	tsh, ch
י	(consonant) y (vowel) i
יִ	i
יי	ey
ײַ	ay
כּ	k
כ, ך	kh
ל	l
מ, ם	m
נ, ן	n
ס	s
ע	e
פּ	p
פֿ, ף	f
צ, ץ	ts
ק	k
ר	r
שׁ	sh
שׂ	s
תּ	t
ת	s

1. Yiddish transliteration rendered according to U. Weinreich's Modern *English-Yiddish Yiddish-English* Dictionary.
2. Hebrew words in Yiddish are usually transliterated according to standard Yiddish pronunciation, e.g., חזנות = *khazones*.

LADINO

Ladino and Judeo-Spanish words written in Hebrew characters are transliterated phonetically, following the General Rules of Hebrew transliteration (see above) whenever the accepted spelling in Latin characters could not be ascertained.

ARABIC

ا ء	a[1]	ض	ḍ
ب	b	ط	ṭ
ت	t	ظ	ẓ
ث	th	ع	c
ج	j	غ	gh
ح	ḥ	ف	f
خ	kh	ق	q
د	d	ك	k
ذ	dh	ل	l
ر	r	م	m
ز	z	ن	n
س	s	ه	h
ش	sh	و	w
ص	ṣ	ي	y
ـَ	a	ـَا ى	ā
ـِ	i	ـِي	ī
ـُ	u	ـُو	ū
ـَو	aw	ـِيّ	iyy[2]
ـَي	ay	ـُوّ	uww[2]

1. not indicated when initial
2. see note (f)

a) The EJ follows the *Columbia Lippincott Gazetteer* and the *Times Atlas* in transliteration of Arabic place names. Sites that appear in neither are transliterated according to the table above, and subject to the following notes.

b) The EJ follows the *Columbia Encyclopedia* in transliteration of Arabic names. Personal names that do not therein appear are transliterated according to the table above and subject to the following notes (e.g., Ali rather than ʿAlī, Suleiman rather than Sulayman).

c) The EJ follows the *Webster's Third International Dictionary, Unabridged* in transliteration of Arabic terms that have been integrated into the English language.

d) The term "Abu" will thus appear, usually in disregard of inflection.

e) Nunnation (end vowels, *tanwīn*) are dropped in transliteration.

f) Gemination (*tashdīd*) is indicated by the doubling of the geminated letter, unless an end letter, in which case the gemination is dropped.

g) The definitive article *al-* will always be thus transliterated, unless subject to one of the modifying notes (e.g., El-Arish rather than al-ʿArīsh; modification according to note (a)).

h) The Arabic transliteration disregards the Sun Letters (the antero-palatals (*al-Ḥurūf al-Shamsiyya*).

i) The *tā-marbūṭa* (o) is omitted in transliteration, unless in construct-stage (e.g., *Khirba* but *Khirbat Mishmish*).

These modifying notes may lead to various inconsistencies in the Arabic transliteration, but this policy has deliberately been adopted to gain smoother reading of Arabic terms and names.

GREEK

Ancient Greek	*Modern Greek*	*Greek Letters*
a	a	*Α; α; ᾳ*
b	v	*Β; β*
g	gh; g	*Γ; γ*
d	dh	*Δ; δ*
e	e	*Ε; ε*
z	z	*Ζ; ζ*
e; e	i	*Η; η; ῃ*
th	th	*Θ; θ*
i	i	*Ι; ι*
k	k; ky	*Κ; κ*
l	l	*Λ; λ*
m	m	*Μ; μ*
n	n	*Ν; ν*
x	x	*Ξ; ξ*
o	o	*Ο; ο*
p	p	*Π; π*
r; rh	r	*Ρ; ρ; ῥ*
s	s	*Σ; σ; ς*
t	t	*Τ; τ*
u; y	i	*Υ; υ*
ph	f	*Φ; φ*
ch	kh	*Χ; χ*
ps	ps	*Ψ; ψ*
o; ō	o	*Ω; ω; ῳ*
ai	e	*αι*
ei	i	*ει*
oi	i	*οι*
ui	i	*υι*
ou	ou	*ου*
eu	ev	*ευ*
eu; ēu	iv	*ηυ*
–	j	*τζ*
nt	d; nd	*ντ*
mp	b; mb	*μπ*
ngk	g	*γκ*
ng	ng	*νγ*
h	–	ʽ
–	–	ʼ
w	–	*Ϝ*

RUSSIAN

А	A
Б	B
В	V
Г	G
Д	D
Е	E, Ye[1]
Ё	Yo, O[2]
Ж	Zh
З	Z
И	I
Й	Y[3]
К	K
Л	L
М	M
Н	N
О	O
П	P
Р	R
С	S
Т	T
У	U
Ф	F
Х	Kh
Ц	Ts
Ч	Ch
Ш	Sh
Щ	Shch
Ъ	omitted; see note [1]
Ы	Y
Ь	omitted; see note [1]
Э	E
Ю	Yu
Я	Ya

1. Ye at the beginning of a word; after all vowels except ***Ы***; and after ***Ъ*** and ***Ь***.
2. O after ***Ч***, ***Ш*** and ***Щ***.
3. Omitted after ***Ы***, and in names of people after ***И***.

A. Many first names have an accepted English or quasi-English form which has been preferred to transliteration.
B. Place names have been given according to the *Columbia Lippincott Gazeteer*.
C. Pre-revolutionary spelling has been ignored.
D. Other languages using the Cyrillic alphabet (e.g., Bulgarian, Ukrainian), inasmuch as they appear, have been phonetically transliterated in conformity with the principles of this table.

GLOSSARY

Asterisked terms have separate entries in the Encyclopaedia.

Actions Committee, early name of the Zionist General Council, the supreme institution of the World Zionist Organization in the interim between Congresses. The Zionist Executive's name was then the "Small Actions Committee."

***Adar**, twelfth month of the Jewish religious year, sixth of the civil, approximating to February–March.

***Aggadah**, name given to those sections of Talmud and Midrash containing homiletic expositions of the Bible, stories, legends, folklore, anecdotes, or maxims. In contradistinction to **halakhah.*

***Agunah**, woman unable to remarry according to Jewish law, because of desertion by her husband or inability to accept presumption of death.

***Aharonim**, later rabbinic authorities. In contradistinction to **rishonim* ("early ones").

Ahavah, liturgical poem inserted in the second benediction of the morning prayer *(*Ahavah Rabbah)* of the festivals and/or special Sabbaths.

Aktion (Ger.), operation involving the mass assembly, deportation, and murder of Jews by the Nazis during the *Holocaust.

***Aliyah**, (1) being called to Reading of the Law in synagogue; (2) immigration to Ereẓ Israel; (3) one of the waves of immigration to Ereẓ Israel from the early 1880s.

***Amidah**, main prayer recited at all services; also known as *Shemoneh Esreh* and *Tefillah.*

***Amora** (pl. **amoraim**), title given to the Jewish scholars in Ereẓ Israel and Babylonia in the third to sixth centuries who were responsible for the **Gemara.*

Aravah, the *willow; one of the *Four Species used on *Sukkot ("festival of Tabernacles") together with the **etrog, hadas,* and **lulav.*

***Arvit**, evening prayer.

Asarah be-Tevet, fast on the 10th of Tevet commemorating the commencement of the siege of Jerusalem by Nebuchadnezzar.

Asefat ha-Nivḥarim, representative assembly elected by Jews in Palestine during the period of the British Mandate (1920–48).

***Ashkenaz**, name applied generally in medieval rabbinical literature to Germany.

***Ashkenazi** (pl. **Ashkenazim**), German or West-, Central-, or East-European Jew(s), as contrasted with *Sephardi(m).

***Av**, fifth month of the Jewish religious year, eleventh of the civil, approximating to July–August.

***Av bet din**, vice president of the supreme court (*bet din ha-gadol*) in Jerusalem during the Second Temple period; later, title given to communal rabbis as heads of the religious courts (see **bet din*).

***Badḥan**, jester, particularly at traditional Jewish weddings in Eastern Europe.

***Bakkashah** (Heb. "supplication"), type of petitionary prayer, mainly recited in the Sephardi rite on Rosh Ha-Shanah and the Day of Atonement.

Bar, "son of . . . "; frequently appearing in personal names.

***Baraita** (pl. **beraitot**), statement of **tanna* not found in *Mishnah.

***Bar mitzvah**, ceremony marking the initiation of a boy at the age of 13 into the Jewish religious community.

Ben, "son of . . . ", frequently appearing in personal names.

Berakhah (pl. **berakhot**), *benediction, blessing; formula of praise and thanksgiving.

***Bet din** (pl. **battei din**), rabbinic court of law.

***Bet ha-midrash**, school for higher rabbinic learning; often attached to or serving as a synagogue.

***Bilu**, first modern movement for pioneering and agricultural settlement in Ereẓ Israel, founded in 1882 at Kharkov, Russia.

***Bund**, Jewish socialist party founded in Vilna in 1897, supporting Jewish national rights; Yiddishist, and anti-Zionist.

Cohen (pl. **Cohanim**), see Kohen.

***Conservative Judaism**, trend in Judaism developed in the United States in the 20th century which, while opposing extreme changes in traditional observances, permits certain modifications of *halakhah* in response to the changing needs of the Jewish people.

***Consistory** (Fr. *consistoire*), governing body of a Jewish communal district in France and certain other countries.

***Converso(s)**, term applied in Spain and Portugal to converted Jew(s), and sometimes more loosely to their descendants.

***Crypto-Jew**, term applied to a person who although observing outwardly Christianity (or some other religion) was at heart a Jew and maintained Jewish observances as far as possible (see Converso; Marrano; Neofiti; New Christian; Jadīd al-Islām).

***Dayyan**, member of rabbinic court.

Decisor, equivalent to the Hebrew *posek* (pl. **posekim*), the rabbi who gives the decision (*halakhah*) in Jewish law or practice.

***Devekut**, "devotion"; attachment or adhesion to God; communion with God.

***Diaspora**, Jews living in the "dispersion" outside Ereẓ Israel; area of Jewish settlement outside Ereẓ Israel.

Din, a law (both secular and religious), legal decision, or lawsuit.

Divan, diwan, collection of poems, especially in Hebrew, Arabic, or Persian.

Dunam, unit of land area (1,000 sq. m., c. ¼ acre), used in Israel.

Einsatzgruppen, mobile units of Nazi S.S. and S.D.; in U.S.S.R. and Serbia, mobile killing units.

***Ein-Sof**, "without end"; "the infinite"; hidden, impersonal aspect of God; also used as a Divine Name.

***Elul**, sixth month of the Jewish religious calendar, 12th of the civil, precedes the High Holiday season in the fall.

Endloesung, see *Final Solution.

***Ereẓ Israel**, Land of Israel; Palestine.

***Eruv**, technical term for rabbinical provision permitting the alleviation of certain restrictions.

***Etrog**, citron; one of the *Four Species used on *Sukkot together with the **lulav, hadas,* and *aravah.*

Even ha-Ezer, see Shulḥan Arukh.

***Exilarch**, lay head of Jewish community in Babylonia (see also *resh galuta*), and elsewhere.

***Final Solution** (Ger. *Endloesung*), in Nazi terminology, the Nazi-planned mass murder and total annihilation of the Jews.

***Gabbai**, official of a Jewish congregation; originally a charity collector.

***Galut**, "exile"; the condition of the Jewish people in dispersion.

*__Gaon__ (pl. **geonim**), head of academy in post-talmudic period, especially in Babylonia.

Gaonate, office of *gaon.

*__Gemara__, traditions, discussions, and rulings of the *__amoraim__*, commenting on and supplementing the *Mishnah, and forming part of the Babylonian and Palestinian Talmuds (see Talmud).

*__Gematria__, interpretation of Hebrew word according to the numerical value of its letters.

General Government, territory in Poland administered by a German civilian governor-general with headquarters in Cracow after the German occupation in World War II.

*__Genizah__, depository for sacred books. The best known was discovered in the synagogue of Fostat (old Cairo).

Get, bill of *divorce.

*__Ge'ullah__, hymn inserted after the **Shema* into the benediction of the morning prayer of the festivals and special Sabbaths.

*__Gilgul__, metempsychosis; transmigration of souls.

*__Golem__, automaton, especially in human form, created by magical means and endowed with life.

*__Ḥabad__, initials of *ḥokhmah, binah, da'at*: "wisdom, understanding, knowledge"; ḥasidic movement founded in Belorussia by *Shneur Zalman of Lyady.

Hadas, *myrtle; one of the *Four Species used on Sukkot together with the **etrog*, **lulav*, and *aravah*.

*__Haftarah__ (pl. **haftarot**), designation of the portion from the prophetical books of the Bible recited after the synagogue reading from the Pentateuch on Sabbaths and holidays.

*__Haganah__, clandestine Jewish organization for armed self-defense in Ereẓ Israel under the British Mandate, which eventually evolved into a people's militia and became the basis for the Israel army.

*__Haggadah__, ritual recited in the home on *Passover eve at seder table.

Haham, title of chief rabbi of the Spanish and Portuguese congregations in London, England.

*__Hakham__, title of rabbi of *Sephardi congregation.

*__Hakham bashi__, title in the 15th century and modern times of the chief rabbi in the Ottoman Empire, residing in Constantinople (Istanbul), also applied to principal rabbis in provincial towns.

Hakhsharah ("preparation"), organized training in the Diaspora of pioneers for agricultural settlement in Ereẓ Israel.

*__Halakhah__ (pl. **halakhot**), an accepted decision in rabbinic law. Also refers to those parts of the *Talmud concerned with legal matters. In contradistinction to **aggadah*.

Ḥaliẓah, biblically prescribed ceremony (Deut. 25:9–10) performed when a man refuses to marry his brother's childless widow, enabling her to remarry.

*__Hallel__, term referring to Psalms 113-18 in liturgical use.

*__Ḥalukkah__, system of financing the maintenance of Jewish communities in the holy cities of Ereẓ Israel by collections made abroad, mainly in the pre-Zionist era (see *kolel*).

Ḥalutz (pl. **ḥalutzim**), pioneer, especially in agriculture, in Ereẓ Israel.

Ḥalutziyyut, pioneering.

*__Ḥanukkah__, eight-day celebration commemorating the victory of *Judah Maccabee over the Syrian king *Antiochus Epiphanes and the subsequent rededication of the Temple.

Ḥasid, adherent of *Ḥasidism.

*__Ḥasidei Ashkenaz__, medieval pietist movement among the Jews of Germany.

*__Ḥasidism__, (1) religious revivalist movement of popular mysticism among Jews of Germany in the Middle Ages; (2) religious movement founded by *Israel ben Eliezer Ba'al Shem Tov in the first half of the 18th century.

*__Haskalah__, "enlightenment"; movement for spreading modern European culture among Jews c. 1750–1880. See *maskil*.

*__Havdalah__, ceremony marking the end of Sabbath or festival.

*__Ḥazzan__, precentor who intones the liturgy and leads the prayers in synagogue; in earlier times a synagogue official.

*__Ḥeder__ (lit. "room"), school for teaching children Jewish religious observance.

Heikhalot, "palaces"; tradition in Jewish mysticism centering on mystical journeys through the heavenly spheres and palaces to the Divine Chariot (see Merkabah).

*__Ḥerem__, excommunication, imposed by rabbinical authorities for purposes of religious and/or communal discipline; originally, in biblical times, that which is separated from common use either because it was an abomination or because it was consecrated to God.

Ḥeshvan, see Marḥeshvan.

*__Ḥevra kaddisha__, title applied to charitable confraternity (**ḥevrah*), now generally limited to associations for burial of the dead.

*__Ḥibbat Zion__, see Ḥovevei Zion.

*__Histadrut__ (abbr. For Heb. **Ha-Histadrut ha-Kelalit shel ha-Ovedim ha-Ivriyyim be-Ereẓ Israel**). Ereẓ Israel Jewish Labor Federation, founded in 1920; subsequently renamed Histadrut ha-Ovedim be-Ereẓ Israel.

*__Holocaust__, the organized mass persecution and annihilation of European Jewry by the Nazis (1933–1945).

*__Hoshana Rabba__, the seventh day of *Sukkot on which special observances are held.

Ḥoshen Mishpat, see Shulḥan Arukh.

Ḥovevei Zion, federation of *Ḥibbat Zion, early (pre-*Herzl) Zionist movement in Russia.

Illui, outstanding scholar or genius, especially a young prodigy in talmudic learning.

*__Iyyar__, second month of the Jewish religious year, eighth of the civil, approximating to April-May.

I.Ẓ.L. (initials of Heb. *__Irgun Ẓeva'i Le'ummi__; "National Military Organization"), underground Jewish organization in Ereẓ Israel founded in 1931, which engaged from 1937 in retaliatory acts against Arab attacks and later against the British mandatory authorities.

*__Jadīd al-Islām__ (Ar.), a person practicing the Jewish religion in secret although outwardly observing Islām.

*__Jewish Legion__, Jewish units in British army during World War I.

*__Jihād__ (Ar.), in Muslim religious law, holy war waged against infidels.

*__Judenrat__ (Ger. "Jewish council"), council set up in Jewish communities and ghettos under the Nazis to execute their instructions.

*__Judenrein__ (Ger. "clean of Jews"), in Nazi terminology the condition of a locality from which all Jews had been eliminated.

*__Kabbalah__, the Jewish mystical tradition:
Kabbala iyyunit, speculative Kabbalah;
Kabbala ma'asit, practical Kabbalah;
Kabbala nevu'it, prophetic Kabbalah.

Kabbalist, student of Kabbalah.

*__Kaddish__, liturgical doxology.

Kahal, Jewish congregation; among Ashkenazim, *kehillah*.

*__Kalām__ (Ar.), science of Muslim theology; adherents of the Kalām are called *mutakallimūn.*

*__Karaite__, member of a Jewish sect originating in the eighth century which rejected rabbinic (*Rabbanite) Judaism and claimed to accept only Scripture as authoritative.

*__Kasher__, ritually permissible food.

Kashrut, Jewish *dietary laws.

*__Kavvanah__, "intention"; term denoting the spiritual concentration accompanying prayer and the performance of ritual or of a commandment.

*__Kedushah__, main addition to the third blessing in the reader's repetition of the *Amidah* in which the public responds to the precentor's introduction.

Kefar, village; first part of name of many settlements in Israel.

Kehillah, congregation; see *kahal.*

Kelippah (pl. **kelippot**), "husk(s)"; mystical term denoting force(s) of evil.

*__Keneset Yisrael__, comprehensive communal organization of the Jews in Palestine during the British Mandate.

Keri, variants in the masoretic (*masorah) text of the Bible between the spelling (*ketiv*) and its pronunciation (*keri*).

*__Kerovah__ (collective plural (corrupted) from **kerovez̦**), poem(s) incorporated into the **Amidah.*

Ketiv, see *keri.*

*__Ketubbah__, marriage contract, stipulating husband's obligations to wife.

Kevuz̦ah, small commune of pioneers constituting an agricultural settlement in Erez̦ Israel (evolved later into *kibbutz).

*__Kibbutz__ (pl. **kibbutzim**), larger-size commune constituting a settlement in Erez̦ Israel based mainly on agriculture but engaging also in industry.

*__Kiddush__, prayer of sanctification, recited over wine or bread on eve of Sabbaths and festivals.

*__Kiddush ha-Shem__, term connoting martyrdom or act of strict integrity in support of Judaic principles.

*__Kinah__ (pl. **kinot**), lamentation dirge(s) for the Ninth of Av and other fast days.

*__Kislev__, ninth month of the Jewish religious year, third of the civil, approximating to November-December.

Klaus, name given in Central and Eastern Europe to an institution, usually with synagogue attached, where *Talmud was studied perpetually by adults; applied by Ḥasidim to their synagogue ("*kloyz*").

*__Knesset__, parliament of the State of Israel.

K(c)ohen (pl. **K(c)ohanim**), Jew(s) of priestly (Aaronide) descent.

*__Kolel__, (1) community in Erez̦ Israel of persons from a particular country or locality, often supported by their fellow countrymen in the Diaspora; (2) institution for higher Torah study.

Kosher, see *kasher.*

*__Kristallnacht__ (Ger. "crystal night," meaning "night of broken glass"), organized destruction of synagogues, Jewish houses, and shops, accompanied by mass arrests of Jews, which took place in Germany and Austria under the Nazis on the night of Nov. 9–10, 1938.

*__Lag ba-Omer__, 33rd (Heb. **lag**) day of the **Omer* period falling on the 18th of *Iyyar; a semi-holiday.

Leḥi (abbr. For Heb. *__Loḥamei Ḥerut Israel__, "Fighters for the Freedom of Israel"), radically anti-British armed underground organization in Palestine, founded in 1940 by dissidents from *I.Z.L.

Levir, husband's brother.

*__Levirate marriage__ (Heb. *yibbum*), marriage of childless widow (*yevamah*) by brother (*yavam*) of the deceased husband (in accordance with Deut. 25:5); release from such an obligation is effected through *ḥaliz̦ah.*

LHY, see Leḥi.

*__Lulav__, palm branch; one of the *Four Species used on *Sukkot together with the **etrog, hadas,* and *aravah.*

*__Ma'aravot__, hymns inserted into the evening prayer of the three festivals, Passover, Shavuot, and Sukkot.

Ma'ariv, evening prayer; also called **arvit.*

*__Ma'barah__, transition camp; temporary settlement for newcomers in Israel during the period of mass immigration following 1948.

*__Maftir__, reader of the concluding portion of the Pentateuchal section on Sabbaths and holidays in synagogue; reader of the portion of the prophetical books of the Bible (**haftarah*).

*__Maggid__, popular preacher.

*__Maḥzor__ (pl. **maḥzorim**), festival prayer book.

*__Mamzer__, bastard; according to Jewish law, the offspring of an incestuous relationship.

*__Mandate, Palestine__, responsibility for the administration of Palestine conferred on Britain by the League of Nations in 1922; mandatory government: the British administration of Palestine.

*__Maqāma__ (Ar. pl. **maqamāt**), poetic form (rhymed prose) which, in its classical arrangement, has rigid rules of form and content.

*__Marḥeshvan__, popularly called Ḥeshvan; eighth month of the Jewish religious year, second of the civil, approximating to October–November.

*__Marrano(s)__, descendant(s) of Jew(s) in Spain and Portugal whose ancestors had been converted to Christianity under pressure but who secretly observed Jewish rituals.

Maskil (pl. **maskilim**), adherent of *Haskalah ("Enlightenment") movement.

*__Masorah__, body of traditions regarding the correct spelling, writing, and reading of the Hebrew Bible.

Masorete, scholar of the masoretic tradition.

Masoretic, in accordance with the masorah.

Meliz̦ah, in Middle Ages, elegant style; modern usage, florid style using biblical or talmudic phraseology.

Mellah, *Jewish quarter in North African towns.

*__Menorah__, candelabrum; seven-branched oil lamp used in the Tabernacle and Temple; also eight-branched candelabrum used on *Ḥanukkah.

Me'orah, hymn inserted into the first benediction of the morning prayer (*Yoz̦er ha-Me'orot*).

*__Merkabah__, *merkavah*, "chariot"; mystical discipline associated with Ezekiel's vision of the Divine Throne-Chariot (Ezek. 1).

Meshullaḥ, emissary sent to conduct propaganda or raise funds for rabbinical academies or charitable institutions.

*__Mezuzah__ (pl. **mezuzot**), parchment scroll with selected Torah verses placed in container and affixed to gates and doorposts of houses occupied by Jews.

*__Midrash__, method of interpreting Scripture to elucidate legal points (*Midrash Halakhah*) or to bring out lessons by stories or homiletics (*Midrash Aggadah*). Also the name for a collection of such rabbinic interpretations.

*__Mikveh__, ritual bath.

*__Minhag__ (pl. **minhagim**), ritual custom(s); synagogal rite(s); especially of a specific sector of Jewry.

*__Minḥah__, afternoon prayer; originally meal offering in Temple.

*__Minyan__, group of ten male adult Jews, the minimum required for communal prayer.

*__Mishnah__, earliest codification of Jewish Oral Law.

Mishnah (pl. **mishnayot**), subdivision of tractates of the Mishnah.

Mitnagged (pl. ***Mitnaggedim**), originally, opponents of *Ḥasidism in Eastern Europe.

*__Mitzvah__, biblical or rabbinic injunction; applied also to good or charitable deeds.

Mohel, official performing circumcisions.

*__Moshav__, smallholders' cooperative agricultural settlement in Israel, see moshav ovedim.

Moshavah, earliest type of Jewish village in modern Ereẓ Israel in which farming is conducted on individual farms mostly on privately owned land.

Moshav ovedim ("workers' moshav"), agricultural village in Israel whose inhabitants possess individual homes and holdings but cooperate in the purchase of equipment, sale of produce, mutual aid, etc.

*__Moshav shittufi__ ("collective moshav"), agricultural village in Israel whose members possess individual homesteads but where the agriculture and economy are conducted as a collective unit.

Mostegab (Ar.), poem with biblical verse at beginning of each stanza.

*__Muqaddam__ (Ar., pl. **muqaddamūn**), "leader," "head of the community."

*__Musaf__, additional service on Sabbath and festivals; originally the additional sacrifice offered in the Temple.

Musar, traditional ethical literature.

*__Musar movement__, ethical movement developing in the latter part of the 19th century among Orthodox Jewish groups in Lithuania; founded by R. Israel *Lipkin (Salanter).

*__Nagid__ (pl. **negidim**), title applied in Muslim (and some Christian) countries in the Middle Ages to a leader recognized by the state as head of the Jewish community.

Nakdan (pl. **nakdanim**), "punctuator"; scholar of the 9th to 14th centuries who provided biblical manuscripts with masoretic apparatus, vowels, and accents.

*__Nasi__ (pl. **nesi'im**), talmudic term for president of the Sanhedrin, who was also the spiritual head and later, political representative of the Jewish people; from second century a descendant of Hillel recognized by the Roman authorities as patriarch of the Jews. Now applied to the president of the State of Israel.

*__Negev__, the southern, mostly arid, area of Israel.

*__Ne'ilah__, concluding service on the *Day of Atonement.

Neofiti, term applied in southern Italy to converts to Christianity from Judaism and their descendants who were suspected of maintaining secret allegiance to Judaism.

*__Neology; Neolog; Neologism__, trend of *Reform Judaism in Hungary forming separate congregations after 1868.

*__Nevelah__ (lit. "carcass"), meat forbidden by the *dietary laws on account of the absence of, or defect in, the act of **sheḥitah* (ritual slaughter).

*__New Christians__, term applied especially in Spain and Portugal to converts from Judaism (and from Islam) and their descendants; "Half New Christian" designated a person one of whose parents was of full Jewish blood.

*__Niddah__ ("menstruous woman"), woman during the period of menstruation.

*__Nisan__, first month of the Jewish religious year, seventh of the civil, approximating to March-April.

Niẓoẓot, "sparks"; mystical term for sparks of the holy light imprisoned in all matter.

Nosaḥ (**nusaḥ**) "version"; (1) textual variant; (2) term applied to distinguish the various prayer rites, e.g., *nosaḥ Ashkenaz*; (3) the accepted tradition of synagogue melody.

*__Notarikon__, method of abbreviating Hebrew works or phrases by acronym.

Novella(e) (Heb. **ḥiddush (im)*), commentary on talmudic and later rabbinic subjects that derives new facts or principles from the implications of the text.

*__Nuremberg Laws__, Nazi laws excluding Jews from German citizenship, and imposing other restrictions.

Ofan, hymns inserted into a passage of the morning prayer.

*__Omer__, first sheaf cut during the barley harvest, offered in the Temple on the second day of Passover.

Omer, Counting of (Heb. *Sefirat ha-Omer*), 49 days counted from the day on which the *omer* was first offered in the Temple (according to the rabbis the 16th of Nisan, i.e., the second day of Passover) until the festival of Shavuot; now a period of semi-mourning.

Oraḥ Ḥayyim, see Shulḥan Arukh.

*__Orthodoxy__ (Orthodox Judaism), modern term for the strictly traditional sector of Jewry.

*__Pale of Settlement__, 25 provinces of czarist Russia where Jews were permitted permanent residence.

*__Palmaḥ__ (abbr. for Heb. *peluggot maḥaz*; "shock companies"), striking arm of the *Haganah.

*__Pardes__, medieval biblical exegesis giving the literal, allegorical, homiletical, and esoteric interpretations.

*__Parnas__, chief synagogue functionary, originally vested with both religious and administrative functions; subsequently an elected lay leader.

Partition plan(s), proposals for dividing Ereẓ Israel into autonomous areas.

Paytan, composer of **piyyut* (liturgical poetry).

*__Peel Commission__, British Royal Commission appointed by the British government in 1936 to inquire into the Palestine problem and make recommendations for its solution.

Pesaḥ, *Passover.

*__Pilpul__, in talmudic and rabbinic literature, a sharp dialectic used particularly by talmudists in Poland from the 16th century.

*__Pinkas__, community register or minute-book.

*__Piyyut__, (pl. **piyyutim**), Hebrew liturgical poetry.

*__Pizmon__, poem with refrain.

Posek (pl. ***posekim**), decisor; codifier or rabbinic scholar who pronounces decisions in disputes and on questions of Jewish law.

*__Prosbul__, legal method of overcoming the cancelation of debts with the advent of the *sabbatical year.

*__Purim__, festival held on Adar 14 or 15 in commemoration of the delivery of the Jews of Persia in the time of *Esther.

Rabban, honorific title higher than that of rabbi, applied to heads of the *Sanhedrin in mishnaic times.

*__Rabbanite__, adherent of rabbinic Judaism. In contradistinction to *Karaite.

Reb, rebbe, Yiddish form for rabbi, applied generally to a teacher or ḥasidic rabbi.

*__Reconstructionism__, trend in Jewish thought originating in the United States.

*__Reform Judaism__, trend in Judaism advocating modification of *Orthodoxy in conformity with the exigencies of contemporary life and thought.

Resh galuta, lay head of Babylonian Jewry (see exilarch).
Responsum (pl. ***responsa**), written opinion (*teshuvah*) given to question (*she'elah*) on aspects of Jewish law by qualified authorities; pl. collection of such queries and opinions in book form (*she'elot u-teshuvot*).
***Rishonim**, older rabbinical authorities. Distinguished from later authorities (**aḥaronim*).
***Rishon le-Zion**, title given to Sephardi chief rabbi of Ereẓ Israel.
***Rosh Ha-Shanah**, two-day holiday (one day in biblical and early mishnaic times) at the beginning of the month of *Tishri (September–October), traditionally the New Year.
Rosh Hodesh, *New Moon, marking the beginning of the Hebrew month.
Rosh Yeshivah, see *Yeshivah.
***R.S.H.A.** (initials of Ger. *Reichssicherheitshauptamt*: "Reich Security Main Office"), the central security department of the German Reich, formed in 1939, and combining the security police (Gestapo and Kripo) and the S.D.
***Sanhedrin**, the assembly of ordained scholars which functioned both as a supreme court and as a legislature before 70 C.E. In modern times the name was given to the body of representative Jews convoked by Napoleon in 1807.
***Savora** (pl. **savoraim**), name given to the Babylonian scholars of the period between the **amoraim* and the **geonim*, approximately 500–700 C.E.
S.D. (initials of Ger. *Sicherheitsdienst*: "security service"), security service of the *S.S. formed in 1932 as the sole intelligence organization of the Nazi party.
Seder, ceremony observed in the Jewish home on the first night of Passover (outside Ereẓ Israel first two nights), when the *Haggadah is recited.
***Sefer Torah**, manuscript scroll of the Pentateuch for public reading in synagogue.
***Sefirot, the ten**, the ten "Numbers"; mystical term denoting the ten spheres or emanations through which the Divine manifests itself; elements of the world; dimensions, primordial numbers.
Selektion (Ger.), (1) in ghettos and other Jewish settlements, the drawing up by Nazis of lists of deportees; (2) separation of incoming victims to concentration camps into two categories – those destined for immediate killing and those to be sent for forced labor.
Seliḥah (pl. ***seliḥot**), penitential prayer.
***Semikhah**, ordination conferring the title "rabbi" and permission to give decisions in matters of ritual and law.
Sephardi (pl. ***Sephardim**), Jew(s) of Spain and Portugal and their descendants, wherever resident, as contrasted with *Ashkenazi(m).
Shabbatean, adherent of the pseudo-messiah *Shabbetai Ẓevi (17th century).
Shaddai, name of God found frequently in the Bible and commonly translated "Almighty."
***Shaḥarit**, morning service.
Shali'aḥ (pl. **sheliḥim**), in Jewish law, messenger, agent; in modern times, an emissary from Ereẓ Israel to Jewish communities or organizations abroad for the purpose of fund-raising, organizing pioneer immigrants, education, etc.
Shalmonit, poetic meter introduced by the liturgical poet *Solomon ha-Bavli.
***Shammash**, synagogue beadle.
***Shavuot**, Pentecost; Festival of Weeks; second of the three annual pilgrim festivals, commemorating the receiving of the Torah at Mt. Sinai.
***Sheḥitah**, ritual slaughtering of animals.
***Shekhinah**, Divine Presence.
Shelishit, poem with three-line stanzas.
***Sheluḥei Ereẓ Israel** (or **shadarim**), emissaries from Ereẓ Israel.
***Shema** ([Yisrael]; "hear… [O Israel]," Deut. 6:4), Judaism's confession of faith, proclaiming the absolute unity of God.
Shemini Aẓeret, final festal day (in the Diaspora, final two days) at the conclusion of *Sukkot.
Shemittah, *Sabbatical year.
Sheniyyah, poem with two-line stanzas.
***Shephelah**, southern part of the coastal plain of Ereẓ Israel.
***Shevat**, eleventh month of the Jewish religious year, fifth of the civil, approximating to January–February.
***Shi'ur Komah**, Hebrew mystical work (c. eighth century) containing a physical description of God's dimensions; term denoting enormous spacial measurement used in speculations concerning the body of the **Shekhinah*.
Shivah, the "seven days" of *mourning following burial of a relative.
***Shofar**, horn of the ram (or any other ritually clean animal excepting the cow) sounded for the memorial blowing on *Rosh Ha-Shanah, and other occasions.
Shoḥet, person qualified to perform **sheḥitah*.
Shomer, *Ha-Shomer, organization of Jewish workers in Ereẓ Israel founded in 1909 to defend Jewish settlements.
***Shtadlan**, Jewish representative or negotiator with access to dignitaries of state, active at royal courts, etc.
***Shtetl**, Jewish small-town community in Eastern Europe.
***Shulḥan Arukh**, Joseph *Caro's code of Jewish law in four parts:
Oraḥ Ḥayyim, laws relating to prayers, Sabbath, festivals, and fasts;
Yoreh De'ah, dietary laws, etc;
Even ha-Ezer, laws dealing with women, marriage, etc;
Ḥoshen Mishpat, civil, criminal law, court procedure, etc.
Siddur, among Ashkenazim, the volume containing the daily prayers (in distinction to the **maḥzor* containing those for the festivals).
***Simḥat Torah**, holiday marking the completion in the synagogue of the annual cycle of reading the Pentateuch; in Ereẓ Israel observed on Shemini Aẓeret (outside Ereẓ Israel on the following day).
***Sinai Campaign**, brief campaign in October–November 1956 when Israel army reacted to Egyptian terrorist attacks and blockade by occupying the Sinai peninsula.
Sitra aḥra, "the other side" (of God); left side; the demoniac and satanic powers.
***Sivan**, third month of the Jewish religious year, ninth of the civil, approximating to May–June.
***Six-Day War**, rapid war in June 1967 when Israel reacted to Arab threats and blockade by defeating the Egyptian, Jordanian, and Syrian armies.
***S.S.** (initials of Ger. *Schutzstaffel*: "protection detachment"), Nazi formation established in 1925 which later became the "elite" organization of the Nazi Party and carried out central tasks in the "Final Solution."
***Status quo ante** community, community in Hungary retaining the status it had held before the convention of the General Jew-

ish Congress there in 1868 and the resultant split in Hungarian Jewry.

*__Sukkah__, booth or tabernacle erected for *Sukkot when, for seven days, religious Jews "dwell" or at least eat in the *sukkah* (Lev. 23:42).

*__Sukkot__, festival of Tabernacles; last of the three pilgrim festivals, beginning on the 15th of Tishri.

Sūra (Ar.), chapter of the Koran.

Ta'anit Esther (Fast of *Esther), fast on the 13th of Adar, the day preceding Purim.

Takkanah (pl. ***takkanot**), regulation supplementing the law of the Torah; regulations governing the internal life of communities and congregations.

*__Tallit (gadol)__, four-cornered prayer shawl with fringes (*ẓiẓit*) at each corner.

*__Tallit katan__, garment with fringes (*ẓiẓit*) appended, worn by observant male Jews under their outer garments.

*__Talmud__, "teaching"; compendium of discussion on the Mishnah by generations of scholars and jurists in many academies over a period of several centuries. The Jerusalem (or Palestinian) Talmud mainly contains the discussions of the Palestinian sages. The Babylonian Talmud incorporates the parallel discussion in the Babylonian academies.

Talmud torah, term generally applied to Jewish religious (and ultimately to talmudic) study; also to traditional Jewish religious public schools.

*__Tammuz__, fourth month of the Jewish religious year, tenth of the civil, approximating to June-July.

Tanna (pl. ***tannaim**), rabbinic teacher of mishnaic period.

*__Targum__, Aramaic translation of the Bible.

*__Tefillin__, phylacteries, small leather cases containing passages from Scripture and affixed on the forehead and arm by male Jews during the recital of morning prayers.

Tell (Ar. "mound," "hillock"), ancient mound in the Middle East composed of remains of successive settlements.

*__Terefah__, food that is not **kasher*, owing to a defect on the animal.

*__Territorialism__, 20th century movement supporting the creation of an autonomous territory for Jewish mass-settlement outside Ereẓ Israel.

*__Tevet__, tenth month of the Jewish religious year, fourth of the civil, approximating to December–January.

Tikkun ("restitution," "reintegration"), (1) order of service for certain occasions, mostly recited at night; (2) mystical term denoting restoration of the right order and true unity after the spiritual "catastrophe" which occurred in the cosmos.

Tishah be-Av, Ninth of *Av, fast day commemorating the destruction of the First and Second Temples.

*__Tishri__, seventh month of the Jewish religious year, first of the civil, approximating to September–October.

Tokheḥah, reproof sections of the Pentateuch (Lev. 26 and Deut. 28); poem of reproof.

*__Torah__, Pentateuch or the Pentateuchal scroll for reading in synagogue; entire body of traditional Jewish teaching and literature.

Tosafist, talmudic glossator, mainly French (12–14th centuries), bringing additions to the commentary by *Rashi.

*__Tosafot__, glosses supplied by tosafist.

*__Tosefta__, a collection of teachings and traditions of the *tannaim*, closely related to the Mishnah.

Tradent, person who hands down a talmudic statement on the name of his teacher or other earlier authority.

*__Tu bi-Shevat__, the 15th day of Shevat, the New Year for Trees; date marking a dividing line for fruit tithing; in modern Israel celebrated as arbor day.

*__Uganda Scheme__, plan suggested by the British government in 1903 to establish an autonomous Jewish settlement area in East Africa.

*__Va'ad Le'ummi__, national council of the Jewish community in Ereẓ Israel during the period of the British *Mandate.

*__Wannsee Conference__, Nazi conference held on Jan. 20, 1942, at which the planned annihilation of European Jewry was endorsed.

Waqf (Ar.), (1) a Muslim charitable pious foundation; (2) state lands and other property passed to the Muslim community for public welfare.

*__War of Independence__, war of 1947–49 when the Jews of Israel fought off Arab invading armies and ensured the establishment of the new State.

*__White Paper(s)__, report(s) issued by British government, frequently statements of policy, as issued in connection with Palestine during the *Mandate period.

*__Wissenschaft des Judentums__ (Ger. "Science of Judaism"), movement in Europe beginning in the 19th century for scientific study of Jewish history, religion, and literature.

*__Yad Vashem__, Israel official authority for commemorating the *Holocaust in the Nazi era and Jewish resistance and heroism at that time.

Yeshivah (pl. ***yeshivot**), Jewish traditional academy devoted primarily to study of rabbinic literature; *rosh yeshivah*, head of the yeshivah.

YHWH, the letters of the holy name of God, the Tetragrammaton.

Yibbum, see levirate marriage.

Yiḥud, "union"; mystical term for intention which causes the union of God with the **Shekhinah*.

Yishuv, settlement; more specifically, the Jewish community of Ereẓ Israel in the pre-State period. The pre-Zionist community is generally designated the "old yishuv" and the community evolving from 1880, the "new yishuv."

Yom Kippur, Yom ha-Kippurim, *Day of Atonement, solemn fast day observed on the 10th of Tishri.

Yoreh De'ah, see Shulḥan Arukh.

Yoẓer, hymns inserted in the first benediction (*Yoẓer Or*) of the morning **Shema*.

*__Ẓaddik__, person outstanding for his faith and piety; especially a ḥasidic rabbi or leader.

Ẓimẓum, "contraction"; mystical term denoting the process whereby God withdraws or contracts within Himself so leaving a primordial vacuum in which creation can take place; primordial exile or self-limitation of God.

*__Zionist Commission (1918)__, commission appointed in 1918 by the British government to advise the British military authorities in Palestine on the implementation of the *Balfour Declaration.

Ẓyyonei Zion, the organized opposition to Herzl in connection with the *Uganda Scheme.

*__Ẓiẓit__, fringes attached to the **tallit* and **tallit katan*.

*__Zohar__, mystical commentary on the Pentateuch; main textbook of *Kabbalah.

Zulat, hymn inserted after the **Shema* in the morning service.